THE ROUGH GUIDE TO
South America
ON A BUDGET

written and rese

Tom Azzopar
Robert Coate
Kaminski, Ste
Meghji, Rosalb
Ben Westwood

ROUGH
GUIDES

roughguides.com

Contents

INTRODUCTION 4

| Where to go | 8 | Ideas | 14 |
| When to go | 12 | Itineraries | 22 |

BASICS 28

Getting there	29	Culture and etiquette	36
Getting around	31	Work and study	37
Accommodation	33	Crime and personal safety	38
Health	34	Travel essentials	39

THE GUIDE 43

1 Argentina	43	7 The Guianas	641
2 Bolivia	153	8 Paraguay	685
3 Brazil	223	9 Peru	711
4 Chile	369	10 Uruguay	829
5 Colombia	485	11 Venezuela	855
6 Ecuador	563		

LANGUAGE 918

SMALL PRINT & INDEX 928

Introduction to
South America

From the palm-smothered tropical beaches of the Caribbean to the wild and windswept archipelago of Tierra del Fuego, South America is a dizzying trove of landscapes, legendary cities and ancient ruins that have fuelled the imagination of adventurers for centuries. Trace Darwin's voyage through the Galápagos, the devastating path of the conquistadors in Peru or Che Guevara's route across the snowcapped peaks of the Andes. Discover Eva Perón's Buenos Aires, a truly beautiful, stylish metropolis, or pick up the trail of Bruce Chatwin across the lonely plains and ice-bound fjords of Patagonia. Whether exploring the elegant cities of Colombia, soaking up Aymara culture in Bolivia, or just chilling on a white-sand Brazilian beach, options for budget travellers remain extensive and highly alluring.

Much of the continent's dynamism is a result of the collision of cultures here over the last five hundred years. Settled at least 10,000 years ago, South American peoples were devastated by European invasion in the sixteenth and seventeenth centuries, not least by the introduction of diseases that killed thousands. Yet **indigenous culture** never entirely disappeared and is especially strong in Peru, Bolivia and Brazil to this day. Indeed, much of the continent's people are proud of their **mestizo heritage**; indigenous, Spanish and Portuguese cultures dominate, but West African, British, Italian, German, French and Dutch influences have also contributed over the years, supplemented more recently by waves of Japanese, Chinese and Middle Eastern settlers. As the Argentine saying goes, "Peruvians come from the Incas; Argentines come from the boats".

This blending of races and cultures across the continent means that South American nations share a lot in common. **Catholicism** has provided a foundation for spiritual life here for centuries – sometimes blurring with far more ancient indigenous beliefs,

ABOVE LAKE TITICACA **RIGHT** IPANEMA BEACH, BRAZIL

especially in the Andes, it has created a legacy of magnificent churches and exuberant fiestas. When it comes to natural wonders the continent is equally blessed, with just about every terrain – from deserts and glaciers, to grasslands, rainforests and wetlands – and a range of **wildlife** found nowhere else: rheas, llamas, giant anteaters, jaguars and armadillos among them. The mighty Amazon River connects the Atlantic with the Brazilian jungle and the Peruvian Andes, while the lofty mountain chain itself runs from Colombia and Ecuador in the north, through Peru and Bolivia to the south of Chile and Argentina. This shared cultural and natural heritage is reflected in the ease of crossing borders, with multi-nation itineraries relatively simple to put together, whether traversing the River Plate between Argentina and Uruguay or the Atacama between Chile and Peru.

Today, South America is booming: Portuguese-speaking Brazil, the largest, richest and most populated country in South America, is a global power in the making, while Peru, Chile, Colombia and Argentina boast fast-growing economies and stable democracies. It's an exciting time to visit; backpackers will still find an extensive range of accommodation on offer, with plenty of options for the tight budget. South America also sports some of the best camping and hammock-slinging spots in the world, as well as many exhilarating **adventure tourism** destinations. Travelling within the continent varies wildly from country to country; sometimes it will require a little patience, initiative and navigating of red tape, but the colourful bus journeys, sunrise ferry crossings and people you'll meet along the way will be impossible to forget.

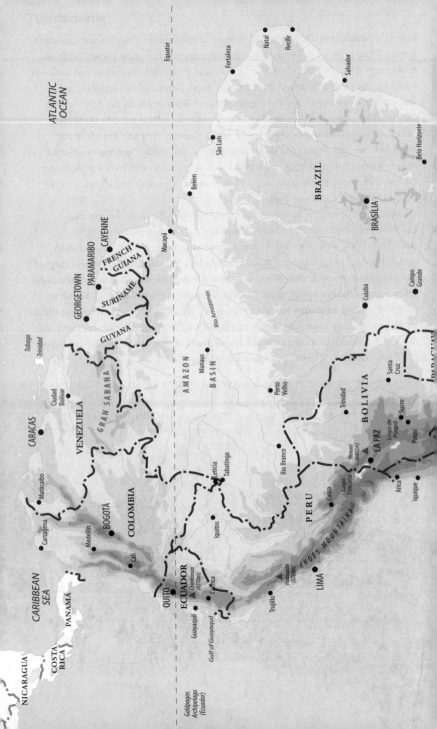

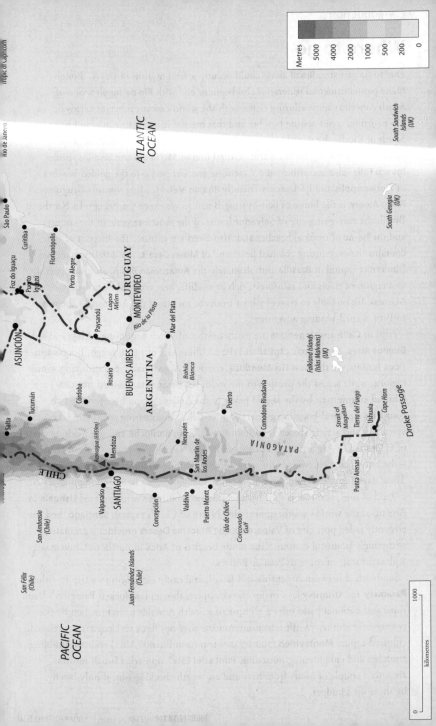

PACIFIC
OCEAN

San Félix
(Chile)

San Ambrosio
(Chile)

Juan Fernández Islands
(Chile)

Salta

Tucumán

Córdoba

Rosario

ASUNCIÓN

CHILE

Valparaíso

SANTIAGO

Mendoza

Aconcagua (6959m)

Concepción

Valdivia

Neuquén

San Martín de
los Andes

Puerto Montt

Isla de Chiloé

Corcovado
Gulf

ARGENTINA

PATAGONIA

Puerto

Comodoro Rivadavia

Bahía
Blanca

BUENOS AIRES

Mar del Plata

Río de la Plata

Paysandú

Lagoa
Mirim

URUGUAY

MONTEVIDEO

Foz do Iguaçu

Puerto
Iguazú

Florianópolis

Porto Alegre

Curitiba

São Paulo

Rio de Janeiro

ATLANTIC
OCEAN

Tropic of Capricorn

Punta Arenas

Strait of
Magellan

Tierra del Fuego

Ushuaia

Cape Horn

Drake Passage

Falkland Islands
(Islas Malvinas)
(UK)

South Georgia
(UK)

South Sandwich
Islands
(UK)

0   1000

kilometres

Where to go

Due to its vast size, **Brazil** alone could occupy several months of travel, though many pan-continental itineraries also begin or end with **Rio de Janeiro**, one of South America's most alluring cities: with the world's most exuberant carnival, hip nightlife, trend-setting beaches and that mesmerizing skyline, it's hard to beat. South of Rio lie the wealthier parts of the country, from the colonial elegance of **Paraty**, the sprawling business and cultural hub of **São Paulo** and awe-inspiring **Iguaçu Falls** (also accessible from Argentina and Uruguay), to the golden beaches of **Florianópolis** and backpacker-friendly **Ilha do Mel**. Heading towards Uruguay, **Porto Alegre** is the home of belt-busting Brazilian *churrasco* (barbecue). In Northeast Brazil, the easy-going city of **Salvador** is one of the most energetic in the country and the home of tropical beaches and Afro-Brazilian culture. The interior of Brazil contains the enchanting colonial heartland of **Minas Gerais**, the unfairly maligned Modernist capital of **Brasília** and ultimately the **Amazonian Basin**, an unimaginably vast region of rivers and rainforest, rich in wildlife, best accessed from Belém or Manaus. It's possible to travel by boat from the mouth of the Amazon all the way to Peru, a spell-binding adventure.

Trips to **Chile** and **Argentina** are easily combined, often beginning with grand old **Buenos Aires**, Argentina's capital and the ravishing city of Evita, tango, Borges and Boca Juniors. To the west sits **Mendoza**, centre of Argentina's ever-improving wine regions, while across the pampas to the south lies **Patagonia**, divided from its Chilean counterpart by the jagged peaks of the Andes. Slicing between the two countries are mind-boggling glaciers and ice-fields, shimmering mountain lakes, volcanoes and activity-based mountain towns, from **Bariloche** and the trekking centre of **El Chaltén** in Argentina, to **Pucón** and **Puerto Natales** across the Chilean border – the latter is the gateway to the jaw-dropping **Parque Nacional Torres del Paine**. These days **Tierra del Fuego** is more a land of penguins, sea lions and flamingos than a "land of fire", and is also split between the two countries, with isolated **Ushuaia** in Argentina the world's southernmost city. North of Chile's capital, **Santiago**, and the elegantly faded port city of **Valparaíso**, the **Atacama Desert** provides a dramatic, witheringly beautiful contrast. The sandy beaches of **Arica** in northern Chile make a pleasant stop en route to Peru or Bolivia.

Sandwiched between Argentina and Brazil, and easily tacked on to a trip to either, **Paraguay** and **Uruguay** lack major showstoppers, though landlocked Paraguay's Jesuit ruins and national parks offer a glimpse of a South America untrammelled by the twenty-first century. While adventure tourists may not flock to Uruguay, its relaxed, cultured capital **Montevideo** (an easy day-trip from Buenos Aires) sports crumbling churches and enlightening museums. **Punta del Este**'s upmarket beach resorts are only a couple of hours from here and are worth checking out, if only briefly, by those on a budget.

RIGHT FROM TOP VALPARAÍSO, CHILE; BRAZILIAN FOOTBALL TEAM

Top ten places to spot wildlife

Beagle Channel (Argentina) Take a thrilling boat trip to see the sea lions, penguins, whales and seabirds of Tierra del Fuego (p.148).

Parque Nacional Madidi (Bolivia) Deep in the Amazonian jungle, this remote park is home to rare monkeys, jaguars, bears, giant otters and thousands of tropical birds (p.220).

Amazonian Basin (Bolivia/Brazil/Ecuador/Peru/Venezuela) Visit any corner of the Amazon and you'll be treated to a wealth of insects, birds, reptiles and mammals (p.216, p.314, p.609, p.825 & p.898).

The Pantanal (Brazil/Paraguay) The world's largest wetland is home to thousands of animal species; giant river otters, giant anteaters, macaws and capybaras among them (p.326 & p.691).

Punta Arenas (Chile) Use this Patagonian city as a base to visit the thriving penguin colonies on Isla Magdalena and Seno Otway (p.462).

Parque Nacional Torres del Paine (Chile) Visit this spectacular mountain park and you are guaranteed to see herds of guanacos (like llamas), rheas (like ostriches) and gliding condors, with pumas lurking in the scrub (p.470).

Galápagos Islands (Ecuador) Charles Darwin's theories on evolution were developed here and it's unsurprisingly one of the continent's biggest attractions; think giant tortoise, marine iguanas, penguins and the flightless cormorant (p.631).

The Chaco (Paraguay) Home of a fascinating peccary breeding project, huge flocks of waterbirds, pumas, tapirs and capybaras (p.691).

Colca Canyon (Peru) Best place in the Andes to see condors, rising up the sides of a mesmerizing canyon wall (p.780).

Los Llanos (Venezuela) This tropical grassland supports hordes of capybaras, crocodiles, anaconda, armadillos, scarlet ibis and over sixty species of waterbirds (p.894).

FROM TOP GIANT TORTOISES, GALÁPAGOS ISLANDS, ECUADOR; GUANACO, CHILE

Bolivia is perhaps the continent's most intriguing destination, encompassing snaggle-toothed peaks, dense jungles and a dynamic indigenous culture, best absorbed in the capital **La Paz**, around **Lake Titicaca**, heartland of the Aymara and especially on the **Isla del Sol**, said to be the spiritual centre of the Andean world. The silver-mining city of **Potosí** funded the kings of Europe for centuries, while **Sucre** is one of the most captivating colonial cities on the continent.

Backpackers continue to flock to **Peru**, globally renowned for the great Inca ruins at **Cusco**, the **Sacred Valley** and especially **Machu Picchu**, the jaw-dropping mountain hideout on which all images of "lost cities" are now based. Many travellers reach the city on foot via the **Inca Trail**, a truly magical experience. Yet Peru has a lot more to offer, from virgin Amazonian jungle protected in parks such as the **Pacaya Samiria National Reserve** and a long dry coastline where ceviche became an art form, to the booming nightlife and innovative culinary scene in **Lima**.

Ecuador has much in common with Peru and is easily combined with a trip to its larger southern neighbour. The highland capital, **Quito**, is crammed with absorbing museums and colonial architecture, while the rest of the country is littered with volcanoes, old Spanish towns and beguiling indigenous markets. Naturalists, however, should head straight for the extraordinary **Galápagos Islands**, home to some of the world's most astonishing wildlife.

At the northern end of the continent, **Colombia** continues to be an up-and-coming travel destination, much safer after years of drug wars and guerrilla insurgencies. Immerse yourself in the salsa-soaked nightlife of **Bogotá**, the coffee-growing landscapes of the **Zona Cafetera** and the romantic colonial towns of **Cartagena** and **Popayán**. The mesmerizing scenery around **Villa de Leyva** is perfect for trekking, while **San Gil** is the base for adventure sports, especially white-water rafting. Far to the north, closer to Nicaragua than South America, the **Isla de Providencia** is part of the remote San Andrés chain, home of palm-fringed Caribbean beaches and a spectacular reef ideal for divers.

Neighbouring **Venezuela** remains a far more challenging country to visit, but the rewards for doing so are considerable; experience untouched and incredibly raw national parks, spectacular Caribbean beaches and the Amazon region of Guayana, which contains the **Angel Falls**, the world's tallest waterfall.

The **Guianas**, comprising the former British and Dutch colonies of **Guyana** and **Suriname** and the French overseas *département* of **French Guiana**, are often overlooked. However, their three vibrant capital cities, Georgetown, Paramaribo and Cayenne respectively, are home to cool bars and colonial wooden architecture in picturesque decay, while French Guiana has the added appeal of the **Centre Spatial Guyanais**, **Devil's Island** (immortalized in *Papillon*) and top-notch French cuisine. English-speaking Guyana offers a taste of West Indian culture – with cricket, rum and rotis, it's more Barbados than Brazil.

When to go

With about two-thirds of South America near the equator or the tropic of Capricorn, visitors to most destinations can expect a tropical or subtropical **climate** all year round. Temperatures rarely drop below 20°C, while rainforest regions average maximum temperatures of about 30°C. As you get further south (and don't forget the southern hemisphere reverses the seasons), you'll find colder winters from June to August and milder summers from December to February, with the extreme south of the continent freezing between April and October. It's important to plan around the **rainy season** in each country, particularly when travelling in the Andes.

Domestic tourism, especially in the richer countries of the south, is booming, meaning that hostels, hotels and transportation can become fully booked during the summer (December to March), especially on the coast, so book ahead if possible. Expect hordes of local tourists to hit the road in any country on major religious holidays, especially **Christmas** and **Semana Santa** (Easter).

Check the "When to go" information at the start of each country chapter for advice about region-specific weather.

Author picks

Scaling snow-tipped volcanoes, trekking through Amazonian jungle and driving some of Patagonia's most challenging and isolated roads, our hard-travelling authors have visited every corner of this vast, magnificent continent – from the islands of Colombia to the pampas of Argentina. Here are their personal favourites:

Argentine Andes Strap on a pair of crampons and trek across the majestic Perito Moreno glacier (p.142), or check out the mesmerizing views from Cerro Catedral (p.121).

Swing those hips Get down with the salsa at El Maní Es Así in Caracas (p.873), or soak up the tango at Buenos Aires' Torquato Tasso (p.65).

Best eats Sample belt-busting Brazilian *churrasco* (barbecue) in Porto Alegre (p.363), or the world's best *ceviche* on Peru's southern coast (p.719).

Amazon ecotourism A thrilling five-hour boat trip from Rurrenabaque to Chalalán ecolodge in Bolivia's Madidi National Park (p.219).

Historic Amazon city From gritty sunshine to acappella renditions of *Silent Night*, the jungle city of Manaus is as compelling as it is unforgettable (p.310).

Hike to the Lost City The trek to the understated ruins of the Ciudad Perdida leads you past sparkling swimming holes, a roaring river and indigenous Kogi villages (p.530).

Chill-out Ecuador's spa town of Baños is the ideal place to relax in the thermal baths that ooze from the mountainside (p.593).

Drinking tereré – Sip Paraguay's ice-cold herbal tea – with the sun setting over the Río Paraguay in Concepción (p.690 & p.707).

Stay with a view A stay or meal at the Ventorrillo de la Buena Vista in Uruguay provides exquisite food, fantastic architecture and spectacular views (p.847).

Off the beaten track Use Iquitos as a springboard to explore the wonders of the Amazon rainforest – you'll need at least five days (p.813).

> Our author recommendations don't end here. We've flagged up our favourite places – a perfectly sited hotel, an atmospheric café, a special restaurant – throughout the guide, highlighted with the ★ symbol.

LEFT CAPOEIRA DISPLAY, BRAZIL **FROM TOP** THERMAL BATHS, ECUADOR; PERITO MORENO GLACIER, ARGENTINA; CEVICHE, PERU

Festivals

1 ROCK AL PARQUE FESTIVAL, BOGOTÁ, COLOMBIA
Page 501
Free rock festival held over three days at Bogotá's Simón Bolívar Park; hosts everything from ska and blues to punk and metal.

2 INTI RAYMI, CUSCO, PERU
Page 750
Join thousands of revellers in honouring the sun god at Cusco's lavish and theatrical week-long Inca festival.

3 FERIA DE MATADEROS, ARGENTINA
Page 60
Mingle with gauchos, snack at parrillas and peruse local crafts at one of Buenos Aires' most exhilarating events.

4 CARNAVAL, RIO, BRAZIL
Page 237
Get ready for some serious partying at this legendary flesh-fest in South America's greatest city.

5 SEMANA SANTA, QUITO, ECUADOR
Page 571
Celebrate Holy Week at Quito's Good Friday parade, where thousands are dressed and veiled in purple garments and conical hats.

6 FIESTA DE LA VIRGEN DEL CARMEN, PAUCARTAMBO, PERU
Page 724
Magical Andean celebration featuring groups of beautifully costumed dancers blending pre-Columbian and Catholic traditions.

Ancient Sites

1 NAZCA LINES, PERU
Page 773

These unforgettable shapes and figures are one of the continent's great mysteries, only visible from the air and tops of the surrounding foothills.

2 CIUDAD PERDIDA, COLOMBIA
Page 529

Marvel at the ruins of this lost city of the Tayrona, only rediscovered in 1972 and accessible via a five-day hike.

3 EASTER ISLAND, CHILE
Page 477

Explore this mysterious, remote Polynesian island in the middle of the Pacific, known for its enigmatic Moai statues.

4 TIWANAKU, BOLIVIA
Page 175

This pre-Inca ruined city is considered by some to have been the cradle of Andean civilization.

5 MACHU PICCHU, PERU
Page 751

Hike the ancient Inca Trail to this precipice-surrounded, awe-inspiring citadel high in the Andes.

6 SAN AGUSTÍN, COLOMBIA
Page 554

A dramatic landscape littered with hundreds of gigantic, elaborately carved, pre-Columbian monoliths.

The Great Outdoors

1 BEACH-HOPPING, BRAZIL
Pages 245, 256 & 276

Swim, snorkel or just lounge on one of Brazil's enticing beaches, from Rio de Janeiro to Arraial do Cabo and Salvador.

2 GALÁPAGOS ISLANDS, ECUADOR
Page 631

Explore this volcanic, natural wonderland, home to giant tortoises, iguanas, sea lions and an abundance of sea birds and marine life.

3 SAN ANDRÉS, COLOMBIA
Page 533

Visit the remote Caribbean islands of San Andrés and Providencia and dive in their crystal clear waters.

4 PARQUE NACIONAL TORRES DEL PAINE, CHILE
Page 470

Ice-walk, fly-fish, kayak and mountaineer in this wild and beautiful national park, home to guanacos and rheas.

5 PUNTA TOMBO, ARGENTINA
Page 132

Get up close to Magellanic penguins at this protected coastal reserve in Patagonia.

6 VOLCÁN COTOPAXI, ECUADOR
Page 589

Climb at midnight for a sunrise at the summit of this active Andean volcano, one of the world's highest at almost 6000m.

Incredible Journeys

1 CARRETERA AUSTRAL, CHILE
Page 456

Wend your way along this spectacular Patagonian highway, rounding ice-fields, vast glaciers and jagged fjords.

2 INCA TRAIL, PERU
Page 755

Tackle the four-day hike between Cusco and Machu Picchu, a spell-binding mountain trek into the Inca past.

3 RUTA 40, ARGENTINA
Page 132

Travel this epic 5000km highway along the Andes, from the Bolivian border to the bottom of Patagonia.

4 RÍO BENI BY BOAT, BOLIVIA
Page 218

Cruise by slow boat to explore the mighty Amazon Basin and its wildlife up close.

5 SERRA VERDE RAILWAY, BRAZIL
Page 349

This enchanting train ride winds around mountains and traverses one of the largest Atlantic Forest reserves in the country.

6 THE CIRCUIT, TORRES DEL PAINE, CHILE
Page 474

This seven- to ten-day hike is the best way to soak up the charms and wildlife of the rugged national park.

Itineraries

You can't expect to fit everything South America has to offer into one trip – or two or three or four, to be fair – and we don't suggest you try. On the following pages a selection of itineraries will guide you through the different countries and regions, picking out a few of the best places and major attractions along the way. For those taking a big, extended trip around the continent you could join a few together, but remember that the distances you'll be covering can be vast. There is, of course, much to discover off the beaten track, so if you have the time it's worth exploring smaller towns, villages and wilderness areas further afield, finding your own perfect hill town, deserted beach or just a place you love to rest up and chill out.

SOUTHERN BRAZIL

❶ Rio The beaches, the samba, the towering statue of Christ the Redeemer looming over it all – Rio has every base covered to kick off your trip in style. **See p.236**

❷ Costa Verde Backed by forested mountain peaks, the coastline between Rio and São Paulo contains hidden gems like colonial Paraty and spectacular beaches at Ilha Grande. **See p.256 & p.257**

❸ Minas Gerais This state inland from Rio offers some of Brazil's most stunning historic towns – none more attractive than Ouro Preto. **See p.260**

❹ Brasília Come see the vision of the future, circa 1960, courtesy of Oscar Niemeyer's Modernist architecture. **See p.317**

❺ The Pantanal If you're not going to make it out to the Galápagos during your travels, consider checking out the huge array of wildlife in this vast wetland. **See p.326**

❻ Ilha de Santa Catarina Some of the best beaches in the country can be found on the coast near Florianópolis. **See p.356**

❼ Serra Gaúcha The mountain bases of Canela and Gramado serve two nearby parks with crashing falls and challenging climbs and hikes. **See p.364 & p.365**

ABOVE CAFÉ CULTURE, BUENOS AIRES

NORTHERN ARGENTINA, PARAGUAY AND URUGUAY

❶ **Buenos Aires** The most cosmopolitan of all South American cities, worthy of a few days of anyone's time. **See p.54**

❷ **Colonia del Sacramento** If you're just going to dip into Uruguay, you can't do better than the historic centre of this charming town. **See p.843**

❸ **Eastern Beaches** Beach getaways to suit every budget, from quiet Cabo Polonio with no roads or electricity to the flashy surf resort of Punta del Este. **See p.848**

❹ **Rosario** The perfect spot to launch yourself into the Paraná Delta. **See p.80**

❺ **Córdoba** Wander from the colonial centre to Nuevo Córdoba, a neighbourhood chock-a-block with cool bars and restaurants in converted mansions. **See p.71**

❻ **Mendoza** Undoubtedly the best stop for wine-lovers, a sophisticated city with great restaurants and hundreds of nearby *bodegas*. **See p.100**

❼ **Cerro Aconcagua** Whether you take two weeks to scale the summit or just see a bit on a day-hike, the tallest mountain in the western hemisphere will sear itself into your memory. **See p.105**

❽ **Salta** Its central plaza is a lovely place to begin an evening stroll. **See p.89**

❾ **Parque Nacional el Rey** The lush cloudforests here hold colourful toucans, as well as other exotic flora and fauna. **See p.93**

❿ **Iguazú Falls** Better to see the crashing waters from the trails and catwalks on the Argentina side. **See p.88**

⓫ **The Ruta Jesuítica** Visit Paraguay's famous Jesuit ruins; Trinidad and Jesús are just a four- to five-hour coach ride from Iguazú Falls. **See p.702**

CHILE AND ARGENTINA: THE LAKE DISTRICTS AND PATAGONIA

❶ **Volcán Villarrica** Skiing, snowboarding, mountaineering – depending on the season, you may be able to experience the smouldering volcano up close. **See p.438**

❷ **Lago Llanquihue** A sparkling blue lake lined with beaches and hemmed in by woods. **See p.442**

❸ **Eastern Chiloé** The less-developed side of the archipelago has no major tourist sights, just some low-key villages and some great coastal hiking. **See p.455**

❹ **San Martín de los Andes** A lower-key version of Bariloche: a hub for getting out to the nearby lakes and Parque Lanín. **See p.114**

❺ **Parque Nacional Nahuel Huapi** Well-marked trails, plentiful campsites and huts, crystal-clear lakes and much more make this the most popular Patagonian park on the Argentine side. **See p.122**

❻ **Península Valdés** Consider an eastern detour here to see abundant birdlife, a sea-lion colony and – if you time it right – whales on their migration route. **See p.130**

NORTHERN ARGENTINA, PARAGUAY AND URUGUAY

CHILE AND ARGENTINA: THE LAKE DISTRICTS AND PATAGONIA

❸ Pisco Elqui This charming village, with views over the Elqui valley, is the perfect place to sample a pisco sour. **See p.406**

❹ Parque Nacional Nevado de Tres Cruces Drive by arid salt flats, spot vicuñas and guanacos, and stay by a lake populated with colourful flamingos. **See p.408**

❺ San Pedro de Atacama There aren't too many sights per se in this pre-Columbian

NORTHERN CHILE AND SOUTHERN BOLIVIA

❼ Perito Moreno Glacier The unquestioned highlight of Parque Nacional Los Glaciares, a calving glacier that provides theatrical drama for onlookers. **See p.132**

❽ Parque Nacional Torres del Paine The most famous destination on the Chilean side of Patagonia – and perhaps the best trekking in the entire region. **See p.470**

❾ Ushuaia If you've made it here you're practically at the end of the world – send a postcard, eat some seafood, ski in winter and dream of Antarctica, 1000km away. **See p.144**

NORTHERN CHILE AND SOUTHERN BOLIVIA

❶ Santiago Not the most dynamic capital city, but a nice enough place to arrive, get oriented and explore some interesting museums and neighbourhoods. **See p.380**

❷ Valparaíso Ride the *ascensores* (funiculars) around the hilly streets by day, then eat, drink and carouse in the gritty port area at night. **See p.393**

settlement, but it's a perfect jumping-off point for the *altiplano* wilderness. See p.411

❻ Salar de Uyuni You'll have to go on a tour, but it's worth the trip to see the flat, white salt "lake", perfectly reflective in summer when covered with water. See p.195

❼ Potosí The colonial architecture and lively cafés are somewhat blighted by the tragic legacy of the nearby silver mines at Cerro Rico. See p.189

❽ Santa Cruz One of the rare places in Bolivia known for its excellent restaurant and club scene. See p.209

ECUADOR, PERU AND NORTHERN BOLIVIA

❶ Guayaquil An alternative introduction to Ecuador than more traditional Quito; the Malecón and nearby beaches make it seem like a different land entirely. See p.621

❷ Otavalo Few can resist the town's famous Saturday market, the ultimate place to purchase a hammock or woodcarving as a keepsake. See p.584

❸ Quito Base yourself in the old town, where plaza after plaza provides a vantage point for historic churches and narrow walkways. See p.571

❹ The Quilotoa Loop Hike for a few days around the peaceful waters of a volcanic crater lake. See p.590

❺ Nariz del Diablo train ride A five-hour journey starting in Riobamba and slicing its glorious way through the Andes. See p.598

❻ Vilcabamba Nurture mind, body and soul in the "Valley of Longevity", where the scenery is beautiful and the climate unbeatable. See p.607

❼ Huaraz This lively city, nestled in a valley, affords you an approach to trekking in both the Cordillera Blanca and Cordillera Huayhuash. See p.786

❽ Lima Love it or hate it, you can nevertheless find plenty to occupy you in the Peruvian capital, and the proximity to the sea makes it a great place to try out *ceviche*. See p.724

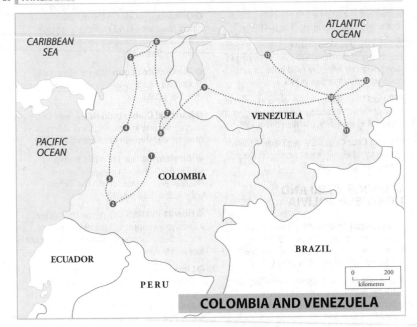

CARIBBEAN
SEA

ATLANTIC
OCEAN

PACIFIC
OCEAN

VENEZUELA

COLOMBIA

ECUADOR

BRAZIL

PERU

0   200
kilometres

COLOMBIA AND VENEZUELA

⑨ Trails to Machu Picchu Discover less expensive and less crowded alternative Inca Trails deep in the imposing jungle. **See p.763**

⑩ Cusco As much of a hub as Lima and closer to many of the country's highlights – though its plazas, museums, restaurants and nightlife certainly stand on their own. **See p.739**

⑪ Lake Titicaca Whether you visit the Uros islands on the Peru side or the sacred Isla del Sol in the Bolivian section, you're certain to be awed by the high-altitude lake. **See p.786 & p.179**

⑫ La Paz Now this is what an Andean capital city should be: delightfully situated high up in a canyon, full of interesting and inexpensive places to eat, drink and stay, and with an undeniable energy all its own. **See p.165**

⑬ Sucre The official capital's beautifully maintained colonial architecture accounts for the nickname "White City", but don't overlook this pretty town's excellent bars. **See p.200**

COLOMBIA AND VENEZUELA

① Bogotá Colombia's densely packed, cosmopolitan capital divides opinion, but is a worthwhile first or last stop for its colonial architecture and raucous nightlife. **See p.495**

② San Agustín A crazy array of monolithic statues, with a lovely mountain landscape serving as a backdrop. **See p.554**

③ Cali This might be Colombia's most fun and freewheeling city, with plenty of salsa clubs and streetlife to balance out the sober array of churches. **See p.548**

④ Medellín From Cali you can travel up to Medellín – an attractive, modern city that's had quite a makeover in the past decade – via Colombia's coffee country. **See p.535**

⑤ Cartagena The jewel of the Caribbean coast, a gorgeous colonial city and a must on any Colombia trip. **See p.515**

⑥ Parque Nacional Tayrona Beautiful beaches, lush flora and pre-Columbian ruins are the highlights of this pristine coastal park, accessed from Santa Marta. **See p.528**

⑦ San Gil Colombia's best spot for adventure sports is known for its white-water rafting, but you can also try out paragliding, kayaking, abseiling and more in the mountains north of Bogotá. **See p.510**

⑧ Villa de Leyva Under an hour from San Gil, this is a thoroughly unmodern and relaxed colonial town; from Villa de Leyva or San Gil you can loop back to Bucaramanga for buses to the border with Venezuela at Cúcuta, though don't linger here. **See p.507**

❾ Mérida Contemplate adventures to nearby mountains, a trip to wildlife-rich Los Llanos or just chill out in this laidback city. **See p.888**

❿ Ciudad Bolívar Venezuela's most lovely colonial town and the gateway to Angel Falls and the Orinoco Delta. **See p.900**

⓫ Angel Falls Journey by boat and on foot to reach this towering waterfall. **See p.904**

⓬ Orinoco Delta Visit the delta jungle region for a truly mind-blowing experience. **See p.908**

⓭ Parque Nacional Henri Pittier A great mix of beaches, wildlife and walking trails – and it's relatively near Caracas, which makes your exit or travel connections easier. **See p.878**

NORTHERN BRAZIL AND THE AMAZON

❶ Chapada Diamantina Some of the best hiking and waterfall hunting in the country is to be found in this canyon-filled national park. **See p.286**

❷ Salvador For candomblé, capoeira or Carnaval, Bahia's capital is practically the country's capital. Seek out fine beaches, diving and surf at nearby Morro de São Paulo. **See p.276**

❸ Olinda You won't find a prettier array of churches, plazas and houses anywhere in the north of the country. **See p.295**

❹ Fortaleza The central market is a sure bet to buy a hammock; take it with you to Jericoara, the best beach in the area. **See p.298**

❺ Belém Great restaurants and bars, but the main reason to come is its location at the mouth of the Amazon. **See p.303**

❻ Manaus After seeing the astounding Teatro Amazonas, grab some of the fine street food on offer and head to the lively port area. **See p.310**

❼ Amazon river trip Float along the Rio Negro to a jungle lodge or even just a clearing where you can string up a hammock – or head along the Amazon all the way to Iquitos in Peru. **See p.314 & p.316**

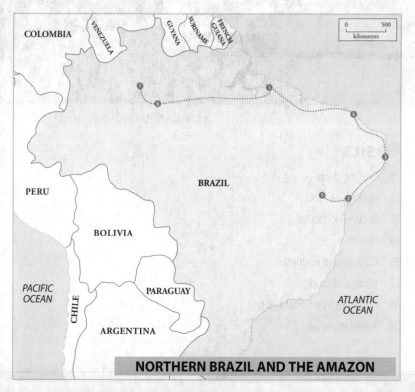

NORTHERN BRAZIL AND THE AMAZON

BUS IN NORTHERN ARGENTINA

Basics

29 Getting there

31 Getting around

33 Accommodation

34 Health

36 Culture and etiquette

37 Work and study

38 Crime and personal safety

39 Travel essentials

Getting there

The easiest way to reach the northern parts of South America is by air via the US, usually through a hub such as Houston, Atlanta or Miami. Flights from Europe alternatively may go via another city in the EU or, for the southern part of the region, stopover in São Paulo or Rio. The national South American airlines, such as Aerolíneas Argentinas, LAN, TACA and TAM, provide a reasonable choice of schedules and routes. Many immigration departments in South America insist that you have an onward or return ticket to enter the country, but the application of such rules is more strict in some countries than in others.

Airfares are seasonal, with the highest around July, August and mid-December to mid-January; you'll get the best prices during the dry winter (May, June and late Sept) and the wet summer (in most of the region Feb–April, excluding Carnaval and Easter). Note also that flying on weekends is often more expensive. You can generally cut costs by going through a specialist flight agent, booking flights well in advance or taking advantage of web-only offers and airline frequent-flyer programmes. Another way to cut costs is to book with a tour operator that can put together a package deal including flights and accommodation, and perhaps tours as well.

Flights from the UK and Ireland

If you book your flight well in advance, flying to South America from the UK will be considerably cheaper than a few weeks before, unless you manage to get a last-minute deal – not always to be banked on. If you're prepared to not fly direct, you'll also get a cheaper price, but this could mean a long stopover in an airport while waiting for a connection. Return flights from the UK and Ireland start at around £400–500. British Airways operates

direct flights to both Rio de Janeiro and São Paulo in Brazil and Buenos Aires in Argentina (for the latter you'll sometimes have to touch down in Brazil but don't have to change planes) – but fares tend to be more expensive than those of their European and South American rivals. The best value-for-money airline depends on the country you are flying to, but generally a flight with a European airline such as Iberia, TAP or Air France, via their main airport in Madrid, Lisbon or Paris, is cheaper than flying via the US.

Flights from the US and Canada

Most South American airlines serving North America operate flights from New York or Miami. US airlines tend to fly out of their hubs: Delta from Atlanta and Continental from Houston. Flying through Miami affords you greater flexibility in travel planning and cheaper prices. There are flights to all major South American cities from at least one of the above. Direct flights from Canada are very limited; it's generally best to transfer at a US hub. From either the US or Canada, return flights are available from around US$450.

Flights from Australia and NZ

The best deals to South America are offered by the major South American airlines Aerolíneas Argentinas and LAN in conjunction with Qantas and Air New Zealand. Aerolíneas Argentinas flies from Sydney to Buenos Aires, with connections across the continent; Qantas has code-shares with LAN via Auckland to Santiago and beyond. There are also plenty of flights via the US, but most are not scheduled through to South America and therefore tend to take longer and cost more, as each sector has to be priced separately. From Australia and NZ expect to pay at least US$1500 – but you can sometimes pay much more. Often airlines will charge more if you wish to stay in South America for longer than a month.

ESTA CLEARANCE

Since January 12, 2009, the US government has required those travellers coming to or through the US on the **Visa Waiver Program** to apply for clearance via **ESTA** (Electronic System for Travel Authorization). This is not something to ignore – if you arrive at the airport without having done it, the airline won't allow you to check in. To apply for clearance visit ⓦcbp.gov /xp/cgov/travel/id_visa/esta/ – make sure you do this at least 72 hours before travelling; you'll need your passport to hand, and the admin fee at the time of publication is US$14. Once a traveller has received clearance, it remains valid for two years.

A BETTER KIND OF TRAVEL

At **Rough Guides** we are passionately committed to travel. We believe it helps us understand the world we live in and the people we share it with – and of course tourism is vital to many developing economies. But the scale of modern tourism has also damaged some places irreparably, and climate change is accelerated by most forms of transport, especially flying. All Rough Guides' flights are carbon-offset, and every year we donate money to a variety of environmental charities.

From Central America

Crossing overland from Panama into Colombia is not recommended as it entails traversing the Darién, a wild, lawless region occupied by guerrillas. The safest option is to fly – Bogotá and Caracas are the main points of entry – or take a boat from Panama to the Caribbean coast of Colombia. There are no ferry services, but boats can be chartered in Colón and San Blas in Panama to Cartagena, Colombia. The journey takes four to six days.

AIRLINES

Aerolíneas Argentinas Ⓦ aerolineas.com.ar
Air Canada Ⓦ aircanada.com
Air Europa Ⓦ aireuropa.com
Air France Ⓦ airfrance.com
Air New Zealand Ⓦ airnewzealand.com
Alitalia Ⓦ alitalia.com
American Airlines Ⓦ aa.com
Avianca Ⓦ avianca.com
British Airways Ⓦ ba.com
Caribbean Airlines Ⓦ caribbean-airlines.com
Delta Airlines Ⓦ delta.com

Gol Ⓦ voegol.com.br
Iberia Airlines Ⓦ iberia.com
KLM Ⓦ klm.com
LAN Ⓦ lan.com
Qantas Ⓦ qantas.com.au
TACA Ⓦ taca.com
TAM Ⓦ tam.com.br
TAP Air Portugal Ⓦ flytap.com
United Airlines Ⓦ united.com

AGENTS AND OPERATORS

Adventure Center US ☎ 1 800 228 8747, Ⓦ adventurecenter.com. Hiking and "soft adventure" specialists with trips deep into most South American countries.
Dragoman UK ☎ 01728 861133, Ⓦ dragoman.com. A range of South American overland trips on a giant 4WD bus, with a choice between accommodation in a hotel or tents.
Exodus UK ☎ 020 8675 5550, Ⓦ exodus.co.uk. Walking and cycling – and everything in between – from Argentina to Venezuela.
Expedia Ⓦ expedia.com. Discount airfares, all-airline search engine and daily deals.
HostelTrail Ⓦ hosteltrail.com. A great source for hostels and budget tour companies in South America.
Hotwire Ⓦ hotwire.com. Last-minute savings of up to forty percent on regular published fares. Travellers must be at least 18 and there are no refunds, transfers or changes allowed. Log-in required to purchase.
Intrepid Australia Ⓦ intrepidtravel.com. Global travel company with almost three decades organizing adventure group travel – also has a "basix" option for those on a budget.
Journey Latin America UK ☎ 020 3432 1550, Ⓦ journeylatin america.co.uk. Knowledgeable and helpful staff, good at sorting out stopovers and open-jaw flights. Also does package tours.
Lastminute.com Ⓦ lastminute.com. Package holiday and flight-only deals available at short notice.
Opodo Ⓦ opodo.com. International flight comparison site where you can also book everything from car rental to hotels.
REI Adventures US ☎ 1 800 622 2236, Ⓦ rei.com/adventures. Climbing, cycling, hiking, cruising, paddling and multi-sport tours to many countries on the continent.
Skyscanner Ⓦ skyscanner.net. International flight comparison site.

AIRPASSES AND ROUND-THE-WORLD TICKETS

If you're visiting South America as part of a world trip, a **round-the-world (RTW) ticket** offers the greatest flexibility – and if your starting point is Australia or New Zealand, it may even be cheaper. Many international airlines are now aligned with one of two globe-spanning networks: "Star Alliance" (Ⓦ staralliance.com), which has 27 members including Air Canada, Air New Zealand, Lufthansa, Avianca/TACA and United; or "One World", which combines routes via twelve airlines including American, British Airways, Cathay Pacific, Iberia, LAN and Qantas. Fares depend on the month, point of origin and number of continents or distance travelled, and in general the more expensive options include South America, but they are worth exploring.

If you plan to do a fair amount of travelling within South America consider buying an **airpass** (see p.32) with your main ticket. These passes offer substantial savings, but can be bought only outside South America when buying an international ticket.

STA Travel UK ☎ 0333 321 0099, ⓦ statravel.co.uk. Low-cost flights and tours for students and under-26s, though other customers welcome.

Trailfinders UK ☎ 020 7368 1200, ⓦ trailfinders.com. One of the best-informed and most efficient agents for independent travellers. Good for round-the-world tickets.

Travel Cuts Canada ☎ 1 800 667 2887, ⓦ travelcuts.com. Canadian student-travel organization.

Tucan Travel Australia ☎ 2 9326 6633, ⓦ tucantravel.com. Specializing in adventure and backpacker holidays – and also has a budget option. Based in Australia but offices worldwide.

Wilderness Travel US ☎ 1 800 368 2794, ⓦ wildernesstravel.com. Adventure travel and wildlife tours throughout South America.

Getting around

Most South Americans travel by bus, and there is almost nowhere that you can't reach in this way. The major routes are comfortable and reliable and always cost-effective. Moreover, you will see more, and meet more people, if you travel by bus. Remember, though, that distances between towns can be huge, and that in more remote areas such as Patagonia there are few bus and no train services. If you have a little spare cash and limited time, you may want to fly occasionally, or rent a car to explore at leisure. There are frequent flights within and between South American countries; the former are generally much cheaper (but budget options are few and far between). Public transport options vary within each country. Most places will have collectivos (which are minibuses that depart when full and take set routes; not to be confused with colectivos, a name for city buses in the south), as well as rickety local buses. There are also mototaxis in some place (similar to those in Thailand and India), which are good for covering short distances within towns.

By bus

This is by far the cheapest way to see the continent. While you can, technically, travel all the way from the tropical north to Tierra del Fuego by bus, there are few direct international services and you usually have to disembark at the border, cross it, then sometimes get on another bus to a large city in the new country. The process is repeated at most border crossings. The best bet for an international service is in capital cities or major hubs near borders; in places with limited transport you may just have to buckle down and take what's on offer.

Terminals are often situated on the outskirts of towns – follow the signs to the *terminal* (in Spanish-speaking countries) or the *rodoviária* (in Brazil). Levels of comfort vary, so a quick visual check in the terminal will give you an idea of which company to go for. With better bus companies on long-distance routes, the **seating options** usually include normal seats, seats that partly recline (*semi-cama*) and seats that recline fully (*cama*) to become beds. They are priced according to the level of comfort, with the most expensive options including on-board meals and drinks. Some of the cheapest companies only have one level of comfort and that can mean anything from wooden seats to standing in an aisle.

By car

South American **roads**, especially outside the major cities, are notorious for their bumpy, potholed and generally poor conditions. Most car rental companies in South America do not allow their vehicles to be driven across borders, making independent exploration of the continent by car difficult.

If you are determined to go it alone and drive around South America, you will find car rental companies at all airports and in most major cities. Hotels can advise you of better-value local places, but often it's better to book in advance online. Costs are high due to skyrocketing insurance rates, but the independence of a car may be worth it. An international driving licence is recommended although most of the time you will probably be able to use the one issued by your country of residence (and may not even be asked for the international one). It's more a question of having it "just in case". Check your **insurance** carefully for exclusions, as car theft, vandalism and general security are renowned problems in many parts of South America, especially Argentina and Brazil, and you may not be covered for these. Damage to tyres or the underside of the car may also be excluded. Consider the state of the roads you'll drive on before choosing your vehicle type.

Rental charges vary from country to country and depend on the model of car. You will be required to present a credit card and valid driving licence. It is worth noting that most international rental companies won't allow you to cross a border with a rental car. Buying can be an option, and with the industry booming in South America – and more cars on the road every day – most countries have competitive secondhand markets. If you want to buy a car, make sure you check the quality of vehicle (standards are lower than in Europe and the US) and your insurance cover. Driving standards are poor, so beware, especially at night. Honk your horn before going round any corner – the locals do this with great gusto, so no one will find you rude. South Americans drive on the right except in Suriname and Guyana. Useful websites for driving in South America include Ⓦ drivetheamericas.com and Ⓦ driveabroad.co.uk.

By air

Several budget airlines have sprung up in recent years, although they are still more expensive than US or European counterparts. You can normally check-in online, but always find out whether flights need reconfirming. Remember that distances are large and may involve a stopover. Budget airlines include Brazil's Gol (Ⓦ voegol.com.br), Chile's Sky (Ⓦ skyairline.cl) and Colombia's EasyFly (Ⓦ easyfly.com.co).

Airpasses

If you plan to do a lot of travelling around South America, consider one of the reasonable **airpasses**. These are a godsend if you want to see as much as possible in a limited time.

All Airpass (Ⓦ allairpass.com) is a useful website for checking the different "airpass" offers out there from regional airlines. The passes are only available to travellers with a scheduled international return ticket and they have to be purchased outside South America. After you have used the first sector on your pass the ticket is non-refundable. Prices range from US$500 to US$1300 depending on the number of stops and area covered.

The **Mercosur Airpass** covers travel in Argentina, Brazil, Chile, Paraguay and Uruguay. Prices are calculated on a kilometres-flown basis. There is a maximum of two stopovers and four flight coupons for each country, and the pass is valid for seven to thirty days. The pass is available directly from the participating airlines (including Gol, Aerolíneas Argentinas and Austral). You can rebook to change dates (but not reroute); contact the individual airlines for more details. Both LAN (Ⓦ lan.com) and TAM (Ⓦ tam.com .br) also offer their own airpasses for routes they fly.

By train

Trains are much less frequent and efficient than South American buses, but if you have a little time to spare they provide a wonderful way to see the countryside and wildlife, as they tend to travel more exotic routes. Typically they are less expensive than buses, but services in popular tourist areas can be pricey. Two of the most famous routes are from Cusco to the start of the Inca Trail (see p.762) in Peru and the Serra Verde Express (see p.349) between Curitiba and the coast in Brazil. There are several types of train, including the fast and efficient *ferrotren*, stopping at major stations only; the average *tren rápido*; the slower *expreso*, which stops at most stations; and the super-slow and amazingly cheap *mixto*, which stops for everyone – and their livestock too.

By boat

There are several ferry and catamaran services on South America's **lakes**, especially in Chile, Argentina, Peru and Bolivia, providing unforgettable views. Those relevant to a single country are explored in the country chapter but there are two cross-border crossings that are recommended: the Southern Lakes Crossing (see p.444) between Argentina and Chile, and the Lake Titicaca Crossing (p.158) between Bolivia and Peru.

One of the finest ways to soak up the slow pace of South American life is to travel some of the continent's **rivers** by boat. Unfortunately, the riverboat industry is in decline, especially on the Amazon, with more passengers flying and cargo-only replacing many travel boats. However, several riverboat services survive, recommended for anyone with time and patience, particularly on the narrower, less-frequented rivers. Shop around, as boats vary hugely in quality. Your ticket will include hammock space and basic food, but drinks are extra and will probably be expensive on board – it's best to bring your own supplies. You should also bring a hammock, rope, insect repellent and a sleeping bag, and aim to be on board well before departure to ensure that you don't get put right next to the toilets.

By bicycle

If you're fit and hardy enough to consider cycling in South America, there are a few common-sense rules. Given the terrain, a mountain bike is best, unless you stick to paved roads and well-travelled routes. Taking on some of the Andean roads, though, is an experience hard to rival. In adventure travel centres, especially in Argentina and Chile, bikes can be rented for short periods, but if you're doing serious cycling, bring your own. Bikes and bike parts tend to be of a lower quality in South America than in other parts of the world, so give your bike a thorough check before you go. Carry a basic repair kit and check the bike daily when you arrive. Weather can be a problem, especially in Patagonia, where winds can reach 80km/hr, and be aware that bicycle theft – particularly in larger towns – is common; bring a good bike lock. Finally, remember that South American drivers can be a hazard, so try to avoid major roads and motorways if at all possible.

Hitchhiking

Hitchhiking is still fairly common in rural South America, and it isn't hard to get a lift if you're on the road early. Be aware, though, that many drivers now expect to be paid – it's only in the Southern Cone (Argentina, Chile and Uruguay) that hitchhiking seems to be understood to be free. Prices are usually around that of a bus fare, but if you head to the local truck park or refuelling station (most towns have one), ask around for the going rate. Hitchhiking in South America, like anywhere in the world, is a potentially perilous enterprise – travellers should be aware that they do so at their own risk. Couples and groups are safest; women should never hitchhike alone.

Accommodation

The range of accommodation available in South America – and the variety of price and quality that goes with it – is enormous and, should you be leaving on a multi-country tour, you'll find that the US$10 that buys you a night's rest in Ecuador won't even stretch to breakfast in the Southern Cone or French Guiana.

Most local tourist offices will provide a list of available accommodation, but bear in mind that establishments often pay to be included on these lists and that they may include little outside the main tourist hotspots. Generally, tourist boards will not recommend specific accommodation, nor book it.

Usually there is no shortage of places to stay, but use common sense if you plan to be somewhere at the time of a local festival, such as in Rio for Carnaval. Obviously, accommodation fills up quickly at these times, prices skyrocket and it's best to book well in advance. While the types of lodging described below offer an overview of your options in South America, names, classifications and prices vary from country to country. For information regarding the nomenclature in a specific country, check the "Accommodation" section of the relevant chapter. Unless alternatives such as dorms or camping are specified, **prices** quoted for accommodation throughout the Guide are for the **cheapest double room in high season**.

A good resource for budget accommodation in South America is Ⓦ hosteltrail.com.

Hospedajes, residencias, albergues and pensiones

These categories of accommodation are all used throughout South America and are interchangeable terms, although **pensiones** (known as *pensões* or pousadas in Portuguese) and **residenciales** are officially the most basic forms of accommodation. Generally, the Andean countries are the least expensive, and you should be able to find a decent room in a *residencial* or *pensión* for under US$15 (US$8 for dorms). For this price you should expect a bed, shared bathroom and intermittent hot water. In Brazil, the room cost will usually include breakfast but most other places are room only. In the south of Argentina and Chile, you can expect to spend around US$45 a night – check out the quality of the local *casas familiares* (family houses where you stay with a local family in a room in their house), which can be the best value for money in these areas.

Hostales, hosterías and haciendas

Hostales tend to fill the gap between the totally basic *pensión* and hotels, and come in many shapes, sizes and forms. Usually they include private bathrooms and hot water, clean towels and maybe a television, and cost from US$5 to US$20 per night. In the southern countries, though, *hostales* may be youth hostels.

Hosterías and **haciendas** are often old, sprawling estates converted into hotels, and are perhaps the grandest places to stay on the continent. They are often furnished in period style and offer excellent home-cooked meals, fires, hot water and maybe a swimming pool. Be aware that *hostería* can also refer to a family-style hotel complex out of town, so check which kind of *hostería* you're getting first.

Camping

Camping is most popular in the southern region of Latin America, particularly in the Southern Cone areas of Argentina and Chile. It is wise to stick to official sites, which are usually well equipped, with hot, running water, toilets, firepits and maybe even a self-service laundry. Camping is not really a popular or viable option in the northern countries unless as part of an organized tour, and is practically non-existent in Colombia, French Guiana and Paraguay.

ACCOMMODATION ALTERNATIVES

Useful websites that provide alternatives to standard hotel and hostel accommodation:

Craigslist ⓦ craigslist.org
CouchSurfing ⓦ couchsurfing.org
Vacation Rentals by Owner ⓦ vrbo.com
Airbnb ⓦ airbnb.com

Youth hostels

Youth hostels are not always the most viable option in South America, but in the more expensive southern countries like Argentina and Chile, they are a more attractive choice: competition means that many have great facilities and offer extras, from free internet to party nights. Prices average US$10–15 per night and most are open all year, although some only open in January and February for the South American summer. If you are planning on using hostels extensively, consider getting an official **HI card**, which will quickly pay for itself in discounted rates.

HOSTELLING ORGANIZATIONS

Argentina Hostelling International Argentina/Red Argentina de Alojamiento para Jóvenes (RAAJ) ☏ 011 4511 8723, ⓦ hostels.org.ar.
Argentina, Brazil, Chile, Peru and Uruguay Che Lagarto ⓦ chelagarto.com. Argentine chain that now also has hostels in other countries.
Brazil Federação Brasileira dos Albergues de Juventude (FBAJ) ☏ 21 2531 1085, ⓦ hostel.org.br.
Chile Asociación Chilena de Albergues Turísticos Juveniles ☏ 02 577 1200, ⓦ hostelling.cl.
Peru Asociación Peruana de Albergues Turísticos Juveniles, Av Casimiro Ulloa 328, Miraflores, Lima ☏ 01 446 5488, ⓦ limahostell.com.pe.
South America Hostelling International ⓦ hihostels.com. Membership cards and worldwide hostel booking.

Health

The potential health risks in South America read like a textbook of tropical diseases and the possibilities could easily deter nervous travellers before they even set out. But if you prepare for your trip carefully and take sensible precautions while travelling, you will probably face nothing worse than a mild case of "Montezuma's revenge" (traveller's diarrhoea) as your system gets used to foreign germs and unhygienic conditions.

It is important to get the best health advice before you travel – prevention is always better than cure. The Centre for Disease Control (see p.36) is worth consulting on each of the countries you wish to visit. About ten weeks before you travel, **vaccinations** can be arranged with your doctor or a specialized tropical diseases clinic. Bring your vaccination record when you travel. If you are taking any prescription drugs, your doctor can prescribe enough for the time you are away, and you should also take a list with you and a covering letter in case of emergencies. Good **medical insurance** (see p.40) is essential. It is important to declare any pre-existing conditions, and also to ensure that you have sufficient cover for all the extra activities you may undertake (particularly diving, extreme sports and hiking at high altitudes).

A common affliction is **heat stroke**, for which you should seek immediate treatment. Avoid dehydration by drinking bottled water and staying off alcohol, and stay out of the sun at the heat of the day (midday until around 4pm).

Pharmacies abound in every town but bringing a basic first-aid kit is sensible. Essentials in remote areas include insect repellent, bandages, painkillers, anti-diarrhoeal tablets and antiseptic cream.

Bites and stings

The general advice is to use an **insect repellent** containing at least 35 percent DEET, especially in rural areas or where malaria is endemic, and to wear light clothes that cover as much of your body as possible. It is wise to use a mosquito net or a mosquito coil containing permethrin at night, especially in the cheaper hotels.

Venomous **spiders and snakes** exist throughout the continent and bites from these, while rare, merit seeking medical advice as soon as possible. Most responsible tour companies carry antivenin, but in the absence of this, prompt medical attention is the only answer. A photo or description of the offending species may be useful, but never attempt to catch or kill it as this can provoke further bites, and don't listen to so-called local knowledge involving tourniquets, sucking venom or anything else – go to hospital.

If travelling to remote areas, consider a rabies vaccination – this will not make you immune to infection, but will buy you time to seek medical treatment after exposure. The majority of reported cases are from contact with dogs, and licks and scratches can be as dangerous as being bitten. If this happens, wash the area thoroughly with soap and water and disinfect it with alcohol or iodine solution. Always seek medical advice.

ALTITUDE SICKNESS

If you don't take care, altitude sickness, known locally as *soroche*, can seriously affect your trip. The most common symptoms are **headache**, **nausea** and **dizziness**, but when climbing at high altitude (above 2400m), symptoms can lead to more serious conditions such as **HAPE** (high altitude pulmonary oedema) or **HACE** (high altitude cerebral oedema), when medical attention should be sought immediately.

Soroche can affect anyone regardless of physical fitness. The key is to allow a few days to **acclimatize** when you arrive in a high-altitude region. When hiking, ascend slowly and follow the rule "sleep low and hike high" (sleep at a lower altitude than you ascended to that day), which allows your body time to recover. Drink plenty of water and eat light food, including carbs. Avoid alcohol and caffeine and, most importantly, pace yourself. Don't attempt to climb a mountain like Cotopaxi or Chimborazo after just a few days at 2800m in Quito – you need a couple of days above 2500m, then a couple more above 3500m before climbing over 4000m. If you are hiking as part of a tour and not dealing well with the altitude, alert your guide. Better to turn back than risk your health. In the Andean region locals swear by "mate de coca" – coca leaf tea – as a cure.

A much more likely nuisance when visiting wilder areas is the itchy **bites** given by tiny black sand flies or painful bites of ants and ticks. Hairy caterpillars are also capable of giving nasty stings similar to burns.

Mosquito-borne diseases

Malaria prevention is two-fold; in addition to avoiding mosquito bites as detailed above, travellers should be sure to take a prescription anti-malarial drug, typically malarone (usually the best option), chloroquine or doxycycline – consult with a doctor before taking any. These should generally be started several weeks before you travel, and the full course must be completed which means continuing to take them after leaving a malaria zone. Symptoms can occur any time up to a year after travel, so it's important to inform your doctor about your travel history.

Yellow fever is a serious disease carried by mosquitoes, which, like malaria, can be avoided by vaccination and taking sensible precautions against insect bites. It is present in most of South America except the far south. You'll need to show a certificate if travelling from one endemic country to another (although you won't always be asked for it, it's best to have one anyway). The following countries are considered the greatest risk areas: Bolivia, Brazil, Colombia, Ecuador, Peru and Venezuela.

Dengue fever is also mosquito-borne and there is no vaccine. The mosquitoes carrying the virus tend to live near stagnant water so it's more of a problem in poor areas. It has become a serious health issue in Brazil, Bolivia, Paraguay and Argentina, but is present in most countries in South America. Symptoms include high fever and aching limbs. Drink fluids, take paracetamol and seek medical attention immediately.

Intestinal problems

Common illnesses such as traveller's **diarrhoea** can be largely avoided by steps such as washing your hands before eating and drinking bottled water. Unpasteurized dairy products and all un-refrigerated food should be avoided and fruit and vegetables should be washed and peeled. Take care with shellfish, lettuce and ice. If you do fall ill, rest and replace the fluids you have lost by drinking plenty of water and an oral rehydration solution. A homemade option is 1tsp salt and 8tsp of sugar in 1 litre of water. An anti-diarrhoeal tablet can usually alleviate symptoms.

Other than diarrhoea that usually lasts no more than a few days there are a number of more serious problems that you can encounter on your travels. **Cholera**, for example, is an acute infection with watery diarrhoea and vomiting; **dysentery** has similar symptoms but includes bleeding. If your diarrhoea persists for a week and your symptoms include a chill or fever or bleeding, or if you are too ill to drink, seek medical help. Typhoid is also a problem in the poorest, most rural areas and is transferred through food or water. Symptoms include fever, headache and occasionally a bleeding nose or spotty rash. Seek medical advice immediately – the fever can be easily treated with antibiotics but is serious if not caught early.

To avoid problems, always use bottled water, even for cleaning your teeth. Avoid buying food from street vendors unless the food is piping hot, and think carefully about swimming in lakes and rivers. If bottled water isn't available, there are various methods of treating water: boiling for a minimum of five minutes is the most effective method. Filtering alongside chemical sterilization is the next best option. Pregnant women or people with thyroid problems should consult their doctors about chemical sterilization formulae.

MEDICAL RESOURCES FOR TRAVELLERS

Before travelling to South America travellers should seek health advice. Useful websites and major organizations are listed below:

UK AND IRELAND

Fit for Travel Ⓦ www.fitfortravel.nhs.uk. NHS website with information about travel-related diseases and how to avoid them.
MASTA (Medical Advisory Service for Travellers Abroad)
Ⓦ masta-travel-health.com. Comprehensive website for medical advisory services for travel abroad. See website for the nearest clinic.
Tropical Medical Bureau Republic of Ireland, see website for different branches Ⓦ tmb.ie.

US AND CANADA

Canadian Society for International Health Ⓣ 613 241 5785, Ⓦ csih
.org. Distributes a free pamphlet, "Health Information for Canadian Travellers", containing an extensive list of travel health centres in Canada.
Center for Disease Control Ⓣ 1 800 232 6348, Ⓦ cdc.gov/travel. US Department of Health and Human Services travel health and disease control department. Offers comprehensive and up-to-date advice on health for travellers. Publishes outbreak warnings, suggested inoculations, precautions and other background information.
International Society for Travel Medicine Ⓦ istm.org. Has a full list of clinics specializing in international travel health.
Travel Health Online Ⓦ www.tripprep.com. Travel Health Online provides an online comprehensive database of necessary vaccinations for most countries, as well as destination and medical service provider information.

AUSTRALIA AND NEW ZEALAND

Travellers' Medical and Vaccination Centres Ⓦ traveldoctor
.com.au. Contains a list of all Travellers Medical and Vaccination Centres throughout Australia, New Zealand and Southeast Asia, plus general information on travel health.

Culture and etiquette

South America is a vast continent and it's difficult to generalize about how to dress or behave; ultimately, you should try to behave unobtrusively and dress modestly if not at the beach.

Cultural hints

People usually shake hands upon introduction and women generally kiss acquaintances on one cheek or two (dependent on the country), although you can defer to a handshake if you prefer. It is common to wish people you meet on the street "Buenos días" ("bom dia" in Brazil) or "buenas tardes" ("boa tarde" in Brazil). Politeness is a way of life in South America, and pleasantries are always exchanged before getting to any kind of business. Dress with respect in official or religious buildings.

Remember that in most South American countries, locals have a lax attitude to **time**, so expect people to arrive late in social situations and don't get annoyed if they do.

Tipping is generally common in restaurants and cafés but is lower than the norms in Europe and the US. If in doubt, ask a local (and not a waiter!).

Shopping

Shops and markets in South America tend to offer a wide range of beautifully crafted goods and antiques for the visitor. Prices are usually reasonable; you can **bargain** in markets and outside the tourist drags, but only do so if you really think the item is worth less than its asking price. If you decide to buy something, be firm – ask the price and confirm it before offering cash. Be polite to street vendors, no matter how annoyed you get with them. Remember that this is their livelihood and smile, saying "no, gracias" or "não, obrigado". Check that you are not purchasing objects plundered from the jungle or made from endangered species.

As a rule of thumb, native crafts are usually of the best quality and cheapest when bought close to the source. Buying such items, rather than mass-produced alternatives, is a good way to help local *artesania* and give something back to the communities you're visiting.

Public holidays and festivals

Travelling through South America entails negotiating a variety of **public holidays** (*feriados* in Spanish and Portuguese) that differ from country to country. The essential ones are listed in the "Opening hours and public holidays" section of each chapter, but bear in mind that, particularly in more remote areas, some towns and villages celebrate saints' days and other local holidays that shut down businesses and make travel difficult. Check with local tourist information offices (where they exist) for more details. South Americans are not known for passing up an excuse to celebrate; find local festivals in the relevant chapters.

Every country in South America has a take on **Carnival** (known in Spanish and Portuguese as *Carnaval*); the exact time varies, but official celebrations usually take place on the days before Ash Wednesday and Lent. There are national variations, of course: in Ecuador, for instance, the festivities are most visibly represented by the water fights throughout the country. There are a couple of locations where Carnaval has become famous internationally, such as Oruro in Bolivia and Encarnación in Paraguay. The most famous Carnaval of all, however, is in Rio de Janeiro, Brazil. This variegated event lasts for weeks before and after the "official" Carnaval time and is an extravagant mix of dance, sweat, drink, laughter and colour.

South America remains a devoutly Catholic continent, although Argentina and Uruguay are the most secular nations – expect lots of festivals around Semana Santa (Holy Week in Easter). Show respect and dress modestly when entering a church or religious site.

Work and study

Opportunities for volunteer and non-profit work abound, but be prepared to pay something towards your upkeep. Paid opportunities are few and far between, and some are likely to be illegal.

Teaching English

Qualified English teachers with a CELTA, TEFL or TESOL should be able to find work, but you are strongly advised to arrange a placement before you travel. Qualified schoolteachers from English-speaking countries can also find teaching opportunities, and if you have a Master's degree, you can teach at university. However, turning up and looking for work is likely to leave you frustrated and/or violating local laws – officially you will require a work permit. The British Council (Ⓦbritishcouncil.org) and the TEFL website (Ⓦtefl.com) each has a list of English-teaching vacancies. Most jobs are in the larger cities.

Language study

South America has long been a hugely popular destination for people wishing to brush up on their **Spanish**: Cusco, Peru; Buenos Aires, Argentina; Sucre, Bolivia; and Quito, Ecuador are the most popular destinations and a huge variety of courses and levels is available. In Brazil, most of the large cities are great locations for learning **Portuguese**. You can also learn **indigenous languages** such as Quechua in Bolivia

or Guaraní in Paraguay. Typically, three types of course are on offer: a classroom-based course, a more active learning course through activities and excursions, or the live-in option with a host family.

LANGUAGE SCHOOLS

Academía Latinoamericana de Espanol Ⓣ 1 801 268 2468 (US), Ⓦwww.latinoschools.com. Spanish classes in Ecuador, Peru and Bolivia.
Amerispan Ⓣ 1 800 511 0179 (US), Ⓦ amerispan.com. Spanish courses and volunteer opportunities.
Apple Languages Ⓣ 703 835 9762 (US), Ⓣ 01509 211612 (UK), Ⓦ applelanguages.com. High-quality Spanish schools throughout South America.
Bridge Linguatec Ⓦ bridge.edu. Spanish and Portuguese classes in Argentina, Chile and Brazil.
Don Quijote Ⓦ donquijote.org. High-quality, internationally recognized courses offered in Argentina, Bolivia, Chile, Ecuador and Peru.
Escuela Runawasi Ⓣ 04 424 8923 (Bolivia), Ⓦ runawasi.org. Quechua, Aymara and Spanish-language and literature lessons in Cochabamba, Bolivia.
Latin Immersion Ⓦ latinimmersion.com. Spanish immersion courses throughout the continent.
Simón Bolívar Spanish School Ⓣ 07 284 4555 (Ecuador), Ⓦ bolivar2.com. Based in Cuenca, Ecuador, with courses based on a study of the country.
Spanish Study Holidays Ⓣ 01509 211612 (UK), Ⓦ www.spanishstudyholidays.com. Courses from one week to nine months.

Volunteering

Volunteer opportunities are available in social, environmental and conservation work in many South American countries, though you will be expected to pay for the privilege. Working alongside local people on a worthwhile project that captures your interest can be an unforgettable experience.

VOLUNTEER ORGANIZATIONS

While many positions are organized prior to arrival, it's also possible to pick something up on the ground through word of mouth. Noticeboards in the more popular backpacker hostels are always good sources of information.
Earthwatch Institute Offices worldwide, Ⓦ earthwatch.org. Long-established research company offering environmental and social volunteer programmes throughout the continent.
Global Volunteer Network Ⓣ 0800 032 5035 (UK), Ⓦ globalvolunteernetwork.org. Volunteer opportunities in eight different community projects in Peru.
i to i Volunteering Ⓣ 0800 011 1156 (UK), Ⓦ i-to-i.com. Offers everything from conservation work in the Galápagos Islands to archeology work in Lima, Peru.
Projects Abroad Ⓣ 01903 708 300 (UK), Ⓦ projects-abroad.co.uk. Teaching, conservation and community projects throughout South America.

Crime and personal safety

South America is a continent that suffers from high levels of poverty. This tends to go hand in hand with crime levels, which, while much magnified by tales in the foreign news media, shouldn't be ignored.

In general, cities are more dangerous than rural areas, although the very deserted mountain plains can harbour bandits. Many of the working-class *barrios* of big cities are "no-go" areas for tourists, as are the marginal areas near them. One of the biggest problems in urban areas is **theft**, and bag snatching, handbag slitting and occasional armed robbery are problems in cities such as Buenos Aires, Lima, Rio, Salvador, Recife, Georgetown, Quito and Cusco. Caracas has also experienced an upsurge in violent crime in the last few years, so extra precaution is recommended there.

Take particular care on the street, in taxis and in restaurants. Any unsolicited approach from a stranger should be treated with the utmost suspicion, no matter how well dressed or trustworthy they may look. There are obvious preventative measures you can take to avoid being mugged: avoid isolated and poorly lit areas, especially at night; never walk along a beach alone at night, or even in a pair if female.

Keep a particular eye out in busy areas and watch out on public transport and at bus stations, where **pickpocketing** is rife. If travelling by bus, keep your valuables in your carry-on luggage rather than stowing them below with your backpack. Make sure that you are given the numbered receipt corresponding to your bag. If you need to hail a taxi, get someone at your hotel to recommend one, or hail a moving one – never get into a "taxi" that just happens to be parked at the kerbside or which has two drivers. Avoid wearing expensive jewellery and watches, dress down, and keep cameras out of sight.

Car-jackings can also be a problem, particularly in certain areas of Brazil. When driving in the city, keep doors locked and windows closed, particularly at night, and be especially vigilant at traffic lights. Kidnapping of tourists in South America is extremely unlikely.

Drugs

Just say no! In South America **drug trafficking** is a huge, ugly and complicated enterprise, and large-scale dealers love to prey on lost-looking foreigners. Don't let anyone else touch your luggage, be sure to pack it yourself and don't carry anything – no matter how innocuous it may seem – for anyone else. You will find that drugs, particularly marijuana and cocaine, are fairly ubiquitous in the region, but you should be aware that they are illegal and that punishments are severe. Tourists are likely to come off much worse than locals at the hands of the South American police, something of which the dealers and pushers are very aware. If you happen to visit a region famed for drug trafficking, stay well away from anything that looks (or smells) like trouble.

The only **legal high** on sale in South America is the leaves of coca (locals will be keen to point out it has nothing to do with chemically produced cocaine), which are particularly popular in Bolivia and Peru. They are usually used to make *mate de coca*, a hugely popular tea in the Andes, and one that's claimed to cure altitude sickness (among other things). Some people chew the leaves as this is meant to produce a mildly intoxicating state, but the taste and texture may well convince you that you can do without the alleged high. If you want to try *mate de coca* or chewing on coca leaves, be aware that there is a possibility that you could test positive for cocaine use in the weeks following your trip.

Reporting crime

In case you are mugged or robbed, you should make sure that you have a photocopy of your passport and plane tickets in a safe place. Call the local police immediately and tell them what happened. It's likely that they won't do much more than take a statement, but you'll need it for insurance purposes. In some South American countries there is a special "tourist police" force, used to dealing with foreigners and, hopefully, able to speak English.

Women travellers

Though violent attacks against women travellers are not very common, many women find that the barrage of hisses, hoots and comments in parts of South America comes close to spoiling their trip. Latin American men are not renowned for their forward-thinking attitudes towards women's emancipation, and genuinely see nothing wrong with the heady sense of machismo that rules much of the continent. You may find that attitudes are less polarized in country areas.

There are measures you can take to avoid being hassled. Don't go to bars or nightclubs alone – this is an activity only undertaken by prostitutes in the region, and you will be considered fair game. If you are approached and feel uncomfortable, try to avoid antagonizing the guy, but make it clear that you're not interested (in Spanish "no estoy interesada" or "não estou interessada" in Portuguese). It's sometimes easier to invent a boyfriend or husband than to get into a protracted dispute. Watch how the local women behave and where they go, and never be afraid to ask for help if you feel lost or threatened.

Solo women travellers should also avoid going to remote locations alone, and if you go as part of an organized visit, check the credentials of the tour company. There are emergency numbers given in individual chapters of this book. However, if you are attacked, you should not only get medical attention and go to the regular police, but also contact the tourist police and your country's embassy.

Travel essentials

Costs

South America is not as cheap as it used to be, but, if approached in the right way, you can still travel for less here than you would on other continents. French Guiana, Suriname, Argentina, Chile and Brazil are the most expensive countries, with prices often comparable to North America, Europe and Australia. Bolivia, Peru and Ecuador still remain budget destinations but the highlights such as the Galápagos Islands, the Amazon jungle and mountain climbing can add a lot of expense to the trip.

Electricity

The standard electrical current in most South American countries is 220V, 50/60Hz. The main exceptions are Colombia, Ecuador and Venezuela, where a 110/120V, 50/60Hz current is used, and Suriname, where 127V is standard. Some major tourist cities also use a 110V, 50Hz current, at odds with the rest of their country, including La Paz and Potosí in Bolivia

---

> ### PRICES
>
> At the beginning of each country chapter you'll find a guide to "**rough costs**", including food, accommodation and travel. These costs are quoted in US$ to make comparison easy: within the chapter itself prices are quoted in local currency. Note that prices and exchange rates change all the time, which may affect the accuracy of those figures we have quoted.

---

and Rio de Janeiro and São Paulo in Brazil. For the most part **plug sockets** are flat two-pin (as in the US), but three-pin sockets are sometimes found. Your best bet if visiting several countries is to travel with a universal adaptor and make sure you check appliances' compatibility before plugging them in to South American sockets.

The South American attitude to safety may be a little more lax than you are used to, and it is not unusual to see plugs that obviously don't fit, forcibly pushed into sockets. Take particular care with electrical showers, common in the poorer countries.

Gay and lesbian travellers

Rural, Catholic South America is not overly welcoming towards homosexuality but there is more acceptance in urban areas. Gay and lesbian travellers would probably be safest following locals' example – public displays of affection between two men or two women could invite trouble on much of the continent.

Things are generally easier in the big cities, though, and there are a couple of major destinations where anything goes. Brazil boasts most of them – Rio de Janeiro, Salvador and São Paulo provide safe and welcoming havens for any sexual orientation, as do Buenos Aires and Santiago. If you are looking for thumping nightlife and a very "out" scene, then these cities are the best on the continent.

BUDGET TIPS
- Take local transport, which means buses and *colectivos* instead of taxis or tourist shuttles.
- Avoid the most touristy destinations. Get off the beaten track and you'll notice the price difference.
- Eat and drink as the locals do. Eat street food from popular vendors and in restaurants choose local staples over the tourist menu. Buy from stores and markets as opposed to hostels or hotels.
- You can make big savings on bottled water, which many hostels will refill for free or a small fee.
- Be prepared to barter – bargaining can be fun. Don't be afraid to confront taxi drivers or chancers who you suspect are trying to rip you off. However, don't be too ruthless – bargaining over a few cents is not cool.

ROUGH GUIDES TRAVEL INSURANCE

Rough Guides has teamed up with Worldnomads.com to offer great **travel insurance** deals. Policies are available to residents of over 150 countries, with cover for a wide range of **adventure sports**, 24hr emergency assistance, high levels of medical and evacuation cover and a stream of **travel safety information**. roughguides.com users can take advantage of their policies online 24/7, from anywhere in the world – even if you're already travelling. And since plans often change when you're on the road, you can extend your policy and even claim online. roughguides.com users who buy travel insurance with Worldnomads.com can also leave a positive footprint and donate to a community development project. For more information go to ⓦ**roughguides.com/travel-insurance**.

Insurance

A typical **travel insurance policy** provides cover for the loss of baggage, tickets and – up to a certain limit – cash, as well as cancellation or curtailment of your journey. Most of them exclude so-called dangerous sports unless an extra premium is paid: this category can include scuba diving, white-water rafting, windsurfing and trekking, though probably not kayaking or jeep safaris. Many policies can be changed to exclude coverage you don't need. If you take medical coverage, ascertain whether benefits will be paid as treatment proceeds or only after your return home, and whether there is a 24-hour medical emergency number. When securing baggage cover, make sure that the per-article limit will cover your most valuable possession. If you need to make a claim, you should keep receipts for medicines and medical treatment and, in the event you have anything stolen, you must obtain an official statement from the police.

Internet

Internet access is now almost ubiquitous in cities and towns across South America (though it is more restricted in the Guianas) and only in rural areas is it difficult to come by. Connection speeds and costs vary from country to country, and in some cases from area to area. Wi-fi is now increasingly common in hostels and hotels, but also in cafés and restaurants (especially in the Southern Cone).

Mail

Post offices in cities and major towns offer a wide range of services; those in villages are much more basic, with shorter opening hours and slow service. It's often quicker and safer to use a courier service – although you'll pay much more. Hotels in capital cities may sell stamps and have a postbox – if you are staying in one, this can be the most convenient way to send a letter home. Expect airmail to take from a week to a month to Western Europe and the US.

Maps

Excellent maps of South America, covering the region at a scale of 1:5,000,000, are produced by Canada's International Travel Maps and Books (ⓦitmb.com). They also publish individual country and regional maps. Once in South America the South America Explorers Club (ⓦsaexplorers.org) is a good point of reference, and often the only source of accurate maps is the military – check at the local tourist offices on where to purchase them. If you'd rather be safe than sorry, buy maps at home and bring them with you.

Money

ATMs are widely available in most large cities, but in smaller towns and rural areas don't expect to rely solely on using international debit cards to access funds. Travellers' cheques are much less widely accepted than they once were, and you'll often get a fixed exchange rate: pre-paid **currency cards** are an excellent alternative, though these, too, require access to an ATM. There is still nothing as easy to use as cash, preferably US dollars, and it makes sense always to carry at least a few small-denomination notes for when all else fails.

Credit card fraud is a problem on the continent, particularly in Brazil and Venezuela; be sure to keep an eye on your card and to retain your copy of the transaction slip. In many countries credit cards will only be accepted in the biggest hotels and shops, and banks will sometimes refuse to offer cash advances against them. Payments in plastic may also incur high surcharges when compared to cash payments.

When **exchanging money**, you should use only authorized bureaux de change, such as banks, cambios and tourist facilities, rather than deal with moneychangers on the streets. For details on each country, consult the "Money and banks" section at the beginning of each chapter. In remote and rural areas, and for shopping in local markets and stalls,

cash is a necessity – preferably in small denominations of local currency. Some countries, including Venezuela and Argentina, having a flourishing black market, which should be approached with caution.

Phones

The mobile phone is causing **public phone boxes** to disappear in many South American countries. Where phone boxes exist, they usually operate with cards, available from newspaper kiosks. There are, however, plenty of *locutorios*, stores originally dedicated to telephone communications, most of which have now branched out into internet access as well. You can make direct-dial international calls from most South American phones, apart from remote areas, where calls must be made through an operator. International phone calls are, in general, expensive from South America, so you're best off trying to buy international calling cards where they exist or using web services such as Skype – most internet cafés will be set up with webcams and headsets.

Mobile phones

If you want to use your **mobile phone** in South America, you'll need to check with your phone provider whether it will work abroad, and what the call charges are (beware of amassing a fortune in data charges and use wi-fi wherever possible). Generally speaking, UK, Australian and New Zealand mobiles should work fine in South America (but double-check the band-width compatibility especially if you have an old model). However, with US mobiles only tri-band models are likely to work outside the States.

You are likely to be charged extra for incoming calls when abroad, as the people calling you will be paying the usual rate. If you're in the country for a while, and assuming your phone is unlocked (most contract phones are locked so that they can only be used on one network – your provider can usually unlock it for a fee), you can buy a **SIM card** from a local telephone company and use it in your phone. These are usually pretty cheap and your calls will be charged at a local rate. If you don't have a mobile phone and are staying a few months in one country, consider buying a local phone, easily done for less than US$50.

Tourist information

The quantity and quality of tourist information varies from country to country, but in general, don't expect too much. While almost every city in Brazil and Argentina will have at least one well-equipped

CALLING FROM ABROAD

To phone abroad, you must first dial the international access code of the country you are calling from, then the country code of the country you are calling to, then the area code (usually without the first zero) and then the phone number. In some South American countries there may be different international access codes for different providers. See below for details.

INTERNATIONAL ACCESS CODES WHEN DIALLING FROM:
Argentina ✆00
Australia ✆0011
Bolivia ✆0010 (Entel), ✆0011 (AES), ✆0012 (Teledata), ✆0013 (Boliviatel)
Brazil ✆0014 (Brasil Telecom), ✆0015 (Telefónica), ✆0021 (Embratel), ✆0023 (Intelig), ✆0031 (Telemar)
Canada ✆011
Chile ✆00
Colombia ✆009 (Telecom), ✆007 (ETB/Mundo), ✆005 (Orbitel)
Ecuador ✆00
French Guiana ✆00
Guyana ✆001
Ireland ✆00
New Zealand ✆00
Paraguay ✆002
Peru ✆00
Suriname ✆002
UK ✆00
Uruguay ✆00
US ✆011
Venezuela ✆00

COUNTRY CODES WHEN DIALLING TO:
Argentina ✆54
Australia ✆61
Bolivia ✆591
Brazil ✆55
Canada ✆1
Chile ✆56
Colombia ✆57
Ecuador ✆593
French Guiana ✆594
Guyana ✆592
Ireland ✆353
New Zealand ✆64
Paraguay ✆595
Peru ✆51
Suriname ✆597
UK ✆44
Uruguay ✆598
US ✆1
Venezuela ✆58

TIME ZONES

Most of South America is spread across only two time zones, with the outlying islands spread across five:

GMT–6: Galápagos Islands and Easter Island

GMT–5: Colombia, Ecuador and Peru

GMT–4.5: Venezuela (a new time zone created by former president Chávez in 2007)

GMT–4: Chile, Bolivia, Guyana, Paraguay, western Brazil and the Falklands

GMT–3: Argentina, Uruguay, French Guiana, Suriname and most of Brazil

GMT–2: Fernando de Noronha (Brazil) and South Georgia

tourist office, they are much thinner on the ground in countries like Paraguay and the Guianas. You should make the most of any operational office you find there. Fortunately, there is a lot of information about South America on the internet that will help you plan your trip and answer questions about history, language and current events. We've listed websites wherever pertinent throughout the guide; the following is a general list of places to begin your research.

SOUTH AMERICA ON THE INTERNET

W **2backpackers.com** Quirky blog from a travel-addicted couple who have journeyed extensively across South America (and pretty much everywhere else).

W **buenosairesherald.com** English-language newspaper, updated weekly.

W **clarin.com** The largest Spanish-language daily newspaper on the continent, printed in Buenos Aires.

W **cotal.org.ar** Confederation of Latin American Tourist Organizations.

W **lapress.org** Non-profit news organization based in Lima, producing independent news and analysis.

W **latinnews.com** Real-time news feed with major stories from all over South America in English.

W **zonalatina.com/ZImusic** Excellent directory of regional music links and information, covering everything from Mariachi and Sertaneja to Shakira.

W **planeta.com** Excellent selection of online ecotravel and ecotourism resources for South America.

W **roughguides.com** Travel articles, apps and guides covering the whole of South America.

W **saexplorers.org** The website of the South American Explorers Club, a non-profit organization with the latest research, travel and adventure information.

Travellers with disabilities

South America is not the friendliest of destinations for travellers with disabilities and many places are downright inaccessible. The more modern the society, the more likely you are to find services for physically challenged travellers – this means that while Bolivia and Paraguay are pretty impenetrable, much of inhabited Chile and Argentina, as well as several cities in Brazil, is more accessible. Unfortunately, though, you may need to compromise over destination – big hotels in major cities that are very much on the tourist trail are much more likely to have facilities to cater to your needs than idyllic cabañas in the middle of nowhere. You might be limited as regards mobility, too, as local buses will probably prove difficult and you might need to settle for taxi services or internal flights. In any case, check with one of the agencies below before planning anything.

Access Travel UK ☎ 01942 888 844, W access-travel.co.uk. Small tour operator that can arrange flights, transfers and accommodation. Personally checks out places and can guarantee accommodation standards in many countries – for places they do not cover, they can arrange flight-only deals.

Directions Unlimited US & Canada ☎ 1 800 533 5343, W www.empressusa.com. Tour operator specializing in custom tours for people with disabilities.

National Disability Services (NDS) Australia ☎ 02 6283 3200, W nds.org.au. Can supply lists of travel agencies and tour operators for people with disabilities.

YOUTH AND STUDENT DISCOUNTS

Various official and quasi-official youth/student ID cards are available and are worth the effort to obtain: they soon pay for themselves in savings. Full-time students are eligible for the **International Student ID Card** (ISIC; W isiccard.com), which entitles the bearer (any student no matter their age) to special air, rail and bus fares and discounts at museums, theatres and other attractions. For Americans, there's also a health benefit, providing up to US$300,000 in emergency medical, plus a 24hr hotline (☎ 1 800 353 1972) to call in.

You have to be 26 or younger to qualify for the International Youth Travel Card, which carries the same benefits. Teachers qualify for the International Teacher Card, offering similar discounts. All these cards are available from student travel specialists including STA (see p.31).

PARQUE NACIONAL LOS GLACIARES, PATAGONIA

Argentina

HIGHLIGHTS

❶ Buenos Aires Tango and football rule in this European-style capital. **See p.54**

❷ Iguazú Falls The world's largest waterfalls are framed by lush, subtropical jungle. **See p.88**

❸ Salta This beautifully preserved colonial city is surrounded by epic mountain scenery. **See p.89**

❹ Bariloche An outdoor adventure hub with stunning mountain vistas. **See p.117**

❺ Glaciar Perito Moreno A frozen lansdscape that splinters and creaks. **See p.142**

❻ Ushuaia The end of the Earth and just 1000km from Antarctica. **See p.144**

HIGHLIGHTS ARE MARKED ON THE MAP ON P.45

ROUGH COSTS

Daily budget Basic US$50, occasional treat US$80

Drink Beer (1ltr) US$4 (shop) US$7 (bar/restaurant)

Food *Asado* beef US$15

Camping/hostel/budget hotel US$10/15/40

Travel Bus/airfare from Buenos Aires to Córdoba US$70/160

FACT FILE

Population 40 million

Official language Spanish

Currency Argentine peso (AR$)

Capital Buenos Aires

International phone code ❼ 54

Time zone GMT -3hr

1

Introduction

Even without the titanic wedge of Antarctica that its cartographers include in the national territory, Argentina ranks as the world's eighth-largest country. Stretching from the Tropic of Capricorn to the most southerly reaches of the planet's landmass, it encompasses a staggering diversity of climates and landscapes: from hot and humid jungles in the northeast and bone-dry Andean plateaux in the northwest, through endless grasslands, to the windswept steppe of Patagonia and the end-of-the-world archipelago of Tierra del Fuego.

A country influenced by generations of immigration from Europe and elsewhere, Argentina offers a variety of attractions, not least the great spectacles of tango and football in the seductive European-style capital **Buenos Aires**. Moreover, the extent and diversity of the country's natural scenery are staggering. Due north of the capital stretches **El Litoral**, a subtropical region of riverine landscapes featuring the awe-inspiring **Iguazú** waterfalls. Highlights of the northwest are the spectacular, polychrome **Quebrada de Humahuaca** gorge and the **Valles Calchaquíes**, stunningly beautiful valleys where high-altitude vineyards produce the delightfully flowery *torrontés* wine.

West and immediately south of Buenos Aires are the seemingly endless grassy plains of the **Pampas**. This is where you'll still glimpse traces of traditional **gaucho** culture, most famously celebrated in **San Antonio de Areco**. Here, too, you'll find some of the country's best *estancias*. As you move west, the **Central Sierras** loom on the horizon: within reach of **Córdoba**, the country's vibrant second city, are some of the oldest resorts on the continent. In the lee of the Andes, the vibrant city of **Mendoza** is the country's wine capital, from where the scenic Alta Montaña route climbs steeply to the Chilean border, passing **Cerro Aconcagua**, the highest mountain in the Americas and a dream challenge for mountaineers from around the world.

To the north of Mendoza, San Juan and La Rioja provinces are relatively uncharted territory but their star attractions are

Parque Nacional Talampaya, with its giant red cliffs, and the nearby **Parque Provincial Ischigualasto**, usually known as Valle de la Luna on account of its intriguing, moon-like landscapes.

Argentina claims the lion's share of the sparsely populated expanses of **Patagonia**, one of the world's biggest deserts, and the frigid isles of **Tierra del Fuego**. An almost unbroken chain of national parks hugs the mountains, making for some of the best trekking anywhere on the planet – certainly include the savage granite peaks of the **Parque Nacional Los Glaciares** in your itinerary. For wildlife enthusiasts the **Peninsula Valdés** is also essential viewing, famous above all else as a breeding ground for southern right whales.

CHRONOLOGY

1516 The first Europeans reach the Río de la Plata and clash with Querandí natives.

1535 Pedro de Mendoza founds Buenos Aires.

1609 The first missions to the Guaraní people are established in the upper Paraná.

1806 The British storm Buenos Aires, only to be expelled within a few months.

1810 The first elected junta is sworn in to replace Spanish leaders.

1816 Independence is officially declared in the city of Tucumán.

1854 The country's first railways are built.

1912 Universal male suffrage is introduced.

1930 Radical Hipólito Yrigoyen is overthrown in a military coup.

1943 A coup led by Juan Domingo Perón results in the ousting of the constitutional government.

1946 Juan Domingo Perón is elected president.

1952 Perón's wife Evita dies at the age of 33.

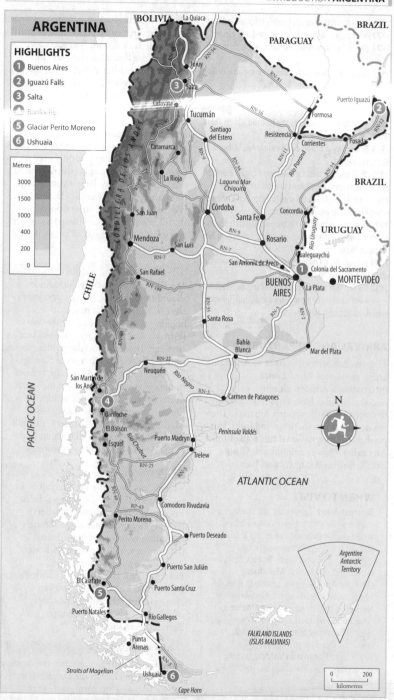

ARGENTINA

HIGHLIGHTS

1. Buenos Aires
2. Iguazú Falls
3. Salta
4. Bariloche
5. Glaciar Perito Moreno
6. Ushuaia

Metres
3000
1500
1000
400
200
0

1

1955 Perón is overthrown in a military coup and exiled.

1973 Perón returns from exile in Spain and is re-elected.

1974 Perón dies and power defaults to his third wife "Isabelita".

1976 Videla leads a military coup against Isabel Perón, marking the beginning of the "Dirty War".

1978 Argentina hosts, and wins, the FIFA World Cup in the middle of a military dictatorship.

1982 A military force invades the Falkland Islands (Islas Malvinas) and is defeated by the British.

1983 Democracy is restored and radical Raúl Alfonsín is elected president.

1989 Neoliberal Peronist Carlos Menem begins a decade as president during which most services are privatized.

2001 President De la Rúa is forced to resign in the midst of economic collapse and violent rioting.

2008 Cristina Fernández de Kirchner is inaugurated as the country's first elected female president, succeeding her husband, Néstor.

2010 The country celebrates two centuries of nationhood with parades and other festivities.

2012 The first year of the second term of Cristina Fernández as president is marred by corruption scandals, rising inflation, mass demonstrations and urban riots.

ARRIVAL AND DEPARTURE

The vast majority of visitors to Argentina arrive at Buenos Aires' **Ezeiza International Airport**, although other major cities also have flight connections to countries within South America. There are no direct international **rail** links, but a plethora of **international bus routes** links Argentina with its neighbours: Chile, Brazil, Bolivia, Uruguay and Paraguay.

> ### WHEN TO VISIT
>
> **Buenos Aires** is probably at its best during spring (October and November), when purple jacaranda trees are in bloom all over the city and the weather is typically sunny and warm. For spectacular autumnal colours, visit **Mendoza** between April and May, or else in early March to witness its international harvest festival. Unless heading to **Bariloche** to ski, Patagonia is best avoided in the depths of winter. Instead, plan a visit between October and April, but if heading to **Peninsula Valdés**, be sure not to miss the whale season, at its peak in early November.

FROM BOLIVIA

There are three entry points into Argentina from Bolivia: Villazón, Bermejo and Yacuiba. You'll need to complete the requisite formalities at Bolivia's migration and customs office on the border and then register on the Argentina side.

FROM BRAZIL

Most people crossing from Brazil to Argentina do so at Foz do Iguaçu. If you're just going for the day you only need to get your passport stamped on the Argentine side, but if going for longer you must pass through both controls. The bus that takes you across the border stops at the Brazilian and Argentine passport controls and waits for passengers to get their passports stamped.

FROM CHILE

Travellers crossing via the high Andes should note that the passes sometimes close in winter. In the north, advance booking is recommended for the San Pedro de Atacama–Jujuy and Salta bus crossing. The most popular border crossing from Chile to Argentina is the Santiago–Mendoza route via the Los Libertadores tunnel. If you're coming from the south, routes in the Lake District include Osorno–Bariloche, and Temuco–San Martín de Los Andes. Further south still are the Puerto Natales–El Calafate and Punta Arenas–Río Gallegos crossings.

FROM PARAGUAY

Visitors can cross the Paraguayan border into Posadas (Argentina) from Encarnación (Paraguay). Travellers crossing here will have to go through migration control at both sides of the border, which are open 24 hours. Another popular option is the Puerto Falcón (Paraguay) to Clorinda (Argentina) crossing, but you can also cross into the Argentine cities of Formosa, Pocitos, Corrientes, Barranqueras and Iguazú.

FROM URUGUAY

From Colonia del Sacramento, the crossing is easy and quick with the Buquebus ferry service (⏷buquebus.com), with a fast service taking an hour and the slower but cheaper service three hours. Otherwise opt for the more scenic route with Cacciola Viajes (ⓦcacciolaviajes.com) from Carmelo to Tigre. If travelling by car, you can cross the border in Fray Bentos further north.

VISAS

Citizens of the EU, US, Canada, South Africa, Australia and New Zealand do not require **visas**, though Argentina charges reciprocal entry fees for nationals of countries that charge Argentine citizens to enter: the US, Canada and Australia are subject to **one-off arrival fees** that need to be paid in advance at ⓦprovinciapagos.com.ar/dnm. Note this fee only applies if you enter Argentina at either of the Buenos Aires airports on an international flight; no fees are payable if you enter via one of the land borders. Tourists are routinely granted ninety-day entry permits – the easiest way to renew your tourist visa is to cross the border into one of the neighbouring countries.

GETTING AROUND

Argentina is a huge country and you are likely to spend a considerable proportion of your budget on travel. Air travel is relatively expensive – and tourists also get charged a much higher rate than local residents – so most people travel by bus (though that is increasingly pricey, too). Car rental is useful in places, but too expensive for most budget travellers, unless they can share the cost. Extra fees are charged for drivers under 25.

BY AIR

Argentina's most important domestic airport by far is Buenos Aires' **Aeroparque Jorge Newbery**. There are connections (with Aerolíneas Argentinas, LAN and LADE) to most provincial capitals and major tourist centres; Andes serves Puerto Madryn and Salta among other destinations. Some cut-price deals booked in advance can work out to be not much more than the bus. One of the best deals is the "Visit Argentina" **airpass** sold by Aerolíneas Argentinas and valid for domestic flights on Aerolíneas and its subsidiary, Austral, covering more than thirty destinations. This pass must be bought abroad; it is not sold in Argentina.

Many smaller airports are not served by public transport, though some airline companies run shuttle services to connect with flights; otherwise, you're stuck with taxis. When leaving the airports of El Calafate, Trelew and Ushuaia you must pay the airport tax (US$38) after checking in.

BY BUS

There are hundreds of private **bus** companies, most of which concentrate on one particular region, although a few, such as TAC, operate pretty much nationwide. Most buses are modern, plush models designed for long-distance travel, and your biggest worry will be what video the driver or conductor has chosen. On longer journeys, snacks and even hot meals are served (included in the ticket price), although these vary considerably in quality. The more luxurious services are usually worth the extra money for long night-rides; some even have waiters. *Coche cama* services have wide, reclinable seats, and *semi-cama* services are not far behind in terms of comfort. Most companies also offer *cama suite* or *cama ejecutivo* services, which have completely reclinable seats and often include an on-board meal.

Buying **tickets** is normally a simple on-the-spot matter, but you must plan in advance if travelling in peak summer season (mid-Dec to Feb), especially if you're taking a long-distance bus from Buenos Aires or any other major city to a particularly popular holiday destination. If in Buenos Aires look for kiosks advertising *venta de pasajes* – these are authorized ticket sellers and will save you having to visit the cavernous Retiro terminal before you leave.

BY CAR

You are unlikely to want or need a car for your whole stay in Argentina, but you'll find one useful if you hope to explore some of the more isolated areas of Patagonia, Tierra del Fuego, the Northwest, and Mendoza and San Juan provinces.

1

To **rent a car**, you need to be over 21 (25 with some agencies); most foreign licences are accepted for tourists. Bring your passport as well as a credit card for the deposit. Before you drive off, check that you've been given insurance, tax and ownership papers. Check too for dents and paintwork damage, and get hold of a 24-hour emergency telephone number. Also, pay close attention to the small print, most notably what you're liable for in the event of an accident: excess normally doesn't cover you for the first AR$5000 or so, and you may not be covered for windscreens, headlights, tyres and more – all vulnerable on unsurfaced roads. Look for unlimited mileage deals, as the per-kilometre charge can otherwise exceed your daily rental cost many times over given the vast distance you're likely to be covering.

BY TRAIN

Argentina's **rail** network, developed with British investment from the late nineteenth century, collapsed in the 1990s with the withdrawal of government subsidies. The few remaining services are generally unsavoury, running on routes that are of limited use for visitors. However, the country's famous **tourist trains**, where the aim is simply to travel for the sheer fun of it, are a major attraction. There are two principal stars: *La Trochita*, the Old Patagonian Express from Esquel; and the *Tren a los Nubes* (April–Nov only), one of the highest railways in the world, which climbs through the mountains from Salta towards the Chilean border.

ACCOMMODATION

You can often tell by a hotel's **name** what kind of place to expect: the use of the term posada for example usually suggests a slightly rustic feel, but generally comfortable or even luxurious. In a similar vein, *hostería* is often used for smallish, high-end hotels – oriented towards the tourist rather than the businessperson. *Hostal* is sometimes used too – but doesn't refer reliably to anything – there are youth hostels called *hostales* as well as high-rise modern hotels.

Residenciales and *hospedajes* are basically simple hotel-style accommodation. Most are reasonably clean and comfortable and a few of them stand out as some of Argentina's best budget accommodation.

A very different experience from staying in a hotel is provided by Argentina's *estancias*, as the country's large ranches are called. **Estancia** accommodation is generally luxurious, and with a lot more character than hotels of a similar price; for around US$250 per person a day you are provided with all meals, invariably including a traditional *asado* or barbecue. At working *estancias* you will have the chance to observe or join in ranch activities such as cattle herding and branding, while almost all of them include activities such as horseriding and swimming in the price. To book *estancia* accommodation, either approach individual establishments directly (they're recommended throughout the text) or try one of the two specialist agencies in Buenos Aires: Comarcas, Laprida 1380 (☎011 4821 1876, ⓦcomarcas.com.ar), and Estancias Argentinas, Diagonal Roque Sáenz Peña 616, 9th Floor (☎011 4343 2366, ⓦestanciasargentinas.com).

HOSTELS AND CAMPSITES

Youth hostels are known as *albergues juveniles*, *albergues de la juventud* or simply *hosteles* in Argentina (you might wish to avoid *albergues transitorios* or motels, which are places that rent rooms to couples by the hour). Accommodation is generally in dormitories, though most places also have one or two double rooms, which are often excellent value. Facilities vary from next to nothing to internet access, washing machines, cable TV and patios with barbecue facilities.

There are plenty of **campsites** (*campings*) – most towns and villages having their own municipal site – but standards vary wildly. At the major resorts, there are usually privately owned, well-organized sites, with facilities ranging from provisions stores to volleyball courts and TV rooms. In less touristy towns, municipal sites can be rather desolate and not particularly secure: it's a good idea to check with locals before pitching your tent.

1

FOOD AND DRINK

Traditionally, Argentine food could be summed up in a single word: **beef**. Not just any beef, but succulent, cherry-red, healthy meat raised on some of the greenest, most extensive pastures known to cattle. The **barbecue** or *asado* remains a national institution, but it's not the whole story.

An *asado* is prepared on a **parrilla** (grill), and this national dish is served everywhere, at restaurants also known as *parrillas*. Usually there's a set menu, but the establishments themselves vary enormously. Traditionally, you start off by eating the offal before moving on to the choicer cuts, but you can choose to head straight for the steaks and fillets. The lightly salted meat is usually served with nothing on it, other than the traditional condiments of *chimichurri* – olive oil with salt, garlic, chilli pepper, vinegar and bayleaf – and *salsa criolla*, similar but with chopped onion, tomato and red pepper added.

Alongside the *parrilla*, pizza and pasta are the mainstays of Argentine cuisine, a reflection of the country's important Italian heritage. Those staying in Argentina for a while may get frustrated by the lack of menu choices, particularly in rustic areas, although the **variety** of restaurants in the cities, especially Buenos Aires, reflects a mosaic of different communities who have migrated to Argentina over the decades: not just Italian and Spanish but Chinese, Middle Eastern, German, Welsh, Japanese and Peruvian. **Vegetarians** will find that there are few options on most menus, but staples such as basic salads, *provoleta* (delicious melted cheese) and *tartas* (a kind of quiche) are almost always available, as well as pastas with meat-free sauces. In larger towns vegetarian restaurants are growing in popularity.

There are plenty of *minutas* or **snacks** to choose from. The *choripán*, a large sausage in a soft roll, is a national favourite, as is the ubiquitous *milanesa*, a breaded veal escalope. Lomitos are grilled steak sandwiches, the local answer to the hamburger. Excellent local-style fast food is also available in the form of *empanadas*, pasties that come with an array of fillings, from the traditional beef or mozzarella cheese to salami, roquefort and chard. *Humitas* are made of steamed creamed sweetcorn, served in neat parcels made from the outer husk of corn cobs. *Tamales* are maize-flour balls, stuffed with minced beef and onion, wrapped in maize leaves and simmered. The typical main dish, *locro*, is a warming, substantial Andean stew based on maize, with onions, beans and meat thrown in.

WHERE TO EAT

Argentines love **dining out** and, in Buenos Aires especially, places stay open all day and till very late: in the evening hardly any restaurant starts serving dinner before 8.30pm, and in the hotter months – and all year round in Buenos Aires – very few people turn up before 10pm. By South American standards the quality of restaurants is high. You can keep costs down by taking advantage of restaurants' *menú del día* or *menú ejecutivo* – good-value set meals for as little as AR$40 served primarily, but not exclusively, at lunchtime. In the evening *tenedor libre* restaurants are just the place if your budget's tight. Here, you can eat as much as you like, they're usually self-service (cold and hot buffets plus grills) and the food is fresh and well prepared, if a little dull.

Cheaper hotels and more modest accommodation often skimp on **breakfast**: you'll be lucky to be given more than tea or coffee, and some bread, jam and butter, though *medialunas* (small, sticky croissants) are sometimes also served. The sacred national delicacy *dulce de leche* (a type of caramel) is often provided for spreading on toast or bread, as is top-notch honey.

DRINK

Fizzy drinks (*gaseosas*) are popular with people of all ages and are often drunk to accompany a meal. Although few beans are grown in the country, good, if expensive, **coffee** is easy to come by in Argentina. In the cafés of most towns and cities you can find a decent espresso, or delicious *café con leche* (milky coffee) for breakfast. *Mate*, the bitter national drink, prepared in a special gourd and drunk through a metal straw

1

known as a *bombilla*, is a whole world unto itself, with special rules of etiquette and ritual involved. It is almost exclusively drunk at home.

Argentina's **beer** is more thirst-quenching than alcoholic and mostly comes as fairly bland lager. The Quilmes brewery dominates the market with lagers such as Cristal; in Mendoza, the Andes brand crops up all over the place; while Salta's own brand is also good. Most breweries also produce a *cerveza negra*, a kind of stout. Patagonia produces some excellent artisanal ales, some of them available in bottles. If you want draught beer ask for a *chopp* or a *liso*.

Argentine **wine** is excellent and reasonably priced – try the Malbec grape variety. The locally distilled *aguardientes* or firewaters are often deliciously grapey. There is no national alcoholic drink or cocktail, but a number of Italian vermouths and digestifs are made in Argentina. Fernet Branca is the most popular, a demonic-looking brew the colour of molasses with a rather bitter, medicinal taste, invariably combined with cola, whose colour it matches, and consumed in huge quantities by students and young people.

CULTURE AND ETIQUETTE

Argentines are generally friendly, outgoing and incredibly welcoming to foreigners. In all but the most formal

---

NATIONAL PARK INFORMATION

The **National Park Headquarters** at Santa Fe 690 in Buenos Aires (Mon–Fri 8am–2pm; ☎011 4311 0303, ⓦparques nacionales.gov.ar) has an information office with introductory leaflets on the nation's parks. A wider range of free leaflets is available at each individual park, but these are of variable quality, and limited funding means that many parks give you only ones with a basic map and a brief park description. Contact the headquarters well in advance if you are interested in voluntary or scientific projects.

---

contexts, Argentines greet with one kiss on the cheek (men included), even on first meeting.

Table manners follow the Western norm and, in general, visitors are unlikely to find any huge culture shock in Argentine etiquette. Service in shops or restaurants is generally very courteous and conversations should be started with "buen día", "buenas tardes" or "buenas noches".

SPORTS AND OUTDOOR ACTIVITIES

Argentina is a highly exciting destination for outdoors enthusiasts, whether you're keen to tackle radical rock faces or prefer to appreciate the vast open spaces at a more gentle pace, hiking or on horseback. World-class fly-fishing, horseriding, trekking and rock-climbing options abound, as do opportunities for white-water rafting, skiing, ice climbing, and even – for those with sufficient stamina and preparation – expeditions onto the Southern Patagonian Icecap. The Patagonian Andes provide the focus for most of these activities – particularly the area of the central Lake District around Bariloche and El Calafate/El Chaltén, but Mendoza and the far northwest of the country, around Salta and Jujuy, are also worth considering for their rugged mountain terrain. If you're keen on any of the above activities (bar angling, of course), take out appropriate insurance cover before leaving home.

ARGENTINE WINE

Argentina is the world's fifth-largest producer of wine, and more than three-quarters of the stuff flows out of **Mendoza**. Enjoying around three hundred days of sunshine a year and a prime position at the foothills of the Andes, Mendoza's high-altitude vineyards are now producing premium vintages on a par with Chile's. The idyllic desert climate (cool nights, little rain and low humidity) works especially well for reds: **Malbec** – brought over from Bordeaux – is Argentina's star grape, producing rich fruity flavours that go down superbly well with the ubiquitous steak.

1

HIKING AND CLIMBING

Argentina offers some truly marvellous **hiking** possibilities, and it is still possible to find areas where you can trek for days without seeing a soul. Most of the best treks are found in the national parks – especially the ones in Patagonia – but you can also find less-known but equally superb options in the lands bordering the parks. Most people head for the savage granite spires of the Fitz Roy region around El Chaltén, an area whose fame has spread so rapidly over recent years that it now holds a similar status to Chile's renowned Torres del Paine, not far away, and is packed in the high season (late Dec to Feb). The other principal trekking destination is the mountainous area of Nahuel Huapi National Park, which lies to the south of Bariloche, centring on the Cerro Catedral massif and Cerro Tronador.

For **climbers**, the Andes offer incredible variety – from volcanoes to shale summits, from the continent's loftiest giants to some of its fiercest technical walls. You do not have to be a technical expert to reach the summit of some of these and, though you must always take preparations seriously, you can often arrange your climb close to the date through local agencies – though it's best to bring as much high-quality gear with you as you can. The climbing season is fairly short – generally November to March, though December to February is the best time. The best-known, if not the most technical, challenge is South America's highest peak, **Aconcagua** (6962m), accessed from the city of Mendoza. In the far south are the Fitz Roy massif and Cerro Torre,

which have few equals on the planet in terms of sheer technical difficulty and grandeur of scenery. On all of these climbs, but especially those over 4000m, you must acclimatize thoroughly, and be fully aware of the dangers of altitude sickness (see p.35).

SKIING

The main **skiing** months are July and August (late July is peak season), although in some resorts it is possible to ski from late May to early October. Snow conditions vary wildly from year to year, but you can often find excellent powder. The most prestigious resort for downhill skiing is modern Las Leñas, which offers the most challenging slopes and once hosted the World Cup; followed by the Bariloche resorts of Cerro Catedral and Cerro Otto. These are the longest-established in the country and are still perhaps the classic Patagonian ski centres, with their wonderful panoramas of the Nahuel Huapi region. It is also possible to ski in Ushuaia, where you can combine the sport with other kinds of sightseeing. Ski gear is widely available to rent. For updates on conditions and resorts, check out the Andesweb website (ⓦandesweb.com).

COMMUNICATIONS

There are Correo Argentino **post offices** throughout the country, and you will also come across *locutorios* offering postal services and phone booths. International post is relatively expensive and not always reliable; use registered post if possible and try to avoid sending items of value.

ARGENTINA ON THE NET

ⓦ**turismo.gov.ar** The official tourist website for Argentina.

ⓦ**welcomeargentina.com** Well-presented website about Argentina, containing information about accommodation and activities, and detailed transport advice.

ⓦ**buenosaires.gov.ar** City government site for Buenos Aires, with up-to-date details on cultural events.

ⓦ**livinginargentina.com** Online magazine with articles in English about Argentine culture and travel.

ⓦ**buenosairesherald.com** Buenos Aires' English-language newspaper, with national and international news updated daily.

1

Making **local phone calls** in Argentina is cheap and easy. In cities and towns, you are never far from a *locutorio*. It's worth asking about phone cards offering cheap minutes if you are planning to make a number of **national calls**. **Mobile calls** are expensive, but mildly cheaper if calling someone with the same phone company. The main ones are Claro, Personal and Movistar. If you're in Argentina for more than a couple of weeks, you may want to buy a pay-as-you-go SIM card (chip) to avoid extortionate roaming fees on your mobile.

Cheap **internet** cafés are everywhere in Argentina and, in all but the most remote areas, the connections are fairly fast. Many cafés and restaurants, as well as most hotels and hostels, have free wi-fi.

CRIME AND SAFETY

Argentina is one of the continent's safest countries and, as long as you take a few basic precautions, you are unlikely to encounter any problems during your stay. Indeed, you'll find many of the more rural parts of the country pretty much risk-free: people leave doors unlocked, windows open and bikes unchained. More care should be taken in large cities and some of the border towns, particularly the northeastern ones, where poverty and easily available arms and drugs make opportunistic crime a more common occurrence. Some potential pitfalls are outlined here, not to induce paranoia but on the principle that to be forewarned is to be forearmed.

By Argentine standards, **Buenos Aires** is currently suffering something of a crime wave, and incidents of violence and armed robbery are definitely on the increase. It's sometimes difficult to know how much local anxiety is due to a genuine increase in crime and how much to middle-class paranoia, a lot of it provoked by sensationalist news channels. But, in general, serious crime tends to affect locals more than tourists. Nevertheless, you should not take unmarked taxis. If possible, it is better to call a radio taxi (hotels and restaurants will be happy to do this for you), or flag

one down, rather than take a waiting cab, particularly in affluent or tourist areas. Avoid walking around the quieter neighbourhoods after dark, and be especially wary near the main bus and train stations in Once, Retiro and Constitución; avoid carrying valuables around with you. In La Boca, stick to the main touristy areas like the Caminito – the non-touristy part is to be avoided and is considered dangerous. In the rare event of being held up at gunpoint, don't play the hero.

Theft from hotels is rare but, as anywhere else in the world, do not leave valuables lying round the room (most have a safe). Some hostels have lockers; it's worth having a padlock of your own.

Drugs attract far more stigma than in most European countries, and Argentine society at large draws very little in the way of a line between "acceptable" soft drugs and "unacceptable" hard drugs. Although they are commonly found in clubs and bars, you're advised to steer clear of buying or partaking yourself – the penalties are stiff if you get caught.

HEALTH

Health issues are rarely a problem in Argentina, which has a generally good health service and clean drinking water. Vaccines are not really needed, but if you're planning on significant travel in rural areas within Salta, Jujuy or Misiones provinces, **malaria** tablets are recommended. **Yellow fever** vaccinations should be considered before visiting forested areas in the north of Argentina, including Iguazú Falls. All travellers over 1 year of age are advised to ensure they have the **hepatitis A** vaccination at least two weeks before arrival. If you're heading off the beaten track, vaccinations against typhoid and rabies are also recommended.

INFORMATION AND MAPS

Argentina's main **National Tourist Office** is at Santa Fe 883 in Buenos Aires (Mon–Fri 9am–5pm; ☎011 4312 2232, Ⓦturismo.gov.ar) and offers maps of the country and general information about getting around. Every province maintains a *Casa de Provincia* in Buenos Aires too, where you can pick up information about what there is to see or do, prior to travelling. The standard of information you'll glean from them varies wildly, often reflecting the comparative wealth of a given province.

The clearest and most accurate **map** of the whole country is the one you can get free from the national tourist office; it's called Rutas de la Argentina and has small but clear inset maps of twenty towns and cities as well as a 1:2,500,000 national map, the ideal scale for most travellers. Another useful resource for route planning is the website Ⓦruta0 .com. The ACA (Automóvil Club, Ⓦaca.org.ar) produces individual maps for each province, which vary enormously in detail and accuracy; the regional maps or route planners the club publishes may be enough for most travellers.

MONEY AND BANKS

The **Argentine peso** is divided into one hundred centavos. In Argentina, it's represented by the dollar sign ($) but to avoid confusion we have used the symbol AR$ throughout this section. Notes come in 2, 5, 10, 20, 50 and 100 peso denominations, and 1 and 2 peso and 5, 10, 25 and 50 centavo coins are also in circulation. Guard your loose change in Buenos Aires as you will need it for the buses. Try to cash large notes in hotels and supermarkets – never in taxis – and look out for counterfeit money. Check your notes for a watermark, and that the number is printed in shiny green.

Argentina has an unpredictable economy, with high inflation and currency controls. The situation is fluid, and it's advisable to check the latest situation before you travel. At the time of writing there were two dollar/peso exchange rates – an official rate, used by **ATM**s (*cajeros automáticos*) and exchange offices, and an increasingly divergent black market ("blue") rate, which you will be offered (illegally) in the street. If you offer to pay cash dollars for services such as hotels, tours etc they will often give you a rate just short of the blue rate, that equates to a substantial discount (as much as 50 percent), so you may wish to take a supply of dollars with you.

ATMs are plentiful in Argentina, though you can sometimes be caught out in very remote places, especially in the northwest. **Travellers' cheques** are not really a viable option as few banks accept them.

At the official rate of exchange, Argentina currently ranks as a fairly expensive destination by Latin American standards, though it's still cheaper than Brazil and, if you travel outside the main tourist areas, you can still find some surprisingly good bargains.

OPENING HOURS AND HOLIDAYS

Most **shops and services** are open Monday to Friday from 9am to 7pm, and Saturday till 2pm, although later in large towns, including Buenos Aires. In smaller towns they may close at some point during the afternoon for between one and five hours – sometimes offset by later closing times in the evening, especially in the summer. Supermarkets seldom close during the day and are generally open much later, often until 8 or 10pm, and on Saturday afternoons. Large shopping malls don't close before 10pm and their food and drink sections (*patios de comida*) may stay open as late as midnight. Most of them open on Sundays, too. **Banks** mostly open on weekdays only, from 10am to 5pm, while casas de cambio

---

STUDENT AND YOUTH DISCOUNTS

An **ISIC card** will entitle students of any age (over 12) to substantial discounts for many museums, travel and cultural events, as well as other services. See Ⓦisic.com.ar for details. For travel discounts, contact Asatej ☎011 4114 7595, Ⓦasatej.com.ar.

1

more or less follow shop hours. In the northeast, bank opening hours may be more like 7am to noon, to avoid the hot, steamy afternoons.

In addition to the national **holidays** listed above, some local anniversaries or saints' days are also public holidays when everything in a given city may close down. Festivals of all kinds, both religious and profane, celebrating local patrons such as Santa Catalina or the Virgin Mary, or showing off produce such as handicrafts, olives, goats or wine, are good excuses for much pomp and partying.

Buenos Aires

With a huge variety of high-class restaurants, hotels and boutiques, as well as an eclectic mix of Neoclassical and modern architecture, **BUENOS AIRES** is deservedly known as the "Paris of South America". The influence of immigrants from all over the world, Italian and Spanish above all, can be seen in its street names, restaurants, aesthetics and

language. Sip a coffee in the famous *Café Tortoni*, visit a dark and romantic tango hall to watch the nation's famous sultry dance, or simply walk the streets of Recoleta and watch the heavily made-up ladies in their fur coats walking tiny dogs on Chanel leads. If you grow weary of the people, noise and buses of the capital you can head out of the city to the waterways of the Paraná Delta, the quiet streets of La Plata or San Antonio de Areco, home of Argentina's gauchos.

WHAT TO SEE AND DO

The city's museums and sights are well distributed between the central areas of Recoleta, Retiro, Palermo and San Telmo, and the *microcentro* lies east of Avenida 9 de Julio between Retiro and San Telmo. The historic *barrio* (neighbourhood) of San Telmo is one of the most interesting for visitors, on account of its atmospheric streets, surviving (if often faded) nineteenth-century architecture, and its Sunday antiques market. The *microcentro* has the greatest concentration of shops and commerce, but Palermo Viejo should also be on every visitor's itinerary for its leafy streets lined with design and fashion shops, and hip bars and restaurants.

Plaza de Mayo

The **Plaza de Mayo** has witnessed the best and worst moments of Argentina's history – host to founding presidents, devastating military coups, the fanaticism of Evita, the dark days of the "Dirty War", and desperate crowds after the economic crisis. It has been bombed by its own military, filled to the brink with patriots, and left deserted, guarded by the federal police, in times of uncertainty, and even now it is still the spiritual home of the **Madres de la Plaza de Mayo**. These women, whose grown-up children "disappeared" during the Military Dictatorship (1976–1983), marched in the plaza every week for over thirty years demanding information about their children's whereabouts. The huge pink building at the river end of the plaza is the **Casa Rosada** (free tours Sat & Sun 10am–6pm; ☎011 4344 3804, ⓦmuseo.gov.ar), home to the offices of

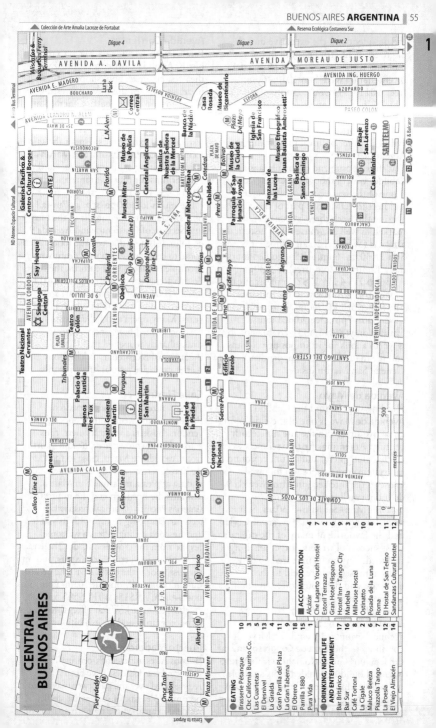

the president and the executive branch of government. To the south of the building is the underground **Museo del Bicentenario** (Wed–Sun 10am–6pm; free; ☎011 4344 3802, ⊛museo.gov.ar), which is basically an extravagant but impressive propaganda exercise in the good of Peronism as compared with the evil of all other political movements in Argentine history.

At the opposite end of the plaza is the **Cabildo**, which, though much altered, is one of the few examples of colonial architecture left in this part of the city. During the week there is a small crafts market, as well as a **museum** of historical artefacts (Wed–Fri 10am–5pm, Sat & Sun 11.30am–6pm; AR$4; guided tours daily 12.30pm, 2pm (free) & 3.30pm; AR$6; ☎011 4334 1782); a pleasant café is open the same hours as the museum. The rather plain **Catedral Metropolitana** (daily 9am–7pm; free guided tours, Spanish only; ☎011 4331 2845), close by, is worth a look for its imposing columns and the **mausoleum** to Independence hero General San Martín inside.

Avenida de Mayo

Heading west behind the Cabildo, **Avenida de Mayo** is one of the city's most attractive streets. In the late nineteenth century, Argentina's first skyscrapers were erected along here, and an underground rail system (the *subte*) soon followed. Close to the intersection with Avenida 9 de Julio, you'll find the famous *Café Tortoni* (Mon–Sat 8am–3.30am, Sun until 1am), with over 150 years of service and the favourite of many of the capital's most successful writers, Jorge Luis Borges included. Within its mirrored golden walls, tango shows are held in the evenings, and delicious coffee and pastries are served during the day.

Avenida 9 de Julio (with sixteen busy lanes) claims to be the world's widest avenue: beyond it, Avenida de Mayo continues to the **Plaza de Congreso**, and the fabulous Greco-Roman-style **Congreso Nacional** building (guided visits available in English Mon, Tues, Thurs & Fri 11am & 4pm, closed Feb; enquire at entrance on south side; ☎011 4010 3000).

Avenida Corrientes

Parallel with Avenida de Mayo to the north, Avenida Corrientes is lined with theatres, cinemas, bookshops and pizzerias. One of the most interesting places to stop is the **Teatro General San Martín** (☎0800 333 5254, ⊛teatrosan martin.com.ar), which hosts plays, festivals and exhibitions. Under the same roof is the **Centro Cultural San Martín** arts space, featuring exhibition spaces and auditoriums for music, drama and film (☎011 4374 1251, ⊛ccgsm.gov.ar).

The much-loved **Obelisco**, a 67m-tall obelisk, stands in the middle of the busy intersection of Corrientes and Avenida 9 de Julio. It is here that ecstatic football fans come to celebrate when their team wins. A couple of blocks to the north, the huge French Renaissance **Teatro Colón** (☎011 4378 7100, ⊛teatrocolon.org.ar) still stands tall after more than one hundred years. Many opera and ballet greats have performed here, and the theatre triumphantly reopened in 2010 – during the national bicentenary celebrations – after extensive refurbishment works.

Calle Florida

Pedestrianized **Calle Florida**, packed throughout the week with shoppers, street vendors, buskers and performers, runs across the downtown area, heading north from Avenida de Mayo, close to the Plaza de Mayo, across Avenida Corrientes and ending at pleasant Parque San Martín. Towards the northern end the impressive **Galerías Pacífico** (⊛progaleriaspacifico .com.ar) shopping centre, with its vaulted and frescoed ceiling, offers a welcome respite from the crowds outside. There is an inexpensive food court downstairs, and on the first floor is the entrance to the **Centro Cultural Borges** (Mon–Sat 10am–9pm, Sun noon–9pm; AR$15; ☎011 5555 5359, ⊛ccborges.org.ar), which offers three floors of photography and art exhibitions.

Puerto Madero

Buenos Aires' nineteenth-century docks, neglected for decades, have been redeveloped over the past twenty years to become a pleasant, if somewhat sterile, residential area, where modern apartment blocks surround bright-red restored warehouses. These are now home to some of the city's most chic restaurants and hotels. One of the capital's best art galleries, the **Colección de Arte Amalia Lacroze de Fortabat**, at Olga Cossettini 141 (Tues–Sun noon–9pm, AR$25; ☎011 4310 6600, ☻coleccionfortabat.org.ar), is housed in a peculiar hangar-style building on the waterfront. Within is an impressive private collection by both national and international artists, including works by Dalí, Warhol and Turner.

Nearby along the river's edge is the **Reserva Ecológica Costanera Sur** (entrance at Av Tristán Achával Rodríguez 1550; Tues–Sun 8am–6pm; free; ☎011 4315 1320), a large expanse of reclaimed and regenerated land. It makes a delightful afternoon stroll, and they hold full-moon tours once a month. In front of the entrance, a small craft market is held on weekends.

Montserrat

Cobblestoned **Montserrat** is one of the oldest neighbourhoods of the city, and the most popular until a yellow fever outbreak in the nineteenth century forced wealthier families to move to Recoleta and Palermo. The *barrio*'s principal street is Calle Defensa, named after the event when residents trying to force back British invaders in the early 1800s poured boiling water and oil from their balconies onto the attacking soldiers.

The neo-Baroque **Basílica de San Francisco** (Mon–Fri 8am–7pm; ☎011 4331 0625), at the corner of Alsina and Defensa, has an intricately decorated interior that can just about be made out through the atmospheric gloom. Nearby is the small **Museo de la Ciudad**, Alsina 412 (Mon–Fri 11am–7pm, Sat & Sun 10am–8pm; AR$1; ☎011 4331 9855), which houses informative and well-presented changing exhibitions about the city. One block west of Defensa is the collection of buildings known as the **Manzana de las Luces** (guided visits daily at 3pm, Sat & Sun also 4.30pm & 6pm; Spanish only; AR$12; info at Perú 272; ☎011 4342 9930, ☻manzanadelasluces .gov.ar), which dates back to 1686.

Originally housing a Jesuit community, it has also been home to numerous official institutions throughout its history, and today it accommodates both the **Colegio Nacional**, an elite high school, and Buenos Aires' oldest church, San Ignacio (daily 8am–8pm; ☎011 4331 2458), begun in 1675.

San Telmo

San Telmo begins further south along Defensa, on the far side of Avenida Belgrano. With its myriad of antique stores and junk shops, as well as a range of busy, late-opening restaurants and bars (especially around the intersection of Chile and Defensa), it's a great place to wander. For fresh food and a variety of eclectic antiques head to the **San Telmo Food Market** (Mon–Sat 7am–2pm & 4.30–9pm, Sun 7am–2pm). The market takes up an entire city block, with an entrance on each side, including one on Defensa near the corner of Estados Unidos.

A few blocks further, **Plaza Dorrego** is a great place to pause for a coffee under the leafy trees, at least on weekdays when it's quieter. On Sundays the area is completely taken over by the **Feria de San Pedro Telmo** (10am–5pm; buses #9, #10, #24, #28 or #86 easily picked up downtown). Vintage watches, posters, antique clothes and jewellery are all on display at this huge open-air antiques market, enlivened by street performers and live tango acts. Another great place for antique-spotting is the **Pasaje de la Defensa**, Defensa 1179, a converted mansion filled with hidden shops, cafés and workshops.

Calle Defensa continues, across the busy, ugly avenues of San Juan and Juan de Garay, to leafy **Parque Lezama**, home to the **Museo Histórico Nacional**, Defensa 1600 (Wed–Sun 11am–6pm; free; ☎011 4307 1182). This small museum has an interesting permanent exhibition on Argentina's history. The collection at the **Museo de Arte Moderno de Buenos Aires (MAMBA)**, at Avenida San Juan 350 (Mon–Fri 11am–7pm, Sat & Sun 11am–8pm; AR$2, Tues free; ☎011 4342 3001, ☻museos.buenosaires.gob.ar),

1

focuses mainly on Argentine art from the 1920s until the present day, and includes pieces by Xul Solar and Antonio Berni.

La Boca

Easily accessible from Parque Lezama, the suburb of **La Boca** is known for the Caminito and as home to one of Argentina's leading football clubs, **Boca Juniors**, arch-rivals of the River Plate team on the other side of town.

The **Caminito** is a small area of brightly coloured buildings along the river, created in the 1950s by the neighbourhood's most famous artist, **Benito Quinquela Martín**. These days the Caminito is a serious tourist trap, though it has an interesting open-air **arts and crafts fair** (daily 10.30am–6pm), street performers, and restaurants and cafés charging tourist prices.

A visit to the Boca Juniors' stadium, **La Bombonera** (Brandsen 805, three blocks west of Av Almirante Brown; ☎011 4362 2050), is definitely worthwhile, even if you can't score tickets to a game. The starting point is the fascinating **Museo de la Pasión Boquense** (daily 10am–6pm; AR$40; ☎011 4362 1100, ⓦmuseoboquense.com), a must for football fans; guided tours of the stadium start from here (daily 11am–5pm hourly; AR$15 extra).

La Boca can be reached by **bus** #29 from Corrientes or Plaza de Mayo, #86 from Plaza de Mayo or #53 from Constitución. Note that La Boca has a bad reputation for **robberies**, so leave your valuables at home and do not stray from the touristy area around Caminito.

Recoleta

Immediately north of the city centre, the wide streets of upper-class Recoleta are most famously home to the **Recoleta Cemetery** at Avenida Quintana and Junín (daily 7am–5pm; free), surrounded by café-lined streets and their designer-clad denizens. Immensely popular, it is the resting place of some of Argentina's leading celebrities, including Evita herself, buried under her maiden name of Duarte. A map is available at the entrance to guide you around the great monuments of dark granite, white marble and gleaming bronze.

Next door are the white walls of the **Basílica de Nuestra Señora del Pilar** (Mon–Sat 10.30am–6.15pm, Sun 2.30–6.15pm; free; ☎011 4803 6793). The eighteenth-century Jesuit building has been beautifully restored, and is much in demand for fashionable weddings: inside, the magnificent Baroque silver altarpiece, embellished with an Inca sun and other pre-Hispanic details, was made by craftsmen from the north of Argentina. Adjacent, the **Centro Cultural de Recoleta** (Tues–Fri 2–9pm, Sat & Sun noon–9pm; free; ☎011 4803 1040, ⓦcentroculturalrecoleta.org), at Junín 1930, is a fabulous art space with interesting temporary exhibitions.

If by now you're in need of a coffee or a shopping fix, head to **Buenos Aires Design**, a shopping centre focusing on chic design products and homeware, which adjoins the cultural centre. The large terrace upstairs overlooks a park, and is a great place for an afternoon drink.

Visible from the terrace of Buenos Aires Design, the **Museo Nacional de Bellas Artes** (Tues–Fri 12.30–8.30pm, Sat & Sun 9.30am–8.30pm; free; ☎011 4803 0802, ⓦmnba.org.ar) is at Avenida del Libertador 1473. Within the imposing, columned building is a traditional art gallery, primarily displaying European paintings but also with a small but valuable collection of colonial and modern Argentine work. For more local artworks, go to the **Museo Xul Solar** (Tues–Fri noon–8pm, Sat noon–7pm; AR$15; ☎011 4824 3302, ⓦxulsolar.org .ar), further to the southwest at Laprida 1212, near the corner of Calle Mansilla, which focuses on the bright and colourful Cubist paintings of twentieth-century Argentine artist Alejandro Xul Solar.

Palermo

Expansive, middle-class **Palermo** stretches around Avenida del Libertador as it heads north from Recoleta, taking in the high-rise apartments near the north of Avenida Santa Fe, the chic cafés and hotels of Palermo Viejo, and the leafy streets and late-night bars of Palermo Hollywood. On or near tree-lined Libertador are three unmissable

PALERMO, BARRIO NORTE & RECOLETA

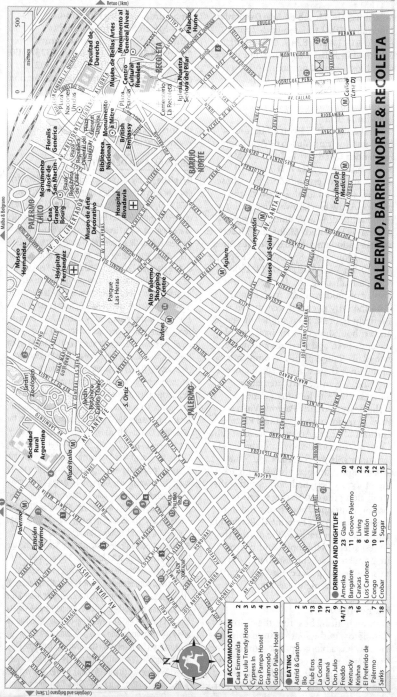

■ ACCOMMODATION	
Casa Esmeralda	2
Che Lulu Trendy Hotel	3
Cypress In	5
Eco Pampa Hostel	4
Giramondo	1
Guido Palace Hotel	6

● EATING	
Astrid & Gastón	2
Bio	5
Club Eros	13
La Cocina	19
Cumaná	21
Don Julio	9
Freddo	14/17
Kentucky	3
Krishna	16
El Preferido de	7
Palermo	
Sarkis	18

● DRINKING AND NIGHTLIFE	
Amerika	20
Bangalore	11
Caracas	8
Los Cardones	24
Congo	12
Crobar	15
Glam	23
Groove Palermo	4
Living	22
Millón	6
Niceto Club	10
Sugar	1

1

museums. The **Museo de Arte Decorativo**, Libertador 1902 (Tues–Sun 2–7pm; AR\$5; ☎011 4801 8248, ⓦmnad.org.ar), is housed in Palacio Errázuriz, one of the city's most original private mansions, with a lovely café in its patio. The collection is of mainly European sculpture, art and furnishings, all beautifully displayed.

At Libertador 2373 you'll find the small and inviting **Museo de Arte Popular Hernández** (Wed–Fri 1–7pm; Sat & Sun 10am–8pm; AR\$1; ☎011 4801 9019, ⓦmuseohernandez.org.ar), whose displays focus on local silverwork and textiles. A few blocks away, in a striking modern building at Avenida Figueroa Alcorta 3415, stands **Malba**, the **Museo de Arte Latinoamericano de Buenos Aires** (Thurs–Mon noon–8pm, Wed till 9pm; AR\$30, on Wed AR\$15; ☎011 4808 6500, ⓦmalba.org.ar). The permanent display of modern Latin American art from the early twentieth century on is a refreshing break from stuffier museums. The art bookshop downstairs is one of the city's best, and the light and modern café (daily 9am–9pm) is recommended. In the foyer there is an excellent cinema showing Argentine and international films (see website for programme).

The heart of trendy **Palermo Viejo** is Plaza Serrano, officially named **Plaza Cortázar** after the Argentine novelist Julio Cortázar, surrounded by cafés, bars and restaurants. Every Saturday and Sunday (10am–8pm) the plaza is host to markets full of locally designed clothes and crafts. Stroll along the connecting streets for fashion boutiques, bookshops and music shops. Even jazzier **Palermo Hollywood** is across the train tracks to the north. The busiest streets, Humboldt and Fitzroy, are home to excellent restaurants and bars, while along Calle Niceto Vega a variety of late-night bars abounds.

Mataderos

Over an hour by bus from the centre, **Mataderos**, in the southwestern corner of the city, has a bloody past as home to the city's cattle slaughterhouses. Today, it is worth a visit for the **Feria de Mataderos**, held on Sunday for most of the year but on Saturday evenings in summer (Jan–March Sat 6pm–midnight, April–Dec Sun 11am–sunset; buses #36, #92 & #126; Mon–Fri; ☎011 4323 9400 ext 2830, weekends 011 4687 5602, ⓦferiademataderos.com.ar). A celebration of all things gaucho, the Feria has stalls selling leatherwork, *mate*, gourds and silver, as well as folk music and displays of horseriding, plus some of the best *empanadas* in the city.

ARRIVAL AND DEPARTURE

By plane Nearly all international flights and a few domestic ones arrive at Ezeiza International Airport (☎011 5480 6111, ⓦwww.aa2000.com.ar), 35km (45min) west of the city centre. Manuel Tienda León runs express buses to and from the airport (every 30min; daily 6am–9pm, less frequent outside these times; AR\$70 one-way; ☎011 4315 5115, ⓦwww.tiendaleon.com.ar), which use its terminal at Av E Madero 1299 (at San Martín) in the Retiro area – for an extra AR\$5 or 10/person you get a transfer from the terminal to a specific address in town. A taxi or *remise* (radio cab) will cost around AR\$220 from Ezeiza to town, a bit less for the return journey. Buenos Aires' domestic airport (also serving some connections with Uruguay and Brazil) is Aeroparque Jorge Newbery (☎011 5480 6111) on the Costanera Norte, around 6km north of the city centre. Local bus #33 (AR\$2) runs from the airport to Paseo Colón, on the fringe of the *microcentro*. Manuel Tienda León shuttles from Aeroparque to downtown are around AR\$30.
Destinations Bariloche (up to 10 daily; 2hr 20min); Córdoba (10 daily; 1hr 15min); Corrientes (1 daily; 1hr 20min); El Calafate (10 daily; 3hr 20min); Jujuy (2 daily; 2hr 10min); La Rioja (1 daily; 3hr); Mar del Plata (up to 5 daily; 1hr 15min); Mendoza (up to 7–9 daily; 1hr 50min); Neuquén (4 daily; 1hr 40min); Puerto Iguazú (up to 10–12 daily; 1hr 50min); Rio Gallegos (3 daily; 3hr 15min); Salta (3 daily; 2hr); San Juan (1 daily; 1hr 50min); San Martín de los Andes (3 weekly; 2hr 20min); Santiago del Estero (1 daily; 1hr 40min); Trelew (4 daily; 2hr); Tucumán (5 daily; 1hr 50min); Ushuaia (6 daily; 3hr 40min).
By bus All domestic and international services use the Retiro bus terminal, at Av Antártida & Ramos Mejía. Taxis are plentiful and the Retiro *subte* (metro) station is just a block away, outside the adjoining train station. Be careful after dark; a large shantytown is located just behind the terminal and pickpockets operate around here. A variety of buses (around AR\$2) leaves from outside, including #5 and #50, to Congreso, and #106 to Palermo Viejo.
Destinations Frequent domestic services to Bariloche (19–25hr); Córdoba (9–11hr); Mendoza (14–16hr); Neuquén (14–19hr); Puerto Iguazú (17–18hr); Puerto Madryn (18–20hr); Rosario (4hr); Salta (20–22hr). Daily international

services to La Paz (48hr); Montevideo (8–9hr); Santiago de Chile (19hr); São Paulo (34hr); Rio de Janeiro (40hr).

By ferry Ferry services to and from Uruguay use the Terminal Dársena Norte (often just known as the Terminal Buquebús) at Viamonte & Costanera Sur, just a few blocks from the *microcentro*. The two main companies are Colonia Express (Pedro de Mendoza 330, Dársena Sur; ☎ 011 4313 5100, ⊛ coloniaexpress.com) and Buquebus (Av Antartida Argentina 821; ☎ 011 4316 6500, ⊛ buquebus.com).

Destinations Colonia (8 daily; 1–3hr); Montevideo (4 daily; 4hr).

By train The main stations are Retiro, Constitución and Once but are mostly used only for urban and provincial travel.

Retiro station (Av Ramos Mejía, just to the east of Plaza San Martín) is the departure point for trains to Tigre and the northern suburbs.

INFORMATION

Tourist information There are a number of *centros de informes* around the city run by the Secretaria de Turismo, including one at Av Alicia Moreau de Justo 200 in Puerto Madero (daily 9am–6pm; ☎ 011 4313 0187, ⊛ bue.gov.ar). Probably the best is on Florida 100, at Av Diagonal Roque Sáenz Peña (daily 9am–6pm). You can also pick up local (and national) information from the well-organized National Tourist Office at Santa Fe 883 (Mon–Fri 9am–5pm; ☎ 011 4312 2232, ⊛ turismo.gov.ar), which has details of the provincial tourist offices within the capital.

GETTING AROUND

By bus Buses (⊛ loscolectivos.com.ar) are one of the most useful (and cheap) ways of getting around the city – and indeed the only way of reaching many of the outlying

districts. Invest in a combined street and bus-route booklet, such as the Guía "T", widely available from street kiosks, to work out the routes. One-way tickets (AR$2) are acquired from a machine on the bus, which gives change for coins (no notes). Many services run all night.

By remise These are radio cabs or minicabs, plain cars booked through an office (and therefore preferred by some wary locals). Not particularly economical for short journeys, they're cheaper than taxis for getting to the airport; try *Remises Uno* (☎ 011 4638 8318). It's safest to call a radio taxi at night. Ask your hostel for their preferred company or try *Taxi Alo* (☎ 011 4855 5555).

By subte The easiest part of the public transport system to get to grips with is the underground railway or *subte*, which serves the central neighbourhoods from 5am until 10.30pm (Mon–Sat) and from 8am to 10pm (Sun & public holidays). There are six lines – Lines A, B, D and E run from the city centre outwards, while lines C and H (still under construction) run between Retiro and Constitución, connecting them all. Tickets cost AR$2.50 for a single trip and are bought from the booths at each station. If you are going to travel a lot, buy a card of 10 tickets – you can share them, and it saves queuing up, or you can buy a pre-pay swipe card.

By taxi The city's black-and-yellow taxis are spectacularly plentiful. The meter starts at AR$9 (charges increase at night), and you should calculate on a ride costing around AR$30 per twenty blocks.

ACCOMMODATION

Finding accommodation in Buenos Aires shouldn't be a problem but advance planning is advised, especially for high season. Discounts can sometimes be negotiated,

BUENOS AIRES TOURS

Walking tours are offered by the city government (free; in English and Spanish) around a given *barrio*, or with themes such as "Evita" or "Carlos Gardel". Ask at a tourism kiosk for the schedule. **Buenos Aires Bus** (daily 9am–5.30pm, every 20min; ⊛ buenosairesbus.com) are city hop-on hop-off bus tours stopping at various points of interest, including Boca, the Reserva Ecológica and the Rosedal in Palermo. $120 per day or $160 for two days represents good value compared to taxis – if you're planning to cover a lot of ground.

TOUR OPERATORS

Agreste Viamonte 1636 ☎ 011 4373 4442. Offers adventurous trips across the country to destinations such as the Saltos de Moconá, Jujuy and the Valle de la Luna.

ANDA tours ☎ 011 3221 0833, ⊛ andatravel.com.ar. Organizes responsible tourist visits with a difference, such as their "Beyond the Caminito" walking tour of Boca, which includes stop-offs at local art collectives and community organizations.

ASATEJ Florida 835, 3rd Floor ☎ 011 4114 7528, ⊛ asatej.com. A young and dynamic travel agency,

offering some of the cheapest flight deals in the city as well as international packages; student discounts available.

Buenos Aires Tur Lavalle 1444, Office 16 ☎ 011 4371 2304, ⊛ buenosairestur.com. Offers city tours of Buenos Aires, including tango shows, and visits to Tigre and nearby *estancias*.

Say Hueque Viamonte 749, 6th Floor ☎ 011 5199 2517, ⊛ sayhueque.com. A professional tour operator covering all of Argentina (and parts of Chile).

1

particularly if you are staying for more than a few days. Most backpackers head for San Telmo, where the hostels are concentrated, but you can also increasingly find good-value, pleasant accommodation in leafier Palermo.

HOSTELS

Most hostels have communal kitchens and offer free or cheap internet, breakfast and laundry.

CENTRAL BUENOS AIRES

★ **Estoril Terrazas** Av de Mayo 1385 (1st & 6th Floors), at Uruguay ☎ 011 4372 5494, ⓦ hostelestoril.com.ar; map p.55. Directly opposite the Palacio Barolo, one of Buenos Aires' most stunning buildings, *Estoril* has to be among the top hostels in the world. Extremely comfortable and always impeccably clean, it offers all amenities and has a roof terrace with perfect views of Av de Mayo and Congreso. Ask for the roof-top dorm. Dorms AR$65, doubles AR$200

Milhouse Hostel Hipólito Yrigoyen 959, at Bernardo de Irigoyen ☎ 011 4345 9604, ⓦ milhousehostel.com; map p.55. A large, lively hostel in a colonial-style building with a huge range of activities on offer. One of the city's most popular, so book well in advance. Full English breakfast AR$20. *Milhouse* also has another outpost at Av de Mayo 1245. Dorms AR$80, doubles AR$300

PALERMO, RECOLETA AND RETIRO

Casa Esmeralda Honduras 5765, at Bonpland ☎ 011 4772 2446, ⓦ casaesmeralda.com.ar; map p.59. Small, friendly hostel with a shady back garden, hammocks and a large living area. Slightly tired-looking, but a good location to kick back and meet people. Dorms AR$90, doubles AR$210

Eco Pampa Hostel Guatemala 4778 ☎ 011 4831 2435, ⓦ hostelpampa.com; map p.59. Dubbing itself the city's first green hostel – the vibrant lime-hued facade sets the tone – *Eco Pampa* is comfortable as well as eco-friendly, with its leafy terrace and low-energy computers. Dorms AR$75, doubles AR$400

Giramondo Guemes 4802 ☎ 011 4772 6740, ⓦ hostelgiramondo.com; map p.59. Spacious Palermo hostel in an early twentieth-century townhouse (discounts for long stays). Has a vast, lower-ground-floor bar area – a great place for partying and meeting fellow travellers. Dorms AR$60, doubles AR$275

SAN TELMO

Che Lagarto Youth Hostel Venezuela 857, at Piedras ☎ 011 4343 4845, ⓦ chelagarto.com; map p.55. Rooms are standard but the sociable atmosphere, cool bar/restaurant (meals AR$40–75) and lovely tree-shaded back garden make *Che* a top traveller hangout. Dorms AR$60, doubles AR$310

Hostel Inn – Tango City Piedras 680, at Chile ☎ 011 4300 5776, ⓦ hitangocity.com; map p.55. Large, fun hostel popular with party animals (there's a themed party every Friday). A plethora of activities is organized, including *asado* nights, Spanish lessons, free walking tours and tango excursions. There's another hostel at Humberto Primo 820. Dorms AR$60, doubles AR$180

Ostinatto Chile 680, at Perú ☎ 011 4362 9639, ⓦ ostinatto.com; map p.55. Falls squarely in the category of "hip" hostel, with cool minimalist design, spacious dorms and extremely friendly staff. Hosts tango shows and film viewings and there's a decent happy hour in the bar from 6–11pm. More expensive than some other hostels, but well worth it. If you feel like treating yourself there are two self-contained apartments, the loft (AR$500) and penthouse (AR$650). Dorms AR$75, doubles AR$350

El Hostal de San Telmo Carlos Calvo 614, at Peru ☎ 011 4300 6899, ⓦ elhostaldesantelmo.com; map p.55. Located in one of the prettiest parts of San Telmo, Buenos Aires' original hostel is cheaper than most, friendly and well kept. Dorms AR$50, doubles AR$150

Sandanzas Cultural Hostel Balcarce 1351, at Cochabamba ☎ 011 4300 7375, ⓦ sandanzas.com.ar; map p.55. One of Buenos Aires' smallest hostels, set slightly off the beaten track. The cosy common room is the setting for a variety of cultural events. Dorms AR$75, doubles AR$290

HOTELS AND B&BS

CENTRAL BUENOS AIRES

Alcázar Av de Mayo 935 ☎ 011 4345 0926, ⓦ hotelalcazar.com.ar; map p.55. This old hotel with a lovely central staircase features basic rooms, all with heating, a fan and private bathroom. AR$280

Gran Hotel Hispano Av de Mayo 861, at Tacuarí ☎ 011 4345 2020, ⓦ hhispano.com.ar; map p.55. Metres from the famous *Café Tortoni*, this family-run classic retains its original Spanish-style architecture. Most rooms are centred on a beautiful old courtyard, while some have balconies looking onto the street below. AR$350

Marbella Av de Mayo 1261 ☎ 011 4383 8566, ⓦ hotelmarbella.com.ar; map p.55. Calm, good-value lodgings (discounts for cash) in a central location. Rooms are modern with cable TV and decent-sized bathrooms, and there is also an economical restaurant. AR$350

Posada de la Luna Perú 565, at México ☎ 011 4343 0911, ⓦ posadaluna.com; map p.55. Attractively decorated B&B set in a colonial townhouse between San Telmo and the Centro. Home-made bread and jam is served with breakfast and there's a jacuzzi and sun deck. No hotel sign outside the door means it's still a relatively well-kept secret. AR$430

Roma Av de Mayo 1413, at Uruguay ☎ 011 4381 4921; map p.55. Low prices and a central location are the draw at the *Roma*. Slightly noisy rooms, some with balconies looking onto Av de Mayo. AR$220

PALERMO, RECOLETA AND RETIRO

Che Lulu Trendy Hotel Pasaje Emilio Zola 5185, at Godoy Cruz, Palermo Viejo ☎011 4772 0289, ⓦchelulu.com; map p.59. On a colourful *pasaje* in Palermo, *Che Lulu* offers a down-to-earth and relaxed experience. AR$300

Cypress In Costa Rica 4828, at Borges ☎011 4833 5834, ⓦcypressin.com; map p.59. Sleek B&B, with designer features and a neat location in the heart of Palermo's "Soho" area. AR$420

Guido Palace Hotel Guido 1780, at Callao ☎011 4812 0674; map p.59. This 60-room hotel is an affordable, no-frills option in upmarket Recoleta, near the cemetery. Triples and quadruple rooms are also available. AR$350

EATING

Buenos Aires has a busy, increasingly diverse, restaurant scene. Many restaurants offer a good-value *menú del día* (lunchtime set menu) on weekdays, usually including a drink; this is an excellent way to sample the best of BA's restaurants at much lower prices. It is wise to book ahead at the more popular places.

CENTRAL BUENOS AIRES

Cbc – California Burrito Co. Lavalle 441 ☎011 4328 3056, ⓦcaliforniaburritoco.com; map p.55. Busy central burrito joint, ideally placed for lunch on the go. White-flour tortillas are packed with seemingly endless combinations of fresh ingredients; portions are enormous. Three burrito and drink special from AR$40. Mon–Fri noon–11pm, Sat & Sun noon–7pm.

Las Cuartetas Av Corrientes 838 ☎011 4326 0171; map p.55. Big, brightly lit theatreland pizzeria, opposite the Gran Rex. Large pizzas from AR$70. Mon–Sat noon–1am, Sun 8pm–midnight.

La Giralda Corrientes 1453 ☎011 4371 3846; map p.55. Brightly lit and austerely decorated Corrientes café, famous for its *chocolate espeso con churros* (thick hot chocolate with fritters, AR$40). A perennial hangout for students and intellectuals, and a good place to observe the *porteño* passion for conversation. Mon–Sat 7am–2am.

La Gran Taberna Combate de los Pozos 95, Montserrat ☎011 4951 7586; map p.55. A popular, bustling and down-to-earth restaurant a block from the Congreso. The vast, reasonably priced menu offers a mixture of Spanish dishes, including a good selection of seafood, *porteño* staples and a sprinkling of more exotic dishes such as *ranas a la provenzal* (frogs' legs with parsley and garlic, AR$205). Many dishes are large enough to share. Mains AR$60–85. Daily noon–4pm & 8pm–2am.

Pura Vida Reconquista 516 ☎011 4393 0093; map p.55. American-style juice and health-food bar serving a mainly business clientele looking for an alternative to beef. Lunch specials include soup and half a wrap (AR$42).

Juices from AR$17 and salads AR$38. Mon–Fri 9am–7pm & Sat 10.30am–5pm.

PALERMO, RECOLETA AND RETIRO

Bio Humboldt 2192 ☎011 4774 3880; map p.59. Vegetarian restaurant with lots of wholesome ingredients – wholemeal *empanadas*, quinoa risotto, tofu salad and so on – with a good-value ($55) lunch with drink. Organic wine and beer are also served. Daily 9am–1am.

★ **Club Eros** Uriarte 1609, Palermo Viejo ☎011 4832 1313; map p.59. Fun, noisy cantina at a neighbourhood sports and social club, offering Argentine standards at bargain prices. Daily noon–4pm and 8pm–midnight.

La Cocina Pueyrredón 1508, Recoleta ☎011 4825 3171; map p.59. Tiny budget place serving *locro* (a filling corn stew from the northeast of Argentina) and a selection of delicious Catamarca-style *empanadas*. Mon–Sat noon–4pm & 7pm–midnight.

Cumaná Rodriguez Peña 1149, Retiro; map p.59. Popular with students and office workers, this is a good place to try *mate*, served from 4pm to 7.30pm with a basket of crackers. There's also a selection of provincial food, such as *empanadas* and *cazuelas* (casseroles).

★ **Don Julio** Guatemala 4699, Palermo Viejo ☎011 4831 9564; map p.59. Excellent *parrilla* with choice cuts of meat, a good wine list and smart, efficient service. *Lomo*, fries, salad and wine will set you back AR$200. Daily noon–4pm & 8pm–late.

★ **Freddo** Branches throughout the city, including Alto Palermo Shopping and Armenia 1618, ⓦfreddo.com.ar; map p.59. Buenos Aires' best ice-cream chain. *Dulce de leche* fans will be in heaven, and the passionfruit mousse flavour (*maracuyá mousse*) is superb. Prices from AR$22. Daily 10am till late.

Kentucky Santa Fe 4602, Palermo Viejo ☎011 4773 7869; map p.59. A Buenos Aires institution that's been around since 1942, serving excellent pizzas and *empanadas*. Expect old-school waiters in white shirts and bow ties, and a grungy clientele. The *empanadas* are large and worth the higher than normal price. Daily noon–4pm & 8pm–late.

Krishna Malabia 1833, Palermo Viejo ☎011 4833 4618; map p.59. Tiny bohemian spot on Plaza Palermo Viejo run by the International Society for Krishna Consciousness and serving tasty vegetarian Indian food. Go for the mixed *thali* with a ginger lemonade. Tues–Sun noon–4pm & 8pm–midnight.

El Preferido de Palermo Borges, at Guatemala, Palermo Viejo ☎011 4774 6585; map p.59. Fun, *pulpería*-style diner with bottles and cans packing the shelves and hams hanging from the ceiling. Menu choices include a lentil and bacon stew and *milanesa* (breaded escalope) with potatoes. Mon–Sat noon–4pm & 8pm–late.

1

Sarkis Thames 1101, Villa Crespo ☎011 4772 4911; map p.59. Excellent tabbouleh, *keppe crudo* (raw meat with onion – much better than it sounds) and falafel at this popular restaurant serving a fusion of Armenian, Arab and Turkish cuisine. Close to Palermo Viejo, and great value for money (very popular so expect long queues). Daily noon–3pm & 8pm–1am.

SAN TELMO AND AROUND

Brasserie Pétanque Defensa 596, San Telmo ☎011 4342 7930, ⓦ brasseriepetanque.com; map p.55. Authentic and chic French-owned brasserie, serving French classics (onion soup, steak tartare, crème brûlée and even snails). Weekday lunch deal AR$70 (main course and drink). Mon noon–4pm, Tues–Sun noon–3pm & 8pm–1am.

★ **El Desnivel** Defensa 855, San Telmo ☎011 4300 9081, ⓦ parrillaeldesnivel.com.ar; map p.55. Classic San Telmo *parrilla* with accessible prices, great meat and a friendly, slightly rowdy atmosphere; popular with tourists. *Lomo* steak AR$85. Mon 8pm–1am, Tues–Sun noon–3pm & 8pm–1am.

Gran Parrilla del Plata Chile 594, San Telmo ☎011 4300 8588, ⓦ parrilladelplata.com; map p.55. Excellent-value steakhouse whose *medallón de lomo* (AR$105) has to be one of the tenderest cuts in town. Mon–Sat noon–3pm & 8pm–1am, Sun 8pm–1am.

El Obrero Caffarena 64, La Boca ☎011 4362 9912, ⓦ bodegonelobrero.com.ar; map p.55. With Boca Juniors souvenirs on the walls and tango musicians moving from table to table at weekends, the atmosphere at the hugely popular and moderately priced *El Obrero* is as much a part of the fun as the simple unfussy food (*lomo* steak AR$45, pasta dishes AR$36). Very popular, so prepare to queue at weekends. Take a taxi as the local area can be unsafe. Mon–Sat noon–3pm & 8pm–1am.

Parrilla 1880 Defensa 1665, San Telmo ☎011 4307 2746; map p.55. Extremely good *parrilla* joint, right opposite Parque Lezama. Its walls are lined with photos and drawings

---

★ **TREAT YOURSELF**

Astrid & Gastón Lafinur 3222 (near Av del Libertador) ☎011 4802 2991; map p.59. A delicious high-end Peruvian fusion restaurant that has branches all over Latin America. Don't be put off by the rather drab paint on the walls; the food – much of it fish – is delicious and delicate on the palate, with the *ceviche* particularly recommended. One of the more expensive restaurants in town, so allow at least AR$350 per head with wine. Book in advance. Mon–Sat 12.30–3pm & 8pm–late.

---

from the restaurant's famous and mostly bohemian clients, and the very friendly owner makes sure everyone is happy. Mains AR$55–90. Tues–Sat noon–3pm & 8pm–1am, Sun noon–4pm.

DRINKING AND NIGHTLIFE

You'll find that Buenos Aires offers a lively nightlife every day of the week. The only exception is perhaps on Monday, when some venues, especially in the centre, tend to close. Wednesday is known as "After Office", and you'll find the city's bars and clubs packed from 6pm. Keep in mind that Buenos Aires starts – and finishes – late, so clubs don't fill up until the early hours. Check out What's Up Buenos Aires (ⓦ whatsupbuenosaires.com) for up-to-date information and articles on the city's cultural and nightlife happenings, or Wipe (ⓦ wipe.com.ar; Spanish only).

BARS AND PUBS

Bangalore Humboldt 1416, Palermo Viejo ☎011 4779 2621; map p.59. Fine traditional pub in Palermo "Hollywood", popular with locals, expats and tourists. Happy hour until 10pm; pints and curries served. Daily.

Bar Británico Defensa, at Brasil, San Telmo ☎011 4361 2107; map p.59. Old men, bohemians and night owls while away the small hours in this traditional wood-panelled bar overlooking Parque Lezama. 24hr.

Caracas Guatemala 4802, Palermo Viejo ☎011 4776 8704; map p.59. Trendy Palermo Viejo venue attracting a cool crowd. Has a lovely roof terrace and serves Venezuelan food. Mon–Sat 6.30pm–4am.

Los Cardones Jorge Luis Borges 2180, Palermo ☎011 4777 1112, ⓦ cardones.com.ar; map p.59. One of the best *peñas* in town – a bar where traditional folk musicians play. Wed–Sat from 9pm.

La Cigale 25 de Mayo 597, Centro ☎011 4312 8275; map p.55. One of Buenos Aires' most happening bars, attracting an up-for-it crowd. Regularly hosts live music and DJs. Mon–Fri from 6pm & Sat from 8pm.

Congo Honduras 5329, Palermo ☎011 4833 5857; map p.59. Sleek interiors and atmospheric lighting at this popular hang-out. Particularly heaving in summer thanks to a stunning outside area. Wed–Sat 8pm–5am.

Milión Paraná 1048, Recoleta ☎011 4815 9925, ⓦ milion .com.ar; map p.59. Grand bar housed in an early twentieth-century townhouse. Overrun with gringos, but a decent place to start the night and another venue with a great garden. Mon–Fri 10am–late, Sat noon–late, Sun 8pm–late.

La Poesía Chile 502, San Telmo ☎011 4300 7340; map p.55. Old-fashioned establishment that feels a bit like a Spanish tapas bar. From the owners of the equally excellent *El Federal* (Carlos Calvo 599), *La Poesía* serves three types of artisan beer (AR$20–25) and does a wide range of *picada* tasting platters (AR$55–105). Daily until 2am.

Sugar Costa Rica 4619, Palermo ☎011 4831 3276, ⓦsugarbuenosaires.com; map p.59. Not the place to come if you're looking for an authentic *porteño* night out. This American-run bar feels more US frat party than BA boozer. But if you fancy a decent hamburger and a ridiculously cheap happy hour (7pm–midnight), then *Sugar* is your bar. Daily noon–late.

NIGHTCLUBS

Amerika Gascón 1040, Villa Crespo ☎011 4865 4416, ⓦameri-k.com.ar; map p.59. The city's biggest gay club, with three dancefloors playing mainly electro. Thurs–Sun from midnight.

Crobar Marcelo Freyres s/n, Paseo de la Infanta ☎011 4778 1500, ⓦcrobar.com.ar; map p.59. Glitzy club near the Hipódromo Argentino that plays commercial dance music and regularly welcomes international DJs like the Godskitchen collective. Fri & Sat from 10pm.

Glam Cabrera 3046, Barrio Norte ☎011 4963 2521, ⓦglambsas.com.ar; map p.59. One of the city's hottest gay bar-discos. Several lounge areas and dancefloors play everything from Latino beats to 1980s classics. Thurs & Sat from 1am.

Groove Palermo Av Santa Fe 4389, Palermo ⓦpalermogroove.com; map p.59. Club specializing in live music, often rock and international bands. Also one of the host venues of legendary alternative rock/reggae nights *Fiesta Clandestina*. Open Sat night for club nights and for live music during the week (see website for listings).

Living M T de Alvear 1540, Centro ☎011 4811 4730, ⓦliving.com.ar; map p.59. Laidback club in a rambling old building with two bars, a coffee stand and a long, narrow dancefloor that gets very packed. Plays a fun, danceable mix of funk, disco and rock music. Thurs from 7pm and Fri & Sat from 10pm.

Maluco Beleza Sarmiento 1728, Centro ☎011 4372 1737, ⓦmalucobeleza.com.ar; map p.55. Long-running Brazilian club, playing a mix of *lambada*, afro-samba and reggae to a lively crowd of Brazilians and Brazilophiles. Wed & Fri–Sun from 10pm.

Niceto Club Niceto Vega 5510, Palermo Viejo ☎011 4779 9396, ⓦnicetoclub.com; map p.59. One of BA's best clubs, *Niceto* has a roster of mainly reggae and electronic music at weekends, with the outlandish Club 69 dance parties on Thurs. See website for schedule.

ENTERTAINMENT

CULTURAL CENTRES

Buenos Aires has a number of excellent and popular cultural centres promoting culture and the arts. Entry is free, although special temporary exhibitions occasionally charge a fee.

Centro Cultural Borges Viamonte 525 ☎011 5555 5358, ⓦccborges.org.ar. Named after Argentina's most famous writer; there's a permanent area dedicated to him,

as well as exhibitions, a cinema and workshops. Mon–Sat 10am–9pm and Sun noon–9pm.

Centro Cultural Recoleta Junín 1930 ☎011 4803 1040, ⓦcentroculturalrecoleta.org. Located next to the famous cemetery, this is an excellent centre with a particular focus on visual arts; it's also the occasional home of anarchic theatre troupe Fuerza Bruta/De la Guarda. Tues–Fri 2–9pm & Sat & Sun noon–9pm.

Ciudad Cultural Konex Sarmiento 3131 ☎011 4864 3200, ⓦciudadculturalkonex.org. Atmospheric cultural centre in converted warehouse, located in the Once part of town. Hosts film and theatre productions as well as live music. Also the home of legendary drumming outfit La Bomba de Tiempo (shows on Mon at 7pm). Daily.

ND Ateneo Espacio Cultural Paraguay 918 ☎011 4328 2888, ⓦndateneo.com.ar. Cultural space and theatre with an emphasis on live music. Has shows from 9pm most evenings and there are also regular evening debates.

TANGO SHOWS

Tango shows are expensive, but they are the best way to see a series of top tango dancers in one evening, and most are well worth the splurge. All the following have nightly shows, and most include dinner. Prices range from around AR$250 (without food) to VIP treatment with haute cuisine for over $1000.

Bar Sur Estados Unidos 299, at Balcarce, San Telmo ☎011 4362 6086, ⓦbar-sur.com.ar; map p.55. This cosy little joint puts on fancy shows and encourages audience participation.

Café Tortoni Av de Mayo 829, Centre ☎011 4342 4328, ⓦcafétortoni.com.ar; map p.55. Buenos Aires' most famous café offers an affordable and rather theatrical tango show downstairs at AR$80–100.

MILONGAS

Milongas – regular dance clubs, usually starting with lessons (beginners welcome) – are popular with tango dancers young and old. They are a great way to try the moves for yourself and to get a feel for the scene for a fraction of the price of a dinner show (entrance usually costs AR$25). Among the city's best *milongas* are **La Viruta** (Armenia 1366, Palermo ☎011 4774 6357); **Salón Canning** (Scalabrini Ortiz 1331, Palermo ☎011 4832 6753); **La Catedral** (Sarmiento 4006, Almagro ☎011 5325 1630); and **Centro Cultural Torquato Tasso** (Defensa 1575, San Telmo ☎011 4307 6506). **Confitería Ideal** (Suipacha 380–384, San Nicolas ☎011 5265 8069), a beautiful if crumbling relic of a dancehall, also holds afternoon classes.

Esquina Carlos Gardel Carlos Gardel 3200, Abasto ☎ 011 4867 6363, ⓦ esquinacarlosgardel.com.ar. Although very touristy, this smart venue, named after the king of tango, remains a classic. Shows from AR$470 (without food).

Piazzolla Tango Florida 165, Microcentro ☎ 011 4344 8200, ⓦ piazzollatangoshow.com; map p.55. Housed in a grand old theatre in the centre, the show here is made up of two singers, an orchestra and a set of tango dancers, with prices starting at US$78.

El Viejo Almacén Av Independencia 300, at Balcarce, San Telmo ☎ 011 4307 6689; map p.55. Dinner and show from 8pm or show only from 10pm.

SHOPPING

Buenos Aires offers some of the best shopping in South America, from high-end designer stores and air-conditioned malls to weekend markets and cutting-edge boutiques. Best buys include leather goods (handbags, belts, shoes), wine, home design and handicrafts (particularly handmade jewellery). Top shopping areas include Avenida Santa Fe, Palermo Viejo and San Telmo. Downtown Calle Florida is a famous shopping street from yesteryear but is a bit of a tourist trap today. Most of the Argentine clothing chains and designers have outlet stores in Villa Crespo, around Gurruchaga and Aguirre; see ⓦ espaciooutlet.con.ar for a full list.

Malls The city's malls house Argentina's most successful brands, as well as big international names; they open every day of the week until 10pm. Try Alto Palermo (Santa Fé and Coronel Díaz, Palermo, ⓦ altopalermo .com.ar), Galerías Pacífico (Florida and Córdoba, Centre, ⓦ progaleriaspacifico.com.ar) or Paseo Alcorta (Salguero 3172 and Figueroa Alcorta, Palermo Chico, ⓦ paseoalcorta .com.ar); the last has a large Carrefour hypermarket downstairs. The largest of all is Unicenter (ⓦ unicenter .com.ar), north of the city in the outer suburbs, full of designer shops, a cinema, and with an IMAX close by. You can get there on the #60 bus from the centre, or by taxi.

Markets The city's *ferias* usually take place on weekends and are an excellent place to pick up inexpensive local handicrafts. The most extensive are: the Feria "Hippy" next to Recoleta cemetery (Sat & Sun); Plaza Dorrego in San Telmo, spreading half a dozen blocks along Defensa (Sun); and on Sat or Sun depending on time of year, the Feria de Mataderos (see p.60). For locally made and designed clothes head to Plaza Serrano in Palermo, weekends from

3pm onwards, when the cafés surrounding the plaza are converted into indoor markets filled to the brim with affordable clothes and jewellery.

DIRECTORY

Banks and exchange The centre has a host of casas de cambio for foreign exchange; shop around for the best rate. Banks will also change to or from dollars.

Embassies and consulates Australia, Villanueva 1400 ☎ 011 4779 3500; Bolivia, Av Corrientes 545, 2nd Floor ☎ 011 4394 1463; Brazil, Cerrito 1350 ☎ 011 4515 2400; Canada, Tagle 2828 ☎ 011 4808 1000; Chile, Tagle 2762 ☎ 011 4808 8601; Ireland, Av del Libertador 1060, 6th Floor ☎ 011 5787 0801; New Zealand, Carlos Pellegrini 1427, 5th Floor ☎ 011 4328 0747; UK, Dr Luis Agote 2412 ☎ 011 4808 2200; United States, Av Colombia 4300 ☎ 011 5777 4533; Uruguay, Av Las Heras 1907 ☎ 011 4807 3040.

Hospitals Private hospitals: Hospital Británico (Pedriel 74 ☎ 011 4309 6400) has English-speaking doctors and 24hr emergency care; for non-emergency visits there is also a more central location at Marcelo T de Alvear 1573 (☎ 011 4812 0040). Hospital Alemán (Av Pueyrredón 1640, between Beruti and Juncal ☎ 011 4827 7000), emergency (enter on Beruti) and non-emergency care; English spoken. Public hospital: Hospital Juan A Fernández (Cerviño 3356, at Bulnes ☎ 011 4808 2600).

Internet Internet cafés are everywhere in Buenos Aires, and many *locutorios* (phone shops) also have internet; rates are inexpensive and they tend to open late.

Laundry Laundries are plentiful and inexpensive (though not usually self-service). Expect to pay around AR$30 for a wash and dry.

Left luggage Retiro bus station and both the domestic and international airports have left luggage services. Your hostel may be prepared to look after your luggage if you have a return booking.

Pharmacies Pharmacies are plentiful. Farmacity (ⓦ farmacity.com.ar) has branches throughout the city, many open 24hr (for example, at Florida 474, between Corrientes and Lavalle, Centre ☎ 011 4322 6559).

Police In an emergency call ☎ 101. Tourist Police, Comisaría del Turista, Av Corrientes 436 ☎ 011 4346 5748 or ☎ 0800 999 5000 (24hr), English spoken.

Post office Correo Argentina has branches all over town (ⓦ www.correoargentino.com.ar).

PALERMO VIEJO

After the economic crash of the early noughties, this low-rise area became a hotbed of creative and design talent, and the streets have since filled to bursting with tiny, beautifully presented boutiques. The area is perfect for browsing but choice boutiques include: **Condimentos** (Honduras 4874) for comely local jewellery designs; **28 Sport** (Gurruchaga 1481) for top-quality shoes for men and women; and **SoldBA** (Costa Rica 4656), cool T-shirt heaven.

Around Buenos Aires

Argentina's most spectacular scenery lies far from the capital but, thankfully, Buenos Aires province offers several rewarding – and easily accessible – destinations for a day-trip from the capital or a peaceful overnighter. The mini-Venice of **Tigre**, just north of Buenos Aires, is the gateway to the watery recreation of the Paraná Delta. A trip to the provincial capital, **La Plata**, is essential for natural history enthusiasts; the city's Museo de la Plata is home to an extraordinary array of megafauna skeletons. And a slice of gaucho life is the draw at **San Antonio de Areco**, where late nineteenth-century houses and cobbled streets

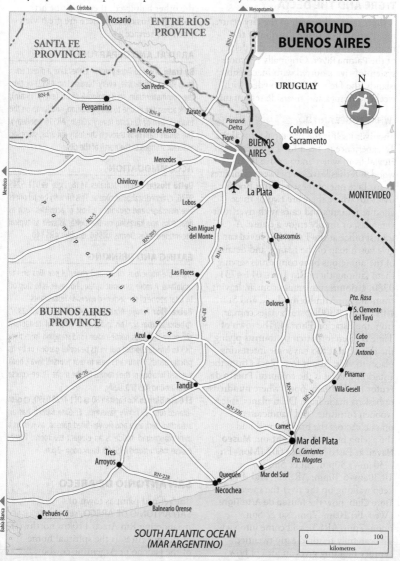

AROUND BUENOS AIRES

Córdoba

Rosario

ENTRE RÍOS PROVINCE

Mesopotamia

SANTA FE PROVINCE

URUGUAY

RN-9

San Pedro

RN-8

Pergamino

Zárate

RN-8

San Antonio de Areco

Paraná Delta

Tigre

BUENOS AIRES

Colonia del Sacramento

Mercedes

Chivilcoy

La Plata

MONTEVIDEO

Lobos

San Miguel del Monte

Chascomús

Las Flores

BUENOS AIRES PROVINCE

Dolores

Pta. Rasa

S. Clemente del Tuyú

Azul

Cabo San Antonio

RP-76

Tandil

Pinamar

Villa Gesell

RN-226

Camet

Tres Arroyos

Mar del Plata

C. Corrientes

Pta. Mogotes

RN-228

Quequén

Mar del Sud

Necochea

Pehuén-Có

Balneario Orense

SOUTH ATLANTIC OCEAN (MAR ARGENTINO)

Mendoza

Bahía Blanca

0   100
kilometres

1

combine with gaucho culture to charming effect. Taking the ferry across the Río de la Plata to **Colonia**, in Uruguay (see p.843), also makes a great day out. Wandering around the old town's cobbled streets – a UNESCO World Heritage Site – and eating in the sunny main plaza can be a welcome relief from hectic Buenos Aires.

TIGRE AND THE DELTA

A short train ride north of the city centre, the river port of **TIGRE** distributes the timber and fruit produced in the delta of the **Paraná River**. Originally a remote system of rivers dotted with inaccessible islands, the Delta is now crowded with weekend homes and riverside restaurants.

WHAT TO SEE AND DO

The river itself is the principal attraction. To experience it, head for Tigre's **Estación Fluvial** from where inexpensive local wooden ferries leave every twenty minutes or so. Take one of these to "Tres Bocas" (AR$40) where there are two or three good restaurants and cafés with riverfront verandas, or simply enjoy a cruise. A tourist office at the Estación Fluvial can give you a map of the islands and details of the numerous boat companies serving them (among them Río Tur ☎011 4731 0280, ⓦrioturcatamaranes.com.ar, leaving from the Los Mimbreros dock; and Sturla ☎011 4731 1300, ⓦsturlaviajes.com.ar, from the Estación Fluvial). The town of Tigre is often forgotten by tourists plying the river, but it too has some interesting places to visit. About four blocks from the Estación Fluvial is the colourful **Puerto de Frutos** (daily 10am–6pm) where hundreds of baskets made from Delta plants, spices, wooden furniture, and handicrafts are on sale. Across the bridge you'll find the ageing but well-thought-out **Museo Naval**, at Paseo Victorica 602 (Mon–Fri 8.30am–5.30pm, Sat & Sun 10.30am–6.30pm; AR$12), and if you keep walking up the river the spectacular **Tigre Club**, now the **Museo de Arte Tigre** (Wed–Fri 10am–7pm, Sat & Sun noon–7pm, AR$3), will come into view. The carefully restored early twentieth-century building gives an idea of how

the other half lived; there is a fine art collection inside and there are great views from the terrace.

ARRIVAL AND DEPARTURE

By train To get to Tigre you can either take a direct train from Retiro (Mitre line, every 10min; 1hr; AR$2) or take the commuter train to Bartolomé Mitre (every 15min); walk across the bridge to Maipú station, and jump on the touristic *Tren de la Costa* (every 20min; AR$16 one-way). This smart train runs through the leafy suburbs, stopping at scenic stations to the north of the city.

ACCOMMODATION

Delta Hostel Coronel Morales 1418, Tigre ☎011 5245 9776, ⓦtigredeltahostel.com.ar. This friendly hostel offers free massages and organizes a host of activities such as boat trips and kayaking on the Delta, as well as typical Argentine *asados*. Dorms **AR$80**, doubles **AR$340**

EATING AND DRINKING

There are numerous cheap and cheerful *parrillas* on the mainland. A more romantic option, however, is to stop off by boat at one of the secluded riverside restaurants.

Beixa Flor Arroyo Abra Vieja 148 ☎011 4728 2397, ⓦbeixaflor.com.ar. This quiet and colourful restaurant serves up delicious home-made food (ranging from river fish to *bife de chorizo*) out in its peaceful garden or by its private beach. If you can't bear to tear yourself away, book yourself into one of their rooms for the night. Three-course meal around AR$170. Daily.

El Gato Blanco Rio Capitán 80 ☎011 4728 0390, ⓦgato-blanco.com. A family favourite, *El Gato Blanco* has an attractive deck area and flower-filled garden, as well as a mini playground. Inside is an elegant tea room. Three-course meal around AR$160. Daily noon–3pm.

SAN ANTONIO DE ARECO

The refined pampas town of **SAN ANTONIO DE ARECO**, set on the meandering Río Areco 110km northwest of Buenos Aires, is the spiritual home of the gaucho or Argentine cowboy.

A robust tourist industry has grown around the gaucho tradition: silver and leather handicraft workers peddle their wares in the town's shops, historic **estancias** (ranches) accommodate visitors in the surrounding countryside and an annual **gaucho festival** draws massive crowds every November. While bicycles rule the streets here, you'll also spot beret-clad *estancia* workers on horseback, trotting about the cobblestones.

WHAT TO SEE AND DO

The leafy town centre is laid out in a grid fashion around the main square, **Plaza Ruiz de Arellano**, and is full of genteel, slightly decaying, single-storey nineteenth-century buildings, many of them painted a blushing shade of pink. On the south side of the square is the plain white **Iglesia Parroquial San Antonio de Padua**, the town's first chapel, dating from 1728. A sculpture of San Antonio graces the exterior. One block north, in a refurbished former power plant at Alsina 66, is the **Centro Cultural Usina Vieja** (Tues–Sun 11am–5pm; AR$5), home to the **Museo de la Ciudad**, with nineteenth-century objects and temporary art exhibitions that depict life in rural Argentina.

Just north of town, across the Río Areco, lies **Parque Criollo**, home to the **Museo Gauchesco Ricardo Güiraldes** (Wed–Mon 11am–5pm; guided visits Sat & Sun 12.30pm & 3.30pm; AR$12). Set in a replica nineteenth-century *estancia*, the museum has a collection of gaucho art and artefacts and pays homage to the

life of author Ricardo Güiraldes, whose classic novel, *Don Segundo Sombra* (1926) – set in San Antonio de Areco – served to elevate the *mate*-sucking, horse-breaking, cow-herding gaucho from rebellious outlaw to respected and romantic national icon. Demonstrations of gaucho feats are held every year in the Parque Criollo during November's week-long **Fiesta de la Tradición** celebrations.

ARRIVAL AND INFORMATION

By bus The bus station (☎ 02326 453 904) is at General Paz & Av Dr Smith, a six-block walk from the town centre along C Segundo Sombra. There are buses to and from Buenos Aires (every 1–2hr; 2hr) and Rosario (6 daily; 4hr).
Tourist information The tourist office, which loans bicycles, is a short walk from the main square towards the river at the corner of Arellano & Zerboni (Mon–Fri 8am–7pm; Sat & Sun till 8pm; ☎ 02326 453 165, ⓦ visiteareco.com).

ACCOMMODATION

While San Antonio de Areco can easily be visited on a day-trip from Buenos Aires, you might well be charmed into staying the night. Book ahead at weekends (the town is a popular destination for *porteños*) and well in advance for the Fiesta de la Tradición in November, or contact the tourist office, which can arrange homestays with families.
Club River ☎ 02326 453 590. This campsite is 1km west of town along Zerboni. The price is for two people. Camping **AR$80**
Hostal de Areco Zapiola 25 ☎ 02326 456 118, ⓦ hostal dearcco.com.ar. Centrally located in a pink colonial build-ing, this B&B has a nice sunny garden and offers decent doubles with private bathrooms. **AR$340**
Hostel Gaucho Zerboni 308 ☎ 02326 453 625, ⓦ hostel gaucho.com.ar. Decent, centrally located option with friendly staff and free access to the all-important barbecue equipment. Dorms **AR$65**, doubles **AR$310**

ESTANCIAS

Reflecting Argentina's changing economic climate, many of the country's **estancias** – vast cattle and horse estates once lorded over by wealthy European settlers – are staying afloat by moving into the tourism market and converting into luxury accommodation. For anyone with latent aristocratic or cowboy aspirations, *estancias* offer the chance to milk cows, ride horses, go fly-fishing, play polo or simply tuck into a juicy slab of steak plucked straight off the *asado* while swanning poolside with a glass of Malbec.

Running the gamut from simple family farmhouses to Pampas dude ranches and ostentatious Italianate mansions, *estancias* are a character-filled throwback to the Argentina of yesteryear. For a list of *estancias* offering accommodation in and around San Antonio de Areco, see ⓦ visiteareco.com or ⓦ sanantoniodeareco.com. For more **information** on *estancias* in other parts of Argentina, visit ⓦ estanciasargentinas.com, ⓦ estanciastravel.com, ⓦ estanciasenargentina.com or ⓦ ranchweb.com.

1

EATING AND DRINKING

Many of San Antonio de Areco's restaurants and bars have been given Old World-style makeovers, and their continued patronage by weathered *estancia* workers gives them an air of authenticity.

Almacén de Ramos Generales Zapiola 143 ☏ 02326 456 376, ⓦ ramosgeneralesareco.com.ar. Old bottles and gaucho paraphernalia line the walls of this delightful *parrilla;* the rabbit and trout specials and waist-softening desserts ensure a steady stream of regulars. Mains around AR$80. Daily.

La Esquina de Merti Arellano 149 ☏ 02326 456 705, ⓦ esquinademerti.com.ar. Dolled up like a traditional corner store, this spacious and atmospheric plaza-side restaurant excels in fast and friendly service. *Parrilla* for two AR$110; pastas around AR$40. Daily until 1am.

La Olla de Cobre Matheu 433 ☏ 02326 453 105, ⓦ laolla decobre.com.ar. A small chocolate factory and sweet shop selling superb home-made *alfajores*. Sample before buying. Closed Tues.

LA PLATA

La Plata became the capital of the province of Buenos Aires in 1880, when the city of Buenos Aires was made the Federal Capital. Close enough to make an easy day-trip, it has a relaxed, small city feel. The geometric design, by French architect Pedro Benoît, and grid-numbered streets, were designed to make navigating the city easy but at times do exactly the opposite.

WHAT TO SEE AND DO

The most famous attractions can be found north of the city centre, next to the zoo, and in the middle of the pleasant lush parkland, **Paseo del Bosque**. The **Museo de la Plata** (Tues–Sun 10am–6pm; AR$6) was the first museum built in Latin America and has a wonderful collection of skeletons, stuffed animals and fossils, set in a crumbling building in the midst of the university. Though desperately in need of refurbishment, the museum is well worth visiting to see the vast whale bones and the models of prehistoric animals.

From the Paseo del Bosque (Av Iraola), avenidas 51 and 53 lead down through the historic centre to the **Plaza Moreno**. On its far side stands the colossal, neo-Gothic brick **Catedral**, with an impressive marble interior of thick columns and high vaulted ceilings. Roughly halfway between the two is **Plaza San Martín**, the lively heart of the city. On the western side, the **Centro Cultural Pasaje Dardo Rocha** (daily 9am–10pm; free) occupies the city's former train station, taking up an entire block between avenidas 49 and 50, 6 and 7. Behind the elegant, French- and Italian-influenced facade are housed a cinema and various exhibition spaces,

---

MAR DEL PLATA

Argentina's **beaches** are somewhat overshadowed by neighbouring Uruguay's golden sands, in particular glamorous Punta del Este (see p.848). Still, a seaside outing in summer is a quintessential Argentine experience – and **Mar del Plata**, boasting some 50km of beach 400km south of Buenos Aires, is the country's number one resort. In the summer season (mid-Dec to March), millions of city-dwellers descend on the place, generating vibrant eating, drinking and entertainment scenes (or overcrowding and overpricing, depending on your point of view).

Though Mar del Plata may have lost some of the lustre of days gone by, glimpses of glamour still abound in the city's restored early twentieth-century mansions (check out French-style Villa Ortiz Basualdo, now the **Museo Municipal de Arte**, at Avenida Colón 1189, and the **Centro Cultural Victoria Ocampo**, Matheu 1851. The renowned **International Film Festival** is held in Mar del Plata in November, showing new Argentine and international films.

Nearby **Cariló** and **Mar de los Pampas** are both eco-resorts that provide a more laidback seaside experience, set within beautiful pine forests. Rent a house or stay in a luxury hotel and chill out for a few days – but be warned, these are boutique resorts for Argentina's rich and famous, so you won't find anything nearing a mid-range or budget accommodation option.

There are numerous daily **buses** from Buenos Aires to Mar del Plata (5–6hr), or (not recommended) you can make the journey less comfortably (from AR$100) by **train**, from Constitución station (3 daily, 6hr), or **fly** across in less than an hour (2–3 daily).

including the excellent **Museo de Arte Contemporáneo Latinoamericano** (daily 9am–10pm; free).

ARRIVAL AND INFORMATION

By bus Buses for La Plata leave from Retiro bus station every 30min (1hr 10min; ARS12 one-way).
Destinations Mar del Plata (12 daily; 5hr); Puerto Madryn (4 daily; 18hr).

By train The train journey from Constitución station is much slower than travelling by bus. Trains leave approximately every 30min (1hr 30min; ARS4).

Tourist information There's a tourist office inside the Pasaje Dardo Rocha cultural centre (daily 9am–5.30pm; ✆0221 427 1535). Many of the best places to eat and drink are just south of here, around the junction of avenidas 10 & 47.

EATING AND DRINKING

Cerveceria Modelo Diagonal 54, 496 ✆0221 421 1321. Old-school classic restaurant and café housed in a century-old building with legs of ham hanging from the ceiling. Serves excellent draught beer; paella and home-made *pan dulce* (sweet buns) are the house speciality. Daily 8am–1am.

Vitaminas Diagonal 74, 1640 ✆0221 482 1106. Colourful vegetarian café serving up healthy meals and snacks including exotic salads and freshly squeezed juices. Mon–Sat 8am–4pm & 8pm–midnight.

Córdoba Province

CÓRDOBA PROVINCE, 700km northwest of Buenos Aires, marks Argentina's geographical bull's-eye. Serene towns dot its undulating **Central Sierras**, the second highest mountain range in Argentina after the Andes, and the region is one of the country's more affordable travel destinations, except perhaps in high season when many city-dwellers flock to its cool heights. Córdoba Province is a relaxed place for exploring the great outdoors – via hikes, horserides or even **skydives** – or just hanging out sipping *mate* with the super-friendly locals.

Most of the action takes place in and around **Córdoba city**, which has the country's highest concentration of bars and clubs outside Buenos Aires. South of Córdoba city in the verdant **Calamuchita Valley**, towns such as **Alta Gracia** and

Germanic, beer-brewing **Villa General Belgrano** have historically served as getaways for Argentina's elite. Northwest of the capital in the **Punilla Valley**, laidback towns such as **Capilla del Monte** are growing in popularity among bohemian *porteños* looking for a clean, green break from city life.

CÓRDOBA

Argentina's second-largest city, unpretentious **CÓRDOBA** boasts some beautifully restored colonial architecture, plentiful restaurants and a legendary nightlife best experienced when the university students are around. It is a good base for exploring the province, though during the city's stiflingly hot summers you'll soon be lured west to the Sierras' cooler elevations.

Plaza San Martín and around

Once the bloody stage for bullfights, executions and military parades, **Plaza San Martín** was converted into a civilized public square, replete with fountains and semi-tropical foliage, in the 1870s. Free tango events are hosted here most Saturday nights at 10pm.

On the square's western side, the two-storey, sixteenth-century **Cabildo** was once the city's colonial headquarters and has now been turned into the **Museo de la Ciudad** (Mon 4–9pm, Tues–Sun 9am–1pm & 4–9pm; free; ✆0351 428 5856). It also hosts concerts, art exhibitions and, in the summer, tango evenings.

Alongside the Cabildo is the **Catedral**, one of the oldest in the country. Construction began in 1577 but wasn't completed for another two hundred years, rendering the cathedral something of an architectural mongrel, with a mix of Neoclassical and Baroque styles and a Romanesque dome thrown in for good measure. Note the trumpeting angels in indigenous dress gracing the bell towers.

Manzana Jesuítica

The seventeenth-century **Manzana Jesuítica** (summer Tues–Sun 9am–1pm & 5–8pm; winter Tues–Fri 9am–1pm & 4–8pm, Sat & Sun 9.30am–12.30pm &

1

3.30–6.30pm; AR$10; ☎0351 433 2075), or Jesuit Block, a short walk southwest of the plaza, is Córdoba's top attraction. A testament to the missionaries who arrived hot on the heels of Córdoba's sixteenth-century colonizers, the **Templo de la Compañía de Jesús**, built in 1640, is Argentina's oldest surviving Jesuit temple. It has a striking Cusqueño altarpiece, and its barrel-shaped vaulted roof is made of Paraguayan cedar. The block also houses a private chapel, the **Capilla Doméstica** (guided visits on request).

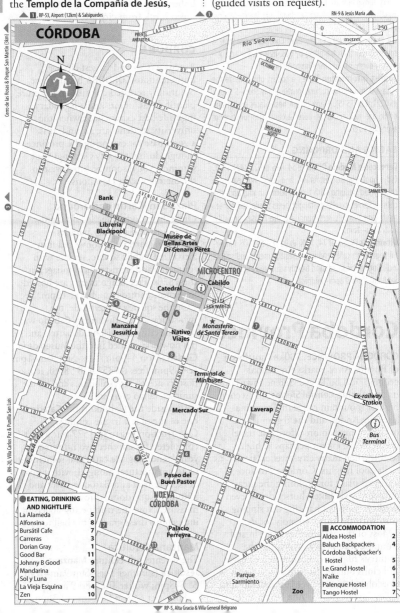

CÓRDOBA

EATING, DRINKING AND NIGHTLIFE

La Alameda	5
Alfonsina	8
Bursátil Cafe	7
Carreras	3
Dorian Gray	1
Good Bar	11
Johnny B Good	9
Mandarina	6
Sol y Luna	2
La Vieja Esquina	4
Zen	10

ACCOMMODATION

Aldea Hostel	2
Baluch Backpackers	4
Córdoba Backpacker's Hostel	5
Le Grand Hostel	6
N'aike	1
Palenque Hostel	3
Tango Hostel	7

Monasterio de Santa Teresa

Southwest of Plaza San Martín at Independencia 146 is the **Iglesia Santa Teresa**, part of a working convent that contains the **Museo de Arte Religioso Juan de Tejeda** (Independencia 122; Wed–Sat 9.30am–12.30pm; AR$10; ☏ 0351 15 671 3218, ✆ museotejedacordoba.com.ar). It has perhaps the finest collection of sacred art in the country, including Jesuit artefacts and religious paintings from Cusco in Peru.

Museo de Bellas Artes Dr Genaro Pérez

The municipal art gallery, the **Museo de Bellas Artes Dr Genaro Pérez**, Avenida General Paz 33 (Tues–Sun 10am–8pm; free; ☏ 0351 434 1646), is housed in a late nineteenth-century French-style mansion and features nineteenth- and twentieth-century Argentine art. The permanent collection has numerous landscape paintings from the **Escuela Cordobesa**, a movement led by master Genaro Pérez.

Nueva Córdoba

The neighbourhood of **Nueva Córdoba**, just south of the historic centre, is full of late nineteenth-century mansions converted into hip bars and restaurants. Diagonal Avenida Hipólito Yrigoyen cuts through the neighbourhood, which extends from Plaza Vélez Sarsfield to Parque Sarmiento (see below). Just over halfway down is the **Paseo del Buen Pastor**, Avenida Hipólito Yrigoyen 325, a former women's prison converted into a culinary and cultural precinct featuring art exhibitions and free concerts. Flanked by fountains and landscaped grassy knolls, it is one of the city's most popular spaces for chilling out in the summer.

Museo Superior de Bellas Artes Palacio Ferreyra

An exemplary art museum, the **Museo Superior de Bellas Artes Palacio Ferreyra**, Avenida Hipólito Irigoyen 511 (Tues–Sun 10am–8pm; AR$10; ☏ 0351 434 3636), features four floors of works in an opulent 1916 palace built in the French classical style. The top floor has rolling contemporary art exhibitions, while the basement level is devoted to photography. In between, some three hundred artists are represented, including Pablo Picasso and Argentina's Fernando Fader and Lino Enea Spilimbergo. A little further south is the hilltop **Parque Sarmiento**, one of the city's most popular green spaces.

ARRIVAL AND DEPARTURE

By plane Córdoba's Aeropuerto Internacional Taravella is 11km north of the city centre. It has domestic flights to Buenos Aires, Bariloche, Mendoza and Rosario, as well as international services to cities in Brazil, Chile and Peru. Taxis (around AR$100) and minibuses connect the airport with the city centre.

By bus The long-distance bus station (☏ 0351 428 4141) is several blocks east of the centre at Blvd Perón 380. Public buses run downtown; a taxi costs around AR$15. Local buses for some provincial destinations leave from the Terminal de Minibuses behind the Mercado Sur market on Blvd Arturo Illia.

Destinations Alta Gracia (every 15min; 1hr); Buenos Aires (frequent; 9–11hr); Capilla del Monte (hourly; 1hr 30min); Mendoza (hourly; 9–10hr); Rosario (hourly; around 6hr); Salta (10 daily; 11–12hr); Villa General Belgrano (every 45min–1hr; 2hr).

INFORMATION AND TOURS

Tourist information The main tourist office is in the Cabildo (daily 8am–8pm; ☏ 0351 434 1200, ✆ cordoba turismo.gov.ar). There are also several smaller (and often more helpful) offices dotted around the city, including at the bus station (daily 7am–9pm; ☏ 0351 433 1982), the airport (daily 8am–8pm; ☏ 0351 434 8390) and the Paseo del Buen Pastor (daily 8am–8pm; ☏ 0351 434 2727).

Tour operators The tourist authority runs regular free walking tours of downtown sights with English-language guides; pop in to the main tourist office to find out what's on during your visit. The privately run City Tour (☏ 0351 424 6605) offers sightseeing tours on a red double-decker

---

★ TREAT YOURSELF

SKYDIVING

Córdoba is the most affordable place in Argentina to jump out of a plane. Tumbling out of the door at 2500m, you get a bird's-eye view, after 20 seconds of face-flattening freefall, of city sprawl, a patchwork of green fields and the Central Sierras. The guys at **Skydive Córdoba** (☏ 0351 15 687 8471, ✆ skydivecordoba .com) have almost 40 years of skydiving experience and charge from AR$690 for a tandem jump.

1

bus starting from the Plaza San Martín near the cathedral. For day-trips and tours of the province, try Nativo Viajes, Independencia 174 (☎0351 424 5341, ⓦcordobanativo viajes.com.ar).

ACCOMMODATION

Córdoba has some of the best-value hostels in the country, as well as the odd decent guesthouse, but its lower-cost hotels are generally pretty poor. All the establishments listed here offer tour-booking services and include internet/wi-fi access, breakfast and use of kitchen in their rates.

★ **Aldea Hostel** Santa Rosa 447 ☎0351 426 1312, ⓦaldeahostelcordoba.com. This bright, ambitious hostel has space for one hundred people and is bursting with extras including two games rooms, a TV lounge, a leafy patio and a roof terrace. Discounts for extended stays. Dorms AR$55, doubles AR$200

Baluch Backpackers San Martín 338 ☎0351 422 3977, ⓦbaluchbackpackers.com. This popular hostel has a cosy lounge area, helpful staff and hosts weekly barbecues on its roof terrace. The dorms sleep up to eight people, and the private rooms have a/c. Late risers, however, might be put off by the ambient street noise. Dorms AR$50, doubles AR$170

Córdoba Backpacker's Hostel Deán Funes 285 ☎0351 422 0593, ⓦcordobabackpackers.com.ar. A lively bar, pool table, tour desk and roof terrace with dead-on cathedral views are just some of the perks of this bustling, centrally located hostel. Dorms AR$55, doubles AR$160

Le Grand Hostel Buenos Aires 547 ☎0351 422 7115, ⓦlegrandhostel.com. The largest hostel on the scene, located in Nueva Córdoba, an area popular with students. There's a chill-out room with huge flat-screen TV, an excellently equipped kitchen and decent outside area. The attached *Le Grand Suites* has smart private en-suite rooms. Dorms AR$60, doubles AR$200

N'aike Fresnal 5048 ☎0351 589 0501, ⓦnaike.com.ar. This friendly, well-run guesthouse is located in the quiet Villa Belgrano neighbourhood, a few kilometres north-west of the centre. There are six colourful rooms, and guests have access to a kitchen, a plunge pool and a Jacuzzi. AR$290

Palenque Hostel General Paz 371 ☎0351 423 7588, ⓦpalenquehostel.com.ar. Noisy but fun hostel in a converted nineteenth-century townhouse. The dorms and private rooms are reasonable value, and the wood-panelled common areas are good for meeting other backpackers. Dorms AR$60, doubles AR$165

Tango Hostel Fructose Rivera 70 ☎0351 425 6023, ⓦtangohostelcordoba.com.ar. In a convenient location, close to the Paseo de las Artes, this hostel has a sociable atmosphere and a collection of decent, no-frills dorms, plus a few private rooms. Dorms AR$60, doubles AR$150

EATING

Córdoba is a real delight for winers and diners. There are restaurants for refined tastebuds, boisterous drinking holes serving pub grub, and plenty of eat-on-the-run *empanada* joints for lining your stomach before a night out on the town. The pick of the fashionable restaurants is in Nueva Córdoba.

La Alameda Obispo Trejo 170. Savour inexpensive Argentine staples like *empanadas* and *humitas* for a few pesos, while sitting outside on wooden benches, or indoors where customers' poetry and art adorn the walls. Mains around AR$25–40. Mon–Sat noon–4/5am.

★ **Alfonsina** Duarte Quiros 66 ☎0351 427 2847, ⓦalfonsinaweb.com.ar. Antique typewriters, exposed brick-work and a jolly crowd of students are the hallmarks of this restaurant-bar, which offers a taste of Argentina's northwest (mains AR$30–60) and is popular for an evening *mate*. There are other branches at Belgrano 763 and Viamonte and Lima. Mon–Sat 8am–2pm & 6pm–2am, Sun 6pm–2am.

Bursátil Cafe Ituzaingo & San Jeronimo ☎0351 571 9971. In Córdoba's small financial district, this café takes its name from the Spanish for "stock exchange". Food includes classics like *locro* (stew) and international dishes such as Caesar salad. Mains from AR$30. Mon–Fri 7am–7/8pm, Sat noon–7/8pm.

★ **Mandarina** Obispo Trejo 171 ☎0351 426 4909. This chilled-out crowd-pleaser is more inventive than the norm, with Chinese, Japanese and southeast Asian dishes, as well as plenty of vegetarian options. The decor includes orange walls and Buddhist symbolism. Mains from AR$30. Daily 8am–2am.

Sol y Luna Av Gral Paz 278 ☎0351 425 1189, ⓦsolyluna online.com.ar. Load your plate with a variety of hot and cold dishes at this lunchtime vegetarian buffet: a good feed costs less than AR$30. There's another branch at Montevideo 66, Nueva Córdoba. Mon–Sat noon–3.30pm.

La Vieja Esquina Caseros & Belgrano ☎0351 424 7940. This tiny local joint serves up excellent *empanadas* (around AR$5), *humitas* and *locro*; you can eat at one of the counters, take them away or even have them delivered to your room. Mon–Sat 11am–3pm & 7.30pm–midnight.

DRINKING AND NIGHTLIFE

Córdoba is no wallflower when it comes to partying, with Nueva Córdoba the late-night venue of choice for the masses. Hipsters gravitate to the revived warehouse district of El Abasto, just north of the centre, for its edgy bars and nightclubs. Further afield, in the Chateau Carreras neighbourhood, chic discos cater to a young crowd who love *cuarteto* music – a Córdoba speciality.

Carreras Av Cárcano and del Piamonte, Chateau Carreras ☎0351 15 676 2342. One of the city's biggest and liveliest clubs, Carreras focuses on house and electro, though early on in the evening the sounds are a bit more varied. Fri & Sat 11pm–6am.

Dorian Gray Blvd Las Heras & Roque Sáenz Peña ☎0351 15 403 1626. Bizarre decor and an alternative ambience draw an eclectic crowd who throw shapes well into the small hours to mostly electro music. Fri & Sat 11pm–6am.

Good Bar Buenos Aires & Larrañaga. The surfboard out the front and white leather lounges might inspire you to slip into Hawaiian-style boardshorts or a white string bikini. You'll certainly wish you had at 2am when you're sweating buckets on the basement dancefloor. Drinks from AR$15–20. Sun–Wed 7pm–3am, Thurs–Sat till 5am.

Johnny B Good Av Hipólito Yrigoyen 320, Nueva Córdoba ☎0351 424 3960, ⊛jbgood.com. This busy, rather cheesy restaurant-bar serves up good US-style food, a wide range of *tragos* (alcoholic drinks; from AR$20) and a rock-dominated soundtrack (live music most weekends). There's another branch at Rafael Núñez 4791, Cerro de las Rosas. Mon–Thurs 7.30pm–2am, Fri 7.30pm–4am, Sat 11am–4am & Sun 6pm–3am.

Zen Av Julio A Roca 730 ☎0351 15 513 9595, ⊛zendisco .com.ar. This renowned gay-friendly club has two throbbing dancefloors and hosts kooky live shows. Fri & Sat midnight–5am.

SHOPPING

Bookshops Librería Blackpool, Deán Funes 395 (☎0351 423 7172, ⊛blackpoolcerro.com.ar). Sells English-language novels and travel guides. Jan Mon–Fri 9am–1pm, Sat 9.30am–1.30pm; March Mon–Fri 8.30am–8.30pm, first and second Sat of the month 9.30am–1.30pm & 4.50–8.30pm; rest of year Mon–Fri 9am–1pm & 4–8pm, Sat 9.30am–1.30pm.

Markets On weekend evenings (5–9.30pm) there is an arts and crafts market at the Paseo de las Artes on the western edge of Nueva Córdoba in the bohemian Güemes neighbourhood, around Belgrano and Archaval Rodriguez streets.

Shopping centres Nuevocentro Shopping, Duarte Quirós 1400 (Sun–Thurs 10am–11pm, Fri & Sat till 1am; ☎0351 482 8193, ⊛nuevocentro.com.ar).

DIRECTORY

Banks Change money at Citibank, Rivadavia 104, or BBVA, 9 de Julio 450. ATMs are everywhere, especially around the Plaza San Martín.

Hospital Hospital Sanatorio Allende, Av Hipólito Yrigoyen 384 (☎0351 426 9200, ⊛sanatorioallende.com).

Laundry Laverap, Chacabuco 313 and Belgrano 76.

Police Colón 1200.

Post office Av General Paz 201.

ALTA GRACIA

The pleasant colonial town of **ALTA GRACIA**, 38km south of Córdoba at the entrance of the Calamuchita Valley, was once a genteel summer refuge for the *porteño* bourgeoisie. Today it continues to bask in the reflected glory of its former residents: Jesuit missionaries, Spanish composer Manuel de Falla and Che Guevara have all left their mark here.

WHAT TO SEE AND DO

Easily walkable on foot, the town centre is dominated by an impressive Jesuit *estancia*, one of the finest examples in Argentina. But it's also a great springboard for walking in the nearby countryside or, for the more adventurous, skydiving.

Plaza Manuel Solares and around

Alta Gracia came into its own after 1643 when it was chosen as the site of a Jesuit *estancia*. When the Jesuits were expelled in 1767, the *estancia* was left to the elements, only briefly re-inhabited in 1810 by Viceroy Liniers. The *estancia* buildings have been well preserved and overlook the town's main square, **Plaza Manuel Solares**. The **Iglesia Parroquial Nuestra Señora de la Merced**, dating from 1762, stands alongside the Jesuits' original living quarters, which have been converted into the UNESCO World Heritage-listed **Museo de la Estancia Jesuítica de Alta Gracia – Casa del Virrey Liniers** (summer Tues–Fri 9am–8pm, Sat & Sun 9.30am–8pm; winter Tues–Fri 9am–1pm & 3–7pm, Sat & Sun 9.30am–12.30pm & 3.30–6.30pm; AR$5; free guided English-language tours on request; ☎03547 421303, ⊛museoliniers.org.ar). Here, a dramatic Baroque doorway leads to a cloistered courtyard and a motley collection of furniture and religious paintings.

Ernesto "Che" Guevara house and museum

A twenty-minute walk uphill from the plaza brings you to the leafy residential neighbourhood of **Villa Carlos Pellegrini**, whose crumbling mansions once served as holiday homes and residences for moneyed socialites. The Guevara family moved within these circles after relocating from Rosario to Alta Gracia in the 1930s in the hope that the fresh mountain air

1

would alleviate the asthma plaguing their four-year-old son, **Ernesto "Che" Guevara**. The family's former home, Villa Beatriz, at Avellaneda 501, has been converted into the **Museo Casa de Ernesto "Che" Guevara** (Jan & Feb daily 9.30am–7pm; March–Dec Mon 2–7pm, Tues–Sun

9am–7pm except Mon from 2pm; AR$75; ☎03547 428579), showcasing Che's personal effects as well as photographs charting his progression from carefree kid to revolutionary icon. Among the museum's highlights are video interviews with Che's childhood

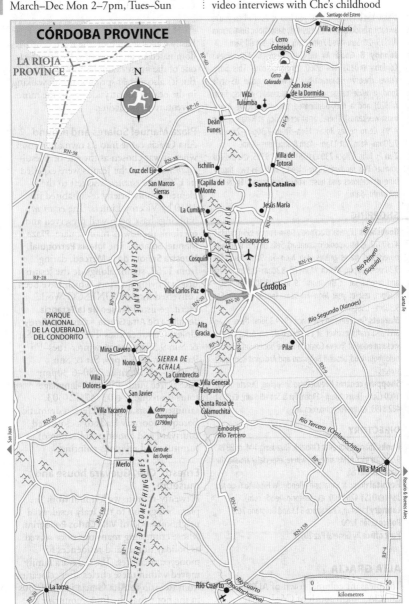

companions, a handwritten resignation letter to Fidel Castro, and photos from a visit Castro and Hugo Chávez made to the house in 2006.

ARRIVAL AND INFORMATION

By bus Regular buses from Córdoba (every 15min; 1hr) and Villa General Belgrano (every 30min–1hr; 1hr) stop at the bus terminal on C P. Butori, at Av Presidente Perón, around eight blocks west of the Tajamar reservoir; minibuses tend to stop nearer the centre on Lucas V Córdoba street.

Tourist information The tourist office is in the clock tower alongside the Tajamar reservoir on Av del Tajamar, at C del Molino (Dec–Feb daily 8am–11pm; March–Nov Mon–Thurs 8am–8pm, Fri–Sun 8am–9pm; 03547 428128, altagracia.gov.ar).

ACCOMMODATION AND EATING

Alta Gracia Hostel Paraguay 218 03547 428810, altagraciahostel.com.ar. A cosy little hostel, five blocks away from the main square, with a basic dorm, a couple of private rooms, a kitchen and a patio area at the back. Dorms AR$60, doubles AR$150

Morena Sarmiento 413 03547 426365. Set in a white, neocolonial house, this restaurant's menu runs the gamut from prawn ravioli to paella and veal in mushroom sauce. The pizzas and fish dishes are also pretty good. Mains from AR$45. Tues–Thurs 8–11pm, Fri–Sun noon–3.30pm & 8–11pm/midnight.

VILLA GENERAL BELGRANO

The twee resort town of **VILLA GENERAL BELGRANO**, 50km south of Alta Gracia, unabashedly exploits its Germanic heritage with all kinds of kitsch. Founded by the surviving seamen of the *Graf Spee*, which sank off the coast of Uruguay in 1939, the town's main street, **Avenida Julio Roca**, comes over like an alpine theme park, with folksy German beer houses and eateries resembling Swiss chalets. You'll either love it or hate it.

WHAT TO SEE AND DO

The best (and some might say only) reason to visit Villa General Belgrano is to sink steins of locally brewed beer at the annual **Oktoberfest**. Held during the first two weeks of October in Plaza José Hernández, it is considered the continent's best celebration of this German tradition. The most popular day-trip from Villa General Belgrano is

30km west to the alpine-flavoured village of **La Cumbrecita**, where there are good opportunities for hiking, abseiling and cooling off in the Río Almbach.

ARRIVAL AND DEPARTURE

By bus The bus terminal is on Av Velez Sarsfield, a 10min walk northwest of the main street, although all buses make drop-offs and pick-ups in the town centre.

Destinations Alta Gracia (every 30min–1hr; 1hr) and Córdoba (every 45min–1hr; 2hr). Pájaro Blanco (03546 461709; call for the latest timetable) runs a minibus service several times a day to and from La Cumbrecita (30min); its bus stop is on Av San Martín, 100m north of Plaza José Hernández.

INFORMATION

Tourist information The tourist office is at Av Julio Roca 168 (daily 8.30am–8.30pm; 03546 461215, vgb.gov.ar).

Mountain bike rental Bike Cerro Negro, Av Julio Roca 625 (03546 462785).

ACCOMMODATION

The hotels in town are generally overpriced, but *cabañas* (self-contained cabins) make a good alternative for groups of four or five – ask at the tourist office for suggestions.

Camping Rincón de Mirlos 9km west of the centre, off the RP-5 03546 15 516 4254, rincondemirlos.com.ar. The best of several campsites around town, *Rincón de Mirlos* has a bucolic riverside setting, clean dorms, isolated camping pitches among the trees, a restaurant-bar, and long stretches of sandy beach. Camping/person AR$35, dorms AR$60

Posada Nehuen San Martín 17 03546 461412, elsitiodelavilla.com/nehuen. This central guesthouse has a selection of comfortable en suites with TVs, mini-fridges and phones, though the decor throughout is a bit old-fashioned. AR$270

★ **Hostel El Rincón** Alexander Fleming 347, 15min walk northwest of the bus station 03546 461323, hostel rincon.com.ar. This laidback, Hostelling International-affiliated hostel offers dorms, en-suite private rooms, and a place to pitch your tent, as well as kitchen access and a small pool. Camping/person AR$20, dorms AR$65, doubles AR$110

EATING AND DRINKING

The town's numerous cafés and restaurants dish up Germanic food of varying quality.

Café Rissen Av Julio Roca 36 03546 464100. Situated on the main strip, this kitsch café is probably the most popular in town. Excellent cakes (from AR$20) and sandwiches are on the menu: the Black Forest (*selva negra*)

gateau, in particular, comes highly recommended. Daily 8am–midnight.

El Ciervo Rojo Av Julio Roca 210 ☎ 03546 461345, ⓦ confiteriaciervorojo.com. Dating back almost 50 years, this appealing restaurant serves up an array of German and Central European dishes (mains AR$40–80) including schnitzel, goulash, spätzle, sausages and sauerkraut. There's live German music on Sat nights. Daily 9am–11pm/midnight.

Viejo Munich Av San Martín 362 ☎ 03546 463122, ⓦ cervezaartesanal.com. The trout, goulash and venison mains aren't too bad, but the beer – nine different varieties, all brewed on-site – is the real star of the show. Free brewery tours Mon, Tues, Fri & Sat 10.45am & 11.45am. Fri–Tues noon–late, Thurs 8pm–late.

CAPILLA DEL MONTE

CAPILLA DEL MONTE attracts more alternative lifestyle-types in summer than you can shake an incense stick at. Situated 102km north of Córdoba city, the idyllic mountain town lies at the base of **Cerro Uritorco**, which, at 1979m, is the Sierra Chica's highest peak and is claimed by many locals to possess an inexplicable magnetic pull.

Set at the confluence of two (often dry) rivers on the northern edge of the Punilla Valley, Capilla del Monte's former glory can be glimpsed in its slowly decaying nineteenth-century mansions. Artisans and New Age healers are the town's more conspicuous residents, and their businesses can be easily visited using the maps and listings provided by the tourist office.

WHAT TO SEE AND DO

Capilla del Monte makes a good base for outdoor adventure sports, including **horseriding** in the surrounding countryside, **rock climbing** the strange sandstone formations around the hamlet of **Ongamira**, **hiking** to the summit of Cerro Uritorco (4hr or so to the top – register at the base of the mountain and start your return by 3.30pm; AR$50; ⓦ cerrouritorco.com.ar), strolling through the multicoloured rock formations of **Los Terrones** (daily 9am–dusk; AR$20; ⓦ losterrones.com) or **paragliding** in the Sierras.

ARRIVAL AND INFORMATION

By bus The bus station is near the centre at Corrientes & Rivadavia. There are regular buses to and from Córdoba (hourly; 1hr 30min).

Tourist information Pick up a map and area information at the tourist office in the old railway station on Av Pueyrredón s/n (daily 8am–8pm; ☎ 03548 481903, ⓦ capilladelmonte.gov.ar).

ACCOMMODATION AND EATING

Calabalumba General Paz s/n ☎ 03548 489601. The closest campsite to town is the riverside *Calabalumba*, which has tent pitches and cabins sleeping up to six. Camping/person AR$20, cabins AR$200

★ **El Duende Azul** Chubut 75, at Aristóbulo del Valle ☎ 03548 15 569667, ⓦ cordobaserrana.com.ar /elduendeazul.htm. A guesthouse in tune with the town's hippy vibe where you can frolic in the big garden or hang out in the common area overrun by pixie and elf figurines. The simple but pretty rooms are en suite and the lovely owners arrange various detox programmes. AR$250

Maracaibo Buenos Aires 182 ☎ 03548 482741. This unpretentious restaurant is a good all-rounder, serving fish, pasta and chicken mains, as well as lots of vegetarian options; the vegetable and corn lasagne is filling and tasty. Mains from around AR$30–40. Fri–Wed 11am–4pm & 7pm–midnight.

Los Tres Gómez 25 de Mayo 452 ☎ 03548 482647, ⓦ hostelencapilladelmonte.com. Hostelling International-affiliated joint with a lurid colour scheme in the communal areas – the dorms and private rooms, by contrast, are plain and a little bare. There's a kitchen, garden and a restaurant-bar. Dorms AR$70, doubles AR$200

THE TRUTH IS OUT THERE

Capilla del Monte hosts an international **UFO convention** every November, organized by local "research" group Centro de Informes OVNI, Juan Cabus 297 (☎ 03548 482485, ⓦ ciouritorco.org – OVNI is Spanish for UFO). **Mystical tourism** is gaining in popularity, with local tour operators jumping on the extraterrestrial bandwagon by offering guided tours to sites of supposed UFO landings as well as night excursions to observe celestial happenings on remote mountaintops. You'll be in good hands with Viajes Ángel (☎ 03548 15 634 532), Diagonal Buenos Aires 183, which does a (fairly) convincing range of otherworldly tours.

1

The Northeast

Sticky summers, *mate* tea and *chamamé* folk music characterize the sultry northeastern provinces of Entre Ríos, Corrientes, Misiones and Santa Fe, an area known as **El Litoral**. Most of the region is wedged between two awesome rivers, the Paraná and the Uruguay, which converge near Buenos Aires as the Río de la Plata. Eclipsing every other attraction in the region are the **Iguazú Falls**, the world's most spectacular waterfalls, framed by lush subtropical forest. Located in the northeastern corner of Misiones Province, the falls straddle the border with Brazil. South of **Iguazú**, the well-preserved Jesuit Mission ruins at **San Ignacio Miní** make for the region's second-biggest draw.

Further afield, in Corrientes Province, the sprawling wetlands of **Esteros del**

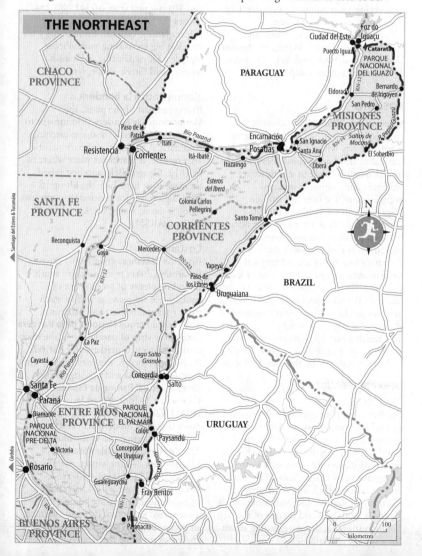

Iberá offer prime wildlife-spotting opportunities. The river-hugging, siesta-loving city of **Corrientes** is increasingly opening itself up to tourism, while Argentina's third-largest city (and the birthplace of Che Guevara), **Rosario**, in Santa Fe Province, has some handsome historic buildings, arresting monuments and a lively weekend party atmosphere. The star of Entre Ríos Province is the **Parque Nacional El Palmar**, with its forest of towering *yatay* palms, an easy day-trip from the resort town of **Colón**.

If you have a problem with heat and humidity, steer clear of this region between December and March, when temperatures in the far north often creep above 40°C.

ROSARIO

Super-stylish **ROSARIO** is a cleaner, greener, less daunting version of Buenos Aires. The city where Che Guevara learned to crawl and Lionel Messi learned to kick a ball is home to a handsome, academic and culturally inclined population of just over one million.

Sprawled on the banks of the **Río Paraná**, Rosario's assets are its riverside beaches, parks, restaurants, bars and museums. For an enjoyable day-trip, the sandy beaches of the subtropical **delta islands** are just a short boat or kayak ride away. There is stylish shopping to be found in Rosario's pedestrianized centre, and free public wi-fi access throughout the city. *Extranjeros* (foreigners) are still very much a novelty here, and whether you're in town to chill or to party, you'll be warmly received by the friendly locals.

WHAT TO SEE AND DO

The leafy parks, historic buildings and excellent shopping opportunities make central Rosario a pleasant place to wander around at any time of year, while the riverfront and beaches are extremely appealing during the summer months. Start your stroll at the Plaza 25 de Mayo and be sure to check out the nearby Catedral de Rosario and Monumento a la Bandera, both postcard images of the city, before hitting the shops or settling down for a spot of sunbathing.

Plaza 25 de Mayo and around

The tree-lined **Plaza 25 de Mayo** lies three blocks west of the river. Here, at the heart of the city, you'll find some of the city's grandest buildings, including the late nineteenth-century **Catedral de Rosario** (daily 9am–12.30pm & 4.30–8.30pm; free), with its striking Italianate marble altar. On the southern side, the **Museo Municipal de Arte Decorativo Firma y Odilio Estévez** (Tues–Fri 3–8pm, Sat & Sun 10am–8pm; free; ☏0341 480 2547) houses the lavish art collection of the Estévez family, Galician immigrants who struck it big cultivating *mate*. Pieces include a Goya painting, a Flemish tapestry and Greek sculptures.

Monumento a la Bandera

Rising just east of the plaza, the **Monumento a la Bandera** (Monument to the Flag) is Rosario's most eye-catching landmark. A stark piece of nationalistic architecture, it marks the place where, in 1812, General Belgrano first raised the Argentine flag. Take the **lift** up its 70m-high tower for panoramic city views (Mon 2–6pm, Tues–Sun 9am–1pm & 2–6pm; AR$5).

Costanera

Rosario's **Costanera** (riverfront) extends for around 20km from north to south, providing plenty of green space to sunbathe or sip *mate*, as well as water-front restaurants, bars and museums. The central **Parque Nacional de la Bandera** – a narrow strip of parkland – is the main setting for regular markets and festivals. As you stroll north, the park merges with **Parque de España** and the large brick **Centro Cultural Parque de España** (Tues–Sun 3–7pm, closed Jan; free; ☏0341 426 0941, ⊚ccpe.org.ar), which hosts changing modern art exhibitions. Half a kilometre north is the **Museo de Arte Contemporáneo de Rosario** (Thurs–Tues 2–8pm winter, 3–9pm summer; AR$5; ☏0341 480 4981, ⊚macromuseo.org.ar), a kitsch temple to modern Argentine art housed inside a converted grain silo, its facade painted in pastel shades. The building – as well as the views from the top floor – outshines

ROSARIO

Río Paraná

Parque
de España

Centro Cultural
Parque de España

Parque Nacional
de la Bandera

Che Guevara's
house

Museo Municipal
de Arte Decorativo

Mercado de
Pulgas del Bajo

Palacio de los Leones

Monumento
a la Bandera

Palacio del Correo

Catedral
de Rosario

Estación
Fluvial

Teatro
El Círculo

Avenida Pellegrini

Parque
Urquiza

Complejo
Astronómico
Municipal

◄ 6. Airport, RN-9, Córdoba & Santa Fe

◄ Bus Terminal & Parque de la Independencia

N

0   500
metres

● EATING, DRINKING & NIGHTLIFE

Bar del Mar	5
La Baska	7
Berlin	6
Café de la Flor	9
La Casa de Nicolás	8
Escauriza	3
La Estancia	11
Gotika City Club	10
Madame	1
Peña Bajada España	4
Petra	12
Via Apia	13
Willie Dixon	2

■ ACCOMMODATION

Anamundana Guesthouse	7
La Casona de Don Jaime I	4
La Casona de Don Jaime Ii	1
Che Pampas	3
Embajador	6
Nuevo City	5
Rosario Inn	2

the displays, while the gallery's riverfront café-bar, *Davis*, is a great place to watch boats floating by over a drink or two.

Most of the summer beach action happens 8km north of the centre at the **Balneario La Florida** (Dec–April 8am–9pm; AR$4; bus #153). Just south of here is the Rambla Catalunya (with a free beach) and Avenida Carrasco, an upmarket restaurant, bar and club strip that is the hub of Rosario's vibrant summer nightlife.

Parque de la Independencia

The **Parque de la Independencia**, 3km southwest of Plaza 25 de Mayo, is one of Argentina's largest urban green spaces. Within its extensive grounds are a football stadium, a racetrack, a theme park, a rose garden and two museums. The **Museo Municipal de Bellas Artes Juan B Castagnino** (Wed–Mon 1–7pm; AR$5; ☎0341 480 2542, ⓦwww .museocastagnino.org.ar), at Avenida

Pellegrini 2202, has an important collection of European and Argentine fine art. West of the lake, the **Museo Histórico Provincial Dr Julio Marc** (Tues–Fri 9am–5pm, Sat & Sun 2–6pm; AR$5; ☎0341 472 1457) is strong on religious artefacts and indigenous ceramics from across Latin America.

Che Guevara's house

Though there's little of the fanfare about it that you might expect given his international icon status, **Ernesto "Che" Guevara** was born in Rosario in 1928. He lived in an apartment on the corner of Entre Ríos and Urquiza until the age of 2, now an office not open to the public, although there's nothing to stop you gawking from the street. One block north and one block east, at the corner of Tucumán and Mitre, a mural of Che's intense and haggard-looking face dominates a small neighbourhood square,

1

while there's a bronze statue of him on a rather forlorn plaza on 27 de Febrero, at Laprida, a full twelve blocks east of Parque de la Independencia.

Alto Delta islands

Just across the river from Rosario, the predominantly uninhabited **Alto Delta islands** are linked to the mainland by regular passenger ferries in the summer (AR$25 return), while a weekend-only service runs in winter. **Ferries** leave from the Estación Fluvial (see below). Some islands have underdeveloped beaches, camping facilities and restaurants. A good way to explore the delta is by taking a **kayak excursion** (see below).

ARRIVAL AND DEPARTURE

By plane Rosario's airport (Islas Malvinas International Airport; ☎0341 451 1226) is 10km northwest of the centre. There are no buses into town; a taxi ride is around AR$70, or take a taxi to the Fisherton neighbourhood, from where buses #115, #116 and #160 run to the bus terminal.

Destinations Buenos Aires (3 daily; 55min); Córdoba (2 daily; 1hr); Mendoza (2 daily; 3hr); Montevideo, Uruguay (daily; 1hr 20min); Santa Fe (3 daily; 1hr).

By bus The Terminal de Omnibus Mariano Moreno is twenty blocks west of the centre, at Santa Fe & Cafferata (☎0341 437 3030). Buses #141 and #146 go to the centre. Bus fares must be paid in exact change or using pre-paid passes.

Destinations Buenos Aires (every 30min; 4hr); Córdoba (every 30min; 6hr 30min); Corrientes (7 daily; 10–12hr); Montevideo in Uruguay (1 daily; 9hr); Puerto Iguazú (3 daily; 19hr); Salta (6 daily; 16hr).

By ferry The Estación Fluvial (☎0341 448 3737), in Parque Nacional de la Bandera, has ferries to the Delta islands. There are services year-round on weekends and a number of inexpensive services daily Dec–March.

By train The train station (☎0800 333 3822) is 3km northwest of the centre.

Destinations Buenos Aires (3 weekly; 7hr).

INFORMATION AND TOURS

Tourist information The riverside tourist office is on the corner of Av Belgrano and C Buenos Aires (daily 9am–7pm; ☎0341 480 2230, ⊚rosarioturismo.com). An information kiosk in the bus terminal has city maps and hotel listings.

Bike Rosario ☎0341 15 571 3812, ⊚bikerosario.com.ar. Cycling tours of the city run by multilingual guides ($120); they also do kayak tours of the Alto Delta islands (AR$170/3hr).

ACCOMMODATION

Rosario has experienced a hostel boom in recent years and at weekends many fill up with party-hard *porteños*. The only time you need to book ahead is on weekends and public holidays, when prices also go up.

HOSTELS

All hostels listed here have double rooms as well as dorms and kitchen facilities. All offer free internet and breakfast.

Anamundana Guesthouse Montevideo 1248 ☎0341 424 3077, ⊚anamundanahostel.com. Attractive guesthouse/hostel run by friendly ex-backpacker Ana, with beautiful stained-glass windows and polished wooden floors, as well as clean dorms with comfortable beds and air conditioning. Dorms AR$60, doubles AR$180

La Casona de Don Jaime I Presidente Roca 1051 ☎0341 527 9964, ⊚youthhostelrosario.com.ar. Hugely popular party hostel whose lively bar, *Roots*, offers late-night reggae music and tasty pizzas. The quieter sister hostel, *La Casona de Don Jaime II*, at San Lorenzo 1530 (☎0341 530 2020), must be one of the few hostels in Argentina to boast its own climbing wall. Staff at both hostels can arrange boating, kayaking and cycling excursions. Dorms AR$70, doubles AR$210

Che Pampas Rioja 812 ☎0341 424 5202, ⊚chepampas .com. Why can't every hostel come with a giant mirrorball, Che Guevara pop art, neon chandeliers and a red PVC throne? In the summer, you'll appreciate the a/c in the dorm rooms. Dorms AR$70, doubles AR$130

★ **Rosario Inn** Sargento Cabral 54 ☎0341 421 0358, ⊚rosarioinn.com.ar. With a fantastic location near the river, this light-drenched hostel has two patios to hang out in and bikes for rent. Tango and theatre classes offered. Dorms AR$60, doubles AR$170

HOTELS

Embajador Santa Fe 3554 ☎0341 438 6367, ⊚hotel embajadorrosario.com. The best of several decent options right in front of the bus station, this spick-and-span-hotel offers rooms with cable TV, wireless internet and a/c. Breakfast included. AR$245

Nuevo City San Juan 867 ☎0341 447 1655, ⊚hotel nuevocity.com.ar. All rooms at this humble hotel have TV, a/c and private bathroom. Request one of the few rooms with external windows. Breakfast included. AR$180

ALTO DELTA ISLANDS

Puerto Pirata ☎0341 15 693 3464, ⊚paradorpuerto pirata.com.ar. Rents out *cabañas* and has a good bar and restaurant with great views over the river from its terrace and long strip of beach. *Cabañas* AR$250, camping AR$20

EATING

The bulk of Rosario's restaurants are clustered along Avenida Pellegrini, although in summer you'll want to take advantage of the waterfront aspect and pull up an outdoor chair at one of the many popular restaurants along the Costanera. Many of these riverfront restaurants open until the small hours during the summer months, although most are closed by around 10pm (later at weekends) during winter.

★ **La Baska** Tucumán 1118 ☎0341 411 1110. The *empanadas* here are piping hot and come with a huge range of heavenly fillings including prawns, tuna, mushrooms and Roquefort cheese. Daily 11am–2pm & 6–11pm.

La Casa de Nicolás Mendoza 937 ☎0341 447 7533. A staggering array of meat-free dishes is served at this inexpensive Asian buffet, and the sushi, stir-fries and soya burgers make a welcome change from barbecued meat. Mon–Sat lunch & dinner.

Escauriza Paseo Ribereño, at Escauriza ☎0341 454 1777. Highly regarded *parrilla* specializing in fish, on the riverfront near the access to the Victoria road bridge. *Surubi* and *dorado* (river fish) are on the menu as well as more conventional meat, and the prices are very reasonable. Daily lunch & dinner.

La Estancia Av Pellegrini, at Paraguay ☎0341 440 7373. Rosario's most popular restaurant is an old-fashioned place with a vast menu. The emphasis is on – you guessed it – beef, and it's fun to watch the impeccably suited waiters rush around with exotic cuts of sizzling cow. Daily 8.30am–1am.

★ **Peña Bajada España** Av Italia, at España ☎0341 449 6801. Restaurant with a tranquil wooden terrace overlooking the river and serving cheap barbecued fish feasts. Access is by elevator. Daily lunch & dinner.

Petra Av Pelligrini 1428 ☎0341 449 8369. For a fixed price, diners can help themselves from the heaving salad bar before loading up on pizza, seafood and grilled meats at this bustling *tenedor libre* (all-you-can-eat buffet). Daily noon–3pm & 6–11pm.

Via Apia Av Pellegrini 961 ☎0341 481 3174. It's easy to miss this small Italian restaurant among the vast neon-lit food palaces of Av Pellegrini, but the crisp stone-baked pizzas are arguably the best in the city. Mon–Sat 6–11pm.

DRINKING AND NIGHTLIFE

Rosario's good-looking locals and party spirit all combine to make it a great place in which to go out. In summer, the clubs and bars in the riverfront Estación Fluvial attract a modish crowd. Summer fun also transfers to Rambla Catalunya, a waterfront avenue in the city's north. Note that nightlife in Rosario doesn't really get going until well after midnight, with some clubs not opening until after 2am.

Bar del Mar Balcarce, at Tucumán. A restaurant-bar with an aquatic theme and colourful mosaics; good for people-watching before painting the town red.

Berlin Pje Zabala 1128, between the 300 block of Mitre & Sarmiento ⓦelberlin.com.ar. Regular events and a steady flow of German beer keep locals coming back to this trendy bar. Thurs–Sun 11pm until late.

Café de la Flor Mendoza 862 ⓦcafedelaflor.com.ar. Live music, DJs and pizza fuel the boisterous alternative crowd at this cavernous joint. Thurs–Sun; shows start around 8pm.

Gotika City Club Mitre 1539. Spacious, gay-friendly club in a converted church; come here when you have some serious energy to burn. Hosts regular shows. Fri–Sun.

Madame Brown 3126. This is *the* club for party animals – a mainstream disco with three dancefloors blaring *cumbia*, reggaeton, electronica and rock. Over-21s only. Fri & Sat 2am until late.

Willie Dixon Suipacha, at Guemes ⓦwilliedixonbluesclub.com. Rock out at this live music venue that hosts quality Argentine acts: a disco follows the band. See website for schedule.

SHOPPING

Bookshop Ameghino, Corrientes 868 (☎0341 447 1147) stocks English-language books.

Clothes The pedestrianized Av Córdoba is a busy shopping street flanked with handsome historic buildings, many of which now function as chic boutiques and department stores. Falabella, at Cordoba & Sarmiento, is a vast department store with good bargains to be found during end-of-season sales.

Markets The Mercado de Pulgas del Bajo flea market is on every weekend afternoon in the Parque Nacional de la Bandera, near Av Belgrano 500. Handmade crafts, used books and antiques are on sale.

DIRECTORY

Banks and Exchange Banco de la Nación Argentina at Córdoba 1026; Branches of HSBC at Santa Fe 1064, San Martín 902 and Córdoba 1770/72. Rosario Transatlantica casa de cambio generally offers decent exchange rates and has branches at Rioja 1198 and Córdoba 1463.

Laundry Lavandería VIP, at Maipú 654.

Post office Buenos Aires & Córdoba on Plaza 25 de Mayo.

PARQUE NACIONAL EL PALMAR

Only after ranching, farming and forestry had pushed the graceful *yatay* palm to the brink of extinction did it find salvation in the **PARQUE NACIONAL EL PALMAR**. The 85-square-kilometre park, on the banks

1

CROSSING FROM COLÓN INTO URUGUAY

Colón, on the Río Uruguay 320km north of Buenos Aires, makes an inviting base for visiting the Parque Nacional El Palmar (see p.83), 50km to the north. Colón is also a prime gateway to Uruguay, and is linked to the city of Paysandú, 16km southeast, by the Puente Internacional General Artigas. It is 8km from Colón to the Uruguayan border (immigration office open 24hr a day) and a further 8km to Paysandú: approximately four buses daily make the journey. Colón's bus terminal is on the corner of Paysandú and 9 de Julio. There are frequent services to Concordia (9 daily; 2hr 15min), passing Parque Nacional El Palmar, and plenty of connections to Buenos Aires (14 daily; 5hr 30min). Colón's helpful tourist office is in the port area on the corner of Avenida Costanera and Gouchón (Mon–Fri 6am–8pm, Sat & Sun 8am–8pm; ☎03447 421 233, ⓦ colon.gov.ar).

of the Río Uruguay, lies 50km north of Colón at Km199 on the RN14, and is a stark, but beautiful, reminder of how large chunks of Entre Ríos Province, Uruguay and southern Brazil once looked. Many of the **palms**, which can grow up to 18m tall, are over three hundred years old. Trails wind through the park, past palm savannas, streams and riverside beaches. Sunset is the perfect time to pull out the camera, when the palms look stunning silhouetted against a technicolour sky. El Palmar's creation in 1966 also did wonders for the habitat of local subtropical **wildlife**, including capybaras, vizcachas, monitor lizards, raccoons and the venomous *yarará* pit viper. Parakeets, egrets, *ñandúes* (large, flightless birds similar to ostriches) and storks are some of the bird species that can be spotted here.

To **get to the park**, catch any Concordia-bound bus from Colón (9 daily; 30min) along the RN14 to the entrance (where you pay AR$12 entry). From here it's a 10km walk, drive or hitchhike to the visitor centre and adjacent **Los Loros campground** (see below).

ACCOMMODATION

Amarello Hotel C Urquiza 865, Colón ☎03447 424063, ⓦ colonentrerios.com.ar/amarello. Plain en-suite rooms in a range of sizes; breakfast included. **AR$190**

Los Loros campground ☎03447 423 378. This campsite in the park has showers and a basic store. Camping **AR$8** plus/person **AR$20**

CORRIENTES

Subtropical **CORRIENTES** is one of the northeast's oldest cities (it was founded in 1588) but doesn't offer much in the way of conventional attractions. That said, its compact historic centre, elegantly crumbling buildings and shady riverside area make it an ideal place for a leg stretch between long bus rides. Party people will be at home here during the heat of summer – Corrientes has been dubbed Argentina's "Capital of Carnaval", and each January and February the city explodes in a riot of colourful costumes and thumping drums.

WHAT TO SEE AND DO

Corrientes' historic core fans out in grid fashion from the shady main square, **Plaza 25 de Mayo**. The square is framed by some of the city's most important nineteenth-century buildings, including the pink Italianate **Casa de Gobierno** and the plain **Iglesia de Nuestra Señora de la Merced** (daily 7am–noon & 4–8pm;

FEELING HOT, HOT, HOT!

Despite the oppressive heat that strikes in summer, the city manages to muster up heroic levels of energy for the annual, Brazilian-style **Carnaval Correntino** (ⓦ carnavalescorrentinos.com), which takes place throughout January and February in the open-air Corsódromo at Avenida Centenario 2800. Raucous street parties, which frequently include bucketloads of iced water being thrown over the sweaty hordes, take place each weekend throughout Carnaval season. Alternatively, if you're in town for the second weekend in December, check out the **Festival del Chamamé** (ⓦ corrienteschamame.com), a celebration of regional folk dancing and music.

free). On the plaza's northeast corner, the **Museo de Artesanías Tradicionales Folclóricas de la Provincia** (Mon–Fri 7am–noon & 4–7pm; free) showcases regional basketwork, leather and ceramics within a whitewashed colonial residence.

One block south of the main square is Corrientes' 2.5km riverside avenue, the **Avenida Costanera General San Martín**, flanked by pretty jacaranda and native *lapacho* trees. It is the favoured haunt of fishermen, *mate-* and *tereré*-sippers, joggers, mosquitoes, daydreamers and courting couples. Locals flock to its promenades on summer evenings after emerging refreshed from siestas. There are a few small riverside **beaches** here, but swimming is not recommended, as the river's currents are notoriously strong.

ARRIVAL AND INFORMATION

By plane Corrientes' airport (☎03783 458 340) is 10km northeast of the city centre. Free shuttle services can take you from the airport to the centre.

Destinations Aerolineas Argentinas (☎03783 458 339) flies to Buenos Aires (2 daily; 1hr 30min).

By bus The bus terminal (☎03783 449 435) is 4km southeast of the city centre. Local buses run frequently between the terminal and the centre; a taxi will set you back around AR$9.

Destinations There are direct bus services to Buenos Aires (6 daily; 12hr); Posadas (9 daily; 5hr; change here for more regular services to Puerto Iguazú); Puerto Iguazú (1 daily; 10hr); Rosario (3 daily; 10hr).

Tourist information The provincial tourist office (Mon–Fri 7am–1pm & 3–9pm; ☎03783 427 200, ⊚turismo corrientes.com.ar) is at 25 de Mayo 1330, and there is also a municipal tourist office where the Costanera meets Pellegrini (daily 7am–9pm; ☎03783 474 702).

ESTEROS DEL IBERÁ

A vast area of marshy swampland, the Esteros del Iberá comprises a series of lagoons, rivers, marshes and floating islands, much of which is protected in the **RESERVA NATURAL DEL IBERÁ**. The islands are created by a build-up of soil on top of a mat of intertwined water lilies and other plants; these in turn choke the flow of water, creating what is in effect a vast, slow-flowing river, draining eventually into the Río Paraná. The wetlands make up nearly fifteen percent of Corrientes

Province – spreading annually in the rainy season and gradually contracting until the rains come again. With the protection of the natural reserve, the area's **wildlife** is thriving, and there's an extraordinary variety: some three hundred species of birds, many brilliantly coloured; forty species of mammals, including capybara, marsh and pampas deer, otters and howler monkeys; and many fish, amphibians and reptiles, including caimans. Take a trip out onto the water, and you can enjoy remarkably close encounters with many of them. For more information on the reserve visit ⊚esterosdelibera.com.

WHAT TO SEE AND DO

Access to the reserve is from the tranquil village of **Colonia Carlos Pellegrini**, on the banks of the Laguna del Iberá. At the approach to the village, immediately before the rickety wooden bridge that is the only way in, former poachers staff the Centro de Interpretación, the reserve's **visitor centre**, which has useful information as well as a fascinating photo display. A nearby forest trail is a good place to spot (and hear) howler monkeys. The **Laguna del Iberá** itself is covered in water lilies, especially the yellow-and-purple *aguapé*, and its floating islands teem with a rich microcosm of bird and aquatic life. Birds include storks, cormorants, egrets, ducks and other waterfowl, while around the edges of the lake lives the *chajá* (horned screamer), a large grey bird with a startling patch of red around the eyes, as well as snakes (including the alarming yellow anaconda) and caimans. The capybara, the world's largest rodent, makes an unlikely swimmer, but in fact spends most of its time in the water – listen out for the splash as it enters.

ARRIVAL AND DEPARTURE

Access to the reserve is from Colonia Carlos Pellegrini. The village has very little to it; a grid of sandy streets around the Plaza San Martín, with very few facilities – bring enough cash to cover your entire stay.

By bus Colonia Carlos Pellegrini is 120km from the village of Mercedes (3hr approx; departures Mon–Sat at noon; AR$50 one-way). Ten buses run daily from Corrientes to Mercedes (3hr). Access to Colonia Carlos is also possible from Posadas, to the northwest, but this is still slower, and frequently impassable in the wet (3 buses weekly with Nordestur, 5–6hr; AR$140 one-way; ☎03722 445 588).

INFORMATION AND TOURS

Tourist information Mercedes has a helpful tourist office (daily 8am–noon & 4–8pm; ☎03773 420 100) and you can also arrange private 4WD transfers from here, through your accommodation in Colonia Carlos.

Tours Guided tours are highly recommended – and obligatory for visiting the lagoon and wetlands. Best organized through your accommodation, they are often included in the price. A variety of trips is on offer, by boat (you'll be poled through the marshier sections, where a motor is useless), on foot or on horseback. There are also moonlit night-time boat tours (Sat nights only) and walks to see the nocturnal species.

ACCOMMODATION

The best accommodation in the village is provided by a handful of gorgeous posadas: they also provide food (often on a full-board basis) and organize tours.

Don Justino Hostel ☎03773 499 415, ✉ibertatours @hotmail.com. Good-quality budget accommodation with both private rooms and dorms. Rooms have a/c and prices include breakfast and towels. Dorms AR$70, doubles AR$210

Posada Ypa Sapukai ☎03773 420 155, ⓦiberaturismo .com.ar. The most affordable of the posadas (cost includes full board/person), this charming lakeside place has a small pool, lookout tower, impeccable rooms and beautiful garden. Excursions can be organized for AR$95 upwards. AR$200

SAN IGNACIO

The riverside town of **SAN IGNACIO** is home to one of the major sights of northern Argentina – the dramatic remains of the Jesuit missions at **San Ignacio Miní**. There's little clue of that in the centre, though, where this is just another hot, sleepy town. If you time the buses right you can visit the missions and move on the same day, but there are a couple of other attractions worth visiting should you be staying longer.

The main street south will lead you past the **Casa de Horacio Quiroga** (daily 8am–7pm; AR$10; ☎03752 470 124), a museum to the Uruguayan-born Argentine writer of Gothic short stories, who made his home here in the early twentieth century. The same road continues to **Puerto Nuevo** on the Río Paraná, a couple

of kilometres away, where a sandy beach offers wonderful views across the river to Paraguay. With a bit more time you could also head to the **Parque Provincial Teyú Cuaré**, some 10km south of the village on a good, unpaved road. Here there are camping facilities and you can seek out the **Peñón Reina Victoria**, a rock face said to resemble Queen Victoria's profile.

San Ignacio Miní

SAN IGNACIO MINÍ (daily 7am–7pm; AR$60; ticket valid for 15 days) was one of many Jesuit missions set up throughout Spanish America to convert the native population to Christianity. Originally established further north in what is now Brazil, the missionaries gradually moved south to avoid attack from Portuguese *bandeirantes* (piratical slave traders), eventually settling here in 1696. The mission became a thriving small town, inhabited by the local Guaraní, but, following the suppression of the Jesuits, was abandoned in the early nineteenth century. Rediscovered around a hundred years ago, the ruins are now among the best-preserved of their kind in Latin America, a UNESCO World Heritage Site with some spectacular Baroque architecture.

At the entrance, at the northeastern end of the village, an excellent **Centro de Interpretación Regional** looks at the life of the mission and its Guaraní inhabitants. Rows of simple *viviendas* (stone-built, single-storey living quarters that once housed Guaraní families) lead down to a grassy Plaza de Armas, overlooked by the **church** that dominates the site. The roof and most of the interior have long since crumbled away, but much of the magnificent facade, designed by the Italian architect Brazanelli, still stands and many fine details can be made out. Twin columns rise either side of the doorway, and the walls are decorated with exuberant bas-relief sculpture executed by Guaraní craftsmen.

ARRIVAL AND INFORMATION

By bus There's no bus station as such in San Ignacio, but all buses drop passengers off at the western end of the main avenue, Sarmiento.

Destinations Posadas (hourly; 1hr); Puerto Iguazú (hourly; 4–5hr).

Tourist information A small Centro de Informes can be found at the corner of Av Sarmiento and RN12, at the entrance to town. Ask here, or at the ruins' entrance, about sound and light shows, held most evenings at San Ignacio Miní.

ACCOMMODATION AND EATING

There's not a great deal of quality when it comes to food, but for budget eats, try one of the pizzerias and snack bars near the ruins. There is a decent supermarket on San Martín, between Av Sarmiento and Belgrano.

Hospedaje El Descanso Pellegrini 270, towards the outskirts of the village around ten blocks south of the bus terminal ☎ 03752 470 207. Smart little bungalows with private bathrooms but no a/c; breakfast AR$6. **AR$140**

Residencial Doka Alberdi 518 ☎ 03752 470 131, ✉ recidoka@yahoo.com.ar. Rooms with a/c, TV, en-suite bathrooms and small kitchens, right next to the ruins. **AR$170**

Residencial San Ignacio San Martín 823, at Sarmiento ☎ 03752 470 047. The largest hotel in town is located right in the centre. Comfortable and modern rooms with TV and a/c. Internet on site. Great value and within walking distance of the ruins. **AR$210**

PUERTO IGUAZÚ

PUERTO IGUAZÚ is an inevitable stop if you're visiting **Iguazú Falls** (see p.88) on a budget – it's a perfectly pleasant town with all the facilities you need, if a little dull. On the western edge of town, the **Hito Tres Fronteras** is an obelisk overlooking the rivers Iguazú and Parana at the point where they meet and form the three-way border between Argentina, Brazil and Paraguay.

ARRIVAL AND DEPARTURE

By plane The airport is 25km southeast of Puerto Iguazú (☎ 03757 422 013). Buses meet flights and run to the bus terminal (☎ 03757 422 962; AR$13 one-way).

Destinations Aerolineas Argentinas (ⓦ aerolineas argentinas.com) has several daily flights to Buenos Aires (1hr 45min). For international destinations, TAM (ⓦ tam.com.br) flies from the larger airport at Foz do Iguacu on the Brazilian side of the border. Taxi drivers will take you from your hotel to the airport at Foz, allowing time for completing visa formalities, for around AR$180.

By bus "El Práctico" buses for the National Park depart from the obelisk at Hito Tres Fronteras every half-hour (7am–7.15pm; 30min; AR$9 each way); you can also pick them up at intervals all the way along the main street, Av Victoria Aguirre. All other national and international bus services arrive at and leave from the bus terminal on Av Córdoba, at Av Misiones. Travellers heading for destinations in Brazil will find that buses departing from Argentina are cheaper and more comfortable than those departing from across the border in Brazil, although it is often necessary to book well in advance. Crucero del Norte (ⓦ crucerodelnorte .com.ar) has regular departures to destinations across Argentina as well as to São Paulo and Rio de Janeiro in Brazil, Asunción in Paraguay, Santiago in Chile and Santa Cruz in Bolivia.

INFORMATION AND TOURS

National Park office Av Victoria Aguirre 66 (Tues–Sun; winter 8am–5pm, summer 8am–6pm; ☎ 03757 420 722).

Tourist information Av Victoria Aguirre 311 (Mon–Fri 7am–9pm, Sat & Sun 8am–noon & 4–8pm; ☎ 03757 420 800). There are also a number of private information booths and travel agents to be found at the bus terminal.

Tour operator Iguazú Jungle (☎ 03757 421 600, ⓦ iguazu jungle.com) offer boat tours from AR$80 for a gentle nature ride to AR$350 for white-water fun.

ACCOMMODATION

There are a number of big resort hotels near the falls, but budget travellers stay in Puerto Iguazú, where there are plenty of good hostels and inexpensive guesthouses. In high season, July and around Easter, reservations are recommended.

CROSSING INTO BRAZIL

To make your trip to Iguazú Falls complete you should really visit the **Brazilian side** (see p.353), where the view is more panoramic, and the photography opportunities are excellent. There are no direct **buses** from Puerto Iguazú to the falls on the Brazilian side – you will need to take one of the regular international buses marked "Brasil" from the main street or bus station (AR$9), which will drop you at the border for immigration formalities. From the border pick up another bus towards Foz, changing to yet another for the falls themselves. If time is short, it's well worth considering sharing a taxi (approximately AR$180 return). Change some Brazilian cash before you go, for bus fares and the like, and bear in mind that, from October to March, Brazil is one hour ahead of Argentina.

1

Lilian Fray Luis Beltrán 183 ☎ 03757 420 968, ✉ hotellilian @yahoo.com.ar. One of the slickest of the budget options, offering spotless modern rooms with good bathrooms. AR$310

Marcopolo Inn ☎ 0375 421 823, ⊛ hostel-inn.com. Recently refurbished HI hostel with six-bed dorms and double rooms. There's a pool, free internet and wi-fi, large kitchen, and friendly ambience. Dorms AR$90, doubles AR$360

Noelia Residencial Fray Luis Beltrán 119, between Moreno and Belgrano ☎ 03757 420 729, ✉ residenciafamiliarnoelia @yahoo.com.ar. Excellent-value, family-run hotel not far from the bus station, with a/c, private baths and a lovely patio where breakfast is served. AR$170

Viejo Americano RN12, 5km from town towards the national park ☎ 03757 420 190, ⊛ viejoamericano.com.ar. Excellent hotel/campsite out of town with beautiful verdant grounds and a large pool. Camping/person AR$60, doubles AR$420

EATING AND DRINKING

With a few exceptions, restaurants in Iguazú serve bland and touristy fare. At the falls there are several cafés, but the food is expensive and uninspiring, so consider packing a picnic.

Las Canitas Av Victoria Aguirre, at Pombero. This lively local *peña* is a little off the main restaurant strip, but worth the walk for the warm welcome, live music and tasty grilled meats. Non-carnivores can tuck into vegetable kebabs and some interesting salads. Mains AR$40–65. Daily 6pm until late.

Gallo Negro Av Victoria Aguirre, at Curupi. Probably the best in town; a good-looking ranch-style *parrilla* on the main street, with outdoor seating on a veranda. Cover charge of AR$14 per person includes unlimited access to the inviting salad bar. Mains AR$45–95. Daily 11.30am–late.

Gustos del Literal Av Misiones 209. This pocket-sized restaurant and bar serves lip-smackingly good dishes from neighbouring Paraguay. Try the *chipá guazú* – a warm, crumbly combination of fresh corn and white cheese; covered here in tangy tomato sauce. Good cocktails too. Mains AR$40–45. Daily 8.30am–midnight.

La Rueda Córdoba 28 ☎ 03757 422 531. Pleasant restaurant, with outdoor seating. Fish is a speciality (mains AR$50–110). Mon–Tues 8pm–midnight, Wed–Sun noon–midnight.

IGUAZÚ FALLS

Around 275 individual cascades, the highest with a drop of over 80m, make up the stunning **IGUAZÚ FALLS** (*Cataratas de Iguazú*, or simply *Las Cataratas*).

Strung out along the rim of a horseshoe-shaped cliff 2.7km long, their thunderous roaring can be heard from many kilometres away, while the mist thrown up rises 30m high in a series of dazzling rainbows. In the Guaraní language Iguazú means "great water", but clearly the Guaraní are not given to over-statement, for there's little doubt that these are the most spectacular falls in the world: only the Victoria Falls in Africa can compare in terms of size, but here the shape of the natural fault that created the falls means that you can stand with the water crashing almost all around you.

This section of the Río Iguazú makes up the border between Brazil and Argentina and the subtropical forests that surround the falls are protected on both sides: by the **Parque Nacional Iguazú** in Argentina, and the **Parque Nacional do Iguaçu** (see p.353) over the border. These parks are packed with exotic wildlife, and even on the busy catwalks and paths that skirt the edges of the falls you've a good chance of seeing much of it. Orchids and serpentine creepers adorn the trees, among which flit vast, bright butterflies. You may also see toucans overhead and – if you're lucky – shy capuchin monkeys. Look out too for the swallow-like *vencejo*, a remarkable small bird, endemic to the area, which makes its nest behind the curtains of water.

Parque Nacional Iguazú

Thanks to an extensive system of trails and boardwalks that lead around, above and below the falls, the Argentine side offers better close-up views of Iguazú, while the Brazilian side has sweeping panoramic views. Everything lies within the **Parque Nacional Iguazú** (daily 8am–6pm; AR$130; ⊛ iguazuargentina. com), whose entrance is 18km southeast of Puerto Iguazú along RN12. Buses drop passengers off here, and the visitor centre just inside can provide a map of the park and various handy leaflets. It's also the departure point of the **Tren de la Selva**, a natural-gas-fuelled train. This leaves every 30 minutes from 8.30am (last at 4pm, 4.30pm in summer) for Cataratas Station, which gives access to the walking trails and the Garganta del Diablo walkway.

Several well-signposted trails (most wheelchair-accessible) take you along a series of boardwalks and paths to the park's highlights. The **Paseo Superior**, a short trail that takes you along the top of the first few waterfalls, makes a good introduction. For more drama, and a much wetter experience, the **Paseo Inferior** winds down through the forest before taking you to within metres of some of the smaller falls. At the bottom of this trail, a regular free boat service leaves for **Isla San Martín**, a rocky island in the middle of the river. Note that the boat doesn't run when water levels are high afer heavy rains. The same jetty is also the departure point for more thrills-oriented boat rides, such as those offered by Iguazú Jungle (see p.87).

At the heart of the falls is the truly unforgettable **Garganta del Diablo** (The Devil's Throat), a powerhouse display of natural forces in which 1800 cubic metres of water per second hurtles over a semicircle of rock into the misty river canyon below. The 1km boardwalk takes you to a small viewing platform within just a few metres of the staggering, sheer drop of water. Often shrouded in mist during winter mornings and early afternoons, the Garganta del Diablo is best visited later in the day, when the views tend to be clearer.

The Northwest

Argentina's northwest is an area of deserts, red earth and whitewashed colonial churches, punctuated with pockets of cloudforest and lush green jungle. The pretty and inviting city of **Salta** is known for its well-preserved colonial architecture and makes a great base for visiting the wonderful natural formations of the **Quebrada del Toro** and **Quebrada de Cafayate**, as well as the stylish wine-producing villages of the **Valles Calchaquíes**, such as **Cafayate**. To the north of Salta loom three jungle-clad **cloudforests** – El Rey above all is worth

a visit – along with the busy market town of **San Salvador de Jujuy**, with its palm trees and wild Andean feel. As you head further north, the seven-coloured **Quebrada de Humahuaca** ravine can be seen from the small mud-brick towns of **Tilcara** and **Humahuaca**.

SALTA

SALTA is one of Argentina's most elegant provincial capitals, with leafy plazas, well-preserved colonial architecture and, thanks to the altitude, a pleasantly balmy climate during the summer. In the winter months temperatures drop dramatically, and snow is not uncommon. Throughout the city, and in its hotels, restaurants and museums, there's a strong emphasis on the culture of the Andes, and you'll notice that the food is spicier than in the south of the country. Attractions include the cable-car ride to the top of **Cerro San Bernardo**; a peach-coloured Neoclassical church; and wonderful *peñas* that mix spicy food and live Andean music.

Salta is a great jumping-off point for the high passes of the **Quebrada del Toro** – ideally viewed from the **Tren a las Nubes** – and for the **Valles Calchaquíes**, where you can stay overnight among the vineyards of **Cafayate**. A less-visited option is the cloudforest national park of **El Rey**, to the east. Salta has scores of good backpacker hostels, but these tend to fill up quickly at weekends and during public holidays, making advance booking essential.

WHAT TO SEE AND DO

The verdant **Plaza 9 de Julio** lies at the heart of Salta, with scenic cafés nestled under its arches – in the evening the whole place is lit up, and half of Salta seems to descend on the square for an evening stroll.

Plaza 9 de Julio

On the southern side of the leafy plaza, the whitewashed **Cabildo** houses the **Museo Histórico del Norte** (Tues–Fri 9am–7pm, Sat & Sun 9.30am–1.30pm & 3–7pm; AR$10, free before 10am Wed; ⊚museonor.gov.ar), which displays an eclectic array of artefacts, from

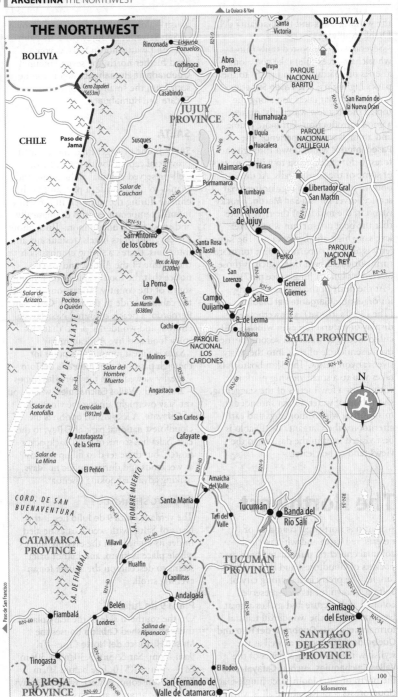

THE NORTHWEST

horse-drawn carriages to everyday objects. The balcony here offers a great view over the goings-on in the square. Facing the museum is the ornate Neoclassical **Catedral**, built in 1882, which has some interesting frescoes inside.

Just east of the plaza, Calle Caseros leads to two more interesting churches. The blood-red **Iglesia y Convento San Francisco**, designed by architect Luigi Giorgi, is one of the most impressive religious buildings in the country. Its exuberance makes a fascinating contrast with the whitewashed walls of the **Convento San Bernardo**, a lesson in simplicity and tranquillity of design.

Archeological museum

MAAM, the **Museo de Arqueología de Alta Montaña** (Tues–Sun 11am–7pm; AR$40; ⓦmaam.gob.ar), is a modern and controversial museum displaying the mummified remains of several high-mountain child sacrifices; many locals argue that the perfectly preserved remains should be laid to rest instead. The beautiful exhibits of Inca clothing and jewellery are well organized and have labels in English.

Cerro San Bernardo

To the east of the microcentro a steep path leads you up **Cerro San Bernardo** hill (1458m; 45min), or you can take the easy option and hop on the **teleférico** (cable car; daily 10am–7.45pm; AR$35 return) from Avenida Hipólito Yrigoyen, between Urquiza and Avenida San Martín, at the eastern end of Parque San Martín. At the top are gardens and a small café with sweeping views over Salta and out to the Lerma valley and Andes mountains beyond.

Calle Balcarce and ethnic art museum

The liveliest part of the city is the area around **Calle Balcarce**, especially the pedestrianized blocks north of Avenida Entre Ríos. Arts and crafts are on sale in the evenings and on weekends, and this is where you'll find the largest number of restaurants, bars, discos and folk-music venues. There is also an outstanding museum of American ethnic art, the **Museo de Arte Étnico Americano Pajcha** at 20 de Febrero 831 (Mon–Sat 10am–1pm & 4–8pm; AR$20; ⓦmuseopajchasalta .com.ar), featuring handicrafts from Argentina and elsewhere in South America, with Mapuche silver jewellery and Andean ceramics the highlights.

ARRIVAL AND INFORMATION

By plane Salta's airport (☏0387 424 2904) is 10km southwest of the city centre. A taxi should cost no more than AR$50.

Destinations Buenos Aires (2–3 daily; 2hr 30min); Córdoba (2–3 daily; 1hr 30min); Tucumán (2–3 daily; 40min).

By bus All buses arrive at the bus terminal (☏0387 401 1143) eight blocks east of the main plaza along Parque San Martín. It has luggage storage, cafés, chemists and bakeries but no internet.

Destinations Regular buses to Buenos Aires (20hr), Rosario (16hr), Córdoba (13hr), Tucumán (4hr), La Quiaca (7hr 30min) and Mendoza (19hr).

By train Bus #5 links the bus terminal with the train station, at Ameghino 690, via Plaza 9 de Julio. The only trains that serve Salta are the tourist *Tren a las Nubes*, which departs twice a week, and infrequent goods and passenger trains to the Chilean border.

Tourist information In a converted Neoclassical building, the city tourist office at Caseros 711 (daily

---

SALTA TOURS

A wide variety of highly professional **tours**, **expeditions** and other **activities** all around the northwest region can be arranged from Salta city.

TOUR OPERATORS

MoviTrack Safaris Buenos Aires 28 ☏0387 431 6749, ⓦmovitrack.com.ar. Lively 1–2-day overland safaris and sightseeing tours.

Norte Trekking Gral Güemes 265, oficina 1 ☏0387 431 6616, ⓦnortetrekking.com. Sightseeing, trekking and mountaineering adventures.

Ricardo Clark Expediciones Mariano Moreno 1950 ☏0387 497 1024, ⓦclarkexpediciones.com. Small eco-tourism company specializing in birdwatching tours.

Salta Rafting Caseros 177 ☏0387 421 3216, ⓦsalta rafting.com. Fun white-water rafting and zipwire excursions on the Río Juramento. Can also arrange horseriding and mountain-biking trips.

1

8am–9pm; ☎0387 421 6285) offers leaflets and a good city map.

ACCOMMODATION

There are plenty of budget accommodation options in Salta, and all are within walking distance of the bus terminal and the central plaza.

HOSTELS

Backpacker's Hostel Buenos Aires 930 ☎0387 423 5910, ⓦbackpackerssalta.com. One of three HI-affiliated hostels in Salta, this lively spot wins points for its free dinners, large pool, LCD TV and fun events such as five-a-side football. Doubles have TV and private bathroom. Dorms AR$50, doubles AR$150

SALTA MICROCENTRO

● EATING & DRINKING
Boliche de Balderrama	6
La Casona del Molino	2
El Corredor de las Empanadas	4
La Estrella Oriental	7
Fili	1
Mercado Central	5
El Solar del Convento	3

■ ACCOMMODATION
Backpacker's Hostel	5
Bloomers Bed & Brunch	2
Los Cardones	1
Corre Caminos	6
Munay	3
Las Rejas	4

Los Cardones Av Entre Rios 454 ☎ 0387 431 4026, ⓦ los cardones.todowebsalta.com.ar. A little out of the centre but close to lots of bars and restaurants, this hostel has five courtyards, hammocks, board games and a friendly welcome. Dorms AR$60, doubles AR$150

Corre Caminos Vicente Lopéz 353 ☎ 0387 422 0731, ⓦ saltahostel.com. Basic rooms and clean bathrooms in this lively hostel with a small garden and pool to enjoy. Dorms AR$60, doubles AR$160

Las Rejas General Güemes 569 ☎ 0387 421 5971, ⓦ lasrejashostel.com.ar. Family-owned and run, this converted 1900 building offers hostel accommodation with dorms and doubles with breakfast, as well as more luxurious accommodation at the adjoining B&B, where rooms start at AR$325. Dorms AR$75, doubles AR$210

HOTELS

★ **Bloomers Bed & Brunch** Vicente Lopéz 129 ☎ 0387 422 7449, ⓦ bloomers-salta.com.ar. Five beautifully decorated rooms, with private bathrooms and a spectacular breakfast (there's an in-house pastry chef), which changes daily. AR$480

Munay San Martín 656 ☎ 0387 422 4936, ⓦ munayhotel .com.ar. Good-quality budget hotel, with basic but clean rooms with private bathrooms. Breakfast included. AR$310

EATING, DRINKING AND NIGHTLIFE

Salta has a good range of budget eating options, ranging from simple snack bars where you can enjoy delicious *empanadas* to atmospheric cafés and lively folk-music *peñas*, with the latter staying open well into the small hours at weekends and during peak tourist seasons; most charge extra for the entertainment.

Boliche de Balderrama San Martín 1126 ☎ 0387 421 1542, ⓦ boliche-balderrama.com.ar. Popular *peña* with local music, and sometimes dancing while you eat.

La Casona del Molino Luis Burela, at Caseros ☎ 0387 434 2835. It's a 30min walk or a quick taxi ride to this rambling old building, but well worth it for the delicious local food and lively atmosphere. The fairly priced menu includes *empanadas*, *locro*, *guashalocro*, *tamales* and *humitas*. The house wine comes by the litre and is dangerously drinkable.

El Corredor de las Empanadas Caseros 117. Pleasant place serving northwestern treats, with an outdoor patio. Try the famous *empanadas*, *humitas* and *tamales*.

La Estrella Oriental San Juan 137. Middle Eastern food that makes a nice change from *empanadas*. Try the hummus and lamb kebabs, followed by *baklawa*.

★ **Fili** Av Sarmiento, at Güemes. This ice-cream parlour, housed in a natty Art Deco building, has been attracting locals for some sixty years with its vast selection of flavours, including a delicious *dulce de leche* with almonds, cinnamon or both.

Mercado Central La Florida, at Av San Martín. Good for lunch, with a range of inexpensive food stalls offering everything from hot dogs and fries to *locro* and *humitas*.

★ **El Solar del Convento** Caseros 444 ☎ 0387 421 5124. Stylish decor, attentive service and thoughtfully prepared traditional dishes combine to make this restaurant a standout on Salta's dining scene. The wine list is extensive, and local "champagne" is served on the house.

DIRECTORY

Banks and exchange There are several banks with ATMS at Plaza 9 de Julio, and Av España is lined with banks including HSBC, Banco Francés, Santander and Citibank. There are further cashpoints and exchange services on España, at Mitre.

Internet Salta Internet, Florida 55.

Post office Deán Funes 170.

LA QUEBRADA DEL TORO

There are several ways to experience the dramatic, ever-changing scenery of the **Quebrada del Toro** gorge and its surrounding town; you can rent a car, take an organized tour or hop on the **Tren a las Nubes** – a fabulous if expensive experience (ⓦ trenalasnubes.com.ar, twice weekly March–Dec only; AR$830). Leaving early from Salta and the Lerma valley, you start to ascend the multicoloured gorge of the Río El Toro, usually tranquil but sometimes torrential in spring. The rail tracks ascend to a dizzying 4200m above sea level, allowing you to experience this exceptional engineering achievement (there are 21 tunnels and more than 13 viaducts, the highlight of them the 64m-high, 224m-long **Polvorilla Viaduct**, almost at the top of the line). Along the way there are various stops and photo opportunities, usually including the town of **Santa Rosa de Tastil**, the pre-Incan site of **Tastil**, and the small mining town of **San Antonio de los Cobres**, where local artists sell their jewellery, clothing and toys by the train station.

PARQUE NACIONAL EL REY

The spectacular cloudforests of the **PARQUE NACIONAL EL REY** (9am–dusk; free) lie just under 200km from Salta. El Rey features an upland enclave covered in lush green vegetation, with high year-round humidity

1

and precipitation but with very distinct seasons – very wet in summer, dry (or at least not so wet) in winter. The park is frequently covered in a low-lying mist, the signature feature of cloudforests, protecting the plants and animals beneath it. El Rey is particularly good for **birdwatching**: the giant toucan is the park's symbol, and is easily spotted, while at least 150 other bird species also live here, as well as jaguar and howler monkeys.

There is just one access road to the park (the RP20). The easiest way to discover the park is on an **organized trip** from Salta (see p.91), but if visiting independently it is advisable that you take a 4WD and check in with the **guardaparques** at the park entrance before you set off. The only option for an overnight stay at the park is to pitch a tent at one of the two official **camping** spots, basic but with toilets and showers. Again, check with the *guardaparques* at the entrance for directions and prices.

VALLES CALCHAQUÍES

To the south of Salta lie the stunning **VALLES CALCHAQUÍES**, the valleys of the Río Calchaquí, fed by snowmelt from the Andes. Here you'll find some of the highest vineyards in the world. You can rent your own car from Salta to explore the area, which allows you to loop round via the amazing **Cuesta del Obispo mountain pass**, visit the wonderful cactus forests of the **Parque Nacional Los Cardones**, stop off in the little towns of **Cachi** and **Cafayate**, and return to Salta via the incredible rock formations of the Quebrada de Cafayate. There are also tours from both Cafayate and Salta – or Cachi and Cafayate are both connected to Salta by bus (though not really near to each other).

CACHI

CACHI lies around 160km southwest of Salta, along an incredibly scenic route with mountainous views across lush valleys. Cachi is small and still quite undiscovered, but what it lacks in services, it makes up for in scenery and location. The permanently snow-covered

Nevado del Cachi (6380m), 15km to the west, looms over the town.

WHAT TO SEE AND DO

Truth is, there's not a great deal to detain you in Cachi other than the tranquil and picturesque nature of the place itself. A small **Plaza Mayor**, shaded by palms and orange trees, marks the centre of town and on the north side you'll find the well-restored **Iglesia San José**. Its bright white exterior gives way to an interior made almost entirely, from pews to confessional, of porous cactus wood. Not far away, the **Museo Arqueológico Pío Pablo Díaz** (Mon–Fri 9am–6pm, Sat & Sun 10am–1pm; AR$2) displays local archeological finds in an attractive building with a wonderful patio. For the more energetic, a hiking track to the west of the village will lead you to **Cachi Adentro** (6km), where you'll have wonderful views of the surrounding landscape and may see the endless fields of drying paprika which line the route from March to May.

ARRIVAL AND DEPARTURE

By bus Buses from Salta (and local buses from nearby villages) drop passengers off at the main square. From there all services are within walking distance. There are frequent services to Salta (2hr) and local destinations.

ACCOMMODATION

There are relatively few budget places to stay in Cachi itself.

Llaqta Mawka Ruíz de los Lanos s/n ☎03868 491 016, ⓦ hotelllaqtamawka.todowebsalta.com.ar. Welcoming inn that has made a concerted effort to respect local building and decoration customs and techniques and offers interesting tours of the immediate region. **AR$280**

Municipal Camping Av Automóvil Club Argentina (at the end) ☎03868 491 053. Basic clean campsite, with cabins on offer. Pool and shaded areas. Camping **AR$30**

> ★ **TREAT YOURSELF**
>
> **El Cortijo** Av Automóvil Club Argentino s/n ☎03868 491 034, ⓦ elcortijohotel.com. In a colonial house at the bottom of the hill, this is good value, with its unusual native-style decor combined with sophisticated neocolonial furnishings and very attentive service. **AR$460**

EATING

ACA Sol del Valle J.M. Castilla. The restaurant of the pricey *ACA Hotel* serves local food, including hearty soups and stews, as well as cakes, sandwiches and pastries at the adjoining café-bar. The setting is wonderful and the staff friendly.

AROUND CACHI

The 157km drive from Cachi to Cafayate takes you through some of the region's most spectacular scenery and some delightful little towns. A short stop in **Molinos** (60km from Cachi) is recommended to view the local crafts, see the picturesque adobe houses and check out a fabulous church, the eighteenth-century **Iglesia de San Pedro Nolasco**. Beyond the town of Angastaco, the red sandstone **Quebrada de las Flechas** gorge is filled with dangerous-looking arrow-head formations. Shortly afterwards the road passes through **El Ventisquero**, the "wind-tunnel", and the natural stone walls of **El Cañón**, over 20m high.

CAFAYATE

The largest town in the region, and the main tourist base, is **CAFAYATE**. Set amid apparently endless vineyards, it makes a perfect place to hole up for a few days while exploring the surrounding area on horseback or sipping the local wines at nearby *bodegas*. The town is lively, filled with inviting plazas and popular restaurants.

WHAT TO SEE AND DO

The pleasure of your visit lies in getting out into the countryside and exploring the vineyards, though there are also craft stalls and a couple of museums to fill the hours. The sleek, modern **Museo de la Vid y el Vino** on Avenida General Güemes (daily 10am–9pm; AR$30) uses poetry and audiovisuals to bring to life the oenologist's craft and explain why the climate in the area is so good for the grapes. The **Museo Arqueológico** (daily 10am–9pm; free; ☎03868 421 054), at the corner of Colón and Calchaquí, is the private collection of late collector Rodolfo Bravo. On display alongside archeological relics are local ceramics, and everyday items from the colonial period.

ARRIVAL AND DEPARTURE

By bus Buses from Salta and nearby villages use the small terminal on Belgrano, east of the plaza, though some will drop you off at your destination as you pass through town. Ask the driver. Buses from Tucumán arrive at the terminal on Güemes Norte & Alvarado.

Destinations Salta (3–4 daily; 5hr); Tucumán (3 daily; 6–8hr).

INFORMATION AND TOURS

Tourist information A kiosk on the plaza (daily 8am–9pm) dispenses information about where to stay, what to do and where to rent bikes or hire horses. Look for the helpful map of the wineries.

Tour operators Puna Turismo, at San Martín 82 (☎03868 421 808), can arrange horserides, trekking, 4WD tours, winery tours and mountain-bike adventures; Turismo Cordillerano, at Camila Quintana de Niño 59 (☎03868 422 137, ⓦturismocordillerano.com.ar), offers trekking and excursions in the valleys.

ACCOMMODATION

The recent boom in tourism has generated a range of options in budget accommodation. All are within walking distance of the plaza, and can advise on winery visits.

Rusty K Hostal Rivadavia 281 ☎03868 422 031, ⓦrustyk hostal.com.ar. Central, friendly hostel with a pleasant garden to relax in. Dorms AR$95, doubles AR$240

Ruta 40 Güermes Sur 178 ☎03868 421 689, ⓦhostel -ruta40.com. The newest and most lively hostel in town, with clean dorms and small doubles. Dorms AR$90, doubles AR$260

Los Toneles Camila Quintana de Niño 38 ☎03868 422 301, ⓦlostoneleshostal.com.ar. Friendly budget hotel half a block from the plaza with barrels of character – literally, with giant beer barrels serving as decoration and as tables in the small patios off each room. A yard with benches that resembles an English pub garden completes the picture. AR$160

★ **Hostal de Valle** San Martín 243 ☎03868 421 039. Large, light spacious rooms, set around a luscious patio. Ask for a room upstairs. AR$300

EATING AND DRINKING

Restaurants and cafés surround the main plaza, where in summer you can join crowds of locals strolling through the city at dusk with an ice cream.

El Almacén Camila Quintana de Niño 59, ⓦelalmacen hostelbar.com. This remodelled house has retained many antique fittings, providing an atmospheric setting

1

WINERY VISITS

There are some world-class wineries around Cafayate and most offer **tours** in English and Spanish with a tasting afterwards. Taking a tour is a great way to see which wines you prefer, and to appreciate the whole process. Ask at the information centre on the small plaza in Cafayate for a winery map of the area.

Two of the most popular are **Bodega Etchart** on RN40 (daily 9am–5pm; ☎03868 421 529, ⓦbodegasetchart.com) and **Bodega La Rosa** on RN68 (Mon–Fri 8am–12.30pm & 1.30–7pm; ☎03868 421 201). Both are within walking or cycling distance, and offer free tours.

for enjoying the house *picadas* and very reasonable *torrontés*, made from vines that grow just behind. The building also houses a decent hostel (dorms $55). Daily noon–late.

Baco Güemes Norte, at Rivadavia. Simple decor and friendly staff make this corner restaurant popular, as do its pizzas, trout and local wines. Daily lunch & dinner.

Carreta de Don Olegario Güemes Sur 20, at Quintana de Niño on the east side of the plaza. Popular for its reasonably priced local dishes, this well-located restaurant features live traditional music as well as hearty goat and veal stews, veggie-friendly tortillas and pasta dishes, and delicious cheeses. There's a good selection of wines from local *bodegas* too. Daily noon–3pm & 7–11pm.

Heladería Santa Barbara Av Güemes, half a block north of the plaza. Gourmet ice creams in exotic flavours; try the famous wine sorbets. Daily noon–8pm.

SAN SALVADOR DE JUJUY

Generally playing second fiddle to its prettier cousin Salta, **SAN SALVADOR DE JUJUY** (known as Jujuy) lies 90km to the north. Although it is the highest provincial capital in the country, at 1260m above sea level, Jujuy is set in a lush pocket of humidity and greenery. It's a busy place, with a frantic, market feel, where crumbling colonial buildings are juxtaposed with neon signs. Most travellers pass through for just one night on their way to the surrounding attractions and small towns of **Tilcara** and **Humahuaca**. The real lure is out of town to the north, in the spectacular colours of the **Quebrada de Humahuaca**.

If you have time to kill in Jujuy, head to the lively **Plaza General Belgrano**, east of the city centre. This large, green open space is generally crowded with young locals, checking out the craftsmen and market sellers who set up stalls here. On the west side of the plaza, the late eighteenth-century **Catedral** (daily 8am–1pm & 5–8pm; free) makes up for a plain facade with a wonderfully decorative interior, above all a spectacular pulpit decorated by local artists over two centuries ago. This has a rival in the intricate pulpit of the nearby **Iglesia San Francisco**, whose tiny human figures, columns and scenes are thought to have been carved in Bolivia.

ARRIVAL AND DEPARTURE

By plane Jujuy's airport (Gobernador Horacio Guzmán International Airport; ☎0388 491 1102) is around 30km southeast of the city. A taxi will cost around AR$150.

By bus Most visitors to Jujuy arrive by bus at the ugly bus terminal (☎0388 422 6299) on Iguazú, at Av Dorrego, just south of the centre across the Río Chico, which serves all local, regional and national destinations, and also offers services to Chile and Bolivia.

Destinations Buenos Aires (3 daily; 22hr); Cordoba (3 daily; 14–15hr); Salta (2 daily; 2hr); Tucumán (regular; 5–6hr).

INFORMATION AND TOURS

Tourist information Dirección Provincial de Turismo, on Plaza General Belgrano (Mon–Fri 7am–10pm, Sat & Sun 9am–9pm; ☎0388 422 1325, ⓦturismo.jujuy.gov.ar).

Tour operators Noroeste, at San Martín 155 (☎0388 423 7565, ⓦnoroestevirtual.com.ar), is a youth travel agency attached to *Club Hostel*.

★ TREAT YOURSELF

Just 19km west of Jujuy are the thermal hot springs of the **Termas de Reyes** and the **Hotel Termas de Reyes** (☎0388 392 2522, ⓦtermasdereyes.com; AR$330 for a day visit, AR$760 for a room overnight). Sinking into a hot mineral spa bath, or relaxing with a mineral mud mask, is just the way to shake off a long bus ride. There are fourteen private thermal baths for three people, with stunning panoramic views, as well as two saunas. The #14 public bus runs to Termas from the main bus terminal (4 daily; 20min).

ACCOMMODATION

★ **Hostal Casa de Barro** Otero 294 ☎ 0388 422 9578, ⓦ casadebarro.com.ar. Wonderful and welcoming, with clean spacious dorms and private rooms, an excellent on-site restaurant and a pleasant common area. Dorms AR$35

Club Hostel San Martín 155 ☎ 0388 423 7565, ⓦ club hosteljujuy.com.ar. Busy, lively hostel with a small pool, within walking distance of the bus terminal and the centre. Dorms AR$100, doubles AR$245

Dublin Hostel y Bar Independencia 946 ☎ 0388 422 9608, ⓦ dublinhostel.com.ar. Long-running Jujuy hostel, recently moved to larger premises. There's a handful of high-ceilinged dorms as well as a couple of doubles, while a bar (which closes at midnight) with a good beer selection is tacked on the side. Dorms AR$60, doubles AR$200

Munay Tierra de Colores Alvear 1230 ☎ 0388 422 8435, ⓦ munayhotel.com.ar. Just north of the centre, this friendly, small hostel has clean, rather dark rooms with private bathrooms. AR$310

EATING AND DRINKING

The open-air market, next to the bus station, is a great place to fill up on *empanadas*, grilled meat sandwiches, coffee, hot chocolate and the like for just a few pesos.

Cacao Sarmiento 330 ☎ 0388 423 2037. Sophisticated formal dining, good tapas and an extensive list of local wines. Around $100 for two courses. Mon–Sat noon–3.30pm & 8pm–2am.

La Candelaria Alvear 1346. West of the city, this *parrilla* is a local institution, and a must for any meat-lover. Tues–Sat noon–3pm & 8.30pm–1am, Sun noon–3pm.

★ **Macedonio** Lamadrid, at Güemes ☎ 0388 424 1606. Wonderful cultural centre and café bar in an 1860s adobe house, with a palm-fringed patio where folk and jazz bands play (Wed–Sat). Inexpensive meals – hearty sandwiches, salads and pasta – are served. Mon 6pm–2am, Tues–Sat 10am–2am, Sun 10am–6pm.

Madre Tierra Belgrano 619. Fresh salads, juices and vegetarian food, with a set menu for AR$60. Lunch only Mon–Sat.

Zorba Belgrano 802. Large, two-storey restaurant serving Greek food, as well as local favourites. Mon–Sat 8am–2am, Sun 6pm–1am.

DIRECTORY

Banks and exchange Alvear is lined with banks that accept foreign cards, including HSBC at Alvear 970.

Car rental Sudamerics, Belgrano 601 (☎ 0388 422 9034, ⓦ sudamerics.com).

Post office La Madrid, at Independencia.

QUEBRADA DE HUMAHUACA

The scintillating, multicoloured **QUEBRADA DE HUMAHUACA** gorge stretches 125km north of Jujuy, past the small village of **Purmamarca** and the town of **Tilcara**, with its pre-Columbian archeological site, all the way to the busy village of **Humahuaca**. From there you can carry on to reach the border crossing with Bolivia at **La Quiaca**, nearly 2000m higher and 150km further on. The region is popular with Argentine holidaymakers, who come to stay in the many swish spas and resorts, to hike and take in the extraordinary mountain scenery.

Purmamarca

As you head north, the first substantial settlement you reach along the RN9 is **PURMAMARCA** at Km61. This small town sits at the foot of the stunning **Cerro de los Siete Colores** (Hill of Seven Colours) and is an ideal base for horseriding and hiking excursions. Purmamarca is popular with Argentine tourists, and home to scores of luxury hotels as well as more budget-friendly options. Despite this tourist influx it retains plenty of rustic Andean charm, thanks to its traditional adobe buildings and colourfully dressed locals. The village has a fantastic seventeenth-century church, the **Iglesia Santa Rosa de Lima**, at its heart – faithfully maintained and still in use today.

Tilcara

The busy tourist town of **TILCARA** is a favourite with holidaymakers for its fantastic restaurants, attractive hotels and a pre-Incan **pukará** or fortress (daily 10am–6pm; AR$30, free Mon). Discovered in 1903 and heavily reconstructed in the 1950s, the site enjoys a wonderful, commanding location, covered in giant cacti. To get here, follow the signposted trail from the centre of town over the bridge across the Río Huasamayo. Keep your entrance ticket for admission to the **Museo Arqueológico** (same hours), on the south side of the square in a beautiful colonial house. The well-presented collection includes finds

1

from the site and further afield, including anthropomorphic vases and a humanoid standing stone from another *pukará*.

Humahuaca

HUMAHUACA is a small, attractive place, originally founded in 1591 and popular with backpackers, with a wider spread of budget accommodation than elsewhere. Numerous shops, restaurants and craft stalls stand all around the leafy plaza. On the east side, the tiny **Iglesia de la Candelaria** (daily noon–1pm; free), constructed in 1631 and rebuilt in the nineteenth century, has some interesting artworks. Beside the church, steps lead up to the base of the **Monumento a la Independencia**, a masculine and dramatic sculpture. There are awesome views from here, pocked by human-size cacti.

ARRIVAL AND DEPARTURE

By bus Buses leave every hour from Jujuy and run up the Quebrada to Purmamarca (1hr), Tilcara (1hr 30min–2hr) and Humahuaca (3hr), dropping off locals at farms and houses along the way. Only certain companies go all the way to La Quiaca – look for El Quiaqueño, Panamericano and Balut. Both Tilcara and Humahuaca have a central bus terminal that offers luggage storage; at other towns you will be dropped off at the main plaza.

INFORMATION AND TOURS

Tourist information The region's best tourist office is in Tilcara, at Belgrano 590 (daily 8am–noon and 1–9pm; ☎0388 495 5720). It has lists of accommodation throughout the region and free maps. Otherwise there is a small tourist office in Humahuaca (Mon–Fri 9–6pm), in the white colonial *cabildo* building on the plaza.

Tour operators Tilcara Tours, at Necochea 250 in Jujuy (☎0388 422 6113), organizes guided tours into the Quebrada de Humahuaca.

ACCOMMODATION

The best budget accommodation is found in Tilcara and Humahuaca, although campsites can be found in nearly every town in the valley.

TILCARA

★ **Malka** San Martín (at the top of the hill) ☎0388 495 5197, ⊕malkahostel.com.ar. It's a strenuous uphill walk to this hostel, which has comfortable *cabañas* for up to six people – great value if travelling in a group – as well as dorms and private rooms. HI discounts. Dorms AR$70, doubles AR$300

Tilcara Hostel Bolívar 166 ☎0388 495 5105, ⊕tilcara hostel.com. A 10min walk from the bus station, this hostel has clean dorms and excellent-value doubles complete with kitchen and private bathroom. Dorms AR$70, doubles AR$200

HUMAHUACA

Hostal Humahuaca Buenos Aires 447 ☎0388 742 1064, ⊕humahuacahostal.com.ar. Located just off the main plaza, this small hostel has slightly dark but cool dorm rooms set around a bright patio. Dorms AR$40, doubles AR$140

Posada el Sol Barrio Medalla Milagrosa (across the river) ☎0388 421 1466, ⊕elsolhosteldehumahuaca.com. Follow the signs from the bus station to this small rustic house on the outskirts of town. Small, comfortable dorms and doubles in peaceful surroundings. Dorms AR$45, doubles AR$170

EATING AND DRINKING

TILCARA

El Nuevo Progreso Lavelle 351. This intimate, candle-lit spot serves delicious Andean cuisine in hearty portions. The llama steaks are good, and there's a decent wine list sourced from local *bodegas*. Live music some evenings. Daily 6–11pm.

Los Puestos Belgrano, at Padilla ☎0388 495 5100. For a meal in exceptionally beautiful surroundings, *Los Puestos* rules supreme: the varied menu features tender grilled llama, mouthwatering *empanadas*, juicy *humitas* and succulent pasta, all at reasonable prices. Daily 11.30am–3pm & 8.30pm–midnight.

HUMAHUACA

Casa Vieja Buenos Aires, at Salta. More regional dishes, including a very substantial *locro*. Daily lunch & dinner.

El Portillo Tucumán 69. This hotel restaurant serves traditional food including llama meat, quinoa and Andean potatoes in a rustic environment. Daily 7pm–midnight.

Mendoza and San Juan

The vast midwestern provinces of **MENDOZA** and **SAN JUAN** are sparsely populated, sun-fried playgrounds for lovers of mountains and vineyards. The highest peaks outside the Himalayas rise to the west, capped by the formidable **Cerro Aconcagua**, whose icy volcanic summit punctures the sky at nearly

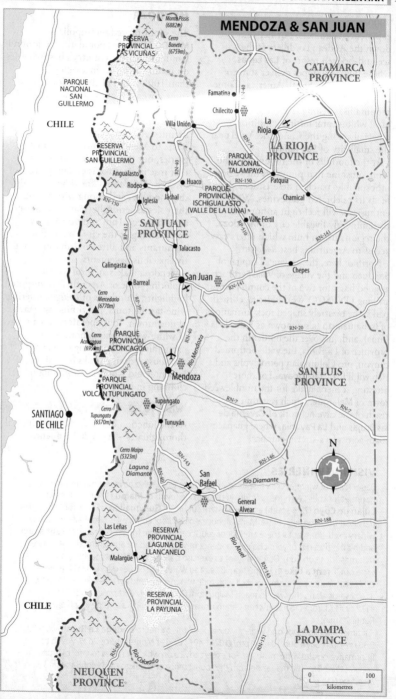

MENDOZA & SAN JUAN

CHILE

CATAMARCA PROVINCE

Monte Pissis (6882m)
Cerro Bonete (6759m)

RESERVA PROVINCIAL LAS VICUÑAS

PARQUE NACIONAL SAN GUILLERMO

Famatina

Chilecito

Villa Unión

La Rioja

LA RIOJA PROVINCE

RN-74

RESERVA PROVINCIAL SAN GUILLERMO

Angualasto

Rodeo

Huaco

RN-40

Jáchal

PARQUE NACIONAL TALAMPAYA

Patquia

RN-150

Chamical

Iglesia

PARQUE PROVINCIAL ISCHIGUALASTO (VALLE DE LA LUNA)

RP-412

Valle Fértil

SAN JUAN PROVINCE

Talacasto

RN-510

RN-141

Calingasta

Chepes

Barreal

Cerro Mercedario (6770m)

San Juan

RN-141

RP-39

Cerro Aconcagua (6951m)

PARQUE PROVINCIAL ACONCAGUA

RN-20

RN-40

Río Mendoza

RN-7

RN-7

Mendoza

SAN LUIS PROVINCE

PARQUE PROVINCIAL VOLCÁN TUPUNGATO

Cerro Tupungato (6570m)

Tupungato

RN-7

RN-7

Tunuyán

SANTIAGO DE CHILE

Cerro Maipo (5323m)

Laguna Diamante

RN-143

RN-146

RN-40

San Rafael

Río Diamante

N

Las Leñas

General Alvear

RN-188

Malargüe

RESERVA PROVINCIAL LAGUNA DE LLANCANELO

Río Atuel

RN-143

CHILE

RESERVA PROVINCIAL LA PAYUNIA

LA PAMPA PROVINCE

RN-40

Río Colorado

RN-151

NEUQUEN PROVINCE

0   100
kilometres

7000m, an irresistible magnet for experienced climbers. Further south down the Andean cordillera is the see-and-be-seen resort of **Las Leñas**, whose powdery slopes deliver some of the best skiing in South America. Come summer, snowmelt rushes down the mountains, swelling rivers and creating ideal **white-water rafting** conditions, especially along the Cañon de Atuel near the small city of **San Rafael**.

At the foothills of the mountains, the same sunshine that pummels the region's inhospitable, parched desertscapes also feeds its celebrated grapevines. Wine enthusiasts will feel right at home in the eminently liveable city of **Mendoza**, the region's urban hub, which offers easy access to Argentina's best *bodegas*.

North of here, the provincial capital of **San Juan** and the village of **Valle Fértil** act as good bases for two of the country's most striking UNESCO World Heritage-listed parks: the bizarrely shaped rock formations of **Ischigualasto** (also known as Valle de la Luna), and, just over the border in the province of La Rioja, the wide-bottomed canyon, pre-Columbian petroglyphs and rich wildlife of **Talampaya**. For more arresting scenery, make for the tumbleweed town of **Malargüe**, which is within easy reach of the cave network of **Caverna de las Brujas** and **La Payunia**, where guanacos roam across lava-strewn pampas.

MENDOZA

The sophisticated metropolis of **MENDOZA**, with a population of around a million, has the country's best wineries on its doorstep. Set in a valley less than 100km east of the Andes' loftiest snow-covered mountains, downtown is characterized by elegant, fountain-filled plazas and wide, sycamore-lined avenues. An earthquake in 1861 laid waste to Mendoza's former colonial glories, but the modern, low-rise city that rose in its wake is certainly no eyesore. *Mendocinos* know how to enjoy the good life, and, along with taking their siestas seriously (many businesses close between 1pm and 4pm), they enjoy dining at the city's many fine restaurants and alfresco drinking along the spacious pavements.

Mendoza makes an ideal base for exploring some of Argentina's undisputed highlights. Hundreds of *bodegas*, offering wine-tasting tours, lie within easy reach of downtown. **Tour operators** run a range of white-water rafting, horseriding, paragliding and skydiving excursions, and those looming peaks offer skiing in winter and world-class mountain climbing in summer.

WHAT TO SEE AND DO

At the junction of the city's two principal thoroughfares – Avenida Sarmiento

---

VISITING WINERIES

Barrel-loads of wineries offer free tours and tastings (some also have restaurants offering gourmet lunches), with the majority in the satellite towns of **Maipú** (15km southeast), **Luján de Cuyo** (7km south) and the eastern suburb of **Guaymallén**, all accessible by public transport from the city centre. Many Mendoza-based tour companies offer half- or full-day winery excursions, but if there are four of you, it can be more fun and cheaper to **rent a taxi** and hit the *bodegas* of your choice independently (call ahead for appointments; also note that most close on Sun). Or if you want to exercise between swills (but maybe spit the wine out?), **rent a bike** in Maipú from Bikes and Wines (AR$60 per day; ☎0261 410 6686, ⊛bikesandwines.com), arm yourself with their winery map, and cycle a 40km circuit, stopping at vineyards along the way. To reach Maipú from downtown Mendoza, catch *colectivos* #171, #172 or #173 from Rioja (between Catamarca and Garibaldi) and ask to be let off at Plazoleta Rutini (45min).

If time only allows for one winery, walk around the corner to **Bodega La Rural** (Mon–Fri 9.30am–5pm, Sat & Sun 10am–1pm, ☎0261 497 2013) at Montecaseros 2625, which has an informative on-site wine museum. For expert advice on which wineries to visit, pick up a free copy of *Wine Republic* magazine from the tourist office or speak to the helpful staff at *Vines of Mendoza* (see p.103).

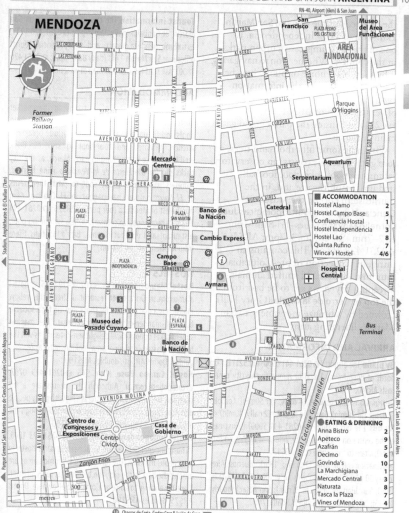

and Avenida Mitre – the spacious **Plaza Independencia** is the physical and cultural heart of Mendoza. Fountains and sycamore trees create an ideal space for chilling out or, over summer, taking in one of the regular outdoor concerts. One block east and south of here, **Plaza España** trumps Independencia in the beauty stakes, thanks to the Andalucian tilework gracing its stone benches, tree-lined paths, pretty fountains and monument to Spain's discovery of South America.

Museo del Pasado Cuyano

The **Museo del Pasado Cuyano** (Mon–Fri 9am–12.30pm; donation), at Montevideo 544, is the city's history museum, housed in a mansion dating from 1873. The collection includes an exhibition on General San Martín along with religious art, weaponry and period furniture.

Parque General San Martín

A four-square-kilometre green space you could easily spend a day exploring, the forested **Parque General San Martín**, 1km west of Plaza Independencia, is one of the most impressive urban parks in the country. Whether you're navigating it by foot, bike, horse or public bus, be sure to grab a map at the **information centre** (daily June–Aug 8am–6pm, rest of year 8am–7pm; ☎0261 420 5052, ext 221) just inside the park's grand gated main entrance.

Within lie some fifty thousand trees, a rose garden, tennis courts, an observatory, swimming pool, lake, zoo, football stadium, amphitheatre and, in the southeastern corner, the **Museo de Ciencias Naturales y Antropológicas Juan Cornelio Moyano** (Tues–Fri 8am–1pm & 2–7pm, Sat & Sun 3–7pm; AR$2; ☎0261 428 7666). This contains an intriguing collection of pre-Columbian mummies, fossils and stuffed animals. Sweeping city views are to be had from the top of **Cerro de la Gloria** (Glory Hill), crowned by a bronze monument to San Martín's liberating army.

ARRIVAL AND INFORMATION

By plane The airport (☎0261 441 0900, ext 521) is 7km north of downtown. A taxi or *remise* to the city centre costs AR$40.

Destinations Buenos Aires (4 daily; 1hr 50min); Córdoba (2 daily; 1hr 20min); Santiago de Chile (2 daily; 40min).

By bus The bus station (☎0261 431 5000) is just east of the centre on Av Gobernador Videla, at Av Acceso Este (RN7); a taxi to the centre costs AR$12.

Destinations Bariloche (2 daily; 18hr); Buenos Aires (every 30min; 17hr); Córdoba (hourly; 10hr); Salta (9 daily; 19hr); San Juan (hourly; 2hr 30min); San Rafael (hourly; 3hr 15min); Santiago de Chile (12 daily; 7hr).

Tourist information The city tourist office is on San Martín, at Garibaldi (daily 9am–9pm; ☎0261 420 1333, ⊛turismo.mendoza.gov.ar), and the provincial tourist office is at San Martín 1143 (daily 8am–9pm; ☎0261 420 2800). Ask staff for a list and map of wineries.

ACCOMMODATION

Mendoza has dozens of outstanding backpacker hostels, the best of which have gardens and swimming pools and fill up fast; all listed here include breakfast, kitchen, internet and tour-booking services. Book well in advance if travelling in early March, as the city packs out for the *Fiesta de la Vendimia* wine festival. Campers will find a shady spot to pitch their tents at *El Suizo* on Av Champagnat in El Challao, 6km northwest of Mendoza (per person AR$25; ☎0261 044 1991, ⊛campingsuizo.com.ar), with a swimming pool, restaurant and outdoor cinema. Bus #115 runs there from Av Alem, at San Martín.

HOSTELS

Hostel Alamo Necochea 740 ☎0261 429 5565, ⊛hostel alamo.com.ar. On a quiet residential street, this yellow mansion is a real godsend for those looking for a sociable but well-mannered backpackers' retreat. The massive supermarket opposite will delight self-caterers, as will the hostel's glassed-in dining area looking onto a Zen-like garden. Dorms <u>AR$80</u>, doubles <u>AR$180</u>

Hostel Campo Base Mitre 946 ☎0261 429 0707, ⊛campobase.com.ar. Although the dorms are a bit cramped, this well-located hostel is a hit with party people and Aconcagua climbers (treks are organized through the affiliated tour company). Dorms only <u>AR$80</u>

Hostel Independencia Mitre 1237 ☎0261 423 1806, ⊛hostelindependencia.com.ar. Boisterous party hostel in a gorgeous mansion. The location and common areas are among the best in the city; the bathrooms, sadly, are not. If you're sensitive to noise or alcohol, go elsewhere. Dorms <u>AR$75</u>, doubles <u>AR$180</u>

MENDOZA TOURS

Mendoza province is not just about wine, and its mountains and rivers offer plenty of opportunities for trekking and adventure sports, for which you'll need the services of the region's highly professional tour operators.

TOUR OPERATORS

Argentina Rafting Potrerillos ☎0262 448 2037, ⊛argentinarafting.com. Runs white-water rafting trips down the Class III–IV rapids of the Mendoza River.

Aymara 9 de Julio 1023, Mendoza ☎0261 420 2064, ⊛aymara.com.ar. Specializes in guided Aconcagua treks.

Bikes and Wines Urquiza 1601, Maipu ☎0261 410 6686, ⊛bikesandwines.com. Organizes bicycle tours to wineries.

Campo Base Peatonal Sarmiento 229, Mendoza ☎0261 425 5511, ⊛campobase.com.ar. Offers adventure excursions that combine trekking, mountain biking and abseiling in one action-packed day.

El Rincón de los Oscuros Av Los Cóndores, Potrerillos ☎0262 448 3030, ⊛rincondelososcuros .com. Horseriding specialists.

★ **Hostel Lao** Rioja 771 ☎ 0261 438 0454, ⊛ laohostel .com. The most inviting of the city's hostels, this English-run place is often full. Chilled-out but buzzing, it has plenty of common space, travel photography graces its walls, there's a large garden with a pool and hammocks, a roof terrace, wi-fi and very clean dorm rooms. Wine flows when the owner is feeling generous. Dorms AR$80, doubles AR$200

Winca's Hostel Sarmiento 717 ☎ 0261 425 3804. This hostel, set in a large, peach-coloured house, has a chef's-quality kitchen and big back yard with swimming pool. The dorms, however, are small and dark. The owners have another hostel at San Lorenzo 19 and fully furnished apartments for rent – a good option for couples or long-term stayers. Dorms only AR$70

HOTELS

★ **Confluencia Hostal** Av España 1512 ☎ 0261 429 0430, ⊛ hostalconfluencia.com.ar. Perfect for couples who want more privacy and sophistication than a hostel, this modern boutique hotel offers spacious doubles (and quadruples) with wooden floorboards and private bathrooms. There's a TV lounge and large roof terrace with mountain views. Breakfast included. AR$220

Quinta Rufino Rufino Ortega 142 ☎ 0261 420 4696, ⊛ quintarufinohostel.com.ar. A B&B offering large rooms with private bathroom and cable TV in a converted villa. It's a short stroll to the city's bar strip. Breakfast included. AR$230

EATING

Mendoza has some exceptional restaurants, many specializing in local produce, Pacific seafood and regional wine.

Anna Bistro Juan B Justo 161 ☎ 0261 425 1818. Cocktail-sipping diners lounge outside on white leather couches amid fragrant foliage and romantic lighting at this top-notch French-run restaurant. The eclectic menu features standouts like seafood pasta (AR$44). Set lunches are good value. Tues–Sun noon–3pm & 8–11pm.

★ **Govinda's** San Martín 453, bus ride or taxi from centre ☎ 0261 424 3799. Simply the best vegetarian restaurant in the city; load up your plate with lovingly prepared dishes from the gigantic buffet (AR$37/kg). No alcohol served. Mon–Sat for lunch (noon–2.30pm) & dinner (6–10pm); lunch only on Sun.

La Marchigiana Patricias Mendocinas 1550 ☎ 0261 423 0751. This airy, family affair is widely considered to be the city's best Italian restaurant and scores extra points for its very fair prices (mains start at under AR$505). Sun–Thurs noon–3pm & 8pm–midnight (Fri until 12.30am, Sat until 1am).

Mercado Central Las Heras between España and Patricias Mendocinas. This bustling indoor market is full of inexpensive cafés offering local dishes such as *humitas* and *empanadas*, and is a great place to try goodies such as Andean goat's cheeses. Most snacks AR$5.

★ **TREAT YOURSELF**

Azafrán Sarmiento 765 ☎ 0261 429 4200. From venison ravioli to Patagonian deer, the dining experience at this lauded restaurant is pure gourmet. The sommelier will guide diners on a rummage in the wine cellar, where more than 450 vintages from 80 different vineyards are stocked. Mains around AR$75. Mon–Sat 12.30–4pm & 8pm–1am.

Naturata Don Bosco 73 ☎ 0261 420 3087. Wholesome vegetarian buffet in light and airy surroundings on a leafy residential street (AR$40 all-you-can-eat or AR$5/kg). Mon–Sat noon–3pm & 7–11pm.

★ **Tasca la Plaza** Montevideo 117 ☎ 0261 420 0603. Flickering candles set off the wooden floorboards, bright-red walls and funky *Mendocino* art at the city's coolest tapas bar and restaurant where you can swill a mojito (AR$25) with your grilled king prawns (AR$45).

DRINKING AND NIGHTLIFE

Mendoza's bar scene is concentrated along trendy Aristides Villanueva, where pavement tables fill with drinkers on summer evenings. The best nightclubs are in outlying neighbourhoods like El Challao to the northwest, Las Heras to the north and Chacras de Coria to the south. Women generally get in free, and while *Mendocinos* like to party late, keep in mind that a city law stipulates that last entry is at 2.30am.

Apeteco San Juan, at Barraquero. A sophisticated crowd packs into this sleek, cavernous club on weekends. Following the midnight live music set, punters lose their cool on the dancefloor to a mixed soundtrack of electronica, rock, reggaeton and salsa. Wed–Sat. Free entry until 11pm, then AR$40 for men.

Decimo Garibaldi 7, 10th floor of Edificio Gómez. Yuppie wine bar and restaurant *par excellence*. Set on the top floor of a downtown apartment block, it offers a winning combination of city and mountain views along with a hundred Argentine wines to wrap your palate around (small bottles from AR$25). Put on your glad rags and live the high life. Mon–Sat 6pm–3am.

Vines of Mendoza Espejo 567 ☎ 0261 438 1031, ⊛ vinesofmendoza.com. A swanky wine-tasting room with more than sixty wines from regional boutique *bodegas*. Let the English-speaking staff talk you through a tasting session (from AR$100) or nurse a glass of *vino tinto* in the wisteria-shaded courtyard. Daily 3–10pm.

DIRECTORY

Banks and exchange Banco de la Nación Argentina accepts foreign cards and has branches across the city,

★ TREAT YOURSELF

Try to make time (and room in the budget) for a trip out of town for a gourmet lunch among the vineyards at a nearby **bodega**: ask at the tourist office or pick up the *Vines of Mendoza* magazine for further listings.

WINERY LUNCHES

Ruca Malen Ruta Nacional 7km 1059, Luján de Cuyo (take a bus to Luján and then a taxi for $AR40) ☎0261 410 6214, ⍟bodegarucamalen.com. The restaurant here looks out on to vineyards and mountains, and lunch is a belly-busting five-course degustation (AR$200), with each delectable plate – from roasted aubergine in plum sauce to *dulce de leche* mousse – perfectly paired with *bodega* wine. Lunch daily.

La Bourgogne Roque Sáenz Peña 3531, Vistalba, Luján de Cuyo (taxi from Luján AR$25); ☎0261 498 9400, ⍟carlospulentawines.com. Attached to the Vistalba winery (producing since 2002), this restaurant prepares French cuisine using regional and seasonal produce. Dishes like veal in mushroom sauce (AR$110) and quince tart with lavender ice cream (AR$45) go down a treat with a bottle of vino (AR$100 upwards). Reserve in advance and ask for a table by the window with cordillera and vineyard views. Closed Sun & Mon.

including San Martín, at Gutierrez, and España 1275. Cambio Express, at Espejo 58, and Cambio Santiago, at Av San Martín 119, will exchange foreign cash.

Car rental Alamo Nacional Rent, Pvo de la Reta 928 (☎0261 429 3111); Avis, Pvo de la Reta 914 (☎0261 429 6403); Hertz, Espejo 415 (☎0261 423 0225); Via Rent a Car, San Juan 931 (☎0261 429 0876).

Internet The WH Internet & Games chain (☎0261 423 3398) has cybercafés at San Martín 1178, Las Heras 61 and Peatonal Sarmiento 219. Only the San Martín branch opens Sundays.

Laundry Lavandería Necochea, 25 de Mayo 1357.

Post office San Martín, at Colón.

Shopping There is a handicraft market on Plaza Independencia every weekend. The upscale Mendoza Plaza shopping mall (⍟mendozaplazashopping.com), at Av Acceso Este 3280 in Guaymallén, to the east of the city centre, has around 200 shops and restaurants, plus a cinema.

Spanish school Intercultural, at Rep de Siria 241 (☎0261 429 0269, ⍟spanishcourses.com.ar), offers one-week courses.

ALTA MONTAÑA

The cathedral-like peaks of the Parque Provincial Aconcagua lie just three hours west of Mendoza, easily visited on a popular day-trip dubbed the **ALTA MONTAÑA ROUTE**. Leaving behind verdant vineyards and climbing into barren hills, this scenic excursion follows the RN7 (the highway to Santiago de Chile), following the former Trans-Andean railway and the Río Mendoza into the spectacular Uspallata Valley, where *Seven Years in Tibet* was filmed.

From the crossroads village of Uspallata (105km west of Mendoza), it's a further 65km to **Los Penitentes**, a winter ski resort with 28 pistes (☎0261 428 3601, ⍟penitentes.com), and, in summer, a base for Aconcagua climbers (see opposite). Some 6km west of Los Penitentes is one of the area's most photographed landmarks, the **Puente del Inca**, a natural stone bridge traversing the Río de las Cuevas at 2700m. Beneath it, thermal waters seep among the ruins of an abandoned 1940s spa resort. The route passes Parque Provincial Aconcagua and ends at the Chilean border where a statue of **Cristo Redentor** (Christ the Redeemer) commemorates the 1902 peace pact between historic enemies.

PARQUE PROVINCIAL ACONCAGUA

At 6959m, **CERRO ACONCAGUA** – "the roof of the Americas" – lords it over the 710-square-kilometre Parque Provincial Aconcagua. The highest mountain in both the western and the southern hemispheres, Aconcagua's faces are ringed by five glistening glaciers. In 1985, the discovery of an **Inca mummy** at 5300m on Aconcagua's southwest face lent further weight to the theory that the Incas worshipped the mountain and offered it human sacrifices.

Nowadays, Inca worshippers have been replaced by ardent mountain climbers, who ascend in droves throughout summer. Only the most experienced attempt the **climb** without a professional guide. Taking into account acclimatization time, it should take at least thirteen days to reach the summit. There are three possible routes – south, west or east – with the least difficult being the western route, leaving from the Plaza de Mulas (4230m). For **route details** and advice on what to take, see ⓦ aconcagua.mendoza.gov.ar. Easier **day hikes** are also possible in the park as well as multi-day treks to base camps and mountain *refugios*.

ARRIVAL AND DEPARTURE

By bus Expresso Uspallata operates four buses daily from Mendoza to the base camps at Los Horcones and Punta de Vacas.

ACCOMMODATION

For accommodation at or near the base camps, there are options at Puente del Inca (where many people spend a couple of days acclimatizing), Las Cuevas and Los Penitentes.
Hostel Campo Base Penitentes Los Penitentes ☎ 0261 425 5511, ⓦ penitentes.com.ar. This lively, 28-bed hostel, with well-equipped kitchen, is a jumping-off point for organized ski trips in the winter and Aconcagua climbs in the summer. Breakfast and dinner included (prices halve Oct–May). Dorms A̅R̅$̅1̅2̅5̅
Refugio Plaza de Mulas ☎ 0261 421 4330, ⓦ refugio plazademulas.com.ar. It is possible to overnight here on day two of the mountain trail. Hot showers and cooked

meals are included in the price. Dorms A̅R̅$̅1̅4̅0̅, doubles A̅R̅$̅4̅5̅0̅
La Vieja Estación Puente del Inca ☎ 0261 452 1103. A hostel with large dorm rooms and communal bathrooms. The restaurant and bar will warm the cockles, and a variety of excursions is offered. Dorms A̅R̅$̅6̅5̅

EATING AND DRINKING

Make the most of hostel kitchens, and bring plenty of food supplies, as refuelling opportunities are few and far between once inside the park itself. During ski season, the resort hotels of Penitentes offer decent, if unspectacular, food, while snacks and hot drinks can be found at Puente del Inca's outdoor market.

SAN RAFAEL AND AROUND

In the heart of wine country, the laidback city of **SAN RAFAEL**, 230km south of the provincial capital, likes to think of itself as a smaller, friendlier version of Mendoza; its wide, flat streets are filled with cyclists and its leafy plazas are squeaky clean. The city itself offers few distractions, and boredom will probably set in once you've become acquainted with the main square, **Plaza San Martín**, and visited the **Museo de Historia Natural** (daily 8am–1pm & 2.30–7pm; AR$2), on Isla Diamante, 6km south of the centre, where the pre-Columbian displays include ceramics from Ecuador and a mummified child dating from 40 AD.

CLIMBING ACONCAGUA

To trek or climb in the Parque Provincial Aconcagua between mid-Nov and mid-March, you need to obtain a **permit** (bring your passport) from the Dirección de Recursos Naturales Renovables (Mon–Fri 8am–6pm, Sat & Sun 9am–1pm; ☎ 0261 425 8751), at San Martín 1143, 2nd floor, in Mendoza. Foreign trekkers pay between US$95 and US$725 between December and March (depending on the date and length of trek). The rest of the year snow cover makes the climb extremely dangerous; the fee at this time is around US$1000 and climbers must apply for a special permit (for update see website ⓦ cerroaconcagua.com/aconcagua/permisos-de-ingreso.asp).

TOUR OPERATORS

Owing to the mountain's unpredictable weather (storms claim lives every year), climbers are advised to go on organized trips with experienced local guides. The following are Mendoza-based operators that specialize in Aconcagua trips. Fernando Grajales Expeditions and Aconcagua Trek can make the arrangements for mule hire.
Aconcagua Trek Barcala 484 ☎ 0261 429 5007, ⓦ aconcaguatrek.com.

Aymara 9 de Julio 1023 ☎ 0261 420 2064, ⓦ aymara .com.ar.
Campo Base Peatonal Sarmiento 229 ☎ 0261 425 5511, ⓦ campobase.com.ar.
Fernando Grajales Expeditions ☎ 0261 428 3157, ⓦ grajales.net.
Inka Expediciones Juan B Justo 242 ☎ 0261 425 0871, ⓦ aconcagua.org.ar.

There are, however, worthwhile sights just beyond the city itself in the San Rafael department, including six hundred square kilometres of vineyards and around eighty **bodegas**. Most of the wineries are small, family-run affairs; the tourist office has a list of those open to the public. For **white-water rafting** enthusiasts, the **Cañon del Atuel**, a short journey to the southwest, is one of the top destinations in the country for riding the rapids.

ARRIVAL AND DEPARTURE

By plane San Rafael Airport is 5km west of downtown, with daily flights to and from Buenos Aires. There are buses to the centre (AR$4); a taxi costs around AR$25.

By bus The centrally located bus terminal is at Coronel Suárez, between calles Almafuerte and Avellaneda.

Destinations Buenos Aires (4 daily; 13hr); Las Leñas (June–Sept 1 daily, Dec–Feb 3 weekly on Tues, Thurs & Sat; 2hr 40min); Malargüe (3 daily; 2hr 30min); Mendoza (hourly; 3hr 15min).

INFORMATION AND TOURS

Tourist information The friendly tourist office is on the corner of avenidas Hipólito Yrigoyen and Balloffet (daily 8am–9pm; ☎ 0260 442 4217, ⌨ sanrafaelturismo.gov.ar).

Tour operator Risco Viajes (Av Hipólito Yrigoyen 284; ☎ 0260 443 6439, ⌨ riscoviajes.com) is a San Rafael-based tour operator for adventurous types. Offers everything from one-day wine-tasting trips (AR$550) and three-day excursions to hot spas (AR$1200 including accommodation), to mountain-biking and climbing adventures in the surrounding peaks.

ACCOMMODATION

San Rafael's accommodation options lack the range and quality found in Mendoza. If you're camping, make for the shady *Camping El Parador* on Isla Río Diamante, 6km south of downtown (AR$12/tent).

Rex Hipólito Yrigoyen 56 ☎ 0260 442 2177. This bright, modern hotel on the main drag has spotless rooms arranged around a quiet courtyard. Cable TV, breakfast and parking included. AR$310

Tierrasoles Hostel Alsina 245 ☎ 0260 443 3449, ⌨ tierrasoles.com.ar. A family-run HI hostel offering modest dorms, a simple breakfast and cheap internet. You have to be a contortionist to use the toilets, though. Dorms AR$88, doubles AR$235

Trotamundos Hostel Barcala 300 ☎ 0260 443 2795, ⌨ trotamundoshostel.com.ar. A relatively new, funky hostel in a converted historical building with a large, open-plan kitchen and plenty of activities laid on for guests. Includes breakfast and wi-fi access. Dorms AR$60, doubles AR$180

EATING AND DRINKING

San Rafael springs to life post-siesta, when locals pack the restaurants, bars, nightclubs and ice-cream parlours along Hipólito Yrigoyen.

La Fusta Hipólito Yrigoyen 538. The best *parrilla* in the city, where you can tuck into a juicy steak (AR$50) and quaff local wine without breaking the bank. Daily noon–3.30pm & 8.30pm–midnight.

Jockey Club Belgrano 330 ☎ 0260 448 7007. Upscale and with an Old-World feel, this much-loved restaurant serves well-prepared, filling mains including good pasta, fish and chicken dishes. Set lunch AR$75. Daily noon–3pm & 7–11pm.

Lorenzo Hipólito Yrigoyen 1850. The dancefloor at this popular bar is often shaking, thanks to a mixed soundtrack of rock, retro and electronica. On steamy nights, the drinking spills into the garden. Occasional live music. Thurs–Sat until late.

Tienda del Sol Hipólito Yrigoyen 1663. A hip, modern restaurant with outdoor tables, serving imaginative beef, chicken and fish mains (around AR$45), along with a wide range of regional wines. Daily 8pm–midnight.

LAS LEÑAS

Some 180km southwest of San Rafael and 445km south of Mendoza, the exclusive ski resort of **LAS LEÑAS** is to winter what Uruguay's Punta del Este is to summer – a chic party playground for *porteño* socialites. Between June and September (snow permitting), they flock here on week-long packages. Beyond après-ski glamour, the setting of Las Leñas is exquisite. The resort, which sits at 2240m, has the dramatic Cerro Las Leñas (4351m) towering over its 29 runs and 13 lifts. Pistes range in difficulty from nursery slopes to hair-raising black runs, with night-time and cross-country skiing also possible.

In summer, Las Leñas transforms into an outdoor action hub, offering horseriding, white-water rafting, trekking, climbing, abseiling, 4WD tours, mountain biking, summer skiing and even scuba diving in high-altitude lakes.

ARRIVAL AND INFORMATION

By bus During the ski season there are daily buses from Mendoza (7hr), Malargüe (1hr 30min) and San Rafael (2hr 40min). Regular direct buses also run from Buenos Aires (14hr; book through the central tourist office).

Tourist information The resort's office for booking ski packages and accommodation is in Buenos Aires at Bartolomé Mitre 401, 4th floor (Mon–Fri 9am–6pm; ☎011 4819 6000, ⓦlaslenas.com).

Lift ticket office Mid-June to late Sept 7.30am–5pm (☎0260 447 1100, ⓦlaslenas.com). Daily lift ticket prices range seasonally from AR$199 to AR$299.

ACCOMMODATION

Las Leñas accommodation needs to be booked through the resort's central Buenos Aires office (see above). Low-priced lodging is non-existent. If you are in a group, the most affordable places are the self-catering apartments known as "dormy houses": *Laquir, Lihuén, Milla* and *Payén* cost around AR$800/night and accommodate up to five people.

José Hostel ☎0260 15 460 0962, ✉josehostel@yahoo .com. The closest hostel to Las Leñas, 18km away in Los Molles. The owner, a ski-patroller, runs a tight ship, with two large dorm rooms, a kitchen, wine bar, fireplace, TV lounge, book exchange and wi-fi. The dorm price including transport to and from Las Leñas is AR$165. Dorms <u>AR$95</u>

EATING AND DRINKING

Innsbruck A log cabin *confitería* in the ski village where you can buy expensive fast food (a steak is AR$75) to enjoy over a beer from a terrace with piste views. Open for breakfast, lunch and dinner, as well as cocktails until the small hours.

El Refugio In the central Pirámide building ☎0260 447 1100 ext 1134. Dip into cheese fondue (AR$130) at this pricey French restaurant. Reservations necessary. Daily 8.30pm–midnight.

UFO Point The appetizing pizzas served here have earned this restaurant a devoted following, but at around AR$90 (serves two), they're not cheap. The restaurant is open for breakfast, lunch and dinner; at night it turns into a club with electronic music.

MALARGÜE

Set at the arid base of the Andes, 186km southwest of San Rafael, **MALARGÜE** is a small, nondescript town that's a jumping-off point for some of Argentina's most remarkable scenery. In winter its *raison d'être* is as an affordable base for **skiing** at the resort of Las Leñas (see opposite), while in summer the surrounding landscape offers ample opportunities for hiking, horseriding, fishing and white-water rafting. Worthwhile day-trips from town are to the underground limestone caves of **Caverna de las Brujas** (73km southwest),

the volcanic wonderland of **La Payunia** (208km south), and to **Laguna de Llancanelo** (65km southeast), a high-altitude lagoon speckled pink with flamingos.

WHAT TO SEE AND DO

Malargüe's flat, compact centre is easy to get your head around: the wide main drag is the RN40, known in town as **Avenida San Martín**. Here you'll find the tourist office, shops and the main square, **Plaza General San Martín**. Just south of the tourist office is the landscaped greenery of **Parque del Ayer** ("Park of Yesteryear"), filled with sculptures and native trees. Opposite, you can take a free guided tour at the **Observatorio Pierre Auger** (Mon–Fri 5–6pm; ☎0260 447 1562, ⓦauger.org.ar), an astrophysics centre that studies cosmic rays.

ARRIVAL AND DEPARTURE

By bus Malargüe's bus terminal (☎0260 447 0690) is on Esquibel Aldao, at Fray Luis Beltrán, four blocks south and two west of Plaza San Martín.

Destinations Mendoza (3 daily; 5hr); San Rafael (3 daily; 2hr 30min); Las Leñas (1 daily during ski season; 1hr 30min).

INFORMATION AND TOURS

Tourist information The tourist office (daily 8am–10pm; ☎0260 447 1659, ⓦmalargue.gov.ar) is on the RN40 four blocks north of the plaza.

Tour operators Many local companies run tours to La Payunia, Laguna de Llancanelo and Caverna de las Brujas, as well as horseriding and other adventure activities. Check out Karen Travel at Av San Martín 54 (☎0260 447 0342, ⓦkarentravel.com.ar), where you can also rent 4WDs.

ACCOMMODATION

Malargüe has plenty of affordable places to stay, including a handful of well-run hostels. Prices rise significantly during the winter, when Malargüe becomes a popular base for skiing at Las Leñas. Some Malargüe hotels offer fifty percent discounts on Las Leñas ski-lift tickets if you stay in town.

Cabañas Newen Mapu Av Roca, at Villa del Milagro ☎0260 447 2318, ⓦnewenmapu.com. Buy yourself some space with a two-storey *cabaña* (sleeps 6) complete with cable TV, full kitchen, fireplace and mountain views. Prices halve in the low season. *Cabaña* <u>AR$850</u>

Camping Polideportivo Capdevila, at Aldao ☎0260 447 0691. This municipal campsite is conveniently located in the north part of town, but is open summer only. <u>AR$28</u>

Hostel La Caverna Cte Rodríguez 445 Este ☎ 0260 447 2569, ⓦ lacavernahostel.com.ar. This hostel has a spacious common area and plenty of dorm beds. The self-catering apartment out back is ideal for groups. Free laundry and internet. Dorms AR$60, doubles AR$230

Ecohostel Colonia Pehuenche I, Finca N. 65, 5km south of town (free transfer from the Choique Turismo Alternativo office on San Martín, at Rodríguez) ☎ 0260 15 440 2439, ⓦ hostelmalargue.com. There's some serious star-gazing and R&R to be had at this rustic HI hostel set on an organic farm. Home-made meals and horseriding excursions offered. Dorms AR$72, doubles AR$221

EATING AND DRINKING

El Bodegón de Maria Rufino Ortega, at General Villegas. Trout and pizza get all the attention at this welcoming rustic-style restaurant. Set lunch AR$45. Daily noon–2.30pm & 7–11pm.

Cuyam-Co 8km west of Malargüe in El Dique. Catch your own meal and have it cooked to perfection at this trout farm. AR$65 for full menu and AR$29 to fish for your dish and then have it cooked. Daily noon–10.30pm.

Río Grande RN40 Norte ☎ 0260 447 1589. The restaurant in this upmarket hotel serves decent steaks (AR$40), pastas (AR$45) and trout ($AR35). Daily for breakfast, lunch & dinner.

AROUND MALARGÜE

Some 65km southeast of Malargüe is the nature reserve of **LAGUNA DE LLANCANELO**, a vast lakeland area famous for its abundant birdlife. Alongside the flamingos that flock here in their thousands, herons and black-neck swans can be easily spotted. Also look out for the *coipo*, a rodent similar in appearance to the capybara but a little smaller in size. The best way to visit the reserve is with a guided tour (see p.107).

The **CAVERNA DE LAS BRUJAS** ("Witches' Cave") is an incredible limestone cave filled with mesmerizing many-coloured rock formations, including **stalactites** and **stalagmites**. The cave, located 73km southwest of Malargüe and 8km along a dirt road off the RN40, is within a provincial park and is staffed by *guardaparques*. Guided visits (AR$30) are restricted to nine people at a time and are the only way to see the various underground chambers. The **temperature** inside the grotto can be 20°C lower than outside, so be sure to wrap up.

Continuing along the RN40, you'll reach the entrance to **LA PAYUNIA** at El Zampal. This expansive, wildlife-rich reserve spans 4500 square kilometres. Flaxen grasslands, black lava flows and eight hundred threatening-looking volcanoes (the highest concentration of volcanic cones in the world) provide a starkly wild backdrop for the guanaco, puma and condor that call it home. The best way to see La Payunia is on an organized **day-trip from Malargüe** (see p.107) that takes in the Caverna de las Brujas along the way.

SAN JUAN

SAN JUAN is a modern, low-rise provincial capital. In 1944, one of South America's most powerful earthquakes (8.5 on the Richter scale) razed the city, killing more than ten thousand people. Essentially a poorer, smaller and less attractive version of its southerly neighbour Mendoza, San Juan is unlikely to capture your imagination. It does, however, make a convenient base for sampling the fruits of nearby wineries as well as for excursions to some of Argentina's most iconic natural wonders – the sculptural desert landscapes of **Parque Provincial Ischigualasto** and the surreal rock formations of **Parque Nacional Talampaya**.

Try to avoid visiting in the summer, when *Sanjuaninos* cope with the midday heat by taking long, sluggish siestas.

WHAT TO SEE AND DO

The leafy Plaza 25 de Mayo, flanked by a couple of inviting cafés, marks the city centre. On its northwestern side, the modern cathedral's 50m-high brick campanile is a nod to St Mark's in Venice. If the mood takes, climb the **bell tower** (daily 9am–1pm & 5–8pm; AR$5) for great city and countryside vistas. Not far away at Sarmiento 21 Sur, opposite the tourist office, is the whitewashed childhood home of former Argentine president **Domingo Faustino Sarmiento** (1811–88), now a museum (Tues–Fri 9am–1.30pm & 5–9.30pm, Mon & Sat 8.30am–1.30pm; AR$3; guided tours every 30min). Although damaged in the 1944 earthquake, the house has been lovingly restored and displays belongings and paraphernalia from Sarmiento's eventful life.

More ancient history is represented in a former train station at the **Museo de Ciencias Naturales** (Av España at Av Maipú; daily 9am–1pm; ARS5; ☎0264 421 6774), the final resting place of the skeleton of the carnivorous **dinosaur**, Herrerasaurus, excavated in the Parque Provincial Ischigualasto (see p.110).

Finally, if all that has left your mouth dry, drop into the historic **Bodega Graffigna** (Tues–Fri 9am–1pm, Sat 9am–8pm, Sun 10am–2pm; free; ☎0264 421 4227), at Colón 1342 Norte, which houses the Museo de Vino Santiago Graffigna, and, perhaps more importantly, a wine bar where you can quench your thirst and sample provincial vintages.

ARRIVAL AND DEPARTURE

By plane Las Chacritas Airport (☎0264 425 4133) is 12km east of the city centre. A taxi downtown costs around ARS30.

Destinations Buenos Aires (daily; 1hr 50min).

By bus The bus station (Estados Unidos 492 Sur; ☎0264 422 1604) is eight blocks east of Plaza 25 de Mayo.

Destinations Buenos Aires (10 daily; 16hr); Córdoba (5 daily; 8hr); Mendoza (hourly; 2hr 30min); San Rafael (2 daily; 5hr 30min); Valle Fértil (3 daily; 4hr). Most long-distance buses, including two daily services to Santiago de Chile, require a change in Mendoza.

INFORMATION AND TOURS

Tourist information The tourist office at Sarmiento 24 Sur has good city and provincial information (Mon–Fri 7.30am–8.30pm, Sat & Sun 9am–8.30pm; ☎0264 421 0004, ⓦturismo.sanjuan.gov.ar).

Tour operators Companies offering Ischigualasto and Talampaya excursions include Algarrobo, at Sarmiento 62 Sur (☎0264 427 2487, ⓦalgarroboturismo.com.ar); and Triassic Tour, at Hipólito Yrigoyen 294 Sur (☎0264 421 9528, ⓦgrupohuaco.com.ar).

ACCOMMODATION

Cheap accommodation is of a reasonable standard in San Juan.

Camping Don Bosco 3km east on RN20 ☎0264 425 3663. A conveniently located campsite with hot showers and a swimming pool. Catch bus #19 from the centre. Camping/person ARS8

★ **Colpa Hostel-Apart** 25 de Mayo 554 Este ☎0264 422 5704. The spotless rooms in this stylish hostel-cum-apartment complex have first-rate beds and – hallelujah – a/c. The price is per person, whether you're sharing or alone. Includes breakfast, two kitchens, swimming pool and TV room. ARS80

Jardín Petit 25 de Mayo 345 Este ☎0264 421 1825. A welcoming hotel with cosy, simple rooms and an inviting patio and pool. Breakfast included and discounts can sometimes be arranged. ARS310

San Juan Hostel Av Córdoba 317 Este ☎0264 4201 835, ⓦsanjuanhostel.com. Helpful staff, a central location and a comfortable common area make up for the depressing dorms and basic bathrooms at this backpackers' pad. Includes breakfast and internet. Dorms ARS55, doubles ARS120

Zonda Hostel Caseros 486 Sur ☎0264 420 1009, ⓦzondahostel.com.ar. Conveniently located four blocks from the bus station, this 35-bed HI hostel has a TV room, patio, kitchen, free internet and breakfast. Dorms ARS50

EATING AND DRINKING

Antonio Gómez Supermercado, General Acha at Córdoba. The heaving paellas (ARS40) draw the lunchtime crowd at this Spanish-centric market stall. Lunch only.

Remolacha Av José Ignacio de la Roza Oeste, at Sarmiento ⓦparrillaremolacha.com.ar. Traditional and hugely popular *parrilla* with a vast range of meaty treats to be enjoyed indoors or alfresco. Vegetarians won't starve either, thanks to some decent meat-free pasta dishes, mixed vegetable grills and interesting salads. Set meals from ARS70. Daily 11am–3pm & 9pm–2am.

El Rincón de Nápoli Rivadavia 175 Oeste. Noisy and cheerful fast-service restaurant whipping up pizza, pasta, burgers and plenty of grilled meat (mains ARS20). Daily noon–midnight.

De Sánchez Rivadavia 55 Oeste. The city's classiest restaurant serves beautifully prepared salmon (ARS70) and beef (ARS55) with a fine selection of local wines by the glass and bottle. After the meal, browse the adjoining book and music shop. Mon–Sat 12.30–3pm & 9pm–midnight.

★ **Soychú** Av José Ignacio de la Roza 223 Oeste. Slip into something elasticated before gorging yourself on one of the continent's best vegetarian all-you-can-eat buffets (ARS35). Don't pass up the offer of a freshly squeezed juice. Mon–Sat lunch & dinner, lunch only Sun.

DIRECTORY

Banks and exchange Several banks on General Acha accept foreign cards, including Banco Macro at Gral Acha 41, HSBC at Gral Acha Sur 320 and Banco de la Nación Argentina at Av Rioja Sur 218.

1

Car rental Renta Auto, San Martín 1593 Oeste (☎ 0264 423 3620).

Internet You're never too far from an internet booth in San Juan. Late opening and good connections at Cyber le Red, Tucumán Norte 910; Cyber 51 at Av Libertador General San Martín Oeste 51; and Upe at Mendoza Sur 21.

Laundry Laverap, Rivadavia 498 Oeste.

Post office Av José Ignacio de la Roza 259 Este.

AROUND SAN JUAN

The UNESCO World Heritage-listed parks of Ischigualasto (better known as Valle de la Luna) and Talampaya lie in the provinces of San Juan and La Rioja respectively. The former is known for its other-worldly rock formations, the latter its red sandstone cliffs. Located close together, both can be visited on day-trips from San Juan, but the sleepy village of **San Agustín de Valle Fértil**, 250km northeast, is a much closer base. Some **tour operators** pack both parks into one day-long excursion, stopping off at Talampaya in the morning when the wind is low and the light best illuminates the red in the sandstone, before journeying 93km to visit Ischigualasto in the mid- to late afternoon.

San Agustín de Valle Fértil

Set in a valley carved out by the Río San Juan and surrounded by olive groves and sheep pasture, **SAN AGUSTÍN DE VALLE FÉRTIL** is a verdant oasis amid desert-like terrain. Take plenty of ready cash as the only cashpoint regularly runs dry and cards are rarely accepted for payment.

ARRIVAL AND INFORMATION

By bus The bus terminal is on Mitre, at Entre Rios; there are three daily services from San Juan (4hr) and three weekly from La Rioja (4hr).

Tourist information The super-friendly tourist office (daily 7am–1pm & 2–10pm; ☎ 02646 420 104, ✉ ischigualasto@sanjuan.gov.ar) is at Plaza San Agustín and can advise on tours and transport to the parks, as well as bicycle and horseriding excursions to view pre-Hispanic petroglyphs in the nearby mountains.

Tour operator Turismo Vesa, at Mitre s/n (☎ 02646 420 143, ✇ turismovesa.com), offers daily trips from Valle Fértil to Ischigualasto and Talampaya.

ACCOMMODATION

Camping Valle Fértil Rivadavia s/n ☎ 02646 420 015. Well-established campsite with plenty of shade. The price includes a tent for up to four people, with a supplement of AR$3/person extra. Camping **AR$16**

Campo Base Valle de la Luna Tucumán between San Luis & Libertador ☎ 02646 420 063, ✇ hostelvalledelaluna .com.ar. This modest but welcoming hostel has a kitchen, TV lounge, free breakfast and tour advice. Dorms **AR$55**

Eco Hostel Mendoza 42 ☎ 02646 226 733. A cooling swimming pool and nightly tango lessons make this basic hostel popular with backpackers. Two blocks from the bus station. Dorms **AR$55**, doubles **AR$105**

★ **Hostería Valle Fértil** Rivadavia 5400 ☎ 02646 420 015, ✇ alkazarhotel.com.ar. The village's most inviting accommodation, thanks to its setting on a breezy hillside overlooking the Dique San Agustín reservoir, though it looks a bit sorry for itself these days. Some of the small, modern rooms have lake views. There's a restaurant and guests can use the swimming pool in the *hostería's cabaña* complex down the hill. **AR$380**

Pension Doña Zoila Mendoza between Rivadavia & Laprida ☎ 02646 420 308. This budget pension has bare-bones rooms and shared bathrooms set around a peaceful, grapevine-shaded courtyard. **AR$170**

EATING AND NIGHTLIFE

There are no bars as such in Valle Fértil, just a couple of shops with games machines and plastic tables and chairs.

La Cocina de Zulma North side of the plaza. Tuck into pesto pasta served with steak for a bargain AR$25. Daily noon–3.30pm & 7.30–11.30pm.

La Florida South side of the plaza. Above-average Argentine fare (mains AR$50) and very attentive service. Daily noon–3pm & 7.30–11pm.

Hostería Valle Fertil The restaurant here is open to non-guests (for dinner only) and serves unpretentious dishes such as omelettes, salads and soups (mains from AR$45). It's the only restaurant in the town to accept credit and debit cards. Daily 7.30–11pm.

Parque Provincial Ischigualasto

Sculpted by more than two million years of erosion, wind and water, the **PARQUE PROVINCIAL ISCHIGUALASTO**, otherwise known as the Valle de la Luna (Moon Valley), is San Juan's most visited attraction. Set in a desert valley between two mountain ranges some 80km north of Valle Fértil, it is considered one of the most significant **dinosaur graveyards** on the planet. Skeletons dating from the Triassic era around two hundred million years ago have been unearthed here.

Given its size (150 square kilometres), you need a **car** to explore the park properly; rangers accompany visitors in convoy on a bumpy 45km circuit of the park's highlights (2–3hr), imparting explanations of its paleontological history, photogenic moonscapes and precarious sandstone rock formations. The southern section of the circuit resembles the arid lunar landscapes of Cappadocia in Turkey, with surreally shaped rock formations dubbed El Submarino (the submarine), El Esfinge (the sphinx) and Cancha de Bolas (bowling alley); while further north on the circuit lie stark white fields strewn with petrified tree trunks. If you're lucky, you might catch a glimpse of some of the park's inhabitants, which include hares, red foxes, armadillos, lizards, guanacos, snakes and condors.

INFORMATION AND TOURS

Park information The park entrance, where there's a helpful *guardaparque* post, is along a signposted road off the RP510 at Los Baldecitos. Entrance (daily April–Sept 9am–4pm, Oct–March 8am–5pm) is AR$100/person and includes a 2hr 30min tour following a ranger in your own vehicle. An extra AR$360 buys you a range of special tours, including 2hr guided bicycle excursions, full-moon night tours and 3hr treks to the top of Cerro Morado (1748m), with tremendous views of the park. Make use of the toilet facilties and cafés at the entrance, as there are none within the park itself.

By bus The easiest way to visit the park is on an organized tour, but if you want to visit independently, Empresa Vallecito buses from San Juan to La Rioja run on Mon, Wed & Fri and pass the Los Baldecitos checkpoint, a 5km walk to the park entrance. It is sometimes possible to accompany rangers on a tour of the park, or hire a vehicle at the entrance, but always check this in advance before showing up.

ACCOMMODATION

Campers can pitch their tents for AR$8 next to the park visitors' centre, where there is also a bathroom and small café. Most people spend the night in nearby Valle Fértil (see p.110) and get a transfer to the park with one of the village's tour operators.

Parque Nacional Talampaya

Familiar from regular appearances on posters promoting Argentine tourism, the smooth sandstone cliffs and surreal rock formations of **PARQUE NACIONAL TALAMPAYA** are even more eye-boggling in reality. The centrepiece of the park is a 220-million-year-old **canyon**, with 180m-high rust-red sandstone cliffs rising on either side, rendering everything in between puny and insignificant. At the centre of the canyon, armadillos and grey foxes scurry among groves of cacti and native trees in a lush **botanical garden**. Elsewhere, erosion has carved out towering columns and gravity-defying **rock formations** where condors and eagles have found nesting sites. Other park highlights include a series of pre-Hispanic **petroglyphs** and **pictographs** etched onto gigantic rock faces. Thought to be around a thousand years old, the etchings depict llamas, pumas, hunters, stepped pyramids and phallic symbols.

INFORMATION AND TOURS

Park information The closest urban centre to the park is Villa Unión, an entirely forgettable town in La Rioja Province, 55km away along the RP26. Organized tours from San Juan, Valle Fértil or Villa Unión are the best option, as private vehicles are not allowed. If you want to visit the park independently, the *guardería* (daily April–Sept 9am–4pm, Oct–March 8am–5pm; AR$40 entrance fee; ☎ 03825 470 397, ✺ talampaya.com) is staffed year-round and you can explore on foot (not recommended) or take an excursion with an official guide in their truck (2hr 30min, AR$145/person; 4hr 30min, AR$240/person).

By bus Buses from Villa Unión to La Rioja and Valle Fértil can drop you off on the main road (check when the last bus goes past or you'll be stuck overnight).

ACCOMMODATION AND EATING

There is a basic, windswept campsite next to the *guardería*; it can get brutally cold at night. A small shop here sells snacks and simple meals.

Lake District

The Argentine **LAKE DISTRICT** in northern Patagonia is an unspoiled region of azure glacial lakes, pristine rivers, snow-clad mountains, extinct volcanoes and verdant alpine forests. Dominated until the late nineteenth century by the indigenous Mapuche people, the Lake District is now Argentina's top year-round vacation destination – the place to go for hiking, camping, fishing, watersports, biking, climbing and skiing.

A series of spectacular national parks runs down the region's serrated Andean spine, providing easy access to the wilderness. The northernmost of Patagonia's national parks is **Parque Nacional Lanín** in Neuquén Province, accessible from both the sleepy fishing town of **Junín de los Andes** or its dressier neighbour **San Martín de los Andes**. As you head south, the dazzling 110km route between San Martín de los Andes and the upmarket village of **Villa La Angostura** affords roadside vistas of snowcapped peaks reflected in picture-perfect lakes as well as the first glimpse of the gigantic **Parque Nacional Nahuel Huapi**.

The route continues south to the lakeside party town of **Bariloche**, the region's transport hub and base for hiking in **Nahuel Huapi** in summer, skiing in winter and gorging on chocolate and locally brewed beer all year round. Further south, in the province of Chubut, the dusty town of **Esquel** is within day-trip distance of the **Parque Nacional Los Alerces**, a dramatic wilderness area of lakes, rivers, glaciers and thousand-year-old alerce trees; it also boasts one of the world's most famous trains, the **Old Patagonian Express**.

PARQUE NACIONAL LANÍN

The imposing snow-clad cone of extinct Volcán Lanín rises 3776m at the centre of its namesake **PARQUE NACIONAL LANÍN** (entrance AR$50). Lanín sits on the Chilean border, spanning 4120 square kilometres of varied Andean terrain. Fishing enthusiasts flock to its glacial lakes and trout-filled rivers, campers enjoy lakeside pitches at free or Mapuche-run campsites, while trekkers take advantage of the park's hiking trails. Forests of monkey-puzzle trees (also known as araucaria or *pehuén*) are the trademark of the northern section of the park. Volcano views are best from **Lago Huechulafquen**, 22km northwest of Junín de los Andes.

Lanín's southern sector is best explored from **San Martín de los Andes** (see p.114), set on the eastern shores of the park's **Lago Lácar**, or on the nearby section of the Seven Lakes Route (see box, p.116). Optimal visiting months are from October to mid-May, when there are organized excursions and regular buses.

JUNÍN DE LOS ANDES

It is impossible to avoid trout in pint-sized **JUNÍN DE LOS ANDES**; they not only populate the Río Chimehuín, but decorate every street sign and dominate every menu. Junín is well positioned for tours to the **Parque Nacional Lanín**, in particular the area around Puerto Canoa, the main base for treks around the volcano and boat trips on **Lago Huechulafquen**. Castelli (☎02972 491 557) runs buses to Puerto Canoa from Junín twice daily (1hr; AR$31), skirting alongside the lake and passing campsites and fishing spots such as the **Boca del Chimehuin** along the way.

For something to do in town, take a stroll around the **Vía Christi** sculpture walkway, which starts at the base of Cerro de la Cruz, a fifteen-minute walk west of Plaza San Martín at the end of Avenida Antártida Argentina. A path winds through a pine-forested hillside dotted with sculptures and mosaics depicting the Stations of the Cross, which fuse Catholic and Mapuche symbolism. If you are thwarted by bad weather, check out the **Paseo Artesanal** instead. Behind the tourism office on the main square various cabins (daily 10am–5pm) sell Mapuche crafts alongside woollen knits and handmade wooden crockery.

ARRIVAL AND INFORMATION

By plane Chapelco Airport (☎02972 428 388), which Junín shares with San Martín de los Andes, is 19km south of town. A taxi to the centre costs around AR$100; on your return, the hourly bus run by Castelli between Junín and San Martín will drop you off at the airport on request (AR$5).

By bus The bus station is three blocks from the main square at Olavarría and F.S. Martín.

Destinations Neuquén (3 daily; 6hr); San Martín de los Andes (12 daily; 1hr).

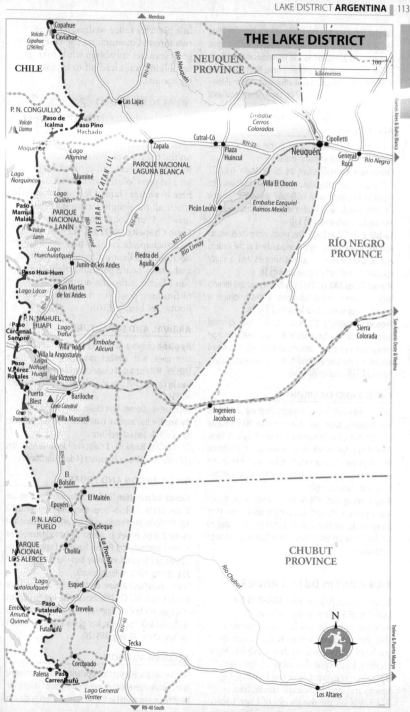

THE LAKE DISTRICT

0 _____ 100
kilometres

1

Tourist information The tourist office is opposite Plaza San Martín (Padre Milenasio, at Coronel Suárez; open 8am–9pm; ☎02972 491 160, ⓦjunindelosandes.gov.ar). Fishing licences can be purchased here. Next door is the helpful Parque Nacional Lanín information office (Mon–Fri 8am–9pm; ☎02972 492 748, ⓦparquenacionallanin .gov.ar).

ACCOMMODATION

Hotel prices hit Andean peaks in the summer, when advance bookings are recommended.

Chimehuín Coronel Suárez, at 25 de Mayo ☎02972 491 132, ⓦinterpatagonia.com/hosteriachimehuin. The rooms in this good-value B&B have windows that look out onto a landscaped garden with porch furniture. Wi-fi and breakfast included. AR$330

La Isla ☎02972 492 029. This pretty campsite is within easy reach of the main plaza, on an island at the eastern end of Gines Ponte. It has hot showers and a shady riverside setting. Camping/person AR$30

Marisa Rosas 360 ☎02972 491 175. A neat and friendly budget option near the bus terminal, this *residencial* is peaceful, despite its central location. AR$250

Tromen Lonquimay 195 ☎02972 491 498, ⓦhostel tromen.com.ar. A characterless but serviceable budget option with a variety of dorm rooms and doubles scattered around a large house. There is a TV room and kitchen. Dorms AR$50, doubles AR$150

EATING AND DRINKING

Junín's culinary offerings are mostly mediocre pizza joints and rotisseries, strung out along the main road. Stock up on fresh produce at the supermarket on 9 de Julio, at Panil.

Panadería La Ideal Gral Lamadrid, at O'Higgins. Seemingly the whole town gathers here each morning for coffee, newspapers and fantastic sweets and sandwiches. Daily 8am–1pm & 4–9pm.

Ruca Hueney Padre Milenasio, at Coronel Suárez ⓦruca -hueney.com.ar. The best restaurant in town serves trout alongside the traditional *parrilla* choices. Less expected are the Middle Eastern dishes such as *hummus*, *tabbouleh* and *baklava*.

SAN MARTÍN DE LOS ANDES

Pleasant but pricey, **SAN MARTÍN DE LOS ANDES** is a smaller version of neighbouring Bariloche, albeit without the gobsmacking vistas, tacky hotels or packs of party-hard students. Alpine-style chalets, boutique chocolate shops and upscale restaurants line the holiday town's impeccably clean streets. San Martín is set on the shores of **Lago Lácar**,

in a peaceful valley wedged between two forested mountains. The lake offers great summer splashing, while hiking and biking trails lead off to lakeside viewpoints.

WHAT TO SEE AND DO

The **Museo de los Primeros Pobladores** (Mon & Wed–Sat 2–6pm; ☎02972 428 676; free), set in a 1930s wooden house on the main plaza, puts the area in a historical context and displays Mapuche art and pre-Columbian artefacts. If you're here in winter (June–Oct) and wondering where all the people are, your answer may lie 19km south on the slopes of **Cerro Chapelco** (☎02972 427 845, ⓦcerrochapelco.com), where there are 29 ski runs, excellent options for beginners and a snowboard park and night skiing. San Martín is also the northern starting or finishing point for the **Seven Lakes Route** (see box, p.116).

ARRIVAL AND DEPARTURE

By plane Chapelco Airport (☎02972 428 388) is 25km from town, with minibus connections to the centre (AR$50). If flying out of Chapelco, the hourly bus to Junín (run by Castelli) will drop you off at the airport on request (AR$5).

Destinations Buenos Aires (daily; 2hr).

By bus The bus terminal is on General Villegas between Juez del Valle and Coronel Diaz.

Destinations Bariloche (3 daily; 4hr); Junín de los Andes (12 daily; 1hr); Villa La Angostura (4 daily; 2hr 30min).

INFORMATION AND TOURS

Tourist information The helpful tourist office is on San Martín, at J.M. de Rosas (open daily 8am–9pm; ☎02972 427 347, ⓦsanmartindelosandes.gov.ar). For trekking and camping maps as well as general park information, head to the Intendencia del Parque Nacional Lanín, on Perito Moreno, at Eduardo Elordi (daily 8am–9pm; ☎02972 427 233, ⓦparquenacionallanin.gov.ar).

Tour operator Pleasure boats run by Naviera Lacar Nonthue (☎02972 427 380), based at the lake pier, depart for excursions to Paso Hua-Hum near the Chilean border (daily; AR$360) and to the bay of Quila Quina on Lácar's southern shore (10 daily; AR$120).

ACCOMMODATION

San Martín's prices reflect its popularity with the Argentine elite. Advance reservations are recommended during the height of summer and in the ski season, when prices can

ACCOMMODATION
Camping Lolen	5
La Colorada	4
Laura	3
Puma	1
Secuoya	2

EATING
Cervecería El Regional	5
Corazón Contento	2
Downtown Matias	1
La Fondue de Betty	3
El Tenedor	4

double. Backpackers can choose from a handful of good hostels, although prices are somewhat inflated.

Camping Lolen 4km southwest of town. The pick of the town's three campsites is run by the Curruhuinca Mapuche community. The site is beautifully positioned on the lake at Playa Catritre. Camping/person **AR$50**

La Colorada Av Koessler 1614 ☎02972 411 041, �🌐lacoloradahostel.com.ar. This hostel, housed in a bright-red cabin, has a fireplace, big back yard and well-equipped kitchen. Some of the dorm rooms have private bathrooms. Breakfast included. **AR$100**

Laura Misionero Mascardi 632 ☎02972 427 271. There's plenty of charm and comfort to the simple little rooms in this unassuming wooden house. Breakfast included. **AR$300**

Puma Fosberry 535 ☎02972 422 443, �🌐pumahostel .com.ar. A serviceable enough hostel with kitchen and laundry and plenty of party potential. Breakfast included. **AR$90**

Secuoya Rivadavia 411 ☎02972 424 485. The welcoming staff, tranquil vibe, spotless kitchen and wooden floorboards make this superb little hostel feel more like a guesthouse. The doubles are a bit pokey, but the three-bed dorm rooms are a treat. Dorms **AR$120**, doubles **AR$180**

EATING AND DRINKING

Dining out is an expensive pastime in San Martín, but generally worth every peso. Restaurants are open daily noon–4pm and 8pm–midnight unless otherwise noted.

★ **Cervecería El Regional** Villegas 965 ☎02972 411 941. This brewery is the local favourite for its familial atmosphere, home-made pilsner on tap and massive *tablas* (antipasti platters) of pâtés, smoked trout, boar sausage and other local delicacies. The deer ravioli with wild mushroom sauce is to die for. You won't get warmer service anywhere else in town.

Corazón Contento San Martín 467 ☎02972 412 750. Bustling café and takeaway offering a wide variety of filling sandwiches and burgers, though the quiche generously stuffed with veggies is most popular with locals (around AR$30 each). Daily 9am–11.30pm.

Downtown Matias San Martín 598 ⓦ downtownmatias .com. This is where all the nocturnal action is – a cool Irish pub and restaurant that shakes its drunken groove well into the small hours. Daily 8pm to late.

La Fondue de Betty Villegas 586 ☎ 02972 422 522. Warm your hands on a fondue pot at this European-style, intimate restaurant. Cheese, meat and chocolate fondue are served up by the owners themselves alongside French favourites like beef bourguignon.

El Tenedor Villegas 745 ☎ 02972 427 597. The cheapest place to fill up on grilled meat. Go nuts with endless refills of *parrilla* and unlimited sides of french fries, salads and *milanesas* – for a few pesos more you also get access to all the *empanadas*, goulash and other appetizers, plus a main course of trout or deer.

VILLA LA ANGOSTURA

A hit with well-heeled Argentines, **VILLA LA ANGOSTURA** is a lovely little wooden village spread loosely along the northern shores of Lago Nahuel Huapi. It makes a tranquil alternative to Bariloche and is the obvious place to overnight before taking a stroll in the unique woodlands of **Parque Nacional Los Arrayanes**. Most of the village's shops and restaurants are in the commercial area known as **El Cruce**, spread along Avenida Arrayanes, a squeaky-clean main street with twee log-cabin buildings. Heading 3km downhill from here, along Boulevard Nahuel Huapi, you'll find a handful of pretty lakeside teahouses known as **La Villa**, as well as two jetties and the entrance to Parque Nacional Los Arrayanes (see below).

Ten kilometres northeast of town is **Cerro Bayo** (ⓦ cerrobayoweb.com), a lovely small winter ski resort that caters for hikers and mountain bikers in the summer. Villa La Angostura is also the southern start (or end) point for the scenic Seven Lakes Route (see box below), which heads north to San Martín de los Andes.

Parque Nacional de los Arrayanes

A mini-park nestled within the mammoth Parque Nacional Nahuel Huapi (see p.122), the **PARQUE NACIONAL DE LOS ARRAYANES** (daily 8am–2pm if arriving by land, 8am–4.30pm by boat; AR$50) lies on Península Quetrihué, which dips into **Lago Nahuel Huapi** from Villa La Angostura. Its key feature is the **Bosque de los Arrayanes** at the peninsula's tip. The *bosque* (wood) hosts the world's last stand of rare *arrayán* myrtle woodland,

---

SEVEN LAKES ROUTE

The **Ruta de los Siete Lagos** is one of South America's most picturesque drives. It winds for 110km between San Martín de Los Andes and Villa La Angostura along the RN40 traversing the dense alpine forests, snowcapped Andean peaks, brilliant blue lakes, trout-stuffed rivers and plunging waterfalls of two magnificent Patagonian national parks – **Lanín** and **Nahuel Huapi**. In summer the road is lined by purple and yellow wild flowers, and the dramatic snow-covered mountains make the view in winter.

Seven principal photogenic **alpine lakes** are visible or accessible from the roadside. From north to south they are: Machónico, Falkner, Villarino, Escondido, Correntoso, Espejo and Nahuel Huapi. You can spend the night en route at numerous free and serviced lakeside campsites as well as at *refugios* and lodges. Camping Lago Falkner (AR$40/person; ⓦ campingfalkner.com.ar) has lots of facilities, including a restaurant and shop, and is popular with Argentine students and young families, who come to cool off in the lake, camp and party. The first half of the road is paved, while the final stretch, between Lago Villarino and Lago Espejo, is a bumpy dirt track, with vehicles spewing up walls of blinding dust in their wake, though tarmac is gradually being applied. Regular buses run the route, though check you are going on the "7 Lagos" route rather than the "Rinconada" alternative route that some buses take between San Martín and Villa Angostura. La Araucana (ⓦ araucana.com.ar) runs two minibus trips daily (AR$50), picking and dropping off on request along the way. Despite obvious hazards from rip-roaring cars and buses, the route is also extremely popular with cyclists. Check in with the tourism office before setting out in winter as parts of the road can be closed due to snow.

where some of the trees are more than 650 years old. The myrtle's corkscrew-like trunks, terracotta-coloured bark and white flowers are a stunning contrast to blue sky or the shimmering lake.

To **get to Bosque de los Arrayanes**, you can either hike, bike or take a boat. To hike, follow the undulating trail (12km one-way) from the park entrance to the end of the peninsula; allow for a five- to six-hour round trip. Cycling is allowed on the trail; bikes can be rented at half a dozen places in Villa La Angostura. Leave early to get to the *bosque* before the catamarans full of tourists arrive at about 11.30am.

ARRIVAL AND INFORMATION

By bus The bus station is at Av Siete Lagos 35, just uphill from the main avenue (☎02944 494 961).

Destinations Bariloche (hourly; 1hr); San Martín de los Andes (4 daily; 2hr 30min).

Tourist information Pick up a map or organize accommodation at the tourist office (daily 8am–10pm; ☎02944 494 124, ⓦvillalaangostura.gov.ar), at Av Siete Lagos 90, across the road from the bus terminal.

GETTING AROUND

By boat Catamarans depart for Bosque de los Arrayanes from the two jetties that are right across from each other in La Villa – Bahía Mansa and Bahía Brava. Futaleufú (☎02944 494 405) runs three daily boat trips from Mansa (AR$210), and Patagonia Argentina (☎02944 494 463) three daily trips from Brava (AR$190). It's also possible to visit the *bosque* on a boat trip from Bariloche, usually stopping off at Isla Victoria on the way (AR$280; ⓦturisur.com.ar).

ACCOMMODATION

Built solely to accommodate tourists, Villa La Angostura is luxury central, with the most exclusive hotels hugging the lakeshore. But there are some reasonable budget options.

Hostel La Angostura Barbagelata 157 ☎02944 494 834, ⓦhostellaangostura.com.ar. It's a short uphill walk west of Plaza San Martín to this enormous green house fronted by wind chimes. The comfortable dorms (AR$90) are en suite and the front room is a huge chill-out space, with pool table, TV lounge and kitchen. Breakfast and wi-fi are included and there are bikes for rent. AR$290

Camping Unquehué 0.5km west of the bus station on Av Siete Lagos ☎02944 494 103, ⓦcampingunquehue.com.ar. This very lovely site is the closest campsite to downtown. Camping/person AR$52 plus/tent AR$20

★ **Italian Hostel** Los Maquis 215 ☎02944 494 376, ⓦitalianhostel.com.ar. Two blocks south of the main

street, this lovely hostel has spacious dorms as well as doubles and triples set in a large wooden-beamed house with plenty of smaller communal nooks to have a chat. Extras include wi-fi, breakfast, bike rental, back-yard hammocks, herb garden and well-equipped kitchen with a recycling system. Dorms AR$90, doubles AR$125

Verenas Haus Los Taiques 268 ☎02944 494 467, ⓦverenashaus.com.ar. The town's most affordable B&B-style option offers six impeccable if dark private rooms (ask for discounts in low season). Board games, wi-fi and a good breakfast are on offer in the living room. AR$420

EATING

Most restaurants in town are of the upmarket variety, although many of the tea houses serve inexpensive sandwiches. That said, it's not impossible to eat full meals on the cheap. All are open daily, approximately noon–4pm and 8pm–midnight.

La Caballeriza Av Los Arrayanes 44 ☎02944 494 248. A good-value restaurant that locals will direct you towards for the best beef. Hard-to-find vegetable *parrilla* with pumpkin, courgettes, peppers and more is big enough to share.

Gran Nevada Av Los Arrayanes 102. This bare-bones eatery is always full because of the gigantic portions of dirt-cheap food.

La Luna Encantada Belvedere 69 ☎02944 495 436. Skip the usual dinners; the draw here is the wood-fired pizza. The locally smoked trout or salmon makes the perfect topping. Closed Sun night and Mon.

BARILOCHE

Set on the southeastern shores of sparkling Lago Nahuel Huapi and framed by magnificent snowcapped Andean peaks, **BARILOCHE** has its breathtaking setting to thank for its status as one of Argentina's top holiday destinations.

1

Argentines will tell you that it is the country's most European or Swiss-tinged city, but Bariloche itself is a rather ugly hotchpotch of high-rise hotels, garish souvenir stores and faux chalets. That said, the lake and surrounding landscape are stunning – snowy evergreens in winter and covered with purple and yellow wild flowers in summer. The lake is at its best when the sun is reflecting off a placid, cobalt-blue surface, but it can rapidly transform into a tempestuous sea, lashing icy wind through the streets and sending every warm-blooded being indoors to drink hot chocolate or huddle around a pot of cheese fondue.

Aside from lake views, Bariloche's forte is as an **outdoor adventure** hub. The town's proximity to the lakes, mountains, forests and rivers of Parque Nacional Nahuel Huapi makes it one of the top spots in the country for white-water rafting, zip-lines through the forest canopy, kayaking, paragliding, mountain biking, trekking and climbing. Come winter, the fun shifts to the nearby pistes of Cerro Catedral (see p.121). To avoid the crowds, come in **spring** or **autumn**.

WHAT TO SEE AND DO

Bariloche's heart is its **Centro Cívico**, a spacious plaza dominated by an equestrian statue of a defeated-looking General Roca. Forming a horseshoe around the square is a set of attractive, mid-twentieth-century public buildings constructed of local timber and green-grey stone, a collaboration between Ernesto de Estrada and famed Argentine architect Alejandro Bustillo, who also built the **cathedral** a few blocks away. Within these buildings is the **Museo de la Patagonia** (Tues–Fri 10am–12.30pm & 2–7pm, Sat 10am–5pm; free), which does an exemplary job of tracing the area's Mapuche and European history. Bariloche's main drag, **Calle Mitre**, runs east of the plaza.

In the height of summer, you might be tempted to dip a toe beneath the lake's icy surface; the most popular **beach** is rocky Playa Bonita, 8km west of town (buses #10, #20, #21 or #22), or, for a

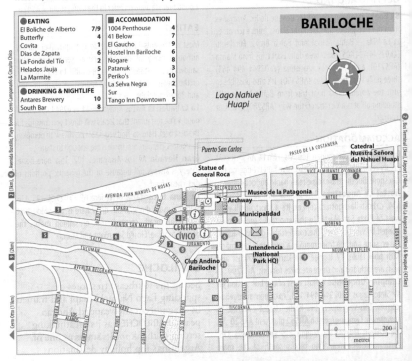

EATING
El Boliche de Alberto	7/9
Butterfly	4
Covita	1
Dias de Zapata	6
La Fonda del Tío	2
Helados Jauja	5
La Marmite	3

DRINKING & NIGHTLIFE
Antares Brewery	10
South Bar	8

ACCOMMODATION
1004 Penthouse	4
41 Below	7
El Gaucho	9
Hostel Inn Bariloche	6
Nogare	8
Patanuk	3
Periko's	10
La Selva Negra	2
Sur	1
Tango Inn Downtown	5

BARILOCHE

Lago Nahuel Huapi

Puerto San Carlos

PASEO DE LA COSTANERA

Catedral Nuestra Señora del Nahuel Huapi

Statue of General Roca

Museo de la Patagonia

Archway

Municipalidad

CENTRO CÍVICO

Intendencia (National Park HQ)

Club Andino Bariloche

warmer and more secluded dip, head 13km southeast to Villa Los Coihues on Lago Gutiérrez (buses #41 or #50). Pick up a map and schedule for the useful network of municipal buses at the tourism office.

ARRIVAL AND DEPARTURE

By plane Bariloche Airport (☎02944 426 162) lies 14km east of the centre. Local bus #72 runs into town every couple of hours; a taxi or *remise* will set you back around AR$90. Agencies including Quetrihue (Inacayal 13 1st floor ☎02944 494 803) operate transfers to Villa La Angostura (AR$180).

Destinations Buenos Aires (6–8 daily; 2hr); El Calafate (daily; 1hr 45min); Esquel (2–3 weekly; 30min); Mar de Plata (weekly; 35min). There are also seasonal flights to Córdoba, Mendoza, Puerto Madryn and Trelew, as well as direct international flights to a number of cities in Brazil and Chile.

By bus The bus terminal (☎02944 432 860) is a couple of kilometres east of the centre. Local buses #10, #20 and #21 run into town along C Moreno; a taxi to the Centro Cívico costs around AR$40. Many intercity buses also drop at the C Moreno stop in the city centre, so check with your driver.

Destinations El Bolsón (11 daily; 1hr 30min); Buenos Aires (6 daily; 21hr); El Calafate (4 weekly; 34hr); Esquel (15 daily; 4hr 30min); Mendoza (2 daily, 18hr); Puerto Madryn (2 daily; 12hr); Puerto Montt in Chile (2 daily; 6hr); San Martín de Los Andes (5 daily; 4hr); Villa La Angostura (hourly; 1hr 30min).

By boat Cruce de Lagos (☎011 5237 1246, ⓦcrucede lagos.com) organizes boat crossings (Sept–April; 12hr; US$280) from Bariloche to Puerto Montt in Chile (see p.445). The scenic journey cruises lakes Huapi, Frieas and Todos Los Santos, with the overland segments traversed by bus. Optional overnight stops at Puerto Blest and Peulla.

INFORMATION AND TOURS

Club Andino Bariloche 20 de Febrero 30 ☎02944 527 966, ⓦclubandino.org. The must-do stop before you set off hiking in Parque Nacional Nahuel Huapi (see p.122). Daily 8am–9pm.

Intendencia del Parque Nacional Nahuel Huapi Av San Martín 24 ☎02944 423 111, ⓦnahuelhuapi.gov.ar. Pick up official national park pamphlets here. Mon–Fri 8am–5pm, Sat & Sun 10am–5pm.

Tourist information The busy tourist office (daily 8am–9pm; ☎02944 429 850, ⓦbarilochepatagonia.info) is in the Centro Cívico.

Tour operators Aguas Blancas, Morales 564 (☎02944 432 799, ⓦaguasblancas.com.ar), runs rafting excursions; Bike Cordillera at Av Bustillo Km18.6 (☎02944 524 828) rents bicycles; Overland Patagonia (☎02944 456 327,

ⓦoverlandpatagonia.com) offers a range of backpacker-friendly excursions, including a four-day Ruta 40 trip to El Calafate in summer; Pura Vida (☎02944 400 327, ⓦpuravidapatagonia.com.ar) offers kayaking trips on the lake; Turisur, at Mitre 219 (☎02944 426 109, ⓦturisur .com.ar), specializes in boat trips.

ACCOMMODATION

Bariloche's accommodation is among the most expensive in Argentina. Bookings are recommended in high season (mid-Dec–Feb & July–Aug), though with so many hotels there is always somewhere with a spare room. Many of the cabins and hotels that lie west of town along Av Bustillo offer great lake views and are a quieter alternative to staying in town. A large number of excellent backpacker hostels have kitchens, internet and tour-booking services.

HOSTELS AND CAMPSITES

1004 Penthouse San Martín 127 ☎02944 432 228, ⓦpenthouse1004.com.ar. Swan around this hostel and take in the panoramic mountain and lake vistas from the tenth floor of an apartment block. Travellers hang out in the mellow living room, or watch the sunset – *vino* in hand – from the balcony. The dorms are not as stylish as the common area. Dorms AR$95, doubles AR$205

★ **41 Below** Juramento 94 ☎02944 436 433, ⓦhostel 41below.com. A chilled, Kiwi-owned hostel with 24 beds, friendly staff and quality music grooving in its common area. Most dorms and doubles have partial lake views, as the hostel has a completely glass front. Dorms AR$90, doubles AR$250

El Gaucho Belgrano 209 ☎02944 522 464, ⓦhostel elgaucho.com. A friendly German/Argentine couple run this spick-and-span operation right downtown. Hanging carpets liven up the rather bare dorms and nicer doubles. Dorms AR$90, doubles AR$160

Hostel Inn Bariloche Salta 308 ☎02944 552 782, ⓦhostelbariloche.com. This HI hostel, smack in the middle of town, offers both breakfast and dinner included in the price. While the atmosphere is a little sterile, one benefit is a number of smaller common areas including a DVD player. Dorms AR$120, doubles AR$380

Patanuk Juan Manuel de Rosas 585 ☎02944 434 991, ⓦpatanuk.com. Right on the lake with its own private pebble beach, this hostel wins hands down in the atmosphere category. The six-bed dorms enjoy gorgeous views and the doubles have private bathrooms, though all rooms have seen better days. Breakfast included and bicycles for rent. Dorms AR$90, doubles AR$350

Periko's Morales 555 ☎02944 522 326, ⓦperikos.com. Recharge at this rustic cabin with a big back yard swinging with hammocks. The four- and six-bed dorms are en suite and there are four bright doubles. Dorms AR$90, doubles AR$280

1

La Selva Negra Av Bustillo 3km west of town ☎02944 441 013. The closest campsite to town is surrounded by forest. Good facilities include a wi-fi area and bar/café. Camping/person __AR$30__

Tango Inn Downtown Salta 514 ☎02944 400 004, ⓦtangoinn.com. A four-storey mega-hostel with stupendous lake views. A good place to come to make friends, as it has a Jacuzzi plus table football and pool tables. Big breakfasts and lounge with wide-screen TV. Dorms __AR$90__, doubles __AR$320__

HOTELS

Nogare Elflein 62 ☎02944 422 438. A welcoming, central budget hotel, with five pleasant blue-and-white rooms with cable TV. Internet is included, as is a hearty breakfast. Discounts in low season. __AR$260__

Sur Beschtedt ☎02944 422 677. This two-star hotel may not be the most beautiful, but it does offer clean hotel rooms with all of the amenities including wi-fi. They can also help arrange excursions. __AR$300__

EATING

Between its decadent chocolate shops and first-rate restaurants, expect to leave Bariloche carrying a little extra weight. Most restaurants are open daily about noon–3pm and 7.30pm–midnight.

El Boliche de Alberto Elflein 347 (☎02944 434 568) and Bustillo 8800 (☎02944 462 285); ⓦelbolichedealberto.com. Make a glutton of yourself at this popular local *parrilla* that serves massive portions; be prepared to wait for a table (they don't take reservations). An outrageously large *bife de chorizo* is AR$60.

Covita Vicealmirante O'Connor 511 ☎02944 421 708. This tiny restaurant does gourmet but affordable takes on dishes like aubergine quiche with borscht, sweet and

---

★ TREAT YOURSELF

Butterfly Hua Huan 7831, Playa Bonita ☎02944 461 441, ⓦbutterflypatagonia .com.ar. "An Irish chef, Argentine hostess and German sommelier walked into a restaurant" may sound like the beginning of a joke but it is the actual story behind this six-table restaurant with a view of the lake. *Butterfly* has caused quite a stir by serving Michelin-worthy meals at a reasonable price. Call ahead to reserve, and let them know of any dislikes and they will craft a meal for you with courses such as Chilean sea-bass carpaccio or pea ravioli with fried bacon and parsley. From AR$350 for seven courses, more with wine pairings. Seatings at 7.45pm and 9.30pm, closed Wednesdays.

---

sour tofu, or Asian curries. Tonnes of vegetarian and vegan options, with a good-value set lunch (AR$50). Mon–Thurs lunch only, Fri & Sat lunch & dinner.

Dias de Zapata Morales 362 ☎02944 423 128. This colourful Mexican-owned restaurant serves mains like quesadillas and tacos, as delicious as they are generous. Arrive before 9pm for cheap cocktails.

La Fonda del Tío Mitre 1330 ☎02944 435 011. Packed to the fluorescent-lit rafters with ravenous locals, this unpretentious, economical diner does outstanding versions of Argentine staples (beef, *milanesas* and pastas).

★ **Helados Jauja** Moreno 18. In a country known for its ice cream, *Jauja* is recognized as the best. Try a scoop of white chocolate, *dulce de leche* with chocolate chips, or blackcurrant. Daily until late.

La Marmite Mitre 329 ☎02944 423 685. This old-fashioned joint hung with antlers is a bit of a wallet-sapper; the traditional afternoon tea or cheese fondue will set you back around AR$150 for two. Closed Sun lunch.

DRINKING AND NIGHTLIFE

Exhaustion after a day on the slopes/rapids/trails leaves many travellers tucked in bed by 10pm, but those with more energy can enjoy any number of bars and after-midnight action in similar lakeside discos such as *Cerebro* (Av Juan Manuel de Rosas 406) and *Roket* (Av Juan Manuel de Rosas 424). Come the winter, most are filled with young Brazilian ski bunnies.

Antares Brewery Elflein 47. Sip the Antares microbrew at a comfortable pub right at the source. Decent pub snacks and a range of artisanal beers (approx AR$25 a pint). Happy hour 7–8.30pm. Daily 7pm to late.

South Bar Juramento 30. Locals and tourists meet at this no-frills Irish bar to share cheap pints and mixed drinks. Stay out late until the tables are pushed aside and the dancing commences. Daily from 8pm.

SHOPPING

Books Cultura Librería, Elflein 74, stocks some English-language books and travel guides.

Chocolate C Mitre has numerous chocolate shops (some the size of supermarkets) selling row upon row of eye-wateringly expensive gourmet chocolate. The local favourite is Mamuschka, at C Mitre 216, though Abuela Goye, at C Mitre 258, is cosier and has shorter queues.

Markets The bustling Fería Municipal (known colloquially as Mercado de Artesanias) is held daily behind the Centro Cívico on Urquiza between Mitre and Moreno, and sells locally made crafts.

DIRECTORY

Car rental Avis, at San Martín 162 (☎02944 431 648, ⓦandesrentacar.com.ar); Budget, at Mitre 717 (☎02944 422 482, ⓦbudgetbariloche.com.ar).

Hospital Moreno 601 (☎ 02944 426 100).
Police Centro Cívico (☎ 02944 422 772).
Post office Moreno 175 and numerous smaller branches.

DAY-TRIPS FROM BARILOCHE

Most day-trips from Argentina's outdoor adventure capital involve conquering – or at least ogling – the nearby mountains, rivers and lakes. Outside the winter months, when **skiing at Cerro Catedral** reigns supreme, the most popular excursions are cycling or driving the scenic **Circuito Chico** route (see below), **white-water rafting** on the class III–IV Río Manson some 80km southwest of Bariloche, and hiking in **Parque Nacional Nahuel Huapi** (see p.122). Local tour operators also offer kayaking, kitesurfing, windsurfing, scuba diving, horseriding, canyoning, rock climbing, mountain biking, parapenting, scenic flights, bus tours on the Seven Lakes Route (see box, p.116) and boating trips.

Shopaholics and beer-lovers will find their spiritual home 123km south of Bariloche in the hippy-ish town of **El Bolsón**, where the outstanding **fería artesanal** (every Tues, Thurs, Sat & Sun 10am–3pm), sells locally crafted wares and food. Afterwards, sample a pint of the local brew at *Cervecería El Bolsón*, at RN258 Km124 (ⓦcervezaselbolson.com), or stay on in the valley for exemplary hiking in the surrounding mountains.

Circuito Chico

The **CIRCUITO CHICO**, a 65km road circuit heading west of Bariloche along the shores of Lago Nahuel Huapi, is a popular day excursion, with a variety of possible stop-offs. It can be explored by bike, rental car, minibus tour (4hr) or by catching a public bus and jumping on and off wherever you fancy. The first point of interest – and a decent half-day excursion on its own – is **Cerro Campanario** at Avenida Bustillo Km18. Take the chairlift (daily 9am–6.30pm; AR\$60) or trail (a 30min steep walk) to the lookout for camera-battery-depleting 360-degree **views**; tours don't usually stop here, so you'll need to come under your own steam. The next point of interest is the luxurious,

mountain-framed **Llao Llao Hotel and Spa** at Km25 (☎02944 448 530, ⓦllaollao .com), an alpine-style creation by architect Alejandro Bustillo. Non-guests can feast on pastries at the hotel's decadent afternoon tea (daily 4–7pm).

Just after the turn-off for the *Llao Llao* is **Puerto Pañuelo**, where boats leave for leisure trips to Puerto Blest, Isla Victoria and the Parque Nacional Los Arrayanes (see p.116). Beyond here the traffic dissipates and the circuit follows an undulating road flanked by thick forest. The scenery is superb, with worthwhile stops at **Villa Tacul**, **Lago Escondido**, **Bahía López** and **Punto Panorámico**, the last of these offering the most recognized postcard shot of the region. For a detour, the pretty Swiss village of **Colonia Suiza** offers an enjoyable opportunity for a lunch or afternoon tea break.

Cycling the circuit allows the flexibility to leave the main road and ride along forested trails to hidden beaches and lakes. As traffic is heavy along the first 20km stretch west of Bariloche, it's best to take a bus (#10, #11, #20 or #22) from downtown to Avenida Bustillo Km18.6, where Bike Cordillera (☎02944 524 828) rents **bicycles**. To see the circuit by **public bus**, take #20 along the lakeshore for *Llao Llao* and Puerto Pañuelo or #10 inland for Colonia Suiza. In summer, #11 does the entire circuit.

Cerro Catedral

Named for a summit (2405m) that resembles the spires of a Gothic cathedral, **CERRO CATEDRAL** (☎02944 409 000, ⓦcatedralaltapatagonia.com) is one of South America's top ski resorts from June to October, offering bedazzling lake and cordillera views, more than fifty runs, forty lifts and descents up to 9km long. **Villa Catedral**, a village just 20km south of Bariloche, lies at the base of the mountain and has hotels, restaurants and ski-hire shops. When the snow melts, Cerro Catedral stays open for trekking; a cable car (AR\$75) and chairlift (free) provide access to **Refugio Lynch** (1870m) and spectacular mountain vistas. A tough but worthwhile trail leads along the ridge and past glacial lakes to **Refugio Frey** (4hr);

1

you can overnight there or push on to descend through spellbinding forest back to Villa Catedral (4hr). Mountain biking, abseiling and horseriding are other popular summertime activities on the mountain. Buses marked "Catedral" leave from Moreno 470 in Bariloche.

PARQUE NACIONAL NAHUEL HUAPI

Spanning a whopping 7050 square kilometres, the magnificent **PARQUE NACIONAL NAHUEL HUAPI** (ⓦnahuelhuapi.gov.ar) is deservedly one of Argentina's most visited national parks. It incorporates both Bariloche and **Lago Nahuel Huapi**, a sapphire-blue glacial lake flanked by forest-quilted slopes. In the park's wild heart lie forests of cypress and beech trees, crystal-clear rivers, cascading waterfalls, lupin-filled meadows, ancient craggy glaciers and formidable snow-capped summits. Nahuel Huapi's crown is **Cerro Tronador**, an extinct volcano whose three icy peaks (around 3500m)

straddle the borders of Argentina and Chile. Wildlife includes Patagonian hares, guanacos and condors, although in the height of summer, humans rule the roost.

WHAT TO SEE AND DO

Nahuel Huapi has three distinct **zones** – northern, central and southern – and helpful *guardaparques* are stationed at key points to advise on trekking, fishing and camping.

The northern zone

The park's **northern zone**, which lies just south of the town of San Martín de los Andes (see p.114), adjoins Parque Nacional Lanín (see p.112). This zone is defined by sky-blue **Lago Traful**, accessible from a turn-off on the Seven Lakes Route (see p.116). Also here is the **Paso Cardenal Samoré**, a popular overland pass into Chile.

The central and southern zones

The **central zone**, which incorporates the pretty Bosque de los Arrayanes (see p.116)

TREKKING IN NAHUEL HUAPI

Parque Nacional Nahuel Huapi has an outstanding network of well-marked trails as well as numerous campsites and *refugios* (basic staffed mountain huts, AR$90–100) to overnight in. Trails link many of these *refugios*, allowing hikers to embark on multi-day treks or return to Bariloche every couple of days for a hit of civilization.

The **hiking season** runs from December to March, although snow at high altitudes sometimes cuts off trails. January and February are the warmest and busiest hiking months, although this is also prime time for *tábanos* – intensely annoying biting horseflies that infest the lower altitudes. Spring in the park can be quite windy, while in autumn the leaves of the *ñire* and *lenga* trees turn a brilliant shade of red. Before heading for the hills, trekkers should visit **Club Andino Bariloche** (see p.119), where knowledgeable staff give out trekking maps and can answer questions about the status of trails, campsites and *refugios* as well as transport to trailheads. They also register solo hikers for safety reasons. Club Andino offers regular guided trekking tours to **Pampa Linda** (AR$250), 90km southwest of Bariloche, from where you can hike to Refugio Otto Meiling, which cowers dramatically beneath Cerro Tronador, nestled between the Castaño Overa and Alerce glaciers.

ACCOMMODATION

All of the park's *refugios* are spectacularly sited in the park's southern zone and have bathrooms with cold water and dorms (bring a sleeping bag, all supplies and a torch). There are authorized campsites at all major park locations, including *Lago Roca* near Cascada Los Alerces, *Los Rápidos* (ⓣ02944 461 861) at Lago Mascardi, and *Los Vuriloches* at Pampa Linda. *Hosterías* within the park are expensive; pleasant *Hostería Pampa Linda*, at the base of Cerro Tronador

(ⓣ02944 490 517, ⓦhosteriapampalinda.com.ar), costs AR$840 half-board.

EATING AND DRINKING

River water is safe to drink untreated, as is the water from *refugio* taps. Fully equipped kitchens in the *refugios* can be used for a small fee, and hot meals, snacks and an impressive selection of alcohol can be purchased (although prices reflect the fact that everything has been lugged up the mountain by porters).

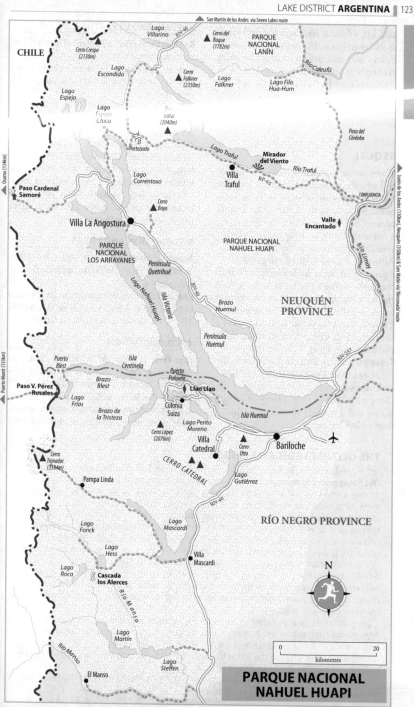

CHILE

San Martín de los Andes via Seven Lakes route

Lago Villarino

RN-40

Cerro del Buque (1782m)

PARQUE NACIONAL LANÍN

Río Caleufú

Cerro Crespo (2130m)

Lago Escondido

Cerro Falkner (2350m)

Lago Falkner

Lago Filo Hua-Hum

Lago Espejo

Lago Espejo Chico

Paso Iratul (2040m)

Paso del Córdoba

El Portezuelo

Lago Traful

Mirador del Viento

Río Traful

Osorno (134km)

Villa Traful

RP-65

CONFLUENCIA

Paso Cardenal Samoré

Lago Correntoso

Cerro Baya

Valle Encantado

Junín de los Andes (130km), Neuquén (350km) & San Martín via 'Rinconada' route

Villa La Angostura

PARQUE NACIONAL LOS ARRAYANES

Península Quetrihué

PARQUE NACIONAL NAHUEL HUAPI

NEUQUÉN PROVINCE

Río Limay

Lago Nahuel Huapi

Isla Victoria

Brazo Huemul

RN-40

RN-237

Península Huemul

Puerto Montt (133km)

Puerto Blest

Isla Centinela

Puerto Pañuelo

Paso V. Pérez Rosales

Brazo Blest

Llao Llao

Isla Huemul

Lago Frías

Brazo de la Tristeza

Colonia Suiza

Cerro López (2076m)

Lago Perito Moreno

Cerro Otto

Bariloche

Cerro Tronador (3554m)

Villa Catedral

CERRO CATEDRAL

Pampa Linda

Lago Gutiérrez

RN-40

RÍO NEGRO PROVINCE

Lago Fonck

Lago Mascardi

Lago Hess

Villa Mascardi

N

Lago Roca

Cascada los Alerces

Río Manso

Río Manso

Lago Martín

0   20
kilometres

Río Manso

Lago Steffen

El Manso

PARQUE NACIONAL NAHUEL HUAPI

El Bolsón (55km) & Esquel (222km)

1

and Isla Victoria, has **Lago Nahuel Huapi** as its centrepiece. In summer, this zone buzzes with tourists on boating, kayaking, cycling and hiking excursions. The southern zone has the best trails and facilities for hikers, and is focused around **Lago Mascardi**, ideal for swimming and diving in summer.

ESQUEL

Cowboys and urban sophisticates should feel equally at home in **ESQUEL**, the main town in the north of Chubut Province. Some 340km south of Bariloche, Esquel means "bog" in the Mapuche language, a name that says nothing of the town's arresting mountainous backdrop. Although Esquel is often relegated to a pit stop en route to Bariloche or Chile, the town makes a perfect base to explore the lush **Parque Nacional Los Alerces** and for riding the historic **Old Patagonian Express** steam train (see box below) on a touristic loop. Other local draws include the tea-house-filled Welsh settlement of **Trevelin**, 23km south, and in winter, the ski resort of **La Hoya** (⊕02945 453 018, ⓦskilahoya.com), 12km northeast, where there are 22km of runs, plenty of off-piste skiing and a season that often extends into early October.

ARRIVAL AND DEPARTURE

By plane Esquel Airport is 21km east of town; a taxi will set you back around AR$80.
Destinations Bariloche (2–3 weekly; 30min); Buenos Aires (daily, less in winter; 3hr); and occasional services to Puerto Madryn.
By bus The bus terminal (⊕02945 451 584) lies eight blocks from the town centre on the corner of A.P. Justo and Av Alvear, the main street.
Destinations Bariloche (15 daily; 4hr 30min); El Bolsón (15 daily; 2hr 30min); El Calafate (daily; 29hr); El Chaltén (daily; 26hr); Comodoro Rivadavia (5 daily; 9hr); Futaleufú in Chile (Jan & Feb 2 daily 3 times a week; rest of year 2 daily twice a week; 2hr); Mendoza (daily; 24hr).
By train The train station from which the *La Trochita* steam train departs is on Roggero, at Brun.

INFORMATION AND TOURS

Tourist information The tourist office is on Av Alvear, at Sarmiento (daily 7am–11pm; ⊕02945 451 927, ⓦesquel.gov.ar).
Tour operator Tours of Parque Nacional Los Alerces can be booked through Gales al Sur (Av Alvear 1871 ⊕02945 453 379) and leave every day according to demand.

ACCOMMODATION

Lago Verde Volta 1081 ⊕02945 452 251, ⓦpatagonia -verde.com.ar. Small but impeccable rooms set behind a quiet family home with a cute rose-filled garden. <u>AR$200</u>
Planeta Hostel Av Alvear 2833 ⊕02945 456 846, ⓦplanetahostel.com. A hostel with delightful owners, wacky artistic touches, an indoor climbing wall and a

---

THE OLD PATAGONIAN EXPRESS

Puffing and chugging its way across the arid Andean foothills at around 25km/hr, the **Old Patagonian Express** is both a museum on wheels and a classic South American train journey. Known as "*La Trochita*" ("little narrow gauge" in Spanish), the locomotive's tracks are a mere 75cm wide. Built in 1922 to connect sheep farmers in isolated, windswept communities with faraway markets for their goods, the train was put out of commission in 1993 when the railways were privatized. Immortalized in Paul Theroux's 1979 train-travel narrative, the express is today mostly involved in short, round-trip tourist jaunts. Passengers pile into antique wooden coaches, complete with wood-burning furnaces and dining cars, to puff from Esquel to a Mapuche community plus museum called **Nahuel Pan** and back (44km return; 3hr; AR$180). Peering out of the window, you might spot guanacos, rheas and hares – and you will certainly see cows. If you are really lucky, you may even see "bandits" that hold up the train on occasion – rest assured that it is an organized part of the experience and no one will be relieving you of your jewellery.

The train leaves throughout the year on Saturdays at 10am and then puts on extra trips depending on the season and demand – up to ten departures a week in high season. Ask the tourist office for the latest schedule or call ⊕02945 451 403. Renovations or strikes sometimes close the line completely, so check that it is running before you come to Esquel if the train ride is the main objective of your journey.

Occasionally, the train makes the 165km journey all the way from Esquel to El Maitén, where there is a museum and railway repair shops.

bright little kitchen. The dorm beds are just what the chiropractor ordered and there's one tiny double room. Internet, wi-fi and breakfast included. Book ahead as there are only four rooms in total. Dorms AR$90, doubles AR$220

Hostel Sol Azul Rivadavia 2869 ☎02945 455 193, ⓦhostelsolazul.com.ar. The cosiest hostel in town boasts a wood-burning stove, heated floors and an all-stone bar. The dorms are small with bunk beds for four and lockers. Dorms AR$80

EATING AND DRINKING

La Barra Sarmiento 638 ☎02945 454 321, ⓦparrilla labarra.com.ar. This *parrilla* serves big juicy slabs of tenderloin accompanied with home-made mayonnaise on lacy tablecloths. Daily lunch & dinner.

Empanadería Molinari Molinari 633 ☎02945 454 687. The delightful owner serves super cheap take-away *empanadas* with beef, vegetable, corn or chicken fillings.

Fitzroya Pizza Rivadavia 1048 ☎02945 450 512. Cheesy, inexpensive pizzas loaded with creative toppings such as broccoli, salmon and trout are delivered piping hot. Daily noon–3pm & 7.30pm–midnight.

Moe Bar Rivadavia 873. Cocktails and classic rock are the orders of the night at this dark and rowdy drinking hole with half a yellow car protruding from its entrance. Tend to your hunger pangs with one of their tasty pizzas or *picadas*. Daily until late.

PARQUE NACIONAL LOS ALERCES

PARQUE NACIONAL LOS ALERCES, 40km west of Esquel, encompasses 2630 square kilometres of gorgeous, glacier-carved Andean landscape (entrance fee AR$50). Although far less visited than Parque Nacional Nahuel Huapi to the north, its network of richly coloured lakes and pristine rivers makes it a prime destination for anglers, while countless hiking trails through verdant forests attract summer walkers and campers. It's easily navigable on a day-trip from Esquel via the very popular lake tour (see below).

The *alerce* (or Patagonian cypress) that grows here is one of the oldest living species on the planet, with some examples surviving as long as 3000 years. In size, they're almost comparable to the grand sequoias of California, growing to 70m tall and 4m wide. Though the *alerce* gives the park its

name, the flora is wildly varied: **Valdivian temperate rainforest** thrives in its luxuriant western zone near the Chilean border, which is deluged by around 3000mm of annual rainfall. Elsewhere, incense cedar, bamboo-like *caña colihue*, *arrayán*, *coihue*, *lenga* and southern beech thrive.

WHAT TO SEE AND DO

Most visitors gravitate towards the park's user-friendly and photogenic **northeast sector** where there is a network of four dazzling lakes – **Rivadavia**, **Verde**, **Menéndez** and **Futalaufquen**. The emerald-hued Lago Verde is often the first port of call for day-trekkers and campers. Spilling over from Lago Verde is the **Río Arrayanes**, crossed by a suspension bridge that marks the start of an easy hour-long interpretive loop walk.

Some hikes, including the trek to the summit of **Cerro Alto El Dedal** (1916m), require registration with the park ranger's office (see below) first. The most popular day excursion is the **boat trip** run by Brazo Sur (Rivadavia 891, Esquel ☎02945 456359, ⓦbrazosur.com.ar), which leaves from either Puerto Limonao (3km north of the ranger's office, 9.30am departure, AR$270) or Puerto Chucao (halfway around the Lago Verde/Río Arrayanes loop trail, 11.30am departure, AR$230). The boats cross Lago Menéndez to visit **El Abuelo** (The Grandfather), a 57m-high *alerce* estimated to be more than 2600 years old.

ARRIVAL AND INFORMATION

By car One main dusty, bumpy road (the RP71) runs through Los Alerces and is usually accessible year-round, although it is occasionally blocked by snow in winter. There is no public transport outside of peak season, so a vehicle is recommended; otherwise, hikers need to walk along the road between trails, enduring clouds of body-coating dust from passing cars and trucks.

By bus Peak season is Jan–Feb, when Transportes Esquel (☎02945 453 529, ⓦtransportesesquel.com.ar) runs a daily bus service to the park; it takes three bumpy hours to reach Lago Verde.

Tourist information The ranger's office (daily 8am–9pm; ☎02945 471 020) is at Villa Futalaufquen, a village on Lago Futalaufquen, 12km past the park entrance point,

1

CROSSING INTO CHILE

Esquel is well placed for crossing into Chilean Patagonia, with several buses weekly making the two-hour trip to the settlement of **Futaleufú**, where there is excellent white-water rafting on its namesake river. Feryval and Lago Espolón buses leave Esquel (travelling south via Trevelin) around four times a week. At the Chilean border (immigration open 8am–8pm), passengers transfer to a minibus for the final 10km to Futaleufú.

with a smattering of shops, public telephones and eating and accommodation options (which close in winter). It can provide information on camping, park accommodation, hiking and fishing, and sells fishing permits.

ACCOMMODATION

A number of cabañas, *hosterías* and campsites lie within the park, including pricey lodges that cater for anglers. There are a dozen free campsites with no facilities at all, some very cheap basic ones with cold-water bathrooms and a handful of slightly more expensive organized campsites with hot water, gas and electricity; enquire at the tourist office in Esquel or at the park ranger's office.

Patagonia

Lonely, windswept and studded with glaciers, **PATAGONIA** has an undeniable mystique, a place where pioneers, outlaws, writers and naturalists have long come in search of open space and wild adventure. When watching a southern right whale swim metres under your boat or strapping on crampons to hike across the Southern Patagonian Ice Cap, you won't care that Argentina's southernmost chunk is now an established tourist destination.

For those short on time, flights allow you to hop between Patagonia's key attractions, but to truly appreciate the region's vastness, it is best to travel overland. After hundreds of kilometres of desolate steppe, nothing quite bedazzles like the sight of serrated Andean peaks rising up on the horizon like a Gothic mirage.

Two main arteries traverse Patagonia. The RN40 runs parallel to the Andes and links some of Patagonia's major sights: the 10,000-year-old rock art of the **Cueva de las Manos Pintadas**; the Fitz Roy sector of **Parque Nacional Los Glaciares** around the town of El Chaltén; and the **Perito Moreno** and **Upsala** glaciers in the park's southern sector, both easy day-trips from El Calafate. To the east, the RN3 loosely traces the Atlantic seaboard, passing the town of **Puerto Madryn**, a launching pad for the marine wildlife-rich shores of **Península Valdés**, before heading south to the Welsh heartland of **Trelew** and **Gaiman**, a short jump to the continent's largest penguin colony, **Punta Tombo**.

December to February are the warmest months to visit Patagonia, but to avoid the crowds, inflated prices and high winds, March and April are better. Tourism all but grinds to a halt come winter, despite the fact that there is less difference between winter and summer temperatures than you might think.

PUERTO MADRYN

Having spent hours travelling through the barren bleakness of the Pampas, you may wonder why you bothered when you first hit **PUERTO MADRYN**. A windy, sprawling, seaside city clinging to the barren coast of northern Patagonia, it has relatively few tourist attractions of its own. But its proximity to one of the world's most significant marine reserves – the **Reserva Faunística Península Valdés**

ESTANCIAS IN PATAGONIA

Patagonia's empty steppe is speckled with isolated *estancias*, many of which open their doors to visitors. While most cater for high-end tourists, others are more modest, and some allow camping in their grounds – a good example is *Estancia Menelik* (see p.133). Contact Estancias de Santa Cruz in El Calafate (Libertador 1215; ☎ 02902 492858, ⓦ estanciasdesantacruz.com) for a comprehensive list of *estancias* in Patagonia.

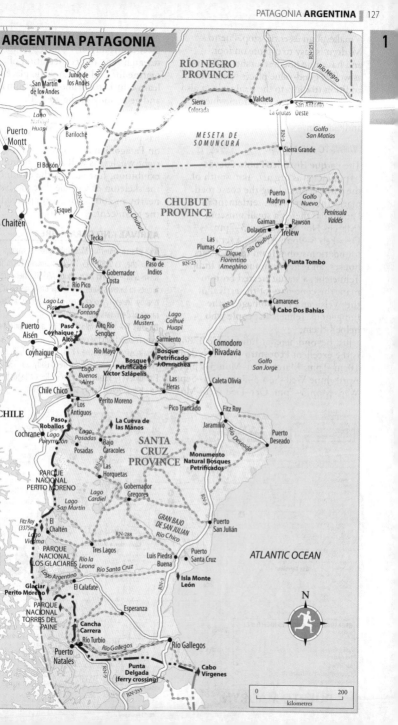

ARGENTINA PATAGONIA

– makes it an essential stop. Puerto Madryn is easy to explore on foot, and has some fine restaurants and bars, as well as good-value places to stay. In addition to tours to the peninsula, it also makes a convenient base from which to explore the nearby Welsh towns of Trelew and Gaiman.

WHAT TO SEE AND DO

The **Parque Histórico Punta Cuevas** (ⓦpuntacuevas.org.ar), 4km south of the town centre along the coast road, marks the first Welsh settlement in Patagonia: there's a small museum (March–Nov Wed–Mon 3–7pm, Dec–Feb 5–9pm; AR$8), a set of foundation stones from the pioneers' houses, and the Monumento al Indio Tehuelche, a statue erected both to mark the centenary of the arrival of the Welsh and pay homage to the indigenous Tehuelche people who helped them.

Just beyond here, at Julio Verne 3784, is the excellent **Ecocentro** (Jan–Feb daily 10am–1pm, March Wed–Mon 3–7pm, April–June Wed–Sun 3–7pm, July–Sept Wed–Mon 3–7pm, Oct–Dec Wed–Mon 3–8pm; AR$55; ⓣ0280 445 7470, ⓦecocentro.org.ar), which promotes research into and conservation of marine life and is a fantastic place to learn a little more about the animals and geography of the area. The three-level building, with stunning views from the reading room at the top, has permanent interactive exhibitions on Patagonian ecosystems and southern right whales, as well as a changing art exhibition. Just outside the entrance is the skeleton of a whale that was beached nearby in 2001. Bus #2 runs here from the town centre.

ARRIVAL AND DEPARTURE

By plane Puerto Madryn's airport (Aeropuerto El Tehuelche; ⓣ0280 445 1909) is around 10km from the town centre; a taxi costs about AR$50. There are regular flights to Buenos Aires and a few other destinations, but nearby Trelew Airport (see p.131) serves a far greater range of destinations.

By bus The bus terminal is at Avila and Independencia, a short walk from the centre.

Destinations Bariloche (1–3 daily; 14hr); Buenos Aires (10–11 daily; 18hr); El Calafate (1 daily; 20–23hr); Puerto Pirámides (1–3 daily; 1hr 15min); Río Gallegos (4–5 daily; 16–19hr); Trelew (every 30min–1hr; 1hr).

PUERTO MADRYN

EATING, DRINKING AND NIGHTLIFE
Ambigú 2
Los Colonos 3
La Frontera 5
Margarita 2
Mr Jones 4
Quemehuencho Churrería 6
Vesta Patagonia 1

ACCOMMODATION
ACA Complejo Turístico Punta Cuevas 1
Casa Patagónica 2
Chepatagonia Hostel 3
El Gualicho 7
El Muelle Viejo 4
Posada del Catalejo 5
El Retorno 6
La Tosca 8

INFORMATION

Tourist information The helpful main tourist office is on Av Roca 223 (☎0280 445 3504, ⊕madryn.gov.ar /turismo; April to mid-Dec Mon–Fri 7am–9pm, Sat & Sun 8am–9pm; mid-Dec to March Mon–Fri 7am–11pm, Sat & Sun 8am–11pm).

ACCOMMODATION

Most accommodation is close to the centre of town and within walking distance of the bus terminal (many hostels will pick you up for free if you call ahead). Prices drop greatly outside the January to March high season. Rates include breakfast unless stated otherwise.

HOSTELS AND CAMPSITES

ACA Complejo Turístico Punta Cuevas Punta Cuevas ☎0280 445 2952, ⊕acamadryn.com.ar. This well-run complex has camping spots (tents provided), simple rooms and self-contained apartments suitable for groups. Breakfast costs extra. Camping/person AR$52, doubles AR$300, apartments AR$670

Chepatagonia Hostel A. Storni 16 ☎0280 445 5783, ⊕chepatagoniahostel.com.ar. Right on the waterfront, this hostel's dorms are not the most stylish but the mattresses are wonderful; private rooms with shared bathrooms are also available. Guests have kitchen access, and tours and bike rental can be arranged. Dorms AR$65, doubles AR$190

⭐ **El Gualicho** Marcos A Zar 480 ☎0280 445 4163, ⊕elgualicho.com.ar. The best hostel in town, *El Gualicho* has four-, six- and eight-bed dorms, comfortable private rooms, a sociable lounge, a communal kitchen and barbecue area, and a pleasant garden. The friendly staff can arrange tours, diving trips and bike rental. Dorms AR$95, doubles AR$420

Posada del Catalejo Mitre 446 ☎0280 447 5224, ⊕posadadelcatalejo.com.ar. A cheerful B&B-type hostel close to the beach and the town centre. The large, brightly painted dorms and private rooms have crisp white sheets and a lovely home-from-home feel. The fireplace in the lounge is perfect for chilly nights. Dorms AR$80, doubles AR$210

El Retorno Bartolomé Mitre 798 ☎0280 445 6044, ⊕elretornohostel.com.ar. A welcoming hostel with small four- to eight-bed dorms and en-suite rooms with TVs, as well as a communal lounge and kitchen, plus laundry facilities. Dorms AR$70, doubles AR$250

La Tosca Sarmiento 437 ☎0280 445 6133, ⊕latosca hostel.com. This hostel may not be the prettiest, but it's friendly, close to the beach and has a nice garden out back. There is a range of economical accommodation options. Dorms AR$80, doubles AR$210

HOTELS AND B&BS

Casa Patagónica Av Roca 2210 ☎0280 445 1540, ⊕casa -patagonica.com.ar. This charming B&B has a handful of

simple, economical rooms with shared bathrooms, plus one en suite. Guests have access to a microwave and fridge (though not a full kitchen), and there's a living room to relax in. AR$250

El Muelle Viejo Av Hipólito Yrigoyen 38 ☎0280 447 1284. Although the decor is pretty dated and the walls a little thin, this budget hotel is a decent choice. The compact rooms are clean and come with attached bathrooms and TVs. AR$350

EATING AND DRINKING

Ambigú Roca & Roque Sáenz Peña ☎0280 447 2541, ⊕ambiguresto.com.ar. The menu at this bustling café-restaurant features everything from steaks and pastas to curries and stir-fries, with most mains starting at around AR$40. *Ambigú* is also popular for its pizzas – the large ones are more than enough for two people. Daily noon–2pm & 8pm–midnight.

Los Colonos Roca & A. Storni ☎0280 445 8486. Located in the hull of a large wooden ship on the main street, this place is just plain fun. The house speciality is seafood; grilled, baked or fried fish goes for around AR$40–50, while the *arroz con mariscos* (a soupy paella) is big enough for two. Daily noon–3pm & 7.30pm–midnight.

Mr Jones 9 de Julio 116 ☎0280 447 5368. A buzzing pub-restaurant, popular with locals and young gringos alike. Most of the diners – who fill up the wooden benches and spill out onto the streetside tables – are here for a beer (from around AR$15) and a *picada* (cold meat and cheese platters). Mon–Sat 6pm–1/2am.

⭐ **Quemehuencho Churrería** Roque Sáenz Peña 212 ☎0280 15 440 4016. *Churros* stuffed with every imaginable filling from the usual *dulce de leche* to home-made jams. This is also a great place for the *mate* novice, as the waiters will explain the different varieties and help you brew the drink. Mon–Fri 8am–noon & 4.30–8pm, Sat & Sun 4.30–8pm.

Vesta Patagonia Punta Cuevas ☎0280 447 0766, ⊕vestarestaurant.com.ar. The best time to come here is at sunset, as the restaurant is located at Punta Cuevas, close to the spot where the Welsh first landed in Patagonia. Grab a drink (from AR$10–15) and a seat on the terrace and enjoy the view. Daily noon–midnight/1am.

NIGHTLIFE

La Frontera 9 de Julio 254 ☎0280 447 2232. Puerto Madryn's most popular club, *La Frontera's* focus is on dance and electro music. It's only open on the weekends, and unless you want the place to yourself, don't even think about getting here before 2am. Fri & Sat midnight–5am.

Margarita Roque Sáenz Peña 15 ☎0280 447 0885. Visit this pub to enjoy some good (and often live) music and rub shoulders with the locals over a few drinks (from AR$15). Also serves fairly pricey but tasty snacks and meals. Happy hour 7.30–9pm. Mon–Sat 7.30pm–2/3am.

DIRECTORY

Banks and exchange Banco Galicia, at Mitre 25 (☎0280 445 2323), changes money and has an ATM, one of dozens in the city.

Internet TeleNetK, Belgrano, at 25 de Mayo.

Laundry Servicios de Lavandería Morenas, Sarmiento, at Marcos Zar (☎0280 445 6969).

DAY-TRIPS FROM PUERTO MADRYN

A visit to the stunning **Península Valdés** marine reserve is a must, and a trip to the penguin colony at **Punta Tombo**, a little further afield, is also worthwhile. Puerto Madryn was originally founded and settled in 1865 by 153 Welsh families who bravely battled the frigid weather and arid land. Despite all odds, the town survived and more settlers arrived, enabling the fledgling community to expand to the southeast, founding **Trelew** (pronounced trey-le-oo) and **Gaiman**. Both are easily reached by bus from Puerto Madryn, and can be combined on a single day-trip.

Península Valdés

PENÍNSULA VALDÉS is brimming with life. More than a million Magellanic penguins make their summer home here, along with a permanent population of 75 colonies of seals and sea lions, and over 2000 dolphins. Topping even that is a breeding colony of southern right whales that can be observed directly from the beach of **Puerto Pirámides**, the peninsula's only town, in winter. You can also board a boat and see the frolicking mammals up close – a truly unforgettable experience. From October to April you can spot groups of orca (killer whales) on the hunt for baby sea lions.

With vast distances between viewing areas and little in the way of public transport, the easiest way to appreciate the place is on a day-trip from Puerto Madryn. You could also rent a car to visit independently, which can be good value if you are travelling in a group, but note that most of the roads are dirt tracks and can be a challenge if it has been raining.

ARRIVAL AND DEPARTURE

By bus There are daily buses from Puerto Madryn to Puerto Pirámides (Mon–Fri departing 6.30am, 9.45am & 4pm, returning 8.10am, 1pm & 6pm; Sat & Sun departing 9.45am, returning 6pm; 1hr 15min; the timetable fluctuates quite a lot, especially in the low season, so double check the latest information before setting off).

ACCOMMODATION

It's much cheaper to stay in Puerto Madryn than within the nature reserve at Puerto Pirámides, but if you prefer the latter, there are a couple of options.

Bahía Ballenas Av de las Ballenas s/n ☎0280 447 4110, ⓦbahiaballenas.com.ar. This hostel is the best bet for backpackers. The two single-sex dorms are clean and

TOURS OF PENÍNSULA VALDÉS

Most people visit on an organized tour (10–12hr round-trip, bring warm clothes), most of which follow the same itinerary, with minor variations according to the season and weather. The first stop, a short drive out of town, is to pay the park entrance fee (ARS$100) and visit the information centre, followed by an impressive look out over the Isla de los Pájaros (Bird Island). Next, across the isthmus on the peninsula proper, you'll stop off in Puerto Pirámides, where sea-lion- and whale-watching boat trips are offered. From here you head north to Punto Norte, at the far tip of the peninsula, to see sea lions, elephant seals and penguins sunbathing on the beach; orcas sometimes make an appearance as well. You'll also see penguins up close at Caleta Valdés, followed by more elephant seals and dolphins at Punta Delgada. Marine life is present year-round but some viewing stations close from Easter to June; optimal viewing is between September and February, but whales can be seen from June to December.

TOUR OPERATORS

Tours cost around ARS$300, excluding an optional whale-watching boat trip (from around ARS$170) and the park entry fee (ARS$100). Recommended operators include:

Tito Bottazzi Brown, at Martín Fierro (☎0280 447 4110).

Argentina Vision Roca 536 (☎0280 445 1427, ⓦargentinavision.com).

For scuba-diving and snorkelling trips in the area contact:

Scuba Duba Brown 893 ☎0280 445 2699.

tidy, though not always the quietest. The owners run the Tito Bottazzi agency (see box opposite) and offer guests discounts on tours. Dorms **ARS45**

La Posta Av de las Ballenas s/n ☎ 0280 449 5036, ⓦ lapostapiramides.com.ar. If you're in a big group, the *La Posta* apartments – sleeping up to six people and featuring kitchenettes and TVs – are a good-value option. Apartments **ARS500**

Trelew

TRELEW doesn't offer a huge amount in the way of sights, but it has good air and bus connections throughout the region, including to the nearby village of Gaiman (see below). The town is proud of its Welsh history – "Trelew" in Welsh means "village of Lewis", in honour of Lewis Jones, the town's founder. It also has, at Fontana & Lewis Jones, the highly acclaimed **Museo Paleontológico Egidio Feruglio** (April–Aug Mon–Fri 10am–6pm, Sat & Sun 10am–7pm; Sept–March daily 9am–8pm; AR$42; ☎ 0280 443 2100, ⓦ mef.org.ar), which houses one of the country's most important paleontological collections; excellent guided tours in English, German and Italian are free on request. The nearby **Museo Regional Pueblo de Lewis** was closed for refurbishment at the time of research, but is due to reopen in the future. It has fascinating displays on the Welsh settlement in the area.

ARRIVAL AND INFORMATION

By plane Trelew Airport, 5km northeast of the town, has flights across Argentina, including to Ushuaia and El Calafate; passengers on all domestic flights must pay a departure tax of AR$32. A taxi to/from the town centre costs about AR$30.

By bus The bus station is next to the Plaza Centenario. Destinations Bariloche (1 daily; 13–16hr); Buenos Aires (11 daily; 19–21hr); Gaiman (every 30min; 25–35min); Puerto Madryn (every 30min–1hr; 1hr); Río Gallegos (4–5 daily; 15–16hr).

Tourist information The main tourist office is on San Martín, at Mitre (☎ 0280 442 6819, ⓦ trelewpatagonia .gov.ar; Mon–Fri 8am–8pm, Sat & Sun 9am–9pm).

ACCOMMODATION AND EATING

Comedor Universitario Luis Yllana Just off 9 de Julio. If you're after an inexpensive breakfast, lunch or early dinner, join the students at this bustling university canteen, which serves simple, hearty dishes (around AR$30-40). Daily 10am–8pm.

★ **Touring Club** Fontana 240 ☎ 0280 443 3997, ⓦ touringpatagonia.com.ar. Antoine de Saint-Exupéry, author of *The Little Prince*, and (reportedly) Butch Cassidy and the Sundance Kid have all stayed at this faded Art Deco hotel. The compact rooms are pretty simple, but the atmosphere – especially in the high-ceilinged café-bar – is a real draw. **ARS250**

Gaiman

Much smaller and prettier than its busy neighbour, **GAIMAN**'s claim to fame is its wonderful **Welsh teas**, so renowned that even the late Princess Diana came to enjoy one in 1995. Served from around 3pm every day in lovely cottages (or their gardens), they consist of freshly brewed tea, home-made cakes (including the famous *torta negra*, a traditional Welsh fruitcake), scones, breads and jams – portions are huge.

ARRIVAL AND INFORMATION

By bus There are regular buses to and from Trelew (every 30min; 25–35min); they arrive and depart from the central square.

Tourist information The tourist office (Mon–Sat 9am–8pm, Sun 11am–7pm; ☎ 0280 449 1571, ⓦ gaiman .gov.ar) is at Belgrano 574, a 5min walk from the main square.

ACCOMMODATION AND EATING

Most tea houses charge around AR$80–90 per person for tea, and are closed on Monday.

Plas y Coed Yrigoyen 320 ☎ 0280 449 1133. The owners have done a good job of re-creating the home-from-home atmosphere that pervaded their original property – Gaiman's first tea house – just around the corner, and there's a spacious living room for guests. **ARS300**

★ **Ty Gwyn** 9 de Julio 147 ☎ 0280 449 009, ⓦ tygwyn .com.ar. Located a block away from the main square and attached to a lovely casa de té, *Ty Gwyn* has clean, compact rooms with wooden floors and partial views of the Río Chubut. **ARS300**

Ty Nain Yrigoyen 283 ☎ 0280 449 1126. This ivy-clad building, dating back to 1890, is one of the most authentic tea houses. The abundant tea is served by a descendant of the first Welsh woman born in Gaiman. There's a tiny museum at the back. Daily except Mon 3–7pm.

Yr Hen Ffordd Michael Jones 342 ☎ 0280 449 1394, ⓦ yrhenffordd.com.ar. Sparsely but charmingly decorated in the best Welsh fashion, this B&B will make you feel you are at high tea all day. Friendly owners preside over this historic brick building. **ARS200**

1

Punta Tombo

Just short of three hours south of Puerto Madryn, the **Reserva Provincial Punta Tombo** (Sept–late March daily 8am–6pm; AR$60), home to the largest penguin nesting site on the continent, makes a perfect spot to get up close to the creatures. Aside from the million or so Magellanic penguins wandering the area – so curious and numerous you may have to step around them on the path – you'll be treated to a vast variety of birds, from rock cormorants to kelp gulls flying overhead. The reserve can be visited independently by car or on a long day's tour (around AR$350) from Puerto Madryn; these tours often include stops at Playa Unión to spot dolphins and in Trelew or Gaiman to sample a Welsh tea.

RUTA 40

Ruta 40 (or RN40) runs from the top to the bottom of Argentina, following the line of the Andes all the way to the far south from the border with Bolivia in the north. It covers 5000km and 11 provinces, crosses 18 important rivers on 236 bridges, and connects 13 great lakes and salt flats, 20 national parks and hundreds of communities. In recent years the section between **El Calafate/El Chaltén**

and **Bariloche** has grown in popularity with backpackers – buses depart several times a week in season along this route – though it still retains a real sense of isolation and adventure. (If you don't want to travel between El Calafate/El Chaltén and Bariloche via RN40, you'll need to catch a bus all the way towards the coast to Puerto Madryn, Trelew or Caleta Olivia, and then head back inland again.) This is classic Patagonian landscape: many kilometres of flat grassland, with hundreds of cattle roaming freely, interrupted only by the occasional village or *estancia*.

There's little to see along the way apart from the stunning deserted grassland landscape itself. However, the ancient **cave paintings** near the unattractive town of Perito Moreno almost justify the journey on their own. With transport of your own, you can also visit the wonderful and isolated **Parque Nacional Perito Moreno**, just off the road along RN37.

PERITO MORENO

With a little over 4000 inhabitants, **PERITO MORENO** is the biggest town in this part of the world. Roughly halfway between El Chaltén and Bariloche, it is a

---

TRAVELLING RUTA 40

The **best time to travel** Ruta 40 from El Calafate/El Chaltén to Bariloche is from November to the end of March. Outside of these months, buses are less frequent and accommodation can be hard to find. The Cueva de las Manos Pintadas can only be visited from December to February.

A handful of companies offer **bus services** between El Calafate and Bariloche, via Perito Moreno, including the well-established **Chalten Travel** (ⓦ chaltentravel.com), which has offices in El Calafate, El Chaltén and Bariloche, and operates between November and the end of March. Note that services (and transport operators) on this route are notoriously prone to change, so it's important to check the latest timetables before planning a trip.

If you have more time and money, plus a sense of adventure, the best way of all to see the region is to rent a **car**. It's a huge territory, much of the road is un-tarmacked and fuel stops are few and far between, but a car gives you the freedom to stop and explore. Two places to break for fuel are Bajo Caracoles, 130km south of Perito Moreno, and Gobernador Gregores, around 440km north. Neither offers anything in the way of attractions, but they are essential for petrol and food.

There is little in the way of budget **accommodation** along the route (especially as the windy, hard plains make camping virtually impossible), but there are a few *estancias* where you can try the local produce, and learn from the farmers about their way of life.

If you want to take an **organized tour** on RN40, try the appropriately named Ruta 40 agency (ⓞ 0294 452 3378, ⓦ ruta-40.com).

typically featureless, spread-out Patagonian settlement whose main point of interest is as a base for excursions to the **Cueva de las Manos Pintadas** (see below). West of town is **Lago Buenos Aires** (the second-biggest lake in South America, after Lake Titicaca) and, towards the Chilean border, the pleasant town of **Los Antiguos**.

ARRIVAL AND DEPARTURE

By bus The bus terminal is a 10min walk north of town. There are buses from here to Río Gallegos (1–2 daily; 14hr), among other destinations.

Destinations Nov–April Chaltén Travel buses (⊛chalten travel.com) stop outside the *Hotel Belgrano*, at the far end of San Martín; the company has services to Bariloche (3–4 weekly; 13hr), El Chaltén (3–4 weekly; 13hr) and Puerto Madryn (3–4 weekly; 14hr). During the same months, Taqsa/Marga (⊛taqsa.com.ar) also runs daily buses to El Chaltén and Bariloche.

INFORMATION AND TOURS

Tourist information The tourist office is on San Martín, at Gendarmería Nacional (daily 8am–10pm; ☎02963 432732).

Tour operators Guanacóndor, Perito Moreno 1087 (☎02963 432303, ✉jarinauta@yahoo.com.ar), run trips to the Cueva de las Manos Pintadas, as well as to Arroyo Feo (Ugly Stream), an area of great beauty and archeological interest, 70km south of town.

ACCOMMODATION

Camping Municipal Mariano Moreno, at Paseo Julio A. Roca ☎02963 432130. This campsite lies off the shore of Laguna de los Cisnes in the southern part of Perito Moreno. As well as spots to pitch your tent, there are small, rustic cabins. Camping/person AR$20, cabaña AR$120

Posada del Caminante Rivadavia 937 ☎02963 432204, ✉posadadelcaminante@yahoo.com.ar. Accommodation in Perito Moreno is neither abundant nor particularly good value, but *Posada del Caminante* is a decent place to stay for a night. Its en-suite rooms are clean, comfortable and popular, so book in advance. AR$250

CUEVA DE LAS MANOS PINTADAS

The **CUEVA DE LAS MANOS PINTADAS** (daily 9am–7pm; AR$50) is an astonishing cave displaying 9000-year-old cave paintings depicting guanacos, abstract figures and, most famously, 829 hand stencils made by ancient local inhabitants. The cave, a UNESCO World Heritage Site, is easily accessible from Perito Moreno via an organized day-trip (around AR$400–450).

ACCOMMODATION

Estancia La Cueva de las Manos 7km off the RN40 ☎011 5237 4043, ⊛cuevasdelasmanos.net. The caves are actually located inside this *estancia's* perimeters. There are dorms, private rooms and a restaurant, and staff can organize transportation, horserides, hikes and trips to nearby Charcamata, another rock-art site. Closed May–Oct. Dorms AR$150, doubles AR$640

Estancia Telken RN40 ☎02963 432079, ✉telken patagonia@yahoo.com.ar. This *estancia*, which dates back to 1915, provides a good insight into life on a working ranch. The rooms are decent and you can also camp in the grounds. Hiking, birdwatching and horseriding trips can be arranged. Closed May–Sept. Camping/person AR$90, doubles AR$400

PARQUE NACIONAL PERITO MORENO

Created in 1937, the **PARQUE NACIONAL PERITO MORENO** covers over 11,500 square kilometres of windy Patagonian steppe and stunning high-mountain landscapes. Not to be confused with the eponymous glacier (see p.142), the national park is located just off Ruta 40 towards the town of Gobernador Gregores. The park is hard to get to unless you have your own transport, and you may find yourself alone among the abundant wildlife, which includes guanacos, flamingos and condors. There are several enjoyable short hikes (self-guided), which are not too challenging. You'll need to register at the park entrance (daily 8am–8pm; free) before you set off.

ACCOMMODATION

There are some basic camping grounds within the park but there are no services and no fires are permitted. Otherwise the two *estancias* which border the park provide comfortable accommodation.

Estancia Menelik 10km outside the park, just off the RN37 ☎011 4765 8085, ⊛cielospatagonicos.com. This English-style *casco viejo* offers cosy, wood-floored rooms with steppe views; dorm beds are provided in two separate buildings. Rates for the former include full board; those for the latter only cover a bed for the night. Closed April–mid-Oct. Dorms AR$140, doubles AR$1700

1

La Oriental 1km from Lago Belgrano ☎ 011 4152 6901, ⓦ estanciasdesantacruz.com. This working *estancia* is beautifully situated, but standards of accommodation and service are not always as high as they should be. Room rates include half board. Closed April–Oct. Camping/person **AR$120**, doubles **AR$450**

PARQUE NACIONAL LOS GLACIARES

The **PARQUE NACIONAL LOS GLACIARES** hugs the eastern slopes of the Andes, extending for 170km along the border with Chile. A UNESCO World Heritage Site, nearly half of the park's 6000 square kilometres consists of virtually inaccessible continental ice fields. Elsewhere, thirteen glaciers sweep down from craggy mountains into two parallel turquoise lakes – Argentino and Viedma – while dry Patagonian steppe and sub-Antarctic forests of *ñire* (Antarctic beech) and *lenga* (lenga beech) trees provide exceptional trekking country and a home for endangered *huemul* deer, red fox and puma.

The park's northern section can be reached from the village of El Chaltén, where the jagged jaws of the Fitz Roy mountain range dominate a skyline as dramatic as anything in Torres del Paine in Chile (see p.470). Tremendous glaciers, including the show-stopping **Glaciar Perito Moreno** (see p.142), are the stars of the park's southern sector, within easy reach of the resort town of El Calafate.

EL CHALTÉN

Argentina's self-proclaimed "national trekking capital", the rapidly growing town of **EL CHALTÉN** lies within the boundaries of the Parque Nacional Los Glaciares, 217km northwest of El Calafate. It is set at the confluence of two pristine rivers, with the granite spires of Monte Fitz Roy (3405m) and Cerro Torre (3102m) protruding like jagged teeth on the horizon. El Chaltén means "smoking mountain", a name given to Monte Fitz Roy by the Tehuelche, who probably mistook the wisps of cloud around its summit for volcanic activity.

El Chaltén is Argentina's youngest town, created in 1985 as an outpost against Chilean encroachment. Since then it has experienced a tourist boom, with campers, hikers and climbers descending in droves every summer, especially in January and February. In the spring the winds are fierce; March is the best month to visit, with fewer tourists and less wind. Most businesses close between Easter and mid-October.

HIKES FROM EL CHALTÉN

The sky-puncturing peaks of Fitz Roy and Torre offer some of the planet's most challenging technical climbing, but there are plenty of paths for beginners. In contrast to Chile's Torres del Paine, those short on time can enjoy a number of day-hikes in the national park with trailheads that start right in town.

The trail most travelled is the relatively flat hike to **Laguna Torre** (11km; 6hr round-trip), which follows the Río Fitz Roy to a silty lake resplendent with floating icebergs, overlooked by Cerro Torre. A more strenuous hike is to **Laguna de los Tres** (12.5km; 8hr), which ascends sharply to a glacial lake with in-your-face views of Fitz Roy; this is impassable in the winter.

For the best panoramic views in the area – of both Fitz Roy and Torre as well as Lago Viedma – hike uphill to 1490m-high **Lomo del Pliegue Tumbado** (12km; 8hr). Shorter walks include those to the **Chorrillo del Salto** waterfall (4km; 2hr) and uphill to the **Los Condores** viewpoint (1km; 1hr 30min) overlooking the town. A classic multi-day hike is the **Monte Fitz Roy/Cerro Torre loop** (3 days, 2 nights), which leaves either from El Chaltén or just beyond the park's boundaries at *Hostería El Pilar* (15km north of town; ☎ 02962 493002, ⓦ hosteriaelpilar .com.ar). There are three free **campsites** (with latrines only) along the route.

Weather in the park is predictably unpredictable, and cloud often obscures the peaks of Fitz Roy and Torre. The park office produces an excellent **free trekking map**, but for something more detailed, the 1:50,000 *Monte Fitz Roy & Cerro Torre* map published by Zagier and Urruty can be purchased in El Chaltén.

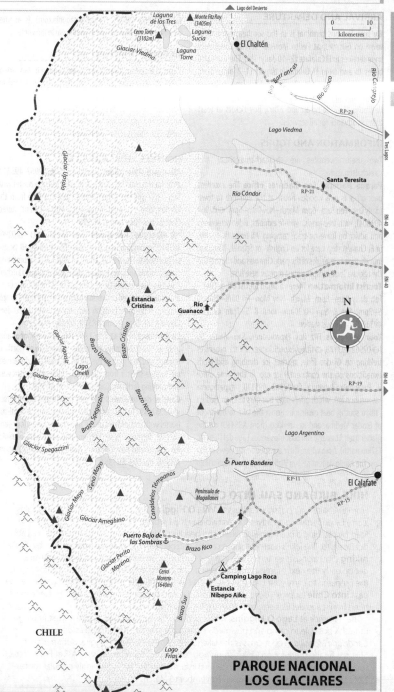

PARQUE NACIONAL
LOS GLACIARES

1

ARRIVAL AND DEPARTURE

By bus The bus terminal is in the southeastern end of town on Güemes, at Perito Moreno. Several companies have services to El Calafate (2–10 daily; 3hr). There are also buses to and from El Calafate's airport (1–3 daily; 3hr), Puerto Natales in Chile (3 weekly; 5hr), and, between November and April, Perito Moreno (1–2 daily; 13hr) and Bariloche (1–2 daily; around 27hr). Buy tickets at least a day in advance for all services.

INFORMATION AND TOURS

Two useful websites are ⓦlacachania.com.ar and ⓦelchalten.com.

Parque Nacional Los Glaciares office The excellent park office is in a wooden house at the entrance to town (daily Dec–Feb 8am–6pm, March–Nov 9am–5pm; ☎02962 493004), with free maps, wildlife exhibits, video screenings and advice on leave-no-trace camping. All buses that arrive in El Chaltén stop here for an English- or Spanish-language introduction to the rules of the park. Climbers and those using the Laguna Torre campsite must register here first.

Tourist information There's a small tourist office (Dec–Feb daily 8am–8pm, March–Nov Mon–Fri 9am–2pm & 5–7pm, Sat & Sun 10.30am–noon & 5–7pm ☎0292 493370) in the bus station.

Tour operators Fitz Roy Expediciones, San Martín 56 (☎02962 493178, ⓦfitzroyexpediciones.com.ar), organizes trekking on Glaciar Torre, teaches ice climbing and leads expeditions on the continental ice cap. In the same office is Patagonia Aventura (☎02962 493110, ⓦpatagonia-aventura.com), which offers daily transfers to Lago Viedma (18km south), boat excursions across the lake to the snout of Glaciar Viedma, and ice-trekking (from AR$440) on the glacier itself. They also run boat trips across Lago del Desierto (37km north), from where there are spectacular views of Fitz Roy. The Anglo-Argentine-run Walk Patagonia, Antonio Rojo

62 (☎02962 493275, ⓦwalkpatagonia.com), is another excellent outfit. Most agencies shut down in the winter.

ACCOMMODATION

Reserve a bed in advance if you are coming in January or February. A number of hostels cater to the young hiking crowd: most offer kitchen facilities, dorms and costly double rooms – couples will find better value at guesthouses. Few places open year-round. Rates for all include breakfast, unless stated otherwise.

HOSTELS AND CAMPSITES

Albergue Aylen-Aike Trevisan 125 ☎02962 493317, ⓦelchalten.com/aylenaike. A bright riverside hostel with four-, six- and eight-bed dorms, superb views from the kitchen, and a relaxed living room with a TV and stereo. Closed April–Oct. Dorms **AR$90**

⭐ **Albergue Patagonia** San Martín 493 ☎02962 493019, ⓦpatagoniahostel.com.ar. This friendly HI hostel, set in a wooden house, has attentive staff, inviting communal spaces, mountain bikes for rent, and a well-equipped kitchen. Downsides are lockers located outside the simple four-person dorms and cramped communal bathrooms. There are simple doubles in the main building and smarter options next door. Closed April–Sept. Dorms **AR$70**, doubles **AR$220**

La Bonanza RP23 ☎02962 493366, ⓦcampingbonanza.com.ar. This charming campsite, around 8km north of town, is situated next to the Río de las Vueltas, where trees offer some shelter from the wind. There are hot showers and cooking facilities. Camping/person **AR$50**

Condor de los Andes Av Río de las Vueltas, at Halvorsen ☎02962 493101, ⓦcondordelosandes.com. A well-run hostel with lots of light in the front room, clean four- and six-bed dorms, a basic kitchen, and staff who organize excursions and lunch boxes. Closed April to Sept. Dorms **AR$90**, doubles **AR$380**

HIKE, BIKE AND SAIL INTO CHILE

From El Chaltén, it's possible to cross to **Villa O'Higgins** (see p.461) in Chile (ⓦvillaohiggins.com) by undertaking an adventurous two-day trip by boat and foot (or bike) in the summer. Start by catching a bus from El Chaltén and heading 37km north to the southern end of Lago del Desierto. The lake's northern shore can be reached either by **scenic boat ride** or by **hiking** (5hr) along its eastern shore to a free campsite. After overnighting at the campsite, get up early the next morning, grab an exit stamp from the Argentine police and hike or cycle (be prepared to carry your bike part of the way along a muddy single-track forest trail) over the pass **into Chile** (approx 16km; allow for a full day and bring plenty of supplies). Horses can be hired from Lago del Desierto to help with the luggage burden.

The trail ends at **Lago O'Higgins**, where you go through the Chilean passport-stamping ritual. It's possible to camp and buy meals here at the lakeside hamlet and *estancia* of *Candelario Mancilla*. A boat crosses the lake to the hamlet of Villa O'Higgins (summer only; 5hr), the final settlement on Chile's stunning 1000km-plus Carretera Austral. Ask at El Chaltén's tourist office for boat schedules and general information on this increasingly popular route. Note the border crossing is only open November to March.

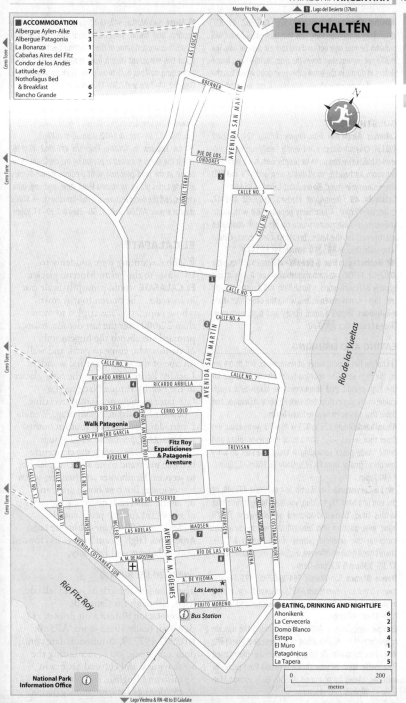

Monte Fitz Roy | Lago del Desierto (37km)

EL CHALTÉN

Cerro Torre

Cerro Torre

Cerro Torre

Cerro Torre

ACCOMMODATION

Albergue Aylen-Aike	5
Albergue Patagonia	3
La Bonanza	1
Cabañas Aires del Fitz	4
Condor de los Andes	8
Latitude 49	7
Nothofagus Bed & Breakfast	6
Rancho Grande	2

LAS LOICAS

BRENNER

AVENIDA SAN MARTIN

PJE DE LOS CONDORES

LIONEL TERAY

CALLE NO. 3

CALLE NO. 4

CALLE NO. 5

CALLE NO. 6

CALLE NO. 7

AVENIDA SAN MARTIN

Río de las Vueltas

CALLE NO. 8

RICARDO ARBILLA

RICARDO ARBILLA

CERRO SOLO

CERRO SOLO

AVENIDA ANTONIO ROJO

CABO PRIMERO GARCIA

Walk Patagonia

RIQUELME

TREVISAN

Fitz Roy Expediciones & Patagonia Aventure

CALLE NO. 12

CALLE NO. 9

CALLE NO. 10

CALLE NO. 11

LAGO DEL DESIERTO

AVENIDA COSTANERA SUR

HENSEN

MCLEOD

LAS ADELAS

AVENIDA M. M. GUEMES

A. M. DE AGOSTINI

MADSEN

HALVORSEN

PIEDRA BUENA

CALLE ROSA SEPÚLVEDA

AVENIDA COSTANERA NORTE

RÍO DE LAS VUELTAS

A. DE VIEDMA

Las Lengas

PERITO MORENO

Río Fitz Roy

Bus Station

National Park Information Office

Lago Viedma & RN-40 to El Calafate

EATING, DRINKING AND NIGHTLIFE

Ahonikenk	6
La Cervecería	2
Domo Blanco	3
Estepa	4
El Muro	1
Patagónicus	7
La Tapera	5

0 — 200
metres

1

Rancho Grande San Martín 520 ☎02962 493005, ⓦranchogrande hostel.com. This less-than-ideal hostel will probably be your only option if you come in June or July. The indifferent owners shut down the main building and house visitors in dorms in the small cabin next door, which has the benefit of some rustic charm. Breakfast is not included, but use of a tiny kitchen is. Dorms <u>AR$100</u>, doubles <u>AR$390</u>

GUESTHOUSES

Cabañas Aires del Fitz Ricardo Arbilla 124 ☎02962 493134, ⓦairesdelfitz.com,ar. Friendly, family-run set of split-level cabañas sleeping up to six people; each has a bedroom, bathroom, kitchenette, small dining area, and a TV and DVD player. Open year-round. No breakfast. Cabaña <u>AR$440</u>

Latitude 49 Güemes, at Madsen ☎02962 493347, ⓦlatitude49.com. A justifiably popular B&B with spick-and-span en-suite rooms, plus a couple of self-contained apartments; for the latter, breakfast costs extra. Closed June–July. Double <u>AR$290</u>, apartment <u>AR$420</u>

★ **Nothofagus Bed & Breakfast** Hensen at Riquelme ☎02962 493087, ⓦnothofagusbb.com.ar. A bright and homely B&B with wooden furnishing and a rustic country feel; three rooms are en suites, while the other four share a bathroom. There's a small library and book exchange. Closed Easter–Oct. <u>AR$250</u>

EATING AND DRINKING

El Chaltén has a good range of restaurants, but prices are on the high side. The opening times given below are for the high season, and should only be taken as a rough guide; many places close between Easter and October, and those that stay open have reduced hours.

Ahonikenk Güemes 23 ☎02962 493070. An unassuming diner that serves huge portions of *milanesas*, pizza and home-made pasta (including a tasty lasagne) at fairly low prices (mains from AR$32). Daily 11.30am–3.30pm & 7–10.30pm.

★ **La Cervecería** San Martín 564 ☎02962 493109. At the end of a hard day's hiking, you have to fight for a seat in this snug, driftwood-adorned microbrewery. They'll bring over popcorn and breadsticks even if you're just sampling the excellent pilsner (from around AR$25). There's good grub on offer too, including *empanadas*. Daily 12.30–3.30pm & 7.30pm–1am.

Domo Blanco San Martín 164 ☎02962 493036. The town's finest ice cream (from AR$15) is served here, as well as an inventive range of panini, sandwiches and wraps. Daily 11am–9/10pm.

Estepa Cerro Solo, at Antonio Rojo. Among the upscale restaurants in town, this is one of the best deals, with Fitz Roy views thrown in. Go gourmet with dishes like roasted Patagonian lamb or your choice of wood-fired pizzas or calzones. Mains from around AR$50. Daily except Mon noon–3.30pm & 7.30–11.30pm.

El Muro San Martín 948 ☎02962 493248. Steak with peppers and bacon, sweet and sour ribs, and salmon *sorrentinos* are just some of the tempting creations dished up at this restaurant (mains from around AR$50). There's a climbing wall out back to help you work up an appetite. Daily 12.30–3pm and 7.30–11.30pm.

Patagónicus Güemes, at Madsen ☎02962 493025. The best pizza in town (starting at AR$26) is served to hungry diners at big wooden tables. There's a good range of beers too. Daily 12.30–3pm & 7–10.30pm. Closed Wed.

★ **La Tapera** Av Antonio Rojo s/n ☎02962 493138. When the menu is recited in person by the chef, you know you're in for food prepared with passion. House staples include tapas plates, lamb and lentil stew, and vegetable crepes, and the decor features a wood-burning stove. Mains start at around AR$50. Daily 12.30–3pm & 7.30–11.30pm.

EL CALAFATE

If global warming were suddenly to lay waste to the Perito Moreno glacier, **EL CALAFATE** would promptly fizzle out in its wake. The brazen tourist town, whose population has tripled to more than 22,000 over the last decade, exists primarily to absorb the huge number of visitors who come to gawk and walk on one of the world's natural wonders. Luckily, Perito Moreno is the only glacier in the nearby Parque Nacional Los Glaciares to show no signs of receding.

Beyond El Calafate's main drag, Avenida Libertador, heaving with tourism outfits, restaurants, supermarkets and a huge casino, the roads leaving the city centre become more and more authentic, leading to wooden farmhouses and pastures where horses graze. But new hotels are going up all the time, each one vying for views of snow-clad Andean peaks and the milky-blue 1600-square-kilometre **Lago Argentino**. High season reaches its crowded peak in January and February.

WHAT TO SEE AND DO

There are few attractions in El Calafate itself, although the **Centro de Interpretación Histórica** on Brown, at Bonarelli (daily 10am–8pm; AR$40; ☎02902 492799, ⓦmuseocalafate.com), does a dramatic job of recounting the area's natural and cultural history in Spanish and English, complete with re-creations of Patagonian megafauna.

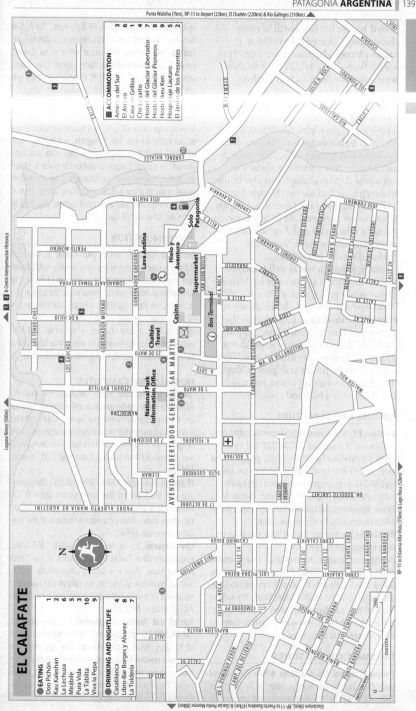

Punta Walichu (7km), RP-11 to Airport (23km), El Chaltén (220km) & Río Gallegos (310km) ▲

EL CALAFATE

● **EATING**
Don Pichón	1
Kau Kaleshan	2
La Lechuza	6
Mirábile	3
Pura Vida	5
La Tablita	10
Viva la Pepa	9

● **DRINKING AND NIGHTLIFE**
Casablanca	4
Libro-Bar Borges y Alvarez	8
La Tolderia	7

■ **ACCOMMODATION**
América del Sur	3
El Arroyo	6
Casa de Grillos	1
Che Lagarto	4
Hostel del Glaciar Libertador	7
Hostel del Glaciar Pioneros	8
Hospedaje Lautaro	9
Hostel Ikeu Ken	5
El Jardín de los Presentes	2

◄ █ **1** █ **2** & Centro Interpretación Histórica

◄ Laguna Nimez (500m)

Glaciarium (6km), RP-11 to Puerto Bandera (47km) & Glaciar Perito Moreno (80km) ▲

RP-15 to Estancia Alta Vista (35km) & Lago Roca (52km) ►

1

A bird reserve lies just north of town (head along C Ezequel Bustillo) at **Laguna Nimez** (daily: summer 9am–9pm, winter 9am–7pm; AR$25), where there are exotic waterfowl such as Chilean flamingos and black-necked swans.

Around 6km west of El Calafate, the **Glaciarium** (daily Sept–April 9am–8pm, May–Aug 11am–7pm; AR$95; ☎02902 497912, ⓦglaciarium.com) is a modern museum that focuses on ice and glaciers, and aims to raise awareness about the impact of climate change. It is also home to Argentina's first ice bar. Shuttle buses (AR$30 return) to the Glaciarium depart from the car park on 1 de Mayo, between Avenida Libertador and Avenida Roca, every hour on the hour, 9am–6pm (reduced service May–Aug).

Finally, although not as well preserved as their counterparts at Cueva de las Manos Pintadas (see p.133), the 4000- to 7000-year-old cave and cliff paintings at **Punta Walichu** (daily guided tours in the summer at 9am & 3pm, winter at 2pm; AR$50), 7km east of town on the shores of Lago Argentino, are worth a visit. They depict animals, people and human hands. Travel agencies run trips here, but you could also rent a bike and cycle here.

ARRIVAL AND DEPARTURE

By plane El Calafate's airport (ⓦaeropuertocalafate.com) is 22km east of town; taxis (AR$80–120) and minibuses run by Ves Patagonia (☎02902 497355, ⓦvespatagonia .com; AR$38) connect it with El Calafate. Las Lengas (☎02962 493023) operates buses direct to El Chaltén.
Destinations Daily flights to Bariloche, Buenos Aires, Trelew, Río Gallegos and Ushuaia. Passengers must pay an AR$38 departure tax for all domestic flights.
By bus The bus terminal is at Av Roca, one block up a flight of steps from Av Libertador.
Destinations Bariloche (summer only; 1 daily; around 30hr); Puerto Natales (Chile; 3–4 weekly; 6–7hr); Río Gallegos (4–5 daily; 4hr–4hr 30min); Ushuaia (via Chile; 1 daily; 16hr). Cal Tur, Chaltén Travel, Taqsa, TPS and Las Lengas all have daily buses to El Chaltén (3hr), normally at 8am and 6pm (and sometimes around 1pm too). Generally only Cal Tur operates a year-round service.

INFORMATION AND TOURS

Parque Nacional Los Glaciares office The national park office, in a historic wooden cabin on Av Libertador 1302, has maps, sells fishing licences and can provide up-to-date information (Mon–Fri 8am–6pm, Sat & Sun 9am–6pm; ☎02902 491545, ⓦparquesnacionales.gov.ar).
Tourist information The tourist office is on Coronel Rosales, just beyond the bridge (daily: summer 8am–10pm, winter 8am–8pm; ☎02902 49190, ⓦturismo.elcalafate.gov .ar). There's also an office in the bus terminal (same hours).
Tour operators Hielo y Aventura, Av Libertador 935 (☎02902 492205, ⓦhieloyaventura.com), offers ice-trekking trips (from AR$640) and boat excursions to see Glaciar Perito Moreno. Solo Patagonia, Av Libertador 867 (☎02902 491298, ⓦsolopatagonia.com), runs boat trips around the Upsala, Spegazzini and Onelli glaciers. *Hostel del Glaciar Pioneros* (see opposite) offers recommended glacier tours that are popular with backpackers. Several operators organize (long and rather rushed) day-trips to Torres del Paine in Chile (see p.470).

ACCOMMODATION

Outside of the high season (Nov–Easter) El Calafate's inflated accommodation prices come down a notch; make sure you reserve in advance for January and February. In addition to *El Arroyo*, you can camp inside the park at the tranquil *Lago Roca* (☎02902 499500; camping/person AR$20), beside the lake of the same name, 50km from town; facilities include showers, a restaurant and bike rental. Rates for all the hostels and guesthouse listed below include breakfast, internet/wi-fi access and kitchen use.

HOSTELS AND CAMPSITES

★ **América del Sur** Puerto Deseado 151 ☎02902 493525, ⓦamericahostel.com.ar. A well-designed, spacious and friendly place with wonderful views of Lago Argentino and knowledgeable staff who can help you organize a wide range of trips. The dorms and private rooms are clean, bright and have under-floor heating. Dorms AR$100, doubles AR$420

El Arroyo José Pantín 151 ☎02902 492233. This camp-site, one block behind the petrol station close to the bridge, has a pleasant riverside setting and is a good shoestring choice during the warmer months of the year. Camping/person AR$40

Che Lagarto 25 de Mayo 311 ☎011 5263 0162, ⓦchelagarto.com. The El Calafate branch of this South America hostel chain is a solid if unspectacular choice, with six- to twelve-bed dorms, en-suite private twins and doubles, a TV lounge and games room, and a bar. Dorms AR$60, doubles AR$320

Hostel del Glaciar Libertador Av Libertador 587 ☎02902 491792, ⓦglaciar.com. A newer and pricier version of its sister hostel *Glaciar Pioneros* (see opposite), this enormous wooden house sleeps more than a hundred, has spotless dorms with private bathrooms and lovely private rooms. There's a recommended in-house travel agency too. Dorms AR$105, doubles AR$435

Hostel del Glaciar Pioneros Los Pioneros 255 ☎02902 491243, ⓦglaciar.com. There are pros and cons to this sizeable HI hostel. The four-bed dorm rooms are cramped, as is the kitchen, but some of the newer double rooms have been tastefully furnished with private bathrooms, and the on-site restaurant does hearty home-style cooking. Dorms AR$83, doubles AR$308

Hostel Ikeu Ken FM Pontoriero 171 ☎02902 495175, ⓦpatagoniaikeuken.com.ar. An intimate but lively hilltop hostel with a balcony that enjoys the afternoon sun and lake vistas. Dorms and bathrooms are pretty ordinary, although the two adjacent fully equipped cabañas, with kitchens and private bathrooms, are highly sought after. Dorms AR$80, cabañas AR$300

GUESTHOUSES

Casa de Grillos Los Condores 1215 ☎02902 491160, ⓦcasadegrillos.com.ar. A peaceful B&B in a two-storey family home with just a handful of comfortable rooms – though they could do with a spruce up – and a self-contained cabin in the garden. Doubles AR$360, cabaña AR$420

Hospedaje Lautaro Espora 237 ☎02902 492698, ⓦhospedajelautaro.com.ar. A super-friendly option where you'll feel just like one of the family, *Hospedaje Lautaro* has a mix of dorms and private rooms, a communal lounge, and free tea and coffee. Dorms AR$97.50, doubles AR$220

★ **El Jardin de los Presentes** Guido Bonarelli 72 ☎02902 491518, ⓦlospresentes.com.ar. You couldn't ask for warmer hospitality or better value than this spotless, family-run B&B. The large doubles have TVs, private bathrooms and partial lake views, while the fully equipped two-storey cabañas sleep up to five. Doubles AR$370, cabañas AR$445

EATING

Restaurant prices are very high throughout El Calafate, and it is difficult to keep to a tight budget unless you self-cater for at least some of your time here. Outside of the high season, most places have reduced opening hours.

Don Pichón Puerto Deseado 242 ☎02902 492577. Top-notch *parilla* on a hill, a 10min walk northeast of the centre (call ahead for a free pick-up), whose wraparound windows offer panoramic views of the city and the lake. Steaks are the big draw, but if you're feeling indulgent, go for the fondue. Mains AR$45–90. Tues–Sun noon–3pm & 7pm–midnight.

Kau Kaleshan Gob. Gregores 1256 ☎02902 491188. This charming vegetarian restaurant/*casa de té* has an inventive menu featuring wraps, pizzas, stir-fries and curries (all AR$35–60). There is also a range of teas, coffees and home-made cakes, ideal for a *merienda* (afternoon snack). Tues–Sun 4pm–midnight.

La Lechuza Av Libertador 1301 ☎02902 491610, ⓦlalechuzapizzas.com.ar. This deservedly popular place serves up good pizzas (AR$45–75) from its wood-fired oven, plus pasta dishes, make-your-own salads and huge sandwiches. There are a couple of other branches around town. Daily noon–midnight.

Mirábile Libertador 1329 ☎02902 492230. This pasta-maker is fronted by an economical (for El Calafate) restaurant. Local families flock here for the wonderful trout or squash ravioli and various types of lasagne and gnocchi. Mains around AR$40–60, and there are often good low-cost specials. Daily noon–3pm & 8pm–midnight.

Pura Vida Av Libertador 1876 ☎0290 493356. The owners provide traditional food with a modern touch in this A-frame cabin. The menu has numerous vegetarian options alongside appetizing dishes such as country chicken pie and "Granny's" lentil stew. Mains around AR$56–76. Daily 7.30–11.30pm. Closed Wed.

La Tablita Colonel Rosales 28 ☎02902 491065. Although the restaurant itself is somewhat lacking in character, the beef and lamb here is some of the best in town. Prices are high, but the huge portions can easily feed more than one person. Mains AR$70–105. Daily noon–3.30pm & 7.30pm–midnight. Closed Wed.

★ **Viva la Pepa** Emilio Amado 833 ☎02902 491880, ⓦvivalapepacalafate.com. Cheerful café with 69 different types of savoury and sweet crepes (AR$36–70), as well as soups, sandwiches, fresh juices and coffee. There's a whimsical air to the place: crudities are served in mini watering cans and children's paintings cover the walls. Daily noon–8pm. Closed Thurs.

DRINKING AND NIGHTLIFE

Casablanca Av Libertador 1202 ☎02902 491402. Buzzing café-bar that serves good coffee and fifteen types of beer (from around AR$20–25), plus tasty *lomitos* (Argentine steak sandwich). Classic film posters and signed hockey and rugby shirts decorate the place. Daily noon–midnight. Closed Wed.

Libro-Bar Borges y Alvarez Av Libertador 1015 ☎02902 491464. This small café-bar is run by, and aimed at, bibliophiles. There's an extensive range of Argentine and South American books (mainly in Spanish) to flick through while sampling a coffee, hot chocolate or *trago* (alcoholic drink). Drinks from AR$12. Daily 11am/noon–2/3am. Closed Wed.

La Tolderia Av Libertador 1177 ☎02902 491443. Those with energy to burn and the opposite sex on their mind flock to this bar/club for live music and a let-it-all-hang-out dancefloor that on weekends throbs until sunrise. Tues–Sun summer noon–5/6am, winter 8pm–5/6am.

DIRECTORY

Banks There are several ATMs including at the Banco de la Nacion, Av Libertador 1133, and Banco de Santa Cruz, Av Libertador 1285.

1

Car rental Avis, Av Libertador 1078 ☎02902 492877, ⓦavis.com; Fiorasi, Av Libertador 1341 ☎02902 495330, ⓦfiorasirentacar.com. Prices start at around AR$500/day.
Internet Locutorio, Av Libertador, at Espora.
Laundry Lava Andina, Espora 88 (☎02902 493980).
Police Av Libertador 835 (☎02902 491824).
Post office Av Libertador 1133.

GLACIAR PERITO MORENO

The **PERITO MORENO GLACIER** is one of Argentina's greatest natural wonders. It's not the longest of the country's glaciers – Upsala is twice as long (60km) – and whereas the ice cliffs at its snout tower up to 60m high, the face of Spegazzini can reach heights double that. However, such comparisons prove irrelevant when you stand on the boardwalks that face this monster: Perito Moreno has a star quality that none of the others rival.

Perito Moreno is considered to be "stable" in the sense that it is neither advancing nor retreating. It has became famous for the way it periodically pushes right across the channel, forming a massive dyke of ice that cut off the Brazo Rico and Brazo Sur from the main body of Lago Argentino. Isolated from their natural outlet, the water in the *brazos* (arms) builds up against the flank of the glacier, flooding the surrounding area, until eventually the pressure forces open a passage into the canal once again. Occurring over the course of several hours, such a rupture is, for those lucky enough to witness it, one of nature's most awesome spectacles.

UPSALA AND OTHER GLACIERS

Although receding fast, **GLACIAR UPSALA** remains the longest glacier in the park and indeed in South America. The same height as Perito Moreno (60m), Upsala is twice as long (roughly 60km), 7km wide and known for carving huge translucent, blue-tinged icebergs that bob around Lago Argentino like surreal art sculptures. Located 45km west of El Calafate, Upsala is accessible by **catamaran excursion** along Lago Argentino's northern arm (boats leave from Puerto Bandera). Full-day tours (AR$560, plus the park entry fee), usually called "All Glaciers" and also taking in the Spegazzini, Onelli and Agassiz glaciers, are run by Solo Patagonia (Av Libertador 867; ☎02902 491298, ⓦsolopatagonia.com). Before booking, remember that your scope for refunds is limited: the weather has to be exceptionally bad for the trip to be cancelled entirely, and the company fulfils its legal obligations if only one main part of the trip is completed; in windy weather especially, icebergs can block the channels, and in recent years, Upsala has frequently been inaccessible.

RÍO GALLEGOS

Grim and windy **RÍO GALLEGOS** is an inevitable stop for travellers heading south to Ushuaia, north towards Puerto Madryn or west to El Calafate or Chile. The capital of Santa Cruz Province, the city lies on the banks of the estuary of the Río Gallegos, a river whose giant,

---

VISITING PERITO MORENO

The **entry fee** for the Perito Moreno section of the park is AR$100 (payable at the park entrance, 30km before the glacier), although some people try to avoid the charge by sneaking in outside the park's opening hours (daily 8am–7pm). Most people visit on a guided **day-trip**, which are offered by virtually all the agencies in El Calafate and allow for around four hours at the ice face. They cost around AR$170–200, excluding the entry fee. To visit independently, take one of the **buses** that leave from El Calafate's terminal (2–3 daily; around 1hr 30min). You could also rent a **taxi** (AR$500, including waiting time) or a **car** (roughly AR$500 per day), taking either the less-travelled RP15 past historic *estancias*, or the less scenic but fully paved RP11.

One-hour **catamaran cruises** (daily Oct–May hourly 10am–4pm, June–Sept noon; AR$100) to see Perito Moreno's southern face leave from Puerto Bajo de las Sombras; regular minibuses shuttle here from the main viewing boardwalks, 6km away. For an even closer view of the glacier, Hielo y Aventura (see p.140) offers **ice-trekking** trips (wearing crampons) across its surface from AR$640, excluding the park entry fee.

sea-going brown trout lure **fly-fishing** enthusiasts from around the world.

WHAT TO SEE AND DO

Río Gallegos' city centre has a couple of worthwhile museums and some nicely restored historical wooden buildings. Housed in an early settler home dating from 1890, at Albedí & Elcano, the **Museo de los Pioneros** (daily 10am–7pm; free; ⓣ02966 437763) is decked out with period furniture and evocative old photos. They also have periodic exhibitions of coins or letters from the early twentieth century. The **Museo Regional Provincial Padre Jesús Molina**, Ramón y Cajal 51 (Mon–Fri 10am–5pm, Sat & Sun noon–7pm; free; ⓣ02966 426427), offers rolling contemporary art exhibitions, a motley collection of stuffed regional fauna, dinosaur models and artefacts from the indigenous Tehuelche. If live animals interest you more, consider a tour of the **penguin colony** at Cabo Vírgenes, a nesting site for around 180,000 Magellanic penguins, 140km southeast of the city; trips are on offer between October and March.

ARRIVAL AND DEPARTURE

By plane Río Gallegos Airport is 7km west of the city. There are no buses to the centre; taxis cost around AR$60–70.

Destinations Daily flights to Buenos Aires, El Calafate and Trelew, and weekly ones to Ushuaia.

By bus The bus station (ⓣ02966 442585) is 2km west of the city at the corner of Av Eva Perón and the RN3. Bus #A runs downtown; a taxi costs AR$30–35.

Destinations El Calafate (4–5 daily; 4hr); Puerto Madryn (7 daily; 18–19hr); Río Grande (3 daily; 9–10hr); Ushuaia (2 daily; 12hr); and, in Chile, Punta Arenas (2 daily; 3hr 30min); Puerto Natales (2 weekly; 4hr).

INFORMATION AND TOURS

Tourist information Río Gallegos has two main tourist offices in the city centre, both helpful and efficient: one at Beccar 126 (Mon–Fri 8am–8pm, Sat & Sun 8am–noon & 4–8pm; ⓣ02966 436920, ⓦturismo.riogallegos.gov.ar) and another in an old (formerly horse-drawn) wagon on the corner of Av Kirchner and San Martín (Mon–Fri 8am–8pm, Sat & Sun 8am–2pm & 4–8pm; closed during the winter; ⓣ02966 422365). There's also a booth in the bus terminal (Mon–Fri 7am–8pm, Sat & Sun 4–8pm; ⓣ02966 442159).

Tour operator Maca Tobiano (Av Kirchner 988; ⓣ02966 422466, ⓦmacatobiano.com) runs day-trips to Cabo Vírgenes.

ACCOMMODATION

Accommodation is generally of fairly poor quality and fills up quickly in summer.

Camping ATSA 500m southwest of the bus terminal on Asturias, at Yugoslavia ⓣ02966 156 7758. Camping/person **AR$20**

Colonial Urquiza, at Rivadavia ⓣ02966 420020, ⓔines_frey@hotmail.com. A warm and chatty *dueña* – a descendant of one of the first settlers in Río Gallegos – runs this rambling old house, in which lurks a hotchpotch of basic, but very clean rooms; all have TVs and some are en suite. **AR$200**

Hospedaje Elcira Pje Zuccarino 431 ⓣ02966 429856. Handy for the bus station, this neat guesthouse is popular with Argentines. It looks like grandma's house, has a TV lounge and the only kitchen open for guests to use in town. Dorms **AR$70**, doubles **AR$180**

Sehuén Rawson 160 ⓣ02966 425683, ⓦhotelsehuen.com. An efficiently run little hotel with a range of decent rooms; each has a TV, phone and boxy private bathroom, as well as a bilingual copy of the New Testament. Breakfast included. **AR$230**

EATING AND DRINKING

As with accommodation, restaurant prices are high in Río Gallegos, but there are a couple of places worth stretching the budget a bit for.

Belfast Alberdi 344. If you fancy a beer (from AR$15), head over to *Belfast*, whose owners have made a decent attempt at creating a pub-like atmosphere. Sun–Thurs 7pm–5am, Fri & Sat 7pm–6am.

British Club Kirchner 935 ⓣ02966 432668, ⓦbritishclub.com.ar. A port of call for Bruce Chatwin, this atmospheric place has more than a hint of a gentleman's club about it. The menu has some inventive lamb and seafood dishes, though prices are on the high side, with few mains under AR$70. An English high tea is served around 5pm. Daily noon–midnight.

Freddo Kirchner 917 ⓣ02966 423302, ⓦfreddo.com.ar. This outpost of the famous Argentina chain serves the top *helado* (ice cream) in Río Gallegos. The coffee is good too, and each cup comes with a little taste of ice cream. Tues–Sun 10am–10pm.

★ **Laguanacazul** Gob Lista, at Sarmiento ⓣ02966 444144. Genial chef Mirko Ionfrida uses locally sourced ingredients (think guanaco and rhea) to cook up memorable haute cuisine at this waterfront restaurant. Lamb is his signature dish. Mains from around AR$60. Tues–Sun noon–3pm & 8pm–midnight.

DIRECTORY

Banks and exchange Thaler, San Martín 484 (ⓣ02966 436052).

Internet Numerous *locutorios* offer internet services.

Post office San Martín, at Av Kirchner.

> ## CROSSING INTO CHILE AND TIERRA DEL FUEGO
>
> Reaching Tierra del Fuego from the Argentine mainland requires travelling through Chilean territory. The journey, which takes the better part of a day (there are no night buses along this route) and involves crossing two borders as well as the Magellan Straits, can feel like a time-wasting exercise in theatrical passport-stamping between two frosty neighbours. The **Chilean border crossing** (no food of any kind is allowed across) is 68km south of Río Gallegos at Monte Aymond. Once in Chile, take the road for **Punta Arenas** (see p.462) and **Puerto Natales** (see p.467). If your destination is Argentine Tierra del Fuego, turn left onto the RN257 at Kimiri Aike, 48km from the border. Follow this road to Primera Angostura, where a **car ferry** takes twenty minutes to cross the narrowest section of the Magellan Straits (ⓦtabsa.cl/Eng/Html/PrimeraAngostura.php; every 45min 7/8am–11pm/midnight; 20–30min; CH$1600 per person, CH$14,000 for a car). If you're headed to Río Grande and **Ushuaia** (see below), the road travels through part of Chilean Tierra del Fuego until reaching **San Sebastián**, the island's first Argentine settlement. If you book a bus ticket from Río Gallegos to Ushuaia or Río Grande (or vice versa), the ferry crossing is included in the ticket price and the bus driver will guide you through the border crossing formalities.
>
> An alternative route to Puerto Natales from Río Gallegos is to head 260km west along the RN40 to the coal-mining town of **Río Turbio**; the Chilean border crossing (open 24hr) is 35km south at Paso Casas Viejas/La Laurita.

Tierra del Fuego

A rugged and isolated archipelago at the extreme southern tip of the continent, **TIERRA DEL FUEGO** (Land of Fire) marks the finish line for South America. Here the Andes range marches into the chilly southern oceans; deciduous forests and Ice Age glaciers lie a stone's throw from a wildlife-rich shoreline, penguins and sea lions huddle on rocky islets, salmon and trout thrash about in the rivers, and sheep and guanacos graze on arid windswept plains.

The archipelago is shared, with historic hostility, by Argentina and Chile, and only about a third of Isla Grande (Tierra del Fuego's main island and the largest in South America) belongs to Argentina. This includes **Ushuaia**, however, the region's top destination. As locals will proudly point out, it is the planet's southernmost inhabited city. It's a jumping-off point for the lakes and mountains of **Parque Nacional Tierra del Fuego**, as well as historic **estancias**, boat trips on the **Beagle Channel**, downhill and cross-country skiing in the winter, and cruises to **Antarctica** in summer.

To the north, a stop in the unattractive town of **Río Grande** may be a necessary evil if you are travelling to or from the Argentine mainland – though it's a destination in its own right for fly-fishermen in pursuit of brown trout.

High season is from December to February, when days are longest and warmest. Spring (Oct to mid-Nov) is beautiful and lush, but even windier than normal. Autumn (late March to April) is, arguably, the best time to visit, when the countryside is lit up in warm shades of red and orange. But Ushuaia's growing status as a winter-sports playground ensures the "uttermost part of the earth" is now a year-round destination.

USHUAIA

USHUAIA is cold, damp and disarmingly pretty, set on a bay on the wildlife-rich shores of the **Beagle Channel** with a backdrop of jagged mountains and glaciers.

The world's southernmost city lies 3500km south of Buenos Aires and just 1000km north of **Antarctica**, a fact you'll have no problem detecting: even in summer you need to wrap up warm (unless you plan to follow the lead of the original inhabitants who got around just fine naked and slathered in seal grease). Another thing you'll need plenty of here is money; as the gateway to Antarctica, Ushuaia is very expensive. Looking back at the city from a boat bobbing in the Beagle Channel, though, with a view of colourful houses stacked up on sloping streets, framed by arresting snow-clad peaks, you'll almost certainly think it's worth it.

WHAT TO SEE AND DO

A former penal colony, Ushuaia is not the best-planned city, but it makes a pleasant place to relax, gorge on seafood and take in some history in the museums and nearby *Estancia Harberton*. Most of the tourist and commercial action is centred on **San Martín** and **Maipú** streets, while boats leave from the Muelle Turístico down by the pier. List-tickers can have their passports stamped in the post office to prove they've made it to the globe's end. For **active pursuits**, there's good hiking in Parque Nacional Tierra del Fuego, ice climbing or trekking on nearby glaciers, horseriding in nature reserves, scuba diving in the chilly harbour, boating to penguin and sea-lion colonies, and in winter dog-sledding or skiing through pristine white valleys.

Museo del Fin del Mundo

The **Museo del Fin del Mundo**, Maipú 173, at Rivadavia (Oct–March daily 9am–8pm, rest of year Mon–Sat noon–7pm; AR$50; ☏02901 421863), offers a good overview of the region's indigenous, maritime and settler history. Exhibits include a quaint reconstruction of an old-style grocery store and a room with stuffed regional creatures. The ticket is also valid for the historic Antigua Casa de Gobierno, Maipú 465 (same opening times; ☏02901 422551).

USHUAIA

EATING
Bambu	1
Bodegón Fueguino	3
Kalma Restó	7
Ramos Generales	8
La Rueda	5
Tante Sara	4
El Turco	6
Volver	9

DRINKING AND NIGHTLIFE
Dublin	2
Kuar	10

ACCOMMODATION
Antarctica Hostel	5
B&B Nahuel	3
Camping Pista del Andino	1
Cruz del Sur	6
Freestyle	4
Galeazzi-Basily B&B	2
La Posta	8
Yakush	7

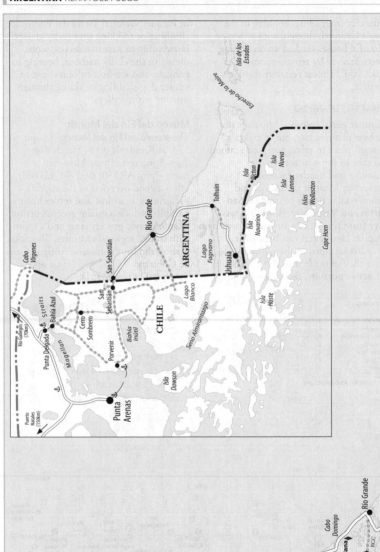

Isla de los Estados

Estrecho de la Maire

Isla Nueva

Isla Picton

Isla Lennox

Islas Wollaston

Tolhuin

Río Grande

ARGENTINA

Isla Navarino

Lago Fagnano

San Sebastián

Cabo Vírgenes

Ushuaia

Cape Horn

Isla Hoste

Isla Hoste

CHILE

Lago Blanco

Bahía Azul

San Sebastián

Río Gallegos (700m)

Cerro Sombrero

Magellan Straits

Punta Delgada

Porvenir

Bahía Inútil

Seno Almirantazgo

Isla Dawson

Puerto Natales (150km)

Punta Arenas

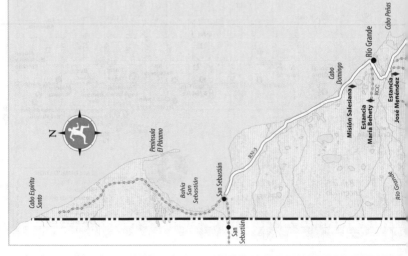

N

Cabo Espíritu Santo

Península El Páramo

Bahía San Sebastián

San Sebastián

Cabo Domingo

Cabo Peñas

Río Grande

Misión Salesiana

Estancia María Behety

RCC

Estancia José Menéndez

San Sebastián

RN3

Río Grande

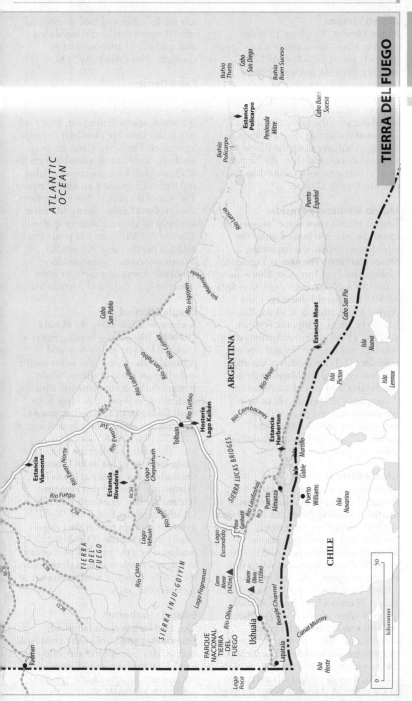

TIERRA DEL FUEGO

ATLANTIC OCEAN

Bahía Thetis

Cabo San Diego

Bahía Buen Suceso

Cabo Buen Suceso

Estancia Policarpo

Península Mitre

Bahía Policarpo

Puerto Español

Río Leticia

Cabo San Pablo

Río Irigoyen

Río Moneta

Río Malengüena

ARGENTINA

Estancia Moat

Río Moat

Cabo San Pío

Isla Nueva

RCI

Río Lainezero

Río San Pablo

Río Eword Sur

Río Turbio

Hostería Lago Kaikén

Río Cambaceres

Estancia Harberton

Isla Picton

Isla Lennox

Tolhuin

SIERRA LUCAS BRIDGES

Isla Gable

Isla Martillo

Estancia Viamonte

Río Eword Norte

RCI

Lago Chepelmuth

Estancia Rivadavia

RCH

Río Lasifashaj

Puerto Williams

Río Fuego

Río Indio

Paso Garibaldi

RCJ

Puerto Almanza

Isla Navarino

RCE

Lago Yehuin

Lago Escondido

RCO

Río Claro

TIERRA DEL FUEGO

SIERRA INJU-GOIYIN

Lago Fagnano

Cerro Alvear (1425m)

Monte Olivia (1328m)

CHILE

RCD

Radman

SIERRA INJU-GOIYIN

PARQUE NACIONAL TIERRA DEL FUEGO

Río Olivia

Ushuaia

Lapataia

Beagle Channel

Canal Murray

Isla Hoste

Lago Roca

0   50
kilometres

Museo Yámana

Museo Yámana, Rivadavia 56 (daily: summer 10am–8pm, winter noon–7pm; generally closed July–Aug; AR$25; ☎02901 422874), is a small gem of a museum exploring the remarkable lifestyle and egalitarian society of the Yámana Indians, who, tragically, were wiped out after the European invasion. Dioramas re-creating their dwellings and fishing techniques along the Beagle Channel demonstrate how the Yámana lived in harmony with nature despite the inhospitable climate.

Museo Marítimo y Presidio

Known around town as the "museo de la carcel" because it is housed inside the city's former prison, the fascinating **Museo Marítimo y Presidio**, at Yaganes & Gobernador Paz (April–Oct Thurs–Tues 10am–8pm, Nov–March daily 9am–8pm; AR$90; free Spanish-language tours April–Oct 11.30am & 6.30pm, Nov–March 11.30am, 4.30pm & 6.30pm; ☎02901 437481, ⓦmuseomaritimo.com), is both a maritime history and a prison museum. There are models of the ships that first explored the Magellan Straits, the Beagle Channel and the Antarctic. Atmospheric old prison cells contain life-size models and recount the lives of former convicts. A wing of the prison has been left bare and makes for poignant wandering.

Glaciar Martial

There are lofty views of Ushuaia and the Beagle Channel from the base of **Glaciar Martial**, a receding glacier that is the source of much of the city's water supply. To get there, walk 7km up Luis Fernando Martial road or take a taxi (AR$35–40) or one of the minibuses that depart from the corner of Juan Fadúl and Avenida Maipú. From here, a chairlift (Nov–March daily 9.30am–4.45pm, June–Oct daily 10am–4.45pm, closed April and May; AR$50) whisks passengers up the mountain; it's then a further one-hour-thirty-minute uphill hike and scramble to the base of the glacier. From the top of the chairlift, three municipal **ski runs** are open in the winter. A charming mountain *refugio*

sells snacks, coffee and mulled wine, and offers dormitory-style accommodation with cold-water bathrooms and no electricity (Nov–March; AR$130).

Cerro Castor

Far from turning into a frozen ghost town over winter, Ushuaia has taken off as a **winter-sports** destination, with a ski season that runs from late May to early September. The Sierra Alvear ranges, northeast of town and accessible from the RN3, are great for cross-country skiing and harbour a growing number of resorts. The pick of the bunch, 26km away from town, is **Cerro Castor**, the world's most southerly ski resort, a blustery spot with 22km of downhill runs (ski passes from AR$220 per day; ☎02901 499301, ⓦcerrocastor.com). Minibuses leave frequently from the waterfront at the corner of Juan Fadul and Avenida Maipú.

Beagle Channel

A scenic boat ride along the **BEAGLE CHANNEL** (the passage heading east from Ushuaia) lets you get up close and personal with the region's marine wildlife, including sea lions, penguins, whales, steamer ducks, cormorants and albatross. Excursions, in vessels that range from small fishing boats to large catamarans, generally last three to four hours (around AR$250, plus a AR$7 dock departure tax). The more popular trips take in the sea-lion colony at **Isla de los Lobos** and the sea-bird-nesting site at **Isla de los Pájaros**, and then sail past **Faro Les Eclaireurs**, often incorrectly dubbed "the Lighthouse at the End of the World". Some longer trips take in the penguin colony at **Isla Martillo** (Oct–May only) or head west into the national park or east to *Estancia Harberton*. Boats leave from the Muelle Turístico, where a number of agencies offer tours.

Estancia Harberton

Tierra del Fuego's oldest farmstead, **Estancia Harberton** (mid-Oct to mid-April daily 10am–7pm; AR$60 – includes a two-hour guided tour and access to the museum; ⓦestanciaharberton.com), perches on a secluded peninsula in a sheltered bay overlooking the Beagle Channel. Built in 1886, this working sheep station lies 85km east of Ushuaia along a scenic road. The land was a government donation to the English missionary Reverend Thomas Bridges in recognition of his work with the local indigenous population and for rescuing shipwreck victims from the channels. His descendants now run the farm, offering guided tours, sugar hits in the tearoom, overnight stays in the cottages and free camping on the property (ask permission first).

The **marine wildlife museum** on the property (ⓦacatushun.org) features an amazing assortment of skeletons of Tierra del Fuego's sea mammals and birds. Minibuses for the *estancia* leave Ushuaia from Juan Fadúl and Avenida Maipú several times daily. Some day-long Beagle Channel boat excursions stop here too.

ARRIVAL AND DEPARTURE

By plane Ushuaia Airport is 4km southwest of the centre of town; a taxi costs around AR\$30–40. Passengers on all domestic flights must pay an AR\$28 departure tax.

Destinations Daily flights to Buenos Aires, El Calafate and Trelew, and less frequent services to Puerto Madryn and Río Gallegos.

By bus There's no central bus terminal; instead buses depart from their company offices. Buses Pacheco (San Martín 1267; ☎02901 437073, ⓦbusespacheco.com) runs buses to Punta Arenas (6 weekly; 12hr) via Río Grande (3hr 30min). Bus Sur (San Martín 245; ☎02901 430727, ⓦbus-sur.cl) has services (4 weekly) to Punta Arenas (12hr) and Puerto Natales (15hr). Tecni Austral also has services to Punta Arenas and a single one to Río Gallegos (daily 5am; 12hr); book through Tolkar (Roca 157, ☎02901 431408, ⓦtolkarturismo.com.ar). Lider (Gob. Paz 921, ☎02901 436421, ⓦlidertdf.com.ar) has (6–8 daily) buses to Río Grande. Taqsa (Godoy 41, ☎02901 435453, ⓦtaqsa .com.ar) has a single daily bus (5am) to Río Gallegos. Note that these are the summer season timetables; out of season, services are reduced drastically.

INFORMATION AND TOURS

Tourist information The main tourist office is at Av San Martín 674 (Mon–Fri 9am–10pm; Sat & Sun 9am–8pm; ☎02901 432001, ⓦturismoushuaia.com). Register here if you plan to go anywhere but the main route through Parque Nacional Tierra del Fuego, as many area trails are poorly marked. There are also tourist offices at the Muelle Turístico (daily 9am–6pm; ☎02901 437666) and the airport (no phone: opens to meet incoming flights).

Parque Nacional Tierra del Fuego office Av San Martín 1395 (Mon–Fri 9am–4pm; ☎02901 421315, ⓦparques nacionales.gov.ar). Fishing licences are available from here.

Tour operators Canal Fun & Nature, 9 de Julio 118 (☎02901 437345, ⓦcanalfun.com), and Rumbo Sur, San Martín 350 (☎02901 421139, ⓦrumbosur.com.ar), both offer a range of tours and day-trips, from kayaking to beaver-spotting. All Patagonia, Juan Fadul 60 (☎02901 433622, ⓦallpatagonia.com), runs Antarctic expeditions, scenic flights and nature and sailing excursions. Patagonia Adventure Explorers, at the Muelle Turístico (☎02901 15 465842, ⓦpatagoniaadvent.com.ar), runs Beagle Channel boat trips in a smaller boat that allows you to get closer to the islands to see wildlife. Ushuaia Divers (☎02901 444701, ⓦushuaiadivers.com.ar) operates diving trips in the Beagle Channel to see shipwrecks, sea lions and king crabs.

ACCOMMODATION

In summer, book accommodation in advance and be prepared for high prices.

HOSTELS AND CAMPSITES

For the budget traveller, a number of excellent hostels offer good services and plenty of *buena onda* (good vibes). All those listed below provide kitchens, free breakfast and internet/wi-fi access.

Antarctica Hostel Antartida Argentina 270 ☎02901 435774, ⓦantarcticahostel.com. This sociable hostel has a light-drenched lounge area, spotless loft kitchen, coin-operated laundry machines and a downstairs bar that takes things up a notch at night. The plain upstairs dorms are a bit of a hike from the downstairs bathrooms. Dorms AR\$90, doubles AR\$290

Camping Pista del Andino 3km uphill at Alem 2873 ☎02901 435890. This site has bay views and good facilities, including a kitchen and bike rental. They offer free pick-up from town. Camping/person AR\$30

Cruz del Sur Deloqui 242 ☎02901 434099, ⓦxdelsur .com.ar. Based in a new building along the road from their former location, this hostel is a reliable choice. The dorms are on the small side but are clean, bright and each one has a view. Dorms only AR\$70

Freestyle Gobernador Paz 866 ☎02901 432874, ⓦushuaiafreestyle.com. *Freestyle* is a delightful hostel with spacious four- and six-bed dorms, swish bathrooms, a beanbag-filled TV room, and a relaxing top-floor lounge that has superb views across the bay. The adjoining *Alto Andino* is a considerable step up in comfort (and price). Dorms only AR\$90

★ **La Posta** Perón Sur 864 ☎02901 444650, ⓦlaposta -ush.com.ar. Too bad it's so far from town (20min walk), because this sparkling hostel ticks every other box: two kitchens, free laundry, well-scrubbed dorms, private rooms and self-contained apartments, plus staff who will

1

bend over backwards to help you. Dorms AR$100, doubles AR$320, apartments AR$490

Yakush Piedrabuena 118 ☎02901 435807, ⓦhostel yakush.com.ar. Spacious and modern yet move-right-in-cosy, this central hostel, which overlooks the main drag, has a piano and owners who know their stuff. The dorms are roomy enough to spread out in, and one of the doubles is en suite. Dorms AR$90, doubles AR$280

GUESTHOUSES

Both the guesthouses listed here include free breakfast and internet/wi-fi access.

B&B Nahuel 25 de Mayo 440 ☎02901 423068, ⓦbybnahuel.com.ar. The bright green exterior makes this B&B easy to spot; inside are cosy, rather frilly rooms (one of which has shocking pink walls you'll either love or hate) with either shared or private bathrooms. There's also a small TV lounge. AR$295

★ **Galeazzi-Basily B&B** Gobernador Valedéz 323 ☎02901 423213, ⓦavesdelsur.com.ar. Run by hospitable English- and French-speaking owners, this large family house on a quiet residential street has small, simple rooms, kitchen access, and hot drinks and cakes on offer all day. The self-contained cabañas in the back yard offer more privacy and sleep up to four. Doubles AR$320, cabañas AR$550

EATING

Prices are very high in Ushuaia, with inexpensive options thin on the ground. Seafood is king here, especially the tasty *centolla* (king crab), though *cordero* (lamb), a Patagonian speciality, is also well represented. Many places operate restricted opening hours during the winter months.

Bambu Piedrabueno 276. You don't often see "vegetarian", "inexpensive" and "Ushuaia" in the same sentence, but this Asian takeaway buffet fits the bill (large portions under AR$20). Mon–Fri 11am–5pm.

★ **Bodegón Fueguino** San Martín 895 ☎02901 431972. Park yourself down on a sheepskin-draped wooden bench in this historic wooden house (built in 1896) and order what this restaurant-bar does best – succulent roast lamb, served with a choice of sauces. Good home-brewed beer too. Mains AR$50–130. Tues–Sat 12.30–3pm & 8pm–midnight.

Ramos Generales Av Maipú 749 ☎02901 424317, ⓦramosgeneralesushuaia.com. An atmospheric bar-café-bakery decked out with an eclectic array of knick-knacks including rows of traditional penguin jugs (used for serving wine) behind the bar. As well as good cakes, sandwiches (AR$40–50) and *picadas* (shared platters) there's a strong wine and beer list. Daily 9am–midnight.

La Rueda San Martín, at Rivadavia ☎02901 436540. If you have a bottomless hunger and are attracted to the various slow-roasting animals (lamb, chicken, beef) turning on the spit over a fire pit in the display window, this is your place. An all-you-can-eat *parrilla* including salads, a soft drink and dessert costs AR$95. Daily noon–11pm.

Tante Sara San Martín 175 ☎02901 433710, ⓦtantesara.com. Popular *confitería* and *panadería*, which does a fine line in cakes, sandwiches and baguettes, as well as decent coffee (AR$12–30). There's another branch on the same road at no. 701. Sun–Thurs 8am–8.30pm, Fri & Sat 8am–9/10pm.

El Turco San Martín 1410 ☎02901 424711. This low-key restaurant serves hearty portions of pizza, pasta, chicken and steak, as well as *empanadas*. The food is nothing to write home about, but prices are reasonable. Mains AR$30–70. Mon–Sat noon–3pm & 8pm–midnight.

Volver Av Maipú 37 ☎02901 444444, ⓦvolverushuaia .com.ar. The usual seafood menu at the usual prices (mains from around AR$70), but the portions are generous and well prepared. *Volver* is an Ushuaia original and the place is dripping with character and bric-a-brac, from faded newspaper cuttings to old tango shoes to a lifesize statue of Che. Tues–Sun noon–3pm & 7.30pm–midnight.

DRINKING AND NIGHTLIFE

Dublin 9 de Julio 168 ☎02901 430744, ⓦdublinushuaia .com. This green-walled, red-roofed pub is a good place for a draught beer (around AR$25), with a buzzing atmosphere and occasional live music. Apart from the Guinness posters, however, there isn't much in the way of Hibernian trappings. Daily 8pm–3/4am.

★ **Kuar** Perito Moreno 2232 ☎02901 437396, ⓦkuar .com.ar. Set in an attractive stone-and-timber building right on the seafront, on the road to Río Grande, this bar-restaurant has stupendous views and a blazing fire, as well as fish and pasta dishes and its own delicious home-brewed pale ale, amber ale and dark porter (each around AR$25). Daily 3pm–4am.

★ TREAT YOURSELF

Kalma Restó Antartida Argentina 57 ☎02901 425786, ⓦkalmaresto.com.ar. It used to be that the best meal in Ushuaia was a fussy presentation in one of the huge restaurants overlooking the harbour. No more, now that *Kalma Restó* has appeared on the scene. The chef himself comes out to explain the dishes, which are often adorned with edible flowers and delicate sauces. Mains (AR$75–145) include lamb cooked three ways, a "Fuegian" paella, and centolla and roasted pumpkin ravioli. Well worth a splurge. Reservations recommended. Mon–Fri 12.30–3pm & 7–11.30pm, Sat 7–11.30pm.

DIRECTORY

Banks and exchange There are numerous ATMs in the city centre. Thaler (Av San Martín 299) exchanges money.
Car rental Avis (☎02901 433323, ⓦavis.com) and Hertz (☎02901 432429, ⓦhetz.com) both have offices at the airport.
Post office Gob. Godoy 118.
Spanish school Finis Terrae Spanish School, Rosas 475 (☎02901 433871).

PARQUE NACIONAL TIERRA DEL FUEGO

Wet and wild **PARQUE NACIONAL TIERRA DEL FUEGO**, 12km west of Ushuaia, stretches from the Beagle Channel in the south to the border with Chile in the west. Encompassing 630 square kilometres of mountains, waterfalls, glaciers, lakes, rivers, valleys, sub-Antarctic forest and peat bog, most of the park is closed to the public, with less than 30km of accessible trails. With a couple of days up your sleeve, you could tackle all the short treks in the park. The most popular is the **Costera Trail** (11km return; 3hr 30min), which follows the shoreline through coastal forest of deciduous beech trees, affording spectacular views of the Beagle Channel, passing grass-covered mounds that were former campsites of the indigenous Yámana and offering birdwatchers prime opportunities for spotting Magellanic woodpeckers, cormorants, gulls and oystercatchers.

For the park's best views, trudge to the top of 970m-high **Cerro Guanaco Trail** (8km return; 8hr). Another popular trail, **Hito XXIV Trail** (5km return; 3hr), is a level path tracing the shores of Lago Roca and ending at a small obelisk that marks the border with Chile (it is illegal to continue beyond here). Guanacos, Patagonian grey foxes, Fuegian foxes, Southern river otters and some ninety bird species are among the park's fauna; introduced Canadian beavers and European rabbits also run amok, wreaking environmental havoc.

The park is open daily 8am–8pm (opening hours are slightly shorter during the winter) and the entry fee is AR$85; if you're planning to visit again the next

PARQUE NACIONAL TIERRA DEL FUEGO

day, let the park staff know, and you won't have to pay twice.

ARRIVAL AND TOURS

By bus Regular buses (20–30min) shuttle throughout the day from the corner of Maipú and Fadul in Ushuaia, not far from the Muelle Turístico, to various points in the park. Services are reduced, and sometimes halted, during the colder months.

By taxi A taxi to the park from the centre of Ushuaia costs around AR$220.

By train El Tren del Fin del Mundo (2–3 departures daily to the park, 1–2 from the park; 40min each way; AR$155 round trip; ticket office at the Muelle Turístico; ☎02901 431600, ⌨trendelfindelmundo.com.ar) departs from its main station, 8km west of Ushuaia, arriving at the park station, 2km from the main gate. Used to transport wood in the days of the penal colony, it's now little more than a tourist toy train.

Tour operators Most travel agencies in Ushuaia offer tours of the park (from AR$200, plus entrance fee).

ACCOMMODATION

There are four rudimentary free campsites plus one serviced campground at Lago Roca. The latter (☎02901 433313, ⌨confiterialagoroca.com.ar) is the only one with any facilities (including hot showers, a café and a shop). It also has a *refugio* with dorm beds and a couple of self-contained cabins. Camping/person AR$45, dorms AR$50, cabañas AR$80

RÍO GRANDE

Trout fishing aside, the only reason to be in dreary, gusty **RÍO GRANDE** is to break the trip between Ushuaia, 230km southwest, and Patagonia. Built on its namesake river, Río Grande consists of grid after grid of flat urban sprawl, its colourful houses and the "promenade of lovers" along the main street the city's only aesthetic saving grace. Sheep and oil are the economic staples, while the **Monumento a la Trucha** – a giant trout statue on the RN3 – explains why high-rolling anglers are drawn to the nearby rivers.

WHAT TO SEE AND DO

The **Museo Municipal Virginia Choquintel**, at Alberdi 555 (Mon–Fri 9am–5pm, Sat 3–7pm; free; ☎02964 430647), has exhibits on the region's indigenous and pioneering history. A twenty-minute ride

out of town is the more interesting museum at the **Misión Salesiana**, at RN3 Km2980 (Mon–Sat 9.30am–2.30pm & 3–7pm, Sun 3–7pm; AR$5; ☎02964 430667), a mission founded in 1899 to catechize the Selk'nam people. The preserved chapel is a charming national historic monument and other buildings house an excellent museum of history, anthropology and natural science, detailing the decline of the Indians in the face of massacres and disease. From town, take bus line "D" from any of the bus stops along San Martín.

ARRIVAL AND DEPARTURE

By plane Río Grande Airport (☎02964 431340) is 5km west of town; a taxi costs around AR$30. Aerolineas Argentina (⌨aerolineas.com.ar) and LADE (⌨lade.com .ar) have irregular flights from here.

By bus Services arrive and depart from the terminal on Finocchio, at Obligado, four blocks from the main avenue, San Martín.

Destinations Punta Arenas in Chile (1–2 daily; 9hr); Río Gallegos (1–2 daily; 10hr); and Ushuaia (every 30min–1hr; 3hr 30min).

INFORMATION

Tourist information The tourist office is on Plaza Almirante Brown, at Rosales 350 (Dec–March Mon–Fri 9am–8pm, Sat & Sun 2–9pm; April–Nov Mon–Fri 9am–5pm; ☎02964 431324, ⌨riogrande.gov.ar).

Fishing licences For fishing licences and information, visit the Asociación Argentina de Pesca con Mosca at Montilla 1040 (☎02964 421268).

ACCOMMODATION

Most hotels are fishing for wealthy anglers, leaving budget travellers very low on options. If you want to brave the relentless wind, try the wooded riverside campsite about ten blocks from downtown on O'Higgins, at Montilla (☎02964 420536; camping/person AR$20).

Hospedaje Noal Obligado 557 ☎02964 427516. Offering great value, this wood-panelled guesthouse has plain, spotless rooms with comfortable beds and TV; some have private bathrooms. AR$150

EATING AND DRINKING

Epa!!! Bar-Café Rosales 445 ☎02964 425334. With leather booths dolled up in 1950s-style shades of purple and yellow, this diner does juices, cocktails, pizzas and, during the day, an inexpensive set menu. Mains from around AR$40. Sun 10am–midnight, Mon–Thurs 9am–3am, Fri & Sat 9am–4/5am.

SALT CONES, SALAR DE UYUNI

Bolivia

HIGHLIGHTS

① Death Road Cycling the spectacular road between La Paz and Coroico. **See p.169**

② Isla del Sol The spiritual centre of the Andean world. **See p.179**

③ Cerro Rico An unforgettable glimpse of the miners' life. **See p.190**

④ Salar de Uyuni The world's largest salt flat. See p.195

⑤ Samaipata Laidback town surrounded by lush cloudforest. **See p.213**

⑥ Parque Nacional Madidi This pristine rainforest protects remarkable diversity. **See p.218**

HIGHLIGHTS ARE MARKED ON THE MAP ON PP.156–157

ROUGH COSTS

Daily budget Basic US$15, with the occasional treat US$28

Drink Small beer US$2

Food Fixed three-course lunch menu US$2

Hostel/budget hotel US$4–6/US$8–10

Travel Bus: La Paz–Copacabana (155km) US$3

FACT FILE

Population 10.3 million

Language Spanish (also more than thirty indigenous languages)

Currency Boliviano, aka Peso (B$)

Capital Sucre is the official capital; La Paz is the de facto capital

International phone code ☎591

Time zone GMT -4hr

2

Introduction

Surrounded by Brazil, Paraguay, Argentina, Chile and Peru, Bolivia lies at the heart of South America. Stretching from the majestic icebound peaks and bleak high-altitude deserts of the Andes to the exuberant rainforests and vast savannas of the Amazon basin, it embraces an astonishing range of landscapes and climates, and encompasses everything outsiders find most exotic and mysterious about the continent.

Three centuries of Spanish colonial rule have certainly left their mark, most obviously in some of the finest colonial architecture on the continent. Yet the European influence is essentially a thin veneer overlying indigenous cultural traditions that stretch back long before the Conquest: while Spanish is the language of business and government, more than thirty indigenous languages are still spoken.

Bolivia is dominated by the mighty **Andes**, which march through the west of the country along two parallel chains. In the north and east, they give way to the tropical rainforests and grasslands of the **Amazon and eastern lowlands**, in the southeast to the dry thornbrush and scrub of the **Chaco**. Yet, despite its extraordinary biodiversity and myriad attractions, Bolivia remains one of South America's least-visited countries.

Most visitors spend a few days in the fascinating city of **La Paz**, which combines a dizzying high-altitude setting with an intermingling of traditional indigenous and modern urban cultures. Close by is the magical **Lake Titicaca**, and the towns of **Coroico** and **Sorata** which serve as a good base for trekking, climbing or mountain biking in the **Cordillera Real**, a range of high Andean peaks that, plunge precipitously down into the Amazon basin through the dramatic, deep valleys of the **Yungas**. The best base for visiting the Bolivian Amazon further north is **Rurrenabaque**, the jumping-off point for exploring the diversity of flora and fauna in the **Madidi National Park**.

South of La Paz, the southern **Altiplano** – the bleak, high plateau that stretches between the Andes – has historically been home to most of Bolivia's population. In **Potosí** you can experience underground life in the mines of **Cerro Rico**, while to the southwest, Uyuni is the gateway to the astonishing landscape of the **Salar de Uyuni** and the **Reserva de Fauna Andina Eduardo Avaroa**. Also well worth visiting are the towns of **Sucre**, with its fine colonial architecture, **Samaipata**, which has designs on Rurrenabaque's crown as the country's best ecotourism base, and **Santa Cruz**, a brash, modern and lively tropical metropolis – and a good base for exploring the rainforests of the **Parque Nacional Amboró** and the immaculately restored Jesuit missions of **Chiquitos**.

WHEN TO VISIT

Climate varies much more as a result of altitude and topography than it does between different seasons.

Winter (May–Oct) is the **dry season**, and in many ways the best time to visit Bolivia, with sunny, trek-friendly highland days and slightly lower temperatures in the generally hot and humid **lowlands**. While highland temperatures hover in the mid-teens most of the year (albeit with chilly winter nights), the summer **rainy season** (December into March and sometimes April) can see lowland temperatures reach 31°C. Rain affects the condition of roads throughout the country, especially in the Amazon, where river transport takes over from often impassable overland routes. The parched Altiplano and mountainsides nevertheless briefly transform into lush grassland, as wild flowers proliferate and the earth comes to life.

CHRONOLOGY

1000 BC Founding of Tiwanaku on the shores of Lake Titicaca, centre of a colonial empire comprising much of modern Bolivia, southern Peru, northeast Argentina and northern Chile.

c.1000 AD Tiwanaku dramatically collapses, most likely as a result of a prolonged drought.

Eleventh to fifteenth centuries The Aymara take control of the Altiplano, maintaining a more localized culture and religion.

Mid-fifteenth century The Aymara are incorporated into the Inca Empire, albeit with a limited degree of autonomy.

1532 Francisco Pizarro leads his Spanish conquistadors to a swift and unlikely defeat of the Inca army in Cajamarca (Bajo), Peru.

1538 Pizarro sends Spanish troops south to aid the Aymaran Colla as they battle both the remnants of an Inca rebellion and their Aymara rivals the Lupaca. Spanish control of the territory known as Alto Peru is established.

1545 The continent's richest deposit of silver, Cerro Rico, is discovered, giving birth to the mining city of Potosí.

1691 San Javier is founded as the first of the Chiquitos Jesuit missions.

1767 The Spanish crown expels the Jesuit order from the Americas.

1780–82 The last major indigenous uprising, the Great Rebellion, is led by a combined Inca-Aymara army of Túpact Amaru and pac Katari.

1809 La Paz becomes the first capital in the Americas to declare independence from Spain.

1824 The last Spanish army is destroyed at the battle of Ayacucho in (Bajo) Peru.

1825 The newly liberated Alto Peru rejects a union with either (Bajo) Peru or Argentina, and adopts a declaration of independence. Bolivia is born.

1879 Chile begins the War of the Pacific by occupying the entire Bolivian coastline and invading Peru.

1899 The Federal Revolution consolidates power of the new tin-mining barons and creates a new administrative capital in La Paz.

1904 Bolivia finally cedes its coastline to Chile, in addition to losing the Acre to Brazil.

1932–35 The Chaco War with Paraguay ends in stalemate and huge loss of life.

1952 The National Revolution sees armed civilians defeat the army in La Paz and the ascension to power of the MNR (Revolutionary Nationalist Movement).

1964 A resurgent army led by General René Barrientos seizes power, beginning eighteen years of military dictatorship.

1967 Che Guevara is captured and executed in the hamlet of La Higuera.

1970s General Hugo Banzer heads a brutal military regime, coinciding with an unprecedented period of economic growth.

1980–81 The most brutal and corrupt regime in modern Bolivian history is led by General Luis García Meza.

1985 Bolivia plunges into a recession as the bottom falls out of the tin market, and the economic vacuum is filled by the production and export of cocaine.

Late 1990s US-backed coca eradication policies provoke widespread resistance, led by indigenous activist Evo Morales.

2005 Evo Morales is elected as Bolivia's first indigenous president with an absolute majority and a programme of nationalization and agrarian reform.

2008 Morales suspends US Drug Enforcement programme, accusing agents of espionage. In retaliation, the US adds Bolivia to its drugs blacklist and suspends trade preferences.

2009 New constitution agreed, giving greater rights to indigenous people. Morales is elected for a second term.

2011 Mass demonstrations lead to a suspension of government plans to build a Brazil-funded highway through the TIPNIS reserve.

2012 The first census for eleven years finds a population increase of over two million.

ARRIVAL AND DEPARTURE

Bolivia isn't the easiest country to fly to. The only direct services are from Madrid in Europe, Miami in the US and from neighbouring South American countries, the most frequent connections being from São Paulo in Brazil, Buenos Aires in Argentina and Lima in Peru. In Bolivia itself the principal international **airports** are: El Alto in La Paz (see p.170) and Viru Viru in Santa Cruz (see p.210); the former boasts the highest airport location in the world. Once you're in Bolivia, **flying** is actually a relatively cheap and convenient way to get around, especially in the rainy season when many roads are impassable. Bolivia has land borders with Argentina, Brazil, Chile, Peru and Paraguay; full details of the main border crossings are given in accounts of relevant departure points.

FROM ARGENTINA

The principal **border crossing** is from La Quiaca in Argentina to Villazón in the southern Altiplano (see box, p.196), with regular bus and train connections to the desert town of Tupiza. There's also a crossing between Pocitos in Argentina and Yacuiba in the Chaco (see p.216), from where it's possible to travel by bus or train to Santa Cruz.

2

BOLIVIA

HIGHLIGHTS

1 Death Road
2 Isla del Sol
3 Cerro Rico
4 Salar de Uyuni
5 Samaipata
6 Parque Nacional Madidi

0 _____ 200
kilometres

N

BRAZIL

Río Guaporé

PARQUE NACIONAL
NOEL KEMPFF MERCADO

SANTA CRUZ

Concepción

Magdalena

Río Blanco

Asención de
Guarayos

Río San Pablo

Trinidad

Río Ichilo

Guayaramerín

Guajará-Mirim

Río Mamoré

San
Ignacio

PARQUE NACIONAL
TERRITORIO INDÍGENA
ISIBORO-SÉCURE

Riberalta

BENI

Santa Ana
del Yacuma

RESERVA DE LA
BIOSFERA DEL BENI

Río Madre de Dios

Río Beni

San Borja

Yucumo

San
Borja

THE
YUNGAS

Caranavi

Coroico
Coripata

Rurrenabaque

Huayna Potosí
(6088m)

PANDO

Brasiléia

Cobija

LLANOS DE MOXOS

PARQUE
NACIONAL
MADIDI

6

Pelechuco

Mapiri
Guanay

Sorata

Achacachi

CORDILLERA
APOLOBAMBA

PERU

Lake
Titicaca

Isla del Sol

2

Copacabana

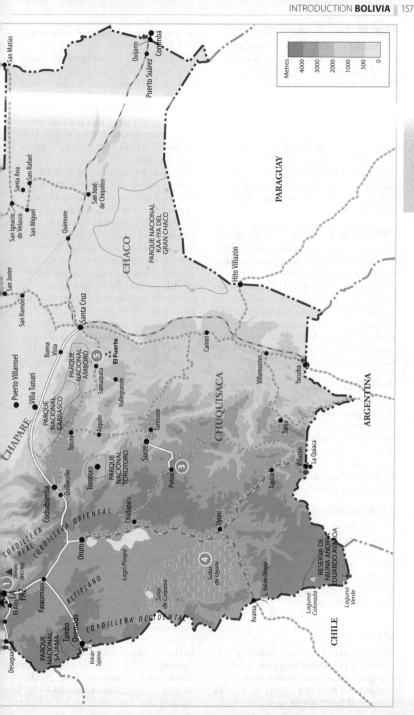

2

FROM BRAZIL

The busiest crossing is the **rail border** at Quijarro (see p.215), near the Brazilian city of Corumbá, where the Bolivian Pantanal meets its more famous Brazilian counterpart. From Quijarro, it's a full day's train journey to Santa Cruz. There are also a couple of borders in **Amazonia**, from Guajará-Mirim (transit point Porto Velho) by boat across the Rio Mamoré to Guayaramerín, from where there are regular onward flights; and from Brasiléia (transit point Rio Branco) to Cobija, the capital of Pando province (see p.221).

FROM CHILE

There are two **trans-Andean routes** which cross from Chile, the most popular being the road up from Arica on the coast to Tambo Quemado (see p.187), and on to La Paz. A more adventurous option is the remote border crossing of **Laguna Verde** (see p.196), at the southern edge of Reserva Eduardo Avaroa, accessible via organized tours from the Chilean town of San Pedro de Atacama.

FROM PERU

The most widely used land border of all is the **Yunguyo-Kasani crossing** (see p.178) at the southern tip of Lake Titicaca near Copacabana, easily accessible from Puno in southern Peru. Less busy but just as easy to get to from Puno is the crossing at **Desaguadero** (see p.175), with regular onward transport to La Paz.

FROM PARAGUAY

For the adventurous only, the **trans-Chaco** border between Bolivia and Paraguay (see p.216) is navigable only in the dry season, during which the route – all the way from Asunción to Santa Cruz – is served by an endurance-testing two- to three-day bus journey.

VISAS

Many visitors to Bolivia – including citizens of the **United Kingdom**, most European countries, **Canada**, **New Zealand** and **Australia** – don't need a visa. Citizens of **South Africa** need a visa but can purchase one on arrival for about US$50 per person.

Citizens of the **United States** can apply for a tourist visa on arrival, at a cost of US$135 per person paid in cash; they're valid for five years and allow visitors to enter Bolivia three times a year, with a maximum of ninety days per year spent in the country. Check ⓦtravel.state.gov for further details of entry requirements for US citizens.

For other nationalities, the situation changes periodically, so always **check** with your local embassy or consulate a month or two before travelling. On arrival, you'll be issued with a **tourist card** (*tarjeta de turismo*) valid for thirty or ninety days, depending on your nationality. Before entry, check the number of days you're allowed to stay and make sure the border officials give you the stamp with the maximum number of days your nationality allows you; if they give you less than the maximum, you can request it on the spot (though there's no guarantee you'll get it) or go to the immigration office in La Paz or the nearest city to your border crossing and receive another stamp. The annual limit, at the time of writing, was restricted to ninety days, and, officially at least, you cannot just cross the border and get another ninety-day card.

GETTING AROUND

Bolivia's topography, size and lack of basic infrastructure mean that getting around is often a challenge, especially in the rainy season. However, buses are very cheap and numerous, and flying within the country is affordable.

BY PLANE

La Paz, Santa Cruz, Sucre and Cochabamba are all connected by **daily flights** (B$550–900), and there are also frequent services to Tarija, Trinidad, Rurrenabaque and a number of remote towns in the Amazon and the eastern lowlands. The principal carriers are Amazonas (ⓦamazonas.com), Aerocon (ⓦaerocon.bo), state-run Boliviana de Aviacion or BoA (ⓦboa.bo) and military-run Transportes Aereo Militar or

TAM (ⓦtam.bo). Busier routes should be booked at least several days in advance. Flights are often cancelled or delayed, especially in the Amazon, where the weather can cause disruption.

BY TRAIN

The sole Andean operator, FCA (Empresa Ferroviaria Andina; ⓦfca.com.bo), runs two passenger lines – *Expreso del Sur* and *Wara Wara del Sur* – from Oruro south across the Altiplano via Uyuni and Tupiza to Villazón on the Argentine border. A separate company, Ferroviaria Oriental (ⓦferroviariaoriental.com), runs two lines in the lowlands: one from Santa Cruz east to the Brazilian border at Quijarro (a service known as the "death train" – a reference to its speed and not its safety record); the other from Santa Cruz south to Yacuiba in the Chaco, on the Argentine border.

BY BUS

Bolivia's **buses** are run by a variety of private companies and ply all the main routes in the country. Road conditions have improved greatly in recent years, but journey times are still unpredictable, and you should always be prepared for major delays, especially in the rainy season. When travelling in the highlands, always bring warm clothing and a blanket or sleeping bag, as journeys can get bitterly cold.

BY BOAT

Although Bolivia is a landlocked country, there are still several regions – particularly Lake Titicaca and the Amazon – where travelling by water is the best way of getting around. There are two main forms of **river transport** in the Bolivian Amazon: dugout canoes, powered by outboard motors, are used to visit protected areas such as the Parque Nacional Madidi; alternatively, more economic but less comfortable cargo boats ply the Río Mamoré, between Trinidad and Guayaramerín on the Brazilian frontier, and the Río Ichilo, between Trinidad and Puerto Villaroel in the Chapare.

BY CAR

Renting a car is an option, though it's often easier and not much more expensive to hire a taxi or *camioneta* to drive you around for a day or longer.

Outside towns, most roads are unpaved and in very poor condition, so **four-wheel drive** (4WD) is essential. Petrol stations are scarce and breakdown services even more so. Generally, you'll pay a flat fee of B$240–400 per day, plus about B$1.75–2.50 extra for each kilometre you drive; 4WDs cost about double. A recommended company with offices at El Alto airport and Santa Cruz (on the second ring road) is Barbol Rent a Car (ⓣ02 2820675, ⓦbarbolsrl.com), while Economica (ⓣ02 2441906, ⓦeconomicacarrental.com) has offices in central La Paz and in Cochabamba. You'll need to be over 25, and to leave a major credit card or large cash deposit as security; most rental companies will include insurance cover with the hire price but it is worth checking.

ACCOMMODATION

While **accommodation** in Bolivia is generally good value, the standard is not particularly high, especially in smaller towns. Room rates vary according to season, rising during the high tourist season (May to September) and on weekends in popular resort towns, and doubling or tripling during major fiestas.

The prices quoted in the chapter are for the cheapest double in high season, and this will often mean you're sharing a bathroom – you can usually get one in a clean, simple hotel for around B$90–130. You will often find, however, that prices are quoted "per person" (*por persona*), and a room for two will be charged at simply twice the price that an individual would pay – no economies of scale here. In some towns there are backpacker-conscious places (not always hostels) that offer low-cost **dorm beds**. Even in the coldest highland cities, heating is usually non-existent; in the lowlands, heat, rather than cold, is often a problem, though all but the cheapest rooms are equipped with a fan. Most places usually have **hot water**, although it's generally intermittent and often courtesy of individual electric heaters that you'll find attached to the

2

tops of showers; don't touch the apparatus while the water is running, as you might get an electric shock. Remember, the less water, the warmer it will be – it requires a delicate balance to get right.

With few designated campsites and an abundance of inexpensive accommodation, few travellers **camp** in Bolivia unless exploring the country's wilderness areas. Beyond the cities and towns, you can camp almost everywhere, usually for free; make sure you ask for permission from the nearest house first; local villages may ask for a small fee of a few bolivianos. In some **national parks** you'll also find shelters where you can stay for a minimal charge.

FOOD AND DRINK

The style of eating and drinking varies considerably between Bolivia's three main geographical regions – the Altiplano, the highland valleys and the tropical lowlands – differences that reflect the produce commonly available in each region and the different cultural traditions of their inhabitants. Each region has *comidas típicas* (traditional dishes). Generally, be wary of street food and take recommendations before trying the real locals' restaurants – food hygiene can be an issue.

Restaurants almost all offer enormously filling good-value set lunches, or *almuerzos*, usually costing between B$12 and B$20, while a smaller number offer a set dinner, or *cena*, in the evening and also have a range of *à la carte* main dishes (*platos extras*), rarely costing more than B$15–30. For B$35–50 you should expect a substantial meal in more upmarket restaurants, while about B$45–65 will buy you most dishes even in the best restaurants in La Paz or Santa Cruz.

FOOD

While Altiplano cuisine is dominated by the humble **potato**, often served in hearty soups (llama and mutton are also common), the valley regions cook with **corn**, often used as the basis for thick soups known as *laguas,* or boiled on the cob and served with fresh white cheese – a classic combination known as *choclo con queso*. Meat and chicken are often cooked in spicy sauces known as *picantes*: a valley mainstay is *pique a lo macho*, a massive plate of chopped beef and sausage fried together with potatoes, onions, tomatoes and chillies. In the tropical lowlands, **plantains** and **yucca** take the place of potatoes; beef is also plentiful – the lowlands are cattle-ranching regions, so beef is of good quality and relatively cheap.

Although Bolivia is obviously not the place to come for seafood, fish features regularly on menus, especially the succulent *trucha* (trout) and *pejerrey* (kingfish) around Lake Titicaca, and the juicy white river fish known as *surubí* and *pucú* in the lowlands. Ordinary restaurants rarely offer much in the way of **vegetarian food**, although you can almost always find eggs and potatoes of some description (usually fried), as well as the ubiquitous potato soup, often cooked without meat. The situation changes a great deal in cities and in popular travellers' haunts, where a cosmopolitan selection of vegetarian dishes, salads and pancakes is widely available, and there's a growing number of wholly vegetarian restaurants.

The most popular snack throughout Bolivia is the **salteña**, a pasty filled with a spicy, juicy stew of meat or chicken with chopped vegetables, olives and hard-boiled egg. It's usually eaten in the mid-morning accompanied by a cold drink and a little chilli sauce if desired.

DRINK

Mineral water is fairly widely available in large plastic bottles – a good thing, as it's best not to drink tap water. The delicious variety of tropical fruits grown in Bolivia is available as juices from market stalls throughout the country, and freshly squeezed orange and grapefruit **juice** is also sold on the streets from handcarts for about B$3 a glass. **Tea and coffee** are available almost everywhere, as well as *mates*, or herbal teas – *mate de coca* is the best known and a good remedy for altitude sickness, but many others are usually available.

Locally produced alcoholic drinks are widely available in Bolivia and drinking is a serious pastime. **Beer** is available almost everywhere – Paceña (half-litre B$8–14), produced in La Paz, is the most popular and widely available, followed by Huari, made by the same company but with a slightly saltier taste. Although not widely consumed, Bolivia also produces a growing variety of exceptional high-altitude – and highly underrated – **wines** (*vinos*), mostly from the Tarija Valley; the best labels are Campos de Solana, Concepción and Kohlberg. A glass of red wine (*vino tinto*) will cost B$8–12. While production is still a fraction of what neighbouring Argentina and Chile achieve, Bolivia's wines deserve – and may yet attract – an equally high profile.

One of the problems the industry has faced is that much cultivation is dedicated to muscat grapes, which, rather than being used for fine **wines**, are used to a produce a white grape brandy called *singani*, the beverage most Bolivians turn to when they really want to get drunk. It's usually mixed with Sprite or 7 Up, which creates a fast-acting combination known as *chuflay*. Finally, no visit to the Cochabamba is complete without a taste of *chicha cochabambina*, a thick, mildly alcoholic yeasty-flavoured beer made of fermented maize and considered sacred by the Incas.

CULTURE AND ETIQUETTE

There isn't really such a thing as an all-encompassing Bolivian culture, as traditions vary widely according to different regions and climates, as well as according to social class and ethnic background. There are around forty official **ethnic groups** in the country, while a distinction is often made between the "camba" (people from the lowlands) and "colla" (those from the highlands). In recent years, tension between the two regions has heightened as a result of sweeping reform on land distribution and nationalization introduced by President Morales.

Spanish is the official language in Bolivia, and it's a great place to brush up on your language skills as Bolivians speak slowly and clearly compared with their Chilean or Argentine neighbours. **Indigenous languages** including Aymara, Quechua and Gurani are also widely spoken. **Catholicism** is the predominant religion though you may find that some festivals and celebrations involve a mishmash of Catholic and native beliefs with offerings made to both the Virgin Mary and Pachamama (mother earth).

Generally speaking, Bolivians are friendly folk and will go out of their way to help you. It is polite and common practice to pepper any requests with "por favor" and "gracias", and greet people with "buenos días" or "buenas tardes" before starting a conversation. There is little concept of personal space in Bolivia and people will typically stand very close when speaking to you.

Chewing **coca leaf** is seen as an integral part of daily life for many Bolivians. The controversial leaf is commonly chewed into a round ball, and kept in the side of the cheek, or used to make herbal tea. It is said to combat tiredness and altitude sickness, and to quell hunger, and is also used in ritual ceremonies.

When eating out at a restaurant, or taking part in a guided tour, a ten percent **tip** is appreciated, and increasingly expected. Many museums and historical landmarks do charge higher fees to foreigners and many tourists find this frustrating. If you are not sure of what you are being asked to pay, it is best to ask around to establish the going rate before assuming you are being ripped off. Haggling is not commonly practised.

SPORTS AND OUTDOOR ACTIVITIES

Dominated by the dramatic high mountain scenery of the Andes, Bolivia is ideal for **trekking**, **mountain biking** and **climbing**; whether you want to stroll for half a day, take a hardcore hike for two weeks over high passes down into remote Amazonian valleys, or climb one of the hundred peaks over 5000m, it's all possible. The best season for outdoor activity is between May and September, while the most pleasant and reliable weather is between June and August.

2

The easiest way to go trekking or climbing is with a tour operator. There are dozens of these in La Paz and in several other cities (see box below). Prices depend on group sizes.

The activity rated by many travellers as one of the highlights of South America is a bike ride down the road from La Paz to Coroico in the Yungas, a thrilling 3500m descent along what was once dubbed the **world's most dangerous road**. There are plenty of tour companies – beware unscrupulous operators – and it is easy to organize as a day-trip from La Paz. You don't need any previous experience, but bear in mind that several bikers have been killed on this route in the past, and though the most dangerous stretch was bypassed in 2007, some

vehicles still use it. Attempting the trip in the rainy season (Nov–March) is not recommended.

COMMUNICATIONS

Airmail (*por avión*) to Europe and North America tends to take between one and two weeks to arrive; mail to the rest of the world outside the Americas and Europe takes longer. Letters cost about B$10–15 to Europe, the US, Canada, Australia or New Zealand. For a small extra charge, you can send letters certified (*certificado*), but even then don't send anything you can't afford to lose.

There are **ENTEL** phone centres in all cities and most towns, where you can make local, national and international

---

ORGANIZED TOURS

Tours to the salt flats, the jungle and Bolivia's national parks are offered by most operators and agencies across the country. Some agencies are less reputable and responsible than others, and it is always worth shopping around before booking a tour.

TOUR OPERATORS

Amboró Tours (based in Santa Cruz but can organize tours by phone or email) C Libertad 417 2nd Floor, Santa Cruz ☎ 03 3390600, ⬢ amborotours.com. Specializes in trips to Amazonian national parks.

America Tours Ground-floor office 9, Edificio Avenida, Av 16 de Julio 1490, La Paz ☎ 02 2374204, ⬢ america -ecotours.com. Efficient and reliable, they're the main booking agent for *Chalalán Ecolodge* in Parque Nacional Madidi, and a good resource for booking internal flights.

Andean Epics Upstairs at C Linares 940 near *Café Illampu* ☎ 71276685, ⬢ andeanepics.com. Excellent option for mountain biking and trekking in the Sorata region. Their April–Dec five-day bike, jeep and canoe trips from Sorata to Rurrenabaque are recommended (around B$2700/person). Travellers already in Sorata can join up with the groups there.

Bolivian Journeys Sagárnaga 363, La Paz ⬢ bolivian journeys.org. Highly regarded mountaineering specialists, offering professionally equipped expeditions into the Cordillera Real.

Crillon Tours Av Camacho 1223, La Paz ☎ 02 2337533, ⬢ titicaca.com. Offer a variety of tours throughout Bolivia, including pricey hydrofoil cruises on Lake Titicaca and tours of Tiwanaku.

Fremen Av 20 de Octubre 2396, Edificio María Haydee, La Paz ☎ 02 2421258, ⬢ andes-amazonia.com. A highly respected agency offering a wide range of tailor-made

tours throughout Bolivia, including river trips on the Río Mamoré on their own floating hotel.

Kanoo Tours C Illampu 832, Zona Rosario, La Paz ☎ 02 2460003, ⬢ kanootours.com. Englishman Phil is fast becoming La Paz's leading source of information for the budget traveller, with quality tours and bookings arranged across the country. Also has branches in the *Loki Hostel*, the *Adventure Brew Hostel*.

La Paz On Foot Prolongación Posnanski 400, in Miraflores near the stadium ☎ 02 2248350, ☎ 71543918, ⬢ lapazonfoot.com. Offers an interesting range of trips in the immediate vicinity of La Paz, not least the "Urban Trek", but also head further afield with an ethos of responsible, rural community-supporting travel.

Ruta Verde Tours C 21 de Mayo 318, Santa Cruz ☎ 03 3396470, ⬢ rutaverdebolivia.com. Pricey but excellent Dutch/Bolivian-run tour operator offering trips to the salt flats and jungle, with sustainability as a priority.

Topas Travel C Carlos Bravo 299, in Hotel El Consulado ☎ 02 2111082, ⬢ topas.bo. A wide-ranging, well-respected operator.

Travel Tracks Sagárnaga 366 & 213 ☎ 02 2316934, ⬢ travel-tracks.com. Run by affable Dutch woman Aly Bakker and specializing in climbing, trekking and Uyuni tours.

Zig Zag C Illampu 867 ☎ 02 2457814, ⬢ zigzagbolivia .com. Climbing and trekking specialists, including the Yunga Cruz trail.

calls. While there are a few coin-operated **telephone booths** in the street, most use **prepaid cards**. These are widely available at street stalls, which often have their own phones for public use or are sited next to booths, and come in denominations of 10, 20 and 50 bolivianos. You might also consider buying a cheap mobile phone handset, or bringing one with you, and buying a Bolivian pay-as-you-go SIM. If you're dialling long-distance within Bolivia, you'll need the respective **area code**, which for La Paz, Oruro and Potosí is ☎02; for Beni, Pando and Santa Cruz ☎03; and for Cochabamba, Chuquisaca and Tarija ☎04. Mobile phone numbers are eight digits wherever you are.

Calling internationally, the cheapest option is via an internet phone or Skype service. **Internet cafés** themselves are ubiquitous in all but the most remote corners of Bolivia, though connections are often slow. Expect to pay about B$3–6 per hour. An increasing number of towns are **wi-fi**-enabled, and lodgings often offer it free, while the Alexander Coffee café chain always has a strong signal. Some towns, including Uyuni, still do not have wi-fi at all.

CRIME AND SAFETY

In recent years, Bolivia's crime levels have risen partly in response to the country's worsening economic situation. If you apply **common-sense precautions**, however, there's no need to be paranoid: the vast majority of crime against tourists is opportunistic theft, and **violence is rare**. An increasingly common method of theft is through the use of **fake police officers** and fake taxi drivers. Fake policemen may approach you on the street and ask to search you or see your documents (before making off with them) or may ask you to go with them in a taxi to the "police station". Be aware that real policemen would never do this, so on no account hand over your documents or valuables and never accompany a stranger in a taxi.

Another trick is for **fake taxi drivers** or even minibus drivers to pick up unsuspecting passengers before either stopping in a deserted part of town where

they and/or their associates rob the victims, or, in even worse scenarios, kidnap and seriously assault the victims to force them to reveal their PINs. Always check the ID of any taxi you take and only ever use official ones; better still, whenever possible ask your hotel to order one for you.

Another common means of theft starts with you being spat on or having some substance spilt on you; a "helpful passer-by" will stop you, point out the offending substance and attempt to clean it off you (while their partner in crime quickly relieves you of your valuables). If this happens to you, don't stop and walk on as quickly as possible before cleaning yourself up.

Political upheaval is a regular feature of everyday life in Bolivia. Keep an eye on the news and ask around before you make travel plans – road blockades are the go-to form of protest for many groups, and can easily disrupt your schedule, while street protests are also common.

HEALTH

Though levels of hygiene and sanitation are generally poor in Bolivia, you can reduce the risk of getting ill. Avoid drinking tap water and watch out for ice in drinks, as well as uncooked or unpeeled fruit and vegetables. Appreciate the risks of buying food from street vendors and always check that food has been properly cooked.

Altitude sickness is a common complaint in La Paz, Potosí and on the salt-flats tour. Mild symptoms include dizziness, headaches and breathlessness. Bolivians swear by coca tea (*mate de coca*), but resting and drinking plenty of non-alcoholic fluids should also help. You can buy small bags of coca leaf around the witches' market area of La Paz for B$2–4. Anyone with more severe symptoms should get immediate medical help.

2

It is advisable to get vaccinated against **yellow fever** before you travel to Bolivia; bring a doctor's certificate with you. Use mosquito repellent with a high DEET content and wear long sleeves and trousers to avoid insect-borne diseases such as malaria and dengue fever.

Bolivia is home to a wide range of venomous **snakes and spiders**. Watch where you step and seek medical advice if you are bitten or stung.

When looking for healthcare, it is always best to opt for **private clinics** (*clínica*) rather than state-run hospitals, which are often overcrowded and poorly equipped.

INFORMATION AND MAPS

Most major cities have a regional **tourist office**, either run by the city municipality or by the departmental prefecture. Tour operators are often a better source of information, and many are happy to answer queries, often in English, though obviously their main aim is to sell you one of their tours.

It's worth buying a good map of the country to take with you, as these are rarely available in Bolivia itself. The best general map is the *Travel Map of Bolivia* (1:2,200,000), produced by O'Brien Cartographics. It's difficult to get hold of, so look out for secondhand copies.

MONEY AND BANKS

The Bolivian currency is the **boliviano**. It's usually written "B$" or "Bs" and is subdivided into 100 centavos. Notes come in denominations of 10, 20, 50, 100 and 200 bolivianos; coins in denominations of 1, 2 and 5 bolivianos, and of 5, 10, 20 and 50 centavos. At the time of writing, the **exchange rate** was roughly B$7 = US$1; B$9.30 = €1; B$10.70 = £1.

US dollars can be **withdrawn at ATMs**, and changed at banks and some hotels, shops and by street moneychangers, so they're a good way of carrying emergency backup funds. Most day-to-day costs will be charged in B$ though tourist-based activities – especially the more upmarket kind – will often be quoted in US$. The easiest way to access funds in cities and larger towns is by using plastic; Visa and MasterCard are most widely accepted. In rural areas and smaller towns carry plenty of **cash**, as plastic and travellers' cheques are fairly useless.

OPENING HOURS AND HOLIDAYS

Public offices in Bolivia have adopted

PUBLIC HOLIDAYS

Jan 1 New Year's Day (*Año Nuevo*)
February/March Carnaval, celebrated throughout the country in the week before Lent. The Oruro Carnaval (see p.187) is the most famous, but Santa Cruz, Sucre and Tarija also stage massive fiestas.
Easter Semana Santa is celebrated with religious processions throughout Bolivia. Good Friday is a public holiday.
May 1 Labour Day.
May/June Corpus Christi. La Paz stages the Señor del Gran Poder, its biggest and most colourful folkloric dance parade.
June 21 Aymara New Year (*Año Nuevo* or *Inti Raymi*). Crowds flock to the Tiwanaku ruins for a colourful ceremony of thanks to the sun and Pachamama (mother earth).
July 16 Virgen del Carmen. Processions and dances in honour of the Virgen del Carmen, the patron saint of many towns and villages across Bolivia.
August 6 Independence Day (*Día de la Patria*). Parades and parties throughout the country, notably in Copacabana.
November 1–2 All Saints (*Día de Todos Santos*) and Day of the Dead (*Día de los Muertos*).
December 25 Christmas Day (*Navidad*).

a new system, *horario continuo*, whereby they work Monday to Friday straight through from 8.30am to 4pm without closing for lunch.

Bank opening hours are generally Monday to Friday from 8.30am to noon and 2.30pm to 6pm; some branches are also open on Saturdays from 9am until noon. ENTEL **telephone** offices usually open daily from around 8am to 8pm, sometimes later.

Bolivians welcome any excuse for a party, and the country enjoys a huge number of national, regional and local **fiestas**, often involving lengthy preparation and substantial expense.

La Paz

Few cities have a setting as spectacular as **LA PAZ**, founded in 1548 as La Ciudad de Nuestra Señora de la Paz – the City of Our Lady of Peace – and now the political and commercial hub of Bolivia. Home to more than a million people, and sited at over 3500m above sea level, the sprawling city lies in a narrow, bowl-like canyon, its centre cradling a cluster of church spires and office blocks themselves dwarfed by the magnificent ice-bound peak of **Mount Illimani** rising imperiously to the southeast. On either side, the steep slopes of the valley are covered by the ramshackle homes of the city's poorer inhabitants, which cling precariously to even the harshest gradients. From the lip of the canyon, the satellite city of **El Alto** sprawls in all directions across the Altiplano, a dirt-poor yet dynamic locus of urban Aymara culture and protest. The fact that its gridlocked main streets control access to La Paz below has often been exploited by the Aymara, with roadblocks used for political leverage.

WHAT TO SEE AND DO

There are still some fine colonial palaces and churches in the centre, with one of the main plazas, **San Francisco**, bisected by the frantic thoroughfare of Avenida Mariscal Santa Cruz and its continuation, Avenida 16 de Julio, collectively known as **El Prado**. While tiny, congested pavements and nose-to-tail traffic make it a challenge just to get from A to B, most visitors are nevertheless enthralled by the energy of La Paz's **street life** and the blazing colour of its indigenous population; once you're used to it, it's easy to explore what is really a very compact city. Though in general the architecture is rather drab and functional, and most of the surviving colonial buildings are in a poor state of repair, their crumbling facades and dilapidated balconies obscured by tangled phone lines and electric cables, there's at least one street, **Calle Jaén**, where you can get a sense of how La Paz used to look. Many of the city's museums are also conveniently situated here. To the west of the Prado, lung-busting lanes sweep up to the travellers' enclave of **Calle Sagárnaga** and the Aymara bustle of **Mercado Buenos Aires** beyond. To the south lies the wealthy suburb of **Sopocachi**, where you'll find some of the city's best nightlife and restaurants. Whatever direction you head in, the far horizon is ever dominated by the majestic, snow-covered, 6439m peak of Illimani.

Plaza Murillo

Though it remains the epicentre of Bolivia's political life, Plaza Murillo – the main square of the colonial city centre – has an endearingly provincial feel, busy with people feeding pigeons and eating ice cream in the shade.

On the south side of the plaza stand two great symbols of political and spiritual power in Bolivia, the **Catedral** (daylight hours; free) – which, with its rather plain facade and relatively unadorned interior, is fairly unremarkable – and the **Palacio Presidencial** (Presidential Palace; closed to public), with its yellow facade, thin, elegant columns and ceremonial guards in red nineteenth-century uniforms. On the east side of the plaza is the **Palacio Legislativo**, the seat of the Bolivian parliament, built in a similar Neoclassical style in the early twentieth century.

2

Museo Nacional de Arte

To the southwest of Plaza Murillo on Calle Socabaya, the Palacio de Los Condes de Arana, one of La Paz's finest surviving colonial palaces, houses the **Museo Nacional de Arte** (Tues–Fri 9.30am–12.30pm & 3–7pm, Sat 10am–5.30pm, Sun 10am–1.30pm; B$15; @mna.org.bo). The palace itself is a magnificent example of Baroque architecture, with a grand portico opening onto a central patio overlooked by three floors of arched walkways, all elaborately carved from pink granite in a rococo style with stylized shells, flowers and feathers.

Contemporary Bolivian artists are represented but the museum's art collection is centred firmly on colonial religious works, featuring several by the great master of Andean colonial painting, Melchor Pérez de Holguín. Look out for the temporary exhibitions programme, which often strays from the colonial theme.

Iglesia Santo Domingo

A block northwest from Plaza Murillo the **Iglesia Santo Domingo** (Calle Ingavi, at Yanacocha; sporadic hours; free) has a richly detailed eighteenth-century facade carved from soft white stone in Mestizo-Baroque style, exemplifying the combination of Spanish and indigenous symbolism characteristic of Andean colonial architecture.

Museo Nacional de Etnografía y Folklore

The small but rewarding **Museo Nacional de Etnografía y Folklore** (Calle Ingavi; Mon–Sat 9am–noon & 3–7pm, Sun 9am–12.30pm; B$20; @musef.org.bo) is housed in an elegant seventeenth-century mansion, with a variety of costumes and artefacts representing three of Bolivia's most distinctive indigenous cultures: the **Aymara** culture, formed of thirty ethnic groups in the Cordillera Oriental; the **Uru-Chipayas**, who subsist in the Altiplano around Oruro; and the Quechua-speaking **Tarabuqueños** from the highlands east of Sucre.

Calle Jaén and its museums

Calle Jaén is the best-preserved colonial street in La Paz and home to no fewer than five municipal museums (all Tues–Fri 9.30am–12.30pm & 3–7pm, Sat & Sun 9am–1pm), all accessed on a single B$4 ticket, sold at the **Museo Costumbrista Juan de Vargas** at the top of the street (the entrance is just around the corner on Calle Sucre). Set inside a renovated colonial mansion, this museum gives a good introduction to the folkloric customs of the Altiplano and history of La Paz, partly by way of some wonderful photographs. Housed in the same building but accessed from Calle Jaén, the **Museo del Litoral Boliviano** is dedicated to one of Bolivia's national obsessions: the loss of its coastline to Chile during the nineteenth-century War of the Pacific (see p.155). Next door, the **Museo de Metales Preciosos**, also known as the Museo del Oro, has a small but impressive hoard of Inca and Tiwanaku gold ornaments, and informative displays explaining the techniques used by pre-Columbian goldsmiths. On the other side of the road, inside the sumptuous mansion which was once the home of the venerated independence martyr after whom it's now named, the **Casa Museo de Murillo** houses an eclectic collection, ranging from colonial religious art to artefacts used in Kallawaya herbal medicine.

Set around yet another pretty colonial courtyard a little further down Calle Jaén, the delightful, independently owned **Museo de Instrumentos Musicales** (daily 9.30am–1pm & 2.30–6.30pm; B$5) features an astonishing variety of handmade musical instruments from all over Bolivia, including the indigenous *charangos*, some of which you can pick up and play. They also host concerts of traditional music (usually B$20).

Plaza San Francisco

Though the frenetic traffic running alongside detracts from its charm, the **Plaza San Francisco** is the focal point for the city's Aymara population. It is one of the liveliest plazas in La Paz, busy with people enjoying snacks and juices or

CENTRAL LA PAZ

Sopocachi, Miraflores & Museo de Textiles Andinos ▲

● EATING, DRINKING AND NIGHTLIFE

100% Natural	15	Ken Chan	14
Alexander	3/19	Oliver's	8
Coffee Shop		Paceña La Salteña	5
Banais Café	6	Pepe's	10
Café Illampu	13	La Quinta	4
El Consulado	16	Sabor Cubano	17
La Cueva	12	Sol y Luna	9
Eli's	11	Star of India	7
Etno	1	TTKos	18
Hotel Gloria	2		

■ ACCOMMODATION

Adventure Brew B&B	4
Adventure Brew Hostel	5
Arcabucero Hostal Inn	12
Bacoo	3
Bash and Crash	15
La Casa Colonial	10
Fuentes	13
Lion Palace Hostel	9
Loki Hostel	11
Hostal Maya Inn	1
Hospedaje Milenio	14
Onieel Inn	2
Residencial Latino	8
Torino	7
Wild Rover	

2

crowding around the many comedians, storytellers, magicians and sellers of miracle cures who come to ply their trade. It's also a focal point for political protest, most of which is peaceful as well as noisy and colourful, although larger demonstrations can sometimes turn violent, and protesting miners are wont to ignite the odd stick of dynamite. Hang on to your bag in this sector of the city, as reports of pickpocketing are common.

Iglesia de San Francisco

On the south side of Plaza San Francisco stands the **Iglesia de San Francisco** (Mon–Sat 4–6pm; free), the most beautiful colonial church in La Paz, first constructed in 1549 and rebuilt in the mid-seventeenth century. The richly decorated facade is a classic example of the Mestizo-Baroque style, showing clear indigenous influence, with carved anthropomorphic figures reminiscent of pre-Columbian sculpture as well as more common birds and intertwined floral designs. Attached to the church is the **Centro Cultural-Museo San Francisco** (Mon–Sat 9am–6pm; B$20 which includes a guided tour; Ⓦmuseosanfranciscobolivia.com), a museum set in a beautiful renovated Franciscan monastery, with a large collection of seventeenth-century Franciscan art and furniture.

Calle Sagárnaga and around

Heading west from Iglesia San Francisco, **Calle Sagárnaga**, La Paz's main tourist street, is crowded with hotels, tour agencies, restaurants, handicraft shops and stalls. It's also the gateway to the main Aymara neighbourhoods of La Paz, one of the most vibrant and distinctive parts of the city, with steep, winding lanes filled with lively markets. The **Mercado de Hechicería** – or Witches' Market – up Sagárnaga on Calle Linares – offers a fascinating window onto the world of Aymara mysticism and herbal medicine. Its stalls are laden with a colourful cornucopia of ritual and medicinal items, ranging from herbal cures for minor ailments like rheumatism or stomach pain to incense, coloured

sweets, protective talismans and dried llama foetuses. The area offers plenty of great photo opportunities, but remember to ask permission or buy a memento.

Museo de la Coca

The small but excellent **Museo de la Coca** (Calle Linares, a block south of Sagárnaga; daily 10.30am–7pm; B$11; Ⓦcocamuseum.com) is dedicated to the small green leaf that is both the central religious and cultural sacrament of the Andes and the raw material for the manufacture of cocaine. The museum gives a good overview of the history, chemistry, cultivation and uses of this most controversial of plants.

Mercado Buenos Aires

A few blocks west of the Witches' Market and Sagárnaga's other tourist honeypots is **Mercado Buenos Aires**, also known as the Huyustus. This vast open-air market sprawling over some thirty city blocks is where La Paz's Aymara conduct their daily business; street after street is lined with stalls piled high with sacks of sweet-smelling coca leaf, mounds of brightly coloured tropical fruit, enormous heaps of potatoes and piles of silver-scaled fish; there are also smuggled stereos and televisions, and endless racks of the latest imitation designer clothes. In the last week of January, the area, as well as most of the rest of the city, is taken over by stalls selling all manner of miniature items during the **Feria de las Alasitas**, which is centred on representations of Ekeko, the diminutive mustachioed household god of abundance.

Museo Tambo Quirquincho

Just northwest of Plaza San Francisco, **Plaza Alonso de Mendoza** is a pleasant square named after La Paz's founder, whose statue stands at its centre. On the southern side of the square on Calle Evaristo Valle, the **Museo Tambo Quirquincho** (Tues–Fri 9.30am–12.30pm & 2.30–7pm, Sat & Sun 9am–1pm; B$5) is one of the most varied and interesting in La Paz, its collection focusing on the city's culture and history,

CYCLING THE DEATH ROAD

One of the most popular trips in Bolivia, and some travellers' sole reason for crossing the border, is a chance to hurtle down the infamous Death Road. This exhilarating 3500m descent along the old road from **La Paz to Coroico**, in the north Yungas, is easy to organize as a day-trip from La Paz. Cyclists have been killed or seriously injured on this rough, narrow track chiselled out of near-vertical mountainsides, and you must choose a tour operator with great care – some are truly unscrupulous. As well as Death Road, there are many other excellent mountain-biking alternatives if you want to get off the beaten track.

TOUR OPERATORS

Gravity Assisted Mountain Biking Ground-floor office 10, Edificio Avenida, Av 16 de Julio 1490 ⓣ 02 2313849, after-hours number ⓣ 77219634, ⓦ gravitybolivia.com. The original and still the best downhill mountain-biking operator, offering daily Death Road trips with excellent US-made bikes and experienced, enthusiastic English-speaking guides. They also offer a range of single-track options for more experienced bikers – their Chacaltaya–Zongo descent plummets 4300m. Gravity helped set up the lower-cost Barracuda (C Illampu 750, office 4, inside Hostal Gloria ⓣ 76728881, ⓣ 02 2459950, ⓦ barracudabiking.com), Zzip (see below) and Urban Rush abseiling in central La Paz (ⓦ urbanrushbolivia.com).

Vertigo Jimenez 836, between Santa Cruz and Sagárnaga ⓣ 02 2115220, ⓦ vertigobiking.com. A recommended agency for cycling the "world's most dangerous road", with top-of-the-range bikes, a good safety record and English-speaking guides.

Zzip the Flying Fox ⓣ 02 2313849, ⓦ ziplinebolivia.com. Situated in Yolosa, the end point of the Death Road trip: 1555m of zip lines – perfect for those craving one final injection of adrenaline. Reservations can be made online, though walk-ins are usually possible.

with exhibits including an extensive collection of grotesque yet beautiful folkloric masks, several rooms full of quaint old photos of La Paz, and a room dedicated to the city's quintessential icon, the **chola**. This is the vernacular term for the ubiquitous Aymara women dressed in voluminous skirts and bowler hats who dominate much of the day-to-day business in the city's endless markets.

Plaza Sucre and the San Pedro Prison

Two blocks southwest of the Prado along Calle Colombia, **Plaza Sucre** lies at the centre of San Pedro, one of the city's oldest suburbs. Also known as **Plaza San Pedro**, the square's tranquil and well-tended gardens surround a statue of Bolivia's first president. On the southeast side of the square rises the formidable bulk of the **Cárcel de San Pedro**. A prison with no guards, San Pedro is essentially controlled by the inmates, who work to pay for cells: those with money can live quite well in luxurious accommodation complete with mobile phones and satellite television, while those without any income sleep in the corridors. There are shops, restaurants, billiard halls and even crèches, as the prisoners' families often live with them. At one time it was possible for tourists to arrange illicit tours of San Pedro, but in recent years the authorities have clamped down on this potentially very dangerous practice.

Museo Nacional de Arqueología and Sopocachi

Shortly before the Prado ends at Plaza del Estudiante, a left turn down the steps and two blocks along Calle Tiahuanaco brings you to the **Museo Nacional de Arqueología** (closed at the time of writing because a neighbouring building has been declared structurally unsound). Set inside a bizarre neo-Tiwanaku building, it has a reasonable collection of textiles, ceramics and stone sculptures from the Inca and Tiwanaku cultures, though it is hoped that the refurbishment will improve the accompanying interpretation boards (previously in Spanish only).

South of Plaza San Francisco, the busy, tree-lined Prado ends at the Plaza del Estudiante, to the south of which lies the relatively wealthy suburb of **Sopocachi**, home to some of the city's best restaurants and a lively nightlife scene.

2

CHOLITA WRESTLING

One of the main reasons to visit El Alto – other than for its airport – is to watch dramatic, Mexican-style wrestling matches featuring the bowler hat-wearing indigenous women known as *cholitas* (Ⓦcholitaswrestling.com). The shows take place on Sundays and can be booked through the hostels or La Paz-based tour operators.

Museo de Textiles Andinos

The **Museo de Textiles Andinos**, Plaza Benito Juarez 488 (Mon–Sat 9.30am–noon & 3–6.30pm, Sun 10am–12.30pm; B$15; Ⓦmuseodetextiles.org), in the student suburb of Miraflores, northeast of the Prado, is a must-see for textile lovers. Set in a beautifully kept house, the museum has an interesting display of textiles from all over the Bolivian Andes. The museum's gift shop sells products made by Quechuan women.

ARRIVAL AND DEPARTURE

BY AIR

Airport International and some domestic flights use the small El Alto airport (flight information on ☎02 2157300, ☎02 2810240), on the rim of the Altiplano, about 11km from La Paz and at over 4000m above sea level.

Transfers The easiest way into town from here is by taxi; they wait right outside the terminal and the half-hour ride should cost B$60–70. Cotranstur also run shuttle mini-buses (*micros*) down into the city and the length of the Prado to Plaza Isabella La Católica (every 10min from 6am–10.30pm; B$1–2/person).

Internal flights Most internal flights with the military airline TAM use the military airport (☎02 2842226), alongside the commercial airport on Av. Juan Pablo II in El Alto, except for flights from Santa Cruz and Cochabamba which arrive at El Alto international airport. Taxis wait here for passengers, but there's no shuttle bus; to get down to La Paz by public transport you'll need to catch any *micro* heading west along Av Juan Pablo II to La Ceja, the district on the edge of the Altiplano above La Paz, and change there. There's a tax of B$15 each way on internal flights.

Destinations Rurrenabaque (5 daily; 40min); Santa Cruz (12 daily; 1hr); Sucre (3 daily; 40min); Tarija (2 daily; 1hr); Uyuni (3 daily; 50min).

BY BUS

Arrivals Buses from southern and eastern Bolivia and international buses arrive at the Terminal Terrestre on Plaza Antofagasta, about 1km northwest of Plaza San Francisco. Buses from Copacabana, Tiwanaku, Sorata and Charazani arrive in the cemetery district, high up on the west side of the city. Plenty of *micros* ply the route to and from the city centre (marked "Cementerio" on the way out), but consider taking a taxi as it's an edgy part of town. Buses from Coroico and Chulumani in the Yungas, and from Rurrenabaque and the Beni, arrive at Minasa Station in the Villa Fátima district, in the far northeast of the city. The different companies all have offices around the intersection of Av de las Américas and C Yanacachi. Again, plenty of *micros* head to and from the city centre, but a taxi is preferable.

Domestic destinations Terminal Terrestre to: Cochabamba (hourly; 7hr 30min); Oruro (hourly, with connections to Uyuni; 3hr 30min); Potosí (every evening, with connections to Sucre, Tarija and Tupiza; 9–10hr). Cemetery District to: Copacabana (regular services throughout the day; 3hr 30min); Sorata (every 30min; 3hr). Villa Fátima to: Chulumani (hourly; 4hr); Coroico (every 30min; 2hr 30min); Rurrenabaque (daily; 18–25hr). Also weekly services to Cobija, Guayaramerín and Riberalta in the dry season.

International destinations Arica (8hr); Buenos Aires (50hr); Cusco (12hr); Lima (27hr).

INFORMATION

Tourist information There's a small office (Mon & Wed 9.45am–noon & 2.30–7pm; Tues, Thurs & Fri 8.30am–noon & 2.30–7pm; ☎02 2371044) on Plaza del Estudiante at the end of the Prado, which has plenty of information on La Paz and the surrounding area. The main tour agencies are the best places to go for information on the rest of the country. An InfoTur office on Av Mariscal Santa Cruz, at Columbia (Mon–Fri 8.30am–noon & 2.30–7pm, Sat & Sun 10am–2pm; ☎02 2453543), also has limited information. The website Ⓦturismolapaz.travel maintains an up-to-date diary of events and exhibitions.

GETTING AROUND

Bus, micro and trufi There are two main forms of public transport in La Paz: city buses and privately owned minibuses, known as *micros*. The names of the *micros'* destinations are written on signs inside the windscreen and bellowed incessantly by the driver's assistants. Your third option is a *trufi* – basically a car operating as a *micro* with a maximum of four passengers and following fixed routes. *Trufis* charge a flat rate of about B$3 in the city centre, *micros* about B$1.30 and buses B$1.30.

Taxi Unlicensed taxis charge about B$4/passenger for journeys anywhere in the centre of town – there are sometimes meters but it's best to agree on the fare at the beginning of the journey. The more reliable marked radio taxis charge about B$10–15 to anywhere in the city centre regardless of the number of passengers.

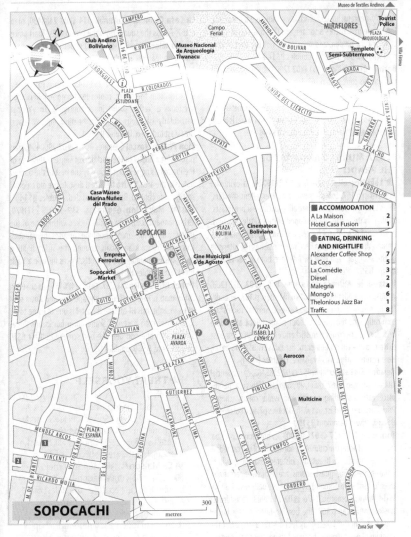

Museo de Textiles Andinos

SOPOCACHI

ACCOMMODATION
A La Maison	2
Hotel Casa Fusion	1

EATING, DRINKING AND NIGHTLIFE
Alexander Coffee Shop	7
La Coca	5
La Comédie	3
Diesel	2
Malegria	4
Mongo's	6
Thelonious Jazz Bar	1
Traffic	8

0   300
metres

ACCOMMODATION

There's plenty of budget accommodation in La Paz, though things get pricier in the peak tourist season from June to August. Most places to stay are in the city centre within a few blocks of Plaza San Francisco, within walking distance of most of the city's main attractions.

NEAR THE BUS STATION

Adventure Brew B&B Av Montes 533 ☎02 2461614, ⓦtheadventurebrewbedandbreakfast.com; map p.167. Dorm beds are offered, but private rooms are the focus at this wood-panelled former hotel. A pancakes-and-coffee breakfast, as

well as daily beer, is included. The rooftop "sky bar" affords excellent views over this gritty patch of the city. Occasional poker nights and free Spanish classes. Doubles B$160

Adventure Brew Hostel Av Montes 503 ☎02 2915896, ⓦtheadventurebrewhostel.com; map p.167. Housed in a refurbished five-storey building, with colourfully tiled bathrooms and a "beer spa"-equipped roof terrace. Breakfast, a microbrewery beer, internet and wi-fi are all included. Socializing is more low-key than their party hostel competition. Dorms B$52

Bacoo Alto de la Alianza 693 ☎02 2280679, ⓦbacoohostel .com; map p.167. Bright yellow walls line the approach to this airy, peaceful hostel, which is well situated for the Calle Jaen museums. There's a social room that gives good views of the city, a garden, and an outdoor hot tub (not always operational). Dorms B$50, doubles B$140

Bash and Crash Ingavi 861 ☎ 02 2280934, ⏍bashandcrash backpackers.com; map p.167. Less slickly managed than the foreign-owned hostels, but part of its appeal is that it is run by a team of welcoming locals. The site – a huge nineteenth-century house – has a ramshackle charm. Peña Mural is in the same building. Dorms B$49, doubles B$144

PLAZA MURILLO AND EAST OF THE PRADO

★ **Loki Hostel** Loayza 420 ☎ 02 2119024, ⏍ lokihostel .com; map p.167. *Loki* has helpful staff, excellent showers, shipshape mattresses, and free all-you-can-eat breakfasts, while private rooms are equipped with a kettle and teas. A self-confessed party hostel, *Loki* hits it hard and loud, though the huge bar area here rarely reaches the intensity of the snugger *Wild Rover's*. Advance booking advisable. Dorms B$52, doubles B$140

Hospedaje Milenio Yanacocha 860 ☎ 02 2281263, ⏍ hospedajemilenio.blogspot.co.uk; map p.167. Friendly family-run place on a cobbled street. Several rooms are comically tiny, most are without natural light and some bed frames are covered in stickers, evidence of their past existence in a child's bedroom. Breakfast is B$8–13 extra. No en-suite bathrooms available. Doubles B$80

Residencial Latino Junin 857 ☎ 02 2285463, ⏍ residencial latino.com; map p.167. Quiet, airy and clean, this is a friendly place with a startling orange and white colour scheme. Prices include breakfast and wi-fi. Doubles (shared bathroom) B$130, private bathroom B$190

Torino Socabaya 457 ☎ 02 2406003, ⏍ hoteltorino.com.bo; map p.167. Facing the crumbling north flank of the cathedral, the site includes a beautiful cloistered courtyard, which, unfortunately, the guest rooms are entirely apart from. Doubles (shared bathroom) B$80, private bathroom B$140

Wild Rover Comercio 1476 ☎ 02 2116903, ⏍ wildrover hostels.com; map p.167. The beating heart of this hostel is its bar – non-drinkers may feel a little alien – but the rambling layout means that you can get beds at a remove from the NYE 1999-pitched boozing. That's not to say that the hostel's other aspects are neglected – this is a tightly run ship. Dorms B$45, doubles B$150

CALLE SAGÁRNAGA AND WEST OF THE PRADO

Arcabucero Hostal Inn Viluyo 307 ☎ 02 2313473; map p.167. A smartly restored old building on the fringe of the city's tourist streets. Quiet, cool, and good value with an inner courtyard and colonial art, but in the past there have been accusations of theft from rooms. Guests can use the kitchen. Doubles B$180

La Casa Colonial C Colombia 314 ☎ 02 2480430; map p.167. Across the square from the prison, this smart place is good value, even if there are cheaper options around. One room features a sculptural bath and there are chunky Andean textile bedspreads throughout. Doubles B$200

Fuentes Linares 988 ☎ 02 2334145; map p.167. Nicely set back from the street, rooms lead onto a gallery that overlooks a (rather plain) inner courtyard. They're not particularly generous with the heating on cold days. Breakfast included. Doubles B$160

Lion Palace Hostel C Linares 1017 ☎ 02 2900454; map p.167. Not a hostel in the backpacker sense – this side of the Prado has none – but arguably the best of the budget hotels in the area, with a fresh feel despite the old colonial setting. Book ahead. Breakfast included. Doubles B$140

Hostal Maya Inn Sagárnaga 339 ☎ 02 2311970, ⏍ hostalmaya.com; map p.167. Tucked within one of the many warren-like mini shopping arcades hereabouts, this place is spick-and-span, though the sickly lighting and garish wallpaper are turn-offs. Prices include a basic breakfast. Doubles B$160

Onkel Inn C Colombia 257 ☎ 02 2490456, ⏍ onkelinn .com; map p.167. Blessedly light and airy and not a shot glass in sight, this HI-affiliated hostel is one to come to for R&R rather than partying. Some dorm bunks are three-storey, with one odd den-like bed screened off for B$20 more. Dorms B$60, doubles B$200

★ TREAT YOURSELF

It's only a half-hour walk or ten-minute taxi ride from the Prado, but the middle-class neighbourhood of Sopocachi feels utterly cocooned from the hectic central area. These two Sopocachi options will bust the budget, but they're worth it.

A La Maison Pasaje Muñoz Cornejo 15 ☎ 02 2413704, ⏍ alamaison-lapaz.com; map p.171. Tucked down the tiniest of cul-de-sacs, this complex of spacious apartments is decorated with a stylish, bohemian touch. Each morning, a bag of fresh juice and bread is left hanging on your door handle. B$350

Hotel Casa Fusion C Miguel de Cervantes 2725 ☎ 02 2141372, ⏍ casafusion.com.bo; map p.171. The affable owner has converted his family home into a lovely, simple hotel. The rooms are not as characterful as the building itself, but they're spotlessly clean and the luxurious bedding is a delight. Prices include a cooked breakfast, served in a pleasant adjoining conservatory. Doubles B$345

EATING

La Paz has an excellent range of restaurants, cafés and street stalls to suit most tastes and budgets – from traditional places that dish up local delicacies to tourist-orientated spots with international menus. For those whose stomachs have adjusted to local food, the cheapest places to eat are the city's markets, where you can get full meals for around B$12. The ubiquitous *salteñas* and *tucumanes* (B$2–4) – delicious pastries filled with meat or chicken and vegetables – make excellent mid-morning snacks, especially if washed down by a freshly squeezed orange and grapefruit juice from a street seller.

CAFÉS

100% Natural Sagárnaga 345; map p.167. Largely vegetarian joint, big on fruit juices (from B$12), soya and the like. Breakfasts from B$24 (sometimes on two-for-one promotions). Daily 8am–9pm.

Alexander Coffee Shop Av 16 de Julio 1832, map p.167; C Potosí 1091, map p.167; Av 20 de Octubre 2463, Sopocachi, map p.171. This serves the city's best coffee in an almost eerily westernized setting, though the C Potosí branch has plenty of atmosphere with a vaulted brick ceiling. Salads from B$20 – try the quinoa option, with broccoli, courgette, and alfalfa sprouts. Daily 9am–1am.

Banaís Café Sagárnaga 161; map p.167. This tourist-hub café has a pleasant central courtyard and good breakfasts, with huge bowls of muesli, cereal and fruit (B$23), and very good-value *almuerzos* (B$28). Strong wi-fi. Daily 7am–10pm.

★ **Café Illampu** Linares; map p.167. Morning sun pours through big colonial windows. Visit for breakfast (B$26); there's home-made bread, good jams and rustic crockery. A couple of tables are squeezed onto the wardrobe-width balcony. No wi-fi.

Pepe's Jimenez 894, just off Linares between Sagárnaga and Santa Cruz; map p.167. Friendly little place with colourful decor and a winning range of sandwiches (the guacamole version comes recommended), pancakes and omelettes. Mains from B$30. The coffee is some of the city's best, and there are old guidebooks for reference. Often closed Sun.

RESTAURANTS

La Coca Rosendo Gutierrez 482; map p.171. Located in the Sopocachi neighbourhood, this is an opportunity to try some Bolivian flavours without risking the real locals' places where food hygiene can be an issue. Red quinoa soup B$13, llama fillet with Bolivian potatoes B$50.

La Comédie Pasaje Medinacelli 2234 ☎02 2423561, ⓦlacomedie-lapaz.com; map p.171. With expensive-looking art on the terracotta-coloured walls and wine glasses on tables, this Sopocachi restaurant is a notch up in class from almost everywhere else in the city. Mains

★ **TREAT YOURSELF**

El Consulado C Carlos Bravo 299, ⓦcafeelconsulado.com; map p.167. This place served as the Panamanian consulate in the mid-twentieth century and it retains a stately grandeur. Stay in one of their guest rooms if you can stretch to it (freestanding baths, original furniture and sky-high ceilings; doubles US$100). Alternatively, treat yourself to a meal or simply afternoon coffee and cake, served in a pretty conservatory or out in the rambling garden – a precious haven of green in this smoky city. Mains from the brief menu come in at around B$50, but they're worth it, from llama in green pepper sauce to trout cannelloni. Tues–Sun 8am–5pm.

are upward of B$50, and the French-influenced cooking is generally exemplary. Mon–Fri noon–3pm & 7–11pm, Sat & Sun from 7pm.

La Cueva C Tarija 210B; map p.167. Part of the "Four Corners" enterprise that has something of a local monopoly, this slip of a restaurant is all terracotta walls, wooden benches and Day of the Dead theming. Chilli, tacos, burritos and quesadillas start at B$34 with generous sharing plates for B$90 (veggie) or B$100. Daily 8am until late.

Eli's Av 16 de Julio, at Bueno; map p.167. This sweetly kitsch place was founded in 1942. The diner-style decor is a shrine to the silver screen, with a portrait of Humphrey Bogart in pride of place. Get into the spirit of the age with huge, Technicolor ice-cream sundaes (all around B$20).

Hotel Gloria Potosí 909; map p.167. Excellent vegetarian lunchtime buffets (B$30) in clean (though hardly atmospheric) surroundings. It's worth coming in for the buffet breakfast too (B$35). Mon–Sat noon–2.30pm.

Ken Chan Batallon Colorado 98; map p.167. On the second floor of the peaceful Japanese cultural centre in a traffic-choked corner of town, the food at *Ken Chan* is some of the city's best, with *gyoza* and *sui mei* at B$19, sushi from B$48 and set meals around B$50. Tues–Fri 11.30am–3.15pm & 6–11pm, Sat & Sun 11.30am–4pm & 6–11pm.

Paceña La Salteña Loayza 233 ⓦpacenalasaltena.com; map p.167. It's a tough call, but this is probably the best of the *salteña* joints in the city, with prices from B$2.50. Mornings only Mon–Sat.

La Quinta C Potosí; map p.167. If you're wary of getting sick but fancy some Bolivian cuisine, then this spotless fast-food take on local cooking is one to try. The *pique a lo macho* (when available – the menu rotates) is just B$25 and resembles something assembled by a drunk student – fries, meat, onions, peppers, hot sauce all slopped together with gravy, ketchup and mayo.

2

Sabor Cubano C Sagárnaga 357, ⓦ saborcubanobolivia .com; map p.167. Excellent-value Cuban cuisine including *almuerzos* (B$25) in a cave of a bar-restaurant plastered in photos and graffiti. There's often live music on Thurs & Fri evenings. Daily 12.30pm– 12.30am.

Star of India C Cochabamba 170; map p.167. A self-proclaimed "British Indian curry house" (albeit one that serves llama tikka masala) with a low-lit interior and tiled floors. They promise their vindaloo is "silly hot". Most curries B$49, naans B$8, *almuerzo* B$35. Mon–Sat 9am– 11pm, Sun 4–11pm.

DRINKING, NIGHTLIFE AND ENTERTAINMENT

Many travellers spend the majority of their partying time in the hostel bars, not moving on until *Loki*, *Wild Rover* and – to a lesser extent – *Adventure Brew* kick out in the small hours. The Sopocachi neighbourhood – a 30min walk or 10min cab ride – is a good option, with venues running the gamut from live jazz to raucous travellers' hangouts. And although La Paz's club scene isn't what it was, you can still find a busy dancefloor heaving to just about any kind of music. For more traditional entertainment, head to one of the folk music venues known as *peñas*, where – with varying degrees of authenticity – you can witness age-old Andean music and dance.

BARS AND NIGHTCLUBS

Diesel Av 20 de Octubre, at Rosendo Gutiérrez; map p.171. Industrial-chic bar with an extraordinary post-apocalyptic design, complete with aircraft engines hanging from the ceiling. Mon–Sat from 7pm until the early hours.

Etno Jaén 722; map p.167. Arty bar/café tucked away in La Paz's most charming street, with dimly lit wooden tables, good coffee and a relaxed vibe. Serves a B$16 *almuerzo* and pizzas from B$14. Mojito B$20. Mon–Sat 11am until late (around 3am).

Malegria Pasaje Medinacelli 2282; map p.171. An Afro-Bolivian band arrives triumphantly into the already buzzing venue late on Thurs nights, which otherwise jumps to Latin sounds, Western club jams, and reggae. Photocopied ID is a must. Thurs–Sat 9pm–2.45am.

Mongo's Hermanos Manchego 2444; map p.171. Not quite the gringo rendezvous it once was, but its cocktail of televised sports, decent food, serious drinking, live music and raucous dancing still pulls a crowd at weekends. Live Cuban music on Tues; it hosts salsa classes too. Daily 6pm until late

Oliver's Murillo 1014; map p.167. Gringo pub above *Sol y Luna* (see p.167) that's ideal for those craving comfort food (the pies and chips are genuinely excellent), televised sports and bar-top dancing. Once the hostel bars kick out, this is often first port of call. Open from 6am, people pop in for been-up-all-night breakfasts.

Sol y Luna Cochabamba, at Murillo ⓦ solyluna-lapaz.com; map p.167. Snug, candlelit bar-café for a laidback evening. There are pool tables, a book exchange, an excellent range of beers, and live music on Mon and Thurs. The food, much of it Dutch, is so-so. Daily 9am–1am.

Thelonious Jazz Bar Av 20 de Octubre 2172; map p.171. A fine little jazz bar, with an intimate basement atmosphere, live music Tues–Sat (not necessarily jazz) and an incredibly convivial owner. B$25–50 cover charge. Closed Sun and Mon.

Traffic Av Arce 2549; map p.171. Long-established crowd-puller with international DJs – mostly from neighbouring countries – and live music. Fridays are particularly good. Mon–Sat 7pm–4am.

TTKOs C Mexico 1555; map p.167. One of the better bars nearer the centre, this basement is an unpretentious hangout for foreigners and locals alike. Often hosts live music, from reggae (Tues) to rock. Cover B$10. Tues–Sat 9pm–3.30am.

CINEMAS AND PEÑAS

Cinemateca Boliviana R. Gutiérrez, ⓦ cinemateca boliviana.org. An excellent arthouse cinema with a café that gives good views north towards Miraflores. Usually showing one or two blockbusters, too.

Cine Municipal 6 de Agosto Av 6 de Agosto 2284 ☎ 02 2442629. Wonderful Art Deco cinema in Sopocachi that bypasses Hollywood for a more engaging programme of Latin American and European film.

Cine Teatro Monje Campero Av 16 de Julio, at C Bueno ☎ 02 2333332. A local landmark, with afternoon and evening showings of the latest releases.

Multicine Av Arce 2631 ☎ 02 2112463, ⓦ 2.multicine.com .bo. A modern, comfortable multiscreen place in Sopocachi, within walking distance of central La Paz. All manner of fast-food joints here, too.

Peña Marka Tambo Jaén 710 ☎ 02 2280041. Hosts the most authentic traditional music and dance show in La Paz from an ideal setting in an old colonial mansion. It also has one of the best-value cover charges in town at B$35. The food, however, is mediocre. Shows start at 10pm.

DIRECTORY

Banks and exchange There are plenty of banks with ATMs in the centre of town, especially on Av Camacho, where many of them are guarded. Keep your wits about you when using the ATMs on Sagárnaga. One of the best places to change cash and travellers' cheques is Money Exchange International, Mercado 990, at Yanacocha (Mon–Fri 8.30am–12.30pm & 2.30–7pm, Sat 9am–12.30pm).

Car rental American, Av Camacho 1574 ☎ 02 2202933; Barbol Rent a Car, Héroes del Kilómetro 7 777, opposite El Alto airport ☎ 02 2820675, ⓦ barbolsrl.com; Economica,

C F Zuazo 1942 ☎ 02 2441906 and El Alto airport ☎ 7627741, ⓦ economicacarrental.com.

Embassies and consulates Argentina, Aspiazu 497 ☎ 02 2417737, ☎ 02 2422912; Australia, Aspiazu 416 ☎ 02 2115655; Brazil, Edificio Multicentro, Av Arce ☎ 02 2440202; Canada, Plaza España, at Sanjinez ☎ 02 2415021; Colombia, C 9, Calacoto 7835 ☎ 02 2784491; Chile, C 14, Calacoto 8024 ☎ 02 2797331; Ecuador, Edificio Hermann, Av 16 de Julio 1440 ☎ 02 2319739; Paraguay, Edificio Illimani, Av 6 de Agosto ☎ 02 2433176; Peru, Edificio Alianza, Av 6 de Agosto 2190 ☎ 02 2440631; UK, Av Arce 2732 ☎ 02 2433424; USA, Av Arce 2780 ☎ 02 2168222/8000; Venezuela, Av Arce 2678 ☎ 02 2432023.

Immigration The *migración* office is on Av Camacho 1480, ☎ 02 2110960 (Mon–Fri 8.30am–4pm), for tourist visa extensions and information.

Internet access The city is crawling with internet cafés, most charging B$1–3/hr. Many bars and cafés have wi-fi.

Laundry Laverap on C Aroma, at C Llampu; Laundry Ballivian, C Ballivian 1286 (closed Sun).

Outdoor equipment There are a number of shops around Sagárnarga selling clothing and equipment for trekking and climbing. The best option is Tatoo at C Illampu 828 ☎ 02 2451265, ⓦ bo.tatoo.ws. Illampu also has lots of outlets selling fake big-name gear.

Pharmacy There is a 24hr pharmacy next door-but-one to Cine Teatro Monje Campero on El Prado.

Police Edificio Olimpio, Plaza Tejada Sorzano, opposite the stadium in Miraflores (daily 24hr; ☎ 02 2225016). This is the place to report thefts for insurance claims.

Post office Correo Central, Av Mariscal Santa Cruz, at Oruro (Mon–Fri 8am–8pm, Sat 8am–6pm, Sun 9am–noon).

Shopping With its many markets, La Paz has a wide range of *artesanía* (handicrafts) on sale from all over the country. You'll find dozens of outlets along Sagárnaga and the surrounding streets selling traditional textiles, leather items, silver jewellery and talismans. Some of the best – and most ethical – are *Artesanía Sorata* on Sagárnaga and *Artesanía Alasita* on Murillo. Most fossils sold on this street are fake.

Telephone centres Punto Cotel on the Prado, opposite the main post office. There are phone booths all over the city which accept cards that you buy at any kiosk or small store. Many internet cafés in central La Paz have Skype.

TIWANAKU

The most worthwhile attraction within a few hours of La Paz is the mysterious ruined city of **TIWANAKU** (also spelled Tiahuanaco), set on the Altiplano 71km to the west. It's Bolivia's most impressive archeological site, and was declared a World Heritage Site by UNESCO in 2000.

Founded some three millennia ago, Tiwanaku became the capital of a massive empire that lasted almost a thousand years, developing into a sophisticated urban-ceremonial complex that, at its peak, was home to some fifty thousand people. Tiwanaku remains a place of exceptional symbolic meaning for the Aymara of the Altiplano, who come here to make ceremonial offerings to the *achachilas*, the gods of the mountains. The most spectacular of these occasions, the **Aymara New Year**, takes place each year at the June winter solstice, when hundreds of *yatiris* (traditional priests) congregate to watch the sun rise and celebrate with music, dancing, elaborate rituals and copious quantities of coca and alcohol.

Though the city of Tiwanaku originally covered several square kilometres, only a fraction of the site has been excavated, and the main ruins (daily 9am–4.30pm; B$80) occupy a fairly small area that can easily be visited in half a day. Two museums by the entrance house many of the smaller archeological finds, as well as several large stone monoliths. The main ruins cover the area that was once the ceremonial centre of the city, a jumble of tumbled pyramids and ruined palaces and temples made from megalithic stone blocks, many weighing over a hundred tonnes. It requires a leap of the imagination to visualize Tiwanaku as it was at its peak: a thriving city whose great pyramids and opulent palaces were painted in bright colours and inlaid with gold, surrounded by extensive residential areas built largely from mud brick (of which little now remains) and set amid lush green fields, rather than the harsh, arid landscape you see today.

ARRIVAL AND DEPARTURE

By bus Local buses (marked "Tiwanaku") depart from the cemetery district in La Paz, at the corner of Kollasuyo and Alquiza (every 45min depending on when buses are full; 1hr 30min; B$15–25 return); on the way back to La Paz, buses leave from the main square in Tiwanaku. They're often quite full as they're coming from Desaguadero, a town bordering Peru, so allow time in the afternoon to get a seat.

2

TOURS

You can hire a guide outside the museum to show you around the ruins for a small fee, but if you want a guided tour – especially one in English – then you're better off coming with an agency from La Paz (see box, p.162); most run one-day tours to the site for about B\$70–90 (plus entrance fee) per person.

Lake Titicaca, Cordillera Real and the Yungas

The region immediately around La Paz is sometimes known as "Little Bolivia", because the variety of landscapes it encompasses can seem like a microcosm of the entire country. To the northwest lies the vast, high-altitude **Lake Titicaca**, with its idyllic islands, **Isla del Sol** and **Isla de la Luna**, and lakeside pilgrimage town of **Copacabana**. East of here is the **Cordillera Real**, the highest and most spectacular section of the Bolivian Andes, easily explored from La Paz, or else from the magical outpost of Sorata. Sweeping down from the Cordillera Real, the **Yungas** is a rugged region of forest-covered mountains, rushing rivers and fertile valleys, with the humid languor of **Coroico** at its heart.

LAKE TITICACA

Some 75km northwest of La Paz, **Lake Titicaca**, an immense, sapphire-blue lake, easily the largest high-altitude body of water in the world, sits astride the border with Peru at the northern end of the Altiplano. The area around the lake is the heartland of the Aymara, whose distinct language and culture have survived centuries of domination, first by the Incas, then by the Spanish.

Titicaca has always played a dominant role in Andean religious conceptions. The Incas, who believed the creator god Viracocha rose from its waters to call forth the sun and moon to light up the world, also claimed their own ancestors came from here. The remains of their

shrines and temples can still be seen on the Isla del Sol and the Isla de la Luna, whose serene beauty is a highlight of any visit to the lake. Nor did Lake Titicaca lose its religious importance with the advent of Christianity: it's no coincidence that Bolivia's most important Catholic shrine can be found in Copacabana, the lakeside town closest to the Isla del Sol.

COPACABANA

The pleasant town of **COPACABANA** overlooks the deep blue waters of Lake Titicaca and is the jumping-off point for visiting Titicaca's sacred islands. It's also the most important Catholic pilgrimage site in the country, as home to Bolivia's most revered image, the Virgen de Copacabana; hordes of pilgrims descend on the city in early February and early August for the two main religious fiestas.

WHAT TO SEE AND DO

The focal point of Copacabana is the imposing **Catedral** (daily 7.30am–8pm; free), set on the Plaza 2 de Febrero six blocks east of the waterfront. Inside the bright, vaulted interior, a door beside the massive gold altarpiece leads to a small chapel housing the beautiful **Virgen de Copacabana** herself. Encased in glass, the lavishly dressed statue is only taken out of the sanctuary during fiestas: locals believe that moving her at any other time might trigger catastrophic floods. Try to catch a "vehicle blessing" ceremony (La Benedición de Movilidades), a ritual where car owners line up outside the cathedral with their vehicles decorated with flowers and ribbons and ask the Virgin to protect them. This usually takes place at about 10am, and usually on weekends.

Another interesting religious site is **Cerro Calvario**, the hill that rises steeply above the town to the north. It's a half-hour walk up to the top along a trail that begins beside the small church at the north end of Calle Bolívar, five or so blocks up from Plaza Sucre. The trail follows the Stations of the Cross up to the summit dotted with ramshackle stone altars where pilgrims light candles, burn

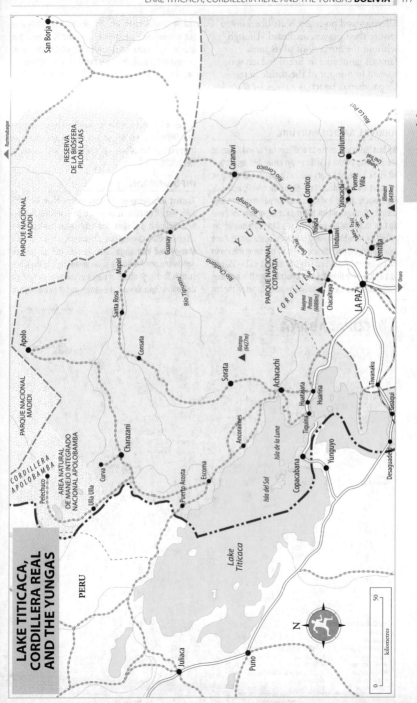

LAKE TITICACA, CORDILLERA REAL AND THE YUNGAS

San Borja

Rurrenabaque

RESERVA DE LA BIÓSFERA PILÓN LAJAS

PARQUE NACIONAL MADIDI

Apolo

PARQUE NACIONAL MADIDI

CORDILLERA APOLOBAMBA

AREA NATURAL DE MANEJO INTEGRADO NACIONAL APOLOBAMBA

Pelechuco

Ulla Ulla

Curva

Charazani

Puerto Acosta

Escoma

PERU

Juliaca

Puno

Lake Titicaca

Isla del Sol

Isla de la Luna

Copacabana

Yunguyo

Ancoraimes

Tiquina

Desaguadero

Tiwanaku

Guaqui

Huarina

Huatajata

Achacachi

Sorata

Illampu (6427m)

Consata

Santa Rosa

Mapiri

Guanay

Río Tipuani

Río Challana

Garanavi

Río Coroico

YUNGAS

Río Zongo

Coroico

Yolosa

PARQUE NACIONAL COTAPATA

Choro Trail

Unduavi

Ventilla

Huayna Potosi (6088m)

Chacaltaya

LA PAZ

Oruro

CORDILLERA REAL

Chulumani

Yanacachi

Puente Villa

Takesi Trail

Mina Cruz Trail

Illimani (6439m)

Río La Paz

N

0   50   kilometres

offerings and pour alcoholic libations to ensure their prayers are heard. Though without the attractions of its more famous namesake in Brazil (which was named in honour of the shrine here), Copacabana's **beach** is a pleasant place for a lakeside stroll and a bite to eat; there are also plenty of pedal boats to rent.

ARRIVAL AND DEPARTURE

By bus Buses and *micros* to and from La Paz and Kasani at the Peruvian border (15min away) arrive and depart just off Plaza Sucre. At Kasani you can get your exit stamp at passport control (daily 8am–9pm) then walk across to Peru, where *micros* and taxis wait for passengers to take them to Yunguyo, which has regular departures for Puno and on to Cusco. Alternatively, you can catch one of the tourist *micros* which travel direct from Copacabana to Puno several times a day; these are run by the companies with offices around Plaza Sucre and, at around B$25–35, cost just a little more than the public *micros*. Note that between Copacabana and La Paz, you will be asked to get off the bus and pay a small fee to cross the lake in a boat, while your bus is transported across on a larger raft. The tourist bus goes to the Terminal Terrestre in La Paz, whilst the cheaper (around B$15) public bus goes to the cemetery district.

Destinations Regular departures to La Paz (every 30min; 3hr 30min) and Puno (daily 9am, 1.30pm & 6pm; 4hr) for onward travel to Cusco (10hr), Arequipa (9hr) and Lima (18hr).

By boat It is also possible to reach Peru by crossing the lake. The best way to do this is by the bus and catamaran tours from La Paz to Puno – or vice versa – with Transturin (see p.180).

INFORMATION

Tourist information The tourist office is on Av 16 de Julio, just off Plaza Sucre (Mon–Fri 8am–noon & 2–6pm) where English is spoken. You might also check out the official website ⓦ visitacopacabana.com.

Money and exchange There are two ATMs on Av 6 de Agosto and another on the main square, next to the police station. To change dollars or travellers' cheques, try the Casa de Cambio Copacabana at the eastern end of Av 6 de Agosto.

COPACABANA

Cerro Calvario

Kusijata & Yampupata

PLAZA DE TOROS

Bullring

AVAROA

BALLIVIAN

COCHABAMBA

MICHEL PÉREZ

BOLIVAR

3 DE MAYO

ORURO

PANDO

Market

ATM

AVAROA

PÉREZ

LA PAZ

AV GENERAL JÁUREGUI

BAPTISTA

ANTONIO GONZÁLES

ZAPANA

PLAZA SUCRE

Buses to La Paz & Kasani

AV 6 DE AGOSTO

PLAZA 2 DE FEBRERO

JOSÉ MEJÍA

Boats to Isla del Sol

Punto Entel

@

ⓘ

5

ATM

BALLIVIAN

5

Lake Titicaca

BUSCH

AV COSTANERA

AV 16 DE JULIO

BOLIVAR

PANDO

Catedral

6

N

MANUEL MEJÍA

R. PAREDES

POTOSÍ

7

8

MURILLO

AV FÉLIX TEJADA

La Paz

0   200
metres

Kasani & Peru

Horca del Inca

■ **ACCOMMODATION**
La Casa del Sol	6
La Cúpula	2
Hostal Emperador	7
Hostal Intihuatana	5
Hostal Leyenda	4
Hostal Las Olas	1
Hostal Sonia	8
Utama Hotel	3

● **EATING AND DRINKING**
Aransaya	5
Café Bistrot	2
El Condor and the Eagle	4
Nemos	3
La Orilla	1

ACCOMMODATION

Owing to its role as a pilgrimage centre, Copacabana has an enormous number of places to stay, though they fill up fast and prices double or triple during the main fiestas.

La Casa del Sol Ballivián ☎ 71586731. Owned by a former mayor of Copacabana (who can impart plentiful insights into local life, should you so wish), this peaceful hotel on the edge of town upholds high standards and irrevocable cleanliness at budget prices. Doubles B$50

Hostal Emperador Murillo 235 ☎ 02 8622083. A good budget option – the place is bright and friendly, though the narrow beds have seen far better days. Rarely has hot water. Breakfast is B$10–15 extra. Doubles B$40

Hostal Intihuatana Ballivián 649 ☎ 02 72071169. There's an Inca theme-park feel here, but it's great value with top-quality bedding and some rooms (all en suite) that overlook the town's eastern edge. Doubles B$60

Hostal Leyenda Av Costanera, at Busch ☎ 07350 8898. The place looks incongruous in its beachside setting, decorated with cement bas-relief sculpture depicting Inca motifs or indigenous characters, and galleried upper floors. The gothic feel is rounded off by a front garden full of stone slabs and rose bushes. Prices include breakfast. Doubles (all en suite) B$150

Hostal Sonia Murillo 256 ☎ 07196 8441, ✉ hostalsonia copacabana@gmail.com. A notch up from nearby *Emperador*, this place has hot water (albeit sporadic), wi-fi, en-suite bathrooms and kitchen facilities. The rooftop terrace has lovely views. Doubles B$80

Utama Hotel Michel Pérez, at San Antonio ☎ 02 8622013, ✉ utamahotel.com. The modern central courtyard has an odd ambience, glowing yellow from the plastic corrugated roof and decorated with huge international flags. But this is a friendly place, with free tea and fruit, en-suite rooms, and breakfast included. Doubles B$200

EATING AND DRINKING

There's no shortage of restaurants in Copacabana, most catering to travellers and pilgrims, and some doubling as bars and evening hangouts. There are also a number of stalls along the waterfront selling decent and cheap local *almuerzos*. At the market you can get a coffee, plus a *pastel* (a bloated, bubbled morsel of fried dough) or *buñuelos* (a sort of doughnut) for around B$3. There are also food stalls that sell *wallaque* fish soup (B$8), a regional delicacy bulked up with dried *chuño* potatoes (most definitely an acquired taste). Despite its tourist hub status, Copacabana is not a party town.

Aransaya Av 6 de Agosto. Said to be the oldest restaurant in town and still serving traditional offerings, from the breaded meat dish *silpancho* (B$30) and *pique a lo macho* (B$40) to good-value fried trout (B$20) and *almuerzos* (B$15). The courtyard improves the otherwise canteen-like atmosphere.

Café Bistrot C Zapana. This first-floor café-restaurant is a great hangout, decorated with all manner of trinkets from hats to musical instruments, though the cooking (plenty of veggie fare on offer) is inconsistent. Wi-fi available to customers who spend over B$15. Daily 7.30am–2pm & 5.30–9pm.

★ **El Condor and the Eagle** Av 6 de Agosto, entered through Residencial Paris. Deservedly popular, with the home-made baked beans on toasted soda bread (B$15) a delight after measly Bolivian breakfasts. The strong coffee (cappuccino B$16) and punchy chocolate cake (B$10) are a treat too. Wed–Mon 7.30am–3pm.

Nemos Av 6 de Agosto. A simple little bar with a good playlist run by a Brit and an Argentine, with Bolivian microbrewery beers including Saya and Ted's Cervecería, plus international favourites like Erdinger. Daily from 5pm.

La Orilla Av 6 de Agosto. They use filtered water here, so you can order their signature stuffed trout safe in the knowledge it won't come back to haunt you. Mon–Sat from 5pm.

ISLA DEL SOL

Just off the northern tip of the Copacabana Peninsula about 12km northwest of Copacabana, the **Isla del Sol** (Island of the Sun) has been attracting pilgrims and visitors for many hundreds of years. Now a quiet backwater, the island was one of the most important religious sites in the Andean world in the sixteenth century, revered as the place where the sun and moon were created

2

and where the Inca dynasty was born. Scattered with **enigmatic ancient ruins** and populated by traditional Aymara communities, Isla del Sol is an excellent place to spend some time hiking and contemplating the magnificent scenery. Measuring 9.5km long and 6.5km across at its widest point, the Isla del Sol is the largest of the forty or so islands in Lake Titicaca, with three main settlements – Yumani, Ch'alla and Ch'allapampa. You can visit the island, along with nearby **Isla de la Luna** (see opposite), on a day- or even half-day trip from Copacabana, but it's really worth spending at least one night on the island to appreciate fully its serene beauty.

WHAT TO SEE AND DO

The best way to see the Isla del Sol is to walk the length of the island from Yumani in the south to Ch'allapampa in the north (or the other way round) – a two- to three-hour hike. When you land, you may be asked to pay a charge of B$5 to the island community. From the lakeshore at **Yumani**, where most boats dock, an Inca stairway, the **Escalera del Inca**, runs steeply up to the village through a natural amphitheatre covered by some of the finest Inca agricultural terracing on the island, irrigated by bubbling stone canals fed by a natural spring believed to have magic powers. About an hour and a half north of Yumani lies the quiet village of Ch'alla, which sits above a calm bay, and from where the path drops to **Playa Ch'alla**, a picturesque stretch of sand. About an hour's walk from Ch'alla is the island's northernmost settlement, **Ch'allapampa**, a pleasant and peaceful village founded by the Incas as a centre for the nearby ceremonial complexes. From here it's

a forty-minute walk northwest along an easy-to-follow path to the **Santuario** (8am–6pm; small fee), a ruined Inca site built around the sacred rock where the creator god Viracocha is believed to have created the sun and moon. Nearby is the **Chincana** (daily 8am–6pm; small fee), an Inca complex of rambling interlinked rooms, plazas and passageways. Broadly, expect to be asked to pay B$10 for exploration of the island's northern sites, and B$5 each for the southern sights and centre.

There's a smaller but evocative multi-roomed Inca site called **Pilko Kaina** (sometimes Pilcocaina) a thirty-minute walk from Yumani. Overlooking the lake, one room, whose small window is aligned with Isla de la Luna, floods with light at sunrise. If you want to experience this, a good option is to lodge with the Pusari family (call Gonzalo on ☎71281710), who live next door to the complex.

ARRIVAL AND DEPARTURE

By boat Full- and half-day boat tours to the Isla del Sol leave every morning from the beach at the end of Av 6 de Agosto in Copacabana – boats usually depart at around 8am for a full day (B$35 return), returning around 5.30pm. Half-day tours to the south (B$25) will only give you a few hours on the island and are hardly worth the effort.

ACCOMMODATION

Yumani is home to the majority of the island's accommodation, most of which offers sporadic (and usually cold) water, and basic conditions. There are also a couple of simple but friendly places to stay in Ch'allapampa. Most places charge B$40–60 per night for private double rooms.

CH'ALLAPAMPA
Alojamiento Nelly Head left from the dock for around a minute and look for the blue door on the right-hand side of the main track. Basic, but well run by a sweet family. Doubles B$50

TOURS

There are numerous private boats and tour companies making the trip to the islands.

TOUR OPERATORS
Crillon Tours Av Camacho 1223, La Paz ☎02 2337533, ⓦtiticaca.com. La Paz agency that runs a variety of pricey one-, two- and three-day tours, with accommodation at their ecolodge on the Isla del Sol.

Transturin Av Arce 2678, La Paz ☎02 2422222, ⓦtransturin.com. One- and two-day catamaran cruises to the Isla del Sol, with a night on board at the north side of the island and a tour of their fascinating Inti Wata "cultural complex".

Hostal Inca Uta Near the northern landing jetty at Ch'allapampa ☎ 71515246, ⍵ hostalincauta.web.bo. Large yellow building with basic rooms, friendly owners and limited electricity. Doubles B$50

YUMANI

Las Cabañas de Aguadulce Leave the dock and turn left. You'll find these three solid, rudimentary buildings with corrugated roofs side by side about halfway up the hillside, above a restaurant that advertises "Hay Pizza" in black-and-white striped writing. Each has a private bathroom. There's no sign, but Franklin Ramos is the owner if you need to ask around. Doubles B$50

Hostal Inti Wayra Near the church, Yumani ☎ 71942015. A little more upmarket, with excellent views and friendly owners. Doubles B$160

EATING

There are plenty of basic restaurants serving pizza, pasta and freshly caught Titicaca trout upon request.

Posada y Restaurant de Manco Kapac Ch'allapampa, turn left from the jetty and it's thirty seconds on your right. Breakfasts, soups and trout at bargain prices.

Las Velas Yumani, high up near the eucalyptus forest. Classy and candlelit *Las Velas* offers wild trout, steamed vegetables and home-made pasta and pizza (mains B$30–50).

ISLA DE LA LUNA

About 8km east of the Isla del Sol, the far smaller **Isla de la Luna** (Island of the Moon) was another important pre-Columbian religious site. For much of the twentieth century, the island was used as a prison for political detainees, yet for the Incas it was a place of great spiritual importance. Known as Coati ("Queen Island"), it was associated with the moon, considered the female counterpart of the sun, and a powerful deity in her own right. The main site on the island – and one of the best-preserved Inca complexes in Bolivia – is a temple on the east coast known as **Iñak Uyu** (daily 8am–6pm; B$10), the "Court of Women", probably dedicated to the moon and staffed entirely by women. From the beach a series of broad Inca agricultural terraces leads up to the temple complex, a collection of stone buildings with facades containing eleven massive external niches still covered in mud stucco, all around a broad central plaza.

ARRIVAL AND DEPARTURE

By boat It takes about an hour by boat from the Isla del Sol to reach the island, and some agencies will include a brief visit to Isla de la Luna with the Isla del Sol tour. A daily public service to the island is planned, leaving at 8.30am from Copacabana and from Yumani at 10am (B$25 return). You could also hire a private sail boat (for about B$90) or private motor boat (around B$200), both including hire of a driver, from Isla del Sol to take you to the island and back.

TREKKING AND CLIMBING IN THE CORDILLERA REAL

The easiest base from which to explore the Cordillera Real is **La Paz**. Many of the best and most popular treks start close to the city, including the three so-called "Inca trails" which cross the Cordillera, connecting the Altiplano with the warm, forested valleys of the Yungas. Two of these ancient paved routes – the **Choro Trail** and the **Takesi Trail** – are relatively easy to follow without a guide; the third, the **Yunga Cruz Trail**, is more difficult – bring at least two days' worth of drinking water. You can do all three of these treks, as well as many other more challenging routes, with many of the adventure tour agencies based in La Paz (see box, p.162).

The other major starting point for trekking is the small town of **Sorata**. From here, numerous trekking routes take you high up among the glacial peaks, while others plunge down into the remote forested valleys of the Yungas. The **Sorata Guides and Porters Association** (see p.182) provides trekking guides, mules and porters. Further afield, the remote and beautiful **Cordillera Apolobamba**, a separate range of the Cordillera Oriental, north of Lake Titicaca and with almost no tourist infrastructure, offers excellent trekking possibilities for the more adventurous traveller. However, due to unpredictable weather conditions and the region's remoteness, it's unadvisable to attempt these treks without a guide.

With so many high peaks, the Cordillera Real is also obviously an excellent place for **mountain climbing**, for both serious and inexperienced climbers. **Huayna Potosí** (6088m), near La Paz, is one of the few peaks over 6000m in South America which can be ascended by climbers without mountaineering experience (albeit with the help of a specialist agency – check carefully that the guide they provide is qualified and experienced, and the equipment adequate).

2

ACCOMMODATION AND EATING

It's possible to camp on the island, but ask permission and bring your own food and drinking water; another alternative is the basic *hostal* next to the ruins, which can put you up. Dorms B$25

THE CORDILLERA REAL

Stretching for about 160km along the northeastern edge of the Altiplano, the **Cordillera Real** – the "Royal Range" – is the loftiest and most dramatic section of the Cordillera Oriental in Bolivia, with six peaks over 6000m high and many more over 5000m forming a jagged wall of soaring, ice-bound peaks separating the Altiplano from the tropical lowlands of the Amazon Basin. Easily accessible from La Paz, the mountains are perfect for climbing and trekking (see box, p.181) – indeed, walking here is the only way to really appreciate the overwhelming splendour of the Andean landscape. Populated by isolated **Aymara communities** that cultivate the lower slopes and valleys and raise llamas and alpacas on the high pastures, the cordillera is a largely pristine natural environment. Here, the mighty **Andean condor** is still a common sight, pumas, though rarely seen, still prowl the upper reaches, and the elusive Andean spectacled bear roams the high cloudforest that fringes the mountains' upper eastern slopes.

SORATA

Set at an altitude of 2695m, **SORATA** is a placid and enchanting little town, and is the most popular base for trekking and climbing in the Cordillera Real. Hemmed in on all sides by steep mountain slopes, often shrouded in clouds and with a significantly warmer climate than La Paz, it was compared by Spanish explorers to the Garden of Eden. There's not a lot to do in Sorata itself except hang out and relax either side of some hard trekking or climbing, or less strenuous walks in the surrounding countryside.

ARRIVAL AND DEPARTURE

By bus Buses from La Paz's cemetery district pull up every hour from 7am until 10pm in front of the bus company,

Transportes Unificada, on the Plaza Enrique Peñaranda. The road is mainly paved but very steep in places, and can be hair-raising. If you're coming from Copacabana, get off at Huarina and wait for a connecting bus to Sorata – you might need to wait a while for one that isn't full. In the past there have been high-season direct services between Copacabana and Sorata.

Destinations La Paz (every 30min until 5pm; 4hr).

INFORMATION

Money There's no ATM but Prodem give cash advances for a 5 percent commission fee.

Tourist information For information and advice on trekking in the surrounding mountains, try the Sorata Guides and Porters Association, whose office lies opposite the *Residencial Sorata*, just off the plaza on Calle Sucre (☏73272763). They can arrange guides for all the main trekking routes around Sorata for around B$200/day; they also organize mule hire and have a limited amount of camping equipment available for rent. La Paz-based Andean Epics offer some fantastic all-action expeditions leaving from Sorata (see p.162).

ACCOMMODATION

There's a good choice of inexpensive places to stay in Sorata, as well as a couple of mid-range options with creature comforts.

Altai Oasis ☏02 2133895, ☏71519856, ⊛altaioasis .com. Follow the path past the *Hostal El Mirador*, take the first right down the hill, then the next right-hand turning to drop steeply down towards the hostel. Alternatively, take a taxi for about B$20. Set by the river, this is an exquisite place to stay, with lush, sprawling grounds, swinging hammocks and a peaceful feel. Camping per person B$30, dorms B$84, doubles B$250

Hostal Jordán III C Murillo, at Bolívar ☏07 3288144, ⊛soratajordan.com. With terraces overlooking the square, this is an excellent place to watch the world go by. Facilities include a kitchen and a comfy DVD room. Continental breakfast available (B$10). Doubles B$90

Hostal El Mirador Muñecas 400 ☏02 2898503. This good-value, popular option is a 5min walk from the plaza. Rooms are basic but there's a lovely terrace with beautiful views, hot showers and a laidback feel. Doubles B$120

Hostal Panchita On the plaza, next to the church ☏02 2134242. A welcoming, simple place with a sunny courtyard and clean rooms (though the "hot" shower doesn't quite live up to its name). Doubles B$140

Las Piedras C 2 near the football field ☏71916341, ⊜laspiedras2002@yahoo.de. A 10–15min walk out of town, *Las Piedras* is a serene place with characterful rooms, balconies with deckchairs and an inviting communal area with games and plenty of cushions. Breakfast with home-made yoghurt and wholemeal bread is available for B$35, and German owner Petra will make you feel at home. Doubles B$80

Residencial Sorata Corner of the main plaza ⊕02 2136672. Set in the delightful, rambling nineteenth-century Casa Gunther, this *residencial* makes you feel you've stepped back in time by at least eighty years. There are lovely gardens, attractive simple rooms and a huge, wonderfully decorated drawing room. Doubles B$100

EATING AND DRINKING

While there's not a huge range of culinary choice in town, the setting more than makes up for it.

Altai Oasis (see above). Vast T-bone steaks, vegetables cultivated in the grounds and beautiful wooden furnishings make it worth the walk or taxi from town, with mains from B$34.

Café Illampu A 15–20min walk across the valley on the road leading to the Gruta de San Pedro. Worth a visit for its delicious breakfasts, milkshakes, bread and pastries, served in a wonderfully relaxing setting. Closed Tues.

Casa Reggae One block west of *Hostal El Mirador*. A basic outdoor bar, with drinks and sandwiches (from B$12) in the evening and a chilled out, hippyish feel. Evenings only.

Pizzeria Italia There are numerous pizza restaurants on the plaza; the best of an uninspiring bunch is the pizzeria attached to *Hostal Panchita*, with fairly decent and quickly turned-out pizza.

Restaurante Jalisco Plaza Enrique Peñaranda. This simple restaurant boasts a rather varied menu of Mexican and Italian food, as well as more traditional dishes. The *enchiladas* are surprisingly tasty (B$24).

THE YUNGAS

East of La Paz, the Cordillera Real drops precipitously into the Amazon lowlands, plunging down through a region of rugged, forest-covered mountains and deep subtropical valleys known as the **Yungas**, abundant with crops of coffee, tropical fruit and coca. Three of the well-built stone roads that linked the agricultural outposts of the Yungas to the main population centres before the Spanish conquest, the so-called "Inca" trails – the **Takesi**, **Choro** and **Yunga Cruz** – are still in good condition, and make excellent three- to four-day hikes from La Paz. The most frequently visited Yungas town is the idyllic resort of Coroico, set amid spectacular scenery and tropical vegetation. From Coroico, the road continues north towards Rurrenabaque and the Bolivian Amazon (see p.216).

COROICO

Rightly considered one of the most beautiful spots in the Yungas, the peaceful little town of **COROICO** is perched on a steep mountain slope with panoramic views across the forest-covered Andean foothills to the icy peaks of the Cordillera Real beyond. It enjoys a warm and pleasantly humid climate, and this, combined with the dramatic scenery and good facilities, makes it an excellent place to relax and recuperate – especially if you've spent the day cycling the "Death Road" (see box, p.169). Most cafés and restaurants are closed on Monday mornings and Tuesdays, and the town is often without electricity on Mondays.

WHAT TO SEE AND DO

Most visitors to Coroico spend much of their time relaxing on the peaceful **Plaza Principal**, lounging by a swimming pool and enjoying the fantastic views. For those with a bit more energy, though, there are some pleasant walks through the surrounding countryside, with forested mountain slopes covered in a lush patchwork of coffee and coca plantations, and banana and orange groves. If you're feeling adventurous, consider a canyoning

---

COCA IN THE YUNGAS

The Yungas is one of Bolivia's major coca-producing regions, a role it has played since the colonial era. Considered sweeter and better for chewing than that produced in the **Chapare** region, Yungas coca still dominates the Andean market, and remains legal for traditional use. It's worth checking on the coca-eradication situation before travelling anywhere off the beaten track in the Yungas; if an eradication campaign starts up before you arrive, strange gringos wandering around the backcountry might be misidentified as undercover US drug-enforcement agents. With President Morales' ongoing attempts to have the coca leaf taken off the official UN narcotics list, however, the situation may become more relaxed.

trip – where anyone looking for their adrenaline fix can clamber and climb their way along a series of river gorges and waterfalls – with community ecotourism agency, El Vagante (☎02 2413065, ⊛elvagante.com; ask at the office on the corner of the main square).

ARRIVAL AND DEPARTURE

By bus Buses and *micros* to and from La Paz use the bus station on the southwest side of town, opposite the football pitch. If you're coming to Coroico from anywhere else, you'll have to catch a pick-up truck for the 15min ride up from the main road at Yolosita – these drop passengers off outside the Mercado Municipal, on Sagárnaga. *Micro* services to La Paz (2hr–2hr 30min) depart every 20min until 6pm.

INFORMATION

Money and exchange Various shops change US dollars; Banco FIE and Pronam offer cash advances on Visa and MasterCard and are open Sat & Sun mornings.

Tourist information The office at the bus station has maps and information on activities and walks around the town. For trekking information, the office on the main square (daily 8am–8pm; ☎06 7108865) next to the police station offers a wealth of local information, with guides available for trips to nearby Afro-Boliviano communities, the Camino del Inca and waterfall hikes.

ACCOMMODATION

For a small town Coroico has a good range of places to stay, aimed primarily at visitors from La Paz. At weekends and on public holidays everywhere gets very full and prices go up, so it's worth booking in advance.

El Cafetal Beside the hospital, about a 10min walk southeast of the town centre ☎07 1954991, ✉danycafetal @hotmail.com. A gorgeous retreat far from the bustle of town, *El Cafetal* has clean, pleasant rooms, a pool, terraces and sweeping grounds. Rooms with private bath open onto balconies with exhilarating views, and there's also a good restaurant (see below). Doubles B$140

Hotel Esmeralda Half a kilometre above the town up Julio Zuazo Cuenca ☎02 2136017. The valley views are really the best thing about this place. It's cheap considering its lofty site, and the rooms and service rather reflect that. Dorms B$75, doubles B$200

Hostal Kory Linares 3501 ☎71564050. The genuinely spectacular views of the valley are the real draw here – you can see Death Road winding its hair-raising way – though the rooms aren't bad at all and the swimming pool is sparklingly clean. Prices include breakfast. Don't be afraid to barter on the room rate – there have been reports of plucked-out-of-the-air quotes. Doubles B$160

★ TREAT YOURSELF

La Senda Verde ☎74722825, ✉vossiop @gmail.com, ⊛sendaverde.com. Situated twenty minutes outside of Coroico (a taxi will usually charge about B$40) and set in a beautiful valley next to a river that you can swim in, this animal sanctuary is the kind of gorgeous hideaway you won't ever want to leave. There are sprawling, lush grounds to wander around, pretty views and a restaurant that serves up home-made pasta and salads. Accommodation is in two- to five-person cabins, which are dotted around the grounds. Prices include breakfast. Doubles B$360

★ **Hostal Sol y Luna** Just under 1km outside town, uphill on Julio Zuazo Cuenca, beyond the *Hotel Esmeralda* ☎71561626, ⊛solyluna-bolivia.com. Tranquil hideaway in beautiful hillside grounds that overlook the valley, with hammocks, fire pits, a yoga room and plunge pools. Cooking facilities are available to guests, but the restaurant does excellent, simple dishes too (daily 8am–10pm). Dorms B$50, doubles B$100, cabins B$300, camping (per person) B$20

EATING AND DRINKING

There's a decent variety of places to eat, from pizza and Mexican food to quality French cuisine, German pastries and even Swiss fondue, plus plenty of places for standard Bolivian fare.

Back-Stube Linares, off the main plaza. A café-restaurant specializing in German dishes such as *Sauerbraten* (B$47) and *Käsespätzle* (from B$37) as well as the all-Bolivian *pique a lo macho* (B$48) and excellent cakes (around B$12). Wonderful views of the valley, too. Wed–Fri 9.30am–2.30pm & 6.30–10pm, Sat & Sun 9.30am–10pm.

Café Internet El Nido del Uchi Main square. There's no internet here, but they do offer uncharacteristically (for Bolivia) hearty breakfasts – try the *desayuno yungueño* which combines steak, egg, rice, fried plantain and tomato, plus juice and coffee for B$30.

El Cafetal See above. The French cliché of snippy service can apply here, but so does the one about good cooking – come for a delicious menu of crêpes, soufflés, fish and meat dishes, plus panoramic views. Closed Tues.

Carla's Garden Pub 50m down the steps beyond *Hostal Kory*. Down a flight of steps that you won't relish climbing back up, *Carla's* is a cute, tucked-away little bar that does good simple food (sandwiches from B$12, pasta from B$32) and a fine range of beers (B$17–20), including the punch-packing "Judas". Wi-fi use is B$5. Tues–Sat 3pm–midnight (sometimes later).

La Casa C Julio Cuenca. German/Bolivian-run restaurant where walls are adorned with an eclectic range of trinkets. Specializes in fondues from B$45. The opening hours (daily 6pm till late) are one benefit in a town which shuts up shop Mon and Tues once the weekending *paceños* have fled.

Villa Bonita C Héroes del Chaco Ⓣ71918298, Ⓔvilla_bonita05@yahoo.com. It's a 10min walk from the plaza, but come for the friendly, boho atmosphere, shady garden, and delicious home-made ice cream and vegetarian dishes. Dorm beds are also available Wed–Sun, and en-suite rooms throughout the week. Daily 8.30am–5.30pm. Dorms B$55, doubles B$130

The Southern Altiplano

South of La Paz, the **Southern Altiplano** stretches 800km to the Chilean and Argentine borders. Set at an average altitude of around 3700m, this starkly beautiful landscape is the image most frequently associated with Bolivia: a barren and treeless expanse whose arid steppes stretch to the horizon, where snowcapped mountains shimmer under deep-blue skies.

The unavoidable transport nexus of the Altiplano is the tin-mining city of **Oruro**, 230km south of La Paz, a grim monument to industrial decline that comes alive once a year during the **Carnaval**. Some 310km further southeast of Oruro is the legendary silver-mining city of **Potosí**, a city of sublime colonial architecture, marooned at 4100m above sea level and filled with monuments to a glorious but tragic past.

The Altiplano grows more desolate still as it stretches south towards the Argentine border. From the forlorn railway town of **Uyuni**, 323km due south of Oruro by road and rail, you can venture into the dazzling white **Salar de Uyuni**, the **world's largest salt lake**. Beyond the Salar in the far southwestern corner of the country is the **Reserva de Fauna Andina Eduardo Avaroa**, a nature reserve of lunar landscapes, brightly coloured lakes and a surprising array of wildlife.

Southeast of Uyuni, the Altiplano changes character. The pleasant little mining town of **Tupiza** is surrounded by arid red mountains and cactus-strewn badlands eroded into deep gullies and rock pinnacles. In the far south of the country lies the provincial capital of **Tarija**, a remote yet welcoming city set in a deep and fertile valley that enjoys a much warmer climate than the Altiplano.

2

PARQUE NACIONAL SAJAMA

Southwest of La Paz, the road to Chile passes through a desert plain from the middle of which rises the perfect snow-capped cone of Volcán Sajama. At 6542m, Sajama is the tallest mountain in Bolivia and the centre of the country's oldest national park, the **Parque Nacional Sajama**.

The mountain's slopes support the highest forest in the world while the surrounding desert is home to pumas, rare Andean deer and the rarely seen, flightless, ostrich-like rheas.

Mountain climbers are drawn by the peak's relative ease of ascent – only permitted between April and October, when the ice is sufficiently frozen. The lower slopes contain bubbling geysers and hot springs which make for excellent hiking.

The administrative centre of the park, where you can register to climb the mountain and arrange guides, mules and porters, is the village of **SAJAMA**.

ARRIVAL AND INFORMATION

By bus There are two ways to reach Sajama by public transport from La Paz. The first is to take any Oruro-bound bus as far as the crossroads town of Patacamaya, from where a *micro* goes directly to Sajama every day at about 1pm (get there a couple of hours early), returning to Patacamaya at 6am the next day. The other way of reaching the park is to get on a bus from La Paz (2–3 daily; 3hr 30min–4hr) headed for Arica in Chile and alight at the village of Lagunillas (Lagunas on some maps), 2.5km beyond the turn-off to Sajama, from where you should be able to hire a taxi to Sajama village for Bs30–50.

Information For pre-trip information, contact SERNAP at Av Mariscal Santa Cruz, Edificio Litoral no. 150 in La Paz (Ⓣ02 2111360, Ⓦsernap.gob.bo). On arrival in Sajama village you must register at the park office (daily 8am–noon & 2.30–7pm) and pay a B$30 entrance fee.

2

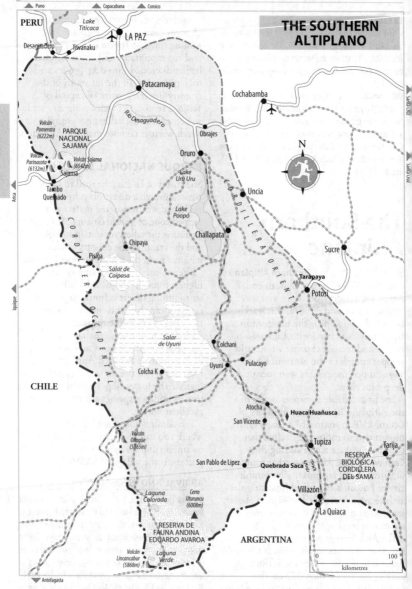

ACCOMMODATION AND EATING

There is very basic accommodation in the village as well as various places serving simple and inexpensive food. Andean Summits (andeansummits.com), based in La Paz, specialize in trips to the park with accommodation at the pleasant, airy *Tomarapi Ecolodge*. Do bring warm clothing – it can get chilly.

ORURO

Huddled on the bleak Altiplano some 230km south of La Paz, the grim mining city of **ORURO** was the economic powerhouse of Bolivia for much of the twentieth century, due to enormous mineral wealth in the surrounding

CROSSING INTO CHILE AT TAMBO QUEMADO

The **border** between Chile and Bolivia is 9km west of the turn-off to Sajama at **Tambo Quemado**. Crossing into Chile is straightforward: there is a Bolivian *migración* (daily 8.30am–6pm) where you get your exit stamp, and a couple of restaurants catering mainly to truck drivers. A couple of kilometres further on from Tambo Quemado is the Chilean border post of Chungara (daily 8am–8pm), where you'll have your passport stamped for entry to Chile. If you're coming from La Paz, the bus will take you all the way through to **Arica** (around 8hr) on Chile's Pacific coast. If you're heading to Chile from Sajama, you can get to the border on the 7am *micro* to Patacamaya (which comes to Tambo Quemado to pick up passengers), then walk across the frontier and pick up transport on the Chilean side.

2

mountains and tin mines established here in the late nineteenth century. Since the fall of world tin prices in 1985, however, Oruro's fortunes have plummeted and more than two decades of economic decline have made it a shadow of its former self.

WHAT TO SEE AND DO

Oruro is a cold and rather sombre place, with the melancholic air of a city forever looking back on a golden age, and there's not much reason to stop here outside of Carnaval time.

Plaza 10 de Febrero and the Casa de Cultura

The town's main plaza, Plaza 10 de Febrero, is a pleasant square shaded by cypress trees. Two blocks east of the plaza, at Avenida Galvarro, the fascinating **Casa de Cultura** (Mon–Fri 8–11.30am & 2.30–6pm; B\$10 including guided tour) is a former home of the "King of Tin" Simón I. Patiño, who was one of the world's wealthiest men when he died in 1947. With the original imported furniture, decadent chandeliers and children's toys all still intact, the museum is an intriguing insight into the luxurious life of one of the few Bolivians who got rich from the country's huge mineral wealth.

Museo Minero

Five blocks west of Plaza 10 de Febrero stands the **Santuario del Socavón** (Sanctuary of the Mineshaft), home to the image of the Virgin del Socavón, the patron saint of miners, in whose honour the Carnaval celebrations are staged. The abandoned mineshaft beneath the church is now home to the **Museo Minero** (daily 9–11.30am & 3–6pm; B\$10), which has an interesting display of equipment explaining the history of mining, as well as two fearsome-looking statues of El Tío, the devil-like figure worshipped by Bolivian miners as the king of the underworld and owner of all minerals.

Museo Antropológico

In the south of the city, at Avenida España, at Urquidi, the **Museo Antropológico Eduardo López Rivas** (Mon–Fri 8am–noon & 2–6pm, Sat & Sun 10am–6pm; B\$5) is home to an extensive archeological and ethnographic

CARNAVAL

Every year in late February or early March, Oruro explodes into life, celebrating its **Carnaval** in what is without doubt one of the most spectacular cultural events in all South America. Tens of thousands of visitors flock here to watch a sensational array of costumed dancers parading through the streets, and there's always a good deal of heavy drinking and chaotic water-fighting. At the centre of the festivities are two events: the **Entrada** on the Saturday before Ash Wednesday, with a massive procession of more than fifty different troupes of costumed dancers passing through the streets, and the **Diablada**, or Dance of the Devils, led by two lavishly costumed dancers representing Lucifer and St Michael, followed by hundreds of devil dancers who leap and prance through the streets. If you're coming to Oruro at this time of year, be sure to book accommodation in advance.

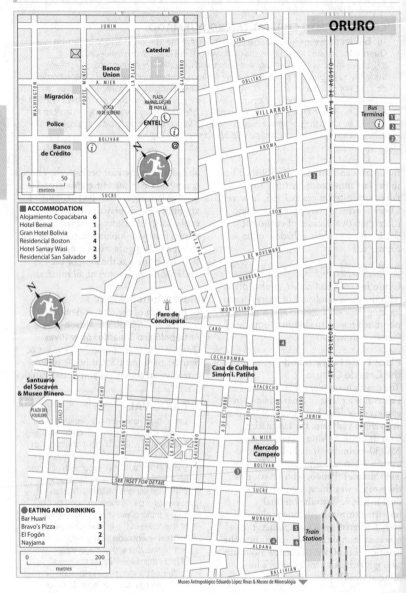

ORURO

ACCOMMODATION

Alojamiento Copacabana	6
Hotel Bernal	1
Gran Hotel Bolivia	3
Residencial Boston	4
Hotel Samay Wasi	2
Residencial San Salvador	5

EATING AND DRINKING

Bar Huari	1
Bravo's Pizza	3
El Fogón	2
Nayjama	4

Museo Antropológico Eduardo López Rivas & Museo de Mineralógia ▼

collection from the Oruro region with displays featuring arrowheads, stone tools, jewellery and a wonderful collection of traditional masks.

ARRIVAL AND DEPARTURE

By bus Almost all long-distance buses pull in at the Terminal Terrestre, ten blocks northeast of the city centre on Av Rajka Bakovic. A taxi into town from here should cost B$6–8/person; alternatively, take any *micro* heading south along Av 6 de Agosto.

Destinations Cochabamba (hourly; 5hr); La Paz (every 30min; 3hr 30min); Potosí (1 daily, between 6–9pm; 8hr); Sucre (1 daily, between 6–9pm; 10hr); several companies run overnight buses to Uyuni (8hr). There are also departures to Iquique in Chile (2 daily at 1pm and 2am; 8hr).

By train The train station is a short walk southeast of the city centre on Av Galvarro (note that the ticket office is closed all day Sat). Only first-class tickets are sold in advance; the rest can be bought the day before travel at the earliest – you'll need to show your passport.

Villazón (3.30pm Tues & Fri with Expreso del Sur, 16hr; 7pm Wed & Sun with Wara Wara del Sur via Uyuni, 7hr, and Tupiza, 13hr).

INFORMATION

Tourist information The office (Mon–Fri 8am–noon & 2.30–6.30pm; ☎ 02 5250144) is on the south side of Plaza 10 de Febrero, though it is rarely open outside of Carnaval. There is also a kiosk at the bus terminal where you might get a map.

ACCOMMODATION

There's a fairly good range of places to stay in Oruro – though a lack of good budget choice. During Carnaval prices go up by as much as five times and most places will only rent rooms for the entire weekend.

Alojamiento Copacabana Av Galvarro 6352 ☎02 5254184. A handy option with a secure feel very close to the train station; rooms are clean though some are tiny. Doubles B$80

Hotel Bernal Av Brasil 701 ☎02 5279468. Near the bus station, this place has seen far better days, but overall it's a steal for the price. Rooms at the front are noisy. Doubles B$160

Gran Hotel Bolivia C Rodriguez 131, between 6 de Agosto and Velasco Galvarro ☎02 5241047. Two blocks from the bus station, it's not grand but it is certainly colourful, with basic rooms set around a fairly cheery central courtyard. Breakfast is available. Doubles B$100

Residencial Boston Pagador 1159 ☎02 5274708. The bright decor of the public areas makes up for slightly dingy rooms, though they're good value and come with or without private bath. Doubles B$100

Hotel Samay Wasi Av Brasil 232 ☎02 5276737, ✉samaywasioruro@hotmail.com. This HI-affiliated modern block near the bus station is a little over budget, but with spick-and-span rooms, good showers and a substantial buffet breakfast included, it's worth it if you need pampering. Doubles B$240

Residencial San Salvador Av Galvarro 6325 ☎02 5276771. Near the train station, the rooms come with private bath and cable TV but can get stiflingly hot. Doubles B$90

EATING AND DRINKING

There are plenty of cheap roast-chicken restaurants and snack bars on Avenida 6 de Octubre, where late on Friday and Saturday night stalls serve the local speciality *rostro asado*, or roasted sheep's head.

Bar Huari Junín, at Galvarro. Near the cathedral, this bar has an old-fashioned vibe (as do many of the customers), but it's a nice laidback option for a quiet beer (B$12–15).

Bravo's Pizza Bolívar, at Potosí. Serves up decent pizza – including one topped with dried llama meat – in a cheerful second-floor restaurant overlooking the plaza. Wi-fi available. Pizzas big enough for two from B$49.

El Fogón Brasil, opposite bus station. This basic place specializes in the local delicacy *charquekan* – llama meat that is first dried then fried in plentiful oil, and served with mote (dried corn), potatoes and white cheese. Mains B$25–45.

Nayjama Pagador, at Aldana. The best restaurant in town, serving huge portions of delicious local food, with specialities including sublime roast lamb and *criadillas* (bull testicles). Mains from B$40.

POTOSÍ

Set on a desolate, windswept plain amid barren mountains at almost 4100m above sea level, **POTOSÍ** is the highest city in the world, and at once the most fascinating and tragic place in Bolivia. Given its remote and inhospitable location, it's difficult to see at first glance why it was ever built here at all. The answer lies in **Cerro Rico** ("Rich Mountain"), the conical peak that rises imperiously above the city to the south and that was, quite simply, the richest source of silver the world had ever seen.

The **silver rush** of Cerro Rico was triggered in 1545 by a llama herder who was caught out after dark on the mountain's slopes. He started a fire to keep warm, and was amazed to see a trickle of molten silver run out from the blaze. News of this discovery soon reached the Spaniards, the rush was soon under way, and its population mushroomed to more than 100,000 over the next twenty years, making it easily the largest metropolis in the Americas.

By the beginning of the seventeenth century, Potosí was home to more than 160,000 people and boasted dozens of magnificent churches, as well as theatres, gambling houses, brothels and dance halls. For the **indigenous workers and African slaves** who produced this wealth, however, the working conditions were appalling. Estimates of the total number who died over three centuries of colonial mining in Potosí run as high as nine million, making the mines of Potosí a central factor in the demographic collapse that swept the Andes under Spanish rule.

WHAT TO SEE AND DO

Potosí is a treasure-trove of colonial art and architecture, with hundreds of well-preserved buildings, including some of the finest churches in Bolivia.

Plaza 10 de Noviembre

The centre of the city is the **Plaza 10 de Noviembre**, a pleasant tree-shaded square with a small replica of the Statue of Liberty, erected in 1926 to commemorate Bolivian independence. On the north side of the square, the site of the original church (which collapsed in 1807) is now occupied by the twin-towered **Catedral**, completed in Neoclassical style in 1836. To the east of the square lies the **Plaza 6 de Agosto**, at the centre of which is a column commemorating the Battle of Ayacucho in 1824, which secured Bolivian independence early the following year.

Casa Real de la Moneda

West of the Plaza 10 de Noviembre on Calle Ayacucho stands the unmissable **Casa Real de la Moneda**, or Royal Mint (Tues–Sat 9–10.30am & 2.30–5.30pm, Sun 9–10.30am; B$20 includes tours in Spanish or English; ⊛bolivian.com/cnm). One of the most outstanding examples of colonial civil architecture in all South America, it is now home to one of the best museums in Bolivia. The collection includes the original minting machinery, some of Bolivia's finest colonial religious art, militaria, archeological artefacts and a display of coins and banknotes.

Built between 1759 and 1773, La Moneda is a truly formidable construction, built as part of a concerted effort by the Spanish crown to reform the economic and financial machinery of the empire to increase revenues. The rambling two-storey complex of about **two hundred rooms** is set around five internal courtyards, and housed troops, workers, African slaves and the senior royal officials responsible for overseeing operations. A vital nerve centre of Spanish imperial power in the Andes, it also served as a prison, treasury and near-impregnable stronghold in times of disorder.

La Torre de la Compañia de Jesus

On Calle Ayacucho, west of the Casa Real de la Moneda, stands **La Torre de la Compañia de Jesus** (Mon–Fri 8am–noon & 2–6pm, Sat & Sun 8.30am–12.30pm & 2.30–6.30pm; B$10), a bell tower which is all that now remains of a Jesuit church originally founded in 1581. Completed in 1707 and recently restored, the grandiose tower is one of the finest eighteenth-century religious monuments in Bolivia and a sublime example of the Mestizo-Baroque style. You can climb to the top, from where there are excellent views of the city and Cerro Rico.

CERRO RICO

Immediately south of Potosí the near-perfect cone of **Cerro Rico** rises above the city, pockmarked with the entrances to the thousands of mines that lead deep into its entrails. Operators in town run regular tours of the mines, but be warned that this is an unpleasant and dangerous environment, where safety precautions are largely left to fate; anyone suffering from claustrophobia, heart or breathing problems is advised against entering. Some also question the ethics of making a tourist attraction of a workplace where conditions are so appalling.

Tours of the mines begin with a visit to the miners' market on and around Plaza El Calvario. Here you can buy coca leaves, dynamite, black-tobacco cigarettes, pure cane alcohol and fizzy soft drinks as gifts for the miners you'll be visiting. Tours should cost B$70–80 per person. Recommended operators are **Koala Tours** (Ayacucho 5 ☏02 6222092, ✉koalabolivia @hotmail.com), with trips run by experienced multilingual guides, and **Big Deal** (Bustillos 1092 near the Casa de Moneda ☏02 6230478, ☏71835516, ✉bigdealtours@gmail.com, ⊛bigdealtours.blogspot.co.uk), whose guides are ex-miners.

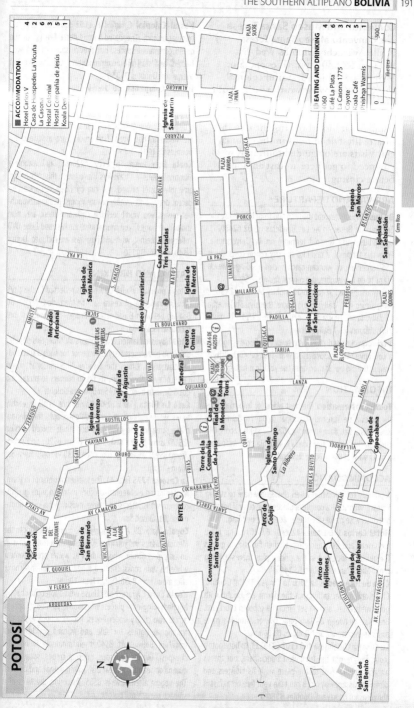

POTOSÍ

2

ACCOMMODATION
Hotel Carlos V 4
Casa de Huéspedes La Vicuña 2
La Casona 6
Hostal Colonial 3
Hostal Compañía de Jesús 5
Koala Den 1

EATING AND DRINKING
4060 4
Café La Plata 6
La Casona 1775 3
Coyote 2
Koala Café 5
Phishqa Warmis 1

0   300
metres

Cerro Rico

Plaza Sucre
Plaza España
Plaza Alonzo
Plaza 10 de Noviembre
Plaza York
Plaza del Estudiante
Plaza a la Madre
Plaza Quiñones

Iglesia de San Martín
Iglesia de Santa Monica
Iglesia de la Merced
Iglesia de San Sebastián
Ingenio San Marcos
Iglesia y Convento de San Francisco
Mercado Artesanal
Museo Universitario
Casa de las Tres Portadas
Teatro Omiste
Catedral
Iglesia de San Agustín
Iglesia de San Lorenzo
Mercado Central
Casa Real de la Moneda
Koala Tours
Torre de la Compañía de Jesús
Iglesia de Santo Domingo
Iglesia de Copacabana
Iglesia de Jerusalén
Iglesia de San Bernardo
Convento-Museo Santa Teresa
ENTEL
Arco de Cobija
Arco de Mejillones
Iglesia de Santa Bárbara
Iglesia de San Benito
La Ribera

ALMAGRO
PIZARRO
BOLIVAR
HOYOS
CHUQUISACA
PORCO
LA PAZ
LINARES
MILLARES
NOGALES
PERIODISTA
BETANZOS
LA PAZ
S. CHACON
SUCRE
OMISTE
MATOS
EL BOULEVARD
PADILLA
CHUQUISACA
TARIJA
INGAVI
BUSTILLOS
CHAYANTA
ORURO
JUNIN
BOLIVAR
QUIJARRO
PLAZA 6 DE AGOSTO
LANZA
FAÑOLA
AV FERRUDO
AV CIVICA
INGAVI
ORURO
FRIAS
AYACUCHO
COCHABAMBA
SANTA TERESA
COBIJA
LANZA
NIKOLAS BENITO
GUZMAN
VILLARROEL
CHICHAS
AV CAMACHO
BOLIVAR
F. QUQUIEL
V FLORES
ARQUEDAS
MEJILLONES
AV RECTOR VASQUEZ
PASAJE DE LAS SIETE VUELTAS

N

2

Convento and Museo Santa Teresa

The **Convento-Museo Santa Teresa** (Calle Ayacucho; Mon & Wed–Sat 9–11am & 2.30–5pm, Tues and Sun 3–5pm; B$21) is a beautiful colonial church and convent worth visiting both for its fine collection of colonial religious painting and sculpture, and for a somewhat disturbing insight into the bizarre lifestyle of nuns in the colonial era. Visits are by guided tour only, so you need to get here at least an hour before closing.

ARRIVAL AND DEPARTURE

By bus All buses (except those to and from Uyuni) use the Terminal de Buses on Av Las Banderas (☎02 6243029). Uyuni buses use the old terminal on Av Universitaria. From the terminal, a taxi into the city centre costs about B$5–8/person, or you can catch *micros* heading towards Plaza 10 de Noviembre, the central square.

Destinations La Paz (up to 10 nightly between 7–9pm; 9hr); Oruro (10 daily; 6hr); Sucre (hourly; 3hr); Tarija (1 daily; 12hr); Tupiza (3–4 daily; 6–7hr); Uyuni (2 daily; 7hr); Villazón (6–7 daily; 12hr).

Taxi A quicker and nicer way to get to Sucre is to take a collective taxi (B$35/person with four people). Drivers wait at the old bus station until the vehicle is full.

INFORMATION

Tourist information The best place for information is the Oficina de Turismo Municipal (Mon–Fri 8am–noon & 2–6pm, Sat 8am–noon; ☎02 6226408), accessible through the arch of Torre de la Compañía on C Ayacucho, a block west of Plaza 10 de Noviembre.

ACCOMMODATION

A primary consideration when choosing where to stay in Potosí is warmth – a couple of places have central heating, but otherwise make sure there's adequate bedding.

Hotel Carlos V C Linares 42 ☎02 6231010. This place feels clean and fresh and offers kitchen facilities to guests (breakfast is included in the price), plus there's a living room-like TV area. Doubles B$140

Casa de Huespedes La Vicuña C Ingavi 184, at Quijarro. Chronically understaffed, but the dorms are bright, with good mattresses, and all set around a cobbled courtyard. Breakfast between 8–9am only. Owner Antonio's mine tours are recommended. Doubles B$100

La Casona Chuquisaca 460 ☎02 6230523, ⓦhotelpotosi .com. They're not the friendliest bunch here, but there's an atmospheric feel to the place with its cloisters and dimly lit passageways. You can take your free breakfast in the pleasant courtyard. Doubles B$80

Hostal Colonial C Hoyos 8 ☎02 6224265, ⓦhostal colonial-bo.com. The dated rooms don't live up to the grand communal spaces, but they're spacious and well heated, and staff are accommodating. Comfortable but overpriced. Doubles B$350

Hostal Compañía de Jesús Chuquisaca 445 ☎02 6223173. The welcome, as frosty as the Potosí nights, is on a par with *La Casona* across the street, but the building, a beautiful colonial conversion, makes up for it. Showers are steaming hot, even if the rooms are a little chilly. Doubles B$100

Koala Den Junín 56 ☎02 6226467, ⓔkoalabolivia @hotmail.com. A travellers' favourite, this charming, amicable hostel owned and run by Koala Tours features decent dorms and inviting private rooms. Heating throughout means you won't feel the chill, and there are great showers, a homely communal area, kitchen and large DVD collection. Internet, wi-fi and breakfast are included. Dorms B$40, doubles B$150

EATING AND DRINKING

Potosí's popularity with travellers is reflected in the city's growing variety of places to eat. The Mercado Central – on Bolívar, between Bustillos and Oruro – is your best bet for cheap local food.

4060 Hoyos 1. Named after Potosí's altitude, this popular café/pub has a pretty, stylish interior for such a spit-and-sawdust town. Offers the dreaded "international" menu (a bit of everything from steaks to burgers to pizza) and good German beer. Mon–Sat 5pm–midnight.

Café La Plata Plaza 10 de Noviembre. With its earthy tones, warm lighting and creaky floorboards, this elegant place screams hot chocolate and their spiced version (B$16) is up to the task. Pizzas (from B$20) and salads (from B$22) available too. Mon 1.30–11pm, Tues–Sat 10am–11pm.

La Casona 1775 Frías 41. The liveliest nightspot in town, housed in an eighteenth-century mansion with graffiti-covered walls. Occasional live music. Mon–Sat 6pm–midnight. Closed Sun.

Coyote Matos 89. A worryingly long menu, but stick to the Mexican dishes and you'll be OK. A long, colourful space with an engaging owner who doubles as waiter and raconteur while his wife cooks. This is a solid if unexceptional choice with mains from B$38. Daily 11am–10pm.

Koala Café C Ayacucho 5. Those who appreciate shabby, higgledy-piggledy places will warm to *Koala*, spread across two creaky upper floors. There's a book exchange, traditional clothes for sale and framed articles about travel in Bolivia. At B$40 their *almuerzo* is not the cheapest, but it's generous, offering crepes, soup (often quinoa or peanut), a meat dish (often llama) and dessert. The veggie alternative is B$35, featuring the likes of a spinach pie or lentil burger.

Phishqa Warmis Sucre 55. The B$30 *almuerzo* (noon–3pm), which includes a salad buffet, is a particularly good reason to come to this smart, warmly decorated place. Other mains include *charquekan*, a Bolivian dish centred on dried llama meat (B$40). There's often Spanish cinema and live music too. Daily 8am–midnight.

DIRECTORY

Banks and exchange The Banco Nacional de Bolivia on Junín changes cash and travellers' cheques, or try Casa Fernandez on Padilla between Bolívar and Matos. Several shops along Bolívar change US dollars. There are several ATMs, including Banco de Crédito, on Bolívar and Sucre.

Cinema Cine Imperial on Padilla between Chuquisaca and Nogales.

Internet There are lots in town, but try the second floor of *Koala Café*, Ayacucho 5 (B$3/hr).

Pharmacy There's a late-night place on El Boulevard, near the junction with Plaza 6 de Agosto.

Post office Correo Central, a block south of Plaza 10 de Noviembre on Lanza, at Chuquisaca. Mon–Fri 8am–8pm, Sat 8am–6pm, Sun 9am–noon.

Telephone centres ENTEL, Cochabamba and Plaza Arce.

UYUNI

Set on the bleak southern Altiplano 212km southwest of Potosí, the cold railway town of **UYUNI** is useful as a jumping-off point for expeditions into the beautiful and remote landscapes of the far southwest. In its heyday, the city was Bolivia's main gateway to the outside world and a symbol of modernity and industrial progress. Today, its streets are lined with a collection of shabby, tin-roofed houses and semi-abandoned railway yards filled with the decaying skeletons of redundant trains. A small town, it holds everything you might need within a few blocks; the effective centre is the nineteenth-century clock tower at the intersection of Avenidas Arce and Potosí. That Uyuni hasn't become a ghost town is due to the ever-growing number of travellers who come here to visit the spectacular scenery of the **Salar de Uyuni** and the **Reserva de Fauna Andina Eduardo Avaroa**, which are usually visited together on a three-day tour.

ARRIVAL AND DEPARTURE

By plane The airport opened in 2011. Between them, Amazonas and TAM (who both have offices in town) run between one and three daily direct flights to La Paz, with onward connections to Sucre, Tarija, Santa Cruz, Rurrenabaque and Cusco.

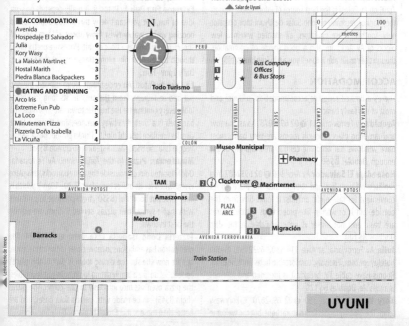

▲ Salar de Uyuni

■ ACCOMMODATION	
Avenida	7
Hospedaje El Salvador	1
Julia	6
Kory Wasy	4
La Maison Martinet	2
Hostal Marith	3
Piedra Blanca Backpackers	5

● EATING AND DRINKING	
Arco Iris	5
Extreme Fun Pub	2
La Loco	3
Minuteman Pizza	6
Pizzeria Doña Isabella	1
La Vicuña	4

N

PERÚ

Bus Company Offices & Bus Stops

Todo Turismo

BOLÍVAR

AVENIDA ARCE

SUCRE

CAMACHO

SANTA CRUZ

COLÓN

Museo Municipal

+ Pharmacy

AYACUCHO

AVAROA

TAM

Clocktower

@ Macinternet

AVENIDA POTOSÍ

AVENIDA POTOSÍ

Amazonas

PLAZA ARCE

Mercado

Migración

Barracks

AVENIDA FERROVIARIA

Train Station

0 ... 100 metres

UYUNI

2

By bus Buses from Potosí, Oruro and Tupiza pull up in front of the various bus company offices, three blocks north of the train station along the partly pedestrianized Av Arce. Todo Turismo (Santa Cruz 155; ☎02 6933337) buses to La Paz are the most comfortable option. Their service (with heating, food and toilet) leaves daily at 8pm. Advance booking recommended.

Destinations La Paz (3–4 nightly at 8pm; 11hr); Oruro (2–3 nightly; 8hr); Potosí (4 daily at 7pm; 4hr); Sucre (4 daily; 10hr; better to take the bus from Potosí); Tarija (1 daily; 18hr); Tupiza (1 daily; 6hr). There are also daily services (at 3am) to Avaroa and Calama in Chile.

By train The train station is on Av Ferroviaria in the centre of town. If you're arriving on a late-night train, most hostels will open their doors to you no matter what time it is. Remember to buy your ticket in advance; you will need your passport as ID. Check ⓦ fca.com.bo for more information.

Destinations Oruro 12.05am Thurs & Sun with Expreso del Sur, 1.45am Tues & Fri; (7hr); Villazón 10.40pm Tues & Fri with Expreso del Sur (9hr); 2.50am Mon & Thurs with Wara Wara del Sur via Tupiza (5hr 30min).

INFORMATION

Internet There's no wi-fi in town and internet connections are often agonizingly slow. Try Macinternet on Av Potosí (B$5/hr).

Money There are a few ATMs on Av Potosí east of the clocktower.

Tourist information Infotur (Mon–Fri 8am–noon & 2.30–7pm) on Av Potosí is the best source of information, though they cannot recommend one Salar de Uyuni tour operator over another. These operators, all situated within a few blocks of Av Arce, are also a good source of information, though their main aim is to sell you a trip (see box, p.195).

ACCOMMODATION

There's a limited range of accommodation in Uyuni and most of it is fairly basic.

Avenida Av Ferroviaria 11 ☎02 6932078. A vast, narrow and rambling place. Though rooms are very basic, most have windows out onto the central area and are bright enough. Doubles B$60

Hospedaje El Salvador Av Arce 346 ☎02 6932407. You can step off your bus and straight into this place, so it's convenient for late-night arrivals. It looks tiny from the outside, but is of warren-like proportions within. Rooms are basic and hot water is only available in the day. Doubles B$100

Julia Av Ferroviaria, at Arce 314 ☎02 6932134, ⓦ julia hoteluyuni.com. Friendly, comfortable hotel with heating. Rooms have cable TV, breakfast is included and internet is available. Doubles B$120

Kory Wasy Av Potosí 350 ☎02 6932670, ⓦ korywasy .com. The gloomy rooms lack natural light, but the welcome

is friendly enough and it's one of the cheapest places in town. Doubles B$100

La Maison Martinet Av Potosí 16 ☎02 2732631, ⓦ lamaisonmartinet.com. The layout is akin to a hotel, but the rooms on offer are actually apartments, each with a mini-kitchen and sitting room. Sleeping three–four people, they work out as good value if you're in a group. The place is decked out with antique apothecary and medicinal artefacts. Apartments B$350

Hostal Marith Potosí 61 ☎02 6932174, ⓦ marithotel .com. A few blocks from the centre, the bright, clean rooms are set round a courtyard (though this is rather spoilt by the plastic sheeting stretched across it). Breakfast included. Doubles B$120

Piedra Blanca Backpackers Av Arce 27 ☎76437643. This rambling, ramshackle place set back from the street has some charm, not least thanks to the row of stained-glass windows down one side of the U-shaped building. Guests get breakfast and can use the kitchen. Private rooms are overpriced. Dorms B$55, doubles B$150

EATING AND DRINKING

As with accommodation, the range of places to eat in Uyuni is pretty limited. The food market on Potosí and Avaroa has cheap and decent local dishes.

Arco Iris Plaza Arce. The best pizzas on this tourist honeypot strip, and, with its brick arches, it's a little more atmospheric than most. Pizzas from B$33, and drinks are relatively cheap.

Extreme Fun Pub Av Potosí 9. It really depends on your idea of fun, but you can't deny this place's dedication to boozing with a wacky twist (how about a "Llama Sperm" shot?). One room has a floor of salt. Prices are pretty high, though there are drinks promotions early in the evening. Daily 2pm–1am.

La Loco Av Potosí. An endearingly weird railroad-themed bar and restaurant. From the outside, its long low block looks every centimetre the frontier town saloon; inside, the bar itself is a riveted railway carriage, and there's a large circular fireplace for cold nights. Drinks promotions 7–8pm. Veggie lasagne B$38, llama steak with quinoa B$55.

Minuteman Pizza In the Toñito Hotel, Av Ferroviaria. Oddly located directly outside the army barracks, this place is renowned for its buffet breakfast (7.30–10am), which is expensive but bountiful (B$50), from porridge to pancakes with maple syrup. Their pizzas, served 5–9pm, are among the best in town.

Pizzeria Doña Isabella C Camacho ☎73759824. The chef-patron has ambitions to move closer to the train station, but for now the strange dining room is part of this place's appeal. Set up like a family sitting room, with just four tables, the pizza oven sits incongruously in one corner. The pizzas (from B$45) can be made with quinoa flour bases, and are better than those at more touristy places. Daily from 6pm.

La Vicuña C Sucre. Set over a few small rooms, this cute, breakfast-only place run by Swedish expat Barbro has an intimate, domestic feel, with a pretty woven wicker lampshade hanging over each table. The food is simple, cheap and good, with prices from B$9 for scrambled eggs and toast. Mon–Sat 6–11am.

SALAR DE UYUNI

One of Bolivia's most extraordinary attractions, the **Salar de Uyuni**, covering some 9000 square kilometres of the Altiplano west of Uyuni, is by far the largest salt lake in the world. The Salar is not a lake in any conventional sense of the word – though below the surface it is largely saturated by water, its uppermost layer consists of a thick, hard crust of salt, easily capable of supporting the weight of a car. Tours will take you to the striking cactus-covered **Isla del Pescado** (also known as Inca Huasi), where a series of paths leads you on a short walk with breathtaking vistas of the vast Salar. The surface is mostly covered by water between December and April, but even then it's rarely more than a metre deep, and usually much less. Driving across the perfectly flat white expanse of the Salar, with the unbroken chains of snowcapped mountains lining the far horizon, the terrain is so harsh and inhospitable it's like being on another planet.

RESERVA DE FAUNA ANDINA EDUARDO AVAROA

The southwesternmost corner of Bolivia is covered by the **Reserva de Fauna Andina Eduardo Avaroa**, a 7147-square-kilometre wildlife reserve, ranging between 4000m and 6000m in altitude and encompassing some of the most startling scenery in Bolivia. Like the Salar de Uyuni, the desolate landscapes of this remote region possess an otherworldly beauty, with glacial salt lakes whose icy waters are stained bright red or emerald green, snowcapped volcanic peaks, high-altitude deserts and a wide range of rare **Andean wildlife** including the world's largest population of the **James flamingo**, the elusive **Andean fox** and herds of **graceful vicuñas**. There is an entrance fee (B$150) into the reserve, which is not usually included in the tour price and

---

VISITING THE SALAR AND THE RESERVE

Pretty much the only way to visit the **Salar de Uyuni** and **Reserva De Fauna Andina Eduardo Avaroa** is on an organized tour, which can be easily arranged from Uyuni. The standard three-day tour price is usually B$800–1000 including food, accommodation, transport and a Spanish-speaking guide. You'll pay more if booking in La Paz, and often significantly more for an English-speaking guide. An additional B$30 is payable for the visit to **Fish Island** (Inca Huasi) and B$150 for entering the reserve. The tour is by 4WD around a circuit comprising the Salar de Uyuni and **Lagunas Colorada** and **Verde** in the reserve; four-day and longer trips are also available. Note that wind-chill temperatures can drop to anything from -25°C to -40°C. You should bring sunblock and sunglasses to counter the possibility of snow blindness, as well as a good sleeping bag, a torch and plenty of warm clothing (your agency should be able to rent you a sleeping bag).

Issues such as late departures, inadequate accommodation and vehicle breakdowns are problems that may occur no matter which agency you choose, but it's definitely worth paying a little more to ensure good safety conditions. The cheaper agencies tend to have older cars, bad food and unfriendly, occasionally drunk drivers. The best method of choosing an agency is to talk to travellers just returned from a tour. If they loved a particular guide, you should ask for that individual when you book. Also request a written contract detailing exactly what you are paying for.

TOUR OPERATORS

Cordillera Traveller Tours Av Ferroviaria ☎02 6933304, ⓦcordilleratraveller.com.
Red Planet Expedition C Sucre between Av

Ferroviaria and Av Potosí ☎72403896, ⓦredplanet expedition.com.
Ruta Verde Santa Cruz ☎03 3396470, ⓦrutaverde bolivia.com.

2

CROSSING INTO ARGENTINA AT VILLAZÓN

The main border crossing between **Bolivia** and **Argentina** is at the dusty ramshackle frontier town of **Villazón**, about 92km south of Tupiza by road or rail. Just walk south from the plaza down to the frontier along Avenida Internacional and get an exit stamp at the Bolivian *migración* office (open 24hrs), then walk across the bridge into Argentina, where immigration is open 7am–11pm. From the Argentine border town of **La Quiaca** there are regular buses to the city of **Jujuy**, from where there are connections to the rest of the country.

paid at a rangers' office at the point of entry. It is possible to cross into Chile at a **border crossing** near Laguna Verde in the far south of the reserve – inform your operator when booking if you wish to do this. Officials at the border post have been known to charge small unauthorized fees for letting you cross.

TUPIZA

Some 200km southeast of Uyuni, the isolated mining town of **Tupiza** nestles in a narrow, fertile valley that cuts through the harsh desert landscape with its cactus-strewn badlands, deep canyons and strangely shaped rock formations and pinnacles. In the late nineteenth and early twentieth centuries, Tupiza was the home of one of Bolivia's biggest mining barons, Carlos Aramayo. His mines were rich enough to attract the attention of the infamous North American gunslingers **Butch Cassidy and the Sundance Kid**, who are believed to have died in a shoot-out in the town of **San Vicente**, some 100km to the northwest. The town draws visitors largely because of the surrounding landscape, ideal for hiking, horseriding or just touring by jeep, activities that are easily arranged through local operators (see box, p.197), who also offer Butch Cassidy-related excursions.

ARRIVAL AND DEPARTURE

By bus The bus terminal is on Av Arraya, three blocks south and two blocks east of the main square, Plaza Independencia. Destinations La Paz (3 daily; 12–13hr); Potosí (2 daily; 5hr); Tarija (several departures between 7pm & 8pm; 6–7hr though much longer in the rainy season); Uyuni (2 daily; 6–7hr); Villazón (4 daily; 3hr).

By train The train station is three blocks east of the main plaza on Plazuela Adolfo Torres del Carpio, just off Av Serrudo. Be sure to buy your ticket in advance. Check ⓦ www.fca.com.bo for more information.

Destinations Oruro (6.25pm Wed & Sat with Expreso del Sur, 7.05pm Mon & Thurs with Wara Wara del Sur; 13hr) via Uyuni (5hr 30min); Villazón (4.10am Wed & Sat with Expreso del Sur, 9.05am Mon & Thurs with Wara Wara del Sur; 3hr).

By taxi The quickest way to reach Villazón is in one of the shared taxis that leave throughout the day from the bus station when full.

INFORMATION

Money and exchange Banco Union and Banco FIE on the main square both have ATMs. Several cambios east of the plaza on C Avaroa will change travellers' cheques, as well as US dollars, Argentine pesos and sometimes Peruvian soles.

Pharmacy Farmacia Nacional on C Avaroa.

Phone Punto Entel on Av Santa Cruz, at C Avaroa.

Tourist information There is no formal tourist office in the town, but the main tour operators (see box, p.197) can tell you all you need to know.

ACCOMMODATION

There is a small range of accommodation in Tupiza, aimed specifically at backpackers on limited budgets. If arriving late, it is best to call ahead.

Mitru Av Chichas 187 ☎ 02 6943001, ⓦ hotelmitru.com. A sunny central courtyard and swimming pool, clean, comfortable rooms and a buffet breakfast make this a popular choice, with prices depending on whether you're in the newer or older parts of the hotel. Run by the same owners are *Anexo Mitru*, C Avaroa (☎ 02 6943002), and *Refugio del Turista*, Av Santa Cruz 244 (☎ 02 6943155), which has dorms and doubles, with use of a kitchen and *Hotel Mitru's* pool. *Mitru*: doubles B$120; *Anexo Mitru*: doubles (with breakfast) B$200; *Refugio del Turista*: dorms B$30, doubles B$90

La Torre Av Chichas 220 ☎ 02 6942633, ⓔ latorrehotel @yahoo.es, ⓦ latorretours-tupiza.com. A friendly place with a handsome black-and-white tiled floor and a homely social area. Kitchen use is offered (though no cooking of eggs, garlic or onions is permitted because of the smell). One room with three beds serves as a "dorm". Dorms B$55, doubles B$100

Hostal Valle Hermoso 2 Av Pedro Arraya ☎ 02 6942592, ⓔ info@vallehermosotours.com. A wood-panelled, HI-affiliated hostel with fresh-feeling dorms and excellent-value

ORGANIZED TOURS FROM TUPIZA

Tupiza's tour agencies all offer broadly similar guided excursions into the desert landscapes around the town. Often referred to as a "triathlon", they combine 4WD excursions, trekking, horseriding and sometimes mountain biking (in the case of Valle Hermoso Tours). The full-day tours usually cost around B$300/person depending on numbers, and half-day tours are often offered for a little over half the price. You can also do longer but not terribly rewarding trips to **San Vicente**, where **Butch Cassidy and the Sundance Kid** are thought to have died. These same agencies organize trips to the Reserva de Fauna Andina Eduardo Avaroa and the Salar de Uyuni, usually as a four-day circuit in a jeep with three to five passengers that should cost about B$1300/person, ending at the town of Uyuni (though returning to Tupiza is usually possible). Reserve entrance fees (B$150), Fish Island entrance fee (B$30) and use of showers (B$10) are payable as extras, as is the luxury of an English-speaking guide. The advantage of doing the trip from Tupiza is that you hit the highlight of the salt flats on the last day.

TOUR OPERATORS

La Torre Tours Hotel La Torre ☎ 02 6942633, ⓦ latorretours-tupiza.com.
Tupiza Tours Av Chichas 187, inside the Hotel Mitru

☎ 02 6943003, ⓦ tupizatours.com.
Valle Hermoso Tours Av Pedro Arraya, inside either Valle Hermoso hostel ☎ 02 6942592, ⓦ vallehermoso tours.com.

---

private rooms. Hot water is gas powered, breakfast is included, plus there's a small roof terrace, free wi-fi and a book exchange. Dorms B$40, doubles B$90

Hostal Valle Hermoso 1 Av Pedro Arraya ☎ 02 6943441. Just up the road (towards the train station) from its sister hostel, this is also a fine choice (though lacks the wood-panelled charm). It's fresh and clean with a large TV room and gas-powered showers, though breakfast is not included. No private rooms available. The huge fig tree climbing up through the central space is a pretty feature. Dorms B$35

EATING AND DRINKING

There's a limited choice of places to eat and drink in Tupiza. As usual, the cheapest place for food is the market, on the first floor of the corner of Calles Chichas and Florida. Local specialities include *asado de cordero* (roast lamb), usually served at weekends, and *tamales* stuffed with dehydrated llama meat – the best are to be found outside the Mercado Negro on Av Chichas.

Alamo Avaroa 203. A bizarre US-diner-style bar/restaurant with walls covered in celebrity pictures. The food is cheap, and served in large portions. Beer B$10. Daily from 5pm.

Il Bambino Florida, at Santa Cruz. Up an easily missed flight of stairs (tall people should mind their head), this lunchtime-only place offers good homely *almuerzos* which include a salad bar and free juice. The ramshackle dining room is enlivened by posters celebrating the local landscape and history. Mon–Sat noon–2pm.

Café del Sur Av Chichas Near the bus station, this is the most stylish place in Tupiza by a long chalk, with half-decent coffee, good cakes and desserts, plus sandwiches and burgers.

Pollo Al Spiedo Petra Av Chichas, near corner with Avaroa. Sure it's a chicken place, but locals adore it and owner Juan Thomas is a true gent. The window-side tables give good views onto the town's comings and goings – a good thing, because the decor is not much to look at. Spit-roasted chicken and sides B$12. Mon–Sat from 6pm.

Tú Pizza Southwest corner of the plaza. The pun's good but the food is better and the surroundings are lovely too, with high ceilings, warm and colourful decor, and an ornament-filled old fireplace. Pizzas from B$20, pasta from B$28. Dangerously cheap cocktails (B$12) and pleasingly incongruous *café turco* (B$5.50) are on offer too. Daily 7–10.30pm.

Urkupiña Just off the main square on C Cholorque. Pretty spit-and-sawdust, but this is the local tip for good *salteñas* (chicken or meat) from B$2. They also do a cheap *almuerzo*. Mon–Sat 9am–noon.

TARIJA

In the far south of the country, the isolated city of **TARIJA** is in many ways a world apart from the rest of Bolivia. Set in a broad, fertile valley at an altitude of 1924m, Tarija is famous for its **wine** production, and the valley's rich soils and mild climate have historically attracted large numbers of Andalucian farmers. The surrounding countryside is beautiful, particularly in the spring (Jan–April), when the vineyards come to fruit and the whole valley blooms.

2

Tarija's tree-lined avenues and temperate climate give the city a laidback ambience. The two main squares, Plaza Luis de Fuentes and Plaza Sucre, are lined with excellent restaurants and cafés – perfect for a glass of the region's increasingly well-known wine. At nightfall, the streets around the Mercado Central, at the corner of Sucre and Bolívar, transform into a bustling street market, and are perfect for picking up bargain food and clothes prior to a trip to the salt flats.

Plazas Luis de Fuentes and Sucre

The centre of town is the tranquil, palm-lined **Plaza Luis de Fuentes**, named after the city's founder, whose statue stands in the middle. The small, charming **Plaza Sucre**, two blocks southeast of the main plaza, is surrounded by restaurants and coffee bars, and is the centre of much of the town's nightlife.

Museo Paleontológico

A block south of the plaza on the corner of Virginio Lema and Trigo, the **Museo Paleontológico** (Mon–Fri 8am–noon & 3–6pm, Sat 9am–noon & 3–6pm; free) offers a fantastic collection of fossils and skeletons from the Tarija Valley. Most of the specimens on display are of mammals from the Pleistocene era, between a million and 250,000 years ago, many of them from species similar to ones that still exist today, such as horses, bears and llamas.

Casa Dorada

On the corner of Ingavi and Trigo is the **Casa Dorada** (Mon–Fri 8.30am–noon & 2.30–6pm; B$5; ⓦcasadelaculturatarija .com), also known as Casa de la Cultura. Built in the nineteenth century in the Art Nouveau style by a wealthy merchant, the house has been restored and declared a national monument. You can wander through its rooms with photo displays depicting the history of Tarija, or check out one of the many cultural events hosted here, including concerts and dance performances.

By train The airport (ⓣ04 4642195) is on the outskirts of town a few kilometres further east along Av Las Américas. A taxi into the town centre from here should cost about B$27, and there are also frequent *micros*. There are regular flights to domestic destinations, with tickets available from Amazonas (Trigo, at Lema ⓣ04 6676800, ⓦamaszonas.com) and TAM (Madrid, at Trigo ⓣ04 6642734, ⓦtam.bo). BoA (Trigo 327 between Lema and Carpio ⓣ04 6111389, ⓦboa.bo) serve domestic destinations, as well as Buenos Aires and São Paulo.

By bus The bus terminal is ten blocks or so southeast of the city centre on Av Las Américas; it's about 20min into the city centre on foot from here, or a short taxi ride (B$6–8). Alternatively, catch one of the frequent *micros* that run along Av Las Américas from the stop opposite the terminal. Destinations La Paz (1–2 daily between 7–8am; 24hr); Oruro (nightly; 20hr); Potosí (3–4 daily; 12hr); Tupiza (2 nightly; 10hr); Villazón (nightly; 10hr). There are also daily services to destinations in Argentina and Chile; the closest border crossing into Argentina is at Bermejo (10 daily; 7hr).

Tourist information There are two tourist information offices in Tarija: the Oficina Departamental de Turismo (Mon–Fri 8am–noon & 2.30–6.30pm; ⓣ04 6672633) and the Oficina Municipal de Turismo (Mon–Fri 8am–noon & 2.30–6.30pm, Sat 8am–noon; ⓣ04 6633581) on Bolívar, at Sucre. Alternatively, speak to Viva Tours (see below).

Tour operators Viva Tours, Bolívar 251 between Campos and Sucre (ⓣ04 6638325, ⓦvivatourstarijabolivia.com), run one-day tours of the city and around the vineyards and *bodegas* of the Tarija Valley with experienced English-speaking guides. Sur Bike, on Ballivián, at Ingavi (ⓣ07 6194200), organizes cycling tours and rents bikes and equipment.

Tarija has a good range of accommodation, almost all in the very centre of town, with a cluster of places around the bus terminal.

Hostal Bolívar Bolívar 256 ⓣ04 6642741. Quiet, clean option set around a pretty courtyard, with reasonable rooms (all have private bath, but those with cable TV are newer and much nicer) and a communal living room. Breakfast included. Doubles B$140

Hosteria España Alejandro Corrado 546 ⓣ04 6641790, ⓔguimediaz@yahoo.com.ar. A relaxed place that's popular with backpackers. It's very simple and the bathrooms could do with a good scrub, but there's an amiable atmosphere and a kitchen. Rooms with private bath also come with cable TV. Dorms B$40, doubles B$140

2

WINE IN THE TARIJA VALLEY

There are some worthwhile excursions close to Tarija in the warm and fertile Tarija valley, which is notable as Bolivia's prime **wine-producing region**. A visit to one of the nearby **bodegas** (wineries) to see how the wines are produced (and sample a few glasses at source) makes an excellent half-day excursion from the city. Generally, you can only visit the closest *bodegas* on an organized trip with a Tarija-based agency, but this can cost between B$100–200 per person depending on the size of the party. However, you can independently visit the lovely **Casa Vieja** *bodega*, about 25km from Tarija. *Micros* marked "v" leave from the corner of Campero and Corrado every half-hour or so (B$4) and will drop you off in the village of Concepción, from where it's a ten-minute walk from the plaza to the *bodega* – ask the driver or anyone in the village for directions. You can taste the wine, wander around the pretty vineyards and eat lunch in the restaurant.

Hostal Miraflores Sucre 920 ☎04 6643355, ☎04 664 4976. Converted colonial house with a sunny central courtyard and helpful and efficient staff. Choose between comfortable (and significantly more expensive) rooms with cable TV, private bath and breakfast, or small, spartan and much cheaper rooms without. Doubles B$170

Residencial El Rosario Ingavi 777 ☎04 6643942. Friendly, sparkling clean and quiet hostel featuring small but decent rooms with comfortable beds. The gas-powered showers are reliably hot. Doubles B$180

Hostal Segovia Angel Calabi, right by the bus terminal ☎04 6632965. Friendly hostel with clean rooms, with or without bath and all with cable TV, conveniently located right by the bus terminal. Doubles B$120

EATING AND DRINKING

Nowhere is Tarija's strong Argentine influence more evident than in its restaurants. Good-quality grilled beef features strongly, ideally accompanied by a glass of local wine, while *Tarijeños* are also justly proud of their distinctive traditional cuisine of meat dishes cooked in delicious spicy sauces – try *ranga-ranga*, *saice* or *chancao de pollo*.

Café Mokka Plaza Sucre. Come for the coffee and cakes (the latter better than the former), though they also offer salads, pizza and burgers, with mains from B$22. Wi-fi available. Mon–Sat 10am–11pm.

Chingos Plaza Sucre. A local favourite, their steaks (served with a heap of chips and salad) are cheaper than other restaurants in town, albeit not the finest quality. Mains from B$40. They also do takeaways (☎02 6632222). Daily 11am–10pm.

El Fogón del Gringo C La Madrid, off Plaza Uriondo (five blocks west of the cathedral). In culinary terms, this is the closest you'll get to Argentina without crossing the border – come for the steaks (upwards of B$55 depending on size and cut) and wines. You can graze at the free salad bar while you wait. Daily 6–11pm.

Taverna Gattopardo Plaza Luis de Fuentes. It may have gringo prices (with most mains upwards of B$40), but it's

worth treating yourself to the delicious food, including steak, served in a lovely, atmospheric restaurant with seating outside on the plaza. Daily 8am–10pm.

XOXO Plaza Sucre. Tarija's see-and-be-seen venue, with walls utterly plastered in Americana and a menu that features a suitably respectable burger. Mains from B$30. Live music, strong wi-fi and drinks promotions seal the deal. Daily 8am–11pm.

DIRECTORY

Banks and exchange The Banco Nacional de Bolivia, opposite the *Hotel Gran Tarija* on Sucre, changes cash and travellers' cheques and has an ATM that takes Visa and MasterCard. There are several other ATMs in town, including one at the Banco de Santa Cruz on Trigo, at Lema.

Cinema Virgina Lema 126 (corner of Plaza Sucre).

Immigration Ingavi 789, at Ballivián. Mon–Fri 8.30am–12.30pm & 2.30–6.30pm.

Internet access There are plenty of places around; try Consultel on Plaza Sucre (B$3/hr).

Post office Correo Central on Lema, between Sucre and Trigo.

Telephone centres ENTEL is on Lema, at Daniel Campos.

The central valleys

East of the Altiplano, the Andes march gradually down towards the eastern lowlands in a series of rugged mountain ranges, scarred with long, narrow valleys and blessed with rich alluvial soils. Both in climate and altitude, the **Central Valleys** are midway between the cold of the Altiplano and the tropical heat of the lowlands.

The administrative and political centre of Bolivia during Spanish rule, and still officially the capital of the republic, **Sucre** is a masterpiece of immaculately preserved colonial architecture, filled with elegant churches and mansions, and some of Bolivia's finest museums. The charms of **Cochabamba**, on the other hand, are more prosaic. Although lacking in conventional tourist attractions, it's a pleasant and interesting city – and not only due to the lack of tourists. It is also the jumping-off point for an adventurous journey south into the **Parque Nacional Torotoro**, Bolivia's smallest national park, boasting labyrinthine limestone caves, deep canyons and waterfalls, dinosaur footprints and ancient ruins.

East of Cochabamba, the main road to Santa Cruz passes through the **Chapare**, a beautiful region of rushing rivers and dense tropical forests, where the last foothills of the Andes plunge down into the Amazon basin. The area has become notorious in recent decades as the source of most of Bolivia's coca crop, so it isn't wise to stray too far off the beaten track.

SUCRE

Set in a broad highland valley on the eastern edge of the Altiplano, **SUCRE**, declared a UNESCO World Heritage Site in 1991, is widely considered the most beautiful city in Bolivia, with some of the finest Spanish colonial architecture in South America and a pleasant, spring-like climate all year round. Neon signs are banned, and a municipal regulation requires all buildings to be whitewashed once a year, maintaining the characteristic that earned Sucre another of its many grandiose titles: "La Ciudad Blanca de Las Américas" – the White City of the Americas. It is also the administrative and market centre for a mountainous rural hinterland inhabited by the Quechua-speaking indigenous communities, particularly renowned for their beautiful weavings. These can be seen – and bought – in the city itself or on a day-trip to **Tarabuco**, a rural town about 60km southeast of Sucre that hosts a colourful Sunday market.

Founded between 1538 and 1540 and initially named Chuquisaca, Sucre's official title subsequently changed to Villa de la Plata (City of Silver). After independence, it was made the capital of the new **Republic of Bolivia** and renamed **Sucre**, but the city's economic importance declined. When the seat of both congress and the presidency was moved to La Paz after the civil war between the two cities in 1899, the transfer merely confirmed long-established realities. Sucre remained the seat of the supreme court and was allowed to retain the title of official or constitutional capital, an honorary position it still holds today.

WHAT TO SEE AND DO

The extravagance of Sucre's silver mine-funded past is immediately evident in the city's beautifully preserved architecture. Most visitors enjoy a few hours wandering the streets and admiring the grandeur of the city centre; the attractive **Plaza 25 de Mayo** is the best place to start. The **Casa de la Libertad** offers an excellent insight into the significance of the city in Bolivia's history. Within easy walking distance of the plaza, you'll find a plethora of lavishly decorated churches, as well as excellent restaurants and some lively bars. When you're ready to explore beyond the city centre, consider a visit to the dinosaur footprints at **Cal Orko**.

Casa de la Libertad

On the northwest side of the Plaza 25 de Mayo stands the simple but well-preserved colonial facade of the original seventeenth-century Jesuit University. Now known as the **Casa de La Libertad** (Tues–Sat 9am–noon & 2.30–6.30pm, Sun 9am–noon; B$15 including guided tours in Spanish, English and French), this was where the **Bolivian act of independence** was signed on August 6, 1825, and it now houses a small but very interesting museum dedicated to the birth of the republic. Inside, a copy of the document proclaiming a sovereign and independent state is on display in the assembly room (with the original displayed every August 6).

SUCRE

■ ACCOMMODATION	
Alojamiento La Plata	7
Casa de Huéspedes San Marco	4
Hostal Charcas	6
La Dolce Vita	1
La Escondida	3
Hostal San Francisco	5
Hostal Wasi Masi	2

● EATING, DRINKING AND NIGHTLIFE	
Abi's Café	4
Amsterdam Café Bar	3
Bibliocafé	8
Café Gourmet Mirador	13
La Casona	10
Churrasquería Cumaná	2
Flavour	11
Florín	6
Joy Ride Café	7
Kultur Café Berlin	9
Las Orígenes	12
Pizzería Napolitana	5
La Taverne	1

The Catedral and Iglesia de San Miguel

Sucre's sixteenth-century Catedral is situated on Plaza 25 de Mayo and is open on Sundays only; next door is the **Museo de la Catedral** (Calle Nicolás Ortiz 61; Mon–Sat 10am–noon & 3–5pm, Sat 10am–noon; B$20), which has a wonderful collection of important religious relics.

Half a block northwest of Plaza 25 de Mayo along Calle Arenales, the modest whitewashed Baroque facade of the **Iglesia de San Miguel** (sporadic opening hours; best to visit during Sunday Mass between 6.30pm and 8pm), completed in 1621, conceals one of the most lavish church interiors in Sucre, with glorious carved Baroque altarpieces covered in gold leaf and an exquisite panelled Mudéjar ceiling.

Museo de Arte Indígena

The fascinating **Museo de Arte Indígena** (Mon–Fri 9am–noon & 2.30–6.30pm; Sat 9.30am–noon & 2–6pm; B$22 including tours; ⊕asur.org.bo/en/museum), at Pasaje Iturricha 314 opposite *Hotel Kolping* in the Zona Recoleta, is dedicated to the distinctive weavings of two local Quechua-speaking indigenous groups, the Jalq'a and the Tarabuqueños, and provides an excellent insight into a distinctly Andean artistic expression.

Museo Universitario Charcas

On Bolívar, at Dalence, is the rambling but worthwhile **Museo Universitario Charcas** (Mon–Fri 8.30am–noon & 2.30–6pm, Sat 9am–noon & 3–6pm; B$15), housed in a delightful seventeenth-century mansion. It is really four museums in one, combining the university's archeological, anthropological, colonial and modern art collections. Visits are by guided tour only (no need to book ahead), mostly in Spanish, and last at least an hour.

Convento-Museo La Recoleta

On the southeast side of Plaza Pedro de Anzures stands the **Convento-Museo La Recoleta** (Mon–Fri 9–11.30am & 2.30–5.30pm, Sat 3–5pm; B$10), a peaceful Franciscan monastery that now houses an interesting little museum of colonial religious art and materials related to the missionary work of the Franciscan order in Bolivia. Visits are by guided tour in Spanish only.

The footprints at Cal Orko

Five kilometres outside Sucre on the road to Cochabamba, the low mountain of **Cal Orko** is home to the world's largest collection of **dinosaur footprints**, discovered in 1994 by workers at a local cement works and limestone quarry. The site has been declared a national monument, and has become a major tourist attraction for its five thousand or so prints from at least 150 different types of dinosaur that cover an area of around 30,000 square metres of near-vertical rock face; it requires a good guide and some imagination to appreciate the footprints, as they're not easy to spot at first sight. The prints are on quite unstable rock, and some are at risk of crumbling away, so visitors are not allowed to get too close. To see them, head to **Parque Cretácico** (Mon–Fri 9am–5pm, Sat & Sun 10am–5pm; tours B$30). *Micros* A and 3 take you to outside

the site; however, the easiest way to visit the park is to take the Dino Truck (B$10 return), a colourful painted pick-up which leaves Mon–Sat at 9.30am, noon and 2.30pm from outside the cathedral.

ARRIVAL AND DEPARTURE

By plane The airport (❶04 6454445) is about 8km northwest of the city; *micros* I and F run from there into the centre of town along Av Siles (30min); alternatively, a taxi should cost about B$25. There are regular flights to La Paz (3 daily; 40min) and Santa Cruz (3 daily; 30min), connecting to other domestic and South American destinations, with Amazonas (Calvo, at Bolívar ❶04 6437000 or at the airport ❶04 6437999, ⓦamazonas.com), TAM (Bustillos 143 between Olañeta and Colón ❶04 6460944, ⓦtam.bo) and BoA (Calvo, at Bolívar ❶04 6912325, ⓦboa.bo).

By bus All long-distance buses use the terminal that's about 3km northeast of the town centre on Ostria Gutiérrez. It's a B$4/person taxi ride to or from the centre of town, or you can catch *micro* A, which serves the Mercado Central, a block north of the main Plaza 25 de Mayo.

Destinations Cochabamba (several daily; 10–12hr); La Paz (4 daily; 12–14hr); Oruro (2 daily; 10–12hr); Potosí (hourly; 3hr); Tarabuco (4 daily; 1hr); Santa Cruz (5–6 daily; 14–16hr).

By taxi Collective taxis for Potosí cost B$35/person with 4 people (2hr 30min); drivers wait just outside the bus station (by the clock) until full. On arrival from Potosí they will drop you off anywhere in the town centre.

INFORMATION

Tourist information There is a wealth of information on offer in Sucre: one office (Mon–Fri 8.30am–noon & 2–6pm; ❶04 6451083, ❶04 6427102) is on the first floor of the Casa de Cultura on C Argentina; the Casa de Turismo is just down the road at C Bustillos 131 (❶04 6452599, ⓦcasadeturismo.com.bo). An Oficina Universitaria de Turismo (Mon–Fri 9am–noon & 3–6pm) on C Estudiantes, just off the Plaza 25 de Mayo, is run by enthusiastic student

---

SUCRE TOUR OPERATORS

Most agencies in Sucre will offer a Sunday tour to the Tarabuco market as well as city tours and trips to the salt flats and mines of Potosí. Some offer more adventurous biking and hiking excursions in the surrounding countryside.

Condor Trekkers Calvo 102, at Bolívar or Loa 457 ❶72891740, ⓦcondortrekkers.org. A not-for-profit tour agency, with the focus on trekking (and good food) over the course of one- to three-day trips (ask about the trip to Maragua). They often use public transport.

Joy Ride Bolivia Next door to the *Joy Ride Café* at Ortíz 2 ❶04 6457603, ⓦjoyridebol.com. Popular

operator offering a wide range of adventurous activities – mountain biking, paragliding, climbing, horseriding – as well as city tours.

Off Road Bolivia Ortíz 30 or at Café Florin ❶04 6437389, ⓦoffroadbolivia.com. Quad and motorbike tours into the countryside around Sucre, including Maragua crater and Yotala. Two-day trips also offered, spending the night at a mountain lodge.

guides, while there's also an InfoTur office on Dalence, at Argentina (Mon–Fri 8am–noon & 2–6pm, weekends 9am–noon & 3–6pm).

ACCOMMODATION

Sucre has a pretty good range of accommodation, almost all of it conveniently located in the heart of the old city centre.

Alojamiento La Plata Ravelo 32 ☎04 6452102. It's really looking dog-eared now, but it's as cheap as the market opposite. Doubles B$55

Casa de Huéspedes San Marco Arce 233 ☎04 6462087. Set back a little from the street, there's a really peaceful atmosphere here, augmented by the plentiful flowers and greenery. It's spick and span and there's a choice of shared or en-suite bathrooms, plus apartments with a kitchen and small additional room. Doubles B$80

Hostal Charcas Ravelo 62 ☎04 6453972. A little gloomy-looking but the friendly welcome really goes a long way to endearing this place to you. Doubles B$80

★ **La Dolce Vita** C Urcullo 342 ☎04 6912014, ⓦdolcevita sucre.com. Central guesthouse run by a friendly, informative Franco-Swiss family with good views from a relaxed terrace and big, nicely decorated rooms. Doubles B$100

La Escondida C Junín 445 ☎04 6435792. The name means "hideaway" and you'll be glad that it is, as it's located down a little passageway that runs off one of the city's most bustling streets. Rooms are smart and peacefully set around a sunny courtyard where you can enjoy the free breakfast. Doubles B$170

Hostal San Francisco Arce 191 ☎04 6462693. The pale yellow and peach colour scheme, as well as bountiful net curtains, creates a sickly sweet look, but it's very well kept, with a pleasant central courtyard. Breakfast not included. Doubles B$120

Hostal Wasi Masi C. Urcullo 233 ☎04 6457463, ⓦwasi -masi.com. A sociable option with an excellent book exchange and basic rooms set around a leafy outdoor space. Doubles B$100

EATING

Sucre is home to an excellent variety of restaurants where you can try everything from the spicy local cuisine to authentic French, Italian and vegetarian food, at reasonable prices. The markets are great places to find cheap, filling lunches: try the second floor of Mercado Central on C Zabelo and the food hall in Mercado Negro on C Junín. Don't miss the huge fresh fruit salads in Mercado Central.

Abi's Café Plaza 25 de Mayo 32. Come to this popular café on the square for two things dear to the traveller far from home – a decent cup of coffee and strong wi-fi. Daily 8.30am–10pm.

Café Gourmet Mirador Pasaje Iturricha 297, Plaza de la Recoleta ☎04 6452330. A B$10 taxi ride from the centre brings you to this shady, dusty length of garden overlooking

the town and strewn with deckchairs. Come for Italian chef Marco Castiglion's home-made pasta (from B$40) as much as the views – the *alfredo* sauce is decadent, while the *ragù bolognese* is also delicious. Breakfast served 9.30–11.30am (muesli, fruit and yoghurt B$25. Daily 9am–8pm.

La Casona Ortiz 70. A good central *churrasquería* for barbecued meat and local dishes, from the diet-busting mound that is *pique a lo macho* to the cow's tongue and spicy pork dish (*mondongo chuquisaqueño*), with an appropriately rugged interior of hefty wooden tables. Mains from B$40. Mon–Sat 10am–8pm.

★ **Churrasquería Cumaná** Plaza Cumaná, Barrio Petrolero. Take a taxi to this steak specialist a little way out of the city centre, with just about your only choice being between different cuts and cooking times. Solo diners might find that the portions, which start at 500g for around B$90, are just too big. The meat comes with salad, chips, pickles and hot sauce (*llajwa*). Tues–Fri 6–11pm, Sat 11.30am–10pm, Sun 11am–9pm.

★ **Flavour** Plaza Cochabamba. Owners Geke and Maaike are breakfast specialists and serve up portions of a generosity rare in Bolivia. Sit inside or at one of the little tables overlooking pleasant Plaza Cochabamba. Try the "Americano" with scrambled eggs and bacon with a great slab of baguette, jam, fresh OJ and well-made coffee for just B$22. Excellent cakes (brownies, banana bread) from B$8. Mon–Sat 8.30am–7.30/8pm.

Kultur Café Berlin Avaroa 326. A winning German-South American fusion, with sauerkraut and sausages, *papa rellena* (mashed potato stuffed with a filling then fried), German beers and cheap *almuerzos*. Daily 8am–midnight (later at weekends).

Pizzeria Napolitana Plaza 25 de Mayo 30. It's a little gloomy inside, but Sucre's longest-established Italian restaurant serves tasty pizza and pasta, home-made ice cream, strong coffee and a daily choice of different set lunches (B$30). Daily except Tues 9am–9pm.

La Taverne Arce 35. Alliance Française-backed restaurant serving classic dishes like *coq au vin*, *boeuf bourguignon* and rabbit with a level of presentation uncommon in Bolivia. Quite pricey (mains around B$60), so consider coming for their generous four-course *almuerzo* (B$45) rather than dinner. Mon–Sat 9am–10.30pm, Sun 7–10.30pm.

DRINKING AND NIGHTLIFE

A high student population and a stream of party-loving backpackers means Sucre has a good range of bars and clubs.

Amsterdam Café Bar C Bolívar 426. This intimate, two-roomed place is heavy on the timber and red brick – the perfect surroundings for their regular live music. Drinks promotions 9–10pm, while food is of the snack variety (panini from B$15, Dutch meatballs B$18), though there's often a daily hot dish. Daily 2pm until late (from 3.30pm weekends).

2

Bibliocafé N. Ortíz 50. Bohemian bar-café attracting a good mix of locals and travellers from early evening until late with its mellow live music and intimate atmosphere. Snacks and light meals are also available.

Florín C Bolívar 567. A booze-focused venue with drinks promotions (mixology quality dips during the 9.30–10.30pm happy hour) and microbrewery beers. There's good food too – try their generous salads (from B$24) or their decent take on *pad thai* (B$38). The decor is pleasant, with antique portrait photographs on the walls. Mon–Thurs 7.30am–2am, Fri & Sat 7.30am–3am, Sun 7.30am–midnight.

Joy Ride Café N. Ortíz 14. Dutch-run place with the feel of a pub, but open from 7am, it's one of the few places welcoming to early morning arrivals. There's a drinking factory vibe come evening, with plentiful promotions. Daily until the early hours.

Las Orígenes Azurduy 473 ☎ 02 6457091. Venue staging a folkoric show with traditional dances from across Bolivia. Not just for gringos, and worth visiting if you're missing out on Carnaval – B$120 with a meal, B$85 without. Shows at 8.30pm Tues–Sun.

DIRECTORY

Banks and exchange Casa de Cambios Ambar, San Alberto 7, and El Arca, España 134, both change travellers' cheques and cash dollars at reasonable rates. There are also plenty of ATMs around town where you can withdraw cash on Visa or MasterCard, including at Banco de Santa Cruz and Banco Nacional de Bolivia, opposite each other on San Alberto, at España.

Car rental Auto Cambio Chuquisaca, Av Jaime Mendoza 1106 ☎ 04 6460984, ☎ 71161229.

Cinema Cine SAS, Juan Jose Perez 331. Shows subtitled new releases. Tickets B$15–20 depending on time of day.

Internet access There are internet cafés all over the city, most of which charge about B$3–4/hr. Try the Punto ENTEL on Bustillo, at Dalence/Olaneta.

Laundry Fast Clean Laundry on Azurduy.

Police If you get into difficulty or need a report for insurance purposes, make for the office on C Bolívar, at Camargo (the continuation of Av Hernando Siles).

Post office Correo Central, Junín, at Ayacucho. Mon–Fri 8am–8pm, Sat 8am–6pm.

Telephone centres Try the Punto ENTEL offices on Bustillo, at Dalence/Olaneta, or on España towards the junction with Urcullo.

TARABUCO

By far the most popular excursion from Sucre is to the small rural town of **Tarabuco**, set amid undulating mountains about 65km southeast of the city. The town itself is an unremarkable collection of red-tiled adobe houses and cobbled streets, but its real claim to fame is the Sunday market. This is the focus for the indigenous communities of the surrounding mountains, the Tarabuqueños, who come to sell the beautiful weavings for which they're famous throughout Bolivia. The market is actually a bit of a tourist trap, but the stalls selling weavings and other handicrafts to tourists are still far outnumbered by those selling basic supplies such as dried foodstuffs, agricultural tools, sandals made from tyres, big bundles of coca and pure alcohol in great steel drums.

ARRIVAL AND DEPARTURE

Buses and trucks to Tarabuco from Sucre (1hr; about B$10) leave most mornings from Av de las Américas returning in the afternoon; however, it's much more convenient to go in one of the tourist buses (they usually charge around B$35 return) organized by hotels and tour agencies in Sucre. Every Sucre tour operator will offer a trip to Tarabuco, some with guided tours in English (see p.202).

COCHABAMBA

Set at the geographical centre of Bolivia, midway between the Altiplano and the eastern lowlands, **COCHABAMBA** is one of the country's most vibrant and youthful cities and the commercial hub of the country's richest agricultural region, the Cochabamba Valley, known as the breadbasket of Bolivia. It's a friendly and unpretentious city, also known as the "City of Eternal Spring" for its year-round sunny climate, matched by the warmth and openness of its population, and is perfect for relaxing in one of the many cafés around Calle España.

WHAT TO SEE AND DO

Though Cochabamba isn't the place for colonial architecture, there are at least a couple of historic sights. Shopaholics will love the huge outdoor market of La Cancha, and there are also opportunities for exploring the understated attractions of the surrounding valleys.

Plaza 14 de Septiembre and the Museo Archeológico

The centre of Cochabamba is **Plaza 14 de Septiembre**, a placid and pleasant square with flower-filled ornamental gardens and plenty of benches where *Cochabambinos* sit under the shade of tall palm trees.

A block south of the plaza on the corner of Calles Aguirre and Jordán stands the extensive **Museo Archeológico** (Mon–Fri 8am–6pm, Sat 8.30am–noon; B$20), which explains the evolution of pre-Hispanic culture in the Cochabamba region.

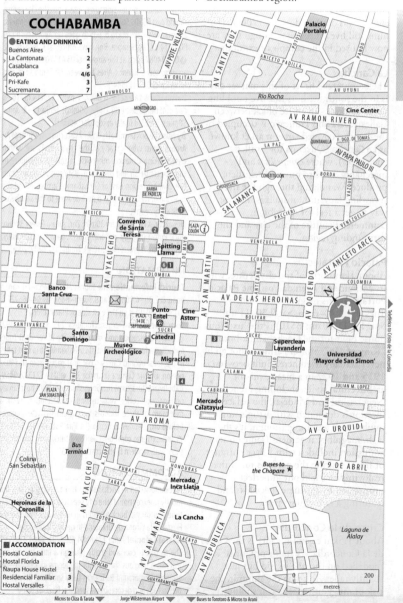

COCHABAMBA

EATING AND DRINKING

Buenos Aires	1
La Cantonata	2
Casablanca	5
Gopal	4/6
Pri-Kafe	3
Sucremanta	7

ACCOMMODATION

Hostal Colonial	2
Hostal Florida	4
Naupa House Hostel	1
Residencial Familiar	3
Hostal Versalles	5

2

Convento de Santa Teresa

The lovely **Convento de Santa Teresa** (Mon–Fri 8.30am–11.30am & 2–5pm; B$20) on Baptista, at Ecuador (the entrance is on Baptista, through the small café) is worth visiting. As well as the convent, this beautiful building houses a church built within a church (the original church was destroyed in the 1700s). The nuns still live on the site, though they are now housed in the complex next door.

La Cancha

The commercial heart of this market city is in the south, with its massive rambling street markets. An entire block between Calles Tarata and Pulucayo is occupied by the massive covered street market known as **La Cancha** (Quechua for "walled enclosure"), where *campesinos* and merchants come to buy and sell their produce. Wandering through the market's sprawling labyrinth of stalls is the best way to get a feel for the vibrant commercial culture of the city and the surrounding region.

Palacio Portales

About 1km north of the city centre, with its entrance off Avenida Posí, the **Palacio Portales** (visits by guided tour only; Tues–Fri 3.30–6pm, Sat 9.30–11am, Sun 11–11.30am; B$10) is the luxurious house built for the Cochabamba-born "King of Tin", Simón Patiño – though he never actually lived here. Built between 1915 and 1922 in a bizarre mix of architectural styles, including French Neoclassical and Mudéjar, the palace's interior is decorated with astonishing opulence. If anything, though, it's the lush, magnificent gardens (same hours; admission included with Palace entrance, or free if visiting the **gardens** only) that really impress, laid out in perfect proportion by Japanese specialists and featuring a rare ginkgo tree.

Cristo de la Concordia

About 1.5km east of the city is the Cristo de la Concordia – a statue of Christ modelled on the one in Rio but just slightly taller. To reach the summit, the risk of muggings means you shouldn't

walk: take the five-minute cable-car ride (Tues–Sat 10am–6pm, Sun 9am–6pm; B$8 return) for excellent views of the city.

ARRIVAL AND DEPARTURE

By plane Cochabamba's Jorge Wilsterman Airport (☎ 04 4120400), served by TAM (ⓦ tam.bo) and BoA (ⓦ boa.bo), is a few kilometres outside town; a taxi into the city centre should cost B$30–50 depending on number of passengers; alternatively, take *micro* B, which goes up Av Ayacucho to Plaza 14 de Septiembre. BoA have offices at C Jordán 202 ☎ 04 4140873 and at the airport ☎ 04 4117098. TAM have an office on C Buenos Aires between Av Santa Cruz and América ☎ 04 4411544/5.

Destinations La Paz (3–6 daily; 35min); Santa Cruz (6–8 daily; 45min); Sucre (2 daily; 30min); Tarija (2–3 daily; 50min); Trinidad (daily except Sat; 40min).

By bus The bus terminal is on Av Ayacucho just south of Av Aroma, from where many of the city's hotels are within easy walking distance; otherwise, a taxi to anywhere in the city centre should cost about B$6/person. Buses from the Chapare region east of Cochabamba arrive around the junction of Av Oquendo and Av 9 de Abril to the southeast of the city centre.

Departures La Paz (every 30min; 7hr); Oruro (every 30min; 4hr); Potosí (nightly at 8pm; 10hr); Santa Cruz (10 daily; 12hr); Sucre (several daily; 10hr); Trinidad (2 daily; 20hr).

INFORMATION

Tourist information The tourist office (Mon–Fri 8am–noon & 2.30–6.30pm, Sat 8.30am–noon; ☎ 04 4662277, ☎ 04 4258030) is on the east side of Plaza Colón.

Tour operators Fremen (Tumulsa 245 ☎ 04 4259392, ⓦ andes-amazonia.com) offer a variety of regional tours including a four-day "Essential Cochabamba" trip that takes in the Torotoro and Carrasco national parks, from US$405/person. Bolivia Cultura (Ecuador 342 ☎ 04 4527272/9459, ⓦ boliviacultura.com) run Spanish lessons with host family options, and offer volunteering opportunities, with a minimum of three months for placements (ⓦ volunteer bolivia.org). Andes Extremo (La Paz 138 ☎ 04 4523392, ⓦ andesxtremo.com) offer Torotoro trips, plus paragliding trips, with tandem flights costing US$55.

ACCOMMODATION

Accommodation in Cochabamba is reasonably priced, but mostly unexceptional (the city sees few tourists). The only time you should book ahead is in mid-August during the Fiesta de la Virgen de Urkupiña in nearby Quillacollo.

Hostal Colonial Junín 134 ☎ 04 4583791, ☎ 04 4221791. The garden is cool and shady (though a little untidy) and features a religious shrine, with the rooms in a cloister-like arrangement around it. They're fairly spacious, though the bedspreads and decor look washed out. Doubles B$80

Hostal Florida 25 de Mayo 583 ☎ 04 4257911. Halfway between the bus terminal and the city centre, this cheap, slightly chaotic place is popular with backpackers and groups. The simple but clean rooms (with or without bath) are set around a sunny courtyard. Doubles Ḇ$90

Ñaupa House Hostel C España 250 ☎ 04 4527723, ☎ 72294592, ✉ ivonne.ortega.fuentes@gmail.com, ⓦ sites.google.com/site/naupahousehostel. The setting is beautiful, with a lovely courtyard garden also shared by *Gopal* restaurant (see below). Rooms at the front are brighter, but those that are set back are quieter (albeit windowless). Kitchen use available. Doubles Ḇ$70

Residencial Familiar Sucre 552 ☎ 04 4227988. Set in a lovely building with decent rooms around a pretty courtyard, this centrally located hostel has atmospherically creaky wooden floors and plenty of character. Doubles Ḇ$130

Hostal Versalles Av Ayacucho 714 ☎ 72724514, ☎ 04 4583315, ✉ hiversalles@yahoo.com. HI-affiliated, though this is not at all like a backpacker hostel, rather a faded hotel. Overall it's a little dingy, choking in the vicinity of the bus station, but the price is right. Doubles Ḇ$100

EATING AND DRINKING

The best places to eat if you're on a tight budget are Cochabamba's many markets, and the choice of restaurants in the city is broad. Boulevar Recolta, a modern pedestrianized strip on the right-hand turning from the roundabout before Av Pando, is a popular night-time place for a meal and a drink; there's an abundance of modern restaurants, bars and a few karaoke joints too.

Buenos Aires Av Ballivián 654. A nice little café-bar with a Parisian boulevard feel, tucked into the side of the wide Avenida Ballivián. Sit out on the pavement terrace and set the world to rights, either over their generous breakfasts (the coffee is pretty good), *almuerzos* (B$20) or evening drinks. Mains from B$30. Daily 8am–11.30pm.

La Cantonata España, at Mayor Rocha. Smart Italian restaurant with tablecloths and flowers on the tables, serving decent pasta, meatballs and carbonara at reasonable prices. Mains from B$35. Daily noon–2.30pm & 6.30–11.30pm.

Casablanca 25 de Mayo 344. Hollywood-themed bar serving cold beer, fruity cocktails and the usual fare of pizzas, pasta, breakfasts and sandwiches to a tourist-heavy clientele. There's a pile of magazines to peruse, plus occasional jazz gigs. Mains B$26–45. Closed Sun afternoon.

Gopal Venezuela near Plaza Colón; España between Ecuador and Colombia. The branch near Plaza Colón is in a house whose colourfully decorated interior is akin to a hippy squat. The other (in the same complex as *Ñaupa House Hostel*) has a pleasant courtyard dining area for their buffet lunch, with twenty different sides to choose from. Mon–Sat 11am–3pm.

Pri-Kafe España, at Venezuela. This simply decorated place – wooden floors, big windows – is jam-packed with young locals, making it a fine contrast to touristy-but-fun *Casablanca*. Daily 5pm–2/3am.

Sucremanta Arce 340. A cool place in this hot town, with white walls and a vaulted ceiling, and otherwise spare but tasteful decoration of old maps, paintings and iron chandeliers. Try the *fritanga* pork stew (B$26/33) or *mondongo* (B$28), which comes as big hunks of pork served with corn. Daily 9am–2pm.

DIRECTORY

Banks and exchange There are exchange offices on the southwest side of Plaza 14 de Septiembre and street moneychangers in the centre of town. There are also plenty of ATMs in the city centre.

Cinema Small Cine Astor on 25 de Mayo, at Sucre, or a multi-screen Cine Center north of Plaza Quintanilla.

Internet access Internet cafés abound and most charge around B$2–3/hr. There are two good places on Arce to the southeast of Plaza 14 de Septiembre.

Laundry Superclean Lavandería, 16 de Julio 392.

Outdoor equipment The Spitting Llama (ⓦ thespittingllama.com) on Ecuador, at España, is a useful place which rents bikes and camping equipment, as well as selling novels and guidebooks. They use their former address at C España 615 as a (partly organic) food store that offers goods from craft beers to imported specialities (ⓦ llamacomelona.com).

Post office Correo Central, Av Ayacucho, at Av Heroínas. Mon–Fri 8am–9pm, Sat 8am–noon.

PARQUE NACIONAL TOROTORO

Some 139km south of Cochabamba, the **Parque Nacional Torotoro** covers just 165 square kilometres and is Bolivia's smallest national park. However, what it lacks in size it makes up for with its powerful scenery and varied attractions – high valleys and deep canyons, ringed by low mountains whose twisted geological formations are strewn with fossils, dinosaur footprints and labyrinthine limestone cave complexes. The park's cactus and scrubby woodland supports considerable wildlife – including flocks of parakeets and the rare and beautiful red-fronted macaw. The main attractions are the limestone caves of **Umajallanta**, the beautiful, waterfall-filled **Torotoro Canyon**, and hiking expeditions to the pre-Inca ruined fortress of **Llama Chaqui**.

ARRIVAL AND DEPARTURE

By bus Buses to Torotoro leave Cochabamba from the corner of Av 6 de Agosto, at Av Republica (daily 6am & 6pm, returning every day except Thurs at 6am; 6–7hr). In the rainy season the journey takes much longer and is sometimes impossible.

INFORMATION

Accommodation There are a couple of simple places to stay in the village, and locals will prepare basic meals for around B$15.

Tourist office On arrival you must head to the tourist office (daily 8am–noon & 2–5pm), on the main street of the village, where you'll need to pay the B$30 park admission fee. The office has basic information about the park and can find you a guide (affiliated with SERNAP) for about B$100 a day for groups of up to five people (slightly more for larger groups).

Tours It's also possible to visit Torotoro on a tour – which is significantly easier but obviously more expensive. Try Fremen Tours (see p.206), or Korysuyo (⊙ korysuyo.com), who offer three-day, all-inclusive packages for about B$2400.

THE CHAPARE

Northeast of Cochabamba, the main road to Santa Cruz drops down into the **CHAPARE**, a broad, rainforest-covered plain in the Upper Amazon Basin and an area of natural beauty. However, it's also Bolivia's largest provider of coca grown to make cocaine, so this is not the place for expeditions far off the beaten track. The peaceful towns along the main Cochabamba to Santa Cruz road are perfectly safe to visit, unless you go during one of the sporadic road blockades by protesting *cocaleros*; these are usually announced in advance, so make sure to look through the local newspapers before your trip.

Villa Tunari

The small, laidback town of **Villa Tunari** is a good place to break a journey between Cochabamba and Santa Cruz and also to get a brief introduction to the Amazon lowlands.

ARRIVAL AND INFORMATION

By bus In Cochabamba, regular minibuses leave from the Av Oquendo, at Av 9 de Abril (4hr); alternatively, you can take a bus heading to Santa Cruz and inform the driver you want to get off just after the Espíritu Santo Bridge.

Money The ATM in Villa Tunari is sporadically operational, so bring sufficient cash.

ACCOMMODATION AND EATING

Hostal Los Cocos Near the church ☎ 04 4136578, ☎ 71771796. A good choice for accommodation, with decent rooms and hot showers. Doubles B$100

Hotel Las Palmas On the main plaza. The best restaurant in town, serving fish from the nearby Chapare River. Mains from B$27.

The eastern lowlands

Stretching from the last foothills of the Andes east to Brazil and south to Paraguay and Argentina, Bolivia's **eastern lowlands** were until recently among the least-known and least-developed regions in the country; however, the area has undergone astonishingly rapid development, while its economy has grown to become the most important in the country, fuelled by oil and gas, cattle-ranching and massive agricultural development. At the centre of this economic boom is the regional capital of **Santa Cruz**, a young, lively city and the ideal base for exploring the many attractions of the surrounding area. A 90-minute drive west of the city are the pristine rainforests protected by the **Parque Nacional Amboró**; the beautiful cloudforest that covers the upper regions of the park can be visited from the idyllic resort town of **Samaipata**. From Samaipata, you can also head further southwest to the town of **Vallegrande** and the nearby hamlet of **La Higuera**, where the iconic Argentine revolutionary, Ernesto "Che" Guevara, was killed in 1967. East of Santa Cruz, the railway to Brazil passes through the broad forested plains of **Chiquitos**, whose beautiful **Jesuit mission churches** bear witness to one of the most extraordinary episodes in Spanish colonial history, when a handful of priests established a semi-autonomous theocratic state in the midst of the wilderness. Finally, south of Santa Cruz, the vast and inhospitable **Chaco**, an arid wilderness of dense thorn and scrub, stretches south to Argentina and Paraguay.

SANTA CRUZ

Set among the steamy, tropical lowlands just beyond the last Andean foothills, **SANTA CRUZ** has emerged in recent decades as the economic powerhouse of Bolivia. An isolated frontier town until the middle of the twentieth century, the city has grown in the last fifty years to become the second biggest in the country, as well as the locus of Bolivia's wealthy right wing. The election of Evo Morales and his plans for constitutional reform have met with increasingly violent opposition here, culminating in the late 2008 expulsion of

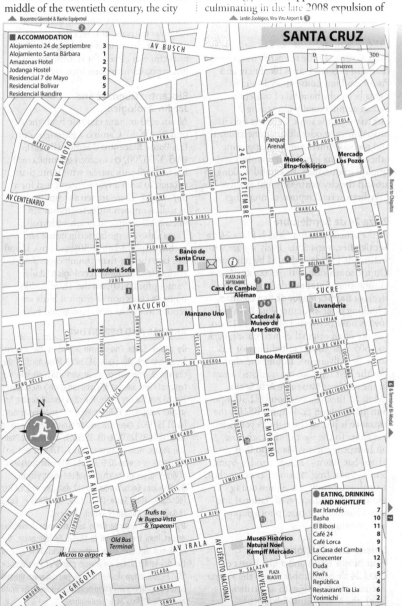

SANTA CRUZ

ACCOMMODATION

Alojamiento 24 de Septiembre	3
Alojamiento Santa Bárbara	1
Amazonas Hotel	2
Jodanga Hostel	7
Residencial 7 de Mayo	6
Residencial Bolívar	5
Residencial Ikandire	4

EATING, DRINKING AND NIGHTLIFE

Bar Irlandés	7
Basha	10
El Bibosi	11
Café 24	8
Café Lorca	9
La Casa del Camba	1
Cinecenter	12
Duda	3
Kiwi's	5
República	4
Restaurant Tía Lia	6
Yorimichi	2

2

the US ambassador, whom Morales accused of fomenting political agitation, and a march on the city by Morales' Aymaran supporters. The city layout consists of a series of rings – called *anillos* – with the colonial city centre inside the Primer Anillo, and almost everything you need within the first two or three.

WHAT TO SEE AND DO

Santa Cruz has little to match the colonial charm of highland cities like Sucre and Potosí, and few conventional tourist sights beyond a handful of museums and an architecturally unexciting cathedral. While some travellers find its unapologetic modernity, commercialism and pseudo-Americanism unappealing, others enjoy its blend of dynamism and tropical insouciance. Be careful walking around the city centre at night as there have been several reports of muggings.

Plaza 24 de Septiembre

At the centre of Santa Cruz is **Plaza 24 de Septiembre**, a spacious, lively square with well-tended gardens shaded by tall trees. On the south side of the plaza stands the salmon-pink **Catedral** (daily 7am–7pm; free), or **Basílica Mayor de San Lorenzo**, a hulking brick structure with twin bell towers built between 1845 and 1915 on the site of an original church dating back to 1605. The cool, vaulted interior has some fine silverwork around the altar, but the best religious art is tucked away in the adjacent **Museo de Arte Sacro** (Mon & Tues 10am–noon & 2.30–6pm, Sun 10am–noon & 4–8pm; B$10); the entrance is just to the right as you face the altar. To the west of the cathedral on Independencia is **Manzano Uno** (Tues–Sat 10am–12.30pm and 4–9pm, Sun 4–9pm; free; ⓦmanzanauno.org.bo), a small exhibition space showcasing some excellent displays of national and international sculpture, photography and painting.

Museo Etno-folklórico

Four blocks north and a block east of Plaza 24 de Septiembre inside the Parque Arenal (a little park with an artificial lake), the **Museo Etno-folklórico** (Mon–Fri 9.30am–noon & 2.30–5.30pm) houses a small but varied collection of artefacts that provides a good introduction to the different indigenous ethnic groups of the eastern lowlands. Exhibits include photographs, samples of traditional dress including feather headdresses worn by dancers at religious festivals, and wooden animal masks. At the time of writing, the museum was closed for refurbishment but expected to reopen by early 2014.

Biocentro Güembé and Jardín Zoológico

About a 30-minute taxi ride from the city centre, at Km7 Camino a Porongo, Zona Los Batos, **Biocentro Güembé** (B$120; ☎03 3700700, ⓦbiocentroguembe.com) is a tranquil park retreat with more than enough to keep anyone entertained for a day or two. There are ten swimming pools, as well as opportunities for mountain biking, kayaking and beach volleyball. There's also a large butterfly house and orchid display (daily 8.30am–6pm). If you can face the less-than-roomy cages and enclosures, the **Jardín Zoológico** (daily 9am–6pm; B$10), on the Third Anillo, houses a collection of tropical birds and reptiles as well as deer, llamas and bears.

ARRIVAL AND DEPARTURE

By plane Santa Cruz's main airport is the modern Aeropuerto Viru-Viru (☎03 3852400) 14km north of the city centre, from where it's around B$50–60 into the centre of town; alternatively, you can catch a *micro* (every 20min) into the city centre. The city's second airport, the smaller Aeropuerto El Trompillo, is still used by Aerocon (☎03 3511200, ✉reservassrz@aerocon.bo) and for some TAM (☎03 3532639, ☎03 3529669, ✉santacruz@tam.bo) flights. With Amaszonas (☎03 3578988) and BoA (Prolongación Aroma 20 ☎03 3348341), who operate out of Viru-Viru, you can reach much of the country by air.
Destinations Cochabamba (10–12 daily; 45min); La Paz (10 daily; 1hr); Sucre (4–5 daily; 30–40min); Tarija (3 daily; 1hr); Trinidad (4–5 daily; 1hr).
By bus Long-distance buses and all trains arrive and depart from the Terminal Bi-Modal de Transporte, the combined bus and train terminal about 2km east of the city centre. There are always plenty of taxis outside (B$12–20 in town); alternatively, you can reach the city centre by catching any *micro* heading east along Av Brasil and marked "Plaza 24 de Septiembre".

Destinations Cochabamba (hourly; 10–12hr; connections to La Paz, Oruro & Uyuni); Potosí (2–3 daily; 18hr); Sucre (4–5 daily; 15hr); Trinidad (4–5 daily; 12hr). There are also daily departures (at 7.30pm) to Buenos Aires.

By train Trains to Quijarro, on the Brazilian border, leave at 11.45am on Tues, Thurs and Sat. There's also a more expensive daily service (Mon–Sat) at 7pm; these are run by the Ferroviaria Oriental company (ⓦferroviariaoriental.com). Trains can be chilly, so wrap up. From the station in Quijarro, it's a 5min taxi ride to the border town of Corumbá (B$5/person).

INFORMATION

Tourist information Santa Cruz's tourist office (Mon–Fri 8am–7pm, Sat & Sun 9am–noon & 3–5pm) is in the government building on the north side of Plaza 24 de Septiembre.

ACCOMMODATION

Most budget accommodation is conveniently located in or close to the old city centre.

Alojamiento 24 de Septiembre Santa Bárbara 79 ☎03 3321992. Centrally located with very basic facilities and shared showers in a clean, if not especially appealing, courtyard. Doubles B$60

Alojamiento Santa Bárbara Santa Bárbara 151 ☎03 3321817, ✉alojstabarbara@yahoo.com. No-frills budget option. The rooms, set around a courtyard, are clean but ultra-basic and equipped with threadbare camp beds. Doubles B$60

Amazonas Hotel Junín 214 ☎03 3334583, ⓦhotelamazonasbolivia.com. Just off the main square, this wi-fi-enabled hotel offers good-value rooms with cable TV and private bathrooms with powerful showers. Doubles B$160

★ **Jodanga Hostel** El Fuerte 1380 (near Parque Urbano) ☎03 3396542, ⓦjodanga.com. If you lug your bag here from the bus terminal rather than taking a taxi, you might want to jump straight into the small but appealing pool. A lovely hostel where they cook your eggs to order in the morning, it's recently been renovated and guests have access to a kitchen, TV room, wi-fi and loads of local info. Dorms B$70, doubles B$170

Residencial 7 de Mayo Av Interradial ☎03 3489634. A gleaming modern establishment directly opposite the new Terminal Bi-Modal de Transporte. It's fine, but definitely more convenient than characterful. Doubles B$60

Residencial Bolívar Sucre 131 ☎03 3342500, ⓦresidencialbolivar.com. Long-standing backpackers' favourite with helpful staff and small but clean dorms and rooms (with fan and private or shared bath) around a cool, leafy patio with hammocks and a resident toucan. Prices include a generous buffet breakfast. Dorms B$85, doubles B$175

Residencial Ikandire Sucre 51 ☎03 3393975, ☎75021954. The building hails from Santa Cruz's early days and has real historic charm, with high ceilings, original doors and a well in one courtyard. The grounds are teeming with local plants, trees and faux naïve art depicting Santa Cruz's history. Breakfast included. Doubles B$160

EATING

Santa Cruz's relative wealth and cosmopolitanism are reflected in the city's wide variety of restaurants.

El Bibosi Independencia. A B$30 all-day buffet very popular with locals, the atmosphere is of eyes-down feeding but the selection is wide and the environment spick-and-span. Daily 11.30am–10pm.

Café 24 Plaza 24 de Septiembre. A cool, old-fashioned, European-style bar with Campari posters, bottles of Pernod, low-hanging cloth lampshades and wooden tables. Mains are overpriced so come for the wi-fi and coffee, which is pretty good (B$12 for a *con leche*). Daily 8am–1am.

La Casa del Camba Av Cristóbal de Mendoza 539. The best of the many traditional *Cruceño* restaurants on this stretch of the Second Anillo, and a great place to enjoy moderately priced *parillada* (barbecued meat), *keperi* (spicy, marinated brisket beef), *majao de charque* (rice with dried meat, fried egg and bananas) and *pacumutu* (massive shish kebab). Daily 11am–1am.

Kiwi's Bolívar 208. The narrow front leads into a big, airy space with a slightly hippy vibe (that's the power of a few carefully placed shisha pipes) and wi-fi access. Salads are good value at B$30 – try the "Samurai" of chicken, beef or tofu with greens, crispy noodles and sesame seeds, or the hefty burgers (B$38) served with excellent fries. Mon–Sat 3pm–midnight.

★ **República** Bolívar 175 ⓦrepublica.com.bo. Contemporary photography and paper sculpture on the walls, well-chosen music, and just-so cooking, with excellent pasta (from B$35) and salads (B$30). The exterior courtyard has a bar. Tues–Sun 10am–midnight.

★ **TREAT YOURSELF**

Yorimichi Busch 548 ☎03 3347717. A cool, modern space with a Japanese garden built into it, you can splurge here in a way that's rarely possible in Bolivia, with portions of sushi reaching beyond B$200. But it's worth it, and if you tend towards the soups and bento box-style platters, that will keep costs down – many of them include a sushi sampler anyway. Mon–Sat 11.30am–2pm & 7–11.30pm.

Restaurant Tía Lía C Murillo 40. It looks like someone's house from outside, with its sliver of a front garden, but inside it's a full-on all-you-can-eat Brazilian buffet (Mon–Sat B$27, weekends B$35) with a couple of big canteen-like rooms and a sunny courtyard with a big *churrasco* grill for meats and plentiful salads plus beans and *farofa*. Daily 11am–4pm.

DRINKING, NIGHTLIFE AND ENTERTAINMENT

The Equipetrol area, to the northwest of the city, is the main area for nightlife. After 10pm, the streets are lined with people going out and cars blaring loud music. Head to clubs on Av San Martín for hedonistic dancing and drink deals, or, for a slightly calmer scene, check out Av Monseñor Rivero, between the First and Second Anillo. Dress up smart for clubs, as doormen will refuse scruffy-looking backpackers. The in-favour nights are always changing, but at the time of writing the hottest central tips were Wed at *Duda* (Florida 228, between España and 21 de Mayo; ⊛ elbar.dudabar.com) and Thurs at *Basha* (Independencia 500, at Salvatierra). The venues below are long-standing favourites.

Bar Irlandés Plaza 24 de Septiembre. On the first floor of the Bolívar shopping centre, with tables overlooking the plaza, this Irish-themed bar gets very lively with locals and travellers in the evenings, especially on weekends. Be warned – they don't serve Guinness. Daily 9am–midnight.

Café Lorca Sucre 8 ⊛ lorcasantacruz.org. Popular café-bar with excellent but expensive food. A good place for a drink in the evenings, and they hold regular art exhibitions, events and live music. Daily 9am (Sun from 4pm) until the early hours.

Cinecenter 2nd Anillo, Av El Trompillo between Monseñor Santiesteban and René Moreno. Big multiscreen complex with fast-food joints and coffee bars, as well as a range of international films (usually subtitled but worth checking individual films).

DIRECTORY

Banks and exchange You can change US dollars and travellers' cheques at the Casa de Cambio Alemán (Mon–Fri 8.30am–noon & 2.30–6pm, Sat 8.30am–noon) on the east side of Plaza 24 de Septiembre, and there are plenty of banks with ATMs: try Banco Mercantil on Av Moreno, at Figueroa.

Internet There are many internet cafés around the city centre (typically B$5/hr), especially in the shopping complex on the east side of the main plaza.

Laundry Hostels are the best bet for laundry, but Lavandería Sofia on C Santa Bárbara is also reliable.

PARQUE NACIONAL AMBORÓ

Forty kilometres west of Santa Cruz, the **Parque Nacional Amboró** covers some 4300 square kilometres of a great forest-covered spur of the Andes jutting out into the eastern plains. Amboró's steep, densely forested slopes support an astonishing biodiversity, including more than 830 different types of bird and pretty much the full range of rainforest mammals, including jaguars, giant anteaters, tapirs and several species of monkey, while its enormous range of plant and insect species is still largely unexplored.

The northern gateway to the park is the picturesque and peaceful town of **Buena Vista**, some 100km northwest of Santa Cruz along the main road to Cochabamba. You can arrange a tour into the park from there, or with one of the operators in Santa Cruz (see box below) or Samaipata (see opposite). Overnight camping trips start

---

TOUR OPERATORS IN THE LOWLANDS

If you plan to head to Amboró National Park, it is cheaper to organize a tour from Samaipata, and you'll get more time in the rainforest for your money. However, the following companies in Santa Cruz are all well established and have good reputations:

Amboró Tours C Libertad 417, 2nd Floor ☏ 03 3390600, ⊛ amborotours.com. A long-established Bolivian firm offering trips to the Jesuit Missions, multi-day trips into the Amboró National Park and cultural tours.

Fremen Tours Beni 79, Edificio Libertador ☏ 03 3338535, ⊛ andes-amazonia.com. Specializes in river tours in Trinidad but can also help with Jesuit Mission trips and other all-inclusive tours in Bolivia and Peru.

Rosario Tours Arenales 196 ☏ 03 3369977, ⊛ rosario tours.com. Standard tours as well as trips to the Bolivian Pantanal.

Ruta Verde Tours C 21 de Mayo 318 ☏ 03 3396470, ⊛ rutaverdebolivia.com. Highly recommended Dutch/Bolivian-run tour operator with excellent local knowledge, who organizes tours to national parks like Amboró and Noel Kempff Mercado National Park, as well as trips further afield.

at US$140 per person each day, depending on duration and number of people in the group.

SAMAIPATA

Some 120km west of Santa Cruz, the tranquil little town of **SAMAIPATA** is enjoying growing popularity as a tourist destination among Bolivians and foreign travellers alike. Nestled in an idyllic valley surrounded by rugged, forest-covered mountains, it's the kind of place where many travellers plan to stay a couple of days and end up staying for a week or longer. Just 9km outside town stands one of Bolivia's most intriguing archeological sites – the mysterious, ruined pre-Hispanic ceremonial complex known as El Fuerte (see box, p.214).

WHAT TO SEE AND DO

At the centre of town lies the small **Plaza Principal**, the core of the grid of tranquil streets lined with whitewashed houses under red-tiled roofs. A few blocks north on Bolívar, the small **Museo Archeológico** (Mon–Fri 8.30am–noon & 2–6pm; Sat & Sun 8.30am-4pm; B$50; including entrance to El Fuerte) shows a short film explaining the significance of El Fuerte, and houses a small collection of archeological finds from all over Bolivia, including beautiful Inca-carved ceremonial *chicha*-drinking cups, Inca stone axes and mace heads, and a range of pottery. Innumerable walking trails run through the surrounding country-side, the beautiful cloudforests of the Parque Nacional Amboró (see opposite) are within easy reach, and most tour companies also offer day-trips to nearby valleys where you might spot condors overhead, climb mountainous ridges for breathtaking vistas, or enjoy an afternoon splashing around in some of the area's spectacular waterfalls.

ARRIVAL AND DEPARTURE

By micro *Micros* leave Av Grigota in Santa Cruz for Samaipata daily at 4pm (3hr) and arrive in Samaipata in the Plaza Principal. Buses to Santa Cruz leave the plaza at about 4am Mon–Fri, with other services on Sun from noon–4pm. Buses to Sucre and Vallegrande pass by the highway, between 6.30pm and 7.30pm for Sucre, and 11.30am–12.30pm and 3.30–4.30pm for Vallegrande. Catch the bus from outside *Restaurant El Turista* on the main Sucre to Santa Cruz highway. You can also buy bus tickets to Sucre from Amboró Tours on Bolívar. They charge B$25 commission, but it guarantees you a seat.

By taxi From Santa Cruz, shared taxis depart from the corner of Chávez Ortiz and Solís de Olguin (B$25–35/ person, with four people in a taxi; 2hr 30min). Returning to Santa Cruz, take one from the petrol station on the main highway (10min from the main plaza). You may have difficulty finding a taxi after 6pm.

INFORMATION

Tourist information For information on Samaipata and the surrounding area, the best place to go is the helpful Ben Verhoef Tours (Campero 217 ☎03 9446365, ✆ benverhoeftours.com), who can organize a variety of tours and activities, including the Amboró National Park, a popular condor-spotting hike, the Ché Guevara route, Jesuit Missions tours, camping and 4WD trips. If you understand Spanish, you might also speak to Jukumari Tours (☎72627202, ✆facebook.com/JukumariTours) on C Bolívar, run by local guide Erwin Acuña Montenegro.

ACCOMMODATION

There's a good range of budget accommodation in Samaipata, including a couple of tranquil tucked-away options. Prices go up at weekends and public holidays, particularly between October and April.

Hostal Andorina C Campero ☎03 9446333, ✆andorina samaipata.com. A meditative place to stay (though beware the mosquitoes), with sunny patios and hammock-strewn balconies, characterful rooms and dorms. A good, generous breakfast is included and there's a library and book exchange. Dorms B$45, doubles B$100

Finca La Víspera ☎03 9446082, ✆lavispera.org. You can camp in this secluded haven with comfortable lodgings, an idyllic location amid orchards and terraced herb, vegetable and flower gardens and a friendly young Dutch-Bolivian couple overseeing the place. Guests can use the kitchen and harvest food from the grounds. Camping (per person) B$30, cabins B$320

Paola Hotel Main plaza ☎03 9446093. Good-value central hotel with clean rooms, hot showers, a kitchen and a large terrace with exhilarating views. Breakfast included. Doubles B$80

★ **La Posada del Sol** Three blocks north of the plaza (look for the sign) ☎03 9446366, ✆laposadadelsol.net. Fresh rooms set in beautiful grounds with views of the mountains bordering Amboró National Park, and there are even dorm beds. Breakfast is served alfresco, and the restaurant is excellent (see p.214). Dorms B$60, doubles B$140

2

EL FUERTE

Located 10km east of Samaipata, **El Fuerte** (daily 9am–5pm; B$50) is a striking and enigmatic ancient site with a great sandstone rock at its centre, carved with a fantastic variety of abstract and figurative designs and surrounded by the remains of more than fifty **Inca buildings**. The easiest way to reach El Fuerte is by taxi from Samaipata (about B$25–30 one-way, or B$80 return with two hours' waiting time), or to join a guided tour with one of the tour agencies in town. While it is possible to walk to the ruins in about two to three hours – follow the road out of town toward Santa Cruz for a few kilometres, then turn right up the marked side road that climbs to the site – it's a tiring, very hot walk, so it's advisable to take a taxi to the site and walk back, otherwise you might be too exhausted to appreciate the ruins.

EATING AND DRINKING

As a resort town with a significant international community Samaipata has a varied range of restaurants and cafés. Many places are closed on Tues.

La Bohème Plaza Principal. A warm welcome from owners Kirsty and Dave, a cool-looking space, and excellent drinks from fresh cocktails to locally brewed beers. if Samaipata becomes the next Rurrenabaque-like ecotourism hub, this bar will be its night-time focal point. Try the *tabla* of goodies including ham, salami, cheese and chutney with a baguette (B$40). Tues–Sun 3pm–midnight (until 3am Fri & Sat).

Café 1900 Plaza Principal. A very simple place overlooking the plaza with strong wi-fi, a laidback atmosphere and decent coffee.

Café Jardin At *Finca La Víspera*. The focus here is on fresh and organic vegetarian food, with much produce grown on their gently sloping terrace plots – when you order, staff will come into the garden to snip herbs and pull up veggies. *Pastel de quinoa* B$40, rhubarb cake B$20. Daily 8am–3pm.

La Luna Verde At *La Posada del Sol*. The reassuringly brief menu changes daily, but the quality of the cooking stays the same (mains with sides B$35). With a Texan in charge, you can imagine how good the steaks and burgers are, but even the sides are prepared with panache, from barbecue baked beans to a surprisingly good strawberry and spinach salad. Tues–Sat 7.30am–10pm, Sun & Mon 2–6pm.

La Oveja Negra Campero. Tiled floors, a high, timbered ceiling and chunky wooden furniture create a feeling of comforting solidity, while the antique stove (from New York) keeps things cosy for board games, darts or perusing the book exchange. Try the *goulash* or pastas, all cooked by a French chef. Daily except Tues, noon–10pm (kitchen), until 1am (bar).

DIRECTORY

Internet *Café 1900* has a decent wi-fi connection, or try internet café *Anyi* on C Campero (B$6/hr).
Laundry Campero. Next door to *La Oveja Negra*.
Money No ATMs, but Western Union a block east of the plaza on C Sucre will give cash advances on credit cards for five percent commission (Mon–Fri 8am–noon & 2.30–6.15pm; Sat 8.30am–12.30pm).
Telephone office The ENTEL office is on the main plaza.

VALLEGRANDE AND LA HIGUERA

West of Samaipata on the old road from Santa Cruz to Cochabamba, a side road leads to the market town of **VALLEGRANDE**. Vallegrande leapt briefly to the world's attention in 1967, when it witnessed the end game of a doomed guerrilla campaign led by Cuban revolutionary hero, **Ernesto "Che" Guevara** (see box below). There is

REVOLUTION CHE

Probably the most famous revolutionary of the twentieth century, Ernesto "Che" Guevara was executed in the hamlet of **La Higuera** about 50km south of Vallegrande on October 9, 1967. Visitors to the area may be surprised to learn that this iconic hero spent his final days hiding out in a remote ravine with only a few bedraggled followers. An Argentine-born doctor, Che became a close ally of Fidel Castro during the Cuban Revolution and then turned his sights to Bolivia, which he hoped would prove to be the kick-off point for a continent-wide revolution.

With a small band of rebel followers, Che tried to drum up support for change, but CIA-backed Bolivian troops were determined to quell any kind of revolution, and he was soon forced into hiding.

When Che was eventually captured, his last words were: "Shoot, coward, you are only going to kill a man". His body was flown to Vallegrande and put on display for the world's press in the town hospital. Today Che's grave and the hamlet of La Higuera attract a steady trickle of pilgrims.

EAST FROM SANTA CRUZ TO THE BRAZILIAN BORDER

From Santa Cruz, the railway line runs some 680km east to the **Brazilian border** across a seemingly endless expanse of forest and tangled scrub, gradually giving way to the vast swamplands of the **Pantanal** as the border draws near.

The last stop on the railway line in Bolivia is **Puerto Quijarro**, a dismal collection of shacks surrounding the station. If you're heading on to Brazil, you're better off pushing on to the border at Arroyo Concepción.

ACCOMMODATION

Tamengo C Costa Rica 57, Puerto Quijarro ☎ 03 9783356, ⓦ tamengo.com. This hostel, six blocks from the train station at Puerto Quijarro, is a good resort-style option if you decide to stay. Dorms B$60, rooms B$240

2

a small **museum** (Mon–Fri 10am–noon, 3–5pm & 7–9pm, Sat 10am–noon; B$10) in the municipal **Casa de Cultura** on the central Plaza 26 de Enero, which houses an unexciting collection of local archeological finds and photographs of Che.

The most comfortable place to stay is the friendly *Hostal Juanita* (☎03 9422231; B$80–100 for room with private bathroom), and the best restaurant is probably the German-run *El Mirador* (evenings only; closed Mon), which offers a daily selection of tasty meat and trout dishes.

La Higuera, the hamlet where Che Guevara met his end, lies about 50km south of Vallegrande and can be reached by taxi or lorry in two to three hours, or by getting buses to Pucará from Vallegrande and getting local transport from there. It's a miserable collection of simple adobe houses with tiled roofs and a one-room **Museo Histórico del Che** (opening hours timed with tours so ask around; B$10), with the atmosphere of a shrine, complete with relics including Che's machete, bullets and ammo clips.

Both Vallegrande and La Higuera can also be visited on a tour; try agencies in Samaipata (see p.213) or Santa Cruz (see p.212). Daily buses run to Vallegrande.

CHIQUITOS: THE JESUIT MISSIONS

East of Santa Cruz stretches a vast, sparsely populated plain which gradually gives way to swamp as it approaches the border with Brazil. Named **CHIQUITOS** by the Spanish, this region was the scene of one of the most extraordinary episodes in Spanish colonial history. In the eighteenth century, a handful of Jesuit priests established a series of flourishing mission towns, where previously hostile indigenous Chiquitanos converted to Catholicism, adopting European agricultural techniques and building some of the most **magnificent colonial churches** in South America. This theocratic, socialist utopia ended in 1767, when the Spanish crown expelled the Jesuits from the Americas. Six of the ten Jesuit mission churches have since been restored and are recognized as UNESCO World Heritage Sites. Their incongruous splendour in the midst of the wilderness is one of the most remarkable sights in Bolivia.

The six missions can be visited in a five- to seven-day loop by road and rail from Santa Cruz. A rough road runs northeast to **San Javier** and **Concepción**, then continues to **San Ignacio** (from where the churches of **San Miguel**, **San Rafael** and **Santa Ana** can all be visited by taxi in a day). From San Ignacio, the road heads south to **San José**. Buses connect all these mission towns as far as San José, from where you can get the train back to Santa Cruz or continue east to the Brazilian border. Alternatively, many agencies organize tours to the missions, including shorter two-day trips that take in San Javier and **Concepción** only; tours can be arranged in Santa Cruz (see p.212).

THE CHACO

South of the Santa Cruz–Quijarro railway line, the tropical dry forest gradually gives way to **the Chaco**, a vast and arid landscape that stretches beyond

2

the **Paraguayan border**. The Chaco is one of the last great wildernesses of South America and supports plentiful wildlife, including jaguars, peccaries and deer – much of it now protected by the 34,000-square-kilometre **Parque Nacional Kaa-Iya del Gran Chaco**, the largest protected area in all South America. There are no organized tourist facilities in the Chaco, so your view of the region will likely be limited to what you can see from the window of a bus or train, either down the region's western edge to the towns of **Villamontes** and **Yacuiba**, which is on the Argentine border, or along the rough **trans-Chaco road** which makes for the Paraguayan border at **Hito Villazón**.

The Amazon basin

About a third of Bolivia lies within the **Amazon Basin**, a vast, sparsely populated and largely untamed lowland region of swamp, savanna and tropical rainforest, which supports a bewildering diversity of plant and animal life. Roads are poor in the best of conditions, and in the rainy season between November and April they are often completely impassable; even in the dry season sudden downpours can quickly turn roads to quagmires.

Linked by road to Santa Cruz, the capital of the Beni – the northeastern lowlands region – is **Trinidad**, the starting point for slow boat journeys down the **Río Mamoré** to the Brazilian border or south into the **Chapare**. From Trinidad, a long and rough road heads east across the Llanos de Moxos, passing through the **Reserva del Biosfera del Beni** before joining the main road down into the region from La Paz at Yucumo.

Just north of Yucumo, the small town of **Rurrenabaque**, on the banks of the Río Beni, is the obvious destination for anyone wanting a taste of the Amazon, given its proximity to the pristine forests of the **Parque Nacional Madidi**, one of Bolivia's most stunning protected areas. From Rurrenabaque, the road continues

north to the city of **Riberalta**, a centre for rubber and brazil nut collection, and on to the Brazilian border and the remote, forest-covered department of **Pando**.

TRINIDAD

Close to the Río Mamoré, some 500km northwest of Santa Cruz, the city of **TRINIDAD** is the capital of the Beni and a modern commercial city dominated by a vigorous cattle-ranching culture and economy. Hot and humid, with few real attractions, Trinidad doesn't really merit a visit in its own right. It is, however, the jumping-off point for adventurous trips into the surrounding landscape.

WHAT TO SEE AND DO

Though most of its buildings are modern, Trinidad maintains the classic layout of a Spanish colonial town, its streets set out in a neat grid around a central square, the **Plaza Ballivián**, shaded by tall trees hiding three-toed sloths. A popular place to go for the afternoon is the river port of **Puerto Varador**, about 13km out of town, where simple restaurants serve up fresh fish. Take a *mototaxi* to the Mercado Campesino on Avenida. Oscar Paz Hurtado, where *micros* leave regularly for the port; it's about a half-hour journey.

ARRIVAL AND DEPARTURE

By plane The airport is located to the northeast of town; a *mototaxi* into the centre should cost B$10–12. Between them, Amaszonas, 18 de Noviembre 267 ☎ 03 4622426, TAM, Bolívar, at Santa Cruz ☎ 03 4622363, and Aerocon, Av 6 de Agosto, at 18 de Noviembre ☎ 03 4624442 ✉ ventastdd @aerocon.bo, cover most destinations.

By bus Buses from Santa Cruz, Guayaramerín and Rurrenabaque arrive at the Terminal Terrestre on Av Mendoza between Calles Viador Pinto Saucedo and Beni. Buses from San Borja arrive just behind the terminal on Av Beni.

Destinations Santa Cruz (roughly hourly depending on road conditions; 10hr). Services to Guayaramerín (25–28hr), and Rurrenabaque (12hr) via San Borja are meant to leave daily in the dry season.

By boat If you are arriving by boat from Guayaramerín to the north, or Puerto Villarroel in the Chapare to the south, you will dock at Puerto Varador, Trinidad's river port, about 13km west. *Mototaxis* ply the 30min route back into town (B$20–25).

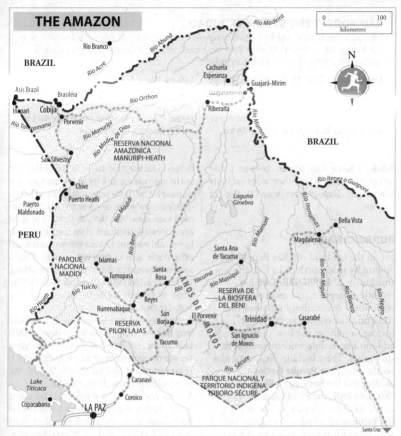

INFORMATION

Money There are a number of ATMs in town; remember to get cash here if you're heading further into the Amazon (though Rurrenabaque also has a couple of ATMs).

Tourist information There's a tourist office on Av 6 de Agosto, next to the *Hotel Campanario* (Mon–Fri 8am–12.30pm & 2.30–6pm).

ACCOMMODATION

Hostal Copacabana Villaviencio 627 ☎03 4622811. Pretty basic and a short distance from the main plaza, but the upstairs rooms with private bath and balcony are spacious and pleasant. Air conditioning also available at additional cost. Doubles B$70

Hostal Palmas La Paz 365 ☎03 4626979. The rooms downstairs are dark and dire, while those upstairs are airier and cooler. All come with fans, and there's a choice of shared or private bath with cable TV. Doubles B$60

Residencial 18 de Noviembre Av 6 de Agosto, at Santa Cruz, two blocks west of the plaza ☎03 4621272. Basic,

good-value place, with a pleasant, hammock-strewn garden and rooms with private or shared bath. Doubles B$50

EATING

There are some pretty good restaurants on and around Plaza Ballivián. The beef in Trinidad is excellent and very good value, while the local speciality is *pacumutu*, great chunks of meat marinated and grilled on a skewer.

Carambar Av 6 de Agosto, between Santa Cruz and Villavicencio. A French-run place with fine crêpes (from B$8) and a buzzy atmosphere. Wed–Sun 5–11pm.

La Casona Plaza Ballivián. Lively and popular place with a great atmosphere and good *almuerzos* as well as steak, hamburgers and fried river fish. Mains B$30–60. Daily 8am–11pm.

Club Social 18 de Noviembre Plaza Ballivián. A vast, elegant dining hall with a rather old-fashioned feel, serving up good-value, filling *almuerzos* and standard Bolivian dishes like *milanesa* (fried meat coated with breadcrumbs) and *pique macho*. Daily: lunchtimes only.

2

RAINFOREST TRIPS FROM TRINIDAD

Trinidad makes a great base for birdwatching excursions into the surrounding wilderness, or as the starting point for river cruises or camping expeditions into an area where tourists rarely venture. Recommended tour operators include:

Fremen Cipriano Barace 332 ☎ 03 4622276, ⓦ andes-amazonia.com. Highly professional operator organizing similar excursions, as well as four- to six-day cruises on the Mamoré aboard a floating hotel, the *Reina de Enín*, starting at about B$2980/person for a three-day trip.

Turismo Moxos Av 6 de Agosto 114 ☎ 71130122, ⓔ moxosibc@hotmail.com. Popular birdwatching excursions with the opportunity of spotting rare blue-bearded macaws. They also offer various one- to three-day trips into the rainforest by motorized canoe.

Heladería Kivon Plaza Ballivián. Ice-cream parlour right on the plaza serving cakes, sandwiches and meaty Bolivian mains. Single ice-cream scoop B$5. Mon–Sat 9am–8pm.

RURRENABAQUE

Set on the banks of the Río Beni about 400km by road north of La Paz, the small town of **RURRENABAQUE** has recently emerged as the most popular ecotourism destination in the Bolivian Amazon. Rurrenabaque, or "Rurre", is close to some of the best-preserved and most accessible wilderness areas in the region. These include the spectacular rainforests of the **Parque Nacional Madidi** and the **Reserva de Biosfera y Territorio Indígena Pilón Lajas**, as well as the wildlife-rich pampas along the **Río Yacuma**, all of which are easily visited with one of Rurrenabaque's numerous tour agencies.

WHAT TO SEE AND DO

Surrounded by rainforest-covered hills, there is little in the way of formal sights in Rurre but it's an enjoyable town to watch the boats go by on the mighty Río Beni or just relax in a hammock. If you've an afternoon to spare, head up to one of the swimming pool miradors, either **Oscar's Butterfly Pool** (B$38), or the nameless, quieter one (B$20) a minute further up the same road. Both have great views of the town and river. Ask a *mototaxi* to take you (B$10).

ARRIVAL AND DEPARTURE

By plane Due to often impassable roads, many people choose to fly to Rurrenabaque – the alternative is a nightmarish bus journey of at least 18 hours. Amazonas

fly from La Paz four times daily while TAM fly Mon, Wed and Fri; make sure you book ahead. Amazonas are more expensive but they're the better option – if your flight is cancelled, as is often the case, their next flight will come round much sooner than TAM's. All flights arrive at the airstrip a short distance north of the town, and are met by free hotel minibuses for those with reservations, and airline shuttle buses for those without, which charge a small fee for transport to their offices in the centre of town. The Amazonas (☎ 03 8922472) and TAM (☎ 03 8922398) offices, on Comercio and Santa Cruz respectively, are marked on the map.

By bus Buses arrive at the Terminal Terrestre, a few blocks away from the centre of town on the corner of Calles Guachalla and 18 de Noviembre; you can get a motorbike taxi into the centre for about B$5. Daily departures to La Paz (minimum of 18hr) and Trinidad (10–20hr), and, when possible, to Guayamerín and Riberalta.

By boat When the road is closed in the rainy season, motorized canoes occasionally carry passengers between Rurrenabaque and Guanay, a small town about 230km northwest of La Paz (6–8hr) and Riberalta (8–10 days). Book in advance with one of the tour agencies.

INFORMATION

Internet The Entel office on Comercio also has internet for B$6/hr.

Money Banco FIE and Banco Union both have ATMs on Comercio.

Tourist information There is a small office at Vaca Diez, at Avaroa (Mon–Sat 8am–noon & 2.30–6pm).

ACCOMMODATION

Rooms can be difficult to find in high season (May–Aug), so book ahead.

Hostal Beni Comercio, at Ancieto Arce ☎ 03 8922408. Clean and modern rooms set around a peaceful patio. Rooms with air conditioning are much pricier. Doubles **B$60**

Hotel Lobo Comercio. Overlooking the Beni River, this grand *palapa*-roofed place looks unfinished, with an empty pool and near-building site of a top deck. But the 11 existing rooms give wonderful views of the steamy Río Beni and San Buenaventura on the far bank – get one on the first floor. Their open sides do not, surprisingly, cause problems with mosquitoes. Doubles B$60

Hotel Rurrenabaque Vaca Diez, at Bolívar ⓣ 03 8922481. This was the first two-storey building in Rurre according to the friendly owners, but it's in good condition, with breakfast and wi-fi included. Doubles B$110

Los Tucanes de Rurre Ancieto Arce, at Bolívar ⓣ 03 8922039, ⓦ hotel-tucanes.com. Popular and spacious hostel with hammocks hung around the grounds, a huge roof terrace, pool table, wi-fi and free breakfast. Doubles B$80

EATING AND DRINKING

A large number of restaurants have sprung up in Rurrenabaque to cater to the ecotourism boom.

Café de la Jungla Comercio. It's all relative, but this tiny place does the best coffee in town, even if the lattes (B$10) come towering with bubbly froth. The strong wi-fi is a boon, as are the B$3 cookies. Breakfasts (with

> ### ★ TREAT YOURSELF
>
> A five-hour boat ride from Rurrenabaque will bring you to the spectacular **Chalalán ecolodge** in the heart of the Madidi National Park. The Chalalán project is run entirely by the rainforest community of San José de Uchupiamonas and is hailed as one of the world's greatest conservation success stories. Trips to the lodge don't come cheap, with a four-day and three-night programme from La Paz (one night in Rurrenabaque, two in the lodge) costing about B$2500 per person, but it is well worth the splurge. Go to ⓦ chalalan.com for a full list of booking agents. Or book direct at the Chalalán office in Rurrenabaque (Comercio; ⓣ 03 8922419), or their office in La Paz (Sagárnaga 189, 2nd floor; ⓣ 02 2311451). Advance booking essential.

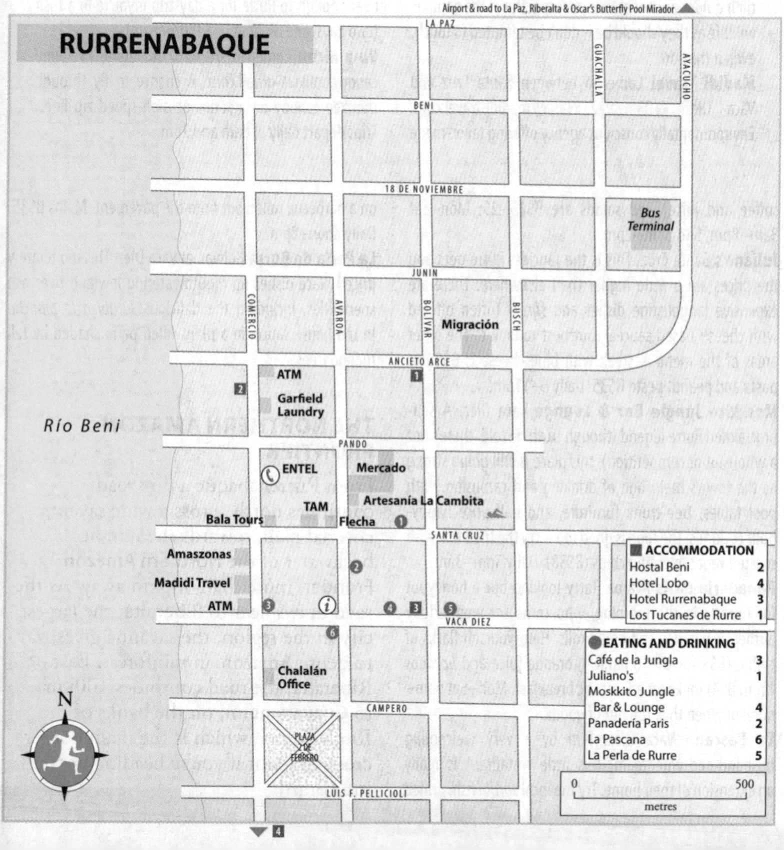
Airport & road to La Paz, Riberalta & Oscar's Butterfly Pool Mirador
RURRENABAQUE
LA PAZ
BENI
18 DE NOVIEMBRE
JUNIN
ANCIETO ARCE
PANDO
SANTA CRUZ
VACA DIEZ
CAMPERO
LUIS F. PELLICIOLI
GUACHALLA
AYACUCHO
COMERCIO
AVAROA
BOLIVAR
BUSCH
Bus Terminal
Migración
ATM
Garfield Laundry
Río Beni
ENTEL
Mercado
Artesanía La Cambita
TAM
Bala Tours
Flecha
Amaszonas
Madidi Travel
ATM
Chalalán Office
PLAZA 2 DE FEBRERO
N
ACCOMMODATION
Hostal Beni 2
Hotel Lobo 4
Hotel Rurrenabaque 3
Los Tucanes de Rurre 1
EATING AND DRINKING
Café de la Jungla 3
Juliano's 1
Moskkito Jungle Bar & Lounge 4
Panadería Paris 2
La Pascana 6
La Perla de Rurre 5
0 500
metres

2

TOUR AGENCIES IN RURRENABAQUE

A growing number of tour agencies offer trips to the rainforest and the pampas lowlands, generally lasting three nights. Most guides speak only Spanish, but agencies can usually arrange an English-speaking interpreter for larger groups. Prices for all-inclusive two-night trips to both the pampas and the jungle start at about B$500 (not including park entrance fees; B$150 for the Santa Rosa reserve on the Pampas Tour, and B$125 for the Madidi National Park) – though expect to pay much more if you want anything more than the most basic accommodation.

TOUR OPERATORS

Bala Tours Av Santa Cruz, at Comercio ☎ 03 8922527, ⓦ balatours.com. Specialize in longer five- to eight-day camping tours into Parque Nacional Madidi, as well as standard *selva* (jungle) and pampas programmes. They're more expensive, but the jungle tours in particular are very highly recommended and they own their own camps.

Flecha Avaroa, at Santa Cruz ☎ 03 8922723, ⓦ flecha-tours.com. Popular agency offering three- to four-day tours of the pampas and rainforest, as well as longer trips into the Parque Nacional Madidi. Be warned that their guides are not always as respectful of the pampas wildlife as they should be – don't be tempted to touch, even if they do.

Madidi Travel Comercio between Santa Cruz and Vaca Diez ☎ 03 8922153, ⓦ madidi-travel.com. Environmentally conscious agency offering tailor-made

tours. Profits go towards conservation and community work.

Mapajo Ecoturismo Indígena Comercio, at Vaca Diez ☎ 03 8922317. Indigenous community-run agency specializing in three-, four- and five-night lodge-based trips into the Reserva de la Biosfera y Territorio Indígena Pilón Lajas; the lodge is fully operated and owned by the Río Quiquibey communities.

San Miguel del Bala Comercio between Vaca Diez and Santa Cruz ☎ 03 8922394, ⓦ sanmigueldelbala. Not the best option for spotting animals but excellent for a cultural experience of a Tacana community, and near enough to Rurre for a day-trip if you're in a rush (two days, one night at US$160/person).

Villa Alcira Comercio s/n ☎ 07 4092054, ⓔ zipline canopy.bolivia@gmail.com. A chance to fly through the tree canopy on a series of high-speed zip-lines. Trips depart daily at 8am and 2pm.

coffee and juice) and salads are B$15–25. Mon–Sat 8am–8pm, Sun 8am–2pm.

Juliano's Santa Cruz. This is the fanciest Rurre gets and the prices are a little higher than elsewhere. There are expensive langoustine dishes and *surubí* (often offered with cheese-based sauces), but best to look to the other areas of the menu – steak with blue cheese is B$50 or pasta and peanut pesto B$35. Daily 6–11pm.

Moskkito Jungle Bar & Lounge Vaca Diez. A self-proclaimed Rurre legend (though truth be told, there's not a whole lot of competition), this place is still going strong as the town's main hub of drinking and carousing, with pool tables, tree-trunk furniture, and half-price happy-hour cocktails. The food is good too – try the fried fish with roasted vegetables and chips (B$38). Daily 3pm–3am.

Panadería Paris Avaroa. Tatty-looking but a honeypot for tourists in the morning, who come for wonderfully authentic pastries and bread rolls. Help-yourself flasks of coffee (B$5 for the "organic"), orange juice and *licuados* (from B$4) make for a fantastic breakfast. Mon–Sat 6am–noon or when they run out of goods.

La Pascana Vaca Diez. Run by a very welcoming husband-and-wife team, this little restaurant is really an extension of their home. Try the local *surubí* fish, grilled

on a barbecue rolled out onto the pavement. Mains B$35. Daily noon–8pm.

La Perla de Rurre Bolívar, at Vaca Diez. This moderately priced place dishes up mouthwatering lowland river fish specialities, including the delicious *surubí a la plancha* in the house sauce, in a plant-filled patio shaded by tall mango trees.

THE NORTHERN AMAZON FRONTIER

From Rurrenabaque a dirt road continues north across a wide savanna-covered plain towards the remote backwater of the **Northern Amazon Frontier**, more than 500km away. As the road draws near to **Riberalta**, the largest city in the region, the savanna gives way to dense Amazonian rainforest. East of Riberalta, the road continues 100km to **Guayaramerín**, on the banks of the Río Mamoré, which is the main border crossing point if you're heading north into Brazil.

RIBERALTA

Set on a bluff above a great sweep of the Río Madre de Dios, sleepy, sun-baked **RIBERALTA** is the second-biggest town in the Amazon lowlands, with a population of about 40,000, largely employed in the processing and export of brazil nuts. At least twelve hours by road from Rurrenabaque when conditions are good in the dry season, there's no great reason to stop unless you're heading for Cobija (see box below) and want to break your journey.

ARRIVAL AND DEPARTURE

By plane The airport is a 10min walk along Av Ochoa from the town centre. TAM (☎03 8522646) flies to La Paz on Wed and to Santa Cruz on Sun, while Aerocon (🌐aerocon.bo) flies daily to Trinidad.

By bus Buses arrive and depart from the offices of various transport companies in the centre of town around República de Brasil. There are 4–5 daily services to Guayaramerín (3hr) and, when possible, services to Rurrenabaque, Trinidad and Cobija.

ACCOMMODATION

Hotel Lazo C Nicolas Salvatierra ☎03 8522352, ☎03 8528326. Basic but clean place which offers a laundry service and cheaper shared-bathroom options a couple of blocks from the plaza. Doubles B$70

Residencial Los Reyes ☎03 8528018. Pleasant hotel near the airport, with a garden, hammocks and pretty tiled walkways creating a cool ambience. Doubles B$80

EATING AND DRINKING

Cabaña Tom Southeast corner of the plaza. *Tom's Cabin* does decent *almuerzos* as well as the two Beni stalwarts: beef steaks and river fish. Mains from B$25.

Club Social Nautico Parque Costanera, on the riverfront. Good Bolivian food and cheap *almuerzos* (B$24); you can also cool off in the swimming pool for B$15.

GUAYARAMERÍN

On the banks of the Río Mamoré some 86km east of Riberalta, **GUAYARAMERÍN** is the main crossing point on Bolivia's northern border, a modern and prosperous frontier town with a distinctly Brazilian flavour and a thriving economy based on duty-free sales. Most people only come here to cross into Brazil (see box below).

ARRIVAL AND DEPARTURE

By plane The airport is four blocks east of the plaza along C 25 de Mayo. TAM (☎03 8553924) flies to La Paz on Mon and to Trinidad on Mon and Thurs.

By bus Buses from Riberalta and beyond arrive at the Terminal de Buses, about 3km from the centre of town along C Beni; a motorbike taxi from here should cost about B$5. Buses to Riberalta leave throughout the day (3hr); in the dry season, services attempt the long journeys to Trinidad (around 30hr), Rurrenabaque (around 26hr) and Cobija (around 15hr) – the length of the journeys varies significantly due to road conditions.

INFORMATION

Money and exchange The *Hotel San Carlos*, a block north and east from the Plaza on Av 6 de Agosto, changes travellers' cheques – the only place in town that does – and also changes dollars and Brazilian reais. There are no ATMs in town but there is a Prodem on the main square.

Tourist information The post office is on C Oruro, three blocks south of the plaza. The ENTEL office is on C Mamoré, two blocks north of the plaza.

CROSSING INTO BRAZIL: GUAJARÁ-MIRIM

From the port at the bottom of Avendia Federico Roman in Guayaramerín, **regular passenger boats** (every 15min; about B$6 each way) make the ten-minute crossing to Guajará-Mirim in Brazil. The Bolivian *migración* (Mon–Fri 8–11am & 2–6pm, Sat 8am–noon) is to the right of the port as you face the river; you should get an exit stamp here if you're continuing into Brazil, but it's not necessary if you're just making a day-trip across the river. If you need a visa, the **Brazilian consulate** (Mon–Fri 11am–3pm) is on Calle Beni, at 24 de Septiembre, a block east of the plaza in Guayaramerín. Note that to enter Brazil you need to have an international certificate of yellow-fever vaccination. From Guajará-Mirim there are frequent buses to Porto Velho, from where there are connections to other destinations in Brazil. You can also cross into Brazil via **Cobija**, capital of the Pando department, a remote and sparsely populated rainforest region that until recently was accessible only by boat; today, a rough road cuts through the rainforest running from just south of Riberalta to Cobija. However, it's much easier to go via Guayaramerín.

ACCOMMODATION AND EATING

There is a reasonable choice of budget hotels and guest-houses in town, though very few tourists choose to stay much more than a night here. The best places to eat are on and around the plaza; the two *heladerías* are good for ice cream, coffee, juices and snacks.

Hotel Anexo Plaza West side of main plaza ☎03 8553650. Long established, but they haven't let their standards – either of cleanliness or friendliness – slip. It's a bit overpriced because of the central location. Doubles B$140

Hotel Santa Ana 25 de Mayo, at 16 de Julio ☎03 8553900. With an inviting garden, located just east of the plaza, this is another reasonable option. Doubles B$90

CHRIST THE REDEEMER, RIO DE JANEIRO

Brazil

HIGHLIGHTS

❶ **Rio de Janeiro** Sunbathing and samba in a stunning urban setting. **See p.236**

❷ **Cidades Históricas** Cobbled colonial streets, architectural gems and great food. **See p.260**

❸ **Salvador** Take in pulsating street life and the Afro-Brazilian martial art Capoeira. **See p.276**

❹ **Chapada Diamantina** Hike canyons and jump waterfalls in the Northeastern interior. **See p.286**

❺ **Iguaçu Falls** Straddling Argentina and Brazil is one of the planet's most impressive natural wonders. **See p.353**

HIGHLIGHTS ARE MARKED ON THE MAP ON PP.226–227

ROUGH COSTS

Daily budget Rio de Janeiro, São Paulo and Brasília: US$55/The North and Northeast: US$45

Drink beer (600ml bottle) US$2

Food *Prato comercial/prato feito* (basic set meal) US$4–8

Hostel/budget hotel US$17–55

Travel Rio–São Paulo (352km) by bus, US$45

FACT FILE

Population 194 million

Language Portuguese

Currency Real (R$)

Capital Brasília (population 2.6 million)

International phone code ☏55

Time zone GMT -3/-4hr

Introduction

Brazil has an energy like no other nation on earth. Unified through open-armed hospitality and the combined passions of football, the beach and all that's beautiful, even the glaring gap between rich and poor somehow fails to distract Brazilians from a determination to succeed – and party hard along the way. It's a huge country (larger than the United States excluding Alaska) with all the diverse scenic and cultural variety you'd expect, from Bahian beaches to Amazonian jungles. But Brazil is cosmopolitan too. You could as easily find yourself dancing samba until sunrise as you could eating sashimi amid a crowd of Japanese Brazilians. Rio and São Paulo are two of the world's great metropolises and eleven other cities each have more than a million inhabitants.

Brazilians are one of the most **ethnically diverse** peoples in the world. In the south, German and Italian immigration has left distinctive European features; São Paulo has the world's largest Japanese community outside Japan; while centred principally in Salvador and Rio is the largest black population outside Africa. Amerindian influence pervades the entire country but is especially evident in Amazonia and the northeastern interior. Enormous natural resources and rapid postwar industrialization have made it one of the world's ten largest economies, but **socio-economic contradictions** mean that this hasn't improved the lives of many of its citizens: there is a vast (and growing) middle class, yet all Brazil's cities are strewn with **favelas** and slums.

Nowhere, however, do people know how to enjoy themselves more – most famously in the orgiastic annual four-day celebrations of **Carnaval**, but also reflected in the lively year-round nightlife you'll find almost everywhere. Brazil's vibrant arts, theatre and design scenes are accompanied by the most relaxed and tolerant attitude to **sexuality**, straight and gay, of anywhere in South America. And the country's hedonism also manifests itself in a highly developed **beach culture**, superb music and dancing, and rich regional cuisines.

WHEN TO VISIT

If **Carnaval** is the main thing on your mind, then try to arrive in Rio, Salvador, Recife or Minas Gerais well before the action – dates change each year from February to early March. This is also the main tourist season and warmest part of the year for most of Brazil (Jan–March), with higher accommodation prices and crowded beaches and hostels. The other big draw is **Reveillon** (New Year), when beds in Rio are especially hard to find. As you go further south it gets noticeably **cooler**, so it's best to visit places like Foz do Iguaçu, Florianópolis and São Paulo between November and April. In the Amazon the less rainy and humid months are between May and October, while the Northeast has pretty good weather all year round.

CHRONOLOGY

1500 Off course, en route to India on behalf of Portugal, Pedro Álvares Cabral lands in Bahia.

1502 Amerigo Vespucci enters Guanabara Bay and calls it Rio de Janeiro.

1549 King João unifies 15 hereditary captaincies under governor-general Tomé de Sousa, who founds Salvador, the first capital. Portuguese settlers begin to flow in.

1555 French take possession of Rio and are finally expelled by the Portuguese in 1567.

1574 Jesuits given control of converted Indians.

1630 Dutch West India Company fleet captures Pernambuco.

1654 Brazilians, without Portuguese aid, defeat and expel the Dutch.

1695 *Bandeirantes* discover gold in Minas Gerais.

1759 Jesuits expelled by prime minister Marquis de Pombal, who grants legal rights to Indians and helps centralize Brazilian government.

1763 Capital shifted from Salvador to Rio.

1789 First rebellion against Portuguese ends in defeat when José Joaquim da Silva Xavier, known as Tiradentes, is executed.

1807 Napoleon I invades Portugal. Portuguese prince regent Dom João evacuates to Brazil.

1808 Dom João declares Rio temporary capital of the empire, opens harbours to commerce and abolishes restrictions on Brazilian trade and manufacturing.

1823 With Dom João (King João IV) in Portugal, his son, Dom Pedro, declares Brazil independent and crowns himself emperor.

1825 Portugal recognizes independent Brazil.

1854 Slave trade abolished, slavery continues.

1864–70 War of the Triple Alliance pits landlocked Paraguay against Argentina, Uruguay and Brazil.

1888 Princess Isabel, acting as regent, signs the "Golden Law" abolishing slavery. The following year Dom Pedro II is overthrown and Brazil becomes a republic.

1907 Brazil and Japan sign a treaty allowing Japanese immigration to Brazil.

1930 Great Depression leads to revolution. Getúlio Vargas rises to power.

1937 Vargas declares himself dictator, creates the "New State", the Estado Novo.

1944 Brazil accepts US aid in return for bases, joins Allies in World War II, and sends Expeditionary Force to fight in Italy.

1956 Juscelino Kubitschek elected president with an ambitious economic programme. Construction of Brasília begins.

1960 Brasília declared capital of Brazil.

1964 Massive population growth, disparity in wealth, economic inflation and fears of a rising proletariat lead to a military coup.

1969 General Emilio Garrastazú Médici assumes presidency. Censorship and torture are routine and thousands are driven into exile.

1983–84 Mass campaign in Rio and São Paulo for direct elections.

1985 Tancredo Neves wins electoral college vote – military rule ends.

1994 Inflation peaks. President Cardoso introduces Real as new currency along with new economic plan.

2002 Liberal former trade union activist Luiz Inácio Lula da Silva elected on promises to curb hunger and create jobs.

2006 Lula re-elected; raises minimum wage by 13 percent and announces new economic plan.

2010 Lula succeeded by Dilma Rousseff, Brazil's first female president, on the promise of continuity assisted by discovery of vast new Atlantic oil reserves.

2013 Buoyed by increasing wealth and infrastructural investments in advance of the World Cup and Olympics, Rousseff's centrist coalition retains sky-high popularity ratings.

ARRIVAL AND DEPARTURE

There are direct **flights** to Rio and São Paulo from Europe, North America, Asia, South Africa, and from most major Latin American cities, while easy connections are available from Australia and New Zealand via Argentina or Chile. Brazil also has a well-developed network of domestic flights. **Overland crossings** are possible from most South American countries, with Colombia and Peru accessed **by boat**, and flights available from Chile, Ecuador and Suriname. If you enter Brazil overland, remember that crossing points can be very remote.

FROM ARGENTINA

Most people crossing between Argentina and Brazil do so at the frontier at **Foz do Iguaçu** (see p.351). Another handy crossing further south is at the Argentine city of Paso de los Libres, across the border from **Uruguaiana**, 694km west of Porto Alegre. There are daily **flights** from Buenos Aires to Brazil's main southern and central cities.

FROM BOLIVIA

You can reach Bolivia's southeastern border by train from the station a few kilometres out of Puerto Suárez or by hourly bus from Quijarro. From the border there's frequent transport to the *rodoviária* in **Corumbá**, where you'll find regular onward buses to Campo Grande (5–7hr), São Paulo (21hr) and Rio de Janeiro (26hr). In the north, passenger boats make the ten-minute crossing to **Guajará-Mirim** in Brazil, where there are frequent buses to Porto Velho, for connections to other destinations in Brazil. There are daily **flights** from La Paz to Rio, Salvador, São Paulo and other Brazilian cities.

FROM THE GUIANAS

It's a bumpy eight-hour bus ride from Georgetown in Guyana to **Lethem**, a quiet border town about 130km northeast of the Brazilian city Boa Vista. There are daily **flights** from Georgetown to Boa Vista, or you can connect via **Paramaribo** in Suriname, from where there are flights to Belém. Crossing to

VENEZUELA

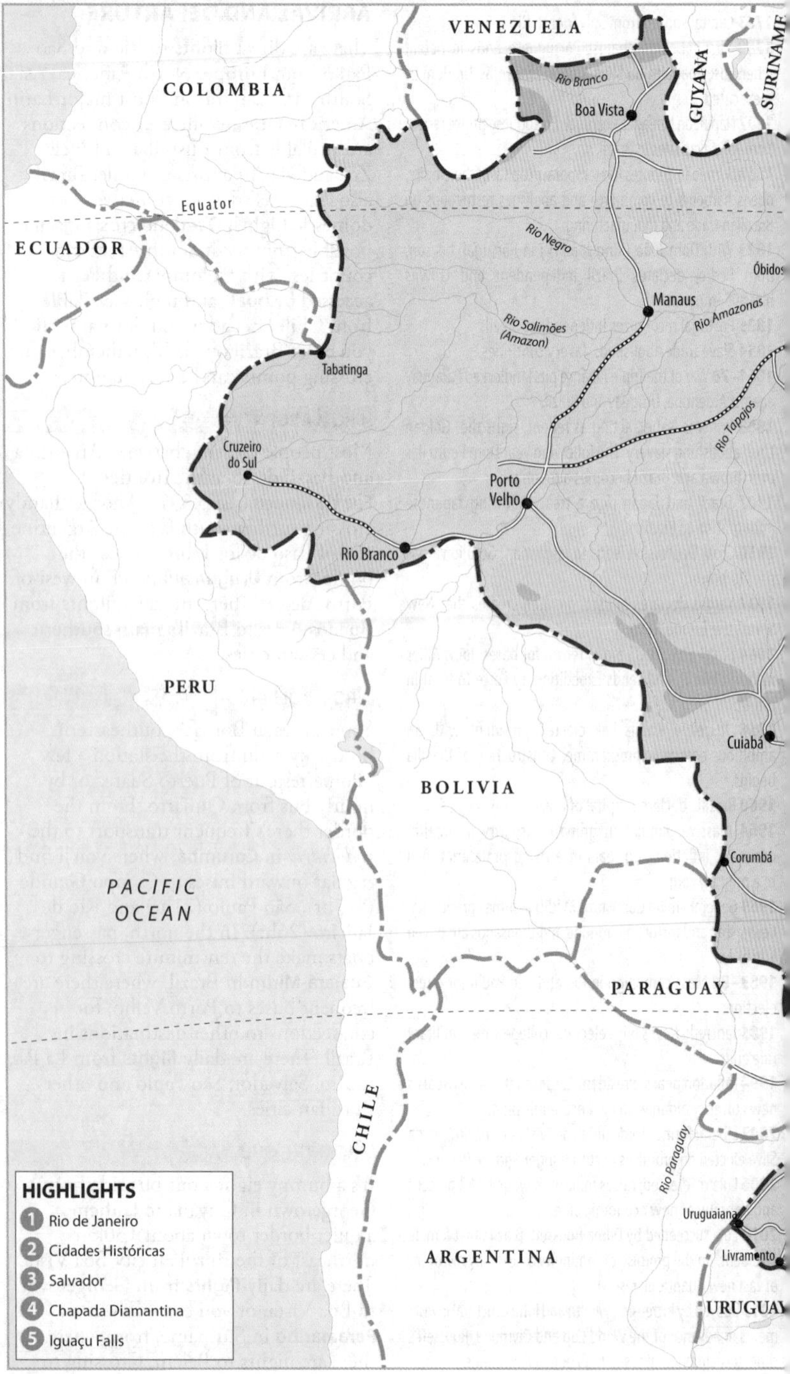

COLOMBIA

Rio Branco

Boa Vista

GUYANA

SURINAME

Equator

ECUADOR

Rio Negro

Óbidos

Manaus

Rio Solimões
(Amazon)

Rio Amazonas

Tabatinga

Rio Tapajos

Cruzeiro
do Sul

Porto
Velho

Rio Branco

PERU

BOLIVIA

Cuiabá

PACIFIC
OCEAN

Corumbá

PARAGUAY

CHILE

Rio Paraguay

Uruguaiana

Livramento

ARGENTINA

URUGUAY

HIGHLIGHTS
1 Rio de Janeiro
2 Cidades Históricas
3 Salvador
4 Chapada Diamantina
5 Iguaçu Falls

3

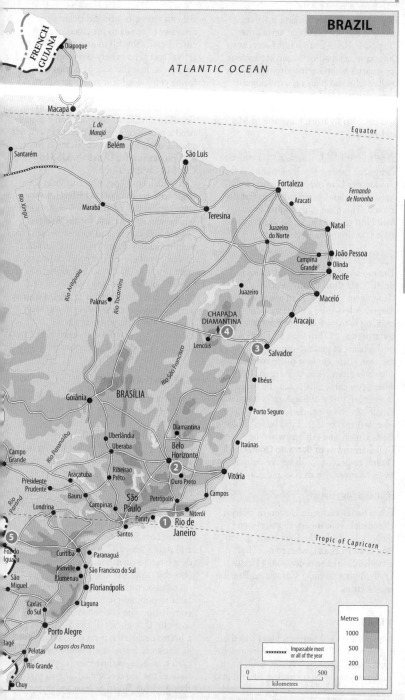

BRAZIL

3

3

Brazil from French Guiana involves taking a dugout taxi-boat across the Oiapoque River from Saint Georges to **Oiapoque**, a small dirt-road settlement. It's smarter to arrive in gritty Oiapoque by daylight and plan on a quick exit; buses depart for the twelve-hour journey to Macapá on the Amazon, twice daily. You can also **fly** from Cayenne to Macapá and Belém.

FROM PARAGUAY

Paraguay's busiest border crossing is from Ciudad del Este over the Puente de la Amistad (Friendship Bridge) to **Foz do Iguaçu**. There are daily **flights** from Asunción to São Paulo, Rio and other major destinations in Brazil.

FROM URUGUAY

The most travelled overland route to Brazil is via **Chuí** (Chuy on the Uruguayan side), 527km south of Porto Alegre. A less-used but more atmospheric crossing is from Rivera to **Santana Do Livramento**, 497km west of Porto Alegre in the heart of gaucho country. Between the two, there are also more complicated crossings from Melo to Aceguá, from where you can easily reach the more interesting town of **Bagé**, or to **Jaguarão**. Finally, in the west, there are international bridges (and buses) linking Bella Unión and Artigas with the Brazilian towns of **Barra do Quarai** and **Quarai** respectively. There are daily **flights** from Montevideo to Rio and São Paulo.

FROM VENEZUELA

From Santa Elena de Uairén in Bolívar (Venezuela's southeastern state) two daily buses make the four-hour trip to **Boa Vista** in Brazil, where you'll find a twelve-hour connection to Manaus. Daily **flights** connect Caracas to Brazil's major cities.

VISAS

Generally, Brazil requires **visas** based on the principle of reciprocity of treatment given to its citizens. Visitors from most European nations, including Britain and Ireland, need only a valid passport and either a return or onward ticket or evidence of funds to purchase one, to enter Brazil. You fill in an entry form on arrival and get a ninety-day tourist visa. Try not to lose the receipt of this entry form; you'll need it if you plan to extend. Citizens from **Australia**, **USA** and **Canada** need visas in advance, available from Brazilian consulates abroad; you'll usually need a return or onward ticket, a passport photo, completed visa application form, and processing fee (Aus$55, US$180 or Can$107 respectively).

In Brazil, entry permits and visas are dealt with by the **Polícia Federal**. Every state capital has a federal police station with a visa section: ask for the *delagacia federal*. You can extend tourist permits for another ninety days if you apply at least fifteen days before expiry; official rules state that you cannot spend more than six months in Brazil in any twelve-month period. A R$76 charge is made on tourist permit and visa extensions. If you stay past the visa date without having extended it you will be charged R$12 per day before you leave the country.

GETTING AROUND

Travel in Brazil is usually straightforward: it's generally by bus or plane, though there are a few passenger trains, too, and given the long distances involved it's usually good value. Hitchhiking over any distance is not recommended. In the **Amazon**, travel is by boat (see p.314), a slow yet fascinating river experience.

BY AIR

Brazil relies heavily on air travel. **TAM** (Ⓦtam.com.br), **GOL** (Ⓦvoegol.com.br) and **Azul** (Ⓦvoeazul.com.br) serve most domestic destinations, while **Webjet** (Ⓦwebjet.com.br) and **Avianca** (Ⓦavianca.com.br) also offer competitive fares to popular cities. A useful flight comparison site is Ⓦsubmarinoviagens .com.br, though you'll almost always get a better deal purchasing on the relevant airline's site (some don't allow foreign card transactions, however, so you may have to use a travel agent). If you plan on flying within Brazil at least four times in thirty days, and don't mind sticking to an itinerary, it makes sense to buy an **airpass** with TAM or Gol. These need to be purchased from an agent before you travel (you can't buy them in Brazil); each costs somewhere between US\$500 and US\$1200 for between five and nine flights. **Departure tax** is included in the price of your international ticket.

BY BUS

Hundreds of bus companies offer services that crisscross Brazil. **Bus travel** prices range from 25 to 75 percent of the cost of air travel, and this is usually the best-value option for journeys of under six hours – although in more remote areas buses tend to be packed and the roads in poor condition. Intercity buses leave from the *rodoviária*, a bus station usually built on city outskirts. **Prices** are standardized even when more than one firm plies the same route, and there are often two levels of bus service: the perfectly comfortable *convencional* and marginally more expensive *executivo*; on the latter you're usually supplied with a blanket, newspaper and snack. **Leitos** are luxury buses that do nocturnal runs between major cities, with fully reclining seats in curtained partitions. All long-distance buses are comfortable enough to sleep in, however, and have on-board toilets. Bring water and a sweater or jacket for the often-cool air conditioning.

For most journeys it's best to buy your ticket at least a day in advance, from the *rodoviária* or some travel agents. An exception is the Rio–São Paulo route, with services every thirty minutes. If you cross a state line you'll get a small form asking for your passport number (*identidade*); give it to the driver before you get on board.

BY CAR

High accident rates, poor signposting, immense urban congestion and heavily potholed rural roads make driving in Brazil hardly a recommendation. Nonetheless, vehicle **rental** is easy, from about R\$120 per day. International companies operate alongside local alternatives like Interlocadora, Nobre,

Localiza and Unidas – offices (*locadoras*) are at every airport and in most towns. An **international driving licence** is recommended: foreign licences are accepted for visits of up to six months but you may find it tough convincing police of this.

Be wary of driving at night as roads are poorly lit and lightly policed – specifically avoid the **Via Dutra**, linking Rio and São Paulo, due to the huge numbers of trucks at night and the treacherous ascent and descent of the Serra do Mar, and the **Belém–Brasília highway**, whose potholes and uneven asphalt make it difficult enough to drive even in daylight. Outside of big cities, service stations don't always accept international credit cards, so bring cash. If you're stopped by police, they can be intimidating, pointing to trumped-up contraventions when they're probably angling for a bribe. If such an on-the-spot **multa**, or fine, is suggested, it's your choice whether to stand your ground or pay up. Whatever you do, always appear polite. If your passport is confiscated, demand to call your consulate – there should always be a duty officer available.

BY TAXI

Metered **taxis** are easy to flag down and relatively inexpensive, though base fares vary from place to place. An alternative is the radiotaxi, a metered cab you can call to pick you up – generally cheaper on airport trips and the like.

ACCOMMODATION

Hostels (*albergues*) usually offer the best value, in most cases with dorms (*dormitórios*) and private rooms (*quartos*). There's an extensive network of Hostel International-affiliated hostels, so it's worth taking out an HI membership (ⓦhihostels.com). In most bigger cities and resorts you'll find numerous **private hostels** for R\$30–45 a night per person. Slightly higher in price are small, family-run hotels called **pensão** (*pensões* in the plural) or *hotel familiar*. *Pensões* are often better in small towns than in large cities. You'll also find **pousadas**, which can be just like a *pensão*, or a small, luxurious or offbeat hotel. In the Amazon and the Pantanal pousadas tend to be purpose-built **fazenda** lodges geared towards upscale ecotourism.

Hotels proper run the gamut from cheap dives to ultra-luxe. The Brazilian star system (one to five) depends on bureaucratic requirements more than on standards – many perfectly good hotels don't have stars. A **quarto** is a room without a bathroom; an **apartamento** or suite is en suite (with private shower); an **apartamento de luxo** is an *apartamento* with a fridge/mini-bar. A **casal** is a double room, a **solteiro** a single. *Apartamentos* normally come with telephone, air conditioning (*ar condicionado*), TV and fan (*ventilador*). Room **rates** vary tremendously by region and season. Generally, for R$80–140 a night you can stay in a reasonable hotel or pousada with private bathroom and fan or air conditioning. In many cases (especially smaller towns) the price of a double or twin room may be little more than two hostel beds – and the breakfast could well be much better. During the off-season hotels in tourist areas offer hefty discounts of around 25 to 35 percent – and even in high season at hotels and pousadas at all times it's worth asking *"tem desconto?"* ("is there a discount?").

Brazilian **campsites** are usually found on the coast near larger beaches. These have basic facilities – running water and toilets, a simple restaurant – and in the south are popular with both Argentines and Brazilians. Elsewhere camping is prohibited in most national parks, and is usually only undertaken on organized jungle treks or with local guides to ensure safety.

FOOD AND DRINK

Brazil has four main **regional cuisines**: **comida mineira**, from Minas Gerais, is based mainly on pork with imaginative use of vegetables and thick bean sauces; **comida baiana** (see box, p.282), from Bahia, has a rich seafood base and an abundance of West African ingredients; **comida do sertão**, from the interior of the Northeast, relies on rehydrated, dried or

> ### RESSACA (HUNG OVER)? TRY ENGOV
>
> *Caipirinhas* go down easily and don't strike at once, which makes getting *bêbado* (drunk) very easy. If you think you're going to overdo it, do what the locals do; stop into a local *farmácia* and buy some gold packets of **Engov tablets**, a cheap, over-the-counter hangover preventative and "cure" whose ingredients, aluminium hydroxide, caffeine, acetylsalicylic acid and pyrilamine maleate, can be found in antacids, aspirin and antihistamines. You're meant to take one before your first drink and another after the last; but trust us, it helps the next day too.

salted meat and regional fruits, beans and tubers; and **comida gaúcha** from Rio Grande do Sul, the world's most carnivorous diet, revolves around *churrasco* – charcoal-grilling every meat imaginable. **Feijoada** is the closest Brazil comes to a national dish: a stew of pork, sausage and smoked meat cooked with black beans and garlic, garnished with slices of orange. Eating it is a national ritual at weekends, when restaurants serve *feijoada* all day.

Alongside regional restaurants, there are **standard meals** available everywhere for about R$9–15: **prato comercial** and **prato feito** (literally, pre-made dish) are two very budget-friendly phrases you'll see on (usually lunchtime) menus, consisting of *arroz e feijão* (rice and beans), a choice of steak (*bife*), chicken (*frango*) or fish (*peixe*), and often served with salad, fries and *farinha*, dried manioc (cassava) flour that you sprinkle over everything. *Farofa* is toasted *farinha*, and usually comes with onions and bits of bacon mixed in. The **prato do dia** (plate of the day) or set-menu **prato executivo** are similarly cheap and usually very filling (R$12–25). Also economical are **lanchonetes**, ubiquitous Brazilian snack bars where you eat at the counter. These serve a range of *salgados* (savoury snacks) like *pão de queijo* (cheese profiteroles), *pastel* (fried pastry with meat or cheese filling) and *coxinha* (shredded chicken in corn dough, battered and fried), or cheap meals like a *bauru* – a basic filling steak meal with egg, fries and salad.

Restaurantes a kilo are the lunch choices of most Brazilian office workers, where you choose from (sometimes vast) buffets and pay by weight (*por kilo*); less lavish ones will cost you anything from R$12–24 for a decent plateful. **Rodizio** restaurants can be fantastic deals – specialized restaurants (such as pizza or sushi), where you pay a set fee and eat as much as you want of the endless supply food waiters bring around. The *churrascaria*, the classic Brazilian **steakhouse**, operates similarly, with a constant supply of charcoal-grilled meat on huge spits brought to your table.

There are more **fruits** than there are English words for them. Some of the fruit is familiar – *manga* (mango), *maracujá* (passion fruit), *limão* (lime) – but most of it has only Brazilian names: *jaboticaba*, *fruta do conde*, *sapoti* and *jaca*. The most exotic fruits are Amazonian: try *bacuri*, *cupuaçu* and *açaí*. The last-named is often served *na tigela* with *guaraná*, crushed ice, sliced bananas and granola – a delicious and ubiquitous filling smoothie – from any *lanchonete*.

DRINK

Brazil is famous for **coffee** and you'll find decent espresso in many cafés, but in lots of local places the coffee comes ready loaded with copious amounts of sugar (Brazilians add it to *everything* and you'll draw looks if you don't follow suit; ask

for it *sem açúcar* to have them offer you a sugar substitute instead). Tea (*cha*) is surprisingly good: try **cha mate**, a strong green tea with a caffeine hit, or one of many herbal teas, most notably that made from *guaraná*. Fruit in Brazil is put to excellent use in *sucos*: fruit is popped into a liquidizer with sugar and crushed ice to make deliciously refreshing drinks. Made with milk rather than water, it becomes a **vitamina**.

Beer (*cerveja*) is mainly of the lager/pilsner type. Brazilians drink it ice-cold, mostly from 600ml bottles. Draught beer is *chopp*. The regional beers of Pará and Maranhão, *Cerma* and *Cerpa*, are generally acknowledged as the best; of the nationally available brands *Skol*, *Brahma*, *Antarctica* and *Bohemia* are all popular, though mild. Despite the undoubted improvement in the quality of Brazilian **wines**, those imported from Chile and Argentina remain more reliable.

As for spirits, stick to what Brazilians drink – **cachaça**, sugar-cane liquor. The best way to drink it is in a **caipirinha** – *cachaça* mixed with fresh lime, sugar and crushed ice – which along with football and music is one of Brazil's great gifts to the world. One thing to remember when enjoying Brazil's beverages: most clubs and some bars will give you an **individual card** when you enter upon which your drinks are tabulated. Don't lose it. Even if you have paid, unless you have the receipt at the door, you will have difficulty leaving and may even have to pay again.

JEITINHO

To make things happen for you in Brazil you first need to understand the concept of *jeitinho*. Literally it means, "a knack", a "fix" or "twist", but in a larger sense it means "a way" and it's how Brazil works. Can't get tickets to the football game two minutes before the match? Go to the head of the line and get creative. Bouncer giving you trouble getting into the club? Smile, joke and get persuasive. In other words start blagging. In Brazil, there's nearly always a way to get what at first glance seems impossible.

CULTURE AND ETIQUETTE

The most widely spoken language in Brazil is **Portuguese**. Educated Brazilians often speak a little English, and there are plenty of Spanish-speakers, but knowing Spanish is of limited help in interpreting spoken Portuguese. You will do yourself a huge favour and likely make several new friends if you learn some Portuguese – even a little effort goes a long way.

On the whole, Brazilians are very friendly, open people (you'll be guided to your stop by passengers on public transport if you ask for help). The pace

3

differs depending on the region. In major cities things operate fairly quickly and on a schedule. Things work in the Northeast too, but in their own special way – you're better off slowing to their pace.

Though attitudes vary regionally, in general it is true that Brazilians are remarkably open with their **sexuality**. Brazil's reputation as a sex destination is not completely without merit – prostitution is legal and you'll see love motels (hourly rates) everywhere. Also be aware that while Brazilians are very accepting of gays and lesbians during Carnaval, Latin machismo still applies here and Brazilians can be as bigoted as anybody. Whatever you do, use protection (a condom is a *camisinha*).

SPORTS AND OUTDOOR ACTIVITIES

Brazilian football (*futebol*) is globally revered and a privilege to watch, at its best reminding you why it's known as "the beautiful game". In fact, you won't really have experienced Brazil until you've attended a match – and the World Cup in 2014 (see box below) could be the ideal time. Stadiums are spectacular sights, games enthralling and crowds are wildly enthusiastic. **Tickets** are not expensive, ranging from R$15 to R$150 depending on whether you stand on the terraces (*geral*) or opt for stand seats (*arquibancada*) – major championship and international matches sometimes cost more. You can usually pay at the turnstile, though there are long last-minute queues. Regional rivalries are strong; fans are seated separately and given different exit routes to prevent fighting. In Rio, **Flamengo** and **Fluminense** have long had an intense rivalry and dominated the city's football; in São Paulo there is a similar rivalry between **São Paulo** and **Corinthians**.

The other major national sport is **volleyball** (*volei*), mostly played on the

---

THE WORLD CUP IN BRAZIL

The 2014 football World Cup risks driving a country already crazy for *futebol* into near elation meltdown – and the spectacle, accompanied by all the arts, music and fiestas Brazil can muster, represents the ideal time to visit. Twelve cities are hosting matches, an unusual deal with FIFA to bring games (and new stadiums) to some of the farthest reaches of the fifth-biggest country in the world.

Porto Alegre, **Curitiba**, **São Paulo**, **Rio de Janeiro** and **Belo Horizonte** make up the host cities of the southern half of the country, while in the northeast **Salvador**, **Recife**, **Natal** and **Fortaleza** are vying to outdo each other in the excitement stakes. Right across the interior, the capital **Brasília**, **Manaus** in the Amazon, and **Cuiabá** near the Pantanal represent a phenomenal variety of landscapes and cultures. This of course means that fans determined to follow all their country's matches almost certainly have to travel large distances – consider buying a domestic air pass (see p.32) alongside your international ticket – but the costs are balanced emphatically by visits to truly diverse locations at their peak of warmth and hospitality. In many places the cost of hostel accommodation is not likely to rise significantly during the tournament, and the Brazilian Football Federation is guaranteeing full stadiums by freeing up cheaper seats nearer to matchday.

To keep travel distance down, consider taking in a few different host cities in one region. You could easily spend a month in the Northeast, moving between group matches and quarterfinals in Salvador, Natal, Recife and Fortaleza. To the south, São Paulo is hosting the opening ceremony on June 12, one semifinal and a handful of other games, and is ideal for visiting Curitiba, Belo Horizonte – and Rio too. São Paulo's interactive new football museum is unmissable, and located in the city's Art Deco Pacaembu stadium (see p.337). But the final on July 13 at Rio's newly renovated temple of football, the Maracanã (p.247), is inevitably drawing the most interest. Memories of Brazil's 2:1 defeat here by Uruguay in the World Cup final of 1950 are a huge blemish on the country's five World Cup-winning record, and this is a match Brazil is not only expected to be at, but to win.

More information is available at ⓦ fifa.com/worldcup.

beach, though the hard-court game is also popular and sand is imported inland for beach volleyball championships elsewhere. In Rio especially, beach **foot-volleyball** (*futevolei*) has gained massive popularity in the last decade.

A full range of **outdoor activities** is available across the country, with regional highlights including hang-gliding in Rio, hiking and waterfall hunting in the coastal forests of the Serra do Mar or Bahia's marvellous Chapada Diamantina, river-based pursuits in the Amazon and Pantanal, and exploration of the lunar-like dune systems of Maranhão's Lençois Maranhenses.

COMMUNICATIONS

There are **internet cafés** (here called *LAN houses*) everywhere in Brazil – even obscure jungle towns have air-conditioned places with web connections – and **wi-fi** is now standard in hotels and cafés in major cities. Prices vary from R$3 to R$7 per hour. Most have headphones and Skype available.

You may wish to buy a **SIM card** to insert in your mobile phone – most telephone company offices and Lojas Americanas stores sell these (R$10–20), though some have laborious bureaucratic requirements; TIM is often the least problematic. Bear in mind that rates will apply only to calls within the same state – calling to and "roaming" within other states is charged at a hefty premium.

Public phones are operated by phonecards (*cartão telefônico*), available at newspaper stands, and are often cheaper for local landline calls than mobile phones. Different phone companies compete within different areas of Brazil, and pay phones display which company code should be used. This doesn't affect **local calls** – just dial the seven- or eight-digit number – but for **long-distance or international calls** (charged at around R$7 per minute), you must first select a phone company (Embratel, code 021, is reliable; from a TIM phone use 041). Dial this code first, then the area or country code. To call Rio from anywhere else in Brazil, for example, dial 021+21 (phone company code + city code) followed by the eight-digit number. For international calls, add an extra zero before the company code. International calls can also be made from booths in a *posto telefônico* – you're billed at the end. A reverse-charge call is a *chamada a cobrar*.

Post offices – *correios* – are identified by their bright yellow postbox signs. International stamps cost R$1.80 for up to ten grams. Airmail letters to Europe and North America take around two weeks, and though generally reliable, it's better not to send valuables.

CRIME AND SAFETY

Brazil's reputation as a rather dangerous place is not entirely undeserved, but it is often overblown, and many visitors arrive with an exaggerated idea of the perils lying in wait. **Street crime** can be a problem, especially in the evenings and late at night (the targeting of tourists is worst in Rio, Salvador and Recife), but the key is to be sensible and not let fear grip you. Criminals are also getting more sophisticated – there has been a reported increase in the **cloning of ATM cards**, so you should check your online account often.

BRAZIL ON THE NET

ⓦ **brasil.gov.br** Government site with information on Brazilian culture, environment and current affairs in English.

ⓦ **visitbrasil.com** Official site of the Brazilian Ministério do Turismo.

ⓦ **brazilmax.com** Self-proclaimed *Hip Guide to Brazil* covering travel, arts and politics across the country.

ⓦ **folha.uol.com.br/internacional** São Paulo newspaper with a helpful English-language version.

ⓦ **gringoes.com** Brazilian culture, arts, sports and travel in English.

ⓦ **riotimesonline.com** Focused on news and entertainment in Rio, but with information for travellers across Brazil.

3

PERSONAL SAFETY

Being a gringo attracts unwelcome attention but it also provides a measure of protection. The Brazilian police can be extremely violent to criminals, and law enforcement tends to take the form of periodic crackdowns. Therefore criminals know that injuries to foreign tourists mean a heavy clampdown, which in turn means slim pickings for a while. If you are unlucky enough to be the victim of an **assalto** (a mugging), remember, it's your possessions that are the targets. Don't resist: your money and anything you're carrying will be snatched, your watch yanked off, but within seconds it will all be over. Most *assaltos* happen at night, in backstreets and desolate areas of cities, so stick to busy, well-lit streets, and where possible take taxis; city buses generally run late too, though mind your belongings when it's crowded.

BUSES, BEACHES AND HOTELS

Long-distance **buses** are pretty secure, but it pays to keep an eye on your things. Get a **baggage check** on your luggage from the person loading it and keep an eye on your possessions until they are loaded. Overhead racks are less safe, especially during night journeys.

On city **beaches**, never leave things unattended; any beachside bar will stow things for you. In tourist areas and busy cities avoid walking on the beach at night. Shared **rooms** in pousadas and hostels usually have lockers (bring a padlock) and even many cheap hotels have **safes** (*caixas*).

POLICE AND DRUGS

If you are robbed or held up, it's not necessarily a good idea to go to the police. Except with something like a theft from a hotel room, they're unlikely to be able to do much, and reporting something will likely take hours even without the language barrier. You may have to do it for insurance purposes, when you'll need a local police report; this could take a full and very frustrating day. If your passport is stolen in a city where there is a consulate, get in touch with the consulate first and take their lead.

Both **marijuana** (*maconha*) and **cocaine** (*cocaína*) are fairly common, but be warned: if the police find either on you, you will be in serious trouble. The following cannot be overstated: under no circumstances do you want to spend any time in a Brazilian jail.

HEALTH

Public healthcare in Brazil varies tremendously from poor to sometimes quite good, but private medical and dental treatment is generally more reliable; costs are significantly less than in North America. Check directories at the end of each section for hospital information and refer to advice from your country's embassy or consulate. Standard drugs are available in *farmácias* (pharmacies) without prescriptions.

INFORMATION AND MAPS

Popular destinations in Brazil have friendly and helpful **tourist offices**, as do most state capitals, many of which distribute free city maps and booklets. Generally the airport information offices have the best English-speakers and are usually open the longest. They also have decent free maps but little else in English. EMBRATUR is the national tourist organization and has a useful website (ⓦ visitbrasil.com).

MONEY AND BANKS

The Brazilian currency is the real (pronounced "hey-al") and is made up of one hundred centavos. Notes are for 2, 5, 10, 20, 50 and 100 reais; coins are 1,

5, 10, 25 and 50 centavos, and 1 real. At the time of writing, US$1 = R$2, £1 = R$3 and €1 = R$2.60. **ATMs** are available all over Brazil, though not all accept foreign cards and many non-airport ATMs are inactive after 8pm or 10pm for security reasons. Banco do Brasil offer the most reliable network of machines, while Bradesco and HSBC also accept foreign cards.

OPENING HOURS AND HOLIDAYS

Basic opening hours for **shops** and **businesses** are weekdays from 9am until 6pm and Saturday 9am to 1pm. Shopping centres are usually open 10am to 10pm, with larger ones also open Sundays from 3–9pm. Banks generally open weekdays from 10am to 4pm. **Museums** and historic **monuments** generally cost just a few reais and follow regular business hours, though many are closed on Mondays. In addition to the public holidays listed, there are plenty of local and state holidays when you'll also find everything closed.

FESTIVALS AND CELEBRATIONS

Carnaval is by far the most important festival in Brazil, and when it comes, the country comes to a halt as it gets down to some of the most serious partying in the world. The most familiar and most spectacular celebration is in **Rio** (see p.237), one of the world's great sights, televised live to the whole country. **Salvador**'s Carnaval (see p.276) is now almost as commercialized, with big headline performers, and a reputation for being even wilder than Rio's. **Olinda** and its winding colonial hilltop streets next to Recife make for a fun and perhaps less frenzied experience, while **Fortaleza**, and **Diamantina** in Minas Gerais, also host great parties.

Reveillon New Year's Eve. Major cities along the coast compete with fireworks displays. Rio's is nearly always the biggest.

Celebration of Yemanjá February 2. Devotees make offerings on beaches along the coast to celebrate the goddess of the sea. Salvador's Praia Vermelha hosts one of the largest.

Lavagem do Bonfim Second Thursday of January. Hundreds of women in traditional Bahian garb clean the steps of Salvador's beloved church with perfumed water (food and music follow).

São Paulo Bienal Biennial in March (next in 2014). The largest arts event in Latin America.

The Passion Play Ten days leading up to Easter. Latin America's largest passion plays are enacted in Nova Jerusalem, outside Recife.

Bumba-meu-boi June 13–29. The people of São Luis re-enact the folk tale of a farmer who, having killed another farmer's ox, must resurrect it or face his own death. Costumes, dancing, *capoeira*, heckling and hilarity ensue.

São João June 13–24. Celebrations of Saint John happen across Brazil, but Salvador, Pernambuco and cities in the Northeast are the most raucous. *Forró*, drinking and eating.

Paraty International Literary Festival (FLIP) Early August. Some of Brazil's and the world's best authors converge on Paraty, with events and talks in Portuguese and English, and performances by top Brazilian musicians. ⓦ paraty.com.br/flip.

Rio International Film Festival October. The country's biggest film festival, showcasing 200 mainstream and independent releases.

Cirio de Nazaré Second Sunday in October. An effigy of the Virgin of Nazaré is carried across the water from Vila de Icoaraci to the port of Belém.

Oktoberfest October 10–27. German-settled Blumenau has all the beer-swilling, German food and traditional garb you'd expect. ⓦ oktoberfestblumenau.com.br.

Grand Prix November. Brazil's Interlagos circuit near São Paulo is one of the most atmospheric Grand Prix venues. ⓦ gpbrasil.com.

PUBLIC HOLIDAYS

In addition to those below, between 1 and 3 further days are offered by each state.

January 1 New Year's Day

February/March (varies) Carnaval. Takes place on the five days leading up to Ash Wednesday

March/April (varies) Good Friday

April 21 Remembrance of *Tiradentes*

May 1 Labour Day

June 11 Corpus Christi

September 7 Independence Day

October 12 Nossa Senhora Aparecida

November 2 Dia dos Finados (Day of the Dead)

November 15 Proclamation of the Republic

December 25 Christmas Day

Rio de Janeiro

The citizens of **RIO DE JANEIRO** call it the *cidade marvilhosa* – and there can't be much argument about that. It's a huge city with a stunning setting, extending along 40km of sandy coast and sandwiched between an azure sea and jungle-clad mountains. The city's unusual name has a curious history: Portuguese explorers arriving at the mouth of Guanabara Bay on January 1, 1502 thought they had discovered the mouth of an enormous river which they named the January River or Rio de Janeiro. By the time the first settlement was established and the error was realized, the name had already stuck.

Although riven by inequality, Rio has great style. Its international renown is bolstered by a series of symbols that rank as some of the greatest landmarks in the world: the **Corcovado** mountain supporting the great statue of Christ the Redeemer; the rounded incline of the **Sugarloaf mountain** standing at the entrance to the bay; the beaches of **Copacabana** and **Ipanema**, probably the most famous lengths of sand

on the planet. Then there's the **Maracanã stadium**, a huge draw for football fans and freshly renovated to host the World Cup final in 2014 and Olympic Games in 2016. It's a setting enhanced by a frenetic nightlife scene and the annual sensuality of **Carnaval**, an explosive celebration which – for many people – sums up Rio and her citizens, the **cariocas**.

WHAT TO SEE AND DO

Rio's sights are scattered across three main sectors of the city, and improved metrô links make getting around fairly straightforward. **Centro** contains the last vestiges of the metropolis's colonial past, and its major sites are easily walkable in one day. The most obvious place to start is historic **Praça XV de Novembro**, while the other main focal point, Cinelândia, has numerous places of interest nearby. Just south of here are the lively *bairros* of **Lapa**, capital of Brazil's samba scene, and bohemian **Santa Teresa** sprawling across the hills above. It's the **Zona Sul** (south zone), however, where you're likely to spend most of your time – in no small part due to the 16km of sandy **beaches** that line its shores – though visits

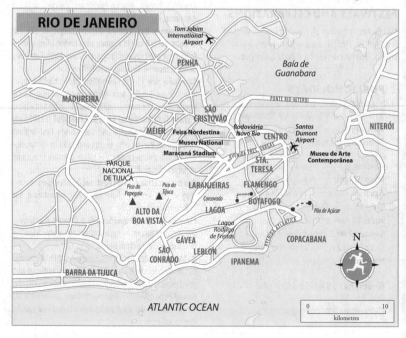

CARNAVAL

Carnaval is celebrated in all of Brazil's cities, but Rio's is the biggest and most famous of all. From the Friday before Ash Wednesday to the following Thursday, the city shuts up shop and throws itself into the world's most famous manifestation of unbridled hedonism. Rio's carnival ranks as the most important celebration on the Brazilian calendar, easily outstripping either Christmas or Easter. In a poverty-stricken city, it represents a moment of release, when *cariocas* unite to express their aspirations in music and song.

THE ACTION

Rio's street celebrations (known as *blocos* and *bandas)* happen all over town from the beaches to the distant suburbs, and you should keep your ears open for the biggest and best parties (W todorio.com has listings), day or night. The processions feature loudspeaker-laden floats blasting out frenetic samba, and thousands of hyped-up revellers. **Avenida Rio Branco** (Metrô Carioca) is the most traditional spot, but Santa Teresa, Laranjeiras, and of course all the beach districts have loads going on. Many neighbourhoods also have their own **samba school**, competing in three leagues, each allowing promotion and relegation. It's a year-round occupation, with schools mobilizing thousands of supporters, choosing a theme, writing the music and learning the dances choreographed by the **carnavelesco** – the school's director. By December, rehearsals have begun and the sambas are released to record stores. From September to February a visit to a samba school is a must (see p.253), while all year round you can check out the *Cidade do Samba* (Rua Rivadávia Correa, Gamboa, Centro W cidadedosambarj.globo.com), a huge complex where carnival floats are constructed and touristic samba spectacles take place.

The main **procession** of *Grupo Especial* schools – known as the **Desfile** – takes place on the Sunday and Monday nights in the purpose-built **Sambódromo** at Rua Marques de Sapucaí (Metrô Praza Onze/Central do Brasil), a concrete structure 1.7km long that can accommodate ninety thousand spectators. Some schools may have thirty thousand participants; they compete for points awarded by judges according to the presentation of their song, story, dress, dance and rhythm. Each school must parade for between 85 and 95 minutes, with the **bateria**, or percussion section, sustaining the cadence that drives the school's song and dance. The **carros alegóricos** (decorated floats) carry prominent figures, and the **porta-bandeira** ("flag bearer") carries the school's symbol. The bulk of the procession behind is formed by the **alas** – each with hundreds of costumed individuals linked to a part of the school's theme.

The **parade** at the Sambódromo starts at 7.30pm, with eight schools (see also p.253) parading on each of the two nights, and it goes on till 8am the following day. *Arquibancada* (high stand) 9 is usually reserved for foreign visitors (from R$600 per night) while stand 3 is the best value for a reasonable view (from R$280). Cheaper stands 4, 6 and 13 all have restricted views (from R$120). **Tickets**, available from Riotur (see p.249), Banco do Brasil and numerous agents and hotels around town, need to be booked well in advance.

Finally, carnival balls (*bailes de Carnaval*) and other live shows are a big feature of festivities before and during the main event. Check out Lapa's *Fundição Progresso* (W fundicaoprogresso .com.br) for appearances by top samba schools in the run-up, and Leblon's *Scala* (W scalario .com.br) for no-holds-barred affairs each night.

to the Corcovado and Sugarloaf mountains will also keep you occupied. Although somewhat run-down, parts of the **Zona Norte** (north and west of Centro) are being renovated in advance of the Olympics: fans of the "beautiful game" should make the pilgrimage to the **Maracanã football stadium**, while for the more culturally minded there's the **Museu Nacional**.

Praça XV de Novembro

"**Praça Quinze**" (10min walk from Metrô Carioca) was once the hub of Rio's social and political life, taking its name from the day in 1889 when Marechal Deodoro de Fonseca, the first president, proclaimed the Republic of Brazil. On the south side of the square is the striking **Paço Imperial** (Tues–Sun noon–6pm; free), which now serves as an exhibition space. It was here in 1808 that the Portuguese monarch, Dom João VI, established his court in Brazil, and the building continued to be used for royal receptions and special occasions: on May 13, 1888, Princess Isabel proclaimed the end of slavery here. Just south is bold,

3

Neoclassical **Palácio Tiradentes**, the Rio state parliament, while to the north is the **Arco de Teles**, constructed on the site of the old *pelourinho* (pillory) in around 1755, and now leading to Rua do Ouvidor and Rua do Mercado, both lively streets with restaurants, cafés, bookshops, and after-work bars and clubs.

On the Rua I de Março side of Praça Quinze, the **Igreja de Nossa Senhora do Carmo da Antigá Sé** (Mon–Fri 9am–5pm) served until 1980 as Rio's cathedral. Inside, the high altar is detailed in silver and boasts a beautiful work by the painter Antônio Parreires. Below, in the crypt, rest the supposed remains of Pedro Álvares Cabral, Portuguese discoverer of Brazil – though his final resting place is more likely to be Santarém in Portugal.

North to São Bento and the port
Heading up **Rua 1 de Março** from the *praça*, you'll pass the church of **Santa Cruz dos Militares** (Mon–Fri 10am–3pm), dating from 1628 and rebuilt in granite and marble by the army in 1780; a display of ecclesiastical and military oddments is to be found inside. The grand interior of the **Centro Cultural Banco do Brasil** (Tues–Sun 10am–9pm; ⓦbb.com.br/cultura), Rio's most dynamic arts centre, is just north of here and well worth a look around. Just beyond, the enormous **Candelária church** (Mon–Fri 7.30am–4pm, Sat–Sun 9am–noon) looms into view, luxuriously decorated inside in marble and bronze. A short way from the entrance a simple wooden cross inscribed with eight names (and with flowers usually laid nearby) commemorates police shootings of street children that took place here in 1993, and serves as an ongoing plea for respect of human rights in Rio. The northward continuation of Rua 1 de Março, the Ladeira de São Bento, leads to the hilltop **Igreja e Mosteiro de São Bento** (daily 7am–6pm, Sun Mass at 9am), founded by Benedictine monks in 1633. The facade is pleasingly simple with twin pyramid-shaped spires, while the interior is richly adorned in gold designs and statues of saints, popes and bishops executed by the deft hand of Mestre Valentim. Further north again is Praça Mauá, now part of the

enormous **Porto Maravilha** redevelopment, featuring cruise ship berths, concert halls, new housing and a light railway, planned for completion before the Olympics.

Museu Histórico Nacional
The **Museu Histórico Nacional** (Tues–Fri 10am–5.30pm, Sat & Sun 2–6pm; R\$6; ⓦmuseuhistoriconacional.com.br), housed in the former military arsenal, is located south from Praça XV de Novembro in the shadow of the Kubitschek flyover. The exhibits contain some pieces of great interest, from furniture, firearms and locomotives to displays on indigenous societies and the sugar, gold, coffee and beef trades. Information about slavery – so important to Brazil's history – is scarce, while the monarchy is granted ample space. There is also very limited information available in English. Despite this, the varied collection makes it one of Brazil's most important museums.

Carioca, Saara and Campo de Santana
The bustling square **Largo da Carioca** (Metrô Carioca) is dominated from above by the cloistered **Igreja e Convento de Santo Antônio** (Mon–Fri 8am–7pm, Sat & Sun 9–11am), though the square's other historical buildings were, sadly, lost to ugly new high-rises. Built between 1608 and 1620, this is Rio's oldest church, a tranquil refuge decorated in marble and Portuguese tiling. Adjoining it, the striking **Igreja de São Francisco da Penitência** (Tues–Fri 1–4pm) contains extensive gold and silver ornamentation. Lively shopping street Rua Uruguaiana heads north from here towards the Candelária, while westwards along ruas Alfândega and Passos takes you through Rio's best (and cheapest) market area, known as **Saara**, originally peopled by Jewish and Arab merchants.

A block south of Saara, the **Igreja de São Francisco de Paula** (Mon–Fri 9am–1pm), the site of the Mass to "swear-in" the Brazilian Constitution in 1831, contains meticulous decoration by Valentim da Fonseca e Silva, known to *Cariocas* as Mestre Valentim, Brazil's most important eighteenth-century sculptor. One of Rio's most impressive ornate interiors is to be found two blocks west, however, at the **Real Gabinete Português de Leitura** (Mon–Fri 9am–6pm), dating from 1887 and containing a library with 350,000 leather-bound volumes. At Saara's western end you come upon a surprisingly peaceful park, the Campo de Santana, where Emperor Dom Pedro I proclaimed Brazil's independence from Portugal in 1822 – now complete with ponds, strutting peacocks and scuttling agoutis (avoid outside of working hours).

Around the Nova Catedral

To the southwest of the Largo da Carioca, the unmistakeable form of the **Nova Catedral Metropolitana** (daily 7.30am–6pm) rises up like some futuristic tepee, 75m high and with a capacity of 20,000. Built between 1964 and 1976, it's an impressive piece of modern architecture, resembling the blunt-topped Mayan pyramids of Mexico. It feels vast inside, its remarkable sense of space enhanced by the absence of supporting columns and four huge stained-glass windows, each measuring 20m by 60m. Over the road is the bizarre Cubist-style **headquarters of Petrobrás**, the state oil company. Immediately behind it is the station (hopefully due to reopen in 2014) for *bondes* (trams) up to Santa Teresa.

Cinelândia: Praça Floriano

At the southern end of Avenida Rio Branco, the dead-straight boulevard that cuts through the centre from north to south, you reach the area known as **Cinelândia** (Metrô Cinelândia), named for long-gone 1930s movie houses. At the centre of impressive square **Praça Floriano** is a bust of **Getúlio Vargas**, still anonymously decorated with flowers on the anniversary of the former dictator's birthday, March 19. At the northern end is the newly renovated **Theatro Municipal** (guided tours in English Tues–Sat 1pm and 3pm; phone to confirm ☎21 2332 9220), modelled on the Paris Opera Garnier – all granite, marble and bronze, with a foyer decorated in Louis XV-style white and gold with green onyx handrails. If you can, come to a performance here (see ⓦwww.theatromunicipal.rj.gov.br) featuring Rio's symphony orchestra and guest ballet schools and singers from across the globe.

Across the road is the superb **Museu Nacional das Belas Artes** (Tues–Fri 10am–6pm, Sat & Sun noon–5pm; R$6, Sun free), a grandiose construction imitating the Louvre in Paris. The European collection includes Boudin, Taunay and Frans Post, but the painting and sculpture by all the modern Brazilian masters are of much greater interest. Neighbouring, the **Biblioteca Nacional** (guided tours Mon–Fri 9am–5pm, Sat 9am–3pm) is also noteworthy, for the high Art Nouveau ceilings of its reading rooms, and its stairway decorated by important artists like Visconti, Amoedo and Bernadelli. Ten minutes' walk southeast, at the edge of the Parque do Flamengo, is the **Museu de Arte Moderna** (Tues–Sun noon–6pm; R$6), which contains a range of twentieth-century Brazilian art. Start upstairs with the pieces from the 1920s.

Lapa

Immediately southwest of Cinelândia is the *bairro* of **Lapa**, a gracefully decaying neighbourhood and the beating heart of Rio's **samba and nightlife scenes** (see p.252). Its **Passeio Público** park (daily 7.30am–9pm) was opened in 1783 and is now a little past its best, but this green oasis still charms – with busts of famous figures from the city's history by Mestre Valentim. Lapa's most recognizable feature is the eighteenth-century aqueduct known as the **Arcos da Lapa**. Built to a Roman design and consisting of 42 wide arches, in its heyday it carried water from the Rio Carioca to the thirsty citizens of the city, though more recently *bondes* (trams) passed across on their way up to Santa Teresa. Each Friday night thousands of people throng the surrounding streets. Just off Rua Joaquim da Silva, a remarkable ascending tiled mosaic lines the **Escadaria Selarón** stairway into Santa Teresa, a feat of obsession by the late Chilean artist, Selarón.

Santa Teresa

Just above Lapa to the southwest is **Santa Teresa**, a leafy *bairro* of labyrinthine,

CENTRAL RIO

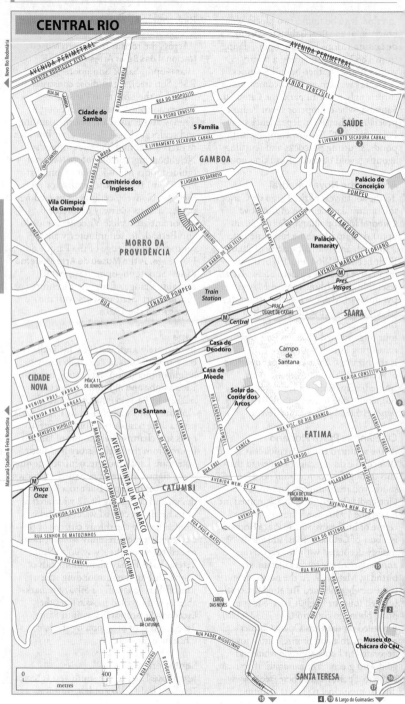

3

Novo Rio Rodoviária

AVENIDA PERIMETRAL
AVENIDA RODRIGUES ALVES
AVENIDA PERIMETRAL
AVENIDA VENEZUELA

RUA DA GAMBOA
R RUA BARÃO DA GAMBOA
R RUABAVIA CORREIA
RUA DO PRÓPOSITO
RUA PEDRO ERNESTO

Cidade do
Samba

S Família

SAÚDE

R LIVRAMENTO SECADURA CABRAL
R LIVRAMENTO SECADURA CABRAL

GAMBOA

RUA CRISTO SANTOS

Cemitério dos
Ingleses

R LADEIRA DO BARROSO

Palácio de
Conceição
POMPEU

Vila Olímpica
da Gamboa

RUA AMÉRICA

MORRO DA
PROVIDÊNCIA

R D ° RIBEIRO
RUA BARÃO DE SÃO FÉLIX
R VISCONDE DA GÁVEA
RUA SENADOR

RUA CAMERINO

Palàcio
Itamaraty

AVENIDA MARECHAL FLORIANO

M
Pres.
Vargas

RUA
SENADOR POMPEU

Train
Station

M
Central

PRAÇA
DUQUE DE CAXIAS

SAARA

Casa de
Deodoro

Campo
de
Santana

Casa de
Moede

RUA DA CONSTITUIÇÃO

CIDADE
NOVA

PRAÇA 11
DE JUNHO

Solar do
Conde dos
Arcos

AVENIDA PRES. VARGAS
AVENIDA PRES. VARGAS

De Santana

RUA VISC. DO RIO BRANCO

AVENIDA G. FREIRE

RUA BENEDITO HIPÓLITO

RUA SANTANA
RUA M. DE POMPAU
RUA GENERAL CALDWELL
CANECA
RUA FREI

FATIMA

RUA DO SENADO

RUA DO INVALIDOS

M
Praça
Onze

Maracanã Stadium & Feira Nordestina

R. MARQUES DE SAPUCAI (SAMBÓDROMO)

AVENIDA TRINTA ULM DE MARCO

DE SÁ

CATUMBI

AVENIDA MEM. DE SÁ

PRAÇA DE CRUZ
VERMELHA

VALADARES

AVENIDA MEM. DE SÁ

AVENIDA SALVADOR

AVENIDA H

RUA DO RESENDE

RUA SENHOR DE MATOZINHOS

RUA PAULA MATOS

RUA REI CANECA

RUA DE CATUMBI

RUA RIACHUELO

RUA MONTE ALEGRE
RUA ANDRÉ CAVALCANTE
RUA JOAQUIM

LARGO
DAS NEVES

LARGO
DE CATUMBI

RUA PADRE MIGUELINHO

Museu do
Chácara do Céu

RUA TIRIPIRU
R COQUEIROS
AV. GUIENTE

SANTA TERESA

0   400
metres

18

4, 19 & Largo do Guimarães

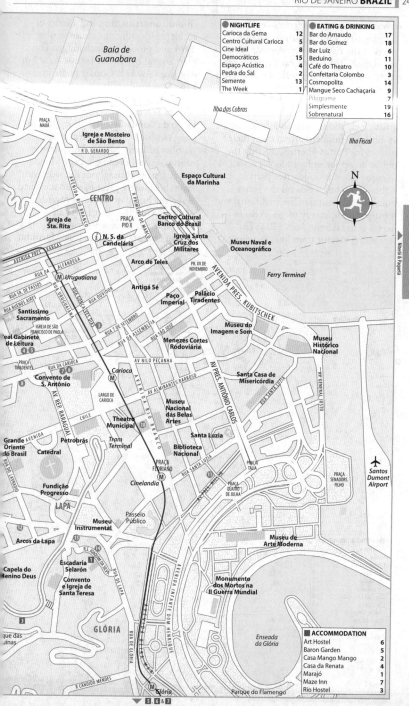

NIGHTLIFE

Carioca da Gema	12
Centro Cultural Carioca	5
Cine Ideal	8
Democráticos	15
Espaço Acústica	4
Pedra do Sal	2
Semente	13
The Week	1

EATING & DRINKING

Bar do Arnaudo	17
Bar do Gomez	18
Bar Luiz	6
Beduino	11
Café do Theatro	10
Confeitaria Colombo	3
Cosmopolita	14
Mangue Seco Cachaçaria	9
Pilograma	7
Simplesmente	19
Sobrenatural	16

ACCOMMODATION

Art Hostel	6
Baron Garden	5
Casa Mango Mango	2
Casa da Renata	4
Marajó	1
Maze Inn	7
Rio Hostel	3

Baía de Guanabara

Ilha das Cobras

Ilha Fiscal

N

3

Niterói & Paquetá

PRAÇA MAUÁ

Igreja e Mosteiro de São Bento

R D. GERARDO

Espaço Cultural da Marinha

CENTRO

Igreja de Sta. Rita

PRAÇA PIO X

Centro Cultural Banco do Brasil

Igreja Santa Cruz dos Militares

Museu Naval e Oceanográfico

(i) N. S. da Candelária

Arco de Teles

PR. XV DE NOVEMBRO

Ferry Terminal

Antigá Sé

Paço Imperial

Palácio Tiradentes

AVENIDA PRES. KUBITSCHEK

Santissimo Sacramento

Museu do Imagem e Som

Museu Histórico Nacional

eal Gabinete de Leitura

IGREJA DE SÃO FRANCISCO DE PAOLA

Menezes Cortes Rodoviária

PRAÇA TIRADENTES

Carioca

AV NILO PEÇANHA

Santa Casa de Misericórdia

Convento de S. Antônio

LARGO DE CARIOCA

Museu Nacional das Belas Artes

Grande Oriente do Brasil

Petrobrás

Theatre Municipal

Santa Luzia

Catedral

Tram Terminal

Biblioteca Nacional

PRAÇA FLORIANO

Santos Dumont Airport

Fundição Progresso

LAPA

Cinelandia

PRAÇA QUATRO DE JULHA

PRAÇA SENADORS. FILHO

Museu Instrumental

Passeio Público

Arcos da Lapa

Museu de Arte Moderna

Capela do Menino Deus

Escadaria Selarón

Convento e Igreja de Santa Teresa

Monumento dos Mortos na II Guerra Mundial

GLÓRIA

Enseada da Glória

que das inas

R. CANDIDO MENDES

(M) Glória

Parque do Flamengo

▼ 5, 6 & 7

cobbled streets and *ladeiras* (steps), clinging to a hillside with stupendous views of the city and bay. Atmospheric but slightly dishevelled early nineteenth-century mansions and walled gardens line the streets; the resident community here enjoys something of a bohemian reputation. Santa Teresa is Rio's main artistic neighbourhood: in July or August around one hundred artists open their studios for **Portas Abertas**, offering the public an opportunity to look (as well as to enjoy an enormous street party) – though on any weekend the *bairro* is buzzing with visitors. The traditional and most picturesque way to get to Santa Teresa is to take the *bonde,* Rio's last remaining **electric tram** line, but due to

chronic underfunding and a series of accidents it's sadly out of use until at least 2014 and probably much longer. For now, ascend on foot or by bus #6, #7 or #14 from Avenida Gomez Freire in Lapa or Avenida Nilo Peçanha in Centro (near Metrô Carioca).

Santa Teresa's tiny centre "square", **Largo do Guimarães**, is a great place to hang out for a drink or meal at any number of lively bars and restaurants nearby – every evening except Monday, but especially throughout the weekend. From here, more great bars are staggered along the bus/tram route westwards, while downhill to the east it's an enjoyable ten-minute walk to art gallery **Museu Chácara do Céu** at Rua Murtinho

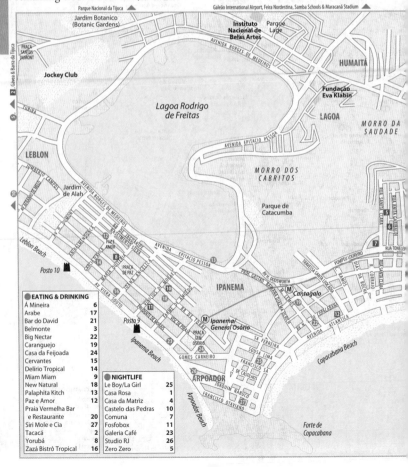

EATING & DRINKING

Á Mineira	6
Arabe	17
Bar do David	21
Belmonte	3
Big Nectar	22
Caranguejo	19
Casa da Feijoada	24
Cervantes	15
Delírio Tropical	14
Miam Miam	9
New Natural	18
Palapita Kitch	13
Paz e Amor	12
Praia Vermelha Bar e Restaurante	20
Siri Mole e Cia	27
Tacacá	2
Yorubá	8
Zazá Bistrô Tropical	16

NIGHTLIFE

Le Boy/La Girl	25
Casa Rosa	1
Casa da Matriz	4
Castelo das Pedras	10
Comuna	7
Fosfobox	11
Galeria Café	23
Studio RJ	26
Zero Zero	5

Nobre 93 (Wed–Mon noon–5pm; ⓦmuseuscastromaya.com.br; R$3), in a modernist building surrounded by gardens. It holds a reasonable, eclectic collection of twentieth-century art, though its best works by Matisse, Picasso, Dalí and Monet were stolen in an audacious raid during Carnaval 2006, the culprits melting into the crowd in fancy dress.

A pathway links the museum to the **Parque das Ruínas** (Wed–Sun 10am–5pm), an attractive public garden with great views and containing the ruins of a mansion that was once home to a Brazilian heiress. Following her death the mansion fell into disrepair but reopened as a cultural and exhibition centre in the 1990s.

Glória and Catete

Heading into the Zona Sul from Centro, it's worth visiting the eighteenth-century **Igreja de Nossa Senhora da Glória do Outeiro** (Tues–Fri 9am–5pm, Sat & Sun 9am–noon), atop the Morro da Glória (5min walk from Metrô Glória). Notable for its innovative octagonal ground plan and domed roof, the latter decked with seventeenth-century blue-and-white *azulejos* and nineteenth-century marble masonry, it's an architectural gem.

At Rua do Catete 153, adjacent to the **Catete** metrô station, the Palácio do Catete houses the **Museu da República** (Tues–Fri 10am–5pm, Sat & Sun 2–6pm; R$6, free Wed & Sun). The displays begin with the period of the

3

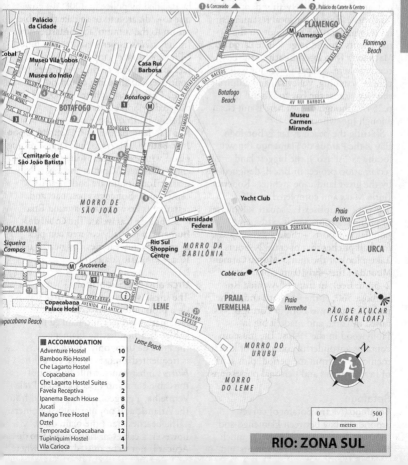

■ ACCOMMODATION	
Adventure Hostel	10
Bamboo Rio Hostel	7
Che Lagarto Hostel Copacabana	9
Che Lagarto Hostel Suites	5
Favela Receptiva	2
Ipanema Beach House	8
Jucati	6
Mango Tree Hostel	11
Oztel	3
Temporada Copacabana	12
Tupiniquim Hostel	4
Vila Carioca	1

RIO: ZONA SUL

establishment of the first Republic in 1888 and end with Presidente Vargas's 1954 suicide, though it's the palace's spectacular Moorish Hall and opulent marble and stained glass that make a visit so worthwhile. Behind the palace is the Parque do Catete, a pleasing tranquil spot, while neighbouring to the south is the **Museu de Folclore Edison Carneiro** (Tues–Fri 11am–6pm, Sat & Sun 3–6pm; R$5), holding a fascinating folkloric collection of leatherwork, musical instruments, ceramics, toys and Afro-Brazilian religious paraphernalia.

Flamengo

Busy during the day, the tree-lined streets of **Flamengo** (Metrô Largo do Machado or Catete) are also lively after dark with residents eating in the local restaurants; it's tranquil enough to sit out on the pavements around large square **Largo do Machado**. The closest **beach** to the city centre is here, a superb place for walking, people-watching, volleyball and admiring the view across the bay to Niterói (see p.254) – though the sea here is not clean enough for swimming.

Skirting the beach as far as Botafogo Bay is the **Parque do Flamengo** (known locally as "Aterro"), the biggest land reclamation project in Brazil, designed by the great landscape architect Roberto Burle Marx and completed in 1960. The park comprises 1.2 square kilometres of prime seafront, and is extremely popular for sports – there are countless football pitches that operate 24-hours. Take a look at the quirky **Museu Carmen Miranda** (Tues–Fri 10am–5pm, Sat 2–5pm; free), in front of Avenida Rui Barbosa 560, at the southern end of the park. Carmen was born in Portugal, raised in Lapa, and made it big in Hollywood in the 1940s. The museum contains a wonderful collection of kitsch memorabilia from the period, plus some of her costumes and personal possessions.

Botafogo

Botafogo (Metrô Botafogo) curves around the bay between Flamengo and the Sugarloaf, a *bairro* known as much for its lively arts scene, restaurants and hostels as its uncomfortably heavy traffic. The bay is dominated by yachts moored near Rio's yacht club, while seven blocks inland the district's top attraction is the **Museu do Índio** (Tues–Fri 9am–5.30pm, Sat & Sun 1–5pm; R$5; ⓦmuseudoindio.org.br) at Rua das Palmeiras 55. Housed in an old colonial building, the museum has broad and imaginative multi-sensory displays, as well as utensils, musical instruments, tribal costumes and ritual devices from many of Brazil's dwindling populations of indigenous peoples, plus an extensive library. A block north of here off Rua São Clemente, the bright colours of *favela* Santa Marta light up the Corcovado mountainside. The first of Rio's *favelas* to be pacified by police in 2008, it's now fine to walk around or to take the cable car up to the summit, for fantastic views. In the *favela*'s upper west area you'll find a life-size bronze sculpture of Michael Jackson, a tribute to the late singer's (then controversial) shooting of the video *They Don't Care About Us* here in 1995, directed by Spike Lee.

To the south of the *bairro*, at the foot of Rua São João Batista, is the **Cemitério São João Batista**, the Zona Sul's largest resting place, with extravagant tombs for the Rio elite – Carmen Miranda and Bossa Nova master Tom Jobim are both near its central area. Botafogo's best bars and restaurants lie westwards around Rua Visconde de Caravelas. The **Cobal de Humaitá**, a partially covered complex of some twenty eateries, lies nearby on Rua Voluntários da Pátria.

Urca and the Sugarloaf

The small, wealthy *bairro* of **Urca** stands on a promontory formed by a land reclamation project and flanked by golden beaches. Facing Flamengo, the **Praia da Urca**, only 100m long, is frequented almost exclusively by the *bairro*'s inhabitants, while in front of the cable-car station (see below) is **Praia Vermelha**, a gorgeous cove sheltered from the Atlantic and popular with swimmers.

The beaches aren't the main draw, however: a cable-car ride up the **Pão de Açúcar** is not to be missed. Rising where

Guanabara Bay meets the Atlantic Ocean, **Sugarloaf** is so named because of its supposed resemblance to the ceramic or metal mould used during the refining of sugar cane (though it actually looks more like a giant termite mound). The **cable-car** station (daily 8am–10pm; every 30min; R$53; ⓦbondinho.com.br) is located at Praça Gen. Tibúrcio (bus "Urca" or "Praia Vermelha" from Centro or #511 and #512 from Zona Sul). The 1325m journey is made in two stages, first to the summit of **Morro da Urca** (220m), then onwards to Pão de Açúcar itself (396m). You can also hike the first section along a clearly marked trail from Praia Vermelha and purchase a cheaper cable-car ticket (R$40) for the second stage. Aim to arrive well before sunset on a clear day and you'll find views as glorious as you could imagine right over the city.

Copacabana and Leme

Leme and **Copacabana** are different stretches of the same 4km beach. At the northeastern end of the Praia do Leme, the Morro do Leme rises up to the ruined Forte do Leme, a thirty-minute cobblestone walk from the army's sports club (8am–5pm daily; R$4), great for more wonderful views of the Zona Sul and Guanabara Bay. Leme morphs into Copacabana at Avenida Princesa Isabel. The **Praia de Copacabana** runs a further 3km to the military-owned **Forte de Copacabana** (Tues–Sun 10am–5pm; R$4), certainly worth a wander around and a drink at its branch of *Confeitaria Colombo*. Immortalized in song by Barry Manilow, the beach is stunning, right down to its over-the-top mosaic

pavements, designed by Burle Marx to mimic rolling waves. The seafront is backed by a line of high-rise hotels and apartments that have sprung up since the 1940s, while a steady stream of noisy traffic clogs the two-lane **Avenida Atlântica**. A strong undercurrent at Copacabana means that it is dangerous even for strong swimmers – don't do anything the locals don't do. Another problem is theft: take only the money and clothes that you will need.

Arpoador, Ipanema and Leblon

On the other side of the point from Forte de Copacabana, the lively waters off **Arpoador** are popular with families and the elderly, as the ocean here is calmer than its neighbours – and the "Arpoador rock" often draws crowds to applaud the sunset. From here, as far as the unkempt and balding greenery of the **Jardim de Alah**, 3km away, you're in **Ipanema**; thereafter lies **Leblon**. The beaches here are stupendous and packed at weekends. Stalls sell fresh coconuts, while for bars and restaurants you'll need to walk a couple of blocks inland. Ipanema's beach is unofficially divided according to the particular interests of beach users; the "rainbow beach" between Rua Farme de Amoedo and Rua Teixeira de Melo is where gay men are concentrated, while posto 9 beyond is firmly for the party crowd; posto 10 is a little more low-key. On Sunday, the seafront road is closed to traffic, and given over to strollers, skateboarders and rollerbladers. At the far end of Leblon, the marvellously located and newly pacified *favela* Vidigal smothers the hillside, and completes the sweep around the bay.

THE GIRL FROM IPANEMA

It was at a bar called **Veloso** in 1962 that master composer-musicians Tom Jobim and Vinicius de Moraes sat down and penned *Garota de Ipanema* – **The Girl from Ipanema** – which put both bossa nova and Ipanema on the global arts map. The song was inspired by 15-year-old local girl Heloisa Paez Pinto, who would pass each morning on her way to the beach. These days the bar has been renamed *A Garota de Ipanema*, and is located at Rua Vinicius de Moraes 49 – changed from Rua Montenegro in honour of the lyricist – while the song has been kept alive through numerous cover versions by the likes of Frank Sinatra and Shirley Bassey. Heloisa posed as a *Playboy* playmate in 1987 and 2003 – the latter at the age of 58 – and now runs a chain of fashion stores (one next door to the bar, at Rua Vinicius de Moraes 53). No prizes for guessing the name.

Since the 1960s, Ipanema and Leblon have developed a reputation as a fashion centre, and are now seen as among the most chic *bairros* in all of Brazil. Try to visit on a Friday for the **food and flower market** on the Praça de Paz, or on Sunday for the **Feira Hippie** bric-a-brac market at Praça General Osório. Bars and restaurants are scattered throughout the two *bairros*, though many of Rio's best restaurants are located around Leblon's Rua Dias Ferreira.

Lagoa, Gávea and Jardim Botânico

Inland from Ipanema's plush beaches is the Lagoa Rodrigo de Freitas, always referred to simply as **Lagoa**. A lagoon linked to the ocean by a narrow canal that passes through Ipanema's Jardim de Alah, Lagoa is fringed by wealthy apartment buildings. On Sundays, its 8km perimeter pathway comes alive with strollers, rollerbladers, joggers and cyclists. Summer evenings are especially popular, with food stalls and live music at parks on the southeastern and western shores of the lagoon.

North of Leblon, heading west from Lagoa's shores, is **Gávea**, home of the **Jockey Club**. Races take place four times a week throughout the year (Mon 6.30–11.30pm, Fri 4–9.30pm, Sat & Sun 2–8pm; shorts not allowed). Any bus marked "via Jóquei" will get you here; get off at Praça Santos Dumont at the end of Rua Jardim Botânico. About 3km northwest of the Jockey Club, at Rua Marquês de São Vicente 476, is the **Instituto Moreira Salles** (Tues–Sun 1–8pm; free; ☏21 3284 7400), one of Rio's most beautiful cultural centres. Completed in 1951, the house is one of the finest examples of modernist architecture in Brazil – and the gardens, landscaped by Roberto Burle Marx, are attractive too.

To the northwest of Lagoa lies the **Jardim Botânico** *bairro*, whose **Parque Lage** (daily 8am–5pm), designed by the British landscape gardener John Tyndale in the early 1840s, consists of primary forest with a labyrinthine network of paths and ponds, as well as its artsy *Café do Lage* inside an Italianate mansion. A little further west is the **Jardim Botânico** itself (daily 8am–5pm; R$5; ⊛jbrj.gov.br), half of it natural jungle, the other half laid out in impressive

---

BARRA DA TIJUCA AND THE OLYMPICS

Rio's answer to Miami, **Barra da Tijuca** occupies the coastal plain of the city's west zone (Zona Oeste) between an inland lagoon system and 23km of almost unbroken white sand. The natural setting is stupendous, but unless you have a love for skyscrapers and shopping malls (Barra Shopping offers a full kilometre of consumer therapy), not to mention your own wheels, you're unlikely to find a trip here very enlightening – or easy on the pocket.

Half the events of the **2016 Olympic Games** will take place in Barra, mainly in a purpose-built Olympic village on the shores of picturesque Lagoa de Jacarepaguá (30km by road west of Leblon), a development which includes the vast RioCentro conference centre, famous for hosting the 1992 UN Earth Summit. Unusually, the main Olympic stadiums are located a good distance away: the Maracanã will host the opening and closing ceremonies and much of the football, while the athletics is scheduled for Engenhão stadium in the Zona Norte (accessed by train from Centro and bus from the Olympic village), an arrangement already rehearsed at the 2007 Pan-American Games.

Controversy has nonetheless followed Barra's land speculation boom in advance of the games. Voracious **development** here monopolized city resources for a quarter century from the late 1960s, yet planners failed to account for the area's working-class builders, maids and other service personnel. As with other areas of Rio, *favelas* grew quickly, the most famous of which is just inland from Barra at Cidade de Deus (City of God), immortalized worldwide in the namesake Oscar-nominated film. While long-standing conflict ended with the implementation of a police "pacification" unit in 2009, removal of other irregular housing around Barra remains a matter of extreme contention – not least because many of their residents were forcibly removed from *favelas* in Rio's Zona Sul under the military dictatorship in the 1970s. New hotels, a golf course, bus routes and metrô extensions offer a mixed bag for a region not known for its social inclusion. Journalists and campaigners are eagerly following Olympic developments: check out the excellent sites ⊛riorealblog.com and ⊛rioonwatch.org.

avenues lined with immense imperial palms that date from the garden's inauguration in 1808. A number of sculptures are dotted throughout, notably the Greek mythology-inspired *Ninfa do Eco* and *Caçador Narciso* (1783), the first two metal sculptures cast in Brazil.

Corcovado and Christ the Redeemer

The unmistakeable Art Deco statue of **Cristo Redentor**, gazing across the bay from the **Corcovado** ("hunchback") hill with arms outstretched in welcome, or as if preparing for a dive into the waters below, is synonymous with Rio de Janeiro. The immense statue – 30m high and weighing over 1000 metric tonnes – was scheduled for completion in 1922 as part of Brazil's centenary independence celebrations. In fact, it wasn't finished until 1931. In clear weather, it's every bit as awe-inspiring as you'd imagine – the journey up to the statue is breathtaking day or night – though what ought to be one of Rio's highlights can turn into a great disappointment if the Corcovado is hidden by cloud. By day the whole of Rio and Guanabara Bay is laid out magnificently before you; after dark, the flickering city lights of this vast metropolis create a stunning visual effect far more impressive than any artificial light show, enhanced by your position at Jesus's feet.

Most people reach the statue by the **Corcovado cog train** (daily every 30min 8.30am–7pm; R$45 return including entrance fee; ⓦcorcovado.com.br), which leaves from the station at Rua Cosme Velho 513 (take any bus marked "Cosme Velho" or take the *Metrô Superfície* bus from Largo do Machado station) and proceeds slowly upwards through lush forest as it enters the **Parque Nacional da Tijuca** (see box below). Taxis (R$30 one-way from Largo do Machado) can drive almost to the mountaintop, at which point you pay the entrance fee (R$20) and switch to a shuttle bus. You can also walk from Parque Lage (above) but it's a steep and gruelling two- to three-hour climb; there hasn't been a robbery along the trail for some years, but it's still advisable to walk in a group.

Maracanã Stadium

Sports fans will not want to miss the **Maracanã** (Metrô Maracanã; Linha 2) – probably the world's most famous football stadium, steeped in soccer history and with a new reformed capacity of 90,000 for the upcoming sports mega events. The real name of this

---

PARQUE NACIONAL DA TIJUCA

The mountains running southwest from the Corcovado are covered with forest, representing the periphery of the **Parque Nacional da Tijuca** (daily 8am–6pm; free). The park offers sixteen walking trails and some excellent views of Rio, and makes an appealing day retreat away from the city. The trails are steep and not for the unfit, but if you have the energy climb 2–3hr for staggering views from coastal Pedra da Gávea (842m; guide essential), or in the far north of the forest, Pico da Tijuca (1021m) above popular picnic spot Bom Retiro. **Public transport** to the park is not especially convenient so it's most easily visited by car, taxi or on a tour. Alternatively, take the metrô to Saens Peña at the end of Linha 1 and catch bus #221 or #233 towards "Barra da Tijuca", asking to be let off at Alta de Boa Vista right by the park entrance. Also accessible on foot from here is the Museu do Açude (Est. do Açude 764; Wed–Mon 10am–4pm; R$2; ⓦmuseuscastromaya.com.br), built by the man responsible for the reforestation of the park, and containing wonderful Chinese bronze sculpture, painted vases and, outside, well-maintained forest trails interwoven with art installations.

Excellent small-group **hiking tours** are run by Rio Hiking (☏21 9721 0594, ⓦriohiking .com.br; full day from R$160/person). For a bird's-eye view take a tandem flight with a **hang-gliding** instructor from the Pedra Bonita ramp above São Conrado near Pedra da Gávea; an experienced and reliable operator is Go Up Brasil (☏21 9177 9234; ⓦgoup.com.br; R$250), with daily flights when weather permits; price includes pick-up and drop-off. If you want to **cycle**, enter the park in the Zona Sul at Rua Pacheco Leão, which runs up the side of the Jardim Botânico to the Entrada dos Macacos and on to the Vista Chinesa, from where there's a marvellous view of Guanabara Bay and the Zona Sul.

monumental arena is actually **Estadio Mario Filho**; *Maracanã* is a nickname derived from the Brazilian word for a macaw and given to a nearby river. But it's not just football that earns the stadium its place in the record books. In 1991 former Beatle Paul McCartney played to a crowd of 180,000 people here, the highest ever concert attendance. It's certainly worth coming to a game (see p.232), but if your visit doesn't coincide with a match, you can tour the stadium and the one-room **Museu dos Esportes** (daily 9am–5pm; R$30), which gives the lowdown on Brazilian football.

Quinta da Boa Vista

The area covered by the **Quinta da Boa Vista** (daily 9am–6pm; Metrô São Cristóvão) was once incorporated in a *sesmaria* (a colonial land grant) held by Jesuits in the seventeenth century, before it became the country seat of the Portuguese royal family in 1808. The park, with its wide expanses of greenery, tree-lined avenues, lakes and games areas, is an excellent place for a stroll, though it can get crowded at weekends. Looking out from a hilltop in the centre of the park is the imposing Neoclassical **Museu Nacional** (Tues–Sun 10am–4pm; R$3; ⊛www.museunacional.ufrj.br). Its archeological section deals with the

human history of Latin America; in the Brazilian room, exhibits of Tupi-Guarani and Marajó ceramics lead on to the indigenous ethnographical section, uniting pieces collected from the numerous tribes that once populated Brazil and with displays on Brazilian folklore and Afro-Brazilian cults. The surprisingly spacious **Rio Zoo** (daily 9am–4.30pm; R$6) is located next door.

ARRIVAL AND DEPARTURE

By plane Tom Jobim International Airport, known as Galeão (☎ 21 3398 5050), is located 15km north of the centre and also handles many domestic flights. Santos Dumont Airport (☎ 21 3814 7070), southeast of (and walking distance from) Centro, handles domestic services only. Frequent executive buses (every 20min 5am–midnight; R$15) link the airports with the *rodoviária* (bus terminal), city centre and the Zona Sul beaches, passing through Flamengo, Botafogo, Copacabana, Ipanema and Leblon. Unless you're arriving at night there's no need to take an overpriced taxi (up to R$100 Galeão to/from the Zona Sul; R$30–40 Santos Dumont to Copacabana/Ipanema).

Destinations São Paulo (every 30–60min; 1hr); Belo Horizonte (every 30–60min; 1hr 30min); Foz de Iguaçu (6–8 daily; 3hr); Salvador (6–8 daily; 3hr); Recife (6–8 daily; 4hr).

By bus Buses arrive at the vast *Rodoviária Novo Rio* (☎ 21 3213 1800), 3km northwest of the centre at Av Francisco Bicalho. Late at night take a taxi (from R$35 to Copacabana/Ipanema), otherwise take either the executive (airport) service (see above) or the (longer) *Metrô Integração* bus to the Largo do Machado metrô

RIO DE JANEIRO TOURS

You can get around most of Rio's sights independently, but for off-the-beaten-track exploring such as to *favelas* and football matches, or for outdoor activities, experienced guides are on hand to help. All operators listed below speak English. Book tours personally rather than through commission-hungry hostels/hotels.

TOUR OPERATORS

Architectur ☎ 21 8115 3703, ⊛favelaarchitectour .com. Astute walking tours through Rocinha run by *favela* residents for R$85.

Cruz the Coast ☎ 21 8076 5743, ⊛cruzthecoast brazil.com. Operates an excellent guided minibus service north to Bahia with a 10-day suggested itinerary including accommodation and numerous excursions (from R$1,450).

Favela Tour ☎ 21 3322 2727, ⊛favelatour.com.br. Responsible, community-approved trips to Rocinha by minibus from R$80.

Heli Rio ☎ 21 2437 9064, ⊛helirio.com.br. Arranges

helicopter trips over the city.

Rio Hiking ☎ 21 9721 0594, ⊛riohiking.com.br. Offers a variety of trips around the city and state, as well as nightlife tours and adventure sports.

Rio's Surf Bus ☎ 21 2539 7555, ⊛surfbus.com.br. 4 daily buses connect Largo do Machado, Botafogo, Copacabana and Ipanema with the top surf spots and gorgeous beaches of Prainha and Grumari west of the city – an ideal day excursion for surfers and non-surfers alike.

Rob Shaw ✉ brazsoc@hotmail.com. For organized trips to football matches, all stadiums and clubs, plus World Cup information.

station (one payment of R$7.50 for bus and train); local buses stop at the Av Francisco Bicalho end of the *rodoviária* concourse, taxis depart from the other end. Book intercity services a couple of days in advance at the *rodoviária* or from the booth inside the "Condo" mall on the south side of Largo do Machado (see p.244).

Destinations Belo Horizonte (8 daily; 8hr); Foz do Iguaçu (2 daily; 22hr); Salvador (3 daily; 18hr); São Paulo (every 30min; 6hr); São João del Rei and Ouro Preto (4 daily; 6hr); Paraty (7 daily; 5hr); Mangaratiba/Angra dos Reis (for Ilha Grande; 7 daily; 4hr). Buses for Petrópolis (hourly; 90min) depart from both the *Rodoviária Novo Rio* and the city terminal at Castelo between Metrô Carioca and Praça XV de Novembro.

INFORMATION

Tourist information Riotur's most helpful office is at Av. Princesa Isabel 183, Copacabana (Mon–Fri 9am–6pm; ☎ 21 2544 7992). Alô Rio is an English telephone informa-tion service (daily 8am–8pm; ☎ 21 2542 8080).

GETTING AROUND

By bus Buses are frequent and many run 24hr; numbers and destinations are clearly marked on the front. Get on at the front and pay the seated conductor; guard your valuables closely. Bus routes/numbers are available at ⊛ vadeonibus .com.br.

By ferry Frequent crossings from the terminal at Praça XV de Novembro to Niterói (see p.254) cost R$2.80 and take 20min.

By metrô Mon–Sat 5am–midnight, Sun 7am–11pm. *Linha 1* (orange) links Ipanema, Copacabana, Botafogo and Flamengo with Centro (downtown) and several stations to the north; *Linha 2* (green) runs from the northern suburbs to Centro and Botafogo. A third line (silver) is under construction linking Ipanema and Leblon to Barra da Tijuca in the west, to be ready for the Olympic Games in 2016. Construction entails the closure of Ipanema General Osório station until early 2014. Tickets are sold as singles (*ida*; R$3.20) with no discount for multiple journeys. Combined metrô and bus tickets (*superficie* or *integração*) are available for various popular routes.

By taxi Rio's taxis come in two varieties: yellow with a blue stripe or white with a red-and-yellow stripe; the latter are pricier, yet more comfortable, radio cabs, which you order by phone. Both have meters and you should insist that they are activated (except from the *rodoviária* or Galeão airport; pick up a ticket at the booth). Try ☎ 21 2252 0054 for Catete/Santa Teresa/Centro or ☎ 21 2560 2022 for Copacabana/Ipanema.

ACCOMMODATION

Rio is by no means cheap, and during Carnaval and *Reveillon* (when you should book well in advance) you can expect to pay way over the odds. That said, there are numerous youth hostels, catering to a massive crowd of budget travellers. Accommodation is cheapest in Botafogo, Catete and Copacabana, with Santa Teresa marginally more and chic Ipanema/Leblon the most expensive. Most options include breakfast; check before you book. For a more authentic *carioca* experience get in touch with *Cama e Café* (daily 9am–4pm; ☎ 21 9638 4850, ⊛ camae cafe.com), who arrange fairly-priced rooms with families in Santa Teresa and elsewhere.

LAPA AND SANTA TERESA

Casa Mango Mango Rua Joaquim Murtinho 587, Santa Teresa ☎ 21 2508 6440, ⊛ casa-mangomango.com; map pp.240–241. A wide range of bright and airy rooms in a large historic house, complete with pool, lounge with wi-fi and guest kitchen. Attractive, great-value dorms. Dorms R$45, doubles R$130

★ **Casa da Renata** Rua Almirante Alexandrino 1086, Santa Teresa ☎ 21 2507 6007, ⊛ casadarenata.com.br; map pp.240–241. Renata's supremely comfortable home is an original Santa Teresa property with all-wooden furnishings. Have breakfast on the overgrown veranda with her resident turtles while she offers tips on the best things to do. R$180

Marajó Rua São Joaquim da Silva 99, Lapa ☎ 21 2224 4134, ⊛ hotelmarajorio.com; map pp.240–241. Excellent choice for budget travellers not keen on the hostel scene. Modern facilities, clean, spacious rooms and friendly service in the heart of vibrant Lapa. Rooms at the front can be noisy at night. R$110

Rio Hostel Rua Joaquim Murtinho 361, Santa Teresa ☎ 21 3852 0827, ⊛ riohostel.com; map pp.240–241. A cool back-packer hangout with a small pool and bohemian feel – plus a great bar serving *caipirinhas* until dawn. Stay seven nights and get one free; cheap packages combined with their sister hostel in Ipanema. Dorms R$40, doubles R$130

CATETE, FLAMENGO AND BOTAFOGO

Art Hostel Rua Silveira Martins 135, Catete ☎ 21 2205 1983, ⊛ arthostelrio.com; map pp.240–241. In a nineteenth-century building near the metrô, this is an artsy place with bags of atmosphere. Ask to see several dorms before choosing one. Café with wi-fi at front, roof terrace and video room. Dorms R$39, doubles R$99

★ **Baron Garden** Rua Barão de Guaratiba, Morro da Glória ⊛ barongarden.com; map pp.240–241. A colonial house with grand views, pool and garden, a short walk from Flamengo beach and Catete Metrô. A real find, aimed more at the 30-plus budget traveller. Dorms R$65, doubles R$140

Oztel Rua Pinheiro Guimarães 91, Botafogo ☎ 21 3042 1853, ⊛ oztel.com.br; map pp.242–243. New on the scene and threatening to shake up Rio's hostel life, Oztel is cosmopolitan designer chic, but thankfully has all the facilities and friendly staff to match. R$50

3

★ **Tupiniquim Hostel** Rua Paulo Barreto 79, Botafogo ☎ 21 2244 1286, ⓦ tupiniquimhostel.com.br; map pp.242–243. Billed as an alternative hostel, there's no denying the facilities on offer: fast internet, pool table, bar, barbecue terrace, and more. Great value, but fills fast. Dorms R$30, doubles R$110

Vila Carioca Rua Estacio Coimbra 84, Botafogo ☎ 21 2535 3224, ⓦ vilacarioca.com.br; map pp.242–243. Small and friendly hostel near the metrô, with neat, balconied dorm rooms, patio and chill-out area. Has internet access and a/c. Dorms R$32, doubles $110

COPACABANA

Bamboo Rio Hostel Rua Lacerda Coutinho 45 ☎ 21 2236 1117, ⓦ bamboorio.com; map pp.242–243. Three blocks from the beach in a quiet, leafy suburb, *Bamboo Rio* is a hostel with refreshingly colourful, a/c rooms, a good pool (though not exactly a "spa" as advertised) and a pleasant garden with wild monkeys. Great value. Dorms R$35, doubles $120

Che Lagarto Hostel Copacabana Rua Barata Ribeiro 111 ☎ 21 3209 0348, ⓦ chelagarto.com; map pp.242–243. They pack them in here, but if big hostels are your thing and you like the price you won't regret staying here. Clean, with numerous facilities and the organization for which the name is known. R$23

Che Lagarto Hostel Suites Rua Santa Clara 305 ☎ 21 2257 3133, ⓦ chelagarto.com; map pp.242–243. This branch of the most established chain of hostels in Rio has gone upmarket, with smart, comfortable rooms and decent facilities, 10min walk from the beach. R$160

Jucati Rua Tenente Marones de Gusmão 85 ☎ 21 2547 5422, ⓦ edificiojucati.com.br; map pp.242–243. On an attractive residential square, this is a bargain if you're travelling in a group (always ask for a discount at booking). Apartments have a double and two bunks, TV, kitchenette and wi-fi. R$200 (four people R$260)

Temporada Copacabana Edificio Av Atlantica 3196 ☎ 21 2255 0681, ⓦ temporadacopacabana.com.br; map pp.242–243. It won't win awards, but if you always dreamt of staying by the beach and can't afford the *Copacabana Palace*, this is your place. No breakfast. R$180

IPANEMA AND LEBLON

Adventure Hostel Rua Vinicius de Moraes 174 ☎ 21 3813 2726, ⓦ adventurehostel.com.br; map pp.242–243. Don't let the name put you off: this is a well-maintained HI hostel, and while they don't have many beds, the rooms are spacious. Dorms R$55, doubles R$170

Ipanema Beach House Rua Barão da Torre 485 ☎ 21 3202 2693, ⓦ ipanemahouse.com; map pp.242–243. Actually three blocks from the seafront, but a welcoming, laidback hostel nonetheless, with hippy-chic rooms and great socializing at the outdoor pool and bar. Dorms R$50, doubles R$160

★ **Mango Tree Hostel** Rua Prudencio de Moraes 594 ☎ 21 2287 9255, ⓦ mangotreehostel.com; map pp.242–243. A block from posto 9 on the beach, this is easily Ipanema's best cheap option. Spacious dorms, grand bathrooms and an overgrown garden with hammocks. Dorms R$55, doubles R$160

EATING AND DRINKING

As you might expect, Rio offers a huge variety of cuisines to discerning diners. In general, *cariocas* eat well at lunch, so you'll find most restaurants in Centro and other office districts only open during the day. At night eating and drinking are always done together, whether in an informal bar with shared *petiscos* (tapas plates) or pricier fine dining. Santa Teresa, Botafogo and Leblon are the city's key districts for innovative eating options.

CENTRO AND LAPA

Bar Luiz Rua Carioca 39; map pp.240–241. This hectic, but essentially run-of-the-mill, restaurant and bar, serving German-style food and ice-cold *chopp*, was founded in 1887 and is quite an institution. Still a popular meeting place for intellectuals, the food is good but a little overpriced; try the *bolinhos de bacalhau* (R$30). Closed Sun.

Beduino Av Presidente Wilson 123; map pp.240–241. Popular and inexpensive Arabic restaurant, which, unlike its rivals, offers a decent meze and falafel meal – great option for vegetarians and carnivores alike. Closed Sun.

Cosmopolita Travessa do Mosqueira 4; map pp.240–241. An excellent Portuguese restaurant established in 1926 with a loyal and bohemian clientele. Fish dishes are firm

---

STAY IN A FAVELA

Contrary to what the media would have you believe, Rio does have safe *favelas*, and staying in one can be an enjoyable, enlightening experience.

Favela Receptiva Estrada das Canoas 610, São Conrado ☎ 21 9848 6737, ⓦ favelareceptiva.com.br; map pp.242–243. A well-organized network of clean and comfortable host homes within small, friendly community Vila Canoas. Good breakfasts included; cultural tours and dance classes available. Price is per person. R$70

The Maze Inn Rua Tavares Bastos 414 Casa 66, Catete ☎ 21 2558 5547, ⓦ jazzrio.com; map pp.240–241. An eccentric, Gaudí-esque pousada/hostel with a truly inspirational view across Guanabara Bay. Huge British-Brazilian breakfast on offer, and also hosts a popular monthly jazz night. Dorms R$55, doubles R$130

★ TREAT YOURSELF

Café do Theatro Praça Floriano; map pp.240–241. Founded in 1894 within Rio's most grandiose Eclectic building, and richly adorned with Assyrian-inspired mosaics. The menu of standard Brazilian *petiscos* is expensive (R$30–60), but the atmospheric setting inside the Theatro Municipal makes it worth every penny. Mon–Fri 11am–4pm.

Confeitaria Colombo Rua Gonçalves Dias 32; map pp.240–241. Take the lift for a peek at the grand *salão* upstairs or indulge in the excellent and huge Franco-Brazilian buffet lunch (R$50). Downstairs relax over coffee or afternoon tea, or in an adjoining room, the *Salão Bilac*; a good-quality budget(ish) set lunch (R$26) is also served. An unmissable Rio institution. Mon–Fri 9am–8pm, Sat 9am–5pm, closed Sun.

favourites (*lula* squid; R$42 for two), as is the Oswaldo Aranha steak, invented here in the 1930s, with heaps of garlic (R$56 for two). Closed Sun.

★ **Mangue Seco Cachaçaria** Rua do Lavradio 23; map pp.240–241. This great bar, offering the twin night-time pleasures of samba and *cachaça*, in the daytime also serves really good meals for a reasonable price (from R$18). Creamy shrimp bobó, grilled fish, or the usual steaks are available, with day specials and seating indoors or on the pavement. Daily.

Pilograma Rua Carioca 53 and 9 other addresses in Centro; map pp.240–241. Just up from *Bar Luiz*, this place is hugely popular with office workers who take advantage of the extensive buffet of eighty different dishes for cheap eats. R$18 for a big plateful. Mon–Sat 11am–4pm.

SANTA TERESA

Bar do Arnaudo Rua Almirante Alexandrino 316; map pp.240–241. An excellent mid-priced place to sample traditional food from Brazil's northeast, such as *carne do sol* (sun-dried meat), *macaxeira* (sweet cassava) and *pirão de bode* (goat meat soup). Closed Mon; Sat & Sun only open till 8pm.

★ **Bar do Gomez** Rua Çurea, at Rua Monte Alegre; map pp.240–241. Santa Teresa's best bar and Portuguese grocery, doing a roaring trade in red wine, *chopp* and *petiscos* (try the succulent *bolinhos de bacalhau*, R$6 each) to a friendly crowd of locals and visitors. On the Paulo Mattos bus and tram route.

★ **Simplesmente** Rua Paschoal Carlos Magno 115; map pp.240–241. Santa Teresa's best bet for an evening drink, with excellent live music and *petiscos* including superb *caldos* (R$6). The friendly Bohemian vibe spills out onto the road. Tues–Fri 7pm–3am, Sat & Sun 2pm–3am.

Sobrenatural Rua Almirante Alexandrino 432; map pp.240–241. Fairly pricey fish restaurant (*moquecas* and Amazonian fish dishes are the highlights; R$80 for two), but nearly always has great live music. Deliberately rustic decor and an inviting place for a leisurely meal. Closed Mon.

FLAMENGO, BOTAFOGO AND URCA

Á Mineira Rua Visconde da Silva 152, Humaitá, Botafogo ☏ 21 2535 2835; map pp.242–243. A great-value unlimited buffet (R$32) introducing the food of Minas Gerais, with soups, grilled meats, vegetarian dishes and desserts. Phone for free pick-up from your hotel/hostel.

★ **Belmonte** Praia do Flamengo 300; map pp.242–243. The first *Belmonte* bar, this is a Rio institution, open all night with crowds occupying the road outside. Good beer and excellent *petiscos* too – try the city's best *pastel de camarão* here (R$25 for 8).

★ **Miam Miam** Rua General Góes Monteiro 34, Botafogo; map pp.242–243. Splashing out here is more than worthwhile, with creative international fusion dishes (R$40) like duck gnocchi or hot-pepper-encrusted tuna, plus superb cocktails served up in friendly, bohemian surroundings.

Praia Vermelha Bar e Restaurante Círculo Militar, Praça General Tibúrcio, Urca; map pp.242–243. Some of the best thin-crust pizza in Rio (from 6pm; R$25) served up in unbeatable surroundings overlooking the beach and Sugarloaf.

Tacacá Rua Barão do Flamengo 39, Flamengo; map pp.242–243. A *lanchonete* (snack bar) with a difference: here you can try delights from the Amazon like tucupi, shrimp and cassava yellow hot pepper soup (R$12), and easily the best *açaí* in Rio, served in large bowls with tapioca and granola (R$8). Mon–Sat 8.30am–10pm, Sun 9am–9pm.

Yorubá Rua Arnaldo Quintela 94, Botafogo ☏ 21 2541 9387; map pp.242–243. Friendly restaurant serving moderately priced Bahian cooking with strong African influences. Service is slow, but the *bobó* and *moquecas* are well worth the wait. Sat & Sun lunch only, closed Mon & Tues.

COPACABANA

Arabe Av Atlântica 1936; map pp.242–243. One of very few good restaurants on Av. Atlântica, this is a reasonably priced Lebanese spot with an excellent-value *por kilo* lunch – heavy on meat though vegetarians won't go hungry. At night have a cold beer and snack on the terrace.

★ **Bar do David** Ladeira Ari Barroso 66, *favela* Babilônia, Leme; map pp.242–243. Officially "pacified" *favelas* are slowly opening up to the business potential of tourism: chef David's had press accolades for excellent shrimp bobó, seafood croquettes, and at weekends his signature seafood *feijoada* – all at knockdown prices.

Big Nectar Av Nossa Senhora de Copacabana 985, at Xavier Silveira; map pp.242–243. A cut above the average *lanchonete* in Copa, serving pretty decent *prato feito* set meals for as little as R$12, and quality juices. Open 24hr.

3

Caranguejo Rua Barata Ribeiro 771, at Rua Xavier da Silveira; map pp.242–243. Excellent, mid-priced seafood – especially the *caranguejo* (crab, from R$30) – served in an utterly unpretentious environment packed with locals and tourists. Closed Mon.

★ **Cervantes** Av Prado do Júnior 335 (restaurant) and Rua Barata Ribeiro 7 (bar); map pp.242–243. Doing a roaring trade day and night (until 5am), this restaurant/bar linked at the rear serves speciality thick-wedge meat sandwiches with a slice of pineapple (the garlic chicken – R$22 – is sublime), plus full meals from R$35 for two. Tues–Sun from noon.

Siri Mole e Cia Rua Francisco Otaviano 50 ☎ 21 2267 0894; map pp.242–243. A rarity in Rio: an excellent Bahian restaurant, serving beautifully presented dishes (many spicy) in an upmarket yet comfortable setting. There are a few tables outside where you can munch on *acarajé* and other Bahian snacks. Mains from R$35. Tues–Sun noon–11pm.

IPANEMA AND LEBLON

Casa da Feijoada Rua Prudente de Morais 10, Ipanema; map pp.242–243. *Feijoada*, traditionally served only on Sat, is available seven days a week here, along with other classic, moderately priced and extremely filling Brazilian dishes, from R$26. Daily.

Delírio Tropical Rua Garcia D'Ávila 48, Ipanema; map pp.242–243. Just a block from the beach and the best value for lunch you'll find anywhere near it. Choose six items from quiches, pastas and salads, fish and meat, for around R$20. Healthy, delicious, and less emphasis on rice and beans.

New Natural Rua Barão de Torre 167, Ipanema; map pp.242–243. Really good vegetarian *por kilo* lunch place that always has a couple of meat choices too. Expect numerous salads, soya dishes and fresh juices. Closed Sun.

★ **Palaphita Kitch** Quiosque 20, Parque do Cantagalo, Av Epitácio Pessoa, Lagoa ☎ 21 2227 0837; map pp.242–243. On the Ipanema side of Lagoa, this is a supremely romantic spot by the water, where you can kick off your shoes by candlelight and enjoy a drink plus great *carpaccio* and other antipastis (from R$25). At weekends phone for a reservation. Tues–Sun 5pm–late.

Paz e Amor Rua Garcia D'Ávila 173, Ipanema; map pp.242–243. One end of this Brazilian bar/restaurant serves the best-value *prato feito* set-plate for miles around. R$12 will buy you a filling heap of rice, beans and a choice of meats/fish *a milanesa*, with salad on the side. Daily until 11pm.

★ **Zazá Bistrô Tropical** Rua Joana Angelica 40, Ipanema ☎ 21 2247 9102; map pp.242–243. Unique, kitsch, South Asian bistro where there's always something different going on. Downstairs is more traditional, upstairs is all cushions, rugs and low Moroccan tables. Inventive cocktails and tropical fruit juices too. Try the phenomenal Argentine *picanha*, the Thai shrimp, or the *namorado* fish with plantain puree (from R$35) – plus inventive cocktails and tropical fruit juices.

NIGHTLIFE

LIVE MUSIC

Lapa is Rio's nightlife heart and the undisputed capital of samba: every Friday night around Avenida Mem de Sá and Rua do Lavradio one of the world's biggest street parties takes place, with numerous bars offering the real deal – some of the best are listed below. Despite Lapa's obvious appeal, be careful walking around after dark; if in doubt, take a taxi. Other currently popular outdoor (free!) parties include samba at Pedra do Sal (off Rua Sacadura Cabral, nr Praça Mauá, Centro; Mon and Fri evenings from 8pm), and street jazz at Praça Tiradentes, Centro (Thurs evening from 10pm). During rehearsals for Carnaval (Sept–Jan), don't miss a trip to a Samba School (see box opposite).

Carioca da Gema Av Mem de Sá 79, Lapa ⓦ barcarioca dagema.com.br; map pp.240–241. Samba bar-cum-pizzeria, this is a more upmarket but very fun place, especially lively on Mon and Fri nights. Mon–Sat from 6pm.

★ **Casa Rosa** Rua Alice 550, Laranjeiras ⓦ casarosa .com.br; map pp.242–243. Sunday evening here (from 6pm) is one of Rio's best treats, with live samba followed by hip-hop/*baile funk* in one room and live rock/reggae/ *forró* in the other, for a flirty 20s–30s crowd. A good *feijoada* dinner is thrown in for just R$3 extra (regular entry R$24). Thurs–Sun.

★ **Centro Cultural Carioca** Rua do Teatro 37, Centro ⓦ centroculturalcarioca.com.br; map pp.240–241. For serious music lovers, this bar/dancehall offers a cross section of the best Brazilian music to a grown-up crowd. Thurs–Sun from 9pm: strictly samba Sat, lively *forró* Sun.

Democráticos Rua do Riachuelo 93, Lapa ⓦ clubedos democraticos.com.br; map pp.240–241. Never short on atmosphere, this traditional *gafieira* (dance hall) has been going since 1867, with popular live *forró* (Wed) and usually samba Thurs–Sat.

Feira Nordestina São Cristovão. A 48hr non-stop party in a stadium every weekend might sound far-fetched, but exactly that has been hosted here for decades. *Forró*, funk and reggae for the Zona Norte and Northeastern Brazilian masses, with food and crafts stalls. Popular in the early hours post-clubbing. Tues–Thurs 10am–6pm, Fri 10am–Sun 9pm 24hr.

Semente Rua Joaquim Silva 138, Lapa; map pp.240–241. A small bohemian bar, but also one of Rio's hottest music spots, where some of the biggest current names in samba cut their teeth. Sun–Thurs only, from 8pm.

NIGHTCLUBS

Rio's vibrant club scene offers a music mix from pop and rock to hip-hop and *funk Carioca*, as well as superb Brazilian electronica, samba and MPB (*Música Popular Brasileira*). Most places don't get going until midnight; entry fees R$20–60.

★ **Casa da Matriz** Rua Henrique Novaes 107, Botafogo

ⓦbeta.matrizonline.com.br; map pp.242–243. Stylish and perennially popular club with different music each night, from rock to reggae and samba to drum 'n' bass.

Castelo das Pedras Favela Rio das Pedras, Jacarepaguá ⓦcastelodaspedras.com.br; map pp.242–243. Rio's premier *funk carioca* venue, with 3000-strong crowds of sweating, gyrating bodies. An hour from the Zona Sul; go on a Sun night tour with ⓦbealocal.com, or if you're confident take a van (around 11pm) from the corner of ruas Bartolomeu Mitre and Conde Bernadotte in Leblon.

Comuna Rua Sorocaba 585, Botafogo; map pp.242–243. A split personality of electronica parties, art exhibitions, film screenings and even food makes this new warehouse-style space a truly communal entertainment centre. Check their facebook page for the latest goings-on.

Espaço Acústica Praça Tiradentes 4, Centro ⓦespaco acustica.com.br; map pp.240–241. Helping along the resurgence of one of Rio's most historic central squares, this is a hip yet unpretentious place to catch some of the best DJ talent in town. Electro/pop/rock/Brazilian mash-up.

Fosfobox Rua Siquiera Campos 143, Copacabana ⓦfosfobox.com.br; map pp.242–243. This small, highly rated and long-standing basement club plays underground techno and alternative music for an animated crowd. Brazil's best DJs often pass through. Thurs–Sun.

Studio RJ Av Vieira Souto, 110, Arpoador ⓦstudiorj.org; map pp.242–243. An eclectic music mix at this new and groovy venue opposite the beach. Alternate weeknights feature live bands (jazz, reggae, soul, Brazilian) at 9pm, otherwise DJs spin 'til late. Tues–Sat.

Zero Zero Av Padre Leonel Franca 240, Gávea ⓦ00site .com.br; map pp.242–243. A trendy club frequented by a wealthy but music-loving crowd. Some of Brazil's top DJs play an eclectic mix. Over-25s only; Sun draws a gay crowd.

GAY AND LESBIAN

Rio has one of the world's liveliest gay scenes, though you may be surprised that many venues are "GLS" ("gay, lesbian and sympathizers") with clubbers of all persuasions hanging out (Fosfobox and Zero Zero listed above, for example). Much action takes place around Rua Farme de Amoedo in Ipanema – ask at gay bar *Bofetada* about circuit parties held all over the city. Gay Pride takes place in Copacabana each September; the wildest weekend on the Gay Rio calendar. For up-to-date information check out ⓦtimeout.com.br/rio-de -janeiro/en/gay-lesbian.

Le Boy/La Girl Rua Raul Pompéia 102, Copacabana ⓦleboy .com.br or lagirl.com.br; map pp.242–243. Separate gay and lesbian clubs for which the partitions are removed late at night. A vast interior with drag shows, podiums and dark rooms. Lively Sun, closed Mon.

Cine Ideal Rua Carioca 64, Centro ⓦcineideal.com.br; map pp.240–241. This young and often-wild GLS club in a former cinema is usually only open Fri/Sat. Open-air terrace and mezzanine, as well as an open bar, and a crowd eager for *beijos* (kisses).

Galeria Café Rua Teixeira de Melo 31, Ipanema ⓦgaleria cafe.com.br; map pp.242–243. Spinning an original music mix from old classics like Chico Buarque to self-styled drum 'n' bossa, this small artistic venue also has theatre and art exhibitions, as well as Sunday's long-standing Café Bazar (noon–9pm) featuring fashion shows and music. Otherwise open Wed–Sat from midnight.

The Week Rua Sacadura Cabral 154, Centro ⓦtheweek .com.br; map pp.240–241. Rio's biggest club, full stop, famous for great house music. GLS crowd on Fri and almost exclusively gay men Sat. Swimming pool and two DJ rooms.

SAMBA

From September to February the ultimate highlight of Rio's nightlife is a visit to a **samba school**, when the emphasis is as much on raising funds for their extravagant Carnaval parade (see p.237) as it is on perfecting routines. Expect drummers and dancers en masse, and thousands of hyped-up revellers. There are many schools, of which a few are listed here; each has its own weekly programme. Check the websites and keep your ear to the ground.

SAMBA SCHOOLS

Beija-Flor Rua Pracinha Wallace Paes Leme 1652, Nilopolis ☎21 2253 2860, ⓦbeija-flor.com.br. Carnaval champions 2011.

Mangueira Rua Visconde de Niterói 1072, Mangueira ☎21 2567 4637, ⓦmangueira.com.br. Probably the most famous and largest school; weekend events attract many tour groups – so while fun, nights out here can sometimes lack a traditional feel.

Portela Rua Clara Nunes 81, Madureira ☎21 3390 0471, ⓦgresportela.com.br. Thought of as a highly

traditional school, with *feijoadas* (usually first Sat of the month) with samba a city highlight.

Salgueiro Rua Silva Telles 104, Tijuca ☎21 2238 5564, ⓦsalgueiro.com.br. Most recently champions in 2009. Easily accessed from the Zona Sul and events here are often a great night out.

Unidos da Tijuca Clube dos Portuários, Av Francisco Bicalho 47, São Cristovão ⓦunidosdatijuca.com.br. Carnaval champions 2010 and 2012; popular with a mixed gay and straight crowd.

3

DIRECTORY

Banks and exchange Banks are located throughout the city, and especially along Av Rio Branco in Centro. Banco do Brasil is best for foreign cards.

Car rental Most agents are located along Av Princesa Isabel in Copacabana. Avis ☎21 2542 3392; Hertz ☎21 2275 3245; Localiza-National ☎800 99 2000.

Consulates Argentina, Praia de Botafogo 228 ☎21 2553 1646; Australia, Av Presidente Wilson 231, Centro ☎21 3824 4624; Canada, Av Atlantica 1130, Copacabana ☎21 2543 3004; UK, Praia do Flamengo 284, Flamengo ☎21 2555 9600; US, Av Presidente Wilson 147, Centro ☎21 3823 2000.

Hospitals Try a private clinic such as Sorocaba Clinic, Rua Sorocaba 464, Botafogo (☎21 2286 0022), or Centro Médico Ipanema, Rua Anibal Mendonça 135, Ipanema (☎21 2239 4647). For non-emergencies, Rio Health Collective has a phone-in service (☎21 3325 9300, ext 44) with details of doctors who speak English.

Police Emergency number ☎190. The beach areas have police posts at regular intervals. The efficient, English-speaking Tourist Police are at Av Afrânio de Melo Franco (opposite the Oi Casa Grande Theatre), Leblon (☎21 3399 7170).

Post office Central branch on Rua 1 de Março (Mon–Fri 8am–noon & 2–6pm, Sat 8am–1pm).

Shopping Rio is replete with high-class shopping malls and designer stores. Budget shoppers however should head to Saara (see p.238), where quality goods are available at reasonable prices, or the Hippie Fair market held every Sun at Praça General Osório in Ipanema, with souvenirs, street shows and typical foods. For handicrafts check out Brasil & Cia, at Rua Maria Quitéria in Ipanema.

Visas The Polícia Federal handles tourist permit and visa extensions at its office in Terminal A at Galeão Airport (Mon–Fri 8am–4pm; ☎21 2203 4000, ⊚dpf.gov.br).

Rio de Janeiro state

Though many travellers dash through the state in order to reach its glorious capital city, there are enough regional attractions to more than reward visitors. Either side of Rio lie two idyllic sections of coast. To the east beyond Rio's neighbouring city **Niterói** is the **Costa do Sol**, an area of gorgeous white beaches peppered with a string of low-key resort towns and three large **lakes**. The trendy and commercial resort town of **Búzios** is popular with the affluent but less of a draw for budget travellers, while nearby Arraial do Cabo offers a slice of beach paradise. To the south of Rio is one of Brazil's most magnificent landscapes, the **Costa Verde**, dotted with charming resort towns and blessed with dreamy stretches of deserted beach. The colonial town of **Paraty** is one of the region's highlights, while **Ilha Grande**'s verdant forests create a stunning unspoilt setting. The mountainous wooded landscape and relatively cool climate of the state's interior make a refreshing change from the coastal heat. Immediately to the north of Rio, high in mist-cloaked mountains, lies the imperial city of **Petrópolis**, with the magnificent **Parque Nacional Serra dos Orgãos** nearby. In the far west lies another breathtaking protected area, the **Parque Nacional Itatiaia**.

NITERÓI

Cariocas have a tendency to sneer at **NITERÓI**, typically commenting that the best thing about the city is the view back across Guanabara Bay to Rio. The vistas are undeniably gorgeous, but there are a few things to see too – without the need to stay overnight.

WHAT TO SEE AND DO

The Oscar Niemeyer-designed **Museu de Arte Contemporânea** (MAC; Tues–Sun 10am–6pm; R$4; ⊚macniteroi.com.br) is Niterói's biggest draw. Opened in 1996 and located just south of the centre on a promontory, the spaceship-like building offers breathtaking 360-degree views of the bay and a worthy, though hardly exciting, permanent display of Brazilian art from the 1950s to the 1990s, plus temporary exhibitions. But the real work of art is the building itself: trademark Niemeyer curves which even his most hardened critics find difficult to dismiss.

Beautiful **Praia de Icaraí** lies near the city's centre, but as the water in the bay is none too clean, take a bus to **Camboinhas** or **Itacoatiara**, long stretches of sand every bit as good as Rio's Zona Sul.

ARRIVAL AND INFORMATION

By bus Services from N.S. de Copacabana and Largo do Machado, via the 14km Rio–Niterói bridge, take you into the centre of Niterói; MAC and Icaraí neighbourhood are a further bus journey (numerous services; look on front of bus) or a 30min walk.

By ferry The best way to get to Niterói is by ferry (see p.249). MAC is just 1.5km from the ferry terminal, passing the Universidade Federal Fluminense en route.

Tourist office Estrada Leopoldo Fróes 773, São Francisco (☎ 0800 282 7755, ⓦ niteroiturismo.com.br).

EATING

A wide selection of eateries is to be found along the seafront in São Francisco *bairro*, beyond Icaraí.

Da Carmine Rua Mariz e Barros 305, Icaraí. Serves the city's best pizzas by far, and, though not cheap, won't break the bank. Lunch Tues–Sun; dinner daily.

★ **Mercado de Peixe São Pedro** Av Visconde do Rio Branco 55. Be sure to visit this small market complex, a 5min walk north from the ferry terminal, with a superb group of low-key seafood restaurants and stalls. Tues–Sun, lunchtime only.

BÚZIOS

The most famous resort on this stretch, "discovered" by Brigitte Bardot in 1964 and nicknamed "Brazil's St Tropez", is Armação dos Búzios, or **BÚZIOS** as it's commonly known. A former whaling town, it's now cashing in on the upscale tourist market. Bardot described the sea here as "foaming like blue champagne", and the seafront promenade, the **Orla Bardot**, now bears a statue of her in homage. From December to February the population swells from 20,000 to 150,000, and boats now take pleasure-seekers island hopping and scuba diving along the very beautiful coastline. If a crowded 24-hour resort full of high-spending beautiful people and buzzing nightclubs is your thing then you're sure to fall for Búzios; if not, give it a miss – at least in high season.

ARRIVAL AND INFORMATION

By bus Direct buses from Rio run at least five times a day, arriving at the *rodoviária* on Estrada da Usina Velha.

Tourist information The helpful tourist office is on Praça Santos Dumont (☎ 22 2623 2099, ⓦ buzios.com.br).

ACCOMMODATION

Búzios Central Hostel Av José Bento Ribeiro Dantas 1475 ☎ 22 2623 9232, ⓦ buzioscentral.com.br. An HI-affiliated hostel with attractive gardens and a plunge pool. Dorms are a little cramped but reasonable, and small doubles the cheapest you'll get in town. Dorms **R$40**, doubles **R$118**

Meu Sonho Av José Bento Ribeiro Dantas 1289, Ossos ☎ 22 2623 0902, ⓦ meusonhobuzios.com.br. The best "budget" pousada in town and just a block from the beach, with clean, basic rooms and a plunge pool. **R$160**

EATING, DRINKING AND NIGHTLIFE

Restaurants in Búzios are, predictably, expensive; cheaper options include the grilled fish stalls on the beaches and numerous pizza places in outlying parts of town.

Bananaland Rua Manoel Turíbio de Farias 50. On a street parallel to Rua das Pedras, this is the best *por kilo* restaurant in Búzios, and one of the cheapest for a good meal (R$28). Outstanding buffet of salads and hot dishes.

Chez Michou Crêperie Rua das Pedras 90. Belgian-owned, this has long been the town's most popular hangout, thanks to its open-air bar, cheap drinks and authentic crêpes. Open until dawn for post-*Pacha* or *Privilège* clubbers.

Pacha Búzios Rua das Pedras 151 ☎ 22 2292 9606, ⓦ pachabuzios.com. The venue of choice for trendy clubbers, Ibiza-based *Pacha* has helped bring Balearic glitz and top-name DJs to Búzios. Fri–Sat from 11pm; entry from R$40.

Privilège Av José Bento Ribeiro Dantas 550 ☎ 22 2620 8585, ⓦ privilegenet.com.br. Despite *Pacha's* rise as venue of choice in the last few years, *Privilège* is still the town's biggest club, has a great party atmosphere, and, at half the price of its rival, is much better value. Fri–Sat from 11pm; entry from R$20.

Sawasdee Av José Bento Ribeiro Dantas 422 ⓦ sawasdee .com.br. Excellent, spicy Thai food, with great vegetarian choices, seafood and meat options (from R$35). Thurs–Tues 6pm–midnight.

3

3

ARRAIAL DO CABO

Tipped by those in the know to have the best beaches east of Rio, the small fishing town of **ARRAIAL DO CABO** has many of the attractions of Búzios, 40km northeast, but without the crowds, nightlife and price tag. The draw here is relaxing on a stunning peninsula between sea, sand dune and lagoon, with beaches like the 23km **Praia Grande** and smaller turquoise gems Praia do Forno (for snorkelling), Prainha da Pontal and Praia Brava (for surfing). All have a rich marine life and excellent diving. Boat trips are available to the beaches of nearby Ilha do Farol and the aptly named Grotto Azul (Blue Grotto), a cavern famous for its deep blue water.

ARRIVAL AND DEPARTURE

By bus Direct buses leave Rio daily at 2 hourly intervals, more frequently early in the morning and after 5pm (4hr; R$42).

Destinations Frequent buses ply the route from Arraial do Cabo to neighbouring Cabo Frio (14km), which is halfway to Búzios.

ACCOMMODATION

Marina dos Anjos Rua Bernardo Lens 145 ☎ 22 2622 4060, ⓦ marinadosanjos.com.br. Drawing mainly Brazilians from Rio and Minas Gerais for the easy-going beach life, this HI hostel is pleasingly social with great communal areas. Dorms R$50, doubles R$130.

ILHA GRANDE

ILHA GRANDE comprises 193 square kilometres of mountainous jungle, historic ruins and beautiful beaches; excellent for some scenic tropical rambling. The entire island, lying about 150km southwest of Rio, is a state park with limits on building development and a ban on motor vehicles.

WHAT TO SEE AND DO

Ilha Grande offers lots of beautiful **walks** along well-maintained and fairly well-signposted trails. As you approach the low-lying, whitewashed colonial port of **Vila do Abraão**, the mountains rise dramatically from the sea, and in the distance there's the curiously shaped summit of **Bico do Papagaio** ("Parrot's Beak"), which ascends to a height of

980m. There's little to see in Abraão itself, but it's a pleasant base from which to explore the island. A 30-minute walk along the coast west are the ruins of the **Antigo Presídio**, a former prison for political prisoners that was dynamited in the early 1960s. Among the ruins, you'll find the *cafofo*, the containment centre where prisoners who had failed in escape attempts were immersed in freezing water. Just fifteen minutes inland from Abraão, overgrown with vegetation, stands the **Antigo Aqueduto**, which used to channel the island's water supply. There's a fine view of the aqueduct from the **Pedra Mirante**, a hill near the centre of the island, and, close by, a waterfall provides the opportunity to cool off.

For the most part the **beaches** – Aventureiro, Lopes Mendes, Canto, Júlia and Morcegoare, to name a few – are wild, unspoilt and most easily reached by boat, though most have some form of basic accommodation or campsites. Araçatiba is home to a sizeable village, accessed by boat direct from Angra dos Reis on the mainland.

ARRIVAL AND INFORMATION

By bus Buses depart from Rio's *rodoviária* to the ferry ports. Mangaratiba (5 daily; 4hr); Angra dos Reis (hourly; 5hr).

By ferry Boats depart from Mangaratiba, leaving at 8am (and 10.30pm Fri), returning at 5.30pm (ⓦ www .grupoccr.com.br/barcas; R$5; 80min). From Angra dos Reis, boats leave at 3.30pm Mon–Fri and 1.30pm at weekends, returning at 10am every day (R$6.50, R$10 at weekends; 1hr 20min).

Tourist information There is a tourist office in Angra dos Reis at Av Ayrton Senna (☎ 24 3365 5186), but no office on the island itself. Online try ⓦ ilhagrande.org. Bring plenty of cash: there's no ATM, nowhere to change money and few places accept credit cards. The Elite Dive Center (☎ 24 3361 5501, ⓦ elitedivecenter.com.br) is the only PADI-registered dive centre on the island.

ACCOMMODATION

Great pousadas are to be found all over Ilha Grande, though Abraão has the largest choice (generally mid-priced). Reservations are essential in the high season, especially at weekends, but prices may be halved off-season. Camping at a designated site is a decent alternative too (expect to pay R$15–20/person). Abraão has a number of basic campsites (ask at the jetty) while nearby Praia das Palmas is a more scenic alternative: ⓦ campingparaiso.com and

ⓦ campingflorestinha.com.br both have facilities such as a restaurant and kitchen. For the more adventurous, try one of the many tiny campsites at stunning and secluded Praia do Aventureiro on the island's southwest coast.

Che Lagarto Praia do Canto, Abraão ☎ 21 3361 9669, ⓦ chelagarto.com. Much like the members of the same chain in Rio (see p.250), this is a well-organized hostel with breakfast served on a glorious wooden sun deck overlooking the sea. Dorms R$36, doubles R$152

Holandês Rua do Assembléia, Abraão ☎ 24 3361 5034, ⓦ holandeshostel.com.br. Always popular, this trendy HI hostel is behind the beach next to the Assembléia de Deus. Accommodation in dorms or lovely chalets (which sleep up to 3) in lush gardens. Dorms R$40, chalets R$130

★ **Lagamar** Praia Grande de Araçatiba ☎ 24 9221 8180, ⓦ pousadalagamar.com.br. Superb-value pousada surrounded by lush jungle in a quiet fishing hamlet at the island's western end. Generous seafood dinners and large breakfast are included. Boat available direct from Angra. R$160

Oásis Praia do Canto, Abraão ☎ 24 3361 5549. Cosy, friendly and one of the nicest pousadas on the island. Rooms are unpretentious and simply furnished. It's located at the far end of the beach, a 10min walk from the jetty. R$160

EATING

Most pousadas serve decent meals, and some gourmet cooking, while there are also independent restaurants where fish and seafood figure heavily. *Rei do Moqueca* at Rua da Praia in Abraão serves reasonably priced meals, while *Rei dos Caldos* offers wonderful fish soups. *Tropicana* at Rua da Praia 28 serves an interesting menu of French dishes with a Brazilian twist (from R$30), in a verdant garden.

PARATY AND AROUND

PARATY, 236km from Rio along the BR-101, is the Costa Verde's main attraction, and rightly so. Inhabited since 1650, Paraty remains much as it was in its heyday as a staging post for the eighteenth-century trade in Brazilian gold. Today, UNESCO considers the city one of the world's most important examples of Portuguese colonial architecture, with all the narrow cobbled streets and churches you'd imagine, and it has been named a national monument. Besides the town's charmingly relaxed atmosphere, the main

PARQUE NACIONAL DO ITATIAIA

On the border with Minas Gerais, 167km west of Rio, the **Parque Nacional do Itatiaia** takes its unusual name from an Indian word meaning "rocks with sharp edges". Holding the distinction of being Brazil's first national park (1937), it's incredibly varied, from dense Atlantic forest in the foothills, through to treeless, grassy summits. The park's loftiest peak, **Agulhas-Negras**, is the second highest in Brazil, at 2789m.

There's no shortage of **walking trails** here, as well as a couple of two-day walks for serious hikers. The better, but more difficult, of the two is the Jeep Trail, which scales the valley and ultimately reaches the peak of Agulhas-Negras. The other is the Tres Picos Trail – easier, but care should still be taken as the path becomes narrow and slippery as it rises. A **guide** is recommended for both trails (available from hotels within the park) and essential for the Jeep Trail, for which you should seek prior permission from the IBAMA office at the park entrance. Itatiaia is also a popular **birdwatching** destination, thanks to its varied terrain and flora: highland species present in the park include the Itatiaia spinetail – a small, brownish, skulking bird that occurs only in this range of mountains.

ARRIVAL AND INFORMATION

Access to the park is via the town of Itatiaia – buses between Rio and São Paulo stop here. Local buses (30min) run from the footbridge in Itatiaia, a short walk from the *rodoviária*, to the park visitors' centre. Staying in the town of Itatiaia is the cheapest way to visit, despite the 30min bus ride.

ACCOMMODATION

Pousada Isa About 500m from the *rodoviária*, Itatiaia. Turn right out of the bus station and look for the "pousada" sign. Best option for budget travellers, as it's basic and not especially attractive, but clean and reliable nevertheless and includes a half-decent breakfast. R$35

Hotel Simon Rodovia Br-485 Km12, PN Itatiaia ☎ 24 3352 1122. A huge hotel within the park boundaries, this is the most convenient place to stay if you are thinking of hiking the park's trails: the Tres Picos trail begins just behind the hotel. Comfortable; some rooms have attractive views over the valleys. R$160

draws are its great restaurants and bars, and stunning surrounding scenery, from rainforest and waterfall to hidden coves, islands and **beaches**. Paraty really comes alive for its annual Literary Festival ("FLIP"; ⊕flip.org.br) in July or August, which in past years has drawn such figures as Tom Stoppard and Brazil's own Chico Buarque, and requires booking accommodation well in advance.

WHAT TO SEE AND DO

One of Brazil's first planned urban projects, Paraty's centre is a warren of narrow, pedestrianized cobbled streets bordered by houses built around quaint courtyards. The cobbles of the streets are arranged in channels to drain off storm water and allow the sea to enter and wash the streets at high tides.

Churches

Paraty's **churches** traditionally each served a different sector of the population. **Nossa Senhora dos Remédios** (daily 9am–5pm), on the Praça da Matriz, is the town's most imposing building. Originally built on the site in 1668, the current construction dates from 1873 with building having begun 84 years earlier. Along Rua do Comércio is the smallest church, the **Igreja do Rosário** (Mon–Fri 9am–5pm), once used by slaves, while at the southern edge of the town, the Portuguese Baroque **Igreja de Santa Rita** (Wed–Sun 10am–noon & 2–5pm) served freed *mulattos* and dates from 1722. The oldest and most architecturally significant of the town's churches, it now houses the **Museu de Arte Sacra de Paraty**, with religious artefacts from all of the town's churches.

Beaches and islands

From the **Praia do Pontal**, across the Perequé-Açu River from town, and from the port quay, boats leave for the **beaches** of Parati-Mirim, Iririguaçu – known for its waterfalls – Lula and Conceição. In fact, there are 65 islands and about two hundred beaches to choose from – ask around for the current favourites. Hotels and travel agents sell tickets for trips out to the islands, typically for around R$40 per person, leaving Paraty at noon, stopping at three or four islands, giving time for a swim, and returning at 6pm. For an hour's **hike**, walk the trail to perfect **Praia do Sono**, 12km southwest of town.

A little way beyond Praia do Sono (21km from Paraty) and reached by a steep winding road is the village of **Trindade** (7 daily buses; 45min). Sandwiched between the ocean and Serra do Mar, it's crammed with backpackers and trippers in peak season, camping on the beaches or staying in one of numerous pousada/ hostels. Famed for its **beaches**, the best are across the rocky outcrops to **Praia Brava** and **Praia do Meio**, some of the most attractive mainland beaches on this stretch of coast, and completely unspoilt.

ARRIVAL AND INFORMATION

By bus The *rodoviária* is about 0.5km from the old town on Rua Jango de Padúa.
Destinations Rio (7 daily; 5hr); São Paulo (5 daily; 5hr); Trindade (7 daily; 45min); Ubatuba (6 daily; 2hr); and Angra dos Reis for Ilha Grande (5 daily; 2hr).
Tourist information On the corner of Av Roberto Silveira and Praça Chafariz (daily 8am–7pm; ☎24 3371 1897).

ACCOMMODATION

Casa do Rio Hostel Rua Antonio Vidal 120 ☎24 3371 2223, ⊕paratyhostel.com. A well-organized HI hostel with a large communal area, social vibe and a variety of dorms – compare a couple before choosing. Helpful staff and tours on offer. Dorms R$34, doubles R$120
★ **Pousada Guaraná** Rua Cinco 13, Portal de Paraty ☎24 3371 6362, ⊕pousadaguarana.com.br. An artistic, spacious, and very good-value pousada 10min from the Centro Histórico. Superb breakfast, free use of bicycles, a pool, plant-filled garden, soft music and attention to detail all make this an ideal choice. R$160
Solar dos Gerânios Praça da Matriz ☎24 3371 1550. Beautiful Swiss-Brazilian-owned place filled with rustic furniture and curios. Rooms are spartan but impeccable, most have a balcony and all are en suite. Great value. Reservations advised; request a room overlooking the *praça*. R$130

EATING AND DRINKING

Café do Armazém Rua Dr. Samuel Costa 18. The best coffee in town, to go with excellent filled tapioca wraps. Amerindian crafts pepper the walls of the shop, while on Sat nights (from 8pm) this is also the home of Paraty's best samba sing-along.

PARQUE NACIONAL SERRA DOS ORGÃOS

The **Parque Nacional Serra dos Orgãos** is breathtakingly beautiful and refreshingly easy to visit from Petrópolis's less attractive neighbour, **Teresópolis**. Dominated in its lower reaches by lush Atlantic forest, the bare mountain peaks that emerge from the trees create a stunning effect against the backdrop of a clear blue sky. It is these peaks that give the park its name, the rocks reminding the early Portuguese explorers of the pipes of cathedral organs.

There are a number of **walking trails** in the park, most of them short, easily accessible and suitable for people who like their hiking easy, though all have uphill stretches. Many of the park's most recognizable landmarks are visible on the horizon from Teresópolis. The most famous of all is the **Dedo de Deus** (Finger of God) – a bare, rocky pinnacle that points skyward – while arguably more picturesque is the **Cachoeira Véu da Noiva** waterfall. The longest and most challenging trail is the **Pedra do Sino** (Stone Bell), starting some distance from the park entrance, passing the bell-shaped rock formation (at 2263m the park's highest point) and emerging some 30km further on (close to the town of Petrópolis) – a guide is strongly recommended.

For **eating**, there's plenty of *por kilo* lunch places for cheap eats, but if you're looking for something a little different, try *Cheiro do Mato* at Rua Delfim Moreira (📞 21 2742 1899). This reasonably priced vegetarian restaurant has a diverse menu that will satisfy even the staunchest meat eater.

ARRIVAL AND INFORMATION

By bus Buses to Teresópolis run hourly from Rio and every 1hr 30min from Petrópolis, arriving at the *rodoviária* on Rua 1 de Maio.

Tourist information Rotariana (daily 8am–7pm; 📞 21 2642 1737, 🌐 portaltere.com). Teresópolis is located right at the edge of the park, the entrance being just to the south of town (head towards the Dedo de Deus). The park office at the entrance (daily 8am–5pm) rents out camping equipment and can provide information on local guides. There is a R$3 entrance charge, increasing to R$8 if you wish to walk the Pedra do Sino trail.

ACCOMMODATION

If you're not camping or walking straight on to Petrópolis, you'll probably want to base yourself in Teresópolis, where there are a couple of reasonable accommodation options.

Pousada Villa Tiroleza Rua da Mariana 144 📞 21 2742 7337, 🌐 pousadatiroleza.com.br. A handsome chalet-style building with a rustic wooden interior and a sauna. Excellent value. R$140

Recanto do Lord Rua Luiza Pereira Soares 109 📞 21 2742 5586, 🌐 teresopolishostel.com.br. An HI hostel, some distance from the centre of town but well worth the trek for the savings you'll make. Great service, with glorious view over town. Dorms R$30, doubles R$130

★ **Camoka** Praça da Bandeira 3. Between the pier and Santa Rita church, genial owner Marcão has found a business niche in inexpensive eats (try the baked *escondidinha* pie, R$15, or *torta vegetarian*, R$12) and good beer served until late at night. Live music or DJ at weekends.

★ **Istanbul** Rua Manuel Torres, Shopping Colonial. Home-cooked Turkish kebabs, rotis, meze, falafel and choice of teas at this friendly and great-value snack bar with tables upstairs, just across from the bus station.

PETRÓPOLIS

Some 66km to the north of Rio, high in the mountains, stands the imperial city of **PETRÓPOLIS**, so named because in the nineteenth century Emperor Dom Pedro II had a summer palace built here, rapidly making the place a popular retreat for Brazilian aristocracy. En route the scenery is dramatic, climbing among forested slopes that suddenly give way to ravines and gullies, while clouds shroud the surrounding peaks. You can easily tour Petrópolis in a day – its cultural attractions and stunning setting make it well worth the trip.

WHAT TO SEE AND DO

The **Palácio Imperial** on Rua da Imperatriz (Tues–Sun 11am–5.30pm; R$8; 🌐 museuimperial.gov.br) is a grandiose colonial structure, set in beautifully maintained gardens. Upon entry, you're given felt overshoes with which to slide around the polished floors of this royal residence, and inside there's everything from Dom Pedro II's crown to the regal commode. The cathedral of **São Pedro de Alcântara** (Tues–Sun 8am–6pm) blends with the surrounding architecture, but is much more recent than its neo-Gothic style suggests – it was finished in 1939. Inside lie the tombs of Dom Pedro himself and several royal personages.

Perhaps the town's most recognizable building is the **Palácio de Cristal** (Tues–Sun 9am–6pm) on Rua Alfredo Pachá, essentially a greenhouse erected for the local horticultural society in 1879, though competing for the honour is the alpine chalet **Casa Santos Dumont** (Tues–Sun 9.30am–5pm), which is well worth visiting for the collection of the personal oddments of the famous aviator.

ARRIVAL AND INFORMATION

By bus Buses leave Rio for Petrópolis every 30min (sit on the left side of the bus for best views), arriving at the *rodoviária* on Rua Dr Porciúncula, from where it's a further 10km by local bus into town.

Tourist information Helpful branches are found around town, at Praça da Liberdade and at the *rodoviária* (both daily 9am–6pm; ☎ 800 241 516).

ACCOMMODATION

There are a few reasonable options in town, though most are very classy former colonial mansions.

Albergue Quitandinha Rua Uruguai 570 ☎ 24 2247 9165, ⓦ alberguequitandinha.com.br. Ten rooms and a dorm within wooden cabins, a bus ride from the *Centro Histórico*. Dorms R$40, doubles R$130

Comércio Rua Dr Porciúncula 55. One of the cheapest options in town, though by no means a bargain. Rooms without bathroom are cheapest. R$100

Pousada 14 Bis Rua Buenos Aires 192 ☎ 24 2231 0946, ⓦ www.pousada14bis.com.br. A themed pousada based on the life of aviator Santos Dumont. Rooms are nothing flashy, but decorated in attractive colonial style. R$140

EATING

Restaurants are surprisingly lacklustre in Petrópolis, most of the best being some distance from town.

Armazem Rua Visconde de Itaboraí 646. Welcoming bar-restaurant with live music most nights and a varied menu of meat and fish that will suit most tastes. Try *camarão com catupiry* (R$24). Daily, lunch and dinner.

Arte Temporada Rua Ipiranga 716 ☎ 24 2237 2133. Based in the converted stable of a beautiful mansion. Offerings include Brazilian local specialities, such as trout and fine salads (from R$30). Wed–Sun lunchtime, Fri & Sat also dinner.

Braganca Rua Raul de Leon 109. In the hotel of the same name, this mid-priced Portuguese restaurant has various lunch options for two people (from R$35). Daily.

Rink Marowil Praca da Liberdade 27. Cheap *por kilo* lunch restaurant right on the square. The food is nothing to write home about but you'll struggle to find better value for money. At night functions as a bar with food à la carte. Daily.

Minas Gerais

Explorers flocked to **MINAS GERAIS** (literally "general mines") following the discovery of gold in 1693, and with the unearthing of diamonds and other gemstones the state has been exploited for these abundant natural resources ever since. For a hundred years the region was by far the wealthiest in Brazil, but as the gold reserves became exhausted so Minas Gerais declined, and by the mid-nineteenth century it was a backwater. Coffee in part served to stem the decline, and alongside extraction of workaday minerals like iron-ore it continues to sustain much of the region today. Visitors flock here, too, enjoying a series of startlingly beautiful towns left behind by the boom.

Minas Gerais's **CIDADES HISTÓRICAS** started life as mining camps, as rough and basic as imagination can make them. But the wealth of the surrounding mountains transformed them, and today they are considered to be among the most beautiful cities in the Americas, with cobbled streets and alleyways, glorious churches encrusted in gold – built in the over-the-top local version of Baroque architecture *Barroco Mineiro* – and beautifully preserved colonial buildings. And all of this is set in an area of rugged natural beauty, with a few towns connected by historic steam trains.

Ouro Preto and **Diamantina** are both UNESCO World Heritage Sites and are the best places for budget travellers to base themselves; **Tiradentes** is pricier though barely less impressive, with attractive and affordable São João del Rei worth a brief visit nearby.

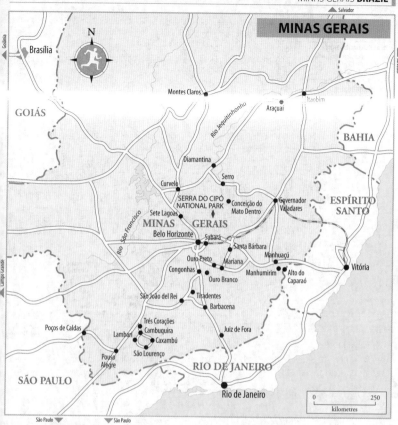

BELO HORIZONTE

Founded at the beginning of the eighteenth century by *bandeirantes* in search of gold and gemstones, **BELO HORIZONTE**, capital of Minas Gerais, nestles between the beautiful hills of the Serra do Curral. The third-largest urban area in Brazil may at first appear daunting and uninspired, but what this cosmopolitan metropolis lacks in aesthetics it makes up for in traditional Minas hospitality, and hidden treasures like eclectic architecture and European-style parks will soon have you enchanted. Thanks to its proximity to the *Cidades Históricas*, Belo Horizonte also serves as a good base to explore the region.

WHAT TO SEE AND DO

For all its size, the centre of Belo Horizonte is fairly easy to explore on foot. Heading south from the *rodoviária*, walk to Praça Raul Soares and then take Rua dos Guajajaras for the bustling **Mercado Central** (Mon–Sat 7am–6pm, Sun 7am–1pm), which has more than four hundred stalls and restaurants selling anything from cheeses to bamboo artefacts and bric-a-brac. Heading east you reach Avenida Afonso Pena, home to the striking **Parque Municipal** (Tues–Sun 6am–6pm). Inspired by the Parisian Belle Époque parks like the beautiful gardens of the Palace of Versailles, its pleasant shaded walkways, lakes and greenery – including two thousand species of tree – are especially busy on Sunday afternoons.

If you are in town on a Sunday morning, don't miss the **Feira das Artes** (Arts and Crafts Fair) on Avenida Afonso Pena, the largest open-air fair in Latin

BELO HORIZONTE

ACCOMMODATION

Lá em Casa Hostel-Pousada	2
Majestyc BH Centro	3
O Sorriso do Lagarto	5
Pousada Sossego da Pampulha	1
Pousadinha Mineira	4

EATING

Bem Natural	2
Bonomi Panificadora	7
La Greppia	3
Kahlúa Light	4
Salumeria Central	1
Vila Árabe	8

DRINKING & NIGHTLIFE

Bombshell Bar	10
Butiquim São Bento	13
Café com Letras	9
CCCP	11
Churrasquinhos do Luizinho	5
Estúdio B	6
Graças a Deus	12
Utopica Marcenaria	14

Brasília & São Paulo

Rodoviária

CENTRO

AVENIDA NOSSA SENHORA DE FATIMA

RUA PECANHA

AV. OIAPOQUE

RUA DOS CAETES

RUA DOS TUPINAMBÁS

RUA DOS CARIJOS

AVENIDA PARANA

RUA DOS TAMOIOS

AVENIDA DO CONTORNO

RUA DOS TUPIS

RUA DOS GOITACAZES

AVENIDA AUGUSTO DE LIMA

BARRO PRETO

RUA DOS GUAJAJARAS

AV. AUGUSTO DE LIMA

PRAÇA RAUL SOARES

Mercado Central

RUA DOS TIMBIRAS

AVENIDA AMAZONAS

Lavanderia Just a Sec

Terminal Turístico JK

RUA DOS GUAJARAS

RUA DOS AIMORÉS

@ Camaleão Lan House

RUA BERNARDO GUIMARÃES

RUA DOS TIMBIRAS

AVENIDA BARBACENA

Diamond Shopping Mall

RUA GONÇALVES DIAS

RUA ALVARENGA PEIXOTO

STO. AGOSTINHO

RUA DOS AIMORÉS

ALVARES

AVENIDA

RUA BERNARDO GUIMARÃES

RUA GONÇALVES DIAS

AVENIDA OLEGARIO MACIEL

RUA SANTA CATARINA

RUA CURITIBA

RUA MARTIM DE CARVALHO

RUA ALVARENGA PEIXOTO

RUA RODRIGUES CALDAS

PRAÇA CARLOS CHAGAS

RUA TOMAS GONZAGA

Museu de Mineralogia

RUA MATIAS CARDOSO

RUA PROF. ANTONIO ALEIXO

Teatro Izabel Hendrix

RUA ANDRE CAVALCANTI

AVENIDA DO CONTORNO

LOURDES

RUA HERCULANO DE FREITAS

AVENIDA DO CONTORNO

RUA LUDGERO DOLABELA

RUA GEN. DIONISIO CERQUEIRA

RUA ANTONIO DE ALBUQUERQUE

RUA AMERICO LUZ

Museu Histórico Abílio Barreto

RUA AMERICO MACEDO

RUA FERNANDES TOURINHO

RUA MAL. BITTENCOURT

AVENIDA DO CONTORNO

CIDADE JARDIM

R. TEIXEIRA MENDES

AVENIDA NOSSA SENHORA DE FATIMA

Vitória

RUA POUSO ALEGRE

AVENIDA BRANDÃO

RUA CERIO DE CASTRO

RUA POUSO ALEGRE

SANTA TEREZA

RUA MÁRMORE

AV SANTOS DUMONT

Train Station
& Museu de
Artes e Ofícios

PRAÇA
DA
ESTAÇÃO

AV ASSIS CHATEAUBRIAND

RUA CURITA

3

2

Igreja
São José

ro-terra
ber Café

Shopping
Metrópole

TELEMIG

Prefeitura

Parque
Municipal

AVENIDA DOS ANDRADAS

AL. ÁLVARO CELSO

RUA DOMINGOS VIEIRA

RUA ÁLVARES MACIEL

STA. EFIGÊNIA

Palácio
da Justiça

Hospital
João XXIII

Centro Cultural
Belo Horizonte

Palácio
das Artes

Escola
da Música

AVENIDA BRASIL

S. LUCAS

AVENIDA FRANCISCO SALES

AVENIDA CARANDAÍ

RUA PADRE ROLIM

6

Museu
Mineiro

Central
Shopping

Catedral da
Boa Viagem

FUNCIONÁRIOS

AVENIDA BRASIL

RUA GONÇALVES DIAS

PRAÇA DE
LIBERDADE

Edifício
Niemeyer

RUA CLÁUDIO MANOEL

AVENIDA GETÚLIO VARGAS

8

7

lácio da
berdade

RUA DOS INCONFIDENTES

RUA STA. RITA DURÃO

AVENIDA AFONSO PENA

AVENIDA DO CONTORNO

SAVASSI

PRAÇA
SAVASSI

RUA TOMÉ DE SOUZA

SÃO PEDRO

RUA PALMIRA

N

AVENIDA DO CONTORNO

RUA MINAS NOVAS

SION

RUA FINO

0   500

metres

Rio de Janeiro & Ouro Preto

Mangabeiras

3

America, with three thousand stalls. More modern artwork can be viewed nearby at the galleries of the **Palácio das Artes**, housed in a fine modern building at Avenida Afonso Pena 1537. Further south you'll reach the **Praça da Liberdade** with its famous **Niemeyer building**, designed by renowned Brazilian modern architect Oscar Niemeyer, before reaching the Neoclassical **Palácio da Liberdade**. Finish your day around **Praça Savassi**, where you can sip a *caipirinha* in one of many trendy bars in the area.

Museu Histórico Abílio Barreto

Just to the south of the centre at Avenida Prudente de Morais 202 in Cidade Jardim, the **Museu Histórico Abílio Barreto** (Tues–Sun 10am–5pm; free) is set within a beautiful colonial mansion, the sole remnant of the small village of Curral del Rey. It is home to some interesting photographs, furniture, sculptures and documents of the time.

Mangabeiras

In the Mangabeiras neighbourhood, southeast of the centre, the **Praça do Papa** has commanding views of the entire city. The monument in the square pays homage to Pope John Paul II, who held a Mass here in 1980. Bus #4103 (or #2001-C) from Avenida Afonso Pena (between Av Amazonas and Rua Tamóios) will get you up here. Stay on the same bus to continue to the mountainous edge of the city, where the vast **Parque das Mangabeiras** (Tues–Sun 8am–6pm), a pleasant spot for a relaxing walk, supports capuchin monkeys and other wildlife in the trees overhead.

Pampulha

Set around an artificial lake, the smart, modernist neighbourhood of Pampulha, north of the city centre (an hour's journey on bus #2215A, B or C from Av Paraná between Rua Tamoios and Rua Carijós), contains some architectural gems, the work of great modern Brazilian designers Oscar Niemeyer and Roberto Burle Marx. The **Museu de Arte de Pampulha** (MAP; Tues–Sun 9am–6pm; R$6), on a peninsula in the lake, is one of the finest; a work of art in itself (though also housing a small collection inside), originally designed to be a casino before becoming a museum in 1957. Also in Pampulha is the compelling **Igreja de São Francisco de Assis** (Tues–Sat 9am–5pm, Sun 9am–1pm; R$3), among the finest works of Niemeyer, Burle Marx and Candido Portinari, who created the beautiful *azulejo* tile facade. Nearby is Belo Horizonte's largest stadium, the **Mineirão**. With a capacity of 90,000, it's the home ground of football team Atlético Mineiro and will serve as a World Cup venue in 2014. At other times a Sunday home derby here against Cruzeiro is unmissable.

INHOTIM

It comes as a bit of a shock to find the world's largest open-air art museum an hour's bus journey from Belo Horizonte. But that's exactly what's on offer at Inhotim Instituto Cultural (Tues–Fri 9.30am–4.30pm, Sat & Sun until 5.30pm; Wed–Thurs R$20; Fri–Sun and holidays R$28; free Tues 🕿 31 3571 9700, 🖳 inhotim.org.br/index.php), an exhibition of 400 pieces of contemporary art across ten galleries and set amid an incredible 106 acres of botanical reserve. Opened officially in 2006, the collection includes paintings, sculpture, photos, videos and installations by both Brazilians and international artists – among them outstanding works by Hélio Oiticica and Amilcar de Castro – dating from the 1960s to the present. Inhotim's appeal goes beyond art, however, with gardens of orchids, palms and rare tropical species landscaped by Burle Marx. The huge surrounding estate also boasts one of the best-preserved sections of Atlantic forest in Brazil.

You'll need a full day (or more) at Inhotim. Buses leave from the *rodoviária* in Belo Horizonte at 9am on Saturday and Sunday (R$16) and return at 4pm. Tuesday to Friday there are hourly buses to Brumadinho (R$12), a small town close to the park from where there's a regular bus service or taxis available. A free bus service exists within the site to outlying artworks and forest trails. Cafés and restaurants on-site.

ARRIVAL AND DEPARTURE

By plane Confins Airport (📞 31 3689 2700), officially called Tancredo Neves, is 38km north of the centre; take the inexpensive a/c bus (1hr) to/from the central *rodoviária* (a pricier though no better *executivo* bus also operates to central BH). First bus daily 4am, last bus around 11pm. For transfers by taxi (R$100), get a fixed rate voucher inside the terminal. Some domestic flights use Pampulha Airport (📞 31 3490 2001), 9km from downtown; take city bus #1202 to the *rodoviária*.

Destinations Brasília (12 daily; 2hr); Rio de Janeiro (12 daily; 1hr); Salvador (5 daily; 3hr); São Paulo (20 daily; 1hr 30min).

By bus *Rodoviária* (📞 31 3271 3000), Praça Rio Branco, at the northern end of the city centre.

Destinations Brasília (4 daily; 13hr); Diamantina (4 daily; 5hr); Ouro Preto (hourly; 2hr 30min); Rio de Janeiro (8 daily; 8hr); São João del Rei (6 daily; 4hr); São Paulo (8 daily; 9hr).

By train The train station (📞 31 3273 5976) at Praça da Estação serves just one route, to Vitória on the coast, with a daily 7.30am departure (14hr) following the valley of the Rio Doce through Minas's industrial heartland.

INFORMATION

The helpful Belotur office is at Rua Pernambuco 284 (Mon–Fri 8am–6pm; 📞 31 3277 9797, 🌐 belohorizonte .mg.gov.br), with branches at the Mercado Central, Parque Municipal (Mon–Fri 8am–7pm, Sat & Sun 8am–3pm; 📞 31 3277 7666), and the *Rodoviária* (daily 8am–9pm). Alô Turismo (📞 31 3220 1310) is Belotur's information hotline. Belotur also publishes a helpful monthly *Guia Turístico*, available at most hotels and information points. Minas's state tourism service Setur (Mon–Fri 8am–5pm; 📞 31 3915 9454, 🌐 turismo.mg.gov .br) is a useful resource, though no longer has an office in Central BH.

ACCOMMODATION

⭐ **Lá em Casa Hostel-Pousada** Rua Capitão Procópio 18F, Santa Tereza 📞 31 3653 9566, 🌐 laemcasahostel.com. A new smart hostel in BH's bohemian quarter, a 10min bus ride from the centre and with numerous traditional botecos nearby. Dorms have 5 beds and an excellent breakfast is included. Dorms R$40, doubles R$90

Majestyc BH Centro Rua Espírito Santo 284, at Rua Caetés, Centro 📞 31 3222 3390, 🌐 hotelmajestyc.com.br. There's nothing majestic about this place at all, but it's centrally located, the simple rooms are cheap and clean, and breakfast is included. R$60

O Sorriso do Lagarto Calle Cristina 791, São Pedro 📞 31 3283 9325, 🌐 osorrisodolagarto.com.br. Good value and friendly, this small hostel is located in trendy Savassi, great for those here for nightlife. Breakfast included, kitchen, wi-fi a little extra. Dorms R$35, doubles R$90

Pousada Sossego da Pampulha Av José Dias Bicalho 1258, São Luiz 📞 31 3491 8020, 🌐 sossegodapampulha .com.br. Close to Pampulha Airport, football stadium and university, this pousada has attractive rooms and a couple of (pricey) dorms, plus sauna and pool. Kitchen for self-caterers (though breakfast is included) and good views. Bus #5401 from Pampulha Airport. Dorms R$49, doubles R$120

Pousadinha Mineira Rua Espírito Santo 604, Centro 📞 31 3273 8156, 🌐 pousadinhamineira.com.br. Institutional yet cheap and reliable hostel with 200 dorm beds, in the centre of town. No breakfast, and sheets R$5 extra. R$25

EATING AND DRINKING

There are plenty of cheap restaurants, *lanchonetes* and *churrascarias* – popular at lunchtime with city workers – on Rua Pernambuco, Rua dos Caetés and around Praça Sete.

⭐ **Bem Natural** Rua Afonso Pena 941, Centro (inside a small plaza), and Rua Alagoas 911, at Rua dos Inconfidentes, Savassi. Not the cheapest *por kilo* in town (expect to pay R$20 for a decent plateful), but plenty of healthy and vegetarian offerings (meat dishes too) plus natural juices. Self-service only; Centro branch Mon–Fri 9am–6pm, Savassi also Sat 11am–3pm.

⭐ **Bonomi Panificadora** Rua Cláudio Manoel 488, Funcionários. This upmarket café/bakery is not strictly budget, but the coffee is the best in town, the bread, cakes and pastries among the best in Brazil, and the sandwiches and soups tasty too. Tues–Sun 8am–10.30pm, Mon noon–10.30pm.

La Greppia Rua da Bahia 1196, Centro. Classic BH 24hr spot for eating and drinking, with great-value tasty Brazilian and Italian meals and snacks, any time day or night. R$25 unlimited lunchtime buffet, or evening pasta *rodizio* with dessert for R$16.80. 24hr.

Kahlúa Light Rua da Bahia 1216, Centro. Pleasant and good-value smartish place with a minimalist design. The *prato executivo* changes daily and will set you back R$16. Mon–Sat 11.30am–3.30pm.

⭐ **Salumeria Central** Rua Sapucaí 527, Floresta. Right by the train station, this Italian-Brazilian restaurant-cum-bar serves salamis, hams, pastas, cheeses and the like from R$20 (try the pork calf cooked for seven hours; R$29), washed down with decent wine or beer. The outdoor seating's great for taking in views of the station square and the arches of the Santa Tereza viaduct. Mon–Sat 6.30pm–1am.

Vila Árabe Rua Pernambuco 781, Savassi. Good value if you opt for the sizeable meze for two (R$38, with vegetarian option), though otherwise moderately priced with an unlimited buffet for R$45 per person. Lunch daily noon–3.30pm, dinner Mon–Sat 7pm–late.

3

3

SERRA DO CIPÓ NATIONAL PARK

In a country of few mountain peaks the upland landscapes of the Serra do Cipó stand out as one of the finest places in the country for outdoor activities. Part of the UNESCO Serra do Espinhaço Biosphere Reserve, this important national park lies 100km northeast of Belo Horizonte, encompassing limestone hills, rugged valleys and grasslands, Atlantic forest and numerous pools and waterfalls – together enticing you to trek, bike, rock-climb, kayak and swim. Rare bird species like the Cipó canastero and hyacinth visorbearer attract serious birders, while other fauna to be sought out includes wolves, jaguars, monkeys and the *sapo de pijama* (pyjama frog).

Eight buses daily (2hr; R$28) ply the route from Belo Horizonte to the small town of Serra do Cipó at the edge of the park – an attractive place for backpackers with a low-key atmosphere, plus bars and pousadas. From here (and with the right gear) it's quite feasible to hike on your own from the park entrance, but there are also guides and organized trips available. Entry to the park is free, and though at weekends the principal trails draw day-trippers in numbers, during the week it's often near-deserted.

ACCOMMODATION

Check the website ⓦ serradocipo.com for more details on accommodation.

Hostel Serra do Cipó Rodovia MG10 Km97 ☎ 31 3718 7296. Attractive and comfortable rooms and a swimming pool. Dorms R$50, doubles R$100

TOUR OPERATORS

Further information on guides and outdoor activities is available from Bela Gerais Turismo (☎ 31 3718 7394, ⓦ serradocipogeraes.com.br) or Cipó Aventuras (☎ 31 9974 0878).

NIGHTLIFE

Savassi is teeming with trendy – if expensive – bars and clubs, while Rua Pium-í continues the trend south of Av Contorno, lined with fashionable hangouts. For slightly more downmarket options, head to Rua da Bahia anywhere between Av Carandaí and Praça da Estação.

Bombshell Bar Rua Sergipe 1395, Savassi ⓦ bombshell bar.blogspot.com. New, contemporary boteco with DJs spinning anything from *funk carioca* to jazz standards or rock/pop: check the schedule. Nice eats for sharing, too. Tues–Fri 6pm–1am, Sat 1pm–1am. Cover R$3.

Butiquim São Bento Rua Kepler 131, Santa Lúcia. A traditional-looking boteco, yet this is a young and friendly bar for unashamed flirting, with live MPB Fri and Sat. Play pool in the back room, sip cocktails or try one of the 28 kinds of beer. Closed Mon.

Café com Letras Rua Antônio de Albuquerque 781, Savassi. Trendy (and a little pricey) bar/bookshop open until the early hours with DJs, great cocktails and a scrumptious menu of crêpes and imaginative vegetarian bites.

★ **CCCP (Cult Club Cine Pub)** Rua Levindo Lopes 358, Savassi. Brand-new spot just off the Contorno that used to be a cinema but now serves international beers on tap. A fun and informal place with frequent gigs and film screenings. 6pm til late; closed Mon; check facebook page for details.

Churrasquinhos do Luizinho Rua Turquesa 327, Prado. Packed on Thursdays with up to 500 people, *Luizinho's* serves the usual drinks and delicious *espetos* (grilled beef on a skewer) – owner Luiz says the secret lies in the sauce,

a recipe of his mother's. Free shot of *cachaça* with your *espetinho* on Mon. Closed weekends.

Estúdio B Contorno 3849, São Lucas ⓦ estudiobmusicbar .com.br. Lively music venue offering anything from samba to rock and salsa to Beatles covers. Tues–Sat until late. Cover charge R$18.

Graças a Deus Rua Padre Odorico 68, São Pedro ⓦ gracas adeus.com.br. Little colourful house from the outside but darker lighting inside, with wooden tables and chilled beats setting the mood. Mean *caipivodkas*. Mon–Fri 7pm– late, Sat–Sun from 4pm.

★ **Utopica Marcenaria** Av Raja Gabáglia 4700, Santa Lúcia ⓦ utopica.com.br. Popular live music venue, located a few kilometres south of Centro. Lively, diverse crowd. Samba Thurs, rock/MPB Fri, funk/soul on Sat and *forró* on Sun. Cover R$12.

DIRECTORY

Banks and exchange Most banks are downtown on Av João Pinheiro between Rua dos Timbiras & Av Afonso Pena.

Car rental Numerous options at the airports; Hertz at Av Prof. Magalhães Penido 101, Pampulha ☎ 31 3492 1919; Alpina Serviços Automotivos at Rua dos Timbiras 2229 ☎ 31 3291 6111; Localiza at Av Bernardo Monteiro 1567 ☎ 31 3247 7956; Localralpha at Av Santa Rosa 100 ☎ 31 3491 3833.

Consulates Argentina, Rua Ceará 1566, 6th floor, Funcionários ☎ 31 3047 5490; Paraguay, Rua Guandaus 60, apt. 102, Santa Lúcia ☎ 31 3344 6349; UK, Rua Cláudio Manoel 26, Funcionários ☎ 31 3225 0950; Uruguay, Av do Contorno 6777, Santo Antônio ☎ 31 3296 7527.

Hospital Ambulance ☎ 192. Pronto Socorro do Hospital João XXIII, Av Alfredo Balena 400, Santa Efigênia (☎ 31 3239 9200).

Internet Camaleão Lan House at Rua São Paulo 1409; Pro-Terra Cyber Café at Av Augusto de Lima 134; at the *rodoviária* try the top floor of the neighbouring shopping mall.

Laundry Lavanderia Just a Sec, at Rua dos Guajajaras 1268, Centro (Mon–Fri 8am–6pm, Sat 8am–1pm).

Police ☎ 190. For visa extensions go to the Polícia Federal at Rua Nascimento Gurgel 30, Gutierrez (☎ 31 3330 5200).

Post office Central Correio, Av Afonso Pena 1270 (Mon–Fri 8am–5pm).

Taxis Coomotaxi ☎ 31 3419 2020; ☎ 0800 39 2020; Coopertáxi/BH ☎ 31 3421 2424, ☎ 0800 97 92424.

OURO PRETO

Founded at the end of the seventeenth century, **OURO PRETO** ("Black Gold") could well be the prettiest town in Brazil. Built on a hill in the Serra do Espinhaço, the former capital of Minas Gerais is home to some of the finest Baroque architecture in the country and was the birthplace of renowned sculptor **Aleijadinho**. The town was also the focal point of the **Inconfidência Mineira**, a failed attempt in 1789 to break from the colony and form a Brazilian republic. People flock to Ouro Preto from all over Brazil for **Semana Santa**, with its grand processions and Passion plays in open-air theatres, while **Carnaval** also attracts large crowds; book in advance at both these times. Other enjoyable festivals in this lively university town include the **Festival do Cinema Brasileiro** in mid-June, **Festival do Jazz** in September and **Festival das Letras**, a literary event, in November.

WHAT TO SEE AND DO

The town is best explored on foot, taking in the cobbled passageways between its handful of stunning churches, two excellent museums, and numerous shopping and eating options – but be prepared for lots of uphill climbing.

Praça Tiradentes

Praça Tiradentes lies at the heart of Ouro Preto, with several sights right on the square. The **Museu da Inconfidência** (Tues–Sun noon–6pm; R$6, students R$3) inside the Paço Municipal describes the town's fascinating local history, and includes the tomb of Tiradentes, leader of the failed *Inconfidência Mineira* rebellion. Numerous documents, torture instruments, Indo-Portuguese images and statuettes – notably nine exquisite figures by Aleijadinho – and other interesting everyday objects bring the eighteenth century to life. On the opposite side of the square, inside the vast **Escola de Minas**, the **Museu de Ciência e Técnica da Escola de Minas** (Tues–Sun noon–5pm; R$3) houses a large geological and mineralogical collection, including gemstones from all over the world. There is also an **astronomical observatory** (Sat 8–10pm).

ALEIJADINHO

The most important sculptor in colonial Brazil, Antônio Francisco Lisboa (1738–1814) was born in Ouro Preto to a slave mother and a Portuguese architect father, Manoel Lisboa. Self-taught, Aleijadinho was exceptionally prolific, turning out scores of profoundly original works, an achievement made all the more remarkable by the fact that from his mid-thirties he suffered from a degenerative disease (presumably leprosy) which led to loss of movement in his legs and hands, eventually forcing him to sculpt using chisels strapped to his wrists while apprentices moved him around on a trolley (the name **Aleijadinho** translates literally as "little cripple"). His extraordinary works reflect his Christian spirituality and abound in many of the *cidades históricas*, particularly Ouro Preto, where the Museu Aleijadinho offers further insights. His most famous works of all, however, sculpted towards the end of his life and credited with introducing greater realism into Baroque art, are the 76 life-size figures at the **Basílica do Senhor Bom Jesus de Matosinhos** in the otherwise utterly unremarkable town of **Congonhas**. Thankfully you don't have to stay there to visit them – Congonhas is a convenient stopoff between Ouro Preto (or Belo Horizonte) and São João del Rei (you may have to change buses in Ouro Branco): leave your baggage at the Congonhas *rodoviária*, from where you'll need about four hours for local bus connections and to make the most of the remarkable site.

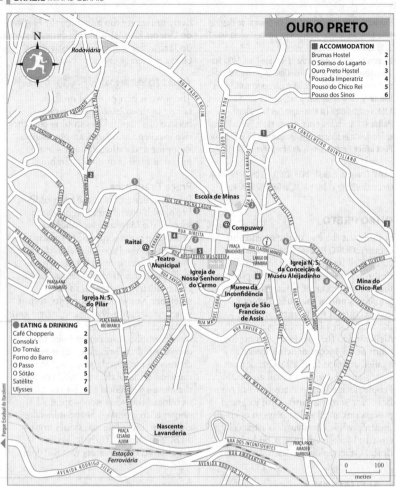

Two churches and Aleijadinho

Arguably the most beautiful church in Ouro Preto, the **Igreja de São Francisco de Assis** (Tues–Sun 8.30am–noon & 12.30–5pm; R$6, including entry to the Museu Aleijadinho), east of Praça Tiradentes, is one of the most important works of Aleijadinho (see box, p.267). The exterior was entirely sculpted by the great master himself and the ceilings decorated by his partner Athayde. The **Museu Aleijadinho** (Tues–Sat 8.30am–noon & 1.30–5pm, Sun noon–5pm), containing many more beautiful works, is located in the **Igreja Matriz de N.S. da**

Conceição. The church was designed by his father and also houses Aleijadinho's simple tomb.

Mina do Chico-Rei

Close to the Igreja Matriz de N.S. da Conceição, at Rua Dom Silvério 108, is the **Mina do Chico-Rei** (daily 8am–5pm; R$10). The abandoned mine has claustrophobic tunnels to explore, and gives a good sense of the scale of the local mining operations (this was only a small mine). It's also an interesting place to learn more about Chico-Rei ("Little King") himself, a legendary figure said to have been an enslaved African king who bought himself and his people out of slavery and became fabulously wealthy.

Teatro Municipal and Igreja do Pilar

A little further west of Praça Tiradentes is the beautiful and still-functioning **Teatro Municipal** (Mon–Fri 9am–5.30pm, Sat & Sun 10am–5pm; R$3), which is worth a look for its simple wooden interior; people used to bring their own chairs to performances. According to the *Guinness Book of Records*, this is the oldest opera house in the Americas, inaugurated on June 6, 1770.

If you continue downhill to the foot of **Rua Brigador Mosqueira**, you'll come to the early eighteenth-century **Igreja Matriz N.S. do Pilar** (Tues–Sun 9–10.45am & noon–4.45pm; R$4), the most opulent church in Minas Gerais, as well as one of the oldest. Over the top even by Baroque standards, it's said to be the second richest in Brazil, with 434kg of gold and silver used in its decoration.

Parque Estadual do Itacolomi

A twenty-minute bus journey outside of town (numerous local buses pass), the **Parque Estadual do Itacolomi** (☎31 8433 2266; Tues–Sun 8am–5pm, last entry 3.30pm; R$7) is a great place to spend a day immersed in nature, with well-organized trails ranging in length from 1.5km to 16km. **Camping** is permitted here if you're feeling adventurous (around R$15; phone to confirm; hiking guides also available).

ARRIVAL AND INFORMATION

By bus The *rodoviária* (☎31 3559 3225) is on Rua Padre Rolim 661, a 15min uphill walk northwest of the city centre. Buses from Mariana stop right by Praça Tiradentes: alight here for accommodations and restaurants.
Destinations Belo Horizonte (10 daily; 2hr); Brasília (daily at 7.30pm; 11hr 30min); Mariana (every 30min; 30min); Rio (daily at 10pm; 7hr); São João del Rei (4 daily; 4hr).
By train An historic steam train (ⓦtremdavale.org) runs between Ouro Preto and Mariana on Fri, Sat & Sun, leaving at 11am and returning at 2pm (1hr; R$18 single, R$30 return). The train station (☎31 3551 7705) is south of town on Praça Cesário Alvim 102.
Tourist information The helpful Centro Cultural Turístico is at Praça Tiradentes 4 (daily 8.15am–7pm).

★ TREAT YOURSELF

Pouso do Chico Rei Rua Brigadeiro Musqueira 90, Centro ☎31 3551 1274, ⓦpousodochicorei.com.br. It's worth paying the extra to stay at this friendly, historic family pousada, formerly graced by pre-eminent Brazilian singers Vinicius de Moraes and Dorival Caymmi. Wooden floorboards provide a rustic touch while the upstairs living room with grandfather clock conveys a home-from-home feel. All rooms are individually furnished and some have commanding views of the Carmo church. A large breakfast is served in the dining room (a cosy room with antiques and fireplace), while complimentary tea and cake is available at any time, as is wi-fi access. R$190

ACCOMMODATION

Make sure that you book in advance in high season and at weekends. Expect substantial discounts midweek and off-season.
Brumas Hostel Ladeira de São Francisco de Paula 68 ☎31 3551 2944, ⓦbrumashostel.com.br. This clean and pleasant HI hostel has a communal area with couches and books. Guest kitchen, laundry service and decent breakfast. Dorms R$36, doubles R$100
O Sorriso do Lagarto Rua Conselheiro Quintiliano 271 ☎31 3551 4811, ⓦosorrisodolagarto.com.br. A 10min walk from Praça Tiradentes, this hostel has big clean dorms with a good breakfast included, brightly decorated rooms and a guest kitchen. Dorms R$35
Ouro Preto Hostel Travessa das Lajes 32, Antônio Dias ☎31 3551 6011, ⓦouropretohostel.com. Grand views and a relaxed feel at this HI hostel a short walk from the Igreja da Conceição. Attractive communal areas and private rooms. Breakfast buffet included. Dorms R$34, doubles R$90
Pousada Imperatriz Rua Direita 179 ☎31 3551 5435. Great value, these very simple but (mostly) spacious double rooms have a TV and, in some cases, a private bathroom. Prime location by the bars below Praça Tiradentes. R$70
Pouso dos Sinos Rua Costa Senna 30 ☎31 3551 1138, ⓦpousodossinos.com.br. This rambling antique-filled building in an ideal location next to the Igreja de São Francisco offers large, attractive rooms with up to five single beds; some have private bath. No internet or breakfast. Dorms R$40, doubles R$110

EATING AND DRINKING

Good cheap places to eat are scattered throughout Ouro Preto. Night-time action is centred on Rua Direita (aka Rua Conde de Bobadella) where students spill out of bars to chat

3

on the street, while there are a couple of options along Rua Barão de Carmargos, and weekly late parties are held at school and university halls elsewhere (look out for flyers).

Café Choperia Real Rua Barão de Camargo 8. A few psychedelic paintings decorate this popular joint with tables on the cobbled street in front, perfect for a *chopp* on a warm evening. Live bossa nova or MPB most nights from 8pm, plus a decent *prato executivo* for R$13. Daily noon–2am.

Consola's Rua da Conceiçao 18, behind the Matriz N.S. da Conceiçao. You can't argue with the value of this place, serving reasonable pizza for R$13, plus the usual steak dinners and excellent (huge) *comida mineira* at R$28 for two. Closed Tues.

Do Tomáz Rua Senado Rocha Lagoa 75. Very simple place with paint wearing off the walls, but the lunch dishes change daily, it's super-friendly and the price hits the spot at R$9. Lunch only, closed Sun.

Forno do Barro Praça Tiradentes 54. Good (if a little salty) range of *mineira* specialities kept warm on the stove; lunch & dinner buffet R$19, plus pizzas and bar vibe at night. Daily.

★ **O Passo** Rua São José 56 ☎ 31 3552 3716. Upmarket dining with excellent large pizzas (R$28) and pastas, buzzing most weekend evenings for a pre- or post-dinner drink on the terrace, often with live jazz. Delivery available. Noon–midnight daily.

O Sótão Rua Direita 124. Fun, colourful paintings decorate this smarter student-friendly place with straw lightshades casting shadows on the walls. Nice cocktails and light bites such as filled pancakes. Live and relaxing bossa nova sets the mood from 8pm. Closed Mon.

Satélite Rua Direita 97. Good place to grab a snack (try the *batatas recheadas* for R$11); gets really lively late at night, with locals sipping on beer and cheap *caipirinhas*. Daily.

Ulysses Rua Bernardo Vasconcelos 25. Family-run place with the cheapest lunches in town (11am–2pm) served on a little terrace for an incredible R$7. You can see the eponymous owner at work in the little kitchen at the back. Closed Mon.

DIRECTORY

Banks and exchange All the major banks with ATMs and exchange facilities are located along Rua São José.

Internet Compuway, Praça Tiradentes 52 (Mon–Fri 8am–9pm, Sat until 6pm); Raitai, Rua Paraná 100 (daily 9am–9pm).

Laundry Ask at your hotel/hostel as there are no laundries downtown. Nacente Lavanderia, at Rua dos Inconfidentes 5 (Mon–Fri 8am–5pm, Sat 8am–noon), picks up and drops off washing.

Shopping The *Feria do Artesanato* on Praça Largo do Coimbra sells a variety of local artefacts made from soapstone.

MARIANA

A thirty-minute bus ride from Ouro Preto, lovely **MARIANA**, founded in 1696 and named after King Dom João V's wife Maria Ana de Austria, is home to two of Minas's most elegant town squares and a beautifully preserved colonial centre. The town can be visited as a day-trip from Ouro Preto, but it's also a great place to stay should you wish to escape the hordes of tourists elsewhere.

WHAT TO SEE AND DO

Once more important than Ouro Preto and home to the first governors of the state, Mariana today is no more than a small town. Head first to the impressive, elaborate **Catedral de N.S. da Assunção** (Tues–Sun 7am–6pm) on Praça Cláudio Manoel. The church was designed by Aleijadinho's father and contains many carvings by the man himself; in addition, the *tapa o vento* door, painted by Athayde, is considered by many to be the most beautiful in South America. Further riches include 365kg of gold and a beautiful German organ with 1039 flutes and a keyboard made of elephants' teeth. **Organ concerts** are held on Friday at 11am and Sunday at noon.

Not far away, at Rua Frei Durão 49, the former bishop's palace now houses the **Museu Arquidiocesano de Arte Sacra** (Mon–Fri 8.30am–noon & 1.30–5pm, Sat & Sun 8.30am–2pm; R$5), a lovely building holding religious treasures and more paintings by Athayde and sculptures by Aleijadinho. Two stunning Baroque churches stand on the **Praça Minas Gerais**: the **Igreja de São Francisco de Assis** (daily 8am–5pm), with more Aleijadinho carving, is the final resting place of Athayde; the relative restraint of the **Igreja do Carmo** (daily 9am–4pm) makes an interesting contrast.

Mina da Passagem

On the outskirts of town in the direction of Ouro Preto, **Mina da Passagem** (daily 9am–5pm; R$26; ⓦ minasdapassagem .com.br) is one of the oldest and richest deep-shaft gold mines in the region. From the beginning of the eighteenth century to the mine's closure in 1985, 35 tonnes of gold were extracted from here. Today it is worth visiting for the roller-coaster journey down into the tunnels alone, in a rickety cart that wobbles along the irregular tracks, taking you 120m below ground. En route you pass caverns where as many as three thousand slaves daily sweated blood and tears at the rock face. You continue on foot, with the option of taking a refreshing dip in a spectacularly clear lagoon. Any bus going between Ouro Preto and Mariana will drop you at the mine.

ARRIVAL AND INFORMATION

By bus Twice-hourly Transcotta buses from/to Ouro Preto drop off and pick up at Praça Tancredo Neves in the heart of town. The *rodoviária* (☎ 31 3557 1215) is a couple of kilometres west of the centre – local buses ply the route.

By train The *Trem da Vale* (see p.269) connects Mariana with Ouro Preto. The station for the steam train from Ouro Preto is right by the *rodoviária*.

Tourist information The excellent Terminal Turístico (daily 8am–5pm; ☎ 31 3557 1158) is on Praça Tancredo Neves.

ACCOMMODATION

Central Rua Frei Durão 8 ☎ 31 3557 1630. Set within a beautiful colonial building and certainly central, this very basic sixty-room hotel has a slightly strange, soulless feel, though it's reliable enough and cheap. R$75

Faisca Rua Antônio Olinto 48 ☎ 31 3557 1206, ⓦhotel faisca.com.br. 35 smart, spotless rooms in the centre of town; excellent value with breakfast and wi-fi included. R$105

Mariana Hostel Rua Mestre Vicente 41 ☎ 31 3557 1435, ⓦmarianahostel.com.br. HI hostel 5min walk from the centre, with sparkling rooms and bathrooms, a communal area, breakfast and wi-fi included. Dorms R$38, doubles R$90

EATING

Cozinha Real Rua Antônio Olinto 34. Next door to the Hotel Faisca, this place offers a good range of *mineira* food (buffet lunch R$21), with friendly staff and live music Fri & Sat nights. Closed Sun.

★ **Pizzaria Dom Silvério** Praça Gomes Freire 242. Top-notch wood-fired pizza in atmospheric surroundings (R$32 for two), while a decent-sized *prato feito mineira* is served at lunchtime (R$8). Open daily; evenings from 6.30pm.

Rancho Praça Gomes Freire 108. Excellent local cuisine kept warm on a wooden stove. Lunchtime buffet (R$18), soups (R$6) and *petiscos* (from R$10) at night. Closed Mon.

SÃO JOÃO DEL REI

Named in honour of Dom João V, king of Portugal, **SÃO JOÃO DEL REI** was one of the first settlements in the region, dating back to the end of the seventeenth century. Today the modern city has a historic centre with imposing Baroque churches surrounded by a less-than-attractive surfeit of post-war apartment blocks; it's one of the few gold towns to have found a thriving place in the modern world. Given that São João's neighbour Tiradentes is the prettier town, you may wish to stay there and visit here for the day; nonetheless the town is overall the more economical option. On Fridays, weekends and public holidays you can ride between the two towns on the *Maria Fumaça* **steam train**.

WHAT TO SEE AND DO

Colonial buildings catch you unawares as you wander through the town: ruas Santo Antônio and Getulio Vargas are particularly well preserved. Right on the town's wide central artery, with a stream running through the middle, the beautiful, classical **Teatro Municipal** on Rua Hemilio Alves (Mon–Fri 8–11am and 1–5pm; R$10) is worth seeking out – or catch one of the regular performances or concerts here; the tourist office has details of current shows. A couple of buildings away is the **Brazilian Expeditionary Force Museum** (Museu FEB; daily 8am–4pm; R$1), which tells the story of the country's involvement in World War II, including combat garbs, radios, photographs, weapons, banknotes and fascinating news clippings from the period. The **Railway Museum**, at the station four blocks east (Tues–Sun 9–11am & 1–5pm; R$1, free with a train ticket), has interesting facts on the origins of the *Maria Fumaça*, and also houses the first engine to run on the track here.

On Rua Getulio Vargas, visit the stunning 1721 Baroque **Catedral de Nossa Senhora de Pilar** (daily 8am–8pm, closed at lunchtime; free), which have extensive gold gilding over the altar and attractive tiling. Close by, the **Museu Regional** on Largo Tamandaré (Tues–Fri noon–5.30pm; Sat & Sun 8am–1pm; R$1) has a rich collection of historical and artistic objects

3

from furniture to paintings, housed in a beautifully restored mansion.

Igreja de São Francisco de Assis

The most impressive and important of the city's churches, the 1774 Baroque **Igreja de São Francisco de Assis** (daily 8am–5.30pm, Sun until 4pm; R$2), gives onto the beautiful Praça Frei Orlando, lined with towering palms. A deceptively large place with carvings by Aleijadinho and his pupils, it also has a graveyard to the rear where President Tancredo Neves is buried. One of Brazil's most revered politicians, he is credited with masterminding the return to democracy in the 1980s.

ARRIVAL AND INFORMATION

By bus The *rodoviária* (☎ 32 3373 4700) is 2km northeast of town; outside, take a local bus from in front of the Drogaria Americana and get off at Av Tancredo Neves. Taxis (☎ 32 3371 2028) charge R$18.

Destinations Belo Horizonte (8 daily; 3hr 30min); Ouro Preto (daily 3am and 6pm; 4hr); Rio (3 daily; 5hr 30min); São Paulo (8 daily; 7hr 30min); Tiradentes (every 30min; 30min).

By train The *Maria Fumaça* leaves São João for Tiradentes on Fri, Sat, Sun and public holidays at 10am and 3pm, returning at 1pm and 5pm (R$20 single, R$34 return).

Tourist information The tourist office (Mon–Fri 8am–6pm ☎ 32 3372 7388) is located right in the centre by the stream on Av Tancredo Neves.

ACCOMMODATION

Brasil Av Tancredo Neves 395 ☎ 32 3371 2804. Facing the river, the biggest hotel in town gives a whole new meaning to faded grandeur, with fifty very simple, clean rooms that surely haven't changed much since the place opened in 1881. Two other equally faded and similarly priced options are close by. R$80

Pousada Estação do Trem Rua Maria Tereza 45 ☎ 32 3372 1985, ⓦ pousadaestacaodotrem.com.br. Wooden furnishings, rugs and soft lighting make this historic house a lovely option, right by the train to Tiradentes. Wi-fi and breakfast included. Good value at R$130

EATING AND DRINKING

Cabana do Zotti Av Tiradentes 805. Drinking spot with snacks and a pleasant atmosphere within a stone, brick and wood setting; busy at weekends. Mon–Sat from 6pm.

Del Rei Cafe Av Tiradentes 553. Open until late, this restaurant-cum-*chopperia* serves reasonable pizza, lunchtime *pratos feitos* and tasty filled crêpes.

Pantanal Rua Getúlio Vargas. A popular joint to have an evening drink close to the Igreja do N.S. do Carmo. Daily 6pm–late.

Pelourinho Rua Hermilio Alves 276. A decent and cheap self-service place with a great variety of *mineira* food, right in the centre of town by the stream. Daily 11am–4pm and 6pm–midnight.

Villeiros Rua Padre José Maria Xavier 132, close to São Francisco church. A relaxed *por kilo* restaurant at lunchtime with a good range of typical *mineira* food. At night there's a more expensive à la carte menu from R$40 for two. Daily 11am–4pm and 7pm–late.

DIRECTORY

Banks and exchange All banks and ATMs are on Av Tancredo Neves.

Internet World Game Internet, at Rua Ministro Gabriel Passos 281 (daily 9am–10pm). The mall adjoining *Del Rei Café* offers free wi-fi.

Post office Av Tiradentes 500 (Mon–Fri 9am–5pm, Sat 9am–noon).

Shopping The *Feira do Artesanato*, held every Sun on Av Presidente Tancredo Neves, sells local crafts.

TIRADENTES

With its quaint historic houses, cobblestone streets and horse-drawn carriages, **TIRADENTES** could be mistaken for a film set. Surrounded by mountains, the charming town is better appreciated during the week, as Brazilian tourists swarm in at weekends for a romantic break or to shop at the many little boutiques around town. Costs here are the most expensive in Minas, but despite this it's worth staying a night or two to fully appreciate the rich atmosphere, explore the town's cobbled alleyways – and, if you like the outdoors – go walking for an hour or two in the surrounding countryside.

WHAT TO SEE AND DO

Despite being described as a *cidade histórico*, modern Tiradentes is little more than a village, which at least ensures that everything is easily found. The chief landmark, pretty much at the highest point in town, is the **Igreja Matriz de Santo Antônio** (daily 9am–5pm; R$5). Among the largest and most gold-laden of Minas Gerais' Baroque churches, it also features some of

Aleijadinho's last works, and the classic view from the church steps is the most photographed in the state. Nearby, at Rua Padre Toledo 190, in the former home of one of the heroes of the *Inconfidência Mineira*, the **Museu Padre Toledo** (Tues–Sun 9am–5pm; R$5) has period furnishings, art and documents dating back to the eighteenth century, and a preserved slave quarters. The slaves themselves built and worshipped at the small, dignified and supremely attractive **Igreja da N.S. do Rosário dos Pretos** (Tues–Sun 10am–5pm; R$2), down the hill, which also contains three sculptures of black saints.

ARRIVAL AND INFORMATION

By bus The *rodoviária* is in the centre of town off Rua Gabriel Passos. Buses leave regularly for São João del Rei (30min), from where you can connect to other destinations.

By train The *Maria Fumaça* departs for São João del Rei on Fri, Sat, Sun and public holidays at 1pm and 5pm. The train station is 1km southeast of the main square.

Tourist information The Secretária de Turismo is on the main square at Rua Resende Costa 71 (daily 9am–5pm; ☏ 32 3355 1212).

ACCOMMODATION

Tiradentes caters primarily for the well-to-do but the addition of a new HI hostel/pousada has made it a little more affordable. Try visiting midweek when pousadas offer discounts – or stay in São João.

Pousada Arco-Íris Rua Frederico Ozanan 340 ☏ 32 3355 1167. Next to the *Pousada da Bia*, this place has clean, spacious rooms with private bath, a big back garden and a little pool. Free internet. R$125

★ **Pousada da Bia** Rua Frederico Ozanan 330 ☏ 32 3355 1173, ⓦ pousadadabia.com.br. Set in a beautiful plot of land with a little herb garden and pool, and offering a variety of comfortable, multicoloured rooms in rustic converted outhouse surroundings. Small charge for wi-fi. R$130

Vila Libertas HI Hostel and Pousada Av Gov. Israel Pinheiro 72 ☏ 32 3355 2256, ⓦ hihostelbrasil.com.br. A little way out of town (beyond the train station) but luckily a bar, cultural centre and nightclub are right on hand. Clean and organized, with a good breakfast. 5-bed dorms R$40, doubles R$130

EATING AND DRINKING

Most restaurants and bars are centred on Largo das Forras, and often feature throngs of affluent Brazilians. Your best bet if in a small group is to share a *comida mineira*, usually

large enough for two or three people. Website ⓦ tiradentes .net offers good what's-on listings (in Portuguese).

Confidências Mineiras Rua Ministro Gabriel Passos 26. Warm, candlelit place serving large (for three) portions of *mineira* delights such as mashed pork and bean Tutú cooked in *cachaça* (R$55), or *petiscos* to accompany your choice of their near-infinite range of *cachaças*. Thurs–Sun noon–midnight.

Divino Sabor Rua Gabriel Passos 300. Popular lunch only place in simple surroundings with wooden tables on a patio outside. *Mineira* buffet for R$18 or reasonable price *por kilo*. Closed Mon.

★ **Libertas Espaço Cultural** Rua Israel Pinheiro 106. A short uphill walk from the railway station (20min from the main square), this is the town's most happening outdoor space for live music and themed festivals, from fashion to *cachaça*. Two bars and a nightclub keep things lively most weekends; ask around town to see what's on. Daily til late.

Mandalun Largo das Forras 88. Although the menu may at first seem expensive, there are some cheap international options among the selection of Lebanese food, such as chunky hamburgers (R$6), sandwiches (R$12) and pizzas (R$16). Daily noon–8pm, Thurs–Sun til 11pm.

Panela de Minas Rua Gabriel Passos 23. Right by the square, the town's most popular lunch spot (daily 11am–4pm) serves typical *mineira* food *por kilo* laid out on a raised hearth, plus decent pizzas on weekend nights.

Viradas do Largo Rua do Moinho 11. On a backstreet a 5min walk behind the *rodoviária*, this is considered the best value in town for good food. While not cheap, the huge portions (R$40–70) serve up to three, most guests seated around large antique tables. Wed–Sun noon–10pm.

DIRECTORY

Banks and exchange All banks with ATMs are located off Rua Gabriel Passos, close to Largo das Forras.

Internet Game Mania Lan House, Rua dos Inconfidentes (daily 9am–10.30pm).

Post office Rua Resende Costa 73 (Mon–Fri 9am–5pm).

DIAMANTINA

Beautiful **DIAMANTINA**, six hours by bus from Belo Horizonte, is the most isolated of the historic towns yet well worth the trip. Nestled in the heart of the Serra do Espinhaço, it is surrounded by a breathtakingly wild and desolate landscape. Named after the abundant diamond reserves first exploited in 1729, the town is rich in history and was designated a UNESCO World Heritage Site in 1999. It retains a lively, friendly atmosphere and is the hometown of visionary 1950s president **Juscelino Kubitschek** who founded Brasília; a statue is dedicated to him on Rua Macau Meio. Diamantina justifies a couple of days' wandering around in its own right, but you should also try to follow a trail outside of town to take in the scenery and nearby waterfalls and rock pools – details of routes and guides can be found at the tourist office (see below).

WHAT TO SEE AND DO

Diamantina's narrow streets are set on two exceptionally steep hills. Fortunately, almost everything of interest is tightly packed into the central area close to the main cathedral square, the Praça Conselheiro Mota. The **Museu do Diamante** (Tues–Sat noon–5pm, Sun 9am–noon; R$2) is right on the square at Rua Direita 14, bringing the colonial period vividly to life through an extraordinary variety of exhibits. They include real gold, real and fake diamonds, mining paraphernalia and reproductions of paintings depicting slaves at work. There are also a number of swords, pistols, guns and torture instruments that were used on enslaved Amerindians and Afro-Brazilians.

Mercado Velho and Casa da Glória

The **Mercado Velho** on Praça Barão de Guaicuí, just below the cathedral square, is an exceptional structure, worth visiting for the building alone; the market itself is held on weekends, a buzzing throng of traders selling *cachaças*, cheese, and ceramics from the Jequitinhonha valley to the north. The wooden arches inspired Niemeyer's design for the exterior of the Presidential Palace in Brasília. Also more worthwhile for the building than its contents is the eighteenth-century **Casa da Glória**, which is uphill from the tourist office at Rua da Glória 298 (Tues–Sun 8am–6pm); it was inspired by Venetian structures. This former residence of diamond supervisors, episcopal see of the first bishops of Diamantina and subsequently a school, is now part of the Centre of Geology and contains a collection of maps, gemstones and minerals.

Two churches

The **Igreja de N.S. Senhora do Carmo** on Rua do Carmo (open sporadically Tues–Sun; not lunchtimes), built between 1760 and 1765, is probably the most interesting of Diamantina's churches, with an exceptionally rich interior including an organ built in 1782 on which Lobo de Mesquita, considered the best composer of religious music of the Americas, performed many of his own works. Just downhill from here, the **Igreja de Nossa Senhora do Rosário dos Pretos** (same opening hours) was built in 1728 to serve local slaves and features an intricately painted ceiling.

ARRIVAL AND INFORMATION

By plane Azul (ⓦ voeazul.com.br) flies to Diamantina from Belo Horizonte from R$180 return.

By bus The *rodoviária* is on a steep hill, about a 10min walk above the centre of town (20min if walking uphill); a taxi costs around R$10. Buses for Belo Horizonte leave at midnight, 6am, 10.45am, 3.30pm and 6pm daily (6hr). There is no service from Diamantina to Brasília.

Tourist information Centro de Atendimento ao Turista, Praça JK 23 (Mon–Sat 9am–6pm, Sun 9am–2pm; ☎ 38 3531 8060).

ACCOMMODATION

Diamantina Hostel Rua do Bicame 988 ☎ 38 3531 5021, ⓦ diamantinahostel.com.br. This HI hostel is spotless and has a great view, yet the rooms are dark and not especially inviting. A 15min (uphill) walk from town and 10min from the *rodoviária*. R$5 discount with HI card. Dorms R$35

JK Largo Dom João 135 ☎ 38 3531 8715, ⓔ hotel_jk @yahoo.com.br. Set in an ugly 1960s building opposite the *rodoviária*, this could be Minas's biggest bargain, with basic but serviceable rooms, friendly staff and breakfast included. Two more basic-ish options lie on the same street. Dorms R$24, doubles R$50

Pousada dos Cristais Rua Jogo da Bola 53 ☎ 38 3531 2897, ⓦ pousadadoscristais.com.br. Lovely pousada with well-decorated spacious rooms, a pleasant patio and pool, with commanding views of the surrounding landscape. Good breakfast included. R$100

EATING AND DRINKING

There's a decent variety of budget options around the town centre, most serving *comida mineira*. Bars around Rua da Quintanda such as *Café A Baiúca* have tables spilling onto the square – perfect to watch life go by as you sip a *chopp*.

AROUND DIAMANTINA

The region surrounding Diamantina, both north to Bahia and southeastwards towards the coast, is rich in history and scenery as well as opportunities for off-the-beaten-track adventure. If you're not pressed for time, bus hopping village-to-village along the rocky ridge-filled terrain of the **Jequitinhonha Valley** is great for those seeking a true taste of the Brazilian interior – though you'll need to be prepared to rough it out in rickety vehicles and basic *dormitórios*. From Diamantina two buses daily depart for **Araçuaí**, five hours northwards and a staging post for the journey onwards to Bahia (see below). The town itself serves as a major marketplace for rural handicrafts and minerals, with tourmaline mined locally. You shouldn't have any trouble finding a bed in one of the town's few basic accommodations.

A more common journey from Diamantina, however, is to return to Belo Horizonte via **Serro** or the waterfall at **Conceição do Mato Dentro**. This creates a week-long circuit northwards from Belo Horizonte or Ouro Preto, stopping a couple of nights in each location. Serro itself is something like a *cidade histórica* without the tourists, and is a great place to relax and take in the atmosphere of small-town Minas founded on gold prospecting. Ninety kilometres from Diamantina, it's just two hours on the bus (5 daily; R$13), and features a number of colonial churches, decently priced crafts stalls, and low-key restaurants and pousadas. A further thirty-minute bus ride brings you to the historic church at **Conceição do Mato Dentro** village, as well as one of the tallest waterfalls in Brazil, the **Cachoeiro do Tabuleiro**. The *Tabuleiro Eco Hostel* (☎ 31 3231 7065, ⊛ www.tabuleiroecohostel.com.br) is the ideal place to stay and enjoy the stunning countryside, with well-organized facilities (camping R$25, dorm R$35, double R$140).

3

★ **Apocalypse** Praça Barão do Guaicuí 78. A popular and classy *por kilo* restaurant across from the market, worth a visit as much for the unintentionally hilarious English translation of the menu (baked namorado fish comes out as "boyfriend to the oven"), as for the genuinely good food: Italian and *comida mineira*, plus sublime desserts (expect to pay R$20). Daily 11am–3pm, Thurs–Sat also 7–11pm.

Grupiara Rua Campos Carvalho. As you walk through the lovely old doors that conjure up images of the town at its height, the garish green, white and orange painted walls come as a bit of a surprise. Good cheap food, though; *por kilo* for lunch and pastas at night. Tues–Sun 11am–late, Mon lunch only.

HS Alimentação Rua da Quitanda 57. The cheapest place in town for reasonably tasty *por kilo* food. Daily 7am–11pm.

Livraria Espaço B Beco da Tecla 31. Just off the cathedral square, this is the place for good coffee and cakes late into the evening, in sophisticated bookshop surroundings. Mon–Sat 8am–late, Sun 9am–2pm.

DIRECTORY

Banks and exchange All banks with international ATMs are located around the central squares.

Internet *Padaria Central*, Rua Joaquim Costa 34 (Mon–Sat 6am–9pm and Sun 6am–1pm), is a cyber-bakery behind the *Mercado Central*.

Post office Praça Monsenhor Neves 59A.

Bahia

Gateway to the Brazilian Northeast (see p.287) and, after Rio, the state drawing the most foreign visitors, **BAHIA** is a clear highlight of South America. The country Brazil began here in the historic capital of **Salvador**, a legacy reflected today in its colonial architecture, political conservatism, and the significant population of Brazilians with African heritage. The syncretism of the African with the European in Brazilian culture is reflected in all aspects of daily life here – but especially in the city's food, music and religion.

Roughly the size of France, Bahia comprises an extraordinary natural landscape, from 1000km of stunning coastline to the vast semi-arid *sertão* of the interior. Rising up at the state's heart, the wide valleys and table-mountains of the **Chapada Diamantina** provide some of the best trekking and climbing possibilities in the country – the perfect antidote to the resorts or laidback hideaways along the coast.

3

SALVADOR

Dramatically set at the mouth of the enormous bay of Todos os Santos, its old city atop a cliff, peninsular **SALVADOR** has an extraordinary energy. Its foundation in 1549 marked the beginning of Brazil's permanent occupation by the Portuguese. It wasn't an easy birth: before they were eventually subdued, the Caeté Indians killed and ate both the first governor and bishop. Then, in 1624, the Dutch destroyed the Portuguese fleet in the bay and took the town by storm, only to be forced out within a year by a joint Spanish and Portuguese fleet.

These days, there's a strange feeling to the old town – the number of tourist shops makes it feel a little like a Brazilian colonial Disneyland. This is Brazil, however, so the crowds of tourists also attract traders, anglers and hustlers who are bound to ensure a colourful stay.

If you tire of the city, go down to the pier and grab a boat for the choppy ride over to **Morro de São Paulo**, an island with beautiful beaches that's just two hours away.

WHAT TO SEE AND DO

Salvador is built around the craggy, 50m-high bluff that dominates the eastern side of the bay and splits the central area into upper and lower sections. The heart of the old city, **Cidade Alta** (upper city, or simply Centro), is strung along its top – this is the administrative, cultural and heavily touristed centre of the city where you'll find most of the bars, restaurants, hostels and pousadas. This cliff-top area is linked to the more earthy financial and commercial district, **Cidade Baixa** (lower city), by precipitous streets, a funicular railway and the towering Art Deco lift shaft of the **Carlos Lacerda elevator** (daily 24hr; R$0.50), the city's largest landmark. Stretching down the cliff and along the coast are beaches, forts and expensive hotels: **Barra** is a quieter neighbourhood where you will find more restaurants and pousadas.

Praça Municipal

Praça Municipal, Cidade Alta's main square overlooking Cidade Baixa, is the place to begin exploring. Dominating the *praça* is the **Palácio do Rio Branco** (Mon–Fri 9am–6pm; free), the old governor's palace, burnt down and rebuilt during the Dutch wars. Regal plaster eagles were added by nineteenth-century restorers, who turned a plain colonial mansion into an imposing palace. The fine interior is a blend of Rococo plasterwork, polished wooden floors, painted walls and ceilings. Inside is a museum, the **Memorial dos Governadores** (same hours; free), with colonial pieces, though it's less interesting than the building itself. Also facing the square is the **Câmara Municipal**, the seventeenth-century city hall.

In the northeastern corner of the square is the **Museu da Misericórdia**, dedicated to

---

IMPORTANT DATES IN SALVADOR

Lavagem do Bonfim (second Thurs in Jan). The washing of the church steps by *baianas* (local Bahian women) in traditional dress is followed by food, music and dancing.

Yemanjá (Feb 2). A celebration of *candomblé*, a popular Afro-Brazilian religious cult, with a procession and offerings to the sound of Afro-Brazilian music.

Carnaval (week preceding Lent). The largest street party in the world takes place in Salvador. There's an accepting atmosphere but it's worth bearing in mind that all-black *blocos* (street bands and groups) may be black culture groups who won't

appreciate being joined by non-black Brazilians, let alone gringos; be sensitive or ask before leaping in.

Festa de Santo Antônio (June 13). The main celebration of the patron saint of matrimony is held at Largo de Santo Antônio.

Dia de São João (June 24). The biggest holiday in Bahia outside Carnaval celebrates Saint John with *forró* (Northeastern Brazilian folk dance), straw hats and traditional food.

Independência da Bahia (July 2). Celebrating the expulsion of the Portuguese and the province's independence since the year 1823.

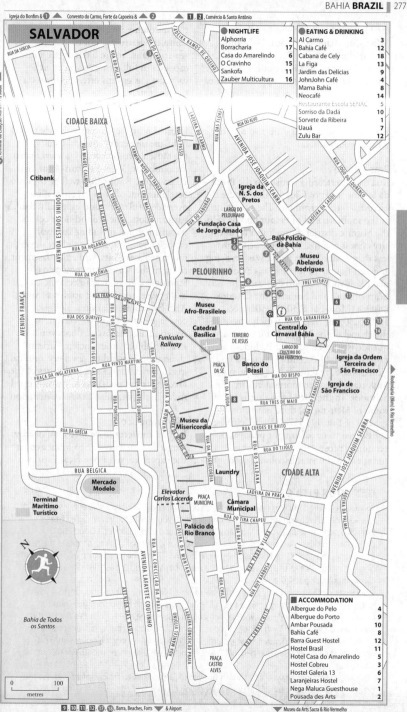

SALVADOR

● NIGHTLIFE

Alphorria	2
Borracharia	17
Casa do Amarelindo	6
O Cravinho	15
Sankofa	11
Zauber Multicultura	16

● EATING & DRINKING

Al Carmo	3
Bahia Café	12
Cabana de Cely	18
La Figa	13
Jardim das Delícias	9
JohnJohn Café	4
Mama Bahia	8
Neocafé	14
Restaurante Escola SENAC	5
Sorriso da Dadá	10
Sorvete da Ribeira	1
Uauá	7
Zulu Bar	12

CIDADE BAIXA

Citibank

Igreja da
N. S. dos
Pretos

LARGO DO
PELOURINHO

Fundação Casa
de Jorge Amado

Balé Folclóe
da Bahia

Museu
Abelardo
Rodrigues

PELOURINHO

Museu
Afro-Brasileiro

Catedral
Basílica

Funicular
Railway

TERREIRO
DE JESUS

Central do
Carnaval Bahia

@ ⓘ

PRAÇA
DA SÉ

Banco do
Brasil

LARGO DO
CRUZEIRO DO
SÃO FRANCISCO

Igreja da Ordem
Terceira de
São Francisco

Igreja de
São Francisco

Museu da
Misericordia

Laundry

CIDADE ALTA

Mercado
Modelo

Terminal
Maritimo
Turistico

Elevador
Carlos Lacerda

PRAÇA
MUNICIPAL

Câmara
Municipal

Palácio do
Rio Branco

Bahia de Todos
os Santos

PRAÇA
CASTRO
ALVES

0	100
metres	

■ ACCOMMODATION

Albergue do Pelo	4
Albergue do Porto	9
Ambar Pousada	10
Bahia Café	8
Barra Guest Hostel	12
Hostel Brasil	11
Hotel Casa do Amarelindo	5
Hostel Cobreu	3
Hostel Galeria 13	6
Laranjeiras Hostel	7
Nega Maluca Guesthouse	1
Pousada des Arts	2

the history of medicine in Brazil (Mon–Sat 10am–5pm, Sun 1–5.30pm; R$5, includes tour in Portuguese only). The main room of this seventeenth-century former hospital, the Salão Nobre, has 170 square metres of painted wood ceilings and walls covered with pretty Portuguese tiles. Magnificent views of the Baía de Todos os Santos are also on offer – bring your camera.

Praça da Sé

Rua da Misericórdia leads into the **Praça da Sé**, the heart of Cidade Alta, where the *executivo* buses terminate. The square lies at the southern end of **Pelourinho** or Pelô, the historic district, home to some of the city's finest colonial mansions, though less than twenty years ago it was decaying and run-down. To the north is a wide plaza known as **Terreiro de Jesus**, the very heart of Pelô, and home to the **Catedral Basílica** (Mon–Sat 8.30–11.30am & 1.30–5.30pm; R$2.50), which was once the chapel of the largest Jesuit seminary outside Rome. Its interior includes an exquisite panelled ceiling of carved and gilded wood, making it one of the most important Baroque monuments in Salvador. To the left of the altar is the tomb of **Mem de Sá**, third governor general of Brazil (1557–72), widely considered to have brought peace and economic prosperity to what was a turbulent and unstable colony – though this inevitably involved the almost complete destruction of the Caeté Amerindians. You're likely to see some capoeira in full swing as you exit the cathedral, as groups often perform on the front steps.

Museu Afro-Brasileiro

Located near the Cathedral in what used to be the university medical faculty, the **Museu Afro-Brasileiro** (ⓦwww.mafro .ceao.ufba.br; Mon–Fri 9am–4pm, Sat 10am–5pm; R$6) could well be the city's best museum, offering an enthralling overview of Brazil's (and especially Bahia's) African roots. The ground floor covers popular culture, including carnival, capoeira, religion, music and art through multimedia exhibits, while the basement contains the **Museu Arqueológico e Etnológico**, given over to ceramics, basketware, textiles and artefacts from Afro-Brazilian burial sites, alongside coverage of the Jesuit conversion of Amerindians. Across all floors you'll see striking objects from ancient African civilizations, including jewellery, musical instruments, masks and sculptures of the *orixás* (African gods), widely worshipped today in the Brazilian *candomblé* religion.

São Francisco

Behind the **Terreiro de Jesus**, on nearby Largo do Cruzeiro de São Francisco, are the superb carved stone facades of two

---

GET YOUR FITA ON

You'll see coloured ribbons reading *Lembrança do Senhor do Bonfim da Bahia* everywhere in Salvador, often with someone trying to give them to you as a "gift". They're called **fitas** (ribbons) and the phrase roughly means "Remembrance of Our Lord of a Good End". Originating in the early nineteenth century, these *fitas* were originally worn around the neck after miraculous cures. Traditionally they were silk and 47cm long (the length of the right arm of an altar statue of Jesus); nowadays they're made of nylon and act as talismans rather than giving thanks for past cures.

Superstitions surrounding *fitas* are many and varied. Everyone agrees, though, that you're not meant to buy your own (hence the "gift" pitch; you get one for yourself free, plus ten for your friends and family that you pay for) and that someone else is meant to tie it in three knots on your left wrist. Each knot gets you one wish. The catch? The wishes only come true when the *fita* breaks – naturally. If you purposefully break it, not only will your wishes go ungranted but you'll also have bad luck. Usually they break after three months or so, but they can last up to a year.

Some say *fitas* identify you as a tourist, but you're just as likely to be identified without the bracelet, and having bought one once at least you can fend off all the other vendors.

SALVADOR'S BEACHES

All of the beaches listed below can be reached by bus (heading to either "Vilas do Atlântico" or "Praias do Flamengo") from Praça da Sé.

Jardim de Alah Perfect for long walks thanks to the large and spacious sandy beach; also good for surfing.

Praia da Onda This beach in Ondina is good for surfing (although watch the rocks) and even fishing.

Praia de Aleuluia The perfect spot to grab some lunch at one of the many bars or restaurants along the beach. Good waves for surfing too.

Praia de Itapoã One of the most scenic beaches, mainly because of its tall, lilting palm trees.

Praia de Jaguanibe Strong winds make this a perfect spot to surf, windsurf and kite-surf.

Praia de Stella Maris Good for long walks as well as surfing.

Praia do Farol da Barra Windswept palms and thatched huts punctuate this small, rocky beach near the lighthouse.

Praia do Porto da Barra The closest swimming beach to historic Salvador is calm and narrow, and just a short bus ride away.

Aldeia Hippie In Arembepe, about 50km from Salvador, the long beach here was made famous by Mick Jagger and Janis Joplin in the 1960s. Though often crowded, there are still peaceful spots to be found, and many people come to take a dip in the Capivara River. Frequent buses from the *rodoviária*.

3

ornate Baroque buildings in a single, large complex dedicated to St Francis: the **Igreja de São Francisco** and the **Igreja da Ordem Terceira de São Francisco** (daily 8am–5pm). The latter was erected at the beginning of the eighteenth century as a display of wealth and power by Portuguese colonizers keen to demonstrate to the world their imperial might in the Americas. Over 100kg of gold was transported here and used to decorate the Baroque interior; the ornate walls display imperious paintings as well as *azulejos* (glazed coloured tiles).

Largo do Pelourinho

The beautiful, cobbled **Largo do Pelourinho**, down narrow Rua Alfredo de Brito, has changed little since the eighteenth century. Lined with solid colonial mansions, it's topped by the Asian-looking towers of the **Igreja da Nossa Senhora do Rosário dos Pretos** (daily 9am–6pm; free), built by and for slaves and still with a largely black congregation. Across from here is the **Fundação Casa de Jorge Amado** (Mon–Fri 9am–6pm, Sat 10am–5pm; free), a museum given over to the life and work of the hugely popular modern novelist, author of 25 works including the critically acclaimed *Captains of the Sands* and *Gabriela, Clove and Cinnamon*; the

displays here are devoted both to the author's life and the contrasting (and controversial) themes of his books, from social realism to sexual mores. You can have fun spotting his rich and famous friends in the collection of photographs.

Mercado Modelo

Cidade Baixa has few sights, but it is well worth the effort to get to the **Mercado Modelo** (Mon–Sat 9am–7pm, Sun 9am–4pm), which is full of Bahian handicrafts, trinkets and beachwear – great for gifts and souvenirs – though be prepared to haggle a little. You'll find it across the street from the bottom of the Lacerda elevator, behind a row of outdoor handicraft stalls.

Colonial forts

Above Pelourinho in Santo Antônio is the **Forte Santo Antônio Além do Carmo** (free), which is now home to several capoeira schools that have rechristened it **Forte da Capoeira**. There are terrific views of the city from inside the fort.

Another fort worth visiting is the **Forte de Santo Antônio da Barra**, past the beach at **Praia do Porto da Barra**, at the end of the peninsula. The site of South America's first lighthouse, it now houses the **Museu Náutico da Bahia** (Tues–Sun 8.30am–7pm, open daily in July; R$6). The sea views and the room of 25 ships-in-bottles by Manecha Brandão are worth the entrance fee alone, but you'll also find fascinating recovered archeological treasures from coastal shipwrecks.

Igreja do Bonfim

The **Igreja do Bonfim** (Tues–Sun 7am–6pm; free), located at the top of the peninsula of Itapagipe, is worshipped at by *Candomblistas* (followers of the Afro-Brazilian religion, *candomblé*) and Catholics alike, an intriguing hotchpotch of city dwellers from *favelados* to wealthy matriarchs and rural mestizos to naval officers. The annual Lavagem do Bonfim procession ends here, when priestesses wash the church's steps. The church houses the **Museu dos Ex-Votos do Senhor do Bonfim** (Tues–Sat 8am–noon & 1–5pm; R$2), lined with heart-wrenching photos of supplicants, written pleas for divine aid and thanks for wishes fulfilled. Hanging from the ceiling are a hundred body parts made of plastic and wood, offerings from the hopeful and the thankful. The church is a thirty-minute bus ride from the centre (take any marked "Bonfim" from the bottom of the Lacerda elevator in Praça da Sé).

ARRIVAL AND DEPARTURE

By plane Dep. Luís Eduardo Magalhães International Airport (☎71 3204 1010) is 23km northeast of the city, connected to the centre by a shuttle express bus service every 15min between 6am & 9pm (5–6am and 9–10pm plus weekends 5–9am, every 30min) to Praça da Sé (45min–1hr 30min depending on traffic, last bus at 10pm; R$6.50) via the beach districts and Campo Grande. A taxi to the centre will cost around R$80.

Destinations Daily flights to Miami, Buenos Aires, Lima, Madrid and Lisbon. Rio (8 daily; 3hr), São Paulo (10 daily; 4hr); other principal Brazilian cities 2–6 flights daily.

By bus The interstate Terminal Rodoviária Armando Viana de Castro, Av ACM 4362, Pituba (☎71 3616 8300), is 8km east of the centre. To get to/from the Cidade Alta an *executivo* bus runs between the Iguatemi shopping centre (across the busy road from the *rodoviária*) and Praça da Sé. The bus costs R$3.20 and makes stately progress via the beach districts of Pituba and Rio Vermelho. Alternatively, take a taxi (about R$25). Useful bus companies are Águia Branca (☎71 4004 1010); Linha Verde (☎71 3450 0321); Real Expresso (☎71 3450 9310).

Destinations Rio (3 daily; 27hr); São Paulo (2 daily; 33hr); Recife (3 daily; 12hr); Belo Horizonte (2 daily; 24hr); Fortaleza (2 daily; 21hr).

By boat Numerous launch services depart from the Terminal Turístico Maritimo, the blue building at the water's edge behind the Mercado Modelo. Popular destinations include the island of Itaparica, visible directly across the bay from Salvador, and Morro de São Paulo (see p.285) on Tinharé.

CRIME AND SAFETY

Salvador is a gritty city that leaves most visitors buzzing with excitement but others feeling that they're perennially being observed by shady characters. Though the latter sentiment can be distinctly counterproductive, as with most large Brazilian cities Salvador does have significant problems with **robberies** and **muggings**. Nonetheless, taking a few **precautions** such as not wandering down poorly lit side streets, leaving valuables in hostel safes, keeping cameras hidden from view or avoiding carrying bags altogether, all certainly help to limit the risks. If you are unlucky enough to be held up, give the assailant exactly what they're asking for. Don't hesitate to take taxis at night, for example getting back to Barra from the Pelourinho if you're unsure about bus times/routes.

The buildings of the tourist-heavy Pelourinho have video cameras perched on them and the area is heavily policed (see p.284) until late at night. That said, stick to the main streets between the squares and on the way up to Santo Antônio Fort – certain parts of the district attract petty thieves and drug addicts for the rich pickings on offer should a less-streetwise visitor stray off the beaten track. The most you're likely to encounter is an attempt by a **pickpocket**, especially on Tuesday evenings when Terça do Bençâo celebrations bring everyone into the district. Remember also that Sunday is the day for the beach; save for the most visited sights the Pelourinho is deserted – as are city buses (the *executivo* bus is a safer Sunday option).

Moving between the Cidade Alta and Cidade Baixa can also be a problem after dark: don't use the Lacerda elevator and avoid walking up and down the winding connecting roads. Give the Avenida do Contorno – the seafront road that runs north from the harbour – a miss too; it can be dangerous even in daylight, so if you want to come to a restaurant here, take a taxi.

INFORMATION AND TOURS

Tourist information The main office of the state tourist agency, Bahiatursa (ⓦwww.bahiatursa.ba.gov.br), is in Pelourinho at Rua das Laranjeiras 12 (daily 8.30am–9pm; ⓣ71 3321 2133). There are also branches at the airport (daily 7.30am–11pm; ⓣ71 3204 1444) and at the *rodoviária* (daily 7.30am–9pm; ⓣ71 3450 3871). Another source of information is the tourist hotline, "Disque Turismo" – call ⓣ71 3103 3103 and you should find an English-speaker at the other end.

Tour operators Salvador Bus (ⓣ71 3356 6425, ⓦsalvadorbus.com.br) operate double-decker buses for various city-tours, with tickets available at hotels and travel agencies; Visão Turismo at the airport (ⓣ71 3204 1300, ⓦvisaotur.com.br) and at Rua Miguel Calmon 506, Comércio (ⓣ71 3319 0800), can help you book budget flights. The Student Travel Bureau (ⓦstb.com.br) is represented locally by Ceu e Mar Turismo, Rua Fonte do Boi 12, Rio Vermelho (ⓣ71 3334 7566), and are helpful for cultural exchanges, language schools, and student travel services.

GETTING AROUND

By bus The bus system is efficient, cheap (R$2.60) and easy to use, running till 11pm on weekdays and 10pm on weekends. To reach the centre, any bus with "Sé", "C. Grande" or "Lapa" on the route card will do. Buses with route card "Flamengo" leave from Praça da Sé passing Barra, and stopping off at all the beaches to the north – the last stop is Ipitanga. Air-conditioned "frescão" buses run most of the same routes, though less frequently (usually R$5.50).

By taxi Taxis are metered and plentiful and are recommended at night, even for short distances within the Cidade Alta. The trip between Pelô and Barra costs around R$30. Chame-Taxi ⓣ71 3241 2266; Elitte Taxi ⓣ71 4009 3000.

ACCOMMODATION

The best area to head for is Cidade Alta, not least because of the spectacular view across the island-studded bay. The exception is if you want to be near the beach, in which case Barra offers great value for money and a good choice of hostels. While pousada prices generally stay within reason, be aware that during Carnaval rates double or even triple. Out of season discounts are nearly always on offer, so make sure you ask for one ("tem desconta?").

PELOURINHO

Pelourinho lies in the heart of the city, and is the perfect spot to base yourself if you want to be at the very centre of the action.

Albergue do Pelo Rua do Passo 5 ⓣ71 3242 8061, ⓦalberguedopelo.com.br. Poky, spartan dorms but management is friendly and the price is pretty reasonable given the central location. Dorms R$25

Hotel Casa do Amarelindo Rua das Portas do Carmo 6, Pelourinho ⓣ71 3266 8550, ⓦcasadoamarelindo.com. Step into a little oasis in the heart of Pelo, with terracotta floors, tropical plants and sculptures of orixas (gods) dotted around the tranquil reception area. It's worth the splurge for the lovely rooms, which have comfy beds and flat-screen TVs, as well as DVD and CD players. There's a small rooftop pool, and a panoramic terrace from which you can soak up the views of the Baía de Todos os Santos. R$398

★ Pousada des Arts Rua Direita de Santo Antônio 90 ⓣ71 3012 5964, ⓦpousadadesarts.com.br. Set in a stunning four-storey colonial mansion dating from 1740, this more upmarket pousada has palatial rooms, some with excellent views of the Santo Antônio Church. *Berimbaus* (percussion instruments) decorate the walls on the ground floor while upstairs local wooden furniture gives the place a warm, cosy touch. Good discounts in low season. R$280

★ Bahia Café Praça da Sé 22 ⓣ71 3322 1266, ⓦbahiacafehotel.com. Rustic doors open onto pleasantly colourful rooms, all of which are en suite. The wooden interiors and side lamps made by local artist Marta give the place a warm and personal touch. Room 8, with views onto the Praça, is the best. R$165

Hostel Galeria 13 Rua da Ordem Terceira 23 ⓣ71 3266 5609, ⓦhostelgaleria13.com. Have an afternoon dip in the pool or unwind in the dimly lit Moroccan chill-out room before heading out on the town at this English-owned hostel with comfy wooden bunks. The two dogs, Spartan and Zulu, pad around the premises keeping you company, and owner Paul is always more than happy to point you in the right direction. Breakfast served until noon. Dorms R$35

Laranjeiras Hostel Rua da Ordem Terceira 13 ⓣ71 3321 1366, ⓦlaranjeirashostel.com.br. Always booked-up HI hostel with long thin dorms that have unbelievably high top bunks. The crêperie in the lobby and mezzanine chill-out area are great for mingling, while the long windows offer the perfect vantage point for people-watching in the colourful cobbled streets below. Dorms R$34, doubles R$96

SANTO ANTÔNIO

Only a 10min walk from Pelourinho, this quiet residential neighbourhood offers a bit of tranquillity and respite from Pelô's hustle and bustle.

Hostel Cobreu Ladeira do Carmo 22 ☎71 3117 1401, ⓦhostelcobreu.com. A steep staircase leads you up to colourful dorms with polished parquet floors. The corridors are decorated with vibrant graffiti by a renowned local artist, as is the little communal chill-out area, which has nice views over town. Dorms R$26, doubles R$65

★ **Nega Maluca Guesthouse** Rua dos Marchantes 15 ☎71 3242 9249, ⓦnegamaluca.com. This Israeli-owned hostel has windy, narrow corridors. Dorms all have deposit boxes for valuables, as well as sockets and lamps above each bed. There's a rooftop terrace with hammocks overlooking the upper part of Salvador, as well as a chill-out area at the back. Dorms R$27, doubles R$75

BARRA AND THE BEACHES

With the beach on your doorstep Barra is the place to stay if you want a mix of ocean calm and party-hostel vibes.

Albergue do Porto Rua Barão de Sergy 197, Barra ☎71 3264 6600, ⓦalberguedoporto.com.br. Comfy hostel with a relaxed vibe, good-sized dorms and hammocks slung in between the rooms. There's also a pool table, PlayStation, big TV and a good selection of films in the living room, as well as a kitchen and a supermarket just next door. Free internet and discount for HI members. Dorms R$38, doubles R$120

Ambar Pousada Rua Afonso Celso 485, Barra ☎71 3264 6956, ⓦambarpousada.com.br. The breakfast room has slightly dreary tablecloths and an old-fashioned feel but the rooms are clean and some open onto the inner courtyard. Staff are helpful and Barra beach is just a 10min walk away. Dorms R$40, doubles R$117

Barra Guest Hostel Rua Recife 234, Barra ☎71 8774 6667, ⓦbarraguesthostel.com. Set in a colonial house, this comfy hostel has clean dorms with lockers and personal reading lamps. There's also cheap European grub, a free *caipirinha* every night at 7pm, as well as weekly barbecue nights and surfboard hire. Free wi-fi. Dorms R$40, doubles R$75

Hostel Brasil Rua Recife 4, Barra ☎71 3264 9637, ⓦhostelbrasil.com.br. Fun and welcoming hostel, 10min from Barra Beach. The spacious dorms all have individual lockers and there's a chill-out area with colourful beanbags that are perfect to sink into after a long day's surfing. Laundry and internet facilities available, and they can also help with travel arrangements. Dorms R$36, doubles R$100

EATING AND DRINKING

Eating out is a pleasure in Salvador. There's a huge range of restaurants and the local cuisine (see box below) is deservedly famous all over Brazil. Street food is fabulous too and readily available all over town, with plenty of vendors selling all sorts of local delicacies (try in Rio Vermelho district where you'll find *acarajé* on every street corner). While Pelourinho has a growing number of stylish, expensive places, it's still relatively easy to eat well for under R$25.

RESTAURANTS

BARRA

Cabana de Cely Av Marquês de Leão, at Rua D. Marcos Teixeira ☎71 3035 0514. A hugely popular seafood restaurant a block from the beach. On Sundays lunch drags on all day, with ample *cachaça*. Try the *caranguejo* (crab) starter or the great *picanha acebolada* (steak with onions; R$42 for two). Tues–Sat 11am–midnight, Sun 11am–6pm.

PELOURINHO

La Figa Rua das Laranjeiras 17 ☎71 3322 0066. Italian-owned trattoria named after a Brazilian good-luck charm. The red and white tablecloths decorating the cobbled street are ideal for eating delicious *spaghetti all'aragosta* (lobster; R$36), while its sister pizzeria (closed Mon) on the same block is renowned for its *pizza alla pescatore* (pizza with fish; R$34). Daily 11am–midnight; closed Sun dinner and Mon lunch.

Jardim das Delícias Rua Maciel de Cima 12 ☎71 3321 1449. A hidden tranquil world within the Pelourinho, this courtyard restaurant offers high-quality ingredients that are definitely worth splashing out for. Try the *badejo Jardim das Delícias* (white fish marinated with herbs and served with plantain) for R$48. Daily 11am–11pm.

COMIDA BAIANA

The secret to Bahian cooking is twofold: a rich seafood base, and traditional West African **ingredients** such as palm oil, nuts, coconut and hot peppers. Many ingredients and dishes have African names: most famous of all is *vatapá*, a bright yellow porridge of palm oil, coconut, shrimp and garlic, which looks vaguely unappetizing but is delicious. Other dishes to look out for are *moqueca*, seafood cooked in the inevitable palm-oil-based sauce; *caruru*, with many of the same ingredients as *vatapá* but with the addition of loads of okra; and *acarajé*, a deep-fried bean cake stuffed with *vatapá*, salad and (optional) hot pepper. Bahian cuisine also has good **desserts**, which are less stickily sweet than elsewhere: *quindim* is a delicious coconut cake, flavoured with vanilla, often with a prune in the centre. Street *baianas*, women in traditional white dress, serve *quindim*, *vatapá*, slabs of maize pudding wrapped in banana leaves, fried bananas dusted with icing sugar, and fried sticks of sweet batter covered with sugar and cinnamon – all gorgeous.

Mama Bahia Rua das Portas do Carmo 21 ☎71 3322 4397. An enjoyable corner restaurant that's good for a bottle of cheap wine and some Bahian standards; choose your dishes carefully and you'll get a feast for just R$30. Daily 11am–10pm.

★ **Neocafé** Rua Santa Isabel 9A ☎71 3321 0849. A funky place with a good vibe serving good-value dishes such as *ostras gratinadas* (oysters au gratin; R$18) and pork chop with mango chutney (R$20). North African lamps and local photography decorate the rooms. Set menu (R$30) at weekends, including tasty Indian and Italian favourites. Tues–Sun noon–late.

★ **Restaurante Escola SENAC** Praça José de Alencar 13/19 ☎71 3324 4553. The municipal restaurant school, set in a restored mansion, may look expensive from outside but it's actually good value – the set-price buffet (R$34) includes forty Bahian dishes and twelve desserts. Mon–Sat 11.30am–3.30pm & 6.30–10pm; Sun 11.30am–3.30pm.

Sorriso da Dadá Rua Frei Vicente 5 ☎71 3321 9642. You certainly won't get much of a *sorriso* (smile) here, but locals still rave about the famous Bahian cuisine on offer here, though you get less for your money than a few years ago. Classic dishes for two will set you back around R$70. Daily 11.30am–midnight.

Uauá Rua Gregório de Matos 36 ☎71 3321 3089. A smarter option with interior decor evocative of the mud huts of northern Brazil. There are plenty of seafood dishes (stewed shrimp and fish in coconut and palm oil R$49 for two) on the menu, alongside meat dishes. Mon–Sat 11am–11pm.

Zulu Bar Rua das Laranjeiras 15 ☎71 8784 3172. Come here if you're craving cheap comfort food or veggie options, including curries and fish and chips. It's lively in the evenings and the high wooden chairs are the perfect spot to enjoy a drink overlooking the street. Try their unique fruity *zumorangi caipirinha* (R$8.50). Daily 11am–2am.

CAFÉS AND ICE CREAM

Al Carmo Rua do Carmo 42, Santo Antônio ☎71 3242 0283. In this tranquil place it's easy to imagine a Portuguese colonialist puffing on a cigar a few centuries ago. Great coffee (R$3.50) away from the heat and bustle of Salvador's streets. There's also an Italian restaurant with a terrace to the rear. Daily 11.30am–1.30am.

Bahia Café Praça da Sé 20, Pelourinho ☎71 3322 1266. Sandwiches, soups and salads (R$8–20) alongside superb coffee (R$3) at this chilled-out internet café in a hotel bang in the centre of town. Drink a bargain *caipirinha* here, too, for R$6. Mon–Sat 10am–10pm, Sun 11am–10pm.

JohnJohn Café Av Estados Unidos 397, Comércio ☎71 3327 0102, ⓦjohnjohncafe.com.br. Bright café with mouth-watering cakes; perfect for a snack as you head

to the nearby Mercado Modelo. Delicious dishes on offer, too, such as lamb burgers (R$18) or quiche (R$6). Mon–Fri 8am–8pm.

★ **Sorvete da Ribeira** Praça General Osório, 87, Ribeira (Cidade Baixa) ⓦsorveteriadaribeira.com.br. Open since 1931, this ice-cream parlour offers numerous flavours including local fruity ones such as tamarind, tapioca, *umbu* and *jenipapo*. Eat your ice cream while watching the fishermen organize their haul in the evenings. Daily 9am–10pm.

NIGHTLIFE

Make sure you're in town on a Tuesday night for Salvador's biggest party, with bands playing Afro-Brazilian music and locals and tourists alike dancing in the streets. The best district for bar hopping and numerous artsy options is Rio Vermelho.

Alphorria Rua Direita de Santo Antônio 97. The restaurant serves good *petiscos* and Brazilian favourites, while later on there is dancing to a *forró*, Latin and Afro soundtrack. *Alphorria* (meaning "liberation") offers reasonably priced drinks and a garden to the rear. 6.30pm–late, closed Wed. R$10 cover if not eating.

Borracharia Rua Conselheiro Pedro Luís 101-A, Rio Vermelho. Make your way through scattered piles of tyres as you enter this club-cum-tyre workshop in Salvador's bohemian district. The music changes depending on the night, but the musical flavours of choice tend to be samba-rock, MPB, soul and hip-hop. Fri & Sat 11pm–late. Entry R$20.

Casa do Amarelindo Rua das Portas do Carmo 6, Pelourinho. Smart, intimate hotel bar with a leafy indoor area serving superb *maracujá caipirinhas* (R$11). Wind your way up the spiral staircase to the terrace, where there's a small pool and lovely views across the bay. Daily 4–11.30pm.

O Cravinho Terreiro de Jesus 5, Pelourinho ⓦwww .ocravinho.com.br. *The* place to kick the night off with a few drinks before heading to *Fundo do Cravinho* at the back to try some frenetic salsa (cover R$4). The speciality here is *cravinhos*, flavoured *cachaça* shots with root infusions (just R$2). Daily 11am–11pm.

★ **Sankofa** Rua Frei Vicente 7, Pelourinho ☎71 3321 7236, ⓦsankofabrasil.com. The hippest African bar and club in town and a true local hangout. Spread over two storeys; the ground floor has live bands as well as DJs spinning anything from reggae to samba-rock and Afro-pop. A more chilled-out area upstairs has a tiny smoking terrace awaits upstairs. Entry R$10. Mon & Wed 7–11.30pm, Tues, Fri & Sat 9pm–3am.

Zauber Multicultura Ladeira da Misericordia 11, Comércio ☎71 3326 2964. Tricky to find but worth it once you get there, this club attracts an alternative crowd. As you cross the small (and very high) bridge, you hear the reggae and samba before you see the large dancefloor;

3

CAPOEIRA

The Brazilian martial art **capoeira** is widely considered to originate from ritual fights in Angola to gain the nuptial rights of young women, though in Brazil it developed into a technique of anticolonial resistance, disguised from slave masters as a dance. Although outlawed for much of the nineteenth century, capoeira is now practised across the country, a graceful, semi-balletic art form somewhere between fighting and dancing. Usually accompanied by the characteristic rhythmic twang of the *berimbau* (single-string percussion instrument), it takes the form of a pair of dancers/fighters leaping and whirling in stylized "combat" – which, with younger *capoeiristas*, occasionally slips into a genuine fight when one fails to evade a blow and tempers fly. There are regular displays on Terreiro de Jesus and near the entrances to the Mercado Modelo in Cidade Baixa, largely for the benefit of tourists and their financial contributions, but still interesting. The best capoeira, though, can be found in the *academias de capoeira*, organized schools with classes you can watch for free. If you want a really cool capoeira experience, leave the Pelourinho and head up to the Forte Santo Antônio, just a short walk up the hill. Inside the renovated white fort are several schools where the setting may make you feel more like a Shaolin monk in training.

CAPOEIRA SCHOOLS

Academia de João Pequeno de Pastinha Largo Santo Antônio, Forte Santo Antônio ☎ 71 3323 0708, ⓦ joao-pequeno.com. You can watch, or if you want to join in, there are classes (Mon, Wed & Fri, 9am, 7.30pm; 2–3hr).

Associação de Capoeira Mestre Bimba Rua das Laranjeiras 1, Pelourinho ☎ 71 3322 0639, ⓦ capoeiramestrebimba.com.br. Probably the most famous *academia*, it sometimes has classes open to tourists.

Forte de Santo Antônio Praça Barão do Triunfo, Largo de Santo Antônio ☎ 71 3117 1488, ⓔ fortesanto antonio@gmail.com. Classes open to tourists.

upstairs is a chill-out loft. Thurs–Sat 10pm–late. R$10; free entry for women before 11pm. Take a taxi as the area's a bit dodgy.

ENTERTAINMENT

A lovely weekly event worth heading to is the jazz concert at MAM, Av Contorno (Museum of Modern Art; ☎ 71 3117 6139; Sat 6–10pm, entry before 9pm; R$5), near the marina in the Cidade Baixa.

Balé Folclórico da Bahia Rua Gregório de Matos 49, Pelourinho ☎ 71 33221962, ⓦ balefolcloricodabahia.com .br. Frantic drumming as radiant dancers in colourful dresses spin around tapping their feet and moving their bodies to Afro-Brazilian music. Performances are on Mon, Wed, Thurs, Fri, Sat at 8pm. Make sure you buy tickets in advance from the box office.

SHOPPING

Instituto de Artesanato Visconde de Mauá Rua Gregório de Matos 27, Pelourinho ⓦ www.maua.ba .gov.br. This place was founded by the government to promote regional artists. You'll find carving, ceramics and hammocks at fixed prices, among other handicrafts. Mon–Fri 10am–6pm.

Mercado Modelo Praça Visconde de Cayru 250. Handicraft market in Cidade Baixa. Mon–Sat 6am–1pm.

Shopping Barra Av Centenário 2992. Large mall that's handy for the Barra beaches. Mon–Sat 9am–10pm, Sun food hall only noon–9pm.

DIRECTORY

Banks and exchange Banks with ATMs are found throughout the city. There's the Confidence Câmbio and Banco do Brasil at the international airport and a Citibank in town on Av Estados Unidos 558, Comércio. There is also a Banco do Brasil on the Terreiro de Jesus square in Pelourinho.

Embassies and Consulates UK, Av Estados Unidos 18B, 8th Floor, Comercio ☎ 71 3243 7399; US, Av Tancredo Neves 1632, Room 1401, Salvador Trade Center, Torre Sul, Caminho das Árvores ☎ 71 3113 2090.

Hospitals Hospital Aliança, Av Juracy Magalhães Jr. 2096, Rio Vermelho (☎ 71 2108 5600); Hospital São Rafael, Av São Rafael 2152, São Marcos (☎ 71 3281 6111).

Internet Bahia Café, Praça da Sé 20 (R$3/hr); Internet do F@rol, Av Sete de Setembro 42, Barra (R$3/hr).

Laundries O Casal at Av Sete de Setembro 3564, Barra (☎ 71 3264 9320); Wash & Dry, Ladeira da Praça 4, Pelourinho (☎ 71 3321 0821).

Left luggage Malubag at the airport (☎ 71 3204 1150; 24hr) has small/large lockers for R$8/10 per day.

Pharmacies Farmácia Sant'ana, Largo Porto da Barra, Barra (☎ 71 3267 8970); Drogaleve, Praça da Sé 6, Pelourinho (☎ 71 3322 6921).

Police The tourist police, DELTUR, are at Praça José de Anchieta 14, Cruzeiro de São Francisco, Pelourinho ☎ 71 3116 6817, ☎ 71 3116 6512.

Post office Largo do Cruzeiro de São Francisco 20, Pelourinho (Mon–Fri 9am–5pm, Sat 9am–1pm).

MORRO DE SÃO PAULO

Still relatively peaceful and undeveloped, the village of **MORRO DE SÃO PAULO** on the island of **Tinharé**, about 75km southwest of Salvador, represents an ideal place to escape frenetic Salvador. Morro has a great atmosphere, with plenty of surfing and diving as well as reggae bars and beach parties that last till the early hours. It's popular among locals and tourists alike, who come here to catch some rays on the pristine beaches and swim the island's clear waters. With no roads (wheelbarrows are used to transport things along the sandy paths), there's a slow and friendly pace of life here, though at the weekends (especially December through March) vast crowds descend.

WHAT TO SEE AND DO

There are four main beaches in Morro (known simply as **First**, **Second**, **Third** and **Fourth beaches**), with the first being the closest (and therefore most popular) to the village centre and the fourth being the furthest away (and thus quietest). Accommodation and restaurant prices increase the further you move towards the Fourth Beach. A good idea is to settle for the Second Beach given its close location to the town centre and party atmosphere.

On arrival, expect to be besieged by tenacious locals offering to be your "guide" – shake them off relatively easily by heading straight to the Tirolesa Zipline (daily 10am–5.30pm), a 70m-high and 350m-long zip-wire that will whizz you down to the First Beach in no time. The 25-second ride from the top of the hill is a great way to check out Morro's beaches from above as well as have a little adrenaline kick before relaxing into the laidback vibe. To get to the zip-line, head along the coastal path up the hill, past the pousadas and the health clinic, and make your way to the back of the lighthouse by the fort. Of course, you can just as easily, if less dramatically, walk to the beach in five minutes from the pier.

ARRIVAL AND INFORMATION

You can reach Tinharé by air or sea. It's obviously much quicker to fly, but it's also far more expensive. At the dock you may have to pay a R$12 Taxa de Turismo, though this is currently in dispute in the courts and may be rescinded.

By plane Aero Star (☎71 3377 4406, ⊚www.aerostar .com.br) and Adey Táxi Aéreo (☎71 3204 1993) fly 2–3 times daily to and from the island from Salvador (around R$300 one-way).

By boat Catamarans to Tinharé depart 3 times daily (9am, 1.30pm and 2pm, returning 9am, 11.30am and 3pm) from Salvador's Terminal Turístico Marítimo (☎71 9195 6744, ☎71 3319 4570), the blue building at the water's edge behind the Mercado Modelo; tickets cost R$75 (Mon–Sat) or R$90 (Sun and holidays) each way – buy tickets at least 30min in advance.

Tourist information The tourist information office, SIT (☎75 3652 1083, ⊚morrosp.com.br), is close to the dock, at the very start of the main path that leads to First Beach. Staff here are friendly, speak some English and can give excellent advice about food and lodging. A good website for the history of the island and information about pousadas, restaurants and nightlife is ⊚morrodesaopaulo .com.br.

ACCOMMODATION

There is plenty of affordable accommodation on First and Second beaches – for R$40 to R$60 you can find a room on the seafront, with a hammock where you can listen to the waves crash all night.

Hostel Morro de São Paulo Rua da Fonte Grande, a 5min walk from the pier and First Beach ☎75 3652 1521, ☎75 9962 1287, ⊚hosteldomorro.com.br. HI hostel with simple but clean dorms and doubles in a leafy, verdant setting. There's a communal kitchen and laundry facilities. Dorms R$48, doubles R$120

Pousada Aradhia Third Beach ☎75 3652 1341, ☎75 8139 6257, ⊚pousadaaradhia.net. Quiet rooms giving onto a small tropical garden, all with a little veranda with hammocks. The pool's the place to mingle with other travellers. R$150

ISLAND ACTIVITIES

You can enjoy all sorts of activities in Morro, from waterskiing and wake-boarding to capoeira and yoga lessons.

Diving enthusiasts or anyone wishing to learn scuba can contact Companhia do Mergulho on First Beach (☎75 3652 1200). They operate day and night dives in fast boats to clear-water areas around the island. **Horseriding** along the beach can be organized by calling ☎75 3652 1070 or 1056. **Surfing** instruction is offered by Morro Surf School (☎75 8836 4042).

3

3

Pousada Estrela do Mar Second Beach ☎ 75 3652 1784, ☎ 75 8805 8554. Spotless, albeit slightly poky, rooms (with a/c and en suite) at this relaxed pousada with a communal terrace with hammocks overlooking Second Beach. You may well catch a glimpse of semi-resident monkey Chico who tends to swing around the premises. `R$60`

EATING AND DRINKING

There are plenty of cheap restaurants lining First and Second beaches – you'll find everything from crêpes and sushi to pizza, fruit, sandwiches and Bahian specialities.

Chez Max Third Beach ☎ 75 3652 1754. This welcoming Italian restaurant has plenty of daily specials to tickle your tastebuds, as well as wood-oven pizzas (from R$22).

Jamaica Second Beach ☎ 75 3652 1669. Bob Marley murals cover the walls of this Bahian *churrascaria* (steak house; R$28), which serves some good-quality meat, grilled right before your eyes.

Mar dos Corais Praça Aureliano Lima 100, town centre ☎ 75 3652 1091. A 10min walk from First Beach, this is the perfect place at any time of day but particularly for breakfast: coffees, fresh juices, as well as all sorts of delectable sweetmeats (R$5–15) and fruit salads (R$3). Daily noon–11pm.

NIGHTLIFE

Clubs, bars, beach and full moon parties – there's always something going on in Morro and you won't need much help in finding it. Second Beach is the place to start (and often end) the evening, with dozens of *caipirinha* vendors and bars playing beats catering to all musical tastes – dancing on the beach goes on until the small hours. To get to the clubs listed below, follow the path through the town centre and head up the hill.

Pulsar Disco Caminho do Forte, ⓦ pulsardisco.com.br. Surrounded by thick vegetation, this three-storey club located on the side of a hill hosts themed nights, from foam parties with house music DJs to "back to the 80s" nights. Tues & Sat only from 11pm. R$30.

Toca do Morcego Caminho do Farol ⓦ tocadomorro .com. Friday night is legendary at this club a 5min walk from the centre. Soak in the sea view as you sip on unbelievably potent *caipirinhas* and groove to dance tunes until the early morning. Tues–Sun. Cover R$35.

THE CHAPADA DIAMANTINA

One of Brazil's most exciting locations for hiking, climbing and rural sightseeing, the **PARQUE NACIONAL DA CHAPADA DIAMANTINA** offers 38,000 square kilometres of awe-inspiring table mountains, jagged rocky peaks and wide-open canyons interspersed with gigantic waterfalls, rivers, scrubland and forest. The region is essentially a natural gateway between the semi-desertified Bahian *sertão* and the vast rocky Brazilian Planalto Central to the south and west. Once here, most visitors undertake a three- or six-day organized trek (guide essential), staying in local houses along the way with meals included. The experience is like no other in Brazil: you gain a glimpse of the slow *sertanejo* pace of life and rural northeastern hospitality while taking in stunning scenery. The challenge of a long hike is not for everyone but guides tailor trips to your ability and fitness. It's advised to come here in the cooler months between April and October – though conversely the region's waterfalls are at their most spectacular in rainy (and high) season, from December to March.

Though the sizeable and attractive ex-diamond-mining town of **Lençóis** provides the most obvious access to the northern half of the park – and offers consummate facilities – most independent/budget travellers choose to go directly on to the community of **Vale do Capão** within the park boundaries itself. Long a bohemian hangout, young people from Salvador come to Capão in numbers to relax by the river, hike, canoe and climb. In recent years smarter pousadas have opened here, adding a new level of alternative-chic with meditation, massage and saunas, and drawing a broader age group.

WHAT TO SEE AND DO

There is almost endless potential for hikes in the national park. Some of the most famous or accessible locations are not too far from Capão or Lençóis and can be visited on day or multi-day excursions. The (guided) hike between the two communities is usually undertaken over three days, though its most famous sight – Brazil's highest waterfall, the Cachoeira da Fumaça (sometimes called the Cachoeira Glass) – can be visited on a circular hike from either location. Here, a stream descends 400m over a cliff face, vaporizing into a fine mist before it reaches the bottom. Jagged overhanging rocks provide dizzying viewing points. Hiking to the base of the waterfall is a somewhat more difficult trek than that of reaching the top, however, and in high season the caves that serve as overnight sleeping spots (camping gear provided or pre-arranged by guides) can get overrun with visitors.

Another famous spot is the **Morro do Pai Inácio**, a 1000m peak with fabulous views over the cactus-strewn tablelands, while the **Gruta do Lapão**, a kilometre-long cathedral of gorge and canyon formed from layered sandstone, lies just 5km north of Lençóis. Further afield, you may wish to follow the trails of the Vale do Patí to spectacular swim-spots like Poço Encantado or marshy Marimbus, great for kayaking.

ARRIVAL AND DEPARTURE

By bus 3 buses run between Salvador and Lençóis each day (6hr; R$70; ⊛realexpresso.com.br), each continuing on to Palmeiras (45min). From there, collective taxis are available for the bumpy 7km ride to/from Capão (30min; R$10).
By plane Azul (⊛voeazul.com.br) flies between Salvador and Aeroporto Coronel Horácio de Matos (☎75 3625 8100; R$100; 1hr), 20km from Lençóis, each Thurs and Sun. Taxis ply the route into town (20min; R$30), with passengers often sharing vehicles.

INFORMATION AND TOURS

Guides are most often arranged by pousadas themselves, but you can arrange your own (see below). Three-day treks cost around R$800 including accommodation, breakfast and a basic but tasty evening meal (stock up on your own food for lunch).
Associação dos Conductores de Visitantes, in Capão (☎75 3344 1087, ⊜acv@valedocapão.com) or Lençóis (Rua 10 de Novembro 22 ☎75 3344 1425).

ACCOMMODATION

Numerous pousadas are located in Lençóis and more are scattered throughout Vale do Capão. Book as far in advance as possible. Capão also offers a few basic restaurants, including a great pizzeria.
Hostel Chapada Rua Boa Vista 121, Lençóis ☎75 3334 1497, ⊛hostelchapada.com.br. Attractive and brightly painted HI hostel in the middle of town. Basic breakfast served and free wi-fi. Dorms R$35, doubles R$85
Pousada Safira Rua Miguel Calmon 124, Lençóis ☎75 3334 1443, ⊛pousadasafira.com. Best-value budget pousada in Lençóis – super-friendly and all rooms have their own bathroom. R$80

★ **Pousada Tatu Feliz** Vale do Capão ☎75 3344 1124, ⊛infochapada.com/pousadatatufeliz.htm. Friendly multilingual service, free wi-fi and an excellent breakfast make this new-ish pousada a really good bet for exploring the park. Dorms (minimum of 3 people required) R$35, doubles R$95
Pousada Verde Vale do Capão ☎75 3344 1083, ⊛pousada verde.com. A large pousada with a good variety of rooms, all featuring TV and fan. Decent breakfast included. R$50, doubles R$90

Northeast

THE NORTHEAST (Nordeste) of Brazil covers an immense area and features a variety of climates and scenery, from dense equatorial forests to palm-fringed beaches. It comprises all or part of the nine states of Maranhão, Piauí, Ceará, Rio Grande do Norte, Paraíba, Pernambuco, Alagoas, Sergipe and the important tourist centre of Bahia (see p.275). Taken together, these form roughly a fifth of Brazil's land area and have a combined population of 36 million.

Notorious for its poverty within Brazil, the region has been described as the largest concentration of poor people in the Americas. Yet it's also one of the most rewarding areas of Brazil to visit, with a special identity and culture nurtured by fierce regional loyalties. The Northeast has the largest concentration of Brazilians of African descent, most of whom live on or near the coast, mainly around Salvador (see p.276) and Recife. In the *sertão* (the semi-arid region inland), though, Portuguese and Amerindian influences predominate in popular culture and racial ancestry. The region also offers more than two thousand kilometres of practically unbroken tropical beaches with white sands, blue sea and palm trees.

NORTHEAST CLIMATE

The rains come to Maranhão in February, in Piauí and Ceará in March, and points east in April, lasting about three months. That said, Maranhão can be wet even in the dry season, and Salvador's skies are liable to give you a soaking any time of year.

3

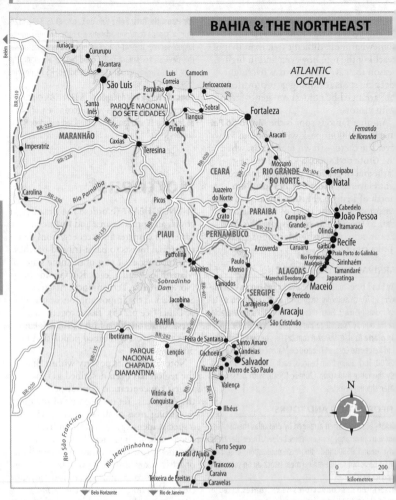

BAHIA & THE NORTHEAST

RECIFE

RECIFE, the Northeast's second-largest city and capital of Pernambuco, appears rather dull at first, but it's lent a colonial grace and elegance by **Olinda** (see p.295), 6km to the north and considered part of the same conurbation. Recife's colonial centre, known as Recife Antigo, is surprisingly pleasant, with a few quiet squares where an inordinate number of impressive churches lie cheek by jowl with the less appealing urban sprawl of the past thirty years. North of the centre are some pleasant leafy suburbs, dotted with museums and parks, and to the

south is the modern beachside district of **Boa Viagem**.

WHAT TO SEE AND DO

Modern Recife sprawls over the mainland, but the heart of the old city, and the epicentre of its nightlife, is **Recife Antigo**, an island connected to its colonial neighbour, Santo Antônio, and to the beach district of Boa Viagem to the south, by numerous bridges over the rivers Beberibe and Capibaribe. While Santo Antônio is home to most of Recife's historic buildings, a number of the city's most fascinating sights are, unhelpfully, located in outlying suburbs. The heart of the modern city, Boa Vista, is your best bet for cheap accommodation and eats.

Recife Antigo

While there's not that much in the way of conventional attractions, the once run-down district of **RECIFE ANTIGO** now has a thriving nightlife scene and is also a pleasant place during the day to walk around. One of the few sites is the **Sinagoga Kahal Zur Israel**, Rua do Bom Jesus 197 (Tues–Fri 9am–4.30pm, Sun 2–5.30pm; R$5; ☏81 3224 2128), built in 1637 when Recife was under Dutch occupation and said to be the first synagogue in the whole of the Americas. When the rather less tolerant Portuguese resumed control of the city in 1654, 23 hardy members of the congregation sailed north to form the first Jewish community in New Amsterdam, soon to become New York.

At the pier south of the synagogue you can hire a rowing boat (R$5 one-way) to take you across the water to a little reef housing the curious **Parque de Esculturas de Francisco Brennand**, where you can see a series of rather phallic statues by renowned local artist Brennand (see p.291).

Praça da República

The broad **Avenida Dantas Barreto** forms the spine of the central island of **Santo Antônio**, and ends in the fine **Praça da República**, lined with majestic palms and home to the governor's palace as well as Recife's most ornate theatre. The centre's narrow, crowded streets make a pleasant contrast to some of the financial district's towering skyscrapers.

Convento Franciscano de Santo Antônio

Perhaps the most enticing of the central buildings on Santo Antônio is the seventeenth-century Franciscan complex known as the **Convento Franciscano de Santo Antônio**, on Rua do Imperador (Mon–Fri 8–11.30am & 2–5pm, Sat 8–11.30am; R$3; ☏81 3224 0530), a combination of church, convent and museum. Built around a beautiful,

small cloister, the museum (Museo Franciscano de Arte Sacra) has some strange but delicately painted statues of saints and other artwork rescued from demolished or crumbling local churches. Santo Antônio's highlight – and Recife's Baroque masterpiece – is the **Capela Dourada** (Golden Chapel). Finished in 1697, the Rococo chapel's jacaranda-carved interior is finished in gold leaf, while its crowning glory is the series of ceiling panels by **Manuel de Jesus Pinto**, an *alforriado*, or freed slave, whose work graces many of the city's finest religious buildings.

Pátio de São Pedro and around

Just off the Avenida Dantas Barreto, the impressive **Concatedral de São Pedro dos Clérigos** (Mon–Fri 8am–noon & 2–4pm; free) stands on the graceful Pátio de São Pedro. Inside there's some exquisite woodcarving and a trompe l'oeil ceiling by Manuel de Jesus Pinto (see above). The colonial buildings that line the square have been beautifully preserved, and in the evenings you can soak up the view over a beer at one of the many bars that set up tables outside. Recife is probably the best big Brazilian city in which to find **artesanato** (crafts), and the area around São Pedro is the place to look for it. Browse the stalls lining the square's adjacent winding streets, or head west to the T-shaped Casa de Cultura, a former prison turned crafts gallery, located on Rua Floriano Peixoto (Mon–Fri 9am–7pm, Sat 9am–6pm, Sun 9am–2pm; ☏81 3224 4017, ⊚casadaculturape.com.br).

Once you've stocked up on souvenirs, head to the **Forte das Cinco Pontas**, off the southwestern end of Avenida Dantas Barreto. Currently housing the **Museu da Cidade do Recife** (Tues–Fri 9am–5pm; free; ☏81 3355 3108), it was originally built in 1630 by the Dutch, the last place they surrendered upon expulsion in 1654. Though the fort is worth visiting for its splendid sea views alone, the museum offers a window onto the city's myriad past lives with an exhaustive collection of old photos, maps and antiques.

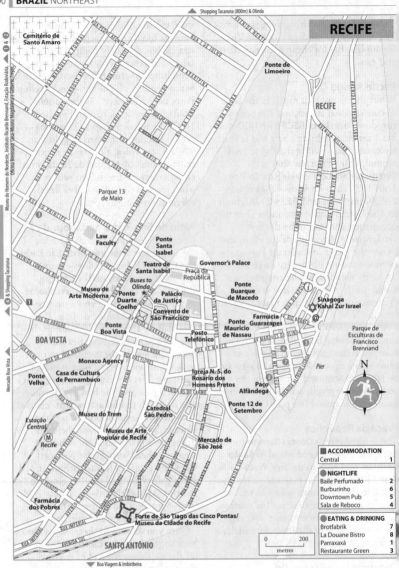

Shopping Tacaruna (800m) & Olinda

RECIFE

RECIFE

ACCOMMODATION	
Central	1

NIGHTLIFE	
Baile Perfumado	2
Burburinho	6
Downtown Pub	5
Sala de Reboco	4

EATING & DRINKING	
Brotfabrik	7
La Douane Bistro	8
Parraxaxá	1
Restaurante Green	3

Boa Viagem & Imbiribeira

Museu do Homem do Nordeste

Though it's a fair distance from Boa Vista (where you catch the bus from), it's worth making the trip to the fascinating **Museu do Homem do Nordeste** in Casa Forte at Avenida 17 de Agosto 2187 (Tues–Fri 8.30am–5pm, Sat & Sun 1–5pm; R$4; ☏81 3224 4017). Founded by Brazilian anthropologist Gilberto Freyre (see opposite) in 1979, the museum depicts everyday life and folk culture with more than twelve thousand exhibits ranging from carriages used by seventeenth-century sugar barons to present-day northeastern carnival costumes. To get here, take the "Dois Irmões – Via Barbosa" bus from the post office or from Parque 13 de Maio, at the bottom of Rua do Hospício in Boa Vista, a pleasant thirty-minute drive through leafy northern suburbs. The museum is on the left, but hard to spot, so ask the driver or conductor where to get off.

Casa-Museu Magdalena e Gilberto Freyre

Anyone with even a passing interest in anthropology, or Brazil's cultural identity, shouldn't miss the chance to root around in the sugar-pink nineteenth-century mansion of Gilberto Freyre, whose 1933 book, *The Masters and the Slaves*, remains one of the most iconic texts ever written on the country. Located a shortish taxi ride away from the Museo do Homem do Nordeste (or via bus #522 or #930 from Av Agamenon Magalhães), at Rua Dois Irmãos 320, Apipucos (Mon–Fri 9am–5pm, R$10; ☎81 3441 1733, ⓦwww.fgf.org.br), the interior is stuffed with his collection of over forty thousand books and all manner of fascinating ethnic antiques and curios.

Instituto Ricardo Brennand

One of Recife's most incongruous attractions is the **Instituto Ricardo Brennand** on Alameda Antônio Brennand in the outlying suburb of Várzea (Tues–Sun 1–5pm; R$15; ☎81 2121 0352, ⓦinstitutoricardobrennand.org.br). This mock-Tudor castle belongs to one of the sons of the city's renowned Brennand family, and is home to an impressive collection of Pernambucan landscapes by Dutch-born painter Frans Post, as well as Greco-Roman mythological figures, suits of armour and a collection of Swiss-army knives with more functions than you can count. To get here, catch bus #040 on Avenida Domingos Ferreira (in Boa

Viagem) or Avenida Agamenon Magalhães (bordering Boa Vista) and take it to the end of the line. Continue on foot to the end of the road, and turn right onto Rua Isaac Buril. The institute is at the end of this road on the left.

Oficina Brennand

A short walk south of the Instituto, on Propriedade Santos Cosme e Damião, you'll find the studio of the Brennand clan's most famous scion, sculptor Francisco. A renovated ceramics factory-cum-Brazilian Parque Güell, Oficina Brennand (Mon–Thurs 8am–5pm, Fri 8am–4pm; R$10; ☎81 3271 2466, ⓦbrennand.com.br) functions as both the artist's workshop and shop window, where you can buy pieces direct.

Boa Viagem

Regular buses make it easy to get down to the district of **BOA VIAGEM** and the beach, an enormous skyscraper-lined arc of sand that constitutes the longest stretch of urbanized seafront in Brazil. Recife, too, was once studded with beaches, but they were swallowed up by industrial development, leaving only Boa Viagem within the city's limits.

The narrow **beach** is packed at weekends and deserted during the week, with warm natural rock pools to wallow in just offshore when the tide is out. Pavilions punctuate the pavement along the noisy road, selling all sorts of refreshing drinks from coconut water to pre-mixed *batidas* (rum cocktails). There have been a small number of shark attacks over the years, but they usually involve surfers far offshore.

CRIME AND SAFETY

Recife and Olinda have a bad reputation throughout Brazil. Everyone has a story about how they were followed, harassed, mugged or intimidated. It's enough to send even seasoned travellers rushing back to their hostels at sundown for fear of turning into flak-jacket-wearing Cinderellas.

While it's true that crime rates are high, if you take the usual **precautions** you should stay safe: be discreet, don't wear fancy watches and jewellery, know where you're going, travel with a friend, take taxis or public transport at night, stick to populated, well-lit areas and be wary of open, free drinks. When withdrawing money, it's best (and safest) to use an ATM in a shopping centre or airport. **CIATUR**, the Tourist Police, patrol areas of the city that tourists normally visit, like Olinda; in Recife call ☎81 3322 4867 (24hr), in Olinda ☎81 3181 1717 (24hr).

3

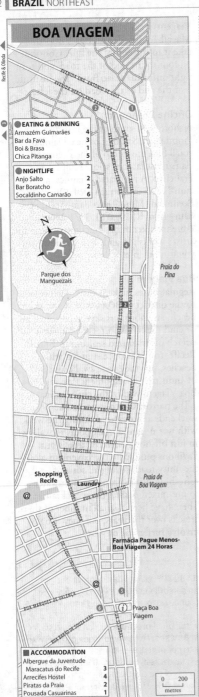

Recife & Olinda

BOA VIAGEM

AVENIDA ENG. ANTÔNIO DE GÓES

AVENIDA HERCÍLIO BANDEIRA

■ EATING & DRINKING
Armazém Guimarães	4
Bar da Fava	3
Boi & Brasa	1
Chica Pitanga	5

■ NIGHTLIFE
Anjo Salto	2
Bar Boratcho	2
Socaldinho Camarão	6

RUA TOMÉ GIBSON

N

Parque dos
Manguezais

Praia do
Pina

RUA PROF. JOSÉ BRANDÃO
RUA PE. BERNARDINO PESSOA
RUA DONA MARIA CAROLINA
RUA ANTÔNIO FALCÃO
RUA MAMANGUAPE
RUA FÉLIX DE BRITO MELO
RUA JAUSTINO
RUA PE CARAPUÇIHO

Shopping
Recife   Praia de
Laundry   Boa Viagem

RUA RIBEIRO DE BRITO

Farmácia Pague Menos-
Boa Viagem 24 Horas

RUA MARQUES DE VALENÇA

(i) Praça Boa
Viagem

RUA BARÃO DE SOUZA LEÃO

■ ACCOMMODATION
Albergue da Juventude	
Maracatus do Recife	3
Arrecifes Hostel	4
Piratas da Praia	2
Pousada Casuarinas	1

0   200
metres

Piedade & 4

ARRIVAL AND DEPARTURE

By plane Recife's modern Aeroporto Internacional dos Guararapes (☎ 81 3322 4353, �🌐 infraero.gov.br) is only 11km from the city centre, at the far end of Boa Viagem; TAM and Gol connect it with the rest of the country.

From the airport You can buy a fixed-price voucher for an airport taxi from the COOPSETA desk at arrivals (☎ 81 3462 1584; ten percent discount for ISIC members). Taxis to Boa Viagem cost R$17, to Santo Antônio R$40 and to Olinda R$63 (R$29, R$48 and R$70 respectively after 10pm). For Boa Viagem hotels, take either the a/c bus #042 from outside the airport (every 20min, 5am–11.55pm; R$2.60), or bus #040 (every 20min, 5am–11.55pm; R$2.15) from nearby Praça Ministro Salgado Filho. For Boa Vista, take bus #163 (every 20min, 5am–11pm; R$2.15) from the same Praça; it terminates on Av Conde da Boa Vista, near *Hotel Central* (see p.293). Another option if you're staying in Boa Vista is to take the overland train, the Metrô (5am–11pm; R$1.60; �🌐 metrorec.com.br) from the airport to the Estação Central terminal ("Recife"), and take a taxi (R$10–15) from there. For Olinda, take bus #040 or #042 to Praça de Boa Viagem, and change for bus #910 (every 20–40min, 4am–9.30pm; R$3.25) to Praça do Carmo, just by Olinda's main post office. Alternatively, take the Metrô to Estação Central and either bus #983 or #993 from there.

Destinations Fortaleza (11–12 daily; 1hr 15min–1hr 30min); Rio (26–32 daily; 5hr 20min–7hr 50min); Salvador (7–10 daily; 1hr 10min–1hr 20min); São Paulo (11–15 daily; 3hr–3hr 30min).

By bus The *rodoviária* or Terminal Integrado de Passageiros (TIP) is about 14km from the centre of town at Rodovia 232, Km15, Coqueiral (☎ 81 3452 1103). From here the Metrô (R$1.60) whisks you through various *favelas* to Estação Central. For Boa Viagem, take any of the buses from Rua Cais de Santa Rita (see below). For Olinda take #983 from nearby Rua do Sol to Praça do Carmo. Alternatively, a taxi from outside Estação Central should cost around R$30 for the 15min journey.

Destinations Guanabara (⌐⍾ expressoguanabara.com.br) serves Fortaleza; Penha (⌐⍾ vendas.nspenha.com.br) serves Salvador; and São Geraldo (⌐⍾ saogeraldo.com.br) serves Rio and São Paulo. Fortaleza (3 daily; 12hr); Rio (2 daily; 38hr); São Paulo (1 daily; 42hr); Salvador (1 daily; 12hr).

GETTING AROUND

By bus Most city buses originate and terminate on the central island of Santo Antônio, on Rua Cais de Santa Rita. They range in price from R$2.15 to R$3.25. To get from the city centre to Boa Viagem, take either bus #042, #039, #032 or #071. For up-to-date timetables see ⌐⍾ www.granderecife.pe.gov.br.

By taxi The bus system is so thorough and comparatively cheap that it rarely makes sense to take a taxi. Though they're metered and straightforward to use, the cost can add up, and it's best to agree a rough price with the driver before you set off; count on paying at least R$10 for even the shortest journey.

INFORMATION AND TOURS

Tourist information The state tourist board (SETUR) runs several information posts, some of which have good English-speakers – most have useful, free maps and event calendars: the most friendly and helpful office is at the airport (24hr; 📞 81 3182 8299), where they can also reserve hotels. There are branches at the *rodoviária* (daily 8am–8.30pm; 📞 81 3182 8298), in Recife Antigo at Rua da Guia (daily 8.30am–9pm; 📞 81 3355 3402) and at Praça de Boa Viagem (8am–8pm; 📞 81 3182 8297). For online info, try the comprehensive 🌐 recife.info, though it's often longer on superlatives than detail.

Tour operators Martur, Rua Dr Nilo Dornelas Câmara 90, Loja 02, Boa Viagem (📞 81 3312 3666, 🌐 martur.com.br), organize flights, cruises and trips to Fernando de Noronha. There's also an office at the airport (📞 81 3213 1404).

ACCOMMODATION

By far the cheapest place to stay is Boa Vista, midway between Boa Viagem, Santo Antônio and Recife Antigo, though most of the city's hotels and hostels are located in Boa Viagem. If you don't mind staying in a soulless high-rise, the beach may compensate for the steep prices. Olinda (see p.295) is also expensive, if offset by the charm of its colonial conversions. As ever, if you want to visit during Carnaval, you'll need to book months in advance.

BOA VISTA

⭐ **Central** Av Manoel Borba 209, Boa Vista 📞 81 3222 2353. The celebrity guests – Carmen Miranda and Orson Welles among them – may have long gone, but this handsomely decaying old hotel still has many of its original features including window shutters, stone steps and cage lift, with a lovely, slightly eccentric staff to match. While the en suites have a/c, the clean, spartan *coletivo* (shared toilet) rooms are probably the best bargain in the city. Ten percent discount if you book two nights or more. Breakfast included. R$60

BOA VIAGEM

Albergue da Juventude Maracatus do Recife Rua Maria Carolina 185 📞 81 3326 1221. Bare but clean and functional tiled dorms, some with leafy views, in a secure setting with friendly staff. A bed sheet costs R$2 extra, towels R$3, and there's no breakfast. Dorms R$30

Arrecifes Hostel Rua João Cardoso Ayres 560 📞 81 3462 5867, 🌐 arrecifeshostel.com.br. One of Boa Viagem's newest hostels, this HI-affiliated place is perfectly pitched between the airport and the beach. The tiled rooms are basic but spotless, with a choice of a/c or fan, and there's

also a kitchen, paved patio with hammocks, a pool table and wi-fi. Breakfast included. Dorms R$50, doubles R$110

Piratas da Praia Av Cons Aguiar 2034 (3rd floor), at Rua Prf. Osias Ribeiro 📞 81 3326 1281, 🌐 piratasdapraia.com. Neat pastel dorms with primary-coloured portraiture and a choice of fan or a/c. Lockers available, discount for HI members, and wi-fi. Also some rooms and small apartments. Breakfast included. Dorms R$40, doubles R$140, apartments R$150

Pousada Casuarinas Rua Antônio Pedro Figueiredo 151 📞 81 3325 4708, 🌐 pousadacasuarinas.com.br. Grab a book and lie back in one of the hammocks in the leafy outdoor area or have a dip in the pool. The pastel yellow rooms have tiled floors, tiny lamps and wooden motifs, and some have an outdoor veranda. Laundry and wi-fi. Single rates are available. Breakfast included. R$195

EATING AND DRINKING

RECIFE ANTIGO, BOA VISTA AND THE SUBURBS

Brotfabrik Rua da Moeda 87, Recife Antigo 📞 81 3424 2250, 🌐 brotfabrik.com.br. Bakery specializing in German rye bread but also selling excellent coffee, *salgados* (R$2), pastries, sandwiches (R$6.70) and bite-sized pizzas (R$6.40), as the constant queue attests. The perfect spot to grab a quick bite as you tour the city. Mon–Fri 7am–8pm.

Parraxaxá Rua Igarassu 40, Casa Forte 📞 81 3463 7874, 🌐 parraxaxa.com.br. A little piece of the desert trans-planted to the city, this celebrated *por quilo* place is themed around the talismanic *sertão* bandit, Lampião, with *cantina*-style tables and chairs, and a daily buffet bulging under the weight of backcountry specialities such as *paçoca*, sun-dried beef and all manner of deliciously stodgy puddings. Prices are per 100g: R$4.29 on weekdays, R$4.49 at weekends. A perfect lunch stop after the nearby Museu do Homem do Nordeste (see p.290). Daily 11.30am–11pm.

⭐ TREAT YOURSELF

La Douane Bistro Paço de Alfândega 35, Recife Antigo 📞 81 3224 5799, 🌐 ladouane .com.br. Located in a shopping centre (see p.295), but don't let this put you off, as the historic building is a beautifully renovated customs house. Waiting staff are immaculately turned out and the food is Mediterranean in flavour with a Brazilian bent – if you're feeling flush, splash out on the *bacalhau gratinado* with garlic purée (R$100); if not, go for the veggie pasta with artichoke and palm heart (R$35.70). Mon–Fri 10am–10pm, Sat noon–10pm, Sun noon–5.30pm.

3

Restaurante Green Rua Gervásio Pires 577, Boa Vista ☎ 81 3221 3531. The food at this friendly neighbourhood *por quilo* joint isn't going to set the world alight but it's cheap (R$18), healthy and largely vegetarian (usually including decent veggie *feijão*), with some chicken and fish options as well. Mon–Fri 11am–3pm.

BOA VIAGEM

Armazém Guimarães Rua Baltazar Pereira 100 ☎ 81 3325 4011, ⓦ armazemguimaraes.com.br. With its Maceió sister branch regularly picking up top awards, this is the place for authentic wood-fired pizza in Recife. What the barn-like interior lacks in romance, the food makes up in quality, with prices in the R$30–40 range. Mon–Thurs 6pm–midnight, Fri & Sat 6pm–1am, Sun 5pm–midnight.

Bar da Fava Rua Padre Oliveira Rolin 37A, Jardim Beira Rio, Pina ☎ 81 3463 8998, ⓦ bardafava.com.br. Renowned for its exquisitely prepared *favas* (broad beans) that accompany virtually every meal, *Bar da Fava* is one of the most consistently popular restaurants in Recife. Most dishes are priced for 2–3 people, though they do an *executivo individual* with *charque* and *feijão verde* for R$18.90, and the grilled cheese starter (R$9) is heavenly. Best take a taxi as it's difficult to locate. Mon 11am–5pm, Tues–Sat 11am–midnight, Sun 11am–6pm.

Boi & Brasa Av Boa Viagem 97, Pina ☎ 81 3466 6334, ⓦ boiebrasa.com.br. Hulking beachfront mega-buffet with a splendid spread that includes mussels and sushi along with all-you-can-eat quality *churrascaria* for R$34.90 (R$29.90 at night). Pricier on Sun (R$44.90). Mon–Thurs noon–4pm & 6.30–11pm, Fri–Sun noon–midnight.

Chica Pitanga Rua Petrolina 19 ☎ 81 3465 2224, ⓦ chicapitanga.com.br. Long one of the most sought-after *por quilo* places in Recife, with a bright, stylish interior and tables that you'll likely have to wait patiently to snag. At R$45.90 (R$50.90 at weekends), it isn't cheap but you get what you pay for, with a dazzling buffet heavy on seafood and always in flux. Mon–Fri 11.30am–3.30pm & 6–10pm, Sat & Sun 11.30am–4.30pm & 6–10pm.

NIGHTLIFE

Recife lives and breathes live music. While Carnaval throbs to *frevo*, *afoxê* and *maracatu*, they've long been hybridized into the city's most famous musical export, *manguebeat*, a style that continues to exert a huge influence on acts you can either see for free, in the Pátio São Pedro (see p.289), or on the big stage at Marco Zero (Recife's official and spiritual central point, marking the spot where the city was founded) or, for a modest fee, in the bars and clubs of Recife Antigo, where tables spill onto the street into the small hours and there's always something going on. Look out, especially, for performances by Orquestra Contem-porânea de Olinda, perhaps the most promising of the area's *manguebeat* inheritors. For upcoming shows see ⓦ acontecenorecife.com.br and ⓦ reciferock.com.br.

RECIFE ANTIGO AND SUBURBS

Baile Perfumado Rua Carlos Gomes 390 ☎ 81 3414 1241, ⓦ baileperfumado.com.br. Recife's newest live music venue, with a capacity of 3,500 and an already impressive list of rock/pop performances including Céu, Arnoldo Antunes and Alceu Valença, as well as local heroes Otto and Mundo Livre S/A and touring foreigners such as Franz Ferdinand. Tickets are usually in the region of R$50. Located well out in the suburbs, so take a taxi.

Burburinho Rua Tomazina 106, Recife Antigo ☎ 81 3224 5854, ⓦ barburburinho.com.br. Long *the* venue in Recife to hear local music in a sweaty nightclub setting, much of it in a tribute vein, this place puts on everything from the new generation of local artists influenced by the 90s *manguebeat* explosion, to homages as diverse as The Cure and Creedence Clearwater Revival. Cover usually R$15. Hours vary, though most shows start at 10pm.

Downtown Pub Rua Vigário Tenório 105, Recife Antigo ☎ 81 3424 6317, ⓦ downtownpub.com.br. Though this place – recently given a swanky makeover and definitely more of a club than a pub – lays it on thick with the Anglophone rock and tribute nights, you can sometimes land lucky with decent live reggae. Good old Latin sexism rules on the cover charge, with men having to cough up R$35, women R$25. Thurs–Sat 10.30pm–5am.

Sala de Reboco Rua Gregório Júnior 264, Cordeiro 264 ☎ 81 3228 7052, ⓦ saladereboco.com.br. If you're really keen to pick up some authentic *forró pé-de-serra nordestino* (Northeastern Brazilian folk dance) skills, then it's worth your while heading out to the suburbs (bus #040 if you're not taking a taxi; ask the driver where to get off) to one of the country's best *casas de forró*, drawing a loyal and passionate crowd as well as some of Brazil's best *forrozeiros*. Thurs–Sat 10pm–late.

BOA VIAGEM

Anjo Solto Galeria Joana D'arc, Av Herculano Bandeira 513, Pina ☎ 81 3325 0862, ⓦ anjosolto.com.br. Sequestered at the back of a tiny boutique gallery (poorly signed and difficult to locate – ask your taxi driver), this stylish, gay-friendly crêperie-cum-bar makes for a mellow start to the evening, with quality wine by the glass starting at R$4.80. The crêpe menu is exhaustive, with many named after customers; try the enigmatic Aimée e Jaguar Ferchado, a feast of buffalo mozzarella and sun-dried tomatoes (R$17.90). Mon– Thurs & Sun 5.30pm–late, Sat & Sun 6pm–late.

Bar Boratcho Galeria Joana D'arc, Av Herculano Bandeira 513, Pina ☎ 81 3327 1168, ⓦ boratcho.com.br. Across a patio from *Anjo Solto*, and with its name practically inviting a good drinking and dancing session, this cool fairy-lit shack is one of the best places in town to hear quality DJs, both local and international, with a recent set from Britain's very own Quantick aka Will Holland. They also do Mexican food, should you need something to soak up all the tequila. Mon–Thurs 7pm–1am, Fri & Sat 7pm–2.30am, Sun 7pm–midnight.

Socaldinho Camarão Av Visconde de Jequitinhonha 106 ☎ 81 3462 9500. If you fancy some footie action, head here and join the locals for a beer over a gripping game of Brazilian *futebol* as you munch on some *peixe à móda* (R$34.95 for three people). Mon–Thurs 11.30am–1.30am, Fri & Sat 11.30am–2am.

SHOPPING

Mercado de São José Rua São José, Santo Antônio. Stock up on some local crafts, or simply peruse the stacks of curious herbal medicines and everyday items as locals go about their daily shopping. Mon–Sat 6am–6pm, Sun 6am–noon.

Shopping Paço Alfândega Rua Alfândega 35, Recife Island ⓦ pacoalfandega.com.br. Chic, refurbished former customs building on Recife Island, housing the typical range of Brazilian chain stores and fast-food outlets as well as the swanky *La Douane Bistro* (see p.293). Mon–Sat 10am–10pm, Sun noon–9pm.

Shopping Recife Rua Pe. Carapuceiro 777, Boa Viagem ⓦ shoppingrecife.com.br. Suburban shopping mall, one of Brazil's largest. Mon–Sat 10am–10pm, Sun noon–9pm.

DIRECTORY

Banks and exchange There are plenty of banks with ATMs in Boa Viagem and Recife including HSBC, though it's safer to use an ATM in one of the shopping centres.

Consulates UK, Av Agamenon Magalhães 4775, 8th floor (☎ 81 2127 0200); US, Rua Gonçalves Maia 163, Boa Vista (☎ 81 3416 3050).

Hospital Real Hospital Português de Beneficência, Av Agamenon Magalhães 4760, Boa Vista (☎ 81 3416 1122).

Internet Caravela's Cyber Café, Rua do Bom Jesus 183, Recife Antigo (daily 8am–6pm; R$3/hr); Espaço Net, Rua Visconde de Jequitinonha, Boa Viagem (Mon–Sat 7am–7.30pm; R$3/hr).

Laundries Aqua Clean Lavanderia, Av Eng Domingos Ferreira 4023, Boa Viagem (☎ 81 3466 0858).

Pharmacies Farmácia Pague Menos, Av Cons Aguiar 4635, Boa Viagem, 24hrs (☎ 81 3301 4209).

Post office Av Guararapes 61, Santo Antônio (Mon–Fri 9am–5pm; ☎ 81 3425 3644).

OLINDA

Designated a UNESCO World Heritage Site, **OLINDA** is, quite simply, one of Brazil's most impressive examples of colonial architecture: a maze of cobbled streets, hills crowned with brilliant white churches, pastel-coloured houses, Baroque fountains and graceful squares. Founded in 1535, the old city is spread across several small hills looking back towards Recife. Besides this historic centre, the city is renowned for its street **Carnaval**, which attracts visitors from all over the country, as well as sizeable contingents from Europe.

Despite its size, Olinda can effectively be considered a neighbourhood of Recife: a high proportion of its residents commute to the city so **transport links** are good, with buses leaving every few minutes.

WHAT TO SEE AND DO

Olinda's colonial highlights include more churches than you could wish to see in an afternoon, and a curious puppet museum. Much of the appeal lies in wandering through the picturesque streets.

Alto da Sé

Olinda's hills are steep, so don't try to do too much too quickly. A good spot to have a drink and plan your attack is the **Alto da Sé**, the highest square in town, not least because of the stunning view of Recife's skyscrapers shimmering in the distance, framed in the foreground by Olinda's church towers, gardens and palm trees. There's always an arts and crafts **market** here during the day, which is busiest in the late afternoon; though there's plenty of good stuff, there's little here you can't get cheaper in Recife or the interior.

The **Igreja da Sé** (daily 8am–5pm; free), on the *praça*, is bland and austere inside – more of a museum than a living church – but is worth a look if only to see the eighteenth-century sedan chair and large wooden sculptures in the small room at the northeast wing. It's also notable for being at the highest point in the region's landscape, making it visible from all the other churches for miles around. The viewing patio at the back right-hand side of the church offers a particularly beautiful view of the city.

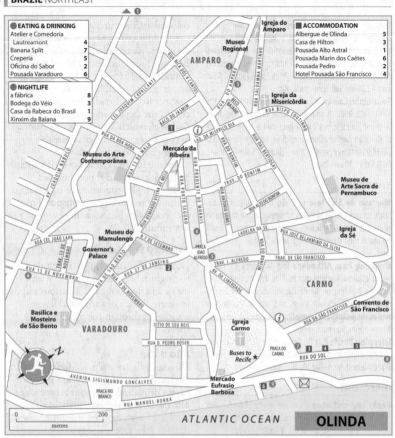

EATING & DRINKING

Atelier e Comedoria Lautreamont	4
Banana Split	7
Creperia	5
Oficina do Sabor	2
Pousada Varadouro	6

NIGHTLIFE

a fábrica	8
Bodega do Véio	3
Casa da Rabeca do Brasil	1
Xinxim da Baiana	9

ACCOMMODATION

Albergue de Olinda	5
Casa de Hilton	3
Pousada Alto Astral	1
Pousada Marin dos Caétes	6
Pousada Pedro	2
Hotel Pousada São Francisco	4

OLINDA

Convento de São Francisco

Olinda is home to eighteen **churches** seemingly tucked away around every corner. The Dutch burned most of them down in the seventeenth century, and left the Portuguese to restore them during the following centuries. If you only have time to visit one, head to the impressive Convento de São Francisco on Rua São Francisco (Mon–Fri 8am–noon & 2–5pm, Sat 8am–noon; R\$3; ☎81 3429 0517), the country's oldest Franciscan convent. It was built in 1585 and is comprised of a chapel, church, cloister and sacristy. Particular highlights are the tiled cloister depicting the lives of Jesus and St Francis of Assisi, and the sacristy's beautiful Baroque furniture carved from jacaranda wood. Behind the convent there's a patio with grand panoramas across the ocean.

Museu do Mamulengo

The fascinating **Museu do Mamulengo**, Rua de São Bento 344 (Tues–Sun 10am–5pm; R\$2; ☎81 3493 2753), houses an excellent collection of more than one thousand traditional puppets, some dating as far back as the eighteenth century, with the upper floor dedicated to *sertão* bandit-cum-folk hero, Lampião. Folk puppets, with diverse outfits and exaggerated faces, played – and still play – an important role in religious festivities and street gatherings, including the famed Carnaval. As well as being an irrepressible guide, curator Enio Mariz de Oliveira is a veritable fount of expert knowledge on all things cultural, Pernambucan and Brazilian, from literature to music to film.

ARRIVAL AND INFORMATION

By bus From Recife, take bus #983 or #993 from Rua do Sol to Praça do Carmo, just by Olinda's main post office and a 2min walk up into the old city. From Boa Viagem, take bus #910.

Tourist information The main tourist office is on Av Da Liberdade (daily 8am–6pm; ☎81 3305 1060, ⊛olindaturismo.com.br), with a branch on Rua Prudente de Morais 472 (Mon–Sat 8am–5pm; ☎81 3429 0244), at either of which you can pick up a decent map. For general info see ⊛olinda.pe.gov.br, and for all Carnaval-related info ⊛carnaval.olinda.pe.gov.br.

Tour operators Victor Tur, Av Sigismundo Gonçalves 732, Carmo, Olinda (☎81 3429 1532, ⊛pousadamarindos caetes.com.br) is an agency run out of the *Pousada Marin dos Caétes* that arranges bus and air tickets and car rentals, as well as city and beach tours.

ACCOMMODATION

Albergue de Olinda Rua do Sol 233, Carmo ☎81 3429 1592, ⊛alberguedeolinda.com.br. Located on a busy main road by the seafront, this bright and tasteful HI hostel has a bucolic little garden with hammocks and a pool, ideal for mingling with other travellers. Rooms are a bit on the plain side with just the bare necessities, but they're clean enough and the place itself has a friendly vibe. Wi-fi. HI discount available. Breakfast included. R$38, doubles R$80
Casa de Hilton Rua do Sol 77 ☎81 3494 2379, ⊛casa dehilton.com.br. The eponymous Hilton rents out a few vibrantly painted rooms in this bright yellow house at an unbeatable price; the tatty furniture has seen better days but the rooms are adequately comfortable for a few nights, and there's also a communal kitchen for those wanting to self-cater. Dorms R$25, doubles R$75
★ **Pousada Alto Astral** Rua 13 de Maio 305 ☎81 3439 3453, ⊛pousadaaltoastral.com. Decorated with naïve art and with a handsome wrought-iron staircase, the staff here are incredibly friendly and the breakfast area (lavish spread included in price) is perfect for socializing. Rooms are warm, wildly painted and superb value, plus there's a pool and wi-fi. Ask for any of the rooms at the back, or, if there are four of you, ask for room eight – spacious and with leafy views over the city. Single rooms available. R$80
Pousada Marin dos Caétes Av Sigismundo Gonçalves 732, Carmo ☎81 3493 1556, ⊛pousadamarindoscaetes .com.br. The petite rooms come in all colours and styles, some like a doll's house, some like a ship's cabin, and each named after one of Pernambuco's great and good. The wooden floorboards are a nice change from tiles, and though the bathrooms are also pretty poky, they're nonetheless clean. Breakfast included. R$70
★ **Pousada Pedro** Rua 27 de Janeiro 95 ☎81 3439 9546, ⊛pousadapedro.com. A spiral staircase leads up to the more expensive rooms in the main house of this charming

pousada, while the cheaper rooms are around the pool area at the back. All have a/c. Breakfast included. R$100
Hotel Pousada São Francisco Rua do Sol 127 ☎81 3429 2109, ⊛pousadasaofrancisco.com.br. Definitely more of a hotel than a pousada, this place has a good-sized pool, a pool table and 45 bright, comfortable rooms, with antique wooden floors and Afro-Brazilian art decorating the walls. All have a/c, fridge, cable TV and wi-fi. Breakfast included. R$180

EATING AND DRINKING

If you want to eat for less than R$20 in Olinda, try the *comida por quilo* places along the seafront and in Novo Olinda. For a bit more, you can eat far better in the old town. Best and least expensive of all, though, is to join the crowds drinking and eating street food at the Alto da Sé, with the best views in town to boot. The charcoal-fired delights sold here can't be recommended too highly; try *acarajé*, from women sitting next to sizzling wok-like pots – bean-curd cakes, fried in palm oil, slit, and filled with salad, dried shrimps and *vatapá* (a paste of coconut milk, dried shrimp, palm oil and ground peanuts).

Atelier e Comedoria Lautreamont Rua Prudente de Morais 249 ☎81 3439 4434. Near the Uruguayan consulate and with a vaguely Uruguayan theme, this crimson-shuttered gallery-cum-restaurant is perfect for a quiet, late afternoon meal when other places are closed. The food's largely regional, though, unusually for this part of the world, they also do a decent Spanish tortilla (R$16). Daily 10am–11pm.

Banana Split Praça do Carmo 5D ☎81 4104 0445. Plenty of tasty snacks to choose from at this tiny German-owned place, including a ricotta and sun-dried tomato sandwich (R$11), soups, including *caldo verde* (R$6), salads (R$16) and tasty fresh fruit juices (from R$2.50). Given the Praça's brutal heat, you might also want to indulge in the house *sorvete* (R$8). Mon–Fri 8am–10pm, Sat & Sun 9am–10pm.

Creperia Praça João Alfredo 168 ☎ 81 3429 2935. This agreeable crêperie is decorated with knick-knacks, local art and exposed brickwork, and has an open-air patio. The scrumptious crêpes come in both sweet (from R$5.80) and savoury (from R$12.90) varieties and they even do a curried version (R$19.50). Daily 11am–11pm.

Pousada Varadouro Rua 15 de Novembro 98 ☎ 81 3439 1163, ⓦ pousadadolindavaradouro.com.br. Tasty, unfussy and cheap *por quilo* food (R$21.99) at this small restaurant set on the ground floor of *Pousada Varadouro*. Locals swarm in on their lunch break so get here early; if you'd rather not sit indoors, head to the back and eat by the pool. Mon–Fri 11.40am–3pm.

NIGHTLIFE

a fábrica Praça do Fortim do Queijo ☎ 71 3429 9258, ⓦ afabricabar.com. Current home to DJ 440's semi-legendary retro-fest, *Terça do Vinil* (vinyl Tuesday), this is Olinda's bar *du jour*, semi-alfresco with a great location close to several hostels on Rua do Sol and a busy schedule that also includes live samba, rock and indie. Cover R$10 and under. Tues–Fri 5pm–4am, Sat & Sun 4pm–4am.

★ **Bodega do Véio** Rua do Amparo 212 ☎ 81 3429 0185. A ridiculously convivial general store-cum-neighbourhood bar of the kind you still find in rural Brazil and Cape Verde, with brooms propped up against the walls and shelves stacked to the ceiling with everything from soap powder to packets of beans and, of course, booze. From mid-afternoon onwards, people are crammed up against the counter and spilling onto the cobbled streets, and there's usually some kind of live music at weekends. An essential Olinda experience. Mon–Sat 9am–11pm.

Casa da Rabeca do Brasil Rua Curupira 340, Cidade Tabajara ☎ 81 3371 8197, ⓦ casadarabeca.com.br. A legacy of the late Mestre Salustiano and a community focal point for the music that made his name, *forró da rabeca*, alongside *maracatu* and other traditional Pernambucan styles; comes into its own during Carnaval. It's a bit out of the way, so best take a taxi. Opening times and cover charge vary (some events are free), though there's usually always something happening Sat nights 9pm–late.

Xinxim da Baiana Avenida Sigismundo Gonçalves 742 ☎ 81 3439 8447. Bahían-themed bar where local *forró de rabeca* stars, Quarteto Olinda, made their name. Still a good place for music new and old, as well as other myriad cultural happenings. Tues–Sun 7pm–3am.

DIRECTORY

Banks and exchange There are no ATMs in Olinda's historical centre so you'll need to take out money in Recife before heading up here; the safest option is to do this at a shopping centre (see p.295).

Pharmacies Farmácia Bicentenária, Rua S Miguel 277, Novo Olinda (☎ 81 3429 2148).

Post office Praça João Pessoa s/n ☎ 81 3439 2203 (Mon–Fri 9am–5pm).

Shopping Crafts aplenty are available at the Mercado da Ribeira, Rua Bernardo Vieira de Melo (daily 9am–6.30pm).

FERNANDO DE NORONHA

Recife is one of the main launch points for this beautiful archipelago 545km off the coast of Pernambuco. It has pristine beaches and it's absolutely terrific for scuba diving; the water is clear for more than 30m in many places, with turtles, dolphins and a wide range of fish species to observe. Since 1988 much of the archipelago has been protected as a marine national park to maintain its ecological wonders (it's also the breeding territory for many tropical Atlantic birds). The main island, **ILHA DE FERNANDO DE NORONHA**, has plenty of gorgeous beaches. While you can no longer swim with the dolphins, you're likely to see quite a few should you visit, though you'll have to wake up early – they enter the bay every day between 5am and 6am.

It's not cheap to get here (from around R$775, two daily flights from Recife with Gol or TRIP/Azul), and you're also charged the **TPA** (Taxa de Preservaçao) **tax** at a *daily* rate of R$43.20 (which goes towards protecting the archipelago), but it can be quite an experience. For more information, including restaurants and places to stay, check the government-run website, ⓦ www.noronha.pe.gov.br.

FORTALEZA

FORTALEZA, the capital city of the State of Ceará, is home to some of the nicest urban beaches in the country, although it's the wild beaches to the north that remain its most popular attraction; crystal-clear waters and palm-fringed beaches are just one selling point – this is any kite- or windsurfer's paradise.

Since the nineteenth century, the city has been the commercial centre of the northern half of the Northeast, and is today Brazil's fifth-largest metropolitan area. Given the city of Fortaleza's lack of any intrinsic appeal, it remains more

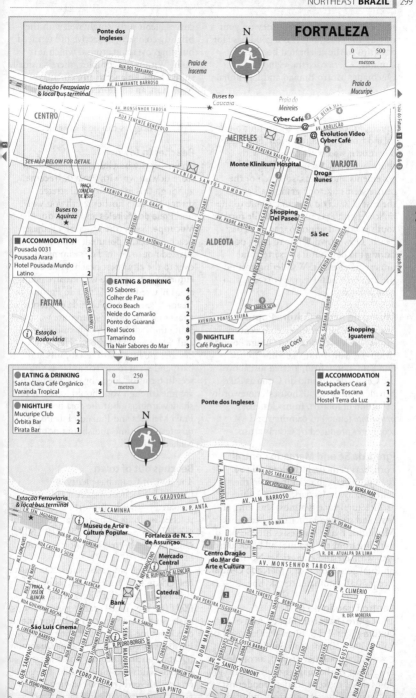

FORTALEZA

0   500
metres

N

Ponte dos
Ingleses

Praia de
Iracema

Praia do
Mucuripe

RUA DOS TABAJARAS

AV. ALMIRANTE BARROSO

Estação Ferroviaria
& local bus terminal

Buses to
Caucaia

Praia do
Meireles

AV. MONSENHOR TABOSA

CENTRO

RUA TENENTE BENEVOLO

Cyber Café

AV. BEIRA MAR

AV. ABOLIÇÃO

Evolution Video
Cyber Café

MEIRELES

RUA PEREIRA VALENTE

VARJOTA

SEE MAP BELOW FOR DETAIL

AVENIDA SANTOS DUMONT

Monte Klinikum Hospital

Droga
Nunes

PRAÇA
CORAÇÃO
DE JESUS

AVENIDA HERACLITO GRAÇA

AV. PADRE ANTÔNIO TOMÁS

Shopping
Del Paseo

Buses to
Aquiraz

R. JOÃO CORDEIRO

RUA ANTÔNIO SALES

AV. BARÃO DE STUDART

ALDEOTA

5à Sec

ACCOMMODATION

Pousada 0031   3
Pousada Arara   1
Hotel Pousada Mundo
Latino   2

FATIMA

AV. VISCONDE DO RIO BRANCO

EATING & DRINKING

50 Sabores   4
Colher de Pau   6
Croco Beach   1
Neide do Camarão   2
Ponto do Guaraná   5
Real Sucos   8
Tamarindo   9
Tia Nair Sabores do Mar 3

RUA ABRÃEN SILVA

AVENIDA PONTES VIEIRA

NIGHTLIFE

Café Pagliuca   7

Estação
Rodoviária

Rio Cocó

Shopping
Iguatemi

Beach Park

3

Airport

EATING & DRINKING

Santa Clara Café Orgânico 4
Varanda Tropical   5

0   250
metres

ACCOMMODATION

Backpackers Ceará   2
Pousada Toscana   1
Hostel Terra da Luz   3

NIGHTLIFE

Mucuripe Club   3
Órbita Bar   2
Pirata Bar   1

Ponte dos Ingleses

N

RUA DOS TABAJARAS

AV. A. TAMANDARÉ

R. DOS POTIGUARAS

AV. BEIRA MAR

Estação Ferroviaria
& local bus terminal

R. G. GRADVOHL

R. A. CAMINHA

R. P. ANTA

AV. ALM. BARROSO

R. DO MAR

Museu de Arte e
Cultura Popular

R. DR. JOÃO MOREIRA

Fortaleza de N. S.
de Assunção

RUA JOSÉ AVELINO

Centro Dragão
do Mar de
Arte e Cultura

AV. MONSENHOR TABOSA

Mercado
Central

RUA CASTRO E SILVA

RUA SÃO PAULO

RUA SEN. ALENCAR

AV. NEPOMUCENO

R. RUFINO DE ALENCAR

Catedral

RUA PEREIRA FILGUEIRAS

Bank

R. GOV.

R. JOSÉ SABOIA

São Luís Cinema

R. PEDRO BORGES

RUA COSTA BARROS

RUA COSTA BARROS

R. DEP. MOREIRA

R. P. CLIMÉRIO

AV. DOM MANUEL

R. PEDRO PEREIRA

RUA PINTO

RUA FRANKLIN TAVORA

RUA SANTOS DUMONT

suited to breaking your journey on your
way up the coast, but it is a good base for
day-trips to the celebrated **beaches:**
Cumbuco, Jericoacoara, Canoa
Quebrada, Morro Branco and Lagoinha.

WHAT TO SEE AND DO

The nerve centre of the city is its largest
square, **Praça José de Alencar**, four blocks
inland from the train station. Fortaleza's
downtown streets are crowded with
shops, with hawkers colonizing
pavements and plazas, so much of the
centre seems like one giant market. To
the east is Praia de Iracema, home to the
bulk of Fortaleza's nightlife, while further
south is Praia do Futuro, the city's best
beach. Downtown is fine to hang out in
during the day, but it's deserted and
unnerving at night. Wandering around
the area on a Sunday by yourself is also
best avoided.

Museu de Arte e Cultura Popular

Situated in a former nineteenth-century
prison, the **Museu de Arte e Cultura Popular**
(Mon–Fri 8am–6pm, Sat 8am–5pm,
Sun 8am–noon; free), located just above
the Centro de Turismo do Ceará at Rua
Senador Pompeu 350, houses a noteworthy
collection of folk art, from Cearense
artesanato (crafts) to paintings and
sculptures produced by Ceará's artists.

Igreja da Sé and Mercado Central

Fortaleza's cathedral, the **Igreja da Sé**,
is an unmistakeable landmark in the
centre of town. Its dark, neo-Gothic
architectural style is almost shocking at
first, and striking rather than beautiful.
Megalithic flying buttresses lift the weird
building from the ground, all black and
grey with age and city grime. Next to it,
on Rua Conde d'Eu, the **Mercado Central**
(see p.303) dominates the skyline.

Centro Dragão do Mar

The **Centro Dragão do Mar de Arte e
Cultura** (Tues–Fri 8.30am–9.30pm, Sat &
Sun 2.30–9.30pm; ☎85 3488 8600,
ⓦwww.dragaodomar.org.br), a couple of
blocks east of the market on Rua Dragão
do Mar 81, makes a strident modernist
landmark in the city; its steel and glass

curves blend surprisingly well with the
brightly coloured, attractive old terraced
buildings over and around which it is
built. Within the complex, there's a small,
shiny-domed planetarium, cinemas, a
bookshop, an auditorium and a couple of
museums. At night the square below is
Fortaleza's most vibrant nightlife spot,
although beggars can be a nuisance.

Beaches in town

The main city beaches begin steps away
from downtown with **Praia de Iracema**,
although this is a pretty dull stretch
during the day; further south you will
find **Praia do Meireles** and **Praia do
Mucuripe**. Sadly, the water off all these
beaches is badly polluted, and you are
advised not to go in. For **swimming**, head
over to the city's best beach, **Praia do
Futuro**. Getting there will involve taking
a bus marked either "Praia do Futuro" or
"Caça e Pesca" from Avenida da Abolição,
a taxi or a minimum 45-minute walk
along the seafront through an industrial
and *favela* neighbourhood. Here the
beaches are lined with restaurants and
bars, and seem to stretch as far as you can
see. In terms of safety, by day the beaches
are fine (though you should look out for
shark warnings), but the area between
Praia Meireles and Praia do Futuro is
unsafe at any time and should not be
walked by night.

Beaches out of town

The state of Ceará has plenty of
incredible beaches on offer if you are
prepared to travel a bit further. All can be
reached on tours or by regular buses from
the *rodoviária*. Lisatur (☎85 3219 5600,
ⓦlisatur.com.br) has transport to those
listed below.

With its emerald-green waters, **Cumbuco**,
only 35km north of Fortaleza, is by far
Brazil's best beach for kite-surfing. *Pousada
0031* (see box, p.301) can organize lessons.
Make sure you go on a **dune-buggy ride** to
check out the area's breathtaking scenery.
Further up is the popular **Canoa Quebrada**
(ⓦcanoa-quebrada.com), which has
dramatic cliffs and fun nightlife that goes
on until the early hours. Heading further
north you come to Ceará's most famous

beach, **Jericoacoara** (ⓦ jeri-brazil.org), with fine white sands and high dunes, especially popular with wind- and kite-surfers. The second half of the trip up here is by 4WD, and it can take up to seven hours to make the 312km journey. Finally, in the opposite direction is Morro Branco, 80km to the south of Fortaleza and renowned for its beaches backed by maze-like cliffs of multicoloured sand.

Beach Park

About 16km from downtown Fortaleza is **Beach Park** at Porto das Dunas (daily 11am–5pm, closed midweek out of season; R$140; ☎ 85 4012 3000, ⓦ beachpark.com.br), which claims to be Latin America's biggest water park. It certainly has some hair-raising rides and makes for a fun day-trip from Fortaleza. Most tour agencies make the trip out here, or – if you're in a group – a taxi (approx 20min; R$50–60) may work out cheaper.

ARRIVAL AND DEPARTURE

By plane Fortaleza's Aeroporto Internacional Pinto Martins (☎ 85 3392 1200) is about 8km from downtown. Buses with the route card Aeroporto/Benfica/Rodoviária (R$2) run regularly to Praça José de Alencar in the centre via the *rodoviária*. Taxis cost about R$30.
Destinations Belém (5 daily; 1hr 50min–3hr 40min); Recife (10 daily; 1hr 15min–1hr 35min); Rio (12–24 daily; 5hr 40min–8hr 15min); Salvador (7–9 daily; 1hr 40min–4hr 20min).
By bus The bus station, Rodoviária Engenheiro João Tomé, Av Borges de Melo 1630 (☎ 85 3230 1111), is about 3km from the centre of town, and served by the same Aeroporto/Benfica/Rodoviária bus (see above).
Destinations Guanabara Express (ⓦ expressoguanabara .com.br) serve Recife and Brasília, while São Geraldo (ⓦ saogeraldo.com.br) and Itapemirim (ⓦ itapemirim .com.br) serve São Paulo, with the latter also serving Rio. Brasília (2–3 daily; 18–19hr); Recife (4 daily; 12–13hr); Rio (1 daily; 46hr); São Paulo (1–2 daily; 52hr).

GETTING AROUND

By bus Fortaleza has plenty of local buses (R$2). Useful routes that take you to the main beaches and back to the city centre are marked "Grande Circular I" and "Caça e Pesca/Centro/Beira Mar".
By taxi Expect to pay in the region of R$20–25 to get anywhere in town. For pre-booked taxis, try Cooperativa Rádio Táxi (☎ 85 3254 5744) or Disque Táxi (☎ 85 3287 7222).

INFORMATION AND TOURS

Tourist information In line with its huge popularity as a domestic holiday destination, Fortaleza boasts a multitude of tourist information outlets including kiosks in the airport (daily 6am–midnight; ☎ 85 3392 1667), *rodoviária* (daily 8am–6pm; ☎ 85 3230 1111) and Centro do Turismo, Rua Senador Pompeu 350 (Mon–Fri 8am–7pm, Sat 8am 3pm, Sun 8am–noon; ☎ 85 3101 5508), as well as offices in the Mercado Central (Mon–Fri 8am–5pm, Sat 8am–noon; ☎ 85 3105 1475), on Praça do Ferreira (Mon–Fri 9am–5pm, Sat 8am–noon; ☎ 85 3105 1444) and on Av Beira Mar near the Anfiteatro Flávio Ponte (Mon–Sat 9am–9pm, Sun 9am–8.30pm; ☎ 85 3105 2670).
Tour operators Lisatur, Av Monsenhor Tabosa 1067, Praia de Iracema (☎ 85 3219 5400, ⓦ lisatur.com.br), has good day-trips to beaches and other attractions.

ACCOMMODATION

The budget hotels, as ever, tend to be downtown, which hums busily during the day but empties at night – it's best to stay elsewhere. Close by is Praia de Iracema, with a decent enough range of accommodation, while Praia Meireles further south is home to more upmarket hotels.

CENTRO

Backpackers Ceará Av Dom Manoel 89 ☎ 85 3091 8997, ⓦ backpacksce.com.br. Somewhat camouflaged until you notice the animated wall painting, this place buzzes with travellers, though it can feel a little impenetrable, with its barbed wire, CCTV and coded locks. Rooms are comfortable, but be ready to battle against the worn-out fans. Wi-fi. Dorms R$20, doubles R$40
Pousada Toscana Rua Rufino de Alencar 272 ☎ 85 3088 4011, ⓦ pousadatoscana.com.br. A pleasant, Italian-owned pousada with a bright-blue exterior and imitation columns in the entrance, as well as a patio-cum-garden at the back. Rooms are simple but rather nondescript. R$70
Hostel Terra da Luz Rua Rodrigues Junior 278 ☎ 85 3082 2260, ⓦ hostelterradaluz.com. This hostel has a cosy

> ## ★ TREAT YOURSELF
> **Pousada 0031** Av das Dunas 2249, Cumbuco ☎ 85 8617 9119, ⓦ 0031.com. A little tropical paradise at this Dutch-run pousada forty minutes from the centre of Fortaleza. Management couldn't be friendlier, the restaurant is the best in town, the rooms – in individually styled thatched-roof apartments – are spotless, the pool refreshing, and the golden sand dunes and pristine beaches only two minutes' walk away; "huge breakfast" included. R$165

atmosphere and scribbled guests' notes coat the upstairs walls. The dorms are clean and colourful, equipped with both a/c and fan, and there's also a communal kitchen and free internet. Breakfast included. Dorms R$42, doubles R$100

PRAIA MEIRELES & PRAIA DO MUCURIPE

Pousada Arara Av Aboliçao 3806, Mucuripe ☎ 85 3263 2277, ⊕ hotelarara.com.br. A friendly hotel in a safe setting, although it's on a main road so not too quiet. Rooms are clean and comfortable although the owners have a penchant for adorning their walls with tropical sunset prints. There's a nice enough pool at the back, as well as a little barbecue area. Wi-fi and breakfast included. R$140

Hotel Pousada Mundo Latino Rua Ana Bilhar 507, Meireles ☎ 85 3242 8778, ⊕ mundolatino.com.br. The breakfast room and communal area are not exactly alluring with their PVC-covered sofas, but staff are helpful and the a/c rooms are spacious. Internet facilities available, plus wi-fi. Breakfast included. R$130

EATING AND DRINKING

Downtown, Praça do Ferreira offers a few *por quilo lanchonetes* (self-service cafeterias), and Iracema has a few good restaurants, while the Centro Dragão do Mar has at least seven pavement cafés overflowing with people having fun. The beaches all have a smattering of good restaurants as well as beach huts offering some of the best deals on seafood; the Centro Dragão do Mar is also a popular spot, particularly in the evenings, with plenty of pavement cafés and a young crowd.

ALDEOTA AND AROUND

Real Sucos Heráclito Graça 1709 ☎ 85 3244 3923, ⊕ realsucos.com.br. Veteran chain serving renowned fresh fruit juices (R$4–10), including *açaí*, *graviola*, *carambola*, tamarind and papaya, as well as lots of sandwich options (R$8); the *cajú* juice is especially good. Mon–Thurs 7am–2am, Fri & Sat 7am–5am, Sun 5pm–2am. Also at Shopping Aldeota ☎ 85 3458 1104, Shopping Benfica ☎ 85 3281 4029, and Centre Um Shopping ☎ 85 3224 0121 (all 10am–10pm).

Tamarindo Rua Araken Silva 296 ☎ 85 3472 1824, ⊕ restaurantetamarindo.com.br. Located down in the leafy *barrio* of Dionísio Torres, this is the rarest of beasts, a wholly organic *por quilo* restaurant, though at R$45.99 you might want to go lightly on the heavier dishes. In addition to fishy favourites like *vatapá* there's plenty for vegetarians including spinach and ricotta quiche, lasagne, brown rice and beans. Mon–Sat 11.30am–2.30pm.

PRAIA DE IRACEMA

Santa Clara Café Orgânico Rua Dragão do Mar 81, Centro Dragão do Mar ☎ 85 3219 6900, ⊕ cafesantaclara .com.br. Try the popular espresso (R$3.25) or sip on a

chocolate-fringed cappuccino (R$8) at Fortaleza's best coffee joint. Tues–Sun 3–10pm.

Tia Nair Sabores do Mar Rua Ildefonso Albano 68, Praia de Iracema ☎ 85 3219 1461, ⊕ tianair.com.br. Despite the menu's unappetizing photos, this seafront place has good food at reasonable prices. A range of ambitious, two- and three-person fish dishes (in the region of R$60) mix it up with shrimp and lobster. Daily 11am–1am.

Varanda Tropical Av Monsenhor Tabosa 714, Praia de Iracema ☎ 85 3219 5195. Open-fronted restaurant on the main road serving a solid range of meat, fish and seafood options, many of which will fill two bellies; if you're on your tod try the shrimps in garlic (R$9.90). Mon–Sat 11am–midnight, Sun 11am–5pm.

PRAIA MEIRELES & PRAIA DO MUCURIPE

50 sabores Av Beira Mar 3958, Mucuripe ☎ 85 3032 5850, ⊕ 50sabores.com.br. This decades-old Fortaleza institution hides its light under a proverbial bushel, with almost double the titular 50 flavours of ice cream, all of which change with the seasons, even if it feels like the weather never does. Try the plum, *caipirinha* or *maracujá* (R$11 for two huge scoops). One of six branches spread around town. Daily 9am–11.30pm.

★ **Neide do Camarão** Av da Abolição 4772 Mucuripe ☎ 85 3248 2680. You buy your shrimp at the door (R$25 *por quilo*), choose how you want it prepared, hand it to the waiter, then eat the crispy shrimp, shell and all, washed down with ice-cold beer. Local, authentic and awesome. Daily 5–11pm.

Ponto do Guaraná Av Beira Mar 3127-A, Meireles ☎ 85 3086 5650. *Guaraná* addicts should head here – there's plenty of flavours to choose from including lemon (R$3), *acerola* (R$3.50) and *açaí* (R$3.50). Sandwiches are also available (R$7). Daily 6am–10pm.

VARJOTA

Colher de Pau Rua Frederico Borges 204 ☎ 85 3267 3773. The "Wooden Spoon" is a popular, family-run restaurant serving up local Cearense cuisine such as sun-dried beef at reasonable prices, with plates (upwards of R$20) you can share with a friend or three. Daily 11am–midnight.

PRAIA DO FUTURO

Croco Beach Av Zezé Diogo 3125 ☎ 85 3521 9600, ⊕ crocobeach.com.br. Probably Futuro's most popular beach restaurant, serving huge sharing platters of seafood (a 1kg pargo with rice and beans for R$72.90) as well as sushi (from R$19.50) and plenty of meat dishes (*carne do sol* R$56.90 for two). Also lays on comedy shows Tues & Thurs (R$20 cover) and DJs/live music at weekends (R$5 cover). Mon, Wed, Fri & Sun 8am–6pm, Tues & Thurs 8am–midnight.

NIGHTLIFE

Fortaleza is justly famous for its *forró*. There's no better way to see what Cearenses do to have fun than to spend a night in a *dancetaria*. One of the busiest nightlife areas is the streets around the Ponte dos Ingleses. Most *dancetarias* open at 10pm, but they don't really get going until about midnight. Other nightlife is mainly out by the beaches: Praia Meireles appeals to a broad cross section of the local and tourist populations, whereas Praia Iracema is slightly younger.

Café Pagliuca Rua Barbosa de Freitas 1035 ☏ 85 3324 1903, ⓦ www.cafepagliuca.com.br. An arty, rustic-bohemian vibe makes this one of the mellowest spots in town for a quiet drink and, from Tues–Sat (9.30pm–midnight), some live jazz, bossa and mpb. There's Chilean red from R$32 a bottle and the food includes a range of authentic Italian risotto (try the house recipe, R$27). R$8.80 cover. Mon–Fri 5.30pm–1am, Sat noon–1am.

Mucuripe Club Travessa Maranguape 108, Centro ☏ 85 3254 3020, ⓦ mucuripe.com.br. Veteran superclub hosting some of the country's biggest DJs, singers and bands in several themed areas including a film-set-like, colonial-style street, a huge "arena" for live shows and a hi-tech clubbing area, with a music policy covering everything from rock, funk and electronica to samba, *axé* and *forró*. No flip-flops or shorts. Cover varies according to event. Wed–Sat 9.30pm–late.

Órbita Bar Rua Dragão do Mar 207 ☏ 85 3453 1421, ⓦ orbitabar.com.br. A Fortaleza institution, with live Brazilian and international indie/alternative, blues, electronica and even – for those who like their twang – a night (Wed) dedicated to the delights of surf-rock. Check out their radio station, ⓦ orbitaradio.com.br. Cover R$10–30. Wed–Sun 9pm–late.

Pirata Bar Rua dos Tabajaras 325 ☏ 85 4011 6161, ⓦ pirata.com.br. The most famous place in Fortaleza, in Brazil and doubtless the world to get your fix of *forró*. By cannily cornering the club-less wilds of *segunda-feira*, this unashamed tourist trap has generated more than its fair share of publicity – the *New York Times* famously called it "the craziest place on earth on a Monday night" and a Brazilian mag rated it as one of the 1001 places to see in the country before you die. Get ready to dance till you drop in a joint that would likely shiver even Captain Jack Sparrow's timbers. Cover R$40. Mon 8pm–very late.

SHOPPING

The Mercado Central on Rua Conde d'Eu, and the nearby shops diagonally across from the cathedral, are the best places in the city to buy a hammock. This huge complex resembles a parking garage crowded with hundreds of small stores.

DIRECTORY

Banks and exchange There are a fair number of ATMs near the beaches and hotels with several HSBC locations: Rua Major Facundo 302, Centro; Av Monsenhor Tabosa 1200, Praia da Iracema; Av Santos Dumont 3581, Aldeota.

Embassies and consulates UK, British Honorary Consulate, Rua Leonardo Mota 501, Meireles (☏ 85 242 0888); US, Torre Santos Dumont, Av Santos Dumont 2828, Suite 708, Aldeota (☏ 85 486 1306).

Hospital Monte Klinikum Hospital, Rua República do Libano 747 (☏ 85 4012 0012, ⓦ www.monteklinikum .com.br).

Internet Evolution Vídeo Cyber Café, Av da Abolição 3230, Meireles (Mon–Sat 8am–6pm; R$4/hr).

Laundry 5 à Sec, Rua Cel Jucá 470, Aldeota (☏ 85 3267 5034).

Pharmacy Farmácia Santa Branca, Av da Universidade 3089, Benfica (☏ 85 3223 0000).

Police The tourist police are open 24/7 and can be found at Av Almirante Barroso 805, Praia da Iracema (☏ 85 3101 2488).

Post office Av Monsenhor Tabosa 1561, Meireles (☏ 85 3248 3030; Mon–Fri 8am–5pm, Sat 8am–noon).

The Amazon

The Amazon is a vast forest – the largest on the planet – and a giant river system, covering over half of Brazil and a large portion of South America. The forest extends into Venezuela, Colombia, Peru and Bolivia, where the river itself begins life among thousands of different headwaters. In Brazil, only the stretch below Manaus, where the waters of the **Rio Solimões** and the **Rio Negro** meet, is actually known as the **Rio Amazonas**. The daily flow of the river is said to be enough to supply a city the size of New York with water for nearly ten years, and its power is such that the muddy Amazon waters stain the Atlantic a silty brown for over 200km out to sea.

BELÉM

Strategically placed on the Amazon River estuary, **BELÉM** was founded by the Portuguese in 1616 as the City of Our Lady of Bethlehem (Belém). Its original role was to protect the river mouth and establish the Portuguese claim to the region, but it rapidly became established as an Indian slaving port and a source of cacao and spices from the Amazon.

Belém prospered following the rubber boom at the end of the nineteenth century but suffered a disastrous decline after the crash of 1914 – it kept afloat, just about, on the back of brazil nuts and the lumber industry. Nowadays, it remains the economic centre of northern Brazil, and the chief port for the Amazon. It is also a remarkably attractive place, with a fine colonial centre.

WHAT TO SEE AND DO

The old town or **Cidade Velha** is at the southern edge of the centre, where the

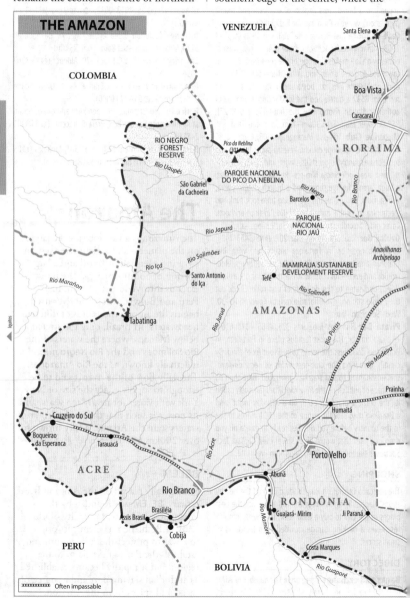

THE AMAZON

VENEZUELA
Santa Elena

COLOMBIA

Boa Vista

Caracaraí

RORAIMA

RIO NEGRO FOREST RESERVE

Rio Uaupés

Pico da Neblina

PARQUE NACIONAL DO PICO DA NEBLINA

São Gabriel da Cachoeira

Rio Negro

Barcelos

Rio Branco

PARQUE NACIONAL RIO JAÚ

Rio Japurá

Anavilhanas Archipelago

Rio Solimões

Rio Içá

Santo Antonio do Içá

MAMIRAUA SUSTAINABLE DEVELOPMENT RESERVE

Tefé

Rio Marañon

Rio Solimões

AMAZONAS

Iquitos

Tabatinga

Rio Juruá

Rio Purus

Rio Madeira

Prainha

Cruzeiro do Sul

Humaitá

Boqueirao da Esperanca

Tarauacá

ACRE

Rio Acre

Porto Velho

Rio Branco

Abuña

RONDÔNIA

Assis Brasil

Brasiléia

Guajará- Mirim

Ji Paraná

Cobija

Rio Mamoré

PERU

Costa Marques

BOLIVIA

Rio Guaporé

xxxxxxxxx Often impassable

cathedral and fort sit around the Praça da Sé. Immediately north on the waterfront lies one of the city's highlights, the **Ver-o-Peso market**, the largest open-air market in Latin America – visit in the morning when the market is bustling, its stalls overflowing with spices, potions, crafts, fish and foodstuffs. Carrying on up the waterfront you reach the **Estação das Docas** cultural centre (Mon & Tues 10am–midnight, Wed 10am–1am, Thurs–Sat 10am–3am, Sun 9am–midnight; ☎91 3212 5525, ⓦestacaodasdocas.com.br) where some

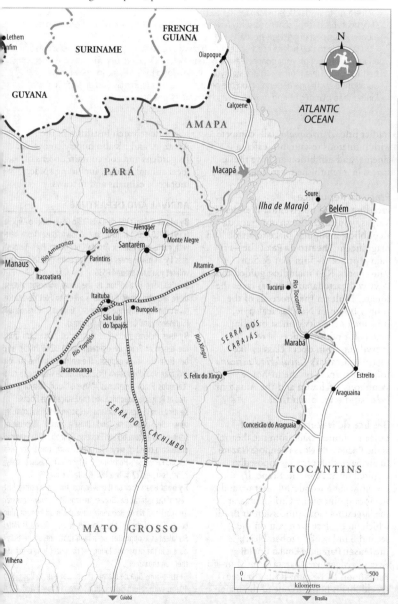

3

TRAVELLING BY BOAT IN THE AMAZON

The range of **boat transport** in the Amazon runs from luxury tourist vessels and large three-level riverboats to smaller one- or two-level boats and covered launches operated by tour companies. Prices are generally calculated per day: as a rule **local boats** are less expensive than **tourist boats** and **launches**. On longer journeys there are different classes; avoid *cabine*, sweltering cabins, and choose instead *primeiro* (first class), sleeping in a hammock on deck. *Segundo* (second class) is often hammock space in the lower deck or engine room. The cheapest tickets (food not included) for the four- to six-day Belém–Manaus trip cost around R$150–200 (for *primeiro* hammock space). Only boats headed to Tabatinga usually have food included in the ticket price (though it gets monotonous; best bring a few treats).

It's sensible to buy tickets in advance, for which you can often get a reasonable discount, and always to get on your boat at least two hours before it's due to depart to secure a decent berth. With all boat journeys, make sure you ask how long the previous journey took as boat durations can change depending on the height of the river (and may end up lasting much longer than planned). Bring provisions, and prepare to practise your Portuguese!

(rather pricey) *artesanato* stalls compete with numerous restaurants, cafés, a cinema, and exhibition and live music spaces in a refurbished warehouse area.

Praça da Republica

Heading inland up Avenida Presidente Vargas, you reach the shady Praça da República, a popular place to stroll. The magnificent **Theatro da Paz** (Tues–Fri 9am–1pm & 2–5pm, Sat & Sun 9am–noon; R$4 including guided tour; ⓦ www.theatrodapaz.com.br) faces the square. Built on the proceeds of the rubber boom in Neoclassical style, it is one of the city's finest buildings; tickets for performances here – everything from opera classics like Pietro Mascagni's *Cavalleria Rusticana* to performances by the in-house symphony orchestra and the Amazônia Jazz Band – are often free.

Basílica de Nazaré and around

Fifteen minutes' walk from the theatre is the **Basílica de Nossa Senhora Nazaré** (daily 5am–8pm; free), supposedly inspired by St Peter's in Rome. It certainly has a wonderful interior, and is the focal point of the Cirio de Nazaré, the largest religious procession in Brazil, which takes place each year on the second Sunday of October. Nearby, the **Museu Paraense Emílio Goeldi** at Avenida Magalhães Barata 376 (Mon–Fri 8am–noon & 1–5pm; R$2; ⓦ museu -goeldi.br) is home to one of the major

scientific research institutes in the Amazon, and it's also hugely enjoyable. Its gardens and zoo contain dozens of local animal species, including spider monkeys, caimans and macaws.

ARRIVAL AND DEPARTURE

By plane Belém's Val-de-Cans/Júlio Cesar Ribeiro Airport (⊕ 91 3210 6000) is 10km out of town. Buses from here with route card "Marex Arsenal" or "Marex Pres. Vargas" pass by all major areas in the city centre (R$2.20). A taxi will set you back around R$35.

Destinations In addition to the usual domestic routes, there are also several flights a week to Fort de France (Martinique), Cayenne (French Guiana), Paramaribo (Suriname) and Georgetown (Guyana).

By bus Belém's *rodoviária* is situated some 5km from the centre at Praça de Operário (⊕ 91 3266 2625); any bus from the stops opposite the entrance to the station will take you downtown (R$2.20); those with route card "Canudos Praça Amazonas", "Arsenal" and "Tamoios" all stop at Praça da Republica and the Estaçao das Docas.

Destinations Transbrasiliana (ⓦ transbrasiliana.com.br) serve Belo Horizonte and Brasília while Itapemirim (ⓦ itapemirim.com.br) and Expresso Guanabara (ⓦ expresso guanabara.com.br) serve Fortaleza, with the latter also serving Recife. Belo Horizonte (1 daily; 43hr); Brasília (1 daily; 33hr); Fortaleza (2 daily; 24hr); Recife (1 daily; 36hr).

By boat Boats dock on the river near the town centre, just east of the Estação das Docas; Amazon Star (ⓦ amazonstar .com.br) and Navio Rondonia have the most comfortable boats. One of the cheapest places to buy tickets is *Hotel Fortaleza* (see opposite), or, failing that, one of the ticket booths in the departure lounge at the port (don't purchase them on the street).

Destinations Ilha de Marajó (Mon–Sat 6am & 2pm, Sun 10am, with return 5pm; 3hr); Macapá (Tues, Wed & Fri

6am; 24hr); Manaus (Tues, Wed & Fri 6pm; 5–6 days); Santarém (Tues, Wed & Fri 6pm; 2–3 days).

INFORMATION AND TOURS

Tourist information In the few short hours they're open, Belémtur are OK for maps but struggle with much else; their deserted-feeling office at Av Gov. Jose Malcher 257 (Mon–Fri 9am–2pm; ☎ 91 3230 3920) is hidden away across a courtyard opposite the municipal library.

Tour operators Valeverde Turismo, in the Estação das Docas (☎ 91 3218 7333, ⓦ valeverdeturismo.com.br), organize good-value river tours around Belém, as well as city tours. Amazon Star Turismo, Rua Henrique Gurjão 210 (☎ 91 3241 8624, ⓦ amazonstar.com.br), is an excellent French-run agency specializing in ecotours, including visits to Ilha de Marajó and various jungle lodges around Manaus.

ACCOMMODATION

Amazônia Rua Ó de Almeida 548 ☎ 91 3222 8456, ⓦ hotelamazoniabelem.com.br. A warren-like tumult of narrow wooden staircases and platforms with a DIY feel, offering a solitary 4-person dorm and some dark-ish rooms. An alternative if *Fortaleza* is full. Dorms R$20, doubles R$45

Amazônia Hostel Av Gov. José Malcher 592 ☎ 91 4141 8833, ⓦ amazoniahostel.com.br. An immaculately kept Hi-affiliated hostel in a lovely old mansion, with polished hardwood floors and stratospherically high ceilings, though the usual colonial layout means rooms give onto a corridor rather than an outside window. There's a kitchen, internet facilities, lockers, free wi-fi and a/c in all dorms. Breakfast included. Dorms R$48, doubles R$75

Fortaleza Travessa Frutuoso Guimaraes 276 ☎ 91 3212 1055. This rambling old colonial house, frayed but with character to spare, is presided over by the formidable Gilda Castro and family, and is often full of French backpackers en route to or from French Guiana. Rooms and dorms are basic but you'll instantly be made to feel at home among the whitewashed walls and old wooden floors. Wi-fi promised soon. Take care at night as the area can be dangerous. Dorms R$20, doubles R$45

★ **Grão Pará** Av Presidente Vargas 718 ☎ 91 3221 2121, ⓦ hotelgraopara.com.br. By far the best mid-range value on Vargas' busy thoroughfare, with a huge modern reception and inviting a/c rooms with desks, lamps, flawless bathrooms and a generally upmarket standard you'd usually only find in a much more expensive business hotel. Breakfast included. R$100

EATING AND DRINKING

Belém boasts plenty of excellent cheap restaurants, which have especially good deals at lunchtime. There's also excellent street food by the main docks, and good *tacacá* (shrimp soup) stalls on Av Nazaré, close to Quintino Bocaiúva. In the evenings, head to the Estaçao das Docas where all places stay open till late.

★ **Govinda** Travessa Padre Prudêncio 166 ☎ 91 3222 2272, ⓦ restaurantegovinda.com.br. Far and away the best quality in town for the price (R$18), with a daily two-course set lunch of delicious vegetarian Indian food (plus salad and *suco*), subtly spiced and – in contrast to the usual Brazilian super-size-me – sensibly portioned. The food changes daily and may include anything from curried sweet potato to dhal to rice with toasted almonds. Don't miss a shot of the heavenly milk-based chai to finish up. Mon–Fri 11.30am–3pm, Sat noon–2.30pm.

Lá em Casa Estação das Docas ☎ 91 3212 5588, ⓦ laemcasa.com. Founded in the early 1970s by the late Slow Food advocate and pioneer of Amazonian cuisine, Paulo Martins, no other restaurant in Belém commands quite the same combination of die-hard local following and international media coverage, with its legendary *paraense* (southern) nosh available as either a lunchtime all-you-can-eat (R$28), or evening à la carte. In among myriad exotic fish and seafood *pratos*, their signature dish is *o pato no tucupi*: duck in an astringent soup (R$45). Mon–Thurs & Sun noon–midnight, Fri & Sat noon–2am.

Nunes Travessa Rui Barbosa 974 ☎ 91 3083 9611. You can't get any more traditional than this – the garrulous owner has pretty much set up shop in his living room. Superb soups for a bargain R$3, while the *prato* of the day costs R$5. Mon–Fri & occasional Sat 10.30am–3pm.

Tapioquinha de Mosqueiro Rua dos Pariquis 1981-B ☎ 91 3242 5240, ⓦ tapioquinhademosqueiro.com.br. If you thought tapioca was a frogspawn-esque hangover from old school dinners, this place might just change your mind. Locals have been lapping up the chewy, almost meringue-like pancakes at this famous *tapiocaria* for years, with both sweet and savoury versions starting at only R$2.50; try the *pupunha* (a selenium-rich palm fruit), if it's in season (R$4.50). Tues–Thurs 6.30am–noon & 3.30–8.30pm, Fri–Sun 6.30am–9pm.

NIGHTLIFE

Belém has some of the most talked-about nightlife in Brazil, with the 80s-pop-cum-primitive synth-rooted *tecnobrega* scene having made headlines around the world, both for its suburban warehouse parties commanded by über-DJs, and for its creative subversion of artistic copyright; the inimitable Gaby Amarantos remains the genre's reigning queen. Most of the action takes place far from the centre of town; ask around for upcoming events. Even during the week you'll see plenty of people hanging out in town having drinks until late; you'll find many bars along Av Almirante Wandekolk and in the Estação das Docas.

Amazon Beer In the Estação das Docas ☎ 91 3212 5401, ⓦ amazonbeer.com.br. Beer-lovers will be in heaven at this bar with an in-house brewery and a mouth-watering selection of artisan recipes on tap; try the Amazon Weiss (R$5.30). Mon–Wed 5pm–midnight, Thurs 5pm–1am, Fri 4pm–2am, Sat noon–2am & Sun noon–midnight.

★ **Bar Palafita** Rua Siqueira Mendes 264, Cidade Velha ☎ 91 3212 6302. One of Belém's most famous treasures: an

atmospheric bar on stilts right on the Amazon River with truly incredible views, especially at sunset. There's great live music Thurs–Sun, though the wildest night is Fri's retro-flavoured Black Soul Samba party. Mon–Wed & Sun noon–midnight, Thurs & Sat noon–1am, Fri noon–4am.

Casa do Gilson Travessa Padre Eutíquio 3172, Condor ☎ 91 3272 7306. For 25 years now, this place has championed the delicate, folky strains of classic *choro* and small-group samba

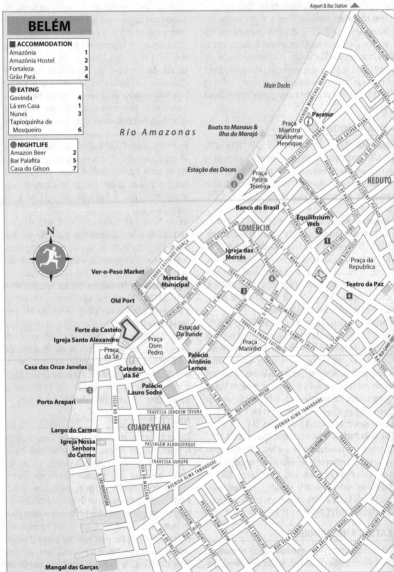

BELÉM

■ **ACCOMMODATION**
Amazônia	1
Amazônia Hostel	2
Fortaleza	3
Grão Pará	4

■ **EATING**
Govinda	4
Lá em Casa	1
Nunes	3
Tapioquinha de Mosqueiro	6

■ **NIGHTLIFE**
Amazon Beer	2
Bar Palafita	5
Casa do Gilson	7

Airport & Bus Station

Main Docks

Paratur

Praça Maestro Waldemar Henrique

Boats to Manaus & Ilha do Marajó

Río Amazonas

REDUTO

Estação das Docas

Praça Pedro Teixeira

Banco do Brasil

Equilibrium Web @

COMÉRCIO

Igreja das Mercês

Praça da República

Ver-o-Peso Market

Mercado Municipal

Teatro da Paz

Old Port

Forte do Castelo
Igreja Santo Alexandre

Estação Do Bonde

Praça Dom Pedro

Praça Marinho

Palácio António Lemos

Casa das Onze Janelas

Praça da Sé

Catedral da Sé

Palácio Lauro Sodré

Porto Arapari

Largo do Carmo

Igreja Nossa Senhora do Carmo

CIDADE VELHA

PASSAGEM ALBUQUERQUE

TRAVESSA GURUPÁ

Mangal das Garças

in the unlikely environs of Belém, with live performances at weekends, including afternoon shows on Sat & Sun. The perfect accompaniment to an ice-cold Cerpa (R$5). Fri 7pm–midnight, Sat & Sun noon–midnight.

DIRECTORY

Banks and exchange There are plenty of banks on Av Presidente Vargas, including Turvicam Cambio at 640, Banco do Brasil at 248, and HSBC at 676, the latter with an ATM that accepts foreign cards.

Hospital Hospital Guadalupe, Rua Arcipreste Manoel Teodoro 734 (☎ 91 4005 9877 or 9820).

Internet Equilibrium Web, Rua Ó de Almeida 533 (Mon–Fri 8am–noon & 2–6pm, Sat 8am–noon; R$3/hr) has flat-screen computers, excellent broadband connection and Skype.

Laundry Lav e Lev, Rua Doutor Moraes 576, Batista Campos (Mon–Sat 8am–8pm).

Post office The central post office (Mon–Fri 9am–5pm) is at Av Presidente Vargas 498. However, as this is frequently crowded, it's often quicker to walk to the small post office at Av Nazaré 319, three blocks beyond the Praça da República (same hours).

Shopping Belém is one of the best places in the world to buy hammocks (essential if you go upriver) – particularly the Ver-o-Peso market, where you can also buy beautiful local crafts.

Taxi Cooperdoca Rádio Táxi ☎ 91 3226 3300; Águia Rádio Táxi ☎ 91 3276 0100.

Tourist police Policia Militar do Estado do Para, Travessa Francisco Caldeira Castelo Branco 393 (☎ 91 3236 2223).

ILHA DE MARAJÓ

The **ILHA DE MARAJÓ** is a vast island in the Amazon delta, opposite Belém, consisting of some forty thousand square kilometres of largely uninhabited mangrove swamps and beaches. Created by the accretion of silt and sand over millions of years, it's a wet and marshy area, the western half covered in thick jungle, the east flat savanna, swampy in the wet season (Jan–June), brown and firm in the dry season (June–Dec). It is home of the giant *pirarucu* fish, which, growing to over 180kg, is the largest freshwater breed in the world. The island is a popular resort for sun-seekers and ecotourists alike.

WHAT TO SEE AND DO

The main port of **Soure** is a growing resort offering pleasant beaches where you can relax under the shade of ancient mango trees. Magnificent empty **beaches** can be found all around the island – the **Praia do Pesqueiro**, about 13km from Soure, is one of the more accessible. If you want to see the interior of the island – or much of the wildlife – you have to be prepared to camp or pay for a room at one of the *fazendas*: book with travel agents in Belém or take your chance on arrival. **Joanes**, with another tremendous beach, is much quieter.

It's wise to take some cash with you from Belém as there's only one ATM on the island (in Soure), and there's no guarantee it'll accept your card.

ARRIVAL

By boat Boats from Belém (see p.306) dock at Porto Camará, about 30km from Soure, and Salvaterra, further south, about 26km away, from where you can grab a bus to any of the island's towns.

ACCOMMODATION AND EATING

In Salvaterra, head to Praia Grande, where there are cheap places to eat spread along the beach.

Ponto Certo Quarta Rua between Travessa 15 & 16, Soure. Friendly and bustling neighbourhood joint serving excellent local food (mains R$10–20).

Pousada O Canto do Francês Sexta Rua at Travessa 8, Soure ☎ 91 3741 1298, ⬤ ocantodofrances.blogspot.com. This beautiful French-owned place is a good choice, offering cool, terracotta-tiled interiors and simple whitewashed rooms fringed in hardwood. R$130

MACAPÁ AND THE ROAD TO FRENCH GUIANA

The main reason to pass through **MACAPÁ**, capital of the impoverished state of Amapá, on the north side of the Amazon across from Ilha de Marajó, is to get to French Guiana. You'll need to take a boat from Belém or fly to get here: the key road in the state then heads north, connecting Macapá with **Oiapoque**, on the river of the same name which delineates the frontier. The road isn't asphalted all the way, but mostly it's pretty good quality; Amazontur (☎ 96 3251 3435, ☎ 96 9112 0892, ⬤ amazontur.com.br) run regular buses to Oiapoque. These are scheduled to take around twelve hours, though the journey can be nearer twenty in the worst of the rainy season.

MANAUS

MANAUS is the capital of Amazonas, a tropical forest state covering around one-and-a-half-million square kilometres. Manaus actually lies on the Rio Negro, 6km from the point where that river meets the Solimões to form (as far as Brazilians are concerned) the Rio Amazonas. Arriving in Manaus may at first seem overwhelming given its near-two million inhabitants, noise and confusion, though it'll have you under its spell soon enough.

Towards the end of the nineteenth century, at the height of the rubber boom, architects were summoned from Europe to redesign the city, which rapidly acquired a Western feel – broad Parisian-style avenues were laid down, interspersed with Italian piazzas centred on splendid fountains. Innovative Manaus was one of the first cities in Brazil to have electricity, trolley buses and sewage systems. However, by 1914 the rubber market was collapsing fast, leaving the city to slumber in past glories for much of the twentieth century. Today, however, Manaus is thriving again: an aggressive commercial and industrial centre for an enormous region.

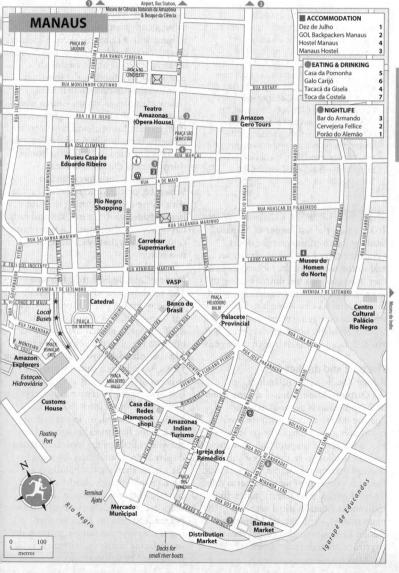

MANAUS

Airport, Bus Station,
Museu de Ciências Naturais da Amazônia
& Bosque da Ciência

■ ACCOMMODATION	
Dez de Julho	1
GOL Backpackers Manaus	2
Hostel Manaus	4
Manaus Hostel	3

● EATING & DRINKING	
Casa da Pomonha	5
Galo Carijó	6
Tacacá da Gisela	4
Toca da Costela	7

● NIGHTLIFE	
Bar do Armando	3
Cervejeria Fellice	2
Porão do Alemão	1

3

ENTERING FRENCH GUIANA

If you are not a citizen of a European Union country, the USA or Canada, you will need a **visa** to enter French Guiana. There is a French consulate in Macapá at the *Pousada Ekinox*, Rua Jovina Dinoa 1693 (☎96 3223 2532), though it's better to arrange visas before you leave home. Buy **euros** at the Casa Francesa Cambio e Turismo either in Belém (Travessa Padre Prudencio 40) or in Macapá (Rua Independência 232); you can get them in Oiapoque but the rates are worse, and you can't depend on changing either Brazilian currency or US dollars for euros in Saint-Georges-de-l'Oyapok. Dug-out taxis are the usual means of transport between Oiapoque and **Saint-Georges-de-l'Oyapok** (see p.678), about ten minutes downriver. Brazilian **exit stamps** can be obtained from the Polícia Federal at the southern road entrance into Oiapoque; on the other side you have to check in with the *gendarmes* in Saint-Georges. From here, regular buses leave for Cayenne.

WHAT TO SEE AND DO

To start with the real flavour of Manaus, head for the riverfront and the **docks**, a constant throng of chaotic activity set against the serenity of the moored ships as they bob gently up and down. During the day there's no problem wandering around the area, and it's easy enough to find out which boats are going where just by asking around. At night, however, the port is best avoided: many of the river men carry guns.

The port and market

Known locally as the Alfândega, the **Customs House** (Mon–Fri 8am–noon & 2–4pm) stands overlooking the floating docks. To cope with the river rising over a 14m range, the concrete pier is supported on pontoons that rise and fall to allow even the largest ships to dock all year round. Across the main road from the port is the **Praça Adalberto Valle**, where there are several craft stalls selling indigenous Amazon tribal *artesanato*. The main **market**, the Mercado Municipal Adolfo Lisboa, is further round the riverfront, though under seemingly eternal renovation.

Teatro Amazonas and around

The sumptuous **Teatro Amazonas** (Mon–Sat 9am–5pm; R$10 including guided tour; ☎92 3622 1880) remains the architectural embodiment of Manaus' rubber boom: a Belle Époque extravagance built with materials brought from Europe and entirely decorated by European artists. Inaugurated in 1896 and famously attracting Enrico Caruso for its opening performance, the place subsequently went silent as boom turned to bust, with a cameo in Werner Herzog's classic, *Fitzcarraldo*, about as much action as it saw for most of the twentieth century. Today, though, the theatre is home to the Amazon Philharmonic (many members of whom – in an ironic postscript to the theatre's origins – hail from Eastern Europe) and hosts regular concerts, including in April the **Festa da Manaus**, initiated in 1997 to celebrate thirty years of the Zona Franca.

The beautiful little **Igreja de São Sebastião**, on the same *praça*, and often with votive candles burning in a stone font outside, was built in 1888 and only has one tower, the result of a nineteenth-century tax payable by churches with two towers.

Museu Casa de Eduardo Ribeiro

This brightly painted rubber boom mansion on Rua José Clemente (Tues–Sat 9am–5pm, Sun 9am–1pm; ☎92 3631 2938; free with guided tour) was once home to the governor responsible for Manaus' original neo-European spending spree. As such, it's a suitably opulent window on how the city's original other half lived, though pretty much everything that you see, apart from the walls, has been re-created, or, in the case of the antique furniture, brought in from elsewhere. Perhaps the most fascinating display is the photograph montage in the garden showing the building's rescue from certain mouldy death (which countless other mansions in the city, sadly, are still heading towards). Likewise poignant to imagine is the original bucolic view of the Rio Negro from the south-facing windows, now entirely obliterated by urban sprawl.

Museu do Índio

The **Museu do Índio**, at Rua Duque de Caxias 356 (Mon–Fri 8.30–11.30am & 2–4.30pm, Sat 8.30–11.30am; R\$5), lies a little way east of the centre off Avenida Sete de Setembro. Run by the Salesian Sisters, whose missions along the Rio Negro have long gone about the dubious work of saving indigenous souls, this dark and slightly oppressive museum unsurprisingly approaches native culture from a paternalistic angle. The exhibits are nevertheless worth the trek from town, ranging from sacred ritual masks and inter-village communication drums to fine ceramics, superb palm-frond weavings, fascinating photos and even replicas of Indian dwellings, as well as more unsettling arrays of surgical instruments and old medical books, echoes of the devastating epidemics that inevitably followed each new contact.

Palacete Provincial

Housed in the former military police headquarters, the Palacete Provincial on Praça Heliodoro Balbi (Tues & Wed 9am–5pm, Thurs, Fri & Sat 9am–7pm, Sun 4–8pm; free; 92 3622 8387, culturamazonas.am.gov.br/programas) is a cultural and educational centre housing a number of curious museums and exhibition halls; among these are the Museum of Image and Sound, the Numismatic Museum and the Archeological Exhibition. The pleasant leafy square and the building itself are also worth checking out.

Museu de Ciências Naturais da Amazônia

The **Museu de Ciências Naturais da Amazônia** (Mon–Sat 9am–noon & 2–5pm; R\$12; 92 3644 2799) on Estrada dos Japoneses s/n, Colcachoeira Grande, is an interesting little museum that's home to various well-preserved insects as well as some rare species of fish, including *pirarucu*, the largest scaled freshwater fish in the world.

Bosque da Ciência

Occupying an area of approximately 32 acres, the **Bosque da Ciência**

(Tues–Fri 9am–noon & 2–5pm, Sat & Sun 9am–4pm; R\$5; 92 3643 3192, www.inpa.gov.br) on Avenida André Araújo 1756, Aleixo, is a plot of forest home to plenty of animals that roam freely within the area, such as monkeys and sloths. A fun way to see the park is with one of the *pequenos guias* (free), children who participate in environmental programmes and act as guides.

The meeting of the waters

The most popular and most widely touted day-trip from Manaus is to the **meeting of the waters**, some 10km downstream, where the Rio Negro and the Rio Solimões meet to form the Rio Amazonas. For several kilometres beyond the point where they join, the waters of the two rivers continue to flow separately, the muddy yellow of the Solimões contrasting sharply with the black of the Rio Negro, which is much warmer, and more acidic. Most one-day river trips stop here (see p.314).

Parque Ecológico do Janauary

Most tours to the meeting of the waters stop in at the **Parque Ecológico do Janauary**, an ecological park some 7km from Manaus on one of the main local tributaries of the Rio Negro. Usually you'll be transferred to smaller motorized canoes to explore its creeks (*igarapés*), flooded forest lands (*igapós*) and abundant vegetation. One of the highlights of the area is the great quantity of *Victoria Amazonica*, the extraordinary giant floating lily for which Manaus is famous, and which reaches a diameter of two metres.

Praia Ponta Negra

At weekends, the river beach at **Praia Ponta Negra**, about 13km northwest of Manaus, is packed with locals. It's an enjoyable place to go for a swim, with plenty of bars and restaurants serving freshly cooked river fish nearby. The bus to Ponta Negra (#120) leaves every thirty minutes; catch it by the cathedral on Praça da Matriz.

3

ARRIVAL AND INFORMATION

By plane The airport (Aeroporto de Eduardo Gomes; ☎ 92 3652 1212) is on Av Santos Dumont, 17km north of town. It is served by both bus #306 ($2.75) and the executive red and white minibus #813 (R$4.20), both of which thread a circular route through the city centre. Many tour operators will offer airport pick-up if you're booked with them, usually a cheaper option than an airport taxi (R$50).

Destinations Belém (4 daily; 2hr 10min–2hr 55min); Cuiabá (6–8 daily; 3hr 45min–10hr).

By regular boat Boats dock right in the heart of the city, either by the Mercado Municipal or a short way along in the floating port. If you're arriving from Peru or Colombia, don't forget to have your passport stamped at the Customs House (see p.312) if you haven't already done so in Tabatinga. Tickets for the regular services on the Amazon (see p.316) can be bought from the ticket windows inside the Estação Hidroviária off Praça da Matriz

(☎ 92 3088 5769, ⊕ portodemanaus.com.br), next to where the boat departure list is posted. Before buying your ticket, ask for a pass (*papel do permissão*), which allows you into the docks (you'll need your passport, too) where the bigger, long-distance riverboats are moored; here you can have a look at the boats before deciding which you want to travel on. Smaller boats with no regular schedules are found in São Raimundo, northwest of the town centre; take bus #101 from Praça da Matriz and ask the attendant to tell you when to get off – turn left at the blue-and-white-tiled community centre and go straight down the hill, where you'll eventually come to the beach. There's no ticket office, or shade (wear a hat); you'll have to ask around for departures. Tanaka operate both regular and express boats to São Gabriel da Cachoeira; in the express boat you have to sit upright in your seat for the whole journey – many end up sleeping in the aisle.

Destinations Belém (Wed & Fri noon; 3–5 days; R$325); Rio Madeira to Porto Velho (Tues 6pm; 4 days; R$170);

JUNGLE TRIPS FROM MANAUS

The nature and quantity of the **wildlife** you get to see on a standard **jungle tour** depends mainly on how far away from Manaus you go and how long you can devote to the trip. Birds like macaws, *jabarus* and toucans can generally be spotted, and you might see alligators, snakes and a few species of monkey on a three-day trip. For a reasonable chance of glimpsing wild deer, tapirs, armadillos or wild cats, a more adventurous trip of a week or more is required. On any trip, make sure that you'll get some time in the smaller channels in a canoe, as the sound of a motor is a sure way of scaring every living thing out of sight. The Rio Negro region has water with high acidity because of the geology of its main sources in the Guyana Shield. Because of this, it tends to have fewer mosquitoes which is an obvious bonus; but it also tends to have less abundant wildlife than some of the lakes and channels around the Rio Solimões. Plenty of tours combine both the Solimões and Negro rivers in their itineraries.

TOUR ITINERARIES

The **one-day river trip**, usually costing R$140–150/person, generally includes an inspection of the famous meeting of the waters (see p.313), some 10km downriver from Manaus. The other most popular jungle river trips tend to be the **three- to five-day expeditions**. If you want to sleep in the forest, either in a lodge, riverboat or, for the more adventurous, swinging in a hammock outside in a small jungle clearing, it really is worth taking as many days as you can to get as far away from Manaus as possible. The usual price for guided tours, including accommodation and food, should be between R$150 and R$200 a day/person (no matter the sales pitch). As well as the itinerary, check that you're getting what you need in terms of security, health and safety, food, sleeping arrangements, guide quality and transfers.

The most commonly operated tours are three-day trips combining both the **Rio Negro** and **Rio Solimões**, although some trips only cover the former, as it is more accessible from Manaus. Four-day trips should ideally also include the **Anavilhanas Archipelago** on the Rio Negro, the second-largest freshwater archipelago in the world with around four hundred isles, as well as a good day's walk through the jungle. On the Solimões, some of the three- to five-day options include trips to Lago Mamori or Manacapuru.

If you want to forgo organized tours entirely and travel independently, note that **commercial boats** are a very inexpensive way of getting about on the rivers around Manaus. The best place to look for these is down on Flutuante Três Estrelas, one of the wooden wharves behind the distribution market, further along the river edge from the Hidroviária (waterway) at the back of the Mercado Municipal. You'll need perseverance and a good grasp of Portuguese to negotiate passage.

Santarém and all ports along the Amazon (Tues & Fri 6am, Wed noon, Thurs 8am, Sat 7am; 2 days; R$159); Rio Negro to São Gabriel da Cachoeira (regular boat Fri 6pm; 3 days; R$240, express boat Tues & Fri 3pm; 28hr; R$300); Rio Solimões to Tabatinga (two each on Wed & Sat 11am & noon; 6 days; R$340).

By express boat If you're in a hurry to get to Tabatinga or Tefé, you might want to consider taking an express boat from Terminal Ajato (☎ 92 3622 6047, ⍟ terminalajato .com.br), located slightly to the northeast of the Mercado Municipal, down a steep flight of iron stairs.

Destinations Tefé (Mon & Thurs 6am; R$220; 12–13hr, Wed, Fri, Sat & Sun 7am; R$200–230; 12–13hr); Tabatinga (Tues & Sun 7am; R$500; 36hr).

By bus The small *rodoviária* is 6km north of the centre, hidden behind a motorway and fiendishly difficult to navigate to or from; the only local bus that leaves from outside, #006, follows a wildly circuitous route into the centre and can literally take hours; save yourself the trouble and splurge on a taxi (R$25). Coming the other way (from the local terminal at Praça Matriz), #005 will get you there direct, eventually, while #500, #640 or #311 all pass the nearby Shell garage; ask the attendant where to get off, otherwise you'll never have a hope of finding it.

Destinations EUCATUR (⍟ www.eucatur.com.br) serve Boa Vista, where you'll find regular connections to Venezuela. For Santa Elena, grab a taxi from Boa Vista's *rodoviária* – it's actually cheaper and less time-consuming than the bus as there are plenty of drivers keen to fill up with cheap fuel in Venezuela. All tourists going to Venezuela must have a yellow-fever vaccination card to buy their tickets – you can get the injection and card at the *rodoviária* or at the main floating harbour for free. Boa Vista (5 daily; 16hr).

Tourist information The tourist office is close to the back of the Opera House at Av Eduardo Ribeira 666 (Mon–Fri 8am–5pm; ☎ 92 3233 0739, ⍟ visitamazonas.am .gov.br); it has helpful, friendly staff who can supply town maps. There's also a small tourist office at the airport (☎ 92 3182 9850; 24hr).

ACCOMMODATION

Dez de Julho Rua Dez de Julho 679 ☎ 92 3232 6280, ⍟ hoteldezdejulho.com. Though sometimes criticized for its noisy a/c and concrete platform beds (albeit with a decent mattress on top), the location is almost perfect and – with rooms fairly dark and internal – it is at least quiet. Staff are friendly and there's a well-respected tour agency, Amazon Gero Tours, just off the reception. Wi-fi and breakfast included. R$90

GOL Backpackers Manaus Rua Barroso 365 ☎ 92 3304 5805, ⍟ golbackapckers.com. One of Manaus' newest hostels, in a fantastic location a mere stone's throw from Teatro Amazonas, with 4–6-bed dorms up a flight of stone steps, plus wi-fi, internet, inclusive breakfast, kitchen and bar. 6-bed dorms R$25, 4-bed dorms R$30

★ **Hostel Manaus** Rua Lauro Cavalcante 231 ☎ 92 3233 4545, ⍟ hihostelmanaus.com. Aussie-owned HI-affiliated hostel with firm comfortable dorm beds with lockers in lovely old high-ceilinged colonial rooms (some dorms with a/c), views of the Palácio Rio Negro from the breakfast table and a sweetly eccentric and eclectic bunch of staff. They proudly boast of having the lowest HI dorm price in Brazil – and all with a bargain laundry service, wi-fi, international call facility and Skype, TV lounge and kitchen, slap-up inclusive breakfast, beer garden and tour agency. Dorms R$27, doubles R$66

Manaus Hostel Rua Costa Azevedo 63 ☎ 92 3231 2139, ⍟ manaushostel.com.br. Pleasant bright-pink hostel in a good location with reasonably clean if slightly poky rooms and bathrooms, a little TV area, a basic kitchen for guests, meagre inclusive breakfast and wi-fi. A half-decent choice if *GOL* or *Hostel Manaus* is full. Dorms R$25, doubles R$70

EATING AND DRINKING

There is plenty of cheap street food everywhere, especially around the docks, the Mercado Municipal and in busy downtown locations like the Praça da Matriz, where a plate of rice and beans with a skewer of freshly grilled meat or fish costs about R$9. There's a Carrefour supermarket on Av Eduardo Ribeiro.

Casa da Pamonha Rua Barroso 375 ☎ 92 3233 1028. All the atmosphere of a doctor's waiting room yet a godsend for vegetarians who don't eat fish/seafood – though slightly pricey, the lunchtime buffet (11am–2pm; R$33.90 *por quilo*) isn't bad at all, with the usual rice, beans, quiche etc, and be sure to help yourself to a bowl of the vegetable soup: thick, salty and delicious. Open for *salgados*, sandwiches, (excellent) coffee and the like the rest of the time. Mon–Fri 7am–7pm, Sat 7am–2pm.

Galo Carijó Rua dos Andradas 536 ☎ 92 3233 0044. One of the best local places for fresh fish and a friendly welcome, with a cavernous corner location and plenty of dishes to choose from, most tacked up on the ancient wall-mounted menu – try the *pirarucu* (R$40 for two), the largest freshwater scaled fish in the world. Mon–Sat 11am–4pm.

Tacacá da Gisela Largo São Sebastião, s/n ☎ 92 8803 4901. One traditional dish you should definitely try when you're here is *tacacá* – a soup that consists essentially of yellow manioc root juice in a hot, spicy dried-shrimp sauce – and this ever-bustling kiosk on Praça São Sebastião is the place to try it (R$12). Daily 4–10pm.

Toca da Costela Rua Barão de São Domingos 268 ☎ 92 3622 0230. Only open during the day and usually packed, this is a great location from which to watch the daily mayhem of the banana market as you feast on superb meat and fish dishes (R$20.99 *por quilo*). Daily 7am–5pm.

NIGHTLIFE

There are some good bars in the centre of town, but if you really want to get immersed in Manaus nightlife, the bulk of the action is on Estrada do Turismo, northwest of the city (taxi R$60), where bars line the avenue. Alternatively, try Praça do Caranguejo in El Dorado (taxi R$40), also home to many bars and restaurants.

Bar do Armando Rua 10 de Julho 593 ☎ 92 3232 1195. As old-school as it gets, this cavernous bar has beer crates stacked high against the back walls and ancient football strips dangling from the ceiling. For forty years now, it's where people have been heading for an ice-cold beer (Brahma R$6) after a tough day's work, with tables spilling out onto the pavement and looking onto the square and the Opera House. Mon–Sat 5/5.30pm–1/2am.

Cervejeria Fellice Studio 5, Festival Mall, Rua Rodrigo Otávio 3555, Distrito Industrial ☎ 92 3216 3400, ⓦ cervejariafellice.com.br. The glass and steel overload – with fermentation tanks looming over the tables – hardly makes for a mellow atmosphere, but this artisan brewery and bar is justifiably proud of its traditional ale, lager and wheat beer; if you've endured one can of Skol too many, a foaming glass of *chopp* will be R$4.50 well spent. Regular live music (cover R$10–20) runs the gamut from samba and *pagode* to Iron Maiden tributes. Mon–Fri 11.30am–late, Sat & Sun 5pm–late.

Porão do Alemão Estrada da Ponta Negra 1986 ☎ 92 3239 2976, ⓦ poraodoalemao.com.br. There's no getting away

from the fact that Brazilians can't get enough of their hoary Anglophone rock, and – with its inimitable logo of the opera house in flames – this place is Manaus' original, hugely popular shrine to the genre. Live music most nights, with the usual mix of tribute acts and young hopefuls; R$20 cover for the bigger shows. Beers start at R$5. Wed–Sat 9pm–late.

SHOPPING

Artesanato Available from the Museu do Índio (p.313) and several shops around the square in front of the Teatro Amazonas. The best selection (and the most fun way to shop) is at the Sunday-morning street market that appears out of nowhere in the broad Avenida Eduardo Ribeira, behind the Teatro Amazonas. Indian crafts are also sold at the Mercado Municipal (under renovation at the time of research) and *artesanato* (including handmade jewellery) at the stalls on Praça Terreira Aranha. Interesting *macumba* and *umbanda* items, such as incense, candles, figurines and bongos, can be found at Cabana Pomba Gira on Rocha dos Santos 92, corner of Rua Miranda.

Hammocks A good hammock shop is Casa das Redes on Rua dos Andradas.

DIRECTORY

Banks and exchange There are ATMs that accept foreign cards at the airport and several banks on Av Eduardo Ribeiro, just a block or two down the street from the tourist office.

THE RIO SOLIMÕES: CROSSING TO PERU AND COLOMBIA

From Manaus to **Iquitos** in Peru (see p.813), the river remains navigable by large ocean-going boats as well as the occasional smaller, more locally oriented riverboats. In spite of the discomforts, such as long delays and frequently broken-down boats, travellers still use this route as it's the cheapest way of travelling between Brazil and Peru.

There are reasonable facilities for visitors in the border town of **Tabatinga**, though most people prefer to stay in the adjacent Colombian town of **Leticia** (see p.560). All boats have to stop at one of these ports, and most will terminate at the border, whichever direction they've come from. If you want to break the journey before you reach the three-way border, you can do so at **Tefé**, around halfway. The main reason to call here is to visit the **Mamiraua Sustainable Development Reserve** (☎ 97 3343 9700, ⓦ mamiraua.org.br), an accessible, beautiful and wild area of rainforest upstream from the town. Entering the reserve is pricey, though – a three-day pass costs R$1290. Another reason for stopping here might be that you really can't face the boat journey any longer: there are flights available (see below) to Tabatinga.

GETTING AROUND

By boat There is a daily express boat service (12– 13hr; R$200–230) connecting Manaus with Tefé. From Manaus to Tabatinga there are regular and express boats running upstream. The downstream journey, which is often very crowded, takes two to four days and costs around R$300; there's also a twice-weekly express service (32hr; R$500). On the other side of the border, there are super-fast powerboats or

standard riverboats connecting Tabatinga to Iquitos (see box, p.821).

By plane Trip/Azul operate daily flights between Tefé and Manaus, as well as weekly flights between Tefé and Tabatinga. If you want to fly from Tabatinga to Iquitos your best bet is flights with the Peruvian air force (PAF) from Caballo Cocha (see box, p.821), a 2hr journey by boat from Santa Rosa, an insignificant Peruvian settlement at the three-way border.

Consulates Chile, Rua Marquês de Caravelas, casa 08, Parque das Laranjeiras (☎92 3236 6888); Colombia, Rua 24 de Maio 220, Ed. Rio Negro Centre, Centro (☎92 3234 6777); UK, Rua Poraquê 240 (☎92 6132 1819); Ecuador, Rua 6 no.16, Conj. Jardim Belo Horizonte, Parque 10 (☎92 3236 3698); Venezuela, Rua Rio Jutaí 839, Vieiralves (☎92 3584 3828).

Hospital For tropical complaints the best is the Instituto de Medicina Tropical, Avenida Pedro Teixeira 25 (☎92 2127 3473).

Internet Cyber Juliana, Av Joaquim Nabuco, at C Bocaiúva (Mon–Sat 8am–11pm, Sun 9am–11pm; R$2/hr), has a/c and a good connection; Mix Internet, Rua 24 de Mayo 345 (Mon–Fri 8am–5pm, Sat 8am–2pm; R$3/hr) is slightly hemmed-in but central.

Pharmacy Drogueria Nossa Senhora de Nazaré, 7 de Setembro 1333 (☎92 3215 2844).

Police The tourist police are located on the lower floor at the airport (24hr; ☎92 3652 1656).

Post office Rua Monsenhor Coutinho 90, by Praça do Congresso; Rua Barroso 226, corner of Rua Saldanha Marinho (both Mon–Fri 8am–4pm, Sat 8am–noon).

Taxis Atlanta Rádio Taxi ☎0800 92 6060, ☎92 3622 2525; Coopertaxi ☎92 3652 1568; Executivo Rádio Taxi ☎92 3611 1000.

Brasília

Much of central Brazil including most of the state of Goiás, the north and west of Minas Gerais and the east of Mato Grosso is dominated by the Planalto Central (central highlands), a largely dry and savanna-like *cerrado*, once covered with low vegetation and now a centre for ranching and plantation agriculture. In this inhospitable landscape almost 1000km northwest of Rio lies **BRASÍLIA**, the largest and most fascinating of the world's "planned cities". Declared capital in 1960 and a UNESCO World Heritage Site in 1995, the futuristic city was the vision of **Juscelino Kubitschek**, who realized his election promise to build it if elected president in 1956. Designed by **Oscar Niemeyer**, South America's most able student of Le Corbusier, it is located in its own federal zone – Brasília D.F. (Distrito Federal) – in the centre of Goiás state.

Intended for a population of half a million by 2000, today the city is Brazil's fastest-growing, with 2.6 million inhabitants. At first glance the gleaming government buildings and excellent roads give you the impression that this is the modern heart of a new world superpower. Look closer and you'll see cracks in the concrete structures; drive ten minutes in any direction and you'll hit kilometres of low-income housing in the *cidades satélites* (poorer satellite cities). This is a city of diplomats, students, government workers and the people who serve them. Prices are high. Still, there are beautiful sunsets, two or three days' worth of things to see (more if you want to take in the best of Goiás), and an exuberant bar and restaurant scene.

3

WHAT TO SEE AND DO

Brasília's layout was designed to resemble an airplane (some say a bird, others a bow and arrow). At its centre is a sloped, grassy plain and two central traffic arteries, the **Eixo Monumental** (north/south) and the **Eixo Rodoviário** or **Eixão** (east/west), which neatly divide the centre into sectors: administrative, shopping, banking, commercial and embassy. These are the treeless (and thus shadeless) parts of Brasília where pavements are provided and you can actually walk between many of the sights. North and south of the centre are self-contained **residential areas** – each with its own shopping, restaurants and nightlife, each one spaced a long way from the next. The city is designed for the car, which means you can end up spending a lot of cash on taxis. To take advantage of better and cheaper food in the city's wings, pick an area with several restaurants and bars, take a bus there and walk between *quadras* (blocks).

Esplanada dos Ministérios

Brasília's *raison d'être* is the government complex known as the **Esplanada dos Ministérios**, focused on the iconic 28-storey twin towers of the **Congresso Nacional** (the nose of the plane or the bird's "beak"). The buildings here, designed by Niemeyer, can all be seen in a day for free (though you'll need to plan carefully around their different opening hours) and are regarded as among the world's finest modernist examples. The white marble, water pools, reflecting glass and flying buttresses on the **Presidential Palace** and **Supreme Court** lend the buildings an elegance made more impressive at night by floodlights. A taxi or bus ride around the Esplanada in the early evening before the commuter traffic (6–8pm), when the buildings glow like Chinese lanterns, is a must.

Praça dos Três Poderes

At the complex's centre is the **Praça dos Três Poderes** (Plaza of the Three Powers), representing the Congress, judiciary and presidency. Two large "bowls" on each side of the Congresso Nacional house the **Senate** (the smaller, inverted one) and the **House of Representatives** (☎61 3303 1581, ☎61 3216 1768). There are free

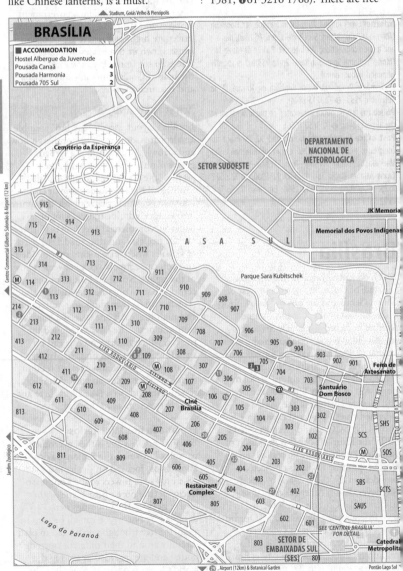

BRASÍLIA

ACCOMMODATION

Hostel Albergue da Juventude	1
Pousada Canaã	4
Pousada Harmonia	3
Pousada 705 Sul	2

guided tours (weekdays every 30min 9am–5pm, weekends 10am, noon, 2pm and 4pm; ask for times of English-speaking tours). There is a strict dress code – men must wear trousers and avoid sleeveless shirts and sandals; women must dress in smart casual attire.

Behind the Congresso Nacional on the *praça*'s northern side, the **Palácio do** **Planalto** houses the president's office (tours Sun only 9.30am–2pm; dress code as above), whose stunning interior is dominated by sleek columns and a curved ramp. On weekdays, visitors must content themselves with a changing of the guard out front (daily 8.30am & 5.30pm).

Also on the *praça*, at its edge near the Avenida das Nações, is the **Panteão da**

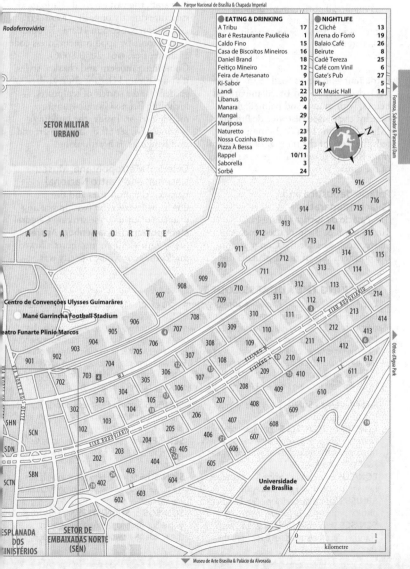

● EATING & DRINKING

A Tribu	17
Bar é Restaurante Paulicéia	1
Caldo Fino	15
Casa de Biscoitos Mineiros	16
Daniel Brand	18
Feitiço Mineiro	12
Feira de Artesanato	9
Ki-Sabor	21
Landi	22
Libanus	20
Manara	4
Mangai	29
Mariposa	7
Naturetto	23
Nossa Cozinha Bistro	28
Pizza À Bessa	2
Rappel	10/11
Saborella	3
Sorbê	24

● NIGHTLIFE

2 Cliché	13
Arena do Forró	19
Balaio Café	26
Beirute	8
Cadê Tereza	25
Café com Vinil	6
Gate's Pub	27
Play	5
UK Music Hall	14

3

Pátria Tancredo Neves (daily 9am–6pm; free), dedicated to ten Brazilian national heroes, with murals and painted glass. Nearby, the **Museu Histórico de Brasília** (Mon–Sat 9am–1pm & 2–5pm; free) tells the story of the transfer of the capital from Rio and features a large-scale model of the city.

Palácio da Justiça and Palácio Itamarati

The **Palácio da Justiça** (Mon–Fri 10am–noon & 3–5pm; dress code as above; free) is beside the Congresso on the northern side of the Esplanada dos Ministérios. The bare facade was covered with fancy – and, to many, elitist – marble tiles during the military dictatorship, but with the return to democracy they were removed, revealing the concrete pillars and waterfalls between them, cascading pleasantly into pools below.

A more worthwhile visit is the **Palácio Itamarati**, the vast external relations structure directly opposite (Mon–Fri 2–4.30pm, Sat & Sun 10am–3.30pm, guided tours by appointment, dress code as above; free; ☎61 2030 8006). Combining modern and classical styles, it's built around elegant courtyards, gardens, and a surfeit of sculptures, including Bruno Giorgi's stunning marble *Meteor*. Inside, the building's spaciousness, set off by modern art and wall hangings, is breathtaking.

Catedral Metropolitana, Museu Nacional and Teatro Nacional

Between the ministries and the downtown *rodoviária* (within walking distance of either), the striking **Catedral Metropolitana Nossa Senhora Aparecida** (daily 7am–6.30pm; no shorts allowed) marks the spot where the city was

CRACKING THE ADDRESS CODES

While initially confusing, Brasília's **address system** does eventually make finding places easier than in cities with named streets. For example: SQN 210, Bloco B – 503, means *superquadra* north no. 210, building B, apartment 503. The *superquadra* number (210) is the location, the first digit the direction east or west of the Eixo Rodoviário, with odd numbers to the west and even numbers to the east; the numbers increase as you get further from the centre. The final two digits give the distance north or south of the Eixo Monumental. The logic also applies to roads: even numbers apply east of the Eixão, odd to the west; a letter in front indicates the side of the Eixão it runs, eg L for east (*leste*) or W for west. Some other helpful terms:

Asa Norte/Asa Sul The city's two "wings" (*asas*), north and south.

CLN/CLS or **SCLN/SCLS** *Comércio Local Norte/Sul.* Shopping blocks interspersed throughout the residential *superquadras* of Asa Norte and Asa Sul.

EQN/EQS *Entrequadras Norte/Sul.* The area between *quadras* at Eixinhos's edge.

SBN/SBS *Setor Bancário Norte/Sul.* Two bank districts, either side of Eixo Monumental.

SCN/SCS *Setor Comercial Norte/Sul.* Two commercial office areas set back from the shopping centres.

SDN/SDS *Setor de Diversies Norte/Sul.* Two shopping centres (*conjuntos*) on either side of Eixo Monumental.

SEN/SES *Setor de Embaixadas Norte/Sul.* The embassy areas east of the bank sectors.

SHIN/SHIS *Setor de Habitaçies Individuais Norte/Sul.* Two peninsulas jutting into Lago Paranoá.

SQN/SQS or **SHCN/SHCS** *Superquadras Norte/Sul.* Individual *superquadras* in the residential wings Asa Norte and Asa Sul.

inaugurated in 1960. Built in the form of an inverted chalice and crown of thorns, its sunken nave lies below ground level though is well lit, and the statues of St Peter and the angels suspended from the ceiling create a feeling of airiness and elevation.

Just to the north, also on the Esplanada, the domed **Museu Nacional Honestino Guimãraes** (Tues–Sun 9am–6.30pm; free), with its suspended curved walkway, looks something like a crashed, white Saturn half-submerged in concrete, and houses visiting art exhibitions.

3

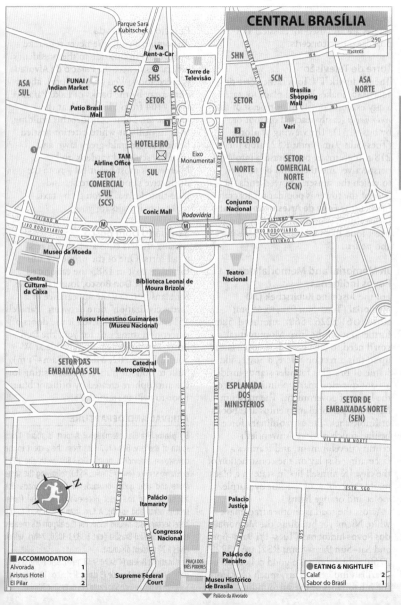

CENTRAL BRASÍLIA

0   250
metres

Parque Sara Kubitschek

Via Rent-a-Car

SHN   W4

ASA SUL

FUNAI / Indian Market

SCS

@ SHS

Torre de Televisão

SCN

Brasília Shopping Mall

ASA NORTE

W3

Patio Brasil Mall

SETOR

SETOR

HOTELEIRO

TAM Airline Office

SETOR COMERCIAL SUL (SCS)

SUL

Eixo Monumental

HOTELEIRO

NORTE

Vari

SETOR COMERCIAL NORTE (SCN)

Conic Mall

Rodoviária

Conjunto Nacional

EIXINHO W

EIXO RODOVIARIO

EIXINHO L

Museu da Moeda

Centro Cultural da Caixa

Biblioteca Leonel de Moura Brizola

Teatro Nacional

Museu Honestino Guimarães (Museu Nacional)

SETOR DAS EMBAIXADAS SUL

Catedral Metropolitana

ESPLANADA DOS MINISTÉRIOS

SETOR DE EMBAIXADAS NORTE (SEN)

VIA E N UM NORTE

SES 803

ESTR. SGO

Palácio Itamaraty

PTP AREA

Congresso Nacional

Palácio Justiça

Palácio do Planalto

PRAÇA DOS TRÊS PODERES

Supreme Federal Court

Museu Histórico de Brasília

Palácio da Alvorada

■ **ACCOMMODATION**
Alvorada	1
Aristus Hotel	3
El Pilar	2

● **EATING & NIGHTLIFE**
Calaf	2
Sabor do Brasil	1

3

Heading up towards the *rodoviária*, on the northern side of the Eixo Monumental, you'll reach the **Teatro Nacional** (Mon–Fri 3–5pm). Built in the form of an Aztec temple, this glass-covered pyramid allows light into the lobby, where there are often art exhibitions, while there are three performance halls inside. Most productions are in Portuguese but the venues are also used for classical and popular music **concerts**.

Torre de Televisão

The landmark TV Tower, the **Torre de Televisão**, makes a good place to start a city exploration, 1km northeast of the *rodoviária* (easily reached on foot or by bus #131). The viewing platform (Tues–Sun 9am–9pm; R\$2) atop the 218m-high tower puts Brasília into perspective, and there's no better spot to watch the sunset. On weekends the base of the tower is popular for its craft market, the **Feira de Artesanato** – great for clothing, souvenirs, and very cheap street food like tapioca, sugar-cane juice and *pasteis*.

JK Memorial and Memorial dos Povos Indígenas

For the **Juscelino Kubitschek (JK) Memorial** (Tues–Sun 9am–5.45pm; R\$10; ☎61 3226 7860), another 1.5km further out on the Eixo Monumental, you'll need to take the bus – dozens head up in this direction. Here, a Soviet-like statue of Brasília's founder stands inside a giant question mark, pointing towards the heart of government. The museum has many personal mementos and books of Kubitschek, the extraordinary force behind much of Brazil's twentieth-century development, and features a fascinating display on the construction of the city. JK himself lies in state in a black marble sarcophagus, backlit by purple, violet and orange lights.

Across the road is another trademark white Niemeyer building, the **Memorial dos Povos Indígenas** (Tues–Fri 9am–6pm and Sat–Sun 9am–5pm; R\$2; ☎61 3223 3760), which houses a good collection of Brazilian indigenous art, much of it from the inhabitants of the surrounding

planalto. Highlights are the ceramic pots of the Warao, beautifully adorned with figures of birds and animals, and vivid, delicate featherwork. Opening hours here are sporadic; if the main entrance is shut, go to the right of the ramp on ground level and bang on the large metal door for security to let you in – it's worth it.

Palácio da Alvorada

To complete your Niemeyer tour take a short taxi or bus ride to the president's official residence, the **Palácio da Alvorada** (guided tours Wed only 3–5pm), about 3km away by the banks of Lake Paranoá (bus #104 from Platform A at the *rodoviária*). Some consider this building, with its brilliant-white exterior nestled behind an emerald-green lawn and carefully sculpted gardens, to be Niemeyer's most beautiful – note the distinctive slender buttresses and blue-tinted glass. If you go by taxi, make sure it waits for you.

Santuário Dom Bosco

Brasília attracts cults and New Agers of all sorts. One of the prime reasons for this is that in 1883 the canonized Italian priest **Don Bosco**, founder of the Salesians, foresaw the appearance of a "great civilization" here between "Parallels 15° and 20° South". Even if the doors of perception thing isn't for you, the **Don Bosco Sanctuary** (easily walkable at W-3 South, Bloco 702; Mon–Sat 7am–7pm), built to honour him, is worth visiting for the atmosphere created by brilliant blue floor-to-ceiling stained glass.

ARRIVAL AND DEPARTURE

By plane Brasília International Airport is about 12km south of the city. Bus #102 runs from the airport to the downtown *rodoviária*, hourly (R\$3.80), with the #113 *executivo* service (every 30min; R\$10) following the same route and also going onwards to the Esplanada dos Ministérios and the Setor Hoteleiro Norte e Sul (hotel sectors north and south). A taxi from the airport to the hotel sector costs around R\$50. For the airport it's cheaper to call Rádio Táxi Brasília (☎61 3323 3030; 24hr), which gives a 20 percent discount.

Destinations Belém (4 daily; 5hr 30min); Belo Horizonte (12 daily; 2hr); Campo Grande (3 daily; 3hr); Rio (12 daily; 3hr); Salvador (4 daily; 4hr); São Paulo (15 daily; 3hr 30min).

ESCAPING THE CITY

There are parks and gardens on the outskirts of the city that can be reached on foot or by local bus. Wilder natural attractions and tourist towns a little further out require renting a car, hiring a taxi or taking a long-distance bus.

CITY PARKS AND GARDENS

Sarah Kubitschek National Park
☎61 3325 1092. If you sicken of all the city concrete, visit this park sprawling west of the TV Tower, which has ponds and walking trails for a quick and easy escape. Daily 5am–midnight; free.

Olhos d'Água Park Asa Norte, entrance by Bloco 414 ☎61 3233 8099. Trails and playgrounds at this park within the residential wing. Take one of the buses running along Eixo Rodoviária Norte to Bloco 213 and walk one block to the park. Daily 6am–8pm; free.

Jardim Zoológico de Brasília Av das Nações, South Exit, Via L4 Sul ☎61 3445 7000, ⓦwww.zoo.df.gov.br. The zoo has more than 250 species of birds, reptiles and mammals. Take one of the buses running along Av das Nações. Tues–Sun 9am–5pm; R$2.

Parque Nacional de Brasília EPIA Highway, North Exit ☎61 3465 2016. Trails and two swimming pools with running mineral water, about 6km northwest of the city centre. Take bus #128 from the *rodoviária*. Daily 8am–4pm; R$13.

Botanical Garden Setor de Mansões Dom Bosco, Module 12 (entrance by QI-23 of South Lake) ☎61 3366 3007. Gardens with more than 100 species of native herbs, a 9km taxi-ride (R$30) southwest of the city centre. Tues–Sun 8.30am–5.30pm; free.

Pontão Lago Sul The beautiful people come to this lakeside area to eat, drink and be seen. They've got the right idea. Walk along the lake and check out the JK Bridge, a series of spectacular modernist arcs. There's no bus so take a taxi (20min; R$40); a line of waiting cabs is there for your return.

FURTHER AFIELD

Chapada Imperial ☎61 9984 4437, ⓦchapadaimperial.com.br. Locals rave about spending weekends camping at this park, which has walking trails and more than thirty natural waterfalls. It's about 50km northwest of the city so renting a car is your best bet.

Pirenópolis In the Serra dos Pireneus mountains, a five-hour drive from Brasília (regular buses ply the route). This attractive market town is a popular weekend retreat

with cobbled streets, pousadas, river swimming, and numerous arts, crafts and hippy/alternative-lifestyle stores.

Goiás Velho One of the prettiest colonial towns in Brazil, entirely unhurried and almost completely surrounded by steep hillsides. Two buses per day operate the six-hour route from the *rodoviária*. Stay a night or two in a pousada to take in the cobbled streets and museums of this UNESCO World Heritage Site.

By bus Long-distance buses arrive at the *rodoferroviária* (although there's no longer a train station here), at the tail of the Eixo Monumental. From here bus #131 runs down the Eixo to the city-centre *rodoviária*.

Destinations Belém (daily; 36hr); Belo Horizonte (3 daily; 13hr); Recife (daily; 48hr); Rio (daily; 20hr); Salvador (daily; 26hr); São Paulo (daily; 16hr).

INFORMATION

Tourist information The official Federal District Tourist Office (☎61 3214 2744, ⓦwww.setur.df.gov.br) is located north of the TV Tower on the second floor of the enormous *Centro de Convenções Ulysses Guimarães* (entrance on northern side) – they're friendly and helpful, and also have a booth at the Praça dos Três Poderes. At the airport the first-floor office (at departures) is more

helpful than that on the arrivals floor, and has free maps. Pick up the daily *Correio Brasiliense* newspaper, with its daily listings supplement on films, exhibitions and live music.

GETTING AROUND

By bus City buses are based at the downtown *rodoviária*. Useful services include the #131, which goes up Eixo Monumental past the TV Tower and JK Memorial to the *rodoferroviária*, and #108 and #104, which run frequently past the Museu Nacional, cathedral, ministries, Praça dos Três Poderes, Congresso Nacional, Palácio do Planalto and the Supremo Tribunal Federal.

By car Lúcio Costa didn't seem to design the city's layout with stoplights in mind; the incredible rush-hour traffic and getting the hang of roundabouts and tunnels may

3

CLAIMING THE RIGHT OF WAY

Brasília has many cars, few traffic lights and an endless number of roundabouts. At most road crossings you'll see a yellow sign on the asphalt near the curb depicting an outstretched hand with the words, "*Dê sinal de vida*", a prompt to claim right of way. If you see approaching cars a fair distance away, do as the locals do and raise your hand with authority. As long as you don't do it at the last second, drivers are well trained to cede the road to you. Trying this elsewhere in Brazil may be your last act.

make renting a car more trouble than it's worth. If you do drive, be aware of the speed cameras.

By metrô Unless you're planning on going to one of the satellite cities (Guarái, Águas Claras, Samambaia, Taguatinga or Ceilândia) the metrô (R$3.10) is currently only useful for getting to the end of Asa Sul, though a new line is under construction to connect the outer reaches of Asa Norte. Starting from the *rodoviária* there are seven city stops.

By taxi Metered and expensive (especially at night and on Sun); expect to pay R$20–25 for quick trips and R$30 wing to wing.

ACCOMMODATION

The centrally located hostels you'll find everywhere else in Brazil must be making up for the lack of them in the capital. The hotel sectors are aimed at diplomats and expense accounts, though many do offer discounts of up to 50 percent at weekends (be sure to ask). In general, the taller the hotel, the more expensive, so go for the squat, ugly ones. Cheaper pousadas (though often very poor quality or even semi-legal) are located in the wings. Easily the best-value accommodations in town are to be found through private B&B rentals on websites like ⓦairbnb.com.

HOTELS

Alvorada SHS Quadra 4 ☎ 61 3222 7068, ⓦalvoradahotel .com.br; map p.321. One of the cheapest central options, a little faded but good value for the area. Can be noisy. R$200

Aristus Hotel SHN Quadra 2, Bloco O ☎ 61 3328 8675, ⓦaristushotel.com.br; map p.321. Small, clean rooms with awkwardly mounted TVs, 1970s design and paintings of boats in the hallways. R$250

El Pilar SHN Quadra 3 Bloco F ☎ 61 3533 5900, ⓦelpilar .com.br; map p.321. Another standard Brasília "budget" option, it has seen better days, but is good value for the area. R$160

HOSTELS AND POUSADAS

Hostel Albergue da Juventude Setor Recreativo Parque Norte (SRPN) Quadra 2, Lote 2, Camping de Brasília ☎ 61 3343 0531, ⓦbrasiliahostel.com.br; map pp.318–319. A bit of a trek from town (bus #143) but this HI hostel is Brasília's only decent (formal) budget accommodation; book well in advance. Dorms R$55, doubles R$120

Pousada Canaã 703 Norte (plus two other locations at 703 Sul and 708 Sul) ☎ 61 3536 3620, ⓦpousadacanaa brasilia.blogspot.com.br; map pp.318–319. A good range of rooms, dorms to smart double suites, in three different houses; bare in mind the nicest rooms have the higher price tag. Dorms R$60, doubles R$100–200

Pousada Harmonia W3 Sul, Quadra 705, Bloco A, Casa 3 ☎ 61 3443 6527; map pp.318–319. This pousada has a good atmosphere and its own attached barbershop as well as gated parking: rooms have cots and fans. R$130

Pousada 705 Sul Bloco M, Casa 184 ☎ 61 3244 6672; map pp.318–319. Marginally better than surrounding "low-budget" options but still very basic. A meagre breakfast is served and a/c costs extra, but the place is clean. R$100

EATING AND DRINKING

There are great restaurants in Brasília, though they're certainly pricey. Eating and drinking is often done in tandem, with restaurants open until at least midnight. Asa Sul is especially popular, peppered with places ranging from Mexican and Chinese to Italian or fondue; good areas are around 206/205, 204/203 and 405/404. The places listed below are all open daily unless otherwise indicated.

RESTAURANTS

A Tribo 105 Norte, Bloco B; map pp.318–319. Excellent organic/vegetarian food including a *por kilo* buffet Tues–Sun lunch only, with a couple of fish/meat options thrown in. Expect to pay around R$25 including a fresh juice.

★ **Bar é Restaurante Paulicéia** CLS 113, Bloco A, Loja 20 ☎ 61 3245 3031; map pp.318–319. A cheap, local dive excellent for *picanha*, salty snacks and for sipping ice-cold beer as smoke from charring meats wafts over the patio. Patrons range from old men to students and office workers. Weekend *feijoada* R$45 for two.

Feitiço Mineiro CLN 306, Bloco B, Lojas 45/51 ⓦfeitico mineiro.com.br; map pp.318–319. Even without the live music at weekends this place would be worth patronizing for the food; a buffet of *comida mineira*, heavy on pork, beans and vegetables, served the traditional way on a wood-fired stove (R$30).

Ki-Sabor SHCN 406, Bloco E, Lojas 20/30/34 ☎ 61 3036 8525; map pp.318–319. Popular student self-service lunch buffet with patio seating. Salads, *feijoada*, grilled meats and decent desserts (from R$21).

Libanus CLS 206, Bloco C, Loja 36 ☏ 61 3597 7575; map pp.318–319. Perennially crowded spot serving up good-value, hearty Lebanese food daily. A young and humming scene at night.

Manara 706/707 Norte, Loja 60, Bloco E ☏ 61 3273 2324; map pp.318–319. Right in front of the university, this is a simple self-service place with good-quality Brazilian and Lebanese food – hummus, *kibe* and the like. Mon–Sat lunchtime only.

Mangai SCES, Trecho 2, Conjunto 41, Asa Sul ⊛ mangai .com.br; map pp.318–319. A really novel spot with a beautiful view of the Paranoá lake, seating for 800, and hammocks waiting for you after you eat. Oh – and there's food, too! – a good Brazilian range *per quilo* (you'll pay R$25 for a decent plate), and delicious juices like cocoa, *cajá* and *caju*. Daily lunch & dinner.

★ **Mariposa** 213 Sul, Loja 5, Bloco B ☏ 61 3245 5534, ⊛ mariposa.com.br; map pp.318–319. Salads, pancakes, crêpes and wraps, all huge, tasty and, more importantly, fairly priced. Mon–Sat noon–midnight (later Fri–Sat), Sun 5pm–midnight.

Naturetto Asa Norte 405 ☏ 61 3201 6223, ⊛ restaurante naturetto.com.br; map pp.318–319. You can eat well here for under R$20/person, selecting from a large menu of vegetarian options, pastas, pizzas, and meat and fish too. Mon–Fri 8am–10pm, Sat–Sun 8am–4pm.

★ **Pizza À Bessa** CLS 214, Bloco C, Loja 40 ☏ 61 3345 5252; map pp.318–319. This excellent pizza *rodizio* serves forty different slices including dessert pizza. It's all-you-can-eat for R$29 so you can try each kind if you dare – though that would be some achievement.

Sabor do Brasil 302 Sul, Bloco A; map p.321. On the edge of the centre, this place offers a bargain evening unlimited buffet for R$22, including salads, soups, *mineira* and Northeastern dishes, and fruit. There's usually a veggie option or two. *Por quilo* option at lunch. Closed Sun.

★ **TREAT YOURSELF**

Nossa Cozinha Bistro SCLN 402, Bloco C, Loja 60 ☏ 61 3326 5207, ⊛ nossacozinhabsb.blogspot.com.br; map pp.318–319. A fantastic find even if we say so ourselves; a small, cosy restaurant hidden at the back of a block in the Asa Norte. Distinctly Brazilian yet with French bistro touches. For lunch enjoy a daily special or delicious steak with chocolate sauce and red wine reduction (R$38), while the barbecue ribs (R$28) are a high point of lunch or dinner. Classic cheesecake for dessert is mouthwatering (R$10). Closed Sun.

CAFÉS, SNACKS, ICE CREAM

Caldo Fino SQN b/n 409/410, Bloco B; map pp.318–319. Great soup served nightly under an open tent that workers put up and take down each night. Try the pumpkin and gorgonzola or the *verde* (potato, leek and sausage).

Casa de Biscoitos Mineiros 106 Sul, Bloco A, Loja 7; map pp.318–319. Decent bakery with bread, cakes, great biscuits and coffee served outside at the rear. Closed Sun.

★ **Daniel Briand** 104 Norte, Bloco A, Loja 26, Asa Norte; map pp.318–319. Patisserie/teahouse serving Brasília's best quiche. Great for coffee, cake, late weekend breakfast or afternoon tea. Closed Mon.

Landi 405 Sul; map pp.318–319. Hot dogs are taken to a new level here, with fresh bread and toppings including tomato, corn and *catupiry* cheese. Evenings only until 11pm; closed Sat.

Rappel CLN 210, Bloco B, Loja 73 or CLS 306, Bloco B, Loja 10; map pp.318–319. Very respectable coffee and a good selection of sweets, *salgados* and ice cream. A nice place to start the day. Closed Sun.

Saborella 112 Norte, Bloco C, Lojas 38/48; map pp.318–319. A smart yet small modern ice-cream parlour with a choice of exquisite flavours; you'll want to taste several before deciding, sadly, on just two, served as standard. Also has decent coffee. Until 10pm.

Sorbê CLN 405, Bloco C, Loja 41 or CLSW 103, Bloco A, Loja 74, Sudoeste; map pp.318–319. Artesanal *sorveteria* that has exotic fruit sorbets and unusual, enticing flavours like tapioca, toasted coconut and cheese. Until 8pm.

NIGHTLIFE

Brasília has plenty of nightlife, scattered throughout each wing. Our list features some mainstream and other off-the-beaten-track ideas.

★ **2 Clichê** CLN 107, Bloco C, Loja 57; map pp.318–319. Around 300 different kinds of *cachaça* line the walls of this *cachaçeria* with funky music and plenty of narghile smoke. Terrific on Sat, when drinks are half price. Local media folks love this place, and the other nearby bars, too. Mon–Fri 5pm–1am or 2am.

Arena do Forró Setor de Clubes Norte, Trecho 3 (next to the Minas) ⊛ arenadoforro.com.br; map pp.318–319. Since its relocation in 2011, *Arena do Forró* is still *the* place for those who love swing from the Brazilian northeast. Every Thurs and other nights as advertised on the website, from 11pm.

Balaio Café CLN 201 Bloco B Loja 19/31 ⊛ balaiocafe.com .br; map pp.318–319. Artsy place for a drink, food and live music from samba to jazz. 9am–2am, Mon til 6pm only.

Beirute 109 Sul, Bloco A, lojas 2/4 and 107 Norte, Bloco D, lojas 19/29; map pp.318–319. Two branches of this all-ages institution where you'll have to wait for a table; the Asa Sul bar has been open for 44 years. Try the best *kibe* (Lebanese lamb) in Brasília, and the mandatory

"Quibeirute" stuffed with cheese – alongside plenty of cold beer, or if you're feeling adventurous the dangerous "Green Devil" cocktail. Daily until 1am; 2am Thurs–Sat.

Cadê Tereza CLS 201 Bloco B, Loja 1 ⓦ cadeterezabar .com.br; map pp.318–319. Get down to some serious dancing at this popular joint for samba, zouk, MPB and much more, alongside the usual choice of food and *cerveja*. Daily 5pm–2am.

Café com Vinil SHCN 413, Bloco E, Lojas 3/5 ⓦ cafecom vinil.com; map pp.318–319. Exactly what it says on the can: 3000 LPs and a good few types of coffee will keep vinyl junkies happy, while fancy food and fine wine completes the sensory experience. Thurs–Sat from 6pm.

Calaf Edifício Empire Centre, Quadra 2, Bloco S, Sétor Bancário Sul ⓦ calaf.com.br; map p.321. Busy after work until late, this is *the* place in Brasília on Mon for samba-rock, or samba Tues and Sat. *Veja* magazine named it the best place in town to flirt. Mon–Sat 11.30am–3am.

Gate's Pub 403 Sul, Bloco B, Loja 34 ⓦ gatespub.com.br; map pp.318–319. This dark London-esque pub has two stages and is bigger inside than it seems, with live rock, pop and blues most nights. Tues–Sun 10pm until late.

Play Club 904 (Asceb), 904 Sul ⓦ projetoplaybsb .blogspot.com.br; map pp.318–319. Current top spot on the Brasília club scene most Fri nights, with an eclectic rock, electro and house soundtrack, gets going at midnight til very late.

UK Music Hall CLS 411, Bloco B ⓦ ukmusichall.com.br; map pp.318–319. Known locally as the "UK-Brasil Pub", this small-ish music venue spins a Brit-rock-leaning music selection with some reggae, blues and soul thrown in for good measure. Most importantly it serves a nice pint of (very non-UK) Murphy's stout. Tues–Sat 8pm–late.

SHOPPING

Brasília Shopping Setor Comercial Norte, Quadra 05. Centrally located mall with a food court, a short walk from the TV Tower. Mon–Sat 10am–10pm.

Conic Opposite Conjunto, parallel and adjacent to the *rodoviária*. This 24hr "alternative" rough-around-the-edges shopping mall has joke T-shirts, comics and much much more, including bars, though it's best avoided late at night.

Conjunto Nacional Opposite Conic parallel and adjacent to the *rodoviária*. Not as flashy as Brasília Shopping but more upmarket than Conic. Open 24hr (Sun until midnight).

Feira de Artesanato The market at the base of the TV Tower sells clothes and crafts, from hammocks to meticulously pin-pricked dried leaves and *capim dourado*, attractive golden-grass jewellery. Stalls and food stands open every day but busiest weekends 8am–6pm.

Pier 21 Setor de Clubes Esportivo Sul, Tr. 02, Conjunto 32. Take a taxi to this lakeside mall which has cinemas and upscale restaurants. Daily 11am–11pm.

DIRECTORY

Banks and exchange Most ATMs take foreign cards; try Banco do Brasil or Bradesco. There's a centrally located *Citibank* near Brasília Shopping. Cambios are located at the airport and at Pátio Brasil Shopping, 1st Floor, Loja 202, Asa Sul.

Car rental Airport branches include: Avis (ⓣ 61 3365 2782); Hertz (ⓣ 61 3365 4425); Interlocadora (ⓣ 61 3365 3656); and Locadora (ⓣ 61 3327 4792).

Crime You'll feel pretty safe walking the streets by day, but at night the central area, with its strikingly lit Niemeyer buildings, is mostly deserted, so take care. Remember, there are few traffic lights outside the centre and crossing main roads north to south requires either entering dodgy tunnels or getting through gaps in traffic: take a taxi instead. Lastly, take care in the *rodoviária* and when using public transport at rush hour.

Embassies and consulates Australia, SES Quadra 801, Conjunto K, Lote 7 ⓣ 61 3226 3111; Canada, SES, Av Naçies, Quadra 803, Lote 16 ⓣ 61 3424 5400; Ireland, SHIS QL 12, Conjunto 05, Casa 09, Lago Sul ⓣ 61 3248 8800; South Africa, Av das Nações, Lote 6 ⓣ 61 3312 9500; UK, Setor de Embaixadas Sul, Quadra 801, Conjunto K ⓣ 61 3329 2300; US, Av das Nações Quadra 801, Lote 03 ⓣ 61 3312 7000.

Hospital Hospital de Base do Distrito Federal, SMHS 101, Bloco A ⓣ 61 3325 5050 (emergency 24hr).

Internet All shopping malls have internet cafés, which change location rapidly.

Laundries No self-service laundries in town but there are *lavanderias* in residential *quadras*, which wash clothes for R$6/item. Try the ubiquitous 5 à Sec, at CLS 309 BL D, s/n Loja 35.

Left Luggage The airport has lockers and baggage storage open 24hr (R$14/day).

Post office SHS 2 Bloco B, Asa Sul (Mon–Fri 9am–5pm); SDN CNB Bloco A, 2nd Loja 2010 (Mon–Fri 9.30am–10pm, Sat 9am–9pm). Branches also at most shopping malls.

The Pantanal

An open, seasonally flooded wetland larger than Spain, extending deep into the states of Mato Grosso and Mato Grosso do Sul, **THE PANTANAL** has some of the most diverse and abundant wildlife in Brazil. The word Pantanal is derived from the Brazilian word *pantano* (meaning marsh) reflecting its general appearance, but originally it was the site of a giant, prehistoric, inland sea. Today, with an area of 195,000 square kilometres, it represents the world's largest freshwater wetland and is one of the most ecologically important habitats in Brazil.

WHAT TO SEE AND DO

Travelling alone in the Pantanal is difficult and the easiest way to experience it is by taking an economical **organized tour** or, if your budget stretches far enough, spending a night or two at a **fazenda-lodge** (called pousadas in the north). The *fazenda*-lodges are generally reached by jeep; those deeper in the interior require access by boat or plane. At least one night in the interior is essential if you want to see animals; three- or four-day excursions will greatly increase your chances of seeing the more elusive species. Most tours enter the Pantanal by road and spend a couple of days exploring in canoes, small motorboats or on horseback from a land base.

There are three main entry points: **Cuiabá** in the north, **Corumbá** in the west and **Campo Grande** in the east. The **best time** to explore the Pantanal is towards the end of the rainy season, around April, when your chances of spotting wildlife are high. Renting a car is not recommended unless you hire a local guide who knows the area well to accompany you – you will need a 4WD.

3

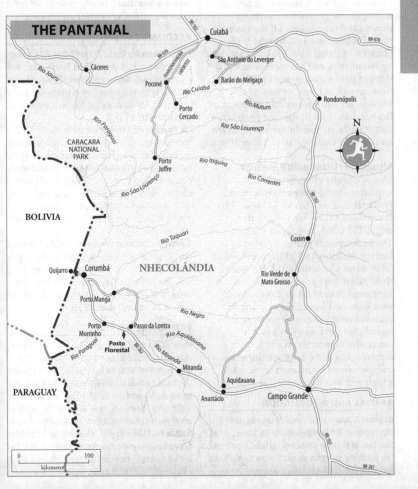

THE PANTANAL

3

CORUMBÁ

CORUMBÁ was founded as a military outpost in 1778 and rose to prominence due to its strategic location on the Paraguay River. Located in the western Pantanal, today it dedicates itself to the more peaceful pursuits of ranching, mining and ecotourism. Of the three main Pantanal towns, **Corumbá** is best placed for getting right into the Pantanal by bus or jeep, and has more than its fair share of guides and agencies to choose from, as well as boats for hire. Oddly enough, the town is more accessible from Bolivia than from Brazil. The town is not safe at night, so you do need to take care and avoid walking the streets after 10pm.

Museu de História do Pantanal

One of the city's highlights is undoubtedly the **Museu de História do Pantanal** on Rua Manoel Cavassa 275, Porto Geral (Tues–Sat 1–6pm; free; ☎67 3232 0303, ☎muhpan.org.br). The museum, designated a national heritage building in 1992, was erected in 1876 when Corumbá was Latin America's third major river port; curiously, most of the materials used for its construction were imported from England. The museum covers over 8000 years of the region's human history in a highly interactive manner, with a variety of archeological and ethnological artefacts complemented by modern resources in a high-tech setting.

ARRIVAL AND INFORMATION

By plane Aeroporto Internacional de Corumbá (☎67 3231 3322) is located 3km from the centre on Rua Santos Dumont. From here, all flights go via the regional hub Campo Grande (see p.329). The bus with route card "Popular Nova" (R$2.40) runs to and from Rua Antonio João in the centre.

By bus The small *rodoviária* is located at Rua Porto Carreiro 750 (☎67 3231 2033), a 10–15min walk south of the city centre.

Destinations Andorinha (☎andorinha.com) serve Campo Grande. Campo Grande (9 daily; 6–7hr).

Tourist information ☎corumba.com.br is a half-decent tourist web portal on the town and surrounding area.

ACCOMMODATION

Laura Vicuna Rua Cuiabá 775 ☎67 3231 5874, ☎hotel lauravicuna.com.br. A peaceful and friendly place, very neat and tidy with clean rooms (all with TV, a/c and wi-fi), and a quirky line in sculpture (look out for the Don Quijote and Sancho Panza), as well as free wi-fi and internet. Breakfast included. R$120

★ **Pousada do Cachimbo** Rua Alan Kardec 4, Bairro Dom Bosco ☎67 3231 4833, ☎pousadadocachimbo.com .br. On the site of a former cattle farm, this delightful colonial pousada is located 5min from Corumbá on the edge of the Bay of Tamengo. It's ideal for a small taster of what the deeper Pantanal will be like, with birds tweeting about as well as the occasional duck strolling around the garden. All rooms have a/c, there's a pool, wi-fi and even a football pitch. R$100

Salette Rua Delamare 893 ☎67 3231 6246. Convenient central location and *muito* atmosphere, with original mosaic tile floors, crisp white linens, handsome period sinks and battered antique beds and furniture. Some rooms with decent views of the cathedral. Breakfast included. TV and a/c R$40 extra. R$50

EATING AND DRINKING

There are plenty of cheap snack bars throughout town, especially on Rua Delamare west of the Praça da República, serving good set meals for less than R$8. Being a swamp city, fish is the main local delicacy, with *pacu* and *pintado* among the favoured species. You'll find bars all over town – the more relaxed are those down on the riverfront, where you can usually get a game of pool with your drink.

Galpão Rua 13 de Junho 797, at Rua Antônio Maria Coelho. A cavernous local with cart-wheel windows and a thatched awning, serving cowboy-sized portions of *comida caseira* at a bargain R$10/person. Mon–Sat 10.30am–3.30pm.

PANTANAL TOURS

Organized tours inevitably include at least some water-based transport and a guide who can tell you about what you see. Numerous tour companies are based out of the main access towns Corumbá, Campo Grande and Cuiabá; as ever, you get what you pay for, and the cheaper options don't always enjoy a good press.

CORUMBÁ TOUR OPERATORS

Águas do Pantanal Av Afonso Pena 367, Miranda ☎ 67 3242 1242, ⓦ aguasdopantanal.com.br. This company organizes programmes in the southern Pantanal, as well as fishing trips and visits to traditional local farms where you can stay overnight. They also own a pleasant pousada offering both upscale and economical rooms in Miranda, between Corumbá and Campo Grande.

CAMPO GRANDE TOUR OPERATORS

Pantanal Tours Rua Terenos 117 ☎ 67 3042 4659, ⓦ pantanaltours.com. Dutch/French-run company offering a wide range of activities and packages from one-week-long 4WD trips exploring the Nhecolândia region to cave diving in Lagoa Misteriosa and the Gruta do Lago Azul.

CUIABÁ TOUR OPERATORS

Ecoverde Tours Pousada Ecoverde, Rua Pedro Celestino 391 ☎ 65 3624 1386 or ☎ 9638 1614, ⓦ ecoverdetours.com.br. Well-established company run by respected guide Joel Souza from his inimitable pousada (see p.331). Keen to foster sustainable ecotourism and offering a variety of nature tours, from birdwatching to jaguar treks deeper into the Pantanal. Stay at a *fazenda*-lodge or camp.

★ **Fiorella Pizza** On the eastern corner of Praça da República and Rua Delamare. In with a shout as the best pizzeria in the Pantanal, with decent prices (R$8–30), alfresco tables in a quiet location, fast, friendly service, delicious wood-fired bases and mouthwatering toppings; try the wonderfully garlicky Buffalo with sun-dried tomatoes. Daily 6–11.30pm.

DIRECTORY

Banks and exchange There's a host of banks including HSBC, some with ATMs, on Rua Delamare west of Praça da República.
Car rental Localiza is at Rua Edu Rocha 969 (☎ 67 3231 6000) and at the airport (☎ 67 3232 6000).
Internet M@bo Cyber Coffee, Rua Antonio Maria Coelho 192 (daily 8am–6pm; R$2.50/hr).
Police Rua Luiz Feitosa Rodrigues 664 (☎ 67 3231 2493).
Post office The main post office is at Rua Delamare 708, opposite the church on Praça da República (Mon–Fri 8.30am–5pm, Sat 8am–11.30pm).

CAMPO GRANDE

Capital of the state of Mato Grosso do Sul, **CAMPO GRANDE** is the most popular gateway into the Pantanal on account of its excellent transport links with the rest of Brazil, plethora of tour companies and good facilities for visitors. The city itself was only founded in 1877 but its growth has been rapid, and today it is a large city with some 800,000 inhabitants.

ARRIVAL AND INFORMATION

By plane Campo Grande's international airport, the Aeroporto Antonio João (☎ 67 3368 6000), is at Av Duque de Caxias. Local bus #408 (R$2.80) will take you into town via central Av Afonso Pena, while a/c minibus #015 (R$8) makes the rounds of the downtown hotels.
Destinations Rio de Janeiro (8–15 daily; 3hr 25min–6hr 30min); São Paulo (6–7 daily; 1hr 45min–6hr 20min).
By bus The new *rodoviária* is 20min south of town at Av Gury Marquis 1215 (☎ 67 3026 6789). Local bus #87 or #85 will take you into the centre (R$2.80) though you'll need a prepaid card, available from the central info kiosk in the station; without a card, you'll need to get off and pay (and wait for another bus) at the nearby Morenão interchange.
Destinations Andorinha (ⓦ andorinha.com) serve Corumbá, Rio and – along with Viação Motta (ⓦ motta.com.br) – São Paulo. Motta and São Luiz (ⓦ viacaosaoluiz.com.br) serve Brasília, and Eucatur (ⓦ www.eucatur.com.br) serve Foz do Iguaçu. All companies serve Cuiabá. Brasília (3 daily; 22–23hr); Corumbá (9 daily; 6–7hr); Cuiabá (21 daily; 11–12hr); Foz do Iguaçu (1 daily; 18hr); Rio (2 daily; 21–22hr); São Paulo (8 daily; 14–15hr).
Tourist information There's a tourist information kiosk at the airport (daily 6am–midnight; ☎ 67 3363 3116), a small office at the *rodoviária* (24hr; ☎ 67 3313 8705) and a large, very helpful downtown office at Av Noroeste 5140, on the corner with Av Afonso Pena (Tues–Sat 8am–6pm, Sun 9am–noon; ☎ 67 3314 9968).

ACCOMMODATION

Anache Rua Marechal Cândido Rondon 1396 ☎ 67 3383 2841, ⓔ hotelanache2007@hotmail.com. A great location,

3

sweet staff and good old-fashioned ceiling fans offset the ill-fitting windows, doors and curtains at this frayed but decent-value hotel. Ask for a rear-facing room. A/c and mini-bar R$10 extra. Parking available and breakfast included. R$80

Hostel Campo Grande Rua Joaquim Nabuco 185 ☎67 3321 0505, ⓦpantanaltrekking.com. Located directly opposite the old bus station, with vivid naïf murals on the walls, a small pool and adjoining breakfast area. The clean, comfy, mini-dorm rooms accommodate up to four people, and there's free internet and wi-fi, and *gratis* airport and *rodoviária* pick-up. English spoken. Dorms R$35

Cosmos Rua Dom Aquino 771 ☎67 3384 4270. One of the friendliest and best-value options among the myriad budget hotels in the environs of the former bus station, with clean, tiled rooms, modern en-suite bathrooms, vintage phones and faux stained-glass windows. Breakfast included and there's also free parking. R$65

EATING

Comitiva Pantaneira Rua Dom Aquino 2221 ☎67 3383 8799. Buzzing, cavernous *por quilo* restaurant (R$35 weekdays, R$40 weekends) that "preserves the culture of our Pantanal", with waiters in cowboy outfits, seriously good meat and fish-based grub sizzling away on an open stove and the odd antique saddle to gee up your appetite. Mon–Fri 11am–2pm, Sat & Sun 11am–3pm.

★ **Fogo Caipira** Rua José Antônio 145 ☎67 3324 1641, ⓦfogocaipira.com.br. Award-winning, modern-rustic shrine to gourmet *comida de fazenda*, with prices that won't break the bank. An inviting and intimate patio-cum-garden is perfect for feasting on the likes of fried spaghetti with cubes of *carne do sol* (R$31.90) and, incredibly for a traditional restaurant in this part of the world, there are even a couple of vegetarian options, and imaginative ones at that. Tues–Thurs 11am–2pm & 7–11pm, Fri 11am–3pm & 7pm–midnight, Sat 11am–midnight, Sun 11am–4pm.

★ **Sabor EnQuilo** Av Afonso Pena 2223 ☎67 3321 4726. An exceptionally hospitable, high-quality cross between a Japanese restaurant and a typical *por quilo* joint, with eat-as-much-as-you-like prices held, at the time of writing, at an incredible R$15 for men and R$13 for women. The spread features everything from freshly prepared sushi to aubergine tempura and four-cheese cannelloni, and they even throw in dessert; try the excellent peach flan if it's on. Mon–Fri 10.45am–2.30pm, Sat 10.45am–3pm, Sun 11am–3pm.

DIRECTORY

Banks and exchange There are ATMs that accept foreign cards at the airport and an HSBC ATM at Av Afonso Pena 2440.

Car rental Lider, Av Afonso Pena 954 (☎67 3029 9009); Renascença Rent A Car, Rua Joaquim Murtinho 4701 (☎67 3348 3400); YES, Av Afonso Pena 829 (☎67 3324 0055).

Consulates Paraguay, Rua 26 de Agosto 384 (☎67 3384 6610).

Hospital Hospital Santa Casa, Rua Eduardo Santos Pereira 88 (☎67 3322 4000).

Internet Cyber Shot, Rua Dom Aquina 1083 (R$2/hr; Mon–Fri 8am–6pm, Sat 8am–3pm).

Pharmacy Drogaria Rui Barbosa, Rua Rui Barbosa 2721 (☎67 3314 3710).

Police Rua Padre João Crippa 1581 ☎67 3312 5700.

Post office Av Calógeras 2309, on the corner with Rua Dom Aquino (Mon–Fri 8.30am–5.30pm, Sat 8am–noon).

PANTANAL WILDLIFE

First-time visitors to the Pantanal will be struck by the sheer quantity of **animals** that populate the region, allowing for some great photo opportunities. Undoubtedly the most visible inhabitants of the region are the **waterbirds**, vast flocks of egrets, cormorants and ibises that flush in the wake of your boat as you cruise the channels – an unforgettable spectacle. The most impressive of the region's waterbirds is the immense **jabiru**, a prehistoric-looking snow-white stork as tall as a man and the symbol of the Pantanal.

Another species that will undoubtedly catch your eye is the **spectacled caiman** (*jacaré*), a South American alligator whose regional populations are estimated at more than ten million. The mammal you'll see most of is the **capybara**, a rodent resembling a huge guinea pig that feeds in herds on the lush plant life, but you will need a bit more luck to see the rare **marsh deer** or the endangered **giant armadillo**. Listen out too for the squeaky calls of the **giant otter**, a species that inhabits the more isolated parts of the Pantanal, but which is often overcome by its own curiosity when approached by a boat-load of tourists.

Jaguar and **puma** are present in the area but are active mainly at night; you will need a huge dose of luck to see either, and you shouldn't count on seeing **maned wolf** or **bush dog** either. **Lowland tapir**, looking something like a cross between a horse and a short-nosed elephant, are sometimes seen bathing in streams. You will likely be serenaded each morning by the far-carrying song of the **black howler monkey**, often observed lying prone on thick branches, while the gallery forests are the preserve of the **black spider monkey**, considerably more svelte and active as they swing acrobatically through the trees.

CUIABÁ

Capital of Mato Grosso and one of the hottest cities in Brazil, **CUIABÁ** is located at the dead centre of the South American continent, broiling home to over half a million people, many of whom speak with one of the country's most distinctive local accents. The city's unusual name is of disputed origin but probably comes from an indigenous term meaning "arrow-fishing", a reference to the local Bororo Indian hunting technique. The installation of Brasília as the nation's capital in 1960 revived Cuiabá's fortunes and its recent growth has been rapid. The city is the main gateway to the northern Pantanal, and is the least frequently used of the three main access points.

ARRIVAL AND INFORMATION

By plane Marechal Rondon International Airport (☎65 3614 2500) is located 10km from the centre at Av João Ponce de Arruda, Varzea Grande. Bus #24 (R$2.95) runs between the airport and the small, turnstyle-controlled mini-terminal on the southeastern corner of Praça Ipiranga. Taxis to the centre cost R$25–30.

By bus The hulking *rodoviária* (☎65 3621 3629) lies west of the centre on Av República do Líbano. Bus #204 and #302 (R$2.95) run between the station and Av Getúlio Vargas, just off Praça Alencastro. Taxis to the centre cost R$15.20, pre-payable at the Ticket Taxi booth (☎65 3621 2829).

Destinations São Luiz (🖥viacaosaoluiz.com.br) serves Brasília, Andorinha (🖥andorinha.com) and Eucatur (🖥eucatur.com.br) serve São Paulo, with the latter also serving Porto Velho and – together with Verde Transportes (🖥viagemverde.com.br) – Cáceres, while Viação Motta (🖥motta.com.br) serve Rio. Most companies serve Campo Grande. Brasília (7 daily; 17–22hr); Cáceres, with connections to Santa Cruz, Bolivia (10 daily; 3–4hr); Campo Grande (22 daily; 11–12hr); Porto Velho (9 daily; 23–24hr); Rio (1 daily; 35hr); São Paulo (6 daily; 26–27hr).

Tourist information There's a Sedtur office at Rua Voluntários de Pátria 118 (Mon–Fri 8am–6pm; ☎65 3613 9313), and also a kiosk at the airport (daily 8am–6pm; ☎65 8419 8310).

ACCOMMODATION

Hostel Pantanal Av Isaac Póvoas 665 ☎65 3624 8999, 🖥portaldopantanal.com.br. Dark and slightly musty HI hostel whose primary colours at least try and lighten it up a bit. There's wi-fi, a half-decent kitchen and basic laundry facilities. Breakfast included. Dorms R$55, doubles R$110

★ **Pousada Ecoverde** Rua Pedro Celestino 391 ☎65 9638 1614, 🖥pousadaecoverde.com.br. Very possibly

unique in Brazil, at least at this price level: a tastefully rambling, shabby-chic, five-room pousada with hospitality and atmosphere to spare, crammed with bric-a-brac and antiques. Cats and hens roam freely around the communal library and book exchange to an original vinyl soundtrack of Herb Alpert, Frank Sinatra and Chico Buarque, while birds peck from feeders in a large, happily un-manicured garden with fruit trees and hammocks. Laundry, cooking facilities and internet (all free) are also available, as well as free airport and *rodoviária* transfers. Highly regarded tours (see p.329) to the Pantanal can be organized. R$60

Ramos Rua Campo Grande 487 ☎65 3624 7472, 🖂hotelramos@hotmail.com. A generally sweet, family-run operation offering clean, comfortable rooms painted in shocking green, with a handy combination of both a/c and ceiling fan to keep the heat at bay, and a well-respected in-house tour agency. Parking, wi-fi and breakfast included, though the latter is hardly lavish, with a cramped clutch of tables in reception. R$80

EATING

Choppão Praça 8 de Abril ☎65 3623 9101. Traditional and hugely popular open-fronted restaurant-bar countering Cuiabá's ferocious heat with a frigid, turbo-charged fan and delicious pints of ice-fortified, hangover-free *chopp* (draught beer). The lunch deal isn't bad, offering a 250g steak with rice and *feijão tropeira* for R$19.50, though give the pizzas a miss. Daily 11am–1pm & 6–11pm.

Empório Alimento Rua Comandante Costa 668, opposite *Hotel Matto Grosso*. Not the most salubrious option, though in the white heat of a city-centre Sun afternoon, when absolutely nothing else moves (not even the drunk slumped in front of his beer), you might just be glad of the dirt-cheap, greasy spoon cuisine (R$8) at this un-signed hole-in-the-wall. Daily 8am–8pm.

Mistura Cuiabana Rua Pedro Celestino 8 ☎65 3624 1127. Set in an airy colonial mansion with handsome old shutters and timber ceiling, this excellent *por quilo* restaurant (R$21.50) hums with activity at lunchtime and has a particularly fine selection of vegetarian and salad options. Mon–Fri 11am–2.30pm.

DIRECTORY

Banks and exchange There are ATMs that accept foreign cards at the airport.

Car rental Localiza, Av Dom Bosco 965 (☎65 3624 7979).

Internet Nameles copy shop inside the same colonial mansion that houses *Mistura Cuiabana* (see above). R$1/15min; Mon–Fri 8am–8pm, Sat 8am–3pm.

Police Av Tenente Coronel Duarte 1044 (☎65 3901 4809; 24hr).

Post office Praça da República (Mon–Fri 9am–5pm, Sat 9am–2pm).

São Paulo

South America's largest city, **SÃO PAULO** – or "Sampa", as the locals call it – makes up for a lack of beach and leisure culture with all the urban buzz and modern grandeur that you would expect from a place that's home to a staggering half of Brazil's industrial output. With an exceptionally vibrant cultural scene, the city boasts 150 theatres and performance spaces, more than 250 cinemas, countless nightclubs and no fewer than 90 museums.

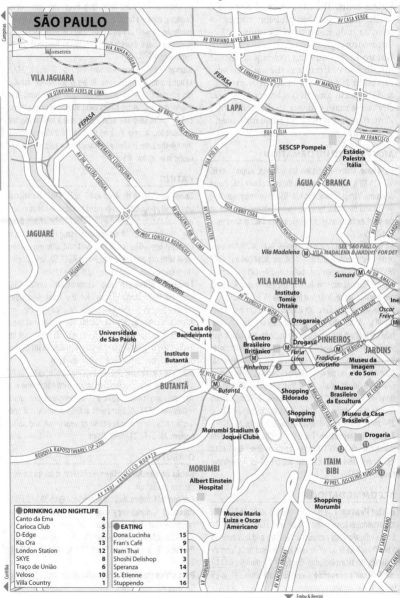

SÃO PAULO

0 ___ 3
kilometres

DRINKING AND NIGHTLIFE	
Canto da Ema	4
Carioca Club	5
D-Edge	2
Kia Ora	13
London Station	12
SKYE	8
Traço de União	6
Veloso	10
Villa Country	1

EATING	
Dona Lucinha	15
Fran's Café	9
Nam Thai	11
Shoshi Delishop	3
Speranza	14
St. Etienne	7
Stuppendo	16

Embu & Berrini

São Paulo is Brazil's New York, and there are echoes of that city everywhere: in Avenida Paulista, it has South America's Park Avenue; in the Edifício Banespa its Empire State Building.

As a city of immigrants, with a heritage of Italian and Japanese influx – it has the largest Japanese population outside Japan – this is easily the best place to eat in Brazil. São Paulo's denizens, known as *Paulistanos*, like to live the good life and party hard at night. While many people will always want to contrast workhorse Sampa with the beauty of Rio, the city

somehow manages its underdog status well, and its friendly population simply gets on with making money – and spending it. If you're someone who gets a thrill out of buzzing cosmopolitan streets and discovering the hottest bar, club or restaurant, then you'll love São Paulo – a city of both pure grit and sophisticated savoir-faire.

WHAT TO SEE AND DO

São Paulo is vast, but the central neighbourhoods and Metrô lines are fairly easy to get a handle on. The focal points downtown are the large squares of **Praça da Sé** and faded **Praça da República**, separated by the wide stretch of **Vale do Anhangabaú**. Just north of Praca da Sé is the seventeenth-century monastery of **São Bento**, and beyond lively shopping streets lead to the unmissable **Mercado Municipal** and the much cleaned-up red-light district of **Luz**. **Bixiga** (also called Bela Vista) and **Liberdade**, to the south, are home to a sizeable chunk of São Paulo's Italian and Japanese immigrants respectively. Rua Augusta is a key yet permanently down-at-heel nightlife district, leading southwards onto imposing commercial artery **Avenida Paulista**, with its sprawling upscale suburb gardens descending the hill on the far side. Heading back uphill west of here is Vila Madalena, another fashionable district with numerous bars and an artistic feel. Superb museums are scattered right across the city, including the palatial **Museu Paulista**, **Museu do Futebol**, **Museu Afro-Brasil**, **MASP art gallery**, and the Niemeyer-designed complex **Memorial América Latina**. A new state-of-the-art stadium, the **Arena de São Paulo** at Itaquera in the east of the city, will host the opening match and one semifinal of the 2014 World Cup.

Around Praça da Sé

The heart of the old part of São Paulo is **Praça da Sé**, a busy, palm-tree-lined square dominated by the large but unremarkable neo-Gothic **Catedral Metropolitana**, completed in 1954. On the opposite side of the square, along Rua Boa Vista, is the whitewashed **Pátio do Colégio**, a replica of the chapel and college founded in 1554 by the Jesuit mission. Next door the run-of-the-mill collection of relics at the **Museu Padre Anchieta** (Tues–Sun 9am–4.30pm, R$6) is best bypassed in favour of its lovely patio café. Around the corner is São Paulo's sole remaining eighteenth-century manor house, the **Solar da Marquesa de Santos** (Rua Roberto Simonsen 136; Tues–Sun 9am–5pm; free), with a few displays telling the story of the city. Of the three colonial-era churches near Sé, the seventeenth-century **Igreja de São Francisco** (daily 7.30am–7pm), two blocks west on Praça da Patriarca, is probably the best preserved and features an elaborate high altar.

Heading northeast towards **São Bento** you'll meet the high-rises of the **Triângulo**, São Paulo's traditional banking district. The **Edifício Martinelli** (Av São João 35) was the city's first skyscraper at thirty storeys, although the views are best from atop the 36-floor **Edifício Banespa** (Rua João Brícola 24; Mon–Fri 10am–5pm; free; ID required), which was modelled after New York's Empire State Building.

A block away, the **Mosteiro São Bento** (Mon–Fri 6am–6pm, Sat–Sun 6am–noon & 4–6pm) has a church dating from 1598, though the impressive complex has been renovated multiple times, and is still home to a community of Benedictine monks who sing Gregorian chants early on Sundays. Take in busy market street Rua 25 de Março before moving on to Rua da Cantareira, where you'll find the city's **Mercado Municipal** (daily 7am–5pm), completed in 1933 and featuring stained-glass windows with rural plantation scenes. Countless food stalls sell exotic fruits plus trademark thick-wedge *mortadella* (ham) sandwiches and *pasteis*. Upstairs are some terrific bars and restaurants – a mob scene at weekends.

Luz

From the Mercado Municipal it's five blocks' walk northwest to **Luz**, a red-light district now in the midst of a huge government renovation project. Close to the metrô at the head of Avenida Cásper

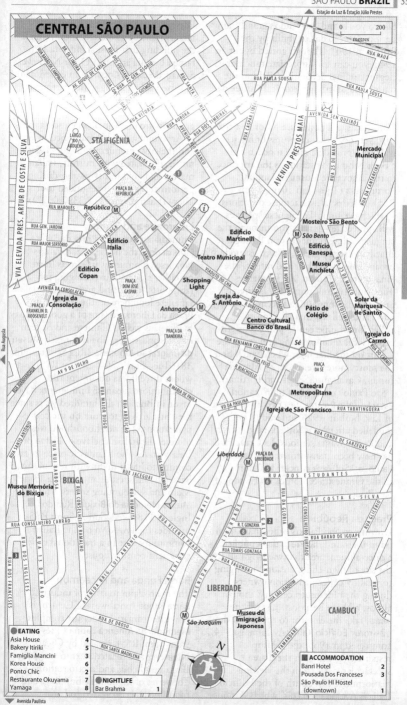

CENTRAL SÃO PAULO

Estação da Luz & Estação Júlio Prestes

0   200
metres

STA IFIGÊNIA

LARGO DO AROUCHE

VIA ELEVADA PRES. ARTUR DE COSTA E SILVA

PRAÇA DA REPÚBLICA

República Ⓜ

Mercado Municipal

Mosteiro São Bento

Ⓜ São Bento

Edifício Martinelli

Edifício Banespa

Edifício Italia

Museu Anchieta

Teatro Municipal

Edifício Copan

PRAÇA DOM JOSÉ GASPAR

Shopping Light

Igreja da Consolação

PRAÇA FRANKLIN D. ROOSEVELT

Igreja da S. Antônio

Pátio de Colégio

Solar da Marquesa de Santos

Anhangabaú Ⓜ

Centro Cultural Banco do Brasil

Igreja do Carmo

PRAÇA DA BANDEIRA

Sé Ⓜ

PRAÇA DA SÉ

AV 9 DE JULHO

Catedral Metropolitana

Igreja de São Francisco

BIXIGA

Museu Memória do Bixiga

Liberdade

PRAÇA DA LIBERDADE

LIBERDADE

CAMBUCI

Ⓜ São Joaquim

Museu da Imigração Japonesa

N

Avenida Paulista

● **EATING**

Asia House	4
Bakery Itiriki	5
Famiglia Mancini	3
Korea House	6
Ponto Chic	2
Restaurante Okuyama	7
Yamaga	8

● **NIGHTLIFE**

Bar Brahma	1

■ **ACCOMMODATION**

Banri Hotel	2
Pousada Dos Franceses	3
São Paulo HI Hostel (downtown)	1

3

3

Líbero you'll find São Paulo's grand train station, **Estação da Luz**, built by the British in 1901. Though gutted by fire in 1946, you can still appreciate much of its elegant original decoration. Behind the station, the startlingly tropical **Parque da Luz** (daily 10am–6pm) was São Paulo's first public garden, dating from 1800. Its bandstands and ponds are proof of a ritzy past, yet today the sculptures lining its walkways provide a more modern feel.

Back behind the station is the entrance to the innovative **Museu da Língua Portuguesa** (Tues–Sun 10am–5pm; R$5). A series of interactive exhibitions – which even non-Portuguese speakers will appreciate – guides you through the language's development from Portugal to Brazilian literary greats, as well as modern urban slang in football and music. The **Pinacoteca do Estado** (Av Tiradentes 141; Tues–Sun 10am–6pm; R$5) is directly opposite the museum, adjacent to the park, and well worth a visit for its collection of nineteenth- and twentieth-century Brazilian painting and sculpture – start on the first floor where you'll find the most impressive pieces by Almeida Junior, Cavalcanti, Segall and Portinari.

São Paulo's other great train station, **Estação Júlio Prestes**, lies two blocks west of Luz, built in 1926 and said to be modelled after New York's Grand Central and Pennsylvania stations. Its Great Hall has now been transformed into **Sala São Paulo**, a 1500-seat concert hall home to the Orquestra Sinfônica do Estado de São Paulo.

Praça da República

Downtown São Paulo's other main focal point is around the **Praça da República**, a once-affluent area that was originally the site of high-end mansions belonging to wealthy coffee plantation owners during the nineteenth century, though almost all have been lost. Just off the *praça*, take the elevator to the top of the 42-storey **Edifício Itália** (Av Ipiranga 344), completed in 1965; the rooftop restaurant is tacky but there are spectacular vistas from the viewing platform (R$15). South of the Edifício Itália is **Avenida São Luis**, which was once

lined with high-class shops and still retains some of its old elegance, though the building that most stands out is famed Brasília architect Oscar Niemeyer's S-shaped **Edifício Copan** – an experiment in mixed urban living with apartments available at all prices.

Three blocks east of the *praça* is the grand **Teatro Municipal**, an enticing mix of Art Nouveau and Renaissance styles and the city's premier venue for classical music, decorated with mirrors, Italian marble and gold leaf (viewable during performances or by free guided tour Tues–Thurs; phone ☎ 11 3397 0327).

Liberdade and Bixiga

Immediately south of **Praça da Sé**, **Liberdade** is the home of São Paulo's Japanese community, its streets lined on either side with overhanging red lampposts. You'll find great traditional Japanese food here on the streets off **Praça da Liberdade** (site of a good Sunday market), as well as Chinese and Korean eateries and stores. There is even a **Museu da Imigração Japonesa** (Rua São Joaquim 381; Tues–Sun 1.30–5.30pm; R$5), whose three floors document the contributions Japanese immigrants have made in Brazil in the hundred years since they first arrived to work on the coffee plantations. The neighbourhood west of here, the Italian enclave of **Bixiga** or Bela Vista, is also a fantastic place to eat, coming to life at night with restaurants, bars and clubs, especially on Rua 13 de Maio and surrounding streets. The **Museu Memória do Bixiga** (Rua dos Ingleses 118; Wed–Sun 2–5pm; R$5) provides the lowdown on the Italian community here in a traditional early twentieth-century house.

Barra Funda and Pacaembu

The main claim to fame of industrial **Barra Funda** (northwest of Centro) is the extraordinary modernist complex **Memorial da América Latina** (Tues–Sun 9am–6pm; R$5), created by Oscar Niemeyer and located next to the giant Barra Funda bus and metrô station. The series of monolithic buildings and monuments is dedicated to Latin

American solidarity, and includes a library, concert hall, permanent outdoor exhibition and sculpture of a giant bloodied hand. Linked by one of Niemeyer's trademark curvaceous walkways, to the south side of the highway is the anthropological museum **Museu Darcy Ribeiro**, containing crafts, bright costumes, and an impressive three-dimensional map of the continent beneath a glass floor.

A bus or taxi ride south from metrô Barra Funda along Avenida Pacaembu brings you to **Estádio do Pacaembu** (also reached by bus #917M from Av Paulista or #177C-10 from Vila Madalena, or a 15min walk from metrô Clínicas), home to Corinthians football club – although from 2014 Corinthians matches will be played at the Arena de São Paulo in Itaquera (see p.334). The impressive 40,000-seat stadium was designed by Brasília's other great designer, Lúcio Costa, at one end of a large square – Praça Charles Miller – named after the Englishman who introduced football to Brazil. The main reason for coming here, however, is the superb **Museu do Futebol** (Tues–Sun 9am–5pm, closed match days; R$7; allow 3hr). Piecing together how it became Brazil's greatest national obsession through enthralling multimedia displays, the museum has an appeal far beyond the game itself, from the players, fans and commentators to the controversies of race and dictatorship in twentieth-century Brazil.

Avenida Paulista and Jardins

South of Bixiga, **Avenida Paulista** is central São Paulo's third major focal point, a 3km stretch that in the early 1900s was lined with Art Nouveau mansions owned by coffee barons. Redeveloped in the 1960s, it's now lined with skyscrapers topped by helipads and TV antennas dramatically lit by different colours at night. The **Casa das Rosas** (Av Paulista 35) gives some sense of what the avenue once looked like, a French-style mansion set in a walled garden that's a huge contrast to the surrounding steel-and-glass hulks, and now a state-run museum. Also worth

a look is the **Museu de Arte de São Paulo** or **MASP** (Av Paulista 1578; Tues–Sun 11am–6pm, until 8pm Thurs; R$15, free Tues), standing on four red stilts floating above the ground and allowing a view of the city behind. Upstairs contains a large collection of Western art, while the basement below has a very enjoyable and reasonable buffet. Opposite MASP make sure you take a stroll along the trails of the eminently peaceful Parque Siqueira Campos, pure Atlantic forest landscaped by Roberto Burle Marx.

Separated from Bixiga by Avenida Paulista is **Jardins**, one of São Paulo's most expensive and fashionable neighbourhoods, modelled in 1915 according to the principles of the British Garden City movement, with cool, leafy streets leading down the hill. Actually a compendium of three smaller neighbourhoods – Jardim America, Jardim Europa and Jardim Paulista – it's home to swanky villas, condos, top-end restaurants and bars. Have a walk on and around **Rua Oscar** and **Rua Augusta**, with their expensive shops and boutiques.

Vila Madalena, Pinheiros and Itaim Bibi

West of Jardins, the *bairro* of **Vila Madalena** is also chock-a-block with nightlife and restaurants, though with a younger, more bohemian feel than its neighbour. Southwards, **Pinheiros** is rougher around the edges but also home to some decent nightlife, and further south, **Itaim Bibi** is a chic neighbourhood with galleries, bars and more good restaurants. **Avenida Brig. Faria Lima** is the main drag here, while the nearby **Museu Brasileiro da Escultura** at Avenida Europa 218 (Tues–Sun 10am– 7pm) is home to travelling exhibits of Brazilian artists and sculptors. Cutting through Pinheiros is Rua Teodoro Sampaio, a street lined with music stores, some of which feature free music performances on weekends. Nearby, and worth driving over (especially when dramatically lit at night), is the 138m-tall, cable-stayed **Octavio Frias de Oliveira Bridge**, a picture-postcard image with separate roadways passing under a giant concrete "X".

SÃO PAULO: VILA MADALENA & JARDINS

ACCOMMODATION

Bali	5
Casa Club Hostel	6
Gold Hotel	3
Paulista Center Hotel	4
Pousada Dona Zilah	2
São Paulo HI Hostel	1

● EATING

Asia House	14	Grão de Soja	4
Bovinu's Grill	7/15	Havanna Café	19
Consulado	10	O Melhor Bolo de	24
Mineiro Restaurante		Chocolate do Mundo	
D.O.M.	25	Sattva	11
Espaço Árabe	22	St. Etienne	2
Figueira Rubaiyat	21	Suco Bagaço	20
Fran's Café	9	Uni Alquimia Culinária	18

● DRINKING AND NIGHTLIFE

All Black	23
A Lôca	5
Bar Filial	6
Chopperia Opção	16
DroSoPhylal	3
Favela da Vila	8
O do Borogodó	17
O'Malley's	12
Posto 6	10
Studio SP	13

Pacaembu Stadium and Museu do Futebol

Oscar Freire (to open 2014)

Fradique Coutinho (to open 2014)

0   500

metres

Butantã and Morumbi

Further west of Pinheiros, near the **Cidade Universitária**, Butantã and Morumbi are accessed via the new metrô line 4 (yellow). Here you'll find the **Casa do Bandeirante**, a preserved, whitewashed adobe homestead from the time of the *bandeirantes*, early colonizers of the Brazilian interior. The Instituto Butantã's **Museu Biológico** at Avenida Vital Brasil 1500 (Wed–Sun 9am–4.30pm) will titillate snake-lovers – it houses rattlesnakes, boas and anacondas among others. Beyond Morumbi to the south, you'll see (or pass through) the impressive new financial district, **Berrini**, within whose skyscrapers the largest sums of money in Latin America are now transferred.

Parque do Ibirapuera

South of Jardins and sandwiched between Itaim Bibi and Vila Mariana, **Moema** is a wealthy district with some really good restaurants, although its main feature is the **Parque do Ibirapuera** (daily 5am–midnight; bus from metrô Brigadeiro), opened in 1954 to celebrate the 400th anniversary of the founding of São Paulo. Outside its main north entrance is the **Monumento às Bandeiras**, a 1953 sculpture by Victor Brecheret that celebrates a *bandeirante* expedition. Inside the park, a triad of inspiring Niemeyer-designed buildings houses the **Museu de Arte Contemporânea** (Tues–Fri 10am–7pm, Sat & Sun 10am–4pm; R$7), with regularly rotated works by twentieth-century European and Brazilian artists; the **Museu de Arte Moderna** (Tues–Sun 10am–6pm; R$6; free Sun), a smaller museum featuring mostly temporary exhibits of Brazilian artists; and the Auditório Ibirapueira concert hall. The **Museu Afro-Brasil** in the northern part of the park (Gate 10, just off Av Pedro Álvares Cabral; daily 10am–5pm; R$5) is an interesting collection exploring the African-Brazilian experience through paintings and artefacts, with sections on religion, slavery and oral history, as well as visiting exhibitions and occasional theatre.

Vila Mariana and Ipiranga

East of the park is the **Museu Lasar Segall**, at Rua Berta 111 (Tues–Sat 2–7pm, Sun 2–6pm; free), which houses the work of the Latvian-born, naturalized-Brazilian painter, originally a member of the German Expressionist movement. In nearby Ipiranga (avenidas Dom Pedro and Nazareth) is the impressive **Museu Paulista** (also known as Museu do Ipiranga; Tues–Sun 9am–5pm; R$4, free Sun; short bus ride or walk from metrô Alto do Ipiranga), modelled on the French Palace of Versailles. Very good exhibitions on the *bandeirantes*, coffee and slavery, alongside paintings and furniture that once belonged to the Brazilian royal family, bring the city's history to life. The museum stands in the park where Brazilian independence was declared in 1822; at its southern end stands the Independence Monument.

ARRIVAL AND DEPARTURE

By plane São Paulo has two airports: Guarulhos, about 25km from downtown, serves international destinations and many domestic flights; and Congonhas, right in the city, for domestic services only. From Congonhas taxis to downtown cost about R$55; from Guarulhos about R$120. An executive bus service (ⓦwww.airportbusservice.com .br) runs between the two airports and from Guarulhos to Tietê bus station (24hr; infrequent at night), and from Guarulhos to the Paulista/Augusta hotel circuit, Praça da República, and other central destinations (every 30min 6am–11pm); all services R$35. Local buses 257 and 299 serve Guarulhos and Tatuape metrô station (5am–midnight; R$5; 1hr 30min), a more difficult option with heavy baggage.

Destinations Flights to Rio and Belo Horizonte depart every 30min–1hr; for Foz, Salvador and Recife 6–8 flights daily.

By bus Almost all inter-state and international buses arrive at the vast Tietê Rodoviária north of the centre, which lies on the metrô line. *Rodoviária* Barra Funda serves towns throughout São Paulo State and some inter-state services to the west, while *Rodoviária* Jabaquara serves Santos and the São Paulo coast (both also on the metrô).

Destinations Ouro Preto (4 daily; 8hr); Belo Horizonte (6 daily; 9hr); Curitiba (hourly; 5hr); Foz do Iguaçu (4 daily; 19hr); Rio de Janeiro (every 30min; 6hr); Paraty (4 daily; 5hr); Salvador (3 daily; 24hr).

3

INFORMATION AND TOURS

Tourist information Available at the Tietê Rodoviária, Congonhas and Guarulhos, though these desks are not especially helpful. You're better off buying a *Mapa Turístico* (R$14.99) at the Laselva Bookstore or heading to the central information booths at Av São João 473, near Praça da República, or Av Paulista 1853, between MASP and Consolação (daily 9am–6pm; ⓦ cidadedesaopaulo.com/sp/en), where they're friendly and have excellent pamphlets and free maps.

Tour operators TurisMetrô (ⓣ 11 7716 5141, ⓦ www.metro.sp.gov.br/cultura-lazer) runs free 3hr city tours (Sat & Sun 9am & 2pm; English spoken) departing from Sé metrô station, with your only expense the metrô ticket. Also check out City Tour São Paulo (ⓣ 11 5182 3974, ⓦ circuitosaopaulo.com.br), who offer city, shopping, culinary and nightlife tours starting at R$60. For football matches and the World Cup contact Futebol Experience (ⓣ 11 3167 7905, ⓦ fxp.com.br) who run expert trips to the three major city clubs: São Paulo, Corinthians and Palmeiras.

GETTING AROUND

Avoid travelling around 4–7pm when the metrô and road network suffer from serious overcrowding.

By metrô Currently five lines but undergoing massive expansion; pick up a metrô map at any station or view at ⓦ www.metro.sp.gov.br. The most useful lines are: Azul (blue, north–south), serving Tietê, downtown, Vila Mariana and Jabaquara; Vermelha (red, east–west) from Barra Funda to downtown and the Arena de São Paulo (World Cup Stadium) at Itapuera; Verde (green, east–west) from Vila Madalena to Av Paulista and Ipiranga; and Amarela (yellow, central–west), downtown to Av Paulista, Pinheiros and Butantã (for USP university). Trains run from 5am–midnight. One-trip tickets cost R$3; a *Cartão Fidelidade* (R$2) will get you 8 trips for R$22 or 20 for R$54; a *Bilhete Único* (free with identification; see ⓦ sptrans.com.br for vendors) allows for up to 4 metrô or bus journeys within 3hr for R$4.65.

By bus Sampa's notoriously congested roads and 1500 bus routes make navigating the city above ground seem unduly complicated; it's best to use buses from metrô stations, where you can ask advice on which lines go to your destination. Standard fares are R$3; buy a *Bilhete Único* (see above) if you are making up to 4 bus/train journeys within 3hr. Buses run from 4am–midnight.

By taxi Taxis are metered and start at R$4. You can also call the following cab companies: Coopertaxi (ⓣ 11 6195 6000), Ligue Táxi (ⓣ 11 3866 3030), Especial Rádio Taxi (ⓣ 11 3146 4000).

ACCOMMODATION

Note that all options serve breakfast unless otherwise indicated.

HOSTELS AND POUSADAS

VILA MADALENA AND JARDIM PAULISTA

Casa Club Hostel Rua Mourato Coelho 973, Vila Madalena ⓣ 11 3798 0051, ⓦ casaclub.com.br; map p.338. A lively hostel in a corner house in this artsy *bairro*; a 25min walk from the metrô and close to nightlife. Great downstairs bar/kitchen under a mango tree. Dorms a little crowded, but wi-fi included. Dorms R$40, doubles R$110

Pousada Dona Zilah Alameda Franca 1621, Jardim Paulista ⓣ 11 3062 1444, ⓦ zilah.com; map p.338. The only real pousada in town: its location near Av Paulista, friendly, family touches and superb breakfast buffet have meant a rise in price. Quad rooms available. Wi-fi and excellent *Zilah Gourmet* restaurant downstairs. R$240, quad R$390

São Paulo HI Hostel (Vila Madalena) Rua Girassol 519, Vila Madalena ⓣ 11 3031 6779, ⓦ hostelsampa.com.br; map p.338. Smarter and cosier than the downtown option, with consummate facilities and close to great bars. HI-discount available. Dorms R$45, doubles R$130

CENTRAL SÃO PAULO AND BIXIGA

Lime Time Hostel Rua Treze de Maio 1552, Bixiga ⓣ 11 2935 5463, ⓦ limetimehostels.com; map pp.332–333. Won't win awards for its dorms but more than makes up for it with friendly vibes: great *caipirinhas*, free use of Macs and wi-fi, kitchen (no breakfast), PlayStation, and guided nights out. Near Bixiga and Av Paulista. Dorms R$35, doubles R$120

Pousada Dos Franceses Rua dos Franceses 100, Bixiga ⓣ 11 3288 1592, ⓦ pousadadosfranceses.com.br; map p.335. More smart hostel than pousada, in an ideal spot near Av Paulista and Bixiga. Fresh, blue rooms, small garden, guest kitchen and a mix of accommodation (wi-fi R$5/day extra). Dorms R$46, doubles R$115

São Paulo HI Hostel (Downtown) Rua Barão de Campinas 94 ⓣ 11 3333 0844, ⓦ hostelsp.com.br; map p.335. The downtown area is grimy but this gigantic hostel is near the metrô, safe, friendly and with numerous facilities, including a roof terrace. HI-discount available. Dorms R$45, doubles R$98

★ **TREAT YOURSELF**

There are ten **Mercure Hotels** (ⓦ mercure.com.br) in São Paulo. They're normally well outside the price range of budget travellers, but offer a range of weekend and national holiday *promoções*, including R$1 nights and the "Diária Cultural", where you buy a ticket to a cinema, theatre or museum and use it to get a room for one night for two people at the weekend for a rate of R$179 (plus tax) including an unlimited buffet breakfast. A great way to take a break from hostels and enjoy a night of luxury!

HOTELS

VILA MADALENA AND JARDIM PAULISTA

Bali Rua Fradique Coutinho 740, Pinheiros ☎ 11 3812 8270, ⓦ hotelbali.com.br; map p.338. The mirrors behind the beds make you wonder if it's not a "love motel" at first, but though basic, it stands up to scrutiny. Near Vila Madalena. R$80

Gold Hotel Alameda Jaú 2008, Jardins ☎ 11 3085 0805, ⓦ hotelgold.com.br; map p.338. On a noisy corner two blocks from Av Paulista, but has some serious personality, with decor that's Greek diner meets kitsch Taj Mahal. Funky red rooms with doors with room service openings. R$110

Paulista Center Hotel Rua da Consolação 2567 ☎ 11 3062 0733, ⓦ paulistacenterhotel.com.br; map p.338. A crisp business hotel just off Paulista. Excellent deals for public holidays, Carnaval and new year. R$160

CENTRAL SÃO PAULO AND BIXIGA

Banri Hotel Rua Galvão Bueno 209, Liberdade ☎ 11 3207 8877; map p.335. There may be cracking plaster in the hallways but this is one hotel where the rooms are better than the public spaces. Good value, almost stylish, and near great Japanese restaurants. R$110

Ibis Rua Vergueiro 1571, Paraiso 1571 ☎ 11 5085 5699, ⓦ ibis.com; map pp.332–333. Right by the metrô near Av Paulista, good value but the last word in characterlessness. All rooms sleep three for the same price as two; breakfast and wi-fi not included. Other Ibis and sister Formule1 hotels dotted around São Paulo. R$160

EATING

São Paulo hosts by far Brazil's best selection of restaurants, and you'll feel the need to splurge. Take advantage of the excellent Mercado Municipal at lunchtimes (its upstairs food court is good value, too). A range of cheap *por quilo* restaurants is located along Rua Augusta, north of Av Paulista. Also keep in mind that at night all bars serve food, with Vila Madalena known for high-quality options. Note that restaurants listed below open daily for lunch and dinner unless otherwise stated.

BRAZILIAN

Bovino's Grill Alameda Santos 2100, Jardins; Rua Augusta 1513, Consolação; map p.338. Cheap-ish *churrascaria* rodízio and *por quilo* restaurants; often packed out. Spend around R$35 for a lunch all-you-can-eat buffet with numerous meats, salads, stews and fish (double the price at night).

Consulado Mineiro Restaurante Praça Benedito Calixto 74, Pinheiros ☎ 11 3064 3882; map p.338. Satisfying fare from Minas Gerais at this popular choice in Jardins/ Pinheiros. Crowded at weekends. Two can share one (huge) portion for around R$65. Daily; Sun lunch only until 6pm.

★ **Dona Lucinha** Av Chibarás 399, Moema ☎ 11 5051 2050; map pp.332–333. Excellent unlimited R$37 lunch

3

★ **TREAT YOURSELF**

D.O.M. Rua Barão de Capanema 549 ☎ 11 3088 0761, ⓦ domrestaurante .com.br; map p.338. One of Brazil's best restaurants, starring celebrated chef Alex Atala. There's no better way to do it than by working your way through the tasting menu, around R$120. Mon–Fri lunch and dinner; Sat dinner only; closed Sun.

Figueira Rubaiyat Rua Haddock Lobo 1738, Jardins ☎ 11 3063 3888; map p.338. Built around a massive, golden-lit, 130-year-old majestic fig tree, this place serves the city's best steak, *feijoada* and Brazilian specialities. Around R$110 per person (unlimited food); great for a splurge. Mon–Sat lunch and dinner; Sun noon–6pm.

buffet (Tues–Sun) at the best *mineiro* restaurant in São Paulo. Try the full range of typical meat and vegetable dishes (vegetarians catered for), *cachaças* and desserts. Double the price at night. Closed Mon; Sun lunch only until 4.30pm.

Ponto Chic Largo do Paissandu 27, Centro Novo ☎ 11 3222 6528; map p.335. Established in 1922, this low-key sandwich shop does a scrumptious *bauru* with roast beef, four cheeses, tomato and pickle on baguette (R$17), plus other meaty goodies. Mon–Sat 7am–8pm.

Uni Alquimia Culinaria MASP, Av Paulista 1578 ☎ 11 3253 2829; map p.338. This basement buffet is not the typical museum cafeteria. For R$36 you can endlessly sample the more than sixty types of salads, hot dishes and desserts. Lunch only daily.

ITALIAN AND ARABIC

For really decent Italian food, head to *bairro* Bixiga, where you can take your pick of at least ten budget places along Rua 13 de Maio.

Espaço Árabe Rua Oscar Freire 168, Jardins ☎ 11 3081 1824; map p.338. This large and welcoming restaurant does great, tasty chargrilled chicken and steak kebabs, hummus and other excellent Middle Eastern food (from R$25).

Famiglia Mancini Rua Avanhandava 81, Bixiga ☎ 11 3256 4320; map p.335. Great antipasti, lasagne and other pasta at this mid-priced and highly popular restaurant, with another branch serving high-quality pizza just opposite. Open until the small hours at weekends.

Speranza Av Sabiá, 786, Moema ☎ 11 5051 1229; map pp.332–333. This labyrinthine pizza house with balcony seating has been open since 1958, and successfully replicates genuine Neapolitan pizza (from R$35). Daily; Mon dinner only.

3

JAPANESE, KOREAN AND THAI

In addition to those below, seek out traditional Korean food along Rua Correia de Melo (*bairro* Bom Retiro) close to Luz.

Asia House Rua da Glória 86, Liberdade; map p.335; Rua Augusta 1918, Jardins; map p.338. Great-value *por quilo* lunch buffet, with a range of Japanese soups, sushi and noodle dishes; expect to pay R$25 for a decent meal. Lunch only; closed Sun.

★ **Korea House** Rua Galvão Bueno 43, Liberdade ☎ 11 3208 3052; map p.335. One of São Paulo's few Korean restaurants, with excellent soups for R$20 and barbecue for R$30 – a nice haven from the busy street downstairs. Closed Wed; until 10pm only.

Nam Thai Rua Manuel Guedes 444, Itaim Bibi ☎ 11 3168 0662, ⓦ namthai.com.br; map pp.332–333. Good Thai food is hard to find in South America, but this smart restaurant serves an authentic range of dishes including excellent *tom-yum* soup, succulent ginger fish and delicious curries (mains from R$40). Closed Sun.

★ **Restaurante Okuyama** Rua da Glória 553 ☎ 11 3341 0780; map p.335. Probably the best-value Japanese place in Liberdade, open for lunch but most popular late at night until 3 or 4am daily. Sushi *executivo* lunches for R$18, plus sushi platters for two for R$37.

Yamaga Rua Thoaz Gonzaga 66, Liberdade ☎ 11 3275 1790; map p.335. Inventive and well-presented Japanese food in an inviting setting, with reasonable (though not budget) lunch specials bringing the cost down to R$23 for sushi/sashimi selection. Excellent ramens too. Closed Wed; Sun until 9pm only.

VEGETARIAN

Grão de Soja Rua Girassol 602, Vila Madalena ☎ 11 3813 2166; map p.338. One of the *bairro*'s best bohemian eating spots, with soya replacing meat in most dishes, from pasta to Brazilian *feijoada*. Lunch only until 5.30pm. Closed Sun.

★ **Sattva** Alameda Itu 1564, Jardins ☎ 11 3083 6237; map p.338. A lunchtime *prato de dia* is served here for R$16, including a juice, though it's in an otherwise expensive part of town. Full evening vegetarian menu; mains from R$25. Daily until 10pm.

CAFÉS, BAKERIES, SNACKS

Bakery Itiriki Rua dos Estudantes 24, Liberdade; map p.335. Brazilian and Japanese pastries and savoury snacks, with upstairs seating. Daily 8am–7pm.

Black Dog "Doguerias" across town, see ⓦ blackdog.com .br. The pressed hot dogs here (from R$10), with oozing *catupiry* cheese and other strange fillings, are perfect after-drinks food but they taste good sober too. 24hr.

Fran's Café Praça Benedito Calixto 191, Jardins; map p.338. Rua Cubatão 1111, Vila Mariana; map pp.332–333. Excellent coffee, and free wi-fi access. 24hr.

Havanna Café Rua Bela Cintra 1829, Jardins/Concolação; map p.338. An airy café perfect for lounging around and reading the paper, with quality coffee and free wi-fi. Try the *empanadas* or foil-wrapped *alfajor* cookies. Daily until 10pm.

O Melhor Bolo de Chocolate do Mundo Rua Oscar Freire 125, Jardins; map p.338. Its name ("the world's best chocolate cake") gives it away – and after tasting their creations here, modelled on those of a renowned Lisbon bakery, you may well agree. Mon–Sat 10am–9pm; Sun 11am–8pm.

★ **Shoshi Delishop** Rua Correia de Melo 206, Bom Retiro; map pp.332–333. In among the Korean eateries is this inexpensive Jewish-Brazilian lunch and snack joint. Super-friendly and ideal if you're visiting museums in Luz. 8.30am–3.30pm; closed Sun.

St. Etienne Al. Joaquim Eug. de Lima 1417, Jardins; map p.338. Rua Harmonia 699, Vila Madalena; map pp.332–333. Busy, unpretentious 24hr cafés/bars with pavement seating, great sandwiches and, if you're really hungry, a variety of unlimited breakfast/lunch/tea buffets.

Stuppendo Rua Canário 1321, Moema; map pp.332–333. A great place for top-notch ice cream, with flavours galore rivalling Italy's best. Daily until 10pm.

Suco Bagaço Rua Haddock Lobo 1483, Jardins; map p.338. Get your *açaí* (or other frozen fruit) fix or grab a quiche and a salad for just R$10.40. Mon–Sat 9am–9pm; Sun noon–8pm.

DRINKING AND NIGHTLIFE

São Paulo's nightlife is fantastic – a good enough reason alone for visiting the city. Options are scattered all over town, with things really getting going after midnight: Rua Augusta north of Av Paulista is the unofficial nightlife (though also red-light) centre; Vila Madalena (corners of Morato Coelho and Aspicquelta) is a more upscale drinking hotspot; nearby Pinheiros is a mix of the more artsy and Brazilian down-at-heel; Barra Funda has big dance music clubs; while Bixiga and Itaim Bibi also both offer good bars and live music. Pick up *Guia da Folha* or *Divirta-Se* (every Fri) at the tourist office or newsstands for entertainment listings. Great-value performances by famous Brazilian singers and dance troupes often take place at Auditório Ibarapuera: see ⓦ auditorioibirapuera.com.br.

BARS AND PUBS

All Black Rua Oscar Freire 163, Jardins ☎ 11 3088 7990, ⓦ allblack.com.br; map p.338. São Paulo's best Irish pub for those dying for a pint of Guinness. Mon–Sat 6pm–late.

Bar Brahma Av São João 677, Centro ☎ 11 3333 3030, ⓦ barbrahmasp.com; map p.335. Yellow-vested waiters serve good food and beer at this famous evening bar where Caetano Veloso wrote his song "Sampa". Live music upstairs; decent Brazilian menu. Daily 3pm–midnight.

Bar Filial Rua Fidalga 254, Vila Madalena ☎ 11 3813 9226; map p.338. Order a *caipirinha vermelha* from a bow-tie-wearing waiter at this smart and busy chequered-floor bar. Daily 5pm–midnight.

Choperia Opção Rua Carlos Comenale 97 ☎ 11 3288 7823; map p.338. Yards from Av Paulista and MASP, this is a really popular after-work place, with an outdoor terrace that's great for watching workhorse Sampa go by. Daily 4pm–late.

DroSoPhyla Rua Pedro Taques 80, Consolação ☎ 11 3120 5535, ⊛ drosophyla.com.br; map p.338. The strange art and bizarre decor contribute to making this funky bar a popular spot, but the good food and drink are what bring people back. Mon–Sat 8pm–late.

Kia Ora Rua Dr. Eduardo de Souza Aranha 377, Itaim Bibi ☎ 11 3846 8300, ⊛ kiaora.com.br; map pp.332–333. A little bit of "down-under" in Brazil; the spacious, wooden bar here has a pool table, live music, cover charge, and a dancing, flirty crowd till late. Tues–Sat 7pm–late.

London Station Rua Tabapuã 1439, Itaim Bibi ☎ 11 3368 8300, ⊛ londonstation.com.br; map pp.332–333. Chic bar/lounge with DJs and live music. Wear that collared shirt or little black dress. Cover R$18–25. Happy hours early evening. Thurs–Sat til late; happy hour 6.30–8.30pm.

O'Malley's Alameda Itú 1529, Jardins ☎ 11 3086 0780, ⊛ omalleysbar.net; map p.338. This cavernous Irish pub has a great happy hour (6–8pm) including food, plus there's pool, darts, free wi-fi and live music/DJs. Daily noon–4am.

Posto 6 Rua Aspicquelta; map p.338. This big corner bar is one of the four mammoth standbys in Vila Madalena and central to Sampa's night scene. Get some *picanha* with your *chopp*, and cook it at your table. Mon–Fri 6pm–very late; Sat from 2pm; Sun noon–midnight.

⭐ **SKYE** Hotel Unique, Av Brigadeiro Luis Antônio 4700, Jardim Paulista ☎ 11 3055 4700, ⊛ hotelunique.com.br; map pp.332–333. This is the place to start your night, on the roof of the "watermelon hotel" sipping a cocktail along with the beautiful people and a 360-degree view of the skyline. Chic and luxurious. Mon–Sat 6pm–midnight; Sun noon–midnight.

Veloso Rua Conceição Veloso 56, Vila Mariana ☎ 11 5572 0254; map pp.332–333. Perennially popular bar voted for serving Sampa's best *caipirinhas* and *coxinha* savouries. Inevitably neither comes cheap, but they are worth it. Tues–Fri 6pm–midnight; Sat 1pm–midnight.

CLUBS

A Lôca Rua Frei Caneca 916, Consolação ⊛ aloca.com.br; map p.338. Crazy-busy, this place gets crammed with people (gay and straight) dancing to electronica of all guises. Cover varies. Tues–Sun from midnight.

Canto da Ema Av Brig. Faria Lima 364, Pinheiros ⊛ canto daema.com.br; map pp.332–333. You can hear the *forró*

outside despite the airlock entrance. Inside, it's all dancing fun and *cachaça*. Cover R$9 women, R$12 men. Wed–Sun from 11pm.

Carioca Club Rua Cardeal Arcoverde 2899, Pinheiros ⊛ www.cariocaclub.com.br; map pp.332–333. This great dance hall (in a slightly seedy area) feels more Northeastern-Brazil than *carioca* (from Rio). Features live *forro*, funk or samba nightly, with friendly people not averse to showing newcomers the ropes. Nightly from 11pm; very busy on Mon. Cover R$25.

D-Edge Al. Olga 170, Barra Funda ⊛ d-edge.com.br; map pp.332–333. Sampa's premier electronica hotspot, with nightly DJs playing anything from techno to (*baile*) funk, and a mixed crowd ready to dance. Mon–Sat from midnight; entry from R$40.

Favela da Vila Rua Mourato Coelho 1272, Vila Madalena 419 ☎ 11 3848 6988, ⊛ faveladavila.com.br; map p.338. Live rock, Brazilian pop (MPB) or samba at this hip and friendly spot. Saturday *feijoada* buffet from 2pm only R$32 for two people, with live samba. Thurs–Sun until late.

Ó do Borogodó Rua Horácio Lane 21, Pinheiros; map p.338. This is the real Brazil: a gritty, authentic samba bar where everybody dances with everybody. R$25 cover. Nightly from 11pm; Sun 7pm–midnight.

⭐ **Studio SP** Rua Augusta 591, Consolação, ⊛ studiosp .org; map p.338. In the heart of the Augusta action this long-standing innovative club moved from Vila Madalena in 2008, and features a varied programme from live rock to Brazilian electronica, or DJs, depending on the night (R$25–35). Open most nights from 10pm, check the programme; advance tickets necessary for bigger named acts, from the venue. Club Vegas next door also has a good vibe.

⭐ **Traço de União** Rua Claudio Soares, Pinheiros ⊛ tracodeuniao.com.br; map pp.332–333. One of the city's top samba venues, mainly famous for its Sat *feijoadas* (R$25–35) from 2pm until late; includes food and great music. But it's busy on Wed and Fri nights, too, with a good vibe. Nightly.

Villa Country Av Francisco Matarazzo 774, Barra Funda ⊛ villacountry.com.br; map pp.332–333. *Sertaneja* (Brazilian country music) is massive right now thanks to a certain Michel Teló, and this 1800-capacity venue needs to be seen to be believed. Expect crowds of cowboy hats and cowgirl hotpants. Cover varies R$20–30. Thurs–Sun from 11pm.

DIRECTORY

Banks and exchange There are *cambios* at the airports and sprinkled throughout the city, including Banco do Brasil, at Rua São Bento 465, Centro, and Bradesco and HSBC along Av Brigadeiro Faria Lima and Av Paulista.

Car rental (Centro) Hertz, Rua Da Consolação 431 ☎ 11 3258 9384; Localiza, Rua da Consolação 419 ☎ 11 3231 3055; Movida, Rua da Consolação 271 ☎ 11 3255 6870.

3

Consulates Argentina, Av Paulista 2313 ☏ 11 3897 9522; Australia, Alameda Santos 700, 9th Floor ☏ 11 2112 6200; Canada, Av das Nações Unidas 12901, 16th Floor ☏ 11 5509 4321; Ireland, Al. Joaquim Eugênio de Lima 447 ☏ 11 3147 7788; South Africa, Av Paulista 1754, 12th Floor ☏ 11 3285 0433; UK, Rua Ferreira de Araujo 741, 2nd Floor ☏ 11 3094 2700; US, Rua Henri Dunant 500 ☏ 11 5186 7000.

Crime São Paulo has high crime. Keep valuables hidden and be careful at all times, especially in crowded areas like bus stations and markets. At night, much of downtown including Luz and Praça da República through to São Bento gets very seedy.

Hospitals Best hospital is Einstein, at Av Albert Einstein 627, Morumbi ☏ 11 3747 1233, ⒲einstein.br. For dental work, Dental Office Augusta, at Rua Augusta 878, Cerqueira César ☏ 11 256 3104; the largest central public hospital with A&E is Clínicas, at Av Dr. Enéas Carvalho de Aguiar 255 ☏ 11 3887 6611.

Laundries Lavesec, Praça Julio Mequita 13, at Sta. Efigênia and Av Castro Alves 437, Aclimação; 5 à Sec, at Rua José Maria Lisboa 1079, and Brigadeiro Luis Antonio 2013, Loja 4.

Left luggage Guarulhos, Congonhas and Tietê Rodoviária have 24hr lockers available (R$15–30/day).

Police Emergencies ☏ 190. DEATUR (tourist police) at Rua Consolação 247 (loja 8) ☏ 11 3257 4475.

Post offices See ⒲correios.com.br. Praça Correio at Av São João (Mon–Fri 8am–7pm); Av Brigadeiro Luis Antonio 996, Bixiga (Mon–Fri 9am–5pm).

Visas To extend a tourist visa, go to the Polícia Federal, at Rua Hugo D'Antola 95, 3rd Floor, Lapa de Baixo (Mon–Fri 8am–2pm; ☏ 11 3616 5000). To get there take suburban train 7 (Ruby) to Lapa from Luz or metrô Barra Funda, from where it's 5 blocks' walk or taxi.

SANTOS

Half the world's coffee, oranges and sugar pass through Santos, Latin America's biggest port. Inevitably a big chunk of the city is given over to industrial complexes and shipyards, but the surprise beneath the grit is a charming historical centre that attests to its foundation by the Portuguese in 1535. Lying on the island of São Vicente, the city is surrounded by water and has some popular beaches that draw the crowds in from São Paulo at weekends (you may wish to give swimming a miss here, however, as the water is not thought to be especially clean). You can see Santos's sights in a few hours, making it great for a day-trip or a stopoff if you're travelling from São Paulo along the coast to Paraty via São Sebastião.

A tourist tram (R$2; closed Mon) is available from outside the *rodoviária* to tour the sights, though the centre is also easy to navigate on foot. Walk past the attractive colonial-era houses on Rua do Comércio towards the nineteenth-century train station. Nearby, the grand Bolsa de Café (Rua XV de Novembro, 95; ⒲museudocafe.com.br; closed Mon; R$6) is Santos's main museum space. It hosts a remarkable permanent exhibition on the history of Brazil's coffee industry, partly responsible for the country's ethnic make-up given its enormous demand for first African slave labour, then Italian, Japanese, and other migrant workers in the late nineteenth and early twentieth centuries. Elsewhere, international football legend Pelé learnt his trade at Santos Futebol Clube, a legacy followed in part today by the club's newest young prodigy, Neymar. The stadium has a small museum on the development of the club and its stars, and makes a worthwhile visit (Rua Princesa Isabel 77; R$7).

ARRIVAL AND DEPARTURE

By bus Buses leave for Santos from São Paulo's Rodoviária Jabaquara (Azul metrô line) every 30min (R$30; 1hr; same frequency returning, avoid rush hour 4–7pm). Santos's *rodoviária* has left luggage (R$15) and tourist information. If you're going onwards to São Sebastião, executive buses depart at 7am, noon and 8pm daily, plus 4pm on Sun (⒲litoranea.com.br; 4hr; R$42).

ACCOMMODATION

HI Santos Hostel Rua Barão de Paranapiacaba 22 ☏ 13 2202 4566, ⒲santoshostel.com.br. Smart, friendly and well organized, it's a 10min taxi ride south of the centre. **R$40**

THE SÃO PAULO COAST

Between São Paulo and Rio the coastline is fantastic, and while Paraty (see p.257) and Ilha Grande (see p.256) get all the credit, a couple of days along the São Paulo section is a really worthwhile diversion. Founded on sugar and fishing, **São Sebastião** is a pretty colonial town popular with Brazilian and Argentine backpackers and trippers. A calming place after the urban clamour of São Paulo, you can also visit the island of **Ilha Bela** from here, home to fantastic beaches and waterfalls – though it's on the radar of São Paulo's rich list and has no budget accommodation aside from camping. Stunning coves and Atlantic forest mark the route onwards to **Ubatuba**, an energetic yet plain town best known for its 72 beaches on nearby islands and inlets. Though some now resemble hotel resorts, they're still the state's best, and numerous secluded spots remain. A car or plenty of time on buses is needed to explore them, but you'll most probably find plenty of like-minded beach seekers to do it with.

ARRIVAL AND DEPARTURE

By bus 13 buses/day ply the route from São Paulo's Rodoviária Tietê (R$47) to São Sebastião, while there are 3/day from Santos (both 4hr). From there, 4 buses/day make the 2hr journey eastwards to Ubatuba (R$20), and beyond, 2 buses daily on from Ubatuba direct to Rio, or 6 (3 on Sun) to Paraty (2hr; R$20).

ACCOMMODATION

HI Maresias Hostel Rua Sebastião Romão Cesar 406, São Sebastião ⊕ 12 3865 6612. A great place to relax after the rigours of the big city, and also lively with Paulista and Argentine surfers in season. **R$35**

HI Tribo Hostel Rua Amoreira 71, Ubatuba ⊕ 12 3842 0585, ⓦ ubatubahostel.com. Consummate facilities include free wi-fi, large buffet breakfast, games and book/DVD rental, while the lively party atmosphere is aided by the Praia do Lázaro right on hand. **R$30**

The South

Southern Brazil – the states of **Paraná**, **Santa Catarina** and **Rio Grande do Sul** – is a land of gauchos, barbecues and beaches. It's also generally considered to be the most developed region in the country and shows little of the obvious poverty found elsewhere. As a result the South can be an expensive place to travel, and hotel and restaurant prices are equivalent to those in Rio de Janeiro. Choose wisely, though, and you can still find good-value places to stay and eat out.

The spectacular **Iguaçu Falls** are deservedly the South's most visited attraction, though it's the subtropical southern coast that provides much of the region's allure in the summer (Nov–March). Building is virtually forbidden on the beautiful islands of the **Bay of Paranaguá** in Paraná – the most frequently visited being the gorgeous **Ilha do Mel**. By way of contrast, tourism has encroached along Santa Catarina's coast, but development has been restrained and resorts around Florianópolis, particularly in the south of the **Ilha Santa Catarina**, remain small and in tune with the region's natural beauty.

Beyond the pretty German enclaves of Gramado and Canela, the highland areas and the pampas of southern **Rio Grande do Sul** are largely given over to vast cattle ranches and latter-day **gauchos** – who share many cultural similarities with their Uruguayan and Argentine neighbours. The haunting remnants of **Catholic missions** pay homage to the brief but productive Jesuit occupation of the area.

CURITIBA

Founded by the Portuguese in 1693, **CURITIBA** was of little importance until 1853 when it was made capital of the newly created state of Paraná. Since then, the city's population has risen steadily from a few thousand to 1.8 million, its inhabitants largely descendants of Polish, German, Italian, Ukrainian and other immigrants. Home to a pristine old town and some enticing art museums, notably the eye-catching **Museu Oscar Niemeyer**, to visit Curitiba is to experience the best of the Brazilian economic boom: on average, *curitibanos* enjoy Brazil's highest standard of living, the city boasts facilities that are the envy of other parts of the country, and its eco-friendly design is a model that many urban planners try to emulate.

WHAT TO SEE AND DO

Most of Curitiba's attractions can be visited relatively easily in a day or so on foot. However, if you have limited time, take the Linha Turismo **bus tour**, which departs from Praça Tiradentes (every 30min Tues–Sun 9am–5.30pm; R$27). Stopping at 25 attractions around the city centre and suburbs, it takes two hours thirty minutes to complete the full circuit. Tickets allow passengers five hop-on hop-off stops.

3

3

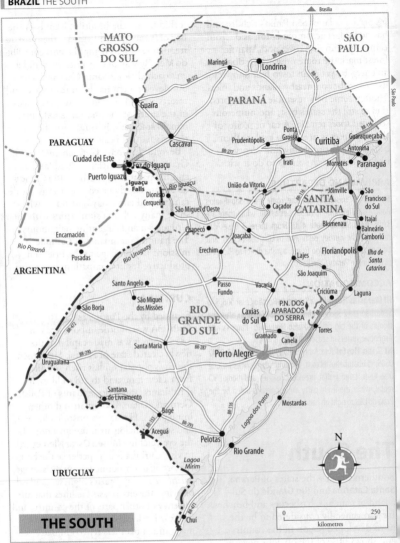

▲ Brasília

MATO
GROSSO
DO SUL

SÃO
PAULO

PARAGUAY

PARANÁ

Maringá · Londrina

Guaíra

Cascavel

Prudentópolis · Ponta Grossa · Curitiba · Guaraqueçaba
Antonina
Ciudad del Este · Foz do Iguaçu
Irati · Morretes · Paranaguá
Puerto Iguazú
Iguaçu Falls

Dionísio · Rio Iguaçu · União da Vitória · Joinville · São Francisco do Sul
Cerqueira
São Miguel d'Oeste · Caçador · SANTA CATARINA

Itajaí
Encarnación · Chapecó · Blumenau · Balneário Camboriú

Joaçaba
Rio Paraná · Erechim · Florianópolis · Ilha de Santa Catarina
Posadas

ARGENTINA · Rio Uruguay · Lajes

Santo Angelo · Passo Fundo · Vacaria · São Joaquim

São Borja · São Miguel dos Missões · Criciúma · Laguna
RIO GRANDE DO SUL · Caxias do Sul · P.N. DOS APARADOS DO SERRA

Santa Maria · Gramado · Torres
Uruguaiana · Canela
Porto Alegre

Santana do Livramento

Bagé · Mostardas
Aceguá · Lagoa dos Patos
Pelotas
Rio Grande

URUGUAY · Lagoa Mirim

N

Chuí

0 ———— 250
kilometres

THE SOUTH

Rua das Flores

The **Rua das Flores** – a pedestrianized precinct section of the Rua XV de Novembro, lined with graceful, pastel-coloured early twentieth-century buildings – is the centre's main late afternoon and early evening meeting point. Few of the surrounding streets are especially attractive, but the former city hall, at **Praça José Borges**, across from the flower market, is well worth a look.

Praça Tiradentes and the historic quarter

A couple of blocks north from Rua das Flores is **Praça Tiradentes**, the site where the city was founded and home to the neo-Gothic **Catedral Basílica de Nossa Senhora da Luz**. From here a pedestrian tunnel leads to Curitiba's **historic quarter**, an area of impeccably preserved eighteenth- and nineteenth-century buildings of Portuguese and central

European design. The **Igreja da Ordem**, on Largo da Ordem, dates from 1737 and is the city's oldest surviving building, dominating the historic quarter. Plain outside, the church is also simple within, the only decoration being typically Portuguese blue and white tiling and late Baroque altar and side chapels. The church contains the **Museu de Arte Sacra** (Tues–Fri 9am–noon & 1–6pm, Sat & Sun 9am–3pm; free), with relics gathered from Curitiba's churches. Opposite is the mid-eighteenth-century **Casa Romário Martins**, Curitiba's oldest surviving house, now the site of a cultural foundation and exhibition centre for regional artists.

A short distance uphill from here, on the same road, is the **Igreja Nossa Senhora do Rosário**, built by and for Curitiba's slave population in 1737, though it was completely reconstructed in the 1930s. The **Museu Paranaense**, nearby on Rua Kellers 289 (Tues–Fri 9am–6pm, Sat & Sun 10am–4pm; free), contains paintings by twentieth-century Paranaense artists as well as arts and crafts made by the region's first indigenous population. Some of the antiquities on show date back 10,000 years.

Modern Curitiba

Some of Curitiba's most unusual and impressive attractions are more contemporary. Among the largest museums in Latin America is the futuristic **Museu Oscar Niemeyer** (Tues–Sun 10am–6pm; R$4; ⓦmuseuoscarniemeyer.org.br), about 3km to the north of Curitiba's old town, on Rua Marechal Hermes. Designed by the Brazilian architect after whom it was named, the building's most notable feature resembles a giant eye. The galleries inside house primarily modernist art, including works by *paranaenses* Alfredo Andersen, Theodoro de Bona and Miguel Bakun, and many by Niemeyer himself, best known for designing much of Brasília (see p.317).

You could also head out to the **Jardím Botânico** (daily 6am–8pm; free) on the eastern edge of town at Rua Ostoja Roguski. Packed with native plants, it centres on an immense **greenhouse**, adopted as one of the symbols of the city.

West of the *rodoferroviária* along Avenida Sete de Setembro is the city's converted former railway station, now the **Shopping Estação**, an atmospheric mall incorporating the small **Museu Ferroviário** (Tues–Sat 10am–6pm, Sun 11am–7pm; free), which houses relics from Paraná's railway era as well as temporary exhibits.

Finally, it's worth a trip out to Curitiba's most popular attraction, the **Torre Panorâmica** (Tues–Sun 10am–7pm; R$3.50) on Rua Prof. Lycio Grein de Castro Vellozo, the only telephone tower in Brazil with an observation deck (109m), offering sensational views across the city.

ARRIVAL AND INFORMATION

By plane The ultramodern Aeroporto Internacional Afonso Pena (ⓣ41 3381 1153) is about 18km from the city centre. Taxis from the airport to the centre (30min) charge about R$55. Regular city buses ("Aeroporto") trundle between the Centro Civico and the airport every 20–30min (6am–11pm; R$2.60); there is also a faster shuttle (every 15–20min; R$10; ⓦaeroportoexecutivo.com.br). The shuttles stop at the *rodoferroviária*, at Rua Visconde de Nacar in front of the old Rua 24 Horas (name of the stop), and Shopping Estação.

Destinations Frequent flights to all major cities in Brazil – including Florianópolis, Foz do Iguaçu, Porto Alegre and São Paulo – and international flights to Paraguay and Argentina.

By bus The main bus station (ⓣ41 3320 3232) – the *rodoferroviária* – is southeast of town, about ten blocks from the city centre on Av Pres. Affonso Camargo.

Destinations Camboriú (22 daily; 2hr 30min); Florianópolis (23 daily; 4–5hr); Foz do Iguaçu (9 daily; 10hr); Paranaguá (hourly; 1hr 30min); Porto Alegre (8 daily; 12–13hr); Rio de Janeiro (4–5 daily; 13hr); São Paulo (hourly; 6–7hr).

By train The train station (ⓣ041 3888 3488) is next to the bus station in the southeast of town. The only passenger train from Curitiba is the Serra Verde Express (see box, p.349), which runs to Morretes and Paranaguá.

Tourist information There's a year-round tourist information booth at the *rodoferroviária* (daily 8am–6pm; ⓣ41 3320 3121, ⓦviaje.curitiba.pr.gov.br).

GETTING AROUND

Curitiba's centre is small enough to be able to walk to most places within the city centre.

By bus City buses (ⓦurbs.curitiba.pr.gov.br) stop at the strange glass boarding tubes you see dotted around town. Pay at the turnstile on entering the tube, not on the bus (R$2.50).

ACCOMMODATION

There are numerous cheap and secure hotels near the *rodoferroviária*. Places in the city centre are within walking distance of most attractions and are generally excellent value.

Ibis Budget Curitiba Centro Rua Mariano Torres 927 ☎ 41 3218 3838, ⊛ hotelformule1.com. Within walking distance of the bus station, this Ibis-run chain offers spotless, standard motel-like rooms that can accommodate up to three people – a good deal. R$109

Knock Knock Hostel Rua Isaías Bevilácqua 262 ☎ 41 3152 6259, ⊛ knockhostel.com. Stylish, modern hostel featuring six dorms, a fully equipped kitchen, laundry, barbecue area and terrace, a 10min walk from the centre. Free breakfast and wi-fi. Taxis from bus station R$14. Dorms $40

★ **Motter Home Curitiba Hostel** Rua Desembargador Motta 3574 ☎ 41 3209 5649. Opened in 2012, this justly popular hostel offers four clean dorms, three private rooms (with shared bathroom), communal kitchen, TV lounge and pool table, all a short stroll from the centre. Breakfast and wi-fi included. Taxis from bus station R$14. Dorms R$35, doubles R$90

Pousada Betânia Monteiro Tourinho 1335 ☎ 41 2118 7900, ⊛ pousadabetaniacuritiba.com.br. Cosy, tranquil accommodation, 20min from the bus station, with compact, modern en-suite rooms. Buffet breakfast and wi-fi included. R$65

Roma Hostel Rua Barão do Rio Branco 805 ☎ 41 3224 2117, ⊛ hostelroma.com.br. A block from the Shopping Estação, midway between the *rodoferroviária* and the centre, this is an older, standard HI hostel (converted from an old 1909 hotel), with dorms, private rooms and an attractive courtyard and garden. Light breakfast and wi-fi included. Discount for HI members. Dorms R$41, doubles R$82

EATING AND DRINKING

Curitiba's prosperity and its inhabitants' diverse ethnic origins have given rise to a good range of restaurants, with the most interesting located in the historic centre. For the cheapest eats check out the food court in Shopping Estação or the Mercado Municipal, Rua Sete de Setembro (Mon 7am–2pm, Tues–Sat 7am–6pm, Sun 7am–1pm).

Bouquet Garni Alameda Doutor Carlos de Carvalho 271 ☎ 41 3223 8490. Excellent veggie restaurant offering lunch buffets of stroganoff chickpeas, spinach lasagne and *feijoada* with onion, turnip and coconut for R$18 Mon–Fri and R$23 Sat–Sun. Daily 11am–3pm.

Mein Schatz Rua Jaime Reis 18 ☎ 41 3076 0121, ⊛ meinschatz.com.br. Next door to the Igreja do Rosário, offering a variable and affordable menu of German and Brazilian dishes in quasi-Bavarian surroundings; the popular starter plates of red and white sausages are R$16 (mains from R$25). Mon–Sat 11.30am–2.30pm, Sun 11.30am–3.30pm.

★ **TREAT YOURSELF**

Durski Rua Jaime Reis 254 ☎ 41 3225 7893, ⊛ restaurantedurski.com.br. Curitiba's only Ukrainian restaurant, located in a renovated house in the heart of the historic centre, looking onto Largo da Ordem. The food (including Polish and Brazilian dishes) is attractively presented and very tasty. The delicious filet mignon with mash and sautéed mushrooms in Madeira wine sauce is R$69. Tues–Thurs 7.45–11pm; Fri & Sat 7.45–11.30pm.

★ **Montesquieu** Rua Des. Westphalen 918 ☎ 41 3233 7065. Legend with students and staff at the technological university (UTFPR), who come to fill up on the famous X-Pastel burgers (R$5.50), X-Montanha (burger with meatloaf; R$6), and other cheap plates. No tables – just sit around the bar. Mon–Fri 9.30am–9.30pm.

Oriente Árabe Rua Kellers 95 ☎ 41 3224 2061, ⊛ orientearabe.com.br. Excellent, reasonably priced Arabic food (the founder was Syrian), with mains starting from R$22. If you want to try a bit of everything go for the *rodízio* buffet (dinner Tues–Fri R$42.50, Sat & Sun R$45). Belly-dancing shows feature in the evenings. Tues–Sat 11am–3pm & 6–11pm, Sun 11am–3pm.

Schwarzwald Rua Claudino dos Santos 63 ☎ 41 3223 2585, ⊛ bardoalemaocuritiba.com.br. Also known as the *Bar do Alemão* (German bar), this pub and restaurant has outdoor seating and a spacious, kitsch interior. A popular evening student meeting point in Largo da Ordem, at the heart of the old town, it serves excellent German food with cold beer (half a litre for R$7.50). A plate of pork knuckle and sausages for two will set you back R$36.90. Daily 11am–2am.

DIRECTORY

Banks and exchange Main offices of banks are concentrated at the Praça Osório end of Rua das Flores.

Hospital In emergencies use the Nossa Senhora das Graças hospital at Rua Prof Rosa Saporski 229, which has a 24hr hotline ☎ 41 3240 6555.

Laundry Auto Serviço Gama at Rua Tibagi 576 (Mon–Sat 8am–8pm; wash from R$12; ☎ 41 3019 1699), near the intersection with Rua Nilo Cairo, is a good central option.

Post office The central office is at Rua Marechal Deodoro 568, by Praça Santos Andrade (Mon–Fri 9.30am–6pm).

PARANAGUÁ

Brazil's second most important port for exports, **PARANAGUÁ**, 92km east of Curitiba, has lost some of its former character, though the colonial-style pastel-coloured buildings along the waterfront retain a certain charm. It was founded in the 1550s on the banks of the Rio Itiberê, making it one of Brazil's oldest cities, but only recently have measures been undertaken to preserve its colonial buildings.

WHAT TO SEE AND DO

The appeal of Paranaguá lies in wandering around the cobbled streets and absorbing the faded colonial atmosphere of the town. Almost everything worth seeing is concentrated along **Rua XV de Novembro**, a block inland from the waterfront. At the corner of Avenida Arthur de Abreu is the very pretty **Igreja São Francisco das Chagas** (daily noon–7pm), a small and simple church built in 1784 and still containing its Baroque altar and side chapels. Further along is the **Mercado Municipal do Café** (Mon–Sat 6am–6pm, Sun 6am–noon), an early twentieth-century building that used to serve as the city's coffee market. Today the Art Nouveau structure contains handicraft stalls and simple restaurants (see p.350) serving excellent, very cheap seafood.

SERRA VERDE EXPRESS

The Serra Verde Express (☎41 3323 4007, ⓦserraverdeexpress.com.br) is one of the most scenic train rides in Brazil, winding around mountainsides, slipping through tunnels and traversing one of the largest Atlantic Forest reserves in the country. It is undoubtedly the most atmospheric way to travel between Curitiba and Paranaguá (for the Ilha do Mel); make sure to sit on the left-hand side of the train for the best views (or on the right if you're not good with heights). The complete five-hour run to Paranaguá departs only on Sundays, leaving Curitiba at 8.15am and returning at 2pm; during the rest of the week the service only goes as far as Morretes. A variety of tickets is available, with coach class (*turístico*) from R$74 one-way (it's another R$57 for the return leg). For cheaper tickets book several days in advance, as they are limited and sell out quickly.

Just beyond the market is Paranaguá's most imposing building, the fortress-like **Colégio dos Jesuítas**. Construction of the college began in 1698, sixteen years after the Jesuits were invited by Paranaguá's citizens to establish a school for their sons. Because it lacked a royal permit, however, the authorities promptly halted work on the college until 1738, when one was at last granted and building recommenced. In 1755 the college finally opened, only to close four years later with the Jesuits' expulsion from Brazil. Today it is home to the **Museu de Arqueologia e Etnologia**, Rua XV de Novembro 575 (Tues–Fri 9am–noon & 1.30–6pm, Sat & Sun noon–6pm; R$3; ⓦwww.proec.ufpr.br). Exhibits concentrate on prehistoric archeological finds, indigenous culture and popular art, and the poor old Jesuits don't even get a mention. Three blocks inland from here on Largo Monsenhor Celso is the town's oldest church, **Igreja de Nossa Senhora do Rosário**, dating from 1578 (daily 8am–6pm; free).

ARRIVAL AND INFORMATION

By bus Buses arrive at the *rodoviária*, in the southwest of town on the waterfront at Rua João Estevão 403. Buses depart for Curitiba hourly (1hr 30min).

By train The *ferroviária* is three blocks from the waterfront at Av Arthur de Abreu 124. The Serra Verde Express to Curitiba departs Sun only at 2pm; 5hr (see box opposite).

By ferry Services depart from the Estação Nautica (Rua General Carneiro 258) to the bay islands, including Ilha do Mel (summer: 7 daily; winter: 2–3 daily; 1hr 45min; R$30 return).

Tourist information The municipal tourist office is on Rua Padre Albino 45, next to the *rodoviária* (Mon–Fri 8am–7pm; ☎41 3420 2940).

ACCOMMODATION

There is no real reason to hang around in Paranaguá, but should you need to, you can choose from a cluster of reasonably priced hotels within walking distance of the major transport terminals.

Hostel Continente Rua Gral. Carneiro 500 ☎41 3423 3224, ⓦhostelcontinente.com.br. Handy HI hostel in front of the Estação Nautica. HI discount for members. Dorms R$38, doubles R$80

Palácio Rua Correia de Freitas 66 ☎41 3422 5655, ⓦhotelpalacio.com.br. Centrally located hotel with clean but spartan rooms for up to four people. A good option for families on a budget. Breakfast, parking and wi-fi included. R$110

3

EATING

Cheap seafood and the local speciality, *barreado* (slow-cooked meat stew baked in clay pots), are the order of the day at most restaurants. There are some excellent inexpensive seafood places in the Mercado Municipal do Café, on Rua General Carneiro at Prof. Cleto, though they are open at lunchtimes only.

Casa do Barreado Rua Antonio da Cruz 78 ☎41 3423 1830, ⓦcasadobarreado.com.br. The best place to try the regional speciality *barreado* (R$25, with dessert included); the lunchtime buffet of Brazilian dishes is also good. Sat & Sun noon–3pm.

Lar do Má Rua João Estevão 574 ☎41 3425 2156. Next to the Colégio dos Jesuítas, this place offers a reasonably priced Chinese lunch buffet (R$20–25), as well as à la carte seafood in the evenings. Daily 11.30am–2.30pm & 7pm–midnight.

ILHA DO MEL

Famed for its golden beaches and tranquil setting, the idyllic **ILHA DO MEL** ("Island of Honey") in the Bay of Paranaguá is a hit with backpackers and surfers looking to enjoy the simpler things in life – and the island's waves. It's an unusually shaped island, to say the least. Its bulbous northern half, a protected Atlantic forest ecological station (entry is prohibited), is joined to the slender south by a bridge of land where the lively main area **Nova Brasilia** is located. The island's other major settlement, **Encantadas**, near the southwest corner, has the atmosphere of a sleepy fishing village. It's little more than 12km from north to south, but given the relief of the island most walks hug the coast. Bear in mind that there are no cars, no public transport and no shops on the island and electricity for only a short period each day – so come prepared.

WHAT TO SEE AND DO

Praia do Farol is the closest beach to Nova Brasilia, curving a wide arc around the northeastern part of the island. It's a 4km walk north along these sands to the Portuguese fort of **Fortaleza Nossa Senhora dos Prazeres** (open daily; free), completed in 1769. Encantadas' nearest beach is **Praia de Fora**. The entire stretch of coastline along the southeast side between Praia de Fora and Praia do Farol is dotted with enchanting coves, rocky promontories and small waterfalls. The rocks are slippery here, so care should be taken, and the three-hour walk along the beach from Praia de Fora as far as Fortaleza should only be attempted at low tide or you risk being stranded. The southern tip of the island, known as **Ponta Encantada**, is where you will find the **Gruta das Encantadas** (Enchanted Cave), focal point for a number of local legends.

ARRIVAL AND INFORMATION

By boat In summer 7 daily ferries (1hr 45min; R$32 return) link Ilha do Mel with Paranaguá. You can also catch a bus from Curitiba (5 daily; 2hr 15min; R$28) or Paranaguá (10 daily; 1hr 30min; R$3.40) to Pontal do Sul, from where boats leave every hour or so from the beach to the island (daily 8am–5pm; 30min; R$27 return; ⓦabaline.com.br); all ferries usually serve Encantadas then Nova Brasilia. There are fewer boats to the island in winter.

Tourist information There is a tourist information booth at the dock in Nova Brasilia (summer: daily 7.30am–8pm).

ACCOMMODATION

If you plan to visit in the height of summer, it's best to arrive during the week and as early as possible, as accommodation books up quickly during the weekends. The island is always full to capacity over New Year and Carnaval, when reservations are essential and are accepted only for minimum stays of four or five nights.

Casadumel Trilha da Gruta Encantada ☎41 3426 9087, ⓦcasadumel.blogspot.com. Rustic self-catering two-bedroom bungalow (with space for up to eight adults) a short walk from Praia de Encantadas, with hammocks in the garden and fully equipped kitchen. **R$130**

★ **Ilha do Mel Hostel** Praia do Farol (Farol), Nova Brasilia ☎41 3426 8065, ⓦilhadomelhostel.com.br. Not really a hostel but a budget hotel with compact but stylish rooms near the main beaches. There is a "cyber lounge" with four computers, Sky TV and breakfast is served on the deck; beach chairs and umbrellas available. **$90**

Pousadinha Caminho do Farol ☎41 3426 8026, ⓦpousadinha.com.br. Popular backpacker hangout with leafy gardens and relaxing hammocks for chilling out. Rooms (*quartos*) are simple but good value, while the newer wood cabins (*apartamento novo*) have more character. Multilingual staff can assist with booking activities. R$70–100. Cabañas **R$120**, doubles **R$80**

Pousada Lua Cheia Praia das Encantadas ☎41 3426 9010, ⓦluacheiatur.com.br. Ten simple en-suite wood cabins that hold up to four people each, equipped with TV, fridge, fan and a/c. Breakfast included. Cabañas **R$100**

FOZ DO IGUAÇU

A classic stop on the backpacker trail, the city of **FOZ DO IGUAÇU** is the Brazilian gateway to the magnificent **Iguaçu Falls**, one of the world's greatest natural wonders, which lie 20km south. Much larger than its Argentine counterpart **Puerto Iguazú** (see p.87), it makes a better base for exploring the falls, with the advantage of decent restaurants and a livelier nightlife.

WHAT TO SEE AND DO

Foz do Iguaçu is a modern city, with no real sights of its own, but there are a couple of attractions on the road to the falls (Av de Cataratas) that are worth checking out. Despite the hefty entrance fee, the parrots and showy toucans at **Parque das Aves**, Km17.1, just 300m from the falls entrance (daily 8.30am–5.30pm; foreigners pay R$32 or US$17; ℗parquedasaves.com.br), are well worth the expense, with enormous walk-through aviaries in dramatic forested surroundings (all birds have been rescued from traffickers and would not survive alone in the wild). There is also a large walk-through butterfly cage – butterflies are bred throughout the year and released when mature. All the butterflies and eighty percent of the eight hundred bird species are Brazilian, many endemic to the Atlantic forest. Around 200m back along the road and along a narrow lane is the **Thermas Parque Aquático Cataratas** (Mon–Fri 8am–6pm, Sat & Sun 8am–7pm; R$15; ☏45 3529 6016), which maintains a series of thermally heated pools supplied with water springing directly from the underground Guaraní aquifer, the largest natural freshwater source in the Americas. It features a series of giant slides, children's pools and a decent grill restaurant.

ARRIVAL AND INFORMATION

By plane Foz do Iguaçu International Airport (☏45 3521 4200) is 13km south of town, halfway along the road to the falls (12km north of the falls themselves). It is served by flights from Curitiba, São Paulo, Rio de Janeiro, Brasília, Salvador and Belém. A taxi into town costs R$45–50, or take a bus from outside the airport ("Aeroporto Parque Nacional"), which shuttles between the falls and the local terminal in town on Av Juscelino Kubitschek (every 25min 5.30am–7pm, then hourly until midnight; 45min; R$2.65).

By bus The *rodoviária* (☏45 3522 2590) is on the northern outskirts of town on Av Costa e Silva; buses #105 and #115 from here, marked "Rodoviária", can take you to the local bus terminal (TTU or Terminal de Transporte Urbano) on Av Juscelino Kubitschek in the city centre (R$2.65); taxis cost around R$16–17. Here you can pick up bus #120 to the falls ("Aeroporto Parque Nacional"; R$2.65).

Destinations Curitiba (9 daily; 9–10hr); Florianópolis (5 daily; 15–16hr); Porto Alegre (8 daily; 14–16hr); Rio de Janeiro (2 daily; 22–23hr); São Paulo (10 daily; 15–17hr).

Tourist information There are tourist offices at the airport (daily 8.30am–8pm; ☏41 3521 4276), the *rodoviária* (daily 7am–6pm; ☏41 3522 1027) and the local bus terminal in town (daily 8am–6pm). The main Foz tourist office is at Av das Cataratas 2330 (daily 7am–11pm; ☏45 3521 1455, ℗www.pmfi.pr.gov.br).

ACCOMMODATION

When choosing where to stay, your main decision will be whether to pick a central option or to go for a place closer to the falls. Central options have the advantage of proximity to good restaurants and bars, while those closer to the falls cut down your travelling time and include a number of excellent hostels and a great campsite.

IGUAÇU FALLS TOURS AND ACTIVITIES

The Iguaçu Falls has become a major adventure travel hotspot with a bewildering range of activities available. Every 15min the **Helisul helicopter** (☏45 3529 7474, ℗helisul.com) takes off just outside the park entrance, offering 10min flights over the falls for US$110 per person (minimum three people); sensational views, but controversial thanks to the noise pollution (which scares wildlife).

TOUR OPERATORS

Macuco Safari ℗macucosafari.com.br. Based within the national park, offers a guided forest safari and a boat trip into the Devil's Throat (see p.353) among its varied programmes.

Martin Travel Travessa Goiás 200 ☏45 3523 4959, ℗martintravel.com.br. A reliable local travel agency that specializes in ecotourism and puts together groups to go canoeing, rafting or mountain biking along forest trails.

3

CENTRAL

★ **Favela Chic Hostel** Rua Major Raul de Mattos 78 ☎ 45 3027 5060, ⓦfavelachichosteliguassu.com. New, spotless hostel opened in March 2012 by friendly English owner, Nick, near the bus stop for the falls. It's all nicely done, with bright, comfy hang-out areas, hammocks and two dorms with a/c and shared bathrooms. Includes cooked breakfast, free yoga classes and wi-fi. Dorm R$30, camping R$14

Iguassu Guest House Rua Naipi 1019 ☎ 45 3029 0242. Short walk from the bus station, this small hostel offers spotless dorms (R$38) but also excellent private en-suite rooms (R$55 per person) with all the amenities (wi-fi, bar, book exchange, pool table).

HI Paudimar Falls Rua Antônio Raposo 820 ☎ 45 3028 5503, ⓦpaudimarfalls.com.br. Run by the same people as the *Paudimar Campestre* (see below), this gives you the same great service and facilities in a central location, and free internet. Dorm R$30, double R$80

Pousada Evelina Navarrete Rua Irlan Kalichewski 171 ☎ 45 3574 3817, ⓦpousadaevelina.com.br. Extremely friendly place with a youth hostel atmosphere that mainly attracts foreign backpackers. Rooms are simple but spotless, breakfasts are adequate, there's internet access (R$2.50/day) and multilingual Evelina goes out of her way to be helpful. Well located for buses to the falls. R$110

Pousada El Shaddai Rua Engenheiro Rebouças 306 ☎ 45 3024 4493, ⓦpousadaelshaddai.com.br. A good, central, hostel-type establishment; rates include a sumptuous Brazilian buffet breakfast. The multilingual staff, pool, internet access and on-site travel agency all help make your stay comfortable. Dorm $28, double R$60

ROAD TO THE FALLS

★ **HI Paudimar Campestre** Av das Cataratas Km12.5 ☎ 45 3529 6061, ⓦpaudimar.com.br. A favourite with backpackers, this excellent HI establishment has superb facilities. Choose from basic shared dorms sleeping six to eight people, family apartments (with double bed, bunk bed, a/c and private bathroom) and pretty cabins for two. The extensive grounds include a swimming pool and bar. Kitchen facilities are available, and they also serve evening meals. The hostel organizes daily trips to the Argentine side of the falls. Dorm R$25–35, private cabin R$80–92, family apartment R$120–184

Camping Clube do Brasil ☎ 45 3529 8064, ⓦcamping clube.com.br. This excellent campsite is at Km17 on the road to the falls; the site is surrounded by jungle, and facilities include a laundry area and a clean swimming pool. Tents can be rented for R$3–8.70. Camping/person R$17.50

EATING AND DRINKING

While it's no gastronomic paradise, Foz do Iguaçu is a good place to eat cheaply, with a proliferation of buffet-style *por kilo* restaurants.

★ TREAT YOURSELF

Ipé Grill Parque Nacional do Iguaçu ☎ 45 2102 7000, ⓦhoteldascataratas.com. The only hotel restaurant worth a splurge. Located by the pool in the Tropical das Cataratas Eco Resort (near the falls), it offers an extensive but very pricey buffet dinner of typical Brazilian dishes and "gaucho" style barbecue for R$120. Even if you can't afford to stay here (rooms start at around R$730), you should take a wander around the hotel grounds just to have a look. Daily 6.30–10am & 7.30–11pm.

La Bella Pizza Rua Xavier da Silva 648 ☎ 45 3574 2285, ⓦlabellapizzafoz.com.br. The best of several pizza *rodízios* on this block, where you can gorge yourself on endless servings of pizza and pasta for just R$14.99. An added attraction is the "sweet pizzas", including white chocolate and caramelized banana flavours. Daily 6–11.45pm.

Capitão Bar Rua Jorge Schimmelpfeng 288 ☎ 45 3572 1512, ⓦcapitaobar.com. One of a series of lively bars on this stretch, this is a particularly popular nightspot on account of its loud music, extensive cocktail menu and affordable pizzas. Outdoor tables fill quickly so arrive early in summer if you want to sit outside. Daily 5pm–3am.

Clube Maringá Rua Dourado 111, Porto Meira ☎ 45 3527 3472, ⓦrestaurantemaringa.com.br. Justly popular among locals for its superb *rodízio de peixe* (R$29) and stunning views of the Iguaçu River. Apart from a selection of local freshwater fish, there's an excellent salad bar and you can pay a little extra for some of the freshest *sashimi* you're likely to come across. Take the "Porto Meira" bus and ask for directions, or a taxi (R$22–25). Mon–Sat 11.30am–11.30pm; Sun till 3pm, reservations advised on Sun.

Recanto Gaúcho Av das Cataratas Km15 (near the falls entrance) ☎ 45 3572 2358, ⓦrecantogaucho.com. It can be a little touristy, but the atmosphere's lively, the meat's excellent and cheap (R$29.90 for all-you-can-eat) and the owner (who dresses in full gaucho regalia) is a real character. Short afternoon horse rides are also included in the price. Turn up soon after 11am; food is served until 3pm. Reservations advised. Sun 10.30am–6pm. Closed Dec & Jan. Taxis R$18–21.

Trigo & Cia Av Paraná 1750 ☎ 45 3025 3800, ⓦtrigoecia .com.br. 10min by bus from the centre of town, this busy café serves tasty savoury snacks, good coffee and the best cakes in Foz (R$5–7). Daily 24hr.

DIRECTORY

Banks and exchange Dollars (cash or travellers' cheques) can be easily changed in travel agents and banks along Av Brasil; the banks have ATMs.

CROSSING THE BORDER TO PARAGUAY AND ARGENTINA

International buses leave every 15min from the *rodoviária* via the local bus terminal, bound for Ciudad del Este in Paraguay (25min; R$4), which is 7km northwest of Foz do Iguaçu. You need to disembark at the Brazilian customs for your exit stamps – the bus will not wait but your ticket is valid for the next one. You will then cross the Friendship Bridge to the Paraguayan customs, where you will again be asked to disembark. Buses for Puerto Iguazu (40min; R$4) leave every 20min from the *rodoviária*; you will have to get your passport stamped to enter Argentina – the bus will stop at customs on the way and wait for you. Taxis will charge R$60–70 to Puerto Iguazu, a bit less for Ciudad del Este. Two things to note: it's unlikely that your Brazilian reais will be accepted across either border, so change money as soon as you can; and that crossing the border on the bus can take up to an hour if it's busy.

Consulates Argentina, Eduardo Bianchi 26 ☎45 3574 2969; Paraguay, Rua Marechal Deodoro 901 ☎45 3523 2898.

Hospital Ministro Costa Cavalcanti, Av Gramado 580, ☎45 3576 8000, is a good private hospital.

Police Tourist police ☎45 3523 3036.

Post office Praça Getúlio Vargas near Rua Barão do Rio Branco (Mon–Fri 9am–5pm).

Taxi Coopertaxi Cataratas ☎45 3524 6464.

IGUAÇU FALLS

The **IGUAÇU FALLS** are, unquestionably, one of the world's great natural phenomena. They form the centrepiece of the vast bi-national **Iguaçu National Park**, which was first designated in 1936 and declared a UNESCO World Heritage Site fifty years later, a long time coming given that the falls were discovered as early as 1542 by the Spanish explorer Alvar Nuñez Cabeza de Vaca. To describe their beauty and power is a tall order, but for starters cast out any ideas that Iguaçu is some kind of Niagara Falls transplanted south of the equator – compared with Iguaçu, Niagara is a ripple. About 15km before joining the Rio Paraná, the Rio Iguaçu broadens out, then plunges precipitously over an 80m-high cliff in 275 separate falls that extend nearly 3km across the river. To properly experience the falls it is essential to visit both sides. The Brazilian side gives the best overall view and allows you to fully appreciate the scale of it; the Argentine side (see p.88), which makes up most of the falls, allows you to get up close to the major individual falls.

The falls are mind-blowing whatever the season, but they are always more spectacular following a heavy rainstorm. Weekends and Easter are best avoided if you don't want to share your experience with hordes of Brazilian and Argentine holidaymakers.

WHAT TO SEE AND DO

At its best in the early morning, a 1.5km cliffside trail runs alongside the falls, offering breathtaking photo opportunities. A stairway leads down from the bus stop to the start of the trail. The path ends by coming perilously close to the ferocious "**Garganta do Diabo**" (Devil's Throat), the most impressive of the individual falls. Depending on the force of the river, you could be in for a real soaking, so if you have a camera with you be sure to carry it in a plastic bag. From here, you can either walk back up the path or take the lift to the top of the cliff and the road leading to the *Tropical das Cataratas Eco Resort* hotel. You'll undoubtedly come across coatis on the trails (though raccoon-like, they are not raccoons, whatever the local guides may say) – don't be fooled by their cute and comical appearance; these little creatures are accomplished food thieves with long claws and sharp teeth.

ARRIVAL AND DEPARTURE

It costs foreigners R$41.10 to enter the park (concessions available for MERCOSUR and Brazilian residents), after which a shuttle bus (included) will deliver you to the trails.

By bus Bus #120 ("Aeroporto Parque Nacional"; $2.65) from Foz do Iguaçu terminates at the entrance to the falls (daily 9am–5pm).

By taxi Taxis charge at least R$50 from town.

ILHA DE SÃO FRANCISCO DO SUL

Travelling 135km south from Curitiba into the state of Santa Catarina the coastline becomes the main attraction, with the beaches of **ILHA DE SÃO FRANCISCO DO SUL** well worth a diversion off the main highway. A low-lying island separated from the mainland by a narrow strait some 40km east of the industrial port city of Joinville and the site of a major Petrobras oil refinery, it might be reasonable to assume that São Francisco should be avoided, but this isn't the case. Both the port and refinery keep a discreet distance from the main town, **São Francisco do Sul**, and the beaches blend perfectly with the slightly dilapidated colonial setting. On the east coast, **Praia de Ubatuba**, 16km from the centre, and the adjoining **Praia de Enseada**, 20km from town, offer enough surf for you to have fun but not enough to be dangerous. A ten-minute walk across the peninsula from the eastern end of Enseada leads to **Praia da Saúde** (or just Prainha), where the waves are suitable for only the most experienced surfers.

São Francisco do Sul

Though the island was first visited by French sailors in 1504, it was not until 1658 that the town of **SÃO FRANCISCO DO SUL** was established by the Portuguese. One of the oldest settlements in the state, it is also one of the very few places in Santa Catarina with a well-preserved historic centre.

WHAT TO SEE AND DO

Dominating the city's skyline is the **Igreja Matriz Nossa Senhora da Graça**, the main church, originally built in 1699 by Indian slaves, but completely reconstructed in 1926. The **Museu Nacional do Mar** on Rua Manoel Lourenço de Andrade in the historic centre (Tues–Sun 10am–6pm; R$5; ⓦ museunacionaldomar.com.br) has a vast maritime collection with an emphasis on southern Brazil and its people. The prettiest beaches, **Paulos** and **Ingleses**, are also the nearest to town, just a couple of kilometres to the east. Both are small, and have trees to provide shade.

Surprisingly few people take advantage of the calm and shallow waters here, which are ideal for weak swimmers.

ARRIVAL AND DEPARTURE

By bus The island is connected to the mainland by two causeways, but the *rodoviário* is inconveniently located outside São Francisco do Sul centre on Rua Dom Fernando Trejo y Sanabria (just off the main highway); you'll need to catch a local bus (R$2.40) to the market in the town centre. Buses to the beaches at Enseada and Ubatuba leave from the market, with the last services in both directions departing at about 9.30pm.

Destinations Curitiba (daily; 3hr); Joinville (hourly; 1hr 20min); São Paulo (daily; 8hr).

ACCOMMODATION

Most of the island's visitors bypass the town altogether and head straight for the beaches to the east, so, even in midsummer, there's rarely any difficulty in finding a central hotel.

Kontiki Rua Babitonga 33, near the market in São Francisco do Sul ⓣ 47 3444 2232, ⓦ hotelkontiki.com.br. Located in the heart of the old town in front of the bay, this comfortable hotel has wonderful views and a "colonial-style" (which basically means indulgent) breakfast. R$82

Pousada Farol da Ilha Enseada, just behind the beach on Rua Maceió 1156 ⓣ 47 3449 1802, ⓦ pousadafarol dailha.tur.br. This little family-run place, only 300m from the beach, also has its own pool. The rooms are decorated in a rustic style and it's particularly popular with couples. There is a discount for rooms with a shared bathroom. R$156

Zibamba Rua Fernando Dias 27, São Francisco do Sul ⓣ 47 3444 2020, ⓦ hotelzibamba.com.br. Relatively luxurious, this attractive colonial-style hotel has its own pool and restaurant. R$160

EATING AND DRINKING

Eating out holds no great excitement, with the *Zibamba's* (see above) restaurant the best of a generally poor bunch serving up a seafood buffet at lunch and typical Brazilian dishes à la carte in the evenings. Enseada does have a lively nightlife, though.

Bar do Banana Av Brasilia at João Pessoa, Prainha ⓣ 47 3444 0785, ⓦ bardobanana.com.br. Popular with twenty-somethings (and cruise-ship passengers) looking for reasonably priced drinks, food and fun by the sea. Daily 11am–11pm.

Surf Bar Av Brasilia 15, Prainha ⓣ 47 3442 4234, ⓦ surfbarsc.com.br. Unpretentious and popular bar hosting regular live music acts and DJs from Floripa (Fri & Sat). Daily 11am–1am.

BALNEÁRIO CAMBORIÚ

If you are travelling in search of the Santa Catarina party scene, look no further than **BALNEÁRIO CAMBORIÚ**, an effervescent resort town 112km south of São Francisco do Sul with a distinctly hedonistic approach to life often dismissed by *cariocas* as the "poor man's Copacabana". Either way it's a popular summer destination with young Brazilians, Paraguayans and Argentines, and the town is packed out during the peak season with sunbathers and fun-seekers.

WHAT TO SEE AND DO

Camboriú has something of a Mediterranean holiday resort feel to it, with its high-rise buildings and pedestrian streets lined with artists peddling souvenirs, and walking around town you could be forgiven for thinking that you were on the Portuguese Algarve. The place is not without its charms – not least its 7km-long **Praia Central**, offering safe swimming and golden sand. **Praia do Pinho**, on the other side of the peninsula west of town, is the site of Brazil's first nudist beach.

Camboriú even has its own 33m-high Rio-style Christ statue, the **Cristo Luz** (April & Sept Wed–Sat 4pm–midnight; Oct, Nov & July Tues–Sat 4pm–midnight; Dec–March Mon–Sat 4pm–midnight; Aug & June Thurs–Sat 4pm–midnight; Sun 10am–midnight year-round; R$10 10am–7pm, R$20 after 7pm; ⏀cristoluz.com.br), illuminated at night and casting a faint greenish glow over the town. On summer evenings the park at the foot of the statue is the site of concerts, theatre and poetry recitals. The forested hillside of Morro da Aguada in the south of town is a nature reserve-cum-theme park, the **Parque Unipraias** (daily 9.30am–6pm; closed Mon Nov–April; ⏀unipraias.com.br). You can reach it via a 3.25km cable car (same hours; R$30) that starts at the Estação Barra Sul on the Praia Central before shooting up to the Estação Mata Atlântica on the summit (240m), offering glorious views over the town, beaches and out to sea. From here you can stroll the

trails in the Parque Ambiental (same hours; included in price), enjoy the 140m canopy trail (Arvorismo; R$20) or the Youhooo! 60km/hr toboggan ride ($15). The cable car continues down to the beach at Praia Laranjeiras.

ARRIVAL AND INFORMATION

By bus Camboriú sits on the main Curitiba–Florianópolis highway (BR-101), and is just 80km north of Florianópolis. Buses arrive at the *rodoviária* (⏀47 3367 2901) on Av Santa Catarina, at the edge of town close to the highway.

Destinations Buenos Aires (1 daily; 28hr); Curitiba (22 daily; 2hr 30min); Florianópolis (38 daily; 1hr 30min); Joinville (26 daily; 1hr 30min); Porto Alegre (9 daily; 8–9hr); São Paulo (13 daily; 8–9hr).

Tourist information There is a tourist information office at Rua 2950 no. 771 (⏀47 3367 8005, ⏀guiacamboriu .com.br).

ACCOMMODATION

You'd be wise to book ahead in the peak season when block bookings take up the majority of the more affordable hotels. That said, there is always the possibility of reductions if you ask around during late afternoon, with hotels desperate to be full to capacity. If you're in a group ask at the tourist office about renting a house – it's cheaper than you might think.

Hotel Arco do Sol Rua Cel. Benjamin Vieira 50 ⏀47 3369 4960. Plain but adequate option in the centre, offering buffet breakfast and free wi-fi. The simple en-suite rooms come with tiled floors, a/c and TV. R$120

Hostel Rezende Rua 3100, no. 780 ⏀47 3361 9815, ⏀hotelpousadarezende.com.br. Standard HI hostel (internet, kitchen, breakfast) a few blocks back from the beach. It's decent value for money, and dorms are small and uncrowded. Dorms R$40, doubles R$89

Hotel Topázio Rua 11, no. 15 ⏀47 3367 1022, ⏀htopazio .com.br. Another small, basic hotel but a great deal and in the centre of town, 50m from the beach. En-suite rooms come with a/c and cable TV, but no internet. R$109

EATING

In addition to the proliferation of fast-food joints and *lanchonetes* that you might expect in a town populated by twenty-somethings, there are also some excellent restaurants around if you look hard enough, with seafood platters featuring heavily on most menus.

Guacamole Av Beira Rio 1122 ⏀47 3366 0311, ⏀guacamolemex.com.br. Charismatic Mexican mini-chain with live music, *mariachis* and *"tequileros"* who are only too happy to wet your whistle. Latin dance shows every Tues night add to the experience. Spicy mains from R$25. Daily 7.30pm–2am.

BEER DRINKING IN BLUMENAU

Founded by German immigrants in 1850, the affluent city of Blumenau is best known today for its annual **Oktoberfest** (Ⓦoktoberfestblumenau.com.br), the biggest German festival in South America, attracting over 500,000 revellers annually to its vast beer tents, folk dancing, shooting matches and German singing contests. Accommodation options can be found at Ⓦblumenau.sc.gov.br, but you'll need to book in advance; the cheapest option (dorms for around R$35) is usually the *Pousada e Hostel Vento Minuano* (Rua Lydia Zwicker 271; ☎47 9191 4422), 9km from the bus station (taxis are around R$15). Blumenau is just one hour thirty minutes from Camboriú, three hours by hourly bus from Florianópolis, and four hours from Curitiba.

O Pharol Av Atlântica 5740 ☎47 3367 3800, Ⓦpharol .com.br. Smart seafood restaurant, well worth the extra reais. The seafood *rodizio* (R$49.90 per person) is something special and includes prawns, lobster, oysters and more. Daily 11.30am–midnight.

NIGHTLIFE

Camboriú has a vibrant nightlife aimed mainly at a young crowd who love loud music, bare flesh and dancing. Most places are on or around Av Atlântica, especially at the southern end, the Barra Sul, where you'll find a huge array of beach bars and discos. Things don't start to get lively until well after midnight and the action continues until after the sun comes up.

Cachaçaria Uai Av Atlântica 2334 ☎47 3367 4978. Bar-style hangout on the beach, specializing in *caipirinhas*, the Brazilian carnival cocktail made with *cachaça* and crushed limes. Daily 6pm–late.

Woods Av Atlântica 4450, Barra Sul ☎47 7812 3475, Ⓦwoodsbar.com.br. This popular country-style pub is a good place to start the evening off, with cold beers served in a beachfront location. Live music. Entry is R$30 (women) and R$60 (men). Wed, Fri & Sat 11pm–5am.

ILHA SANTA CATARINA

Joined to the mainland by suspension bridges, **ILHA SANTA CATARINA** is noted throughout Brazil for its gorgeous scenery and beaches, ideal climate, attractive fishing villages and the city of **Florianópolis**, the small and prosperous capital of Santa Catarina state (half of the city lies on the mainland and the other half on the island). Fifty percent of Ilha Santa Catarina has been placed under a permanent national preservation order, ensuring that its timeless appeal will survive at least for the foreseeable future.

The island is peppered with resorts – the **north** of the island is the most developed while the extreme **south** remains the quietest and most unspoilt – and **Lagoa da Conceição** is a great spot for good-value accommodation and bar hopping. There are 42 **beaches** around Ilha Santa Catarina, which means even the most crowded are rarely unbearably so. Anywhere on the island can be reached by bus within an hour or so from Florianópolis, although **renting a car** (see p.358) is a good idea if you have limited time, allowing you to explore the island more thoroughly. Note, however, that parts of Santa Catarina are notorious for bad traffic, especially on the weekends and in the summer. Also, locals often refer to the whole island as Florianópolis, with the city known simply as *centro*.

Florianópolis

Founded in 1675 by Francisco Dias Velho, **FLORIANÓPOLIS** (aka "Floripa") boomed 75 years later thanks to an influx of immigrants from the Azores. With the construction of the bridges linking the island with the mainland, Florianópolis as a port has all but died, and today it thrives as an administrative, commercial and tourist centre. It's a modern city, but the late nineteenth-century pastel-coloured, stuccoed buildings of the old town still have a whiff of old-world appeal, and it's worth taking time to have a look around. Few people visit Ilha Santa Catarina for the express purpose of seeing the city, however, and to truly experience the natural beauty for which the island is renowned, it's best to head out of the urban centre.

WHAT TO SEE AND DO

On the former waterfront, you'll find two ochre-coloured buildings: the 1889 **Mercado Público** (Mon–Fri 7am–7pm & Sat 7am–3pm), which contains some excellent bars and small restaurants, and the **Alfândega** (Mon–Fri 2am–6pm & Sat 9am–noon), a former customs house dating from 1875 that has been converted for use as a crafts market. Most sights of interest, however, are centred on the lush square, **Praça XV de Novembro**, at the centre of which is the enormous, gnarled "Centenary Fig" tree. According to legend, walking three times around the tree will guarantee you fame and fortune.

On one side of the square is the **Palácio Cruz e Souza**, an imposing pink building built between 1770 and 1780 as the seat of provincial government – it houses the **Museu Histórico de Santa Catarina** (Tues–Fri 10am–6pm, Sat & Sun till 4pm; R$2; ⊕fcc.sc.gov.br/mhsc/) whose nineteenth-century interior is more engaging than its collection of military memorabilia. The **Catedral Metropolitana** (Mon–Fri 6.15am–8pm, Sat 8am–noon & 4–8pm, Sun 7am–noon & 4–9pm), overlooking the square, dates back to the eighteenth century but has been modified many times since; the only church in the city centre virtually unchanged since the colonial era is the **Igreja de Nossa Senhora do Rosário**, built 1787 to 1830 and approached by a flight of steps at Rua Marechal Guilherme 60, two blocks north of the Praça.

ARRIVAL AND INFORMATION

By plane The airport (⊕48 3331 4000) is 12km south of the city, with daily flights from Buenos Aires, São Paulo, Rio and Porto Alegre. You can get into the centre by taxi (20min; R$40–50) or catch green bus #183 or #186 (every 10–30min and labelled "Corredor do Sudoeste"; R$2.90), which will end up at the Terminal de Integração Centro (TICEN) in the centre (around 45min).

By bus Buses arrive at the Terminal *Rodoviária* Rita María (⊕48 3212 3100) at the foot of the road bridge that links the island to the mainland. Cross Av Paulo Fontes and it's a short walk to the centre; the local bus terminal (TICEN; see below) is one long block east at Paulo Fontes 701.

Destinations Blumenau (hourly; 3hr); Curitiba (hourly; 4–5hr); Foz do Iguaçu (6 daily; 14–16hr); Joinville (hourly; 2.5–3hr); Porto Alegre (12 daily; 6–7hr); São Paulo (10 daily; 11–12hr).

Tourist information There's a tourist information kiosk (daily 8am–6pm; ⊕48 3228 1095, ⊕guiafloripa.com.br) at the *rodoviária*. Santa Catarina's state tourist board is based at Rua Felipe Schmidt 249, on the 9th floor (Mon–Fri 8am–7pm; ⊕48 3212 6300, ⊕www.santur.sc.gov.br).

GETTING AROUND

By bus The island has several local bus terminals, so be prepared to change if travelling extensively by bus (transfers are free). The central local bus terminal is Terminal de Integração Centro (or TICEN) at Paulo Fontes 701, which serves most of the island (fares are R$2.90). If you buy a stored-value card (*cartão magnético*) the rate drops to R$2.70. Faster, air-conditioned yellow minibuses – called *executivas* (R$5) – also zip between the main beaches.

Destinations From Terminal de Integração Centro (TICEN): #311, #330 or #320 to Lagoa da Conceição (TILAG); #231 or #233 to Canasvieiras (TICAN); From Lagoa da Conceição (TILAG): #360 to Barra da Lagoa; #363 to Joaquina via Praia Mole; #842 to Canasvieiras (TICAN); From Canasvieiras (TICAN): #276 to Balneário Canasvieiras.

ACCOMMODATION

Most tourists choose to stay at the beaches and resorts around the island (see p.360), but staying in Florianópolis itself has the benefit of direct bus services to other parts of the island. It's not cheap, though, and accommodation is snapped up quickly in high season.

Hotel Central Sumaré Rua Felipe Schmidt 423 ⊕48 3222 5359, ⊕hotelcentralsumare.com.br. The cheapest of the central hotels, in a secure area of town. The minimal rooms are nothing to write home about, but will do if you'd rather spend your money on enjoying yourself than on your digs. There is an R$25 discount for the rooms with shared bathrooms and cheaper single rates. R$100

HI Hostel Florianópolis Rua Duarte Schutel 227 ⊕48 3225 3781, ⊕floripahostel.com.br. Everything you would expect from an HI hostel, though as in the rest of town, you'll find yourself paying more than elsewhere. It fills rapidly in summer, so get here early. Dorms R$40, doubles R$105

Valerim Center Rua Felipe Schmidt 554 ⊕48 3225 1100, ⊕hotelvalerim.com.br. The largest of the mid-range hotels, with clean comfortable rooms (some of which sleep up to six people), all with a sleek modern design, a/c, TV and minibar. R$106

EATING AND DRINKING

Getting a snack in Florianópolis is no problem, but finding a decent meal sometimes can be, and many of the better restaurants are some way from the centre along Av Beira Norte (take bus #134 from the local bus terminal) – expect prices similar to upmarket areas of Rio de Janeiro. The best place for cheap eats is the Mercado Público (see p.356).

Botequim Floripa Av Rio Branco 632 ⊕48 3333 1234, ⊕botequimfloripa.com.br. Pub-style place with a lively happy hour and cold beer on tap. Serves up a Brazilian classic *feijoada* on Sat (R$29.90). Mon–Fri 5.30pm–1am & Sat 4.30pm–1am.

3

Box 32 Mercado Público ☎ 48 3224 5588, ⓦ www.box32 .com.br. Seafood specialist and meeting place of the local glitterati who come to slurp oysters and munch prawns. That said, it's not as expensive as you might fear, with most meals setting you back R$25–30. Mon–Fri 10am–8pm & Sat till 3pm.

Mini Kalzone Rua Felipe Schmidt 706 ☎ 48 3024 3106, ⓦ minikalzone.com.br. If you're hungry, broke and in a hurry, this chain is the answer to your prayers. Top-notch, bite-sized fold-over *calzones* come with a wide variety of meat and vegetarian fillings (from R$4.90). For a good healthy bet try the *Joaquina*: spinach, ricotta and parmesan in a wholemeal casing. Mon–Fri 9am–10pm & Sat till 6pm.

Scuna Bar Osvaldo Rodrigues Cabral 1251 ☎ 48 3225 3138, ⓦ scunabar.com.br. A fashionable bar and club in the old 1907 port building, near the bridge that links the island to the mainland. Live music and a dancefloor – though this is not the place to look for an all-night rave. Tues & Thurs 10pm–3am, Fri & Sat 10pm–4.30am.

Vida Restaurante Natural Rua Visconde de Ouro Preto 298 ☎ 48 3223 4507. Lovely carrot-coloured colonial building with vegetarian buffet (R$14) for those who like their food to be predominantly green. Mon–Fri 11.30am–3.30pm.

DIRECTORY

Banks and exchange Banks are located on Rua Felipe Schmidt and by Praça XV de Novembro.

Boat trips Scuna Sul, Av Osvaldo Rodrigues Cabral s/n (☎ 48 3225 1806, ⓦ scunasul.com.br), offer boat trips around the island for around R$50/person.

Car rental Avis, Av Deputado Diomicio Freitas s/n ☎ 48 3331 4176; Hertz, Rua Bocaiuva 2125 ☎ 48 3224 9955; Localiza, Rua Henrique Valgas 112A ☎ 48 2107 6464; YES, Av Deputado Diomicio Freitas ☎ 048 3236 0229. Advance reservations recommended in summer.

Consulates Argentina, Av Rio Branco 387 ☎ 48 3024 3036; Uruguay, Rua Walter de Bona Castelon 559 ☎ 48 3222 3718.

Internet Gaming café Adrenaline Lan House at Rua Tenente Silveira 155 has a decent, cheap connection (R$3/hr; Mon–Fri 9am–6am, Sat & Sun 1pm–6am).

Pharmacies Farmacia Bela Vista, Rua Tenente Silveira 110. For homeopathic remedies try Farmacia Homeopática Jaqueline, Rua Felipe Schmidt 413.

Post office The main post office is at Praça XV de Novembro 242 (Mon–Fri 9am–5pm, Sat 8am–noon).

Lagoa da Conceição

A large saltwater lagoon in the centre of the island, **Lagoa da Conceição** is popular for swimming, canoeing and windsurfing, with the artsy downtown area known as **Centrinho da Lagoa** at the southern end. The town is both an attractive and convenient place to stay: there are good bus services from here into the centre of Florianópolis and to the east coast beaches, and the main road is lined with restaurants and bars. This is arguably the liveliest nightspot on the island during the summer and at weekends throughout the year, with restaurants always crowded and people overflowing into the streets from the bars. The east coast beaches are close by; cross the lagoon bridge from Centrinho and it's 3.5km to Praia Mole (see p.360).

ACCOMMODATION

Lagoa da Conceição has plenty of good-value options, although you'll need to book ahead in high season.

433 Backpackers Hostel Av Prefeito Acácio Garibaldi 433 ☎ 48 3232 4537, ⓦ backpackers433.com. Located on the road to Joaquina beach (3km from Centrinho), this popular hostel offers two comfy dorms, delicious breakfast and free wi-fi. Private rooms come with TV and a/c. Not much English spoken. Dorms R$30, doubles R$60

Estrela do Mar Rua Antônio da Silveira 282 ☎ 48 3232 1079, ⓦ estreladomar.net. Bright and kitsch *residencial* complete with Disney character gnomes in the garden. The six apartments, which all have kitchens, cable TV and free wi-fi, are named after different species of fish. Apartments R$130

Lagoa Hostel Rua José Henrique Veras 469 ☎ 48 3234 4466, ⓦ lagoahostel.com.br. Friendly hostel where staff make you feel part of the extended family, convenient for the local bus station (TILAG) in Centrinho. There's a sundeck, jacuzzi, pool table, huge widescreen TV and free wi-fi. Dorms (with a/c) R$35, doubles (with a/c) R$120

Pousada e Camping Lagoa da Conceição Av das Rendeiras 1480 ☎ 48 3232 5555, ⓦ pousadaecamping lagoadaconceicao.net. Decent campsite shaded by trees, with hot showers, outdoor barbecues and free wi-fi. Camping/person R$15

★ **Tucano House Backpackers** Rua das Araras 229 ☎ 48 3207 8287, ⓦ tucanohouse.com. Popular place with six dorms and five doubles, some with lagoon views and private bathrooms (R$140). The hostel serves meals (R$15) every night in an outside patio area, a great place to meet fellow travellers. There are also half-price drinks at the bar between 5pm and 7pm. Other services include a pool, free internet and free surfboard hire. Dorms R$50, doubles (shared bath) R$120

Hostel Way2Go Rua Rita Lourenço da Silveira 139 ☎ 48 3364 6004, ⓦ hostelway2go.com. Well-located hostel near the bridge in Centrinho. Washing machines available for guests' use and excellent kitchen space. The private rooms are rather boxy, but functional. Dorms R$35, doubles R$110

EATING AND DRINKING

The Black Swan Rua Manoel Severino de Oliveira 592 ☎ 48 3234 5682, ⓦ theblackswan.com.br. Faux-English pub and sports bar run by a British expat, popular with Brazilians and an international crowd. Standard priced local beer on tap, plus a range of expensive imported beer from Europe. Happy hour 5–9pm. Sun–Thurs 3.30pm– midnight, Fri 3.30pm–2am, Sat noon–2am.

Confraria Chopp da Ilha Av Afonso Delambert Neto 671 ☎ 48 3334 3696, ⓦ confrariachoppdailha.com.br. A bar that regularly offers live Brazilian music and often does promotions on beer (eg a bucket of Stella for R$35). A decent place to watch sport. Daily 7.30pm–4am (or the "last guest").

DNA Natural Rua Manoel Severino de Oliveira 680 ☎ 48 3207 3441, ⓦ dnanatural.com.br. Chain specializing in natural, healthy foods, including tasty wraps and huge mixed salads. There's also an exhaustive range of tropical juices and shakes (from R$4.25). Daily 8am–midnight.

Miyoshi Av Afonso Delambert 101 ☎ 48 3232 5959, ⓦ miyoshi.com.br. One of the finest restaurants for sushi on the island. It's pricey, but sushi is self-service and weighed by the kilo (R$7–8 per 100g), so exercise some restraint and you can eat cheaply. There's usually an all-you-can-eat promotion most nights (R$53.90 for men, R$43.90 for women). Sun–Thurs 6.30–11pm, Fri & Sat 6.30–11.30pm.

Querubim Av Henrique Veras do Nascimento 255 ☎ 48 3232 874. Arguably the best-value place to have lunch in Centrinho. The delicious buffet includes chicken, beef, shrimp and salads (R$26.90 per kilo or R$18.90 all-you-can-eat). Lunch 11.30am–3.30pm & afterwards for snacks until 4am.

3

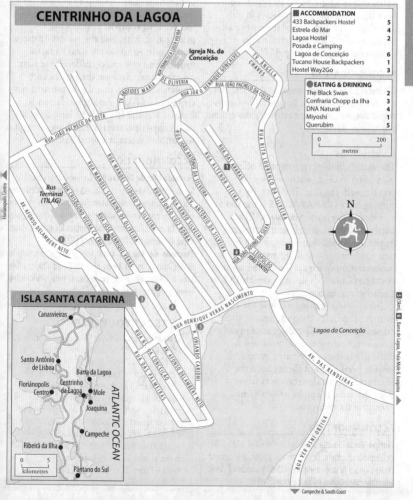

CENTRINHO DA LAGOA

■ ACCOMMODATION	
433 Backpackers Hostel	5
Estrela do Mar	4
Lagoa Hostel	2
Posada e Camping Lagoa de Conceição	6
Tucano House Backpackers	1
Hostel Way2Go	3

● EATING & DRINKING	
The Black Swan	2
Confraria Chopp da Ilha	3
DNA Natural	4
Miyoshi	1
Querubim	5

0 — 200
metres

Igreja Ns. da Conceição

Bus Terminal (TILAG)

N

Lagoa da Conceição

ISLA SANTA CATARINA

Canasvieiras
Santo Antônio de Lisboa
Barra da Lagoa
Florianópolis Centro
Centrinho da Lagoa
Mole
Joaquina
Campeche
Ribeirã da Ilha
Pântano do Sul

ATLANTIC OCEAN

0 — 5
kilometres

▼ Campeche & South Coast

3

East coast beaches

Just 4km from Centrinho da Lagoa, **PRAIA MOLE** is one of the most beautiful beaches in Brazil, slightly hidden beyond sand dunes and beneath low-lying cliffs. Despite its popularity commercial activity has remained low-key, probably because there's a deep drop-off right at the water's edge. Approached by a road passing between gigantic dunes, the next beach as you head south is at **JOAQUINA**, attracting serious surfers. The water's cold, however, and the sea rough, only really suitable for strong swimmers. If you have the energy, climb to the top of the dunes where you'll be rewarded with the most spectacular views in all directions. The beaches of the east coast are accessed via the bus terminal in Centrinho (TILAG; see p.357).

ACCOMMODATION

Cris Hotel Estrada Geral da Joaquina 1 ☏ 48 3232 5104, ⊛ crishotel.com.br. A/c rooms for up to five people overlooking Joaquina beach – the more expensive options have balconies. R$140

Canasvieiras

The island's built-up **north coast** offers safe swimming in calm, warm seas and is popular with families. The long, gently curving bay of **CANASVIEIRAS** is the most crowded of the northern resorts (27km north of Floripa), largely geared towards Argentine families who own or rent houses near the beach. By walking away from the concentration of bars at the centre, towards **Ponta das Canas**, it's usually possible to find a relatively quiet spot.

Unless you're renting a house for a week or more (agencies abound, among them ⊛ ibiubi.com.br and ⊛ aluguetemporada .com.br), finding accommodation is difficult, as the unappealing hotels are usually booked solid throughout the summer. The local **restaurants** mostly offer the same menu of prawn dishes, pizza and hamburgers.

ACCOMMODATION

Floripa Hostel Rua Dr João de Oliveira ☏ 48 3225 3781, ⊛ floripahostel.com.br. Decent budget option, with shared kitchen, colour TV and eating area offering wonderful views across the coast. Dorms R$30, doubles R$80

Hostel & Camping Canasvieiras Rua Tertuliano Brito Xavier 521 ☏ 48 9111 9574, ⊛ hostelcampingcanasvieiras .blogspot.com.br. This rustic camping option boasts a pool and grill areas, as well as simple dorms. Open Dec–Feb only. Dorms R$20; camping/person R$20

West coast beaches

The principal places of interest on the west coast are **SANTO ANTÔNIO DE LISBOA** to the north of Florianópolis and **RIBEIRÃO DA ILHA** to the south. These are the island's oldest and least spoilt settlements, their houses almost all painted white with dark blue sash windows, in typical Azorean style, and both villages have a simple colonial church. Fishing, rather than catering to the needs of tourists, remains the principal activity, and the waters offshore from Santo Antônio are used to farm mussels and oysters, considered the best on the island. Because the beaches are small and face the mainland, tourism has remained low-key. Accommodation is limited and the few visitors here tend to be on day-trips, staying just long enough to sample oysters at a local bar.

ACCOMMODATION

Pousada Mar de Dentro Rua Caminho dos Açores 1929, Santo Antônio ☏ 48 3235 1521, ⊛ pousadamardedentro .com.br. A lovely setting right on the beach, and with a tiny pool. Offers apartments with at least two bedrooms, a/c, cable TV and balconies, so good option for groups. Rates halve in low season (March–Nov). R$230

Pousada do Museu ☏ 48 3237 8148, ⊛ pousadado museu.com.br. In the heart of Ribeirão da Ilha, try this simple option, which has some rooms with glorious sea views and a decent restaurant. R$180

★ TREAT YOURSELF

Ostradamus Rodovia Baldicero Filomeno 7640 ☏ 48 3337 5711, ⊛ ostradamus.com .br. For a splash-out meal in Ribeirão, the rather kitsch restaurant serves up creative dishes such as a dozen oysters with martini and lemon (R$32), as well as delicious mains – despite the high prices and long waits for tables this is easily one of the island's best places to eat. Try the seafood risotto, washed down with local wine (mains $65–99). Tues–Sat noon–11pm, Sun noon–5.30pm.

PORTO ALEGRE

The capital of Rio Grande do Sul, **PORTO ALEGRE** lies on the eastern bank of the Rio Guaíba some 450km south of Florianópolis. Founded in 1772 by settlers from the Azores, it's a hard-working industrial city with run-down charm – and a lively bar and restaurant scene – but it's best to avoid the business centre and area around the bus terminal after dark and take taxis at night.

WHAT TO SEE AND DO

The city centre is a little shabby but everything worth seeing is within an easy walk, and a day or so is enough to visit most places of interest. For city tours, the tourist board operates "Linha Turismo", an open-top double-decker bus with two circuits that take in the historic centre and southern zone. Tours leave from outside the main office, Travessa do Carmo 84 (ⓦportoalegre.travel; Tues–Sun 9am–4pm every hr; R$15).

Mercado Público and around

The golden-coloured **Mercado Público** (Mon–Sat 7.30am–7.30pm) stands at the heart of the lower town, located alongside Praça Rui Barbosa and Praça XV de Novembro. A replica of Lisbon's Mercado da Figueira, this imposing building contains an absorbing mix of stalls selling household goods, food and regional handicrafts. Upstairs are restaurants offering traditional Brazilian all-you-can-eat lunch buffets which stay open after the market stalls shut. Next to the market is

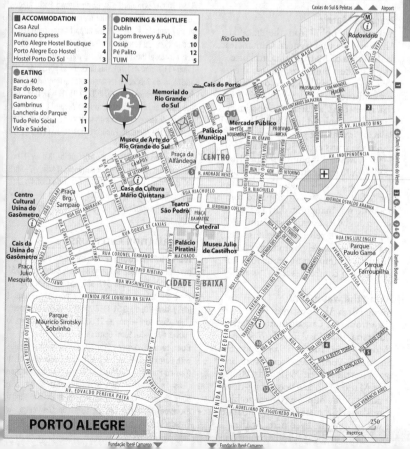

◼ ACCOMMODATION	
Casa Azul	5
Minuano Express	2
Porto Alegre Hostel Boutique	1
Porto Alegre Eco Hostel	4
Hostel Porto Do Sol	3

◯ EATING	
Banca 40	3
Bar do Beto	9
Barranco	6
Gambrinus	2
Lancheria do Parque	7
Tudo Pelo Social	11
Vida e Saúde	1

◯ DRINKING & NIGHTLIFE	
Dublin	4
Lagom Brewery & Pub	8
Ossip	10
Pé Palito	12
TUIM	5

PORTO ALEGRE

3

the ochre **Palácio Municipal**, the old *prefeitura* (town hall), built in Neoclassical style between 1898 and 1901, its impressive proportions an indication of civic pride and self-confidence during Porto Alegre's golden age.

West of here along Rua Sete de Setembro is the pleasantly verdant **Praça da Alfândega**, home of the grand **Museu de Arte do Rio Grande do Sul** (ⓦwww.margs.rs.gov.br; Tues–Sun 10am–7pm; free). You can spend an hour or so admiring the local modern art here, combined with a visit to the **Memorial do Rio Grande do Sul** next door (ⓦwww.memorial.rs.gov.br; Wed–Sat 10am–6pm, Sun 1–5pm; free), which houses pictorial exhibitions on the history of the state.

Praça da Matriz

A short walk uphill from the Praça da Alfândega via Rua General Câmara leads to the **Praça da Matriz**, home to Porto Alegre's oldest buildings, though they have been so heavily altered over the last few centuries that few retain their original character (the Catedral Metropolitana was only completed in 1986). The **Palácio Piratini** (the state governor's residence; tours every 30min Mon–Fri 9–11.30am & 2–5pm; free) dates from 1898, while the **Teatro São Pedro** (tours by reservation only; Tues–Fri noon–6pm, Sat & Sun; free; ⓦteatrosaopedro.com.br) opposite was inaugurated in 1858. Surprisingly, its Portuguese Baroque appearance, all velvet and gold inside, has remained largely unmolested, and the theatre is an important venue for local and visiting companies.

Along the waterfront

Along Porto Alegre's spruced-up waterfront, the **Casa de Cultura Mário Quintana**, Rua dos Andradas 736 (Mon 2–9pm, Tues–Fri 9am–9pm, Sat & Sun noon–9pm; free; ⓦccmq.com.br), was a hotel between 1918 and 1980; the poet Mário Quintana was a long-time resident. Pride of place is given to his room, which is maintained in the state it was in when he lived here. At the western tip of the peninsula, housed in a converted 1920s power plant, is the **Centro Cultural Usina do Gasômetro** (Tues–Sun 9am–9pm; free; ⓦportoalegre .rs.gov.br/smc) which hosts frequent exhibitions, recitals and shows.

Fundação Iberê Camargo

South of the centre, the **Fundação Iberê Camargo**, on Avenida Padre Cacique 2000 (Tues–Sun noon–7pm, & Thurs noon–9pm; free; ⓦwww.iberecamargo .org.br), has an impressive range of artwork from the renowned Brazilian artist, occupying a modernist building designed by Portuguese architect Álvaro Siza.

ARRIVAL AND DEPARTURE

By plane Aeroporto Internacional Salgado Filho (ⓣ51 3358 2000), 6km northeast of downtown Porto Alegre, receives flights from all major national destinations and nearby capitals. A taxi from the airport to the centre costs about R$25–30 (confirm the price before you get in), or you can take the metrô a short walk from Terminal 2 (5am–11.20pm; R$1.70); this links the airport, *rodoviária* and Mercado Público on its single line (ⓦtrensurb.gov.br).

By bus The *rodoviária* (ⓣ51 3210 0101) is northeast of the centre at Largo Vespasiano Júlio Veppo 11, but within walking distance; after dark it's safer, and easier, to ride the metrô to the Mercado Público or take a taxi (ⓣ51 3352 6166, ⓣ51 3319 5100).

Destinations Canela (hourly; 2hr); Curitiba (8 daily; 11hr); Buenos Aires (1 daily; 18hr); Florianópolis (14 daily; 7–8hr); Foz do Iguaçu (8 daily; 14–16hr); Gramado (hourly; 2hr); Montevideo (1 daily; 11hr); Rio de Janeiro (1–2 daily; 24–25hr); Santo Ângelo (13 daily; 6–7hr); São Paulo (4 daily; 18hr).

INFORMATION AND TOURS

Tourist information The main municipal office is in the city centre at Travessa do Carmo 84 (daily 8am–6pm; ⓣ51 3289 6700, ⓣ51 0800 517 686, ⓦportoalegre.travel). There are also tourist information offices at the airport (daily 8am–10pm; ⓣ51 3358 2048), Usina do Gasômetro (Tues–Sun 9am–6pm; ⓣ51 3289 8146) and Mercado Público (Mon–Sat 9am–6pm; ⓣ51 3211 5705).

Boat tours Excursions (1hr 30min) on the Rio Guaíba with Barco Cisne Branco leave from the tour-boat berth (Cais do Porto) on Av Mauá 1050, near the train station (Tues–Fri 10.30am, 3pm & 4.30pm, Sat & Sun also 6pm; ⓦbarcocisnebranco.com.br). There are also similar excursions from the Cais da Usina do Gasômetro, Av Presidente João Goulart 551 (Tues–Fri 3.30pm & 5.30pm; Sat & Sun 7 daily).

ACCOMMODATION

Hostels are scattered all over the city centre, but it's a relatively small area and it's possible to walk to most places – though you should take a taxi after dark.

Casa Azul Rua Lima e Silva 912 ☏51 3084 5050, ⍟casaazulhostel.com. Popular hostel in a house in Cidade Baixa with bar open to the public (Tues–Sun 7pm–midnight). There's a spacious outside area, flat-screen TV, pool table and friendly staff who can organize excursions. Dorms R$30, doubles R$90

Minuano Express Av Farrapos 31 ☏51 3226 3062, ⍟minuanohotel.com.br. Despite the ugly high-rise building in which they are housed, rooms here are pleasant and surprisingly modern, and the sound-proof windows ensure a good night's sleep regardless of the traffic outside (it's a short walk from the bus station). Free wi-fi and filling buffet breakfast. R$99

Porto Alegre Hostel Boutique Rua São Carlos 545 ☏51 3228 3802, ⍟hostel.tur.br. Great location, and though not really a "boutique", the rooms here are a step up from a normal HI hostel; all en suite in a historic mansion, with a/c and TVs. Free wi-fi and buffet breakfast, with laundry and communal kitchen on site. Discount for HI members. Dorms R$50, doubles R$120

Porto Alegre Eco Hostel Rua Luiz Afonso 276 ☏51 3019 2449, ⍟portoalegreecohostel.com.br. Justly the most popular hostel in the city, with excellent staff and comfy dorms right in Cidade Baixa. Extras include a swimming pool, free wi-fi, games room, garden and bike rental. Breakfast included. Dorms R$37, doubles R$100

Hostel Porto Do Sol Rua Mariante 958 ☏51 3330 1324, ⍟hostelportodosol.com.br. One of the quieter hostels, but a hike from the centre (R$10–12 by taxi). Mixed and female-only dorms with tiled floors, fans and free wi-fi – a simple breakfast is served on the patio. Pool table, TV room (with DVDs) and kitchen available. Dorms R$27, doubles R$80

EATING

As the home of Brazilian *churrasco* (barbecue), Porto Alegre has some great places to eat, especially in the Cidade Baixa and Moinhos de Vento neighbourhoods. As always, the best-value places to eat are buffets (especially in the Mercado Público), serving a plentiful range of food and usually offering good lunchtime deals.

★ **Banca 40** Mercado Público Loja 40 ☏51 3226 3533. Open since 1927, this local institution is justifiably lauded for its *bomba royal* ice-cream dessert (R$8.90); regular scoops of ice cream start at R$3.50. Mon–Sat 8am–7.30pm.

Bar do Beto Av Sarmento Leite 811 ☏51 3332 9390, ⍟bardobeto.com.br. Cidade Baixa restaurant that heaves at lunchtime due to its R$15 buffet special, when waiters walk round tables offering different cuts of beef and chicken. Dinner is à la carte only (mains R$25–55). Daily 11am–2am.

Barranco Av Protásio Alves 1578 ☏51 3331 6172, ⍟restaurantebarranco.com.br. Meat lovers' paradise since 1969 – try the celebrated (and huge) *vazio*, the classic steak cut of the south (R$45 – two can share). An all-you-can-eat "salad sidecar" trundles around the restaurant (R$11). Daily 11am–2am.

★ **Gambrinus** Mercado Público Loja 85 ☏51 3226 6914, ⍟gambrinus.com.br. Visit the city's oldest restaurant (since 1889) for an old-fashioned southern Brazil experience, sampling some real classics: *rabada* (oxtail), a *filé* of beef with fried eggs or salted cod. Dishes R$25–35. Mon–Fri 11am–9pm, Sat 11am–4pm.

Lancheria do Parque Av Osvaldo Aranha 1086 ☏51 3311 8321. Knocking out cheap eats for over 30 years in Bom Fim, this diner does a good "lunch" buffet (11am–9pm; R$12), huge juices (R$3.30), X Salada (cheeseburger), steak sandwiches and chicken soup. Daily 6am–1am.

Tudo Pelo Social Rua João Alfredo 448 ☏51 3226 4405, ⍟restaurantetudopelosocial.com.br. Hugely popular restaurant that serves Brazilian classics such as rice, beans and meat. Lunchtime buffet is a bargain at R$7/person, while the à la carte *picanha* "for two" (steak; R$28) comes with huge portions of chips, rice and salad, and easily feeds three to four people. Mon–Sat 11am–2.45pm & 6–11.45pm, Sun 11am–2.45pm.

Vida e Saúde Rua Gral. Câmara 60 ☏51 3012 5841. Vegetarian, lunchtime-only buffet, offering all the healthy vegetable options you may well be craving in a town obsessed with beef. Buffet R$13, including fruit juices. Mon–Fri 11am–3pm.

NIGHTLIFE

Porto Alegre boasts a lively nocturnal scene, with two main centres for nightlife: the more flashy action revolves around Moinhos de Vento, and the hub of Rua Padre Chagas, while the Cidade Baixa offers more traditional samba joints and bohemian bars in the streets around Rua da República and Av João Pessoa.

Dublin Rua Padre Chagas 342, Moinhos de Vento ☏51 3268 8835, ⍟dublinpub.com.br. Every city must have one: this is your standard faux-Irish bar and the current place where well-to-do "gauchos" look to enjoy themselves. Live bands play daily and an entry fee is charged after 9pm (Sun–Wed R$7; Thurs–Sat R$10 for women, R$20 for men). Sun–Wed 6pm–3am, Thurs–Sat 6pm–5am.

Lagom Brewery & Pub Rua Bento Figueiredo 72 ☏51 3062 5045, ⍟lagom.com.br. Porto Alegre's first brew pub serves a range of tasty ales, stouts and IPAs on a seasonal basis – top tipples include the amber ale and oatmeal stout. Mon–Sat 6–11pm.

Ossip Rua da República 677, Cidade Baixa ☏51 3224 2422. Lively and colourful Cidade Baixa hangout, with samba and bossa nova most nights. Good pizza. Daily 6pm–1.30am.

Pé Palito Rua João Alfredo 577 ☎ 51 9962 8851. Colourfully decorated club hosting Brazilian live music sessions, from samba-rock to bossa nova. The more chilled-out sister bar next door, *Boteco do Pé*, is just as colourful and popular (but shuts earlier, at midnight). Thurs–Sat 11pm–5am.

TUIM Rua General Câmara 333 ☎ 51 9962 8851, ⓦ barchopptuim.kit.net. Just off Praça de Alfândega, this pocket-sized pub in the centre is ideal for a cool, quiet beer. *TUIM* also has an impressive variety of spirits, including quality *cachaça*. Try their famous anchovy and mustard sandwich (R$5). Mon–Fri 10am–9pm.

DIRECTORY

Banks and exchange There are banks and casas de câmbio (Mon–Fri 10am–4.30pm) along Rua dos Andradas and Av Senador Salgado Filho near Praça da Alfândega, and there are ATMs everywhere.

Consulates Argentina, Rua Coronel Bordini 1033 (Mon–Fri 10am–4pm; ☎ 51 3321 1360); Paraguay, Rua Dr. Barcelos 2237 (Mon–Fri 9am–noon & 1.30–5pm; ☎ 51 3241 9576); Uruguay, Av Cristóvão Colombo 2999 (Mon–Fri 9am–5pm; ☎ 51 3325 6197); UK, Rua Antenor Lemos 57/conjunto 303 (Mon–Fri 9am–noon, by appointment only; ☎ 51 3232 1414); USA, Av Assis Brasil 4320, Store 84 (Boulevard Strip Mall), Parque Sao Sebastiao (by appointment only; Mon–Fri 9am–1pm; ☎ 51 3226 3344).

Hospital Hospital Municipal de Pronto Socorro (HPS), Largo Teodore Herzl (Av Osvaldo Aranha) ☎ 51 3289 7999.

Internet Free wi-fi is available at the Mercado Público, Praça da Alfândega and Usina do Gasômetro.

Post office In the *centro historico* at Rua Siqueira Campos 1100 ☎ 51 3220 8800 (Mon–Fri 9am–6pm, Sat 9am–noon), and inside the *rodoviária* (Mon–Fri 9am–6pm; ☎ 51 3225 1945).

GRAMADO

Some 120km north of Porto Alegre, **GRAMADO** is Brazil's best-known mountain resort – famous for its Natal Luz (Christmas lights) and its annual film festival (ⓦ festivaldegramado.net), held in August. Architecturally, Gramado tries hard to appear Swiss, with "Alpine" chalets and flower-filled window boxes the norm. It's a mere affectation, though, since hardly any of the inhabitants are of Swiss origin – the town was settled by the Portuguese in 1875 and only a small minority is of German extraction (most locals today are of Italian ancestry). The most pleasant time to visit the area is in spring (Oct and Nov) when the parks, gardens and roadsides are full of flowers.

At 825m Gramado is high enough to be refreshingly cool in summer and positively chilly in winter.

WHAT TO SEE AND DO

Gramado's chief appeal lies in its clear mountain air and generally relaxed way of life – things that inhabitants of Brazil's major cities rarely get to enjoy. There really isn't much to do in town other than to admire the houses, enjoy the food and stroll around the large and very pretty flower-filled **Parque Knorr** (daily 10.30am–9.30pm; free; during the festive season the kitsch Santa Claus village is R$16). The surrounding region is magnificent, best appreciated at the **Ecoparque Sperry** (entrance just off Av das Hortênsias on the way to Canela; Tues–Sun 9am–5pm; R$10; ☎ 54 9629 8765; ⓦ ecoparquesperry.com.br). Here you'll be guided along forest trails and past waterfalls by the English-speaking owner, a font of knowledge on the local flora. Roads in the mountainous areas around Gramado are unpaved and can be treacherous after rain, so **guided tours** are a safer bet – ask at the tourist office for recommendations.

ARRIVAL AND INFORMATION

By bus Buses from Porto Alegre arrive every 1hr 30min at the *rodoviária* (☎ 54 3286 1302) on Av Borges de Medeiros 2100, a couple of minutes' walk south from the town centre.

Destinations Canela (local buses every 20min; 15–20min; R$1.80); Porto Alegre (every 30min; 2hr); São Francisco de Paula (7 daily; 2hr).

Tourist information The tourist office at Av Borges de Medeiros 1674 is open daily (9am–7pm; ☎ 54 3286 1475, ⓦ gramado.rs.gov.br).

ACCOMMODATION

Accommodation is expensive and you should book ahead during peak periods. Outside busy times many hotels offer discounts during the week.

Gramado Hostel Av Das Hortências 3880 ☎ 54 3295 1020, ⓦ gramadohostel.com.br. About 1.5km outside town on the road to Canela (20min walk or R$1.80 on the Canela bus), this HI hostel is decent value (discounts for members) with dorm rooms and some doubles. Dorms R$55, doubles R$140

Pousada Belluno Rua Nilo Dias 50 ☎ 54 3286 0820, ⓦ pousadabelluno.com.br. The best of the cheaper hotels

★ **TREAT YOURSELF**

La Caceria Av Borges de Medeiros 3166 ☎54 3295 7575, ⓦcasadamontanha.com .br. An intriguing but expensive restaurant in the classy *Hotel Casa da Montanha*, specializing in game dishes (mains R$43–79) with unusual tropical fruit sauces that complement the often strong-tasting meat. Daily 7pm–midnight.

in downtown, with elegantly furnished, heated rooms, free wi-fi, LCD TVs and floor-to-ceiling windows. The substantial buffet breakfast will set you up for the day. R$86

EATING

Gramado is noted for its handmade chocolate and has some good restaurants (especially fondue places), but expect to pay through the nose for anything resembling a good meal; aim for the buffets or "café colonial" places to fill up for a reasonably good price.

★ **Bela Vista Café Colonial** Av das Hortências 4665 ☎54 3286 1608, ⓦbelavista.tur.br. One of Gramado's classic Alpine-style cafés, offering fabulous "café colonial" spreads of cakes, pastries and meats for R$45. Mon–Fri 11am–11pm, Sat & Sun 10am–11pm.

ITA Brasil Av São Pedro 1005 ☎54 3286 3833. Off the main drag, but well worth seeking out for the cheap lunch buffets (R$14 or R$23 per kilo) of classic Italian-Brazilian food, fresh juices, strong coffee and home-made *cachaça* (liquor made from fermented sugar-cane juice). Wed–Mon 11.15am–2.30pm.

CANELA

Marginally cheaper than Gramado, but arranged very much along the same lines, **CANELA** (which means "cinnamon"), 8km further east, is another mountain retreat popular with holidaying Brazilians and better located for visits to the nearby national parks.

ARRIVAL AND INFORMATION

By bus Buses arrive at the *rodoviária* (☎54 3282 1375), a short walk from the centre.

Destinations Gramado (local buses every 20min; 15–20min; R$1.80); Porto Alegre (15 daily; 2hr); São Francisco de Paula (8 daily; 2hr).

Tourist information The tourist office, at Largo da Fama 227 (☎54 3282 2200, ⓦcanelaturismo.com.br) in the town centre, can put you in touch with a host of tour companies arranging adventure-style trips to the national

parks; buses to Parque Estadual do Caracol also run from here. Daily 8am–7pm.

ACCOMMODATION

Accommodation can be hard to come by during peak periods, when you should book ahead. Though it's cheaper than Gramado, it is not cheap per se, and the town can be easily visited on a day-trip from Porto Alegre.

Hostel Viajante Rua Ernesto Urbani 132 ☎54 3282 2017, ⓦpousadadoviajante.com.br. Right next to the *rodoviária*, this is the best budget choice, with economical dorms and neat and tidy doubles – perfect for travellers winding down after a hard day's bungee jumping. Dorms R$45, doubles R$110

EATING

You can forget about finding truly cheap eats in Canela, but there are some interesting restaurants around town that make it worth investing the extra few reais; Canela is especially known for its apple strudel and other German-inspired sweet treats.

Churrascaria Espelho Gaúcho Baden Powel 50, at Av Danton Corrêa ☎54 3282 4348, ⓦespelhogaucho.com .br. Meat, meat and more luscious barbecued meat. In fact all the meat you can eat for a one-off R$30.90. Daily 11.30am–3pm & 6–11pm.

Strudelhaus Rua Baden Powell 246 ☎54 3282 9562, ⓦstrudelhaus.de. This German-inspired restaurant is the place to sample that schnitzel, wurst and *apfelstrudel*. Mains R$15–25. Tues 8–10.30pm, Wed–Fri noon–2.30pm & 8–10.30pm, Sat noon–3pm & 8–11pm, Sun 11.45am–3pm.

Toca da Bruxa Praça da Matriz 50 ☎54 3282 9750, ⓦtocadabruxa.com.br. A pizza house styled like a witch's den. Serves a series of savoury and sweet pizzas (from R$15.90) with haunting names such as the "Furiosa" and the "Sinistra", the latter with a healthy serving of chilli peppers. Tues–Sun 7–11pm.

PARQUE ESTADUAL DO CARACOL

Just 7km outside Canela on RS-466 (aka Estrada do Caracol), the highlight of the **PARQUE ESTADUAL DO CARACOL** (daily 8.45am–5.45pm; R$12) is the spectacular **Cascata do Caracol**, a stunning waterfall on the Río Caracol that plunges dramatically over a 131m-high cliff of basaltic rock in the middle of dense forest. The hike to the foot of the falls involves climbing down (and then up) over 700 exhausting steps. Alternatively, skip the walk and take a lift (*elevador panorâmico*) up the 27m-high

3

3

Observatorio Ecológico (daily 8.30am–6pm; R$20; ⓦobservatorioecologico.com.br) near the park entrance, which will give you a 360-degree bird's-eye view of the park and falls over the tree-tops. Binoculars are available for close-up sightings of flora and fauna.

For even more scintillating views of the waterfall take the 830m Teleférico de Canela 500m beyond the park entrance, a nerve-jangling **chair lift** (daily 9am–5pm; 20min; R$25; ☎54 3504 1405). Yet further along the road (Km15) is the entrance to the **Parque Vale da Ferradura** (daily 8.30am–5.30pm; R$8; ⓦwww.valedaferradura.com.br), where three viewpoints cover the dramatic 420m "horseshoe" canyon of the Río Santa Cruz.

Heading back to Canela you'll pass the araucaria wood **Castelinho** (RS-466 Km3; daily 9am–1pm & 2.20–5.40pm; R$8; ⓦcastelinhocaracol.com.br), a fairy-tale German-style mansion dating from 1915 and now a memorial to German immigration to the area (as well as serving incredible *apfelstrudel* in the tea rooms).

ARRIVAL AND INFORMATION

By bus Buses run from the *rodoviária* in Canela to the park entrance (departs daily at 8.15am & noon; returning at 12.20pm and 6pm; R$1.80), or take a taxi.

Tourist information The admission fee (R$12) should be paid at the excellent visitors' centre (daily 8.45am–5.45pm; ☎52 3278 3035). Here you will find details about walking trails and adventure activities such as rock-climbing, abseiling and bungee jumping.

PARQUE NACIONAL DOS APARADOS DA SERRA

Around 150 million years ago, lava slowly poured onto the surface of the Brazilian Shield, a vast **highland plateau**, developing into a thick layer of basalt rock. At the edge of the plateau, vast canyons puncture the basalt and the largest of these is protected within the predominantly untouched wilderness of the **Parque Nacional dos Aparados da Serra** (Tues–Sun 8am–5pm; R$6), some 100km east of Canela.

WHEN TO VISIT

The Parque Nacional dos Aparados da Serra can be visited throughout the year, but is at its best during spring (Oct and Nov) when the blooming flowers create a spectacular effect. In the winter (June to Aug), it can get very cold, though visibility is often excellent. Summers are warm, but heavy rainfall sometimes makes the roads and trails impassable and fog and low-level cloud sometimes completely obscure what should be spectacular views. Avoid April, May and September, the months with the most sustained rainfall.

Approaching the park from any direction, you pass through rugged cattle pasture, occasionally interrupted by the distinctive umbrella-like araucaria pine trees and solitary farm buildings. As the dirt road enters the park itself, forest patches appear, suddenly and dramatically interrupted by a canyon of breathtaking proportions. Some 5.8km in length, between 600m and 2000m wide and 720m deep, **Itaimbézinho** is a dizzying sight. On the higher levels, with relatively little rainfall, but with fog banks moving in from the nearby Atlantic Ocean, vegetation is typical of a cloudforest, while on the canyon's floor a mass of subtropical plants flourishes.

Three trails are open to visitors, the most difficult of which is the **Trilha do Rio do Boi** (8hr) – an option for experienced hikers that must only be attempted with a guide. It involves a 5m vertical descent of a rock face by rope and a complete descent to the rocky river in the canyon floor. Rather easier is the **Trilha do Vértice** (1.4km), which affords views of Itaimbézinho and two spectacular waterfalls **Véu da Noiva** and **Andorinhas**. If this isn't challenging enough for you, try the **Trilha do Mirante do Cotovelo** (6.3km), which runs along the rim of the canyon and provides some glorious photo opportunities.

ARRIVAL AND INFORMATION

By bus Getting to the park via public transport is tough. First, take a bus from Gramado or Canela to São Francisco de Paula (every 30min; R$7.50–8.50). From São Francisco you need to take another bus 60km northeast to Cambará do Sul (daily 9.15am & 5pm; R$13.15) and ask to be let off at the entrance to the park (Citral has one daily bus to Cambará from Porto Alegre at 6am that takes five hours; R$32). From Cambará it's a further 15km to Itaimbézinho (taxi: ☎ 54 3251 1320). Buses occasionally run between São Francisco or Cambará and Praia Grande (which has a couple of basic hotels, one on the main square and the other at the *rodoviária*), on the Santa Catarina side of the state line. These will drop you just 3km from Itaimbézinho but you'll need to walk the difference – there is no bus service to the canyon.

By car If you intend to make the trip in your own vehicle it is imperative that you call ☎ 54 3251 1230 for up-to-date information on local road conditions.

INFORMATION AND TOURS

Tourist information There is a visitors' centre (☎ 54 3251 1262, ⓦ guiaaparadosdaserra.com.br) and a snack bar at the main entrance. Only 1000 visitors are permitted to enter the park each day, so it's advisable to phone the visitors' centre in advance to reserve a place.

Tour operators Trying to visit the park on your own is difficult and barely cheaper than doing it with a tour. Try ecotourism specialists Canyons do Sul (ⓦ canyonsdosul .com.br).

ACCOMMODATION

Camping is prohibited in the park, so if you decide to visit independently, you'll need accommodation – the most convenient place is Cambará do Sul, aka the "capital of honey" thanks to its numerous bee farms.

Pousada Pôr-do-Sol Rua Pe. João F. Ritter 1150 ☎ 54 3251 1390, ⓦ pousadapordosol.tur.br. Solid option in the centre of Cambará, with small but clean and cosy modern doubles with heating and TVs (has quadruples for R$180). R$120

ROTA MISSÕES (MISSION ROUTE)

Though less well known than those in Argentina and Paraguay, Rio Grande do Sul is home to no fewer than seven **Jesuit Missions**, with four of the ruins in an excellent state of preservation and grouped together on what is called the **ROTA MISSÕES** (ⓦ rotamissoes.com.br). The Jesuits arrived here in 1626 determined to convert the Guarani Indians, with the missions founded between 1682 and 1706 in nominal Spanish territory. In fact the region was virtually independent of both Spain and

3

CROSSING THE BORDERS TO URUGUAY AND ARGENTINA

Most overland travellers cross the southern Brazilian borders via long-distance bus – in this case formalities are fairly straightforward and you just need to know the entry requirements for Uruguay (see p.831) and Argentina (see p.47). The borders here are generally open, meaning anyone can just walk across – if you are a foreigner, however, you need to find the nearest immigration post to have passports stamped.

TO URUGUAY

Chuí/Chuy (340km northeast of Montevideo). By far the most travelled route, 527km south of Porto Alegre. Buses entering and leaving Brazil stop at an immigration office a short distance north of the town itself (Chuí/Chuy is actually divided by the border) on BR-471. The Uruguayan customs is 3km further south on Rte-9.

Santana do Livramento (497km west of Porto Alegre). There's no duty-free here or passport controls – the town simply merges into the Uruguayan city of Rivera (500km north of Montevideo). Before leaving Livramento you'll need a Brazilian exit (or entry) passport stamp from the Polícia Federal, at Rua Uruguai 1177, near the central park, and a stamp from Uruguay's Dirección Nacional de Inmigración, at Av Presidente Viera s/n. If you have any problems, head for the Uruguayan consulate in Livramento at Av Tamandaré 2101, 4th floor (☎ 55 3242 1416).

TO ARGENTINA

Most people heading to Argentina from Brazil cross the frontier at Foz do Iguaçu (see p.351), but if you find yourself in the south of the country, **Uruguaiana** (694km west of Porto Alegre) is the most convenient crossing – with Paso de los Libres on the other side (around 740km north of Buenos Aires). Customs formalities take place at either end of the 1400m-long road bridge across the Rio Uruguai. Accommodation and restaurant options are both better on the Argentine side of the border. The Argentine consulate is at Rua 13 de Mayo 1674 (☎ 55 3412 1925).

Portugal, a state of affairs ended by the 1750 Treaty of Madrid when the missions became definitively Portuguese; this led to the Guarani War of 1756, devastating the region (and dramatized in the film *The Mission*).

The best place to base yourself is the town of **SANTO ÂNGELO** in the far southwest of the state, where there is a cluster of accommodation options around Praça Rio Branco. The most accessible and best of the missions is **SÃO MIGUEL ARCANJO** (daily 9am–noon & 2–6pm, Oct–Feb to 8pm; R$5; ⓦmissoesturismo.com.br), founded in 1687 in the village of São Miguel da Missões. Guided tours are available, and the small Museu das Missões (same times) and a kitschy nightly light show (Aug–Feb 9pm; March & April 8pm; May–July 7pm; R$9) brings the story of the Jesuits to life.

GETTING AROUND

By bus 8 daily buses run from Porto Alegre to Santo Ângelo (7hr 30min). 4 daily buses run the 53km southwest from Santo Ângelo to São Miguel (1hr).

ACCOMMODATION

There are also decent options in Santo Ângelo.

Missões Hostel ☎55 3381 1202, ⓦpousadatematica .com.br. Next to the São Miguel Arcanjo ruins is an excellent themed hostel, which has dorm rooms as well as doubles and a pool to relax in. Dorms R$52 doubles R$106

SALAR DE SURIRE, NORTE GRANDE

Chile

HIGHLIGHTS

❶ **Valparaíso** Fantastic nightlife and bohemian culture. **See p.394**

❷ **The Elqui Valley** Laidback villages, pisco tasting and stargazing. **See p.404**

❸ **San Pedro de Atacama** Fascinating desert landscapes. **See p.411**

❹ **Iquique** Chile's top paragliding destination. **See p.416**

❺ **Pucón** Volcano climbing, white-water rafting and hot springs. **See p.435**

❻ **Parque Nacional Torres del Paine** Hiking amid majestic scenery. **See p.470**

HIGHLIGHTS ARE MARKED ON THE MAP ON P.371

ROUGH COSTS

Daily budget Basic US$40

Drink Pisco sour US$3

Food *Pastel de choclo* US$8

Camping/hostel/budget hotel US$10/20/40

FACT FILE

Population 16.5 million

Languages Spanish; indigenous languages Aymará, Huilliche, Kawéscar, Mapudungun, Quechua, Rapanui and Yámana

Currency Chilean Peso (CH$)

Capital Santiago (population: 6.0 million)

International phone code ❼56

Time zone GMT -4hr; GMT -3hr from second Sunday in October to second Sunday in March

Introduction

Chileans will tell you that when God created the world, he had a little bit of everything left over, and put pieces of desert, rivers, lakes and glaciers together to make Chile. From the world's driest desert – the Atacama – in the north to the volcanic peaks and verdant landscapes of the Lake District, down to the icy wilderness of Patagonia, this is perhaps the most geographically diverse and fascinating country in Latin America. Snaking between the snowcapped Andes and the Pacific Ocean, it's a fantastic playground for lovers of the outdoors, and for adrenaline junkies, with world-class skiing, surfing, white-water rafting, climbing and paragliding, while the country's plentiful national parks and nature reserves also boast an astounding array of plant and animal life.

Today, in spite of its troubled past, Chile is among the most politically and economically stable of all Latin American countries, and the memory of the tainted Pinochet dictatorship is gradually fading. For the most part, it is westernized and affluent, and its excellent bus network makes it an easy country to navigate.

Cosmopolitan **Santiago** is a very manageable starting point, with plentiful excellent bars, hostels and restaurants, as well as easy access to superb ski resorts and the vineyards of **Middle Chile**. In the nearby coastal city of **Valparaíso**, ride the *ascensores* (funiculars), or relax on the sandy beaches of neighbouring **Viña del Mar**. Head further north to the **Norte Chico** to knock back a pisco sour in the sublime **Elqui Valley**, or gaze at the stars in some of the world's clearest skies,

while further north still the **Norte Grande** is where the strong breaks of the Pacific Ocean meet the moonscape scenery of the Atacama Desert. Visit gleaming lagoons and steaming geysers in the backpacker oasis of **San Pedro de Atacama**, and get your fill of sun and surf in the beach towns of **Iquique** and **Arica**.

South from Santiago, the **Lake District** – a region of lush forests and snow-capped volcanoes – exudes opportunities for rafting, cycling and mountaineering, while the mysterious island of **Chiloé** has beautiful wooden churches. Towering granite pillars and blue-tinged glaciers draw thousands of visitors to **Chilean Patagonia**, and the excellent trekking routes of **Parque Nacional Torres del Paine**. Last, but definitely not least, for serene beauty, ancient mystery and giant Moai statues, head to the world's most remote island of **Rapa Nui** (Easter Island).

WHEN TO VISIT

If you want to experience the whole of Chile in all its diversity you'll need to come prepared for both extreme cold and extreme heat. The **Lake District**, **Patagonia** and **Tierra del Fuego** are best explored from October through to April, since the Chilean winter effectively shuts down much of the south and transport can be very limited. **Norte Grande**, **Norte Chico**, **Middle Chile** and the **Pacific island** territories, however, can be accessed all year round.

CHRONOLOGY

1520 Ferdinand Magellan is the first European to sail through what is now the Magellan Strait.

1536 Expedition from Peru to Chile by conquistador Diego de Almagro and his four hundred men ends in death for most of the party.

1541 Pedro de Valdivia, a lieutenant of Francisco Pizarro, founds Santiago de Chile; a feudal system in which Spanish landowners enslave the Indian population is established.

1808 Napoleon invades Spain and replaces Spanish King Ferdinand VII with his own brother.

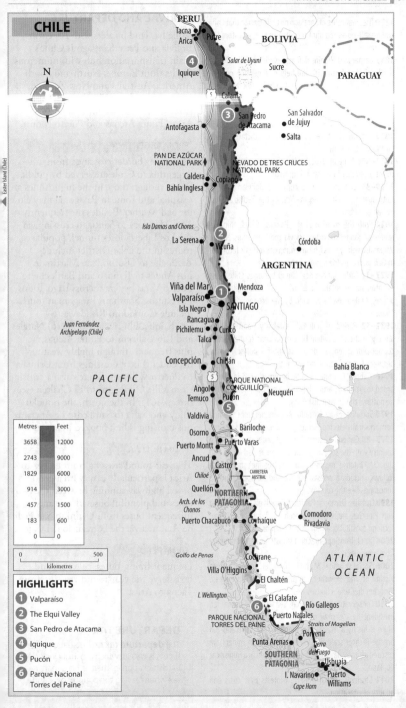

CHILE

N

PACIFIC OCEAN

ATLANTIC OCEAN

PERU
BOLIVIA
PARAGUAY
ARGENTINA

Tacna
Putre
Arica
Iquique
Salar de Uyuni
Sucre
Calama
San Pedro de Atacama
San Salvador de Jujuy
Antofagasta
Salta
PAN DE AZÚCAR NATIONAL PARK
NEVADO DE TRES CRUCES NATIONAL PARK
Caldera
Copiapó
Bahía Inglesa
Isla Damas and Choros
La Serena
Vicuña
Córdoba
Viña del Mar
Valparaíso
Mendoza
SANTIAGO
Isla Negra
Rancagua
Pichilemu
Curicó
Talca
Concepción
Chillán
Angol
Temuco
PARQUE NATIONAL CONGUILLÍO
Neuquén
Pucón
Valdivia
Bariloche
Osorno
Puerto Montt
Puerto Varas
Ancud
Castro
Chiloé
CARRETERA AUSTRAL
Quellón
NORTHERN PATAGONIA
Arch. de los Chonos
Puerto Chacabuco
Coyhaique
Comodoro Rivadavia
Golfo de Penas
Cochrane
Villa O'Higgins
El Chaltén
I. Wellington
El Calafate
PARQUE NACIONAL TORRES DEL PAINE
Puerto Natales
Río Gallegos
Straits of Magellan
Porvenir
Punta Arenas
Tierra del Fuego
SOUTHERN PATAGONIA
Ushuaia
I. Navarino
Puerto Williams
Cape Horn
Bahía Blanca

Easter Island (Chile)
Juan Fernández Archipelago (Chile)

Metres	Feet
3658	12000
2743	9000
1829	6000
914	3000
457	1500
183	600
0	0

0   500
kilometres

HIGHLIGHTS

1 Valparaíso
2 The Elqui Valley
3 San Pedro de Atacama
4 Iquique
5 Pucón
6 Parque Nacional Torres del Paine

4

1810 The *criollo* elite of Santiago de Chile decide that Chile will be self-governed until the Spanish king is restored to the throne.

1817 Bernardo O'Higgins defeats Spanish royalists in the Battle of Chacabuco with the help of Argentine general José San Martín, as part of the movement to liberate South America from colonial rule.

1818 Full independence won from Spain. O'Higgins signs the Chilean Declaration of Independence.

1829 Wealthy elite seizes power with dictator Diego Portales at the helm.

1832–60s Mineral deposits found in the north of the country, stimulating economic growth.

1879–83 Chilean troops occupy the Bolivian port of Antofagasta, precipitating the War of the Pacific against Bolivia and Peru.

1914 With the creation of the Panama Canal, shipping routes no longer need to pass via the Cape, thus ending Valparaíso's glory days. The invention of synthetic fertilizers in Germany ends the nitrates boom.

1927–31 Carlos Ibáñez del Campo becomes Chile's first dictator, founding the corps of *carabineros* (militarized police); Chile is badly affected by the economic crash of 1929.

1932–52 Period of political instability: land belongs largely to the elite, while US corporations control Chile's copper production. Seeds are sewn of a political divide between left and conservative right.

1946 Gabriel González Videla becomes president of a broad coalition of parties; bowing to pressure from the US, he outlaws the Communist Party.

1970 Socialist leader Salvador Allende becomes the first democratically elected Marxist president by a slim margin.

1973–89 General Augusto Pinochet seizes control of the country with the support of the Chilean armed forces and the CIA. Intense repression of the regime's opponents follows, including arrests, torture and "disappearances"; thousands flee the country.

1990 Christian Democrat Patricio Aylwin is elected president and Pinochet steps down peacefully, though not before securing constitutional immunity from prosecution.

2004 The Chilean Supreme Court strips Pinochet of immunity from prosecution.

2006 Socialist leader Michelle Bachelet, former torture victim of the Pinochet regime, is elected president. Pinochet dies under house arrest.

2010 Conservative businessman Sebastián Piñera named president by a narrow margin. On February 27, Middle Chile is hit by a massive earthquake that measures 8.8 on the Richter scale. In October, 33 Chilean miners are rescued after 69 days trapped underground in a mine near Copiapó.

2011 Students launch massive protests over costs and quality of education.

ARRIVAL AND DEPARTURE

Chile has land borders with Argentina, Bolivia and Peru. Santiago is Chile's main transportation hub with numerous flights from Europe, North and South America, Australia and New Zealand. You can also fly to Chile's neighbours from several smaller airports such as Arica, Punta Arenas and Puerto Montt.

FROM ARGENTINA

Numerous **border crossings** from Argentina to Chile are served by public buses, though those in the high Andes are seasonal and some in Patagonia may close for bad weather. Besides the frequently used Mendoza to Santiago crossing via the Los Libertadores tunnel, popular routes in the Lake District include Bariloche to Osorno, San Martín de Los Andes to Temuco and Bariloche to Puerto Varas by ferry across Lago Todos Los Santos. Southern Patagonian routes include Comodoro Rivadavia to Coyhaique, El Calafate to Puerto Natales and Río Gallegos to Punta Arenas, plus frequent (though highly weather-dependent) boat crossings from Ushuaia to Puerto Williams. There's also a crossing from Villa O'Higgins to El Chaltén (see box, p.461). In the north, the popular Jujuy and Salta to San Pedro de Atacama bus crossing is best booked in advance.

FROM BOLIVIA

The year-round crossing from La Paz to Arica is particularly easy, with a good paved highway running between the two cities and plentiful buses. There are infrequent buses from Uyuni to San Pedro de Atacama via the Portezuelo del Cajón.

FROM PERU

Frequent trains, buses, *colectivos* and taxis serve the year-round crossing from Tacna to Arica.

DEPARTURE TAX

The **departure tax** on international flights is US$30, which is usually included in the ticket price. There is no departure tax when leaving the country overland.

VISAS

Citizens of the European Union, the United States, Canada, South Africa, Australia and New Zealand do not require **visas**, though citizens of the United States (US$160), Canada (US$132) and Australia (US$95) are subject to **one-off arrival fees**, valid for the life of the passport. Tourists are routinely granted ninety-day entry permits and must surrender their tourist cards upon departure. In theory, visitors can be asked to produce an onward ticket and proof of sufficient funds, though that rarely happens. Ninety-day **visa extensions** can be granted by the Departamento de Extranjería, San Antonio 580, Piso 2, Santiago Centro (Mon–Fri 8.30am–2pm, calls taken 9am–4pm; ☎600 6264222, ⍵www .extranjeria.gov.cl/ingles at a cost of US$100, although it may be cheaper and easier simply to cross the border into a neighbouring country and back again. If you lose your tourist card, you can get a replacement from the Policía Internacional, Morande 672, Santiago (☎2 26901010).

GETTING AROUND

The majority of the population in Chile travels by bus, and it's such a reliable and inexpensive option that you'll probably do the same. However, domestic flights are handy for covering long distances in a hurry.

BY PLANE

Several airlines offer frequent and reasonably priced flights within Chile. You'll often find better fares by booking locally, rather than in advance from home. The flight from Santiago to Arica (2hr 30min) costs around CH$70,000, and the Santiago to Puerto Montt flight (1hr 30min) around CH$50,000. Return tickets are often much cheaper than two singles. **LAN** (☎600 5262000 in Chile, when abroad call ☎56 26872400, ⍵lan.com) is the most established airline with efficient online booking, last-minute discounts and a good-value "Visit South America Air Pass". **Sky Airline** (☎600

6002828, ⍵skyairline.cl) competes with LAN price-wise, with daily flights between Chile's major cities. Punta Arenas-based **Aerovías DAP** (☎61 2616100, ⍵aerovias dap.cl) flies to various destinations in Chilean and Argentine Patagonia and Tierra del Fuego; it's best to book tickets directly at the airline offices as their website is inefficient.

BY TRAIN

Travelling by **train** is a good option if you plan to stop off in Middle Chile. A reliable and comfortable service operated by Terra Sur (⍵terrasur.cl) usually runs several times a day between Santiago and Chillán, with stops at intermediate stations including Rancagua, and Talca. On the cheapest seats, the three-hour trip from Santiago to Talca costs about CH$5600, and from Santiago to Rancagua (1hr) around CH$3600.

BY BUS

Bus travel is popular, affordable and convenient. The level of comfort depends on how much you are prepared to pay for your ticket, with the *cama* buses being the plushest, their seats reclining almost horizontally. The cheapest seats from Santiago to Arica cost around CH$40,000, from Santiago to Puerto Montt CH$24,000, and from Santiago to Mendoza CH$17,000.

Bus tickets are valid only for specified buses, and the major bus companies, such as **Tur Bus** (☎600 6606600, ⍵turbus.cl) and **Pullman** (☎600 3203200, ⍵pullman .cl), require you to buy your ticket before you board – though for the majority of routes you'll have no trouble purchasing tickets at a bus station kiosk shortly before your departure. That said, south of Puerto Montt, and especially during the peak months, demand outstrips supply, so it is advisable to book in advance if you are on a tight schedule. Bus station kiosks are the easiest option – online booking services are available but cannot usually process foreign credit cards. If crossing **international** borders by bus, remember that it's prohibited to transport animal and plant matter to neighbouring countries, and luggage searches are frequent.

4

4

Smaller **local buses** and minibuses (*micros*) connect city centres with outlying neighbourhoods and smaller towns with villages. In some parts of Chile, especially in the north, *colectivos* (shared taxis with fixed fares) provide a faster and only slightly pricier service between towns than local buses.

BY FERRY

South of Puerto Montt, where Chile breaks up into a plethora of islands and fjords, you will have to take a **ferry**, whether to continue along the Carretera Austral or to work your way down to Southern Patagonia. Travelling south by boat is more expensive than going by bus, but it allows you access to some of the remotest and most beautiful parts of Chile. Popular routes include Puerto Montt to Puerto Natales, Puerto Montt to Chacabuco and Chacabuco to Laguna San Rafael.

BY CAR

Car rental is costly (CH$19,000–35,000 per day) and complicated, with expensive insurance due to the varying condition of the dirt roads. Carrying spare tyres, a jack, extra petrol and plenty of drinking water is essential for driving around more remote parts of Chile, and punctures are frequent. Since public transport is perfectly adequate in most parts of the country, the only places where it may make sense to rent a **4WD vehicle** is on Easter Island, and perhaps to some national parks. To rent a car, you need to be over 21 years old; take your passport as ID, and have a national driver's licence and major credit card on hand.

HITCHING

Hitchhiking is popular in Chile and widely practised by locals, especially in rural areas. While it's never an entirely safe method of travel, Chile is the safest country in Latin America in which to hitch, although it's always best to do so at least in pairs.

BY BIKE

Cycling can be a good way of getting to the more remote national parks, some of which are inaccessible by public transport. It's a good idea to carry spare parts, although bike repair shops are found in most medium-sized towns. While in the south of Chile **drinking water** can typically be acquired from streams, in the northern half of the country it is highly advisable to carry your own, and essential if cycling anywhere in the arid Atacama region. There are few cycle lanes, and for the most part cyclists share the road with motorists; at least traffic outside cities tends to be light. Stray dogs can also be a nuisance in populated areas.

PACHAMAMA BY BUS

The hop-on, hop-off **Pachamama by bus** service is especially tailored for independent travellers and designed to cover the most scenic spots in the Lake District and the Atacama Desert. You purchase a pass for the number of days you wish to travel – a seven-day pass costs CH$119,000 – and you can stay at any of the given stops for as long as you want. You are responsible for booking your own accommodation, which the guides can assist with. There are weekly departures on both routes; check the website for exact dates. To book a pass, contact the office inside the *Casa Roja* hostel in Santiago at least 48 hours in advance (see p.388; ☎ 2 26888018, ⓦ pachamamabybus.com).

ACCOMMODATION

Chile has a wide range of **budget accommodation**, often of great quality, occasionally not so great. Prices are highest during the peak season from December to February, when Chileans go on summer holiday; in shoulder seasons, they generally drop by around twenty percent. Many lodgings in the south of Chile close down during the winter months, so check ahead. Prices are normally listed inclusive of tax but it is best to establish this at the start of your stay.

RESIDENCIALES, CABAÑAS AND REFUGIOS

Residenciales are the most commonly available budget lodgings, found in both large cities and villages. Typically they consist of furnished rooms in someone's home, often with breakfast included; not surprisingly, the quality varies enormously. A basic double room will cost about CH$12,000–20,000; single rooms can cost as much as two-thirds the price of doubles.

Cabañas are usually found in well-visited spots, particularly by the ocean. They tend to come with a fully equipped kitchen, bathroom and bedrooms, and can be a great option for those travelling in groups. Depending on the time of year, a cabaña for two people costs about CH$20,000–30,000. Lower rates can be negotiated for larger groups.

Refugios are cheap (except those in Torres del Paine National Park), bare-bones lodgings found in national parks, usually consisting of several bunk beds in a wooden hut. Most have clean bedding, showers and flushable toilets; some require you to bring your own sleeping bag. Costs are around CH$8000–10,000 per person. Many *refugios* stay open year-round, but if you are planning on wilderness trekking, or on travelling in the south of Chile in the winter, try to arrange lodgings by calling the local **Conaf** office (⟨conaf.cl⟩), Chile's national forestry service, in advance; individual offices are listed on its website.

HOSTELS AND CAMPING

Hostel and camping options are plentiful across the country, especially in well-visited cities and popular outdoor destinations. Some independent hostel groups compile booklets listing the best hostels, which are worth picking up. **Backpackers Chile**, for example, who have both a booklet and website (⟨backpackerschile.com⟩), offer a reliable benchmark for high-quality hostels. The booklet is available from any of the hostels listed on the site, and at major information offices. Also worth picking up is the **Get South** booklet (⟨getsouth.com⟩), which offers discounts and freebies for various hostels across Chile, as well as Argentina and Uruguay.

Most major cities and key tourist centres have a **Hostelling International**-affiliated hostel (⟨hihostels.com⟩), for which member discounts will be available. The quality of HI hostels is not necessarily better than independent hostels, though they do tend to meet basic standards, so can be preferable to some budget hotels.

Note that in some widely visited places, such as Pucón and San Pedro de Atacama, a **hostal** may not necessarily mean a bona fide youth hostel – in many cases they simply turn out to be family homes.

Chile has marvellous opportunities for **camping**, with a proliferation of both fully equipped campsites (which can be somewhat pricey) and beautiful wilderness spots. There is ample free camping on empty beaches, although in most national parks you should only camp in designated spots. *Campings y Rutas Chile*, published only in Spanish by Turistel, and updated annually, has an extensive, though not entirely complete, list of campsites around Chile.

FOOD AND DRINK

Despite the abundance of fresh produce, **food** in Chile can seem somewhat bland as few spices are used; exceptions are *pebre* (a spicy salsa served with bread) and *ají chileno*, served with barbecued meat. **Breakfast** (*desayuno*) consists of coffee and the ubiquitous pockmarked bread with butter and jam. **Lunch** (*almuerzo*) is the main meal of the day, typically made up of three courses; at lunchtime most restaurants offer a good-value fixed-price *menú del día*. **Dinner** (*cena*) is usually served late, rarely before 9pm, and in Chilean households is often replaced by a lighter **evening snack** (*once*). Restaurants open from around 7pm but don't start to fill up until around 9pm.

Chicken and beef are the commonest **meats**, the latter often served boiled or grilled with a fried egg on top (*lomo a lo pobre*) or as part of a *parillada* (mixed grill). Two dishes found on menus across the country are *cazuela*, a hearty meat casserole, and *pastel de choclo*, a sweet-tasting corn and beef pie. When in Patagonia, do not miss the *asador patagónico*, spit-roasted lamb (*cordero*) and wild boar (*jibali*) steaks, while llama and alpaca steaks and stew are a staple of

4

4

EATING ON A BUDGET

Prices at some upmarket restaurants in Santiago and Valparaíso could give the impression that you have to break the bank to enjoy good food in Chile, but there are cheaper options. In coastal towns, you can pick up superb fish at bargain prices at little **marisquerías**, rustic fish eateries usually found at the busiest point of the seafront. In most large cities, look out for the **market** area where you'll get excellent deals on fruit and vegetables.

Small **kiosks** along city streets and country roads will often sell delicious and filling snacks like *empanadas* (savoury pasties filled with meat or fish) and *humitas* (ground corn wrapped in leaves).

American-style **diners** and home-grown fast-food chains across Chile sell huge *completos* (hot dogs), and *italianos*, hot dogs covered in mayonnaise, ketchup and avocado, as well as a range of sandwiches, like *Barros Jarpa* (melted cheese and ham), as alternative cheap eats.

---

altiplano cuisine in the north of Chile. Both the island of Chiloé and Easter Island serve up *curanto*, an elaborately prepared dish of meat and seafood.

There is a fantastic range of **fish and seafood**, and trendy sushi bars are springing up everywhere. Fish are typically served *frito* (battered and deep-fried), or *a la plancha* (grilled) with different sauces. Alternatively, try the *ceviche* – raw fish marinated in lemon juice with coriander. Excellent seafood dishes include *machas a la parmesana*, baked razor clams covered with parmesan cheese, *chupe de locos*, creamy abalone casserole topped with breadcrumbs, and *paila marina*, seafood soup.

Some excellent vegetarian restaurants have appeared in recent years, but vegetarian cuisine may be hard to find outside major cities and tourist destinations. Delicious **fruit and vegetables** are abundant in most parts of Chile, barring Patagonia and Tierra del Fuego. The north of the country grows exotic delights like scaly green *chirimoya* (custard apple), papaya, *tuna* (cactus fruit) and melon-like *pepino dulce*. Easter Island cuisine incorporates Polynesian tubers such as the *camote* (sweet potato).

DRINK

Tap water is generally drinkable all over Chile, with the exception of the Atacama, though Santiago tap water may upset some stomachs unaccustomed to the high mineral content. **Mineral water** is inexpensive and comes *sin gas* (still) or *con gas* (carbonated). **Soft drinks** (*gaseosas* or *bebidas*) are plentiful and very popular, and freshly squeezed **fruit juices** (*jugos*)

are abundant, especially in the fertile region of Middle Chile; beware that most Chileans like their juice sweetened, so if you don't want a half-juice, half-sugar concoction, ask for it *sin azúcar* (without sugar). *Licuados* are fruit smoothies mixed with water or *leche* (milk). *Mote con huesillo*, a drink made from boiled, dried apricots, is popular, especially in Middle Chile.

It can be difficult to find real **coffee** (*café de grano*) in smaller towns, as Nescafé seems to be the drink of choice, but coffee bars are appearing thick and fast across Santiago and other cities. In the Lake District and Patagonia, due to the proximity to Argentine culture, you are likely to encounter *yerba mate*, an antioxidant-rich, energizing herb drunk from a gourd through a metal straw.

Chile has several generic lager **beers** including Escudo, Cristal and Austral; the best beers come from microbreweries, with Kunstmann being the pick of the bunch. Chileans often start meals with a refreshing **pisco sour**, the national drink (see box, p.405).

Chilean **wine**, renowned worldwide, features on many restaurant menus. Wine tourism is also on the rise, with the Rutas del Vino (Wine Routes) in the Maule and Colchagua valleys giving visitors easy access to both the process of wine-making and the sampling of many different varieties.

CULTURE AND ETIQUETTE

Chilean city lifestyle, superficially at least, has more similarities with Europe than with neighbouring Bolivia. When eating out, a ten-percent **tip** in restaurants is normal and appreciated. Bargaining is not common and rarely done, even in marketplaces, though Chileans are often excellent at seeking out bargain prices.

Chileans are family- and **child-oriented**, and young people tend to live with their parents until they get married. The predominant religion is **Catholicism**, though the Church is not as influential as it used to be. Machismo is not as prevalent here as in other parts of Latin America; **women** are more respected and a lone woman travelling around the country is not likely to encounter any trouble beyond catcalls. While **homosexuality** is still frowned upon, it is tolerated, and there is a thriving gay scene in larger cities.

Chileans are very **sociable** people and will go out of their way to greet you in the street if they know you. If arranging to go out with Chileans, be aware that they may turn up later than the arranged time. When it comes to topics of conversation, Pinochet's rule is still very much a divisive subject, so unless you wish to be drawn into a heated discussion, steer clear.

SPORTS AND OUTDOOR ACTIVITIES

While Chile is not quite in the same league as Argentina or Brazil when it comes to **football**, the game is taken very seriously and attending a live match in Santiago (CH$4000–13,000) is very worthwhile for the atmosphere alone. Be aware, though, that the passion for football can turn aggressive, and be ready to make an exit. Santiago team Colo Colo has the largest and most enthusiastic following.

Every year, over three hundred **rodeos** are staged during the season (Sept–May) in Middle Chile and Aisén in particular. Evolved from the rural *huaso* (cowboy) culture, the rodeo is a spectacle worth going out of your way for.

La cueca, Chile's national **dance**, is also firmly rooted in *huaso* culture; it re-enacts the courting ritual between a rooster and a hen. Men and women clad in traditional outfits dance largely to guitar-led ballads, though the tempo and the instruments vary from region to region. *La cueca* is most commonly seen during the Chilean independence celebrations in September, when troupes perform on streets and stages across the country, though Chileans often take little persuading to show off their beloved dance whatever the opportunity.

WATERSPORTS

The mighty rivers of the Lake District and Patagonia offer excellent **white-water rafting** and **kayaking**, with Río Trancura, Río Petrohué and Río Futaleufú offering class 5 challenges. Futaleufú in particular is hailed as one of the top white-water runs in the world.

Sea kayakers can choose between multi-day paddling in the Patagonian fjords, shorter trips to small islands off the coast of Chiloé and wildlife-viewing on Isla Damas near La Serena.

Surfers head to Chile's top spot, Pichilemu, just south of Santiago, though there are excellent surfing and **windsurfing** opportunities all along the coast north of the capital, around Iquique in particular, and year-round swells on Easter Island.

In the northern half of the country, lack of rain makes for good visibility and abundant marine life for **divers** and **snorkellers**, while Easter Island and the Juan Fernández Archipelago both have world-class dive spots.

HIKING, CLIMBING AND SKIING

Hiking in the Torres del Paine National Park, on Isla Navarino or anywhere in the south is limited to the summer, spring and autumn, but the rest of Chile can be visited at any time of year. There are currently 55 **Rutas Patrimoniales** (ⓦbienesnacionales.cl – click on Rutas Patrimoniales in the left-hand column) covering the whole of Chile as part of a government initiative to preserve and develop land that has natural and historical value. These can all be explored on foot, by bike or on horseback. Another ambitious project, **Senderos de Chile** (ⓦsenderodechile.cl), consists of 35 trail sections intended to span the whole of Chile, including its Pacific islands. Once completed, it will become the longest trekking route in the world, but progress on the project is currently slow.

Ice climbers will find excellent **climbing** routes in the Central and Patagonian Andes from November to March, with plenty of accessible glaciers, while the granite towers of Torres del Paine rank among the world's most challenging rock climbs. Middle Chile and the Lake District, however, have the greatest variety of climbing and mountaineering spots.

Along with Argentina, Chile has world-class powder snow, with some of the best **skiing** spots found within easy reach of Santiago (see box, p.392). The Lake District's Villarica-Pucón and Osorno give you the opportunity to whizz down the slopes of volcanoes.

BIKING

Spectacular **biking** terrain can be found from Norte Grande to Tierra del Fuego, though you will need a sturdy mountain bike to cope with the potholed trails. While the best time to cycle around much of Chile is between October and March, Norte Chico and Norte Grande can be explored year-round, though altitude is often a consideration, especially if you're planning on exploring Parque Nacional Lauca. Norte Chico offers easy and enjoyable coastal rides, while the Lake District and Chiloé have the greatest variety of cycling routes, and the Carretera Austral is a challenging undertaking that rewards with amazing scenery.

COMMUNICATIONS

Overseas mail sent from any part of Chile via Correos de Chile, Chile's **postal service**, generally takes two or three weeks to reach its destination. Important shipping to Chile is best sent via registered mail. The larger post offices have a *lista de correos* (alphabetical list) for collecting *poste restante* (general delivery).

Chile has a number of different telecoms operators, and in order to make an **international call**, you dial the three-digit carrier code of the telecom,

CHILE ON THE NET

ⓦ **chile.travel** The international section of the official website of Sernatur – Chile's government-run tourist board – covers regional attractions, places to stay and restaurants.

ⓦ **conaf.cl** Information on Chile's protected natural areas (in Spanish only).

ⓦ **gochile.cl** Online travel agency covering the whole of Chile (available in English).

ⓦ **santiagotimes.cl** Online version of the capital's English-language newspaper.

ⓦ **turismochile.cl** Descriptions of regional attractions (mostly in Spanish).

ⓦ **conadi.cl** Site for indigenous affairs (Spanish only).

ⓦ **puntogay.cl** Information on gay nightlife and more.

ⓦ **dibam.cl** Plenty of detail on cultural attractions and museums.

followed by 0, then the country code and finally the phone number itself. Most local numbers consist of seven or eight digits, preceded by the city/area code; if dialling from the same area, drop the city or area code and dial the six or seven digits directly. During 2013, the government will complete the roll-out of a new numbering system, adding a 2 to the start of every fixed line number, so beware that some businesses may not have updated their details. Mobile phone numbers start with 07, 08 or 09, followed by seven digits; drop the 0 when calling mobile-to-mobile. Calls abroad from the numerous **centros de llamadas** to most European countries and North America cost around CH$150 per minute, although prices vary from area to area. Setting up a **Skype** account is cheap and convenient, as many internet cafés in Chile are Skype-equipped. Alternatively, get a Chilean **SIM card** for an "unlocked" mobile phone for around CH$6000, and all incoming calls are free.

Internet is widely available across Chile. Most towns and villages have broadband-equipped **internet cafés**, where access costs around CH$500 per hour, although on Isla Navarino and Easter Island it is considerably pricier.

CRIME AND SAFETY

The risk of **violent crime** in Chile is very low; in larger cities pickpocketing and petty thievery are minor concerns, but assaults are practically unknown, and there is very little corruption among Chilean police.

HEALTH

There are no compulsory **vaccinations** for Chile, though there have been reported incidents of mosquito-borne **dengue fever** on Easter Island; use insect repellent. **Hantavirus**, caused by inhaling or ingesting rat droppings, is uncommon but deadly: when staying in rural buildings that could potentially have rodents, air them out thoroughly and do not sleep on the floor. Chile has two species of **spider** with a venomous and potentially dangerous bite: the black widow (found in parts of Torres del Paine National Park, among other areas) and the Chilean recluse spider (found throughout Chile). The recluse – or *araña del rincón,* literally "corner spider" – is commonly found in houses. Though bites from either spider are relatively rare, they can prove fatal – if you think you may have been bitten, seek medical help immediately.

INFORMATION AND MAPS

Official **Sernatur** tourist offices (Servicio Nacionalde Turismo; ⓦsernatur.cl) are found in all the major cities and towns. They produce a plethora of brochures on local attractions, accommodation and outdoor activities, though some are better stocked than others. Some regions may also have a **municipal tourism office** run by the regional authorities. For information on Chile's natural attractions, as well as maps and up-to-date trekking conditions for specific areas, you should head to the local **Conaf** office (Corporación Nacional Forestal, ⓦconaf.cl), again found in most towns.

JLM Cartografía maps are usually accurate and helpful, and can be found in most bookshops; they cover both cities and trekking routes in Chile. The Instituto Geográfico Militar (ⓦigm.cl) produces detailed topographic maps of the entire country, but they can be pricey. **TurisTel guidebooks**, published by Telefónica Chile, are an excellent source of information on the country (in Spanish); they come in three volumes, covering the south, Middle Chile and Santiago, and the north, and are updated annually.

MONEY AND BANKS

The **peso** is the basic unit of Chilean currency, and it comes in 1000, 5000, 10,000 and rare 20,000 denomination notes, and 10, 20, 50, 100 and 500 peso coins. It is usually represented with the $ sign, not to be confused with US$. Few places will accept US dollars or other foreign currencies, though some hostels and hotels may suggest you pay in dollars to avoid the nineteen percent IVA tax (value added tax) on accommodation, from which foreigners are exempted when paying in dollars. Chile is fairly expensive compared to its Latin American counterparts (besides Brazil), with prices comparable to those in North America and Europe.

4

PUBLIC HOLIDAYS

Jan 1 New Year's Day (*Año Nuevo*)

Easter (*Semana Santa*) national holidays on Good Friday, Holy Saturday and Easter Sunday

May 1 Labour Day (*Día del Trabajo*)

May 21 Navy Day (*Día de las Glorias Navales*) marking Chile's naval victory at Iquique during the War of the Pacific

June 29 St Peter and St Paul (*San Pedro y San Pablo*)

July 16 Our Lady of Mount Carmel (*Solemnidad de la Virgen del Carmen, Reina y Patrona de Chile*)

Aug 15 Assumption of the Virgin Mary (*Asunción de la Virgen*)

Sept 17 If it falls on a Monday, an extension of Independence celebrations

Sept 18 National Independence Day (*Fiestas Patrias*) celebrates Chile's proclamation of independence from Spain in 1810

Sept 19 Armed Forces Day (*Día del Ejército*)

Sept 20 If it falls on a Friday, an extension of Independence celebrations

Oct 12 Columbus Day (*Día del Descubrimiento de Dos Mundos*) celebrates the European discovery of the Americas

Nov 1 All Saints' Day (*Día de Todos los Santos*)

Dec 8 Immaculate Conception (*Inmaculada Concepción*)

Dec 25 Christmas Day (*Navidad*)

At the time of writing, the exchange rate was £1 = CH$714; US$1 = CH$474 and €1 = CH$618.

Large and medium-sized cities have plentiful **banks** and **ATMs**; Banco de Chile and Santander are good bets for withdrawing cash with debit cards. Santiago and most of the more visited destinations have casas de cambio which can change travellers' cheques and foreign currencies at a reasonable rate. Some smaller towns (and Easter Island) only have Banco Estado ATMs, which accept just Cirrus and MasterCard. If you are heading to small towns off the beaten track, it's wise to carry enough cash to cover a few days as ATMs are not always reliable. **Credit cards** can also be widely used to pay for purchases, especially in larger towns, though budget lodgings and eating places rarely accept them.

OPENING HOURS AND HOLIDAYS

On weekdays, most services and **shops** tend to be open from 9 or 10am to 6 or 7pm; Saturday hours are usually 10 or 11am to 2pm. In smaller towns, **restaurants** are often closed in the afternoon between the lunchtime hours of 1 to 3pm and the dinnertime hours of 8 to 11pm. An increasing number of restaurants, bars and shops open on Sundays, but smaller places, particularly in more rural areas, generally remain closed.

Banks typically operate from 9am to 2pm on weekdays only, while post offices generally open Monday to Friday from 9am to 6pm; in larger towns, they also open Saturdays from 9am to 1pm. Monday is a day off for most **museums**; they are, however, usually open on Sundays, often with free entry. Shops and services are closed during national holidays, local festivals and on local and national election days.

Santiago

Towered over by the snow-streaked Andes, the buzzing metropolis of **SANTIAGO** has a distinctly European feel. Its rich pockets of culture and history are often overlooked by travellers frustrated by a lack of iconic sights, and put off by the smog that hangs over the city. Yet those prepared to venture beyond the grid of central shopping streets will be rewarded with quirky, vibrant neighbourhoods filled with a huge variety of lively bars and excellent restaurants. Streetscapes flit between elegant colonial buildings and high-rise office blocks. The city is a microcosm of the country's contrasting ways of life, with ramshackle markets, smart office buildings, rough-and-ready bars and plush shopping malls all just a short metro ride from the main square.

Home to more than a quarter of Chile's population, the capital is crowded but easy to navigate with a clean and efficient metro system. And even if the city itself fails to impress, Santiago is an excellent base from which to explore, with world-class ski resorts, sun-kissed beaches and beautiful vineyards all within easy reach.

WHAT TO SEE AND DO

Downtown Santiago is loosely bordered by the **Río Mapocho** to the north, and the central thoroughfare of Avenida Libertador Bernado O'Higgins – commonly known as **La Alameda** – to the south. The city's accommodation and most inviting *barrios* are all a short distance from this central section. Bohemian **Barrio Lastarria** is home to a wealth of art museums and characterful boutique shops. North of the river, **Barrio Bellavista** offers trendy cafés as well as the city's best viewpoint at **Cerro San Cristóbal**. In the west, down-to-earth **Barrio Brasil** and **Barrio Yungay** are home to many budget hostels and good restaurants, while out east, upmarket Providencia and plush Las Condes make up in shopping malls what they lack in character.

Plaza de Armas

Pedro de Valdivia, the city's founder, intended the lush tree-studded **Plaza de Armas** to be the epicentre of Chile, surrounding it with splendid colonial architecture. The oldest building on the west side of the plaza is the **Catedral Metropolitana** (1748), its Neoclassical facade designed by the Italian architect Joaquín Toesca. To the north is the **Palacio de la Real Audiencia** (1804), housing the Museo Histórico Nacional, and the **Correo Central**. A lively gathering point since the mid-1800s, the plaza's flower gardens and the fountain in the centre honouring Simón Bolívar attract a multitude of chess players, mimes, buskers, vagrants, stray dogs, soap-box preachers, strolling families and giggling children, making the square an ideal place to linger on a bench and people-watch.

Mercado Central and La Vega

By the south bank of Río Mapocho lies the lively **Mercado Central** (daily 6am–4pm), a mass of stalls spilling over with wondrous fish and seafood, dotted with busy little *marisquerías* whose delicious smells draw crowds of customers at lunchtime. All of this is gathered inside an elaborate metal structure prefabricated in Birmingham, England, and erected in Santiago in 1868. Cross the Río Mapocho and you reach **La Vega** (daily: roughly 6am–5pm), an enormous roofed market surrounded by outdoor stalls, selling all kinds of fresh produce, with fruit and vegetables at rock-bottom prices. La Vega is full of local character, giving you a glimpse of "real" Santiago: fragrant, pungent and chaotic. It is also the best place in town to grab a giant fruit smoothie, as well as excellent seafood.

Museo Chileno de Arte Precolombino

The excellent **Museo Chileno de Arte Precolombino** (Tues–Sun 10am–6pm; CH$3000, guided tours must be pre-booked, call ☎2 29281522, ⓦmuseoprecolombino.cl), at Bandera 361, is housed in the elegant late-colonial Real Casa de Aduana (Royal Customs House, 1807). The unparalleled collection of pre-Columbian artefacts spans a time period of around ten thousand years and covers the whole of Latin America, from Mexico down to the south of Chile. More than 1500 examples of pottery, finely woven textiles and jewellery are on display, including permanent collections from the Andes, Mesoamerica, the Amazon and the Caribbean, and there are outstanding temporary exhibitions. Currently closed for renovation, the museum is due to reopen towards the end of 2013.

La Moneda

The restored **Palacio de la Moneda**, on the large **Plaza de la Constitución**, is the presidential palace and site of the dramatic siege that brought Pinochet to power on September 11, 1973, and led to the death of President Salvador Allende. A wide, squat Neoclassical construction, originally built to house the Royal Mint, the palace stages an elaborate **changing of**

the guard every other day at 10am, featuring white-jacketed officers, cavalry and an inspired brass band. The palace's inner courtyards can be accessed through the North Gate (Mon–Fri 10am–6pm) and the basement features a huge relief map of Chile that allows visitors to get an accurate impression of the country's size. There are four free tours each day (e visitas@presidencia.cl). The **Centro Cultural Palacio La Moneda** (daily 9am–9pm; exhibitions CH$2000; w ccplm.cl), a smart, arty space home to exhibitions, craft shops and cafés, is

SANTIAGO

ACCOMMODATION

Casa Bonita	6
Casa Condell	1
La Casa Roja	2
EcoHostel	5
Hostel Cienfugos	3
Landay Barceló	4

accessed by steps to the left and right of the palace's main frontage.

Cerro Santa Lucía

Six blocks east of Palacio de la Moneda along the Alameda, Santiago's main thoroughfare (officially Avenida Libertador Bernardo O'Higgins), the splendidly landscaped **Cerro Santa Lucía** (Dec–Feb 9am–8pm; rest of the year 9am–7pm; free; register passport details at the entrance), is the historically significant promontory where Pedro de Valdivia defeated the indigenous forces

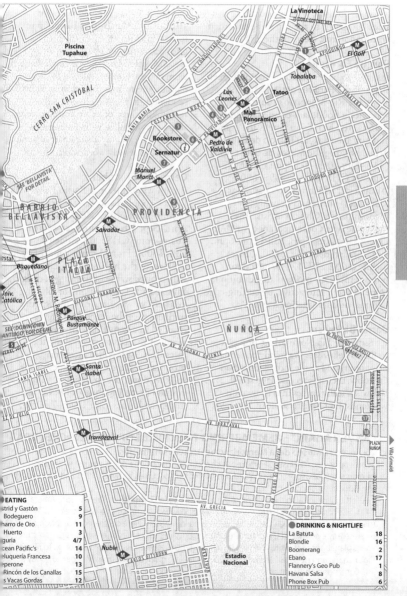

● EATING

strid y Gastón	5
Bodeguero	9
harro de Oro	11
Huerto	3
guria	4/7
cean Pacific's	14
eluquería Francesa	10
eperone	13
Rincón de los Canallas	15
s Vacas Gordas	12

● DRINKING & NIGHTLIFE

La Batuta	18
Blondie	16
Boomerang	2
Ebano	17
Flannery's Geo Pub	1
Havana Salsa	8
Phone Box Pub	6

(to whom it is known as Huelén – "the curse"), and where Santiago was officially founded on February 12, 1541. The barren hill was transformed into a lush retreat through the labour of 150 prisoners in the 1870s. The park's peaceful winding footpaths and the ornate Terraza Neptuno fountain draw amorous couples, while visitors take the steep footpaths to the top to be rewarded with **panoramic views** of the city.

Parque Forestal

It's hard to believe that the tranquil green space of the **Parque Forestal**, stretching along the Río Mapocho's south bank, was once a floodplain covered in rubbish dumps. Top attraction here is the grand and airy Neoclassical **Palacio de Bellas Artes**, housing the **Museo de Bellas Artes** (Tues–Sun 10am–6.50pm; CH$600, students CH$300; ☎2 24991600, ⓦmnba.cl), which features paintings, sculptures, prints and drawings by predominantly Chilean artists. The **Museo de Arte Contemporáneo**, or **MAC** (Tues–Sat 11am–7pm, Sun 11am–6pm; CH$600, students CH$400; ⓦmac .uchile.cl, ☎2 29771741), next door, offers temporary modern art exhibitions, some of them interactive, by cutting-edge national and international artists.

Barrio Bellavista

Crossing the Pío Nono bridge brings you to **Barrio Bellavista**, the trendy bohemian neighbourhood at the foot of **Cerro San Cristóbal**, the city's second-largest hill. Bellavista really comes into its own on weekends; it's home to some of Santiago's best **bars** and **restaurants**, which sit along quiet, tree-lined streets. There are also several good nightclubs and raucous beer-and-burger joints lining Pío Nono, the main street. You'll find **La Chascona**, one of the three residences of Chile's most famous poet, **Pablo Neruda**, down the little side street of Márquez de la Plata (Márquez de la Plata 0192, Tues–Sun: Jan–Feb 10am–7pm, March–Dec 10am–6pm; tours CH$3500; ☎2 27778741, ⓦfundacionneruda.cl). Named after Neruda's wife Matilde, "the tangle-haired woman", the house is faithful to the nautical theme that characterizes all his residences, its creaking floorboards resembling those of a ship and strangely shaped rooms filled with a lifetime of curios. You can only visit as part of a tour, which is extremely worthwhile.

Cerro San Cristóbal

A path winds up from Barrio Bellavista's Plaza Caupolicán to Terraza Bellavista, passing Santiago's modest zoo (daily: April–Sept 10am–6pm, Oct–March 10am–7pm; CH$3000, students CH$1500). From Terraza Bellavista you walk up to the hill's summit, crowned with a huge statue of the Virgen de la Immaculada Concepción and offering excellent views of the city, though the outlying neighbourhoods might be clouded in a gentle haze of smog. The many dirt tracks running along the forested hillsides offer excellent mountain-biking opportunities, while walking down the spiralling road brings you to **Piscina Tupahue** (mid-Nov to mid-March Tues–Sun 10am–7.30pm;

"NEVER AGAIN" – REMEMBERING THE CRIMES OF THE PINOCHET ERA

The excellent **Museo de la Memoria y los Derechos Humanos** at Matucana 501 (Tues–Sun 10am–6pm; free; ⓦmuseodelamemoria.cl; Metro Quinta Normal) documents the chilling human rights abuses, repression and censorship that occurred between 1973 and 1990 under the Pinochet dictatorship.

Another memorial to the victims of the regime is **Villa Grimaldi** at Avenida José Arrieta 8401, a secret torture and extermination centre now transformed into a Park for Peace (daily 10am–6pm; free; ⓦvillagrimaldi.cl). The buildings here were destroyed in an attempt to erase any evidence of the centre's existence, but among a series of memorials to its victims are explanations of the site's original layout. To get there, take bus 513, or D09, or go to Metro Plaza Egaña and get a taxi (about CH$6000). There are guided tours from Monday to Friday at 10.30am, noon and 3pm.

DOWNTOWN SANTIAGO

Providencia & Las Condes

EATING

Emporio La Rosa	4
Cotopardo	7
Kintaro	3
Mercado Central	2
El Rápido	5
Sur Patagonico	9

DRINKING & NIGHTLIFE

Ciré Caribe	6
Ciré Escondido	8
Ciré Haiti	10
Confitería Las Torres	11
La Piojera	1

ACCOMMODATION

Hostal 168	4
Andes Hostel	1
Footsteps Backpackers	5
Hostal Forestal	3
Happy House Hostel	6
París	6

4

BELLAVISTA

Estación Mapocho

La Vega

Río Mapocho

Puente Cal y Canto

Parque Recoleta

La Bicicleta Verde

Palacio de Bellas Artes

Museo de Arte Contemporáneo

Parque Forestal

Netcenter

Cyber Online

Mercado Central

Palacio de la Real Audencia

Pl de Armos

PLAZA DE ARMAS

Catedral

Cine Hoyts

Feria Mix

Museo Chileno de Arte Precolombino

PLAZA DE CONSTITUCIÓN

Palacio de la Moneda

PLAZA DE LA LIBERTAD

PLAZA BULNES

PLAZA DEL LIBERTADOR O'HIGGINS

Terminal Los Héroes

Los Héroes

Moneda

Universidad de Chile

Univ. de Chile

Iglesia San Francisco

Teatro Municipal

Centro de Exposición de Arte Indígena

Biblioteca Nacional

Feria Artesanal Santa Lucía

Santa Lucía

CERRO SANTA LUCÍA

Universidad Católica

Diego Portales Convention Centre

Clínica Universidad Católica

Cine Arte Alameda

Parque Gómez Rojas

Parque San Borja

PLAZA BAQUEDANO

Baquedano

AV. VICUNA MACKENNA

AV. GEN. BUSTAMANTE

Parque Quinta Normal

Airport

Roadside Expediciones

Palacio Cousiño

500
meters

N

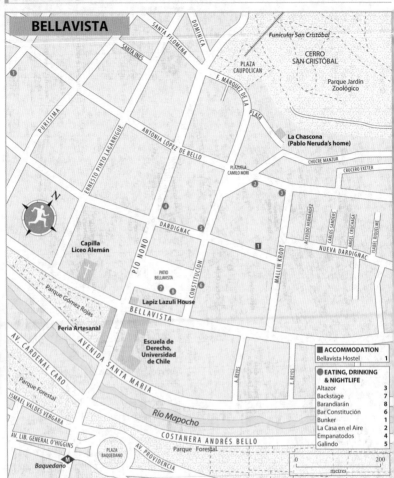

BELLAVISTA

SANTA FILOMENA
DOMINICA
SANTA INÉS
PLAZA CAUPOLICÁN
F. MÁRQUEZ DE LA PLATA
Funicular San Cristóbal
CERRO SAN CRISTÓBAL
Parque Jardín Zoológico
PURÍSIMA
ERNESTO PINTO LAGARRIGUE
ANTONIA LÓPEZ DE BELLO
La Chascona (Pablo Neruda's home)
CHUCRE MANZUR
CRUCERO EXETER
PLAZUELA CAMILO MORI
Capilla Liceo Alemán
DARDIGNAC
PÍO NONO
ACEVEDO HERNÁNDEZ
CARLOS SANDERS
ÁNGEL CRUCHAGA
ISABEL RIQUELME
NUEVA DARDIGNAC
MALLIN KRODT
CONSTITUCIÓN
PATIO BELLAVISTA
Parque Gómez Rojas
Lapiz Lazuli House
BELLAVISTA
Feria Artesanal
AV. CARDENAL CARO
AVENIDA SANTA MARÍA
Escuela de Derecho, Universidad de Chile
A. REYES
E. REYES
Parque Forestal
ISMAEL VALDÉS VERGARA
Río Mapocho
COSTANERA ANDRÉS BELLO
AV. LIB. GENERAL O'HIGGINS
AV. PROVIDENCIA
PLAZA BAQUEDANO
Baquedano
Parque Forestal

ACCOMMODATION
Bellavista Hostel 1

● **EATING, DRINKING & NIGHTLIFE**
Altazor 3
Backstage 7
Barandiarán 8
Bar Constitución 6
Bunker 1
La Casa en el Aire 2
Empanatodos 4
Galindo 5

0 ———————— 200
metres

CH\$6000), a popular open-air swimming pool and picnicking spot amid monkey puzzle trees. You can either return by the same route or continue down to the Estación Pedro de Valdivia in Providencia.

Barrio Brasil

West of the Vía Norte Sur, downtown's western boundary, **Barrio Brasil** is centred around the nicely landscaped Plaza Brasil, with a surreal-looking playground and a tall monkey puzzle tree reaching for the sky. In the early twentieth century this was a prestigious residential neighbourhood; now its elegant streets have faded and it

has morphed into a lively area with good restaurants and bars, popular with backpackers and Santiago's students.

Ñuñoa

Southeast of central Santiago, the laidback neighbourhood of **Ñuñoa**, with the attractive **Plaza Ñuñoa** at its heart, is overlooked by many visitors to the city, though it has a lively **nightlife** due to the proximity of two university campuses. Football fans also flock here to watch the matches at the **Estadio Nacional**, at Avenida Grecia 2001. The stadium has a grim past – it was once used by Pinochet as a torture centre and prison.

ARRIVAL AND DEPARTURE

By plane Aeropuerto Arturo Merino Benítez (☏2 26901752, ⊛aeropuertosantiago.cl), 30min from the city centre, has useful facilities including ATMs, currency exchange, tourist information kiosk and mobile phone rentals. The blue Centropuerto bus (Mon–Fri every 10min, weekends every 15min: daily 6am–11.30pm; CH$1600 one-way), just outside the terminal doors, is the cheapest way to get to the city centre and stops at the Los Héroes metro station. Tur Bus has transfers to the Terminal Alameda (every 20min; daily 6am–10.30pm; CH$1900; ☏2 28227448), while TransVip (☏2 26773000) and Transfer Delfos (☏2 29138800) charge from CH$5500 to drop you off at your destination.

Destinations LAN, Aerolíneas del Sur and Sky Airline have multiple daily flights to all major Chilean destinations: Arica (hourly; 2hr 45min); Calama (every 30min; 2hr 5min); Iquique (hourly; 2hr 25min); La Serena (hourly; 1hr 5min); Puerto Montt (every 30min; 1hr 40min); Punta Arenas (every 30min; 3hr 25min).

By train Estación Central, at Alameda 3322 (ticket sales ☏2 25855000, ⊛efe.cl), is served by TerraSur trains from various destinations in Middle Chile. Trains leave five times a day for Chillán, stopping at Rancagua, San Fernando, Curico and Talca among other Central Valley towns.

Destinations Trains head south from Estacion Central as far as Chillán: Chillán (4 daily; 4hr 30min); Curicó (4 daily; 2hr); Rancagua (4 daily; 1hr); Talca (6 daily; 2hr 50min); all are served by TerraSur (⊛terrasur.cl). A slower Metrotrén has hourly departures to Rancagua (6.55am–10pm; 1hr 20min).

By bus The main bus station is the Terminal Buses Estación Central – also known as Terminal Santiago – (☏2 23761755), at Alameda 3850, near the Universidad de Santiago metro station, which handles international routes, and journeys to the west and south. The Terminal Alameda, next door at Alameda 3750 (☏2 28227400), is served by Pullman and Tur Bus, who also have some international departures. The two terminals have ATMs, snack shops and luggage storage, as well as easy access to public transport along Alameda. Buses from northern and central Chile use Terminal San Borja (☏2 27760645), at San Borja 184, near the Estación Central metro station, while the smaller Terminal Los Héroes, at Tucapel Jiménez 21 (☏2 24200099), near the Los Heroés metro station, serves a range of destinations in both northern and southern Chile.

Destinations Arica (8 daily; 28hr); Chillán (8 daily; 6hr); Copiapó (5 daily; 10hr); Iquique (10 daily; 24hr); La Serena (15 daily; 7hr); Pucón (every 30min; 12hr); Puerto Montt (8 daily; 13hr); Rancagua (every 15min; 1hr); Valparaíso and Viña del Mar (every 10min; 1hr 45min). Terminal Buses Estación Central has international departures to various South American countries including Argentina (Buenos Aires, Mendoza), Brazil (Saõ Paulo, Río de Janeiro) and Peru (Lima, Cusco, Tacna, Arequipa).

INFORMATION

Listings For entertainment listings, check Friday's "Recitales" page in *El Mercurio* or in *La Tercera*, Santiago's main newspapers.

Tourist information An excellent source of tourist information (with bilingual staff) is the municipal tourism office found on the north side of the Plaza de Armas (Mon–Fri 9am–6pm, Sat & Sun 10am–4pm, ☏2 27136745). There is also a small municipal office at the foot of Santa Lucia on Terraza Neptuno. The main Sernatur office is at Av Providencia 1550, near the Manuel Montt metro station, east of the city centre (Mon–Fri 9am–6pm, Sat 9am–2pm; ☏2 27318300). It provides maps of the city and is well stocked with brochures on the surrounding area. Conaf has an office at Av Bulnes 265 (Mon–Thurs 9am–5.30pm, Fri 9am–4.30pm; ☏2 26630125, ⊛conaf.cl), which provides information on national parks and reserves, as well as some pamphlets and inexpensive maps.

Tours Free walking tours of the city start in front of the cathedral, and are a good way to take in the city's main sights (Mon–Sat 10am; 4hr; free, though tips appreciated). Bike tours are also a good option (see box, p.391).

GETTING AROUND

By bus Fleets of white-and-green "TranSantiago" (⊛transantiago.cl) buses run around the city. To use them, you need to purchase a "BIP" transit card (CH$1350), sold in most metro ticket booths, which you can then add credit to (at the same booths, and at BIP centres across the city). Bus destinations are posted on window signs and at marked stops; a standard fare is CH$590.

By colectivo Slightly pricier than buses, *colectivos* have their destinations displayed on their roofs and carry passengers on fixed itineraries, reaching their destination slightly quicker than regular transport, though you need to know where you are going; useful for destinations outside the city centre.

By metro Metro (Mon–Fri 6am–11pm, Sat 6.30am–11pm, Sun 9am–10.30pm; ⊛metrosantiago.cl) is the quickest way to get around the city, with just five lines that are easy to navigate, though it gets rather cramped during rush hour. BIP cards (see above) are the easiest way to use the metro, with each journey costing CH$560–670 depending on the time of day. Single-use tickets are also available at metro stations.

ACCOMMODATION

There are a number of accommodation options in Santiago to suit budget travellers although really cheap places are scarce. Good inexpensive lodgings are mostly to be found in the city centre and Barrio Brasil.

CENTRAL SANTIAGO

Hostal 168 Santa Lucía 168, Metro Santa Lucía ☎2 26648478; map p.385. Welcoming hostel just beneath Cerro Santa Lucía with excellent facilities, free internet and breakfast included. Dorms CH$8000, doubles CH$30,000

Andes Hostel Monjitas 506, Metro Bellas Artes ☎2 26329990, ⓦandeshostel.com; map p.385. Centrally located hostel with modern decor, bright dorms complete with individual lockers, and a whole range of facilities – guest kitchen, lounge with pool table and cable TV, free internet, laundry service and a fully stocked bar. Dollars preferred. Can get noisy. Dorms CH$11,000, doubles CH$39,500

Casa Condell Condell 114, Metro Baquedano ☎2 27178592, ⓦcasacondell.com; map pp.382–383. Brightly coloured and spotlessly clean guesthouse with very good breakfasts (included), and a congenial hostess. Situated on a quiet street just off bustling Avenida Providencia. Doubles CH$25,000

EcoHostel General Jofré 349B, Metro Universidad Católica ☎2 22226833, ⓦecohostel.cl, ⓔinfo@ecohostel.cl; map pp.382–383. With its clean and spacious dorms, chilled-out common areas and fully equipped guest kitchen, this hostel and its environment-friendly ethic attracts mostly younger travellers. Lockers, internet, good breakfast and knowledgeable bilingual staff are a big plus. Dorms CH$7000, doubles CH$25,000

Footsteps Backpackers Almirante Simpson 50, Metro Baquedano ☎2 26347807, ⓦfootsteps.cl; map p.385. Well located for downtown and Bellavista, this cheerful hostel offers colourful dorm rooms and relaxed communal spaces. Internet included. Dorms CH$7000, doubles CH$27,500

Hostal Forestal Coronel Santiago Bueras 122, Metro Baquedano ☎2 26381347, ⓦhostalforestal.cl; map p.385. Perpetually popular, *Hostal Forestal* throws impromptu barbecues and the bilingual staff can advise on sightseeing. Luggage storage, outdoor patio, guest kitchen and lounge with cable TV are some of the perks. Dorms CH$7000, doubles CH$26,000

★ TREAT YOURSELF

Casa Bonita Pasaje República 5, Metro República ☎2 26727302, ⓦbbcasabonita.com; map pp.382–383. If you're tired of night buses, and in need of good coffee, try a few nights at this beautifully restored, centrally located bed and breakfast with spotless rooms. It's owned by a Dutch-Chilean couple, who are only too happy to help their guests make the most of Santiago. Doubles CH$49,000

París París 813, Metro Universidad de Chile ☎2 26640921, ⓔcarbott@latinmail.com; map p.385. Atmospheric, centrally located budget hotel with cheaper rooms to suit backpackers and a newer annexe featuring comfortable rooms and spotless bathrooms. Continental breakfast CH$1500 extra. Doubles CH$24,000

BELLAVISTA

Bellavista Hostel Dardignac 0184, Metro Bellavista ☎2 28997145, ⓦbellavistahostel.com; map p.386. It's easy to see why this hostel is extremely popular with younger travellers – a stone's throw from some of Santiago's best eating and nightlife, it's cosy, colourful, run by helpful bilingual staff and has all the standard backpacker conveniences. Dorms CH$7000, doubles CH$22,000

BARRIO BRASIL

La Casa Roja Agustinas 2113, Metro República ☎2 26964241, ⓦlacasaroja.cl; map pp.382–383. Sprawling, Aussie-owned converted mansion firmly established as backpacker party central, with spacious dorms and rooms. There's a jacuzzi, poolside barbecues, large common areas, free internet, kitchen and an on-site travel agency. A top budget choice, though not a place to catch up on your sleep; breakfast not included in dorms (CH$1,800). Dorms CH$8000, doubles CH$26,000

Hostel Cienfuegos Cienfuegos 151, Metro Los Héroes ☎2 26718532, ⓦhostelcienfuegos.cl; map pp.382–383. Large, professionally run, HI-affiliated hostel with clean dorms, plush bunk beds, spacious dining room and bonuses including on-site travel agency, internet and wi-fi, book exchange, breakfast and laundry service. Dorms CH$7500, doubles CH$25,200

Happy House Hostel Moneda 1829, Metro Los Héroes ☎2 26884849, ⓦhappyhousehostel.cl; map p.385. Travellers are made to feel really welcome at this beautifully decorated, spacious hostel, with large private rooms, attractive common areas, large kitchen, terrace bar and pool. Breakfast and internet included. Dorms CH$10,000, doubles CH$37,000

Landay Barceló Erasmo Escala 2012, Metro Los Héroes ☎2 26710300, ⓦlandaybarcelo.cl; map pp.382–383. Beautifully renovated house with gleaming bathrooms, wooden floors, colourful rooms with lockers, and a comfy DVD room. Breakfast and internet included. Dorms CH$8000, doubles CH$32,000

EATING

Santiago has a proliferation of good restaurants. Most are concentrated in Downtown, Bellavista and Providencia, with some good options, popular with backpackers and students, in Barrio Brasil and up-and-coming Barrio Yungay.

TRAITORS' CORNER

For an unusual eating experience, try **El Rincón de los Canallas** ("Traitor's Corner"), at Tarapacá 810 (entry only by prior reservation on ☎ 2 26325491; map pp.382–383). It was once a secret meeting place for the opposition during Pinochet's dictatorship, and though this is not the original site, you still need a password to enter. When asked, "Quién vive, canalla?", respond "Chile libre, canalla." (Pinochet called his detractors "canallas", so the exchange roughly means: "Who's there, traitor? Free Chile, traitor.") Against a nostalgic backdrop including wall-to-wall rallying slogans, this intimate bar offers traditional Chilean grub served up under names like Pernil Canalla ("Traitor's Ham", a roasted leg of pork). Mains CH$4000–7000.

DOWNTOWN

Emporio La Rosa Merced 291, near the corner of Lastarria; map p.385. Café and ice-cream haven with tables out onto the street. Good coffee, too, and the hot chocolate comes highly recommended. One ice-cream scoop CH$2600.

Gatopardo Lastarria 192; map p.385. Excellent Chilean and Mediterranean cuisine, good value at lunchtimes, served in an attractive interior. The stuffed calamari are particularly tasty. Fixed-price lunch CH$7000. Closed Sun.

Kintaro Monjitas 460; map p.385. Tasty and authentic sushi, along with teriyaki and udon dishes, all at very reasonable prices. Very popular at lunchtimes. Chicken katsu CH$3900. Closed Sun.

Mercado Central See p.381; map p.385. The best place for large portions of inexpensive fish and seafood, the fish market's bustling eateries offer such delights as *pastel de jaiva* (creamy crab pie) (CH$4800) and *machas a la Parmesana* (CH$4500); *Donde Augusto* is a popular spot. Lunch only.

El Rápido Bandera 371; map p.385. Established *empanadería* serving perfectly prepared *empanadas* and sandwiches; a snack counter rather than a restaurant. *Empanadas* from CH$850.

Sur Patagonico Lastarria 96; map p.385. Well-prepared Patagonian-style lamb and other tasty dishes served within a cosy, rough-hewn wood interior (Magellanic lamb with smoked polenta CH$9900).

BELLAVISTA AND PROVIDENCIA

Backstage Patio Bellavista; map p.386. Half bar, half decent pizzeria, popular *Backstage* has an open-air patio, perfect for enjoying live jazz on Sat nights. Pizza from CH$4000.

★ TREAT YOURSELF

Astrid y Gastón Antonio Bellet 201 ☎ 2 26509125, ⓦ astridygaston.com; map pp.382–383. Flawless fusion cuisine with Peruvian, Spanish, French and Japanese influences by Lima's famous chef, Gaston Acurio. The tuna steak (CH$16,800) borders on divine. Reservations required.

Barandiarán Patio Bellavista; map p.386. Spicy and flavourful Peruvian concoctions, including superb *ceviche* and sea bass dishes; the pisco sours stand out, too. *Ceviche* CH$5700.

El Bodeguero Manuel Montt 382; map pp.382–383. Rough-and-ready bar with cheap lunch deals: an excellent place to experience eating and drinking like a Santiago student. Three-course lunch including *bife a lo pobre* (steak with chips, fried onion and fried egg) CH$3400.

Empanatodos Pío Nono 153; map p.386. Bustling takeaway doing brisk business, turning out 33 types of delicious *empanadas* including delicious *manjar*-filled ones. From CH$1000.

Galindo Constitución; map p.386. Perpetually packed spot serving traditional Chilean food, such as hearty *pastel de choclo*, *cazuela* and *lomo a la pobre*, along with beers until late, even on weekdays. If sitting outside, you *will* be entertained by street musicians. *Pastel de choclo* CH$4500.

El Huerto Orrego Luco 054; map pp.382–383. An excellent choice for a wide variety of lovingly prepared vegetarian dishes, such as hearty burritos. Omelette CH$5300.

Liguria Av Providencia 1373; map pp.382–383. Large portions of Chilean and Italian dishes are on offer in this ever-popular and charming bar-bistro, as well as large sandwiches, good salads and superb pisco sours. Clams in parmesan cheese CH$7800. Also has a sister restaurant at Pedro de Valdivia 047.

BARRIO BRASIL AND BARRIO YUNGAY

Charro de Oro Av Ricardo Cumming 342A; map pp.382–383. Spicy and inexpensive Mexican tacos (from CH$1000) and burritos served in an intimate, no-frills setting. Open evenings only, until 1.30am Fri & Sat; closed Sun.

Ocean Pacific's Av Ricardo Cumming 221; map pp.382–383. Popular restaurant serving consistently good fish dishes (though not the cheapest), including an excellent salmon platter for two. Check out the elaborate puffer fish decorations. Mains CH$5000–10,000.

Peluquería Francesa Compañía de Jesús 2789 ☎ 2 26825243; map pp.382–383. Take a trip back in time at this charming restaurant above a nineteenth-century hair salon, where each table literally bursts with quirky memorabilia. Excellent French cuisine (*coq au vin* CH$6500), and good cocktails.

4

Peperone Huérfanos 1954; map pp.382–383. Excellent *empanadería* dishing out baked *empanadas* with myriad fillings, including scallops. Cheese and crab *empanada* CH$1400.

★ **Las Vacas Gordas** Cienfuegos 280 ☎ 2 26971066; map pp.382–383. Probably the best restaurant for carnivores in the city, with steaks grilled to perfection at very reasonable prices. Extremely popular, especially on weekends. Veal medallions with pancetta CH$7890. Closed Sun night.

DRINKING AND NIGHTLIFE

Santiago is not a 24-hour party town, and compared to other Latin capitals can seem rather tame. However, Thursdays, Fridays and Saturdays are lively, with crowds pouring into the streets and bars of the nightlife *zonas*.

DOWNTOWN

Café Escondido Pasaje Rosal 346; map p.385. If you want cheap beer and bar snacks in a less than raucous environment, this intimate bar is the perfect spot. Open until 2.30am. Closed Sun.

La Piojera Aillavilú 1030; map p.385. Carve your name into the wooden tables at this rough-and-ready bar with a loyal clientele, and knock back a *terremoto* (earthquake) – a powerful wine and ice-cream mix. Drinks CH$1800.

BELLAVISTA AND PROVIDENCIA

Altazor Antonia López de Bello 0189 ☎ 2 27323934; map p.386. Popular bar packed on weekends, often featuring live folk music and blues. Cover CH$1500.

Bar Constitución Constitución 67, near Patio Bellavista ☎ 2 22444569, ⓦ barconstitucion.cl; map p.386. A friendly international bar-cum-club with a dancefloor that fills up every Fri and Sat night to an eclectic choice of music. Free entry until 12.30am, and then CH$3000. Open Tues–Sat until 5am.

Boomerang Holley 2285; map pp.382–383. Lively Australian-run watering hole with nightly drinks specials, popular with foreign travellers and locals alike. Open until late Tues–Sat.

Bunker Bombero Núñez 159 ☎ 2 27371716; map p.386. Giant dancefloor with varied alternative music events. A devoted young following makes this one of the most popular places on the gay night scene. Cover CH$5000 on Fri, CH$6000 on Sat.

La Casa en el Aire Antonia López de Bello 125 ☎ 2 27356680, ⓦ lacasaenelaire.cl; map p.386. Inviting candlelit venue offering poetry reading, contemporary theatre performances, film screenings and folk music; check the website for listings.

Flannery's Geo Pub Encomenderos 83 ☎ 2 22336675, ⓦ flannerys.cl; map pp.382–383. Extremely popular with expats, this pub has authentic Irish charm and a welcoming staff. While the exotic cocktails are not their strong suit, it's

---

COFFEE WITH LEGS

In downtown Santiago you may encounter the strange phenomenon of **café con piernas**, or "coffee with legs" – cafés where besuited businessmen are served coffee by skimpily clad waitresses. *Café Caribe*, at Ahumada 120, and *Café Haiti*, at Ahumada 336, are both tamer examples of the genre. At the raunchier cafés, customers are offered more than just coffee.

---

a great spot for a beer and surprisingly tasty fajitas. Mon–Fri noon–2.30am, Sat 5.30pm–3am, Sun 5.30pm–12.30am.

Havana Salsa Dominica 142 ☎ 2 27371737, ⓦ havana salsa.cl; map pp.382–383. If you want to shake your hips to some salsa beats, this is the place. Cover and Cuban-style buffet dinner CH$9900. Fri & Sat until 4am.

Phone Box Pub Av Providencia 1652 locals 1 & 2 ☎ 2 22359972; map pp.382–383. Relaxed and lively pub, popular with expats, offering a wide selection of beers, including the delectable Kunstmann. Mon & Tues until 1am, Wed & Thurs until 2am, Fri & Sat until 3am; closed Sun.

BARRIO BRASIL

Blondie Alameda 2879 ⓦ blondie.cl; map pp.382–383. Large and popular four-floor dance club featuring techno, goth, indie and other musical styles (depending on the night), as well as occasional live music. Admission CH$3500.

Confitería Las Torres Alameda 1570 ☎ 2 26680751; map pp.382–383. Elegant, nineteenth-century building hosting spellbinding live tango shows on weekends to accompany the expertly cooked traditional Chilean dishes. Dishes CH$6900–10,000. Closed Sun.

PLAZA ÑUÑOA

La Batuta J. Washington 52 ⓦ batuta.cl; map pp.382–383. A thriving gem of Santiago nightlife, where Chilean and British rock music attract a dedicated following. Vodka and Red Bull CH$4000. Open Thurs–Sat 11pm–4am.

Ebano Jorge Washington 176 ☎ 2 24534665, ⓦ ebano cocinasoul.cl; map pp.382–383. Upmarket bar with smart wooden tables; staff make great cocktails and there is an excellent choice of wine. Mojito CH$3500. Mon–Fri 7pm–2am.

ENTERTAINMENT

Cine Arte Alameda Alameda 139, Metro Baquedano ⓦ centroartealameda.cl. An arts cinema showing independent and avant-garde films.

Cine Hoyts Moneda 835, Metro Santa Lucía ⓦ cinehoyts .cl. Multiplex cinema showing the latest releases; English-language films tend to be subtitled.

Teatro Municipal Agustinas 794, Metro Universidad de Chile ☎ 2 24638888, ⓦ municipal.cl. You can find the best of Chile's classical music inside this magnificent historical building. Special productions take place throughout the year.

SHOPPING

Artesanías de Chile Av Bellavista 0357, ⓦ artesanias dechile.cl. High-quality crafts from Chile's indigenous communities, including Aymará textiles, Mapuche silver-work and woodcarvings. There are also outlets in the La Moneda Cultural Centre (see p.382) and the Los Dominicos craft market. Mon–Sat 10am–2pm & 3–6pm.

Bookstore Av Providencia 1652, local 3b. Good selection of secondhand English-language books.

Centro de Exposición de Arte Indígena Alameda 499. Alongside Cerro Santa Lucía, this *feria artesanal* stocks some excellent Mapuche, Rapanui and Aymará crafts. Mon–Sat 10am–7pm.

Feria Artesanal Santa Lucía, Cerro Santa Lucía. Large crafts market stocking indigenous crafts, tie-dyed clothing and T-shirts featuring the Chilean flag. Mon–Sat 10am–7pm.

FeriaMix Ahumada 286. A large branch of the ubiquitous music store stocking a wide variety of Chilean music as well as international rock and pop. It also sells books and electronic goods. Mon–Fri 10am–9pm, Sat 10am–8pm.

Lapiz Lazuli House Bellavista 08, Barrio Bellavista ⓦ lapislazulihouse.cl. One of the better places to buy the expertly crafted lapis lazuli jewellery for which Chile is famous.

Patio Bellavista Between Constitución and Pío Nono, Barrio Bellavista ⓦ patiobellavista.cl. Open-air space with a concentration of gift shops selling high-quality crafts and clothing, postcards, jewellery and home-made honey. A bookshop by the Constitución entrance stocks a plethora of guidebooks and maps. Daily 11am–10pm.

Tatoo Av Los Leones 81 ☎ 2 22946008. Second branch in the Mall Sport at Av Las Condes 13451 (daily 10am–9pm). Adventure shop specializing in trekking and climbing gear as well as sleeping bags and backpacks. Mon–Fri 10.30am–8pm, Sat 10.30am–7pm.

La Vinoteca Manuel Montt 1452 ⓦ lavinoteca.cl. Great if you're looking for some of Chile's best wines to take home with you – the knowledgeable staff here can help locate some of the rarer vintages, and will even wrap up a case so that you can check it in at the airport.

DIRECTORY

Banks and exchange There are plenty of ATMs down-town, especially along Huérfanos, Agustinas, Bandera, Moneda and Av Alameda, as well as at the large bus termi-nals. There are several exchange houses on Agustinas, between Ahumada and Bandera, which give a reasonable rate on foreign currencies and travellers' cheques (Mon–Fri 9am–2pm & 4–6pm, Sat 9am–2pm).

Embassies and consulates Argentina, Miraflores 285 ☎ 2 25822500, ⓦ ehile.mrecic.gov.ar; Australia, Isidora Goyenechea 3621 ☎ 2 25503500, ⓦ chile.embassy.gov.au; Bolivia, Av Santa María 2796, Providencia ☎ 2 22328180, ⓦ consuladobolivia.cl; Brazil, Padre Alonso de Ovalle 1665 ☎ 2 28763400, ⓦ embajadadebrasil.cl; Canada, Nueva Tajamar 481, 12th floor ☎ 2 26523800, ⓦ canada international.gc.ca/chile-chili; New Zealand, Isidora Goyenechea 3000, 12th floor ☎ 2 26163000, ⓦ nzembassy .com/chile; Peru, Bucarest 162, Providencia ☎ 2 28731700, ⓦ conpersantiago.cl; South Africa, Av 11 de Septiembre 2353, 17th floor, Providencia ☎ 2 28200300, ⓦ embajada -sudafrica.cl; UK, Av El Bosque Norte 125 ☎ 2 23704100, ⓦ ukinchile.fco.gov.uk/en; US, Av Andrés Bello 2800 ☎ 2 2330 3000, ⓦ chile.usembassy.gov.

4

SANTIAGO TOUR OPERATORS

Attractions around Santiago include wineries, thermal baths, the outdoor enthusiast's paradise of the mountainous Cajón del Maipo valley and more.

La Bicicleta Verde Loreto 6, at Av Santa María, Bellavista ☎ 2 25709338, ⓦ labicicletaverde.com. See Santiago at a different pace with a range of bike tours in the city, and around nearby vineyards. Also arranges bike rental. Morning tour of Santiago's sights CH$18,000/person.

Fueguinos ☎ 2 27373251, ☎ 9 1624707, ⓦ fueguinos .cl. Full-day nature tours around Santiago; destinations include the Cajón del Maipo valley, Parque Nacional La Campana and the San Francisco glacier. CH$60,000/person for one-day hike, includes transportation, meals and entry to national parks. English and French spoken.

Monteagudo Aventura ☎ 2 23469069, ⓦ monte agudoaventura.cl. Experienced outfit running full-day horseriding and white-water rafting trips in the Cajón del Maipo, as well as treks to the San Francisco and Morado glaciers and night excursions to the Colina thermal baths. Full-day horseriding including an *asado* (barbecue) CH$80,000/person.

Rockside Expediciones Constantino 96 ☎ 2 27796366, ⓦ rockside.cl. Adrenaline-filled outdoor adventure, including rafting, kayaking, rock climbing and mountain biking in the Cajón del Maipo. Half-day rafting trip to Maipo River CH$17,500/person.

SKIING NEAR SANTIAGO

It's easy to arrange day-trips from Santiago to experience some world-class powder snow. The **ski season** lasts from mid-June to early October. All resorts rent ski equipment and clothing, and day passes cost CH$20,000–33,000. High in the Andes Mountains, 36km east of Santiago, three large **ski resorts** are clustered in the Tres Valles area: El Colorado, La Parva and Valle Nevado; all three can be accessed from Farellones, a village at the foot of Cerro Colorado (3333m). A fourth resort, Portillo, is set on the banks of the stunning Laguna del Inca on the Argentine border, a two-hour drive from Santiago.

OPERATORS

Ski Total Av Apoquindo 4900, local 40-46 🕿 2 22460156, 🖳 skitotal.cl. Operates daily departures to all four resorts, and is a good choice for renting equipment and clothing.

Ski Van 🕿 2 22192672, 🖳 skivan.cl. Daily departures to El Colorado, Valle Nevado and La Parva, from General Bustamante 10, just off Plaza Italia.

RESORTS

El Colorado 🖳 elcolorado.cl. The resort boasts 19 chairlifts and 21 runs, most of intermediate level, between elevations of 2430m and 3333m.

La Parva 🖳 laparva.cl. The Cerro Franciscano (3608m) and Cerro La Falsa Parva here offer thirty runs for skiers of all abilities, with some excellent long advanced runs, as well as extensive backcountry skiing and heli-skiing.

Portillo 🖳 skiportillo.com. Chile's most exclusive resort boasts 23 runs between altitudes of 2590m and 3322m that cater to intermediates and experts alike, along with ample backcountry terrain and heli-skiing opportunities.

Valle Nevado 🖳 vallenevado.com. With the best skiing conditions in Tres Valles and geared towards foreign visitors, this luxury resort has a good mixture of advanced and intermediate runs, as well as a snow-board park and half-pipe along with extraordinary terrain for heli-skiing.

Hospitals Clínica Las Condes, Lo Fontecilla 441 🕿 2 22104000; Clínica Universidad Católica, Marcoleta 367, downtown 🕿 2 26334122, Clínica Alemana, Av Vitacura 5951, Vitacura 🕿 2 22101111.

Internet There are plenty of internet cafés, and most youth hostels also offer free internet use. Try Netcenter, at Merced 615 (🖳 cafenetcenter.cl), or CyberOnline, Jose M. de la Barra 414, which offers freshly ground coffee while you surf.

Language schools Bridge Linguatec Language Center, at Los Leones 439, Providencia (🕿 2 22334356 or 🕿 +1 303 495 5963 in the US, 🖳 bridgechile.com), offers intensive immersion Spanish courses, group tutorials and private lessons. Instituto Chileno-Suizo de Idioma, at José Victorino Lastarria 93, 2nd floor (🕿 2 26385414, 🖳 chilenosuizo.tie.cl), combines Spanish language courses of varying intensity with homestays, city tours and an introduction to Chilean culture.

Laundry Try Lavandería Autoservicio, Monjitas 507, or Lavanderia Lolos, Moneda 2296, Barrio Brasil.

Pharmacies There are plenty of Farmacias Ahumada and Cruz Verde pharmacies all over Santiago; Farmacia Ahumada at Av Portugal 125 is open 24hr.

Post offices Correo Central, Plaza de Armas 559 (Mon–Fri 8am–7pm, Sat 9am–2pm). Other branches are at Moneda 1170, near Morandé; Local 503, Exposición 51 Paseo Estación; and Av 11 de Septiembre 2092.

Telephone centres There are numerous *centros de llamados* run either by Entel, whose largest branch is at Morandé, between Huérfanos and Compañía, or by Telefónica CTC Chile, located inside metro stations, such as Universidad de Chile and Moneda, and on the streets.

Valparaíso and Viña del Mar

Draped in a crescent shape around the Bahía de Valparaíso, the UNESCO World Heritage-listed city of **Valparaíso** is just 120km from Santiago. "Valpo" – as it's affectionately known – is Chile's principal port and naval base, and also perhaps the country's liveliest and most vibrant city. The **nightlife** and excellent seafood attract much of Santiago to its bars and restaurants at the weekend, as does the nearby beach resort of **Viña del Mar**. Viña's attractions are wide, white beaches surrounded by expensive high-rise apartments, casinos and pricey, touristy restaurants. It has none of the character that distinguishes Valparaíso – the good news is that since they're so close together, it's easy enough to stay in Valparaíso and visit Viña's beaches for the day.

VALPARAÍSO

Few travellers can fail to be inspired by the ramshackle beauty of **VALPARAÍSO**, whose mishmash patchwork of brightly coloured houses is built across a series of hills; steep stairways and the city's famous ascensores (elevators) link the hills to the port area. Still a major port today, the city came into its own during the California Gold Rush, and in the mid-nineteenth century was the main hub for ships crossing between the Atlantic and Pacific oceans. Valparaíso's narrow labyrinth of atmospheric alleyways offers glimpses of the city's decline from the grandeur of its former glories.

WHAT TO SEE AND DO

Valparaíso is effectively split into two halves: the hills (*cerros*), and the flat El Plan. Most restaurants and hostels can be found on **Cerro Concepción** and **Cerro Alegre**. Visitors usually spend their time here meandering along the winding passageways, and enjoying the spectacular views from the rickety *ascensores*. **El Plan**, which includes the busy port area, is home to an extensive nightlife quarter as well as the shopping and administrative districts, all linked by traffic-choked narrow streets.

The hills

Without a doubt, Valparaíso's biggest attraction is its **hills**. Few pastimes are as enjoyable as meandering up and down the area's winding narrow streets, or riding its antique funiculars (see box below). Visitors can stop to marvel at the impressive views of the city from a multitude of **miradores** (viewpoints), or duck into little shops and cafés to admire the colourful **murals** – a striking example of the city's bohemian culture. It is easy to see how Valparaíso has produced more writers, artists and poets than any other Chilean city.

Cerro Concepción and **Cerro Alegre** are the best known of the hills, with the highest concentration of churches and museums, but they are by no means the only gems. Nearby **Cerro Panteón**, reached by a network of winding paths, is home to three colourful cemeteries, the most interesting of which is the **Cementerio de Disidentes**, resting place of non-Catholic European immigrants. Nearby **Cerro Cárcel** is the site of a former prison, now decorated with colourful graffiti and a hangout for artists and thespians. Its **Parque Cultural** (Mon–Fri 9am–7pm, Sat & Sun 11am–7pm; ☎322 258567) sometimes hosts outdoor theatre performances.

La Sebastiana

La Sebastiana, Ferrari 692, off Alemania (Tues–Sun: Jan & Feb 10.30am–6.50pm; March–Dec 10.10am–6pm; CH$3500; ☎322 256606, ⓦfundacionneruda.org),

---

LOS ASCENSORES DE VALPARAÍSO

Once numbering thirty-three and now down to about a dozen, Valparaíso's **ascensores**, or funiculars, were built between 1883 and 1916. As well as being one of the city's enduring attractions, they remain an essential way of getting about. After years of neglect, many are undergoing much needed renovation so some may be closed. Most run daily from 7am to 11pm and cost between CH$100 and CH$300 per journey.

Ascensor Polanco The only *ascensor* that is an actual elevator, Polanco is reached through a long underground tunnel from Calle Simpson, off Avenida Argentina. It rises vertically through the yellow tower to a *mirador* offering excellent views of the port.

Ascensor Concepción (also known as Ascensor Turri). The city's oldest funicular, built in 1883 and originally steam-powered, is one of the most popular. It climbs up to Paseo Gervasoni on Cerro Concepción,

a delightful residential area and the start of many walking tours that cover Cerro Alegre as well. The lower entrance is opposite the Relój Turri clock tower.

Ascensor Artillería Extremely popular with visitors, this funicular rivals Ascensor Barón for views. It runs from Plaza Aduana up to Cerro Playa Ancha, and offers a beautiful panoramic view of the city and coastline, with Viña del Mar in the distance. The Museo Naval y Marítimo (see p.396) is nearby.

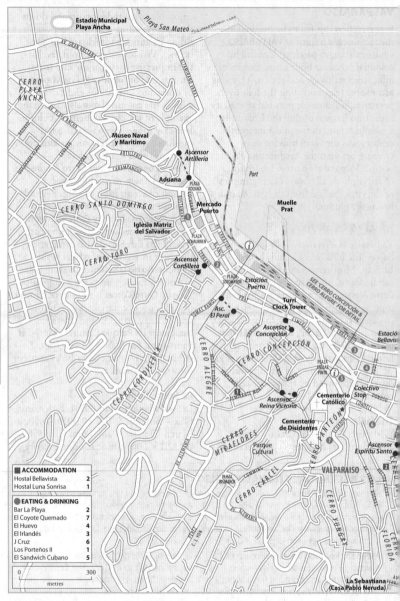

ACCOMMODATION

Hostal Bellavista	2
Hostal Luna Sonrisa	1

EATING & DRINKING

Bar La Playa	2
El Coyote Quemado	7
El Huevo	4
El Irlandés	3
J Cruz	6
Los Porteños II	1
El Sandwich Cubano	5

was the least lived-in of the poet **Pablo Neruda**'s three residences, but it offers incredibly picturesque views of the city and the interior design reflects the poet's quirky tastes. Like his other homes, the five-storey house has a nautical theme and is crammed with random knick-knacks that Neruda picked up on his travels; unlike the others, you can explore this one without a guide. The vista from his bedroom window is nothing short of spectacular. To get here, take a short ride on *colectivo* #39 from Plaza Ecuador or bus #612 from Avenida Argentina.

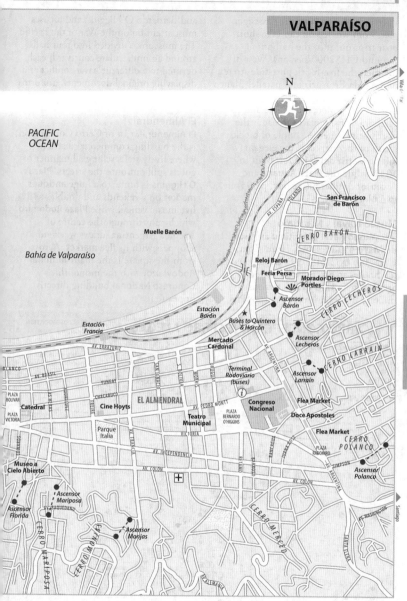

VALPARAÍSO

N

PACIFIC OCEAN

Bahía de Valparaíso

Muelle Barón

San Francisco de Barón

CERRO BARÓN

AV. ESPAÑA

Reloj Barón

Feria Persa

Morador Diego Portles

Ascensor Barón

CERRO LECHEROS

Estación Barón

Estación Francia

Buses to Quintero & Horcón

Ascensor Lecheros

AV. ERRAZURIZ

Mercado Cardonal

Ascensor Larraín

CERRO LARRAÍN

AV. BRASIL

YUNGAY

CHACABUCO

Terminal Rodoviario (buses)

AV. ARGENTINA

PLAZA BOLIVAR

BLANCO

Catedral

Cine Hoyts

EL ALMENDRAL

AV. PEDRO MONTT

Congreso Nacional

Flea Market

Doce Apostoles

PLAZA VICTORIA

Teatro Municipal

PLAZA BERNARDO O'HIGGINS

Flea Market

CERRO POLANCO

Parque Italia

VICTORIA

PLAZA RADOAIRO

Ascensor Polanco

Museo a Cielo Abierto

AV. INDEPENDENCIA

AV. COLON

AV. SIMPSON

Ascensor Mariposa

Ascensor Florida

AV. BAQUEDANO

Ascensor Monjas

CERRO MARIPOSA

CERRO MONJAS

CERRO MERCEDO

AV. COLON

AV. WASHINGTON

AV. ALEMANIA

4

Viña del Mar ▶

Santiago ▶

Barrio Puerto

El Plan consists of long east–west streets, crossed by shorter north–south streets leading into the hills, and is divided into two halves, with **Barrio Puerto** located northwest of Cerro Concepción. Its centrepiece, the pedestrianized **Plaza Sotomayor**, is lined with a mixture of modern concrete blocks and grand early twentieth-century buildings, and is home to the **Primera Zona Naval**, the country's naval headquarters. At the port end of the plaza, near the Metrotrén Estación

Puerto, is **Muelle Prat**, the passenger pier, from where you can take short boat trips out into the harbour (around CH$2000/person). West of the pier, the five-block port-side stretch of Avenida Errázuriz and parallel Blanco make up Valparaíso's principal nightlife district, with **Mercado Puerto** and its plethora of fishy places to eat at the northwest corner. A couple of blocks south of the market is the elegant **Iglesia Matriz del Salvador**, built in 1842, while the **Plaza Aduana** and Ascensor Artillería (see box, p.393) lie two blocks west.

Museo Naval y Marítimo

The **Museo Naval y Marítimo** at Paseo 21 de Mayo 45 (Tues–Sun 10am–5pm; CH$700; ☎32 2437018, ⓦmuseonaval.cl) houses an extensive collection of artefacts related to Chile's famous military figures, including Arturo Prat and Bernardo O'Higgins, and focuses most attention on the War of the Pacific. The museum is divided into four halls around an immaculate courtyard, each devoted to a different naval conflict and displaying original documents, uniforms and medals.

El Almendral

El Almendral, east of Cerro Concepción, is the bustling commercial district, where lively stalls selling all manner of goods spill out onto the streets. **Plaza O'Higgins** is home to a huge **antiques market** on weekends and doubles as a live music venue, while **Plaza Rodomiro**, which runs through the centre of Avenida Argentina, draws weekend shoppers with its **flea market**. Across from the square is the main **Terminal Rodoviario**, with the monolithic **Congreso National** building directly opposite it.

CERRO CONCEPCIÓN & CERRO ALEGRE

EATING, DRINKING & NIGHTLIFE

Alegretto	3
Café Con Letras	5
El Desayunador	6
Destajo	4
Pasta e Vino	2
Valparaíso Eterno	1

ACCOMMODATION

Álecon Fine Hostel	3
Casa Aventura	5
Hostel Casa Valparaíso	2
La Maison du Filou	1
Residencia en el Cerro	4

Train Station

ERRÁZURIZ

GÓMEZ CARREÑO

MARTÍNEZ

MELGAREJO

BLANCO

BLANCO

ESMERALDA

Turri Clock Tower

PLAZA SOTOMAYOR

COCHRANE

URRIOLA

CLAVE

PRAT

Ascensor Concepción

PASEO GERVASONI

PAPUDO

CERRO CONCEPCIÓN

PASEO ATKINSON

PLAZA ANÍBAL PINTO

Lutheran Church

CONCEPCIÓN

ABTAO

Lavandería Jerasalem

CUMMING

Ascensor El Peral

PASEO YUGOSLAVO

URRIOLA

TEMPLEMAN

PASAJE GÁLVEZ

PILCOMAYO

St Paul's Anglican Church

ALMIRANTE MONTT

Ascensor Reina Victoria

CERRO ALEGRE

MONTE ALEGRE

LEIGHTON

Pasaje Templeman

Pasaje Bavestrello

ABTAO

ALMTE MONTT

PASEO DIMALOW

ELÍAS

MIRAMAR

ALEGRE

– – – Walking Tour

0   100
metres

ARRIVAL AND DEPARTURE

By bus Long-distance buses arrive at the Terminal Rodoviario, Pedro Montt 2800 (☎ 32 2939695), a 20min walk from Cerro Alegre and Cerro Concepción. There are snack shops, an ATM and luggage storage inside.
Destinations Arica (5 daily; 24hr); Iquique (5 daily; 24hr); Isla Negra (every 30min; 1hr 30min); La Serena (5 daily; 7hr); Puerto Montt (6 daily; 16hr); Santiago (every 10min; 1hr 45min).

By train Frequent trains from Viña del Mar stop at the stations along the waterfront. Barón is the closest station to Terminal Rodoviario, while Bellavista and Puerto are the handiest for Cerro Alegre and Cerro Concepción.

INFORMATION

Tourist information There are tourist information kiosks on Muelle Prat and in the bus terminal (daily 10am–2pm & 3.30–5.30pm). The municipal tourism office is at Condell 1490, first floor (Mon–Fri 8.30am–2pm & 3.30–5.30pm; ☎ 32 2939262, ⓦ ciudaddevalparaiso .cl). Fundación Valparaíso, Héctor Calvo Cofre 205, Cerro Bellavista (☎ 32 2593156, ⓦ fundacionvalparaiso.cl), runs various restoration projects around the city; its "Bicentennial Heritage Trail" guide is full of curious trivia about the city.

GETTING AROUND

By bus, colectivo and micro Frequent transport of all sorts runs to and from Viña del Mar; look for "Viña" displayed in the window. In El Plan, buses labelled "Aduana" run west towards the centre along Pedro Montt while "P. Montt" buses run back to the bus station; one-way fares range between CH$230 and CH$400.

By metrotrén Fast, frequent, air-conditioned commuter trains run to Viña del Mar and beyond from the stations along the harbour (Mon–Fri every 12min, 6.15am–11pm; Sat every 12min, 7.30am–11pm; Sun every 18min, 8am–11pm; ⓦ merval.cl); you have to make a one-off purchase of a swipe card (CH$1200) on top of the fares.

By tram Antique German trams offer limited but cheap service around El Plan; just look for the rails (CH$250).

ACCOMMODATION

Álecon Fine Hostel Abtao 684, Cerro Concepción ☎ 9 76823055, ⓦ alecon.cl. Wonderfully friendly family-run guesthouse with airy single rooms, doubles, triples and quads; excellent breakfast and internet are included and the hostel offers a free Spanish language course to long-term guests. Doubles CH$25,000

Hostal Bellavista Pasaje Santa Lucía 5, Subida Ferrari, Cerro Bellavista ☎ 32 2121544, ⓦ arthostalbellavista.cl. Arty hostel covered with murals and rooms named after painters. Internet and breakfast included. To reach it, walk up Av Ferrari for about 300m and take the stairs going up

to your right, or take Ascensor Espíritu Santo and walk downhill for 200m. Doubles CH$25,000

Casa Aventura Pasaje Gálvez 11, Cerro Alegre ☎ 32 2755963, ⓦ casaventura.cl. Hostel with friendly and knowledgeable staff, spotless dorms, a sunny lounge, kitchen privileges and internet; popular with backpackers. Dorms CH$9000, doubles CH$22,000

Hostel Casa Valparaíso Pasaje Gálvez 173, Cerro Alegre ☎ 32 3194072, ⓦ casavalparaisohostel.blogspot.com. Cheerful, family-run hostel with homely communal spaces, wi-fi and a hearty breakfast included. Dorms CH$7000

Hostal Luna Sonrisa Templeman 833, Cerro Alegre ☎ 32 2734117, ⓦ lunasonrisa.cl. Professional hostel run by *Footprint* guide author; fully equipped kitchen, tranquil lounge with book exchange and large rooms with tall ceilings in a central location make it a top choice. Good breakfast included. Dorms CH$9000, doubles CH$29,500

La Maison du Filou Papudo 579, Cerro Concepción ☎ 32 2124681, ⓦ lamaisondufilou.overblog.com. Colourful double and twin rooms with high ceilings and wonderful views; kitchen privileges, laundry service, book exchange, wi-fi and breakfast included. French and a smattering of English spoken. Doubles CH$20,000

Residencia en el Cerro Pasaje Pierre Loti 51, Cerro Concepción ☎ 32 2495298, ⓦ residenciaenelcerro.cl. Large, wonderfully friendly family-run place, with a good breakfast, internet and a number of cats to keep you company. Dorms CH$9000, doubles CH$24,000

EATING

Alegretto Pilcomayo 529, Cerro Concepción. Complete with an entertaining vintage jukebox, this Italian spot serves good pizza and excellent gnocchi. Medium pizza CH$6400.

Café Con Letras Almirante Montt 316, Cerro Alegre. A popular artsy café with quirky decor and a book exchange; serves a good range of real coffee, too. Espresso CH$1500.

El Desayunador Almirante Montt 399, Cerro Alegre. This informal place offers generous servings of all-day breakfast from 8.30am onwards. *Energetico* breakfast CH$4550.

Destajo Cumming 55. Takeaway offering excellent *empanadas* with myriad meat, fish and vegetable fillings – perfect for a late-night snack. Open all evening except Sun. *Empanada* CH$750–1350.

4

Los Porteños II Cochrane 102. Specializing in fresh fish and seafood, this cheerful option is an extension of the equally popular *Los Porteños* across the street. *Pastel de jaiba* (crab pie) CH$5950.

El Sandwich Cubano O'Higgins 1221. Small and very popular lunchtime stop serving excellent-value plates of tasty *ropa vieja* (beef dish) with *moros y cristianos* (rice and beans) for CH$2000.

DRINKING, NIGHTLIFE AND ENTERTAINMENT

Bar La Playa Serrano 567 ☎ 32 2259426. This historic bar with a wood-panelled interior is an excellent spot for a quiet beer in the afternoon, and at night transforms into a buzzing dance spot. Thurs 10am–2am, Fri & Sat 10am–5am.

Cine Hoyts Pedro Montt 2111 ⊛ cinehoyts.cl. A five-screen cinema showing the latest blockbuster releases.

El Coyote Quemado Subida Ecuador 144 ☎ 32 2493478. Dark two-tiered bar playing heavy rock. Packed with a younger crowd. Daily 7pm–4am.

El Huevo Blanco 1386, ⊛ elhuevo.cl. Huge five-level nightclub with different music on each one, packing a student crowd. Entry CH$3000–5000. Mon–Sat from 9pm.

El Irlandés Blanco 1279 ☎ 32 2543592, ⊛ elirlandes.cl. A fairly raucous Irish pub run by an actual Irishman, and offering a large selection of beers. Chilean stout Szot CH$2900. Daily 5pm–4am.

J Cruz Condell 1466 ☎ 322 211225. Along a graffiti-covered passageway lies a somewhat legendary bar with glass cabinets filled with all kinds of strange memorabilia. It's an excellent place to enjoy a glass of wine and share a greasy pile of *chorrillana* (meat with fries, onion and fried egg). Mon–Sat noon–late.

Valparaíso Eterno Señoret 150, 2nd floor. Besides offering reasonably priced meals and beers, this joint has heaps of personality; some Sat nights a singer-songwriter belts out Communist tunes. Fri & Sat 9.30pm–4am.

DIRECTORY

Banks and exchange Prat has a number of banks, ATMs and cambios; Banco de Chile, at Prat 698, also has an ATM and there is a cambio at Plaza Sotomayor 11 which offers a decent exchange rate (Mon–Fri 9am–6pm Sat 10am–1pm).

Hospital Hospital Carlos van Buren, San Ignacio 725, has modern facilities (☎ 32 2364000).

Internet There are several internet cafés on Cerro Concepción and Cerro Alegre; most hostels have access as well.

Language courses Interactive Spanish School, C Elias 571, Cerro Cárcel ☎ 9 2864973, ☎ 32 2735351, ⊛ interactive -spanish.cl. Spanish lessons of varying intensity offered with or without homestay options.

Laundry Lavanderia Jerusalem, Condell 1176, Local 3 ☎ 32 2219216. Efficient launderette which washes by the kilo. Five kilos wash and dry CH$4500.

Post office Prat 856 (Mon–Fri 9am–6pm, Sat 10am–1pm).

VIÑA DEL MAR

Though only fifteen minutes from Valparaíso by public transport, **VIÑA DEL MAR** could hardly be more different from its grittier neighbour. Purpose-built in the late nineteenth century as a weekend getaway for wealthy Santiago and Valparaíso residents, it draws thousands of local holidaymakers during the summer and on weekends. Viña makes for an enjoyable day-trip to the beach, and is especially worth a visit during the week-long **Festival de la Canción**, held in the second or third week of February, which draws top Latino and international artists. The city also hosts spectacular Año Nuevo (New Year) celebrations, drawing thousands of Chileans. Other festivals include the two-week-long **Feria del Libro** (Jan), which attracts important literary figures and hosts live readings, and the acclaimed **Festival Cine Viña del Mar** film festival (Oct or Nov; ⊛ cinevina.cl).

WHAT TO SEE AND DO

The city is split in two by the broad, none-too-clean **Marga Marga** estuary, with a largely residential area to the south and most of the beaches in the northern half. **Avenida San Martín**, parallel to the beach, and the side streets off it feature numerous dining and nightlife options. At the heart of Viña lies the large, shady **Plaza Vergara**, a popular spot with the occasional busker or *capoeira* demonstration and horse-drawn carriages parked around it. Several blocks of **Avenida Valparaíso**, Viña's main thoroughfare, which runs from the square's southwest corner, have been pleasantly pedestrianized, with a number of shops and places to eat.

The beaches

Playa Caleta Abarca lies in a sandy cove south of **Castillo Wulff**, an impressive castle-like structure built on a rocky

VIÑA DEL MAR

■ ACCOMMODATION

Che Lagarto Hostel	3
Jaguar Hostel	1
Kalagen Hostel	2
My Father's House	4

■ EATING

Anayak	7
Amura Cafe	5
Fellini	6
El Gaucho	2
Jerusalem	8
Only Sushi	1

■ DRINKING & NIGHTLIFE

Café Journal	9
Stingray	4
Tutix	3

0 ———— 250
metres

PACIFIC OCEAN

4

outcrop at the mouth of the estuary by a Valparaíso businessman in 1906. Located next to the large **Reloj de Flores** ("flower clock"), the beach draws a lively picnicking crowd on weekends. Just north of the estuary, Avenida Perú runs parallel to the sea, past the brash **Casino Viña del Mar**. Beyond you will find an almost unbroken line of sandy beaches, backed by high-rise apartment buildings, stretching all the way to the smaller resort of **Reñaca**, which itself has more good beaches and nightlife.

Quinta Vergara

The one spot besides the beaches where you might want to spend some time in Viña del Mar is the lovely **Quinta Vergara** park (daily 7am–7pm), where the manicured grounds are home to a vast array of exotic imported plants. It is located a couple of blocks south of Plaza Vergara behind the Metrotrén Estación Viña, with the futuristic-looking **Anfiteatro**, home to the annual music festival, as its centrepiece.

ARRIVAL AND INFORMATION

By bus Long-distance buses pull up at Terminal Rodoviario (☎ 32 2752000) at Av Valparaíso 1055; it has a tourist information booth and an ATM.

Destinations Arica (5 daily; 24hr); Iquique (5 daily; 24hr); La Serena (5 daily; 7hr); Osorno (6 daily; 14hr); Puerto Montt (6 daily; 16hr); Santiago (about 20 daily; 1hr 45min).

By metrotrén The commuter train from Valparaíso stops at Estación Miramar, Estación Viña del Mar and Estación Hospital along Alvares; Miramar is the closest station to the beaches. You need to buy a metro card (CH$1200).

Tourist information The main tourist office is at Arlegui 715 (Mon–Fri 9am–2pm & 3–7pm, Sat & Sun 10am–2pm & 3–6pm; ☎ 32 2185709, ⓦ visitevinadelmar.cl). Staff are helpful and can provide maps, and advise on accommodation and camping options.

ACCOMMODATION

Che Lagarto Hostel Diego Portales 131 ☎ 32 2625759, ⓦ chelagarto.com. Clean dorms, a pleasant garden, kitchen use, communal lounge, free internet and wi-fi are all pluses at this hotel – but it attracts a young backpacker crowd and can get noisy. Dorms CH$6200, doubles CH$26,000

Jaguar Hostel Pasaje Massot 12, small street off 2 Poniente, between 4 Norte and 5 Norte ☎ 9 97279219, ⓔ residenciaeljaguar@gmail.com. Elegant house in a quiet neighbourhood just five blocks from the beach. Dorms CH$12000, doubles CH$35000

Kalagen Hostel Av Valparaíso 618 ☎ 32 2991669, ⓦ kalagenhostel.com. Smart, large and lively hostel on Viña's main shopping drag, with spacious communal areas, wi-fi, internet and organized tours. Expect parties. Dorms CH$9900, doubles CH$37,000

My Father's House Gregorio Marañón 1210 ☎ 32 2616136, ⓦ myfathershouse.cl. Spacious, quiet single, double and triple rooms, swimming pool, internet and gracious owners. The only drawback is that it's about 2km from the centre of town; catch colectivo #31, #82 or #131. Doubles CH$28,000

EATING

Amura Cafe Av Peru, off Plaza Colombia. Simple café with seating outside offering very good-value lunch deals. Sandwich, cake and coffee CH$4500.

Anayak Quinta 134. A good, unpretentious spot for cake, light snacks and real coffee. Large coffee CH$1900.

Fellini 3 Norte 88 ☎ 32 2975742. Bustling Italian serving up exquisite pasta dishes in an intimate setting with superb presentation and service. Worth booking ahead. Mains CH$8000–9500.

El Gaucho San Martín 435 ☎ 32 2693502. The ideal place to satisfy your carnivorous cravings, this Argentine-style steakhouse doesn't come cheap but serves succulent steaks, chorizo and sweetbreads, among other offerings. Steak CH$7900.

Jerusalem Quinta 259. Tasty Middle Eastern cuisine is dispensed from this tiny food counter; the falafel is excellent (CH$2490).

Only Sushi San Martín 560. This simple sushi bar offers reasonable Japanese cuisine at affordable prices, and offers delivery across town. Eighteen-piece tabla CH$5500.

DRINKING, NIGHTLIFE AND ENTERTAINMENT

Café Journal Agua Santa 2 ☎ 32 2666654, ⓦ cafejournal .cl. Thriving university student haunt, complete with pub grub and regular live music. Mon–Thurs 10am–4am, Fri & Sat 10am–5am, Sun 7pm–4am.

Cinemark 15 Norte 961, Local 224. Multiplex cinema showing the latest releases.

Stingray 5 Norte, between 4 Poniente and 5 Poniente. With space to drink, and a dancefloor, this is the latest place to attract the weekend, party-going crowds. Entry CH$2000–3500.

Tutix 6 Poniente, corner with 5 Norte, next to Starbucks. White leather sofas and wooden tables adorn the bar area; the dancefloor gets heaving later on. Electronic dance music dominates. From 9pm until late.

DIRECTORY

Banks and exchange Numerous banks, most with ATMs and cambios, are found along Av Arlegui.

Hospital Hospital Gustavo Fricke is on Álvarez 1532, at Simón Bolívar (☎ 32 2675067); for emergencies call ☎ 32 2652328.

Internet access and telephone centre There are several internet cafés and telephone centres along Valparaíso.

Post office Plaza La Torre 32, just off the main square (Mon–Fri 9am–7pm Sat 10am–1pm).

ISLA NEGRA

The seaside village of **ISLA NEGRA** (which, incidentally, is not an island), about 80km south of Valparaíso, was the site of Pablo Neruda's favourite and most permanent home. The **Casa Museo Pablo Neruda**, at Calle Poeta Neruda s/n (Tues–Sun: Jan & Feb 10am–8pm; March–Dec 10am–6pm; CH$3500 including tour in English; students CH$1500, reservations essential in summer; ☎ 35 461284, ⓦ fundacionneruda.org), lies down a wooded trail by the sea, a short walk from the main road. Larger than his other two homes, Isla Negra is fascinating for the sheer amount of **exotic objects** that

Neruda accumulated here, and the degree of thought that went into every aspect of the design – from the arrangement of wooden ships' figureheads in the living room, to the positioning of blue glass bottles along the seaward side of the house. The poet's exotic collection of objects includes African wooden carvings, ships in bottles, a gigantic *moai kavakava* statue from Easter Island (see p.479) and an amazing array of seashells, housed in a purpose-built room that Neruda designed but never completed. A strong nautical theme runs throughout; there is even a small boat out on the terrace so that the poet could be "a sailor on land".

ARRIVAL AND DEPARTURE

By bus Pullman Peñuelas run from Valparaíso to San Antonio (every 40min: 6.35am–10pm; 1hr 40min); ask to be dropped off in Isla Negra. To return to Valparaíso, wait at the bus stop on the other side of the road, and buy your ticket on the bus. Pullman buses also pass by Isla Negra direct from Santiago.

Norte Chico

Dominated by dry scrubland and sparse vegetation, the **Norte Chico** region, which stretches roughly from the northern tip of Santiago to the southern reaches of the Atacama, might seem unremarkable from a bus window. Visitors are, however, drawn here for its **stargazing**, long sandy beaches, and trips to its far-flung national parks. The biggest population centre is the relaxed seaside town of **La Serena** with its bustling market and colonial-style architecture, while the fertile **Elqui Valley**, which once inspired Nobel-Prize-winning poet Gabriela Mistral, is now the focal point for the country's favourite tipple, pisco. The islands of **Damas** and **Choros** brim over with seals, penguins and cormorants. Further north, the mining town of **Copiapó**, currently undergoing one of its regular copper-induced booms, is the jumping-off point for the stunning kaleidoscopic landscapes of **Parque Nacional Nevado de Tres Cruces**, and **Parque Nacional Pan de Azúcar**. Horse-riding, trekking and kayaking are all

attractions which are likely to keep tourists in this region longer than they expected.

LA SERENA

LA SERENA, 474km north of Santiago, is considered one of Chile's prime **beach resorts**, though its charms also include an impressive number of churches and several worthwhile museums. It is also an excellent base for exploring the surrounding countryside. The city was founded in 1544, and during the following century it was the target of multiple raids by the French and English, including the pirate Francis Drake.

Downtown La Serena

With a tranquil vibe to its central streets, La Serena is an easy place to wander around on foot. Exploring its peaceful churches is a good way to get to know the town. The largest church is the Neoclassical **Iglesia Catedral**, at the corner of Los Carrera and Cordovez, off the Plaza de Armas, which has a beautiful, marble-decorated interior. **Iglesia de San Francisco**, Balmaceda 640, was the first church to be built out of stone, and **Iglesia Santo Domingo**, Cordovez s/n, dates back to 1673.

The **Casa Gabriel González Videla**, Matta 495, on the west side of the Plaza de Armas (Mon–Fri 10am–6pm, Sat 10am–1pm; CH$600), is well worth a visit. Originally the home of former president González Videla, who was born in the town, it is now a museum housing an impressive collection of fine art and contemporary painting. About two blocks west from the square, the tranquil and beautifully sculpted Japanese-style **Jardín El Corazón** (daily 10am–6pm; CH$1000) is the perfect place to while away a sunny afternoon.

At the junction of Cienfuegos with Cordovez, the recently renovated **Museo Arqueológico** (Tues–Fri 9.30am–5.50pm, Sat 10am–1pm & 4–7pm, Sun 10am–1pm; CH$600, Sun free, ticket also valid for Casa Gabriel Gonzáles Videla) displays elaborate Diaguita ceramics, as well as a 2.5m *moai* statue from Easter Island and lapis lazuli jewellery.

4

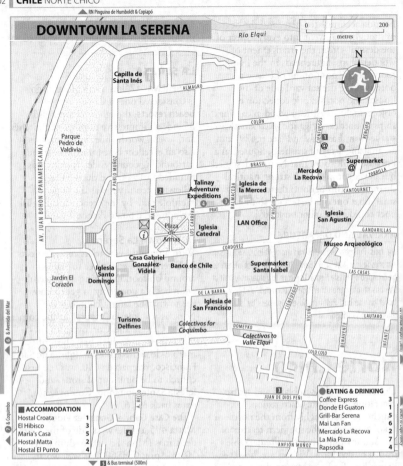

DOWNTOWN LA SERENA

Río Elqui

RN Pinguino de Humboldt & Copiapó

Capilla de Santa Inés

ALMAGRO

COLÓN

Parque Pedro de Valdivia

BRASIL

Mercado La Recova

Supermarket

ZORRILLA

CANTOURNET

Talinay Adventure Expeditions

Iglesia de la Merced

PRAT

LAN Office

Iglesia San Agustín

GANDARILLAS

Plaza de Armas

Iglesia Catedral

Museo Arqueológico

CORDOVEZ

LAS CASAS

Casa Gabriel González-Videla

Banco de Chile

Supermarket Santa Isabel

Jardín El Corazón

Iglesia Santo Domingo

DE LA BARRA

LAUTARO

Iglesia de San Francisco

Turismo Delfines

Colectivos for Coquimbo

DOMEYKO

Colectivos to Valle Elqui

COLO COLO

AV. FRANCISCO DE AGUIRRE

JUAN DE DIOS PEÑI

● **EATING & DRINKING**
Coffee Express	3
Donde El Guaton	1
Grill-Bar Serena	5
Mai Lan Fan	6
Mercado La Recova	2
La Mia Pizza	7
Rapsodia	4

■ **ACCOMMODATION**
Hostal Croata	1
El Hibisco	3
Maria's Casa	5
Hostal Matta	2
Hostal El Punto	4

ANFIÓN MUÑOZ

& Bus terminal (500m)

& Avenida del Mar

& Coquimbo

The beaches

While reasonably crowded in the summer, the **beaches** are quiet for the rest of the year. The nearest beach area is a half-hour walk west from the city centre from Jardín El Corazón along Francisco de Aguirre.

Between La Serena and the town of Coquimbo, a **cycle lane** runs beside a dozen or so wide, sandy beaches lined with pricey condominiums, hotels and restaurants – an easy and enjoyable day-trip. **Bikes** are available for rent in the city centre at Vicente Zorilla 990 (☏51 227939; $6,000/4hr). Most of the beaches are suitable for swimming and windsurfing, although Playa Cuatro Esquinas is known to have strong rip currents.

ARRIVAL AND INFORMATION

By plane Aeropuerto La Florida is 5km east of town along Ruta 41; catch a taxi or *micro* to the centre (CH$2000–2500).
Destinations Antofagasta (3–4 daily; 1hr 25min); Santiago (4–5 daily; 1hr 5min).

By bus The main bus terminal is located on corner Amunátegui, at Av El Santo, a 20min walk south of the centre. Destinations Via Elqui serves: Pisco Elqui (6 daily; 2hr) and Vicuña (8 daily; 1hr); 24hr Elqui Valley pass costs CH$4500. Other destinations: Antofagasta (8 daily; 13hr); Arica (7 daily; 23hr); Copiapó (8 daily; 5hr); Iquique (7 daily; 19hr); San Pedro de Atacama (1 direct Tur Bus overnight; 17hr); Santiago (7hr; 8 daily); Valparaíso (6 daily; 6hr 30min).

By colectivo Coquimbo (frequent daily departures from Av Francisco de Aguirre, between Los Carrera and Balmaceda; CH$700, 20min); Elqui Valley (several departures daily from Domeyko in the centre; CH$1700, 1hr).

Tourist information Sernatur, Matta 461, Plaza de Armas (Mon–Fri 9am–6.30pm, Sat 10am–2pm; summer daily 9am–9pm; ☎ 51 2225199, ⊛ turismoregiondecoquimbo .cl). Conaf has an office at Regimiento Arica 901, Coquimbo (☎ 51 2230437).

ACCOMMODATION

Hostal Croata Cienfuegos 248 ☎ 51 2224997, ⊛ hostal croata.cl. Cosy rooms, some en suite, all with internet, breakfast and cable TV, in a warm setting. Central location; bike rental available for CH$5000/day for guests. Doubles CH$31,250

El Hibisco Juan de Dios Peñí 636 ☎ 51 2211407, ⊜ hostal elhibisco@hotmail.com. Guesthouse with a relaxed family atmosphere and wooden-floored rooms, kitchen access, laundry service and good breakfast; excursions organized. Dorms CH$8000, doubles CH$20,000

Maria's Casa Las Rojas 18 ☎ 51 2229282 or ☎ 8 2189984, ⊛ hostalmariacasa.cl. Small guesthouse with an effusive hostess, kitchen access, free internet, breakfast and a relaxing garden; popular with backpackers. A 3min walk from the main bus station – good for late arrivals. Dorms CH$9000, doubles CH$18,000

Hostal Matta Matta 234 ☎ 51 2210014, ⊛ hostalmatta .cl. Large and airy family-run house with comfortable rooms around a patio. Some rooms are windowless; includes library, cable TV and grill. Tours are organized too. Breakfast CH$1500 extra. Doubles CH$24,000

★ **Hostal El Punto** Andres Bello 979 ☎ 51 2228474, ⊛ hostalelpunto.cl. German-run hostel with friendly and knowledgeable staff, daily excursions, an on-site café, wi-fi in the courtyard, laundry service and spotless rooms; popular with travellers of all ages. Call ahead if arriving later than 10pm. Dorms CH$8500, doubles CH$26,000

EATING AND DRINKING

The city's main places to eat are along Calle Prat. Coquimbo, however, is livelier for drinking and nightlife.

Coffee Express Balmaceda, at Prat. A large, popular spot for coffees and sandwiches. Coffee and cake CH$2790.

Donde El Guaton Brasil 750. Popular *parilla* serving excellent grilled meat. *Parillada* for two CH$10,800.

Grill-Bar Serena Eduardo de la Barra 325. For excellent and reasonably priced seafood dishes, look no further. Lunchtime specials CH$4000.

Mai Lan Fan Av Francisco de Aguirre 0109, about three blocks west of the Parque Jardín del Corazón. This restaurant has a plush interior, serving generous portions of well-prepared Chinese food; noodle dishes are particularly good (CH$6000).

Mercado La Recova Though touristy, the upstairs eateries serve excellent seafood *empanadas*, cheap fish dishes and *cazuela*. Try *3 As* restaurant for superb fish. *Corvina* (sea bass) CH$4500.

La Mia Pizza Av del Mar 2100. Seafront pizzeria that offers excellent fish dishes as well as large portions of tasty pizza. Pizzas from CH$5000.

Rapsodia Prat 470 local 19. Dine *alfresco* on expertly prepared meat and fish dishes in one of La Serena's traditional courtyards. Set lunch CH$4000. Closed Sun.

COQUIMBO

A fifteen-minute *colectivo* ride south from La Serena lies its rougher, livelier twin: **Coquimbo**, the region's main port. The beautifully restored historical district of **Barrio Inglés** comprises several lively plazas, and has a far more

---

STARGAZING IN CHILE

With an average of 360 cloudless nights per year, northern Chile has some of the clearest skies in the world, so it's little wonder that it's home to some of the world's most powerful telescopes. The larger observatories allow public visits free of charge during the day, allowing you to view the equipment, though not to use it. There are an ever-increasing number of small centres offering nocturnal stargazing facilities expressly for tourists, though the best set up for visits are **Cerro Mamalluca** (see p.405) and Cerro Collowara in the Elqui Valley, and **Cielo Austral** (see box, p.413) near San Pedro de Atacama.

The following places are the best of the big Elqui observatories; there is no public transport other than organized tours and you need to reserve in advance.

OBSERVATORIES

Cerro Paranal ☎ 55 435335; ⊛ eso.org. 130km south of Antofagasta, the observatory sports four VLTs (Very Large Telescopes), each with an 8m mirror. Tours Sat 10am & 2pm. Contact visits@eso.org.

Cerro Tololo Office at Casilla 603, La Serena ☎ 51 205200, ⊛ ctio.noao.edu. Some 70km east of

La Serena, this Inter-American observatory features an impressive 8.1m Gemini telescope. Tours Sat 9am & 1pm. Reservations necessary.

La Silla ⊛ eso.org. 147km northeast of La Serena, and home to 14 telescopes. Tours Sept–June Sat 1.30pm; to register email ⊜ contactvisits@eso.org.

TOUR OPERATORS

From La Serena, a number of tour companies run excursions in the surrounding area. Popular tours of the **Elqui Valley** include *pisco*-tasting (around CH$20,000), stargazing at the **Observatorio Mamalluca** (CH$15,000) and penguin-watching at **Isla Damas** (CH$30,000).

Daniel Russ ☎9 94546000, ✉jeeptourlaserena @gmail.com, �🌐jeeptour-laserena.cl. An experienced and extremely knowledgeable man (with a jeep), who runs standard excursions for small groups, as well as trips to Paso del Agua Negra (CH$50,000) and tailor-made outings. German and English spoken.

Kayak Australis ☎2 23342015, 🌐kayakaustralis .com. Specializes in multi-day sea-kayak trips around Chile, including one to Isla Damas (CH$300/person for three days). Book through their Santiago office at El Bosque Sur 65, Piso 2, Oficina 3, Las Condes, or by email ✉info@kayakaustralis.cl.

Mundo Caballo Km27, along the road between La Serena and Vicuña ☎9 2197872, ✉mundocaballo @gmail.com, 🌐mundocaballo.cl. Stables 20km outside La Serena offering various horseriding trips, including one at night (CH$9000/hr). Best contacted by phone.

Talinay Adventure Expeditions Prat 470 Local 22 ☎9 83606464, ✉contacto@talinaychile.com. Horse-riding (CH$80,000/person), diving, sea kayaking and multi-day trekking and volcano-climbing expeditions, as well as visits to observatories including La Silla.

Turismo Delfines Matta 655 ☎51 2223624, 🌐turismodelfines.cl. Established operator specializing in bilingual guided trips to Isla Damas.

exciting eating and nightlife scene than La Serena. Coquimbo's only real drawback is the lack of budget accommodation, though there is one exception.

The most striking landmark, looming over town, is a huge 93m cross, the **Cruz del Tercer Milenio** (🌐cruzdeltercermilenio .cl). This slightly bizarre construction, the base of which provides a great viewpoint over town, was funded by the King of Morocco for the benefit of the town's Lebanese Muslim community.

ACCOMMODATION

Hostal Nomade C Regimento Coquimbo 5 ☎51 2315665, ☎9 3695885, 🌐hostalnomade.cl. HI-affiliated hostel in the large and rambling former residence of the French ambassador, which has a slightly haunted house feel. It has friendly and informative staff, large rooms with exceptionally high ceilings, internet, kitchen facilities and other backpacker conveniences. Dorms from CH$10,000, doubles (private bath) CH$25,000

EATING, DRINKING AND NIGHTLIFE

With many fish restaurants, Coquimbo is a seafood lover's paradise, and also comes alive at night with lively pubs and clubs – a popular drinking area is along Alduante between Freire and Argandoña.

La Barceloneta Alduante 726 ☎9 84212372. Offers an exquisite menu featuring fish dishes with a Mediterranean flavour, and transforms into a trendy bar at night, opening until late. Set lunch CH$3000.

Caleta Pescadores Av Costanera, about three blocks down from the Plaza de Armas at the end of Borgoño. Bustling, loud and smelly: a superb fish market on the seafront. Fish dishes from CH$2000.

Restaurant Coquimbo Bilbao 210. Giant portions of excellent-value fish, as well as superb seafood *empanadas*. *Merluza* and chips CH$3000.

ELQUI VALLEY

East of La Serena, the 62km journey to **Vicuña** is a scenic trip with breathtaking vistas of the tranquil **Elqui Valley**. Its fertile greenery contrasts greatly with the valley's sandy sides, its slopes a spectrum of red, green and gold due to the mineral-rich soil. The ribbon of the highway, lined with pink peppercorn trees, runs along the valley floor, past vineyards and grapes drying on canvas sheets by the roadside. Tours of the valley typically take in the giant dam and man-made **Lago Puklara**, popular with windsurfers and kitesurfers, the historical village of **Vicuña**, the laidback community of **Pisco Elqui** and a pisco-tasting distillery, before finishing with stargazing at the **Observatorio Mamalluca**.

Vicuña

Sleepy **Vicuña** makes a convenient stopover for exploring the Elqui Valley.

Formerly home to Nobel Prize-winner **Gabriela Mistrál**, it has a **museum** at Gabriela Mistrál 759 (Jan & Feb Mon–Fri 10am–7pm, Sat 10.30am–7pm, Sun 10am–6pm; March–Dec Mon–Fri 10am–5.45pm, Sat 10.30am–6pm, Sun 10am–1pm; CH$600), dedicated to her. **Planta Capel** (daily: March–Nov 10am–12.30pm & 2.30–6pm; Dec–Feb plus public holidays 10am–6pm; CH$1000; ☎51 2411251, ⓦpiscocapel .cl), the valley's largest **pisco distillery**, lies just south of town, and has half-hourly bilingual tours tracking the Muscatel grape's journey from the vine to the pisco bottle, culminating in a small free sample at the end.

ARRIVAL AND INFORMATION

By bus Vicuña's main terminal is one block south of the Plaza de Armas, on O'Higgins, at Prat (☎51 2411348). For Santiago and other major cities, it is easiest to return to La Serena.

Destinations Via Elqui buses go to La Serena (20 daily; 1hr 15min); Coquimbo (20 daily; 1hr 30min); and Pisco Elqui (20 daily; 1hr).

By colectivo From La Serena stop across the street from the main bus terminal. *Colectivos* to La Serena and Coquimbo leave from the bus station when full (daily 7am–9pm).

Tourist information Inside the Torre Bauer, San Martín s/n, in the northwest corner of the Plaza de Armas (Mon–Fri 8.30am–5.45pm, Sat 9am–6pm, Sun 9am–2pm; ☎51 2670308).

ACCOMMODATION

Hostal Donde Rita Condell 443 ☎51 2419611, ⓦhostal donderita.com. A homely set of rooms surrounded by a leafy garden, complete with pool and terrace area. Overseen by a charming German hostess, who prepares delicious breakfasts. Doubles CH$26,000

Hostal Valle Hermoso Gabriela Mistrál 706 ☎51 2411206. Family-run, beautifully refurbished colonial-style house with small, clean rooms, some without windows. Excellent fresh breakfasts included. Doubles CH$25,000

EATING

Halley Gabriela Mistrál 404. Vicuña's best-known restaurant serving roast *cabrito* (baby goat; CH$8900) in a rather formal setting.

Restaurant Solar de Villaseca Punta Arenas s/n, Villaseca. This famous place, 6km from town in the village of Villaseca (take a *colectivo* from the bus station; about CH$700), cooks up traditional cuisine in ten solar ovens – for obvious reasons, daylight hours only. Closed Mon.

Soledad y Yo Carrera 320. A typical *picada* or family restaurant, popular with locals, serving up substantial servings of Chilean favourites. Three-course lunch CH$4500.

Observatorio Cerro Mamalluca

The **Observatorio Cerro Mamalluca** is located 9km northeast of Vicuña. Compared to those in other observatories in the area, its 30cm telescope is tiny, but it still offers magnification of 150 times – sufficient to look closely at the craters on the moon and to view nebulas, star clusters and Saturn. There are two tours offered (both CH$4500; 2hr 30min; 4 nightly in summer from 8.30pm, 4 nightly in winter from 6.30pm): "Basic Astronomy" and "Andean Cosmovision", looking at the night sky as seen by the pre-Columbian inhabitants of the area. Shuttles to and from the observatory (CH$1500 return) depart from the Cerro Mamalluca office in Vicuña (Gabriela Mistrál 260, office 1; Mon–Fri 8.30am–9pm, Sat & Sun 10am–9pm; ☎51 2670330, ✉reservas@mamalluca .org, ⓦmunivicuna.cl/mamalluca) half an

4

PISCO

The climatic conditions in the Elqui Valley are ideal for growing the sweet Muscatel grapes from which the clear, brandy-like **pisco**, Chile's national drink, is derived. Pisco is a constant source of **dispute** between Chile and Peru. Peru claims that the drink originates from the Peruvian port of the same name, and some historical records demonstrate that pisco has been consumed in that area since the Spaniards introduced vineyards in the early 1600s.

Chileans claim that they have also been producing pisco for centuries, that their pisco is of better quality and that it plays a greater role in Chilean society. In both Chile and Peru, pisco is normally consumed in a **pisco sour** – a mix of pisco, lemon juice, sugar syrup, egg white, crushed ice and a drop of angostura bitters. It goes down deceptively smoothly, but packs a real punch.

4

hour before the tour starts. Reserve tickets in advance, especially in the peak months from December to February.

Pisco Elqui

The green and laidback village of **PISCO ELQUI** boasts a beautiful hillside setting alongside the Río Clara, with unparalleled views of the Elqui Valley. The shaded **Plaza de Armas**, with its brightly painted Gothic church, hosts the **Mercado Artesanal** in the summer. A block away, the Destileria **Pisco Mistral** is Chile's oldest pisco distillery, and offers guided tours (O'Higgins 746; daily: Jan–Feb 11.30am–7.30pm; March–Dec 10.30am–6pm; CH$5000; ☎51 451358) complete with tastings. **Los Nichos** (daily tours at 1pm and 3.30pm, CH$1,000) is an old-fashioned distillery 3km south of Pisco Elqui, and worth visiting to see pisco processed by hand.

Be warned there are no ATMs in town, so bring plenty of cash.

ARRIVAL, INFORMATION AND ACTIVITIES

By bus Via Elqui buses stop in front of the Plaza de Armas. Via Elqui run to La Serena and Coquimbo (more than 20 daily; 2hr 15min) via Vicuña.

Horseriding *Alcohuaz Expediciones*, based in Monte Grande, 4km before Pisco (☎9 87881978, ✉alvarezhuasco @yahoo.com, ⓦcaballo-elqui.cl), is run by a genuine *huaso* (Chilean cowboy) and offers excellent horseriding trips in the area.

Tourist information Hostel owners will be able to help you with information, but an excellent option for local knowledge of the area is the tour agency Turismo Migrantes, O'Higgins s/n (☎51 2451917, ☎9 8295630, ⓦturismomigrantes.cl), where Bárbara and Pablo organize pisco tours, horseriding and bike rides in the surrounding area, and even stargazing tours at their own home.

ACCOMMODATION

El Tesoro de Elqui Prat s/n ☎51 2451069, ⓦtesoro -elqui.cl. Cosy adobe dorms and rooms – one with a skylight for stargazing – and excellent food. The owners can help organize motorbike hire and tours. Dorms CH$11,000, doubles CH$37,000

Hostal Triskel Baquedano s/n ☎9 94188680, ⓦhostal triskel.cl. Lovingly decorated rooms and decent breakfasts. They can arrange hiking, biking and horseriding too. Doubles CH$24,000

EATING

Los Jugos Plaza de Armes. Delicious fruit juices and large portions of pizza (CH$3000).

El Ranchito de Don René Centenario s/n, just up from the church. Serves Chilean classics, such as *pastel de choclo* (CH$4900), on a shaded patio.

RESERVA NACIONAL PINGÜINO DE HUMBOLDT

The **Reserva Nacional Pingüino de Humboldt** is a remarkable marine wildlife reserve 110km north of La Serena, which comprises three islands jutting from the cold Pacific waters: Isla Chañaral, Isla Choros and Isla Damas. The islands are home to *chundungos* (sea otters), a noisy colony of **sea lions**, the **Humboldt penguin**, four species of cormorants, clamouring **Peruvian boobies** and countless seagulls.

Unless you plan to stay the night at Punta de Choros (see below), it is much easier to visit as part of a tour (see box, p.407). **Boats** sail (CH$8000 per person; sailings dependent on conditions) from **Caleta de Choros**, the small fishing community closest to the islands, along the steep jagged coastline of **Isla Choros**. You get close enough to see the wildlife in great detail, and on the way to the island, pods of curious **bottlenose dolphins** often frolic around the boat; it's also possible to spot humpback, blue and killer **whales**. On the way back, visitors are allowed a short ramble on sandy **Isla Damas**, whose pristine beaches are home to a smaller penguin population.

INFORMATION

Tourist information There is a Conaf-run Centro de Información Ambiental (Mon–Thurs, Sat & Sun 8.30am– 5.30pm, Fri 8.30am–4.30pm) at Caleta de Choros, with informative displays on local flora and fauna, and another smaller one at Caleta Chañaral.

ACCOMMODATION

Camping There are opportunities for wild camping at Punta de Choros in the summer (mid-Dec to mid-March); reserve in advance with Conaf (☎09 5443052). Be sure to give names, dates (the maximum stay is three days and two nights) and the number of campers (CH$12,000/ site for up to six people). Bring all necessary supplies, including water.

COPIAPÓ

The prosperous mining town of **COPIAPÓ**, 333km north of La Serena, was founded in 1744 and benefited greatly from the **silver boom** of the 1830s. Today, Copiapó still makes its living from mining, nowadays for **copper**. It will forever be linked in many people's minds with the 2010 rock collapse at the nearby San José mine, which left 33 miners ("Los 33") trapped underground for 69 days before the world cheered their safe rescue.

At the heart of Copiapó is the large **Plaza Prat**, dotted with pepper trees; handicraft stalls line the plaza's east side, facing the mall. The Neoclassical **Iglesia Catedral Nuestra Señora de Rosario** graces the southwest corner, while half a block from the northwest corner of the square, at the corner of Colipí and Rodriguez, is the worthwhile but poorly labelled **Museo Mineralógico** (Mon–Fri 10am–1pm & 3.30–7pm, Sat 10am–1pm; CH$500; ☎52 2206606), with an impressive mineral collection including copper, silver ore, part of a meteorite which landed in the Atacama Desert, and massive chunks of semi-precious stones, such as malachite, onyx, jasper and amethyst.

ARRIVAL AND DEPARTURE

By plane Aeropuerto Desierto de Atacama is 45km west of the city; take Transfer Casther (CH$5000) to Copiapó or a *colectivo* (CH$3000) to Caldera. Airport transfers are operated by Buses Casther (☎52 2235891).
Destinations Antofagasta (2 weekly); Arica (2 weekly); Calama (2 daily); Iquique (2 weekly); Santiago (10 daily; 1hr 30min).

By bus The Tur Bus terminal is at Freire and Colipí; Terminal Torreblanca, with numerous carriers, is directly opposite. The Pullman bus terminal is a block south, at Colipí 109; buses Casther and Recabarren leave from Caldera stop just east of the Hiper Líder supermarket at Buena Esperanza 552.
Destinations Antofagasta (6 daily; 5hr); Arica (5 daily; 16hr); Calama (about 5 daily; 10hr); Iquique (6 daily; 13hr); La Serena (5 daily; 5hr); San Pedro de Atacama (at least 6 daily; 11hr).

INFORMATION

Tourist information Los Carrera 691 (Mon–Fri 8.30am–6pm, Sat 9am–1pm; Jan–Feb also Sun 10am–1pm; ☎52 2231510, ✉infoatacama@sernatur.cl). Extremely helpful staff, and good stock of maps and leaflets. Conaf has an office at Juan Martínez 55 (Mon–Thurs 8.30am–5.30pm, Fri 8.30am–4.30pm; ☎52 2237042, ✉oirs@conaf.cl). Excellent source of information on Nevado de Tres Cruces and Pan de Azúcar.

ACCOMMODATION

Residencial Ben Bow Rodriguez 541 ☎52 2217634. Clean, no-frills rooms around a narrow courtyard. Doubles **CH$22,000**
Residencial Chañarcillo Chañarcillo 741, a block from the Tur Bus bus station ☎52 2213281. A convenient stopover, with dark but tidy rooms and friendly owners. Doubles **CH$20,000**

EATING

Café Columbia Plaza Prat on Colipi, at Carrera. Pricey but excellent, this place serves good coffee and delectable cake. Breakfasts from CH$4000.
Flor de la Canela Chacabuco 710 ☎52 2219570. Popular but pricey Peruvian restaurant serving up favourites like *lomo saltado, cebiche. Aji de gallina* CH$7200.

COPIAPÓ TOUR OPERATORS

Since the area's national parks are difficult to get to without a sturdy vehicle of your own, it is easier to go as part of a tour. Day-trip prices are typically around CH$45,000 per person to the Parque Nacional Pan de Azúcar and CH$60,000 to Parque Nacional Nevado Tres Cruces, including lunch and entrance fees.

Atacama Chile Maipú 580 ☎9 98723652, ⊛atacamachile.com. Reputable bilingual company running separate day-trips to Laguna Santa Rosa and Laguna Verde, as well as 4WD, dirt-biking and sandboarding trips in the Atacama Desert and diving excursions off the coast.
Atacama Expeditions Infante 661 ☎52 2223640, ☎9 98918212, ⊛atacamaexpeditions.cl. Standard and tailor-made tours of the area for small groups

offered by the extremely knowledgeable local guide, Ovidio Rodríguez; includes both Laguna Verde and Laguna Santa Rosa in a day-trip to Nevado Tres Cruces. Spanish only.
Aventurismo Vallejos 771 ☎52 2232455, ⊛aventurismo.cl. Mountaineering outfit specializing in multi-day ascents of the Ojos de Salado volcano between November and March.

4

Okasama Av O'Higgins 799. This intimate, multi-roomed restaurant serves surprisingly good sushi and offers excellent lunchtime discounts. Six California rolls CH$4800.

AROUND COPIAPÓ

The landscape surrounding Copiapó is astonishingly varied, with the salt flats of the **Parque Nacional Nevado de Tres Cruces**, mesmerizing **Laguna Verde**, active volcano **Ojos de Salado** and, to the west, the fine white sands of **Bahía Inglesa** and **Caldera**.

Parque Nacional Nevado de Tres Cruces

Remote and ruggedly beautiful **Parque Nacional Nevado de Tres Cruces** is located east of Copiapó via Ruta 31, which winds through the mercilessly desolate desert landscape. The road climbs steeply before reaching the **Salar de Maricunga** – a great field of white crystals on the edge of the park, dotted with emerald-coloured salt pools – and continuing on towards **Paso San Francisco** on the Argentine border.

The park consists of two separate parts. The larger is the 490-square-kilometre **Laguna Santa Rosa** sector, 146km east of Copiapó at an altitude of 3700m, which comprises half of the salt flat and the namesake lake, with roaming herds of **vicuñas** and **guanacos** feeding on the abundant grasslands. The pale blue lagoon, dotted with flamingos and giant coots, is set against a backdrop of snow-streaked volcanoes, including the grand **Nevado Tres Cruces** (6749m). On the west side of the lake is a small and very rustic Conaf-run *refugio*, consisting of bare floorspace, basic cooking facilities and a privy out back.

Cutting across a vast expanse of parched brown land, dotted with hardy yellow *altiplano* plants, you reach the 120-square-kilometre **Laguna del Negro Francisco** sector, around 85km south. In summer it becomes a sea of pink and beige, thanks to the presence of eight thousand or so Andean, Chilean and James **flamingos** that migrate here from neighbouring Argentina, Bolivia and Peru. On the west side of the lake, Conaf's *Refugio Laguna del Negro Francisco* has beds and kitchen facilities; make reservations with Copiapó's Conaf office (CH$8000 per person).

Laguna Verde and Volcán Ojos de Salado

The magnificent spectacle of the misnamed **Laguna Verde** lies 65km beyond Laguna Santa Rosa, at a whopping altitude of 4325m. The first flash of its brilliant turquoise waters, around a bend in the road, is breathtaking. On the lake's salty white shore are some rustic and relaxing **hot springs** inside a little wooden shack. It's possible to camp here: you must bring all necessary supplies with you, including water, and remember that night-time temperatures drop well below freezing. Beyond the lake loom three volcanoes, including the second-highest peak in Latin America – **Ojos de Salado**. At an elevation of 6887m, it trails just behind Argentina's 6962m Aconcagua as the tallest mountain in the Americas. It is also the world's highest active volcano, with recent eruptions in 1937 and 1956.

Caldera and Bahía Inglesa

The towns of Caldera and Bahía Inglesa, 7km apart and 75km west of Copiapó, are both popular **beach resorts** famous for their large, delicious **scallops**. **Caldera** itself is an unremarkable little town, though the Gothic **Iglesia San Vicente** (1862) on the pretty Plaza Condell is worth a look. Pedestrianized **Gana**, lined with craft stalls in the summer, makes for a nice stroll between the square and the waterfront **Costanera** (pier) – home to the oldest railway station in Chile, dating back to 1850, and now a museum and events centre. The pier is the best place to sample inexpensive seafood *empanadas* and other fishy delights.

Caldera's main beach, small seaweed-tinted Copiapina, is not the best in the area; for crystal-clear turquoise waters and long stretches of fine white sand, head to nearby **Bahía Inglesa**, either by *colectivo* or along the cycle path parallel to the road. Bahía Inglesa is immensely popular with locals in the summer, and it's easy to see why: the laidback atmosphere, the proximity of the ocean and an abundance of cheap seafood *empanadas* sold by vendors along the seafront entice you to linger longer. There are several small and sheltered beaches along the main Avenida El Morro, with the wide crescent of Playa Las Machas stretching into the distance.

ARRIVAL AND INFORMATION

By bus Buses arrive at the main plaza in Caldera; Copiapó-bound Casther and Recabarren buses stop at Ossa Varas 710 (every 30min; 1hr 30min).

Colectivo Those to Copiapó leave from Cifuentes, just south of Ossa Varas. *Colectivos* from the plaza regularly make the 15min journey to Bahía (CH$1000).

Tourist information On Plaza Carlos Condell in Caldera (daily 9am–2pm & 4–7pm; ☎ 52 2316076, ⓦ caldera.cl).

ACCOMMODATION AND EATING

All these options are in Bahía, which has a greater selection of accommodation than Caldera, though it tends to be overpriced during peak season.

Camping Bahía Inglesa Off Playa Las Machas, just south of the town ☎ 52 2316399. An excellent place to camp, with hot showers, picnic tables and restaurants. Pitch for up to six people CH$18,000

Domo Bahía Inglesa Av El Morro 610, on the waterfront ☎ 9 8162 8642, ⓦ domobahiainglesa.cl. Has bizarre but comfortable tent-like dome rooms (private or shared). Doubles CH$42,000

El Plateao El Morro 756 ☎ 9 88260007. Restaurant-bar with a terrace overlooking the beach, good service and an innovative menu offering exceptional seafood dishes. Seafood risotto for two CH$9000.

PARQUE NACIONAL PAN DE AZÚCAR

About 180km north of Copiapó, **Parque Nacional Pan de Azúcar** entices visitors with its spectacular coastal desert landscape, which alternates between steep cliffs, studded with a multitude of cactus species, and pristine white beaches. A small gravel road leads into the park from the compact town of Chañaral and continues past Playa Blanca and Playa Los Piqueros to **Caleta Pan de Azúcar**, a small fishing village inside the park. **Isla Pan de Azúcar**, home to Humboldt penguins, sea lions, sea otters and a wealth of marine birds, lies a short distance offshore. Although landing on the island is forbidden, fishing boats (March–Nov 9am–6pm; Dec–Feb 9am–7pm; CH$50,000 for up to ten people, or whatever deal you can strike) get visitors close enough to see (and smell) the wildlife at close quarters. A 9km trail runs north from the village to the **Mirador Pan de Azúcar**, a lookout point offering staggering panoramic views of the coastline. Also heading north from the village, towards Ruta 5, is a dirt road with a 15km trail branching off to the west that leads you through the arid landscape to **Las Lomitas**, an outlook point often visited by inquisitive **desert foxes** and shrouded in rolling *camanchaca* (sea mist), the main water source for all the coastal vegetation.

ARRIVAL AND INFORMATION

By bus There are no public buses to the park, though northbound buses from Copiapó can drop you off in Chañaral, the nearest town. Ask around at the bus terminal in Chañaral, and you should be able to get someone to take you to the park. Taxis cost CH$10,000 each way – worth it for a group. Alternatively, take a day-trip tour from Copiapó (see box, p.407).

Tourist information Conaf's Centro de Información Ambiental (daily 8.30am–12.30pm & 2–6pm) is opposite Playa Los Piqueros and has maps and information on the park, as well as a display of local cacti. The park fee of CH$4000 is payable here; no fee is charged if entering the park from the east.

ACCOMMODATION AND EATING

Camping is available at several sites in the park (☎ 2 1960626, ☎ 9 94444169), costing CH$5000/person, and includes twenty litres of drinking water, picnic tables, showers and WC use. Groups of four to six people may prefer to rent beachside cabañas complete with kitchen facilities (CH$30,000 for two). Both cabañas and camping can also be reserved through the Conaf office in Copiapó. For food, there are a number of places in the village cooking up the day's fresh catch.

Norte Grande

In some parts of the vast Atacama Desert, which covers almost all of the Norte Grande region, there are areas where no rainfall has ever been recorded. With such an inhospitable landscape, it is no wonder that most of the population is squeezed into the more moderate climes along the coast. The sprawling port city of **Antofagasta** is the largest population centre, while other major towns include the beach resort of **Iquique** – popular with surfers and paragliders – and **Arica**, home to the iconic cliff of El Morro, a fantastic viewpoint from which to survey the area's long stretches of sandy beach. The best base from which to enjoy the spectacular desert scenery is the laidback backpacker haven of **San Pedro de Atacama**, where visitors flock to whizz down dunes on sandboards, admire the steam rising from geysers in the early morning sun, and spot flamingos on Chile's largest salt flat.

ANTOFAGASTA

ANTOFAGASTA is the biggest city in northern Chile; a busy industrialized port and major transportation hub, it has few attractions to detain travellers, though it's a good place to stock up on necessities. James Bond fans may recognize flashes of the city from the 2008 film *Quantum of Solace*, part of which was filmed here.

WHAT TO SEE AND DO

Antofagasta's compact centre boasts the surprisingly lovely **Plaza Colón**, the apparent British influence accentuated by its centrepiece, the **Torre Reloj**, a small-scale Big Ben replica. To the north, three blocks of Arturo Prat are pedestrianized and feature shops and cafés, while three blocks south along Matta is a large pedestrian square presided over by the impressive pink, grey and cream **Mercado Central**, with its evocative smells of fresh produce and frying fish.

At the port end of Bolívar, you'll find the oldest building in the city, the former **Aduana**, now housing the **Museo Regional** (Tues–Fri 9am–5pm, Sat & Sun 11am–4pm; CH$600), with exhibitions on regional natural history, archeology and the War of the Pacific, and an outstanding mummified babies exhibit. *Colectivos* (CH$700) run along Matta to the often-crowded Balneario Municipal,

and further south to the Balneario El Huáscar and Caleta Coloso. These are Antofagasta's better **beaches**, lined with places to eat, bars and discos, though not really suitable for swimming.

La Portada

Much featured on postcards, the natural monument of **La Portada**, 15km north of Antofagasta, is a giant rock eroded into a natural arch. To get there, take a Mejillones-bound bus and ask to be dropped off at the junction (10min), from where it is a half-hour walk towards the ocean.

ARRIVAL AND INFORMATION

By plane The Cerro Moreno airport is 25km north of the city on Ruta 1; the Aerobús shuttle will drop you off at your destination. Alternatively, take a bus into the city centre. Buses to the airport are infrequent. Transvip (☎02 26773000) will pick up across town (from downtown CH$6000).
Destinations Calama (2 daily; 45min); Iquique (3 daily; 55min); Santiago (10 daily; 1hr 55min).
By bus Most buses now come through the modern Terminal de Buses Cardenal Carlos Oviedo Cavada on Pedro Aguirre Cerda, at Paihuano.
Destinations Arica (6 daily; 10hr); Calama (about 8 daily; 3hr); Copiapó (8 daily; 7hr); Iquique (6 daily; 6hr); La Serena (8 daily; 12hr); San Pedro de Atacama (at least 6 daily; 5hr); Santiago (10 daily; 18hr).
Tourist information Prat 384, on Plaza Colón (Mon–Fri 8.30am–7pm, Sat 10am–2pm; ☎55 2451819, @infoantofagasta@sernatur.cl); helpful staff provide city maps and information on local attractions.

ACCOMMODATION

Hostal del Norte La Torre 3162 ☎55 2251265, ☎9 88692570. Spotless place with pleasant rooms and a family atmosphere, located just a few blocks from the centre. Breakfast available if requested the night before. Doubles CH$26,000
Residencial El Cobre Arturo Prat 749 ☎55 2225162 Centrally located option with a grubby-looking exterior and no-frills rooms, with shared bathrooms. Double CH$16,000
Rocomar Hotel Baquedano 810 ☎55 2261139, @hotel rocomar@hotmail.com. Pricier, but this place offers clean cosy rooms with private bathroom and cable TV, and basic breakfast included. Doubles CH$32,000

EATING AND DRINKING

Bavaria Latorre 2618. Two-tiered grill-cafeteria, the latter serving inexpensive fast food, and the former specializing in tasty *panrilladas* and German-style meat-and-vegetable dishes. Roast pork and mashed potato CH$6,200.

Mercado Central Matta, between Maipú and Uribe. Besides fresh produce, the market's eateries cook up fishy delights for a reasonable price. *El Sureño* comes recommended. Grilled fish CH$2800.

Raconto Arturo Prat 645. Very popular restaurant offering good steaks, pizzas, sandwiches and ice creams. Lasagne CH$3990.

CALAMA

The busy city of **CALAMA**, at the heart of the Atacama **copper mining** industry, is a convenient transportation hub and an almost inevitable stop for travellers heading to San Pedro de Atacama.

WHAT TO SEE AND DO

Calama may lack the natural marvels of San Pedro de Atacama, but it does boast the giant Chuquicamata copper mine. State copper company Codelco offers free tours, including views of the kilometre-deep open pit and the now abandoned company town. Bilingual English and Spanish tours leave from Calama at 1pm and last approximately two hours (book in advance; call ☎55 2322122 or email ☎visitas@codelco.cl).

ARRIVAL AND DEPARTURE

By plane Aeropuerto El Loa (☎55 2342348) is 6km south of the city. Transfer Licancabur (☎55 2543426) will take you from the airport direct to San Pedro (CH$12,000 one-way). To get into Calama, a taxi (around CH$5000) is the only option.

Destinations Antofagasta (3 daily; 45min); Santiago (16 daily; 2hr 5min).

By bus There is no central bus terminal – Turbus and Pullman arrive at separate terminals – and bus companies are either clustered near the train station to the east of the city centre, or lie to the north of it. The lack of a central terminal makes bus travel in Calama slightly chaotic. All major cities are covered by Tur Bus (tickets at Granderos 4219), and Pullman, who have their own terminal at Granaderos 3048, out of town. Buses Atacama 2000 (Antofagasta 2088; ☎55 2316664) run to San Pedro de Atacama and to Ollagüe (4 weekly; 3hr) on the Bolivian border, from where it's possible to get an ongoing connection to Uyuni. Géminis, at Antofagasta 2239 (☎55 2892043), have Tues, Fri and Sun morning departures for Salta and Jujuy between them.

Destinations Antofagasta (6 daily; 3hr); Arica (5 daily; 9hr); Iquique (5 daily; 7hr); Santiago (8 daily; 22hr); San Pedro de Atacama (every 30min; 1hr 30min).

ACCOMMODATION

Hostal Claris Loa Avenida Granaderos 1631 ☎55 2311939. Clean but dark rooms, most with TV, set around a central patio and catering largely to mineworkers. Doubles CH$16,000

Residencial Toño Vivar 1970 ☎55 2341185. Secure and spacious rooms with cable TV. The walls are thin so it can get noisy. Doubles CH$23,000

EATING

Café del Sol Abaroa 1688. A. Delightful little tearoom with a laidback feel: a perfect spot for recovering after a long bus journey, with coffee, cake and sandwiches. Large latte CH$1100.

Restaurant Palador Vivar con Sotomayor. A carnivore's paradise in quite a plush setting. Offers an excellent three-course lunch and drink deal (CH$4900).

SAN PEDRO DE ATACAMA AND AROUND

SAN PEDRO DE ATACAMA, a little oasis town of single-storey adobe houses and unpaved streets, is situated 75km east of Calama, the nearest city. No other northern destination can compete with the sheer number of natural attractions in the surrounding area: the stunning *altiplano* scenery draws scores of travellers year-round, while volcanoes, sand dunes, geysers and lagoons will keep any nature lover busy.

One of the oldest settlements in Chile, San Pedro was originally a stop on a pre-Columbian trade route between the highland and coastal communities; in 1547, the Spanish established their first mission here and subjugated the locals. The town later became an important rest stop for cattle drives from Salta, Argentina, when the nitrate industry took off in Chile and fresh meat was needed for the workers.

Despite being somewhat crowded during the peak season, San Pedro retains a friendly and relaxed vibe, and has an excellent assortment of budget accommodation and facilities for visitors, as well as the widest range of cuisine north of Santiago.

SAN PEDRO DE ATACAMA

ACCOMMODATION	
Hostal Elim	6
Hostelling International San Pedro	2
Hotel & Camping Takha Takha	5
Mama Tierra	3
Pozo 3	4
Hostal Sonchek	1

EATING, DRINKING & NIGHTLIFE	
Blanco	2
Cafe Esquina	1
La Estaka	3
Sala de Té O2	5
Tierra Todo Natural	4

WHAT TO SEE AND DO

The centre of town is the cheery little **Plaza de Armas**, framed by *algarrobo* and pink peppercorn trees. The whitewashed **Iglesia de San Pedro** (1641) stands on the west side of the square, while most places to eat and other services are found along nearby Caracoles.

Museo Arqueológico Gustavo Le Paige

The intriguing **Museo Arqueológico Gustavo Le Paige** (Mon–Fri 9am–6pm, Sat 10am–6pm; CH$2500), located northeast of the square, is well worth a visit, though it no longer displays its famous prehistoric mummy exhibit. Founded by a Belgian Jesuit, after whom it is named, it is home to more than 380,000 clearly labelled pre-Columbian artefacts, perfectly preserved in the dry desert air, including ceramics, gold work and a wide range of tablets and straws for the ritual inhalation of hallucinogenic cacti.

ARRIVAL AND DEPARTURE

By bus The Tur Bus terminal is on Domingo Atienza, at Licancábur; Buses Frontera, Buses Atacama 2000, Buses Géminis and Pullman stop further east on Licancábur. Most travellers will choose to cross the border to Uyuni in Bolivia on a tour, though it's possible to do so by public transport on a bus from Calama to the border town of Ollagüe.

Destinations Antofagasta (6 daily; 5hr); Arica (1 daily; 14hr); Calama (6 daily; 1hr 45min); Salta and Jujuy (Tues, Fri & Sun 7am & 11am; 14hr); Santiago (1 daily; 22hr); Socaire (1 daily at 7.30pm; 2hr); Toconao (4 daily; 1hr 30min).

INFORMATION

Bike rental Bikes can be rented (around CH$1000/hr) from the internet café at the southeast corner of Plaza de Armas, as well as from most hostels.

Money Bring plenty of cash as the ATMs along Caracoles are frequently out of order. Money exchanges on Toconao change foreign currency at a poor rate; tour agencies running trips to Salar de Uyuni can provide better rates for Bolivianos.

Tourist information Toconao s/n, northeast corner of Plaza de Armas (Mon–Fri 9am–9pm; ☎ 55 2851420). The office provides maps of the town centre, and the visitor book is a good source of information from other travellers. Also check out ⓦ sanpedroatacama.com, an excellent source of information on the area.

ACCOMMODATION

Hostal Elim Palpana 6 ☎ 55 2851567, ⓦ hostalelim.cl. Quiet hostel whose friendly owners offer ten lovingly decorated and furnished doubles, quads and family rooms, with private bathrooms, in a garden setting with fruit trees and hammocks. Prices include breakfast and internet; laundry service available. Doubles CH$46,410

Hostelling International San Pedro Caracoles 360 ☎ 55 2564683, ⓔ hostelsanpedro@hotmail.com, ⓦ hostelling sanpedro.cl. Bustling HI branch with member discounts, three-tiered bunk beds in dorms, clean singles and doubles, a shaded courtyard, free internet and breakfast. It also organizes a plethora of tours in the area and rents out bikes and sandboards. Dorms CH$9000, doubles CH$36,000

Hotel & Camping Takha Takha Caracoles 101 ☎ 55 2851038, ⓦ takhatakha.cl. Camping sites in a shaded area and clean rooms with private or shared bathrooms, set in a tranquil oasis of vegetation. Popular with travellers of all ages, and there's also a good café on the premises. Camping/person CH$10,500, doubles CH$47,250

Mama Tierra Pachamama 615 ☎ 55 2851418, ⓔ mamatierra@sanpedroatacama.com. Popular with backpackers and a 10min walk from the centre, this tidy

hostel offers dorms, singles and doubles with private or shared bathrooms. Extras include laundry service, and the congenial hostess can help organize volcano climbs in the area. Dorms CH$11,000, doubles CH$38,000

Pozo 3 ☎ 9 62044475. About 4km out of town, this campsite boasts the best views in all of San Pedro, with the volcanoes in the distance. Ask around at the bus terminal for a taxi to take you there (CH$5000). A pool (CH$3000 for non-guests, included for guests) with hot showers, picnic tables and barbecue facilities are pluses. Camping/person CH$5000

★ **Hostal Sonchek** Gustovo Le Paige 198 ☎ 55 2851112, ⓔ soncheksp@hotmail.com. With a welcoming and helpful English- and French-speaking hostess, this extremely popular and conveniently located hostel has cosy rooms, kitchen use, a courtyard with hammocks, laundry service and an excellent café next door. Dorms CH$8000, doubles CH$34,000

EATING, DRINKING AND NIGHTLIFE

The no-frills food stalls by the Atacama 2000 bus stop on Licancábur s/n are a good place to fill up on *cazuela*, fried chicken, hot dogs and other budget options. Meals are all under CH$3000.

Blanco Caracoles 195. Although fairly pricey, the imaginative chicken and salmon dishes in this trendy bar-restaurant are worth the splurge. Fixed-price lunch menu CH$5500.

Café Esquina Caracoles s/n. Small café dishing out delicious *empanadas* (CH$1300) and wonderfully refreshing ginger lemonade (CH$2200), as well as simple sandwiches and snacks.

La Estaka Caracoles 259. A rustic bar-restaurant that features nightly live music, complimentary pisco sours and a range of expertly prepared if pricey meat and

---

SAN PEDRO TOUR OPERATORS

Choosing a reputable **tour operator** in San Pedro can be difficult, but at least the intense competition keeps prices fairly stable. Talk to other travellers who have done the tours recently, and look at the comment book in the tourist information office. Expect to pay around CH$25,000 for a tour of the *altiplano* lagoons and villages, CH$10,000 to visit Valle de la Luna, CH$20,000 to visit the El Tatio geysers and CH$10,000 for a three-hour sandboarding trip (including an instructor and board rental); trip prices normally exclude entrance fees. The following are reliable:

Know Chile Gustavo Le Paige 534 ☎ 9 4981280, ⓦ knowchiletour.com. Cheery and knowledgeable Erich prides himself on seeking out the less well-trodden path. English spoken.

Maxim Experience Caracoles 174C ☎ 55 2424724, ⓔ maximexperience@hotmail.com, ⓦ maximexperience .cl. Sandboarding and trips to the Ojos de Salar lagoons, among others.

Observatorio del Cielo Austral Caracoles 166 ☎ 55 2851935, ⓦ spaceobs.com. French astronomer Alain Maury brings the night sky to life during the tours at his home in the desert, where he has set up several powerful telescopes (times vary; 2hr 30min; CH$18,000/person). Tours are conducted in English, French and Spanish. Warm clothes are essential.

4

vegetarian dishes. Home-made cannelloni with smoked salmon CH$8900.

Sala de Té 02 Caracoles 295B. Unpretentious place serving excellent quiches alongside standard fast food, as well as a range of teas, and the best breakfasts in town. Scrambled eggs and coffee CH$2500.

★ **Tierra Todo Natural** Caracoles 46. Fantastic daily set menus that always include imaginative vegetarian dishes. Evening service can be slow. Fixed menu CH$7000.

DAY-TRIPS FROM SAN PEDRO

Beyond San Pedro, the scenery is dramatic, dominated by large volcanic peaks, **Valle de la Luna**'s magnificent lunar landscape, the red rock of the **Valle de la Muerte**, the famous **El Tatio geysers**, Chile's largest salt flat **Salar de Atacama** and dazzling **lagoons**. With the exception of the village of **Toconao**, and

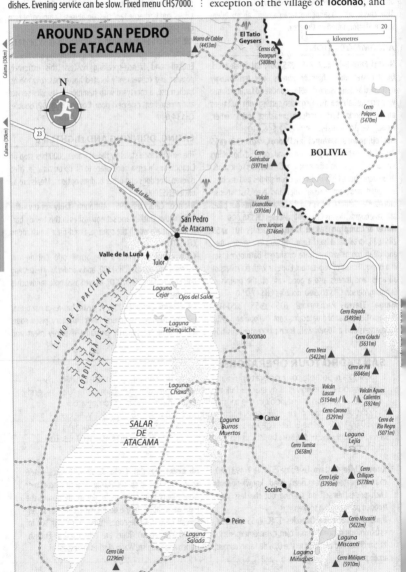

AROUND SAN PEDRO DE ATACAMA

Calama (30km)

Calama (30km)

0   20
kilometres

N

23

Valle de La Muerte

San Pedro de Atacama

Valle de la Luna
Tulor

LLANO DE LA PACIENCIA

CORDILLERA DE LA SAL

Laguna Cejar

Ojos del Salar

Laguna Tebenquiche

Laguna Chaxa

SALAR DE ATACAMA

Laguna Burros Muertos

Camar

Cerro Tumisa (5658m)

Socaire

Peine

Laguna Salada

Cerro Lila (2296m)

Laguna Miñiques

Morro de Cablor (4453m)

El Tatio Geysers

Cerros de Tocorpuri (5808m)

BOLIVIA

Cerro Polques (5470m)

Cerro Sairécabur (5971m)

Volcán Licancábur (5916m)

Cerro Juriques (5746m)

Toconao

Cerro Rayado (5493m)

Cerro Colachi (5631m)

Cerro Heca (5422m)

Cerro de Pili (6046m)

Volcán Lascar (5154m)

Volcán Aguas Calientes (5924m)

Cerro Corona (5291m)

Cerro de Río Negro (5071m)

Laguna Lejía

Cerro Lejía (5793m)

Cerro Chiliques (5778m)

Cerro Miscanti (5622m)

Laguna Miscanti

Cerro Miñiques (5910m)

Paso Sico

Valle de la Muerte and Valle de la Luna, both of which can be visited by bike, these places are only accessible on a tour.

Valle de la Muerte
The easiest attraction to cycle to – only 3km from San Pedro – is the **Valle de la Muerte**, with its narrow gorges, peculiar **red rock formations** and 150m-high **sand dunes**. It is also a prime **sandboarding** destination, with scores of enthusiasts whizzing down the slopes in the early mornings and late afternoons. The rest of the time an exquisite silence reigns over the still sand and rocks, and you can often enjoy the views of the snow-peaked volcanoes in the distance entirely undisturbed.

Valle de la Luna
Most people come here at sundown with one of a plethora of tour groups, but the lunar landscape of **Valle de la Luna** (Moon Valley; entry CH$2000), at the heart of the Cordillera del Sal, is equally impressive at sunrise, when the first rays of sunlight turn the surrounding jagged red peaks various shades of pink and gold. Though the effect is even more intense at sunset, at dawn there are far fewer spectators, and after making your way up the giant sand dune along a marked trail, you can walk up the crest of the dune for a better vantage point. If cycling the 14km to the valley, go west along Caracoles out of town, turn left at the end and carry straight on; plenty of water, sunscreen and a torch are essential.

Toconao
Toconao, 38km from San Pedro, is a small village nestled in an idyllic spot surrounded by sandy hills, with houses built entirely of volcanic liparita stone. A cool stream runs through the valley and the surrounding fertile soil supports lush vegetation, including fig, pear and quince trees, as well as a hallucinogenic type of cactus. The site has been inhabited since 11,000 BC, and its present population of around seven hundred villagers make traditional crafts. It is possible to stay in several rustic *hospedajes* here, and there are delicious *humitas* (corn paste wrapped

in corn leaves) for sale. Buses Atacama and Buses Frontera each run twice-daily bus services to Toconao from San Pedro.

Salar de Atacama
The edge of Chile's largest salt flat, the Salar de Atacama, lies 50km south of San Pedro. It may disappoint those expecting a sparkling white field, but still makes an unforgettable spectacle: a jagged white crust, resembling dead coral, created by water flowing down from the mountains, stretches as far as the eye can see. Several shallow lakes dot the Salar, including **Laguna Chaxa**, made bright by the resident Andean, Chilean and James flamingos, which spend up to fourteen hours a day feeding on tiny saltwater shrimp. Many excursions will also take in **Laguna Cejar** (CH$2000) – where salt content is so high that you can float on the surface – and gleaming **Laguna Tebenquiche**. Also look out for the two **Ojos del Salar** (entry CH$2500) – two small, and almost perfectly round, cold-water pools set amid the arid plain.

El Tatio geysers
The **El Tatio geysers**, 90km north of town, are a morning attraction, with tours setting off at 4am in order to reach them by sunrise, when the fumaroles that spew steam and the jets of scalding water that shoot up from the geysers are at their most impressive. At dawn, there is a surreal quality to the plateau: dark shadowy figures move through the mist and the sunlight glints on patches of white ground frost. When walking around, stick to marked paths, since the ground crust can be very fragile – breaking it might result in a plunge into near-boiling water. The temperature here, at the world's highest geothermal field (4320m), is often below freezing, so warm clothes are essential. A soak in the nearby thermal pool is a must.

Lagunas Miscanti and Miñiques
These two *altiplano* **lagoons** (entry CH$2500) lie 134km from town, at an elevation of around 4200m. Visitors here are left breathless not just by the altitude, but also by the first sight of the huge

4

shimmering pools of deep blue, ringed with white ribbons of salt. There's abundant bird and animal life as well, and it is possible to see both flamingos and the inquisitive *zorro culpeo*, a type of **fox** that often approaches the area's picnic site to look for scraps.

IQUIQUE

The approach to the busy coastal city of Iquique is unforgettable, especially if coming from the east. The highway along the plateau suddenly gives way to a spectacular 600m drop, looking down onto the giant **Cerro Dragón** sand dune which in turn towers over the city. At sunset, the dune and the surrounding cliffs turn various shades of pink and red, giving the city an almost unearthly feel.

Almost 500km north of Antofagasta, Iquique prospered in the nitrate era, between 1890 and 1920. Most of the grand old buildings in the city's historical centre date back to that heyday. The town's biggest draws nowadays are its **beaches**, though the huge duty-free Zona Franca in the north of the city also draws locals and visitors alike. The city is also one of the top destinations in Latin America for **paragliders**.

Plaza Prat

At the heart of Iquique's historic centre lies **Plaza Prat**, lined with banks and restaurants, with the tall white **Torre Reloj**, the city's symbol, built in 1877, as centrepiece. On the south side of the square stands the Neoclassical **Teatro Municipal**. The **Casino Español**, a 1904

IQUIQUE

ACCOMMODATION

Backpacker's Hostel Iquique	4
Casa de Huespedes "Profesores"	1
Hostel La Casona 1920	3
Hostal Cuneo	2
Flight Park	5

EATING, DRINKING & NIGHTLIFE

Canto del Mar	2
Casino Español	1
Doña Lucy	5
Mercado Centenario	6
M.Koo	4
Otaku	9
Sala Murano	8
El Tercer Ojito	7
El Viejo Clipper	3

Moorish-style wooden building with an opulent interior, graces the northeast corner of the square and is worth a visit both for the interior decorations and for the delicious pisco sours.

Calle Baquedano

Heading south from Plaza Prat towards Playa Bellavista, quiet pedestrianized **Calle Baquedano**, with its elevated boardwalks and grand wooden buildings, is strikingly different from the modern parts of Iquique, with a faded colonial feel about it. The **Museo Regional**, at no. 951 (Tues–Fri 10am–5.30pm, Sat 9.30am–6pm; CH$1000), is home to a number of curious pre-Columbian artefacts, the most impressive of which are the Chinchorro mummies and skulls, deliberately deformed by having bandages wrapped tightly around them. The natural history section features a sea-lion embryo pickled in formaldehyde and an informative exhibition on nitrate extraction in the area, along with a scale model of the ghost town of Humberstone.

The beaches

Iquique's most popular beach, **Playa Cavancha** is sheltered in a bay alongside the busy main thoroughfare of Avenida Arturo Prat, about 2km from the main plaza. It is particularly popular with sunbathers and boogie-boarders and is safe for swimming. The boardwalk, which winds along the beach amid the palm trees and giant cacti, is always teeming

with bikers, rollerbladers and scores of sun worshippers; in the evenings a relaxed atmosphere prevails. At the north end of Playa Cavancha lies rocky **Playa Bellavista**, with several good surf breaks, while the large stretch of **Playa Brava**, lined by fun-fairs and themed restaurants, is south of the Peninsula de Cavancha, and is a popular landing spot for paragliders. The less crowded **Playa Huayquique** is located to the very south of the city; it also has good waves for surfers and can be reached by *colectivos* from the centre.

ARRIVAL AND INFORMATION

By plane Aeropuerto Diego Arecena lies 41km south of Iquique; Aerotransfer (☎57 2310800) drops you off at your door for CH$5000.

Destinations Arica (2 daily; 45min); La Paz (8 weekly; 1hr 5min); Santiago (up to 6 daily; 2hr 20min).

By bus The main terminal is inconveniently located at the north end of Patricio Lynch; numerous *colectivos* run to the city centre (CH$1500) and some bus companies pick up passengers at their central offices around Mercado Centenario. The Tur Bus terminal is slightly more central, on Esmeralda, at Ramírez.

Destinations Arica (10 daily; 4hr); Calama (4 daily; 6hr); Colchane (2 daily; 6hr); Copiapó (6 daily; 15hr); La Serena (6 daily; 18hr); Pica (13 daily; 1hr 30min); San Pedro de Atacama (1 daily; 8hr); Santiago (8 daily; 24hr).

Tourist information Aníbal Pinto 436 (Mon–Fri 10am–6pm, Sat 10am–2pm; ☎57 2419241, ✉infoiquique @sernatur.cl). Staff can advise on city attractions and provide maps of the city. The Conaf office at Juan Antonio 2808 (Mon–Fri 8.30am–1.30pm & 3–5pm; ☎57 2432085) can provide information on the Volcán Isluga National Park and arrange accommodation there.

PARAGLIDING IN IQUIQUE

Few things compare to the sheer rush of running off the cliff at **Alto Hospicio** on the plateau above Iquique. Once the butterflies settle, you find yourself soaring gently with white-headed eagles as tiny houses with minute turquoise swimming pools, ocean-side high-rises, beaches and the giant sand dune of Cerro Dragón spread out beneath you. **Paragliding** feels entirely different from flying in an aeroplane, and the views from above are nothing short of incredible. You fly in tandem with an experienced instructor, who guides you through the entire procedure, from take-off to landing. Recommended operators are **Altazor Sky Sports** (☎57 2380110, ☎9 88261860, ⓦaltazor.cl), and **Puro Vuelo**, Baquedano 1440 (☎57 2311127, ☎9 95350157, ⓦpurovuelo.cl), which both offer paragliding courses as well as tandem flights. Puro Vuelo also provide a CD of pictures of you during, before and after your flight (optional: CH$13,000). Flights typically cost CH$40,000 for half an hour; transport to and from the paragliding site is included. If you want to enjoy a beer with some of the world's best paragliding talent, consider staying at *Flight Park Altazor* (see p.418). For the more faint of heart, tour companies will also help you organize a **sandboarding** trip on the dunes.

ACCOMMODATION

★ **Backpacker's Hostel Iquique** Amunátegui 2075, about 2km south of Plaza Prat ☎57 2320223, ⓦhostel iquique.cl. With English-speaking staff who help organize trips in the area, a friendly atmosphere and a superb beachside location, this hostel remains a firm backpacker favourite. Kitchen facilities, free internet and frequent barbecues are part of the draw. Dorms CH$6500, doubles CH$25,000

Casa de Huéspedes "Profesores" Ramírez 839 ☎57 2314475, ⓔinfo@hostalcasadelprofesor.cl. Friendly guesthouse with internet and wi-fi, laundry service, bike rental and a tour agency. Rooms by the patio have been recently refurbished. Dorms CH$9000, doubles CH$21,000

Hostel La Casona 1920 Barros Arana 1585 ☎57 2413000, ⓦcasonahosteliquique.cl. Excellent, welcoming hostel in the childhood home of charming owner Isabel, offering spotless rooms with good lockers, spacious communal areas and a family atmosphere. No private bathrooms. Dorms CH$8000, doubles CH$20,000

Hostal Cuneo Baquedano 1175 ☎57 2428654, ⓔhostal cuneo@hotmail.com. Cosy, quiet and conveniently located family-run *residencial*, with tidy rooms for up to four, and dorms, many with cable TV, some en suite; breakfast included. Doubles CH$25,000

Flight Park Via 6, Manzana Am Sitio 3, Bajo Molle, about a 15min bus ride from town ☎57 2380110, ⓣ9 98862362, ⓦaltazor.cl. Built almost entirely of ship containers, the rooms at this international paragliding centre are surprisingly inviting, with shared kitchen, internet access and chilled-out communal areas. Check their website for directions. Doubles CH$18,000, camping/person CH$4000

EATING

Canto del Mar Baquedano, at Thompson. Popular and bustling restaurant on the plaza, serving filling meat and fish dishes and good daily specials. Grilled fish CH$5500.

Doña Lucy Vivar 855, local 4. Pleasant café to while away an afternoon or wait for a bus, with huge slices of cream-filled cake (CH$1700).

Mercado Centenario Barros Arana. This market is the place for fresh produce and generous helpings of fish and seafood for lunch; *Sureña II* and *La Picada* are very popular. Fish with side dish CH$4200.

M.Koo Latorre 600. An excellent central spot for takeaway *pastel de choclo* and *humitas*, as well as tasty *empanadas* and *chumbeques* (local sweet biscuits). *Empanada* CH$600.

Otaku Av Arturo Prat 3082 ☎57 542850. Small but excellent and reasonably priced sushi restaurant with takeaway on Playa Brava; open late. Six California rolls CH$3500.

★ **El Tercer Ojito** Patricio Lynch 1420, between Perez and Riquelme ☎57 2426517. One of the best restaurants in town, set in a pretty courtyard, with sublime fish dishes, delicious bread and sushi in the evenings. Vegetarian lasagne CH$6500.

El Viejo Clipper Baquedano 796. Popular pub/restaurant with outdoor terrace on pedestrianized Baquedano, offering meat, fish, pasta and pizza. Pizzas from CH$3600.

DRINKING AND NIGHTLIFE

Casino Español Plaza Prat 584. The food here is pricey, but it's worth a visit for some of the best pisco sours in Chile. Pisco sour CH$3000.

Sala Murano Bajo Molle Km7 ⓦsalamurano.com. Two-tiered dancefloor mostly playing dance and pop music. Entry CH$3000–5000. Wed–Sat midnight–5am.

AROUND IQUIQUE

The nitrate pampas inland from Iquique is dotted with **ghost towns** left over from

---

IQUIQUE TOUR OPERATORS

Apart from sandboarding and **paragliding** on Cerro Dragón, and **surfing** all along Iquique's coast, the area around the city has a wealth of attractions on offer, including trips to the **ghost town** of Humberstone, the Gigante de Atacama **geoglyph**, the **hot springs** of Mamiña and the Pica oasis, the **burial site** of an Inca princess at the village of La Tirana, and the sobering **mass graves** from the Pinochet era at the tiny settlement of Pisagua. The cheapest – though perhaps not the most satisfying – tours combine a whistle-stop trip through all these attractions in a day (about CH$20,000). We recommend the following operators:

Avitours Baquedano 997 ☎57 413334, ⓦavitours .cl. Day-trips to the local hot springs, geoglyphs and ghost towns as well as longer excursions to Parque Nacional Volcán Isluga and multi-day trips to Parque Nacional Lauca and Reserva Las Vicuñas, finishing either in Arica or in Iquique.

Civet Adventure Bolívar 684 ☎57 2428483,

ⓔecivetcor@vtr.net, ⓦcivet-adventure.cl. Customized 4WD trips to *altiplano* destinations with an expert guide and an all-new desert buggy.

Turismo Santa Teresita Ramírez 839 ☎57 2314475. Arranges paragliding sessions and runs day-trips to the hot springs, Pisagua, La Tirana and other regional attractions.

the area's mining heyday, with the biggest and best-preserved example being **Humberstone** (daily: March–Nov 9am–6pm; Dec–Feb 9am–7pm; CH$1000; 45km to the east. Established in the middle of parched desert land in 1862, this once-thriving mining town bears the name of its British manager, James Humberstone. Visitors can wander the eerie streets where squalid and partially wrecked worker barracks contrast sharply with the faded glamour of the theatre and the well-maintained church. Workers here, mostly Chilean but some foreign, earned a pittance by putting in long hours in a hot and dangerous environment.

The thermal springs at **Pica**, 114km southeast of Iquique, are well worth a visit for a relaxing splash around; the most popular is **Cocha Resbaladero** (daily 8am–9pm; CH$1000). The small, pre-Hispanic town is also famed for producing limes widely believed to make the perfect pisco sour, and the pretty **Iglesia de San Andrés**.

ARICA

ARICA, Chile's northernmost city, 316km north of Iquique, benefits greatly from tourism, with foreign visitors flocking to its pleasant sandy beaches in the summer, and with a smattering of good museums. The city was the principal port exporting silver from Bolivia's Potosí mines until 1776, and only became part of Chile in the 1880s after the War of the Pacific. Aside from its own attractions, Arica makes a good base for the beautiful Parque Nacional Lauca (see p.423).

WHAT TO SEE AND DO

The compact city centre is easy to explore on foot, though a visit to Arica isn't complete without climbing **El Morro**, the dramatic cliff that looms high over the city.

El Morro

A steep path leads to the top of **El Morro** from the southern end of Calle Colón. From the clifftop, home to a number of turkey vultures and a giant Jesus statue

that lights up at night, you can enjoy a magnificent panoramic view of the entire city. Also up here, with cannons stationed outside, is the **Museo Histórico y de Armas** (daily 8am–8pm; CH$600), with displays of weaponry, uniforms and other artefacts from the War of the Pacific.

The city centre

Below El Morro is the large, palm-tree-lined **Plaza Vicuña Mackenna**, and alongside that lies Avenida Máximo Lira, the main coastal road. On the east side is the attractive **Plaza Colón**, decorated with pink flowers and ornate fountains. The plaza is home to one of Arica's most celebrated buildings, the Gothic **Iglesia de San Marcos**, designed by Gustave Eiffel (of Eiffel Tower fame), made entirely out of iron and shipped over from France in 1876. Eiffel was also responsible for the grand 1874 **Ex-Aduana** building nearby, alongside the Parque General Baquedano. This now houses the Casa de Cultura, and regularly hosts art and photo exhibitions. The main thoroughfare, **21 de Mayo**, heads east from here before becoming a pedestrian strip, lined with restaurants and banks. Just off it, at Sangra 315, the **Museo del Mar** (Mon–Sat 11am–7pm; CH$2000) houses the impressive, personal collection of Nicols Hrepic Gutunic, who has spent much of his life collecting more than one thousand species of shells from Chile and across the globe. To the west is the bustling **Terminal Pesquero**, where sea lions compete with pelicans for scraps from the dockside fish stalls.

The beaches

North of the centre and west of the bus terminals lies the popular **Playa Chinchorro**, which is ideal for swimming, sunbathing and body-boarding. The city's northernmost beach, **Playa Las Machas**, is not suitable for swimming due to the strong undertow but has some good surf breaks. A twenty-minute walk south of the centre will bring you to the sandy **Playa El Laucho** and **Playa La Lisera**, both popular with sun worshippers and good

4

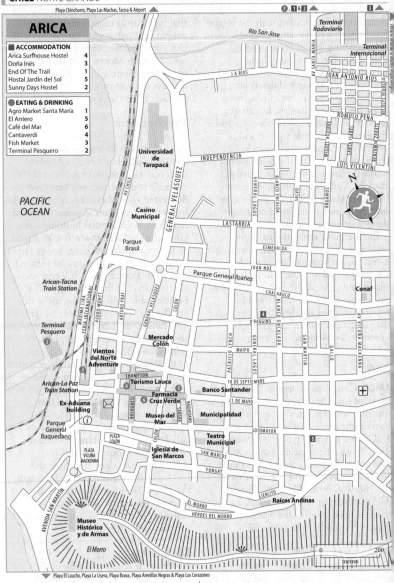

ARICA

ACCOMMODATION

Arica Surfhouse Hostel	4
Doña Inés	3
End Of The Trail	1
Hostal Jardín del Sol	5
Sunny Days Hostel	2

EATING & DRINKING

Agro Market Santa María	1
El Arriero	5
Café del Mar	6
Cantaverdi	4
Fish Market	3
Terminal Pesquero	2

for swimming, followed by the pretty **Playa Brava** and the dark-sand **Playa Arenillas Negra**, which has rougher waves. Finally, there's **Playa Los Corazones**, a beautiful expanse of clean sand flanked by cliffs 8km south of town. The southern beaches can be reached by *colectivo*, though these tend to run only during the summer season.

Museo Arqueológico

The excellent **Museo Arqueológico** (daily: Jan–Feb 10am–7pm; March–Dec 10am–6pm; CH$2000) lies 12km from Arica in the green **Azapa Valley**. The museum traces the history of the valley's inhabitants, from the earliest hunter-gatherers, via a remarkably thorough collection of regional pre-Hispanic artefacts. Most impressive of these are the four elaborately prepared **Chinchorro mummies** – a male, a female and two young children, which are believed to be around seven thousand years old, making them by far the oldest mummies in the world. To get there, catch one of the yellow *colectivos* labelled "Azapa" which run along Avenida Diego Portales past the bus terminals.

ARRIVAL AND DEPARTURE

By plane Aeropuerto Internacional Chacalluta is 18km north of Arica; a radio taxi downtown costs around CH$6000, or a *colectivo* CH$4000.
Destinations Iquique (2 daily; 45min); Santiago (4 daily; 2hr 40min).
By train The Arica–Tacna train station is located at Máximo Lira 889, on the northwest edge of the city centre, but services have been suspended since April 2012 and are not likely to resume before 2014.
By bus Terminal Rodovario, at Diego Portales 948, is the main stop for local arrivals, plus a few international; inside there are cash machines and snack kiosks. Terminal Internacional is immediately adjacent, with arrivals from La Paz and numerous *micros* and *colectivos* crossing the border from Tacna, Peru.
Destinations Antofagasta (6 daily; 10hr); Arequipa (daily 8am; 12hr); Cusco (daily 10am; 20hr) and Lima (daily at noon; 20hr); Calama (several daily; 9hr); Copiapó (several daily; 16hr); Iquique (frequent daily departures; 4hr); La Paz (4–5 daily, morning departures; 7hr); La Serena (6 daily; 19hr); Parinacota (1 daily Tues–Fri; about 5hr); San Pedro de Atacama (1 overnight; 11hr); Santiago (4–6 daily; 28hr); Salta and Jujuy, Argentina (Mon, Thurs & Sat at 10pm; 25hr).

INFORMATION

Tourist information The tourist office is at San Marcos 101 (March–Dec Mon–Thurs 9am–6pm, Fri 9am–5pm; Jan–Feb Sat & Sun 9am–5pm also; ☎ 58 2252054, ✉ infoarica @sernatur.cl). Helpful staff provide maps of town and a plethora of brochures on arica. Conaf has an office at Av Vicuña Mackenna 820 (☎ 58 2201200). Staff provide information on, and maps of, local national parks; reserve beds at regional Conaf *refugios* here.

ACCOMMODATION

You can camp for free at the Playa Las Machas.
Arica Surfhouse Hostel O'Higgins 661 ☎ 58 2312213, ⓦ aricasurfhouse.cl. This centrally located hostel has spacious rooms, and caters well to its surfer clientele, as well as organizing other activities including horseriding and paragliding. Dorms CH$10,000, doubles CH$27,000
Doña Inés Manuel Rojas 2864 ☎ 58 2248108, ✉ hiarica @hostelling.cl. The inconvenient location of this hostel is compensated for by the owner's hospitality, knowledge and insatiable enthusiasm. Pluses are free internet, bike rental, and a cosy common room with TV. To get there, take *colectivo* #4 from the bus station to Chapiquiña (corner of Blest Gana); the hostel is on the left. Dorms CH$9500, doubles CH$22,000
End of the Trail Esteban Alvarado 117 ☎ 58 2314316, ☎ 9 77863972, ⓦ endofthetrail-arica.cl. A congenial American owner runs this brand-new hostel, which has comfortable, quiet rooms around an indoor courtyard, amazing showers and a specially designed roof that keeps the house cool. Breakfast included. To get there from the bus station, walk two blocks west on Diego Portales, then four blocks south on Pedro de Valdivia. Dorms CH$9000, doubles CH$26,000
Hostal Jardín del Sol Sotomayor 848 ☎ 58 2232795, ⓦ hostaljardindelsol.cl. Central *hostal* run by a very helpful

---

TOUR OPERATORS AROUND ARICA

A number of tour companies offer trips into the **national parks** outside Arica. The standard three- to four-day trip takes in Parque Nacional Lauca, Reserva Nacional Las Vicuñas, Salar de Surire and Parque Nacional Volcán Isluga, with overnight stops in the *altiplano* villages of Putre and Colchane. Most tours either return to Arica or drop passengers off in Iquique. Normally, a minimum of two people is required per tour and a three-day all-inclusive package costs around CH$196,000; the price reduces the more people join on the trip. Tour operators do offer day-trips taking in Parque Nacional Lauca, and Putre, but this is not recommended as the altitude change is extreme, and is at best likely to make you feel queasy.

Raíces Andinas Héroes de Morro 632 ☎ 58 2233305, ⓦ raicesandinas.com. Tour operator with close links to the local Aymará communities, promoting ecotourism and Aymará culture. Also operate Parinacota Expediciones (ⓦ parinacotaexpediciones.cl), who offer a trip

through Parque Nacional Lauca into Bolivia.
Turismo Lauca Thompson 200, at Bolognesi ☎ 58 2220067, ⓦ turismolauca.cl. Standard trips around the national park circuit, as well as city tours, and archeological interest trips.

and welcoming couple who organize all manner of outdoor activities for guests. Most rooms are en suite; shares arranged. Kitchen, lounge, wi-fi, cable TV, bicycle rent and laundry service are some of the bonuses. Breakfast included. Doubles CH$22,000

★ **Sunny Days Hostel** Tomas Aravena 161 ☏ 58 2241038, ⊚ sunny-days-arica.cl. Extremely friendly and knowledgeable Kiwi-Chilean hosts preside over travellers of all ages in this custom-built hostel. Free internet, excellent breakfast, kitchen and lounge facilities and a relaxed communal atmosphere all add to its appeal. Dorms CH$9000, doubles CH$26,000

EATING AND DRINKING

Agro Market Santa Maria Av Santa Maria, at Diego Portales. Chilean and Peruvian cuisine goes to *mano a mano* in this packed, bustling food hall, just one block from bus terminal and some popular hostels. Try Manos Peruanas. *Ceviche* CH$4500.

El Arriero 21 de Mayo 385. Atmospheric steakhouse with fantastic grilled meat and expertly prepared fish dishes; slightly pricier than the competition. Steak in pepper sauce CH$7990.

Café del Mar 21 de Mayo 260. Popular restaurant with a bargain *menú del día*, plus large salads and good quiches. Quiche CH$2500.

Cantaverdi Bolognesi 453. Attractive, much frequented pub with a pleasant buzz, serving snacks and pizzas along with a wide range of drinks. Salads CH$2500.

Fish market Av Máximo Lira, at C 21 de Mayo. Excellent place to pick up some inexpensive sea bass *ceviche* (CH$1000).

Terminal Pesquero Off Av Máximo Lira, across from entrance to C 21 de Mayo. Several no-frills oceanside eateries here cook up hearty portions of inexpensive fish dishes; *Mata Rangi*, in particular, stands out. Set lunch CH$5200.

PUTRE

The highland village of **PUTRE** sits at an altitude of 3500m and provides an ideal acclimatization point for venturing into the Parque Nacional Lauca. Populated by the indigenous Aymará people, Putre consists of basic stone houses centred around a square. It is a tranquil place to spend a few days, and is becoming an increasing must-see on the backpacker trail, with a growing number of accommodation options. Note that the only bank, in the square's southeast corner, does not accept Visa.

ALTITUDE SICKNESS

Known here as *puna* or *soroche*, **altitude sickness** affects roughly a quarter of all travellers who venture above the altitude of about 2500m, regardless of age or fitness, though people with respiratory problems tend to suffer more. It is rarely life-threatening, though is dangerous for people suffering from hypothermia. Symptoms include vertigo, headaches, nausea, shortness of breath, lethargy and insomnia. Keeping properly hydrated and taking aspirin can alleviate some of the symptoms; **mate de coca** (tea brewed from coca leaves) is also widely believed to help. Avoid alcohol consumption, overeating and over-exertion; if symptoms persist, try to move to a lower elevation. The best way to avoid altitude sickness is to acclimatize gradually by breaking up your journey to higher regions into segments.

ARRIVAL AND INFORMATION

By bus La Paloma buses (☏ 58 2222710) depart daily from Arica to Putre at 7am from German Riesco 2071, returning to Arica from in front of Putre's *Hotel Kukuli* at 2pm (CH$3500).

Tourist information The tourist office is on the south side of the square (Mon–Fri 10am–2pm & 3–6pm). The Conaf office is at Teniente Del Campo, between La Torre and O'Higgins (☏ 9 77733032).

ACCOMMODATION

La Chakana A 20min walk from the plaza; head downhill past the church ☏ 9 97459519, ⊛ la-chakana.com. German-Chilean-run option, with comfy beds, filling breakfasts and a homely atmosphere. Dorms CH$10,000, doubles CH$32,000

Hostal Kali Baquedano 399 ☏ 9 85438716. Spare but clean rooms off central alley, breakfast available on request. Doubles CH$25,000

EATING

Cantaverdi Arturo Perez 339 East side of the square. Simple and centrally located restaurant, serving up large, inexpensive meals, often accompanied by a football game on TV. Set lunch CH$3500.

Kuchu Marka Baquedano. Homely stews and filling dishes are on offer at this traditional restaurant. Lunch menu CH$3800.

PARQUE NACIONAL LAUCA

From Putre, Ruta 11 leads up onto the *altiplano* to the **Parque Nacional Lauca**, a region of rich flora and fauna, shimmering lakes and snowcapped volcanoes 4300m above sea level. The most visited village at these dizzying heights is the little whitewashed settlement of **Parinacota**, accessible by public transport, though it's far easier to see the sights of Lauca on an organized tour.

Las Cuevas

The Conaf-run **Las Cuevas** *refugio* is located 9km into the park, and the nature trail near it is the best place to see **viscachas**, the long-tailed, rabbit-like relatives of chinchillas, as they use their powerful hind legs to leap from boulder to boulder. The well-watered *bofedal* (alluvial depression) here provides permanent grazing for herds of **vicuñas**, the wild relatives of llamas and alpacas, which are also commonly seen. In addition, you'll find numerous examples of the *llareta* plant, which takes three hundred years to grow to full size; the plant looks like a pile of oddly shaped green cushions but is actually rock-hard. The local Aymará break up the dead plants with picks for use as firewood. Just off the *refugio*'s nature trail are some rustic thermal baths.

Parinacota

The **Conaf** headquarters (daily 9am–12.30pm & 1–5.30pm) are located in the tiny Aymará village of **Parinacota**, 19km east of the Las Cuevas *refugio*. Parinacota is worth a stop for its cheerful, whitewashed little **church**, reconstructed in 1789, and for the stalls opposite, selling colourful local **artesanía**. Besides a fetching bell tower with a tiny doorway, the church (ask around for the guardian of the key) has murals depicting scenes of Jesus being borne to the cross by soldiers resembling Spanish conquistadors, as well as sinners burning in hell. A small wooden table is tethered to the wall to the left of the altar; legend has it that the table wandered around the village, causing the death of a man by stopping in front of his house – the chain prevents the table from escaping again.

Parinacota can be reached by **public bus** from the Terminal Internacional in Arica (departs Tues–Fri at 11am, returning at 9am the following day). It may be possible to rent a very basic **room** from a villager, or stay in the basic hostel opposite the church (ask at Raíces Andinas in Arica).

Lago Chungará

Some 18km east of Parinacota, at a breathtaking altitude of 4600m, lies the stunning **Lago Chungará**. With its brilliant blue waters perfectly reflecting the towering snowcapped cone of **Volcán Parinacota** (6350m), this is undoubtedly one of the highlights of the national park. The roadside **Conaf refugio** here has six basic beds (CH$5500 per person), kitchen facilities and three **camping** spaces (free). There is a short lakeside **nature trail**, which provides a good vantage point for viewing the giant coots, flamingos and Andean geese that nest here.

RESERVA NACIONAL LAS VICUÑAS AND SALAR DE SURIRE

A southbound turn-off from Ruta 11 by Lago Chungará heads through the 2091-square-kilometre **Reserva Nacional Las Vicuñas** towards the Salar de Surire salt lake. The *reserva* is made up of seemingly endless marshes and grasslands where herds of vicuñas can be seen grazing in the distance.

At an altitude of 4295m, the enormous, dirty-white **Salar de Surire** is home to up to ten thousand **flamingos** – mostly Chilean, but with a smattering of James and Andean species. Surire means "place of the rhea" in Aymará, and it's also possible to catch glimpses here of these swift, ostrich-like birds. On the southeast side of the salt flat are the **Termas de Polloquere**, several hot thermal pools amid a small geyser field, which are a good spot to soak and pamper yourself using the mud at the bottom of the pools. It is possible to **camp** at a rustic site near the pools.

There is no public transport to either the *reserva* or *salar*, and a tour is the easiest option.

4

PARQUE NACIONAL VOLCÁN ISLUGA

South of Las Vicuñas, the dirt track drifts eastwards, passing by large herds of **llamas** and their shorter and hairier **alpaca** cousins, as well as tiny, seemingly deserted Aymará hamlets. All these are overshadowed by the towering **Volcán Isluga** (5218m), from which the park takes its name. The little village of **Enquelga** is home to a small Conaf-run **refugio** with five beds and hot showers (CH$5500 per person), as well as a free **campsite** (1km east of town) with Conaf-maintained shelters alongside a stream and some hot springs. One warm pool here, against the impressive backdrop of the volcano, is large enough for swimming.

Just outside the park, the small farming settlement of **COLCHANE**, surrounded by fields of bright red quinoa and *kiwicha* (a highly nutritious local staple), has several basic **guesthouses** providing simple home-cooked food. It is possible to get on a bus from Iquique to Colchane (daily 1pm & 9pm; 3hr), and get dropped off at the park, but it is best to contact Conaf in advance for advice. For drivers, the road condition is poor and requires a 4WD vehicle.

Middle Chile

As the southernmost reaches of Santiago's sprawling suburbs fade away, a vast expanse of fertile fields, orchards and vineyards serves as a transition area between the bustling metropolitan borough and the natural landscapes of the Lake District. This is Chile's most fertile region, and home to the country's world-famous **wineries**, which are accessible by day-trip from Santiago but are much less rushed if taken from the quaint town of **Santa Cruz**. West of Santa Cruz is the country's surf capital of **Pichilemu**, where some of the world's biggest breaks crash along vast sandy beaches. Further south, **Concepción**, Chile's second-largest city, was the epicentre of a massive **earthquake** in

2010, which left more than 500 dead across the country. The worst affected towns were **Talca** and **Curicó**, which are likely to show the scars of the destructive quake for some years to come. They both serve as good bases for some excellent wine tours, however, and for trips to see the waterfalls and lush forests of the **Parque Nacional Radal Siete Tazas**, and the diverse wildlife of **Parque Nacional Nahuelbuta**.

RANCAGUA

RANCAGUA is a busy agricultural city that lies 87km south of Santiago. The best time for a day-trip here is either in April, to witness the **National Rodeo Championships**, or the last weekend in March, during the **Fiesta Huasa**, a three-day celebration of cowboy culture held in the main square, involving traditional food and wine. Alternatively, if you are coming in November, try to catch the **Encuentro Internacional Criollo**, a demonstration of spectacular horse-breaking and lassoing skills from expert riders from all over Latin America.

ARRIVAL AND INFORMATION

By bus The Terminal O'Higgins (☎72 2225425), hub for long-distance destinations, lies northeast of town, just off Ruta 5. Tur Bus, at O'Carrol 1175, has a more convenient, central location. Expreso Santa Cruz and Pullman Del Sur run buses on to Santa Cruz.

By train The hourly Metrotrén from Santiago and the faster train to Chillán stop at the Estación Rancagua (☎600 5855000), on Av Estación, between O'Carrol and Carrera Pinto, at the western edge of downtown.

Tourist information The helpful Sernatur office at Germán Riesco 277, 1st floor (Mon–Thurs 8.30am–5.30pm, Fri 8.30am–4.30pm; ☎72 2230413, ⊛turismo libertador.cl), can provide plenty of information on the city and its festivals.

SANTA CRUZ

About 90km southwest of Rancagua, the attractive little town of **SANTA CRUZ** lies at the heart of the fertile Colchagua Valley, home to Chile's best-organized *Ruta de Vino*. The hot climate here has proved to be perfect for growing Carmenère, Cabernet, Malbec and Syrah grapes. The ideal time to visit is during the first weekend in March, when the **Fiesta de La Vendimia del Valle de Colchagua** (grape harvest festival) is held, allowing you to sample the best wines and the region's typical dishes.

WHAT TO SEE AND DO

The heart of Santa Cruz is the gorgeous **Plaza de Armas**, dotted with araucarias, conifers and palm trees, with an ornate fountain at its centre and drinking fountains around its periphery. Within a couple of blocks of the plaza are numerous places to eat and *hospedajes*.

The excellent, privately run **Museo de Colchagua**, at Errázuriz 145 (daily: Dec–Feb 10am–7pm; rest of the year 10am–6pm; CH$5000, students CH$2000; ⓦmuseocolchagua.cl), displays the unmatched private collection of Carlos Cardoen, which includes pre-Columbian artefacts from around Latin America, conquistador weaponry, exquisite gold work, Mapuche weavings, a re-creation of the San José mine rescue and much more. Cardoen himself is a highly controversial figure: still wanted by the FBI for allegedly selling weapons to Iraq in the 1980s, the former arms dealer has transformed himself into a successful businessman and philanthropist with extensive interests in wine and tourism.

ARRIVAL AND INFORMATION

By bus Terminal Municipal is on Casanova, four blocks southwest of the Plaza de Armas.
Destinations Pichilemu (10 daily; 2hr); Santiago (more than 10 daily; 2hr 30min).
Tourist information The Ruta de Vino headquarters on the east side of the Plaza de Armas 298 (Mon–Fri 9am–6pm, Sat & Sun 10am–6pm; ☎72 2823199, ⓦrutadelvino.cl) is an excellent source of information on the Valle Colchagua (see box below).

ACCOMMODATION

Gomero Capellania 327 ☎72 2821436. Unremarkable hotel with clean but not particularly inviting rooms, and friendly staff. Breakfast included. Rooms CH$25,000

EATING AND DRINKING

Café Sorbo Casanova 158, on the 2nd floor of a cultural centre. Extremely friendly café/restaurant with quality coffee, and great choice for vegetarians. Soya hamburger CH$6800.
Pizzeria Refranes Diaz Besoain 176. Opposite the fire station. Traditional Chilean dishes combine with an excellent range of *empanadas* and divine slabs of pizza in a pleasant ambience. Large pizza CH$4990.

PICHILEMU

The drive to the surfing magnet of **PICHILEMU**, 90km west of Santa Cruz, is particularly scenic. The road meanders past sun-drenched vineyards before snaking in and out of patches of pine

---

RUTA DEL VINO DE COLCHAGUA

The **Colchagua Valley** has some of the best red wines in the world, not to mention the best-organized **wine route** in Chile. There are fourteen **wineries** in all, including both large, modern producers and small-scale, traditional *bodegas*; many of them can be visited on a drop-by basis or at short notice. The Ruta del Vino headquarters in Santa Cruz organizes full-day and half-day tours that commence at 10.30am, taking in two or three wineries, along with lunch and a visit to the Museo de Colchagua. Rates depend on the number of people and type of tour; a half-day tour without lunch will cost around CH$39,000, while full-day tours start at CH$75,000.

WINERIES

Viña Casa Silva Hijuela Norte s/n Angostura, Km132, Ruta 5, San Fernando ☎72 2913117, ⓦcasasilva.cl. Award-winning winery set in a colonial-style hacienda, using modern technology to produce Carmenère, as well as the less common Viognier, Sauvignon Gris and Shiraz. Tours CH$10,000/person.
Viña Laura Hartwig Camino Barreales s/n ☎72 2823179, ⓦlaurahartwig.cl. Small, family-owned,

boutique winery producing only reserve-quality wines; the owners directly oversee each stage of production. Book in advance. Tours CH$10,000/person.
Viña Viu Manent Carretera del Vino Km37 ☎72 2858751, ⓦviumanent.cl. Family-owned winery famous for its excellent reds, especially Malbec, offering horse-drawn carriage tours as part of its attraction. Tours including carriage ride CH$14,000/person.

4

forest. "Pichi", as it's known, was originally planned as an upmarket vacation spot by the local land baron Agustín Ross Edwards, though in recent years it's become ever more popular with a motley crew of **surfers** and local beach bums.

WHAT TO SEE AND DO

A spread-out town, Pichilemu has numerous guesthouses and places to eat concentrated along the east–west Avenida Ortúzar, and the north–south Aníbal Pinto, a couple of blocks from the sea.

Playa Las Terrazas

Avenida Costanera Cardenal Caro runs alongside the black-sand expanse of **Playa Las Terrazas**, Pichilemu's principal beach. Good for both sunbathers and surfers, it has a cluster of places to eat and **surf schools** concentrated towards its southern end, at the rocky promontory of La Puntilla. Steps lead up to the meticulously landscaped **Parque Ross**, dotted with palm trees and boasting an excellent view of the coast.

Punta de Lobos

Chile's most famous wave, **Punta de Lobos**, where the National Surfing Championships are held every summer, can be found 6km south of downtown Pichilemu; to get there, take a *colectivo* along Jorge Errázuriz (CH$800), or cycle down Comercio until you reach the turn-off towards the coast and make your way to the end of the jutting, cactus-studded headland. At the tip of the promontory, intrepid surfers descend via a steep dirt path before swimming across the short churning stretch of water to **Las Tetas**, the distinctive sea stacks, and

catching the powerful, consistent left break just beyond.

ARRIVAL AND INFORMATION

By bus The main Terminal Municipal is located on Millaco, at Los Alerces, though unless you're staying in Pichi's southeastern quarter it's more convenient to disembark at the bus stop on Angel Gaete. There are hourly departures to Santiago (daily 4.30am–6.40pm; about 3hr 30min; Buses Cruz Mar and Buses Nilahue stop in Santa Cruz and Rancagua). Buy your ticket at the bus offices on Angel Gaete at Aníbal Pinto, and catch them at the bus stop on Santa María, four blocks northeast.

Spanish school Pichilemu Languages Institute (☎72 2842449, ⓦstudyspanishchile.com) offers short- and longer-term Spanish classes.

Tourist information There is a helpful booth on Angel Gaete, between Montt and Rodríguez (Mon–Fri 8am–1pm & 2.30–7pm; ⓦpichilemu.cl), which gives out maps of town and can help with accommodation.

ACCOMMODATION

Hostal Casa Verde Camino Vecinal 295, opposite Dunamar Cabanas, on Playa Hermosa Pasaje San Alfonso s/n; walk up the track opposite Verde Mar supermarket, ☎9 92998866, ☎9 81291274, ⓦhostalcasaverde.cl. About 3km from town, this small but popular hostel has good breakfasts, surfing classes, free bike rental, and a chilled-out vibe. Dorms CH$12,000, doubles CH$34,000

Hotel Chile España Av Ortúzar 255 ☎72 2841270, ⓦchileespana.cl. Smart, central guesthouse with clean and comfortable rooms; breakfast is included and there's a pleasant patio area. Doubles CH$50,000

La Higuera Angel Gaete 467 ☎72 2841321. This long-standing guesthouse in town has a messy-looking court-yard with basic rooms but it is well located just up from the bus drop-off point. Dorms CH$7000

EATING, DRINKING AND NIGHTLIFE

El Balaustro Av Ortúzar 289. Conveniently located, two-tiered pub which serves excellent lunchtime specials, both meat and fish, and has nightly drinks deals. Set lunch CH$4900.

SURF'S UP!

Budding surfers wanting to get in on the action can hone their skills with the help of several surfing schools:

Lobos del Pacífico Av Costanera ☎9 5062127, ⓦlobosdelpacifico.cl. Experienced surfing instructor charges CH$12,000 per lesson (2hr 30min), which includes board and wetsuit rental. Equipment rental alone costs CH$8000.

Manzana 54 Surf School Av Costanera, next to *Waitara Restaurant* ☎9 5745984, ⓦmanzana54.cl. Professional surf school and equipment rental offering lessons for CH$18,000 (2hr), all equipment included. Equipment rental alone is CH$7000–8000 for a full day.

La Casa de las Empanadas Aníbal Pinto, between Aguirre & Acevedo. Takeaway with amazing range of excellent *empanadas* (CH$1200).

Disco 127 Av Angel Gaete s/n. Pounding venue that acts as a magnet for Pichilemu's youth and surfing population. Doesn't kick off until after midnight.

Waitara Av Costanera 1039d ☎ 72 2843004, ⊕ waitara .cl. The restaurant here is more appealing than the cabañas – its lunchtime menu features tasty and well-cooked fish dishes. Mains CH$5000.

CURICÓ

The garden city of **CURICÓ**, 56km south of Santa Cruz along the Panamericana highway, makes for a good brief stop if you want to visit the nearby wineries or the Reserva Nacional Radal Siete Tazas. The **Plaza de Armas** is shaded by a variety of native trees, with several modern sculptures to add character. The **Vinícola Miguel Torres** (daily: April–Oct 10am–5pm; Nov–March 10am–7pm; CH$6000; ☎ 75 2564100, ⊕ miguel torres.cl), a Spanish-owned vineyard just south of Curicó, is a good spot for a drop-in visit, with an informative video on wine production followed by a sampling of the many wines available; there is also an excellent restaurant on-site. Molina-bound *colectivos* can drop you off very near the entrance.

ARRIVAL AND INFORMATION

By bus Most long-distance carriers arrive at the Terminal de Buses Rurales on Montt, at O'Higgins.
Destinations Chillán (6–8 daily; 2hr 30min); Santiago (every 30min; 3hr); Talca (every 15min; 1hr); Temuco (5 daily; 8hr). Minibuses shuttle to Santa Cruz (every 30min; 2hr).
By train The station for services between Chillán and Santiago is at Maipú 657 (☎ 600 5855000).
Destinations Chillán (6 daily; 2hr 30min); Santiago (6 daily; 2hr); Talca (6 daily; 50min).
Tourist information A new and enthusiastic municipal tourist information office has opened at Av Manso de Velasco 449, Corporacion Cultural building 2nd floor (Mon–Fri 10am–1.30pm & 3.30–6pm; ☎ 075 2543045). Information on the Ruta del Vino Curicó is available at the helpful office at Prat 301-A (☎ 75 2328972, ⊕ rutadelvino curico.cl).

ACCOMMODATION AND EATING

Plaza Bonissimo Yungay 615. Just off the plaza, this place serves up an excellent three-course lunch (CH$2500),

and transforms into a busy bar in the evenings with good drinks deals.

Hotel Prat Peña 427 ☎ 75 2311069. Clean and comfortable rooms around a courtyard, free internet access, breakfast and cable TV. Doubles CH$35,000

PARQUE NACIONAL RADAL SIETE TAZAS

Some 73km southeast of Curicó, the **Parque Nacional Radal Siete Tazas** (daily: April–Nov 8.30am–5.30pm; Dec–March 8.30am–8pm; CH$4000) is named after an astonishing natural phenomenon in which the crystalline Río Claro has carved the basalt rock face into a series of "cups", interconnected by seven **waterfalls**, plummeting from high above. Though the waterfall run is a favourite of expert **kayakers** during the spring snowmelt, the reserve otherwise gets few visitors outside the summer holidays and weekends. From the Conaf Administration, a short trail runs through a lush forest to a **mirador** overlooking the "teacups". Longer hikes to Cerro El Fraile and Valle del Indio are also possible.

> ### ★ TREAT YOURSELF
> **Casa Chueca** Camino Las Rastras s/n ☎ 71 1970096, ☎ 9 94190625, ⊕ trekkingchile.com. The best place to stay in the area by far is the *Casa Chueca*. Located on the banks of the Río Lircay, a short distance out of Talca, this German/Austrian-run guesthouse is a peaceful retreat, with comfortable and charmingly decorated rooms for one to three people, delicious, home-cooked, mainly vegetarian meals and a swimming pool set amid its lush gardens. Franz Schubert, its knowledgeable owner, also runs excellent guided excursions into the little-visited and underappreciated protected areas nearby.
>
> To get here, take a "Taxutal A" bus from the bus stop at the southeast corner of the main bus terminal to the end of the route; if possible, call the guesthouse beforehand so that they can pick you up. Otherwise, follow the dirt road from Taxutal for about twenty minutes. Closed Easter–Sept 18. Dorms CH$10,000, doubles CH$41,000

ARRIVAL AND INFORMATION

By bus Public buses run year-round from Curicó to Radal, at the western tip of the park, via the village of Molina (Mon–Sat 8am–5.30pm). In summer, Buses Radal 7 Tazas runs to Parque Inglés (mid-Dec to Feb: 8 services Mon–Sat 10am–8pm; 6 services Sun 7.45am–9pm).

Conaf Conaf Administration is located in the western Parque Inglés Sector, where the park fee of CH$4000 is collected. There are talks on the flora and fauna at the Centro de Información on Sat (times vary).

ACCOMMODATION

Camping Los Robles ☎ 71 228029. Of several campsites, this large one at Parque Inglés is the pick, with hot showers, toilets, picnic tables and fire pits in an attractive spot, surrounded by native forest and within walking distance of several waterfalls; the site at Radal tends to be rather dirty during peak season. Pitch **CH$12,000**

TALCA

The agricultural city of **TALCA** makes a good base for exploring the nearby **Valle del Maule** and its **Ruta de Vino**, though the town itself has few attractions and was severely damaged in the February zolo earthquake.

The city's streets are on a numbered grid, making it very easy to navigate. Most of the commercial activity revolves around the **Plaza de Armas**, dominated by the cathedral, between 1 Norte, 1 Sur, 1 Poniente and 1 Oriente. Banks and pharmacies line 1 Sur, and there are numerous inexpensive places to eat and *completo* stands within a couple of blocks of the square. Unfortunately, the Museo O'Higgiano, at 1 Norte 875, where the national hero Bernardo O'Higgins spent his childhood and signed the Declaration of Independence in 1818, remains closed due to severe damage suffered in the 2010 quake.

ARRIVAL AND DEPARTURE

By train The station (**☎** 2 2585 5927) is at 11 Oriente 1000; there is no luggage storage.

Destinations Curicó (6 daily; 45min); Santiago (6 daily; 3hr); Chillán (6 daily; 1hr 50min).

By bus Most long-distance and local buses arrive at the Terminal Rodoviario at 2 Sur 1920 (**☎** 71 2243270), ten blocks east of the Plaza de Armas; the Tur Bus terminal (**☎** 71 2414807) is at 13 Oriente No 1962 on the corner with 3 Sur. Frequent *colectivos* go back and forth along 1 Sur to and from the train and bus stations.

Destinations Chillán (every 30min; 2hr); Puerto Montt (5 daily; 10hr); Santiago (hourly; 3hr 30min); Temuco (8 daily; 6hr).

INFORMATION

Tourist information The well-stocked and very useful Sernatur office is found in the Correos, on the east side of Plaza de Armas, at 1 Oriente 1150 (Mon–Fri 8.30am–5.30pm, Sat 10am–2pm; **☎** 71 2233669, **e** infomaule @sernatur.cl). The helpful Conaf office, at 2 Poniente/3 Sur (**☎** 71 2228029), has information on the Reserva Nacional Altos de Lircay and Radal Siete Tazas.

ACCOMMODATION

Hostal del Puente 1 Sur 407 **☎** 71 2220930, **e** hotel delpuente@gmail.com. Small but elegant rooms set around a beautiful leafy courtyard, in a traditional adobe house just two blocks from the Plaza de Armas. Doubles **CH$28,000**

Refugio del Tricahue w refugio-tricahue.cl, **e** refugio .tricahue@yahoo.fr. Run by French-Belgian couple Betty and Dimitri, this nature lover's retreat has simple wooden

---

RUTA DEL VINO DEL MAULE

Valle del Maule is rapidly developing a **Ruta del Vino** involving fifteen wineries, most of which require reservations to visit. The Ruta del Vino del Maule headquarters at Avenida Circunvalacion Oriente No 1055 in the lobby of Talca's casino (Mon–Sat 8.30am–2pm & 5–8pm; **☎** 9 81579951, **w** valledelmaule.cl) can help to arrange full-day and half-day visits to the nearby wineries. Good options include:

Viña Balduzzi Av Balmaceda 1189, San Javier, **☎** 73 2322138, **w** balduzzi.cl. Operating since the seventeenth century, this family winery runs interesting guided tours (CH$5000/person) and tastings in English, and is the easiest to visit by public transport: take the San Javier bus from Talca. No need to reserve. Mon–Sat 9.30am–6.30pm.

Viña Gillmore Camino a Constitución Km20, San Javier **☎** 73 1975539, **w** gillmore.cl. A boutique winery producing Cabernet Franc, Carignan, Malbec, Syrah, Carmenère and Merlot that doubles as a luxury agro-tourism resort, complete with a "winotherapy" spa. Call to arrange a tour.

chalets set against a beautiful backdrop of tree-covered mountains, with opportunities for fishing, trekking and cycling. Take Bus Interbus from Talca terminal towards Armerillo (7 buses daily; 1hr 30min). Email ahead to make a reservation. Camping/person CH$3500, dorms CH$6000, doubles CH$14,000

EATING

La Buena Carne 1 Norte 1305. Large restaurant specializing in grilled meat, owned by the butchers on the opposite corner. Excellent cuts at bargain prices. *Lomo vetado* (Ribeye) CH$2990.

Restaurant Via Lactea 1 Sur 1339, local 10. Restaurant serving a range of meat and fish dishes and an excellent selection of ice cream. Tables fill up in the evenings. Mains CH$3500–CH$7000.

CHILLÁN

CHILLÁN lies 150km south of Talca in the middle of the green **Itata Valley**. A nondescript town rebuilt time and time again after earthquake damage and Mapuche attacks, Chillán is famous as the birthplace of Chile's national hero and founding father, Bernardo O'Higgins. It also boasts an excellent market, overflowing with an abundance of fresh produce and authentic Mapuche handicrafts. The centre of town is the **Plaza Bernardo O'Higgins**, featuring a towering 36m cross commemorating the thirty thousand victims of the 1939 earthquake, which largely destroyed the city. **Escuela Mexico**, a school built with Mexico's donations in the wake of the earthquake, draws visitors with its frescoes, painted by the famous **Mexican muralists** David Alfaro Siqueiros and Xavier Guerrero. They depict famous figures from Latin American history.

ARRIVAL AND INFORMATION

By bus Most long-distance buses arrive at the Terminal María Teresa at Av O'Higgins 10 (☎42 2272151), while the regional firm Linea Azul operates its own terminal at Constitución 1 (☎42 2203800). Buses from local destinations, such as the Valle Las Trancas, arrive at the rural bus terminal at the market.

Destinations Concepción (8 daily; 1hr 30min); Curicó (every 30min; 2hr); Santiago (every 50min; 6hr); Talca (8 daily; 3hr).

By train The station is at Av Brasil s/n (☎600 5855000). Trains run six times a day between Santiago and Chillán, stopping at several Central Valley towns.

Destinations Santiago (6 daily; 4hr 30min); Talca (6 daily; 2hr 20min).

Tourist information The helpful and well-stocked Sernatur office is located at 18 de Septiembre 455 (March–Nov Mon–Fri 8.30am–5pm; Dec–Feb Mon–Fri 8.30am–8pm, Sat 10am–8pm, Sun 10am–2pm; ☎42 2223272).

ACCOMMODATION

Hostal Canadá Av Libertad 269 ☎42 2234515. A welcoming hostess presides over spotless rooms with cable TV. Doubles CH$16,000

Residencial 18 18 de Sept 213 ☎42 2211102. Family-run hotel with friendly owners offering slightly tatty but clean rooms with a simple breakfast included. Doubles CH$20,000

EATING

Arcoiris Roble 525. Excellent vegetarian restaurant specializing in delicious juices, crêpes and salads. Veggie burger CH$2500.

Mercado Municipal Bordered by Roble, Riquelme, Prat and 5 de Abril. Inexpensive, traditional Chilean dishes, such as *pastel de choclo* and *completos*, are served at the multitude of *cocinerías* here. *Longaniza y pure* (Chilean bangers and mash) CH$2500.

AROUND CHILLÁN

One of the biggest attractions of the area is the hot-springs resort of **Termas de Chillán** (☎42 2434200, ⊛termaschillan.cl), which with 29 runs, most of intermediate level, becomes a bona fide **ski resort** in the winter. There is also ample off-piste terrain, ideal for **snowboarders**, who are not allowed on some of the resort's runs. During the summer, in the valley overlooked by the looming **Volcán Chillán** (3212m), hiking, horseriding and downhill biking are all popular activities.

ARRIVAL AND DEPARTURE

By bus Regular Rem Bus (☎42 2229377) services go to nearby Valle Las Trancas between 6.50am and 7.20pm from Chillán's rural bus terminal; the last bus departs Las Trancas at 7pm.

ACCOMMODATION AND EATING

The majority of holidaymakers stay at the cheaper lodgings in Valle Las Trancas, which offers a scattering of *hospedajes*, campsites and restaurants, surrounded by immense mountains.

Chill'In Km72.5, Valle Las Trancas ☎42 2247075. Brand-new place with its own pizzeria, attractive dorms and Skype-equipped free internet. Dorms CH$9000, doubles CH$20,000

4

CONCEPCIÓN

CONCEPCIÓN is Chile's second-largest city, a bustling sprawl some 112km southwest of Chillán. It has little in the way of tourist sights, though its huge student population ensures a high concentration of lively bars. Founded in 1550, the city was the administrative and military capital of colonial Chile. It suffered considerable structural damage in the huge 2010 earthquake.

WHAT TO SEE AND DO

The heart of Concepción's walkable city centre, lined with a mixture of elegant old buildings and modern concrete blocks, is the carefully landscaped **Plaza de la Independencia**. Partially pedestrianized Barros Arana, the main thoroughfare, has shops and places to eat, while at the western end lies the lively **Barrio Estación**, whose trendy bars and restaurants are centred around **Plaza España**, across Calle Prat from the new **train station**. A four-block walk south from the Plaza de la Independencia along Aníbal Pinto brings you to the long green stretch of **Parque Ecuador**.

Galería de la Historia

Three blocks west of the Parque Ecuador, at the corner of Lamas and Lincoyán, is the **Galería de la Historia** (Mon 3–6.30pm, Tues–Fri 10am–1.30pm & 3–6.30pm, Sat & Sun 10am–2pm & 3–7pm; free), which showcases the region's turbulent history through a series of interactive dioramas, with voice-overs dramatizing the scenes. There's also a large collection of ornate silver maté gourds.

Casa del Arte

Three blocks south of the Plaza de la Independencia, you can catch a *colectivo* eastwards to the **Casa del Arte** (Tues–Fri 10am–6pm, Sat 11am–5pm, Sun 11am–2pm; free), on the corner of Plaza Perú. This museum displays a modest collection of Chilean art and hosts captivating modern art exhibitions in its basement, but its highlight is the giant **mural**, *La Presencia de América Latina*, by Mexican muralist Jorge Gonzáles Camarena. Latin America – its conquest, its cultural and agricultural wealth – is captured in a series of densely packed images oriented around the main figure of an *indígena* (a native woman). Interwoven throughout are colourful ribbons representing every Latin American flag and numerous national symbols.

ARRIVAL AND INFORMATION

By plane Aeropuerto Internacional Carriel Sur (☎41 2732000) is 5km northwest of downtown; a door-to-door airport transfer service is available (CH$5000; ☎41 2248776).
Destinations Santiago (5–6 daily, 1hr 5min) with LAN (☎600 5262000) and Sky Airline (☎41 2218941).
By train Estación Concepción (☎41 2868015) is located across Prat from Barros Arana. Fast commuter trains run to nearby Talcahuano, Hualqui and Lomas Coloradas.
By bus Most long-distance buses arrive at the Terminal de Buses Collao, Tegualda 860 (☎41 2749000), from where numerous local buses run downtown.
Destinations Angol (6–8 daily; 2hr); Chillán (every 50min; 1hr 30min); Los Ángeles (hourly; 1hr 30min); Santiago (every 30min; 7hr); Talca (6–8 daily; 4hr).
Tourist information The Sernatur office is at Aníbal Pinto 460 (Mon–Fri 8.30am–1pm & 3–6pm; ☎41 2741415, ⓦdescubrebiobio.cl) and has plenty of information on the region surrounding Concepción. Conaf has an office at Barros Arano 215 (Mon–Fri 8.30am–1pm & 2.15–5.25pm).

ACCOMMODATION

Apart Hotel Don Matías Colo Colo 155 ☎41 2256846, ⓦaparthoteldonmatias.cl/inicio.html. An attractive B&B with friendly service, large rooms, some with private bathrooms, and a good breakfast. Doubles CH$40,000
Residencial O'Higgins O'Higgins 115, 2nd floor ☎41 2221086. Centrally located guesthouse with basic but clean rooms. Dorms CH$7000
Hostal San Martín San Martín 949 ☎41 2981282, ⓦhostalsanmartin.cl. Smart and slightly sterile hotel with professional service, spacious rooms and breakfast included. Doubles CH$40,000

EATING, DRINKING AND NIGHTLIFE

Hiper Lider on Prat/Freire is a massive supermarket with an excellent selection of fresh produce, as well as rare Thai and Chinese cooking ingredients.
Mercado Central Rengo, between Maipú and Freire. The informal *cocinerías* here are a good spot for inexpensive Chilean standards, such as *cazuela* (CH$3000).
Il Padrino Barros Arana, at Plaza España. Bustling Italian restaurant and bar, serving generous portions of pasta and pizza. Mains CH$6000–8000. Closed Sun.
La Suite Barros Arana, at Serrano. Café/restaurant with *tablas*, beers and live music, offering *chorrillanas* (a huge portion of chips, covered with sausagemeat and fried onions).

4

El Tablon/Barrabirra Plaza España 532. To catch the latest match and knock back a beer, try this popular bar with nightly drink specials and pizza. Beers CH$2000.

DIRECTORY

Banks and exchange There are numerous banks with ATMs on Barros Arana and O'Higgins; Afex, at Barros Arana 565, Local 57, changes foreign currencies.
Hospital Hospital Regional is on San Martín, at Av Roosevelt (☎ 41 2722500).
Internet access There are several internet cafés around Concepción's centre; Fonossa Internet, at the corner of Freire and Lincoyán, has broadband and Skype-enabled computers (CH$500/hr).
Laundry Try Limposco y Lavenderia, Colo Colo 148.
Pharmacy Numerous pharmacies can be found along Barros Arana.
Post office Colo Colo 417 (Mon–Fri 9am–7pm, Sat 9.30am–1pm).
Telephone centres Entel, Barros Arana 541, Local 2, is the best phone centre.

PARQUE NACIONAL NAHUELBUTA

High in the Cordillera de Nahuelbuta, 35km west of the frontier town of Angol, lies the remote **Parque Nacional Nahuelbuta** (daily: Jan–Feb 8.30am–8pm; March–Dec 8.30am–6pm; CH$4000). The park is 1600m at its highest point and benefits from coastal rainfall, creating a **rare ecosystem** that sustains both *coigüe* and *lenga* trees, common to temperate coastal areas, and the araucaria trees of the mountains. The area is a haven for **diverse wildlife**, including *pudú* (pygmy deer), Chilote fox and puma, not to mention many species of birds.

From the park administration at Pehuenco, 5km from the park entrance, a dirt trail snakes its way through monkey puzzle trees to the 1379m pinnacle of **Piedra de Aguila**, presenting awesome panoramic views of the distant volcanoes to the north and the endless blue of the Pacific to the west. From the *Refugio Coimallín*, 3km north of the park administration, a shorter trail leads up to the *mirador* **Cerro Anay**, at the top of a 1450m peak, which offers similarly impressive views of the park and the wilderness beyond. The best time to visit is from October to April, when there is less rainfall.

ARRIVAL AND INFORMATION

By bus To access the park, you'll need to reach Angol first. Daily buses go from Angol's Terminal Rural, Ilabaca 422 (☎ 45 2712021), to Vegas Blancas, a village 7km from Portones at the park's eastern boundary, and in Jan and Feb Buses Angol have a Sun return service to Pehuenco. In Angol, Terminal Rodoviario, Oscar Bonilla 428 (☎ 45 2711854), serves long-distance destinations; Terminal Rural (☎ 45 2712021), at Ilabaca 422, serves local destinations.
Conaf There are five Conaf *guarderías* (ranger stations) in the park, at Portones (where the entrance fee is paid; ☎ 402 1960244), Pehuenco, Coimallin, Pichinahuel and Cotico. In Angol, the office is at Prat 191, 2nd floor (☎ 45 2711870), and has up-to-date information on the park.

ACCOMMODATION

Camping You can camp in relative isolation, either by the park administration at Pehuenco, where there are eleven pitches with picnic tables, fire pits, showers and rustic toilets (CH$12,000/pitch for up to six people; ☎ 2 1960244 ext 245), or at a smaller campsite by Coimallín's Centro de Información Ambiental; you'll need to bring all your food and supplies with you.

4

The Lake District

Stretching south from the end of the Río Bío Bío to the large port of Puerto Montt, **THE LAKE DISTRICT** falls within the region of La Araucanía, one of the last parts of Chile to be colonized by Europeans thanks to fierce resistance by the Mapuche that lasted until 1880. While not as challenging as Patagonia, the area's multitude of snowcapped volcanoes, sparkling lakes and dense forest make it a vastly rewarding place to explore. And after you've hiked, kayaked, climbed and rafted yourself to a state of exhaustion, you can soak your weary bones in the numerous hot springs here, sipping Kunstmann, Chile's best beer, brewed in Valdivia.

TEMUCO

The busy market city of **TEMUCO** was founded in 1881 towards the end of the "pacification" of the Mapuche, the indigenous minority who still inhabit the area – Temuco remained a frontier town well into the early twentieth century, when poet Pablo Neruda grew up here (he departed for Santiago in 1921). You may well have to change buses in Temuco, but there's little of interest in the city itself besides the lively and extensive **Feria Libre** (daily: summer 8.30am–6pm, winter 8.30am–5pm), a Mapuche fruit and veg **market** that stretches for several blocks of Aníbal Pinto between Lautaro/Barros Arana and Balmaceda. The **Mercado Municipal** (summer Mon–Sat 8am–8pm & Sun 8am–3pm, winter Mon–Sat 8am–5pm), at Manuel Rodríguez 960 between Bulnes and Aldunate, also stocks a wide array of Mapuche **crafts**, ranging in quality from tacky to exquisite.

ARRIVAL AND DEPARTURE

By plane Tiny Aeropuerto Maquehue is 5km southwest of Temuco; LAN and Sky Airline shuttle back and forth from Santiago, with Sky also serving Concepción and Puerto Montt. Transfer Aeropuerto Temuco (☎45 334 033) minibuses will whisk you into the city centre and the bus stations for CH$2500, while taxis charge CH$6000 (taxis charge CH$50,000 to Pucón).

By bus The JAC bus terminal at Balmaceda 1005 is best for central Temuco, and for regular buses to Pucón and Villarrica; most other companies use the main bus station (aka Terminal Rodoviario de la Araucanía), 5km north of the city centre on Vicente Pérez Rosales – taxis, buses and micros run every few minutes to the city centre. The Terminal Buses Rurales is near the Feria Libre at Aníbal Pinto 032, serving smaller destinations in the region.

Destinations Concepción (4 daily; 5hr); Pucón (every 30min; 2hr); Puerto Varas (hourly; 5hr); Santiago (every 30min; 9hr); Valdivia (every 30min; 2hr 30min); Villarrica (every 30min; 1hr 30min).

PARQUE NACIONAL CONGUILLÍO

A vast expanse of old lava fields, extending from the very active Llaima volcano, pristine lakes and araucaria forest, the **PARQUE NACIONAL CONGUILLÍO** (daily 8.30am–6pm; high season CH$4500, low season CH$2000) is all the more rewarding because of the difficulty of access by pitted dirt road (it's 120km northeast of Temuco). If you make it that far, you're rewarded with a variety of hiking trails, ranging from short day-hikes to wilderness expeditions of several days.

ARRIVAL AND DEPARTURE

By bus and 4WD To get to the park, it's best to rent a 4WD, but failing that, you can take Nar Bus (☎45 257074) from Temuco's Terminal Buses Rurales to Melipeuco (8 daily; 2hr), where, in high season, the tourist office can help arrange transport to the southern entrance of the park via taxi. To reach the northern entrance at Laguna Captrén, take Buses Flota Erbuc (☎45 233958) from Temuco's Terminal Buses Rurales to Curacautín (frequent; 1hr 30min), from where a shuttle runs to the *guardería* (ranger station) at Captrén (Dec–Feb, Mon & Fri only at 6am and 5pm).

INFORMATION

Tourist information You can pick up maps of the park at the Conaf-run Centro de Información Ambiental (Oct–March daily 9am–1pm & 3–6.30pm; ☎65 972336) by Lago Conguillío.

ACCOMMODATION

La Baita ☎045 416410, ⓦ labaitaconguillio.cl. Camping is the main form of accommodation in the park, but you can also stay in the cabañas run by the La Baita ecotourism project in the southern section: meals are available during high season. Between January 15 and February 15, the minimum stay is four nights. Cabaña CH$45,000

Camping El Hoyón y La Caseta ☎65 972336, ⓔ reservas@parquenacionalconguillio.cl. The tranquil Hoyón campsite is located on the shores of Laguna Conguillío, 2km from the main entrance – each of the ten pitches has its own bathroom. Adjacent *La Caseta* offers ten similar pitches on the lake, also with private bathrooms. Open Nov–March. Pitch for up to 5 people CH$35,000

Camping Los Ñirres, El Estero y Los Carpinteros ☎65 972336, ⓔ reservas@parquenacionalconguillio.cl. These three campsites are located a short walk away from the lake, in the forest, all with shared bathrooms. *El Estero* also has a basic backpacker dorm. Open Nov–March. Camping/pitch CH$20,000, dorms CH$5000

VILLARRICA

Some 87km southeast of Temuco on the tranquil shores of Lago Villarrica, the colonial town of **VILLARRICA** was destroyed several times by volcanic eruptions and abandoned after being captured by the Mapuche in 1603. What you see today has been built since the 1880s, when Swiss, German and Austrian immigrants resettled the area. Thanks to the railway completed in 1933, the town was attracting

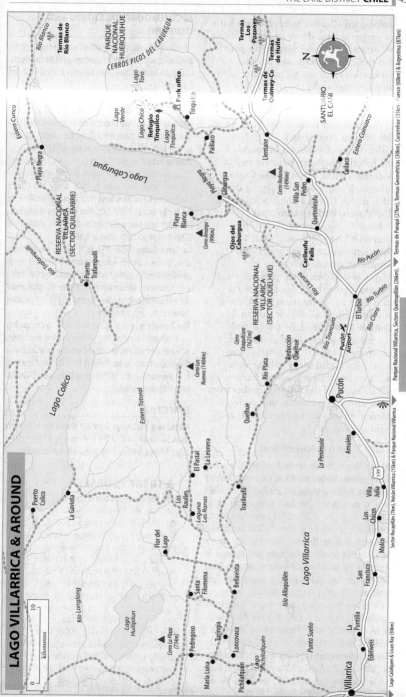

LAGO VILLARRICA & AROUND

0 — 10 kilometres

4

well-heeled Chilean holidaymakers with its gorgeous lakeside views of the Volcán Villarrica long before Pucón (see p.435), and these days foreign visitors and backpackers are coming in greater numbers, drawn by the slower pace of life than its adrenaline-charged neighbour – the distinctive squawking of the local buff-necked and white-faced ibis adds an exotic touch.

The centre of the town surrounds the junction between Valdivia and Alderete/Henríquez, with the Costanera bike track and footpath hugging the lakeside for 1.8km a few blocks north. The **Museo Histórico Municipal** (Mon–Sat 9am–1pm & 3.30–7pm; free; ☎045 415706), next door to the tourist office at Valdivia 1050, showcases a small collection of Mapuche artefacts. Plenty of Mapuche arts and crafts shops dot the centre; next door to the museum on Valdivia, at Zegers, the stalls of the **Centro Cultural Mapuche** (daily 9am–5pm) sell silver jewellery, local cheese and cheap *empanadas* (CH$300) around a *ruka* – a traditional dwelling with walls and roof tightly woven from reeds. Many of the former vendors from here have set up shop at the nearby Mercado Fritz, across Acevedo (also with its own *ruka*).

ARRIVAL AND INFORMATION

By bus Most of the bus terminals cluster along Anfion Muñoz between Valdivia and Bilbao, just east of Alderete/ Henríquez. Tur Bus at Muñoz 657 and Pullman (opposite) serve all major central Chile destinations on the way to Santiago. Buses JAC at Bilbao 610 serves Lake District destinations, notably Pucón (from CH$800) and Temuco (CH$2000), while Igi Llaima at Valdivia 615 crosses the border to San Martín de Los Andes and Bariloche in Argentina; the same terminal serves second-class Buses Villarrica (just CH$1000 to Temuco), Condor and cheap minibuses to Lican Rey and Pucón (CH$850).

Destinations Pucón (every 30min; 45min); Puerto Montt (hourly; 6hr); Santiago (4 daily; 9hr); San Martín de Los Andes (4 weekly; 10hr); Temuco (every 30min; 1hr); Valdivia (7 daily; 2hr 15min).

Tourist information The helpful tourist office, at Pedro de Valdivia 1070 (Mon–Fri 8.30am–1pm & 2.30–6pm; Sat & Sun 9am–1pm & 3.30–5.30pm; ☎45 206619, ⓦvisitvillarrica.cl), offers free maps of the town.

ACCOMMODATION, EATING AND DRINKING

Several supermarkets are conveniently located in the centre of Villarrica, with the largest Supermercado Eltit on Valdivia, at General Körner (Sun–Thurs 8.30am–9.30pm, Fri & Sat 8.30am–10pm).

Hostal Don Juan Körner 770 ☎45 411833, ⓦhostal donjuan.cl. Boasting great views of Volcán Villarrica, this cosy hotel has an assortment of rooms and cabañas, plus table tennis and table football for the guests. Doubles (private bath) CH$24,000, shared bath CH$16,000

Huerto Azul Henríquez 341 ☎45 413148, ⓦhuertoazul .cl. Serves the finest frozen yogurt, Belgian artisan choco-late and Italian ice cream in Chile, tangy and creamy concoctions laced with fresh fruit all made locally from old family recipes (CH$1200). Also produces marmalade, jam, fruit juice and sauces (cakes CH$1300–1500). Daily 9.30am–9.30pm (café closes at 8pm).

La Torre Suiza Bilbao 969 ☎45 411213, ⓦtorresuiza .com. The Swiss owners here welcome you into their wood-panelled haven for outdoor lovers, particularly cyclists. There's a book exchange, kitchen privileges, bike rental, good break-fast and tons of helpful advice. Dorms CH$10,000, doubles (private bath) CH$20,000

The Travellers Letelier 753 ☎45 413617, ⓦthetravellers .cl. A top spot for coffee, beer or meals of any description, with a relaxed outdoor terrace and woodsy, cabin interior – the eclectic menu features dishes from all over the world, from Mexican burritos to Thai curry. Mains from CH$6500. Daily 9.30am–midnight.

DIRECTORY

Banks and exchange There are several banks (Bank of Chile, Santander) with ATMs and money exchange places along Valdivia, between the tourist office and Alderete.

★ TREAT YOURSELF

Hostería de la Colina Casilla 382, Las Colinas 115 ☎45 411503, ⓦhosteriadelacolina.com. On a hill overlooking Lago Villarrica, set in a beautiful sculpted garden alive with blossoms and flitting hummingbirds, you'll find the *Hostería de la Colina*. Not only are the expat Oregonian owners legendary for their hospitality, but their food is made from fresh local ingredients (such as steak, elk, wild boar and smoked salmon; mains CH$6000–7000), they make their own sumptuous ice cream (try the ginger, CH$900) and they hand out excellent hiking maps that they produce themselves. CH$55,000

Internet Try the Centro de Llanados y Internet at Valdivia 658 (Mon–Sat 9am–8.30pm, Sun 10am–2.30pm; CH$500/hr), near the bus stations.

Pharmacy Plenty of Cruz Verde branches can be found in the centre (including one at Valdivia and Henríquez).

Post office Anfión Muñoz 315 (Mon–Fri 9am–2pm & 3.30–7pm, Sat 9am–1pm).

PUCÓN

On a clear day, you will spy the mesmerizing snowy cone of the **Volcán Villarrica** long before the bus pulls into

PUCÓN, 25km east of Villarrica. This small lakeside resort town, awash with the smells of wood smoke and grilled meat, has firmly established itself as a top Chilean and backpacker destination in the last decade. Each November to April season brings scores of adventure sports fanatics looking to climb the volcano, brave the **rapids** on the Río Trancura and Río Liucura or explore the nearby Parque Nacional Huerquehue. A day outdoors is usually followed by eating, drinking and partying in the town's

4

PUCÓN

● EATING AND DRINKING

Arabian Café	5
Cassis	3
¡école!	4
Latitude 39°	2
La Maga	1
Mama's and Tapas	7
Rap Burger	8
Trawen	6

■ ACCOMMODATION

La Bicicleta	3
Camping Parque La Poza	6
Donde Germán Hostal	5
Hostal La Maison	1
Hostal el Refugio	4
Tree House Hostel	2

▼ Volcán Villarrica (15km)

restaurants and bars, or by a soak in the nearby **thermal springs**.

Pucón's wide, tree-lined streets are arranged in a compact grid, and most tour companies, supermarkets, banks and bars are located along frenzied **Avenida O'Higgins**, which bisects the town. O'Higgins ends by **La Poza**, a black-sand beach on the lake. If you follow Calle Lincoyán to its northern end, you will reach **Playa Grande**, with a multitude of pedalos, jet-skis and rowing boats for hire. Try to avoid February and even January if you can, when central Pucón can make parts of downtown Santiago seem fairly tranquil in comparison.

ARRIVAL AND INFORMATION

By plane There are twice-weekly flights between Santiago and Pucón airport (5km east of the town), with both LAN and Sky Airline, between December and February. The closest airport otherwise is at Temuco (see p.432).

By bus The three main long-distance carriers have separate terminals: Buses JAC (and Condor), Palguín 505 (📞 45 990880), serves Villarrica (CH$1000), Temuco (CH$2700), Valdivia (CH$5200) and Puerto Montt (CH$11,700); Pullman Bus, Palguín 555 (📞 45 443331), and Tur Bus, O'Higgins 910 (📞 45 443328), offer similar services. Smaller carriers such as Igi Llaima (Palguín 595) and Buses San Martín (Colocolo 612) have services to Argentina within a couple of blocks of the main bus terminals; Buses Caburgua (Uruguay 540, at Palguín) serves Parque Nacional Huerquehue (one-way CH$2000, return CH$3600; 8.30am, 1pm, 4pm) and the Ojos de Caburgua.

Destinations Buses JAC to: Puerto Montt (4 daily; 5hr 30min); Puerto Varas (4 daily; 5hr); Temuco (every 20min; 1hr); Valdivia (6 daily; 3hr); Villarrica (every 20min; 45min). Buses Vipu Ray to: Curarrehue (every 30min; 45min). Buses San Martín to: San Martín de Los Andes (Tues–Sun 10.35am; 5hr). Igi Llaima to: San Martín de Los Andes (daily at 9.45am; 5hr). Pullman Bus to: Santiago (2 nightly at 9pm and 9.30pm; 11hr).

Tourist office The Oficina de Turismo Municipal is on the corner of O'Higgins, at Palguín (March–Nov daily 8.30am–4pm; Dec–Feb daily 8.30am–10pm; 📞 45 293002, 🌐 pucononline.cl).

Travelaid Ansorena 425, Local 4 (Mon–Sat 10am–1.30pm & 3.30–7pm; 📞 45 444040, 🌐 travelaid.cl).

OUTDOOR ACTIVITIES

Pucón operators offer a vast range of adventure tours and activities; the nearby **Río Trancura** offers a popular Class III run on the lower part of the river, with the more challenging Class VI, upper Trancura run made up almost entirely of drop pools; some operators allow you to combine the two. Since the activities on offer involve an element of risk, it is important to use a reliable operator like those listed below. We don't recommend Trancura, the largest agency, due to its poor safety record.

TOUR OPERATORS

Aguaventura Palguín 336 📞 45 444246, 🌐 aguaventura.com. Established French outfit specializing in rafting trips, canyoning and watersports (such as hydrospeeding for CH$27,000), as well as winter activities. English spoken.

Antilco Campo Antilco, S-919 (12km northeast of Pucón) 📞 9 7139758, 🌐 antilco.com. This operator is recommended for horse treks in the valleys around Pucón with bilingual guides. Half-day CH$25,000; two days' riding with barbecue CH$90,000.

Bosque Aventura Arauco 611, at O'Higgins 📞 45 444030, 🌐 canopypucon.cl. The most reliable operator for zip-lining tours, with an emphasis on safety. Whiz around one of 11 lines (40–240m long) up to 25m high. Canopy tour with transport CH$13,000/person (tours daily 10am, 12.30pm, 3pm & 5pm; 1hr 30min).

Elementos Pasaje Las Rosas 640 📞 45 441750, 🌐 elementos-chile.com. This friendly, German-run operator offers tours with an emphasis on small group size and safety, offering mini-volcano trekking as well as the standard volcano tour and half- and full-day rafting. Volcano tour CH$52,000.

Kayak Chile O'Higgins 524 📞 45 441584, 🌐 kayak chile.net. Established American-run outfit specializing in kayaking trips on the Río Liucura. Learn the Eskimo roll in Lago Villarrica (CH$34,000 half-day/CH$53,000 full day), take to the Class III rapids in a double kayak with a guide (CH$20,000) or run the river in a ducky (CH$20,000).

Paredon Andes Expeditions Variante Internacional, Pasaje Artemio Carrillo s/n 📞 45 444663, 🌐 paredonexpeditions.com. A small team of expert trekking and mountaineering guides leads small group ascents up Volcán Villarrica (Sept–April) and other Lake District volcanoes, and also offers tailor-made excursions around Chile. English and French spoken. Volcano ascent CH$45,000 (plus CH$7000 chairlift ticket); minimum 3 people & 14 years of age.

Knowledgeable Swiss-run travel agency that sells guidebooks and maps of Chile, and can help you book passage on the Navimag tour boat (see p.446). English and German spoken.

ACCOMMODATION

La Bicicleta Palguín 361 ☎45 444583, ✉labicicleta pucon.com. The owners go out of their way to make you feel welcome at this family-run hostel right in the centre of town. You can organize all your tours, dine at the on-site café and use the free internet; the only downsides are the queues to the shared bathrooms and the noise at times. Doubles CH$26,000

Camping Parque La Poza Costanera Roberto Geiss 769 ☎45 444982, ✉campinglapoza.com. Large, shaded campsite near the lake with hot showers, a well-equipped cooking hut/dining area, and a picnic table per camping site. Popular with overland expeditions, cycling tourists and backpackers (it's the only site open year-round). Per person CH$4000

Donde Germán Hostal Las Rosas 590 ☎45 442444, ✉dondegerman.cl. Comfy beds in cosy rooms with rustic wooden decor, a fully equipped kitchen, an inviting common area with satellite TV and an in-house tour agency are just some of the perks at this welcoming guesthouse. Walk four blocks south of the centre until you see people relaxing on the outdoor terrace and by the pool. Doubles CH$12,500

Hostal La Maison Lincoyán 261 ☎45 443138, ✉hostal lamaison.com. Hosted by the friendly Franco-Chilean Etienne, this justly popular budget option in a lovely historic house has just two simple rooms with shared bathroom. Guests share a living room with fireplace, dining table and flat-screen TV, as well as a small kitchen; breakfast extra CH$3000. Doubles CH$20,000

Hostal el Refugio Palguín 540 ☎45 441596, ✉hostal elrefugio.cl. This friendly, efficiently run hostel has wooden interiors, one clean eight-bed dorm and three private rooms, as well as a kitchen and free internet. Dorms CH$10,000, doubles CH$12,000

Tree House Hostel Urrutia 660 ☎45 444679, ✉tree housechile.cl. Run by two knowledgeable, bilingual Journey Latin America guides, this chilled-out hostel is the place to organize all manner of outdoor activities, particularly the volcano ascent, and get a good night's sleep on the orthopaedic beds. Relax in the garden hammocks, or join in an impromptu barbecue. Dorms CH$12,000, doubles CH$36,000

EATING AND DRINKING

Supermercado Eltit (daily 8.30am–10.30pm) is conveniently located in the centre of town on O'Higgins, with a vast range of fresh fruit and veg, breads and pastries. Cheap cafés and snack stalls cluster around the bus stations on Palguín.

Arabian Café Fresia 354 ☎45 443469. For those who've eaten their fill of Chilean staples, this authentic Middle Eastern restaurant offers falafel, hummus, tasty stuffed vegetables and nicely grilled kebabs. Mains from CH$5000. Daily noon–4pm & 7.30pm–midnight.

Cassis Fresia 223, at Alderete ☎45 449 088. This trendy café is often full; the clientele come not just for the free wi-fi, but also for the filling multigrain sandwiches and the impressive array of desserts. Try the crêpe cassis – a pancake you'll have to excavate from under a caramel brownie piled high with chocolate and *dulce de leche* ice cream. Desserts CH$3200–4000. Daily 8.30am–midnight.

★ **¡école!** Urrutia 592 ☎45 441675, ✇ecole.cl. Established vegetarian restaurant serving consistently superb, hearty dishes made from local organic produce, accompanied by home-made multigrain bread. Try the sublime vegetable lasagne, or the yellow Thai vegetable curry with quinoa. Mains from CH$4500. Daily 8am–11pm.

Latitude 39° Alderete 324 ☎09 74300016. Low prices (mains from CH$1800), speedy wi-fi, cheap beer, happy-hour deals and friendly service make this a justly popular pit stop, with US comfort food ranging from Tex-Mex tacos and breakfast burritos to burgers and fries. Daily 9.30am–11.30pm.

La Maga Alderete 276, at Fresia ☎45 444277, ✇lamaga pucon.cl. Sate all your carnivorous cravings here. While not budget, this Uruguayan steakhouse really delivers when it comes to expertly cooked *bife de chorizo*, and the service is excellent. Steak from CH$9000. Daily noon–4pm & 7.30pm–midnight.

Mama's and Tapas O'Higgins 587 ☎45 449002. A well-established watering hole that consistently entices a large clientele nightly with their excellent selection of beers (from CH$1500), nightly drinks specials and not-half-bad Mexican food. Sun–Thurs noon–1am, Fri & Sat noon–2am.

Rap Burger O'Higgins 619 ☎45 443336. Decent Chilean-style burgers (*churrasco* steak and crispy baps) from just CH$3400 (or CH$3900 with fries and drink), with outdoor seating.

★ **Trawen** O'Higgins 311 ☎45 412024. One of the friendliest places in town, this offbeat restaurant tantalizes your tastebuds with imaginative organic and locally inspired dishes such as Antarctic krill (a bit like tiny shrimp) and ricotta ravioli (CH$7400), excellent wholewheat *empanadas* (CH$3200–3900) and filling breakfasts (CH$4000–5000). Mains such as trout, steak and venison CH$6000–9000. Daily 8am–11.30pm.

DIRECTORY

Banks and exchange There are several banks with ATMs and money exchange places along O'Higgins, between Fresia and Ansorena, and a good exchange desk inside the Supermercado Eltit (daily 8.30am–10.30pm).

4

Bike rental Sierra Nevada on O'Higgins 524a (☎45 444210) rents mountain bikes in good condition. Full day (9am–8pm) CH$7000; 5hr CH$5000.

Hospital Hospital San Francisco, Uruguay 325 (☎45 441177).

Internet Cyber Unid@d on O'Higgins 415 has fast and reliable connections (CH$250/10min; CH$700/hr). There's also Cyber ZP (CH$200/15min, CH$700/1hr) on Fresia just south of O'Higgins.

Laundry Lavandería Oasis on Lincoyán 272 (Mon–Sat 10.30am–1.30pm & 4–7pm); CH$3900 for 1–3kg. There's an excellent bakery attached. Lavandería Magda on Brasil 420 offers similar rates.

Pharmacy Cruz Verde is at O'Higgins 400 (Mon–Fri 8.30am–10.30pm, Sat 9am–10.30pm, Sun 9.30am–10pm).

Post office Fresia 183 (Mon–Fri 9am–1pm & 2.30–6pm, Sat 9am–2pm).

PARQUE NACIONAL VILLARRICA

The **Volcán Villarrica** (2847m) is the crown jewel of the **PARQUE NACIONAL VILLARRICA** (daily 8.30am–6pm; CH$1000 entry; ascent CH$4000, Villarrica traverse CH$8000; fees included in guided hikes) and undoubtedly Pucón's biggest attraction; in the winter it becomes a ski and snowboard destination. To do the climb, unless you have mountaineering experience, you should go with a guide (see p.436); they will provide all the necessary equipment and transportation. It's a fairly challenging four- to five-hour ascent (plus 3hr down), starting at the chairlift at the base of the volcano (at the end of the road), with much of the walking done on snow. If the chairlift (CH$7000) is running, it cuts an hour off the climb. At the top, by the lip of the (sometimes) smoking crater, you'll be rewarded with unparalleled views across the Lake District, with lakes and distant volcanoes stretching out before you. The sulphuric fumes mean you cannot linger long over the spectacle though. Check the weather forecast before embarking on the climb, as many tour companies take groups out even in cloudy weather, only to turn back halfway.

OJOS DEL CABURGUA

The azure **Ojos del Caburgua** pool, fed by several small but enchanting waterfalls (Oct–March daily 8am–8pm; cars CH$2000; bicycles/individual CH$500), is relatively easy to access via the Caburgua bus from Pucón. There are two privately managed viewing points (both charge the same), but the second is by far the best (get off the bus at "El Cristo", a statue of Christ on the cross on the main road, and follow the signs for around 2km; some buses may take you to the entrance). The loop also makes an excellent day-trip for bikers; follow the road out of town towards Caburgua, then take a left turn along the dirt road by the "El Cristo" cross, 18km away. The signposted dirt trail winds along the Río Liucura, passing the falls, before emerging at the Pasarela Quelhue (hanging bridge) 8km later, and just 2km from the paved road back to Pucón.

PARQUE NACIONAL HUERQUEHUE

The compact but dazzling 125-square-kilometre **PARQUE NACIONAL HUERQUEHUE** (daily 8.30am–6pm, till 8pm high season; high season CH$4500, low season CH$2000) comprises densely forested **precordillera** (foothills), highland araucaria groves, several waterfalls and many entrancing **lakes**, making it a perfect destination for day-hikes.

The prettiest of the lakes – Chico, Toro and Verde – are accessed via the popular **Sendero Los Lagos** trail, which climbs steeply to a height of 1300m from the park office at Lago Tinquilco, past two waterfalls (14km return) – expect sensational views back towards the **Volcán Villarrica** on a clear day. You can extend the loop by taking in the tiny Lago de los Patos and Lago Huerquehue (2hr extra) before rejoining the main path, or you can continue along the **Sendero Los Huerquenes** to Termas de San Sebastián and the stunning Renahue viewpoint overlooking the lakes below. It's possible to hike to the Termas in one day (23km, 8–9hr), since much of the Sendero Los Huerquenes is downhill, and stay at the excellent campsite here (see below).

ARRIVAL AND INFORMATION

By bus About 30km northeast of Pucón (and 14km of the Caburgua highway via gravel road), Huerquehue is accessible by Buses Caburgua (one-way CH$2000, return CH$3600; daily 8.30am, 1pm, 4pm; return 9.30am, 2.10pm, 5.10pm; less frequently out of season). At the Conaf guardería at the Lago Tinquilco entrance, you'll find a trail map; all the trails are clearly signposted.

ACCOMMODATION

Cabañas San Sebastián Termas de San Sebastián ☎ 45 381279, ⓦ termassansebastian.cl. Serene campsite and cabañas at the end of the Sendero Los Huerquenes; the rustic wood cabins can accommodate two or five people, all equipped with bathrooms and showers supplied by the hot springs. Day use CH$4000; cabañas from CH$35,000; camping/person CH$5000

Parque Nacional Huerquehue Camping ☎ 09 61574089, ⓔ parque.huerquehue@conaf.cl. If not headed to the Termas de San Sebastián, you can camp at the basic but pretty Conaf-run campsite at Lago Tinquilco, near the entrance (toilets and hot showers included); pay Conaf at the park entrance. Pitch CH$15,000

Refugio Tinquilco ☎ 569 2789831, ⓦ tinquilco.cl. Excellent, airy wooden guesthouse in a beautiful stream-side location a 2km hike from the park entrance, with home-cooked meals (breakfast included), a sauna and even a book exchange. Bunks in cabins CH$11,500, doubles from CH$27,900

CURARREHUE

This small Mapuche settlement 48km east of Pucón, the last stop before the Argentine border, feels like a frontier town, with its sleepy streets and handful of local restaurants. Those interested in **Mapuche culture** will want to stop by the **Aldea Intercultural Trawupeyüm** (daily 10am–8pm; donation), the small museum of Mapuche artefacts and cultural centre found behind the bright green Municipalidad buildings on the plaza (Héroes de La Concepción 21, just off the main drag, O'Higgins). Exhibit labels are in Spanish and Mapuche only.

ARRIVAL AND DEPARTURE

By bus Minibuses Vipu Ray runs from Pucón (Palguín 550) to Curarrehue every 30min or so (45min). You can catch onward buses to Argentina with Buses San Martín on O'Higgins.

EATING

Mapu Iyagl Camino internacional s/n ☎ 08 7887188, ☎ 09 85141783. If you have time, try and eat at this lauded restaurant, 1km on the main road back to Pucón, home of celebrity Mapuche chef Anita Epulef; her Mapuche dishes utilize local pine nuts (piñónes), herbs, sopapillas and seasonal vegetables. Daily noon–3pm (call ahead to confirm).

El Tropero O'Higgins 346 ☎ 45 1971561. Several cafés serve up local and Chilean dishes on the main street, but this is the best, set in an old wooden cabin and offering several computer terminals with free internet for customers. Expect typical dishes such as roast lamb, fried salmon, corn cakes and chicken with peas (from CH$2000). Mon–Sat 11am–7pm.

VALDIVIA

From 1848, thousands of German immigrants passed through the port of **VALDIVIA**, initiating an industrial boom that lasted well into the twentieth century. Founded in 1552 by Pedro de Valdivia, it is one of Chile's oldest cities,

---

TOP THREE HOT SPRINGS IN THE LAKE DISTRICT

Termas Geométricas 16km northeast of Coñaripe towards Villarrica National Park ☎ 9 74771708, ☎ 2 2141214 in Santiago, ⓦ termasgeometricas.cl. With a Japanese feel to the beautiful design, there are seventeen thermal pools here, connected by winding boardwalks around a ravine overflowing with greenery, as well as three cold plunge pools, two waterfalls and an excellent café. Jan–late March 10am–11pm; rest of the year 11am–8pm; CH$14,000 (10am–1pm), CH$16,000 (1–11pm), cash only.

Termas de Panqui 58km east of Pucón ☎ 45 442039, ⓔ panquihotsprings@hotmail.com. Unconventional hot springs offering three pools of varying temperature, as well as relaxing mud baths, a vegetarian restaurant, a chance to join in full-moon celebrations, and camping spots and tepees to stay in. Daily 9am–9pm; CH$9000; more with accommodation.

Termas Los Pozones 34km east of Pucón, past Termas de Huife ☎ 9 1972350. Probably the most-visited thermal baths near Pucón, especially on night tours, these consist of hot riverside pools at the end of a steep and sometimes muddy descent (bring a torch); there are wooden changing rooms above the pools from which you descend via a trapdoor. Daily 11am–3am; 11am–8pm CH$5500; 8pm–3am CH$6500.

4

though it was razed to the ground by the Mapuche in the sixteenth century and largely destroyed by the devastating earthquake of 1960, which accounts for the hotchpotch of buildings from every era and architectural style here. Today Valdivia remains an energetic university city that lies at the confluence of the Río Valdivia and Río Calle Calle, 145km southwest of Pucón.

Most of the action centres on the **waterfront**; you'll smell the fishy **Mercado Fluvial** and hear the noise before you reach it. The real highlight here is the resident colony of monstrously sized **sea lions**, which spend much of their day lounging on the river behind the market feeding on scraps (competing with a motley horde of clamouring seagulls, cormorants, vultures and pelicans). While the colony has become somewhat acclimatized to humans, they remain wild, so keep a healthy distance, even when they waddle onto the market floor. The waterfront is also a departure point for numerous boats offering entertaining half-day cruises up the river to the fort ruins (see below) for CH$15,000–35,000, though commentary is Spanish only.

WHAT TO SEE AND DO

Just on the other side of the Río Valdivia from the fish market, in a tranquil section of Isla Teja, the **Museo Histórico y Antropológico** (Jan & Feb daily 10am–8pm; March–Dec Tues–Sun 10am–1pm & 2–6pm; CH$1500, CH$2500 with Philippi museum; ☎63 212872, ⊛museosaustral.cl) offers a rare glimpse of nineteenth-century Chile.

VALDIVIA

ACCOMMODATION
Airesbuenos Hostel	3
Hostel Bosque Nativo	2
Cabañas y Hostal Borde Río	4
Hostal Totem	1

EATING & DRINKING
Café Haussmann	3
Café Palace	5
La Calesa	1
Cervecería Kunstmann	2
Entrelagos	6
Mercado Municipal	4
La Última Frontera	7

Isla Teja

Río Calle Calle

Dreams Hotel & Casino

Bus stop for Niebla

Mercado Municipal

Museo Historico

Mercado Fluvial

Feria Artesanal

Plaza Pedro de Valdivia

Unimarc Supermarket

Cyber Central

Scotia Bank

Banco de Chile

Banefe

Catedral

PLAZA DE LA REPÚBLICA

Banco Santander

LAN

Centro Cultural El Austral

Torreón de los Canelos

Iglesia de San Francisco

Plaza de Los Ríos

Unimarc Supermarket

Bus Terminal

Río Valdivia

Museo R.A. Philippi de la Exploracíon & Niebla (20km)

N

0   200
metres

Built in 1861 as the Casa Anwandter for one of the city's wealthiest men (German-born Don Carl Anwandter established the brewing industry here in the 1850s), its period rooms contain an odd assortment of historic curios (one room has the cane used by Lord Thomas Cochrane when he captured the city in 1820), while upstairs galleries are filled with Mapuche artefacts and prehistoric finds (some English labelling). Nearby is the **Museo R. A. Philippi de la Exploración** (same hours and admission fees) in the Casa Schüller (dating from 1914), a tribute to German-born naturalist Rudolph Philippi, who worked here in the 1850s (some English labelling).

Las Fuertes (forts)

In 1645 the Spanish started building elaborate fortifications at **Corral**, **Niebla** and **Isla Mancera**, where the Río Valdivia and Río Tornagaleones meet the Pacific Ocean, to protect Valdivia from opportunistic attacks by British, French and Dutch privateers. If the weather is good, a trip to the ruins can make for a refreshing day out; take the Niebla-bound bus #20 from Carampanque, at O'Higgins (25min; CH$500; frequent), and get off at the little ferry pier 18km from the city. From here boats (Mon–Sat 5 daily, Sun 4 daily; seasonal changes possible; CH$300) ply their way to Isla Mancera and the ruins of the **Castillo San Pedro de Alcántara** (Jan & Feb daily 10am–8pm, March–Dec Tues–Sun 10am–1pm & 2–6pm; CH$700).

You can also take a ferry (daily 9am–5.40pm; 30min; CH$650) across the Bahía de Corral to the **Castillo San Sebastián de la Cruz** (Nov–March daily 10am–6pm, April–Oct Tues–Sun 10am–5.30pm; CH$1300), reinforced in the 1760s; it's the most intact of all the forts, and a short walk from the pier in Corral.

To get an overview of the whole system visit **Fuerte Niebla**, 2km beyond the ferry pier (ask the bus driver to drop you off), built between 1647 and 1672 and now the **Museo de Sitio Castillo de Niebla** (April–Oct Tues–Sun 10am–5.30pm, Nov–March Tues–Sun 10am–7pm; CH$600;

☎63 282084, ⓦmuseodeniebla.cl). Only the battlements, a battery of rusty cannons and a few grassy foundations remain, but the views of the bay are magnificent and the museum, in the restored commander's house, covers colonial military history in detail (Spanish text only). The fort saw action only once – in 1820, when it was captured by Lord Cochrane's naval flotilla.

ARRIVAL AND INFORMATION

By plane Aeropuerto Pichoy lies 32km northeast of the city; a Transfer Valdivia minibus (☎63 225533) into town will set you back CH$5000. Sky Airline serves Puerto Montt (weekly, summer only; 25min), while LAN serves Santiago (2 daily; 1hr 35min).

By bus The main Terminal de Buses (☎63 220498, ⓦterminalvaldivia.cl) is located at Anfión Muñoz 360, by Río Calle Calle. Most Santiago buses depart 7–10am, and 7–11pm.

Destinations Bariloche (1 daily at 8.45am; 7hr); Osorno (every 15–30min; 1hr 45min); Pucón (5–6 daily; 3hr); Puerto Montt (every 15–30min; 3hr 30min); Santiago (32 daily; 11hr); San Martín de Los Andes, Argentina (Wed, Fri & Sun 7.30am; 8hr); Villarrica (4–5 daily; 2hr 15min).

Internet Try Ciber Centro on Chacabuco between Henríquez and Caupolicán (CH$500/hr).

Laundry Lavandería y Lavaseco Fenix 3, Picarte 3135 (Mon–Sat 9am–6pm; ☎63 225122; CH$1900/kg).

Tourist information There is a helpful Sernatur office at Arturo Prat s/n (on the Costanera, just north of the fish market; Mon–Fri 9am–6pm, Sat & Sun 10am–4pm; ☎63 239060, ⓦvaldiviaturismo.cl).

ACCOMMODATION

Airesbuenos Hostel García Reyes 550 ☎63 222202, ⓦairesbuenos.cl. Well-run HI-affiliated and eco-friendly hostel, bustling with younger travellers, with bright, cheery dorms at a central location, complete with internet, TV lounge and guest kitchen, as well as friendly staff on hand to help and advise. Dorms CH$8500, doubles CH$23,000

Hostel Bosque Nativo Fresia 290 (off Janequeo) ☎63 433782, ⓦhostelnativo.cl. Newish hostel in a beautifully restored 1920s house with cosy rooms, kitchen, lounge and rooftop terrace. Profits go towards the preservation of native Chilean forest and foreigners get discounted room prices. The staff couldn't be friendlier. Dorms CH$9500, doubles CH$20,000

Cabañas y Hostal Borde Río Henríquez 746 ☎63 214069, ⓦvaldiviacabanas.cl. Most of the colourful rooms have small sofas, the bathrooms are larger than in most hostels, and you can arrange kayaking trips here. Doubles CH$28,000

4

Hostal Totem Carlos Anwandter 425 ☎63 292849, ⓦturismototem.cl. Quiet guesthouse with clean, spacious, en-suite rooms. Cable TV, wi-fi and breakfast are included. Doubles CH$30,000

EATING AND DRINKING

Grab basic food supplies at the Unimarc supermarket, behind the Mercado on Yungay; for fresh fruit and vegetables the Mercado Fluvial is your best bet.

Café Haussmann O'Higgins 394 ☎63 213878, ⓦhaussmann.cl. Tiny canteen with four small booths, founded by Don Ricardo Haussmann in 1959 and harking back to Valdivia's German roots with its specialities of *crudos* (steak tartare) on toast (CH$1800 each), Kunstmann beer (CH$1700) and excellent cakes (küchen) from CH$1400. Mon–Sat 8am–9pm.

Café Palace Pérez Rosales 580 ☎63 213539. Old-fashioned Valdivian diner, which hasn't changed much since it was founded in 1954. Try the hefty and delicious "palace sandwich", and grab some real coffee (mains from CH$1900). Smoking allowed. Daily 7am–11pm.

La Calesa O'Higgins 160 ☎63 225467. Peruvian restaurant in a quiet neighbourhood putting some spice in your life with its *ají de gallina* (spicy garlic chicken stew), and excellent *ceviche*. Mains CH$6000–9000. Tues 7–11.30pm, Wed–Sat 1–4pm & 7–11.30pm, Sun 1–4pm (April–Dec closed Tues and Wed–Fri lunchtime).

★ **Cervecería Kunstmann** 950 Ruta T-350 ☎63 292969, ⓦlacerveceria.cl. German beerhall serving monster portions of meat, sauerkraut and potatoes to accompany its beers (from CH$1950); order the sampler for CH$2600. Finish off with a beer ice-cream sundae (CH$2600). To get here, take bus #20 bound for Niebla (CH$500). Daily noon–idnight (brewery tours Nov–March daily noon–9pm; hourly; April–Oct call ahead to confirm; CH$6900).

Entrelagos Pérez Rosales 622 ☎63 212047. Lauded chocolatier and bakery selling all sorts of delectable cakes, pastries, chocolates and *gelato* (CH$1000 per scoop). Next door is the sit-down "salon de the" which serves the cakes but also full meals and tea sets. Shop Mon–Fri 9.40am–1.30pm & 3.30–8pm, Sat 10am–1.30pm & 4–7pm, Sun 4–7pm; café Mon–Fri 9am–9pm, Sat 9am–10pm, Sun 11am–9pm.

Mercado Municipal Prat s/n. Try the large servings of fresh fish (salmon), razor clam or mussel dishes at these busy little eateries inside the craft market overlooking the river (the third floor is cheapest). Mains CH$2000–3000. Daily 8am–8.30pm.

La Última Frontera Pérez Rosales 787 ☎63 235363. Laidback clapboard café popular with students. It's decorated with local artwork and serves excellent sandwiches and tasty crêpes with a variety of fillings (including vegetarian options) late into the evenings; wash them down with fresh fruit juice or a Kunstmann beer. Crêpes CH$4000. Daily 11.30am–11pm.

LAGO LLANQUIHUE

Some 170km south of Valdivia lies dazzling **LAGO LLANQUIHUE**, the second-largest lake in Chile, its shimmering blue waters framed by thick forest and the peaks of snow-tipped volcanoes. The lake draws local and foreign visitors alike to its appealing **beaches**, the best found in the German lakeside town of **Frutillar** (ⓦfrutillar .com). People also come for the ample natural attractions around the resort town of **Puerto Varas**, and to experience the laidback lifestyle of lakeside villages such as **Puerto Octay** (ⓦpuertoctay.cl), where the Swiss-Chilean-run *Hostal Zapato Amarillo* (☎64 210787, ⓦzapatoamarillo.cl; dorms CH$10,000, doubles CH$30,000) is a huge budget-traveller draw in itself, providing a welcoming place to stay amid stunning scenery.

PUERTO VARAS

Dominating the southwestern corner of the lake, sprawling **PUERTO VARAS** has become a popular resort town and backpacker haunt, with unparalleled sunset views of the two nearby volcanoes, Osorno and Calbuco. Rivalling Pucón in terms of nearby **outdoor attractions**, Puerto Varas does not feel too crowded despite its popularity, and makes an excellent base for volcano-climbing, white-water rafting, kayaking and cycling; it also serves as a popular stopover on the way to Patagonia. Though the town is spread out over 3km of lakefront, most services, hostels and restaurants are located within a couple of blocks of the little Plaza de Armas.

ARRIVAL AND INFORMATION

By plane The nearest airport is at Puerto Montt, but you can book your flights with LAN at Gramados 560 (Mon–Fri 9am–1.30pm & 2.30–6.30pm, Sat 9.30am–1.30pm; ☎600 5252000) or with Sky Airline at San Bernardo 430 (Mon–Fri 9am–1pm & 3–7pm, Sat 10am–1pm; ☎65 234252). Taxis to the airport charge CH$18,000, but shared transfers are CH$12,000.

By bus Bus Norte (with services to Bariloche, Argentina), Pullman and Cruz del Sur (serving Chiloé and the Lake

District up to Santiago) share a bus station at San Francisco 1317, a few blocks south of the centre. Tur Bus, Intersur, JAC, Tas Choapa, Andersmar and Cóndor Bus all share the terminal at El Salvador 1093 (☎65 234163).

Destinations Ancud (8 daily; 2hr 30min); Castro (8 daily; 4hr 30min); Puerto Montt (every 15–30min; 35min); Santiago (6 daily; 18hr); Valdivia (2–3 daily; 3hr).

By minibus Those for Ensenada (1hr; CH$1200), Frutillar (40min), Petrohué and the Saltos de Petrohué (45min; both CH$2000), leave from San Bernardo 240, just north of Walker Martínez; frequent minibuses to Puerto Montt (CH$850) and the beach at Puerto Chico (CH$450) stop along San Francisco and at Del Salvador between Santa Rosa and San Pedro; less frequent buses to Puerto Octay (1hr 15min) also depart here.

Tourist information The official Casa del Turista is found at the foot of a pier (Muelle Piedraplan) on Av Costanera (Mon–Fri 9.30am–6.30pm, Sat & Sun 10am–6.30pm; ☎65 237956, ⓦpuertovaras.org), though they charge for maps. The municipal tourist office is at Del Salvador 320 (Mon–Fri 9.30am–6.50pm, Sat & Sun 10am–2pm & 3–7pm) – other places claiming to be a "tourist office" are usually fronts for organized tours and activities.

ACCOMMODATION

Casa Azul Manzanal 66, at Rosario ☎65 232904, ⓦcasa azul.net. Firm backpacker favourite a short walk uphill from the centre, run by a German-Chilean couple who offer comfortable rooms, kitchen privileges and an excellent breakfast buffet that includes muesli and home-made bread (CH$3000 extra). Dorms CH$9000, doubles (shared bath) CH$24,000

Casa Margouya Santa Rosa 318 ☎65 237640, ⓦmargouya.com. Lively backpacker hostel with guest kitchen, comfortable lounge area and a big emphasis on outdoor adventures. Bathroom queues are the only drawback. Dorms CH$9000, doubles CH$23,000

★ **Compass Del Sur** Klenner 467 ☎65 232044, ⓦcompassdelsur.cl. Large wooden guesthouse with airy dorms and rooms, communal breakfast (muesli, eggs and real coffee; CH$1500 extra), internet, book exchange, kitchen use and laundry service. The helpful Chilean-Swedish owners are happy to organize all manner of tours. Camping/pitch CH$8000, dorms CH$10,000, doubles CH$30,000

Hospedaje Ellenhaus San Pedro 325 ☎65 233 577, ⓦellenhaus.cl. Identified by "Hospedaje" sign and tiny

4

PUERTO VARAS

EATING & DRINKING

Caffé El Barista	2
Dane's Café & Restaurant	5
Donde El Gordito	4
Garage	1
Trattoria Di Carusso	3

ACCOMMODATION

Casa Azul	2
Casa Margouya	3
Compass Del Sur	1
Hospedaje Ellenhaus	4
Hostal Margouya II	6
Hostal Melmac	5

Puma Verde

Centro Cultural Estación

Lago Llanquihue

Yak Expediciones

Casa de Turista

Tierra Outdoors & Ko'Kayak

Jac Bus Office

Cruz del Sur Office

Campo Aventura

Turis Tour

Buses to Petrohué

Centro Médico

Casino

Lavandería Alba

Banco Santander

Buses to Frutillar & Llanquihue

Sky Airlines

LAN

Mercado

Banco de Chile

Buses to Puerto Montt & Puerto Octay

Fruit Stalls

Banco Santander

Ciber Patagonia

Supermarket Express Líder

Supermarket Santa Isabel

Farmacia Ahumada

Iglesia del Sagrado Corazón de Jesús

Tur Bus/Tas Choapa/ Buses JAC terminal

0	300
	metres

Panamericana, Cruz del Sur Bus Terminal, Osorno, Temuco (north) & Puerto Montt (south)

Beach & Puerto Chico

Al Sur (Rafting) & Pachamagua

4

TAKING THE BOAT TO ARGENTINA

Puerto Varas lies on the well-beaten path between Puerto Montt and Bariloche in Argentina. If you're Argentina-bound, a **lake crossing** that allows you to experience the beauty of Chile's oldest national park – **Parque Nacional Vicente Pérez Rosales** – is an excellent alternative to a long bus journey. Starting out at 8.30am, you are first driven along the banks of Lago Llanquihue to **Petrohué**, before boarding the ferry that takes you across **Lago Todos Los Santos**, a spacious expanse of clear blue-green water. As you sail along the densely forested shores, the volcanoes Osorno (2660m) and Puntiagudo (2190m) loom to the north, with the majestic Tronador (3491m) to the east. After going through **Chilean customs** at Peulla, you then cross the Argentine border at Paso Pérez Rosales, and get stamped in at tiny Puerto Frías. At this point you'll board the ferry again for the short crossing of Laguna Frías, then transfer by bus to Puerto Blest and your final nautical leg of the journey, a boat across the stunningly beautiful **Lago Nahuel Huapi** (departing around 6pm), arriving at Puerto Pañuel. From here another bus should get you into Bariloche around 8.30pm. Book in advance, especially during the peak season, with Turismo Peulla (☎65 437127, ⊛traveladventure.cl; CH$135,000).

---

entrance next to post office. Central location and rock-bottom prices make this warren of immaculately clean, tiny rooms a top budget choice. The only drawbacks are not being able to find your way out and the lack of central heating. Dorms CH$5000, doubles CH$15,000

Hostal Margouya II Purísima 681 ☎65 237695, ⊛margouya2.com. Doubling up as a language school, the second branch of *Casa Margouya*, housed in a historic 1932 building, offers spacious, quiet rooms, with priority given to those wishing to study Spanish. Dorms CH$8000, doubles CH$19,000

Hostal Melmac Walker Martínez 561 ☎65 230863, ⊛melmacpatagonia.com. Self-proclaimed "hostel from another world" offering yoga and painting workshops, as well as the standard outdoor excursions. The beds are new and comfortable, there are lockers for your valuables and kitchen access, and the owner sometimes throws barbecues in the garden. Dorms CH$9000, doubles CH$20,000

EATING AND DRINKING

There are two major supermarkets in the centre: Santa Isabel on Del Salvador (Mon–Sat 9.30am–10pm) and Express Lider on Gramados (Mon–Sat 8.30am–10pm, Sun 9am–10pm).

Caffé El Barista Martínez 211 ☎65 233130, ⊛elbarista .cl. Bright, trendy café serving excellent Italian coffee (from CH$1500), sandwiches (CH$2700–3200) and cakes (CH$1000–2200). They also serve wine and decent pisco sour (CH$2500). Wi-fi available. Daily 9am–10.30pm.

Dane's Café & Restaurant Del Salvador 441 ☎65 232371. This established favourite reflects the town's hybrid history, their *empanadas de horno* sitting alongside the superb *apfelstrudel*. A great spot for coffee with cake (around CH$1700) or an inexpensive lunch. Daily 7.45am–1am.

Donde El Gordito San Bernardo 560 ☎65 233425. Busy little café inside the market serving large portions of

inexpensive fish and seafood to hungry locals. Try the conger eel, any of the fish plates (CH$5500–7500), and their infamous Don Guillermo pisco sour. Cash only. Daily 11am–10pm.

Garage Martínez 220 ☎65 232856. A bar/club that's located in an, erm, garage, that comes alive after 11pm, with its mixture of jazz and rock or wherever the mood takes them. Mon–Sat 8pm–4am.

Trattoria Di Carusso San Bernardo 318, at San José ☎65 233 478, ⊛dicarusso.cl. Family-run Italian restaurant with a wood-fired oven inside the *Hosteria Outsider*, with chequered tablecloths and heaped portions of delicious home-made pasta. *Menú del día* from CH$5200, seafood CH$6000–7000. Daily 1pm–12.45am.

DIRECTORY

Banks and exchange There are several banks with ATMs downtown, including the reliable Banco de Chile at Del Salvador 201 and Santander at San Francisco and Del Salvador.

Hospital Centro Médico Puerto Varas is at Walker Martínez 576 (☎65 232792).

Internet Try Ciber Patagonia inside the Dona Natalia shopping gallery off Del Salvador, half a block from the Plaza (Mon–Fri 9am–9.30pm, Sat 10.30am–9.30pm, Sun 11.30am–7pm; CH$250/15min; CH$600/1hr).

Laundry Lavandería Alba at Walker Martinez 511 (Mon–Fri 9am–1pm, 3–7.30pm; Sat 9.30am–1.30pm; self-service CH$1500 or CH$1900/kg.

Post office San José 242, at San Pedro (Mon–Fri 9am–1.30pm & 3–6pm, Sat 9am–1pm).

SALTOS DE PETROHUÉ

Chile boasts hundreds of waterfalls, but none quite like the **Saltos de**

Petrohué (daily: summer 8.30am–7pm; winter 9am–6pm; CH$1500; parking CH$270 per 20min). Some 50km from Puerto Varas, these is a series of boiling, churning rapids and falls that shoot through eroded lava tubes and bizarrely shaped rocks. With the Osorno volcano as a backdrop, it's hard to imagine a more enchanting location. According to local legend, these rapids are the home of a monster, Cuchivilu, which resembles a giant puma with a claw on the end of its tail. Regular minibuses run here from Puerto Varas (every 30min; 45min; CH$2000) on the way to **Petrohué**. Save money by skipping the jetboat ride offered at the entrance (you won't see much more of the falls).

LAGO TODOS LOS SANTOS

From the **Saltos de Petrohué** the road turns to gravel and continues for another 6km to the tiny village of **Petrohué** itself, embarkation point for boat trips around the mesmerizing waters of **Lago Todos Los Santos** inside the **Parque Nacional Vicente Pérez Rosales** (trips from CH$5000–15,000). Minibuses connect Puerto Varas with the falls and **Petrohué** (CH$2000).

PUERTO MONTT

Established in the 1850s by German settlers, **PUERTO MONTT** is beautifully situated on the **Seno de Reloncaví** (Strait of Reloncaví), with snowcapped mountains clearly visible beyond the sound on a good day. Though perhaps not deserving its "Muerto Montt" ("Dead Montt") moniker, Puerto Montt is a large, busy city with traffic-choked streets; a place to stock up on provisions and equipment on the way to Patagonia and a major transport hub, but little else.

The town stretches along the bay, with Avenida Diego Portales running east along the seafront towards the **Plaza de Armas** – the centre, surrounded by banks, cheap bars and restaurants. West of the main bus terminal, Avenida Costanera takes you to the busy passenger port with a **feria artesanal** (craft market) and the Angelmó fishing district.

ARRIVAL AND INFORMATION

By plane Aeropuerto El Tepual (☎65 294161, ⓦaeropuertopuertomontt.cl) is located 16km northwest of the city, with ATMs and car rental desks in the terminal. Buses ETM (☎65 294294, ⓦbusesetm.cl) meets flights and drops you off at the main bus terminal (CH$1900). Taxis charge CH$10,000 into the centre and CH$18,000 to Puerto Varas (shared transfers CH$5000 and CH$12,000

4

PUERTO VARAS TOUR OPERATORS

The area around Puerto Varas offers a variety of outdoor adventures, from challenging climbs up the nearby volcanoes Osorno and Calbuco to rafting on the turbulent turquoise waters of the Río Petrohué and exploring the surrounding Parque Nacional Vicente Pérez Rosales on horseback. The operators listed below are reputable.

Al Sur Aconcagua, at Imperial ☎65 232300, ⓦalsur expeditions.com. Top rafting adventures along the Class III rapids of the Río Petrohué, with half-day and full-day trips available.

Campo Aventura San Bernardo 318 ☎65 232910, ⓦcampoaventura.cl. The place to go for horse-trekking, from one day to ten days into the foothills of Cochamó valley near the Estuario de Reloncaví. Customized options, like veggie meals, are available, and canyoning and rafting are also among activities on offer. Day horserides from CH$50,000. Mid-Oct to early April only.

Ko'Kayak San Pedro 210 ☎9 93105272, ⓦkokayak .cl. Excellent outfit with fun-loving bilingual guides and an emphasis on safety, specializing in half- to four-day rafting trips in the Lake District as well as

one- or three-day sea-kayaking trips, and more challenging multi-day expeditions in the Patagonian fjords. Half-day rafting on the Río Petrohué CH$32,000.

Pachamagua Del Rosario 1111 ☎65 542080, ⓦpachamagua.com. A reliable and professional canyoning specialist arranging adrenaline-filled excursions; half-day from CH$33,000; full day from CH$54,000. They can also arrange ascents of the Osorno volcano (CH$139,000), horseriding (CH$49,000) and rafting on Río Petrohué (CH$30,000).

Yak Expediciones ☎9 83320574, ⓦyakexpediciones .cl. Long-standing operator specializing in outstanding sea-kayaking excursions – from one-day trips to Lago Todos Los Santos (CH$60,500) to multi-day adventures in the fjords around Parque Pumalín.

4

respectively). Buy tickets for transport in the baggage claim area. Daily flights serve Santiago (1hr 50min), Punta Arenas (2hr 10min), Balmaceda (Coyhaique; 1hr 10min) and Temuco (45min) with LAN, at O'Higgins 167 (☎600 5262000), and Sky Airline, at Benavente 405, Local 4 (☎600 6002828).

By bus Both long-distance and local buses arrive at the large Terminal de Buses (☎65 283 000, ⊛terminalpm.cl), at Av Diego Portales 1001 on the waterfront, a 10min coastal walk from the city centre. The bus station has an information office, ATMs, café and luggage storage. Bus companies include: Cruz del Sur (☎65 252872; Transchiloé (☎65 252872); Buses Turibus (☎65 254731); Tur Bus (☎65 253329); Pullman Bus (☎65 316561); Tas-Choapa (☎65 254828); and Inter Sur (☎65 259320). Minibuses to Puerto Varas (CH$850) depart from the eastern side of the terminal.

Destinations Ancud (every 30min; 2hr); Bariloche, Argentina (2 daily; 6hr); Castro (every 30min; 3hr 30min); Coyhaique (4 weekly; 24hr); Futaleufú (2 weekly; 12hr); Osorno (every 30min; 1hr 30min); Pucón (hourly; 7hr); Puerto Varas (every 15–20min; 30min); Santiago (every 30min; 14hr); Valdivia (every 30min; 3hr).

By ferry The Terminal de Transbordadores lies at Angelmó 1735, several blocks west of the main bus terminal; Navimag (☎65 432300, ⊛navimag.com) and Naviera Austral (☎65 270430, ⊛navieraustral.cl) ferries have offices here. Navimag has departures to Puerto Chacabuco (July–April 1–4 weekly; 24hr; CH$23,500–CH$27,500 for shared cabin) and Puerto Natales (1–2 weekly at 4pm; 3 days; CH$200,000 for shared cabin). Check the website for updated timetables and prices.

Tourist information There is a small tourist information kiosk at the main bus terminal and a well-stocked and helpful Turismo Municipal office on the Plaza de Armas, on Varas at San Martín (Dec–March daily 9am–9pm; April–Nov Mon–Fri 9am–1pm & 2.30–6.30pm, Sat 9am–1pm; ☎65 223027; ⊛puertomontt.cl).

ACCOMMODATION

Casa Perla Trigal 312 ☎65 262104, ⊛casaperla.com. The uphill walk is worth it: this is one of the friendliest homes in town, where you're treated like one of the family. The owners speak good English and German and offer Spanish lessons, you can use their kitchen and internet, and even camp in the yard. Camping/person CH$5500, doubles CH$23,000

Hospedaje Rocco Pudeto 233 ☎65 272897, ⊛hospedaje rocco.cl. Enjoy a warm welcome from Argentine hostess Veronica Rocco and her dogs. The dorms and rooms are cosy, though a little overpriced, but the breakfast is excellent and you can use the internet and kitchen. Located just five blocks from the Navimag. Cash only. Dorms CH$12,000, doubles CH$25,000

Hospedaje Vista Al Mar Francisco Vivar 1337 ☎65 255625, ⊛hospedajevistaalmar.unlugar.com. Justly popular guesthouse offering excellent value, especially for single travellers (CH$13,000), with cosy en-suite rooms overlooking the city, TVs and wi-fi. Doubles CH$24,000

EATING AND DRINKING

For cheap food and drink, stock up at the vast Unimarc supermarket in the basement of Paseo Costanera mall, or make for the line of kiosks at Gallardo and Varas, where *empanadas*, burgers and *salchi* (fried hot dogs on fries) are just CH$800–900.

Café Haussmann San Martín 185 ☎65 293380. This perpetually busy café (a franchise of the Valdivia original) is a good spot to sample *crudos* (steak tartare on toast with lemon juice, capers and minced onion; CH$1800), or indulge in some of the delicious cakes on display. Smoking is permitted. Mon–Sat 9.30am–8.30pm, Sun 11am–8.30pm.

★ **Mercado Angelmó** Av Angelmó, to the west of the ferry terminal; catch any of the Angelmó-bound *colectivos* along Av Diego Portales if you don't want to walk (CH$400). Don't miss this lively fish market and the nearby two-storey cluster of cheap *marisquerías*, an ideal place to sample super-fresh fish and seafood dishes, such as *chupe de locos* (abalone chowder) and *curanto* (clams, giant mussels, potatoes, dumplings, ham hocks, sausage and chicken in steaming fish broth; the broth served separately), all for under CH$5000. Daily noon–8pm.

Sherlock Varas 542, at Rancagua ☎65 288888. Named after the fictional detective, though the legend that he visited Puerto Montt is an invention of a Chilean author, not Conan Doyle. It's still the best pub in town, serving excellent food (fajitas "Sherlock"; CH$2500), good sandwiches and a wide range of Kunstmann beers (from CH$1900) in a dark, cosy setting (there's also seating on the street in summer). Mon–Sat 9am–5am, Sun 9am–2am.

Tablón del Ancla Varas 350, at O'Higgins ☎65 367555, ⊛tablondelancla.cl. Slide into a booth at this sports diner decorated with caricatures, and fill up on massive hamburgers and grilled meats. Or if you're particularly hungry, a *pichanga* – mountain of chips strewn with bits of meat and chorizo – should sort you out. Mains from CH$4000. Daily 10am–2am.

DIRECTORY

Banks and exchange There is an ATM at the main bus terminal and several banks with ATMs downtown; try BBVA on Urmeneta, at O'Higgins, or Santander on Urmeneta, at Montt. Also try AFEX, at Portales 516 (Mon–Fri 8.30am–5.30pm, Sat 10am–2pm), which accepts American Express travellers' cheques.

Hospitals Clínica Puerto Montt, at Panamericana 400 (☎65 484800, ⊛clinpmontt.cl), and Hospital Regional, Seminario s/n (☎65 490213), handle medical emergencies.

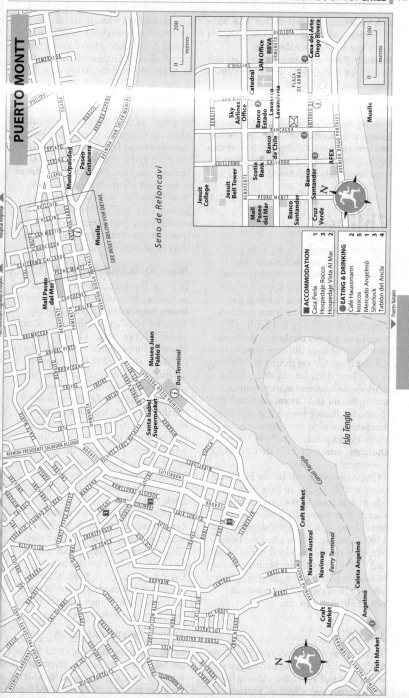

PUERTO MONTT

Seno de Reloncaví

SEE INSET BELOW FOR DETAIL

Isla Tenglo

Canal Tenglo

ACCOMMODATION
Casa Perla	1
Hospedaje Rocco	3
Hospedaje Vista Al Mar	2

● EATING & DRINKING
Café Haussmann	2
kioscos	5
Mercado Angelmó	1
Sherlock	3
Tablón del Ancla	4

Municipalidad
Paseo Costanera
Muelle
Mall Paseo del Mar
Museo Juan Pablo II
Bus Terminal
Santa Isabel Supermarket
Craft Market
Naviera Austral
Navimag
Ferry Terminal
Angelmó
Caleta Angelmó
Craft Market
Fish Market

INSET

Casa del Arte Diego Rivera
Catedral
LAN Office
BBVA
Sky Airlines Office
Banco Estado
Lavasecco
Lavandería
Banco de Chile
Jesuit College
Jesuit Bell Tower
Scotia Bank
Banco Santander
AFEX
Banco Santander
Cruz Verde
Mall Paseo del Mar
PLAZA DE ARMAS
Muelle

0 — 200 metres

0 — 100 metres

4

Puerto Natales

Laundry Lavaseco y Lavandería Fast Clean, at San Martín 167 (inside the building), charges CH$1900/kg (Mon–Fri 9am–1.30pm & 3–8pm; Sat 9.30am–2pm).

Pharmacy There are numerous pharmacies along Urmeneta; Cruz Verde is on Pedro Montt, at Varas (Mon–Fri 8.30am–10pm, Sat 8.30am–9.30pm).

Post office Rancagua 126 (Mon–Fri 9am–7pm, Sat 9.30am–1pm).

Shopping The best shopping mall is the towering Paseo Costanera on the waterfront, with its extensive food court, multi-screen cinema and an "Andesgear" outlet, which stocks high-quality (though not cheap) outdoor and camping gear. Unimarc supermarket is in the basement.

Chiloé

As the ferry ploughs through the grey waters of the Canal de Chacao that separates the **CHILOÉ** archipelago from the mainland, an island appears out of the mist. **Isla Grande de Chiloé** is the second-largest island in South America, a patchwork of forests and fields, with traditional villages nestling in sheltered inlets. Its residents still largely make a living from salmon fishing and farming, as they have done for centuries. Today Chiloé draws visitors to its two main towns, **Ancud** and **Castro**, crammed with distinctive shingle houses and waterside *palafitos*, as well as more remote national parks and its precious cache of clapboard **churches**, many of which are UNESCO monuments.

Originally populated by the Huilliche (southern Mapuche) Indians, most of whom died from a smallpox epidemic shortly after European contact, Chiloé was colonized by the Spanish as early as 1567. Scores of refugees fled the fierce Mapuche on the mainland to the island, and Chiloé's very distinct culture evolved in relative isolation, resulting in a diverse and rich mythology that permeates people's lives to this day.

ANCUD

Tucked away on Chiloé's northern coast, **ANCUD** is the island's second-largest settlement and a pleasant place to linger. Its importance as a Spanish fortification was highlighted when it became the royalists' last stronghold, holding out against hostile forces for almost a decade after Chile's declaration of independence in 1818. Much of the action these days centres on the lively little **Plaza de Armas**, where there are crafts and book stalls in the summer and locals chill out in the evenings. At the Mercado Municipal, a block north, there are numerous bustling *marisquerías* and craft stalls. Overlooking the town at the northern end of the harbour, the **Fuerte Real de San Antonio** (Mon–Fri 8.30am–9pm, Sat & Sun 9am–8pm; free) was erected on a promontory in 1779, but is little more than a ruined gun battery today. This is where the last Spanish troops in Chile were finally defeated in 1826.

WHAT TO SEE AND DO

In the southwest corner of the Plaza de Armas, the small but illuminating **Museo Regional de Ancud** (Jan–Feb Mon–Fri 10.30am–7.30pm, Sat & Sun 10am–7.30pm; March–Dec Tues–Fri 10am–5.30pm, Sat & Sun 10am–2pm; CH$600; ☎65 622413, ⚐museoancud .cl) features a relief map of Chiloé and small displays on just about every episode of the island's history, from the little-known Dutch occupations of 1600 and 1643 to the devastating earthquake of 1960 – labels are in Spanish only. Don't miss the replica of the *Goleta Ancud* outside, the locally built ship that led the expedition to take control of the Straits of Magellan for Chile in 1843.

Make time also for the **Iglesias de Chiloé Centro de Visitantes** (daily 9.30am–7pm; free; ⚐iglesiasdechiloe.cl) at Errázuriz 227, housed in the beautifully preserved Ex Convento de la Inmaculada Concepción of 1875. Models, carved doors, windows and explanation boards (much in English) introduce the island's beloved wooden churches.

ARRIVAL AND INFORMATION

By bus Long-distance buses (Cruz del Sur, Pullman Sur and Trans Chiloé) arrive at the conveniently located Terminal de Buses at Los Carrera 850 (☎65 622249), a 10min walk from the plaza; Castro is served frequently

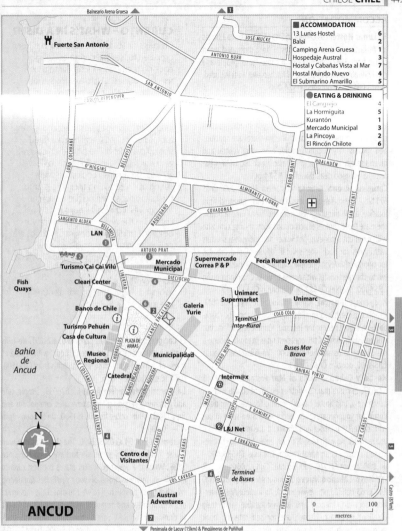

ACCOMMODATION

13 Lunas Hostel	6
Balai	2
Camping Arena Gruesa	1
Hospedaje Austral	3
Hostal y Cabañas Vista al Mar	7
Hostal Mundo Nuevo	4
El Submarino Amarillo	5

EATING & DRINKING

El Cangrejo	4
La Hormiguita	5
Kurantón	1
Mercado Municipal	3
La Pincoya	2
El Rincón Chilote	6

ANCUD

Península de Lacuy (15km) & Pinqüineras de Puñihuil

(CH$2000) and bus tickets to and from the mainland (Puerto Montt is CH$4000) include ferry passage (otherwise the ferry is CH$10,000/car, CH$1600/bicycle; 30–40min, frequently; 24hr). Buses from villages across Chiloé pull up at the Terminal Inter-Rural on Colo Colo, above the Unimarc supermarket (they stop in the street, there's no actual bus station), or in the less convenient Terminal Municipal, at the end of Prat. See relevant sections for specific bus details.

Destinations Castro (every 15–30min; 1hr 15min); Dalcahue (6.05pm; 1hr); Osorno (10 daily; 3hr 30min); Puerto Montt (every 30min; 1hr 30min–2hr); Puerto Varas

(5 daily; 2hr 30min); Quellón (16 daily; 4hr); Santiago (daily 6.35pm & 7.35pm; 16hr); Valdivia (7 daily; 5hr);

Tourist information The well-stocked Sernatur office at Libertad 665, on the west side of the Plaza de Armas (Dec–Feb Mon–Fri 8.30am–7pm, Sat & Sun 9.30am–7pm; March–Nov Mon–Thurs 8.30am–6pm, Fri 8.30am–5pm; ☎65 622800), has very helpful staff, maps of town and lists of accommodation and attractions, as well as a list of families participating in Agroturismo Chiloé, the opportunity to stay in rural family homes. If Sernatur is closed, try the tourist information kiosk underneath the plaza bandstand (aka Glorieta) or check out ⓦchiloe.cl.

ACCOMMODATION

13 Lunas Hostel Los Carrera 855 ☏ 65 622106, ⊛ 13lunas
.cl. Attractive, clean, modern hostel (in a renovated wood
house from 1947), with dorms for four to six people and
comfy doubles, breakfast, use of kitchen and wi-fi included.
Dorms `CH$9500`, doubles `CH$24,000`

Balai Pudeto 169 ☏ 65 622541, ⊛ hotelbalai.cl. "Quirky
and whimsical" comes to mind when you walk in and make
yourself at home among the boat figureheads, wooden
carvings and models of ships. The en-suites are spacious
and spotless, the location couldn't be more central and
given the extras thrown in – basic breakfast, wi-fi – the
prices are a good deal. Doubles `CH$24,000`

Camping Arena Gruesa Costanera Norte 290 ☏ 65
623428, ⊛ hotelarenagruesa.cl. At this great clifftop
location, a few minutes' walk from the Arena Gruesa beach,
there are three choices of accommodation: a large campsite
with excellent sea views, hot water and individual shelters
with lights for each site; several fully equipped cabañas
for two/four/six/eight people; and well-kept rooms in the
white-shingled hostel with access to wi-fi. Camping/person
`CH$4000`, doubles `CH$22,000`, cabañas `CH$33,000`

Hospedaje Austral Aníbal Pinto 1318 ☏ 65 624847,
⊛ ancudchiloechile.com. Friendly wood-pannelled backpacker hangout near to the Terminal Municipal (the local bus
station), with some of the cheapest rates in town (though a
basic breakfast is another CH$1000). Wi-fi included. Dorms
`CH$8000`, doubles `CH$18,000`

Hostal y Cabañas Vista al Mar Costanera 918 ☏ 65
622617, ⊛ vistaalmar.cl. Another excellent choice with an
ocean view, this hostel has something for everyone: clean
dorms for younger travellers and spacious en-suite rooms
with cable TV. Internet and breakfast are included, and if
you're travelling with friends a fully equipped two- or five-
person cabaña is an ideal choice. Cabañas `CH$35,000–
44,000`, dorms `CH$10,000`, doubles `CH$32,000`

★ **Hostal Mundo Nuevo** Salvador Allende (Costanera)
748 ☏ 65 628383, ⊛ newworld.cl. An impeccable waterfront location, friendly and knowledgeable staff, truly
excellent breakfast, kitchen use for self-caterers, book
exchange, wi-fi, and spotless airy rooms and dorms all
make this Swiss-owned hostel the most popular choice
for backpackers. Dorms `CH$12,000`, doubles (shared
bath) `CH$31,000`, private bath `CH$39,000`

El Submarino Amarillo Las Américas 958 ☏ 65 620436,
⊛ subamarillo.net. One of the newer hostels in Ancud, the
"yellow submarine" is set in an old Chiloé-style house with
clean dorms, free wi-fi and Ikea-like furnishings. Dorms
`CH$10,000`, doubles `CH$20,000`

EATING AND DRINKING

Ancud contains a huge Unimarc supermarket (on Prat,
behind the Feria Rural & Artesanal), open daily 9am–10pm.
Many restaurants in Ancud shut for half or all day on Sun.

> ## CURANTO – WHAT'S IN A DISH?
>
> Chiloé's signature dish, **curanto**, has been
> prepared for several centuries using
> cooking methods very similar to those
> used in Polynesia. First, extremely hot
> rocks are placed at the bottom of an
> earthen pit; then, a layer of shellfish is
> added, followed by chunks of meat,
> *longanisa* (sausage), potatoes, *chapaleles*
> (potato dumplings) and *milcaos* (fried
> potato pancakes). The pit is then covered
> with *nalca* (Chilean wild rhubarb) leaves,
> and, as the shellfish cooks, the shells
> spring open, releasing their juices onto
> the hot rocks, steaming the rest of the
> ingredients. *Curanto en hoyo* is slow-
> cooked in the ground for a day or two,
> but since traditional cooking methods are
> only used in the countryside, you will
> probably end up sampling *curanto en olla*,
> oven-baked in cast-iron pots. The dish
> comes with hot broth, known to the locals
> as "liquid Viagra", that you drink during
> the meal.

El Cangrejo Dieciocho 171 (2/F) ☏ 65 623091. No-frills
seafood restaurant on the second floor, with a decent
menu of fish and shellfish stews and grills from CH$3500.
Daily 10am–10pm.

La Hormiguita Pudeto 44 ☏ 65 626999. Simple café
and *pastelería*, serving giant sandwiches, *empanadas* and
fruit-filled cream cakes from CH$1500. Daily noon–3pm
& 7–10.30pm.

Kurantón Prat 94 ☏ 65 623090. The slogan on the wall
reads: "Curanto: helping people to have good sex since
1826". When the bow-tied waiter places the best *curanto
en olla* in town in front of you, you'll be wondering
whether those people had to wait to digest the mountain
of shellfish, meat and potato dumplings first. Don't forget
to drink your "liquid Viagra" – the potent shellfish stock
that comes with your dish. *Curanto* CH$6000. Daily 12.30–
3pm & 7–10.30pm.

Mercado Municipal The basic cafeterias in the courtyard
behind the market, and the slightly better places above
it, tend to be packed at lunchtime if the weather's good.
They all serve a variety of inexpensive fish and seafood
dishes; *Rincon Sureno* (2/F) and *La Pica de la Corita* (at the
back) are good bets. *Empanadas* from CH$1000, fish dishes
from CH$4000. Daily 8am–8pm.

La Pincoya Prat 61 ☏ 65 622613. Opposite *Kurantón*,
La Pincoya overlooks the harbour and serves excellent
salmon *ceviche*, *curanto* and delicious *cancato* (steamed
salmon stuffed with sausage, cheese and tomatoes). *Ceviche*
CH$4500; *curanto* CH$6000. Daily 1–3pm & 7–11pm.

El Rincón Chilote Pudeto 115. Hole-in-the-wall on the plaza, selling cheap *empanadas*, tortillas and coffee. Next door *La Estación* serves better coffee (closed Sun). Mon–Sat 9am–7pm.

DIRECTORY

Banks and exchange There is an ATM in Banco de Chile at Chorillos 621 (Plaza de Armas).
Hospital Almirante Latorre 301 (☎65 622355). 24hr medical service.
Internet and telephone Most hostels now offer internet access and wi-fi (the Mercado Municipal usually has free wi-fi). Try L&J Net at Errázuriz 342 (daily 10am–7pm; CH$500/hr), or Interm@x on Maipú between Pudeto and Ramírez (similar hours and rates).
Laundry Clean Center, Pudeto 45 (Mon–Sat 9.30am–1pm & 3–7.30pm).
Post office Pudeto, at Blanco Encalada (Mon–Fri 9am–6pm, Sat 9am–12.30pm).
Shopping The Feria Rural & Artesanal on Prat and the Mercado Municipal have a number of stalls selling woollen goods and woodcarvings, as well as home-distilled liqueurs such as the bright golden *licór de oro* – a traditional Chilote drink, the recipe for which is guarded jealously.

Pingüineras de Puñihuil

Don't leave Ancud without taking a half-day tour of the **Pingüineras de Puñihuil** (@pinguineraschiloe.cl), a large colony of Humboldt and Magellanic **penguins** spread over three tiny islands off the coast some 24km southwest of Ancud. The last 10km is on a rough gravel road to the little fishing village of **Puñihuil**, where local collective Ecoturismo Puñihuil runs half-hour zodiac trips (Spanish commentary, with English information; Sept–March 10.30am–5.45pm, every 30min;

CH$6000; ☎09 8 317 4302, @ballenaschiloe.cl). You are likely to catch sight of sea lions and sea otters, as well as the penguins and a wealth of seabirds from the boats – in the summer months (late Jan–April), you might also see a large pod of endangered blue **whales**: the same outfit that runs boats to the penguin colony arranges whale-watching trips (CH$95,000). The easiest way to see the penguins is on a tour from Ancud (around CH$15,000; see box below), but to save money use Buses Mar Brava at Aníbal Pinto 356 (6.45am, noon & 1pm; CH$1500), and ask to get off at the colony (you'll still have to walk 2km).

VALLE DE CHEPU

Around 25km south of Ancud, a turn-off leads to the **Valle de Chepu**, a large stretch of wetlands created during the 1960 tsunami, whose sunken forest provides a thriving habitat for hundreds of bird species and superb hiking trails as far as the Parque Nacional Chiloé.

ARRIVAL AND DEPARTURE

By bus To get here, take the Buses Peter service (☎8 3831172) from the Petrobras petrol station at the corner of Arturo Prat and Goycolea in Ancud (6.45am; buses return around 5pm), or if you plan to stay the night, the 4pm bus from the Terminal Inter-Rural (Mon, Wed & Fri only; these buses pass *Chepu Adventures*).

ACCOMMODATION

Chepu Adventures ☎09 93792481, @chepuadventures .com. A superb, self-sufficient eco-campsite; you can either cook for yourself or stay in one of the two nearby *agroturismo* homes for some superb home cooking. The welcoming

---

ANCUD TOUR OPERATORS

Aki Turismo Mercado Municipal (on Dieciocho, at Libertad) ☎65 545253, @akiturismochiloe.cl. Established outfit running daily tours to see the penguins at Pingüineras de Puñihuil (Dec–Feb 10am & 4.30pm; CH$15,000, minimum 2 people), as well as day-tours taking in Chiloé's most famous wooden churches. Reserve a day ahead and you will be picked up from your hostel.
Austral Adventures Costanera (Salvador Allende) 904 ☎65 625977, @austral-adventures.com. While this reputable operator run by an extremely knowledgeable

American-Peruvian couple generally caters for the upper end of the market, specializing in multi-day tours of Patagonian fjords and the Chiloé archipelago aboard the *Cahuela*, they also offer excellent day-trips around Chiloé – from visiting the penguin colonies (CH$35,000, with full-day coastal trek) to kayaking and trekking parts of the Sendero de Chile. Day-kayak trip on the Bay of Ancud including lunch CH$35,000.
Turismo Pehuén (see p.455) has an office at the Plaza de Armas.

owners offer dawn kayaking trips as well as ecologically sensitive nature walks along the coast to the large but endangered Ahuenco penguin colony. Camping/person CH$4500, dorms CH$7000, doubles CH$35,000

CASTRO

The third-oldest continuously inhabited city in Chile, **CASTRO** was founded by the Spanish in 1567 and survived a number of calamities through the centuries: being pillaged by English and Dutch pirates, numerous fires and the great earthquake of 1960, which largely destroyed it. These days it's the bustling capital of Chiloé – though it's about the same size, it feels a lot more developed than Ancud.

WHAT TO SEE AND DO

A large **Plaza de Armas** surrounded by bars and restaurants is Castro's focal point; in summer, outdoor musical events are staged here. The yellow-purple neo-Gothic **Iglesia San Francisco** (daily 9.30am–12.30pm & 3–8.30pm) stands on the northeastern corner of the plaza – this version was completed in 1912, with its all-wood interior well worth admiring. The **Museo Regional** (Jan–Feb Mon–Fri 9.30am–7pm, Sat 9.30am–6pm, Sun 10.30am–1pm; March–Dec Mon–Fri 9.30am–1pm & 3–6.30pm, Sat 9.30am–1pm; donations) is on Esmeralda, just half a block south of the plaza, and features everything from exhibits on the indigenous Chonos and Huilliche (a branch of the Mapuche), to black-and-white photos of the 1960 earthquake and its devastation. Two blocks from the plaza, steeply downhill, lies Eusebio Lillo, the coastal road that's home to a number of **seafood restaurants**, with the large **Feria Artesanal** (daily 9am–6pm) by the water selling all sorts of woollen goodies and other crafts; though not as famous as the Sunday market at Dalcahue, this one is almost as good, and you can try salmon *ceviche* with red peppers for a spicy breakfast at the restaurants behind. The summer-only **Museo de Arte Moderno** in the Parque Municipal de Castro (Pasaje Díaz 181; Jan–March daily 10am–6pm; donations; ☎65 635454, ⓦ mamchiloe.cl), housed in a shingled farmhouse, is a

Spartan contemporary art space featuring Chilote artists.

Palafitos

Though deemed unsanitary by some locals, Chiloé's famous **palafitos** are still found at several locations around Castro. Perched precariously on stilts above the water, these brightly painted, traditional wooden fishermen's dwellings are an unforgettable sight. The idea was that you could moor your boat at your back door and walk out onto the street through the front one. The most impressive examples are found at the north end of town, off Pedro Montt, where they are perfectly reflected in the mini-lake by the roadside. More *palafitos* are found slightly south along the same street, while others are used as restaurants at the southern end of town, by the Feria Artesanal. A final batch can be seen from the western end of Eusebio Lillo, across the Río Bamboa, and you can even stay in one (see p.454).

ARRIVAL AND INFORMATION

By bus Cruz del Sur (☎ 65 632389) has its own bus terminal at San Martín 486, which serves numerous long-distance destinations up to and including Puerto Montt (CH$5500) and Santiago, as well as Punta Arenas in the south, Bariloche in Argentina, and Ancud (CH$2000) and Quellón in Chiloé. The Terminal de Buses Municipal, at San Martín 667, serves ETM (buses to Santiago), Trans-Chiloé (Puerto Montt) and also has services to smaller destinations around Chiloé, including Cucao (Parque Nacional Chiloé). Ancud is cheaper from this bus station (CH$1300).

Destinations Cruz del Sur terminal to: Ancud (hourly; 1hr 15min); Puerto Montt (frequent; 3hr); Puerto Varas (15 daily; 3hr 45min); Punta Arenas (2 weekly; 32hr); Quellón, for Parque Tantauco (hourly; 2hr 15min); Santiago (5.05pm & 6.10pm; 18hr); Valdivia (7 daily; 8–9hr). Terminal Municipal to: Ancud (frequent; 1hr 15min); Cucao (4–6 daily from 8.30am; 1hr 15min); Dalcahue (every 30min; 30min); Puerto Montt (frequent; 3hr); Santiago (5.10pm & 7pm; 18hr).

By ferry Naviera Austral (ⓦ navieraustral.cl) runs one weekly ferry (Jan & Feb only) to Chaitén on the mainland (from CH$16,000) from the passenger terminal (in the port on Av Pedro Montt); from Chaitén you can connect with buses south into Aysén (see p.457).

Tourist office The tourist information centre (daily 10am–8pm; ⓦ municastro.cl) on the Plaza de Armas has plenty of information on the area (though it's all behind the counter, so you have to know what to ask for) and scale models of Chiloé's famous wooden churches.

ACCOMMODATION

Hostal Central Los Carrera 316 ☎ 65 637026, ⓦ hostalcentraldecastro.com. Quiet central hotel with brightly painted bathrooms and spotless rooms, some en-suite, all with cable TV and wi-fi, though some are windowless. Ask for a room on the top floor, with the best view. Doubles (shared bath) CH$18,000

Hostal Cordillera Barros Arana 175 ☎ 65 532247, ⓦ hostalcordillera.cl. Run by a gregarious hostess who really makes you feel at home, this central hostel has clean, cosy rooms and an outdoor deck with sea views to chill out on. Breakfast, internet/wi-fi and luggage storage are all included, and the owners can help organize tours of the island. Doubles (no bath) CH$28,000, triples (with bath) CH$50,000

Hostal Entretenido Almirante Latorre 139 ☎ 65 531677, ⓦ hostalentretenido.blogspot.com. Small, centrally located hostel with simple doubles, shared bathrooms, free wi-fi,

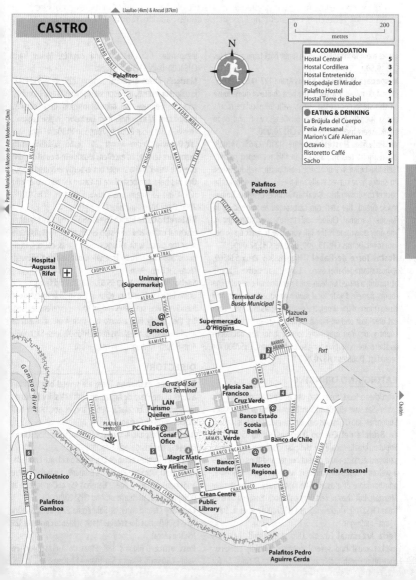

CHILOTE CHURCHES

It is impossible to visit Chiloé and not be struck by the sight of the archipelago's **wooden churches**, some of which have a vaguely Scandinavian rather than Spanish look. In 2001 UNESCO accepted sixteen of them on to its prestigious World Heritage list. The outside of the churches is almost always bare, and the only thing that expresses anything but functionality is the three-tiered, **hexagonal bell tower** that rises up directly above an open-fronted portico. The facades, doors and windows are often brightly painted, and the walls clad with plain clapboard or wooden tiles. The roofs are built like traditional Chilote boats and then turned upside down. The ceilings are often painted too, with allegorical panels or golden constellations of stars painted on an electric blue background. For more information on Chiloé's churches, check out the informative ⓦinterpatagonia.com/iglesiaschiloe.

games room with cable TV and a sunny back terrace. Doubles CH$19,500

Hospedaje El Mirador Barros Arana 127 ☎65 633795, ⓦhostalelmiradorcastro.cl. The best choice of guesthouse on this steep pedestrian street, with immaculate rooms and a friendly host. Kitchen privileges, wi-fi and good breakfast are included. Doubles CH$20,000

★ **Palafito Hostel** Riquelme 1210 ☎65 531008, ⓦpalafitohostel.com. Staying in this revamped *palafito* feels like being in a boat: the eight plush, well-furnished en-suites have curved walls and there's a little deck at the back of the dining area. Breakfast includes delicious home-made bread, the staff can help organize horseriding in Parque Nacional Chiloé and there's wi-fi throughout. The only downside is the hill you have to walk up to into town. Dorms CH$13,000, doubles CH$32,000

Hostal Torre de Babel O'Higgins 965 ☎65 534569, ⓦhostaltorredebabel.com. Large, attractive house attracting a mixed Chilean and international clientele. The rooms, panelled with local *mañío* wood, are spacious and clean (most of the time), the owner throws in all-you-can-eat breakfast and wi-fi and organizes group trips into the countryside. You may have to queue for the bathroom as there are only two for the eight rooms. CH$2000 for breakfast. Doubles CH$20,000

EATING AND DRINKING

Grab cheap food, fruits and veg at Unimarc on O'Higgins (Mon–Sat 9am–9.30pm; Sun 10am–9pm) or the smaller Supermercado O'Higgins outside the municipal bus station.

La Brújula del Cuerpo O'Higgins 308 ☎65 633225. Popular, bustling café on the plaza, serving milkshakes, sandwiches, pizza and decent burger-and-fries combos – a welcome sight for travellers who can't bear to look at another plate of mussels. The fajitas may not be terribly Mexican, but they're certainly palatable. Burger and fries from CH$2700; chicken fajitas CH$2700. Free wi-fi. Daily 11am–midnight.

Feria Artesanal Eusebio Lillo s/n. Behind the crafts market you'll find several *palafitos* housing cafeterias that fill up with locals at lunchtime. Try *El Caleuche* for inexpensive fish, seafood and *curanto*. Mains from CH$3000. Daily 11.30am–10pm.

Marion's Café Aleman Serrano 325 ☎8 3524342. Excellent breakfasts, real espresso, light meals and especially addictive German-style cakes/*apfelstrudel* in a homely, relaxed café (Marion hails from Germany; English spoken). Free wi-fi. Mon–Sat 8.30am–7pm, Sun 10.30am–7pm.

★ **Octavio** Pedro Montt 261 ☎65 632855. With exemplary service, an excellent location in a *palafito* right over the water and a simple but expertly executed menu, this has been the best place in Castro for *curanto en olla* (CH$4500) for many years now. Fish mains CH$4000–7000. Daily 10am–midnight.

Ristoretto Caffè Blanco 264 ☎65 532769. Castro's other essential coffee and cake stop is this modern, stylish café near the plaza, with a huge range of teas, coffees, fresh juices and sandwiches. Free wi-fi, but smoking allowed. Mon–Sat 8am–9pm.

Sacho Thompson 213 ☎65 632079. This old favourite still draws both locals and travellers in the know with its mix of friendly service, sea views and, of course, excellent seafood. Try the *pulmay* (like *curanto* but with more shellfish) or anything with clams. Mains from CH$5500. Tues–Sat noon–4pm & 8pm–midnight, Sun noon–4pm.

DIRECTORY

Banks and exchange There are several banks within a block of the Plaza de Armas, all with ATMs. Try Banco de Chile on Blanco Encalada, at Serrano, or Scotiabank half a block north on Serrano.

Hospital Hospital Augusta Rifat, on Freire 852 (☎65 632445), has basic medical facilities.

Internet Try the Centro de Llamados on Blanco Encalada, half a block from the Plaza (it's primarily a gaming centre and open late), PC Chile at Gamboa 452 or Don Ignacio at O'Higgins 626 (all charge around CH$500/hr).

Laundry Clean Center, at Balmaceda 220, does laundry (CH$1500/kg), as does Magic Matic at Blanco Encalada 329 (on the plaza).

Post office O'Higgins 388, Plaza de Armas (Mon–Fri 9am–1.30pm & 3–6pm, Sat 10am–12.30pm).

Tours Altué Expeditions in Dalcahue (📞9 4196809, 🌐seakayakchile.com) offer multi-day trips around the Chiloé archipelago complete with lodging at their kayak centre near Dalcahue. Multi-activity combination trips in the Lake District and Patagonia are also on offer. Turismo Pehuén on Esmeralda 198 (📞65 635254, 🌐turismopehuen.cl) organizes city tours, summer boat-trips to the uninhabited islets off the east coast, day-trips around Chiloé as well as in-depth multi-day programmes. Newcomer Chiloétnico at Riquelme 1228 (📞65 630951, 🌐chiloetnico.cl) specializes in trekking across Chiloé's national parks.

EASTERN CHILOÉ

The east coast of Chiloé between Ancud and Castro remains a bastion of traditional village life, and the location of many of those famed wooden churches. Some are only accessible by car – the enigmatic and isolated **San Antonio de Colo**, for example – but you can visit several via public transport from Castro. Frequent buses run to the Sunday craft market and the Nuestra Señora de los Dolores church in **Dalcahue** (20km from Castro), where ferries (every 30min; foot passengers free, cars CH$2000; 10min) shuttle across to the elongated Isla Quinchao. The island is home to Chiloé's oldest church, the ancient-looking **Iglesia de Santa María de Loreto in Achao**, dating back to 1740. The coast road continues from Dalcahue for another 30km to the tiny fishing village of Tenaún, location of the most dazzling church on the island, the blue and white Nuestra Señora del Patrocinio (completed in 1902 but almost completely rebuilt in 2011). The road north to Quicaví and the sleepy fishing town of Quemchi is rough gravel (though slowly being paved), and best tackled by car.

ARRIVAL AND DEPARTURE

By bus Most of the east coast is accessible by minibus from Castro, departing the Terminal de Buses Municipal, San Martín 667 (Quemchi is the only town serviced by regular buses from Ancud). Always check the latest schedule (and return bus) before departing.

Destinations Castro to: Curaco de Vélez/Achao (every 30min; 1hr 50min); Dalcahue (frequently; 30min); Quemchi (8.20am; 12.25pm & 6.30pm; 1hr); Quicaví (3 daily Mon–Fri, 2 Sat, 1 Sun; 1hr 30min); Tenaún (Mon–Sat 3 daily, Sun 2 daily; 1hr).

PARQUE NACIONAL CHILOÉ

On the island's mountainous western coast, the **PARQUE NACIONAL CHILOÉ** comprises vast areas of native evergreen forest, covering the slopes and valleys of the **Cordillera de Piuchén**, as well as wide deserted beaches and long stretches of **rugged coastline**, home to dozens of seabird species, penguins and sea lions. The dense vegetation hides the elusive *pudú* (pygmy deer) and the shy Chilote fox. The park is divided into three sectors, though by far the easiest to access is Sector Anay.

Sector Anay

To reach Sector Anay, take a bus to the tumbledown village of **Cucao** from Castro's Terminal Municipal (4–6 daily in peak season; 1hr). Pay the park entrance fee at **Chanquín** (daily 9am–7pm; CH$1500), across the river from the village, where Conaf's **Centro de Visitantes** provides visitors with a detailed map of the park. Though you can pick up some supplies at Cucao (there are several guesthouses of varying quality here also), and buy fresh catch from the fishermen, you'll need adequate food to explore the park properly.

There are some attractive **short walks** from the visitors' centre – the 750m Sendero El Tepual winds its way through humid, slippery *tepú* woods, and the Sendero Dunas de Cucao switches between patches of dense vegetation and sand dunes, before arriving at a white beach. The 25km Sendero Chanquín–Cole Cole runs to the Conaf *Refugio Cole Cole*, alternating between stretches of beach and forest, with dramatic views of the coastline, pounded by the fierce Pacific surf.

ACCOMMODATION

Camping Chanquín 📞9 6442489. This campsite 200m beyond the visitor centre has twenty camping sites, fire pits, showers and picnic tables. Wild camping is free on the beach and along the trails. Camping/person CH$4500, cabins CH$35,000

PARQUE TANTAUCO

At the very south of Chiloé, the remote private reserve of **PARQUE TANTAUCO**, created by the current president of Chile,

Sebastián Piñera, is completely uninhabited apart from the fishing hamlet of **Caleta Inío** on the southern coast. The park consists of Zona Norte, accessible only by 4WD, and Zona Sur, accessible only by boat from Quellón, with 150km of trails between the two. While it's possible to do some **day-hikes** in Zona Norte, it's more rewarding to spend a week, hiking all the way from the first campsite at Lago Chaiguata, 20km from the ranger station (Dec–March 9am–4pm; park entry CH$6000) at the entrance of the park, down to Caleta Inío. Here you can camp (CH$3500/person) or stay in some family-owned accommodation (full board CH$35,000), explore the coastal caves and trails and then catch a boat back to Quellón (Jan & Feb Wed, Fri, Sun noon; 2–3hr; CH$30,000), spotting local marine life such as sea lions and sometimes even blue whales along the way. For more **information** on the park, contact the Oficina de Parque Tantauco in Quellón, at Avenida La Paz 68 (☎65 685064, ⓦparquetantauco.cl), which can help to arrange bus transportation to Lago Chaiguata from Quellón (Jan & Feb Mon, Wed, Fri 9.30am; 3hr; CH$8000) and book your boat passage to or from Caleta Inío.

Northern Patagonia: Aysén

Comprising the northern half of Patagonia, **AYSÉN** is the wildest, least populated and least visited of all of Chile's regions, a land of spell-binding glaciers, soaring fjords and snowcapped mountains. The **Carretera Austral**, the partially paved, partly dirt-and-gravel "Southern Highway", stretches for 1240km down from Puerto Montt to tiny **Villa O'Higgins** – a popular destination for cyclists – interrupted in places by various bodies of water and supplemented by short ferry rides. This really is the end of the road – to get further south you'll need to fly, take

a boat or travel through Argentina. The only town of any size on the way is **Coyhaique**, a good base for exploring the surrounding area, though you'll need a car to make the most of Aysén – you can try to tackle the region by bus (see box opposite). Stock up with cash; only Coyhaique, Chile Chico and Cochrane have banks (there are none in Villa O'Higgins or El Chaltén, though the latter has an ATM). Note also that Aysén is best explored between November and March, as transport tends to be scarce at other times of year, and travel is very susceptible to changes in the weather at all times.

FUTALEUFÚ

The fast-flowing, crystal-clear waters of Río Futaleufú have made this modest village, nestling between snow-tipped mountains, one of the top **white-water rafting** destinations in the world. Though threatened by the Spanish-owned hydroelectricity company ENDESA's proposed plans to dam Río Futaleufú, at the moment, the challenging Class III – V rapids still draw the crowds here from December to February; outside those months, the place can feel like a ghost town.

RAFTING OPERATORS

The following reputable operators offer half- (from CH$55,000) and full-day (from CH$90,000) rafting trips down the Futaleufú and the less challenging Río Espolón (from CH$25,000).

Earth River Expeditions ☎1 800 6432784, ⓦearthriver.com. Long-established operator with four camps along the river and a host of rafting, rock climbing, mountain biking and canyoning packages from the US (8–10 days from US$3400).

Expediciones Chile Mistral 296 ☎65 721386, ⓦexchile.com. Experienced operator that specializes in multi-day rafting and kayaking on the Futa, though day-excursions are also possible.

Futaleufú Explore O'Higgins 772 ☎65 721527, ⓦfutaleufuexplore.com. Established outfit that runs rafting and kayaking trips from its own luxury riverside camp.

THE BEST OF AYSÉN – BY BUS

Aysén is a vast, remote region but potentially one of the most rewarding in the whole of South America for travellers – the landscapes here are truly mesmerizing. To do it justice you'll need to take at least two weeks and rent a car, preferably a 4WD – not a cheap proposition. However, you can still get a taster of the region by bus, though there are no services from Puerto Montt south along the Carretera Austral; buses from central Chile all make the journey to **Coyhaique** through Argentina via Osorno and Bariloche (figure on at least CH$30,000 from Puerto Montt). If you are determined to travel north–south without doubling back, take a Naviera Austral ferry from Castro to Chaitén (see p.452), or take a bus to Futaleufú (see p.456) from the Argentine side, and head south from either place. Once in Coyhaique, which is also accessible by plane or ferry (see p.458), you can take buses up or down the Carretera Austral, stopping along the way, though it's crucial to confirm bus times in advance as they often change. Here are the highlights (assuming a Coyhaique start):

NORTH OF COYHAIQUE

Reserva Nacional Río Simpson On the road to Puerto Aysén, 37km from Coyhaique, this scenic gorge of craggy cliffs and plunging waterfalls is best experienced on a long day-trip from Coyhaique. Take any bus to Aysén and ask to get off at Cascada de la Virgin, 1km from the Conaf park office, or the thunderous Velo de la Novia, 8km further on – check when the return buses are due to pass by and flag them down (you'll have to hitch back otherwise – safe and not so unusual here). Reckon on CH$1000 for the bus.

Parque Nacional Queulat A five-hour bus ride north of Coyhaique lies this little-explored national park, its crowning feature the stunning Ventisquero Colgante (CH$3500), or "hanging glacier", a frozen blue-white mass spilling over a rock face, while a mighty waterfall fed by the melting ice roars into the Laguna Los Tempanos below. You can stay at the fully equipped campsite (☎67 314250; CH$3500/person) by the guardería at the park's southern entrance. There is no public transport to the glacier; you can ask any northbound bus to drop you off at the park entrance (around CH$7000 from Coyhaique), though it can be difficult to flag them down afterwards. Alternatively, aim to stay in Puyuhuapi and arrange a visit from there.

Puyuhuapi This beautifully located village was founded by Germans in the 1930s: reckon on CH$8000 for the bus fare from Coyhaique. The main attraction is the posh hot springs nearby (🌐patagonia-connection.com) but a cheaper option is the Termas Ventisquero, 6km south of town (Dec–Feb daily 9am–11pm; CH$12,000).

Futaleufú Rafting capital of the Americas. From here there are buses across to Argentina (Esquel), or on to Chaitén, where there is a ferry to Castro (see p.452) in January and February.

SOUTH OF COYHAIQUE

Laguna San Rafael Trips here are mesmerizing but expensive (see box, p.460).

Villa Cerro Castillo Some 57km south from Coyhaique, buses pass through the pristine Reserva Nacional Cerro Castillo, but stay on the bus to Villa Cerro Castillo (CH$4500), where you can hike back up to the Cerro Castillo, view another hanging glacier and find relatively cheap camping (CH$4000/person) maintained by Conaf. You can also visit the Monumento Nacional Manos de Cerro Castillo (Dec–April; CH$1000), a cave of enigmatic handprints, thought to have been made by Teheulche people five thousand years ago.

Puerto Río Tranquilo and Capilla de Mármol South of Castillo (118km) the highway is interrupted by the dark blue Lago General Carrera, then passes the attractive village of Puerto Río Tranquilo (CH$8000 by bus from Coyhaique), on the lake's northern shore; stop here to visit the "marble chapel", a vast limestone cliff streaked with blue marble and dotted with caves (CH$25,000/boat). Visiting Villa O'Higgins is another possibility (see p.461).

ARRIVAL AND INFORMATION

By bus Most buses drop off and pick up passengers on Prat, at Balmaceda, while some stop by the post office on the Plaza de Armas. Buses Becker runs to Coyhaique (Sun at 8am, more frequently in peak season; 12hr); Buses Transaustral to Esquel in Argentina several times a week and Puerto Montt via Argentina and Osorno (Mon at 8am; more frequently in peak season; 12–14hr).

Information Visitor services, such as the tourist office at O'Higgins 536 (summer only; daily 9am–8pm), the Banco Estado ATM (which doesn't accept Visa) and post office are all located around the Plaza de Armas.

ACCOMMODATION, EATING AND DRINKING

Burger stand Next to the Telefónica Sur on Cerda. If you happen to be passing through during the off-season, this is one of the very few places open. Huge burgers CH$1800. Daily 7–11pm.

Cara del Indio Carretera Austral, 4km from Puente Futaleufú (35km from Futaleufú) ☎ 2 1964239, ⊛ caradel indio.wordpress.com. Riverside campsite managed by the affable Toro-Meza family, offering tent pitches, basic *refugios* and more comfortable cabañas. The on-site restaurant is pretty good. Camping/person CH$3000, shelters CH$3000, cabañas for up to 6 CH$25,000

Hospedaje Adolfo O'Higgins 302 ☎ 65 721256, ⊜ hospedajeadolfo@gmail.com. Popular family home offering five warm, clean rooms (shared bathroom) and two cabins for up to six people. Breakfast includes home-made bread. Doubles CH$20,000

Hospedaje Carahue O'Higgins 332 ☎ 65 721221, ⊛ carahue.guiapatagonia.net. The wooden floors may be uneven and creaky, but Don Carlos and his family are very welcoming and helpful. Shared bathrooms, but breakfast included (full board available). Doubles CH$16,000

Sur Andes Cerda 308 ☎ 65 721405. Real coffee, freshly squeezed juice and good vegetarian options contribute to this café's popularity. Mains from CH$3500. Daily 9.30am–11pm.

COYHAIQUE

The town of **COYHAIQUE**, 634km south of Puerto Montt, boasts a spectacular setting nestled in the shadow of the great slab of Cerro Macay, at the confluence of the Simpson and Coyhaique rivers in the heart of the Patagonian Andes. It is the capital of Aysén and a surprisingly dynamic and affluent pocket of civilization compared to the smaller hamlets and villages along the Carretera Austral. The **transport hub** for the entire area, Coyhaique has departures up and down the Carretera, as well as neighbouring Argentina.

The heart of the city is the hexagonal **Plaza de Armas**, which resembles a wheel with ten spokes stretching out in various directions, making navigation confusing even for people who have maps. Most places to eat and drink are to be found within a few blocks of the plaza, and the small **Feria de Artesanos**, between Dussen and Horn, on the plaza's western side, sells regional handicrafts. The small **Museo Regional** inside the Centro Cultural (on Baquedano, at Lillo) should be open again in 2013 after a major renovation.

ARRIVAL AND INFORMATION

By plane Aeropuerto de Balmaceda is 55km south of town; all flights are met by several minibus companies that do door-to-door drop-offs (all CH$4000/person; CH$7000 to Puerto Aysén). Daily flights service Puerto Montt and Santiago with LAN (office Moraleda 402; Mon–Fri 8am–1pm & 3–6.45pm, Sat 9.30am–1.30pm) and Sky Airline (Prat 203; Mon–Fri 9am–7pm, Sat 7.30am–1pm), and there are weekly flights to Punta Arenas. Aeródromo Teniente Vidal, 7km out of town, handles charter flights to Villa O'Higgins (Mon & Thurs 9am, return 11am; 1hr 15min; around CH$50,000) and Cochrane (CH$35,000) via Transportes Aéreos Don Carlos (Subteniente Cruz 63; ☎ 67 231981).

By bus Most buses arrive at the main Terminal de Buses on Lautaro 109, at Magallanes, five blocks from the Plaza de Armas. Opposite the bus terminal, Aguilas Patagónicas (☎ 67 211288) runs buses to Cochrane (Tues & Sun 9am, return Mon & Thurs 8am); it also sells tickets for Acuario 13 buses from Cochrane to Villa O'Higgins Thurs & Sun 8am (return Mon & Fri 10am).

Destinations (Terminal de Buses) Buses Acuario 13 (☎ 67 522143) runs to Cochrane Wed & Fri 9am, Sun 10am (returning Tues, Thurs & Sat 8am; 10hr); Buses São Paolo (☎ 67 255726) serves Cochrane, Puerto Cisnes and Puerto Aysén (Mon–Fri every 1–2hr; 1hr); Buses Becker (☎ 67 232167) serves Chaitén (Tues–Sat 9am, return Wed–Sun 10am; 12hr); Queilén Bus (☎ 67 240760) serves Osorno, Puerto Montt, Ancud and Castro via Bariloche in Argentina (Thurs 2pm; more Dec–Feb; 20/24/28hr), with transfers to Temuco and Santiago; and Transaustral (☎ 67 232067) goes to La Junta via Puyuhuapi (for Parque Queulat; daily 3pm; 5hr), Puerto Cisnes (Mon–Fri 5pm; Sat & Sun 4pm; 5hr) and Comodoro Rivadavia (Mon & Fri at 9am; 9hr), in Argentina.

By ferry Navimag ferries from Puerto Montt (24hr) and Naviera Austral boats from Quellón (24hr) arrive at Puerto Chacabuco's Terminal de Transbordadores, 82km from Coyhaique and served by frequent buses via Puerto Aysén. The Navimag office in Coyhaique is at Paseo Horn 47-D (Mon–Fri 9am–1pm & 3–6.30pm, Sat 10am–1pm; ☎ 67 223306); Naviera Austral is opposite. Navimag has three weekly departures to Puerto Montt during high season; C berths, high season/low season CH$57,000/

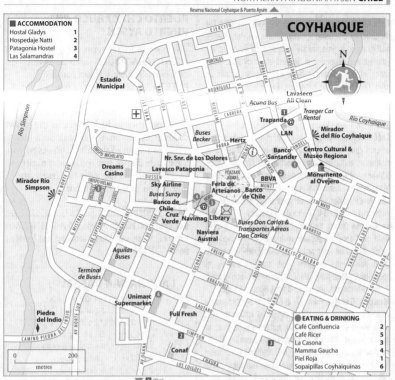

COYHAIQUE

■ ACCOMMODATION

Hostal Gladys	1
Hospedaje Natti	2
Patagonia Hostel	3
Las Salamandras	4

● EATING & DRINKING

Café Confluencia	2
Café Ricer	5
La Casona	3
Mamma Gaucha	4
Piel Roja	1
Sopaipillas Coyhaiquinas	6

49,000; check ⓦ navimag.com and ⓦ navieraustral.cl for updated timetables.

Tourist office The well-stocked and super-helpful Sernatur office at Bulnes 35, just off the Plaza de Armas (Dec–Feb Mon–Fri 8.30am–9pm, Sat & Sun 10.30am–6pm; March–Nov Mon–Fri 8.30am–6pm, Sat 8.30am–2pm; ☏ 67 240290, ⓦ recoreeaysen.cl, ⓦ exploreaysen.com), dishes out detailed maps of town an Carretera Austral, and is able to advise on accommodation and travel in the area.

ACCOMMODATION

Hostal Gladys General Parra 65 ☏ 67 245288, ⓦ hostal gladys.cl. Welcoming, quiet, central guesthouse with 12 spotless rooms (most with bathrooms), complete with cable TV, breakfast and wi-fi, run by a friendly family. Doubles CH$35,000

Hospedaje Natti Almirante Simpson 417 ☏ 67 231047, ⓦ nattipatagonia.cl/hospedaje.html. Guesthouse popular with backpackers and bikers, with small rooms, some windowless. There's a separate guest kitchen and eating area, space for a couple of tents and a handy laundry service next door. Camping/person CH$5000, doubles CH$18,000

★ **Patagonia Hostel** Lautaro 667 ☏ 9 62406974, ⓦ patagonia-hostel.com. The only genuine hostel in town is almost always full – book ahead. There are two double rooms and one dorm with six beds; use of common room, computers, wi-fi and healthy breakfast included. Dorms CH$10,000, doubles CH$30,000

★ **Las Salamandras** Carretera Teniente Vidal, Km1.5, towards the airport ☏ 67 211865, ⓦ salamandras.cl. The friendly owners of this large, attractive lodge can assist with planning your outdoor adventures. Comfortable rooms and fully equipped cabañas come complete with breakfast, laundry service, kitchen use, a TV loft and ample common spaces. Camping/person CH$6000, dorms CH$8500, doubles CH$20,000, with private bath CH$28,000

EATING AND DRINKING

Stock up with cheap food and drink at the Unimarc or Full Fresh (Sun–Thurs 9am–10pm, Fri & Sat 9am–11.30pm) supermarkets south of the plaza on Lautaro. Grab a *sopaipilla* (fried doughy bread, topped with ketchup; CH$200) at the *Sopaipillas Coyhaiquinas* stall outside Unimarc, a nutritionally void but genuinely tasty snack favoured by local students.

Café Confluencia 25 de Mayo 548 ☎67 245080. The menu at this arty bistro actually features fresh vegetables, not to mention imaginative dishes, such as *ají relleno* (stuffed hot pepper) and Spanish-style tortillas. Huge range of teas, decent coffees and stronger drinks on offer. On Fridays and Saturdays, live music kicks off at 11pm. *Menú del día* CH$5500, sandwiches from CH$3000. Smoking allowed (but non-smoking room available). Sun–Thurs 10am–11pm, Fri & Sat 10am–2am.

Café Ricer Horn 48 ☎67 244917. Perch on a sheepskin-covered chair at this gringo-friendly wi-fi-enabled café-restaurant and enjoy ample portions of Chilean staples (chicken with peas, or shredded beef with *merkén*, a Mapuche chilli seasoning), sandwiches and pasta – they also serve local beers. It's all competently cooked and filling, with most mains CH$4000–5000. Daily 10am–11.30pm.

La Casona Obispo Vielmo 77 ☎67 423365. In a quiet residential area and popular with both tour groups and locals, this white-linen restaurant counts delicious grilled lamb and *pastél de jaiba* (crab soufflé) among its specialities. Mains from CH$6000. Mon–Sat noon–3pm & 7.30pm–midnight, Sun noon–3pm & 8pm–midnight.

Mamma Gaucha Horn 47 ☎67 210721, ⓦ mamma gaucha.cl. The pizzas at this congenial Italian-themed place are so-so (CH$4400–7900) but it's a good place to grab a beer at all hours: draught Austral (from CH$1200), local brews such as D'Olbeck (CH$2000) and Kunstmann (CH$2000), though they can sometimes run out – check before sitting down. Mon–Sat 10am–2am.

Piel Roja Moraleda 495 ☎67 244 917, ⓦ pielroja.cl. An excellent spot for a beer and snack, this lively pub with a quirky interior serves up good burgers and quesadillas. Strut your stuff on the upstairs dancefloor (bar and disco open until 4am). Daily 6pm–4am.

DIRECTORY

Banks and exchange Banco de Chile, BBVA and Santander, all located along Condell, have global ATMs.

Hospital Jorge Ibar 168 (☎67 219100) for 24hr emergencies.

Internet *Café Ricer* and many other restaurants have free wi-fi access; also try Trapanda at General Parra 65, opposite *Hostal Gladys* (Mon–Fri 10am–1pm & 3–9pm) or the Centro de Llamados at Horn 51 (which closes early) and the Sociedad Bíblica Chilena inside the passage behind it (Mon, Tues, Thurs & Fri 9.30am–9pm, Wed 9.30am–7.30pm, Sat 10am–9pm). All charge around CH$700/hr.

Laundry Lavasco All Clean (Mon–Fri 9am–1pm & 3–7pm, Sat 9am–2pm; ☎67 219635), next to *Hostal Gladys* on General Parra, charges CH$1500/kg; you'll find similar rates and times at Lavasco Patagonia (☎8 4095244) at Dussen 340.

Post office Cochrane 22 (Mon–Fri 9am–6.30pm, Sat 9.30am–1pm).

PUERTO CHACABUCO AND PUERTO AYSÉN

The port and ferry terminal of **PUERTO CHACABUCO** lies 82km west of Coyhaique, and 16km south of **PUERTO AYSÉN**. While the road to the two ports cuts through the stupendous scenery of the **Reserva Nacional Río Simpson**, there is little to see in the towns themselves. If you're planning on taking a trip to **Laguna San Rafael**, however, you have little choice but to spend a night or two here due to the early departure and late arrival of the catamaran.

ACCOMMODATION

Residencial El Puerto O'Higgins 80 ☎67 351147. Worn but cheap rooms with shared bathroom and breakfast. Doubles CH$8000

LAGUNA SAN RAFAEL

If you only see one glacier in Latin America, make it **Laguna San Rafael**, 200km southeast of Coyhaique and only accessible by **boat** or **plane**. It is estimated that in the next twenty years or so it will be completely gone.

As you pass through the tight squeeze of Río Témpanos ("Iceberg River"), and sail past the silent, densely forested shores of the long, narrow inner passage of **Estero Elefantes**, you catch numerous glimpses of marine wildlife. Nearing the impossibly huge glacier, over 4km in width and 60m in height, the boat dodges massive bobbing icebergs, some the size of small houses. From time to time you'll hear a loud crack as a massive slab of blue ice calves from the glacier face, temporarily disturbing the still waters. Most boat trips allow the passengers to get close to the glacier in inflatable **Zodiacs**, and one of the trip's highlights is drinking whisky on the rocks – using the millennia-old ice, of course.

Catamaranes del Sur (☎67 351112, ⓦ catamaranesdelsur.cl) run high-speed catamaran day-trips (4–5hr each way) from Puerto Chacabuco's *Hotel Loberías del Sur* to the glacier (Dec–Feb Tues & Sat; fewer days Sept–Nov & March–April 7.30am–10pm; US$299); book several weeks in advance through a travel agent such as Chile Tours (ⓦ chile-tours.com).

VILLA O'HIGGINS

Continuing south to **VILLA O'HIGGINS**, a cluster of wooden houses huddled against a sheer mountain face, the Carretera Austral narrows to a single lane, ribboning its way around hairpin bends with sheer drops and spectacular vistas of glacial rivers cutting through endless forest. Once here, there are two choices: turn back, or cross the lake into Argentina. You are likely to linger longer than intended, partly because of the scarcity of public transport, and partly to enjoy the relaxed pace of life, small-town hospitality and the hiking and horseriding opportunities the rugged scenery provides.

The town is built on a simple grid around the Plaza de Armas. The Carretera Austral runs along the western side of the village all the way down to the boat landing on **Lago O'Higgins**, 7km away. A footpath off Calle Lago Cisnes runs through Parque Cerro Santiago up to a *mirador* overlooking the village; from there, the path continues on towards the ice "tongue" of the **Ventisquero Mosco**, the nearest hanging glacier, though the trail is sometimes impassable. Several glaciers, including the pristine **Ventisquero O'Higgins**, spill into Lago O'Higgins, but these can only be accessed via boat trips in the summer (Nov–April). Robinson Crusoe (☎67 431821, ⊛hielosur.com), Carretera Austral Km1240, has up-to-date timetables for the Lago O'Higgins crossing (see box below) as well as boat trips to the glaciers (from CH$80,000/person).

ARRIVAL AND INFORMATION

By plane Transportes Aéreos Don Carlos has charter flights from Coyhaique (Mon & Thurs 9am, return 11am; 1hr 15min; around CH$50,000) to the airstrip just to the west of town.

By bus There is no direct bus between Coyhaique and Villa O'Higgins – you need to change in Cochrane. Buses Acuario 13 runs from Cochrane Sun and Thurs at 8am (CH$12,000 one-way; 7hr) to the Supermercado San Gabriel on C Lago O'Higgins, returning on Mon and Fri at 10am; buy tickets in advance from the Supermercado, as the bus is usually full.

TO ARGENTINA

The 130km border crossing between Villa O'Higgins and Argentina's El Chaltén is still remote and challenging, yet more and more hardy travellers are prepared to take on the lake crossing, followed by a strenuous hike over the border. The sixty-passenger *Quetru* leaves Bahía Bahamóndez at 8.30am (Dec Wed & Sat; Jan–Feb Mon, Wed & Sat; Nov & March Sat only; CH$40,000; excursion Glaciar O'Higgins an extra CH$25,000) and arrives at the hamlet of **Candelario Mancilla** at around 11.15am. Here there's no-frills accommodation (doubles CH$6000) and basic camping spots with no facilities, and you'll get your passport stamped by **Chilean border control**. Beyond, a wide gravel track runs slightly uphill through patches of woodland to the international border; on the way, you will either have to ford the shallow, glacial **Río Obstáculo**, or cross it on some rickety planks. Beyond the border, the 7.5km stretch of trail to the **Argentine border control** on the banks of the **Laguna del Desierto** becomes a narrow, muddy footpath snaking its way through hilly forest and scrubland; cyclists have to push and sometimes carry their bikes.

After being stamped into Argentina, you can either pitch a tent at *Camping Laguna del Desierto* (CH$2500/person), catch the *Huemul* motor launch across the lake from Punta Norte (daily at 1.30pm, 4.45pm & 6.30pm; 30–45min; CH$13,000, bicycles CH$5000 extra) or hike the remaining 15km (5hr) along a thickly forested path on the left side of the lake, emerging at the *guardería* by the pier on the south side. Minibuses meet the arriving boats at Punta Sur, the last one leaving for town at 7.30pm (CH$13,000) and arriving around 9pm.

While it is possible to complete the border crossing in a day, boat schedules are weather-dependent, so pack enough food for several days. To book a guide and pack horses (CH$20,000 per pack horse), and for up-to-date information on the trek, visit the helpful website ⊛villaohiggins.com.

Do the crossing while you can: there are plans to make it more accessible by creating a proper road between the lakes and using larger boats to carry vehicles, which, while making it easier to go from Villa O'Higgins to Puerto Natales, will destroy the frontier feel that currently exists.

By ferry The ferry to Argentina (and the Ventisquero O'Higgins) docks at the Bahía Bahamóndez, 7km east of town (see box, p.461); a private minibus charges CH$2000/person from Villa O'Higgins (CH$3500 return).

Tourist information Helpful staff run the small tourist office on the plaza (summer only; Mon–Fri 9am–5.30pm; no tel, ⓦ villaohiggins.com) and provide plenty of information on the town and the surrounding area. The public library, just off the plaza, has free internet (the whole town is covered by slow, but free, wi-fi). There are no banks in town, so bring plenty of cash with you.

ACCOMMODATION, EATING AND DRINKING

Camping Los Ñires Hernan Merino s/n ☏ 67 431811. Just south of *Hostal Runín*, this spacious, tree-lined campsite has indoor cooking facilities and hot showers, though the ground can be muddy. Per person CH$3000

Entre Patagones Carretera Austral s/n ☏ 67 431819, ⓦ entrepatagones.cl. Excellent family-run restaurant, busy after 8pm, serving tasty Patagonian favourites such as *asadór patagónico* (spit-roasted lamb) and hearty *cazuela* in a homely environment. To reach it, follow Carretera Austral to the northern end of town. Dinner CH$6000. Mon–Sat 7.30–11pm, Sun 1–3.30pm. Also has cosy cabañas for CH$60,000

Hospedaje Patagonia Río Pascua 191 ☏ 67 431818. A comfortable, family-run choice by the plaza that offers clean, basic rooms with shared bathroom. Breakfast CH$2500 extra; lunch or dinner CH$5000. Doubles CH$16,000

Hostal Runín Pasaje Vialidad s/n ☏ 67 43170, ⓔ runin @villaohiggins.com. Tranquil, popular guesthouse with welcoming rooms, hot showers, tasty home-cooked breakfasts and the occasional BBQ (other meals extra). Dorms CH$8000, doubles (shared bath) CH$24,000

Southern Patagonia

Enormous glaciers calving icebergs the size of houses, pristine fjords and dozens of islands make up the other-worldly vistas of Magallanes province, or **SOUTHERN PATAGONIA**. Add in forbidding craggy peaks, impossibly blue glacial lakes, a wealth of wildlife and the sheer size and majesty of the internationally renowned **Torres del Paine** national park, and it's easy to see why Patagonia captures the imagination.

Cut off from the rest of Chile by the giant Campo de Hielo Sur (Patagonian Ice Fields) to the northeast, the locals have a strong camaraderie with their counterparts across the Andes; many consider themselves to be Patagonians first, Chileans or Argentines second.

PUNTA ARENAS

On the shores of the turbulent Magellan Strait, **PUNTA ARENAS** is Patagonia's largest city, with a booming economy and flourishing tourism industry thanks to its proximity to penguins, glaciers and Tierra del Fuego. Established in 1843, nearby Forte Bulnes was Chile's first outpost in the region, but the city itself has its roots in a penal colony founded five years later. The port provided a convenient stopover for ships heading to California during the gold rush of 1849, and then grew in size and importance with the introduction of sheep from the Falkland Islands to the Patagonian plains. Punta Arenas emerged as a wool empire, drawing migrant workers from Croatia, Italy, Spain and especially Britain. Following the decline of the wool economy after World War II, the city benefited from the discovery of petroleum in Tierra del Fuego in the 1940s, and now makes its living from a combination of petroleum production, commercial fishing and tourism.

WHAT TO SEE AND DO

The city centre is compact and easy to navigate, its streets laid out in a grid, and most services and conveniences lie within a few blocks of the main square. Taxis charge a flat fare of CH$350 anywhere in the centre (CH$400–450 at night).

Plaza Muñoz Gamero

The heart of the city is this tranquil, shady square lined with lofty Monterrey cypresses and craft stalls. In the centre stands a fierce-looking statue of **Ferdinand Magellan**, donated by Spanish-born wool magnate José Menéndez in 1920 to commemorate the 400-year anniversary of the explorer's voyage (a bust of Menéndez stands on the north side of the plaza). A statue of a **Patagonian Indian** sits at the foot of the monument; it is believed that if you touch or kiss his big toe, you will one day return to Punta Arenas. The plaza is surrounded by several grand Art Nouveau mansions, evidence of the great wealth accumulated here in the 1890s.

Palacio Sara Braun (Club de la Unión)

A visit to this opulent Neoclassical French palace on the plaza (Mon 10am–1pm, Tues–Fri 10am–1pm & 5–8.30pm, Sat 10am–1pm & 6–8.30pm; CH$1000), built for wealthy widow Sara Braun between 1895 and

▲ Cemetery main enterance, Ferry Terminal (5km) & Airport (20km)

PUNTA ARENAS

ACCOMMODATION
Backpackers' Paradise	3
El Conventillo	5
Hostal La Estancia	4
Hospedaje Independencia	6
Imago Mundi	2
Hostel Keokén	1

Streets and landmarks:
ANGAMOS, AV MANUEL BULNES, MAIPÚ, Museo Maggiorino Borgatello, Bulnes Statue, Santuario María Auxiliadora, SARMIENTO DE GAMBOA, CHILOÉ, A SANHUEZA, BORIES, H DE MAGALLANES, CROACIA, MEJICANA, Unimarc Supermarket, SAMPAIO, JORGE MONTT, Ciber Center @, Lavasco Josseau, CARRERA PINTO, Cruz Verde, Río de las Minas, O'HIGGINS, Buses Fernández/Pinguino & Turibus', Pullman Bus, Central de Buses, Buses Pacheco, AV COLÓN, AV ESPAÑA, Bus Sur, Unimarc, LAN, NAVARRO, Aerovías DAP, Castillo Millward, British School, St James, Palacio Sara Braun, Banda Aneha, Club Militar, Museo Regional Magallanes, JOSÉ MENÉNDEZ, Buses Ghisoni, Queilen, Techni Austral & Transfer, Hertz, Lavanderia Record, Europacar, WALDO SEGUEL, PEDRO MONTT, Banco Santander, Palacio de la Góbernación, PLAZA MUÑOZ GAMERO, 21 DE MAYO, Residencia Blanchard, Banco de Chile, Museo Naval y Marítimo, KORNER, PLAZA WILLIAMS, Catedral, FAGNANO, Banco Santander, ROCA, Sky Airlines, Palacio Montes Pello, Whalesound, ERRÁZURIZ, NOGUEIRA, Dreams Casino, Port, Magellan Strait, BALMACEDA, COSTANERA DEL ESTRECHO, O'HIGGINS, AV INDEPENDENCIA

EATING & DRINKING
Brocolino	7
Café Almacén Tapiz	8
Café Montt	6
Kiosko Roca	9
Lomito's	4
La Marmita	2
Pub Olijoe	10
Sabores	1
Santino	3
Taberna del Club de la Unión	5

0 — 200 metres

4

▼ Fuerte Bulnes (51km)

1905 (it's been the posh Club de la Unión since 1960), provides a fascinating glimpse into the homes of the city's elites during the boom years. The reception room, music room (with portraits of Braun and her millionaire Portuguese husband, José Nogueira), the upstairs balcony and billiard room, as well as the public areas of the Hotel Nogueira (which now occupies half the mansion), are a feast of richly carved ceilings, frescoes, dark wood and artwork – all imported from Europe.

Mirador Cerro La Cruz and Castillo Milward

A five-block walk along Calle Fagnano from the southeast corner of the plaza brings you up to the *mirador*, offering a stupendous view of the brightly coloured, galvanized metal rooftops of Punta Arenas and the deep blue Magellan Strait beyond. Nearby, at España 959, stands a red-brick tower with Gothic windows – **Castillo Milward**, the house built in 1924 for eccentric sailor Charley Milward (it's now the offices of the local newspaper, Diario El Pingüino), relative of the writer Bruce Chatwin and described in his travel memoir *In Patagonia*.

Palacio Braun-Menéndez

Completed in 1906 half a block northeast of the plaza at Magallanes 949, the **Palacio Museo Braun-Menéndez** is the former family residence of Sara Braun's younger brother, Mauricio Braun, and the daughter of José Menéndez, Josefina (a marriage that united the two wealthiest and most powerful families in Punta Arenas). The house reopened in 2013 as the renovated **Museo Regional de Magallanes** (Oct–April Wed–Mon 10.30am–5pm; May–Sept Wed–Mon 10.30am–2pm; CH1000; ⓦmuseodemagallanes.cl), with displays on the maritime and farming history of the region.

Museo Naval y Marítimo

Two blocks east of the plaza, at Pedro Montt 981, lies the small but illuminating **Museo Naval y Marítimo** (Tues–Sat 9.30am–12.30pm & 2–5pm; CH$1200), with a focus on Punta Arenas's naval history and exploration of the southern oceans. The ground floor features a multitude of scale models of famous ships, including Sir Ernest Shackleton's *Endurance*, as well as a block of Antarctic ice, while the first floor is decked out as a ship, complete with nautical equipment, radio room, maps and charts.

Museo Salesiano Maggiorino Borgatello

Located seven blocks north of the plaza, at Avenida Bulnes 336, **Museo Salesiano Maggiorino Borgatello** (Tues–Sun 10am–12.30pm & 3–5.30pm; CH$2000; ⓦmuseomaggiorinoborgatello .cl) provides an enlightening introduction to local flora, fauna, geology and history. One room is entirely devoted to a life-size replica of the **Cave of Hands** in Argentina, decorated with prehistoric rock paintings (see p.133), and there are galleries dedicated to the Kawéskar (Alacaluf), Selk'nam (Ona), Yámana (Yagán) and Tehuelche cultures.

Cementerio Municipal

A stroll through the darkly impressive **Cementerio Municipal** (daily: summer 7.30am–8pm; winter 8am–6pm; free), its straight alleys lined with immaculately sculpted cypresses, offers a fascinating glimpse into the city's immigrant history, cultural diversity and social hierarchy. The monumental marble tombs of the city's ruling families, elaborately engraved with the English and Spanish names, mingle with the Croatian and Scandinavian names of immigrant labourers, etched on more modest grave spaces the size of lockers. Look out for the stern gravesite of German Admiral Graf von Spee, killed fighting the British in 1914 at the Battle of the Falkland Islands, and the grand Italianate tomb of José Menéndez. The illustrious Sara Braun has her own elegant Russian-style chapel (she emigrated from Latvia with her parents in 1874, and died here in 1955).

ARRIVAL AND INFORMATION

By plane Aeropuerto Presidente Ibáñez is 20km north of town. Flights are met by Buses Fernández (CH$3000) and taxis (CH$8000; CH$9000 at night). LAN (Mon–Fri 9.15am–1pm & 3–6.45pm, Sat 10am–1pm) and Sky Airline offer daily flights to Santiago, Puerto Montt and Balmaceda/Coyhaique, but not Ushuaia. Aerovias DAP (Mon–Fri 9am–12.30pm & 2.30–6.45pm, Sat 9am–1pm & 3–6pm; w aeroviasdap.cl) has flights to Puerto Williams (Mon–Sat 10am; 1hr 15min) and Porvenir (Mon–Sat 2–3 daily; 12min), as well as charter flights to Antarctica.

By bus There is no central bus station (despite the name, the Central de Buses on Av Colón, at Magallanes, ☎ 61 245811, is just an office selling tickets for several companies), though all buses arrive within four or five blocks of the Plaza de Armas. Note that if you are taking a bus to Ushuaia (see p.144) it's crucial to book ahead in the summer and there may be a long wait to cross the Magellan Straits if the sea is rough (the ferries and buses simply wait till things calm down, sometimes up to 5 hours; ferries run daily 8.30am–11.45pm; CH$13,900/car, CH$1600/person, included in bus fare); try to get some Argentine pesos before you leave, as there is nowhere to change money at the border, and make sure you have accommodation booked in advance.

Destinations Buses Pacheco (Colón 900) to: Río Grande (Mon–Sat 9am; 8hr 30min; CH$17,000), where you can connect with Ushuaia buses – the bus goes direct on Tues, Thurs & Sun (CH$27,000); Río Gallegos (Mon, Wed, Thurs & Sun 11.30am; 5–7hr); Buses Fernández (Sanhueza 745) to: Puerto Natales (8 daily; 3hr; CH$5000); Bus Sur to: Ushuaia (Mon, Wed, Fri & Sat at 8.30am; 12–14hr; CH$30,000); Río Gallegos (daily 11am; 5–7hr); Puerto Natales, with connections to Torre del Paine (daily 10am, 3pm, 5.15pm & 7pm; 3hr; CH$4000); Pullman (Colón 568) to: Osorno and Puerto Montt (Mon, Wed & Fri 9am; 34–36hr); Buses Ghisoni (Navarro 971) to: Río Gallegos (Mon, Wed, Thurs, Fri & Sat 11am; 5–7hr; CH$9000); Ushuaia (Wed & Sat 8.30am; 12–14hr); Tecni Austral (Navarro 975) to: Ushuaia (12–14hr; from CH$25,000) via Río Grande (8hr 30min; CH$15,000) Tues, Thurs & Sun.

By ferry Ferries from Puerto Williams and Porvenir arrive at the Terminal Tres Puentes 5km north of the plaza; frequent *colectivos* (CH$800) shuttle between the docks and the centre. Transbordadora Austral Broom, at Juan Williams 6450 (Mon–Fri 8.30am–12.15pm & 2–6.15pm; ☎ 61 728100, w tabsa.cl), operates ferries to Puerto Williams (Wed only; US$258 for a berth, US$186 for a Pullman seat; 28hr, subject to weather conditions) and Porvenir (1 daily; 2hr 30min; CH$5500).

Tourist office There's a tourist information kiosk on the south side of Plaza Muñoz Gamero, but this was being renovated at the time of writing; your best bet is the helpful and well-stocked Sernatur office at Navarro 999, at Pedro Montt (April–Sept Mon–Fri 8.30am–6pm; Oct–March Mon–Fri 8.30am–8pm, Sat & Sun 9am–1pm & 2–6pm; ☎ 61 24130).

ACCOMMODATION

Backpackers' Paradise Ignacio Carrera Pinto 1022 ☎ 61 240104, e backpackersparadise@hotmail.com. Run by an effusive hostess and perpetually popular with younger travellers, this hostel offers very cheap bunks in two large, open-plan rooms. Laundry service, free hot drinks, secure luggage storage, kitchen facilities, internet access and bike rentals are among the extras. Dorms CH$6000

El Conventillo Korner 1034 ☎ 61 242311, w hostal elconventillo.com. Spotlessly clean bathrooms and cosy dorms for 4–6 people. Use of fridge and microwave in kitchen, but otherwise not really a self-catering option. Breakfast included, free wi-fi (one computer for shared use), cable TV in lounge and welcome pisco sour on arrival. Dorms CH$8500

Hostal La Estancia O'Higgins 765 ☎ 61 249130, w estancia.cl. At this perpetually popular hostel, you're well looked after by the bilingual Alex and Carmen, who can arrange your outdoor adventures. The restored 1920s house has spacious rooms and comfortable common areas. Book in advance, even in the off-season. Dorms CH$12,000, doubles CH$30,000

Hospedaje Independencia Independencia 374 ☎ 61 227572, w chileaustral.com/independencia. This hostel, six blocks from the centre, is popular with hikers and bikers; there's a homely feel to the rooms, which are small but warm and comfortable (shared bathroom). The friendly young family has camping spaces in their front yard (use of bathroom included) and rent camping equipment; they also organize tours of the area and let you use their kitchen. Camping/person CH$2000, doubles CH$10,000

★ **Imago Mundi** Mejicana 252 ☎ 61 613115, w imago mundipatagonia.cl. Environmentally conscious travellers and outdoor junkies alike flock to this popular little hostel run by a brother-sister team. There are just eight cosy bunk beds in two en-suite rooms, as well as an on-site climbing gym for pros and beginners alike, an excellent café (full-board is possible) and an attached cultural centre that often features live music. Dorms CH$10,000, doubles CH$25,000

Hostel Keokén Magallanes 209 ☎ 61 244086, w hostel keoken.cl. Comfortable rooms (en suite and shared bath), a book exchange and kitchen privileges are all on offer at this welcoming family-run guesthouse a few blocks from the plaza. English, French and Italian are spoken and the owners can help you with further travel arrangements. Doubles (shared bathroom) CH$22,000

EATING

Unimarc supermarket has several branches in the centre, with the largest at Bories 647 (Mon–Sat 9am–10pm, Sun 10am–9pm), with a cheap café upstairs.

★ **Brocolino** O'Higgins 1055 ☎61 710479. The unassuming exterior hides some of the best food in Patagonia by chef Héctor Gálvez; don't miss "aphrodisiac soup" (CH$5500), made with the freshest seafood, *centolla* (king crab; CH$8000) or steak "in the style of Paris Hilton" (CH$8500), whatever that means. Daily 1–3pm & 7–11.30pm.

Café Almacén Tapiz Roca 912 ☎9 77693359, ⓦcafe tapiz.cl. Fashionable café set in a lovely old building from 1930, serving all sorts of delicious pies, cakes and sandwiches. Mon–Sat 10.30am–6pm, Sun 11am–5pm.

Café Montt Pedro Montt 976 ☎61 220381. A (small) book exchange and wi-fi are available in this cosy coffee shop, as well as a good selection of teas and coffees. Particularly good is the caffeine-fuelled creation with condensed milk (CH$1700). Mon–Fri 8am–8pm, Sat 8am–2pm.

Kiosko Roca Roca 875 ☎61 223436. Elbow your way to the counter at this legendary joint packed with locals (its been here since 1932) and grab a banana milkshake (CH$200) or *choripán* (a sort of mini-burger with chorizo and cheese) for CH$350–450. Daily 8am–7pm.

Lomito's Menéndez 722 ☎61 243399. Classic Chilean version of a US diner-cum-sports bar, open until the wee hours and one of the few places open on Sun; chefs knock out all manner of burgers and grilled sandwiches in the centre, while locals sip beers and watch the football at the bar or from tables. The surly servers are part of the experience, so be prepared for a wait. Mains from CH$4000. Daily 10am–2.30am.

★ **La Marmita** Plaza Sampaio 678 ☎61 222056, ⓦmarmitamaga.cl. If you can tear your gaze away from the decor, order one of the imaginative dishes made from organic produce, such as the exotic *ceviche* with coconut milk, or the tasty *caldillo de congrio* (conger eel soup). The pisco sours, served in martini glasses, are the best in Patagonia, and the calafate berry and chocolate dessert is a work of art. Mains from CH$6500. Mon–Sat 12.30–3pm & 6.30–11.30pm.

Sabores Mejicana 702 ☎61 227369, ⓦrestaurant sabores.com. Cosy spot with Croatian owners offering such bargains as the two-course *menu ejecutivo* (CH$3850), which includes a choice of home-made pasta or hearty seafood stews, drink and dessert. Daily 10.30am–midnight.

DRINKING

Pub Olijoe Errázuriz 970 ☎61 223728. Decked out like a classy English pub, with its leather and dark wood, this pub serves a good selection of beers, though its speciality is the *glaciar*: a potent mix of pisco, milk, *horchata* and curaçao. It may take a while to catch the barman's eye. Daily 6pm–2am.

Santino Colón 657 ☎61 710882, ⓦsantino.cl. Spacious, welcoming Italian-owned bar offering typical Chilean food, such as *lomo a la pobre*, as well as good sandwiches, pasta and live music on Sat. Beers CH$1300; mains CH$5500. Daily 6pm–3am.

Taberna del Club de la Unión Palacio Sara Braun, Plaza Muñoz Gamero ☎61 241317. Travellers can't resist this darkly elegant basement drinking venue – once part of the posh Club de la Unión and gathering point for the town's most powerful men. Free wi-fi. Daily 6.30pm–3am.

DIRECTORY

Banks and exchange There are several banks with global ATMs around Plaza Muñoz Gamero, including Banco Santander and Banco de Chile. There are cambios along Roca and Lautaro Navarro.

Hospital Hospital Regional at Angamos 180 (☎61 205000) deals with 24hr emergencies.

Internet and phone Try Internet Banda Ancha, at Menéndez 787 (daily 9am–11pm; CH$700/hr), or the similarly priced Ciber Center at Carrera Pinto 674.

Post office Bories 911 (Mon–Fri 9am–6.30pm, Sat 10am–1pm).

PUNTA ARENAS TOUR OPERATORS

Turismo Pali Aike ☎61 615750, ⓦturismopaliaike .com. A variety of nature-watching trips, including daily trips to Isla Magdalena, Seno Otway and Estancia Lolita, as well as full-day canopy trips, transfers to the nearby Reserva Nacional Magallanes and excursions. Day-trip to Pali Aike park CH$70,000.

Turismo Yámana Errázuriz 932 ☎61 321172, ⓦyamana.cl. Intrepid single- and multi-day kayaking trips on and around the Strait of Magellan, taking in seal and penguin colonies, as well as multi-day trekking and riding excursions in Tierra del Fuego. Nine-day kayak expedition from US$3460.

Whalesound Navarro 1163, 2nd floor ☎61 221076, ⓦwhalesound.com (office Mon–Fri 9.30am–1pm & 2.30–6.30pm). Responsible operator offering study-based kayaking trips to the Coloane Marine Park and humpback whale-watching trips from December to May. All-inclusive trip (2 days, 1 night) US$900.

ISLA MAGDALENA

In the middle of the stormy Magellan Strait lies **Isla Magdalena** – the largest Magellanic **penguin colony** in all of Chile, with an estimated 120,000 nesting birds residing on a one-kilometre-square cliff by the old lighthouse. The monogamous birds spend the September to March breeding season here, living in burrows in the ground. The female lays two eggs in October, with both parents taking turns looking after the chicks once they've hatched in December, while the other fishes for food. In early February you'll find the grown chicks huddled near the sea, as large as their parents but still growing the adult feathers necessary for swimming. The **best time to visit** the colony is January, when the population is at its largest. Though you have to stick to the designated walking routes, the penguins don't fear humans and will come quite close to you. You can visit the colony with the large ferry *Melinka*, run by **Turismo Comapa** (Magallanes 990 ☏61 200200, ⊛comapa.com, late Nov–Feb Tues, Thurs & Sat 5–10pm from Tres Puentes Terminal, with around one hour on the island; CH$28,000), or with **Solo Expediciones** (Nogueira 1255; ☏61 243354; ⊛soloexpediciones.com), which has excursions to the island in a small but faster Zodiac boat (mid-Oct to mid-April daily 7–11am, depending on weather conditions, includes 1hr on island; CH$39,000), passing Isla Marta on the way (home to a colony of 1,000 sea lions that use nearby Isla Magdalena as their local takeaway).

PINGÜINERA SENO OTWAY

If you can't make the boat trip to Isla Magdalena, then don't miss the land-based excursion to the colony of **Seno Otway**, 70km northwest of Punta Arenas. Hosting around ten thousand Magellanic penguins at its peak, the breeding site is fenced off and visitors are obliged to stick to the 1.5km wooden boardwalk that runs between the penguin burrows. While not as up-close-and-personal as Isla Magdalena, you still get excellent views of the penguins, especially at the viewpoint by the beach, where you can watch them frolic in the waves just a few metres away. Several tour operators run tours at 3pm daily mid-Oct to March, with two hours at the colony, returning 7.30pm (CH$25,000; CH$5500 entry charge and CH$1500 toll road fee not included).

PUERTO NATALES

Some 241km northwest of Punta Arenas, the town of **PUERTO NATALES** is situated in relative isolation on the **Seno Última Esperanza** ("Last Hope Sound"). Officially founded in 1911, it was used primarily as a port for exporting wool and beef from the nearby Puerto Prat cattle *estancia*, built by German explorer **Hermann Eberhard** in 1893. Though the export trade has since declined, the town's proximity to one of the continent's most gasp-inducing national parks – Torres del Paine – as well as the magnificent Serrano glacier, combined with the popular Navimag ferry from Puerto Montt, has led to a tourist boom that has firmly established Puerto Natales as one of Patagonia's top destinations for outdoor enthusiasts and backpackers, with hostels on almost every corner.

Faced with a motley collection of tin and wooden houses, a visitor's first impression of Puerto Natales is invariably coloured by the weather. On a clear day, Seno Última Esperanza, bordering the town's west side, is a remarkably vivid, tranquil blue, with magnificent views of the snowcapped **Cordillera Sarmiento** and **Campo de Hielo Sur** visible across the bay.

WHAT TO SEE AND DO

The town is centred on the **Plaza de Armas**, with its main commercial thoroughfares north–south Baquedano and east–west Bulnes. The worthwhile **Museo Histórico** at Bulnes 285 (Dec–Feb Mon–Fri 8.30am–1pm & 3–8pm, Sat & Sun 2.30–6pm; rest of the year Mon–Thurs 8am–5.30pm, Fri 8am–4.30pm; CH$1000), less than two blocks from the plaza, has attractive bilingual exhibits on the region's **native tribes**, illustrated with artefacts and black-and-white photos of

4

4

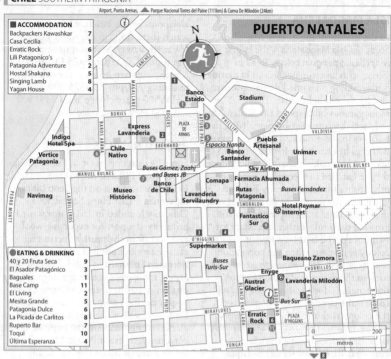

PUERTO NATALES

■ ACCOMMODATION
Backpackers Kawashkar	7
Casa Cecilia	1
Erratic Rock	6
Lili Patagonico's	3
Patagonia Adventure	2
Hostal Shakana	5
Singing Lamb	8
Yagan House	4

● EATING & DRINKING
40 y 20 Fruta Seca	9
El Asador Patagónico	3
Baguales	1
Base Camp	11
El Living	2
Mesita Grande	5
Patagonia Dulce	6
La Picada de Carlitos	8
Ruperto Bar	7
Toqui	10
Última Esperanza	4

Aónikenk (Tehuelche) and Kawéskar Indians, as well as on European settlement and natural history, including the story of the Milodon's cave.

ARRIVAL AND INFORMATION

By plane The tiny airport is 5km out of town, on the road to Torres del Paine. Some Sky Airline (Bulnes 682; Mon–Fri 9am–1pm & 3–7pm, Sat 10am–1pm) flights serve Santiago in the summer, but it's much more reliable to fly on Punta Arenas. Taxis meet flights.

By bus Puerto Natales has no central bus station, with buses departing from their company offices. Services to El Calafate (Argentina) and Torres del Paine only operate Oct–April. Of the main players, Bus Sur (Baquedano 668) serves Punta Arenas, El Calafate and Ushuaia; Buses Fernández (Ramírez 399) serves Punta Arenas; Buses Pacheco (Ramírez 224) runs to Punta Arenas and Ushuaia; Buses Gómez (Prat 234) and Turismo Zaahj (Prat 236) to Torres del Paine. Turismo Zaahj also runs to El Calafate (daily 8am & 6pm; 5hr 30min).

Destinations El Calafate (2–3 daily; 5hr 30min); Punta Arenas (hourly; 3hr); Río Gallegos (3 weekly; 5hr); Torres del Paine (4–6 daily; Laguna Amarga 2hr 15min; Pudeto 3hr 15min; Park Administration 3hr 15min); Ushuaia (4 weekly; 14hr).

By ferry The Navimag ferry terminal (Pedro Montt 308 ☎ 61 414300, ⊛ navimag.cl) is five blocks west of the Plaza de Armas. MV *Magallanes* sails to Puerto Montt (Tues 4am, embark by Mon 9pm; from CH$200,000; 4 days). Book a couple of weeks in advance in summer.

Tourist information Sernatur is at Pedro Montt 19, on the shore of the Seno Última Esperanza (Mon–Fri 8.30am–1pm & 2.30–6pm; summer also Sat & Sun 10am–5pm; ☎ 61 412125, ⊛ sernatur.cl), with very helpful staff. Erratic Rock (⊛ erraticrock.com) at Baquedano 719 holds excellent bilingual daily talks at 3pm at the *Base Camp* pub next door on hiking in Torres del Paine, covering logistics as well as park etiquette and required gear. If you want anything booked, from bus tickets to tours to accommodation in Argentina, look no further than the English-speaking Austral Glacier office at Baquedano 695 (Mon–Sat 10am–1pm & 3–8pm, Sun 3–8pm; ☎ 09 9357 8558, ⊛ australglacier.com).

ACCOMMODATION

Backpackers Kawashkar Encalada 754 ☎ 61 414553. Incredibly chilled-out backpacker haunt, run by the knowledgeable Omar. Kitchen privileges, breakfast and lockers are included; it's possible to camp out back and Omar helps to organize your stay. Dorms CH$9000
Casa Cecilia Tomás Roger 60 ☎ 61 613560, ⊛ casacecilia hostal.com. The rooms at this long-established guesthouse

are on the small side, but the helpful owners are good for trekking info. Guests have use of the kitchen and the good breakfast includes home-made bread. Doubles CH$20,000

Erratic Rock Baquedano 719 ☎ 61 414317, ⓦ erraticrock .com. Excellent long-term favourite, with a laidback vibe, legendary breakfasts and an in-house tour agency that provides top-notch advice on Torres del Paine. Comfy rooms, free wi-fi and a large kitchen. Dorms CH$10,000, doubles CH$26,000

★ **Lili Patagonico's** Prat 479 ☎ 61 414063, ⓦ lili patagonicos.com. Contender for the best hostel in town, this lively place features an indoor climbing wall, an excellent breakfast, wi-fi and book exchange, and the owners organize half- and full-day trips into the surrounding area. The doubles are particularly plush. Dorms CH$8000, doubles CH$20,000

Patagonia Adventure Tomás Rogers 179 ☎ 61 411028, ⓦ apatagonia.com. Brightly decorated central hostel run by young owners; a good breakfast is included and other bonuses include internet, a camping gear outlet next door and the hostel's own adventure outfit for kayaking enthusiasts. Dorms CH$10,000, doubles CH$24,000

★ **Hostal Shakana** Miraflores 798 ☎ 61 413291. Small and personal: your host, Torres del Paine guide Chacana, will personally cook you eggs for breakfast (and real coffee) over a wood stove, offer advice and generally organize your trip. His rooms are compact, warm and cosy. Free wi-fi. Doubles CH$16,000

Singing Lamb Arauco 779 ☎ 61 410958, ⓦ thesinging lamb.com. Justly popular hostel with especially comfy single beds in both dorms (no bunks), spotless showers and filling breakfasts. Eco-friendly touches include composting, recycling and rainwater collection. Free wi-fi and use of computer. Dorms CH$11,000

Yagan House O'Higgins 584 ☎ 61 414137. Highly recommended hostel, with comfy beds, a fire blazing in the welcoming lounge and owners who can arrange all manner of tours (bike rental for CH$7000/day). Dorms CH$10,000, rooms CH$25,000

EATING

40 y 20 Fruta Seca Baquedano 443 ☎ 61 210661. Aka "the dried fruit guy", this is the place to stock up on a bewildering array of dried fruit and nuts for the forthcoming hike. Dried mango is especially good. CH$500/100g. Mon–Sat 10am–8pm.

El Asador Patagónico Prat 158 ☎ 61 413553. Like most hikers, you'll be drawn into this excellent restaurant catering primarily to carnivores by the sight of the *asador patagónico* – a lamb being spit-roasted in front of you, Patagonian style. The expertly cooked steaks are just as good; bring your appetite, as the portions are ample. Mains CH$8500. Daily noon–3pm & 7–11.30pm.

★ **El Living** Prat 156 (on the plaza) ☎ 61 413609, ⓦ el-living.com. Not just an excellent vegetarian restaurant, with changing daily specials, but also the town's most popular café/lounge, playing chilled-out tunes, and featuring the best local book exchange too. Smoothies, sandwiches and salads stand out, and the owner makes excellent cakes, too. Mains from CH$3900. Late Oct to mid-April daily 11am–10pm (11.30pm Thurs).

★ **Mesita Grande** Prat 196 ☎ 61 411571, ⓦ mesita grande.cl. Hordes of hungry hikers stage a daily invasion of the best pizzeria in Patagonia, drawn by the generous portions of superb thin-crust pizzas (CH$2300–5900), home-made pasta and sumptuous desserts (including sweet pizza with *dulce de leche*). Customers sit along two long wooden tables, which encourages conversation and creates a communal dining experience. Daily noon–midnight.

Patagonia Dulce Arana 233 ☎ 61 415285, ⓦ patagoniadulce.cl. Those with a sweet tooth shouldn't miss out on the home-made chocolates and ice cream in this little gingerbread-house-like café (cakes and pies CH$1500; chocolate "tasting" CH$1500). They say that if you eat calafate berries, you'll return to Patagonia; whether the same is true of calafate berry ice cream (CH$2500) is not clear, but it's worth a try. Mind-blowing range of hot chocolates (CH$2500). Mon–Sat 10am–9pm, Sun 2–8pm.

La Picada de Carlitos Encalada 444 ☎ 61 415496. Ever-popular place famed for its hearty Chilean dishes, such as the *cazuela de pollo* (chicken stew), as well as the big sandwiches. *Menú del día* CH$3000. Daily 10am–11.45pm.

Toqui Banquedano 699 ☎ 9 94013486. Excellent family-run budget option, with no-frills sandwiches (CH$2800–3800), burgers and more substantial fish dishes (CH$3000–4000). Daily noon–9pm.

Última Esperanza Eberhard 354 ☎ 61 413626. Come early to get seats in this extremely popular restaurant, which serves some of the tastiest fish and seafood in southern Chile (CH$4500–7500). Splash out on the *chupe de locos* (abalone chowder) for CH$8000. Daily noon–3.15pm & 6.30–11.30pm.

DRINKING

Baguales Bories 430 ☎ 61 411920, ⓦ cervezabaguales .cl. If the one thing that would make your Patagonian hiking experience complete is returning to a cosy brewery that serves ample platters of tasty buffalo wings (CH$5500), quesadillas (CH$4400) and other assorted Tex-Mex food, accompanied by rice and beans and home-made guacamole, then you're in luck: look no further than this Californian-Chilean pub on the Plaza de Armas. Beers CH$1700. Mon–Sat 6pm–2am.

Base Camp Baquedano 719 ☎ 61 411920. This pub draws the crowds, with the backpackers from *Erratic Rock* next door raising the roof during the odd rock and reggae gig, or enjoying a post-hike beer or three. Daily noon–1am.

4

PUERTO NATALES TOUR OPERATORS

Baqueano Zamora Baquedano 534 ☎61 613531, ⓦbaqueanozamora.com. Horse-trekking trips of varying length in Torres del Paine National Park. Half-day horseriding CH$25,000; full-day CH$45,000.

Erratic Rock Baquedano 719 ⓦerraticrock.com. Equipment rental, informative talks on Torres del Paine and multi-day trekking expeditions to Cabo Froward and Isla Navarino, among others.

Fantastico Sur Esmeralda 661 ☎61 614184, ⓦfantasticosur.com. Specializing in guided treks (W Circuit from US$344) and *refugios* in Torres del Paine; gives free talks on hiking 10.30am and 6pm (daily; check ahead).

Vertice Patagonia Ladrilleros 209 ☎61 412742, ⓦverticepatagonia.com. Up-and-coming operator offering ice-hiking on the glacier in Torres del Paine National Park (CH$246,200 for 4 days, 3 nights).

BALMACEDA & SERRANO GLACIERS

It's not cheap (typically CH$70,000; boats run between 8am and 5.30pm daily in summer), but a trip to the Serrano Glacier (with views of the Balmaceda Glacier), on the edge of Parque Nacional Bernardo O'Higgins, via stunning fjords, cormorant and sea-lion colonies and gliding condors, is still one of Chile's most scintillating experiences. Boats take four hours to reach the glacier dock, where you walk the last 1km to the base. The companies below offer similar services, with Turismo 21 de Mayo usually running bigger boats.

Agunsa (Punta Alta) Blanco Encalada 244 ☎61 415940, ⓦagunsapatagonia.cl.

Turismo 21 de Mayo Eberhard 560 ☎61 614420, ⓦturismo21demayo.cl.

4

Ruperto Bar Bulnes 371 ☎61 413921, ⓦrupertobar.com. Popular bar with loud music, Guinness and pool tables, drawing a younger crowd – a good spot for a post-hike beer or mojito. Daily 6pm–3am (Fri & Sat 4.30am).

DIRECTORY

Banks and exchange Banco Santander, on Blanco Encalada, at Bulnes, and Banco de Chile, at Bulnes 544, both have ATMs.

Hospital Hospital Puerto Natales (☎61 411583), at Pinto and O'Higgins, handles basic medical emergencies, but the facilities in Punta Arenas are better.

Internet Try *Café Reymar*, at Hostal Reymar, Baquedano 414 (CH$1000/hr; minimum CH$400/20min), or Cyber Café Enyge at Baquedano and Chorrillos. Lots of cafés have wi-fi.

Laundry The cheapest place is Lavandería Servilaundy at Prat 332 (daily 9am–10pm; CH$1600 per load); try also Lavandería Milodón, Baquedano 642 (Mon–Sat 10am–noon & 2.30–8pm).

Post office Eberhard 429, on the plaza (Mon–Fri 9am–1pm & 3–6pm; Sat 10am–1pm).

PARQUE NACIONAL TORRES DEL PAINE

The great massif contained within the **PARQUE NACIONAL TORRES DEL PAINE**, 112km northwest of Puerto Natales, with the sheer granite towers of **Las Torres** to the east, and the multicoloured **Los Cuernos** to the west, is one of Patagonia's most jaw-dropping sights. The park offers incomparable opportunities for backcountry hiking, as well as animal spotting; you are likely to see **guanacos** – wild relatives of llamas – and *ñandú* or rhea (similar to an ostrich). Pumas also live in the park, though they're shy, as well as foxes, the elusive *huermúl* deer and condors. There are also challenging scrambles to the park's *miradores* and a host of other outdoor activities – from ice-trekking on Glacier Grey to horseriding in the outlying hills; the most popular trekking route is the "W" (see box opposite).

Pudeto

After Laguna Amarga (see p.474), buses stop one hour later at the northern tip of **Lago Pehoé**, near the catamaran pier at Pudeto. From here it's a fifteen-minute walk uphill to **Salto Grande**, a thundering waterfall fed by melting glacial waters, with views of Los Cuernos in the distance. There's also an easy hour's walk along the lakeside to another **viewpoint**, offering a spectacular vista of the Cuernos del Paine, reflected in the icy blue waters of Lago Nordenskjöld. You can commence on the "W" by taking the Hielos Patagónicos catamaran (see p.474) from the pier across Lago Pehoé to the *Paine Grande Lodge* (see p.475).

HIKING THE "W"

Though Torres del Paine offers numerous hiking trails, the most popular is undoubtedly the "W", a four- to five-day hike that takes in the park's highlights: the massive Glacier Grey, steep Valle Francés and, finally, the *mirador* Las Torres. It makes sense to hike the "W" from west to east, tackling the steepest ascent first, especially if you're carrying camping gear, as you will have eaten most of your provisions by the time you approach the challenging *mirador*, and will have grown used to the rigours of the hike.

Glacier Grey

From the pier at the *Paine Grande Lodge*, a clearly marked trail runs north through the scrubland, past a small lagoon and into a *lenga* forest, crisscrossed with narrow, icy streams. The trail meanders before emerging at the **Quebrada de los Vientos** ("Windy Gorge"), an hour or so into the hike, where your first glimpse of **Glacier Grey** stops you in your tracks. For the next couple of hours, you walk across exposed terrain, beside the pale water of Lago Grey and its house-sized chunks of blue ice. The glacier peeks from behind the dark rock of **La Isla Nunatak** on the lake's far side.

The trail then descends steeply through the silent *lenga* woods, almost doubling back on itself and crossing a wooden bridge over a gushing torrent, before emerging on the lakeshore. Ten minutes before arriving at a shaded lakeside clearing housing the **Refugio y Camping Grey**, another short trail branches off from the main path, leading you to a

LAGO GREY BY BOAT

From the *Hostería Lago Grey* it's possible to take a spectacular three-hour **boat ride** up Lago Grey to Glacier Grey (Nov–March; daily 8am, noon & 3pm; CH$45,000, minimum 8 people; check ahead for the current departure times). If short of time you can also hike the easy 2.2km trail along the beach to see the icebergs and the glacier looming in the distance – climb the cliff trail for the best views. Note, however, there is no public transport to Lago Grey.

rocky outcrop with a spectacular close-up of the glacier's gigantic ice crystals. The hike lasts three or four hours; *Refugio y Camping Grey* marks the end of the first leg of the "W", from where you either double back to Lago Pehoé or continue north if doing the "Circuit" (see p.474).

Valle Francés

Back at the *Paine Grande Lodge*, a two-hour-long, eastbound trail heads through scrubland and prickly calafate bushes along Lago Pehoé before leading north with glimpses of **Lago Skottsberg** on your right-hand side. As you round the imposing 3050m Paine Grande massif, look up, as there is a known condor nest near the peak. A wobbly hanging bridge brings you to the *Campamento Italiano*, where you can leave most of your gear before scrambling up the steep rocky path leading up the **Valle Francés**, the middle part of the "W". The turbulent **Río del Francés** churns on your left-hand side and there are spectacular views of Glacier Francés and Glacier Los Perros.

After two hours hiking through enchanted-looking woods, you reach the very basic *Campamento Británico*, from where it's an hour's hike up to the steep lookout that gives you an excellent close-up view of the multicoloured Los Cuernos, rising from dense forest to the east, as well as the aptly named 2800m-high **Fortaleza** ("fortress"), northeast of the *mirador*. The descent can be somewhat treacherous, so hiking poles are useful. From *Campamento Italiano*, allow two hours for the hike through the forested backcountry to the *Refugio y Camping Los Cuernos*; it's a long, steep descent on a scree-strewn trail followed by a brief stretch along the pale blue waters of Lago Nordenskjöld.

Los Cuernos to Las Torres

From the *refugio*, the trail runs through hilly scrubland, crossing several small streams, with Lago Nordenskjöld on your right. Shortly after you depart Los Cuernos, you come to the **Río del Valle Bader**, a rushing glacial stream that can be difficult to cross without hiking poles. This sector of the hike takes around four

4

4

Puerto Natales (116km)

Laguna Azul

Laguna Azul

Laguna Amarga

Laguna Goic

Laguna Amarga

1.5hrs (7km)

Cascada Paine

4.5hrs (10km)

Laguna Smock

Laguna Blanquillos

Laguna Escondida

Laguna Cebolla

Laguna Vega

Río Paine

Horse trail

4hrs (9km)

Las Torres

Hostería Las Torres

Serón

Valle y Río Ascencio

2hrs

Laguna Inge

4hrs (11km)

Lago Paine

Torres

Chileno

1.5hr (5km)

Japonés

1hr (4km)

Mirador las Torres

1hr

Cerro Almirante Nieto (2668m)

Río de los Calqueres

Río Paine

3hrs

Nido de Cóndor (2243m)

8hrs (19km)

Valle del Silencio

Torre Norte Monzino (2600m)

Torre Central (2600m)

Torre Sur Di Agostini (2650m)

Río Bader

Cuerno Este (2200m)

Cuerno Norte (2400m)

Horse trail

Cerro Fortaleza (3000m)

Mirador Valle de Frances

0.5hr (2 km)

2.5hrs (5.5km)

Cuerno Principal (2600m)

Lago Quemado

Dickson

Britanico

Valle y Río del Francés

Glaciar

Lago Dickson

Río de los Perros

4hrs (9km)

Cerro Paine Grande (3248m)

Lago Escondido

Glacier Los Perros

Los Perros

John Gardner Pass (1241m)

9hrs (12km)

Paso

2hrs (6km)

Los Guardas

Grey

1hr (4km)

La Isla Nunatak

Glacier Grey

Serviced campsite

Unserviced campsite

Guardería (ranger station)

Refugio (mountain refuge)

PARQUE NACIONAL TORRES DEL PAINE

hours and there is a clear track that crosses a bridge over the Río Asencio just before you reach the *Hostería Las Torres*.

Mirador Las Torres

To see the sunrise at the famous **Mirador Las Torres**, some make their way up the Valle Ascencio from the *Hostería Las Torres* the night before, spending the night at the basic, unserviced *Campamento Torres*. The hike itself is a steep, three-hour thirty-minute ascent alongside the Río Ascencio. You'll need to rise before daybreak to tackle the steepest part of the journey – an hour-long scramble up boulders – to witness the spectacle of the sun's first rays colouring the magnificent Torres, perfectly reflected in the still waters of **Laguna Torres**. Alternatively, you can break your journey by staying at the *Refugio y Camping Chileno*, halfway up the trail. Or take the hike further up the Valle Ascencio to *Campamento Japonés*, then up another steep yet spectacular climb along the aptly named **Valle del Silencio** to a less-visited *mirador*. The "W" ends with a short trek or minibus ride from *Hostería Las Torres* back to Laguna Amarga and the park entrance.

The "Circuit"

The "Circuit" is an extended version of the "W", a seven- to ten-day hike that leads you around the back of the Torres, giving you respite from the inevitable crowds during peak season, and offering unique glimpses of the park, which you may be able to experience in complete solitude. You can either start from the *Paine Grande Lodge* and head straight for the Valle Francés, or you can stay on the bus past Lago Pehoé, get off at the Park Administration, and do the scenic five-hour walk before commencing on the Circuit (this is called "doing the Q"). Alternatively, you can follow the trail directly from **Laguna Amarga**, from where it's a mostly flat five-hour hike along Río Paine to *Camping Serón*. You can also pick up the trail from the *Hostería Las Torres*. Since there is only one *refugio* along the Circuit, you will have to stop at unserviced campsites most of the way, bringing food and camping supplies with you – most people opt for an organized hike with a guide (see box, p.470).

ARRIVAL AND INFORMATION

By bus Buses from Puerto Natales stop at the Laguna Amarga park administration building (2hr 15min), then at Pudeto (the catamaran departure point; 3hr 15min) and finally at the Administration building (4hr 15min). Out of season, when the catamaran is no longer running, the buses stop first at Administration and then at Laguna Amarga. Minibus transfers (CH$2500) meet the buses at Laguna Amarga and run to *Refugio y Camping Las Torres*.

By ferry A Hielos Patagónicos catamaran (☎61 41138C CH$12,000 one-way, CH$19,000 return) crosses Lago Pehoé from Pudeto, returning from Paine Grande 30min later. Pudeto departures are at 9.30am, noon and 6pm (Nov 16–March 15); noon & 6pm (March 16–March 31 & Oct 16–Nov 15); or noon only (Oct 1–Oct 15 & April 1–April 30); there is no service the rest of the year.

Conaf The Conaf *guardería* at Laguna Amarga has basic information on the park's fauna and flora, as well as basic trekking maps. You must register and pay your CH$18,000/8,000 peak/off-peak entrance fee here. Ranger stations at Lago Sarmiento, Laguna Azul, Lago Grey and Laguna Verde also have basic information on the park. The Conaf-run Centro de Visitantes (Dec–Feb daily 8.30am–8pm; ☎61 691931) at the Lago del Toro Park Administration building has small displays on the park fauna and flora.

REFUGIOS IN TORRES DEL PAINE

Most of the park's campsites and **refugios** are open only from September to May. Some basic refugios are run by Conaf, but most of the decent sites belong either to Vertice Patagonia or Fantástico Sur, both in Puerto Natales (see p.467). At these *refugios* you can rent bedding (CH$17,000–26,500 for a basic bed; camping CH$3500/person) and enjoy pricey hot meals (around CH$6000 for breakfast, CH$8000 for lunch and CH$10,500 for dinner). Try to book your *refugio* space in advance, especially in the peak season from December to February. You can rent camping equipment at most serviced sites: tents CH$7000; sleeping bags CH$5500; mats CH$1500. There are several unserviced campsites in the park which are free of charge and consist of a clearing with a fire pit; these include *Campamento Paso*, *Campamento Italiano*, *Campamento Británico* and *Campamento Torres*. Wild camping inside the park is not permitted.

ACCOMMODATION

Camping Los Perros (Vertice). Halfway between the John Garner pass and the *Refugio Dickson*, this campsite comes equipped with hot showers, a food shop and equipment rental; meals have to be reserved in advance. Camping/person CH$3500

Camping Serón (Fantástico Sur). Partially shaded campsite on the Circuit beside the Río Paine; hot showers, toilets, and a *guardería* on-site. Camping/person CH$4000

Mountain Lodge & Camping Grey (Vertice). A small popular *refugio* a stone's throw from Glacier Grey; book meals in advance. Campsite includes hot showers and a small on-site grocery store. Camping/person CH$3500, basic beds CH$17,300

Mountain Lodge & Camping Paine Grande (Vertice). The campsite, where you can rent gear, has an indoor cooking area, hot showers and bathrooms. The popular lodge has great views of Lago Pehoé, as well as a small grocery store, café-bar and restaurant, though the food is decidedly uninspiring. Camping/person CH$4800, basic beds CH$26,500

Refugio & Camping El Chileno (Fantástico Sur). A popular stop halfway along the Valle Ascencio, this *refugio* offers kitchen privileges after certain hours as well as hot meals. Camping/person CH$6000, basic beds CH$23,500

Refugio & Camping Los Cuernos (Fantástico Sur). *Refugio* serving good meals, with kitchen privileges after 10pm; campers share bathroom facilities with *refugio* guests. Camping spots are sheltered among vegetation. Camping/person CH$8000, basic beds CH$23,500

Refugio & Camping Las Torres (Fantástico Sur). Near the entrance to the park, this *refugio* is split between two buildings and has comfortable bunks as well as decent food. Camping spots have hot showers, picnic tables and fire pits. More upmarket eating can be found at the excellent restaurant at nearby *Hostería Las Torres*. Camping/person CH$6000, basic beds CH$22,500

Shelter & Camping Dickson (Vertice). On the shore of Lago Dickson, this *refugio* offers hot showers and hot meals, and has a small grocery kiosk and equipment rental. Camping/person CH$350, basic beds CH$17,300

Tierra del Fuego

The most remote of Chile's land territories, **TIERRA DEL FUEGO** was named "Land of Fire" by Fernando Magellan, who sailed through the strait that now bears his name in 1520, and saw a multitude of cooking fires lit by the native hunter-gatherers. From then on until the opening of the Panama Canal in 1914, the frigid waters around Cape Horn – the largest ship graveyard in the Americas – formed a link in the perilous yet lucrative trade route from Europe to the west coast of the Americas.

Tierra del Fuego's Isla Grande is split between Chile and Argentina: the Chilean half features the nondescript town of **Porvenir**, settled by a mixture of Chilote and Croatian immigrants in the late nineteenth century, as well as a number of remote sheep-rearing *estancias*. The Argentine half includes the lively town of **Ushuaia** (see p.144), the base for Antarctic voyages. The region's biggest natural draw is southern Tierra del Fuego – a scattering of rocky islands, separated by labyrinthine fjords, home to the craggy Darwin Range and the southernmost permanently inhabited town in the world – Isla Navarino's **Puerto Williams**.

PUERTO WILLIAMS

Although Argentine Ushuaia, on the north side of the Beagle Channel, loudly proclaims its "end of the world" status, that title rightfully belongs to **PUERTO WILLIAMS**. Home to just over two thousand people and the last remaining **Yámana people** (relocated here in 1941), the windblown town has a desolate quality to it even in the height of the brief summer. In contrast to the weather, the people of Puerto Williams are exceptionally warm and welcoming; you get a real sense of a close-knit community. Many travellers come to Puerto Williams to complete the challenging 70km **Los Dientes de Navarino Circuit** – a strenuous four- to seven-day clockwise trek in the Isla Navarino wilderness for experienced hikers only (see box, p.476).

WHAT TO SEE AND DO

The worthwhile **Museo Antropológico Martin Gusinde**, at Aragay 1 (Nov–March Tues–Fri 9.30am–1pm & 3–6pm, Sat & Sun 2.30–6.30pm; April–Oct Tues–Fri 9.30am–1.30pm & 2.30–5.30pm, Sat 2.30–5.30pm; donations; ☎61 621043,

ⓦmuseoantropologicomartingusinde.cl), is named after a German clergyman and anthropologist who spent 22 months among the native tribes of Tierra del Fuego between 1918 and 1924. Located on the west side of town, it features informative and well-laid-out displays on the native Kawéskar, Selk'nam and Yámana Indians, complete with a replica of a Selk'nam ritual hut, as well as exhibits on local geology, flora and fauna.

ARRIVAL AND INFORMATION

By plane The tiny airport receiving Aerovías DAP flights from Punta Arenas lies a short distance from Puerto Williams; flights are met by local minivans that double as taxis (CH$2000). Aerovías DAP has its office at Centro Comercial Sur 151 (ⓦaeroviasdap.cl).

By boat A popular (but not cheap) way to reach Puerto Williams is from the Argentine city of Ushuaia (Sept–March, depending on the weather; 30min; one-way US$65–125, plus US$23 fee for Ushuaia departures and US$10 for Navarino); Zodiac boats via Zenit Explorer (depart Ushuaia daily at 8.30am, return 4.30pm; ⓦzenitexplorer.com.ar) and Ushuaia Boating (Mon–Sat 9.30am–10am; ⓦushuaiaboating.com.ar) cross the Beagle Channel and dock at tiny Puerto Navarino where visitors have to check in with Chilean immigration authorities; minibus transfers take passengers to their *residenciales* in Puerto Williams, an hour's drive (52km) across the island (another US$20; allow 90min for whole trip). The boats do not sail in extreme conditions, so be prepared to spend an extra day or two on either side of the channel.

By ferry The Transbordadora Austral Broom ferry (☎61 621015, ⓦtabsa.cl) sails to Punta Arenas (every Sat night; seat/berth US$186/258; 38hr).

Tourist information Inside the Municipalidad on O'Higgins (Mon–Fri 8.30am–1pm & 2.30–5pm). Check out ⓦimcabodehornos.cl for more information. The post office is located inside the Centro Comercial, by Plaza O'Higgins; Banco de Chile has a global ATM on a narrow passageway towards the waterfront from the Centro Comercial.

ACCOMMODATION

Hostal Bella Vista Teniente Muñoz 118 ☎61 621010, ⓦvictory-cruises.com. Hostel with incredible views of the Beagle Channel, run by an American-Chilean family. Warm rooms (some en suite), with laundry service, wi-fi and discounts at the internet café and the minimart. Sailing trips to Cape Horn and Antarctica on their yacht S/V *Victory* are on offer. Doubles CH$17,500

Hospedaje Akainij Austral 22 ☎61 621173, ⓦturismo akainij.cl. Simple but calm and cosy guesthouse, with single, double and triple rooms, private bathroom, wi-fi, satellite TV and breakfast included. Doubles CH$28,000

Refugio al Padrino Costanera 276 ☎61 621136, ⓔceciliamancillao@yahoo.com.ar. Barebones but snug backpacker joint, with friendly owner, comfy bunks, shared kitchen, wood-burning stove and info on bike rentals and horseriding. Dorms CH10,000

Residencial Pusaki Piloto Pardo 222 ☎61 621116, ⓔpattypusaki@yahoo.es. Another backpacker favourite, run by an extremely hospitable family (try Patty's king crab soufflé; see below), this hostel has warm, cosy rooms with shared bath as well as a common lounge and kitchen. Dorms CH$12,000, doubles CH$26,000

EATING AND DRINKING

Micalvi Costanera s/n. This former Navy ship is a nightly gathering point for travellers, local sailors and Antarctic explorers; open late. Drinks are not cheap, but the congenial atmosphere and bizarre location make up for it. Nov–March Mon–Sat 9pm–2am.

★ **Residencial Pusaki** Piloto Pardo 222 ☎61 621116 Even if you're not a guest here, give the owner a couple of hours' warning and come try some of her delicious home cooking at dinnertime; *centolla* night is the best when Patty makes filling king-crab stew. CH$7000.

ISLA NAVARINO TOUR OPERATORS

Outdoor activities on and around Isla Navarino tend to be on the expensive side and not for the faint-hearted, but if you've had fantasies about yachting to Cape Horn or tackling some of the most challenging hiking in Latin America, several experienced tour operators in Puerto Williams can help you realize your dream.

SIM Expeditions Casilla 6 ⓦsimexpeditions.com. Intrepid German-Venezuelan operator organizing hiking and horseriding on Isla Navarino and Cordillera Darwin, as well as sea-kayaking trips and multi-day yacht excursions around Cape Horn and even to South Georgia and Antarctica.

Turismo Shila O'Higgins 322 ☎09 78972005, ⓦturismoshila.cl. Luis and family run trekking trips around Isla Navarino (including the Dientes circuit) and fishing excursions to Lago Windhond, Lago Navarino and Laguna Rojas; they also rent outdoor gear.

Easter Island

One of the most remote island territories on earth, over 2000km from the nearest inhabited part of the world, **EASTER ISLAND** entices visitors with the enduring mystery of its **lost culture**. A remarkable civilization arose here, far from outside influence on an island only 163 square kilometres in extent. It apparently declined rapidly and had all but disappeared by the time Europeans first arrived here. Originally known as "Te Pito O Te Henua", or "the navel of the world", due to its isolation, and now called "Rapa Nui" by its inhabitants (*Pascuenses*), the island is home to a culture and people with strong Polynesian roots and a language of their own, which sets it well apart from mainland Chile. Archeological mysteries aside, the island has much to offer: year-round warm weather, excellent diving and surfing conditions and plenty of scope for leisurely exploration of the more out-of-the-way attractions, both on foot and on horseback. Welcoming people, excellent food and a laidback atmosphere seal the deal.

HANGA ROA

The island's only settlement and home to around four thousand people, **HANGA ROA** is a dusty village spread out along the Pacific coast. At night there is limited street lighting and the sky, lit with endless stars, is spectacular. North–south Atamu Tekena is the main road, lined with small supermarkets, cafés and tour agencies. Much of the action is centred on the pier, Caleta Hanga Roa, overlooked by **Ahu Tautira**, the only *moai* site in the town proper. Restaurants spread from here along oceanside Policarpo Toro and east–west Te Pito O Te Henua, which

4

A BRIEF HISTORY OF EASTER ISLAND

500–800 AD Easter Island is settled by King Hotu Matu'a and his extended family, who come from either the Pitcairn Islands or the Cook or Marquesas Islands in Polynesia. The island is divided between *mata* (tribes), each led by a male descendant of the original king.

800–1600 Population grows to an estimated 20,000–30,000. Island culture evolves into a complex society and flourishes; *ahu* (ceremonial platforms) are built and *moai* (stone statues) are erected all over the island.

1600–1722 Natural resources are depleted and deforestation takes its toll. Two warring factions form: the Ko Tu'u Aro, who rule the island's western half, and the Hotu Iti, who populate its eastern half. *Moai* construction stops, the population declines and the Birdman cult develops.

1722 Dutch admiral Jacob Roggeveen lands and names the island after the day of his arrival – Easter Sunday.

1770 The expedition of Felipe Gonzáles de Haedo claims Easter Island for King Carlos III of Spain.

1774 Captain James Cook visits; he finds the *moai* in ruins and the population bedraggled.

1862 Nearly one thousand islanders are kidnapped to work as slaves in the guano mines of the Chincha Islands off the coast of Peru, including the island's king and all the priestly elite. Later, one hundred islanders are shipped back to Easter Island; the final fifteen survivors of this voyage infect the islanders with smallpox and the population is reduced to a few hundred.

1870 The island is purchased for a pittance by Frenchman Jean Baptiste Dutroux-Bornier, who wages war on missionaries. Most islanders agree to be shipped to Tahiti rather than work in indentured servitude.

1888–1953 Easter Island becomes part of Chile and is leased to the Compañía Explotadora de la Isla de Pascua, a subsidiary of the sheep-rearing Scottish-owned Williamson, Balfour and Company. Villagers are confined to Hanga Roa.

1953 Company's lease is revoked; Easter Island comes under the control of the Chilean Navy.

1967 Mataveri Airport is built. Islanders are given full rights as Chilean citizens.

1967–present day The island undergoes material improvement and the Rapa Nui language is no longer suppressed. Disputes with the Chilean government over ancestral land rights, however, continue.

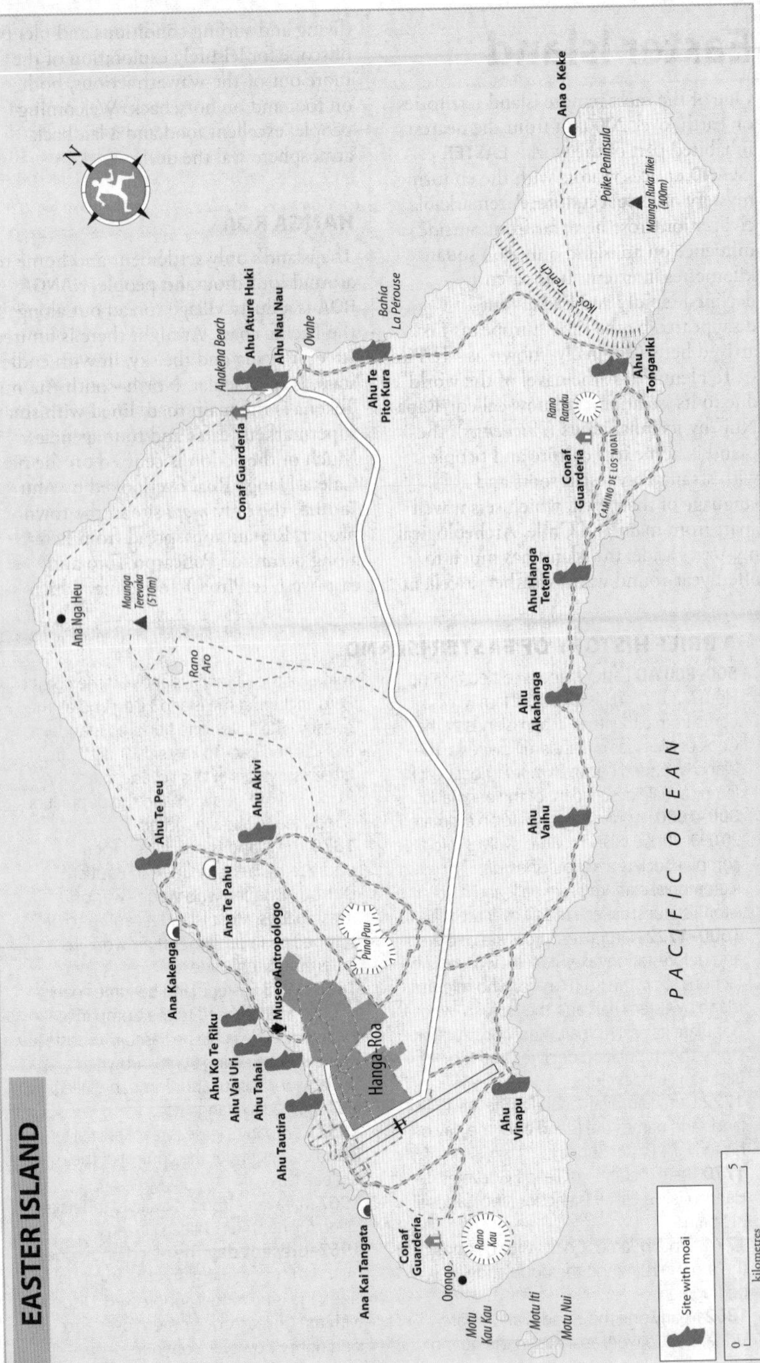

EASTER ISLAND

N

Ana o Keke

Poike Peninsula

Maunga Tuka Tikei (400m)

Poike Isthmus

Ana Ature Huki
Ahu Nau Nau
Anakena Beach
Ovahe
Bahia La Pérouse

Ahu Te Pito Kura

Ahu Tongariki

Conaf Guarderia

Rano Raraku

Conaf Guarderia

CAMINO DE LOS MOAI

Ahu Hanga Tetenga

Ana Nga Heu

Maunga Terevaka (510m)

Rano Aro

Ahu Akahanga

Ahu Vaihu

PACIFIC OCEAN

Ahu Te Peu

Ahu Akivi

Ana Kakenga

Ana Te Pahu

Museo Antropólogo

Puna Pau

Ahu Ko Te Riku
Ahu Vai Uri
Ahu Tahai

Hanga Roa

Ahu Tautira

Ahu Vinapu

Ana Kai Tangata

Conaf Guarderia

Rano Kau

Orongo

Motu Kau Kau
Motu Iti
Motu Nui

Site with moai

0   kilometres   5

takes you past the small Plaza Policarpo Toro before ending at the Iglesia Hanga Roa, a Catholic **church** decorated with elaborate woodcarvings.

WHAT TO SEE AND DO

Just south of the pier and opposite the tourist office lies tiny **Playa Pea**, a rock pool safe for swimming, cordoned off from the stretch of ocean popular with surfers and bodyboarders. Avenida Policarpo Toro heads north, past the Hanga Roa **cemetery** with its colourful crosses, to three main sites, particularly spectacular at sunset. First is **Ahu Tahai**, with a single large *moai*, then **Ahu Vai Uri**, with five standing *moai* in various states of repair, and finally the much-photographed **Ahu Ko Te Riku**, a single *moai* with a *pukao* (topknot) and intact, pensive-looking coral eyes. Also in this direction, amid gentle hills dotted with numerous *hare paenga* (boat-shaped foundations of traditional houses), lies the **anthropological museum**. To the south, Policarpo Toro heads towards the extinct Rano Kau volcano.

Museo Antropológico Padre Sebastián Englert

Off the coastal road just north of Ahu Tahai, this excellent **museum** (Tues–Fri 9.30am–5.30pm, Sat & Sun 9.30am–12.30pm; CH\$1000) students free; ☎ 32 5512032, ✉ museorapanui.cl, Spanish labels only, with English-language handouts available) is not to be missed, as it gives a thorough and informative introduction to the island's geography, history, society, Birdman cult (see box, p.481) and the origins and significance of the *moai*. The displays include a rare female *moai*, a wooden carving of a *moai kavakava* – a gaunt figure, believed to represent the spirits of dead ancestors – and replica *rongorongo* tablets (no original examples remain on the island). *Rongorongo* script is one of only four written languages in the world that developed independently of outside influence; the tablets were first mentioned in the nineteenth-century accounts of French missionary Eugene Eyraud, and their purpose remains unclear. It seems that only a

---

THE RISE AND FALL OF THE MOAI OF EASTER ISLAND

The giant stone statues, around 887 of which litter the island, are a unique symbol of a lost civilization, whose existence raises many questions. Why were they made? By whom? How were they transported around the island and erected without the benefit of machinery? Why was their construction suddenly abandoned?

Believed to be representations of **ancestors**, the statues range from 2m to 10m in height, with an average weight of 12 tonnes. The majority of the *moai* share a similar appearance: elongated features and limbs, prominent noses, heavy brows and rounded bellies. Most are male, and some wear *pukao*, topknots carved of red stone in a separate quarry. Most *moai* once had coral-and-rock eyes, though now the only intact example is Ahu Ko Te Riku.

Carved from the slopes of the **Rano Raraku quarry**, the *moai* were buried upright in earthen pits so that their sculptors could shape their facial features with basalt *toki* (chisels), and then lowered down the volcano's slopes, presumably using ropes. Most archeologists believe that to transport them to the coastal *ahu* (platforms) the islanders used wooden rollers or sledges – a practice which resulted in complete deforestation – and that once at the foot of the *ahu*, the *moai* were lifted into place using wooden levers. All *moai*, apart from those at Ahu Akivi, were positioned around the coast facing inland, so as to direct their *mana* (life energy) towards their creators and to bless them with plentiful food and other bounties.

It is known that at the height of Easter Island's civilization (800–1500 AD), the tiny island supported a large and complex multi-tiered society, with a ruling class who worshipped **Make-Make**, the creator, and oversaw the construction of these statues. A phenomenal amount of energy must have gone into their creation and transportation, fatally depleting the island's resources and causing acute food shortages. Full-scale warfare erupted when farmers and fishermen couldn't or wouldn't support the *moai*-carving workforce any longer. The carving ceased and the *moai* were toppled from their pedestals. That which gave the civilization purpose was ultimately also its undoing.

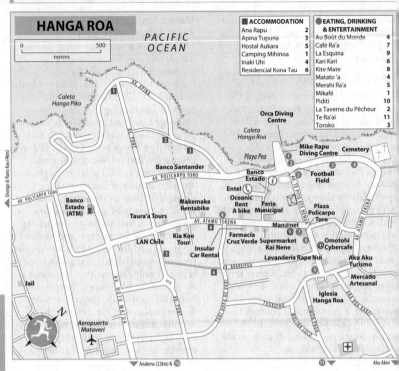

PACIFIC OCEAN

Caleta Hanga Piko

Caleta Hanga Roa

Playa Pea

Orca Diving Centre

Mike Rapu Diving Centre

Cemetery

Banco Santander

Banco Estado

Football Field

AV. POLICARPO TORO

Entel

AV. POLICARPO TORO

Banco Estado (ATM)

Makemake Rentabike

Oceanic Rent A bike

Feria Municipal

Plaza Policarpo Toro

Taura'a Tours

AV. ATAMU TEKENA

Man@net

Kia Koe Tour

LAN Chile

Farmacia Cruz Verde

Supermarket Kai Nene

Omotohi @Cybercafe

Insular Car Rental

Lavanderia Rapa Nui

Aku Aku Turismo

AV. AVAREIPUA

Mercado Artesanal

Jail

Iglesia Hanga Roa

Aeropuerto Mataveri

ACCOMMODATION	
Ana Rapu	2
Apina Tupuna	3
Hostal Aukara	5
Camping Mihinoa	1
Inaki Uhi	4
Residencial Kona Tau	6

EATING, DRINKING & ENTERTAINMENT	
Au Boût du Monde	4
Café Ra'a	7
La Esquina	9
Kari Kari	6
Kite Mate	8
Matato'a	4
Merahi Ra'a	5
Mikáfé	1
Piditi	10
La Taverne du Pêcheur	
Te Ra'ai	11
Toroko	3

Orongo & Rano Kau (4km)

Anakena (22km) & 10

Ahu Akivi

4

small priestly elite was literate and that the knowledge perished with them during the slave raids and smallpox epidemic of the early 1860s. The script remains undeciphered to this day.

Rano Kau crater and Orongo ceremonial village

South of Hanga Roa, a dirt road climbs steeply past a *mirador* offering an excellent panoramic view of the island, to one of Easter Island's most awe-inspiring spots – the giant crater of the extinct **Rano Kau volcano**. The dull waters of the volcano's reed-choked lake contrast sharply with the brilliant blue of the Pacific, visible where a great chunk of the crater wall is missing. You pay the CH$30,000 entry fee (CH$10,000 for Chilean residents) at the Conaf ranger station just before you reach **Orongo ceremonial village**; it is valid for one visit each to the two main sights of **Parque Nacional Rapa Nui** which comprises much of the island: Orongo and Rano Kau.

The Orongo site of the Birdman cult consists of 53 restored houses with tiny doorways, made of horizontally overlapping flat stone slabs, hugging the side of the cliff. A winding labelled footpath leads past them to the edge of Rano Kau, where a cluster of **petroglyphs** depicting the half-bird, half-human Birdman, as well as Make-Make, the creator, overlooks a sheer drop, with the islets Motu Kao Kao, Motu Iti and Motu Nui jutting out of the azure waters below.

THE SOUTHERN COAST

Heading east out of Hanga Roa, Hotu Matu'a leads you towards the **southern coast**. A right turn at the end, followed by an almost immediate left by the fuel storage tanks, takes you to **Vinapu**, an important site consisting of three *ahus* (stone platforms) with a number of broken *moai* scattered around. The *ahus* are made of overlapping stone slabs, seemingly similar in construction to those built by the Inca in Cusco, Peru, leading some archeologists to believe that Easter Island culture has Latin American roots. Continuing east along this coast you reach **Ahu Vaihu**, with its eight toppled *moai* and their scattered *pukao* (stone topknots). Up the road, the large **Ahu Akahanga** is widely believed to be the burial place of Hotu Matu'a, the first king of the island. The site features a dozen *moai*, lying face down, with petroglyphs carved into one of the platforms. There are also the remains of a village, consisting of *hare paenga* outlines, as well as a number of *pukao*.

Another 3km east, the almost utterly ruined **Ahu Hanga Tetenga** consists of two toppled and shattered *moai*. Beyond, the road forks, the northern branch looping inland toward Rano Raraku, while the east-bound branch continues to **Ahu Tongariki**, one of the island's most enduring and awe-inspiring images. Consisting of fifteen *moai*, one significantly taller than the rest and another sporting a topknot, the island's largest *moai* site was destroyed by a tsunami in 1960, and re-erected by the Japanese company Tadano between 1992 and 1995.

Rano Raraku

Just inland of Ahu Tongariki lies the unforgettable spectacle of **Rano Raraku** – the gigantic quarry where all of Easter Island's *moai* were chiselled out of the tuff (compressed volcanic ash) that makes up the sides of the crater. From the Conaf ranger station, a dirt path leads up to the volcano's slopes, littered with dozens of completed *moai*, abandoned on the way to their *ahus*. The right branch meanders between the giant statues, buried in the ground up to their necks, their heads mournfully looking out to sea. You pass *moai* in various stages of completion, including the largest one ever carved, **El Gigante**, 21m tall and 4m wide, its back still joined to the stone from which it was carved. The east end of the path culminates in the kneeling,

round-headed **Moai Tukuturi**, the only one of its kind, discovered by Thor Heyerdahl's expedition in 1955.

To the west, the trail winds its way up between wild guava trees into the crater itself, with a dirt path running through knee-high shrubbery alongside the large reed-strewn lake. You may take the footpath up to the crater's eastern rim for unparalleled views of the bay and Ahu Tongariki in the distance, but only if accompanied by a ranger or a guide. There has been increased concern regarding visitor behaviour ever since a Finnish tourist was caught in 2008 while trying to break an ear off a *moai* to take home as a souvenir.

Ovahe Beach

This small, sheltered **beach** is located off a dirt road just before Anakena Beach, on the other side of the Maunga Puha hillock. Backed by tall cliffs, its pristine sands are very popular with locals who come here to picnic, swim and snorkel. It's best earlier in the day, before the cliff blocks the afternoon sun.

Anakena Beach

Easter Island's largest and most popular beach is found on the northeast side of the island, and can be reached directly by the paved, cross-island road. A white-sand beach dotted with coconut trees, it has picnic tables and fire pits, public toilets and showers, as well as food stands offering drinks and snacks. The beach is also home to the largest *hare paenga* (boat-shaped house) on the island and is believed to have been the landing point for the legendary King Hotu Matu'a. To the east stands the large, squat *moai* on **Ahu Ature Huki**, re-erected by Thor Heyerdahl's expedition of 1955 with the help of some islanders, while nearby stand the seven *moai* of **Ahu Nau Nau**, four sporting *pukaos* and two badly damaged. The best time for photographers to visit is in the mid-afternoon.

4 THE NORTHERN COAST AND THE INNER LOOP

Heading up the coast from the north end of Hanga Roa, a rutted dirt-and-gravel road takes you past **Ana Kakenga**, or Caverna Dos Ventanas – a cave set in the cliff with a spectacular view of the coast. Look for two offshore **islets**, Motu Ko Hepko and Motu Tautara; the cave is directly opposite them, with a cairn indicating the location. Bring a torch if you wish to explore. Further along, at the site of Ahu Tepeu, the road turns inland while a path carries on up to a copse of trees. The inland road leads you along fenced-off pasture land to **Ana Te Pahu** on your right-hand side – one of many underground **lava caves** on the island, used as a *manavai* (underground garden) to cultivate bananas, sweet potatoes, taro and other tropical plants due to its moisture and fertile soil.

At the southwestern base of **Maunga Terevaka**, the island's highest point (507m), is **Ahu Akivi**, with seven intact *moai*, the only ones on the island to be looking out to sea. As the road heads south to link up with the island's main thoroughfare, a dirt track to the west takes you to **Puna Pau**, the quarry where the *pukao* were carved.

ARRIVAL AND INFORMATION

By plane Aeropuerto Mataveri is located on Hotu Matu'a, southeast of Hanga Roa; most *residenciales* provide free transfers. Flights to Easter Island tend to be in the region of US$700–900 return, unless you buy your ticket very much in advance and also in conjunction with a long-distance LAN flight. LAN (☎ 600 5266000) is the only airline with commercial flights to Easter Island, and flies direct from Santiago seven days a week; some flights continue onto Papeete, Tahiti. Flights are often full, so book well in advance. Some travellers have complained that due to overbooking, they have been bumped off their return flight, so it may be worth confirming flights at Hanga Roa's LAN office or checking in for the afternoon flight in the morning

Conaf Mataveri Otai s/n, south of Hanga Roa (Mon–Fri 8am–4.30pm; ☎ 32 2100236, ⓦ conaf.cl), has information on the Rapa Nui National Park. Conaf ranger stations are found at Rano Raraku, Anakena Beach and Orongo ceremonial village.

EASTER ISLAND TOUR OPERATORS

There is a proliferation of tour operators in Hanga Roa, and touring the archeological sites with a knowledgeable guide, especially if you have limited time on Easter Island, can be very worthwhile. If you are not thrilled at the idea of being cooped up in a minivan, horseriding can be an excellent way of seeing the sites instead. A full-day car tour costs around CH$30,000, while a day's horseriding can set you back around CH$35,000.

Aku Aku Turismo Av Tu'u Koihu s/n ☎ 32 2100770, ⓦ akuakuturismo.cl. Established operator offering standard guided day- and half-day tours of the island's sites, both in 4WDs and on horseback.

Cabalgatas Pantu ☎ 32 2100577, ⓦ pantupikerauri .cl. Reputable operator offering half- and full-day horseback tours of the west and north coasts, including the ascent of Maunga Terevaka, the island's highest point.

Kia Koe Tour Atamu Tekena s/n ☎ 32 2100852, ⓦ kia koetour.cl. Bilingual archeological tours of the island.

Taura'a Tours Atamu Tekena s/n ☎ 32 2100463, ⓦ tauraahotel.cl. Excellent operator offering full-day, small-group tours of the south coast, including Anakena Beach as well as the principal sites, or the west coast, incorporating the inland *moai* site of Ahu Akivi. English and French spoken; tailor-made tours possible.

Tourist office Policarpo Toro at Tu'u Maheke (Mon–Fri 8.30am–6pm; ☎32 2100255). Helpful staff provide detailed information on the island's attractions and can help you organize camping, activities such as horseriding, and vehicle rental; some English and French is spoken. There is a tourist information booth at the airport providing brochures on the island.

ACCOMMODATION

Ana Rapu Apina Iti s/n ☎32 2100540, ⓦanarapu.cl, ⓔinfo@anarapu.cl. Accommodation at this seafront guesthouse, set in a garden overflowing with lush vegetation, ranges from camping spots to large, airy en suites and cabañas. It's possible to arrange horseriding and scuba diving with Ana herself, and her son Joaquín. Camping/person **CH$7500**, doubles **CH$30,000**, cabañas **CH$80,000**

Apina Tupuna Apina Nui Policarpo Toro s/n ☎32 2100763, ⓦhostalapinatupuna.com, ⓔinfo@hostalapinatupuna.com. Oceanside *residencial* popular with backpackers and surfers, offering six bright rooms around a large communal area, decorated with the owner's own artwork; alternatively, you can rent one of the 2- 3-person cabañas. Breakfast and fully equipped kitchen included; camping allowed on the lawn. Camping/person **CH$7000**, doubles **CH$28,000**, cabañas **CH$45,000**

Hostal Aukara Av Pont s/n ☎32 2100539, ⓦaukara.cl, ⓔaukararapanui@gmail.com. Follow the signs for the Aukara art gallery, which showcases the owner's pieces, to this small guesthouse, lost in the midst of the beautiful garden. The six rooms are basic but comfortable, there's a small kitchen for guests and guided tours of the gallery are available. Doubles **CH$60,000**

Camping Mihinoa Pont s/n ☎32 2551593, ⓦmihinoa.com. Large campsite with an excellent ocean view, run by a friendly family, with adjoined showers, kitchen facilities, dining room, internet access and car rental; a complete lack of shade is the only drawback. The adjoining guesthouse has basic, clean rooms and a five-bed dorm; it's also possible to rent camping equipment. Camping/person **CH$5500**, dorms **CH$8,000**, doubles **CH$25,000**

Inaki Uhi Av Atamu Tekena s/n ☎32 2100231, ⓦinakiuhi.com, ⓔpaatan@entelchile.net. As central as it gets, this guesthouse consists of two self-contained apartments (for two and four people) and 13 pristine rooms and fully equipped kitchens in two low-slung buildings, with an attractive garden/sitting area in between and a dining area upstairs where breakfast is served. What the rooms lack in character, the owners more than make up for by being extremely accommodating. Doubles **CH$60,000**

Residencial Kona Tau Avareipua s/n ☎32 2100321, ⓦkonatau.com. HI-affiliated hostel in a large family home with a friendly atmosphere, with thirteen comfortable dorm beds, as well as basic en-suite rooms set in a mango-strewn garden. Large breakfasts are a bonus, but the staff can be hard to find. Dorms **CH$17,500**, doubles **CH$45,000**

EATING

Café Ra'a Atamu Tekena s/n, near Plaza Policarpo Toro. Popular café with outdoor terrace, excelling in light dishes. The tuna *ceviche* (CH$10,000) is divine and the fresh fruit juices are excellent (if pricey).

La Esquina Te Pito O Te Henua, at Tu'u Koihu. For epic fruit juices, come to this chilled-out place popular with locals. The pizza and the *empanadas* aren't half bad either. Fresh fruit juice CH$2500; pizza CH$4500.

Kite Mate Plaza Policarpo Toro. This bright-green shack serves some of the best *empanadas* on the island (CH$1500–3000); try the *atún y queso*.

Merahi Ra'a Te Pito O Te Henua s/n. This is the place to come for large servings of the freshest grilled fish, the *mahi mahi* (dorado) being particularly tasty. Fish dishes from CH$10,000.

Mikafé Caleta Hanga Roa s/n. Tiny café with outdoor seating overlooking the bay featuring the tastiest home-made ice cream on the island, as well as exotic fruit juices from CH$3000 (try the *guayaba*), and banana cake to die for. Coffee and cheesecake CH$5000.

La Taverne du Pêcheur Av Te Pito O Te Henua s/n. Sit on the attractive terrace at the (formerly) best restaurant in town and dig into expertly prepared fish, accompanied by island tubers. The desserts are also superb, though the pleasure doesn't come cheaply, and the quality of the service depends on the mood of the chef. Mains from CH$12,000; desserts CH$4000.

DRINKING AND ENTERTAINMENT

Kari Kari Atamu Tekena s/n, opposite Tuku Haka He Vari. Extremely entertaining traditional dance-and-music show, featuring talented young dancers and musicians in elaborate costumes. Be warned that there is usually some audience participation. Tues, Thurs & Sat at 9pm; CH$12,000.

Matato'a Av Policarpo Toro s/n ☎9 62213196. At a venue next to *Au Bout Du Monde*, this internationally renowned band with vividly painted bodies and faces turns up the heat with its energetic music and dance – a mix of

---

★ TREAT YOURSELF

Au Boût du Monde Policarpo Toro s/n, north of Caleta Hanga Roa. Enjoy excellent sunset views from the extensive upstairs terrace while tucking into inspired dishes such as tuna steak in Tahitian vanilla sauce accompanied by island vegetables. The chocolate mousse is also superb. Mains CH$10,000–13,000; cake CH$5000. Closed Tues.

4

traditional and modern, accompanied by "umu", or typical Rapa Nui cuisine. Wed, Fri & Sun at 9pm.

Piditi Av Hotu Matua s/n, by the airport. Smaller club that gets packed with an older crowd on weekends; action kicks off after midnight. Thurs–Sat until 6am.

Te Ra'ai Kaituoe s/n ☎ 32 2551460. Highly recommended island banquet, accompanied by a traditional singing and dancing performance of the Haha Varua dance group on Mon, Wed and Fri nights. Book ahead for pick-up from your guesthouse.

Toroko Av Policarpo Toro s/n, opposite Ahu A Rongo. Popular club with a mellow atmosphere that attracts young islanders on a Sat night.

DIRECTORY

Banks and exchange There are two banks on the island. Banco Estado, at Tu'u Maheke s/n (Mon–Fri 8am–1pm), has an adjoining ATM which only accepts MasterCard. Another Banco Estado ATM can be found at the Puna Vai gas station which doubles as another exchange office, at the west end of Av Hotu Matu'a. Banco Santander, at Av Apina s/n (Mon–Fri 9am–1pm), just south of the Sernatur office, has an ATM that accepts Visa cards. You can change US dollars at both banks. Many establishments accept US dollars and credit cards.

Car, scooter and bicycle rental Most agencies and bike rentals are found along Av Atamu Tekena and Av Te Pito O Te Henua. Oceanic Rent a Car and Insular rent hardy 4WDs (from CH$30,000/24hr), as well as quad bikes (CH$30,000/24hr), motorbikes (CH$25,000/24hr), scooters (CH$20,000/24hr) and mountain bikes (CH$10,000/24hr). Makemake Rentabike, at Atamu Tekena s/n, rents well-maintained bikes (CH$10,000/24hr) and gives out handy maps of various bike routes around the island. There is no insurance on the island, and to rent a scooter, dirt bike or motorbike, you need a valid motorbike licence.

Festivals Tapatai Rapa Nui, a ten-day cultural celebration in February, involving traditional dance and music, statue-carving competitions, canoe races and more, is the most popular time to visit Easter Island. Semana Santa (Easter week) has lively celebrations at Hanga Roa's Iglesia Parroquial de la Santa Cruz. The Ceremonia Culto al Sol is a feast that takes place on June 21 for the winter solstice, and Día de la Lengua Rapa Nui, a celebration of the Rapa Nui language, is held in late November.

Hospital The brand-new Hospital Hanga Roa on Simón Paoa s/n (☎ 32 2100215), southeast of the church, means islanders no longer have to travel to the mainland for all but the most basic procedures.

Internet and phone Internet cafés in Hanga Roa tend to be expensive, charging CH$1500/hr. Man@net on Akamu Tekena s/n (Mon–Sat 9am–10pm, Sun 10am–10pm) has wi-fi, while similarly priced Omotohi Cybercafé on Te Pito O Te Henua s/n doubles as a call centre and you can hook up your laptop to a cable, though you won't get charged any less. When dialling a Rapa Nui number, all local numbers are preceded by a "2", making them seven-digit numbers.

Laundry Lavandería Rapa Nui, on Te Pito O Te Henua s/n, near the church (Mon–Sat 9.30am–1pm & 4.30–7pm).

Pharmacy Farmacía Cruz Verde, Akamu Tekena s/n, opposite Tu'u Maheke (Mon–Sat 9am–1pm & 4.30–8pm).

Post office Te Pito O Te Henua s/n (Mon–Fri 9am–1pm & 3pm–6pm).

Shopping There are two crafts markets in town: Feria Municipal, at Tu'u Maheke at Atamu Tekena, and Mercado Artesanal, at Tu'u Koihu at Ara Roa Rakei; the latter is larger and better-stocked. Local crafts, and woodcarvings in particular, tend to be expensive; a cheaper option is to seek out the local jail (off Manutara, behind the airport), as local craftsmen sometimes outsource to inmates.

Surfing and diving Surfing schools near Playa Pea offer lessons to beginners, and Hare Orca, next to the Orca Diving Centre, rents surf- and boogie boards (CH$12,000/9000 for 3hr). The established and reputable Orca Diving Centre on the Caleta Hanga Roa (☎ 32 2550877 ⊛seemorca.cl) and Mike Rapu Diving Centre next door (☎ 32 2551055, ⊛mikerapu.cl) both offer day and night dives (CH$30,000–45,000), as well as introductory dives for complete beginners (CH$40,000).

OLD CITY, CARTAGENA

Colombia

HIGHLIGHTS

❶ **San Gil** The best white-water rafting in Colombia. **See p.510**

❷ **Cartagena's old city** Spain's most enduring architectural legacy in Latin America. **See p.517**

❸ **Parque Nacional Tayrona** A paradise of white sandy beaches and falling coconuts. **See p.528**

❹ **Providencia** Experience the unique Raizal culture on this tiny island. **See p.534**

❺ **La Zona Cafetera** Stay on an authentic coffee plantation and go hiking in the lovely Valle de Cócora. **See p.544 & p.547**

❻ **San Agustín** Ponder the mystery behind the Parque Arqueológico's curious statues. **See p.554**

HIGHLIGHTS ARE MARKED ON THE MAP ON P.487

ROUGH COSTS

Daily budget Basic US$50, occasional treat US$90

Drink Fresh fruit juice US$2

Food *Pargo frito con arroz con coco* (fried snapper with coconut rice) US$8

Hostel/budget hotel US$20/40

Travel Bogotá–Cartagena bus (663km; 19hr) US$75

FACT FILE

Population 46.3 million

Languages Spanish (official), plus various indigenous languages

Currency Colombian peso (C$ or COP$)

Capital Bogotá (population: 7.6 million)

International phone code ☎57

Time zone GMT -5hr

5

Introduction

Home to a traumatic but rich history, stunning scenery and some of the continent's most welcoming and sophisticated people, Colombia is a natural draw for travellers to South America. Despite its four-decade-long civil war and reputation for violence, improved security conditions have led to a sharp increase in tourism. Foreigners and Colombians alike are now far more able to explore this thrilling paradise of cloudforested mountains, palm-fringed beaches and gorgeous colonial cities. The only country in South America to border both the Pacific and the Caribbean, Colombia offers a huge range of ecosystems, from the Amazon rainforest near Leticia to the snowcapped mountains of the Sierra Nevada de Santa Marta and the tropical islands of San Andrés and Providencia.

Cosmopolitan **Bogotá** is, like most capitals, a busy commercial centre, with a vibrant cultural scene and festive nightlife. The two other major cities, **Medellín** and **Cali**, are also lively but less overwhelming. Better still are the small towns scattered throughout the country that could turn out to be the highlight of your visit. **Popayán** and **Mompox**, for example, are famed for raucous Semana Santa (Easter week) celebrations, and Mompox has a timeless beauty to it. Colombia's coffee-growing region, the **Zona Cafetera**, offers breathtaking walks

in the foothills where the bean is grown, accommodation in authentic *fincas* (coffee farms) and excellent trekking.

Most visitors make time – and rightfully so – to head north to the Caribbean for the sun. Just a stone's throw from the beach, the walled city of **Cartagena** is the biggest Spanish colonial port in South America. A few hours east, the less scenic **Santa Marta** and fishing village of **Taganga** are near **Parque Nacional Tayrona**, whose picturesque sandy beaches are unrivalled. The two are also great bases for a five-day trek to the archeological ruins of **La Ciudad Perdida**, the Lost City.

Almost un-Colombian in their feel, the remote Caribbean islands of **San Andrés** and **Providencia** both offer great diving, crystal-clear waters and – particularly in Providencia's case – a unique Raizal culture.

As you head north from Bogotá through the Andes to **Bucaramanga**, picturesque colonial villages like **Villa de Leyva** give way to more tropical, river-fed bastions of adventure tourism such as **San Gil**.

In the southeast, Colombia's stake of the Amazon, centred on **Leticia**, may not be as well known as Peru's or Brazil's but it offers a slice of jungle adventure and a gateway into the neighbouring countries. The southwest, near Popayán, boasts some wonderful scenery as well as the monumental stone statues and burial chambers of the forgotten cultures of **San Agustín** and **Tierradentro**.

WHEN TO VISIT

Colombia's proximity to the equator keeps regional **temperatures** stable throughout the year, around 24°C (75°F) along the coast and 7–17°C (45–63°F) as you move higher inland. However, **rainfall** does vary with the seasons. In the Andean region there are two dry and two wet seasons per year, the driest months being from December to March and July to August. In low-lying areas, especially southern Colombia, rainfall is more constant but showers never last very long. The Amazon climate is uniformly wet the entire year. Bear in mind that the most intense **tourist seasons**, with the highest prices, are from December to February and Semana Santa (Easter Week), the week before Easter.

CHRONOLOGY

10,000 BC Earliest evidence of human habitation at El Abra in present-day Bogotá.

1200 BC–1525 AD Indigenous cultures – including the Tayrona, Calima, Muisca, Quimbaya, Nariño and others – live scattered across the country.

700 AD The Tayrona build the Ciudad Perdida – their largest city.

1499 Alonso de Ojeda sets foot at Cabo de la Vela.

1525 Rodrigo de Bastidas establishes the first Spanish settlement in Santa Marta, kicking off the hunt for El Dorado.

1533 The Spanish found Cartagena.

1537–38 Spanish conquistador Gonzalo Jiménez de Quesada wrests power (and staggering amounts of gold and emeralds) from the native Chibchas and founds Santa Fe de Bogotá, now known simply as Bogotá.

1717 The Spanish consolidate their colonial holdings, creating the viceroyalty of Nueva Granada from the land now occupied by the independent nations of Colombia, Ecuador, Panama and Venezuela.

1819 Simón de Bolívar overthrows Spanish rule and founds Gran Colombia, comprised of Colombia, Ecuador, Venezuela and Panama. He becomes its first president, thus fulfilling his desire for a united, independent South America.

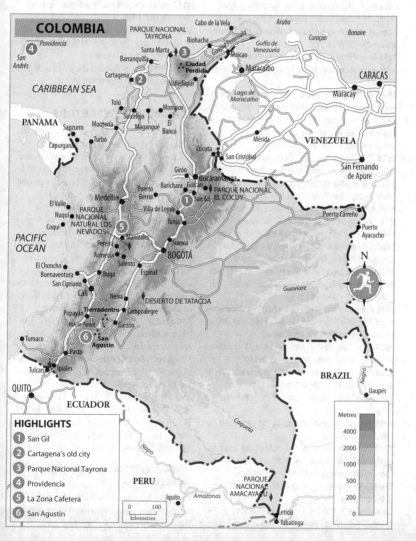

HIGHLIGHTS

1 San Gil
2 Cartagena's old city
3 Parque Nacional Tayrona
4 Providencia
5 La Zona Cafetera
6 San Agustín

5

1830 Ecuador and Venezuela secede from Gran Colombia. Bolívar dies in self-imposed exile in Santa Marta.

1853 Colombia adopts a constitution that includes a prohibition against slavery.

1886 Nueva Granada becomes the Republic of Colombia, after Christopher Columbus.

1899–1902 The War of a Thousand Days, the bloody three-year-long civil war born of escalated antagonism between the Conservative and Liberal political parties.

1903 With the support of the US Navy, Panama secedes from Colombia.

1948 The assassination of the working class's greatest advocate, Bogotá's populist mayor, Jorge Eliécer Gaitán, begins the massive rioting known as *El Bogotazo*, which catalyzes a decade of partisan bloodletting, *La Violencia*, leaving 200,000 dead.

1953 General Rojas Pinilla leads a military coup and begins negotiations to demobilize armed groups and restore peace and order.

1954 The group that would develop into Communist-linked Fuerzas Armadas Revolucionarios Colombianos (FARC) forms among the countryside peasants as a response to the violence and repression suffered by the rural population at the hands of the military.

1958 The Conservative and Liberal parties become a united National Front, agreeing to share power, with each party holding office alternately for four years.

1964 US-backed military attacks lead to violent clashes between the government and armed guerrilla groups. The leftist National Liberation Army (ELN) and Maoist People's Liberation Army (EPL) are founded and civil war erupts.

1982 Gabriel García Márquez wins the Nobel Prize in Literature. Pablo Escobar is elected as a Congress member.

1984 The government intensifies efforts to do away with drug cartels, as violence by narco-trafficker death squads and left-wing terrorists escalates.

1985 Members of radical leftist guerrilla group Movimiento 19 de Abril (M-19) take over the Palace of Justice, killing eleven judges and nearly a hundred civilians.

1986 Pope John Paul II visits Colombia. A grandiose cathedral is built in preparation in Chiquinquirá.

1990 Drug cartels declare war on the government after it signs an extradition treaty with the US.

1993 Drug kingpin Pablo Escobar is shot dead evading arrest.

1995 San Agustín and Tierradentro are recognized as UNESCO World Heritage Sites.

1999 Plan Colombia, aimed at tackling the country's cocaine production, is launched, with backing from the US. Spraying destroys coca fields and food crops alike.

2002 Álvaro Uribe Vélez is elected president on a platform of law and order.

2006 Around 20,000 AUC paramilitaries claim to disarm in return for lenient sentences for massacres and other human rights abuses. In practice, they reform as neo-paramilitary groups such as Los Rastrojos and the drug trafficking, murders and land grabbing continues.

2008 The US and Venezuela assist in a government-orchestrated operation to free high-profile kidnapping victims. French-Colombian presidential candidate Ingrid Betancourt, held hostage for six years, and fifteen other captives are liberated. FARC founder Manuel Marulanda dies.

2010 Following Uribe's failed attempt to run for a third term, former Defence Minister Juan Manuel Santos is elected president.

2011 Former leader of the M-19 guerrillas, Gustavo Petro, becomes mayor of Bogotá.

2012 The FARC announce that they shall no longer kidnap people. Negotiations between the FARC and the Colombian government commence in Cuba.

2013 FARC ceasefire ends in January, and some hostilities against the Colombian government resume.

ARRIVAL AND DEPARTURE

Colombia's biggest international **airport** is Bogatá's Aeropuerto Internacional El Dorado (ⓦwww.elnuevodorado.com). Direct services **from Europe** to Bogotá are offered by Iberia (Madrid and Barcelona), Air France/KLM (Paris), Avianca (Barcelona and Paris) and Lufthansa (Frankfurt). Avianca also operates flights from Madrid to Cali and Medellín.

In **North America**, Air Canada connects Toronto to Bogotá, Lan and American Airlines connect Bogotá with Miami, while Delta links Bogotá with New York, Chicago and Atlanta, and Jet Blue flies to Bogotá from Orlando and Fort Lauderdale. It's also possible to fly from Miami directly to Santa Marta, Cartagena and Medellín.

In **South and Central America**, Lan links Bogotá with Lima, Santiago and Quito; Copa offers regular flights from the capital to Panama City, and Tam links the capital to São Paulo. Avianca also flies to Buenos Aires, Caracas, Guayaquil, Lima, Mexico City, Panama City, Quito, Rio de Janeiro, Santiago (Chile) and São Paulo.

OVERLAND FROM ECUADOR AND VENEZUELA

Frequent bus services cross Colombia's borders into neighbouring Venezuela and Ecuador, though there can be security issues with both borders, so check in advance. Ormeño buses cover several international routes to and from Bogotá, including Quito, Caracas and Lima.

There are three main overland **border crossings** with Venezuela (see box, p.515), the most popular being Cúcuta–San Antonio/San Cristóbal. The **Maicao–Maracaibo** crossing at Paraguachón is useful if you are travelling directly to or from Colombia's Caribbean coast. Expreso Brasilia (wexpresobrasilia .com) operates a coastal bus service between Cartagena, via Barranquilla and Santa Marta, which passes through Maicao in the remote Guajira Peninsula to Maracaibo (1 daily at 7am; 20hr; COP$220,000).

The Panamerican Highway runs south into **Ecuador**, with the Ipiales–Tulcán crossing being the most popular and straightforward, though slow (see box, p.558).

There is no overland crossing between Colombia and Panama due to the presence of drug traffickers, paramilitaries and smugglers, and the threat of kidnapping in the Darién Gap.

BY BOAT TO/FROM BRAZIL, PERU AND PANAMA

From the Amazon region it's possible to cross to or from Colombia into Manaus, Brazil, and Iquitos, Peru, by taking a **riverboat** (see p.316).

From Cartagena, adventurous travellers with plenty of time on their hands can take a sailboat to Puerto Lindo or Colón in Panama via the remote tropical islands of the San Blas archipelago (see p.520). Trips take four to five days and cost around COP$750,000 per person. Rough seas can make travelling between November and February dangerous.

VISAS

A passport and onward ticket are the sole entry requirements for nationals of most of Western European countries, Canada, the US, Australia, New Zealand and South Africa.

Upon arrival, all visitors receive an entry stamp in their passports, usually for **sixty days**. You can request up to ninety days but this is rarely granted. Double-check the stamp straightaway for errors. Make sure you get an entry stamp if coming in overland and that you get a departure stamp upon exiting to avoid trouble.

Thirty-day extensions cost COP$72,350 and can be obtained at the former DAS (Departamento Administrativo de Seguridad) offices from the Ministerio de Relaciones Exteriores (wwww.cancilleria.gov.co). You'll need two passport photos with a white background, copies of your passport and entry stamp as well as the original, and an onward ticket.

GETTING AROUND

Colombia's generally reliable and numerous **buses** are your best bet for intercity travel, though increased competition between domestic airlines means that **air travel** is frequently only slightly more expensive than travel by bus and far faster and more comfortable.

BY BUS, PICK-UP TRUCK AND JEEP

With **buses**, the wide range of options in comfort and quality is compounded by the size and diversity of the country; it's a good idea to shop around at different companies' kiosks within larger stations. Generally, the larger, long-distance buses have reclining seats, toilets, loud cheesy music and videos; wear warm clothing as air conditioning is guaranteed to be arctic. Some recommended companies are: Expreso Bolívariano (wbolivariano .com.co), Expreso Brasilia (wexpreso brasilia.com), Expreso Palmira (wexpresopalmira.com.co), Berlinas (wwww.berlinasdelfonce.com), Copetran (wcopetran.com.co) and Flota Magdalena (wflotamagdalena.com), though different companies cover different parts of the country. Long-distance buses tend to stop at *requisas* (military checkpoints), sometimes at night; the soldiers sometimes search everyone's possessions and make everyone disembark and show their ID. Each city has a *terminal de buses* (bus terminal) where the intercity buses arrive; Bogotá has more than one.

5

For shorter trips, you're better off sacrificing comfort and price for speed by buying a ticket on a *buseta*, *colectivo* or any similarly sized minibus or minivan that departs when full. If you don't want to be waiting around for ages, don't hand over your luggage or pay unless you can see that a bus is nearly full and ready to depart.

In the coffee-growing areas in particular, the most common mode of transport is the hardy **Willy jeeps**, with two rows of seats in the covered interior and more passengers clinging to the back. These tend to be inexpensive, but the ride can be bumpy and you are squeezed in with mounds of luggage.

BY PLANE

There are more than half a dozen domestic airlines. Avianca (Ⓦavianca .com) serves the greatest number of domestic destinations. Copa (Ⓦcopaair .com), the second-largest airline, covers largely the same destinations and flies to San Andres. Satena (Ⓦsatena.com) offers flights to the Amazon, the Pacific coast and between San Andrés and Providencia.

Budget carrier EasyFly (Ⓦeasyfly.com.co) serves Bogotá, Barranquilla, Cartagena, Cúcuta, Medellín and Santa Marta; Lan (Ⓦlan.com) flies to all the major cities as well as smaller regional destinations, while new VivaColombia (Ⓦvivacolombia.co) is the only one to connect Medellín directly to Santa Marta.

Booking in advance doesn't necessarily guarantee a low fare (except during Semana Santa). A one-way fare between Santa Marta and Bogotá purchased a day – or a month – in advance costs about COP$120,000–155,000 (in high season).

ACCOMMODATION

Accommodation ranges considerably, but given the country's relative prosperity you'll be pleasantly surprised at the bargains available. **Backpacker hostels** are prolific, particularly in larger cities such as Bogotá, Medellín, Cali and Santa Marta, and prices start at around COP$19,000 for dorms and COP$43,000 for double rooms. Comfortable beds, shared kitchens, free wi-fi, book exchanges, laundry, cable TV

and stacks of DVDs are common, and hostels are often the best places to find out about local attractions; some rent bicycles and even horses. **Guesthouses** rarely cost more than COP$70,000 for a double room with private bathroom.

Camping is an option in some rural areas and national parks, particularly Parque Nacional Tayrona on the Caribbean coast and Parque Nacional Cocuy in the highlands. Be aware that many campsites don't have tents (or rent substandard ones), so it's best to bring your own if you plan to camp regularly. If you hike to the Ciudad Perdida (see p.529) you'll get to sleep in hammocks with mosquito nets.

In the coffee-growing region, you can stay on one of the stately **fincas**, coffee-growing plantations that have barely changed over the decades. Though these farms range from tiny to sleek, modernized operations, the majority are small estates that offer comfortable accommodation for a moderate price (COP$25,000–45,000 per room). Meals prepared from locally grown food as well as numerous outdoor activities, like farm tours and horseriding, are often included or available.

FOOD AND DRINK

Whether it's a platter full of starch or a suckling pig stuffed with rice, Colombian **food** is anything but light. Breakfast usually consists of *huevos pericos*, scrambled eggs with onion and tomatoes, accompanied by a fried maize pancake (*arepa*) stuffed with chopped pork, rice, potatoes and more. The midday *almuerzo* or *comida corriente* consists of soup, a main course and dessert. Dinners, after 6pm, also tend to involve meat or fish.

In Bogotá and other major cities there is an excellent array of Western and international cuisine.

LOCAL SPECIALITIES

Each region in Colombia has its own local speciality. The national dish is the *bandeja paisa* – an enormous platter of ground beef, chorizo, beans (*frijoles*), rice, fried banana (*plátano*), a fried egg, avocado and fried pork – usually found at inexpensive **market stalls** (*fondas*).

In rural areas, vegetarians will be hard-pressed for options, but in medium and large cities you can find a decent spread of vegetarian dishes.

Other Colombian favourites include *ajiaco* (a thick chicken stew replete with vegetables, maize, three types of potato, cream, capers and sometimes avocado), and *mazamorra* (a similar meat and vegetable soup but with beans and corn flour). Both are often served with *patacón*, a mashed and heavily salted cake of fried plantain.

More unusual regional specialities include *hormigas culonas* – fried giant ants, found in the Santander area. In Cali and southern Colombia, grilled guinea pig, known as *cuy* or *curí*, sometimes crops up on the menu. The coast is renowned for its fish and shellfish, served with aromatic *arroz con coco*, slightly sweet rice with caramelized coconut, while the Amazon is known for its unusual and delicious fish. The islands of San Andrés and Providencia specialize in locally caught crab dishes and lobster.

DRINKING

Though Colombia used to export its best **coffee**, demand from travellers has led to a proliferation of Juan Valdéz café branches; good coffee is now available in other establishments as well, though the majority of Colombians still drink heavily sugared, watered-down black coffee (*tinto*).

If there's one thing you'll pine for when you've returned home it's Colombia's exotic variety of **fresh fruit juices**. Some are completely foreign to Western palates and lack English translations. Worth trying are *guanábana*, *lulo*, mango, *feijoa*, *maracuyá*, *mora* and *guayaba*.

Beer is reasonably good and inexpensive (try light, fizzy lagers like Dorado, Club and Aguila). Far more popular among locals is the anise-flavoured *aguardiente*, pure grain alcohol, and rum (*ron*), both of which are drunk neat. Brave souls won't want to pass up any offer to try *chicha*, a frothy drink, often prepared with maize or yucca, found in rural areas and made with the fermenting enzyme found in saliva: pieces of the peeled root are chewed, spat into a bowl and the juice is left to ferment.

CULTURE AND ETIQUETTE

In Colombia you will notice a great disparity between the wealthiest members of society – who live a lifestyle akin to that of their counterparts in Europe's capitals – and the rest of the population: the poor city residents who live in dangerous neighbourhoods, and below them on the poverty scale the rural poor, particularly those who live in isolated areas where armed conflict still goes on.

When interacting with Colombians, Westerners will note that sincerity in expression, often expressed via good eye contact, is valued more highly than the typical steady stream of pleases and thank-yous.

TROPICAL FRUIT TREAT

Dotting the country's streets are vendors who will happily blend drinks for you from the juicy bounty in their baskets, either with milk (*con leche*), or the standard ice and sugar (*con agua*).

Corozo A round, maroon-skinned fruit, not unlike a cranberry in tartness.

Guanabaná Pulpy, yellow fruit that tastes like a mild guava, with a touch of grapefruit.

Lulo Resembling a vivid yellow persimmon, this tangy fruit is perfectly balanced sweetness and tartness.

Mora Close cousin of the blackberry.

Níspero This combination of pear and papaya is rich and musky, and goes really well with milk.

Tomate de árbol Literally, "tree tomato", this orange-red fruit blurs the line between fruit and vegetable, being sharp and only faintly sweet.

Zapote This luscious orange fruit's uncanny resemblance to sherbet is confirmed by the tendency of some locals to freeze its pulp to eat as dessert.

LOCAL SLANG

Colombians take much joy in their particular style of linguistic acrobatics and slang. Colombians freely convert verbs to nouns and vice versa, so take each word as a fluid concept.

Un camello (n), **camellar** (v) Work, or working. A good way to refer to a particularly trying task.

La/una chimba (adj) Used to describe a situation or thing that is wonderful. Roughly synonymous with the youthful American usage of "awesome". Variations include "Qué chimba!" ("Nice!").

Chucha (n) Body odour. A crass but still useable term.

Elegante (adj) "Cool", loosely. Used to describe the subset of cool things – or happenings – that's particularly classy, well executed or elegant. Think football passes or a good outfit. *Chevere* and *bacán* are other words for "cool".

Paila (adj) "That really sucks". Used in response to a comment or situation that's aggressively bad or heavy.

Perico (n) Cocaine. Regional translations include scrambled eggs, coffee with milk or (as here) a parakeet.

Al pelo (adj) Common response to a question like "How was your day?" that means "Good!" or "Perfect!"

Tipping ten percent at mid-range restaurants is the norm; some establishments will ask you if you'd like for the tip to be included when you ask for the bill, while some add it on automatically. For short taxi trips, round up to the nearest thousand pesos.

The **machismo** often ascribed to Latin American culture is present in Colombia, though a significant number (around 30 percent) of politicians and diplomats are female. The country's Catholic roots run quite deep and are apparent in sexual attitudes among both men and women, though there is some flexibility – and contradiction – in views toward gender and sexual orientation.

SPORTS AND OUTDOOR ACTIVITIES

Adrenaline junkies might hyperventilate when they discover Colombia. From almost every vantage point there's a snowcapped peak to climb, an untamed river to ride or some sunken coral reef to explore.

Colombia's waters are a good (and cheap) place to learn to **scuba dive**. All along its 3000km of coastline, but especially around Santa Marta and Taganga, and also on the islands of San Andres and Providencia – home to the world's third-largest barrier reef – operators offer week-long PADI certification courses for around

COP$650,000. Be sure to enquire about the reputation of dive operators before signing up, check their PADI or NAUI accreditation, the instructor-to-student ratio and ask for recommendations from other divers. Snorkelling is also particularly good on the islands.

There is a concentration of Class II–IV rapids among the many rivers in the *departamento* of Santander – three intersect near San Gil – that offer some spectacular challenges to **white-water rafting** enthusiasts (see p.510), while the river near San Agustin gives you a somewhat tamer ride.

Hiking in Colombia is second to none: there are demanding week-long adventures in Parque Nacional de Cocuy (see p.513), jungle treks to the spectacular ruins of Ciudad Perdida (see p.529), and shorter but no less attractive rambles around Manizales and Salento in coffee country.

Football is the national sport and Colombians have a reputation for being some of South America's most skilled players. **Cycling** is also a common passion – the mountainous land here is made for rugged biking – and Colombians regularly compete in the Tour de France.

COMMUNICATIONS

Sending a postcard or a **letter** abroad can be done for COP$5500–6500 from almost anywhere in the country, using the efficient 4-72 (ⓦ4-72.com.co).

COLOMBIA ON THE NET

Ⓦ **colombiareports.com** Latest news, sports, culture and travel in English.

Ⓦ **colombia.travel** Colombia's official tourism site, with plenty of photos, good background and some practical information.

Ⓗ hosteltrail.com/colombia Budget accommodation and local attractions.

Ⓦ **parquesnacionales.gov.co** Portal to Colombia's national parks.

Packages are best sent via private companies such as Avianca (Ⓦavincaexpress.com) and Deprisa (Ⓦdeprisa.com).

The three major **mobile phone** networks are Movistar, Claro and Tigo, and it's inexpensive to purchase a local mobile phone: a basic handset will set you back around COP$50,000–60,000; if you have an unlocked phone, a SIM card will set your back around COP$12,000, with around COP$5000 worth of credit, with top-up credits sold in every corner shop. However, it's cheapest to make **domestic long-distance calls** using the mobile phones in corner stores that buy minutes in bulk (look for the word "*minutos*"). Call centres (*telecentros*) allow you to make inexpensive calls both to local numbers and abroad, though Skype is by far the cheapest way to go, given the proliferation of free wi-fi.

Internet cafés can be found even in small towns (from COP$3000/hr), and free wi-fi spots are becoming easier to find.

CRIME AND SAFETY

Colombia today is far safer and more accessible than it has been in decades. That said, pockets of guerrilla activity remain in remote parts of the country, particularly the jungle – a haven for drug-running activities – both by the rebels and particularly by the paramilitary groups who have the tacit support of the government, and who have been criticized for using techniques as dirty as those employed by the rebels. The FARC have renounced **kidnappings** for financial or political ends, but it remains to be seen whether they'll remain true to their word. Although, reassuringly, tourists have not been targeted specifically in the country's civil war, **certain areas should still be avoided**, including the Chocó, parts of Nariño, Putumayo, Meta, Arauca and rural parts of Cauca. Most guerrilla/paramilitary activity is confined to rural areas near the border with Panama and Venezuela. However, it's imperative that you stay abreast of current events: for up-to-date travel advice check Ⓦwww.travel.state.gov or Ⓦwww.gov.uk/fco.

Violent crime does exist, particularly in poor neighbourhoods of the big cities, but visitors are far more likely to encounter pickpockets, so keep a sharp eye on your belongings. Beware of **scams** – such as criminals posing as plain-clothes policemen and asking to inspect your passport and money, allegedly in search of counterfeit notes, which they then confiscate. Counterfeit notes do exist, so ask locals how to identify them.

When out and about, take only as much cash as you need for the outing, and leave the rest (as well as your passport) in a safe in your lodgings. Always carry **a photocopy of your passport** with you – the main page and the page with your entry stamp. Local police have a mixed reputation for corruption.

Drugs are widely available in Colombia, cocaine and marijuana in particular. Possession of either is illegal and could result in a prison sentence, and being caught with drugs while trying to cross a border can have serious consequences. If you do decide to take drugs, be very careful: they are much stronger than in Europe and the US. Do not accept drinks, snacks or cigarettes from strangers as there have been reports of these being spiked with the tasteless and smell-free drug *burundanga,* or "zombie drug", that leaves victims conscious but incapacitated and susceptible to robbery and rape.

EMERGENCY NUMBERS

Police/ambulance/fire ☎123

HEALTH

Vaccinations against hepatitis A, hepatitis B and typhoid are strongly recommended and rabies should also be considered; consult a travel health clinic weeks in advance. Vaccinations against **yellow fever** are necessary if visiting coastal national parks; some countries, such as Australia and Brazil, will not let you into the country without a yellow fever certificate if you're travelling directly from Colombia. Insect-borne diseases such as **malaria** and **dengue fever** are present, particularly in the Amazonas, Chocó, Antioquia, Córdoba, Bolívar, Putomayo and Atlántico departments – bring plenty of mosquito repellent (50 percent DEET, unavailable in Colombia) and cover up with long sleeves and trousers. **Altitude sickness** (*soroche*) may affect travellers at altitudes over 2500m, including those flying directly to Bogotá – take time to acclimatize before continuing your journey, drink plenty of water and avoid alcohol.

Colombia offers some of the best healthcare in South America; all major cities have **hospitals**, while in rural areas healthcare is more difficult to come by. In the case of serious health issues, you may be transferred to a larger hospital with more specialized doctors and facilities.

INFORMATION AND MAPS

Despite the significant rise in tourism to Colombia in recent years, the practical information available at tourist offices is often rudimentary. Almost every town has a tourist office, although their staff often don't speak English, and hostels are often much more useful for gathering information.

In Colombia, the annually updated (Spanish only) *Guía de Rutas*, sold at

PUBLIC HOLIDAYS

January 1 New Year's Day (*Año Nuevo*)
January 6 Epiphany (*Día de los Reyes Magos*)
March 21 St Joseph's Day (Father's Day)
March or April Easter (*Semana Santa*)
May 1 Labour Day (*Día del Trabajo*)
May Ascension Day (the Monday six weeks and a day after Easter Sunday)
May/June Corpus Christi (the Monday nine weeks and a day after Easter Sunday)
June 29 Saint Peter and Saint Paul (*San Pedro y San Pablo*)
July 20 Independence Day
August 7 Battle of Boyacá
August 15 Assumption of the Virgin Mary (*Asunción de la Virgen*)
October 12 Columbus Day (*Día de la Raza*)
November 1 All Saints' Day (*Día de Todos los Santos*)
November 11 Independence of Cartagena
December 8 Immaculate Conception (*Inmaculada Concepción*)
December 25 Christmas Day (*Navidad*)

PLAN COLOMBIA

On August 7, 2010, **Juan Manuel Santos** was inaugurated as the fortieth president of Colombia, following a failed attempt by former President **Álvaro Uribe** to run for an unprecedented third term in office. Uribe was first elected in 2002 on a platform of law and order and turned to the US for help in dealing with the country's perpetual cycle of violence by tipping the military balance in their favour. Under **Plan Colombia**, the US has committed around US$7 billion in foreign aid, most of it to the military, to root out illegal drug trafficking and the guerrilla protectors that allow it to blossom. Largely intended to eradicate the growing of **coca**, Plan Colombia funded crop spraying on a large scale. Since the early 2000s coca production has declined dramatically – with the security situation improving as well – and Peru has now surpassed Colombia in coca production. However, coca farming has also adapted, for example by being planted in smaller areas, and the people who suffer the most from Plan Colombia have often been the impoverished farmers whose food crops have been sprayed alongside the coca plants and who have received no compensation from the Colombian government. Under Uribe drug-related crime declined and Santos has vowed to continue his predecessor's hardline **security** policies.

COLOMBIA'S FESTIVAL PLANNER

Colombia knows how to party and does so year-round. You can join in the following:

January *Carnaval de Blancos y Negros.* Pasto's un-PC celebrations dating back to the days of slavery, with revellers with whitened and blackened faces throwing chalk and flour over each other

February *Carnaval de Barranquilla.* Second-biggest carnival in South America, complete with parades, dancing, drinking and music, held forty days before Easter

March *Semana Santa.* Holy Week celebrated with nighttime processions by the faithful; particularly impressive in Popayán and Mompox

June/July *Rock al Parque.* Massive free thee-day pop/rock/funk/metal/reggae concert in Bogotá's Parque Simón Bolívar.

August *Feria de las Flores.* Medellín's big bash, culminating in a parade of peasants bearing flowers down from the mountains.

September *Festival Mundial de Salsa.* Cali's salsa festival, with the hottest moves on show at the Teatro al Aire Libre Los Cristales

November *Reinado Nacional de Belleza.* Cartagena crowns Miss Colombia amid parades, street dancing and music

December *Feria de Cali.* Epic street parties.

March 21 St Joseph's Day (Father's Day).

tollbooths and some tourist offices, has excellent maps, as well as potential road-trip routes and extensive local listings.

MONEY AND BANKS

Colombia's national currency is the **peso (COP)**, divided into 100 centavos. Coins are for 50, 100, 200, 500 and 1000 pesos and notes for 1000, 2000, 5000, 10,000, 20,000 and 50,000 pesos. At the time of writing, rates were: US$1=COP$1800; £1=COP$2700; €1=COP$2300.

Changing large notes can be problematic outside big cities.

ATMs are plentiful, with at least one even in small towns. For **changing money**, casas de cambio offer slightly better rates, have more flexible hours and provide quicker service than most banks. Travellers' cheques can also be exchanged at casas de cambios and banks, but few businesses accept them. Using moneychangers on the street is not recommended.

OPENING HOURS

Shops are open 8am until 6pm, Monday to Friday. Many businesses also often open on Saturdays until mid-afternoon. Outside Bogotá many businesses close at noon for a two- or three-hour siesta. Commercial hours in cities in warmer areas such as Cali often get started and end earlier. Government offices often follow the same pattern. Banks open around 9am and close at 4pm. Casas de cambio stay open later.

Bogotá and around

Colombia's capital, **BOGOTÁ**, is a city that divides opinion. Its detractors cite poverty, gridlock traffic and crime, as well as depressingly regular rain, and with 7.6 million tightly packed inhabitants and some decidedly drab neighbourhoods, Bogotá rarely elicits love at first sight. Given a day or two, however, most people do fall for this cosmopolitan place with its colonial architecture, numerous restaurants and raucous nightlife. Besides, love it or hate it, odds are you'll have to pass through it at some stage during your travels in Colombia.

Situated on the **Sabana de Bogotá**, Colombia's highest plateau at 2600m, the city was founded on August 6, 1538 by Gonzalo Jiménez de Quesada in what was a former citadel belonging to the Muisca king **Bacatá**, from whom the city's name is derived. For many years, Bogotá's population did not expand in step with its political influence, and even in the 1940s the city had just 300,000 inhabitants. That all changed in the second half of the twentieth century, thanks to industrialization and civil war, which prompted a mass exodus of peasants from rural areas who live in dire conditions in the slums on the southern approach to the city – in marked contrast to the affluent neighbourhoods in the northern part of town. Today, Bogotá is South America's fourth-largest city and home to one of the continent's most vibrant cultural scenes.

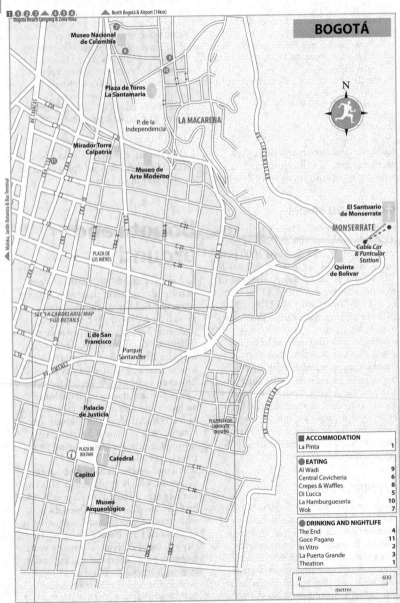

BOGOTÁ

North Bogotá & Airport (14km)
Bogota Beach Camping & Zona Rosa

Museo Nacional de Colombia

Plaza de Toros La Santamaria

P. de la Independencia

LA MACARENA

Mirador Torre Colpatria

Museo de Arte Moderno

El Santuario de Monserrate

MONSERRATE

Cable Car & Funicular Station

Quinta de Bolivar

PLAZA DE LOS NIEVES

SEE LA CANDELARIA MAP FOR DETAILS

I. de San Francisco

Parque Santander

Palacio de Justicia

PLAZOLETA DEL CHORRO DE QUEVEDO

PLAZA DE BOLÍVAR

Catedral

Capitol

Museo Arqueológico

Maloka, Jardin Botanico & Bus Terminal

N

ACCOMMODATION	
La Pinta	1

EATING	
Al Wadi	9
Central Cevicheria	6
Crepes & Waffles	8
Di Lucca	5
La Hamburgueseria	10
Wok	7

DRINKING AND NIGHTLIFE	
The End	4
Goce Pagano	11
In Vitro	2
La Puerta Grande	3
Theatron	1

0   400
metres

5

A WORD ON GETTING AROUND

Getting around Bogotá – and all Colombian cities for that matter – is facilitated by a foolproof **numbering system**, derived from the original Spanish grid layout, which makes finding an address virtually arithmetic. The names of the streets indicate their direction: **calles** (abbreviated C) run at right angles to the hills, from east to west, while **carreras** (abbreviated Cra) run from north to south. Addresses are a function of both, with the prefix indicating the cross street. For example, the address Cra 73 No. 12–20 can be found on Carrera 73 at number 20, between calles 12 and 12B. To make matters a little confusing, in La Candelaria, C 13 doesn't follow C 12; there are streets labelled 12 A–12 D in between.

WHAT TO SEE AND DO

The city's historic centre, **La Candelaria**, is full of colourfully painted colonial residences. It begins at Plaza de Bolívar and stretches northward to Avenida Jiménez de Quesada, and is bordered by Cra 10 to the west and the mountains to the east. **Downtown Bogotá** is the commercial centre, with office buildings and several museums, while **North Bogotá**, a catch-all term for the wealthier neighbourhoods to the north of the centre, offers stylish shopping districts and enough dining options to suit most palates and wallets.

Plaza de Bolívar

The heart of La Candelaria is the **Plaza de Bolívar**, awhirl with street vendors, llamas, pigeons and visitors; in the evenings, street-food carts set up shop by the cathedral. A pigeon-defiled statue of El Libertadór himself stands in the centre of the square, surrounded by monumental buildings in disparate architectural styles spanning more than four centuries, most covered with political graffiti.

On the west side of the cathedral stands the Neoclassical **Capitol**, where the Congress meets, with its imposing, colonnaded stone facade. On the plaza's north side is the modern **Palacio de Justicia**, which was reconstructed in 1999 after the original was damaged during the army's much-criticized storming of the building in 1985, in response to the M-19 guerrilla takeover, with more than a hundred people killed in the raid.

Every Friday from 5pm, Cra 7 is closed to traffic from Plaza de Bolívar all the way to C 26, and the streets fill with performers, food vendors and *cachacos* (Bogotá natives). The **Septimazo**, as it is called, is people-watching at its best.

Catedral

Looming over the Plaza de Bolívar, Bogotá's Neoclassical **Catedral** (Tues–Sun 9am–5pm; free; ⓦcatedraldebogota.org) allegedly stands on the site where the first Mass was celebrated in 1538. Rebuilt over the centuries after several collapses, it was completed in 1823, and while its interior is gold-laced, it's still relatively austere compared to the capital's other churches. You'll find the tomb of Jiménez de Quesada, Bogotá's founder, in the largest chapel.

Casa de Nariño

A couple of blocks south of Plaza de Bolívar, between Cra 7 and 8, is the heavily fortified presidential palace and compound, **Casa de Nariño** (ⓦwww .presidencia.gov.co), done in the style of Versailles. This is where President Santos currently lives and works. To take part in a guided visit (3–6 visits daily), book online – look for "Visitas Casa de Nariño" on the website. It's also possible to watch the ceremonial changing of the guard three times a week (Wed, Fri & Sun at 4pm) – best viewed from the east side of the palace.

Museo Botero

Housed in a fine colonial mansion surrounding a lush courtyard, the **Museo Botero** (C 11 No. 4–41; Mon–Sat 9am–7pm, Sun 10am–5pm; free; ⓦbanrepcultural.org/museo-botero) contains one of Latin America's largest collections of modern and Impressionist art, donated in 2000 by Colombia's most celebrated artist, Fernando Botero. There

5

are no fewer than 123 paintings and sculptures by Medellín-born Botero himself, which rather upset the residents of his home city. Botero's trademark is the often satirical depiction of plumpness – he claims to find curvy models more attractive than slim ones – and here you will find fatness in all its forms, from a chubby Mother Superior to rotund guerrilla fighters.

Also on display are works by Picasso, Miró, Monet, Renoir and Dalí, as well as a sculpture room featuring works by Henry Moore and Max Ernst.

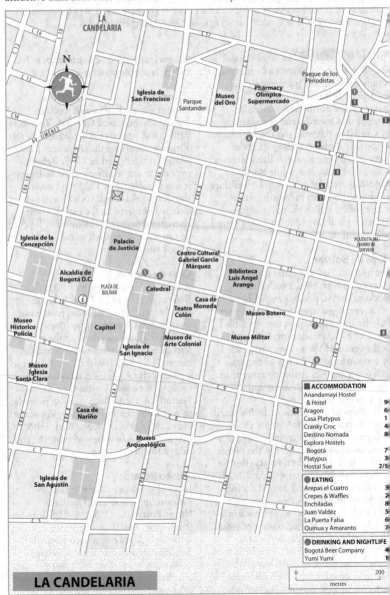

■ ACCOMMODATION	
Anandamayi Hostel & Hotel	9
Aragon	6
Casa Platypus	1
Cranky Croc	4
Destino Nomada	8
Explora Hostels Bogotá	7
Platypus	3
Hostal Sue	2/5

● EATING	
Arepas el Cuatro	3
Crepes & Waffles	2
Enchiladas	8
Juan Valdéz	5
La Puerta Falsa	6
Quinua y Amaranto	7

● DRINKING AND NIGHTLIFE	
Bogotá Beer Company	4
Yumi Yumi	1

LA CANDELARIA

0   200
metres

Casa de Moneda

The stone-built **Casa de Moneda**, or mint (C 11 No. 4–93; Mon–Sat 9am–7pm, Sun 10am–5pm; free; wwww .banrepcultural.org/museos-y-colleciones /casa-de-la-moneda), is home to the **Colección Numismática**, its displays chronicling the history of money in Colombia from the barter systems of indigenous communities to the design and production of modern banknotes and coins. Ramps lead to the **Colección de Arte**, featuring a permanent exhibition of works owned by the Banco de la República. The predominant focus here is on contemporary Colombian artists, but the pieces on display range from seventeenth-century religious art through to modern canvases by twentieth-century painters. Behind the permanent collection is the **Museo de Arte**, a modern, airy building that houses free, temporary exhibitions of edgy art, photography and challenging installations.

Museo de Arte Colonial

Set around a beautiful, leafy courtyard, the **Museo de Arte Colonial** (Cra 6 No. 9–77; Tues–Fri 9am–5pm, Sat & Sun 10am–4pm; COP$3000) displays fine colonial-era religious and portrait art, as well as sculptures and furniture. A highlight is the exhibition about the life and work of seventeenth-century Baroque painter Gregorio Vásquez de Arce y Ceballos.

Museo Histórico Policía

Friendly young English-speaking police offer free guided tours of the Museo Histórica Policía (C 9 No. 9–27; Tues–Sun 8am–5pm; free), which are really worthwhile just to hear about their experiences. The basement is largely given over to a display on the notorious 499-day police hunt for drug lord Pablo Escobar, and includes his Bernadelli pistol, also known as his "second wife", and there's a great view across the city from the roof.

Museo Militar

Run by the military, the **Museo Militar** (C 10 No. 4–92; Tues–Sun 9am–4pm; free) showcases weaponry through the ages, jaunty military uniforms, model battleships, anti-aircraft guns and other articles relating to the art of war. You need ID to enter.

Plazoleta del Chorro de Quevedo

Nowhere is La Candelaria's grittier, bohemian side better captured than on the streets surrounding the **Plazoleta del Chorro de Quevedo** (C 12 B and Cra 2). The tiny plaza is said to be the site of the first Spanish settlement, though the tiled-roof colonial chapel on the southwest corner was built much later.

THE CHURCHES OF LA CANDELARIA

In addition to its cathedral, La Candelaria is teeming with some of the best-preserved colonial-era **churches and convents** found in Latin America:

Museo Iglesia de Santa Clara Cra 8 No. 8–91 (Mon–Fri 9am–5pm, Sat & Sun 10am–4pm; COP$3000; wwww.museo iglesiasantaclara.gov.co). Overlooking Palacio Nariño, the austere exterior, built in the early part of the seventeenth century and formerly part of the convent of Clarissa nuns, contrasts sharply with its opulent gold-plated interior and Day of the Dead-looking anaemic Christ.

Iglesia de San Francisco Cra 7 at Av Jiménez (Mon–Fri 6am–7pm, Sat & Sun 7am–1pm; free; wwww .templodesanfrancisco.com). Across from the Gold Museum, San Francisco is appropriately noted for its particularly splendid golden altar.

Iglesia de la Concepción C 10 No. 9–50 (Mon–Sat 8am–6pm, Sun 6.30am–1pm; free). The soaring vault here is a fine example of the Moorish-influenced Mudéjar style popular in the sixteenth century.

Iglesia de San Ignacio C 10 No. 6–35 (Mon–Sat, 9am–4.30pm, Sun 11am–1pm; free). The largest and most impressive of the colonial-era churches is the domed San Ignacio founded in 1610 as the first Jesuit church in Nueva Granada.

5

Monserrate

Perched above La Candelaria is the rocky outcrop that is one of Bogotá's most recognizable landmarks: **Cerro de Monserrate**. The hilltop, crowned by **El Santuario de Monserrate** church, offers spectacular views back down on the seemingly endless urban sprawl that is Bogotá. It is easily reached by the frequent *teleférico* cable car (Mon–Sat noon–midnight, Sun 9am–5pm; COP$15,400 before 5.30pm, COP$17,000 after, Sun COP$9000; ⓦwww.cerromonserrate .com) or by funicular railway (Mon–Sat 7.45am–11.45pm, Sun 6am–6.30pm; prices same as *teleférico*). Alternatively, it's a ninety-minute trek up the 1500-step stone path that begins at the base of the hill and leads to the summit 600m above.

Be aware that there are reports of **robberies** both on the way up the hill and on the walk between the Quinta and its base. The safest (and cheapest) time to go is Sunday, when you'll be accompanied by thousands of pilgrims hoping for miracles from the church's dark-skinned Christ.

Quinta de Bolívar

At the foot of Monserrate is the **Quinta de Bolívar** (C 20 No. 2–91 Este; Tues–Fri 9am–5pm, Sat & Sun 10am–4pm; COP$3000, audioguide COP$1000), a spacious colonial mansion with beautiful gardens where Simón Bolívar lived sporadically between 1820 and 1829. The informative museum retells the story of Bolívar's final, desperate days in power before being banished by his political rivals, in a collection that includes a plethora of Bolívar paraphernalia including his military medals, billiard table and bedpan. One object you won't see here is the sword El Libertadór used to free the continent from four centuries of Spanish rule. It was stolen in 1974 from the collection in the now legendary debut of urban guerrilla group **M-19**. When they handed in their arsenal in 1991, the sword was quickly shuttled into the vaults of the Banco República.

Museo del Oro

On the northeastern corner of Parque de Santander, at Cra 6 and C 16, is Bogotá's must-see **Museo del Oro**, or Gold Museum (Tues–Sat 9am–6pm, Sun 10am–4pm; COP$3000, Sun free; ⓦwww.banrepcultural.org/museo-del-oro). The world's largest collection of gold ornaments, some 55,000 pieces strong, is spread out over three floors, with extensive displays on Colombia's indigenous cultures, cosmology and symbolism, techniques used in working with gold, and a region-by-region breakdown of the use of various pieces. Note the recurring symbolism of animals (jaguars, birds, monkeys, human/animal hybrids), the very fine filigree earrings, gold offerings used in rituals and elaborate ornamentation worn by chieftains and those who communed with deities. Free one-hour tours in Spanish and English take place from Tuesday to Saturday at 11am and 4pm, respectively.

Museo Nacional de Colombia

Inside a fortress-like building, the **Museo Nacional de Colombia** (Cra 7, at C 28; Tues–Sat 10am–6pm, Sun 10am–5pm; free; ⓦwww.museonacional.gov.co) provides a detailed chronological look at the country's tumultuous history. The converted jailhouse's most impressive exhibits relate to the conquest and the origins of the beguiling El Dorado myth that so obsessed Europe. The second floor houses an extensive collection of paintings by modern Colombian artists, including Fernando Botero, while on the third floor, don't miss the exhibit on Jorge Gaitán, the populist leader assassinated in 1948. Descriptions are in Spanish only, but you can pick up English-language placards.

Mirador Torre Colpatria

Fantastic 360-degree views can be had from the **Mirador Torre Colpatria** (Cra 7, No. 24–89; Fri 6–9pm, Sat & Sun 11am–5pm; COP$3500), Colombia's tallest skyscraper (162m). Here you can catch a glimpse of the **Plaza de Toros La Santamaría**, the Moorish-style bullring where the Temporadas Taurinas (bullfights) take place each January and February.

5

BOGOTÁ FESTIVALS

Colombia's capital has no shortage of festivals. The year begins with the **Bogotá Feria Taurina** (bullfighting festival; Jan–Feb), with matadors from Spain and Mexico flown in for the occasion, while **Semana Santa** (Holy Week; March or April) brings processions, re-enactments and religious pomp. Every other year around Holy Week the city also hosts the **Ibero-American Theater Festival**, one of the continent's biggest festivals of theatre, a fortnight of international performing art and street processions. Perhaps the highlight of the annual calendar is **Rock al Parque** (Rock in the Park; June/July; ⑩ rockalparque.com.co), South America's biggest rock music festival, which lasts three days, before the **Festival de Verano** (summer festival; Aug) to commemorate Bogotá's founding and **Salsa al Parque** (Salsa in the Park; Aug) heats things up. September heralds the **Festival de Jazz** at the *Teatro Libre*, followed by the **Festival de Cine** (film festival; Oct), which includes open-air screenings. Soon after that, the city begins gearing up for a truly South American **Christmas**.

Museo de Arte Moderno

The **Museo de Arte Moderno** (C 24, at Cra 6; Tues–Sat 10am–6pm & Sun noon–5pm; COP$4000; ⑩ www .mambogota.com) has the largest collection of contemporary Colombian art in the country, running the gamut from photography and painting to sculpture and graffiti. Frequently changing exhibits tend to focus on Latin American artists, such as the psychedelic works of Jairo Maldonado. There's also a bookshop and a *cinemateca* that projects art films on weekends between 3 and 5pm.

ARRIVAL AND DEPARTURE

By plane Most international flights land at El Dorado International Airport (⑩ www.elnuevodorado.com), 14km northwest of the city centre, currently being rebuilt, though some domestic flights use the Puente Aéreo terminal, 1km from the international one. A taxi downtown costs around COP$20,000; buy a ticket at one of the authorized stands and make sure the taxi meter is turned on. Bus rides into town cost COP$1500 and can take about an hour (do not attempt if you have a lot of luggage). The airport is served by the following domestic airlines: Avianca, Copa, EasyFly, LAN and Satena.

Destinations There are multiple flights daily to Bucaramanga (1hr); Cali (1hr); Cartagena (1hr 20min); Leticia (1hr 50min); Manizales (50min); Medellín (40min); Pasto (1hr 30min); Pereira (50min); Popayán (1hr 15min); San Andres (2hr); Santa Marta (1hr 30min). International routes include: Buenos Aires (6hr); Caracas (2hr); Frankfurt (10hr); Guayaquil (1hr 50min); Lima (3hr); Santiago (6hr); São Paulo (5hr).

By bus The huge long-distance bus terminal, Terminal de Transporte (Diagonal 23 No. 69–60, off Av de la Constitución; ⑪ 1 423 3600, ⑩ terminaldetransporte.gov.co), is around 5km southwest of the city centre. It's divided into five hubs, three of them colour-coded, roughly serving destinations north (No.3; red), south (No. 1; yellow), east and west of the city and international departures (No. 2; blue). A taxi to the centre costs about COP$12,000. You can also get into town by hailing any *buseta* from Cra 10 between C 17 and 26, marked "Terminal" (COP$1500).

Destinations from No. 1 (yellow) Cali (hourly; 8–10hr); Medellín (hourly; 8–9hr); Pasto (8 daily; 18–20hr); Pereira (hourly; 7–9hr); Popayán (7 daily; 12–16hr); San Agustin (11 daily; 9–10hr).

Destinations from No. 2 (blue) Domestic: Cali (hourly; 10hr); Cartagena (14 daily; 12–19hr); Manizales (10 daily; 18hr); Medellín (hourly; 8–9hr); Popayán (7 daily; 12–16hr); Santa Marta (11 daily; 16–18hr). International: Buenos Aires (Tues & Sun; 6 days); Caracas (Thurs; 32hr); Lima (Tues & Sun; 2.5 days); Quito (Tues & Sun; 28hr); Santiago (Tues & Sun; 5 days).

Destinations from No. 3 (red) Cartagena (14 daily; 12–19hr); Cúcuta (several daily; 15–16hr); Manizales (10 daily; 8–9hr); San Gil (3 daily; 6–7hr); Santa Marta (11 daily; 16–18hr); Villa de Leyva (4 daily; 4hr).

INFORMATION

Tourist information Bogotá's tourist bureau produces city maps complete with Transmilenio bus routes. The most useful *Puntos de Información Turística* are at the airport, bus station and the southwest corner of Plaza Bolívar at Cra 8 No. 10–65 (Mon–Sat 8am–6pm, Sun 10am–4pm; ⑪ 1 283 7115).

National park information For up-to-date safety information on Colombia's 51 national parks and protected areas, visit the ecotourism office of Unidad de Parques Nacionales at Cra 10 No. 20–34 (Mon–Fri 8am–5.30pm; ⑪ 1 353 2400, ⑩ parquesnacionales.gov.co).

Publications Pick up a copy of *Plan B* (⑩ planb.com.co) – a monthly what's-on publication. On Fri, Bogotá's leading newspaper, *El Tiempo*, publishes *Qué Hacer*, a weekend entertainment guide. The monthly free English-language *The City Paper* (⑩ thecitypaperbogota.com) is also a useful resource.

GETTING AROUND

Most of Bogotá's attractions are in or near La Candelaria and can be reached on foot (unless you're staying uptown). **Buses** Besides the chaotic minibuses, Bogotá is covered by an extensive, efficient and ever-spreading bus system called TransMilenio (Mon–Sat 5am–11pm, Sun 10am–6pm), with a flat fare of COP$1400 (COP$1700 during rush hour) per journey; buy a card to be loaded up with credit at any of the stations and pick up a bus route map from the tourist office. Bus lines are a little confusing, as some express buses miss out a number of stops. The most useful routes include the J buses, which run to Candelaria (otherwise change at Jiménez), and the B lines running north-south along Av Carcas to Portal del Norte via the Zona Rosa. Best avoided during rush hour.

Taxis Taxis in Bogotá are yellow, small and relatively inexpensive. Fares correspond to the number of units on the taxi meter, with a small surcharge levied between 7pm and 7am, on Sun and holidays; ask the driver to turn the taxi meter on and check the fare table as some drivers overcharge. It's safer to call a taxi company rather than grab one off the street; you'll need to give the driver the passcode – the last two digits of the phone number you call from. Try Radio Taxi (☎ 1 288 8888), Taxi Real (☎ 1 333 3333) or Taxi Express (☎ 1 411 1111).

ACCOMMODATION

Most budget accommodation is concentrated in La Candelaria; all accommodation reviewed apart from one hostel is in La Candelaria. All offer free internet and/or wi-fi. Most have private rooms with either shared or private bathrooms; prices below are for doubles with shared bathroom in high season (single rooms are often around two-thirds the price of a double).

Anandamayi Hostel & Hotel C 9 No. 2–81 ☎ 1 341 7208, ⓦ anandamayihostel.com; map p.498. This hostel is pure Zen, set in a restored colonial house around three flower-filled, hammock-strung courtyards frequented by hummingbirds. Rustic dorms and private rooms come with lockers, and shared bathrooms have spacious stone showers. At night, guests gather around the woodfire stove in the communal kitchen. Dorms COP$30,000, doubles COP$140,000

Aragon Cra 3 No. 14–13, La Candelaria ☎ 1 342 5239; map p.498. While this bare-bones hotel has zero atmosphere, the warm rooms with shared bathrooms are clean, most have wi-fi access and cost far less than their youth hostel equivalent. Singles COP$25,000, doubles COP$40,000

Cranky Croc C 12D No. 3–46 ☎ 1 342 2438, ⓦ crankycroc .com; map p.498. A friendly, Australian-owned place with sparklingly clean dorms, basic rooms around a courtyard, a well-equipped shared kitchen, Fri-night barbecue and daily group outings. Free wi-fi plus computer terminals. Dorms COP$23,000, doubles COP$66,000

Destino Nomada C 11 No. 00–38 ☎ 1 352 0932, ⓦ destinonomada.com; map p.498. This hostel is guaranteed to leave you breathless (thanks to the uphill walk). A compact place with guest kitchen and plenty to occupy you on those rainy Bogotá nights: small bar/pizza place, table football, TV lounge, and the on-site tour desk helps you plan your time. Dorms COP$21,000, doubles COP$57,000

★ **Explora Hostels Bogotá** C 12C No. 3–19 ☎ 1 282 9320, ⓦ explorahostels.com; map p.498. An unassuming exterior hides this appealing hostel with an indoor hammock-festooned common space, café that cooks up breakfast and bar with nightly happy hour. The colourful, spacious rooms face the covered courtyard and dorms feature nice touches such as large lockers and individual reading lights. Dorms COP$19,000, rooms COP$65,000

La Pinta C 65 No. 5–67 ☎ 1 211 9526, ⓦ www.lapinta .com.co; map p.496. If you want to be closer to the night-life, then this wonderfully friendly hostel (complete with two labradors) on the outskirts of the Zona Rosa is a safe bet. Bunks and rooms are comfortable (though don't expect to get much sleep on weekends), a good breakfast is thrown in, and while the hostel's a 15min walk from the

---

BOGOTÁ TOURS

The cheapest way to tour the city is to devise a self-guided **bus** tour. For the price of a single Transmilenio ticket, you can ride the buses for as long as you like as long as you don't leave the stations. The contrast between the likes of wealthy Zona Rosa in the north of the city and the poverty-stricken slums in the south are very much indicative of the great disparity between Colombia's wealthiest and poorest citizens.

Bogotá Graffiti Tour ☎ 321 297 4075, ⓦ bogota graffiti.com. This excellent three-hour walking tour takes in Bogotá's not inconsiderable collection of street art on Tues, Thurs and Sat (COP$4000); reserve ahead.
Cycling Every Sun morning (until 2pm), there is much good-natured fun to be had as many of Bogotá's

main roads close to traffic in a civic attempt to get people cycling, known as *Ciclovía*. Bogotá Bike Tours rents bikes (Cra 3 No. 12–72; COP$18,000/30,000 per half/full day; ☎ 1 281 9924, ⓦ www.bogotabiketours .com), and runs informative guided tours of the city (COP$30,000, 4hr approx).

★ TREAT YOURSELF

Casa Platypus C 12F No 28, La Candelaria ☎ 1 281 1801, ⓦ casaplatypus.wix.com; map p.498. Located in a beautiful colonial house overlooking Parque de los Periodistas, *Casa Platypus* (same owner as the hostel *Platypus*) combines many of the comforts of a boutique hotel with backpacker-friendly facilities. Rooms are compact but stylish and there's a huge dining room/lounge where a hefty breakfast including fresh fruit and juice, eggs, granola and yoghurt is served up (included in room rate). Add to this a roof terrace, upscale communal kitchen, free coffee, wi-fi and public computers, cold beers on an honour system plus all the information and friendly advice that an independent traveller could hope for from super-knowledgeable owner Germán, and you really do have the best of both worlds. Dorms COP$40,000, doubles COP$150,000

nearest Transmilenio stop, regular minibuses along Cra 7 connect it to La Candelaria. Dorms COP$24,000, doubles COP$90,000

Platypus C 12F No. 2–43, La Candelaria ☎ 1 341 3104, ⓦ platypusbogota.com; map p.498. An institution, mostly because the English/French/German-speaking owner Germán warmly shares knowledge of Colombia accumulated from extensive travels. Comfortable shared and private rooms with kitchen facilities. Dorms COP$22,000, doubles COP$44,000

Hostal Sue C 12F No. 2–55 ☎ 1 334 8494, ⓦ suecandelaria.com; map p.498. This well-maintained hostel with a party vibe has just about everything a backpacker could want: neat dorms, three doubles with TVs, on-site bar, bean-bag-stacked TV lounge, kitchen, free coffee, laundry service, ping-pong table and regular pub crawls. Has a second location in La Candelaria at Cra 3 No. 12C–18 (☎ 1 341 2647). Dorms COP$22,000, doubles COP$60,000

EATING

While the traditional highlander diet consists of meat and starch, middle-class *cachacos* prefer the same cosmopolitan cuisine as their counterparts in London or New York. Bogotá has four main restaurant zones, from south to north: gritty La Candelaria; yuppie La Macarena (Cra 4 between calles 23 & 28); gay-friendly Chapinero, also called the "G-Zone" (between calles 58 & 72 and carreras 8 & 7); and upmarket Zona Rosa (concentrated in the "T Zone" at C 82 and Cra 12).

Al Wadi C 27 No. 4A–14, La Macarena; map p.498. A compact, cave-like Middle Eastern place serving heaped plates of falafel and moussaka with the trimmings, as well as shwarma and good, tooth-achingly sweet baklava for dessert. Mains COP$15,000. Daily noon–10pm.

Arepas el Cuatro Cra 4 just off Parque de los Periodistas; map p.496. This bare-bones café also has a hole-in-the-wall selling excellent *arepas* with delicious shredded meat (COP$3500) or cheese (COP$1900). Be sure to season yours with some spicy *ají* sauce from the counter. Open until midnight, and great for soaking up that one beer too many.

Central Cevicheria Cra 14 No. 85–14, Zona Rosa; map p.496. Look no further to sate your cravings for fish and seafood – be it laced with spicy sauce or cut into thin *tiradito* slices. Busy and popular, it also serves cooked mains such as prawn curry. Expensive, but so, so worth it. Ceviche from COP$17,000. Daily noon–10pm.

Crepes & Waffles Av Jimenez No. 4–55; map p.498; Cra 12 No. 83–40 in the Zona Rosa; map p.496; and more than 30 other city outlets ⓦ www.crepesywaffles.com. A hugely popular chain restaurant that fulfils every savoury and sweet craving with a monster menu of crêpes and waffles, plus naughty ice-cream sundaes. Savoury crêpes COP$9500–30,000, sweet treats start at $4500.

Di Lucca Cra 13 No. 85–33, Zona Rosa; map p.496. Munch on wood-fired pizzas, home-made pasta and expertly cooked risotto at this smart Italian restaurant. Given its trendy Zona Rosa location, the prices are extremely good value and dishes such as sepia pasta with seafood sauce stand out. Mains from COP$17,000. Daily noon–10pm.

Enchiladas C 10 No. 2–12, La Candelaria; map p.498. Tuck into enchiladas, burritos and other Mexican staples at this colourful spot festooned with Day of the Dead paraphernalia and black-and-white film photos. The home-made salsas have a real kick to them and the *sopa de tortilla* really hits the spot. Mains from COP$12,000. Sun & Mon noon–5pm, Tues–Sat noon–10pm.

La Hamburgueseria Cra 4A No. 27–27, La Macarena ⓦ www.lahamburgueseria.com; map p.496. This great little chain offers international takes on gourmet hamburgers: think Greek, Italian, Thai… Choose from five home-made sauces and relishes to complement the glorious patty. Burgers from COP$12,000. Daily noon–11pm.

Juan Valdéz Cra 7 at C 11, La Candelaria; map p.498. Colombia's answer to Starbucks, with good hot and cold caffeine offerings, muffins, sandwiches and more. Be prepared to pay top dollar for it, though. Also has wi-fi. Coffees COP$5000. Mon–Sat 9am–8pm, Sun until 5pm.

La Puerta Falsa C 11 No. 6–50, La Candelaria; map p.498. This is where the good citizens of Bogotá come for snacks such as *chocolate completo* (hot chocolate with cheese and bread) and colourful sweets that beckon you through the window. Snacks COP$2000. Daily 11am–5pm.

5

★ **Quinua y Amaranto** C 11 No. 2–95, La Candelaria; map p.498. A tiny place with an open kitchen and delicious, largely organic and vegetarian set lunches (COP$13,000). Sample dishes include black bean soup and mushroom risotto. Also sells wholewheat *empanadas*, bread, eggs and coffee. Tues–Fri 8am–7.30pm, Mon & Sat 8am–4pm.

Wok Cra 13 No. 82–74, Zona Rosa, also next to the Museo Nacional ⊕ www.wok.com.co; map p.496. This chain of trendy restaurants has all-white modern decor and a menu that was clearly constructed by someone who knows about Asian food. Choose from heaped noodle salads, Thai curry, sushi, tempura and much more. The shrimp speared on sugar-cane stalks with Vietnamese dipping sauce are seriously tasty and the lemonade is among the best in town. Spice fans should ask for extra chilli. Mains start around COP$17,000.

DRINKING AND NIGHTLIFE

Rumbear, literally to dance the rumba, is how locals refer to a night's partying, which invariably involves heavy doses of dancing. Bars and discos in La Candelaria attract a somewhat bohemian, often studenty crowd, while their fluorescent-lit counterparts in the Zona Rosa in North Bogotá (around C 83 and Cra 13) appeal to the city's beautiful people. Virtually everywhere shuts down at 3am. Take taxis to and from your destination.

Bogotá Beer Company C 12D No. 4–02, La Candelaria; map p.498; Cra 12 No. 83–33, Zona Rosa ⊕ bogotaeer company.com. Artisan brews including stout and wheat beer, served in bottles and on tap, fourteen seasonal microbrews, plus excellent pub grub to soak them up. One of the few places that is busy even on a Mon night. Daily noon–2am.

The End Aparte Suites Tequendema, Cra 10 No. 27–51; map p.496. After all the clubs close and Bogotá's night owls go home, *The End* (aka Piso 30) is where the after-party continues until past sunrise. With great views of the city from its 30th-floor location, this spot attracts a diverse crowd. Fri & Sat 8pm–very, very late.

Goce Pagano Cra 13A No. 23–97, Downtown; map p.496. Less is more in this divey watering hole, which has a simple dancefloor and Bogotá's largest rack of golden-era salsa LPs. Owner Gustavo is a throwback to the era when the revolution was fought listening to salsa; you won't forget your visit. Take a taxi as the area is unsafe at night. Thurs–Sat only.

In Vitro C 59 No. 6–38 ⊕ www.invitrobar.com; map p.496. Popular with local students, this aquamarine-lit lounge changes moods with the hour, from quiet cocktail bar early on to late-night dance joint embracing diverse musical styles on different days of the week, including electronica on Thurs and salsa on Fri. Shows locally produced short films on Tues & Wed.

La Puerta Grande Cra 12 No. 93–64, Zona Rosa; ⊕ www .lapuertagrande.net; map p.496. With different Spanish themes throughout, this eclectic venue is a restaurant serving excellent traditional tapas with DJ/live music areas scattered throughout. Wed is live flamenco night, Thurs is live rock, and DJs hit the decks on the weekend. Cover COP$16,000. Mon–Sat noon–3am, Sun noon–5pm.

Theatron C 58 No. 10–42, Chapinero ⊕ www.theatron depelicula.com; map p.496. A neon-lit wonderland, this colossal gay club is spread over three floors and six rooms, some of which are men only. Also hosts live shows, which attract a mixed audience. The COP$25,000 cover charge on Sat night gets you a cup and access to an open bar (until 2am).

Yumi Yumi Cra 3A No. 16–40; map p.498. A pint-sized cocktail bar on Parque de Los Periodistas offering delicious but potent drinks. Try the coconut mojito or the *maracuyá caipiroska*. Dangerously, cocktails are always 2-for-1 (around COP$16,000). Also does food until 9pm, including chunky imaginative sandwiches and cheap, tasty Thai curry on Tues & Wed. Has a second (more expensive) branch in the Zona Rosa on the corner of Cra 13 and C 84.

★ **TREAT YOURSELF**

Andrés Carne de Res C 3 No. 11A–56, Chía ⊕ andrescarnederes.com. Suburban legend *Andrés Carne de Res* must be seen to be believed. A 1000-capacity restaurant and salsa club that looks like something from a Tim Burton film, it is the biggest all-singing, all-dancing party in the Colombian capital. The four floors (Hell, Earth, Purgatory and Heaven, the last with large roof terrace) are decked out in a kind of gothic burlesque, with live salsa music and staff dressed as circus performers and coquettish chambermaids who parade around dragging non-dancers to their feet. The menu is 62 pages long and features no fewer than nine pages of alcoholic drinks as well as countless eating options, such as the steaks they are famous for. There's live music, and the party runs until 3am Fri & Sat (cover COP$20,000), finishing a bit earlier the rest of the week (COP$10,000 after 10pm Thurs). The location is far out – 23km north of the city, and if you don't want to splurge on a taxi (around COP$190,000 return, including waiting time), many hostels run party buses to Andrés on Saturday nights; for COP$50,000, you get the transport there and back and booze along the way. For those who can't make it to the original and best, there's a more sedate version at C 82 No. 12–21, Zona Rosa.

SHOPPING

Artesanías de Colombia Cra 2 No. 18A–58 🌐 artesanias decolombia.com.co. Not cheap, but has beautiful, high-quality handicrafts and jewellery from all over Colombia that's far nicer than the tat you'll find in the tourist traps around the Museo del Oro. Two other branches in north Bogotá.

Authors C 70 No. 7–53 🌐 authors.com.co. A bookshop with a café and two floors of English-language books. Daily 10am–8pm (until 6pm Sun).

Flea markets Some gems to discover amid the more rough-and-ready Sun flea markets at Parque de los Periodistas and Mercado de San Alejo on Cra 7 (between calles 24 & 26), where you can find anything from a secondhand tuba to clothes and souvenirs.

Paloquemao C 19 & Cra 24. The largest and most bustling market in the city, where you can stock up on supplies to cook at your hostel. Fantastic veg and tropical fruit, a somewhat gory meat section and plenty of dry goods. Tues and Fri are when the flower-sellers show up: get there by about 8am to catch the best of their displays. It's safe enough to take a camera if you are sensible with it: be discreet and ask permission before taking photos of people.

DIRECTORY

Banks and exchange ATMs are available throughout the city – along Cra 2A in La Candelaria and all over the Zona Rosa. Currency exchanges are found at most hotels, the airport, and on Cra 2A, right near the Museo de Oro.

Embassies Australia, C 69 No. 7–51, Apt 302 (☎1 694 6320); Brazil, C 93 No. 14–20, 8th floor (☎1 218 0800); Canada, Cra 7 No. 115–33, 14th floor (☎1 657 9914); Ecuador, C 67 No. 7–35 (☎1 317 53289); Peru, C 80A No. 6–50 (☎1 257 0505); UK, Cra 9 No. 76–49, 9th floor (☎1 326 8300); US, C 24 No. 48–50 (☎1 315 0811); Venezuela, Av 13 No. 103–16 (☎1 636 4011).

Hospital Clínica Marly at C 50 No. 9–67 (☎1 343 6600; 🌐 marly.com.co) is a well-equipped medical facility accustomed to attending foreigners.

Immigration For visa extensions (COP$72,350) visit the Ministerio de Relaciones Exteriores (see p.489) which has replaced the DAS at C 100 No. 11B–27 (Mon–Fri 7.30am–4.30pm; ☎1 595 3525 🌐 ancilleria.gov.co).

Internet All accommodation options reviewed offer free internet and/or wi-fi. There are several internet cafés in La Candelaria.

Pharmacy There is a pharmacy in the Olimpica supermarket at Av Jimenez No. 4 (Mon–Sat 7am–9pm, Sun 9am–4pm).

Police Headquarters of the tourist police is at Cra 13 No. 26–62 (daily 7am–noon & 2–7pm; ☎1 337 4413).

Post The main post office is in La Candelaria; Cra 8 and C 12A. A popular option is 4-72 (🌐 4-72.com.co), which has offices around town including at Cra 7 No. 12–13.

DAY-TRIPS FROM BOGOTÁ

The **Zipaquirá salt cathedral** and the up-and-coming adventure sports town of **Suesca** are both within easy day-trip distance of the capital.

The Zipaquirá salt cathedral

The most popular day-trip from Bogotá is a visit to the salt cathedral of **ZIPAQUIRÁ** (daily 9am–6pm; COP$20,000; 🌐 www .catedraldesal.gov.co), some 50km north of the city. Inaugurated in 1995 to great fanfare – having replaced an earlier one that closed because of collapse – the cathedral lies completely underground, topped by a hill that was mined by local Indians even before the Spanish arrived in the seventeenth century. As you descend 180m into the earth, you'll pass fourteen minimalist chapels built entirely of salt that glow like marble in the soft light, each a different combination of colours. The main nave is a feat of modern engineering, complete with the world's largest subterranean cross, and the vast salty cavern is impressive, though the changing lighting is very gimmicky.

Above ground, there's a **museum** (same hours as cathedral) explaining the history of salt extraction; more expensive ticket combinations include museum entry. You must enter the salt cathedral with a **guided tour** that's included in the entrance fee, but once inside, you're free to escape. To get there from Bogotá, take the TransMilenio to the Portal del Norte station at the end of the B line and from here a *buseta* (COP$3500) to Zipa or Zipaquirá. From the centre of Zipaquirá, it's a short taxi ride or fifteen-minute walk to the entrance.

Suesca

Some 65km north of Bogotá, the small town of **SUESCA** is one of Colombia's top rock-climbing destinations. Adventure-sports enthusiasts of all persuasions will feel at home here, but it is the sandstone cliffs on the town's doorstep that steal the show, offering traditional and sport rock-climbing with more than six hundred routes including multi-pitch.

The majority of the rock-climbing and adventure-sports operators are located at

5

the entrance to the rocks, a fifteen-minute walk from the town centre. Try Dealturas (day climb COP$125,000; ☎315 826 2051, ⓦwww.dealturas.com).

To get to Suesca from Bogotá, take the TransMilenio to the northern terminus at Portal del Norte and then jump on one of the regular buses marked "Alianza" or "Ayacucho" (40min).

ACCOMMODATION

El Vivac Hostal Autopista Norte ☎ 311 480 5034, ⓦwww .elvivachostal.com. Fifteen minutes on from the rocks, this is a cosy place to stay and recharge, with a communal kitchen, fireplace, good mattresses and camping pitches. Tents COP$20,000, dorms COP$25,000, doubles COP$65,000

North of Bogotá

Away from Bogotá, the smog and busy streets give way to the bucolic countryside of Colombia's central Andean departments Boyacá, Cundimarca and Santander, which mark the geographical heart of the country. First inhabited centuries ago by the gold-worshipping Muisca Indians, these mountainous highlands played a pivotal role in forging Colombia's national identity. **Tunja**, one of Colombia's oldest cities, is famous for its architecture, while an hour further northwest is one of Colombia's best-preserved colonial towns, **Villa de Leyva**, its surrounding countryside studded with archeological treasures.

Tiny **Barichara**, just a steep 22km from the burgeoning adventure centre of **San Gil**, is a compact colonial beauty. Further north again, the modern city of **Bucaramanga** or the colonial town of **Girón** are both decent midway points if you're heading to Venezuela or the coast. Follow a different road from Bogotá, and eight hours later you arrive at the high-altitude splendours of **Parque Nacional El Cocuy**, with its glacial lakes and snowcapped peaks.

TUNJA

Founded in 1539 on the ruins of the ancient Muisca capital of Hunza, **TUNJA**

is not the region's most exciting city, though its historic centre is one of the foremost preserves of the country's colonial heritage, and is worth a quick stop on the way to Villa de Leyva.

WHAT TO SEE AND DO

The mansions around the Plaza de Bolívar are particularly splendid. The **Casa del Fundador Suárez Rendón** (Cra 9 No. 19–68; Wed–Sun 8am–noon & 2–6pm; COP$2000), home of the town's founder, was built in the Moorish Mudéjar style in 1540 and features interesting scenes on its ceiling, while the **Casa de Don Juan de Vargas** (C 20 No. 8–52; Tues–Fri 9am–noon & 2–5pm, Sat & Sun 10am–4pm; COP$2000) also stands out for its eighteenth-century ceiling frescoes. The motifs are a curious mishmash of imagery – from Greek gods to exotic animals and coats of arms, combined in unusual settings.

The town's churches are no less interesting, with **Iglesia de Santo Domingo** (Cra 11 No. 19–55) known for its Rosario Chapel, richly decorated with religious paintings and magnificent gilded woodcarving by Gregorio Vásquez de Arce y Ceballos. **Iglesia y Convento de Santa Clara de Real** (Cra 7 No. 19–58; daily 8am–noon & 2–6pm; COP$3000) was the first convent in Nueva Granada, and combines indigenous and Catholic imagery in its elaborate decor; note the sun on the ceiling – the main god of the Muisca.

About 16km south of Tunja on the main road back to Bogotá is a reconstructed colonial-era bridge, **El Puente de Boyacá**, commemorating the Battle of Boyacá of August 7, 1819, which cleared the way for Bolívar and his freedom fighters to march triumphantly into Bogotá. Any Bogotá–Tunja bus will drop you off/pick you up (provided there's room).

ARRIVAL AND DEPARTURE

By bus The bus terminal is on Av Oriental, several blocks uphill from Plaza de Bolívar. Buses north to Bucaramanga (hourly; 6–7hr), the main jumping-off point for the Caribbean coast, travel via San Gil (4hr 30min). Small buses – some direct, some not – to Villa de Leyva leave every 15min (45min), while Bogotá departures are every 15min (3hr).

ACCOMMODATION

Hotel Casa Real C 19 No. 7–65 ☎ 8 743 1764, ⓦhotel casarealtunja.com. Atmospheric place with attractive en-suite rooms in an old colonial building between the bus station and Plaza de Bolívar. **COP\$70,000**

VILLA DE LEYVA

Tucked against the foot of spectacular mountains, scenic **VILLA DE LEYVA**, founded in 1572, is a must-see showcase of colonial architecture. The untroubled ambience and mild, dry climate make it a perfect place to relax – sitting in the 400-year-old plaza drinking sangria, you'll be able to appreciate why many describe it as Colombia's most beautiful town. In the mountains around (see p.509), you can go hunting for fossils, or enjoy the countryside on horseback. The narrow streets throng with day-trippers from Bogotá on weekends, but the rest of the time, this lovely town reverts to its former tranquil, timeless self.

WHAT TO SEE AND DO

Villa de Leyva looks and feels immaculately preserved, right down to hand-painted tiles prohibiting horseback riding and car traffic along the main plaza. A lively **market**, mostly featuring fruit, veg and clothing, is held in the Plaza de Mercado on Saturday morning.

Plaza Mayor

The impressive **Plaza Mayor** is one of the largest in the Americas, paved with large cobblestones, centred on a stone Mudéjar well and surrounded by attractive colonial buildings. Dominating the plaza is the huge stone portal of the seventeenth-century **Catedral**, rebuilt after an 1845 earthquake.

Casa-Museo Luis Alberto Acuña

Facing the Plaza Mayor is the **Casa-Museo Luis Alberto Acuña** (daily 9am–6pm; COP\$4000), which houses the most comprehensive collection of sculptures

Santuario de Iguaque, Arcabuco & Museo Paleontológico

VILLA DE LEYVA

● **EATING & DRINKING**
La Bonita	3
Carnes y Olivas	1
Dortkneipe	4
Restaurante Savia	2
La Wafflería	5

AV CIRCUNVALAR

CRA 17

CRA 11A

CRA 11

Casa Museo Luis Alberto Acuña

Museo del Carmen

Monasterio de las Carmelitas

VIA ARCABUCA

CRA 10

Parque el Carmen

PLAZA MAYOR

Colombian Highlands

VIA ARCABUCA

Bus Station

Parque Nariño

Catedral

Casa de Antonio Ricaurte

Parque Ricaurte

CRA 9

CRA 8

CRA 7

CRA 2

CRA 6

PLAZA DE MERCADO

CRA 5

0   100
metres

■ **ACCOMMODATION**
Casa Viena	3
Hospedería La Roca	2
Hostal Renacer	4
Zona de Camping	1

5

and other artwork by influential, avant-garde twentieth-century artist Luis Alberto Acuña, who lived here for the last fifteen years of his life. The large, colourful murals in the courtyard, depicting Muisca mythological figures, are a highlight.

Museo del Carmen

Facing the imposing **Monasterio de las Carmelitas** and its attached church is the **Museo del Carmen** (Plazuela del Carmen; Sat, Sun & hols only 10am–1pm & 2–5pm; COP$2500), justifiably famous for its collection of religious art. Here you'll find large numbers of wooden icons from the Church's early years of proselytizing in the New World, as well as altarpieces and paintings that date back to the sixteenth century.

Casa de Antonio Ricaurte

Once home to a national hero who fought for Bolívar, and operated by the Colombian armed forces since 1970, the house where Antonio Ricaurte was born (Wed–Fri 9am–noon & 2–5pm, Sat & Sun 9am–1pm & 2–6pm; free) contains some personal objects and documents (in Spanish only), plus modern military paraphernalia, but the best reason for coming here is the beautiful garden.

ARRIVAL AND INFORMATION

By bus The bus station is three blocks southwest of the Plaza Mayor, towards the road to Tunja. Direct buses run to Bogotá (6–8 daily; 4–5hr) between 5am and 5pm, and plentiful minibuses connect Villa de Leyva with Tunja (every

---

LOCAL FIESTAS

The town plays host to two spectacular annual festivals. The larger is the **Festival de Luces** (Festival of Lights; Dec 6–8), a fireworks extravaganza that gathers the best of the region's pyrotechnicians, while the popular **Festival de las Cometas** (Kite Festival; Aug) sees the country's finest kite-flyers compete in a variety of categories as spectators shout encouragement. There are also smaller festivals, including foodie-friendly **Festival Gastronómico** (Sept): ask at the tourist information office for details.

15min; 45min). To continue north to San Gil or Bucaramanga, it's better to backtrack to Tunja and catch a bus from there as they are more frequent, though it's also possible to go via Arcabuco or Chiquinquirá and transfer there.

Tourist information The helpful tourist information office at Cra 9 No. 13–04 (Mon–Sat 8am–12.30pm & 2–6pm, Sun 9am–1pm & 3–6pm; ☎8 732 0232) has maps and lots of information. The nearby headquarters of Colombian Highlands, at Cra 9 No. 11–02 (daily 9am–noon & 1–8pm; ☎8 732 1201, ⓦcolombianhighlands .com), is an excellent first stop to pick up information on a variety of outdoor excursions.

GETTING AROUND AND TOURS

Taxis You can hire a taxi for the day to drive you from site to site around the city (approx. COP$20,000 per site, but negotiate). Alternatively, you can travel by horseback or walk to some sites, though the winding roads can be dangerous for unwary pedestrians.

Tours Colombian Highlands (see above) can organize an array of excursions, including hiking, abseiling and on horseback, and offers ten percent discounts to those who stay at their hostel.

ACCOMMODATION

There are several campsites around town, but you need your own tent. Discounts of up to thirty percent are often available during the week; book early for weekends and holidays.

Casa Viena Cra 10 No. 19–114 ☎8 732 0711, ⓦcasaviena .com. Friendly little hostel – two doubles, a single and a three-bed dorm – run by Hans and his family, complete with Austrian (and Indian) dishes on the menu, and home comforts. It's on the same road as *Hostal Renacer* and they'll also refund you the taxi fare from the bus station (COP$4000). Dorms COP$18,000, doubles COP$50,000

Hospedería La Roca Plaza Mayor ☎8 732 0331. This place has a fantastic location on the main square, plus a pretty courtyard and 23 rooms (including one for up to six people) with private bathrooms and TV. Breakfast COP$5500. Prices drop twenty percent outside high season. COP$100,000

★ **Hostal Renacer** 1.2km northeast of Plaza Mayor ☎8 732 1201, ⓦcolombianhighlands.com. Owned by Oscar Gilède, the English-speaking biologist behind Colombian Highlands (see above), *Hostal Renacer* is a haven surrounded by trees and mountain views. A TV room, hammocks, free wi-fi and hot drinks, a fridge full of beer and heaps of information, plus rooms with huge windows and comfortable beds, make it popular with backpackers, and you can also camp. The location, about 1km uphill from the centre, is a bit of a pain, but if you call when you arrive in town they'll pay for your taxi. Camping per person with own tent COP$10,000, without tent COP$20,000, dorms COP$38,000, doubles COP$130,000

Zona de Camping C 11, at Cra 10 ☎ 311 530 7687. No-frills camping, with a wall set up around a large patch of grass and a basic toilet/shower block. Great mountain views. Per person COP$11,000

EATING AND DRINKING

If you can spare the pesos, you will eat very well here, as the food scene is very diverse; the best gourmet food courts are Casona La Guaca (Cra 9 between C 13 & C 14) and Casa Quintero (Cra 9 at C 12). The nightlife is centred on Plaza Mayor.

★ **La Bonita** Casa Quintero, Cra 9 at C12. If you're craving some spice, then get your fix at this colourful, genuine Mexican restaurant. There is some real heat to the salsas, and while the mains are not cheap (around COP$25,000), you can't go wrong with the sublime *cochinita pibil* (slow-roasted pork), and the soups and tacos are very affordable (from COP$15,000). Daily noon–5pm.

Carnes y Olivas Cra 10 No. 11–55 ☎ 8 732 1368. Offers a fantastic value, three-course *menu del día* (COP$8000), including traditional dishes such as tender braised *sobrebarriga* (flank steak), cooked with considerable skill and flair. Also international dishes such as pizza and hamburgers. Daily 9am–9pm.

Dortkneipe Cra 9, Plaza Mayor. The nicest bar on the main square draws beer connoisseurs with its selection of unusual beers on tap, as well as the ubiquitous Aguila. Daily from 6pm.

Restaurante Savia Casa Quintero, Cra 9 at C 12. The organic dishes at this fantastic little spot will delight vegetarians and vegans alike. Huge mains (big enough for two) include the likes of vegetable and lentil quinoa and mega salads. Mains from COP$13,000. Thurs–Sun noon–10pm.

La Waffleria La Casona de Arroyo, Cra 9 No. 14–14. Cute little café dishing up all the crêpes and waffles your heart may desire. Choose sweet, savoury or both. Waffles from COP$7000. Daily 11.30am–6pm.

AROUND VILLA DE LEYVA

Attractions surrounding Villa de Leyva include giant fossils, archeological sites, nature reserves and a town specializing in local crafts. They can be reached on horseback, by bicycle, bus or taxi or via a tour. If making an arrangement with a taxi, make sure the driver knows exactly which sites you want to see, and agree on the price beforehand.

El Fósil

The arid desert highlands surrounding Villa de Leyva attract trekkers, but 120 million years ago the huge flood plain would have been better suited to scuba diving. The ocean waters have since retreated, leaving the country's largest repository of **fossils**. Five kilometres out of town along the road to Santa Sofía, the star of the **El Fósil** museum (daily 9am–5pm; COP$6000; ✆ museoelfosil .com) is the most complete fossil of a 120-million-year-old baby kronosaurus, a prehistoric marine lizard found by a *campesino* here in 1977. The 12.8m-long lizard is one of only two in the world excavated in its entirety, but on display you'll find it without the 5m tail, which was lost.

Estación Astronómica Muisca

Also known as El Infernito, this **Muisca observatory** (Tues–Sun 9am–noon & 2–5pm; COP$5000), dating back to early centuries AD and located around 2km on from El Fósil, is Colombia's answer to Stonehenge. Pathways run between the 115-odd stone monoliths, the larger ones strongly resembling enormous stone phalluses. The Muisca used to decide when to start planting crops by measuring the length of the shadows between the stones.

El Santuario de Iguaque

Around 15km north of town, the large nature reserve of **El Santuario de Iguaque** has excellent hiking. It's named after the park's most sacred lake, Laguna de Iguaque – believed by the native Muiscas to be the birthplace of humanity – which can be visited as a day-trip; there are eight lakes altogether in the park at an altitude between 3550m and 3700m, and it can be cold and wet (the best time to come is Jan, Feb, July & Aug), so come equipped accordingly.

A **visitor centre**, 12km northeast out of Villa de Leyva, offers basic shared accommodation (COP$35,000 per person), a camping area (COP$8000 per person) and food. The entrance fee for the reserve is COP$35,000 for foreigners. Take one of the buses that leave for Arcabuco (up to 7 daily) and ask to be dropped off at Casa de Piedra (aka Los Naranjos) at Km12; from here it's a 3km walk to the visitor centre.

5

Ráquira

Tiny **Ráquira**, 25km from Villa de Leyva to the west, is famous countrywide for its pottery. If you're looking for crafts to take home, besides perusing the many pottery workshops, you can raid the craft shops around the main square for hammocks, jewellery, woodcarvings and ponchos. Sunday is **market day** and a particularly good time to visit. Ráquira can be reached by bus from Villa de Leyva (4–5 daily; 45min) or by taxi (around COP\$35,000 one-way).

SAN GIL

An adventure-sports hotspot, **SAN GIL** is one of the biggest backpacker draws in northern Colombia. The compact town is a premier destination for white-water rafting and paragliding, as well as other outdoorsy activities that take place in the surrounding countryside, and also for day-trips to quiet colonial Barichara. For those craving a spot of culinary adventure, fried *hormigas culonas*, or fat-bottomed ants, a Santander delicacy, can be bought from a few places around town including the market and the street by the river.

San Gil's main attractions lie outside town, but if you want a quiet moment in between adventures, make your way to the large riverside **Parque El Gallineral** (8am–5.30pm; COP\$5000), its trees atmospherically festooned with tendrils of "old man's beard" moss. There's a natural spring-fed swimming pool, and the entrance fee gets you a wristband that means you can go in and out of the park all day. To get here, head to the river and turn left along the Malecón to its end.

ARRIVAL AND DEPARTURE

By bus San Gil has several bus stations, though the main terminal is around 2km southwest of town; a taxi to the centre costs around COP\$3500. Buses to Barichara (every 30min; 45min) leave from the terminal at C 15 and Cra 10, while Bucaramanga-bound buses (every 30min; 2hr 30min) leave from the terminal at Cra 11 and C 8, and Bogotá-bound buses depart from the main terminal (several daily; 6–8hr).

ACCOMMODATION

⭐ **Macondo Guesthouse** C 8 No. 10–35 ☎ 7 724 8001, ⓦ macondohostel.com. Australian-owned *Macondo* has a homey, laidback atmosphere, with guests relaxing in the jacuzzi after an adrenaline-packed day. An excellent place to organize your outdoor adventures, and with all the backpacker-friendly creature comforts to boot. Dorms COP\$18,000, doubles COP\$46,000

La Mansión de Sam Gil C 12 No. 8–71 ☎ 7 724 6044, ⓦ hotelmansionsangil.com. There's no stopping Sam of *Sam's VIP* (see below): this colonial mansion on the corner of Parque Central features attractive singles and doubles arranged around a central courtyard. There's a decent gastropub downstairs too. COP\$50,000

Sam's VIP Cra 10 No. 12–33 ☎ 7 724 2746, ⓦ samshostel .com. This lively hostel with particularly attractive decor has a balcony overlooking the main square, poker table and even a small swimming pool. Dorms are on the small side, but there's a superb guest kitchen and the double rooms downstairs are great value. Dorms COP\$17,000, doubles COP\$50,000

ADVENTURE SPORTS

Adrenaline junkies are spoilt for choice by the array of **adventure sports** on offer in San Gil. There are two main **white-water rafting** routes: a hair-raising day-trip down the Class IV/V (depends on the season) Río Suarez costs about COP\$130,000, while a more sedate half-day on the Río Fonce is COP\$35,000. **Abseiling** down the Juan Curí waterfalls will set you back COP\$40,000, or you can take flight with a tandem **paraglide** (COP\$65,000–175,000 depending on location). **Spelunkers** have the choice of several caves to explore (around COP\$25,000). Other sporty options include kayaking, horseriding and extreme mountain biking.

Most accommodation can arrange any of the above, and you should pay the same as if you book direct. The staff at *Macondo Guesthouse* are particularly helpful if you're trying to decide what to opt for. Alternatively, **recommended operators** are:

Colombian Bike Junkies C 12 No. 8–35 ☎ 316 327 6101, ⓦ colombianbikejunkies.com.
Colombia Rafting Expediciones Cra 10 No. 7–83

☎ 311 283 8647, ⓦ colombiarafting.com.
Páramo Santander Extremo Cra 4 No. 4–57 ☎ 7 725 8944, ⓦ www.paramosantanderextremo.com.

Hostel Santander-Aleman C 12 No. 7–63 ☎ 7 724 2535, ⓦ hostelsantanderalemantv.com. With great views from its terrace, this hostel with a sociable atmosphere appeals to those who want a quiet night after the day's adventures. Great open-air shower and a DVD player plus film collection (including in English). Breakfast from COP$5500. Dorms ~~COP$17,000~~, doubles ~~COP$45,000~~

EATING AND DRINKING

By far the liveliest place to drink on most evenings is the main plaza, which is usually full of families and young people. In the evenings, vendors grill meat skewers and corn on the cob. The central market between calles 13 and 14 is the best bet for self-catering supplies, as well as fresh fruit juice, and is open until 2pm daily. By the riverside park, vendors sell a local speciality – fried giant ants.

Donde Betty Cra 10, cnr Parque Central. The best place for fruit juices (COP$2500) and superb scrambled eggs, each portion cooked and served in its own miniature frying pan; try the *huevos rancheros* (with fresh tomato, chorizo and coriander) or the *huevos Israeelis* (with onions and spinach). Mains COP$3000. Mon–Sat 8.30am–3pm.

★ **Gringo Mike's** C 12 No. 8–35. Sooner or later, everyone makes their way to this candlelit courtyard for the mega breakfast burritos, brie-and-bacon burgers the size of your head, doorstop sandwiches and that old gringo dessert favourite, brownie with ice cream. Mains COP$17,000. Daily 8am–noon & 5–11pm.

El Maná C 10 No. 9–12. Ask a local for advice on restaurants and you'll probably be directed here: *El Maná* is extremely popular for its dependable set meals (COP$10,000), which come with a choice of dishes such as grilled trout and *carne asado* (grilled meat). You shan't leave hungry. Mon–Sat 11am–2.30pm & 6–9pm, Sun 11am–3pm.

AROUND SAN GIL

Cascadas de Juan Curí

For a spectacular swim in a natural pool at the base of a 180m-high waterfall, or to abseil down its face (see box, p.510), take a trip out of town to the **Juan Curí waterfalls**. Take a bus to Charalá (30min) from Calle 10 on the east side of the bridge, and ask to be let off at the *Las Cascadas* sign. From here it's a 25-minute walk to the waterfalls along either of the two trails; you might be asked to pay COP$5000 by the owners of the land.

Parque Nacional del Chichamocha

About an hour from San Gil on the road to Bucaramanga, Colombia's newest **national park** (Tues–Thurs 9am–6pm,

Fri–Sun 10am–7pm; COP$13,000; ⓦ parquenacionaldelchicamocha.com) holds a collection of tacky, forgettable attractions situated next to a beautiful canyon. The *teleférico*, a cable car which runs down into the canyon and over to the other side, is the best way to get sweeping views (Wed & Thurs 9–11am & 1–5.30pm, Fri–Sun 9am–4.30pm; park entrance with *teleférico* COP$38,000). You can also watch the scenery whizz by at much higher speed while hurtling along a zipline (COP$26,000), or get a bird's-eye view by paragliding above the valley (COP$180,000), though it is far more expensive than at Curiti, which is nearer town.

BARICHARA

With its undulating stone-slab roads, clay-tiled *tejas* roofs draped in bougainvillea blossoms and single-storey adobe homes, the sedate colonial town of **BARICHARA** looks like it hasn't changed much in its 250 years. So well kept is the town that it was declared a national monument in 1978 and, with its historical buildings restored, it now makes a popular set for Spanish-language films. Barichara is considerably less crowded than similarly picturesque Villa de Leyva, making it a peaceful, if expensive, resting spot for travellers. Indeed, the town's name comes from an Indian word, *Barachala*, meaning "a good place to rest". Alternatively, it makes for a great day-trip from San Gil.

WHAT TO SEE AND DO

Barichara's quiet streets, lined with beautiful architecture, combined with a tranquil vibe, are its biggest attraction. Once you've checked out the striking **Catedral de la Inmaculada Concepción** which stands on fluted sandstone columns on the Parque Principal, the leafy main square, take a look at the elaborate marble tombs at the **Capilla de Jesús Resucitado** cemetery. Surrounding an attractive patio at **Casa de la Cultura** (Mon–Sat 9am–noon & 2–5.30pm, Sun 9am–1pm; COP$1000) is a collection of regional

5

photos, Guane pottery, fossils and various early twentieth-century paraphernalia.

Very popular with hikers is the 9km **Camino Real**, an ancient stone-paved trail used by the indigenous Guane people, leading down through a cactus-filled valley with great mountain views to the tiny village of **Guane** (2hr one-way).To join the path, head uphill along C 5 from the cathedral before taking a left along Cra 10 to the edge of Barichara. From Guane, there are five buses daily back to Barichara, the last leaving at 6pm; bring plenty of water and wear sturdy footwear.

ARRIVAL AND DEPARTURE

By bus Buses run between Barichara's Parque Central and San Gil's local bus terminal every 30min between 5am and 6.30pm (30–45min).

ACCOMMODATION

Costs drop considerably outside high season; otherwise, a day-trip from San Gil is a better option for those watching their wallets.

Casa de Hercilia C 3 No. 5–33 ☎ 315 641 1841, ⓦ lacasa dehercilia.com. A light and airy guesthouse that oozes tranquillity, with hammocks, beanbags and leafy pot plants liberally scattered throughout. Also has a well-equipped communal kitchen. No dorms, but in low season it's worth asking about renting a single bed in one of their bigger rooms. COP$100,000

EATING

Some restaurants only open at weekends, and everything is shut on Tuesdays.

★ **Color de Hormiga** C 8 No. 8–44 ☎ 7 726 7156. The giant ants above the gate give the game away: yes, the speciality at this lovely, airy restaurant is *medallones de lomito en salsa de hormiga culona* (essentially steak in ant sauce, COP$25,000), but it's far nicer than you imagine – the steak is perfectly cooked and the ants are reminiscent of popcorn in texture and taste. Plus, there are insect-free options too. Daily 12.30–4.30pm.

Panadería Central C 6, at Cra 6. This bakery on the main square selling bread, cheese, ham and cream-filled puffs and doughnuts is a useful spot for walkers in search of picnic provisions, and self-caterers. Daily 7am–9pm.

BUCARAMANGA

Founded in 1622, **BUCARAMANGA** has shed much of its colonial heritage and evolved into one of Colombia's largest, most modern cities. The centre might be low on attractions, but it makes a great jumping-off point for visits to nearby Girón, the mountains surrounding the city make for superb paragliding, and it makes a convenient stopover for anyone travelling to the coast or Venezuela.

WHAT TO SEE AND DO

Simón Bolívar (El Libertadór) spent a grand total of seventy days living in Bucaramanga in 1828, enough for the locals to rename the beautiful house where he stayed, at C 37 No. 12–15, **Casa de Bolívar** (Mon–Fri 8am–noon & 2–6pm, Sat 8am–noon; COP$2000). It now contains a small historical museum, the highlight of which is the Guane mummies and artefacts. Across the street another colonial mansion houses the **Casa de la Cultura** (Mon–Fri 8am–noon & 2–6pm, Sat 8am–noon; free), which holds displays of regional art. Also of interest to art lovers is the **Museo de Arte Moderno** (C37 No. 26–16; Mon–Fri 8am–noon & 2–6pm, Sat 8am–noon; free), featuring temporary exhibitions of contemporary painting and sculpture.

Bucaramanga is justifiably taking off as a **paragliding** destination, thanks to Colombia Paragliding (☎ 312 432 6266, ⓦ colombiaparagliding.com), which now offers everything from one-off fifteen-minute tandem flights (COP$50,000) to fifteen-day courses for those who want their international licence (COP$1,900,000). The owners, who also run *Kasa Guane* (see below), also have a hostel at their flight site outside town, which means you can be airborne within about ten minutes of getting out of bed.

ARRIVAL AND DEPARTURE

By plane Palonegro International Airport lies about 30km southwest of the downtown area. The taxi fare to downtown is fixed at COP$30,000. You can also take one of the *colectivos* that run to and from Parque Santander on Cra 20 (COP$10,000). Alternatively, your accommodation can arrange a lift in a shared taxi. There are ten flights daily to Bogotá (1hr).

By bus The Terminal de Transportes is about 5km southwest of the city, and is accessible by city bus marked "Terminal" from Cra 15, or by taxi (COP$6500).

Destinations Bogotá (every 15min; 10hr); Cartagena (8 daily; 12hr); Cúcuta (several daily; 6hr); Santa Marta (2 daily; 9hr).

ACCOMMODATION

Balmoral Corner C 21 & Cra 35 ☎ 7 630 4663. Lacking in style, but has very cheap double rooms which are clean, secure and have private bath and TV. Many also have fridges, and there's internet and a restaurant serving cheap breakfasts and lunches on the ground floor. **COP$40,000**

⭐ **Kasa Guane** C 49 No. 28–21 ☎ 7 657 6960, ⌨ kasa guane.com. The backpacker hostel that Bucaramanga desperately needed, *Kasa Guane* has airy dorms, basic doubles, a good communal kitchen, TV area, hammocks, a pool table, free wi-fi and enthusiastic staff happy to share with you the wonders of the surrounding area, including hikes in the nearby mountains. The top-floor bar is great if you want to socialize. Its sister hostel, *Nest*, perched on a hilltop, is more expensive, but there's no better base if paragliding is your passion. Dorms **COP$21,000**, doubles **COP$50,000**

EATING AND DRINKING

Keep an eye out for regional specialities such as *cabra* (goat). You'll find a proliferation of bars near Parque Las Palmas.

Govinda Cra 20 No. 51–95. Cheap-as-chips Hare Krishna spot, offering good-value set vegetarian meals, with a daily main and side dishes costing you no more than COP$6500. Mon–Sat 8am–3pm.

Guru Food & Drink Cra 29 No. 42–44. Decor consists of fairy lights and rock posters, the menu is a mismmash of Tex-Mex, Thai and Colombian dishes, and the waiting staff live on Zen time, but the food ain't bad. Steer clear of anything that sounds too ambitious, though. Mains COP$15,000. Mon–Sat 2.30–11pm.

Rio Palma Cra 29 at C 48. An extremely popular two-storey bar with live music upstairs at weekends and canned tunes the rest of the week. Full of lively groups swigging beer from early in the evening. Open until 2am.

El Viejo Chiflas Cra 33 at C 34. *Comida típica* including *cabro en salsa* (goat in sauce; COP$20,000) and nibbles such as chorizo or *papas criollos* (COP$5500). Open 24hr, so perfect for night owls.

GIRÓN

With its whitewashed colonial buildings, leafy main square, stone bridges and elegant churches, pretty **GIRÓN** makes for a great day-trip from nearby Bucaramanga, and is particularly worthwhile for those who don't have time to visit other colonial gems like Villa de Leyva and Barichara. The pace of life here is extremely relaxed, and the narrow cobbled streets are perfect for a wander. Keep an eye out for the main **Catedral del Señor de los Milagros** and the attractive eighteenth-century **capilla de las Nieves** on the tiny namesake square.

ARRIVAL AND DEPARTURE

By bus Buses from Bucaramanga drop you off on the corner of Cra 26 and C 32 and pick you up from C 29 and Cra 26.
By taxi A taxi from Bucaramanga's bus terminal to Girón costs COP$12,000; from the airport it's around COP$24,000.

ACCOMMODATION AND EATING

Girón Chill Out Cra 25 No. 32–06 ☎ 7 646 1119, ⌨ www .gironchillout.com. The Italian-run hotels offers cosy rooms. **COP$90,000**
Restaurante Balcón Real de Girón Plazuela de Las Nieves. A good place for people-watching over big portions of local dishes (goat with yucca COP$20,000) or a cold beer.

PARQUE NACIONAL EL COCUY

Rising to a high point of 5330m above sea level, and taking in 32 glacial lakes and 22 snowcapped peaks on the way, **PARQUE NACIONAL EL COCUY** (entrance for foreigners COP$34,000) is a hiker's dream come true. Tourism is increasing but, for now at least, you can hike for a week surrounded by natural splendours with little contact with other people. Be prepared for any climatic conditions and be aware that at night it gets bitterly cold, so pack plenty of warm gear and a four-season sleeping bag (you can rent sleeping bags from tour companies, but they may not be as warm as you need). Pack reasonably light, as you'll be carrying your own gear for much of the trek. By far the best weather is from December to February, when the park is at its busiest.

The starting points for any trip to the park are the towns of **El Cocuy** and **Güicán**.

WHAT TO SEE AND DO

You can do day-long forays into the park from the gateway villages, or from a few mountain cabañas inside the park itself that can be used as bases for day walks, or as a place to acclimatize to the altitude before embarking on a longer hike.

Cabañas Sisuma (☎ 311 557 7893; COP$35,000 per person), near Las Lagunillas at the south end of the park, is a good base for walks to the beautiful **Laguna de la Plaza**, a beautifully situated glacial lake, and **El Pulpito del Diablo**

5

(The Devil's Pulpit), a column of rock that sits dramatically in the middle of a glacier.

However, to really experience the park it's extremely worthwhile to do the six- to seven-day ciruit between the two. Since the trail is not always obvious, it's highly recommended that you do the long trek with a guide (see below).

The trek from Güicán to El Cocuy

Güicán is the starting point for the six- to seven-day circuit. On **day one**, you hike for five hours or so to the cabañas; it's possible to continue on the same day to the top of Ritacuba Blanco (5hr), but better to stay for a night to acclimatize and then hike up early in the morning of **day two**. From Ritacuba Blanco it's then a couple of hours' walk to the Río Cardenillo creek and a two-hour ascent to the Boquerón del Carmen pass (4300m), from which you descend to the Laguna Grande de los Verdes (4100m), where you camp.

On **day three** it takes around seven hours to hike between Laguna Grande de los Verdes and Laguna del Avellanal – a spectacular climb up to the Boquerón de los Frailles pass (4200m), then past a couple of lakes and up again to the Boquerón de la Sierra pass (4650m). The descent brings you down to the lake, where you camp for the night either on the shore or in a cave nearby. From here it takes around seven hours on **day four** to reach Laguna del Pañuelo. You pass through the Valle de los Cojines, and past several waterfalls before climbing to the Laguna del Rincón (4350m), from where it's another hour's ascent to the Boquerón del Castillo pass (4530m), offering spectacular views of the valley below. If the pass is foggy, wait until the fog clears before descending to the Laguna del Pañuelo. **Day five**'s section to Laguna de la Plaza is around six or seven hours' hike, made more difficult by the lack of trail, so having a guide is imperative. There are no major descents or ascents; you keep roughly level until you reach Laguna Hoja Larga in around five hours, with your destination – the splendid Laguna de la Plaza – roughly an hour later. On **day six** you follow the trail from here up

to the Boquerón de Cusiri (4410m), the last pass you'll have climb, then descend for an hour to the chain of attractive small lakes – lagunillas – where you'll find the park's busiest campsite. You can either camp here or press on to the Alto de la Cueva – a straightforward four-hour walk to the main road. If hiking as part of a tour, then you may have pre-arranged transport waiting; otherwise, it's another four hours' walk to El Cocuy.

ARRIVAL AND DEPARTURE

By bus From Bogotá, there are around six El Cocuy-bound buses daily, the first leaving around 8.30am (11hr). Returning from El Cocuy, overnight Libertadores buses to Bogotá depart at 8pm daily from the main square, while Concorde buses leave at 4pm and 6pm and cheaper and Fundadores minibuses leave from Cra 5 No. 5–38 (3 daily). From Bogotá there are morning departures for Güicán with either Libertadores or Fundadores (12hr), the return buses leaving Güicán's main square around 7pm. To get from El Cocuy to Güicán there are three Cootradatil buses daily (30min).

To the park From Güicán it takes five hours to hike to the park entrance, while hiring private transport to take you up there will set you back around COP$85,000–100,000. It's cheaper to hitch a ride on a *lechero* (milk truck, COP$6000–10,000) to the mountain farms; they depart from the main square in Güicán at 5.30am, then at 6am from El Cocuy plaza. Since there are several milk trucks, ask around to make sure you're going to the right place, they tend to drop you off at the intersection nearest to the cabañas, so you'll have to hike the rest of the way.

GUIDES

Ecoturismo Comunitario Sisuma 314 348 9718, elcocuyboyaca.com. You can hire guides and horses from this guide cooperative within the park boundaries – for around COP$85,000 per day for an accredited guide for up to six people, while horses will cost you around COP$35,000 per day.

Colombia Trek 320 339 3839, colombiatrek.com Bilingual climber Rodrigo Aria comes highly recommended; he rents out equipement and arranges personalized packages, with a week-long trek costing around COP$1,500,000 per person for a group of three people and a guide (cheaper if it's just a Spanish-speaking guide).

ACCOMMODATION

The village of Güicán makes for a closer and easier hike into the park, while El Cocuy has the lion's share of facilities (including an ATM) and accommodation. Most places to eat are inside hotels.

CROSSING INTO VENEZUELA: CÚCUTA

The only reason to visit the border town of **Cúcuta** is if you're heading by land to Venezuela. The city is polluted, hot and crime-ridden and not a place to linger, with a dodgy bus station to boot, so exercise utmost caution. Frequent buses and *colectivos* run across the border from Cúcuta's bus terminal and also from the corner of Av Diagonal Santander and Calle 8 to Venezuela's San Antonio de Táchira or San Cristóbal, one hour from Cúcuta (around COP$3000), or else you can take a taxi (COP$17,000). The border is open 24hr, seven days a week. At the time of writing, citizens of the US, Canada, Australia, New Zealand, the UK and much of Western Europe do not require visas to enter Venezuela (see p.859). You must disembark at the DAS post just before the bridge to get your Colombian exit stamp. Once over the border, remember to put your watch forward thirty minutes and pick up a tourist card at the DIEX office on Carrera 9 between Calles 6 and 7.

It's best to take as much cash in US dollars to Venezuela as you can (see p.858).

From San Cristóbal there are up to seven overnight departures daily for **Caracas** (14hr), all leaving late afternoon or early evening.

GÜICÁN

Brisas del Nevado Cra 5 No. 4–5 ☎ 310 629 9001. Quite possibly the best hotel in town, complete with restaurant serving delicious takes on local specialities and private baths in most rooms. COP$30,000

Hotel El Eden Transversal 2 No. 9–58 ☎ 311 808 8334. Family-run guesthouse popular with travellers, with assorted wildlife in the garden and (mostly) en-suite rooms filled with the smell of pine. It's a 10min walk from the main square; turn right onto the dirt road from Cra 4 past the basketball court, then first right and second left. Campsite COP$6000, rooms per person COP$27,000

EL COCUY

Hotel Casa Muñoz Cra 5 No. 7–26 ☎ 8 789 0328, ⓦ hotelcasamunoz.com. Modern, not terribly memorable hotel on the main square, with functional, clean rooms around a flower-filled courtyard and reliable hot showers. Rooms per person COP$25,000

La Posada del Molino Cra 3 No. 7–51 ☎ 310 494 5076 ⓦ elcocuycasamuseo.blogspot.com. An allegedly haunted colonial mansion featuring a handful of en-suite rooms with some period furniture and unusual bathrooms. Rooms per person COP$35,000

Cartagena and the Caribbean

Ever since Rodrigo de Bastidas became the first European to set foot on Colombian soil in Santa Marta in 1525, there's been a long history of foreigner fascination with the country's Caribbean coastline, and hundreds of thousands – Colombian holidaymakers chief among them – follow in his footsteps annually. In addition to hot weather and cool breezes, **Cartagena** boasts splendours from the town's past role as the main conduit for the Spanish crown's imperial plundering. For its extensive fortifications and colonial legacy, the walled city was declared a UNESCO World Heritage Site in 1984.

The 1600km coast holds a wide variety of landscapes from the inaccessible dense jungles of the **Darién Gap** on the border with Panama to the arid salt plains of the **Guajira Peninsula**. If it's a tropical paradise you're after, try the white, jungle-fringed beaches of **Tayrona National Park** near **Santa Marta**. The translucent waters around the fishing village of **Taganga** number among the most inexpensive places in the world to learn to scuba dive. Inland, travel back to the sixteenth century in sleepy **Mompox** and cross paths with coca-chewing Kogis on a mesmerizing five-day trek to the **Ciudad Perdida**.

While the vast majority of travellers come straight to Cartagena by night bus from Medellín, it's possible to break your journey in the appealing beach town of **Tolú** and do a day-trip to the Islas de **San Bernardo archipelago**.

CARTAGENA DE INDIAS

Without a doubt the Caribbean's most beautiful city, **CARTAGENA DE INDIAS** offers stunning colonial architecture, gourmet dining, all-night partying and beaches. Cartagena literally embodies Colombia's Caribbean coast, with many of the city's

5

colourful, weathered buildings built using coral from the surrounding reefs.

Founded in 1533, Cartagena was one of the first Spanish cities in the New World and served as the main port through which the continent's riches were shipped off to the mother country. Not surprisingly, the city proved an appetizing target for English pirates prowling the Caribbean, and it suffered several dreadful sieges in the sixteenth century, the most infamous led by Sir Francis Drake in 1586, during which he held the town hostage for more than a hundred days. After "the Dragon" was paid a hefty ransom to withdraw, the Spaniards began constructing the elaborate

CARTAGENA

Airport, Bus Station & Playa de Marbella ▲

CARIBBEAN SEA

● EATING	
El Bistro	6
La Cevicheria	3
Crepes y Waffles	8
Ganesha	1
I Balconi	12
Restaurante Café Oh! lá lá	7
Tabetai	4

● DRINKING & NIGHTLIFE	
Café Havana	11
Café del Mar	5
El Coro Lounge Bar	2
Donde Fidel	10
Mister Babilla	13
Tu Candela	9

N

Las Bovedas

Laguna del Cabrero

Hotel Santa Clara Sofitel

PLAZA DE SAN DIEGO

SAN DIEGO

SERREZUELA

7 INFANTES

PORTOBELO

Iglesia de Santo Toribio de Mangrovejo

SANTISIMO PLAZA DE JOSE FERNANDEZ DE MADRID

QUERO

S. J. MARTIN

MERCED

AGUARDIENTE

SERGENTO MAYOR

TABLADA

CRUZ

MONEDA

AVENIDA VENEZUELA

SOLEDAD

SAN AGUSTIN

ESCALON

GASTELBONDO

MANTILLA

ESTRELLA

Iglesia de Santo Domingo

PLAZA DE SANTO DOMINGO

AYOS

COLISEO

GARCIA

TABLON

ESTRIBOS

Palacio de la Inquisición

Catedral

Puerto del Reloj

PLAZA DE LOS COCHES

C. BOLOCA

Plaza de Bolivar

Museo del Oro

i PLAZA DE LA ADUANA

Parque del Centenario

AVENIDA SANTANDER

DIOS

RONDA

PLAZA DE SAN PEDRO CLAVER

Iglesia & Convento San Pedro Claver

Convention Centre

GETSEMANÍ

PLAZA DE LA TRINIDAD

LARGA

SAN JUAN

SAN ANTONIO

ANCHO

ARSENAL

ANGOSTO

MEDIA LUNA

Bahía de las Animas

Laguna de San Lázaro

PUENTE ROMAN

■ ACCOMMODATION	
Blue House	1
Casa Baluarte	6
Hotel Casa Villa Colonial	5
The Chill House Backpackers	4
Makako Chill Out Hostel	3
Media Luna Hostel	7
El Viajero Cartagena	2

0   100
metres

▼ Bocagrande

fortifications that are now the city's hallmark. Cartagena's monopoly on the Caribbean slave trade in the early seventeenth century is evident in its diverse population, the rhythms of its music, its songs, dances and traditions.

WHAT TO SEE AND DO

Bursting with history, Cartagena's supremely photogenic walled **Old City** is a colourful assault on the senses and where the bulk of the sightseeing is. The greatest pleasure here is wandering the narrow streets, lined with colonial buildings painted in bold colours with their wrought-iron detail, bougainvillea tumbling down from balconies, peddlers trying to sell you all manner of tat, and horse-drawn carriages passing by. You might get a little lost, but the city's many **plazas** can guide you, acting not only as convenient landmarks but as distinct social hangouts. You can take in the city by strolling the 11km of stone **ramparts** that encircle it, though it's best to avoid this late at night.

San Diego, home to a good number of mid-priced *hostals* and several hostels, offers a more mellow, though still lively, version of the Old City. Grittier **Getsemaní**, in pockets of which shirtless men play dominoes and *cumbia* music blasts out in the plazas, lacks some of the architectural grandeur of the walled city but offers a better taste of local life. The most raucous nightlife and nearly all budget accommodation are found here. South of the Old City is **Bocagrande**, Cartagena's modern tourist sector, a thin isthmus dotted with high-rise hotels catering to Colombian holidaymakers.

Plaza de los Coches and around

The city's main entranceway is the triple-arched **Puerta del Reloj**, which gives way to the **Plaza de los Coches**, a triangular former slave-trading square. Today, it's where horse-drawn carriages can be hired for romantic tours around the city, and the stage for street performances. In the centre stands a statue of the city's founder **Pedro de Heredia**. In the plaza's covered arcade, **Portal de los Dulces**, vendors adeptly

pluck sweets of your choice out of a sea of huge glass jars. In the evening, several lively bars open up above the arcade.

Plaza de la Aduana and around

The largest and oldest square, the Plaza de la Aduana, formerly used as a parade ground, features the restored Royal Customs House, which is now the City Hall, and a statue of Columbus.

Convento and Iglesia de San Pedro Claver

Standing on the quiet plaza of the same name, the imposing **Convento de San Pedro Claver** (Mon–Sat 8am–5pm, Sun 8am–4.30pm; COP$9000) was founded by Jesuits in 1603, and is where Spanish-born priest Pedro Claver lived and died, in 1654. Called the "slave of the slaves" for his lifelong ministering to the city's slaves, aghast at the conditions in which they lived, the ascetic monk was canonized two centuries after his death. His skull and bones are guarded in a glass coffin at the altar of the adjacent **church** (9.30am–noon & 3–5pm; free). The convent itself is a grand three-storey building surrounding a large courtyard bursting with greenery; besides exhibits of religious art and pre-Colombian ceramics, there's a superb display on the top floor featuring colourful, contemporary Haitian art and intricate African wooden masks and carvings.

Plaza de Bolívar

Locals and tourists alike come to find respite from the heat in this leafy, shaded square, with a statue of **Simón de Bolívar** as its centrepiece. Formerly the Plaza de Inquisición, the square is surrounded by some of Cartagena's most opulent buildings.

Palacio de la Inquisición

On the west side of Plaza de Bolívar stands the **Palacio de la Inquisición** (Mon–Sat 9am–6pm, Sun 10am–4pm; COP$15,000), a splendid block-long example of late colonial architecture. The seat of the dreaded Inquisition for two hundred years from 1611 onwards, it wasn't completed until 1776, and is

5

believed to be the site where at least eight hundred people were sentenced to death. Heretics were denounced at the small window topped with a cross, around the corner from the entrance, and culprits found guilty of witchcraft and blasphemy were sentenced to public *autos-de-fé* (executions) until independence in 1821. The museum within features a particularly interesting display of torture implements favoured by the Inquisition, as well as scale models of Cartagena, pre-Columbian pottery and displays on the city's history.

Museo de Oro

If you're haven't yet visited Bogotá's larger counterpart, this excellent **gold museum** (Tues–Fri 10am–1pm & 3–7pm, Sat 10am–1pm & 2–5pm, Sun 11am–4pm; free), off the Plaza de Bolívar, will whet your appetite. The displays feature the intricate gold creations of various pre-Columbian cultures, particularly the Zenú. Look out for their intricate "woven" earrings and mammal-bird hybrids, as well as the elaborate gold and copper figures of the Tayrona and the schematic representations of shamans from the San Jacinto range.

Catedral

Looming above the northeast corner of the Plaza de Bolívar is the fortress-like **Catedral** (Tues–Sun 10.30am–7pm; COP$13,000), whose construction began in 1575, but which wasn't completed until 1612 due to setbacks such as its partial destruction by cannon fire in 1586 by Sir Francis Drake when Cartagena was slow to come up with the extortionate ransom he demanded. The interior is airy and pleasantly austere and the compulsory audioguide tour very worthwhile.

Iglesia de Santo Toribio de Mangrovejo

The compact church of **Iglesia de Santo Toribio de Mangrovejo** on Calle del Sargento Major, built between 1666 and 1732, has a particularly attractive interior, with splendid Mudéjar panelling and a striking altar. During the failed attack on the city by Vernon in 1741, a cannonball

landed inside the church but didn't cause casualties; you can see it in a glass display case on the left wall.

Iglesia de Santo Domingo

On the lively **Plaza de Santo Domingo** and fronted by Fernando Botero's voluptuous *La Gorda* sculpture, the church of **Santo Domingo** (Tues–Sat 9am–7pm, Sun noon–8pm; COP$13,000) constitutes the plaza's main draw. Completed in 1579, the fortress-like structure's austere interior belies its status as Cartagena's oldest church. On the Baroque altar there's a sixteenth-century carved Christ, and the audioguide immerses you in the history of the church.

Las Bovedas

In the northeast corner of the walled city, these mustard-coloured dungeons, built into the city walls between 1792 and 1796, have been used variously as munitions storage, a jail and – their current incarnation – as craft shops.

Convento de la Popa

For a bird's-eye view of Cartagena, take a taxi (30–45min; around COP$50,000 return, haggle) up the hill 2km northeast of the Castillo de San Felipe to the **Convento de la Popa** (Mon–Fri 8am–5pm; COP$9000), outside the city's walls. Don't walk: robberies have been reported along that zigzagging road. The restored whitewashed chapel, built in 1608, is clearly visible from almost anywhere in the city. In addition to offering spectacular panoramic views of the city, photos of Pope John Paul II's 1986 visit to Cartagena are also on display in the small chapel. On February 2, when the city celebrates the day of its patron saint, the **Virgin of Candelaria**, protector against pirates and the plague, a candle-lit procession of pilgrims storms the hill.

Castillo de San Felipe de Barajas

More than a single, uniform wall, Cartagena is surrounded by a series of impressive fortresses, most of which are still standing. The largest and most important was **Castillo de San Felipe de**

Barajas (daily 8am–6pm; COP$17,000), a towering stone fort just east of the walled city along Avenida Pedro de Heredia. The sacking of the city by Sir Frances Drake highlighted the need for protection, and so this mighty fort was built between 1656 and 1798 with plans from a Dutch engineer. The fort is an ideal spot from which to watch the sunset, and getting the audioguide is well worth it, as you can walk around the fort walls and underground passages at your leisure, learning about its history, functions and other important landmarks, such as the leper hospital. Alternatively, you can talk to one of the guides who hang around at the entrance.

Other forts

The majority of Cartagena's other remaining defences, most of them nearer to the sea than San Felipe, were built much later, during the dawning of the Spanish Empire in the late eighteenth century. Visible on excursions to Islas del Rosario (see below), the **Fuerte de San Fernando** on Tierrabomba Island was built to seal off Bocachica, which, after a sandbar blocked Bocagrande in 1640, was the only access to the city's harbour. As part of the complex engineering feat, a heavy bronze chain was dangled across the entrance, beneath the water, to the restored fort **Batería de San José**. Boats to Tierrabomba Island depart every 30–45 minutes from the Muelle Turística (10min; COP$7000).

Islas del Rosario

At least fifty minutes out to sea from Cartagena, 35km southwest of the city, lies an archipelago of small coral islands known as the **Islas del Rosario**, sunk in transparent turquoise waters. In total there are 27 islands, many of them private islets barely large enough for a bungalow. Not technically part of the chain, **Playa Blanca**, on Barú island, is one of the more popular beach spots.

For **day-trips by boat**, all of which depart in the morning around 8–9am and return around 4–6pm, you can either book through your accommodation (around COP$40,000) or head straight to the **Muelle Turística**, the wharf across from the Convention Center. For COP$70,000 you can get a round-trip ride on a large boat to Playa Blanca with about twenty others, plus a tasty lunch of fried fish, *patacones* (smashed, fried plantains), rice and salad. Larger boats, such as the *Alcatraz*, tend to be slower, and you do spend a lot of time on the boat, while smaller boats whizz around too quickly (several have sunk), so make your choice carefully.

All the boats sail through Bocachica Strait, passing between Fuerte de San Fernando and Batería de San José (see above), and stopping for lunch on Playa Blanca on Isla de Barú where you're let loose for a couple of hours.

If you want to **stay** on the island and enjoy the peace once day-trippers return to Cartagena, there are a few basic accommodation options, with hammocks available for around COP$10,000. Snorkelling costs COP$20,000 extra – COP$5000 if you bring your own gear – and entrance to the open-water aquarium that's a stop on some trips (ask ahead) is COP$25,000. A COP$12,000 park fee applies to all those leaving from the port.

Volcán de Lodo El Totumo

The small, mud-blowing **Volcán de Lodo El Totumo**, 50km northeast of Cartagena, makes for another popular day-trip. You can clamber down into the crater for a refreshing wallow in the mud (COP$5000) that allegedly has therapeutic properties, while helpful locals gather nearby, offering to photograph you in your *Creature From the Black Lagoon* guise, and to give you an energetic but not terribly professional massage. Most hostels arrange this trip (around COP$50,000).

ARRIVAL AND INFORMATION

By plane Cartagena's Rafael Nuñez International Airport is 10min by taxi (COP$12,000) or a slightly longer bus ride (COP$1600) from the city centre.

Destinations Multiple flights daily to Bogotá (1hr 20min), Cali (1hr 25min) and Medellín (1hr 20min). Twice-daily flights to San Andrés (2hr).

By bus The city's large bus terminal is 45min by bus northwest from the city centre; a taxi will set you back COP$15,000; otherwise catch one of the frequent green-and-red Metrocar buses from Av Santander (40min; COP$2200).

5

Destinations Barranquilla (every 30min 5am–10pm; 2hr); Bogotá (every 2hr 6am–7pm; 22hr); Caracas (1 daily at 7am; 20hr); Medellín (6 daily 5am–9pm; 13hr); Mompox (1 daily at 7.30am; 8hr); Riohacha (every 2hr 5am–8pm; 7hr); Santa Marta (every 1–2hr 4.30am–8pm; 4hr).

By boat Sailboats run between Cartagena and Puerto Lindo or Colón in Panama via the remote islands of the San Blas archipelago. Trips take 4–6 days and cost around COP$800,000 per person. Rough seas can make travelling between Nov and Feb dangerous. Since there are no regular scheduled departures, ask at your hostel for more information or check hostel noticeboards.

Tourist information Turismo Cartagena de Indias (daily 9am–1pm & 2–6pm; ☎5 660 1583, ⓦwww.turismo cartagena.com) is located in Plaza de la Aduana and stocks maps of the city.

GETTING AROUND

Most visitors will get around by foot, though the streams of available taxis make a trip to the other end of town after a long night out easy.

ACCOMMODATION

Budget lodgings are spread out equally over the attractive San Diego neighbourhood in the heart of the historical centre, as well as grittier Getsemaní, a short walk from the Old City. Prices during the high season (Dec–Feb) usually surge ten to twenty percent.

★ **Blue House** Parque Fernández Madrid, No. 38–08, San Diego ☎5 668 6501. For wonderfully friendly, personalized service, a great central location and supremely comfortable rooms, look no further than this pint-sized boutique hostel, consisting of just two doubles and a spacious dorm. The showers are possibly the best you'll see in Colombia, breakfast is served in the tiny downstairs café, there are bikes for rent and you certainly can't miss the bright blue exterior. Dorms COP$30,000, doubles COP$300,000

Casa Baluarte C Media Luna No. 10–81, Getsemaní ☎5 664 2208, ⓔadmin@hostalbaluarte.com. One of the more airy and upmarket guesthouses in the area, housed in an attractive colonial building. The 24 a/c suite rooms with terracotta floors are well kept and there is a decent restaurant on-site. COP$82,000

Hotel Casa Villa Colonial C de la Media Luna No. 10–89, Getsemaní ☎5 664 5421, ⓦwww.casavilla colonial.com. Quiet colonial house with spacious en-suite rooms, friendly staff and attractive communal areas to lounge around in. The small kitchen dispenses free coffee all day long. Doubles COP$120,000

The Chill House Backpackers C de la Tablada No. 7–12, San Diego ☎5 660 2386, ⓦchillhousebackpackers.hostel .com. In a wonderfully central location, overlooking a small leafy square, this compact hostel's chilled vibe is reflected in its decor – retro posters, hammock in the indoor chillout area – and the good bars and restaurants are just footsteps away. Dorms COP$22,000, doubles COP$84,000

Makako Chill Out Hostel C Quero No. 9–54, San Diego ☎5 660 6231. Located along one of the loveliest streets in the historical centre, this spacious colonial house – all polished tiled floors and relaxed ambience – is a great place to kick back and relax. Wonderfully tranquil yet also close to the action. Dorms COP$25,000, doubles COP$90,000

★ **Media Luna Hostel** C Media Luna No. 10–46, Getsemaní ☎5 664 3423, ⓦwww.medialunahostel.com. Popular with young travellers, this smart super-hostel (with 160 beds) offers all the services discerning backpackers have come to expect. The rooms and dorms all overlook the central courtyard with pool and have good beds, there are plenty of tours on offer, and bicycles for rent (COP$3000/hr). Frequent parties on the enormous roof terrace – with a bar open until 4am – go on until the early hours. Dorms COP$25,000, doubles COP$100,000

El Viajero Cartagena C 7 Infantes No. 7–35, San Diego ☎5 660 2598. At this sociable hostel, the a/c rooms and dorms, decked out with comfortable beds, are clustered around a narrow inner courtyard where everyone meets to socialize, so don't count on getting much sleep on weekends. The place is well run, but somewhat impersonal, wi-fi doesn't always work, and the basic doubles are rather overpriced for what they are. Dorms COP$29,000, doubles COP$140,000

EATING

Among Cartagena's greatest charms is its array of fine restaurants catering to all palates, though many are not cheap.

El Bistro C de Ayos No. 4–46, El Centro ⓦel-bistro -cartagena.com. German-owned bistro and bakery, serving a French-leaning set menu of soup and a main course as well as curries prepared by the excellent Bangladeshi chef – a fantastic deal at COP$12,000–15,000 per main. Mon–Sat 8am–11pm.

★ **La Ceviceria** C Stuart No. 7–14, San Diego. Small, smart *cevicheria* with lively outdoor seating, with music from passing street musicians filling the air. Innovative takes on *ceviche* – including shrimp, octopus and squid combos in coconut-lime and mango sauces. The Vietnamese-style grilled seafood on brown rice is nothing short of inspired. Mains around COP$40,000. Daily 5–11pm.

Crepes y Waffles C Baloco, at C Sta Teresa. A variety of crêpes, sweet and savoury, plus ice-cream sundaes and sweet waffles with a choice of toppings. Avoid on weekends when the harried staff find it difficult to keep up with orders. Waffles from COP$6000. Mon–Sat 10am–10pm, Sun 11am–6pm.

★ **Ganesha** C de la Bóvedas No 39–91, San Diego. Do your tastebuds a favour and treat yourself to authentic southern Indian food at this appealing courtyard restaurant. Veggie options – such as *chana masala* and vegetable *chettinadu* – abound, and if you order the beautifully flavoured fish *chettinadu*, you will find yourself in spice-tinged heaven. Mains from COP$19,000. Daily noon–3pm & 7–10pm.

I Balconi C del Guerrero No. 29–146, Getsemaní. At what may be the best pizza place in Colombia you'll find woodfired pizzas topped with the likes of mozzarella, anchovies and other hard-to-get ingredients that the Italian owner insists on having. Mains around COP$16,000. Daily noon–3pm & 7–11pm.

Restaurante Café Oh! lá lá C de Ayos Cra 5 No. 4–49. Attentive Colombian/French couple Carolina and Gilles serve fresh, innovative food that reflects their respective cultural backgrounds, including imaginative soups and the likes of slow-cooked ribs. Mains COP$15,000–33,000. Closed Sun.

Tabetai C Segunda de Badillo No. 36–63. Perch yourself on a low seat in this thimble-sized sushi joint and order some freshly prepared, imaginative sushi rolls, melt-in-your-mouth sashimi, or crispy tempura. Best Japanese food in the city. Mains from COP$19,000. Daily noon–3pm & 7–10pm.

DRINKING AND NIGHTLIFE

A concentration of tourist bars and dance clubs above the Portal de los Dulces overlooks the Plaza de los Coches; most charge a small cover. Locals gather at the cheaper clubs in Getsemaní along Calle del Arsenal. Another option for a night out is a *chiva* ride – essentially a party bus in an old-fashioned, luridly decorated trolley that takes you on a late-night city tour fuelled by rum or red wine, fried regional finger foods, and *vallenato* music. *Chivas* depart at 8–8.30pm from Bocagrande locations such as *Hotel Capilla del Mar*, at Cra 1 No. 8–12 (☎5 650 1500; rides around COP$30,000, return at midnight).

Café Havana C de la Media Luna, at C del Guerrero, Getsemaní. You'll be transported to Old Havana at this packed Getsemaní spot, where black-and-white photos of Cuban music legends line the walls and thumping live Cuban beats get the crowd's hips swinging. Excellent mojitos (COP$14,000). Thurs–Sun 7pm–4am.

Café del Mar Baluarte de Santo Domingo, Old Town. Perched on the city's stone fortress walls, with spectacular 360-degree views of the Caribbean and the Old City's elegant colonial buildings, this is the perfect spot to lounge on an open-air couch with a sunset martini (COP$14,000) surrounded by cool locals. Food is served until 1am and DJs take over from 10pm. Dress nicely. Mon–Wed & Sun 5pm–3am, Fri & Sat until 5am.

Donde Fidel Portal de los Dulces No. 32–09, Old Town. These outdoor tables, between the city wall and the Plaza de los Coches, are the place to people-watch over a beer. Pounding Cuban music from the owner's extensive salsa collection is the soundtrack to which couples get romantic. Open until 2am.

Mister Babilla Av del Arsenal No. 8B–137, Getsemaní. The tacky jungle-themed decor aside, this massive multi-floor club will get you dancing to at least one of its music genres, be it salsa, rock or house. The party usually extends until the wee hours of the morning. Entry COP$12,000. Tues–Sat 7pm–4am.

Tu Candela Above the Portal de los Dulces No. 32–25, Old City. One of Cartagena's wildest and most popular clubs, frequented by tourists and Colombian jet-setters, who dance the night away predominantly to salsa, though reggeaton, *merengue* and other guests creep onto the playlist. Entry COP$13,000. Daily 8pm–4am.

DIRECTORY

Banks and exchange Several banks with 24hr ATMs and casas de cambio are on the Plaza de la Aduana and adjoining streets, as well as along Av San Martín in Bocagrande.

Embassies and consulates Canada: Cra 3 No. 8–129 (☎5 665 5838); UK: Edificio Inteligente Chambacú, Cra 13B No. 26–78 (☎5 664 7590); US: Centro, Cra 3 No. 36–37 at C de la Factoría (☎5 660 0415).

Immigration For visa extensions, DAS has an office in the airport and at Calle Gastelbondo near the ramparts. Otherwise dial ☎153 for any immigration-related emergencies.

Medical Hospital Bocagrande on C 5 and Cra 6 (☎5 665 5270).

5

TOLÚ

Popular with holidaying Colombians but practically undiscovered by overseas travellers, the seaside town of **TOLÚ** is a pleasant spot to break your journey from Medellín to Cartagena. The laidback vibe is exemplified by the proliferation of bicycles rather than cars, though the brightly decorated *bicitaxis*, each one blaring its own choice of upbeat music, make up in volume for the lack of motorized traffic. While Tolú's beaches are nondescript in comparison to the ones in Parque Nacional Tayrona (see p.528), you can reach those 20km south, near Coveñas, by *colectivos* from the corner of Cra 2 and C 17 in Tolú. The town's malecón, lined with restaurants, craft stalls and bars, makes for a nice stroll, but Tolú's main attraction – the Islas de San Bernardo (see box below) – lies off the coast.

ARRIVAL AND DEPARTURE

By bus The bus station is on the southwest side of Plaza Pedro de Heredia.

Destinations Bogotá (2 daily at 8am & 5.30pm; 19hr); Cartagena (several daily; 3hr); Medellín (5 daily; 10hr); Santa Marta (2 daily at 7.30am & 5.30pm).

ACCOMMODATION AND EATING

There are plenty of informal eateries along the malecón, most serving fried fish and *ceviche*, while around the main plaza there are several bakeries and *arepa* stalls.

LAS ISLAS DE SAN BERNARDO

The ten archipelagos of tiny islands that make up the **Islas de San Bernardo** are wonderfully tranquil (when not overrun by Colombian holidaymakers), and their teal waters and blinding-white beaches make for a great day-trip. Boats leave Tolú's Muelle Turístico at around 8.30am, returning around 4pm. Tours (COP$40,000) take in **Santa Cruz del Islote** – an island populated by fishermen – **Isla Tintípan**, the largest of the islands, and mangrove-fringed **Isla Múcura**, where you get to linger the longest – around three hours – to have lunch, sip a cold beer or go snorkelling. Tours finish on **Isla Palma**, which is the best of the lot when it comes to snorkelling, with greater visibility and an abundance of fish.

El Velero Cra 1 No. 9–26 ☎ 5268 0058, ⊛ hostalelvelero .com. With a great waterfront location, this guesthouse is nautically themed down to the various-shades-of-blue colour scheme and paintings of boats in the impeccable, tiled rooms, each equipped with fridge and TV. There's also a sunny deck from which to watch the waves. **COP$75,000**

Villa Babilla C 20 No. 3–40 ☎ 312 677 1325, ⊛ villa babillahostel.com. A few minutes' walk from the waterfront, this German-owned guesthouse features airy, spotless rooms named after locations around the world. The ones on the first floor are somewhat pricier, but they do come with a nice terrace. There's free coffee all day and they'll wash your dirty togs, too. **COP$80,000**

MOMPOX

Marooned on a freshwater island in the vast low-lying wetlands of the Rio Magdalena's eastern branch, **MOMPOX** (also spelt Mompós) was founded in 1537 by Don Alonso de Heredia (brother of Cartagena's founder). It served as the lynchpin for the mighty river's trade network between coastal Cartagena and the country's interior, and remained one of Colombia's most prosperous commercial centres until the silt-heavy river changed its course in the late nineteenth century and Mompox was left to languish as a forgotten backwater. Simón Bolívar raised an army here and Mompox was later the first town in Colombia to declare complete independence from Spain in 1810.

Its beauty has remained practically untouched ever since and **UNESCO** declared it a World Heritage Site in 1995 in recognition of its outstanding colonial architecture. It was also the setting for **Gabriel García Márquez**'s classic novella *Chronicle of a Death Foretold*. Time seems to stand still here: locals unhurriedly putter around the unpaved streets, cats doze in the shade of the tombs at the cemetery and fishing boats ply the network of rivers and lakes. The town's remoteness has kept it out of mainstream travel but its appeal as the "anti-Cartagena" – architecture to rival the coastal city but none of the hustle – has seen a recent influx of visitors.

WHAT TO SEE AND DO

Mompox's grid of streets stretches out alongside the river and is easy to explore on foot. Its sprawl of grand Catholic churches and elaborate colonial mansions is a constant reminder of the town's faded glory and wealth. The town is also famous for its **wooden rocking chairs**, which residents drag on to the streets in the evenings to watch the world go by, as well as **filigree silver and gold** work sold around Calle Real del Medio, and Vinimompox – fruit wines made from banana, guava, orange and tamarind.

The best way to explore is to wander the streets, peeking at the whitewashed colonial houses with wrought-iron grilles, intricately carved doorways, clay-tile roofs and fragrant flower-draped balconies.

The churches

Of its six churches, the finest is **Iglesia de Santa Bárbara**, at the end of Calle 14 on the riverfront plaza of the same name. With its Baroque octagonal bell tower and Moorish balcony adorned with ornate mouldings of flowers and lions, it resembles a fancy cake. **Iglesia de San Agustín**, on Calle Real del Medio, houses several richly gilded religious objects, most notably the Santo Sepulcro, used in the traditional Semana Santa procesions.

Cementerio Municipal

Hiding behind Mompox's most attractive leafy square, the atmospheric **cemetery** (C 18; daily 8am–noon & 2–5pm), where elaborate white marble tombs stand alongside more modest graves in the unkempt grass, will appeal to those with a taste for the macabre.

Museo Cultural

The **Museo Cultural**, at Cra 2 No. 14–15 (Mon–Fri 8am–noon & 2–5pm, Sat & Sun 8am–5pm; COP$3500), where Simón Bolívar once stayed, has a small collection of religious art. Bolívar's statue graces the small namesake square, while the inscription on the plinth of another Bolívar-related statue in a tiny nearby square reads (in Spanish): "To Caracas I owe my life but to Mompós I owe my glory."

Boat tours

Particularly worthwhile if you're interested in local birds and wildlife, **boat trips** are a great way to spend an afternoon and are best booked through *La Casa Amarilla*. Tours leave around 3pm, generally take four hours and cost COP$25,000–30,000, depending on the number of people. Your guide will point out numerous animals and birds that live alongside the river, such as giant iguanas, monkeys, herons, fishing eagles and kingfishers, and there's usually an opportunity for a swim in one of the lakes, such as the **Ciénaga de Pjinon**, reachable by narrow channels from the main waterway. Returning by boat to Mompox after a quick sunset dip, you'll be greeted by a sixteenth-century vision of how the town would have appeared to new arrivals (if you discount the anachronistic mounds of twenty-first-century trash on the riverbank), with all six of its imposing churches facing the river to welcome you.

ARRIVAL AND INFORMATION

By bus Buses arrive and depart from the Expreso Brasilia/ Unitransco terminal, on the riverfront next to *La Casa Amarilla*. From Bogotá take a bus to El Banco, Magdalena (1–3 daily; 14hr), followed by a 4WD to Mompox (1hr). From Bucaramanga take a night bus to El Banco (3 daily; 9hr), then a 4WD. From Cartagena a direct bus leaves at 6.30am (8hr); for a faster route (5–6hr), take a direct bus to Managué, then a *chalupa* water taxi to Bodegá-Mompox (30min).

By van A door-to-door van ("puerta a puerta") can be arranged from Cartagena with Toto Express (☎ 310 707 0838; COP$75,000), and a different company from Santa Marta (6–10hr; COP$80,000) and Taganga (6–10hr; COP$50,000), with 3am or 11am pick-up. Call *La Casa Amarilla* to book, or ask for more information at your hostel.

Tourist information There is no tourist office but Richard McColl at *La Casa Amarilla* is very knowledgeable about the area. The ATM on Plaza Bolívar often runs out of money so arrive with plenty.

ACCOMMODATION

★ **La Casa Amarilla** Cra 1 No. 13–59 ☎ 5 685 6326, ⓦ lacasaamarillamompos.com. Hands down the best place to stay in Mompox, this scenic hostel in a beautifully restored, riverfront colonial building has ten clean and stylish rooms, ranging from dorms to luxury suites, with comfortable beds and colourful murals. The bright, plant-filled courtyard is great for an afternoon hammock snooze, and the open-air shared kitchen, rooftop terrace, bike rental, book exchange, cable TV and stacks of DVDs make

5

backpackers feel welcome. The owner – British journalist Richard McColl – is an excellent source of information and can arrange transport and tours. Dorms COP$18,000, doubles COP$90,000

Casa Hotel La Casona Cra 2 (C Real del Medio) No. 18–58 ☎5 685 5307. The place to go if *La Casa Amarilla* is full, this atmospheric colonial building has a maze of communal areas, including pretty courtyards, lots of scattered rocking chairs and basic rooms. COP$40,000

EATING AND DRINKING

In the evenings, Plaza de Concepción is the best place to people-watch while sitting in one of the rocking chairs next to the huddle of open-air restaurants and sipping an ice-cold beer, while Plaza Santo Domingo bustles with popular food stands, selling juice, beer, pizzas, grilled meats and more.

★ **Comedor Costeño** Cra 1 (Calle de la Albarrada). Informal outdoor eatery on the breezy riverfront serving excellent-value set meals. Try the mouthwatering *bagre* (catfish) with coconut rice, fried plantain and yucca, which comes with a fish soup starter and drink (COP$12,000). Daily noon–4pm.

Dely Bros C 18 No. 2B–19 (opposite Colegio Pinillos) ☎5 685 5664. Colombian classics at a reasonable price. Try the steak served with salad and plantain (COP$17,000). Daily 8am–10pm.

Luna de Mompox Cra 1, Albarrada de Los Angeles. This lively bar on the riverfront can get cramped but has tables outside and is fun for a late-night drink. Daily until 1am, later on weekends.

BARRANQUILLA

Despite being Colombia's fourth-largest city and main port, **BARRANQUILLA**, on the mouth of the Río Magdalena, would be all but overlooked if it were not for its annual **Carnaval** (ⓦcarnavalde barranquilla.com) – Colombia's biggest street party. For four days at the start of each March, this swelteringly hot, industrial city drapes itself in a riot of vibrant colours, playful costumes and pulsating music: salsa, *cumbia*, *vallenato* and African drumming. Preparations begin much earlier, in mid-January, and once the festivities begin, the town converts into one huge street party, kicked off by traditional parades like the "Battle of the Flowers" and "Dance of the Caiman". Parallel to the festivities, the city-sponsored gay Carnaval, though less publicized, is equally bacchanalian. Although barely known outside Latin America, Barranquilla's festivities are second only to Rio's Carnaval in size. Outside festival time, you'll be wanting just to pass through here on the way to either Cartagena or Santa Marta without stopping.

ARRIVAL AND DEPARTURE

By bus The bus terminal is 7km out of the city centre (COP$16,000 by taxi; 30min).
Destinations Bogotá (several daily; 18hr); Cartagena (every 30min; 2hr); Santa Marta (every 30min; 2hr).

ACCOMMODATION

Arrange accommodation well in advance if you visit during Carnaval. The centre can be unsafe at night but this is where you'll find the cheapest options.

MAGICAL MACONDO

Before you came to Colombia, you may have read about the town of **Macondo** in *One Hundred Years of Solitude* by Gabriel García Márquez. Now you can visit it. Yes, officially it's called **Aracataca**, but the birthplace of the author seems to blur the lines between reality and magical realism, largely through the efforts of one Aan't Goor (a.k.a. Tim Buendía). Goor is an eccentric 2m-tall" Dutchman who wears a dress around town, claims to be the last surviving member of the Buendía family from the novel and whose enthusiasm for the book knows no limits. His colourful hostel (see below) is named after Melquíades, the character who introduces ice to Macondo, and Goor/ Buendía has even built Melquíades's tombstone, to be visited as part of his hugely entertaining day-long tour of the town (COP$99,000), which takes in a plethora of García Márquez-themed attractions, including the re-creation of the author's family home.

Regular **buses** run to Aracataca from Santa Marta's market (1hr 30min).

ACCOMMODATION

The Gypsy Residence Cra 6 No. 6–24, Barrio Nariño, Aracataca (Macondo) ☎321 251 7420, ⓦthegypsyresidence.com. Aan't Goor's colourful hostel. Dorms COP$20,000, doubles COP$60,000

Hotel Barahona 72 Cra 49 No. 72–19 ☎ 5 358 4600; ⓦ www.hotelesbarahona.com In the upmarket neighbourhood of El Prado, rooms here are well priced for the area and comfortable. COP$111,000

Hotel Colonial Inn C 42 No. 43–131 ☎ 5 379 0241. A reasonable bet in the centre, with clean and simple rooms; Carnaval parades pass nearby. Doubles COP$45,000

EATING

Sancochos y Asados de la 74 C 74 No. 49–10. Serves generous portions of Colombian favourites (mains COP$14,000–17,000).

SANTA MARTA AND AROUND

Although Colombia's oldest city, founded in 1525, **SANTA MARTA**'s colonial heritage was all but swept away at the hands of English and Dutch pirates. The result is a busy beach city geared to middle-class Colombians on holiday, and international backpackers in search of jungle adventure. Though its narrow streets are clogged with traffic, restoration in the city centre over the past few years has manifested itself in attractive public spaces, such as the Parque de los Novios, the pedestrian area around it bustling with restaurants, and an international marina full of yachts.

Not far away are some of the country's best beaches, particularly in and near **Parque Nacional Tayrona**, Colombia's most popular national park. Also close by is the fishing/party village of **Taganga**, ultra-popular with backpackers, hippies and holidaying Colombians. Santa Marta also acts as the hub for organizing hikes (see p.531) to the **Ciudad Perdida**.

WHAT TO SEE AND DO

Although better known as the jumping-off point for the region's attractions, Santa Marta does have several sights of its own.

Casa de la Aduana and Museo del Oro

A striking building with wooden garrets underneath a pitched tile roof, the well-maintained **Casa de la Aduana** (Customs House; C 14 & Cra 2; Mon–Fri 8–11.45am & 2–5.45pm; free) is the city's oldest building, dating from 1531. Simón Bolívar stayed here briefly, and his body lay in state in an upstairs gallery after his death. On its ground floor, the **Museo del Oro** has extensive displays on ancient Tayrona culture and its modern-day descendants – the Kogis, Arhuacos and Arsarios. A large-scale model of the Ciudad Perdida provides a valuable introduction for anyone planning to visit the ruins.

Quinta de San Pedro Alejandrino

Whether or not you have a particular interest in Colombia's liberation hero, the hacienda and sugar plantation 5km south of town where Simón Bolívar spent his last agonizing days makes for a great visit (daily 9.30am–5.30pm; COP$12,000; guided tours in Spanish included in admission price). The lush grounds, complete with an enchanted forest of twisted trees and creeping vines, are a pleasure to wander and you are very likely to spot numerous giant iguanas perched on the trees. Peek into the various mustard-coloured buildings for a glimpse of the Libertadór's personal effects – an Italian marble bathtub, miniature portraits of the Bolívar family and military badges. Just to the right of the imposing Altar de la Patria memorial, the **Museo Bolívariano** features contemporary works by artists from countries liberated by Bolívar – Colombia, Peru, Bolivia, Ecuador, Panama and Venezuela. Buses leaving the waterfront main drag (Cra 1) for the Mamatoco suburb will drop you off at the Quinta if you ask the driver (COP$1400), or take a taxi for COP$4000–5000.

Catedral

The large whitewashed **catedral** (Cra 4, at C 17) is the oldest church in Colombia, but the current structure, with its bulky bell tower and stone portico, dates mostly from the seventeenth century. Just to the left of the entrance are the ashes of Rodrigo de Bastidas, the town's founder. Simón Bolívar's remains were kept here until 1842, when they were repatriated to his native Caracas.

5

ARRIVAL AND INFORMATION

By plane Santa Marta's Simón Bolívar airport is 16km south of the city centre. Taking a taxi to the airport costs COP$25,000.

Destinations Bogotá (12 daily; 1hr 30min); Medellín (3 daily; 1hr 30min).

By bus The Terminal de Transportes (main bus station) lies 5km to the southeast of the city centre and taxis cost around COP$5000.

Destinations Barranquilla (hourly; 2hr); Bogotá (hourly 2–8pm; 17hr); Bucaramanga (3 daily; 10hr); Cartagena (hourly 5am–8pm; 4hr); Medellín (11 daily; 15hr). Buses run between Taganga and Cra 1C in Santa Marta every 10min from 5am–10pm.

Taxi A taxi to Taganga costs COP$9000.

Tourist information There is a tourist office at C 16 No. 3–120 (Mon–Fri 8am–1pm & 2–6pm; ☎5 438 2587, ⓦ www.turismocartagena.com), on the Plaza de la Catedral. You can pick up free maps here; the staff don't speak much English and are of limited assistance.

ACCOMMODATION

Hostels are numerous, but book in advance in December and January. Prices can double in peak season.

★ **Aluna** C 21 No. 5–72 ☎5 432 4916, ⓦ alunahotel.com. Feel well looked after and rested at this peaceful hostel, beautifully designed by Dublin-born architect and owner Patrick Flemming. Paintings by local artists line the walls, rooms are spotless and fresh, thanks to wooden slats that allow air to circulate, and a bamboo roof offers welcome shade from the blazing midday sun. Excellent book exchange and a great little café on the premises. Pricier rooms have a/c. Dorms COP$20,000, doubles COP$60,000

★ **La Brisa Loca** C 14 No. 3–74 ☎5 431 6121, ⓦ labrisaloca.com. This sprawling converted mansion, named after Santa Marta's wild coastal wind, is owned by two party-loving Californian dudes and has firmly established itself as a backpacker haven, with spacious dorms, a roof terrace, lively late-night bar, billiards and a well-used pool. Attracts a mostly younger international crowd and the helpful bilingual staff are a plus. Dorms COP$18,000, doubles COP$60,000

★ **The Dreamer** C 51 No. 26D–161, Magdalena ☎5 433 3264, ⓦ thedreamerhostel.com. Some 5km out of town but more than worth it for the atmosphere, this huge backpacker favourite has a pool in a hammock-bedecked courtyard, Italian food on the menu and a plethora of day-trips (including Bahía Concha and diving outings) organized by friendly staff. Take a Mamatoco-bound bus (COP$1200) or a taxi (COP$5000). Dorms COP$18,000, doubles COP$60,000

Hostal El Noctámbulo C 20 No. 6–55 ☎5 431 7643. After years of backpacking, the French owners of this small hostel have figured out what people really want, and their attention to detail creates a relaxing, sociable atmosphere. Tables are clustered together on the patio to encourage lone travellers to grab a cocktail from the outdoor bar and get chatting to guests. Dorms COP$20,000, doubles COP$90,000

Hostal Parque Real C 21 No. 2A–05 ☎5 431 0016, ⓦ hostalparquereal.com. You won't find lively common areas here or that backpacker vibe, but you will find three floors of spotless, tiled, en-suite a/c rooms with cable TV and excellent wi-fi on every floor – more a hotel than hostel. Ideal for a quiet stay and for getting away from the backpacker scene. COP$150,000

EATING, DRINKING AND NIGHTLIFE

★ **Agave Azul** C 14 No. 3–58. New York-trained chef Michael McMurdo uses locally sourced ingredients to prepare a quality spin on Mexican food at reasonable prices. You can't go wrong with the *ceviches* (COP$18,000), fish tacos with mango salsa (COP$23,000) or the cocktails with a twist (try the lulo daiquiri). Tues–Sat noon–10pm.

Crêpes Expresso Cra 2 No. 16–33. Gorge yourself on tasty sweet and savoury crêpes (from COP$6500) at this authentic French-owned crêperie. Mon–Sat from 4pm.

Lulo Cra 3 No. 16–34 ⓦ lulocafebar.com. Friendly owners Melissa and David whip up fantastic breakfasts for around COP$9000 at this excellent café. Try the delicious "Lula la Ranchera" *arepa* made from natural corn, served with egg, beans and chorizo. Great smoothies from COP$3800, happy-hour cocktails Mon–Fri 5–7pm and free wi-fi. Mon–Fri 8am–10pm, Sat 9am–11pm.

La Placita C 20 No. 3–16. Gourmet burgers attract locals and visitors alike to this small, friendly joint. Choose from the likes of lamb burger and beef burger stuffed with caramelized onion and melted cheese, with spicy potato wedges or fries on the side. Mains COP$17,000. Daily 5–11pm.

La Puerta C 17 No. 2–29. Local students and foreign backpackers in their 20s and 30s frequent this jam-packed, sexy club. Salsa, electronica and international club hits will have you sweating on the narrow dancefloor that

---

★ **TREAT YOURSELF**

Tierra Negra at C 15 No. 1C–40, 2nd floor; ☎5 422 8421, ⓦ tierranegra.co. The most exciting new place to eat in town, classy without a hint of pretentiousness, this airy restaurant serves internationally inspired dishes, flavourful and full of flair. The steak is expertly seared, the *arroz con mariscos* (seafood rice) features the freshest of scallops, squid and octopus, and the *limonada de coco* is the best in town. Mains from COP$32,000.

snakes into one of the club's many nooks and crannies. Cool off on the outdoor patio if the crowd gets too much. Tues & Wed 6pm–1am, Thurs–Sat 6pm–3am.

TAGANGA

Although no longer as pristine as it used to be, the lively fishing village of TAGANGA, 4km north of Santa Marta (between it and Parque Nacional Tayrona), is where backpackers come to party, both before and after they tackle the Ciudad Perdida hike (see p.530). Built on the side of a mountain, the town has an uncanny Mediterranean feel, with incongruously pleasant unpaved dirt streets, busy beach, and arid hills surrounding the horseshoe-shaped bay. For budget travellers, it's a great alternative to Santa Marta when exploring the surrounding area's attractions.

WHAT TO SEE AND DO

Everything here is pretty much water-related, whether diving (see box below), or hitting the beach. Fishermen ply an easy alternative access route to Tayrona National Park's southern beaches, the most popular being the crystalline waters of **Bahia Concha**, about an hour away by boat. Costing at least COP$120,000, this is a good excursion for small groups. Accessible by boat (5min, COP$5000) and foot (20min) is the much closer **Playa Grande**, which is modestly sized, heavily touristed and a bit pebbly, but still has the makings for a day of sun and sea. Taganga's main beach is awash with small boats, many available for hire, though you'll find people swimming at the southern end.

Conveniently, Ciudad Perdida treks and a whole manner of adventure travel options are on offer too at bigger shops on the main drag, along the beach.

ARRIVAL AND INFORMATION

By plane A taxi from Santa Marta's Simón Bolívar Airport (14km) will cost around COP$35,000.

By boat A daily speedboat runs to Cabo de San Juan in Parque Nacional Tayrona from the waterfront by the tourist information kiosk at 10.30am (COP$40,000; 1hr); book in advance at your hostel as spaces are limited.

By bus Frequent buses (COP$1200; every 10min 6am–9pm; 15min) run along Cra 2 to Santa Marta's Cra 1C. Daily minibus transfers to Parque Nacional Tayrona (COP$17,000 one-way) are arranged through your accommodation.

By taxi A taxi between the centre of Santa Marta and Taganga costs COP$9000. If you're coming from the bus terminal, it will be around COP$13,000.

Tourist information There's a tourist information kiosk on the waterfront (8.30am–6pm) where you can pick up maps of Taganga. The one and only ATM, on Cra 2 next to the police station, often runs out of money, so it's best to load up in Santa Marta.

ACCOMMODATION

Casa de Felipe Cra 5A No. 19–13 ☎5 421 9101, ⓦlacasadefelipe.com. Three blocks uphill from the beach, with beautiful views of the bay and a lush, greenery-filled garden, the rustic rooms at this long-time backpacker fave fill up quickly so book in advance. Plenty of information on exploring the area available. Dorms COP$25,000, rooms COP$75,000, private apartments for 2 people COP$90,000

★**Casa Holanda** C 14 No. 1B–75 ☎5 421 9390, ⓦmicasaholanda.com. Quiet terraces with hammocks and bay views, perfect for reading, and bright, spotless rooms with comfortable beds and crisp white sheets. A two-for-one happy hour in the bar daily from 9 till 10pm livens things up. Breakfast included. COP$90,000

DIVING IN TAGANGA

One of the cheapest spots in the world for **scuba** certification, both PADI and NAUI, Taganga has so many dive shops that the prices and services offered by each are pretty competitive. A four- to six-day certification course costs about COP$650,000 and often includes basic accommodation, English- or Spanish-speaking dive masters, and six dives (four open water, two pool). Quality-focused **Aquantis Dive Center** (C 18 No. 1–39; ☎5 421 9344, ⓦaquantisdivecenter.com) offers the best service in town, with the highest standard of professional instruction and a great awareness of the needs of both new and experienced divers. If you decide to opt for one of the other schools, don't just be tempted by cheap deals: check their PADI or NAUI accreditation, your instructor's credentials, the instructor-to-student ratio, and ensure that equipment is well maintained.

5

Hostel Divanga B&B C 12 No. 4–07 ☎ 5 421 9092, ⊕ divanga.com. This French-run hostel has a small pool lined with hammocks, an upstairs bar, a sociable vibe and wonderfully friendly staff. Rooms are compact but spotless and the restaurant on the premises is one of the best in town. There's another branch a block away, aimed squarely at the backpacker crowd. Dorms COP$30,000, doubles COP$100,000

Hostal Techos Azules Sector Dunkarinca, cabaña No. 1–100 ☎ 5 421 9141, ⊕ techosazules.com. Sitting high above Taganga, just off the main road to Santa Marta, this rambling blue-roofed guesthouse offers a plethora of rooms for individuals and groups and great views of the town. Some rooms have kitchenettes, some share bathrooms, and all have access to the airy, hammock-festooned patio. The road leads steeply down to the beach. More expensive with a/c. Dorms COP$25,000, doubles COP$58,000

EATING, DRINKING AND NIGHTLIFE

The waterfront is lined with fresh fruit juice and fried snack sellers, as well as *palapas* specializing in fish-heavy lunches. The menus (*ceviche*, fried fish, *arroz de coco*) are comparable, but *Estrella del Mar #3* stands out.

Baba Ganoush Cra 1 No. 18–22. Huge diner overlooking the sea featuring the culinary creations of chef Patrick, who whips up everything from Thai green curries to Mediterranean-inspired dishes. Daily 6–11pm.

Los Baguettes de María C 18 No. 3–47. Stuff yourself with giant 30cm-long chicken, tuna or beef baguettes (COP$10,000) and thirst-quenching giant fruit juices before stumbling into one of the hammocks at this backpacker treat. Sun–Thurs 10am–10pm, Fri 10am–6pm, Sat 6–10pm.

★ **Café Bonsai** C 13 No. 1–7 ⊕ cafebonsai.com. This cool Swedish-run café serves delicious home-made treats (around COP$2500), including brownies in chocolate sauce, fresh sandwiches on crusty home-baked bread, healthy muesli breakfasts with yogurt and blackberry jam (from COP$10,000), organic local coffee and an array of over twenty teas. Happy-hour cocktails (5–8pm) and mains are around COP$17,000. Mon–Sat 9am–9.30pm.

Estrella del Mar #3 On the waterfront. The best of the *palapas*, this one does great daily specials for COP$10,000 and the fish is always wonderfully fresh. Daily 11.30am–5pm.

El Mirador Cra 1 No. 18–117. The frisson sparked by the mix of locals and backpackers that fill this club favourite makes this place taxi-worthy even if you're staying in Santa Marta. A disco with a great view, this spot throbs with mainstream pop. Wed–Sat 8.30pm–3am.

★ **Pachamama** C 16 No. 1C–18. Off a quiet backstreet, this Tiki bar-cum-tapas bar serves some of the most imaginative offerings in town. The dishes (COP$8000–10,000) are small, so you can have quite a few. Choose from the likes of kefta (spiced lamb meatballs), prawns wrapped in bacon, fish in passion-fruit sauce, scallop tartare and grilled camembert. Mon–Sat 6–11pm.

PARQUE NACIONAL TAYRONA

Colombia's most unspoilt tropical area, **PARQUE NACIONAL TAYRONA**, a 45-minute drive east of Santa Marta, is a wilderness of beaches, with lush jungle running right down to the sand. Silhouettes of swaying palm trees set against sunsets complete the cinematic image. The laidback attitude of the place makes it feel like a paradisiacal summer camp, though it does get overcrowded during the holidays.

The park gets its name from the Tayrona Indians, one of South America's greatest pre-Columbian civilizations. This area was a major trading centre for the Tayrona, whose population once exceeded a million. With the arrival of the Spanish, however, their peaceful existence came to an end. The Spanish governor ordered their annihilation in 1599 on the trumped-up charge that the Tayrona men practised sodomy; the brutal massacre that followed forced the remaining Tayronas to seek refuge high in the Sierra Nevada de Santa Marta, whose foothills flank the park to the south. Rising from sea level, these snowcapped sierras reach their apex just 42km from the coast, at the 5775m-high **Cristóbal Colón**, Colombia's tallest peak. Tayrona stretches over 120 square kilometres on land, with an additional 30 square kilometres of marine reserve, but since much of the park isn't easily accessible, visitors find themselves sticking largely to the string of beaches that stretch for around 8km from the entrance of the park, bounded by **Cañaveral** to the east and ending with **Cabo San Juan** to the west.

Beaches

Tayrona's beaches and the jungle that edges them are the irrefutable stars of the park. If arriving by boat, you'll get dropped off at **Cabo San Juan**, an attractive palm-fringed beach where many budget visitors stay; further west into the park from here are two more beaches, the second being a **nudist beach** (30min). Twenty minutes' walk east of Cabo San Juan brings you to **La Piscina**, a beach good for swimming and snorkelling, with calm, deep water. From there, it's another twenty-minute stroll east to **La Aranilla**, a narrow strip of sand framed by huge boulders, fine for swimming, followed almost immediately by the long, beautiful, wave-lashed stretch of **Arrecifes** where signs warn you that over two hundred tourists have drowned here; swimming is extremely dangerous due to rip tides and strong currents. Another forty minutes or so east along a wooded, muddy trail takes you to **Cañaveral** and the entrance to the park, where the beach is good for sunbathing but the rip tides make it unsuitable for swimming.

Pueblito

A clear and physically demanding uphill path leading from Cabo San Juan brings you to the archeological site of **Pueblito**, a former Tayrona village with a large number of terrace dwellings, sometimes called a mini Ciudad Perdida. Although it's possible to complete an Arrecifes–Cabo San Juan–Pueblito circuit in one long, strenuous day, the trip is better made as part of a multi-day stay on the beaches in the park. From Pueblito, you can also hike two hours through the jungle back down to the road and catch a bus back to Santa Marta from that park exit point, instead of traversing your original route back to Cabo San Juan. That said, you may be better off hiring a guide for this hike out, which has no signs and is quite taxing.

ARRIVAL AND INFORMATION

By boat Regular speedboats run from Taganga to Cabo San Juan, arriving at around 11am and departing at around 4pm (see p.527). Rangers collect the park entrance fee (COP$38,000) when you disembark. From Cabo San Juan it's around a 4hr walk east to the park entrance via various beaches.

By bus Buses run from Santa Marta (every 30min; 1hr) from the market at the corner of Cra 11 and C 11 to El Zaino, 35km away, which is the main entrance to Tayrona, where your passport will be checked, and entrance fee (COP$38,000) collected. From here, take one of the jeeps that regularly traverse the 4km to the entrance proper at Cañaveral for COP$2000. From Cañaveral to Cabo San Juan the walk takes around 4hr. From Taganga, hostels arrange daily minibus transfers to Tayrona for around COP$17,000.

Park information Bring plenty of cash – only the Aviatur-run restaurant and accommodation accept credit cards – and lots of insect repellent.

ACCOMMODATION AND EATING

The two beaches offering accommodation are Arrecifes and Cabo San Juan, both offer the option of renting tents and hammocks, and cabañas are a good alternative for medium to large groups at Arrecifes. There are basic restaurants at Cabo San Juan, food shacks at La Aranilla, serving *empanadas* and *ceviche*, and another restaurant at Arrecifes.

CABO SAN JUAN

Cabo San Juan de la Guía The downside to the hammocks here – both on the beach and in a gazebo on a small hillock – is that they offer no mosquito netting, so bring your own, and it can get quite chilly at night. Seek out the information hut next door to the restaurant (mains from COP$12,000), the only real building in sight. Camping COP$15,000, hammock on the beach COP$15,000, hammock in gazebo COP$25,000

ARRECIFES

Finca El Paraiso Rents hammocks and tents close to the beach, and has a basic restaurant and shop. Hammocks COP$15,000, tent for two COP$26,000, with own tent COP$13,000

Yuluka Has options of hammocks, camping and five-person cabañas with luxury bathrooms. Also has a well-priced restaurant – the only one in the park that accepts credit cards; mains are around COP$15,000. Hammocks COP$20,000, camping per person COP$12,000, cabaña for five COP$355,000

CIUDAD PERDIDA

The "Lost City" of the Tayronas, **CIUDAD PERDIDA** ranks among South America's most magical spots. More than a lost city, it's a lost world. Although its ruins are more understated than those found at Machu Picchu in Peru, thanks to its geographic isolation the once-teeming city perched high in the Sierra Nevada de Santa Marta manages to preserve the natural allure that the overrun Inca capital lost years ago to tourism. While steadily climbing the sierra's luxuriant foothills, you'll get a chance to bathe in idyllic rivers, visit inhabited indigenous villages and marvel at the swarms of monarch butterflies and beautiful jungle scenery.

5

Built sometime after 500 AD, the Tayrona capital is less than 50km southeast of Santa Marta and is believed to have been home to around four thousand people before the Spanish wiped the Tayrona out. The ruins weren't "discovered" until the early 1970s, when a few of the more than ten thousand *guaqueros* (tomb raiders) from Santa Marta chanced upon the city while scavenging for antiquities. Perched atop a steep slope 1300m high in the vast jungle, the site consists of more than a thousand circular stone **terraces** – with more still being uncovered – that once served as foundations for Tayrona homes. Running throughout the city and down to the Buritaca river valley is a complex network of paved footpaths and steep stone steps – more than 1350, if you're counting – purportedly added later to obstruct the advance of Spanish horsemen.

The hike

The trek covers 40km, with most hikers opting for the five-day version. You get picked up in Santa Marta for the three-hour drive to **Machete**, the village where the hike begins after lunch. From here it's four to five hours to **Camp 1** – mostly a steep uphill slog with a long, steep descent towards the camp. There's a swimming hole close to the start of the trail and another at Camp 1, where

there are hammocks with mosquito nets. **Day two**'s four- to five-hour hike to Camp 2 is an hour's ascent, a steep hour's descent, and an attractive flat stretch that takes you past a Kogi village. At the camp there's good swimming in the river and relatively comfortable bunks with mosquito nets. **Day three** consists of a four-hour hike that includes a narrow path overlooking a sheer drop and ups and downs along a narrow jungle trail, and a bridge across the main river. Camp 3, Paraíso, tends to be the most crowded, and has hammocks, bunks and musty tents with mattresses. Weather permitting, some groups press on to the Ciudad Perdida in the afternoon (four-hour round trip), an hour's ascent from Camp 3, most of it up a very steep bunch of uneven and slippery stone steps – particularly challenging on the way down. And then it's there – your prize – stone terrace upon stone terrace, tranquil and overgrown with jungle, with splendid views of the main terrace from the military outpost. The alternative is to hike to Ciudad Perdida on the morning of day four. On your return, you either stay overnight in Camp 2 at the end of **day four** or, if you made it to Ciudad Perdida on day three, you make the eight- to nine-hour hike from Camp 3 back to Camp 1. **Day five** is then either a very early start and a gruelling seven-hour hike from Camp 2 back to Machete

---

THE KOGI INDIANS

Although now uninhabited, Ciudad Perdida is in many respects a living monument. It's surrounded by villages of **Kogi Indians**, who call the revered site Teyuna. You may be able to interact with the Kogis as they drift on and off the main trail you'll traverse as part of the trek. As it comprises only a fraction of the wilderness they call home, they are increasingly less present on this popular tourist trail. The men are recognizable by their long, black hair, white (or off-white) smocks and trousers, a woven purse worn across one shoulder and trusty *pópor*o, the saliva-coated gourd holding the lime that activates the coca leaves they constantly chew. Women also dress in white, and both women and girls wear necklaces; only the men own *pópor*o. About nine thousand Kogis are believed to inhabit the Sierra Nevada.

When flower power was in full bloom in the US in the 1970s, the Sierra Nevada became a major marijuana factory, and an estimated seventy percent of its native forests were burned to clear the way for untold amounts of the lucrative Santa Marta Gold strand. As the forest's prime inhabitants, the Kogis suffered dearly from the arrival of so many fast-buck farmers, one of the reasons why they're sceptical of the outside world; while Kogi children may well approach you, asking for sweets, don't take pictures of adults without their permission.

CIUDAD PERDIDA: TOUR GUIDES AND TIPS

As of 2008, the area has been safe from paramilitaries, but you can only do the hike as part of an **organized group**. There are four tour companies authorized to lead tours, all with offices in Santa Marta, the most reputable being **Magic Tour** (C 14 No. 1B–50, Taganga; ☎5 421 9429, ⓦwww.trail.com/magictour), though you may find that guides from different companies swap clients to accommodate those who wish to do the tour in more or fewer days, and during low season the four companies pool clients. The official price of the tour is set at COP$650,000 and includes all meals, accommodation along the trail, the entrance fee to the ruins and transport to and from the trailhead. Guides generally don't speak English. Groups consist of four to twelve hikers.

The hike can be done all year; the driest period is between late December and March, while during the wet months from May to November the trail can get exceedingly muddy. It's a reasonably challenging trek lasting four to six days, and a reasonable level of **physical fitness** is required.

Expect to get wet at any time of the year and pack everything you'll need, especially: **sturdy footwear** suitable for river crossings (either waterproof trekking sandals or hiking boots and flip-flops); 50 percent DEET **insect repellent** (not available in Colombia); **water-purifying tablets**; **anti-malarial prophylactics** (there's low risk of malaria but if you want to err on the side of caution); **waterproof bag** and poncho, and **sunscreen**.

before lunch or – if you're already at Camp 1 – a somewhat less gruelling four-hour slog, with the steepest part at the very beginning. Hearty victory lunch at Machete follows, and a transfer back to Santa Marta.

THE GUAJIRA PENINSULA

Colombia's northernmost point, **Guajira Peninsula** has a hostile desert climate that has kept it largely isolated since colonial times. As a result it's one of those special places where independent travellers can still feel as if they're leaving fresh tracks. Some 240km long and no more than 50km wide, the barren peninsula is empty except for the semi-nomadic Wayuu, a beguiling mix of desert and sea, a smugglers' haven that English pirates once tried to conquer. More challenging to explore than the rest of the Caribbean coast, the Guajira Peninsula rewards those who make the effort with the end-of-the-world feel of **Cabo de la Vela** and **Punta Gallinas**. Cabo de la Vela is a remote Wayuu fishing village, 180km northwest of **Riohacha**, the capital of the Guajira Peninsula in itself is 175km northeast of Santa Marta. On the journey to Cabo you pass through a landscape of sand, baked mud huts of the Wayuu and goats grazing under the sparse shade of the acacia trees.

Cabo de la Vela

A dusty one-street settlement strung out along an aquamarine bay, **CABO DE LA VELA**'s main draw is the spectacular landscape: a long sliver of beach, rocky cliffs and cactus-studded arid plains. In December and January the village is inundated with holidaying Colombians, but the rest of the year it's a tranquil spot for sunset viewing, particularly from the westernmost hill at the far end of the bay, El Faro, kitesurfing and lazing on the sand.

ARRIVAL AND INFORMATION

By bus Catch an early morning bus from Santa Marta's Terminal de Transportes to Riohacha (3hr); from Riohacha, Cootrauri (C 15 No. 5–39; ☎5 728 0000) runs shared cars to Uribia (COP$15,000;1hr) where the driver will drop you off at the pick-up truck departure point. The last trucks head for Cabo at 1pm at the latest (COP$15,000; 2hr). Coming back, trucks leave Cabo between 4 and 4.30am.

ACCOMMODATION AND EATING

There's plentiful accommodation consisting of hammocks (CH$15,000), traditional Wayuu *chinchorros* (warmer hammocks; COP$20,000), Wayuu huts made of *yotojoro* (the inner core of the cactus) and basic concrete rooms (around COP$30,000 per person). Showers tend to be bucket-style affairs. Most guesthouses have generators that only work between 6 and 10pm, and many double as restaurants serving goat and locally caught fish and lobster.

5

Punta Gallinas

If Cabo is insufficiently remote, then perhaps **Punta Gallinas** will suffice. Consisting of a turquoise bay fringed by what is perhaps Colombia's most beautiful beach, home to a large colony of pink flamingos and around sixty Wayúu, Colombia's northernmost tip is only reachable by organized tour. Contact **Kaí Ecotravel** in Riohacha (☎311 436 2830, ⊛www.kaiecotravel .com), a reputable operator that also runs trips to Cabo.

San Andrés and Providencia

A world apart from the rest of Colombia, both geographically and culturally, the San Andrés and Providencia islands sit in the Caribbean sea near Nicaragua, with Providencia atop the third-largest barrier reef in the world. Visitors come all this way for the fantastic beaches, the best diving in Colombia, and the unique Raizal culture; 300-year-old ties to England mean that the residents of **Providencia** in particular speak an English-based Creole with a Caribbean lilt. On larger, busier **San Andrés** the Raizal culture is much more diluted, and for many Colombians, one of the island's draws is its duty-free status, making it a much cheaper place to shop than the mainland.

SAN ANDRÉS

Seahorse-shaped **SAN ANDRÉS** is a lively island with gorgeous (if often crowded) white-sand beaches, surrounding azure waters, fantastic diving (see box opposite) and other natural attractions. Budget accommodation is concentrated in **San Andrés Town**, the capital – a busy whirl of unpretty concrete buildings, duty-free shops and careering scooters.

WHAT TO SEE AND DO

Though San Andrés Town has an attractive main beach of its own, the best beach is on **Johnny Cay**, the palm-shaded, iguana-inhabited island visible directly across the water. Numerous boats depart from San Andrés beach for Johnny Cay in the mornings around 9am; a return trip costs around COP$20,000, with the last boats returning around 5pm (make sure you remember on which boat you came). Visits to Johnny Cay can be combined with a stop at **Acuario** – a sliver of sand off the east coast of the island, where the water is swimming-pool clear – though on busy days you'll find yourself fighting for space among the other visitors, hawkers selling stuffed crab shells and piña coladas and stalls renting snorkelling gear; trips to both places cost around COP$50,000.

If you rent a bicycle or scooter, you can do an easy loop around the island, following the coastal road. Along the west coast, south of El Cove, you'll pass **Piscinita**, a beachside restaurant and snorkelling combo: for COP$2000 entry, you can swim with the many fishes who'll eat out of your hand. At the southern tip of the island is **Hoyo Soplador** – a natural blowhole; when the tide and wind conditions are right, a jet of water shoots up to 20m up out of the hole in the rock. On the east side of the island, you're often likely to have the white-sand, windswept beaches of **San Luis** all to yourself.

ARRIVAL AND DEPARTURE

By plane San Andrés airport, a short walk from San Andrés Town, is served by numerous daily Avianca and Copa flights from the mainland and is connected to neighbouring Providencia by Satena flights. You have to buy a tourist card (COP$47,000) on the mainland before checking in for your San Andrés flight. Taxis from the airport to the heart of San Andrés Town cost COP$10,000, or else you can walk in 10min.

Destinations Bogotá (2 daily; 3hr); Cartagena (daily; 2hr); Cali (daily; 2hr 45min); Medellín (daily; 2hr 30min); Providencia (2–4 daily; 30–40min).

GETTING AROUND AND INFORMATION

Buses Local, not terribly frequent buses leave from near the *Hotel Hernando Henry* and cost COP$1300 per ride. The "San Luis" bus runs all the way to the Hoyo Soplador.

Bicycle/scooter Several outlets in San Andrés Town rent bicycles (COP$20,000/day) and scooters (COP$60,000/day). Cycling is a good way to explore the rest of the island, as the roads are paved and there's not much traffic. Most scooter rental places won't ask you for your licence and they won't provide you with a helmet, either; be prepared for some erratic local driving.

Tourist information On Av Newball, almost directly opposite *Restaurante La Regatta* (Mon–Fri 8am–noon & 2–6pm; ☎ 8 513 0801).

ACCOMMODATION

The Rock House Cabinas Altamar, entrada al Vivero ☎ 316 579 1342, ⓦ therockhouse1.webs.com. In a quiet residential area behind the airport, a 25min walk to town, the Luz family greets you with open arms for a bit of homey comfort. The en-suite rooms are spotless and the atmosphere just wonderful. Singles `COP$30,000`, doubles `COP$60,000`

Sheyla's Place II Los Almendros, Manzana 4, casa 10 ☎ 315 467 8873. In an apartment building a 10min walk behind the airport, this is a light, bright flat with several spacious en-suite private rooms, shared kitchen and an airy lounge for socializing. The owner is not always there, so agree on time of arrival. Singles `COP$30,000`, doubles `COP$60,000`

El Viajero San Andrés Av 20 de Julio No. 3A–12 ☎ 8 512 7497, ⓦ www.sanandreshostel.com. Thoughtfully designed, this upscale hostel occupies an entire multi-storey building. Expect a/c dorms and doubles, and all the perks you can think of – daily tours organized, a movie

room, chillout bar area, large guest kitchen, balconies to hang out on – all within a slick, dark interior. Dorms `COP$30,000`, doubles `COP$120,000`

EATING

The town's fruit-and-veg market on the corner of C 2 and Cra 11, where self-caterers can stock up, is open daily but liveliest Saturday to Monday when the *campesinos* come to sell their wares.

Fisherman Place Av Colombia, just behind the airport. Large, casual, open-air restaurant, serving the best of the local catch every lunchtime. The grilled fish in garlic sauce with all the trimmings comes in a heaped platter, the *rondon* (spicy seafood cooked in coconut milk) is flavourful and filling, and lobster is very reasonably priced. Mains from COP$13,000. Daily noon–4pm.

Mahi Mahi Hotel Casablanca, Av Colombia ☎ 8 512 4115. Perch in the alfresco seating area of this stylish restaurant and savour the view of San Andrés Town's best beach alongside your Mediterranean-inspired main or super-fresh *ceviche*. The fruit juices are not the cheapest, but they are the best in town. Mains COP$20,000. Daily noon–3pm & 7–10pm.

Miss Celia O'Neill Taste Av Colombia, at C 2. The decor gives the game away at this friendly little place: the fishing nets hanging from the ceiling, nautical memorabilia and plastic fish aplenty suggest that the specialities here come from the sea. You can't go wrong with the curry crab (or any other curried seafood, for that matter) and the service is relaxed and friendly. Mains from COP$16,000. Daily noon–10pm.

THE BEST OF ISLAND DIVING

The islands' biggest attractions are to be found under the sea, and both Providencia and San Andrés have several reputable diving outfits who can introduce you to a whole new world, even if you're a first-time diver.

GREAT DIVE SITES

Cantil de Villa Erica Turtles, manta rays and eagle rays to be found around this reef southwest of San Andrés; 12–45m depths.

Manta's Place Southern stingrays (rather than mantas) congregate at this Providencia spot.

Palacio de la Cherna Exciting wall dive that drops from 12m to over 300m, with reef and nurse sharks, lobster and king crab among its denizens; southeast of San Andrés.

Piramide Large numbers of morays, octopus and shoals of fish make this shallow reef dive in San Andrés one of the most exciting.

Tete's Place An abundance of schoolmasters, goat fish, parrotfish and more makes you feel as if you're swimming in a giant aquarium southwest of Providencia.

DIVE OPERATORS ON SAN ANDRÉS

Banda Dive Shop Av Colombia, San Andrés Town ☎ 8 513 1080, ⓦ bandadiveshop.com. A friendly, central choice.

San Andrés Divers Av Circunvalar Km9 ☎ 312 448 7230, ⓦ sanandresdivers.com. Particularly recommended for their professional approach.

DIVE OPERATORS ON PROVIDENCIA

Felipe Diving Shop in Aguadulce ☎ 8 514 8775, ⓦ www.felipediving.com.

Sirius Dive Shop Bahía Suroeste (Southwest Bay) next to *Sirius Hotel* ☎ 8 514 8213.

5

PROVIDENCIA

Tiny **PROVIDENCIA** is the antithesis of its sister island: a quiet place with a population of around five thousand, where everyone knows everyone else, where most speak an English-based Creole; with a mountainous interior covered with lush vegetation, and the world's third-largest barrier reef beckoning divers from all over the world. It's difficult not to fall in love with Providencia; many do, and end up staying far longer than they intended.

WHAT TO SEE AND DO

Providencia is circled by a 16km loop of a coastal road, so it's easy to see all the sights along it. At the north tip of the island is **Santa Isabel**, the main "town", with ATMs and other services. A pedestrian bridge takes you across to the minute **Santa Catalina Island** – after dark, it's possible to see manta rays swimming under the bridge. On Santa Catalina Island, a footpath leads past the labelled mangroves to Morgan's Cannon on the right, while a slightly longer walk to the left leads you up to Fort Warwick and down to **Morgan's Cove** where it's possible to snorkel.

Back on Providencia and heading clockwise, a road loops off from the main coastal road through Maracaibo, where the pricey but good seafront restaurant, *Deep Blue*, is a fantastic spot for an oceanside drink. Directly across the water is **Cayo Cangrejo**, a tiny island with some superb snorkelling and a great view of Providencia from the top (boat trips to Cayo Cangrejo are easily arranged through your accommodation).

Heading south past the airport, you eventually pass Haley's Point – a lookout spot with an all-encompassing view of the reef beyond. In the south of the island, a hiking trail leads from **Casabaja** village up **El Pico** (360m), the island's only mountain, with superb 360-degree views from the top. The hike takes around ninety minutes one-way; be sure to ask for directions and bring plenty of water.

From Casabaja, another road leads south to **Bahía Manzanillo** (Manchineel Bay), the liveliest of the beaches, with a bar and restaurants. Further west long

the coastal road, you pass the turn-off to **Bahía Suroeste** (Southwest Bay), with a couple of hotels and places to eat. On the west side of the island, **Aguadulce** is a scattering of shops and services, while between Aguadulce and Santa Isabel, there are a couple of turn-offs to beaches, particularly in the Catalina Bay area.

ARRIVAL AND INFORMATION

By plane Several Satena (ⓦsatena.com) flights daily (30min) connect Providencia with San Andrés only; there are no flights from the mainland. Be sure to reconfirm your return flight upon arrival in Providencia. Luggage allowance is 10kg. Pick-up trucks meet flights and will drop you off anywhere on the island for a non-negotiable COP$23,000; if there are several people going to the same place, costs are shared.

GETTING AROUND AND INFORMATION

By bike/colectivo/scooter To get around the island, you can either rent a bicycle, a scooter (around COP$60,000 from operators in Aguadulce and Santa Isabel), or you can flag down passing vehicles who can give you a lift for around COP$2000 (negotiate).

Tourist information There's a helpful tourist booth in Santa Isabel by the bridge to the Santa Catalina island (daily 8am–5pm).

ACCOMMODATION

Mr Mac Aguadulce ⓣ8 514 8283. Large, simple rooms right by the water. Ideal for self-caterers, as rooms come with kitchenettes; discounts for solo travellers. Doubles **COP$50,000**

Refugio De La Luna El Bluff ⓣ8 514 8460, ⓔcarmenicoa@gmail.com. At this lovely posada on the south side of the island, Carmeni and her son Bruce go out of their way to make you feel welcome. Up to three people can stay in the apartment below the owners' house, you can snorkel in the bay below, and dinner is cooked on request. The location is a little isolated, but you can rent transport through Bruce. Three people **COP$240,000**

Sirius Hotel Bahía Suroeste (Southwest Bay) ⓣ8 514 8213, ⓦwww.siriushotel.net. Chilled-out beachside hotel whose owner is happy to organize diving and boating outings for you (the dive shop is on the premises). The a/c rooms are clean and spacious and several friendly dogs roam the property; hefty discounts for solo travellers. Doubles **COP$200,000**

EATING AND DRINKING

The liveliest part of the island is Bahía Manzanillo (Manchineel Bay), where there are a couple of basic beachside eateries serving heaped portions of curry crab and more.

5

★ **Café Studio** 200m along the main road from Bahía Suroeste to Aguadulce. The best restaurant on the island, run by a Canadian-Raizal couple; try anything in Creole sauce and don't leave without sampling either the cappuccino pie or the lemon pie. Mon–Sat 11am–10pm.

Old Providence Taste Signposted off the road from Aguadulce to Santa Isabel in the Pueblo Viejo area (if you pass a bus stop shaped like an octopus, you've gone too far). Friendly beachside restaurant serving a fantastic-value *menú* for COP$12,000, which includes soup and a heaped plate of fish or curry crab with all the trimmings. Daily noon–4pm.

Roland Roots Bar Bahía Manzanillo (Manchineel Bay). This Rasta-themed bar rocks to a thumping reggae soundtrack and there are even swings from which to fling yourself into the sea.

Tierra Paisa

Nominally a slang term to describe anyone from the mountainous region of Antioquia, **paisas** are alternately the butt of jokes and the object of envy for many Colombians. What makes them stand out is their rugged individualism and reputation for industriousness. Their fame dates back to the early nineteenth century, when they cleared Colombia's hinterland for farming in exchange for the government's carrot of free land. Perhaps the biggest *paisa* contribution to Colombia is its role in the spread of coffee.

The heart of *paisa* country is the metropolis of **Medellín**, which has made a remarkable turnaround since its days as Colombia's murder capital in the early 1990s, and turned into an attractive cosmopolitan city. The picturesque coffee-growing *fincas* near the modern cities of **Manizales** and **Pereira** were almost all established by *paisa* homesteaders and some growers have opened their estates to tourists, who during harvest time can partake in the picking process. Easily accessible from Pereira, the incredibly photogenic village of **Salento** is the gateway to some great hiking in the misty **Valle de Cócoro**. The so-called **Zona Cafetera**, or "Coffee Zone", is the base for exploring one of Colombia's most postcard-perfect national parks, **Parque Nacional Natural Los Nevados**.

MEDELLÍN

It's hard to think of a city that was more in need of a public relations makeover than **MEDELLÍN**. When turf wars between rival drug gangs became public in the 1980s and 1990s, Colombia's second-largest city was rampaged by teenage hitmen, called *sicarios*, who, for as little as US$30, could be hired to settle old scores.

COFFEE AND COCAINE

It's hard to say which of Colombia's two cash crops garners more international attention, the white or the black one. One thing is for certain: both are synonymous with quality. The country's first bumper crop was **coffee**. Colombia is the second-largest producer of hand-picked mild Arabica coffee after Brazil and the third-largest overall coffee producer in the world (behind Vietnam and Brazil). High temperatures, heavy rainfall and cool evening breezes make Colombia the bean's ideal habitat, though changes in weather patterns have led to poor crops in recent years: 7.8 million bags were produced in 2011 following torrential downpours, fungus and flooding, well below the average of around 12 million.

Cocaine was perceived as an innocuous stimulant until the twentieth century. Two US presidents, several European monarchs and even a pope were early addicts (and vocal advocates) of Vin Tonique Mariani, a nineteenth-century liqueur made from coca extract. The "real thing" that Coca-Cola initially pushed on its customers was cocaine. For Sigmund Freud, a spoonful of coke each day was the cure for depression. Plan Colombia (see p.494) has seen some decline in coca cultivation, though coca growers have merely moved on to producing hardier coca crops that give four times as much yield and grow far faster than old crops, though the cocaine-related cartel violence that used to plague the cities of Medellín and Cali has recently been "exported" to Mexico, where drug trade-related murders have risen dramatically in the last few years.

MEDELLÍN: CENTRE

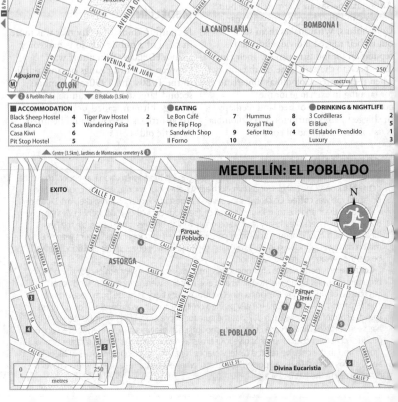

■ ACCOMMODATION		● EATING			● DRINKING & NIGHTLIFE	
Black Sheep Hostel	4	Tiger Paw Hostel	2	Le Bon Café	7	Hummus	8	3 Cordilleras	2
Casa Blanca	3	Wandering Paisa	1	The Flip Flop		Royal Thai	6	El Blue	5
Casa Kiwi	6			Sandwich Shop	9	Señor Itto	4	El Eslabón Prendido	1
Pit Stop Hostel	5			Il Forno	10			Luxury	3

MEDELLÍN: EL POBLADO

But when cocaine kingpin **Pablo Escobar** was snuffed out in 1993, Medellín began to bury its sordid past, though the notorious Mr Escobar remains an infamous attraction (see p.538). These days, the increasing number of travellers who come here find an inviting, modern city with one of the country's best climates – year-round temperatures average 24°C.

WHAT TO SEE AND DO

Pleasant green spaces, interesting museums, a bustling centre and thriving commercial areas make Medellín an exciting place to explore, while top-notch restaurants, vibrant bars and a pumping club scene provide non-stop fun until the early hours. The reliable metro makes it easy to get around. **El Poblado**, an upmarket area in the southeastern part of Medellín, has the highest concentration of lodgings, restaurants and nightlife.

Museo de Antioquia

Medellín is the birthplace of sculptor and painter **Fernando Botero**, known for his satirical representation of all things fat – oranges, priests, even a chubby Mona Lisa who appears to have eaten all the pies. Although Medellín residents felt miffed by Botero's donation of his extensive European art collection to the Museo Botero in Bogotá (see p.497), the highlight of the **Museo de Antioquia** (Cra 52 No. 52–43; Mon–Sat 10am–5.30pm, Sun 10am–4.30pm; COP$10,000) is the largest collection of his works, including painting, sculpture and sketches. Another twenty Botero sculptures are on display outside the museum in the busy **Plaza Botero**, including a rotund Roman legionary.

Basílica Nuestra Señora de la Candelaria

A few churches from the late colonial era survive. The most important is the **Basílica Nuestra Señora de la Candelaria** (Cra 50, at C51 Boyacá), whose Baroque interior dates from 1776. Its most impressive feature is a German pipe organ that made its way here on the backs of long-suffering horses.

Catedral Metropolitana

The fortress-like **cathedral** (between Cra 48 & 49), four blocks from Basílica de la Candelaria, along a pedestrian walkway, at **Plaza Bolívar**, was constructed between 1875 and 1931 and claims to be the largest church in the world built entirely of bricks – 1.2 million, if you're counting. A large **handicraft fair** is held on the first Saturday of every month in the plaza.

Parque San Antonio

If your appetite for Botero isn't sated, check out his *Pájaro de Paz* (Bird of Peace) sculpture at **Parque San Antonio**, on Carrera 46 between calles 44 and 46. When a guerrilla bomb destroyed the bronze sculpture in 1996, Botero ordered the skeleton to be left in its shattered state and a replica of the original was placed alongside it as an eloquent protest against violence.

Museo de Arte Moderno de Medellín

Housed in an attractively restored industrial warehouse in the Ciudad del Río neighbourhood, the **Museo de Arte Moderno de Medellín** (Cra 44 No. 19A–100; Tues–Fri 9am–5.30pm, Sat 10am–5.30pm, Sun 10am–5pm; COP$7000; ⓦwww.elmamm.org; metro Poblado) features an impressive selection of contemporary art by international and national artists, including prolific Medellín painter Débora Arango.

Pueblito Paisa

The geographical limitations of so many people living in a narrow valley have forced residents to live in overcrowded conditions, with many homes running up 45-degree slopes. Within the city centre itself there's a huge shortage of open recreational spaces. An exception is **Pueblito Paisa** at C 30A No. 55–64 (daily 6am–midnight; free), a replica of a typical Antioquian village that's situated atop Cerro Nutibara, a hilly outcrop downtown that offers fabulous panoramic views of the city. At the bottom of the hill is the **Parque de las Esculturas**, a sculpture park where the imagination of South American artists takes on abstract form. The closest metro station is

5

5

Industriales, from where it's a ten-minute walk up Cerro Nutibara.

Jardín Botánico de Medellín Joaquín Antonio Uribe

This lush **botanical garden** (C 73 No. 51D–14; daily 9am–5pm; free; ✪www.botanicomedellin.org; metro Universidad) is one of Colombia's oldest, dating from 1913 and home to over six hundred plant species as well as a butterfly enclosure. Don't miss a visit to the stunning Orchideorama – a weaving structure of steel trunks and towering wooden petals – where plants are showcased and the garden's annual orchid exhibition is held in August during the Feria de las Flores flower festival.

Parque Arví

On the eastern slopes of the Aburrá Valley, **Parque Arví** (Tues–Sun 9am–6pm; ✪www.parquearvi.org) is an ecological nature reserve and archeological site. It forms part of the network of pre-Hispanic trails of Parque Ecológico Piedras Blancas (see p.540), which can be reached from the park in an hour on foot. Other attractions include canopy ziplines and a butterfly enclosure, and you can easily spend the day exploring this welcome bit of wilderness. The park is connected to downtown Medellín via the Cable Arví Metrocable (Linea L; closed for maintenance on Mon) from the Metro Santo Domingo inter-change (COP$3500); the 15-minute ride up glides over the mountain ridge and into the park, affording spectacular views of the city.

ARRIVAL AND INFORMATION

By plane Medellín's futuristic José María Córdova Airport (☎4 562 2828) lies a hilly 28km from the city along a scenic highway; it services all international and most domestic flights. Taxis to the city cost COP$57,000. Conbuses, at Cra 50a No. 53–13 (☎4 311 5781), run every 20min from roughly 5am to 9pm between the *Nutibara Hotel*, across the street from Plaza Botero, and the airport (1hr; COP$8000). The city's smaller second airport is Olaya Herrera (☎4 365 6100), located beside the southern bus terminal and serving domestic destinations; taxis to El Poblado cost around COP$6000.

Domestic destinations Barranquilla (12 daily; 1hr 45min); Bogotá (hourly; 50min); Bucaramanga (6 daily; 50min); Cali

---

ESCOBAR'S LEGACY

Few individuals have had as great (and negative) an impact on Medellín in recent history as **Pablo Escobar Gaviria** – the most successful of the cocaine barons. After years of inflicting violence on the city's civilians because of the Medellín cartel's rivalry with the Cali cartels and his willingness to blow up a plane just to get at a single passenger, Escobar was unceremoniously shot down on the roof of a house on December 2, 1993, while on the run from the police.

ESCOBAR TOURS

Though many Medellín citizens find the idea of this godfather of crime posthumously becoming a major tourist attraction distasteful, a number of **tours** have sprung up since his death that take you around the city to various Escobar-associated sights. You get to see the building he lived in, apartment blocks he built, the rooftop on which he was shot, and, finally, his gravestone at the Jardines de Montesacro cemetery. Tours cost around COP$55,000 per person and the best of the operators is **Paisa Road** (☎317 489 2629, ✪www.paisaroad.com), known for their sensitive and balanced tours.

ESCOBAR'S HIPPOS

Escobar is also the reason why there are feral hippos in the mountains around Medellín. To find out why, you can visit one of the more bizarre sites in Colombia – **Hacienda Nápoles** (COP$27,000; ☎1800 510 344, ✪www.haciendanapoles.com), the huge farm that was once Escobar's private kingdom, complete with mansions, menagerie of exotic animals, bullring and more. Once Escobar was on the run, the abandoned hippos broke out of their enclosure, fled into the wild and bred, thus giving rise to dangerous non-native mammals in Colombia. This strange attraction sits halfway between Medellín and Bogotá, off the highway 1km from Dorodal. Today you can wander through the abandoned mansion, check out the displays on Escobar's reign of terror, and there are even some rides for children.

★ TREAT YOURSELF

Medellín's cool mornings and warm days create thermal updraughts that are ideal for **paragliding**. A number of gliding schools have taken off in recent years, offering short tandem flights 45 minutes from the city centre over the Aburrá Valley with sensational views back to Medellín. Recommended operator Zona de Vuelo (☏ 4 388 1556; ☝ zonadevuelo.com) offers tandem flights (from COP$85,000/105,000 for 15/30min). Buses leave Medellín's northern bus terminal (metro Caribe) every half-hour for the town of San Felix. Ask the driver to let you off at "parapente".

(2 daily; 50min); Cartagena (3 daily; 1hr 20min); Manizales (2 daily; 30min); Pereira (7 daily; 35min); San Andrés (1 daily; 1hr 50min).

International destinations Caracas (daily; 2hr); Lima (daily; 4hr 30min); Quito (1–2 daily; 1hr 30min).

By bus Depending on which part of the country you're coming from, long-distance buses arrive either at the Terminal del Norte (Metro Caribe) or Terminal del Sur, almost equidistant from the centre. Terminal del Norte handles traffic from the north, east and southeast, while Terminal del Sur has departures for destinations south and west. A taxi from the northern terminal to El Poblado, where most of the hostels are, costs about COP$12,000, but it is cheap and easy to get the metro (station: metro Polado). A taxi from the southern terminal to El Poblado is COP$6000.

Terminal del Norte destinations Bogotá (every 30min; 9–10hr); Cartagena (15 daily; 13hr); Ipiales (5 daily; 20–22hr); Magangué for Mompox (2 daily; 12hr); Santa Marta (12 daily; 16hr).

Terminal del Sur destinations Cali (50 daily; 9hr); Manizales (hourly; 5hr); Pasto (5 daily; 18hr); Pereira (twice hourly; 5hr); Popayán (3–4 daily; 10hr).

Tourist information There are information stands at both airports as well as a small tourist office inside the Palacio de Exposiciones at Cl 41 No. 55–35 (daily 9am–5pm; ☏ 4 385 6966).

GETTING AROUND AND TOURS

Metro The city's excellent metro system (Mon–Sat 4.30am–11pm, Sun 5am–10pm; COP$1600; ☝ www.metrodemedellin.gov.co) is clean and efficient; included in the price of a metro ride are cable cars that leave from Acevedo, Santo Domingo and San Javier metro stations, carrying passengers high above the city for remarkable views of the city and close-up views of the hilltop shanty towns.

Buses The safety and efficiency of the metro means that you're far less likely to use buses, but at COP$1500 a ride they're a cheap – though not recommended – option after the metro closes. Bus #133 runs between Parque Berrío and Calle 10 in El Poblado, and to get from the Zona Rosa to Metro Poblado, just hop on any bus running along C 10A.

Taxi Taxis are cheap and plentiful and there is no surcharge for journeys to the bus terminal, airports or at night.

ACCOMMODATION

Most of the recommended budget accommodation is close to the night-time action in El Poblado and Patio Bonito.

HOSTELS

★ **Black Sheep Hostel** Transversal 5A No. 45–133, Patio Bonito ☏ 4 311 1589, ☝ www.blacksheepmedellin.com. This sociable backpackers' pad has all bases covered, including Spanish classes, high-pressure showers and weekly barbecues. The affable Kiwi owner has travelled extensively in Colombia and is happy to share his knowledge. Single rooms available. Dorms COP$21,000, doubles COP$60,000

Casa Blanca Transversal 5A No. 45–256 ☏ 4 586 5149, ☝ casablancamedellin.com. In a quiet, attractive neighbourhood, only 15min walk to the Zona Rosa, you can take advantage of the little extras that this homey hostel offers – from free Spanish classes to the sociable barbecues on Sun. Dorms COP$20,000, doubles COP$75,000

Casa Kiwi Cra 36 No. 7–10 ☏ 4 268 2668, ☝ casakiwi.net. Owned by a motorcycle-loving American, this excellent 55-bed party hostel has clean dorms, DVD room, pool table, kitchen, bicycles for rent, laundry service, and an adjoining luxury wing with fancy doubles, some en suite. Dorms COP$20,000, doubles COP$60,000

Pit Stop Hostel Cra 43E No. 5–110 ☏ 4 352 1176, ☝ pitstophostel.com. Right near the Zona Rosa, this lively place is aimed at the travellers who play hard – with pool and basketball court complemented by the chillout areas – one with steam room, another with hammocks. Dorms COP$21,000, doubles COP$60,000

Tiger Paw Hostel Cra 36 No. 10–49 ☏ 4 311 6079, ☝ tigerpawhostel.com. Right in the middle of the Zona Rosa, this is one of the liveliest hostels in town, with its own bar, lounge and pool table. The rooms are colourful but a bit basic – not that it matters, since you won't be spending much time sleeping. Dorms COP$19,000, doubles COP$50,000

Wandering Paisa C 44A No. 68A–76 ☏ 4 436 6759, ☝ wanderingpaisahostel.com. A little out of the way, this hostel goes the extra mile when it comes to arranging social events for its guests. There's an on-site bar to assist with the social lubrication. Dorms COP$19,000

5

EATING

Paisa cuisine, among Colombia's most distinctive, is heavy on the *frijoles* (black beans), grilled meat, plantains and rice. Perhaps no dish is more characteristic of the region than the *bandeja paisa*, a large bowl filled with ground beef, chorizo sausage, *frijoles*, rice, fried green bananas, a fried egg, avocado and fried pork. The city's trendiest restaurants are around leafy Parque Lleras in El Poblado, also known as the Zona Rosa.

Le Bon Café C 9 No. 39–09. Excellent pastries and 32 types of coffee are on offer at this El Poblado café, which has several other locations throughout the city. Mon–Sat 4.30am–11pm, Sun 5am–10pm.

★ **The Flip Flop Sandwich Shop** Cra 36 No. 8A –92. Homesick travellers (or anyone in search of real bacon) gravitate towards this excellent breakfast/sandwich joint. Chris, the owner, is a treasure trove of local information, his sandwiches (try the Buffalo) hit the spot and the vibe is wonderfully relaxed. Sandwiches COP$7,000. Mon–Sat 9am–3pm.

Il Forno Cra 37A No. 8–9. A modern, open-air Italian place and El Poblado institution with plenty of mood lighting and satisfying pizza, home-made pasta and salads. Mains COP$12,000–18,000. Daily noon–10pm.

★ **Hummus** C 6 No. 43C–12. Not only are there plenty of vegetarian options at this classy Lebanese restaurant, but their *limonada de coco* is easily the best in town, and if you're extra hungry, go for the *mixto platter* – complete with *kofta, tabouleh, swarma, kibbeh* and rice. Mains from COP$20,000. Daily noon–3pm & 7–10pm.

★ **Royal Thai** C 8A No. 37A–05. Though there are Japanese elements to the decor upstairs, the food here is authentic Thai. The curries, though not cheap, are beautifully flavoured and hit that spice spot, and the dessert menu features the classic sticky rice with mango. Mains COP$25,000. Mon–Sat noon–3pm & 7–11pm.

Señor Itto C 9 No. 43B–127. For a taste of beautifully prepared raw fish, try what is considered to be the best sushi joint in town. The "Dinamita Especial" deserves applause and there are plenty of noodle and teriyaki dishes for those who like their food cooked. Lunch *menú* COP$12,000, mains COP$20,000. Mon–Sat noon–3pm & 7–10pm.

DRINKING AND NIGHTLIFE

A cluster of thumping bars and clubs – most of them catering to a young clientele – is in El Poblado. If you fancy something a bit more authentic, start with a beer on Calle 70 (Metro El Estadio) and listen to local musicians playing *vallenato* before heading on to Calle 33 (Metro Floresta) for a dance. Bars usually close around 2am Mon–Wed and 4am Thurs–Sat.

3 Cordilleras C 30 No. 44–176 ☎ 4 444 2337. If you take beer seriously and want to learn a thing or two about how

it's made, this brewery offers weekly tours (COP$18,000), including five free beers, to help you appreciate Medellín's finest. Thurs only 5.30–9pm.

El Blue C 10 No. 40–20. Giant speakers pump hard electro beats to a student and backpacker-centric crowd who wave along to flashing green laser lights. Thurs–Sat until late. Entry COP$10,000.

★ **El Eslabón Prendido** C 53 No. 42–55. Renowned for its live music on Tues nights, when the tightly packed crowd goes wild to Colombia salsa. Tues–Sat 8pm–2am. Entry COP$5500.

Luxury Cra 43G No. 24–15. This is where a young, tipsy crowd gets down and dirty to reggaeton, hip-hop and more. Luxury it ain't, but it sure is lively. Thurs–Sun 9.30pm–3am. Entry COP$20,000.

DAY-TRIPS FROM MEDELLÍN

A few nearby parks make good if not absolutely essential stops within range of Medellín.

Parque Ecológico Piedras Blancas

The **Parque Ecológico Piedras Blancas** (daily 9am–5pm; free), 26km east of the city, serves as the lungs of Medellín. Set at the cool height of 2500m, much of this nature reserve has been reforested with native species, attracting butterflies and birds such as the brilliant blue soledad and the toucanet. Well-preserved pre-Columbian stone trails constructed between 100 BC and 700 AD weave through the park, while there is a butterfly gallery and a slick **insect museum** close to the official entrance.

To **get to the park**, board a bus from the corner of Ayacucho and Córdoba in the city centre (leaves every 30min) to the village of Santa Elena (30min), where another bus runs (every 30min) to the park. The metro cable car that runs from Santo Domingo to Parque Arví (see p.538) also connects the city to the park.

Piedra del Peñol and Guatapé

Bearing a freakish resemblance to Rio de Janeiro's Sugar Loaf Mountain, **Piedra del Peñol**, or simply "the rock", rises spectacularly from the edge of Embalse del Peñol, an artificial lake some 70km east of Medellín, studded with islands. Locals may tell you that the 200m granite and quartz monolith is a meteorite.

Whatever geological or intergalactic anomaly brought it here, it's well worth climbing the 649 stone steps to the rock's peak for phenomenal 360-degree views of emerald green peninsulas jutting into the azure Embalse del Peñol – a hydroelectric dam that submerged the original town of El Peñol in the 1970s.

There is a handful of restaurants and tourist stalls at the base of the rock, but it's better to walk or take a jeep (COP$3500 per person) to the delightful lakeside village of **Guatapé**, 3km away, which is full of restaurants serving trout fresh from the lake. The palm-lined main square, Plaza Simón Bolívar, is well preserved, with its crowning glory the Iglesia La Inmaculada Concepción; throughout the town you'll find colourful colonial houses adorned with intricate artistic motifs.

The best places to eat are along the lakefront Avenida Malecón (also known as Calle 32) and include *Vaso é Leche*, at C 32 No. 26–35, where you'll get filling trout mains with a salad, plantain and fries for COP$12,000. **Buses** leave for Guatapé roughly every half-hour from Medellín's northern bus terminal (2hr). Ask the driver to let you off at "La Piedra".

MANIZALES AND AROUND

Founded in 1849 by migrating *paisas*, **MANIZALES** developed in the late nineteenth century with the growth of the coffee industry. One legacy is the numerous Neoclassical buildings in the city centre, which has been declared a national monument. This high-mountain city (altitude 2150m) sits at the base of the snowcapped Nevado del Ruiz volcano (see p.543), which, on a clear day you can sometimes see burping vapour from the bridge in front of the Teatro Los Fundadores. Manizales owes its hilly topography to the geologically volatile earth beneath it, and earthquakes occur with some frequency.

WHAT TO SEE AND DO

Much of the town's charm lies in its large student population, who help create a festive atmosphere, with night-time entertainment centred mostly on Cable Plaza. The party comes to a head in the first weeks of January during the **Fería de Manizales**, when there are colourful parades, a beauty pageant in search of a new Coffee Queen and bloody bullfights staged in the Plaza de Toros (C 8 and Cra 27). Manizales also makes an excellent base for exploring the surrounding **coffee farms** (see p.544) and the **Parque Nacional Natural Los Nevados** (see p.543).

Plaza de Bolívar

In the centre of the city, the main square is dominated by the vast **Catedral de Manizales** (tower Mon & Thurs–Sun 9am–noon & 2–6pm; COP$3000), made of reinforced concrete and featuring a virtigo-inducing, 106m-tall tower that you can ascend with a guide; tours start on the hour. In the centre of the plaza stands an obligatory **statue of Simón Bolívar**, but with a twist – *Bolívar-Cóndor*, the creation of Rodrigo Arenas Betancur, is half-man, half-condor.

Torre al Cielo

In the northwest suburb of Chipre, on a high bluff at the end of Avenida 12 de Octubre, the 45m-tall **Torre al Cielo** (Mon–Wed 11am–10pm, Thurs–Sat 11am–2am, Sun 10am–10pm; COP$3000) is the town's best lookout. On a clear day you can see seven *departamentos* and three mountain ranges. Buses run to Chipre from the Cable Plaza along Avenida Santander every minute or so.

Reserva Ecológica Río Blanco

Around 3km northeast of Manizales, the **Reserva Ecológica Río Blanco** is home to 362 bird species, 350 butterfly species and more than forty mammals. Tranquil orchid-lined uphill hikes through impressive cloudforest reveal dense jungle flora entwined in a battle for a place in the sun; if you are lucky, you may catch a glimpse of the reserve's endangered spectacled bear. There is also a hummingbird farm. You'll need to request permission to enter the reserve from the Fundación Ecológica Gabriel Arango Restrepo (Av Kevin Angel No. 59–181; Mon–Fri 8am–4.30pm; ☎6 887 9770,

5

ⓦfundegar.com). They will book the compulsory guides (COP$20,000 for up to fifteen people). A taxi to the entrance costs around COP$20,000 (20min); arrange a return trip.

Recinto del Pensamiento

Butterflies and birds are the main attraction at this nature park (Tues–Sun 9am–4pm; COP$11,000, COP$15,000 including cable-car ride; ☎6 874 4157, ⓦrecintodelpensamiento.com), 11km from Manizales. As well as visiting the colourful butterfly enclosure, you can also wander through a medicinal herb garden, relax in the Japanese Zen garden, enjoy a stroll through the orchid forest and marvel at the gigantic *guadua* bamboo gazebo, used for conventions and wedding ceremonies. Guides are compulsory and included in the admission price. Buses (marked Sera Maltería; 30min; COP$1600) leave Cable Plaza every 15min; or you can catch a taxi (10min; COP$9000) or take the cable car.

ARRIVAL AND DEPARTURE

By plane La Nubia Airport is 8km southeast of the city centre. A taxi costs around COP$11,000 or you can jump on one of the frequent buses for COP$1500.
Destinations Bogotá (10 daily; 50min); Cartagena (daily; 1hr 20min); Medellín (2 daily; 30min).
By bus The bus terminal (☎6 878 7858, ⓦterminal demanizales.com) is at Cra 43 No. 65–100. Ride the cable car to the centre of town from where regular buses (COP$1500) run to Cable Plaza, or jump in a taxi (COP$5000–6000).
Destinations Bogotá (hourly; 8–9hr); Cali (hourly; 5hr); Medellín (hourly; 4hr 30min); Pereira (every 5min; 1hr 20min).

GETTING AROUND AND INFORMATION

Cable car The city's flashy new cable-car line runs from the bus station (Cambulos stop) to Cra 23 in the centre of town (Fundadores stop) in less than 10min and costs COP$1500.
Tourist information Parque Benjamin López on the corner of Cra 22 and C 31 (daily 7.30am–7.30pm; ☎6 873 2901) dishes out maps.

ACCOMMODATION

★ **Base Camp** Cra 23 No. 32–20 ☎6 882 1699, ⓦbasecamphostel.com. Just steps from the cable car's Fundadores stop, this spacious hostel is a great city-centre

option, immaculately clean and with a stylish retro design. The roof terrace has stunning views across the city and is perfect for a sunset beer. Owners Carolina and Victor are outdoor enthusiasts and can organize multiple-day hikes to Los Nevados. Dorms COP$20,000, doubles COP$50,000
Manizales Hostel C 67 No. 23A–33 ☎6 887 0871, ⓦmanizaleshostel.com. *Mountain House*'s sister hostel has the same friendly management, facilities and excellent tourist information but its smaller capacity makes it more low-key and a good choice if you want to wind down. Helpful owner Cristina Giraldo goes out of her way to enhance your stay in the city, and several tours can be booked through both hostels. Dorms COP$20,000, doubles COP$60,000
★ **Mountain House** C 66 No. 23B–91 ☎6 887 4736, ⓦmountainhousemanizales.com. On a quiet suburban street just two blocks from the buzzing Zona Rosa, this lively backpackers' hostel has comfortable dorms, a cosy TV room stocked with DVDs, free breakfast, kitchen, a large back yard with a barbecue area, bike and mountain gear rental, and – best of all – all kinds of outdoor ventures organized by helpful staff. Dorms COP$22,000, doubles COP$50,000
Pit Stop Hostel C 65 No. 23B–19 ☎6 886 5866, ⓦpit stophostel.com. This hostel likes a party and its on-site jacuzzi, large terrace and popular bar with regular DJs draws an energetic bunch. Dorms COP$18,000, doubles COP$60,000

EATING, DRINKING AND NIGHTLIFE

The city centre clears out at night and most eating and drinking is done in the suburbs. The liveliest area, popular with students, is around Cable Plaza, between calles 60 and 75 along Cra 23 (the Zona Rosa), where you'll find the best selection of restaurants, bars and places to dance.
★ **La Clave del Mar** C 69A No. 27–100, Barrio Palermo ☎6 887 5528. Excellent fresh seafood delivered from Tumaco or Buenaventura on the Pacific coast. Try the delicious *Cazuela de mariscos* seafood casserole (COP$27,000) or the *Sancocho del bagre* (COP$20,000), a potato, cassava and catfish soup. Mon–Sat 10am–9.30pm, Sun 10am–4.30pm.
★ **Juan Sebastian-Bar** Cra 23 No. 63–66. Charismatic owner Elmer Vargas has a passion for jazz and an awesome CD collection. Popular with artists, writers and university lecturers, this intimate spot has great views of the city and fine cocktails. Mon–Sat 7pm–2am.
Restaurante y Asadero Típico El Zaguán Paisa Cra 23 No. 31–27. Enter through the never-ending bamboo corridor for a hearty *menú del día* (COP$5000); it's conveniently located for the cable car to the bus station. Daily 11.30am–9pm.
Santelmo Cra 23B No. 64–80. Heaving with students who down cocktails (COP$13,000) and jugs of sangria (COP$33,000), then dance the night away between the tables. Wed–Sat until late.

Spago C 59 No. 24A–10 ☎ 6 885 3328. A stylish Italian restaurant that offers great home-made pasta, wood-fired pizza and expertly cooked meats. Mains COP$18,000. Mon–Sat noon–10.30pm, Sun until 3pm.

La Suiza Cra 23B No. 26–57. Superb bakery where you can grab breakfast or a light lunch – crêpes, pastries, sandwiches – or treat yourself to home-made chocolates. Mon–Sat 9.30am–8pm, Sun 10am–7.30pm.

Valentino's Gourmet Cra 23 No. 63–128. Excellent hot chocolates (COP$4000) and an extensive coffee, cocktail and ice-cream menu. Daily 10am–10pm.

PARQUE NACIONAL NATURAL LOS NEVADOS

Indisputably one of the crown jewels in Colombia's national parks system, the **PARQUE NACIONAL NATURAL LOS NEVADOS** (entry COP$57,000, including guide), 40km southeast of Manizales, protects some of the last surviving snowcapped peaks in the tropics. Three of the five volcanoes are now dormant, but **Nevado del Ruiz** – the tallest at 5321m – remains an active threat, having killed 22,000 people and buried the now extinct town of Armero when it erupted in 1985. Sadly, though, for a park whose name, Nevado, implies perpetual snow, climate change has lifted the snow line to almost 5000m on most peaks. The best months to visit are January and February – clear days make for spectacular views of the volcanic peaks. March, July, August and December can also be ideal, while the rest of the year sees a fair amount of rain.

WHAT TO SEE AND DO

The park's **northern sector** is the more touristy and is easily accessible from Manizales. Though it's of little compensation, because of the severe melt, it's now possible for even moderately fit armchair adventurers to reach Nevado del Ruiz's summit in a long day's journey from Manizales. Although not technically difficult – with good weather you can climb in regular hiking shoes – a **guide** (see below) is required to navigate the confusing path and assist in the event of altitude sickness.

At the time of writing, the Nevado Del Ruiz volcano was showing some activity,

so the park was off-limits. Instead, *Mountain House* (see opposite) offers an alternative: hiking down through stunning mountain scenery, past mountain villages. The hostel arranges for its guests to meet a milkman's cart at an assigned point at 4.30am; the milkman then drives up the mountain road to the starting point of the hike and picks up the hikers further down the road a couple of hours later, having finished his rounds. The outing costs around COP$50,000. Wear warm clothing as you'll be going up to a high altitude in the middle of the night.

The dramatic **southern end**, where a dense wax-palm forest slowly metamorphoses into *páramo* near the cobalt-blue **Laguna del Otún** (3950m), can only be accessed on foot. Reaching Laguna del Otún from Manizales involves an initial four-hour drive, taking in park highlights such as the extinct Olleta crater, Laguna Verde and Hacienda Potosí, before culminating in a two-hour trek to the trout-stuffed lagoon (fishing permitted). You can also approach from the Valle de Cócora in Salento (see p.546) .

There is no public transport to the park. Many visitors come as part of a day-trip, which doesn't allow a great deal of time for hiking. To explore the park at your leisure, it's possible to sign up for a day-trip and then arrange to stay overnight, to be picked up by the same tour company the following day.

Contact a tour operator to see whether Parque Nacional Los Nevados is still off-limits.

TOUR OPERATOR

Ecosistemas Cra 21 No. 23–21 Local 108 ☎ 6 880 8300. Runs a daily 12hr trip from Manizales, leaving at 7.30am, for COP$140,000, including transport, breakfast, lunch, park entrance, the ascent of Ruiz and a visit to the thermal baths at the park's entrance.

PEREIRA

Just 56km south of Manizales, **PEREIRA** makes an equally suitable base for exploring the Zona Cafetera. The region's largest city, it shares Manizales' history as a centre for the coffee industry. Its historic

5

centre has been repeatedly destroyed by earthquakes, the most recent striking in 1999. However, it's closer to many of the region's coffee *fincas* and thermal springs.

Pereira's **Plaza de Bolívar** is unique among the uniformly named central plazas of Colombia for its modern sculpture of Bolívar Desnudo – the El Libertadór nude on horseback, a controversial pose when it was unveiled in 1963 but now a beloved city symbol. Also on the plaza is the town's magnificent **Catedral**, built in 1875. Nondescript from the outside, the Catedral's single-nave interior is supported by an elaborate latticework of twelve thousand wooden beams forming a canopy like a spider's web.

ARRIVAL AND INFORMATION

By plane Pereira's international Aeropuerto Matecaña (☎ 6 326 0021) is 5km west of the city centre. A taxi downtown costs around COP$10,000, or jump on one of the frequent buses for COP$500.
Destinations Bogotá (8 daily; 50min); Cali (4 daily; 30min); Medellín (5 daily; 35min).

By bus The bus terminal (☎ 6 321 5834) lies 1.5km south of the city centre at C 17 No. 23–157. A taxi to the centre is COP$4000; a bus will set you back COP$500.
Destinations Armenia (every 10min; 1hr); Bogotá (hourly; 9hr); Cali (hourly; 3hr 30min); Manizales (every 15min; 1hr 15min); Medellín (hourly; 6hr); Salento (3 daily, hourly on weekends; 50min); Santa Rosa de Cabal (every 10min; 45min).
Tourist information The tourist office (Mon–Fri 8.30am–noon & 2–6pm; ☎ 6 325 8753, ⓦ risaralda.com.co) is on the corner of C 17 and Cra 10 on the first floor of the Centro Cultural Lucy Tejada.

ACCOMMODATION

Pereira has few accommodation options for budget travellers, so it's worth staying at one of the converted *fincas*, many of them former coffee plantations, between 5km and 35km from the city (see below). Most have swimming pools, offer meals and are accessible by bus from Pereira.
Hotel Cumanday Cra 5 No. 22–54 ☎ 6 324 0416. Solid downtown option, with reliable hot showers, cable TV and a place to wash your dirty togs. If you ask nicely, the staff will let you cook in their kitchen. <u>COP$55,000</u>
Kolibrí Hostel C 4 No. 16–35 ☎ 6 331 3955, ⓦ www.kolibri hostel.com. New hostel run by a wonderfully friendly Dutch–Colombian couple. The rooms are bright, the atmosphere

---

STAYING ON A COFFEE FARM

Coffee is the planet's most-traded commodity after oil and Colombia is one of its largest producers, with 500,000-plus growers and the unique benefit of two annual harvests. Recognized for producing world-class coffee, **coffee fincas** in the Zona Cafetera are now following in the footsteps of the wine industry and opening their doors to curious tourists.

Fincas range from traditional estates still attended by their owner to deceptively modern rural hotels where the only coffee you'll find comes served with breakfast. Scenically, the farms look out on lush slopes, overgrown with the shiny-leaved coffee shrubs and interspersed with banana plants and bamboo-like *guadua* forests. Many will also arrange horseriding and walks, and they make an ideal base to explore the region's many attractions.

To locate the best *fincas* for your needs, ask other travellers; you can also enquire at the local tourist offices or hostels in Manizales (see p.542) or Pereira (see above).

FINCAS

Hacienda Guayabal Cra 3 No. 15–72 Chinchiná ☎ 314 772 4856, ⓦ www.haciendaguayabal.com. Runs tours, in English, of their postcard-perfect coffee farm (COP$30,000). Guests can stay in the main house, and the price includes a tour, three meals and use of the swimming pool. To get there, take a bus from Manizales or Pereira to Chinchiná (30min) and then travel the last 3km by taxi or catch a bus from in front of the church to the farm. Per person <u>COP$50,000</u>
★ **Hacienda Venecia** C 59 No. 24A–18 ☎ 6 885 0771, ⓦ haciendavenecia.com. This fourth-generation, family-owned working coffee farm is an essential stop

for anyone who wants to learn more about coffee production, roasting techniques, trade and aromas. Proud owner Juan Pablo exports coffee as well as roasting for the domestic market. Tours (COP$30,000 including pick-up from Manizales) of his sprawling plantation allow visitors to observe the production process from start to finish. Spend a night at the guesthouse, swinging in a hammock on the veranda, firefly-spotting and listening to the croaks of happy frogs in the swimming pool. Breakfast included. To get there, catch a taxi (COP$35,000) or take a jeep from the Plaza de Mercado in Manizales (3 daily at 6am, midday and 5pm; COP$3000). Per person <u>COP$30,000</u>

sociable and the location is great for going out in the Sector Circunvalar. Dorms COP$20,000, doubles COP$60,000

Hotel Mi Casita C 25 No. 6–20 ⊙ 6 333 9995. Close to Parque El Lago Uribe and used to dealing with travellers, this no-frills option is one of the better budget spots in town, with cable TV and a garish colour scheme. Free wi-fi. COP$69,000

EATING AND DRINKING

The majority of good eating and drinking options are located in the Sector Circunvalar, on or near the Av Circunvalar.

Crepes & Waffles Cra 8 No. 19–17. Branch of the ubiquitous chain where the myriad sweet and savoury offerings are always a crowd-pleaser. Waffles from COP$6000. Daily 11am–8pm.

★ **Leña y Carbón** This Argentine-style steakhouse specializes in what is possibly the best grilled meat in Colombia. You are presented with a beautifully cooked cut of your choice with all the trimmings by smartly attired waiters and it's all amazing value for the quality and quantity. Steaks COP$16,000. Daily noon–11pm.

Maria La Mexicana C 9A No. 15–14. Perch on one of the colourful chairs on the patio and choose from authentic quesadillas (COP$12,000), overflowing burros (COP$9500), tacos (COP$5000) and other beautifully cooked Mexican food. When you're done, add a scribble to the happy customer wall. Daily noon–10pm.

★ **El Parnaso** Cra 6 No. 23–35. Enjoy a cocktail (COP$12,000) in this cool outdoor garden bar, with fairy lights strung between guava trees, to a rock-indie soundtrack over which you can still make yourself heard. Closed Sun.

DAY-TRIPS FROM PEREIRA

Pereira makes a good base for striking out on numerous ventures to the nearby hot springs, hiking trails and coffee *fincas*.

Termales Santa Rosa

Sitting at the foot of a 25m-high waterfall and surrounded by lush greenery, these attractive **hot springs** (daily 9am–midnight; COP$14,000; ⓦtermales.com.co) consist of four thermal pools and a visitor centre with cafeteria and massages on offer, and you can also take a dip in the natural pool directly beneath the waterfall. Just a little further down the dirt road are the **thermal springs** (daily 9am–10pm; COP$36,000; ⓦtermales.com.co) attached to the *Hotel Termales*, which resembles an alpine chalet, with one large pool and two thimble-sized hot tubs available to non-guests, set against a spectacular backdrop of three tall waterfalls. There's also a lavish spa on site.

The springs are easily reachable from Santa Rosa de Cabal, 9km west. Frequent buses run from Pereira to Santa Rosa de Cabal (COP$2500, 40min). From the corner of Santa Rosa's *la galería* (marketplace), opposite the police station, *chivas* and buses (try to catch a *chiva* if possible) leave for the hot springs at 7am, 10am, noon, 3pm and 5pm (COP$3000, 45min; double-check timetables before departure), coming back pretty much straight after. If you miss the bus, one of the Willy Jeeps parked by the market will take you there for COP$20,000.

Termales San Vicente

These lavishly landscaped **hot springs** (daily 8am–1am; COP$25,000; ⊙6 333 6157, ⓦsanvicente.com.co), 35km northeast of Pereira via the town of Santa Rosa de Cabal, feature a selection of steaming medicinal thermal pools scattered across some five square kilometres of cloudforest, river, waterfalls and luxuriant countryside. At 2330m, it gets pretty chilly up here, so it helps that the average pool temperature is 38°C. A variety of spa treatments is offered, including massage (COP$40,000) and mud therapy (COP$20,000). If you want to **spend the night** at the springs, the most cost-effective option is camping (COP$85,000 including entrance fee and breakfast). Further up the accommodation ladder are cabañas (COP$180,000).

The easiest way to get to San Vicente is with one of the direct daily buses that leave at 9am from the thermal springs' office in Pereira at Cra 13, No. 15–62, returning at 5pm. This service only runs during the week if there is a minimum of ten people. The price, including entrance, transport and lunch, is COP$55,000. Alternatively, you can make your own way to the spa by catching a bus to Santa Rosa from the bus terminal in Pereira and grabbing a seat on a Willy Jeep (ex-US military 4WD) from *la galería* (market) for Termales San Vicente (CP$50,000/80,000 one-way/return).

5

SALENTO

In the heart of coffee country, the adorable village of **SALENTO** is one of the region's earliest settlements, and its slow development means the original lifestyle and buildings of the *paisa* journeymen who settled here in 1842 have barely been altered since. Rural workers clad in cowboy hats and *ruanas* (Colombian ponchos) are a common sight. The colourful, wonderfully photogenic one-storey homes of thick adobe and clay-tile roofs that surround the plaza are as authentic as it gets.

WHAT TO SEE AND DO

Salento is a popular destination for weary backpackers who linger here to soak up the town's unpretentious charms and hike in the spectacular Valle de Cócora or to use the town as a base to explore the rest of the Zona Cafetera. Salento is also the second most popular weekend destination in the country for Colombians, and on Saturdays and Sundays the main plaza hosts a **food and handicrafts fair**. Salento's annual fiesta falls in the first week of January, when the town kicks up its heels for a week of horse processions, mock bullfighting and folk dancing.

From the top of Calle Real, steps lead to **Alto de la Cruz**, a hilltop *mirador* offering unbeatable vistas of the Valle de Cócora and, on a clear day, the peaks of snow-clad volcanoes in Parque Nacional Natural Los Nevados (see p.543).

ARRIVAL AND INFORMATION

By bus Buses arrive and depart from Salento's main plaza. Willy Jeeps (daily at 6.10am, 7.30am, 9.30am, 11.30am; 20min) run to Cócora. They return when full at around 3 or 4pm.

Destinations Armenia (every 20min from 6am–9pm; 1hr); Pereira (3 daily at 7.50am, 2.50pm & 5.50pm, more frequent on weekends; 50min). Going to/from Pereira, you can also take an Armenia-bound bus to the Las Flores junction and then catch one of the frequent buses from Armenia to Salento or Pereira.

Tourist information The English-speaking staff at *Tralala* and *Plantation House* (see below) are particularly knowledgeable about the area.

Bank The ATM on the main square often runs out of money, so it's best to arrive with cash.

ACCOMMODATION

Book ahead if you plan to visit during the annual fiesta at the start of January.

Hostal Ciudad de Segorbe C 5 No. 4–06 ☎6 759 3794, ⓦhostalciudaddesegorbe.com. Stylish rooms offer stunning views of the Valle de Cócora and balconies overlook the spacious flower-filled central courtyard, which is a great place to unwind with a book. There's also a Spanish bar with a good selection of wine and the owners are just wonderful. Dorms COP$22,000, doubles COP$65,000

Plantation House C 7 No. 1–04 ☎316 285 2603, ⓦtheplantationhousesalento.com. An old colonial house set on a picturesque coffee plantation, this British/

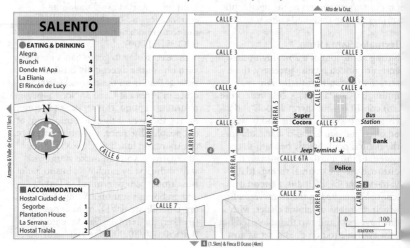

SALENTO

● EATING & DRINKING

Alegra	1
Brunch	4
Donde Mi Apa	3
La Eliania	5
El Rincón de Lucy	2

■ ACCOMMODATION

Hostal Ciudad de Segorbe	1
Plantation House	3
La Serrana	4
Hostal Tralala	2

▲ Alto de la Cruz

CALLE 2

CALLE 3

CALLE 4

CALLE 5

CALLE 6

CALLE 7

CARRERA 2

CARRERA 3

CARRERA 4

CARRERA 5

CALLE REAL

Super Cocora

PLAZA

Jeep Terminal ★

CALLE 6TA

Bus Station

Bank

Police

CARRERA 6

CARRERA 7

0   100
metres

Armenia & Valle de Cócora (11km)

▼ ◀ (1.5km) & Finca El Ocaso (4km)

Colombian-run hostel is a good place to meet fellow travellers and provides excellent tourist information. An adjacent building accommodates guests when the main house is full and the owners can let you stay on their coffee farm. Dorms are plain and some rooms are en suite. Dorms COP$18,000, doubles COP$50,000

★ **La Serrana** Via Palestina Km1.5 ☎ 316 296 1890, ⨁ laserrana.com.co. Eco-friendly working farm and hostel with faux-rustic rooms, 1.5km from Salento, with spectacular views of the surrounding Cócora mountains and valleys. Horseriding, mountain biking, fishing, rafting and paragliding are all offered. End your day on a comfy sofa enjoying the great music selection. Call to arrange a pick-up from town. Dorms COP$20,000, doubles COP$55,000

★ **Hostal Tralala** C 7 No. 6–45 ☎ 314 850 5543, ⨁ hostel tralalasalento.com. Friendly Dutch owner, Hemmo Misker, has worked hard to convert this traditional *paisa*-style house into a beautiful, modern hostel. The spotless rooms with ultra-comfortable beds and smart bathrooms retain original features, like the wooden floors with furnishings made by local artisans. Bonus features include a fully equipped guest kitchen, DVD lounge, library and sun terrace. Dorms COP$20,000, doubles COP$60,000

EATING AND DRINKING

Fresh trout is on the menu in all the town's restaurants and is usually served with big crunchy *patacones* (fried plantains). The main square has several lively bars with outside tables. Or meet locals to play *tejo* – which involves throwing metal weights into a clay pit to trigger gunpowder explosions for points – at Cra 4, C 3–32.

Alegra C 6 No. 7 Esq. Delicious home-made cakes, veggie burgers, chutneys and jams. Owner Jaime Eduardo has a passion for local organic produce and paintings by Salento artists. Homecooked pasta, pizza and salad mains from COP$12,000. Daily noon–9pm.

★ **Brunch** C 6 No. 3–25 ⨁ brunchsalento.com. This American-run spot has been winning rave reviews from an international crowd for its burgers, fajitas and delectable peanut butter brownies, among other things. The friendly owner will whip up packed lunches for Cócora-bound hikers and there's even a little cinema room for nightly screenings. Daily 7am–9pm.

★ **Donde Mi Apá** Cra 6 No. 5–24, main square. Perfect for people-watching on the square and hanging out with drunk locals. The interior is packed with stacked vinyls, old photos and a glaring stuffed bull's head. Mon–Thurs 4pm–midnight, Fri 4pm–2am, Sat 1pm–2am, Sun 11am–midnight.

La Eliania Cra 2 No. 6–65. If you're craving proper Indian curry, gourmet pizza or doorstop sandwiches with inventive fillings, look no further. Given the high cooking standards, the prices are a bargain. Mains from COP$7000. Daily 8am–1pm & 4–9pm.

★ **El Rincón de Lucy** Cra 6 No. 4–02. A whizz in the kitchen, Lucy serves the best set lunches in town. For COP$6500 you get juice, soup and a heaped plate of beans, vegetables and fish or meat. Daily 6am–3pm.

DAY-TRIP FROM SALENTO: VALLE DE CÓCORA

Salento sits atop the **VALLE DE CÓCORA**, which contains a thick forest of the skyscraper wax palm, Colombia's national plant, which grows up to 60m high. The valley, which offers picturesque hikes, is easily explored in a day-trip from Salento. The hamlet of **Cócora**, with a handful of restaurants, small shops and hotels, lies 11km east of Salento. From Cócora a well-trodden path leads into misty, pristine cloudforest, scattered with the remains of pre-Columbian tombs and dwellings. Orchids, bromeliads and heliconias are just some of the plant species that thrive here, and the fauna includes spectacled bear, native deer and puma, along with hundreds of bird species such as toucans, eagles and motmots.

A five- to six-hour **loop walk** starts from the blue gate in Cócora; the muddy track passes a trout farm and runs through farmland for around 45 minutes before reaching the park entrance, after which you're following an uneven, slippery trail through cloudforest. The trail eventually branches, with one track leading up to the extremely worthwhile **Reserva Acaime** (entrance COP$3000), home to eighteen species of hummingbirds that flock to its bird feeders. The price includes a large mug of revitalizing hot chocolate and a chunk of locally produced cheese. You then retrace your steps to the main trail that crosses nine rickety wooden Indiana Jones-style bridges over the Río Quindío before the Finca La Montaña branch culminates at a mountain-top viewing platform with exhilarating valley views. The way down along a wide gravel road takes you past a cluster of wax palms – Colombia's national tree.

To **get to Cócora**, take one of the four Willy-Jeeps (ex-US military 4WDs) that leave daily from Salento's main plaza (daily at 6.10am, 7.30am, 9.30am,

5

11.30am; 20min; COP$3000 one-way). They return when full at around 3 or 4pm. Jeeps can also be hired for COP$24,000 one-way.

The southwest

Leaving the snowy white caps of the "Coffee Zone" behind, the Cauca River Valley descends south and widens until you reach **Cali**, gateway to Colombia's southwest and the self-proclaimed world capital of salsa music. A knuckle-whitening detour from Cali takes you to the tiny town of **San Cipriano**. Further south, the Panamerican Highway stretches past steamy fields of sugar cane to the serene, colonial town of **Popayán**, known for its blindingly white Rococo colonial architecture. The verdant rolling countryside around **San Agustín** is some of Colombia's finest, and would be worth a visit even without the enigmatic stone statues – remnants of a mysterious civilization – that pepper the hillsides. **Tierradentro**'s ancient tombs are less well known but no less fascinating. Heading further south from the overlooked town of **Pasto**, you ascend a ridge dominated by volcanoes all the way to Ecuador.

CALI

Colombia's third-largest city, with a population of 2.3 million, **CALI** was founded in 1536 but only shed its provincial backwater status in the early 1900s, when the profits brought in by its sugar plantations prompted industrialization. Today it's one of Colombia's most prosperous cities, in part because of its central role in the drug trade since the dismantling of the rival Medellín cartel in the early 1990s; however, Cali is now more famous for its salsa dancers than white powder.

The low-lying and extremely hot city (with temperatures routinely surpassing 40°C) straddles the **Río Cali**, a tributary of the Río Cauca, surrounded by the sugar plantations of the marshy Cauca Valley. The large numbers of African slaves brought to work the sugar mills left a notable impact on Cali's culture, nowhere more so than in its music.

Parts of central Cali are **unsafe** to walk around; be sure to get up-to-date advice on where not to go.

WHAT TO SEE AND DO

The city stakes a powerful claim to being Colombia's party capital, and you'll hear Cuban-style **salsa** music blaring from the numerous *salsatecas* throughout the day and night. If you're here in September, don't miss the Festival Mundial de Salsa.

Plaza de Caycedo and around

The city's centre is **Plaza de Caycedo**, which has a statue of independence hero Joaquín de Caycedo y Cuero in the middle. On the plaza's south end is the nineteenth-century **Catedral San Pedro**, with its elaborate stained-glass windows.

Iglesia de la Merced

The oldest church in the city is the **Iglesia de la Merced**, on the corner of Cra 4 and C 7, built from adobe and stone shortly after the city's founding. In the adjoining former convent – Cali's oldest building – is the **Museo Arqueológico la Merced** (Mon–Sat 9am–1pm & 2–6pm; COP$4000), which has displays of pre-Columbian pottery including funerary urns and religious objects unearthed throughout central and southern Colombia.

Museo del Oro

This small museum at C 7 No. 4–69 (Mon–Sat 10am–5pm; free) has a well-presented collection of gold and ceramics from the Calima culture from the region northwest of Cali.

Museo de Arte Moderno La Tertulia

Cali's **Museo de Arte Moderno La Tertulia** (Av Colombia No. 5–105 Oeste; Tues–Sun 10am–6pm; COP$4000; ⓦmuseolatertulia.com) shows changing exhibitions of contemporary photography, sculpture and painting, sometimes featuring high-profile international names, as well as arthouse film screenings in the adjoining *cinemateca*. Walk along

CALI

● EATING

Café Macondo	8
Chocolatino	4
Crepes y Waffles	3
Litany	6
Mister Wings	10
El Solar	7

● DRINKING & NIGHTLIFE

Changó	1
Kukaramakara	2
Lulu	5
Tin Tin Deo	9

■ ACCOMMODATION

Iguana	2
Jardin Azul	5
Jovita's Hostel	3
Pelican Larry	1
Tostaky	4

Río Cali for fifteen minutes from the city centre to get here.

ARRIVAL AND INFORMATION

By plane The best way to and from Cali's Aeropuerto Palmaseca (☎ 2 666 3200), 16km northeast of the city, is to catch one of the regular minibuses that run to and from the bus terminal (40min; COP$4300).

Destinations Bogotá (daily; 50min); Cartagena (daily; 1hr 25min); Medellín (4 daily; 40min); Pereira (4 daily; 30min); Pasto (2 daily; 1hr); San Andrés (daily; 2hr). Also international departures for Lima, Panama City, Madrid and Miami.

By bus The city's gigantic bus terminal at C 30N No. 2AN–29, 2km north of the centre, is connected to downtown by Mio, the efficient integrated bus system (see below). A taxi

into downtown costs COP$6000. There's a left luggage office at the terminal (24hr; COP$2700/12hr).

Destinations Armenia (hourly; 4hr); Bogotá (hourly; 12hr); Manizales (hourly; 5hr); Medellin (8 daily; 9hr); Pasto (hourly; 9hr); Pereira (several daily; 4hr); Popayán (every 30min; 3hr).

Tourist information The Secretaria de Cultura y Turismo, inside the Gobernación building at Cra 7 between C 9 and 10 (Mon–Fri 8.30am–4pm; ☎ 2 886 0000).

GETTING AROUND

Much local sightseeing can be done on foot, provided you're staying in the Granada or San Antonio neighbourhoods and are prepared to walk a lot.

By bus The main route of the efficient Mio network of electric buses (☎ www.metrocali.gov.co), akin to Bogotá's

5

TransMilenio, runs along the river, and also passes through the centre and along the Av Quinta (Av 5). It costs COP$1500 per ride; you need to buy a swipecard.

By taxi Some outlying attractions are best reached by inexpensive taxi. Always take a taxi at night. Try Taxi Libre (☎ 2 444 4444) or Taxi Libre Aeropuerto (☎ 2 555 5555).

ACCOMMODATION

Cali's backpacker hostels are concentrated in two clusters, one around the Granada neighbourhood with good access to nightlife on Avenida 6N and the restaurants around Avenida 8N, and the other in the characterful (but slightly less secure at night) colonial neighbourhood of San Antonio.

Iguana Av 9N No. 22N–46 ☎ 2 660 8937, ⓦ iguana.com .co. A friendly, Swiss-run youth hostel with all the vital backpacker facilities spread over two houses: garden barbecues, plus loads of information on the region and free salsa lessons for those with two left feet. A short walk from Granada. Dorms COP$17,000, doubles COP$45,000

Jardin Azul Cra 24A No. 2A–59 ☎ 2 556 8380, ⓦ jardin azul.com. A wonderfully friendly guesthouse in a quiet neighbourhood a short ride from the centre on the Mio. The bilingual proprietress is super-helpful, and the large, bright rooms and small swimming pool make this a great place to unwind after the heat of the city. Breakfast included. Wi-fi access patchy. Doubles COP$100,000

Jovita's Hostel Cra 5 No. 4–56 ☎ 2 893 8342, ⓦ jovitas hostel.com. If you're serious about your dance moves, then this salsa school/hostel/yoga centre is for you. The attractive be-hammocked common areas make up for the lack of windows in several rooms. If you don't wish to be stacked into the three-tiered bunkbeds, opt for a private room. Dorms COP$16,000, doubles COP$40,000

Pelican Larry C 23N No. 8N–12 ☎ 2 392 1407. The big beds, DVD room and twice-weekly barbecues at this fabulous location in Granada make this hostel popular with younger backpackers who are in Cali to party. Dorms COP$22,000, doubles COP$66,000

Tostaky Cra 10 No. 1–76 ☎ 2 893 0651, ⓦ tostakycali .com. There's a refined atmosphere at this French-run hostel in San Antonio, which probably has something to do with the coffee bar complete with chess sets in the front room. Guest kitchen for self-caterers is a bonus. Dorms COP$17,000, doubles COP$40,000

EATING

Café Macondo Cra 6 No. 3–03 ☎ 2 893 1570, ⓦ macondo cafe.blogspot.com. This cosy café with a jazz and blues soundtrack offers sandwiches, salads and burgers (from COP$10,000) plus delicious carrot muffins with an oozy *mora* centre (COP$2500) and a decent list of coffees and stronger tipples. Free film screenings every day bar Sat. Mon–Thurs 11.30am–11pm, Fri & Sat 11.30am–11pm, Sun 4.30–11pm.

Chocolatino Av 8N, at 17N. Marvel at the elaborate cake slices in their chilled counter, order à la carte (mains around COP$26,000) or enjoy a better class of set lunch (from COP$15,000) at this minimalist café. Also does brunch at weekends. Daily 11am–11pm.

Crepes y Waffles Av. 6AN No. 24A–70. Everyone's favourite crêpe and waffle joint, serving a predictably good array of sweet and savoury offerings and ice creams. Waffles from COP$6000. Mon–Sat 11.30am–8pm, Sun 11.30am–5pm.

★ **Litany** C 15AN No. 9N–35 ☎ 2 661 3736, ⓦ restaurante litany.com. Flavour-starved foodies should make a beeline for this acclaimed Lebanese restaurant, which serves up mouthwatering platters featuring *tabouli*, falafel, vine leaves (COP$25,000) and top-notch *shawarma* (around COP$20,000). Better still, you can BYO alcohol for no charge. Closed Fri & Sun night.

Mister Wings Cra 34 No. 4–12 Esq ⓦ misterwings.com. True to its name, this joint serves several styles of wings (we dare you to try the *endiabladas*), ribs, heaped platters of nachos with all the works, slabs of steak and jalapeño cheese sticks – enough to make anyone homesick for the US. You're guaranteed not to leave hungry. Wings from COP$11,800. Daily noon–11pm.

El Solar C 15N No. 9–62. Imagine a large courtyard filled with greenery. Now imagine some of the best seafood pasta and wild mushroom risotto appearing before you, with a tall, frothy glass of *limonada de coco* to wash it down with. This is it. Mains from COP$18,000. Mon–Sat noon–11pm.

DRINKING AND NIGHTLIFE

Much of the late-night action is just beyond the city limits. Cover charges, where they exist, are usually converted into drinks vouchers. The clubs around Avenida 6N are liveliest at the weekends. Single male travellers should find themselves a mixed group to go out with or risk being refused entry. For up-to-date information about what's hot and what's on, see ⓦ rumbascali.com.

★ **Changó** Vía Cavasa Km2, Juanchito ⓦ chango.com .co. Named after the African god of virility and leisure, infamous *Changó* overlooks the Río Cauca at the entrance to Juanchito. Skilled salsa dancers regularly fill its two dancefloors, and the clientele are less forgiving of gringos with two left feet than at some other places. Taxi around COP$17,000.

Kukaramakara C 28N No. 2bis–97 ⓦ kukaramakara .com. There's rock, pop and electronica at this large, rowdy disco, but the live bands, who usually blast out salsa, are the biggest draw. Cover COP$12,000. Thurs–Sat.

Lulu C 16N No. 8–42 ⓦ www.luludisco.com. You better be coming here to dance rather than to just lounge around looking gorgeous, as there's practically nowhere to sit down. Gay-friendly and fun.

★ **Tin Tin Deo** C 5 No. 38–71 ⓦ tintindeo.com. Unpretentious salsa temple where the odd reggae tune also sneaks onto the playlist and dancers sing along to the music. Particularly popular with foreigners on Thurs. Entrance is COP$5000 for women, COP$10,000 for men. Thurs 7pm–2am, Fri & Sat 7pm–3am.

SAN CIPRIANO

Cali is a good springboard from which to launch yourself to the unusual riverside village of San Cipriano, en route to the Pacific coast (see p.559). Set in the sweltering tropical jungle 128km northwest of Cali, the straggly jungle community of **SAN CIPRIANO** offers an entertaining change of pace for those who need time out from city life. The crystalline river here provides plentiful secluded cooling-off opportunities, but it is the unique journey to the 300-strong community of African slave descendants that has put San Cipriano on the traveller's map. There's no road and only a forest-flanked railway line linking San Cipriano with the town of Córdoba, 6km away, and since it sees very little train action, to bring visitors from Córdoba, inventive locals have attached motorcycle-powered wooden carts to the tracks. The journey down is nothing short of hair-raising and exhilarating; since it's a single-track railway, and there might be traffic coming the other way, be prepared to leap off in case of emergency.

San Cipriano lies at the confluence of the Escalarete and San Cipriano rivers and there are nine sites for safe **river swimming**, as well as opportunities for **tubing** (COP$6500). Follow the only road out of the settlement (the river will be on your right); well-signed tracks positioned every few hundred metres lead down to the river.

ARRIVAL AND DEPARTURE

To reach San Cipriano, catch any Buenaventura bus from Cali's bus terminal and ask to be let out at the junction to Córdoba (3hr). Walk down the hill (10min) to the train tracks from where carts leave roughly every hour. The carts leave when they are full; agree the price of your cart trip before setting off (around COP$10,000 return). San Cipriano is just inland from the port city of Buenaventura, making it a convenient stopover for adventurous souls heading to the Pacific coast.

ACCOMMODATION AND EATING

A number of restaurants serve meals and many also offer basic accommodation. If you do plan to spend the night here, bring a mosquito net.
Hotel David ☏ 312 815 4051. The rooms here come with fans, and shared or private bathrooms with cold water only; the food is hearty and tasty. Per person COP$12,000

POPAYÁN

Although less illustrious than Cartagena, Colombia's other open-air colonial museum, **POPAYÁN**, has little reason to envy its more celebrated rival. Founded in 1537 by Sebastián de Belálcazar on his

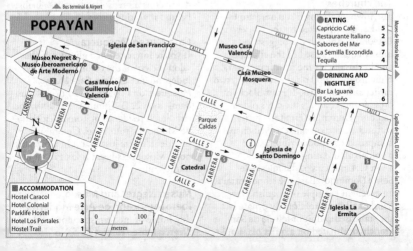

▲ Bus terminal & Airport

POPAYÁN

Iglesia de San Francisco

Museo Negret & Museo Iberoamericano de Arte Moderno

Casa Museo Guillermo León Valencia

Museo Casa Valencia

Casa Museo Mosquera

Parque Caldas

Iglesia de Santo Domingo

Catedral

Iglesia La Ermita

Museo de Historia Natural

Capilla de Belén, El Cerro ▶ de las Tres Cruces & Morro de Tulcán

EATING
Capriccio Café	5
Restaurante Italiano	2
Sabores del Mar	3
La Semilla Escondida	7
Tequila	4

DRINKING AND NIGHTLIFE
Bar La Iguana	1
El Sotareño	6

ACCOMMODATION
Hostel Caracol	5
Hotel Colonial	2
Parklife Hostel	4
Hotel Los Portales	3
Hostel Trail	1

0   100
metres

5

march northward from Quito, the "White City" was a powerful counterweight to Bogotá's dominance during the colonial era and a bastion of Spanish loyalty during the wars of independence. Unlike Cartagena, which saw its influence wane after independence, Popayán's aristocrats remained very active in politics, and no fewer than eleven presidents have emerged from their ranks.

When a disastrous earthquake destroyed most of the historic centre in 1983, collapsing the cathedral's roof onto the worshippers just before the Maunday Thursday celebrations, residents banded together to rebuild. The result is one of the most attractive cities in Colombia, its streets flanked by single-storey houses and whitewashed mansions and its churches lit up beautifully at night. During Easter week the city is cordoned off to make way for thousands of parading worshippers brandishing candles and colourful flowers. Popayán's Semana Santa celebrations are the second largest in the world, after Seville in Spain.

WHAT TO SEE AND DO

Besides its attractive architecture and leafy main square, most of Popayán's attractions lie outside the city. The museums are of limited interest to visitors, though you can kill a couple of hours on a rainy day there.

The churches

The town's leafy main square, Parque Caldas, is overlooked by the whitewashed **Catedral**. Although the biggest and most frequently used of the churches, architecturally it's the least important, built around 1900 on the site where two earlier structures stood. Four blocks east, on C 5 and Cra 2, is the city's oldest standing church, **La Ermita**, which features an austere single-naved chapel comprised of wooden ribbing and a golden altar dating from 1564.

On C 4 and Cra 5, the **Iglesia de Santo Domingo**'s Baroque stone portal is an excellent example of Spanish New World architecture. Equally ornate is the staircased pulpit of **Iglesia de San Francisco**, situated on a quiet plaza on

C 4 and Cra 9, where several of Popayán's patrician families are buried. La Ermita and Iglesia de Santo Domingo are beautifully lit up at night.

Museo de Historia Natural

A few blocks east of the historic centre, the **Museo de Historia Natural** (Cra 2 No. 1A–25; 9am–noon & 2–5pm; COP$3000; ⓦ museo.unicauca.edu.co) is worth visiting to see its rich collection of taxidermied animal and bird species, many of which are endemic to Colombia – just to see what they look like, as it's difficult to spot many of them in the wild.

Morro de Tulcán, El Cerro de las Tres Cruces and Capilla de Belén

For a tremendous view of the town, follow Cra 2 north to the **Morro de Tulcán**, once the site of a pre-Columbian pyramid and now a hill capped by an equestrian statue of Sebastián de Belalcázar, who founded Popayán in 1537. Near El Morro is **Pueblito Patojo**, a slightly bizarre set of buildings that are smaller copies of Popayán's most famous landmarks. From the top of El Morro, a path continues to the three crosses of **El Cerro de las Tres Cruces** and on to the hilltop chapel of **Capilla de Belén**, accessible via a steep cobbled path from the eastern end of C4; the entire walk takes a couple of hours. There are usually people on El Morro, whereas the Capilla de Belén is more isolated; leave valuables behind if visiting either.

Casa Museo Mosquera

If you're interested in a glimpse of the salon society of the colonial and early independence era, the **Casa Museo Mosquera** on C 3 No. 5–14 (Tues–Sun 8am–noon & 2–5pm; COP$2000), the childhood residence of Tomás Cipriano de Mosquera, four times Colombia's president, offers just that. On a macabre note, Mosquera's heart is kept in an urn in the wall.

Museo Negret and Museo Iberoamericano de Arte Moderno

The home of modernist sculptor Edgar Negret, **Museo Negret** (C 5 No. 10–23;

Tues–Sun 8am–noon & 2–5pm; COP$2500) is now a museum exhibiting his work. Next door the **Museo Iberoamericano de Arte Moderno** (same opening hours; included in entry to Museo Negret) exhibits Negret's private collection of works by Picasso and other important artists from Spain and Latin America.

ARRIVAL AND INFORMATION

By plane Popayán's airport is just a 20min walk north of the centre of town, opposite the bus terminal.
By bus The bus station is a 15min walk north of the centre along Autopista Norte and opposite the airport.
Destinations Bogotá (5 daily; 12hr); Cali (every 15min; 2–3hr); Pasto (hourly; 6hr; travel during daylight hours); San Agustín (6 daily; 5–6hr); Silvia (every 30min; 1hr 30min); Tierradentro (4 daily; 5–6hr).
Taxi Within town, taxis should cost COP$3600, or COP$4200 at night and on Sun.
Tourist information The tourist office is at Cra 5 No. 4–68 (daily 9am–12.30pm & 2–6pm; ☎ 2 824 2251). Staff hand out a good free city guide/map, bus and flight timetables, and can help arrange guided tours in the region.

ACCOMMODATION

Popayán boasts a good selection of budget options, including several excellent hostels. Accommodation is particularly expensive during Semana Santa; book well ahead.
Hostel Caracol C 4 No. 2–21 ☎ 2 820 7335, ⓦ hostelcaracol.com. *Hostel Trail*'s offshoot, popular with travellers who like a quiet place to retreat to at the end of the day, offers cosy rooms clustered around a covered courtyard and all the information you need on the area, courtesy of the helpful staff. Dorms COP$17,000, doubles COP$45,000
Hotel Colonial C 5 No. 10–94 ☎ 2 831 7848, ⓦ hotelcolonialpopayan.com. A comfortable central hotel with clean and bright en-suite double rooms with cable TV. Upstairs rooms are naturally brighter. COP$65,000
Parklife Hostel C 5 No. 6–19 ☎ 300 249 6240, ⓦ parklifehostel.com. Besides its super-central location right on the main square, *Parklife* is appreciated for its many perks (attractive glassed-over communal space, movie night, large kitchen...), as well as its colour-coded private rooms and large (though dark) dorms. Dorms COP$17,000, doubles COP$42,000
Hotel Los Portales C 5 No. 10–125 ☎ 2 821 0139. A great-value hotel in an attractive colonial building. The 29 rooms all come with cable TV and private bathrooms, and are nicely set around three pretty patios. Cheaper to pay cash. COP$55,000

★ **Hostel Trail** Cra 11, No. 4–16 ☎ 314 696 0805, ⓦ hosteltrail.com/hostels/hosteltrail. Friendly Scottish owners Tony and Kim run an excellent hostel with clean, bright rooms, free coffee, DVD room and a sociable atmosphere. There's heaps of information on the walls about Popayán and the region, and cycling trips are organized, as well as visits to a local coffee farm. Dorms COP$17,000, doubles COP$42,000

EATING

For self-caterers, there's an enormous *Exito* supermarket next door to the bus station.
Capriccio Café C 5 No. 5–63. Fabulous *granisados* (iced coffee drinks) and more at this little café that roasts its own coffee beans. Daily 8.30am–12.30pm & 2–8.30pm.
Restaurante Italiano C 4 No. 8–83 ☎ 2 824 0607. A two-floor, Swiss-owned restaurant serving good Italian standards as well as fondues – expect a leisurely meal. Good-value set lunch COP$9000, mains from COP$15,000. Mon–Sat noon–3pm & 5.30–10pm, Sun noon–11pm.
Sabores del Mar C 5 No. 10–97. Decked out with all sorts of nautical paraphernalia, this little place lures you in with delicious smells. Unusually for a *menú del día* you can enjoy decent fish or seafood. Lunch COP$6000. Mon–Sat 11am–7pm, Sun 11am–4pm.
★ **La Semilla Escondida** C 5 No. 2–28. A self-styled slice of France in a small Colombian town, *La Semilla* serves sweet and savoury crêpes, chunky sandwiches and Colombian lunch specials, with the likes of *crème brûlée* sneaking onto the dessert menu. Free wi-fi. Crêpes COP$6500. Daily noon–10pm.
Tequila C 5 No. 9–25. A jaunty Tex-Mex café that is not going to win any fine-dining awards, but does get a prize for its burritos (COP$6500), quesadillas (COP$6000), cheap beer, good cocktails, lively music and very friendly service. Mon–Thurs 5–10pm, Fri & Sat 5pm–midnight.

DRINKING AND NIGHTLIFE

Bar La Iguana C 4 No. 9–67. This dimly lit bar has a good cocktail list (around COP$10,000), funky salsa soundtrack, projector screen for showing videos, and trendy clientele.
★ **El Sotareño** C 6 No. 8–05. Head through *El Sotareño*'s swing doors and the first thing you'll see is the owner quietly sitting behind his compact bar, surrounded by a vinyl collection of vintage salsa, tango and other Latin music. Order a cold beer, bag one of the booths then sit back and listen as the tunes are spun. Mon–Sat until 1am.

AROUND POPAYÁN

The colourful market village of Silvia, an outstanding national park and some invigorating thermal springs are all within 60km of Popayán.

5

Silvia

Well worth a detour is the rural village of **SILVIA**, 60km northeast of Popayán, which fills up with Guambiano Indians, with the men in blue skirts with fuchsia trim and bowler hats (don't take photos as they can become aggressive), every Tuesday morning for market day. The market itself focuses on fruit, veg and basic household goods rather than tourist-friendly handicrafts, but the presence of the Guambiano, who arrive from their homes in the mountain villages above Silvia, makes it a great opportunity for people-watching. **Buses** (every 30min; 1hr 15min) leave for Silvia from Popayán's bus terminal. If coming from Cali, take a Popayán-bound bus to Piendamó (2hr), then grab a bus to Silvia (30min). Once here, it's possible to hire horses (COP$6000/hr) by the small lake and ride up to the village of Guambia (1hr) where the Guambiano cook up fried trout, plucked fresh from nearby trout farms.

Parque Nacional Natural Puracé

The high-altitude **Parque Nacional Natural Puracé** (daily 8am–6pm; COP$19,000), 58km east of Popayán, encompasses 860 square kilometres of volcanoes, snowcapped mountains, sulphurous springs, waterfalls, canyons, trout-stuffed lagoons and grasslands. The park's literal high point is **Volcán Puracé** (4700m), which last blew its top in 1956. It's a lung-straining four-hour climb to the steaming crater where, on a clear day, there are sensational views of Cadena Volcánica de Los Coconucos – a chain of forty volcanoes. There are also less strenuous trails, including an orchid walk, and thermal baths. Enquire at the visitor centre near the park entrance if you want to hire a guide. The weather is best for climbing the volcano in December to January; it is worst in June to August.

Four **buses** daily leave Popayán for the park entrance at El Cruce de San Juan (2hr), though if you're planning a day-trip you should catch the bus at 4.30am or 6.30am; double-check timetables before departure. Sometimes one of the early buses is cancelled at the last minute, which makes a day-trip challenging. The last bus back to Popayán passes El Cruce at 5pm.

For a more relaxed ascent of the volcano, it's best to **overnight** in the park in basic cabañas (☏ 2 823 1212; COP$33,000 per person; order meals in advance), some with fireplaces, or camp (COP$8000), which includes use of a bathroom with cold showers.

Thermal springs at Coconuco

The village of **Coconuco**, 26km from Popayán, is a short hop to two rudimentary outdoor thermal baths. The better maintained and more pleasant of the two is **Termales Agua Tibia** (daily 8am–6pm; COP$10,000; ☏ 315 578 6111, ⓦ termalesaguatibia.com), 5km southwest of Coconuco on the road to San Agustín. Set at the base of a steep-sided valley with great views, the complex has five lukewarm pools, a bottom-jarring concrete waterslide and a mud spring rich in rejuvenating minerals. There is no place to lock up valuables.

The indigenous-run **Agua Hirviendo** (Tues–Sun 24hr; COP$8000), 3km east of Coconuco, is less picturesque than Agua Tibia but it's open around the clock, its sulphur-reeking pools are far toastier, and the on-site waterfall is a refreshing shock to the system. Basic cabins are available for rent and a restaurant serves meals until late.

To **get to either baths**, take the bus from Popayán to Coconuco (hourly, more frequently on weekends; 45min; COP$3000), from where it's a short walk to Agua Hirviendo and about thirty minutes to the Termales Agua Tibia; a *mototaxi* will take you for COP$2000, or hire a jeep for COP$7000. The owners of *Hostel Trail* in Popayán organize cycling trips that involve driving you and a rented bicycle to the thermal baths for COP$40,000. Having enjoyed the waters, you can then pedal your way back to town, mostly downhill.

SAN AGUSTÍN AND PARQUE ARQUEOLÓGICO

The thoroughly laidback little town of **SAN AGUSTÍN**, 140km southeast of Popayán, has everything a budget traveller could want: awesome landscape, cryptic remains of a forgotten civilization, bargain-basement prices and a plethora of outdoor activities – from white-water rafting to horseriding. There's plenty to discover here, in particular the **archeological park**. Some 3300 years ago the jagged landscape around the town was inhabited by masons, whose singular legacy is the hundreds of monumental fanged stone statues comparable in detail to the more famous Moai statues found on Chile's Easter Island.

Much mystery still surrounds the civilization that built the monoliths, though the surreal imagery of sex-crazed monkeys, serpent-headed humans and other disturbing zoomorphic glyphs suggests that the hallucinogenic San Isidro mushroom may have been working its magic when the statues were first created. What is known is that the priestly culture disappeared before the Spanish arrived, probably at the hands of the Inca, whose empire stretched into southern Colombia. The statues weren't discovered until the middle of the eighteenth century.

To see San Agustín and its surroundings properly, you ideally need three days: one for the archeological park, one for a day-long jeep tour of the outlying sights, such as the Alto de los Idolos, and one for a horseback tour of El Tablón, La Chaquira, El Purutal and La Pelota.

Parque Arqueológico

Unmissable for its wealth of statues, the **Parque Arqueológico**, which was declared a UNESCO World Heritage Site in 1995 (daily 8am–6pm; COP$15,000), sits 2.5km west of San Agustín. The park contains over a hundred stone creations, the largest concentration of statues in the area. Many of them are left as they were found, linked by trails A, B and C, while others, like the ones in the wooded sector known as the **Bosque de las Estatuas**, are rearranged and linked by an interpretative trail. The statues are beguiling – their fanged faces, the animal-human hybrids, the stylized animal carvings – and they are all very much intact, though their purpose remains a mystery. Don't miss the **Fuente de Lavapatas**, a maze of terraced pools, covered with clearly visible images of reptiles and human figures, thought to

have been used for ritual ablutions. Further along, and up, is the furthest point of the park, **Alto de Lavapatas**, the oldest of the sites, with statues sitting forlornly on a hilltop, their brooding gaze sweeping over the countryside.

There's also a Museo Arqueológico (8am–5pm) featuring pottery, jewellery, smaller statues and background information on the San Agustín culture; visit it before hitting the statue sites if possible.

El Tablón, La Chaquira, La Pelota and El Purutal

Hundreds more statues are littered across the colourful hillside on either side of the Río Magdalena. Some of the most popular destinations are **El Tablón**, **La Chaquira**, **La Pelota** and **El Purutal**, which most visitors see as part of a four-hour horseriding tour. While the four sites are also doable as part of a day-long hike from town, riding through spectacular scenery is one of the highlights of San Agustín, and knowledgeable guides, booked through your accommodation, can shed some light on what you are seeing. Of the four sites, La Chaquira is the most impressive, with deities carved into the sheer rock above the beautiful Río Magdalena gorge.

Alto de los Ídolos, Alto de las Piedras and around

Alto de los Ídolos (daily 8am–4pm; COP$10,000 or combination ticket with Parque Arqueológico COP$16,000) is the area's second most important site after the Parque Arqueológico, and its two hills lined with tombs are home to the region's tallest statue, 7m high. Four kilometres southwest of the village of San José de Isnos (26km northeast of San Agustín), it can be reached by joining a day-long **jeep tour** (around COP$35,000 per person), which is easily arranged through your accommodation. Jeep tours also take in the **Alto de las Piedras**, another important archeological site, its highlight being *Doble Yo*, a statue that is half-man, half-beast. If you look closely, you'll see that there are four figures carved on that rock. Other stops include Colombia's tallest waterfall and a smaller waterfall viewpoint.

5

White-water rafting

Though they play second fiddle to the archeological attractions, **white-water rafting** and **kayaking** are also popular in San Agustín, thanks to ready access to the Class II–IV Río Magdalena. Magdalena Rafting (☎311 271 5333, ⍟magdalenarafting.com) offers excursions (COP$45,000 for a half-day); trips can be arranged via your guesthouse.

ARRIVAL AND INFORMATION

By bus Buses arrive and depart in the centre of town near the corner of C 3 and Cra 11, where there is a cluster of bus company offices.

Destinations Bogotá (5 daily; 10–12hr; afternoon and evening only); Neiva (5 daily; 4–5hr); Pitalito (several daily; 45min); Popayán (at least 7 daily; 6–7hr). The road to Popayán is still pretty ghastly, so if you're planning on visiting both Popayán and Tierradentro, go to Tierradentro first. Getting to Tierradentro from San Agustín involves two bus transfers, which can extend the journey time to around 7hr. The first transfer is at Pitalito, then at La Plata (after 3hr). From La Plata it's 2hr 30min to El Cruce de San Andrés, then a 20min walk to the museum in Tierradentro. There are many more buses to destinations (including Bogotá) from Pitalito.

Tourist information The helpful tourist office (C 3 at Cra 12; Mon–Fri 8am–noon & 2–5pm; ☎8 837 3062) is inside the town hall.

ACCOMMODATION AND EATING

There is an abundance of budget accommodation in San Agustín, including some fantastic-value *fincas* in stunning locations just outside town.

DESIERTO DE TATACOA

The bizarre **Tatacoa Desert** makes for a worthwhile detour en route from Bogotá to San Agustín or Tierradentro. Measuring just 300 square kilometres, tiny Tatacoa's arid topography – complete with cracked earth, giant cacti, orange-and-grey soil and towering red rock sculptures – is all the more astonishing because it lies only 37km northeast of Neiva, a city encircled by fertile coffee plantations. Scorpions, spiders, snakes, lizards, weasels and eagles have all found a home here, while fossils indicate that the area was an ancient stomping ground for monkeys, turtles, armadillos and giant sloths.

Some of the fossils are on display at the paleontology museum (daily 8.30am–noon & 2–5pm; COP$2000), on the main plaza in the village of **Villavieja**, 4km from the desert. Villavieja has a few basic hotels and restaurants, but since one of Tatacoa's chief attractions is the amazing night sky, it pays to stump up for one of the basic four-walls-and-a-corrugated-iron-roof deals in the desert itself; accommodation is scattered along the road just past the **observatory**, the desert's focal point. In the evenings, don't miss local astronomer Javier Fernando Rua Restrepo's star show, where you get to observe the night sky from his three powerful telescopes (weekends 7–9.30pm; by appointment on weekdays; COP$10,000; ☎310 465 6765). Across the road from the observatory, there's a lookout point over the Laberintos de Cusco – the maze of otherworldly red rock formations. A 45-minute trail runs down from the red-roofed bar through this labyrinth to the main road; a number of locals also offer guided **desert tours** by car, *mototaxi* or horseback. The best time to explore the desert is early morning before the heat becomes intolerable (temperatures frequently reach 43°C).

Villavieja is an hour **by bus** from Neiva, which in turn is 6hr by bus from Bogotá and 5hr from San Agustín on the main Bogotá–San Agustín road. Buses and vans from Neiva (COP$6000, 1hr) run frequently early in the morning and late in the afternoon; a taxi from Neiva to Villavieja costs COP$60,000 and COP$70,000 to the desert itself; since a *mototaxi* from Villavieja to the desert costs a stiff COP$15,000–20,000 for up to three people, it pays to take a taxi all the way to the desert if you've taken it from Neiva to Villavieja.

ACCOMMODATION

Accommodation tends to be basic and overpriced for what it is, though with some negotiation you can bring the prices down.

Estadero Doña Lilia ☎313 311 8828. 400m past the observatory; camping also possible and meals available on request. Shared room COP$15,000,

doubles COP$50,000

Noches de Saturno ☎313 305 5898. A little further up the road from the observatory, with very basic rooms and camping; there's a small swimming pool for COP$3000 per use. Rooms for around COP$30,000, camping COP$15,000

La Casa de Francois 250m along Via El Tablón ☎ 8 837 3847, ⓦ lacasadefrancois.com. Situated on a bluff overlooking the city, this ecologically friendly and sociable place offers airy dorms (one with fantastic views), an excellent communal kitchen and a couple of private doubles. The enthusiastic owner offers home-made bread, jam and other goodies, plus hearty breakfasts (COP$8000). There's also a camping area. Camping COP$800, dorms COP$17,000, doubles COP$40,000

Casa de Nelly Via la Estrella 1.5km along Av 2 ☎ 310 215 9057, ⓦ hotelcasadenelly.co. Tricky to find, as the route along a poorly lit dirt track from town is not brilliantly signposted, but lovely once you've made it. Romantic cabins surrounded by trees make this a great spot for those who want to hide away and relax for a couple of days. Has a restaurant serving breakfasts and "whatever's available" for dinner. Dorms COP$18,000, doubles COP$50,000

★ **Finca El Maco** 750m along the road to the Parque Arqueológico and then 500m up a rough road ☎ 8 837 3437, ⓦ elmaco.ch. This working organic farm with a gaggle of friendly dogs offers a range of sleeping options from camping and simple dorms to luxurious *casitas* (literally "small houses"). The restaurant serves up good-value Thai curries, great crêpes and massive breakfasts. Alternatively, you can buy home-made bread, cheese, pasta sauces and yoghurt and make your own meals in the basic communal kitchen, then retire to a hammock and admire the surrounding hills. Camping COP$8000, dorms COP$16,000, doubles COP$33,000

El Hogar de San Agustín Cra 14 No. 4–03 ☎ 8 837 3185; ⓦ www.hotel-san-agustin.com. The beautiful garden at this comfortable posada makes it a good option for those who want both greenery and an in-town location. There's an attractive adobe colour scheme in the spotless rooms, a living room with TV/DVD and a book exchange, and the on-site pastry shop sells those French baked goods. Doubles COP$40,000

EATING

The town's fruit-and-veg market on the corner of C 2 and Cra 11, where self-caterers can stock up, is open daily but liveliest Sat–Mon when the *campesinos* come to sell their wares.

★ **Donde Richard** 750m along the road to the Parque Arqueológico at C 5 No. 23–45. The best spot to chow down in town serves high-quality, carnivore-friendly food such as barbecued pork, chicken, beef and fish, all cooked on a big grill at the front of the restaurant (mains COP$20,000). Don't miss the Sunday special of *asado huilense* (slow-cooked pork marinated overnight). Daily noon–8pm.

El Fogón C 5 No. 14–30. Extremely popular restaurant that serves up a better-than-average *menú del día* (COP$7000) to scores of hungry locals every day of the week. Daily 6am–11pm.

Restaurante Italiano Vereda el Tablón. A short taxi ride out of town (COP$4500), this authentic Italian spot with the most imaginative name ever delivers consistently good dishes, including home-made pasta, that have earned the praise of Italian and non-Italian travellers alike. Mains from COP$15,000. Mon–Sat noon–10pm.

TIERRADENTRO

After San Agustín, **Tierradentro** is Colombia's most treasured archeological complex, though far less visited. Its circular tombs, some as deep as 9m and reachable by steep, smooth original steps through trapdoors, are decorated with elaborate geometric iconography and are as impressive as San Agustín's statues. Monumental statues have also been found here, indicating a cultural influence from San Agustín, though again little is known about the tomb-building civilization other than that it flourished around 700–900 AD, with the statue phase occurring around 500 years later.

No large population centres have been discovered, lending credence to the belief that the original inhabitants belonged to a dispersed group of loosely related farmers. The modern **Paez Indian** population, 25,000 of whom live in the surrounding hillside, is not thought to be related to the creators of the tombs.

Tierradentro means "Inner Land", an appropriate nickname to describe the rugged countryside of narrow valley and jagged summits. The area receives far fewer visitors than San Agustín, thanks to the poor quality of the road from Popayán, though that's likely to change, given the ongoing road improvements and with the area currently safe from guerrillas.

WHAT TO SEE AND DO

The main village is tiny **San Andrés de Pisimbalá**, 4km from El Cruce de San Andrés, the junction on the main Popayán–La Plata road. San Andrés has a picturesque thatched-roof chapel that dates from the seventeenth-century mission. Two kilometres along the road to San Andrés, where you'll find a smattering of guesthouses, starts

5

the **Parque Arqueológico Tierradentro** (daily 8am–4pm; COP$10,000), which comprises the five burial sites. The trail begins behind the **Museo Etnográfico** (daily 8am–4pm), where you pay the park entry fee and receive a wristband, valid for two days. The well-presented displays in the museum focus on the history and customs of the indigenous Paez, while the **Museo Arqueológico** across the road has an archeological display including funerary urns, some statuary and information about the park's tombs; both are worth visiting before you visit the sites.

It's possible to visit all five sites, spread out over a sublime landscape, on a full-day, 14km walk that runs in a loop from the Museo Etnográfico and the Museo Arqueológico, with San Andrés making a convenient lunch stop. Be sure to bring your own torch to explore the tombs, as some are unlit, as well as plenty of water, and wear sturdy footwear. The guards at each site who open the tombs for you can answer most questions (in Spanish). It's best to do the loop anticlockwise, since a clockwise route would mean tackling a long, tough uphill climb first thing.

Start with **Segovia** (20min walk uphill), the most important of the tomb sights. There are 29 of them; you descend into the trapdoors and down large, steep stone steps to peer into the gloom; note the black, red and white patterns that have survived the centuries. From here, it's fifteen minutes up to **El Duende**, a smaller site with four tombs and very little colour on the walls of the tombs. It's then a 25-minute walk to **El Tablón** – where you'll fine nine weather-worn stone statues which look similar to the ones found in San Agustín (see p.554). To get here, go up to the main road and head left; El Tablón will be well signposted on your left. From here you can either take the main road into the village or else descend down the muddy trail that joins the other road that runs up into San Andrés from the two museums.

The best place for lunch is *La Portada* (see opposite), after which you can pick up the trail again along the side of the restaurant. A ten-minute walk gets you to **Alto de San Andrés**, its six tombs boasting well-preserved wall paintings. From here, it's a good hour and a half to the last and most remote site, **El Aguacate**, with spectacular views of the valley and a style of tomb painting not found in the others. Allow plenty of daylight time for the hour-and-a-half walk down to the museums as in the past there have been several robberies along this isolated trail.

CROSSING INTO ECUADOR: PASTO

Pasto is the commercial hub of southern Colombia – a bustling town devoid of major sights and likely to be visited only in passing on the way to Ecuador, 88km further south along the Panamerican Highway, unless you happen to be travelling through during the Carnaval de Blancos y Negros (see p.495).

The Colombian town of **Ipiales**, a 2hr bus ride from Pasto, is 2km from the **Rumichaca Bridge**, which has Colombian and Ecuadorian border control offices on either side. Border formalities heading into Ecuador take far longer than the other way round, so you may be here for several hours. You will need to cross into Ecuador on foot and take a new *colectivo* from there; the town of **Tulcán** is 2km from the bridge (see box, p.587), and from there you can connect to Quito, Otavalo and elsewhere. Check the **safety** situation on the Ecuadorian side before travelling. There are moneychangers on both sides of the border on and close to the bridge. From Ipiales, you can catch a minibus (which leaves when full from half a block north of the marker on C 14) or a *colectivo* (COP$1500; departs from the bus terminal near the corner or C 14 and Cra 10) to the border, which is open 5am to 10pm.

ACCOMMODATION IN PASTO

Koala Inn C 18 No. 22–37 ☎ 2 722 1101. If you have to stay overnight in Pasto, this long-established backpackers' hostel two blocks from the main square is a convenient spot. Dorms COP$15,000, doubles COP$30,000

ARRIVAL AND DEPARTURE

By bus Tierradentro is 113km from Popayán along a rough mountain road that's currently undergoing improvement. There is one direct bus at 10.30am daily (5hr 30min) from Popayán (COP$18,000) and three daily (5am, 8am &1pm) that pass El Cruce de San Andrés – a road junction. From here it's a 2km walk to the museums and 4km uphill to San Andrés de Pisimbalá. There's a direct bus to Popayán daily from San Andrés at 6am, and from El Cruce de San Andrés at 9am, 11am & 1pm. Buses and pick-ups run from San Andrés to La Plata (6.30am, 8.30am, 1pm; 2hr) where you can pick up connections to San Agustín and Bogotá via Neiva (and Tatacoa).

ACCOMMODATION AND EATING

There are several basic guesthouses of comparable standards right near the two museums; meals available on request in most places.

★ **La Portada** ☎ 311 601 7884. Located along the main road in the village, *La Portada* has attractive, clean rooms with reliably hot showers. The excellent, home-cooked food on offer in the pretty restaurant (breakfast COP$4500, lunch and dinner COP$6000) is the best in town and the gregarious owner is a treasure trove of local knowledge. Doubles COP$35,000

Hotel El Refugio ☎ 312 811 2395. A 2min walk from the museums, this hotel with a pool and somewhat musty rooms is the swishest option besides *La Portada*. Doubles COP$40,000

Residencias Ricabet ☎ 312 795 4636. A short walk up from the museums, with small, basic rooms with shared or private bath, set around a pretty cobbled courtyard. Doubles COP$25,000

The Pacific coast

One of the least-visited parts of the country, and a ruggedly beautiful one at that, the Pacific coast is where the jungle and ocean meet alongside grey-sand beaches, where you can go whale- and dolphin-spotting, or stay in small villages, the majority of whose residents are of African descent. You will need plenty of time and patience to explore this region, as the majority of the settlements, such as laidback **El Valle**, are reachable only by boat from the main port of **Buenaventura**.

BUENAVENTURA

A busy, gritty and charmless port city, **BUENAVENTURA** is the only gateway to the region, so you will end up overnighting here. The boats to various coastal destinations run from the *muelle turístico* (tourist wharf); the area around it is reasonably safe (which is more than can be said for much of the rest of town), and you'll find a number of guesthouses and eateries nearby.

Buenaventura doesn't lend itself to sightseeing, though if you're a surfer it's well worth visiting **Ladrilleros**, an hour's boat ride north, where enormous 2–3m waves lash the shore during the August to November rainy season and where you can stay in a number of basic digs. To reach Ladrilleros, take a boat to Juanchaco, from where you can either walk the 2.5km or get a ride on the back of someone's motorbike.

ARRIVAL AND DEPARTURE

By bus Numerous buses run between Buenaventura and Cali (3–4hr) and you can stop in San Cipriano (see p.551) on the way.

By boat Speedboats for various coastal destinations leave from the *muelle turístico*.

ACCOMMODATION AND EATING

In Buenaventura, as the cheapest digs in town are downright unsavoury, it's worth paying a little more for comfort. Cheap eats are to be had at *la galería* (market) in Pueblo Nuevo; the stalls on the second floor serve the likes of fish stewed in coconut milk and other coastal specialities. A taxi here costs around COP$3500.

Hotel Titanic C 1A No. 2A-55 ☎ 2 241 2046. Conveniently located just a block from the *muelle turístico*. Comfortable rooms come with a/c, cable TV and internet, though many lack windows, and the rooftop restaurant is good for people-watching. Doubles COP$60,000

EL VALLE AND AROUND

Way north up the coast, and near **Bahía Solano**, a town famous for sports-fishing and whale-watching, compact **EL VALLE** is a good spot for surfing, as well as visiting **Parque Nacional Natural Ensenada de Utría**, where it's possible to see whales close to the shore during calving season. Entry to the park costs COP$15,000 and you can stay overnight in one of the cabins in the park (COP$120,000 per person); group trips can be arranged from El Valle, with boats costing around COP$300,000.

5

In En Valle itself, there's some good **surfing**, and between September and December it's possible to see **turtles** nesting at Estación Septiembre, a sanctuary (COP$10,000) 5km south along the coast. You can also do a day hike through the jungle to the **Cascada del Tigre**, a splendid waterfall with a refreshing waterhole (guide necessary).

ARRIVAL AND DEPARTURE

By plane To reach El Valle, you can fly from Medellín with Satena into Bahía Solano's tiny airport, with flights very much weather-dependent, and then take a Jeep from opposite the school (around COP$10,000; 1hr).

By boat Catch one of the many cargo boats out of Buenaventura (at least 1 daily; 24hr; around COP$120,000) to Bahía Solano and then a Jeep.

ACCOMMODATION

Humpback Turtle on Playa Almejal, El Valle ☏312 756 3439, ⊛humpbackturtle.com. Complete with beach bar, hammock room, rustic camping, a plethora of tours, surfboard rental and even an on-site restaurant. Dorms COP$20,000

Amazonas

Accounting for around a third of Colombia in size and largely inaccessible to visitors, the **Amazon basin** feels unlike any other part of the country, with its pristine rainforest, fantastic wildlife and indigenous groups living deep in the jungle, their cultures still preserved intact. The capital of the Amazonas province, the bustling jungle town of **Leticia**, is only accessible by air and river, and thus retains a somewhat isolated feel. Travellers come to Leticia for a taste of jungle adventure and also to cross over into Brazil or Peru, as this is where the three countries meet.

LETICIA

This compact riverside town, its partially unpaved streets abuzz with a fleet of scooters and motorcycles – the local transport of choice – has worn many hats during its lifetime. Founded in 1867, **LETICIA** was part of Peru until it was awarded to Colombia in 1933 in a ceasefire agreement following a war between the two countries in 1932. A den of iniquity and sin (well, drug trafficking) in the 1970s, Leticia had to clean up its act when the Colombian army moved in, though visitors are still warned not to wander out into the outskirts of Leticia after dark. Today it's a hot, humid, yet relatively tranquil place, with a lively waterfront and houses hidden amid the greenery. It makes a good base for short trips up the Amazon and for crossing over into Brazil or Peru.

WHAT TO SEE AND DO

The main attractions lie outside the town, but in Leticia proper you can stop by the **Museo Etnográfico Amazónico** (Cra 11 No. 9–43; Mon–Fri 8.30– 11.30am & 1.30–5pm, Sat 9–11am; free) to check out the collection of indigenous weaponry, splendid (and scary) ceremonial masks, pottery and more. For high-quality crafts made by local indigenous tribes, the best selection is at the **Galería Arte Uirapuru** (C 8 No. 10–35; Mon–Sat 9am–12.30pm & 3–7pm, Sun 9am–12.30pm).

ARRIVAL AND INFORMATION

By plane Leticia is served by several flights daily from Bogotá (2hr) with LAN and Copa. All visitors must pay COP$19,000 tourist tax upon landing at the tiny Aeropuerto Nacional Alfredo Vásquez Cobo. From the airport, you can catch a taxi (COP$7000) or a *mototaxi* (motorbike taxi; COP$2000) into town. Tabatinga International Airport, 4km south of Tabatinga (take *colectivos* marked "Comara" from Leticia), has daily flights to Manaus with TAM and Trip.

By boat (see box, p.562).

Tourist information The helpful tourist office (C 8 No. 9–75; Mon–Fri 8am–noon & 2–5pm; ☏8 592 7569) can provide onward transport info and maps.

Visas Both locals and foreigners are allowed to move between Leticia, adjoining Tabatinga, and Peru's Benjamin Constant without visas or passport control (though you have to have your passport on you). To head further afield, you must get a Colombian exit stamp from the Ministry of Foreign Relations office at Leticia Airport. If heading into Brazil and/or Peru overland, you'll need an entry stamp from the Brazilian Policía Federal in Tabatinga (Av de Amizade 650; 8am–noon & 2–6pm; ☏97 3 412 2180 in Brazil). Some nationalities need a visa to enter Brazil;

try to get it before coming to Leticia; otherwise, visit the Brazilian consulate (C9 No. 9–73; 8am–noon & 1–3pm; ☎8 592 7530). All travellers require a yellow fever certificate to enter Brazil.

ACCOMMODATION

★ **Amazon B&B** C 12 No. 9–30 ☎8 592 4981, ⓦamazonbb.com. If you have just got off the boat from Brazil or Peru, this lovely hotel will seem like paradise. Think minimalist chic, silent a/c, crisp white sheets and plenty of space in both rooms and bungalows to throw your gear about. Doubles COP$102,000

La Jangada Cra 9 No. 8–106 ☎312 361 6506, ⓦlacasadefrancois.com. This Swiss-Colombian run hostel wins extra points for friendliness and helpfulness; the fan-cooled rooms are basic but clean, you can book your jungle adventures here and the kitchen whips up breakfast for an extra fee. Dorms COP$25,000, doubles COP$65,000

Mahatu Jungle Hostel C 7A No. 1–40 ☎311 539 1265, ⓦmahatu.org. On the outskirts of town, this hostel boasts its own lake and lush grounds filled with fruit trees and the odd animal. Gustavo the owner is a no-nonsense character with a wealth of local knowledge, the rooms are somewhat musty and pricey for what they are, but there's a large guest kitchen and it's a great spot to meet fellow travellers. Dorms COP$20,000, doubles COP$50,000

EATING

In Leticia you'll find culinary delicacies you won't encounter elsewhere in Colombia – an abundance of river fish and a vast variety of fruit juices. The most delicious fish include *gamitana* and *pirarucu*, though the latter is best avoided out of season so as to discourage overfishing. Places to eat are concentrated along C 8 and Cra 10, off C 8.

★ **Tierras Amazónicas** C 8 at Cra 10. Unpretentious open-air restaurant serving huge slabs of perfectly cooked fish with *patacones* (plantain fritters) for COP$17,000, and *bandeja paisa* (COP$14,000). Wash it down with *borojó* or *copoazú* juice. Daily noon–9pm.

AROUND LETICIA

Amazonas' biggest attractions are found outside Leticia. These include the abundant wildlife of Parque Nacional Natural Amacayacu, jungle hikes and stays in Puerto Nariño, upstream of Leticia – a great base for dolphin-spotting trips.

Jungle trips

There are numerous tour agencies in Leticia that can organize **jungle and river trips** of virtually any length, taking in flora, fauna and the area's indigenous

---

EXPLORING THE UNKNOWN

While parts of Peruvian and Brazilian jungle are quite well trodden by now, Colombian jungle remains pristine, and Leticia can be your launching point for multi-day jungle adventures: just you, your indigenous guide, and indigenous communities as yet virtually untouched by the outside world. **Travel The Unknown** (☎44 20 7 183 6371, ⓦtraveltheunknown .com) can help you arrange your jungle trip, including local guide.

---

communities. However, that also means that there are a number of unscrupulous operators, so make sure you've agreed on exactly what's included and avoid pushy "guides" who approach you in the street. Since the Amazon is such a vast area, odds are, you won't see any big mammals, but you're very likely to see monkeys and numerous bird species, and a three-day stint in the jungle is great exposure to a unique environment. Recommended operators include Amazon Jungle Trips (Av Internacional No. 6–25; ☎8 592 7377, ⓦwww.amazonjungletrips.com.co), going strong after more than 25 years, and Tanimboca (Cra 10 No. 11–68; ☎8 592 7679, ⓦwww.tanimboca.org), both with English-speaking guides.

Parque Nacional Natural Amacayacu

Around ninety minutes upstream from Leticia, the 3000-square-kilometre **Parque Nacional Natural Amacayacu** is a spectacular slice of wilderness, home to five hundred bird species, plenty of crocodiles, anacondas and other reptiles and 150 mammal species, including big cats. Here you can go hiking, kayaking and birdwatching, but come prepared for squadrons of mosquitoes. Entry costs COP$35,000, and it's very expensive to spend the night here: the park's only facilities are run by the Decameron hotel chain and a bunk bed would set you back around COP$200,000 in high season. You can visit the park on the way to Puerto Nariño from Leticia; any boat travelling between the two can drop you off at the visitor centre. To get back, flag down one of the high-speed boats

5

INTO BRAZIL AND PERU BY BOAT

Many travellers come to Leticia en route to Brazil or Peru. To get to the former, you need only head to the port of **Tabatinga**, just across the border, which has virtually fused with the Colombian town; there are no checkpoints between the two and all you have to do is walk south along Av Internacional.

Boats leave for **Manaus** from Tabatinga's port on Wednesdays and Saturdays at around 2pm (double-check times in advance and remember that the time in Tabatinga is 1hr ahead of Leticia time), taking three days and four nights and costing around R$180 if you have your own hammock, or around R$1000 for a double cabin. The reverse journey (upstream) takes around six days and is more expensive.

High-speed passenger boats connect Leticia and **Iquitos** in Peru, leaving from Isla Santa Rosa; since the boats depart early in the morning, it's easiest to stay in Tabatinga the night before, especially since in dry season boats can only cross over to Isla Santa Rosa from Tabatinga's Porta de Feira. Boats depart daily around 4am (double-check departure times), with daily Transtur (☎973 412 2945, ⓦwww.transtursa.com) services, while Transportes Golfinho (☎973 412 3186, ⓦwww.gransportegolfinho.com) leave Tabatinga on Tuesdays and Thursdays, coming back on Wednesdays and Sundays. Price includes breakfast and lunch. Don't forget to get an exit stamp and relevant visa (see p.228 & p.713) before departing Leticia.

---

returning to Leticia (around 11.30am and 4.30pm); if the boats are full, flag down one of the motorized canoes or cargo ships.

Puerto Nariño

Eco-friendly **PUERTO NARIÑO** sits around 75km upstream of Leticia and makes a great base for spotting the Amazon's pink dolphins; half-day excursions to Lago Tarapoto cost around COP$55,000 for up to three people. You can learn more about the endangered creatures at the riverfront Fundación Omacha (ⓦomacha .org), located right near the docks. The village itself, peopled mostly by the indigenous Yagua, Tikuna and Cocoma, is a shining example of recycling, organic waste management and rainwater collection; other Colombian towns could learn a great deal here, and this may well be the only Colombian settlement with zero motorized traffic.

ARRIVAL AND DEPARTURE

By boat Three high-speed boats run daily from Leticia at 8am, 10am and 2pm (COP$30,000; 2hr), returning at 7.30am, 11am and 4pm. Bring plenty of cash, as there are no banks here.

ACCOMMODATION AND EATING

Las Margaritas C 6 No. 6–80. This thatch-roofed place does a great home-cooked buffet.
Moloka Napü C 4 No. 5–72 ☎310 488 0998. The friendliest place to stay, with sparse yet cosy rooms, and some of the best showers in Colombia. <u>**COP$25,000**</u>

MARKET DAY, SAQUISILÍ

Ecuador

HIGHLIGHTS

❶ **Quito** Explore the capital's preserved colonial squares, churches and monasteries. **See p.571**

❷ **Volcán Cotopaxi** A magnificent cone-shaped volcano. **See p.588**

❸ **Baños** Thermal baths, adventure sports and a stunning location. **See p.593**

❹ **Vilcabamba** Chill out in the valley of longevity. **See p.607**

❺ **The Northern Oriente** Rainforest with diverse wildlife and indigenous cultures. **See p.610**

❻ **Galápagos Islands** Witness the miracle of evolution. **See p.631**

HIGHLIGHTS ARE MARKED ON THE MAP ON P.566

ROUGH COSTS

Daily budget Basic US$25, occasional treat US$40

Drink Cerveza Pilsener US$1

Food Set menu two-course lunch US$2.50

Hostel/budget hotel US$6–12

Travel Quito–Baños: 3hr 30min, US$4

FACT FILE

Population 14.9 million

Language Spanish

Currency US dollar

Capital Quito (population: 1,600,000)

International phone code ☎ 593

Time zone GMT -5hr

6

Introduction

In Ecuador it's possible to wake up on the Pacific coast, drive through the snowcapped Andes and reach the edge of the Amazon jungle by sundown. Although Ecuador is only slightly larger than the UK, its vastly different terrains have enough to keep visitors occupied for months. It's one of the world's most biodiverse countries, with some 25,000 species of plants, more than the species found in all North America, and 1600 species of birds. It's entirely fitting, therefore, that the Galápagos Islands, where Charles Darwin developed his theory of evolution, belong to Ecuador.

Mainland Ecuador is divided into three geographically distinct regions: coast, jungle and highlands. The most popular region is the highlands, with **Quito** the most convenient starting point. The Ecuadorian capital's historic sights, range of day-trips and excellent facilities can keep you busy for over a week.

Northwest of Quito are the cloudforest reserves around **Mindo** and to the northeast the indigenous market town of **Otavalo**, whose *artesanía* crafts are a shopper's dream.

South of Quito is Ecuador's most dramatic mountain scenery, including **Volcán Cotopaxi**, the highest active volcano in the world, and the extinct volcanic lake **Laguna Quilotoa**. Further south is the popular spa town of **Baños** and **Riobamba**, the best base to explore Ecuador's highest mountain, **Chimborazo** (6310m), and the **Nariz del Diablo** train ride. In the southern highlands are Ecuador's best-preserved Inca ruins, **Ingapirca**, its beautiful third city **Cuenca** and the relaxing "Valley of Longevity", **Vilcabamba**.

Excursions deep into wildernesses of primary jungle, including **Cuyabeno Natural Reserve** and **Yasuní National Park**, can be arranged via the unsightly oil towns of **Lago Agrio** and **Coca**, while shorter trips and stays with indigenous communities are best via **Puyo** and **Tena**, Ecuador's white-water-rafting capital and the most appealing jungle town.

On the coast, visit Ecuador's largest city **Guayaquil** to see its regenerated waterfront, then head for the beach: eco-city **Bahía de Caráquez**, surfer

hangouts **Montañita** and **Canoa**, or the unspoilt beaches of **Parque Nacional Machalilla** and **Mompiche**.

Some 1000km west of mainland Ecuador lie the country's tourism crown jewels, **the Galápagos Islands**, which remain among the world's top destinations for watching wildlife and are easy to explore independently.

CHRONOLOGY

4000 BC The first evidence of humans in Ecuador is the Valdivia culture in Santa Elena.

1460 AD Tupac Yupanqui leads the first Inca invasion of Ecuador.

1495 Huayna Capac conquers Ecuador, establishing centres in Quito and Ingapirca.

1526 Civil war erupts between Huayna Capac's sons Huascar and Atahualpa; the latter triumphs.

1532 Spaniard Francisco Pizarro arrives in Ecuador, captures and executes Atahualpa the next year, and conquers Peru by 1535.

1541 Francisco de Orellana journeys down the Amazon and reaches the Atlantic.

1820 On October 9, Guayaquil declares independence, supported by Simón Bolívar.

1822 On May 24, Quito wins independence at the Battle of Pichincha. Bolívar's dream of a united continent dies and Ecuador becomes fully independent in 1830.

1861 Conservative Gabriel Garcia Moreno seizes power, quashes rebellions and makes Catholicism a prerequisite for all citizens. He is assassinated in Quito in 1875.

1895 Liberal Eloy Alfaro becomes president and introduces sweeping reforms, ending the connection between church and state and legalizing divorce. He is assassinated in 1912.

1941 Peru invades Ecuador and forces a treaty giving Peru 200,000 square kilometres of Ecuadorian jungle.

1967 Oil is discovered in the Ecuadorian Oriente, prompting an oil boom in the 1970s.

1979 Left-winger Jaime Roldós is elected president, ending military rule. He confronts the oil-rich hierarchy and dies in a mysterious plane crash two years later.

1996 Self-styled *loco* (crazy) Abdalá Bucharam wins the presidency then raises taxes and records an album. He is ousted by Congress a few months later for "mental incapacity" and escapes to Panama.

1998 President Jamil Mahuad and Peruvian President Fujimori sign a peace treaty, which ends the long-running border dispute.

2000 The sucre plummets from 6000 to 25,000 to the dollar in under a year. President Mahuad is ousted in a coup but his successor Gustavo Noboa presses ahead with dollarization.

2001 Ecuador qualifies for the FIFA Football World Cup for the first time, sparking wild national celebrations.

2002 Former coup leader Lucio Gutiérrez wins the presidency but is removed in 2004 after infuriating his left-wing base with neo-liberal policies and attempts to increase presidential powers.

2007 Rafael Correa, friend of Venezuelan President Hugo Chavez, becomes Ecuador's seventh president in ten years. He refuses to pay Ecuador's national debt, engages in a war of words with the rich, replaces Congress with a new Assembly and introduces a new constitution.

2010 Following his re-election in April 2009, Correa endures a series of crises, and on September 30, a police protest escalates into an attempted coup. Six people are killed as the president is dramatically rescued by his own army from a police hospital in Quito.

2011 Correa wins a narrow victory in a referendum of ten questions on issues ranging from judicial and penal reform to bans on bullfighting and casinos. He announces his intention to run for re-election in 2013.

ARRIVAL AND DEPARTURE

Arriving by **air**, most travellers enter Ecuador via Quito's airport (see p.576), though Guayaquil's new José Joaquín de Olmedo (see p.624) is more convenient for the Galápagos and the beach. Airlines with regular services from Europe include: Air Europa, Air France, Avianca, Iberia, KLM, LAN and Lufthansa. From North America: Air Canada, American Airlines, Continental Airlines, Delta, COPA and LAN (see p.30). Note when flying out of Ecuador, departure tax must be paid in cash. In Quito, it's $44 and in Guayaquil $28.

OVERLAND FROM PERU

You can reach Ecuador by **bus** from Peru via Tumbes and Huaquillas on the coast, which is easier. It's also possible to cross via Macará or Zumba in the highlands, which are more scenic.

OVERLAND FROM COLOMBIA

Travelling to and from Colombia overland is only possible via Tulcán in the northern highlands. The border region has a troubled history, so many travellers fly to Cali from Tulcán.

PASSPORTS AND VISAS

Visitors to Ecuador require a passport valid for over six months and can stay for **ninety days** on an automatic 12-X tourist visa. Visitors receive a T3 tourist card, which must be kept until departure. Officially, you should bring proof of sufficient funds to support yourself and a return ticket or proof of onward travel, but it's rarely demanded.

It's possible to extend to 180 days but you must go to the immigration office on the day the visa expires and the decision is at officials' discretion. If the visa expires, it's a $200 fine. Given this, it's preferable to leave the country within ninety days and then re-enter.

WHEN TO VISIT

Because of Ecuador's diverse landscapes, the best time to visit varies by region. On the **coast**, temperatures are typically 25–35°C. The rainy season is dramatic, with downpours between January and April. This is the hottest time of the year, at times uncomfortably humid, but also the best months for the beach. It's cooler and cloudier between June and December. In the **highlands**, the temperature is on average 15°C but due to the altitude it gets hot at midday and cold at night, particularly above 2500m. The driest, warmest season is June to September. In the **Oriente** the temperature is generally 20–30°C with high levels of rainfall and humidity. The driest season is December to March. In the **Galápagos**, the temperature peaks at over 30°C in March and cools to the low 20s in August. It's best to avoid the rough seas and cold between June and September.

6

ECUADOR

Metres	
	3000
	2000
	1200
	900
	600
	300
	0

HIGHLIGHTS

1 Quito
2 Volcán Cotopaxi
3 Baños
4 Vilcabamba
5 The Northern Oriente
6 Galápagos Islands

GETTING AROUND

BY BUS

Ecuador's cheap **buses** are the preferred form of public transport, reaching just about everywhere there's a road. The **Panamericana** forms the backbone, linking all major highland towns. The government has poured investment into the roads, which have improved markedly recently. However, poor driving conditions, particularly in the rainy season, often result in **delays**; the worst roads tend to be in Esmeraldas and the Oriente.

Public buses are typically about $1–1.50 per hour of travel, but quality varies so if

possible check the bus you're going to travel on before buying. For longer bus rides at peak periods, buy tickets in advance. Avoid bus travel at night if possible as **crime** is more common. Also note that pickpocketing is rife on public buses, especially popular tourist routes out of Quito. Never stow valuables in your bag above your head or under your seat – always keep them on you.

BY CAR AND TAXI

Renting a car is possible but not recommended because of the expense. Rental charges are $300–500 per week, with an alarming excess of $1000 in case of damage. A better option is a **taxi**. In bigger cities this is certainly the best way to get around, though always check credentials, avoid unmarked cabs and use the meter (if there isn't one, negotiate in advance). The safest option in cities is to use a prebooked cab from a reputable company – your hotel can recommend some. Short trips around small towns cost $1–2. In Quito, many taxis use a meter and short trips cost $2–4. In Guayaquil prices are a little higher and meters rarely used. Taxi drivers in tourist towns will often offer longer trips, but rates are obviously higher than for buses.

BY AIR

It's tempting for those pushed for time or weary of the bus to **fly**. Prices of internal flights range from $50–100 one-way. TAME (☎02 2397 7100, ⊛www.tame .com.ec) offers reasonable deals from Quito to Coca, Cuenca, Esmeraldas, Galápagos, Guayaquil, Lago Agrio, Loja, Machala, Tulcan and Cali, Colombia. There are flights from Guayaquil to Coca, Cuenca, Esmeraldas, Galápagos, Loja and Cali. Icaro (☎02 244 8626, 02 245 0928) and Aerogal (☎02 294 2800) both serve Quito, Guayaquil and Cuenca, and are often cheaper than TAME. Chilean airline LAN (☎02 299 2300, ⊛lan.com) also offers flights between Quito, Guayaquil and Cuenca, as well as to the Galápagos.

ACCOMMODATION

Ecuador has a wide variety of **accommodation**, from dirt-cheap rickety shacks to comfortable mid-range hotels and luxury high-rise options. A basic dorm in a cheap *pensión*, *residencial* or *hostal* can cost just $5. The mid-range is where Ecuador offers best value. In most destinations $20–40 gets you a good-sized double room with comfortable beds, private bathroom, hot water and cable TV. The $40–100 range gets you a swankier international city hotel, a colonial hacienda or a secluded jungle lodge.

Cities such as Quito, Guayaquil and Cuenca are slightly more expensive but competition keeps the prices down.

On the coast, air-conditioning costs extra, and budget places sometimes have no hot water, although the climate renders it unnecessary. Consider bringing your own mosquito net if you plan to spend time in the jungle or on the coast during the rainy season. Deep in the jungle, budget options are harder to find so expect to pay more as part of a tour. **Camping** is not widely available but possible in some areas for $5 per person, but you must usually bring your own gear unless you book a tour.

FOOD AND DRINK

There's a lot more to Ecuadorian cuisine than roasted guinea pig. Rice and beans are the staple, so don't be surprised to be served rice with everything. Note that use of oils and animal fats can make the food surprisingly unhealthy. Budget travellers can enjoy cheap set menu *almuerzos* (lunches) and *meriendas* (dinners), which serve a soup, main course and drink for $2–3. *Sopa* (soup), *caldo* (broth) and *seco* (stew) are cheap ways to stay full. *Locro de papa* is a blend of cheese, pasta and potato; *chupe de pescado* is a thick fish-and-vegetable soup. *Seco de pollo* (chicken stew with coriander) or *lomo salteado* (salted beef steak) are common main courses, whereas *caldo de pata* (cow's foot soup) is for the more adventurous. In the highlands and Oriente the fish of choice are tilapia and river trout. The famous *cuy* (guinea pig) and *hornado* (giant pigs) are a local delicacy and are often roasted whole on a spit.

On the Ecuadorian coast, the **seafood** is among the best in the world. *Ceviche*, a cold seafood dish marinated with lemon and onion, is excellent. *Encebollado*, a fish and onion soup, is often eaten to stave off a hangover. A more interesting option is *cazuela*, a seafood and vegetable broth made with plantains and peanut. In Manabi try *biche*, a sweeter fish soup with corn and *maduros* (sautéed plantains). The best white fish is *corvina* (sea bass), which can be *frito* (fried), *apanado* (breaded), *a la plancha* (grilled) or *al vapor* (steamed). Note that shellfish is a common cause of illness, so take care.

6

If you're on a tight budget, **snacks** come in handy, but avoid meat cooked on the street and avoid hot snacks sold on public transport. Popular treats from bakeries include *empanadas* (meat- or cheese-filled pastries), *tortillas de verde* (fried mashed green bananas) or *yucca* (a local root vegetable) and delicious *humitas* (mashed corn with cheese wrapped in a corn husk and steamed). *Pan de yuca* (yucca bread), eaten with yogurt, is a common snack.

Always buy **bottled water** and never drink from the tap. It's best to avoid ice in cheaper places. Ecuador's abundant tropical fruits make fresh *jugos* (juices) and *batidos* (milkshakes) great breakfast options. Alongside pineapple, melon, papaya and banana are more unusual fruits such as *naranjilla* (a sour orange) and *tomate de árbol* (a sweet tomato). Sodas are everywhere, while coffee is of variable quality. The most common beers are the standard local Pilsener and slightly more expensive Club Verde. Whisky, rum and the local firewater *Agua Ardiente* are cheap and strong enough to give you a stonking hangover. *Chicha*, made from fermented corn or potato, is drunk by indigenous people across Ecuador. If you are offered some, it is generally considered impolite to refuse. Note that when going out at night, in Ecuador the expression "nightclub" means brothel, so don't get caught out! Use the word discoteque.

CULTURE AND ETIQUETTE

A highlight of Ecuador is the hospitable, fun-loving people. Ecuador's population of more than fourteen million is divided equally between the coast and highlands, with 5 percent in the Oriente. Some 65 percent are *mestizo* (mixed race), 25 percent indigenous, 3 percent Afro-Ecuadorian and 7 percent white. While many of the Indians hold on to traditional customs and dress, the mainstream population dress like Americans. This aspiration has led to nearly two million emigrants in the past twenty years.

More than ninety percent of Ecuadorians are Roman Catholic, although evangelical Christianity is increasing. Rivalry between the mountains and coast is fierce. Many *Costeños* consider *Serranos* (mountain people) to be conservative, uptight and two-faced. *Serranos* sometimes call *Costeños* "monos" (monkeys) and consider them rude, uncultured, immoral gossips. The rivalry ranges from banter to deep resentment.

Ecuadorians' lax attitude to time is legendary. At social gatherings, add at least an hour to the agreed meeting time or bring a book and patience. However, scheduled departures such as buses and tours are usually punctual, so don't be caught out.

Greetings are essential for Ecuadorians – a kiss on each cheek for women and a handshake between men. If you don't know any Spanish, it's worth learning basic greetings and pleasantries.

Tipping is not essential in most situations but advisable in higher-end hotels for bellboys (50 cents to $1). If your guide is good, show your appreciation. Supermarket bag carriers and parking attendants require a tip (up to $1).

SPORTS AND OUTDOOR ACTIVITIES

FOOTBALL

Football is the number one sport in Ecuador and watching a local match at a stadium in Quito or Guayaquil is unforgettable. During big matches the cities grind to a halt. Quito has three major teams: Liga, Nacional and Deportivo Quito, while Guayaquil has two: Emelec and Barcelona.

HIKING AND CLIMBING

The highlands' open spaces offer the widest range of **hiking** – the Quilotoa Loop, Parque Nacional Cotopaxi, Mindo cloudforest, the hills around Baños, Parque Nacional Cajas and Vilcabamba are but a few. On the coast, Parque Nacional Machalilla and Cordillera Chongón near Montañita also offer good hiking. The best **climbing** is on Cotopaxi and Chimborazo, although ensure you are fit, acclimatized and with a qualified guide.

WATERSPORTS

For watersports, including **rafting** and **kayaking**, Tena and Baños are best for trips on fast-flowing rapids and gentler tributaries. The best **surfing** is at the resorts of Montañita, which holds a famous surfing competition around Carnaval, or Canoa and Mompiche. **Scuba-diving** and **snorkelling** opportunities are limited on the mainland. Parque Nacional Machalilla has a few operators but the best place by far is the Galápagos Islands, whose amazing marine life makes it one of the world's top underwater destinations.

WILDLIFE

Birdwatching enthusiasts should head to the cloudforests of Mindo, which have more than 400 bird species and 250 species of butterfly. The tiny hummingbirds are a highlight, commonly seen in the cloudforests and the jungle. The Andean condor is a rare but unforgettable sight, occasionally seen in Parque Nacional Cotopaxi. For other **wildlife-watching**, the Oriente offers opportunities to observe sloths, otters, caymans, tapirs and many species of monkey. The Galápagos is of course unbeatable for wildlife.

COMMUNICATIONS

The **postal** system in Ecuador is very unreliable; your postcard will either reach its destination late or never. Receiving mail is worse, so if you need to send or receive something important, use an international courier service such as DHL or Fedex, but bear in mind there is a minimum charge of about $50.

Ecuador's **phone** system is improving and international calls are cheap. There are countless phone offices in towns. These are the best places for conventional calls, useful for calling hotels or tour operators. There are also cellular public phones, which use prepaid phone cards available at shops or kiosks. Calling North America costs as little as $0.10–0.20 per minute and Europe $0.30–0.40 per minute, but there is usually a connection charge. Most travellers staying longer than a few weeks invest in a mobile phone

from Claro or Movistar. Phones start at $35 and SIM cards from $4.

You're never far from **internet cafés** in tourist towns, and even remote places have a connection. Expect to be charged $1–1.50 per hour, although many good hotels have free wi-fi. Skype calls are obviously far cheaper than telephone but connections can be poor.

CRIME AND SAFETY

Sneak theft is common for travellers across Ecuador. Expert pickpockets target tourists, particularly in Quito. Be vigilant in crowded areas and on public transport, keep your money out of sight and be wary of strangers engaging you in conversation, a common diversionary tactic. Don't carry large amounts of cash. **Armed robbery** is less common but increasing. Sadly the tourist district of Mariscal Sucre in Quito is now the most common place for tourists to be mugged. There have also been some reports of violent attacks on tourists. Gangs look for easy targets, so don't wander around alone and always take a licensed taxi back to your hotel at night, no matter how close it is. Other crime hotspots in Quito include parts of the Old Town, the walk up to El Panecillo (take a taxi) and Parque Carolina.

In Guayaquil, be extra vigilant at night, particularly downtown. Esmeraldas and Atacames also have problems with theft and robbery; avoid the northern coastal town of San Lorenzo completely. Drug smuggling, Colombian guerrilla activity and risk of kidnappings in the northern border areas have made areas of Sucumbíos (capital Lago Agrio), Carchi (capital Tulcán) and Esmeraldas (capital Esmeraldas) provinces unsafe. On the southern border, the Cordillera del Cóndor, southeast of Zamora, contains landmines from the conflicts with Peru.

By law you must carry **identification** – this means your passport. If you can't produce it, you may be detained by the police. Carry **drugs** in Ecuador and you may end up in jail for up to fifteen years, so avoid contact with drug dealers. Foreigners are sometimes vulnerable to drug set-ups and a bail-out is an easy way for corrupt police officials to make money.

6

HEALTH

Vaccinations that are recommended include typhoid, hepatitis A and yellow fever. Others to consider are hepatitis B and rabies. **Malaria** is present (but rare) in the Oriente and on the northern coast. Wear long sleeves, light-coloured clothes and use repellent to avoid mosquito bites. Malarone is the best anti-malarial medication, and must be taken daily. **Dengue fever** is spread by day-biting mosquitoes, mainly during the rainy season, and is an increasing problem in urban areas on the coast. There is no vaccine, so seek medical help immediately if you show symptoms (high fever, aching limbs, vomiting and diarrhoea).

The most common problem is **travellers' diarrhoea**. Minimize risks of bacterial and parasitic infections by avoiding bus vendor/street food; also try to eat in clean restaurants. Tap water, ice, salad, ice cream, unpeeled fruit and seafood are common culprits. Eat plenty of carbohydrates, drink water and pack oral rehydration and Imodium.

Another common problem is **altitude sickness**, which can be dangerous. When arriving at altitudes over 2000m (most of the highlands), don't over-exert yourself, avoid alcohol and don't attempt to climb mountains without sufficient time to adjust to the altitude.

Sunburn and **sunstroke** are also very common because the equatorial sun is fiercely strong. Apply sunblock regularly and don't be fooled by cool temperatures in the mountains – because of the altitude, the sun is stronger.

Note Ecuador's health system is poor and **emergency care** particularly bad. Travelling with valid insurance is essential. If you have an emergency, try to head for a private hospital. In Quito, Hospital Metropolitano is good, and in Guayaquil, Clínica Kennedy has several branches. Pharmacies will dish out medicines without prescription, so you are responsible for knowing what you're taking.

INFORMATION AND MAPS

Ministry of Tourism iTur offices (Ⓦecuador.travel), in provincial capitals

> ### EMERGENCY NUMBERS
>
> Call ☎911 for police, fire and ambulance services.

and the main tourist centres, supply maps, lists of hotels, restaurants and sights. The website is a good source of information. Quito's tourist office is the best in Ecuador, with a very good website (Ⓦquito.com). Mid-range hotels often have leaflets and brochures about surrounding attractions.

El Instituto Geográfico Militar in Quito, Senierges, at Paz y Miño, sells topographical maps for $3 and a giant map of Quito for $10 (bring your passport as ID to enter the institute). The best general map of Ecuador is the 1:1,000,000 International Travel Maps Ecuador map (Ⓦitmb.com). There are also maps of the Galápagos and Quito available.

MONEY AND BANKS

Ecuador replaced the plummeting sucre with the **US dollar** as its currency following an economic crisis in 2000. There are 1, 5, 10, 25, 50 cent and 1 dollar coins. Notes come in 1, 5, 10 and 20 dollars. Avoid 50 and 100 dollar bills, and even 20 dollar bills cause problems in small towns. Dollarization has made Ecuador more expensive but it's still cheap; you can get by on $25 per day staying in budget hotels, eating set menus and taking buses. For $30–40 per day you get a higher level of accommodation, restaurants and taxi rides. The climbing, birdwatching and jungle-trekking tours push costs up to $50–100 per day.

Carry enough cash for a few days; a credit card is recommended as backup. Visa, MasterCard, Cirrus and Maestro are commonly accepted at ATMs. In larger agencies, you can pay for tours with a credit card but you may be charged five to ten percent more. Note rates of exchange for currencies outside South America (eg British pounds) are often poor, so bring cash and travellers' cheques in US dollars wherever possible.

PUBLIC HOLIDAYS

Most of the following are national holidays, although some are celebrated in certain areas of the country. Note that the government habitually changes the dates of national holidays to tag them onto the weekend.

January 1 New Year's Day (*Año Nuevo*).
January 6 Epiphany (*Reyes Magos*). Celebrated mainly in the highlands.
February/March Carnival (*Carnaval* – literally "goodbye to meat"). The week before Lent is Ecuador's biggest party. Monday and Tuesday are holidays. The beaches are packed and in the highlands Ambato and Guaranda are famous for celebrations. Don't be surprised to get wet, as throwing water is part of the fun.
March/April Holy Week (*Semana Santa*). The big processions in Quito are on Good Friday, a public holiday.
May 1 Labour Day (*Día del Trabajo*).
May 24 Battle of Pichincha (*La Batalla del Pichincha*). Celebrating the decisive battle for independence in 1822 (highlands only).
July 24 Birthday of Simón Bolívar, the man who dreamed of a united South America and helped liberate Ecuador.

August 10 Quito Independence Day (*Día de la independencia*).
October 9 Independence of Guayaquil (Guayaquil only).
October 12 Columbus Day (*Día de la Raza*).
November 2 All Souls' Day or Day of the Dead (*Día de los Muertos*).
November 3 Independence of Cuenca (Cuenca only).
December 6 Foundation of Quito. Bullfights are the order of the day (Quito only).
December 25 Christmas Day (*Navidad*). Most Ecuadorians celebrate Christmas on Christmas Eve night and relax on Christmas Day.
December 31 New Year's Eve (*Nochevieja* or *Años viejos*). New Year rivals Carnival as the country's biggest party. Locals burn effigies of well-known characters. Note that safe use of fireworks is absent.

OPENING HOURS AND HOLIDAYS

Most shops and public offices are open Monday to Saturday 9am to 5pm or 6pm, but family-owned businesses open at the owner's discretion. Most banks are open 8 or 9am to 4pm Monday to Friday. Call centres open 8am to 10pm. Restaurant and bar opening hours vary and museums are usually open weekends and closed Mondays. On Sundays and public holidays most shops and official buildings are closed.

The majority of national holidays mark famous historical events as well as Catholic festivals. Ecuadorians love to party with lots of food, drink and late nights, so it's a great experience. Note that tourist resorts, especially beach towns, are extremely busy on national holidays, with sky-high prices.

Quito

At a dizzying elevation of 2850m, **QUITO** is the second-highest capital city in the world after Bolivia's La Paz. It has a dramatic location, with active Volcán Pichincha, which covered the city in ash in 1999, looming to the west and Valle de los Chillos descending east towards the Amazon basin. If the altitude doesn't leave you breathless then the architecture will. Founded by the Spanish in 1534, Quito rapidly became a major colonial centre and its churches, monasteries, cobbled streets and wide plazas have been beautifully preserved. The warmest, driest time is June to September, but the rest of the year can be chilly, especially at night, with frequent rain in the afternoons.

WHAT TO SEE AND DO

Although most visitors stay in the New Town, the **Old Town**, also known as "El Centro Histórico", is what makes Quito special. Highlights include the two main squares **Plaza Grande** and **Plaza San Francisco**, the **Palacio del Gobierno**, the **Catedral**, the gaudy gold church **La Compañia** and the **Church of San Francisco**. For great views, take a taxi up to the top of **El Panecillo** or climb the stairs of the gothic **Basílica del Voto Nacional**.

6

The **New Town** has a huge range of accommodation, restaurants and bars around Avenida Amazonas in Mariscal Sucre. This thriving tourist district is where most visitors base themselves and has such an international feel that it's nicknamed "gringolandia", although safety is a problem, especially at night. The New Town has plenty of attractions, but they are spread out, which makes sightseeing more complicated than in the Old Town. Highlights include Ecuador's best museum, **El Museo del Banco Central**, Oswaldo Guayasamín's extraordinary work of art **La Capilla del Hombre** and a trip up to 4100m on the **Teleférico**.

Plaza Grande and around

This picture-perfect sixteenth-century plaza forms the political and religious focal point of Quito, containing the cathedral, Presidential Palace, Archbishop's Palace and city hall. Visitors can enter the **Palacio del Gobierno** (Presidential Palace; tours Tues–Sun 10am–5pm, except when the government is in session; free) on a guided tour to see the state rooms, a stunning mosaic and various indigenous artefacts. On the other side of the square is the **Catedral**, entered through the museum (entrance on Venezuela; Mon–Fri 9.30am–4pm, Sat 10am–4pm; $1.50, Sun services free). Inside is a collection of seventeenth- and eighteenth-century religious art, the tomb of liberator Mariscal Sucre and

SIX OF THE BEST VIEWS OF QUITO

Quito's stunning location in a valley surrounded by volcanoes means you are spoilt for choice for the finest views of the city. Here are six of the best. All are best visited by taxi (except La Basílica which is easily accessible).

1. El Panecillo, Old Town
2. La Basílica, Old Town
3. Centro Cultural Itchimbia, Old Town
4. Guápulo, New Town
5. Parque Metropolitano, New Town
6. El Teleférico, north of the city

a memorial to conservative president Gabriel García Moreno, who was assassinated in Plaza Grande and is buried below the Catedral.

On the corner of García Moreno and Espejo is the **Centro Cultural Metropolitano**, with regular exhibitions and performances in its courtyard. The centre also houses the **Museo Alberto Mena Caamaño** (Tues–Sun 9am–5pm; $1.50), which has waxwork depictions of Quito life from 1700 to 1830, including the battles for independence.

Walk half a block south from Plaza Grande along Calle García Moreno to reach Quito's most extravagant church, **La Compañía de Jesús** (Mon–Fri 9.30am–5pm, Sat 9.30am–4pm, Sun 1.30–4pm; $3), built by Jesuits in the seventeenth and eighteenth centuries. It took 163 years to construct, with seven tonnes of gold to cover the interior from top to bottom. It's a wonder to behold, despite bordering on opulence gone mad.

Continue south down García Moreno to reach the **Museo de la Ciudad** (Tues–Sun 9.30am–4.30pm; $3). If you can navigate the confusing layout, it's a rewarding experience, depicting life in Quito through the centuries in a series of scale models.

Plaza San Francisco

From La Compañía head northwest to Plaza San Francisco, one of Ecuador's most beautiful squares. The sixteenth-century **Iglesia de San Francisco** is Quito's oldest church and its twin bell tower is one of the city's most famous sights. The altar of the church has been undergoing years of painstaking restoration, but the rest of the interior is visible. Behind the impressive facade on the northwest side is the largest religious complex in South America. The **Museo de San Francisco** (Mon–Sat 9am–5pm, Sun 9am–12.30pm; $2) is housed among the cloisters and has an impressive collection of religious sculptures, paintings and furniture. Through the museum, you can enter the choral room of the church with a statue of the "dancing virgin" and depictions of planets on the ceiling.

6

QUITO: OLD TOWN

LA CHILENA

San Juan Monasterio

Basílica del Voto Nacional

La Alameda

La Alameda

New Town

SANTA PRISCA

Banco Central

Parque La Alameda

Plaza Hermano Miguel

CIUDAD VIEJO

Museo Arte Colonial

Santa Barbara

Museo Camilo Egas

Hermano Miguel

Banco Central

La Merced

Casa de Benalcazar

Carmen Bajo

Teatro Sucre

San Blas

Mercado Ipiales

Inmaculada Concepcion

Palacio Arzobispal

Sucre Theatre

Museo San Francisco

Palacio Gobierno

Plaza Grande

Alcaldia Municipal

Monasterio de San Agustin

SAN BLAS

San Francisco

Plaza San Francisco

Centro Cultural Metropolitano

Plaza Grande

La María

Carmen de San Jose

La Compañía de Jesús

Bolivar Theatre

Santa Catalina

Plaza Marin

Casa de Sucre

Museo de la Ciudad

SAN MARCOS

Plaza Santo Domingo

PLAZA SANTO DOMINGO

Iglesia Santo Domingo

San Marcos

MANOSALVAS

LA TOLA

SAN SEBASTIAN

Plaza M. Saenz

Cumandá

LA LOMA

Bus Terminal

Ecovía

Trole

● EATING, DRINKING & NIGHTLIFE

El Búho	5
Café Sibari	9
Caféto	6
Las Cuevas de Luis Cardelas	1
Frutería Monserrate	8
Govindas	2
La Guaragua	7
Pedro y Pablo	3
Tianguez	4

EL PLACER

La Recoleta

■ ACCOMMODATION

Auca Continental	6
Catedral	1
Hostal Sucre	5
Plaza del Teatro	2
La Real Audiencia	8
San Francisco de Quito	7
Secret Garden	3
Vienna Hotel Internacional	4

0   200
metres

Ichimbía Park

Train Station

Plaza Santo Domingo and La Ronda

Follow Simón Bolívar east of Plaza San Francisco to reach Quito's third impressive square, Plaza Santo Domingo, dominated by the sixteenth-century **Iglesia Santo Domingo**. From this square take Guayaquil to reach the narrow alley of **La Ronda**, one of Quito's oldest streets. This working-class neighbourhood has been completely renovated; the result is a pleasant walkway of tiny art galleries, bakeries and traditional cafés. La Ronda has become a popular spot at night to listen to live music or have a quiet drink.

6

El Panecillo

Old Quito's skyline is dominated by the 40m-high statue of the **Virgin de Quito**, on the hill known as El Panecillo ("little bread loaf") to the southwest. It's not safe to walk, so take a taxi (about $3 single from the Old Town or $8 return including waiting time). From the top, the view over the city is spectacular and the close-up of the statue with a chained dragon at her feet is equally impressive. You can climb up the statue for $1 (daily 9am–5pm).

Basílica del Voto Nacional

Take Calle Venezuela uphill from Plaza Grande to admire the gothic grandeur of the **Basílica del Voto Nacional** (daily 9am–5pm; $2). Construction has taken place over the past century, beginning in 1892. Instead of gargoyles, the church has iguanas and Galápagos tortoises protruding from its sides. Climbing the steep stairs and ladders up the 115m towers is unnerving, so take the lift if you're afraid of heights. The views across the city are fantastic.

Itchimbia Park and Cultural Centre

Perched high on a hill east of the Old Town, this cultural centre inside the park hosts occasional exhibitions, but the main draw is the view and a chance to escape the city on footpaths winding through the extensive natural landscape. A taxi from the Old Town costs $2–3.

La Casa de la Cultura

Next to the Parque El Ejido in the New Town, the large oval building of **La Casa de la Cultura** (Patria between 6 de Diciembre and 12 de Octubre; ☎02 222 3392, ⍟cce.org.ec) contains cinemas, theatres, auditoriums and, of most interest to tourists, the **Museo del Banco Central** (Tues–Fri 9am–5pm, Sat & Sun 10am–4pm; $2). This is Ecuador's best museum, with an astonishing collection of pre-Columbian ceramics and artefacts as well as colonial, republican and modern art. The museum is divided into four rooms: archeology, colonial art, contemporary art and the Gold Room, which displays a majestic Inca sun-mask, the symbol of the Banco Central.

Museo Fundación Guayasamín and the Capilla del Hombre

Oswaldo Guayasamín is Ecuador's most famous contemporary artist, and Quito's Bellavista district, where he used to live, houses two collections of his art. The **Museo Fundación Guayasamín** (Jose Bosmediano 543; Mon–Fri 10am–5pm; $3; ⍟guayasamin.org) exhibits many paintings as well as his enormous collection of pre-Columbian ceramics and colonial religious art. A further ten-minute walk up the hill is the far more impressive **Capilla del Hombre** or "Chapel of Man" (Tues–Sun 10am–5.30pm; $3, or $2 with museum entrance ticket), one of South America's most important works of art. This was Guayasamín's final great project, initiated in his last years and not fully completed until after his death in 1999. From the museum you can walk up to the garden of Guayasamín and see where his ashes are buried under the "Tree of Life". Just up from the Capilla del Hombre is the **Parque Metropolitano**, Quito's largest park, with forested trails, picnic areas and sweeping views. There are occasional buses up to Bellavista but it's best to take a taxi ($2).

Parque Carolina

The best place to relax in Quito's New Town is **Parque Carolina**. This is where locals come to walk, play sports and eat. The park contains a beautiful set of **Botanical Gardens** (Tues–Sun 9am–5pm; $3.50), which showcases Ecuador's biodiversity with an array of plants and trees, including more than five hundred orchid species in greenhouses. Next door, the **Museo de Ciencias Naturales** (Mon–Fri 8.30am–4.30pm; $2) has a huge collection of dead insects and arachnids. The park also contains **The Vivarium** (Tues–Sun 9.30am–5.30pm; $2.50), with more than forty species of reptiles including caimans, turtles and snakes. The highlights are the 6m-long python and the boa constrictor, which you can be photographed holding ($3).

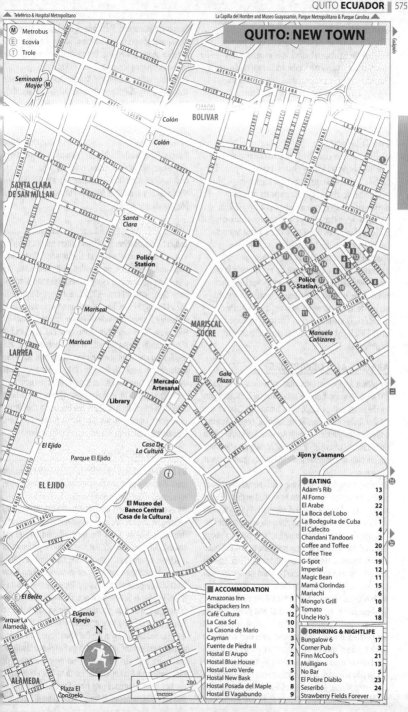

QUITO: NEW TOWN

M   Metrobus
E   Ecovía
T   Trole

ACCOMMODATION

Amazonas Inn	1
Backpackers Inn	4
Café Cultura	12
La Casa Sol	10
La Casona de Mario	13
Cayman	3
Fuente de Piedra II	7
Hostal El Arupo	2
Hostal Blue House	11
Hostal Loro Verde	5
Hostal New Bask	6
Hostal Posada del Maple	8
Hostal El Vagabundo	9

EATING

Adam's Rib	13
Al Forno	9
El Arabe	22
La Boca del Lobo	14
La Bodeguita de Cuba	1
El Cafecito	4
Chandani Tandoori	2
Coffee and Toffee	20
Coffee Tree	16
G-Spot	19
Imperial	12
Magic Bean	11
Mamá Clorindas	15
Mariachi	6
Mongo's Grill	10
Tomato	8
Uncle Ho's	18

DRINKING & NIGHTLIFE

Bungalow 6	17
Corner Pub	3
Finn McCool's	21
Mulligans	13
No Bar	5
El Pobre Diablo	23
Seseribó	24
Strawberry Fields Forever	7

6

Guápulo

Northeast of the New Town, this pretty hillside neighbourhood is a world away from the city. With cobbled streets, historic houses and pleasant cafés, it's a relaxing place. The focal point is the beautiful seventeenth-century Iglésia de Guápulo which houses a collection of colonial art.

The Teleférico

Quito's most dizzying tourist attraction is the **Teleférico** (Sun–Thurs 10am–7pm, Fri & Sat 10am–10pm; $4), a cable-car ride high above the city. The main attraction is the fifteen-minute ride up to 4100m, from where the views are spectacular on a clear day. At the top, take in the views, relax in the café or tackle the hike to Ruca Pichincha, 3km away (do not attempt this walk alone as robberies have been reported). Bring warm clothes and take care not to over-exert yourself at this altitude if you've just arrived in Quito. Teleférico shuttles run from Río Coca, at 6 Diciembre (Ecovía) and Estación Norte (Trole).

ARRIVAL AND DEPARTURE

By plane Aeropuerto Internacional Mariscal Sucre (☎ 02 294 4900, ⓦ quiport.com) is in the town of Tababela 18km to the northeast of Quito. This brand-new airport has regular flights to Europe, North America, Central America and other destinations in South America. The journey from Quito (30min) costs $20–25 by taxi. At the time of writing, it is unconfirmed whether there will be any specific airport bus services.

By train Trains from Quito leave from Chimbacalle station, south of the old town, which can be reached on the trolleybus or via a taxi from La Mariscal District ($4–5). Advanced booking is advised, as the services are very popular. The Latacunga service (Thurs–Sun 8am; 4hr) passes through Machachi and Boliche, but there are separate services to each of these towns on weekends (see ⓦ ferrocarrilesdelecuador .gob.ec). The train (see box, p.591) should run to Riobamba and all the way to Guayaquil by 2014.

By bus Quito has three bus terminals. For all destinations from the south, including the coast and jungle, use the main terminal, Quitumbe, in the far south of Quito. It's complicated, involves changes and takes over an hour to reach the New Town by trolleybus, so consider a taxi ($8–10). From Otavalo and the northern highlands, you arrive at Carcelén terminal, at the northern end of the Metrobus line. From Mindo, you arrive at Ofelia in the far north on the Metrobus line. It takes an hour to get to the New Town

from these stations by Metrobus or taxi ($5–7). However, some private bus companies have offices in the New Town, which are more convenient. The biggest is Panamericana (Reina Victoria, on Colon ☎ 02 255 7133).

Destinations from Quitumbe Ambato (hourly; 2hr 30min); Atacames (daily; 7hr); Baños (hourly; 3hr); Coca (daily; 9hr); Cuenca (hourly; 9hr); Guaranda (daily; 5hr); Guayaquil (hourly; 8hr); Lago Agrio (daily; 9hr); Latacunga (hourly; 1hr 30min); Santo Domingo (hourly; 3hr); Tena (hourly; 5hr).

Destinations from Carcelén Atacames (daily; 7hr); Ibarra (hourly; 2hr 30min); Los Bancos (indirect to Mindo, daily; 2hr); Otavalo (hourly; 2hr); Tulcan (hourly; 5hr).

Destinations from Ofelia Cayambe (hourly; 1hr 30min); Mindo (direct, daily; 2hr); Mitad del Mundo (via Metrobus line, hourly; 1hr 30min).

INFORMATION

Tourist information The Quito Visitors Bureau (ⓦ quito .com.ec) has several offices in the city with brochures, maps and information on Ecuador. In the Old Town the office is on Venezuela, at Espejo, on Plaza Grande (Mon–Fri 9am–6pm, Sat 10.30am–9.30pm, Sun 9am–5pm; ☎ 02 257 2445). In the New Town there's an office in the Casa de La Cultura Ecuatoriana (6 de Diciembre, at Patria; Mon–Fri 9am–5pm, Sat & Sun 10am–4pm; ☎ 02 222 1116) and in Mariscal Sucre (Reina Victoria, at Luis Cordero; ☎ 02 255 1566). Also check out the travellers' club South American Explorers on Jorge Washington 311, at Leonidas Plaza (Mon–Fri 9.30am–5pm & Sat 9am–noon, open until 8pm Thurs; ☎ 02 222 5228, ⓦ saexplorers.org), which has a huge amount of information on Quito and Ecuador in the form of trip reports, and free information sheets for non-members. Membership costs from $60 per year ($90 for couples).

GETTING AROUND

By bus These are very hit and miss but useful for travelling short distances up main avenues such as 12 de Octubre, Amazonas, 10 de Agosto and Colón.

By electric bus There are three main electric bus routes running north to south, with designated stations and car-free lanes, making them the most efficient way to get around. All charge $0.25 flat fare (bought at kiosks or machines in advance). Note that the three services rarely link up, so changing routes often involves walking a few blocks. They generally run every 10min Mon–Fri 6am–midnight, Sat & Sun 6am–10pm. El Trole is the modern trolleybus system that runs down 10 de Agosto to the Old Town; stops are easy to spot because of their distinctive green raised platforms. In the Old Town buses travel south along Guayaquil and return north on Flores and Montufar. Ecovía are dark red buses that run mainly along 6 de Diciembre from Río Coca in the north to Plaza la Marín in the Old Town. Metrobus runs from Carcelén bus terminal down Avenida América to Universidad Central. Note that pickpocketing is a chronic problem on Quito's trolleybuses so be vigilant and don't carry valuables.

By car Many reputable international rental companies have offices outside the international terminal of the airport, including Avis (☎02 244 0270) and Hertz (☎02 225 4258).

By taxi It's often easier to take a taxi and is recommended at night. Quito is the only city in Ecuador where taxis use a meter. Check that the meter is reset when you get in. It's very cheap – from the Old Town to the New Town should be only $2–3. Fares increase at night, when most drivers don't use the meter (in which case, agree the price beforehand). It's safer to use a pre-booked service; most hoteliers have numbers of trusted companies. Reliable 24hr services include Central Radio Taxis (☎02 250 0600) and Teletaxi (☎02 222 2222).

ACCOMMODATION

Most visitors stay in La Mariscal in the New Town, which is geared up for tourists with a wide selection of hotels, restaurants, bars, tour operators, internet cafés and laundry. La Mariscal gets very noisy at the weekends and can be dangerous, especially at night. There are quieter, safer alternatives in Guapulo and La Floresta. Staying in the Old Town is a better option than it used to be and convenient for sightseeing – though there are fewer tourist amenities.

NEW TOWN

Amazonas Inn Joaquín Pinto 471, at Av Amazonas ☎02 222 5723; map p.575. Friendly hotel with comfortable if compact rooms with private bath and cable TV. $26

Hostal El Arupo Juan Rodriguez E7-22, at Reina Victoria ☎02 255 7543, �🌐hostalelarupo.com; map p.575. An attractive renovated house with TV room, free internet and colourful rooms. Breakfast included. $45

Backpackers Inn Juan Rodríguez 245, at Reina Victoria ☎02 250 9669, �🌐backpackersinn.net; map p.575. A very popular budget option situated on one of the quieter, more pleasant streets in Mariscal. Dorms $8, doubles $16

Hostal Blue House Pinto, at Diego de Almagro ☎02 222 3480, �🌐bluehousequito.com; map p.575. Very popular new backpacker hostel with a kitchen, bar, free internet and breakfast included. Dorms $9, doubles $30

La Casa Sol Calama 127 ☎02 223 0798, �🌐lacasasol.com; map p.575. Cosy, quiet, brightly coloured guesthouse with comfortable rooms set around an attractive courtyard. Breakfast included. $68

La Casona de Mario Andalucia 213, at Galicia ☎02 254 4036, �🌐casonademario.com; map p.575. If Mariscal is not for you, stay in the quieter neighbourhood of La Floresta. This welcoming home away from home run by an Argentine has a communal kitchen and comfortable lounge area. $20

Cayman Juan Rodríguez 270, at Reina Victoria ☎02 256 7616, �🌐hotelcaymanquito.com; map p.575. Attractive

renovated old house with a huge fireplace, large garden and good restaurant. Free wi-fi and breakfast. $53

★ **Fuente de Piedra II** Juan Mera, at Baquedano ☎02 290 0323, ⍑ecuahotel.com; map p.575. Take a step up from Mariscal's budget options and treat yourself at this colonial-style mid-range hotel. It's elegantly furnished and has attentive service, wi-fi and a gourmet restaurant (breakfast is included). A sister hotel is on Tamayo, at Wilson. $56

Hostal Loro Verde Juan Rodriguez, at Diego de Almagro ☎02 222 6173; map p.575. A hotel as colourful as its name (green parrot), with indigenous artefacts and comfortable rooms. $30

Hostal New Bask Lizardo Garcia, at Diego de Almagro ☎098 188 5575; map p.575. The cheapest, friendliest place in the New Town. A great deal but fills up fast. Dorms $6, doubles $16

Hostal Posada del Maple Juan Rodriguez ☎02 290 7367; map p.575. A small but inviting budget place with a plant-filled courtyard and balconies. Dorms $9, doubles $26

Hostal El Vagabundo Wilson E7-45 ☎02 222 6376; map p.575. A dependable budget option with a friendly atmosphere, small café and table tennis. $25

OLD TOWN

Auca Continental Sucre OE-414, at Venezuela ☎02 255 3953; map p.573. Clean, no-frills budget option with firm beds, private bath and TV. $20

Catedral Mejia 638, at Benalcazar ☎02 295 5438, ⍑hotelcatedral.ec; map p.573. Recently upgraded hotel in the heart of the Old Town with comfortable rooms, cable TV, sauna and steam room. $55

Plaza del Teatro Guayaquil, at Esmeraldas ☎02 295 9462; map p.573. Great-value mid-range choice with a plush reception and charming if slightly worn rooms. $24

La Real Audiencia Bolívar 220, at Guayaquil ☎02 295 0590, ⍑realaudiencia.com; map p.573. Try this upmarket Old Town option with stylish rooms, black-and-white photography and a fabulous view of Plaza Santo Domingo from the restaurant (open to non-guests). Breakfast included. $55

★ **San Francisco de Quito** Sucre 217, at Guayaquil ☎02 228 7758, ⍑sanfranciscodequito.com.ec; map p.573. The pick of the Old Town mid-range options with

> ### ★ TREAT YOURSELF
>
> **Café Cultura** Robles 513, at Reina Victoria ☎02 222 4271, ⍑cafecultura.com; map p.575. The most elegant place to stay in the New Town, this restored colonial mansion mixes grandeur with intimacy. The roaring fires in the lounge, the large bathtubs and a gourmet café are the perfect repose after a hard day's sightseeing. $122

6

pleasant rooms set around a cosy courtyard, a fountain, rooftop patio and great views. Breakfast included. $47

Secret Garden Antepara E4-60, at Los Rios ☎099 602 3709, ⓦsecretgardenquito.com; map p.573. Hidden away southeast of the historic centre in a listed building, this is a great Aussie-run budget hostel set on five floors with basic rooms and a rooftop terrace serving big breakfasts. There's also a Spanish school and tour operator. Dorms $9, doubles $24

Hostal Sucre Bolívar, at Cuenca ☎02 295 4025; map p.573. The cheapest option in the Old Town by a long way. Basic, tatty rooms but a friendly atmosphere, lounge and great views of Plaza San Francisco. Dorms only $8

Vienna Hotel Internacional Flores, at Chile ☎02 295 4860; map p.573. A good-quality three-star hotel with well-appointed rooms set around an enclosed courtyard. $40

EATING

Quito boasts the best selection of international restaurants in Ecuador – from Asian to Middle Eastern and Mediterranean. Most are found in the New Town, with Old Town eating options restricted. For those on a budget, fill yourself up at lunch, as most restaurants offer specials for $2–4. Most places are closed on Sundays unless indicated.

NEW TOWN

Adam's Rib Calama, at Reina Victoria; map p.575. The best place for barbecued meat – ribs, steak, kebabs and even sautéed chicken livers. Mains $6–8.

Al Forno Moreno, at Diego de Almagro; map p.575. Seek out the biggest choice of pizzas in town ($5–10) with an incredible fifty different varieties.

El Arabe Reina Victoria 627, at Carrion ☎02 254 9414; map p.575. The best place in town for kebabs, falafel and pitta. Open daily.

La Bodeguita de Cuba Reina Victoria N26-105; map p.575. Tasty Cuban specialities ($4–5) with live Cuban music on Thurs nights, when drinking and dancing continues into the early hours.

El Cafecito Luis Cordero 1124; map p.575. Cosy café with great coffee, home-made cakes, crêpes and vegetarian meals for around $3–5. Open daily.

Chandani Tandoori Juan Mera, at Luis Cordero; map p.575. Head here for authentic Indian food at low prices. *Masala, korma, dupiaza, balti* and hot *vindaloo* – all the classics are done well for only $3–5. Lunchtime only Sun.

Coffee and Toffee Calama, at Diego Almagro; map p.575. Start the day with breakfast or the evening with cocktails, lounging on armchairs and surfing the net in this relaxed café. Daily 24hr.

Coffee Tree Foch, at Reina Victoria; map p.575. A long-standing café on Plaza Foch, great for people-watching over a coffee or cocktail. Daily 24hr.

G-Spot Diego de Almagro, at Calama; map p.575. Its name may leave you nonplussed but this fast-food joint has

cheap burgers with trimmings galore ($2–3). Open daily.

Imperial Juan Rodriguez, at Reina Victoria; map p.575. Eat alfresco in this restaurant's garden terrace. Choose from an imaginative menu of mainly chicken and meat dishes ($5–6) and a great-value set lunch ($2). (Simple rooms with bath upstairs for $20.)

Magic Bean Foch, at Juan Mera; map p.575. Hugely popular café with a small garden. Great breakfasts, pancakes and fresh juices from $3–6. Open daily.

Mamá Clorindas Reina Victoria 1144; map p.575. Well-prepared but pricey Ecuadorian specialities. Try half a guinea pig (*cuy*) for $9.

Mariachi Foch, at Juan Mera; map p.575. A good Mexican place – burritos, chimichangas, fajitas, etc, for $5–8, all washed down with cocktails and sangria.

Mongo's Grill Calama; map p.575. This hugely popular Mongolian barbecue offers sizzling meat and vegetable dishes such as chicken teriyaki and lamb in spicy yogurt, all cooked in front of you. Excellent-value buffets from $4–6.

Tomato Juan Mera, at Calama; map p.575. A great place for pizza ($5–7) and pasta. The *calzone* is particularly good. Open daily.

★ **Uncle Ho's** Calama 166-E8-29; map p.575. Vietnamese restaurant run by a friendly Irish guy who serves up a range of great cocktails, followed by a feast of Asian food – from coconut curry to Imperial rolls and beef noodle soup. Mains $5–7.

OLD TOWN

El Búho Jose Moreno, at Espejo; map p.573. Inside the Centro Cultural Metropolitano, this is a pleasant stop for soups, salads, sandwiches and pasta. $3–6. Lunchtime only Sun.

Caféto Chile, at Guayaquil; map p.573. Little gem of a café at the entrance to San Agustín Monastery specializing in coffee and hot chocolate served with *humitas, tamales, empanadas* and cakes for $3–5. Open Sun mornings.

★ **Las Cuevas de Luis Candelas** Benalcazar, at Chile; map p.573. One of the best restaurants in the Old Town, snuggled in a cosy basement offering gourmet Ecuadorian and International food. Paella and Fondu Bourguignonne are two specialities. Mains $6–10.

Frutería Montserrate Espejo 0e2-12; map p.573. The perfect place to take a break from sightseeing with an extravagant helping of fruit salad and ice cream ($2–5). Cheap *almuerzos* and sandwiches also available.

Govindas Esmeraldas 853; map p.573. The best vegetarian option in the Old Town. Healthy breakfasts and specialities such as veggie risotto for lunch. Mains $2–4.

La Guaragua Espejo Oe2-40; map p.573. Appealing little restaurant just down from Plaza Grande. Ecuadorian specialities such as *seco de pollo* (chicken stew) and *chuleta* (fried pork chops); the great-value set lunches will set you back $3–6.

Pedro y Pablo Chile, at Plaza Grande; map p.573. Just one of the many cafés in a delightful food court hidden in a historic building on Plaza Grande, serving mainly seafood. Mains $4.

Tianguez Plaza de San Francisco; map p.573. Under the church on the plaza, this is a perfectly situated café in which to take a break from sightseeing. Well-prepared local specialities and indulgent desserts are slightly pricey ($3–8) but worth it for the great setting.

DRINKING AND NIGHTLIFE

NEW TOWN

Mariscal in the New Town has a vibrant nightlife scene and gets packed on weekends. The most happening area is along José Calama and Foch between avenidas Amazonas, Juan León Mera and Reina Victoria. Bars are busy from 8pm onwards with the clubs filling up towards midnight and winding down around 3am. Remember to take a taxi at night. Mariscal is quiet and feels dangerous on Sundays, when most police take the day off.

⭐ **Bungalow 6** Calama, at Diego Almagro; map p.575. A mixture of locals and tourists flock to enjoy the great atmosphere and dance to Latin and pop classics in this hugely popular bar/disco (entrance $5 including one drink).

Corner Pub Amazonas, at Calama; map p.575. A small new bar on the corner of Mariscal's main drag, popular with expats and locals alike.

Finn McCool's Almagro, at Pinto; map p.575. The most popular expat pub with draught beer, pool, quiz nights, movie nights and plenty of rock music.

Mulligans Calama, at Reina Victoria; map p.575. Very popular Irish bar with draught beer, football on the big screen and traditional gut-busting food. Guinness is extortionate though, at $12.

No Bar Calama 380; map p.575. Raucous Mariscal disco with a large dancefloor. It gets very loud and crowded at weekends (entrance $5 including one drink).

El Pobre Diablo Isabel La Católica, at Galavis; map p.575. A Quito institution in La Floresta with a bohemian atmosphere, cocktails, a good restaurant and live music.

Seseribó Edificio El Girón, Veintimilla, at 12 de Octubre; map p.575. A long-time Quito favourite and the best place to dance salsa and *merengue*, or just stand back and watch the experts. Thursday nights are particularly good.

Strawberry Fields Forever Calama E5-23; map p.575. A world away from *No Bar* next door, this tiny rock bar, brimming with Beatles memorabilia, is great to escape the disco craziness.

OLD TOWN

Café Sibari La Ronda; map p.573. Just one of the many café options along regenerated La Ronda. Catch live music at weekends or have a quiet drink during the week.

DIRECTORY

Banks and exchange There are plenty of banks near Av Amazonas in the New Town but fewer in the Old Town. They are normally open Mon–Fri 8.30am–4pm and Sat mornings. Try Banco de Guayaquil on Reina Victoria, at Colón, or Banco del Pacífico, on 12 de Octubre, at Cordero.

Books The English Bookshop (Calama, at Diego de Almagro) is the best place in Mariscal to pick up fiction and travel books, to buy, sell or borrow. Libri Mundi (J Mera, at Wilson; ☎ 02 223 4791, ⊕ librimundi.com) is the best place for new books, and Confederate Books (Calama, at Mera; ☎ 02 252 7890) is also good for secondhand books.

Embassies and consulates Argentina, Amazonas 21–147, at Roca ☎ 02 250 1106; Bolivia, Eloy Alfaro 2432, at Fernando Ayarza ☎ 02 244 6652; Brazil, Amazonas 1429, at Colón, Edificio España ☎ 02 256 3086; Canada, 6 de Diciembre 2816, at Paul Rivet, Edificio Josueth González ☎ 02 250 6162; Chile, Juan Pablo Sanz 3617, at Amazonas ☎ 02 224 9403; Colombia, Colón 1133, at Amazonas, Edificio Arista ☎ 02 222 2486; Ireland, Antonio de Ulloa 2651, at Rumipamba ☎ 02 245 1577; Peru, República de El Salvador 495, at Irlanda ☎ 02 246 8411; UK, Naciones Unidas, at República de El Salvador, Edificio Citiplaza, 14th floor ☎ 02 297 0801, ⊕ ukinecuador .fco.gov.uk; US, 12 de Octubre, at Patria ☎ 02 256 2890, ⊕ ecuador.usembassy.gov; Venezuela, Cabildo 115, at Quito Tenis ☎ 02 226 8635.

Hospital Hospital Metropolitano, Av Mariana de Jesús, at Av Occidental ☎ 02 226 1520, emergency and ambulance ☎ 02 226 5020.

Internet Quito's New Town is full of internet cafés, charging about $0.70–$1/hr. Friendly, comfortable places include Papaya Net (Calama, at JL Mera; ☎ 02 255 6574) and Sambo. net (JL Mera, at J Pinto; ☎ 02 290 1315).

Police La Policía de Turismo (Reina Victoria, at Roca; ☎ 02 254 3983).

Post offices The most convenient office for La Mariscal is on the corner of Reina Victoria, at Colón (Mon–Fri 8am–7pm, Sat & Sun 8am–noon; ☎ 02 250 8890).

Shopping Mercado Artesanal (Juan Mera, at Jorge Washington, New Town), weekend market at Parque El Ejido, and Mercado Ipiales (Chile, at Imbabura, Old Town).

Telephones CNT (⊕ www.cnt.com.ec) has its main office on Eloy Alfaro near 9 de Octubre and branches around the city. In Mariscal there is an office on Reina Victoria. You can also buy Porta and Bell South phonecards at most larger shops.

6

6

DAY-TRIPS FROM QUITO

There are many interesting destinations that can be reached on a day-trip from Quito: Otavalo, Mindo and Cotopaxi are all less than three hours from the city.

La Mitad del Mundo

The most popular day-trip is **LA MITAD DEL MUNDO** tourist complex ("The Middle of the World"; Mon–Fri 9am–6pm, Sat & Sun 9am–8pm; $3, ⓦwww.mitaddel mundo.com) on the equator, 22km north of Quito. The centrepiece is the 30m-high **monument** (an extra $3 to go inside), topped by a brass globe. Climb to the top and then descend the stairs through the **Ethnographic Museum**, which has fascinating displays of Ecuador's richly varied indigenous populations. There are various other small exhibitions dotted around the complex, the highlight being the France building with a good exhibition on the discovery of the equator by Charles Marie de La Condamine. The **plaza** is a pleasant place to relax and have lunch, with music and dance at weekends. Although everybody wants to get a photo of themselves straddling the equator in front of the monument, this is not actually the real equator, which lies approximately 300m along the main road to the east at the **Museo Solar Inti Ñan** (daily 9.30am–5pm; $3, ⓦmuseointinan.com.ec). It's particularly fun to see the experiments to prove you are standing on the equator. There's an interesting exhibition of indigenous housing and, bizarrely, a guide on how to make a shrunken head. To get to Mitad del Mundo, take the Metrobus on Avenida America north to the Ofelia terminal and then a green Mitad del Mundo **bus** ($0.50). The trip from the New Town takes about an hour.

Pululahua Crater and Reserve

Just 5km north of La Mitad del Mundo the extinct volcanic crater of **Pululahua** has been turned into a 32-square-kilometre nature reserve. On clear days it is a spectacular sight and very pleasant hike. It takes about three or four hours to hike to the bottom and back up. There are occasional buses from Mitad del Mundo, or take a taxi.

ACTIVITIES IN QUITO

After a few days of sightseeing and acclimatization, you will be ready to take advantage of the huge range of activities in the mountains near the city. The most popular one-day tours are cycling and horseriding. For **cycling**, Cotopaxi National Park and Ilinizas are firm favourites (average cost $65 per day). There are numerous locations south of Quito offering **horseriding** (average cost $45 per day). For **rafting and kayaking**, day tours in valleys north and west of Quito cost $70–80. The most popular **trekking** route is around Lake Quilotoa (see p.590). One- and two-day tours can be booked from Quito. If you fancy **climbing**, the easier peaks include Pasochoa (4199m), El Corazón (4788m) and the more challenging Iliniza Norte (5126m). All cost $65 for a one-day tour. Cotopaxi (5897m), Cayambe (5790m), Antisana (5755m) and Chimborazo (6310m) are tough and can all be climbed by well-prepared, fit people on two-day tours ($175–215).

TOUR OPERATORS

The following tour operators offer many of the above tours as well as a range of other tours throughout Ecuador:
Alta Montaña Jorge Washington 8–20 ☎02 255 8380. Climbing and trekking.
Biking Dutchman Foch 714, at Juan Mera ☎02 254 2806, ⓦbiking-dutchman.com. Mountain-biking tours.
Ecuadorian Alpine Institute Ramírez Dávalos 136, at Amazonas ☎02 256 5465, ⓦvolcanoclimbing.com. Top-class climbing tours.
Enchanted Expeditions De las Alondras N45-102, at Los Lirios ☎02 334 0525, ⓦenchantedexpeditions

.com. Wide range of tours. Specialists in Galápagos yachts and haciendas in the highlands.
Gulliver JL Mera, at Calama ☎02 252 9297, ⓦgulliver .com.ec. Popular Mariscal operator with climbing, hiking, biking and jungle tours as well as Galápagos visits.
Sierra Nevada Expeditions J Pinto, at Cordero E4-150 ☎02 255 3658, ⓦsierranevada.ec. Climbing and river-rafting specialist.
Yacu Amu Foch 746, at Juan Mera ☎02 290 4055, ⓦyacuamu.com. White-water rafting and kayaking specialist.

The Pichinchas

The twin peaks that give the province its name dominate the landscape (both are over 4700m). **Rucu**, meaning Elder in Kichwa, and **Guagua** (baby) make good hikes, but each has their problems. Rucu, which is easily accessed from the top of the *teleférico*, has suffered from crime problems in recent years but there is usually police presence on the trail at weekends. Guagua is badly behaved and a violent eruption showered Quito in ash in 1999. It is still officially active and harder to climb. Ask at a tour operator in Quito for the latest situation.

Papallacta

About 65km (two hours) from Quito, the road to Lago Agrio and Tena passes through the town of **Papallacta**, home to the best thermal baths in Ecuador. The entrance to **Las Termas de Papallacta** (daily 6am–9pm; $7; ☎02 232 0040) is a twenty-minute walk up a dirt road, so consider a taxi. The complex is impressive, with 25 baths of different temperatures. On clear days there are great views over the town and snowcapped Volcán Artisana. Note that at 3300m it gets cold outside the baths, so bring warm clothes.

ACCOMMODATION

Choza de Don Wilson ☎06 232 0627. A great budget option in town which has decent rooms, great views and a good restaurant serving a $4 set menu. Trout is a speciality and breakfast is included. $30

The Northern Highlands and Western Andean slopes

North of Quito lie two dramatically different regions. To the northwest are verdant **cloudforests**, filled with birdlife. The small town of **Mindo** is the best base to explore the forest's biodiversity and indulge in adrenaline-pumping adventure sports. To the northeast, magnificent Andean scenery populated by proud indigenous cultures extends to the Colombian border. Passing the snowcapped **Volcán Cayambe**, the most popular destination is **Otavalo**, whose colourful Saturday market is one of the largest in South America and heaven for lovers of indigenous crafts and clothing. Some 30km north are the stately squares of La Ciudad Blanca, **Ibarra**, the largest city in the region. North of Ibarra is mainly visited by those crossing into Colombia via **Tulcán**.

MINDO

Snuggled in a cloudforest at a pleasant elevation of 1200m, **MINDO** is a truly idyllic destination. Whether you want to watch for some of the 400 species of birds and 250 species of butterfly, swing above the forest canopy on zip-lines, plunge down the rivers on rubber tubes or simply gaze at the waterfalls, there's something for everyone. The cool climate means that this is a far more comfortable region to explore pristine forest than the Oriente. Tourism has developed relatively slowly in Mindo so you can usually avoid the crowds in this sleepy town, although weekends get busy with day-trippers. Many attractions listed above are a one- or two-hour walk from town. To save time, share a taxi for $5–10.

Mariposas de Mindo

The town is surrounded by the Bosque Protector Mindo-Nambillo cloudforest but most accessible areas are due south. The dirt road leading out of town forks after about 1km. To the left is the butterfly farm **Mariposas de Mindo** (9am–6.30pm; $5; ⊕mariposasdemindo .com), which breeds 25 species, including the Brown Owl Eye and the Peleides Blue Morpho, the latter with a wingspan of 20cm. The guide shows the lifecycle from egg to caterpillar, pupa to butterfly. Come in the early morning and you may be lucky and see them hatch.

Mindo Canopy Adventure

Take a right when the dirt road out of town forks to **Mindo Canopy Adventure**

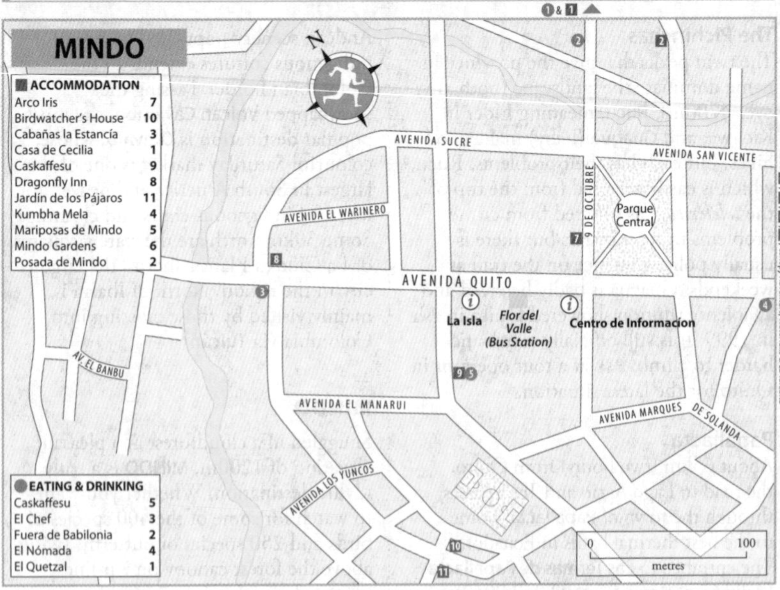

6

($10; ☎098 542 8758, ⓦmindocanopy.com). Adrenaline lovers can get their fix by zinging along cables from 20m to 400m in length, high above the forest. Go solo or be accompanied by a guide. It's great fun and the lines and harnesses are tested by experts. The thirteen-line circuit takes about one hour thirty minutes ($10), or do three lines for $5.

About 1km up the hill is a more relaxed way to traverse the treetops. **La Tarabita** cable car ($5/person) cruises 150m above a river basin. On the other side are trails to seven waterfalls. The paths are confusing in places but you can't really get lost as there is only one exit – wear boots as it's muddy. The entire circuit takes two hours and goes deep inside the cloudforest; hiring a birdwatching guide is a great way to learn more. Most charge $50 per half-day and $100 per full-day. It's cheaper in a group.

Tubing and canyoning

For adventure-sports lovers, there's plenty in Mindo. An unusual alternative to rafting is tumbling down river rapids in an inflatable **tube** ($8 for a couple of hours including transport). **Canyoning** is also available ($10/half-day).

ARRIVAL AND DEPARTURE

By bus Cooperativa Flor del Valle (☎02 252 7495, ⓦflordelvalle.com.ec) leaves Quito's Ofelia bus station daily at 8am, 9am, 3pm and 4pm, returning at 6.30am, 1.45pm and 3pm (Sat & Sun more frequent services); 2hr. If you miss the morning bus from Quito, go to Carcelén terminal and take any bus heading to Los Bancos and ask the driver to let you off at the turn-off to Mindo, where you can usually hire a taxi to town ($1–2).

INFORMATION AND TOURS

Information The Centro de Información is on Quito near the main plaza (8.30am–12.30pm and 1.30–5pm Wed–Sun). It has lists of recommended guides and brochures.

Tours The owner of *Birdwatcher's House* (see below) is an experienced guide. Other recommended tour operators who can organize all the activites from Mindo include *La Isla Mindo* (☎02 217 0481, ⓦlaislamindo.com) and *Mindo Bird* (☎099 735 1297, ⓦwww.mindobirds.com.ec), both on the main Avenida Quito.

ACCOMMODATION

Mindo has a wide selection of accommodation but it's a more enjoyable and authentic experience to stay in one of the lodges on the edge of town, surrounded by cloudforest.

Arco Iris Quito, at 9 de Octubre ☎02 390 0405. A dependable option in town, with comfortable rooms and a central location on the main square. **$18**

Birdwatcher's House Los Colibres ☎02 217 0204, ⓦbirdwatchershouse.com. On the western edge of town, this home from home has stunning photography in the rooms, hummingbirds in the gardens and an outdoor jacuzzi. $\overline{\$30}$

Cabañas la Estancia ✆099 878 3272, ⊕mindo hosterialaestancia.com. Cross the rickety bridge to these spacious cabins, set in landscaped gardens with outdoor restaurant, a swimming pool and even a waterslide. $\overline{\$30}$, camping from $\overline{\$3}$

Casa de Cecilia End of 9 de Octubre ✆02 217 0243. On the eastern edge of town, these great-value rustic cabins stand on the banks of a roaring river. $\overline{\$14}$

Caskaffesu Sixto Duran, at Quito ✆02 217 0100, ⊕caskaffesu.com. This American-owned place is arguably the best accommodation in the centre of town. A friendly atmosphere, pleasant café and imaginatively decorated mid-range rooms. $\overline{\$32}$

Dragonfly Inn Quito, at Sucre ✆02 217 0426, ⊕dragonflyinn-mindo.com. This wooden cabin-style hotel is one of the best options in town, with balconies overlooking a garden patio along the river and a very good restaurant. $\overline{\$46}$

Jardin de los Pájaros Los Colibres ✆099 175 6688. Well-presented hotel with carpeted rooms, and a balcony lounge with hammocks and outdoor swimming pool. $\overline{\$26}$

Kumbha Mela ✆099 405 1675. Deep in the forest with a selection of cabins and rooms nestled in extensive gardens. There's a good restaurant, swimming pool and even a private lagoon. Dorms $\overline{\$16}$, doubles $\overline{\$42}$

Mariposas de Mindo ✆02 224 2712, ⊕mariposas demindo.com. Pleasant cabins 2km from town near the butterfly farm (entrance included in price, as well as breakfast). $\overline{\$58}$

Mindo Gardens ✆099 733 1092, ⊕mindogardens.com. One of Mindo's most popular mid-range hotels, 1km past the butterfly farm and set in a private reserve of forest and waterfalls. Brightly coloured cabins sit beside the river and there's a comfortable lounge and games area. Breakfast included. $\overline{\$65}$

Posada de Mindo End of Vicente Aguirre ✆02 217 0199. One of the most comfortable options in town, these new spotless cabins have a good restaurant attached. $\overline{\$40}$

EATING AND DRINKING

There are plenty of restaurants on the main street in the centre of town offering Ecuadorian standards for $5. Many lodges out of town listed above also have good restaurants. Most restaurants are open noon–2pm for lunch and 6–10pm for dinner, often staying open all day at weekends. Mindo has very little nightlife so have a few beers in a restaurant after dinner. There is usually one nightclub open on Saturday night but location varies.

Caskaffesu Sixto Duran, at Quito. One of the more refined options in town. Choose from steak, fish and vegetarian dishes for $4–8.

El Chef Quito. One of the best restaurants in Mindo. The set lunch ($2.50) is outstanding value. To treat yourself, try the speciality *lomo a la piedra* (barbecued steak). Mains $4–8.

Fuera de Babilonia 9 de Octubre. An alternative bar with assorted Indian artefacts on the walls, misshapen tables, a wide-ranging menu (dishes $4–7) and live music at weekends.

El Nómada Quito. On the eastern edge of town, this is the best place to fill up on carefully prepared pizza and pasta dishes, from $6–10.

El Quetzal 9 de Octubre. Head to this organic restaurant for vegetarian specialities, big breakfasts, fresh juices and tasty snacks. Mains $6–8.

CAYAMBE

Between Quito and Otavalo, the little town of **CAYAMBE** is the centre of Ecuador's important flower industry. It's also well known for its *bizcochos*, a type of buttery cookie, and is a quieter base than Otavalo to explore surrounding peaks, notably the volcano the town is named after. Cayambe celebrates the festival of Inti Raymi fervently in late June.

ARRIVAL AND DEPARTURE

By bus There are direct buses to Cayambe from Quito's Ofelia terminal (hourly; 1hr 20min). There are also regular buses from Otavalo hourly; 45min.

ACCOMMODATION

Hotel El Refugio Teran, at 10 de Agosto ✆02 236 3700. Small basic rooms in the centre of town. $\overline{\$10}$

Hotel La Gran Colombia Av Natalia Jaran ✆02 236 1238. More comfort just south of the centre with TV, private bathrooms and a playground at the back (get in touch with your inner child). $\overline{\$15}$

CAYAMBE COCA RESERVE AND VOLCAN CAYAMBE

This is the second-largest Andean reserve in the country, ranging in altitude from 600m to 5790m at the top of Cayambe itself – Ecuador's third-highest peak, and the highest point in the world that straddles the equator. It's a tough climb, possibly the most difficult in the country, so is for advanced climbers only. It's a seven-hour trek from the refuge through constantly changing terrain and frequent snowstorms. Contact Alta Montaña in Quito (✆02 252 4422) to arrange a trek. Highlights of the surrounding reserve include more than 80 lakes and 900 species of birds, among them condors and toucans.

OTAVALO

If you love wandering around markets and picking up *artesano* bargains, then **OTAVALO** is your town. The famous **Saturday market** spreading across town from the Plaza de Ponchos (from 7am) is easily the best in Ecuador and possibly South America. There is a wide range of handicrafts, clothing, hammocks, weavings, carvings, jewellery, ceramics and oddities such as fake shrunken heads. The *Otavaleño* traders are friendly and greet you as "amigo"; behind the smiles, they're savvy salespeople. Take your time gauging the prices and then knock them down by

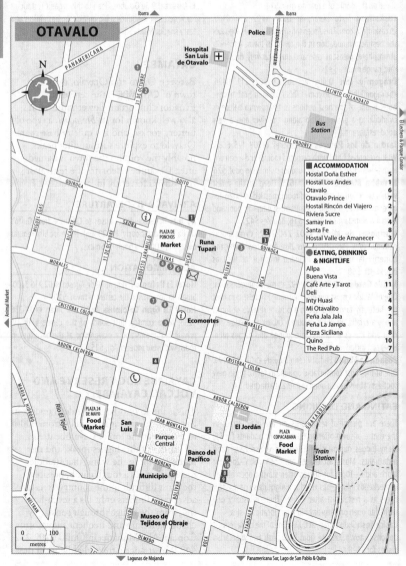

OTAVALO

ACCOMMODATION
Hostal Doña Esther	5
Hostal Los Andes	1
Otavalo	6
Otavalo Prince	7
Hostal Rincón del Viajero	2
Riviera Sucre	9
Samay Inn	4
Santa Fe	8
Hostal Valle de Amanecer	3

EATING, DRINKING & NIGHTLIFE
Allpa	6
Buena Vista	5
Café Arte y Tarot	11
Deli	3
Inty Huasi	4
Mi Otavalito	9
Peña Jala Jala	2
Peña La Jampa	1
Pizza Siciliana	8
Quino	10
The Red Pub	7

a few dollars, but bear in mind that while this is part of the fun, the extra dollar means more to the locals than to you.

During the week the town is quieter but the market is open. Outside the market, the **Museo de Tejidos el Obraje** (Mon–Sat 9am–1pm & 3–5pm; $2) is worth a visit for its demonstrations of textile production. Otavalo's surroundings are also impressive – the town is nestled between the extinct volcanic peaks of Imbabura and Cotacachi on opposite ends of town. Some 4km out of town is the **Parque Condor** (Tues–Sun 9.30am–5pm; $2.50; ☎02 292 4429, ⓦparquecondor.org), which rehabilitates owls, eagles, falcons and condors. It is a pleasant walk with views over Otavalo. Start from the south end of town along Piedrahita and follow the signs past a eucalyptus grove and up a hill. Along the way is **El Lechero**, a tree revered by locals for its healing powers, named because of the milky liquid found in its leaves. Note that robberies have been reported on this route and it can be hard to find so consider a taxi ($4).

ARRIVAL AND INFORMATION

By bus Buses to Otavalo leave from Quito's Carcelén terminal several times each hour (2hr). There are also services from Ibarra (hourly; 40min). The bus station is on Atahualpa, at Neptalí Ordoñez, a couple of blocks northeast of the central Plaza de Ponchos market. It's a short walk to the centre from the bus station but take a taxi for $1 if you're laden with luggage or if you arrive at night.

Tourist office For information and maps, try the Cámara de Turismo office (Quiroga, at Modesto Jaramillo; Mon–Fri 8.30am–1pm & 2.30–5.30pm, Sat 9am–2pm, Sun 9am–noon; ☎06 292 7230).

GETTING AROUND

Otavalo is small and compact enough to walk around, but a taxi across town costs just $1 and is recommended at night. Taxis to surrounding attractions like Peguche, Parque El Condor and Laguna San Pablo cost $3–4. A taxi to attractions further away, including Lagunas de Mojanda, costs $10/hr.

SPORTS AND ACTIVITIES AROUND OTAVALO

Otavalo is surrounded by stunning scenery that can be explored independently or on guided tours. While most travellers come to Otavalo for a day or two, you could easily fill a week exploring mountains and valleys, and trying out adventure sports.The nearest attraction is the **Laguna de San Pablo**, fifteen minutes from town by bus from the terminal (take any bus heading to Araque). Hike around the lake, visit small indigenous communities or arrange watersports. It's very popular with locals at weekends.

Of the many indigenous communities near Otavalo, the best known is **Peguche**, a five-minute journey by bus (Coop Imbaburapac at the terminal does this route). The town is famed for its weavers and musicians, and for a 20m-high waterfall. Peguche, the waterfall and surrounding weaving communities can be visited on a tour ($30/person) with Runa Tupari (see below). Further afield are the three **Lagunas de Mojanda**, considered sacred by many locals. There are trails around the lakes and up to the peak of **Fuya Fuya** (4275m), which is good practice for climbing higher peaks. Another popular trip is the stunning **Laguna Cuicocha**, a 3km-wide extinct volcanic crater lake with steep forested islands in the middle. It sits at the foot of Cotacachi Volcano and can be reached by taxi from Cotacachi (a 30min bus ride from the Otavalo terminal). Tours to Mojanda and Cuicocha can be organized with tour operators in Otavalo for $25. Hiking or cycling tours cost $30–40.

The valleys and rivers around Otavalo offer great adventure-sports opportunities. **Canyoning** is possible in Peguche and in Taxopamba ($30–35). There is class 3–4 **white-water rafting** in Río Chota, Río Mira and Río Intag ($30). The best **mountain-biking** tour descends into the Intag Valley to the west ($50). For those well acclimatized and fit, the mountains around Otavalo offer unforgettable climbing. **Imbabura** (4690m, $60) is the easiest climb, **Cotacachi** (4944m, $80) has technical climbing at the summit, and **Cayambe** (5789m, $190) is Ecuador's third-highest peak and takes a minimum of two days.

TOUR OPERATORS

Runa Tupari Plaza de Ponchos ☎06 292 2320, ⓦrunatupari.com.

Ecomontes Sucre, at Morales ☎06 292 6244, ⓦecomontestour.com.

6

ACCOMMODATION

Otavalo has a lot of hotels for such a small town, most of which are empty during the week but fill up at weekends (it's recommended to book ahead for Friday or Saturday night). The area near the market can be noisy and the best hotels are found in the south of town.

Hostal Doña Esther Montalvo 4–44 ☎06 292 0739, ⓦotavalohotel.com. Owned by a Dutch family, this small colonial-style hotel has friendly service, a verdant courtyard and a great restaurant with Mediterranean specialities. $40

Hostal Los Andes Roca, at Juan Montalvo ☎06 292 1057. One of the cheapest options in town, overlooking the market. Great view but the simple rooms can be noisy. $15

Otavalo Roca, at Juan Montalvo ☎06 292 3712. Quiet, colonial-style hotel with a spacious peach-coloured interior and immaculate rooms for a great price. $44

Otavalo Prince Sucre, at García Moreno ☎06 292 3200. Extravagant exterior but cosy interior with low ceilings. The low prices mean this place fills up fast. $24

Hostal Rincón del Viajero Roca 11-07 ☎06 292 1741. This is a hospitable option for budget travellers, with artwork on the walls, a TV lounge with fireplace, rooftop terrace with hammocks, games room and restaurant. Includes breakfast. $24

Riviera Sucre Roca, at García Moreno ☎06 292 0241, ⓦwww.rivierasucre.com. Relaxing lounge area, beautiful garden and colourful, comfortable rooms. $26

Samay Inn Sucre, at Colon ☎06 292 1826. One of the best options in the centre, with hot water, firm beds, cable TV, small balconies and a family atmosphere. $20

Santa Fe Roca, at García Moreno ☎06 292 3640, ⓦhotel santafeotavalo.com. The quiet location, excellent-quality rooms furnished in pine and eucalyptus, good restaurant and reasonable prices make this one of the best deals in town. $30

★ **Hostal Valle del Amanecer** Roca, at Quiroga ☎06 292 0990, ⓦwww.valledelamanecer.com. The most pleasant budget accommodation in town with rooms set around a cobbled, leafy courtyard. Outdoor fireplace and hammocks. $20

EATING

Alli Allpa Plaza de Ponchos, at Salinas. Endearing little café with great-value Ecuadorian meals and fresh lemonade. Three-course set lunch $4.

Buena Vista Plaza de Ponchos, at Salinas. From the balcony you can observe the market from afar and choose from a wide-ranging menu. The brownies are a speciality. $4–6.

Café Arte y Tarot García Moreno, at Bolívar. A quirky, creative atmosphere and a range of tasty crêpes ($3–5). The most popular spot is the toilet seat at the upstairs table.

★ **Deli** Quiroga, at Bolívar. Little gem of a café a block from the market specializing in Tex-Mex and Italian (main dishes $4–8). Also crêpes, desserts and delicious hot chocolate with marshmallows. Sun–Thurs 9.30am–9pm, Fri–Sat 9.30am–11pm.

Inty Huasi Plaza de Ponchos, at Salinas. Locals head to this well laid-out, large restaurant to fill up on meat and seafood dishes priced around $5–7.

Mi Otavalito Sucre, at Morales. The best place in town to enjoy well-presented Ecuadorian dishes ($5–7) in an elegant but cosy setting. Live Andean music at weekends.

Pizza Siciliana Morales, at Sucre. Out of all the pizza places in town, this has the best reputation with a rustic atmosphere and roaring fire. Pizzas $5–10.

Quino Roca, at García Moreno. If you're craving seafood, try the *ceviche* and fresh mountain trout here. Juices, cocktails and mulled wines are also good. Mains $5–8.

DRINKING AND NIGHTLIFE

Peña Jala Jala 31 de Octubre. Head north of the centre to catch live music and dance the night away to a mix of local and international tunes. Fri–Sat 7pm–2am.

Peña La Jampa 31 de Octubre. Three blocks north of the market, this is another great place to catch energetic live performances from traditional Andean bands. Fri–Sat 7pm–2am.

The Red Pub Morales, at Jaramillo. English-style pub with plenty of beer, rock music and live bands at weekends. Daily 4pm–late.

IBARRA

Thirty minutes by bus northeast of Otavalo lies **IBARRA**, the largest town in the northern highlands, known as La Ciudad Blanca (white city). Ibarra is the biggest commercial town in the region and of less interest to tourists, but it does have some beautiful squares and a fantastic ice-cream store.

WHAT TO SEE AND DO

Parque La Merced is impressive, fronted by the nineteenth-century Basílica La Merced, but eclipsed in terms of beauty by **Parque Pedro Moncayo**, dominated by the Baroque-influenced **cathedral** adorned with a golden altar. The **Museo Banco Central** on Sucre and Oviedo (Mon–Fri 8.30am–1.30pm & 2.30–4.30pm; $0.50) has an exhibition of archeology from prehistory to Inca times. A **train service** that used to run all the way to San Lorenzo on the north coast is under reconstruction.

It currently runs 45km from Ibarra's train station (❶06 295 0390) to Salinas at 7.30am Friday to Sunday. A return costs $6.50. Another popular excursion is to **Laguna Yahuarcocha**, which means Lake of Blood due to its violent history (tens of thousands of dead Cara soldiers were dumped into the lake after an Incan victory in 1495). You can rent boats or just walk around the beautiful setting. Buses run regularly at weekends from the obelisk on Sanchez and Cifuentes.

ARRIVAL AND INFORMATION

By bus Aerotaxi and Expreso Turismo have regular services to and from Quito's Carcelén terminal (hourly; 2hr 30min) and Atacames (daily; 9hr); Trans Otavalo goes to and from Otavalo (hourly; 35min); Expreso Turismo and Flota Imbabura head to and from Tulcán for the Colombian border (hourly; 2hr 30min). Services depart from the terminal 1km out of town, so to/from the centre take a bus ($0.25) or a taxi ($1).
Internet Zonanet, Moncayo 5–74 ($1/hr).
Tourist information García Moreno on Parque La Merced (Mon–Fri 8.30am–1pm & 2–5pm; ❶06 295 5711) supplies free maps and general information.

ACCOMMODATION

Most tourists stay at hotels in the historic centre of town, which are more pleasant than the cheap hotels near the train station southwest of the centre, an area that feels unsafe at night.
Hostal El Retorno Pedro Moncayo, at Sucre ❶06 295 7722. A very good deal for the price: decent rooms with TV and private bath. $̄16
Hotel Imbabura Oviedo 9–33, at Chica Narváez ❶06 295 0155. A friendly, comfortable budget choice with laundry service, internet and basic, clean rooms set around a pleasant courtyard. $̄10
Hotel Madrid Pedro Moncayo 7–41, at Olmedo ❶06 295 6177. This quiet hotel feels slightly more upmarket with slickly decorated, well-appointed rooms. $̄16
Hotel Montecarlo Rivadeneira 5–61, at Oviedo ❶06 295 8266. One of the few upmarket hotels in the centre of Ibarra. Well-appointed rooms with cable TV, a small pool and spa at weekends. $̄44
★ **Hotel Nueva Estancia** Garcia Moreno 7–58, at Parque La Merced ❶06 295 1444. Treat yourself at this ideally located hotel across from Basílica La Merced. It has spacious, carpeted rooms, cable TV, laundry service and a good restaurant. Breakfast included. $̄31

EATING AND DRINKING

There are plenty of cheap restaurants serving filling almuerzos and meriendas for $2.

Antojitos de mi Tierra Plaza de la Ibarreñidad. Traditional Ecuadorian dishes and tasty snacks such as humitas and quimbolitos ($1–3).
Cafe Arte Salinas 5–43, at Oviedo. A wide variety of international food – from burgers to tacos to filet mignon – in a vibrant setting, with live music at weekends. Mains $3–6. Mon–Sat 5pm till late.
Casa Blanca Bolívar, at Moncayo. A dependable choice for breakfast and a great-value lunch ($3), popular with locals.
D'Gloria Oviedo, at Sucre. A good place for breakfast and snacks. Choose from crêpes, fruit pies and salads for $3–6.
Donde El Argentino Plaza de la Ibarreñidad. A tiny place that specializes in barbecued meats, ideal for eating alfresco on sunny days. Mains $5–9.
★ **Heladería Rosalía Suárez** Oviedo, at Olmedo. Ibarra is famous for its sorbet and this is the best place to try it. Ice creams $0.50–3.
El Horno Rocafuerte, at Flores. Great pizza (from $5) cooked in a clay oven.

TULCÁN

The border between Ecuador and Colombia is a problematic region and the only recommended place to cross is via **TULCÁN**. Don't wander out of town, and take care at night. There's little reason to stay here long, and, with Otavalo and Ibarra only three hours south by bus, staying in Tulcán overnight is unnecessary. One sight worth a visit is the incredible cemetery near Parque Ayora, whose

> ### CROSSING INTO COLOMBIA
> Seven kilometres east of Tulcán, the **Rumichaca Bridge** marks the busy **Colombian border**, open daily 6am–10pm. To cross the border, obtain an **exit stamp** from Ecuadorian customs, in the Migración building, and an **entry stamp** from the Colombians on the other side of the bridge. The entry stamp for Colombia is valid for 90 days (arriving from Colombia, the Ecuadorians will also give you up to 90 days and a tourist card, which you retain until you leave the country). **Buses to the border** leave from Parque Isidro Ayora (15min; $0.80), while a taxi costs about $4. From the border, **Ipiales** is the nearest town with decent hotels. It is 3km away and you can take a taxi shuttle ($1), bus ($0.50) or taxi (around $2). Official **moneychangers** abound on the border, but check the calculations before handing money over.

topiary gardens feature trimmed bushes and hedges sculpted into pre-Columbian figures, animals and geometric shapes.

ARRIVAL AND INFORMATION

By bus There are regular buses to and from Ibarra (2hr 30min) and Quito (5hr). The bus terminal on Bolívar is 1.5km from the centre so take a taxi (about $1).

Embassies The Colombian Consulate is on Bolívar, at Junín (☎ 06 298 0559; Mon–Fri 8am–1pm & 2–3pm).

Money exchange To exchange dollars, you should get a slightly better rate in Tulcán than at the border so try the official moneychangers on Plaza de la Independencia, where there are also ATMs.

Tourist information The Cámara de Turismo office (☎ 06 298 6606; Mon–Fri 9am–12.30pm and 2.30–6pm) is on Bolívar & Ayacucho.

ACCOMMODATION

Internacional Torres de Oro Sucre, at Rocafuerte ☎ 06 298 0296. The best budget option. Clean rooms with private bath and TV, and a restaurant attached. $24

EATING

There are several decent restaurants close to the main plaza.

Mama Rosita Sucre, at Chimborazo. Filling but simple Ecuadorian staples for $3.

El Patio Bolívar, near 10 de Agosto. Large portions of Colombian specialities such as *bandeja paisa* (pork, sausage, egg, fried bananas, avocado, beans and rice). $3–5.

The Central Highlands

South of Quito lies Ecuador's most dramatic Andean scenery, where the Panamericana winds between two parallel mountain chains. Eight of Ecuador's ten highest peaks are here so it's unsurprising that nineteenth-century German explorer Alexander von Humboldt named the region "the Avenue of the Volcanoes". On the eastern side, the most popular peak to visit (and climb if you're fit enough) is **Cotopaxi** (5897m), which dominates the surrounding valley. To the southwest lies the turquoise luminescence of **Lake Quilotoa**, one of Ecuador's most stunning natural sights. The region's principal towns are **Latacunga**, **Ambato** and **Riobamba**, all of which sit at an altitude

of 2800m and provide convenient bases. The spa town of **Baños**, with its ideal climate, beautiful setting, thermal baths and adventure sports, is a highlight. Nearby **Volcán Tungurahua** has been erupting regularly for the past decade and is an attraction in itself. South of Riobamba, the relaunched **Nariz del Diablo train ride** remains popular. By late 2013 it may be possible to travel by train all the way from Quito to Riobamba.

PARQUE NACIONAL COTOPAXI

About 60km south of Quito, **Volcán Cotopaxi** (5897m) is everybody's idea of a picture-perfect volcano, its symmetrical cone-shaped peak dominating the region. But Cotopaxi's beauty belies its destructive heritage – it has erupted on ten occasions since 1742, destroying Latacunga several times. Luckily for local inhabitants, it has been quiet since 1904, although it's still officially active, with plumes of smoke visible to climbers reaching the crater. As well as being Ecuador's most photogenic volcano, **Parque Nacional Cotopaxi** (8am–5pm; $10) is also Ecuador's most-visited park. The volcano offers a spectacular climb (see box opposite), but for a more relaxed experience, the surrounding *páramo* (Andean grasslands) offers great opportunities for trekking and cycling. Inhabitants of the park include deer, rabbits, foxes, pumas and ninety species of birds, among them the elusive Andean condor.

INFORMATION AND TOURS

Most people take a guided tour from Quito, Latacunga, Riobamba or even Baños. A one-day hiking and cycling tour costs $50, taking in the museum, Limpiopungo Lake and the mountain refuge. A two-day climbing tour costs from $170 and the better three-day tour about $200–250. A good tour operator in Latacunga is **Volcán Route** (2 de Mayo, at Guayaquil ☎ 03 281 2452, ✉ volcanroute @hotmail.com). In Quito, try **Gulliver** (JL Mera, at Calama ☎ 02 252 9297, ⊛ gulliver.com.ec). All of the accommodation options listed below can arrange tours.

ACCOMMODATION

Cuello de Luna El Chasqui, Panamerican Highway South Km44 ☎ 099 970 0300, ⊛ cuellodeluna.com. The "neck of the moon" is just 6km from the park entrance and offers

6

CLIMBING COTOPAXI

Climbing Cotopaxi can be done with little technical mountaineering experience. However, it's not a challenge to be taken lightly. You must be in good physical shape, acclimatized and travel with a qualified guide, preferably certified by ASEGUIM (Asociación Ecuatoriana de Guías de Montaña) and arranged through a tour operator (see p.592).

The importance of acclimatization cannot be stressed enough. If you're pushed for time and feeling bold, it's tempting to get up in the morning and think "let's climb a volcano today". Unscrupulous guides won't hesitate in taking your money and going to the high-altitude refuge. But above 3000 metres you need to ascend slowly over a few days. A couple of days in Quito (2800m) is not enough to immediately tackle Cotopaxi (5897m). Lake Quilotoa (3800m) is good preparation and a three-day, rather than two-day, climbing tour of Cotopaxi is recommended.

The best preparation is to climb lower peaks first. The most popular option is Rumiñahui (4712m), mainly a steep hike. You can also try Corazon (4788m) or the more challenging Illiniza Norte (5126m).

When climbing Cotopaxi itself, beginning from the José Rivas refuge at 4800m, it's six to eight strenuous hours to the top, negotiating snow, ice and several crevices. The views of Ecuador's other major peaks are breathtaking, as is the view down into the steaming crater. The descent takes three to four hours. December to April is usually the best time to climb Cotopaxi, when the snow is hardest, but it can be climbed year-round.

simple dorms or private rooms with fireplaces. Dorms $18, doubles $50

Hostería La Ciénega ☎03 271 9052, ⊕hosteria lacienega.com. A 400-year-old hacienda, 2km from Lasso, with period furnishings and a good restaurant. Breakfast included. $88

Secret Garden Cotopaxi ☎099 357 2714, ⊕secret gardencotopaxi.com. An ecolodge set in the foothills of Pasochoa, near the village of Pedregal, overlooking the national park. The price includes three meals, snacks, drinks and use of mountain bikes. Many rooms have their own fireplace to keep warm. Meals included. Dorms $38, doubles $65

SAQUISILÍ

SAQUISILÍ is gaining popularity for its Thursday market, a lesser-known and more authentic indigenous market than Otavalo. On market day, eight plazas in the centre flood with tradespeople selling foodstuffs, herbal remedies, household goods and live animals. It's also a social gathering for the locals, many of whom arrive in their best traditional dress and felt hats. For tourists, the main attraction is the shopping. There are also plenty of tasty *tortillas de maíz* to snack on.

Saquisilí is a few kilometres off the Panamericana, two hours south of Quito. Ask the bus driver to drop you at the junction and take another bus – or catch a regular bus from Latacunga (30min).

LATACUNGA

Some 30km south of Cotopaxi National Park, **LATACUNGA** doesn't look inviting from the highway, but venture towards the centre of town with quaint cobbled streets and friendly people. There's not a huge amount to do, but the town serves as the best base to explore **Quilotoa** and **Cotopaxi**, with good local tour operators (see p.592) and decent accommodation.

WHAT TO SEE AND DO

The town has been rebuilt in colonial style after being destroyed several times by Cotopaxi's eruptions. The main square – **Parque Vicente León** – forms the town's focal point, flanked by the cathedral and town hall. A few blocks to the west, next to the river Cutuchi, is **Museo de la Casa de la Cultura** (Vela, at Salcedo; Tues–Fri 8am–noon & 2–6pm; $0.50), which has a small ethnography and art museum. In late September and again in early November (usually the Saturday before November 11) Latacunga parties hard for **La Fiesta de la Mama Negra**, which features a parade of colourful costumed characters and culminates in the arrival of the Mama Negra, a man dressed up as a black woman in honour of the liberation of African slaves in the nineteenth century. The November celebration is secular and more raucous.

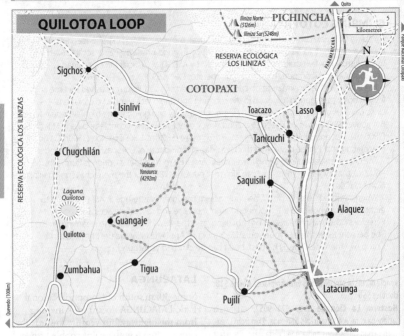

QUILOTOA LOOP

ARRIVAL AND INFORMATION

By bus Latacunga's bus station is on the Panamericana, five blocks west of town. If Latacunga is not the final destination of your bus, you'll be dropped off 400m further west (take a taxi to the centre for $1, or walk over the bridge). There are hourly services from the bus station to Quito's Quitumbe terminal (1hr 30min) and Ambato (1hr). For the surrounding indigenous villages there are buses to Saquisilí (hourly; 20min). To get to Quilotoa, there is only one direct bus per day (around noon). If you miss it, take a bus to Zumbahua and take a taxi from there.

By train The Quito–Latacunga train service (4hr; $15 return, $10 one-way; ⓦ ferrocarrilesdelecuador.gob.ec) passes through Machachi and Boliche. Services are more frequent Fri–Sun and often don't run the rest of the week. The route is popular so book in advance at the train station.

Tourist information Captur (Orellana, at Guayaquil ☎ 03 281 4968).

ACCOMMODATION

Hotel Central Orellana, at Salcedo ☎ 03 280 2912. Along with *Hotel Cotopaxi* next door, this is the best-located budget option in Latacunga. Rooms have private bathroom, cable TV and some have a great view of the main square. **$20**

Rodelu ☎ 03 280 0956, ⓦ rodelu.com.ec. This upmarket hotel has wood panelling, indigenous motifs, free internet and an excellent restaurant. **$44**

Rosim Quito 16–49 ☎ 03 280 2172, ⓦ hotelrosim.com. A quieter option than the *hostals* on the main square, with well-equipped rooms and high ceilings. Good value. **$26**

Hostal Tiana Vivero, at Ordoñez ☎ 03 281 0147, ⓦ hostal tiana.com. This friendly backpacker favourite has a range of colourful new rooms and its own tour operator. Breakfast included. Dorms **$9.50**, doubles **$22**

EATING

Chifa Miraflores Salcedo, at 2 de Mayo. The best Chinese restaurant with a wide range of soup, rice, noodles and sweet and sour for $3–5.

El Copihue Rojo Quito 14–38. Charming restaurant tucked away behind the cathedral, specializing in grilled meats for $6–8.

La Mama Negra Ordoñez, at Rumiñahui. The best place to try the local speciality *chugchucara* (fried pork with fried potatoes, plantains and corn). $6–7.

Pizzeria Bon Giorno Orellana, at Maldonado. A friendly place in which to escape the highland staples, with great lasagne and large pizzas ($5) to share.

LAKE QUILOTOA AND THE QUILOTOA LOOP

The luminous turquoise water of volcanic crater lake **Laguna Quilotoa** is one of Ecuador's most awe-inspiring sights. The lake was formed 800 years ago by a massive eruption and subsequent collapse of the volcano. The caldera is 3.2km wide and the lake 250m deep. You can visit from Latacunga on a day-trip but it's better to at least stay overnight or spend a couple of days hiking parts of the **Quilotoa Loop**.

WHAT TO SEE AND DO

The first town after leaving Latacunga is **Tigua** (3500m), famous for indigenous arts and handicrafts. Another 30km further is **Zumbahua**, a small village that gets boisterous at the weekend with its busy Saturday market and accompanying merriment. A further 14km north is the sleepy village of **Quilotoa** (3800m), perched above the lake. A great base for exploring, it costs $1 to enter the village, including unlimited access to the lake. You can hike down into the crater to the waterside in forty minutes (it's an hour to come back up). The water's high sulphurous content makes it unsuitable for swimming but there are canoes for rent. For a longer walk to appreciate the lake from all angles, allow four hours to walk around the perimeter. The most popular hike on the Quilotoa Loop is the dramatic route from Quilotoa to Chugchilán. It takes about five hours but don't attempt it alone and do not set off after 1pm.

GETTING AROUND

The biggest problem in this region is getting around because public transportation is infrequent and often full. During the rainy season, bus routes are sometimes cancelled and roads impassable. It is strongly advised that you don't attempt parts of the loop alone because of the remoteness of the region.

By bus The Latacunga–Zumbuhua–Quilotoa–Chugchilán bus leaves Latacunga daily at noon. It is 2hr to Quilotoa and a further 1hr 30min to Chugchilán. If you miss the bus from Latacunga, get the first bus to Zumbahua, and hire a taxi to Quilotoa (about $5/person). Coming back, the Chugchilán–Quilotoa–Zumbuhua–Latacunga bus leaves Chugchilán at 4am. There are buses later in the morning on Sundays only, otherwise take a taxi to Zumbuhua ($35 from Chugchilán, $10 from Quilotoa), where there are more frequent buses back to Latacunga (hourly; 2hr).

ACCOMMODATION

Quilotoa has a few accommodation options run by friendly indigenous people. All *hostals* provide two meals.

Hostal Cabanas Quilotoa ☏ 099 212 5962. The best budget option in Quilotoa is owned by local artist Humberto Latacunga. It has comfortable rooms, hot showers and wood burners (it gets very cold at night). $16

Hostal Cloudforest ☏ 03 281 4808. A backpacker favourite in Chugchilán, with simple rooms and a common room with fireplace to warm up. $24

Mama Hilda ☏ 03 281 4814, ⓦ mamahilda.com. Another good-value option in Chugchilán, with cosy rooms. $34

Princesa Toa Another simple, budget option in the village of Quilotoa, with warm, comfortable rooms just across from the best lake-viewing area. $16

★ **Quilotoa Crater Lake Lodge** ☏ 02 252 7835, ⓦ quilotoalodge.com.ec. The only mid-range accommodation option in Quilotoa is perched above the lake, with spectacular panoramic views. Comfortable rooms, a warm common room area with large fireplace and an international restaurant makes this a well-earned treat after a hard day's hiking. Includes breakfast. $40

BACK ON TRACK

Ecuador's **rail network** took nearly forty years of toil before completion in 1908, when President Eloy Alfaro rode triumphantly from Guayaquil to Quito. But as the twentieth century rolled on, Ecuador's train service rolled backwards; by the 1990s one of the few lines still running was the short section along the famous Nariz del Diablo (Devil's Nose) south of Riobamba (see p.598).

All this has changed recently. Current President Rafael Correa, for whom Eloy Alfaro is a hero, announced ambitious government plans to revitalize the entire rail network and relaunch the journey from Durán (near Guayaquil) to Quito, and from Quito to San Lorenzo on the north coast. Work began in 2008 and is expected to finish in 2014, when the two-day journey from Guayaquil to Quito will be launched.

At the time of writing the following services are running. Prices are for the return fare and durations for the outbound journey only. For further information visit ⓦ ferrocarrilesdelecuador .gob.ec.

Quito–Latacunga (via Machachi and Boliche): 4hr; $15
Alausi–Sibambe (La Nariz del Diablo): 2hr 30min; $25
Durán–Yaguachi: 1hr; $10
Ibarra–Salinas: 1hr 30min; $10

6

TOURS TO QUILOTOA

If you're travelling alone or want to see Quilotoa without the inconvenience of relying on public transport, take a **guided tour** from Latacunga. A one-day tour to the lake costs $40, or three days to do the entire loop costs $130.

TOUR OPERATORS
Tierra Zero Padre Salcedo, at Quito ☎ 03 280 4327.
Tova Expeditions Guayaquil 5–38, at Quito ☎ 03 281 1333.

Volcan Route 2 de Mayo, at Guayaquil ☎ 03 281 2452, ✉ volcanroute@hotmail.com.
All these operators also offer hiking and climbing tours to Cotopaxi.

AMBATO

Some 47km south of Latacunga, most tourists pass through **AMBATO** en route to Baños or Riobamba. There's little to hold your interest for more than a few hours and the downtown area suffers from traffic problems, which can ruin the experience of wandering around what is, in parts, a beautiful city.

WHAT TO SEE AND DO

Of most interest in the **Parque Juan Montalvo** is the **Casa de Montalvo** (Mon–Fri 9am–noon & 2–6pm, Sat 10am–1pm; $1), the former residence of Ambato's most famous literary son. A liberal, he was forced into exile by conservative president Gabriel García Moreno in 1869. The house has a collection of photos, manuscripts, clothing and a life-size portrait. Unnervingly, Juan Montalvo's body is on display in the mausoleum. His face is covered by a death mask but his decayed fingers are visible. On the other side of the park is the city's huge but rather ugly modern **cathedral**, rebuilt after the devastating 1949 earthquake. The interior is more impressive, with huge bronze statues and fabulous acoustics during Mass. Escape the city's bustle by visiting the riverside gardens of **La Quinta de Juan León Mera** (Av Los Capulíes; Wed–Sun 9.30am–5.30pm; $1), just 2km from the centre (30min walk or $1 taxi ride).

ARRIVAL AND INFORMATION

By bus Ambato's bus station is 2km north of the centre and an important hub. There are regular services to and from Quito, Guayaquil, Latacunga, Riobamba, Puyo, Cuenca and Loja. To get to the centre of town costs $1.50 by taxi or you can catch a local bus. Note that buses to

Baños don't leave from the bus station. Take a taxi ($1.50) to Mercado Mayorista where buses to Baños pass several times per hour (45min; $0.80).
Tourist information The tourist office on Guayaquil, at Rocafuerte (☎ 03 282 1800), is open Mon–Fri 8am–5pm and has maps and brochures.

ACCOMMODATION

Accommodation in Ambato tends to cater for the business community, so mid-range hotels are more expensive, while cheaper options tend to be seedy. You're better off heading to Baños or Riobamba.
Hotel Ambato Guayaquil, at Rocafuerte ☎ 03 242 1793, ⊚ hotelambato.com. The best in town with spectacular views of the river and a gourmet restaurant. Breakfast included. $68
Pirámide Inn Av Cevallos, at Mariano Egüez ☎ 03 242 1920. Well-appointed rooms with hot water, private bathroom and cable TV. Breakfast included. $30

EATING AND DRINKING

Café Marcelos Castillo, at Rocafuerte ☎ 03 282 8208. Renowned locally as one of the best places to eat in town. Choose from a wide range of meats, snacks and delicious ice cream. $6–10.
Café la Catedral Bolívar. This friendly little café, in a small mall opposite the cathedral entrance, is ideal for good-value lunches ($2.50–4).
La Fornace Av Cevallos 17–28. Delicious pizza baked in a massive brick oven as well as great pasta dishes ($3–6).
Parrilladas El Gaucho Bolívar, at Quito. The best spot to pig out on huge portions of steak and barbecued meats ($7–10).

SALASACA

On the road between Ambato and Baños, it's worth stopping at **SALASACA**, famous for its tapestries. The indigenous people who live here look noticeably different, dressed in black ponchos and white hats. They originate from Bolivia, driven here by the Incas in the fifteenth century. There is a craft market every Sunday; on other days, it's best to browse the tapestry stores. About 6km from Salasaca is **Pelileo**, with surely more cut-price jeans per square metre than anywhere in South America. To visit Pelileo and Salasaca, hop off the bus from Ambato to Baños. There are several buses per hour.

BAÑOS, TUNGURAHUA

Even if you're only in Ecuador for a short time, **BAÑOS** is one place you shouldn't miss. With an ideally warm climate, a stunning location in a verdant valley surrounded by steep hills, an excellent choice of hotels and restaurants, great walking and adventure sports, plus of course, the thermal baths that give the town its name, Baños is mainland Ecuador's most

idyllic destination. There are four sets of public baths around town and many of the better hotels have their own, although they don't draw on volcanic spring water. Be aware that Baños is only 8km from the active **Volcán Tungurahua** (see p.596), which has been erupting regularly for the past decade. Luckily, the crater is on the opposite side to the town and Baños has been relatively unaffected.

WHAT TO SEE AND DO

In town, don't miss the **Basílica de Nuestra Señora de Agua Santa** on the main Ambato street. This massive church is dedicated to the Virgin Mary, credited with several miracles including saving the town from Tungurahua's eruption in 1773. The building is spectacular when lit up at night, dominating the town's skyline. Inside the church are ten huge

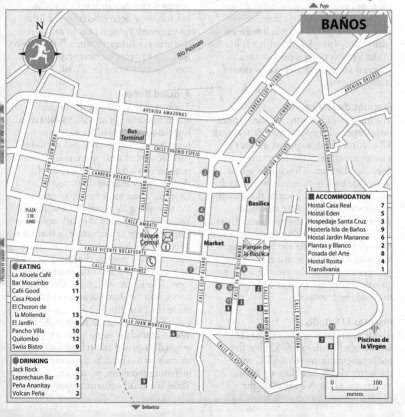

6

THE ROAD FROM BAÑOS TO PUYO

One of Ecuador's most beautiful routes, the road from Baños to Puyo, drops nearly 1000m following the Río Pastaza down from lush Andean foothills, through cloudforest to the edges of the tropical jungle. It's best admired from the saddle of a bike, which can be hired from any agency in Baños for $8/day, including helmet, map and repair kit. A guided tour costs $40. Leaving Baños you cross the Agoyan hydroelectric project and it's about forty minutes until the impressive **Manto de La Novia** (Bride's Veil) waterfall. You can take the cable car ($2) 500m across the river gorge for a closer look. The second waterfall in the same location was caused by a landslide here in 2010. A 25-minute ride then brings you to the village of Río Verde, where you can lock your bike and hike 15 minutes downhill to see the even more spectacular **Pailón del Diablo** (Devil's Cauldron) waterfall. View it from a rickety suspension bridge or pay $1.50 to get a closer look from the panoramic balcony. There is also a path cut into the rock so you can go inside the cave behind the waterfall. Cycling half an hour uphill from Río Verde, you reach **Machay**. From here, hike a 2.5km trail into the cloudforest past eight waterfalls, the most beautiful of which is Manantial del Dorado. Finally, from Machay, it's downhill to **Río Negro** where the surroundings begin to feel tropical with bromeliads, giant tree ferns and colourful orchids. Start early if you want to cover the entire 61km but bear in mind the route is far more scenic than the end destination of **Puyo**, an unimpressive jungle town. Most people hop on a bus back to Baños from Río Verde or Río Negro. Note that in February 2010 two locals were killed by a landslide in Río Verde, so exercise caution visiting during the rainy season.

paintings depicting the Virgin saving the town and its citizens from various calamities. Upstairs is a small **museum** (daily 8am–4pm; $0.50) with a collection of the Virgin's processional clothes, religious art and a bizarre collection of stuffed animals.

Piscinas de la Virgen

The most popular baths are the **Piscinas de la Virgen** (daily 5am–4pm & 6–10pm; $2 daytime, $3 at night) at the foot of a small waterfall to the eastern end of Avenida Martínez. The cloudy yellow waters are high in minerals and make for a very relaxing soak. Next to the changing rooms you can see where the boiling waters emerge from the rock face. There are three pools – freezing cold, warm and hot (45°C: just a little too hot to linger for more than a few minutes). The baths get very busy at weekends so it's best to go either early morning or early evening to avoid the crowds.

Piscinas El Salado

About 2km out of town, **Piscinas El Salado** (daily 5am–5pm; $3) has five pools ranging from 16 to 42°C with the water visibly bubbling up from underground. In August 2008 the

complex was damaged by a landslide but has since been rebuilt by the local government, though bear in mind that this area is vulnerable when there is heavy rain. It's a twenty-minute walk from town, or take a taxi for $1.50.

Around Baños

The best way to take in the town's stunning setting is to walk to **Bellavista**, high above the town. It's a steep forty-minute climb up a rocky, muddy path, rewarded with spectacular panoramic views over Baños and the Pastaza valley leading down to the Oriente. There are a couple of cafés at the top selling light lunches and drinks. You can continue on the path uphill for a further hour to the village of **Runtun** at 2600m, then loop around to the other side of Baños, passing the statue of La Virgen del Agua Santa and back to town. The entire walk takes about four hours. You can **hire horses** to see this route ($12 for 2hr, $22 for 4hr, including guide). On the edge of town is the **San Martin Zoo** (daily 8am–5pm; $1.50), originally opened as a refuge for sick animals. It has birds and mammals including monkeys, pumas and a jaguar. There is a small aquarium opposite.

ARRIVAL AND INFORMATION

By bus Baños's bus terminal is a few blocks north of the main square surrounded by stalls selling *jugo de caña* (sugar cane juice). Baños is so compact that you can walk everywhere, and a taxi across town costs just $1.

Destinations There are services to Puyo (hourly; 2hr), Riobamba (hourly; 2hr 30min) and Ambato (hourly; 1hr). For most other destinations, including Quito (several daily; 4hr) and Guayaquil (several daily; 6–7hr), there are hourly services by changing at Ambato. The direct road to Riobamba is often closed due to Tungurahua's eruptions.

Tourist information Purchase guidebooks and pick up free maps at the municipal tourist office on Haflants near Rocafuerte (Mon–Fri 8am–12.30pm & 2–5.30pm; ☎03 274 0483, ⟐banos-ecuador.com) on the east side of Parque Central.

ACCOMMODATION

Hostal Casa Real Montalvo, at Pasaje Ibarra ☎03 274 0215, ⟐banios.com/casareal. This is a good-value mid-range option close to the waterfall. Rooms are simple but brightened up by murals of wildlife. Breakfast included. **$26**

Hostal Eden 12 de Noviembre ☎03 274 0616. This hostel has comfortable rooms with cable TV set on a small garden courtyard. There's a cheap restaurant next door. **$20**

Hospedaje Santa Cruz 16 de Diciembre ☎03 274 0648. A funky little place with simple but colourfully decorated rooms. **$19**

Hostería Isla de Baños Halflants, at Montalvo ☎03 274 0609, ⟐isladebanios.com. An excellent-value mid-range option with comfortable rooms, balconies, a leafy garden and spa ($10/person). **$42**

Hostal Jardin Marianne Montalvo, at Halflants ☎03 274 1947. Brand new rooms with balconies in a quiet, leafy courtyard setting are the best-value mid-range deal in town. **$30**

★ **Plantas y Blanco** Martínez, at 12 de Diciembre ☎03 274 0044. This backpacker favourite is the ideal place to swap stories with kindred spirits. Relax on the rooftop terrace, make your own meals in the kitchen, and soak in the Turkish baths. There's also free internet. Rooms are small but adequate. Dorms **$6.50**, doubles **$19**

Posada del Arte Pasaje Ibarra ☎03 274 0083, ⟐posadadelarte.com. As its name suggests, this homely place offers a feast of South American art. The invitingly colourful rooms all have fireplaces with chimneys. The restaurant is very good and worth a visit even if you don't stay. **$56**

Hostal Rosita 16 de Diciembre, at Martínez ☎03 274 0396. One of the best-value budget options in town, with free internet. There are two larger apartments for longer stays. **$14**

ACTIVITIES AND TOURS

Adventure sports are popular in the Pastaza valley between Baños and Puyo. **Rafting** is particularly good. A half-day on the class 3 part of the Rio Pastaza costs $30 including transport, equipment, licensed guide and lunch. A half-day on the faster class 4 part of the river costs $45. Other adrenaline-filled activities include **Bridge Jumping** (rather like bungee except you swing like a pendulum) off the 100m Puente San Francisco for $20, as well as zipping across the valley on **canopy lines** ($10–15). You can also rent *Cuadrones* (quad bikes) and motorbikes for about $8 per hour ($20 for 3hr). Canyoning trips cost $30, taking in four waterfalls. You can book tours to many jungle destinations including Coca and Lago Agrio, but these generally go through Quito so it's better booking there. For a more accessible jungle experience, there are good trips via Puyo. For more information on jungle trips, see the chapter on the Oriente (see p.609).

TOUR OPERATORS

Cordova Tours Maldonado, at Espejo ☎03 274 0923, ⟐cordovatours.banios.com.

Expediciones Pailontravel 12 de Diciembre, at Montalvo ☎03 274 0899.

Geotours Ambato, at Thomas Halflants ☎03 274 1344, ⟐geotoursbanios.com. In the business for nearly 20 years and highly recommended.

Rainforestur Ambato, at Maldonado ☎098 446 9884, ⟐www.rainforestur.com.ec. Jungle tour specialist.

Sebastian Moya Expediciones Oriente, at Halflants ☎03 248 4287. Jungle tour specialist.

Wonderful Ecuador Maldonado, at Oriente ☎03 274 1580.

MASSAGE

Baños has many skilled professionals and you can get all types of massage treatments here from soothing aromatherapy to reflexology, deep tissue treatments and physiotherapy. Most charge around $20 for an hour's massage and $15 for a facial.

Chakra Alfaro, at Luis Martinez ☎03 274 2027.

Stay in Touch Montalvo ☎03 274 0973.

6

Transilvania 16 de Diciembre, at Oriente ☎ 03 274 2281, ⊛ hostal-transilvania.com. If you can get past the rather bizarre name, you'll find this Israeli-owned *hostal* a great deal, with bright, simple rooms and a café where big breakfasts are served on petrified wooden tables. There's also a pool table and a Middle Eastern menu. It's popular and fills up fast. Breakfast included. **$15**

EATING

Baños has many top-quality restaurants and offers some of the best international cuisine outside Quito. Most of the finest are away from the main street. The town is also great for those with a sweet tooth, famous for dozens of stalls selling *membrillo* (a gelatinous red block made with guayaba) and *milcocha*, chewy sugar-cane bars that you can watch being made, swung over wooden pegs. Outside the market, there's also the memorable sight of *cuy* (guinea pig) being roasted on a spit.

La Abuela Café Ambato, at 16 de Diciembre. Many of the restaurants on the main street are uninspiring but this is one of the best options, with a wide-ranging menu and a balcony to watch the world go by. Mains $6.

Café Good 16 de Diciembre ☎ 03 274 0592. Specializes in vegetarian and Asian food. The Indian curry is good. Mains $3–7.

★ **Casa Hood** Martinez, at Alfaro ☎ 099 462 0269. This is a great place for a meal or a drink, with a vibrant atmosphere and a wide-ranging menu of international food including Mexican, Middle Eastern and Asian dishes, plus smoothies and hot drinks. Mains $4–5. Closed Tues.

El Chozón de la Molienda Montalvo, at Pasaje Ibarra ☎ 03 274 1816, evenings only. Enjoy excellent barbecued dishes such as *lomo volcánico* (steak in ginger sauce) served in a thatched hut set in a large garden. Mains $5–8.

El Jardín 16 de Diciembre. A popular place to eat breakfast or afternoon snacks alfresco in the leafy garden, with a wide selection of dishes and an economical set menu. Mains $6–9.

Pancho Villa Martinez, at 16 de Diciembre ☎ 03 274 2138. Run by a friendly local couple, this is the best Mexican in town with great *enchiladas, fajitas, tacos* and *burritos*. Mains $5–8.

Quilombo Montalvo, at 12 de Noviembre ☎ 03 274 2880. A quirky, humorous place set in a wooden cabin decked out with eclectic decor, from hammocks to horseshoes and even a broken bicycle. The menu comes on cubes in little bags and the barbecued steaks and chicken dishes ($6–8) are cooked to perfection.

★ **Swiss Bistro** Martínez, at Alfaro ☎ 099 400 4019. One of the best places in Ecuador for a sumptuous fondue. The cow skins on the walls and even cow-patterned lampshades place you in the heart of the Swiss Alps. The cheese and meat fondues ($6–8) are fabulous, rounded off by stewed pears in red wine for dessert.

NIGHTLIFE

Nightlife in Baños has improved in recent years. Although it's still rather sleepy during the week, it can get very busy at weekends, particularly on Saturday night. Most of the best places are situated on the stretch of Alfaro north of Ambato.

Jack Rock Ambato. Start the evening off with some rock classics at this bar, which is decked out with music memorabilia.

Leprechaun Bar Ambato. A popular spot with backpackers. It has a dancefloor that gets busy at weekends and a roaring bonfire out back.

Peña Ananitay 16 de Diciembre, at Espejo. The best place in town to catch some traditional folk music.

Volcan Peña Ambato. Stands out on Ambato for offering more of an authentic flavour with mainly Latin music. It's popular with locals.

VOLCÁN TUNGURAHUA

Tungurahua, which means "throat of fire", has a troubled relationship with Baños. The volcano supplies the **hot springs** that make the town famous, but eruptions have caused regular alerts in recent years. The volcano awoke from years of dormancy in October 1999 with a spectacular eruption that covered Baños in ash. However, because the crater is on the opposite side, the town escaped further damage. There have been subsequent eruptions in August 2006 and at regular intervals in 2008, 2009 and in May 2010, when a 10km-high ash cloud reached as far as Guayaquil, over 200km away. The volcano remains highly active at the time of writing.

Bañenos have been living in Tungurahua's shadow for centuries, but it's important to check on the current state of activity before visiting the town. Check the national press, Instituto Geofísico's Spanish website (⊛ igepn.edu.ec) or the Smithsonian Institution's English site (⊛ volcano.si.edu). When Tungurahua is erupting, it becomes a star attraction. The best views of the volcano are from the town of Runtun above Bellavista (see p.594). Most agencies in town charge $5 for a night tour but good views are rare.

RIOBAMBA

The main draw of **RIOBAMBA** is that it's the starting point for the dramatic **Nariz del Diablo** (Devil's Nose) train ride, but this traditional town's nineteenth-century architecture and wide avenues lined with huge palm trees make it a pleasant stopover for a day or so. It's also the best base to climb towering Volcán Chimborazo, Ecuador's highest mountain.

WHAT TO SEE AND DO

The best sightseeing is centred around **Parque Maldonado**. The **Catedral** is the only building in town that survived the 1797 earthquake, and was painstakingly moved and reconstructed when the town was rebuilt in a new location. The **Basilica**, nearby on Parque La Libertad, is the only round church in Ecuador. A couple of blocks further north, inside the Monasterio de las Conceptas, the **Museo de Arte Religioso** has a large collection of religious art (entrance on Argentinos; Tues–Sat 9am–12.30pm & 3–6.30pm; $3). On Saturdays, Riobamba has one of the largest **markets** in the region, spreading out northeast of Parque de la Concepción. On clear days, walk up the hill to **Parque 21 de Abril** for views of Chimborazo.

ARRIVAL AND DEPARTURE

By bus Riobamba's main bus terminal is 2km northwest of the centre. From the Oriente (and from Baños if the road passing Tungurahua is open) you arrive at the Terminal Oriental (Espejo, at Luz Elisa Borja); take a regular bus ($0.25) to the centrally located train station. A taxi into town from the terminal costs $1.

Destinations Ambato (hourly; 1hr); Baños (hourly via Ambato; 2hr); Cuenca (hourly; 6hr); Guayaquil (hourly; 4hr 30min); Quito (hourly; 4hr).

By train See box, p.598.

ACCOMMODATION

Most accommodation is situated close to the train station. The area can be noisy so it's best to stay off the main road or ask for a back room.

★ TREAT YOURSELF

Troje Km4.5 Via Riobamba a Chambo ☎ 03 262 2201, ⓦ eltroje.com. If you have spare cash, go south of town to enjoy the sauna and spacious grounds of this upmarket *hostería*. Breakfast included. **$55**

Imperial 10 de Agosto, at Rocafuerte ☎ 03 296 0429. One of the best deals in town, with colourful decor, spacious rooms, friendly service and surprisingly low prices. **$12**

★ **El Libertador** Av Daniel León Borja 29–22 ☎ 03 294 7393. The best mid-range deal. For more comfort, this colonial-style hotel has spacious, tastefully furnished rooms with cable TV. **$25**

Montecarlo 10 de Agosto 25–41 ☎ 03 296 1557, ⓦ hotel montecarlo-riobamba.com. To treat yourself, try this restored historic house around a pleasant flower-filled courtyard. Breakfast included. **$33**

Ñuca Huasi 10 de Agosto 10–24 ☎ 03 296 6669. For those on a very tight budget, try these basic rooms in a tatty but characterful old building. **$10**

Oasis Veloz, at Almagro ☎ 03 296 1210. South of the Basilica in a quiet area of town, this is an excellent mid-range choice. Tastefully decorated rooms, with a garden, courtyard and kitchen. Book in advance as there are only eight rooms. **$24**

Los Shyris 10 de Agosto, at Rocafuerte ☎ 03 296 0323. An excellent budget deal with private baths, cable TV and hot water. **$18**

6

THE DEVIL'S NOSE TRAIN RIDE

As the name suggests, this train ride is not for the faint-hearted, but it's an exhilarating experience. Riobamba is the starting point and the 100km line stretches from there southwest via Alausí to Sibambe. The journey is relatively laidback at first, with sweeping views of Andean valleys. The final part of the ride is the main event – a hair-raising 800m descent through a series of tight switchbacks carved out of the steep mountainside. Tourists used to ride on the roof to get the full dramatic effect but the authorities have banned this after the deaths of two Japanese people in 2007.

After a long period of renovation, this service resumed in 2012. The train leaves Riobamba Tuesday to Sunday at 6.30am and takes around five hours to get to Sibambe. It returns to Riobamba at 5pm. **Tickets** ($30) can be purchased from Riobamba's train station (☎03 296 1909). The section between Alausí and Sibambe is the most interesting part of the trip so if you want the shortened version, board the train in Alausí (daily 8am, 11am and 3pm; $25; 2hr 30min including lunch). A cheaper Devil's Nose trolleybus service runs Friday to Sunday at 9am ($7) but is extremely popular and fills up fast. Visit ⓦecuadorbytrain.com for further information on all routes.

Tren Dorado Carabobo 22–35, at 10 de Agosto ☎03 296 4890. A popular option for travellers, with compact but perfectly adequate rooms and a friendly atmosphere. A filling buffet breakfast ($3) is available in the café at 5.30am on train days. **$22**

EATING AND DRINKING

El Delirio Primera Constituyente 28–16 ☎03 296 6441. This traditional colonial house is the perfect place for a romantic meal accompanied by live music, set inside a sleepy courtyard with a log fire to ward off the chills. Book in advance. Mains, including filet mignon, $6–9.

★ **Pizzeria d'Baggio** Av Leon Borja 33–24 ☎03 296 1832. Unbeatable for sumptuous pizzas and *calzone* hand-made in front of you. Pizzas $4–8.

El Rey de Burrito Borja 38–36 ☎03 295 3230. The best bet for burritos and enchiladas with plenty of vegetarian options. $3–5.

San Valentín Av Leon Borja, at Torres ☎03 296 3137. For something cheap and cheerful, try the Tex-Mex and varied fast food served in an informal atmosphere. Mains $3–5.

Sierra Nevada Primera Constituyente 27–38 ☎03 295 1542. A good-value eatery offering imaginative seafood and meat dishes. Mains $5–7.

El Tentadero Av León Borja. Nightlife is limited in Riobamba but this club, just up from *San Valentín*, pumps out reggaeton, *merengue* and salsa until late (Thurs–Sat; $2).

VOLCÁN CHIMBORAZO

Just 30km northwest of Riobamba, the extinct **Volcán Chimborazo** looms large. At 6310m, it's Ecuador's highest peak and the furthest point from the centre of the Earth due to the equatorial ridge. The mountain has good roads so is easily visited from Riobamba. On a day-trip you can walk from the lower refuge (4800m) to the second refuge (5000m), but bear in mind that the climb in altitude from Riobamba could leave you suffering. For experienced mountaineers planning to tackle the summit, there are several tour operators in Riobamba charging $220 for a two-day tour. Recommended operators include: Alta Montaña, on Avenida Daniel León Borja at Diego Ibarra (☎03 294 2215); and Andes Trek, on Colón 22–25, at 10 de Agosto (☎03 294 0964, ⓦandes-trek.com).

For non-climbers, enjoy the unworldly moonscapes and sweeping *páramo* that are home to thousands of alpaca, vicuñas and llamas. This enormous park stretches over 580 square kilometres in three provinces. It also contains Carihuairazo (5020m), used as a preparation climb. One-day hiking tours to Chimborazo National Park cost from $50 per person with tour operators in Riobamba. Alternatively, take a bus to Guaranda and ask to be let off near the refuge (8km from the main road) or take a taxi from Riobamba ($35).

ALAUSÍ

This small town is back on the tourist map with the regeneration of the train line. Situated in a verdant valley with steep hills rising up on all sides, Alausí is a very pleasant town to base yourself for the most exhilarating train ride in

Ecuador: the **Devil's Nose train ride** (see box opposite). Although the train runs from Riobamba, it's worth picking it up here to experience the best part of the journey. The town itself is not filled with attractions but the walk up to the huge statue of Saint Peter ten minutes from the centre offers excellent views over the town and valley. For even better views, head up to Hosteria Pircapamba and hire horses to ride around the hills.

ARRIVAL AND DEPARTURE

By bus There are regular bus services (quicker and cheaper than the train) to Alausí from Riobamba (hourly; 2hr) and Cuenca (daily; 4hr); Quito (daily; 5hr); and Guayaquil (daily; 5hr).
By truck or taxi To begin the Inca Trail to the south, occasional trucks head to Achupallas from 5 de Junio, or you can take a taxi.

ACCOMMODATION

Hotel Europa 5 de Junio ☎03 293 0200. Dependable budget option on the main street but fills up fast. Choose from shared or private bath. **$12**
Hostal San Pedro 5 de Junio ☎03 293 0089, ⓦhostal sanpedro.com.ec. The newest hotel in the centre, these comfortable rooms with private bath and cable TV are great value. **$30**

EATING

Alausí has plenty of budget eateries but few stand out. If money is tight choose from various set menus on the main street. The restaurant under *Hostal San Pedro* is probably the best of these.
Chifa Pekin 5 de Junio. A break from the usual Andean fare. Choose from noodles, fried rice and a range of Chinese soups. Mains $3–6.
El Meson del Tren Ricaurte, at Eloy Alfaro ☎03 293 0243. The best restaurant in town offers a wide range of meat and fish specialities. Try the tilapia, pork chops or roast lamb at weekends. Mains $5–7.

★ TREAT YOURSELF

Hosteria Pircabamba Villalva, at Pedro de Loza ☎03 293 0180, ⓦpircapamba .com. The best-located hotel in Alausí is this friendly, family-run place high above the town with breathtaking views of the valley. Horseriding and hiking will keep you busy during the day, and for the evening there are piping-hot showers and a games room. Breakfast included. **$46**

The Southern Highlands

South of Riobamba, the majestic mountains of the Central Highlands fade from view to be replaced by undulating green hills. The tourist hub of the region is **Cuenca**, Ecuador's third-largest city and possibly its most beautiful. Cuenca is also the best base to explore the Incan archeological site **Ingapirca**, and the rugged moors and lakes of **Parque Nacional El Cajas**.

South of Cuenca, distances between towns lengthen and the climate warms up. The historic plazas and award-winning parks of the provincial capital of **Loja** are worth visiting before heading to the relaxing backpacker favourite of **Vilcabamba**, nicknamed the "Valley of Longevity". Recharge your batteries and take advantage of great hiking and horseriding trails in the surrounding hills.

INGAPIRCA

Between Riobamba and Cuenca lies the site of **Ingapirca** (daily 8am–6pm; $6 including guide), Ecuador's only major Inca ruins. Those who've already visited Peru may be disappointed by this modest site; however, the complex boasts the Inca Empire's sole remaining sun temple. The site's strategic position is impressive, at a height of over 3200m with panoramic views over the surrounding countryside.

Ingapirca was built at the end of the fifteenth century by Huayna Capac on top of the ruins of a Cañari city. The stone of the Cañari moon temple, which the Inca preserved from its earlier construction, is still visible. Sadly, much of the site is now little more than stone foundations and it takes imagination and a guided tour to bring it to life.

WHAT TO SEE AND DO

Points of interest include the **calendar stone** and sacrificial site, but the highlight is the well-preserved **Temple of**

6

6

THE INCA TRAIL TO INGAPIRCA

Though by no means as famous or impressive as the trail in Peru, keen hikers can make the most of the countryside between Alausí and Cuenca by hiking this three-day trail. The start of the trail is at **Achupallas**. To get there, take a bus from Riobamba towards Cuenca and get off at La Moya, 10km south of Alausí. From there, it's a steep climb – or you can hitch a ride to Achupallas. Alternatively, a taxi from Alausí direct to Achupallas costs $7. On the first day, head south down the Río Cadrul valley and through a narrow gap between two hills, Cerro Mapahuiña and Cerro Callana Pucará. Continue towards Laguna Tres Cruces and camp nearby. This hike is about six hours in total.

On day two, continue southwest and up along Cuchilla Tres Cruces, which commands great views of the Quebrada Espíndola valley. Descend into the valley to the left of the final peak, Quillo Loma. There are remains of an Inca road and the foundations of an Inca bridge. You'll also find a trail to Laguna Culebrillas and more ruins at **Paredones**.

On day three, head southwest from Paredones on the 7m-wide Inca road. After the village of **San José** turn right to **El Rodeo**, then follow the road to **Ingapirca**. It takes nearly five hours in total. Take plenty of food, water and camping equipment and ensure you are prepared as the entire trail is not well marked. Alternatively, take a guided tour. Several tour operators based In Riobamba and Cuenca (see p.602) operate tours.

---

the Sun, constructed with more than three thousand intricately carved blocks. It's entertaining to stand in the sentry posts of the temple and hear your whispers reverberate through the walls. Just outside the complex is a **museum** (included in the entrance fee), which houses a small collection of objects found at the site.

ARRIVAL

By bus To get to Ingapirca, take a Transportes Cañar bus from Cuenca's bus terminal (9am & 1pm; 2hr). The return service is at 1pm & 4pm (weekends 1pm only). Guided tours from Cuenca cost $45/person. If you're travelling south from Alausí, get off the bus at El Tambo.

ACCOMMODATION

Options to stay overnight are limited and a day-trip is most common.

Hostal Inti Huasi ✆07 229 2940. Very basic rooms in Ingapirca village, 5min from the site. Bring warm clothes, as it gets cold at night. **$12**

★ **TREAT YOURSELF**

Posada Ingapirca ✆07 282 7401, ⍟posadaingapirca.com. A beautiful converted farmhouse overlooking the ruins, adorned with indigenous art and with a decent restaurant offering a range of Ecuadorian and European specialities. Breakfast included. **$73**

CUENCA

CUENCA is Ecuador's third-largest city, with a population of 330,000, but it doesn't feel that way, retaining the atmosphere of a traditional Andean town. The Incas established **Tomebamba** in the late fifteenth century, one of the most important cities in the Inca Empire. It was destroyed shortly afterwards by the civil war between brothers Atahualpa and Huascar, and the Spanish later founded Cuenca in 1557. Little remains of the city's Inca past, although ruins have been excavated behind the **Museo Pumapungo** (see p.602). Note that most museums and restaurants are closed on Sundays, which is the best day to take a trip outside the city to **Cajas**, **Ingapirca** or **Baños**.

WHAT TO SEE AND DO

The cobbled streets, charming squares, colonial architecture and magnificent cathedral make the historic centre a delight to explore; Cuenca was declared a UNESCO World Heritage Site in 1996.

The historic city centre

The focal point of Cuenca's centre is **Parque Calderón**, an elegant square filled with flower beds and palm trees, dominated by the towering eighteenth-century **Catedral Nueva**. The interior is relatively bare except for the stunning

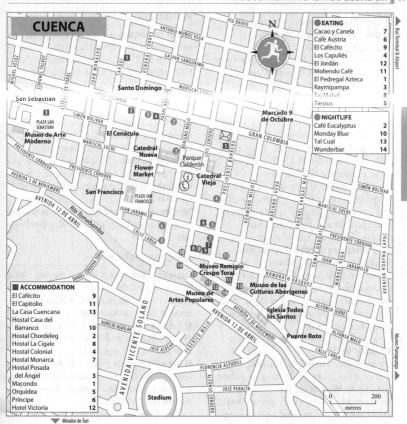

CUENCA

● EATING

Cacao y Canela	7
Café Austria	6
El Cafécito	9
Los Capuliés	4
El Jordán	12
Moliendo Café	11
El Pedregal Azteca	1
Raymipampa	3
Taj Mahal	8
Tiestos	5

● NIGHTLIFE

Café Eucalyptus	2
Monday Blue	10
Tal Cual	13
Wunderbar	14

■ ACCOMMODATION

El Cafécito	9
El Capitolio	11
La Casa Cuencana	13
Hostal Casa del Barranco	10
Hostal Chordeleg	2
Hostal La Cigale	8
Hostal Colonial	4
Hostal Monarca	7
Hostal Posada del Ángel	3
Macondo	1
Orquidea	5
Príncipe	6
Hotel Victoria	12

6

gold-leaf altar and the massive sky-blue domes, best viewed from the side or rear. To the left of the cathedral entrance, along Calle Sucre on the Plazoleta del Carmen, is a flower market. Turn left along Padre Aguirre to the ramshackle clothes market on **Plaza San Francisco** and the peach-and-white **Iglesia San Francisco**. Five blocks west on a quiet square is the seventeenth-century **Iglesia San Sebastián**. Opposite is the **Museo de Arte Moderno** (Mon–Fri 9am–1pm & 3–6.30pm, Sat 9am–1pm; free), which houses temporary exhibitions of Latin American modern art.

Along the Río Tomebamba

From the historic centre, head south to the riverside, where there are several interesting museums along Calle Larga. Beginning at the west end is **Museo del Sombrero** (Mon–Fri 9am–6pm, Sat 9.30am–5pm, Sun 9.30am–1.30pm; free) where you can learn about the process of making Panama hats, which originated in Ecuador. The **Museo Remigio Crespo Toral** (Mon–Fri 8.30am–1pm & 3–6pm, Sat 10am–noon; free) exhibits pre-Columbian ceramics as well as colonial and modern art in a restored nineteenth-century house. A couple of blocks further east, the excellent **Museo de las Culturas Aborígenes** (Mon–Fri 8.30am–6pm, Sat 9am–1pm; $2) has an enormous collection of pre-Hispanic artefacts – second only to Museo Banco Central in Quito – from Stone Age tools to Inca ceramics. Calle Larga has three staircases, the largest of which is **La Escalinata**, down to the riverbank, pleasant for a stroll. East is the **Puente Roto** (Broken Bridge), part of a bridge that once spanned the river.

6

Museo Pumapungo

Museo Pumapungo (C Larga, at Huayna Capac; ☎07 283 1255, ⓦpumapungo.org; Mon–Fri 9am–6pm, Sat 9am–1pm; $3) is easily Cuenca's best museum and worth the twenty-minute walk east of the centre (taxi $1.50). The museum is spread out across three floors and includes a large collection of colonial art, an archeology room and an exhibition of indigenous costumes and masks. The highlight is the **ethnographic** exhibition of Ecuador's indigenous cultures with animated dioramas, re-created dwellings and a stunning display of five *tsantsas* (shrunken heads) from the Shuar culture. Entrance includes access to the **Pumapungo archeological site** behind the museum, where the most important buildings of the Inca city of Tomebamba were located, although mainly only foundations remain. Below the ruins are landscaped gardens and a bird rescue centre.

Mirador de Turi

For great views over Cuenca, take a taxi ($3) or a bus from 12 de Abri, at Solano ($0.25), to **Mirador de Turi**, a lookout point on a hill 4km south of the centre. Views are particularly good on evenings when the churches are lit up.

ARRIVAL AND DEPARTURE

By plane Cuenca's airport (Mariscal Lamar International Airport) is 2km northeast of the centre. There are daily flights to and from Quito and Guayaquil by Tame (Av Florencia Astudillo; ☎07 288 9581, ⓦtame .com.ec), LAN (Bolívar 9–18, at Benigno Malo; ☎07 282 2783, ⓦlan.com) and Aerogal (Av España 1114; ☎07 286 1041, ⓦwww.aerogal.com.ec). Icaro also operates regularly to Quito (Av España 11–14; ☎07 280 2700, ⓦicaro.aero.com). Prices start at about $70 one-way. From the airport buses run on Av España to the northern edge of central Cuenca or it's a 10min walk to the main bus terminal.

By bus The bus terminal is near the airport, northeast of the centre.

Destinations Quito (hourly; 10hr); Guayaquil (hourly; 4hr 30min); Ambato (hourly; 7hr); Riobamba (hourly; 6hr); and Loja (hourly; 5hr).

Taxi Taxis cost about $2 from the airport to Cuenca. Minimum charges around town are $1.25.

INFORMATION

Tourist information Go to the iTur office on the main square (Mariscal Sucre; Mon–Fri 8am–8pm, Sat 8.30am–1.30pm; ☎07 282 0521, ⓦwww.cuenca.gov.ec), which has friendly staff providing maps and regional information.

TOUR OPERATORS

The following offer tours to Ingapirca, Cajas and elsewhere. Trips to Cajas and Ingapirca cost $40–50/person.
Expediciones Apullacta Gran Colombia 11–02, at General Torres ☎07 283 7815, ⓦapullacta.com.
Metropolitan Touring Mariscal Sucre 6–62, at Hermano Miguel ☎07 283 1463, ⓦmetropolitan-touring.com.
Río Arriba Expeditions Hermano Miguel 7–14, at Córdova ☎07 283 011.
Terra Diversa Travel and Adventure Hermano Miguel 5–42, at Honorato Vásquez ☎07 282 3782, ⓦterradiversa .com.

ACCOMMODATION

Cuenca has a wide range of hotels in charming colonial buildings. The best area to stay is south of the centre on the north bank of the river. Consider booking ahead at weekends and on national holidays.
El Cafécito Honorato Vasquez 7–36, at Cordero ☎07 283 2337, ⓦcafecito.net. A friendly café with basic rooms at the back. Dorms $7, doubles $25
El Capitolio Hermano Miguel 4–19 ☎07 282 4446. Opposite *La Casa Cuencana*, this is an equally good budget option offering decent, basic rooms with shared bathroom in a quiet home from home. $16
La Casa Cuencana Hermano Miguel 4–36 ☎07 282 6009. With terracotta walls adorned with artwork, and a friendly family atmosphere, these simple rooms with private bathrooms are excellent value for the price. $16
Hostal Casa del Barranco C Larga 8–41, at Cordero ☎07 283 9763, ⓦcasadelbarranco.com. Many of the hotels on Calle Larga come at a premium, but this historic house displaying paintings by local artists is a great-value mid-range option. Breakfast included. $31
Hostal Chordeleg Gran Colombia, at General Torres ☎07 282 2536. An attractive converted colonial home on a corner in the city centre with decent mid-range rooms set around a pleasant courtyard and garden. Breakfast included. $40
Hostal La Cigale Vasquez, at Cordero ☎07 283 5308. Simple rooms and the popular Café Goloso attached. Dorms $8, doubles $22
Hostal Colonial Gran Colombia 10–13, at Padre Aguirre ☎07 2841 644. Compact mid-range rooms in an eighteenth-century house set around a small courtyard. Breakfast included. $34
Hostal Monarca Borrero 5–47, at Honorato Vasquez ☎07 283 6462. Loud, bright decor but a quiet family

★ **TREAT YOURSELF**

Hotel Victoria C Larga 6–93, at Borrero ⊕ 07 282 7401. Splash out on one of Cuenca's finest hotels and stay in a beautifully restored colonial building overlooking extensive gardens. Most of the spacious, elegantly furnished rooms have views of the river. The sister hotel, *Posada Ingapirca*, is also the best place to stay in Ingapirca (see p.600). **$91**

atmosphere, with great-value budget rooms and shared bathroom. **$14**

Hostal Posada del Ángel Bolívar 14–11, at Estevez de Toral ⊕ 07 284 0695, ⓦ hostalposadadelangel.com. It's difficult to paint a hotel orange and blue and still maintain a charming elegance, but this endearing place pulls it off. Free internet and breakfast served in the spacious, enclosed courtyard. **$57**

★ **Macondo** Tarqui 11–64, at Mariscal Lamar ⊕ 07 284 0697. Another colonial-style favourite with artwork on the walls, a spacious lawn in the back garden and a choice of private or shared bathrooms. Breakfast included. **$31**

Orquidea Borrero 931, at Bolívar ⊕ 07 282 4511. A converted colonial home in the centre of the city, and one of the cheapest mid-range options. **$24**

Príncipe J Jaramillo 7–82, at Cordero ⊕ 07 284 7287. Charming, elegantly furnished rooms in a traditional colonial house with artwork on the walls of the spacious dining area. Breakfast included. **$54**

EATING

The sweetness of the *Cuencanos* temperament extends to their palates. You're never far from a stall or bakery selling cakes and confectionery, including the ubiquitous *membrillo* (a gelatinous red block made with guayaba). Cuenca has the best choice of restaurants outside Quito, offering diverse international and local cuisine. Note that most places are closed on Sundays (unless otherwise indicated).

★ **Cacao y Canela** Jaramillo, at Borrero. Snug little café serving a huge selection of hot chocolate drinks ($2–3) – rum, cinnamon, almonds and mozzarella are just a few of the flavours available. Great cakes and snacks too. Mon–Sat 4pm–late.

Café Austria Benigno Malo 5–95, at Juan Jaramillo. Tasty Central European specialities such as roulade and goulash, plus tasty cakes and ice creams for dessert. Open on Sunday too. Mains $6–8. Daily.

El Cafécito Honorato Vasquez 7–36, at Luis Cordero. A backpacker hangout, this is a good place to meet like-minded travellers over a coffee and a game of chess.

Burgers, pasta and Tex-Mex are great value at around $3. Daily.

Los Capuliés Córdova, at Borrero. Well-priced Ecuadorian specialities ($4–6) served in a pleasant enclosed courtyard.

El Jordán C Larga 6–111, at Borrero ⊕ 07 285 0517. Middle Eastern specialities such as *moussaka* with *falafel*, served attentively in a formal setting with French and Moorish decor. Perfect for a romantic meal. Mains $6–9.

Moliendo Café Honorato Vásquez 6–24. Huge selection of cheap Colombian *arepas* (corn tortillas) and filling *almuerzos* ($2–4).

El Pedregal Azteca Colombia 10–33 ⊕ 07 282 3652. The best place in town for high-quality Mexican fare. Especially good is the *mole poblano* (chicken with chocolate, chillies and almonds). $5–10.

Raymipamba Benigno Malo, at Bolívar, Parque Calderón. Bustling café under the colonnaded arches of the Catedral Nueva, offering large portions of filling Ecuadorian staples and sweet and savoury crêpes for $4–6. Daily.

★ **Taj Mahal** Larga, at Benigno Malo. *Jalfrezi*, *Biryani* and a range of Indian dishes are done extremely well in this friendly Pakistani-run place. They also do good kebabs. Don't miss the traditional yogurt or the Bollywood on the big screen. $3–5. Daily.

NIGHTLIFE

It's not as raucous as Guayaquil or Quito but there are enough options, mostly south of downtown and along Calle Larga. All places listed below are closed Sundays.

★ **Café Eucalyptus** Gran Colombia, at Benigno Malo. Lively, fun café-bar with a diverse tapas menu (dishes $5–6), draught beer, couches to lounge on and live music Wed–Sat.

Monday Blue C Larga, at Cordero. Funky little bar with walls covered in art and eclectic memorabilia, serving cheap Mexican and Italian food.

Tal Cual C Larga 7–57. This popular bar pulls in the crowds at weekends when it turns into a lively disco, playing mainly salsa and *merengue*. Tues–Sat.

Wunderbar Escalinata, off C Larga. Popular German-owned place in a large red-brick building with a small garden nestled above the river. The bar is lively in the evenings with occasional live music.

★ **TREAT YOURSELF**

Tiestos Jaramillo, at Borrero. One of Cuenca's best and most popular restaurants. Gourmet dishes cooked to perfection and served in style with a range of side dishes. Try the beef tenderloin or the langoustines followed by one of the indulgent desserts. Book in advance. Shared mains $15.

DIRECTORY

Banks and exchange Banco de Guayaquil on Mariscal Sucre, at Hermano Miguel; Banco de Austro on M. Sucre, at Pdte A Borrero; Banco de Pacifico on Benigno Malo 9–75.

Hospitals Hospital Santa Ines on Av Daniel Cordova Toral 2–113, at Augustian Cueva (☎ 07 281 7888); Hospital Monte Sinai at Miguel Cordero 6–111, at Av Solano (☎ 07 288 5595).

Internet Cuenc@net at C Larga, at Hermano Miguel; ExploreNet on Padre Aguirre 10–96, at Lamar.

Police Main station at Benigno Malo & Antonio Muñoz (☎ 07 281 0068).

Post offices Main post office on Presidente Borrero, at Gran Colombia; Fedex on Miguel Cordero 350, at Alfonso Cordero.

Telephone Pacifictel on Benigno Malo, at Cordoba.

BAÑOS (CUENCA)

The ideal way to relax after sightseeing is to visit the small town of **BAÑOS**, a fifteen-minute drive southwest of Cuenca, although the mineral content of the baths is debatable and the town doesn't rival its namesake in the Central Highlands (see p.593). There are two sets of baths: the *Balneario Durán* (Av Ricardo Durán) has two warm pools ($2.50); and there are upmarket facilities up the road at the *Hostería Durán* (Av Ricardo Durán; ☎ 07 289 2485, ⊕ hosteriaduran.com). Use of the warm pool (36°C) and steam rooms costs $5.50. Massages cost $25 per hour.

ARRIVAL

By bus The bus ($0.25) departs from Vega Muñoz, at Padre Aguirre or Av 12 de Abril, at Av Fray Vicente Solano, south of the river.

By taxi A taxi from Cuenca to Baños costs $4–5.

PARQUE NACIONAL EL CAJAS

Just 30km northwest of Cuenca, the enormous **PARQUE NACIONAL EL CAJAS** (daily 6am–5pm; $2) spans nearly 300 square kilometres of spectacular moor-like *páramo*. With two hundred lakes shining beneath rugged hillsides, this is one of Ecuador's most compelling wildernesses, offering great hiking and trout-fishing opportunities. Highlights include wild llamas, which were introduced to the park in the late 1990s. There are eight hiking trails, ranging from three hours to two full days. The short hike around Laguna Toreadora is the most popular, while the trail to Laguna Totoras takes six hours. However, the wind, rain and fog can often make visits uncomfortable so come prepared with rainproof gear, snacks, warm clothing and walking boots. Most of the park lies above 4000m so ensure you are properly acclimatized before tackling long hikes.

It's easy to visit independently by taking a Cooperativa Alianza bus from the terminal (1hr) and walking 100m to the Laguna Toreadora refuge station, which has maps and information on popular hiking trails. The station also has a few beds, or you can camp in the recreation area for about $5 per person, but it gets very cold. Cuenca-based tour operators (see p.602) offer guided tours costing about $40 per person.

VILLAGES AROUND CUENCA

There are several interesting indigenous villages close to Cuenca, famous for handicrafts. **Gualaceo** (45min east of Cuenca; $0.60 by bus from the terminal) has the largest indigenous market in the area on Sundays with a range of woven textiles – from shawls to tapestries. **Chordeleg** is 5km further and renowned for jewellery. A further 15 minutes by bus ($0.25) is **Sigsig**, well known for the Panama hat factory on the edge of town, where you can make considerable savings on hats compared with Cuenca. On a separate route, southeast of Cuenca, the village of **San Bartolome** (30min by bus; $0.50) is famous for handmade guitars.

LOJA

South of Cuenca, there is little to catch the visitor's attention until **LOJA**, some 200km away. Loja was founded in 1548 and today boasts a well-preserved historic centre, thriving music scene and spectacular parks.

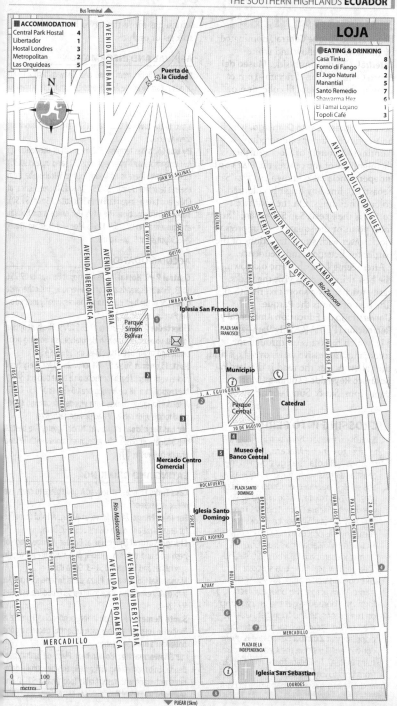

Bus Terminal ▲

LOJA

■ ACCOMMODATION
Central Park Hostal	4
Libertador	1
Hostal Londres	3
Metropolitan	2
Las Orquideas	5

● EATING & DRINKING
Casa Tinku	8
Forno di Fango	4
El Jugo Natural	2
Manantial	5
Santo Remedio	7
Shawarma Hez	6
El Tamal Lojano	1
Topoli Café	3

N

Puerta de
la Ciudad

AVENIDA CUXIBAMBA

JUAN DE SALINAS

JOSE F. VALDIVIESO

18 DE NOVIEMBRE

SUCRE

QUITO

BOLIVAR

AVENIDA IBEROAMÉRICA

AVENIDA UNIBERSITARIA

AVENIDA LAURO GUERRERO

RAMON PINTO

JOSE MARIA PEÑA

AVENIDA ORILLAS DEL ZAMORA

AVENIDA AMILIANO ORTEGA

AVENIDA ZOILO RODRIGUEZ

Río Zamora

BERNARDO VALDIVIESO

OLMEDO

JUAN JOSE PEÑA

IMBABURA

Iglesia San Francisco

Parque
Simón
Bolívar

COLÓN

PLAZA SAN
FRANCISCO

Municipio

Parque
Central

Catedral

J. A. EGUIGUREN

10 DE AGOSTO

Museo del
Banco Central

Mercado Centro
Comercial

Río Malacatus

18 DE NOVIEMBRE

SUCRE

ROCAFUERTE

PLAZA SANTO
DOMINGO

Iglesia Santo
Domingo

MIGUEL RIOFRÍO

BERNARDO VALDIVIESO

OLMEDO

JUAN JOSE PEÑA

PASAJE SINCHINA

24 DE MAYO

AVENIDA LAURO GUERRERO

RAMON PINTO

JOSE MARIA PEÑA

NICOLAS GARCIA

AVENIDA IBEROAMÉRICA

AVENIDA UNIBERSITARIA

AZUAY

BOLIVAR

MERCADILLO

MERCADILLO

PLAZA DE LA
INDEPENDENCIA

Iglesia San Sebastian

LOURDES

0   100
metres

▼ PUEAR (5km)

6

WHAT TO SEE AND DO

Begin at the **Parque Central**, dominated by the towering yellow and white **Catedral**. On the south side, **Museo del Banco Central** (Mon–Fri 9am–1pm & 2–5pm; free) has a small collection of pre-Columbian ceramics and religious art. Walk south on Bolívar, passing the beautiful **Iglesia Santo Domingo**, which houses more than one hundred oil paintings. A couple of blocks further is the highlight of the centre, the **Plaza de la Independencia** (also known as Plaza San Sebastián), lined by brightly coloured colonial buildings. On the southwest corner is the **Iglesia San Sebastián**. The focal point of the square is an impressive clock tower with stone depictions of the battles for Ecuador's independence.

After seeing Loja's historic old town, the best thing to do is visit the parks, easily reached by a short taxi ride ($2). The best option is the **Parque Universitario de Educación Ambiental y Recreación** (PUEAR, daily 9am–4pm; $1), which has trails up through the forest and impressive views over Loja and the valley. Across the road is the **Jardín Botánico Reynaldo Espinosa** (Mon–Fri 9am–4pm, Sat & Sun 1–6pm; $0.60), which has more than two hundred species of orchids.

ARRIVAL AND INFORMATION

By plane Flights from Quito and Guayaquil (from $80 one-way) arrive at the Aeropuerto La Toma, 33km west in the town of Catamayo. A shared taxi (about $5/person) is the only way to get directly to Loja from the airport, or take a taxi to the town of Catamayo ($2) and take a bus from there to Loja.

By bus Loja's bus terminal is 2km north of the centre on Av Cuxibamba, with plenty of taxis ($1) and buses ($0.30) to the centre. There is an hourly bus to Vilcabamba from the bus terminal (75min, $1.25). Or go to Iberoamerica, at Chile, and take a shared taxi with Taxi Ruta (45min; $1.50).

Tourist information The city's iTur office is on Bolívar, at Eguiguren (☎07 258 1251; Mon–Fri 8.30am–1pm, 2–6.30pm & Sat 9am–1pm).

ACCOMMODATION

Central Park Hostal 10 de Agosto, at Bolívar ☎07 256 1103. Pink bedspreads are not for everyone, but otherwise this is one of the best mid-range choices, ideally located on the Parque Central. **$33**

Libertador Colon 14–30 ☎07 256 0779. The best option to treat yourself, with plush decoration, swimming pool, sauna and steam bath. Breakfast included. **$65**

Hostal Londres Sucre 07–51 ☎07 256 1936. Very basic rooms with shared bath for those on a tight budget. **$10**

Metropolitan 18 de Noviembre 06–31 ☎07 257 0007. A solid mid-range choice, with wooden floors and good-sized rooms with cable TV and private bath. **$24**

★ **Las Orquideas** Bolívar, at 10 de Agosto. The best of the budget options, with clean, neat rooms with TV and private bathroom. **$18**

EATING AND DRINKING

Casa Tinku Lourdes, at Bolívar. A good place to catch live music at weekends.

Forno di Fango 24 de Mayo, at Azuay. A local favourite for great pizza and pasta dishes at $3–7. Daily.

El Jugo Natural Eguiguren, at Bolívar. A huge range of fresh fruit and vegetable juices, plus fresh bread, veggie specialities and ice cream. $1–3. Open daily.

Manantial Bolívar near Plaza de la Independencia. An informal, inexpensive place to fill up on Ecuadorian staples for $2–4.

Santo Remedio Plaza de la Independencia. Nightlife is limited in Loja, but this bar with delightful decor is a good option for a drink and dance.

★ **Shawarma Hez** Bolívar near Plaza de la Independencia. Enjoy something different in this beautifully decorated restaurant with tasty Arabic food (mains $2–4) and seating on traditional floor cushions. Closed Sun.

CROSSING INTO PERU

If you're in the southern sierra, it's better to cross to Peru via **Macará**, 190km southeast of **Loja**, than go down to the coast and cross via frenetic Huaquillas. A bus service operated by Cooperativa Loja (☎07 257 9014) travels from Loja to Piura in Peru via Macará (7am, 1pm & 11pm; 6hr). Buy tickets in advance if possible. The company has offices in Loja's bus terminal and next to Vilcabamba's bus terminal. From Vilcabamba take a bus to Loja and change. In Macará the bus stops at the 24-hour *Migración* office for your exit stamp. Walk across the bridge, which forms the border, to get the entry stamp on the other side and then get back on the bus. An alternative route is gaining popularity at **Zumba** because it is more convenient if visiting the Chachapoyas ruins in Peru. There are three night buses from Loja to Zumba via Vilcabamba (6hr), and one bus passing Vilcabamba at 6am.

6

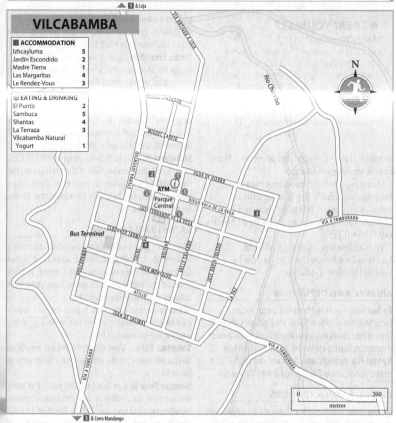

VILCABAMBA

ACCOMMODATION

Izhcayluma	5
Jardin Escondido	2
Madre Tierra	1
Las Margaritas	4
Le Rendez-Vous	3

EATING & DRINKING

El Punto	2
Sambuca	5
Shantas	4
La Terraza	3
Vilcabamba Natural Yogurt	1

El Tamal Lojano 18 de Noviembre. The best place to sample local specialities like *humitas*, *tamales* and *empanadas* for $1–2. Another branch on 24 de Mayo.

Topoli Café Bolívar, at Riofrio. Sandwiches, burgers, crêpes, cakes and ice cream, all for less than $4.

VILCABAMBA

VILCABAMBA has been attracting travellers for years in search of relaxation and the apparent secret to a long, healthy life. Backpackers, hikers and hippies flock to the "Valley of Longevity" to enjoy the region's perfect climate and spectacular scenery. The town itself is not brimming with tourist attractions; the main draw is in the surroundings, which offer great **hiking** and **horseriding** opportunities.

Vilcabamba has also long been associated with the hallucinogenic San Pedro cactus, which grows in this region.

Be warned that consuming San Pedro is illegal and local police may deal severely with anyone found taking it.

WHAT TO SEE AND DO

Perhaps the most impressive hiking trail is up to the jagged hill **Cerro Mandango**. Walk south of town along Avenida Eterna Juventud to find the trail entrance ($1.50). It's a steep 45-minute climb to the first peak and then an unnerving trek across the very narrow ridgeline to the second peak. You can loop around descending slowly towards town, which means the entire walk is about four hours. To shorten it, retrace your steps back down from the first peak.

Easier trails are found at Rumi Wilco Nature Reserve (@rumiwilco.com), just ten minutes east of town. There are half

6

★ TREAT YOURSELF

Madre Tierra ☎ 07 264 0269, ⓦ madretierra.com.ec. For more comfort, stay at this award-winning spa hotel 1km north of town. Enjoy the view from the balcony of your comfortable cabin and take advantage of the jacuzzi, pool and huge range of spa treatments on offer. Breakfast and soft drinks included. **$39**

---

a dozen trails through the protected forest beside the river Chamba.

Many hotels have excellent **massage** facilities attached; the best option in town is Karina at Massage Beauty Care (Diego Vaca de Vega, at Bolívar; $15/hr; ☎ 07 264 0359).

To hire **horses**, contact Caballos Gavilán (see below), which is run by a friendly New Zealander.

ARRIVAL AND DEPARTURE

By bus Buses run to and from Loja (every 30min; 75min) from the corner of Av de la Eterna Juventud and C Jaramillo. To go to Peru, buses to the crossing at Zumba pass through Vilcabamba. To cross via Macará, take a bus from Loja.
By taxi Pick-up trucks act as taxis and charge $1–1.50 to most of the accommodation in and around Vilcabamba.

INFORMATION AND TOURS

Money Note that there is a Banco de Guayaquil cash machine on the main square in Vilcabamba but no bank; the nearest is in Loja. The machine frequently runs out of money at weekends.
Tourist information The tourist office, on the northeast corner of Parque Central (open daily 8am–1pm & 3–6pm; ☎ 07 264 0090), provides maps and information on hikes and excursions around Vilcabamba.
Tour operators Caballos Gavilán (Sucre, at Diego Vaca; ☎ 07 264 0281) organize half-day/full-day ($20/30) horse-riding tours with a guide, and two- and three-day tours to a cloudforest cabin in Podocarpus; Monta Tour (☎ 098 914 4812) next door and Apache Tour on Sucre (☎ 07 264 0415) also offer tours to Podocarpus.

ACCOMMODATION

Expect to pay a little more for accommodation in Vilcabamba than in other parts of Ecuador unless you stay at one of the town's grubbiest dives.

★ **Izhcayluma** ☎ 07 264 0095, ⓦ izhcayluma.com. About 2km south of town, this friendly German-owned *hostería*, whose name means "between two hills" in Inca, has rustic cabins, a small spa and a great view. The owners have

mapped out trails around Vilcabamba for hikers. Don't miss the Bavarian stroganoff or the German Weissbier in the restaurant. Breakfast included. Dorms **$10**, doubles **$26**
Jardín Escondido Sucre, at Diego Vaca ☎ 07 264 0281. Simple but spacious rooms around a garden with lemon trees, a small pool and jacuzzi. The hotel's Mexican restaurant is excellent and the service friendly. **$25**
Las Margaritas Sucre, at C Jaramillo ☎ 07 264 0051. This large white house feels like a family residence, with a cosy atmosphere and well-maintained rooms. Excellent value for the price, and breakfast is included. **$20**
Le Rendez-Vous Diego Vaca de la Vega ☎ 099 219 1180, ⓦ rendezvousecuador.com. East of the town centre, this French-owned guesthouse has good-value, comfy rooms with hammocks on the terrace overlooking the garden. Breakfast included. **$20**

EATING AND DRINKING

Many hotels have good restaurants attached, particularly Mexican food at *Jardin Escondido* (see above) and German food at *Izhcayluma* (see above). After dinner, nightlife is almost non-existent in Vilcabamba. Many restaurants outside the hotels are closed Sundays.

El Punto Sucre, at Diego Vaca. Popular café with expats, ideal to watch the world go slowly by over pizza, local fare, a coffee, juice or dessert ($3–5).
Sambuca Bolívar. Good choice for organic vegetarian specialities, soups, salads, Mexican and a wide range of juices. $4–7.
Shantas Diego Vaca de la Vega. Going east out of town, this informal place offers a wide selection of dishes, including trout and frog's legs ($4–6). The more adventurous can try snake juice ($2), made from pickled coral snake, sugar cane and *aguardiente*.
La Terraza Parque Central. This restaurant serves good *almuerzos* as well as tasty Mexican, Italian and Chinese dishes ($5–7). The set lunch ($2.50) is great value.
Vilcabamba Natural Yogurt Bolívar. One of the cheapest places in town, great for crêpes, burgers, breakfasts, home-made yogurt and juice for $2–3.

PODOCARPUS

Ecuador's southernmost national park contains remarkable diversity spanning different terrain, from high to tropical jungle. The park is comparatively remote, but visitors are rewarded with hillsides covered in cloudforest, waterfalls, and thousands of species of plants. There are six hundred species of birds, including 61 species of hummingbirds, as well as spectacled bear, tapirs and deer, although you will be lucky to see them.

ARRIVAL AND TOURS

Cajanuma ranger station between Loja and Vilcabamba is the most popular and accessible entrance to the park (entrance fee $2).

By Bus Buses from Vilcabamba drop you on the main road 9km from the entrance (tell the driver you are going to Podocarpus).

By taxi A taxi from Vilcabamba is approximately $15.

Tours There are hikes ranging from one hour to several days. If you are planning to stay longer, you are better off arranging a tour in Vilcabamba.

The Oriente

East of Quito, the Andes drop dramatically and snowcapped mountains give way to verdant swathes of tropical rainforest stretching 250km to the Colombian and Peruvian borders. Ecuador's chunk of the Amazon basin, known as the Oriente ("The East"), constitutes almost half of the country's

6

JUNGLE TOURS

If you dream of striking out on your own and hacking through dense jungle like a modern-day explorer, dream on. Unguided travel is strongly discouraged by the government and not advisable, considering how inhospitable and inaccessible parts of the Oriente remain. **Guided tours** are the best option and are relatively cheap, costing $30–50 per person per day. Prices rise if you stay in a luxurious lodge or air-conditioned river cruiser, but bear in mind that some discomfort is part of the jungle experience. Always check that your guide has a **permit** from the Ministry of Tourism. Generally the larger the number of people in your group, the lower the price. Solo travellers usually have to share a cabin or pay a higher rate for a separate room. Tours range from two to eight days and can often be booked at the last minute. For tours around Puyo and Tena, a couple of days will give you an insight into life in the Oriente, but if you are travelling deep into the jungle, more than four days is recommended, because nearly two days will be spent travelling.

You must prepare thoroughly and pack **essentials** before heading into the jungle. Take plenty of insect repellent, long-sleeved tops, trousers, waterproofs, a torch and boots. A first-aid kit is also advisable, although the guide will carry one. Anti-malarials and yellow fever vaccinations are recommended (see p.35). You must carry your original **passport**, as copies are not sufficient at military checkpoints.

TOUR OPERATORS

It's easiest to book your tour in Quito, particularly for those going via Coca and Lago Agrio. For shorter tours to secondary jungle, operators in Tena and Baños are also useful (see listing for those towns). Booking locally in Coca and Lago Agrio is more difficult so it's better to make arrangements beforehand. The following Quito operators are recommended:

Dracaena J Pinto E4-453, at Amazonas ☏ 02 254 6590, ⓦ amazondracaena.com. Offers tours of Cuyabeno, staying at *Nicky Amazon Lodge and Dracaena Camp Site* (5 days; $240).

Gulliver Travels Juan Mera N24-156 ☏ 02 252 9297, ⓦ gulliver.com.ec. Tours in Cuyaben from $220 for four days.

Kem Pery Tours Pinto 539, at Amazonas ☏ 02 222 6583, ⓦ kempery.com. Offers trips to the Huaorani reserve staying in *Bataburo Lodge* (4 days $350, plus $20 donation to the Huaorani). Trips also to Napo Wildlife Centre, Yuturi Lodge, Sacha Lodge and Tapir Lodge.

Magic River Tours 18 de Diciembre, at C Primera, Pacayacu ☏ 02 262 9303, ⓦ magicrivertours.com. German-owned company specializing in canoe trips in the Cuyabeno reserve. Five days from $330.

Neotropic Turis J Pinto E4-340 near Amazonas and Wilson ☏ 02 252 121, ⓦ neotropicturis.com. Four-day tours to Cuyabeno Reserve, staying in *Cuyabeno Lodge*, from $350.

Rainforestur Amazonas 410, at Robles ☏ 02 223 9822, ⓦ rainforestur.com. Wide range of jungle tours throughout the Oriente via Lago Agrio, Coca, Puyo and Tena. Four days in Jamu Lodge from $220.

Safari Tours Reina Victoria N25-33, at Av Colon ☏ 02 255 2502, ⓦ safari.com.ec. Wide range of jungle tours through Puyo, Tena, Coca and Lago Agrio.

Tropic Ecological Adventures Av República 307, at Almagro, Edif Taurus ☏ 02 222 5907, ⓦ tropiceco.com. Tours and ecotourism projects throughout the Oriente. Four days on the edge of Yasuní from $670 in *Sani Lodge*; from $860 in *Huaorani Eco Lodge* (not including flights from Puyo). Indigenous community stays available.

6

territory, although only five percent of the population lives here in oil towns and remote indigenous communities. However, due to oil exploration and improved roads, the population is expanding fast. Sadly areas of pristine jungle remain as under threat here as elsewhere in South America.

The **Northern Oriente** offers the most spectacular opportunities for visitors to encounter an array of flora and fauna in primary rainforest. The highlights are two huge protected areas – **Parque Nacional Yasuní** and the **Reserva Faunística Cuyabeno**. Unfortunately, reaching these unforgettable wildernesses usually involves travelling through the forgettable hubs of **Lago Agrio** or **Coca**. For those with limited time seeking an accessible experience, more pleasant towns of **Tena**, **Puyo** and **Macas** are surrounded by secondary rainforest with chances to stay with **indigenous communities**. The higher elevation of these towns makes **white-water rafting** and **kayaking** popular activities in rapids tumbling down to the Amazon basin.

LAGO AGRIO

LAGO AGRIO, also known as Nueva Loja, was used by Texaco in the 1960s as a base for oil exploration in the Oriente and takes its name (meaning "sour lake") from the company's original headquarters in Texas. The town epitomizes the power struggle between oil companies keen to get their hands on the "black gold" underneath the jungle and tour operators keen to preserve the once

---

THE ROAD TO LAGO AGRIO

The bus ride from Quito to Lago Agrio (8hr) is long and arduous and you might consider flying. If you take the bus, it makes sense to break the journey up with visits to **Papallacta** (see p.581) and **San Rafael Falls**, Ecuador's largest waterfalls. These are located three hours after Baeza, 2.5km along a trail from the main road (ask the bus driver). You should allow yourself about one hour thirty minutes to walk down to the falls and back.

---

pristine forests of the **Cuyabeno Reserve**. More worryingly, the infiltration of Colombian FARC guerrillas along the border just 21km to the north makes this a **dangerous area**. A FARC leader and 16 rebels were killed in a bombing raid just north of Lago Agrio in March 2008 and two tourists were kidnapped (and released) in 2012. It's best not to hang around waiting for a tour; book from Quito and consider flying in or out to avoid spending time in the area. If you are staying in Lago Agrio, don't wander from the centre (most hotels, restaurants and tourist agencies are located along Av Quito), and take care at night. At the time of writing, the British Foreign Office advises travellers to avoid Lago Agrio and all areas in Succumbios Province bordering Colombia.

ARRIVAL AND DEPARTURE

By plane The airport is located 4km east of Lago Agrio. TAME (9 de Octubre, at Orellana; ☎06 283 0113) has a morning flight Mon–Sat from Quito ($70 one-way). Take a taxi to the town centre ($3) unless your tour operator has arranged a transfer.

By bus The bus station is 2km northeast of the town centre.

Destinations Quito (hourly; 8hr); Tena and Puyo (overnight).

ACCOMMODATION

D'Mario Av Quito 1–171 ☎06 283 0172. A popular option with bar, cable TV, swimming pool, a/c and free internet. Breakfast included. $27

Gran Colombia Av Quito 265 ☎06 283 1032. Well-equipped but rather characterless rooms with fans (a/c extra) and cable TV. $28

RESERVA FAUNÍSTICA CUYABENO

This beautiful reserve (admission $20) of unique **flooded rainforest** spreads out over 6000 square kilometres east of Lago Agrio, extending to the Peruvian border. It contains an astonishing biodiversity of plants, trees, mammals and aquatic wildlife. Meandering down the Río Aguarico, a tributary of the Amazon, through huge areas of inundated forest and passing countless lagoons, is unforgettable. Pink freshwater **dolphins**, white and black **caiman**, **giant otters** and many species of **monkeys** are commonly

TEN OF THE BEST JUNGLE LODGES

Prices include all accommodation, food, guides and tours. Transfers are extra. Contact details given are for the Quito offices of each operator. Most lodges do last minute deals when you can save up to thirty percent.

Bataburo Lodge Ramirez Davalos, at Amazonas Edificio Turismundial ☎02 250 5600, ⓦkempery.com. Thatched cabins on the Tinguino River, eight hours by bus and canoe from Coca, deep in Huarorani territory in primary jungle. Proceeds of tours stay with the local tribe. Four days from $340.

Cotococha Lodge Amazonas, at Wilson ☎02 223 4336, ⓦcotococha.com. Located on the Napo River between Tena and Puyo, with 21 comfortable bungalows and a lounge area. Five days from $435.

Cuyabeno Lodge Pinto, at Amazonas ☎02 252 121, ⓦneotropicturis.com. The first lodge in Cuyabeno Reserve, these simple eco-cabins are still one of the cheapest ways to experience primary jungle. Four days from $250.

Jamu Lodge Calama, at Reina Victoria ☎02 222 0614, ⓦcabanasjamu.com. One of the best-value budget lodges in the jungle, with nine thatched cabins in the Cuyabeno Reserve. Five days from $260.

Kapawi Lodge Mariscal Foch, at Reina Victoria ☎02 600 9333, ⓦkapawi.com. High-end ecolodge owned by the Achuar people and situated on the Pastaza River near the Peruvian border. Five days from $999.

Misahualli Jungle Lodge Ramirez Davalos, at Paez ☎02 252 0043, ⓦhosteriamisahualli.com. Comfortable

lodge near Tena with swimming pool and restaurant. Four days from $243.

Napo Wildlife Center Av de la Prensa, at Av de America ☎02 600 5893, ⓦnapowildlifecenter.com. Ten deluxe cabins and a 15m viewing tower two hours from Coca by boat. Part-owned by the Quichua Añargu community. Four days from $839.

Sani Lodge Roca, at Amazonas ☎02 255 8881, ⓦsanilodge.com. Cabins owned by the Quechua community, set on a secluded lagoon on the Napo River, three hours from Coca. Four days from $670 (camping from $440).

La Selva Jungle Lodge San Salvador E7-85, at Carrion ☎02 255 0995, ⓦlaselvajunglelodge.com. One of the cheaper options deep in primary jungle next to Yasuní National Park. Its location on a lake is spectacular and the food is particularly good. Four days from $720.

Yachana Lodge Vicente Solano, at Oriental ☎02 256 6035, ⓦyachana.com. Award-winning higher-end lodge with comfortable accommodation on the Napo River near Coca. Four nights from $660.

Yarina Lodge Av Amazonas, at Av Colon ☎02 250 4037, ⓦyarinalodge.com. Ecolodge in Yasuní National Park with 24 huts. Five days from $450.

6

seen, while the famous anaconda and jaguar will likely prove elusive.

The borders of the reserve were expanded in the early 1990s, partly in response to damaging oil exploration. Sadly, areas of Cuyabeno have been badly polluted but vocal indigenous protest has improved the situation and there remain areas of unspoilt jungle to explore. The remoteness of the region means that you need a guided tour (see p.614).

COCA

The capital of Orellana province has grown rapidly since the 1970s into a sprawling oil town. It's more pleasant than Lago Agrio, but there's little to tempt you to stay long. **COCA** is the last major town on the Río Napo, the gateway to the enormous **Parque Nacional Yasuní**, and is also emerging as a route

over the border to Peru via **Nuevo Rocafuerte**. Local operators are thin on the ground so it's best to organize a tour from Quito.

ARRIVAL AND DEPARTURE

By plane Tame (☎06 288 1078) and Icaro (☎06 288 0997) both operate daily flights from Quito to Coca (from $65 one-way), which is tempting to avoid the gruelling bus ride. The airport is 2km north of town (taxi $1).

By boat Coop de Transportes Fluviales Orellana (☎06 288 0087) has an office on the riverside and operates boat services to Nuevo Rocafuerte on the Peruvian border (Sun, Tues, Thurs & Fri at 7am; 10hr). Advance booking advised. The office doubles as a tourist information point.

By bus Coca's bus terminal is 500m north of town but most bus companies have offices in the centre of town. Trans Baños (Napo & Bolívar) offers several services daily to Quito (9hr), Tena (5hr) and Baños (7hr). Transportes Loja and Transportes Esmeraldas also go to Quito.

By taxi Taxis will take you from the terminal and around town from $1.

6

YASUNÍ ITT PROJECT

In 2007, Rafael Correa's government launched one of its most ambitious and innovative projects, **Yasuní ITT**. The basic idea is that Ecuador will be paid around $3.6 billion over thirteen years in exchange for not drilling the estimated one billion barrels of oil in the Ishpingo, Tambococha and Tiputini (ITT) fields under Yasuní National Park, a biodiversity hotspot. The government's reasoning is that oil has been a key income for Ecuador for the past thirty years and, now that supplies are dwindling, there is increasing financial pressure to drill under protected rainforest. To resist this pressure, the country deserves compensation for preserving a unique biosphere, protecting indigenous communities and helping efforts to curb global warming.

Initially, the project received a very favourable response from international media and governments. However, in the global economic crisis, it has proved difficult to get firm commitments to invest. President Correa has also been reluctant to accept conditions on how the money is spent. At the time of writing, the project succeeded in raising the initial $100 million set by the president as essential to prevent exploration. It remains to be seen whether the initiative will succeed in the long term. Visit ⓦ yasuni-itt.gob.ec or ⓦ sosyasuni.org.

ACCOMMODATION

El Auca Eloy Alfaro, at Napo ⓣ 06 288 0127. Choose from rustic cabins or upscale hotel rooms with a garden courtyard and good restaurant. $44

La Misión Camilo de Torrano ⓣ 06 288 0260, ⓦ hotel mision.com. Next to the river, this is one of Coca's more upscale hotels, with well-tended rooms, swimming pool, steam baths, good restaurant and monkeys roaming the grounds. $38

Oasis Camilo de Torrano ⓣ 06 288 0206. The pick of the cheap options. Rooms are basic and don't face the river, but the terrace does. $12

EATING AND DRINKING

El Auca Napo, at Rocafuerte. The best upscale place in town, with a varied menu – from shrimps in garlic to pork chops with pineapple. $8–11.

La Casa de Maito Espejo. Good place for cheap, delicious fish. $4–6.

Dayuma Hosteria La Mision Camilo de Torrano. Wide range of meat, fish and salads on the riverside terrace. $6–12.

Emerald Forest Blues Bar Espejo, at Napo. A place to drink with fellow jungle-seekers at this backpacker hangout.

PARQUE NACIONAL YASUNÍ

YASUNÍ (park entrance $20) is one of Ecuador's last great wildernesses and the country's largest mainland national park. The terrain of nearly 10,000 square kilometres ranges from upland tropical forest to seasonally flooded forest, marshes, swamps, lakes and rivers. This region was untouched by the last Ice Age and has staggering biodiversity – more than five hundred species of **birds** and sixty percent of Ecuador's **mammals**, including jaguar, puma and tapir. A highlight is the spectacle at the clay licks where dozens of parrots and parrakeets congregate daily to feed.

UNESCO declared it an International Biosphere Reserve in 1979 but this didn't prevent oil exploration. The construction of a road, Vía Maxus, through the park and pollution from irresponsible oil companies has damaged some areas. However, large sections remain unscathed and Yasuní still offers the best opportunities in Ecuador to experience pristine rainforest. Most tours coming through Coca include a visit to the park.

TENA

TENA is the most pleasant town in the Oriente to be based for a few days. Rather than being merely a gateway to the jungle, it's a destination in itself, with a slightly cooler climate, good hotels and restaurants, and an impressive setting on the river surrounded by lush forest.

Aside from wandering around the centre and relaxing in a riverside restaurant, the main attraction in town is **Parque Amazónico La Isla** (daily 8.30am–6pm; $1), just south of the main pedestrian bridge. This park has several self-guided forested trails, diverse plants and wildlife.

ARRIVAL AND INFORMATION

By bus The terminal is 1km south of the centre. A taxi from here or anywhere in town costs $1.

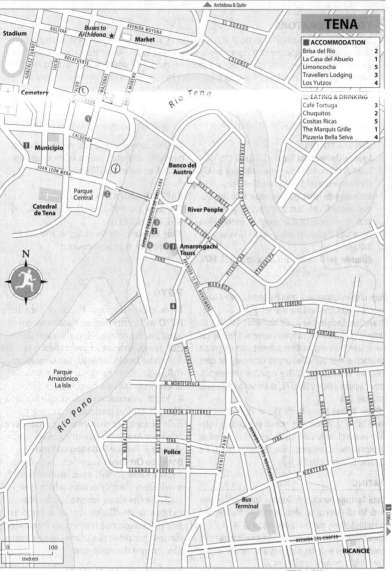

TENA

■ ACCOMMODATION

Brisa del Rio	2
La Casa del Abuelo	1
Limoncocha	5
Travellers Lodging	3
Los Yutzos	4

◻ EATING & DRINKING

Café Tortuga	3
Chuquitos	2
Cositas Ricas	5
The Marquis Grille	1
Pizzería Bella Selva	4

6

Destinations Quito via Baeza (hourly; 5hr); Puyo (hourly; 2hr 30min); Baños (daily; 4hr); Coca (daily; 4hr 30min).

Tourist information Agusto Rueda (Mon–Fri, 7.30am–12.30pm & 2–5pm; ☎ 06 288 8046).

ACCOMMODATION

Brisa del Rio Av Francisco de Orellana ☎ 06 288 6444. One of the best-located budget hotels on the river, as well as a friendly owner. Pricier rooms have a/c, cable TV and private bath. $16

La Casa del Abuelo Sucre 432 ☎ 06 288 8926. This mid-range choice is as cosy and friendly as the name ("grand-father's house") with well-furnished rooms, high ceilings and a pleasant rooftop terrace. Rooms upstairs are better. $24

Limoncocha Av de Chofer ☎ 06 288 7583. A popular back-packer option is this German-run *hostal* on the southeast

6

TOUR OPERATORS

The following Tena-based operators offer jungle tours in addition to rafting and kayaking. Most tours are all-inclusive of transport, accommodation, food and guides. As well as offering plenty of jungle tours, Tena is also the best place in Ecuador for **white-water rafting** and **kayaking** on the countless tributaries surrounded by spectacular jungle scenery. There are plenty of tour operators in town, but ensure you book with an experienced, well-equipped organization, ideally accredited by AGAR. The most famous stretches of river are the Jondachi and Jatunyacu or Upper Napo (both class III) and the wilder Misahuallí and Hollin (class IV). Day-trips are generally $55–70 and longer trips with overnight accommodation are from $130.

JUNGLE TOURS

Agency Limoncocha Sangay 533 ☏ 06 288 7583. Based in the *hostal* of the same name (see p.613); offers jungle tours of 1–4 days at $35–45/day.

Amarongachi Tours 15 de Noviembre ☏ 06 288 6372, ⓦ amarongachi.com. Tours staying in Cabañas Amarongachi or, preferably, Cabañas Shangri-La, perched 100m above Napo River commanding wonderful views. From $40/day.

Ricancie Av El Chofer, at Cuenca ☏ 06 288 8479, ⓦ ricancie.nativeweb.org. Coordinates ten indigenous community ecotourism projects in the upper Napo region. Tours cost around $30/day.

RAFTING AND KAYAKING

Rios Tarqui 230 ☏ 06 288 6727 or Quito ☏ 02 290 4054, ⓦ riosecuador.com.

River People 15 de Noviembre, at 9 de Octubre ☏ 06 288 8349, ⓦ gecodeko.com/river.

edge of town (20min walk from the centre), with a travel agency, guest kitchen and free internet. **$16**

Travellers Lodging Av 15 de Noviembre 438, at 9 de Octubre ☏ 06 288 7102. Budget travellers will feel right at home here. The rooms in three different price ranges are good value, with hot water, private bathroom and cable TV. River views cost extra. The reputable Amarongachi travel agency (☏ 06 288 6372, ⓦ amarongachi.com) is attached. **$14**

★ **Los Yutzos** Agusto Rueda 190, at 15 de Noviembre ☏ 06 288 6717. The riverside location and spacious, tastefully decorated rooms make this the best mid-range option. Lounge on the balcony overlooking the river or relax in the gardens. Breakfast included. **$40**

EATING

Café Tortuga Francisco de Orellana. Travellers' favourite with friendly service, an ideal location on the river and great fresh coffee, snacks and desserts for $2–4.

Chuquitos Off Parque Central. An excellent riverside position, with a wide-ranging menu and attentive service. The fish is particularly good. Mains $6–7.

Cositas Ricas Av 15 de Noviembre, at 9 de Octubre. This cheap, cheerful place serves tasty Ecuadorian staples ($2–6) and is a good option for the cheap set lunch.

★ **The Marquis Grille** Amazonas, at Olmedo. The ideal choice to treat yourself, and one of Tena's few upmarket restaurants. Specialities include trout, paella and filet mignon. Mains $8–20.

Pizzeria Bella Selva Francisco de Orellana. The best place in town for pizza and large plates of pasta. They sell pizza by the slice for those on a tight budget (mains $2–14).

PUYO

If you're arriving from Baños or even Tena, **PUYO** will at first sight be a disappointment, as the centre is less than attractive. But 3km southeast of town (take a taxi for $1) is the **Jardín Botánico Las Orquídeas** (Mon–Sat 8.30am–4pm, Sun 8.30am–noon; $5 book in advance; ☏ 03 288 4855, ⓦ jardinbotanicolasorquideas.com). These botanical gardens, set among lush hills, boast more than two hundred species of native Amazonian orchids. Also worth visiting is **Parque Pedagógico Etno-Botánico Omaere** (Tues–Sun 9am–5pm; $3; ☏ 03 288 7656), a ten-minute walk north from the city centre, which has guided tours along forested paths past indigenous dwellings. Part of the park is primary jungle and it offers an interesting glimpse for those not planning to venture further into the rainforest.

ARRIVAL AND DEPARTURE

By bus The bus station is 1km west of the centre, a 15min walk or $1 by taxi.

Destinations Baños (every 30min; 1hr 30min); Tena (hourly; 2hr 30min).

INFORMATION AND TOURS

Tourist information There are two tourist offices, one on Atahualpa, at Marin, the other next to the market on Orellana, at 9 de Octubre.

Tour operators Most travellers book tours from Quito or Baños but there are a few good tour operators in Puyo offering tours to communities close to town. Other communities, such as the Huaorani, are only reachable by light aircraft from the Shell airport 10km west of town; these tours are more expensive. Further information about Huaorani communities can be obtained from the political body ONHAE (☏ 03 288 6148). Amazonía (Atahualpa, at 9 de Octubre; ☏ 03 288 3219) offers a range of tours to indigenous communities close to Puyo from $35/day. Papangu (27 de Febrero, at Sucre; ☏ 03 288 3875, ⊛ sarayaku.com) is an indigenous-run agency offering tours to nearby Quechua communities and further afield to Sarayacu and Río Curaray (travel by light aircraft). Tours $65/day not including flights. Selva Vida (Ceslao Marin, at Atahualpa; ☏ 03 288 9729, ⊛ selvavidatravel.com) offers two- and three-day jungle trips from $35/day, plus five-day trips deeper into the rainforest.

ACCOMMODATION

You didn't come to Puyo to stay in the bland, central hotels, so it's best to avoid these options and stay on the outskirts of town or head straight to a jungle lodge.

Hostal Araucano Ceslao Marín, at 27 de Febrero ☏ 03 288 5686. Worn, weathered rooms but very friendly service in this cosy, basic budget option in town. Breakfast included. **$16**

★ **El Jardín** Barrio Obrero ☏ 03 288 6101, ⊛ eljardin .pastaza.net. North of the centre towards Parque Omaere, this rustic wooden building, set in a large garden with chirpy parrots, is a real find. The restaurant is award-winning and one of the best in the region. Breakfast included. **$66**

Las Palmas 20 de Julio, at 4 de Enero ☏ 03 288 4832. This pleasant yellow building on the edge of town has economical rooms and breakfast included. **$24**

EATING

El Fogon Atahualpa. Barbecued meat dishes and jungle specialities, including *guanta* (a type of Amazonian rodent). Mains $4–6.

★ **El Jardín** Barrio Obrero. In the lodge of the same name, this is the best restaurant with specialities including *pollo ishpingo* (chicken with cinnamon). Mains $5–10.

MACAS

MACAS is Ecuador's southernmost and most remote jungle town, five hours south of Puyo and seven hours northeast of Cuenca. Most travellers enter the jungle via the northern towns but quieter Macas has a certain charm. In the midst of Shuar territory, a people once renowned for headhunting, indigenous pride burns strongly here and there have been recent confrontations with the government. Tourists can only visit the traditional villages that surround Macas with approved guides. Local tour agencies also arrange jungle treks.

WHAT TO SEE AND DO

In the centre of Macas, the main attraction is the large modern **Catedral** on Parque Central, which commands good views of the town. A block southwest of the park is the small **archeological museum** at the Casa de la Cultura (10 de Agosto, at Soasti; Mon–Fri 8am–5pm; free), which has Shuar exhibits including headdresses, blowpipes and a replica of a shrunken head. To the north is the **Parque Recreacional**, which has even better views than the cathedral.

CROSSING INTO PERU: NUEVO ROCAFUERTE

For adventurers wanting to emulate Francisco de Orellana and float deeper down the Río Napo into the Amazon Basin, improved relations between Ecuador and Peru in the past decade have made it easier to cross the border via Nuevo Rocafuerte. There are even plans afoot to make the trip possible all the way to Brazil's Atlantic coast, although it remains to be seen if and when this will happen. This is not a trip for those who like comfort, as it's some eight hours downstream from Coca. Boats leave Coca at 7am Sunday, Tuesday, Thursday and Friday ($15 one-way), usually stopping off at Pañacocha. (On the return journey from Nuevo Rocafuerte to Coca there are usually departures Wednesday and Sunday.) Come prepared with adequate supplies of food, water purification tablets and insect repellent. In Nuevo Rocafuerte there are a few very basic, cheap places to stay but nowhere good enough to linger long. From Nuevo Rocafuerte you receive an **exit stamp** and boats cross the border to Pantoja, where you get an **entry stamp**. Pantoja also has a small amount of basic accommodation. Boats leave to Iquitos (Peru) from Coca via Nuevo Rocafuerte only once a month, a trip that takes six days.

6

ARRIVAL AND INFORMATION

By plane Tame (☎ 02 397 7100) flies Mon–Fri to Macas from $50 one-way.

By bus The bus terminal is on Amazonas, at 10 de Agosto, in the centre.

Destinations There are several daily buses to Cuenca (7hr), Puyo (3hr) and Quito (8hr).

By taxi Taxis around town cost $1.

Tourist information There is a new tourist office on Comin (Mon–Sat 8am–noon; ☎ 07 270 1606, ⓦ www.macas.gov.ec).

ACCOMMODATION

Casa Blanca Soasti, at Sucre ☎ 07 270 0195. Has decent rooms with private bath, cable TV and breakfast included. $25

La Orquidea 9 de Octubre, at Sucre ☎ 07 270 0970. A basic boarding house with firm beds, run by a friendly family. $22

EATING AND DRINKING

La Maravilla Soasti, at Sucre. Adorned with indigenous artefacts, and serving a variety of meat dishes and snacks (mains $3–6).

La Napolitana Amazonas, at Tarqui. Serves pizza, pasta and barbecue as well as great fish dishes, including tilapia and trout. Mains $3–8.

The northern coast and lowlands

Travelling up the Ecuadorian coast, the scenery gets greener and the vibe more Caribbean. The Afro-Ecuadorians who make up a large part of the population of **Esmeraldas** province give the region a different cultural feel to the rest of the country. The locals are exuberant, extrovert and talkative, a refreshing change from the mountains.

The main route from the Sierra descends dramatically via **Santo Domingo de los Colorados**, an unattractive transport hub. Avoid the dangers of grim **Esmeraldas** town and head south to a string of beach resorts. **Atacames** is the most popular party town. Further south, the beautiful beach at **Mompiche** is emerging as a popular spot for budget travellers. In the

province of **Manabí**, head to **Canoa**, a haven for surfers and sunseekers. Nearby, the elegant resort **Bahía de Caráquez** juts out dramatically on a slim peninsula, close to mangroves and tropical forest. Further south is Ecuador's second-largest port, **Manta**, a bustling city that is unfortunately plagued by security problems.

SANTO DOMINGO DE LOS COLORADOS

This transport hub is the most convenient route from the Sierra to the coast. From here you can head north to Esmeraldas and Pedernales or south to Bahía de Caráquez, Manta and Guayaquil. Parts of town are dangerous so take care at night. Try to begin your journey early so that an overnight stop becomes unnecessary, since Santo Domingo has little to offer.

ARRIVAL

By bus The bus terminal is 1.5km north of the town centre (take a taxi for $1 or a public bus).

ACCOMMODATION

Hotel Diana Real Corner 29 de Mayo, at Loja ☎ 02 275 1380. The best mid-range option in the centre, with spacious rooms and a restaurant attached. $24

EATING

Gran Hotel Santo Domingo Río Toachi, at Galápagos ☎ 02 276 7950. This hotel has a good restaurant *La Tonga* inside. Choose from veggie, local and international food for around $5.

Timoneiro Av Quito. Just one of the good restaurants east of the centre serving chicken, soups and filling set meals. $3–5.

ATACAMES

ATACAMES is the busiest, brashest beach resort on the north coast and, along with Salinas, the most popular in Ecuador. Most hotels, restaurants and bars are situated on the thin peninsula, which forms the **Malecón**. The long sandy beach is lined with bamboo bars serving up fruit shakes by day and cocktails by night. During the week it's relatively quiet and a bit depressing, with staff desperately trying to lure you into their empty bars, but at the weekends and on national holidays Atacames turns into a heaving party town. Boom boxes pump out ear-splittingly loud salsa and reggaeton, while bars are packed with revellers until dawn. Note that tourists, particularly women, get hassled more here than in the southern resorts. **Muggings** have also been reported so avoid taking valuables onto the beach, take taxis at night and stay in well-lit areas.

WHAT TO SEE AND DO

There are a few interesting excursions, including boat trips to nearby **Isla Encantada** ($3), which has abundant birdlife. From June to September, you can watch humpback whales off the coast; tours can be organized through *Le Castell Hotel*, on the Malecón (☎06 273 1442). The town of Atacames is inland over the bridge but it's a dusty unpleasant place, which only necessitates a visit if you need a bank.

ARRIVAL AND INFORMATION

By bus There are buses to and from Quito (several daily; 7hr) and Guayaquil (several daily; 8hr). If you can't get a direct bus to or from Quito or Guayaquil, change at Esmeraldas (the bus station is a few kilometres outside of the city, which it's preferable to avoid). Use Trans Esmeraldas, Aerotaxi or Trans Occidentales (offices across the footbridge). Bear in mind that at weekends and during national holidays you must book in advance as demand is high. Atacames has no central bus terminal so you usually need to stand on the dusty main street inland to hail one. Trans La Costeñita and Trans Pacífico buses run several times an hour to Súa, Same and Muisne (1hr 30min). For Mompiche (2hr 30min), there are three or four direct buses a day, or you can catch a bus heading to Pedernales and be dropped off nearby.

By tricycle taxi The town is compact enough to walk around, but if you're laden with luggage and particularly at night, take one of the motorized tricycle taxis ($0.50).

Tourist information There is a small iTur office stocked with brochures on the corner of the main road inland from Malecón.

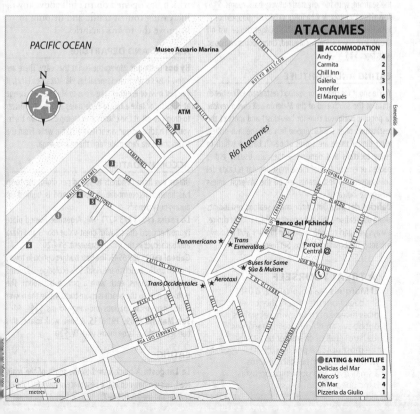

ATACAMES

PACIFIC OCEAN

N

Museo Acuario Marina

ATM

Río Atacames

Banco del Pichincho

Panamericano ★ Trans Esmeraldas

Parque Central @

Buses for Same
Súa & Muisne

Trans Occidentales ★ Aerotaxi

Esmeraldas

■ **ACCOMMODATION**
Andy	4
Carmita	2
Chill Inn	5
Galería	3
Jennifer	1
El Marqués	6

● **EATING & NIGHTLIFE**
Delicias del Mar	3
Marco's	2
Oh Mar	4
Pizzeria da Giulio	1

0   50
metres

Internet There are several internet cafés inland in town on Rua Luis Cervantes and opposite the Parque Central.

ACCOMMODATION

Atacames has a vast amount of accommodation ranging from dirt-cheap cabins to luxurious tourist complexes. It can be surprisingly hard to find anything decent during peak periods so book ahead. Note that prices can rise by around fifty percent in high season.

Andy Malecón, at Los Ostiones ☎06 276 0221. This beachfront hotel is cleaner than other budget options and has good, well-kept rooms (for the price) with fans and TV, although it gets noisy. $\overline{\$20}$

Carmita Las Taguas, at Malecón ☎06 273 1784. For a quieter stay just off the seafront, this *hostal* is good value with cable TV and a/c. $\overline{\$20}$

Chill Inn Los Ostiones, at Malecón ☎06 276 0477, ⓦ chillinnecuador.com. Comfortable rooms, communal TV, kitchen for guest use and a small bar make for a homely atmosphere at this new Swiss-run hostel. There are only four rooms so book in advance. $\overline{\$20}$

Galería Malecón ☎06 273 1149. The cheapest place on the seafront, with friendly staff but very basic rooms. $\overline{\$15}$

Jennifer Malecón, at C La Tolita ☎06 273 1055, ⓦ hostal jennifer.com. Another dependable budget choice just off the Malecón, with peach-coloured, clean rooms equipped with fans. $\overline{\$15}$

EATING AND NIGHTLIFE

You're spoilt for choice for seafood restaurants. The beach stalls at the south end of the Malecón sell cheap *ceviche* (a popular hangover cure for breakfast) and most of the restaurants offer similarly good fish and shellfish dishes. After dinner there are scores of beach bars in which to enjoy cocktails and dancing – they are usually either packed or empty. One of those most popular is Caida del Sol (sunset). All restaurants are on the Malecón unless otherwise indicated.

Delicias del Mar Out of the many seafood restaurants along the seafront, this is the most popular budget choice, always jam-packed with locals and tourists wolfing down fish soup and breaded shrimps. Set menu just $3.

> ### ★ TREAT YOURSELF
>
> **El Marqués** Malecón ☎06 276 0182. Set back from the beach, the towering glass facade of this new hotel stands out above anything else in Atacames. It's hardly full of character but it's the most upscale place in town, with spacious, impeccable rooms, a small gym and pool, plus breakfast is included. $\overline{\$73}$

★ **Marco's** For something a bit more intimate, try *Marco's*, where a delightful lady serves up large portions of sumptuous seafood dishes such as *encocado* (seafood cooked in coconut and garlic) and *cazuela* (fish and plantain casserole) in an elegantly furnished setting (mains $4–7).

Oh Mar Principal. For a feast of seafood in a more refined setting head a block inland. *Ceviche, encocado*, shrimps, as well as steaks and pork chops all cooked well. $6–9.

Pizzeria da Giulio For a break from seafood, head to this Italian-Ecuadorian place, which takes pride in offering sumptuous fresh pizza and pasta dishes (mains $4–12).

MOMPICHE

The tiny little village of **MOMPICHE** is home to one of the most beautiful beaches in Ecuador. This, combined with great surfing conditions, has increased its popularity recently. The backpacker community is supplemented by a different class of tourist thanks to a new luxury hotel, *Royal Decameron*, which has opened on the hill above town, increasing tourist traffic and helping to improve the town's facilities.

ARRIVAL AND DEPARTURE

By bus Getting to Mompiche is not that easy. There are a few buses daily from Esmeraldas via Atacames (3hr). If you just miss one, either take a bus to Muisne and change at El Salto, or take a bus to Pedernales and ask the driver to drop you off at the entrance to Mompiche. From there, you can hitch a ride or sweat it on a 30min walk. From the south travel via Pedernales and then Chamanga.

ACCOMMODATION

Unless you have hundreds to spend per night, the town has limited accommodation options and is booked up during busy periods.

La Facha ☎098 873 4271. This Argentine-owned place is another good choice, with great-value rooms and pizza and barbecues in the small restaurant. $\overline{\$14.20}$

Gabeal ☎099 969 6543. The best budget option in town, located up the beach to the right. This ecolodge has rooms in bamboo cabins, each with a private bathroom. The building next to the beach is more basic, while the newer building has more spacious mid-range rooms. $\overline{\$25}$

San Marena ☎099 191 6115. A 5min walk inland, this budget hotel has large rooms with TV. $\overline{\$20}$

EATING

La Langosta A block inland to the south of the main road, this is renowned as the best place in town for lobster, *ceviche* and fried fish. $4–7.

6

★ TREAT YOURSELF

Royal Decameron Mompiche ☎ 02 602 5602, ⓦ decameron.com. Blow your budget completely on the newest, swankiest hotel on the Ecuadorian coast. Perched on a headland above town, it boasts six swimming pools, four restaurants, and boats to a private beach on island Portete. Discounts for longer stays. **$150**

El Punto Encuentro You can get your seafood fill at any of the restaurants on the beachfront. This is a dependable option. $4–6.

CANOA

CANOA is rather like the Montañita of ten years ago – a quiet fishing village that has developed into a laidback resort by virtue of its beautiful beach and great surfing conditions. It has a dramatic setting, with waves crashing upon long stretches of sand flanked by steep cliffs. At present, it's probably Ecuador's best beach resort for budget travellers without the overblown craziness of Atacames or Montañita, but it's changing fast and can get pretty crowded on high season weekends.

An interesting excursion from Canoa is **Río Muchacho Organic Farm**, where you can see sustainable farming in practice and learn about the culture of the *Montubios* (coastal farmers). Guided hikes, horseriding and birdwatching are available.

ARRIVAL

By bus From Quito there are now direct buses with Transvencedores and Reina del Camino from Quitumbe bus station (daily; 7hr). There are more regular buses from Quito to Bahía de Caráquez; from there take a bus to Canoa (twice hourly; 20min). The opening of an impressive new bridge makes it easier to reach Canoa from Bahia, although you can still take the ferry across the bay and a bus from San Vicente. From Pedernales, there are buses to Canoa every 30min or so.

INFORMATION AND TOURS

Tourist information There is no tourist office, though the Rio Muchacho Office a block inland on Av 3 de Noviembre, at Javier Santos, has plenty of information and friendly staff. The guys at *Surf Shak* (see p.620) are also full of advice on local tours.

Tour operators Guacamayo Bahiatours offers all-inclusive tours (1 day $30, 3 days $115). Its offices are in Bahia de Caráquez (Bolívar 902; ☎ 05 269 1412) and Canoa (☎ 099 147 9849).

ACCOMMODATION

Accommodation prices are seasonal. The following prices are for high season (Dec–April & national holidays). They are about 50 percent cheaper out of season.

Bambú ☎ 098 926 5225, ⓦ hotelbambuecuador.com. At the north end of the beach is Canoa's most happening hotel. Rooms are small but the vibrant atmosphere and beautiful beachfront gardens make up for it. The restaurant is worth visiting even if you don't stay. Surfboards are available for rent. Camping **$3.50**, doubles **$22**

Canoa's Wonderland Malecón, at C San Andre ☎ 05 261 6363, ⓦ hotelcanoaswonderland.com.ec. This hotel stands out as one of the few plush options in Canoa, with a pleasant bar, restaurant, rooftop terrace, swimming pool and a/c rooms. **$90**

Coco Loco ☎ 099 544 7260, ⓦ hostalcocoloco.weebly.com. Two blocks left of the junction with the beach are these basic rooms in a large thatched bamboo house with fans, hammocks on the balconies, kitchen, bar with cocktails and a friendly atmosphere. Dorms **$6**, doubles **$18**

★ Pais Libre ☎ 05 261 6387. This very popular hotel is run by friendly local surfer Favio Coello. Rooms are well kept, the hotel is decorated with artwork, there's a disco/ bar next door and a small pool set in leafy gardens. Dorms **$6**, doubles **$20**

Posada Olmito Javier Santos ☎ 099 553 3341. An endearing Dutch-owned place with basic rooms in an intricately constructed wooden building. **$20**

Sundown Beach Hostel Km2 Via San Vicente ☎ 099 981 5763, ⓦ ecuadorbeach.com. A 20min walk from town, this quiet beachfront hostel is a good spot to get away from it all, with private patio, garden and communal atmosphere. Dorms **$8**, doubles **$24**

La Vista Hotel ☎ 098 647 0222. Next to *Coco Loco*, this mid-range beachfront hotel offers more comfortable, airy rooms, all with sea view and private bathroom. **$24**

EATING AND NIGHTLIFE

Canoa has plenty of restaurants – mainly informal beach-front places offering fresh seafood, though some new options have opened recently. Nightlife is restricted but quite busy in the bars on the main street at weekends and on national holidays.

Amalur C San Andres. A few blocks from the beach, this is one of Canoa's few upmarket options and specializes in Spanish food such as tortillas, meatballs and octopus (dishes $5–8). They've just opened a small but great-value hotel at the back ($20).

Café Flor Malecón. A block or so behind *La Vista Hotel*, this cosy café serves a range of Mexican, Italian and vegetarian dishes in an informal setting. They also have real ales. $5–10.

6

Cevicheria Saboreame Malecón. The best seafood in town according to locals – and they should know. Seafood soups and *encocado*, all delicious. Mains $3–5.

Coco Bar Javier Santos. On the main street leading to the beach, this is the hub of Canoa's nightlife – dead during the week but hot at weekends and in high season, with a packed dancefloor and free-flowing cocktails.

★ **Surf Shak** Malecón. This American-owned place is fast turning into the centre of the expat community in Canoa. Choose from big breakfasts, big burgers, pizzas and fresh coffee. Wi-fi is available as well as plenty of advice on tours from Pete the owner. Mains $3–6.

BAHÍA DE CARÁQUEZ AND AROUND

The most dramatic location of Ecuador's coastal resorts, **BAHÍA DE CARÁQUEZ** sits on a slim sand peninsula jutting out from the mouth of the River Chone into the Pacific. The city, known simply as Bahía to locals, endured two disasters in 1998, when the El Niño rains washed away roads and triggered massive landslides before an earthquake in August destroyed two hundred buildings and left twenty people dead. The city recovered, however, and introduced a wide-ranging environmental programme, converting itself into an "eco-city" with recycling, sustainable development and reforestation. The result is that, unlike many of Ecuador's resorts, Bahía is a clean and pleasant place to stroll around. The completion of an impressive new bridge (the longest in the country) across the bay has improved access to Bahía, and made journeying up and down the coast easier.

WHAT TO SEE AND DO

The **Museo Banco Central** (Wed–Sat 10am–5pm, Sun 11am–3pm; $1) has a very good collection of pre-Columbian artefacts including tools, gold pectorals and ceramics. The **Mirador La Cruz**, a large cross above the south end of town, offers wonderful views over the city and surrounding bay. Some 15km south of town is the **Chirije archeological site**, which has countless ancient artefacts such as ceramics and burial sites dating from 500 BC. Inland from Bahía, the River Chone has some excellent unspoilt

mangroves inhabited by abundant birdlife, including a colony of frigate birds to rival those found in the Galápagos.

ARRIVAL AND DEPARTURE

By boat It's a short walk to the passenger ferry dock, which has regular boats speeding across the bay to San Vicente, from where you can continue north up the coast.

By bus Buses to the terminal run up and down Malecón. There are regular services to and from Portoviejo, Manta and Guayaquil, and four a day from Quito (or travel via Pedernales). Reina del Camino is the biggest bus company with the best services.

By taxi There are plenty of tricycle taxis to get around town (most fares $0.50–$1).

INFORMATION AND TOURS

Tourist information The new tourist information office is on Bolívar, at Malecón (☎ 05 269 1044). The next best thing is to visit Guacamayo Tours (see below).

Tour operators The Chirije archeological site can be visited through Bahía Dolphin Tours (Bolívar 1004; ☎ 05 269 2097, ⊛ bahiadolphintours.com), which owns the site. A half-day nature tour with Guacamayo Tours (Bolívar 902, at Arenas; ☎ 05 269 1412, ⊛ guacamayotours.com) costs $25/person.

ACCOMMODATION

Most budget travellers prefer to stay in Canoa, but Bahía is a pleasant alternative. Accommodation ranges from cheap and basic to rather overpriced at the higher end. Hotels fill up quickly during high season (Dec–April) and on national holidays.

Bahia Bed and Breakfast Inn Ascazubi 316, at Morales ☎ 05 269 0146. The best rock-bottom budget option in town, with basic rooms with fans and cable TV in the lounge. $10

★ **Hostal Coco Bongo** Intriagi, at Arenas ☎ 098 544 0978, ⊛ cocobongohostal.com. Run by a friendly Aussie lady, this converted house overlooking the park has rooms with hot water, private bath, wi-fi and cable TV. It´s a good

---

★ TREAT YOURSELF

La Herradura Bolívar, at Daniel Hidalgo ☎ 05 269 0266, ⊛ laherradurahotel.com. At the northwest end of town, this charming old Spanish house is a delight. Nooks and crannies are filled with colonial artefacts from wagon wheels and saddles to statues and artwork. Rooms are comfortable with a/c and cable TV, and the restaurant is renowned as one of the best in town. Book in advance, 50 percent discount in low season. $80

place to hang out and the breakfasts are top-notch. Dorms $6, doubles $20

Hotel Italia Bolívar, at Checa ☎ 05 269 1137. A cut above the budget options, this mid-range place has clean, simple rooms with private baths and a café downstairs. $25

EATING AND DRINKING

Arenabar Pizzeria Marañon, at Bolívar. Good pizza and lasagne ($5–7) plus eclectic celebrity decor.

Colombus Bolívar. A cheap place for set lunches of chicken and fish ($2–3).

Muelle Uno Malecón. One of a string of restaurants on the pier near the docks, serving man-sized barbecue platters and seafood dishes for $4–8.

Puerto Amistad Malecón. This place is owned by an American sailor and offers *quesadillas* and crêpes as well as meat and fish dishes ($5–10).

Tropihelados Bolívar. Indulgent ice-cream sundaes and filling fast food ($2–3).

MANTA

Ecuador's second port used to be a pleasant expat haven, but a deteriorating security situation means that the city is best avoided. There are far better beaches elsewhere too. However, you may need to pass through Manta on your way up or down the coast and change at its unsightly bus terminal in front of the fishing boat harbour on Calle 7 and Avenida 8.

ARRIVAL AND DEPARTURE

By bus There are regular services to Bahía de Caráquez (hourly; 3hr), Puerto López (hourly; 2hr) and Montañita (daily; 3hr 30min), as well as departures to Guayaquil (hourly; 4hr) and Quito (hourly; 8hr). There are also daily buses up the coast to Esmeraldas.

Guayaquil

GUAYAQUIL is Ecuador's largest city and its economic powerhouse, handling most of the country's imports and exports. The heat, dirt and danger used to be reasons enough to stay away, but the city has undergone quite a facelift in the past decade and the waterfront and city centre have enough to keep visitors occupied for a day or two.

Arriving from the mountains, the contrast is striking between Quito's cool colonial charms and Guayaquil's hot, humid vivacity. *Guayaquileños* (or *Guayacos*) are fiercely proud of their city and they have a centre that is worth showing off. Guayaquil's 3km-long **Malecón** and renovated artistic district of Las Peñas are great achievements, as are the new airport, bus terminal and museums.

WHAT TO SEE AND DO

Be aware that the heat and traffic pollution can make sightseeing an uncomfortable experience, so get up early. The weekend, when the city is quieter, is the best time to explore. Outside the centre, Guayaquil is not picturesque and remains dangerous, particularly at night.

El Malecón

The **Malecón** (daily 7am–midnight) running alongside the river is a public space that is easily the highlight of the city – enclosed, pedestrianized and patrolled by security guards. The best point to enter is **La Plaza Cívica** at the end of 9 de Octubre. Start at **La Rotonda**, a statue of South America's liberators, José de San Martín and Simón Bolívar, shaking hands in front of a semicircle of marble columns. Past the plush Guayaquil Yacht Club is the 23m-high Moorish Clock Tower, and further south **The Henry Morgan**, a replica of a seventeenth-century pirate ship, is docked. A one-hour trip on the river costs $5 (hourly departures afternoons and evenings).

Further south is **Plaza Olmedo**, with its contemplative monument of José Joaquín de Olmedo (1780–1847), the first mayor of Guayaquil. The southern end of Malecón reaches La Plaza de la Integración and an artisans' market, selling traditional indigenous clothing and crafts.

Botanical gardens

North from La Rotonda is a large children's play area packed with families at weekends. Further on is a stunning set of **botanical gardens** with more than three hundred species of coastal vegetation. The gardens are divided into four zones: ornamental trees, humid forest, palms and coniferous. There are two plazas within the gardens: the Pre-Columbian Plaza,

6

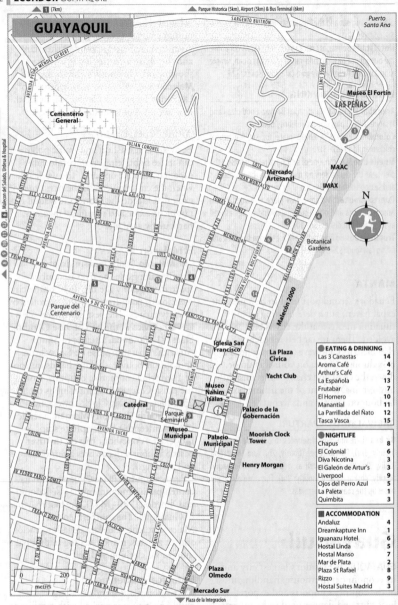

GUAYAQUIL

Puerto Santa Ana

(7km)

Parque Historica (5km), Airport (5km) & Bus Terminal (6km)

SARGENTO BUITRÓN

Cementerio General

Museo El Fortín

LAS PEÑAS

JULIÁN CORONEL

LOJA

Mercado Artesanal

MAAC

IMAX

Botanical Gardens

Malecón 2000

Parque del Centenario

Iglesia San Francisco

La Plaza Cívica

Yacht Club

Museo Nahim Isaías

Catedral

Parque Seminario

Palacio de la Gobernación

Museo Municipal

Palacio Municipal

Moorish Clock Tower

Henry Morgan

Plaza Olmedo

Mercado Sur

Plaza de la Integración

0 200 metres

● EATING & DRINKING	
Las 3 Canastas	14
Aroma Café	4
Arthur's Café	2
La Española	13
Frutabar	7
El Hornero	10
Manantial	11
La Parrillada del Ñato	12
Tasca Vasca	15

● NIGHTLIFE	
Chapus	8
El Colonial	6
Diva Nicotina	3
El Galeón de Artur's	3
Liverpool	9
Ojos del Perro Azul	5
La Paleta	1
Quimbita	3

■ ACCOMMODATION	
Andaluz	4
Dreamkapture Inn	1
Iguanazu Hotel	6
Hostal Linda	5
Hostal Manso	7
Mar de Plata	2
Plaza St Rafael	8
Rizzo	9
Hostal Suites Madrid	3

with Manteña balsa wood and palm trees, and the Neoclassic Plaza, with a bronze fountain surrounded by lanterns. Above the gardens is a set of 32 transparent panels with the names of some 48,000 citizens who contributed to the construction of the Malecón.

IMAX and Museo Guayaquil en La Historia

At the north end of Malecón is an **IMAX cinema** (☎04 256 3078, ⊛imaxmalecon2000.com) with a 180-degree screen. Below the cinema is **Museo Guayaquil en La Historia** (daily

10am–6.30pm; $2.50), which condenses a compact history of the city in English and Spanish, from prehistory to the present day, into fourteen dioramas.

Museo Antropológico y de Arte Contemporáneo

The north end of Malecón culminates in the spacious **Museo Antropológico y de Arte Contemporáneo (MAAC)** (Tues–Sat 10am–6pm, Sun 10am–4pm; $1.50, Sun free), which has regular exhibitions and a huge collection of pre-Columbian ceramics and first-rate modern art.

Mercado Artesanal (Artisans' market)

A couple of blocks inland along Calle Loja is the huge, enclosed **Mercado Artesanal** (Mon–Sat 9am–7pm, Sun 10am–5pm), which has a wide selection of traditional handicrafts and clothing. Prices are slightly higher than in the Sierra and haggling is obligatory.

Malecón del Salado

At the opposite end of 9 de Octubre (a 20min walk or short taxi ride) is the **Malecón del Salado**, next to the Estero Salado, a tributary of the river Guayas. It is a picturesque place to stroll, and for great views of the river you can cross the bridges (which tower over 9 de Octubre). Otherwise, take a boat trip or relax in one of the seafood restaurants.

Las Peñas

Rising above the north end of Malecón is the colourful artistic district of **Las Peñas**, a formerly run-down area that's been revamped. Like the Malecón, it's patrolled by security guards. Round the corner to the right of the steps is the historic, cobbled street of Numa Pompillo Llona, named after the *Guayaco* who wrote Ecuador's national anthem. The street leads from old to new, reaching **Puerto Santa Ana**, the city's latest grand project with waterfront shops, restaurants, luxury apartments and an extensive marina. There are a couple of interesting museums, the best of which is **Museo de la Musica Popular Julio Jaramillo** (Wed–Sat, 10am–1pm & 2–5pm; free), dedicated to the city's most famous musician. Next

door is **Museo Pilsener** for everything on Ecuador's most popular beer.

For spectacular views of Guayaquil, climb the 444 steps up Las Peñas to the peak of **Cerro Santa Ana** (en route, there's a wide selection of craft shops, restaurants, cafés and bars). At the top of the hill in the Plaza de Honores is a new colonial-style chapel and the **Lighthouse** (free), based on Guayaquil's first, built in 1841. Also here is the open-air **Museo El Fortín del Santa Ana** (free), which holds the foundations of the Fortress of San Carlos. The fortress, which defended the city from pirates, has original cannons and replicas of Spanish galleons. The highlight is the sweeping panoramic view over the rivers Daule and Babahoyo, downtown Guayaquil and, across the river, the reserve of Santay Island.

Parque Seminario and Catedral

Three blocks behind the grand **Palacio Municipal** (town hall) is the small **Parque Seminario**, also known as Parque Bolívar or, more aptly given that dozens of urban iguanas reside here, Parque de las Iguanas. At the centre of the park is an imposing monument of liberator Simón Bolívar on horseback. The huge white neo-Gothic **Catedral**, reconstructed in 1948 after a fire, towers over the west side of the square.

Northeast, Plaza San Francisco is dominated by the church of the same name, a statue of Pedro Carbo, the nineteenth-century liberal politician and writer, and a large fountain.

Museo Municipal

One block southeast from the park is the **Museo Municipal** (Sucre, at Chile; Tues–Sat 9am–5pm; free). This is the oldest museum in Ecuador and the city's best. The Pre-Hispanic room has fossils, including the tooth of a mastodon, dating back 10,000 years, as well as sculptures created by the Valdivia – Ecuador's oldest civilization – and a huge Manteña funeral urn. Upstairs is a room of portraits of Ecuadorian presidents, nicknamed "the room of thieves", plus a small exhibition of modern art. There are five shrunken

6

heads on display in a closed room, which is only viewed on guided tours. Free tours in English are recommended because the museum has no English information.

Parque Histórico

Across the bridge in the wealthy district of Entre Rios, the **Parque Histórico** (Wed–Sun 9am–4.30pm; free; ☎04 283 3807) is worth the trip out of town. The park is divided into three zones. Created out of the natural mangroves of the River Daule, the **wildlife zone** provides a snapshot of the Ecuadorian jungle with deer, tapirs, monkeys, sloths, ocelots, tortoises, parrots, toucans, caimans and fermenting termite mounds. The **traditions zone** depicts the rural way of life via haciendas, "peasant" houses and crops. At weekends, there are boisterous music and comedy shows. In the **urban architecture zone**, some of Guayaquil's late nineteenth-century buildings are reproduced. The colonial-style *Café 1900* is the perfect place to gaze out over the river. To **get there**, catch bus #81 from the terminal or get a taxi from downtown ($4–5).

ARRIVAL AND DEPARTURE

By plane Guayaquil's José Joaquín de Olmedo airport, about 5km north of downtown (☎04 216 9000, ⓦtagsa .aero), is Ecuador's only international airport outside Quito. There are regular flights to and from Quito, the Galápagos, Cuenca, Loja and Esmeraldas. The airport has an exchange bureau and ATM. Take a taxi to your hotel, as Metrovia and public buses are not best tackled with luggage.

By bus The bus terminal is 6km north of downtown, with food courts and shopping malls. The cheapest way to get into town from here is the Metrovia ($0.25), a rapid transit bus system modelled on Quito's. It runs from Terminal Río Daule opposite the bus station through downtown to the south. Get off at La Catedral stop for the main tourist sights. Watch your belongings as pickpockets are common. Destinations Bahía de Caráquez (hourly; 7hr); Baños (3 daily; 6–7hr); Canoa (2 daily; 7hr); Puerto López (8 daily; 4hr); Montañita (3 daily; 3hr 30min); Quito (hourly; 9hr); Salinas (hourly; 2hr).

By taxi There are plenty of taxis but few of them use a meter, so negotiate the price first. Taxi drivers In Guayaquil will nearly always try to overcharge foreigners. You should pay $3–4 from the bus terminal to the centre and $4–5 from the airport. Avoid unmarked cabs. Short taxi rides around the city centre should cost about $2–3.

INFORMATION AND TOURS

Tourist information The Dirección Municipal de Turismo office on Ballen, at Pichincha, near the Parque de las Iguanas (Mon–Fri 9am–5pm; ☎04 259 9100; ⓦvisit aguayaquil.com), has friendly staff and up-to-date maps and brochures. The tourist office also produces two guidebooks – a general tourist guide and a gastronomic guide. Another useful website is ⓦinguayaquil.com.

Tour operators Canodros (Urb. Santa Leonor Mz 5 Solar 10 ☎04 228 5711, ⓦcanodros.com); Chasquitur (Acacias 605, at Las Monjas ☎04 288 8988); Ecoventura (Miraflores Av Central 300A ☎04 283 9390, ⓦecoventura.com); Metropolitan Touring (Artarazana C 11A NE103; ☎04 232 0200, ⓦmetropolitan-touring.com).

ACCOMMODATION

Guayaquil has plenty of hotels but is still not well geared up for the backpacker market. Many of the budget hotels are of a very poor standard in unappealing areas, while the top-end hotels charge high rates for foreigners. It's best to stay near to Parque Bolívar or Parque Centenario. The centre can get very noisy so ask for a back room or a higher floor. It doesn't make much sense to stay in the suburbs because there are few tourist sights, although there is one good backpacker hostel, *Dreamkapture Inn* (see below).

★ **Andaluz** Baquerizo Moreno, at Junín ☎04 230 5796. Located just a few blocks from Malecón and 9 de Octubre, this bright, breezy hotel has comfortable rooms with a/c and hot water, a splash of artwork on the walls, a relaxing rooftop terrace and a lounge area with leather sofas and TV. $40

Dreamkapture Inn Alborada Doceava Etapa ☎04 224 2909, ⓦdreamkapture.com. A few kilometres from the centre, this is one of the city's few backpacker haunts. Secure, well maintained and friendly, the comfortable rooms have a/c and there's a small pool. The hostel also owns its own travel agency. Dorms $10, doubles $25

Iguanazu Hostal Cuidadela La Cogra ☎04 220 1143, ⓦiguanazuhostel.com. The hilltop location of this hostel offers a different experience of Guayaquil, with friendly service, charming wooden-floored rooms and a great view. Dorms $15, doubles $55

Hostal Linda Lorenzo de Garaicoa 809 ☎04 256 2495. New hotel overlooking Parque Centenario with marble floors and plush, well-furnished rooms. $40

Hostal Manso Malecón 1406, at Aguirre ☎04 252 6644, ⓦmanso.ec. A slice of Arabian boutique chic in Guayaquil with individually designed rooms, seated cushions and regular performances in the lounge area. $42

Mar de Plata Junín 718, at Boyacá ☎04 230 7610. Many of Guayaquil's budget hotels border on intolerable but this is a good deal. Rooms are basic but clean and come equipped with fans, cable TV and private bathrooms (a/c $5 extra). $20

Plaza St Rafael Chile 414 ☎04 232 7140. Smallish but

comfortable rooms with a/c, cable TV and hot water. Breakfast included. $35

Rizzo Clemente Ballén, at Chile ☎ 04 232 5210. Adequate rooms, some with small balconies, ideally situated next to Parque Bolívar. $44

Hostal Suites Madrid Quisquis 305, at Rumicacha ☎ 04 230 7804, ✉ hostalsuitesmadrid.com. Not the best location but certainly one of the best-value options in the city, with colourful decor, patterned bedspreads, spacious rooms, background music, a feast of artwork covering the walls and very friendly service. $25

EATING AND DRINKING

Guayaquil has a wide range of restaurants spread around the city. Downtown, there are plenty of cheap, basic places, while restaurants attached to hotels are overpriced. Las Peñas is the most pleasant area to eat, with a cluster of traditional cafés. An alternative is to take a taxi ($2–3) to the fashionable neighbourhood of Urdesa, where there's a wide range of restaurants along the main street Victor Emilio Estrada.

Las 3 Canastas Velez, at Chile. This colourful, informal café specializes in pastries, fruit salads, ice creams and traditional Ecuadorian meals. It's cheap, clean and portions are big (mains $3–4). There's a smaller sister café on Pedro Carbo, at Clemente Ballen.

⭐ **Aroma Café** Jardines del Malecón 2000. The best place to eat on the Malecón, with a wide selection of Ecuadorian specialities ($5–8) served in the cool, shaded atmosphere of the botanical gardens.

Arthur's Café Numa Pompillo, Las Peñas. Dramatically located restaurant perched over the river. The open windows make for a fresh, breezy experience and the menu offers local staples such as grilled fish, *ceviche* and fried pork chops for $6–9.

La Española Junín, at Boyaca. Excellent bakery with a wide selection of delicious cakes, pastries, sandwiches and big breakfasts for $1–3.

Frutabar Malecón, at Martínez. Misshapen tables, surfboards, tropical murals, a huge selection of *batidos* (fruit shakes) and imaginative burgers and sandwiches make this the perfect repose after a hard morning's sightseeing. $4–6.

El Hornero Estrada 906, Urdesa. Delicious pizzas baked in a large clay oven. Portions from $2.

Manantial Estrada 520, Urdesa. Large, popular café with benches, serving a wide range of Ecuadorian specialities (mains $5) and pitchers of beer. Service is a bit surly.

La Parillada del Ñato Estrada, at Laureles, Urdesa. Treat yourself to a huge plate of barbecued meats in this enormously popular Urdesa institution. There's a branch in the centre at Luque, at Pichincha. Mains $5–12.

Tasca Vasca Ballén 422, Parque Bolívar. Beautifully laid-out Spanish restaurant with a cosy cellar-like ambience and waiters in traditional dress. Large menu of tapas and Spanish specialities with mains at $6–10.

NIGHTLIFE

Guayaquileños love to party, so it's no surprise that the city has a nightlife to rival Quito's. Las Peñas has a wide selection of café-bars and Urdesa is also a good place for a few drinks after dinner. To hit the dancefloor, go to the Zona Rosa, between downtown and Las Peñas, around Rocafuerte and Pánama. Most bars open at 8pm and clubs at 10pm. Bars stop serving alcohol at midnight Mon–Thurs and at 2am Fri–Sat and most discos only open Thurs–Sat. There's usually a minimum consumption charge of $10 for discos, which includes entrance.

Chappus Estrada, Urdesa. A Guayaquil institution. Have a few drinks on the wooden balcony or hit the dancefloor – one of the few in Urdesa.

El Colonial Rocafuerte, at Imbabura, Zona Rosa. A traditional Peñas bar with Ecuadorian specialities and live music at weekends.

Diva Nicotina La Escalinata, Las Peñas. At the bottom of the steps of Las Peñas, you can catch some great live music here – from Cuban Habanera to jazz – accompanied by whisky and cigars.

El Galeón de Artur's La Escalinata, Las Peñas. With its maritime decor and live music at weekends, this is a good place for a drink and a light meal.

Liverpool Av Las Monjas 402, Urdesa. Bright, vibrant café-bar packed with Beatles memorabilia. Live music Tues–Sat.

Ojos del Perro Azul Panama, at Padre Aguirre. The name alone (eyes of the blue dog) make this worth a visit. It's a good place to catch live rock and latin music at weekends.

⭐ **La Paleta** Numa Pompillo Llona, Las Peñas. One of the city's most aesthetically pleasing watering holes with a bohemian atmosphere, cosy corners and bars on two floors.

Quimbita Galeria La Escalinata, Las Peñas. At the bottom of the steps, this art gallery doubles as a café-bar with live folk music at weekends.

DIRECTORY

Banks and exchange The most convenient downtown banks are Banco del Pacífico, Banco de Guayaquil and Banco Pichincha, all on Icaza and Pichincha.

Consulates Australia, San Roque, at Av Francisco de Orellana, Ciudadela Kennedy Norte ☎ 04 601 7529; Canada, Edificio Nobis Executive Centre, 702 Av Joaquin Orranita, at Av Juan Tanca Marengo ☎ 04 215 8333; UK, General Córdova 623, at Padre Solano ☎ 04 256 0400; US, 9 de Octubre, at García Moreno ☎ 04 232 3570.

Hospital Clínica Kennedy on Av del Periodista, Kennedy ☎ 04 228 6963.

Internet Internet 50C, Rumicacha, at Rendon.

Post office The main office is on Pedro Carbo, at Ballén, just off the Parque Bolívar.

The south coast beaches

At weekends, *Guayacos* flee the city's heat in droves and head west to the cooler Pacific beaches of the **Ruta del Sol**. It gets very crowded in peak season between Christmas and Easter, when the weather is hottest. Among the beach resorts, **Playas** is the closest to Guayaquil, **Salinas** is the playground of wealthy *Guayacos*, and surfer hangout **Montañita** draws in backpackers. Further north is the beautiful province of Manabí, which contains Ecuador's only protected coastal area, the **Parque Nacional Machalilla**. The port of **Puerto López** is the most convenient base to explore the park and Isla de la Plata, billed as the "poor man's Galápagos" because of its birdlife. **Whale-watching** is a highlight between June and September.

PLAYAS AND PUERTO EL MORRO

PLAYAS, one hour thirty minutes from Guayaquil by bus, attracts lower-middle-class *Guayacos*. Like all south-coast resorts, it's jammed in high season and quiet the rest of the year. The beach is very long but not sheltered and currents are strong, so take care in the water.

A few kilometres east of Playas is the small port of **Puerto El Morro**, which makes a great day-trip. To get here from Guayaquil, change at Playas. The main attractions are mangroves, birdlife and dolphins in the estuary, as well as Islas de los Pájaros, which has a large population of magnificent frigatebirds and pelicans.

TOUR OPERATOR

Ecoclub Los Delfines ☎ 04 252 9496, 🌐 puertoelmorro .blogspot.com. Arranges tours of Puerto El Morro (1hr 30min, $5; 3hr, $8). A short tour takes in the mangroves, lets you see dolphins and even do a spot of fishing, and a longer tour includes an extended boat trip and a walk on the Isla de los Pájaros.

ACCOMMODATION

There are plenty of well-priced hotels on the Playas water-front should you choose to stay.

Hostal Cattan Malecón ☎ 04 276 0179. This cheapie budget hotel is past *Dorado* (see below). **$20**
Hotel Dorado Malecón ☎ 04 276 0402. A good mid-range choice with a/c, private bath and cable TV. **$35**

EATING

Cabins line the beach selling great fresh seafood.
Los Ajos Jaime Roldos, at C 8. One of the best in town, with a more upscale atmosphere and range of fish, chicken and meat dishes. $8–12.
La Cabaña Tipica Malecón. A cosier alternative to the beach, doing seafood specialities at $4–6.

SALINAS

To new arrivals **SALINAS** looks like a wannabe Miami Beach with high-rise apartment blocks and expensive yachts. But it's worth stopping here, at least for a day-trip, to walk along the attractive waterfront and swim in the calm waters. The resort has plenty of great restaurants and nightlife. West of the Malecón is a second beach, **Chipipe**, which is quieter and has a plaza, church and park.

ARRIVAL AND INFORMATION

By bus Comfortable CLP buses run to and from Guayaquil (hourly; 2hr 30min); most come equipped with a/c, TV and seat belts. Change at Santa Elena for Montañita.
Tourist information The tourist information office (Enriquez Gallo, at C 30 ☎ 099 623 6725) is open sporadically in high season.

ACCOMMODATION

Book hotels ahead in high season, particularly at weekends and on national holidays. Hotels on the waterfront come at a premium, while inland from the waterfront, Salinas is rather ugly.
Cocos Malecón, at Fidón Tomala ☎ 04 277 2609, 🌐 cocos -hostal.com. The most economical of the options on the waterfront, with a restaurant, bar, disco and games room. **$40**
Francisco II Enríquez, at Rumiñahui ☎ 04 277 3544. A dependable mid-range option, with a/c and a small pool. The sister hotel, *Francisco*, is located behind. **$50**
Oro del Mar I C 23, at General Enrique ☎ 04 277 1334. One of the most economical choices, but like most of the cheap accommodation in Salinas, it's a bit shabby. There are three hotels of the same name dotted around town. **$30**
Yulee Eloy Alfaro, at Mercedes Molina ☎ 04 277 1334. In the more pleasant area of Chipipe, this brightly painted colonial-style hotel is a break from the high-rise concrete.

It has three levels of rooms and you won't find a cheaper option. $\overline{\$16}$

EATING

You're spoilt for choice on where to eat, particularly seafood. Avoid the seafood stalls, nicknamed "Cevichelandia", as sanitation is a problem. Salinas' nightlife hots up in high season.

Amazon Malecón ☎ 04 277 3671. International cuisine in a rustic ambience with mains for around $6–10.

La Bella Italia Malecón ☎ 04 277 1361. For a break from Ecuadorian fare, watch mouth-watering pasta and pizza prepared in front of you in this comfortable restaurant – and then devour. Mains $4–7.

La Ostra Nostra Eloy Alfaro, at Las Almendras ☎ 04 277 4028. Choose from a wide range of seafood, soups and meat (mains $5–10) at this extremely popular restaurant out towards Chipipe. Oysters ($12 per dozen) are a particular speciality.

MONTAÑITA

Perhaps there should be a sign at the entrance to **MONTAÑITA** that reads: "You are now leaving Ecuador". Such is the international vibe that you could be anywhere. At first sight, the town feels like countless backpacker havens, but whether you love it or hate it, you can't deny the place's infectious energy. The surfing contingent has been joined in recent years by hippies and partygoers, making it the coast's most buzzing resort for budget travellers. Many people stay for months, while others get out after a couple of excessive nights – if you're seeking a relaxing beach break, go elsewhere. Surfers can enjoy rideable breaks most of the year, frequently 2–3m on good days. It's not the best place to learn but there are plenty of experienced teachers. There's a renowned international surf competition around Carnaval (Feb/March).

ARRIVAL

By bus The bus stop is a couple of blocks inland from the beach on the corner of Rocafuerte. Comfortable CLP buses leave Guayaquil at 5am, 1pm and 5pm (3hr 30min). If you can't catch one of these, take a bus from Guayaquil to Salinas (hourly; daytime only) and ask the driver to drop you at Santa Elena (1hr) to catch a connection. Buses north to Puerto Lopez pass hourly (1hr). For Quito, go to Manta or Puerto Lopez and change.

TOUR OPERATORS

Carpe Diem Guido Chiriboga, at Rocafuerte ☎ 04 206 0043. Offers a wide range of tours – everything from kayaking, horseriding and snorkelling, to organized tours of Machalilla and even the jungle.

Sweet Surf C Quatro ☎ 099 738 9089. Run by a friendly Swedish-Ecuadorian couple, *Sweet Surf* offers surfboard rentals for $15/day ($4/hr) and 2hr lessons for $15, as well as tours ranging from day-trips to a week-long surf tour of the coast.

ACCOMMODATION

Montañita has a huge amount of accommodation and where you stay depends mainly on how much sleep you want to get. You can find a basic room for $5–7/person, but bear in mind the centre is often very noisy and at weekends partying continues until after dawn. The north end is quieter with the best-quality mid-range accommodation. Prices double on high season weekends and it's hard to find a room in the centre. You can negotiate prices in low season.

Abad Lounge Av Costanera, at Malecón ☎ 04 230 7707. Right on the beach, this new family-run hotel has tidy rooms, many with sea views and balconies. $\overline{\$20}$

★ **Casa del Sol** ☎ 099 248 8581, ⓦ casadelsolsurfcamp .com. Walk north all the way to the point to this very popular hangout run by a Californian surfer. The rooms are bright and breezy, and there's a great restaurant and bar area. Sea view costs extra. $\overline{\$40}$

El Centro de Mundo Malecón, at Rocafuerte ☎ 099 728 2831. Look no further for cheap, basic rooms than this three-storey, wooden beachfront building, just to the right of the junction of Rocafuerte with the beach. Dorms $\overline{\$3.50}$, doubles $\overline{\$14}$

Charos Malecón between 15 de Mayo & Rocafuerte ☎ 04 206 0044, ⓦ charoshostal.com. Just inland to the left of the beachfront. This is the most comfortable place to stay in the centre, with a/c rooms, a bar, restaurant and small pool. $\overline{\$45}$

Kamala Hostería ☎ 099 942 3754, ⓦ kamala-hosteria .minihostels.com. Escape the noise of Montañita completely at this hippy haven just north of Manglaralto. The individual cabins are set around a small swimming pool in front of the beach and there's also a bar, restaurant and dive school. $\overline{\$30}$

Hostal Pakaloro Av Costanera at the north end of Chiriboga ☎ 04 206 0092. A great budget deal, featuring newly refurbished rooms with private bath and cable TV. $\overline{\$18}$

Paradise South ☎ 04 290 1185. For something quieter and more upmarket, go north of town (past the second bridge) to enjoy the comfortable thatched cottages and large lawns of this tranquil, welcoming place. $\overline{\$25}$

6

EATING

There are scores of good restaurants in the centre of town. Montañita throws quite a party at weekends, particularly in high season (Dec–April). Most bars on the main street, Guido Chiriboga, offer two-for-one happy hours on cocktails ($3), but take it slow until things get going towards midnight.

Cañagrill Av Costanera. Round the corner from the main street Guido Chiriboga, this is the town's busiest disco, with two dancefloors playing a mix of electronic and Latin music. It gets packed in the early hours and the partying continues until after dawn. From 10pm at weekends; entrance $5.

★ **Hola Ola** 10 de Agosto. Two blocks inland, *Hola Ola* is turning into the centre of the town's social scene. Big breakfasts in the morning, a wide range of cocktails in the evening, parties at weekends and great international food in between. Mains $5–10.

Karukera Guido Chiriboga. A great choice for breakfast, this place specializes in crêpes and also serves up Caribbean cuisine such as fish in orange sauce. Mains $4–8.

Papillon Guido Chiriboga, at Rocafuerte, on the corner of the main street. Indulge in a range of sweet and savoury pancakes or relax with an ice-cream sundae. Mains $4–8.

Tiki Limbo Guido Chiriboga. This backpackers' favourite takes pride in its food ($6–9) and you´re bound to find something tantalizing on its imaginative, eclectic menu. Asian and vegetarian dishes are particular specialities. The brightly coloured rooms in the hostel upstairs are very popular ($20).

DOS MANGAS

DOS MANGAS is the best base to explore the tropical dry forest of the Cordillera Chongón. This community of 950 people makes a living from crafts and agriculture. It has a small information centre, and two paths through the forest to waterfalls and natural pools. Trucks from the main coast road head to Dos Mangas every hour and you can hire guides and horses (around $10 per person). The park entrance fee is $1. Alternatively, book a tour in Montañita.

OLÓN

This tranquil village on the other side of the point is developing as a quiet alternative to Montañita; it has a long beach and a few good hotels and restaurants. The sea isn't suitable for surfing but you could just about swim in it.

ACCOMMODATION

Hostería N&J ☎ 04 239 0643. This friendly place is on the beachfront. Breakfast included. $25

Quimbita ☎ 04 278 0204. The most interesting accommodation option is this charming, colourful hotel with a permanent art exhibition. $20

MONTAÑITA TO PUERTO LÓPEZ

Head north from Montañita and cross into the province of **Manabí**. This is probably the most beautiful stretch of Ecuador's coastline – so if you prefer peace to partying and watching wildlife rather than people this is the place to come. On the road to Parque Nacional Machalilla, you pass a succession of fishing villages – **Ayampe**, **Las Tunas**, **Puerto Rico** and **Salango**. Tourist facilities are still underdeveloped, but the area does contain some good-quality accommodation and the beaches are often deserted.

ACCOMMODATION

Between Montañita and Puerto Lopez there are several highly recommended *hosterías*.

Hostería Alandaluz ☎ 04 278 0690. Near Puerto Rico this award-winning eco-resort has a great location in front of the beach, enclosed by a garden, orchard and bamboo forest. Those on a budget can camp. Camping/person $7, doubles $40

★ **La Barquita** ☎ 04 278 0051, ⊛ hosterialabarquita .com. Near the tiny village of Puerto Rico. The main attraction is the wooden, boat-shaped restaurant, worth a visit even if you don't stay. The rooms are set in idyllic gardens with a small adventure playground and swimming pool. $20

Cabañas La Tortuga ☎ 04 278 0613, ⊛ latortuga.com .ec. These comfortable cabins are the only beachfront accommodation in Ayampe. For those on a budget there are bunk beds with shared bath and camping. Camping/ person $10, dorms $10, doubles $30

PUERTO LÓPEZ

PUERTO LÓPEZ is the tourism hub for the Machalilla area and the best base to explore **Parque Nacional Machalilla** and **Isla de la Plata**. The town boasts one of the most attractive locations on the coast, set in a wide bay surrounded by the green hills of Ecuador's largest protected coastal forest. The dusty Malecón has a certain beaten-down charm, and in the morning the sight of fishermen heading out from the bay gives the town a vibrant feel. Note that the town gets very busy on weekends during the whale-watching season (June–Sept), so booking accommodation in advance at that time is advisable.

ARRIVAL AND INFORMATION

By bus Buses drop passengers by the terminal on the main road, General Córdova, from where it's a short walk to the waterfront. Alternatively you can take a tricycle taxi ($0.50).

Destinations There are regular buses to Jipijapa (hourly; 1hr 30min), where you change to get to Guayaquil, La Libertad (daily; 3hr) or Salinas; Manta (hourly; 2hr). Reina del Camino (☎05 230 0207) offers comfortable secure services to Quito (8am and 8pm; 10hr).

Tourist information The local iTur office on Av Machalilla, at Atahualpa (open daily; ✉turismo@puertolopez.gov.ec), is two blocks inland and has plenty of leaflets and attentive service.

ACCOMMODATION

Hostal Itapoa Malecón ☎099 314 5894, ⊛hosteltrail .com/hosteriaitapoa. North of town, these Brazilian-run cabins set in a small garden are an endearing budget hide-away. **$20**

★ **Hosteria Mandala** ☎05 230 0181, ⊛hosteria mandala.info. North of town along the Malecón is this very popular travellers' option with beachfront cabins set in beautiful gardens, plus a games room, small library and a good restaurant. **$45**

Hosteria Nantu Malecón ☎099 781 4636. This new hotel is excellent value, offering mid-range rooms at a low price. Firm beds, hot water as well as a small pool and games room to keep you busy. **$30**

Piedra del Mar ☎05 230 0011. Boutique style at budget prices at Puerto Lopez's newest hotel. The colonial-style courtyard, pebble-dashed walls and small pool mark this out as the most interesting option in the centre of town. **$50**

Ruta del Sol Malecón, at Mariscal Sucre ☎05 230 0236. Comfortable hotel on south end of the Malecón with well-equipped rooms with a/c, hot water, cable TV, restaurant, postal service and friendly staff. **$30**

Sol Inn Juan Montalvo, at Eloy Alfaro ☎05 230 0248. The basic, wooden cabins and laidback vibe are ideal for those on a tight budget. Camping/person **$3**, dorms **$6**, doubles **$14**

EATING AND DRINKING

Espuma del Mar The decor is a bit tacky but this spacious restaurant does most dishes well, from breakfasts to snacks and evening meals. Mains $4–5.

Patacón Pisa'o General Córdova. For something different, try Colombian specialities such as *arepas* at this friendly little place where mains are $3–5.

Restaurant Carmita Stands out from the cluster of restaurants along the Malecón with a great selection of seafood (mains $5) in a polished setting.

★ **The Whale Café** At the south end of Malecón, this is a great place to eat and chat. The friendly American owners whip up everything from Thai noodles to pancakes and veggie specialities for around $6–9. Home-made bread for breakfast too.

PARQUE NACIONAL MACHALILLA

Ecuador's only coastal national park was set up in 1979 to preserve the rapidly disappearing tropical dry forest that once stretched north all the way to Costa Rica. It's a dramatic setting with thickly forested hills crowned by candelabra cacti, dropping down to pristine, peaceful beaches. The park headquarters (daily 8am–5pm; ☎05 230 0102) is based in Puerto López, opposite the market, just off the town's main road. This is where you pay your entrance fee (valid for five days; mainland only $12; Isla de la Plata only $15; combined ticket $20).

WHAT TO SEE AND DO

The best place to explore the park's dry forest is **Agua Blanca**, a village inhabited by some 280 indigenous people and an important archeological site of the Manteño culture that lived here from 800 to 1500 AD. Getting to Agua Blanca involves either taking a bus north from Puerto López and then walking the unpleasant 5km trail up a dirt track, or hiring a mototaxi ($5 one-way, $10 return). The museum houses an interesting collection of sculptures, funeral urns and pickled snakes. A guided tour ($5) includes museum entry followed by a two-hour forest walk. Highlights include the towering ceibos, barbasco and fragrant Palo Santo trees whose wood is burnt as incense and to repel mosquitoes. Take in the spectacular views up to San Sebastián before a refreshing soak in a pungent but relaxing sulphur pool, considered sacred by local indigenous people.

6

San Sebastián

The landscape rises to 800m inland, where the dry forest turns into the cloudforest of **San Sebastián**, where lush vegetation includes orchids, bamboo and wildlife such as howler monkeys, anteaters and 350 species of birds. This virgin forest can be explored on a 20km hike with a mandatory guide hired in Agua Blanca ($20). You can camp overnight or stay with local villagers.

Playa Los Frailes

A few kilometres further north is the entrance to **Playa Los Frailes**, a stunning virgin beach, often deserted in early mornings. Present your park ticket or pay the entrance fee at the kiosk, then either head straight for Los Frailes on a thirty-minute hike or take the 4km circular trail via the black-sand cove of La Payita and Playa La Tortiguita. To get straight to the beach, take a taxi from Puerto Lopez ($5 one-way).

ISLA DE LA PLATA

The tag of "poor man's Galápagos" is unfair to this small island 37km from Puerto López. **ISLA DE LA PLATA** will inevitably come up short in comparison with the world-famous archipelago, but it is worth a day-trip to see its birdlife or for whale-watching in the summer months. The island is home to numerous blue-footed boobies, masked boobies and frigate birds and these are the species most frequently on view. Red-footed boobies and waved albatrosses are also seen from April to October. The island has a small colony of sea lions, though it's rare to see them. Note that you can only visit the island with a tour operator (see opposite).

WHAT TO SEE AND DO

From the landing point in Bahía Drake, there are two circular **footpaths** around the island, the 3.5km Sendero Machete and the 5km Sendero Punta Escaleras.

CROSSING THE PERUVIAN BORDER

The only significant coastal town between Guayaquil and the Peruvian border is the transport hub, Machala. Some 75km south of here is the grubby border town of **Huaquillas**, the busiest crossing point from Ecuador to Peru. Spend as little time as possible here; Cuenca and Guayaquil are both at an easy distance by bus so there should be no need to stay overnight.

Grand Hotel Hernancor 1 de Mayo 323, at Hualtaco, Huaquillas ☎07 299 5467. This hotel has decent guest rooms with private bath and a/c. **$24**

La Habana T. Córdovez, at Santa Rosa, Huaquillas. A good choice for Ecuadorian meat and fish dishes and a filling set meal ($2.50).

INTO PERU

Crossing the border is a fraught business but you need to ensure you do it right. If you don't get the correct stamps on your passport, you're in big trouble. Keep your wits about you, a close eye on your belongings and avoid changing money here as the rates are bad. The border crossing is a bridge over the Río Zarumilla, but before crossing the border, get the **exit stamp** from the **Ecuadorian immigration office** (open 24hr; ☎07 299 6755), inconveniently located 3km north. If you're coming from Machala, ask the driver to stop here, otherwise take a taxi ($1.50). Then take a bus or taxi to the bridge, which must be crossed on foot, and get your passport checked by Peruvian officials on the other side. Note that the **entry stamp** is usually obtained at the main **Peruvian immigration office** at **Zarumilla** 2km away ($1 by mototaxi). There are regular direct buses to Tumbes, Piura, Trujillo or Lima. A taxi to Tumbes costs $5–7.

INTO ECUADOR

For those arriving in Ecuador, **buses** from Huaquillas leave from depots a few blocks from the international bridge. Co-op CIFA (☎07 293 0260, ⓦcifainternacional.com) goes to Machala (several/hr; 1hr), the closest city. CIFA also goes to Guayaquil (4hr 30min), as does Ecuatoriano Pullman (☎07 293 0197) and Rutas Orenses (☎07 293 7661). Panamericana (☎07 293 0141) has comfortable buses to Quito (6 daily; 12hr). For Cuenca (8 daily; 5hr) use Trans Azuay (☎07 293 0539). If you intend to go to Loja, it's better to cross from Peru at Macará.

The hikes are about three hours long and there's no shade, so bring sunscreen and a hat. The close encounters with the friendly boobies, which peer at you with mild curiosity, are the main highlight, but also watch out for colourful caterpillars crossing your path. Cool off after the hike with some snorkelling among an array of marine life including parrotfish and clownfish. Peak season is June to September (particularly July–Aug) when humpback whales arrive for the mating season, which is an awesome spectacle.

TOUR OPERATORS

The day-trip to Isla de la Plata can be arranged at several local tour operators and hotels on the Malecón in Puerto López. It generally costs $35–40/person including guide and light lunch but not including the park entrance fee. Recommended companies include:

Bosque Marino ☎ 099 707 1320, ⓦ bosquemarino.com.

Exploramar Diving ☎ 05 256 3905, ⓦ exploradiving.com (which also offers diving trips along the coast).

Naturis ☎ 05 230 0218, ⓦ machalillatours.com (specializes in community tourism and offers a wide range of multi-activity trips including kayaking, fishing and snorkelling ($25/person) as well as tours to San Sebastián).

The Galápagos Islands

Charles Darwin developed his monumental theory of evolution after travelling to the **GALÁPAGOS** in the 1830s, and it's no exaggeration that the creatures of these unworldly volcanic islands, 1000km west of the Ecuadorian coast, were fundamental in changing the way we view ourselves.

The array of **wildlife** in the Galápagos is spellbinding. From giant tortoises to marine iguanas, sea lions to sharks and blue-footed boobies to magnificent frigate birds, it's hard to know which way to turn. Nowhere else on earth can you view wild mammals, reptiles and birds that are utterly unconcerned by human presence – a legacy of there being few natural predators on the islands.

Visiting the Galápagos independently is now relatively easy and last-minute deals are better than ever. However, a week in the Galápagos will cost considerably more than one on the Ecuadorian mainland. The **low season** is May/June and September/October, while December to mid-April and July/August is high season, though cheap deals can still be found.

The Galápagos is a year-round destination, but conditions are best between December and April, with calmer seas and sunny weather with occasional rain on larger islands. From June to October the weather is cooler and the sea rougher. Whenever you choose to visit, you can only see a tiny percentage of the islands because 97 percent of the area is protected by the national park and the 70 registered visitor sites comprise only 0.01 percent of the landmass, a comforting fact for environmentalists.

ARRIVAL AND DEPARTURE

By plane Return flights to San Cristóbal or Baltra cost about $350 from Guayaquil and $400 from Quito with TAME (Quito ☎ 02 397 7100, Guayaquil ☎ 04 231 0305) or Aerogal (Quito ☎ 02 294 2800, Guayaquil ☎ 04 231 0346). Chilean airline LAN (☎ 1800 101075, ⓦ lan.com) has recently launched flights at slightly cheaper rates. In San Cristóbal it's a $2 taxi ride to the port, Puerto Baquerizo Moreno. If arriving on Balra, it's more complicated. To get to the main port Puerto Ayora involves a 10min bus ride south, a 10min ferry crossing and then a $2.50 bus (45min) or $15 taxi (40min). Note that to return to the airport from Puerto Ayora, the last bus usually leaves about 9.30am, after which a taxi or private transfer is the only option.

INFORMATION AND TOURS

Tourist information The Ministry of Tourism (☎ 05 252 6174, ⓦ www.turismo.gob.ec) has iTur offices in Puerto Ayora, Puerto Baquerizo Moreno and Puerto Villamil. Alternatively contact the Galápagos National Park (☎ 05 252 6511, ⓦ galapagospark.org). The Galápagos National Park entrance fee is $100, payable in cash on arrival. There is also a $10 transit card, which must be purchased in Quito or Guayaquil airport, that regulates the length of stay in the archipelago (3 months maximum).

Tour operators The price of tours, accommodation and cruises varies hugely. When booking from abroad, tours cost $2000–5000 for a week. Booking last-minute in Quito and Guayaquil brings the prices down to $500–1500 (not including flights). However, the most common way for backpackers to visit is to buy flights, stay in budget accommodation ($10–20/night), eat at cheap restaurants

6

6

WHERE TO SEE WILDLIFE IN THE GALÁPAGOS

Blue-footed boobies Most easily viewed on North Seymour, Punta Pitt (San Cristóbal), Española or Genovesa.

Frigatebirds Try Seymour Norte, Punta Pitt or Española.

Galápagos penguins Colonies on Floreana, Bartolomé, Fernandina and Isabela.

Giant tortoises Try the Charles Darwin Station on Santa Cruz or the larger breeding centres on Isabela and San Cristóbal.

Green sea turtles The best-known nesting sites are Bartolomé, Tortuga Bay (Santa Cruz) and Gardner Bay (Española).

Iguanas The marine variety is found on all major islands; see their land cousins on Seymour Norte, South Plaza or Santa Fé.

Sea lions To see them underwater, the best snorkelling spots are Champion Island (Floreana) and La Isla de los Lobos (San Cristóbal). Or walk among a colony at South Plaza or La Lobería (San Cristóbal). Males are territorial, so keep your distance.

Sharks Docile white-tipped and black-tipped reef sharks are best viewed off Floreana, North Seymour, Bartolomé and Leon Dormido (San Cristóbal), while hammerhead sharks are mainly seen by divers (also at Leon Dormido).

Waved albatross Exclusively found on Española from April to November.

and pick up day-trips locally ($50–150/day). Doing it this way, it's possible to spend a week on the islands for less than $1200 total, including flights.

GETTING AROUND

By plane The airline EMETEBE (Santa Cruz ☎ 05 252 6177, San Cristóbal ☎ 05 252 0615, Isabela ☎ 05 252 9255; ⓦ emetebe.com) flies small eight-seater planes between San Cristóbal, Baltra and Isabela (several times per week; $160 one-way or $260 return, plus $15 taxes).

By ferry Daily services on small launches connecting Santa Cruz with San Cristóbal and Isabela (all routes $25 one-way; 2hr–2hr 30min). The ferries leave Isabela at 6am and San Cristóbal at 7am, and depart Santa Cruz for both islands at 2pm. There are usually two boats, but you should book one day in advance at a registered agent in the main ports. Note that it's a bumpy ride, particularly at 2pm.

ISLA SANTA CRUZ

This is the most developed island in the Galápagos and its capital **PUERTO AYORA** is the central tourism hub where most visitors arrive. It's by no means the most interesting island, but the central location and wide range of hotels, restaurants and tour operators make it the best base to explore surrounding islands.

Puerto Ayora

In Puerto Ayora you can arrange tours and pick up last-minute deals. A visit to the Charles Darwin Research Station to see the tortoises is worth it, and there are some interesting short hikes out of town.

WHAT TO SEE AND DO

There are various attractions close to Puerto Ayora but to see them you need to take the **Bay Tour** ($35 from most local operators). The tour takes in La Lobería, where you can snorkel with sea lions, Playa de los Perros, where marine iguanas and various birds are seen, Las Tintoreras, channels where sharks are often found, and Las Grietas (see opposite).

A fifteen-minute walk east of town is the **Charles Darwin Research Station** (daily 7am–6pm; free; ☎ 05 252 6146, ⓦ darwinfoundation.org), which contains an information centre and a museum. The highlight is the giant tortoise enclosure where you can view the Galápagos giants close-up. Of the original fourteen subspecies, eleven have survived. "Lonesome George" was the most famous resident until his death in 2012 meant the extinction of his Pinta island subspecies. Note that the station gets quite busy with tour groups so come early if possible, and you can actually see more tortoises at the breeding centres in San Cristóbal and Isabela.

If you're in Puerto Ayora at the beginning or end of your trip and want to kill a few hours, then the best option is **Tortuga Bay**. Follow the trail from the western edge of town along a paved path through cactus forest (a 45min walk with little shade). The first bay is not actually Tortuga Bay, but one of the longest beaches in the archipelago, popular with surfers but dangerous to swim. Walk to the end of this beach and cross over to a lagoon to find the bay where marine turtles come to lay their eggs. Note that the beach closes at 5pm so leave the port earlier than 3pm to have time to enjoy it.

Las Grietas

Another side trip from the port with a relaxing dip at the end is the walk to **Las Grietas**, a crevice in the rocks that supplies the port with much of its fresh water. Take a water taxi ($0.60) across the bay towards Playa de Los Alemanes, then venture along rocky trails for a further twenty minutes to reach Las Grietas. Fissures in the lava rocks have created two layers of brackish water – saline and fresh. It's a beautiful, sheltered place for a swim. Be aware that the rocky trails are a bit tricky; walking shoes will come in handy.

The highlands

The highlands offer a very different experience to the beaches on Santa Cruz and it's worth venturing inland to see the diversity of the island. At El Chato, you can observe giant tortoises in their natural habitat in the reserve (entrance $3 including guide). Nearby are the lava tunnels, which are naturally formed and have lighting so you can walk through them. Note that you need to crawl under a low wall to get out unless you walk back to the entrance. Either side of the main road which cuts through Santa Cruz are the Gemelos (twins), collapsed 30m-deep craters. The sheer drop into the craters, covered in vegetation, makes them an impressive sight; tour groups often stop on the way to or from the airport. All of the attractions above can be seen on a guided tour with any of the tour operators in Puerto Ayora ($80 for groups up to 14), or, to save money, hire a taxi in the port to take you to all of them ($30), which can be done in two or three hours.

Las Bachas

On the north coast, **Las Bachas**, once a base for the US military, is a long white-sand beach often covered in

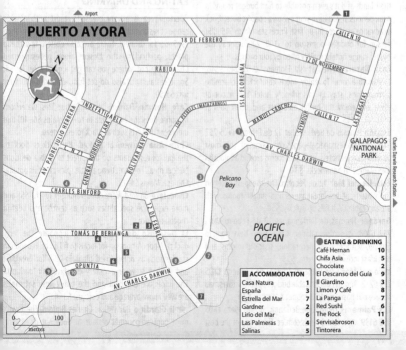

PUERTO AYORA

Pelicano Bay

GALÁPAGOS NATIONAL PARK

Charles Darwin Research Station

PACIFIC OCEAN

0   100
metres

■ **ACCOMMODATION**

Casa Natura	1
España	3
Estrella del Mar	7
Gardner	2
Lirio del Mar	6
Las Palmeras	4
Salinas	5

● **EATING & DRINKING**

Café Hernan	10
Chifa Asia	5
Chocolate	2
El Descanso del Guía	9
Il Giardino	3
Limon y Café	8
La Panga	7
Red Sushi	6
The Rock	11
Servisabroson	4
Tintorera	1

6

Sally Lightfoot crabs; flamingos also abound in the lagoons inland. Tour operators often combine a visit here with other excursions such as North Seymour (see p.635).

ACCOMMODATION

Santa Cruz has the largest selection of accommodation on the islands and it's even possible to find budget rooms in peak periods. If you have your eye on a specific hotel, book in advance as places fill up fast. Prices start from $15–25/person for budget rooms up to $100–200/night in the higher-range hotels, mainly filled by tour groups.

Casa Natura Petrel, at Isla Floreana ☎02 246 9846, Ⓦ vianatura.com. To enjoy more comfort in charming surroundings, stay at this friendly hotel 10min out of town and enjoy the buffet breakfast and small pool at the back. $145

España Thomas de Berlanga, at 12 de Febrero ☎05 252 6108, Ⓦ hotelespanagalapagos.com. One of the most popular budget hotels, with neat rooms around a colourful courtyard with hammocks. $30

Estrella del Mar 12 de Febrero. The cheapest hotel on the waterfront has great views and simple rooms with a/c and cable TV. It fills up quickly. $50

Gardner Thomas de Berlanga, at 12 de Febrero ☎05 252 6108, Ⓦ gardnergalapagoshotel.com. Next door to *España*, with elegant decoration, spacious rooms and breakfast included. A/c extra. $35

Lirio del Mar Islas Plaza, at Thomas de Berlanga ☎05 252 6212. Another dependable budget option with a small terrace but basic, no-frills rooms. A/c extra. $30

Las Palmeras Thomas de Berlanga, at Islas Plaza ☎05 252 6139, Ⓦ hotelpalmeras.com.ec. This is one of the best

mid-range options in town. Rooms are plushly decorated and there's a large pool on the terrace and even a small disco downstairs at weekends. $85

Salinas Islas Plaza, at Thomas de Berlanga ☎05 252 6212. Across from *Lirio del Mar*, this is a well-established budget hotel. Ground-floor rooms are very basic, with more comfort and higher prices on the upper floors. $35

EATING AND DRINKING

Puerto Ayora is a very pleasant resort with a wide range of restaurants, mostly in the slightly higher range ($15–25 for dinner). There are also quite a few cheap places, particularly the *kioskos* along pedestrianized Charles Binford, where you can get a good meal for $5. Some restaurants also do set lunches and dinners for just $3.50.

Café Hernan Darwin, at Av Baltra. This waterfront favourite does the best pizza in town (mains $6–10) and indulgent desserts such as black forest gateau.

Chifa Asia Darwin, at Binford. Backpackers flock to the *kioskos* restaurants on this street to grab a delicious budget meal. For something a little spicier try this popular Chinese. Mains $4–6.

Chocolate Binford. Very good-value set lunch ($5) and more expensive specialities such as *ceviche* and beef in chocolate sauce.

El Descanso del Guía Darwin (opposite the ferry docks). A popular option for locals to fill up on Ecuadorian staples such as *bolon* (fried plantain ball) for breakfast and chicken stew or a variety of white fish for lunch. The juices are excellent and the two-course set meals are well above average and cost just $3–4.

★ **Il Giardino** Darwin, at Charles Binford. The town's most popular gourmet restaurant does not disappoint, with a menu featuring home-made panini and crêpes, plus delicious ice creams and sorbets. Mains $6–10.

Limon y Café Darwin, at 12 de Febrero. Friendly, popular bar to start the evening with music, chat, pool and cards.

La Panga Darwin, at Thomas de Berlanga. The town's main disco, which pumps out Latin and international music until 2am. *Bongos*, the bar upstairs, is a more laidback place for a drink.

Red Sushi Red Mangrove Inn, Darwin. Treat yourself to an indulgent platter of sushi ($10–20) at this upscale restaurant on the waterfront.

The Rock Darwin, at Islas Plaza. Named after the first Galápagos bar set up on Baltra in the 1940s, this endearing place serves up a feast, from Mexican *quesadillas* to teriyaki fish fillets ($6–10). The wide variety of juices, shakes and cocktails washes it all down.

Servisabroson Binford. One of the many cheap and informal places on the *kioskos* offering filling plates of chicken, pork and seafood (mains $4–7). The fish in coconut is particularly popular.

Tintorera Darwin, at Floreana. A great place for a healthy organic breakfast or snack. Vegetarian specialities ($3–6) are popular and the set lunch ($4) is a good deal.

AROUND ISLA SANTA CRUZ
Isla North Seymour

Off the north coast of Santa Cruz is the tiny island of **NORTH SEYMOUR**, which offers some of the best opportunities in the archipelago to watch frigatebirds and get close to blue-footed boobies. Follow the 2.5km circular trail around the island to see frigates nesting and the amusing courtship of the boobies. Sea lions and iguanas are also common. A day tour is comparatively pricey ($125/person with Puerto Ayora tour operators) due to restricted access.

Islas Plazas

Off the east coast of Santa Cruz are the two tiny islands of **Plazas**, home to a large sea-lion colony and a great place to observe these animals up close on land. You can only visit the south island, where a 1km trail around the cliffs offers good views of birdlife including pelicans and

---

CRUISES

Although many budget travellers now choose to travel independently and stay in hotels, in many ways the best way to see the Galápagos is on a **cruise**. If you can deal with the seasickness, which is likely on all but the most luxurious boats, then you'll be rewarded with more quality time at sites and be spared the daily return journey to a port. There are also many sites only accessible to cruise boats.

Vessels that tour the Galápagos range from small boats to luxury cruise yachts carrying ninety passengers. Five-day tours allow visitors to explore the islands close to Santa Cruz, while eight-day tours include islands further afield. Single-cabin supplements are usually very high. If you have some flexibility, you can make substantial **savings** on cruises by booking last-minute in Quito or Guayaquil. Prices are even lower booking last-minute in Puerto Ayora and you could be lucky enough to get the higher-level cruises on the cheap. Always check the official grading of the boat before booking. Prices below are full prices for eight days based on two sharing (note last-minute discounts can be as little as 50 percent of these prices). Boats listed are not necessarily recommended. The rock-bottom economy-class boats have all but disappeared as budget travellers increasingly opt for land-based tours.

Tourist class boats cost $1100 per week or $125 per day and offer a basic level of comfort. They have Class 2 guides with a good level of knowledge and English-language skills. Boats include *Pelikano*, *Rumba*, *Sea Man* and *Yolita*.

Tourist-superior boats cost $1600 or $150 per day and have more comfortable cabins, better food and Class 2 guides. Boats include *Spondylus*, *Free Enterprise*, *Aida Maria*, *Angelique* and *Encantada*.

First-class yachts cost $2000–3500 or $250–300 per day, can travel faster and have

a decent level of comfort, high-quality food and Class 3 guides, the highest level of accreditation. Boats include *Eric*, *Letty*, *Flamingo*, *Galápagos Adventure*, *Monserrat*, *Beagle*, *Tip Top* and *San José*.

Deluxe vessels cost $3500–5000 or over $500 per day. These are the largest yachts and ships with the most stability and have extra facilities such as jacuzzis and more spacious social areas. Boats include *Galápagos Legend*, *Galápagos Explorer* and *Santa Cruz*.

frigatebirds. There's also a sea-lion bachelor colony, where defeated males congregate. Like north Seymour, day tours cost $125/person, combined with Punta Carrion.

Isla Santa Fé

6

Southeast of Puerto Ayora, the small island of **SANTA FÉ** has great snorkelling as well as opportunities to see white-tipped reef sharks, marine iguanas, sea lions and stingrays. Santa Fe land iguanas laze around the trails that wind through a forest of 10m-high *Opuntia* cacti. Access to the island's land sites is restricted to cruise boats, but there are day-trips from Puerto Ayora (around $60), which are of limited appeal because you can only visit selected offshore sites and are not permitted to land on the island itself.

ISLA SAN CRISTÓBAL

The most easterly island of the archipelago, this is the administrative centre of the islands. It's quieter than Santa Cruz, which may appeal to you, and the large population of sea lions in the main port is a particular highlight.

WHAT TO SEE AND DO

The most popular boat trip ($60) combines Isla de Los Lobos, where you can snorkel with playful sea lions, and Leon Dormido, one of the best snorkelling and diving sites in the archipelago, with great opportunities to see reef sharks, turtles, stingrays and even hammerhead sharks. Inland, highlights include El Junco Lagoon, one of the few freshwater lakes in the islands, with abundant birdlife. Nearby is the Galapaguera, a giant-tortoise reserve set in dry forest. To visit these two attractions as well as nearby beach Puerto Chino, either take a guided tour ($50) or hire a taxi. On the far east of the island is Punta Pitt, an excellent dive site, visited only by cruises.

Puerto Baquerizo Moreno

The capital is smaller than Puerto Ayora and it has the feel of a quieter tourism hub with hotels, restaurants, tour operators, and a pleasant waterfront and beach usually covered in sea lions.

A fifteen-minute walk north of town past the small, popular Mann Beach is the **Centro de Interpretación** (8am–5pm daily; free), which provides a more in-depth overview than the exhibition at Charles Darwin Station in Puerto Ayora. Learn about the islands' history, development and current environmental problems, split into three galleries. Continue walking past the centre and you will find a forked path that leads to Cerro Tijeretas (Frigatebird Hill) to observe the birds and enjoy sweeping views over the bay below. Then take the other path down to Playa Cabo de Horno, which has good snorkelling. On the opposite end of town, it's a forty-minute walk to La Lobería, a large sea-lion colony, which is not technically part of the national park. There's also good surfing nearby (taxi from port $2).

TOUR OPERATORS

Tours to Leon Dormido and the highlands can be arranged with most tour operators in town, including Sharksky (Española; ⓣ 05 252 1188, ⓦ sharksky.com), Chalo's (Española; ⓣ 05 252 0953) and Galakiwi (Darwin; ⓣ 05 252 1562, ⓦ southernexposuretours.co.nz). The best diving option is Dive and Surf Club (Melville; ⓣ 099 409 5450, ⓦ divesurfclub.com).

ACCOMMODATION

Casa Blanca Malecón, at Melville ⓣ 05 252 0392, ⓦ casablancagalapagos.com. This Moorish Moroccan throwback is the most elegant mid-range place in town with rustic a/c rooms, wide balconies and an art gallery downstairs. $50

Hostal Leon Dormido José de Villamil, at Malecón ⓣ 05 252 0169. The best-value budget option – clean rooms with private bath, fans and TV. $40

Hotel Mar Azul Alsacio Northia, at Esmeraldas ⓣ 05 252 0139. The inland location on the main road is not ideal, but cheap rooms with a/c and cable TV make it worth a look. $33

Hostal San Francisco Malecón ⓣ 05 252 0304. A cheap option with no-frills, basic rooms, ideal for those on a tight budget. $20

Suites Bellavista Malecón, at Melville ⓣ 05 252 0352. This is an excellent mid-range option with smart, a/c rooms on the waterfront. $50

6

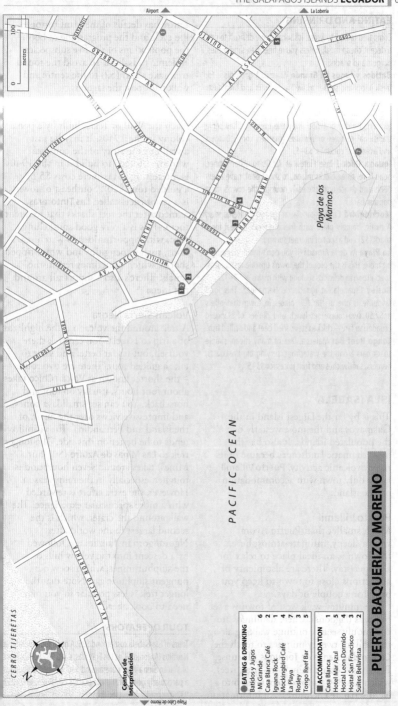

PACIFIC OCEAN

Playa de los Marinos

PUERTO BAQUERIZO MORENO

Airport

La Lobería

CERRO TIJERETAS

Centros de Interpretación

Playa Cabo de Horno

0 — 100 metres

● **EATING & DRINKING**

Batidos y Jugos	6
Mi Grande	2
Casa Blanca Café	1
Iguana Rock	4
Mockingbird Café	7
La Playa	3
Rosley	5

Tongo Reef Bar

■ **ACCOMMODATION**

Casa Blanca	1
Hotel Mar Azul	5
Hostal Leon Dormido	4
Hostal San Francisco	3
Suites Bellavista	2

6

EATING AND DRINKING

Compared to Puerto Ayora, it's surprisingly difficult to find a decent cheap meal, unless you're fine with sandwiches, burgers and snacks.

Batidos y Jugos Mi Grande Villamil. A good place for fresh juices and shakes as well as burgers and breakfasts for $1.50–3.

★ **Casa Blanca Café** Malecón, at Melville. Good place to start the day or while away the evening. They serve traditional *tamales* or *humitas* (mashed corn), burgers and a range of cocktails. $3–5.

Iguana Rock J Jose Flores, at Av Quito. After dinner, head here, three blocks inland, to shoot pool, have a few beers and dance until the early hours at the town's most popular bar.

Mockingbird Café Española, at Ignacio de Hernández. A rustic, homely place with friendly service, ideal for a snack ($2) and a spot of internet surfing.

La Playa Av de la Armada. If you don't mind spending a bit more, this is the pick of the town's upscale restaurants, specializing in delicious seafood with mains at $7–12.

Rosley Española, at Ignacio de Hernández. This local favourite is one of the few places in town that offers a $2.50 two-course set lunch and dinner of standard Ecuadorian fare – chicken stew, fried beef and grilled fish.

Tongo Reef Bar Malecón. One of many cheap, simple snack bars along the waterfront, serving big breakfasts, burgers, sandwiches and fruit juices for $3–5.

ISLA ISABELA

This is by far the largest island in the Galápagos and the most westerly of the populated islands. It also has the most dramatic landscapes because of its recent volcanic activity. **Puerto Villamil** is the only town with accommodation on the island.

Puerto Villamil

Much smaller than Puerto Ayora, with a sleepy, intimate atmosphere, this town is an ideal place to relax for a longer stay. There are also plenty of attractions close to town to keep you busy for a couple of days.

Five minutes' walk west of town is a set of pozas (lagoons), where flamingos are commonly seen. Continue walking along the trail for twenty minutes to reach the **Centro de Crianza de Tortugas** (Tortoise Breeding Centre; daily 9am–5pm; free), which has 850 tortoises separated into eight separate enclosures. An information

centre has details of the giant tortoise's life cycle and the programme to boost the populations of the five subspecies endemic to Isabela. To avoid the round trip, take a taxi ($2) to the centre and walk back past the lagoons.

Continuing along the coast to the west, it's a pleasant but longer walk to reach the Wall of Tears, built by a penal colony in the 1940s. It may be just a wall but the story of the convicts who were forced to build it in the 1940s is interesting (a taxi here costs $5 or a guided tour $20). Southeast of town is a set of islets called **Las Tintoreras**, named after the reef sharks that frequent them. This is a very good snorkelling spot, with opportunities to watch sea lions, turtles, penguins and white-tipped sharks, which sometimes rest in the canals. There's also a short trail around the islets.

Volcán Sierra Negra

A trek around the volcano is the highlight of a trip to Isabela. You can trek there yourself, but it's far better and safer to take a guided tour. There are two routes – the shorter known as **Volcán Chico** takes about four hours, usually on foot and horseback. You can see small lava cones and impressive views over the north of the island and Fernandina. The visibility tends to be better on this side. The longer trek to **Las Minas de Azufre** (Sulphur Mines) takes around seven hours and is tougher, especially in the rainy season. However, the extra effort is rewarded with a more spectacular experience. The walk around the crater, which is the second largest in the world after Ngorongoro in Tanzania, is followed by a descent into the yellow hills of the sulphur mines, which spew out pungent sulphuric gas. Note that the longer trek is less popular so you may need to book ahead.

TOUR OPERATORS

Tours of Isla Isabela cost around $25. A good tour operator is Nautilus (Antonio Gil, at Las Fragatas; ☎ 05 252 9076). Tours of Volcán Sierra Negra are around $40. Wilmer Quezada is a particularly good local guide (☎ 098 687 8626, ☎ 05 252 9326) or use Nautilus (see above).

ACCOMMODATION

There is quite a large accommodation offering for such a small town and it may be possible to negotiate because hotels don't fill up that often. Accommodation on the beach tends to be a bit more expensive than inland.

Dolphin House Antonio Gil ☎ 05 252 9138. Great for dramatic views of the ocean, but beware of the insistent cockerels guaranteed to wake you before dawn. Rooms are adequate – you're paying extra for the location. Breakfast included. **$45**

Posada del Caminante Near Cormoran ☎ 05 252 9407. For those on a tighter budget in search of an informal atmosphere, try this place, a 15min walk inland. Most rooms have a kitchen and there's a communal fridge and free laundry. **$20**

Rincon de George 16 de Marzo, at Antonio Gil ☎ 05 252 9214. Offers comfortably furnished rooms with firm beds, a/c and hot water. **$30**

San Vicente Cormorant, at Escalacias ☎ 05 252 9140. This mid-range inland hotel, popular with tour groups, has a quiet courtyard, good restaurant and comfortable rooms. **$60**

EATING AND DRINKING

Bar Beto Antonio Gil. At the far end of the main road, one of the few open-air bars in town; a place where you can sip pricey cocktails on wooden tables overlooking the beach.

★ **La Choza** Antonio Gil (in front of the park). Puts on a barbecued feast (mains $8–15) in a colourful, rustic setting.

El Encanto Antonio Gil. A good option for seafood at $5–7. *Ceviche* to breaded shrimps and grilled fish.

Tres Hermanos Antonio Gil. A cheaper option on Antonio with simple but good meals, ranging from breakfasts, burgers and sandwiches to fish with *patacones*, rice and salad ($3–6).

NORTHERN ISLANDS

Isla Santiago

Northwest of Santa Cruz are the blackened lava fields of **ISLA SANTIAGO**, also known as San Salvador, only accessible to cruises. Highlights of the island include the lava trails of **Sullivan Bay**. On the western side is **Puerto Egas**, the best landing point to hike along the lava flow and watch countless crabs and marine iguanas. On the southeastern tip of Santiago, the waters around the volcanic cone of **Sombrero Chino** are also excellent for snorkelling.

Bartolomé, just off the east coast, is available on day-trips. It contains the Galápagos's most famous landmark, **Pinnacle Rock**, a partially eroded lava formation. Climb up 108m to a viewpoint commanding spectacular views over the 40m-high rock with two horseshoe-shaped beaches in the foreground and the blackened lava of Santiago's Sullivan Bay beyond. There's very good snorkelling below and opportunities to see the Galápagos penguins and marine turtles. Bartolomé can be visited on a day-trip from Puerto Ayora ($125 per person with Puerto Ayora tour operators).

Genovesa

This is one of the remotest northern islands, only included on cruises. However, it is worth the eight-hour overnight trip to see the largest red-footed booby population in the archipelago. The two visitor sites are Darwin Bay Beach, with a trail to see boobies and frigates, and a boat trip along the cliffs at Prince Philip steps, named after a royal visit in the 1960s.

SOUTHERN ISLANDS

Isla Floreana

The southern island of **FLOREANA** has a small population at Puerto Velasco Ibarra. It was actually the first island to be populated due to its freshwater supply, and a descendant of the German Wittmer family runs Hotel Wittmer (☎ 05 252 0150; $50), but the infrequent transportation and strict regulations mean that the most practical way to visit is on a cruise or a day tour. Post Office Bay is the most common landing point for cruises, with its quirky post office barrel – leave a postcard, hoping a fellow tourist will post it, and take letters to post in your country. In the highlands, there is a small tortoise-breeding centre and caves that were inhabited by pirates in the sixteenth century. Punta Cormorant is a good place to observe flamingos and various wading birds. The islands of Enderby and Champion are excellent spots for snorkelling, while

6

6

TOUR OPERATORS

In Quito Galapagos Tours (Amazonas 2331, at Veintimilla; ☎02 254 6028, ⓦgalapagostours.net); Metropolitan Touring (Av Amazonas N20–39, at 18 de Septiembre; ☎02 250 6650, ⓦmetropolitan-touring .com); Ninfa Tour (Av Amazonas N24–66, at J Pinto; ☎02 222 3124); Nuevo Mundo Expeditions (Av Coruña N26–207, at Orellana; ☎02 250 9431, ⓦnuevomundo expeditions.com); Parir (General Baquedano, at JL Mera; ☎02 222 0892).

In Guayaquil Centro Viajero (Baquerizo Moreno 1119, at 9 de Octubre; ☎04 230 1283); Ecoventura (Miraflores Av Central 300ª; ☎04 220 7177, ⓦecoventura.com); Metropolitan Touring (Artarazana C 11A NE103; ☎04 228 6565, ⓦmetropolitan-touring.com); Ninfa Tour

(Córdova 646, at Urdaneta; ☎04 230 0182); Via Natura (Junín 114, at Malecón, Ed. Torres del Rio, Floor 7; ☎04 256 9052, ⓦvianatura.com).

In Puerto Ayora Galapatour (Av Rodriguez Lara) ☎05 252 6088); Galapagos Deep (Indefatigable, at Matazarno; ☎05 252 7045; Galapagos Voyager (Av Charles Darwin, at Colono; ☎05 252 6833); Moonrise Travel (Av Charles Darwin; ☎05 252 6348); Scuba Iguana (Av Charles Darwin; ☎05 252 6497); Galapagos Sub-Aqua (Av Charles Darwin; ☎05 252 6350, ⓦgalapagos -sub-aqua.com); Metropolitan Touring (Finch Bay Eco Hotel; ☎05 252 6297, ⓦmetropolitan-touring.com); We are the Champions Tours (Av Charles Darwin; ☎05 252 6951, ⓦwearethechampionstours.com).

---

nearby Devil's Crown, a half-submerged volcanic cone, is one of the top snorkelling and diving sites in the archipelago, with reef sharks, turtles and rays. A day-trip from Puerto Ayora costs about $75, but only includes the highlands, Enderby and Champion. The tour misses out many of the most famous sites, which are restricted to cruises.

Isla Española

ESPAÑOLA is the southernmost island and can only be visited via a cruise. The island is the sole place in the Galápagos with a colony of waved albatrosses, which flock here between April and November. Seeing them land at one of the "albatross airports" is quite a sight. As well as sea lions, iguanas and boobies, there are opportunities to see the rare hood mockingbird and the finches made famous by Charles Darwin's studies.

Punta Suárez is the most popular landing point, and there is excellent snorkelling at Turtle Island.

ISLA FERNANDINA AND OUTLYING ISLANDS

West of Isabela is the volcanic **FERNANDINA**, which can only be visited on a cruise. The highlight is the huge population of marine iguanas sunning themselves on the rocks of **Punta Espinoza**, the only visitor site; there are also trails through the recently formed lava fields. Fernandina's volcano La Cumbre was the most recent eruption in the Galápagos, in April 2009. Further north are the tiny, remote islands of **Darwin** and **Wolf**. These are restricted to specialist diving trips to see large populations of hammerhead and whale sharks.

KAIETEUR FALLS

The Guianas

HIGHLIGHTS

❶ **Kaieteur Falls** One of the world's highest single-drop waterfalls. **See p.653**

❷ **Rupununi Savannah** Friendly Amerindian villages and fantastic wildlife viewing. **See p.654**

❸ **Awarradam** Unique Saramaccan culture and jungle walks. **See p.668**

❹ **Galibi Nature Reserve** An important turtle-nesting beach. **See p.669**

❺ **Centre Spatial Guyanais** View a space rocket being launched into orbit. **See p.679**

❻ **Îles du Salut** Spot monkeys and peacocks at these former French prison islands. **See p.680**

HIGHLIGHTS ARE MARKED ON THE MAP ON PP.644–645

ROUGH COSTS

Daily budget Basic G: US$65; S: US$45; FG: US$100
Drink Beer G: US$1.70; S: US$1.50; FG: US$5
Food G: *Pepperpot* (stew) US$4; S: *Saoto soep* US$3; FG: *Blaff* (soup) US$12
Guesthouse/budget hotel G: US$15–60; S: US$18–50; FG: US$50–80
Travel Georgetown–Lethem, bus: 18hr, US$60

FACT FILE

Population G: 751,000; S: 524,000; FG: 203,000
Official languages G: English; S: Dutch; FG: French
Currencies G: Guyanese dollar (G$); S: Suriname dollar (SRD); FG: Euro (€)
Capitals G: Georgetown; S: Paramaribo; FG: Cayenne
International phone codes G: ☎592; S: ☎597; FG: ☎594
Time zones GMT -3hr (-4hr in Guyana)

Introduction

The Guianas, which comprise the independent nations of Guyana and Suriname and the French overseas département of French Guiana, feel more Caribbean than South American. As a result of colonial legacies the official languages are English (Guyana), Dutch (Suriname) and French (French Guiana), and each has an ethnically diverse population, a mix of indigenous peoples, descendants of European colonizers and their slaves, East Indians, Indonesians, Southeast Asian refugees and Haitians.

Tucked between Brazil's Amazonian region and the continent's northeast coast, the verdant Guianas are criss-crossed by rivers; indeed, the Amerindian word *guiana* means "land of many waters". Between eighty and ninety percent of the area is covered by dense tropical forests. Jaguars, pumas, caimans, iguanas, ocelots, tapirs and other diverse wildlife thrive in this environment, making the Guianas an ecotourism haven. That said, wildlife can remain stubbornly elusive, and though you're bound to see birds, monkeys and small rodents, you'll be very lucky to spot a big cat. It's worth the expense to stay in a **jungle lodge**, to take a **river trip** down some of its majestic waterways, or to witness **sea turtles** laying their eggs.

The towns take a back seat to nature in the Guianas, but the capital cities of **Georgetown** (Guyana), **Paramaribo** (Suriname) and **Cayenne** (French Guiana) have a certain charm and are worth exploring for a day or two. Paramaribo is the best preserved, Georgetown has wonderful wooden architecture, and edgy Cayenne offers a mainland France-style nightlife. These three capitals comprise the main **international gateways** from the Caribbean, North America and Europe. Within South America, you can fly directly to all three from **Belém** and **Boa Vista** in Brazil.

Borders between the Guianas are marked by imposing rivers, and crossing involves taking infrequent **ferries** and **motorized boats**. From Guyana to Suriname, you'll need to cross the Corentyne River from **Molson Creek** to **South Drain** near Nieuw Nickerie (see box, p.659); and from Suriname to French Guiana, the Maroni River from **Albina** to **Saint-Laurent du Maroni** (see box, p.684). Overland travel between the three countries, although lengthy, is relatively straightforward.

WHEN TO VISIT

Temperatures in the Guianas vary little from one month to the next: generally 20°C to 33°C, with a mean temperature of around 27°C (slightly hotter in the interior owing to the absence of the cooling coastal trade winds). This makes deciding when to plan a trip much more dependent on the dry and wet seasons. While the tropical forest is lush and green during the wet season, navigating the many unsealed roads that govern land access to the interior can be extremely difficult (if not impossible). The main **rainy seasons** in the region are generally between May and August and from around mid-November to mid-January. As such, late summer/early autumn and late winter/early spring are the optimum times for a visit – the latter particularly, as this is when many carnival celebrations take place.

COUCH SURFING

The Guianas are not a traditional budget destination so you may want to consider staying with locals by joining an online **hospitality site** such as ⓦ couchsurfing .org (see p.34).

Guyana

GUYANA, the largest and most populous nation of the three Guianas, is a rum-drinking and cricket-loving country, and the only English-speaking nation in South America. **Georgetown**, the capital, typifies this with its cosmopolitan mix of black, white, East Indian, Asian and Amerindian ethnicities and a Caribbean feel.

Unlike the Caribbean, however, Guyana's principal attractions are its rainforests (part of the Guyana Shield and some of the oldest and most pristine on earth), its wildlife and its indigenous culture. One of Guyana's greatest natural wonders is the majestic **Kaieteur Falls** – among the tallest and most powerful in the world – made all the more dramatic by their isolated location in a tree-covered mountain range.

Going down the middle of the country from north to south is the **Iwokrama Rainforest**, where millions of acres of rainforest have been reserved for conservation, research and sustainable ecotourism. Further southwest, the jungle gives way to the wide-open spaces of the **Rupununi Savannah**, dotted with Amerindian villages. Here you can immerse yourself in indigenous culture and go in search of caimans, giant anteaters and giant river otters.

CHRONOLOGY

10,000 BC Amerindians arrive, having crossed a land bridge from Asia.

3000 BC Agriculture – cassava farming – used to supplement hunting and gathering.

1492 Christopher Columbus sets foot in the region. Unsuccessful Spanish exploration in search of the Lost City of Gold.

1595 Sir Walter Raleigh visits Guyana and publishes *The Discoverie of the Large, Rich and Bewtiful Empyre of Guiana*, igniting European interest in the region.

1613–21 The Dutch found Fort Kyk Over Al, build trading posts, and establish sugarcane plantations.

1650s African slaves replace Amerindian ones; Amerindians assist the Dutch in capturing runaway slaves.

1763 Slave revolt led by Guyana's national hero, Cuffy. Revolt finally quelled in 1764; 125 slaves executed.

1796 Dutch lose control of colony to the British.

1802 Dutch regain control of Guyana.

1814 Treaty of Paris formally grants the British control of the area.

1823 Demerara slave revolt brutally suppressed.

1834 Slavery abolished. Thousands of indentured labourers from India, China, England, Ireland, Portugal and Africa are brought to Guyana to work the sugar-cane plantations.

1870s Charles Barrington Brown is the first European to find Kaieteur Falls. Gold found in Guyana's interior.

1950 The People's Progressive Party (PPP) is established.

1953 PPP wins first elections allowed by British. Jagan becomes leader. Britain suspends constitution and sends in troops, fearing plans to establish Guyana as a communist state.

1955 PPP splits and Burnham forms the People's National Congress (PNC).

1957 Elections permitted and PPP wins. Jagan becomes first premier in 1961.

1966 Guyana achieves independence.

1978 More than 900 members of Rev. Jim Jones' People's Temple religious sect commit mass suicide in Jonestown (see box, p.649).

1980 Guyana gets a controversial new constitution and Burnham becomes president.

1985 Burnham dies; Prime Minister Hugh Desmond Hoyte becomes president.

1992 Cheddi Jagan's PPP wins election.

1997 Jagan dies. His American widow, Janet Jagan, is elected president.

1999 Janet Jagan resigns and is succeeded by Bharrat Jagdeo.

2001 Violent demonstrations follow the elections.

2009 Norway agrees to invest US$250m to preserve Guyana's rainforests.

2010 Guyana chosen as one of the hosts of the Twenty20 cricket World Cup.

2012 Protests in Linden leave three people dead. Police questioned over killings.

ARRIVAL AND DEPARTURE

Guyana's **Cheddi Jagan International Airport**, 41km from Georgetown, receives direct **flights** from Suriname, Brazil, Barbados, Trinidad, New York, Miami, Fort Lauderdale and Toronto. Some flights from Suriname and domestic flights arrive at the smaller **Ogle International Airport**, some 7km east of the capital.

OVERLAND FROM BRAZIL

Travellers arriving overland from Brazil enter Guyana at the town of **Lethem**,

7

about 130km northeast of the Brazilian town of Boa Vista. It is a cramped and bone-jarring eighteen-hour **minibus** ride (see p.652) from Lethem to Georgetown along a dirt logging road that slices the country in half. There are also several daily flights from Lethem to Georgetown.

OVERLAND FROM SURINAME

Travellers from Suriname must board a **ferry** at South Drain, near Nieuw Nickerie, and make the thirty-minute journey across the Corentyne River to **Molson Creek** on the Guyana border before taking a local minibus to Georgetown (see box, p.659). It's possible to arrange direct transport

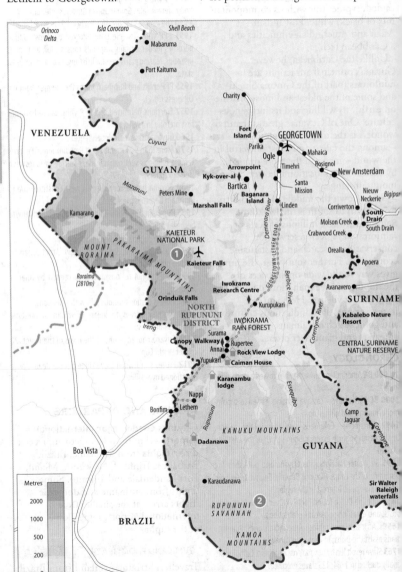

from Paramaribo to Georgetown (total travel time 10hr).

VISAS

You must have a passport with six months' validity and a return ticket if arriving by air. Guyanese immigration grants visitors stays of up to ninety days. To extend your stay, contact the Ministry of Home Affairs (6 Brickdam St ☏226 2445, ⓦmoha.gov.gy) or the Central Office of Immigration (Camp St ☏226 4700), both in Georgetown.

Visas are required for all visitors except those from Commonwealth and

THE GUIANAS

HIGHLIGHTS

1 Kaieteur Falls
2 Rupununi Savannah
3 Awarradam
4 Galibi Nature Reserve
5 Centre Spatial Guyanais
6 Îles du Salut

N

ATLANTIC OCEAN

Totness
Zorg en Hoop
Leonsburg
Matapica Beach
Nieuw Amsterdam
WIA WIA NATURE RESERVE
GALIBI NATURE RESERVE
PARAMARIBO
Meerzorg
Alliance
Christiaankondre
Langamankondre
Plage les Hattes
Awala-Yalimapo
Zanderij
COMMEWIJNE
Moengo
Mana
Javouhey
Iracoubo
Colakreek
Jodensavanne
Albina
St Laurent du Maroni
Sinnamary
Space Centre
Brownsweg
Blakawatra
Brokopondo
Apatou
Voltaire Falls
Kourou
CAYENNE
Îlet la Mère
Witagron
BROWNSBERG NATURE RESERVE
Blonnestein Meer
Montsinéry Tonnegrande
Remire-Montjoly
Matoury
Pokigron
Voltzberg
RALEIGHVALLEN NATURE RESERVE
Cacao
Roura
Kaw
Cabo Orange
...ELBERG ...ATURE ...ERVE
Tafelberg (1026m)
Kajana
Botopasi
Grand Santi
FRENCH GUIANA
Regina
Cisame
Approuague River
Ouanary
...Top ...m)
3 Awarradam
Palumeu
Jai
Maroni
Maripasoula
Saül
Saint-Georges-de-l'Oyapok
Oiapoque
SURINAME
...EILERTS DE ...AN NATURE ...RESERVE
Kasikasima
St Maroni (635m)
Camopi
BRAZIL

Coppename

Oyapok

0   100
kilometres

7

CARICOM (Caribbean community) countries, plus USA and most Western European countries. Contact your nearest Guyanese embassy/consulate for more details.

GETTING AROUND

Privately owned **minibuses** operate to nearly all destinations accessible by road, including Lethem close to the Brazilian border (US$60). Roads are paved from Georgetown to towns along the coast and inland as far as Linden; beyond, it's dirt roads only, which sometimes become impassable during rainy season. There is a possibility that the road from Georgetown to Lethem will be paved by 2015, courtesy of the Brazilian government.

Independent travel in the interior requires either hiring a 4WD with a driver or hopping on the back of someone's motorcycle (see box, p.655). Daily **flights** in small aircraft connect Georgetown to settlements in the Rupununi and elsewhere; these are reliable and relatively cheap (US$100 to Lethem).

Travel along Guyana's main rivers involves **river taxis** (speedboats), whereas locals tend to use dugout canoes and motorboats when travelling along the smaller rivers.

ACCOMMODATION

There are plenty of good, reasonably priced **guesthouses** and **hotels** in Georgetown, where G$7000 will get you a spacious, clean room with a mosquito net, TV, running water and air conditioning. Prices are cheaper outside the capital, but accommodation more limited. In the Rupununi Savannah there are several excellent ecolodges and ranches that offer an introduction to traditional savannah life as well as outdoor pursuits such as wildlife-watching and fishing; these range from rustic to luxurious, and there are also cheaper guesthouses in some villages. Most villages will have a *benab* (wooden shelter with thatched roof) where you can hang your hammock (bring your own, cost/night US$10); in the absence

of a *benab*, you may well be able to hang it on someone's porch.

In Guyana a "single room" will usually have a double or queen-sized bed and a "double room" may come with two beds of varying sizes. Not all establishments accept foreign credit cards, so check when making a booking. Call rather than email.

FOOD AND DRINK

Curries, roti, cassava, rice and coconut milk reign over **Guyanese cuisine**. Chicken, pork and beef are fried Creole-style, curried with East Indian spices or flavoured with Chinese spices. **Rice** is ubiquitous, boiled with coconut milk, black-eyed peas, lentils, *channa* (chickpeas), okra or *callaloo* (spinach). Other staples include roti and *dhal puri* (akin to a tortilla wrap).

Black pudding (a sausage filled with rice mixed with cow's blood) is popular, and is often eaten with *sour*, a hot, tangy sauce, and *souse* – pickled pork, pig's skin, chicken's feet, cow's heel, cow's face or fish. The Amerindian contribution to Guyanese cuisine is *pepperpot* – made with stewed meat (or fish), coloured, preserved and flavoured with *cassareep* (a thick dark sauce made from cassava juice), cinnamon and hot peppers. Other Amerindian food includes cassava bread and *farine* (grated, dried cassava).

Locals consider **wild meat** a delicacy and adventurous eaters should try deer, iguana, wild pig, *manicou* (opossum) and *labba* or agouti (jungle rat).

Snacks such as patties, buns, potato balls, *pholouri* (seasoned flour and lentil balls), pineapple tarts, *salara* (red coconut rolls) and *cassava pone* (like bread pudding but made with coconut and cassava) are sold in bakeries (G$200–300 each).

In Georgetown you'll also find Brazilian and Chinese restaurants as well as Western-style international cafés and eateries. A hot meal **costs** G$400–500 from a market *cook shop*; in local cafés it costs twice that and in upmarket restaurants you'll spend over G$1300.

DRINK

Alcoholic drinks worth trying include local award-winning **Banks Beer** (G$300) and Banks DIH's 10-year-old or Demerara Distillers' El Dorado 15-year-old Special Reserve rums.

Fizzy soft drinks (many from Brazil) are sold everywhere, along with regional brands such as Busta and I-Cee. Chilled drinks like Mauby (a tree bark-based beverage), Cherry and Sorrel (each flavoured with their eponymous ingredient) are very refreshing, as is **coconut water**. In spite of an abundance of fresh fruit, fresh fruit juice is practically unheard of. Drinking tap water is inadvisable.

CULTURE AND ETIQUETTE

English is the national **language** but locals tend to converse in Guyanese *Patwah* (patois), an English-based Creole influenced by the Amerindian, African, Dutch and Indian languages. The nine Amerindian communities speak several dialects including Arawak, Macushi and Warao, while the prominent Brazilian population speaks Portuguese. The three dominant **religions** are Christianity, Hinduism and Islam.

Women can expect to get plenty of loud comments and persistent kissing noises. It's best not to wear excessively revealing clothing or respond to such advances. Guyanese dress stylishly for work, church, visiting government offices and dining out. **Tipping** is not compulsory though it is appreciated.

SPORTS AND OUTDOOR ACTIVITIES

The country's national sport is cricket, though visitors are more likely to come for the outdoor activities such as canoeing, birdwatching, wildlife-spotting and mountain climbing in the interior. **Horseriding** in the Rupununi Savannah is easily accessible and a visit to the annual **Rupununi Rodeo** in Lethem (see p.657) is recommended.

COMMUNICATIONS

Sending **letters and postcards** from Guyana is cheap (G$80–180) but slow. For urgent deliveries, try FedEx.

> **GUYANA ON THE NET**
> Ⓦ**exploreguyana.org** Directory of accommodation, restaurants, airlines and travel agencies run by the Tourism and Hospitality Association of Guyana.
> Ⓦ**guyanalive.com** Social site providing forums and info on festivals and events.

Guyana's country code is 592. Local, national and international **phone calls** can be made with phonecards issued by GT&T and Digicel, available from most shops and pharmacies. To use your **mobile phone**, get it unlocked, then purchase a local SIM card from either GT&T or Digicel outlets.

In Georgetown, there are several **internet cafés**. Internet and/or **wi-fi** is available in most hotels and guesthouses (mostly for free) and some cafés, but is less readily available outside the capital.

CRIME AND SAFETY

Most visits to Guyana are trouble-free. Still, opportunistic **petty crime** (particularly theft) is rife, particularly in Georgetown, so avoid displaying valuable items. Pickpockets are said to be particularly active around Stabroek Market. Occasional muggings also occur, so it's highly recommended that you take taxis everywhere after dark and avoid walking alone down deserted, sparsely lit streets. Steer clear of areas such as Albouystown and Tiger Bay (near Main St, Georgetown). Dangerous driving is also an issue, both in and around Georgetown.

HEALTH

There is one public and several private **hospitals** in Georgetown. Rural and outlying areas are served by municipal hospitals and health centres; Medivac services (emergency air ambulance) are also available in emergencies. Medical facilities at Georgetown public hospital (see p.654) are rather limited; serious injury or illness may require an airlift to Port of Spain, Trinidad.

7

Avoid drinking tap, creek or river **water**, and pack sunscreen, as well as rehydration mix for severe cases of travellers' diarrhoea.

Consult your doctor regarding vaccinations; advice currently includes hepatitis A and B, typhoid, tetanus-diphtheria and rabies. A yellow fever certificate is required to enter Guyana if coming from endemic areas. Malaria is found in all parts of the interior; bring anti-malaria tablets (such as Malarone, mefloquine or doxycycline) with you. Pack insect repellent that's at least 50 percent DEET, as mosquitoes also transmit dengue fever. If you experience flu-like symptoms, seek medical assistance, as malaria symptoms are very similar.

In the interior, travellers must be wary of several types of venomous snakes as well as black caimans.

INFORMATION AND MAPS

There is no tourist information office as such in Guyana, but the **Tourism and Hospitality Association of Guyana (THAG)** (157 Waterloo St; Mon–Fri 8.30am–5pm; ☎225 0807, ⓦexploreguyana.org) produces the annual **magazine**, *Explore Guyana*, full of **general information** about the country. G.E.M.S. Inc also publishes a pocket-sized listings guide called *Guyana: where & what*. Both are available at hotels and tourism agents around the city. **Permits** are required to visit Amerindian villages, arranged by tour operators for organized trips. Independent travellers should contact the Ministry of Amerindian Affairs, at 251–252 Quamina, at Thomas (☎227 5067, ⓦamerindian.gov.gy).

The best city map of Georgetown is produced by Advertising & Marketing Services Ltd, obtained from THAG and various tour operators. The *Guyana, Suriname & French Guiana* map by International Travel Maps provides an overview of the three countries, though not without errors.

MONEY AND BANKS

The unit of **currency** is the Guyanese dollar (G$), available in 20, 100, 500 and 1000 notes and 1, 5 and 10 coins. Licensed currency exchanges (cambios) offer better exchange rates than banks. A few businesses and hotels accept foreign currency (US$ or euros). While major **credit cards** such as MasterCard, Visa and American Express are accepted in some restaurants and hotels, take plenty of Guyanese dollars if travelling in the interior. Scotiabank has one of the few ATMs that accepts foreign cards. At the time of writing, US$1=G$203, €1=G$261, £1=G$325.

OPENING HOURS

Banks: Mon–Thurs 8am–2pm, Fri 8am–2.30pm. Government offices: Mon–Thurs 8am–noon and 1–4.30pm, Fri 8am–noon and 1–3.30pm. Shops and businesses: Mon–Fri 8.30am–4pm, Sat 8am–noon.

GEORGETOWN

GEORGETOWN is the colourful, gritty, commercial and administrative heart of Guyana. Set on the east bank of the Demerara estuary, the capital is a grid city designed largely by the Dutch in the eighteenth century, originally nicknamed "The Garden City" because of its parks, tree-lined streets and an abundance of flowers. Today, there is still a definite charm despite its rubbish-strewn streets – with musicians on street corners and gently decaying colonial architecture, Georgetown is the gateway to Guyana's true attractions and likely to be your base for several days.

WHAT TO SEE AND DO

The capital is worth exploring for its diverse cultural, religious and historical landmarks.

Main Street and around

One of downtown's most distinctive buildings, the towering **St George's Cathedral** on Church Street is one of the world's tallest freestanding wooden structures at 44m, with an attractive, airy interior (daily 9am–2pm except public holidays). A couple of blocks south along the Avenue of the Republic is the turreted City Hall, built in the Victorian Gothic style.

The **Walter Roth Museum of Anthropology** (61 Main St; Mon–Thurs 8am–4.30pm, Fri 8am–3.30pm; entry by donation) is a good introduction to the culture of Guyana's nine Amerindian tribes, showcasing everything from cassava-processing, traditional fishing and hammock-making to the medicinal use of plants and ceremonial wear, which includes some splendid macaw-feather headgear.

The **Guyana National Museum** (North Rd; Mon–Fri 9am–4.30pm, Sat 9am–noon; entry by donation) showcases the history of slavery in Guyana, the gold-mining industry (including a demonic-looking figure of a "pork-knocker"), and stuffed and pickled wildlife, including an impressive baby aparaima (the largest freshwater fish on earth).

Stabroek Market and around

The busy-as-bedlam focal point for *higglers* (fruit and vegetable sellers), moneychangers, beggars and pickpockets, **Stabroek Market** (near Water St) is dominated by its four-faced, non-functioning clock tower. Originally the site of the slave market where the exhausted survivors of the Middle Passage

JONESTOWN MASSACRE

The chilling events of November 18, 1978, when more than 900 members of a sect died in an apparent mass suicide in northwestern Guyana, about 80km southwest of the town of Mabaruma, have been the subject of many books and theories. In 1974, American **Reverend Jim Jones**, the leader of a sect called **The People's Temple**, chose Guyana to establish a self-sufficient community of about 1100 based on utopian socialist ideals, which he humbly named Jonestown. Referring to an unnamed enemy that would come to destroy Jonestown, he told his flock that "revolutionary suicide" was the only way to combat this threat. When US Congressman Leo Ryan and a party of journalists and concerned family members visited Jonestown in November 1978 to investigate alleged human rights abuses, the enemy had apparently arrived. Ryan and others were shot and killed at Port Kaituma airstrip as they tried to leave, while back at Jonestown the men, women and children were instructed to drink poison. A total of 913 people died, although a coroner's report suggested that many were forcibly killed, including at least 200 children. A few managed to escape and later wrote about their experiences. Today the Jonestown site is overrun by bush and there is no monument or other reminders of its existence.

first faced a hostile New World, Stabroek now supports slavery of the sweatshop variety, spilling over with knock-off designer gear, jewellery and watches. It's also a great place for a cheap lunch at a *snackette*. East of Stabroek, off North Street, is the small but lively **Bourda Market**, a colourful shantytown filled with fruit and vegetable vendors.

The National Art Gallery and around

Located in Castellani House on Vlissengen Road – once the official residence of the prime minister of

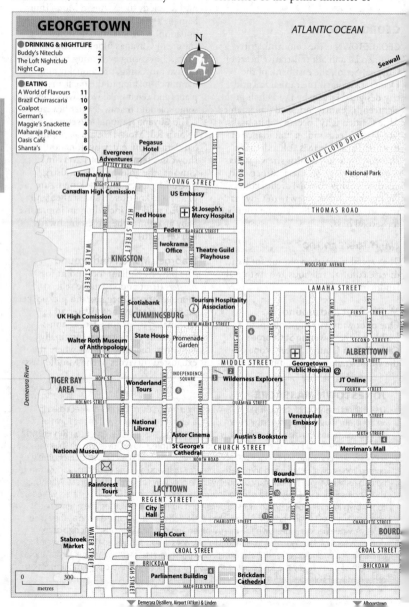

GEORGETOWN

ATLANTIC OCEAN

Seawall

● **DRINKING & NIGHTLIFE**
Buddy's Niteclub	2
The Loft Nightclub	7
Night Cap	1

● **EATING**
A World of Flavours	11
Brazil Churrascaria	10
Coalpot	9
German's	5
Maggie's Snackette	4
Maharaja Palace	3
Oasis Café	8
Shanta's	6

Evergreen Adventures
Pegasus Hotel
Umana Yana
BATTERY ROAD
WIGHTS LANE
Canadian High Comission
CLIVE LLOYD DRIVE
National Park
CAMP ROAD
SIDE STREET
YOUNG STREET
US Embassy
THOMAS ROAD
Red House
St Joseph's Mercy Hospital
HIGH STREET
DUKE STREET
FORT STREET
Fedex
BARRACK STREET
Iwokrama Office
PARADE STREET
Theatre Guild Playhouse
KINGSTON
COWAN STREET
WATER STREET
WOOLFORD AVENUE
LAMAHA STREET
Scotiabank
Tourism Hospitality Association
FIRST STREET
CUMMINGS STREET
ALBERT STREET
UK High Comission
CUMMINGSBURG
NEW MARKET STREET
THOMAS STREET
EAST STREET
SECOND STREET
State House
Promenade Garden
CAMP STREET
ALBERTTOWN
Walter Roth Museum of Anthropology
BENTICK
MIDDLE STREET
THIRD STREET
Georgetown Public Hospital @
TIGER BAY AREA
HOPE ST
CARMICHAEL ST
WATERLOO STREET
INDEPENDENCE SQUARE
Wilderness Explorers
JT Online
FOURTH STREET
Wonderland Tours
MAIN STREET
HOLMES STREET
QUAMINA STREET
National Library
Venezuelan Embassy
FIFTH STREET
Demerara River
Astor Cinema
Austin's Bookstore
SIXTH STREET
National Museum
St George's Cathedral
CHURCH STREET
Merriman's Mall
NORTH ROAD
ROBB STREET
WELLINGTON ST
CAMP STREET
Bourda Market
Rainforest Tours
LACYTOWN
ALEXANDER STREET
BOURDA STREET
ORANGE WALK
CUMMINGS STREET
LIGHT STREET
REGENT STREET
City Hall
AVENUE OF THE REPUBLIC
KING STREET
CHARLOTTE STREET
CHARLOTTE STREET
BOURD
Stabroek Market
High Court
SOUTH ROAD
WATER STREET
CROAL STREET
CROAL STREET
HIGH STREET
BRICKDAM
BRICKDAM
Parliament Building
Brickdam Cathedral
HADFIELD STREET

0   300
metres

N

7

Guyana – is the **National Art Gallery** (Mon–Fri 10am–5pm, Sat 2–6pm; free). The collection features African-inspired masks, carvings and paintings, including the psychedelic works of celebrated local artist Philip Moore. Don't miss the collection of *balata*

(hardened, shaped tree sap) Amerindian figurines in the attic, taking part in traditional pastimes such as hunting and cassava processing. Just south of the gallery is the **1763 Monument**, a 5m-high bronze memorial to Cuffy, an African slave who led an unsuccessful

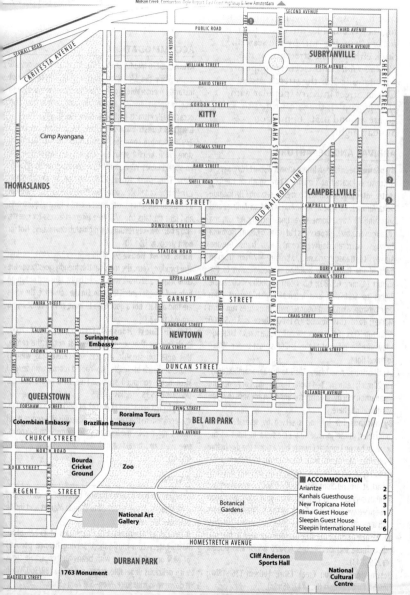

ACCOMMODATION

Ariantze	2
Kanhais Guesthouse	5
New Tropicana Hotel	3
Rima Guest House	1
Sleepin Guest House	4
Sleepin International Hotel	6

slave rebellion in 1763. North of the art gallery are the botanical gardens (daily 9.30am–5.30pm).

The seawall

Georgetown is bounded to the north by the Dutch-built **seawall**, which keeps the Atlantic Ocean at bay. A popular spot for post-work jogging, on Sunday nights it seems like the whole town is *liming* (hanging out) by the seawall. Stick either to the stretch near the *Pegasus Hotel* in the centre (popular with families) or the stretch east of Queen Street in Kitty (popular with young people); the safest times to go are around 4.30–6pm or on Sunday nights.

ARRIVAL AND DEPARTURE

By plane Cheddi Jagan International Airport (w cjairport-gy.com) is located at Timehri, 41km south of the city centre. International carriers currently serving CJIA include Delta Airlines, Caribbean Airlines, LIAT, Meta Airlines and Suriname Airways. Domestic airlines include Air Guyana (w airguyana.biz), Air Services Ltd (w aslgy.com), Roraima Airways (w roraimaairways.com) and Trans Guyana Airways (w transguyana.net). Minibus #42 runs from in front of the Parliament building in Georgetown to the airport (45min; G$280); taxis cost G$4000–5000. Some flights to Suriname and internal flights depart from Ogle airstrip, 8km from Georgetown; minibuses run from Market; taxis cost around G$1500. There is a G$4000 departure tax for international departures. Luggage allowance on internal flights is 20lbs (just under 10kg), so travel light.

Destinations Annai (daily; 1hr 30min); Karanambu (daily; 1hr 20min); Lethem (3–4 daily; 1hr 30min). For Annai and Karanambu you must notify the airline in advance that you want to alight here.

By minibus The interior is served by several minibus companies; these include Guy-Braz from in front of the Brazilian bar on Light, at Church; buy a ticket the day before if possible. Minibuses from Georgetown to Lethem leave around 6pm, while those travelling in the opposite direction depart at around 5pm (G$12,000/US$60). Several private minibus services offer pick-ups from your accommodation in Georgetown to Molson Creek by the Surinamese border with a reciprocal arrangement with a Surinamese operator on the other side of the river, so you only need to buy one ticket. These include Bobby's (t 226 8668) and Douglas (t 226 2843).

Destinations Molson Creek (3hr); Lethem (16–18hr); Timehri for CJ Airport (bus #42; 45min).

GETTING AROUND

By minibus Privately owned minibuses run all over Georgetown from Stabroek Market (G$80–100). They tend to be packed, drive very fast and are impossible to board during rush hour.

By taxi Taxis are unmetered, plentiful and cheap; most are painted yellow and display number plates beginning with "H". Always agree to a price before starting your journey; fares tend to be G$250–300 for a short hop, G$400 within the city and G$500 or more outside the city limits.

ACCOMMODATION

Ariantze 176 Middle St t 225 4634, w ariantzesidewalk.com. While the a/c rooms at this central hotel are not instantly memorable, pool access sweetens the deal, and weekly entertainment at the *Sidewalk Café & Jazz Club* occasionally attracts highbrow clientele. **US$67**

Kanhais Guesthouse 210 Charlotte St, Lacytown t 223 2393, w kanhais.com. Secure guesthouse above a hardware store, with helpful staff and clean but characterless a/c en-suite doubles. Wi-fi available. Breakfast included. **US$40**

New Tropicana Hotel 177 Waterloo St t 227 5701, w newtropicanahotel.com. *Tropicana*, aka *Jerrie's*, is a bit of a catch-all operation, with basic rooms with mosquito nets and fans upstairs (no a/c), free internet access for guests, and a bar/low-key restaurant/nightclub downstairs. Not for light sleepers. **US$20**

Rima Guest House 92 Middle St t 225 7401, e rima@networksgy.com. The rooms at this friendly guesthouse are comfortable and clean, with shared baths, fans and mosquito nets and a great central location. On the downside, the walls are thin and it's not a good idea to leave any valuables lying around. **US$20**

Sleepin Guest House 151 Church St t 231 7667, w sleepinguesthouse.com. Somewhat out of the centre, this quiet guesthouse attracts self-caterers as well as those in search of simple, fan-cooled rooms, with several kitchenette-equipped studios. Free wi-fi and breakfast. Doubles **US$35**, studios **US$65**

Sleepin International Hotel 24 Brickdam t 227 3446, w sleepininternationalhotel.com. Spacious city-centre hotel with comfortable, modern en-suite rooms with balconies, free wi-fi and breakfast included. Outdoor pool and bar. **US$40**

EATING

Georgetown has a wide range of bakeries, *snackettes* and *cook shops* – many attached to Bourda Market and inside Stabroek Market.

A World of Flavours 125 Carmichael St t 225 8556. Rasta-eatery-cum-music-shop, serving heaped portions of only one dish – rice with beans and vegetable stew, with delicious vegetable *achar* (pickle) G$280/360. Wash it down with fruit juice. Mon–Sat 7am–5pm.

★ **TREAT YOURSELF**

Maharaja Palace 207 Sheriff St ☎ 225 5301. This three-storey restaurant, aglow with neon, does Chinese food and sushi too, but it's the Indian dishes that steal the show. You can't go wrong with the likes of fragrant, beautifully flavoured tandoori specials or the curries (mains from G$2500 but big enough for two).

★ **Brazil Churrascaria** 208 Alexander St, Lacytown ☎ 231 1268. Meat is what these guys do best, so the carnivorously inclined will enjoy skewers of expertly seasoned grilled meats, steak and more. Mains G$1000. Daily noon–10pm.

Coalpot 125 Carmichael St ☎ 225 8556. Here you can enjoy *metagee*, *pepperpot* and Creole dishes such as red snapper steamed in banana leaf – with a great view of the cathedral to complement your meal. Mains from G$800. Daily 11am–3pm & 6–11pm.

German's 8 New Market, at Mundy St ☎ 227 0079. Busy lunchtime restaurant famed for its legendary cow-heel soup (G$1000) and Creole dishes. Located in a sketchy part of town, so take a taxi. Daily 11.30am–3pm & 6–11pm.

Maggie's Snackette 224 New Market St. Busy eatery with delicious cakes, pastries, black pudding and *souse* (G$200–400) plus lunch specials (G$1100). Around 10am–10pm.

Oasis Café 125 Carmichael St ☎ 226 9916, ⊛ oasiscafegy .com. Georgetown's answer to Starbucks, only much nicer, this is an air-conditioned, erm, oasis where expats and locals alike linger over the iced caramel lattes (G$650), salads and inventive lunchtime mains (from G$2000). Free wi-fi. Mon–Sat 9am–5pm (also open for dinner on Fri).

Shanta's 225 New Market St. Besides curries, this great corner joint serves excellent *dhal puri* with a range of tasty fillings, meat and vegetable stews, samosas and more. Meals around G$1200. Daily 11am–10pm.

DRINKING AND NIGHTLIFE

The bars and clubs are mostly concentrated along Sheriff and Main streets. The real action in the clubs starts around midnight on weekends.

Buddy's Niteclub 137 Sheriff St ☎ 231 7260. A multi-storey hotspot attracting a young crowd with "Shooter Fridays": a melange of hip-hop, r'n'b, chutney (the music style, not the condiment) and reggae. Bring your confidence. Free entry before 10.30pm. Thurs–Sat.

The Loft Nightclub 110 Third St. Spacious venue offering a mix of dance, *soca* and reggae. The bar is well stocked and tasty snacks are on the menu. Wed–Sat.

★ **Night Cap** 8 Pere St, Kitty ☎ 231 8644. An enchanting garden bedecked with Christmas lights, nestling inside the walls of the Russian embassy. Swing in a hammock, lounge on the patio, or sit in the wi-fi-enabled a/c cool of the café. Order peanut butter frappes and espresso margaritas, accompanied by inventive wraps and sandwiches. Daily 5–11pm.

DIRECTORY

Banks and exchange Bank of Nova Scotia, at 104 Carmichael St, also Robb St at Av of the Republic. There are also ATMs at Pegasus Hotel, Seawall Rd and Courtyard Mall, Robb St. Ask about the cambio nearest to your lodgings.

Embassies and Consulates Brazil, 308 Church St (☎ 225 7970); Canada, High at Young St (☎ 227 2081); Suriname, 171 Peter Rose St at Crown St (☎ 226 7844); UK, 44 Main St (☎ 226 5881); US, Young St at Duke St (☎ 226 3938); Venezuela, 296 Thomas St (☎ 226 1543).

7

KAIETEUR FALLS

Almost five times the height of Niagara Falls and twice the height of Victoria Falls, 226m **Kaieteur Falls** are in a cavernous gorge surrounded by the dense rainforest of the **Kaieteur National Park**. Their isolation and pristine surroundings make them one of the world's most appealing waterfalls and Guyana's biggest natural attraction: seeing them from above is heart-stopping.

Operators (see p.654) offer flights to Kaieteur Falls in twelve-seater planes, combined with visits to the smaller Orinduik or Marshall Falls. A day-trip usually involves a brief guided tour of the three viewpoints from which you can admire the sight of 30,000 gallons of water crashing down into the valley below (with the more intrepid visitors crawling to the cliff edge to watch the rainbows play on the water spray). Your guide will point out interesting animal life, such as the tiny golden frogs, the toxins from which are used in Haitian voodoo ceremonies.

Alternatively you can take a five-day/four-night overland journey involving a 4WD drive, boat trip and a fairly strenuous hike, with rustic accommodation thrown in along the way. If you want to visit independently, the only overnight accommodation is a rustic lodge near the falls (G$4000/person), booked through Air Services Ltd (⊛ aslgy.com). You will be rewarded with views of the falls at dusk and dawn without the crowds. Air Services Ltd, together with Roraima Airways (⊛ roraimaairways.com), are responsible for flights to the falls. Day-trips from Georgetown (including flight from Ogle, park entrance fees and lunch) start from US$195; it's easiest to arrange a trip on a weekend when there are plenty of people to fill up flights.

Hospital St Joseph's Mercy Hospital, 130–132 Parade St (🕿 227 2072). Private hospital with 24hr emergency room.
Internet All accommodation options reviewed offer internet and/or wi-fi. Otherwise try JT Online Internet Café at 38 Cummings St.
Pharmacies Medi-care Pharmacy at 18 Hinck St or The Medicine Chest at 315 Middle St.

DAY-TRIPS FROM GEORGETOWN

Georgetown makes a good base for ventures into the interior to visit **Kaieteur Falls** – one of the most impressive waterfalls in the world – as well as trips up Essequibo River for an appreciation of the country's colonial past and mining present, and to Santa Mission, for a taste of Amerindian life.

Essequibo and Mazaruni rivers

This popular day-trip involves a boat journey on the **Essequibo**, one of Guyana's main waterways. First stop is the market town of Parika, then a visit to **Kyk Over Al**, a seventeenth-century Dutch fort, and a stopover in **Bartica**, a gritty gold-mining town and a wonderful place to get an insight into one of Guyana's main trades. This is followed by a boat trip up the smaller Mazaruni River to the Bara Cara Falls or else Marshall Falls

– both great spots for a dip – and a short hike through the jungle for a chance to see some of the country's fabled wildlife.

Santa Mission

Though it's no substitute for visiting the Amerindian villages of the interior, a boat trip up Kumuni Creek to the **Santa Mission** village is a good introduction to Amerindian culture for those who have little time. Here you learn about traditional pastimes such as hunting and cassava processing and you can pick up good-quality woodcarvings and woven handicrafts. A swim in the Black Creek is usually thrown in for good measure.

THE INTERIOR: IWOKRAMA RAINFOREST AND THE RUPUNUNI SAVANNAH

Visitors come to Guyana for two things: pristine nature and Amerindian culture. Both are found away from the colourful chaos of Georgetown, in the interior, reachable either by Guyana's main highway that runs all the way to the Brazilian border, or by frequent flights made by small aircraft. Much of the road passes through some of the oldest and most pristine jungle on earth, home to

---

TOURS OF THE INTERIOR

While travels in the interior are cheapest if you have the time and flexibility to arrange it all independently (see box opposite), there are several reputable tour operators in Georgetown who specialize in nature and adventure tours throughout Guyana's hinterland and who can also arrange day-trips to Kaieteur Falls and other destinations within easy reach of the capital. Prices are roughly as follows: tour of the city (US$30–40); day-trip to Bartica (US$120); day-trip to Santa Mission (US$120); flight to Kaieteur Falls (US$195–240).

TOUR OPERATORS

Bushmasters ⓦ bushmasters.co.uk. Jungle survival courses in pristine jungle and cowboy adventure tours in the Rupununi Savannah.
Evergreen Adventures Pegasus Hotel, Seawall Rd 🕿 225 4484, ⓦ evergreenadventuresgy.com. City tours, four types of Kaieteur Falls trips, day-trips up Essequibo River and to Berbice.
Rainforest Tours 5 Av of the Republic, 1st floor 🕿 231 5661, ⓦ rftours.com. This longest-standing, helpful operator specializes in overland treks to Kaieteur Falls. Flights to the falls, Santa Mission and up the Essequibo River also arranged.

Roraima Tours 8 Eping Av, Bell Air Park 🕿 225 9648, ⓦ roraimaairways.com. Linked with Roraima Airways and offering the cheapest flights to Kaieteur Falls (US$195). Kaieteur/Arrowpoint day tours also available.
Wilderness Explorers Cara Suites, 176 Middle St 🕿 227 7698, ⓦ wilderness-explorers.com. Renowned operator specializing in custom-made adventure tours of Guyana, but they also do shorter jaunts.
Wonderland Tours 85 Quamina St 🕿 225 3122, ⓦ wonderlandtoursgy.com. Trips to Kaieteur Falls, day-trips up Essequibo and Mazaruni rivers, culinary tours and more.

INDEPENDENT TRAVEL IN THE INTERIOR

Independent travel in Guyana's interior requires forward planning, time and flexibility, but it's possible to visit every single attraction mentioned in this chapter without having to go with a tour operator. To visit most Amerindian villages (barring Annai and Rupertee), you would first have to get permission from either the Amerindian Affairs office (see p.648) in Georgetown or its equivalent in Lethem if coming over from Brazil. Guyana takes the needs of its indigenous communities seriously and you can't just turn up, though if you've booked accommodation there in advance, that automatically takes care of things. If travelling overland, it is essential that you have your passport with you, as there are several police checkpoints in the interior.

GETTING AROUND

By plane see p.646.

By minibus Georgetown–Lethem minibuses can stop en route at Annai or drop you at the turn-offs to Surama or the Iwokrama Research Centre and Canopy Walkway (make arrangements to be picked up from the turnoff or walk in). Since minibuses tend to overflow with passengers and luggage, to board a bus from a location in between Lethem and Georgetown, reserve a seat in advance by calling the minibus company directly or through your lodgings. Take your passport with you, as there are several police checkpoints along the way.

By 4WD and boat There is no public transport from the main "highway" to remote lodges and villages, so you have to hire a 4WD (around US$200/day; less for short distances) or motorbike (see below). In the rainy season, you will find yourself travelling more by motorboat. 4WDs are easy to arrange in Lethem,

but all lodges can help you with onward travel arrangements.

By motorbike The least expensive way of getting around the Rupununi is on the back of someone's motorbike. Most people own one, and wherever you may be staying, it's always possible to arrange onward transport by motorbike just by asking around. It's considerably cheaper than going by 4WD, especially if you're a solo traveller: several hours' ride or hiring someone to take you around for a day will set you back no more than US$40. You have to travel light, though!

By bicycle Most Amerindians in the Rupununi cycle long distances on their sturdy, fixed-gear Brazilian bikes. While cycling from Georgetown to Lethem has been done by several intrepid travellers, there is a long stretch of uninhabited jungle between Linden and Kurupukari, and you have to carry all the water you need. Cycling around the Rupununi Savannah is a possibility in the dry season, though.

jaguar, tapir, ocelot, puma, peccary and anaconda. In the heart of the country lies Guyana's only official nature reserve: the vast **IWOKRAMA RAINFOREST**, known for the incredible biodiversity of its plant, bird and animal species. Beyond Iwokrama, dense jungle dramatically gives way to the **RUPUNUNI SAVANNAH**, Guyana's cowboy country – scrubland and grassland that stretches as far as the eye can see, punctuated with giant anthills, the odd cattle ranch and a smattering of thatched roofs, which announce the presence of an Amerindian village. Here you can sling your hammock in the hospitable villages of Annai, Yupukari, Shulinab and Nappi, linger in the friendly frontier town of Lethem or go wildlife-spotting from one of the local ecolodges. The savannah's grasslands abound with giant anteaters, while the many rivers are home to the black caiman, giant river otter and aparaima.

Iwokrama Research Centre and Canopy Walkway

The pristine, 400-square-kilometre **Iwokrama Rainforest** is home to a staggering 474 bird species, 130 different mammals, 420 types of fish and 132 species of reptile. It's possible to stay at the eight attractive solar-powered riverside cabins at the **Research Centre** itself (rooms US$120; meals $39/day; ☎225 1504, ⓦiwokrama.org), an internationally funded project to research forest management and sustainable development, with active participation from local Amerindian communities. Visitors share lodgings and meals with visiting biologists, botanists and journalists, and can take part in visits to nearby Amerindian villages, night-time caiman spotting, and multi-day excursions into the jungle and up Turtle Mountain.

7

A ninety-minute drive from the Research Centre is the **Canopy Walkway** (ⓦiwokramacanopywalkway.com), a 140m network of aluminium suspension bridges set amid the treetops, 30m from the forest floor. Its three observation platforms provide excellent vantage points to spot birds, howler monkeys and other fauna within the forest canopy – but only if you're there at dusk or dawn, when animal life is at its most active. An overnight stay at the luxurious **Atta Rainforest Camp**, at the foot of the canopy walk trail, costs US$260 for a room, including all meals, the canopy user fee and a trained guide. Day visitors pay G$5000. Booking in advance is vital.

Surama Village and Ecolodge

A 45-minute drive west of the Canopy Walkway is the turn-off for **Surama Village** (ⓣ548 9262, ⓦsuramaecolodge .com). A spread-out Makushi settlement of some 300 people and thatch-roofed huts connected by dusty paths, Surama is an ecotourism success story. You can stay in one of the two ecolodges in the village, each consisting of several traditional huts (rooms US$150), learning about medicinal plants from local guides, or hiking up Surama Mountain (230m) and wildlife-watching along the Burro Burro River. Alternatively, camp in one of the two basic camps along the river (US$15) and go jungle trekking.

Annai and Rupertee

The first Makushi village you reach after emerging from the jungle is **Rupertee**, famous for its craft shop (if it's closed, ask around for Gloria Duarto) where you can pick up carvings made of a local red hardwood, as well as intricate woven goods and bows and arrows (still very much used for hunting in these parts). Jeep tracks and footpaths connect it to **Annai**, around 2km off the main road – a compact, attractive village of around 300 people. Across the road from *Oasis* (see below) is the Uncle Dennis Trail (45min) that snakes up the forest-covered hill; from the top there's a splendid view of the savannah.

ACCOMMODATION

Oasis The budget-friendly sister to *Rock View Lodge* (see below) is a 10min walk away. Just off the main road, it's a popular stop for minibuses. Comprises spacious, airy en-suite rooms with mosquito nets, a hammock *benab* and an eatery with simple, inexpensive meals. Doubles US$70, hammocks US$15

Rock View Lodge ⓦrockviewlodge.com. This plush option has clean and comfortable en-suite rooms and is set in large grounds with a swimming pool. Owned by local character Colin Edwards, even if you don't stay here, he will help arrange all manner of activities, including visits to the nearby village of Wowetta. Wi-fi when the generator is running. Triples make this option a little more affordable for groups. Doubles US$300, triples US$360

Yupukari and Caiman House

Yupukari (ⓦrupununilearners.org) is a mostly Makushi village of around 500 inhabitants, a couple of hours' drive along a rutted dirt track from Annai; it's also possible to reach it by boat along the Rupununi River from Guinep Landing, 21km west of Annai (2hr). The main attraction here is the **Caiman House Field Station**, whose main purpose is to study the black caiman. If you're lucky, you will join the local caiman research crew in the evening when they go out to capture, weigh, measure and tag the fearsome creatures.

ACCOMMODATION

Caiman House This guesthouse has en-suite rooms with mosquito nets, a hammock *benab* and some of the best

---

★ TREAT YOURSELF

Karanambu Lodge ⓦkaranambulodge .com. Sitting in a clearing near the Rupununi River, this one-of-a-kind lodge consists of six luxurious cabins. A bell summons guests to the table, presided over by the formidable 82-year-old Diane McTurk – a local legend, best known for her work with orphaned giant river otters. Wild animals abound in the savannah, wetlands and rainforest around the lodge, and there's a good chance of seeing jaguars, giant anteaters, tapirs and caimans during guided walks and river trips. The meals are excellent, the rate is inclusive of everything and the staff are just wonderful. You can either fly into Karanambu or take a boat from Guinep landing (1hr 30min); Karanambu is 30min by boat from Caiman House. Cabañas US$200

home-cooked food in the savannah (meals are included). The place is a constant hub of activity, with knowledgeable Fernando to talk to and a lively learning centre for the local children next door (book donations very welcome). Doubles US$85, hammocks US$30

LETHEM AND AROUND

With its wide dirt streets, unhurried pace of life and an everybody-knows-everybody-else feel, **LETHEM** is a great little place to linger en route to Brazil or Venezuela and a good base from which to launch your exploration of the southern **Rupununi Savannah**. Moco Moco and Kumu Falls (30min drive each) are both great for swimming and it's possible to arrange horseriding near the Kumu Mountains at the village of **Shulinab** (1hr 30min drive). There's easy access to the village of **Nappi**, 30km away – a great place for wildlife watching – and you can live out your cowboy fantasy at the remote Dadanawa Ranch.

Lethem really comes alive during Easter weekend, when cowboys from all around (including the Brazilian *vaqueros*) gather in town for bull-riding, calf-roping and stallion-taming competitions (book accommodation weeks in advance).

ARRIVAL AND INFORMATION

By plane Four airlines fly between Lethem and Georgetown (up to 4 departures daily; 2hr), and all four offices are located next to the airstrip. TGA and Roraima airlines will stop at Annai and Karanambu on request. Ticket prices (one-way) vary between US$98 and US$125. Confirm departure time the day before and check in two hours before the flight. Flying is sometimes the only mode of travel between Georgetown and Lethem during the rainy season, when sections of the main "highway" become impassable for days.

By minibus Various minibus companies from Georgetown arrive and depart from different places around town. Guy Braz is probably the most convenient one, as its office is the most central (10min walk from the airstrip). Buses for Georgetown leave between 5pm and 7pm and reach their destination at around noon–2pm. The journey takes around 18hr because, aside from the paved stretch between Georgetown and Linden, the rest of the "highway" is unpaved and rutted, and since the car ferry at Kurupukari runs only between 6am and 6pm, the minibuses break their journey near the ferry dock. Most passengers end up sleeping in the cramped bus.

Tourist information Your one essential contact in Lethem is Shirley Melville, usually found either in the craft shop next to the airstrip or in the grocery store next door. She produces maps of Lethem and has started her own tour company, so she'll either be able to personally assist you in your onward travels, or will at least point you in the right direction.

ACCOMMODATION AND EATING

Betty's Snackette & Creole Corner The lovely Betty cooks up a roti storm at her little *cook shop* on the corner. Portions are generous, the curries are great and there are fruit juices, snack and pastries if you're not looking for a full-on meal (meals GS600–800). Sun–Fri.

Dadanawa Ranch ☎ 0044 7961 521 951 (UK number), ⊛ rupununitrails.com. Situated against the dramatic backdrop of the Kanuku Mountains, this is the largest and most isolated ranch in Guyana, a 3hr drive southeast of Lethem. You're treated like family by Sandy, Duane and their team of workers and guides, and the ranch is a good base to help cowboys work the cattle, as well as for trekking, horseriding, nature walks, birdwatching, swimming and fishing. Meals included. US$120

Maipaima Eco-Lodge ⊛ wildrupununi.com. Surrounded by pristine rainforest and located at the foot of the Kanuku Mountains, 10km south of Nappi village, this lovely spot consists of traditional wood-and-thatch buildings on stilts and a central *benab* for dining. There's limited electricity and the rustic setting is perfect for wildlife-watching:

CROSSING INTO BRAZIL

To get from Lethem to the Brazilian town of Bonfim, cross the Takutu River Bridge about 1.5km north of Lethem either on foot or by taxi. Pick-ups from the airstrip to the crossing cost around GS1200. **Guyanese immigration formalities** should be completed either at the airstrip when there are flights, or at the Lethem immigration office. Get your passport stamped on the Brazilian side of the border before you make your way to Bonfim, from where there are buses to Boa Vista, some 150km away, with connections to Manaus (Brazil) and Caracas (Venezuela).

There is a GBTI **bank** in Lethem (Lot 121; Mon–Fri 8am–1pm), which offers foreign exchange. **Moneychangers** on the Lethem side of the river will also change Guyanese dollars for Brazilian reais and vice versa. Make sure that you have enough reais to get you to Bonfim, if not Boa Vista.

jaguar, monkeys and tapir have been sighted in the near vicinity. Stays include a village tour and introduction to balata craft – making figurines and scenes out of hardened tree sap. US$125

Ori Hotel ☎ 772 2124. The loveliest hotel in town, with wonderfully friendly service and en-suite, wi-fi-enabled rooms hidden within a tranquil blooming garden. The restaurant serves delicious Creole dishes. G$6000

Restaurante 2 Nações Grab a spot on the patio of this informal Brazilian joint by the airstrip and order the grilled meat skewers with an enormous helping of rice and beans. Stews, fried chicken and other daily specials available (meals G$700–1000).

Takutu Hotel ☎ 772 2034. ✉ morsha@electricity.gov.gy. Friendly hotel 5min from the airstrip, with spic-and-span, tiled en suites with a/c and wi-fi and a bar/restaurant in a flowering garden. You can meet some interesting characters on karaoke nights. G$$5500

Suriname

SURINAME, formerly Dutch Guiana, is one of South America's smallest nations and it shares some traits with Guyana – a brutal history of slavery, for one. Though it attracts predominantly tourists and volunteers from Holland, English-speaking travellers are also made to feel welcome. The capital, **Paramaribo**, is the most attractive city in the Guianas, with much of its eighteenth- and nineteenth-century wooden architecture still intact; it also makes a good base for visiting the former plantations nearby and river dolphin-watching on the Commewijne River.

While ecotourism is still in its fledgling state, and facing constant challenges (thirteen percent of Suriname's land surface area is under official environmental protection but that hasn't stopped "unofficial" gold mining), there are two excellent ecolodges in the interior – *Awarradam* and *Palumeu* – that act as springboards for exploration of the unique Amerindian and Saramaccan (Maroon) communities. There's great hiking and wildlife-watching to be done at the Central Suriname Nature Reserve, while on the coast **Galibi Nature Reserve** offers the chance to observe giant sea turtles laying their eggs. If you're short of time, **Brownsberg Nature Park**, easily accessible from Paramaribo, gives you a taste of Suriname's wilderness.

CHRONOLOGY

10,000 BC Suriname's earliest inhabitants are thought to be the Surinen Indians after whom the country is named.

1498 Columbus sights Surinamese coast.

1602 Dutch begin to settle the land.

1651 England's Lord Willoughby establishes first permanent settlement – Willoughbyland, with 1000 white settlers and 2000 slaves.

1654 Jews from Holland expelled from Brazil arrive.

1667 Suriname becomes Dutch Guiana with the Treaty of Breda, after conquest of Willoughbyfort (now Fort Zeelandia) by Dutch Admiral Crynssen.

1700s & 1800s Slavery under the Dutch particularly harsh, with rape, maiming and killing of slaves common. Many run away into the interior and form Maroon communities, conducting occasional murderous raids on the plantations and their owners.

1799 Suriname reconquered by the British.

1814 Suriname given back to Holland as part of the Treaty of Paris.

1853 Chinese plantation labourers arrive.

1863 Formal abolition of slavery (though slaves not released for another 10 years as part of transition period).

1873 Labourers from India, and later Indonesia, arrive.

1941 US troops occupy Suriname to protect bauxite mines.

1949 First elections based on universal suffrage held.

1975 Suriname wins independence.

1980 Military coup led by Sergeant Major Dési Bouterse topples government. Socialist republic declared.

1982 Fifteen prominent leaders of re-democratization movement executed.

1986 Civil war begins between military government and Maroons, led by Bouterse's former bodyguard, Ronnie Brunswijk. At least 39 unarmed inhabitants of the N'Dyuka Maroon village, Moiwana, mostly women and children, are murdered by military.

1987 Civilian government installed with new constitution for Republic of Suriname, but Bourtese remains in charge of army.

1990 Bourtese dismisses civilian government with phone call in "telephone coup".

1991 Bourtese holds elections under international pressure. The New Front coalition wins; Ronald Venetiaan is elected president.

1996 National Democratic Party (founded by Bouterse in 1987) wins election.

1999 Bourtese convicted of drug smuggling in Holland in absentia.

2000 Venetiaan and the New Front coalition regains presidency (and again in 2006).

2004 Surinamese dollar introduced as currency.

2007 UN maritime border tribunal awards both Guyana and Suriname a share of the potentially oil-rich offshore basin under dispute.

2008 Trial begins of Bouterse and others accused of involvement in executions of opponents of military regime in 1982.

2010 Bouterse elected president.

2012 Fire in Paramaribo destroys a number of historical wooden buildings.

ARRIVAL AND DEPARTURE

Johan Adolf Pengel International Airport (also known as Zanderij), an hour south of Paramaribo, receives direct **flights** from Aruba, Amsterdam, Belém and Boa Vista (Brazil), Cayenne (French Guiana), Curaçao, Georgetown, Miami and Port of Spain (Trinidad). **Zorg en Hoop**, a smaller airport about fifteen minutes from the capital, receives small domestic aircraft, as well as six flights a week from Guyana.

OVERLAND FROM GUYANA

From Georgetown it's a three-hour **bus** ride to the **ferry** port at Molson Creek, with two crossings per day, then a three-hour **bus** ride from South Drain to Paramaribo (see box below).

OVERLAND FROM FRENCH GUIANA

Travellers from French Guiana must cross the Marowijne Maroni River from St Laurent du Maroni to Albina by **ferry** or motorized **dugout canoe**, before continuing the three- to four-hour drive by **minibus** or **taxi** to Paramaribo (see box, p.684).

VISAS

Visas are required for all visitors except nationals from CARICOM countries, and a few Asian and South American countries. Visitors may instead apply for a Tourist Card, valid for thirty days, single entry only (US$25). Tourist Cards may be obtained at Paramaribo airport (Johan Adolf Pengel International Airport) on arrival, whereas overland travellers need to secure theirs in advance at the consulates in Guyana (see p.645) and French Guiana (see p.676); same day processing. For stays of longer than thirty days or multiple entry, visas must be obtained (from US$45 upwards); unlike Tourist Cards, these may not be processed on the same day for travellers of certain nationalities. For updated information on visa requirements, check Ⓦ surinameembassy.org.

GETTING AROUND

While commuting around the capital and outlying areas is reasonably easy, there are no major highways in Suriname except for the Oost–Westverbinding (East–West Highway) that runs between Albina and Nieuw Nickerie; large stretches of this road (between Paramaribo and Albina) are still under repair following the civil war in the mid-1980s, though work looks set to be completed in late 2013. Scheduled state-run buses and private minibuses run to most destinations, though for many remote interior destinations you'll need to travel by 4WD, small plane or motorized dugout canoe (or a combo of all three); it's cheaper and easier to go as part of a tour.

CROSSING BETWEEN SURINAME AND GUYANA

Getting to Guyana involves crossing the Corantijn (Corentyne) River on the ferry, with daily departures at 11am (SRD10 single) from **South Drain**, an hour west of Nickerie. Numerous minibuses run to the ferry from Paramaribo (3–4hr; SRD70); some minibus companies work in partnership with Guyanese tour companies (see p.652 & p.665). You will need time to clear customs and a valid passport. Once you arrive at **Molson Creek, Guyana**, you must clear customs again and get your passport stamped before taking one of the waiting minibuses for the three-hour journey to Georgetown (G$2500–3000). There is no currency exchange or ATM at South Drain or Molson Creek, but euros or US$ (preferably the latter) can be easily exchanged at either location with unofficial moneychangers for Surinamese/Guyanese dollars, respectively. If going from Guyana to Suriname, most minibus companies pick up passengers at around 4–4.30am in order to make the 9.30am ferry to Suriname.

7

BY PLANE

There are some **scheduled internal flights**, but tour operators tend to charter planes to visit parks and reserves, and this limits their frequency to the number of tourists wishing to make a trip. Suriname Airways (Ⓦwww.slm.firm.sr) offers organized tours to Kasikasima, Palumeu and Awarradam through its tour division METS (see p.665).

BY BUS

Brightly decorated, crowded **private minibuses** are numbered and run along assigned routes both between the capital and smaller cities near the coast, and to Paramaribo's various neighbourhoods. These display their prices on the door and do not leave until they are full, but are more frequent than the scheduled state-run services and stop wherever you want along the road. Getting on board is a bit of a free-for-all, so shared taxis (see below) are a better option if travelling long distances with a lot of luggage. The plainer **state-run buses** (*staatsbus*) have a dedicated bus station, follow a schedule and use bus stops. See Ⓦnvbnvsuriname.com.

BY SHARED TAXI

Shared taxis (essentially private vehicles) run to Albina and are far more comfortable than minibuses (your guesthouse can recommend a reliable operator).

ACCOMMODATION

Accommodation in Paramaribo consists of **guesthouses** (including the closest thing Suriname has to a youth hostel) and mid-range hotels. Almost all rooms will come equipped with running water, fans and/or air conditioning and mosquito nets. Outside the capital, besides a couple of hotels in Nieuw Nickerie, accommodation is rather basic, unless you count several resorts. A comprehensive list of guesthouses can be found at Ⓦsuriname-tourism.org.

If you travel into the interior, you're likely to stay in **lodges** in Suriname's nature parks and reserves – which vary from rustic (a place to hang your hammock and shared facilities) to the more luxurious (en-suite rooms with mosquito nets). This is usually on an all-inclusive basis and bookings are best made through tour operators.

FOOD AND DRINK

The food in Suriname is fairly inexpensive, tasty and influenced by its ethnically diverse population. Informal Indonesian eateries known as **warungs** (in the Blauwgrond area) and Hindustani **roti shops** sit alongside Chinese, European-style and Creole restaurants. Meals cost around SRD15–25.

Kip (chicken) is very popular and typical Surinamese dishes include *moksie alesie* (rice, beans, chicken and vegetables) and *pom* (chicken baked with a root vegetable). Indonesian specialities include *saoto* (chicken soup, beansprouts, potatoes and a boiled egg), *bami* (fried noodles) and *nasi goreng* (fried rice). Two tasty peanut soups are *pindasoep*, made with tom-tom (plantain noodles), and *petjil*, made with vegetables. *Bakabanna* (plantain slices, dipped in a pancake batter and fried) is an established crowd-pleaser. Traditional Dutch favourites like *bitterballen* (breaded and fried minced meat balls) and *poffertjes* (sugared pancakes) are plentiful. If travelling in the interior, you may well get to try various game dishes.

DRINK

Suriname has its own **rum** industry and both Borgoe and Black Cat are worth a try; the lethal 90 percent proof stuff is usually used to mix cocktails. Imported and local beer (*Parbo* is the very drinkable local tipple of choice), soft drinks and bottled water are widely available, as is **dawet**, a very sweet, pink concoction of coconut milk and lemongrass. In Paramaribo you can also find decent **coffee**.

CULTURE AND ETIQUETTE

Suriname's diverse population is 37 percent Hindustani (the local term for

East Indian); 31 percent Creole (people of mixed European and African origin); 15 percent Javanese; 10 percent Maroon (Bush Negro); 3.7 percent Amerindians; Jews, Chinese, Portuguese, Lebanese and Brazilians make up the rest. The main **religions** are Hinduism, Christianity and Islam.

The official **language** in Suriname is Dutch but the common language is Sranan Tongo (Surinamese Creole), also known as Takitaki. Several Maroon languages, including Saramaccan and Aukan, are spoken, as are Amerindian languages such as Carib. A reasonable number of people speak some English, particularly in Paramaribo. Always check with your guide and ask permission before taking pictures of people, buildings and sacrificial areas, especially when visiting Maroon villages. For **tipping**, ten percent is the norm if a service charge hasn't been included.

COMMUNICATIONS

Postal services are provided by the Central Post Office, Surpost, near RBTT in Kerkplein 1. The country code is 597. Public **telephone booths** in Suriname do not accept coins, so you can either buy **phone cards (**denominations of US$3, 5 and 10) from newsagents, shops and hotels, or else use Skype. To use your **mobile phone**, get it unlocked, then purchase a Telesur or Digicel SIM card and some prepaid charge cards costing SRD5, 10, 20 or 50. **Internet cafés** are dying out due to proliferation of (mostly) free internet/wi-fi in many hotels/guesthouses.

SURINAME ON THE NET

ⓦ **suriname-tourism.org** The Suriname Tourism Foundation has info on what to do, where to stay and how to get around in Suriname.

ⓦ **ci-suriname.org** Info on Suriname's protected areas by Conservation International.

ⓦ **whc.unesco.org/en/list/940** Info on Paramaribo's historic city centre.

EMERGENCY NUMBERS

Fire services ☎ **110**
Ambulance ☎ **113**
Police ☎ **115**

CRIME AND SAFETY

Locals are proud of saying that tourists can walk safely from one end of Paramaribo to the other at night. Take this with a pinch of salt; as in most cities, burglary, armed robbery and other **petty crime** does take place. Avoid flaunting valuables and don't walk down inadequately lit streets after dark.

Travel to the interior is usually without incident, although there have been some reports of independent tourists being robbed. Be careful on the **roads**, as drivers can be reckless, and mopeds, scooters and motorcycles always have the right of way.

HEALTH

Medical care is limited, as is the small ambulance fleet. **Academisch Ziekenhuis** (Fluestraat; ☎ 113, ⓦ azp.sr) has the only 24-hour emergency room service in Paramaribo as well as general practitioners who speak English. Tap water is allegedly safe to drink in Paramaribo, but, where possible, drink bottled water. Insect repellent is essential as there are reported cases of mosquito-borne dengue fever. Consult your doctor regarding malaria tablets (malaria is present in some parts of the interior) and the various **vaccinations** required, which include hepatitis A, hepatitis B, yellow fever, typhoid, tetanus-diphtheria and rabies.

INFORMATION AND MAPS

Staff at the Toeristen Informatie Centrum (Tourist Information Centre), at Fort Zeelandia Complex, Waterkant 1 (Mon–Fri 8am–3.30pm; ☎ 479 200), are very helpful and speak English. They provide free maps and information in Dutch and English on transport, restaurants, nightlife, day-trips and tours, as well as the latest copy of *Suriname's Destination Guide*.

7

MONEY AND BANKS

The unit of **currency** is the Suriname dollar (SRD), which comes in 1, 2.50, 5, 10, 20, 50 and 100 notes and 1, 5, 10, 25, 100 and 250 cent coins. Prices are often given in euros, which are readily accepted (as are US$), and cambios (money exchanges) offer better exchange rates than banks. Major **credit cards** are accepted by most tour operators and in some restaurants and hotels in Paramaribo. Some **ATMs** in Paramaribo accept foreign bankcards; elsewhere ATMs are sparse, so carry extra **cash**. At the time of writing, €1=SRD4.30, US$1=SRD3.27 and £1=SRD5.29.

OPENING HOURS AND HOLIDAYS

Government institutions open Mon–Fri 7am–2.30pm. **Shops** and other businesses open Mon–Fri 9am–4.30pm and Sat 9am–1pm; Chinese corner shops tend to be open daily. **Banks** are open Mon–Fri 9am–2pm.

PARAMARIBO

PARAMARIBO ("Parbo" to the locals) is by far the most pleasant of the three Guyanese capitals. Originally a Dutch trading post, Parbo's historic inner city became a UNESCO World Heritage Site in 2002. Its streets are lined with attractive eighteenth- and nineteenth-century colonial Dutch, British, Spanish and French wooden buildings, you can take refuge from the heat in the beautiful palm tree grove that is Palmentuin (Palm Garden), and the riverfront near the historical **Fort Zeelandia** is a romantic spot at sunset. The town's houses of worship reflect the melange of cultures that make up Suriname – from the wooden churches and whitewashed synagogue to the characteristic domes of the mosque and the swastikas in their original meaning decorating the Hindu temples. You can eat well in Parbo, as this mix of cultures is also reflected in the capital's diverse cuisine.

The Waterkant (waterfront), the bus station and the markets seem just as colourful and chaotic as their equivalents in the two neighbouring countries, but Paramaribo is generally **safe**. Steer clear of the unlit Palmentuin after dark, as well as the residential area east of Van Sommelsdijkstrant Straat and its intersection with Kleine Dwarsstraat. Taxis are the best way to get around town in the evening.

WHAT TO SEE AND DO

Paramaribo's principal charm lies in the unhurried exploration of its Old Town. It's easy to organize cycling tours of nearby plantations, as well as river dolphin-spotting on the Commewijne River.

PUBLIC HOLIDAYS

January 1 New Year's Day
March Holi Phagwa (Hindu festival; date varies)
March/April (varies) Good Friday
March/April (varies) Easter Monday
May 1 Labour Day
July 1 Keti Koti (Emancipation Day)
August 8 Emancipation of the Javanese

August 9 Day of the Indigenous People
September Eid Ul Fitr (Muslim festival; date varies)
November 25 Srefidensi. Independence Day
December 25 Christmas Day
December 26 Second Christmas Day

FESTIVALS AND CELEBRATIONS

In addition to national holidays, many important events are celebrated among the resident ethnic communities. These include Chinese New Year (Feb); Jewish New Year (Sept); Loweman Dei, celebrating all things Maroon (Oct); and Diwali (Nov). Other festivities include the Brazilian carnival (Feb); French Music Festival (June); Back to School Festival (Sept); Salsuri Music and Suriname Jazz Festivals (Oct); and Surifesta, the end of year festival (Dec). On New Year's Eve (Owru Jari) there is a spectacular fireworks display in the capital. In 2013 it was Suriname's turn to host the all-Caribbean culture and music extravaganza that is **CariFesta**, check the website for future host countries (Ⓦ carifesta.net).

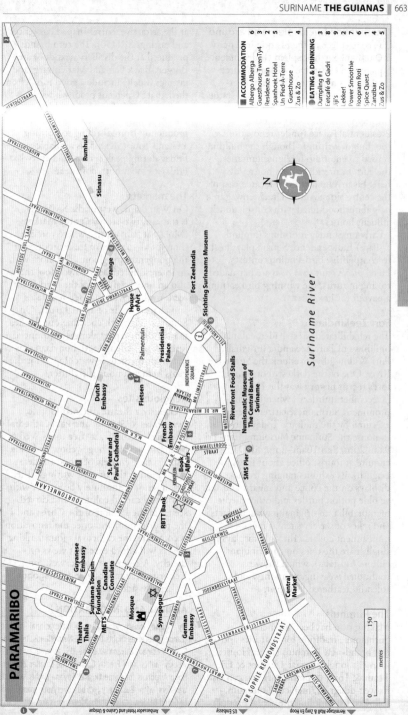

PARAMARIBO

Ambassador Hotel and Casino & Unique ▲
US Embassy ▲
Hermitage Mall & Zorg En Hoop ▲

■ ACCOMMODATION	
Albergo Alberga	6
Guesthouse TwenTy4	3
Residence Inn	2
Spanhoek Hotel	5
Un Pied-A-Terre	1
Guesthouse	
Zus & Zo	4

● EATING & DRINKING	
Dumpling #1	3
Eetcafé de Gadri	8
Jiji's	9
Lekker!	2
Power Smoothie	7
Rooipram Roti	6
Spice Quest	1
Zanzibar	4
Zus & Zo	5

Rumhuis

Stinasu

Orange

House of Art

Palmentuin

Presidential Palace

Fort Zeelandia

Stichting Surinaams Museum

Suriname River

Dutch Embassy

Fietsen

French Embassy

Independence Square

Riverfront Food Stalls

Numismatic Museum of The Central Bank of Suriname

St. Peter and Paul's Cathedral

Book & Affairs

SMS Pier

RBTT Bank

Guyanese Embassy

Suriname Tourism Foundation

Canadian Consulate

Mosque

Synagogue

German Embassy

Central Market

Theatre Thalia

METS

N

0   metres   150

7

Onafhankelijkheidsplein and around

The centrepiece of the historic inner city is **Onafhankelijkheidsplein** (Independence Square), an expanse of well-manicured green lawns near the Waterkant overlooked by several state buildings, a statue of a rather round Johan Adolf Pengel (former prime minister) and the **Presidential Palace** (under renovation at the time of writing). Though the building is used to entertain foreign dignitaries, the current president does not reside here: his private fortress is located east of the centre along Anton Drachtenweg in a neighbourhood filled with conspicuously affluent houses.

Early on Sunday mornings (around 7–8am) Independence Square plays host to competitive **bird-singing contests**. Here, *picolets* and *twa twas* are persuaded to sing in turns, the winning bird earning a payout for its owner.

Fort Zeelandia

The rehabilitated, tree-shaded colonial buildings of Fort Zeelandia (originally Fort Willoughby) overlook the Suriname River. One of the darkest spots in the fort's recent history was the 1982 "December murders", when fifteen prominent Surinamese citizens were executed by the military. Today it is used to house the **Suriname Museum** (Tues–Fri 9am–2pm, Sun 10am–2pm; SRD15; enquire at tourist office about tours in English), its exhibits ranging from displays on the coffee and sugar trade and ye olde potion bottles and other medical memorabilia, to original Jewish artefacts and relics of slavery such as metal punishment collars. The only displays in English are the ones on Amerindian culture (upstairs), which showcase traditional weaving, weaponry, and splendid feathered headgear.

The Rumhuis

Making rum has been a venerable Surinamese tradition for centuries and at this brand-new **Rumhuis** (Rum House; Cornelis Jongbawstraat 18; Tues & Fri 11am & 1pm; ⊙ rumhuis.sr) you can visit its well-designed interactive museum, followed by sampling the actual product

at the attractive, barrel-shaped bar (entry and tastings SRD50). The rum brands produced at the distillery next door are Borgoe, Black Cat and Mariënburg, and tastings usually include a good mix – from the lethal 90 percent proof white rum to the venerable fifteen-year-old Borgoe. For those wanting to see every step of the production from distilling to bottling, a Grand Tour (SRD65) is available every Friday during peak season, and every last Friday of the month outside it.

The markets

On Waterkant, west of the SMS pier, is the vast, two-storey **Central Market** (Mon–Sat 5am–4pm), where you can shop for all manner of fresh produce in the pungent semi-gloom. For those with an interest in fetishes and voodoo, there's also an unofficial "under the market" section where Maroons sell necklaces and charms made of animal parts. On Sundays, it's worth checking out the flea market (8am–1pm) along Tourtonnelaan, just east of Verlengde Mahonylaan – as much for the people-watching as for the gems hidden among the clutter.

Religious sites

Previously a theatre, the neo-Gothic, twin-towered **St Peter and Paul Cathedral** on Henck Arronstraat (free tours Wed & Sat mornings) is a huge yellow and blue edifice made entirely of wood (under renovation at the time of writing). The airy interior is absolutely beautiful, with intricately carved columns and carved scenes of the Passion of the Christ and the resurrection, and once the renovation is complete, the cathedral's four flanking towers will afford excellent views of the city. A couple of blocks west, on Keizerstraat, a **mosque** and **synagogue** sit happily side by side.

ARRIVAL AND INFORMATION

By plane Johan Adolf Pengel International Airport (Zanderij) receives flights from the Netherlands, Trinidad, Brazil, Curaçao, Guyana and the US, as well as twice-weekly flights from French Guiana. The smaller Zorg en Hoop Airport is for domestic and Guyana flights. Airport transfers with Buscovery (⊙ buscoverytours.com) and Le Grand Baldew (⊙ legrandbaldew.com) take around 1hr and cost US$20; book in advance. The cheap but infrequent state bus (*staatsbus*) will drop you off at the Heiligenweg bus station in Knuffelsgracht (3 daily services except Sun; 1hr 30min; SRD2.50; w nvbnvsuriname.com), or you can catch the more frequent private minibuses, which will drop you in Maagdenstraat (Line POZ, less than SRD10). From Zorg en Hoop, minibus lines #8 and #9 pass near the airport and drop you at Steenbakkerijstraat (less than SRD10). Unmetered taxis from JAPI to the city centre (45min) cost around SRD120–140. Taxis from Zorg en Hoop cost around SRD20–25 and take about 15min.

Destinations Scheduled domestic flights operated by Gum Air (w gumair.com) and Blue Wing (w bluewing airlines.com; note that this airline has a poor safety record) depart to Kajana (2 weekly on Mon & Fri; 50min) and Palumeu (2 weekly on Mon & Fri; 1hr 5min). Trans Guyana Airways (w transguyana.net) and Blue Wing both fly from Zorg en Hoop to Guyana (daily except Sun; 1hr 20min).

By minibus From South Drain (Guyana river crossing) and Nieuw Nickerie (car park next to market), private minibuses (2–3hr; SRD60) will offload you at Dr. Sophie Redmondstraat, opposite *Hotel Ambassador* (some may drop you off at your lodgings). The state-run bus (2 daily except Sun; 3hr; SRD15) drops you at the Heilgenweg bus station in Knuffelsgracht. From Albina (French Guiana border) several daily minibuses and two daily state-run NVB minibuses (one service on Sat and Sun; 3–4hr; SRD8.50) drop you at Waterkant and the Heiligenweg bus station in Knuffelsgracht.

For NVB buses, arrive at least an hour in advance to get a number from the ticket office; you then present the number to the minibus driver and pay for your seat when you board. Private minibuses such as Lada & Son have a reciprocal arrangement with minibus companies in Guyana, so you can buy a ticket all the way to Georgetown if you use their services to get to South Drain.

Destinations Albina (NVB state bus from Heiligenweg, minibus #PA from Central Market; 3–4hr); Nieuw Nickerie and South Drain (NVB state bus from Heiligenweg or minibus #PN from Dr. Sophie Redmondstraat; several daily; 2hr–3hr 30min).

By taxi To and from South Drain unmetered taxis cost SRD70–200 depending on passenger numbers (2–3hr). Taxis to Albina (for the French Guiana border crossing) cost SRD70–200 depending on passenger numbers (3hr); ask your guesthouse to book a reputable one.

Tourist information The Toeristen Informatie Centrum is at Fort Zeelandia Complex, Waterkant 1 (see p.661).

GETTING AROUND

By bicycle You can rent bikes from €3.50/day from Fietsen, at Grote Combeweg 13a (w fietseninsuriname .com), or from €2.50/day from Cardy Adventures at Cornelis Jongbawstraat 31 (w cardyadventures.com).

By bus The larger, cheaper but less frequent scheduled state buses (*staatsbus*) leave from the bus station at Heiligenweg in Knuffelsgracht. Fares in and around Paramaribo cost about SRD1.50.

By taxi Taxis wait for passengers in front of Central Market (Waterkant). Registered, unmetered taxis use fixed rates. Trips within the city should cost SRD7.50–15; always agree a fare with your driver in advance. Recommended taxi firms include Djo's Taxi (☎ 471 048) and Sheriff Taxi (☎ 410 241).

ACCOMMODATION

All accommodation options below have a/c and wi-fi, unless stated otherwise.

Albergo Alberga Mr F.H.R. Lim A Postraat 13 ☎ 520 050, w guesthousealbergoalberga.com. Lovely nineteenth-century wooden house in the city centre with a button-sized swimming pool. Rooms (some with a/c) are bright but could be cleaner. **€24**

SURINAME TOURS

In the off-season, the tour operators work together and share customers in order to make up minimum group numbers. Price-wise, there isn't much difference between operators. Unless you have a lot of time to spare, you'll need a tour operator for excursions into the interior.

TOUR OPERATORS

Fietsen Grote Combeweg 13A ☎ 520 781, w fietsen insuriname.com. From day-long cycling tours of the plantations to multi-day cycling challenges.

METS Dr. J F Nassylaan 2, Parbo ☎ 477 088, w suriname vacations.com. One of longest-running, reputable operators; specializes in visits to the interior and manages jungle lodges in Awarradam, Kasikasima and Palumeu, but also does day-trips around Parbo.

Myrysji Tours Griegstraat 41 ☎ 456 611, w myrysji tours-suriname.com. The only Amerindian tour operator

in Suriname, based in Christiankondre; specializes in trips to Galibi.

Orange Van Sommelsdijkstraat 1 ☎ 421 984, w orange suriname.com. Professional, English-speaking staff, and a plethora of tours – from day-trips to Brownsberg and the Commewijne River to multi-day adventures in Galibi, Central Suriname Nature Reserve and much more.

STINASU Cornelis Jongbawstraat 14, Parbo ☎ 476 597, w stinasu.com. This government agency is in charge of Suriname's protected areas, but the independent operators above have a better reputation.

7

Guesthouse TwenTy4 Jessurunstraat 24 ☎ 420 751, ⓦ twenty4suriname.com. Under the same management as *Zus & Zo* (see below), this comfortable guesthouse is a little bit plusher (most rooms are en suite) but also feels quite isolated in spite of its central location. Friendly staff can help arrange tours and there's a small bar open until 11pm. €25

Residence Inn Anton Dragtenweg 7 ☎ 521 414, ⓦ resinn.com. Yes, it's a chain, but a good one at that: the en-suite rooms and cabins are not terribly memorable but guests have use of the swimming pool within a pleasant garden and there's a decent restaurant serving a mix of Surinamese and international dishes. US$60

Spanhoek Hotel Domineestraat 2–4 ☎ 477 888, ⓦ spanhoekhotel.com. Stylish rooms with all mod cons, warm accents and nice touches, such as fresh flowers – all in a very central location. Buffet breakfast included in price. €110

Un Pied-À-Terre Guesthouse Costerstraat 59 ☎ 470 488, ⓦ un-pied-a-terre.com. A quaint guesthouse just blocks away from all the action. Breezy veranda and rooms with four-poster beds draped with mosquito nets, and breakfast from SRD14. For a cheaper option, hang a hammock in the garden (€2 discount if you hang your own). Rooms €25, hammocks €12

★ **Zus & Zo** Grote Combéweg 13a ☎ 520 905, ⓦ zusenzosuriname.com. This is the traveller hub of Parbo, comprising several compact, brightly painted rooms with shared bath, helpful staff, tour agency, bike rental agency next door and one of the best eateries/chillout spots in town. Clientele varies between international travellers and screeching Dutch teenagers. €25

EATING AND DRINKING

Take a taxi to the Blauwgrond neighbourhood to eat at one of the many *warungs* (Javanese restaurants) here. Check ⓦ eteninsuriname.com for a restaurant list and online menus.

Dumpling #1 Nassylaan 168 ☎ 477 904. Breezy Chinese restaurant in a courtyard set back from the tree-lined street, serving dumplings, grilled seafood and more. Meals from SRD35. Tues–Sat 9.30am–3pm & 6–11pm; Sun 8am–1pm & 6–11pm.

Eetcafé de Gadri Zeelandiaweg 1 ☎ 420 688. Generous portions of Creole and Indonesian food (SRD15–30), served at tables overlooking the Suriname River. Mon–Fri 8am–10pm & Sat 11am–10pm.

Jiji's SRD Pier, Waterkant 2nd floor. At this breezy location overlooking the river, this is the best of the eateries, serving generous portions of Surinamese and international dishes. Meals around SRD30. Daily 5–11pm.

Lekker! Johannes Mungstraat 8 ☎ 430 661. Aptly named, trendy café and bistro ("lekker" is Dutch for "delicious"), with the best coffee in town, create-your-own-salad

★ **TREAT YOURSELF**

Spice Quest Nassylaan 107 ☎ 520 747. One of the capital's most stylish restaurants, set in a tropical garden with a lovely ambience. You'll find yourself paying over the odds for Vietnamese spring rolls, crispy Chinese duck and various fusion dishes, but it's all delicious and beautifully presented. Meals around SRD90. Mon 6–11pm, Tues–Sun 11am–3pm & 6–11pm.

option, toasties and treats such as bagels with grilled goat's cheese and honey and real lemonade. You can linger with your laptop, too. Mon–Fri 7.30am–4pm & Sat 7.30am–5pm.

Power Smoothie Zwartenhovenbrugstraat at Wilhelminastraat. Tiny spot churning out excellent smoothies, including "healthy" ones and a few potent, alcohol-tinged ones. There are sandwiches and wraps if you're looking for more than liquid refreshment. Smoothies from SRD8. Daily 10am–6pm.

Roopram Roti Several sites across town including Saturnusstraat 44. Visit for generous portions of roti (Indian pancake) stuffed with various curried meats (or vegetables) with all the trimmings for around SRD15. Daily 9am–10pm (varies by location).

Zanzibar Van Sommelsdijkstraat 1. This lively outpost with a DJ (Fri & Sat) has outdoor seating and an open-air bar serving food and delicious cocktails from SRD8. Daily 6pm until late.

★ **Zus & Zo** Grote Combéweg 13a ☎ 520 905. This garden café decorated with Christmas lights serves great international tapas (grilled plantain, flavourful *sate*, *patatas bravas*) as well as more substantial mains – noodles, grilled meats and more, accompanied by tangy ginger juice and Parbo beer. Wednesday night is movie night and the little stage hosts live music on the weekends. Daily 9am–11pm.

SHOPPING

Book Affairs Kerkplein 8. Run by the wonderful Debby, this small secondhand bookshop may have what you need.

Zus & Zo (see above). Quality Saramaccan and Amerindian handicrafts – from carved, decorated calabashes to intricate jewellery and woodcarvings.

DIRECTORY

Banks and exchange Several RBTT ATMs in the centre accept foreign cards. A convenient cambio is on Kleine Waterstraat, at Van Sommelsdijkstraat: outside working hours, you can exchange your cash directly at the ATM-like exchange machine next to it.

Embassies and Consulates Brazil, Maratakastraat 2 (☎400 200); Canada, Wagenwagstraat 50 (☎424 527); France, Henck Arronstraat 5–7 (☎475 222); Guyana, Gravenstraat 82 (☎477 895); Netherlands, Van Roosevelt-kade 5 (☎477 211); UK, c/o VSH United Bldgs, Van't Hogerhuysstraat 9–11 (☎402 558); US, Dr. Sophie Redmondstraat 129 (☎472 900).

Internet All accommodation options reviewed offer internet and/or wi-fi.

Pharmacies Ali's Drugstore & Apotheek, at Tourtonnelaan 127; Apotheek Sibilo, at Koningstraat 90.

DAY-TRIPS FROM PARAMARIBO

From Paramaribo you can do numerous interesting day-trips; some destinations are reachable by public transport, whereas others are more easily accomplished by organized tours (see p.665).

Brownsberg Nature Park

About 130km south of Paramaribo on the Mazaroni Plateau, **BROWNSBERG NATURE PARK** is the only protected area in Suriname that can be visited from Paramaribo as a day-trip (10hr). On a lucky day, you might see howler and spider monkeys, deer, agouti and birds such as woodpeckers, macaws and parrots. There are also fine views from the plateau of the rainforest and the vast **Van Blommestein Lake**, created to provide electricity for the Alcoa aluminium industry (which typically resulted in the displacement of several Maroon villages and inadequate government compensation for its residents). Several tour companies, including Orange (see p.665), offer day-trips to the reserve (US$60), with transport, lunch and a hike to one of the three waterfalls included (bring your bathing suit). It's technically possible to stay overnight, as STINASU (see p.665) operates a lodge on the plateau (rooms from SRD400), as well as hammock and camping facilities (SRD35–45); however, travellers have complained about the run-down rooms and inadequate cleanliness of the facilities.

Suriname and Commewijne rivers

Paramaribo stands on the banks of the Suriname River, which joins Commewijne River a short distance east. The area is littered with the remnants of plantations (alongside a few working ones) and wonderful colonial architecture. The dilapidated **Pepperpot Plantation** is an old coffee and cocoa plantation that's great for birdwatching, and Frederiksdorp Plantation has stone and wooden buildings that have been fully renovated and converted into a delightful hotel and restaurant. The star-shaped **Fort Nieuw Amsterdam** (Mon–Fri 9am–6pm, Sat & Sun 10am–6pm; SRD10; ⓦfortnieuw amsterdam.com) is located at the meeting point of the Commerwijne and Suriname rivers. It houses an entertaining open-air museum with highlights including the Coach House, the temporary art/ photography exhibitions held in the former jail cells and the impressive American World War II cannons.

North of Fort Nieuw Amsterdam, near the mouth of Suriname River, is **Matapica Beach**, a reserve established in 1966 to protect the nesting places of the sea turtles. Nowadays, much of the beach has eroded, though some turtles still visit the shores to lay their eggs between April and August and it is also the habitat of many species of waterfowl. Since the only accommodation on the beach has been swept away, staying overnight to watch the turtles is problematic, even if you can arrange boat transport out there. Still, it's worth enquiring about.

To explore the rivers and plantations you can either go by organized **boat tour** (see p.665), which typically includes Fort Nieuw Amsterdam, lunch at Frederiksdorp and a spot of dolphin-watching (the rivers are home to pink river dolphins), by **bike** (see p.665), either as a group tour or solo (both Fietsen and Cardy Adventures can help with maps and independent trip planning), or by **public transport** (see ⓦnvbnvsuriname.com for bus schedules within Commewijne).

Jodensavanne

Jodensavanne, 70km south of Paramaribo on the east bank of the Suriname River, is named after the Jews who settled in this savannah area around 1650 after fleeing from the Inquisition.

NIEUW NICKERIE AND BIGIPAN

Though easily bypassed if you're taking a direct minibus between the border and Paramaribo, the orderly grid of Nieuw Nickerie's streets with its palm tree-lined boulevard is worth an overnight stay, if only to visit Bigipan, a coastal area overgrown with mangroves, known for its abundance of birds, particularly the scarlet ibis. If you have your own wheels, you can try asking the local fishermen in the area to take you birdwatching. METS (see p.665) offer two-day tours of the Bigipan area and the coast west of Paramaribo (US$260). Nickerie is reachable by NVB state buses and private minibuses from Paramaribo (2hr–3hr 30min) and by minibus from South Drain (1hr).

Residence Inn R. B. Bharostraat 84 ☏ 210 950, ⓦ resinn.com. This centrally located hotel is a good place to stay. There is a decent fusion restaurant and the helpful staff can arrange a day-trip to Bigipan. **US$60**

Little remains of the village, but ruins of the graveyard and the **synagogue** – the oldest remaining in the Americas – really come alive if you visit the place with a knowledgeable guide. By infrequent state bus it's possible to get as far as the village of Carolina (1hr 30min) 5km away, where you can pay a boatman to take you across the river and then walk the rest of the way, but you get much more out of the trip if you join forces with Marina La Costa (Algerstraat 28, Paramaribo; €95; ☏ 498 407, ✉ flair@tip-suriname.com), an expert in Jewish history in Suriname who can provide you with the background and regale you with stories of key figures.

Colakreek

Just 5km from the international airport lies **COLAKREEK** (SRD12.50–15), a recreation park centred around a river the colour of Coca-Cola. The well-managed site is great for swimming and there are also water bikes for rent, a good cafeteria and overnight facilities including five-person cabins (SRD295) and camping sites (SRD20/person). To **get here**, take one of the state buses (or a taxi) to the airport, from where you can either walk or take another taxi.

AWARRADAM AND PALUMEU

One of Suriname's greatest highlights is a visit to the Saramaccan and Amerindian villages in the country's interior. **AWARRADAM** is a community made up of eight villages populated by Saramaccan Maroons, descendants of runaway plantation slaves who fled deep into the

jungle; it lies in the Gran Rio River near a rapid of the same name. There is a wonderful ecolodge located on an island in the river, consisting of a number of self-contained huts with mosquito nets owned by METS (see p.665) and run by members of a local Saramaccan village. From here a knowledgeable guide can take you wildlife-spotting along the river, swimming in the nearby rapids and to the four Saramaccan villages nearby – a slice of Africa in the depths of the Surinamese jungle. The women still carry large loads on their heads, and the Saramaccan tongue spoken is based on the dialects spoken in Ghana over 300 years ago; most of the villages still follow traditional religions and practise traditional dance (which you may be able to see – and participate in). While modernity is creeping in (many men now work in Paramaribo or in the gold mines and many villages now have mobile phone reception), it's still a unique culture and tours of the villages are very sensitively conducted.

PALUMEU is a village located at the beginning of the Tapanahony River, deep within the Amazon rainforest, populated by Trio and Wajana Amerindians. Visitors stay in the METS-owned traditional lodge by the airstrip and activities offered include a boat trip along the Tapanahony River to Poti Hill, hikes in the rainforest and a two-day trip by dugout canoe to Mount Kasikasima.

ARRIVAL AND TOURS

By plane There are flights to both Awarradam and Palumeu on Mon and Fri from Zorg en Hoop airport.

Tour operators Trips to either community are usually booked through METS (see p.665), which offers four-/five-day stays at either location (combo visits to both can be arranged), though if you're looking to hike up Mt Kasikasima, it's an eight-day trip.

THE CENTRAL SURINAME NATURE RESERVE

Created in 1998 by amalgamating the Ralleighvallen, Tafelberg and Eilerts de Haan nature reserves, the **CENTRAL SURINAME NATURE RESERVE** occupies 16,000 square kilometres of southwestern Suriname, some nine percent of the country's total surface area. Though there are complaints of STINASU mismanagement (the foundation for nature conservation allegedly turned a blind eye to gold-mining inside a designated protected area), it is nevertheless a staggeringly beautiful part of the country, home to diverse fauna such as spider monkeys, ocelot and the world's largest-known species of the cock-of-the-rock bird. Natural highlights include Ralleighvallen (Raleigh Falls) and Voltzberg mountain. It's a three-hour hike to the base of Voltzberg, then another 240m or so to the summit, which affords good views of the surrounding forest canopy.

Visitors stay at the basic lodge on Foengoe Island next to Ralleighvallen, reachable either by short flight (50min) or else by five hours in a 4WD, followed by a two-hour ride up the river in a motorized canoe. Tours can be organized through Orange (see p.665), among others.

GALIBI NATURE RESERVE

Situated in the northeastern corner of Suriname at the mouth of the Maroni River, the **GALIBI NATURE RESERVE** is a major nesting ground for leatherback and green turtles between March and August. Several tour operators (see p.665) run two- to three-day trips to Galibi (€165–200), which involve a bus ride to Albina, followed by a three-hour boat trip, with overnight accommodation in the Amerindian village of Christiankondre. The visit to the Galibi site itself is at night, when the newly hatched baby turtles make a break for the water. Sadly, some travellers have complained about tour guides (not from the tour companies we have listed) picking up the baby turtles, and some locals continue to take and sell turtle eggs, in spite of the turtles' endangered status.

French Guiana

FRENCH GUIANA is a strange beast. It's a tropical corner of France, with its laws, customs, language and outlook largely mirroring those of the motherland, despite many of its citizens coming from Caribbean stock. It's also one of the most expensive countries to visit in South America.

A notorious penal colony for much of its existence, French Guiana's muggy, oppressive climate, malaria-ridden forests and inhospitable terrain were considered an ideal way to punish French criminals (as well as WWII prisoners of war). French Guiana next came to international attention in the 1960s, when the European Space Agency cleared a patch of jungle and built a **space centre** to launch satellites into orbit from the town of **Kourou**. A rocket launch is one of the country's biggest attractions, along with the **Îles du Salut**, rocky islets that were once home to the prison population.

French Guiana is perfect for adventurous travellers; it helps to have your own transport and to speak a little French. You'll find Cayenne, the edgy capital, along with Kourou and St Laurent, fairly straightforward to visit. The attractions of the Hmong village of Cacao and the turtle-watching beach, Plage Les Hattes, lie in the interior or somewhat off the beaten path. Finally, there are expeditions down the country's rivers deep into the jungle and visits to remote Amerindian communities – which means flights by tiny plane, nights in hammocks and long boat journeys into the unknown.

7

7

CHRONOLOGY

10,000 BC Originally settled by various Amerindian groups, such as the Arawak and the Caribs.

1498 AD Columbus briefly sets foot in Guiana and dubs it "the land of pariahs".

1604 First attempts at French settlement made difficult by tropical diseases and native resistance.

1643 Cayenne founded but French soon forced out by hostile Amerindians.

1664 Cayenne finally established as a permanent settlement.

1665 Dutch occupy Cayenne.

1667 Colony awarded to France under the Treaty of Breda. All inhabitants now French citizens.

1676 Brief Dutch occupation and expulsion.

1763–65 France sends around 12,000 immigrants as part of the Kourou Expedition to develop the region, but 10,000 die of yellow fever and typhoid.

1809 Combined Anglo-Portuguese naval force captures the colony for Portugal.

1814 Guiana restored to France as part of the Treaty of Paris but Portuguese remain until 1917.

1848 Slavery is abolished. The colony's fragile plantation economy collapses. Ex-slaves establish Maroon communities in the jungle.

1852 Region designated a penal colony by Napoleon; more than 70,000 French convicts transported to the area.

1853 Gold discovered in the interior.

1946 French Guiana becomes an overseas *département* of France.

1947 Penal colony abolished but the last convicts only leave in 1952.

1964–68 ESA (European Space Agency) establishes space station in Kourou to launch communications satellites.

1974 French Guiana gains own *Conseil Régional* with some autonomy in social and economic matters.

1997 Independence leader Jean-Victor Castor arrested by police, leading to civil violence in Cayenne.

2000 Riots occur in Cayenne following an organized march calling for greater autonomy.

2008 President Sarkozy dedicates 1000 troops to combat growing immigration problems.

2009 The largest space telescope yet created is launched from Kourou.

2010 The option of increased autonomy rejected in referendum.

2011 Russian rocket "Soyuz" launched from Kourou.

ARRIVAL AND DEPARTURE

French Guiana's main international airport, **Aéroport de Félix Eboué**, is some 17km south of Cayenne, near the town of Matoury. It receives direct flights from France, Martinique, Guadeloupe,

Haiti, Brazil, Suriname and the Dominican Republic.

OVERLAND FROM BRAZIL

Travellers arriving from Brazil enter French Guiana via a boat across the Oyapok River to the town of **Saint-Georges** (see p.678) and then continue their journey via road by bus or car.

OVERLAND FROM SURINAME

Travellers from Suriname must take a **ferry** or **dugout canoe** across the Maroni River to **St Laurent du Maroni** (see box, p.684) then continue via road by bus or car.

VISAS

As French Guiana is an overseas department of France, **visas** are only required for those travellers who would also need a visa for France. Non-EU nationals unsure of their visa requirements should check ⓦdiplomatie .gouv.fr/en.

GETTING AROUND

Public transport in French Guiana is limited and expensive. St Laurent, Kourou, Cayenne and Saint-Georges are connected by *taxis collectifs* (shared minibuses) that only leave when full. **Private taxis** within the three main towns are difficult to find and pricey.

Scheduled (though infrequent) TIG **buses** (ⓦcg973.fr/Lignes-de-transport -prevues) connect Cayenne and St Laurent with destinations such as Roura, Mana, Saint-Georges, Kourou and Iracoubo; few bus routes operate on weekends.

Hitchhiking is widely practised by locals outside Cayenne; common-sense precautions apply.

Renting a car is relatively inexpensive and pretty much essential if you wish to travel beyond the coastal towns or even around Cayenne and Kourou. Car rental works out cheaper than the bus if there are two of you sharing the costs. Prices start from around €30 per day and you can rent cars in Cayenne, Saint Laurent and at Félix Eboué Airport. The main roads are paved and well signed. Keep your passport with you, as there are occasional *gendarme* checkpoints.

Travel into and within the interior involves taking tiny planes and motorized *pirogues* (dugout canoes). Your *pirogue* travel will usually be part of an organized tour.

ACCOMMODATION

Accommodation in French Guiana is rather limited, with the budget end geared towards independent, adventurous travellers with their own transport. In large towns, you're likely to be confined to unremarkable business-oriented hotels (from €50/double). On the outskirts of towns and in rural areas you'll find *gîtes* (family-run lodgings), which range from simple to fairly luxurious (from €30/double). Adventurous and particularly budget-conscious travellers may choose to opt for *carbets* – wooden shelters for hammocks, which are found throughout the country. Many are unmanned and free of charge, located by the sides of roads or on beaches, and have no facilities attached; for these you'll need your own hammock (easily purchased in Cayenne). Others are found in villages and even in some towns; some come with an attached shower/toilet block and provide own hammocks at extra cost (€10–15/night).

FOOD AND DRINK

Those on a tight budget will look to street vendors, markets, well-stocked supermarkets (in Cayenne) and small takeaway joints. There is inexpensive Chinese food and pizza on offer in the main towns, as well as proper coffee, *croque monsieurs*, crêpes and croissants in the capital's cafés and bakeries. Cayenne offers the best variety of cuisines, with French, Laotian, Chinese, North African, Indonesian, Japanese, Vietnamese, Brazilian and Creole options (although you may find yourself paying Parisian prices), some of which you'll also find in St Laurent and Kourou. The best Laotian food is found in the Hmong village of Cacao (see p.677).

Fish dishes are plentiful, one of the more typical being *blaff*: a stock heavily seasoned with onion, garlic, celery, basil and spices. Another popular stock, used mostly at Easter and the Pentecost, is *bouillon d'awara*, made from the *awara* palm tree fruit and cooked with chicken, shrimp, crab and vegetables. *Fricassée* and *colombo* are typical Creole stews, the latter a meat- and vegetable-based curry stew. Wild meat like capybara, peccary and paca can also be found on the menu.

DRINK

The authentic drink here is the sweet French aperitif Ti' punch: lime, sugar-cane syrup and rum – without ice, downed in one – and there's an excellent selection of French wines also. Fresh fruit juices are popular and found at the Cayenne market, in Cacao and in some restaurants.

CULTURE AND ETIQUETTE

Amerindian tribes and Maroons largely maintain their own cultural traditions, as does the immigrant population of Hmong from Laos in villages such as Cacao and Javouhey. The majority of the population is **Creole**, and mixed-Creole culture is dominant in the metropolitan areas; there is also an increasing number of immigrants from Brazil and other South American countries, whose presence is evident in Cayenne and St Laurent. All teachers, police and *gendarmes* are recruited in mainland France, hence the sizeable French population. Note that the French generally don't **tip**.

LANGUAGE

French is the most widely spoken language, though a significant proportion of the population also speaks a French-based patois or Creole, with Chinese, *Neg Maron* (Bush Negro or Maroon), Portuguese and Amerindian languages spoken in certain areas. In St Laurent, due to the number of Surinamese and Guyanese immigrants, some English is also spoken, and the one language common to all three Guianas – Taki-Taki – is spoken along the rivers.

7

COMMUNICATIONS

The efficient postal system is integrated with that of metropolitan France, which makes deliveries to Europe quick and cheap. Public **telephone** booths that accept France Telecom cards for local calls are almost obsolete, replaced by mobile phones. To use your **mobile phone**, get it unlocked, then purchase a local SIM card from operators such as Digicel and Orange. When calling French Guiana from abroad you must dial 594 (country code) followed by a nine-digit number also beginning 594 (or 694 for mobiles). For international calls it's better to buy phone cards that work with PINs (*libre service*), available from convenience stores, or else opt for Skype. Most hotels offer wi-fi and there are internet cafés in both Cayenne and St Laurent.

CRIME AND SAFETY

There are certain areas of Cayenne that are best avoided after dark, such as the area immediately south of Avenue de Liberté and the smaller, poorly lit side streets in the centre. The area around Canal Laussat and the market can be sketchy and it's best to stick to well-lit main streets such as Avenue du Général de Gaulle and Rue Lalouette as much as possible. Drug addicts and beggars can be a nuisance both in Cayenne and in St Laurent. If sleeping in a *carbet* on a deserted beach, mind your valuables.

HEALTH

Malaria prophylactics are recommended for all areas, though the risk is thought to be low along the coast. A number of vaccinations, including hepatitis A, hepatitis B, typhoid, yellow fever, tetanus-diphtheria and rabies, are also strongly recommended. Vaccination against yellow fever is compulsory if

EMERGENCY NUMBERS

Ambulance ☎ 15
Police ☎ 17
Fire service ☎ 18

FRENCH GUIANA ON THE NET

Ⓦ **tourisme-guyane.com** Official site providing information on accommodation, transport, tour agencies and life in French Guiana.

Ⓦ **cg973.fr** Culture, sport and a general overview of French Guianese life.

Ⓦ **terresdeguyane.fr/guyane** News, politics, history, nature and some helpful links.

you're arriving from certain South American countries. There have also been recent outbreaks of dengue fever and Q fever, so mosquito repellent is essential.

Tap water is drinkable throughout the coastal area but avoid drinking creek or river water. European-standard **medical care** is available in Cayenne, Kourou and St Laurent du Maroni. The European Health Insurance Card (Ⓦ www.ehic.org .uk) that allows travellers to receive free medical treatment in participating member states works in French Guiana.

INFORMATION AND MAPS

Printed information (mostly in French) is readily available in tourist offices in Cayenne and St Laurent, where you will also find good city maps. Ask for a copy of *Le Guide*, a handy, annual, easy-to-carry guide, which lists hotels, restaurants, bars and clubs throughout French Guiana in French and English. The internationally available *Guyana, Suriname & French Guiana* by International Travel Maps is useful for a general overview of the country but contains errors. If you can read French, it's well worth buying the *Guide Guyane* by Philippe Boré – a labour of love and a detailed and entertaining guidebook to French Guiana.

MONEY AND BANKS

The currency of French Guiana is the **euro** (€), and credit/debit cards are widely accepted in the urban centres. **ATMs** generally accept Visa, MasterCard and Eurocard (and occasionally American

PUBLIC HOLIDAYS

January 1 New Year's Day
February Ash Wednesday (varies)
March/April Good Friday (varies)
March/April Easter Monday (varies)
May 1 Labour Day
May 8 WWII Victory (VE) Day
May/June Ascension Day (varies)
May/June Whit Monday (varies)

June 10 Abolition of Slavery Day
July 14 Bastille Day
15 Aug Assumption Day
1 Nov All Saints' Day
October Cayenne festival (varies)
November 11 Armistice (Remembrance Day)
December 25 Christmas Day

FESTIVALS AND NATIONAL CELEBRATIONS

The major festival in French Guiana is **Carnival**, which begins after Epiphany in the first week of January and goes on for about two months until Ash Wednesday. On Friday and Saturday nights during Carnival you can witness the tradition of **Touloulou balls**, when women (*Touloulou*), heavily disguised and wearing masks, are given the sole, non-reciprocal right to ask the men to dance; guys are not allowed to refuse. Women disguise their faces, bodies and voices so the men are incapable of recognizing even their own wives. Mardi Gras (Carnival Monday and Tuesday) takes place during the last five days of Carnival, which ends on Ash Wednesday. It features colourful street parades with music, dancing, exotic costumes and merriment.

Express). Few banks have foreign exchange facilities; Cayenne has more than one bureau de change but St Laurent has none. At the time of writing, US$1.34=€1, £0.86=€1.

OPENING HOURS AND HOLIDAYS

Many businesses and shops shut for two to three hours over lunch. Most **shops** are open Monday to Saturday 8/9am to 1pm and 3/4 to 6.30/7pm. Supermarkets remain open until around 9pm and open on Sunday 9am to 12.30pm. **Banks** open Monday to Friday 7.30am to noon & 2.30 to 5.30pm.

CAYENNE

In your travels around French Guiana **CAYENNE** is likely to be your base for exploration of the surrounding sights. This sprawling city of a myriad roundabouts has a compact centre with an attractive central square, vibrantly painted cathedral and eighteenth-century colonial buildings, a lively market (see box, p.677), and a more continental feel than the rest of the country.

WHAT TO SEE AND DO

The view overlooking Cayenne and the ocean from the hill at the end of Rue de Rémire, west of the Place des Palmistes, is the best place to get your bearings before exploring.

Place des Palmistes and around

Place des Palmistes, on Avenue du Général de Gaulle, is a refreshing green space covered sparsely with palms, where you can catch an impromptu football game or live music performance some weekends. It includes a statue of Felix Éboué (1884–1944), a black French Guianese who governed various French territories in Africa and the Caribbean. Just off the square, the **Musée Départemental**, at 1 Avenue du Général de Gaulle (Wed 8am–1.15pm & 3–5.45pm, Thurs 8am–1.45pm, Fri 8am–1.45pm & 3–5.45pm, Sat 9am–1.15pm; €3.50), offers exhibits on French Guiana's history as a penal colony, paintings by local artists and some particularly impressive taxidermied examples of local fauna, as well as an impressive butterfly collection.

Fort Céperou

For a sweeping view of Cayenne, climb up the hill at the end of Rue de Rémire to the crumbling remains of **Fort Céperou**, the first building to appear in Cayenne after the Compagnie de Rouen purchased the hill from a Galibi Amerindian chief named Céperou in 1643.

Musée des Cultures Guyanaises and around

For a good introduction to Amerindian, Maroon and Creole languages and culture through the mediums of artefacts, crafts, costume and art, check out the **Musée des Cultures Guyanaises**, at 78 Rue Madame-Payé (Mon–Fri 9am–1pm & 3–5.45pm except Wed & Fri 9am–1pm, Sat 8am–11.45am; €3.50). Brochures in English are available.

ARRIVAL AND INFORMATION

By plane Félix Eboué International Airport (ⓦwww .guyane.cci.fr/fr/aeroport) is in Matoury, 17km south of Cayenne. Taxis to Cayenne cost €30–35.

Destinations Air France (ⓦairfrance.com) has regular flights to Paris, Guadeloupe and Martinique; Air Caraibes (ⓦaircaraibes.com) flies to Brazil and France and connects French Guiana with Haiti, Martinique, Guadeloupe and the Dominican Republic; Surinam Airways (ⓦslm.nl) connects Cayenne to Paramaribo twice weekly. Air Guyane (ⓦairguyane.com) provides domestic services to Maripasoula, Saül and St Laurent du Maroni.

By bus TIG buses arrive at the Cayenne bus station (*gare routière*) opposite Canal Laussat. For frequency and prices visit ⓦcg973.fr/Lignes-de-transport-prevues.

Destinations Kaw (bus #15; 1hr 50min); Kourou (bus #5A/5B; 1hr 15min); Matoury (bus #15/15R; 45min); Rémire Montjoly (bus #11B; 45min); Roura (bus #15/15R; 40–50min); Saint-Georges de l'Oyapock via Régina (bus #17 to Regina, 1hr 30min; then bus #18 to Saint Georges, 1hr); Saint Laurent du Maroni via Iracoubo (bus #9 to Iracoubo, 1hr 30min; then bus #3 to St Laurent, 1hr 40min).

Tourist information Comité du Tourisme de la Guyane, at 12 Rue Lallouette (Mon, Tues & Thurs 7.30am–1pm & 2.30–5.30pm; Wed & Fri 7.30am–1pm; ☎594 296 500, ⓦtourisme-guyane.com), has helpful staff and a plethora of maps and brochures.

GETTING AROUND

By bus SMTC, 2682 Route de la Madeleine (☎594 254 928), runs a small network of local buses around Cayenne (Mon–Sat); call for details. Most of the buses leave from Place du Coq near the market.

By taxi Taxis in Cayenne are metered; there's a taxi stand just off the Place de Palmistres. Rates are around €1.75 to hire, plus €0.65/km (double on Sun and between 7pm and 6am).

ACCOMMODATION

Budget accommodation is limited. Solo travellers end up paying almost as much for single occupancy as for a double. All accommodation reviewed below has a/c and en-suite bathrooms.

Hôtel Des Amandiers Place Auguste-Hort ☎594 289 728. Rambling colonial house complete with confused staff, worn but serviceable rooms and wi-fi on the terrace, all overlooking a pleasant park. Plenty of parking space – a rarity in Cayenne. €60

Best Western Hôtel Amazonia 28 Av du Général de Gaulle ☎594 310 000, ⓦbestwestern.fr. Efficient, central hotel with unmemorable rooms, swimming pool and overpriced restaurant. Good option for groups of three or more as triple rooms are good value. Wi-fi. Doubles €100, triples €120

Central Hôtel Rues Molé & Becker ☎594 256 565, ⓦcentralhotel-cayenne.fr. The central location, friendly service and clean, tiled rooms make this place an under-stated winner; kitchenettes in some rooms are a bonus for self-caterers. €78

Le Dronmi 42 Av du Général de Gaulle ☎594 317 770, ⓦledronmi.com. A nineteenth-century bordello in a previous incarnation, this is now Cayenne's most stylish hotel, its nine chic rooms boasting flat-screen TVs, kitchenettes and wi-fi. Great value for groups and its location is either a boon or a bane, depending on whether you enjoy living just a short stagger up the stairs from the city's most popular bar. Doubles €115, triples €135

Hôtel Ket Tai 72 Blvd Jubelin ☎594 289 777, ✉g.chang @wanadoo.fr. Brazilian *telenovelas* in the lobby, friendly service and compact, featureless, tiled rooms with struggling a/c. If every other hotel in town is full, there's a good chance you can still find a bed at this cheapie. Wi-fi extra. €55

Oyasamaïd 2313 Route de la Madeleine ☎594 315 684, ⓦoyasamaid.com. The four spacious tiled rooms at this delightfully friendly four-bed family pension may be simple but boast nice touches, such as Jacuzzi bathtubs, microwaves, wi-fi on the patio and swimming pool for guest use. The only drawback is the location – about 4km south of the centre. Meals extra. €60

EATING

Self-caterers will find fresh produce at the market, fresh bread in the *boulangerie* next to the market, and pretty much everything else at the enormous *Carrefour* and *Geant* supermarkets on the southern approach to town. In the centre, there are small shops with limited choice. Many restaurants are closed on Sun.

Crêp In 5 Rue Lieutenant Becker. It just wouldn't be France without crêpes, and this little place serves up a fine choice, along with a good selection of fresh fruit juice, *croque monsieurs* and salads. Meals €8. Mon–Sat 8am–8pm.

Centre Hospitalier Andre-Rosemon de Cayenne, Motel Beauregard & Break Club

CAYENNE

■ **ACCOMMODATION**
Hôtel Des Amandiers	1
Best Western Hôtel	3
Amazonia	4
Central Hôtel	2
Le Dronmi	5
Hôtel Ket Tai	6
Oyasamaïd	

● **EATING**
Crép In	9
Le Café de la Gare	3
L'Entracte	8
Flunchy Foods	6
Laotian market stalls	10
Paris Cayenne	4
La Petite Maison	5
La Rivière Imperiale	1

■ **DRINKING & NIGHTLIFE**
Le Bistrot	7
Jungle Pub	2
Le Latino Bar	11

RN 1, RN 2 & Airport (17km

7

7

★ TREAT YOURSELF

Paris Cayenne 59 Rue Lalouette ☎ 594 317 617. All dark-wood-meets-anaconda-skin chic and giant prints on the walls; this eclectic bar/restaurant is *the* place to be on a Friday night. Some of the dishes are more inspired than others (it's difficult to go wrong with the tournedos – the house special) and the staff seem to live on Zen time, but it's worth stopping by for the ambience and the signature Paris-Cayenne cocktail alone. Meals around €40, cocktails €10. Mon–Sat noon–3pm & 8–10.30pm; closed Mon & Sat lunch.

Le Café de la Gare 48 Rue Héder. This playful establishment wears many hats: café, restaurant (serving the likes of lamb in mango sauce; mains around €12), live music venue (in the evenings) and even karaoke bar. Daily noon–3pm & 7–11pm.

L'Entracte 65 Rue Justin Catayée ☎ 594 300 137. At this pseudo-Italian joint you can consume (actually pretty decent) pizza, pasta and salads under the watchful eyes of Marlon Brando and Brigitte Bardot. A number of veggie options on the menu. Mains from €8. Daily noon–2.30pm & 6–10.30pm.

Flunchy Foods 24 Rue Rouget de Lisle ☎ 594 281 038. Hole-in-the-wall takeaway serving up heaped portions of curry and rice, *porc caramel*, spring rolls and more; delivery available. Mains €7.50. Daily 10am–3pm & 6.30–10.30pm.

★ Laotian market stalls Av du Président Monnerville. Feast on *nems* (spring rolls), *phô* soup and other Laotian dishes at the market. Portions are generous and the dishes are full of flavour, with plenty of fresh herbs. Meals from €5. Wed, Fri & Sat, lunchtime only.

★ La Petite Maison 23 Rue Félix Eboué ☎ 594 385 839. Imaginative changing menu of *nouvelle* French cuisine

served in a beautifully restored Creole colonial mansion. There is a cosy nook upstairs that's simply perfect for a tête-à-tête. Meals around €25.

La Rivière Imperiale 10 Rue J. Catayée. Crispy *nems* (spring rolls), noodles, *fricassée* and conch stew are all on the menu at this small, friendly restaurant specializing in Vietnamese, Creole and Haitian dishes. Daily noon–2.30pm & 7–11pm; closed Sun evening & Wed.

DRINKING AND NIGHTLIFE

Le Bistrot 42 Av du Général de Gaulle. Perch on the terrace of Cayenne's most popular bar for an afternoon beer, a pre-dinner short drink, or even a liquid breakfast (coffee, that is). There is a small dancefloor with an adjoining chillout lounge. Daily 7am–1am.

Jungle Pub 10 Blvd Jubelin. Not the place for a quiet drink, this lively joint with a continental feel (read: white clientele) specializes in reggae and rock with salsa classes on Thurs nights. Daily 7pm–1am.

Le Latino Bar 493 Route de la Madeleine. True to its name, this is the place to show off your salsa and *merengue* moves (or else watch someone else's moves over a cocktail). Karaoke some nights. Tues–Sun 6pm–1am.

DIRECTORY

Banks and exchange ATMs along Av du Général de Gaulle and on the corner with Rue Mole. Change Caraïbes offers good exchange rates at 64 Av de Général de Gaulle (Mon–Fri 7.30am–12.30pm & 3.30–6.30pm, Sat 8am–12.30pm).

Car rental Avis, 58 Blvd Jubelin (☎ 594 302 522); Budget, 55 Artisanal Zone Galmot (☎ 594 351 020); Europcar, ZI Collery Ouest (☎ 594 351 827); Hertz Auto Guyane, Zi Collery Building, Route de la Madeleine (☎ 594 296 930).

Embassies and Consulates Brazil, 444 Chemin Saint-Antoine (☎ 594 296 010); Suriname, 3 Av Leopold Héder (☎ 594 282 160); UK, Honorary British Consul, 16 Av du Président Monnerville (☎ 594 311 034).

FRENCH GUIANA TOURS

If you wish to explore Guiana's jungle and rivers, virtually the only way to do so is to join an **organized excursion**, although it's cheaper to hire local guides by asking around.

TOUR OPERATORS

Couleurs Amazone 21 Blvd Jubelin, Cayenne ☎ 594 287 000, ⊚ couleursamazone.fr. Dynamic agency specializing in multi-day trips along the Maroni, Oyapock and Approuague rivers (from €550) as well as overnight stays in the Cisame jungle camp (€198).

JAL Voyages 26 Av du Général de Gaulle, Cayenne ☎ 594 316 820, ⊚ jal-voyages.com. Specializes in birdwatching river trips to Kaw and the Maroni aboard

floating *carbets* (houseboats with both hammock spaces and cabins) but also arranges trips to Kourou's space centre, Cacao and Îles du Salut.

Takari Tour 2 Rue Lallouette, Cayenne ☎ 594 311 960, ⊚ takaritour.com. The oldest of the tour operators, offering everything from a three-hour history tour of Cayenne (from €20), trips to Îles du Salut and Cacao (from €45) to multi-day adventures on the Oyapock and Maroni rivers (from €550).

TO MARKET, TO MARKET!

The best place to shop for crafts and souvenirs is the **market** on Avenue du Président Monnerville (Wed, Fri & Sat from dawn until early afternoon), surrounded by colourful fruit and vegetable stalls. Inside, you'll find African-style wall prints, jewellery, carved calabashes, assortments of local spices and home brews – from peanut punch and passion fruit liquor to rums. In between browsing, quench your hunger and thirst at the Laotian food stalls (see opposite).

Hospital Centre Hospitalier de Cayenne Andrée Rosemon, 3 Av des Flamboyants (☎594 395 050, ⓦ ch-cayenne .com).

Internet Copy'Print Cybercafe, at 22 Rue Lalouette.

Laundry Rue Catayée at Rue Lalouette.

Pharmacies Pharmacie Benjamin-Agapit, 23 Av du Général de Gaulle.

Post office Opposite Place Léopold Heder near Place des Palmistes (Mon–Fri 7.30am–1pm; Sat at 11.30am).

DAY-TRIPS FROM CAYENNE

There are a number of varied attractions outside Cayenne that make for easy day-trips – from a sloth sanctuary, monkey island and morass rich with birdlife to a Hmong Laotian village – though having your own wheels is necessary to access most of them.

Sloth sanctuary

What moves at 2m per minute, hangs upside down from a tree, digests its food for a month and wears a beatific smile? If your answer is "sloth", you are correct, and if you've ever seen a sloth cross a road, you'll understand the need for this sanctuary (Wed & Thurs 1.45–4pm; €5; ☎694 906 923, ⓦ www.chouai.free.fr) that takes in injured and orphaned sloths and nurses them back to health before releasing them. Here you get to cuddle several of its three-toed members (the *ai*), and learn about the less cuddlesome, larger and omnivorous two-toed sloths (the *unau*). To **get here** from Cayenne, take the bridge across the Cayenne River towards Kourou and take the first left immediately, then turn right.

Îlet la Mère

This small island, 13km from the coast and reachable from Cayenne's Marina de Degrad-des-Cannes (to the east of the city centre), has recently opened to the public and is home to an abundance of squirrel monkeys, iguanas, caimans and red ibis. You can either walk around the island's perimeter (3.5km; 1hr 30min), with its various viewpoints and picnic spots, or else hike up to the 88m peak (2.5km; 1hr 15min) to admire the environs. Or both. Count on making this a day-trip, since the boat (€35; ☎694 222 253) departs the marina at around 8–8.30am and returns at around 4pm.

Cacao

A slice of Asia in Guyana's interior, about 75km southwest of Cayenne, **CACAO** was settled in 1977 by refugees from Laos. Since then, this small Hmong community has become the fruit and vegetable basket of the *département* due to the extensive cultivation of Cacao's steep hillsides. The village draws visitors with its Laotian-style architecture and an excellent market (particularly good on Sunday mornings) where you can pick up fresh produce and high-quality Laotian embroidery before sitting down to large bowls of *phô*, *porc caramel*, spring rolls and other outstanding Laotian dishes. Don't miss the wonderful **Le Planeur Bleu** museum (Sun 9am–1pm & 2–4pm; other days by appointment; ☎594 270 034; €3.50), opposite the market, where you'll gape in wonder at the wealth of insects and butterflies, hold live tarantulas and get a brief introduction to gold mining, Hmong handicrafts and other aspects of French Guiana's culture.

ARRIVAL AND DEPARTURE

By car Take the RN2 towards Saint-Georges before turning off along the beautiful, winding, signposted road to Cacao.

ACCOMMODATION

Quimbe Kio ☎594 270 122, ✉infos@quimbekio.com. Overnight stays on a wooded hill near the centre, either in a *carbet* (€5 discount if you bring your own hammock) or in one of the en-suite rooms (breakfast included). Kayaking, boat and quad tours available. Doubles €45, carbets €10

7

7

CROSSING INTO BRAZIL

From Cayenne, take bus #17 to Régina and then switch to bus #18 to **Saint-Georges** (check timetable in advance). *Do not* drive between Cayenne and Saint-Georges at night or pick up hitchhikers along the Régina/Saint-Georges road; French authorities periodically clamp down on those seen to assist illegal immigrants. Saint-Georges is a small border town with a lively Brazilian feel, used as the jumping-off point for Brazil and tours (see p.676) of local Amerindian villages along the Oyapok River.

To cross over to Brazil, non-EU passport holders must get their passport stamped at the **Douane** by the river (8am–6pm; closed for lunch). Then take one of the **motorized canoes** across the river to Oiapoque in Brazil (15–20min; €4–6; negotiate price beforehand). Once in Brazil, get your passport stamped by the **Policia Federal**; follow the main street until you see a road to your left with a church in its middle. The office is on the right side of the road, past the church. **Moneychangers** operate on the Brazilian side of the river, but not in Saint-Georges.

If travelling further into Brazil, there is a morning bus and an evening bus daily from Oiapoque to Macapá (10hr); pack a sweater as they tend to crank up their a/c.

OVERNIGHT IN SAINT-GEORGES

Chez Modestine ☎ 594 370 013. Clean a/c en-suite rooms in a traditional house on the main square; book in advance. **€45**

Ilha do Sol ☎ 694 407 311. Take a boat (5min) to the tiny Ilha do Sol to swing a hammock at their *carbet* or stay in a basic double. Doubles **€25**, *carbets* **€12**

ROURA AND KAW

Some 75km east of Cacao, across the heavily forested Kaw Hills, is an Everglades-style swamp called **MARAIS DE KAW**, which covers around one thousand square kilometres. The surrounding hills make for some stunning vistas – especially when covered with mist during the wet season – and this is an excellent place to spot water birds, including flamingos. Tour operators in Cayenne such as JAL Voyages (see p.676) offer wildlife-spotting boat trips along the river, after-dark *pirogue* trips to spot black caiman and overnight stays in a floating *carbet*. When driving to Kaw, you pass through the pleasant village of Roura, where it's possible to arrange boat trips to various destinations, including the Îlet la Mère (see p.677).

ARRIVAL AND DEPARTURE

Visitors to Kaw arrive either as part of an organized tour, by rented car or via the limited TIG bus service.

By bus Bus #15 goes to Kaw from Cayenne via Roura (Mon–Fri 2 daily; 2hr), and there are two additional daily services from Roura to Cayenne (1hr).

ACCOMMODATION AND EATING

If staying overnight, arrangements must be made in advance; Kaw is not a place to turn up on spec.

Auberge de Camp Caïman PK 36, Route de Kaw ☎ 594 307 277. In between Roura and Kaw, this eco-friendly large wooden hostel with a library offers basic doubles and a large *carbet*. Butterfly-catching, marsh walks and caiman-spotting trips on demand. Meals available on request. Closed Wed. Doubles **€35**, *carbets* (including hammock rental) **€17**

★ **Malou** Route de Kaw ☎ 694 210 712. A short distance east of Roura, this new roadside eatery has a breezy terrace overlooking the large garden where they grow their own fruit for the fresh juices. The crêpes are perfection and there's a nice little sandwich selection too. Wed–Sun 10am–5pm.

KOUROU

KOUROU is a sprawling, artificial town with no discernible centre, built largely to service the **Centre Spatial Guyanais** – the space station that employs the majority of its residents. If your timing is right, you can witness one of the most impressive spectacles you're ever likely to see: the fiery passage of a rocket into space.

French Guiana's next biggest tourist attraction – the **Îles du Salut** – can be reached by catamaran from Kourou's jetty.

Centre Spatial Guyanais

The sight of the launch towers surrounded by tropical forest at the

CENTRE SPATIAL GUYANAIS (3hr guided tours Mon–Thurs 8.15am & 1.15pm, Fri 8.15am; free but advance reservation by phone is *essential* due to the tours' popularity, visitors must be over 8 years old and provide ID; ⓦcnes-csg.fr, ☎594 326 123) is like something out of a Bond film. The CSG occupies an area of 850 square kilometres and has sent more than five hundred rockets (most carrying satellites) into orbit since Véronique blasted off on April 9, 1968. **Tours** include a film charting the site's history and a visit to the Jupiter Control Centre, though no tours take place on launch days. There are three types of tours: one takes in all three rocket sites, Ariane 5, Vega and Soyuz; another focuses on just the Soyuz site (Mon & Wed pm); while a third takes you to the Ariane 5 and Vega sites (Tues & Thurs pm).

The partially interactive, state-of-the-art **Musée de l'Espace** (Mon–Fri 8am–6pm, Sat 2–6pm; €7 or €4 if on a guided tour of the CSG), next to the CSG welcome centre, introduces visitors to space exploration, with exhibitions on human space flight, the history of the base, the universe and more, through a mix of multimedia animations, space-related artefacts and temporary exhibits. The museum is sometimes closed on launch days.

Unless visiting the CSG via a tour operator, make your own way by car, or else take a bus (see below) from Cayenne to Kourou and then a taxi to the site.

ARRIVAL AND INFORMATION

Kourou is difficult to navigate on foot, with no public transport to speak of.

By bus TIG buses connect Kourou with Cayenne and St Laurent (via Iracoubo); departures and arrivals at Shell service station (Av de France, at Av Vermont Polycarpe).
Destinations Cayenne (bus #5A/5B 8–10 daily; 1hr 15min); St Laurent via Iracoubo (bus #4R Mon–Fri 4 daily; 1hr 30min) then change at Iracoubo (bus #10 2–5 daily; 1hr 30min).

Tourist information Place de l'Europe, C2 Rue Palika (Mon, Tues & Thurs 8am–1.30pm, Wed & Fri 8am–2pm; ☎594 329 833, ✉tourisme@kourou.info). Impressive collection of information in French and English on the space centre, Îles du Salut and Kourou.

BLASTOFF! VISITING A ROCKET LAUNCH

Few spectacles compare to the excitement of a countdown, followed by a mighty roar and blast of light, as a rocket detaches itself from the earth and makes its fiery passage into the sky. There's a launch pretty much every month, usually scheduled on a weekday night (visit ⓦcnes-csg.fr for details and requirements), and the one you're most likely to see is Ariane 5 – the French rocket that frequently launches satellites into orbit. The Centre Spatial Guyanais has seven official observation sites from which you can watch the rocket launch: Agami, Carapa, Venus, Ibis, Jupiter, Colibri and Toucan; access is limited and by invitation only. To obtain an **invitation** (you must be over 16), email either ✉liza.greene@cnes.fr (in English or French) or ✉helene.hernandez-garcia@cnes.fr (in French), giving your full name, date/place of birth, passport number and contact details, including address, email and telephone number, or else send a written request to CNES, Centre Spatial Guyanais, Communication Service, BP 726, 97387 Kourou Cedex, including the same details. Once you've obtained an invitation, either ask for it to be emailed to you (you'll need to print it out) or pick it up from the assigned point (usually the Musée de l'Espace) the day before the launch. Even if you have an invitation, it's possible that the launch may be delayed by a few days – or even a week or two – often with little notice, so it helps if your schedule is flexible. On the day of the launch, visitors typically assemble at the Médiathèque du Kourou, from where they are taken to the assigned observation sites by a convoy of coaches. Few visitors make it to the Jupiter Control Room (the spaces tend to be snapped up by family and friends of the space station employees), so you'll most likely end up at Agami, Toucan or Colibri (5.5–7.5km from the launch site), where you'll watch the countdown on the giant screen and have an unobstructed view of the rocket itself for a spectacle lasting between seven and thirty minutes. Finally, even if you can't obtain an invitation, it's possible to drive up the Montagne des Singes, just to the southwest of Kourou, where anyone can view the launch from one of two observation spots, connected by a twenty-minute hiking trail.

7

ACCOMMODATION

Budget travellers into swinging (in hammocks) can stay at the *carbets* on the attractive beach off Av des Roches. Accommodation is more limited than in Cayenne and tends to be booked up weeks in advance if there's a rocket launch due.

Hôtel Le Ballahou 1–3 Rue Amet-Martial ☎ 594 220 022, ⓦballahou.com. Those who succeed in finding this friendly hotel in the warren of tiny streets behind the Camp Militaire will be rewarded with spic-and-span en-suite rooms and eight studios fully equipped with kitchen facilities. Reception open noon–2pm & 6–8pm. Studios **€70**, doubles **€50**

Résidence le Gros Bec 56 Rue D. Floch ☎ 594 329 191, ⓔhotel.legrosbec@wanadoo.fr. Only three blocks from the catamaran departure point for the Îles du Salut, this is a brightly painted, family-friendly place offering studios equipped with kitchenettes. Studios **€69.90**

Typic Accueil 1 Résidence St Exupéry ☎ 594 324 370, ⓔtypic.accueil@orange.fr. This quiet, secure, family-run establishment has five studios with a/c, TV, microwave and en-suite facilities. Great if you have your own wheels; otherwise all the way across town from the catamaran launch. Minimum two night stay. Studios **€50**

EATING

You'll find a number of places to eat, drink and be reasonably merry in Le Vieux Bourg, along Av du Général de Gaulle, and there are some good options scattered around town.

Le Baraka 37 Av du Général de Gaulle ☎ 594 323 323. This inviting spot lit with Christmas lights serves Moroccan tagines and the like from €15. Daily 12.30pm–11pm.

L'orchidée Off Av F. Kennedy, opposite the post office. Heaped portions of delicious Vietnamese food. It's difficult to go wrong with the *phô* or any of the noodle dishes. Mains from €10. Daily noon–10.30pm.

Le Cupuaçu 38 Av du Général de Gaulle ☎ 694 912 146. Colourful Brazilian *churrascaria* serving sizzling skewers of well-seasoned meats, as well as chicken and fish dishes. Meals from €15. Daily noon–10pm.

ÎLES DU SALUT

The **ÎLES DU SALUT**, 15km off the coast, comprise three beautiful islands shaded with coconut trees and surrounded by azure waters: **Île Royale**, **Île Saint-Joseph** and **Île du Diable**. Their English name – Salvation Islands – is an ironic misnomer, given their use as a penal colony responsible for the deaths of over 50,000 of its 70,000 prisoners between 1852 and 1953. Thanks to Henri Charrière's book, *Papillon*, which recounts the horrors of life in the colony and his various attempts at escape (though it is now thought that he'd incorporated other prisoners' exploits into the story and passed them off as his own), the islands are the country's most popular attraction.

WHAT TO SEE AND DO

Most catamaran tours take in all three of the islands; though the virtually inaccessible **Île du Diable** is off-limits to visitors, you can catch a glimpse of the ruined prison buildings as you sail past. It was once reserved for political prisoners – most famously Alfred Dreyfus, who was arrested but later cleared for passing military secrets to the Germans.

Île Royale, the main and most-visited island, was used for administration and housing common-law criminals. You can peer at the ruins of old buildings and go swimming either off the small pier (on the opposite side of the island from the boat landing) or in the small bay sheltered from the sea by rocks. The fearless wildlife is another attraction; you

---

ÎLES DU SALUT TOURS

One-day tours (from €42) include visits to Île Royale and Île Saint-Joseph, and while on weekends it's possible to turn up and get a ticket, for weekdays you must make reservations in advance. If you wish to stay overnight, make arrangements with the Royal Ti' Punch/Îles du Salut operator, directly connected to the island's lodgings. Catamarans leave from Kourou's *appontement des pêcheurs* (fishermen's jetty) at the end of Avenue du Général de Gaulle at around 8–8.30am and depart the islands around 4pm.

TOUR OPERATORS

Albatros ☎ 594 321 612, ⓔhalliercatherine @wanadoo.fr.

La Hulotte ☎ 594 323 381, ⓦwww.lahulotte -guyane.fr.

Royal Ti'Punch/Îles du Salut ☎ 594 321 100, ⓦilesdusalut.com.

may well spot some monkeys and agouti. Île Royale is home to the islands' only hotel and excellent restaurant (see below), as well as the small Musée du Bagne (10.30am–12.30pm & 2.30–4pm; free), which showcases the history of the penal colony (in French).

"Incorrigible" convicts and those who tried to escape were sent to **Île Saint-Joseph**. Today it's home to a small naval base, and visitors can take the tranquil, coconut-tree-lined path around the perimeter of the island, passing the ruins of the penal colony overgrown with vegetation, a pebble beach and a small seafront naval cemetery – a tranquil spot to see out eternity.

ACCOMMODATION

Auberge des Îles Île Royale ☎ 594 321 100, ⓦilesdusalut.com. At the only lodgings on the islands, you have a choice between delightfully clean, bright and breezy rooms, cheaper digs in the renovated former guards' barracks, or else a space to sling your hammock (with access to bathroom facilities). Even if you're not staying here, stop by for the excellent meals (three-course lunches €26; mains €15) with an emphasis on Poseidon's subjects. There are inexpensive sandwiches at the bar, too. Doubles **€60**, hammocks **€10**

SAINT LAURENT DU MARONI

Outside **SAINT LAURENT DU MARONI**'s tourist office is a statue of a convict with his head in his hands – an apt monument to despair, given that this town was a transportation camp for prisoners until the middle of the twentieth century. Saint Laurent is less homogeneous than the capital, thanks to the porous border between French Guiana and Suriname; the large number of illegal Surinamese, Brazilian and Guyanese residents account for the melange of languages spoken and the laidback feel of this riverside frontier town, so likeable compared to Cayenne. Visiting the former penitentiary is undoubtedly the focus of your stay here, but the town also makes a good base for trips to nearby **Amerindian and Maroon communities**, excursions on the **Maroni River**, or the beautiful **Voltaire Falls**.

SAINT LAURENT FESTIVALS

Unlike Cayenne, Saint Laurent has a festival or three happening pretty much every month. Festivities not to miss include January's **Carnaval**, October's **Les Journées de la Culture Bushinengué** (a celebration of traditional Maroon culture) and November's biennial **Le Festival des Transamazoniennes**, an international extravaganza that spans the music of South America and the Caribbean (the next dates for the diary are 2013 and 2015).

WHAT TO SEE AND DO

Saint Laurent has some fine colonial architecture in the triangular "Petit Paris" area north of Rue du Lieutenant-Colonel Chandon. A stroll through this district to view the old bank and the town hall will nicely complement your visit to the former prison camp.

Camp de la Transportation

The **Camp de la Transportation**, where prisoners were processed before being moved on (or executed), is an imposing complex; fortress-like stone walls surround the cell blocks, chapel and other buildings. You can walk around the grounds and check out the permanent free exhibition of photos in the camp's former kitchen and chapel, but access to the cells is by guided tour only and not to be missed (daily at 9.30am, 11am, 3pm & 4.30pm; Mon 3pm & 4.30pm only & Sun 9.30am & 11am only; 1hr 15min; €5; tours in English available some days). A peek into the grim solitary confinement cells, the punishment cells where convicts were shackled to the wooden bed, the mass holding cell where fifty to sixty inmates would sleep in cramped conditions, and the cells of the condemned, awaiting execution by guillotine, puts everything into chilling context. Cell no. 47 allegedly once held Papillon, though that is now in dispute. Tickets for the tour are sold at the tourist office (see p.682). Less morbidly, the grounds are sometimes used for concerts.

7

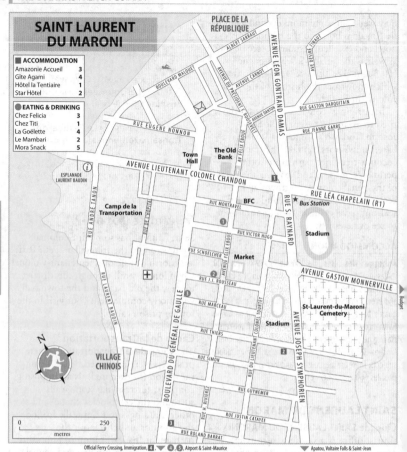

SAINT LAURENT DU MARONI

■ ACCOMMODATION
Amazonie Accueil	3
Gîte Agami	4
Hôtel la Tentiaire	1
Star Hôtel	2

● EATING & DRINKING
Chez Felicia	3
Chez Titi	1
La Goëlette	4
Le Mambari	2
Mora Snack	5

Official Ferry Crossing, Immigration, 4, ▼ ● 5, Airport & Saint-Maurice   ▼ Apatou, Voltaire Falls & Saint-Jean

ARRIVAL AND DEPARTURE

By plane There are four flights weekly to/from Cayenne with Air Guyane (ⓦ airguyane.com).

By boat See box opposite.

By bus TIG buses arrive at and depart from the bus station (*gare routière*) on Rue Léa Chapelain, near the stadium in the centre of the town.

Destinations Awala-Yalimapo (bus #1 via Mana; Mon–Fri 4 daily; 45min–1hr 10min); Cayenne & Kourou (bus #2, #3 or #10 to Iracoubo, 1hr 25–1hr 40min; then bus #9 from Iracoubo to Cayenne via Sinnamary and Kourou; 2–8 daily; 2hr 30min).

INFORMATION

Tourist information The Office du Tourisme at 1 Esplanade Laurent Baudin (Mon 2.30–6pm, Tues–Sat 8am–12.30pm & 2.30–6pm, Sun 8.30am–12.30pm; ☎ 594 342 398, ⓦ www .ot-saintlaurentdumaroni.fr) provides the excellent *Discover Saint-Laurent du Maroni* booklet, as well as other useful information in English and French on St Laurent's restaurants, lodgings, activities and excursions. Some staff speak English.

ACCOMMODATION

Amazonie Accueil 3 Rue R Barrat ☎ 594 343 612. Two centrally located guarded *carbets*, which come with a hammock (€5 discount if you hang your own) and mosquito net. Laundry service and meals available. *Carbets* **€15**

Gîte Agami Pk 10, Rte St Jean, Village Espérance ☎ 594 347 403. Hang your hammock in a beautiful garden overflowing with banana trees and treat yourself to excellent Amerindian cuisine at the restaurant of the same name. Espérance village is just south of Saint Laurent. *Carbets* **€10**

Hôtel la Tentiaire 12 Av Franklin Rossevelt ☎ 594 342 600, ⓔ tentiarie@wanadoo.fr. The nicest hotel in the centre of town, complete with attractive rooms (some with balconies), friendly service, swimming pool and wi-fi. Advance booking advised, as this place is the first to fill up. **€55**

EXCURSIONS FROM SAINT LAURENT

The **Maroni River** lends itself to a variety of activities – from visits to Amerindian and Maroon villages by *pirogue* to swimming, fishing, wildlife-spotting and jungle trekking. Trips range from two-hour to multi-day adventures.

Apatou is an Aluku Maroon village, about 70km upriver from St Laurent, and is a great place to experience Maroon culture, food and lifestyle. Although now accessible by road, there is no public transport (though you can conceivably hitch a ride with a "bush taxi", i.e. hitchhike). Maroni Tours (see below) arrange visits to the village as well as longer stays.

A visit to the secluded **Voltaire Falls**, about 73km south of St Laurent, is very rewarding. Getting there involves a 4WD journey through dense forest via the Route de Paul Isnard and Route d'Apatou forest roads, followed by a one-hour-thirty-minute hike. You can stay either at **L'Auberge des Chutes Voltaire** (w aubergechutesvoltaire.com; doubles €60, *carbets* €12–17; advance bookings only), on the banks of the Voltaire River, close to Voltaire Falls, or else you can hang your hammock for free further up the hiking trail.

TOUR OPERATORS

Agami Village Espérance ☎ 594 347 403.

Maroni Tours Village de Saint-Jean ☎ 594 341 175,

w maronitours.com.

Tropic Cata 1 Esplanade Laurent Baudin Saint Laurent ☎ 594 342 518.

7

Star Hôtel 26 Thiers ☎ 594 341 084. This central hotel won't win any architectural prizes, but the anonymous tiled rooms are spotless and guests have use of the large swimming pool. Free wi-fi. €58

EATING AND DRINKING

At dusk, things get lively at the waterfront, just south of the immigration office. The beer shacks and food stands are a great place to watch the sun set over the Maroni River (just don't bring any valuables along).

★ **Chez Felicia** 23 Av de Général de Gaulle. A local institution, still going strong after 25 years. The basic menu focuses on generous portions of Creole dishes, such as *fricassée*, and wild game. Mains €9–12. Closed Sun evening.

Chez Titi 18 Av Félix Eboué. Open-air pizzeria with outdoor tables, pizza that's decent without wowing, and an assortment of French, Creole and grilled dishes (mains €10–20). A bakery attached to the restaurant will give you love handles. Closed Sun & Mon.

★ **La Goëlette** Balaté Plage ☎ 594 342 897. This boat-cum-restaurant, complete with frolicking cats and dogs, is the most atmospheric place for a meal for miles around. The quality of the Creole and French dishes matches the ambience and there are music sessions on Sun nights. Mains €13–17. Closed Mon, Tues lunch and Sun lunch.

Le Mambari 7 Rue Jean Jacques. Perch at one of the picnic-style tables outside or prop up the bar at this new French/Creole joint; mains €8–18. DJs on Thurs, while on Fri and Sat it's time for "soirée NO STRESS". Closed Sun & Mon.

Mora Snack Rue Louise Orsini. Pull up a plastic chair at this informal little spot, decked out in Christmas lights, and chow down on the excellent *saté*, burgers and sausages (but avoid the insipid French fries). Mains €3–4. Daily 5–11pm.

DIRECTORY

Banks and exchange BFC, at 11 Ave Félix Eboué; BRED, at 30 Rue Thiers. There is no currency exchange in St Laurent.

Car rental Budget (☎ 594 340 294, w budget-guyane .com) has an office by the Texaco service station (closed between noon and 3pm).

Internet Upgrade Computer, at 25 Rue Félix Eboué.

Pharmacy Pharmacie Centrale, at 22 Av du Général de Gaulle.

CONVICT ART

If you happen to be driving between St Laurent and Cayenne, you'll invariably pass through Iracoubo. The **Eglise Saint Joseph d'Iracoubo** by the roadside is a church famed for its amazing interior covered with brightly coloured frescoes, painted by French convict and painter Pierre Huguet between 1892 and 1898. Well worth getting out of the car for.

PLAGE LES HATTES

From roughly March to July, the wide, clean stretch of sand that is **PLAGE LES HATTES**, situated at the mouth of the Maroni River a few kilometres from the Suriname border, is French Guiana's best place to view endangered **leatherback turtles** laying their eggs. Leatherbacks are massive – they can grow up to 2m in length and weigh almost 900kg. During the peak of the egg-laying season, it is estimated that up to 200 of these giants

7

CROSSING BETWEEN FRENCH GUIANA AND SURINAME

The **ferry** runs between Saint Laurent and **Albina** in Suriname 3–7 times daily (7am to 5.30pm; €4 one-way for foot passengers; motorbike/car €15/€33; euros only). Unless you have a vehicle, however (and rental vehicles may not cross borders), the quickest way to cross the Maroni River is to take one of the many **motorized dugout canoes** (10–15min; €5 or SRD15). When crossing the river in either direction, ask to be dropped off either at the **Surinamese Immigration office** (daily 7am–6pm) or the **French Immigration office** (daily 6am–7pm) – both located at the ferry piers – to get your visa checked and passport stamped. For Suriname, most passport holders require either a visa or a Tourist Card (see p.659). You'll find that non-tourists travelling across the river tend to ignore border formalities, but if you're looking to travel further into either country, your paperwork must be in order.

There is a **cambio** at the Albina ferry terminal, which gives good rates when exchanging Suriname and US dollars for euros: change your money here, as in Saint Laurent there are no money-changing services. The French Immigration office is around 2km south of the centre of Saint Laurent; taxis are hard to find, so you may have to walk for twenty minutes. Unlike Saint Laurent, Albina is not a town to linger in; minibuses (SRD50–70) and taxis (SRD70–250) meet the ferries and take passengers to Paramaribo (3–4hr). State buses (see p.665) between Albina and Paramaribo run from the centre of Albina; take a taxi (SRD5) to and from the pier.

crawl up onto the beach each night to lay their eggs. In August and September thousands of baby turtles can be seen hatching at night and dashing towards the water to escape predators.

The small Amerindian village of **Awala-Yalimapo** is situated 4km away from the beach. Unless you are part of an organized tour, it's best to rent a car and base yourself here, or in the pleasant town of Mana 20km away. You can also stay on the beach itself (in which case bring food, water, a hammock and mosquito protection).

ARRIVAL AND DEPARTURE

By bus Bus #1R goes from St Laurent to Awala-Yalimapo (55min) via Mana; bus #9 from Cayenne goes to Iracoubo (2hr), followed by bus #2 to Mana (40min).

By car Plage Les Hattes is some 60km from St Laurent, accessible via a turn-off along the D9 from the RN1 via Mana and then a 20km single-track access road to Awala-Yalimapo.

ACCOMMODATION AND EATING

Several local spots in Awala-Yalimapo, such as *Chez Judith et Denis* and *Yalimalé*, offer *carbets* with basic facilities.

★ **Le Buffalo** Rue A. M. Javouhey, Mana ☏ 594 344 280. An unexpectedly sophisticated restaurant in small-town Guiana that would give Cayenne's best a run for its money: great service, steak and other French delights cooked to perfection, complemented by a good range of French wines and cocktails. Dessert? Profiteroles to die for. Mains €12–15. Closed Mon.

Hôtel Le Samana Mana ☏ 694 382 294, ✉ lesamana hotel@hotmail.fr. This cheery yellow hotel near the bridge is a real find: the spotless en-suite rooms and studios all have facilities for self-caterers, there are pleasant common areas for lounging around with a laptop, and some rooms offer river views. Studios **€70**, doubles **€60**

Simili Youth Hostel Route de Yalimapo, Awala-Yalimapo ☏ 594 341 625. Beachside accommodation to suit all tastes, from basic bungalows sleeping 2–6 people to a large *carbet* with hammocks (mosquito net extra €8 each); meals provided on request. Reservations must be made in advance as the place is deserted outside turtle season. Bungalow/person **€15**, carbets **€7**

JAGUAR

Paraguay

HIGHLIGHTS

❶ **Laguna Blanca** A crystal-clear lake, perfect for birdwatching. **See p.691**

❷ **Asunción** Learn about Paraguay's history by day and bar-hop by night. **See p.693**

❸ **The Ruta Jesuítica** Stargaze at remote Jesuit missions and explore under-threat Atlantic Forest. **See p.702**

❹ **Ciudad del Este** Use this crazy consumerist city as a cheap base for Iguazú Falls and the mighty Itaipú Dam. **See p.704**

❺ **The Chaco Mennonites** This Mennonites share this immense wilderness with indigenous tribes and jaguars. **See p.709**

HIGHLIGHTS ARE MARKED ON THE MAP ON P.687

ROUGH COSTS

Daily budget basic US$30, occasional treat US$50

Drink 1 litre Pilsen beer US$3

Food *Sopa paraguaya* US$0.75, *asado* US$10

Hostel/budget hotel US$10–15/US$25–40

Travel Asunción–Encarnación (365km): bus US$15

FACT FILE

Population 6.4 million

Language Guaraní and Castellano (Spanish). The blending of the two languages is known as *Jopará*.

Currency Guaraní (Gs)

Capital Asunción (population: 2.3 million)

International phone code ☎ 595

Time zone GMT -4hr

Introduction

Paraguay is billed as the "Heart of South America", but perhaps "South America's forgotten corner" is more appropriate. Despite being one of the most traditional countries on the continent and the only one with an indigenous tongue as its official language (Guaraní), Paraguay is far too often passed over by travellers. Those who do stop here may find themselves pleasantly surprised by the rich culture, host of under-promoted natural attractions, fascinating and bloodthirsty history and real feeling of being "off the beaten track".

Paraguay combines the scorching, arid wilderness of the **Chaco** – one of the best places in South America to see large mammals – with the wet and humid **Atlantic Forest** of eastern Paraguay; the rampant commercialism of **Ciudad del Este** with the muted, backwater feel of colonial towns like **Concepción**. Paraguay is difficult to pin down in part due to its mixed immigrant intake over the past century; you're as likely to stumble across a colony of Japanese migrants, Mennonites or Australian socialists as you are to meet an indigenous tribe. Paraguay is not lacking in attractions – it is part-owner of the second-largest hydroelectric dam in the world and home to superbly preserved **Jesuit-Guaraní missions** – but tourism is undeveloped. Don't let this deter you, though; if you've a sense of adventure and crave a real, uncommercialized South American experience, get off the beaten path in Paraguay.

CHRONOLOGY

1537 The Spanish found the city of Nuestra Señora de Asunción.

1609 Jesuit missionaries arrive with the aim of converting indigenous tribes.

1767 The Jesuits are expelled from Paraguay by King Charles III of Spain.

1811 Paraguay declares its independence from Spain in a bloodless revolution.

1814 Dr José Gáspar Rodríguez de Francia is chosen as the first president and takes Paraguay into a period of isolation and industrialization.

1816 Rodríguez de Francia declares himself "El Supremo" – dictator for life, becoming progressively more arbitrary through his reign, suppressing the Church, isolating the country and taking to torturing opposition.

1844 Rodríguez de Francia is succeeded by Carlos Antonio López and Paraguay enters its period of greatest prosperity.

1862 Francisco Solano "Mariscal" López takes over as president from his ailing father, who leaves him with the deathbed advice that the pen is mightier than the sword.

1865–70 López launches Paraguay into the disastrous War of the Triple Alliance against Brazil, Argentina and Uruguay, which saw the country lose much of its territory and suffer many losses.

1927 The first Mennonites arrive in Paraguay, part of a campaign to colonize the Chaco.

1932–37 The Chaco War breaks out after rumours of undiscovered oil reserves provoke a violent reaction from the Paraguayan government at Bolivian army presence in the Paraguayan Chaco.

1954 After 22 presidents in 31 years, General Alfredo Stroessner seizes power and goes on to become the longest-lasting dictator in South American history, holding power for 34 years.

1989 Stroessner is driven into exile and Paraguay declares itself a Republic.

1993 The first democratic elections are held, and are won by the quasi-liberal Colorados, effectively returning Stroessner's political party to power.

1999 Eight protesters are shot dead by snipers during pro-democracy protests during a month of unrest now referred to as the Marzo Paraguayo.

2008 Fernando Lugo, an ex-Catholic priest with a socialist agenda, defeats the Colorado Party candidate, ending 61 years of Colorado party rule.

2012 Lugo is impeached in 24hr period in what many consider to have been a "parliamentary" coup d'état. His vice president, Federico Franco, continues the presidency until the 2013 general elections.

ARRIVAL AND DEPARTURE

A **passport** valid for six months after entry is required by all visitors, except residents of Argentina or Brazil who can use their national identity documents. Australian, Canadian and US citizens need to get an **entry visa** before travelling; Western European, UK and Japanese citizens do not (see ⓦworldtravelguide .net/paraguay/passport-visa for a list of countries not requiring visas).

If you're **arriving by land**, be aware that buses frequently cross the border without stopping at the customs post. It is your responsibility to get exit stamps from Bolivia, Brazil and Argentina and the required entry stamp for Paraguay or you risk a substantial fine – inform your driver that you need stamps and take your bags with you as buses won't always wait. The entry stamp entitles you to a ninety-day stay in Paraguay and this can be renewed once without cost at an immigrations post. A **yellow fever certificate** may also be demanded at border control.

BY PLANE

Those arriving on international flights will land at Aeropuerto Internacional Silvio Pettirossi (☏021 688 2000, ⓦwww.dinac .gov.py), 15km northeast of Asunción in the suburb of Luque. The main **airlines** operating in and out of Paraguay are: TAM (flies internally to Ciudad del Este and externally to Brazil, Bolivia, Argentina and Chile; ⓦtam.com.br); Aerolineas Argentinas (to Buenos Aires; ⓦaerolineas .com.ar); Copa (to Panama where there are connecting flights within Central America; ⓦcopa.com); Taca (Lima only; ⓦtaca.com); GOL (to Buenos Aires and various Brazilian cities; ⓦvoegol.com.br); and Buquebus has just started flying to Uruguay (ⓦwww.flybqb.com). It's a good idea to confirm your flight 24 hours in advance, as there are often cancellations on intercontinental departures. Check before

PARAGUAY

8

HIGHLIGHTS

1 Laguna Blanca
2 Asuncion
3 The Ruta Jesuitica
4 Ciudad del Este
5 The Chaco Mennonites

flying that your ticket includes the US$41 **departure tax** (*tasa de embarque*) or you'll have to pay at the window at the airport.

OVERLAND FROM ARGENTINA

Argentina wraps around all of southern Paraguay and is easily accessible. From Asunción many international buses make a quick exit out of Paraguay across the river headed towards Formosa, Resistencia and Corrientes in Argentina. The border city of Encarnación sits across the River Paraná from **Posadas**; international buses connect the terminals on each side of the border. Similar buses run from Ciudad del Este in Paraguay to **Puerto Iguazú**, making day-trips to the falls – or onwards into Argentina – easy (see p.706).

OVERLAND FROM BOLIVIA

Land crossings from Bolivia are fairly straightforward in good weather, less so during heavy rains. A paved road branches off from the Trans-Chaco to cross the border at **Fortín Infante Rivarola**; international buses stop here en route from Santa Cruz to Asunción, but there is no passport control, so border formalities need to be done in another town (see p.710).

OVERLAND FROM BRAZIL

The busiest border crossing with Brazil is the **Puente de la Amistad** ("friendship bridge") linking Ciudad del Este with Foz do Iguaçu. Regular buses make the short crossing, and it is also possible to cross by taxi or even on foot (see p.706). Many other border crossings with Brazil, such as that at Pedro Juan Caballero, are popular smuggling routes and considered unsafe.

GETTING AROUND

Buses in Paraguay are cheap and easy, although they may stop short of national parks, *estancias* or other isolated attractions. Renting a car is extremely expensive and many provisions need to be taken if driving alone. It is not recommended for non-Spanish speakers.

BY BUS

The easiest and cheapest way to get around Paraguay is by **bus**; there are frequent and affordable services daily between the major cities. Visiting areas away from the major cities is more difficult and bus services – when they exist – are uncomfortable. Journey durations and departure times tend to be erratic, as buses leave when they are full and may pick further passengers up en route.

Asunción is the country's major transport hub and there are so many companies at the main "Terminal" (see p.696) that, outside of the holiday seasons, there is no need to book tickets in advance. The quality of service varies greatly: in general, you get what you pay for. Pluma (ⓦwww.pluma.com.br) offers services to Brazil, NSA (ⓦwww.nsa.com .py) offers national bus services as well as international routes to Argentina, while Crucero del Norte (ⓦcrucerodelnorte .com.ar) is an Argentine company whose bus services link up most of the southern half of the continent.

BY CAR

Renting a **car** is possible only in Asunción, Ciudad del Este or Encarnación, and a 4WD is necessary for the dirt roads that crisscross the country away from the national highway system. Rental is expensive (around Gs800,000 per day or more for a 4WD with unlimited mileage), making it difficult to

---

WHEN TO VISIT

Paraguay is an extremely hot country for most of the year. Eastern Paraguay can be very humid, while the Chaco (northwest) is dry. The hottest time is from November to February, when daytime temperatures can peak at around 45°C (or hotter in the Chaco) and high atmospheric pressure makes just walking along the street a tough task. Winter (June–Aug) is often pleasantly warm during the day (around 20–25°C), generally sunny and dry, though can get as cold as 5°C. Between September and November spectacular electric storms become more frequent and travelling off-road can be difficult.

see more remote areas of the country cheaply, though petrol costs are low (around Gs6000 a litre for unleaded). An **international driving licence** is required.

Heading off the Ruta Trans-Chaco on your own is strongly discouraged. If you plan on going deeper into the Chaco than the Mennonite colonies, you should take a guided tour (see p.710) – many tourists come to grief by embarking on poorly planned journeys in an effort to save a little money. Once past the Mennonite colonies there is nowhere to stay or buy food, and very few places to refuel.

There are rental agencies at the airport in Asunción, including international chains, but the only company that currently serves all three of the main cities is Localiza (☎0800 979 2000, ⊕www.localiza.com); 24hr breakdown cover is provided by the Touring y Automovil Club Paraguayo (TACPy; ☎021 210 550, ⊕tacpy.com.py).

BY TAXI

Taxis are well organized in Paraguay and there is not as much need to barter. *Taxistas* are assigned a rank to wait at, and these are clearly marked in towns by a yellow shelter saying "Taxi". Ask for the meter (*contadora*) to be switched on (*prendida*), or at least agree on a price before embarking. Journeys in small towns or around central Asunción will cost around Gs10,000–25,000, while trips out of towns or to airports may be up to Gs100,000.

BY BOAT

Most of the **boats for tourists** in Paraguay are very expensive. For the budget traveller there is just one boat trip from Asunción up the Río Paraguay to Concepción (or the reverse). From Concepción it is possible to take another cheap boat further upstream into the Paraguayan Pantanal.

ACCOMMODATION

On the whole **accommodation** in Paraguay is good value for money, and you'll usually get a/c, TV, en-suite bathroom and breakfast included. You don't usually need to book in advance, except in Caacupé during the weeks surrounding the Immaculate Conception (Dec 8), during the Carnaval in Encarnación (Feb) and in the Mennonite colonies during the Trans-Chaco Rally (last weekend in Sept), when prices are higher.

In Asunción there are ten or so **youth/ backpacker hostels** that have opened in recent years. Don't bank on **camping** in Paraguay as campsites are few and far between and in rural areas most land is in private hands and you risk being accused of trespassing if you do not have the permission of the landowner. Times are changing, however, and SENATUR is trying to develop a camping culture to attract tourists, so it's always worth asking them for updates if you're determined.

FOOD AND DRINK

At first glance, **Paraguayan cuisine** may appear to be based entirely on junk-food joints selling hamburgers, *milanesas* (schnitzels) and pizza. However, a little exploring will uncover a number of excellent restaurants, at least in the major cities. The mainstay of the Paraguayan diet is **asado** – essentially barbecue – almost always accompanied by *mandioca* (manioc, also known as cassava or yucca). The best cuts are *tapa de cuadril*, *corte Americano* and *colita de cuadril*. Those with a weak stomach should avoid *mondongo* (tripe), *lengua* (tongue), *chinchulín* (small intestine) and *tripa gorda* (large intestine). *Morcilla* is black pudding and *chorizo* is sausage – but no relation to Spanish chorizo. *Pollo asado* (grilled chicken) is often sold on roadside grills, and don't forget to try *corazoncitos* (chicken hearts).

Fish is generally expensive and at least twice the price of beef, *surubí* being the most frequently available. For a cheap, tasty snack *empanadas* (pasties) are widely available and there is almost always somebody selling **chipa** (cheese bread made with manioc flour) – it is best when hot (*caliente*). Oddly, *chipa* in Asunción is frequently disappointing, so don't let it

8

put you off trying it elsewhere. *Sopa Paraguaya* is not soup, but a savoury cheese cornmeal cake, delicious when warm. *Chipa Guazu* is similar, but made with fresh corn and egg. Both come as accompaniments to meals.

Ask around for unmarked eating houses, which local people always know about, where you may be able to find home-cooked Paraguayan food such as *bori-bori* (soup with corn balls), *guiso de arroz* (a sort of Paraguayan paella) and *so'o apu'á* (meatball soup).

Paraguayan **desserts** include *ensalada de frutas* (fruit salad), which you can buy from street sellers after lunch, the sandwich spreads *dulce de leche* and *dulce de guayaba*, as well as *dulce de batata con queso paraguayo* (a candied sweet potato accompanied with cheese).

DRINK

Wondering what those wildly decorated thermos flasks contain? It's **tereré**, or ice-cold *yerba mate*, a refreshing and addictive herbal tea, undoubtedly the most widely consumed drink in Paraguay. It is sometimes drunk mixed with fruit juice (*tereré Ruso*) or with milk and desiccated coconut (*tereré dulce*). Look out for street vendors with baskets of **yu-yos**: native plants with medicinal properties. Whether you have a hangover or want to lose weight, let the vendor know and he'll add the appropriate plant mix to your *tereré*. Ask a "*yuyera*" if they sell the *tereré por el vaso* (by the cup) if you want to try some.

The preferred **local beer** is Pilsen. *Chopp* is a generic term for draught beer, although beer is more widely available in returnable litre bottles.

CULTURE AND ETIQUETTE

Paraguay is generally a safe, informal and laidback country. Men greet each other with a shake of the hand and women are greeted with a kiss on each cheek. The main **religion** is Roman Catholicism. As in many Latin American countries, there is a typically macho attitude to **women**, who may be seen as "fair game" when travelling alone; try to avoid any

behaviour or clothing that may be misconstrued as "flirty", especially away from the major cities. Equally, it's not considered normal or appropriate for women to be drunk in public. If you wish to take a photo of somebody, ask permission and don't offer payment if it's not asked for.

Tipping is not expected but is always appreciated. A tip of Gs2000–3000 is appropriate for an ordinary meal, and as most museums are free, a tip to the guide is always welcome.

SPORTS AND OUTDOOR ACTIVITIES

As in most South American countries, **soccer**, or *fútbol*, is the main sporting obsession and Paraguay's special claim is that it now houses the **Museo de Fútbol Sudamericano**, near Asunción's airport (Autopista Aeropuerto Internacional Km12, Luque; Mon–Sat, call in advance; free; ☎02 164 5781; bus #30 from Oliva/ Cerro Corá). For football fans this museum has become a pilgrimage to see the trophy room containing all the most important cups South American teams play for. Regular matches are played on Sundays and the two biggest clubs are Olimpia and Cerro Porteño. Tickets to see games are bought at the stadium upon entry. **Motor racing** fans will want to look into the **Trans-Chaco Rally**, one of the most demanding motor races on earth (see p.709).

COMMUNICATIONS

Postal services, run by Correo Paraguayo (ⓦwww.correoparaguayo.gov.py), are unreliable, so important mail should always be sent registered (*certificado*) or by international courier. There are no post boxes – you have to go into the post office. Making **telephone calls** in Paraguay can be tricky as there are no street payphones; you need to look out for *cabinas telefónicas*, telephone booths inside a shop. Copaco (ⓦwww.copaco .com.py) are the national phone company and they have an office in most towns with *cabinas* that tend to open roughly

PARAGUAY'S DIFFICULT NATURAL WONDERS

The immense range of **flora and fauna** in Paraguay should be drawing tourists from all over the world; the Chaco is one of the best places in South America to see large mammals, while the Atlantic Forests of eastern Paraguay are the most threatened natural habitat on the planet. Paraguay also has a sizeable slice of the mighty Pantanal, a wildlife wonderland normally associated with Brazil. Paraguay suffers from aggressive deforestation and encroaching agrarian interests, but luckily, people are starting to catch on that this is a country that needs protecting. All of the options below are well worth investigating, but many – in the Chaco in particular – are notoriously difficult to access. **Fauna Paraguay** (w faunaparaguay.com) provide an impressive number of ecologically sensitive tours with extremely knowledgeable English-speaking guides to suit pretty much any wildlife-related need (including all of the below). Many of the Asunción-based tour companies (see p.696) will also arrange wildlife tours.

Central Chaco Lagoons Correctly the Cuenca del Riacho Yacaré Sur, these are a series of temporal saline lakes east of the Mennonite colonies, whose presence depends on rainfall in previous months. In winter they may be occupied by ducks and Chilean flamingos, while from September to December, huge flocks of sandpipers and plovers are attracted to the water. To visit without a tour agency, get in touch with the Mennonites (see p.709) who may be able to provide transport, accommodation and food (upwards of US$200 per day).

Laguna Blanca This is one of the most beautiful and peaceful places in Paraguay, with crystal-clear water offering much-needed "beaches" in this landlocked country. Activities such as birdwatching (with a chance of seeing the world's rarest bird, the white-winged nightjar), kayaking, snorkelling, fishing and horseriding are available and accommodation is either in cabins, or camping. You are only allowed in with prior arrangement, but it's all bookable via w lagunablanca.com.py, and accessible with public transport. Those particularly interested in animals should get in touch with conservation group Para la Tierra (w paralatierra.org), who welcome people who want to stay for longer as volunteers.

Bosque Mbaracayú This forest reserve, consisting of over 640 square kilometres of Atlantic Forest and *cerrado* habitat, is accessible to tourists (though not cheap) thanks to the Fundación Moises Bertoni (Prócer Carlos Argüello 208, Asunción; t 021 608 740, t 034 720 147, w www.mbertoni .org.py). It's home to over 400 bird species, and 89 different mammals, including pumas and jaguars. FMB run a lodge for tourists, and you can hike, canoe, abseil or mountain bike with guides. Buses from Asunción go to Villa Ygatimi, 25km from the forest, where FMB can pick you up (Gs10,000 to enter forest; Gs200,000 per night B&B for two, or Gs35,000 to camp; pickup from Villa Ygatimi costs Gs250,000).

The Pantanal Paraguay's part of this enormous marshland spanning Brazil and Bolivia is difficult to reach, and not tourist-friendly. However, thanks to its remoteness, people who do make it here will be rewarded with many of nature's giants, including giant otters, giant armadillos, giant tegus and giant anteaters. Again, you're best off going with Fauna Paraguay between April and September – the roads are impassable at other times.

Parque Nacional San Rafael Set in 730 square kilometres of Atlantic Forest, this national park contains some 300 species of bird, along with big mammals such as pumas, ocelots and tapirs, nestling in a unique ecosystem where you'll also find rare orchids. Pro Cosara (t 076 829 5046, w procosara.org) are the main NGO working here and they can provide food and accommodation (US$25/day full board in cabins plus US$8 transportation into the park from nearest town; minimum two-day stay) as well as guided tours of the park. If you need an English-speaking guide, organize it through Fauna Paraguay.

Parque Nacional Teniente Enciso As this national park is just off the Trans-Chaco, almost at the Bolivian border, it's the most accessible of the region's national parks. It was established to protect a series of trenches dating from the Chaco War and to conserve the Chaco peccary. You may also see puma, tapir and a host of endemic bird species. It is possible to go it alone by taking a NASA bus from Filadelfia (see p.709) – there is basic accommodation available – but you'd need supplies of everything, including ice. If you go with Fauna Paraguay you'll get much more out of it. The best time of year is May–Sept, when temperatures are more manageable.

8

8

between 8am and 8pm. If you are going to be in the country a while, think about getting a pay-as-you-go **mobile phone** (from around Gs180,000) which may include some credit.

Internet access is ubiquitous in the major cities and very cheap (around Gs4,000/hr), with generally good connections; most hotels and hostels offer wi-fi. The most popular **newspapers** (*diarios*) are the tabloids *Crónica* and *Popular*, both written in Jopará, a mixture of Spanish and Guaraní. For a more serious read try *ABC* or *Última Hora*.

CRIME AND SAFETY

Paraguay is generally a safe country to visit; with so few tourists around they are rarely targeted by thieves. The usual precautions regarding personal safety and protecting your belongings should be taken, and it's unwise to wander alone after dark in unpopulated areas of the capital. If you report a crime, don't expect the **police** to offer more assistance than the taking of your statement for insurance purposes.

The border area in **Ciudad del Este** is occasionally unsafe and you should take a taxi if you have all your belongings with you. Further afield, the vast, largely unpopulated wilderness of the **Chaco** is an extremely desolate and hostile environment, and you should not go off the beaten track without a local guide and substantial preparation and supplies.

HEALTH

Travellers coming to Paraguay should be **vaccinated** against diphtheria, yellow fever and hepatitis A. Your doctor may also recommend malaria, rabies, hepatitis B and typhoid vaccines, depending on your travel plans. Take the usual precautions against mosquitoes; while malaria is uncommon, dengue fever is

on the rise here. The tourist board says all running **tap water** is safe; however, bottled or sterilized water is preferable and essential in more rural areas, where you may also want to avoid eating prepared salads.

Bed bugs are an increasing problem internationally, so scour mattresses for signs of them; they hide in the seams and you might notice blood spots from bites.

INFORMATION AND MAPS

The tourist board is run by **SENATUR** (Secretaría Nacional de Turismo; ⓦwww .paraguay.travel). They produce some good leaflets and maps; be sure to drop into their Asunción office (see p.696). Asatur's website (ⓦasatur.org.py) lists all tour agents in Paraguay. Fauna Paraguay (see box, p.691) provides accurate lists and image galleries of the majority of the species present in the country.

For detailed **maps**, try the Touring y Automovil Club Paraguayo (TACPy; 25 de Mayo, at Brasil, Asunción; ☎021 210 550, ⓦwww.tacpy.com.py). Most Paraguayans locate places by landmarks, so addresses are often vague. Paraguayans know places by being "almost at" a crossroad (usually indicated by the word *casi*, shortened to c/), or, if they are at a street corner, the address will say *esquina* (or esq.).

MONEY AND BANKS

The **guaraní** has been relatively stable in recent years. Notes are issued in denominations of 1000, 5000, 10,000, 20,000, 50,000 and 100,000. Coins come in denominations of 50, 100, 500 and 1000. There is very little forged money in circulation. Note that the Gs2000 note is plastic currency, while other notes are paper. It is almost impossible to change the guaraní outside Paraguay. **Credit cards** are not widely accepted outside the capital and incur a charge of five to ten percent – plan on paying in cash wherever you go. There are 24hr **ATMs** which will accept international cards in all sizeable towns and cities, though an administration charge of Gs20,000–30,000 is usually applied.

You'll get the best exchange rates if you **exchange money** midweek at a casa de cambio; prices tend to rise at weekends. Do not use street moneychangers – when you are dealing with hundreds of thousands of guaraníes you can be easily tricked. The chain MaxiCambios (ⓦ maxicambios.com.py) has branches in Asunción and Ciudad del Este and is reliable for both exchanging money and cashing travellers' cheques.

OPENING HOURS

Opening hours for shops are generally Monday to Friday 8am until 6pm, plus Saturday until early afternoon. Restaurants are open around 11.30am to 2.30pm and 6.30pm to midnight. Banks are typically open Monday to Friday 8am to 1pm and closed at weekends, though ATMs can be used at any time. Many **museums** are only open in the mornings, or not at all unless you find the guide or guardian, but persevere.

PUBLIC HOLIDAYS

In addition to the national holidays listed below, some local anniversaries or saints' days are also public holidays, when everything in a given town may close down.

January 1 New Year's Day (Año Nuevo)

February 3 Day of San Blas, patron saint of Paraguay (Día de San Blas)

March 1 Heroes Day (Día de los Héroes)

March/April Easter and Holy Week (Pascua y Semana Santa)

May 1 Labour Day (Día del Trabajador)

May 15 Independence Day (Día de la Independencia Patria)

June 12 Commemoration of the end of the Chaco War (Paz del Chaco)

August 15 Founding of Asunción (Fundación de Asunción)

December 8 The Immaculate Conception and the Virgin of Caacupé (Concepción Immaculada y la Virgen de Caacupé)

December 25 Christmas Day (Navidad)

Asunción

Less intimidating than many South American capital cities, **ASUNCIÓN** sits astride a broad bay on the Río Paraguay. Once the historic centre of government for the Spanish colonies of Río de la Plata, the city declined in importance with the founding of Buenos Aires, while the impenetrable Chaco prevented it from becoming the envisioned gateway to the riches of Peru. The quirky city brims with the history of its despots and dictators, but the real stars are its friendly and accommodating citizens, whom you'll meet if you take advantage of the city's fun nightlife.

WHAT TO SEE AND DO

While Asunción offers the usual dichotomy of Latin American cities with a crumbling historical centre and modern, wealthy suburbs, its personality shines through once you start getting your head around the country's crazy history. The **historic centre**, or *casco histórico*, is spookily deserted in the evenings and at weekends, but it provides enough cultural attractions for at least a couple of days of wandering. The action is centred around the **Plaza Uruguaya**, the **Plaza de los Héroes** and the **waterfront**. Many of the city's high-end restaurants are in the area around the mammoth **Shopping del Sol** complex in the suburb of **Villa Mora**, but the old centre is still the best place to look for cheap accommodation, as well as cutting-edge nightlife. Those seeking more tranquil surroundings will find solace in the arty towns around the peaceful **Lago** (**Lake**) **Ypacaraí**, easily reached as a day-trip from the city.

Note that in the historic centre, the street names running east–west change after Independencia Nacional, which cuts them north–south, so Cerro Corá and Oliva, for example, are the same street.

Plaza de los Héroes

The *casco histórico* is easy to explore on foot and a good starting place is the main square, **Plaza de los Héroes**. A lively and vibrant place, filled with *lapacho* trees that bloom a dramatic pink in July and August, it is a frequent concert venue and

8

CENTRAL ASUNCIÓN

ACCOMMODATION

Arandú Hostal	3
Black Cat Hostel	1
Hostel B&B Ñande Po'a	5
El Jardín Hostal	4
Palmas del Sol	2

EATING

Bar San Roque	7
Café de Acá	6
Lido Bar	1
Nat Salud	10
Sukiyaki	11
Taberna Española	2
La Vienesa	3

DRINKING & NIGHTLIFE

Britannia Pub	8
Hollywood Dance	9
Kilkenny	5
Planta Alta	4

attracts tourists, protesters and pedlars alike. It is, in fact, made up of four squares, each with its own name, but generally referred to as a whole as the Heroes' Square thanks to the redoubtable **Panteón de los Héroes** (daily 8am–6pm; free) in its northwestern corner. In a country lacking in postcard-perfect moments, it is Paraguay's most instantly recognizable monument and it contains the remains of former presidents Carlos Antonio López, his son Francisco Solano López and the dictator Dr Rodríguez de Francia. The Panteón faces onto the busy commercial and shopping street **Palma**, where you'll find plenty of *artesanía* stalls.

The waterfront

A right turn on Juan de Ayolas, a few blocks up Palma from the Plaza de los Héroes, will bring you down to the **waterfront** on the banks of the Río

Paraguay where the squat, yet overblown, **Palacio de Gobierno** will come as something as a shock. Often referred to as the Palacio de los López, the seat of government was started in the 1850s by the elder of the López dictators who wanted to bring a touch of Europe to Paraguay. He hired an English contractor to whip up a palace with a touch of Versailles, the White House and Westminster, but for all its grand pretensions, the resulting building is almost friendly and, thanks to the lack of fencing, you can walk almost right up to it.

A few blocks west of the Palace, down El Paraguauo Independiente, brings you to the **puerto** (port; at the corner with Colón), where it is possible to catch boats across the Paraguay (daily 6.30am–7pm; Gs3500 one-way; 30min) to the small town of Chaco'i from where you'll get lovely views of Asunción, as well as respite from its smog. Once a week boats also leave for Concepción in the north (see p.696).

Immediately opposite the palace is a terrace of old buildings with Italianate facades which are known collectively as the **Centro Cultural Manzana de la Rivera** (Ayolas 129; daily 8am–6pm; free; ☏021 442 448, ⊚centroculturalmanzanarivera .blogspot.com), a series of restored houses dating from 1750, housing the **Museo Memoria de la Ciudad**, with artefacts from the city, a gallery space with temporary exhibitions, a library and a bar which fills with people having after-work drinks overlooking the beautifully lit palace.

Plaza de Armas

A two-block walk east along El Paraguayo Independiente from Palacio de Gobierno will bring you to the unofficially named **Plaza de Armas** (also known as the Plaza Mayor, Plaza de la Independencia, the Parque de la República or the Plaza del Marzo Paraguayo). This square, home to some of the most important buildings in the city, feels sleepy and almost forgotten. It is dominated by the **Cabildo**, which housed the national congress until 2004 when a modern building was completed just off the northwestern corner of the square along Avenida República. Built in the 1840s, the Cabildo now houses the **Centro Cultural de la República** (Mon–Fri 9am–7pm, Sat & Sun 10am–5pm; free; ☏021 443 094, ⊚www.cabildoccr.gov.py), which exhibits important historical pieces, such as the López's presidential throne alongside displays about famous national musicians and actors, while there are often free concerts and talks in the evenings. On the southeastern corner of the plaza stands the uninteresting Neoclassical **Catedral** (unreliable opening hours, officially Mon–Fri 9.30am–noon & 1–5pm, Sat & Sun 10am–noon), built in the same decade as the Cabildo. It's not safe for tourists to walk in the slums that lead from this plaza down to the bay.

A few blocks away, the **Casa de la Independencia** (14 de Mayo esq. Presidente Franco; Mon–Fri 7am–6pm, Sat 8am–1pm; free; ☏021 493 918, ⊚casadelaindependencia.org.py),

dating back to 1811, is one of the oldest and most important buildings in the country. It was here that the architects of Paraguayan independence secretly met to discuss their plans. Today it houses a museum with artefacts from the time of the declaration of independence, and there is a lovingly preserved colonial alleyway alongside.

Plaza Uruguaya

The leafy **Plaza Uruguaya** has several bookshops in the middle and its gentle pace is encapsulated in the nostalgic and elegant **Estación de Ferrocarril** (México 145, entrance on Eligio Ayala; Mon–Fri 7am–5pm; Gs10,000; ☏021 447 848, ⊚www.ferrocarriles.com.py), the city's old railway station, which dates back to 1861. It now serves as a museum to Paraguay's historic railway, with grand old carriages in the station hall to wander around. Things get slightly seedier in the Plaza at night, but the surrounding streets become the centre of the city's nightlife.

Other museums in the centre

Five blocks east along Eligio Ayala from the Plaza Uruguaya is the modest **Museo de Bellas Artes** (Eligio Ayala 1345, at Curupayty; Tues–Fri 7am–6pm, Sat & Sun 8am–2pm; free; ☏021 211 578), primarily displaying artworks collected by Paraguayan intellectual Juan Silviano Godoy (1850–1926), including some European art, but the strong selection of national art evoking a bygone Paraguay is the real draw.

A little further out of the centre, in an unassuming terraced house, sits the former torture house of the Stroessner dictatorship, now housing the moving **Museo de las Memorias: Dictadura y Derechos Humanos** (Chile 1066 between Manduvirá and Jejuí; Mon–Fri 9am–4pm; free; ☏021 493 873). The museum's displays are based on the "terror archives" discovered in 1992 detailing the human rights abuses carried out under the 35-year dictatorship. You'll see the cells where up to a hundred people at a time were kept, as well as a bath tub used for water torture and other gruesome implements used by the regime.

8

Villa Mora and the Museo del Barro

Like many other Latin American countries, Paraguay's elite have left the crumbling splendour of the historic centre for flashy modernity at arm's length from their past. Most buses going away from the centre up España will go through the neighbourhood of **Villa Mora** and its beating heart; the mall **Shopping del Sol** (see p.698), as well as Paseo Carmelitas, which has restaurants and bars and is popular in the evening.

If you're not a shopaholic, the best reason to make the trip here is to visit arguably Paraguay's best museum, the **Museo del Barro** (Grabadores del Cabichuí 2716; free; Wed & Thurs 3.30–8pm; Fri & Sat 9am–noon & 3.30–8pm; 021 607 996, museodelbarro.org; bus #28, #30 or #56 from any corner of Oliva, which becomes Cerro Corá). Dedicated to Paraguay's indigenous, folk and urban/contemporary visual arts, it is housed in an interesting modern building with a good shop selling folk art. Don't miss the eighteenth-century *ñandutí* (spiderweb lace specific to Paraguay). The museum is a couple of blocks east after Shopping del Sol. Av España splits in two; take the left fork – Aviadores del Chaco – two blocks further, and turn right down Cañada.

ARRIVAL AND DEPARTURE

By plane Aeropuerto Internacional Silvio Pettirossi (021 645 600, 021 645 605) is 15km northeast of the city along Av España and its continuation Aviadores del Chaco. Taxis from the airport are extremely expensive (Gs100,000 to central Asunción); if you arrive by day, walk to the avenue outside the airport and take a taxi there (approx. Gs60,000 to city centre), or even better, get the bus (#30; approx 30min–1hr depending on traffic; Gs2300), which takes you directly into the centre.

By bus The two-tiered intercity bus terminal (021 551 740, 021 551 741, www.mca.gov.py/webtermi.html), at the junction of Fernando de la Mora and República de Argentina, is in the southeast of the city. A taxi from the terminal to the centre will cost around Gs40,000. Several international bus companies depart from here.

International destinations Buenos Aires (several daily; 21hr); Córdoba (2–5 weekly; 20hr); Rio de Janeiro (weekly; 26hr); Santa Cruz, Bolivia (daily; 20hr); Santiago (2 weekly; 30hr).

Domestic destinations Ciudad del Este (hourly; 4–5hr); Concepción (hourly; 7hr); Encarnación (hourly; 6hr); Filadelfia (2–3 daily; 8hr); San Bernardino (every 1–2hr; 2hr); San Cosme y San Damian (daily; 6hr); San Ignacio (5 daily; 4hr).

By boat There are expensive cruise boats (such as Crucero Paraguay; cruceroparaguay.info) that have all the mod cons, leave infrequently and often require large group bookings. The Cacique II (021 492 829), however, is for locals and goes from Asunción to Concepción once a week at 7pm on a Tuesday from the Puerto Botánico (near the botanic gardens), in theory: it's best to go down to the port in advance and enquire in person.

INFORMATION AND TOURS

Tourist information The Turista Róga (Palma 468, at 14 de Mayo; daily 7am–7pm; 021 494 110, paraguay .travel), run by SENATUR, is packed with maps, information and high-quality handicrafts. Staff are extremely helpful, speak English, and there are computers with internet access to use free of charge. SENATUR also run a booth at the airport (daily 10am–6pm; 021 645 600).

Tour operators DTP, Gral. Brúguez 353, at 25 de Mayo (021 221 816, dtp.com.py); and Mavani, Palma, at 14 de Mayo Galeria Palma, Local 39 (021 493 580, 021 446 654, mavani.com.py). Both offer some of the best tours all over the country as well as Asunción and Lago Ypacaraí tours, and both also have offices in Ciudad del Este; DTP is also in Encarnación. Pyporé (pypore.com.py) offer extensive tours of towns around Asunción.

GETTING AROUND

The city centre is compact and easily walkable, as is Mercado 4. You'll want to take a bus to the Villa Mora area.

APPRECIATING MERCADO 4

Asunción's **Mercado Cuatro** (4) is one of those sprawling Latin American markets where you can buy anything and everything (not to mention delicious and dirt-cheap street food). There are seemingly endless passageways in and out of this part-covered, part-street market and it's easy to get lost in the bustle. In 2012, a film based entirely in the market, *7 Cajas* (Maneglia & Schémboli), or "7 Boxes" as it's known in English, brought the world's attention to Paraguay's great market. As with any market, keep your wits about you and belongings close (or leave them in the hostel). The market is a twenty-minute uphill trudge from the centre via Pettirossi, or hop on any bus going southwest with "Mercado" in the window.

Buses You can flag down buses at all street corners. Destinations are advertised on the front and there is a flat fare of Gs2300. From the centre, buses to most parts of town run along Oliva, which becomes Cerro Corá. Buses #31 and #8 go to the bus terminal; #30 goes to the airport via Villa Mora; #31, #12, #28 and #56 all go to Villa Mora from the centre; #21 and 27 go from Herrera/Haedo in the centre to Mercado 4.

Taxis A journey within the centre shouldn't come to more than about Gs25,000; there are ranks every few streets in the centre, and in the Plaza de los Héroes.

ACCOMMODATION

For people on a budget, there is far more choice and quality in the historic centre than Villa Mora. The capital is also currently the only place in Paraguay to find backpacker hostels. Breakfast, internet and/or wi-fi, a/c and hot water is included unless otherwise stated.

Arandú Hostal 15 de Agosto 783, at Humaitá ⊕021 449 712, ⓦaranduhostal.com. A new hostel in the owner's refurbished family home, with lovely facilities including robust generous bunks each with locker, a roof terrace with great views west over the city and cosy communal areas. Dorms Gs70,000, rooms Gs160,000

Black Cat Hostal Eligio Ayala 129, between Yegros and Indepencia Nacional ⊕021 449 827, ⓦhostelblackcat .com. While the *Black Cat* – Paraguay's first backpacker hostel – is shabbier than some of the newcomers, it boasts all the features backpackers love, including a roof terrace with barbecue and a/c in every room; there's even a small pool. The mother–daughter outfit running the place speak good English, provide great customer service and help organize tours. Dorms Gs45,000, rooms Gs170,000

Hostel B&B Ñande Po'a Manuel Dominguez 489, cnr México ⊕021 449 480, ⓔhostelnandepoa@gmail.com. You are welcomed in as the "missing star" of this home of a Uruguayan family (with limited English), which is more of a B&B than a hostel. Set around a verdant courtyard in a colonial-style building. Dorms Gs60,000, rooms (up to three people) Gs155,000

★ **El Jardín Hostal** Azara 941, between EEUU and Tacuary ⊕098 486 0340, ⓔeljardinhostal@hotmail.com. Run by a creative Paraguayan–Swedish couple, whose garden generates a convivial atmosphere between guests. Rooms are adorned with interesting fabrics and Paraguayan *artesanía*, while bathrooms have some of the best showers around. Friendly policies, like no checkout time, and singles not having to pay double for a private room (write rather than use a booking website), set this place apart. Dorms Gs53,000, rooms (for two) Gs180,000

★ **Palmas del Sol** España 202, at Tacuary ⊕021 449 485, ⓦhotelpalmasdelsol.com. Reminiscent of complexes in the Mediterranean, this German-run place offers incredible value for the price, as well as a sanctuary from noisy, grimy Asunción. Immaculately kept rooms, some with balconies, look out over courtyards either filled with greenery, or with a small pool. Rooms Gs231,000

EATING

At lunchtime it is easy to find cheap filling food – simply look out for the barbecues springing up outside restaurants all over the centre, chalk boards displaying the *menú del día*, or head over to Mercado 4 (see box opposite).

Bar San Roque Eligio Ayala 792, cnr Tacuary. Classic Paraguayan food in a classic Paraguayan restaurant – it claims to be the oldest in the country. Service by the bow-tied waiters is slow, but sometimes the best things are worth waiting for. Mains from Gs35,000. Mon–Sat 9am–3pm & 7pm–midnight, Sun lunch only.

★ **Café de Acá** Tte Vera 1390, cnr Dr Mora. A delightful café with art on the walls, a bougainvillea-filled garden and featuring delectable desserts, Italian coffee, artisan Paraguayan snack foods and microbrewed Paraguayan ales. You can also try *mate* and *tereré* here. It's out of the centre behind Paseo Carmelitas on Av España. Daily 8am–11pm.

★ **Lido Bar** Av Mariscal José Felix Estigarribia, cnr Chile. Make this your first stop in Asunción to get a taste for Paraguayan food and the locals. It is as central as you can get – right in front of the Panteón de los Héroes – and is packed day and night. It has a diner-style interior with everyone sitting around the bar barking their orders at gingham-capped waitresses who are a vision in peach. Empanada Gs8000, mains Gs30,000. Daily 7.30am–1am.

Nat Salud Pettirossi 443, at Perú. Vegetarian restaurant and health-food shop with more inventive options than elsewhere in the city. Lunch buffet Gs29,000/kg. Mon–Thurs 7am–6.30pm, Fri 7am–3pm.

Sukiyaki Constitución 763, at Pettirossi. Walkable from the centre, towards Mercado Cuatro, this is a genuine sushi restaurant that offers some of the best food in Asunción for decent prices. Bento box Gs45,000. Closed Sun.

Taberna Española Ayolas 631, at Gral. Díaz. Excellent tapas, hearty portions of paella and flowing sangría at this cosy and eccentrically decorated Spanish restaurant. Plate of mixed tapas Gs50,000. Open daily.

La Vienesa Alberdi, cnr Oliva. For a refined coffee-and-cake stop, you can't do better than this upmarket café and patisserie with lowbrow prices. Also does salads, sandwiches and cocktails and has wi-fi. Smoothie and cake Gs20,000. Daily 7am–11pm.

DRINKING AND NIGHTLIFE

Asunción has a thriving nightlife, especially at weekends, though things only really get going after midnight. The centre offers the coolest and most exciting places, while the biggest live music events are held at the Jockey Club, also known as the Hipódromo at Eusebia Ayala Km4.5 (⊕021 553 376, ⓦjcp.com.py).

8

★ **Britannia Pub** Cerro Corá 851, between EEUU and Tacuary ⓦ britannia-pub.com. There are two other good bars on this block of Cerro Corá, but Britannia is the best; despite being over twenty years old, this British-themed pub still heaves with Asunceños. Unlike most Asunción nightspots it's busy on weeknights and the action starts earlier than elsewhere. 2.5lt "tower of beer" Gs35,000. Tues–Thurs from 6.30pm, Fri–Sun from 8pm.

Hollywood Dance Independencia Nacional, at Tte. Fariña ⓦ facebook.com/HWDdanceclub. Not Asunción's only gay club, but certainly the best, with a friendly crowd, huge dancefloor and cheap drinks to make up for entrance fee (from Gs25,000 depending on night and if there's a show). Fri & Sat from 11.30pm.

Kilkenny Malutín, at Av España alongside Paseo Carmelitas ⓦ kilkenny.com.py. Every city must have one, and this is a typical faux-Irish bar with drunken revelry guaranteed. Although themey and expensive, good for the live music, rowdy atmosphere and huge beer menu. Beer from Gs8000. Daily 6pm–5am.

★ **Planta Alta** Caballero 294, at Mcal. Estigarribia. Hip as anywhere in Berlin, Brooklyn or East London, climb the stairs to enter a world of modern art (all for sale), jazz (sometimes live), roaming cats and a legendary roof terrace with views over Asunción. Gay-friendly. Small entrance fee depending on live music. Cocktail or pizza Gs12,000. Mon–Sat 5pm–1am.

SHOPPING

Artesanía The website ⓦ artesania.gov.py has a run-down of arts and crafts by department. Good and high-quality selection sold at the Turista Róga (see p.696); cheapest in Asunción is in Mercado 4 (see box, p.696), clustered inside market close to Pettirossi at Gral. Aquino.

Bookshops Many in and around the Plaza Uruguaya, but not much in English. Books (ⓦ libreriabooks.com.py), with one shop in the centre on Mcal. López 3791, at Dr. Morra, and in Shopping del Sol, Local 154, has a good variety of English-language titles, including guidebooks and Paraguay fiction and non-fiction.

Shopping centres Asunción has many "shoppings" (malls): Shopping del Sol (Av Aviadores del Chaco, cnr Prof. Delia González; ⓦ www.delsol.com.py), the most famous, will fulfil your every consumer dream.

DIRECTORY

Banks and exchange You can find branches of all the major banks in Shopping del Sol. In the centre there's 24hr ATMs at BBVA, Yegros 435, cnr 25 de Mayo; HSBC, J.E.O'Leary 302, cnr Palma; Sudameris Bank, Independencia Nacional 513. The casas de cambio are clustered around Palma and Aberdi. There's a MaxiCambios in Shopping Asunción Super Centro at Oliva, cnr 14 de Mayo, as well as in Shopping del Sol; the chain changes travellers' cheques.

Embassies and consulates *The Quick Guides*, produced by SENATUR, have a full embassy list. Canada, Prof. Ramirez, at J. de Salazar (ⓣ 021 227 207); New Zealand, O'Leary 795, cnr Humaitá (ⓣ 021 496 951); South Africa, Fulgencio R. Moreno 509 – Piso 8 (ⓣ 021 441 971); UK, J. Eulogio Estigarribia 4846, at Mons. Bogarín (ⓣ 021 210 405); USA, Mariscal López 1776 (ⓣ 021 490 686).

Hospital Centro Medico Bautista, Av República de Argentina, cnr Andrés Campos Cervera ⓣ 021 200 171, ⓦ cmb.org.py.

Internet Easy Internet on Plaza Uruguaya, 25 de Mayo, at Antequera, has internet and telephone *cabinas* (Gs15,000/hr; closed Sat pm & all day Sun). There is free wi-fi in any plaza where you see the wi-fi/Tigo sign.

Language school Idipar, Manduvirá 979/963, at Colón (ⓣ 021 447 896, ⓦ idipar.edu.py), provide individually tailored lessons in Spanish and Guaraní.

Laundry Lavandería Shalom, 15 de Agosto 230.

Pharmacy Punto Farma is a slick chain with 24hr delivery service (ⓣ 021 607 500, ⓦ puntofarma.com.py), and many stores open 24hr. Central branch: Estrella 480, at 14 de Mayo (daily 7am–midnight).

Phone Copaco, 14 de Mayo, at Oliva.

Police Tourist police, Chile, cnr Presidente Franco ⓣ 021 446 608.

Post office 25 de Mayo, cnr Yegros (Mon–Fri 7am–7pm, Sat 7am–noon).

DAY-TRIPS FROM ASUNCIÓN

Respite from Asunción's oppressive heat is easier than you might imagine, and just a short distance from the city limits the buildings clear and the pace of life slows to a more typically Paraguayan tempo. The lushness of the area is immediately striking, a textbook image of fertile South America. Two of the most interesting nearby towns are situated on the cool (but contaminated) waters of **Lago Ypacaraí**, a huge lake with attached national park. Although it's easy (and cheap) to hop on local buses between the towns if you speak Spanish (you can see them both in a day), tours are available (see p.696).

Areguá

A pleasant town full of big old houses located among the lush hills above the lake, arty **AREGUÁ** is noted for its ceramics, but has drawn all kinds of artists and literary types over the years. It has a small "**beach**" by the lake (a 5min walk down Mcal.

Estigarribia) with a picturesque pier, which becomes crowded from December to February with Asuncéños escaping the city on day-trips. It is also known for its huge strawberry (*frutilla*) crops and every September it holds the Festival de las Frutillas. Don't miss the outstanding craft shops El Cántaro (Mcal. Estigarribia, cnr La Candelaria; ⊛el-cantaro.com) and the Centro Cultural del Lago (Yegros 855, at Mcal. López; ⊛ccdl.com.py). There is **tourist information** at La Candelaria 515 (☎0291 4335 00). To get there, catch bus #203 from Dr R. de Francia via Mercado 4, where you could also take the #11 (Gs2700; 1hr 30min).

San Bernardino

From Areguá you can get two buses (changing at the main crossroads in Ypacaraí town; takes less than 1hr), or in summer, a boat, to the shady village of **SAN BERNARDINO**, or "SanBer" as it's locally known, on the eastern shore of the lake. Founded in the 1880s by five German families, the town has retained an orderly feel. In the winter it is a ghost town full of exotic birdsong, bromeliads, and sprinklers maintaining the perfect lawns of Asunción's elite's second homes, but in summer it springs to life, although predictably prices soar. Outside town there's fantastic walking in the mix of valleys and wooded slopes, while in town

there are rowing boats and pedalos for rent, as well as craft stalls at Playa la Rotonda near the main square. **Tourist information** is at Casa Hassler on Luís F. Vaché one block from the plaza (☎051 223 2974, ⊛sanbernardino.gov.py), and Aventura Xtrema (Ntra. Señora de la Asunción, cnr Hassler; ⊛aventuraxtrema. com.py) can sort out all your extreme sporting needs, including waterskiing, even when their shop shuts in winter. Buses depart every one to two hours from Asunción's main terminal (see p.696).

ACCOMMODATION

Brisas del Mediterraneo ☎051 223 2459, ⊛paraguay -hostel.com. Hostel with dorms and space to camp 2km north of town, still on the shores of the lake. Dorms (at weekend in high season, when two-night min) <u>Gs170,000</u>

East of the Paraguay

8

The Río Paraguay slices the country into two distinct landscapes. The wild west of the Chaco couldn't be more different to the populous, diverse east. Some 97 percent of the population live on this side of the river, and it holds the majority of Paraguay's tourist draws. Whether you experience the human influence of the **Jesuit missions**, the **Itaipú hydroelectric dam**, Encarnación's fabulous **Carnaval**, or the under-promoted and under-explored wildlife of the Atlantic Forest, in either the **Parque Nacional San Rafael** or **Bosque Mbaracayú** (see box, p.691), you'll leave wondering why more people don't come to Paraguay. The exquisite **Laguna Blanca** (see box, p.691), and the tranquil town labelled the "pearl of the north", **Concepción**, will only confirm the feeling that you've stumbled across some of the world's last secret spots.

ENCARNACIÓN

Known as the "Perla del Sur" (Pearl of the South), **ENCARNACIÓN** is Paraguay's third-largest, but second-wealthiest city outside of the capital, and you'll notice some extraordinary houses as you walk

---

★ **TREAT YOURSELF**

Hotel del Lago Tte. Weiler 401 esq. Mcal. López; ☎051 223 2201, ⊛www .hoteldellago.org. Built in 1888, the *Hotel del Lago* on the main plaza boasts a formidable history, tinged with dark Nazi associations, alongside a who's who of Paraguay's rich and famous. It has recently been tastefully restored in its full Victoriana glory, and includes a museum, a treetop adventure circuit. It exudes an irresistibly nostalgic air, and watching the sunsets from its fern-laden terrace overlooking its beautiful grounds rolling down to the lake will be a highlight of any trip to Paraguay. En-suite doubles <u>Gs400,000</u>, two nights (per night) <u>Gs280,000</u>, four nights or more <u>Gs200,000</u>

8

CARNAVAL

For most Paraguayans, Encarnación is synonymous with **Carnaval** (🌐carnaval. com.py), a spectacular celebration transforming the city into a whirlpool of frivolity during four weekends from January to February. Some claim the Carnaval here is better than Rio's thanks to the crowd and community participation. Things begin to hot up during the week with bands of children roaming the streets armed with spray-snow and water balloons, looking to make a fool out of the unwary, but the main events are the weekend *corsos* (parades) in the Sambodromo on Av Rodriguez de Francia. The action begins around 9pm each night in the Sambódromo on the Costanera, and lasts through to the early hours. Tickets (Gs30,000–150,000) sell out rapidly so book ahead via the tourist office, or in person at the TIGO store at Mcal. Estigarribia, at Av Caballero, or at their store in Asunción, Av Mcal. López, at República de Argentina.

around its streets. However, unlike its commerce-hungry fellow border town of Ciudad del Este, Encarnación has a laidback modernity that makes it much more likeable.

WHAT TO SEE AND DO

Although it's a pleasant, cosmopolitan town, there's not much to do here outside of **Carnaval** (see box above) but enjoy the benefits of the town's immigrant populations – which include Germans, Eastern Europeans and Japanese – in the city's **restaurants**, and become a river-beach bum lazing on the sandy **beach** looking over to Posadas in Argentina. If you're visiting in winter, you're probably better off experiencing the countryside and staying nearer the reductions (see p.702), but it's worth stopping by to get some good food and to visit the tourist information, specializing in the Jesuit missions.

ARRIVAL AND DEPARTURE

By bus Most visitors arrive at the bus terminal on General Cabañas at Mariscal Estigarribia, six blocks downhill from the Plaza de Armas. If you're coming from Argentina you'll arrive at the San Roque González International Bridge in the south of the city.

Destinations Asunción (hourly; 5–6hr); Ciudad del Este (6 daily; 4–5hr); Posadas (every 15min; 1hr); San Cosme (3 daily; 2hr).

INFORMATION AND TOURS

Tourist information Good English is spoken at the Ruta Jesuítica tourist office run by SENATUR, Mcal. Estigarribia 1015, at Curupayty (daily 7.30am–6pm; ☎071 205 021, ✉lamisiongroup@gmail.com). They can help with booking Carnaval tickets, reserving posadas and luggage storage. There is another office at customs at Puente San Roque González de Santa Cruz (daily 7.30am–5.30pm; ☎098 579 4595). Good road maps can be bought at Touring and Automovil Club Paraguayo (Gral. Artigas, at Villarrica).

Tour operators Most of the tour operators in Asunción will do one- or two-day tours to the Jesuit ruins, but they tend to be prohibitively expensive unless you are in a large group. The tourist information office can provide an English-speaking guide to take you on public transport to the missions, for a fee.

Taxi Central Encarnación is easily walkable, but there are taxi ranks every few streets; no journey within the city should cost more than Gs25,000. Taxista Diosnel Cabral has a nice taxi fully equipped with seat belts. He'll do a return trip to Jesús and Trinidad for Gs250,000 (one-way Gs120,000).

ACCOMMODATION

Book well ahead for Carnaval, when prices rise considerably. Avoid the hotels around the bus terminal (except *Germano*) and those along Tómas Romero Pereira in the centre. The former attract an undesirable clientele, the latter have serious noise issues at weekends.

Casa de la Y Carmen de Lara Castro, at Yegros ☎071 203 981, ✉cvfb77@hotmail.com. Doña Yolanda will make you feel like part of the family in this cosy homestay with dorms. Space is tight, and booking ahead is essential, but a good choice for a bed with breakfast in a city with slim pickings on the accommodation front. **Gs80,000**

CROSSING TO ARGENTINA

Buses between **Encarnación** and **Posadas** in Argentina originate from Ruta 1 at the junction with Caballero (opposite *Camelot Pub*) and go down Mallorquín through the centre where you can catch the bus on most corners every 10min (5am–11pm; 1hr; Gs5000). Make sure to get off the bus at both ends of the bridge for **customs** formalities. The bus won't wait for you to get your stamps, but your ticket remains valid for the next service.

ENCARNACIÓN

ACCOMMODATION
Casa de la Y	3
Ciudad	1
Germano	2

EATING & DRINKING
Benndo	1
Camelot	1
Hiroshima	2
La Piccola Italia	1

8

Ciudad Mcal. Estigarribia, cnr 25 de Mayo ☎071 202 155. Recently refurbished, bright and often wild decor with animal prints and textured materials, far more pleasant than other options, with TV, breakfast, a/c and wi-fi. En-suite __Gs180,000__

Germano General Cabañas, at C.A. López ☎071 203 346. Conveniently located right in front of the bus station, this is the city's best-value budget option. It is basic (fans only, no a/c and price does not include breakfast), but it's a good place to get your head down for the night. Shared bath __Gs70,000__, en-suite __Gs100,000__

EATING AND DRINKING

There are surprisingly good eating options in Encarnación, thanks to its multicultural population. For cheap food fast, the *comedor* (dining hall) behind the bus station has lots of little restaurants with a central seating area, as does La Placita indoor market. Encarnación's nightlife revolves around one or two bars for most of the year, but during the summer everything moves to the beach and there are always new pop-up bars there.

Benndo 25 de Mayo, at Tte. Horario Gonzalez. With a huge array of sandwiches, *empanadas*, Mexican food and pizza, *Benndo* is a cheesy-meaty-carb-lover's dream. Pizzas from Gs20,000.

Camelot Ruta 1, at Caballero ⓦ camelotrestopub.com. Next to *La Piccola Italia*, and run by the same people, this is the most consistent bar/disco in town and is always popular. Open from 9pm.

★ **Hiroshima** 25 de Mayo, cnr Lomas Valentinas, also runs a pop-up restaurant by the beach in summer. What this place lacks in character, it makes up for with good service, fresh ingredients and excellent quality. Superb selection of bento boxes. Mains Gs30,000–50,000.

La Piccola Italia Ruta 1, at Caballero. Faux Mediterranean surroundings and a cheery Paraguayan/Italian host at this popular trattoria. Pig out on huge portions of quasi-authentic pizza and pasta – one plate is easily enough for two. Mains Gs30,000.

DIRECTORY

Banks and exchange Sudameris Bank and Banco Familiar on the Plaza de Armas both have ATMs.

Hospital Clínica Tajy, Gral. Artigas 1772, at Constitución ⓦ clinicatajy.com.

8

THE ENTRANCE AND EXIT OF THE JESUITS

The **Jesuits**, a religious order of Catholic missionaries, came to Paraguay in 1607 and based seven of their *Treinta Pueblos* (the thirty towns they built in South America between Brazil, Argentina, Bolivia and Paraguay) within the modern borders of the country. In the missions, or reductions as they are also known, isolated from the colonial world, the arts flourished and the Jesuit-Guaraní partnership was best known for its music, printing press (the first in South America), sculpture and architecture. The missions survived and grew for 160 years, but the Jesuits were finally expelled in 1768 having plagued the colonial rulers for too long for their insular governance and protection of the indigenous community from exploitation. The Oscar-winning film *The Mission* (Roland Joffe, 1986), starring Robert De Niro, explores many of the reasons for their expulsion.

Laundry Salon de Belleza Meri, Gral. Cabañas, at C.A. López.
Post office Nuevo Circuito on the Ruta Internacional, at San José.
Tourist Police Wear light blue shirts with chequered hat; the main police station is at Tte. H. Gonzalez, cnr 25 de Mayo.

THE RUTA JESUÍTICA

No trip to Paraguay is complete without visiting at least a few of the seven towns which make up the **RUTA JESUÍTICA** (Jesuit route; ⓦrutajesuitica.com.py, comprehensive website of museums and ruins, as well as accommodation), so dubbed by SENATUR to promote the route between Asunción and Encarnación via those towns with Jesuit history. There are four such towns in the department of **Misiones** (see box, p.704), while in neighbouring Itapúa, there are the remains of three **Jesuit-Guaraní missions**. While **Trinidad** is the most well known, neglecting its neighbour **Jesús**, or the further-afield **San Cosme**, the other side of Encarnación, would be a great loss. It's worth timing trips to Trinidad and San Cosme for an evening as both have evening events. There is a **joint ticket**

(Gs25,000) for all three as long as you go within 72 hours. The best places to stay are in posadas (see box opposite), or one of the fancy or unusual hotels (see box opposite) along the way. There are no ATMs in any of the mission villages, so be sure to carry cash.

Trinidad

One of the many joys of Paraguay's most famous tourist attractions is the extraordinary feeling of having UNESCO World Heritage Sites to yourself. The mission of **Trinidad**, or **La Santísima Trinidad del Paraná** to give it its full unwieldy name (English-speaking guides available; daily 7am–7pm, Luz y Sonido show Thurs–Sun 7/8pm; Gs25,000 joint ticket; ⓣ098 577 2803, ⓔtrinidad @senatur.gov.py) is the most complete and important of all the *Treinta Pueblos*, and retains its magic (despite being just 700m from Ruta 6) thanks to its hilltop location. It best provides a sense of how full life would have been for the inhabitants of the missions. The most impressive structure is the **Iglesia Mayor**, filled with fantastically ornate stone carvings, the most famous being the **frieze of angels** stretching around the altar (look up). Try and time your visit to see the *Luz y Sonido* which, at nightfall, provides – you've guessed it – lights and sounds re-creating daily life in the mission.

Trinidad is easily reached on **public transport** travelling in either direction on Ruta 6 (ask to be dropped at Trinidad at Km31, clearly signposted next to an incongruous power plant). Buses and *colectivos* to Trinidad leave the Terminal in Encarnación regularly (hourly; 30min–1hr). It's 250km from here to Ciudad del Este and you can flag down any of the larger buses, which will probably be heading there.

Jesús

Some 13km from the ruins at Trinidad lie those of **Jesús** (Jesús del Tavarangüe; daily 8am–5.30/7pm; ⓣ071 270 038, ⓣ098 573 4340, ⓔjesus@senatur.gov.py), in rolling agricultural lands punctuated by palm trees and the simple wooden

8

STAYING IN A POSADA

To help local communities and tourists alike, the **posadas** scheme was established as a way of integrating the two. To open as a posada, the homeowner must have an en-suite guestroom, sometimes away from the rest of the house, which offers tourists some privacy, but with an opportunity to get to know locals better if you wish. The rooms cost Gs40,000–70,000, and SENATUR lists the posadas on their website ⓦwww .paraguay.travel. There are posadas in both the villages of Jesús and Trinidad. It's always best to call ahead to book; if you can't speak Spanish, call or email the Encarnación tourist office (see p.700), who can help.

houses, painted in shades of blue and green, which are characteristic of the Paraguayan countryside. The mission is, again, set on a hill above the modern village and has enough original buildings to give visitors a feel for how the inhabitants lived. Although there would have been a great workforce living here to make the mission, it was not completed before the expulsion of the Jesuits, and the church is unfinished, but it was on track to be one of the greatest.

To get between the sites, men with *mototaxis* hover (20–30min; Gs40,000 round trip), or there are *colectivos* that leave from the petrol station on Ruta 1, at the turning to Jesús, every hour or two (Mon–Sat 8am–7pm; Gs5000).

San Cosme

From Santiago in Misiones department, it will soon be possible to get to **SAN COSME Y SAN DAMIÁN** (to give it its full name) along a new road from Ayolas, making a full circuit of Jesuit missions easier without doubling back. Until then, access is via Ruta 1 (turning off at Km333, then 30km) in a meander of the Paraná. The **mission** here (buy tickets from the planetarium; there is usually a peace corps volunteer in town who can help translate into English if you let the staff know in advance; on the main plaza; daily 7am–5pm; ☎098 573 2956) is well

worth the detour as it has two unique draws. Firstly, it is the only working mission from that period: the main building, dating to 1760, is still used as the town's main church. Still standing is a restored doorway (don't miss the cheeky bat guarding the top) and the original structure of most of the mission. You'll see original painted wooden ceilings, as well as the only ironwork left in any of the missions on one of the windows.

The second attraction here is the **Centro Astronómico Buenaventura Suárez** (daily 7am–8pm or later in summer; included in joint ticket), which promotes the work of the eponymous Jesuit astronomer who worked from this mission and developed the incredibly accurate sundial in the mission's plaza, among other celestial discoveries. You'll be shown a documentary on the Guaraní understanding of the stratosphere and then taken to a little **planetarium**. Spending time in San Cosme's plaza or down by the river, experiencing the enormity of the sky here, is an unforgettable Paraguayan experience.

There are direct **buses** from Encarnación (2–3 daily; Gs50,000; 2hr), or catch a *colectivo* (every 1hr 30min–2hr, 6am–6pm; Gs20,000) to San Cosme from Coronel Bogado's bus terminal (any bus passing along Ruta 1 between Asunción and Encarnación will stop in Coronel Bogado).

★ TREAT YOURSELF

There are two really good hotels on the road between Encarnación and Ciudad del Este, after Jesús and Trinidad. All buses heading between the two cities pass both hotels.

Papillon Ruta 6, Km45 ☎076 724 0235, ⓦpapillon.com.py. With modern facilities, a lovely pool and pretty grounds, locals prefer this spotless choice. **Gs300,000**

Hotel Tirol Ruta 6, Km17 ☎071 202 388, ⓦhoteltirol.com.py. Set within Atlantic Forest, its grounds are home to capuchin monkeys and some 190 bird species. Even if you don't stay here, you can use the (four) pools and walk around the forest for a minimal fee (Gs10,000). **Gs250,000**

8

THE MUSEUMS OF MISIONES

It's all well and good roaming the ruins of Itapúa department – these are Paraguay's stellar attractions after all – but if these have piqued your interest in the Jesuits, there is a lot more to see in the neighbouring Misiones department with its four **museums** containing some of the finest remaining Jesuit-Guaraní art of all the *Treinta Pueblos*. There are five designated buses daily to San Ignacio, or any bus heading south along Ruta 1 will drop you there too (3–4hr from Asunción). From here it's easy to hop on local *colectivos* to the other towns, or alternatively, taxis between the towns will cost upwards of Gs75,000.

Museo Diocesano del Arte Jesuítico Guaraní Two blocks from Ruta 1 South at Iturbe 870, San Ignacio ☎097 291 0669, ✉museoartejesuitico@hotmail.com. San Ignacio was the first Jesuit-Guaraní mission established in Paraguay. The museum here contains art and history from this mission and is housed in a seventeenth-century adobe building, which was the Jesuit college then and, amazingly, now. Mon–Sat 2–5pm. Gs10,000.

Museo de Santa María de Fe To the right of the church in the fenced building in Santa María ☎0781 283 332, ☎098 578 8011. In nearby Santa María, the unrivalled collection of carved wooden statues displays the Guaraní Baroque style at its best, and you can see the differences between the carvings done by the Italian–Jesuit masters and those done by their indigenous pupils. Daily until 5pm – you need to ask for a guide from their home across the plaza to get in. Gs10,000.

Loreto Chapel On Santa Rosa's main square ☎0858 285 221. The village of Santa Rosa has the only remaining Jesuit Loreto Chapel, with beautiful, muralled walls and some more fine carved pieces, as well as a full terrace of *casas de indios* from the original mission and a surviving high bell tower. Mon–Sat 7.30–11.30am; ask at the parochial office next door for it to be opened. Free.

Museo Tesoros Jesuíticos 18km south of Ruta 1 on the road to Ayolas, in the village of Santiago next to the church on the main plaza ☎097 576 2008. Museum where the only remaining wooden altarpiece of any of the Jesuit ruins is displayed, along with other Jesuit treasures. Mon–Sat 8–11am & 2–5pm, Sun 9–11am. Gs10,000 for the guide.

ACCOMMODATION

★ **Santa María Hotel** Opposite the museum across the plaza in Santa María ☎0781 283 311, ⊛santamariahotel.org. The best place to stay in Misiones department, started by a Brit with the aim of generating employment for locals, this pint-size hotel has great food, excellent English is spoken, and country-wide tours are offered. Includes American breakfast. Rooms (per person) <u>Gs140,000</u>

Coronel Bogado is a sizeable town with ATM and money-changing facilities. San Cosme's only **accommodation** option (and a good one) is its posada (see box, p.703).

CIUDAD DEL ESTE

Commercial, tacky, frequently intimidating and occasionally sordid, **CIUDAD DEL ESTE** ("city of the east") is a shock to the system for many entering Paraguay for the first time; you'd be forgiven if your first instinct is to escape across the Puente de la Amistad into Brazil. Paraguay's second city, with a population of some 220,000, is hard to love, but do stick around and explore the sights: it does get better. Founded in 1957 as a garden city named Puerto Presidente Stroessner, it grew rapidly as people flocked to the jobs and homes created by the **Itaipú Dam**. Capitalizing on its position on the triple frontier, the town provides cheap duty-free – and frequently contraband – goods to Brazilians and Argentines hungry for bargains; almost everything is priced in US dollars.

WHAT TO SEE AND DO

The city's relative modernity means that it has little in the way of sights, but you might want to whizz round the small **Museo el Mensú** (Pioneros del Este between Paí Pérez and Eusebio Ayala; Mon–Fri 7am–1pm; ☎06150 170 610) based in CDE's first house, now enclosed in the summer-camp-like Municipality complex.

CDE's **malls**, or *shoppings*, as they are known, provide the real entertainment, with shops, bars, clubs, arcades and cinemas. **Shopping Zuni** and **Shopping Corazón**, both on Avenida San Blas alongside the Ruta Internacional, are two of the best for entertainment (Corazón has better eating and drinking, Zuni has one of Paraguay's only cinemas out of the capital). The real attractions, however, lie in the surrounding area, including the dam and numerous nature reserves.

ARRIVAL AND INFORMATION

By plane Aeropuerto Internacional Guaraní, 30km west of town on Ruta 7, has regular flights to Asunción, as well as nearby destinations in Brazil and Argentina (🌐 tam.com .br), but suffers from frequent unexplained cancellations. A taxi to most points in the city costs Gs150,000.

By bus The bus terminal (☎ 061 510 421) is some way south of the centre on Chaco Boreal y Capitán del Puerto, adjacent to the Estadio P. Sarubi on Gral. Bernadino Caballero. There are *colectivos*, but if you arrive with luggage it's safer to take a taxi (Gs25,000 to Centro). Destinations Asunción (hourly; 5hr); Encarnación (hourly; 4–5hr); Foz do Iguaçu (every 15min, 45min if no traffic); Puerto Iguazú (every 30min–1hr, 1hr if no traffic).

Tourist information SENATUR's office (daily 7am–7pm; ☎ 061 511 626, ✉ senaturcde@senatur.gov.py) is at the end of Av Jara in the Centro, behind Arco Iris supermarket, or just off the Ruta Internacional down Av del Lago next to the bus stands opposite Shopping Corazón. They have good free maps of the city. Good road maps can be bought at Touring and Automovil Club Paraguayo (Av San Blas Km1.5 in petrol station).

Tours Mariza Martinez (☎ 098 365 4619, ✉ mariza @cosmos.com.py) organizes tours for two agencies and can arrange English-speaking guides to most of the surrounding places if you write in advance. You could also

try Mavani, who work in CDE with Exchange Tours (offices next to each other in Edificio Saba, Av Nanawa 90, at Jara, ☎ 061 509 586, 🌐 mavani.com.py).

ACCOMMODATION

Mid-range accommodation in Ciudad del Este is widely available, but cheap options are thin on the ground and seedy. Avoid the area around the bus station and head for the cluster of decent hotels that line E. R. Fernández, two blocks north of the Ruta Internacional near the bridge. All prices include breakfast, wi-fi, TV and a/c unless stated.

★ **Austria** E. R. Fernández 165 ☎ 061 504 213, 🌐 hotel austriarestaurante.com. Excellent rooms with TV, minibar and a spacious terrace with majestic views out over the river. The restaurant is also recommended even if you do not plan to stay, for its pleasant faux-alpine ambience and good range of food. **Gs200,000**

Florestal Tte. Manuel Cabello 525, between Alejo Garcia and C.A. López ☎ 061 511 473, ☎ 061 500 252. Someone once had grand plans for a luxury hotel with a pool, jacuzzi and outdoor grill, but this tired old place with mismatched decor and grubby walls doesn't quite live up to them. The rooms with windows are bearable (it's worth asking to see a few rooms as they're all so different), though, and staff are friendly. **Gs150,000**

Venecia E.R. Fernández 209 ☎ 061 500 375. Rooms are basic and a bit old-fashioned, but they are set around a delightful patio with lush valley views. **Gs150,000**

EATING AND DRINKING

Thanks to its international clientele, food tends to be pricier here than elsewhere in Paraguay. For cheap food, try the *comedor* for workers between the southbound Ruta Internacional and Av Monseñor Rodriguez. Restaurants in the Centro tend to close around 9pm.

★ **Época** Av Rogelio Benítez 439, approx 700m up Av Bernardino Caballero from the Centro ☎ 061 514 984, 🌐 epoca.com.py. Not cheap, but this 1950s Americana themed bar/restaurant is a stand-out bar in distinctly

8

CIUDAD DEL ESTE ORIENTATION

The **Ruta Internacional**, running east–west through the centre of town, leads to the rest of Paraguay one way, and Brazil via the bridge, over the Río Paraná, the other. It is flanked by **Av San Blas** going east and **Av Monseñor Rodríguez** going west. Nearly all the malls, markets and shops are based along this mammoth avenue. At the roundabout, just before the Ruta leads down to the bridge, **Pioneros del Este** runs south and splits around one of the parks into Alejo Garcia and Gral. Bernadino Caballero (which goes to the bus station). Most hotels and restaurants are based in the **Centro**, which comprises the blocks south of the Ruta Internacional and east of Pioneros del Este running to the river – Gral. A. Jara is the main street in the Centro – or **San Blas** neighbourhood, which is immediately north of the Centro across the Ruta Internacional. **E.R. Fernández** is packed with hotels with stunning views over the Río Acaray at its juncture with the Paraná. The Centro becomes deserted in the evenings as trading stops, and nightlife is based in the **Boquerón** neighbourhood, southwest of the centre off Gral. Bernardino Caballero.

8

CROSSING TO BRAZIL AND ARGENTINA

The Puente de la Amistad (Ponte da Amizade in Portuguese, or Friendship Bridge), across the Río Paraná, marks the border with the Brazilian town of **Foz do Iguaçu**. Immigration formalities take place at either end of the bridge. This is Paraguay's busiest border crossing, and there are frequently huge queues in either direction (if crossing by bus, try to go as early as possible). A local bus runs from the bus terminal along Av Gral. Bernardino Caballero, Pioneros del Este, then to the Ruta Internacional to the terminal in "Foz", as it's known locally (every 15min; duration depends on bridge traffic; Gs8000). Often crossing on foot is quicker, but be sure to obtain all necessary entrance and exit stamps; you need them even if you are just visiting the waterfalls. Traffic police do not help matters by putting pressure on buses to speed up their crossing, occasionally directing them away from the customs checkpoint.

The company Río Uruguay runs buses daily between CDE and **Puerto Iguazú** in Argentina (every 30min–1hr, 7am–6pm, duration depends on bridge traffic; Gs10,000 or AR$10). It starts from the Terminal, but you can catch it anywhere along Av Gral. Bernardino Caballero, or on the Ruta Internacional. You'll have to get stamps before the bridge to leave Paraguay, and again at the Argentine border, some 20min later. You do not need to get stamps to go in and out of Brazil if you do not plan to get off the bus before Argentina. Even if the buses tell you they will not wait, be sure that your paperwork is in order; another bus will come along.

un-cool Paraguay. There's a dancefloor with mirror-ball, stage and live music (with small entrance fee), and the food has names like the "Steak 'n' Shake" while cocktails are named after movies. Worth booking a table if you want to go for the music. Tues–Sat 6pm–late.

Gouranga Av Pampliega, at Eusebio Ayala, behind the Municipalidad complex. An Indian vegetarian restaurant with bargain set lunches (Gs20,000) including veggie takes on Paraguayan classics and inventive fresh juices. Daily 7.30am–2.30pm.

Miu Miu Boquerón, at Av Jara. A decent Chinese in a little row of oriental restaurants, with a great range of food (including plenty for vegetarians) and good-value set menus. All US$5–15 (menu in dollars).

Patu's Bar Av Bernardino Caballero 480 ⓦ patusbar.com. Lively open-air bar-restaurant overlooking the parks, with a large list of cocktails to accompany pizza, steaks and salads. Cocktail and burger Gs40,000.

Tia Lily Carlos Antonio López, at Oscar Rivas. A great place to sample exactly the kind of typical – and cheap – Paraguayan food that can be hard to find elsewhere, like *Caldo de Surubí* (fish stew) and *Chipa Guazú* (an eggy corn bread). This also serves as a relaxed bar in the evening, when tables spring up on the street. Mains Gs20,000. Daily 6am–11pm, closes 4pm Sun.

SHOPPING

Not for nothing is CDE known as the "Supermarket of South America", and just about everything you can think of can be purchased here at prices well below market rates. Electronics, alcohol and perfumes provide the best deals, but beware of substandard goods and do not be afraid to haggle – it is expected. Compare prices before completing any transaction and ask for the product to be tested; not all dealers are honest. The maze of shops and stalls on either side of the Ruta Internacional is where the bulk of the bargains are, though the area also attracts petty thieves – do not carry valuables with you.

DIRECTORY

Banks and exchange On Av Jara there are multiple options.

Car rental Various options at the airport, or Localiza (ⓣ 021 683 892) on Av San Blas (Ruta Internacional) Km4.

Hospital Fundación Tesai on Av Caballero behind the bus terminal.

Internet *Hotel Venecia* (see p.705) has computers for Gs5000/hr.

Laundry At least three laundries along E.R. Fernandez two blocks north of the Ruta Internacional.

Post office Alejo Garcia and Centro Democrático (Mon–Fri 7am–6pm, Sat 7am–noon).

AROUND CIUDAD DEL ESTE

The main reasons for staying in CDE are to visit **Iguazú Falls** – both the Brazilian (see p.353) and Argentine (see p.88) sides are an easy day-trip from here – and the **Itaipú Dam**, the second-largest dam in the world (but still the largest producer of hydroelectric power), and an extraordinary engineering feat. The Itaipú Dam company also oversees the management of eight small nature reserves, but if you have time, head straight for the **Reserva Bosque Mbaracayú** (see box, p.691).

Itaipú Dam

Sited 20km north of Ciudad del Este, ITAIPÚ (in Hernandarias 10km from CDE; ☏061 599 8040, ⊚www.itaipu.gov.py) was once referred to as one of the seven wonders of the modern world. With a maximum height of 195m and generating up to 75,000GWh of energy per year (and fulfilling 87 percent of Paraguay's energy needs), it's still something to behold. Visits are by **guided tour only** (daily on the hour 8am–5pm; free, passport required; 1hr 30min), with a short documentary shown first. There are tours from the Brazilian side where you can pay to see the inner workings of the colossal 1km-long machine room, which is fantastic, but as tours from the Paraguay side are free, those on a budget will be more than satisfied with the enormous vistas outside. There are also spectacular light shows on Friday and Saturday nights at 7.30pm (free, but reserve with passport details).

The project's backers had to invest heavily in ecological damage limitation projects, establishing several nature reserves as well as the **Centro Ambiental** (Tues–Sun 8am–6pm; free), a few kilometres south of the dam's entrance (back towards CDE) and easily reached by taxi. It contains a good museum about the Guaraní peoples, as well as an excellent zoo by South American standards, set up to house animals rescued from the flooding. The Dam also runs several **nature reserves** in this area, but these are really only worth looking into if you won't have time to make it to Mbaracayú or San Rafael (see box, p.691).

The Dam is easily accessed by **public transport**; simply jump on any bus marked "Hernandarias" from the bus stands next to the SENATUR office (Gs3000; 20min) and get off at Km17 where you'll see the entrance on your right. There is also a taxi stand here for the return journey.

CONCEPCIÓN

From CDE it's possible to catch a connecting bus from transport hub Coronel Oviedo up to **CONCEPCIÓN**, although it's a comfier journey from Asunción. A cultured, peaceful and historic port town on the bank of the Río Paraguay, Concepción is the main trading centre in the northeast of the country. It has a wealth of **museums** for a town of its size and more recently it has become popular with tourists as a centre for rustic but picturesque river trips along the Río Paraguay to the Paraguayan **Pantanal** (see box, p.691).

WHAT TO SEE AND DO

Concepción is perhaps best known by Paraguayans for its graceful Italianate and Art Deco turn-of-the-twentieth-century **mansions**, with Villa Heyn (set back from C.A. López between Brasil and Otaño), housing the regional government, arguably the finest example. The bulk of the tourist sights are in the centre, concentrated on the main street Avenida Pinedo, which runs north–south, with east–west streets running from Pinedo to the river. Presidente Franco goes from Pinedo to the port and is mainly commercial, Mariscal Estigarribia and Mariscal López run parallel to the south of Franco, and have three plazas between them, containing the bulk of the museums and old buildings; there are some old signs outside the museums and important buildings with a map of town to help orientate you. While here, don't miss hanging out at the port at sunset with a *termo* of *tereré*, watching locals swimming in the river and the sun setting over the Chaco.

The museums

The town's small but high-quality museums are mostly only open in the morning. The ones not to miss include the **Museo del Cuartel de Villa Real** (Mcal. Estigarribia, cnr C.A. López; Mon–Sat 8am–noon; free), with a motley collection of historical artefacts (including the wheels to Eliza Lynch's carriage) housed in a refurbished part of the army barracks dating back to the triple alliance war, and a rather good **contemporary art museum** in the delightful Art Deco Mansión Otaño (Mcal. Estigarribia, cnr Cerro Corá; Mon–Fri 8am–noon; free), which includes a room dedicated to the art of Concepción-born artist Carlos Colombino, who also made the altarpiece in the Catedral.

8

Nearby is the stately yellow and white **Palacio Municipal** dating from 1898 (pop in to see two enormous murals in the main hall), and one block south of here, on Mcal. López between Cerro Corá and Gral. Garay, is the **Teatro Municipal**, which currently houses not only the theatre, but the tourist information office and, temporarily, the collection of the **Museo Municipal**, a fascinating haul of paintings, fossils, musical instruments, items of clothing and furniture.

ARRIVAL AND INFORMATION

By boat The Aquidabán (☎033 124 2435) goes upriver to Bahía Negra in the Paraguayan Pantanal once a week. In theory it leaves Concepción every Tues around 11am, arriving at dawn on Fri. It costs Gs100,000, or Gs180,000 with a bed (you'll need to take a hammock if not). Boats are uncomfortable, and while they should have basic food available to buy, it's best to take your own food and water with you. The *Cacique II* leaves on Sun nights for Asunción (see p.696).

By bus Buses arrive at the terminal on Asunción, between Gral. Garay and Andrés Miancoff, eight blocks north of the town centre.

Destinations Asunción (7 daily; 7hr); Campo Grande, Brazil (4 daily; 7–10hr); Coronel Oviedo (daily; 6–7hr); Filadelfia (daily; 8hr); Pedro Juan Caballero (11 daily; 4–5hr); Vallemí (2 daily; 5hr); Sao Paulo, Brazil (daily; 24hr).

Tourist information Tourism is currently run by Elva Ruíz on behalf of the municipality, at the Teatro Municipal (Mon–Fri 8am–1pm), though there are plans to start a dedicated tourist office. She speaks good English and Italian, and can offer the best service if you email or call her in advance (☎097 124 7648, ☎098 399 4372, ✉eruizmendez @yahoo.com). She is able to help with booking accommodation, and provides information on the Pantanal.

ACCOMMODATION

There is a good range of accommodation in town, as well as two great country escapes to *estancias*. All hotels listed below include breakfast, TV, wi-fi and a/c unless specified.

IN TOWN

Francés Franco, cnr C.A. López ☎0331 242 383, ⓦhotel francesconcepcion.com. The best bet in town, in a charming old building with a swimming pool and a good restaurant. Rooms with fan Gs120,000, a/c Gs150,000

Victoria Franco and Pedro Caballero ☎0331 242 256. While sparklingly refurbished on the outside, the rooms may have seen better days, but it's great value, with a patio with orchids and ferns and two decent restaurants. Rooms with fan Gs90,000, with a/c Gs140,000

ESTANCIAS NEAR CONCEPCIÓN

Estancia Primavera ☎0331 242 045. Run by the parents of Elva Ruíz who runs the tourist office (see above), 40km from town on the banks of the River Aquidabán, you can stay in the family home on this private ranch with its own white-sand beaches as well as horseriding and fishing facilities. Pick-up from town can be arranged. Room, full board and activities Gs70,000, camping only Gs20,000

Granja El Roble Km16 towards Belén ☎098 589 8446, ⓦparaguay.ch. This farm offers treehouses, camping space or cabins, and is very well set up for tourism. The owner offers all kinds of excursions – including the Chaco – as well as rafting and fishing. The website is in English and gives excellent details on how to get there. Camping Gs45,000, cabins Gs90,000

EATING AND DRINKING

For snacks, there are numerous *copetíns* (snack bars) in town which serve juices, *empanadas*, croquettes and sandwiches for next to nothing. There is a market two blocks east of Pinedo on Don Bosco (extension of Franco) and there's a supermarket at the corners of Pinedo and Estigarribia.

Hotel Victoria & La Quincha de Victoria Franco and Pedro Caballero. The lunchtime restaurant is in the hotel itself and is a pleasant place for a Gs15,000 set lunch. The evening restaurant is right across the street, and is a popular outdoor spot to have a grill, steak, burger or beer, and listen to Paraguayan music. Mains Gs15,000-45,000.

Palo Santo restaurant and chopería Franco, at Pedro Caballero, next to the *Hotel Victoria*. Brazilian-run place serving the best caipirihnas in town, but with erratic opening hours.

★ **Toninho y Jandira** Mcal Estigarribia between Iturbe and Cerro Corá, in front of the Municipalidad. An excellent Brazilian restaurant where a set price of Gs50,000 gives you a simple choice of beef or fish accompanied with a personal feast of rice, beans and five types of salads and vegetables. One portion is more than enough for two people. Closed Sun.

DIRECTORY

Banks and exchange Avenidas Franco and Pinedo are lined with casas de cambio and banks, most of which have 24hr ATMs that accept international cards.

Hospital State-run hospital at Guillermo Cabral, cnr Doctor Macial Roig.

Internet Cyberplanet on Gral. Garay between Brasil and Mayor Julio Otaño. Gs4000/hr.

Laundry On Gral. Garay between Mayor Julio Otaño and Tte. 1 Eugenio Aguero.

Phone Copaco office on Franco between Pinedo and Yegros. Daily 7am–8.45pm.

Post office Correo Paraguayo, 485 Mcal. J.F. Estigarribia, at Gral. Garay.

West of the Paraguay

West of the Río Paraguay lies the area of the country that accounts for over sixty percent of the land, but with just two to three percent of the population, **THE CHACO**. The main route north from the capital is Ruta 9 – the "Trans-Chaco" – which takes you straight up through this "inferno verde", or "green inferno", as it is popularly known, and beyond to Bolivia. It is split into three departments, Presidente Hayes, Alto Paraguay and Boquerón, but it is more helpful to think of it as two climate zones – the **lower Chaco** being humid, and the **upper Chaco** being dry. Where they meet in the central Chaco there is a cluster of fascinating **Mennonite colonies** which provide the only real urban tourism in the whole place.

Vast swathes of the Chaco are uninhabited and this, along with the extreme heat, makes it very dangerous to travel around for even those who live here; locals always travel in groups. **Guided tours** are the easiest (and safest) way to see the highlights, which include stunning birdlife at the **Central Chaco Lagoons** and isolated, wildlife-packed national parks (see box, p.691); however, these can be cripplingly expensive and difficult to organize unless booked well in advance. Exploring independently is not recommended and renting a vehicle and obtaining all the necessary survival gear will work out no cheaper. There are, however, some limited public transport options. You'll get the most out of a visit to the Chaco if you plan everything (including getting in touch with tourist information offices) in advance.

THE MENNONITE COLONIES

While indigenous tribes still make up just over fifty percent of the Chaco's denizens (some 28,000 people), the German Mennonites, who first came to Paraguay in 1927 as a group of just 1700 or so to escape discrimination, persecution, or enforced participation in national service (Mennonites are pacifists), are now the largest minority group here. Despite their early struggles, today the Mennonites here are some of the most prosperous people in Paraguay. They are the major dairy producers in the country and their three colonies operate with a clinical efficiency that belies their isolated location, with beautifully kept gardens, ruler-straight streets and solidly made brick houses, interspersed with parks and pavements. The Mennonites here are relatively liberal, modern and open, and have embraced tourism and relish the opportunity to show off their achievements to the few visitors who pass through.

WHAT TO SEE AND DO

The **three Mennonite colonies** who settled here each established one of the central Chaco towns, and the only thing to do in the towns, other than seeing how the Mennonites, indigenous peoples, and *mestizo* Paraguayans rub along together, is to visit the interesting **Mennonite museums**, symbolic monuments and cooperative supermarkets in each.

Unless you are a motor-racing fanatic, the area is best avoided in the last week of September when it becomes gripped by **Trans-Chaco Rally** fever (⑩transchacorally .com.py). Billed as one of the toughest motorized events on earth, it is accompanied by a considerable hike in hotel prices and you will have to book well in advance.

Filadelfia

Thanks to its proximity to the Ruta Trans-Chaco, **FILADELFIA**, home to the Fernheim Colony, has grown to be the capital of the Boquerón department and receives all the long-distance buses, as well as being the hub for "local" buses, for the Chaco. Of all the colonies, it also has the most to do in town, with several museums and monuments, most on or around the main Avenida Hindenburg. In a prim park at the corner of Calle Unruh sit the **Museo Jakob Unger**, which houses taxidermied Chaco wildlife, and the **Museo de la Colonia** (both Mon–Sat 7–11.30am; free; ☎0491 417 380), housed in the only surviving building from the original pioneers. In the same park is a **tourist information** office run by very helpful Gati Harder, who speaks perfect English (daily 7–11am; ☎0491 417 380, ✉turismo@fernheim.com.py) and will happily give talks on Mennonite history, and her other speciality, the trees of the Chaco.

Loma Plata and Neu Halbstadt

The largest of the Mennonite towns is **LOMA PLATA**, home to the Menno Colony, whose Chortitzer Cooperative makes Paraguay's largest dairy brand, Trébol, but other than the small **Museo de Historia Mennonita** (next to the cooperative on the main street; daily 7am–noon & 2–6pm; free; ☎098 356 9922), it's the least interesting of the colonies. The Neuland Colony's main town, **NEU HALBSTADT** (also referred to as Neuland), has more to offer tourists thanks to its dynamic tourist officer Heinz Weiber (information office next to the coop; ☎097 170 1634, ☎0493 240 201, ✉hwiebe@neuland .com.py). Although he only speaks Spanish, if you get in touch with him before you go he can arrange a translator for his tours of all three colonies.

ARRIVAL AND INFORMATION

Although all three Mennonite cities are populous (and growing rapidly), all maintain a very suburban feel with wide streets and huge blocks. They are tiring to walk around and can feel inaccessible at times, but people tend to be very helpful. There are ATMs which accept foreign cards on the principal avenue in each town, and each has a post office and a supermarket.

By bus There is a bus terminal in Filadelfia, of sorts, on Chaco Boreal, one block west of Hindenburg. Most services from Filadelfia pass through Loma Plata en route to the capital.

Destinations Asunción (5 daily; 8hr); Concepcion (daily; 8–10hr); Mariscal Estigarribia (2 daily); Neuland & Loma Plata (2 daily to each; 30min); Parque Nacional Teniente Enisco (3 weekly).

Taxi There is a taxi rank on Hindenburg in Filadelfia of 4WDs who charge some Gs14,000 to Loma Plata, Gs200,000 to Neuland, or Gs30,000 within town.

Tours The best local people to ask are Norbet Epp, who runs Gran Chaco Turismo (☎098 122 3974, ⊚granchaco turismo.net), and Walter Ratzlaff (☎098 120 2200, ✉walterrat@hotmail.com); both take tourists around when they can, but contact them in advance. Also worth looking into is Paraguay Salvaje ⊚paraguay-salvaje.com .py, ⊚chaco-wildlife.org.

ACCOMMODATION

The Mennonites run mid-range, spotless, efficient hotels in all three colonies. All are en-suite, have wi-fi, TV, a/c, and offer very good buffet breakfasts, as well as having dining options.

Boquerón Opposite the Coop on main street Av 1 de Febrero, Neu Halbstadt ☎049 324 0311, ✉hotel@neuland .com.py. A very pleasant Mennonite hotel with lawns and flower beds flanking spacious rooms with pine beds. ̲G̲s̲1̲3̲0̲,̲0̲0̲0̲

Estancia Iparoma ☎098 194 0050, ✉estanciaiparoma @gmail.com. Worth investigating if you want to stay out in the Chaco without straying so far you could put yourself in danger, this Mennonite-run working farm, 19km from Filadelfia, provides accommodation, food, horseriding and other activities. Best organized through Gati at the Filadelfia tourist office (see above). B&B ̲G̲s̲5̲0̲,̲0̲0̲0̲

Golondrina Hindenburg 365-Sur, at Palo Santo, Filadelfia ☎049 143 3111, ⊚hotelgolondrina.com. Run by Para-guayans, laid out in a motel style, with clean but soulless rooms; it's the cheapest you can get for B&B with wi-fi in Filadelfia. En-suite rooms ̲G̲s̲1̲4̲5̲,̲0̲0̲0̲

EATING AND DRINKING

Boquerón Boquerón, cnr Miller, Filadelfia. Big and bright restaurant with good choice of food including everything from Mexican to pizza, and from buffet (Gs60,000/kg) to burgers (Gs18,000). Open daily from 7pm.

Girasol Unruh, at Hindenburg, Filadelfia. Regarded as the best restaurant in the colonies, this place does a great range of grills, as well as a buffet (Gs62,000/kg). It's open for lunch and dinner, and its garden is nice for drinks, too.

CROSSING TO BOLIVIA

At the small town of **La Patria**, a fully paved road (formerly Picada 108) branches off the Trans-Chaco to the border crossing of **Fortín Infante Rivarola**. There is a small guard post here that does not have exit stamps; you have to stop in Mariscal Estigarribia en route to do immigration formalities. This border point is extremely isolated and a popular smuggling route, so you are not advised to attempt to cross the border here by yourself. International buses (1–2 daily; 30hr) run between Asunción and Santa Cruz in Bolivia via the bus companies Yacyretá, Pycasu and Río Paraguay.

MACHU PICCHU

Peru

HIGHLIGHTS

❶ **Machu Picchu** Walk the Inca Trail to these legendary ruins. **See p.757**

❷ **Nazca Lines** Dazzling geometric designs etched into the desert. **See p.773**

❸ **Colca Canyon** At its deepest point the canyon reaches 4km. **See p.780**

❹ **Huaraz** Trek the stunning snowcapped peaks of the Andes. **See p.786**

❺ **Cajamarca** Outstanding architecture, great food and the Northern Highlands. **See p.806**

❻ **Madre de Dios** Lush rainforest home to the world's largest macaw clay lick. **See p.822**

HIGHLIGHTS ARE MARKED ON THE MAP ON PP.714–715

ROUGH COSTS

Daily budget Basic US$25, occasional treat US$35

Drink Cristal beer US$1–2

Food Lunchtime menu US$3–5

Hostel/budget hotel US$7–12

Travel Tumbes–Lima: 18hr, US$20–40, Lima–Cusco: 22hr, US$25–55

FACT FILE

Population 29.5 million

Language Spanish, Quechua, Aymara

Currency Nuevo Sol (S)

Capital Lima (population: 8.5 million)

International phone code ❼51

Time zone GMT -5hr

9

Introduction

Peru is the most varied and exciting of all the South American nations, with a combination of mountains, Inca relics, immense desert coastline and vast tracts of tropical rainforest. Dividing these contrasting environments, the Andes, with its chain of breathtaking peaks, over 7km high and 400km wide in places, ripples the entire length of the nation. So distinct are these regions that it is very difficult to generalize about the country, but one thing for sure is that Peru offers a unique opportunity to experience an incredibly wide range of spectacular scenery, a wealth of heritage and a vibrant living culture.

Hedonists will head for the beaches of **Máncora**, the nightclubs of **Lima** and the bars of **Cusco** – the latter a city where a cosmopolitan lifestyle coexists alongside pre-Columbian buildings and ancient festivals. Just as easily, you can retreat from civilization, travelling deep into the remote parts of the **Peruvian Amazon**, searching for jaguars or taking part in hallucinogenic *ayahuasca* (jungle vine) ceremonies. Or you can walk in the footsteps of the Incas, taking on the challenge of the **Inca Trail** to reach the ancient citadel of **Machu Picchu**, take a flight over the **Nazca Lines** to ponder the meaning of the giant figures etched into the desert, or hike the canyons and snow-tipped peaks around **Arequipa** and **Trujillo**.

In the more rural parts of Peru, local life has changed little in the last four centuries and many people lead humble, traditional lives, though roads and tracks now connect almost every corner of the country, making travel quite straight-forward. Nevertheless, you should be prepared to accept the occasional episode of social unrest or travel delays caused by natural disasters with the good humour of the locals.

CHRONOLOGY

c.40,000–15,000 BC The first Peruvians, descendants of nomadic tribes, cross into the Americas from Asia during the last ice age.

2600 BC The complex civilization at the site of Caral develops, lasting for an estimated 500 years.

200–600 AD Emergence and growth of the Moche and Nazca cultures.

1200 The Inca Empire begins to emerge.

1438–70 Pachacutec becomes ruler of the Inca Empire. Machu Picchu and the Inca capital of Cusco are constructed.

1500–30 The Inca Empire stretches over 5500km, from southern Colombia right down to northern Chile.

1532 Francisco Pizarro leads his band of 170 conquistadors from Tumbes to Cajamarca, capturing the Inca ruler Atahualpa and massacring thousands of Inca warriors.

1533 Atahualpa is executed and the Spaniards install a puppet Inca ruler, Manco Inca.

1535 Lima is founded by Pizarro as the "City of Kings".

1538–41 Conquistadors fight for control of the colony. Diego de Almagro is executed by Pizarro, who in turn is assassinated by Almagro's son.

1542 The Viceroyalty of Peru is established by Spain's King Charles I, with Lima as its capital.

1571 Unsuccessful rebellion by the last Inca, Túpac Amaru, results in his execution.

1821 Argentine general José de San Martín declares Peruvian Independence on July 28.

1824 The last of the Spanish forces defeated at the battles of Junín and Ayacucho. Peru becomes an independent state.

1879–83 The War of the Pacific with Chile. Chile is victorious, annexing a large chunk of southern Peru, including the nitrate-rich northern Atacama desert.

1911 Hiram Bingham discovers Machu Picchu.

1948–56 The economy spirals into ruin and a military junta takes control.

1969–75 Massive economic crisis occurs after General Juan Velasco nationalizes foreign-owned businesses, bans foreign investors and gives all the hacienda land to workers' cooperatives.

1980–92 The Maoist Sendero Luminoso ("Shining Path"), led by Abimael Guzman, carries out terrorist attacks against the government. The conflict causes 69,000 deaths and "disappearances", at least 75 percent of them Quechua-speaking highlanders.

1985 Socialist candidate Alan García comes to power. Financial reforms cause massive hyperinflation and trigger the worst economic crisis Peru has ever experienced.

1990 Surprise presidential victory by Alberto Fujimori over renowned author Mario Vargas Llosa. Privatization of state-owned companies improves economic conditions.

1994 Amnesty offered to Shining Path members; more than 6000 surrender.

2000 Fujimori re-elected amid allegations of electoral fraud, but flees to Japan shortly after due to revelations of corruption, extortion, arms trafficking and human rights abuses.

2001–06 Alejandro Toledo becomes Peru's first full-blooded indigenous president. Protests against the US-backed eradication of coca plantations and nationwide strikes ensue, but the economy remains stable.

2007 Massive earthquake devastates the coastal province of Ica, killing 520 people.

2007–09 Fujimori extradited to Peru. After a lengthy public trial he is convicted to 25 years in prison for authorizing death squad killings in 1991–92.

2010 Mario Vargas Llosa wins the Nobel Prize for Literature.

2011 Ollanta Humala wins the presidential election in a run-off vote.

2012 Shining Path faction leader Artemio is captured and charged with terrorism and drug trafficking.

WHEN TO VISIT

The best time to visit Peru will depend upon which areas of the country you intend to visit, and what activities you plan on doing. **The coast** tends to be mostly dry year-round, but sits under a blanket of fog from April to November each year (especially in Lima); the driest, sunniest months here (Dec–March) tend to coincide with the rainiest weather elsewhere.

In the **Andes** the seasons are more clearly marked, with heavy rains from December to April and a relatively dry period from June to September, which, although it can be cold at night, is certainly the best time for trekking and most outdoor activities. In much of the **jungle**, rainfall is heavier and more frequent, and it's hot and humid all year. In the lowland rainforest areas around Iquitos water levels are higher between December and January, which offers distinct advantages for spotting wildlife and accessing remote creeks by canoe.

Those wishing to avoid the crowds will prefer to visit during the shoulder seasons of May and September to November, as from May to August many popular tourist attractions are packed with tour groups.

ARRIVAL AND DEPARTURE

Peru has land borders with Chile, Ecuador, Bolivia, Brazil and Colombia. While the borders with Chile, Ecuador and Bolivia are easily negotiated, the borders with Brazil and Colombia are deep in the jungle and less easily reached. Lima is a major transport hub with international flights from the US and Europe; there are also good connections from Lima to other South American countries. International flights within South America tend to be expensive, while national flights within Peru average around US$90 to any destination. Save money by crossing borders by land and only flying within Peru.

Major operators include LAN Peru and Taca; also American Airlines from the US, Iberia from Europe via Madrid, and KLM from Europe via Amsterdam. Local airlines include Star Peru and Peruvian Airlines. US citizens are required to show a return ticket if flying in.

If crossing land borders from Chile, Bolivia or Ecuador, aim to take a long-distance bus that goes directly to your destination across the border – it may be a little pricier, but that way you avoid hanging around dodgy border crossing areas and the drivers can assist you with border formalities.

VISAS

EU, US, Canadian, Australian and New Zealand citizens can all stay in Peru as tourists for up to 183 days without a visa; for other nationalities, check with your local Peruvian embassy. You're typically given ninety days upon entry, so if you're planning to stay a long time in Peru, make sure to ask for the maximum time allowance, as it is no longer possible to extend tourist visas.

All nationalities need a **tourist or embarkation card** (*tarjeta de embarque*) to enter Peru, which is issued at the border or on the plane before landing. In theory you have to show an outbound ticket (by air or bus) before you'll be given a card, but this is almost never checked. Keep a copy of the tourist card and your passport on you at all times – particularly

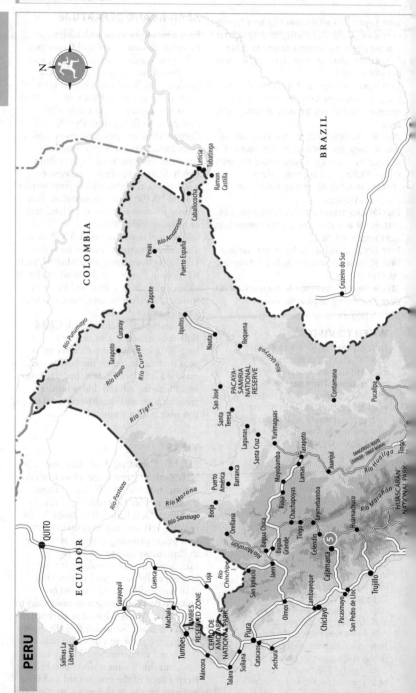

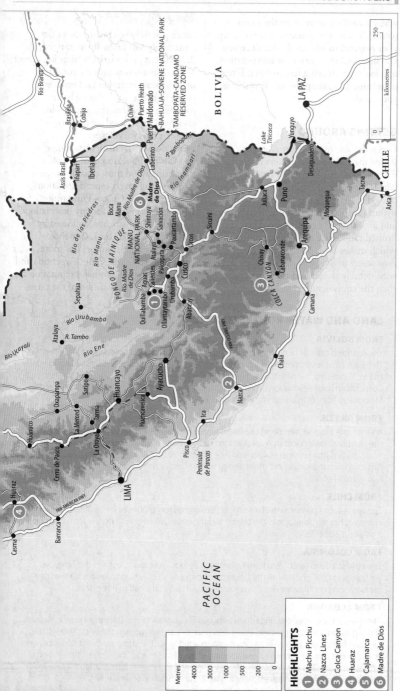

PACIFIC
OCEAN

HIGHLIGHTS

1. Machu Picchu
2. Nazca Lines
3. Colca Canyon
4. Huaraz
5. Cajamarca
6. Madre de Dios

Metres
4000
3000
1000
500
200
0

when travelling away from the main towns. It is very important that you keep your original tourist card safe, since you will be asked to return it to immigration officials when leaving the country. Fines of around S15 are applicable if you lose your card.

GETTING AROUND

Given the size of the country, many Peruvians and holiday-makers fly to their destinations, as all Peruvian cities are within a two-hour flight from Lima. Most budget travellers get around the country by bus, as these go just about everywhere and are extremely good value. There is a limited rail service along some routes, which makes for a change from the monotony of long bus rides, despite being considerably slower and more expensive than the equivalent bus journey.

BY BUS

Peru's privately operated buses offer remarkably low fares. Buses range from the efficient and relatively luxurious *cama* or *semicama* buses with air conditioning, snacks/meals included and on-board entertainment, to the more basic *económico* buses, to the scruffy old ex-school buses used on local runs between remote villages.

Cruz del Sur (Ⓦcruzdelsur.com.pe) and Oltursa (Ⓦoltursa.com.pe) offer the plushest and most reliable buses; Cruz del Sur covers most destinations (though not the Cusco–Puno route), while Oltursa is best for any destination along the Panamericana, followed by Cial (Ⓦexpresocial.com). Ormeño (Ⓦgrupo-ormeno.com.pe) has routes as far as Colombia, Brazil, Chile, Argentina and Bolivia, though it also has a reputation for lateness, and the condition of the buses

LAND AND WATER ROUTES TO PERU

FROM BOLIVIA

The southern cities of Puno, Cusco and Arequipa are easily reached overland from Bolivia. There are two crossings: Yungayo from Copacabana on Lake Titicaca, and Desaguadero from La Paz; Yungayo is marginally less chaotic. Regular buses run direct to Puno (and some to Cusco) from both destinations. It's difficult, though not impossible, to take a boat to Puerto Maldonado from Bolivia's Puerto Heath via Puerto Pardo.

FROM BRAZIL

It's a simple bus journey along the Interoceanic Highway and across the bridge from the Brazilian border post of Assis Brasil to the Peruvian village of Iñapari, which is three hours by bus from Puerto Maldonado (see p.823). You can also reach Iquitos via the Amazon from the small port of Tabatinga via the border post of Santa Rosa, just like from Colombia's Leticia.

FROM CHILE

The Arica–Tacna border in the far south of Peru causes few problems for travellers. Taxi *colectivos* run regularly across the border and the driver will help with border formalities for a small tip. See p.780.

FROM COLOMBIA

The easiest way to reach Peru from Colombia is by bus via Ecuador, but if in the Amazon, you can also take a boat from the Colombian border town of Leticia to Iquitos via the small immigration post of Santa Rosa; river journeys take two and a half to three days.

FROM ECUADOR

There are three border crossings open between Ecuador and Peru. The most commonly used is the Tumbes–Machala crossing along the Panamerican Highway on the coast, though the crossing from Loja to Piura via La Tina is also straightforward, as there are direct buses between major destinations in each country, stopping at the Peruvian and Ecuadorian immigration offices en route. The third crossing – from Vilcabamba to Jaén – is further inland where roads are not so good, and it involves changing basic transportation several times.

has declined over the years. Reliable companies covering the north of Peru include **Movil Tours** (ⓦmoviltours.com.pe), **Línea** (ⓦlinea.pe) and **Tepsa** (ⓦwww.tepsa .com.pe), while the south is covered by the cheaper **Flores** (ⓦfloreshnos.net), **TransMar** (ⓦtransmar.com.pe) and **Soyuz** (ⓦwww .soyuz.com.pe). For intercity rides, it's best to buy tickets in advance direct from the bus company offices; for local trips, you can buy tickets on the bus itself.

If storing main luggage in the hold, you should get a receipt. You'll need to hand this in at the end of your journey to claim your luggage. Keep your hand luggage with you at all times, particularly if travelling on cheaper buses like Soyuz.

BY TAXI, MOTOTAXI AND COLECTIVO

Taxis are easily found at any time in almost every town. Any car can become a taxi simply by sticking a taxi sign up in the front window; a lot of people take advantage of this to supplement their income. However, in recent years this has led to an increase in crime, so if possible call a radio taxi from a recommended company. Always fix the price in advance, since few taxis have meters. Relatively short journeys in Lima generally cost around S6, but it's cheaper elsewhere. Taxi drivers in Peru do not expect tips.

In many towns, you'll find small cars and *mototaxis* (**motorcycle rickshaws**). The latter are always cheaper than taxis, if slightly more dangerous and not that comfortable. Outside Lima, you will almost never pay more than S5 for a ride within a town.

Colectivos (shared taxis) are a very useful way of getting around. They look like private cars or taxis but run a fixed route; each has a small sign in the window with the destination and can squeeze in up to six passengers. They connect all the coastal towns, and many of the larger centres in the mountains, and tend to be faster than the bus, though they often charge twice as much. *Colectivos* can be found in the centre of a town or at major stopping places along the main roads. The price is generally double that of *combis* (see below), depending on distance travelled. *Colectivo* minibuses, also known as

combis, can squeeze in twice as many people, or often more. They cost on average S5 per person, per hour travelled. Do keep in mind that in the cities, particularly in Lima, *colectivos* (especially *combis*) have a poor reputation for safety. They frequently crash, turn over and knock down pedestrians.

BY TRAIN

Peru's spectacular train journeys are in themselves a major attraction. **Peru Rail** (ⓦperurail.com) runs passenger services from Puno to Cusco, from where another line heads down the magnificent Urubamba Valley as far as Machu Picchu (see box, p.762). The world's second-highest railway route, from Lima to Huancayo, is considered to be among the most scenic in the world, but it only runs once a month or so; check departure dates and times at ⓦwww.ferrocarrilcentral .com.pe.

Trains tend to be slower than buses and considerably more expensive, but they do allow ample time to enjoy the scenery, and are quite comfortable. If you're planning on visiting Machu Picchu but don't intend to hike the Inca Trail, you have no option but to take a tourist train priced in US dollars.

At the time of writing, the Cusco–Puno service costs S436, while a bus costs S40; a "backpacker" train to Machu Picchu costs US$78. If possible, tickets should be bought at least a day in advance, and a week in advance on the Cusco–Machu Picchu route.

BY AIR

Peru is so vast that the odd flight can save a lot of time, and flights between major towns are frequent and relatively inexpensive. The most popular routes usually need to be booked at least a few days in advance (more at the time of major fiestas). For the best fares to popular destinations, either book your flights in advance with Chilean-owned LAN (ⓦlan.com), the main airline, or with the smaller Peruvian subsidiaries of Star Peru (ⓦstarperu.com), Peruvian Airlines (ⓦperuvianairlines.pe) or LC Perú (ⓦlcperu.pe).

9

Some places in the jungle, such as Iquitos, are more easily accessible by plane, as land and river routes take much longer and can cost as much as a plane ticket.

Flights are sometimes cancelled, delayed or leave earlier than scheduled, so it is important to reconfirm your flight 48 hours before departure. If a passenger hasn't shown up twenty minutes before the flight, the company can give the seat to someone on the waiting list.

BY BOAT

There are no coastal boat services in Peru. In the jungle, river travel is of enormous importance, and cargo boats are an excellent way of travelling along the Amazon – though you have to have plenty of time at your disposal. The facilities are basic (bring your own hammock to hang on deck or rent a cabin), as is the food. The most popular routes are either from Pucallpa or Yurimaguas to Iquitos, from where you can then go on to Colombia or Brazil. On smaller rivers, motorized dugout canoes are the preferred local mode of transport and come in two basic forms: those with a large outboard motor, and slow and noisy *peke-peke* (the name describes the sound of the engine).

ACCOMMODATION

Peru has the typical range of Latin American accommodation, from top-class international hotels to tiny rooms at the back of someone's house for around ten soles a night. Virtually all upmarket accommodation will call itself a hotel or, in the countryside regions, a posada. Lodges in the jungle can be anything from quite luxurious to an open-sided, palm-thatched hut with space for slinging a hammock. *Pensiones* or *residenciales* tend to specialize in longer-term accommodation and may offer discounts for stays of a week or more.

GUESTHOUSES AND HOTELS

Budget **guesthouses** (usually called *hospedajes* or *hostales* and not to be confused with youth hostels) are generally old – sometimes beautifully so, converted from colonial mansions with rooms grouped around a courtyard – and tend to be quite central. At the low end of the scale, which can be basic with shared rooms and a communal bathroom, you can usually find a bed for S20–30, the price often including breakfast. Rooms with private bath tend to cost S10–15 more. *Hostales* can be great value if you're travelling with one other person or more; you can often get a good, clean en-suite room for less than two or three bunk beds in a youth hostel. A little haggling is often worth a try, particularly in the low season.

HOSTELS AND CAMPING

A list of the HI-affiliated **youth hostels** in Peru is at ⒲hihostels.com/dba/country -Peru-PE.en.htm. These are relatively cheap and reliable; expect to pay around S15–25, more in Lima. All hostels are theoretically open 24hr. There are also many non-HI-affiliated hostels throughout the country (try ⒲hostels .com, ⒲hostelbookers.com or ⒲hostelworld.com). While these are great for meeting people, they are often not the cheapest option, as dorm beds cost S10–25, the same price as a room at a budget hotel. **Camping** is possible all over Peru. In towns and cities you may be charged the same amount to put up a tent in the grounds of a hostel as for a dorm bed. Organized campsites are gradually being established on the outskirts of popular tourist destinations, though these are still few and far between. Outside urban areas, apart from some restricted natural reserves, it's possible to camp amid some stunning scenery along Peru's vast coast, in the mountains and in the jungle. It's best not to camp alone, and if you are setting up camp anywhere near a village or settlement, ask permission or advice from the nearest farm or house first.

FOOD AND DRINK

Peruvian cuisine is wonderfully diverse, and essentially a *mestizo* creation, merging indigenous Indian cooking with Spanish, African, Chinese, Italian and Japanese influences. Along the coast, *ceviche* is the classic Peruvian seafood dish, consisting of raw fish, assorted seafood or a mixture of the two, marinated in lime juice and chilli and with corn, sweet potato and onions. You'll also find *arroz con mariscos* (rice with seafood), *tiradito* (like sashimi, served with a spicy sauce), *conchitas a la parmesana* (scallops baked with cheese) and fish prepared a dozen different ways. In coastal areas you'll also find numerous *chifas* (Chinese eateries) serving ample portions of inexpensive Chinese dishes, including vegetarian options.

Food in the Andes includes delicious, hearty soups, such as *sopa de quinoa* (quinoa soup), *chupe de camarones* (shrimp chowder) and *sopa criolla* (beef noodle soup with vegetables). Peru is home to hundreds of potato varieties, the standout dishes from which include *ocopa* (potato with spicy peanut sauce), *papa a la Huancaína* (potato in a spicy cheese sauce) and *causa* (layers of mashed potato with countless fillings). Other popular dishes include *lomo saltado* (stir-fried beef), *ají de gallina* (chicken in a mild chilli sauce), *arroz con pato* (rice with duck, simmered in dark beer with coriander) and the ubiquitous *cuy* (seared guinea pig).

In the jungle, the succulent local fish, such as *dorado* and *paiche*, comes grilled, as *patarashka* (spiced, wrapped in banana leaves and baked on coals) or as *paca* (steamed in a banana tube). Fried and mashed plantain figures highly, along with *yuca* (a manioc rather like a yam) and *juanes* (banana leaves stuffed with chicken,

---

TAX HOAX

If any restaurant tries to add an extra "tax" to your bill, be aware that in Peru, the 19 percent VAT is automatically added to the cost of the dishes and that you shouldn't have to pay anything extra. Also, for a bill to be legal, it has to be either a *boleto de venta* or a *factura*, with the name and address of the restaurant on it. Should any establishment insist that you pay an illegal bill or tax, you have the right to report them to SUNAT, the local regulating board (Ⓦ www.sunat.gob.pe).

WHERE AND WHEN TO EAT

In Peru, lunch is the main meal of the day, and the time to grab the best food bargains. In coastal areas, some of the best food is found in *cevicherías*, simple seafood restaurants open at lunchtime only. Ask for the *menú marino* – a lunchtime seafood menu that typically consists of two courses, such as *ceviche* and *arroz con mariscos*, and costs around S15–20. Elsewhere, most restaurants will offer a *menú* – a three-course set lunch from S10 upwards.

---

rice and spices). There is often game on the menu, but beware of eating turtle or other endangered species. It is best not to eat fish along the River Tambopata due to the high levels of mercury used extensively in river mining activities.

In big cities, there are numerous vegetarian restaurants, though vegetarian food may be quite difficult to find elsewhere. If you ask for your dish *sin carne* (without meat), that may only exclude red meat, but not chicken or fish.

Dessert-wise, Peru offers a wide array of tropical fruit, such as *lúcuma*, *chirimoya* (custard apple) and *grenadilla* (passion fruit), as well as *mazamorra morada* (purple corn pudding with cloves and pineapple) and *suspiro limeño* (caramelized condensed milk topped with meringue).

DRINK

In Peru you can find all the popular soft drink brands, though Peruvians prefer the neon-yellow Inca Kola, which tastes like liquid bubblegum. Fresh fruit juices (*jugos*) are abundant, with *jugerías* (juice stalls) in markets and elsewhere offering a variety of flavours, such as papaya, *maracuyá* (passion fruit), *plátano* (banana), *piña* (pineapple) and *naranja* (orange); specify whether you want yours *con azúcar* (with sugar) or *sín azúcar* (without sugar). Another excellent non-alcoholic drink is *chicha morada*, made from purple corn – not to be confused with *chicha*, home-made corn beer popular in the Andes (look out for a red flag outside homes).

Surprisingly for a coffee-growing country, Peruvians tend to drink either *café pasado* (previously percolated coffee mixed with hot water to serve) or simple powdered Nescafé, though it is possible to find good coffee in big cities. A wide variety of herbal teas is also available, such as *menta* (mint), *manzanilla* (camomile) and the extremely popular *mate de coca* – tea brewed from coca leaves that helps one acclimatize to high altitude.

Peru brews some excellent beer, the most popular brands being *Cristal*, *Pilsen* and *Cusqueña* – all light lagers, though you can also get Pilsen *cerveza negra* (dark beer). Good regional brews include *Arequipeña* and *Trujillana* (named after the cities they're brewed in). Most Peruvian wine tends to be sweet and almost like sherry. Among brands more attuned to the Western palate are *Tabanero*, *Tacama* and *Vista Alegre*. The national beverage and a source of great pride is pisco, a potent grape brandy with a unique and powerful flavour. Pisco sour – a mix of pisco, lime juice, ice and sugar – is a very palatable and extremely popular cocktail found on menus everywhere.

CULTURE AND ETIQUETTE

Due to the huge variety of geographical conditions found within Peruvian territory, culture and traditions tend to vary between regions. On the whole, coastal people tend to be more outgoing and vivacious, while the mountain people of Quechua descent are more reserved and modest. The jungle is still home to many indigenous groups who keep their ancestral traditions and way of life. All Peruvians are family-oriented and tend to be close to large extended families. *Machismo* is alive and well in Peru, though women travelling alone are not likely to encounter much trouble.

Note that whistling in the north of Peru can be a greeting rather than an attempt at harassment.

One of the most common things travellers do that offends local people is to take their picture without asking – so always ask first, and respect a negative answer. At tourist sites all over Peru, you'll encounter women and children in stunning traditional dress who expect a tip for having their photo taken (1–2 soles is a reasonable amount). In the highlands in particular there is a strong culture of exchange, meaning that if you receive something, you are expected to give in return. This can be as simple as giving someone coca leaves in exchange for directions on a trail.

Tipping is becoming the norm in more upmarket restaurants, where a ten percent gratuity is expected and sometimes automatically added to the bill; in cheap local eateries, tips are received with surprise and gratitude. It's worth bearing in mind that some unscrupulous travel agencies pay their guides very low wages, meaning that they rely on tips, as do freelance guides in museums (agree on a fee before a tour). You should always tip your guide and porters on the Inca Trail (see box, p.756).

SPORTS AND OUTDOOR ACTIVITIES

When it comes to exploring the wilderness, few of the world's countries can offer anything as varied, rugged and colourful as Peru.

PERU'S CULINARY SUPERSTAR

No foodie should come to Peru without sampling the gastronomic delights of **Gastón Acurio**, the chef who put Peruvian cuisine on the world map. His restaurants include *ChiCha* in both Cusco and Arequipa, *La Trattoria del Monasterio* in Arequipa, *La Mar* in Lima and his flagship restaurant, *Astrid y Gastón*, also in the capital. The food ranges from superb takes on regional cuisine to original and innovative fusion creations. Not to be missed.

TREKKING AND HIKING

Peru offers a spectacular variety of trekking routes; the main hiking centres are Cusco and Arequipa in the south and Huaraz in the north. The most popular trekking route is, of course, the famous Inca Trail, but other trails in and around the Sacred Valley are rapidly gaining popularity, partly because you get to experience fantastic Andean scenery without being overrun by hordes of tourists. From Arequipa, you can descend into two of the world's deepest canyons – Cañón de Colca and the more remote Cañón de Cotahuasi, which are accessible all year, unlike the Sacred Valley. The Cordillera Blanca near Huaraz lures hikers and climbers alike with its challenging peaks, many of them over 5000m high.

Guides are required for some trekking routes, such as the Inca Trail, and for some challenging routes you'll need to hire mules and *arrieros* (muleteers). You can rent trekking gear or join guided treks at all the major hiking centres; good topographic maps are available from the Instituto Geográfico Nacional (IGN) or the South American Explorers' Club (see p.723). Always make sure you're properly equipped, as the weather is renowned for its dramatic changeability, and properly acclimatized.

MOUNTAIN BIKING

Bike shops and bicycle repair workshops are easy to find throughout Peru, though you should bring your own bike if you're planning on some major cycle touring, as mountain-bike rental is pretty basic. Various tour companies (see p.746) offer guided cycling tours, which can be an excellent way to see the best of Peru. Huaraz and Cusco are both popular and challenging destinations for experienced bikers, while the Colca Canyon is a better bet for novices.

WATERSPORTS

Cusco is one of the top white-water rafting and kayaking centres in South America, with easy access to a whole range of river grades, from Class II to V on the Río Urubamba (shifting up grades in the rainy season) to the most dangerous white water on the Río Apurímac, only safe for rafting during the dry season. Río Chili near Arequipa offers good rafting for beginners, with half-day trips passing through Class II and III rapids. A superb multi-day rafting expedition from Cusco goes right down into the Amazon Basin on the Tambopata River.

Bear in mind that rafting is still not a regulated sport in Peru, so it's very important to go with a responsible and eco-friendly operator (see p.746). Also see Ⓦperuwhitewater.com.

SURFING

Surfing is a popular sport in Peru, with annual national and international championships held in Punta Rocas, south of Lima. You can find good breaks even in Lima itself, particularly in the Miraflores area, though Punta Hermosa, further south, is less crowded. Peru's north coast offers some world-class breaks, with Puerto Chicano boasting the world's longest left-hand wave, whereas Santa Rosa and Pacasmayo outside Chiclayo also have excellent waves. Equipment rental is abundant and it's possible to take surfing lessons. Check out Ⓦperuazul.com or Ⓦvivamancora.com for more information.

SANDBOARDING AND DUNE BUGGYING

The best places to ride the sand are in Nazca (see p.773), home of the world's largest dune – Cerro Blanco – and Huacachina, near Ica (see p.769). You can either rent a board from the numerous agencies or go out on the dunes with one

GAY AND LESBIAN TRAVEL IN PERU

Being gay in Peru is still very much frowned upon due to a culture infused with *machismo* and fervent Catholicism, though tolerance is slowly improving. **Epicentro** (Jr. Jaén 250A, Barranco, Lima; Ⓣ01 247 4158, Ⓦepicentro.org.pe) is a not-for-profit community centre that also produces the regular publication *Guía Antena* (available to download free from the website), which includes gay-friendly hostels, bars, clubs, health services and shopping in Lima, as well as gay clubs nationwide.

9

of them; snowboarding experience is helpful but not necessary. Also in Huacachina, you can experience the stomach-churning adrenaline rush of dune-buggy rides. While in Nazca they are used as the most efficient means of reaching distant desert sites, in Huacachina they are used for the thrill alone.

COMMUNICATIONS

Postal services are slow and very expensive but quite acceptable for normal letters and postcards.

All public phones are operated by coins or phone cards (*tarjetas telefónicas*), which are available in 3, 5, 10, 15, 20, 40 and 50 sol denominations. You can buy cards at little *tiendas* (corner shops) or at *farmacias* (pharmacies) or on the street from cigarette stalls in the centres of most towns and cities. Both 147 and Hola Peru cards are good for local, national and international landline calls. A number of shops, restaurants and corner shops in Peru have a phone available for public use, which you can use for calls within Peru only. If you need to contact the international operator, dial ☎103. Collect calls are known either simply as *collect* or *al cobro revertido*.

If you have an unlocked mobile phone, it's cheap and easy to get a Peruvian SIM card (S15); alternatively, you can buy a cheap mobile for the duration of your stay (S80). The networks with the most extensive coverage of the country are Movistar and Claro; the latter allows you to send free text messages via their website.

Peru has good internet connections, with internet cafés abundant in big cities and found even in the most unlikely of small towns (though the connection may be

slow). Many hotels, hostels and cafés now have free wi-fi as well. The general rate is S1 per hour, though in touristy places you may end up paying as much as S5.

CRIME AND SAFETY

Perhaps the most common irritants are the persistent **touts** found at bus stations and other tourist spots, offering anything from discount accommodation to tours; be very wary of accepting their services, and don't give them money up front. Also don't take **unlicensed taxis** if possible.

You're most likely to come into contact with **police** at the border posts. While they have a reputation for being corrupt, they will mostly leave tourists alone, though some travellers may experience petty harassment aimed at procuring a bribe. If they search your luggage, be scrupulously polite and be aware that possession of any drugs is considered an extremely serious offence in Peru – usually leading to at least a ten-year jail sentence.

Violent crime, such as muggings, is relatively rare. Robberies occasionally occur on overnight buses and there have been isolated attacks on hikers in the area around Huaraz, so it's best not to hike alone. It's not advisable to travel at night between Abancay and Ayacucho, around the Apurímac Valley near Ayacucho or in the Río Huallaga area in the north, between Tingo María and Juanjui, as those areas are notorious for drug trafficking. If you're unlucky enough to have anything stolen, your first port of call should be the **tourist police** (*policía de turismo*), from whom you should get a written report. Bear in mind that the police in popular tourist spots, such as Cusco, have become much stricter about investigating reported thefts, after a spate of false claims by dishonest tourists. This means that genuine victims may be grilled more severely than expected, and the police may even come and search your hotel room for the "stolen" items.

PERU ON THE NET

ⓦ **andeantravelweb.com/peru** Links to a whole range of travel-related features and listings.
ⓦ **perulinks.com** English-language pages on art, entertainment and travel.
ⓦ **virtualperu.net** Peruvian geography, history and people, plus satellite photos, maps and other information.

EMERGENCY NUMBERS

All services ☎105

HEALTH

In most cities there are **private clinics** (*clínicas*) with better medical facilities than general hospitals, and if given the choice in a medical emergency, opt for a *clínica*. The EsSalud national hospitals have undergone drastic improvements in the last few years, and although they are supposed to be for Peruvians who pay into an insurance scheme with them, they can take independent patients (who pay a higher price). Even in relatively small villages there is a *posta médica* where you can get basic medical attention and assistance in getting to a larger medical facility. The South American Explorers' Clubs in Lima and Cusco as well as iPerú offices can provide you with a list of recommended doctors and clinics.

INFORMATION AND MAPS

The government iPerú offices present in every large city are useful for basic information and advice, as well as free local maps and leaflets (24hr hotline: ☎01 574 8000, Ⓦperu.info); they are also the place to go if you need to make a formal complaint about dishonest guides, tour companies not meeting their obligations, and so on.

Good bookshops stock the Lima 2000 series, which produces the best maps of the major cities as well as the best road map of Peru. For excellent topographic maps of remote places, try Lima's Instituto Geográfico Nacional (Ⓦign.es).

MONEY AND BANKS

The current Peruvian currency, the **nuevo sol**, whose symbol is S/, is simply called a "sol" on the streets and has so far remained relatively steady against the US dollar. The bills come in denominations of 10, 20, 50, 100 and 200 soles; there are coins of 1, 2 and 5 soles, and the sol is divided into céntimos, in values of 5, 10, 20 and 50. Beware of counterfeit bills, which feel smooth and glossy to the touch, rather than crisp and coarse; genuine bills should have watermarks and thin ribbons when held up against a light source, and when tilted from side to side, the reflective ink on the number denomination should change colour.

Changing foreign currencies is easy in all major cities; you will find casas de cambio around the Plaza de Armas or along the main commercial streets. They readily change euros and British pounds, though the preferred currency is US dollars. You'll find that some tour companies and hotels still quote prices in US dollars, and happily accept them as long as the notes are new; few places will accept US$100 bills.

Banks and ATMs are numerous in cities; if travelling to remote villages, take plenty of cash in small denomination bills and coins with you. BCP (Banco de Crédito) accepts all major credit cards and is the best bank for cash withdrawals, as it doesn't charge a fee for the transaction, whereas the Global Net network can charge up to US$2.50 per withdrawal.

OPENING HOURS AND HOLIDAYS

Most shops are open from around 9am to 9pm, and many are open on Sunday as well, if for more limited hours. Peru's more important ancient sites and ruins usually have opening hours that coincide with daylight – from around 7am until 5pm or 6pm daily.

PUBLIC HOLIDAYS

January 1 New Year's Day.

March/April Easter Semana Santa (Holy Week). Maundy Thursday and Good Friday are national holidays, Easter Monday is not.

May 1 Labour Day.

July 28–29 National Independence Day. Public holiday with military and school processions.

October 8 Anniversary of Battle of Angamos.

November 1–2 Day of the Dead, and All Souls' Day.

December 8 Immaculate Conception.

December 25 Christmas Day.

FESTIVALS AND CELEBRATIONS

Peru is a country rich with culture and traditions, and on any given day there is a town or village celebrating their anniversary or similar occasion. Festivals can be spectacular events with processions, usually with live music and dancing, and a proud usage of traditional dress. Carnival time (generally late February) is especially lively almost everywhere in the country. During fiesta times small towns become completely booked up, hotel prices go up significantly, transport services stop running or prices double, and often most people will stop work and celebrate for a few days either side of the festival. Below are some of the major events:

February Carnaval. Wildly celebrated immediately prior to Lent, throughout the whole country.

February 2 Virgen de la Candelaria. Celebrated in the most spectacular way in Puno (known as the folklore capital of the country) with a week of colourful processions and dancing.

March/April Semana Santa (Holy Week). Superb processions all over Peru (the best are in Cusco and Ayacucho), the biggest being on Good Friday and Easter Saturday night.

Late May/early June Q'oyllor Riti. One of the most breathtaking festivals in Peru; thousands of people make the overnight pilgrimage up to Apu Ausangate, a shrine located on a glacier just outside of Cusco.

Early June Corpus Christi. Takes place nine weeks after Maundy Thursday and involves colourful processions with saints carried around on floats and much feasting. Particularly lively in Cusco.

June 24 Inti Raymi is Cusco's main Inca festival.

June 29 St Peter's Day. Fiestas in all the fishing villages along the coast.

July 16 Virgen del Carmen. Celebrated in style in the town of Paucartambo, on the road between Cusco and Manu Biosphere Reserve. Dancers come from surrounding villages in traditional dress for the celebration, which lasts several days. There's a smaller celebration in the Sacred Valley town of Pisac.

August 13–19 Arequipa Week. Processions, firework displays, plenty of folklore dancing and craft markets in Arequipa.

August 30 Santa Rosa de Lima. The city of Lima stops for the day to worship their patron saint, Santa Rosa.

Late September Spring Festival. Trujillo festival involving dancing, especially the local Marinera dance and popular Peruvian waltzes.

October 18–28 Lord of Miracles. Festival featuring large and solemn processions (the main ones take place on October 18, 19 & 28); many women wear purple.

November 1–7 Puno Festival. Celebrates the founding of Puno by the Spanish and of the Inca Empire by Manco Capac. Particularly colourful dancing on the fifth day.

November 1–30 International Bullfighting Competitions. Spectacular in the Plaza da Ancho in Lima.

Lima

LIMA, "City of Kings", was founded in 1535 by **Francisco Pizarro** and rapidly became the capital of a Spanish viceroyalty that included Ecuador, Bolivia and Chile. By 1610 its population had reached 26,000 and it had become an international trading port, the city's centre was crowded with stalls selling produce from all over the world and it was one of the most beautiful and wealthy cities in Spanish America. It then grew steadily until the twentieth century, when the population exploded. Today, many of its eight and a half million inhabitants are *campesinos* (rural folk) who fled their homes in the countryside to escape the civil war that destroyed many Andean communities in the 1980s and 1990s.

Some say that Lima is Peru. And given its wealth of museums, nightlife, architecture and world-class food, plus its position as the nation's transport hub, the city makes the perfect base from

9

which to explore the rest of the country. Ignore Lima's grey and polluted facade, ride the *combis* and get stuck in – no visit to Peru is complete without time well spent in Lima.

Lima is very much a city of neighbourhoods, and it's worth visiting several before making up your mind about this huge capital. You can't beat **Central Lima** for sights or architecture. **San Isidro** and neighbouring **Miraflores** are certainly the most modern and commercial areas of the city and you'll find many designer stores, gourmet restaurants and sophisticated lounge bars here, as well as some of the best tourist attractions and nightlife. Arty and colourful **Barranco** feels like a sleepy seaside town by day, and is fantastic for escaping the chaos of central Lima, but at night comes alive and is packed with bars and clubs.

The Plaza Mayor

Lima's main square, known as the **Plaza Mayor** or the Plaza de Armas, boasts UNESCO World Heritage status due to its former colonial importance – Lima was capital of the Spanish Empire in South America – and its colours and famous wooden balconies are kept in beautiful condition accordingly. It is one of the largest squares in South America and has some of the most important government and religious buildings in Peru.

On the eastern corner of the plaza stands the austere Renaissance-style **Catedral** (open for Mass Sat 9am & Sun 11am). The interior retains some of its appealing Churrigueresque (highly elaborate Baroque) decor and it houses the **Museo de Arte Religioso** (Mon–Fri 9am–5pm & Sat 10am–1pm; S10; ☎01 427 9647), which contains paintings from the seventeenth century as well as the remains of Francisco Pizarro.

The original **Palacio del Gobierno** was built on the site of Pizarro's adobe house, where he spent the last few years of his life until his assassination in 1541. The present building was only built in 1938 (the older palace was destroyed by an earthquake). It's possible to arrange a free tour, on Saturdays only, although this can take a few days to sort out (contact the Jefatura de Turismo, English spoken, on ☎01 311 3900 extension 523; ✉scuadros@presidencia .gob.pe). The **changing of the guard** takes place outside (daily 11.45am & 5.45pm), which always draws a crowd to watch the marching soldiers and listen to the military brass band.

Museo de la Iglesia y Convento San Francisco

East of the Palacio del Gobierno along Jr. Ancash is the majestic **Museo de la Iglesia y Convento San Francisco** (daily 9.30am–5.30pm; S7 for 40min guided tour; ☎01 426 7377, ⊛museocatacumbas .com). The ticket combines seeing the large seventeenth-century church and its attached **monastery**, which contains a superb library, a room of paintings by (or finished by) Rubens, Jordaens and Van Dyck, some pretty cloisters and the main highlight: vast crypts with gruesome **catacombs**, which contain the skeletons of some seventy thousand people – well worth a visit.

Museo de la Inquisición

A couple of blocks southeast of San Francisco, the **Museo de la Inquisición y del Congreso**, at Jr. Junín 548 (daily 9am–5pm; free, by regular guided tours only, available in English; ☎01 311 7777, ⊛www.congreso.gob.pe/museo.htm), was the headquarters of the Inquisition for the whole of Spanish America from 1570 until 1820. The museum includes the original tribunal room, with its beautifully carved mahogany ceiling, and beneath the building you can look round the dungeons and torture chambers, which contain a few gory, life-sized human models.

Mercado Central and Chinatown

Walk south on Avenida Abancay from the Museo de la Inquisición, take a left on Ucayali and after a couple of blocks you'll see the fascinating **Mercado Central** on your left, where you can buy almost anything (keeping one eye open for

9

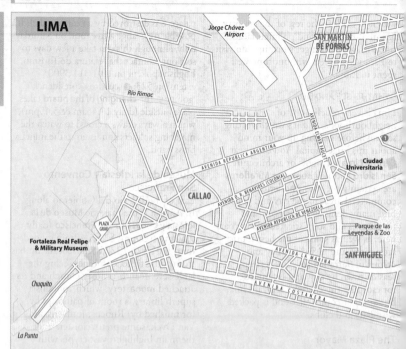

LIMA

Jorge Chávez
Airport

SAN MARTIN
DE PORRAS

Río Rimac

AVENIDA ELMER FAUCETT

AVENIDA REPUBLICA ARGENTINA

Ciudad
Universitaria

CALLAO

AVENIDA O. R. BENAVIDES (COLONIAL)

AVENIDA REPUBLICA DE VENEZUELA

PLAZA
GRAU

AVENIDA LA MARINA

Parque de las
Leyendas & Zoo

**Fortaleza Real Felipe
& Military Museum**

SAN MIGUEL

Chuquito

AVENIDA COSTANERA

La Punta

PACIFIC

N

■ **ACCOMMODATION**
Aquisito	2
Domeyer	3
The Point	1

● **EATING & NIGHTLIFE**
Anticuchos Tío Jhony	3
El Grifo	1
Expreso Virgen de Guadalupe	7
La Candelaria	9
Mi Carcochita	8
La Noche	5
Punto Azul	2
De Rompe y Raja	4
Wahio's Bar	6

0   2
kilometres

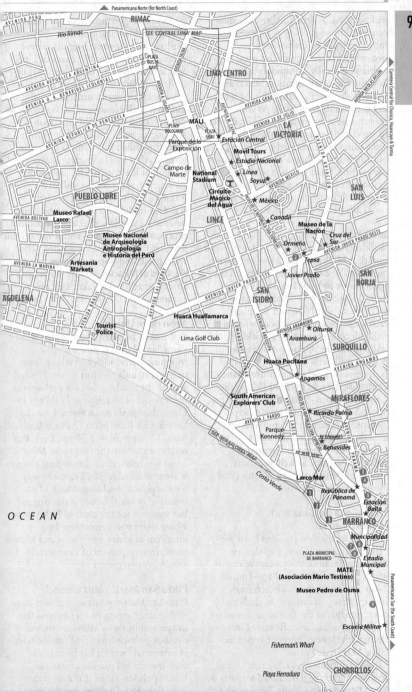

Panamericana Norte (for North Coast)

RIMAC

Río Rimac

SEE 'CENTRAL LIMA' MAP

PLAZA
DOS DE
MAYO

LIMA CENTRO

AVENIDA PERU

AVENIDA REPUBLICA ARGENTINA

AVENIDA O. R. BENAVIDES (COLONIAL)

AVENIDA REPUBLICA DE VENEZUELA

AVENIDA PALMA

AVENIDA GRAU

AVENIDA NICOLAS AYLLON

Carretera Central for Chosica, Huancayo & Tarma

AVENIDA 28 DE JULIO

LA
VICTORIA

AVENIDA WILSON / AVENIDA GARCILASO DE LA VEGA

AVENIDA TACNA

AVENIDA ALFONSO UGARTE

MALI

PLAZA
BOLOGNESI

PLAZA
GRAU

Estación Central

Movil Tours

Parque de la
Exposición

Campo de
Marte

National
Stadium

Estadio Nacional

Linea
Soyuz

AVENIDA MEXICO

SAN
LUIS

Circuito
Mágico
del Agua

México

PUEBLO LIBRE

AVENIDA BOLIVAR

Museo Rafael
Larco

AVENIDA BRASIL

LINCE

Canadá

Museo de la
Nación

Cruz del
Sur

PASEO REPUBLICA VIA EXPRESA

AVENIDA REPUBLICA DE PANAMA

Museo Nacional
de Arqueología
Antropología
e Historia del Perú

Ormeño

Tepsa

AVENIDA JAVIER PRADO OESTE

AVENIDA AVIACION

AVENIDA LA MARINA

Artesania
Markets

AVENIDA SALAVERRY

Javier Prado

SAN
BORJA

MAGDALENA

AVENIDA BRASIL

Tourist
Police

Huaca Huallamarca

SAN
ISIDRO

AVENIDA JAVIER PRADO ESTE

Lima Golf Club

COMANDANTE ESPINAR

AVENIDA AREQUIPA

Avenida Aramburu

Oltursa

AVENIDA ARAMBURU

Aramburú

SURQUILLO

Huaca Pucllana

AVENIDA ANGAMOS

AVENIDA EJERCITO

Angamos

South American
Explorers' Club

AVENIDA LARCO

MIRAFLORES

Ricardo Palma

PASEO REPUBLICA VIA EXPRESA

SEE 'MIRAFLORES' MAP

AVENIDA J. PARDO

Parque
Kennedy

AV. BENAVIDES

AV. 28 DE JULIO

Benavides

AVENIDA REPUBLICA DE PANAMA

Costa Verde

O C E A N

Larco Mar

República de
Panamá

Estación
Balta

BARRANCO

Municipalidad

PLAZA MUNICIPAL
DE BARRANCO

Estadio
Muncipal

MATE
(Asociación Mario Testino)

Museo Pedro de Osma

Panamericana Sur (for South Coast)

Escuela Militar

Fisherman's Wharf

Playa Herradura

CHORRILLOS

9

pickpockets). A little further east, an ornate Chinese gateway ushers visitors into Lima's **Barrio Chino**. This pedestrianized section of the street is, rather graphically, commonly referred to as Calle Capón (Castration Street) after some of the practices the Chinese used to fatten up their animals. As you'd expect, this is where many of Lima's best (from cheap to super swanky) Chinese restaurants are, crammed into a few bustling streets. There's also an indoor mall selling Asian goods, and don't forget to look down at the modest walk of fame paying tribute to many *Limeños* who could afford to pay for a tile.

Jirón Ucayali

Walking back towards Plaza Mayor, you'll find that Jr. Ucayali has a few interesting buildings. The **Iglesia San Pedro**, on the corner with Jirón Azángaro (Mon–Sat 9.30–11.30am & 5–6pm; free), was built by the Jesuits in 1636 and the plain exterior is completely at odds with its richly decorated interior, a world of gold leaf, ornate tiles and impressive altars. A short walk west on the corner with Jr. Lampa is the excellent **Museo Banco Central de Reserva del Perú** (Mon, Tues, Thurs, Fri 10am–5pm, Wed 10am–7pm, Sat & Sun 10am–1pm; free; ⓦbcrp .gob.pe), whose permanent collection includes textiles, ceramics and a security-heavy room full of gold and precious artefacts, as well as a short history of Peruvian painting with good information in English.

Santa Rosa de Lima and Las Nazarenas

Heading west down Jr. Lima from the Plaza Mayor you'll pass the **Iglesia y Convento Santo Domingo** on the corner with Camaná (Mon–Sat 8am–1pm & 2–6pm; monastery S5, church free). It's here that you can see the skull and other remains of the first saint canonized in the Americas, Santa Rosa de Lima, along with those of another Peruvian saint, Martín de Porres.

If you continue on to Avenida Tacna, you'll come to the terracotta **Santuario de Santa Rosa de Lima** (daily 7am–noon & 5–8pm; free), birthplace of the saint. Directly behind the church, a small garden (9am–1pm & 3–6pm) offers a pleasant escape from the chaos of Lima and many Peruvians come here to drop cards with their wishes down the well.

A few blocks south on Tacna, at the junction with Huancavelica, is the **Iglesia de Las Nazarenas** (daily 6am–noon & 4–8.30pm; free), small and outwardly undistinguished but with an interesting history. After the 1655 earthquake, a mural of the crucifixion, painted by an Angolan slave on the wall of his hut, was apparently the only object left standing in the district. Its survival was deemed a miracle – the cause of popular processions ever since – and it was on this site that the church was founded. The widespread and popular processions for the **Lord of Miracles**, to save Lima from another earthquake, take place every autumn (Oct 6, 7, 18, 19, 28 & Nov 1).

Jirón de la Unión

The stretch between Plaza Mayor and Plaza San Martín is now the main shopping street, with everything from designer brands to thrift stores. Nestled among the modern shops is perhaps the most noted of all religious buildings in Lima, the **Iglesia de La Merced**, on the corner with Jirón Miro Quesada (daily 8am–12.30pm & 4–8.30pm; free). Built on the site where the first Latin Mass in Lima was celebrated, the original church was demolished in 1628 to make way for the present building. Much of its beautiful colonial facade is not original, but look out for the **cross of Padre Urraca**, whose silver staff is smothered by hundreds of kisses every hour and witness to the fervent prayers of a constantly shifting congregation.

Plaza San Martín and around

Plaza San Martín is virtually always busy, with traffic tooting its way around the square and buskers, mime artists and soapbox *políticos* attracting small circles of interested faces. It has been (and continues to be) the site of most of Lima's political rallies. Of note is the huge **Gran Hotel Bolívar**, not for its rooms but for its streetside bar *El Bolivarcito*, which serves arguably the best pisco sour in Lima.

One block east of the Plaza, Avenida Nicolás de Piérola runs towards the **Parque Universitario**, with the grand old buildings of the first university in the Americas, San Marcos. The buildings now house the **Centro Cultural de San Marcos** (Mon–Sat 9am–1pm & 2–5pm; free or S5 with guided visit of historic building; ⓦccsm-unmsm.edu.pe), the cultural centre of the modern university, now sited in Pueblo Libre. It hosts many interesting talks and events and also contains a gallery, focusing on

Peruvian folk and contemporary art, and an archeological and anthropology museum with rotating exhibits on different aspects of Peruvian history, as well as a permanent collection of textiles and ceramics.

Plaza Grau and around

The Jr. de la Unión becomes Jirón Belén and leads down to the **Plaza Grau** and the **Paseo de la República** (also known as the Vía Expresa), an enormous dual carriageway that cleaves through the city. Underneath the plaza is the Estación Central of the Metropolitano bus service (see p.733).

CENTRAL LIMA

ACCOMMODATION	
Hostal Belén	4
Hostal España	3
Europa	2
Pensión Ibarra	1

EATING	
Antigua Pastelería y Panedería Huérfanos	10
Bodega Cafetería Santa Isabel	4
El Cordano	2
Esbari	3
Queirolo Café Bar Restaurant	7
Tanta	1
Wa Lok	9

NIGHTLIFE	
El Bolivarcito	6
Etnias Bar Cultural	8
El Mirador	5
Munich	11
Rincón Cervecero	12
Vichama	13

9

Just south of the plaza at Paseo Colón 125 is the **Museo de Arte Lima** (MALI; Tues–Sun 10am–8pm, Sat until 5pm; S12; ⓦmali.pe), housed in the former International Exhibition Palace built in 1868 and designed by Eiffel. It contains interesting collections of colonial art and many fine crafts from pre-Columbian times, and also hosts frequent temporary exhibitions of modern photography and other art forms, as well as lectures and film screenings. MALI sits in the **Parque de la Exposición** (daily 8am–10pm; free), a pleasant green space with duck ponds and some pretty bandstands.

Through the park is the **Estadio Nacional** (National Stadium) and just beyond that lies Lima's most eccentric attraction, the **Circuito Mágico del Agua**, at Avenida Petit Thouars at the corner of Jr. Madre de Dios (Wed–Sun & holidays 3–10.30pm; S4; ⓦparquedelareserva .com.pe). It's a park showcasing thirteen different fountains, including one over 80m tall and one sprouting arches you can walk under, all choreographed to pop music and coloured lights.

Museo de la Nación

The **Museo de la Nación**, at Avenida Javier Prado Este 2465 (Tues–Sun 9am–5pm; free; ☎01 476 9933, ✉mnacion@mcultura.gob.pe) in

San Borja, a district southeast of the centre, is one of the country's largest and most important museums and has an outstanding and very moving exhibition about the devastation caused by the Sendero Luminoso group, which terrorized the country in the 1980s and 1990s (see p.712).

To **get here**, take the Metropolitano bus from the centre or from Miraflores to the huge intersecting Avenida Javier Prado. Then take any bus east marked "todo Javier Prado" and ask for the museum.

Miraflores

Miraflores, its streets lined with cafés and flashy shops, is the major focus of Lima's gastronomy and nightlife as far as affluent locals and most tourists are concerned – along with San Isidro, further north, which has even more exclusive boutiques and lounge bars. To get here from the centre, either take the Metropolitano at Jr. de la Unión and Avenida Emancipación and get off at Puente Ricardo Palma, or take take a *combi* (line A; purple and white coloured) on Avenida Tacna.

The attractive **Parque Kennedy** at the end of Avenida Arequipa has a small craft and antiques market every evening (6–10pm). Avenida Larco, which runs along the eastern side of the park, leads to the ocean and to **Larcomar** (ⓦlarcomar.com), a popular clifftop mall with great sea views. From here you can walk north along the Malecón through the small parks and flower gardens, as many others do at weekends. At the **Parque El Faro** (the lighthouse park) you can take tandem paraglides (daily 10am–6pm; S150 for 10min; ☎01 726 8023) from the clifftop down to the beach.

Barranco

Barranco, scattered with old mansions as well as colourful smaller homes, was the capital's seaside resort during the nineteenth century and is now a kind of *limeño* Left Bank, with young artists and intellectuals taking over many of the older properties. To get here take any *combi* along the Diagonal

MIRAFLORES

● EATING
La Lucha	1
La Luchíta	2
Manolo	6
La Máquina	
Café y Cultura	5
Patagonia: Soul Food	7
Punto Azul	9
Thani Wasi	4

● NIGHTLIFE
Downtown Vale Todo	3
Jazz Zone	8

■ ACCOMMODATION
Casa del Mochilero	1
Explorer's House	3
Flying Dog Hostels	7/8/9
The House Project	5
HQ Villa	4
Kokopeli Backpackers	6
The Lighthouse	2

beside Parque Kennedy (about 10min), or take the Metropolitano to the Municipalidad stop.

The best museum here is the pleasant **Museo Pedro de Osma**, at Avenida Pedro de Osma 421 (Tues–Sun 10am–5.30pm; S20; ☎01 467 0141, ⌽museopedrodeosma.org), which houses a good collection of religious art, silver and antique furniture in a stunning French-style mansion with stained-glass windows designed by the eponymous collector. Another highlight is the **Associación Mario Testino**, or MATE, at Avenida Pedro de Osma 409 (Tues–Sat 11am–8pm & Sun

11am–6pm; S20; ⌽mate.pe), housed in another beautifully restored colonial townhouse and the first permanent exhibition to the UK-based fashion photographer in his home town.

A walk across the **Puente de Suspiros** (The Bridge of Sighs) to the cliffside bars and cafés is a favourite pastime for locals – as well as checking out some of the colourful houses, often daubed with graffiti, on streets such as Calle Cajamarca – but otherwise there's little else to see specifically; the main highlight of Barranco is its bars, clubs and cafés clustered around the attractive **Plaza Municipal**.

9

Pueblo Libre

This upcoming neighbourhood, southwest of the centre, hosts two world-class museums. The **Museo Nacional de Arqueología, Antropología e Historia del Perú** (Plaza Bolívar s/n; Tues–Sat 9am–5pm, Sun 9am–4pm; S10; ✉ mnaahp@mcultura.gob.pe) has an extensive collection of pre-Hispanic and colonial artefacts, helpfully laid out in chronological order. It also houses the two most important relics from the Chavín de Huántar site near Huaraz: the Raimondi Stela, a 2m-tall piece of granite with intricate carvings, and the Tello Obelisk, which once lurked underground, worshipped by priests of the Chavín cult. Part of the museum is in a mansion once inhabited by the liberators Simón Bolívar and José de San Martín.

Follow the (sometimes worn) blue line outside the museum for a pleasant 25-minute walk to the expensive but excellent **Museo Rafael Larco** at Avenida Bolívar 1515 (daily 9am–10pm; S30; guided tour in English S25, reserve in advance; ☎ 01 461 1835, ⦿ museolarco.org). Situated in a viceroy's mansion, which in turn was built on a pre-Columbian pyramid, it displays the enormous private collection of Peruvian archeologist Rafael Larco, which includes textiles, jewellery, gold, silver and ceramics. Best of all, you can explore the vast storage rooms, packed to the rafters with more than 45,000 pre-Columbian objects. It's also famous for an extensive erotic ceramics section.

These museums are close to both the **artisan stalls** on blocks 6–8 of Avenida La Marina known as the Mercado Inca (9am–8.30pm) and the **Parque de las Leyendas** at Avenida Las Leyendas 580 (daily 9am–6pm; S10; ⦿ leyendas.gob.pe), a family-orientated zoo landscaped to represent the three zones in Peru – coast, mountains and jungle. The site also contains more than thirty pre-Columbian *huacas* (see box below), all in differing stages of excavation, as well as a botanical garden and boating lake.

ARRIVAL AND DEPARTURE

BY PLANE

All flights leave and depart from **Jorge Chávez Airport** (⦿ www.lap.com.pe) in Callao, 10km northwest of the city centre – departure and arrival taxes are included in the price of tickets. The two main carriers serving the rest of the country are LAN (⦿ lan.com) and the cheaper StarPerú (⦿ starperu.com).

FROM THE AIRPORT INTO TOWN

By taxi The quickest and safest way to get into central Lima (45min) is to take an official taxi from one of the

---

HUACAS

There are reminders of Lima's pre-Columbian past all over the capital in the form of adobe **huacas** – sacred places – also referred to as pyramids. They are mostly associated with the Lima culture, which dominated in the area from 200 to 700 AD. Two of the most impressive sit wonderfully at odds with the modern monstrosities around them. The **Huaca Pucllana**, at General Borgoño block 8, Miraflores (Wed–Mon 9am–4pm; S12; ☎ 01 617 7138, ✉ huacapucllana@hotmail.com), the larger of the two, was thought to have been a major administrative centre. It's a short walk from Av Arequipa at block 44 (off to the right if you're coming from central Lima). **Huaca Huallamarca**, at Nicolás de Ribera 201, San Isidro (Tues–Sun 9am–5pm; S5), is three blocks from Camino Real along Choquehuanca. It's thought to be a little older than Pucllana and pertains to the Hualla tribe. The spaceship-like ramp can be scaled to get great views of the neighbourhood. Both tickets include entrance to small site museums.

The most wonderful of all Lima's *huacas*, **Pachacamac**, lies just outside the city at Km31.5 off the Antigua Panamericana Sur, Lurín (Tues–Sun 9am–5pm; S8; ☎ 01 430 2115, ✉ museopachacamac@mcultura.gob.pe). It's easily reached by public transport – you can do it in half a day. Get there from Lima centro by catching the brown *combi* marked San Bartolo from outside MALI and double-check that it's going to Lurín. Alternatively, you can get this same *combi* nearer Miraflores by taking any bus marked "todo Benavides" from Miraflores to the Panamericana; go down the steps to the busy motorway and wait at the stop under the bridge. From here it's about 30min away and you can be dropped right outside the Museo de Sitio (site museum).

companies with desks at the airport – pay there and you'll be assigned a driver. Green Taxis is the cheapest (S45–55 to downtown). The family-run RGM Secure Taxi service is also recommended; the father and sons are very knowledgeable about the city (S40–55; English spoken; ☎ 997 380 389).

DESTINATIONS

Arequipa (10 daily; 1hr 20min); Cajamarca (5 daily; 1hr 20min); Cusco (15 daily; 1hr 15min); Iquitos (8 daily; 1hr 45min); Tumbes (daily; 1hr 50min).

BY BUS

Unfortunately Peru doesn't have central terminals – each bus company has its own private terminal. Buses to Lima usually arrive and depart in the district of La Victoria, near central Lima, or at the other end of La Victoria on Av Javier Prado. Whichever terminal it's best to hail the first decent-looking taxi you see and fix a price – about S12–15 from or to anywhere in the centre, or S15–18 from or to anywhere else in Lima. Many buses can't be booked online, so you'll have to visit the office in person – it's worth booking in advance if you want the best seats (ie *cama*, with fully reclining seats). A good option is to find a decent travel agent – the in-house agency in the *Hotel España* (see p.734) is recommended and they can advise you about different companies, hours and prices.

BUS COMPANIES

The following bus companies have the best fleets and services. **Cruz del Sur** Av Javier Prado 1109 (☎01 311 5050, ✪www.cruzdelsur.com.pe); **Línea** Av Paseo de la República 941–959 (☎01 424 0836, ✪linea.pe); **Movil Tours** Paseo de la República 749 (☎01 716 8000, ✪moviltours.com.pe); **Oltursa** Av Aramburu 1160, San Isidro (☎01 708 5000, ✪oltursa.pe); **Ormeño** Av Javier Prado Oeste 1057 (☎01 472 1710); **Soyuz Perú** Av México 280 333 (☎01 205 2370, ✪www.soyuz.com.pe); **Tepsa** Av Javier Prado Este 1091 (☎01 617 9000, ✪www.tepsa.com.pe).

DESTINATIONS

Ayacucho (9hr 30min): Cruz del Sur (3 daily), **Arequipa** (15hr): Cruz del Sur (7 daily), Oltursa (6 daily), Ormeño (1 daily), Tepsa (2 daily); **Cajamarca** (14hr): Cruz del Sur (1 daily), Línea (2 daily), Tepsa (1 daily); **Chachapoyas** (20hr): Movil Tours (1 daily); **Chiclayo** (12hr): Cruz del Sur (4 daily), Línea (2 daily), Movil Tours (2 daily), Oltursa (4 daily), Tepsa (3 daily); **Cusco** (22hr): Cruz del Sur (2 daily), Oltursa (1 daily), Movil Tours (1 daily), Tepsa (2 daily); **Puno** (20hr): Ormeño (1 daily); **Huaraz** (7hr 30min): Cruz del Sur (4 daily), Oltursa (4 daily), Movil Tours (5 daily); **Nazca** (7hr 30min): Cruz del Sur (5 daily), Oltursa (3 daily), Ormeño (2 daily), Soyuz Perú (hourly),

Tepsa (3 daily); **Tacna** (19hr): Cruz del Sur (2 daily), Oltursa (2 daily), Tepsa (1 daily); **Trujillo** (9hr): Cruz del Sur (4 daily), Oltursa (3 daily), Línea (9 daily), Movil Tours (1 daily), Tepsa (2 daily); **Tumbes via Máncora** (18–20hr): Cruz del Sur, Línea, Oltursa, Ormeño, Tepsa (all 1 daily).

BY TRAIN

Apart from a small local service, the only train from Lima goes to Huancayo twice a month (see p.717). It departs from Desamparados station (Jr. Ancash 207).

GETTING AROUND

By bus *Combis* race from one street corner to another along all the major arterial city roads. Wave one down and pay the flat fare (S1–1.50 within Lima, depending on distance) to the driver or *cobrador* (conductor). A fantastic unofficial map of Lima's most useful and safe *combis* (many are more than a little ropey) can be purchased for US$2.50 at ✪rutasrecomendables.com.

By colectivo A useful form of transport for getting to outer districts of the capital such as Chosica and Comas, mostly leaving from Plaza Bolognesi (S4–8).

By taxi Taxis should not cost more than S30 within the city (except to/from the airport). Most are unofficial, although the yellow ones with a licence plate number on the side are, in theory, regulated. It is, perhaps, better to look at the condition of the car and always agree on a price beforehand as they don't have meters. As a guide, taxis within a district (eg anywhere within central Lima) should be S4–7, while Miraflores to the centre should be S12–15. Private companies are few and far between, change numbers regularly and charge a lot more.

METROPOLITANO

Lima may be one of the largest cities in the world without an underground metro, but it now has the very modern **Metropolitano** bus service (daily 6am–9.50pm, express service during rush hours 7–9.30am & 5–8.30pm; ✪metropolitano.com.pe). This bus runs through the city north to south and connects the main tourist areas of Barranco, Miraflores and San Isidro along the Paseo de la República with central Lima. It uses a rechargeable card which subtracts S1.50 per ride, and it's the quickest, easiest and certainly the safest way to get around Lima as the buses use special lanes and the fleet is new. Check the website (under "rutas") for any changes before you use it.

9

INFORMATION

Tourist information The municipal tourist office is just off the Plaza de Armas behind the Palacio Municipal (Pasaje Los Escribanos 145; Mon–Fri 8.30am–6pm, Sat & Sun 9am–5pm; ☎ 01 314 1542). iPerú is the national tourist info provider, and can also help if you need to make a complaint, visit the police or simply book accommodation. iPerú has desks in Lima airport (open 24hr; ☎ 01 574 8000) and Miraflores (Larcomar, stand 10; daily 11am–2pm & 3–8pm; ☎ 01 445 9400), as well as San Isidro (Jorge Basadre 610; daily 9am–1pm & 2–6pm; ☎ 01 421 1627). Callao has a basic tourist information booth on the road between Plaza Grau and Chuquito (daily 10am–5pm), which has information about the museums in the area. The South American Explorers' Club, at C Piura 135, Miraflores (Mon–Fri 9.30am–5pm, Sat 9.30am–1pm; ☎ 01 444 2150), has good information including maps, listings and travel reports available to non-members for a higher fee.

TOUR OPERATORS

Bike Tours of Lima C Bolívar 150, Miraflores ☎ 01 445 3172, ⓦ biketoursoflima.com. Does what it says on the tin, as well as bike rentals.

Ecocruceros Av Arequipa 4960, Miraflores, and a stand by the port in Callao ☎ 01 226 8530, ⓦ islaspalomino.com. Runs trips to the Islas Palominos.

Fertur Peru Jr. Junín 211, Central Lima ☎ 01 427 2626, ⓦ fertur-travel.com. Offers nationwide package tours and some local tours.

Kolibri Expeditions ☎ 01 273 7246, ⓦ kolibriexpeditions .com. Recommended for birdwatching tours locally and across Peru.

Lima Vision Jr. Chiclayo 444, Miraflores ☎ 01 447 7710, ⓦ limavision.com. The best choice for Lima tours, including Pachacamac and the museums.

Mirabús Stalls in both Parque Kennedy and Plaza Mayor ☎ 01 242 6699, ⓦ mirabusperu.com. Runs open-top bus tours of Lima by day/night, as well as Callao (Sun only 10.15am). Also does boat trips to the Islas Palominos (bi-monthly) and a land and sea excursion (Thurs, Fri & Sat 2pm).

ACCOMMODATION

There are good budget options throughout the city, although Central Lima works out slightly cheaper and offers hostels within walking distance of some of the most important tourist sights. Barranco has a relaxed bohemian atmosphere and is close to the sea, but the most popular district for tourists is still Miraflores; with bright lights and fast-food joints on every corner, it has a cosmopolitan feel, plus plenty of chain backpacker hostels providing mainly dorm-style accommodation. There are no campsites, official or otherwise.

CENTRAL LIMA

Hostal Belén Nicolás de Piérola 953, Plaza San Martín ☎ 01 427 7391, ⓔ ryexport2000@yahoo.es; map p.729. One of the best-value budget options in Central Lima – a well-maintained colonial gem with a restaurant (Mon–Sat) serving bargain set lunches. Try to get a room with views of the plaza. **S60**

★ **Hostal España** Jr. Azángaro 105 ☎ 01 428 5546, ⓦ hotelespanaperu.com; map p.729. The main courtyard, filled with antique oil paintings, marble statues and trailing pot plants, is quite stunning. There's also a verdant rooftop patio where breakfast is served (S6–6.50) – look out for peacocks strutting about. *España* is perhaps a little old-school, but it's secure and has wi-fi, a book exchange and a tour operator service for onward travel anywhere in the country. Dorms **S20**, doubles **S50**

Europa Jr. Ancash 376 ☎ 01 427 3351; map p.729. A very basic and slightly run-down building opposite the San Francisco church, with a pretty internal courtyard. The rooms are worthy of a monastery in their simplicity (most have shared bathroom), but it's good value (although can be cold in winter). **S35**

Pensión Ibarra Av Tacna 359 apt.1402 ☎ 01 427 8603, ⓔ pensionibarra@gmail.com; map p.729. For a different type of experience, try staying with the very welcoming Ibarra couple in two apartments on the fourteenth and fifteenth floor. The rooms are simple but the views are spectacular and the place is kept tidy. Breakfast (S8–10) and laundry can be arranged, use of the kitchen is permitted and there's no curfew. Very cheap rates can be arranged for long stays. **S35**

MIRAFLORES

Casa del Mochilero Jr. Cesareo Chacaltana 130a, upstairs ☎ 01 444 9089, ⓔ pilaryv@hotmail.com; map p.731. This safe place is remarkably good for the price, with hot water, cable TV and a newly refurbished kitchen. It's not right at the centre of Miraflores's action, but it's close enough. Don't confuse it with the similarly named and decorated hostel next door; ask for Pilar or Juan to be sure you're in the right place (it's the green building). Dorms **S15**, doubles **S40**

Explorer's House Av Alfredo Leon 158 ☎ 01 241 5002, ⓔ evaaragon_9@hotmail.com; map p.731. Out of the centre of Miraflores but close to the sea, *Explorer's House* is a good old-fashioned hostel. Breakfast is included and internet, wi-fi, hot water and a rooftop terrace add to the charm; there's also a small kitchen for guests to use. Book ahead as it is small and popular. Dorms **S21**, doubles **S50**

Flying Dog Hostels ⓦ flyingdogperu.com; map p.731. The *Flying Dog* is the most established backpacker joint in the city, with several outlets: *Backpackers*, at Diez Canseco 117 (includes breakfast); *Bed and Breakfast*, at C Lima 457; *Hostel*, at Olaya 280. All locations offer cheap accommodation, kitchen use, TV room, storage service and internet access, as well as being hugely popular and therefore a great place to meet people. Dorms S30, doubles S75

The House Project Bellavista 215 ☎01 446 2941, thehouseproject.pe; map p.731. A newly opened backpacker option near the Miraflores strip with a focus firmly on having a party (there's even an earplug dispenser by the front door). Has other nice touches, too, such as a BBQ, pizza oven and an outdoor bar. Dorms US$13, doubles US$40

★ **HQ Villa** C Independencia 1288 ☎01 651 2320, hqvilla.com; map p.731. While this is a bit out of the way in a quiet residential neighbourhood – in between Miraflores and San Isidro, parallel to Cuadra 40 of Arequipa and about a 20min walk to the centre of either neighbourhood – it's worth it. A British/Peruvian-owned boutique hostel with loads of character, including a huge garden and open-plan kitchen/living area with moodily lit bathrooms, chandeliers, photography and a packed social calendar, on top of all the usual extras. Dorms US$6

Kokopeli Backpackers C Berlin 259 ☎01 242 5665, hostelkokopeli.com; map p.731. Another top spot for meeting people, with the social life revolving around a rooftop bar that is always buzzing. Dorms S30, doubles S80

★ **The Lighthouse** Jr. Cesareo Chacaltana 162 ☎01 446 8397, thelighthouseperu.com; map p.731. Spacious comfortable rooms in this B&B (one with a balcony) with cable TV – for those looking for a more tranquil stay. A patio with BBQ plus a communal area with DVDs, books and internet offer the budget traveller some real creature comforts. Kitchen use and a generous breakfast all add to the homely experience. Book in advance as there are only six rooms. US$20

BARRANCO

Aquisito Av Centenario 114 ☎01 247 0712, aquisito.com.pe; map pp.726–727. Cosy little bed and breakfast with a family feel. There are also computers and wi-fi, a patio space, luggage storage and airport transfers. S95

Domeyer C Domeyer 296 ☎01 247 1413, domeyerhostel.net; map pp.726–727. This hostel has a bohemian feel (there's normally one or two long-stayers here), shared kitchen and living room plus laundry service (and a decent breakfast included with room price). Rooms include cable and wi-fi, and there is a cheaper dorm room. Gay friendly. Dorms S40, doubles S180

The Point Malecón Junín 300 ☎01 247 7997, thepointhostels.com; map pp.726–727. Boasts lots of facilities including internet, TV room and kitchen, as well as the on-site *Pointless Bar*, a great place to meet other travellers and have a good time. Relaxed garden with hammocks is a boon. Dorms S27, doubles S70

EATING

Lima has seen its gastronomy boom in the past few years, partly thanks to Peruvian celebrity chef and international restaurateur Gastón Acurio (see box, p.720); the swell in national pride surrounding Peruvian cuisine is palpable, nowhere more so than in Lima. Many of the more upmarket restaurants fill up very quickly, so it's advisable to reserve in advance.

CENTRAL LIMA

There is a Metro supermarket on Jr. Cusco 245 (between Lampa and Augusto Wiese) and two enormous supermarkets opposite each other on Alfonso Ugarte, where it is crossed by Uruguay. Most *chifas* (Chinese restaurants) in Chinatown are good and very cheap. There is also a whole street full of vegetarian restaurants one block from the Plaza de Armas on Camaná.

★ **Antigua Pastelería y Panedería Huérfanos** Azángaro ☎01 428 6273; map p.729. This cake shop has been here for over one hundred years – and is easily the best place in central Lima for bread. It also makes its own fresh pasta and you can buy pastries and biscuits by weight. Also has a small restaurant. Plate of lasagne with wine and bread S19.80.

★ **Bodega Cafetería Santa Isabel** Jr. Carabaya 520 ☎01 426 0058; map p.729. Recharge after sightseeing in this tiny *huarique* that serves some of the best coffee in Lima. Excellent chocolates and liquors are available, and they also specialize in regional cheeses and hams – their sandwiches and *empanadas* (S3) are excellent. Mon–Sat 8am–8.30pm.

El Cordano Jr. Ancash 202 ☎01 427 0181, restcordano@hotmail.com; map p.729. Beside the Palacio del Gobierno, this is one of the city's last surviving traditional bar-restaurants, open since 1905. The food is overpriced, but go for a drink, soak up the atmosphere and feel yourself slip back in time. Does a roaring trade in local ham sandwiches (S10). Daily 8am–8pm.

Esbari Jr. de la Unión 574; map p.729. Primarily an ice-cream parlour with fabulous flavours and sundaes (S13.50), good coffee and cheap food – look for the "ofertas" section in the back of the menu where everything is less than S10. Daily 8am–11.30pm.

Queirolo Café Bar Restaurant Quilca 201; map p.729. Arguably there is no place that better represents old bohemian Lima; this bar has seen every artist and writer in the city come through its doors for lunch or drinks since 1880. They serve a good set lunch (S9), as well as sandwiches and the usual *criolla* favourites. Mon–Fri 9am–11pm.

Tanta Pasaje Nicolás de Rivera 142–148 ☎01 428 3115; map p.729. If you can't afford a whole Gastón Acurio meal, his café chain *Tanta* can give you a taste of what he has to offer. This one, opposite the tourist information office, is a very pleasant place to refuel while sightseeing. Serves

9

breakfasts, sandwiches, soups, salads and mains. Try the *ají de gallina* (S29) or the fruit juice mixes (S12–14). Mon–Sat 9am–10pm, Sun 9am–6pm.

Wa Lok Jr. Paruro 864, Chinatown ☎01 427 2656; map p.729. An excellent and traditional Chinese restaurant, consistently recommended by many Peruvians. It offers a range of authentic *chifa* dishes, and although it's not the cheapest, there are good vegetarian and dim sum options under S20. Come for an early dinner as it closes at 9pm.

MIRAFLORES

Eating options tend to be a little more expensive out of the centre, but there are a lot of good set menus for S8–12 in the small passage connecting Manuel Bonilla to Esperanza off the Parque Kennedy in Miraflores (go for the ones that are full of locals). There is also a huge food market between the Ovalo Parque Kennedy and Paseo de la Republica at Jr. Eledoro Romero, and supermarkets everywhere.

La Lucha & La Luchíta Av Diagonal at the corner with Pasaje Olaya & Pasaje Champagnant 139, Miraflores; map p.731. These two sandwich joints just around the corner from each other may be diminutive, but their oversized sandwiches with a variety of meaty fillings and sauces certainly aren't – the *chicharrón* (deep-fried pork) is particularly delicious at S9.10 for a large. Mon–Thurs 8am–1am, Fri & Sat 8am–3am, Sun 8am–1am.

Manolo Larco 608 ☎01 44 2244, ⓦmanolochurros.com; map p.731. This Miraflores institution is all about the Spanish-style *churros con chocolate* – a thin doughnut that comes with hot chocolate for dipping; heaven for just S12.80. Also does breakfasts, mains, burgers and the like. Mon–Fri 7am–1am, Sat & Sun 7am–2am.

★ **La Máquina Café y Cultura** Alcanfores 323 ☎01 243 8707; map p.731. Achingly trendy café with reading material, games, rock and electronic music, fairy lights and a huge picture of David Bowie. Try the incredible cocktails or the pisco hot chocolate (S6). There is a good lunchtime menu, as well as sandwiches and salads (S10–12). Mon–Fri 10am–11pm, Sat & Sun 5pm–late.

Patagonia: Soul Food C Bolívar 164 ☎01 446 8705, ⓦpatagoniarestaurant.net; map p.731. Colourful mixture of Peruvian and Argentine influences (the owner is from Buenos Aires so expect everything from juicy steaks to *chifa*) – there are bright Andean throws, walls crammed with photos and a rooftop terrace. Does an excellent lunchtime menu for S25. Mon–Sat noon–2.30am, Sun noon–4pm.

★ **Punto Azul** Benavides 2711 and San Martín 595, Miraflores ☎01 445 8078, ⓦpuntoazulrestaurante.com; maps p.726 & p.731. This *cevichería* is a real gem. As well as *ceviche* (S23) it serves other Peruvian classics involving fish or seafood, such as *causas* (tuna with mashed potato and lime) and *chupes* (chowder). The original site, a *huarique* on the busy Javier Prado in San Isidro, has you sitting on stools

★ **TREAT YOURSELF**

El Grifo Av Oscar R. Benavides (ex-Colonial) 2703, near the crossroad with Universitaria ☎01 564 7789, ⓔrestaurante.elgrifo@gmail.com; map pp.726–727. Literally called "the petrol station", this chic Lima restaurant is on an old petrol forecourt. It serves some of the best versions of classic Peruvian dishes in Lima, including mouth-watering *lomo saltado* (S24) – marinated steak, their speciality – and original fusions such as the delicious *fettuccini a la Huancaína con lomo* (S27), as well as stunning desserts. The standard of food and service is impeccable, more than worth the price. Take a taxi. Breakfasts S10–20, Mains S20–40. Daily 8am–5.30pm.

outside, while those in Miraflores are more restaurant-like. Tues–Sun 11am–4pm.

Thani Wasi C Manuel Bonilla 176; map p.731. Serving tasty and healthy food, locals pack out the small wooden tables at lunchtime thanks to its good-value menus (S8–12), featuring everything from *bistec a la pobre* (steak, egg and chips) to *trucha* (trout). Daily 11.30am–9pm.

BARRANCO AND OTHER SUBURBS

Anticuchos Tio Jhony Catalina Miranda 101, at Av Paseo de la República; map pp.726–727. This authentic *huarique* serves some of the best *anticuchos* (beef heart kebabs) in the capital. Don't be put off by the unusual meat – *anticuchos* are the most flavourful beef you'll ever try, especially here (S15–30). "Uncle" Jhony's special chilli sauce is spectacular. Daily 5.30pm–1am.

Expreso Virgen de Guadalupe Av Prolongación San Martín 15-A, next to the Municipalidad ☎01 252 8907; map pp.726–727. A unique vegetarian restaurant in an old tram car right on the main square. Lunchtime buffet S16 (S18 at weekends) for a great selection of meat-free and some vegan dishes. Mon–Thurs & Sun 9am–2am, Fri & Sat 9am–3am (live music most nights from 10pm).

Mi Carcochita Av Pedro de Osma 30, at Malecón Castilla ☎01 248 7826; map pp.726–727. Friendly corner bar and café that does a good range of snacks, sandwiches and juices – but the main draw is the fact that it's open 24hr. Lunch menu S14 (S15 at weekends).

NIGHTLIFE

The daily newspaper *El Comercio* provides good entertainment listings and its Friday edition carries a comprehensive supplement on Lima's nightlife. The Plaza San Martín is, at present, the newest hotspot for nightlife, with enough bars and clubs there to take you through until dawn

Barranco is also trendy and the liveliest place to hang out at weekends, while Miraflores has the highest concentration of cheap bars around the Parque Kennedy. Good places for live music can be found in all three areas. As you would expect, Friday and Saturday nights are the most popular, and many bars and clubs only open on those days. Most bars have Facebook pages to check what's on.

BARS AND CLUBS

The distinction between a bar and a club in Lima is often blurred, as bars become dancefloors and stay open all night. A good guide as to which is which is the opening times – many of the clubs only open at weekends. Lima has a fun and rapidly growing gay and lesbian scene; see ⓦ lima .queercity.info for current information about what's on.

El Bolivarcito Jr. de la Unión 926, Central Lima ⓦ gran hotelbolivar.com.pe; map p.729. Come to the "catedral" of pisco sour, part of the *Gran Hotel Bolívar*, for probably the best in Lima (the classic house pisco will set you back S20). Also does an excellent set lunch (S14; except Sun). Mon–Sat noon–midnight and Sun noon–11pm.

Downtown Vale Todo Pasaje Los Pinos 168, Miraflores ⓦ peruesgay.com; map p.731. The name means "everything's allowed downtown" and it certainly is here at Lima's most established gay/lesbian club. Often has live drag or strip shows. Usually free Mon–Thurs, entrance fee at weekends. Daily from 9pm.

Etnias Bar Cultural Jr. Carabaya 815, Central Lima; map p.729. A highly atmospheric multipurpose space with muralled walls, folk art and a chequered dancefloor. *Etnias* is a café/nightclub which often has live world music/ reggae or film showings. Thurs–Sat 9.30pm until dawn.

★ **El Mirador** Jr. de la Unión 892, 7th floor, Central Lima ⓦ barelmirador.com; map p.729. Without doubt the bar with the best view in Lima. Walk confidently up to the bouncer and take the lift up to the seventh floor, where you'll find a cool crowd listening to a mix of rock and Latin music surrounded by incense and Hindu imagery. Get there before 10pm to grab a table with views of the plaza. Entry S10. Thurs–Sat 8pm until dawn.

Munich Jr. de la Unión 1044, Central Lima; map p.729. German-themed underground piano bar with a barrel for a doorway and bar food, a live pianist and nostalgic European landscapes on the walls. Mon–Sat 7pm–3am.

Rincón Cervecero Jr. de la Unión 1045, Central Lima ☎ 01 428 1422, ⓦ rinconcervecero.com.pe; map p.729. Another German-themed bar opposite *Munich*, where you can order beer in containers of all forms, including a 5-litre barrel (S77), from Peruvian waiters in lederhosen. Mon–Thurs 3pm–midnight, Fri & Sat noon–3am (closed Sun).

Vichama Jr. Carabaya 945, Central Lima; map p.729. A seriously cool rock bar/club in a huge colonial space, with many small art-filled rooms containing a mix of shabby-chic furniture. Free entry. Thurs–Sat 10pm until very late.

Wahio's Bar Pasaje Espinoza 111 on the Plaza de Bomberos ☎ 01 247 2592; map pp.726–727. Cosy bar club with several rooms playing different sounds, though you'll mostly hear reggae and electronic pop. Walls are packed with photos and artwork, there's comfy seating and bar food is served. Free entry. Thurs–Sat from around 9.30pm until the last people leave.

LIVE MUSIC

The great variety of traditional and hybrid sounds is one of the most enduring reasons for visiting the capital. The best place to go for an evening's entertainment is a *peña* – a live music spectacular featuring many styles of national song and dance with an MC, live band, some audience participation and much dancing. *Peñas* are great fun for all ages – they start late and the dancing can last all night. The Lima versions are very expensive compared to the rest of the country (you can pay up to S60 just to enter) – so if you can't go here, be sure to seek one out elsewhere.

La Candelaria Av Bolognesi 292, Barranco ☎ 01 247 1314, ⓦ lacandelariaperu.com; map pp.726–727. Impressive costumes, choreography and plenty of audience participation mark this place out as one of Barranco's most popular *peñas*. The amazingly decorated room adds to the atmosphere. Entrance fee (depending on the show) S35–45, including a pisco sour. Shows Thurs and Sat starting at 9.30pm.

Jazz Zone Av La Paz 646, Pasaje El Suche, Miraflores ☎ 01 241 8139, ⓦ jazzzoneperu.com; map p.731. Live music (most often rock, jazz and *música criolla*) from local and international groups in this atmospheric joint upstairs. Entrance fee varies depending on the show. Tues–Sat from 8pm.

★ **La Noche** Av Bolognesi 307, at El Boulevard, Barranco ⓦ lanoche.com.pe; map pp.726–727. At the top end of the Boulevard, this bar is really packed at weekends and is the top nightspot in the neighbourhood. There's a section with a stage for live music, with free jazz sessions on Mon eve. Free entry to bar, cover charge for live music. Mon–Sat from 7pm.

De Rompe y Raja C Manuel Segura 127, Barranco ☎ 01 247 3271, ⓦ derompeyraja.pe; map pp.726–727. This moodily lit *peña* is especially famous for Afro-Peruvian rhythms, but you'll hear salsa and *música folklórica* too. Entry is S30, but always check the website as flyers can be printed off for discounts. Lunchtime shows with food included are cheaper. Thurs–Sun from around 10pm.

SHOPPING

All types of Peruvian *artesanía* are available in Lima, including woollen goods, crafts and gemstones. Some of the best in Peru are on Av Petit Thouars, which is home to a handful of markets between Av Ricardo Palma and Av Angamos, all within easy walking distance of Miraflores centre. Often considerably cheaper are the artisan markets on blocks 9 and 10 of Av La Marina in Pueblo Libre, as well

9

as the good craft and antique market in the Miraflores Park between Diagonal and Av Larco, which takes place every evening (6–9pm). In central Lima the Artesanía Santo Domingo, opposite the church of the same name, houses a range of suppliers to suit all budgets, just a stone's throw from the Plaza Mayor; it is especially good for loose beads.

For clothing, Polvos Azules (Av Paseo de le República, 2 blocks from Plaza Grau) and Gamarra (Prolongación Gamarra 712, La Victoria) are huge shopping centres/markets where you can pick up very cheap branded clothing and footwear. Both areas can be dangerous and are rife with pickpockets so take only the money you want to spend and try to visit early in the morning.

DIRECTORY

Banks and exchange Central Lima, Miraflores, Barranco and San Isidro all have several casas de cambio, and Interbank will change money and travellers' cheques. Moneychangers on the streets will often give a slightly better rate but will try all sorts of tricks, from doctored calculators to fake money. Often the best way to change money in Lima is by buying things in supermarkets with large US$ notes and asking them for the change in soles – they usually give the best rates.

Embassies and consulates Australia (Av La Paz 1049, 10th floor, Miraflores ☎01 630 0500); Canada (Bolognesi 228, Miraflores ☎01 319 3200); Ireland (consulate) (Av Paseo de la Republica 5757b, Miraflores ☎01 242 9516); South Africa (Av Víctor Andrés Belaunde, Edificio Real 3, Office 801, San Isidro ☎01 440 9996); UK (Torre Parque Mar, Av Larco 1301, 22nd floor, Miraflores ☎01 617 3000); USA (Av La Encalada, block 17, Surco ☎01 618 2000).

Internet Internet cafés are available throughout the capital, most equipped for chat, with several 24hr places in Miraflores. A large percentage of bars, restaurants and accommodation also have wi-fi access.

Police Tourist Police, at Jr. Moore 268, Magdalena del Mar (☎01 460 1060 or ☎980 121 462, ✉divtur@pnp.gob.pe). English spoken.

Postal services Not overly reliable, the principal postal company is SERPOST whose main office is on Pasaje Piura s/n off Jr. de la Unión, one block from the Plaza de Armas (open 8am–8.30pm; ☎01 511 5110). SERPOST also has an office in Miraflores at Petit Thouars 5201. FedEx, DHL and UPS all have offices in Lima – check their websites for details.

CALLAO

Still the country's main commercial harbour, and one of the most modern ports in South America, **Callao** lies about 14km west of central Lima. Its main attraction is the pentagonal **Fortaleza del Real Felipe**, on Plaza Independencia, which houses the **Museo del Ejército** (Military Museum; Tues–Sun 9.30am–4pm; S15 by 1hr 30min guided tour in Spanish or English; ☎01 429 0532). The collection of eighteenth-century arms and rooms dedicated to Peruvian heroes are interesting, but the real star is the fort itself, a superb example of the military architecture of its age. A short walk from the fort, at the dock on Plaza Grau, you can take **boat tours** (see p.734) out around local islands. Book ahead for trips further out to the **Islas Palomino** (4hr; around S115), where you'll see sea birds, dolphins and sometimes whales.

A twenty-minute walk southwest of the fort are the crumbling but charming neighbourhoods of **Chuquito** and **La Punta**, where you can dream away an afternoon on the pebble beach, eat mouth-wateringly fresh *ceviche* or go for a rowing-boat ride out to sea.

ARRIVAL

By bus or colectivo To get to Callao from central Lima, take a *colectivo* from Plaza Dos de Mayo running down Avenida Oscar R. Benavides, or a bus from Avenida Tacna (line Roma 1). Note that Callao can be dangerous in the evening.

Ayacucho

Beautiful **AYACUCHO** (2761m) played a vital role for the fifteenth-century Spanish conquistadors, thanks to its strategic location between Lima and Cusco and between Potosí (Bolivia) and Antofagasta (Chile-Argentina), home to gold, silver and mercury mines. Ayacucho attracted rich miners and landowners who financed the construction of the beautiful churches and colonial buildings that are still standing today. More recently, the region was one of the worst hit in the 1980s when the Maoist revolutionary movement Sendero Luminoso, or Shining Path, launched mass internal conflict leading to the death of thousands. The city's isolation and its recent turbulent history mean that the area has mostly remained off the backpacker trail. Nonetheless, since the late 1990s, the region has become as safe as the rest of Peru and travellers have begun to explore the city's treasures and enjoy the surrounding Andean landscape.

WHAT TO SEE AND DO

The heart of the city is the Plaza Mayor, with its sixteenth- and seventeenth-century buildings characterized by stone arches, pillars with balustrades and red brick clay roofs. The Plaza is home to the seventeenth-century **Catedral**, which combines Renaissance and Baroque elements. Despite its somewhat sombre facade, its rich interior is home to ten beautiful gold-leaf altarpieces.

Visitors should not miss the **Museo de la Memoria** (Prolongación Libertad 1229; Mon–Fri 9am–1pm & 3–6pm, Sun call in advance; S2; ⓣ066 317 170), which focuses on the socio-political violence inflicted by the Shining Path revolutionary movement in the 1980s and 90s. The little museum is home to a number of displays including photographs of the dead and missing, as well as artworks on the conflict and a replica of a torture cell. A wall chart details the history of ANFASEP, the non-profit organization that runs the museum. Mothers and wives of the deceased and missing meet here regularly to share their experiences and lend support to one another. You can purchase the women's handmade clothes and crafts in the little shop upstairs.

ARRIVAL AND DEPARTURE

By plane The Alfredo Mendivil Duarte airport is a 10–15min taxi ride (S8) east of town. There are major plans to renovate the runway and to open a larger more modern airport, but at the time of research, the only destination was Lima, operated by Star Peru and LC (3 daily; 45min).

By bus The Terrapuerto bus station is at Av Javier Pérez de Cuellar s/n (ⓣ066 311 710).

Destinations Lima (8am & 11am, thereafter nightly services only; 9–10hr); Ica (3 nightly; 6–7hr); Huancayo (3 nightly; 8–9hr). Expreso Turismo Los Chancas (ⓣ066 401 943) runs daily services to Cusco (18hr) via Andahuaylas, where you will have to wait an hour or so before boarding a new bus to Cusco. Note that the road to Cusco is currently being paved; once this has been completed travel time should substantially decrease.

INFORMATION

Tourist information The friendly and helpful iPerú office is on the eastern side of the main plaza (ⓣ066 318 305, ⓔiperuayacucho@promperu.gob.pe). Mon–Sat 9am–6pm, Sun 9am–1pm.

ACCOMMODATION

La Colmena Cusco 140 ⓣ066 311 318, ⓔcesarde95@hotmail.com. Formerly the home of a Spanish General, La Colmena has clean tiled rooms spread out over three levels, most giving onto a leafy interior courtyard. All have private bath and rates include breakfast and wi-fi. There's also a pleasant outdoor restaurant serving creole dishes. **S50**

Tres Máscaras Jr. Tres Máscaras 194 ⓣ066 312 921, ⓦhoteltresmascaras.galeon.com. Colouful birds tweet in cages as two little dogs supervise the premises of this welcoming hostel with a pleasant open courtyard. Rooms are spacious and all have TV and private bath. Free wi-fi. **S60**

EATING

La Miel Portal Constitución 11–12. The toothsome cakes (S5.50) can be enjoyed with a freshly squeezed juice (S5). Health buffs can top up their vitamin count with a great fruit salad. Daily 10am–10pm.

Via Via Portal Constitución 4. This welcoming Belgian-owned restaurant/café with great views over the square serves an excellent-value lunch menu (S9). Dishes are made using local produce – try the tasty quinoa risotto (S17). Free wi-fi. Daily 7.30am–midnight.

DIRECTORY

Banks and exchange BCP and Banco Continental are both on the northern side of the square; both have ATMs. There are casas de cambio and money exchangers just by La Miel café.

Internet Try Adis at Cusco 132 (Mon–Sat 8am–9pm, Sun 9am–1pm; S1/hr).

Laundry LHL, Garcilazo de la Vega 265 (Mon–Sat 8am–9pm).

Police The tourist police are at 2 de mayo 113 (ⓣ066 315 845).

Post office Asamblea 293 (Mon–Sat 8am–7pm).

Cusco and around

The former capital of the Inca empire, modern **CUSCO** is an exciting and colourful city, enclosed between high hills and dominated by the imposing ceremonial centre and temple of **Sacsaywamán**. It's one of South America's

9

biggest tourist destinations, thanks to its narrow whitewashed streets, thriving culture, lively nightlife, substantial Inca ruins and architectural treasures from the colonial era.

Once you've acclimatized to the 3400m altitude, there are dozens of enticing destinations within easy reach. For most people the **Sacred Valley** is the obvious first choice, with the citadel of **Machu Picchu** as the ultimate goal. The mountainous region around Cusco boasts some of the country's finest trekking, and beyond the **Inca Trail** to Machu Picchu are hundreds of lesser-known paths into the mountains, including the **Salcantay** and **Ausungate** treks, which are even more stunning and challenging. Cusco is also a convenient jumping-off point for the exploration of the lowland **Amazon rainforest** in Madre de Dios, such as the Tambopata-Candamo Reserved Zone, or the Manu Biosphere Reserve, among the most biodiverse wildernesses on Earth.

SOME HISTORY

Legend has it that Cusco was founded by **Manco Capac** and his sister **Mama Occlo** in around 1100 AD. Over the next two centuries, the **Cusco Valley** was home to the Inca tribe, but it wasn't until **Pachacutec** assumed power in 1438 that Cusco became the centre of an expanding empire. The new ruler designed the city in the shape of a puma, with its head incorporating some of its most important sites. Of all the Inca rulers, only **Atahualpa**, the last, never actually resided in Cusco, and even he was en route there when the conquistadors captured him at Cajamarca. **Francisco Pizarro** reached the native capital on November 15, 1533,

after holding Atahualpa to ransom, then killing him anyway. The city's beauty surpassed anything the Spaniards had seen before in the New World, the stonework was better than any in Spain and precious metals were used in a sacred context throughout the city. As usual, they lost no time in looting it.

Like its renowned art, the Cusco of today is dark yet vibrantly coloured, reflecting its turbulent legacy. It's a politically active, left-of-centre city where the streets are often alive with fiestas and demonstrations.

WHAT TO SEE AND DO

The city divides into several distinct zones, with the **Plaza de Armas** at the heart of it all.

The **Boleto Turístico** Tourist Ticket (see box opposite) will give you an idea of some of the most popular city and sacred valley sites, but it does not include entry to the one unmissable Cusco site, the Inca sun temple at **Q'orikancha**. Around the city there are opportunities for tours, hikes and extreme sports, as well as the fascinating Inca sites of **Sacsaywamán** and **Tambomachay**.

Plaza de Armas

Cusco's ancient and modern centre, the **Plaza de Armas**, corresponds roughly to the ceremonial *Huacaypata*, the Incas' ancient central plaza, and is a constant hub of activity, its northern and western sides filled with shops and restaurants. Here you'll be approached by touts, waiters and shoe-shine boys, and here is where you'll come to watch the parades during Cusco's festivities. You'll see two flags flying here – the Peruvian one and the rainbow flag of Tuhuantinsuyo, which represents the four corners of the Inca empire (not to be confused with the gay pride flag). On the northeastern side stands the imposing cathedral, flanked by the Jesús María and El Triunfo churches, with the Compañía de Jesús church on the eastern side.

La Catedral

The plaza's exposed northeastern edge is dominated by the fortress-like

WHEN TO VISIT

The best time to visit the area around Cusco is during the dry season (May–Sept), when it's warm with clear skies during the day but relatively cold at night. During the wet season (Oct–April) it rarely rains every day or all week, but the heavy downpours trigger landslides, making it difficult and dangerous to travel in the nearby mountains.

THE CUSCO TOURIST TICKET AND BOLETO INTEGRAL

The **Boleto Turístico** (S130 for ten days, students with ISIC card S70) is a vital purchase for most visitors, as you can't visit most important sites without it. It covers the Sacsaywamán, Q'enqo, Pukapukara and Tambomachay ruins near the city, as well as those in Ollantaytambo, Chinchero, Písac, Moray, Tipón and Pikillacta, plus the optional extras of Museo Histórico Regional, Museo de Arte Contemporaneo, Museo de Arte Popular, Centro Qosqo de Arte Nativo, the Pachacutec monument and the Q'orikancha site museum (though not the Q'orikancha itself). It's available from all of the sites on the ticket, or from the issuing COSITUC offices at Avenida Sol 103, office 102 (📞 084 261 465, 🌐 www.cosituc.gob.pe). You can also buy three partial *boletos*, valid for two days (S70), one covering the ruins immediately outside Cusco, another the above museums, and the third, the Sacred Valley ruins. The **Boleto Religioso** (S50 or S25 for students; valid for ten days), which must be purchased at one of the following sites, covers the star attractions of the Catedral and the Iglesia de la Compañía de Jesús, as well as the Iglesia de San Blas, Museo Quijote (contemporary art) and the Museo de Arte Religioso.

Baroque-style **Catedral** (daily 10am–6pm; S25). Inside you'll find some of the best examples of art from the *Escuela Cusqueña* (Cusco School): look out for *The Last Supper*, with Christ sitting down to a feast of *cuy* (guinea pig), and the portrayals of the Virgin Mary as Pachamama (Mother Earth). Also check out the cathedral's finely carved granite altar and oldest surviving painting in Cusco, depicting the terrible 1650 earthquake, as well as a Neoclassical high altar made entirely of finely beaten embossed silver. Ten smaller chapels surround the nave, including the Chapel of El Señor de los Temblores (The Lord of Earthquakes) which houses a 26kg crucifix made of solid gold and encrusted with precious stones.

Iglesia de la Compañía de Jesús

As you look downhill from the centre of the plaza, the **Iglesia de la Compañía de Jesús** (daily 9–11.30am & 1–5.30pm; S10) dominates the skyline, and is often confused with the cathedral on first glance due to the splendour of its highly ornate facade. First built in the late 1570s, it was resurrected after the earthquake of 1650 in a Latin cross shape, over the foundations of Amara Cancha – originally Huayna Capac's Palace of the Serpents. Cool and dark inside, with a grand gold-leaf altarpiece and a fine wooden pulpit displaying a relief of Christ, its transept ends in a stylish Baroque cupola.

Museo Inka

North of the cathedral, slightly uphill, you'll find one of the city's most beautiful colonial mansions, **El Palacio del Almirante** (The Admiral's Palace), which now houses the **Museo Inka** (Mon–Fri 8am–7pm, Sat 9am–4pm; S10). The museum itself is the best place in Cusco to see exhibits of Inca pottery, textiles, trepanned skulls, finely crafted metalwork (including miniature metal llamas given as offerings to the gods) and the largest range of wooden *quero* vases in the world. There's excellent interpretative information in Spanish only, but you can hire a guide at the entrance for a small fee.

Monasterio de Santa Catalina

Leading away from the Plaza de Armas, Callejón Loreto separates La Compañía from the tall, stone walls of the ancient **Acclahuasi**, a temple where the Sun Virgins used to make *chicha* beer for the Inca ruler. Today, the building is occupied by the **Monasterio de Santa Catalina**, built in 1610, with its small but grand side entrance half a short block down Calle Arequipa; just under thirty sisters still live and worship here. Inside the convent is the **Museo de Arte** (Mon–Sat 8.30am–5.30pm, Sun 2–5pm; S8), with a splendid collection of paintings from the *Escuela Cusqueña*.

Q'orikancha

If you visit one site in Cusco it should be **Q'orikancha**. The Convento de Santo Domingo at the intersection of Avenida

9

El Sol and Calle Santa Domingo rises imposingly but rudely from the impressive walls of the Q'orikancha complex (Mon–Sat 8am–5pm; S10), which the conquistadors laid low to make way for their uninspiring Baroque seventeenth-century church. Before the Spanish set their gold-hungry eyes on it, the temple must have been even more breathtaking, consisting of four small sanctuaries and a larger temple set around the existing courtyard, which was encircled by a cornice of gold made of seven hundred solid gold sheets (Q'orikancha means "golden enclosure"). Below the temple was an artificial garden in which everything was made of gold or silver and encrusted with precious jewels, from llamas and shepherds to the tiniest details of clumps of earth and weeds, including snails and butterflies. The Incas used the Q'orikancha as a solar observatory to study celestial activities, and archeologists believe that the mummies of the previous Incas were brought here and ritually burned.

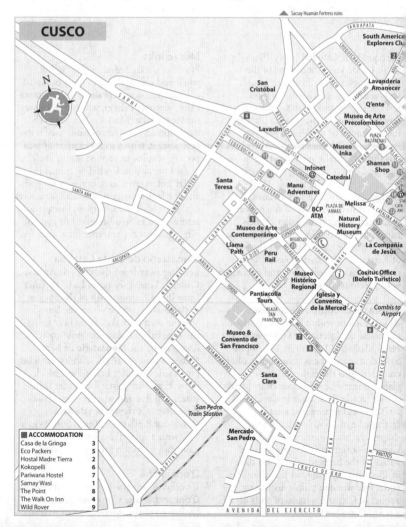

CUSCO

▲ Sacsay Huamán Fortress ruins

ACCOMMODATION

Casa de la Gringa	3
Eco Packers	5
Hostal Madre Tierra	2
Kokopelli	6
Pariwana Hostel	7
Samay Wasi	1
The Point	8
The Walk On Inn	4
Wild Rover	9

Visitors need to use their imagination when they enter the courtyard inside the site, although surviving sections of the original Inca wall, made of tightly interlocking blocks of polished andesite, stand as firmly rooted as ever, completely unshaken by the powerful earthquakes that have devastated colonial buildings.

Museo de Sitio del Q'orikancha

The underground **Museo de Sitio del Q'orikancha** (daily 9am–6pm; entry with Boleto Turístico) consists of five rooms,

containing various relics such as pottery shards, Inca weaponry, mummies and a section on the practice of trepanning, complete with medical instruments and several examples of trepanned skulls from the Paracas area. Guides are available for a small fee.

Iglesia y Convento de La Merced

Just southwest from the Plaza de Armas along Calle Mantas is the **Iglesia y Convento de La Merced** (Mon–Sat 8am–noon & 2–5pm; S6). Founded

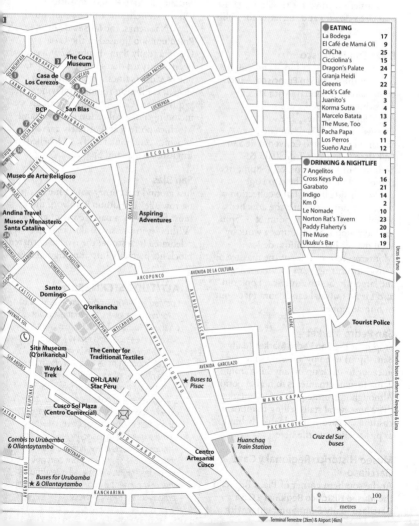

EATING	
La Bodega	17
El Café de Mamá Oli	9
ChiCha	25
Cicciolina's	15
Dragon's Palate	24
Granja Heidi	7
Greens	22
Jack's Cafe	8
Juanito's	3
Korma Sutra	4
Marcelo Batata	13
The Muse, Too	5
Pacha Papa	6
Los Perros	11
Sueño Azul	12

DRINKING & NIGHTLIFE	
7 Angelitos	1
Cross Keys Pub	16
Garabato	21
Indigo	14
Km 0	2
Le Nomade	10
Norton Rat's Tavern	23
Paddy Flaherty's	20
The Muse	18
Ukuku's Bar	19

The Coca Museum

Casa de Los Cerezos

BCP San Blas

Museo de Arte Religioso

Andina Travel
Museo y Monasterio Santa Catalina

Aspiring Adventures

Santo Domingo

Q'orikancha

Tourist Police

Site Museum (Q'orikancha)

The Center for Traditional Textiles

Wayki Trek

DHL/LAN/ Star Perú

Buses to Pisac

Cusco Sol Plaza (Centro Comercial)

Combis to Urubamba & Ollantaytambo

Buses for Urubamba & Ollantaytambo

Centro Artesanal Cusco

Huanchaq Train Station

Cruz del Sur buses

Urcos & Puno ▶

Ormeño buses & others for Arequipa & Lima ▶

0 — 100
metres

▼ Terminal Terrestre (2km) & Airport (4km)

9

in 1536, it was rebuilt after the 1650 earthquake in a rich combination of Baroque and Renaissance styles. While its facade is exceptional, the highlight is a breathtaking 1720s **monstrance** standing a metre high; it was crafted by a Spanish jeweller using more than six hundred pearls, 1500 diamonds and 22kg of solid gold. The monastery also possesses a fine collection of *Escuela Cusqueña* paintings, and entombed in the church on the far side of the cloisters are the bodies of the two Diegos de Almagro, father and son, the former executed for rebelling against Francisco Pizarro and the latter for killing Pizarro in revenge.

Plaza San Francisco

Continue on another block and you'll come to the **Plaza San Francisco**, which comes alive on Sundays with street performers and food stalls selling traditional favourites. The square's southwestern side is dominated by the simply decorated **Convento de San Francisco** (Mon–Sat 7–8.30am & 5–8pm, Sun 7am–noon & 5–8pm; free), completed in 1652. The two large cloisters inside have a large collection of colonial paintings, while the attached **Museo** (Mon–Fri 9am–noon & 3–5pm, Sat 9am–noon; S5) features a work by local master Juan Espinosa de los Monteros, responsible for the massive oil canvas measuring 12m by 9m – allegedly the largest in South America. Look out also for an unusual candelabra made out of human bones.

San Pedro Market

Stop in at the **San Pedro Market** (daily 8am–5pm) to enjoy a freshly squeezed juice, or to stock up on anything from llama toenail ornaments to herbal potions. Although it is principally a food market, there are several stalls selling traditional costumes. Leave your valuables behind, as pickpockets are rife here.

Museo Histórico Regional y Casa Garcilaso

At the southern corner of Plaza Regocijo, the **Museo Histórico Regional y Casa Garcilaso** (daily 8am–5pm; entry with Boleto Turístico) is home to fascinating pre-Inca ceramics, plus a Nazca mummy with 1.5m-long hair, and a number of Inca artefacts such as bolas, maces, and square water dishes that functioned as spirit levels. The museum also displays some gold and silver llamas found in 1996 in the Plaza de Armas when reconstructing the central fountain, golden figurines from Sacsaywamán and wooden *quero* drinking vessels and dancing masks from the colonial era.

Museo de Arte Precolumbino

On the western side of the small, quiet Plaza Nazarenas, the **Museo de Arte Precolumbino** housed in the Casa Cabrera (daily 8am–10pm; S20) has an open courtyard that's home to *MAP Café*, one of Cusco's finest restaurants, and elegant exhibition rooms displaying some exquisite pre-Columbian works of art, including a fine collection of Nazca and Mochica pottery and ornately carved Mochica ceremonial staffs, all labelled in English, French and Spanish.

San Blas

Just around the corner you come to the narrow alley of **Hathun Rumiyoq**, the most famous Inca passageway of all. Within its impressive walls lies the celebrated **Inca stone**; the twelve-cornered block fits perfectly into the original lower

---

ALTITUDE SICKNESS

Located at 3400m above sea level, Cusco is, for most travellers, the highest point on their trip. *Soroche*, or acute mountain sickness (see p.35), is a reality for most people arriving by plane from sea level. Cusco's mountainous location also means that a number of the city's steep streets, in particular high up in San Blas, will quickly leave you breathless as you explore town. Make sure to take it easy for the first couple of days, even sleeping a whole day just to assist acclimatization. Although Cusco's lively nightlife is an obvious draw, stay away from bars at least on the first night. Virtually all guesthouses offer complimentary coca tea, a traditional remedy for altitude sickness.

wall of what used to be the Inca Roca's old imperial palace.

Walking up the Cuesta de San Blas, you come to the Plazoleta de San Blas, which hosts a Saturday handicrafts market (9am–4pm). Also on the tiny square is the small **Chapel of San Blas** (daily 8am–6pm; S15 or free with Boleto Religioso). The highlight here is an incredibly intricate pulpit, carved from a block of cedar wood in a complicated Churrigueresque style by an indigenous man who allegedly devoted his life to the task and whose skull rests in the topmost part of the carving.

Museo de la Coca

Just up Calle Suytuqatu from Plazoleta San Blas lies the fascinating little **Museo de la Coca** (daily 9am–7pm; S10), devoted to the history of the coca leaf through the ages. The exhibits explore the significance of the plant in Peru from its first known ceremonial use by the Andean people to the present day through a series of displays, from ancient ceramic figures with cheeks bulging from chewing coca leaves to nineteenth-century texts on research into the medical use of cocaine. The curator is happy to answer any questions you may have.

ARRIVAL AND DEPARTURE

By plane Cusco Airport (Alejandro Velasco Astete International Airport; ☎084 222 611) is 4km south of the city centre. You can either take a taxi from outside the arrivals hall (S10–15 to the city centre), or hop on a Correcaminos *colectivo* (S0.60) from outside the airport car park, which goes along Av Sol to C Ayacucho, two blocks from the Plaza de Armas.

Destinations LAN, Star Peru and TACA have regular flights to major national destinations, including Lima (every 20min between 7.35am–3.30pm; 1hr 20min), Puerto Maldonado (4 daily between 11.50am–1.20pm; 55min), Arequipa (daily; 2hr 15min) and Juliaca (for Puno; daily; 1hr). AeroSur flies to La Paz (daily; 1hr 55min) and Santa Cruz (daily; 5hr 25min) in Bolivia.

By bus Most international and inter-regional buses use the Terminal Terrestre (☎084 224 471) at Vía de Evitamiento 429, 2km southeast of the centre. *Colectivos* from the nearby Pachacutec monument uphill run between the station and the Plaza San Francisco or the Plaza de Armas (S0.60); a taxi will set you back S5–8. There is an embarkation tax of S1.50, which you pay before getting on. Recommended bus companies include: Cruz

del Sur, which has its own bus depot at Av Industrial 121 (☎084 243 261); Ormeño (☎084 227 501); Inka Express (☎084 247 887); Tour Peru (☎084 236 463); Litoral (☎084 281 920); Movil Tours (☎084 262 526); Cial (☎084 256 216); San Martín (☎097 970 9615).

Destinations Arequipa (hourly between 6–9am and 7pm–midnight; 10hr); Arica, Chile (twice weekly; 2 days) La Paz, Bolivia (daily at 10pm; 12hr); Lima (at least hourly; 20hr); Nazca (hourly; 12–14hr); Puerto Maldonado (10pm and 5–6 daily between 6.30–9pm; 7hr); Puno (4 early departures between 7 and 8am, one departure at 10pm; 8hr). Cruz del Sur to: Arequipa (daily at 8pm & 8.30pm; 9hr); Lima via Nazca (daily at 2pm & 6pm; 18hr).

By train If you're coming from Puno, you'll arrive at the Wanchaq station in the southeast of the city. From here you can hail a taxi on the street outside (around S5 to the centre), catch the airport *colectivo*, or walk the eight or nine blocks up a gentle hill to the Plaza de Armas. If you're coming by train from Machu Picchu, you'll disembark at Estación Poroy, east of the centre; arrivals are met by a bus (S8) that can drop you off at the Plaza Regocijo, or else take a taxi (S15–20).

Destinations Wanchaq station to: Puno (Mon, Wed, Fri & Sat at 8am, April–Oct; Mon, Wed & Sat Nov–March; 10hr). Poroy station to: Machu Picchu (Vistadome daily at 6.53am; Expedition daily at 7.42am; Hiram Bingham daily at 9.10am; 4hr). Peru Rail has an office in town at Plaza Regocijo 202 (daily 7am–10pm), though it's also easy to buy tickets directly through Perú Rail (ⓦperurail.com). For Machu Picchu, it's best to buy a week in advance in peak season.

INFORMATION

Tourist information The main tourist office (Dircetur) at Mantas 117–A (Mon–Sat 8am–8pm, Sun 9am–noon; ☎084 222 032, ⓔ cusco@dircetur.cusco.gob.pe) has limited information on the city as well as free maps, though the staff are friendly and helpful. iPerú, at the departures hall at the airport (daily 6am–5pm; ☎084 237 364), offers a decent amount of information on the area as well as free maps and brochures. There is also a small iPerú kiosk at the arrivals area, which meets incoming flights.

South American Explorers' Club (Atoqsaycuchi 670; Mon–Fri 9.30am–5pm, Sat 9.30am–1pm; ☎084 245 484, ⓦ saexplorers.org) is by far the best source of information about Cusco and around, with trip reports compiled by fellow travellers, as well as good trekking maps and a good book exchange.

Andean Travel Web (ⓦ andeantravelweb.com) also has up-to-date information about events and festivities in the Cusco area.

GETTING AROUND

By bus and colectivo The city bus and *colectivo* networks are incredibly complicated, though cheap and fast once you learn your way around, and charge S0.60 per person. If

9

TOURS IN AND AROUND CUSCO

Tours in and around Cusco range from a half-day city tour to a full-on adventure down to the Amazon. Service and facilities vary considerably, so check exactly what's provided. **Standard tours** around the city, Sacred Valley and to Machu Picchu range from a basic bus service with fixed stops and little in the way of a guide, to luxury packages including guide, food and hotel transfers. The two- to four-day **Inca Trail** is the most popular of the **mountain treks**; many agencies offer trips with guides, equipment and fixed itineraries; do a lot of research deciding when and how to do the Inca Trail (see p.755).

Other popular **alternative Inca trails** (see p.763) are around the snowcapped mountains of Salcantay (6264m) to the north and Ausangate (6372m) to the south, a more remote trek, which needs at least a week plus guides and mules. You can also rent out **mountain bikes** for trips to the Sacred Valley and around, and some operators arrange guided tours. Many **jungle trip** operators are also based in Cusco (see p.825).

TOUR OPERATORS

The Cusco area is an adrenaline junkie's paradise, with a huge range of adventure sports on offer. As well as trekking expeditions in the Sacred Valley, there's world-class river rafting on the Apurimac River, climbing and canyoning in the nearby mountains, and mountain biking.

Amazonas Explorer Av Collasuyo 910, Miravalle ☎084 252 846, ⓦamazonas-explorer.com. Internationally renowned operator offering multi-activity trips, combining hiking and rafting on the Apurimac, as well as mountain biking and horseriding excursions.

Aspiring Adventures Qolla 467 ☎958 257 042, ⓦaspiringadventures.com. Aspiring offers gastronomic and "off-beat Cusco" tours to discover more about the city's hidden attractions, as well as unique 3–4-day trips to mysterious religious festivities such as Qoyllur Riti where entranced costume dancing goes on for days.

Andina Travel Plazoleta Santa Catalina 219 ☎084 251 892, ⓦandinatravel.com. Andina are the pioneers in real alternative treks and are constantly working at opening and developing new alternatives to remote areas. Part of the profits goes towards community projects including building new schools.

Big Foot Triunfo 392, 2nd floor ☎084 233 836, ⓦbigfootcusco.com. Specialists in multi-day expeditions, such as trekking in Ausangate and to Vilcabamba (see p.766).

Llama Path San Juan de Dios 250 ☎084 240 822, ⓦllamapath.com. One of the newer Inca Trail trekking operators in town, Llama Path has quickly established itself as a more affordable, high-quality, responsible outfit.

Q'ente Choquechaca 229 ☎084 222 535, ⓦqente.com. Responsible adventure travel company specializing in alternative treks as well as the traditional Inca Trail.

Wayki Trek Av Pardo 506 ☎084 224 092, ⓦwaykitrek.net. Professional company supporting many community projects in the area and offering some off-the-beaten-trail treks. Also offers a "wayki option" on the Inca Trail whereby groups spend the night in a porter community prior to starting the trail.

you don't have much luggage, you can take a Correcaminos *colectivo* from the eastern side of C Ayacucho, half a block south of Av El Sol, to the airport and the Terminal Terrestre.

By taxi Rides within Cusco cost around S3 or S6–10 for trips to the suburbs or up to Sacsaywamán and Q'enqo (some *taxistas* may charge S20 and wait for you, in which case give them half in advance and half later).

ACCOMMODATION

There are numerous budget options around the Plaza de Armas and in the quieter San Blas area uphill from the square.

Casa de la Gringa Tandapata, at Pasñapaqana 148 ☎084 241 168, ⓦcasadelagringa.com. Cactus pots and a colourful mural decorate the hall of this pleasant guesthouse. Try and stay in the main building as the annexe has darkish rooms. There's a kitchen for guests' use and a communal area with TV and wi-fi. Rates include breakfast. **S68**

★ **Eco Packers** Santa Teresa 375 ☎084 231 800, ⓦecopackersperu.com. This fun and colourful hostel has clean dorms set around a leafy interior courtyard. There is table football and billiards to unwind, as well as a laidback bar with live rock music on Sat evenings. Wi-fi enabled rooms and breakfast included. Dorms **S26.50**, doubles **S95**

Hostal Madre Tierra Atoqsaycuchi 647 ☎084 248 452, ⓦhostalmadretierra.com. A wonderful little guesthouse offering brightly coloured doubles, all with private bath, set on two floors. The interiors are decked out in local wood and fireplaces add to the homelike atmosphere. Staff are friendly and helpful, and there's free wi-fi and all-day coca tea. **S153**

Kokopelli San Andres 260 ☎084 224 473, ⓦhostelkokopelli.com. Set in a beautiful colonial house, this new addition to town has female only and mixed dorms, as well as doubles with private bath. There's table tennis, mini-football, a TV lounge, billiards and a cosy wooden bar. Wi-fi and breakfast included. Dorms S21, doubles S95

Pariwana Hostel Mesón de la Estrella 136 ☏ 084 233 751, ⊛ pariwana-hostel.com. A long-standing favourite among backpackers, *Pariwana* has dorms and doubles set around a lovely interior courtyard dotted with colourful beanbags. Table tennis, mini-football, TV lounge, book exchange and drinking games are sure to keep you busy. Wi-fi, free breakfast and 24hr security. Dorms S25, doubles S95

★ **Samay Wasi** C Atoqsaycuchi 416, San Blas ☏ 084 253 108, ⊛ samaywasiperu.com. This wonderful little place high up in San Blas has clean and tidy rooms set on two floors. All have private bath, there's a kitchen for guests' use, all-day coca tea, wi-fi, free continental breakfast and free airport pick-up. Ask for a room on the second floor, from where there are spectacular views over Cusco. Dorms S28, doubles S68

The Point Mesón de la Estrella 172 ☏ 084 252 266, ⊛ thepointhostels.com. Cusco's party hostel hits it hard every night at the lively bar upstairs. Luckily there's a verdant garden at the back to get some air and come back to your senses in the morning. Dorms are mostly dark as they all give onto the interior courtyard and the premises could do with a bit more of a clean. Dorms S22

The Walk On Inn Suecia 504 ☏ 084 235 065, ⊛ walkoninn.com. This well-established hostel has spacious dorms and rooms set around a light interior space. There's all-day coca tea, wi-fi and laundry service. Staff can help book tickets to Puno with Cruz del Sur and Transzela. Dorms S25, doubles S75

Wild Rover C Matará 261 ☏ 084 221 515, ⊛ wildroverhostels.com. Cusco's other lively party hostel has a fiesta every night. Rooms at the back are slightly quieter although lack sunlight; on the plus side, this means they are the perfect spot to kick that hangover. Free wi-fi and breakfast included. Dorms S21, doubles S70

EATING

There are dozens of stalls at the Mercado San Pedro where you can get hearty dishes for a bargain S4. Self-caterers can stock up on fresh produce here too, as well as at Orion Supermarket, just opposite the San Pedro market.

★ **La Bodega** Herrajes 138. This welcoming restaurant attracts a young, laidback crowd who enjoy the pizzas (S29) and pastas (S25) in little partitioned dining areas. The salads (S19) are made with organic ingredients from the Sacred Valley, and the delicious tiramisú (S12) is large enough to share. Mon–Sat 8am–10.30pm.

El Café de Mamá Oli Plazoleta Nazarenas 199. This family-run place is the perfect spot for breakfast or afternoon tea. Top up your vitamin count with a generous helping of fruit salad (S8), or opt for a heartier breakfast (S14). The home-made cakes (S5) are a must. Mon–Sat 8.30am–8pm, Sun 10am–4pm.

★ **Dragon's Palate** Arequipa 167. Part restaurant, part art gallery, *Dragon's* serves a fusion of international and Peruvian dishes in a wonderful open-air courtyard. Blues, soul and folk bands liven the scene on Thurs, Fri & Sat afternoons between 2 and 4pm. There's also a TV room for rainy days. Mains S15–35. Mon–Sat 9.30am–9.30pm.

Granja Heidi Cuesta San Blas 525. This German-run place offers all sorts of delights for dairy lovers, from hot and cold "milky way" drinks (S10) to a variety of natural yogurt combos (S22–29), as well as sweet and savoury crêpes (S19). Mon–Sat 11.30am–9.30pm.

Greens Santa Catalina Angosta 235, 2nd floor. Once a laidback informal hangout, Greens has become more of an affected establishment in recent years. A farm in the Sacred Valley supplies the organic food, and there are plenty of veggie dishes to choose from. Mains S30–45. Free wi-fi. Daily 11.30am–10.30pm.

★ **Jack's Cafe** Choquechaca 509. A real gringo hangout – don't be surprised to see customers standing in line. The ingredients here come from local suppliers and the coffee is family grown. Plenty on offer, from English breakfasts (S18) to hearty home-made soups (S15). Daily 7.30am–11pm.

Juanito's Qanchipata 596. This tiny sandwich joint serves the best sandwiches (S10–22) in town – just point at what ingredients take your fancy and it'll all come nicely served in a large bun. It's the perfect spot to grab a sandwich before a long bus journey. Mon–Thurs 11am–11pm, Fri & Sat 11am–midnight.

Korma Sutra Tandapata 909, San Blas. Cusco's Indian restaurant attracts crowds of Brits itching for generous portions of onion bhajis (S12) and chicken tikka masala (S22), all to be washed down with a refreshing mango lassi (S8). More adventurous types can go for the crispy tandoori guinea pig (S22). Mon–Sat 1–10pm.

Marcelo Batata Palacio 121. The real draw at Marcelo's is the wonderful roof terrace with breathtaking views of the town, where you can enjoy a postprandial pisco (S15). Try the house speciality, the charbroiled alpaca tenderloin. Mains S35–39. Daily noon–10pm.

The Muse, Too Tambopata 917, San Blas. Sister restaurant to The Muse, this smaller joint with an upstairs seating area offers home-made Western cooking and a range of vegetarian dishes, all rustled up with organic greens; try the veggie lasagne (S20). Take your bottle and get a filtered water refill for just S1. Live music Fri, Sat & Sun at 8.30pm. Daily 8am–midnight.

Pacha Papa Plazoleta San Blas 120. Set in a pleasant courtyard, *Pacha Papa* is one of Cusco's few restaurants with outdoor seating. The cuisine is Peruvian, with a variety of meats, including the ubiquitous *cuy horneado* (S60) grilled in the outdoor clay oven. Mains S40. Daily 8am–11pm.

9

Cicciolina's C Triunfo 393, 2nd floor ☏ 084 239 510. The Argentine chef here rustles up a fantastic selection of Mediterranean fusion dishes, all lovingly prepared with local ingredients. The wooden beams along with the dried garlic and chilli strands hanging from the ceiling give the interior a cosy rustic touch. Try the *carpaccio de alpaca* (S22.) Book ahead. Daily noon–3pm & 6–10pm.

ChiCha Plaza Regocijo 261, 2nd floor. Gastón Acurio's swish eatery has superb takes on traditional cuscqueño dishes, such as *anticuchos de corazón* and *chicharrónes*, as well as expertly executed fusion dishes. The *ceviche* really is heaven on a plate. Mains S25–60.

Los Perros Tecsecocha 436. This relaxed restaurant/bar with dark red undertones, hanging lamps and comfortable sofas is the perfect spot to while away an evening. The international menu includes wontons (S17), crunchy potato skins (S17) and burgers (S24). Daily 11am–midnight.

Sueño Azul Teqseqocha 171. This itty-bitty Israeli place serves Middle Eastern favourites including hummus and falafel (S12), shakshuka (S7) and kebabs (S13). Service is lethargic and carefree, but the S10 menu makes it worth the wait. Mon–Sat 11am–9.30pm.

DRINKING AND NIGHTLIFE

Apart from Lima, no Peruvian town has as varied a nightlife as Cusco. Clubs open early, around 9pm, but don't start getting lively before 11pm, and close in the wee hours. Pubs and clubs alike often offer 2-for-1 drink deals during happy hour. Beware of your drink being spiked in crowded nightspots.

PUBS AND BARS

Cross Keys Pub C Triunfo 350, 2nd floor. British memorabilia dots the premises of this English pub, owned by the British Consul. Catch up on the latest sports on one of the screens, play darts or sink into the sofas by the fireplace on a cold rainy day. There are English beers and ciders on offer, as well as great pub food, including fish and chips (S30). Daily 10am–1.30am.

Indigo Tecsecocha 415. It's always happy hour at this laidback bar with swinging chairs and comfortable couches. The Thai food (S20–27), hookahs, board games, background classics and friendly staff will ensure you stay for a good while. Free wi-fi, too. Daily 4pm–2am.

Norton Rat's Tavern Santa Catalina Angosta 116, 2nd floor, Plaza de Armas. This spacious, low-key pub/bar with flags draped on the ceiling attracts crowds of young blokes keen for a game of darts or billiards. The beer is home-brewed (S12), the burgers (S12) are some of the best in town, and the chile con carne burrito (S14) sells like hot cakes. Daily 7am–2am.

Paddy Flaherty's Triunfo 124. At 3347m, Paddy's proudly boasts that it is the highest 100-percent Irish owned pub on the planet. The pub attracts a melting pot of Peruvians and tourists alike and the menu offers all sorts of home faves, such as shepherd's pie (S16), at very reasonable prices. Happy hour 8–9pm and 10.30–11pm. Daily 10am–late.

CLUBS AND LIVE MUSIC

7 Angelitos San Blas 638. Up in San Blas, 7 Angelitos hosts national and international bands nightly (10pm), playing an assorted mix of reggae, grunge and Beatles tracks. The bar has two happy hours (7–9pm and 10.30–11.30pm) and proudly claims to have the best mojito in the universe. Mon–Sat 7pm–3am.

Garabato Plateros 316, just by Ukuku's. *Cusqueños* head here to boogie to national tunes; join the locals before hitting the dancefloor and knock back a shot of *té piteado* (S7), black tea with alcohol. Cocktails S15–23. Daily 8pm–4am, Fri & Sat until 6am.

Km 0 Tandapata 100, Plaza San Blas. This chilled-out bar with a relaxed lounge area upstairs hosts live bands (daily at 10pm) playing an eclectic mix from reggae to funk. Hookahs (S15), darts, tapas (from S6) and more substantial mains (S18–24), as well as happy hour 4–10pm. Daily 4pm–2am.

Le Nomade Choquechaca 124. Sample some home-made rum with soaked fruits and relax with a hookah as you enjoy some quechua jazz, rock, funk or blues tunes played nightly (9pm) at this laidback French bar. It's happy hour all evening from 5pm. Daily 8am–midnight.

The Muse Triunfo 338, 2nd floor. Belt your favourite songs out in the karaoke room, catch up on some footie or hit the dancefloor at this popular joint. A great Cuban salsa band kicks off at 11.30pm on Wed, Fri and Sat, and it livens up substantially on weekends. Mains S20–25. Daily 9am–late.

Ukuku's Bar Plateros 316. This is one of the oldest and largest bars in town, with a world collection of liqueur bottles dating back over one hundred years. It really gets going at 10.30pm, with live music and dance shows. Profits go towards preserving the Andes by planting native trees, as well as helping children in local communities. Happy hour 7.30–10.30pm. Drinks start at S9. Daily 7.30pm–4am.

SHOPPING

The best shopping area is around Plazoleta San Blas – Tandapata, Cuesta San Blas and Carmen Alto.

Books The best bookshops with extensive English-language sections are Jerusalén at Heladeros 143, with a large book exchange (if you give two books you can take one) and guidebooks, and the smaller SBS Bookshop on Av El Sol 781A.

Clothing Buy quality T-shirts with unique designs at Andean Expressions on Choquechaca 213; makes for a nice change from the standard T-shirts advertising Inka Kola or Cusqueña beer.

Crafts Mercado Modelo de Huanchac stocks a good range of crafts and you can find quirky gifts at Mercado San Pedro. Try Aymi Wasi on Nueva Alta for handmade fairtrade gifts – anything from jewellery to ceramics to art.

Food Self-caterers can stock up on fruit and veg at the Mercado de Wanchaq on Av Garcilazo, at Huascar (daily 6am–6pm). The best supermarket is Orion, just opposite the Mercado San Pedro.

Textiles Centro de Textiles Tradicionales del Cusco, on Av El Sol 603A (daily 7.30am–8.30pm), promotes traditional weaving techniques, so not only can you purchase textiles of excellent quality, but you may also watch weavers demonstrate their skill.

DIRECTORY

Banks and exchange BCP has a global ATM (Plateros, at Espaderos on the Plaza de Armas), and there are ATMs in the BCP and BBVA bank branches along Av El Sol. Up in San Blas, there is a BCP on Plazoleta San Blas. The best place to exchange foreign currency is along Av El Sol, where there are dozens of money exchangers. *Cambistas* (moneychangers along the pavement) may offer slightly better rates than foreign-exchange bureaus, but rip-offs are common.

Camping equipment Most tour agencies rent out tents, sleeping bags, sleeping mats and cooking equipment. There are also several shops on Procuradores and Plateros. Try Camping Equipment Rosly, C Produradores 394 (☎084 248 042). Make sure to always thoroughly check the equipment before renting.

Consulates Most embassies are in Lima, though there are several honorary consul representatives in Cusco: UK (☎084 239 974); US (☎084 231 474); Finland (☎084 252 721); Germany (☎084 235 459); Holland (☎084 224 322).

Hospital and pharmacies Clínica Peruana Suiza (☎084 237 009) on C Oswaldo Baca J–8, Urb. Magisterio 1ra Etapa, and Clinica Hampi Services on Av Collasuyo A–8B, Urb. Manuel Parto (☎084 224 575), are both well equipped to deal with 24hr emergencies. There are pharmacies along Av El Sol.

Internet Café-Internet Melissa, C Triunfo 338, 2nd floor, has a good internet connection (daily 8.30am–9pm; S2/hr); alternatively, try Infonet at Procuradores 340 (daily 8.30am–11.30pm; S2/hr). Most hostels, as well as plenty of cafés and restaurants, offer wi-fi.

Laundry The cheapest laundry places are along C Choquechaca. Try Lavandería Amanecer at Choquechaca 216 (Mon–Sat 8am–8.30pm; S3/kg). Alternatively, Casa de Los Cerezos, Suytucato 681, San Blas (S4/kg), is open 24hr – just knock at the blue gate; or try Lavaclin, Suecia 400 (daily 8am–8pm; S4/kg).

Police The 24hr tourist police is at Plaza Tupac Amaru s/n (☎084 235 123).

Post office The main office is at Av Sol 800 (Mon–Sat 8am–8pm; Sun 9am–1pm).

Taxis Reliable companies include AloCusco (☎084 222 222).

Tourist police Plaza Túpac Amaru s/n (☎084 249 654); 24hr.

INCA SITES OUTSIDE CUSCO

There are four major Inca sites, all an energetic day's **walk** from Cusco: the megalithic fortress of **Sacsaywamán**, which looms high above the city, the great *huaca* of **Q'enqo**, the fortified hunting lodge of **Pukapukara** and the nearby imperial baths of **Tambomachay**. To start from the top and work your way downhill, take one of the regular **buses** to Pisac leaving from Avenida Tullumayo or Calle Puputi every twenty minutes throughout the day and ask to be dropped off at the highest of the sites, Tambomachay, from where it's an easy two-hour walk back into the centre of Cusco, visiting the above sites in reverse order. The **opening times** for all the sites below are daily 7am–6pm and entry is by Boleto Turístico only (see box, p.741).

Sacsaywamán

From central Cusco, it's quite a steep 2km climb up to the ruins of Sacsaywamán from the Plaza de Armas. Take Calle Suecia, then the first right along Huaynapata until it meets the even narrower Pumacurco going steeply up (left) to a small café-bar. From there, follow the signposted steps all the way up to the ruins.

Because **SACSAYWAMÁN,** was protected by such a steep approach from the town,

9

it only needed defensive walls on one side, and three massive parallel walls zigzag together for some 600m. Little of the inner structures remains, yet these enormous ramparts stand 20m high, unperturbed by past battles, earthquakes and the passage of time. The strength of the mortar-less stonework – one block weighs more than 300 tonnes – is matched by the brilliance of its design: the zigzags expose the flanks of any attackers trying to clamber up. The Inca Pachacutec began work on Sacsaywamán in the 1440s, although it took the labour of some twenty thousand men and nearly a century of work to finish it.

A flat expanse of grassy ground divides the temple from a large outcrop of volcanic rock, called the **Rodadero** ("precipice"), which is used today during the colourful spectacle of the **Inti Raymi festival** held annually during the summer solstice in June.

Q'enqo

From the warden's hut on the northeastern edge of Sacsaywamán, take the track towards the Cusco–Pisac road; **Q'ENQO** is just over the other side of the main road.

This great stone or *huaca* revered by the Inca is carved with a complex pattern of steps, seats, geometric reliefs and puma designs, and illustrates the critical role of the Rock Cult in the realm of Inca cosmological beliefs; the name of the temple means "zigzag" and refers to the patterns carved into the upper western edge of the stone. At an annual festival priests would pour *chicha* or sacrificial llama blood into a bowl at the serpent-like top of the main channel; if it flowed out through the left-hand bifurcation, this was a bad omen for the fertility of the year to come. If, on the other hand, it continued the full length of the zigzag and poured onto the rocks below, this was a good omen.

Pukapukara

A relatively small ruin named **PUKAPUKARA** ("Red Fort", due to the pinkish hue of the rock) is situated right beside the main Cusco–Pisac road, a two-hour cross-country walk uphill from Q'enqo. Although in many ways reminiscent of a small European castle, Pukapukara is more likely to have been a hunting lodge, or out-of-town lodgings for the emperor, than simply a defensive position. Thought to have been built by the Emperor Pachacutec, it commands views towards glaciers to the south of the Cusco Valley.

Tambomachay

TAMBOMACHAY, otherwise known as "El Baño del Inca" ("The Bath of the Inca"), less than fifteen minutes' walk away along a signposted track from Pukapukara, is an impressive temple, evidently a place for ritual as well as physical cleansing and purification.

The ruins consist of three tiered platforms. The top one holds four trapezoidal niches that may have been used as seats; on the next level, underground water emerges directly from a hole at the base of the stonework, and from here cascades down to the bottom platform, creating a cold shower just about high enough for an Inca to stand under. On this platform the spring water splits into two channels, both pouring the last metre down to ground level. The superb quality of the stonework suggests that its use was restricted to the higher nobility, who perhaps used the baths only on ceremonial occasions.

Tipón

Around 25km east out of Cusco, the town of **TIPÓN** is famous for its Sunday lunches, featuring oven-roasted *cuy* (guinea pig), and its ruins – a large structure made up of several terraces and one of the few working examples of Inca irrigation systems, with fountains and water channels covering the area. From the town, it's a steep one-hour-thirty-minute climb (or 20min taxi ride; S20 each way) to the ruins. To get here take an Urcos-bound *colectivo* from Avenida de la Cultura, one block west of the Hospital Regional, and ask to be let out at the Tipón turn-off (45min; S5). To get back, squeeze onto a passing bus on the main road.

Pikillaqta and Rumicolca

One of the few well-preserved pre-Inca sites in the area, **Pikillaqta** was built by the Wari culture and comprises a sprawling residential compound surrounded by a defensive wall in the midst of rolling grasslands. It is the earliest example in the region of two-storey buildings. Further on, on the opposite side of the road, is **Rumicolca**, the huge Inca gateway to Cusco, built on top of what used to be a massive Wari aqueduct. The contrast between the fine Inca stonework and the cruder earlier constructions of the Wari is quite striking. You can easily visit this site together with Tipón in a day-trip from Cusco; otherwise, stay on an Urcos-bound bus for an extra 5km; the site is 1km from the main road.

The Sacred Valley and Machu Picchu

The Río Urubamba valley, also known as El Valle Sagrado or the **Sacred Valley**, traces its winding, astonishingly beautiful course to the northwest of Cusco. Standing guard over the two extremes of the Sacred Valley road, the ancient **Inca citadels** of Pisac and Ollantaytambo are among the most evocative ruins in Peru, while the small Andean towns of Pisac and Chinchero really come into their own on Tuesdays, Thursdays and Sundays – market days – when villagers in colourful regional dress gather to sell their crafts and produce.

Beyond Ollantaytambo the route becomes too tortuous for any road to follow, the valley closes in around the rail tracks, and the Río Urubamba begins to race and twist below **Machu Picchu** itself, the most famous ruin in South America and a place that – no matter how jaded you are or how commercial it seems – stops you in your tracks.

Unless you're walking the Inca Trail, you will inevitably spend at least one night in Machu Picchu town, commonly referred to as **Aguas Calientes**. Given the town's brutalist architecture and overpriced accommodation and eating establishments, it is advised not to linger here for too long.

A plethora of tour companies runs day-trips to Machu Picchu (which have to be booked in advance), as well as whirlwind day tours of the Sacred Valley (from S30 upwards, plus entry to the sites). While guiding standards vary, it's a good way of seeing sights that are far apart, especially if you don't have much time, though it's more rewarding to linger and explore the valley at your leisure.

PISAC

A vital Inca road once snaked its way up the canyon that enters the Sacred Valley at **PISAC**, and the ruined citadel that sits at the entrance to the gorge controlled a route connecting the Inca Empire with Paucartambo, on the borders of the eastern jungle. Nowadays, the village is best known for its Tuesday, Thursday and Sunday craft **market**, held on the town's main square, the Plaza Constitución, though most stalls are open all week, with fewer crowds on non-market days. The main local **fiesta** – Virgen del Carmen (July 15–18) – is a good alternative to the simultaneous but more remote and raucous Paucartambo festival of the same name, with processions, music, dance groups, the usual fire-cracking celebrations, and food stalls around the plaza.

WHAT TO SEE AND DO

It takes roughly two hours to climb directly to the **citadel** (daily 8am–5pm; entry by Boleto Turístico), heading up through the agricultural terraces still in use at the back of Plaza Constitución. A better option is to take a taxi to the top of the ruins (20min; from S20 one-way, or negotiate a return fare with waiting time) and then walk back down, visiting all four archeological complexes on the way.

Set high above a valley floor patchworked by patterned fields and rimmed by centuries of terracing amid

9

giant landslides, the stonework and panoramas at the citadel are magnificent. On a large natural balcony, a semicircle of buildings is gracefully positioned under row upon row of fine stone terraces thought to represent a partridge's wing (*pisac* means "partridge"). In the upper sector of the ruins, the main **Temple of the Sun** is the equal of anything at Machu Picchu. Above the temple lie still more ruins, largely unexcavated, and the honeycombed cliff wall opposite the fortress is the handiwork of agile grave robbers who desecrated the cliff tombs.

ARRIVAL AND DEPARTURE

By bus From Cusco, Calca-bound buses via Pisac leave from Tullumayo 207 (5am–7pm, every 15min; 1hr), returning from the main street where they drop you off in Pisac throughout the day.

ACCOMMODATION AND EATING

Blue Llama Plaza de Armas. Part restaurant, part shop, the calm pink and blue shades and soothing music here make for a relaxed spot to grab a meal (S13–21). There's also a vegetarian menu (S18). Free wi-fi. Daily 7.30am–8.30pm.

Club Royal Inca ☏ 084 203 064, ⊛ hotel-royal-inca -sacred-valley.com. An excellent place to camp, 1.5km out of town. Not only do you get access to the club's facilities, such as the restaurant and Olympic-sized pool, but each fenced-off camping area comes with barbecue, an electricity plug and a light. Camping S̲2̲0̲

Samana Wasi Plaza de Armas 509 ☏ 084 203 133. Located right on the main square, this guesthouse offers clean tiled rooms and wi-fi throughout. Those with shared bath have lovely views over the square. The in-house restaurant offers plenty of trout dishes (S20), as well as meat favourites (S14–20). S̲4̲5̲

Ulrike's Café C Pardo 613. Set over two floors and a roof-top terrace, this German-run restaurant with wi-fi is a pleasant place to hang out. Thin-crust pizzas are baked in the wood-burning oven on Tues, Thurs, Sat and Sun, although the burgers (S13) remain their bestseller. Set menu S20. Daily 8am–9pm.

URUBAMBA AND AROUND

Spread-out **URUBAMBA** lies about 80km from Cusco via Pisac or around 60km via Chinchero. Although it has little in the way of obvious historic interest, the town has numerous connections to other parts of the Sacred Valley and is situated in the shadow of the beautiful Chicon and Pumahuanca glaciers.

The attractive Plaza de Armas is laidback and attractive, with palm trees and a couple of pines surrounded by interesting topiary. At the heart of the plaza is a small fountain topped by a maize corn, but it is dominated by the red sandstone **Iglesia San Pedro**. At weekends there's a large **market** on Jirón Palacio, which serves the local villages.

WHAT TO SEE AND DO

Urubamba makes an ideal base from which to explore the mountains and lower hills around the Sacred Valley, which are filled with sites. The eastern side of the valley is formed by the **Cordillera Urubamba**, a range of snowcapped peaks dominated by the summits of Chicon and Veronica. Many of the ravines can be hiked, and on the trek up from the town you'll have stupendous views of Chicon. **Moray**, a stunning Inca site, lies about

6km north of Maras village on the Chinchero side of the river, within a two- to three-hour walk from Urubamba. Make a circuit to include the spectacular Maras salt flats.

ARRIVAL AND DEPARTURE

By bus From Cusco, buses leave from Av Grau 525, while frequent *colectivos* depart from along Pavitos; both arrive at the Urubamba Terminal Terrestre on the main highway, 1km west of town via either Pisac or Chinchero (5am–7pm; every 20min; 1hr–1hr 30min). Buses depart every 15min from Urubamba to Cusco (1hr 30min), Pisac (1hr) and Ollantaytambo (40min). A *mototaxi* into town will set you back S1.

ACCOMMODATION

Hostal Los Perales Pasaje Arenales 102 ☎ 084 201 151, ⓦ ecolodgeurubamba.com. This pleasant guesthouse features six neat rooms set around a large overgrown garden. There's table tennis and a billiards table, and an internet café arriving soon. The congenial owner, who speaks some English, also offers apartments sleeping six, all fully equipped with kitchen. **S50**

Misky Illary Wasi C Belen Cuadra 6 ☎ 084 201 332, ⓔ inturduran@hotmail.com. Rooms here have cable TV, private bath and wi-fi, although the decor is a bit on the chintzy side. There's also a kitchen for guests' use. **S45**

EATING

Los Geranios Av Cabo Conchatupa s/n ☎ 084 201 093. Secluded booths at this restaurant/hostel are set around an interior garden humming with caged canaries, parakeets and parrots. The food is local and good value, with dishes such as *pollo a la plancha* (grilled chicken) and *trucha frita* (fried trout; S17). There are also rooms for rent (S70). Daily 11am–5pm.

Tres Keros Av Sr de Torrechayoc. Located on the top floor of a pleasant wooden building, this is probably Urubamba's best restaurant. Try the much-sought-after *lomo saltado*

flambeado con Pisco (fillet steak flambéed with pisco; S38). Wed–Mon noon–3.30pm & 6.15–9.30pm.

OLLANTAYTAMBO

On the approach to **OLLANTAYTAMBO** from Urubamba, the river runs smoothly between a series of fine Inca terraces that gradually diminish in size as the slopes get steeper and rockier. Built as an Inca administrative centre rather than a town, it's hard not to be impressed by the two huge Inca ruins that loom above the village, or by the foundations that abound in the cobbled backstreets radiating up from the plaza, especially in Calle Medio. Laid out in the form of a maize corncob – and one of the few surviving examples of an Inca grid system – the plan can be seen from vantage points high above it, especially from the hill opposite the fortress. Ollanta is an attractive, laidback village, and a wonderful place in which to linger.

WHAT TO SEE AND DO

The hubs of activity in town are the main **plaza** – the heart of civic life and the scene of traditional folk dancing during festive occasions – and the Inca fortress. Off the central plaza, down Patacalle, there's the recently refurbished **Museo CATCCO** (Mon–Sat 9am–6pm; S5), a small but very interesting museum containing interpretative exhibits in Spanish and English about local history, culture, archeology and natural history. It also has a ceramic workshop where you can buy some good pottery.

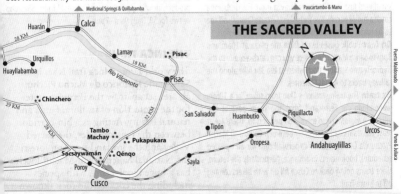

9

Downhill from the plaza, just across the Río Patacancha, is the old Inca Plaza Mañya Raquy, dominated by the town's star attraction – the astonishing Inca ruins atop some steep terraces. Climbing up through the **fortress** (daily 7am–5pm; entrance with Boleto Turístico, see box, p.741), the solid stone terraces, jammed against the natural contours of the cliff, remain frighteningly impressive and the view of the valley from the top is stupendous. Not only was this the site of a major battle in 1536 between the Spaniards and the rebellious Manco Inca, who fought them off before being forced to retreat to the jungle stronghold in Vilcabamba, but this was also a ceremonial centre; note the particularly fine stonework towards the top of the ruins.

Directly across, above the town, are rows of **ruined buildings** originally thought to have been prisons but now believed to have been granaries. To the front of these it's quite easy to make out a gigantic, rather grumpy-looking profile of a face carved out of the rock, possibly an **Inca sculpture** of Wiracochan – commonly referred to as Tunupa – the mythical messenger from Wiracocha, the major creator god of the Incas. It's a stiff forty-minute climb to the viewpoint; follow the signpost from Waqta, off the Plaza de Armas.

ARRIVAL AND DEPARTURE

By bus and colectivo From Cusco, several buses daily go via Urubamba from Av Grau 525, as well as numerous *colectivos* and *combis* from Pavitos in Cusco (between 6am–5pm; 1hr 30min–2hr) and Urubamba (30min). From Ollanta, Cusco-bound tourist buses (2hr) leave from the small yard just outside the railway station. For Urubamba catch a *combi* or *colectivo* from the Mercado Central, off the southeastern corner of the plaza (every 15min; 30min).

On foot Public buses leave from the plaza at 10am and 3pm to Santa María; from here you can catch a *combi* to the HydroElectric Station, from where it is a 3hr hike along the railway tracks to Aguas Calientes.

By train The train station is 1km from town, or a 10min walk along Av Ferrocarril from the main part of the village. A *mototaxi* into town is S1 per person. There are at least ten trains daily each way between Cusco and Machu Picchu via Ollanta (check ⊛perurail.com for an updated schedule); book tickets in advance, particularly the return, since trains going back to Cusco fill up with hikers coming off the Inca Trail.

ACCOMMODATION

Chaska Wasi Plaza de Armas s/n ☎084 204 045, ⊛hostalchaskawasi.com. Named after Chaska, the cat who roams the premises, this hostel has colourful single-sex and mixed dorms with feline murals. The rooftop terrace has great views over town and the nearby Inca ruins. Rates include breakfast and there's wi-fi and a book exchange. Dorms S̲2̲5̲, doubles S̲5̲0̲

KB Tambo Hostal Ventiderio s/n ☎084 204 035, ⊛kbperu.com. This welcoming guesthouse offers a range of spacious rooms, some with views over the surrounding mountains and Inca ruins, others overlooking the leafy flower garden that attracts an array of tweeting humming-birds. Their popular hiking and mountain-biking tours are worth checking out. S̲6̲0̲

Hostal El Tambo C del Horno s/n ☎084 385 770, ⊛hostaleltambo.com. The rooms at this wonderful place are set on two floors and look over a pleasant interior garden with hammocks. Local fabrics and paintings decorate the interiors, all with beautiful hardwood floors. Rates include breakfast and wi-fi. Discounts for large groups. S̲5̲0̲

EATING

La Esquina Plaza de Armas. Baked goods fresh from the oven every day, including *empanadas*, breads and cakes, while the coffee is sourced from a local artisanal producer. Salads (S10–15), soups (S10) and sandwiches (S9–17), as well as all-day breakfasts (S5–15), are on offer. Free wi-fi. Daily 7am–8pm.

★ **Hearts Café** Av Ventiderio s/n. This wonderful little café serves chunky home-made soups (S10), huge salads (S10) and a range of international dishes (mains S14–24.50), including plenty of veggie options. The bread is freshly baked and the cookies and pies (S8) are all home-made. Profits go out to the local community. Free wi-fi. Daily 7am–8.45pm.

★ **Tutti Amore** Av Estación s/n. This little ice-cream joint produces over eighty flavours a year, solely using local produce including all manner of seasonal fruits. S5/scoop or two for S8. Daily 9am–7pm.

THE INCA TRAIL

The world-famous **Inca Trail** is set in the **Sanctuario Histórico de Machu Picchu**, an area set apart by the Peruvian state for the protection of its flora, fauna and natural beauty. Acting as a bio-corridor between the Cusco Andes, the Sacred Valley and the lowland Amazon forest, the National Sanctuary of Machu Picchu has a huge biodiversity, with species including the cock-of-the-rock (known

THE INCA TRAIL: WHEN AND HOW TO DO IT

Consider the **season** when booking your Inca Trail. The dry season runs approximately from May to October – expect blistering sun during the daytime and sub-zero temperatures at night. During the rainy season of November to April the temperature is more constant but, naturally, the path is muddier and can be slippery, and afternoon thunderstorms are the norm. The trail is closed for restoration during the entire month of February.

In recent years, due to the growing popularity of the Inca Trail, the sanctuary authority, the Unidad de Gestión del Santuario Histórico de Machu Picchu, has imposed a **limit of 500 people a day** on the Inca Trail, and they must be accompanied by a registered tour operator. By law, permits must be purchased thirty days before departure on the trail with the name and passport number of each trekker. In practice, however, it is usually necessary to book four to six months in advance to make sure you get a space on the trail. Currently permits cost around US$100 per person, including entrance to Machu Picchu – this permit should always be included in the price of your trek. Check the government website Ⓦ www.machupicchu.gob.pe for permit availability. Always carefully research the **tour company** (see p.746) that you choose, and make sure you know exactly what you are paying for, as well as what conditions your porters will be working under (see box, p.756). Make sure you enquire about the toilets used on the trek, as more reliable companies use portable toilets, thereby avoiding the facilities at the campsites that are used by hundreds of people every day.

Prices vary considerably between US$300 and US$750, and although a higher price doesn't always reflect genuine added value, usually the better and more responsible companies will have higher expenses to cover (for better food, equipment, fair wages, and so on). Check what's included in the price: train tickets (which class), quality of tent, roll mat, sleeping bag, porter to carry rucksack and sleeping bag (or if not, how much a personal porter will cost), bus down from ruins, exactly which meals, drinking water for the first two days, and what transport to the start of the trail.

As far as **preparations** go, the most important thing is to acclimatize, preferably allowing at least three days in Cusco if you've flown straight from sea level, because altitude sickness will seriously ruin your travel plans.

If you don't want to hike for four days, the **two-day Inca Trail** is a good option. It starts at Km104 of the Panamerican Highway, 8km from Machu Picchu; the footbridge here leads to a steep climb (3–4hr) past Chachabamba to reach Wiñay Wayna (see p.756), where you join the remainder of the Inca Trail.

as *tunkis* in Peru), spectacled bear (*tremarctos ornatus*) and condor (*vultur gryphus*). Although just one of a multitude of paths across remote areas of the Andes, what makes the 33km Inca Trail so popular is the fabulous treasure of **Machu Picchu** at the end.

SETTING OFF AND DAY ONE

An early departure from Cusco (around 5am) is followed by a three-hour drive to Ollantaytambo (where you can buy last-minute supplies, including recycled walking sticks). The trail begins at **Piscacucho**, at Km82, where you cross the Urubamba River after signing in at the first checkpoint on the trail. The first day consists of a 12km stretch, beginning at an elevation of 2600m and gaining 400m during the course of the day. The gentle incline of the trail first follows the river and passes a viewpoint with the terraced Inca ruins of the **Llaqtapata** fortress below, before it descends past rock formations to the first night's campsite at **Huayllabamba**. Along the way you pass the villages of Miskay and Hatunchaca, where you can buy (overpriced) snacks and water, as well as *chicha* (traditional fermented corn beer).

The campsite at Huayllabamba is very basic, and there are no showers, though you may consider bathing in the icy stream. If you haven't acclimatized and don't feel well, then Huayllabamba is the last place from which it's fairly easy to return to Cusco; beyond, it's nearly impossible.

9

PORTER WELFARE

Even though the Peruvian government has recently introduced regulations, stipulating that the Inca Trail porters must be paid a set minimum wage and only carry a set amount, abuses of staff by unscrupulous tour agencies still occur, especially on the alternative trails, where you may find your porters eating leftovers, carrying huge weights and sleeping without adequate cold-weather gear. Avoid doing the Inca Trail for the cheapest price possible, and be prepared to pay more by going with a reputable company that treats its staff well (see box, p.746). When trekking, keep an eye on the working conditions of the porters, offer to share your snacks and water, ask the porters about how they are treated, and don't forget to tip them at the end of the trek (around US$20 per porter is fair; a bit more if you had a personal porter). If you find evidence of abuse, don't hesitate to report it at your nearest iPerú office.

DAY TWO

The second day is the toughest part of the hike – an ascent of 1100m to the Abra Huarmihuañusca, or **Dead Woman's Pass** (4200m), the highest point on the trail, followed by a steep descent to the second night's campsite at Paq'aymayo. There is little shade or shelter, so prepare for diverse weather conditions, as cold mist sometimes descends quickly, obscuring visibility.

After an hour or so, you reach the campsite of Ayapata (where some groups camp on the first night), where there are bathrooms and a snack stall. Another one hour thirty minutes to two hours along a combination of dirt path and steep stone steps through mossy forest takes you up to the second campsite of Llulluchapampa, your last chance to purchase water or snacks.

The views from the pass itself are stupendous, but it gets cold rapidly. From here the trail drops down into the Paq'aymayo Valley. The descent takes up to two hours, but you're rewarded by sight of the attractive **campsite** by the river (3600m), complete with showers (cold water only).

DAY THREE

This is the longest day but also the most enjoyable, with some of the loveliest scenery. It takes forty minutes up the steep, exposed trail to reach the ruins of the Inca fortress of Runkurakay, then another twenty minutes of stone steps and steep dirt track before you pass the false summit with a small lake before arriving at the **second pass** – Abra de Runkuracay (3950m), from which you

can see the snow-covered mountains of the Cordillera Vilcabamba.

About an hour's descent along some steep stone steps leads to the Inca ruins of **Sayaqmarka**, a compact fortress perched on a mountain spur, overlooking the valley below. From Sayaqmarka you make your way down into increasingly dense cloudforest where delicate orchids begin to appear among the trees, and then up to the Chaquicocha campsite, where some groups break for lunch. The one-hour hike between Chaquicocha and the **third pass** – Abra de Phuyupatamarka (3650m) – is the loveliest bit of the hike; the trail runs through stretches of cloudforest, with hummingbirds flitting from flower to flower and stupendous views of the valley. The trail winds down to the impressive ruin of **Phuyupatamarca** – "Town Above the Clouds" – where there are five small ceremonial baths and, in the wet season, fresh running water. Some groups camp here on the third night and wake to a starry milky way at 4am, followed by breathtaking views of the surrounding range of glaciers at sunset.

It's a rough two- to three-hour descent to the final campsite. The first section comprises steep stone steps for forty minutes, followed by gentler stretches of dirt track. When you come to the fork in the trail, the right branch goes down to the next ruin, a citadel almost as impressive as Machu Picchu, **Wiñay Wayna** ("Forever Young"), where most groups will spend their third night. There is basic **accommodation** here and a large restaurant/bar area where you can treat your group and porters to a round of drinks. Most groups will **camp** outside the structure, but still enjoy the hot showers.

To reach **Intipunku** ("The Sun Gate") for sunrise the next day, most groups form a bottleneck at the Wiñay Wayna guard post long before it opens at 5.30am; groups are no longer allowed to leave the campsite any earlier. A well-marked track from Wiñay Wayna skirts the mountain, leading you along some gentle ups and downs for about an hour before you reach a spectacularly steep set of stone steps – the last ascent of the hike – which leads to a pathway paved by the Inca. This in turn culminates in a large stone archway, Intipunku, where you catch your first sight of Machu Picchu – a stupendous moment, however exhausted you might be. From Intipunku, to reach the main ruins, it's an easy thirty- to forty-minute descent.

MACHU PICCHU

The most dramatic and enchanting of the Inca citadels lies suspended on an extravagantly terraced saddle between two prominent peaks. **MACHU PICCHU** (daily 6am–5pm; S120) is one of the greatest of all South American tourist attractions, set against a vast, scenic backdrop of forested mountains that spike up from the deep valleys of the Urubamba and its tributaries.

With many legends and theories surrounding the position of Machu Picchu (meaning "ancient mountain"), most archeologists agree that the sacred geography of the site helped the Inca Pachacutec decide where to build it. Its intactness owes much to the fact that it was never discovered by the Spaniards, and the atmosphere, as you wander around, drinking it all in, is second to none.

Unknown to the outside world, for many centuries the site of Machu Picchu lay forgotten, except by local Quechua people. In the 1860s it was first looted by a pair of German adventurers and then rediscovered by the US explorer **Hiram Bingham**, who came upon it on July 24, 1911.

It was a fantastic find, not least because it was still relatively intact, without the usual ravages of either conquistadors or tomb robbers. Bingham was led to the site by an 11-year-old local boy, and it didn't take long for him to see that he had come across some important ancient Inca terraces. After a little more exploration Bingham found the fine white stonework, which led him to

---

ARRIVING AT MACHU PICCHU

If coming from the Inca Trail, you'll need to descend to the main entrance and register your entrance ticket before doubling back to the ruins. Or, if you're arriving from Aguas Calientes, you can either hike up to the ruins (1–3hr, depending on how fit you are) along a clearly marked footpath that's much shorter than following the winding paved road, or take one of the **buses** that run throughout the day (every 10min, 5.30am–5.30pm).

If you're travelling independently, it's best to buy your **entrance ticket** to Machu Picchu at the INC (Instituto Nacional de Cultura) office in the main square before going up to the ruins; that way you'll avoid the long queues at the ticket office at the site itself.

There is no **accommodation** near Machu Picchu itself apart from the hideously overpriced *Machu Picchu Sanctuary Lodge*, located right at the entrance to the ruins. The lodge serves up a good lunchtime buffet that will set you back US$35; otherwise, there are expensive sandwiches (S20–25) to be had at the café by the gate. It's best to bring your own pack-lunch from Aguas Calientes, although bear in mind you must consume your food outside the ruins. Water bottles are allowed in.

There are two **left-luggage** offices: one next to the entrance to the ruins (S5) and one just as you go inside (S3); you must check in any large rucksacks and camping equipment. There are toilets just outside the entrance (S1) and this is where you can also hire a guide (approximately S100 for a 2hr tour, per group), though they tend to be of varying quality.

When walking around the ruins, stick to the designated trails, or the zealous wardens will blow their whistles at you.

9

believe (incorrectly, as it transpired) that Machu Picchu was the lost city of Vilcabamba, the site of the Incas' last refuge from the Spanish conquistadors. Bingham returned in 1912 and 1915 to clear the thick forest from the site and in the process made off with thousands of artefacts; the Peruvian government is currently trying to reclaim them from Yale University, where they are kept.

While archeologists are still not clear as to what Machu Picchu's purpose was, there is a general consensus that it was an important religious and ceremonial centre, given the layout and quantity of temples, as well as the quality of the stonework. The citadel may have been built as an administrative, political and agricultural centre, while the existence of numerous access routes to Machu Picchu has led others to believe that it was a trading post between the Andes and the Amazon. Conflicting theories aside, there is no denying Machu Picchu's great importance to the Inca culture.

WHAT TO SEE AND DO

Though more than 1000m lower than Cusco, Machu Picchu seems much higher, constructed as it is on dizzying slopes overlooking a U-curve in the Río Urubamba. More than a hundred flights of stone steps interconnect its palaces, temples, storehouses and terraces, and the outstanding views command not only the valley below in both directions but also extend to the snowy peaks around Salcantay. Wherever you stand in the ruins, spectacular terraces (some of which are once again being cultivated) can be seen slicing across ridiculously steep cliffs, transforming mountains into suspended gardens.

Unless you're coming off the Inca Trail, you'll be following the footpath from the main entrance to the ruins proper. For a superb view of the ruins, take the staircase up to the thatched guardian's hut and the **funerary rock** behind it; this is thought to have been a place where mummified nobility were laid due to its association with a nearby graveyard where Bingham found evidence of many burials, some of which were obviously royal.

Temple of the Sun and the Royal Tomb

Entering the main ruins through the ancient doorway, you soon come across the **Temple of the Sun** on your right, also known as the *Torreón* – a wonderful, semicircular, tower-like temple displaying some of Machu Picchu's finest stonework and built for astronomical purposes. Its carved steps and smoothly joined stone blocks fit neatly into the existing relief of a natural boulder, which served as some kind of altar. During the June and December solstices, the first rays of the sun shine directly into the eastern and western windows respectively, illuminating the tower perfectly. The temple is cordoned off, but you can appreciate it from above.

Below the Temple of the Sun is a cave with a stepped altar and tall niches, known as the **Royal Tomb**, despite the fact that neither graves nor mummies have ever been found here. Along the staircase leading up to the Temple of the Sun, you'll find sixteen small **fountains**, the most beautiful at the top.

The Sacred Plaza

Another staircase ascends to the old quarry, past the **Royal Area**, so-called due to the imperial-style Inca stonework. Turn right and cross the quarry to reach the **Sacred Plaza**, flanked by an important temple complex. Dominating the southeastern edge of the plaza, the attractive **Three-Windowed Temple** has unusually large windows, perfectly framing the mountains beyond the Urubamba river valley. Next to it is the **Principal Temple**, so-called because of the fine stonework of its three high main walls; the damage to the rear right corner was caused by the ground sinking, as opposed to a construction flaw. Directly opposite the Principal Temple, you'll find the **House of the High Priest**.

Intihuatana

An elaborately carved stone stairway behind the **Sacristy** brings you to one of the jewels of the site, the **Intihuatana**, loosely translated from Quechua as the "hitching post of the sun". This fascinating carved rock, sometimes mistakenly referred

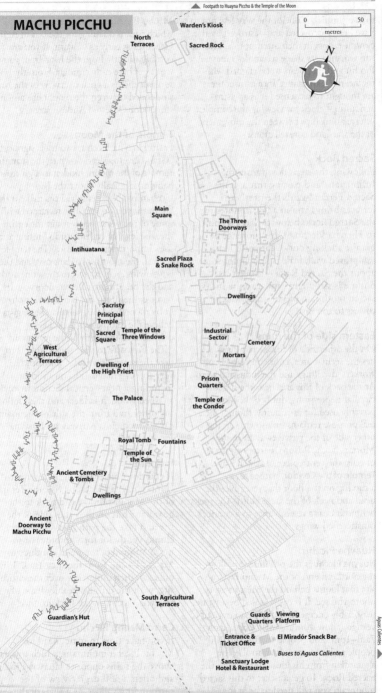

MACHU PICCHU

Warden's Kiosk

North Terraces

Sacred Rock

0   50
metres

N

Main Square

The Three Doorways

Intihuatana

Sacred Plaza & Snake Rock

Dwellings

Sacristy

Principal Temple

Sacred Square

Temple of the Three Windows

Industrial Sector

Cemetery

West Agricultural Terraces

Mortars

Dwelling of the High Priest

Prison Quarters

The Palace

Temple of the Condor

Royal Tomb

Fountains

Temple of the Sun

Ancient Cemetery & Tombs

Dwellings

Ancient Doorway to Machu Picchu

South Agricultural Terraces

Guards Quarters

Viewing Platform

Guardian's Hut

Entrance & Ticket Office

El Miradór Snack Bar

Buses to Aguas Calientes

Funerary Rock

Sanctuary Lodge Hotel & Restaurant

Aguas Calientes

Machu Picchu Mountain, Inti Punku gateway, Inca Trail & Wiñay Wayna

9

to as a sundial, is one of the very few not to have been discovered and destroyed by the conquistadors in their attempt to eradicate sun worship. Its shape resembles Huayna Picchu and it appears to be aligned with the nearby mountains. Inca astronomers are thought to have used it as an astro-agricultural clock for viewing the complex interrelationships between the movements of the stars and constellations.

Sacred Rock
Following the steps down from the Intihuatana and passing through the Sacred Plaza towards the northern terraces brings you in a few minutes to the **Sacred Rock**, below the access point to Huayna Picchu. A great lozenge of granite sticking out of the earth like a sculptured wall, little is known for sure about the Sacred Rock – though its outline is strikingly similar to the Inca's sacred mountain of Putukusi, which towers to the east.

Eastern side of the ruins
On the other side of the Sacred Plaza lies the secular area, consisting largely of workers' dwellings and the industrial sector. At the back of this area lie some shallow circular depressions, dubbed the **Mortars**, possibly used for astronomy, though their real purpose remains unknown. On the other side of the passageway from the Mortars lie the **Prison Quarters** – a maze of cells, the centrepiece of which is the **Temple of the Condor**, named after a carving on the floor that resembles the head and neck of the sacred bird. The rocks behind it bear a resemblance to a condor's outstretched wings.

Huayna Picchu
Huayna Picchu is the prominent peak at the northern end of the Machu Picchu site that looms behind the ruins in every photo you see. It is easily scaled by anyone reasonably energetic and with no trace of vertigo (allow 40min–1hr); access (daily 7am–1pm; 200 people at 7am and 200 people at 10am; free) is controlled by a guardian from his kiosk just behind the Sacred Rock. To get a ticket to this sacred mountain you will need to be at the Machu Picchu gate when it opens, which means queuing for the bus in Aguas Calientes as early as 4.30am. If you are coming directly from the Inca Trail, you won't get here early enough. From the summit there's a great overview of the ruins suspended between the mountains among stupendous forested Andean scenery.

Temple of the Moon
From Huayna Picchu, two trails signposted "Gran Caverna" lead down to the stunning **Temple of the Moon**, hidden in a grotto hanging magically above the Río Urubamba. Not many visitors make it this far, but if you do you'll be rewarded with some of the best stonework in the entire site, the level of craftsmanship hinting at the site's importance to the Inca. The temple is set in the mouth of a dark cave and there is a flowing, natural feel to the stonework and the beautifully recessed doorway. Its name comes from the fact that it is often lit by moonlight, but some archeologists believe the temple was most likely dedicated to the spirit of the mountain.

The best way to visit the temple is to take the steep downhill trail from the very top of Huayna Picchu (30min, including a near-vertical section involving a lashed wooden ladder) and then follow the other trail from the side of the main cave, which ends partway up Huayna Picchu (1hr).

Intipunku
If you don't have the time or energy to climb Huayna Picchu or visit the Temple of the Moon, simply head back to the guardian's hut on the other side of the site and take the path below it, which climbs gently for forty minutes or so up to **Intipunku**, the main entrance to Machu Picchu from the Inca Trail. This offers an incredible view over the entire site, with the unmistakeable shape of Huayna Picchu in the background.

Cerro Machu Picchu
If you have time to spare, head for Machu Picchu mountain, which towers above the ruins opposite Huayna Picchu and offers a 360-degree view of the surrounding valleys, as well as of the

ruins and Huayna Picchu. It's a longer climb; most people take one hour twenty minutes to two hours to reach the top, but the trail is not as vertigo-inducing as Huayna Picchu and you can climb at your leisure; there are no daily quotas and you will have the view largely to yourself (as opposed to the overcrowded Huayna Picchu). Take the path towards Intipunku and then follow the signpost to the right before leaving the ruins.

Inca drawbridge

If you don't suffer from vertigo, there's an excellent scenic and level twenty-minute walk that you can take from the Hut of the Caretaker of the Funerary Rock through the cemetery to the Inca drawbridge. Follow the narrow path along the tops of the southern terraces, along the side of the cliff, and over a man-made ledge until you reach the barrier several hundred metres above the bridge, which spans the gap in the Inca road that was built on a sheer cliff face. You're no longer allowed to get close to it, as someone fell

to their death from it a few years ago, but it's certainly an impressive sight.

AGUAS CALIENTES

Anyone wishing to come to Machu Picchu will invariably pass through the settlement of **AGUAS CALIENTES** (the official name is "Machu Picchu Pueblo", though it never stuck), which is connected to the ruins by bus, though the town itself is only accessible by train from Cusco via the Sacred Valley. Its warm, humid climate and surrounding landscape of towering mountains covered in cloudforest make it a welcome change to Cusco, though it has even more of a touristy feel to it: every other building in this little town seems to be either a hotel, restaurant or a souvenir shop and you constantly run the gauntlet of persistent touts. If you wish to see Machu Picchu at sunrise and to enjoy the surrounding scenery when it is not overrun by day-trippers, you'll be staying here for at least one night.

AGUAS CALIENTES

0 — 50 metres

N

Mariana (Laundry)

Hot Springs

Parque Wiñay Wayna

Banco de La Nación

Police

Bank

PLAZA

School

Market

Buses for Machu Picchu ★

INC Office: Machu Picchu Tickets

i I-Peru

Bus Ticket Office

Río Aguas Calientes

Caja Municipal

Football Field

Mercado Artesanal

Train Station

Train Ticket Office

AVENIDA IMPERIO DO LOS INCAS

Río Vilcanota

Río Alcamayo

WIÑAY WAYNA

CHASKA TIKA

ACCOMMODATION
Camping Municipal	4
Margarita's House	6
Pirwa	2
Hostal Quilla	3
Rupa Wasi Condor House	1
Super Tramp Hostel	5

EATING & DRINKING
Bistro Indio Feliz	3
La Boulangerie de Paris	7
Captain's Bar	3
Cupido	6
Govinda	2
Inka Wasi	5
Ollantay	4
Toto's	8
Tree House	1

Sacred Valley (Cusco)

9

TRAIN JOURNEY TO MACHU PICCHU

The new, improved service offered by PeruRail between Cusco and Machu Picchu enhances the thrill of riding tracks through such fantastic scenery even further by offering good service and largely comfortable carriages. If you can afford to, pay the extra US$24 for a Vistadome seat; not only do you get a better view, but there's also leg room – something conspicuously absent from the "backpacker" carriages.

Daily rumbling out of **Cusco** (see p.745), the train zigzags its way through the backstreets, where little houses cling to the steep valley slopes. It takes a while to rise out of the teacup-like valley, but once it attains the high plateau above, the train rolls through fields and past highland villages before eventually dropping rapidly down into the Urubamba Valley using several major track switchbacks, which means you get to see some of the same scenery twice. It reaches the Sacred Valley floor just before getting into **Ollantaytambo**, where you can already see scores of terraced fields and, in the distance, more Inca temple and storehouse constructions. The train continues down the valley, stopping briefly at Km88, where the Inca Trail sometimes starts, then following the Río Urubamba as the valley gets tighter and the mountain more forested and precipitous. The end of the line these days is usually the new station at **Aguas Calientes** (see below).

WHAT TO SEE AND DO

The town's main attraction (besides Machu Picchu) is the natural **thermal bath** (daily 5am–8pm; S10), which is particularly welcome after a few days on the Inca Trail. Several shops rent towels and bathing suits near the entrance.

There is also a **hiking trail** (around 90min each way; closed at the time of writing) up the sacred mountain of Putukusi, starting just outside of town, a couple of hundred metres down on the left if you follow the railway track towards the ruins. The walk offers stupendous views of the town and across to Machu Picchu, but watch out for the small, venomous snakes. It is also not for the faint-hearted as the trail is very steep in parts (some sections have been replaced by ladders) and very narrow.

ARRIVAL AND DEPARTURE

By train You are most likely to arrive in Aguas Calientes by train (see box above). To get to the heart of the town, walk through the market and cross one of the bridges. Trains connect Aguas Calientes with Poroy (for Cusco) via Ollantaytambo. The options to Cusco are Backpacker/New Backpacker, 8 daily between 9.56am and 9.45pm, S99–174; Vistadome, daily at 3.20pm, S206; Hiram Bingham, daily except Sun, S853. All take 3–4hr.

INFORMATION

Tourist information iPerú (Mon–Sat 9am–1pm & 2–6pm, Sun mornings only; ☎084 211 104) has an office just off the main plaza and informative leaflets about the area plus photocopied maps. Next door is the INC office (daily 5.20am–8.45pm) where it's best to buy your entrance ticket to Machu Picchu, as the queues at the site itself are very long.

ACCOMMODATION

Although there is an overwhelming choice of accommodation options, most hostels in Aguas Calientes lack charm; there can be a lot of competition for lodgings during the high season (June–Sept) and the better places need booking a week or two in advance. The check-out time at most hostels is 9–9.30am.

Camping Municipal The municipal campsite is just before the bridge over the Río Urubamba, a 20min walk from Aguas Calientes. The campsite has toilets, showers with intermittent hot water, and cooking facilities. Camping S̄15̄

Margarita's House C Chaska Tika 107 ☎084 211 069, ✉mandorturismo@hotmail.com. Just a short walk away from the train station, Margarita offers simple rooms with private bath. Most are dark as they face the interior courtyard. Rates include breakfast and wi-fi. S̄70̄

Pirwa Tupuc Yupanqui 103 ☎084 244 315, ⓦpirwa hostelscusco.com. No-frills hostel with dorms and doubles, some with private bath. There's a kitchen for guests' use, free breakfast and wi-fi. Call ahead and a staff member will pick you up from the train station. Dorms S̄35̄, doubles S̄100̄

Hostal Quilla Av Pachacutec s/n ☎084 211 009, ⓦcusco places.com/hostalrestaurantquilla. This pleasant little guesthouse has clean and tidy rooms, all with private bath, decorated with local fabrics and ceramic lamps. There's a cosy adjoining restaurant, free wi-fi and computers for guests. S̄80̄

Super Tramp Hostel C Chaska Tika, at Plaza de la Cultura ⓦsupertramphostel.com. This friendly hostel offers a range of dorm rooms sleeping 8–12. Doubles, all with shared bath, are small but comfortable. There's a communal kitchen, a lounge area with cable TV, book exchange, wi-fi and all-day coffee and tea. Dorms <u>S20</u>, doubles <u>S55</u>

EATING AND DRINKING

Since there is enormous competition for customers, you'll perpetually find yourself running the gauntlet of over-eager waiters, all trying to entice you into their particular restaurant, which looks and offers exactly the same dishes as most eateries within sight. Below are the exceptions.

★ **Bistro Indio Feliz** Lloque Yupanqui 3y4 M-12 ☏ 084 211 090. The best restaurant in town has been going for over two decades, serving top-notch French and Peruvian dishes in a unique nautical setting. The set menu (S59) is exceptional value and the pisco sours the largest you'll ever come across. Book ahead. Daily 11am–10pm.

La Boulangerie de Paris Jr. Sinchi Roca. This French-run bakery serves superb freshly baked sweet and savoury pastries, including *empanadas* (S8). With sandwiches (S5–15), quiches (S8), lasagne (S12) and fresh buns (4 for S1), this is a great spot to pick up a packed lunch for Machu Picchu. Daily 7am–9pm.

★ **Captain's Bar** Lloque Yupanqui 3y4 M-12. Located just above Bistro Indio Feliz, this welcoming bar-cum-crêperie is the perfect spot for a drink or two. Pick up one of the instruments or sit at the piano and share your musical talents with the other guests. Happy hour 6–7.30pm. Daily 6pm–2am.

Cupido Alameda Los Artesanos L-1. Statues of Incas with wings and arrows decorate the premises of the town's main club. Split over two floors, the musical flavour here is mainly disco music with a pinch of pop. Cocktails S16. No cover charge. Daily 8pm–3am.

Govinda Pachacutec 20. The only veggie place in town rustles up some tasty dishes blending local produce and all manner of Indian spices. Favourites include the curry rice (S21) and the deliciously fresh natural yogurt (S6–14). Mon–Sat 9am–9pm, occasionally Sun.

★ **TREAT YOURSELF**

Rupa Wasi Condor House C Huanacaure 180 ☏ 084 211 101, ⊛ rupawasi.net. The young conservationist owners here have tried to preserve the original design of the house and maintain the surrounding natural environment; the result is a beautiful eco-friendly lodge with avocado, walnut and native trees. The rustic *Tree House* restaurant is one of the best in town, featuring *novoandina* cuisine, which combines local ingredients with international influences to great effect. They also offer cooking lessons (S108). <u>US$86</u>

Inka Wasi Av Pachacutec 112. This warm and welcoming restaurant-cum-pizzeria serves a range of pizzas (S21–42) cooked in front of your very eyes, as well as pricier local favourites such as *cuy al horno* (roasted guinea pig; S80). Daily 9am–10.30pm.

Ollantay Av Pachacutec 112. This eclectically decorated bar/lounge with an eagle made entirely of nails, and *taitas* (shaman-like dolls) safely locked away in glass cabinets, serves ten flavours of *chilcano* (pisco). There's a darts board, billiards table and the Peruvian game of *sapito*. Cocktails S18. Happy hour 6–10pm. Daily 2pm–late.

Toto's Imperio de los Incas s/n. This warm, rustic restaurant with a crackling open fire to grill meats and views over Urubamba River offers a huge buffet lunch (noon–4pm; S65). There's a popular evening show upstairs (Mon–Fri at 8pm; 45min), featuring a contemporary circus performance. Daily 10am–10pm.

DIRECTORY

Banks BCP on Av Los Incas, next to *Toto's*, Banco de la Nación on Av Los Incas by the police station and Caja Municipal by the Mercado Artesanal all have ATMs, but sometimes run out of money, especially at weekends.

Hospital Ministerio de la Salud by the Mercado Artesanal has a 24hr emergency room (☏ 084 211 161). There's a 24hr pharmacy on the plaza.

Internet Cyber World, on the plaza, has reliable internet (daily 8.30am–10pm; S3/hr). Most restaurants offer wi-fi.

Laundry Mariana on the eastern end of Av Pachacutec (Mon–Sat 7am–9pm; S8/hr).

Police Av Imperio de Los Incas 401 (☏ 084 211 178).

Post Office On the western end of the plaza (Mon–Fri 9am–8pm, Sat 9am–1pm).

ALTERNATIVE INCA TRAILS

As permits to walk the famous Inca Trail become more expensive and the Trail more crowded, many tour operators and individuals have started exploring **alternative Inca Trails**. Many of these offer stunning scenery to rival that of the Inca Trail, as well as ecological biodiversity and in some cases archeological sites larger than Machu Picchu itself. Of the several established alternative trails, only one (Salcantay) takes you close to the site of Machu Picchu. At the time of writing all of these trails can still be done independently, apart from the Salcantay trail that joins the Inca Trail, although it may still be necessary to purchase a **permit** from the INC office in Cusco prior to setting off, and plans are afoot to

9

enforce stricter regulations. For most of them, it is recommended to hire local guides, *arrieros* (muleteers) and mules (around S60 per day for each). For information about requirements to walk the trails see the South American Explorers website ⓦ saexplorers.org.

Salcantay

The most popular of the alternatives, this five- to seven-day hike takes you either as far as the hydroelectric plant (from where it's a short bus and train ride to Aguas Calientes), or to the village of Huayllabamba, where you can join the regular Inca Trail. Beginning in Mollepata, the **first day** is a gentle climb through winding cloudforest trails to Soraypampa. On the **second day** there's a steep climb up to the only high pass on the trail (4750m), at the foot of the Salcantay glacier; the landscape here is sparse and dry. From the pass you descend into cloudforest with views of the verdant canyon below, camping that evening at Colcapampa. On the **third day** a five-hour walk takes you to the jungle town of La Playa, and then it's either an hour's bus ride to the town of Santa Teresa, or a six- to seven-hour walk. From Santa Teresa, you walk along the valley to the hydroelectric plant, from where there are trains to Aguas Calientes (check for the latest schedules).

Alternatively, on the second day you'll descend along the right-hand side of the pass into the valley towards the village of Huayllabamba, and join the Inca Trail there. Buses run from Cusco's Avenida Arcopata to Mollepata every morning (hourly from 5.30am; 3hr).

Choquequirao

A trek to the archeological site of **Choquequirao** and back will take four or five days. Believed to be much larger than Machu Picchu, Choquequirao is only forty percent uncovered, and is a much more authentic experience as it still receives few visitors and you can find yourself wandering alone among huge ruined walls covered with cacti and exotic flowers. There are four trekking options, all starting at **Cachora**, which involves

crossing the Apurimac Canyon. Day one is a steep descent of around 2000m, and day two a steep climb up the other side. It is recommended to spend one whole day (day three) at the ruins, and then either return on the same route, or via Huanipaca. It is also possible to link this trail to the last day of the Salcantay via Yanama, or to Hancacalle, returning to Cusco via Quillabamba (allow at least eight days for these options).

Hiring *arrieros* and mules is highly recommended for the above treks, as the area is very remote. To **get to Cachora**, take an Abancay-bound bus from Cusco and ask to be dropped off at the Cachora turn-off (4hr), from where you can catch a taxi to the village, where there is basic accommodation, *arrieros* and mules for hire.

Ausangate

This incredible high-altitude trek takes five to six days, plus two more days for travel, and provides the chance to see herds of vicuña wander among glacial lakes with the imposing snowcapped **Ausangate mountain** towering above you. The entire trek is above 4000m and includes several high passes over 5000m. Beginning at the town of **Tinqui**, you make a loop around the Ausangate mountain, in either direction, passing through small Andean villages with great views of nearby glaciers. There are morning buses to Tinqui from Cusco's Calle Tomaso Tito Condemayta at around 10am (5hr).

Lares

There are several options for trekking in the **Lares valley**, lasting two to five days, and all offer splendid views of snow-capped peaks and green valleys. The hikes allow you to properly experience village life in the Andes. You'll pass through communities where you can stay with local families and purchase traditional crafts. The hot springs in Lares make for a relaxing end to any trek in the area. Some tour operators sell a three-day Lares trek with a day-trip to Machu Picchu on the fourth day, but do not be misled; in most cases you will still need to travel

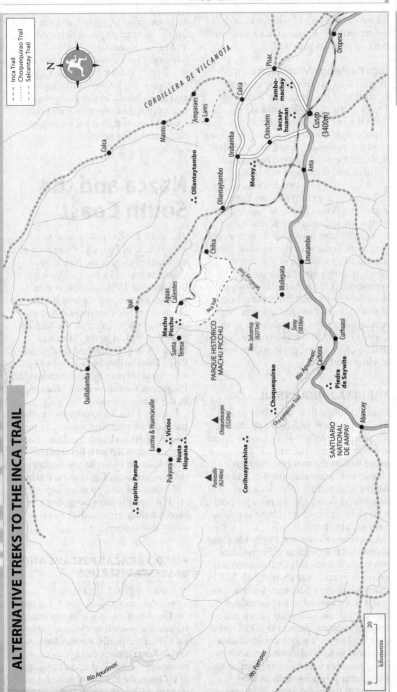

ALTERNATIVE TREKS TO THE INCA TRAIL

9

for two to five hours by bus and/or train before arriving at Aguas Calientes from the end point of your trail.

Espíritu Pampa/Vilcabamba

To visit the least frequented but most rewarding of the alternative Inca Trails, Espíritu Pampa or **Vilcabamba**, believed to be the last stronghold of the Inca, deep in the jungle and as remote as it gets, you need ten to sixteen days. Only accessible in the dry season, the trail begins at Huancacalle, 60km east of Machu Picchu, from where you can visit the sites of Vitcos (a huge fortress) and Yurac Rumi (the White Rock – a huge rock with steps and seats carved into it, thought to have been used for ceremonial purposes). It usually takes around three days to trek to the site of Vilcabamba, which is mostly covered by jungle vegetation. It is a further day's walk to the village of **Kiteni**, from where there is regular transport to Quillabamba (6hr); regular buses from Quillabamba go to Cusco (7–9hr). It is highly recommended that you hire a local guide and *arrieros* in Huancacalle.

THE INKA JUNGLE TRAIL

The Inka Jungle Trail lasts three to four days, going south to Machu Picchu via the peaceful jungle towns of Santa Teresa and Santa María. The name is a misnomer, as the trail runs through cloudforest rather than jungle. Tours consist of a mixture of walking and mountain biking, and are ideal for people who want activity but without spending too much money.

A great way to save some extra soles is to do the trail independently. From Cusco you take a bus towards Quillabamba and get off at Santa María (5–6hr; S15; S30 by minivan); the town is pretty unattractive and it is not advised to stay overnight. Instead, you can easily hop onto a taxi heading to Santa Teresa (1hr; S15), where there is plenty of cheap accommodation and some wonderful natural hot springs (S10) outside town. Combis (30min; S2) from Santa Teresa run daily to take workers to the hydroelectric plant and

meet the trains to Aguas Calientes (check for the latest schedule), which then go on to Machu Picchu.

If you're with a tour, on the first day you'll go by private bus to Abra Málaga, the high point between Ollantaytambo and Santa María, before going on an exhilarating four-hour downhill ride to Santa María and then proceeding to Santa Teresa the next day.

Nazca and the South Coast

The south has been populated as long as anywhere in Peru and for at least nine thousand years in some places. With the discovery and subsequent study, beginning in 1901, of ancient sites throughout the coastal zone, it now seems clear that this was home to at least three major cultures: the **Paracas** (500 BC–400 AD), the influential **Nazca** (500–800 AD) and finally, the **Ica** or **Chincha Empire** (1000–1450 AD), which was overrun by and absorbed into Pachacutec's mushrooming Inca Empire in the fifteenth century.

The area has a lot to offer the modern traveller: the enduring mystery of the enigmatic **Nazca Lines**, the desert beauty of the **Paracas National Reserve** and wildlife haven of the **Ballestas Islands**, as well as the tranquil oasis of **Huacachina** – the essential stop on the gringo trail around Peru for **dune-buggying** and **sandboarding** trips on the immense dunes that surround it.

PISCO, PARACAS RESERVE AND BALLESTAS ISLANDS

The town of **PISCO**, devastated by a powerful earthquake in 2007, has little to offer the visitor, as it is largely industrial. It's possible to use it as a jumping-off point for visiting the nearby **Paracas Reserve** and **Ballestas Islands**, though it's more convenient to stay in the seaside village of **El Chaco**, the launching point for boat tours to the islands, inside the reserve itself.

TOURS OF THE PARACAS RESERVE AND BALLESTAS ISLANDS

There are several local **tour operators** running standard speedboat tours to the Ballestas Islands, leaving Pisco early in the morning and returning a couple of hours later. Many people choose to do an afternoon tour of the Paracas National Reserve with the same operator, making a whole day trip. The boat trips to the **Ballestas Islands** cost S40–50, not including the S1 entrance fee, to be paid on the pier. They last two hours and take in the giant Candelabra geoglyph on the northern part of the Paracas Peninsula, 124m tall and 78m wide, before bobbing very close to the islands to give you the full measure of the impressive stench, the rocks alive with wildlife and the sky dark with birds. You can sometimes see sea lions, penguins and bottlenose dolphins.

Excursions into the **Paracas Reserve** typically cost S25, not including the S5 entry fee or lunch. Tours begin at around 11am to coincide with the return of the boats from the Ballestas Islands and take in a stretch of desert with 40-million-year-old fossils, two attractive beaches, the popular "La Catedral" rock formation just off the shore, which collapsed after the 2007 earthquake, and a couple of fantastic viewpoints overlooking the desert scenery. Tours end with lunch at the tiny fishing village of Lagunillas (*menú marino* S25).

It's best to buy **tickets** the day before, as boats leave at around 8am and you can arrange to be picked up at your hotel if you already have tickets.

TOUR OPERATORS

Most companies also organize cycling, camping and dune-buggying trips into the reserve, as well as tours to other nearby attractions, such as Tambo Colorado – adobe ruins built by the Chinca culture – and dune-buggy excursions into the desert.

Paracas Overland San Francisco 111, Pisco (☏ 056 533 855, ⊛ paracasoverland.com.pe/home.htm), or El Chaco, just as you enter the village (☏ 056 533 625). **Paracas Explorer** Paracas 9, El Chaco (☏ 056 531 487, ⊛ paracasexplorer.com).

The Paracas Reserve

Founded in 1975, the **PARACAS NATIONAL RESERVE** covers an area of approximately 3350 square kilometres; with a large area of ocean within its boundaries, it also includes red-sand beaches, stunning cliffs and islands. The reserve is Peru's principal centre for marine conservation and is home to dolphins, whales and sea lions, as well as many birds including pelicans, flamingos, penguins and cormorants. The name Paracas comes from the Quechua "raining sand", and the reserve is constantly battered by strong winds and sandstorms. Despite the harsh climate, the area has been inhabited for around nine thousand years, most notably by the pre-Inca culture known as the Paracas.

The Ballestas Islands

Around twenty minutes offshore, the **Islas Ballestas**, one of the most impressive marine reserves in Latin America, are protected nesting grounds for vast numbers of sea birds. They are sometimes referred to as the Guano Islands, due to the intensive guano mining that used to take place here, since they are completely covered in guano or bird droppings. Today the islands are all alive with a mass of sea lions soaking up the sun, and birds including pelicans, Humboldt penguins, Inca terns, Peruvian boobies and cormorants.

ARRIVAL AND DEPARTURE

Just 4hr south of Lima, the Paracas Reserve is easily reached via the Panamerican Highway.

By bus Only two bus companies, Oltursa and Cruz del Sur, operate in Paracas proper, at the village of El Chaco. The rest drop you off at Cruz del Pisco, in the middle of the Panamericana, from where you will first have to take a *colectivo* to Pisco (S3) and then another *colectivo* (S3) or taxi (S15) to El Chaco. If travelling from Ayacucho, buses drop you off at San Clemente, from where you will need to catch a *colectivo* to Cruz del Pisco first. Oltursa has an office in town at Av Paracas 6 (☏ 994 616 492), while Cruz del Sur stops at the northern entrance to the village (☏ 056 536 636).

Destinations Oltursa to: Nazca (daily at 11am; 3hr 30min) via Ica; Arequipa (daily at 11am; 14hr) via Ica and Nazca; Lima (daily at 10am and 8pm; 2hr 30min); Ica (daily at 11am; 1hr 15min). Cruz del Sur to: Lima (5 daily only in the afternoon; 3hr); Nazca (3hr 30min); via Ica (5 daily; 1hr); Arequipa (daily at 10am; 12hr).

9

By colectivo *Colectivos* to Paracas leave from outside Pisco's central market about every 20min or when full, throughout the day (20min; S3). To head back into Pisco, grab a *colectivo* at the entrance of El Chaco.

ACCOMMODATION

As Pisco is a rather unattractive dusty town, it is best to base yourself in the laidback fishing village of El Chaco. All guesthouses here can arrange trips to the Ballestas Islands and the Paracas Reserve.

Hospedaje Backpacker Soler Av Paracas s/n ☎ 056 798 200, ✉ hospedajesolerparacas@hotmail.com. This airy hostel with wind chimes gently singing in the sea breeze offers accommodation in rustic wooden and bamboo huts. All have shared bathrooms and wi-fi. Ask for a dorm *descuento* in low season. Dorms S̲2̲0̲, doubles S̲4̲0̲

Paracas Backpackers House Av Los Libertadores s/n ☎ 056 773 131, 🌐 paracasbackpackershouse.com.pe. Cheaper accommodation here is in little wooden huts with clean, shared bathrooms, while the tiled en suites with marine-themed blankets are at the back in a concrete block. There's a sandy chill-out area with deckchairs, a communal kitchen and wi-fi. Dorms S̲1̲5̲, doubles S̲4̲0̲

Hostal Santa María Av Paracas s/n ☎ 056 775 799, 🌐 hostalsantamariaparacas.com. The plusher choice, this lovely secure guesthouse has light and airy wi-fi enabled rooms (ask for one on the top floor). The premises are spic-and-span, there are computers for guests' use

and there's a pleasant rooftop terrace. Rates include breakfast. S̲1̲0̲0̲

EATING AND DRINKING

Aqua Marina On the street behind the seafront. This is the only place in El Chaco offering desserts, including ice cream (three scoops S6), crêpes (S12) and fruit salad (S6–8), as well as breakfasts (S6–7) and sandwiches (S5–8). Daily 7am–noon & 5–10pm.

Brisa Marina Right on the seafront. The most Peruvian of all the touristy restaurants along the seafront, this place serves a variety of *pescados a la plancha* (grilled fish; S22–27), chicken dishes (S19) and a limited selection of vegetarian options, which mostly comprise salads (S5–17). A *menú marino* will set you back S25. Daily 7.30am–8.30pm.

Cevicherías Off the southern end of the Malecón El Chaco (boardwalk). This row of no-frills fish and seafood eateries offers the cheapest set menus in town and they usually include *ceviche* followed by a fish or seafood main (*menú marino* S15–20).

ICA

The city of **ICA** lies 50km inland, in a fertile valley surrounded by impressive sand dunes. It suffered considerable damage in the 2007 earthquake and several buildings were completely

PARACAS, ICA & NAZCA

ICA AND HUACACHINA TOURS

Most hostels in Huacachina rent out **sandboards** and run **dune-buggy tours**. Those looking to cut costs may want to rent a board and go it alone, but bear in mind that it soon gets very tiring dragging a board up a sand dune in the scorching sun.

TOUR OPERATORS

Irresponsible dune-buggy drivers are known to drive quite recklessly, so it's best to book your trip with a responsible agency such as the following:

Desert Adventures Hostal Desert Nights ☎ 056 228 458, ⓦ desertadventure.net. An established Huacachina-based tour company, offering the standard half-day dune-buggy tours of the dunes (S40), with sandboarding included (with the option of using professional boards for a S10 surcharge), as well as 1hr quad-biking tours (S140). Also runs vineyard tours (S40) and two-day trips with a night spent camping in the desert (S140).

Curasi Balneario de Huacachina 197 ☎ 056 216 989, ⓦ huacachinacurasi.com. A reliable outfit running sandboarding and dune-buggy tours (S35 plus S3.65 entry tax payable as you enter the dunes), bodega tours (S30), one-night camping trips in the desert (S110), as well as tours to the Ballestas Islands (S60).

---

destroyed, including almost one entire side of the Plaza de Armas. In the city itself, the **Museo Regional** warrants a visit, and the surrounding area offers **vineyard tours** with plenty of wine-tasting opportunities. Note that it's better to stay in nearby Huacachina (see below).

WHAT TO SEE AND DO

Ica's busy streets do not lend themselves to leisurely strolls; however, it is easy to get around using the numerous *tico* taxis that will take you anywhere in the city for around S4.

Museo Regional de Ica

Located in an Ica suburb, the superb **Museo Regional** (Jr. Ayabaca, block 8; Mon–Fri 8am–7pm & Sat–Sun 8.30am–6.30pm; S10) is one of the best in Peru, housing important Nazca, Ica and Paracas cultural artefacts. The exhibits range from mummies (including those of children and parrots), trophy heads and trepanned skulls to examples of Nazca pottery and Paracas weavings; a scale model of the Nazca lines is out back. To get there, take a *mototaxi* from the centre of Ica (S3).

Bodega and vineyard tours

Ica's main tourist attraction and principal industry is the many *bodegas* and vineyards nearby, which can be visited on organized tours, both from the city and from Huacachina, and usually involve a look around the vineyard followed by wine tasting and the chance to buy. Tours most commonly visit one or more of the following vineyards: Bodega Ocucaje (ⓦ ocucaje.com), Bodega Vista Alegre (ⓦ vistaalegre.com.pe), Bodega Tacama (ⓦ tacama.com), Bodega Lazo (ⓦ bodegalazo.com) and Bodega El Catador (☎ 056 403 427), where the visitors are allowed to join in the stomping of the grapes in February and March.

ARRIVAL AND DEPARTURE

By bus Most bus companies have their own terminals in the unsavoury area along Manzanilla and Lambayeque; there are numerous departures in both directions along the Panamericana during the day. Recommended companies include Cial, Av Fernando León de Vivero 110 (☎ 056 207 6900); Ormeño, Lambayeque 180 (☎ 056 215 600); Cruz del Sur, Fray Roman Rojas (☎ 056 223 333), and Oltursa, Av Ayabaca 974 (☎ 056 211 960); if travelling with Soyuz (Av Manzanilla 130 ☎ 056 224 138), watch your belongings. Destinations Arequipa (several daily; 10–12hr); Lima (12 daily; 4hr 30min); Nazca (6 daily; 2hr 30min); Paracas (5 daily; 1hr 15min).

By mototaxi A *mototaxi* to Huacachina will set you back S4.

HUACACHINA

Since Ica itself is not terribly attractive, it's preferable to base yourself at the nearby village of **HUACACHINA**, as it's just as easy to do *bodega* tours from here. This once peaceful oasis, nestled among huge sand dunes and boasting a lake with curative properties, has recently been overrun with travellers, eager for adrenaline-packed adventures (in particular **sandboarding** and **dune-buggying**) and all-night parties

9

around dimly lit pools. If the picture-postcard lagoon looks familiar, that's because you've seen it on the S50 notes.

ARRIVAL AND DEPARTURE

By colectivo *Colectivos* run every 30min, or until full, from near the kiosks at the entrance of the lagoon in Huacachina to the Plaza de Armas in Ica (S2).

By mototaxi A *mototaxi* between Ica and Huacachina should cost no more than S5.

ACCOMMODATION

All hostels below either run their own sandboarding, dune-buggy and *bodega* tours, or they can organize them for you. Much of the nightlife in Huacachina revolves around the hostels, which usually have their own restaurants and bars, and throw raucous pool parties in the evenings.

Casa de Arena Perotti s/n ☎056 215 274, ⟨w⟩casadearena.net. Huacachina's party hostel has raucous nightly pool parties and an affiliated club (with free entry for guests) playing electronica and Peruvian tracks. The party goes on all night, as does the noise – join in or bring earplugs. The simple yet colourful wi-fi enabled rooms are mostly set around the pool and there's a large eighteen-bunk dorm too. Dorms **S25**, doubles **S60**

Curasi Balneario de Huacachina 197 ☎056 216 989, ⟨w⟩huacachinacurasi.com. Slightly less backpackery than the other options in that it is a quiet three-star hotel including more of a Peruvian clientele, the secure *Curasi* has neat and tidy rooms giving onto a pleasant pool area with deckchairs. **S100**

Hostal Desert Nights By the lagoon ☎056 228 458, ⟨w⟩bookingbox.org.uk/desertnights. Right by the lagoon, this popular backpacker choice has four eight-bunk dorms (no doubles) and a perpetually packed restaurant serving international grub such as burgers (S15–20; veggie burger S15) and sandwiches (S6–15). Thirsty gullets can opt for a jug of pisco sour (S35). Dorms **S22**

EATING

La Casa de Bamboo Perotti s/n, behind the *Hostería Suiza*. This laidback family-run veggie restaurant with tables dotted around the garden offers healthy breakfasts (S9), delicious chocolate fudge brownies (S8) and green tea (S5). Veggie and vegan dishes include Thai curry (S18) and pasta dishes (S12–16), as well as exquisite home-made hummus (S8). Mon–Sat 8.30am–3pm; Thurs, Fri & Sat also open 6–10pm.

Curasi As you enter the lagoon. Tourism only hit Huacachina a decade ago but this place has been going for five; the elderly owners serve tasty *ceviche* (S20), soups (S8–20), cheap breakfasts (S8–9) and all manner of mains (S10–28). Daily 9am–6pm.

NAZCA AND AROUND

The small, sun-baked town of **NAZCA** spreads along the margin of a small coastal valley. Although the river is invariably dry, Nazca's valley remains green and fertile through the continued application of ancient subterranean aqueducts. These days, the town is one of Peru's major attractions, and though most travellers come here solely to take a flight over the enigma that is the Nazca Lines (see p.773), other local attractions include the excellent **Museo Didáctico Antonini**, the adobe Inca ruins of **Paredones** on the outskirts, and the popular (if somewhat macabre) outlying archeological sites, such as the nearby **Chauchilla Cemetery** and the **Cahuachi pyramids**, an hour's drive into the desert.

WHAT TO SEE AND DO

The **Plaza de Armas** is the heart of Nazca. Jr. Bolognesi is the main street leading away from it and there are numerous restaurants, bars and hostels to be found within a couple of blocks of the Plaza de Armas and Plaza Bolognesi, three blocks to the west.

Museo Didáctico Antonini

If you head east from the Plaza de Armas along Avenida de La Cultura you soon come to the fascinating **Museo Didáctico Antonini** (daily 9am–7pm; S15). The museum stretches for six long blocks from the Plaza de Armas along Bolognesi and presents excellent interpretative exhibits covering the evolution of Nazca culture, with superb examples of pottery, household tools and trophy skulls with pierced foreheads. There's a good audiovisual show and scale-model reconstructions of local ruins such as the Templo del Escalonado at Cahuachi. The museum complex includes an archeological park that contains the Bisambra aqueduct (once fed by the Bisambra reservoir higher up the valley) and some burial reconstructions. The exhibit labels are in Spanish but you can pick up translation booklets at the front desk.

Didáctico Museo Antonini & Cantayoc Aqueducts ▲

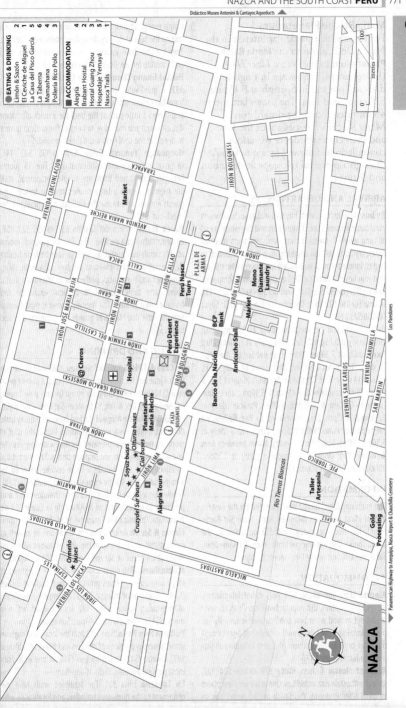

● EATING & DRINKING	
Limón & Sazón	2
El Ceviche de Miguel	1
La Casa del Pisco García	5
La Taberna	6
Mamashana	4
Pollería Rico Pollo	3

■ ACCOMMODATION	
Alegría	4
Brabant Hostal	2
Hostal Guang Zhou	3
Hospedaje Yemayá	5
Nasca Trails	1

NAZCA

▶ Panamerican Highway to Arequipa, Nasca Airport & Chauchilla Cemetery

▶ Los Paredones

9

María Reiche Planetarium

For those with a particular interest in the Nazca Lines, a trip to the **María Reiche Planetarium** in the *Nazca Lines Hotel* (Bolognesi 147, showings in English daily at 7pm and in Spanish at 8.15pm; S20) is a good idea. The shows last about 45 minutes, focusing primarily on María Reiche's theories about the Lines, and their correspondence to various constellations, followed by a quick look through a powerful telescope at the moon and Saturn.

ARRIVAL AND DEPARTURE

By bus There isn't a central bus terminal as such, although most bus companies are clustered around the western end of Lima where it meets Bolívar. Persistent touts meet all buses, trying to sell you anything from accommodation to flights; ignore them, as well as any taxi drivers who tell you that your hostel is dirty/too far/has closed down. Companies include Cial (☎ 056 523 960); Cruz del Sur (☎ 056 523 713); Oltursa (☎ 056 522 265); Ormeño (☎ 056 522 058); Soyuz (☎ 056 523 713).

Destinations Cial to: Arequipa (daily at 10pm; 11hr); Cusco (daily at 9.15pm; 14hr); Lima (daily at 1.30am; 7hr); Tacna (daily at 7.30pm; 14hr). Cruz del Sur to: Arequipa (3 daily, 10hr); Ica (4 daily; 2hr); Lima (4 daily; 7hr); Paracas (4 daily; 3hr). Oltursa to: Arequipa (daily at 3pm & 10pm; 9hr); Ica (daily at 4.45pm & 6.30pm; 2hr); Lima (daily at 6.30am & 4.45pm; 6–7hr); Paracas (daily at 6.30am & 4.45pm; 2hr). Ormeño to: La Paz, Bolivia, via Arequipa and Puno (daily at 5pm; 21hr); Tacna (daily at 5.30pm; 14hr). Soyuz to: Ica (every 30min between 6am & 10pm; 2hr); Ormeño to: Arequipa (daily at 3.30pm; 10hr); Tacna (daily at 10pm; 12hr).

INFORMATION

The main municipal tourist office, located on the eastern end of Plaza de Armas (Mon–Fri 8am–8pm, Sat 8am–noon), has maps and very limited information on the town. There's also a municipal kiosk (Mon–Fri 8am–8pm, Sat 8am–3.30pm) where Lima meets Bolognesi.

ACCOMMODATION

Alegría Lima 166 ☎ 056 522 702, ⊛ hotelalegria.net. An upmarket option, this popular hotel has clean en-suite rooms set around a verdant pool; service is friendly yet professional and the hotel's well-established agency next door can organize all manner of tours, including flights over the Nazca Lines. **S175**

Brabant Hostal C Juan Matta 878 ☎ 056 524 127, ⊛ brabanthostalnasca.webklik.nl. One of the very few places in town offering dorms, this Dutch-owned hostel has six simple rooms, all with cable TV, set on two floors; ask for a pad on the second floor as those downstairs are a bit dark. There's a little book exchange, a communal kitchen, wi-fi and a rooftop terrace. Dorms **S15**, doubles **S50**

Hostal Guang Zhou Fermín de Castillo 494 ☎ 056 521 391. A good-value central option, this Chinese-owned hotel has clean rooms with a/c or fan. All have private bath and there's a little pool at the back for a quick afternoon dip, although you may have to head to the rooftop terrace to dry off as the pool lacks a suitable surround. **S40**

Hospedaje Yemayá Callao 578 ☎ 056 523 146, ⊛ nascahospedajeyemaya@hotmail.com. The 15 rooms here, all with shared bath, are simple yet central, staff are friendly, there's a large shaded rooftop terrace and guests are welcome to use the facilities and showers after check-out. **S42**

Nasca Trails Fermín del Castillo 637 ☎ 056 522 858, ⊛ nascatrails@terra.com.pe. The freshly painted rooms at this family-run hostel, all with private bath and cable TV, are set around a pleasant outdoor area with sofas, armchairs and hammocks, perfect for an afternoon siesta. There's also table football, wi-fi, book exchange and home-cooked dinners. The friendly owner is multilingual and the little dog Margaret guards the premises day and night. **S56**

EATING AND DRINKING

La Casa del Pisco García Bolognesi 298. Head to this bar with a juke box for some home-made pisco, a potent pisco sour (S12) or an excellent tuna frozen (prickly pear frozen; in season only, Dec & Jan; S14). Mon–Sat 6pm–midnight.

★ **El Ceviche de Miguel**. Tucked away off a dusty little dirt road, *Miguel's* is a local institution. Watch the chef at work as he lovingly prepares mouth-watering *ceviche* and all manner of fish and seafood dishes. The menus are excellent value and include a large *ceviche* followed by a huge main dish. Try the exquisite *menu parihuela* (S24). Follow Miguel in December 2013 as he changes name and premises to *La Ballena Azul* in Altura de la Cuadra 13 de Juan Mata, Urbanización Amaprovi. Wed–Mon 8am–4pm.

Limón & Sazón Av Los Incas s/n. Great *ceviche* as well as creole dishes are rustled up at this airy restaurant with *peña* shows at lunchtime on Sat and Sun. Daily 8.30am–10pm.

Mamashana Bolognesi 270. On the main restaurant strip, *Mamashana* serves great fish and seafood dishes (S24–34) and meat mains (S20–35); there are also plenty of vegetarian options (S10–18). Try the mild *fish a lo macho* (S33). Mon–Fri 8am–11pm, Sun noon–11pm.

Pollería Rico Pollo Lima 190. Join the locals and dig into some generous portions of chicken and fries (1/4 chicken S13), chorizo (S12) or *salchipapas* (S10) at one of Nazca's most popular pollerías. Daily 10am–1am.

La Taberna Lima 321. The scribbled walls here are testament to the numerous travellers and locals alike who

TOURS AROUND NAZCA

Some well-established companies arrange **tours** to the major sites around Nazca, all offering similar trips to Los Paredones, Cantalloc, Cahuachi, Chauchilla and the Lines. Tours around Chauchilla Cemetery last 2hr 30min for about S20–30, while a trip to the viewing tower and the Casa Museo María Reiche also takes 2hr 30min and costs around S50–60. Tours out to the ruined temple complex in the desert at Cahuachi (see p.774) are 4hr and cost around S120 person, depending on group size; these need to be arranged in advance.

TOUR OPERATORS
The best companies are:
Alegría Tours Lima 168 ☎056 522 444, Ⓦalegria toursperu.com. Well-established company.
Perú Nasca Tours Bolognesi 449 ☎056 523 300,

Ⓦperunascatours.com
Perú Desert Experience Bolognesi 299 ☎56 523 466, Ⓦperudesert.com. For sandboarding tours and buggy rides.

---

have stopped by this family-run place for a great-value *menú de casa* (S8.50–10), washed down nicely with a *chicha morada* (fermented maize drink). There's a veggie menu too (S13.50). Daily 10am–4pm & 6–10pm.

DIRECTORY

Banks and exchange BCP at Lima and Grau, and Banco de la Nación just next door.
Hospital Callao s/n ☎056 522 010.
Internet Try Cheros at Ignacio Morseski 408 (daily 8am–11pm; S1/hr).
Laundry There's a real shortage of *lavanderías* in Nazca so prices are high; try inside Mono Diamante Guesthouse at Lima 660 (S7/kg; open 24hr).
Post office Castillo 379 (Mon–Fri 9am–5.30pm, Sat 8am–3.30pm).
Tourist police Av Los Incas 1, s/n Km447 ☎056 522 105.

THE NAZCA LINES

One of the great mysteries of South America, the **NAZCA LINES** are a series of animal figures and geometric shapes, none of them repeated and some up to 200m in length, drawn across some 500 square kilometres of the bleak, stony Pampa de San José. Each one, even such sophisticated motifs as a spider monkey or a hummingbird, is executed in a single continuous line, most created by clearing away the brush and hard stones of the plain to reveal the fine dust beneath. Theories abound as to what their purpose was – from landing strips for alien spaceships to some kind of agricultural calendar, aligned with the constellations above, to help regulate the planting and harvesting of crops. Perhaps at the same time some of the straight lines served as

ancient sacred paths connecting *huacas*, or power spots. Regardless of why they were made, the Lines are among the strangest and most unforgettable sights in the country.

At Km420 of the Panamerican Highway, 20km north of Nazca, a tall metal **viewing tower** (or *mirador*; S2) has been built above the plain, from which you get a partial view of a giant tree, a pair of hands and a lizard, though the experience does not compare to a **flight** over the Lines (see box, p.774).

Around 5km further along the Panamericana from the *mirador*, you'll find the **Museo María Reiche** (daily 8am–6pm; S5), the former home of the German mathematician who made research into the Lines her life's work. Here you can see her possessions and sketches and visit her tomb.

AROUND NAZCA

Chauchilla and Cahuachi, after the Lines the most important Nazca sites, are both difficult to reach by public transport, so you may want to consider an organized tour.

Cerro Blanco
You can easily see **Cerro Blanco**, the world's largest sand dune, from anywhere in the city. Formerly used as a religious centre, it's now the site for extreme dune-buggy rides and sandboarding. Several tour agencies (see box above) run morning trips here, typically leaving at 5am and returning at lunchtime.

9

FLYING OVER THE NAZCA LINES

A spectacular way of seeing the Lines is to **fly** over them. Flights leave from Nazca airstrip, about 3km south of Nazca, and cost from US$100 per person, lasting around 30min. Note that flights only take off when the skies are clear; this can sometimes mean a delay at the airport until the weather conditions improve. Depending on the time of day, the Lines appear different due to the angle of the sun, although both morning and afternoon departures have their own particular charm. In the winter months of July and August it is best to fly in the afternoons, while in January, February and March early morning (6–11am) and late afternoon (3–5pm) take-offs are best. Those who suffer from motion sickness may want to skip breakfast as it is not unlike being on a roller coaster when the small plane zips around the sky, turning tight circles around each giant figure so that people on both sides of the plane get a good look.

TOUR OPERATORS

You will be assaulted with offers of flights the moment you arrive in Nazca, but since they are not likely to sell out, it's best not to accept the first offer you get, as it's likely to be marked up. Any hotel/hostel will help you organize your flight.

The most popular operators are Aeroparacas (Teodoro Cardenas 470, Lima ☎ 01 265 8073, ⓦ aeroparacas .com) and Alas Peruanas (Lima 168, Nazca ☎ 056 522 497, ⓦ alasperuanas.com). Both have an excellent safety record and well-maintained planes. Pay the S25 airport tax before boarding your flight.

Chauchilla Cemetery

Roughly 30km south of Nazca, **Chauchilla Cemetery** is an atmospheric sight. Scattered about the dusty ground are literally thousands of graves, dating back to the Nazca culture (400 BC–800 AD), which have been cleaned up in recent years and organized for visitors, though bits of human bone and broken pottery shards still litter the ground, left there by grave robbers from decades ago.

There are clear walkways from which you must not stray, and open graves have roofs built over them to save the mummies, skeletons, shroud fabric and lengths of braided hair from the desert sun. The mummies with the longest hair are the chiefs, and the Nazca mummified animals as well; look for a child's pet parrot. It is an impressive experience, intensified by the curator's decision to arrange the mummies into positions intended to represent their daily lives. Tours of the cemetery last around three hours and take in a pottery workshop and a gold-processing centre on the way back to town.

Cahuachi

Currently being excavated by an Italian archeological team, **Cahuachi** is an enormous ceremonial centre of great importance to the Nazca culture, consisting of 44 pyramids, only one of which has been renovated; the rest are still hidden under the sand. There is also a llama cemetery and a site called Estaquería – a possible place of mummification. It lies in the middle of the desert, 25km west of Nazca along a dirt track; on the way, you pass ransacked ancient graveyards with scattered human remains. Tours normally take place in the morning, as sandstorms can pick up in the afternoon.

Paredones and Aquaductos de Cantallo

These two sites are normally seen as part of one tour as they are close together. The **Paredones ruins**, 2km southeast of town, are the crumbling remains of an Inca fortress and administrative centre (and now home to desert owls). The **Cantallo Aqueducts** lie 5km further on; constructed by the Nazca, they consist of stone spirals going deep into the ground and are still used to irrigate the nearby fields. It used to be possible to enter the aqueducts through the *ventanas* (windows) – the holes out of which the water would come out – but this has been forbidden since the last earthquake.

Arequipa and around

The country's second-biggest and arguably, after Cusco, most attractive city, **AREQUIPA** sits some 2400m above sea level with **El Misti**, the dormant volcano poised above, giving the place a rather legendary appearance. An elegant yet modern city, with a relatively wealthy population of more than 750,000, it has a relaxed feel and maintains a rather aloof attitude towards the rest of Peru.

The spectacular countryside around Arequipa rewards a few days' exploration, with some exciting trekking and rafting possibilities (best in the dry season, May–Sept). Around 200km to the north of the city is the **Colca Canyon**: called the "valley of marvels" by the Peruvian novelist Mario Vargas Llosa, it is nearly twice the size of Arizona's Grand Canyon

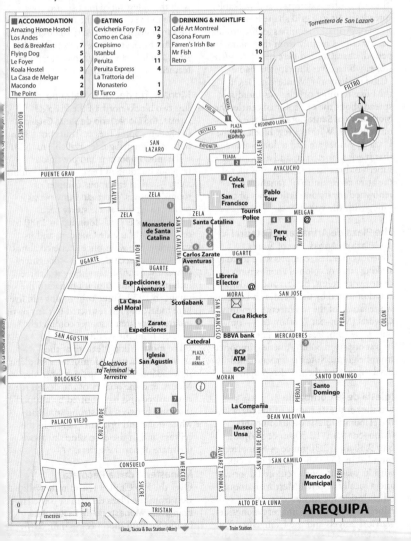

■ ACCOMMODATION		● EATING		● DRINKING & NIGHTLIFE	
Amazing Home Hostel	1	Cevichería Fory Fay	12	Café Art Montreal	6
Los Andes		Como en Casa	9	Casona Forum	2
Bed & Breakfast	7	Crepísimo	7	Farren's Irish Bar	8
Flying Dog	5	Istanbul	3	Mr Fish	10
Koala Hostel	3	Peruita	11	Retro	2
Le Foyer	6	Peruita Express	4		
La Casa de Melgar	4	La Trattoria del			
Macondo	2	Monasterio	1		
The Point	8	El Turco	5		

Lima, Tacna & Bus Station (4km)   Train Station

AREQUIPA

9

and one of the country's most extraordinary natural sights. Further north, the remote **Cotahuasi Canyon** offers even more remote and challenging treks for those with plenty of time. Around 120km west of Arequipa, you can see the amazing petroglyphs of **Toro Muerto**, perhaps continuing on to hike amid the craters and cones of the **Valley of the Volcanoes**.

WHAT TO SEE AND DO

The city centre is compact and walkable, spreading out in a grid shape from the Plaza de Armas. Arequipa's architectural beauty comes mainly from the colonial period, characterized here by white *sillar* stone, which gives the city the name "Ciudad Blanca" ("White City"). Of the huge number of religious buildings spread about the old colonial centre, the **Monastery of Santa Catalina** is the most outstanding. Within a few blocks of the Plaza de Armas are half a dozen churches that merit a brief visit, and a couple of superb old mansions. You can walk to the attractive suburb of **Yanahuara**, renowned for its dramatic views of the valley with the volcanoes.

The Plaza de Armas and Catedral

The **Plaza de Armas**, one of South America's grandest, comprises a particularly striking array of colonial architecture, dotted with palms, flowers and gardens. It is dominated by the arcades and elegant white facade of the seventeenth-century **Catedral** (Mon–Sat 7–10am & 5–7pm, Sun 9am–1pm; free), which has one of the largest organs in South America, imported from Belgium. Note the serpent-tailed devil supporting the wooden pulpit.

Iglesia de la Compañía

On the southeast corner of the plaza lies the elaborate **Iglesia de la Compañía** (Mon–Sat 9am–12.30pm & 3–6pm, Sun 9.30am–12.30pm & 3–6pm; free), founded in 1573 and rebuilt in 1650, with its magnificently sculpted doorway, and a locally inspired Mestizo-Baroque relief. Inside the former sacristy, the cupola depicts jungle imagery alongside warriors, angels and the Evangelists. You

can also enter the fine **Jesuit Cloisters**, their pillars supporting stone arches covered with intricate reliefs showing more angels, local fruits and vegetables, seashells and stylized puma heads.

Other churches

Other notable churches within a few blocks of the Plaza include **Santo Domingo** (Mon–Sat 6–9am & 3–7.45pm, Sun 5.30am–1pm; free), two blocks east of La Compañía, built in 1553 by Gaspar Vaez, with the oldest surviving Mestizo-style facade in the city; and the imposing **Iglesia de San Francisco** (Mon–Fri 10am–noon & 3–5pm; free), at the top of its namesake street, built in the sixteenth century and featuring an unusual brick entranceway.

Monasterio de Santa Catalina

Just two blocks north of the Plaza de Armas, the **Monasterio de Santa Catalina** (daily 8am–5pm, Tues & Thurs until 8pm; S35, multilingual guides available for S20) is the most important and prestigious religious building in Peru – a citadel within a city – and its enormous complex of rooms, cloisters, streets and tiny plazas is perfect to explore at a leisurely pace.

The monastery was founded in 1580 by the wealthy María de Guzmán, and its vast protective walls once sheltered almost two hundred secluded nuns – daughters of wealthy Spanish families – and three hundred servants until it opened to the public in 1970. Some thirty nuns still live here today; though restricted to their own quarter, they are no longer completely shut off from the world.

The most striking feature of the architecture is its predominantly Mudéjar style, adapted by the Spanish from the Moors, and the quality of the design is emphasized and harmonized by a superb interplay between the strong sunlight, white stone and brilliant colours in the ceilings and in the deep blue sky above the maze of narrow streets.

Monasterio de La Recoleta

Over the Río Chili, a ten-minute walk west from the Plaza de Armas, is the large Franciscan **Monasterio de La Recoleta** (Mon–Sat 9am–noon & 3–5pm; S10), founded in 1648 by Franciscan friars. If you duck into the rooms leading off the cloisters, you will come across a collection of art and ceramics made by pre-Inca cultures, as well as trepanned skulls and several mummies.

Bibliophiles will appreciate the impressive **library** on the second floor, housing more than 20,000 antique books and maps, which are only used by researchers with special permission from the Father. You can visit the library for fifteen minutes, at 45 minutes past the hour.

The **Amazonian section** of the museum is a must-see; one room houses jungle jewellery collected by the Franciscan monks on their early missions, as well as photographs of their first encounters with the "natives". The second room displays a large variety of stuffed birds and animals from the Amazon, as well as traditional weapons, some still used today, and maps of early exploration of the Manu and Madre de Dios areas.

Museo Santuarios Andinos

Often referred to as the "Juanita" or "Ice Princess" museum after its most famous exhibit – the immaculately preserved mummy of a 12- to 14-year-old girl sacrificed to a mountain deity around five hundred years ago – the superb little **Museo Santuarios Andinos** lies just off the plaza at Calle La Merced 110 (Mon–Sat 9am–6pm, Sun 9am–3pm; S20). After a dramatic twenty-minute National Geographic video about the discovery of Juanita, a multilingual guide talks you through the exhibits related to the sacrificial and burial practices of the Incas before finally unveiling the museum's star attraction. The intricate tiny offerings to the gods, made of gold and precious stones, are particularly fine and ice-covered Juanita is very well preserved. Bring warm clothes, as it's rather cold inside, and don't forget to tip the guide.

Museo Arqueológico UNSA

A block and a half south of the Plaza along Álvarez Thomas, you'll find the small yet fascinating **archeological museum** (Mon–Fri 9am–4pm; S2), which gives a glimpse into the local pre-Inca culture. The displays, labelled in Spanish only, feature Nazca, Chiribaya and Wari pottery; Nazca mummies and ritually deformed skulls; fine cloaks adorned with parrot feathers; and Inca and Spanish weaponry.

TOURS, TREKKING AND CLIMBING AROUND AREQUIPA

Most companies offer trips of one to three days out to the **Colca Canyon** for S90–250 (sometimes with *very* early morning starts) or to the petroglyphs at **Toro Muerto** for S60–120. Trips to the **Valley of the Volcanoes**, as well as specialist adventure activities (such as rafting in the Colca Canyon, mountaineering or multi-day trekking), can cost anything from S180 up to S1200 for a three- to six-day outing.

TOUR OPERATORS

Carlos Zarate Adventures Santa Catalina 204 ☎054 202 461, ⓦzarateadventures.com. Knowledge-able guide Carlos offers climbs of nearby peaks, canyoning, and cycling excursions, as well as archeological tours.

Colca Trek Jerusalén 401b ☎054 206 217, ⓦcolcatrek.com.pe. An excellent trekking, climbing, mountain-biking and canoeing operator that special-izes in customized tours permitting a mix of these, as well as three-day tours of the Colca Canyon. Also sells maps and has equipment rental for independent trekkers.

Expediciones y Aventuras Santa Catalina 219 ☎054 221 653, ⓦexpedicionesyaventuras.com.

Specialists in rafting and kayaking trips along the Chili River, the Canyon del Colca and Cotahuasi. They also offer personalized tours.

Pablo Tour Jerusalén 400 ☎054 203 737, ⓦpablo tour.com. Run by friendly multilingual Edwin who took over the family business from his father Pablo, this company runs all manner of tours, from 4WD trips to the salt lake Laguna de Salinas, to trekking and cultural trips into the Colca Canyon using new alter-native routes, thereby avoiding the crowds.

Sacred Road Jerusalén 400 ☎054 330 408, ⓦsacred road.com. This company offers a wide range of tours to satisfy all tastes: mountain biking, canyoning, rock climbing, trekking and mountaineering, as well as the standard Colca Canyon tours.

9

Mercado Municipal

For a taste of local life, check out the covered **market** (Mon–Sat 6am–7.30pm, Sun 6am–5pm), which takes up an entire block between San Camillo and Alto de la Luna. Lose yourself amid the stalls piled high with local produce, the smells of cooking, *juguerías*, the vendors of jungle potions and wandering musicians. Just leave your valuables behind.

The views: Yanahuara and Mirador de Carmen Alto

A jaunt across the Río Chili via Puente Grau followed by a fifteen-minute uphill stroll brings you to the attractive plaza of the Yanahuara neighbourhood. It features a **viewing point** (*mirador*), with a postcard panorama of Misti framed behind by the white stone arches. The elaborately carved facade of the small eighteenth-century **Iglesia San Juan Bautista** nearby is a superb example of Mestizo art.

From here, a five-minute taxi ride (S5–8) takes you to the Mirador del Carmen Alto, which features a stupendous view of the city and all the volcanoes surrounding it.

ARRIVAL AND DEPARTURE

By plane Flights land at Arequipa airport (☎054 443 464), 7km northwest of the town. A taxi from the airport to downtown Arequipa will set you back S20.

By bus There are two main bus terminals in Arequipa: the Terminal Terrestre (☎054 427 798), Av Cáceres, at Arturo Ivañez, which mainly receives buses from Puno, Cusco and the Colca Canyon; and the Terrapuerto (☎054 348 810), just next door at Av Arturo Ivañez, with buses travelling mainly west to destinations such as Lima and Nazca. Leaving from the Terrapuerto for destinations including Lima, Nazca and Cusco are Cruz del Sur (☎054 427 375) and Cial (☎054 429 090). Flores (☎054 431 717) has its own terminal just opposite the Terminal Terrestre and has numerous services to Puno and to Lima via Nazca and Ica. If you're going to the Colca Canyon, use Andalucía (☎054 445 089), Milagros (☎054 298 090) or Reyna (☎054 430 612). Both terminals are around 4km from the centre of town; a taxi to the Plaza de Armas should cost no more than S6. Regular *colectivos* run to the Terminal Terrestre from the corner of Bolognani and Cruz Verde.

Destinations Cusco (8 daily, mostly with night-time departures; 9–11hr); Desaguadero (4 daily; 8–9hr); La Paz, Bolivia (daily; 12–14hr); Lima (hourly; 16hr) via Nazca (9hr 30min) and Ica (12hr); Puno (7 daily; 6–7hr); Tacna (hourly; 6–7hr).

INFORMATION

Tourist information There is an iPerú kiosk in the arrivals halls of the airport which meets oncoming flights. The iPerú office in town is at Portal de La Municipalidad 110, Plaza de Armas (Mon–Sat 9am–6pm, Sun 9am–1pm; ☎054 223 265, ✉iperuarequipa@promperu.gob.pe), which has helpful staff, free maps of the city and information on sights, cultural events and accommodation. There's also a municipal tourist office right next door (Mon–Fri 8am–4pm, ✉ofturisticamunicipalidad@hotmail.com). For topographic maps of the Colca Canyon, try Colca Trek (see box, p.777), while Librería El Lector on San Francisco 213 has an extensive English-language book section, as well as detailed city maps.

ACCOMMODATION

Amazing Home Hostel Plaza Campo Redondo 100 ☎054 222 788, ⊛amazinghomeaqp.com. Rooms, randomly named after Italian cities, are decked out in dark furniture and parquet floors; the spartan corridors give the place a bit of an institutional feel, but staff are helpful and there's a pool table, table tennis, a book exchange, board games, a communal kitchen, wi-fi and laundry service. Dorms S̲2̲3̲, doubles S̲6̲0̲

Los Andes Bed & Breakfast La Merced 123 ☎054 330 015, ⊛losandesarequipa.com. This welcoming place has spacious wi-fi enabled rooms with parquet flooring and a rooftop terrace with views over town. Self-caterers will delight at the huge open-plan kitchen with a large outdoor seating area, complete with TV lounge. Rates include breakfast. S̲5̲0̲

★ **Flying Dog** Melgar 116 ☎054 231 163, ⊛flyingdogperu.com. Misti the dog and Chacani the cat patrol the premises of this pleasant hostel located in a colonial building just a couple of blocks east of the Monastery of Santa Catalina. Rooms are warm and clean, there's a kitchen for guests' use and a lounge area with a pool table, as well as a bar for evening drinks. Dorms S̲3̲0̲, doubles S̲9̲0̲

Le Foyer Ugarte 114 ☎054 286 473, ✉hostallefoyer @yahoo.com. The neat rooms here are set on two floors around a sunny interior courtyard, and there's a lounge with DVDs and a Play Station to unwind; two jacuzzis and a barbecue area on the rooftop terrace are soon to come. The happening bar downstairs, El Escondido de las Monjas, means lots of fun, although things can stay quite loud till the early hours. Free wi-fi. Dorms $\overline{S25}$, doubles $\overline{S70}$

Koala Hostel Av Puente Gráu 108 ☎ 054 223 622, ⓦ koalahostel.com. Friendly and helpful staff at this quiet little hostel want guests to sit back and relax. Rooms are small and colourful, there's a kitchen, wi-fi and plans to build a bar and a rooftop terrace. $\overline{S60}$

★ **Macondo** Puente Grau 109 ☎ 054 405 350, ⓦ booking .com/macondo. More of a B&B than a hostel, this friendly Italian-owned place has neat and tidy colourful rooms, most with shared bath. The little rooftop terrace has great views over St Francisco Church and the surrounding volcanoes. Staff are extremely helpful and will happily recommend sights, restaurants and more. Dorms $\overline{S25}$, doubles $\overline{S60}$

The Point Palacio Viejo 325 ☎ 054 286 920, ⓦ thepoint hostels.com. Part of the chain of party hostels popular with backpackers throughout Peru, the Arequipa branch is more intimate, with just four dorms. There's a pool table, table tennis and games and trivia on weekday nights, as well as Spanish language classes on offer. Breakfast and wi-fi included. Dorms $\overline{S19}$

EATING

★ **Cevichería Fory Fay** Thomas 221–223. This family-run place prepares up to 20kg of fish daily for its savvy clientele who flock here to tuck into Arequipa's best *ceviche*. Try the excellent *ceviche mixto* (S23). Wed–Mon 10am–4pm.

Como en Casa Piérola 106-A. Owned by a gastroenterologist, the emphasis at this little vegetarian place is on wholesome food. Following the healthy soup of the day, you're encouraged to take your pick of four mains, all generously served and followed by a nutritious dessert. Set menu S9. Mon–Sat noon–4pm.

Crepísimo Santa Catalina 208. This Swiss-run café serves one hundred varieties of sweet and savoury crêpes to be enjoyed with a refreshing home-made Andean ice tea (S4). Try their bestselling crêpe with strawberry ice cream (S18). Daily 8am–midnight.

Istanbul San Francisco 321. This café/lounge serves Middle Eastern fare such as hummus (S12), falafel (S7.50), kofte (S7.50) and mezze (S29) to share. Drinks are reasonably priced at S11, with a refreshing strawberry mojito (S14) as their signature drink. Mon–Sat 8.30am–1am, Sun 10am–10pm.

Peruita Palacio Viejo 321A. One of southern Peru's very few Italian-run pizzerias, here you will see the Italian *pizzaiolo* spinning all sorts of exotically flavoured thin-crusted (or more thickly so, depending on customers' preference) pizzas (S15–33), nicely washed down with an authentic Italian Peroni beer (S8). Mon–Fri 12.30–3pm & 5.30–10.30pm, Sat 5.30–11pm.

★ **TREAT YOURSELF**

La Trattoria del Monasterio Santa Catalina 309 ☎ 054 204 062. Three intimate dining areas located in the grounds of the Santa Catalina Monastery, offering sumptuous fusion dishes with the best of *arequipeño* and Italian flavours. As is to be expected, the exquisite pasta here is all home-made; try the *ravioli de camarones en salsa de cauche arequipeño* (S37). Mon–Sat noon–4pm & 7–11pm, Sun noon–4pm.

Peruita Express Jerusalén 123. Head here for some authentic and exquisite Italian *pizza al taglio* (slices of pizza) on the go as you explore town, or to regain your senses on a Saturday night after a pisco sour too many. Mon–Fri 9am–1pm, Sat open all night.

El Turco San Francisco 223. Crawl over to this Turkish-owned joint after a heavy night out to soak up the booze with a good old kebab (S5.90). Daily 7.30am–midnight, open 24hr on Thurs, Fri & Sat.

DRINKING AND NIGHTLIFE

Café Art Montreal Ugarte 210. This cavernous vaulted bar with brick walls hosts saxophone and *trova* (Cuban guitar music) bands on Thurs at 9pm, while *arequipeño* bands take the stage at 10.30pm on Fri and Sat for some 1980s tracks. Beer S6, cocktails S11. Happy hour 5–11pm. Mon–Sat 4pm–3am.

★ **Casona Forum** San Francisco 317. This three-storey complex houses some of Arequipa's best nightspots, such as *Zero Pub & Pool*, with pool tables, and the *Terrasse* lounge restaurant, offering a combo of fine dining and stunning views of the city through 360-degree windows. The jewel in the crown – the basement *Forum* disco – is the place to see and be seen among young *arequipeños*, with a lively tropical decor including palm trees, pools and a large artificial waterfall.

★ **Farren's Irish Bar** Pasaje Catedral 107. Just behind the plaza, this little Irish bar/pub with outdoor seating is the perfect spot to grab a refreshing beer as you explore town. There's a screen for sporting events, and if you're around on St Patrick's Day you can enjoy a few pints of Guinness. Local beers (S6), as well as Belgian and English brews (Old Speckled Hen S18). Happy hour 6–10pm. Mon–Sat 10am–midnight.

Mr Fish Av Variante Uchumayo s/n. This large club located on the outskirts of Arequipa is now the city's hottest nightlife spot. Young *arequipeños* dance away on Thurs from as early as late afternoon, on Fri it's creole music while on Sat revellers go wild to club beats. Entry S60. Thurs 3pm–5am, Fri & Sat 9pm–5am.

9

CROSSING INTO CHILE

The **border with Chile** (Mon–Fri 8am–midnight, Sat & Sun 24hr) is about 40km south of Tacna (a 6–7hr bus ride from Arequipa). Regular buses and *colectivos* to **Arica** (see p.419) leave from the modern bus terminal on Hipolito Unanue in Tacna; the *colectivos* (S20) are a particularly quick and easy way to cross the border. For a small tip, the drivers will assist you with border formalities. **Coming back into Peru** from Arica is as simple as getting there; *colectivos* run throughout the day from the Terminal Internacional de Buses on Diego Portales 1002.

Retro San Francisco 317. Located in the Casona Forum, this is Arequipa's only bar hosting bands early on in the week. Rock groups hit the stage Tues through to Sat at 10pm, occasionally backed up by some salsa, reggaeton, and 1970s, 80s and 90s combos. Mon–Sat 7pm–2am.

DIRECTORY

Banks and exchange BCP at San Juan de Dios 125 and Scotia Bank on Moral, at San Francisco, have ATMs and can change/dispense US dollars. There are *cambios* on the Plaza de Armas, on Jerusalén and on San Juan de Dios.
Hospital Clínica Arequipa, Av Bolognesi con Puente Grau (☎054 599 000).
Internet Try Cyber Espacio at Rivero corner Melgar (Mon–Sat 7am–9pm; S1/hr) or Internet Señor de Huanca at Jerusalén 201G (Mon–Sat 9.30am–8pm; S1/hr).
Laundry Lavandería Santa Catalina at Santa Catalina 302 (Mon–Sat 8am–8pm; S3/kg); Laundry at Peru Trek, Jerusalén 302B (Mon–Sat 7.30am–7pm; S3/kg).
Pharmacy Mifarma on C Arequipa 121, at Moral (daily 7am–11pm).
Police The tourist police is at Jerusalén 315 (☎054 201 258).
Post office Moral 118 (Mon–Sat 8am–8pm, Sun 9am–1pm).
Taxi Reliable companies include Alo 45 (☎054 454 545) and Turismo Arequipa (☎054 458 888). Make sure to book over the phone, as there have been reports of drivers using fake car signs purporting to work for taxi companies.

THE COLCA CANYON

The sharp terraces of the **COLCA CANYON**, the world's deepest at more than 4km from cliff edge to river bottom, are still home to more-or-less traditional Indian villages, despite the canyon's growth into one of Peru's most popular tourist attractions. The **Mirador Cruz del Condor** is the most popular viewing point – the canyon is around 1600m deep at this point – from where you can almost guarantee seeing condors circling up from the depths against breathtaking scenery (best spotted 7–9am; in May, June and July sightings are best 9–11am).

The entry point for the Colca Canyon is the market town of **Chivay**, 150km north of Arequipa (3–4hr by bus). The pleasant little town of **Cabanaconde** (3300m) serves as an excellent base to descend into the canyon, and is about 10km further down the road.

You'll need a couple of days to begin exploring the area and three or four to do it any justice, but several tour companies offer punishing one-day tours as well as extended trips with overnight stops. When you enter the canyon, you need to purchase the Boleto Turístico (Tourist Ticket; S70) from the control point just before the entrance to Chivay. Only buy tickets from Autocolca authorities, as counterfeit tickets do exist.

Chivay

This is the largest village in the canyon, located by its entrance. Its attractions include the hot springs, 3km northeast of town (4am–7pm; S15), with a zip-line (ⓦcolcaziplining.com) next to it. *Colectivos* run from the Plaza de Armas (S1; 7min). There are also several hiking trails here, although as **CHIVAY** is not so attractive, most visitors continue on to the laidback village of Cabanaconde.

ARRIVAL AND DEPARTURE

By bus Regular buses connect Chivay with Arequipa (every 2hr or so; 3hr) and Cabanaconde (6 daily; 2hr 30min). The bus companies 4MM and Sillustani have daily departures to Puno (6hr) leaving around lunchtime.

ACCOMMODATION

Hostal El Caminante Av Siglo XX s/n ☎959 464 783. A good option with eleven clean rooms in a concrete block just a short walk from the main square. All have cable TV and private bath and there's wi-fi too. ~~S40~~
La Pascana A pleasant respite from the endless concrete blocks, *La Pascana* has rooms giving onto a central flowering courtyard, although these could do with a splash of paint and a quick revamp. Rates include breakfast. Free wi-fi. ~~S70~~

COLCA CANYON

Sepregina (5432m)
Bomboya (5200m)

Metalled road
Dirt track
Trekking trail

map not to scale

N

Catarata de Huaruro
Tocallo
Fure
Mirador de Tocallo
Llatica
Río Huaruro
Mirador Apacheta
Tapay
Malata • Coshñirwa
Paclla
San Juan de Chuccho 2300m
Pallca
Geyser
Colca Canyon
Río Colca
Chuirca
Sangalle Oasis
Mirador Cruz del Condor
Pinchollo   Yanque   Chivay
Cabanaconde
Mirador Tapay
Nevado Huaca Huaca (6025m)
Volcano Sabancaya (5976m)
Lago Mucurca
Ampato Glacier (6425m)
Arequipa

Nazca, Lima, Tacna & Chile

EATING

El Horno Av 22 de Agosto s/n. Only open for dinner, this place attracts locals and tourists alike who both get happily involved in the daily *peña* shows. Choose from pizza, international and local dishes. The set menu will set you back S25, or opt for the à la carte menu if the former doesn't tickle your fancy. Daily 6–10pm.

Urinsaya Francisco Bolognesi 1026. Serving one of the best all-you-can-eat lunchtime buffets (S25), the grub here includes a variety of hearty soups, as well as fish and meat dishes. Daily 11am–3pm.

Cabanaconde

An attractive village in the heart of the canyon, surrounded by Inca terracing, **CABANACONDE** makes an excellent base for hiking down into the canyon. Follow fellow hikers through the fields to a steep trail leading down to Sangalle Oasis – a splotch of blue and green amid parched scenery. Halfway down, the path splits in two; take the right-hand turn, which leads to the oasis below. The trek takes about three

hours, and, while it's possible to ascend on the same day, it's far more rewarding to either camp or stay in one of the basic huts at Sangalle; each campsite has its own swimming pool.

Another popular route is Cabanaconde–San Juan de Chuccho–Coshñirhua–Malata–Sangalle Oasis (approx 6hr). However, between San Juan de Chuccho and Coshñirhua thick vegetation at times covers the path, and smaller diverging trails can be confusing. You might lose your way temporarily before joining the main path again.

It is strongly advised to tackle all other routes with a guide, in particular given that there have been reported accidents and even deaths of tourists who have ventured off unaccompanied into the canyon.

ARRIVAL AND DEPARTURE

By bus There are several daily departures to Arequipa (6hr) via Chivay (2hr 30min).

9

ACCOMMODATION AND EATING

La Casa de Santiago ☎ 054 203 737, ⓦ lacasadesantiago .com. This calm little oasis with clean and tidy rooms has a verdant garden with hammocks and wonderful views over the surrounding mountains. Dorms S̄15, doubles S̄50

Pachamama ☎ 054 767 277, ⓦ pachamamahome.com. The main area of this hostel is warm and welcoming with a wood-fire pizza oven that keeps the room toasty and plenty of board games and a book exchange to keep travellers happy. Rooms here are pleasant, while those in the two annexes down the street are basic and lack charm; those with a private bath will set you back a bit more. S̄35

★ **Valle del Fuego** ☎ 054 668 910, ⓦ valledelfuego .com. Laidback and friendly owner Yamil will welcome you with a potent pisco sour ("the authentic pisco sour, not the one for tourists…"). The brick and stone rooms, all with private bath, are warm and welcoming and command lovely views over the surrounding mountains. You can rent mules and horses here (S60), as well as mountain bikes. Breakfast included. Their rustic family-run restaurant and bar just a few doors down serves pizzas and sandwiches (S10–15) as well as set menus for S10. Dorms S̄10, doubles S̄40

Puno and Lake Titicaca

An immense region both in terms of its history and the breadth of its magical landscape, the **Titicaca Basin** makes most people feel as if they are on top of the world. The skies are vast and the horizons appear to blend away below you. With a dry, cold climate – frequently falling below freezing in the winter nights of July and August – **Puno** is a breathless place (at 3870m above sea level), with a burning daytime sun in stark contrast to the icy evenings. On the edge of the town spreads the vast **Lake Titicaca** – enclosed by white peaks and dotted with unusual **floating islands**. The lake is home to the Uros culture, as are the beautiful island communities of **Amantani** and **Taquile**, which can all be visited by boat from Puno.

PUNO

The first Spanish settlement at **PUNO** sprang up around a silver mine discovered by the infamous Salcedo brothers in 1657, a camp that forged such a wild and violent reputation that the Lima viceroy moved in with soldiers to crush the Salcedos before things got too out of hand. In 1668 he created Puno as the capital of the region and from then on it developed into Lake Titicaca's main port and an important town on the silver trail from Potosí. Rich in traditions, Puno is also famed as the folklore capital of Peru. During the first two weeks of February, fiestas are held in honour of the **Virgen de la Candelaria** – a great spectacle, with incredible dancers wearing devil masks, which climaxes on the second Sunday of February.

WHAT TO SEE AND DO

Puno is a congested, chaotic but friendly town, compact enough to walk around. Most travellers use it as a stopover on their way to see the islands, but there are a couple of sites of interest in the town itself. There are four main points of reference in Puno: the spacious **Plaza de Armas**, the cosmopolitan strip of **Jirón Lima** on which most restaurants and bars can be found, tiny **Parque Pino** and the bustling **port** area.

The Plaza de Armas and around

The seventeenth-century **Catedral** on the Plaza de Armas (Mon–Fri 8am–noon & 3–6pm, Sat 8am–noon & 3–7pm, Sun 7.30am–noon & 3–5pm; free) is surprisingly large, with an exquisite Baroque facade and, unusually for Peru, a very simple interior, in line with the local Aymara Indians' austere attitude to religion. High up, overlooking the town and Plaza de Armas, **Huajsapata Park** sits on a prominent hill, a steep ten-minute climb up Jirón Deustua, right into Jirón Llave, left up Jirón Bolognesi, then left again up the Pasaje Contique steps. Huajsapata offers stupendous views across the bustle of Puno to the serene blue of Titicaca and its unique skyline, though there have been some reported muggings here, so be careful.

The Yavari

Moored in the dock of the *Hotel Sonesta Posada del Inca*, the nineteenth-century British-built steamship **Yavari** (daily 8am–6pm; admission by donations; ☏051 369 604, ⓦyavari.org) is the oldest working single-propellor iron ship in existence. In 1862, the 2766 pieces of the ship were transported from the Peruvian coast on the backs of mules and llamas, many of whom perished during the trip, and with the help of eight thousand men the *Yavari* was reconstructed on Lake Titicaca. *Yavari* started life as a Peruvian navy gunship but ended up rusting on the lake's shores after being decommissioned. In 1982, Englishwoman Meriel Larkin formed the Yavari Project in a bid to save it. The project aims to repair the ship sufficiently to make it possible to take trips around the lake on it by 2015. Guests can stay on board in beautiful wooden cabins for US$45 a night, inclusive of breakfast.

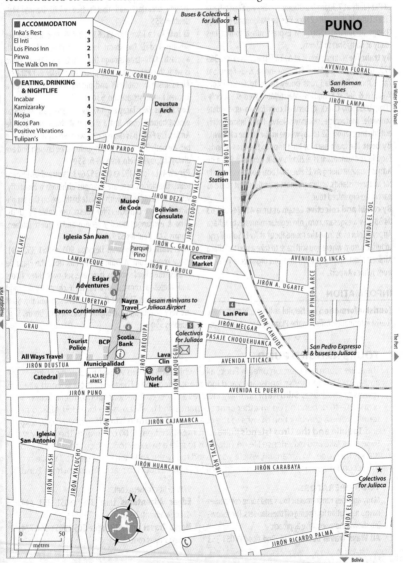

PUNO

■ ACCOMMODATION
Inka's Rest	4
El Inti	3
Los Pinos Inn	2
Pirwa	1
The Walk On Inn	5

● EATING, DRINKING & NIGHTLIFE
Incabar	1
Kamizaraky	4
Mojsa	5
Ricos Pan	6
Positive Vibrations	2
Tulipan's	3

Buses & Colectivas for Juliaca
Low Water Port & Yavari
AVENIDA FLORAL
JIRÓN M. H. CORNEJO
San Roman Buses
JIRÓN LAMPA
Deustua Arch
AVENIDA LA TORRE
JIRÓN PARDO
JIRÓN INDEPENDENCIA
Train Station
JIRÓN TARAPACÁ
JIRÓN DEZA
JIRÓN TEODORO VALCARCEL
Museo de Coca
AVENIDA EL SOL
Bolivian Consulate
Iglesia San Juan
Parque Pino
JIRÓN C. GRALDO
ILLAVE
LAMBAYEQUE
Central Market
AVENIDA LOS INCAS
JIRÓN F. ARBULU
Edgar Adventures
JIRÓN A. UGARTE
JIRÓN PINEDA ARCE
JIRÓN LIBERTAD
Nayra Travel
Gesam minivans to Juliaca Airport
Lan Peru
JIRÓN CAHUIDE
Banco Continental
GRAU
Tourist Police
BCP
Scotia Bank
JIRÓN AREQUIPA
Colectivos for Juliaca
JIRÓN MELGAR
PASAJE CHOQUEHUANCA
San Pedro Expresso & buses to Juliaca
All Ways Travel
JIRÓN DEUSTUA
Municipalidad
Lava Clin
AVENIDA TITICACA
Catedral
PLAZA DE ARMES
@ World Net
JIRÓN MOQUEGUA
AVENIDA EL PUERTO
JIRÓN PUNO
JIRÓN LIMA
Iglesia San Antonio
JIRÓN CAJAMARCA
JIRÓN ANCASH
JIRÓN AYACUCHO
JIRÓN HUANCANE
JIRÓN TACNA
JIRÓN CARABAYA
Colectivos for Juliaca
AVENIDA EL SOL
JIRÓN RICARDO PALMA
Huajsapata Park
The Port
N
0   50
metres
Bolivia

9

ARRIVAL AND DEPARTURE

If you arrive in Puno from sea level, you'll immediately be affected by the altitude and should take it easy for the first day or two.

By bus The bus terminal is at Jr. Primero de Mayo 703 (☎ 051 364 733). A taxi to the centre is S4. Recommended companies include: Cruz del Sur (☎ 051 368 524), Ormeño (☎ 051 352 780), Transzela (☎ 051 353 822) and Flores (☎ 051 366 734). The bus terminal departure tax is S1.

Destinations Arequipa (hourly; 6hr); Cusco (hourly; 6hr); La Paz (daily at 7.30am & 2.30pm; 6–7hr) via Copacabana (3hr); Lima (4 daily; 18–21hr); Puerto Maldonado (3 daily; change at Juliaca; 15hr). 4M Express run a tourist bus (daily at 6am; 5hr) to Chivay.

By train The train station is at Av La Torre 224 (☎ 051 369 179; ticketing office Mon–Fri 7am–noon & 3–6pm, Sat 7am–3pm). Peru Rail runs pricey trains to Cusco (Mon, Wed, Fri & Sat at 8pm; Nov–March Mon, Wed & Sat only; 10hr; US$150). Check ⓦ perurail.com for an up-to-date schedule. Motorcycle rickshaws leave from immediately outside the station (S2 to anywhere in the centre of town).

By boat The main port for boat trips to the Uros Islands, Taquile and Amantani is a 20min walk from the Plaza de Armas, straight along Av El Puerto. Local boats leave daily for all three islands, although most travellers visit these as part of an organized tour.

By combi and colectivo Gesam at Lima 419 (☎ 051 63 04 38, ⓦ viajesgesam.com) run regular minivans to Juliaca Airport. Colectivos from the roundabout at Av El Sol only go to Juliaca, from where you will have to take a taxi to Juliaca Airport. Most hospedajes in Puno can organize a pick-up from Juliaca Airport.

INFORMATION

Tourist information The helpful and friendly staff at the tourist information office on the Plaza de Armas (Deustua,

at Lima; Mon–Sat 9am–6pm, Sun 9am–1pm; ☎ 051 365 088, ⓔ iperupuno@promperu.gob.pe) can provide photo-copied town plans, leaflets and other information.

ACCOMMODATION

★ **Inka's Rest** Psje. San Carlos 158 ☎ 051 368 720. This welcoming place has spacious, comfortable dorms and doubles, all with individual communal areas with sofas, TV, kitchen, computers and all-day coca tea. Staff can organize pick-up from Juliaca Airport for S15. Rates include breakfast and there's free wi-fi. Dorms S̲1̲8̲, doubles S̲5̲5̲

El Inti Av La Torre 137 ☎ 051 778 756, ⓔ intibackpacker @hotmail.com. The decor in the rooms is frilly with a splash of chintz, although the premises are clean, there is wi-fi throughout and the price is virtually unbeatable. All rooms have cable TV and private bath, and there's a kitchen for guests' use too. S̲3̲0̲

Los Pinos Inn Tarapacá 182 ☎ 051 367 398, ⓔ hostal pinos@hotmail.com. Just a short walk from the Plaza de Armas, Los Pinos has clean rooms with woolly blankets and private bath. The friendly staff speak some English and are always happy to help. Free wi-fi. S̲5̲0̲

Pirwa Av La Torre 492 ☎ 051 352 693, ⓦ pirwahostelsperu .com. The dorms here are spacious although a bit stuffy, while the doubles, all with private bath, are on the simple side. There are computers for guests' use, cable TV, DVDs, a book exchange, laundry service and a guest kitchen. Dorms S̲2̲8̲, doubles S̲7̲5̲

The Walk On Inn Jirón Deustua 901 ☎ 051 352 631, ⓦ walkoninn.com. A 2min uphill walk from the Plaza de Armas, the simple rooms here are set over three floors and there's a communal area with chintzy sofas and all-day coca tea. The hot showers work sporadically. Staff are very helpful and can organize bus tickets. Dorms S̲2̲0̲, doubles S̲5̲0̲

TOURS AROUND PUNO

There are four main tours on offer in Puno, all of which will reward you with abundant bird and animal life, immense landscapes and indigenous traditions. The trip to the ancient burial towers or chullpas at **Sillustani** normally involves a three- to four-hour tour by minibus and costs S30–40 depending on whether or not entrance and guide costs are included. Most other tours involve a combination of visits to the nearby **Uros Floating Islands** (half-day tour; S30) and **Taquile and the Uros Islands** (full day from S60, or from S100 overnight). The best way to see the lake and experience life on Titicaca is to take a two-day tour, which stops at the Uros Islands then goes to Amantaní, where you spend the night, and then continues to Taquile on the second day; a day-trip is very rushed, as it takes three hours to reach Amantaní from Puno.

TOUR OPERATORS

Many agencies run formulaic tours and some companies have a reputation for ripping off the islanders. The following show a more sensitive approach:

All Ways Travel Deustua 576, 2nd floor ☎ 051 353

979, ⓦ titicacaperu.com.

Edgar Adventures Lima 328 ☎ 051 353 444, ⓦ edgaradventures.com.

Nayra Travel Lima 419, office 105 ☎ 051 364 774, ⓦ nayratravel.com.

EATING, DRINKING AND NIGHTLIFE

Incabar Lima 348. This place fills up in the early evenings when customers pour in for an aperitif (S15) and some *novoandina* cuisine such as kingfish with fried vegetables and a red curry sauce (S32). Soups (S15), salads (S16–25) and sandwiches (S13–16) too. Free wi-fi. Daily 8am–10pm.

Kamizaraky Grau 158. This dark, cavernous bar has live music on Fri and Sat from 9pm. The main musical flavour is rock, although bands also play reggae, country, jazz and blues. Cocktails S13. Daily 5pm–midnight.

★ **Mojsa** Lima 635, 2nd floor ☎ 051 363 182. It translates as "delicious" in Aymara and so it is – local and international dishes here are prepared using highland produce, and the pizzas (S12–38) are cooked in the wood-fire oven that keeps the place snug on cold winter evenings. Try the *trout ceviche* (S28). The bar upstairs has wonderful views over the plaza. Book ahead. Daily 10am–10pm.

Ricos Pan Jr. Moquegua 334. A local favourite, this café/bakery serves all manner of tasty pies (S5), cakes (S6), hot chocolate (S3.50) and teas (S1.50), as well as breakfasts (S8) and freshly baked *empanadas* (S2.50). Mon–Sat 6am–9pm, Sun 3–9pm.

Positive Vibrations Lima 378. This well-established bar has nightly DJs playing all sorts from electronica to reggae. After a few drinks, the neon lighting at the back will wreak havoc with your retinas. Happy hour 4–7pm. Beer S5, cocktails from S12. Daily 6am–3am.

Tulipan's Lima 394. Sit in the open-air courtyard during the day or huddle up by the wood-fired oven at this restaurant serving thin-crust pizzas. The menu includes a range of local and international dishes, from healthy soups (S10) to trout (S26), all cooked with Andean herbs. Mon–Sat 7am–9pm, Sun 4–10pm.

DIRECTORY

Banks and exchange Banco Continental, Lima at Libertad, and BCP, at Lima 444, both have ATMs. There are plenty of casas de cambio along Lima.

Consulate Bolivia, Arequipa 136, 2nd Floor (Mon–Fri 8am–2pm; ☎ 051 351 251).

Hospital Tourist Health, Moqueua 191 (☎ 051 365 909).

Internet Try World Net on Arequipa, at Deustua (Mon–Sat 9am–10pm; S1.50).

Laundry Lava Clin, Deustua 323 (Mon–Sat 8am–noon & 2.30–7pm; S6/kg).

Post office Moquegua 269 (Mon–Fri 8am–7.30pm, Sat 8am–noon).

Tourist police At Deustua 538, open 24hr (☎ 051 352 303).

LAKE TITICACA

An undeniably impressive sight, **Lake Titicaca**'s skies are vast, almost infinite, and deep, deep hues of blue; below this

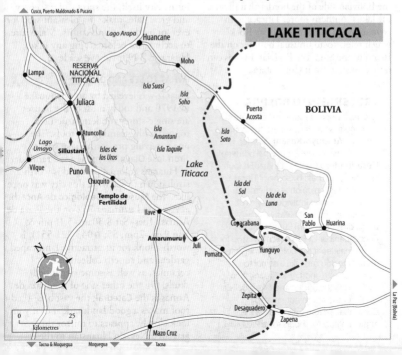

Cusco, Puerto Maldonado & Pucara

LAKE TITICACA

BOLIVIA

La Paz (Bolivia)

N

0   25
kilometres

Tacna & Moquegua   Moquegua   Tacna

9

sits a usually placid mirror-like lake, reflecting the big sky back on itself. A national reserve since 1978, the lake has more than sixty varieties of birds, fourteen species of native fish and eighteen types of amphibians. It's also the world's largest high-altitude body of water, at 284m deep and more than 8500 square kilometres in area.

The unique, man-made **Uros Floating Islands**, which have been inhabited since their construction centuries ago by Uros Indians, are an impressive sight. Tour groups only visit a couple of the islands where the people are used to tourism; they will greet you, offer you handicrafts for sale and possibly suggest a tour on one of their boats, made from the same totora reeds as their island homes, for a small fee. For a more authentic experience, visit the communities who live on the fixed islands of **Taquile** and **Amantaní**, who still wear traditional clothes and follow ancient local customs. There are, in fact, more than seventy islands in the lake, the largest and most sacred being the **Island of the Sun** (see p.179), an ancient Inca temple site on the Bolivian side of the border that divides the lake's southern shore. Titicaca is an Aymara word meaning "Puma's Rock", which refers to an unusual boulder on the Island of the Sun. The Bolivian islands can only be visited from Copacabana.

CROSSING INTO BOLIVIA

The most popular routes to Bolivia involve overland road travel, crossing the frontier either at **Yunguyo/Kasani** (best for Copacabana) or at the principal border of **Desaguadero** (best for La Paz). En route to either you'll pass by some of Titicaca's more interesting colonial settlements, each with its own individual styles of architecture. By far the easiest way is to take a direct bus from Puno to either Copacabana or La Paz, which will stop for the formalities at the border. Otherwise, from Puno you can take a *combi* to Yunguyo, then another to Kasani, then walk across the border and take a Bolivian *combi* for the ten-minute ride to Copacabana. From Copacabana it is approximately five hours to La Paz.

Huaraz and the Cordillera Blanca

Sliced north to south by the parallel **Cordillera Blanca** and **Cordillera Negra** (the white and black mountain ranges), the department of Ancash offers some of the best hiking and mountaineering in the Americas. Its capital **Huaraz** – eight hours by bus from Lima – is tourist-friendly, has a lively atmosphere and makes an ideal base for exploring some nearby lagoons, ruins, glaciers and remote trails. Through the valley known as the Callejón de Huaylas is the pretty town of **Caraz**, which offers a taste of traditional Andean life.

HUARAZ

With glaciated peaks and excellent trekking nearby, **HUARAZ** is a place to stock up, hire guides and equipment, and relax with great food and drink after a breathtaking expedition. While there are only a couple of tourist attractions to visit in the city itself, the spectacular scenery and great cafés make it a pleasant stop for even non-adventurous spirits. Make sure to acclimatize before trying any hikes; Huaraz is 3090m above sea level.

WHAT TO SEE AND DO

Huaraz was levelled by an earthquake in 1970 and today most of the houses are single-storey modern structures topped with gleaming tin roofs. The one surviving pre-earthquake street, **Jiron José Olaya**, serves as a sad reminder of Huaraz's colonial past and is worth a stroll down to see what this city was once like. The **Museo Arqueologico de Ancash**, at Avenida Luzuriaga 762 on the Plaza de Armas (Tues–Sat 8.30am–5.15pm & Sun 9am–2pm; S5; ☎043 721 551), is worth a look for its attractive landscaped gardens and superb collection of ceramics, as well as some trepanned skulls. On the other side of the Plaza de Armas is the **Catedral**; the vast blue-tiled roof makes a good landmark and, if you look closely, appears to mirror the glaciated Nevado Huanstán to the east.

There's an easy day trek (7km; 3hr) from Huaraz to the remains of a Wari mausoleum, **Wilcawain** (Mon–Sat 9am–5pm & Sun 9am–2pm; S5). From here there's a non-covered road that leads to the nearby thermal springs at **Monterrey**, a relaxing afternoon. Be sure to check details with the tourist office before you go, as attacks on tourists have been reported on this route.

ARRIVAL AND DEPARTURE

By plane LC Perú operates daily flights from Lima. The small airstrip is close to the village of Anta, some 23km north of Huaraz; a 30min ride into the city by *combi* (S2.50).

By bus Most bus companies have terminals a street or two from the main drag of Av Luzuriaga on Jr. Comercio which becomes Jr. Lucar y Torre.

Destinations Lima (18 daily; 8hr); Chimbote (3 daily; 7hr); Trujillo (4 daily; 9hr).

GETTING AROUND

Av Luzuriaga is the north–south axis of the town centre, where most of the restaurants, nightlife and tour operators are based. Much of Huaraz town can be negotiated on foot once you've acclimatized to the altitude; however, some of the more remote sectors around the urban area should not be walked alone at night.

By taxi For short journeys within the city, the best option is to use one of the regular *taxi colectivos* that run on fixed routes along Av Luzuriaga and Av Centenario (S0.80). A taxi ride anywhere in the city should not cost more than S3–4.50. Companies include Phono Taxi (043 428 800) and Taxi Plus (043 792 111).

INFORMATION

Tourist information iPerú, at Pasaje Atusparia just off the Plaza de Armas (Mon–Sat 9am–6pm, Sun 9am–1pm; ☎ 043 428 812). Make sure to pick up the free mini-booklet *Map Guide Huaraz-Peru*, produced by ⓦ andeanexplorer.com. It contains excellent information on local treks and lots of maps; it's also available in many of the tourist restaurants in Huaraz.

HUARAZ

Airport (23km) ▲   ▲ Monterrey, Anta, Yungay, Caraz & Wikahuain

ACCOMMODATION

B&B My House	6
Benkawasi Albergue	7
Churup Guest House	5
El Jacal Guest House	4
Jo's Place	1
Hostal Raimondi	2
The Way Inn	3

EATING, DRINKING & NIGHTLIFE

La Brasa Roja	9
Café Andino	5
California Café	8
Chilli Heaven	7
El Horno	1
Portal de Los Andes	2
El Tambo	4
Xtreme Bar	6
Zion Bar	3

Mirador de Rataquena ▼

9

TOURS AND ACTIVITIES IN AND AROUND HUARAZ

Most of the tour operators in Huaraz can be found along Avenida Luzuriaga, or the two small squares that join it to the Plaza de Armas, and are open from 7am until late, closing between 1pm and 4pm. Most specialize in hiking and mountaineering. Popular excursions include the 8hr **Llanganuco Lakes** (see p.790), the 9–11hr **Chavín de Huantar** (see p.789) and the edge of the **Pastoruri Glacier** at 5240m (8hr). Most operators can also arrange trips to the Monterrey **thermal baths** (2hr) and some offer **adventure activities** in the area. Costs usually exclude entrance fees and food; make sure your guide can speak English if you need them to. If you're hiring your own guide, always check for certification and that they're registered at the Casa de Guías (see below). iPerú can help with any complaints.

TREKKING

If you're organizing your own trek in Huascarán National Park, register beforehand with the Park Office (see below), where you should buy your permit (S65; valid for six days) to enter the park; if you're trekking with an agency then they should sort all of this for you. In theory you're not meant to enter the park without one of these agencies – unless you're a professional. Also visit the Casa de Guías (Parque Ginebra 28-G ☎043 421 811, ⓦcasadeguias.com.pe) for the best information about local trails, current climatic conditions and advice on hiring guides, equipment and mules – they also organize rock- and ice-climbing courses. They have a useful noticeboard, worth checking to see if there are any groups about to leave on treks that you might want to join, and they sell detailed trekking maps.

TOUR OPERATORS

★ **Andean Kingdom** Parque Ginebre 120 ☎043 425 555, ⓦandeankingdom.com. Argentine-run tour operator specializing in climbing and trekking. Has its own centre out in the Cordillera Negra, where they offer lodging and rock-climbing courses.

Galaxia Expeditions Parque del Periodista, Lote 36 ☎043 425 355, ⓦgalaxia-expeditions.com. The biggest and most popular tour office in town offers a variety of treks, mountaineering trips and day tours as well as horseriding, mountain biking and canyoning. Also owns a guesthouse (*Aldo*; see Galaxia website). Four-day Santa Cruz trail US$120 all-inclusive; a day trek to Laguna 69 costs US$35–50. Open 6am–10pm.

Mountain Bike Adventures Jr. Lucar y Torre 530, 2nd floor (one block east of Av Luzuriaga) ☎043 424 259, ⓦchakinaniperu.com. Customizable guided bike tours and hikes, with English-speaking guides. Also rents bikes and sells local artesanía in the office. Good reputation for safety.

Huascarán National Park office Jr. Federico Sal y Rosas 555 (Mon–Fri 8.30am–1pm & 2.30–6pm, Sat 9am–noon; ☎043 422 086).

Tourist police Av Luzuriaga 724, at the Plaza de Armas (daily 8am–8pm; ☎043 421 351). Some English spoken.

ACCOMMODATION

Even in high season, around August, it's rarely difficult to find accommodation at a reasonable price and except during high season it's definitely worth bargaining.

B & B My House Av 27 de Noviembre 773 ☎043 423 375, ⓦmicasahuaraz.jimdo.com. A pleasant family-run B&B with a flower-filled courtyard and bright dining room. S̄80

★ **Benkawasi Albergue** Parque Santa Rosa 928 ☎043 423 150, ⓦhuarazbenkawasi.com. This hostel is run by a friendly Huaraz family who have done a lot for the area – the owners built Huaraz's first hotel after the 1970 earthquake (now *Andino Club Hotel*). The communal areas are pleasant, with table tennis and games, and there's a shared kitchen. If you're into adventure sports, owner Benquelo Morales is the man to see. Dorms S̄10, doubles S̄50

Churup Guest House Jr. Amadeo Figueroa 1257 ☎043 424 200, ⓦchurup.com. A good base for trekkers, with luggage storage as well as reference maps and a book exchange. Although it's an uphill walk from the centre, they'll pick you up from the bus station for free and the views from the terrace are great. Breakfast included. Dorms S̄28, doubles S̄99

★ **El Jacal Guest House** Jr. José de Sucre 1044 ☎043 424 612, ⓦjacalhuaras.com. This place is amazing value, with friendly owners and lots of extras like laundry, wi-fi, kitchen use and cable TV. But above everything (literally) there's a terrace with unbelievable 360-degree views. S̄40

Jo's Place Jr. Daniel Villaizan 276 ☎043 425 505, ⓦhuaraz.com/josplace. Although ramshackle and somewhat chaotically managed, *Jo's Place* is a die-hard backpacker joint, with functional rooms and dorms, some with wonderful views. It's always popular and there's internet, wi-fi, a common room with TV and a terrace with hammocks. Full

English breakfast (S10), thanks to the British owner. Camping/person S10, dorms S15, doubles S35

Hostal Raimondi Av Raimondi 820 ☎043 421 082. An old-fashioned place with real character. Large rooms that stay cool in summer. Those on a tight budget can take the cheaper rooms without hot water. S40

★ **The Way Inn** Carretera Huaraz–Pitec Km22 ☎043 466 219, ⓦthewayinn.com. Built and owned by a Brit, this mountain lodge about 40min from the city offers a true alternative from normal hostels, with orthopaedic beds, down duvets, a climbing wall and a sauna. Camping/person S15, dorms S35, doubles S230

EATING

There's no shortage of restaurants in Huaraz, with a huge number of budget options, but the places aimed at tourists tend to be better (albeit pricier). Mercado Central is good for cheap fresh food and there are a few mini-marts on Luzuriaga.

La Brasa Roja Av Luzuriaga 915 ☎043 427 738. Very popular and always busy, serving cheap and generous plates of chicken, pizza, grills and hamburgers. Pasta dishes from S15; chicken and chips with salad S19.50. Daily noon–midnight.

★ **Café Andino** Jr. Lucar y Torre 530 ⓦcafeandino.com. This top-floor café with amazing views is a true gem. It serves a range of international dishes and great breakfasts with pizza-sized pancakes. There's wi-fi and not only a book exchange, but a substantial library of guides on the area, as well as maps. Try the *shara shara* herbal tea for altitude sickness; mains S8–25. Daily 7am–10pm.

★ **California Café** Jr. 28 de Julio 562 ⓦhuaylas.com. One of several very pleasant cafés in town, this one predictably has West Coast vibes and it makes a relaxing spot to refuel at any time. The food, including American breakfasts, soups, salads and sandwiches (mains S11–17; American-style pancakes S13), is great, and they also have a good book exchange as well as games, wi-fi and maps. Daily except Wed 7.30am–6.30pm, Sun 7.30am–2pm.

Chilli Heaven Parque Ginebra ☎043 396 085. Fun, popular place that draws an international crowd, run by a Peruvian/British couple. Spicy dishes from around the world are on the menu, including Indian and Thai curries (mains S18–40). Owner Simon is also a motorbike fanatic and organizes tours. Daily 10am–10pm.

El Horno Parque del Periodista (off the 6th block of Luzuriaga) ☎043 424 617, ⓦelhornopizzeria.com. The best wood-fired pizzas in town, as well as charcoal grills and a mean pasta carbonara. Pizzas S17.50–21.50. Mon–Sat noon–11pm.

Portal de Los Andes Jr. José de la Mar 437 ☎043 426 983. This place is a gem for a good set lunch at either S5, S7 or S12. You won't find any gringos here – this is as real as it gets. Enjoy the enormous portions of tasty traditional

Peruvian food and Andean music playing in the background. Daily 7am–9.30pm.

DRINKING AND NIGHTLIFE

El Tambo Jr. José de la Mar 776 ☎043 423 417. One of Huaraz's best nightspots, spinning Western music with Latino beats and occasional live music. Food also served. Daily 11am–2am.

★ **Xtreme Bar** Av Luzuriaga 646, 2nd floor. This is a true Huaraz institution, run by the owners of Benkawasi. There's often live music, food and a quirky rock'n'roll shrine to icons such as Bob Marley and Amy Winehouse. Daily 5pm–late.

Zion Bar Jr. José de la Mar 773. A French/Peruvian-run bar that aims to be the most chilled-out space in town. Friendly atmosphere, cheap drinks and plenty of reggae make this place a good bet. Drinks two for S15 before 10pm. Daily from 7pm.

CHAVÍN DE HUANTAR

One of the most popular day-trips from Huaraz is to **Chavín de Huantar** (Tues–Sun 8.30am–1pm & 2.30–5pm; S10; ☎043 454 042), a mysterious stone temple complex that was at the centre of a puma-worshipping religious movement some 2500 years ago. The pretty village of **Chavín**, with its whitewashed walls and traditional tiled roofs, is a gruelling but stunning drive from Huaraz; from here the complex is a few hundred metres away. The same distance in the other direction is the accompanying **museum** (same hours; free), which displays some of the most important finds from the site, including most of the famous tenon heads that originally adorned the walls of the temple.

Most people arrive on a **full-day tour** (S45 excluding lunch and entrance), although the distance can make visits feel rushed and many agencies only provide Spanish-speaking guides. To visit independently, take one of the buses that leave Huaraz for Chavín daily around 8am (3–4hr; S10) from small terminals on Jr. Andres Avelino Cáceres. Buses return from Chavín more or less on the hour from 3–6pm. It's a small village, but there are a couple of hostels, and you can camp by the Baños Quercos thermal springs, a twenty-minute stroll from the village.

9

THE CORDILLERA BLANCA

The highest range in the tropical world, the **Cordillera Blanca** consists of around 35 peaks poking their snowy heads over the 6000m mark, and until early in the twentieth century, when the glaciers began to recede, this white crest could be seen from the Pacific. Above Yungay, and against the sensational backdrop of Peru's highest peak, **Huascarán** (6768m), are the magnificent **Llanganuco Lakes**, whose waters change colour according to the time of year and the movement of the sun.

Fortunately, most of the Cordillera Blanca falls under the auspices of the **Huascarán National Park**, and the habitat has been left relatively unspoiled. Among the more exotic **wildlife** are viscacha (Andean rabbit-like creatures), vicuña, grey deer, pumas, foxes, the rare spectacled bear and several species of hummingbirds.

To get here without an organized trek, take a *combi* along the valley to Yungay or Caraz and ask around for recommended guides (check them out first with the Casa de Guías in Huaraz).

CARAZ

Further along the valley north from Huaraz are the distinct settlements of **Yungay** and the much prettier and friendly **CARAZ**. The town sits at an altitude of 2285m, making it much warmer than Huaraz, and palm trees and flowers adorn a classic colonial **Plaza de Armas**. While most people come for the hiking or cycling trails around the town, there's enough here to divert you for a day or so, most notably the pre-Chavín era remains of **Tumshukayko** (daily 8am–5pm; free), an archeological structure about 1km uphill from the Plaza de Armas (turn right once you hit Av 28 de Julio). This impressive series of stone walls, stairways and terraces (the layers have been dated to between 2500 BC and 300 AD) needs a huge amount more excavation to make greater sense of it, but is nevertheless fascinating to wander around. Finally, no stay in Caraz would be complete without careful consideration of the dessert menu: Caraz is famous for its **manjar blanco** – a caramel-like substance similar to *dulce de leche*; all bakeries in town sell it.

HIKING IN THE HUARAZ REGION

Given the scope of the mountain ranges and the passion of mountaineers, it's not surprising that there is an enormous range of **hikes** and guides in the area. Anyone interested in really getting stuck in should arm themselves with good maps and detailed guidebooks, and talk to everyone in town, from hostel owners to expats. Wherever you end up, be sure to pay heed to the rules of **responsible trekking**: carry away your waste, particularly above the snow line, where even organic waste does not decompose. And always carry a camping stove – campfires are strictly prohibited in Huascarán National Park. It's also vital to be fit, particularly if you are going it alone.

It's essential to spend at least a couple of days **acclimatizing** to the altitude before attempting a hike; if you intend high mountain climbing, this should be extended to at least five days. Although Huaraz itself is 3060m above sea level, most of the Cordilleras' more impressive peaks are over 6000m.

HIRING A GUIDE

Going hiking alone without an agency is possible, but not recommended to anyone but the most experienced hikers and climbers, and you'll likely end up paying a lot more as you'll be shouldering the costs alone. Be very careful when hiring an independent guide and always check them out with the Casa de Guías (see p.788), which has a list of all qualified guides in the area. On top of the national park fee (S65) and guide's fee (around US$60 per day for someone certified), you'll be expected to foot the bill for return transport, accommodation and food for everyone hired to help. Auxillary porters, mule drivers (*arrieros*) and cooks will each cost you around US$10 a day, plus an additional US$10 per day per pack-carrying mule or llama.

ARRIVAL AND DEPARTURE

By plane Anta Airport is 45km from Caraz and has a daily flight to and from Lima (50min). There's a regular bus service to town (S5) or Pony Exhbitions can organize a minibus (for groups).

By bus Most of the bus terminals are along Daniel Villar and Córdova, within a block or two of the Plaza de Armas. From anywhere in the Callejón de Huaylas, it's best to go back through Huaraz and down the main road to the coast. The only other alternative is to take the road north from Caraz via the Cañon del Pato down to Chimbote on the coast, where you'll have to change buses.

Destinations The main routes are Chimbote via Cañon del Pato (2 daily; 7–10hr); Lima (7 daily; 8hr); Trujillo (5 daily; 8–10hr).

GETTING AROUND

By mototaxi Everywhere in Caraz is walkable; don't let the *mototaxis* charge you more than S1 for anywhere in town (S2 to bus terminals outside the centre).

By combi *Combis* pull in at Av Sucre, three blocks south of the Plaza de Armas.

INFORMATION AND TOURS

Tourist office In the municipality building on the Plaza de Armas. Keeps sporadic hours, but try it for maps and brochures covering the attractions and hikes in the area.

Pony Expeditions Jr. Sucre 1266, at Plaza de Armas. ☎ 043 391 642, ⓦ ponyexpeditions.com. A professional and knowledgeable organization good for local information. Offers tours of the area (including the stunning Cañón del Pato) as well as guides for trekking. Prices get cheaper the larger the groups are.

ACCOMMODATION

Hostal La Casona Jr. Raimondi 319 ☎ 043 391 334. Shabby but full of character, this place is set around a nice courtyard and the prices cannot be argued with – although if you do you'll find they become even cheaper. __S20__

★ **Los Pinos Lodge** Parque San Martín 103 ☎ 043 391 130, ⓦ lospinoslodge.com. This hostel on a little plaza five minutes' walk from the centre has colourful and tastefully decorated common areas with a retro feel. The bedrooms are not as impressive, but offer basic accommodation at reasonable rates. Also offers camping space and wi-fi. Breakfast included. Camping/person __S20__, doubles __S120__

San Marco Jr. San Martín 1133 ☎ 043 391 558. Just off the plaza, this hostel in a pretty colonial building has somewhat dark rooms, but the gorgeous courtyards more than make up for it, and all rooms have private bath and TV. Breakfast not included. __S40__

EATING

Eating in Caraz is basic. The small daily market, three blocks north of the plaza, is good for fresh food and traditional Andean goods.

Café de Rat Above Pony Expeditions on Jr. Sucre 1266 ☎ 043 391 642. It may sound unsanitary, but Cafferata is the owner's surname and the place has the joint appeal of cheap, good food (including vegetarian) and a cosy feeling like that of being in someone's kitchen. The little balcony overlooks the main square. Best for pizza (S15–29) and breakfasts (S5–12). Has wi-fi too. Mon–Sat 8am–11am & 6–10pm.

Café La Terraza Jr. Sucre 1107 ☎ 043 301 226, ⓦ hostal carazdulzura.com. Probably the best place in town to grab a cappuccino or espresso. Also does excellent artisan ice cream (S2) using regional fruits. Daily 7am–11pm.

Restaurant Jeny Plaza de Armas ☎ 043 391 101. Offers tasty good-value set menus (S6) as well as some traditional and Chinese dishes plus sandwiches and breakfasts. Daily 8am–9pm.

Trujillo and the North

Pizarro, on his second voyage to Peru in 1528, sailed by the ancient Moche site of **Chan Chan**, then still a major city and an important regional centre of Inca rule. He returned to establish a Spanish colony in the same valley, naming it **Trujillo** after his birthplace in Extremadura. Despite two Inca rebellions, the Spanish hold was lasting and Trujillo grew to become the main port of call for the Spanish treasure fleets. It still boasts one of the most impressive colonial centres in Peru, as well as some of the grandest pre-Inca remains, but this city of more than one million feels modern and there's plenty to keep visitors occupied.

North of Trujillo the vast desert stretches all the way to the Ecuadorian frontier just past **Tumbes**, passing the modern city of **Chiclayo** as well as Peru's liveliest beach resort, **Máncora** – and some genuinely unspoilt stretches for the adventurous. This area has an incredible wealth of pre-Inca pyramids, tombs and temple sites to explore, as well as world-class museums, many of which can be easily visited in day-trips from the main cities. Including some of the

9

Northern Highland cities in your trip, especially **Cajamarca**, often referred to as the Cusco of the North, and the tropical **Chachapoyas**, with its nearby ruins at **Kuelap**, will give you a totally different angle to travellers only doing the traditional gringo trail.

TRUJILLO

Traditionally a trading point for coastal and jungle goods, **TRUJILLO** retains a cosmopolitan atmosphere and a welcoming attitude towards visitors. The climate is usually pleasant all year, although in winter it can be grey and sometimes fresh.

WHAT TO SEE AND DO

From the graceful colonial mansions and Baroque churches at its heart, Trujillo's commercial buildings, light industry and shantytown suburbs give way to rich sugar-cane fields that stretch far into the neighbouring Chicama Valley. Everything within the circular **Avenida España** is considered the centre and this is where most of the colonial buildings and museums lie. **Gamarra** is the main commercial street, dominated by modern buildings, shops, hotels and restaurants. The other main street, older and more attractive, is **Jirón Pizarro**, which has been pedestrianized from the eighth block to the pleasant **Plazuela El Recreo**. But it is the large and graceful **Plaza Mayor** that is the deserved star and heart of the city.

The city also boasts the largest mural in Latin America; it runs along the walls of the Universidad de la Nación (worth seeing at night when lit up).

Around Plaza Mayor

Trujillo's **Plaza Mayor** (Plaza de Armas) is often packed with street vendors

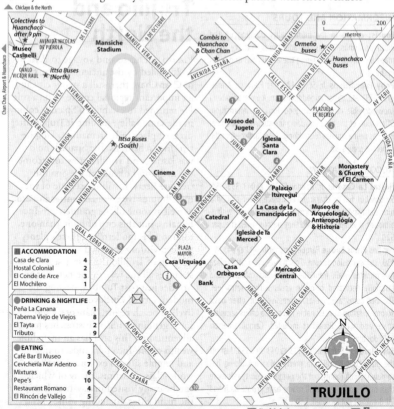

ACCOMMODATION

Casa de Clara	4
Hostal Colonial	2
El Conde de Arce	3
El Mochilero	1

DRINKING & NIGHTLIFE

Peña La Canana	1
Taberna Viejo de Viejos	8
El Tayta	2
Tributo	9

EATING

Café Bar El Museo	3
Cevichería Mar Adentro	7
Mixturas	6
Pepe's	10
Restaurant Romano	4
El Rincón de Vallejo	5

TRUJILLO

and entertainers. The city's **Catedral** (daily 8am–noon & 5–8pm; free), built in the mid-seventeenth century and then rebuilt the following century after earthquake damage, sits in one corner of the plaza. Beside the cathedral is its **museum** (Mon–Fri 9am–1pm & 4–7pm, Sat 9am–1pm; S4), which exhibits a sombre range of mainly eighteenth- and nineteenth-century religious paintings and sculptures.

Also on the square at Jr. Pizarro 313 sits the **Casa Urquiaga** (Mon–Fri 9.30am–3pm; free), a colonial mansion owned by the Peruvian Central Reserve, which is worth a visit – despite the rather rigid thirty-minute tour you have to take – for its well-kept interiors and historical importance. Simón Bolívar stayed here while he organized his final push for liberation.

East of Plaza Mayor

East of the plaza, on the corner of Jr. Pizarro and Gamarra, stands another of Trujillo's impressive mansions, **La Casa de la Emancipación**, at Jr. Pizarro 610 (Mon–Fri 9am–1pm & 4–8pm; free). The building is now head office of the Banco Continental but hosts contemporary art displays in its colonial rooms, where the enormous windows make for great people-watching.

Further down the same road, two blocks east of the Plaza Mayor, is the **Palacio Iturregui**, at Jr. Pizarro 668 (Mon–Fri 10.30am–8pm; S5), a striking mid-nineteenth-century mansion whose highlight is a pseudo-Classical courtyard, with tall columns and an open roof. The courtyard is encircled by superb galleries.

At the eastern end of Jr. Pizarro, five blocks from the Plaza Mayor, there's a small but attractive square known as the **Plazuela El Recreo** where, under the shade of some vast 130-year-old fig trees, a number of bars and food stalls provide a place to meet in the evenings for young couples. The waterworks for colonial Trujillo can be seen in the plaza, where the Spaniards extended Moche and Chimu irrigation channels to provide running water to the city.

Central museums

The **Museo de Arqueología, Antropología e Historia**, at Jr. Junín 682 (Mon–Sat 9am–5pm, Sun 9am–noon; S5; ☎044 474 850), is housed in a colonial mansion; among the highlights are some beautiful anthropomorphic ceramics. The entry fee includes a guide (some speak English).

A short walk along the same street brings you to the quirky **Museo del Juguete**, at Jr. Junín 713 on the corner with Jr. Independencia, upstairs (Mon–Thurs & Sat 10am–6pm, Fri 10am–10pm, Sun 10am–1pm; S5; ☎044 208 181). This was South America's first museum dedicated to toys, and the few well-laid-out rooms are crammed with antiques from all over the world, including mini Routemaster buses from the UK, Meccano sets and a large doll collection. There's also a display of toys belonging to pre-Hispanic cultures.

Museo de Arte Moderno

The substantial and beautiful **Modern Art Museum**, at Avenida Villarreal just after the crossroads with the carretera Industrial (Mon–Sat 9am–5pm; S10), was opened in 2006 by one of Peru's most successful artists, Gerardo Chávez, who lives next door (also the man behind the Museo del Juguete). A world-class gallery with colonial and postmodern architecture set in lush grounds, the permanent collection includes work by Chávez, Klee and Giacometti, as well as showcasing artists from all over the Americas, and there's also a decent café and shop. There's a tram service that runs from the Museo del Juguete (from 9am; two museum entrance fee package and transport S25), otherwise your best bet from the centre is via a taxi (S12), or *combi* "B" from Avenida España, which doesn't take you right to the door – hop off at the crossroads mentioned above and walk from there.

ARRIVAL AND INFORMATION

By plane Flights arrive and depart from Carlos Martínez de Penillos Airport, near Huanhuaco (☎044 464 197). LAN, at Jr. Almagro 490 on the Plaza Mayor (☎0801 1234), has three flights daily to Lima. Taxis into the city will cost

9

around S25, or you can get a bus, which leaves every 20min from Av Del Aeropuerto at a stop called "El Cruce" (10–15min walk from aiport), for around S1.50. You can also take a taxi direct to Huanchaco from the airport for S10.

By bus Most of the buses have terminals close to the centre of town near the Mansiche Stadium, southwest of it on Av Daniel Carrión or Av España, or east of it along Ejército. If you decide to stay in Huanchaco you'll have to return to Trujillo to get an onward connection. Note that some companies have two terminals: one for buses north and the other south.

Destinations Cajamarca (9 daily; 6hr); Chachapoyas (1 daily; 13hr); Chiclayo (every half hour; 4hr); Huaraz (4 daily; 9hr); Lima (hourly; 8hr); Máncora (6 daily; 7hr); Tumbes (7 daily; 10hr). Ormeño runs buses from Trujillo straight to Quito in Ecuador (2 weekly; 30hr; US$85) or to Guayaquil, Ecuador, via Piura, Máncora and Tumbes (daily; 18hr; US$55).

By combi and taxi *Combis* cannot enter within Av España, but if you walk to this boundary you can find one to most places. If you're arriving by day it's fine to walk to the city centre, though at night it's best to take a taxi (around S3.50 for a ride within Trujillo, S15 to Huanchaco, S25 to the airport). Navy blue and white coloured *combis* go to Huanchaco. Of the taxi companies, Tico Taxi (☎ 044 282 828) and Tele Taxi (☎ 044 694 747) are two recommended by iPerú.

Tourist information iPerú, at Jr. Diego de Almagro 420 on the Plaza Mayor (Mon–Sat 9am–6pm, Sun 10am–2pm; ☎ 044 294 561).

ACCOMMODATION

The majority of Trujillo's hotels are within a few blocks of the central Plaza Mayor; however, there are surprisingly few good-value hotels for a city this size. Many people prefer to stay in the nearby (11km north) bohemian beach resort of Huanchaco (see opposite), which has a much wider variety of accommodation, including some good budget options.

Casa de Clara Jr. Cahuide 495 ☎ 044 299 997. Jr. Orbegoso in the centre becomes Jr. Huayna Capac, where at about the fifth block there's a little green space, on one side of which is this hostel (it's around a 10min walk from the centre). Hot showers, wi-fi and spacious rooms in a place with a family feel. $\overline{S30}$

★ **Hostal Colonial** Jr. Independencia 618 ☎ 044 268 261, ⊛ hostalcolonial.com.pe. A central place where some English is spoken – the highlight here is the stunning colonial building. Rooms are cosy and come with TV, plus there's internet, a patio and a café that does a decent breakfast. Also has a cheap tour agency and taxi service. $\overline{S90}$

El Conde de Arce Jr. Independencia 577 ☎ 044 295 117, ⊜ elcondedearce@hotmail.com. Small guesthouse in a great location, just off the Plaza de Armas. Rooms are basic but comfortable, there's lots of outdoor patio space,

packed with plants, and there is wi-fi. Breakfast S5–9. Dorms $\overline{S20}$, doubles $\overline{S45}$

El Mochilero Jr. Independencia 887 ☎ 044 297 842. An oasis in the heart of the city, this is the only backpacker place in Trujillo and it has a lovely patio with a tropical feel, including hammocks, sofas and even two cabin rooms on a bamboo mezzanine. Internet, laundry service and breakfast provided. Tours can also be organized. Cabins/ person $\overline{S25}$, dorms $\overline{S20}$, doubles $\overline{S40}$

EATING

There's no shortage of restaurants in Trujillo. Jr. Pizarro has a huge assortment of cafés and a Metro supermarket at number 700. A speciality of the area is seafood, which is probably best appreciated on the beach at the nearby resort of Huanchaco (see below).

★ **Café Bar El Museo** Jr. Independencia, at Jr. Junín ☎ 044 324 374. In the same building as the Museo del Juguete, this plush café-bar with an old-world vibe is cluttered with posters and features a saloon bar. The menu is limited to sandwiches (S10–14), coffee, juices and alcohol but it's worth it for the atmosphere alone (expect an ever-so-cool jazz soundtrack). There's also a small art gallery in an adjoining room. Mon–Sat 9am–midnight.

Cevichería Mar Adentro Jr. Diego de Almagro 311. Look for the sample plates of food on a pavement table and then follow the passageway to a bright, large room with cheap *ceviche*, as well as other classic Peruvian dishes. *Ceviche* S6, set lunch S4. Daily 10am–4.30pm.

Mixturas Jr. de Orbegoso 319 ☎ 044 205 946. This café-bar serves good Peruvian snacks – try the fried yucca (S4) – and is decorated with colourful local artworks. There's a relaxing garden to escape from Trujillo's busy centre. Set lunch S12. Mon–Sat 8am–11pm.

Pepe's Jr. Ayacucho 214. This basic place packed with locals only does evening meals and it only does meat, but it does it well; the steak is wonderful. All mains under S13.50. Mon–Sat 6–11pm.

Restaurant Romano Jr. Pizarro 747 ☎ 044 252 251. Small, friendly restaurant specializing in Peruvian and Italian dishes. Good-sized portions and tasty food make this a popular place. Mains S15. Daily 8am–11pm.

El Rincón de Vallejo Jr. Orbegoso 303 ☎ 044 476 628. Cesar Vallejo, Peru's most famous poet, was brought up in the house next door to this cramped and characterful corner café. Really good *criollo* food that couldn't be cheaper, so predictably this place gets packed and rushed at lunch. Set menu S6.90–8.90. Mon–Sat 7am–3pm & 5–11pm, Sun 7am–3pm.

DRINKING AND NIGHTLIFE

★ **Peña La Canana** San Martín 791 ☎ 044 295 422. A highly popular restaurant-*peña* serving excellent meals, with a great atmosphere and shows with bands, dancing and audience participation, usually culminating in a disco. The music and dances are fantastic and you'll be amazed at Peruvian stamina. Meals from S16, cocktails S20. Wed– Sat from 6pm for food, from 10.30pm for show until the last people leave.

Taberna Viejo de Viejos Jr. San Martín 323. This rustically decorated place is a truly Peruvian experience; a specialist pisco serving cocktails as well as local wines. Try the "Viejo" deals: from S50 you get a whole bottle of pisco and everything else you need to make various cocktails, and you'll be shown how to make them at your table. Great for groups. Tues–Thurs 7pm–2am, Fri & Sat 6pm–3am.

El Tayta Jr. Pizarro 926 (in Plazuela El Recreo). Bar-restaurant with soft rock vibes and art on the walls. Drinks are good value, and while main dishes are a little pricier, there are plenty of sandwiches under S10. Daily 6pm–midnight.

Tributo Jr. Pizarro 389 ☎ 949 711 045. Featuring live music nightly with regular drinks specials, this is one of the most happening places in Trujillo. Thurs 10pm–4am, Fri & Sat 10pm–5am.

DIRECTORY

Banks and exchange Banco Continental, at Jr. Pizarro 620; BCP, at Jr. Gamarra 562; Scotiabank, at Jr. Pizarro 314; Interbank, at Jr. Gamarra 463; Banco de la Nación, at Av Almagro s/n, BBVA, at Real Plaza mall and Av Pizarro 620. There are also several casas de cambio on the Pizarro side of the Plaza Mayor, and further up on block 6 of Pizarro.

Embassies and consulates UK (consulate), at Jr. Alfonso Ugarte 310 (☎ 044 245 935).

Hospital Hospital Belén de Trujillo, at Jr. Bolívar 350 (☎ 044 245 281). Open 24hr.

Internet Places are numerous. Try Jr. Orbegoso 348 (no name).

Laundry Lavandarias Unidas, at Jr. Pizarro 683.

Post office SERPOST, at Jr. Independencia 286.

Telephones There are many *locutorios* on Jr. Pizarro and Jr. Gamarra.

Tourist police Jr. Independencia 630 (☎ 044 291 705).

HUANCHACO

A traditional fishing village turned popular surfing resort, **HUANCHACO** is the perfect base for exploring nearby ruins while relaxing by the beach and enjoying excellent seafood. Just fifteen minutes from the centre of Trujillo, Huanchaco has exploded in terms of popularity and growth in the last thirty years. While prices do rise in the summer, it's nowhere near as overpriced as some other beach towns.

WHAT TO SEE AND DO

It's impossible to miss the multitude of **surf and language schools** in town; Espaanglisch (ⓦ espaanglisch.com) does both and is recommended (English spoken). If you're not a surfer, another way to catch some waves is with a local fisherman in their traditional *caballitos de mar* – hand-made reed fishing boats first used by the Moche culture; you'll see them lined up along the front. There is a long beachfront promenade and a rickety pier, as well as an unusual church-less Plaza de Armas away from the seafront. Reggae parties on the beach are commonplace, and Latino music blasts from the many beachfront restaurants.

ARRIVAL AND DEPARTURE

By taxi or combi Taxis to and from Trujillo should cost no more than S15, or it's easy enough to take any one of the frequent *combis* (yellow & orange) from Av España on the corner with Jr. Junín (S1.50). *Combis* come in along Av La Rivera, by the sea.

ACCOMMODATION

Every other house in Huanchaco seems to offer lodging of some sort. For those on a really tight budget, there are many no-frills places that charge S10 per person for small and often dark rooms with shared bath. Los Pinos, the street that all the buses turn down away from the sea, has a few hostels and many signs saying *alquilo habitaciones* ("I rent rooms"). Prices drop outside high season. Many places do not have hot water – fine in the summer but miserable in winter.

Las Brisas Ricardo Palma 120 ☎ 044 461 186. Good-value clean, comfortable rooms with private bath (hot water) and fan; a couple have sea views. Internet available. In high season breakfast is included and in low season discounts are available. S̲8̲0̲

★ **La Casa Suiza** C Los Pinos 308 ☎ 044 461 285, ⓦ casasuiza.com. Popular budget accommodation with many of the extra services loved by backpackers – internet, cable TV, laundry, book exchange and a barbecue balcony. Also has hot water and a friendly atmosphere. Dorms S̲2̲5̲, doubles S̲7̲5̲

★ **Naylamp** Av Victor Larco 1420 ☎ 044 461 022, ⓦ hostalnaylamp.com. A well-deserved favourite in Huanchaco. Offers great value for the setting, with bungalow-style accommodation as well as dorm rooms and a camping area with kitchen, all set around pleasant hammock-filled gardens. Camping/person S̲1̲0̲, dorms S̲1̲5̲, doubles S̲6̲0̲

9

★ TREAT YOURSELF

El Kero La Rivera 612 ☎ 044 461 184.
A modern and chic lounge bar-restaurant not to be missed. The three-storey building contains a restaurant with seafront dining on a balcony, with an impressive range of sumptuous seafood and traditional Peruvian dishes. You can come here at any time of day really, as they do breakfasts, amazing cocktails (S18–20), have a huge wine list and there's a dancefloor too. Mains S33–38. Mon–Fri 8am–1am, Sat 8am–2am, Sun 8am–midnight.

EATING

There are restaurants all along the front in Huanchaco, many of them with balconies overlooking the beach. Not surprisingly, seafood is the local speciality, including excellent crab; *ceviche* is traditionally only served at lunch.

★ **Chocolate Café** Av La Rivera 752 ☎ 044 462 420. Really good Peruvian hot chocolate for the low season when Huanchaco gets pretty cold. Breakfasts, soups, wraps and inventive sandwiches are served up in a cheerful incense-scented café with locally made *artesanía*. Full English breakfast S15. Organizes a tea party on Thurs where Peruvians and foreigners can practise each others' language. Owner Choco also organizes archeological tours. Wed–Mon 8.30am–8.30pm.

Estrella Marina Av Larco 740. Very good, fresh *ceviche* (S15) served in a seafront restaurant, which often plays loud salsa music and is popular with locals. Daily 10am–11pm.

Menu Land C Los Pinos 250. Run by a friendly German-Peruvian couple, the name refers to the set lunch *menú* you'll find all over Peru. Food is basic, but you won't find bigger or cheaper portions anywhere else; great for refuelling on a very tight budget. Daily 8am–10pm.

DRINKING AND NIGHTLIFE

Huanchaco has a buzzing nightlife, with many bars and clubs. Always ask around to see if there's a pop-up party on the beach going on, or to find the coolest bar (these can open and close quickly). Outside of peak season nightlife will certainly be calmer.

Da Beach House Out of town along Av La Rivera on the beach. The most popular of the beach hangouts in town, this open-air place has live music, club nights and plays everything from reggae and rock to electronica. Has a bar area with sofas and projector. A cover charge sometimes applies. Tues–Sun from 5pm.

My Friend C Los Pinos 533 ☎ 044 461 080. A good restaurant as well as a cheap hostel, but it is definitely

the most well-known meeting spot in town and serves cheap drinks. Daily 8am–10.30pm; happy hour 7–10.30pm (Thurs evening, all cocktails are S3).

Sabes? Av Larco 804 ⌨ sabesbar.com. This place is either great fun or fairly quiet, as it's right down at the end of the main drag past *Big Ben* restaurant. When it's the former it's a fantastic place to meet people, relax on the outdoor terrace with a happy-hour cocktail and munch on a pizza (S25–30). Mon–Sat 7pm–1am.

ANCIENT SITES AROUND TRUJILLO

One of the main reasons for coming to Trujillo is to visit the numerous **archeological sites** dotted around the nearby Moche and Chicama valleys. For anyone even remotely interested in Peruvian history these should not be missed.

Huacas del Moche

Five kilometres south of Trujillo, beside the Río Moche in a barren desert landscape, are two temples that really bring ancient Peru to life. The stunning complex known as the **HUACAS DEL MOCHE** (daily 9am–4pm; S10 including guided tour in English or Spanish; ☎ 044 297 430, ⌨ huacasdemoche.pe) is believed to have been the capital, or most important ceremonial and urban centre,

ANCIENT SITES

Most companies offer tours to **Chan Chan** (see p.798) and to the **Huacas del Moche** (see above) (the Huaca del Sol and Huaca de la Luna). These cost around S20 each (half-day), or S30–35 for both (full day), but prices change depending on the season; expect to pay more for an English-speaking guide. All operators have slightly different programmes, so shop around. Tours can also be organized from Trujillo for Chiclayo sites, and even sites as far away as Kuelap near Chachapoyas.

TOUR OPERATORS

Established operators include:
Muchik Tours C Santa Teresa 146 depto. 203, La Merced ☎ 044 243 022, ⌨ muchiktours.com.
Trujillo Tours Diego de Almagro 301 ☎ 044 233 091.
Colonial Tours Independencia 616 ☎ 044 291 034, ⌨ hostalcolonial.com.pe.

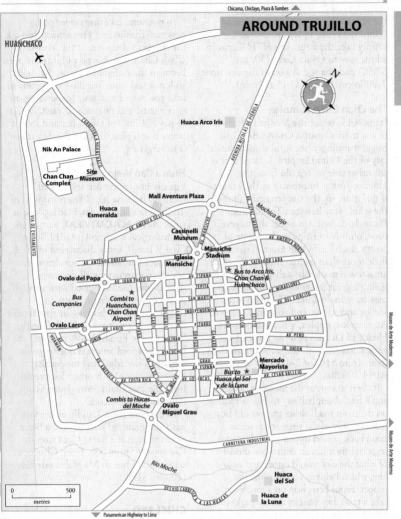

AROUND TRUJILLO

HUANCHACO

Chicama, Chiclayo, Piura & Tumbes

Huaca Arco Iris

Nik An Palace

Chan Chan Complex

Site Museum

Mall Aventura Plaza

Huaca Esmeralda

Cassinelli Museum

Mochica Baja

Iglesia Mansiche

Mansiche Stadium

AV. AMÉRICA NORTE

AV. SALVADOR LARA

Ovalo del Papa

AV. ANTENOR ORREGO

AV. JUAN PABLO II

AV. AMÉRICA OESTE

★ Bus to Arco Iris, Chan Chan & Huanchaco

AV. ESPAÑA

ZEPITA

AV. MIRAFLORES

Bus Companies

★ Combi to Huanchaco, Chan Chan Airport

SAN MARTÍN

INDEPENDENCIA

AV. DEL EJÉRCITO

AV. SANTA

Ovalo Larco

AV. LARCO

AV. JR. JUNÍN

PIZARRO

BOLÍVAR

AV. PERÚ

JR. UNIÓN

AYACUCHO

HUAMÁN

AV. AMÉRICA SUR

AV. COSTA RICA

GRAU

AV. ESPAÑA

AV. LOS INCAS

Mercado Mayorista

AV. CÉSAR VALLEJO

★ Bus to Huaca del Sol y de la Luna

★ Combis to Huacas del Moche

Ovalo Miguel Grau

AV. AMÉRICA SUR

CARRETERA INDUSTRIAL

Río Moche

DESVÍO CARRETERA A LAS HUACAS

Huaca del Sol

Huaca de la Luna

Panamerican Highway to Lima

Museo de Arte Moderno

Museo de Arte Moderno

0 500 metres

for the **Moche** (Mochica) culture at its peak between 400 and 600 AD. It contains two temples: the **Huaca del Sol** (Temple of the Sun) is perhaps the most impressive of the many pyramids on the Peruvian coast, set over 12,000 square metres. Its twin, **Huaca de la Luna** (Temple of the Moon), is smaller, but more complex and brilliantly frescoed; it's thought to have been a sacrificial centre. For now, it's not possible to go inside the Huaca del Sol, still being studied by archeologists, but it's an

amazing sight from the Huaca de la Luna, 500m away. In between the two you can see the remains of a town in the midst of excavation, and there's also an excellent **museum** (S3) across from the site, displaying objects found here and explaining Moche culture.

To **get here** from Trujillo, walk down Avenida Almagro from the centre, which turns into Avenida Moche once you cross Avenida España (a 20min walk), and take the small "CM" or "SD" *combis* from Ovalo Grau, which will take you all

9

the way to the car park of the Huacas (20min; S1.40). From Huanchaco, simply take the larger *combi* "H Corazón" all the way to Ovalo Grau (30min; S1.50) and change. A taxi to the site from Trujillo costs around S15 (20min).

The Chan Chan complex

It's possible to see the Moche influence in the motifs around **CHAN CHAN**, the huge, stunningly beautiful ruined capital city of the **Chimú Empire**, located across the other side of Trujillo from the Huacas. Just as impressive as the Huacas, if not more so, the site stretches almost the whole way between Trujillo and Huanchaco and represents the largest pre-Columbian ruins in the whole of South America. While most of the area is little more than melted mud walls, there are a few remarkably well-preserved areas, giving a great insight as to what the city may have looked like. The main areas to see are spread out and comprise the Nik An temple complex, a site museum, the Huaca El Dragon and the Huaca La Esmeralda (all with the same hours: daily 9am–4pm; S10 for 2-day pass to all sites; ☎044 206 304).

It's best to start at the **museum**, which you'll find about halfway to Huanchaco on the main road, although you can buy tickets at any of the sites. It has some good background information, but most importantly it has an enormous model of what the city would once have looked like, which helps as you tour the site proper. From here, hop on a *combi* or take a taxi (they wait in the car park) to the **Nik An Palace**, a series of open-air temples and passageways with some extraordinarily beautiful patterns and lattice-work. Not far away, the **Huaca Arco Iris** (The Rainbow Temple; also referred to as Huaca El Dragón, or Dragon Temple) was a ceremonial or ritual pyramid rather than a citadel, and sports more geometric and zoomorphic designs, especially of dragons and rainbows. On the other side of this enormous city, **Huaca La Esmeralda** was similar in function to Arco Iris but is much older (around 1100 years old) and has intricate designs, which have been restored with relish if not historical perfection.

To **get here**, take any *combi* going between Trujillo and Huanchaco and ask the driver to drop you at the Museo de Chan Chan. There is no public transport between the different sites on the ticket, so hire a taxi from Trujillo (see p.794) to take you round and wait (depending on sites visited and distance covered, expect to pay S30/hr), or take a hat and lots of water if you plan to walk; the desert sun is unforgiving.

Huaca Cao Viejo

Equally impressive but less visited (perhaps because it's 60km northwest of Trujillo) lies another fascinating Moche ruin, the **HUACA CAO VIEJO**, part of an archeological site known as "El Brujo" (The Wizard). Only discovered in 2006, the huaca contained a mausoleum in which an extremely well-preserved woman was found, buried with enough pomp to suggest that she was an important Moche leader (the first female discovery of this type in Peru). The site is run by the Fundación Wiese, and the heavily tattooed *señora* is due to go on display in the adjoining modernist museum, along with other discoveries from the area (daily 9am–5pm; S10; ⓦfundacionwiese.com).

To **get here** from Trujillo either visit with an organized tour or take a bus or *colectivo* from the Santa Cruz stop to Chocope (45min; S3). From Chocope take another bus to Magdalena de Cao (20min; S1.50).

CHICLAYO

Apart from building a few convents the Spanish never really bothered with **CHICLAYO**, and tourists, too, would be forgiven for missing out Peru's fourth-largest city if it were only for the city itself. Though not an unpleasant place to spend a day or so, it's full of casinos, banks and bus stations and not much else. The attractions here are the remarkable **archeological finds** in the nearby countryside, which are of huge importance to Peruvian culture and identity. It's well worth spending at least a few days in the area getting to grips with the different groups that formed part of the pre-Inca landscape here, and seeing their intriguing tombs, temples and pyramids, many still in the process of being uncovered.

WHAT TO SEE AND DO

The **Plaza de Armas**, or **Parque Principal**, is still very much the centre of Chiclayan life, with the huge commercial Avenue Balta running north to the fascinating witches' market and south to the main bus stations.

The only real point of interest in town is the **Mercado Modelo** – a good general market, but if you turn left on Arica, walk another block and enter where you see the plants outside, you'll reach the **witches' market**. Here the stalls sell shaman's tools, elixirs, swords, taxidermied snakes and voodoo aids. Avoid the northern end of the market as it's seedy, and watch out for pickpockets.

ACCOMMODATION	
Muchik Hostel	1
Sol Radiante	3
Hostal Victoria	2

EATING, DRINKING & NIGHTLIFE	
900's Café	4
La Esquina	8
Mixtura del Norte	6
La Naturaleza	5
Rico Mar	1/2/3
Romana	7

CHICLAYO

9

ARRIVAL AND INFORMATION

By plane The airport is 2km east of town and is served by TACA and LAN which connect with Lima (3 daily; 1hr 15min). From here, a taxi to town should cost S10. Chiclayo Taxi is recommended by the tourist board (☎074 265 410).

By bus Most bus companies have terminals along Av Bolognesi, the main road at the end of Av Balta Sur. From here it's a 10min walk to the Plaza de Armas.

Destinations Cajamarca (8 daily; 6hr); Chachapoyas (2 daily; 9hr); Lima (every 30min; 10hr); Piura (every 30min; 4hr); Trujillo (every 30min; 3.5–4hr); Tumbes (3 daily; 10hr).

Tourist information iPerú, on C 7 de Enero 579 (Mon–Sat 9am–6pm, Sun 9am–1pm; ☎074 205 703). English spoken.

Tour operators Moche Tours, at C 7 de Enero 638 (☎074 788 535, ⊛www.mochetourschiclayo.com.pe), offers reliable tours around the area with good English-speaking guides and their own transport.

GETTING AROUND

By combi *Combis* skirt around the centre; simply walk down Balta to Bolognesi, or east from the Plaza to Av Sáenz Peña, to pick one up (S1 within town).

By taxi or mototaxi Taxis should cost no more than S3.50 anywhere within the city. Always go for one with the municipal shield stencilled on the doors, as these should be officially licensed. *Mototaxis* are not allowed in the centre, so walk out to the post office or the Av Bolognesi at the end of Balta Sur to find one. Within the city limits they should cost no more than S1.50–2.50.

ACCOMMODATION

Muchik Hostel Jr. Vincente de la Vega 1127 ☎074 272 119, ⊛muchikhostel.com. This place is really trying to set itself up as the backpackers' choice in Chiclayo. It's the only place with a dorm and some other traveller conveniences like lockers, free internet and a laundry service. Other rooms are bright, clean and the whole building's very safe. Private rooms are all en suite and come with cable TV. Dorms S̲2̲5̲, doubles S̲6̲0̲

Sol Radiante Manuel María Izaga 392 ☎074 237 858, ✉radianteteti@hotmail.com. Slightly old-fashioned but functional hotel in a bright building. All rooms have TV and private bathrooms (and there's wi-fi). S̲7̲0̲

Hostal Victoria Av Izaga 933 ☎074 225 642, ✉victoria star2008@hotmail.com. Pleasant, friendly hostel with cable TV, laundry service, wi-fi, a luggage depot and communal kitchen. All rooms are en suite and there are homely touches everywhere. Book ahead as can be popular. S̲3̲5̲

EATING, DRINKING AND NIGHTLIFE

Go to Centro Comercial (CC) Real Plaza on the edge of town for all the Western chain restaurants, as well as

shopping. Good local specialities include *tortilla de raya* (ray omelette), *arroz con pato* (duck with rice) and *King Kong*, a pastry thick with *manjar blanco* (caramel), peanuts and pineapple flavouring.

★ **900's Café Bar** Av Izaga 900 ☎074 209 268, ⊛cafe900.com. A really pleasant place any time of day, this café-bar does good breakfasts, snacks, salads, pastas, *criollo* mains (S17.50–28; try the *spaguetti a la huancaina con lomo al pisco*) and cocktails. But better than anything, this place has truly great coffee – there are around 25 different concoctions on the menu. Mon–Sat 8am–3.30pm & 5.30–11pm (open until 1am Fri & Sat).

La Esquina Jr. Juan Cuglievan 598 ☎074 274 987. A little corner café good for most things, from mains and set lunches to much cheaper breakfasts than you'll find in the restaurants on the Plaza de Armas. Excellent range of juices from S1.50 and lots of *platos típicos* (S7–15). Mon–Sat 8am–10pm, Sun 8am–3pm.

Mixtura del Norte M María Izaga 421. A simple but popular place that does a good range of Peruvian dishes with a focus on northern cuisine. Luchtime menus S5–8. Mon–Sat 8am–10pm.

La Naturaleza Jr. Juan Cuglievan 619 ☎074 233 060. A good little vegetarian place – one of few places in town – that serves breakfast, lunch and dinner, and, in theory, a wide range of veggie takes on classic Peruvian dishes. Does a good set menu that includes salad, soup and a drink (S7). Mon–Fri 8am–9pm, Sat 8am–3pm.

Rico Mar Saenz Peña 841, San José 476, at Elias Aguirre 241. A chain of *cevicherías* with a good range of little dishes, ideal for trying different classic Peruvian starters like *papa rellena* (stuffed potato), *tamales* and of course *ceviche*. Lunch from S3.50. Daily 9am–4pm.

Romana Av Balta 512. This place specializes in northern Peruvian cuisine (with a sister restaurant in Chachapoyas) and is a solid choice for good food and a buzzing atmosphere. Classic dishes include *arroz con pato* (duck with rice) and *ceviche*, plus there's a cheaper set lunch and good-value sandwiches. Mains S15–25. Daily 7am–midnight.

DIRECTORY

Banks and exchange You'll find all the banks and moneychangers by walking south on Balta from the Plaza de Armas. It's always better to exchange in a bank – count money carefully if on the street.

Hospital Hospital Nacional Almanzo Aguinaga Asento, at C Hipólito Unanue 180 (☎074 237 776). Open 24hr; you'll need to present insurance documents for treatment.

Laundry Lavandería Burbujas, at C 7 de Enero 639.

Post office Jr. Elías Aguirre 140.

Tourist police Av Saenz Peña 830 (☎074 235 181). Open 24hr.

AROUND CHICLAYO

There are several sites around Chiclayo that are definitely worth seeing, all offered on organized tours, though it can get confusing as some sites have several names, while different places have similar names. The most easily confused are **Sipán**, where remains from the **Moche** culture were discovered, and the **Sicán** (or Lambayeque) culture. Add to the mix the fact that several Sipán sites are located in the town of Lambayeque and it all becomes too much. Save to say that the sights below are essential viewing, but be warned – there are many, many more. Details are given on how to get to the sights independently, but it will be easier and cheaper to go with a tour company.

Huaca Rajada

The Moche culture (100–800 AD) was based all along the coast in northern Peru. The tombs found at the **Huaca Rajada** in Sipán (site museum daily 9am–5pm; S8) are vital to Moche history, as unlike the *huacas* near Trujillo, they were never plundered by treasure hunters. Excavation began in 1987 and continues to this day. Walk around the site to see the archeologists at work and the real tombs, where the extraordinary treasures now mostly displayed at the Museo

Tumbas Reales in Lambayeque (see below) were discovered. There's a small museum documenting the digs, but it is best combined with a visit to the larger museum. It's fascinating to think that there's still so much more to be found.

To **get to Sipán**, take a *combi* from the Terminal EPSEL on Avenida Nicolás de Piérola in Chiclayo (45min; S2.50).

Lambayeque museums

The treasures from the Huaca Rajada's multiple tombs are displayed at the world-class **Museo Tumbas Reales de Sipán** in Lambayeque (Av Juan Pablo Vizcardo y Guzmán; Tues–Sun 9am–5pm; S10; ⓦmuseotumbasrealessipan.pe). Although the museum is quite an eyesore from the outside, it is impossible to do justice to the wonders within. The hauls from the various digs are laid out as they were discovered, and there are an overwhelming number of sacred objects all intricately made from precious metals, shells and stones.

The **Bruning National Archeology Museum**, also in Lambayeque (Parque Infantil; daily 9am–5pm; S8; ☎074 282 110), contains displays on all Peru's ancient cultures and spans five millennia. Housed in a modernist building, the collection is displayed over four floors

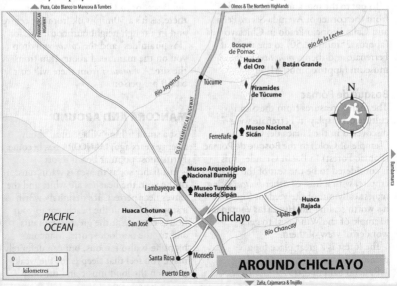

AROUND CHICLAYO

9

and even has a "Sala de Oro" (room of gold), full of Sipán and Sicán treasures.

To **get to Lambayeque**, take a *combi* from the corner of Calle San José (leading off the northwest corner of the Plaza de Armas) with Avenida Leonardo Ortíz (15min). The museums are within walking distance of each other and everyone in town knows where they are.

Museo Nacional Sicán

Little is known about the Sicán, or Lambayeque, culture, even though it existed as recently as the fourteenth century AD. Some suggest Sicán culture was simply an extension of Moche culture, which makes it fascinating to compare the haul at the **Museo Nacional Sicán** in Ferreñafe (Tues–Sun 9am–5pm; S8; ☎074 286 469, ✉museosican @hotmail.com) with its counterpart in Lambayeque, as it's clear there are similarities between the two in terms of their belief and adornment. Although this museum is the less well-presented of the two and the treasures fewer, the metalwork here is finer and the use of semi-precious stones just as remarkable. There's also a reconstruction of the surreal tomb of the Señor de Sicán; his body was discovered decapitated, upside down and with huge gauntlets laid out beside him.

To **get to the museum**, take a *combi* from the corner of Avenida Sáenz Peña and Calle Leoncio Prado in Chiclayo (approx 25min; S2.50) to the town of Ferreñafe and then a *mototaxi* to the museum (approx 5min; S1.50).

Bosque de Pómac

The major treasures from the Sicán culture on display in Ferreñafe were discovered in the Huaca del Oro (Temple of Gold) in the **Bosque de Pómac** (Pomac Forest) in Batán Grande. This is considered to be the seat of the Sicán empire, with a host of other *huacas* rising majestically out of the verdant forest – it's worth scaling the **Huaca las Ventanas** (Temple of the Windows) to get a wonderful view of them.

The forest is a great place for a picnic, birdwatching or horseriding – Rancho Santana (☎979 712 145, ✉cabalgatasperu.com) offers different riding tours of the area from S45 for four hours. Don't miss the **Árbol Milenario**, an ancient, enormous carob tree which locals believe has magic and religious powers; it's situated along the main road through the forest.

Tours will take you here from Chiclayo, usually combined with a visit to one or two of the museums above, but if you want to go alone, get a *combi* from the Terminal EPSEL in Chiclayo (45min; S5) and head for the Centro de Interpretación, at the entrance to the forest on the main road from Chiclayo, for information.

Valle de los Pirámides

The Sicán culture was also responsible for the extraordinary **Valle de los Pirámides** (Valley of the Pyramids) at Túcume (museum daily 8am–4.30pm; S8; ☎074 830 250, ✉museodesitiotucume.com). This site consists of a cluster of a few of the 26 trapezoidal structures that fan out around the countryside here – you can see many of them for miles around if you scale the tallest in the complex. There's a small museum and a great craft shop selling individual pieces made by locals.

Combis to Túcume cost S2.50 and leave from the Terminal Leguía at the Ovalo del Pescador in Chiclayo (take a taxi there, as it's a 30min walk from the centre and in a rough neighbourhood). Ask for "los pirámides" and the *combi* will drop you on the main road about 1km from the site. A *mototaxi* from there will cost S1.50 per person.

MÁNCORA AND AROUND

Just a small fishing village until about twenty years ago, **MÁNCORA** has become Peru's most popular beach resort – justifiably so, as the sea is warm most of the year, the beaches are white and the waves near perfect. It's definitely worth a stop to relax on the beach, eat to your heart's content at the great restaurants and try the outdoor sports. Máncora's **nightlife** is also famous, but can definitely make you feel that sleep is for the weak. Between the loud music and the busy main road, *la bulla* (the ruckus) puts many off, but there are more peaceful resorts along this stretch of coast between here and Tumbes – such as Pocitas, Vichayito, Cabo Blanco and Canoas de Punta Sal – where it's possible to find quieter, unspoilt stretches of coastline.

WHAT TO SEE AND DO

Máncora itself is a small settlement based along Avenida Piura (the stretch of the Panamericana that passes through Máncora) and the few side roads and passageways (many without an official name) that lead to the beach. There are no real **sights** other than some small mud baths about forty minutes away by *mototaxi*; hit the waves, wander around the multitude of *artesanía* stalls along the main avenue, have a cocktail and watch the spectacular sunsets. Check the site ⓦvivamancora.com for up-to-date information on everything in the area, including upcoming surfing events.

Outdoor activities

Long famed for its **surf**, the area is rapidly becoming a world-class destination for **kite-surfing**, and regularly hosts national and international competitions. The long beach and warm water make for a great place to learn how to surf and there's no shortage of teachers. You can rent gear and take lessons from several places along the beach from around S50 per hour for surfing or US$45 per hour for kite-surfing (both work out cheaper if you buy package deals).

Horseriding is also popular, and you'll see touts along the beach offering ragged-looking ponies for S15–30 per hour; it's preferable to go through your hostel or use a tour agency listed with the tourist office as the animals may be better treated. It's also possible to arrange tours to see marine wildlife, including **Humpback whale spotting** (see below) in August to October.

ARRIVAL AND DEPARTURE

By plane Tumbes Airport is 2hr by bus.
By bus Most of the buses have terminals at the northern end of town where Av Piura becomes Av Prolongación Grau. All are a 15min walk or less to most parts of town.

Destinations Buses to Lima (18hr) and other destinations all originate from Tumbes (2hr) or Piura (3hr 45min) and come via Máncora. Most buses to Lima (9 daily; 17–20hr) leave Tumbes in the afternoon and may stop at Máncora (2hr), Piura (6hr), Chiclayo (8hr), Trujillo (10hr), or go straight there. International buses go to Machala, Ecuador (8 daily; 1hr 30min once through immigration).

By colectivo and combi *Colectivos* depart every 30min 4am–7pm from EPPO, at Av Grau 470, to nearby beach Los Organos (20min; S1.50) and most resorts south to Piura (4hr). *Combis* drive up and down Av Piura throughout the day, picking up passengers until they are full for the trip to Tumbes (2hr; S7). There are also companies along Av Piura offering a comfortable trip to Piura or Tumbes in modern people carriers; much faster than coaches, but they cost a lot more (eg to Piura S35).

INFORMATION AND TOURS

Tourist information There's a small office on Av Piura 352 (daily 8am–1pm & 2–4pm). Alternatively, the main iPerú office in Piura can supply information (☎073 320 249, ⊜iperupiura@promperu.gob.pe).

Tour operators Iguana's Trips (Av Piura 233 ☎073 632 762, ⓦiguanastrips.com) offers horseriding, hikes to national parks and trips to mud baths; Eco Fundo La Caprichosa (Av Grau s/n ☎073 258 574, ⓦecofundolacaprichosa.com) is a great one-stop shop – they have an eco-lodge and also specialize in adventure tourism, including motorbike rental (S250/hr with kit and instructors).

GETTING AROUND

By mototaxi *Mototaxis* are a standard S1–2 per journey within town, although many will try to charge you double to *The Point* hostel – fix a price before riding. Don't take one of the taxis without an official-looking sticker on the front, especially if you are going out of town, as there have been incidences of tourists getting robbed.

ACCOMMODATION

Those looking for peace and quiet will do better staying on the edges of town, although take care when returning late at night, as attacks on tourists are not unheard of. Note that prices are given for high season (Nov–March, plus Easter week and Independence Day weekend) where prices at least double in soles or may even be changed to US dollars.

Balsa y Totora Av Piura 452 ☎073 258 630, ⓦbalsay totora.com. Simple, perhaps, but a much more pleasant place than those of a similar price, with friendly owners. Rooms have cable TV, fans, private bathrooms and some have sea views. **S60**

Kokopeli Beachpackers Av Piura 209 ☎073 258 091, ⓦhostelkokopeli.com. Comfortable bunks and en-suite dorms at this chain hostel. An outdoor bar is located at one

9

end of the pool so you can swim over to get that ice-cool beer. Dorms **S30**, doubles **S95**

The Point Playa del Amor ☏073 706 320, ⓦthepoint hostels.com. Although this hostel is a little out of town (20min walk along the beach or S2 in a *mototaxi*), it has a lot going for it. There's a variety of dorms, a good bar, a chill-out pool and they serve food. Be sure to use a licensed *mototaxi* if coming for a party at night. Breakfast included. Dorms **S22**

★ **Waltako Beach Town** Av Panamericana Norte Km1199, Canoas de Punta Sal ☏998 141 976, ⓦwaltako peru.com. For those looking for an unspoilt stretch of beach away from the craziness of Máncora, this is a sure bet. Here it's all about eating fresh *ceviche*, chilling in hammocks and enjoying the bungalows, complete with kitchen, cable TV and fans. For more adventurous types, the owners organize trekking and mountain biking. Take a bus from Máncora towards Tumbes and ask to be dropped in Canoas de Punta (30min); from here it's a short *moto* ride (S5). Camping/person **S20**, bungalows **S120**

EATING

Many of the restaurants aimed at gringos are along the Panamericana and serve excellent international cuisine, but none is cheap. Better-priced grub can be found towards the market at the north end of town, where Av Piura becomes Av Prolongación Grau. Here you can find S5 menus, *pollo a la brasa* (spit-roast chicken) joints, *ceviche* for S2, and fresh fruit and veg.

El Ají Pasaje 8 de Noviémbre s/n (between Papa Mo's & Del Wawa) ☏968 247 189. Down a little passageway that leads to the sea – from the beach looking back towards the main drag it's to the right of *Birdhouse*. A tiny little Mexican restaurant that serves great burritos, tacos and quesadillas for around S23, not forgetting some mean cocktails. Daily12.30pm–11pm.

La Bajadita Av Piura 424 ☏073 258 385. For a decent espresso and a huge selection of home-made cakes and desserts, this place can't be beaten. Also serves reasonably priced sandwiches, cocktails and combos. Main courses S25–28. Tues–Sun 10.30am–10pm.

Birdhouse complex Sitting on a balcony overlooking the sea next to *Hostal Sol y Mar* is this colourful three-in-one restaurant with wi-fi access. *Green Eggs and Ham* (open 7am–5pm) does the best breakfasts in town, including waffles and fantastic American pancakes (S12); *Papa Mo's* (open all day) does milkshakes and nothing but milkshakes; and *Surf & Turf* is open for lunch and dinner and does, as the name suggests, fish and steak plates (S25–35).

La Espada Av Piura 501 & 655 ☏073 258 334. This restaurant with two locales is the best for very large portions of seafood such as *ceviche* and *parihuela espada* (stew). Mains average S20–30, daily lunch menu for S15. Daily 8am–11pm.

★ **Tao** Av Piura 228 ☏073 258 056. This place gets packed every night, as word is spreading about its great Thai and Chinese food. The tuna steak pad thai (S35) is exquisite and the service excellent. Mains S20–40. Daily 11am–11pm.

DRINKING AND NIGHTLIFE

Eating might be expensive in Máncora, but drinking certainly is not. Every bar in town has a very flexible "happy hour", which usually runs all night; you can get two cocktails or beers for S10 in many bars. Strangely, the after-hours nightlife tends to take place in the hostels, especially *Sol y Mar*, *Loki* and *The Point*, whose full-moon party every month has become a town fixture.

Iguana's Bar Av Piura 223 ☏073 632 762. The oldest bar in town and a friendly place to have a drink, where every hour is happy hour. Daily 6pm–3am.

Surfers Bar Block 3 of Av Piura. One of the few bars in Máncora that isn't just a roadside shack, this place has Elvis posters and kitsch on the walls, and rock and pop on the stereo. Happy hour is two drinks for S15. Daily from 6pm.

DIRECTORY

Banks and exchange Banco de la Nación, at Av Piura 525–527; Globalnet ATM outside Minimarket Marlon, on Av Piura 520.

Health Clínica Emergencias, at Av Piura 641 (☏073 258 713). Open 24hr.

Laundry Mil@net, at Av Piura 408, will do your laundry cheaply, but it takes a couple of days; make sure it's your own clothes you get back.

Police Av Piura block 5, next to Banco de la Nación.

TUMBES

Unlike most border settlements, tropical **TUMBES**, about 30km from the Ecuadorian border, is a surprisingly friendly place. Although the tourism infrastructure around here is in its infancy, Tumbes is close to some of Peru's finest **beaches** and three national parks of astounding ecological variety: the arid **Cerros de Amotape**, the mangrove swamps of the **Santuario Nacional Manglares de Tumbes** and the tropical rainforest of the **Zona Reservada de Tumbes**. Unfortunately, as so few tourists explore this part of Peru, tours can be hard to come by and expensive.

WHAT TO SEE AND DO

Tumbes is good for a stroll to see its bright, almost gaudy modern architecture around the centre. The large **Plaza de Armas** feels very tropical, with sausage trees, a huge rainbow archway and a stripy cathedral. Next to the plaza runs the pedestrianized **Paseo de la Concordia** (also known as Av San Martín), which has huge sculptures and more colourful architecture. **Calle Grau**, which leads east off the plaza, has unusual rickety wooden buildings, while the southern end leads to the *malecón* (boardwalk) along the river. To get to the national parks without a tour company, you need to talk to SERNANP and the tourist information office (see below).

ARRIVAL AND INFORMATION

By plane There's a daily flight from Lima with LAN to and from Tumbes (1hr 45min). Note that Tumbes Airport is often very quiet, particularly at night, when there's no access to food or drink. A taxi into town should cost S40; it's about a 20min journey.

By bus or colectivo Most buses and *colectivos* coming to Tumbes arrive at offices along Av Tumbes Norte. From here it's a couple of blocks to the Plaza de Armas.

Tourist information iPerú (Malecón III Milenio, 3rd floor Mon–Sat 8am–1pm & 2–6pm, ☎072 506 721). If you're venturing into the national parks or reserves (though not the mangrove swamps), you'll need permission from SERNANP (Av Panamericana Norte 1739; Mon–Fri 8am–4pm; ☎072 526 489). They are also good for helping you find a guide if you want to explore the area without a tour company.

Tour operators Mayte Tours (Jr. San Martín 131 ☎072 782 532, ⓦmaytetours.com); Preference Tours (Calle Grau 427 ☎072 525 518 ✉turismomundial@hotmail.com) and Tumbes Tours (Av Tumbes Norte 355 ☎072 524 837, ⓦtumbestours.com) all offer trips to the mangroves and the national parks, but none is cheap.

ACCOMMODATION

While there are many budget hotels in Tumbes, few of them are recommendable. If you don't have mosquito repellent, go for places with windows that close and fans.

Hospedaje Amazonas Av Tumbes Norte 317 on the corner of the Plaza de Armas ☎072 525 266. One of the more pleasant of the budget places, with cable TV, fans and light en-suite rooms. S10 extra for hot water. **S̲3̲0̲**

Hospedaje Tumbes Jr. Filipinas 311–01 (just off Av Grau) ☎072 522 164. Has definitely seen better days, but nevertheless the rooms are big enough and have fans. Cold water only, though this is rarely a problem here; you can pay extra for a TV. **S̲3̲5̲**

CROSSING INTO ECUADOR

Crossing the border from Tumbes is complicated and has caught many tourists, especially non-Spanish-speaking ones, adrift in a no-man's land with a lot of canny locals trying to make as much as they can fleece you for. Remember to change your money well before you get to the border, as exchange rates in **Aguas Verdes** (the closest town to the border) can be extortionate.

By far the easiest way to cross the border is to take an **international bus service** from Tumbes, such as Ormeño, Cruz del Sur or the Ecuadorian company Cifa, which take you straight through to Machala in Ecuador (S6–20), only stopping directly outside each immigration office. If you can't do this, you'll have to go it alone. From Tumbes, **combis** (40min; S2) and **colectivos** (30min; S3.50) for the border leave from Calle Mariscal Castilla – ensure that they'll drop you at the **Complejo Inmigraciones** (Immigration Complex; open 24hr), 3km before Aguas Verdes, where you get an exit stamp and tourist card for your passport. After getting stamped, pick up a *mototaxi* that will take you on to the border (S2). Once there, walk over the bridge to the Ecuadorian border town of Huaquillas (see p.630), where you'll find the Ecuadorian immigration office (open 24hr). A **taxi** from Tumbes will cost S40–50, and for this amount the driver should wait for you while you get your stamp at immigration and then take you on to the border.

If you're coming into Peru from Ecuador, it's simply a reversal of the above procedure – note that Tumbes is a much nicer place to stay than Aguas Verdes – and in both directions the authorities occasionally require that you show an onward ticket out of their respective countries. **Do not take photographs** anywhere near the border or immigration offices.

9

EATING AND DRINKING

Tumbes is the best place in Peru to try *conchas negras* – the black clams found only in these coastal waters, where they grow on the roots of mangroves.

Bahía Lounge Av Grau 307 ☎072 526 038, ⓦbahia loungetumbes.com. All a bit swanky for a border town really – this place bills itself as serving international and fusion cuisine on top of Peruvian staples. Mon–Sat 8am–1am & Sun 8am–4pm.

★ **Bohemia/Eduardo (El Brujo)** Jr. Malecón Benavides 850 ⓦeduardoelbrujo.com. One of the best restaurants in this part of the world, this place serves exquisite seafood in a light, open restaurant spanning two floors, including a rooftop terrace with river views. Try the fantastic *sudado de conchas negras*, a thick seafood stew served with rice, with supposedly aphrodisiac properties. A little pricey (mains S30–40), but portions are big enough to share. Mon–Sat 9am–midnight.

Misky Bologneisi 221 ⓦmiskytumbes.com. Good-value snack bar offering breakfasts, snacks, burgers, sandwiches, milkshakes, juices, cakes, sundaes and smoothies. Everything less than S15. Daily 7am–11pm.

DIRECTORY

Banks and exchange All banks are along C Bolívar (to the left of the cathedral). Moneychangers can also be found on this street at the crossroads with Av Piura.

Post office San Martín 208.

The Northern Highlands

The **Northern Highlands** offers some of the least-explored areas in Peru. The two main cities, **Cajamarca** and **Chachapoyas**, are welcoming and peaceful compared to other cities more geared up for tourism. Each offers accessible stopping points before striking out into the stunning countryside, ranging from lush pastures to craggy mountaintops and cloudforest.

CAJAMARCA

Nestling in a fertile rolling valley of eucalyptus and pine, 2720m above sea level, **CAJAMARCA** is a charming colonial town shrouded in legend, most famously – or infamously – known as the place of **Atahualpa's last stand** against Pizarro in 1532, signalling the end of the Inca

Empire. While its Spanish ambience, along with its one remaining Inca building and Andean location, have earned it the title "the Cusco of the north", Cajamarca has a character all of its own. Relatively small until Peru's largest gold mine (within driving distance) was discovered, the city's population has grown rapidly in the last decade to around 350,000, and the influx of money and expats is reflected in the modern restaurants and watering holes. Despite this, Cajamarca is still surprisingly low-key, and the lack of hassle will come as a welcome relief if you've come from the gringo trail in the south, or Máncora in the north.

WHAT TO SEE AND DO

Cajamarca's sights either lie in the centre around the **Plaza de Armas**, in the swish suburb of **Baños del Inca** – where you'll find the eponymous thermal springs – or **outside the city**, where the attractions are all accessible on half-day tours. Note that all the main tourist attractions in the centre, as well as many shops, close for lunch between 1 and 3pm.

Around the Plaza de Armas

The **Plaza de Armas** lies at the centre, and most of the sights in the city are located nearby in the easy-to-navigate surrounding streets. On the plaza sit the **Catedral** (open during Mass times Mon–Sat 6pm, Sun 7.30am, 11am & 6pm) and the **Iglesia San Francisco** (daily 10am–noon & 4–6pm). The adjoining **Convento San Francisco** (Mon–Sat 9am–noon & 4–6pm; S5), whose entrance is on Amalia Puga, houses an interesting selection of religious art in a rambling run of rooms, crypts and cloisters in a working monastery.

Just a couple of blocks from the main square, and run by the national university, is the eccentric and compact **Museo Arqueológico Horacio Urteaga**, at Jr. Del Batán 289 (Mon–Fri 8am–3pm; free, though donations welcome). It houses an unusual variety of pots, some excellent textiles, colonial furniture, a couple of mummies and a cabinet with erotic ceramics.

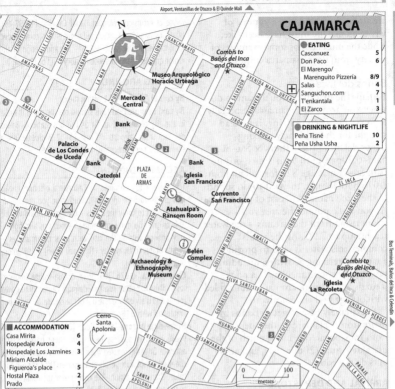

CAJAMARCA

● EATING
Cascanuez	5
Don Paco	6
El Marengo/	
Marenguito Pizzería	8/9
Salas	4
Sanguchon.com	7
T'enkantala	1
El Zarco	3

● DRINKING & NIGHTLIFE
Peña Tisné	10
Peña Usha Usha	2

■ ACCOMMODATION
Casa Mirita	6
Hospedaje Aurora	4
Hospedaje Los Jazmines	3
Miriam Alcalde	
Figueroa's place	5
Hostal Plaza	2
Prado	1

Cerro Santa Apolonia

Looking south from the Plaza de Armas, your eyes will immediately be drawn to the pretty white church on the hill of **Cerro Santa Apolonia**, and the large crucifix looming behind it. The walk up Jr. 2 de Mayo is steep but there's plenty to see on the way – the undulating steps are filled with amorous couples, children playing and people making jewellery and other crafts. At the church, you can pay S1 (daily 7am–6pm) to go right to the top through pretty gardens, and see the rock formation known as the **Silla del Inca** (Inca chair), reputed to be a place the Inca King would sit and gaze out over his empire.

Atahualpa's Ransom Room and the Belén Complex

One **joint ticket** (S5, available from the tourist office in the Belén Complex) gives you entrance to a trio of sights (all:

Tues–Sat 9am–1pm & 3–6pm, Sun 9am–1pm). The most famous is the only surviving Inca structure in Cajamarca – a modest stone room known as **El Cuarto del Rescate** (the ransom room), at Jr. Amalia Puga 722. It is the room, legend has it, that Atahualpa was forced by the conquistadors to fill with gold in order to save his life, although in reality it is probably just the room in which he was held prisoner.

The joint ticket also includes entrance to the gorgeous Baroque **Complejo Belén**. This complex includes two colonial hospitals – one now an archeology and ethnography museum, and the other a large space with small alcoves that would have been the patients' beds, which now hosts rotating art exhibitions – that sit either side of the **Iglesia Belén**, on the corner of Calle Belén and Jr. Junín. The church is the most attractive in Cajamarca, worth seeing for its ornate carved interiors and painted chubby angels. The hospitals

9

are atmospheric and give a glimpse of what colonial life must have been like, while the museum has some examples of pottery from the Cajamarca culture.

Baños del Inca

Perhaps the first thing you'll want to do when you arrive in Cajamarca, especially if you've just been trekking, is to head straight for the sublimely relaxing **Baños del Inca** (Tues–Thurs & Sat–Sun 5am–6.30pm, until 5pm Thurs; private bath S4–7, massage S20 for half an hour; ☎076 348 385), in the well-to-do suburb of the same name 6km east of the centre. As you walk around the area you'll see steam rising from the streams – the water reaches up to 72°C. At the tourist complex this water is used to provide a range of relaxing activities, including private and communal baths, a pool, jacuzzis and even an aromatic sauna filled with orange peel and eucalyptus.

It's extremely easy to get to Baños by *combi* from Cajamarca – they depart from Jr. Sabogal, one block north of the Plaza de Armas (20min; S1), and arrive outside the baths.

ARRIVAL AND DEPARTURE

By plane The small airport, 5km out of town, is served by LC Perú and LAN. There are three flights a day to Lima (1hr 10min).

By bus Most of the buses have terminals close to the centre of town, between blocks 2 and 3 of Av Atahualpa, about 1.5km east of the main plaza. A taxi from here to the centre is S3.50.

Destinations Chachapoyas via Celendín, Leymebamba and Tingo (2 daily around 5.30am; 12hr); Chiclayo (3 daily; 4hr); Lima (6 daily, all in the evening; 14hr); Trujillo (8 daily; 6hr).

INFORMATION AND TOURS

Tourist information The very helpful tourist office is run by DIRCETUR and is next to the Iglesia Belén on Calle Belén (Mon–Sat 7.30am–1pm & 3–5pm; ☎076 362 903). Some English spoken.

Tour operators All the companies offer pretty much the same array of tours, and most of them will pool clients. Bike Cajamarca (☎076 506 354, Ⓦbikecajamarca.blogspot.com) offers mountain-bike trips in the surrounding mountains; Catequil Tours (☎076 363 958 Ⓦcatequiltours.com) organizes everything from guided city tours to community tourism in the nearby countryside; Cumbe Mayo Tours (Jr. Amalia Puga 635 ☎076 362 938) offers the normal range of excursions; Manuel Portal Cabellos (☎097 696 8016, Ⓔmanueljpc11@hotmail.com) is a recommended local guide who speaks English – his knowledge of the region and Peruvian indigenous history can't be beaten.

GETTING AROUND

By combi *Combis* cost S1 within the city.

By taxi or mototaxi Taxis should cost no more than S3 in the city centre and as far as the bus stations. Baños del Inca or the airport will cost S6–12. *Mototaxis* are a standard S2 per journey within the city.

ACCOMMODATION

There are a few families in Cajamarca offering cheap homestays (*turismo vivencial*), which give you the opportunity to get to know the locals – the tourist board will be able to give you more information about this and homestay options outside the city with local communities – most notably in Huayanay (1hr from town) and Namora (40min from town).

Casa Mirita ☎076 369 361, Ⓦcasa-mirita.blogspot.com. This homestay run by Edelmira Calderón has two rooms and is a *mototaxi* ride out of the centre. Includes hot water and wi-fi. **S15**

Hospedaje Aurora Amalia Puga 1014 ☎076 367 878. If you're bored of soulless rooms, this new hostel is the antidote. Brightly coloured walls, towels and sheets provide cheer, while hot water, cable on flatscreen TVs and wi-fi add value. There is an atrium-like ceiling over the main space, so the communal areas are light. **S60**

★ **Hospedaje Los Jazmines** Jr. Amazonas 775 ☎076 361 812, Ⓦhospedajelosjazmines.com.pe. The prettiest of the budget choices, this is in a renovated colonial building with a green courtyard and a small café. Rooms are simple, but lots of pine furniture makes them feel bright, and they all have cable, hot water and wi-fi. It's for a good cause too – this is a non-profit hotel (money goes towards helping cancer patients who can't afford treatment). **S80**

Miriam Alcalde Figueroa's place Ayacucho 319 ☎076 362 932, Ⓔaraujo.alcalde@hotmail.com. This homestay is very central, with six dorm-like rooms – and there's hot water and space to do laundry. Dorms **S15**

Hostal Plaza Amalia Puga 669 ☎076 362 058. The most central and best-value place in town. Rooms are basic but generous – be warned, though, it's seriously chintzy with plastic flowers and teddy bears in some rooms. But there's a charm to it, with flourishes like a communal TV, wi-fi and free tea/coffee. A multitude of room choices with or without bathroom (note, hot water only in mornings and evenings). **S30**

Prado Jr. La Mar 582 ☎076 344 772, Ⓦhotelpradocajamarca.com. Looks crummy from the outside, but inside it does the job. Offers cleanliness, bright rooms, hot water, TV, free internet and wi-fi; they'll even store luggage. **S70**

EATING

Cajamarca is famous for its dairy products – including some of the best cheese in Peru. It's often served as *choclo con queso*, where you literally get a slab of cheese with a big cob of corn – a delicious snack. Other dishes include *caldo verde* (green broth) – something of an acquired taste – made from potato, egg, herbs and quesillo cheese, and *picante de papas con cuy* (potatoes with peanut and chilli sauce with fried guinea pig). There is a mall housing a supermarket – El Quinde, at Av Hoyos Rubios blocks 6 and 7, a 20min walk from the Plaza de Armas.

Cascanuez Amalia Puga 554 ☎076 946 089. The best coffee and cake in town, in a refined café. Also good for snack foods and good range of breakfasts (S12–14).

Don Paco Puga 726 ☎076 362 655. A popular hangout that bills itself as the pioneer of *novoandina* cuisine in Cajamarca. Has a decent range of salads and veggie options too. Fried trout sets you back S18 while the lunchtime menu costs S8. Daily 9am–10pm.

El Marengo/Marenguito Pizzeria Jr. Junín 1201 ☎076 368 045, & Junín 1184 ☎076 344 251. This pizzeria is so popular it has two locales around the corner from each other; both get packed with locals after the best pizza in town (around S15). Also serves up some Mexican dishes. Daily 5–11pm.

Salas Amalia Puga 637 ☎076 362 867. *Salas* has been around since 1947 and is still run by the same family. Not the cheapest, but regarded as the best restaurant in town. The *cuy* with potato and rice stew (S23.50) is delicious; try it here if you've not been brave enough elsewhere. Set lunch S14. Daily 7am–10.30pm.

Sanguchon.com Jr. Junín 1137 ☎076 343 066, ⊛sanguchon.com.pe. As the opposite of the diminutive "ito", the suffix "ón" in Spanish signifies that something is enormous, and these sandwiches certainly live up to their name. Try the *sanguchón* extreme – hamburger, sausage, double cheese, egg, salad and chips stuffed inside a baguette (S11.90). Mon–Sat 5–11pm.

T'enkantala Amalia Puga 237 ☎076 364 125. Incredibly good value, fresh-tasting Chinese set meals from S6, which includes soup, fried wanton, rice, main and a drink. Huge variety and a decent option for vegetarians. Daily noon–4pm & 6–11pm.

El Zarco Jr. Del Batán 170. An old-fashioned canteen-like restaurant with a huge choice of soups, grills, Chinese meals, desserts and juices that is very popular with locals. Set menu from S9, juices from S1.50. Daily 7am–11pm.

DRINKING AND NIGHTLIFE

★ **Peña Tisné** Jr. San Martín 265. This is neither a real *peña* nor a real bar, but a one-of-a-kind Peruvian experience that should not be missed. Knock on the unmarked door and Don Victor will lead you through his house to his bohemian back garden, full of cosy tables and memorabilia soaked in Cajamarcan history. Everyone is welcome here, from tourists to poets to the mayor. Try the home-made *macerado* – a delicious liquor made from fermenting tomatillo (an exotic fruit) and sugar (pitcher S14). Daily 9am–midnight.

Peña Usha Usha Amalia Puga 142. Not at all like other Peruvian *peñas* (which put on a structured show), *Usha Usha* is a one-man show improvised on the night, with singing and music in an intimate kerosene lamp-lit room. Atmospheric, but don't come if you want to chat, as the action is very much centred on the show. Entry S5. Tues–Sun 9pm–3am; busiest Fri & Sat.

SHOPPING

Cajamarca is known for its high-quality pottery, and the general standard in some of the small shops here is excellent – there is some unique craftwork you'll not find elsewhere. There are plenty of stalls selling the usual stuff along Jr. 2 de Mayo up to Cerro Santo Apolonia, but the shops listed below offer higher-quality workmanship.

Cajamarca Colors & Creations Jr. Belén 628 ☎076 343 875, ⊛cajamarcacyc.com. Wonderfully imaginative jewellery, ceramics, shawls and gifts for children.

Quinde Ex Jr. 2 de Mayo 264 ☎942 025 555 ✉quinde .ex.cajamarca@gmail.com. Colourful textiles, cushion covers and handbags made of Andean woven belts.

DIRECTORY

Banks and exchange Banco de Crédito, at Jr. Apurímac 717; Interbank, at Jr. 2 de Mayo 546 (good for changing money); Banco de La Nación, at Jr. Pisagua 552; Banco Continental, at Jr. Tarapaca 747.

Hospital Mártires de Uchuracay, at Larry Johanson (recently opened and without an official phone number at the time of going to press).

Post office SERPOST, at Jr. Apurímac 626 (☎076 364 065).

Tourist police Jr. El Comercio 1013 (☎076 507 826).

DAY-TRIPS FROM CAJAMARCA

There are several sites of interest easily accessible from Cajamarca. One is the fascinatingly precise aqueduct of **Cumbe Mayo**, thought to be perhaps the oldest man-made structure in South America. It's possible to walk there (4–5hr), or you can take the 6am *combi* from the top of Cerro Santa Apolonia towards Chitilla (around 1hr; S5) and then walk back (2–3hr; take your own supplies). Most will prefer to go with a tour (around S25), as there is no obvious route around the huge area.

9

Another interesting half-day excursion is to the **Ventanillas de Otuzco** (daily 9am–5pm; S5), a hillside necropolis whose graves resemble little alcoves or windows (*ventanillas*). *Combis* go here from Plaza de la Recoleta in Cajamarca (20min; S1), or you can take an organized tour.

CHACHAPOYAS

Few tourists make it as far as **CHACHAPOYAS**, the capital of the Amazonas department in the *selva alta* (high jungle) – those who come for thick rainforest will be surprised, as the altitude and rolling sierras (mountains) around town don't fit the Amazonian cliché. There is a surprising amount of activities on offer, however, not least the marvellous remains of the **Kuelap** fortress. The city itself is a colonial delight and its citizens are known for their friendliness. But what "Chacha", as the locals call it, really offers is the chance to get well off the gringo trail and see some extraordinary sights that easily rival their southern counterparts.

WHAT TO SEE AND DO

While the city is certainly a pleasant place to stay, with many good cafés and restaurants and a couple of small **museums**, most people use it as a base to explore the remains of ancient cultures littering the Utcubamba valley. Most famous of all the sights in this region is **Kuelap** (see p.812), the cloud citadel second only to Machu Picchu in terms of location and magnificence (although it is significantly older). **Birdwatching** is also a big draw, partly as this is one of the few jumping-off places to see the very rare marvellous spatuletail hummingbird. Other popular trips are to the waterfall at **Gocta** and the mysterious 1000-year-old sarcophagi at **Karajía**.

The museums

The two museums are the only real tourist attractions within Chachapoyas. The **Museo Gilberto Enorio**, at Ayacucho 904 on the Plaza de Armas (Tues–Sat 9am–1pm & 3–5.45pm; free; ☎041 477 045), run by the Instituto Nacional de Cultura (INC), is just two tiny rooms with some ceramics and a couple of

CHACHAPOYAS

EATING & DRINKING	
Café Fusiones	1
Ciomara Café & Arte	3
El Eden	2
Panificadora San José	5
Romana	7
Silvias Pub	4
Terra Mia	6

ACCOMMODATION	
Hostal Karajía	3
Kuelap	4
Hostal Revash	2
Hostal Rumi Huasi	1

0   100 metres

Cajamarca via Chiclayo

mummies, but it does let you get up close to one of the sarcophagus heads from Karajía.

The **Museo de Santa Ana**, at Jr. Santa Ana, block 10 (Mon–Sat 9am–1pm & 3–6pm, Sun 10am–1pm & 3–5pm; S5; ☎041 943 869), has some local costumes, religious garments, ceramics and local history on display. There is also a memorable *mirador* (viewpoint) that you can reach if you walk west from the Museo de Santa Ana to the end of the road and take the steps.

ARRIVAL AND DEPARTURE

By bus Most companies have their own separate terminals on block 9 of Av Salamanca, or a few blocks north from the Plaza on Grau, Libertad and Ortiz Arrieta. A taxi anywhere in town from the bus stations costs S2–3.
Destinations Cajamarca (2 daily; 12hr); Chiclayo (4 daily; 10hr); Lima (2–3 daily; 20hr); Trujillo (daily; 12hr). Many of the buses to Chiclayo will stop in Pedro Ruíz (1hr 30min, or ask around for *combis* or *colectivos*), where you can catch buses to Tarapoto and Yurimaguas for boats to Iquitos (see p.816). There is a new minibus service direct to Tarapoto from Chachapoyas with Tursimo Selva (Jr. Salamanca 956, ☎961 659 443; S34). Departs at 6.30am & 10am (8hr) – make sure to book a seat in the front next to the driver as the roads are winding.
By combi There are no *combis* that run within the city – everywhere is walkable and taxis are cheap – but there are minivans and *colectivos* servicing nearby towns such as Huancas and Pedro Ruíz. Their terminals are along Jr. Ortiz Arrieta, north of the Plaza de Armas.

INFORMATION AND TOURS

Tourist information Jr. Ortiz Arrieta 5 (Mon–Sat 9am–6pm, Sun 9am–1pm; ☎041 477 292). Run by iPerú; English spoken.
Tour operator Turismo Explorer, at Jr. Grau 509 on the plaza (☎041 478 162, ⊕turismoexplorerperu.com), is highly recommended and the guides speak excellent English.

ACCOMMODATION

Hostal Karajía Jr. 2 de Mayo 546 ☎041 312 606, ✉jjchdosio@hotmail.com. Their tagline claiming "elegance" may be overstretching things a little, but this is a nice budget hostel with homely touches. All rooms have private bath, hot water and cable TV. **S30**
Kuelap Jr. Amazonas 1057 ☎041 477 136, ⊕hotelkuelap .com. A big rambling colonial building that also has a new part tacked on (the old part is much more atmospheric but can get damp so best to inspect first or stay in the modern wing). **S20**

★ **Hostal Revash** Jr. Grau 517, Plaza de Armas ☎041 477 391. Right on the plaza, this hostel in a colonial building has good-value spacious rooms, some looking out on the plaza, around a tropical patio (there are plans under way to expand the garden and open a library and add computers). There's also wi-fi and TV in all rooms, plus an in-house tour company, Andes Tours, a great source of info. Does a decent breakfast too (S10). **S70**
Hostal Rumi Huasi Ortiz Arrieta 365 ☎041 791 100. In keeping with its name (literally "stone house"), this place is a bit bare, but it's clean, light, has hot water, a laundry service, wi-fi, TV in all rooms and is pretty good value too. **S40**

EATING AND DRINKING

You'll find the Mercado Central one block north of the Plaza de Armas between Grau and Ortiz Arrieta; small, but with plenty of fresh produce.

★ **Café Fusiones** Chincha Alta 445 ☎041 479 170. A chilled-out café serving excellent espresso (S3.50), along with breakfasts, snacks, juices and shakes. Also offers wi-fi, a book exchange and local handicrafts. The owner speaks English, and is a good person to ask about volunteer projects in the area. Daily 7am–1pm & 2–9pm.
Ciomara Café & Arte Jr. Ortiz Arrieta 524, Plaza de Armas. Overflowing with art, magazines, records and even some sculptures, this quirky place is a delight. Breakfasts served (from S4), as well as juices (around S2.50), sandwiches, burgers, *tamales*, etc. Daily 7am–3pm & 4–10pm.
El Eden Jr. Grau 448 ☎041 478 644. A vegetarian restaurant that's good enough and ridiculously cheap. Also sells health-related books. Breakfast from S2, lunch menu S4.50. Sun–Fri 7am–9pm.
Panificadora San José Ayachucho 816. You can't get better (or much cheaper) than this bakery/café for bread, breakfasts and snacks. Fruit salad S5. Daily 6.30am–1pm & 3–10pm.
Romana Jr. Amazonas 1091 ☎041 477 212. For a very good set lunch (Mon–Sat) – three courses and bread roll for S8 – also does an excellent range of *ceviche*. Daily 7am–10.30pm.
Silvias Pub Jr. Ayacucho 822. A time warp of a bar, with posters of John Lennon, Kurt Cobain and Bon Jovi on the walls, and English-language pop on the sound system. Go for their good selection of locally made *macerado* (fermented fruit rum). Daily 9pm–1am.
★ **Terra Mia** Jr. Chincha Alta 557 ☎041 477 217. A cultured hangout with an artistic air – walls are painted a deep red hue and there are colourful Andean cushions. But what marks this place out are the breakfasts (from S12) – a welcome change from bread, juice and coffee. Try the spinach and cheese omelette or yogurt with honey and cereal. Daily 7am–10.30pm.

DIRECTORY

Banks and exchange Banco de Crédito, on Plaza de Armas next to iPerú office.

Hospital The public hospital (open 24hr) is on the corner of the plaza (☎ 041 477 017).

Police Half a block from the plaza on Jr. Amazonas 1040 (☎ 041 477 017).

Post office Jr. Salamanca (block 9), two and a half blocks from Plaza Mayor.

DAY-TRIPS FROM CHACHAPOYAS

There is so much to see in the department of Amazonas that the real problem is choosing where to go. There are many remote ruins dotted around the stunning countryside ripe for exploring, but the sights below are the most popular, for good reason.

Kuelap

If you only see one sight in the northern highlands, make it **KUELAP** (daily 8am–5pm; S15). This impressive pre-Inca fortress, 3100m up in the clouds, was built around 600 AD and would have housed more than three thousand people in circular thatched huts. Although rediscovered in the mid-1800s, it's only just being properly uncovered; it is beautifully overgrown with trees, bromeliads and mosses, and you may see archeologists at work while here. One of the most interesting buildings is called *El Tintero* ("the ink well"), a temple that, as its name suggests, has nothing but a hole through its middle, open at the top. It's thought that it was used for astrology or sacrifices.

It takes around three hours to cover the 40km between Chachapoyas and the site, due to poor road quality, so it's a long day however you do it. Coming with a tour company (see p.811) from Chachapoyas is the easiest way to get here, but if you're in a group and don't want a guide, consider hiring a taxi (around S150 to take you there and wait for you). You can also get there as part of a four-day trek that passes by the ruins known as **Gran Vilaya** – the tour companies in Chachapoyas all run excursions (around S120 per person per day and includes food, accommodation and transport).

Cateratas de Gocta

About a two-hour road trip from Chachapoyas, the waterfalls at **GOCTA** were only measured officially in 2005, and there has since been much debate concerning their place in the scale of the world's tallest waterfalls – they could be anywhere between the third and fourteenth tallest. Whatever the truth, they are indisputably impressive. Taking a tour is the best option as it's mandatory to go with a guide, though if you get a taxi to the entrance you'll find guides (S5) and even horses to rent (S30) – without them it's a two-hour walk through lush forest each way from the entrances (either at Cocachimba or San Pablo).

AYAHUASCA CEREMONIES

Shaman ceremonies involving the **ayahuasca** jungle vine are popular with visitors all over Peru, particularly in the jungle areas and Cusco. *Ayahuasca* is a powerful hallucinogen traditionally used for medicinal purposes, never for recreation. Ceremonies need to be prepared for with a special diet (many places in town have special menus) and are typically an all-night affair. It is not a comfortable experience; the visions can be intense and profound and are often accompanied by nausea, vomiting and diarrhoea – part of the cleansing process.

Due to the strength of some people's reactions to the vine, ceremonies should only be undertaken with a reputable **shaman**. In Cusco these include the Shaman Shop on Triunfo 393 and Lesley Myburgh at the Casa de la Gringa, at the corner of Tandapata and P'asñapacana. In Puerto Maldonado, *ayahuasca* ceremonies can be arranged through *Tambopata Hostel* (see p.824). In Iquitos, there is a plethora of shamans and lodges specializing in learning about the vine. Some will take visitors for long work-stays to reduce the cost. Don Lucho and Carlos Tanner are recommended and can be reached via ⓦ ayahuascafoundation.org. Ron Wheelock (ⓦ ronwheelocksayahuascacenter.com), known as "the gringo shaman of the Amazon", also has a good reputation.

Karajía and the Pueblo de los Muertos

Day tours are offered to see Karajía and the Pueblo de los Muertos ("town of the dead"), two different cliff-side mausoleums where important figures in Chachapoya society were once buried. The six sarcophagi at **KARAJÍA** are the more famous; standing over 2m high, their flattened faces, deep-set eyes and painted bodies give them distinct and eerie personalities. Built in the twelfth and thirteenth centuries, they still manage to conjure up an ancestral presence. The **PUEBLO DE LOS MUERTOS** is similarly interesting, with more sarcophagi and also burial houses, again perched precariously on a ledge with a huge drop into the valley below. While these sites lie relatively close to Chachapoyas (46km west and 30km northwest of the city respectively), **getting there** is complicated by the condition of the roads (or lack of). By far the easiest way is with a tour from Chachapoyas (though you'll still have to walk a fair bit), or else take a *combi* to either Luya, where it's a 2hr 30min to 3hr walk to Karajía (ask for directions to Shipata where the path starts), or to Lamud for the Pueblo de los Muertos (approx. 3hr walk each way).

It's often possible to supplement one of these destinations for the **CAVERNA DE QUIOCTA** (10km northwest of Lamud; 2hr walk each way), an impressive cave with jaw-dropping stalagmites and stalactites, also the site of pre-Inca archeological findings.

The Northern Jungle

Although far easier to access by air from Lima or by boat from Brazil, you can get here from the northern Peruvian coast via an adventurous, increasingly popular four-day boat journey up the Río Marañon from Yurimaguas. This will take you close to a national reserve the size of many European countries, **Pacaya Samiria**, which has much unexplored jungle.

IQUITOS

The largest city in the world not accessible by road (the only motorway stretches 100km south to Nauta), **IQUITOS** began life in 1739 when the Jesuits established settlements on the Río Mazán. By the end of the nineteenth century, it was, along with Manaus in Brazil, one of the great rubber towns – as depicted in Werner Herzog's 1982 film *Fitzcarraldo* – but during the last century has oscillated between prosperity and depression. Yet its position on the Amazon – making it accessible to large ocean-going ships from the distant Atlantic – and the nearby three-way frontier with Colombia and Brazil (see box, p.821) has ensured both its economic and strategic importance; there is a strong military presence.

Iquitos is a busy, cosmopolitan town of about 500,000 and growing (people from smaller jungle villages flock here looking for a better life), with elegant architectural reminders of the rubber boom years, eccentric expats and the atmospheric *barrio* of **Puerto Belén**, at whose market you can buy just about anything.

WHAT TO SEE AND DO

Iquitos is easily overlooked in favour of its wild and exotic surroundings, but don't be too quick to dismiss this jungle

WHEN TO VISIT

Unlike most of the Peruvian *selva*, the **climate** up north is little affected by the Andean topography, so there is no rainy season as such; instead, the year is divided into "high water" (Dec–May) and "low water" (June–Nov) seasons. The upshot is that the weather is always hot and humid, with temperatures averaging 23–30°C and an annual rainfall of about 2600mm. Most visitors come between June and August, but the high-water months can be the best time for **wildlife**, because the animals are crowded into smaller areas of dry land and more rivers can be navigated.

The city of Iquitos is good to visit year-round. When the water is high it's a better time to see Puerto Belén and the floating houses, though during low-water season there are more nearby beaches available.

9

THE JUNGLE

Whether you look at it up close from the ground, or from a boat, or fly over it in a plane, the Peruvian *selva* (jungle) seems endless, though it is actually disappearing at an alarming rate. Over half of Peru is covered by rainforest, with its eastern regions offering easy access to the world's largest and most famous jungle, the **Amazon**. Of the Amazon's original area, around six million square kilometres (about eighty percent) remains intact, fifteen percent of which lies in Peru. It's the most biodiverse region on earth, and much that lies beyond the main waterways remains relatively untouched and unexplored. Jaguars, anteaters and tapirs roam the forests, huge anacondas live in the swamps and indigenous tribes live deep within the thick jungle, many surviving primarily by hunting and gathering, as they have done for thousands of years.

WHERE TO VISIT

Given the breadth and quality of options, it's never easy to decide which bit of the jungle to head for. Your main criteria will probably be budget, time, ease of access and the nature of experience you're after. Flying to any of the main jungle towns is surprisingly cheap and, once you've arrived, a number of **excursions** can be easily arranged, such as a camping expedition or travel by canoe or speedboat deep into the wilderness. A costlier, but rewarding, option, mainly restricted to a few operators based in Iquitos, is to take a river cruise on a larger boat.

metropolis. It has a few sights, more than its fair share of quirks and some surprisingly good food.

Plaza de Armas

The only real sight in the **Plaza de Armas** is the unusual **Casa de Fierro** (Iron House). Originally created by Eiffel for the 1889 Paris exhibition, it was shipped out to Iquitos in pieces by one of the rubber barons and erected here in the 1890s. Unfortunately, there is now a pharmacy downstairs, so the only way to see the interior is to check out the overpriced (but fine) restaurant above.

Along the river

The two best sections of the **old riverfront** run parallel to the Plaza de Armas. Malecón Maldonado, locally known as **El Boulevard**, is the busier of the two, especially at night, as it's full of bars and restaurants and there's a small dugout amphitheatre where some kind of entertainment occurs most nights. The other section, **Malecón Tarapaca**, has fine old mansions with Portuguese *azulejos* (tiles), brilliantly extravagant in their Moorish inspiration. The municipal **Museo Amazónico** (Malecón Tarapacá 386, Mon–Fri 9am–12.30pm & 2–5pm; free, though a guide may try to take you round, in which case a tip will be expected; 065 234 031) has very few

exhibits on offer, though look out for the collection of fibreglass statues modelled on more than eighty people from different ethnic groups residing in the jungle surrounding Iquitos.

Próspero and around

Strolling along the main shopping street off the Plaza de Armas, **Próspero**, you'll see many fine examples of *azulejo*-covered buildings; a useful one is the **Casa Cohen**, the biggest supermarket in the centre. The name serves as a reminder that the boom drew a Jewish community to Iquitos in the early 1900s. There is, in fact, a small Jewish cemetery within the main Peruvian **cemetery** (Av Alfonso Ugarte, at Av Fanning; daily 8am–7pm), and both cemeteries are worth a visit, the former for its elegant tiled and Art Deco graves and the latter for wildly colourful and unusual ones – don't miss the tug boat or the castle.

Puerto Belén

Simply follow Próspero south for nine blocks (or take a *motokar*, the brand name for *mototaxis* here), turn left towards the river and you'll see the most memorable *barrio* in Iquitos, **Puerto Belén**. It consists almost entirely of wooden huts raised on stilts and houses constructed on floating platforms, which rise and fall to accommodate the changing water levels.

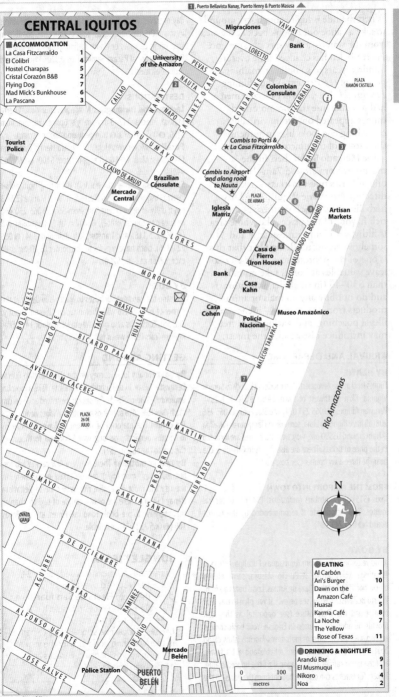

CENTRAL IQUITOS

ACCOMMODATION
La Casa Fitzcarraldo	1
El Colibrí	4
Hostel Charapas	5
Cristal Corazón B&B	2
Flying Dog	7
Mad Mick's Bunkhouse	6
La Pascana	3

EATING
Al Carbón	3
Ari's Burger	10
Dawn on the Amazon Café	6
Huasaí	5
Karma Café	8
La Noche	7
The Yellow Rose of Texas	11

DRINKING & NIGHTLIFE
Arandú Bar	9
El Musmuqui	1
Nikoro	4
Noa	2

9

When the tide is high enough, ask around to take a canoe out to look back at the area from the water – a very special experience. Puerto Belén has changed little over its hundred years or so of life, remaining a poor shanty settlement. While filming *Fitzcarraldo* here, Werner Herzog merely had to make sure that no motorized canoes appeared on screen: virtually everything else looks like an authentic slum town of the nineteenth century.

The **Mercado Belén** (best in the mornings from around 7am–1pm) is one of Peru's finest markets – ask for directions to Pasaje Paquito, the busy herbalist alley, which synthesizes the very rich flavour of the place. The whole area is filthy, yet highly atmospheric and somehow beautiful. Remember that this is one of the poorest areas of the city, so leave valuables at home, take no more than S30–40 (in small denominations) and do not buy any animals or animal products from the market – it encourages illegal poaching, and setting them free may introduce disease into the forest.

ARRIVAL AND DEPARTURE

BY PLANE

Flights land at the Aeropuerto Internacional Francisco Secada Vigneta, 8km southwest of town. LAN (☏ 080 111 234), Peruvian Airlines (☏ 065 231 074) and Star Perú (☏ 065 236 208) all have flights to Lima, some go via Tarapoto or Pucallpa – from around US$90 one-way. Departure taxes are included in the price of tickets. There are also flights to Caballo Cocha near the three-way frontier (see box, p.821).

FROM THE AIRPORT INTO TOWN

Taxis (S15) and motokars (*mototaxis*) (S8) run to central Iquitos. Taxi Aeropuerto is recommended by the tourist board (☏ 065 241 284).

BY BOAT

If you've come by boat from Yurimaguas, Pucallpa, Leticia or Tabatinga, you'll arrive at Puerto Masusa, some eleven blocks northeast of the Plaza de Armas. Local boats go from Puerto Bellavista Nanay (see below). If you plan to travel by boat, email the iPerú office (see opposite) as they can provide detailed information in English. Your basic choices are *rápidos* (speedboats) or *motonaves/lanchas* (slow cargo boats), the former being more reliable and a lot faster, and the latter calmer and cheaper, if a little unpredictable. Tickets for *lanchas* can only be bought from the ports on the

day of travel, while the speedboat companies have offices in town. On the Yurimaguas–Iquitos route, it's possible to stop off in Lagunas or Nauta to find guides and tours to Reserva Nacional Pacaya Samiria (see p.820). Prices should include all meals.

DESTINATIONS

Lagunas and Yurimaguas: Motonaves Eduardo, at Puerto Masusa, Punchana (2–3 days; daily at 6pm except Sun; from S100; ☏ 065 351 270, ✉ transpeduardo@hotmail.com).

Pucallpa: Motonaves Henry, at Puerto Henry, Punchana (4–5 days; Mon, Wed & Fri at 6pm; from S100; ☏ 065 263 948).

Santa Rosa (three-way border): departing from either Puerto Pesquero or Puerto Masusa, at Av La Marina (2.5–3 days; daily at 6pm except Sun; from S60; ☏ 065 250 440 or speak to tourist office); Golfinho, at Jr. Raimondi 378 (☏ 065 225 118), and Transtur, at Jr. Raimondi 384 (☏ 065 221 356), both have *rápidos* to the border (8–10hr; daily except Mon at 6am; S200).

BY BUS

The stop for Trans del Sur buses to Nauta is in Belén at the corner of Jr. Prospero with Prolongación Libertad (hourly; 2hr; S8). *Colectivos* also go to Nauta from block 14 of Elias Aguirre (cars leave when full; 1hr 40min; S10).

GETTING AROUND

By boat For any local journey on the river, head to Puerto Bellavista Nanay, in the suburb of Bellavista. Take a *motokar* (*mototaxi*) (10min; S3–4). Canoes can be rented and you can catch river *colectivos* to islands and other villages nearby.

By combi The majority of the unusual wooden *combis* in Iquitos generally go one-way back and forth out of the city to the airport (S1).

By taxi or motokar There are very few cars in Iquitos, but *motokars* (*mototaxis*) can be taken everywhere. In the city the most expensive ride would be to Bellavista Nanay (S3–4). There are only a couple of taxi companies that you have to pre-book; Fono Taxi Flores, at Calle Pevas 169 (☏ 065 232 014), is reliable.

> ### JUNGLE FIESTA
>
> At the end of June (supposedly June 24, but actually spread over three or four days), the main **Fiesta de San Juan** takes place across the Peruvian jungle. It is believed that, on this date, Saint John blesses all local rivers; locals flock to bathe in them to bring good luck for the year to come. In Iquitos, dancing, parades and a feast mark the festival.

INFORMATION

Tourist information Loreto, at Raymondi (Mon–Sat 9am–6pm, Sun 9am–1pm; ☎ 065 236 144, ✉ iperuiquitos @promperu.gob.pe). Staff can advise on lodges, tour operators and guides, and can help book accommodation in Iquitos. They also provide free advocacy should you run into any problems with tour companies, or need the police or your embassy. The monthly English-language newspaper *The Iquitos Times* (✆ iquitostimes.com) is also a good source of information, and is available at most hotels and restaurants.

Tourist permits If you are planning a trip into the jungle with just a guide (as opposed to a group) or to Pacaya Samiria National Reserve, then talk to SERNANP (☎ 065 223 555), located at C Jorge Chávez 930–942 (behind the military base).

ACCOMMODATION

El Colibrí Jr. Nauta 172 ☎ 065 241 737, ✆ hostalelcolibri .net. A modern, clean and pleasant construction right in the centre. Rooms have cable TV and private bath with hot water, as well as a/c or fans. There's also a decent breakfast (S6–7). **S55**

Hostel Charapas Raimondi 156 ☎ 065 272 859, ✆ hostelcharapas.com. Newly opened hostel right in the heart of town and catering exclusively for back-packers – this place only does dorms. There's a TV room, laundry service and internet (plus breakfast included). Dorms **S20**

Cristal Corazón B&B C Nanay 130 ☎ 065 222 070, ✆ cristalcorazon.com. A cosy B&B with orthopaedic beds, healthy breakfasts, a large communal kitchen and a patio. Mosquito nets and repellent can be provided. Host Miguel Pizango can organize expeditions, lodge stays and *ayahuasca* ceremonies. **S50**

Flying Dog Malecón Tarapacá 592 ☎ 065 242 476, ✆ flyingdogperu.com. As the quality of accommodation in Iquitos can be so variable, you may feel more at ease staying with this reputable chain. The building overlooks the river and is very central. Breakfast included. Dorms **S30**, doubles **S75**

Mad Mick's Bunkhouse Putumayo 163 (upstairs 202) ☎ 992 193 726, ✉ michaelcollis@hotmail.com. British expat Mad Mick will welcome you with a smile to his one room with eight beds, behind the office for his jungle supplies store. Not for those who need personal space, but you can't fault it at the price. Dorms **S10**

La Pascana Pevas 133 ☎ 065 235 581, ✆ pascana.com. Very friendly little place with book exchange and on-site agency. Slightly run-down rooms with private bath and fans are on either side of a flower-filled garden, with tables for soaking up the atmosphere or an early evening drink. BYO mosquito protection. **S55**

EATING

Food in Iquitos is exceptionally good for a jungle town; fish dishes are a speciality here, but most tastes are catered for. As always, the dirt-cheap food can be found at markets like Belén, where a *menú* can be as little as S2.50.

Al Carbón Condamine 115 ☎ 065 223 292. A good, clean and popular place for grills, with a wide range of choices. Tenderloin kebabs S17; glass of wine S10. Daily 5.30pm–1am.

Ari's Burger Prospero 127 ☎ 065 241 124. An American-style diner serving more than just burgers, including a mind-boggling variety of jungle superjuices (from S9) as well as traditional dishes. The most popular meeting spot in Iquitos and good for late-night munchies. Burger combo from S15. Daily 7am–2am.

Dawn on the Amazon Café Malecón Maldonado 185 ☎ 065 234 921, ✆ dawnontheamazoncafe.com. Next to its associated tour company, this riverfront restaurant comes highly recommended. Exquisite juice combinations, all-day lunches or breakfasts, as well as main courses for dinner are all offered, as is the *ayahuasca* diet. The food is free from artificial ingredients and only purified water is used in food preparation – there's everything from Mexican to Chinese and Peruvian cuisine on offer. Mains around S15. Mon–Sat 7.30am–10pm.

★ **Huasaí** Jr. Fizcarrald 131 ☎ 065 242 222. Family-run traditional Peruvian restaurant, always heaving with locals. Serves an excellent and huge S12 lunch *menú* including starter, main and jug of juice. Simply delicious. Daily 7am–4.30pm (sometimes later).

★ **Karma Café** Napo 138 ☎ 065 600 576. Come for the free wi-fi (which lots of places don't have because of the isolated location), but stay for the large range of cocktails (S14) and other drinks, sandwiches (S12) and excellent Thai curries (S26). Sofas, bean bags, lava lamps, cosmic art and chill-out music make this a great place to relax. Also offers board games, a small library with guidebooks and a book exchange. Has a happy hour 7–9pm. Tues–Sun 12.30pm–midnight.

La Noche Malecón Maldonado 177 ☎ 065 222 373. A safe bet for a meal or drink at any time of day – and less crammed with gringos than nearby *Dawn on the Amazon Café*. Has a small balcony looking out on the river and comfy sofas inside. Mains average S25–30. Daily 7am–midnight.

The Yellow Rose of Texas Putumayo 180. Run by a non-Texan from the USA, this place just off the Plaza de Armas is a true Iquitos establishment, a jungle anomaly, and the most popular gringo meeting spot. Very tasty range of international and Peruvian dishes (mains around S30) – there are a staggering 400 items on the menu – in a Texas-themed atmosphere, including saddles for bar stools and a sports bar upstairs. Owner Gerald used to work with the tourist board so is also a great source of local knowledge. Downstairs open 24hr.

DRINKING AND NIGHTLIFE

Arandú Bar Malecón Maldonado 113. With a prime location on the Boulevard, this bar is often packed in the evenings, with seating spilling outside. Serves a range of drinks (pisco sour S14, large beer S7) and a few snacks. Daily 4pm–midnight.

★ **El Musmuqui** Raymondi 382. A specialist in exotic cocktails, this tiny but lively bar is packed with locals every night of the week. Come here to try traditional jungle liquors, many of which have strong aphrodisiac properties (S4–7). Try the *charapita ardiente*, it's a house speciality. Also serves snack food. Sun–Thurs 5pm–midnight, Fri & Sat 5pm–3am.

★ **Nikoro** Down the steps at the end of Pevas. This is one special bar; a huge wooden hut on the river (though in low water; you're 15m up on stilts) serving jungle drinks and cocktails (S10). Sit on the balcony for unrivalled views of the river and the stars. Iquitos' most bohemian and diverse crowd can be found here, from hippies to botanists to doctors. Daily 7pm–1am.

Noa Fitzcarrald 298 ☎ 065 222 555, ⊛ noadisco.com. Easily identified after midnight by the huge number of flashy motorbikes lined up outside, this is the most popular and lively of the clubs in Iquitos. It has five bars and plays lots of Latino music. S15 entrance includes one beer. Thurs–Sat 10pm–7am.

DIRECTORY

Banks and exchange Banco de Crédito, at Jr. Próspero with Putumayo; BBVA Banco Continental, at Jr. Próspero 961. Use Interbank, at Jr. Próspero 330, for exchanging money, as the moneychangers on Próspero can't always be trusted.

Consulates Brazil, Sargento Lores 363 (☎ 065 235 151); Colombia, C Calvo de Araujo 431 (☎ 065 236 246); UK, C San Jose 133 (☎ 065 253 364).

Health Clínica Ana Stahl, at Av La Marina 285 (☎ 065 252 535; ⊛ clinicaanastahl.org.pe). Open 24hr.

Immigration Migraciones, at Av Mariscal Cáceres block 18, Moronacocha (☎ 065 235 371).

Internet Jr. Putumayo block three (has the quickest connection in Iquitos; S2/hr).

Jungle supplies Mad Mick's Trading Post, Putumayo 184b. Provides everything you need for a jungle trip, for purchase or rent, including rubber boots, rainproof ponchos, sunhats and fishing tackle.

Post office SERPOST, at Jr. Arica 402.

Tourist Police Jr. Sargento Lores 834 (☎ 065 242 081).

INDIGENOUS JUNGLE TRIBES

Outside the few main towns there are hardly any sizeable settlements, and the jungle population remains dominated by 59 different ethnic groups and 14 different linguistic families, all with distinct customs and dress. After centuries of external influence, many jungle Indians speak Spanish and live pretty conventional, westernized lives, preferring jeans, football shirts and fizzy bottled drinks to their more traditional clothing and a fermented alcoholic drink made from manioc (the tasty, filling and nutritious *masato*). Other tribal groups chose to retreat further into the jungle to avoid contact with outside influences and maintain their traditional way of life.

For most of the traditional or semi-traditional tribes, the jungle offers a **semi-nomadic** existence. Communities are scattered, with groups of between ten and two hundred people, and their sites shift every few years. For subsistence they depend on small, cultivated plots, fish from the rivers and game from the forest, including wild pigs, deer, monkeys and a range of edible birds. The main species of edible jungle fish are *sabalo* (a kind of oversized catfish), *carachama* (an armoured walking catfish) and the giant *zungaro* and *paiche* – the latter, at up to 200kg, being the world's largest freshwater fish. In fact, food is so abundant that jungle-dwellers generally spend no more than three to four days a week engaged in subsistence activities.

DAY-TRIPS FROM IQUITOS

For those who want to experience a bit of the jungle without straying too far from the city, there are several easy day-trips from Iquitos. It's simple to hop over to a nearby island for a taste of landlocked beach life or to experience wildlife in safe confines; at the Amazon Animal Orphanage you'll be able to get up close with many rescued jungle species. The following sites can all be done in a day or less, and the Iquitos iPerú office has good maps of how to get to them.

Amazon Animal Orphanage

One of the most popular day-trips from Iquitos is to the **Amazon Animal Orphanage and Pilpintuhuasi Butterfly Farm** in Padre Cocha (Tues–Sun 9am–4pm; S20; ☎965 932 999, ⍟amazonanimalorphanage.org). The

life's work of Austrian expat Gudrun (she speaks excellent English), this is a butterfly farm and also a sanctuary for jungle animals bought illegally and subsequently confiscated (many of the jungle's most endangered species are under one roof here). **To get here**, take a *peke peke* (river *colectivo*) from the Bellavista Nanay port in Iquitos heading for Padre Cocha (S3; 20min); once there, it's a fifteen-minute signposted walk or a S1 *motokar* journey. Some touts at Bellavista – in order to get you to take a tour with them – might tell you the place is shut (ignore their quips).

River beaches

From the Bellavista Nanay port you can set out by canoe ferry for **Playa Nanay**, a beach resort where bars and cafés are springing up to cater for the

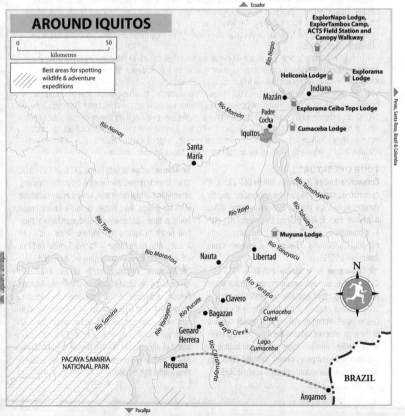

AROUND IQUITOS

0   50
kilometres

/// Best areas for spotting wildlife & adventure expeditions

Ecuador

ExplorNapo Lodge, ExplorTambos Camp, ACTS Field Station and Canopy Walkway

Río Napo

Heliconia Lodge

Explorama Lodge

Mazán

Indiana

Río Momón

Padre Cocha

Explorama Ceiba Tops Lodge

Iquitos

Cumaceba Lodge

Pevas, Santa Rosa, Brazil & Colombia

Río Nanay

Santa María

Río Tamshiyacu

Río Itaya

Río Tahuayo

Río Tigre

Muyuna Lodge

Río Marañón

Río Yanayacu

Nauta

Libertad

Río Yarapa

N

Río Pucate

Clavero

Río Yanayacu

Bagazan

Mayo Creek

Cumaceba Creek

Genaro Herrera

Río Samiria

Lago Cumaceba

PACAYA SAMIRIA NATIONAL PARK

Requena

Río Ucahuayta

BRAZIL

Angamos

Pucallpa

9

weekend crowds. Be aware that currents here are pretty strong and, although there are lifeguards, drownings have occurred.

The best beaches are by **Santa Clara**, also west of Iquitos on the Río Nanay, at a turn-off near the airport (S6 by *motokar* to the turn-off; 20min). From here the road is sand, so you'll either have to negotiate another price with often-reluctant drivers from the city (S4 more to go the whole way to the beach) or pick up another ride with a more willing local *colectivo* that leaves when full (S1.50 per person). Note the beaches can only be visited in summer when the river is low (July to Oct).

Moronacocha and around

On the western edge of Iquitos, a tributary of the Nanay forms a long lake called **Moronacocha**, a popular resort for swimming and waterskiing. Near the airport, still on the Nanay, is the agricultural and fishing village of **Santo Tomás** (renowned for its *artesanía*), where you can swim and canoe from the beach.

PACAYA SAMIRIA NATIONAL RESERVE

RESERVA NACIONAL PACAYA SAMIRIA, around 130km southwest of Iquitos, covers over 20,000 square kilometres

---

IQUITOS TOURS AND JUNGLE LODGES

The massive river system around Iquitos offers some of the best access to indigenous villages, lodges and primary rainforest in the entire Amazon. You can go it alone with the *colectivo* boats that run more or less daily up and down the Amazon River, but it's usually best to travel with one of the many lodges or tour companies (see below). Note that many tours include a visit to a jungle tribe who put on the same show multiple times a day, specially donning traditional dress that they long ago stopped wearing, and tourists are often disappointed.

When choosing a lodge, consider its distance from Iquitos, the company's commitment to conservation, the level of comfort you want and what's included in the price. Most lodge itineraries will include dolphin-watching, fishing, visiting a local village and night walks. While you can often book when you turn up in Iquitos and barter, the best companies should be booked in advance, have fixed prices and never tout for business in the street. Prices below are based on a three-day/two-night stay for two people, per person, and the addresses included are for the Iquitos-based booking offices. Companies mostly fix prices in US dollars, so prices in soles may change according to the exchange rate. A lot of lodges also do day visits, which include lunch, a jungle walk and sometimes a visit to an animal sanctuary.

TOUR OPERATORS

Cumaceba Lodge Putumayo 184 ☎ 065 232 229, ⓦ cumaceba.com. A highly recommended slightly cheaper option on the Río Yanayacu, some 40km downriver from Iquitos (45min by speedboat), with accommodation in private rustic bungalows with individual bathrooms. Also runs an explorer camp downriver. US$303.

★ **Explorama** Av la Marina 340 ☎ 065 252 530, ⓦ explorama.com. Explorama is the top operator in the region and has a good reputation for responsible tourism; not cheap but worth it. It has four sites in the jungle (see website) offering everything from remote camping to the most luxurious lodge in the Amazon. It's possible to go between sites and tailor your stay to include an excursion to the company's canopy walkway. Ceiba Tops (the most luxurious option, with a/c & pool) US$455.

Heliconia Lodge Ricardo Palma 242 ☎ 065 231 959, ⓦ amazonriverexpeditions.com. A reputable company offering traditional lodge trips as well as birdwatching stays for groups, boat cruises (it has a luxury house boat), or time split between the lodge and one of their two hotels in Iquitos (the *Victoria Regia* and *Hotel Acosta*). Also has a lodge in Pacaya Samiria and can offer access to Explorama's canopy walkway. US$330.

★ **Muyuna** Putumayo 163 ☎ 065 242 858, ⓦ muyuna.com. Located close to the Pacaya-Samiria Reserve, and one of the furthest lodges from Iquitos, *Muyuna* offers rustic but comfortable accommodation and very good service. The lodge works hard to distinguish itself as a protector of wild animal rights; and staff are proud to tell you that they will not take you to visit a pre-prepared tribe who will perform then ask for tips. S1,060.

CROSSING INTO COLOMBIA OR BRAZIL: THE THREE-WAY FRONTIER

Leaving or entering Peru via the Amazon is an intriguing adventure; by river this inevitably means experiencing the **three-way frontier**. The cheapest and most common route is by river from Iquitos to **Santa Rosa**, some ten to twelve hours by *rápida* (speedboat; S200 one-way) or 2.5–3 days in a standard riverboat (from S80 hammock one-way; cabin from S130). Remember if going for a cheaper hammock space, you need to bring your own. Boats will drop you off at immigration, where you must obtain an **exit stamp** from Peru if you're leaving (you must show your tourist card to do this), or get an **entry stamp and tourist card** if arriving. Larger boats may take you all the way to Tabatinga (Brazil) or Leticia (Colombia), in which case an immigration official may board the vessel and do the paperwork there and then.

There are few hostels and cafés in Santa Rosa; the small *La Brisa del Amazonas* is both, and the owner is a useful source of information. Once through immigration, ferries (10min; around S6) connect the town with Tabatinga and Leticia (they're pretty much extensions of the same city).

It's possible to **fly from Iquitos** to near the three-way frontier. There are currently no direct flights to Santa Rosa, although the route tends to be run by small airlines that come and go – so your best bet is to check in with the tourist office for the latest information. There are currently flights with the Peruvian air force (FAP) to **Caballo Cocha** bookable through travel agency Contactus (Jr. La Condamine 493; ☏065 608 828; one-way from S200). Departures are on Mon, Wed & Fri. From Caballo Cocha you can hop on a *rápido* (2hr) to Santa Rosa.

(about 1.5 percent of the landmass of Peru and the size of Israel) and is home to the Cocama tribe. The reserve is a swampland during the rainy season (Dec–March), when the streams and rivers all rise; as such you'll see very different wildlife in the high-water and low-water seasons (both good in different ways). Athough it can end up costing more than lodge stays in Iquitos, for anyone interested in wildlife this reserve offers an unbelievable quantity and variety of flora and fauna; more than a thousand types of vertebrates exist here, including nearly a third of the bird species of Peru and one percent of the reptile species of the world.

Note that while it's possible to visit the reserve via an operator in Iquitos, you'll need at least five days to explore it properly, and it won't be cheap (lodges cost double or more than ones nearer Iquitos). The cheapest way to do it is to go to the town of **Lagunas** (one day upstream from Yurimaguas) and find a tour/guide going from there – although it's best to call in advance and organize something. You can do the same from **Nauta** if coming from Iquitos, though this tends to be a little more expensive. It's recommended that you go with a licensed operator from Iquitos; if you do, the entry fee to the park (S60 for 3 days;

S120 for 7 days) will be included. If you are determined to go alone, talk to SERNANP before you go, as it provides maps and information on the region – you're meant to be accompanied by a guide at all times. You should, of course, bring mosquito nets, hammocks, insect repellent and all the necessary food and medicines.

The Southern Jungle

Part of the Peruvian Amazon basin – a large, forested region with a searingly hot and humid climate, punctuated with sudden cold spells (*friajes*) between June and August – the **southern selva** regions of Peru have only been systematically explored since the 1950s and were largely unknown until the twentieth century, when rubber began to leave Peru through Bolivia and Brazil, eastwards along the rivers. Cusco is the best base for trips into the jungles of the southern selva, with road access to the frontier town of **Puerto Maldonado**, itself a good base for budget travellers. The nearby forests of Madre de Dios are rich in flora and fauna, especially in the **Manu Biosphere Reserve**.

9

MADRE DE DIOS

Named after the broad river that flows through the heart of the southern jungle, the still relatively wild *departamento* of **MADRE DE DIOS** is changing rapidly, with agribusinesses moving in to clear mahogany trees and set up brazil nut plantations, and prospectors panning for gold dust along the riverbanks. Nearly half of Madre de Dios *departamento*'s 78,000 square kilometres are accounted for by national parks and protected areas such as **Manu Biosphere Reserve**, **Tambopata-Candamo Reserved Zone** and **Bahuaja-Sonene National Park**, between them containing some of the richest flora and fauna in the world.

Madre de Dios still feels very much like a frontier zone, centred on the rapidly growing river town of **Puerto Maldonado**, near the Bolivian border, supposedly founded by legendary explorer and rubber baron Fitzcarraldo.

Puerto Maldonado

Despite its position firmly on the Interoceanic Highway, connecting the Peruvian and Brazilian coasts, the jungle town of **PUERTO MALDONADO** still has a raw, chaotic feel to it. Puerto's wide streets often culminate in pitted dirt tracks, which are barely passable in the rainy season and where a multitude of beeping *mototaxis* raise clouds of dust at other times of year. With an economy based on gold panning, logging, cattle ranching and brazil-nut gathering, it has grown enormously over the last twenty years, becoming the thriving capital of a region that feels very much on the threshold of major upheavals, with a rapidly developing ecotourism industry.

The traffic-choked **León de Velarde** is the town's main artery, culminating in the attractive **Plaza de Armas**, near one of the town's bustling ports, and with an attractive if bizarre Chinese pagoda-style clock tower at its centre; every Sunday

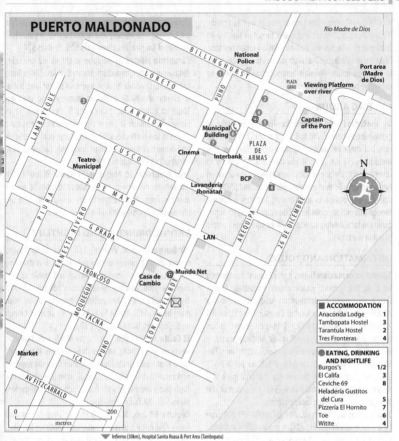

PUERTO MALDONADO

Río Madre de Dios

National Police ❶

Port area (Madre de Dios)

PLAZA GRAU

Viewing Platform over river ❷

Captain of the Port

Municipal Building ❻ ❼

PLAZA DE ARMAS

Cinema Interbank

Teatro Municipal

BCP

Lavandería Jhonatán ❹

LAN

Casa de Cambio Mundo Net

■ **ACCOMMODATION**	
Anaconda Lodge	1
Tambopata Hostel	3
Tarantula Hostel	2
Tres Fronteras	4

● **EATING, DRINKING AND NIGHTLIFE**	
Burgos's	1/2
El Califa	3
Ceviche 69	8
Heladería Gustitos del Cura	5
Pizzería El Hornito	7
Toe	6
Witite	4

Streets: BILLINGHURST, LORETO, PUNO, CARRION, LAMBAYEQUE, CUSCO, 2 DE MAYO, G PRADA, ERNESTO RIVERO, PIURA, J TRONCOSO, MOQUEGUA, TACNA, ICA, PUNO, AV FITZCARRALD, LEON DE VELARDE, AREQUIPA, 26 DE DICIEMBRE

0 — 200 metres

N

▼ Infierno (30km), Hospital Sanita Roasa & Port Area (Tambopata)

morning, military parades are held here, reminding you of the town's strategic position near the Bolivian and Brazilian borders. Ten blocks from the plaza is the large, bustling **market**, which covers an entire block, and if you follow Fitzcarraldo beyond it, you'll reach the **Obelisco** (Mon–Fri 8am–9pm, Sat 8am–8pm, Sun noon–8pm; S2), a viewpoint offering an expansive panorama of the entire city and the jungle beyond.

ARRIVAL AND DEPARTURE

By plane Puerto Maldonado International Airport (☎ 082 571 531) is 4km from the centre of town. *Mototaxis* cost around S7 for the ride. LAN, Taca and Star Peru have daily flights to Cusco (50min) and Lima. If flying, technically you have to go through a yellow-fever vaccination checkpoint at Puerto Maldonado's small but modern airport, though it's closed most of the time.

By bus Puerto Maldonado's Terminal Terrestre is located 2km away from the airport, along Carretera Tambopata, and this is the arrival point for all buses. The most reliable company is Movil Tours.

Destinations Cusco (two departures at 10am and then every 30min between 6–9pm; 10hr); Arequipa (every 30min between 2–6pm; 13hr) and Juliaca (for Puno; every 30min between 2–6pm; 10hr). Movil Tours also runs buses to Rio Branco in Brazil (Tues & Fri at noon; 10hr); regular *colectivos* travel to the Brazilian border from the market (every 30min between 5am–10pm; 3hr).

By boat Puerto Maldonado has two main river ports: one on the Río Tambopata, at the southern end of León de Velarde, the other on the Río Madre de Dios, at the northern end of León de Velarde. From the latter you can hire a boatman and canoe for a river trip (S90 person/day, for a minimum of 2 people). From the Tambopata dock there are twice-weekly passenger boats that go as far as the indigenous community of Baltimore and can drop people off at lodges along the way, though you'll need

9

your SERNANP permit (see below) first, as well as a guide. It's significantly cheaper and easier to get in touch with local guides (see below) and go with an organized tour. From the Río Madre de Dios dock you can hire private boats to take you to the Bolivian border, although this is an expensive option (S500; 6hr).

GETTING AROUND

By mototaxi and motorbike The quickest way of getting around town is to hail a *mototaxi* (S2 in-town flat rate, but check before getting on) or passenger-carrying motorbikes (S1 flat rate). If you have a lot of ground to cover in town, try one of the places along Prada between Puno and Velarde that rent mopeds for around S5/hr (no deposit, but passports and driving licences required), though this option might be a little intimidating for some, given the local driving standards. Make sure there's ample petrol in the tank.

INFORMATION AND TOURS

Tourist information There's a small tourist information kiosk at the airport which meets oncoming flights; they have limited information on jungle lodges in the area. The inconveniently located Dirsetur office (Mon–Fri 7am–1pm & 2–4pm; ☎082 571 164) on Fonavi, at San Martín, a 5min ride from the Plaza de Armas, stocks very basic information on Puerto Maldonado's attractions. The SERNANP office at Av 28 de Julio, 8th block (☎082 573 278), has handouts on the nearby national park and reserve; it collects entrance fees (S30) for a permit, for those planning on going independently.

Tour operators *Tambopata Hostel* (☎082 574 201), run by a former Rainforest Expedition guide, offers authentic backpacker jungle tours between one and five days and popular trips to Lago Sandoval and Lago Valencia, as well as *ayahuasca* ceremonies at the indigenous community of Infierno. *Anaconda Lodge* organizes kayak tours and trips to Sadoval Lake, Tambopata and Madre de Dios. *Tarantula Hostel* (see below) also offers a range of tours in the area.

ACCOMMODATION

★ **Anaconda Lodge** 600m away from the airport, along Av Aeropuerto s/n ☎082 792 726, ⓦanaconda junglelodge.com. Occupying an area of just under four acres, this Swiss-Thai lodge is home to rustic bungalows surrounded by a verdant tropical garden. Monkeys, sloths, porcupines, agoutis and armadillos – to name a few – roam the premises and there's a little pool at the back to cool off. The restaurant offers superb Thai food. Breakfast included. S̲8̲0̲

Tambopata Hostel 26 de Diciembre 234 ☎082 574 201, ⓦtambopatahostel.com. Tambopata has rooms set around an interior courtyard, while those on a tighter budget can kip in the hammocks at the back (S20). There's a washing

machine and kitchen for guests' use. Wi-fi and breakfast are included. The friendly and helpful owner organizes all manner of jungle tours. Hammocks S̲2̲0̲, doubles S̲7̲0̲

Tarantula Hostel Av Aeropuerto s/n ☎082 632 334, ⓦtarantulahostel.jimdo.com. Located at just 500m from the airport, *Tarantula* is set on a verdant plot of land, home to plenty of wildlife including monkeys and macaws. Those on a tight budget can camp in the garden (tents provided) or snooze in one of the hammocks. Guests have access to the barbecue, kitchen and large pool. Free wi-fi and airport pick-up. Breakfast included. Camping S̲2̲0̲, hammocks S̲1̲5̲, doubles S̲1̲0̲0̲

Tres Fronteras Jr. Arequipa 357 ☎082 300 011. The nineteen rooms, all with private bath and cable TV, are set over two floors; all have interior windows, which give the place a slightly institutional feel. Wi-fi. S̲8̲0̲

EATING, DRINKING AND NIGHTLIFE

★ **Burgos's** Leon Velarde 127. This open-fronted restaurant with woven prickly-pear lamps and dangling clay pots serves a range of regional and creole dishes; there's a good selection of vegetarian options (S8–14). Try the *palta rellena con palmito* (avocado stuffed with palm hearts; S13). Mains S20–28. There's another branch on Billinghurst. Daily 10am–11.30pm.

El Califa Jr. Piura 266. This Puerto Maldonado favourite has been going strong for over three decades. It serves all manner of meats (including exotic ones from the jungle – make sure to check which are legal), as well as *ceviche*. The fresh juices are made with fruits from the back garden. Mains S17–20. Daily 9am–5pm.

Ceviche 69 2 de Mayo, at Madre de Dios. Set on two floors, *Ceviche 69* is part of a wider chain with a/c interiors, serving good *ceviche* (S22–26) and plenty of fish and seafood mains (S20–29). Daily 10am–10pm.

Heladería Gustitos del Cura Velarde 474. Run by a Swiss priest, the profits at this pleasant café help fund a local orphanage. Friendly staff serve a selection of homemade ice creams (S2/scoop) in seventeen exotic fruit flavours, as well as delicious cakes (S5). Free wi-fi. Daily 8am–11pm.

Pizzería El Hornito Carrión 392. This rustic pizzeria with red brick walls and wooden tables serves wood-fired pizzas, which come in various sizes (from S16.50). There's another larger branch on the Plaza de Armas. Daily 6pm–midnight.

Toe On the western side of Plaza de Armas. Named after an ingredient of the hallucinogenic jungle vine *ayahuasca*, *Toe* is a lively bar attracting partygoers before they head for a big night out to club *Witite* up the road. Cocktails S10–15, beers S7. Mon–Fri 4pm–3am, Sat–Sun 11am–3am.

Witite Velarde 151. This popular club packs with twenty-somethings for some pop, rock and salsa tunes on Fri & Sat nights and keeps going until the early hours of the morning. Entry S10. Daily 11pm–6am.

DIRECTORY

Banks and exchange BCP on Plaza de Armas has an ATM and changes US dollars. Casa de Cambio on C Prada, at C Puno, changes foreign currency at good rates (Mon–Sat 8am–8pm).

Hospital Hospital Santa Rosa at Cajamarca 171 (☎082 571 019).

Internet Mundo Net on León Velarde 613 (Mon–Sat 7am–midnight; Sun 10am–midnight; S2/hr).

Laundry Lavandería Jhonatan, C Cusco s/n (Mon–Sat 7.30am–9pm; Sun 8.30am–9pm; S5/kg).

Police Billinghurst s/n (24hr).

Post office Velarde 675 (Mon–Sat 8am–8pm).

Visas Oficina de migraciones, Av 28 de Julio 467 (Mon–Fri 8am–1pm & 2–4pm; ☎082 571 069). Get your passport stamped here if leaving for Bolivia by river.

PUERTO MALDONADO TOURS AND JUNGLE LODGES

Compared with independent travel, an **organized excursion** saves time and adds varying degrees of comfort. It also ensures that you go with someone who knows the area, who speaks English and can introduce you to the flora, fauna, culture and regions. It's best to book a trip in Cusco directly through the lodge offices or online before travelling to Puerto Maldonado. There are several daily flights from Cusco to Puerto Maldonado, and most Cusco agencies will organize plane tickets (US$90–110) for you if you take their tours. The cheapest option is a two-day and one-night tour, but you will spend most of your time travelling and sleeping, so it's best to allow at least three to four days.

A stay at one of the many rustic lodges around Puerto Maldonado, mainly on the ríos Madre de Dios and Tambopata, offers a good taste of the jungle, and the cost typically includes full board (though not tips for guides or drinks), transfers and bilingual guides. The quality of wildlife sightings depends on the location; the further you travel from Puerto Maldonado, the more likely you are to see large mammals.

TOUR OPERATORS

Eco Amazonia Lodge C Garcilaso 210, office 206, Cusco ☎084 236 159; Enrique Palacios 292, Miraflores, Lima ☎01 242 2708; Puerto Maldonado ☎082 573 491; ⊛ecoamazonia.com.pe. Less than 2hr downriver from Puerto Maldonado, this large establishment offers basic bungalows with hammocks. Packages include visits to Monkey Island, the secluded "Cocha Perdida" oxbow lake, hikes in the rainforest and wildlife spotting along the Madre de Dios tributaries. A shamanic session involving the hallucinogenic jungle vine *ayahuasca* is also on offer. From US$280 per person for three days and two nights.

Explorer's Inn Plateros 365, Cusco ☎084 235 342; Alcanflores 459, Miraflores, Lima ☎01 447 8888; Puerto Maldonado ☎082 572 078; ⊛explorersinn .com. Located 58km south of Puerto Maldonado in the Tambopata reserve and featuring en-suite rustic doubles and triples. It offers 38km of forest trails, canoeing on the oxbow lake of Cococcocha (inhabited by giant otters), and visits to a macaw clay lick, accompanied by experienced naturalist guides. English, French and German spoken. From US$220 per person for three days and two nights.

Posada Amazonas Lodge Contact through Rainforest Expeditions, Aramburu 166, Miraflores, Lima ☎01 421 8347; Portal de Carnes 236, Cusco ☎084 246 243; or Puerto Maldonado ☎082 572 575; ⊛peru nature.com. Run by the local Ese'eja community, Posada is the perfect choice for culture travellers who want to learn more about the native community. The lodge features a medicinal farm where guests can partake in *ayahuasca* ceremonies with the guidance of a local shaman. There are comfortable en suites with hammocks, plus excellent food served in a rustic dining hall. Similar is Refugio Amazonas, located further up the river. There are plenty of activities on offer such as kayaking, stand-up paddle boarding, mountain biking, tree climbing, as well as excursions to a fruit farm and a 30m canopy nearby. From US$375 per person, minimum three days and two nights.

★ **Tambopata Research Centre** Contact through Rainforest Expeditions (see above). One of the most remote lodges in South America, TRC lies at the heart of the Tambopata National Reserve. Guests can interact with macaw researchers and visit the world's largest clay lick, located just 1km from the lodge. Birds supplement their diet with sodium in the clay, resulting in colourful flashes of hundreds of macaws every morning. Chances of seeing wildlife here are greatly increased: peccaries, monkeys, wild boars, over 500 species of birds and even jaguars are commonly spotted. Fantastic photography tours using high-end equipment are also offered. From US$745 per person, minimum of four days.

9

Wildlife reserves around Puerto Maldonado

Madre de Dios boasts spectacular virgin lowland rainforest and exceptional wildlife. Brazil-nut-tree trails, a range of lodges, some excellent local guides and ecologists plus indigenous and colonist cultures are all within a few hours of Puerto Maldonado. There are two main ways to explore: either by arranging your own boat and boatman, or by taking an excursion up to one of the lodges, which is more expensive but also more convenient.

Less than one hour downriver from Puerto Maldonado (1hr 30min return) is **Lago Sandoval**, a large oxbow lake, home to caimans, giant otters and a host of birds. It's best to stay here overnight and do a boat ride on the lake in the early morning – the best time for wildlife-spotting, though it's also possible to do the lake as a day-trip. Take one of the recommended tours (see p.824) or hire a boat (around S120) to drop you off at the start of the trail (about 1hr to the lake) and to pick you up later. Bring your own food and water.

Further along the river, 60km from Puerto Maldonado, lies the huge **Lago Valencia**. It takes at least two days to visit, and its remoteness increases your chances of seeing wildlife, both while gliding through the still lake and along the hiking trails around it; the lake also features excellent fishing opportunities.

South of Puerto Maldonado, Río Tambopata flows into the heart of the **Reserva Nacional Tambopata**, where you'll find several excellent lodges, as well as the indigenous communities of Infierno and Batimore. The remote **Parque Nacional Bahuaja-Sonene** is even further upstream (6hr minimum) and features some of the best wildlife in the Peruvian Amazon as well as the Tambopata Research Centre, located next to the Colpa de Guacamayos – one of the largest macaw clay licks in the Amazon. To visit the reserve and the national park, you will need to book a guided tour at one of the lodges.

MANU BIOSPHERE RESERVE

Encompassing almost 20,000 square kilometres (about half the size of Switzerland) on the foothills of the eastern Andes, **MANU**, declared a Biosphere Reserve by UNESCO in 1977, features a uniquely varied environment of pristine rainforest, from crystalline cloudforest streams and waterfalls down to slow-moving, chocolate-brown rivers in the dense lowland jungle. Manu is one of the most biologically diverse places in South America; rich in macaw clay licks and otter lagoons, it's also home to thirteen species of monkey and seven species of macaw.

Manu is reachable via an arduous six-hour bus journey from Cusco along a bumpy dirt road, followed by several hours along Río Madre de Dios, making it a destination for serious jungle enthusiasts with at least a week to spare. The reserve is divided into three parts: the **cultural zone**, encompassing the bus route and several villages within the cloudforest; the **reserved zone**, with the jungle lodges and oxbow lakes, located along Río Madre de Dios and Río Manu, accessible only as part of a guided tour (see box, p.828); and the **restricted zone**, consisting of pristine jungle, home to several indigenous communities and uncontacted tribes, and completely off-limits to visitors.

WHAT TO SEE AND DO

The highlights of most visits to Manu include the trail network and lakes of **Cocha Salvador** (the largest of Manu's

WHEN TO VISIT

Any expedition to Manu is very much in the hands of the gods, thanks to the changeable jungle environment. The region experiences a **rainy season** from December to March, when the road into the park is particularly susceptible to landslides, so is best visited between May and August when it's much drier, although at that time the temperatures often exceed 30°C/86°F. Bring a jacket just in case, as roughly once a month the jungle experiences several days of *friaje* – a cold spell that can bring the temperature down as low as 12°C/54°F.

oxbows) and **Cocha Otorongo** – bountiful jungle areas rich in animal, water and birdlife, both located along Río Manu. Cocha Otorongo is best known for the family of **giant otters** that live here. Other wildlife includes the plentiful **caimans** – the white alligators and rarer black ones – and you can usually see several species of **monkey** (dusky titis, woolly monkeys, red howlers, brown capuchins and the larger spider monkeys). Sometimes big mammals such as **capybara** or **white-lipped peccaries** also lurk in the undergrowth, and the fortunate have been known to see a jaguar. Also along Río Manu you'll find the Manu Wildlife Centre, located near a clay lick popular with tapirs, while further along the river to the east, a short boat ride and hike away, is a large clay lick, frequented by colourful flocks of macaws.

The **flora** of Manu is as outstanding as its wildlife. Huge cedar trees can be seen along the trails, covered in hand-like vines climbing up their vast trunks, as well as the giant Catahua trees, traditionally the preferred choice for making dugout canoes, and the "erotic palm" with its suggestive-looking roots.

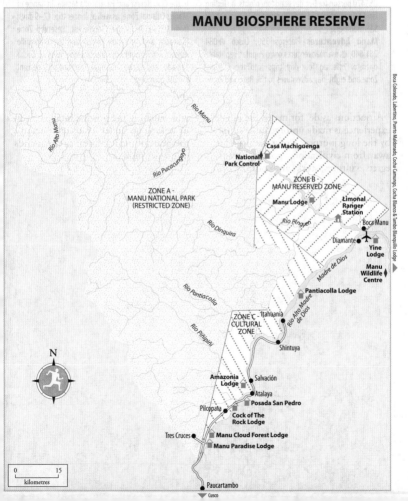

MANU BIOSPHERE RESERVE

Boca Colorado, Laberinto, Puerto Maldonado, Cocha Camungo, Cocha Blanco & Tambo Blanquillo Lodge

Río Manu

Río Pucacungoyo

Río Alto Manu

Casa Machiguenga

National Park Control

ZONE B – MANU RESERVED ZONE

ZONE A – MANU NATIONAL PARK (RESTRICTED ZONE)

Manu Lodge

Limonal Ranger Station

Río Pinguen

Río Dinquira

Boca Manu

Diamante

Yine Lodge

Madre de Dios

Manu Wildlife Centre

Río Pantiacolla

Pantiacolla Lodge

Río Alto Madre de Dios

ZONE C – CULTURAL ZONE

Itahluania

Río Pinipini

Shintuya

N

Amazonia Lodge

Salvación

Atalaya

Posada San Pedro

Pilcopata

Cock of The Rock Lodge

Tres Cruces

Manu Cloud Forest Lodge

Manu Paradise Lodge

0 — 15 kilometres

Paucartambo

Cusco

MANU TOURS

The companies below have a responsible attitude towards the Manu reserve and are keen to keep the impact of tourism to a minimum. Transport here is by land from Cusco.

TOUR OPERATORS

Atalaya Reserva Ecológica Chontachaka, Jardines del Inka G6, Cusco ☎084 228 327, ⓦatalayaperu .com. One of the few companies offering combined Manu and Tambopata tours, as well as ecological volunteer placements in the jungle. Atalaya has its own reserve, but uses the indigenous-owned and -run *Casa Matsiguenka* for accommodation on many of its tours. Also offers programmes where you can experiment with the hallucinogenic *ayahuasca* vine, and a course in the use of medicinal plants. From US$470 person for five days and four nights, including land transport in and out. Discount of 10 percent for SAE members.

Manu Adventures Plateros 356, Cusco ☎084 261 640, ⓦmanuadventures.com. Popular, reputable operator offering four-day trips into the Cultural Zone and eight-day adventures to the Reserved Zone.

Optional extras include rafting, zipping down a canopy line and a visit to the clay lick near their own *Erika Lodge* in the Cultural Zone, as well as visits to the oxbow lakes during the longer trip. Five-day "esoteric" trips are also available and involve shamanic rituals using medicinal and hallucinogenic plants. From US$760 for eight days.

Pantiacolla Tours Garcilaso 265, 2nd floor, Cusco ☎084 238 323, ⓦpantiacolla.com. A company with a reputation for serious eco-adventure tours. This company offers three- to five-day trips (from US$410) to the Cloudforest and Pantiacolla Mountain Range of Manu's Cultural Zone, as well as longer trips (7–9 days; from US$1370) to the Cloudforest, Reserved Zone (Salvador and Otorongo Lakes) and the Blanquillo macaw lick. Longer trips also include visits to Cocha Salvador and Cocha Otorongo. Discount of 5 percent for SAE members.

Attractions aside, for many, the jungle experience is made unforgettable simply by the long journeys along the river, far away from civilization, spotting herons, egrets, vultures, storks and toucans, and watching the pristine jungle pass by, or waking up under a mosquito net in the heart of the rainforest to the sounds of howler monkeys.

PUNTA DEL ESTE

Uruguay

HIGHLIGHTS

❶ **Montevideo** Eclectic architecture, sweeping beaches and hip nightlife. **See p.835**

❷ **Colonia del Sacramento** Picturesque town with excellent food. **See p.843**

❸ **Minas** Ride with gauchos through Uruguay's vast interior. **See p.846**

❹ **Punta del Este** Flashy beach resort with surf and celebrities. **See p.848**

❺ **Cabo Polonio** A remote community without electricity or roads. **See p.852**

HIGHLIGHTS ARE MARKED ON THE MAP ON P.831

ROUGH COSTS

Daily budget Basic US$30, occasional treat US$50

Drink Pilsen beer (1 litre) US$3

Food *Asado de tira* steak US$10

Hostel/budget hotel US$15–40

Travel Montevideo–Colonia del Sacramento (150km) by bus: 2hr 45min, US$11

FACT FILE

Population 3.3 million

Language Spanish

Currency Peso Uruguayo (UR$)

Capital Montevideo (population: 1.3 million)

International phone code ☎598

Time zone GMT -3hr

Introduction

If, as the saying goes, countries get the government they deserve, then President José Mujica is a great fit for Uruguay – modest, but sure of himself, progressive, but totally laidback; it's no wonder that this country is often referred to as the Switzerland of South America.

10

Through misfortune and good times, Uruguayans maintain their traditionally laidback and cheerful attitude, and it's not hard to see why. From the secluded **surfing beaches** of the Atlantic coast, to the rolling pastoral land of the interior tended by **gauchos**, or the picturesque streets of **Colonia del Sacramento** and the buzzing nightlife of **Montevideo**, theirs is a gem of a nation set between the South American giants of Brazil and Argentina. "*Tranquilo*" (peaceful) could be Uruguay's national motto, and, after witnessing the beauty of the land and the relaxed kindness of its people, you are unlikely to be in any hurry to leave.

CHRONOLOGY

Pre-1600 Uruguay is home to the Charrúa Indians, a hunter-gatherer people hostile to the European invaders.

Early 1600s Spanish settlers introduce cattle to Uruguay and the gaucho lifestyle of cattle-ranching develops.

1680 The Portuguese establish Colonia del Sacramento as the first major colony in Uruguay.

1726 The Spanish retaliate by founding Montevideo in an attempt to cement their power in the region. Their wars with the Portuguese continue for the next century.

1811 José Artigas begins an independence campaign against the Spanish, who finally leave Uruguay in 1815, only for Brazil and Argentina to fight over control of the territory.

1820 Artigas, defeated by the Portuguese, is exiled to Paraguay, where he stays until his death.

1825 Juan Lavalleja leads the legendary Treinta y Tres Orientales (a group of 33 revolutionaries) to a major victory over the Brazilians. Uruguay gains its independence a year later.

1831 Uruguay's 500 remaining Charrúa are massacred by the government.

1834–51 Uruguay plunged into civil war pitting the Colorados against the Blancos, names that have survived as political parties to this day.

1903–15 President José Batlle y Ordoñez of the Colorado Party makes sweeping social reforms, effectively making Uruguay South America's first welfare state.

1950–60s Inflation and political corruption leads to the stagnation of Uruguay's industries, and social unrest ensues.

1973 The Congress is dissolved and the army takes control of the government. Twelve years of military dictatorship ensue.

1984 The military allows free elections to take place. Colorado Dr Julio Sanguinetti becomes president and holds office until 1989 only to return to power from 1995 until 2000.

2000 Personal possession and use of marijuana is legalized.

2001 The economic crisis in Argentina leads to a collapse in the value of the Uruguayan peso; inflation and widespread unemployment ensues.

2009 José Mujica, a former militant leftist taken prisoner and tortured during the military regime, easily wins the presidency.

2012 Uruguay becomes the second Latin American country, after Cuba, to legalize abortion.

ARRIVAL AND DEPARTURE

The majority of visitors to Uruguay arrive via **ferry** from Buenos Aires to Colonia del Sacramento as an easy day-trip. Those **flying** into Uruguay usually arrive at Montevideo's **Aeropuerto de Carrasco** (see p.838); check online for the full list of airlines flying here (ⓦaeropuertode carrasco.com.uy). Those coming by bus will be dropped at Tres Cruces bus terminal (ⓦtrescruces.com.uy) in downtown Montevideo.

WHEN TO VISIT

One of Uruguay's main draws is its beaches, so it's best to visit from November to February when it's warm, although bear in mind that prices in beach towns soar. Winters in Uruguay can be downright frigid, with cold wet air blowing in from the ocean, but you should still get some sunny days.

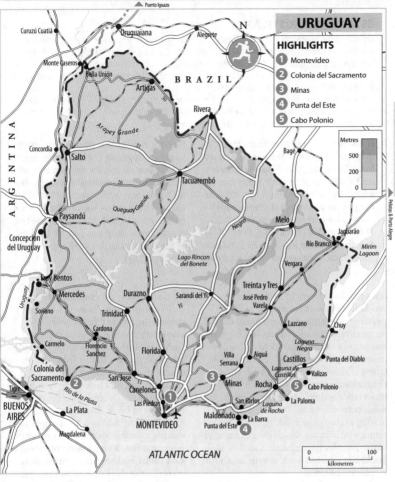

URUGUAY

HIGHLIGHTS
1. Montevideo
2. Colonia del Sacramento
3. Minas
4. Punta del Este
5. Cabo Polonio

Metres
500
200
0

VISAS

Citizens of the EU, US, Australia, New Zealand, South Africa and Canada, among others, do not need a visa to visit Uruguay. Check ⓦwww.dnm.minterior .gub.uy/visas.php for a full list of countries.

GETTING AROUND

BY BUS

The most convenient and cheapest means of transport in Uruguay are **intercity buses**, which operate from the bus terminal (*terminal de ómnibus*) in most towns. Montevideo's main terminal Tres Cruces

has an excellent website (ⓦtrescruces.com .uy) with details of all the companies and timetables operating there.

BY CAR

Uruguay is an easy country to drive around; all the major routes are asphalted, well signposted, and, outside of summer along the coast, there are very few drivers on the roads. Non-paved roads off the numbered routes tend to be in pretty good shape, except after rain when they may become too muddy without a 4WD. Even Montevideo is fairly straightforward to get in and out of, thanks to the coastal road (the *ramblas*) linking the airport with the

10

ESTANCIAS TURÍSTICAS

No visit to the interior of the country would be complete without a stay or at least a daytime visit to an *estancia* – a working ranch – but although staying overnight can be magical, the experience does not come cheap and there is a huge variation in authenticity; note that *estancias turísticas* are essentially rural hotels (you can download a comprehensive list at Ⓦturismo.gub.uy/informacion-turistica/folletos-para-descargar).

If you can't afford to stay overnight, most will arrange (much cheaper) day stays which will include horseriding, farm activities and a meal or two. The following are a couple of suggestions and demonstrate the huge variety you can choose from:

El Galope 50km from Colonia near Colonia Suiza, Ⓦelgalope.com.uy. One of the few *estancias* run with backpackers in mind, owners Miguel and Mónica (who speak English) aim to provide "a holiday from your holiday", offering R'n'R, Uruguayan style. With horse-riding, a sauna and great food all priced separately, you can choose how much or how little you do (meals US$8–12, horseriding US$35). Dorms US$25, doubles US$70
Guardia del Monte Ruta 9, Km261.5, Ⓦguardia delmonte.com. If you can shell out for a night at a traditional *estancia*, none offers a better location (overlooking Laguna de Castillos) or more rugged elegance than this one. The cosy farmhouse, with fantastic birdwatching and horseriding opportunities, is a taxi ride from Castillos (around UR$300), 10km down a dirt track. English is spoken, and while it is relatively expensive, you'll get an incomparable taste of rural Uruguay. Closed May–Sept. Full board with all activities per person (less if B&B only, or without activities) US$160

---

centre and old town. In low season you can find **rental cars** for as little as UR$35 per day (all the major international car rental companies have offices in Uruguay), but petrol costs are equivalent to European prices. Fines for speeding are extortionate (from US$500), so be sure to adhere to the national speed limits of 45km/hr in inner cities and 90km/hr on the main roads between towns. **Taxis** tend to be safe as long as they're licensed, but look out for remises (minicabs), which sometimes offer better rates for fixed distances as they are booked in advance – ask at your hostel for reliable companies.

BY BIKE

With a predominantly flat landscape and good-quality roads, Uruguay is a tempting place for cyclists.

Accommodation is never more than 50km apart along the coast (although in the interior and north facilities are much more sparse) and there are repair shops in many cities. As with elsewhere in South America, however, you must beware of the recklessness of local drivers.

ACCOMMODATION

Uruguay's coastal towns are full of **youth hostels** and other towns will offer basic hotels for those on a budget. Off the main tourist routes, however, places to stay can be few and far between and it's also worth checking if your trip coincides with a public holiday as accommodation can book up fast; tourist information offices are usually happy to help find accommodation. During the summer holidays from December to February it's necessary to book ahead, and prices soar, so that a dorm bed can be as expensive as sharing a double room in a basic hotel. Note that hotels and hostels often have a set dollar exchange rate, rather than going by the daily rate, which can mean you'll be slightly better off paying in dollars than pesos.

FOOD AND DRINK

Uruguay may not provide the most cosmopolitan of culinary experiences, but if you enjoy **beef** or most kinds of **seafood**, you will not go hungry. Uruguayan steakhouses (*parrillas*) serve steaks that are larger and (as the locals insist) more tender than their Argentine counterparts, with the most popular cuts being the ribs (*asado de tira*) and tenderloin (*bife de chorizo*).

The best dining option for **vegetarians** tends to be the ubiquitous pizza and pasta restaurants. **Desserts** (*postres*) also bear an Italian influence and Uruguay's *confiterías* (patisseries) and *heladerías* (ice-cream parlours) are bursting with delicious treats. *Dulce de leche* is an irresistible type of caramel that you'll find in almost any form on dessert menus (and as part of your hostel breakfast to spread on toast). The national snack is the **chivito**, essentially a whopping burger stacked with fried egg, ham, cheese and bacon, but with a whole steak instead of ground beef.

Uruguayans don't really do breakfast – most cafés open around 10am, but almost all hotels and hostels provide a basic breakfast for tourists. Lunch is eaten early, between noon and 1pm, making time for the *merienda* or *te*: a sumptuous afternoon tea – usually advertised for two – full of sweet and savoury snacks along with tea or coffee, which is taken around 5pm. Thanks to this tradition, dinner is always late; you'll normally be eating on your own if you arrive at a restaurant before 9pm.

Restaurant **prices** are fairly high for South America: the average price for a lunch set menu is around US$10 in Montevideo, and *à la carte* prices can be much higher than this.

DRINK

Mate (pronounced mah-tey) is the national drink and involves a whole set of paraphernalia to partake in drinking it (see box below). Coffee is the other non-alcoholic drink of choice here, and teas and bottled water are always available, along with fresh juices and smoothies (*licuados*).

When not clutching their thermos, Uruguayans enjoy the local beers – especially the ubiquitous **Pilsen** – which come in one-litre bottles (UR$5) fit for sharing. Uruguayan wine is becoming more prominent, especially the Tannat grape which makes a fine red (*tinto*). You may also see wine offered as *medio y medio* which is a blend of sparkling and slightly sweet white wine. **Tap water** is fine to drink.

10

CULTURE AND ETIQUETTE

Uruguayans of all ages tend to be warm, relaxed people, fond of lively conversation over a beer or barbecue (*asado*). As a nation in which the overwhelming majority of people are descended from Italian and Spanish immigrants, Uruguay also maintains some conservative **Catholic** religious and social practices, especially in the countryside, although the coastal towns are very liberal by South American standards. Uruguayans display a rugged sense of independence that recalls the romantic figure of the **gaucho**, the cowboys who still roam the grassy plains of the interior. Women and men alike greet each other with one kiss on the cheek. It's usual to leave a ten percent **tip** anywhere with table service.

SPORTS AND OUTDOOR ACTIVITIES

Ever since the first World Cup in 1930 was held in Uruguay and won by the national team, **football** has been the sport to raise the passions of the normally laidback Uruguayans. In the countryside, **horseriding** (*cabalgata*) is more a part of working life than a sport, but there are now many opportunities for tourists to go riding – many hostels and most *estancias* (see box opposite) offer

THE ART OF DRINKING MATE

You are unlikely to walk down a single street in Uruguay without seeing someone carrying the thermos, pots and metal straw (*bombilla*) required for **mate**. In a tradition that goes back to the earliest gauchos, Uruguayans are said to drink even more of the grassy tea than Argentines, and a whole set of social rituals surrounds it. At the close of a meal, the *mate* is meticulously prepared before being passed round in a circle; the drinker makes a small sucking noise when the pot needs to be refilled, but if this is your position, beware making three such noises: this is considered rude.

10

horseriding. **Cycling** is a popular way of seeing the cities (many hostels provide free or cheap bikes), while **fishing** is another favoured afternoon pursuit.

Surfing is increasing in popularity, thanks to fantastic Atlantic waves, and many beach hostels will rent out boards or advertise lessons.

A widely accepted translation of the Guaraní word *uruguay* is "river of painted birds", so it's no surprise that the country offers fantastic **birdwatching** opportunities, including flamingos, vultures, hawks, rheas and Magellanic penguins. Tourist information offices have excellent leaflets about twitching in Uruguay.

COMMUNICATIONS

The **national post office**, *Correo Uruguayo* (ⓦcorreo.com.uy), provides an expensive and sometimes unreliable service for international mail; for urgent deliveries, you are much better using a private mailing company like FedEx, at Juncal 1321 in Montevideo's old town. There are no postboxes on the street; you either need to go to a post office branch, or in Montevideo most museums have *buzones* (boxes) in their foyers. Antel run the **public phone** service and you'll find street phones and *cabinas telefónicas* (booths inside shops) wherever you go. You can buy phone cards (*tarjeta telefónica*), available wherever you see the Antel signs, or use change.

Internet cafés charge UR$20–50 per hour and are present in all towns.

CRIME AND SAFETY

Uruguayans pride themselves on how safe their country is, although statistically crime is on the rise. **Thefts** from dorms, as well as pickpocketing, do occur, especially in Montevideo and the

---

EMERGENCY NUMBERS

☎911 is the general emergency number for the police, ambulance and fire services. You may need to dial ☎42911 from mobiles.

---

beach resorts during the summer months. Store your valuables in lockers whenever possible, but you shouldn't feel worried carrying valuables around with you during the day. The Uruguayan police are courteous, but unlikely to speak English. As well as the emergency phone number (see box below), there is a national number for **tourist police** ☎08008226.

HEALTH

Uruguay's public healthcare system is in pretty good shape; there are adequate public **hospitals** in the major cities. Contact your embassy, or ask locals, for advice on the best facilities, and check that they will accept your insurance.

INFORMATION AND MAPS

The national **tourist board**, run by the Ministerio de Turismo y Deporte (Minitur; ☎02 1885100, ⓦturismo .gub.uy), is branded as **Uruguay Natural**, and they run offices in all of Uruguay's major towns, alongside local tourist offices run by the municipality. Uruguay Natural in Montevideo (see p.839) can give you free maps of every department, or you can buy high-quality road maps in petrol stations and bookshops. Uruguayans often write addresses using the abbreviations "esq.", meaning "at the corner with", and "c/", meaning "almost at", or "nearby".

MONEY AND BANKS

The unit of currency is the **peso uruguayo** (UR$). Coins come as 50 centimos and 1, 2, 5, and 10 pesos; notes as 10, 20, 50, 100, 200, 500 and 1000 pesos. At the time of writing, the **exchange rate** was £1 = UR$30, €1 = UR$26 and US$1 = UR$19.

Money changing is completely stress-free as everyone has to buy at the same rate, which varies slightly day to day (you can always find it displayed on the front of the daily newspapers). Breaking large banknotes is less of a problem than in most South American countries, though you are still advised to carry smaller notes in the countryside.

While major **credit cards** are widely accepted, and **ATMs** are common in cities (look out for the Banred ATMs which accept international cards), you should always carry a relatively large supply of **cash** for places where this is not the case. This applies especially to the beach villages of Eastern Uruguay, such as Punta del Diablo, which don't have ATMs. ATMs charge around UR$85 per withdrawal.

OPENING HOURS AND HOLIDAYS

Most **shops and post offices** open on weekdays from 8am until noon, before closing for lunch, reopening around 4pm until 7 or 8pm. Most businesses work at least a half-day on Saturday, but most close on Sundays. Banks are usually open Monday to Friday 1 to 5pm and closed at weekends. The exception to this is many shops in Montevideo, the main coastal tourist centres, and **supermarkets** in general; the latter are often open as late as 11pm during the week.

Most **museums and historic monuments** are open daily, though times vary, and tend to close once a week for maintenance (check with each attraction when theirs is). **Public holidays** are: January 1, January 6, Good Friday, Easter Monday, April 1, May 1, May 18, June 19, July 18, August 25, October 12, November 2, December 25.

Montevideo

With a population of around 1.6 million, over fifteen times larger than the second city of Paysandú, **Montevideo** is Uruguay's political, economic and transport hub. Founded in 1726 as a fortress against Portuguese encroachment on the northern shore of the **Río de la Plata**, it had an excellent trading position and, following a turbulent and often violent early history, its growth was rapid. The nineteenth century saw mass immigration from Europe – mostly Italy and Spain – that has resulted in a vibrant mix of architectural styles and a cosmopolitan atmosphere.

CARNAVAL

You will not truly understand the lure of Montevideo unless you experience **Carnaval**. It's a three-month celebration of Uruguayan culture with parades, neighbourhood stages known as *tablados* which host *murgas* (street bands where singing groups are accompanied by wild drumming – *candombe* – originating in the African rhythms brought over by slaves), plays, parodists and comedians, all wildly dressed and there to entertain. The spectacular opening and closing parades take place on Avenida 18 de Julio and many of the biggest events are held at the **Teatro de Verano** (see p.842). If you know you'll be in Montevideo during Carnaval, email the tourist office to find out key dates.

10

Far more relaxed, but less affluent than its Argentine neighbour across the river, the Uruguayan capital has nevertheless seen an economic improvement in recent years, and wisely invested in its culture, infrastructure and beaches. Montevideo may appear humble at first, but this is a seriously cool, confident city.

WHAT TO SEE AND DO

Montevideo can sometimes be overshadowed by its snazzier neighbour Buenos Aires, but this, Uruguayans will tell you, is the true home of the **tango**, with plenty of free classes and *milongas* – bars playing traditional music – not to mention the best place to experience South America's longest **Carnaval** season (see box above). There are tons of quirky **museums**, especially in the charming **Ciudad Vieja** and east to the **Centro**, based around Avenida 18 de Julio. Close to here, **Calle Tristan Narvaja** is filled with independent bookshops and cultural spaces, and holds a huge weekly flea market (see p.838). You may well stay in **Barrio Sur** – a traditionally Afro-Uruguayan neighbourhood where **candombe** drumming was cultivated – or chic and affluent areas **Punta Carretas** or **Pocitos**, where you'll find some of the best food and nightlife.

10

Ciudad Vieja

If you've ever seen a fictionalized version of Havana on TV or film, it's quite possible it was actually shot in Montevideo's **Ciudad Vieja**, so reminiscent are its streets of those in the Cuban capital. Dotted among the crumbling houses and cobbled streets are endearingly bizarre (and mostly free) **museums** and galleries, while the highlight is the glorious **Mercado del Puerto**.

Plaza Independencia and around

A good place to start a walking tour of the Ciudad Vieja is the **Puerta de la Ciudadela**, dating to 1746, marking the original site of the Citadel of Montevideo on the **Plaza Independencia**. This square commemorates the emergence of Uruguay as a sovereign nation, and a 17m-high statue and mausoleum (under the statue; daily 9am–5pm) of **José Artigas**, the man credited with kick-starting Uruguay's independence campaign against Spain and Portugal, stands aptly in the centre.

The area around the plaza contains eclectic architectural styles from different periods, from the pretty ugly **Torre Ejecutiva** where the president performs his duties, to the bulbous tower of the **Palacio Salvo**, built on the reported site of the first ever performance of tango.

Tucked behind the plaza's southwestern corner is the celebrated **Teatro Solís** (see p.842), the most prestigious theatre in the country, completed in 1856 and remodelled a few times thereafter. The guided tours (Tues & Thurs 4pm, Wed & Fri–Sun 11am, noon and 4pm; UR$20 in Spanish, or free on Wed; UR$40 in English, arrange in advance) are a fun way to see behind the scenes, but to experience its full splendour, you really have to watch a performance.

On the south side of the plaza, the old Presidential palace, a Neoclassical building from 1873, now houses the intriguing **Museo Casa de Gobierno** (Mon–Fri 10am–5pm; free; ☎02 1515902), which charts the history of the country via its often eccentric presidents.

Plaza de la Constitución and around

Lively pedestrian boulevard **Sarandí** cuts through the centre of the old city – starting at the Puerta de la Ciudadela – with its street-sellers, artisans, buskers and frequent parades, to the **Plaza de la Constitución**. Also referred to as the Plaza Matríz, this is Uruguay's oldest square, dating back to 1726. It's dominated by the **Catedral Metropolitana**, also known as the Iglesia Matríz, which, despite dating back to 1790, is underwhelming by Latin American standards.

Museo Torres García and Museo Gurvich

Sarandí is home to two of Uruguay's finest art galleries. At No. 683 the **Museo Torres García** (Mon–Fri 10am–7pm, Sat 10am–6pm; UR$65; ☎29162663, ⊚torresgarcia.org.uy) is devoted to the work of Uruguay's visionary artist, Joaquín Torres García, who championed the creation of a Latin American art form and created the upside-down image of South America that is so prevalent in *artesanía* in Uruguay. Torres García's most famous pupil is honoured on the Plaza Matríz next to the cathedral (due to move along Sarandí in 2013) at the excellent **Museo Gurvich** (Mon–Fri 10am–6pm, Sat 11am–3pm; UR$65, free on Tues; ☎29157826, ⊚museogurvich.org). Lithuanian Jewish immigrant José Gurvich gained fame in his own right with elaborate murals and sculptures, reminiscent of Chagall and Miró.

Around Plaza Zabala

Named for the founder of Montevideo, leafy **Plaza Zabala** may be passed by if it weren't for the **Palacio Taranco** on the north side. An opulent private home that was designed by Charles Louis Girault and Jules Leon Chifflot – the same French team who created the Arc de Triomphe – it now holds the **Museo de Artes Decorativas** (entry at 25 de Mayo 376; Mon–Fri 12.30–5.30pm; free; ☎29151101, ⊚cultura.mec.gob.uy). The beautifully displayed collection includes Uruguayan art and an expansive world pottery collection.

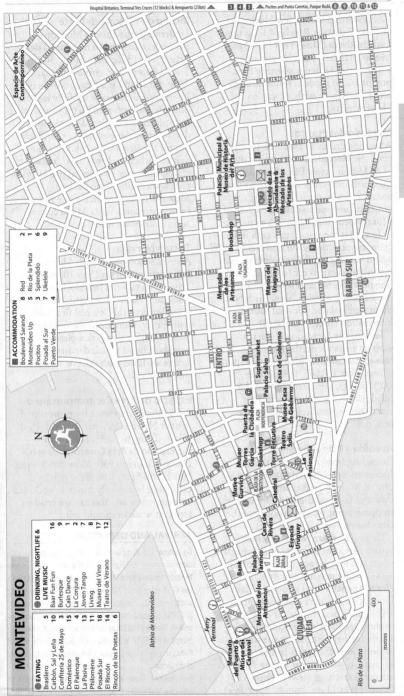

10

MONTEVIDEO

● **EATING**

Brasilero	5
Carbón, Sal y Leña	10
Confitería 25 de Mayo	3
Domestico	15
El Palenque	4
La Pasiva	13
Philomène	11
Posada Sur	18
El Rincón	14
Rincón de los Poetas	6

● **DRINKING, NIGHTLIFE &**
LIVE MUSIC

Baar Fun Fun	16
Burlesque	9
Caín Dance	1
La Conjura	2
Joven Tango	7
Living	8
Museo del Vino	17
Teatro de Verano	12

■ **ACCOMMODATION**

Boulevard Sarandí	8
Montevideo Up	5
Pocitos	1
Posada al Sur	3
Puerto Verde	4
Red	2
Rio de la Plata	5
Splendido	6
Ukelele	9

Espacio de Arte
Contemporáneo

Palacio Municipal & Museo de Historia
del Arte

Mercado de la
Abundancia &
Mercado de los
Artesanos

BARRIO
SUR

Bookshop

Mercado
de los
Artesanos

Manos del
Uruguay

PLAZA
CAGANCHA

PLAZA
FABINI

CENTRO

Supermarket

Casa de Gobierno

Puerta de
la Ciudadela

Palacio Salvo

Bookshop

Museo
Torres
García

Torre Ejecutiva

Museo Casa
de Gobierno

PLAZA
INDEPENDENCIA

Teatro
Solís

La
Pasionaria

Museo
Gurvich

Catedral

Casa de
Rivera

Esencia
Uruguay

PLAZA
CONSTITUCIÓN

PLAZA
MATRIZ

Palacio
Taranco

Bank

Mercado de los
Artesanos

PLAZA
ZABALA

CIUDAD
VIEJA

Ferry
Terminal

Mercado
del Puerto &
Museo del
Carnaval

Bahía de Montevideo

Río de la Plata

RAMBLA MONTEVERDE

0   metres   400

N

10

Also worth a look, a few blocks east of Plaza Zabala at Rincón 437, is the **Casa de Rivera** (Mon–Fri 11am–5pm; free; ☎29151051, ⓦmhn.gub.uy), which traces Uruguay's history from prehistoric to modern times through art and artefacts, with a focus on the life of Artigas.

Mercado del Puerto

A foodie's dream and an architectural gem, the **Mercado del Puerto** (at the end of pedestrian street Pérez Castellano by the port; open daily for lunch, some restaurants also open for dinner; ⓦmercadodelpuerto.com.uy) is one of Montevideo's highlights. It's so popular, in fact, that the restaurants cash in by charging extortionately; however, it's well worth soaking up the atmosphere, even if you don't stay to eat (see box, p.841). The **port** (*puerto*) and ferry terminal is on the northern edge, along with both the municipal and national **tourist information offices** (see p.839).

Set into the Mercado del Puerto, with its entrance on the Rambla is the **Museo del Carnaval** (daily 11am–5pm, closed Wed; UR$65, free on Tues; ☎29165493, ⓦmuseodelcarnaval.org), filled with colourful exhibits from the city's Carnaval celebrations (see box, p.835).

Avenida 18 de Julio and around

Extending from the eastern end of Plaza Independencia, **Avenida 18 de Julio** is central Montevideo's main shopping thoroughfare and the most important stopping point for the majority of the city's buses.

Try to pass **Plaza Fabini**, a verdant square along the avenue, on a Saturday when you'll come across people of all ages dancing tango (from 4pm). The **Plaza Cagancha** (also known as Plaza Libertad) is the next grand square on 18 de Julio; pass through it on your way to the huge **Palacio Municipal** building a little further east. Ask at the tourist information office at its feet for a ticket to enter, as the **mirador** on the 22nd floor offers far-reaching views over the city (Mon–Fri at 11am, 2pm & 3pm; free).

Museo de Historia del Arte

Underneath the Palacio Municipal the underrated **Museo de Historia del Arte** (Ejido 1326; Tues–Sun 1.30–5.30/7.30pm; free; ⓦmuseomuhar .blogspot.co.uk) is a treasure-trove of international items, beautifully laid out, but you'll soon notice that much of what is displayed are copies, designed to demonstrate the evolution of art; look out for the items with red dots telling you they're authentic. It has a particularly strong collection of original pre-Hispanic pieces, including Peruvian and Mesoamerican ceramics, some huge urns from Argentina's Santa María culture, and Guatemalan textiles.

Tristan Narvaja

A street synonymous with Montevideo's largest **street market** (Sun 10am–3pm), Tristan Narvaja is a few blocks east from the Palacio Municipal. Spanning several streets, this is a real flea market selling everything from antiques to pets. On other days, it's a pleasant neighbourhood to wander around as the streets are lined with eclectic independent shops and cafés.

Espacio de Arte Contemporráneo

A few blocks northeast from the top of Tristan Narvaja, in a partly refurbished prison dating to 1888, you'll find the **Espacio de Arte Contemporráneo** (Arenal Grande 1930; Mon–Sat 3–8pm, Sun 11am–5pm; free; ⓦeac.gub.uy), exhibiting beautifully curated, world-class contemporary art. You can see resident artists at work in the old cells.

ARRIVAL AND DEPARTURE

By plane The Aeropuerto de Carrasco (ⓦaeropuertode carrasco.com.uy) is 25km east of the city centre. Eschew the extortionately priced taxis (30min; UR$1000) and take a bus (1–3 every hour; 24hr with reduced service overnight and at weekends; 25min; UR$120) run by COT (ⓦcot.com.uy) or COPSA (ⓦcopsa.com.uy) to Tres Cruces bus station (see below). There is a US$36 tax on international flights (with the exception of US$17 to Buenos Aires), and US$2 on internal flights, usually included in your ticket price, but if not, payable at the airport.

Destinations There are long-distance direct flights to Asunción (daily; 3hr); Lima (daily; 5hr); Miami (daily; 9hr);

CROSSING THE RÍO DE LA PLATA

Every day, two Buquebus **ferries** leave from Montevideo (in the morning and late afternoon) to Buenos Aires (2hr 30min; UR$400–1000 one-way). For a more frequent service, both Buquebus and Seacat do a combined bus and ferry ticket to Colonia del Sacramento (see p.843), where there are ferries every couple of hours which take just one hour (around the same price) to the Argentine capital. Although less convenient and less used, the most picturesque ferry crossing is operated by Cacciola between Tigre, a northern suburb of Buenos Aires, and Carmelo, a one-hour bus ride to the west of Colonia (daily; 2hr 30min; UR$630 one-way; w cacciolaviajes .com). They also do connecting buses to Montevideo. Note that there is a one-hour time difference between the countries, so check which time is being quoted on the websites.

10

Madrid (3 weekly); Panama City (daily; 7hr 30min); Rio de Janeiro (daily; 2hr 40min); Santiago, Chile (4 daily; 2hr 40min); São Paulo (4 daily; 2hr 30min). There are several daily flights with Aerolineas Argentinas (w aerolineas .com.ar) and SOL (w sol.com.ar) to Buenos Aires' Aeroparque and Ezeiza airports (Aeroparque is better for central BA). Buquebus (w flybqb.com) run the only internal flights.

By bus All intercity buses operate out of Tres Cruces bus station (w trescruces.com.uy), 2km northeast of the centre. From here bus CA1 (every 15min; 15min; UR$11) goes to the centre, down Av 18 de Julio to the Plaza Independencia, loops around the Ciudad Vieja, then returns via the same route.

Destinations International: Asunción, Paraguay (2 weekly; 22hr); Buenos Aires, Argentina (3 daily; 8–10hr); Córdoba, Argentina (daily; 15hr); Porto Alegre, Brazil (daily; 12hr); Rosario, Argentina (daily; 8–10hr); Santiago, Chile (weekly; 28hr). National: Cabo Polonio (daily; 5hr); Carmelo (hourly; 3hr 30min); Colonia del Sacramento (hourly; 2hr 45min; 4hr); Minas (hourly; 1hr 40min–2hr 30min); Punta del Diablo (every 2hr; 5hr); Punta del Este (every 30min–every 2hr, 24hr a day; 2hr); Valizas (3 daily; 4–5hr).

Backpacker bus Summer Bus (t 42775781, w summer bus.com) is a beach-hopping backpacker bus which conveniently picks you up from your hostel during summer months (Nov–April; hop-on-hop-off ticket to 12 beaches US$75).

By ferry (see box above).

INFORMATION

Online The website w descubrimontevideo.uy is aimed at Spanish-speakers, but it has comprehensive tourist information, including an excellent downloadable guide in English (under Montevideo – *Guía Práctica* – *Guía en Inglés*). Look out for the guide *Friendly Map Magazine* at tourist information offices for LGBT listings. The government site w cultura .montevideo.gub.uy (only in Spanish) is great for cultural listings.

Tourist information The Minitur office on La Rambla 25 de Agosto de 1825 at the end of Yacaré (daily 8am–10pm; t 021885100, w turismo.gub.uy) has the best range of maps, leaflets and information in English in Uruguay. There are also information kiosks at the airport (t 26040386), and at Tres Cruces bus station (t 21185801). There are municipal tourist offices (daily: April–Nov 9am–5.30pm; Dec–March 11am–5pm; t 29168434) on the port side of the Mercado del Puerto, as well as outside the Palacio Municipal (t 19501830).

Tour operators LB Tour (18 de Julio 1044, office 702, t 29007159, w lbtour.com.uy) run some of the most popular city tours in Montevideo and Colonia, while Travel Montevideo (t 096614267, w travelmontevideo.com.uy) offer good walking tours around the city for around US$15. Soccer fans won't do better than Fanaticos Fútbol Tours (t 099862325, w futboltours.com.uy), who live and breathe the beautiful game. *Hostel Posada al Sur* (see p.840) have responsible tourism in mind with tours that benefit locals.

TOUR URUGUAY

Uruguay's vast countryside makes it difficult to tackle without a car, but there are some excellent tour operators who can get you out in the sticks.

TOUR OPERATORS

Biking Uruguay (t 27090636, w bikinguruguay .com) & **Bike Tours Uruguay** (t 099591519, w biketoursuruguay.com). Both companies run cycling tours in Montevideo and Punta del Este.

Caballos de Luz t 099400446, w caballowsdeluz .com. Recommended, good-value horseriding tours in Rocha department.

Lares W. Ferreira Aldunate 1322, office 14, Montevideo t 29019120. The most popular nationwide tour operator, specializing in outdoor activities and nature.

The Wine Experience t 097348445, w thewine -experience.com; prices depend on number of people in tour. South African Ryan runs raved-about gourmet food and vineyard tours from both Montevideo and Colonia.

10

GETTING AROUND

Most of the points of interest in the city are within walking distance of Plaza Independencia, while Pocitos and Punta Carretas are easily reached by bus. Note that the roads crossing Av 18 de Julio north–south change names either side of the main road.

By bus There are no route maps available, but there is a bus journey planner at ⓦ montevideo.gub.uy/aplicacion /como-ir and a list of inner-city route numbers with destinations at ⓦ cutcsa.com.uy/informacion/facrecorridos.php . You can catch buses to most parts of the city from outside the Teatro Solís. Buses heading for the centre are marked "Aduana" or "Ciudad Vieja". Ask for a "centrico" ticket (UR$11) if you're only going within the centro, or a "común" (UR$19) otherwise. Buses run regularly from 6am until midnight, when the service starts to thin out dramatically.

By bike Renting a bike is a popular way to see the city, and the lovely Ramblas hugging the estuary beaches makes it easy. Most hostels rent bikes cheaply.

By taxi Journeys within the confines of the city rarely amount to more than UR$200 in hailed street taxis or *remises* (minicabs). Note that the meter does not give the fare but rather the distance, which corresponds to a prefixed rate (taxis should always have the rates displayed for the passenger).

ACCOMMODATION

Although the Ciudad Vieja is dotted with cheap hotels and hostels, away from the pedestrianized Sarandí it can be unsafe at night. The Barrio Sur is a good bet for character and excellently placed for the old town and nightlife hotspots, while Punta Carretas and Pocitos are best for safety, shopping, beaches and partying. Hostels will usually offer bikes for rent and tango classes, and you can also assume that breakfast, internet and wi-fi, a/c and heat are provided unless otherwise mentioned. Prices are given for the cheapest bed or double room in high season, which starts in mid-Nov.

BARRIO VIEJO AND CENTRO

Boulevard Sarandí Sarandí 405, at Zabala ☎ 029153765, ⓦ boulevardsarandihostel.com. This friendly family-run hostel on Ciudad Vieja's pedestrian drag has a cosy layout and is outfitted with gaucho items. The living room has a bar and holds events such as jam sessions. Dorms UR$320, doubles UR$1000

★ **Posada al Sur** Pérez Castellano 1424 ☎ 29165287, ⓦ posadaalsur.com.uy. The most ethical choice in Montevideo, with organic breakfasts and community-oriented tours. Light common areas enhance the *buena onda* ("good vibes"). Its location close to the port is great during the day, but you might want to take a taxi back at night. Dorms UR$350, doubles UR$1050, en-suite apartment UR$1580

Red San José 1406 ☎ 29088514, ⓦ redhostel.com. Up a grand staircase in a building with nice architectural flourishes, this hostel is a 20min walk to the old city, but still very central, just off Av 18 de Julio. With various communal areas, including a roof terrace and living room with fireplace, it is a nice place to relax. Dorms UR$400, doubles UR$1450

Río de la Plata Av18 de Julio 937 ☎ 29085174. A six storey old-fashioned basic hotel, complete with caged elevator, that's stacked with character. The antique furniture, as well as the rock-bottom prices, makes up for the occasional sagging mattress. The best rooms face the street. No breakfast. Doubles UR$600

★ **Splendido** Bartolomé Mitre 1314 ☎ 29156171, ⓦ splendidohotel.com.uy. This budget hotel with retro styling is truly splendid. All rooms have balconies overlooking Teatro Solís, and each has a different shabby-chic personality. There's a kitchen you can use and the breakfast is good; the only downside is that it's above the most popular bars in the Ciudad Vieja, so bring earplugs. Rooms sleep 1–5 people. Doubles UR$900

Ukelele Maldonado 1183 between Micheline and Ruíz ☎ 29027844, ⓦ ukelelehostel.com. You can really relax in what was the family home of owner Patricia. This enormous house with soaring ceilings eschews the institutional feel that you find in many hostels, and, unusually for Montevideo, has a pool and nice patio garden. With no heating, the place becomes a little fridge-like in winter, though. Dorms UR$350, doubles UR$1040

POCITOS AND PUNTA CARRETAS

Montevideo Up Riachuelo 175 ☎ 27123463, ⓦ montevideoup.com.uy. A somewhat chaotic place run by a likeable family who make you feel welcome with no set times for breakfast and free use of the washing machine. In a pleasant neighbourhood just one block from the water. Dorms UR$440, doubles UR$1100

Pocitos Sarmiento 2641 ☎ 27127780, ⓦ pocitoshostel .com. Let the good times roll in one of the city's most likeable – if cramped – backpacker joints, with a lovely garden and good rates on private rooms. The young owners also have a hostel in Colonia. Dorms UR$360, doubles UR$600

Puerto Verde José M. Montero 2948, Punta Carretas ☎ 27126172, ⓦ puertoverdehostel.com. A Chilean-run petit hostel in wealthy Punta Carretas in a delightful house filled with light and art. There's a common room with a fireplace and a small patio. Dorms UR$320

EATING

Café culture is big in Montevideo, with several galleries and design stores doubling as cafés and small restaurants. There are some truly great eating experiences to be found. Restaurants open noon–4pm and 8pm–midnight unless stated.

BARRIO VIEJO AND CENTRO

⭐ **Brasilero** Ituzaingó 1447 ⓦ cafebrasilero.com.uy. Established in 1877, this is the most classic café in Montevideo, with cosy dark wooden walls and furniture. With its good, fresh food and huge selection of tea and coffee, it's no wonder it has been favoured by Uruguayan literary giants such Mario Benedetti and Eduardo Galeano. Coffee and cake UR$75.

Confitería 25 de Mayo 25 de Mayo 655, at Bartolomé Mitre. A patisserie/bakery with an unbeatable selection of snacks and takeaway lunches, but what it's really known for are the mouth-watering pastries, sold by weight, adorning the windows. *Menú del día* UR$180.

⭐ **Doméstico** Reconquista 587. This gourmet café, beloved among the city's arty crowd, serves fresh, seasonal and inventive dishes and is tucked away in La Pasionaria (see p.842). Mains UR$250.

La Pasiva Sarandí 600, Plaza de la Constitución. A national institution for one thing and one thing only; *panchos* (hot dogs) and beer at the bar. This one is the original, but it is now a nationwide chain offering other reliable fast food. Daily 8am–2am.

Posada Sur Paraguay, at Gardel. A neighbourhood *parrilla* whose terrace has glimpses of the river, and whose walls and food are infused with Uruguayan gaucho tradition. For the less carnivorous there is fish, pasta and salads too. *Parrillada* for two (plenty for three!) UR$595.

El Rincón Rincón, at Zabala, Ciudad Vieja & Buxareo 1321, Pocitos. Those really on a shoestring cannot do better than this *empanada* joint where whatever you choose is made to order and arrives piping hot. There are twenty fillings to choose from, both savoury and sweet. The molten *dulce de leche* filling is divine. *Empanadas* UR$25–40.

Rincón de los Poetas San José 1312, at Yaguarón. For big, cheap plates of comfort food, try this popular lunch

---

⭐ **TREAT YOURSELF**

The fantastically atmospheric Mercado del Puerto (see p.838) has become a victim of its own success with most restaurants offering overpriced and distinctly average food. While **El Palenque** (ⓣ 29170190, ⓦ elpalenque.com.uy) may be a little overpriced (the UR$80 cover charge could almost buy you a whole meal elsewhere), it bucks the trend by serving truly excellent food. You'll end up spending at least UR$500 for the fresh seafood and meat, cooked on the grill in front of you, but it's worth it. Usually open for lunch and dinner Mon–Sat, lunch only on Sun; closed Sun or Mon (depending on time of year).

---

and dinner spot above the artisan market in the beautiful old Mercado de la Abundancia. *Menú del día* UR$140–200. Closed Sun.

PUNTA CARRETAS AND POCITOS

Carbón, Sal y Leña España 2688, at Fco. Aguilar, Pocitos. A highly recommended *parrilla* run by a friendly husband and wife who cook arguably the best steak in the city on their wood-fired grill. Imaginative sides, stir-fries and home-made pasta too. Mains UR$200–400. Mon–Sat from 8pm. Closed Jan.

Philomène Solano García 2455, at Miñones. An elegant, but cosy, French-style café serving some great light bites – including gourmet soups, sandwiches and salads (UR$160) – as well as the finest real tea in the city. Closed Sun.

DRINKING AND NIGHTLIFE

There are a number of good bars in the Ciudad Vieja, mainly along Bartolomé Mitre and Ciudadela. The area known as the "World Trade Centre" in Pocitos (Av Dr. Luís A. de Herrera leading up from the Rambla República del Perú) has a huge number of bars and clubs, but they tend to be more expensive than in the centre. Bars open in the early evening and close in the early hours, when, at weekends, clubs will open.

BARS AND CLUBS

Baar Fun Fun Ciudadela 1229 ⓦ baarfunfun.com.uy. Open since 1895, *Fun Fun* is a small place steeped in the history of tango, visited by guests from the president of Chile to Bryan Adams. You can watch some top tango singers and dancers while you try the house speciality drink, *uvita* (similar to grappa), for just UR$80. Open Tues–Sat, see board outside for what's on.

Burlesque Av Dr. Luís A de Herrera 1136. One of the most popular bars in Pocitos, this Americana-themed bar has a massive range of whiskies (over 70), good Tex-Mex food and is a great place to start – or finish – on this buzzing nightlife boulevard. Daily from 6.30pm.

Caín Dance Cerro Largo 1833 ⓦ caindance.com. Uruguay is one of the most gay-friendly countries in South America and *Caín* is the most friendly gay club in town, getting its groove on every Fri and Sat night. Opens at midnight, though no one goes before 3am.

Living Paulier 1050. A chilled-out grungy bar, between the centre and Pocitos, that will make you feel at home in Montevideo. The staff will join you for a shot of the house Grappamiel (UR$60), and DJs might take over the downstairs room. Open Wed–Sun 9pm–3/6am.

⭐ **Museo del Vino** Maldonado 1150 ⓣ 29083430, ⓦ museodelvino.com.uy. Despite its name this is no museum but a wine (only national wines are sold) and tango bar. Live music can command covers of up to UR$250, but the ambience is well worth it. There are free *milongas* (community tango dances) every week. Tues–Sat from 9pm; tango classes Wed 8pm.

LIVE MUSIC AND CULTURE

★ **La Conjura** Tristán Narvaja 1634, at Uruguay ☎ 24021245. A secondhand bookstore selling locally made clothes with a cheap café (daily noon–8pm; *menú del día* UR$70), also with live *Candombe*, tango and Afro-Uruguayan beats (Thurs–Sat from 10.30pm & Sun lunchtime).

Joven Tango Mercado de la Abundancia, San José 1312 ⓦ joventango.org. If you are a tango enthusiast, head to the food court of this market (see below), which is converted into a dancefloor for classes followed by dancing most nights of the week.

Teatro Solís ☎ 219503323, ⓦ teatrosolis.org.uy. Uruguayans are very cultured and justly proud of their historic theatre. Shows the best of Uruguayan opera, music and theatre at subsidized prices. Tickets start at around UR$150.

Teatro de Verano Rambla Wilson, at Cachón ☎ 2712 4972, ⓦ teatrodeverano.org.uy. For some of the biggest moments during Carnaval and to see international music stars, try this big outdoor amphitheatre in Parque Rodó.

CINEMAS

Most films are shown in their original language with Spanish subtitles. You can find all the theatres in the country (there aren't many) listed at ⓦ cartelera.com.uy under "Cine por sala". Tickets cost UR$120–180. There are small movie theatres in the centre, but the best choice of films is at Casablanca (21 de Septiembre 2838, at Ellauri ☎ 27123795) in Punta Carretas, and the enormous Movicenter in Montevideo Shopping (Luis Alberto de Herrera 1290 ☎ 29003900, ⓦ movie.com.uy) in Pocitos.

SHOPPING

Av 18 de Julio is Montevideo's main commercial street, while there are some large malls located in the richer neighbourhoods of Pocitos and Punta Carretas.

Bookshop Central shops at Sarandí 640 and at 18 de Julio 1296 with Yaguarón (shops 4–5). See ⓦ bookshop.com.uy for locations ("sucursales"). Stocks a good range of English-language novels.

Esencia Uruguay Sarandí 359. If you can't get out to the *bodegas* in the countryside, sampling Uruguay's fine wine selection at this pleasant shop may well be the next best thing.

Manos del Uruguay San José 1111. The discount store of the international brand with a range of high-quality woollen clothes, all of which are handmade in Uruguay.

Mercado de los Artesanos Mercado de la Abundancia, San José 1312; Mercado Plaza, Plaza Cagancha; Espacio Cultural Rafael Barradas, Pérez Castellano 1542,

ⓦ mercadodelosartesanos.com.uy. Three excellent indoor artisan markets where you can find original, high-quality souvenirs.

La Pasionaria Reconquista 587 ⓦ lapasionaria.com.uy. A sophisticated multipurpose art complex housing a design store, boutique clothing shop, small gallery, and the excellent café *Doméstico* (see p.841).

DIRECTORY

Banks and exchange You'll find ATMs in Tres Cruces Terminal, and branches of all the major banks along Av 18 de Julio in the centre, or at the World Trade Centre in Pocitos. Exchange rate, by law, is the same everywhere, so change your money wherever you see casas de cambio.

Embassies and consulates Argentina, Cuareim 1470–11 ☎ 29028166; Australia, Cerro Largo 1000 ☎ 29010743; Brazil, Blvr Artigas 1328 ☎ 27072003; Canada, Plaza Independencia 749, office number 102 ☎ 29022030; South Africa, Dr. Gabriel Otero 6337 ☎ 26017131; UK, Marco Bruto 1073 ☎ 26223630; US, Lauro Muller 1776 ☎ 217702000.

Hospital Hospital Britanico, near the Tres Cruces Bus Station on Italia 2400 (☎ 24871020), offers good private healthcare.

Internet and phone Phone Box, Av 18 de Julio, at Andes, is open 24hr.

Laundry Most of the hostels have cheap laundry services available. There are no self-service laundrettes but La Lavanderia, at Andes 1333, charges UR$100 to wash and dry a backpack full of clothes.

Left luggage There is 24hr left-luggage at Tres Cruces bus terminal (UR$120/24hr). Most hostels will let you store things for free.

Pharmacies 24hr pharmacy just off Plaza Independencia at 843 Av 18 de Julio.

Post office Misiones 1328 (Ciudad Vieja), at Ejido, between San José and Soriano (central).

Tourist Police Uruguay 1667, at Minas (☎ 08008226). Look out for the police officers in high-visibility vests.

Supermarket Chain Ta-Ta has a central store at 880 Av 18 de Julio (daily 9am–10pm).

Western Uruguay

Although Western Uruguay in general has often been neglected by visitors heading for the eastern beaches, **Colonia del Sacramento**, just one hour away from Buenos Aires, is the most common point of entry for tourists – especially Argentine day-trippers – as well as being one of the most beautiful and intriguing towns on the whole continent.

COLONIA DEL SACRAMENTO

Originally a seventeenth-century Portuguese smuggling port designed to disrupt the Spanish base of Buenos Aires across the Río de la Plata, **COLONIA DEL SACRAMENTO** (often referred to simply as "Colonia") is a picturesque town with charming little museums, plenty of outdoor activities and some of the best foodie culture in Uruguay. Despite an increasing number of tourists visiting the town, it retains a sleepy indifference to the outside world and merits more than just a day-trip to get to know it better.

WHAT TO SEE AND DO

Start your trip at **BIT**, the "Uruguay experience", the country's flagship tourist information centre (Odriozola 434; daily 10am–7pm; ☎45221072, ⊛bitcolonia .com; free wi-fi), two blocks from both the bus terminal and ferry port. It's architecturally interesting – built in a modernist glass box at the old railway station, beautifully integrated with the disused tracks – and is also a fantastic source of information for both Colonia and the whole country. From there it's an easy stroll around the atmospheric **Barrio Histórico** (old quarter), or there's an easy half-day excursion on foot or by bus to the eerie abandoned resort of **Real de San Carlos**.

Around the Plaza Mayor

At the southwestern corner of the plaza is the **lighthouse** (daily noon–6pm; UR$15), which affords great views from the cupola, while at the southeastern corner lie the remains of the old (if heavily restored) city gateway, the **Portón de Campo**. Once charged with protecting the important trade centre from invading forces, now they permanently separate old Colonia from the "new" city.

A few blocks north of the plaza, along Vasconcellos, the **Iglesia Matríz** claims to be the oldest church in Uruguay, with some columns from the original Portuguese building constructed in 1730.

The central museums

Dotted around the Barrio Histórico, a UNESCO World Heritage Site, is a series of eight modest **museums** (all open

10

COLONIA DEL SACRAMENTO

Río de la Plata

▲ Real de San Carlos (5km)

ACCOMMODATION
El Capullo — 3
Rivera — 4
Sur — 1
El Viajero B&B Posada — 5
El Viajero Hostel & Suites — 2

EATING
La Bodeguita — 5
Buen Suspiro — 7
Lentas Maravillas — 3
Mi Carrito — 2
Viejo Barrio — 6

DRINKING & NIGHTLIFE
Matamala — 4
Tr3s Cu4tro — 1

Feria de los Artesanos

Bastión del Carmen

Museo del Período Español

Motorent

Mini-Market

El Abrazo

Iglesia Matríz

PLAZA 25 DE AGOSTO

Police

Hostel Colonial

Motorent

Museo Municipal Casa Nacarelo

Lighthouse

PLAZA MAYOR HENRIQUEZ DE LA PEÑA

Portón de Campo

Museo del Período Portugés

Bus Terminal

B.I.T

Ferry Terminal

Port

Colonia Shopping (1km)

N

0   100
metres

10

11.15am–4.30pm, each closed one day a week on different days; joint ticket UR$50; ⓦ museoscolonia.blogspot.com). The **Museo Municipal** (closed Thurs) on the west side of Plaza Mayor, is the only place you can buy the joint ticket. It houses town treasures and a small natural history museum and is worth a peek around. A few of the other museums deserve a look if you have time, especially the restored **Casa Nacarello** (closed Tues), next to the Museo Municipal, whose tiny rooms, with period furnishings, give you a taste of colonial life. The **Museo del Período Histórico Portugés** (between De Solís and De los Suspiros on the Plaza; closed Fri) is also worth a visit; you'll find some fine *azulejos* here, and the internal walls are constructed in rectangular and diagonal brick patterns, dating back to around 1720.

The similarly named **Museo del Período Histórico Español** (De España, at De San José; closed Wed), at the north end of the Barrio Histórico, also exhibits colonial items, but, most interestingly, has seven evocative oil paintings by Uruguay's most famous contemporary painter, Carlos Páez Vilaro, creator of Casapueblo (see p.850), depicting important moments in Colonia's history.

Bastión del Carmen

Wandering along the piers on the northern edge of the Barrio Histórico, you'll notice the striking red-brick **Bastión del Carmen** (Rivadavia 223; daily 10am–8pm; free; ☎ 45227201), with walls dating from the time of Governor Vasconcellos (1722–49). Once a fortress, it was converted into a factory producing soap and gelatine products in the 1880s, and a chimney from that period still stands. Today it operates as a cultural centre, with a theatre, gallery and a small museum dedicated to its history.

Real de San Carlos

Outside of Colonia's touristic centre, the only attraction in town is the **Real de San Carlos**. Originally the brainchild of millionaire Nicolas Mihanovic, who conceived the idea of an exclusive tourist complex for rich Argentines, it now lies largely deserted. Between 1903 and 1912, he constructed a magnificent bullring, which was used only eight times in two years, a *frontón* (Basque pelota) court which now lies decaying, and a racecourse, which is the only part of the resort still operational.

Regular **horse races** take place, and the horses can frequently be seen exercising along the nearby beach. If you fancy a ride yourself, the *Hostel Colonial* organizes **horseriding** trips for up to four hours (UR$1000) to forests and wineries outside town. To get there either walk the 5km north along the *rambla*, or catch a bus (10min) from the bottom end of Avenida General Flores.

ARRIVAL AND DEPARTURE

By bus and ferry The terminal and port are located next to each other three blocks to the south of Av General Flores (the main street). The town centre is a 10min walk to the west along Manuel Lobo.

Destinations by bus Carmelo (every 2hr Mon–Sat, 3 daily Sun; 45min–1hr 30min); Montevideo (every 1–2hr; 2hr 45min).

INFORMATION

Tourist information Colonia has no shortage of tourist information centres. Head to BIT first (see p.843), then to the branch in the historical centre on Manuel Lobo by the Portón de Campo, run by the Intendencia (daily 9am–6pm; ☎ 45228506, ⓦ coloniaturismo.com), if you still need information. There are smaller offices in both the bus and ferry terminals.

Tour operators Local operator Minitur (van often parked outside tourist information office on Lobo; ☎ 093724893, ⓦ coloniaescondida.com) can take you on city tours, as well as to vineyards and to Parque Anchorena – the historic country home of the president which has its own nature reserve – for around US$25/person. City walks with professional guides start at the tourist information office on

Lobo daily at 11am and again at 3pm (UR$100 in Spanish or UR$150 in English with prior reservation; ⓣ 099379167).

ACCOMMODATION

The standard of budget accommodation in Colonia is dire and prices are higher than elsewhere. On the other hand, most are very central, but it's worth investigating the out-of-town estancia *El Galope* (see box, p.832). Breakfast is included unless otherwise stated.

HOSTELS

★ **Sur** Rivadavia 448, at Mendez ⓣ 45220553, ⓦ surhostel.com. The lovely lads who run this and *Pocitos Hostel* in Montevideo have made it their mission to spread *buena onda* ("good vibes") among their guests, and the staff are always on hand to socialize and give a local perspective. Dorms UR$340, doubles UR$1000

El Viajero Hostel & Suites/B&B Posada W. Barbot 164 ⓣ 45222683; Florida 269 ⓣ 45228645, ⓦ elviajerohostels.com. Success has made this Uruguayan chain of HI hostels feel a little formulaic and institutional, but it is always a reliable choice. In Colonia, there is a hostel with some "suites" (private rooms), and around the corner is a "B&B Posada" offering very nice private rooms with TV and DVDs, some with river views. Dorms UR$400, suites UR$1600, *B&B Posada* doubles from UR$1900

HOTELS

The hotels below provide rooms with TV, private bathrooms and a free breakfast. For a comprehensive list of hotels and hostels by star rating, try ⓦ hotelesencolonia.com.

★ **El Capullo** 18 de Julio 219 ⓣ 45230135, ⓦ elcapullo.com. Run by a British-American couple, this boutique hotel is stylish yet cosy, with a gorgeous garden and a great breakfast buffet. At the pricier end of budget, but head and shoulders above other places which charge only a couple of hundred pesos less. Doubles UR$2200

Rivera Rivera 131 ⓣ 45220807, ⓦ hotelrivera.com.uy. A comfy hotel with an Alpine feel, conveniently located a block from the bus terminal and port. Doubles UR$1700

EATING

Although the restaurants in the Barrio Histórico are pricey, the quality on the whole is excellent and the ambience is hard to beat. Restaurant opening hours are 11am–midnight unless otherwise noted. Contact details are given where booking is recommended.

La Bodeguita Del Comercio 167. Buzzing, stylish place whose three terraces overlooking the river get crowded with people who've heard rumours of the best pizzas in town (UR$110). Tues–Sun from 8pm; Sun also 12.30–3.30pm.

Buen Suspiro C de los Suspiros 90 ⓣ 45226160. On the most photographed street in Uruguay, only recognizable by a discreet sign, this foodie heaven specializes in fine wines, cheeses, charcuterie and preserves attractively served on platters for sharing (as a main for two UR$490). Closed Wed.

★ **Lentas Maravillas** Santa Rita 61. If you've got an afternoon to relax you won't find a cosier way to do it than perusing owner Maggie's English-language books in front of the fire or on the riverside deck. Inventive baked goods, gourmet sandwiches (UR$280) and hot drinks. Daily noon–8pm, weekends only April–Nov.

★ **Mi Carrito** Lavalleja between Rivadivia and Dr. D. Fonseca. There is nowhere locals rave about for budget food more than this food truck selling the best bad food you'll ever eat. Try the epic *milanesa* for two with every topping imaginable (UR$170), or the *pancho* wrapped in bacon with mozzarella (UR$60). Daily 11.30am–4pm & 8pm–1am except Sun (lunch only).

Viejo Barrio Vasconcellos 169. This otherwise decent Italian restaurant serves the best veal *milanesas* (like a schnitzel) this side of Vienna, including one stuffed with ham and cheese (UR$240). Thurs–Mon 11am–midnight, Tues & Wed 11am–4pm.

DRINKING AND NIGHTLIFE

Matamala Ituzaíngo 222. A surprisingly sophisticated bar which would be rather more at home in Brooklyn, with stylish furniture, chilled alternative music, Belgian bottled beers and a refined liquor collection (UR$100 for a generous measure). Thurs–Sat from 9pm.

Tr3s Cu4tro Alberto Mendez 295, ⓦ trescuarto.com. Their website says it all: "one building, two courtyards, three dancefloors, four bars, steaming hot". A great Uruguayan "*boliche*" (bar/nightclub), good for just a few drinks, or for staying up all night. There is an entry fee (UR$50–100), but once you get in, food and drinks are reasonably priced. There's often live music too. Fri & Sat from 11pm.

SHOPPING

The Barrio Histórico is littered with fashionable, pricey boutiques selling locally made as well as more generic leather goods, but the best deals for handicrafts are to be found either at the *feria* or artisans' market (Dr. Daniel Fosalba; daily 10am–6pm).

El Abrazo Flores 272. A commendable little shop selling Uruguay-specific books, including English translations of national authors Bennedetti and Galeano, music, and locally made gifts and clothes.

Colonia Shopping Roosevelt 458, ⓦ coloniashopping.com.uy. A brand-new mall with all the expected facilities, including a cinema.

DIRECTORY

Av General Flores is the main commercial street and has many banks, casas de cambio and ATMs as well as pharmacies. If you can't find what you're looking for, try at Colonia Shopping (see above).

10

Hospital 18 de Julio between Rivera and Mendez.

Internet Free wi-fi in the Plaza 25 de Mayo, computers either at the main Antel office (see below), or there's an internet café at Flores 172, open until 9pm every night.

Laundry Arco Iris on Suárez between Flores and 28 de Julio.

Left luggage Facilities at the bus terminal, and at BIT (see p.843).

Post office and telephone Correo Uruguayo and Antel have main offices next to each other on Lavalleja on Plaza 25 de Agosto, and share an office in the ferry terminal.

Taxi A 24hr service is run from the corner of Flores with Mendez (☎45222920).

Tourist Police At the main *comisaría* on Flores opposite Plaza 25 de Mayo (☎45223348).

Supermarket El Económico mini-market, Flores 290, at Barboto; Micro Macro, Flores, at Rivera.

The Interior

Some of South America's most undiscovered natural beauty awaits you in Uruguay's **INTERIOR**. This is real gaucho country and it's easily accessible, if little known about. While most of the interior is unknown to tourists, largely due to the fact it's mostly covered in vast ranches, some of Uruguay's finest and least explored pastoral landscapes are within reach of **Minas**, a small town with a big history.

MINAS

Just 120km from Montevideo, but far from the usual backpacker trail, **MINAS**, the capital of the Lavalleja department, is an excellent base for exploring the rolling hills and romantic traditions of Uruguay's interior – you won't have to go far before you see a genuine mounted gaucho wearing a poncho and clutching his *mate*. Delving into this region's history can give you a deeper understanding of the Uruguayan mentality and the nation's history.

WHAT TO SEE AND DO

In Minas, there are some interesting **museums** worth visiting, as well as pleasant parks, but around Minas is where the real fun lies. **Parque del Salto**

Penitente, in craggy moor-like countryside, offers outdoor adventures aplenty, while **Villa Serrana** is a copse of isolated houses offering complete rest and relaxation in pretty surrounds.

Central Minas

Most of the region's draw lies in the rolling hills surrounding the town, but there are some cultural surprises here that warrant a pause before heading out into the countryside. The city is easily navigated; the main shopping street, 18 de Julio, is parallel with Avenida Treinta y Tres which runs along the north side of the main square, the **Plaza Libertad**, and onwards to the bus terminal. Full of palm trees and with a horseback statue of the national hero Juan Lavalleja who lends his name to the department, the Plaza Libertad is a pleasant place to sit and enjoy a pastry from one of the country's most renowned patisseries (see opposite).

Casa de Cultura

One block south of the main Plaza is the excellent series of museums housed in the **Casa de Cultura** (Lavalleja, at Rodó; daily noon–6pm; free), including rooms displaying gaucho artefacts from the nineteenth century and a room dedicated to Uruguayan composer Eduardo Fabini. Independence leader Lavalleja's childhood house sits in the central courtyard; one of the forty original houses from the town's foundation, it has been restored, but its original ceiling beams made from palm trees are intact.

Teatro Lavalleja

The city's most surprising building is the grand old **Teatro Lavalleja** (Batlle y Ordóñez between Florencio Sánchez y Sarandí), a magnificent brick construction finished in 1909, with regular productions and also housing the odd **Museo del Humor y la Historieta** (Mon–Fri noon–5.30pm; free), the only museum in the world dedicated to caricatures.

Cerro Artigas

The city is surrounded by some very pleasant parks. **Cerro Artigas** is worth visiting for its great views of the city and surrounding hills, as well as its imposing 10m-high concrete statue of the liberator Artigas on his horse; said to be one of the largest equine statues in the world. Avenida Varela goes all the way to Cerro Artigas from central Minas – around a 45-minute walk – or a taxi costs UR$100.

Parque del Salto Penitente

At the heart of this private natural reserve is a delicate waterfall, the eponymous **Salto del Penitente**, which falls some 60m before following its course. Here there is a restaurant (open daily for lunch), precariously cantilevered off the hillside over the falls, as well as a hostel and terrace affording graceful views across the park, all under the same management (☎44403096, ⓦsaltodelpenitente.com). Sleeping is in shared wood cabins (UR$300/400 with/without linen), or you can camp, and there's a rustic common room with an open fire. For those who decide to stay, activities include horseriding, rock climbing, zip-wiring and abseiling (all UR$150–200), as well as hiking and birdwatching. It's tricky to get to without a car, but the management can collect you from Minas or a taxi is around UR$800.

Villa Serrana

With zero amenities, other than a couple of places to stay, it's hard to even award **Villa Serrana** village status; it's more a cluster of houses 25km from Minas. However, its location is Elysian, perching on top of a horseshoe string of hills around a lake, with splendid walking, fishing and horseriding opportunities – not to mention magical sunsets. Its other major attraction is a remarkable historic hotel, the **Ventorrillo de la Buena Vista** (☎44402109, ⓦventorrillodela buenavista.com.uy), designed by Uruguayan architect Julio Vilamajó, which attracts architecture fans from across the world. Built in 1946, its brilliance lies in its synthesis with its surroundings, and it has been tastefully restored to run as a splendid inn (see p.848). There are just four **buses** a week

from Minas to Villa Serrana (9am & 5.30pm on Tues & Thurs, returning shortly after that; 30min), but if you're staying there you'll probably be able to arrange a lift with your hosts. Taxis cost UR$1000.

ARRIVAL AND INFORMATION

Bus Intercity and local buses arrive and depart from the Terminal de Omnibuses (☎44423178), three blocks west of Plaza Libertad on Treinta y Tres between Claudio Williman and Sarandí.

Destinations Montevideo (hourly; 1hr 40min–2hr 30min); Punta del Este (4–7 daily; 2hr); Villa Serrana (4 weekly; 30min).

Taxi 24hr service from the Plaza Libertad (☎099844159). Set prices to surrounding areas.

Tourist information At the bus station (daily 8am–7pm; ☎44429796, ⓦwww.minascity.com/turismo & ⓦlavalleja.gub.uy).

ACCOMMODATION

It's worth booking ahead; accommodation is limited and fills up fast, especially during Minas' large festivals over nine days in October and on April 9.

Camping Arequita 10km north of town on Ruta 12 ☎44402503, ⓦwww.lavalleja.gub.uy/web/lavalleja /campingarequita. Set in pleasant grounds at the foot of Cerro Verdún (a grand rocky peak with caves to explore), each plot has electricity and a barbecue. Horseriding can be arranged, but there's no internet. 12km from town; buses from Minas run Dec–Feb. Self-catering cabins UR$900, mini-cabins (beds only) UR$350, camping/ person UR$90

Posada Verdún Dr. Washington Beltrán 715 ☎44424563, ⓦhotelposadaverdun.com. The same family has run this posada, the best-value place in town, for more than two decades. The rooms are clean with private bathrooms and TV; there's also a recommended restaurant. Doubles (includes breakfast) UR$1000

★ **Villa Serrana B&B** The green thatched house in Villa Serrana ☎098280811, ⓦvillaserrananp.com. Owned by the exuberant Zen, who speaks fluent English, the house has three spacious rooms and is decorated with flea-market finds and bright colours. There is also an adjacent self-catering bungalow for groups. Horseriding and other day-trips in the country can be arranged. Breakfast included and other meals can be provided. Doubles UR$1400 (cheaper without breakfast), bungalow (up to 6 people) UR$2000

EATING

Nightlife is limited to drinking in restaurants.

★ **Confitería Irisarri** Treinta y Tres 618, Plaza Libertad ⓦconfiteriairisarri.com.uy. A family business originating

10

in 1898, this confectionery shop and tearoom is one of the great treats in the region. Try their speciality – *yemas* – bonbons designed to look like egg yolks. Selection of pastries with coffee UR$50. Daily 9am–9pm.

Ki-Joia Domingo Pérez 489, Plaza Libertad. A surprisingly modern, good-value *parrilla* with quick and friendly service and alfresco tables overlooking the plaza. The meat is good and the home-made pasta (with real parmesan cheese) is excellent. Mains UR$150–500. Daily from 6pm; *parrilla* open from 8pm.

★ **Ventorrillo de la Buena Vista** Villa Serrana (see p.847). The name means "Good View Inn", and if you can't afford the UR$2000 for a double designer room (each has a living room with working fireplace as well as bed and bath), at least eat at the restaurant and enjoy one of the best views and meals in Uruguay (mains UR$200–300). Try the *Borego Confitado* – lamb, date and walnuts with beetroot pasta. Mon–Fri 10am–7pm, or 11pm at weekends for dinner.

DIRECTORY

Av 18 de Julio is the main commercial street and has many banks, casas de cambio and ATMs as well as pharmacies and laundries.

Hospital On Av Pedro Varela between Maldonado and Dighiero ☎ 44422058.

Internet Cyber Peatonal on 25 de Mayo charges UR$12/hr and there's free wi-fi in Plaza Libertad.

Left luggage Facilities at the bus terminal (see p.847).

Phone Antel office at Treinta y Tres 589, just off Pza. Libertad.

Police Off Pza. Libertad down Vidal y Fuentes.

Post office Correo Uruguayo, Wáshington Beltrán, at 25 de Mayo.

Supermarket Las Palmas, 18 de Julio, at Sarandí.

The eastern beaches

Uruguay's biggest draw is its vast, and largely unspoilt, coastline. Humans have made their mark with *balnearios* (coastal resorts or villages), each with a very different feel to them.

Between Maldonado and Rocha departments you can choose between the hedonistic party life in **Punta del Este**, the isolated and rugged **Cabo Polonio**, the blissful beaches and dunes of **Valizas** or wild surfing and nightlife in **Punta del Diablo**, all with

shimmering **lagoons** full of birdlife in between.

The towns are easy to hop between, especially in the summer, but be warned that they change drastically off-season; holidaymakers can increase the population in these tiny towns to twenty times their normal numbers in high season, but in winter everything shuts down and they can feel completely deserted. Other than in luxurious Punta del Este, be sure to come with enough **cash** to fuel your stay; there are no banks or ATMs in the smaller villages.

PUNTA DEL ESTE

Situated on a narrow peninsula 140km east of Montevideo, **PUNTA DEL ESTE** – often written as PdE – is a jungle of high-rise hotels, expensive restaurants, casinos and designer stores bordered by some of the finest beaches on the coast. Exclusive, luxurious and often prohibitively expensive, between this and the nearby towns of **La Barra** and **José Ignacio**, this is *the* place to be seen for many South American celebrities in summer.

WHAT TO SEE AND DO

The best thing to do in PdE is what everyone else does: go to the beach during the day and go drinking at night. Within striking distance and well worth the trip is the whitewashed **Casapueblo**, a remarkable villa and art gallery.

The beaches

These are what attract most visitors to Punta del Este, and two of the best are on either side of the neck of the peninsula. **Playa Mansa** on the bay side is a huge, arcing stretch of sand, with plenty of space for sunbathing and gentle waves, while **Playa Brava** on the eastern side is where you go if you're serious about **surfing**, or simply to compare your height to the fingers of the uncanny **Hand in the Sand** sculpture, one of Uruguay's most famous sights. Both sides are commonly referred to by these names, although there are actually many beaches with their own names.

Off the coast

From Playa Mansa, there are excellent views out to the wooded **Isla de Gorriti**, once visited by Sir Francis Drake (boats daily in high season if sufficient demand; UR$300/person). Slightly further off the coast lies the **Isla de Lobos**, home to one of the largest **sea-lion colonies** in the world. Calypso (opposite *La Galerna* at the entrance to the harbour; ☎42446152)

offer expensive tours, though if you just want to see sea lions, it's worth heading down to the port itself in the early morning: they are often out sunbathing as the fishermen set sail.

On the peninsula

Life on the peninsula itself offers a glimpse of what the town must have been like when it was a modest holiday village

10

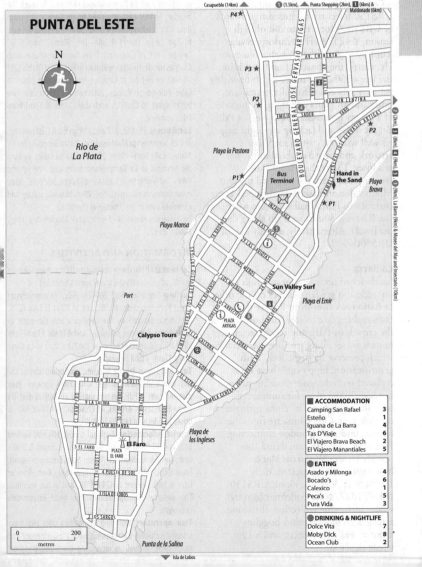

PUNTA DEL ESTE

Casapueblo (14km) ▲   ❶ (1.5km), ▲ Punta Shopping (2km), ❶ (6km) & Maldonado (6km)

❷ (2km), ❸ (8km), ❹ (9km), ❺ (9km), La Barra (9km) & Museo del Mar and Insectario (10km)

Rio de La Plata

Playa la Pastora

Playa Mansa

Port

Calypso Tours

Playa de los Ingleses

El Faro

PLAZA EL FARO

Bus Terminal

Hand in the Sand

Playa Brava

Sun Valley Surf

Playa el Emir

PLAZA ARTIGAS

Punta de la Salina

▼ Isla de Lobos

0   200
metres

■ ACCOMMODATION

Camping San Rafael	3
Esteño	1
Iguana de La Barra	4
Tas D'Viaje	6
El Viajero Brava Beach	2
El Viajero Manantiales	5

● EATING

Asado y Milonga	4
Bocado's	6
Calexico	1
Peca's	5
Pura Vida	3

● DRINKING & NIGHTLIFE

Dolce Vita	7
Moby Dick	8
Ocean Club	2

10

a few decades back – the **port** area up to **Plaza el Faro** is charmingly old-world and the houses represent a host of architectural styles not present in the identikit luxury developments that have sprung up all along the adjacent coastal roads.

Casapueblo

The area's best sight is the vision of Uruguayan artist Carlos Páez Vilaró – **Casapueblo** (daily 10am–sunset; UR$150 for entry to museum; upwards of UR$4000 for a room out of high season; ☎42578041, ⓦcarlospaezvilaro .com.uy & ⓦclubhotelcasapueblo.com). He started the construction himself in the late 1950s, and today it's an unwieldy yet strangely beautiful villa, restaurant, hotel and art gallery clinging to the side of a craggy peninsula 15km west of PdE. Bright white and lacking any right angles, it's well worth a visit to see Vilaró's artwork and have a cocktail in the bar at sunset. To get there from PdE, take any bus from the terminal towards Montevideo and ask to be dropped at the entrance to Punta Ballena, from where you'll have a 30min walk up along the peninsula. Alternatively, a taxi will cost UR$500–600.

La Barra

Sandwiched between forested hills on one side and golden beaches on the other, **La Barra** took over from PdE as the fashionable place to stay for those tired of the crowds of PdE, and its characterful houses are set along tree-lined dirt tracks which preserve its rustic feel. With gentrification, hippy cafés have been replaced with designer clothing stores, but it's still the place for summer nightlife, with new "it" clubs springing up each year. One kilometre from the famous **undulating bridge** connecting PdE with La Barra, you'll find the frankly bizarre **Museo del Mar & Insectario** (well signposted; daily 10.30am–5.30pm/8.30pm; UR$150; ☎42771817, ⓦmuseodelmar.com.uy), whose intriguing collection of marine artefacts includes a mind-boggling array of seashells, insects, and a 19m whale skeleton.

ARRIVAL AND DEPARTURE

Addresses are often given by their *parada* – or bus stop number – which you'll see on poles in the middle of the large dual carriageway – the Costanera – which hugs the coast either side of PdE. The streets in the peninsula have names and numbers, but addresses usually give their numbers.

By bus Punta del Este's bus station lies at the top end of Av Gorlero, just past the roundabout, at the neck of the peninsula. It's a 10min walk to the port along Av Gorlero, or a 5min walk to Playas Mansa or Brava. To reach the beaches further east, you need to get back to the main Ruta 9 by catching the #1 or #2 bus from Punta del Este to San Carlos (every 15min–1hr; 50min) from C 20 (winter), or C 26 (summer). From there most buses with Chuy as the destination will stop in Punta del Diablo (2hr 30min), or get off at Castillos for connecting buses to Cabo Polonio or Valizas. Alternatively, there are two buses direct to Castillos each day (11am & 5pm) from PdE's terminal.

Local buses #9, #12, #17 and #19 go from C 20 (winter), or C 26 (summer) to Maldonado via Punta Shopping (every 30min; daily 6am–11pm; 20min). Codesa buses go from the terminal to La Barra, Manantiales and José Ignacio (Mon–Sat hourly from 5.20am–midnight; Sun 6am–9pm; more buses in summer). See ⓦmaldonado.gub.uy and ⓦcodesa.com.uy for timetables (*horarios*).

Destinations Minas (4–7 daily; 2hr); Montevideo (every 30min; 2hr).

INFORMATION AND ACTIVITIES

Car rental All the major international firms have agencies in PdE, otherwise try the travel agents listed below.

Surfing Sunvalley Surf (☎42448622, ⓦsunvalleysurf .com) have two stores in PdE, one at Playa El Emir (C 28, at Rambla Artigas) on the peninsula and the other at Playa Brava, between *paradas* 3 and 4 (daily 11am–7pm all year), and another opposite the Nike shop in La Barra (daily 11am–11pm all year).

Taxi Taxi stands by the beaches, on Gorlero and at the bus terminal. Minicabs are sometimes cheaper than metered cabs – PdE can get snarled up with traffic. Try Punta Remises at Artigas, at Chiverta (☎42498585), or driver José Techera (☎098447000).

Tourist information National tourist office at Gorlero 942, at C 30 (high season: daily 10am–1.30pm & 2.30–6pm; low season: Mon–Sat 10am–5pm, Sun noon–4pm). Local tourist office in Plaza Artigas (daily 8am–5pm or later in high season; ☎42446510), and in bus terminal. The website ⓦvivapunta.com has good information in English.

Tour operators Most tour companies offer city tours (usually including Casapueblo), boat trips, vineyard and ranch tours, as well as organizing motorized transport such as Segways and quad bikes, or renting cars or bikes. Hostels generally provide the most backpacker-friendly tours, but try A.G.T. (☏42490570, ⊛alvarogimenoturismo .com) in the bus terminal, or DW Service (Artigas, at Chiverta; ☏42491749, ⊛dwservice.com.uy) if you want to go it alone. Nationwide tour operators covering PdE are also worth checking out (see box, p.839).

ACCOMMODATION

In the summer months (Dec–Feb) accommodation is wildly overpriced (you may pay upwards of US$50 for a dorm bed), yet this does not put people off; book at least a month in advance. In winter you won't need to book and prices will be affordable again, but most hostels close down completely. Options listed here are open year-round (except the campsite), but do check online if you're going in summer. If you're stuck, try the tourist information offices, who can help with accommodation.

CAMPING

San Rafael Aparicio Saravia (no number), 800m from Parada 30 ☏42486715, ⊛campingsanrafael.com.uy. Set in pleasant woods, this campsite has a minimart and wi-fi, and lies just 1km from La Barra. Closed April–Oct. It's 15 percent cheaper off season and there are other discounts for longer stays. Camping/person UR$250, self-catering cabin (sleeps 4) UR$2000

HOSTELS

Several buses run every hour (and throughout the night in high season) to La Barra and Manantiales (10min). Dorm beds in Jan will cost upwards of UR$1000, but quickly fall back to normal prices after that. Prices are given for the cheapest dorm beds and doubles in Jan, breakfast included.

Iguana de La Barra C 8, at Ruta 10, La Barra ☏42772947, ⊛iguanadelabarra.com. The friendly owners have made their home welcoming and relaxing, with built-in beds instead of bunks in private rooms, and a fireplace downstairs. Dorms UR$1200, en-suite twins UR$3000

Tas d'Viaje C 26, at 27 ☏42445734, ⊛playa.tasdviaje .com. A very nice addition to the hostel scene in PdE, which can be grotty. This place feels like home and is probably the best located of all the hostels, right in the centre of the peninsula. Dorms UR$660

El Viajero Brava Beach Francia, at Charrua ☏42480331, ⊛elviajerohostels.com. Part of the successful Uruguayan chain, this house on the edge of the peninsula has a large common room with a pool table and fireplace. In high season a second hostel opens at Manantiales beach (Ruta 10 Km164, just past La Barra), 11km away from PdE, which, outside of Dec–Jan, can be around half the cost. Dorms UR$550, en-suite twins UR$3000

HOTELS

Hotel rates (as well as everything else) are typically more reasonable in Maldonado, 20min by bus from PdE (take the #10 from C 20).

Esteño Sarandí 881, Maldonado ☏42229828, ✉hotel esteno@hotmail.com. An old-fashioned hotel with modern touches like a/c and wi-fi. Ask for a room with its own balcony (same price). Price includes breakfast. Doubles UR$2000

EATING

The peninsula is packed with expensive restaurants, and even the best-value places are pricey, though there are bargains if you look around. Restaurants usually go by standard Uruguayan opening hours (see p.835) out of season, but in summer you can eat until about 2am. For very cheap fast food, head to Av Gorlero, where places are open 24hr in high season. Cheap seafood is not available in restaurants here, so try the stalls below the port for the freshest hauls and cook at your hostel.

Asado y Milonga Joaquín Lenzina between Francia and Artigas. The big wagon wheel outside characterizes this rustic *parrilla*, popular with locals, which serves tasty grilled meat and pastas at fair prices. Mains UR$250–400.

Bocado's C 24, at 25. One of PdE's only real budget options, this takeaway place serves fantastic home-made quiches, *empanadas*, pastas and sandwiches, as well as a *menú del día*. Everything UR$100 or less.

★ **Calexico** Paseo de la Cadena, at Dunkerque, just off the third roundabout up Artigas from the bus terminal ☏42491190, ⊛restocalexico.com. Inviting Mexican-American restaurant adorned with pretty ceramics that does some of the best food in the city at excellent prices (chicken fajita UR$400). Book in high season. Daily noon–midnight; low season Tues–Sat noon–3pm & 7pm–midnight.

Peca's Golero, at Las Focas. Better than its rivals across the street, and slightly cheaper (ice cream: two flavours and two toppings UR$70), *Peca's* also serves breakfasts and has free wi-fi. Daily 9am–late.

★ **Pura Vida** Ruta 10 Km160, behind the petrol station in La Barra. Informal but elegant restaurant with a slow food ethos and a huge range of interesting dishes, including plenty for vegetarians. Well worth the trip to La Barra (mains UR$200–400). Closed Tues.

DRINKING AND NIGHTLIFE

Punta is home to a wild nightlife scene; most bars serve drinks from midday onwards, but the real parties only start at around 2am and rarely end before sunrise. The top clubs change every season, so do some research once you arrive.

Dolce Vita C11, at Rambla Artigas, underneath *Boca Chica* restaurant ⊛dolcevitapunta.com. This dark and sweaty basement room hosts raucous club nights (entry UR$200), mainly for a young crowd. Sat only, from midnight.

10

10

Moby Dick Pub Artigas 650. The only reliable and down-to-earth watering hole in town, albeit with inflated prices. There's a good range of cocktails (UR$300) to sip outside as you watch the ships go by, and there's also live music and food. Daily from noon; low season daily from 5pm.

Ocean Club Parada 12, Playa Brava ⊛ oceanclub.com.uy. A multi-room venue right on the beach, and one of just two clubs that are open year-round (women free before 2am, men around UR$200), this place is flashy and loud, playing pop, rock and house. Dress to impress. Opens midnight Fri–Sat.

DIRECTORY

Between Av Gorlero and the huge mall **Punta Shopping** (Roosevelt between Los Alpes and Gattas; ⊛ puntashopping .com), you'll find most services you'll need. There's a pleasant artisan market (daily in summer, weekends only in low season, 10am–6pm) in Plaza Artigas.

Banks ATMs and major banks available along Gorlero, with further branches in Punta Shopping.

Cinema Multiplex cinema, arcades and bowling at Punta Shopping.

Hospital Hospital de Maldonado, in Maldonado (Continuación Ventura Alegre; ☎ 42559137, ⊛ hospital demaldonado.com).

Internet Many (expensive) internet cafés on Gorlero; around UR$45/hr.

Language school Spanish Uruguay (☎ 094264473, ⊛ spanishuruguay.com) runs classes and can organize home-stays and tours for their students. Also in Montevideo.

Laundry Espumas del Virrey, C 28, at 18.

Pharmacy Farmacia Campus (Gorlero 920); open until 3am in summer.

Phone Antel office at corner of streets 24 & 25.

Police Colonia 1021 (☎ 08008226, or ☎ 911 for emergencies).

Post office Correo Uruguayo, Golero 1037, near the roundabout.

Supermarket Large Tienda Inglesa in Punta Shopping (see above).

CABO POLONIO

Moving east from brash Punta del Este can be quite a shock to the system – the *balnearios* thin out and become increasingly rustic – but even the most hardy rural-dweller would find the lack of infrastructure in **CABO POLONIO** surprising. Originally no more than a few fishermen's huts, the settlement consists of some eighty permanent residents who still live in extremely rustic dwellings; the cape with its dunes and forests is protected as a national park and camping is not allowed.

There's nothing to see or do other than soak up the beauty of the cape, spot **sea lions** near the 120-year-old **lighthouse**, or hike (you can walk unobstructed both ways along the coast to Valizas 10km to the east, or as far as La Pedrera 43km to the west). Ask around to arrange horseriding, or trips to the **Laguna de Castillos** with its strange ombú trees. Although in high season it can be inundated with tourists during the day, it still exudes a dreamy, other-worldly isolation, thanks to its lack of roads and electricity, that is best experienced by staying overnight.

To get to the cape from Valizas it's possible to hike, ride or pay someone with a rowing boat, but most guests arrive via the newly opened visitor centre (☎ 095643217, ⊛ turismorocha.gub.uy) at the entrance to the national park at Km264.5 of Ruta 10. This is where any bus from Montevideo (daily) or Castillos (at least 3 daily; more during summer) selling you a ticket to Cabo Polonio will drop you (if you've rented a car, leaving it in the car park costs UR$185/24hr). From here it's necessary to walk the final 7km (over sand), or pay for one of the 4WD drivers to take you (30min drive; hourly from around 8.30am–11pm Dec–Feb, less frequent March–Nov; UR$170 round trip).

ACCOMMODATION

Cabo Polonio Hostel ☎ 099445943, ⊛ cabopoloniohostel .com. A rustic place with solar-powered electricity and a pedal-powered washing machine. Meals can be arranged here, at other lodging/restaurants in the village, or bring your own supplies. Dorms UR$775, doubles UR$1350

BARRA DE VALIZAS

In the summer, Cabo Polonio's slightly more grown-up next-door neighbour, **VALIZAS** (as it's more commonly known), feels like you're at one big festival. You'll either love or hate the hazy, dreadlocked, guitar-strumming vibes, with people practically living on the enormous and ancient sand dunes from Christmas until Carnaval in February, but it's worth staying both for its beauty and because in January, when prices along the coast soar, you'll find better value here. Out of season you'll have the sweeping sun-bleached beaches completely to yourself.

ARRIVAL AND DEPARTURE

By bus There are local buses from Castillos (every 2–3hr; 30min) and Montevideo (6 daily; 4–5hr).

ACCOMMODATION

Lucky Valizas No address; simply stroll across the football pitch one block to the right of where the bus will drop you ☎ 44754070, ⓦ luckyvalizas.com. Stay with Lucky in her home-turned-eco-hostel; she knows everyone in town and can arrange horseriding or boats to Cabo Polonio. Prices include breakfast and are halved, or more, off-season. Dorms <u>UR$400</u>, cabins for two <u>UR$1300</u>, camping/pitch <u>UR$200</u>

EATING

El Rabuk By the lake. The only restaurant open year-round, this husband-and-wife wife team serve excellent fresh fish at bargain prices. Grilled fish with salad UR$150).

PUNTA DEL DIABLO

For a similar mix of remoteness and natural beauty to Cabo Polonio but within reach of a supermarket, electricity and heady nightlife, **PUNTA DEL DIABLO** is the place to go. Stay in a hostel or beach cabin; relax in a hammock or go out and hit the waves.

WHAT TO SEE AND DO

During the summer months the population swells from some 1,500 inhabitants to over 20,000 and you'll find pop-up businesses, hostels and internet facilities appear – they even wheel in an ATM. The rest of the year you're pretty much stuck with a handful of restaurants by the **Playa Pescadores**, the main beach strewn with fishing boats (a tourist information office springs up here during summer months).

The **surfing** is excellent all year, and the hostels are the best place to rent gear out of season. There are other beaches either side of Pescadores; northeast the **Playa Grande** is vast and will lead you to the **Parque Santa Teresa** 10km away (around a 3hr walk), a small national park with some easy forest treks and an impressive fort. Along the southwest edge of town, the **Playa de la Viuda** tends to get the biggest waves, although all are good for surfing and the abundance of wide beaches means it never gets unbearably crowded.

Don't miss the twenty-minute walk up Avenida Central (starts at the northern end of the Playa Pescadores) until the houses start to thin out. Keep looking to your right, and soon you'll come across **La Casa Mágica** –the Magic House. Built by a local woodworker, it's in the shape of a head, the steps leading up to the door from the tongue, and entirely made from carved wood and found objects. When someone's in, you'll be welcomed inside to admire the workmanship and artwork.

ARRIVAL AND DEPARTURE

By bus At the time of writing there was some debate about where the exact location of the new bus stop would be, but you'll be dropped somewhere along the only paved road in and out of town; it ends at Av los Pescadores, which leads to the main beach, from where you'll be able to spot

---

CROSSING THE BRAZILIAN BORDER

Crossing the border is straightforward if you catch an international **bus** from Montevideo or any major town (the last of which is San Carlos) on the Ruta 9 heading north: the bus driver will take your passport details at the start of the journey and get all the required stamps for you en route. If you want to stop in Chuy itself (a haven for duty-free shops and not much else), or are planning to cross the border from any of the beach towns on the northern coast, it becomes more complicated. It is essential that you receive all necessary **entrance and exit stamps** from both the Uruguayan and Brazilian border controls before entering Brazil.

All local buses heading north stop at the Brazilian border, 2km to the north of Chuy, but Uruguayan bus drivers do not routinely stop at the Uruguayan border control, so you'll have to ask to get off. The **tourist office at customs** (daily 9am–5pm; ☎ 44744599, ⓦ turismorocha .gub.uy) can assist with information regarding crossings.

the hostels off to the right when you look back at town. There are offices for all the bus companies which serve the town, but again, these are in the process of moving.

Destinations Chuy (5 daily; 2hr); Montevideo (3 daily; 5hr); Rocha (4 daily; 2hr); San Carlos (for Punta del Este; 1 daily; 3hr).

ACCOMMODATION

Hostels have sprung up like mushrooms in the last few years; check online before you go for hostels which open seasonally. Locals throughout the town also rent out their cabañas for tourists – look out for the signs saying *se alquila*, but these are generally only a better-value alternative to the hostels if you're in a large group. As elsewhere, prices stated are for the cheapest bed in high season, but expect the prices to be more than halved outside of Dec–April.

Botella al Mar ✉ marosierras@gmail.com, ⓦ marosierras .blogspot.com. Two sweet white cabins just 150m from the Playa Pescadores right in the centre of town; one sleeps 2 and the other 4. They come fully equipped (apart from sheets and towels), and have sea views. Cabin for two per day, min stay 7 days UR$1900

★ **La Casa de las Boyas** C 5 s/n, also access from Av Central ☎ 44772624, ⓦ lacasadelasboyas.com. This really well-equipped hostel – the oldest in town – sprawls over several buildings all connected with wooden walkways. Kitchenettes in the dorms furthest away from the house, lots of bathrooms and reading lights, as well as a swimming pool, elevate this from the rest. Dorms UR$600, room (sleeps up to 4) with kitchenette UR$3600

★ **El Diablo Tranquilo Hostel & Suites** Hostel on Av Central, Suites opposite on beach ☎ 44772647, ⓦ eldiablotranquilo.com. Bright red hostel with open-plan common areas and a fun terrace kitchen with sea views, which compensate for the rather cramped dorms. There are boutique en-suite rooms and dorms in both locations; the newer building is on the beach with a funky bar for guests. Dorms UR$700, doubles UR$900–1700

EATING AND DRINKING

The best place to start for food or drink is the Av los Pescadores, leading down to Playa Pescadores. In high season bars and clubs open down by Playa de la Viuda and at the top of Av Central (there are huge parties held near the old bus). Everywhere runs on less than reliable opening hours out of season, but they are more or less the same as elsewhere in Uruguay. In summer everything opens late and closes late to cater for the nocturnal lifestyle.

Desigual Opposite the police station, Av los Pescadores. A funky restaurant and bar with torn-up magazines plastering the walls. It serves decent, cheap pizza, pastas and other fast foods. Pizza and a beer UR$200.

Lo de Olga Av los Pescadores. Olga has over 30 years' experience serving up the freshest fish in town with an excellent range of seafood, fish, pastas and Uruguayan staples like *chivitos*, all under UR$350. Ask for the *menú túristico*, which will be much cheaper than *à la carte*.

Mirjo Av los Pescadores. A classy joint serving fine food and Italian coffee right by the beach. Grilled fish with side dish UR$300.

ORINOCO DELTA

Venezuela

HIGHLIGHTS

❶ Mérida A high-altitude adventure sports paradise. **See p.888**

❷ Los Llanos Endless horizons, stunning wildlife, and cowboys. **See p.894**

❸ Amazonas Tropical rainforest and other-worldly geography. **See p.896**

❹ Angel Falls The world's tallest waterfall. **See p.904**

❺ Orinoco Delta A vast region of waterways and indigenous tribes. **See p.908**

❻ Parque Nacional Mochima Deserted beaches and the mainland's best snorkelling. **See p.911**

HIGHLIGHTS ARE MARKED ON THE MAP ON P.857

ROUGH COSTS

Daily budget Basic US$60, occasional treat US$70 – at official exchange rate (see box, p.858)

Drink Polar beer (300ml) US$2.30

Food *Arepa* US$5

Budget hotel US$35

Travel Caracas–Mérida (680km) by bus, US$48

FACT FILE

Population 28 million

Language Spanish

Currency Bolívar Fuerte (BsF)

Capital Caracas (population: 3.5 million)

International phone code ☏58

Time zone GMT -4hr 30min

Introduction

Deterred by an unjustly poor international reputation, many visitors to South America choose to avoid Venezuela. In fact, some of the continent's most rewarding and varied attractions are here, packed into a relatively small space. An outdoor-lover's paradise, Venezuela boasts nearly every natural environment: towering mountains, mini-deserts, endless plains, Caribbean beaches, lush green jungle and wildlife-rich wetlands. You'll also find a passionate and welcoming people, proud of their nation and keen to showcase it to foreign visitors. Although the FCO still advise against travel to the border areas with Colombia, security has improved greatly since the increase in tourist traffic to the neighbouring country. The time to explore is now, as Venezuela's unique brand of socialism may not be around for much longer.

11

With 43 **national parks** and many private nature reserves, Venezuela's prime attractions lie outside its major urban areas. Its capital **Caracas** is a lively and cosmopolitan city, although given its high prices and shoddy budget accommodation it does little to encourage backpackers. Most visitors explore at least part of Venezuela's stunning 2600km-long Caribbean **coast**. Several hours east of the capital, **Parque Nacional Mochima** boasts red-sand beaches, fishing villages, fantastic seafood and playful dolphins, while **Parque Nacional Henri Pittier**, about three hours west, offers wildlife-spotting opportunities, crystal-clear lagoons and a lively social life. Further west is **Parque Nacional Morrocoy**, which features picturesque white-sand cays. More exclusive, the **Los Roques Archipelago** in the Caribbean is actually an extension of the Andes range, and contains

the country's most pristine beaches with fewer crowds, given the off-mainland transport issues.

An overnight bus ride from the coast will take you to **Mérida**, in the northern extent of the continent-spanning Andes range. Mérida is also the best place to arrange trips to **Los Llanos**, the extensive plains that provide some of the best wildlife and birdwatching opportunities on the continent. The enormous region of **Guayana** encompasses most of the south and east portions of the country and boasts a number of adventure-based attractions. Here you'll find the **Orinoco Delta**, a labyrinth of jungle waterways formed as the enormous river reaches the Atlantic Ocean. Further up the Orinoco, the historic town of **Ciudad Bolívar** is the most economical base from which to explore **Parque Nacional Canaima**,

---

WHEN TO VISIT

Venezuela can be visited year-round, but you are most likely to get the best out of visiting during the November to May **dry season**. On **the coast**, there is less rain and fewer mosquitoes, if slightly higher temperatures. Wildlife spotting in **Los Llanos** is much better in the dry season, when animals congregate at the few watering holes, while the abundance of mosquitoes during the wet season makes walking very unpleasant. Travel in the **Guayana** region is more comfortable during the dry season, though Angel Falls tends to be fuller and therefore more spectacular during the wet season.

If you are after beach time, it is best to come outside the national holiday periods of Easter, Carnaval (which begins at the end of Feb or beginning of March), Christmas (Dec 15–Jan 15) and the summer holidays (July 15–Sept 15). Venezuelans tend to spend their holidays at the beach and the hordes drive prices up significantly.

VENEZUELA

CARIBBEAN SEA

HIGHLIGHTS
1 Mérida
2 Los Llanos
3 Amazonas
4 Angel Falls
5 Orinoco Delta
6 Parque Nacional Mochima

Aruba
Bonaire
Punto Fijo
Curaçao
Los Roques Archipelbo
Golfo de Venezuela
Coro
Malcao
Chichiriviche
Isla de Margarita
Porlamar
Tobago
PARQUE NACIONAL MORROCOY
Choroní
Puerto La Cruz
Santa Fe
Chacopata
Guiria
Maracaibo
Barquisimeto
Maracay
CARACAS
Barcelona
Caripe
Trinidad
Lago de Maracaibo
Trujillo
PARQUE NACIONAL HENRI PITTIER
PARQUE NACIONAL MOCHIMA
6
Maturín
El Vigia
Mérida
Barinas
1
Tucupita
5
Orinoco Delta
Cúcuta
San Cristóbal
San Fernando de Apure
2
Los Llanos
Puerto Ordáz
San Félix
Bucaramanga
Apure
Orinoco
Ciudad Bolívar
11
La Paragua
PARQUE NACIONAL CANAIMA
Puerto Páez
Puerto Carreño
Angel Falls
4
Tunja
Puerto Ayacucho
3
Canaima
GUYANA
COLOMBIA
Mt Roraima (2810m)
Santa Elena de Uairén
Metres
4000
2000
1000
500
200
0
N
Boa Vista
BRAZIL
San Carlos de Río Negro
San Simón de Cocuy
0   100
kilometres

where **Angel Falls**, the world's highest waterfall, plunges a vertical kilometre into the jungle below.

CHRONOLOGY

C.13,000 BC–1498 AD Roughly 500,000 indigenous peoples live in the area today covered by Venezuela, belonging to three principal ethno-linguistic groups: Carib, Arawak and Chibcha.

1498 Christopher Columbus arrives August 4 at the eastern tip of the Paria Peninsula and continues south to the Orinoco Delta.

1502 Italian Amerigo Vespucci sees the Arawak houses on wooden stilts in Lake Maracaibo and calls the place Venezuela, or "little Venice". Enslavement of the indigenous population for pearl harvesting begins around this time.

1521 The first European settlement is established at Cumaná, on the northeast coast, serving as a base for Catholic missionaries and further exploration of the mainland.

Late 1500s The Creoles, Spanish descendants born in the New World, accumulate slaves, agricultural wealth and a large degree of autonomy.

1819–21 Simón Bolívar, a wealthy Creole landowner from Caracas, wins several naval battles against the Spanish and liberates the territory of Colombia. Bolívar proclaims the new Republic of Gran Colombia, an independent nation made up of modern-day Venezuela, Colombia and Ecuador. He subsequently liberates Peru and Bolivia.

1829 Gran Colombia disbands in the face of irreconcilable internal disputes, and Bolívar, bitterly disappointed by the dissolution of his dream, succumbs to tuberculosis.

1859–63 A power struggle between Liberals and Conservatives, known as the Federal War, results in Liberal control of Venezuela until the turn of the century.

1908–35 General Juan Vicente Gómez rules the country and becomes one of Venezuela's most brutal dictators. Press and public freedoms are curtailed and political dissidents murdered.

1918 Oil is discovered in Venezuela along the Caribbean coastline, and ten years later the country is the largest producer in the world. Gómez pays off all foreign debts and invests in roads, ports and public buildings.

1973 Carlos Andrés Pérez is elected and governs Venezuela through one of its most prosperous periods, during which

11

OFFICIAL VS. BLACK MARKET EXCHANGE RATES

One of the most common mistakes among first-time visitors to Venezuela is not informing themselves of the advantages of cash (US dollars and euros in particular), over ATMs and credit cards. Though illegal, money can be exchanged on the black market – *mercado negro, oscuro* or *paralelo* – at rates that are around triple the official value. In fact, inflation is so rampant, and foreign currency so undervalued by the federal bank, that Venezuela is almost prohibitively expensive if you travel on ATM and credit cards alone – you can easily end up paying more for goods and services than you would at home.

The main downside of the black market – besides the fact that it's illegal – is that it requires you to carry your money in cash, a risky venture in a country known for high crime rates. Do not change money at the airport as police watch the area and you'll normally get landed with a very poor rate. It is generally possible to pay in foreign currency until you have the chance to exchange securely and comfortably, usually with a hotel or travel agency. You will generally get the best rates for US dollars and euros in either Caracas or Mérida. For an accurate daily calculation of the *paralelo* rate see ⓦ lechugaverde.com.

Here's what to bring depending on where you're coming from:

Colombia: Colombian pesos are virtually worthless in comparison to the Bolívar Fuerte. Travellers entering from Colombia should exchange local currency for US dollars in the closest major city to your border crossing (Bucaramanga for Cúcuta, Cartagena for Paraguachón).

Brazil: Brazilian reais can be exchanged in Santa Elena de Uairén (see p.905) for a better rate than you would get for US dollars or euros. Stock up from an ATM in Manaus or at the Brazilian side of the border in Pacaraima.

Outside South America: US dollars or euros are the most widely changed currencies. You do not have to declare carrying cash up to the value of US$10,000 when entering the country.

---

the petroleum industry is nationalized, quadrupling the price of oil and filling the country's coffers.

Late 1970s–80s Increased oil production in other countries sends prices spiralling downwards. Inflation and unemployment increase as foreign capital drops off significantly, and Venezuela sells much of its precious oil reserves to pay its debts.

1992 A mid-level military officer named Hugo Chávez launches an unsuccessful coup attempt against Pérez and is imprisoned; soon after, Pérez is found guilty of corruption charges.

1994 Chávez is pardoned for his coup attempt and continues gathering support around the country.

1998 In a landslide victory over former Miss Universe Irene Sáez, Chávez is elected president and, through national referendum, establishes a new constitution that dismantles the Senate, increases state control over the oil industry and grants the military greater autonomy.

2000 Chávez wins a new election.

2002 Government officials and the middle class, angered by Chávez's controversial reform laws and a weakening economy, incite massive, violent protests on April 11; the next day, Chávez is taken into military custody. Two days later the interim government collapses and Chávez regains control.

2007 Chávez attempts to pass, by national referendum, another constitutional reform that would facilitate federal expropriation of private property, give him unfettered

control of the national bank and, most controversially, allow him to be re-elected indefinitely. Shortly after, Chávez turns the clocks back a half-hour, claiming it will increase the country's productivity.

2010 The opposition overturns Chávez's two-thirds majority in Parliament, reducing the president's sway on the National Assembly.

2012 Hugo Chávez wins his third presidential election, defeating his closest challenger yet, Henrique Capriles Radonski. The victory extends Chávez's term as president until 2018, although he misses his January inauguration due to ill health.

2013 The fifth devaluation of the Bolívar Fuerte since Chávez's administration took control of the exchange rate sees the official rate for the currency drop from BsF1 equalling US$4.3 to US$6.3. A month later Hugo Chávez's death is announced by the Venezuelan government.

ARRIVAL AND DEPARTURE

Venezuela can be entered by air, most likely through Maiquetía International Airport in Caracas; by land from neighbouring Colombia and Brazil, but not from Guyana to the east; and by sea, usually through Isla de Margarita (see p.914) from surrounding Caribbean islands.

BY AIR

Nearly all international flights land at Simón Bolívar International Airport in Maiquetía (often known simply as **Maiquetía Airport**), between 45 minutes and an hour from central Caracas. Services and public transport are available at the airport (see p.868).

If you know someone in Venezuela, you can save an enormous amount on your airfare by having them book your ticket for you and then paying them in foreign currency at the *paralelo* exchange rate (see box opposite). Given the national currency's instability, many Venezuelans have foreign bank accounts in Europe and the US, which makes immediate payment possible through bank transfers. It is essential that you only do this with someone you trust.

BY BUS

Long-distance international buses arrive from neighbouring Colombia and Brazil and head for Caracas, nine to fifteen hours from the Colombian border crossings, depending on where you cross (see box, p.886), and up to 24 hours from the main Brazilian crossing. Border formalities for international bus passengers are generally straightforward, though you are responsible for arranging any necessary visas, vaccinations and exit/entry stamps.

PASSPORTS AND VISAS

Citizens of the US, Canada, Australia, New Zealand, South Africa, Ireland, the UK and other EU countries do not need a **visa** to enter Venezuela – just a tourist card, provided by the airlines, that lets you stay for ninety days. Entry by bus or car can be more complicated: you'll be issued with a tourist card by the border office where your entry is processed. This card acts as your exit form and will be required for your eventual departure stamp. You may be asked for a certificate of yellow fever vaccination. You will need to present a passport valid for at least six more months and sometimes they will also ask to see an onward ticket.

To extend your stay for an additional ninety days, go to SAIME, the country's immigration agency, in Caracas (see p.865). Bring your passport, two photos and your return or onward ticket. The process takes a maximum of 72 hours (although it is usually issued the same day) and costs roughly US$50.

GETTING AROUND

Travellers are best off using the convenient and inexpensive public transport system of buses and *por puestos*. Internal flights are an unreliable alternative if you wish to avoid the longer overland routes.

BY AIR

Flying within Venezuela is neither cheap nor convenient; domestic air travel is plagued by delays and cancellations. Always call to confirm flight times, and arrive at airports up to two hours in advance, as queues can be formidable. Domestic flights usually require a *tasa* (tax) of around BsF60.

BY BUS

Buses are the primary mode of transport throughout Venezuela and invariably the cheapest. Tickets go on sale on the day of departure and are bought from the various private company ticket booths in the bus terminals. Venezuelans book all bus travel with their national identification numbers, for which you should use your passport number. It helps to have it memorized. You'll usually have to pay a *tasa*, or tax, on top of the bus fare. Usually around BsF4, the *tasa* is a ticket bought from the dedicated terminal booth and presented when you board the bus or depart the terminal. Most regional bus services end at around 6pm or 7pm; overnight services to more distant destinations sometimes depart as late as midnight or 1am.

Local buses, or *busetas*, are minibuses recognizable for the myriad destination cards stuck to the inside of the windscreens and can be hailed from roadsides along their routes. If you want to get off at a specific point, shout "parada!" (meaning "bus-stop") at the driver, who will let you off at the nearest

11

possible place, payment is usually given when you alight. Economical buses, or *servicio normal* (roughly BsF12/hr), are common for shorter distances. These are often cramped, with no toilet or air conditioning; when choosing your seat, try to select one away from the sound system as music is often blasted at deafening volumes. More comfortable executive buses, or *servicio ejecutivo* (about BsF20/hr), run longer distances and have toilets. Air conditioning, however, is so intense that you'll need a blanket or sleeping bag to stave off hypothermia. If you're travelling overnight, be sure to take a *bus-cama*, with almost fully reclinable seats, more comfortable but more expensive (about BsF25/hr).

BY POR PUESTO

Another economical option is the ubiquitous **por puesto** or **carrito**. Essentially shared taxis, *por puestos* are gas-guzzling American sedans in which you pay for one of four or five places and depart when the car is full. They are generally twice the price of a bus ride, but take half the time and are sometimes the only available option. "¿Cuanto falta?" is a useful expression to ask how many places are still to be filled before the car can depart.

BY TAXI

Taxis never have meters, so you should agree on a price before your journey. In towns where public buses are rare, taxis are the established way of getting around. In these cases, fares within the town are set; ask a local beforehand. Don't get into the car until you've agreed upon the price.

ACCOMMODATION

Naturally enough, you'll find Venezuela's best low-end **accommodation** in the towns that attract the most backpackers. Consequently Mérida (see p.888),

---

VENEZUELA TOURS

For better or for worse, Venezuela has yet to develop a budget travel infrastructure on the level of Brazil's or Peru's, meaning that independent travellers often turn to **agencies** for assistance in arranging trips and activities to the country's top attractions. Booking tours is always done cheapest in the closest town to the attraction itself – see each attraction's account for local tour prices – but if your time is limited, or if you're looking for a multi-destination tour, the following Caracas- and Mérida-based companies can arrange trips anywhere. All accept credit cards, though for the best rates you should pay in US dollars (see p.858); many have foreign bank accounts, allowing you to pay at *mercado paralelo* rates through bank transfer if you didn't bring cash.

TOUR OPERATORS

Akanán C Bolívar, Ed Grano de Oro, Ground Floor, Chacao ☎0212 715 5433, ⌨akanan.com. Akanán's office has plenty of material for researching trips, and Rough Guide readers can use the internet for free. Clients who opt not to hire a guide are lent a mobile phone for use on their travels.

Andes Tropicales ☎0274 263 8633, ⌨andes tropicales.org. A Mérida-based company devoted to helping local communities protect the natural environment while promoting tourism in remote areas.

Angel Eco-Tours Av Casanova, at 2da Av de Bello Monte, Ed La Paz, Oficina 51, Sabana Grande ☎0212 762 5975, ⌨angel-ecotours.com. An excellent agency specializing in slightly more luxurious travel than affiliate Osprey (see below). The company also manages a

non-profit organization assisting the indigenous Pemón community of Parque Nacional Canaima (see p.903).

Hans Peter Zingg Res. Bravamar, Urb. Caribe, Estado Vargas ☎0414 322 8798, ✉hpzingg@hotmail.com. Hans Peter Zingg and his team offer a highly recommended pick-up service from Caracas airport (US$40), in order to allay fears of safety and unnecessary hassle. They also offer other tourist services including travel advice and advance purchase of inter-city bus tickets. Payment is in US dollars.

Osprey Expeditions Same office as Angel Eco-Tours ☎0212 762 5975 or ☎0414 310 4491, ⌨osprey expeditions.com. The most economical option for backpacker-friendly, nationwide trips, with exceptionally friendly staff. They can also organize pick-ups from Caracas airport.

Choroní (see p.879) and Ciudad Bolívar (see p.900) have excellent budget options. Cheap accommodation is generally poor in larger cities such as Caracas and Puerto La Cruz, where tourism is not adapted to suit backpackers. It's not uncommon for budget hotels in larger towns to rent out rooms by the hour, and although this is no cause for safety concern, it may offer a clue as to how backpacker-friendly your hotel is. Nevertheless, you can always expect clean sheets and towels. Hot water is rare outside Mérida and other Andean towns.

Dormitories are not common, while youth hostels are virtually non-existent; solo travellers are often stuck paying for a *matrimonial* (for couples), cheaper than a twin but more expensive than a single. Quality is much higher beyond the big cities and usually appears in the form of **posadas**, affordable family-owned guesthouses, often with lots of individual character. Many posadas and backpacker spots are run by French and German expats who have started families in Venezuela.

Camping hasn't caught on among Venezuelans, and in general is not recommended due to robberies, even on isolated beaches and cays. The safest time to camp is on weekends and during national holidays. For more information, contact Inparques (☎0212 273 2701, ⊛inparques.gob.ve).

FOOD AND DRINK

Venezuelan cuisine, like that of most of the Caribbean, centres around **meat**, with the most common accompaniments being rice, beans and plantains. PAN corn flour, a brand ubiquitous throughout the country (although it's now manufactured in Colombia), is a large component of many Venezuelan staples, most notably the **empanada** (fried savoury turnover), the **cachapa** (a sweet-meal pancake folded over a slab of cheese) and the **arepa**. The latter, the most typically Venezuelan of all, is a fried savoury corncake, stuffed with fillings which depend on the time of day. Among the most common fillings are *carne*

mechada (shredded beef) and *reina pepeada* (avocado and a mixture akin to coronation chicken).

Though rather difficult to find, **vegetarian food** (*comida vegetariana*) and health food (*comida dietética*) are usually available in larger cities, often in restaurants dedicated to these cuisines.

Breakfasts are generally small, usually little more than an *empanada* or *cachapa*, and always accompanied by a thimble-sized cup of scalding-hot coffee. Lunch is generally lighter – a good economic choice is the *menú ejecutivo* (soup, main dish and a drink) which many restaurants offer. Common dinner options include fried fish, rotisserie chicken, southern-fried chicken or any number of international dishes, including pizza and pasta.

The Venezuelan national dish is **pabellón criollo**, which consists of shredded beef, avocado, plantain, cheese, rice and beans; a breakfast version of this is the *desayuno criollo*. *Pabellón*-stuffed *empanadas* are particularly good and should be sampled if stumbled upon. You'll also find delicious burgers sold at street kitchens, whose plastic tables and chairs line the pavements in the evening. The ocean, abundant rivers and mountain lakes afford plenty of fresh **fish**, the most common varieties being *mero* (grouper), *dorado* (dolphin fish), *pargo* (red snapper), *trucha* (trout), *corvina* (sea bass) and *corocoro* (grunt).

Common **desserts** are strawberries and cream, *dulce de leche* (caramel) and sweets made from guava or plantains. Venezuelan *cacao* (cocoa) is considered among the best in the world but, as nearly all of it is exported to Europe, Venezuelan chocolate is difficult to find. However, the Nestlé *Savoy* chocolate bars are pretty good.

Restaurants tend to open around 6am for breakfast and stay open for dinner, which ends around 8pm. Although restaurants close early, burger and hotdog stands keep serving until around midnight in most towns. In most restaurants, it's customary to leave a tip of around ten percent. Restaurants may also add the 13.5 percent tax to the bill.

11

DRINK

Fruit juices, or *jugos* (also known as *batidos*), are delicious, inexpensive and safe to drink; combined with milk and whipped, they become *merengadas*. The most common flavours are *lechosa* (papaya), *parchita* (passion fruit), mango, *piña* (pineapple), *guayaba* (guava), *guanábana* (sour sop) and *tamarindo* (tamarind). Another sweet, refreshing drink is *papelón con limón* (lemonade made with unrefined brown sugar). Bottled water is inexpensive and available everywhere.

Coffee in Venezuela is served very strong, black, sweetened and in small amounts. The tiny red straws that come with the drink are for stirring rather than drinking through. If you want it with milk, ask for *marrón* (brown). Although you can always depend on being served an ice-cold one, Venezuelan **beer** is bad compared to what you'll drink elsewhere. The major brand is Polar, with several varieties: the green-bottled Solera, Polar Pilsen, referred to as negra (black), and Zulia being among some of the more drinkable. Beer generally costs around BsF6–8 in a liquor store or BsF10 in a bar. Draught beer is a very rare sight. Bottles are endearingly small – Venezuelans preferring to drink up before it loses its chill. Dark rum (such as Cacique) is generally the liquor of choice – this part of the world producing some of the best – while whisky is popular among the more affluent set (particularly Johnny Walker Black Label).

CULTURE AND ETIQUETTE

Thanks to its location at the crown of South America, Venezuela combines distinctive elements of Caribbean and Latin American **culture**. Visitors familiar with these regions won't be surprised to find the country a fairly relaxed place, whose warm, cheerful nationals place a high value on socializing, recreation, food and (loud) music. By the same token, **machismo** is an inescapable aspect of Venezuelan society, and while women travelling solo needn't expect any more harassment here than elsewhere, groups of drunken men loitering around liquor stores and on street corners are a common sight, particularly on weekends.

Understandably, given their government's notoriety, Venezuelans are **politically aware** and eager to discuss their thoughts about their country. Even in death, President Hugo Chávez excites both zealous fervour and fearful hatred throughout the country. Venezuelans will listen with good grace to anything you may have to say on the subject of politics, but it's best to be asked before sharing and to keep any strong opinions to yourself. Political demonstrations can flare up at a moment's notice and should be avoided.

SPORTS AND OUTDOOR ACTIVITIES

Resulting from its proximity to Caribbean nations such as Cuba and the Dominican Republic, Venezuela's primary sporting obsession is **baseball**. You'll see fans across the country wearing gear from both Venezuelan and American Major League Baseball teams. There is a long history of players heading to the major leagues in the US; the Detroit Tigers are particularly favoured due to Venezuela's large representation on the team. The LVBP (Liga Venezolana de Beisbol Profesional) consists of eight teams, the most prominent being the Caracas Leones and Valencia's Navegantes del Magallanes. The regular season runs from October until December, and attending a game (see p.874) is an excellent experience.

Despite baseball's dominance, **football** has a large following, particularly when the national side plays, nicknamed the *Vinotinto* (red wine) due to the colour of their strip. Bullfighting also exists, although it is becoming increasingly controversial.

The country is also an **outdoor** enthusiast's paradise, with a variety of landscapes and climates offering the ideal conditions for hiking, paragliding, snorkelling, scuba diving, white-water rafting and more. Most outdoor activities are concentrated in the few backpacker-friendly destinations, namely Mérida (p.888), Caripe (p.913), Ciudad Bolívar (p.900) and Santa Elena de Uairén (p.905), and tours generally require a minimum number of people.

VENEZUELA ON THE NET

Ⓦ **caracasvirtual.com** Everything you could possibly want to know about life in Venezuela's cosmopolitan capital, affectionately known to cynical locals as "Crack-ass".

Ⓦ **inatur.gob.ve** Official site of the government's tourism arm, with current, tourism-related news and links to similar federal agencies.

Ⓦ **inparques.gob.ve** Official site of the national parks agency, with contact info and descriptions of parks and reserves.

Ⓦ **miropopic.com** Website for the publisher of Venezuelan maps and reference books, with an online "gastronomic guide".

Ⓦ **venezuelatuya.com** Decent overview of travel and accommodation in Venezuela, with a smattering of country facts.

Ⓦ **valentinaquintero.com.ve** An extensive and detailed guide covering all parts of the country, particularly useful for out-of-the-way towns away from the tourist trail.

COMMUNICATIONS

Venezuela is relatively technologically savvy, and call centres and cybercafés are found in all major towns; except in the most remote outposts, you should have no trouble finding a reasonable **internet** connection. Rates are BsF7/hr on average.

Movistar and CANTV are the most visible **telecommunications** providers, while Movilnet is government-owned and therefore the cheapest. All three have call centres and outlets in most towns and cities. Pre-paid SIM cards cost around BsF90 and come with a cheap phone. These can be topped up online, by street vendors or in your provider's store. Calls are inexpensive: around BsF1.40 per minute within the country, BsF2.50 per minute for international. Street vendors often have mobile phones you can use, usually for around BsF2 per minute. To place an international call, first dial 00 and then the code of the country you are calling.

Ipostel, the Venezuelan national **postal service**, is fairly unreliable. If you have an important letter or package to send, do so through an international carrier like MRW or DHL, which have offices in most major cities. Ipostel charges BsF1.70 for a postcard to the US, BsF2 to Europe and BsF2.20 to the rest of the world. Ipostel branches are typically open weekdays from 8am to 4pm.

CRIME AND SAFETY

While Venezuela is a relatively **safe** place to travel, the western border with Colombia is not a pleasant region to spend any amount of time due to international tensions and the over-zealous police force, who see backpackers as easy targets for extortion. Urban law enforcement in Caracas has heightened in recent years, although the capital can still be dangerous (see box, p.872). Police corruption is a fact of life in Venezuela: if you are asked to pay a fine by the police, always ask for the official paperwork and never offer bribes.

Never accept help at an ATM – anyone who offers is virtually guaranteed to be a **con artist** – and keep a close eye on your bank, debit and credit cards.

Illegal drugs are common in Venezuela, most notably *creepy* (a potent strain of

11

LANGUAGE

Not many Venezuelans speak English – a general knowledge of Spanish will serve you well. Venezuelan Spanish is notable for its dropped "S" and the constant use of the diminutive, the most notable example being "*ahorita*", a diminuation of "*ahora*" (meaning "now"). European-Spanish speakers should note that the personal pronoun "*vosotros*" is not generally used, "*ustedes*" being the standard for third person plural.

Slang is a major feature of Venezuelan Spanish; some of the most common words are "*chévere*" (pronounced che-ver-ey, meaning great or excellent), "*chamo*" (meaning dude) and "*chimbo*" (meaning bad or uncool).

11

USEFUL NUMBERS

All-purpose, nationwide emergency
hotline ☏ 171
All-purpose, nationwide information
hotline ☏ 131

cannabis), cocaine and *base* (unrefined
cocaine). Although it's unlikely that you
will be offered drugs, illicit substances
should be avoided due to unpredictable
police searches and serious penalties
for possession.

HEALTH

The main illnesses in Venezuela are
dengue fever, yellow fever, hepatitis A,
hepatitis B and malaria. Make sure
you consult a doctor before travelling;
they will be able to recommend which
vaccinations to get pre-trip. You may
be asked for a certificate of **yellow-fever**
vaccination when entering the country.
The vaccination should be procured four
weeks in advance to ensure effectiveness.
Malaria is a risk in rural parts of the
country, so if you're planning on staying
in remote areas such as the Orinoco
Delta, a course of anti-malarials and
sufficient repellent is advisable.

Good **medical care** is available in
Venezuela, although this tends to be of
a higher standard in Caracas than in the
rest of the country. It may be very hard
to find a hospital with good facilities,
let alone good doctors, in remote areas.
Foreigners tend to rely on private clinics,
which offer high-quality service.

INFORMATION AND MAPS

What Venezuela's tourism officials
– Inatur (⚇inatur.gob.ve), Venetur
(⚇venetur.gob.ve) and Mintur (⚇mintur
.gob.ve) – lack in useful knowledge for
budget travellers, they make up for with
charm and enthusiasm. Unfortunately,
many offices don't abide by any logical
schedule. Additionally, each state has its
own tourism entity located in its capital
city. Tourist offices are listed under
"Information" throughout the guide.
Though information provided by private

tour agencies is rarely unbiased,
independent travellers will find them
useful, as they are more in touch with
current public transport schedules and
black market exchange rates.

A variety of country and regional **maps**
is available in Venezuela, the best being
Miro Popic's *Guia Vial de Venezuela/Atlas
de Carreteras* and individual city maps.
Elizabeth Klein's guidebooks to Venezuela
are also an excellent source of information, and these, along with maps, are
available in most bookshops.

MONEY AND BANKS

Money – and how to get the most value
from it – is likely to be your biggest
concern while in Venezuela. The country's
economy is extremely volatile, with a
devaluation in 2013, in the aftermath of
the 2012 presidential elections. Rather
than leaving it to the country's stock
exchange, the Bolívar Fuerte's official
value is dictated by the government at
rates vastly higher than the reality.
Consequently, Venezuelans and foreigners
alike resort to foreign currency
transactions through the **black market**,
or *mercado paralelo* (see p.858). Very
importantly, all prices given in
Venezuelan currency in this chapter are
based on the **official exchange rate**.

Bank hours vary hugely, but are
generally open Monday to Friday,
8am to 4pm, and many offer 24-hour
access to ATMs. VISA and MasterCard
are the most widely accepted bank cards.
Two reliable banks are Banco Coroní
(⚇bancocoroni.com.ve) and Banco
Mercantíl (⚇bancomercantil.com),
both found in most sizeable towns.
Exchange houses, such as Italcambio,
also exist, though their exchange rates
are worse than the banks; they do
however exchange travellers' cheques
for a commission.

OPENING HOURS AND HOLIDAYS

Most **shops** are open from 8am until
7pm on weekdays, often closing for lunch
from around 12.30pm until 2 or 3pm.
Shopping centres, however, generally stay

PUBLIC HOLIDAYS

In addition to the events listed here, Caracas celebrates the anniversary of its foundation every year from July 21 to July 29 with a series of cultural events that include theatre presentations, painting and sculpture exhibits, concerts and sports.

Reyes Magos Jan 6. Twelfth Night or Epiphany. Choroní (see p.879), Mucuchíes and Caracas (see p.865).

Carnaval Feb (no fixed date). The most famous celebrations are in Carupano and El Callao.

Nuestra Señora de La Candelaria Feb 2. Virgin of the Candlemas, with offerings and folk singing. Mérida (see p.888) and Caracas (see below).

Semana Santa March (no fixed date). Large processions involve re-enactments of Jesus' last days and resurrection; most Venezuelans, however, celebrate by heading to the beach. Several small towns in the state of Mérida, as well as El Hatillo (see p.868).

San Isidro Labrador May 15. Honours agriculture and animal husbandry; produce is carted through the streets and animals are blessed.

Corpus Christi Late May or early June (no fixed date). The most famous celebration on this day – one of the country's definitive festivals – is Diablos Danzantes (Dancing Devils) in San Francisco de Yare (see p.877).

Día de San Juan Bautista June 24. Choroní, El Higuerote and Ocumare del Tuy. Venezuelans celebrate the arrival of the summer solstice and rejoice the birth of San Juan, with drumming and dancing on the streets.

Día de Todos los Santos and Día de los Muertos Nov 1–2. All Saints' Day. Venezuelans pay tribute to the deceased by adorning their tombs with flowers and offerings.

La Navidad Dec 24. Christmas – the entire country essentially shuts down for a week.

11

open until 9 or 10pm. In addition to their regular business hours, **pharmacies** operate on a "turno" system, with a rotating duty to stay open all night; the designated pharmacy will advertise *turno* in neon. All **banks** take a bank holiday on one Monday each month, although these off-days have no fixed timings since they are often scheduled to coincide with other public holidays. Businesses are generally closed on Sunday, while hours are unpredictable if they do open – don't expect to get much done.

Festivals, most with a religious basis, seem to occur constantly. Some are national, while others are local, as each town celebrates its patron saint.

Caracas

The Venezuelan capital gets something of a bad rap, and while expensive living costs, poor budget accommodation and higher crime rates than the rest of the country have tended to deter visitors, this cosmopolitan capital nevertheless has some diverting attractions. *Caraqueños* are proud of their vibrant city with its excellent artistic, culinary and social scenes; you'll be surprised at how readily and enthusiastically they are willing to help a foreign traveller.

Caracas's most famous native, **Simón Bolívar**, was born to an influential creole (Spanish descendent) family in 1783. After several years abroad he returned in 1813 and captured the city from the Spanish. He had to abandon it a year later, but Bolívar had already earned the epithet "El Libertador". When Venezuela became fully independent in 1830, Caracas was made the capital of the new nation. Since then, various political eras have left their mark on the city's architecture, though the predominant aesthetic is the mid-twentieth-century concrete high-rise.

WHAT TO SEE AND DO

The bustling and attractive district of **El Centro** has some excellent museums and budget restaurants, perfect for getting an authentic taste of Venezuela if Caracas is your first port of call in the country. Street vendors and heavy traffic along the wider arteries can be an irritation, but the area is interesting enough for a day's wandering. Sightseeing

11

around this area is best kept to daylight hours as it has a reputation for street crime after dark. Away from El Centro, visitors can take in the gritty street life of **Sabana Grande**, enjoy the business end of town in **Altamira**, and immerse themselves the restaurant and bar scene around residential **Los Palos Grandes**. Slow the pace slightly with a trip to the arty suburb of **El Hatillo**, or treat your lungs to some fresh air with an excursion to **Parque Nacional El Ávila**.

Plaza Bolívar

As with all Venezuelan towns, the **Plaza Bolívar** is the main square, and Caracas's version, a leafy hub northeast of the Capitolio/El Silencio metro station, is a good starting spot for a walking tour. The south side of the square features the **Consejo Municipal** (City Hall), which doubles as the **Museo Caracas** (Tues–Sat 9am–4pm; free), containing artefacts from the city's history as well as seasonal art exhibitions.

Built in 1575, the colonial-style **Catedral de Caracas** on the east side of the plaza houses Bolívar's parents and wife, who are buried in a chapel on the right-hand side. Next door at the **Museo Sacro de Caracas** (Mon–Sat 9am–4pm; BsF15; ☎0212 861 6562) you'll find a greater collection of artwork with summaries in English. The serene *Café del Sacro* (see p.872) inside is well worth a visit.

Museo Bolivariano and around

If you're interested in learning more about the man who lends his name to seemingly every aspect of Venezuelan life, the **Museo Bolivariano** (Mon–Fri 9am–4.30pm, Sat & Sun 10am–4pm; free) has its entrance on the western side of Plaza Venezolano, one block southeast of the Plaza Bolívar. It contains portraits of El Libertador and his family, carefully preserved relics from his life, and gangs of children on school trips. Next door is the painstakingly reconstructed **Casa Natal** (Mon–Fri 9am–4pm, Sat & Sun 10am–3.30pm; free), where Bolívar was born and lived until the age of nine. There are portraits and some original furniture, but little in the way of explanation. At his final resting place, the **Panteón Nacional**, five blocks north of Plaza Bolívar, soldiers stand guard over Bolívar's tomb.

The **Iglesia de San Francisco**, on the south side of Avenida Universidad, is one of Venezuela's oldest churches. Its principal claim to fame is as the place where Bolívar was proclaimed "El Libertador" in 1813.

Parque Central

Not really a park, **Parque Central** is a long concrete strip filled with vendors selling pirated CDs, DVDs, video games, jewellery and miracle herbs. More importantly, the district is the city's cultural hub, and home to Caracas's best

11

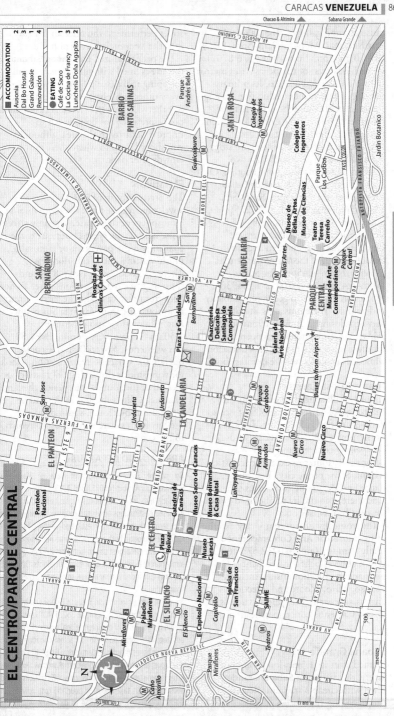

EL CENTRO/PARQUE CENTRAL

■ ACCOMMODATION	
Ausonia	2
Dal Bo Hostal	3
Grand Galaxie	1
Renovación	4

● EATING	
Café de Sacro	1
La Cocina de Francy	3
Lunchería Doña Agapita	2

Chacao & Altimira

Sabana Grande

BARRIO
PINTO SALINAS

SANTA ROSA

Parque
Andrés Bello

Colegio de
Ingenieros

Colegio de
Ingenieros

Museo de Bellas Artes
Museo de Ciencias

Teatro
Teresa
Carreño

Parque
Los Caobos

Jardín Botánico

SAN
BERNARDINO

Hospital de
Clínicas Caracas

LA CANDELARIA

Bellas Artes

PARQUE
CENTRAL

Museo de Arte
Contemporáneo

Parque
Central

San José

San
Bernardino

Plaza La Candelaria

Charcutería
Delicatesses
Santiago de
Compostela

Galería de
Arte Nacional

Buses to/from Airport

LA CANDELARIA

Urdaneta

Urdaneta

Parque
Carabobo

EL PANTEON

Panteón
Nacional

Fuerzas
Armadas

Nuevo
Circo

Nuevo Circo

EL CENTRO

EL SILENCIO

Palacio
Miraflores

El Silencio

Catedral de
Caracas

Museo Sacro de Caracas

Museo Bolivariano
& Casa Natal

LaHoyada

Plaza
Bolívar

Museo
Caracas

Capitolio

El Capitolio Nacional

Iglesia de
San Francisco

SAIME

Parque
Miraflores

Caño
Amarillo

Teatros

VIADUCTO NUEVA REPUBLIC

500
metes
0

N

museums and galleries. The **Galería de Arte Nacional** (Mon–Fri 9am–5pm, Sat & Sun 10am–5pm; free; ☎0212 576 8707) is one block west of the Bellas Artes metro station on Avenida México. Its primary offering is a permanent exhibition tracing Venezuelan art throughout the last five centuries, while visiting exhibitions often feature household names.

A block east from the same metro stop, the oval Plaza de los Museos has two excellent museums facing one another. On the northern side, the **Museo de Bellas Artes** (Mon–Fri 9am–5pm, Sat & Sun 10am–5pm; free; ☎0212 578 0275) houses temporary exhibitions by Venezuelan and international artists. Opposite, the more modern and child-friendly design of the **Museo de Ciencias** (Mon–Fri 9am–4.45pm, Sat & Sun 10am–4.45pm; free; ☎0212 573 4938) focuses on Venezuelan geography, habitats and wildlife. These museums alternate between closing at 2pm and 9pm on Fridays. To find out which is open late, and for more information, visit the Fundación Museos Nacionales website ⊕fmn.gob.ve.

Teatro Teresa Carreño

A quick walk south brings you to the **Teatro Teresa Carreño** (box office 9am–8pm, free guided tours Tues–Fri until 5pm; ☎0212 574 9122), whose compelling concrete and black-glass design contributes to excellent acoustics within. Some of the city's best music, dance and theatre performances take place here; enquire by phone or in person for details of what's on.

The ironically un-contemporary exterior of the **Museo de Arte Contemporáneo** (daily 9am–4.30pm; ☎0212 573 4602, ⊕fmn.gob.ve) belies an excellent permanent collection inside, including Picasso, Miró, Moore and infectiously enthusiastic staff. The gallery is across Teatro Carreño's concrete pedestrian walkway.

Sabana Grande

Named after its 1.5km-long commercial artery, the district of **Sabana Grande** is filled with cheap restaurants, locals promenading their latest purchases and street performers who offer an insight into the Venezuelan sense of humour.

The pedestrianized **Bulevar de Sabana Grande** is lined with numerous specialist shopping malls (see p.875), as well as every other conceivable trade, legitimate or otherwise, on street level. A heightened police presence has done much to improve security in the area, although you should keep to where there are crowds after dark.

El Hatillo

The pretty suburb of **El Hatillo** provides a welcome respite from the more intense atmosphere of the centre. The only street noise here is gallery and boutique owners chatting on the pavement or faint salsa music wafting out of café doorways. There are good eating (see p.873) and shopping (see p.875) options here. To **get here** from Caracas, take the forty-minute metrobus ride from Avenida Sur below Altamira metro station (Mon–Fri 5.30am–11pm; every 30min; BsF1.50). On weekends, *busetas* (BsF4) leave from outside the Chacaíto metro station – look for windshields displaying "El Hatillo". Get off at the roundabout beside the large pharmacy. The suburb is at the end of a circuitous bus route, so simply catch the bus from where you got off to return to the centre.

ARRIVAL AND DEPARTURE

By plane 26km northwest of Caracas, Maiquetía International Airport (☎0212 303 1329) is the country's primary hub for international flights, and also serves domestic destinations across the country. The airport has two terminals, one for domestic and another for international, although both are in the same building. Visitors leaving Venezuela must pay an exit tax of BsF225, while an airport tax of BsF45 is levied for domestic flights. Often the tax will be included in your airfare, so be sure to check with your airline.

From the airport into town Buses to Parque Central (daily 5am–10pm; 1hr; BsF25; ☎0212 352 4140) leave every 20min from in front of the international terminal. From the bus stop, it's best to continue to your accommodation by taxi. Red Sitssa buses (hourly 7.30am–9pm; BsF8) also connect the airport to Hotel Alba in Parque Central, from where Bellas Artes metro station is two blocks away. Official taxis to and from the airport take about an hour and cost upwards of BsF200 depending on the time of day. Taxis waiting at

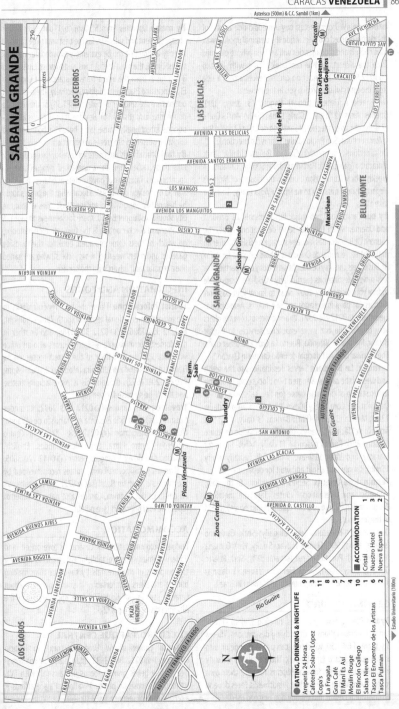

SABANA GRANDE

Asterisco (500m) & C.C. Sambil (1km) ▲

11

● **EATING, DRINKING & NIGHTLIFE**

Arepería 24 Horas	9
Cafetería Solano López	3
Copa's	11
La Fragata	8
Gran Café	5
El Maní Es Así	7
Moulin Rouge	4
El Rincón Gallego	10
Sabas Nieves	1
Tasca El Encuentro de los Artistas	6
Tasca Pullman	2

■ **ACCOMMODATION**

Cristal	1
Nuestro Hotel	3
Nueva Esparta	2

Estadio Universitario (100m) ▲

arrivals are 4WD *camionetas*; buy a prepaid ride at one of the clearly marked counters inside the terminal upon arrival. Many hotels and tour agencies will arrange private pick-ups from the airport, or you can book ahead with Teletaxi (☎0212 952 8780). Under no circumstances accept a ride from the touts who approach you in the terminal.

Destinations (international) Bogotá (3 daily; 1hr); Buenos Aires (2 daily; 10hr); Lima (daily; 4hr); Quito (2 daily; 4hr w/connection); Santiago de Chile (2 daily; 9hr w/connection); São Paulo (daily; 10hr w/connection).

Destinations (domestic) Ciudad Bolívar (daily; 1hr); Maracaibo (daily; 1hr); Porlamar (daily; 50min); Canaima (4 weekly; 5hr w/connection). Due to the closure of Mérida's airport, visitors must fly to nearby El Vigia (daily; 1hr) and take a bus.

By bus Caracas has two major bus terminals, La Bandera and Oriente, which together serve destinations across the country. La Bandera has luggage storage for BsF2/hr after an initial BsF10, Terminal de Oriente will hold luggage for BsF5/hr. Bus tickets can only be bought on the day of departure. For less-served destinations (particularly Mérida) it is advisable to buy your ticket early. You'll need to know your passport number (or have it to hand) to book tickets. Aeroexpresos Ejecutivos (☎0212 266 2321, ⊛aeroexpresos.com.ve) offers very comfortable but more expensive services to Ciudad Bolívar, Maracaibo, Valencia, Puerto La Cruz and other cities. The terminal is on Av Principal de Bello Campo in Chacao.

Terminal La Bandera Serves destinations to the south and west of the capital. Situated two blocks uphill from the metro station of the same name (on line 3).

Destinations Coro (every 30min; 9hr); Maracaibo (4 daily; 12hr); Mérida (3 daily; 15hr); Barinas (3 daily; 8hr); San Antonio del Táchira (2 daily; 20hr); San Fernando de Apure (3 daily; 8hr); Puerto Ayacucho (1 daily; 14hr). Buses for Maracay and Valencia leave when full (usually every 15min); simply take a seat and wait for departure.

Terminal de Oriente Serves destinations to the east, southeast and international routes. Take the metro to Petare station, where you can take a 15min *buseta* (BsF5) to the terminal.

Destinations Barcelona (several daily; 5hr); Carúpano (several daily; 10hr); Ciudad Bolívar (5 daily; 9hr); Cumaná (6 daily; 8hr); Puerto La Cruz (several daily; 5hr); Puerto Ordáz (5 daily; 10hr); Santa Elena de Uairén (1 daily at 3.45pm; 22hr); which continues on to Manaus in Brazil.

GETTING AROUND

By bus Olive-green metrobuses, running 5.30am–11pm, connect metro stations with outlying destinations. There's a set fare of BsF1.50, which you can pay in change or with an *abono integrado* (see below). There is also a virtually infinite number of unofficial *busetas* running their own routes, with stops listed on their windshields. Fares depend on distance travelled, but usually don't exceed BsF6.

By metro Operates from 5.30am to 11pm daily and is cheap, efficient and safe – by far the best way to get around the city, although it can be extremely crowded during peak times. Line 1, the most useful, runs east to west. Lines 2 and 3 run south from the line 1 transfer stations of Capitolio/El Silencio and Plaza Venezuela respectively. The best ticket options are the single-ride *boleto* (BsF1.50) or the ten-ride *abono integrado* (BsF13.50). Beware at peak hours as pick-pockets intentionally cause jams between boarding and alighting passengers to create a distraction.

By taxi Official taxis are white with yellow licence plates; take these rather than their unmarked *pirata* ("pirate") counterparts. Taxis do not have meters and fares should be agreed before you get in. Ask a local what the price should be before bartering with a *taxista*. Most rides within the city should cost under BsF50, more for journeys at night. A cheaper and quicker option is the two-wheeled *mototaxi*, on which helmets come provided. Look for the roadside gazebos and riders wearing hi-vis jackets (who are hailed like a regular taxi) advertising the service.

INFORMATION AND TOURS

Tourist information There are two Venetur desks in the airport's international terminal (both 7am–midnight; ☎0212 355 1326 or ☎0212 355 1765) and another in the domestic terminal (7am–8pm). There's also an office in Caracas, on the first floor of the Torre Venetur, on Av Francisco de Miranda in Altamira (Mon–Fri 8.30am–4pm; ☎0212 208 4652), though this is more administrative and they'll be surprised to see you.

Travel agents Candes (☎0212 953 1632, ⊛candes turismo.com) in Edificio Roraima Av Francisco de Miranda; Club del Trotamundo (☎0212 283 7253) in Centro Comercial Centro Plaza, Los Palos Grandes. English-speaking taxi driver Eustoquio Ferrer (☎0412 720 3805, ✉ferrermiranda@hotmail.com) comes recommended by the owners of *Nuestro Hotel* (see p.872) and can take you on day-trips out of town. Caracas also has a number of reputable tour operators (see p.860).

ACCOMMODATION

Budget accommodation in Caracas is overpriced and underwhelming, many establishments existing more for the purposes of room rentals by the hour than making budget travellers comfortable. If you're nervous about Caracas, stay at *Dal Bo Hostal* (see opposite) or in the Altamira district (see p.872).

EL CENTRO/PARQUE CENTRAL

Ausonia Corner of Av Urdaneta (next to Palacio Miraflores) ☎0212 864 3931; map p.867. A spanking-clean lobby belies grimier rooms upstairs (all with TV), although the position beside Miraflores Palace affords it a certain level of security. BsF310

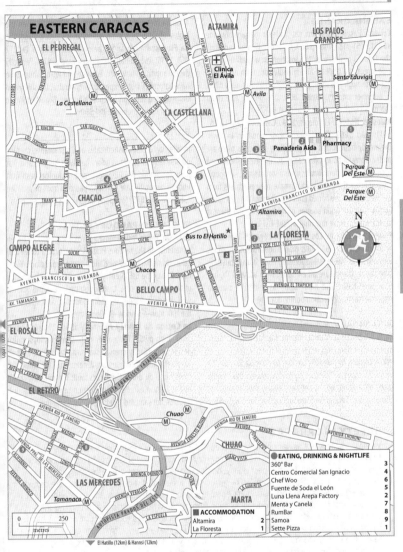

EASTERN CARACAS

EATING, DRINKING & NIGHTLIFE

360° Bar	3
Centro Comercial San Ignacio	4
Chef Woo	6
Fuente de Soda el León	5
Luna Llena Arepa Factory	2
Menta y Canela	7
RumBar	8
Samoa	9
Sette Pizza	1

ACCOMMODATION

Altamira	2
La Floresta	1

El Hatillo (12km) & Hannsi (12km)

★ **Dal Bo Hostal** Av Sur 2, at Av Universidad ☎ 0424 215 0799; map p.867. Gustavo Dal Bo's homestay hasn't been outside the hostelbookers World Top Ten since he opened two years ago. Right in the centre of town, on the first floor of a building next door to a shoe shop, there's capacity for six, while the apartment is equipped with every imaginable gadget. Gustavo has a couple of pleasant surprises including lending out pre-paid mobile phones. You must book ahead, preferably through ⓦ hostelbookers.com. Breakfast included. Dorm **US$35**

Grand Galaxie Av Baralt Truco, at Caja de Agua ☎ 0212 864 9011; map p.867. This basic hostel has a bustling lobby, wi-fi throughout and a good bakery next door; the rooms themselves have a/c and hot water. **BsF290**

Renovación Av Este 2, 154 ☎ 0212 571 0133, ⓦ hotel renovacion.com; map p.867. The upside is the proximity of the city museums, the downside is putting up with the sour-faced staff. Some of the rooms (all en suite) have comically ostentatious bathtubs and there's a great place to eat on the nearby corner. **BsF400**

11

SABANA GRANDE

Cristál Pasaje Asunción, at Bulevar Sabana Grande ☎0212 761 9131; map p.869. A good option for sampling the Caracas nightlife as the location on a graffiti-strewn side street is a popular and friendly spot with numerous bars, although you should avoid it if getting an early night is a higher priority. Expect adequate service and clean rooms, all with a/c, en suite and TV. <u>BsF290</u>

Nuestro Hotel C El Colegio, at Av Casanova ☎0212 761 5431; map p.869. The cheapest accommodation in town, the starkly basic rooms in this security-conscious place are pretty grimy, although you can guarantee clean sheets and towels. The reception doubles up as a sort of shop – although anyone other than guests must make their purchases from the other side of the barred entrance. Some of the staff speak English and are good sources of information, and there is wi-fi. Do not venture downhill on foot. <u>BsF150</u>

Nueva Esparta Av Los Manguitos between Libertador & Solano ☎0212 761 5732; map p.869. The ostentatious entrance sets this pristine lodging back from a bustling side street. Rooms are all en suite, with a/c and TV, but otherwise basic. The hotel also has a decent pizzeria opposite the tiny reception booth. <u>BsF300</u>

ALTAMIRA

Caracas's business district, Altamira is far safer to walk around after dark than other areas of the city.

★ **Altamira** Av José Félix Sosa, at Av Altamira Sur ☎0212 267 4255; map p.871. Secure, stylish and relaxed, this friendly place on a quiet side street has homely rooms with hot showers, a/c, TV and wi-fi throughout. A short walk from Altamira metro station, the rates are a bargain given the high-end nature of accommodation in the area. <u>BsF360</u>

La Floresta Av Ávila Sur below Plaza Altamira ☎0212 263 1955, ⓦhotellafloresta.com; map p.871. Perfectly decent rooms all have a/c, en suite and wi-fi, while some have balconies. Don't expect quality service; the shifty and disinterested staff can be comically rude. Breakfast in the hotel restaurant included. <u>BsF590</u>

EATING

In addition to established cafés and restaurants, there is no shortage of street vendors hawking burgers and hot dogs for around BsF30. Street food, including fresh fruit juice, is generally safe when prepared in front of you. See "Shopping" (p.875) for good places to buy picnic supplies.

EL CENTRO/PARQUE CENTRAL

Café de Sacro Inside Museo Sacro; map p.867. A haven of serenity on the raucous Plaza Bolívar. Grab a coffee and cake and sit back to admire the pretty surroundings. You'll have to pay the BsF15 entry fee whether you're interested in the art gallery or not, although the peace and quiet is well worth it. Mains are more gourmet, and start from BsF100. Mon–Fri noon–3.30pm.

La Cocina de Francy Ave Este 2, at Sur 11 ☎0212 576 9849; map p.867. This corner restaurant employs stylish design and smartly dressed staff who take pride in their work. The menu focuses on Venezuelan fare while the chefs focus on doing the basics well. The *pabellón criollo* (BsF105) is an excellent introduction to the national dish if you've not sampled it yet. Mon–Sat 9am–6pm.

SAFETY IN CARACAS

While Caracas is not as dangerous as its dreadful international reputation would have you believe, crime rates in the capital are the country's highest and robberies are not uncommon. Simple common sense is the best policy: don't carry around excessive cash or anything you can't afford to lose. Don't venture up deserted side streets and stick to where there are crowds after dark, especially in and around El Centro and Sabana Grande. Dress down; wearing overtly touristy clothes will earn you odd looks even from those who don't pose a threat, though grimy backpacker-chic is best saved for towns more accustomed to budget travellers. Change money calmly, in a secure place, and only once you've had a chance to gauge current *paralelo* rates (see p.858). Don't change money in the street; you'll be an easy target for passing opportunists and could also get landed with fake notes.

While not as overtly aggressive as in previous years, the Caracas **police** are a constant presence. Street-level officers are usually very helpful, while the bored staff manning the red or blue police gazebos in pedestrianized areas (particularly common in Sabana Grande) are best avoided; giving them a wide berth is usually enough to avoid unwanted interaction. Spot searches are rare, but if you are unlucky enough to be pulled into a gazebo for an inspection, insist that you unpack your things yourself, one item at a time – things are less likely to go missing if you don't allow yourself to be rushed. Never offer bribes. If you are asked to pay a fine, always ask for the official paperwork.

All that said, there is no reason for paranoia; Caracas is one of South America's friendlier capital cities; exercise your common sense, don't take unnecessary risks, stay alert to your surroundings at all times and you're likely to have an incident-free stay.

★ **Luncheria Doña Agapita** Av Sur 13 south of Plaza la Candelaria; map p.867. If you've not eaten a *cachapa* (sweet-meal pancake folded over a thick slab of cheese), this is the place to have your first. Grab a seat, enjoy the banter between the staff and their patrons, and watch your meal cooked on the hot plate at the entrance. BsF35 for a *cachapa con queso de mano*. Mon–Sat 7am–8pm.

SABANA GRANDE

★ **Arepería 24 Horas** Av Casanova, at Av Las Acacias ☎0212 793 7961; map p.869. Open 24hr for when you need your *arepa* fix, this open-fronted diner brims with colourful characters. Look behind the glass counters to select your fillings, which include octopus, tuna and roast pork (BsF35–45). For more leisurely dining, the table service area has slick waiters and sports channels rolling on the numerous TVs, although the other patrons are far more interesting. Also does excellent *batidos* from BsF18. 24hr.

Cafetería Solano López Av Francisco Solano López, across from Tasca Pullman ☎0212 761 6417; map p.869. Wobbly fans and pumpkins on the bar; this place is as *caraqueño* as they come. The coffee is strong and a surprisingly extensive menu includes *pabellón criollo* (BsF60), which the regulars vouch for as the definitive. The blue-shirted staff and their patrons welcome gringos with quizzical but not unfriendly looks. Mon–Sat 6.30am–6.30pm, Sun 7am–2pm.

Gran Café Bulevar de Sabana Grande, at C Pascual Navarro ☎0212 763 6792; map p.869. Grand it ain't, but this popular lunch destination serves potent coffee, sandwiches (around BsF40 with fries), ice cream, pastries and more. Mon–Sat 7am–6pm, Sun 7am–3pm.

El Rincón Gallego Av Francisco Solano López, at C Los Manguitos ☎0212 762 8307; map p.869. The unstoppably chatty owner Lola emigrated from Spain over fifty years ago and is still dishing out traditional favourites from her homeland as well as friendly security advice. A cosy place that stays open until the early hours if the punters are having fun. Paella BsF130 per person. Mon–Sat noon–late.

Sabas Nieves C Pascual Navarro ☎0212 763 6712; map p.869. On a backstreet, in what looks like your grandma's sitting room, the vegetarian health-conscious menu here alternates daily. Look for the green security bars rather than a sign and squeeze into a seat beside the super-friendly regulars. A BsF40 lunch ticket buys you a fresh juice and as much food as you can load onto your plate. Takeaway for BsF5 extra. Mon–Sat noon–3.30pm.

ALTAMIRA/LOS PALOS GRANDES

Chef Woo 1ra Av above Av Francisco de Miranda, Los Palos Grandes; map p.871. Students and businessmen alike flock to this Chinese restaurant (and neighbouring *Lai Cen*) for cheap beers, lively conversation and sometimes even Chinese food, though this is usually lower down the list of priorities. Closes 11pm.

Luna Llena Arepa Factory 2da Transversal, at 2da Av Los Palos Grandes ☎0212 285 1125; map p.871. They've fixed what isn't broken with artesanal, slim or wholemeal *arepa* options, although the staff admit nothing beats the original. The fillings menu is extensive (BsF26–45), while a yummy local favourite is the *capresa con queso planchado* (BsF42), a caprese salad with grilled cheese. Bag a seat first and order at the counter. 8am–9pm Mon–Thurs, until 1pm Fri–Sun.

Menta y Canela Av Avila Sur next to *La Floresta* (see p.872) ☎0212 261 6571; map p.871. The secret garden feel of this boho-chic deli, a good breakfast option for those staying in the area, is a welcome respite from the busy road without. Daily specials (from BsF75) follow a Mediterranean regimen while cooked breakfasts and custom omelettes (all BsF55) are popular throughout the day. Daily 7am–8pm.

Sette Pizza 4a Av between 2da & 3ra Transversals, Los Palos Grandes ☎0212 283 6608; map p.871. Down a side street, this over-staffed pizza joint stone-bakes tasty artisan pizzas to compensate for underwhelming service. The pasta menu operates on a "choose your shape, choose your sauce" basis. Individual pizza from BsF79, family-size from BsF196, pasta dishes from BsF85. There's live music from Thurs–Sat with a BsF40 cover charge. Daily 2pm–midnight.

EL HATILLO

Dulces Criollos C La Paz on Plaza Bolívar ☎0212 961 3198. Come in for a gawp at the sweets and pastries that run three rows deep at this rustically contemporary (or contemporarily rustic) cake shop. A slice of cake is BsF25 and the coffee is excellent. Scoff it down at a bar stool or enjoy it outside in the leafy Plaza Bolívar. Daily 8am–11pm.

DRINKING AND NIGHTLIFE

Caracas has bars and clubs for virtually anyone, and at any time – many establishments stay open until the last patron leaves. Being a large and cosmopolitan city, it also has a decent selection of gay and lesbian nightspots. Check ⊛rumbacaracas.com for a variety of club and event listings. As most streets empty out after dark, especially in the western districts, it's wise to take taxis to and from your destination.

SABANA GRANDE

El Maní Es Así C El Cristo; map p.869. This self-proclaimed "temple of salsa" is a Caracas legend where they relish gringos getting involved. Thurs to Sat sees live bands fill the wide dancefloor from 9pm while the enormous sound system thumps out salsa the rest of the time. Tues–Sat 7pm–3am; arrive early for occasional salsa lessons.

11

11

Moulin Rouge Av Francisco Solano ⓦ moulinrouge
.com.ve; map p.869. With a giant, two-dimensional
windmill for a facade, you can't miss this ever-popular
dive bar, where the city's rockers, ravers and gutter-
punks convene for live alternative music. Mon–Thurs
10pm–2am, Fri–Sun until 5am; see the website for
who's performing soon.

Tasca El Encuentro de los Artistas Pasaje la Asunción;
map p.869. This is the best of the bars along a street lined
with many. Take a seat at the long bar and talk politics,
or head upstairs for the DJ sets from 8pm. Many punters
get their drinks to go, preferring the reveller-filled street
without. Ice-cold beers (BsF12) are fished out of the cooler
by staff who are always keen to talk politics. Daily
4pm–1am, until 3am Fri & Sat.

ALTAMIRA/LOS PALOS GRANDES

360° Bar Hotel Altamira Suites, 1ra Av at 1a Transversal;
map p.871. While you don't access this rooftop bar via the
classiest route (you go up in the rickety service elevator),
the under-lit interior lazes to a chilled vibe and there
are fantastic city views. Throw yourself into a hammock,
order a delicious coconut mojito (BsF70) and feel glad
you're not negotiating the Caracas traffic surging below.
Daily 5pm–late.

Centro Commercial San Ignacio Av Blandín ⓦ centro
sanignacio.com; map p.871. An upmarket shopping centre
with a wide selection of bars and clubs where wealthy
caraqueños come to show off their latest moves and
fashionable purchases. Try *Suka*, which has a pan-Asian
design and regular DJs, or neighbouring *Pi'Sko* which has a
chintzy Inca theme. There are plenty of eating options here
too. Opening hours vary, although generally daily from
7pm until late.

Fuente de Soda el León 2da Transversal de la Castellana
☎ 0212 263 6014; map p.871. A popular bar (and pizzeria)
where the waiters keep the drinks coming. Grab a seat at
the wide outdoor patio, relax and watch the Venezuelan
motorists crossing the poorly designed roundabout nearby.
Keep note of how many beers you've had, as the waiters
have been known to add a couple to the bill. Daily until 3am.

LAS MERCEDES

RumBar C Nueva York, at C Madrid; map p.871. Sweaty,
crowded and excellent fun; party to salsa, reggaeton and
merengue. An outdoor patio offers a breather from the
constantly rammed dancefloor. It's at its best from Thurs
onwards. Tues–Sat 9pm–late.

Samoa Av Principal de Las Mercedes, at C Mucuchíes
☎ 0212 261 6949; map p.871. An increasingly popular
chain of bars, *Samoa* stands out for its bizarre South Pacific
theme, where the locals go crazy for the plastic palm trees,
looped surf videos and swings instead of seats at the bar.
Daily 5pm until late.

GAY AND LESBIAN

Copa's C Guaicaipuro, close to Chacaíto metro station
☎ 0212 951 3947; map p.869. Caracas's best (possibly
only) lesbian spot, the overzealous security is worth
putting up with for the friendly crowd, which has become
more mixed in recent years. BsF50 cover charge. Wed–Sat
10.30pm–6.30am.

La Fragata C Villa Flor, Sabana Grande; map p.869. This
popular club brings in a friendly, mostly male clientele,
although the good location and party-hard reputation are
beginning to attract a fun-loving straight crowd as well.
Excuse the cheesy, neon-heavy decor and focus instead on
the cheap drinks and crowded dancefloor. Daily 6pm–3am.

TAKE ME OUT TO THE BALL GAME

It won't take you long to notice Venezuela's baseball obsession, with what seems like every
fifth person sporting club gear. If you're in town during the October to December season,
attending an LVBP (Liga Venezolana de Beisbol Profesional) game in the capital is a good way
to see what all the fuss is about. The two local teams, the Leones and Tiburones (Lions and
Sharks), share the Estadio Universitario in Sabana Grande, and there are games on most days
of the week. The biggest fixture of the year pits the Caracas Leones against their fiercest rivals,
Valencia's Navegantes del Magallanes.

Tickets can be bought in advance at one of the numerous Leones merchandise shops
around town; there's one in the Centro Comercial Sambil in Chacao (see p.875). You can also
buy them online at ⓦ leones.com, although you'll need a local friend to reserve them, as the
site doesn't accept international credit cards.

Alternatively, you can buy tickets from the stadium box office from 9am on game days. Arrive
early as service at the four ticket windows is slow. Tickets for the *tribuna* (main stand) start at
BsF50, unreserved-seating tickets for the *grada* (terrace) around the outfield are cheaper and
you can jump the queue to buy them.

The stadium is a ten-minute walk south of Plaza Venezuela metro station. Walk to *Arepería 24
Horas* and you'll see the floodlights. Check ⓦ lvbp.com for upcoming fixtures.

Tasca Pullman Av Francisco Solano, Sabana Grande; map p.869. One of Caracas's oldest gay bars, and still sporting a distinctly Eighties vibe, this dimly lit place draws a friendly, working-class crowd and the occasional drag queen. Mostly male, though women are welcome. Daily until late.

SHOPPING

Shopping culture in Caracas is dominated by mega-malls, where your chances of finding unique, inexpensive crafts are virtually nonexistent. Street shopping is a bit more promising, at least in terms of prices, and the Hannsi crafts outlet in El Hatillo (see p.868) is your best source for souvenirs.

Centro Artesanal Los Goajiros Next to Chacaíto metro station. This alleyway of stalls is the closest Caracas gets to backpacker-chic and the place to come if you have a pressing need for Hugo Chávez baseball caps. Mon–Sat 7am–7pm, Sun 9am–4pm, although individual vendors keep their own hours.

Centro Comercial Lido Av Francisco de Miranda. A good place to get things done; services include Continental, Copa and Santa Barbara airline offices, major phone network outlets and various ATMs. *South Beach* is a good spot to stock up on women's beachwear before a trip to the coast. Mon–Sat 10am–7pm.

Centro Comercial Sambil Chacao. The most famous of the city's malls, this mind-bogglingly enormous complex hosts every conceivable amenity, including top international brands. Mon–Sat 10am–9pm, Sun & holidays noon–8pm.

Hannsi C Bolívar No 12, El Hatillo ⓦ hannsi.com.ve. This enormous craft shop sprawls through several buildings, filled throughout with astonishing amounts of chintzy junk, although the occasional gem is buried beneath it all. You can choose your own coffee beans to grind at the café, which also has wi-fi, pastries and savoury snacks. Daily 10am–1pm, 2.30–7pm.

Libreria Tecni-Ciencias In Centro Comercial Sambil and around the city ⓦ tecniciencia.com. The prices are a bit high, but this chain is one of the best options for books in Caracas, with more than a dozen outlets (including one in Centro Lido in El Rosal).

SBS Sports Business In Centro Comercial Sambil or Centro Comercial El Recreo. Come here for official Caracas Leones baseball gear, including jerseys, T-shirts, caps, pins, stickers and game tickets (see box opposite).

DIRECTORY

Banks and exchange In a city as shopping-obsessed as Caracas, you can't walk ten steps without passing a bank. For safety reasons, try to use ATMs in shopping centres or the lockable booths on Bulevar Sabana Grande. The international airport terminal has a Banco de Venezuela (and others), as well as an Italcambio for exchanging travellers' cheques; visit ⓦ italcambio.com for other locations around town.

Embassies and consulates Brazil, Av Mohedano, at C Los Chaguaramos in La Castellana (Mon–Fri 9am–1pm; ☎0212 981 6000, ⓔ brasembcaracas@embajadabrasil .org.ve); Canada, Av Francisco de Miranda at Av Sur, Altamira (Mon–Thurs 7.30am–4.30pm, Fri 7.30am–1pm; ☎0212 600 3000, ⓦ caracas.gc.ca); Colombia, 2e Av de Campo Alegre at Av Francisco de Miranda, Torre Credival (Mon–Fri 8am–1pm; ☎0212 515 9596, ⓔ ecaracas @cancillera.gov.co); Guyana, Av El Paseo, Quinta Roraima in Prados del Este (Mon–Thurs 8.30am–3.30pm, Fri 8.30am–3pm; ☎0212 977 1158, ⓔ embaguy@cantv .net); Ireland, Av Venezuela, Torre Clement, 2nd Floor, Office 2-A in El Rosal (Mon–Fri 8am–12.30pm; ☎0212 951 3645, ⓔ irlconven@cantv.net); South Africa, Centro Profesional Eurobuilding, P-4, Office 4B-C in Chuao (Mon– Fri 9am–1pm; ☎0212 991 4622, ⓔ rsaven@ifxnw.com .ve); UK, Av Principal de La Castellana, Torre La Castellana 11th Floor (Mon–Fri 8am–4.30pm; ☎0212 263 8411, ⓦ ukinvenezuela.fco.gov.uk); USA, Colinas de Valle Arriba, C F at C Suapure (Mon–Fri 8am–5pm; ☎0212 975 6411, ⓦ caracas.usembassy.gov).

Hospitals Two recommended clinics are Hospital de Clínicas Caracas, on Av Panteón, at Av Alameda in San Bernardino (☎0212 508 6111, ⓦ clinicaracas.com), and Clinica El Ávila, on Av San Juan Bosco, at 6ta Transversal in Altamira (☎0212 276 1111, ⓦ clinicaelavila.com).

Immigration office SAIME (El Servicio Administrativo de Identificación, Migración y Extranjería) at Av Baralt in front of Plaza Miranda opposite Teatros metro station (Mon–Fri 8.30am–3.30pm; ☎0212 483 2070, ⓦ saime .gob.ve).

Internet There are numerous internet cafés in Caracas, especially in pedestrian-heavy Sabana Grande. Most charge BsF10/hr. Two reliable options are MSX Cybershop, at C San Antonio above Bulevar de Sabana Grande and Ciberplace, at C Villa Flor below Bulevar de Sabana Grande. Both daily 8.30am–8.30pm.

Laundry Many hotels will do your laundry (generally for around BsF50/load). Otherwise, try Maxiclean (ⓦ grupo maxiclean.com), which has branches around the city including on Av Casanova in Sabana Grande.

Left luggage Both La Bandera and Oriente bus terminals (see p.870) offer luggage storage. Most accommodation will hold luggage for you as well.

Pharmacy Pharmacies are just as ubiquitous as banks and internet cafés. On Bulevar de Sabana Grande, Farmacia Saas is at C Villa Flor. In Altamira, Farmacia San Andrés is on the corner of 3a Av at 2da Transversal.

Phones CANTV, Digicel and Movistar have shops through-out the city for buying SIM cards and credit; all three have outlets around Plaza Bolívar, and the latter also has phone booths and photocopiers (8am–4pm). There's a CANTV office (8am–5pm) on C San Antonio above Av Francisco Solano, which also offers internet.

11

11

Post office Ipostel beside the cathedral in Plaza la Candelaria (Mon–Fri, 8am–noon & 1–4pm). There's another post office at the international airport, and others in *Puntos de Gestión* (administration offices) around the city. Locals will warn you against using state-run Ipostel for anything important; private alternatives include MRW (ⓦmrw.com.ve) and DHL (ⓦdhl.com.ve), both of which have numerous offices around the city.

DAY-TRIPS FROM CARACAS

For a quick escape from the hustle and bustle of Caracas, ride the cable car that ascends the slopes of **Parque Nacional El Ávila**, with its spectacular views and hiking trails. If you've got more time, consider visiting **Colonia Tovar**, a Black Forest-style village built by nineteenth-century German immigrants. On the other side of the coastal range, Caracas boasts some fabulous beaches, particularly popular with surfers from the capital.

Parque Nacional El Ávila

Based along the lush mountain ridge that separates Caracas from the coast, **PARQUE NACIONAL EL ÁVILA** (ⓦel-avila.com) is a popular day-trip from the urban mayhem for *caraqueños*. On clear days there are stunning views of the city to the south and the Caribbean to the north.

There are several ways to explore the park. From Caracas, there are four well-marked hiking trails accessible via Avenida Boyacá, the city's northernmost east-to-west thoroughfare. It is also possible to drive to the top in a 4WD. However, the most popular option is the **teleférico** (box office Tues noon–6pm, Wed–Sun 9.30am–6pm, closed Mon; BsF45; last return 10pm), a high-speed cable car. To get to the base station, go to Colegio de Ingenieros metro station and take a BsF20 taxi from outside the entrance. There's an ice-rink at the top as well as some more predictable attractions, while a steep trail leads down to the pretty village of **Galipán**. Jeeps wait at either end to ferry passengers up and down the trail for BsF8 each way. Numerous roadside stands sell strawberries and cream and local honey, while restaurants in the village have superb views.

To explore the park further contact Akanán Tours (see p.860). Alternatively, take a taxi to San Bernadín at the foot of the hill at weekends, where jeeps leave for Galipán when full (BsF15/ person one-way).

The northern coast

The coast of Vargas state, separated from Caracas by Parque Nacional El Ávila (see above), provides a good sample of Venezuela's **beaches** if you don't have time to visit anywhere else on the coast. The surfing here is particularly good, with some of the best breaks at Anare, Los Caracas and Playa Pantaleta. To **get here** under your own steam, catch the bus (see below) from Parque Central to the airport and continue 35km by taxi to La Guaira or Macuto (around BsF180). Here you can flag down one of the numerous *busetas* that ply the seaside highway in both directions; hop off and on wherever you choose.

Colonia Tovar

Founded by German immigrants in 1843, the small mountain village of **COLONIA TOVAR**, 60km west of Caracas, is still inhabited by their ancestors. Most of the houses have been built in traditional Black Forest style, and restaurants selling German-style bratwurst line the main roads of the village. Sadly, production of Cerveza Tovar has moved from the village microbrewery to the nearby town of La Victoria, but the end result is still readily available. "Colonia" is a popular weekend destination, when it becomes packed with bemused *caraqueños*, who turn the whole place into a Deutsch Disneyland. The **Museo de Historia y Artesanía** (weekends and festivals 9am–6pm; BsF10) features a small collection of documents, clothes, tools, guns and other relics of the village's early days.

ARRIVAL AND DEPARTURE

By metro and buseta To get here from Caracas, take the metro to La Yaguara station. Join the queue around the

★ TREAT YOURSELF

An underwater extension of the Andes range, the **Los Roques** archipelago is Venezuela's closest thing to desert-island paradise. Populated mostly by posada owners and boatmen, the high cost of flying to Los Roques has helped keep them both exclusive and unspoilt. Most Caracas travel agencies (p.870) and tour operators (see p.860) offer package trips, but you'll save a lot of money organising things yourself.

Trips are cheaper during the week, and the major carrier for the archipelago, Aereotuy (w tuy.com), offers return flights and a night's accommodation for BsF1600/person Mon–Fri. Chapi Air (☎ 0212 355 1965, w chapiair.com) serves Los Roques with two flights daily each way.

Two good **posadas** are El Botuto (☎ 0416 621 0381, w posadaelbotuto.com; $85/person with breakfast), which has great service and lovely outside showers, and Doña Carmen (☎ 0414 318 4926, w turismodonacarmen.com; BsF300/person with dinner).

Camping is a safer option than on the mainland, although you'll need a permit from the Inparques office (at the far end of town from the landing strip). Camping is restricted to a designated area on Gran Roque and a few of the smaller, uninhabited islands, for a maximum of eight days. Contact Libya Parada (☎ 0414 291 9240, e libyapara@hotmail.com) for tent rentals.

A boatmen's cooperative for transport around the islands operates out of Oscar Shop next to the landing strip, which also rents snorkelling gear (BsF50/day). Arrecife Divers, near Inparques, runs **scuba-diving** trips and courses. There are **no ATMs**, so take plenty of cash. Tourist numbers and prices rise substantially in the June to September high season.

11

corner for a *buseta* to El Junquito (every 15min; 1hr). Onward buses to Colonia Tovar (every 15min; 1hr) depart from where the El Junquito bus stops. On weekends, everyone else on the bus is usually heading to Colonia Tovar too.

To return to Caracas, *busetas* leaving Colonia Tovar depart 300m outside the village on the road to El Junquito; many of them go directly to Caracas for BsF30. The last *buseta* leaves Colonia at 6pm. If you want to move on to the western coast, take a *buseta* to La Victoria from the other end of town. From La Victoria buses leave regularly for Maracay, the access point for Parque Nacional Henri Pittier (see p.878).

TOUR OPERATORS

Douglas Pridham ☎ 0416 743 8939, w vivatrek.com. An expert paraglider who can get you airborne from the steep hillsides around Colonia Tovar (BsF450). His outfit also offers guided excursions into Parque Nacional Henri Pittier (see p.878).

Rustic Tours ☎ 0244 355 1908, e rustictours@cantv.net. One of several companies with stalls around the village, which run jeep outings through the mountainous country-side (2hr; BsF70).

EATING

Lunchería Schmuk 100m uphill from the church. Specializes in German-style meats, which come in a variety of forms ranging from simple hot-dogs (BsF20) to the *Plato Especial Schmuck* sausage-fest (BsF75). Daily 6am–9pm.

Zu Hause Next to the car park. Offers good-value breakfasts, again involving sausages, and lunch combos such as *sandwich de pernil* (BsF65), all of which include a drink. Fri–Sun 8am–5pm.

FESTIVAL DE LOS DIABLOS DANZANTES

The otherwise nondescript town of **San Francisco de Yare**, 60km southeast of Caracas, is the site of one of Venezuela's most famous spectacles, the **Festival de los Diablos Danzantes** ("dancing devils"). In observance of the Catholic holy day Corpus Christi (in late May or early June; check with Caracas tourism offices for exact dates), townspeople don elaborate devil costumes and engage in highly ritualized performances. While similar festivals occur in other parts of Venezuela, including Ocumare de la Costa, Chuao, Naiguatá and Cuyagua, Yare's is considered the definitive.

GETTING THERE

By metro and bus To get here from Caracas, take the metro to the Nuevo Circo station and walk one block to the bus terminal of the same name. From here, buses (1hr 30min) leave every 15min until 9pm for Ocumare del Tuy from the designated stand. From the Ocumare terminal, frequent *busetas* to Santa Teresa drop passengers at Yare's Plaza Bolívar (20min). To return to Caracas, Ocumare-bound *busetas* pass one block northeast of the Plaza Bolívar. Buses from Ocumare to Caracas leave every 15min until 9pm.

The northwest coast

Venezuela's **northwest coast** gets much less press than the Caribbean offshore islands of Aruba, Bonaire and Curaçao, but offers similarly spectacular beaches alongside some of the Caribbean's prettiest colonial towns and two fine national parks.

Parque Nacional Henri Pittier, roughly 150km from Caracas, has palm-lined sands, striking mountain ranges and four vegetation zones, which are home to a tremendous array of birds and plant life. If taking a speedboat to the beach appeals, then **Parque Nacional Morrocoy** a few hours to the west is popular for its offshore cays surrounded by crystalline water. Three hours closer to Colombia from Morrocoy, the well-preserved colonial town of **Coro** serves as a good breather between the coast and the Andes. For those heading directly to Colombia this is the most backpacker-friendly spot en route to the border (see p.886) 360km away.

PARQUE NACIONAL HENRI PITTIER

Created in 1937, **PARQUE NACIONAL HENRI PITTIER** was Venezuela's first national park, named after the Swiss geographer and botanist who classified more than thirty thousand plants in Venezuela. Despite the park's great biodiversity, the vast majority of visitors come for its **beaches**, which can be overrun at weekends but are generally quiet the rest of the time.

Pittier's wide array of **flora and fauna** is a result of the relatively short space in which it climbs from sea level to 2430m, producing distinct vegetation zones. The park's wildlife is best experienced from the Universidad Central de Venezuela's **Estación Biológica**. The area is renowned among birdwatchers, having one of the highest densities of birds in the world, with at least 582 species (6.5 percent of the world's total), including the Venezuelan bristle-tyrant.

The park also has large reptile and mammal populations; noteworthy residents include sea turtles, jaguars, pumas, spider monkeys and rattlesnakes.

Entry to the park is free, and most people access the towns of **Choroní** and **Ocumare de la Costa**, beach communities at the ends of the only two roads, by bus from the terminal in **Maracay**, a town which offers tourists little of interest. Choroní, on the eastern side of the park, is the nicer of the two beach communities, with lots of places to stay and a lively atmosphere. Ocumare is neither pretty nor particularly lively, but is worth a visit for the stunning La Ciénaga lagoon nearby. Guided tours of the park are organized from either Choroní or Ocumare, rather than Maracay on the outside.

Estación Biológica Rancho Grande

The park can be explored along hiking trails from Choroní (see below), but the best base for serious wildlife-spotting is the atmospheric **Estación Biológica Rancho Grande** (open 8am–4pm if the research team are here, otherwise contact Oskar Padilla; see below), a large complex which the jungle has enveloped to create something Lara Croft would come across in *Tomb Raider*. At about 1100m, this research station for the Universidad Central de Venezuela has lots of trails from which visitors are likely to see an incredible variety of fauna including sloths, anteaters and howler monkeys (if you are particularly lucky). The station also offers very rustic dormitory **accommodation** (BsF30), but guests must bring their own sheets or a sleeping bag, as well as food to cook in the communal kitchen.

ARRIVAL AND DEPARTURE

By bus Maracay is the access point for Henri Pittier and has a busy terminal serving country-wide locations. The Estación Biológica's entrance is a nondescript gate beside a bus stop on the road between Maracay and Ocumare de la Costa; to get there board the hourly bus heading in either direction and ask the bus driver to let you off at Rancho Grande. To get away, hail a passing bus from beside the entrance.

Destinations from Maracay Caracas (every 20min; 1hr 30min); Valencia (every 15min; 45min); Coro (several daily; 7hr); Maracaibo (2 daily; 9hr); Mérida (3 daily; 12hr); San Cristóbal (3 daily; 12hr); Puerto la Cruz (2 daily; 10hr); Puerto Ordaz (2 daily; 14hr); San Fernando de Apure (3 daily; 6hr). Buses for Choroní and Ocumare de la Costa depart from the terminal when full (usually every 30min) until 9pm.

INFORMATION AND TOURS

Tourist information The park's beaches can be accessed from Choroní (see below) and Ocumare (see p.881). Don't show up to the Estación Biológica unannounced, as it's likely that you'll find the gates locked and the building unoccupied. You need permission from Inparques in Maracay (☎0243 889 3242) to walk the trails and from the university (☎0412 871 7319) to stay overnight, although you're better off getting in touch with Oskar Padilla (see below).

Tour operators Oskar Padilla, a helpful, experienced and English-speaking guide (☎0412 892 5308, ✉oskarpadilla@hotmail.com) offers hiking and birdwatching around Rancho Grande, and will happily arrange permits for you. *Casa Luna Espinoza* in Choroní (see p.880) can also arrange stays and activities at the research centre.

CHORONÍ

Choroní actually consists of two parts: the colonial town of **CHORONÍ**, notable for its winding streets and colourful houses, but otherwise dull; and **PUERTO COLOMBIA**, a beach town 2km away where the action is concentrated. Puerto Colombia's beating heart is its lively **malecón** (seafront promenade) where the fishing boats dock, revellers congregate and on weekends it's common to see *tambores*, a coastal tradition of African drum-playing, singing and dancing.

WHAT TO SEE AND DO

The **Mirador de Cristo** on the eastern headland (named *Papelón*, or Sugar Loaf) offers a view over the tiny town and stunning relief surrounding it. A path weaves towards it from the Playa Grande side of the bridge.

The one beach easily reached on foot is **Playa Grande**, a sheltered bay of jungled hills and a curving sandbar, which consequently attracts the most visitors.

About the same distance to the west, but harder to reach (and thus less crowded), **Playa El Diario** is a 45-minute walk from the village. To get here from the midpoint

of the main Choroní–Puerto Colombia road, follow Calle Cementerio past the cemetery, bear left at the split and follow it around the headland to the sea.

To access the other nearby beaches you will need to take a *lancha*, which can be arranged at the malecón. To the east, the closest beach is **Playa Valle Seco** (BsF50/person return), which has some coral reefs and decent snorkelling. Farther east, **Playa Chuao** (BsF60/person return) offers postcard good looks and a path that runs inland to Chuao town. Some of the world's best cacao is grown here. If you don't visit, you can still stock up on their fantastic chocolate from Sabor A Cacao (see p.881) in Puerto Colombia. Still farther east is equally nice **Playa Cepe** (BsF80/person return), which is generally the least crowded.

11

PUERTO COLOMBIA

CARIBBEAN SEA

Playa Grande

■ ACCOMMODATION	
Casa Luna Espinoza	2
Hostal Colonial	3
Habitaciones Mayitas	1
Posada Los Guanches	4

Police station

Mirador del Cristo

lancha

Pharmacy

Coop. Alcatours

Pc Acción

CONCEPCIÓN

JOSÉ MARTÍN

LOS COCOS

UNIÓN

LOS COCOS

TRINO RANGEL

PUERTO COLOMBIA

N

● EATING & DRINKING	
Bar La Playa	2
Brisas del Mar	3
Coco Café Cacao	5
Jalio	4
Oasis	7
Pescaíto	1
Restaurant Araguaneyes	6

Bus Terminal

0 — 100
metres

Playa El Diario (1.5km) ▼

To combine these beaches in a single trip, negotiate a price (aim for around BsF700 for the day) with the *lanchero*. Pack a lunch.

ARRIVAL AND DEPARTURE

By bus The only road to Choroní is from Maracay. Buses (every 2hr; 2hr) leave when full until 8pm and cost BsF30. Puerto Colombia is a safe 15min stroll from the bus terminal. Take a left out of the entrance and follow the other passengers.

By boat If you're coming from or going to Ocumare de la Costa, a rapid and scenic alternative is to negotiate a ride with a *lanchero* from either end. The price should be around BsF300 and the trip takes an hour.

By taxi Taxis from Maracay cost around BsF250 and take half the time. Alternatively, take a seat in a *por puesto* (shared taxi) for BsF60. Both depart regularly from the Maracay terminal.

INFORMATION AND TOURS

Claudia, the owner of *Casa Luna Espinoza* (see below), can organize tours of the park, the chocolate plantations in Chuao and speedboat trips to various beaches along the coast.

ACCOMMODATION

Camping isn't especially worthwhile as there is a good selection of budget accommodation in Puerto Colombia. Reservations are recommended in the high season.

PUERTO COLOMBIA

Casa Luna Espinoza C Morillo ☎0243 951 5318, ⓦjungletrip.de. Knowledgeable German *dueña* Claudia speaks English, while her surly Venezuelan staff barely speak at all. This hostel is a good choice with a communal kitchen, dining table, wi-fi and hammocked courtyard, although the dormitory is next to the noisy main road. Also runs two other posadas in town and can sort out an exploration of Henri Pittier. Don't be surprised if the needy cat gets into bed with you in the morning. Dorms __BsF70__, doubles __BsF120__

★ **Hostal Colonial** C Morillo ☎0243 431 8757, ⓔcolonialchoroni@gmail.com. Rooms are stylish, good value and numerous at this friendly guesthouse with fountains, wi-fi and a good restaurant. The affable staff speak English, Italian and German while the spacious rooms (some with en suite and a/c) are fan-cooled and thankfully set back from the noisy main road. __BsF100__

Habitaciones Mayitas C Rangel 12 ☎0243 991 1141. Look for the dolphins stencilled on the wall rather than a sign in this cluttered family-run homestay. The friendly atmosphere and over-equipped kitchen makes up for the five rather cramped rooms, some with a/c, ranging in size from a double to a sextuple. __BsF120__

Posada Los Guanches C Colón. The only noise you'll be disturbed by in this mercifully cool building is your own echo. Run by the welcoming family that lives on the opposite side of the flowery backstreet, rooms are fan-cooled, en suite and basic. Have a browse of the odd bamboo jewellery on sale. __BsF130__

EATING

The following options are all in Puerto Colombia (all but one on Av Los Cocos), and here you'll also find a small courtyard opposite the malecón where kitchens open in the evenings and serve up excellent hamburgers and hotdogs. There are numerous shacks lining the path to Playa Grande that sell plates of fish, rice and salad for around BsF30 until the foot traffic coming back from the beach slows down.

PUERTO COLOMBIA

Brisas del Mar ☎0243 991 1268. Not the most peaceful place in town to eat, being next to *Bar La Playa* (see below), but *Brisas* offers calamarí five ways (all BsF70) as well as non-seafood options such as *pabellón* and pasta. Locals also recommend the soups at *Restaurant Puerto Colombia* next door. Daily 8.30am–11pm.

★ **Coco Café Cacao** C Union at Plaza Bolívar ☎0426 833 7920. The pastries, cakes and coffee are good here, but people queue up for the signature ice creams (BsF10). You can choose from a variety of flavours, but given that they use the locally grown cacao to make the chocolate popsicle, it's a good test of free will. Puts a percentage of its profits into local community projects. Daily 8am–10pm, Sat until midnight.

Oasis ☎0243 711 1666. Anglophile owner Raúl, who studied art in London in the 1980s, whips up delicious seafood dishes from his bamboo-walled kitchen. Excellent Creole breakfasts (BsF40), fresh juices (BsF15) and healthy touches such as bran *arepas*. His artwork adorns the walls of the attractive covered courtyard. Daily 8am–10pm.

Restaurant Araguaneyes ☎0243 991 1166. Enjoy huge portions of fresh fish and seafood (BsF70) on the large upstairs terrace while listening to music that for once isn't salsa. Also open for breakfast. Daily 8am–11pm.

DRINKING

Nightlife, if you can call it that, is very casual – most people just buy a few beers and drink them on the malecón.

PUERTO COLOMBIA

Bar La Playa At the beach end of Av Los Cocos. By day, holidaymakers laze about in the plastic chairs on the covered patio, sipping beers and watching the fishermen come and go. At night, the focus is on rum, high-volume salsa and getting flirty. Daily until late.

Jalio C Concepción. The most upscale option in town, promising tapas by day and cocktails by night. Thurs–Sat, if the owners feel like it.

Pescaíto Along the path to Playa Grande. The closest that Puerto Colombia gets to a club, atop a low hill across the bridge. Open until dawn when the fishermen head out to catch the nightspot's namesake.

SHOPPING

For food to cook in your posada's kitchen, you can buy fish directly from the fishermen on the malecón or go to Pescaderia Choroní down the side of *Bar La Playa*. There are numerous fruit and veg stands at the sea-end of Av Los Cocos.

Cooperativa Alcatours C Morillo, at Independencia ☏ 0414 237 0797, ✉ alcatours14@hotmail.com. Interesting "cacao-arte" and *artesanía* made by the husband-wife owners. Daily 8am–6pm.

Sabor A Cacao C José Maitín ☏ 0243 673 1449. Excellent chocolate products, including cocoa butter lip-salve from nearby Chuao. Daily 9am–1pm, 3–7pm.

DIRECTORY

Bank There is a BNC ATM at the bus terminal. You can change dollars at some hotels.

Internet *Hostal Colonial* has a computer you can use for BsF4/hr until 10pm, or wi-fi which you can jump onto for free if you're nice to the owner.

Pharmacy A small pharmacy next door to *Brisas del Mar* (see opposite) is open Mon–Sat 8.30am–9pm.

Phones Movistar, C Concepción, for mobile phone credit. Otherwise, ask at your accommodation or head for the malecón, where there will usually be someone with a phone on a plastic table to rent by the minute.

Post office Half a block south of the Plaza Bolívar in Choroní. Theoretically open Mon–Fri 10am–4pm.

OCUMARE DE LA COSTA

The beach at nearby **El Playón** is the most diverting feature of **OCUMARE DE LA COSTA**, not that it's anything special. However, various spots nearby which are worth a look make Ocumare the best place to base yourself if snorkelling, waterfalls and lagoons pique your interest. Only accessible by *lancha*, **La Ciénaga** is a beautiful lagoon nearby where day-trippers go to sunbathe, swim and lounge about the picture-postcard scenery. For those of a more active disposition the lagoon offers some of the area's best snorkelling.

Around 5km east of El Playón is **Playa Cata**, which is attractive but rather sullied by the irresponsible placement of some ugly high-rises. **Playa Catica**, an hour-long hike or short boat ride (BsF25/person) from Cata, is smaller and less crowded. Farther east, legendary surfing beach **Playa Cuyagua** can get fairly large waves, so swimmers should exercise caution.

ARRIVAL AND DEPARTURE

By bus Buses run to and from Maracay (hourly; 90min), but the ride is a rough one, so if there's enough of you, share a taxi.

By taxi Taxis (BsF250) from Maracay depart from the gas station outside the terminal entrance (*por puestos* don't operate this route).

GETTING AROUND

By bus All buses stop at Ocumare de la Costa's main plaza. Buses depart regularly to Playa Cata (every 20min; 30min) and Playa Cuyagua (every 20min; 40min).

By boat *Lanchas* to La Ciénaga and Playa Cuyagua depart from La Boca at the eastern end of Ocumare's malecón and should cost around BsF300 for the day (negotiate depending on where you want to go). The staff at *Eco-Lodge* (see below) can arrange trips for you.

ACCOMMODATION

Eco-Lodge ☏ 0243 993 1986, ⊕ ecovenezuela.com. The best accommodation in El Playón is the luxurious *Eco-lodge* at the western end of the malecón. This posada also runs *Coral Lagoon Lodge* (see box below). Breakfast included. **BsF625**

★ TREAT YOURSELF

Coral Lagoon Lodge La Ciénaga ⊕ corallagoonlodge.com. Located right on the shores of La Ciénaga lagoon, *Coral Lagoon Lodge* might just be the most relaxing place on Venezuela's northwest coast. An all-inclusive overnight package here includes boat transfers, kayaks and snorkelling equipment, fantastic meals involving plenty of fresh fish and drinks. For two days, life won't get any more taxing than deciding between a swim, early morning turtle-spotting or that hammock under a tree. During the week, particularly outside the July–Sept school holiday season, you'll probably have the whole magical lagoon virtually to yourself. If your budget won't stretch to an overnight stay, note that the owners at Ocumare's *Eco-Lodge* organize day-trips to La Ciénaga. Package/person **US$180**

Habitaciones Caribe C Vargas ☎0243 993 1496. Resembling the set of a slasher film, this bare-minimum establishment offers the cheapest rooms in town, although it's still vastly overpriced. A good option if you don't intend spending much time in your hotel, the rooms all have private showers, fans and clean, if moth-bitten, sheets. BsF150

Hotel Monte Mar C Vargas ☎0243 993 1173. A motel-style complex set around a wide courtyard, this colourful and relatively quiet hotel is a short stroll from the beach. All rooms have en suite and wi-fi, while rooms on the upper floors have a/c. Ocumare's best mid-range option. BsF290

PARQUE NACIONAL MORROCOY

Gorgeous white-sand cays surrounded by azure water are the highlights of **PARQUE NACIONAL MORROCOY**, one of the most popular national parks in Venezuela. The 300-square kilometre reserve, spread primarily over water, was created in 1974, but today it doesn't feel much like a national park. Several areas have been irresponsibly developed and the numerous beachgoers are careless with their litter. The park is home to nearly four-fifths of Venezuela's aquatic **bird species**, as well as several types of mammal.

Chichiriviche and **Tucacas** both serve as bases for forays into the park. Neither is particularly attractive, although the profusion of decent budget accommodation options and restaurants in Chichiriviche makes it a better base for further exploration.

WHAT TO SEE AND DO

There is a total of 22 **cays**, or cayos, in the park, most differing only in size and facilities. Day-trips can be arranged by most posadas for no extra charge, while *lancheros* hawk trips from the malecón end of Calle Zamora in the mornings. If you want snorkelling gear it should come included in the journey price for no extra charge. Prices listed are for the boat, not per person, and include return; all are negotiable and a jokey attitude will be a great help when bargaining.

Dotted with shade-giving palms, **Cayo Sombrero** (BsF300), halfway between Chichiriviche and Tucacas, is the most popular of the cays, although with beaches on all sides you can still find uncrowded parts. There are numerous food stands as well as *lancha*-restaurants, boats with rudimentary kitchens that bring the meal directly to your sun lounger. Food is expensive, however, so it's a good idea to pack a lunch. There are some good snorkelling spots, although it's generally better around **Cayo Sal** (BsF180). *Lanchas* also make trips to cayos Muerto (BsF200), Pelón (BsF140), Peraza (BsF140) and Varadero (BsF200). You can combine multiple spots on either a short (BsF1000) or long (BsF1500) day-tour, which includes the two-hundred-year-old shipwrecked *Barco Hundido*, the questionably romantic "tunnel of love" through thick mangroves and Piscina Los Juanes, sapphire-blue shallows where you can hunt for clams.

CHICHIRIVICHE

Chichiriviche's spread-out format, inordinately numerous *liquorerías* and gritty street style render it an unexceptional town. It nevertheless attracts plenty of tourists who come for its useful proximity to the cays. Calle Zamora, the town's main artery, dead-ends at the malecón, where most activity is centred. By day it's bustling with *lancha* passengers headed to the cays; by night hippie street vendors descend to sell handmade jewellery, strum guitars and watch the fishing boats rocking beside the sea wall.

ARRIVAL AND INFORMATION

By bus Only three destinations are served from Chichiriviche, of which Valencia has the most onward connections, serving Caracas, Mérida, Coro and other major cities. Buses arrive and depart 500m inland on C Zamora. Sanare is a junction where a road breaks off from the Coro–Maracay highway and heads to Chichiriviche. For routes between Coro and Chichiriviche, ask your driver to let you off here. Move to the corresponding bus stop, where you shouldn't have to wait more than half an hour to hail a passing bus for either destination.

Destinations Barquisimeto (every 30min; 45min), Valencia (every 30min; 1hr) and Puerto Carreño (every 30min; 45min). All pass through Sanare junction.

Tourist information There's a red-roofed Corfaltur kiosk outside the petrol station 50m inland from where the bus stops on C Zamora, though it has no reliable schedule of opening hours.

CHICHIRIVICHE

ACCOMMODATION
Capri	4
Morena's Place	1
Posada La Negra	2
Posada Villa Gregoria	3

EATING & DRINKING
Panadería El Centro	4
Rancho Andino	1
Restaurant La Esquina de Arturo	2
Txalupa	3

CARIBBEAN SEA

11

ACCOMMODATION

Most accommodation is within a couple of blocks of the malecón, a generally safe part of town with lots of foot traffic. *Panadería El Centro* and *Rancho Andino* also have rooms (see below). Camping in the national park has been banned in recent years, but if you are keen to do it contact the Falcón State Inparques office (☎ 0268 252 4198) to enquire about the current policy.

Capri C Zamora ☎ 0259 818 6026, ✉ hotelcaprica @yahoo.com. A proud boast from the friendly management is that with eight water tanks on the roof, the showers never run dry. Some rooms have psychedelic beach-scene murals, while all come with en suite and a/c. Wi-fi on site. BsF200

Morena's Place Sector Playa Norte ☎ 0259 815 0936, ✉ posadamorenas@hotmail.com. Just one street in from the beach, *Morena's* has the only dorms in town, making this a good-value spot for solo travellers. A friendly English-speaking family runs the place, and can prepare meals on request. There's a laundry service, communal kitchen, barbecue and relaxed atmosphere. Dorms BsF80, doubles BsF150

Posada La Negra C Mariño ☎ 0259 815 0476. The place to come if you need a bed or a haircut, *La Negra* is the only posada-hairdressers you're likely to encounter on your trip. Friendly, brightly coloured rooms around a communal kitchen come with a/c, en suite and TVs. There's a five-person apartment for BsF300. BsF180

★ **Posada Villa Gregoria** C Mariño ☎ 0259 818 6359.

A secure Mediterranean-style building with coconut trees in the wide courtyard, a profusion of hammocks and aloe vera plants, useful if you've skimped on the sunscreen. English-speaking staff provide spotless rooms (a/c, TV, en suite) and showers, which although cold, amount to more than pipes sticking out of the wall. Also has apartments for five (BsF550) and seven (BsF650). BsF200

EATING AND DRINKING

Chichiriviche's nightlife amounts to hanging around the liquor stores while they're open and drinking on the malecón when they're closed. Your best bet for a drink in more relaxed settings is *Txalupa* (see p.884) and its neighbouring seafront restaurants.

Panadería El Centro C Zamora opposite *Hotel Capri* ☎ 0259 818 6906. Now on the corner next to the old shop, impressively moustachioed José serves up good coffee and inexpensive bread. The mini cinnamon rolls, enormous bags of crisps and bottled juices will be all you need for a trip to the cays. Rooms available upstairs for BsF150, with capacity for eighty people. Daily 7am–9pm.

★ **Rancho Andino** C Mariño ☎ 0259 815 0897. The town's most chilled-out restaurant is positioned away from the *lancha* touts and serves up excellent *batidos* (BsF15). Manuel, the Colombian owner, stakes a claim to the town's best *pasta marinera* (BsF60) and makes a passable stab at a full English breakfast (BsF40). Rooms in town are available for BsF100. Daily 8am–9pm, closed Thurs in low season.

Restaurant La Esquina de Arturo C Plantél. "Art's Corner" is a good place to sit and watch the world go by, positioned as it is on the town's busiest intersection. Good *comida criolla* comes cheap and the set breakfasts (around BsF50) include juice. The *desayuno marinero* is particularly good, while there's a great-value *menu del día* (BsF50) for every day of the week, served from noon. Daily 7.30am–6pm.
Txalupa Av Principal, at C Zamora ☎ 0259 818 6425. The portions are big but pricey at this first-floor balcony restaurant overlooking the malecón. If you don't want to spend BsF100 on dinner, beers are BsF10 and the staff are happy to keep them coming. Daily noon–10pm.

DIRECTORY

Banks and exchange Bancoro, C Plantél, at C Calvario; Banco Industrial (and others) on C Zamora.
Internet Byte Quest, on the south side of Paseo Bolívar (daily 8am–8pm; BsF8/hr). Multiple computers, plus wi-fi, scanner, photocopier. Sells camera memory cards and recordable DVDs.
Pharmacy Several options on C Zamora, one next to Oasis Sport (daily 8am–9pm).
Phones Comunicación los Cayos, on the west side of C Zamora (daily 8am–8pm), offers calls, internet access, and sells mobile phone credit for all the major networks. There's also a Movistar call centre about 100m further inland (Mon–Sat 8am–noon & 3–7pm).
Post The nearest post office is in Tucacas.

CORO

CORO, Venezuela's prettiest colonial town, was named a national monument in 1950 and a World Heritage Site in 1993. A pleasant stopover between the coast and the mountains, Coro contains some of the country's best backpacker accommodation. The town is at its prettiest in the **casco histórico**, where a number of colonial mansions have opened their doors to the public as museums. The nearby **Parque Nacional Médanos de Coro** lies on the edge of town; a mini-desert of golden sand dunes and wild goats.

WHAT TO SEE AND DO

You only need wander the sleepy streets of central Coro to get a flavour of the town's Spanish imperial heritage, but for a closer look, there are museums, mansions and churches to be visited. If you're in town on a Tuesday, head over to the Museo de Arte de Coro at 6pm, when **Cine en la**

Calle hosts a weekly showing of classic movies in a makeshift street cinema.

Churches

The centre of the *casco histórico* is the Plaza Bolívar, on the east end of which stands Venezuela's oldest **Cathedral**, begun in 1583 and finished in 1634. Two blocks north on Plaza San Clemente, the **Iglesia San Clemente** was originally built in 1538 by the town's founder, Juan de Ampíes. Totally rebuilt in the eighteenth century, San Clemente is one of three churches in the country built in the shape of a cross. Beside it, a small monument contains the **Cruz de San Clemente**, the wooden cross used in the first Mass after the town was founded.

Colonial mansions

El Balcón de los Arcaya (Mon–Sat 9am–noon & 2.30–5.30pm, Sun 9am–noon; free) at the western edge of the Plaza San Clemente on Calle Zamora is a mansion once owned by the affluent Arcaya family; it houses impressive mastodon excavations and some less-than-scientific diagrams. Further down the road, the **Casa de las Ventanas de Hierro** (Tues–Sun 9am–5pm; free) is a colonial museum where the staff are kitted out in period dress. The work of local artists is displayed at the **Casa del Tesoro** (Tues–Sun 9am–5pm; free), another stately mansion next door. A block and a half to the northeast of Plaza Bolívar on Avenida Talavera, the **Museo de Arte de Coro** (Mon–Sat 9am–6pm, Sun 9am–1pm; free) has temporary exhibits featuring international names in a beautifully restored eighteenth-century townhouse.

Parque Nacional Médanos de Coro

A short taxi ride (BsF25) will take you to the entrance of the eighty-square-kilometre **Parque Nacional Médanos de Coro**, a mini-desert where you can stroll the sand dunes, spy on wild goats or go sandboarding with the staff of *Posada El Gallo* (see p.886). To get back to town try hitching a ride with any of the numerous visitors at the entrance, otherwise it's a 500m stroll to the main road where you can hail a taxi. Robberies have occurred here, so don't linger long after dark and be discreet with any valuables.

ARRIVAL AND DEPARTURE

It is possible to cross into Colombia from this region (see box, p.886).

By bus The bus terminal is 2km east of town on Av Los Médanos. Taxis to and from the *casco histórico* should cost BsF25. There's an exit tax of BsF2 to pay, with three booths dotted around the terminal. There's an ATM but no luggage storage.

Destinations Caracas (several daily; 9hr); Mérida (daily at 6pm; 10hr); Maracay (several daily; 7hr); Maracaibo (several daily; 3hr); San Cristóbal (2 daily; 12hr); Puerto La Cruz (daily at 6.30pm; 12hr). *Por puestos* run regularly from the terminal until around 5pm for closer destinations like Punto Fijo and Maracaibo.

INFORMATION AND TOURS

Tourist information The Corfaltur kiosk beside the old cross (Paseo Alameda; ☎0268 251 8033) has maps, English-speaking staff and very unreliable opening hours. There's an identical kiosk at the entrance to Parque Médanos de Coro, although opening hours are similarly lax. The website ⓦcoroweb.com is your best bet for reliable information, although the English pages didn't work at the time of going to press.

Tour operators Araguato Expeditions (☎0426 866 9328, ⓦaraguato.org), in *La Casa del Mono* (see p.886), does day-trips to the Paraguaná Peninsula, San Luís mountains (including the "Spanish trail", a jungle path once used by European explorers), Maracaibo's flea market and the eerie *catatumbo lightning* (see p.891). *Posada El Gallo* can take you sandboarding on the Parque Médanos de Coro dunes.

11

CORO

ACCOMMODATION
La Casa del Mono	1
Casa Tun Tun	3
Posada El Gallo	2

EATING & DRINKING
La Gran Costa Nova	3
El Guaro	5
Sabor Latino	4
Shangrila	1
El Tinajero	2

ACCOMMODATION

La Casa del Mono C Federación 16 ☎0268 251 1590, ✉info@araguato.org. A well-equipped and attractive posada run by Araguato Expeditions (see p.885). Stylishly decorated rooms (with shared or private bathrooms) come with mosquito nets, and there is a courtyard with hammocks, kitchen, public computer and wi-fi. **BsF150**

Casa Tun Tun C Zamora ☎0268 404 4260, ✉casatuntun @hotmail.com. A relaxed atmosphere generated by Parisian owner Damien and his wife Norka, *Tun Tun* has everything you could want from a posada: hammocks,

wi-fi, kitchen, barbecue, clean rooms with a/c (some with en suite) and a good selection of board games. The only room without a/c is a triple, costing BsF140, a particularly good deal for groups. **BsF200**

★ **Posada El Gallo** C Federación 26 ☎0268 252 9481, ✉posadaelgallo@gmail.com. This beautiful French-run colonial townhouse is a popular spot for backpackers (including non-guests) to hang out in. Beer is on the honour system and there is an abundance of hammocks to swing in. Two dorm rooms are useful for solo travellers, while the intimate doubles are fan cooled, some with

---

CROSSING INTO COLOMBIA

There are three main **border crossings** between Venezuela and Colombia. The northernmost, at Paraguachón, offers the best connections to coastal cities like Cartagena; Cúcuta has onward services to Bogotá. Before leaving Venezuela you must pay the BsF90 **exit tax** (in bolívares) and get your passport stamped by the nearest SAIME emigration office. Once you cross the border, immediately visit the nearest Colombian immigration office for an entry stamp and set your watch back a half-hour.

Relations between Venezuela and Colombia are volatile, and can deteriorate at short notice. It is wise to seek up-to-date advice on the current political situation, and on **security**, before using any of the three crossings.

PARAGUACHÓN (MARACAIBO–MAICAO)

Take a *por puesto* from the **Maracaibo** terminal to **Maicao**, Colombia (several daily until 4pm; 3hr). From here you can switch to a bus for Santa Marta (4hr), Cartagena (8hr) and other destinations. Expect numerous police checks on the way to the border and don't be surprised if they decide to search you. The Venezuelan and Colombian passport stamping points are 200m apart on the border itself. However, the point for purchasing the BsF90 *tasa de salida* is 2km before the border, so make sure you ask your driver to stop briefly so you can buy it. Set off in the morning to ensure that you arrive in Maicao with plenty of time to catch an onward bus.

CÚCUTA

Open 24 hours, this border is more popular with shoppers, so the lack of border formalities can make it trying for those leaving Venezuela. Take a bus to **San Cristóbal**, which is served from numerous destinations including Mérida and Caracas. From the San Cristóbal terminal take a bus or *por puesto* to **Cúcuta** in Colombia (1hr). On Mon–Sat 8am–6pm you can pay your exit tax and get your stamps at the border; outside these times you'll need to go to the SAIME office in **San Antonio del Táchira** (Carrera 9 between calles 6 and 7; ☎0276 771 4453; open 24hr), buy your exit tax at the print shop opposite. From Cúcuta buses run to major Colombian cities; Bucaramanga (3hr); Bogotá (12hr); Medellín (12hr) and Cali (18hr).

PUERTO CARREÑO/CASUARITO

These are two separate crossings, both accessible from Puerto Ayacucho (see p.897), although the difficulty of onward transport in Colombia makes this the worst option of the three. No exit tax or border fees are collected at this border. Go to the SAIME office on Avenida Aguerrevere in Puerto Ayacucho to get your Venezuelan exit stamp; Colombia entry stamps are obtained across the border in Puerto Carreño. From the Puerto Ayacucho bus terminal, catch a *por puesto* for El Burro (45min); from here you can take a *lancha* across the Orinoco to the Colombian city of Puerto Carreño (10min). Alternatively, take a five-minute ferry across the river from Puerto Ayacucho's port to the small village of Casuarito. From here there are two daily departures downriver for Puerto Carreño at 7am and 3pm, making this a less reliable option. The onward journey by road from Puerto Carreño to Bogotá is long and only feasible in the December–March dry season. Outside of these months the only option is to fly, with three weekly departures (Tues, Wed & Fri) for Bogotá (see p.495) with Satena (☯satena.com).

en suite. The friendly owners organize sandboarding (BsF140) and other trips throughout the area. Dorms BsF80, doubles BsF140

EATING AND DRINKING

There are a number of inexpensive restaurants in Coro, many doubling as bars in the evening, although opening hours are generally lax. Be sure to try *chivo* (goat), the regional speciality.

La Gran Costa Nova Av Manaure opposite *Hotel Intercaribe*. This *panadería* makes good coffee and bakes great bread, *pastelitos* and cakes. It's also a good spot to stock up on provisions for your posada's kitchen. If you're eating in, pay at the till first and give your receipt to the staff behind the counter. Daily 6am–9pm.

El Guaro C Ampiés, at Maparari ☎0268 989 0333. This bright-green eatery is a popular place five blocks south of the cathedral, taking pride in the authenticity of its local cuisine. You'll have to come on a Thurs to sample the *chivo*, while the chicken is particularly good the rest of the week. Daily 6am–3pm, although the menu is more limited on Sun.

★ **Sabor Latino** Paseo Alameda ☎0268 252 4139. Miniature houses and marginally amusing jokes scrawled across the walls (test your Spanish to see how many you understand) at this popular joint, which takes its *Latin Flavour* name from more than the food. Staff are friendly and the grub is cheap. The *chivo* (BsF35) comes a few different ways, while the juices (BsF7) are bigger and better than you'll get in the street. Mon–Fri, 6am–4pm, until 8pm Fri.

Shangrila Av Josefa Camejo, at C Toledo ☎0416 360 2832. Taiwanese Tony Lee runs this no-nonsense vegetarian joint, where you can have your plate filled with noodles, dumplings or plantain for BsF7 per serving. Also does ice-cold *frappés* for BsF10 if the air conditioning isn't sufficient respite from the heat outside. Mon–Sat 7am–3pm.

El Tinajero C Zamora next to *Casa Tun Tun* ☎0268 460 0135. The food doesn't resemble the ambitiously gourmet photos on the menu, but big servings of chicken, beef or fish (BsF40) washed down with cheap beers (BsF6) don't leave much room for complaint. Locals prop up the bar to take advantage of the latter and will be happy for you to join them after you've eaten. Mon–Sat 11am–11pm.

SHOPPING

Artesanía There are a few places selling *artesanía* in Coro, though none of it is very compelling. Local potters sell their wares in Plaza Falcón, and the Centro Artesanal next to Plaza San Clemente has a momentarily diverting array of paintings, dioramas and *dulce de leche* made from goat's milk. Officially, it's open daily 9am–6pm, though the vendors tend to operate on their own schedules.

Market There's a small food market on C Garcés at C Colón (daily until about 7pm), where you can pick up supplies for self-catering.

DIRECTORY

Banks and exchange Banco Venezuela on Av Talavera, Banco Mercantil on C Falcón.

Internet *Hotel Intercaribe* opposite La Gran Costa Nova on Av Manaure has a popular internet café next door, BsF5/hr. Daily 8am–8pm.

Laundry All the listed accommodation choices have laundry services. Otherwise, Lavatín on C Falcón (☎0268 251 671) has an English-speaking owner and will wash clothes for BsF30/load. Mon–Fri 8am–6pm, Sat until 2pm.

Pharmacy Farmacia Santa Catalina, C Federación, on Falcón, Mon–Fri 8am–3pm. There's another two blocks south of *La Gran Costa Nova* on Av Manaure.

Phones Movistar call centre at C Falcón between Plaza Falcón and Av Manaure, Mon–Sat 8am–6pm. Also Digitel, at Paseo Talavera.

Post Ipostel, Casa de las 100 Ventanas, C Ampiés. Mon–Fri 8am–4pm.

11

Mérida and the Andes

Occupying the northernmost limit of the Andes range, the mountainous state of **Mérida** is a region of lofty peaks and raw natural beauty. The region has long been Venezuela's most popular backpacker destination, and facilities for budget travellers are among the best in the country. The state capital, also called Mérida, has a sizeable student population, resulting in some of the country's most entertaining nightlife; an excellent way to blow off steam after any of the various adventure sports the region is known for. To the city's south and east, the **Parque Nacional Sierra Nevada**, dominated by the famed Pico Bolívar (5007m) and Pico Humboldt (4920m), offers some of the finest hiking opportunities in the region. To the north, the Carretera Transandina, or the Trans-Andean Highway, passes several charming mountain towns on its weaving way to Barinas, including **Apartaderos**, which has one of the world's highest observatories, the **Observatorio Astronómico Nacional**.

MÉRIDA

From the bottom of a deep valley, the city of **MÉRIDA** enjoys stunning views of the surrounding mountains without ever becoming uncomfortably cold. Based in Mérida, **La Universidad de los Andes** is one of the country's most prestigious universities and runs numerous international exchange programmes, adding undergraduates of all backgrounds to its already sizeable student population. Despite its cosmopolitan sensibilities, Mérida offers reasonable prices, safe streets and a block numbering system that makes the town easily navigable.

Owing to its natural endowment as well as the efforts of several excellent tour operators, Mérida's chief attraction is **adventure sports** (see box, p.890). However, if you've got some down time, or if you're allergic to adrenaline, the city offers a couple of sights, as well as some diverting **day-trips**.

WHAT TO SEE AND DO

The old town around Plaza Bolívar makes for a pleasant half-day's wandering. The town has a small old-fashioned zoo at its northern limit with some impressive species on show.

The Old Town

Walking the streets of the **old town** to admire its colonial houses, pretty parks and inordinate number of shoe shops will only take a few hours. Right on the Plaza Bolívar, the impressive **Catedral** was only completed in 1958, after over 150 years of stalled construction. Of the several decent museums in the area, the most interesting is the **Museo Arqueológico** (Tues–Sun 8–11.30am & 2–5.30pm;

EATING, DRINKING & NIGHTLIFE

La Astilla	1	El Hoyo de Queque	4
El Ático del Cine	14	Mercado Principal	6
Birosca Carioca	5	La Nota	13
La Botana	15	Poco Loco	2
Buona Pizza	11	Restaurant La Montaña	8
La Cucaracha	7	Taperio Café	9
Delicias Mexicanas	12	El Vegetariano	3
Heladería Coromoto	10		

MÉRIDA

ACCOMMODATION

Posada Alemania	1
Posada Casa Sol	2
Posada Guamanchi	7
Posada Jama Chía	8
Posada La Montaña	5
Posada Suiza	3
Posada Yagrumo	6
Sueño Dorado	4

BsF1) on Avenida 3 at the Plaza Bolívar. It presents pre-Columbian artefacts from the region, augmented by thorough historical descriptions.

Parque Zoologico

The zoo (open 8am–5pm, daily in the high season, closed Mon in low season; BsF10) at the northeastern limit of the town has a good selection of native and foreign animals including a tiger, a lion, a condor recently brought down from the refuge above Apartaderos (see p.893), and a spectacled bear, which is pictured on the BsF50 note. To get here take a bus (BsF2.50) bound for Los Chorros from the intersection of Avenida 5 and Calle 23.

The teleférico

Being refurbished at the time of research, Mérida's greatest attraction, the world's highest and longest **teleférico** (cable car), is scheduled to open by the end of 2013. The base station is situated at Parque Las Heroínas (☎0274 252 5080), from where the car climbs 3000m vertically and 12.5km horizontally across three intermediate stations to the **Pico Espejo** (4865m). It is a good idea to pause for acclimatization at the penultimate, Loma Redonda (4045m), as the rapid changes in height can cause mild altitude sickness.

From Loma Redonda, you can also follow various hiking trails (4hr) to the small Andean town of **Los Nevados** 13km away, which contains several posadas and places to eat. You can do this walk on your own, but should notify Inparques beforehand, whose main office is at the base station.

ARRIVAL AND INFORMATION

By plane Mérida's Alberto Carnevalli airport (☎0274 263 4352), which is 3km southwest of the town, has been closed for some time with no indication of when it will reopen. The closest domestic flights land at El Vigia, which is an hour away by bus (BsF15) or taxi (BsF200).

Destinations Caracas (4 weekly); Porlamar (3 weekly); Bogotá (3 weekly) and others. Conviasa (☎conviasa.aero) is the main operator to El Vigia.

By bus The bus terminal is 2km outside the city centre. Take a bus (BsF2.50) into town from the stop on the opposite side of the main road to the terminal. Buses back to the terminal pass via Av 2 beside the bridge.

Destinations Caracas (several daily; 13hr); San Cristóbal (every half hour; 5hr); Maracaibo (several nightly; to go by day take a *por puesto*; 6hr); Maracay (several daily; 8hr); Coro (1 night bus; 10hr); Puerto La Cruz (daily at 10am; 18hr) with Expresos Mérida (☎0414 737 1075). For Ciudad Bolívar you have to change at Puerto La Cruz or Barinas, although onward connections are far more reliable from the former.

Tourist information Cormetur (☎0274 263 4701) has offices in several locations around town, including the bus terminal, the airport and the Mercado Principal on Av Las Américas. The most reliable booth is the one in the bus terminal, which is open daily 7am–7pm. You'll find the town's main central tourist office at the base station of the teleférico, as well as the Inparques office.

ACCOMMODATION

Mérida has a good selection of budget hostels and posadas. Most of the cheapest options are conveniently found near Parque Las Heroínas, a sort of backpacker ghetto where nearly all the tour agencies have their offices. Mid-range options can be up to forty percent cheaper during the Nov–June low season, although the posadas tend to remain the same price year-round. Unlike the rest of the country, hot water is taken as given in Mérida. To camp in the surrounding national parks, contact the Inparques office at the *teleférico* (see opposite).

Posada Alemania Av 2 between calles 17 & 18 ☎0274 252 4067. A hangout at the back with communal kitchen, hammocks and chunky furniture gives this otherwise basic posada a friendly feel. Spacious dorm beds go for BsF100, there's wi-fi, a computer for those who didn't bring their own technology, and the friendly owners cook up big breakfasts from BsF38. **BsF200**

★ **Posada Guamanchi** C 24 between Av 8 & Parque las Heroínas ☎0274 252 2080, ☎guamanchi.com. This three-floor building has a nice location beside Parque las Heroínas. The wi-fi reaches to the top-floor terrace, which contains some of the hammocks that are slung throughout. Probably the only place in the country you can snag a

11

★ TREAT YOURSELF

Posada Casa Sol Av 4 between calles 15 & 16 ☎0274 252 4164, ☎posadacasasol .com. Mérida's best attempt at the boutique hotel, this haven of serenity has an excellent restaurant, balconies suited to Shakespearean soliloquy and an interesting water feature full of carp. Rooms are elegant, the wi-fi reaches throughout, beds are super-soft and showers are excellent; the perfect spot to reward yourself after an arduous trek or bus journey. Breakfast included. **BsF480**

11

ADVENTURE SPORTS AND TOURS

Mérida's surrounds provide the perfect conditions for an astounding range of **adventure sports**. There's an equally amazing array of tour companies in town, so it's a good idea not to jump at the first tour offered (usually by your accommodation). Companies compete particularly hard for your business outside of the July–September high season, and the more you shop around, the more likely you are to find an itinerary, group or price that suits you better.

Tour prices generally decrease as more customers register, so ask your company about joining an existing group. Many trips require a minimum number of customers, so it's a good move to check availability before you arrive in town, easily done through the companies' websites. Paying in cash is the most cost-efficient option, but bank transfers can be expertly arranged for better rates than you would pay on a credit card. Except on one-day trips, all meals and accommodation are included in tour prices.

Due to Venezuela's volatile economy and fierce competition among companies, **prices** listed here are approximate. For the latest rates, contact the tour operators directly. Most operators offer all of the following activities, though some claim individual specialities.

CANYONING

An increasingly popular adrenaline sport involving abseiling, scrambling and climbing around and under waterfalls. Full-day rates are BsF580 per person, typically with a two-person minimum.

CLIMBING AND TREKKING

There are numerous less challenging treks than the popular Pico Humboldt (see p.894) and Pico Bolívar (see p.894) routes. These include Pico Pan de Azúcar (BsF600 per day) or Los Nevados (BsF600 per day); both routes take three to four days to complete.

It is possible for experienced hikers to trek independently, although they should notify Inparques at the base station of the teleférico beforehand.

MOUNTAIN BIKING

Many companies rent out good bikes for BsF150 per day, and will happily indicate where to head for the best routes. If you want to go guided, day tours cost from BsF400–600 per person depending on whether you choose to use a jeep to access the more remote trails. Some companies also offer horseriding for similar rates.

PARAGLIDING

The slopes above Mérida are the jumping-off point for a thrilling thirty-minute descent by paraglider. Tandem rates are around BsF500 per person. Be sure to bring a jacket and

---

double bed in a dormitory. Also has a posada in Los Nevados (see p.889). Dorms BsF100, doubles BsF200

Posada Jama Chia C 24 across from the *teleférico* base ☎ 0274 252 5767. Look for the gold-painted metalwork on this unmarked posada overlooking the *teleférico* and run by affable owner Benedicta. Communal bathrooms, a light-filled seating area and cheaper rates for those who will be in town longer (BsF1500/month is negotiable). Posadas *Paty* and *Mara* in the same block are similarly decent and cheap fall-back options. Dorms BsF80, doubles BsF150

Posada La Montaña C 24 No 6–47 ☎ 0274 252 5977, ⓦ posadalamontana.com. *La Montaña* looks rather like a posada that set up shop in a botanical garden; bursting with greenery, its upper-balcony rooms have stunning views of the even lusher scenery without. Rates drop significantly in the low season and there's a very nice restaurant on the ground floor. BsF300

Posada Suiza Av 3 between calles 17 & 18 ☎ 0274 252 4961, ⓦ colibri-tours.com. Professional and friendly staff run the Colibrí tours company from the large reception, while a courtyard at the back is ringed by dorms and pleasant rooms, all with colourful tartan blankets and en suite. There's wi-fi and it's a short walk back from the bars. Dorms BsF80, doubles BsF260

Posada Yagrumo C 24, at Av 8, next door to *Posada Guamanchi*. ☎ 0274 252 9539, ⓦ posadayagrumo.com. The cheapest dorm in town is found in sterile settings where you'll also find en-suite doubles without natural light. Cable TVs, communal kitchen, wi-fi, laundry service and a few internet booths for BsF5/hr which stay open until 11pm. Dorms BsF60, doubles BsF200

Sueño Dorado Av 6 between calles 19 & 20 ☎ 0274 251 1192, ⓦ hotelsuenodorado.com.ve. A smart hotel with steel banisters and plate glass cleverly designed into more rustic architecture. Rooms upstairs have great views of the

don't eat before going if you're prone to motion sickness. Some agencies also offer paragliding courses.

RAFTING

Rivers in Mérida and Barinas states have Class III to V rapids. Rafting season is from June to November, it's possible in December but companies don't generally take advance bookings due to unpredictable water levels. Two-day trips cost around BsF1300 per person for five people; four-day trips cost double. Some agencies have private camps in Barinas where you'll spend the night.

LOS LLANOS AND CATATUMBO

Mérida is the main staging point for guided trips to Los Llanos (see p.894), the wildlife-filled wetlands east of the Andes. Prices for a four-day trip, which often include some rafting, are around BsF2000. The natural phenomenon of the Catatumbo lightning occurs on average three out of every four nights of the year. Most companies only go for one night and prices are around BsF1400. If you want to double your chances of seeing it, Alan Highton (see below) goes for two nights.

11

TOUR OPERATORS

Colibrí In Posada Suiza ☎ 0274 252 4961, ⓦ colibri-tours.com. This expert outfit is one of Mérida's oldest and can sort out every activity including tailor-made trips. Ask about the owner's signature Jají day-trip and he'll draw you a map.

Fanny Tours C 24 between Av 8 & Parque Las Heroínas ☎ 0274 252 2952, ⓦ fanny-tours.com. No sniggering about the name! Specializes in mountaineering; also offers trips to Los Llanos. Multiple languages spoken, including English.

Gravity Tours C 24 between avenidas 7 & 8 ☎ 0274 251 1279, ⓦ gravity-tours.com.ve. Offers a popular two-day combo of mountain biking and rafting for BsF1300, as well as trips throughout the country. Very helpful, English-speaking staff.

Guamanchi Expeditions C 24 between Av 8 & Parque Las Heroínas ☎ 0274 252 2080, ⓦ guamanchi.com. With more than 20 years of experience in the Andes and Los Llanos, this company supplies quality equipment for its specialities of climbing and trekking. Also offers day-trips to Laguna Negra (see p.894) and birdwatching tours.

Alan Highton ☎ 0414 756 2575. Local community worker who runs the best available tour to the Catatumbo lightning, a three-day/two-night expedition for BsF1400. Alan's also a butterfly expert and will share his passion with you: he's even had a species named after him.

Tony Martin ☎ 0416 973 1682. A Los Llanos native and jack-of-all-trades, Tony is an experienced, enthusiastic and knowledgeable English-speaking guide who runs four-day trips to his home region.

---

mountains as well as safes and cable TV. The restaurant downstairs is a good place for a coffee break while wandering the hilly backstreets. Breakfast included. <u>BsF320</u>

EATING

The cuisine from Mérida and the Andes is famous throughout the country. Some specialities include *arepas de trigo* (made from wheat flour), *queso ahumado* (smoked cheese) and *trucha* (trout). *Vino de mora* is wine made from blackberries.

★ **La Astilla** C 14 between avenidas 2 & 3 ☎ 0274 251 0832. They eventually decided on every colour when they chose the paint scheme for this place. Positioned on the leafy Plaza Milla, much of the vegetation has made its way inside. Friendly staff, tiled tabletops, local specialities like trout (BsF85), pizza (BsF36) and the best *batidos* you'll find in town. Across the way, *El Andino* is another good option in less colourful settings. Daily 8am–10pm.

Buona Pizza Av 7 between calles 24 & 25 ☎ 0274 251 2420. Chunks of gooey mozzarella on crunchy-crusted pizzas follow *Nonna's* original recipe. This long-standing restaurant dresses itself up for the holidays and offers some quirky toppings; who knew guava was good on a pizza? There's an "Express" version across the street for takeaway. Daily noon–11pm.

Delicias Mexicanas Ground floor of *Hotel Altamira*, C 25 between avenidas 7 and 8 ☎ 0274 252 8677 (for hotel reception). Pricey, but if you need your taco fix this stylish eatery is the place to come. Does the Tex-Mex classics alongside a few interesting attempts at Andean-fusion, mainly involving trout. Daily noon–10pm.

★ **Heladería Coromoto** Av 3 between calles 28 & 29. This Mérida institution holds the Guinness World Record for the most ice-cream flavours (860!), although with a menu including sardines-in-brandy, *pabellón criollo* and beer, the importance of the record clearly got a bit out of hand. A quintessential Mérida experience, only around 60 flavours are available daily. BsF10 for 2 scoops. Tues–Sun 2.15–9pm.

Mercado Principal Av Las Américas, at Viaducto Miranda. If shopping for blackberry wine and magic herbs works up your appetite, the fun food court on the second floor has competitive outlets serving up good set menus for around BsF35. The area becomes rammed at lunchtime. Mon–Sat 7am–5pm, Sun until 1.30pm.

La Nota Av 8 by Parque las Heroínas, beside the bus terminal and several other locations about town. Popular local chain which *Mérideños* promote as "how McDonald's should be" (although the excellent street-level burger stands do just as good a job). Does meal combos for BsF55 alongside subs, teriyaki and steaks. Daily until 11pm.

★ **Restaurant La Montaña** In *Posada La Montaña* (see p.890). Roses on the tables, an open-fronted kitchen and an excellent *menú del día* for BsF45 at lunch make this modest trattoria-style place a fine-dining choice for relative peanuts. The menu changes daily, scrawled on the blackboard out front. Daily 8am–9.30pm.

Taperio Café Av 3, at C 29. An atmospheric street-corner joint with iron grille walls and a café-culture crowd. A very chilled spot for a beer in the evening; there's live music on the weekends and tasty food, while the *merengadas* are big and bad in a good way. Mon–Sat 11am–10pm.

El Vegetariano Av 4, at C 18. This small, split-level place features a far more interesting menu than usual for an all-veggie venue. You can also buy artisan honey and other high-quality consumables from behind the counter. Menu options include aubergine carpaccio with pumpkin and pesto (BsF55) and an appealing list of salads. Mon–Sat 7.30am–8.45pm.

DRINKING AND NIGHTLIFE

In large part because of the immense student population, Mérida enjoys an active nightlife, particularly between Wednesday and Saturday. Expect to pay a cover charge of around BsF20 in the evenings, although this often includes a drink.

El Atico del Cine C 25 next to *La Nota*. Beer comes in coffee mugs and the cocktails are named after classic movies (see if you can translate them all) in this trendy little café-bar. Plays a wide range of music and is a popular kickstarter for students on a night out. Does a good late-lunch menu for BsF35. Mon–Sat 4–11pm.

Birosca Carioca Av 2 at C 24. Pounding samba and students define this friendly, ever-popular club, as do the red buckets of "La Bomba", a rum and beer concoction for sharing. Open until the crowd goes home – it's situated on a shady street so be careful outside when leaving. Daily from 5pm.

La Botana Parque las Heroínas, beside the *Mercado Artesanal*. A Bob Marley-themed bar popular for its pizza,

which they keep producing even when it's rammed. A good bar to spend the evening at if you can secure one of the few tables. Tues–Sun 6.30pm–12.30am.

La Cucaracha In Centro Comercial Las Tapias on Av Urdaneta. One of Mérida's oldest nightspots, this large but always crowded disco has two floors, one with techno and the other with salsa and *merengue*. The chain caters to various budgets and clienteles around town. Daily until late.

★ **El Hoyo de Queque** Av 4, at C 19. You can't miss Mérida's most popular student bar a few blocks up from the Plaza Bolívar; for starters it's painted bright purple. DJs pack the place from 8pm, while the draught beer and a *menú ejecutivo* for BsF35 make it a good spot for an easy afternoon. If you're peckish after hours, numerous burger stands accumulate outside. Mon–Sat noon–1am.

Poco Loco Av 3 between calles 18 & 19. Although it's a little odd for a bar in Andean Venezuela to be staunchly FC Barcelona, this is Mérida's best alternative venue, with cheap draught beer and a friendly crowd. Dare you to show up in a Real Madrid shirt. Mon–Sat 1pm–1am, DJs from 8pm.

SHOPPING

Mérida is a decent place to buy souvenirs or stock up on travel essentials.

Antiques You can find a number of antique shops along the road to Apartaderos (see opposite), which specialize particularly in wooden furniture, preserves and fruit liquers.

Food and drink For food to cook at your posada, there's a nameless *frutería* on the corner of Av 7 and C 24, while Panadería Roma (Mon–Sat 7am–8pm, Sun until noon) next to Posada Yagrumo is a useful spot for supplies as well as breakfast, especially since they do Western-sized coffees.

Markets The most renowned destination among bargain-hunters is the green-and-yellow-striped Mercado Principal. This three-storey, tourist-oriented market (Mon–Sat 7am–6pm, Sun until 1.30pm) on the other side of the river sells quality Andean produce and there's a good food court (see above) on the second floor for lunch. More *artesanía* can be found at the much smaller Mercado Artesanal in front of Parque Las Heroínas, where a permanent installation of stalls sells ceramics, jewellery, blackberry wine, leather goods and woodcarvings.

DIRECTORY

Banks and exchange Banco de Venezuela, at Av 4 between calles 23 & 24; various ATMs dotted around town and in the bus terminal. Various agencies and hotels around town offer international bank transfers for vastly superior rates.

Camping equipment Cumbre Azul, at Av 8 between calles 23 & 24, is a good place to rent or buy camping and hiking equipment.

Internet and phones Several useful *centros de conexiones* offer internet, phone services and photocopying. There's a CANTV centre (Mon–Sat 7am–5pm) beside *Posada Guamanchi*. There's another *centro* in the bus terminal, and a handful more internet cafés around the *teleférico* base. Internet costs around BsF5/hr.

Language study Iowa Institute on Av 4, at C 18 ☎0274 252 6404, ⌨iowainstitute.com.

Laundry An unnamed laundry on Av 6, between C 19 & *Hotel Sueño Dorado*, does a same-day service for BsF24/load (Mon–Sat 8am–noon & 2–6pm). Most accommodation will wash guests' clothes for around BsF50.

Medical care A reputable clinic with some English-speaking doctors is Clínica Mérida (☎0274 263 0652) on Av Urdaneta next to the airport.

Pharmacy Farmacía Central (daily) on Av 3, at Plaza Bolívar; Farmacía 6ta Avenida (Mon–Sat) on Av 6, at C 22. Both 8am–7pm.

Police The main station is on Av Urdaneta, adjacent to Parque Gloria Patrias (☎0274 263 6722).

Post office Ipostel, C 21 between avenidas 4 & 5, and in the bus terminal. Mon–Fri 8am–4.30pm.

APARTADEROS AND AROUND

Most of the quaint Andean towns northeast of Mérida are set alongside the Carretera Transandina (Trans-Andean Highway), with beautiful views of the Sierra Nevada range to the south and the Sierra Culata range to the north. Two hours up the valley, the mountain town of **APARTADEROS** makes a diverting day-trip from Mérida, although you should head out early as it tends to rain in the afternoons. The strip of houses here looks a lot like a town in the Scottish Highlands; there are fabulous views of the valley below when it's clear, although, like bonny Scotland, the town is utterly dismal when the rain comes down.

The nearby **Refugio del Cóndor**, best accessed by hailing a passing cab from the main road (daily 7am–5pm; no phone – contact Inparques in Mérida for more details), is home to the Andean condor conservation and research project. Only one condor remains in the dome-cage at the top of the mountain road. It's one of only fifteen remaining in Venezuela, all of which live in captivity around the country. If you want to see a condor without making the trip, Mérida Zoo (see

p.889) recently inherited a condor from this project, although it's not as large as the fully-fledged adult at the refuge. Visitors are shown an instructional five-minute video in English or Spanish.

Two kilometres away, the **Observatorio Astronómico Nacional** (☎0274 245 0106, ⌨cida.gob.ve) opens its doors to the public annually during August and September (daily 5–11pm) to showcase its work in one of the world's highest observatories.

The Carretera Transandina highway eventually crosses the highest driveable summit in Venezuela, at Pico El Águila, and begins the spectacular descent to Barinas and Los Llanos (see p.894).

ARRIVAL AND DEPARTURE

By bus From the Mérida terminal buses for Apartaderos (every 15min; 2hr) leave from the designated platform until 6pm. You don't need to pay a *tasa de salida* to ride this route. To return to Mérida, flag down one of the buses which pass along the route every 20min or so until 6.30pm.

By taxi From Apartaderos taxis will take tourists to the condor refuge or the observatory for BsF30. Getting back is as simple as walking the kilometre (or paying anyone with a car to drive you) back to the bus route (see above).

PARQUE NACIONAL SIERRA NEVADA

Looming above Mérida to the south and east, the Sierra Nevada runs northeast along the Carretera Transandina and through the 2760-square-kilometre **PARQUE NACIONAL SIERRA NEVADA**. There is great diversity in flora and fauna here, but the park's most famous inhabitant, the threatened spectacled bear, is a shy creature that you'll be lucky to see, although Mérida's zoo (see p.889) has one if you're interested. The park features the country's highest mountains, which reach over 5000m, as well as its best **adventure activities**. You can easily explore the lower reaches on your own, but guides (see box, p.890) are recommended for the two higher peaks unless you are an experienced mountaineer.

Just inside the northern entrance to the park, a few kilometres along the highway from Apartaderos, is **Laguna Mucubají**. Camping is allowed here; you will need

11

permission from the Inparques office near the entrance. A good hiking trail connects Laguna Mucubají with **Laguna Negra**, a trout-filled lake with dark water. The beautiful hike takes two hours, and you can continue another one hour thirty minutes to the pretty **Laguna Los Patos**. In the wet season, it's best to leave early to avoid rain and fog that could limit visibility considerably. Just outside the park entrance is Refugio Mucubají, a restaurant that sells good picnic supplies as well as excellent *arepas*, soups and coffees.

Pico Bolívar

At 5007m, **Pico Bolívar** is the country's highest and most hiked peak. There are multiple routes up, varying in difficulty and length of ascent. When the *teleférico* is operational, many walkers get off at the last station, Pico Espejo, and make the five-hour ascent along the Ruta Weiss. This is not very technical in the dry season (Dec–May). The Ruta Sur Este and North Flank are two more challenging routes, which involve ice-climbing and require ice axes and crampons. Views from the top are spectacular – on a clear day, you can see the city of Mérida, the Colombian Andes and the vast expanse of Los Llanos.

Pico Humboldt

Another renowned peak, **Pico Humboldt**, can be combined with a climb of Pico Bolívar or tackled on its own. Starting at the entrance of Parque Nacional La Mucuy, about 10km to the northeast of Mérida, the first day's ascent is 1000m; after the six-hour, 9km walk, most people camp around the picturesque Laguna Coromoto. The ascent on the second day is shorter but steeper as you get into the rocky terrain above the tree line. The final day's ascent to the peak and return to the campsite usually takes at least eight hours, depending upon your ice-climbing ability. The fourth day is for the descent back to La Mucuy.

ARRIVAL AND DEPARTURE

By bus The park entrance is on the Apartaderos route from Mérida; simply stay on the bus for a few kilometres after Apartaderos. To get back to Mérida or onwards to Barinas, flag down a passing bus in either direction, which pass every 20min or so until 6.30pm.

INFORMATION AND TOURS

Tourist information As well as the Inparques offices in Mérida at the base station of the *teleférico* (see p.889), there is one near the park entrance that can issue camping permits and dispense advice (Spanish only).

Tour operators Companies (see box, p.890) organize groups on a one guide to two clients ratio; cost is BsF600 per day and all equipment is included. Routes (Weiss, Sur Este, North Flank) can be selected depending on experience and generally take six days, a time which can be cut to four with higher levels of expertise.

Los Llanos

Taking up nearly a third of the country, the immense plains and wetlands of **Los Llanos** are one of the continent's premier wildlife-viewing areas. Some of the most abundant species are alligators, anacondas and capybaras, the world's largest rodent. Other common species are river dolphins, jaguars, pumas, howler and capuchin monkeys and anteaters. However, the livelihood of the region's human inhabitants, the llaneros, is most closely linked with domesticated animals. Los Llaneros are extremely skilled horsemen and work in secluded groups on **hatos** (see box, p.896), enormous ranches with cattle often numbering in the tens of thousands.

Los Llanos has two very pronounced **seasons**. During the wet season, from May to November, much of the land becomes flooded and extremely verdant. In the dry season the land becomes parched and dusty, and vegetation changes colour to match the dry surroundings. The best wildlife viewing comes when water is scarce, when animals congregate at the few watering holes.

Unless you have a wad of cash to spend on a stay at one of the *hatos*, you'll most likely visit Los Llanos as part of a **multi-day tour** from Mérida (see p.891). If you're determined to see the region on your own, or are passing through Los Llanos to another part of the country, the backwater city of San Fernando de Apure is the region's hub, though there's no reason to visit the town itself.

SAN FERNANDO DE APURE

Founded as a missionary outpost in the seventeenth century, **SAN FERNANDO DE APURE** is now an important trading centre. There's virtually nothing here to detain tourists, but some pass through on the way to the southern *hatos* or to Amazonas.

WHAT TO SEE AND DO

Most of the action is concentrated along the wide Paseo Libertador, while three blocks to the west, the mercifully calm Plaza Bolívar is towered over by the **Catedral de San Fernando**. Designed by a German architect, the church looks more like an Art Deco aircraft hangar than a place of worship, although the acoustics are excellent within. Another marginally diverting sight is the bizarre fountain at the roundabout of Paseo Libertador and Miranda, featuring caimans that spout water when the city occasionally turns it on.

ARRIVAL AND DEPARTURE

By bus The terminal is three blocks northwest of the hotels listed below, although a taxi is a good idea after dark. Buses for Puerto Ayacucho and Valencia depart when full; simply grab a seat and wait. There are no direct buses to Ciudad Bolívar; you must first go to Puerto Ayacucho, then change buses.

Destinations Barinas (several daily; 8hr); Caracas (several daily; 8hr); Maracay (hourly; 7hr); Puerto La Cruz (daily at 4.30pm; 12hr); San Cristóbal (daily at 5pm; 13hr); Valencia (hourly; 7hr); Puerto Ayacucho (hourly; 7hr).

ACCOMMODATION

Budget accommodation in San Fernando de Apure is shoddy and overpriced, but sufficient for a short stopover.

La Fuente Av Miranda, west of Paseo Libertador ☎ 0247 342 3233. With clean rooms (all en suite) which supply nothing more than the basics, *La Fuente* is a passable option in a useful location close to the bus terminal. Open the reception booth door rather than speaking through the mouse-hole in its black glass. Rooms all have a/c, while the illegible numbers scrawled on the doors may make finding yours tricky. **BsF180**

La Torraca Paseo Libertador 8 ☎ 0247 342 2777. Check out what looks like the world's first electronic computer in the reception and the lift with carpeted walls. Rooms are basic, although all come with a/c, TV and en suite. The tour agency in reception has long been closed. **BsF190**

EATING

Eating here is a slightly more promising endeavour, with a number of restaurants serving famed llanero beef.

Panadería San Bernardo Av Carabobo, 3 blocks west of the Monumeto Páez ☎ 0424 314 3602. Very popular place specializing in quantity rather than quality, with *arepas*, *empanadas*, beans and other predictably Venezuelan fare purchased by the kilo (BsF80) from the cheerful staff. The coffee is particularly good (BsF4). Daily 7am–10pm.

Restaurant Independencia C Independencia, at Av Carabobo ☎ 0247 341 3446. Everything is carved out of wood at the town's most popular steak spot, including, it seems, the no-nonsense burly kitchen staff. Serving the best *churrasco* (BsF60) in town, this is the place to sample the excellent llanero beef, which comes straight from the ranches. Also does a good *carne guisada* (BsF35). Daily 7am–3pm.

Rueda Caiman Av Miranda, opposite *Hotel La Fuente*. It's not what the doctor would order, but it's exactly what you'll want after the long bus ride in. This popular street vendor

11

LOS LLANEROS

Many comparisons have been drawn between the **llaneros** and the cowboys of the American West. Known for being tough and independent, both are portrayed as embodying the spirit of their countries. Other similarities include their legendary penchants for drinking, gambling and singing sad ballads.

The mixed-blood llaneros captured the nation's imagination during the **war of Independence** as word of their ferocity spread. Their role in the struggle was integral, and their switch of allegiance in the middle of the war was one of the principal reasons for Bolívar's victory.

The llaneros preserve a strong culture; living and working in secluded groups on ranches for much of the year, they hold various competitions to showcase their fierce machismo. One of the most popular is **coleo**. Riding horseback, competitors race to grab a running bull or calf by the tail and use it to make it stumble; the one who takes the animal down wins. Another popular pastime is **contrapunteo**, during which two llaneros compete by rapping improvised insults at one other to the beat of *música llanera*, a regional music distinctive for its employment of harps, ukelele-like guitars and persistent wailing.

HATOS AND MÓDULOS

Many of the vast cattle ranches of Los Llanos, called **hatos**, double as incredible wildlife sanctuaries and rustic resorts. They offer activities such as truck rides, canoe trips and hikes on their property, and trained guides usually speak good English. High-season rates are around BsF600 per person with all meals and tours included; reservations are almost always required. Call for details on prices and transport to the ranches. The country's three largest *hatos* (El Cedral, Frío and Piñero) are all state-owned, and two are open for tourism.

A cheaper alternative is to stay in **módulos**, smaller ranches with much more basic accommodation, also home to abundant wildlife. Both options listed below offer various activities including boat tours along the Río Guaritico, night safaris, piranha fishing and horseriding. To get to both *módulos*, catch a bus from San Fernando de Apure to the little town of Mantecai (4hr) where the *módulo* owners will collect you. Make sure you call in advance to organize pick-up, and take a mosquito net with you in the wet season. Prices include food.

HATOS

Hato El Cedral ☎0212 718 8995, ⊛elcedral.com. Home to abundant wildlife, this sprawling ranch has more than 340 bird species and the country's highest concentration of capybaras. Three hours from both San Fernando de Apure and Barinas. Room only BsF400.

Hato El Piñero ☎0243 242 0966 or ☎0212 991 8935. Stylish posada with ten rooms, all with a/c, offering some excellent wildlife tours as well as conservation projects in the area. Two nights with full board and all tour activities BsF1350.

MÓDULOS

Rancho Grande Vecindario El Palmar, Mantecal ☎0416 873 1192. Traditional-style cabins provide temporary lodging by the river; tours are in Spanish. Guamanchi Expeditions (see p.891) in Mérida come here for their Los Llanos tours. 3-day/2-night tours BsF2000.

Yopito Vía Los Módulos, Carretera Quintero, Mantecal ☎0416 573 8644, 0426 747 1745 or 0240 808 0284. Across the river from Colombia, El Yopito has hammocks and beds in twelve-person cabañas. There's also a pool. 3-day/2-night tours BsF1800.

serves up enormous "pimp-my-snack"-style *rueda* burgers (BsF100) and *caiman* hotdogs (BsF90) for sharing. Take a seat beside the preparation area and gawp. Daily 4pm–2am.

DIRECTORY

Banks and exchange Banco Coroní, by the fountain. There are two Banco Mercantil ATMs in the bus terminal.

Internet Full Internet, first floor, Paseo Libertador, by the pharmacy. Mon–Sat 8am–6pm (BsF4/hr).

Pharmacy FarmaLlano, Paseo Libertador, two blocks south of *Hotel La Torraca*.

Phones Movistar, Paseo Libertador, by the pharmacy.

Police Paseo Libertador, behind the Monumento Páez. Daily 8am–8pm.

Post Ipostel, C 24 de Julio, at C Bolívar.

Guayana

Covering the southern and southeastern half of Venezuela, **Guayana** (not to be confused with the country Guyana) is comprised of three of Venezuela's largest states – Amazonas, Bolívar and Delta Amacuro. The region is extremely important economically, containing a tremendous wealth of natural resources such as gold, iron ore, bauxite and diamonds. It also supplies hydroelectricity for the entire country and even exports it to Venezuela's neighbours. Despite the immensity of Guayana, there are only two real cities, **Puerto Ordáz** and **Ciudad Bolívar**, which are vastly outnumbered by indigenous communities belonging to the Yanomami, Pemón, Warao and Piaroa, all of whom have retained many of their customs.

The region is estimated to have been above sea level for three billion years; the resulting landscape is the area's biggest tourist draw, although the immensity of the landscape means the individual sights are spread far apart. Attractions include the **tropical rainforests** of the Amazon, the mighty **Orinoco Delta**, the breathtaking **Angel Falls** and the magnificent *tepuis*, or flat-topped mountains. *Tepuis* means "Houses of the Gods" in the indigenous Pemón language, and of these, **Mount Roraima** was the inspiration for Sir Arthur Conan Doyle's *The Lost World*.

PUERTO AYACUCHO

A sleepy town that's home to half the inhabitants of Amazonas, **PUERTO AYACUCHO** is the state's only major municipality, founded in 1924 as a port for shipping timber downriver. Across the Orinoco from Colombia, it is the access point for the most southerly of the three Colombian border crossings (see box, p.886), although the difficulty of onward transport makes it the least convenient. Puerto Ayacucho is also the principal entry point for the Amazon region.

WHAT TO SEE AND DO

Like many other Venezuelan municipalities, Puerto Ayacucho itself has almost no intrinsic appeal, but there are several nearby attractions, including, of course, the jungle. In town, the **Museo Etnológico de Amazonas** (Tues–Fri 8.30am–noon & 2.30–5.45pm, Sat until noon; BsF4), on Avenida Río Negro, showcases the culture and history of the region's indigenous tribes. In front of the museum is **Plaza de los Indios**, a market selling local handicrafts including *catara*, a delicious hot sauce made from leafcutter ants; like peanut butter, it comes either crunchy or smooth.

One block east of the plaza on Avenida Amazonas is the **Centro Cultural Amazonas** (Mon–Sat 8am–6pm; free), where the art gallery has an indigenous-themed permanent exhibit. Styles range from classical to quasi-pornographic absurdism. Ask the friendly staff for what's on at the amphitheatre next door.

The town's most popular attraction lies 30km away at the **Parque Tobogán de la Selva**, where a natural waterslide has been dammed at the bottom to create a rustic infinity pool. A return trip in a taxi to the park costs about BsF200 – make sure you arrange for pick-up.

11

PUERTO AYACUCHO

▲ Border at Casuarito (1km)

ACCOMMODATION
Gran Hotel Amazonas	2
Posada Manapiare	4
Residencia Internacional	3
Residencias Michelangelli de Pozo	1

Mercado Municipal

Laundry

Pharmacy

Centro Cultural Amazonas

Museo Etnológico de Amazonas

SAIME Office

Coyote Expediciones

PLAZA DE LOS INDIOS

Banesco

Pharmacy

Bank

Bank

El Mercadito

Banco de Venezuela

Cerro Perico

Río Orinoco

N

Bank ▶ (1km), ⓑ Hospital (2km), Bus Terminal (4km) & Eco-Destinos

EATING & DRINKING
Café Rey David	5
El Guariqueño	3
El Mercadito	4
Panadería Amazonas	2
Royal Pool	1

0 ————— 200
metres

▼ Mercatradona (300m), El Mirador (700m), Airport (6km) & Tourist Info

11

ARRIVAL AND INFORMATION

You can cross into Colombia (see box, p.886) or Brazil (see box, p.907) from this region.

By plane Puerto Ayacucho Airport is 6km southeast of town. Conviasa (☏ conviasa.aero) operates flights to and from Caracas (3 weekly; 1hr 30min). Buses from the airport into town are rare; it's much easier to take a taxi (roughly BsF50).

By bus The bus terminal is 4km east of the centre and has nowhere to leave luggage. Taxis into town are hailed from the road outside the main entrance and cost BsF15.

Destinations Caracas (daily at 6pm; 15hr); Ciudad Bolívar (hourly with several night buses; 12hr); San Fernando de Apure (several daily until 5pm; 6hr); Valencia (daily at 6.30pm; 13hr).

Tourist information The Secretaría de Turismo is based at the airport ☏ 0248 521 0033, Mon–Fri 8am–5pm.

GETTING AROUND

By taxi Although Puerto Ayacucho does have city buses, you rarely see them and schedules are unpredictable. Consequently, most locals take taxis (in and around town BsF10); look for the "taxi" window-stickers rather than the rooftop signs. Mototaxis are a good option for when traffic clogs the city streets at peak hours.

ACCOMMODATION

Gran Hotel Amazonas Av Emilio Roa, at C Amazonas ☏ 0248 521 5633. The best hotel in town isn't that expensive. An attractive Amazon-themed reception is decorated with wooden parrots, tribal masks and tropical flowers, with spacious rooms set around the perimeter. There's a big swimming pool at the back, which you can pay BsF50 to use if you aren't staying there. BsF320

★ **Posada Manapiare** Urb Alto Parima, Entrada No 2 ☏ 0248 686 0062, ☏ posadamanapiare.com.ve, ☏ posada manapiare@gmail.com. You'll have to remember your animal rather than room number at this stylish posada between the bus terminal and town. Nice rooms are set around a terracotta-roofed courtyard and the restaurant is popular even with non-guests. Book ahead, preferably via email. Breakfast included. BsF250

Residencia Internacional Av Aguerrevere 18 ☏ 0248 521 0242. A colourful and cheap option in a quiet part of town. Some rooms have a/c and private bathrooms for BsF30 extra, and there's a matriarchal atmosphere from the indulgent grandmother who runs the place. A good panadería two doors down is a prime breakfast option. BsF150

Residencias Michelangelli de Pozo C Evelio Roa 35 ☏ 0248 521 3189. You may find yourself showering out of a bucket, since the plumbing occasionally gives out at this otherwise peaceful posada. Rooms (some with a/c) are very basic and set around a courtyard that's more concrete than greenery. BsF140

EATING AND DRINKING

In addition to the range of inexpensive restaurants about town, there is a string of food stalls along Av Aguerrevere,

---

AMAZON TOURS

Squeezing all of the Amazon's wonders into a three-day tour is impossible, but a few companies in Ayacucho do their best. The classic tour is a three-day/two-night trip up the Sipapo and Autana rivers to **Cerro Autana**, a 1200m-high tepui seen from an adjacent vantage point. You'll spend the nights in hammocks with an indigenous community, explore waterways in small boats and fish for exotic species which you can eat for dinner if successful. More in-depth and expensive options include the ten- to twelve-day **Ruta Humboldt**, following in the footsteps of the famous explorer, and even longer journeys to meet the Yanomami and other isolated tribes.

All-inclusive prices, for groups of four or more people, are US$60–80 per day per person for three or four days, usually more for longer trips. Companies provide any necessary jungle access permits and can often help you plan a journey into Brazil.

Finally, a **disclaimer**: many people expect to see amazing wildlife in the Amazon, but in reality the density of the jungle and the reclusiveness of the animals makes this quite difficult. If you're set on wildlife-watching, save your money for a trip to Los Llanos (see p.894).

TOUR OPERATORS

Coyote Expediciones Av Aguerrevere 75 ☏ 0414 486 2500, ☏ coyoteexpedition@cantv.net. Rarely in the office, Luis Coyote is better contacted by phone. He arranges tours throughout the region as well as trips along the narrow Río Casiquiare, on which the indigenous Báquiro live, a good alternative to Autana

if the weather isn't cooperating.

Eco-Destinos Ent. Urbanización Bolivariana, Quinta Los Abuelos ☏ 0416 448 6394 or 0248 521 3964, ☏ amazonasvenezuela.com. Lets customers fully customize trips, for instance by suggesting they bring and prepare their own food to mitigate expenses.

west of Av Orinoco, hawking *empanadas*, burgers, fried chicken and fish each evening.

Café Rey David Av Orinoco, south of the *mercadito* ☎0248 521 0074. Self-titled "King David" is something of a silver fox, and regally presides over his popular open-fronted place positioned right in the thick of it. Tasty *pollo asado* (BsF30), sandwiches (BsF15), *empanadas* (BsF15) and *arepas* (BsF18). Mon–Sat 7am–11pm.

El Guariqueño Av 23 de Enero ☎0248 521 4940. A popular place with *Ayacuchans* thanks to its big portions of *pollo al ajillo* or *pollo a la plancha* (both BsF75). Numerous ceiling fans make this an excellent spot to duck out of the heat and grab a refresher from the long list of juices (BsF12). Mon–Sat 10am–6pm.

El Mercadito Between Av Orinoco & Av Amazonas, south of Av 23 de Enero. The destination of choice for workers on lunch-break. Various indoor restaurants at the east end of the market serve inexpensive *comida criolla*, but for the real deal slurp down a steaming bowl of *sopa de gallina* (around BsF20) surrounded by knock-off DVD salesmen in the market itself.

Panadería Amazonas Av Rómulo Gallegos south of C Constitución. Regarded as the best *panadería* in town, the bread and pastries are nothing to write home about. However, the coffee is excellent and the gossipy staff provide ample entertainment. Daily 6.30am–8.30pm.

Royal Pool C Evelia Roa next to *Residencias Michelangelli*. The friendly and excitable patrons at this pool hall knock back cheap beers while casual games of pool, dominoes or cards proceed until late. There's a little-used *jenga* set behind the bar that will inspire fierce competition and jubliant celebration. Mon–Sat 6pm–1am.

DIRECTORY

Banks and exchange Banesco, Av Orinoco south of Av Aguerrevere; Banco de Venezuela on Av Orinoco south of Av 23 de Enero.

Hospital Clínica Amazonas, Av Rómulo Gallegos ☎0248 521 2454; Clínica Zerpa, Av 23 de Enero ☎0248 521 2815.

Immigration SAIME, Av Aguerrevere 60 (Mon–Fri 8am–4.30pm). If you need a Colombian visa (see p.489), the consulate is at C Yapacana, Quinta Beatriz ☎0248 521 0789 (Mon–Fri 8am–1pm & 3–6pm).

Internet Don't expect to be streaming YouTube in Ayacucho as connections are extremely slow if they work at all. Inversiones Friends (no sign), above CANTV, Av Orinoco, at Av Aguerrevere (Mon–Fri 8am–6pm; BsF4/hr); Servinet, C Atabapo, at Evelio Roa (daily 8am–8pm).

Laundry Lavandería Automática Acuario, Av Aguerrevere next to *Residencias Internacional*. Mon–Fri 8am–noon & 2–6pm, Sat 9am–noon & 2–5pm.

Pharmacy Farmacia Autana, Av Río Negro, at C Evelio Roa. Mon–Sat 8am–8pm; FarmaLlanos, Av Orinoco south of Av Aguerrevere. Both Mon–Sat 8am–6pm, on Sun only one of the two pharmacies is open, following the *por turno* system of opening hours on alternating weekends.

Phones CANTV, Av Orinoco, at Av Aguerrevere; Movistar, Av Orinoco south of C Carabobo; Movilnet, C Evelio Roa, at C Atabapo.

Post Ipostel, Av Amazonas, at C Roa (Mon–Fri 8am–noon & 2–5pm).

Shopping Mercatradona on Av Orinoco, at C Constitución (daily 8am–8pm, Sun until 1pm), is a Wal-Mart-sized monster for everything you might need. For local artesan jewellery head to Plaza de los Indios (Mon–Sat 8am–6pm, Sun until noon).

PUERTO ORDÁZ

Most of the visitors who pass through **PUERTO ORDÁZ** are on their way to Ciudad Bolívar, a much better jumping-off point for the main attractions in the state. The town is the base for Venezuela's aluminium, steel and iron industries, as well as a large producer of hydroelectric power from various dams in the area. It is consequently of little interest to the backpacker and is more of a transport hub. Nearby **San Félix**, an indecorous and seedy town, is best avoided entirely.

WHAT TO SEE AND DO

Built on an industrial scale, Puerto Ordáz's few sights are spread kilometres apart. Taxis are the easiest and safest way to look around and cost around BsF30 for rides within town; public transport is not advised.

The **Ecomuseo de Caroní** (☎0286 960 4464; Tues–Sun 9am–5pm; free), next to the 23 de Enero dam, has temporary exhibitions, all with a conservational theme, as well as a large window through which you can see the dam's gargantuan generators. A taxi from the centre is about BsF50.

Parque Llovizna, just across from the museum, and **Parque Cachamay** features expanses of life-affirming greenery and some nice waterfalls. You can combine both on a half-day tour with Piraña Tours (BsF250; ☎0286 923 64478, ⑩pirañatours.com), in the lobby of *Hotel Venetur* at Avenida Guayana beside Parque Punta Vista.

11

11

ARRIVAL AND INFORMATION

By plane The airport (Manuel Carlos Piar Guayana Airport) is located along the road to Ciudad Bolívar. A taxi into the centre is BsF60; bus routes are inconvenient. Avior (ⓦavior airlines.com) operates the most flights to and from the city.
Destinations Daily flights to Barcelona (30min); Caracas (1hr); Porlamar (50min); Maracaibo (2hr); and Valencia (50min).
By bus Puerto Ordáz's terminal is on Av Guayana, a 10min BsF50 taxi ride into town; *taxistas* wait at the entrance. There is nowhere to leave luggage in the terminal. Some buses arrive in nearby San Félix (keep a close eye on your belongings), from where it's a 15min taxi ride to Puerto Ordáz (BsF70).
Destinations Ciudad Bolívar (every 30min; 1hr); Caracas (hourly; 12hr); Cumaná (4 daily; 8hr); Maracay/Valencia (several daily; 12hr); Puerto La Cruz (4 daily; 7hr); Santa Elena de Uairén (4 daily, mostly night buses; 10hr); Tucupita (3 daily; 4hr).
Tourist information The main tourist office is in the *Hotel Venetur* on Av Guayana (ⓣ0286 713 1244, Mon–Sat 8am–5pm); the Secretaría de Turismo has an office at the airport (ⓣ0426 695 8109).

ACCOMMODATION

La Casa del Lobo Villa Africana, Manzana 39, Casa 2 ⓣ0286 961 6286 ⓦlobo-tours.de. Friendly German owner Wolfgang, who goes by the name of Lobo, runs the only backpacker-friendly place in town and has a travel story or two to tell of his own. The house he built himself has three rooms, all with en suite, in a separate part of the house for guests. His tour company Lobo Tours organizes trips to his excellent *campamento* in the Orinoco Delta (see p.909). <u>BsF150</u>

EATING

In addition to a couple of good places around town, the Orinokia Mall (see below) is safe after dark and has plenty of restaurants open until late.
Chiquito's Av Las Américas, Local 8 & 9, Centro Comercial Anto ⓣ0286 923 4056. Local café and bakery serving a range of sweet and savoury pastries (BsF25) as well as coffees (BsF9). Mon–Sat 7am–7pm, Sun until 1pm.
El Rincón del Chivo Av Loefling, Sector La Esperancita ⓣ0414 870 3230. An excellent barbecue house with long benches and a party atmosphere fuelled by the mouth-watering smells of the open grill-pit area. Enormous hunks of meat (steaks BsF80), *cachapas* (BsF40) and a big selection of sides keep the ravenous and friendly crowd happy. Open Tues–Sun 11am–3pm (until 5pm on weekends).

DIRECTORY

Banks BBVA, Carrera Upata, at Av Ciudad Bolívar. Banco Coroní, Carrera España at Vía Venezuela.

Internet There are plenty of cybercafés (BsF5/hr) in the Centro Comercial Trebol I, II and III on C Upata. Mon–Sat 9am–8pm, Sun till 2pm.
Phones Movistar, across the street from *Hotel Rayoli* on Paseo Caroní.
Post DHL, C El Palmar at C Santa Elena (Mon–Fri 8am–5pm, Sat 8am–noon; ⓣ0286 923 8756).
Shopping For a dose of commercialist perversity (and some good ol' US-style fast food), check out the massive Orinokia Mall, bordered by Av Las Américas & Av Guayana, Mon–Sat 10am–10pm, Sun noon–10pm.

CIUDAD BOLÍVAR

Sitting on the south bank of the Orinoco at one of its widest points, state capital **CIUDAD BOLÍVAR** is the jumping-off point for the region's numerous attractions, and is one of Venezuela's most backpacker-friendly places. The city is attractive, easily walkable, and its various highlights can be seen in a single day. To the city's south lie the endless expanses of **Parque Nacional Canaima** (see p.903) and the **Gran Sabana** (see p.908).

WHAT TO SEE AND DO

Ciudad Bolívar's cobbled streets, well-preserved colonial buildings and compact size make it a pleasant place to explore on foot. There are a couple of historic sites to bone up on Venezuelan history, while nature lovers will want to visit the botanical gardens. While you'll see the town at its prettiest in the historic centre, its lifeblood flows alongside Venezuela's mightiest river on the **Paseo Orinoco**. This noisy riverside boulevard has shopping centres, food stalls and jewellery vendors spilling out onto the busy road.

Casco histórico

Most of the city's colonial architecture is in the **casco histórico**, a ten-block area built on a mound on the Orinoco's southern bank, centred on the **Plaza Bolívar**. On the east side of the plaza, the bright yellow 1840 **Catedral** has an interior which, while not particularly ornate, offers a cool escape from the intense year-round heat that Bolívar is known for.

CIUDAD BOLÍVAR

Río Orinoco

Buses to terminal

PASEO ORINOCO

Casa Correo Del Orinoco

Pharmacy

Val Web

Pharmacy

Bank

C. VENEZUELA

Bank

Bank

Casa del Congreso de Angostura

C. BOLÍVAR

PLAZA BOLÍVAR

Catedral

AMOR PATRIA

C. ROSARIO

C. CONCORDIA

C. MERCEDES

C. PROGRESO

C. DEMOCRACIA

C. 23 DE OCTUBRE

Jardín Botánico

Parque el Porvenir

11

●EATING
El Caribeño	1
Comidas Margarita	4
Mini-lunch Arabian Food	5
Restaurant Vegetariano	6
Restaurante Caribe	2
Tostadas Juancito's	3

■ ACCOMMODATION
La Casa Grande	2
Posada Amor Patrio	5
Posada Don Carlos	4
Posada Doña Carol	3
Posada Turística Sousa	1

0   200
metres

Post Office (2km), Airport (2km) & Museo de Arte Moderno Jesús Soto (2km) ▼

To the west of the plaza, the **Casa del Congreso de Angostura** (Tues–Sun 9am–5pm; free) is the site where Bolívar and the Angostura Congress founded Gran Colombia, the post-imperialist super-state which encompassed modern-day Venezuela, Colombia and Ecuador.

Museo de Arte Moderno Jesús Soto

The works of Jesús Soto, Venezuela's most famous contemporary artist and a Ciudad Bolívar native, are displayed in the excellent **Museo de Arte Moderno Jesús Soto** (Tues–Sun 9am–5pm; free). Many of his paintings and sculptures make use of optical illusions, and you can ask to be accompanied by one of the guides who will point out the visual tricks. Taxis here from the centre cost BsF40; to return, catch a bus from the *McDonald's* across the street.

Jardín Botánico

The city's **Jardín Botánico** (Mon–Sat 8am–5pm, Sun till noon; free) is a popular spot for picnicking locals, while deeper into the gardens, which should be toured with a guide (free, although a BsF10 tip is appropriate), is an impressive array of plants from around the world. The park's main entrance is on Avenida Bolívar at the intersection with Calle Caracas.

ARRIVAL AND INFORMATION

By plane The airport (Tomás de Heres Airport; ☎0285 632 6635) is at the southeastern edge of town, on Av Táchira, at Av Aeropuerto. Taxis to and from the *casco histórico* cost around BsF40. Buses displaying Ruta 1 or Ruta 2 in the windscreen go via the airport and cost BsF4; hail one from the shopping side of the Paseo Orinoco.

11

GUAYANA TOURS

Most of the Ciudad Bolívar agencies listed here also sell tours of the Orinoco Delta (see p.909) and Gran Sabana (see p.908), although for the latter you'll find better tour prices in Santa Elena. All agencies offer pretty much the same packages so make sure you shop around for the best deal.

ANGEL FALLS

While it's possible to cobble together a trip to Angel Falls (see p.904) on your own, the small amount of money you save hardly warrants the effort of arranging all the various components (flights, boats, accommodation, food, etc). Local tourism operates on the basis of package tours arranged elsewhere (usually Ciudad Bolívar), and the needs of maverick travellers are generally an afterthought. The standard three-day/two-night budget tour, with flights in and out of Canaima, should cost around BsF2500. Prices are all-inclusive except for the BsF150 national park fee payable when you land in Canaima, and the Ciudad Bolívar airport tax (BsF30).

TOUR OPERATORS

Amor Patrio In *Posada Amor Patrio* (see below) ☎0414 854 4925, ⓦ posadaamorpatrioaventura.com. Specializes in Río Caura trips, rugged camping and visits to indigenous villages.

Eco-Adventures In the bus terminal ☎0285 651 9546, ⓦ adventurevenezuela.com. Often mistaken for a pirate outfit due to its location, it's actually a great option for travellers who are keen to get things sorted once they've hopped off the bus.

Energy Tours At the airport ☎0285 617 4530, ⓦ energytour.com. Italian-owned company that offers Angel Falls trips combined with other destinations, usually the Gran Sabana, Orinoco Delta, Isla Margarita and Los Roques. Office hours are not strictly kept and they are best contacted through the website.

Excursiones Don Carlos In *Posada Don Carlos* (see below) ☎0285 632 6017, ⓦ posada-doncarlos.com.

Organizes tours throughout the country with reputable operators, as well as offering bank transfers at *mercado paralelo* rates if you're running short on cash.

Excursiones Salto Ángel C Libertad 31 ☎0412 190 5084, ⓦ saltoangel.com.ve. English-speaking Rodman covers the whole state with a range of activities, although, as the name suggests, he specializes in the waterfalls. Tailor-made packages range from luxury to basic.

Sapito Tours At the airport ☎0285 632 7989, ⓦ sapitotours.com. The tour agency arm of *Campamento Bernal* in Canaima, specializing in tourism around the village.

Turi Express Dorado At the airport ☎0285 634 1243. Long-established company that has been operating for over two decades, offering the usual packages as well as tours of Ciudad Bolívar itself.

Destinations Caracas (daily; 1hr); Maturín (daily; 1hr). For Canaima, numerous companies fly daily for BsF1300 return; tickets can be bought in advance at the airport or organized by your hotel.

By bus The terminal lies southwest of the centre on Av República, at Av Sucre. Taxis to or from the centre cost BsF30, while buses heading to the terminal can be hailed from the river side of Paseo Orinoco. Tickets can only be bought on the day of departure, so for less-served destinations (particularly Santa Elena and Barinas) you should buy your night bus ticket in the morning.

Destinations Caracas (several daily; 9hr); Puerto Ayacucho (several daily; 14hr); Puerto La Cruz (4 daily; 5hr); Puerto Ordáz (half-hourly; 1hr); Valencia (several daily; 10hr); Santa Elena de Uairén (6 daily, mostly night buses; 12hr); Barinas (2 daily; 15hr).

Tourist information The Secretaría de Turismo and its extremely enthusiastic staff are in the main entrance of the Jardín Botánico (☎0800 674 6626,

ⓔ secretariadeturismoyambiente@gmail.com); there's also a Venetur desk at the airport (☎0800 462 8871). Both daily 8am–5pm.

ACCOMMODATION

Ciudad Bolívar is rivalled only by Mérida in its selection of great, cheap accommodation.

Posada Amor Patrio C Amor Patrio, at the Plaza Bolívar ☎0414 854 4925, ⓦ posadaamorpatrioaventura.com. In a building that's nearly 300 years old, this German-owned posada rocks a chilled vibe throughout. Rooms are named after exotic locations across the globe and the atmospheric *salón del ritmo* brims with Caribbean personality. There's a kitchen, laundry service and internet (but no wi-fi). Also has its own tour agency. BsF130

★ **Posada Don Carlos** C Boyacá, at C Amor Patrio ☎0285 632 6017, ⓦ posada-doncarlos.com. You can just picture Venezuelan gentry sipping on some dark rum at the bar of this characterful posada. Rooms are off the large colonial courtyard, dotted with all sorts of nineteenth-century knick-knacks. There's a dormitory/balcony area with bunk beds and hammocks for BsF100. Also runs a reputable tour agency. **BsF180**

Posada Doña Carol C Libertad 28. ☎ 0285 634 0989. Wacky grandma Doña Carol welcomes you into her oddly decorated house with a friendly smile. There's a bright colour scheme, wi-fi, five spotless rooms (some with a/c) and a balcony upstairs that overlooks the surrounding roofs. **BsF150**

Posada Turística Sousa C Libertad, at C Venezuela ☎ 0426 799 7663. The cheapest rooms in town, although you may find yourself with neighbours who are paying by the hour. Nevertheless, tight security makes it a safe option. **BsF70**

EATING

Ciudad Bolívar is not particularly noted for its food, but a few decent options exist. Local fish such as *dorado*, *palometa* and *sapoara* are fresh and tasty.

El Caribeño C Igualdad between Paseo Orinoco & C Venezuela ☎ 0285 444 8166. A very simple, very cheap cafeteria serving breakfasts (*pastelitos, empanadas, jugos*) and full meals (*pollo a la brasa, bisteck, pescado*) with sides of rice, salad, yucca and more – nothing over BsF45. Daily 6am–7pm.

★ Comidas Margarita C Bolívar, at C Libertad ☎ 0285 617 8424. The juice (BsF8) comes in jam jars and the coffee comes free at this bright blue lunch option. Grab a spare seat at one of the few tables and browse the day's menu on the whiteboard out front. Chat with the friendly lunchers or watch the world go by while you tackle the big portions (all BsF35). Mon–Sat 6.30am–3pm.

Mini-lunch Arabian Food C Amor Patrio, at C Igualdad ☎ 0285 632 7208. A little corner café that provides a fix of Middle Eastern fare for when you can't handle beans

and rice any more. Beef, chicken or mixed *shawarma* goes for BsF40, while the large platter of falafel, *kibbe*, tabbouleh, meat and hummus is BsF80. Mon–Sat 7am–7pm, occasionally Sun.

Restaurant Vegetariano C Amor Patrio, at C Dalla Costa ☎ 0285 632 6381. A four-course vegetarian meal for BsF50 is not to be sniffed at, while the friendly owner runs four daily yoga classes for which contributions are encouraged but not enforced. An oasis of patrician calm; grab a few guavas from the tree in the courtyard on your way in or out. Mon–Fri noon–3pm.

Restaurante Caribe C Libertad 33 ☎ 0416 697 4707. Two large rooms full of tables occupy the front of this family home, where you can bang on the door after hours as they're usually willing to feed you. Basic food at basic prices: soups BsF25, mains BsF35. Mon–Sat 11am–8pm.

Tostadas Juancito's Av Cumaná, at C Bolívar. Fun and friendly outdoor terrace with stone tables, offering cheap and tasty street food, including *arepas* (BsF25), *pabellón criollo* (BsF35) and *pollo a la brasa* (quarter BsF30). Pay at the cash register first and hand your ticket to the counter staff. Mon–Sat 7am–6pm.

DIRECTORY

Banks and exchange Banco de Venezuela, Paseo Orinoco, at C Constitución; Banesco, C Dalla Costa, at C Venezuela.

Hospital Hospital Ruiz y Páez, Av Germania ☎ 0285 632 0041.

Internet Val Web, C Venezuela, at C Libertad, Mon–Fri 8am–5.30pm, BsF6/hr.

Pharmacy Numerous around town, *por turno* (only one open at a time, look for the illuminated "turno" sign to ascertain which) on Sun. Farmacia Unión, C Venezuela, at C Libertad, Mon–Sat 8am–6pm; Hospifárma, Paseo Orinoco at C Carabobo, Mon–Sat 8am–5.30pm.

Phones Movistar, Paseo Orinoco between calles Dalla Costa & Libertad. There's another *centro de llamadas* on C Dalla Costa between calles Venezuela & Bolívar.

Police Located in the Jardín Botánico by the tourist office, daily 8am–8pm, no phone.

Post Ipostel, Av Táchira, 1km south of the *casco histórico*.

Shopping For groceries there's a fruit/veg market along C Venezuela until 4pm daily; numerous stands and shops along the Paseo Orinoco sell *artesanía*, cheap clothing and electronics.

PARQUE NACIONAL CANAIMA

One of the world's largest national parks, **PARQUE NACIONAL CANAIMA** is Venezuela's number one tourist attraction, due entirely to the world's tallest waterfall, the astonishing Salto

11

Ángel, or **Angel Falls**. The park is inhabited by roughly twenty thousand Pemón Indians, made up of three major tribes: Kamakoto, Arekuna and Taurepan. Most live in small villages of between 100 and 200 people. At the centre of it all is **Canaima Village**, originally a small Pemón settlement that is now the hub of a tourism industry vastly superior to those you are likely to witness elsewhere in Venezuela. The falls are a world-class attraction without the accompanying crowds – perhaps due in part to a reliance on local guides and agencies that have garnered reputations for unprofessionalism.

Canaima Village

The most visited village in the park, **Canaima** is the principal base for trips to Angel Falls. On the other side of **Laguna de Canaima** from the lodges are four postcard-worthy waterfalls – **Salto Ucaima**, **Salto Golondrina**, **Salto Guadima** and **Salto Hacha** – the latter being the largest, discharging enough water to fill an Olympic-sized swimming pool in a single second. The lagoon has a sandy beach and palm trees jutting out of the water, at the end of which the hydroelectric power station that supplies the village and surrounding area with electricity is visitable at all hours, but usually seen on the way to the jetty above the falls from where the boats depart upriver.

Tour packages (see box, p.902) include a short excursion to another nearby waterfall, **Salto El Sapo**, which you can actually walk right behind (make sure you protect your camera properly, as you will get soaked).

Angel Falls

At nearly a vertical kilometre (980m), **ANGEL FALLS** (Salto Ángel in Spanish) is the world's tallest waterfall – around sixteen times the height of Niagara Falls and twelve times the height of Iguazú Falls (see p.353). It is created by the Churún River, which makes a dramatic plunge from the edge of the enormous Auyantepui and into the verdant jungle below.

Seeing the falls is one of the highlights of a trip to Venezuela, and you can arrange a visit through tour agencies in Ciudad Bolívar (see p.902) and even Caracas (see p.860). The first leg of the trip is a three-hour, 70km and very wet boat ride up the Caroní and Carrao rivers from Canaima Village; the second leg is an hour's hike through the jungle, ending at the falls' principal vantage point. The falls themselves are generally fuller, and therefore more spectacular, during the rainy season; the trade-off is less visibility, as the top of the falls can be covered in clouds during those months.

In the **dry season** (Jan–May), low water levels in the access rivers can complicate the journey, sometimes requiring passengers to unload and push the boat. Tour agencies are usually diligent about warning customers of such conditions, but it's a good idea to ask anyway.

ARRIVAL AND TOURS

By plane Canaima is primarily accessed by small planes and in most cases, moving on is simply a matter of boarding your pre-arranged return flight to Ciudad Bolívar. The airstrip is on the village's main road. The main airline is Transmandu (*transmandu.com*); if you're arranging your own transport expect to pay BsF1300 return from Ciudad Bolívar. Tickets can be purchased at the airport's various airplane desks. In theory you can charter a plane to Santa Elena, although the high prices and five-passenger minimum make the twelve-hour overnight bus ride (see p.906) from Ciudad Bolívar a more viable option. There are no direct flights to Caracas.

Destinations Ciudad Bolívar (4 daily; 1hr 30min) and Puerto Ordáz (2 daily; 2hr).

Tour operators If you've come to Canaima on a tour, a guide will have been arranged for you; if you're on your own, seek out English-speaking Materson Nathaniel (*0426 997 2879*, *kaikuse_68@yahoo.es*) or Yosmary López (*0416 852 1558*, *amanon983@gmail.com*), who both run tours to Angel Falls and Salto el Sapo, as well as to other lesser-known sights around the region.

ACCOMMODATION

Like transport, accommodation in Canaima is included in pre-arranged tour packages. All lodgings, save the exclusive luxury ones, are *campamentos* of varying simplicity. On the excursion to Angel Falls you'll spend the night in one of the various camps built close to the falls, usually around an hour's walk to the viewing point. The cheapest *campamentos* are listed here, and they charge per person rather than per room. Note that tour prices from Canaima exclude flights.

Tiuna ☎ 0414 864 0033, **✉** tiunatours@hotmail.com. By far the most receptive option (as well as the cheapest) for independent travellers, *Tiuna* has a serene location at the edge of Canaima Lagoon. Breakfast is BsF50, lunch and dinner BsF100; 3-day/2-night Angel Falls tour is BsF1000. Hammocks BsF50, dorms BsF200

Wey Tupuy ☎ 0414 191 8708, **✉** weytupui@hotmail .com. Expanding to triple in size at the time of research, this high-capacity place beside the lagoon has perfectly decent rooms and a good restaurant. An extra BsF300 if you want three square meals. BsF200

EATING AND DRINKING

Food is included in tour prices; vegetarians should notify the agency when purchasing a tour. Should you get hungry between scheduled meals, *Posada Kusari* (which is a poor accommodation option for BsF300) close to *Tiuna* (see above) runs a general store, though prices are outrageous since all stock is flown in. As a tourist hub, Canaima has a fairly decent social life, with locals, tourists and guides always up for a party.

Bar Morichal At *Campamento Morichal*. A beach bar popular with the locals, guides and tourists alike. The dancefloor has disco lights, an impressive sound system and DJs. If your salsa isn't up to scratch, grab a few unsurprisingly expensive beers from the bar, take a seat in one of the parked boats and watch the waterfalls across the lagoon. Open daily from noon until the last patron leaves.

Salon Ikupai At *Venetur Campamento Canaima*. Occupying the best spot on the lagoon, the state-owned resort's restaurant and bar has unreal views of Canaima's waterfalls across the water. Come to watch the sunset from the specially designed viewing terrace, order a cocktail and soak it all in. Beers BsF20, cocktails BsF40. Daily 6am–midnight.

SANTA ELENA DE UAIRÉN

SANTA ELENA DE UAIRÉN grew significantly when the paved road connecting it with the rest of the country was completed, but, with a population of only eighteen thousand, it's still a quiet town. Many of its inhabitants are originally from Brazil, whose border is just 15km away. The town serves as a good base for exploring the awe-inspiring *tepuis*, as well as being a **good access point for Brazil** (see box, p.907), where Manaus is the closest major city. Although there's little to do, Santa Elena is a very backpacker-friendly town, with reasonably priced accommodation and restaurants. Two blocks southeast of the Plaza Bolívar a baseball field hosts local matches in the evenings, where the party atmosphere is fun, beers are cheap and gringos are warmly welcomed whether or not they can follow what's going on. The town is the best place to book tours to the **Gran Sabana** (see p.908) and up **Mount Roraima** (see p.908).

ARRIVAL AND INFORMATION

By plane Flights arrive from Ciudad Bolívar and Puerto Ordáz, though schedules are unpredictable and planes tend to be relatively old and very small.

EXCHANGING BRAZILIAN REAIS FOR BOLÍVARES

The Brazilian town of Pacaraima's designation as "**puerto libre**" – permitting visitors across the border without immigration formalities if they return the same day – allows you to replenish funds without resorting to Venezuela's unfavourable official exchange rate at an ATM or bank. The border is open 7am–10pm.

Grab your passport and bankcard and head to the intersection of calles Peña and Zea, where *por puestos* leave regularly for the border (20min; BsF15). In the unlikely event that you're stopped when crossing, explain to officials that you're returning to Venezuela the same day; make sure they **do not stamp** your passport (if they do, you'll have to wait a day to return to Venezuela). Once you're over, visit one of several available ATMs and withdraw Brazilian reais at the current exchange rate of US$1 = R$2.

Back in Santa Elena, head to the intersection of calles Urdaneta and Bolívar, where unofficial moneychangers congregate. You can change cash on the street, although they often have better rates at the open-fronted offices where you can sit and take your time over the transaction. You should be able to exchange R$1 for at least BsF6, tripling the value of your money within Venezuela.

11

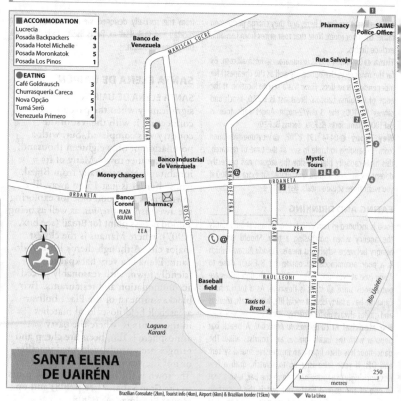

SANTA ELENA DE UAIRÉN

■ ACCOMMODATION	
Lucrecia	2
Posada Backpackers	4
Posada Hotel Michelle	3
Posada Moronkatok	5
Posada Los Pinos	1

● EATING	
Café Goldrausch	3
Churrasquería Careca	2
Nova Opção	5
Tumá Serö	1
Venezuela Primero	4

Brazilian Consulate (2km), Tourist info (4km), Airport (6km) & Brazilian border (15km) ▼ ▼ Vía La Línea

By bus The bus terminal is 3km from the town centre, a short BsF20 taxi ride; there are no city buses. From Ciudad Bolívar there are two checkpoints on the way to Santa Elena as well as a full baggage search when you arrive at the terminal, so keep your passport handy.

Destinations Caracas (daily; 22hr); Ciudad Bolívar (4 daily; 12hr), stopping in Puerto Ordáz; Puerto la Cruz (2 daily; 16hr); Manaus (daily at 1pm; 12hr).

Tourist information Vía La Línea, on the way to the Brazilian border ☎ 0414 998 7167.

ACCOMMODATION

The best places, along with most other backpacker services, are on C Urdaneta between C Icarabú and Av Perimetral.

Lucrecia Av Perimetral ☎ 0289 995 1105, ⊛ hotellucrecia .com.ve. Popular with Brazilians and Venezuelans, big-haired Lucrecia presides over this spacious plot. The rooms are pleasant, and there's a good-sized swimming pool out back. BsF250

★ **Posada Backpackers** C Urdaneta ☎ 0289 995 1430, ⊛ backpacker-tours.com. Easily the best spot in town for backpackers, this colourful German-owned posada is

covered with murals, has spotless rooms and dormitories on the upper floor, and shares the building with an excellent bar. There's a reputable tour agency (see p.908) and wi-fi. Dorms BsF60, doubles BsF120

Posada Hotel Michelle C Urdaneta ☎ 0289 416 1257. Another good choice on the backpacker strip with clean, although somewhat gloomy, rooms. Laundry service (BsF15/kg), kitchen and book exchange. BsF120

Posada Moronkatok C Urdaneta ☎ 0289 995 1518. The staff here aren't exactly sure what the place is called, there being no sign; just look for a gated entrance with red pillars across from Lavandería Pereira. There's a communal kitchen surrounded by decent rooms, all with cable TV and some with hot water. BsF150

Posada Los Pinos ☎ 0289 995 1430 or ☎ 0414 886 7227, ⊛ posadapinos.com. Under the same management as *Posada Backpackers*, this pricier option a 10min walk from town has eleven rooms, with eight more under way at the time of research, each individually inspired by Indian tribes and Venezuelan plants. There's also a fun Flintstones-esque pool with a slide. BsF210 extra to include dinner and breakfast. BsF440

EATING

Santa Elena has some good eating options, particularly if you want to sample authentic Brazilian fare. After dark, numerous burger stands set up along C Icabarú between calles Urdaneta & Zea and serve up tasty grub until around midnight.

★ **Café Goldrausch** C Urdaneta ☎ 0289 995 1576. Adjacent to *Posada Backpackers*, this chilled café and restaurant with an outdoor terrace is the perfect spot to meet other travellers. Tasty food like the excellent *lomito salteado* (BsF50) alongside ice-cold beers. There's an internet café inside if you can't take advantage of the posada's free wi-fi (BsF7/hr). Daily 7am–11pm, Sun from 5pm.

Churrasquería Careca Av Perimentral, at C Urdaneta ☎ 0426 294 2336. You'll know you're not far from Brazil when the mouthwatering aroma of the wood-fired oven reaches you. Load up with sides from the buffet trolley, but leave room for the skewer-toting staff who slice pork, chicken, beef, fish and whatever else they might have directly onto your plate. BsF70/person. Daily 11am–5pm.

Nova Opção Av Perimentral ☎ 0289 995 1013. Don't expect the same quality of food that you'd get in a Brazilian "per kg" restaurant, but do expect all sorts of meats, rice, beans, *farofa*, flan and even *guaraná*. BsF90/kg with meat, BsF85 without. Food runs out quickly so make sure you get there early. Daily 11am–3pm.

★ **Tumá Serö** Between calles Roscio & Bolívar. An indoor food-alley, with numerous restaurants and their pushy representatives hollering for your business. A good choice for a quick bite or a slap-up meal. If you're adventurous and like spicy food, ask your kitchen owner for *catara*, a delicious hot sauce made from ants. Daily 6am–10pm, although it's rare that more than half the stalls will be open at any one time.

Venezuela Primero Av Perimentral ☎ 0289 995 1149. Ironically, *paella* is a speciality at this restaurant. The smartly dressed staff are lackadaisical although the food covers a wide range of cuisines. Mon–Sat 11am–3pm & 6–10pm, Sun 11am–2pm.

DIRECTORY

Banks and exchange Banco de Venezuela, C Bolívar north of C Urdaneta; Banco Coroní on the east side of the Plaza Bolívar. Unofficial moneychangers at the intersection of calles Urdaneta & Bolívar accept dollars, euros and Brazilian reais.

Consulate Brazilian Consulate (see box below).

Hospital Hospital Santa Elena, Av Perimentral ☎ 0289 995 1155.

Internet In the *Café Goldrausch* (Mon–Sat 7am–11pm, BsF7/hr); Megacyber, C Urdaneta at Peña, with another branch one block south on C Zea (daily 8am–10pm, BsF6/hr).

Laundry Lavandería Pereira, C Urdaneta across from *Posada Moronkatok* (Mon–Sat 7am–7pm; BsF25/kg). *Hotel Michelle* (see above) also has a same-day laundry service.

Pharmacy Farmacía Vecimar, C Bolívar, at Urdaneta, daily 8am–10pm, Sun until 3pm.

11

CROSSING INTO BRAZIL

There are two main border crossings between Venezuela and Brazil. The primary crossing is at **Santa Elena de Uairén** (see p.905), a simple affair with good onward connections to Manaus. The other, at **San Simón de Cocuy**, involves a twelve-day boat journey only possible from November–May at around US$150/day. For more information on this trip see ⓦ selvadentro.com.

Citizens of the US, Canada and Australia need a visa to enter Brazil; European, South African and New Zealand nationals do not, although citizens of Spain must register at the nearest police station upon entry. For a list of all countries' visa requirements, visit ⓦ dpf.gov.br. All visitors must have a valid yellow-fever vaccination certificate. Advance your watch half an hour when entering Brazil (or 1hr 30min depending on daylight saving time).

SANTA ELENA DE UAIRÉN

The Brazilian Consulate in Santa Elena, on C Los Castaños (Mon–Fri 8am–2pm; ☎ 0289 995 1256), supplies visas within 72 hours, although they usually process them the same day. You must provide a passport photo and give the address for your first port of call in Brazil. Visa fees vary by country of citizenship. If you have a problem, there's a SAIME office behind the police station in Santa Elena.

The border at Santa Elena is open from 7am–10pm. There is one daily bus at 1pm from Santa Elena to Manaus in Brazil (16hr; BsF200).

From within Brazil regular buses run to Manaus from Boa Vista, the terminal of which you can get to from the border in a taxi for R$40. TAM (ⓦ tam.com.br) also flies from Boa Vista to Manaus (daily; 1hr; R$133).

You can also cross the border simply to change money (see box, p.905).

Phones Movistar/Centro de Comunicaciones Marcos, C Zea between calles Roscio & Peña (Mon–Fri 8am–9pm, Sat & Sun till 8pm).

Police The police station (☎0289 995 1556; open 24hr) is on C Akarabisis, a colourful building facing *Ruta Salvaje* (see below).

Post Ipostel, in the orange brick building on C Urdaneta west of C Roscio (Mon–Fri 8am–noon & 1–4.30pm). Consider yourself lucky if you happen upon stamps.

LA GRAN SABANA AND RORAIMA

The vast area that extends southeast to the Brazilian border technically includes Angel Falls and most of Parque Nacional Canaima, although trips to the 35,000-square-kilometre **GRAN SABANA**, or Great Savannah, do not. At the triple frontier of Venezuela, Brazil and Guyana lies the area's principal attraction: the beautiful and climbable **MOUNT RORAIMA**, a flat-topped mountain with 400m-high cliffs protecting its summit, which is renowned for its otherworldly landscape and was the inspiration for Sir Arthur Conan Doyle's *The Lost World* and the Disney Pixar film *Up*. The entire region is filled with other magnificent *tepuis* and waterfalls, separated by vast expanses of grasslands.

One of the most famous waterfalls is **Quebrada de Jaspe**, noted for its bright red jasper rock. Other well-known waterfalls in the region include the 105m-high **Salto Aponguao**, where you can swim in the nearby **Pozo Escondido**, and **Quebrada Pacheco**, two pretty falls with natural waterslides.

THE ORINOCO DELTA

A unique phenomenon, the enormous **Orinoco Delta** is formed as Venezuela's mightiest river reaches the Atlantic below Trinidad, finishing its 2736km course through the country. It is here that it divides and seeps through a 44,000-square-kilometre area of jungle,

---

GRAN SABANA AND RORAIMA TOURS

The classic six-day trek to the top of **Mount Roraima**, considered by many to be one of the best hikes in South America, costs US$400–600. Since the price is based on distance rather than time, agencies are usually willing to add or subtract a day to fit your schedule. Multi-day **Gran Sabana** tours cost US$90/day/person, typically with a minimum of five people and with meals included. One- or two-day trips to **El Paují**, **El Abismo**, **Salto Aponguao** and other specific sites cost around US$100/day/person, meals included, although prices drop as group size increases. If you want to visit multiple sites on the same day, rates increase considerably. The following are operators in Santa Elena:

TOUR OPERATORS

Backpacker Tours Av Urdaneta ☎0289 995 1430, ⓦbackpacker-tours.com. The most expensive of the bunch, but has a permanent guide staff, sells air tickets and supplies its own equipment, including high-quality tents, bicycles and trucks. Offers shorter alternatives (Mantopai and Chiricayén) to the six-day Roraima trek that costs BsF3500.

Mystic Tours Av Urdaneta ☎0289 416 1081 or ☎0289 416 0686, ⓦmystictours.com.ve. Said to be along one of the world's major energy meridians, which also passes through Machu Picchu and Stonehenge, Gran Sabana has caused many visitors to experience extremely lucid dreams, spiritual rejuvenations and even to see UFOs. Mystic Tours has built a solid reputation on its unique mystical approach to the Gran Sabana and in particular to Roraima – the owner is a scholar of the paranormal and has written guidebooks on the area.

Ruta Salvaje Av Mariscal Sucre, at C Akarabisis ☎0289 995 1134 or ☎0414 889 4164, ⓦrutasalvaje .com. From a hut beside the police station, Ruta Salvaje sells art painted by the owner's family and organizes adrenaline-boosting activities around the Gran Sabana including paragliding (BsF500), rafting (BsF600) on class I to IV rapids and paramotoring (BsF1000) on all-inclusive day tours. Prices listed are per person for a group of two; rates go down the larger the group gets.

Turísticos Álvarez In the bus terminal ☎0414 385 2846, ⓦsaltoangelrsta.com. Francisco Álvarez has wallpapered his bus terminal office with information flyers, and can be found inside organizing trips for budget-conscious travellers. Sorting out bare-bones packages, he also rents tents and offers trips to Gran Sabana from just BsF250/day.

ORINOCO DELTA TOURS

There are various lodges within the delta, which you can contact directly, as well as agencies throughout the country that organize trips in the region. Activities generally include visiting indigenous Warao villages, canoeing through the small *caños*, fishing for piranha and observing local flora and fauna on jungle walks. Packages cost US$100–140 per person per day and are all-inclusive. The lodges and operators listed here are the most reliable.

TOUR OPERATORS

Orinoco Queen ☎ 0414 871 9339, ⊕ lobo-tours.de. Built and run by the owner of *Casa del Lobo* in Puerto Ordáz, the Orinoco Queen is the smallest and most personal of the numerous camps in the area. A three-night stay, one of them spent in the hammocks at a nearby Warao village, costs US$300 and includes all food and activities; piranha fishing, jungle walks and expeditions in dugout canoes. Can also organize customized tours throughout the country.

Tucupita Expeditions Boulevard Playa El Agua, Isla Margarita ☎ 0295 249 1823 or ☎ 0414 794 0172, ⊕ orinocodelta.com. Margarita Island-based company

operating trips to the Orinoco with stays in three different lodges, some more rustic than others. English-speaking guides available. Free pick-up from Maturín, Puerto Ordáz or Tucupita.

Waro Waro Lodge ☎ 0424 162 1960, ⊕ orinoco deltatours.com. Named after the Warao word for the electric-blue butterflies that flutter around the region, this intimate rustic French-Argentine owned lodge is located on the Jaropuna channel northwest of the delta. It's easily accessible from San José de la Buja, and they can also organize a free pick-up from various locations, including Ciudad Bolívar and the northeast coast.

11

forming a network of navigable waterways (known as *caños*) on which the Warao Indians have lived for millennia. Trips to the Orinoco Delta go to tourist *campamentos* built on the riverbanks, although all are very basically equipped.

The northeast coast and islands

The **northeast coast** is home to some of the country's most ruggedly beautiful coastline, where sleepy fishing villages lie unperturbed by the proximity of some of the country's most energetic cities. **Puerto La Cruz**, a high-rise fast-food paradise, is the coastline's main hub, and makes for a diverting afternoon's people-watching on the seafront. A short ferry ride away is **Isla Margarita**, Venezuela's largest island, whose mega-resorts and island vibe are a huge magnet for Venezuelans taking a break from the mainland.

Between Puerto La Cruz and Cumaná (the continent's very first European settlement, although there's little to see) is the **Parque Nacional Mochima**, loved for its uninhabited cays and under-the-radar

charm. Still further east, **Caripe** is a pretty mountain town nestled away at chillier altitudes, where mountain sports, volunteer work and the astonishing Cueva del Guácharo are excellent diversions.

PUERTO LA CRUZ

The bustling collection of high-rises that calls itself **PUERTO LA CRUZ** isn't that long removed from being a fishing village. Not that you'll notice much to give away its rural past; it acts primarily as a hub for tourists heading to Parque Nacional Mochima (see p.911) or taking the ferry to Isla Margarita (see p.914). There's little reason to spend long here, although the wide seafront promenade makes for an enjoyable afternoon of strolling and people-watching, especially when there's a cool breeze rolling in off the Caribbean.

WHAT TO SEE AND DO

There's really nothing much to see in Puerto La Cruz itself – the city doesn't particularly cater to international tourism and most **activities** take place outside the urban limits. For beaches and boat rides in Parque Nacional Mochima, you'll be better off organizing excursions from Santa Fe or Mochima within the park itself.

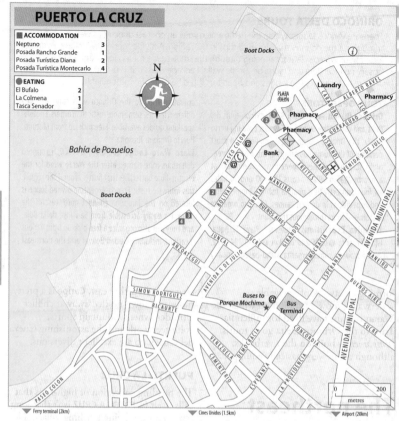

PUERTO LA CRUZ

■ ACCOMMODATION
Neptuno	**3**
Posada Rancho Grande	**1**
Posada Turística Diana	**2**
Posada Turística Montecarlo	**4**

● EATING
El Bufalo	**2**
La Colmena	**1**
Tasca Senador	**3**

Bahía de Pozuelos

Boat Docks

Boat Docks

PLAZA COLÓN

Laundry

Pharmacy

Pharmacy

Pharmacy

Bank

Buses to Parque Mochima

Bus Terminal

0		200
		metres

▼ Ferry terminal (2km) ▼ Cines Unidos (1.5km) ▼ Airport (20km)

Los Altos de Sucre

A more do-it-yourself diversion is to head to the bus terminal for the frequent jeeps (40min; BsF10) to **Los Altos de Sucre**, a small community hidden in the hills above Puerto La Cruz, near the border of Anzoátegui State. The lush, rural roads couldn't be further in spirit from the city's mayhem, and are known for their numerous pastry and *artesanía* shops and spectacular views of the bay below. Shout "¡parada!" at the bus driver wherever you want to get off along the Via Principal de los Altos.

ARRIVAL AND INFORMATION

By plane The nearest airport is in Barcelona, roughly 20km southwest of Puerto La Cruz and served by frequent buses. From the Barcelona terminal, numerous local bus routes cover the airport. Alternatively, a taxi from Puerto la Cruz costs around BsF150.

Destinations Caracas (6 daily; 45min); Maracaibo (2 daily except Sat; 3hr); Mérida (daily except Sun; 2hr 30min with 1 connection); Porlamar (2 daily; 30min); Puerto Ordáz (2 daily; 40min); Valencia (3 daily Sun–Fri, 1 daily Sat; 40min). Avior flies to Miami at 9.30am on Wed–Fri and Mon.

By bus The bus terminal is on C Democracia at C Concordia, an easy walk from most accommodation. Playa Colorada, Santa Fe and Mochima are all served along the same route. *Busetas* depart from 6am–8pm when full from C Democracia beside the liquor shop outside the terminal.

Destinations Caracas (hourly; 6hr); Barinas (3 daily; 12hr); Maracaibo (4 daily; 15hr); Ciudad Bolívar (8 daily; 5hr) also serving Puerto Ordáz; Coro (daily at 3pm; 11hr); Cumaná (half-hourly; 2hr); Mérida (daily at 10am; 17hr); Santa Elena de Uairén (daily at 3pm; 18hr); Barquisimeto (4 daily; 5hr); Valencia (several daily; 7hr).

By ferry The port terminal is about 3km west of the town centre. Ferries arrive and depart daily from Isla Margarita with Conferry (☎ 0281 267 7847, ⓦ conferry.com), Naviarca/ Gran Cacique (☎ 0281 267 7286, ⓦ grancacique.com.ve) and Navibus (☎ 0295 500 6284, ⓦ navibus.com.ve).

Tourist information In the lobby of *Hotel Venetur* (Paseo La Cruz y El Mar; Mon–Fri 9am–noon & 1–5.30pm; ☎ 0281 500 3675, ⓦ venetur.gob.ve).

ACCOMMODATION

Most of the centre's budget accommodation is strung along Paseo Colón, putting you right in the middle of the action.
Neptuno Paseo Colón south of C Juncal ☎ 0281 268 5413. Rooms are clean, all with a/c and en suite, while the furniture is on its last legs. The hotel lobby has an internet café and is, bizarrely, football themed. BsF220
Posada Rancho Grande Paseo Colón between calles Buenos Aires & Sucre ☎ 0414 093 4020. You'll need to bang on the door of this posada in the morning as they don't turn the bell on before lunch. The outlandish owner is a bit of a wheeler-dealer and will happily bargain a discount for a multiple-night stay. Small, clean rooms (en suite, TV, a/c), although none with windows facing outside. BsF200
Posada Turística Diana Paseo Colón, just north of C Sucre ☎ 0281 265 3517. Rooms in this sparsely decorated posada all lack natural light, but are otherwise clean with en suite, a/c and TV. BsF150
Posada Turística Montecarlo Paseo Colón 119 ☎ 0281 268 5677. The chirping canaries in the lobby do little to drown out the thundering a/c in this rather brown posada. Rooms are perfectly decent, all with en suite, although showers amount to little more than a cold dribble. BsF160

EATING

Curiously, Paseo Colón is lined with numerous, nearly identical Lebanese restaurants serving good-value *shawarma*, *kibbe* and *tabbouleh*. These tend to stay open very late.
El Bufalo Paseo Colón 49 ☎ 0281 267 2210. You can't miss *El Bufalo*, due in part to the massive angry bovine stuccoed above the wide entrance. They import some of their more gourmet cuts from Argentina, while the outside terrace is a popular nightspot for cheap beers, sea views and live music on the weekends. Daily 11am–midnight.
La Colmena Paseo Colón, west of C Miranda ☎ 0281 265 2751. A little health-food shop serving up vegetarian food in the back at lunchtime only. Mon–Fri 11.30am–2.30pm.
Tasca Senador C Miranda north of C Alberto Ravel ☎ 0414 825 8044. This restaurant has a rather sultry atmosphere, which nonetheless attracts plenty of office workers on their lunch break for a good-value *menú ejecutivo* (BsF40). Has a DJ on Fri & Sat, when things get rowdy. Mon–Thurs noon–midnight, Fri noon–3am, Sat 8pm–3am.

DIRECTORY

Banks and exchange Banco de Venezuela, C Libertad, at C Miranda; Banco Banesco, C Freites, at C Bolívar.
Hospital Policlínica Puerto La Cruz, Av 5 de Julio at C Arismendi, open 24hr (☎ 0281 265 6833).

Internet In *Hotel Neptuno*, open 8am–9pm. Sky Intern @tional, C Maneiro, at Paseo Colón (daily 9am–9pm, Sun from 1pm). Both cost BsF6/hr.
Laundry There is a nameless *lavandería* on Av Ravél, between calles Carabobo & Las Flores (Mon–Fri 7.30am–6pm, Sat till 3pm, closed Sun).
Pharmacy Meditotal, Paseo Colón across from Plaza Colón, open 24hr.
Phones Movistar and CANTV are both on Paseo Colón between calles Maneiro & Buenos Aires. You can also make international calls from Sky Intern@tional (see above).
Police Located at Av Municipal by the Centro, Comercial Regina (☎ 0281 266 1414).
Post Ipostel, C Freites, at C Libertad, Mon–Fri 8am–4pm.
Shopping There are numerous souvenir shops on the road to Los Altos de Sucre. Dulcería Alicia on this stretch sells delicious tarts and cheesecakes. Taller Artesanal Bogar in Sector Vuelta de Culebra makes local liquor, sweets and preserves.

PARQUE NACIONAL MOCHIMA

The 950-square-kilometre **PARQUE NACIONAL MOCHIMA** was created in 1973 to protect 36 uninhabited cays and the surrounding coastal area. Teeming with coral, dolphins and pelicans, and with laidback locals providing a genial social life, this area is one of Venezuela's most undervalued. While the beaches, some of which are deep-red in colour, aren't as postcard-perfect as those you'll find in Morrocoy (see p.882) and Henri Pittier (see p.878), the snorkelling and scuba-diving opportunities are far superior.

There are limited services and no banks or ATMs in Playa Colorado, Santa Fe or Mochima – stock up on cash in Puerto La Cruz (see p.909) or Cumaná (see p.909).

Playa Colorada

In a protected cove lined with swaying palm trees, **PLAYA COLORADA** is rather winding down from the glory days of Venezuelan tourism, but nevertheless offers a welcome retreat from the more intense coastal towns. Deriving its name from the stretch of terracotta sand, few day-trippers ever venture to the other side of the highway where the town's numerous posadas and single restaurant are to be found. The sandbar's visitors triple at the weekends, but during the week you'll be left pretty much alone.

11

11

ARRIVAL AND DEPARTURE

By bus Buses operating the coastal highway between Puerto La Cruz, Santa Fe and Cumaná all pass through Playa Colorada. Shout "¡parada!" at the driver to alight when you see the red sand. Buses from Puerto La Cruz depart from beside the liquor store on C Demoncracia outside the terminal. To get out of town, simply hail a passing bus (every 30min) in the direction you need.

ACCOMMODATION

Most of Playa Colorada's accommodation consists of purpose-built posadas that rent budget rooms and apartments for longer stays.

★ **Jakera Lodge** On the main highway across from the beach ☎0293 808 7057, ⓦjakera.com. Resembling the secret retreat from *The Beach*, Scottish-owned *Jakera Lodge* looks and feels every centimetre the backpacker accommodation. There are hammocks (BsF175 with a private locker), dorms and doubles are clean, and mosqutio nets are provided. Prices are per person and include breakfast and dinner. Spanish courses are also on offer. Dorms **BsF210**, doubles **BsF350**

Posada Jaly C Marchán ☎0293 808 3246 or ☎0416 681 8113. French-Canadian owner Jacques, who speaks French and English, is running this posada in his retirement. The house is surrounded by a big garden, with a shared kitchen, book exchange and five spacious rooms, all with en suite and a/c. **BsF250**

Villa Nirvana C Marchán ☎0293 808 7844, ⓔrita.pascal@hotmail.com. Straight-talking owner Rita built this beautiful posada after moving from Zurich. She offers the cheapest rooms in town, with apartments, roomy doubles and two little units without a/c for those on a tight budget. Apartments **BsF400**, doubles **BsF200**

EATING

Other than the stalls lining the beach, there's only one place in the village at which to eat.

Las Carmitas 3a Transversal ☎0416 322 8887. There are only five tables, so waiting for a seat is often necessary at the weekends. Not that grabbing a beer and chatting with the other waiting people is much of an inconvenience. Serves pretty good burgers (BsF25), sandwiches (BsF20), pizzas (BsF55) and the like. Daily noon–8.30pm.

Santa Fe

One of the best spots along Venezuela's coastline, **SANTA FE**'s thin strip of sand is lined with good-value accommodation, crystal-clear water and hordes of pelicans whose signature fishing style is very entertaining to watch. The atmosphere is a little sketchier away from the well-populated seafront, and you should stick to the beach and road behind it (Calle Cochaima) after dark. At the far end of the beach, Santa Fe's bright-blue **market** makes for entertaining wandering, as well as a good spot to shop for fresh produce for your posada's kitchen.

The area's best attraction is a day's island-hopping in which you'll cruise alongside dolphins, snorkel in coral reefs, visit island fishing outposts and barbecue your lunch on a secluded beach. You can also hop across to popular individual destinations such as **Isla Arapo** and **La Piscina** from the *lancheros* (return trips cost around BsF60/person) outside the market.

ARRIVAL AND TOURS

By bus The terminal is a 500m walk from the beach on C La Plata. *Busetas* come and go regularly from 5am–7pm. Destinations Cumaná (half-hourly; 1hr) passing via Mochima 30min away; Puerto La Cruz (half-hourly; 40min) passing Playa Colorada 10min away.

Tour operators You can arrange island-hopping through your posada; one excellent guide is Jhonny (☎0293 808 0793) at *Posada Bahía del Mar* (see below), who does full-day trips for BsF70 per person. Local guide Sergio (☎0293 231 0058, ⓔsergioj38@hotmail.com) offers tours of the land behind Santa Fe for around BsF70/person. He takes tourists to coffee, mango and cacao plantations as well as visiting local Indians and swimming at a beautiful waterfall.

ACCOMMODATION

Camping on the beach is discouraged for safety reasons. All listings below are on the C Cochaima beach road. *Café del Mar* also runs a posada (see opposite).

Hotel Cochaima ☎0293 642 0728. Matriarch Margot runs the town's first posada, which has cheap rooms and a family atmosphere. Numerous white-tiled rooms (a/c, en suite) are faded but spotless, while the upper floor has excellent sea views. Discounts negotiable for multiple nights and guests. **BsF180**

★ **Posada Bahía del Mar** ☎0293 231 0073, ⓦposadabahiadelmar.com. Charming French couple Mado and Jean (and their friendly pets) run this delightful posada with its entrance right on the beach. Rooms are nicely decorated, clean and spacious; ask for No 7 or No 8, open-fronted doubles with fantastic views. Fast wi-fi, delicious smells from the outdoor kitchen *and* the laundry service comes included in the room fee. **BsF200**

Posada Sierra Inn ☎0293 231 0042, ⓔposadasde amigos@gmail.com. The family atmosphere is infectious in this colourful beach posada where chunky rocking chairs are favoured. There's a communal kitchen below an outpost-like beach lookout, decent rooms with a/c and hot water when the electricity permits. **BsF160**

EATING AND DRINKING

Seafood lovers are in for a treat in Santa Fe, where the produce is freshly caught daily.

Café del Mar Far end of the beach ☎0293 231 0009. With tables on top of the sand, this palm-roofed restaurant serves up delicious platters made with fresh ingredients from the market nearby. Does soups from BsF35, but the real triumph is the *parrilla café del mar* (BsF65), a seafood platter that you'll be thinking about until dinnertime the next day, when you'll probably be back. Also runs a posada upstairs with doubles for BsF130. Tues–Sun, 11am–9pm.

El Mercado On the beach past *Café del Mar*. An excellent breakfast option, as well as a place to stock up on supplies for your posada's kitchen. Numerous stands where *empanadas* and *arepas* are made to order while you sit back and watch the pelicans sneaking up on the fishermen. Daily breakfast & lunch.

DIRECTORY

Internet *Posada Bahía del Mar* has a computer you can use for BsF6/hr until 8pm, or for free if you're staying there.

Pharmacy Medicinas Santa Elena, C Las Mercedes, east of Av Principal (daily 7am–7pm, although they take a siesta from around noon–2.30pm).

Police Station at beach end of Av Principal.

Shopping The food market on the beach; you can buy fish directly from the fishermen outside in the mornings.

Mochima

The village after which the national park is named occupies a pretty inlet 3km from the main coastal road. Originally a fishing village, **MOCHIMA** has a lively malecón, from where boat trips to the park's cays depart. The village has no beach and is tricky to get to.

The main activity in Mochima is, once again, **boat trips** to the cays of the national park, all of which depart from the Terminal de Lanchas in the town centre. Prices for each destination are written on a board above the booth where you buy your tickets. If there's a group of you, you may want to rent a *lancha* (speedboat) for the day (BsF800 on the weekends, less during the week). Alternatively, consider the friendly Los Buzos dive centre (☎0293 416 0856, ✉mochimadivecenter@hotmail.com), which offers kayaking, trekking, climbing, rafting and dolphin-spotting in addition to one-day scuba trips (BsF600) and a four-day scuba SSI certification course (BsF3200, accommodation included).

ARRIVAL AND DEPARTURE

By bus The road to Mochima breaks off from the main coastal highway (heading towards Puerto La Cruz or Cumaná) beside various food stands; shout "¡parada!" at the bus driver to let you off, or hail a bus from the roadside to get on. Walking the road to Mochima is not recommended as robberies have occurred.

By jeep Intermittent jeeps and *busetas* (BsF15) shuttle back and forth along the road daily until 8pm. Otherwise, drivers who know the road's reputation are usually happy to give you a lift if you flag them down.

ACCOMMODATION

Casa Cruz ☎0293 416 0810, ✉posadacasacruzmochima @hotmail.com. Plenty of fish motifs to remind you of the beach location at this welcoming little posada with five rooms. Also has a separate house for groups of six for BsF600. Book ahead. BsF300

Posada El Mochimero ☎0293 643 5797. An oversized ceramic toad, elevated views from the big rooftop terrace and a trippy painting of marine life brighten up this otherwise dull posada. Rooms are clean, all with a/c; ask for room No 10 or No 17 as they have natural light. All rooms are triple. BsF180

EATING

Restaurant El Mochimero ☎0293 644 3200. They boast a Basque chef (which means delicious food) at this pleasant waterside restaurant, who serves up excellent seafood and grumbles over anything land-based, although the menu is extensive. Daily 11am–9pm.

Restaurant Puerto Viejo ☎0293 416 0810. Right next to the jetty, you'll get splashed at your table if a boat roars away quickly enough. The three-in-one platter serves up fresh octopus, squid and shrimp for BsF120. Also mixes up an excellent *piña colada* if your vitamin C count is running low. Daily 11am–8pm, open Thurs–Sun in low season.

CARIPE

Tucked away in the mountainous state of Monagas, the rounded limestone hills and lush forest around **CARIPE** offer respite from the heat of the coast. The town is famous for the **Cueva del Guácharo**, a 10km-long cave home to screeching nocturnal birds that add an unearthly atmosphere to an astonishing natural phenomenon.

WHAT TO SEE AND DO

The pretty town centre is easily walkable and safe at all times of day. The region is renowned across the country for its

11

fruit; make sure you sample the strawberries and cream on offer from vendors around town.

Venezuela's first national monument, the **Cueva del Guácharo** is a cave set deep in the limestone mountainside inhabited by oilbirds. You can take a tour (daily 8am–4pm; BsF30; ☎0291 641 7543) through the first 1200m of the cave, during which gas-lamp-toting guides point out distinctively shaped rock formations. At the entrance there's a museum dedicated to Alexander Von Humboldt, who first made oilbirds known to science.

Taxis will take you to the entrance of Parque Nacional El Guácharo from the centre for BsF30.

Hiking opportunities abound in Monagas and a popular walk is the **Cerro Turumiquire**, the region's highest point at 2600m. Contact Viajes y Turismo WM (Av Enrique Chaumer; ☎0292 415 0428) in the *centro comercial* for more information on activities.

ARRIVAL AND DEPARTURE

By bus The bus terminal is a BsF25 taxi ride from the centre. Buses run every two hours from 6.30am–4pm (BsF30) to state capital Maturín, which has connections throughout the country. To head directly to Puerto Ordáz or Cumaná, *por puestos* depart intermittently from the terminal. To get here from the coast, take a bus from Cumaná in the morning (3 daily until 1pm; 3hr). If you miss the direct morning buses, *por puestos* leave irregularly from Cumaná bus terminal, or you can take a bus to Maturín from where buses run regularly to Caripe.

ACCOMMODATION

Campamento Kenya Sector El Guácharo ☎0416 396 8376, ✉kenya002@hotmail.com. Friendly tour guide and local legend Carlos Kenya runs his "Lost Boys"-style homestay close to the Guácharo cave. There's a dormitory and four cosy doubles with en suite. Carlos also runs tours and volunteering projects throughout the region. Dorms BsF40, doubles BsF120

Hotel El Nuevo San Fransisco Av Enrique Chaumer, at Plaza Bolívar ☎0414 996 9047. Clean rooms have hot showers, cable TV and fans. The hotel is opposite the Plaza Bolívar, giving a very central location, useful for the weekend when locals converge on the area to drink and socialize. You won't see the hotel's name displayed anywhere on this brown-tiled building, only the word "hotel" written a number of different ways. BsF150

EATING AND DRINKING

On weekends, welcoming revellers tend to hang out with bottles of rum in the pedestrianized middle of C Bolívar until the early hours.

Ké Pollo C Ribero ☎0412 498 9244. Two colourful – if not artistically adept – murals are signature features at the town's most popular chicken joint. Whole (BsF110), half (BsF70) or quarter (BsF30) bird servings come accompanied with mini *arepas* and fries; also does excellent juices. Daily 11am–8pm.

Neno's Pizza C Bolívar ☎0292 808 8478. A pizzeria that's very popular with the locals. Excellent deep-dish-style pizzas come with all the usual toppings and boxes for takeaway. Personal size from BsF50, family size from BsF90. Daily noon–10.30pm.

DIRECTORY

Bank Banco Coroní on C Bolívar has a 24hr ATM.
Internet Centro de Conexiones, C Bolívar. Daily 8am–8pm, BsF5/hr.
Pharmacy Farmacia El Cristo, Av Enrique Chaumer. Daily 8am–4pm.
Police Av Guzman Blanco, daily 8am–8pm.
Shopping You can buy artesan jewellery in the pedestrian park in the middle of C Bolívar beside the Plaza Bolívar most evenings.

ISLA DE MARGARITA

On the ferry to **ISLA DE MARGARITA** from the mainland you're unlikely to see more than one or two backpackers, as the 940-square-kilometre island is primarily visited by well-to-do Venezuelans. While prices are inflated and any cultural authenticity has been supplanted by rampant commercialism, Margarita can still provide an entertaining taste of mainstream Venezuelan-style tourism.

WHAT TO SEE AND DO

Isla de Margarita has innumerable beach communities and just a few developed urban centres, **PORLAMAR** being the largest and containing the lion's share of inexpensive services. It's therefore best to base yourself here and take day-trips to the island's other attractions.

Ten kilometres north of Porlamar lies the more peaceful town of **Pampatar**. Founded in 1530, it was one of the first settlements in Venezuela, and even today it retains some of its former charm, with the remains of a Spanish fortress, Castillo de San Carlos Borromeo, completed in 1684 (daily 8am–5pm; free).

Margarita's most famous beach, **Playa El Agua** (1hr from Porlamar by bus), is 3km of white sand, palm trees and plenty of tourists. Less rammed beaches around the island include playas Manzanillo, El Yaque, Caribe, Guayacán, Puerto Abajo and Cardón.

ARRIVAL AND INFORMATION

By plane Santiago Mariño Airport is about 27km southwest of Porlamar; a taxi ride into town costs BsF180.
Destinations Caracas (several daily; 45min); Barcelona (3 daily; 30min); Maracaibo (4 daily; 2–3hr with connection); Puerto Ordáz (2 daily; 1hr); and San Antonio del Táchira (1 daily; 3hr with connection).
By ferry The cheapest way to get to and from Isla de Margarita is by ferry (see box below). Buses to Punta de Piedras (which stop at the top of the jetties) come and go from the new bus terminal five blocks west of the Plaza Bolívar between calles Velasquez & Igualidad until 7pm. A taxi either way costs BsF120 after hours. Keep in mind that ferry companies leave from different jetties at Punta

de Piedras, so ensure you tell your bus driver which company you are travelling with.
Tourist information Corpotur, Centro Artesanal Gilberto Menchini in Los Robles (☎0295 262 2322 or 262 3638, ⓦcorpoturmargarita.gov.ve), roughly 3km from the centre. There's also an information point at the airport, daily 5am–11pm (☎0295 400 5057).

GETTING AROUND

By bus The cheapest way to explore the island (no more than BsF7/ride). The primary bus terminal is five blocks west of the Plaza Bolívar, serving Punta de Piedras and various locations in the north of the island. Otherwise, bus stops throughout Porlamar's centre correspond to the island's more popular locales; buses run 6am–9pm daily.
By taxi Taxis within Porlamar cost around BsF30 during the day, BsF40 at night. Otherwise the city's centre is easily walkable.

ACCOMMODATION

PORLAMAR
Porlamar is the undisputed commercial centre of the island and rocks a distinctly more Caribbean vibe than the mainland. It's also the best spot for reasonably priced

---

BOAT TRANSPORT TO AND FROM ISLA DE MARGARITA

The three ferry companies which operate to the island depart from either Puerto La Cruz or Porlamar on the mainland, the towns at either end of Parque Mochima. All ferries dock on the island at Punta de Piedras, an hour's bus ride from Porlamar. Speedboats, which are half the price and twice as bumpy, are also an option and depart from the mainland's closest point at Chacopata, arriving at El Faro dock in Porlamar. Fares listed are one-way only. All companies run two-hour "express" services, while Conferry and Naviarca run the cheaper five-hour "conventional" trips, although they're scheduled at inconvenient times. You're asked to arrive 1hr 30min prior to departure to "confirm" your ticket at a company booth. Like bus tickets, you'll need your passport number to book a ticket. Rates are the same both to and from the island.

FROM PUERTO LA CRUZ
Puerto La Cruz's port is roughly 3km west of the centre, to which a taxi from the town should cost BsF20. Naviarca/Gran Cacique (☎0281 267 7286, ⓦgrancacique.com.ve) has four daily express services (BsF126). Conferry (☎0281 267 784, ⓦconferry.com) has three daily express boats (BsF88) and two daily conventional boats (BsF44). Navibus (☎0295 500 9284, ⓦnavibus.com.ve) runs two daily express boats (BsF128).

FROM CUMANÁ
Cumaná's terminal is 1km from the town's centre, from which Naviarca/Gran Cacique and Navibus operate. Both have two daily express boats to and from the island (BsF128), while Naviarca has three conventional boats (BsF90). An additional departure is added to each type of service in the high season.

FROM ISLA DE MARGARITA
From Isla de Margarita, Conferry has three daily express departures for Puerto La Cruz and four daily conventional services. Naviarca/Gran Cacique has three daily express returns to Puerto La Cruz in the high season, and two during the low season. If you didn't buy a return ticket on the mainland, make sure you visit a ferry office in Porlamar a day before you wish to leave.

You can also take cheaper *lanchas* (speedboats) for BsF60, which act like *por puestos*, departing when full between Porlamar and Chacopata on the mainland. The ride takes about an hour and boats operate from 6am–2pm daily, arriving and departing from the El Faro dock in Porlamar. *Por puestos* serve Chacopata from Maturín and Cumaná bus terminals.

11

11

accommodation and dining options. Make sure to ask for low-season discounts outside the island's peak periods of Dec–Jan and Easter.

Contemporáneo Av Santiago Mariño between calles Igualdad & Velásquez ☎0295 988 4978. A decent option in a safe setting, although you'll have to shout upstairs to be let in. The rooms (en suite, a/c, TV) are made darker by windows that don't open, and making a reservation over the phone can prove troublesome. Nevertheless, its location beyond the centre is a plus. **BsF150**

España C Mariño, at Av La Marina ☎0295 261 2479. An alarm clock is unnecessary in this friendly establishment as the frisky canaries (and one mad parrot) don't shut up after their covers come off. The rooms are decent enough, with fan, TV and en suite, and there's also free wi-fi. Get your beers from the Chinese restaurant up the street after the off-licences close. **BsF130**

★ **Il Teramano** C Marcano between calles Narváez & Hernández ☎0424 811 6485. Larger-than-life owner Walter has travelled extensively and knows what backpacking's all about. His spanking-clean establishment shows it. With three floors of dorms, private rooms and a communal kitchen, this is a good, secure option a short walk from the centre. Dorms **BsF80**, doubles **BsF200**

Posada Bahía del Rey C Fermín, at Av Raúl Leoni ☎0295 264 8947, ✉posadabahiadelrey@gmail.com. Bright yellow posada away from the chaos of the city, and only five steps from the seashore. Catch some rays on their lounge chairs on the beach before heading back to the warm and welcoming rooms (en suite, TV). There are plans to build a four-person apartment and swimming pool. **BsF260**

EATING

PORLAMAR

Los Caratos C Marcano, at C Fajardo. A tiny juice joint selling delicious, freshly made *merengadas* and *batidos* (BsF12–18). Also does a good *cachapa* (sweetmeal pancake) (BsF12). Mon–Sat 7am–7pm.

La Casa de Rubén C Santiago Mariño ☎0295 264 5969. Rubén, whose smiling countenance grins at you from all over his establishment, is the author of several traditional Venezuelan cookbooks. The eatery serves meat, but the

PORLAMAR

ACCOMMODATION	
Contemporáneo	3
España	4
Il Teramano	1
Posada Bahía del Rey	2

● EATING	
Los Caratos	2
La Casa de Rubén	5
Cooperativa Nutrioriente	3
Hamburguesa	4
Punto Criollo	1
Restaurant Mérida	6

emphasis is on the locally sourced seafood (BsF90–160). Mon–Sat 11am–6pm.

Cooperativa Nutrioriente C Santiago Mariño, at C Igualidad. A very clean, very cheap self-service restaurant, with plates of beef, vegetarian, chicken, fish and sides for BsF40. As the name suggests, some options are healthy and low-fat. Mon–Sat 7.30am–5pm.

Hamburguesa C Marcano between Ortega & Campo Sur. The absolute definition of a burger shack, owner Magali has been dishing out excellent burgers, steaks and other delights from this front garden patch for years. Grab your food to go or sit down at the rickety street-side furniture to tuck in immediately. Burgers BsF25. Mon–Sat 6–10pm.

★ **Punto Criollo** C Igualdad, at C Fraternidad ☎0295 263 6745. Towering plates of mixed seafood and *comida criolla* at every table of this constantly packed local joint. Meat dishes feature heavily (*bistec* BsF80, *medallones* BsF100, beef stroganoff BsF87), the seafood is excellent (from BsF87) and the choice of sides is endless. Daily 10.30am–10pm.

Restaurant Mérida C Arismendi, south of C Maneiro. Though naming an island restaurant after Venezuela's most renowned mountain town was an odd decision, this is a friendly budget option with communal atmosphere. Tuck into the day's menu (BsF30) scribbled on a board, as you share a table with other diners in the pleasant courtyard of the owners' home. Mon–Sat 10am–3pm, closed Sun.

DRINKING AND NIGHTLIFE

Night owls are in for a treat on the island. Most action takes place in Pampatar or in the Centro Comercial Costa Azul, a 2km taxi ride east of Porlamar (BsF30). Most clubs have no cover charge.

★ **TREAT YOURSELF**

El Fondeadero C Joaquin Maneiro beside the castle, Pampatar ☎0295 267 1526. Sitting in a prime spot between the castle and the beach, *El Fondeadero* is recognized not only as one of Venezuela's best restaurants, but one of Latin America's top seafood eateries. For all the praise it receives, the menu is surprisingly reasonable, with chunky fillets of red snapper, swordfish and island specialities such as the delicious *mojito de pescado* (BsF60) emerging at intervals from the open-fronted kitchen. If you're not feeling peckish, it's worthwhile grabbing a seat at the stylishly tiled bar, ordering a beer (BsF20) or a *batido* (BsF22) and watching the crystal-clear sea through the wide windows. Live music Wed–Sat from 8pm, open 11am–midnight.

CENTRO COMERCIAL COSTA AZUL

Aldea Beach Complejo Margarita Village, behind the Centro Comercial Costa Azul. The main musical flavour is electronica at this open-air club by the seashore with three dance areas. Thurs–Sat 9am–3pm.

British Bulldog ☎0295 267 1527. You've gotta give the place credit for trying so hard with the pub theme – with memorabilia, advertisements for drinks they don't serve and an enormous Union Jack. At weekends, local bands play amazingly accurate renditions of European and American hard-rock classics. Mon–Wed 9pm–midnight, Thurs–Sat till 4am.

Opah ☎0295 262 8186. Your best bet for traditional salsa dancing with a local crowd, though the giant video screen and fog machines remind you that you're in the twenty-first century – or maybe the 1980s. Thurs–Sat 9pm–3am.

PAMPATAR

Beach Bar C El Cristo, La Caranta ☎0295 267 2392, ⓦ beachbar.com.ve. Have a few refreshing cocktails *après-plage* at this laidback bar with bamboo gazebos facing the beach. Tues–Sun 7pm–3am.

Latitud Diez °59 C El Cristo, Sector La Caranta ☎0295 267 1850, ⓦ latituddiez59.com. Snazzy club with an outdoor terrace where you can have a boogie or a cocktail as you check out the view. Thurs–Sat until late.

DIRECTORY

Banks and exchange Banco Universal, C Marcano between C Santiago Mariño & C Malave; Banco Mercantil, C San Nicolás, at C Mariño.

Hospital Clínica Margarita, C Marcano, at C Díaz ☎0295 264 9158.

Internet Grafica Multicolor (BsF6/hr), C Fajardo between calles Marcano & Igualdad, Mon–Sat 8.30am–5.30pm.

Laundry Lavandaria HR, C Marcano, at C Santiago Mariño (Mon–Fri 8am–5.30pm, Sat till noon; BsF15/kg; ☎0295 264 9158); Edi's Lavandería, C Marcano between calles Campo Sur & Fermín (self service; Mon–Sat 7.45am–7.30pm, Sun until 1pm), also has an internet café while you wait (BsF6/hr).

Pharmacy FarmaSigo, C Marcano, at C Díaz, daily 8.30am–6.30pm.

Phones There are plenty of cheap calling places on Boulevard Guevara and Boulevard Gómez.

Police Station on C Arismendi, just south of C Maneiro ☎0295 264 1494.

Post Ipostel, C Maneiro between C Fraternidad & Bulevar Gómez.

Shopping Margarita is famed for its duty-free shopping. Two pedestrianized streets, Bulevar Gómez and Bulevar Guevara, are lined with vendors selling mostly knockoff items and pirated CDs – though the occasional used-book vendor may be holding some treasures.

11

Language

919 Spanish

924 Portuguese

Spanish

Although there are dozens of indigenous tongues scattered throughout South America – some thirty in the Peruvian Amazon alone – this is, in general, a Spanish-speaking continent (see pp.924–927 for a Portuguese primer). The Spanish you will hear in South America does not always conform to what you learned in the classroom, and even competent speakers of peninsular Spanish will find it takes a bit of getting used to. In addition to the odd differences in pronunciation – discussed in detail below – words from native languages as well as various European tongues have infiltrated the different dialects of South American Spanish, giving them each their own unique character.

For the most part, the language itself is the same throughout the continent, while the pronunciation varies slightly. In parts of Argentina, for example, the *ll* and *y* sound like a *zh* (the English equivalent is the *s* in "treasure"), while the final *s* of a word is often not pronounced.

Spanish itself is not a difficult language to pick up and there are numerous learning products on the market. You'll be further helped by the fact that most South Americans, with the notable exception of fast-talking Chileans, speak relatively slowly (at least compared with Spaniards) and that there's no need to get your tongue round the lisping pronunciation. *Spanish: The Rough Guide Phrasebook* is a concise and handy **phrasebook**.

Pronunciation

The rules of Spanish **pronunciation** are pretty straightforward. All syllables are pronounced. Unless there's an accent, words ending in d, l, r and z are **stressed** on the last syllable, all others on the second last. All **vowels** are pure and short.

A somewhere between the "A" sound of back and that of father.

E as in get.

I as in police.

O as in hot.

U as in rule.

C is soft before E and I, hard otherwise: cerca is pronounced "serka".

G works the same way: a guttural **H** sound (like the ch in loch) before E or I, a hard G elsewhere – gigante becomes "higante".

H is always silent.

J is the same sound as a guttural **G**: jamón is pronounced "hamón".

LL sounds like an English **Y**: tortilla is pronounced "torteeya".

Ñ is as in English unless it has a tilde (accent) over it, when it becomes NY: mañana sounds like "manyana".

QU is pronounced like an English **K**.

R is rolled, RR doubly so.

V sounds more like **B**, vino becoming "beano".

X is slightly softer than in English – sometimes almost SH – except between vowels in place names where it has an "H" sound – for example México (Meh-Hee-Ko) or Oaxaca.

Z is the same as a soft **C**, so cerveza becomes "servesa".

There is a list of a few essential words and phrases over the page, though if you're travelling for any length of time a dictionary or phrasebook is obviously a worthwhile investment.

WORDS AND PHRASES

The following will help you with your most basic day-to-day language needs.

BASIC EXPRESSIONS

Yes, No	Sí, No
Please, Thank you	Por favor, Gracias
Where, When?	¿Dónde, Cuándo?
What, How much?	¿Qué, Cuánto?
Here, There	Aquí, Allí
This, That	Este, Eso
Now, Later	Ahora, Más tarde/Luego
Open, Closed	Abierto/a, Cerrado/a
Pull, Push	Tire, Empuje
Entrance, Exit	Entrada, Salida
With, Without	Con, Sin
For	Para/Por
Good, Bad	Buen(o)/a, Mal(o)/a
Big, Small	Gran(de), Pequeño/a
A little, A lot	Poco/a, Mucho/a
More, Less	Más, Menos
Another	Otro/a
Today, Tomorrow	Hoy, Mañana
Yesterday	Ayer
But	Pero
And	Y
Nothing, Never	Nada, Nunca

GREETINGS AND RESPONSES

Hello, Goodbye	Hola, Adios
Good morning	Buenos días
Good afternoon/night	Buenas tardes/noches
See you later	Hasta luego
Sorry	Lo siento/Discúlpeme
Excuse me	Con permiso/Perdón
How are you?	¿Como está (usted)?
What's up?	¿Qué pasa?
I (don't) understand	(No) Entiendo
Not at all/You're welcome	De nada
Do you speak English?	¿Habla (usted) inglés?
I (don't) speak Spanish	(No) Hablo español
My name is …	Me llamo …
What's your name?	¿Como se llama usted?
I am English/American	Soy inglés(a)/ americano(a)
Cheers	Salud

ASKING DIRECTIONS, GETTING AROUND

Where is…?	¿Dónde está…?
…the bus station	…la estación de autobuses
…the train station	…la estación de ferrocarriles
…the nearest bank	…el banco más cercano
…the post office	…el correo
…the toilet	…el baño/sanitario
Is there a hotel nearby?	¿Hay un hotel aquí cerca?
Left, right, straight on	Izquierda, derecha, derecho
Where does the bus to … leave from?	¿De dónde sale el autobús para…?
How do I get to…?	¿Por dónde se va a…?
I'd like a (return) ticket to…	Quiero un boleto (de ida y vuelta) para…
What time does it leave?	¿A qué hora sale?

ACCOMMODATION

Private bathroom	Baño privado
Shared bathroom	Baño compartido
Hot water (all day)	Agua caliente (todo el día)
Cold water	Agua fría
Fan	Ventilador
Air-conditioned	Aire-acondicionado
Mosquito net	Mosquitero
Key	Llave
Check-out time	Hora de salida
Do you have…?	¿Tiene …?
… a room …	…una habitación
… with two beds/ double bed …	…con dos camas/ cama matrimonial…
It's for one person (two people)	Es para una persona (dos personas)
…for one night …	…para una noche…
…one week	…una semana
It's fine, how much is it?	¿Está bien, cuánto es?
It's too expensive	Es demasiado caro
Don't you have anything cheaper?	¿No tiene algo más barato?

NUMBERS AND DAYS

1	un/uno/una
2	dos
3	tres
4	cuatro
5	cinco
6	seis
7	siete
8	ocho
9	nueve
10	diez
11	once
12	doce
13	trece
14	catorce
15	quince
16	dieciséis
20	veinte

21	veintiuno
30	treinta
40	cuarenta
50	cincuenta
60	sesenta
70	setenta
80	ochenta
90	noventa
100	cien(to)
200	doscientos
500	quinientos
1000	mil

Monday	lunes
Tuesday	martes
Wednesday	miércoles
Thursday	jueves
Friday	viernes
Saturday	sábado
Sunday	domingo

USEFUL WORDS

Barrio	Suburb, or sometimes shantytown
Carretera	Route or highway
Cerro	Hill, mountain peak
Colectivo	Shared taxi/bus
Combi	Small minibus that runs urban routes
Cordillera	Mountain range
Criollo	"Creole": a person of Spanish blood born in the American colonies
Entrada	Ticket (for theatre, football match, etc)
Estancia	Ranch, or large estate
Farmacia	Chemist
Gaucho	The typical Argentine "cowboy", or rural *estancia* worker
Gringo	Foreigner, Westerner (not necessarily a derogatory term)
Hacienda	Large estate
Mestizo	Person of mixed Spanish and indigenous blood
Micro	City bus
Mirador	Viewpoint
Peña	Venue with live music
Soroche	Altitude sickness

A SPANISH MENU READER

While menus vary by country and region, these words and terms will help negotiate most of them.

BASIC DINING VOCABULARY

Almuerzo	Lunch
Asada	Barbecue
Carta (la)/Lista (la)	Menu
Cena	Dinner
Comida típica	Typical cuisine
Cuchara	Spoon
Cuchillo	Knife
Desayuno	Breakfast
La cuenta, por favor	The bill, please
Merienda	Set menu
Plato fuerte	Main course
Plato vegetariano	Vegetarian dish
Tenedor	Fork

FRUIT (*FRUTAS*)

Cereza	Cherry
Chirimoya	Custard apple
Ciruela	Plum
Fresa/frutilla	Strawberry
Guayaba	Guava
Guineo	Banana
Higo	Fig
Limón	Lemon or lime
Manzana	Apple
Maracuyá	Passion fruit
Melocotón/durazno	Peach
Mora	Blackberry
Naranja	Orange
Pera	Pear
Piña	Pineapple
Plátano	Plantain
Pomelo/toronja	Grapefruit
Sandía	Watermelon

VEGETABLES (*LEGUMBRES/VERDURAS*)

Aguacate	Avocado
Alcachofa	Artichoke
Cebolla	Onion
Champiñón	Mushroom
Choclo	Maize/sweetcorn
Coliflor	Cauliflower
Espinaca	Spinach
Frijoles	Beans
Guisantes/arvejas	Peas
Hongo	Mushroom
Lechuga	Lettuce
Lentejas	Lentil
Menestra	Bean/lentil stew
Palmito	Palm heart

Patata	Potato
Papas fritas	French fries
Pepinillo	Gherkin
Pepino	Cucumber
Tomate	Tomato
Zanahoria	Carrot

MEAT (*CARNE*) AND POULTRY (*AVES*)

Carne de chancho	Pork
Cerdo	Pork
Chicharrones	Pork scratchings, crackling
Chuleta	Pork chop
Churrasco	Grilled meat with sides
Conejo	Rabbit
Cordero	Lamb
Cuero	Pork crackling
Cuy	Guinea pig
Jamón	Ham
Lechón	Suckling pig
Lomo	Steak
Pato	Duck
Pavo	Turkey
Pollo	Chicken
Res	Beef
Ternera	Veal
Tocino	Bacon
Venado	Venison

OFFAL (*MENUDOS*)

Chunchules	Intestines
Guatita	Tripe
Hígado	Liver
Lengua	Tongue
Mondongo	Tripe
Patas	Trotters

SHELLFISH (*MARISCOS*) AND FISH (*PESCADO*)

Anchoa	Anchovy
Atún	Tuna
Calamares	Squid
Camarón	Prawn
Cangrejo	Crab
Ceviche	Seafood marinated in lime juice with onions
Corvina	Sea bass
Erizo	Sea urchin
Langosta	Lobster
Langostina	King prawn
Lenguado	Sole
Mejillón	Mussel
Ostra	Oyster
Trucha	Trout

COOKING TERMS

A la parrilla	Barbecued
A la plancha	Lightly fried
Ahumado	Smoked
Al ajillo	In garlic sauce
Al horno	Oven-baked
Al vapor	Steamed
Apanado	Breaded
Asado	Roast
Asado al palo	Spit roast
Crudo	Raw
Duro	Hard boiled
Encebollado	Cooked with onions
Encocado	In coconut sauce
Frito	Fried
Picant	Spicy hot
Puré	Mashed
Revuelto	Scrambled
Saltado	Sautéed
Secado	Dried

DRINKS (*BEBIDAS*)

Agua (mineral)	Mineral water
Con gas	Sparkling
Sin gas	Still
Sin hielo	Without ice
Aguardiente	Sugar-cane spirit
Aromática	Herbal tea
Manzanilla	Camomile
Menta	Mint
Batido	Milkshake
Café (con leche)	Coffee (with milk)
Caipirinha	Cocktail of rum, lime, sugar and ice
Cerveza	Beer
Chicha	Fermented corn drink
Gaseosa	Fizzy drink
Jugo	Juice
Leche	Milk
Limonada	Fresh lemonade
Mate de coca	Coca leaf tea
Ron	Rum
Té	Tea
Vino blanco	White wine
Vino tinto	Red wine
Yerba (hierba) mate	Herbal infusion with *mate*

FOOD GLOSSARY

Aceite	Oil
Ají	Chilli
Ajo	Garlic
Arroz	Rice
Azúcar	Sugar
Galletas	Biscuits

Hielo	Ice
Huevos	Eggs
Mantequilla	Butter
Mermeleda	Jam
Miel	Honey
Mixto	Mixed seafood/meats
Mostaza	Mustard
Pan (integral)	Bread (wholemeal)
Pimienta	Pepper
Queso	Cheese
Sal	Salt
Salsa de tomate	Tomato sauce

SOUPS

Caldosa	Broth
Caldo de gallina	Chicken broth
Caldo de patas	Cattle-hoof broth
Crema de espárragos	Cream of asparagus
Locro	Cheese and potato soup
Sopa de bolas de verde	Plantain dumpling soup
Sopa del día	Soup of the day
Yaguarlocro	Blood sausage (black pudding) soup

SNACKS (*BOCADILLOS*)

Bolón de verde	Baked cheese and potato dumpling

Chifles	Banana chips/crisps
Empanada	Cheese/meat pasty
Hamburguesa	Hamburger
Humitas	Ground corn and cheese
Omelet	Omelette
Palomitas	Popcorn
Patacones	Thick-cut dried banana/plantain
Salchipapas	Sausage, fries and sauces
Sanwiche	Sandwich
Tamale	Ground maize with meat/cheese wrapped in leaf
Tortilla de huevos	Firm omelette
Tostada	Toast
Tostado	Toasted maize

DESSERT (*POSTRES*)

Cocados	Coconut candy
Ensalada de frutas	Fruit salad
Flan	Crème caramel
Helado	Ice cream
Manjar de leche	Very sweet caramel made from condensed milk
Pastas	Pastries
Pastel	Cake
Torta	Tart

Portuguese

The great exception to the Spanish-speaking rule in South America is, of course, Portuguese-speaking Brazil (that is, putting the Guianas to the side). Unfortunately, far too many people – especially Spanish-speakers – are put off going to Brazil solely because of the language, while this should actually be one of your main reasons for going. Brazilian Portuguese is a colourful, sensual language full of wonderfully rude and exotic vowel sounds, swooping intonation and hilarious idiomatic expressions.

The best **dictionary** currently available is *Collins Portuguese Dictionary*, which has a pocket edition. For a **phrasebook**, look no further than *Portuguese: The Rough Guide Phrasebook*, with useful two-way glossaries and a brief and simple grammar section.

Pronunciation

Although its complex pronunciation is far too difficult to be described in detail here, for the most part, Brazilian Portuguese is spoken more slowly and clearly than its European counterpart. The neutral vowels so characteristic of European Portuguese tend to be sounded out in full; in much of Brazil outside Rio the slushy "sh" sound doesn't exist; and the "de" and "te" endings of words like *cidade* and *diferente* are palatalized so they end up sounding like "sidadgee" and "djiferentchee".

WORDS AND PHRASES

You'll also find that Brazilians will greatly appreciate even your most rudimentary efforts, and every small improvement in your Portuguese will make your stay in Brazil much more enjoyable.

BASIC EXPRESSIONS

Yes, No	Sim, Não
Please	Por favor
Thank you	Obrigado (men)/ Obrigada (women)
Where, When?	Onde, Quando
What, How much?	Que, Quanto
This, That	Este, Esse, Aquele
Now, Later	Agora, Mais tarde
Open, Closed	Aberto/a, Fechado/a
Pull, Push	Puxe, Empurre
Entrance, Exit	Entrada, Saída
With, Without	Com, Sem
For	Para/Por
Good, Bad	Bom, Ruim
Big, Small	Grande, Pequeno
A little, A lot	Um pouco, Muito
More, Less	Mais, Menos
Another	Outro/a
Today, Tomorrow	Hoje, Amanhã
Yesterday	Ontem
But	Mas (pronounced like "mice")
And	E (pronounced like "ee" in "seek")
Something, Nothing	Alguma coisa, Nada
Sometimes	Às vezes

GREETINGS AND RESPONSES

Hello, Goodbye	Oi, Tchau (like the Italian "ciao")
Good morning	Bom dia
Good afternoon/night	Boa tarde/Boa noite
Sorry	Desculpa
Excuse me	Com licença
How are you?	Como vai?
Fine	Bem
I don't understand	Não entendo
Do you speak English?	Você fala inglês?
I don't speak Portuguese	Não falo português
My name is …	Meu nome é …
What's your name?	Como se chama?
I am English/American	Sou inglês/americano
Cheers	Saúde

ASKING DIRECTIONS, GETTING AROUND

Where is…?	Onde fica…?
…the bus station	…a rodoviária
…the bus stop	…a parada de ônibus
…the nearest hotel	…o hotel mais próximo
…the toilet	…o banheiro/sanitário
Left, right, straight on	Esquerda, direita, direto
Where does the bus to … leave from?	De onde sai o ônibus para…?
Is this the bus to Rio?	É esse o ônibus para Rio?
Do you go to…?	Você vai para…?
I'd like a (return) ticket to...	Quero uma passagem (ida e volta) para…
What time does it leave?	Que horas sai?

ACCOMMODATION

Do you have a room?	Você tem um quarto?
…with two beds	…com duas
…with double bed	…camas/cama de casal
It's for one person/ two people	É para uma pessoa/ duas pessoas
It's fine, how much is it?	Está bom, quanto é?
It's too expensive	É caro demais
Do you have anything cheaper?	Tem algo mais barato?
Is there a hotel/ campsite nearby?	Tem um hotel/ camping por aqui?

NUMBERS AND DAYS

1	um, uma
2	dois, duas
3	três
4	quatro
5	cinco
6	seis
7	sete
8	oito
9	nove
10	dez
11	onze
12	doze
13	treze
14	quatorze
15	quinze
16	dezesseis
17	diecisiete
18	dieciocho
19	diecinueve
20	vinte
21	vinte e um
30	trinta
40	quarenta
50	cinquenta
60	sesenta
70	setenta
80	oitenta
90	noventa
100	cem
200	duzentos
300	trezentos
500	quinhentos
1000	mil

Monday	segunda-feira (or segunda)
Tuesday	terça-feira (or terça)
Wednesday	quarta-feira (or quarta)
Thursday	quinta-feira (or quinta)
Friday	sexta-feira (or sexta)
Saturday	sábado
Sunday	domingo

USEFUL WORDS

Azulejo	Decorative glazed tiling
Boîte	Club or bar with dancing
Candomblé	African-Brazilian religion
Capoeira	African-Brazilian martial art/dance form
Carimbó	Music and dance style from the north
Carioca	Someone or something from Rio de Janeiro
Dancetaria	Nightspot where the emphasis is on dancing
Favela	Shantytown, slum
Fazenda	Country estate, ranch house
Feira	Country market
Ferroviária	Train station
Forró	Dance and type of music from the Northeast
Frevo	Frenetic musical style and dance from Recife
Gaúcho	Person or thing from Rio Grande do Sul; also southern cowboy
Gringo/a	Foreigner, Westerner (not necessarily derogatory)
Latifúndios	Large agricultural estates
Leito	Luxury express bus
Louro/a	Fair-haired/blonde – Westerners in general
Maconha	Marijuana
Mirante	Viewing point
Paulista	Person or thing from São Paulo state
Rodovia	Highway
Rodoviária	Bus station
Visto/visa	Visa

A BRAZILIAN MENU READER

BASIC DINING VOCABULARY

Almoço/lonche	Lunch
Café de manhã	Breakfast
Cardápio	Menu
Colher	Spoon
Conta/nota	Bill
Copo	Glass
Entrada	Hors d'oeuvre
Faca	Knife
Garçon	Waiter
Garfo	Fork
Jantar	Dinner, to have dinner
Prato	Plate
Sobremesa	Dessert
Sopa/Caldo	Soup
Taxa de serviço	Service charge

FRUIT (*FRUTAS*)

Abacate	Avocado
Abacaxi	Pineapple
Ameixa	Plum, prune
Caju	Cashew fruit
Carambola	Star fruit
Cerejas	Cherries
Côco	Coconut
Fruta do conde	Custard apple (also *ata*)
Goiaba	Guava
Laranja	Orange
Limão	Lime
Maçã	Apple
Mamão	Papaya
Maracujá	Passion fruit
Melancia	Watermelon
Melão	Melon
Morango	Strawberry
Pera	Pear
Pêssego	Peach
Uvas	Grapes

VEGETABLES (*LEGUMES*)

Alface	Lettuce
Arroz e feijão	Rice and beans
Azeitonas	Olives
Batatas	Potatoes
Cebola	Onion
Cenoura	Carrot
Dendê	Palm oil
Ervilhas	Peas
Espinafre	Spinach
Macaxeira	Roasted manioc
Mandioca	Manioc/cassava/yuca
Milho	Corn
Palmito	Palm heart
Pepinho	Cucumber
Repolho	Cabbage
Tomate	Tomato

MEAT (*CARNE*) AND POULTRY (*AVES*)

Bife	Steak
Bife a cavalo	Steak with egg and *farinha*
Cabrito	Kid (goat)
Carne de porco	Pork
Carneiro	Lamb
Costela	Ribs
Costeleta	Chop
Feijoada	Black bean, pork and sausage stew
Fígado	Liver
Frango	Chicken
Leitão	Suckling pig
Lingüiça	Sausage
Pato	Duck
Peito	Breast
Perna	Leg
Peru	Turkey
Picadinha	Stew
Salsicha	Hot dog
Veado	Venison
Vitela	Veal

SEAFOOD (*FRUTOS DO MAR*)

Acarajé	Fried bean cake stuffed with *vatapá*
Agulha	Needle fish
Atum	Tuna
Camarão	Prawn, shrimp
Caranguejo	Large crab
Filhote	Amazon river fish
Lagosta	Lobster
Lula	Squid
Mariscos	Mussels
Moqueca	Seafood stewed in palm oil and coconut sauce
Ostra	Oyster
Pescada	Seafood stew, or hake
Pirarucu	Amazon river fish
Pitu	Crayfish
Polvo	Octopus
Siri	Small crab
Sururu	A type of mussel
Vatapá	Bahian shrimp dish, cooked with palm oil, skinned tomato and coconut milk, served with fresh coriander and hot peppers

COOKING TERMS

Assado	Roasted
Bem gelado	Well chilled
Churrasco	Barbecue
Cozido	Boiled, steamed
Cozinhar	To cook
Grelhado	Grilled
Mal passado/Bem passado	Rare/well done (meat)
Médio	Medium-grilled
Milanesa	Breaded
Na chapa/Na brasa	Charcoal-grilled

SPICES (*TEMPEROS*)

Alho	Garlic
Canela	Cinnamon
Cheiro verde	Fresh coriander
Coentro	Parsley
Cravo	Clove
Malagueta	Very hot pepper, looks like red or yellow cherry

DRINKS (*BEBIDAS*)

Água mineral	Mineral water
Batida	Fresh fruit juice (sometimes with *cachaça*)
Cachaça	Sugar-cane rum
Café com leite	Coffee with hot milk
Cafézinho	Small black coffee
Caipirinha	Rum and lime cocktail
Cerveja	Bottled beer
Chopp	Draught beer
Com gás/sem gás	Sparkling/still
Suco	Fruit juice
Vinho	Wine
Vitamina	Fruit juice made with milk

FOOD GLOSSARY

Açúcar	Sugar
Alho e óleo	Garlic and olive oil sauce
Arroz	Rice
Azeite	Olive oil
Farinha	Dried manioc flour beans
Manteiga	Butter
Molho	Sauce
Ovos	Eggs
Pão	Bread
Pimenta	Pepper
Queijo	Cheese
Sal	Salt
Sorvete	Ice cream

Small print and index

928 Small print

930 Index

941 Map symbols

A ROUGH GUIDE TO ROUGH GUIDES

Published in 1982, the first Rough Guide – to Greece – was a student scheme that became a publishing phenomenon. Mark Ellingham, a recent graduate in English from Bristol University, had been travelling in Greece the previous summer and couldn't find the right guidebook. With a small group of friends he wrote his own guide, combining a highly contemporary, journalistic style with a thoroughly practical approach to travellers' needs.

The immediate success of the book spawned a series that rapidly covered dozens of destinations. And, in addition to impecunious backpackers, Rough Guides soon acquired a much broader readership that relished the guides' wit and inquisitiveness as much as their enthusiastic, critical approach and value-for-money ethos.

These days, Rough Guides include recommendations from budget to luxury and cover more than 200 destinations around the globe, as well as producing an ever-growing range of eBooks and apps.

Visit **roughguides.com** to see our latest publications.

HELP US UPDATE

We've gone to a lot of effort to ensure that the third edition of The Rough Guide to South America on a Budget is accurate and up-to-date. However, things change – places get "discovered", opening hours are notoriously fickle, restaurants and rooms raise prices or lower standards. If you feel we've got it wrong or left something out, we'd like to know, and if you can remember the address, the price, the hours, the phone number, so much the better.

Please send your comments with the subject line "Rough Guide South America on a Budget update" to ✉ mail@uk.roughguides.com. We'll credit all contributions and send a copy of the next edition (or any other Rough Guide if you prefer) for the very best emails.

Find more travel information, connect with fellow travellers and plan your trip on ⦿ roughguides.com

Rough Guide credits

Editors: Rachel Mills, Alice Park and Lucy Cowie
Layout: Nikhil Agarwal
Cartography: Rajesh Mishra
Picture editor: Marta Bescos
Proofreader: Jan McCann
Managing editor: Mani Ramaswamy
Assistant editor: Jalpreen Kaur Chhatwal
Production: Charlotte Cade
Cover design: Marta Bescos, Nikhil Agarwal

Editorial assistant: Olivia Rawes
Senior pre-press designer: Dan May
Design director: Scott Stickland
Travel publisher: Joanna Kirby
Digital travel publisher: Peter Buckley
Operations coordinator: Helen Blount
Publishing director (Travel): Clare Currie
Commercial manager: Gino Magnotta
Managing director: John Duhigg

Publishing information

This third edition published September 2013 by
Rough Guides Ltd,
80 Strand, London WC2R 0RL
11, Community Centre, Panchsheel Park,
New Delhi 110017, India
Distributed by the Penguin Group
Penguin Books Ltd,
80 Strand, London WC2R 0RL
Penguin Group (USA)
375 Hudson Street, NY 10014, USA
Penguin Group (Australia)
250 Camberwell Road, Camberwell,
Victoria 3124, Australia
Penguin Group (NZ)
67 Apollo Drive, Mairangi Bay, Auckland 1310,
New Zealand
Penguin Group (South Africa)
Block D, Rosebank Office Park, 181 Jan Smuts Avenue,
Parktown North, Gauteng, South Africa 2193
Rough Guides is represented in Canada by Tourmaline
Editions Inc. 662 King Street West, Suite 304, Toronto,
Ontario M5V 1M7
Printed in Singapore by Toppan Security Printing Pte. Ltd.

Photo credits

All photos © Rough Guides except the following:
(Key: a-above; b-below/bottom; c-centre; f-far; l-left; r-right; t-top)

Index

Maps are marked in grey

ABBREVIATIONS

(A)	Argentina
(B)	Bolivia
(Br)	Brazil
(Ch)	Chile
(C)	Colombia
(E)	Ecuador
(FG)	French Guiana
(G)	Guyana
(P)	Paraguay
(Pe)	Peru
(S)	Suriname
(U)	Uruguay
(V)	Venezuela

A

accommodation 33
  Argentina 48
  Bolivia 159
  Brazil 229
  Chile 374
  Colombia 490
  Ecuador 567
  French Guiana 671
  Guyana 646
  Paraguay 689
  Peru 718
  Suriname 660
  Uruguay 832

Venezuela 860
Aconcagua, Cerro (A) 51, 104, 105
Aguas Calientes (Pe) ... 761–763
Aguas Calientes 761
air passes 30, 32
airlines 30
Alausí (E) 598
albergues 33, 229
Aleijadinho 295
Alta Gracia (A) 75
Alta Montaña (A) 104
altitude sickness 35, 422, 494, 790
Alto de la Piedras (C) 555
Alto de los Idolos (C) 555
Amantaní (Pe) 786
Amazon Animal Orphanage 819
Amazon Basin, the....... 216–222
Amazon Basin, the............ 217
Amazon, the 27, 303–317, 814, 898,
Amazon, the 304–305
Amazonas (C) 560
Ambato (E) 592
Ancud (Ch) 448
Ancud................................. 449
Angel Falls (V) 902, 904
Annai (G) 656
Antarctica 160
Antofagasta (Ch) 410
Apartaderos (V) 893

Aquaductos de Cantallo (Pe) ...774
Areguá (P) 698
Arequipa (Pe) 775–782
Arequipa 775
ARGENTINA 23, 43–152
Argentina 45
Argentina, Northeast 79
Argentina, Northwest 90
Argentina Patagonia 127
Arica (Ch) 419–422
Arica 420
Arraial do Cabo (Br) 256
Asunción (P) 693–699
Central Asunción 694
Atacames (E) 616
Atacames 617
ATMs 40
Ausangate (Pe) 764
Awarradam (S) 668
Ayacucho (Pe) 738
ayahuasca ceremony 812
Aymara New Year 175
Aysén (Ch) 456–462

B

Bahia (Br) 275–287
Bahía de Caráquez (E) 620
Bahía Inglesa (Ch) 408
Bahuaja-Sonene National Park (Pe) 826
Ballestas Islands (Pe) 767

Balneário Camboriú (Br).........355
Baños, Cuenca (E)......................604
Baños, Tungurahua (E)
.... **593–596**
Baños 593
barbecue 49
Barichara (C).............................511
Bariloche (A) 117–121
Bariloche 118
Barra de Valizas (U) 852
Barranquilla (C)........................524
Bartica (G)................................654
baseball, Venezuela 862, 874
Beagle Channel 148
beef..49
Belém 303–310
Belém 308–309
Bellavista (E)............................594
Belo Horizonte (Br) 261–267
Belo Horizonte 262–263
bicycles....................................32
Bigipan (S)................................668
bikes..32
birdman cult, Easter Island 481
bird-singing contests (S).........664
birdwatching (E) 569, 691, 834
bites and stings.........................34
black market (V) 858,
864
Blumenau (Br).........................356
Boa Viagem (Br)......................291
Boa Viagem 292
boats.......................................32
BOGOTÁ (C) 495–505
Bogotá 496
La Candelaria 498
accommodation...................502
addresses...........................497
airport 501
arrival and departure..........501
banks.................................505
Botero, Fernando 497
buses...........................501, 502
cafés..................................503
Capitol...............................497
Casa de Moneda..................499
Casa de Nariño 497
Catedral..............................497
climbing 502
cycling 502
drinking 504
eating 503
embassies...........................505
exchange 505
festivals..............................501
flights 501
hospitals.............................505
hostels................................502
hotels.................................502
immigration........................505
information.........................501
internet...............................505
La Candelaria.......................497
La Candelaria, churches 499
Mirador Torre Colpatria.......500
Monserrate 500
Museo Botero......................497
Museo de Arte Colonial.......499
Museo de Arte Moderno......501
Museo del Oro 500
Museo Histórico Policía........499
Museo Militar......................499

Museo Nacional de Colombia.....500
national park information 501
nightlife..............................504
Palacio de Justicia................497
pharmacies.........................505
Plaza de Bolívar...................497
Plaza de Toros La Santamaría......500
Plazoleta del Chorro de
    Quedevo..........................499
police.................................505
post....................................505
publications........................501
Quinta de Bolívar 500
restaurants..........................503
shopping.............................505
taxis...................................502
tourist information...............501
tours...................................502
transport.............................502
Boleto Turístico (P)..................741
Bolívar, Simón 857, 865
BOLIVIA......................... 153–222
Bolivia 156–157
Bolivia, Central Valleys
.... **199–208**
Bolivia, Northern..................... 25
Bolivia, Southern 24
border crossings
Argentina–Brazil...................87
Argentina–Chile 126, 144
Argentina–Uruguay 84
Bolivia–Argentina 155, 196
Bolivia–Brazil 158, 215, 221
Bolivia–Chile 158, 196
Bolivia–Paraguay.................158
Bolivia–Peru.......................158
Brazil–Argentina..........353, 367, 225
Brazil–Bolivia 225, 328
Brazil–Colombia 316
Brazil–French Guiana ...310, 312
Brazil–The Guianas..............225
Brazil–Paraguay 228, 353
Brazil–Peru..........................316
Brazil–Uruguay 228, 367
Brazil–Venezuela.................228
Chile–Argentina 372, 444, 461
Chile–Bolivia 372
Chile–Peru..........................372
Colombia–Brazil 489, 562
Colombia–Ecuador.......489, 558
Colombia–Peru 489, 562
Colombia–Venezuela....489, 515
Ecuador–Colombia.......565, 587
Ecuador–Peru ...565, 606, 615, 630
French Guiana–Brazil............678
French Guiana–Suriname 684
Guyana–Brazil..........643, 657
Guyana–Suriname................644
Paraguay–Argentina......688, 700
Paraguay–Bolivia 688, 710
Paraguay–Brazil......688, 700, 706
Peru–Bolivia 716, 786
Peru–Brazil................. 716, 821
Peru–Chile 716, 780
Peru–Colombia....................821
Peru–Ecuador............. 716, 805
Suriname–French Guiana 659
Suriname–Guyana................659
Uruguay–Argentina..............839
Uruguay–Brazil....................853
Venezuela–Brazil..........905, 907
Venezuela–Colombia............886
BRASÍLIA (Br) 317–326
Brasília.......................... 318–319
Central Brasília................. 321

accommodation....................324
address system.....................320
airports...............................322
banks.................................326
buses..................................323
cafés..................................325
car rental............................326
Catedral Metropolitana Nossa
    Senhora Aparecida 320
Chapada Imperial 323
Congresso Nacional 317
consulates...........................326
crime..................................326
Dom Bosco Sanctuary..........322
Don Bosco 322
drinking 324
eating 324
embassies...........................326
Esplanada dos Ministérios.....317
exchange 326
flights 322
gardens...............................322
Goiás Velho 323
hospitals.............................326
information.........................323
internet...............................326
JK Memorial 322
laundries.............................326
left luggage.........................326
Memorial dos Povos Indígenas.322
metrô..................................324
Museu Histórico de Brasília....320
Museu Nacional..................321
nightlife..............................325
Palácio da Alvorada.............322
Palácio da Justiça 320
Palácio do Planalto..............319
Palácio Itamarati..................320
Panteão da Pátria Tancredo
    Neves.............................319
parks..................................323
Pirenópolis..........................323
post office 326
Praça dos Três Poderes.........318
restaurants..........................324
safety.................................326
Santuário Dom Bosco...........322
shopping.............................326
taxis...................................324
Teatro Nacional...................322
Torre de Televisão 322
tourist information...............323
transport.............................352
websites..............................320
BRAZIL 223–368
Brazil............................ 226–227
Brazil, Northeast............... 288
Brazil, South...................... 346
Brownsberg Nature Reserve (S)
....667
Bucaramanga (C)......................512
budget tips 39
Buenaventura (C).....................559
BUENOS AIRES (A) 54–66
Central Buenos Aires......... 55
Buenos Aires, around........ 67
Palermo, Recoleta & Retiro... 59
accommodation....................61
arrival and departure............60
arts and crafts fair 58
Avenida Corrientes...............56
Avenida de Mayo.................56
B&Bs...................................62
banks.................................66
bars...................................64

Basílica de Nuestra Señora del
  Pilar 58
Basílica de San Francisco 57
Boca Juniors 58
Bombonera, La 58
Buenos Aires Design 58
buses 60, 61
Cabildo 56
Calle Florida 56
Caminito 58
Casa Rosada 54
Catedral Metropolitana 56
cemetery, Recoleta 58
Centro Cultural Borges 56
Centro Cultural de Recoleta 58
Centro Cultural San Martín 56
Colección de Arte Amalia
  Lacroze 57
Colegio Nacional 57
Congreso Nacional 56
consulates 66
crime and safety 52
cultural centres 65
drinking 64
eating 63
embassies 66
exchange 66
Feria de Mataderos 60
Feria de San Pedro Telmo 57
ferries 61
flights 60
food 63
Galerías Pacífico 56
hospitals 66
hostels 62
hotels 62
Iglesia de San Ignacio 57
information 61
internet 66
La Boca 58
laundry 66
left luggage 66
Madres de la Plaza de Mayo 54
Malba 60
malls 66
Manzana de las Luces 57
market, San Telmo 57
markets 66
Martín, Quinquela Benito 58
Mataderos 60
milongas 65
Monserrat 57
Museo de Arte Decorativo 60
Museo de Arte Latinamericano de
  Buenos Aires 60
Museo de Arte Moderno
  (MAMBA) 57
Museo de Arte Popular
  Hernández 60
Museo de la Ciudad 57
Museo de la Pasión Boquense 58
Museo del Bicentenario 56
Museo Histórico Nacional 57
Museo Nacional de Bellas Artes ...58
Museo Xul Solar 58
nightclubs 65
Obelisco 56
Palermo 58
Palermo Hollywood 60
Palermo Viejo 60, 72
Parque Lezama 57
Pasaje de la Defensa 57
pharmacies 66
Plaza Cortázar 60
Plaza de Congreso 56
Plaza de Mayo 54

Plaza Dorrego 57
police 66
post office 66
pubs 64
Puerto Madero 58
Recoleta 58
Recoleta Cemetery 58
remises 61
Reserva Ecológica 57
restaurants 63
San Telmo 57
shopping 66
subte 61
tango 65
taxis 61
Teatro Colón 56
Teatro General San Martín 56
tour operators 61
tourist information 61
tours 61
trains 61
transport 61
buses 31
Butch Cassidy and
  the Sundance Kid 196
Buzios (Br) 255

C

Cabo de la Vela (C) 531
Cabo Polonio (U) 852
Cacao (FG) 677
caçhaca 231
Cachi (A) 94
Cafayate (A) 95
Cahuachi (Pe) 744
caipirinhas 231
Cajamarca (Pe) 806–809
Cajamarca 807
Cal Orko (B) 202
Calama (Ch) 411
Caldera (Ch) 408
Cali (C) 548–551
Cali 549
Callao (Pe) 738
camping 33
Campo Grande (Br) 329
Canaima Village (V) 904
Canasvieiras (Br) 330
Canela (Br) 365
Canoa (E) 619
Capilla de Mármol (Ch) 457
Capilla del Monte (A) 78
CARACAS (V) 865–877
Eastern Caracas 871
El Centro & Parque
  Central 867
Metropolitan Area 866
Sabana Grande 869
  accommodation 870
  airport 868
  arrival and departure 868
  banks 875
  baseball 874
  buses 870
  Casa Natal 866
  Catedral 866
  consulates 875
  crime 872
  drinking 873

  eating 872
  El Hatillo 868
  embassies 875
  exchange 875
  flights 868
  Galería de Arte Nacional 868
  gay nightlife 874
  hospital 875
  Iglesia de San Francisco 866
  immigration 875
  information 870
  internet 875
  laundry 875
  left luggage 875
  metro 870
  Museo Bolivariano 866
  Museo Caracas 866
  Museo de Arte
    Contemporáneo 868
  Museo de Bellas Artes 868
  Museo de Cincias 868
  Museo Sacro de Caracas 866
  nightlife 873
  Panteón Nacional 866
  Parque Central 866
  pharmacy 875
  phone 875
  Plaza Bolívar 866
  police 872
  post office 876
  restaurants 872
  Sabana Grande 868
  safety 872
  shopping 875
  taxis 870
  Teatro Teresa Carreño 868
  tourist information 870
  tours 870
Caraz (Pe) 790
CariFesta 662
Caripe (V) 913
Carnaval 37
Carnaval (B) 209
Carnaval (Br) 224, 235, 295
Carnaval (P) 701
Carnaval (U) 835
Carnaval Correntino 84
Carnival 37
carnival (FG) 673
cars 31
Cartagena (C) 515–521
Cartagena 516
Cascades de Juan Curí (C) 511
Castro (Ch) 452
Castro 453
Casuarito (V) 886
Catatumbo (V) 891
Cateratas de Gocta (Pe) 812
Cayambe (E) 583, 585
Cayambe Coca Reserve (E) 583
Cayenne (FG) 673–677
Cayenne 675
Central Chaco Lagoons (P) 691
Central Suriname Nature
  Reserve (S) 669
Centre Spatial Guyanais (FG)
 678
Centrinho da Lagoa (Br) 358
Centrinho da Lagoa 359
Cerro Concepción & Cerro
  Alegre 396

Cerro Autana (V)...........................898
Cerro Blanco (Pe)........................773
Cerro Castor (A)...........................148
Cerro Catedral (A)........................121
Cerro de los Siete Colores (A)...97
Cerro Mandango (E)..................607
Cerro Rico (B)..............................190
Ch'allapampa (B).........................180
Chachapoyas (Pe) 810–812
Chachapoyas...................... 810
Chaco, the 215, 709
Chan Chan complex (Pe) 798
Chapada Diamantina,
  the (Br)....................................286
Chapare, the (B) 208
Chauchilla cemetery (Pe).......774
Chávez, Hugo..............................858
Chavín de Huantar (Pe).............789
Che Guevara...................75, 81, 214
Chichiriviche (V) 882–884
Chichiriviche 883
Chiclayo (Pe) 798–800
Chiclayo 799
Chiclayo area....................... 801
CHILE...........................23, 369–484
Chile 371
Chile, Northern 24
Chillán (Ch)...................................429
Chiloé (Ch)........................ 448–456
Chincana (B)................................180
Chiquitos (B)...............................215
cholera...35
Choquequirao (Pe)....................764
Chordeleg (E)..............................604
Choroní (V) 879–881
crafts...36
credit-card fraud..........................40
cricket (G).....................................647
crime..38
  Argentina....................................52
  Bolivia.......................................163
  Brazil...233
  Chile..379
  Colombia...................................493
  Ecuador.....................................569
  French Guiana...........................672
  Guyana......................................647
  Paraguay...................................692
  Peru...722
  Suriname...................................661
  Uruguay....................................834
  Venezuela.................................863
cruises, Galápagos Islands 635
Cúcuta (C)....................................515
Cuenca (E) 600–604
Cuenca 601
Cuesta del Obispo (A) 94
Cueva de las Manos
  Pintadas (A)..............................133
Cuevo del Guácharo (V).........914
Cuiabá (Br)...................................331
culture..36
Cumbe Mayo (Pe).......................809
Curarrehue (Ch).........................439
Curicó (Ch)...................................427
Curitiba (Br) 345–348
Cusco (Pe) 739–749
Cusco........................... 742–743
Cusco Tourist Ticket..................741
cycling...32

Colón (A) 84
Colonia Carlos Pellegrini (A) 85
Colonia del Sacramento (U)
.... 843–846
Colonia del Sacramento 843
Colonia Suiza (A)........................121
Colonia Tovar (V)........................876
Commewijne River (S) 667
Concepción (Ch)........................430
Concepción (Pe).........................707
Copacabana (B)..........................176
Copacabana 178
Copiapó (Ch)...............................407
Coquimbo (Ch)...........................403
Cordillera Blanca (Pe)...............790
Cordillera Blanca,
  hiking in the (Pe)....................790
Cordillera Real, the (B) 182
Córdoba (A)........................ 71–75
Córdoba 72
Córdoba Province (A).......71–78
Córdoba Province 76
Coro (V) 884–887
Coro 885
Coroico (B)...................................183
Corrientes (A)............................... 84
Corumbá (Br)...............................328
Costa do Sol (Br) 254
Costa Verde, the (Br) 254
Cotacachi (E)...............................585
Cotopaxi, Volcán (E)..................588
country codes...............................41
Coyhaique (Ch)...........................458
Coyhaique 459

D

Dalcahue (Ch) 455
Darwin, Charles...........................631
dengue fever......35, 79, 379, 494,
  864
Desierto de Tatacoa (C) 556
Devil's Nose (E) 597, 598
Diamantina (Br)...........................273
diarrhoea..35
dinosaur tracks, Cal Orko........202
disabled travellers......................42
Dos Mangas (E)...........................628
driving..31
drugs...40
dune-buggying.......721, 769, 773
dysentery..35

E

Easter Island (Ch) 477–484
Easter Island....................... 578
ECUADOR 25, 563–640
Ecuador................................ 566
El Calafate (A) 138–142
El Calafate 139
El Chaltén (A) 134–138
El Chaltén 137
El Fósil (C)....................................509
El Fuerte (B) 214
El Litoral (A) 79
El Misti (Pe)..................................775
El Morro (Ch) 419
El Santuario de Iguaque (C)...509
El Tablón (C).................................555
El Tatio geysers (Ch).................415
El Valle (C)....................................559
electricity..39
Elqui Valley (Ch) 404
emergency numbers
  Argentina....................................52
  Bolivia.......................................163
  Brazil...234
  Chile..379
  Colombia...................................493
  Ecuador.....................................571
  French Guiana...........................672
  Guyana......................................648
  Paraguay...................................692
  Peru...722
  Suriname...................................661
  Uruguay....................................834
  Venezuela.................................864
Encarnación (P) 699–702
Encarnación 701
Ernesto Che Guevara 75, 81,
  214
Escalera del Inca (B)..................180
Escobar, Pablo.............................538
Esmeraldes (E).............................616
Espíritu Pampa (Pe)...................766
Esquel (A).....................................124
Essequibo River (G)...................654
ESTA clearance............................ 29
Estación Astronómica
  Musica (C).................................509
Estancia Harberton (A) 148

Coca (E) 611
coca..183
cocaine....................................38, 535
Cochabamba (B) 204–207
Cochabamba 205
Coconuco (C)...............................554
coffee fincas (C).........................544
Colca Canyon (Pe).......... 780–782
Colca Canyon 781
Colchagua Valley Ruta de
  Vino (Ch) 425
COLOMBIA..............26, 485–562
Colombia 487

Chaco, the
Cidades Históricas (Br).............260
Circuito Chico (A).......................121
Ciudad Bolívar (V) 900–903
Ciudad Bolívar 901
Ciudad del Este (P)........692, 700,
  704
Ciudad Perdida (C)....................529
climate..12
  Argentina....................................46
  Bolivia.......................................154
  Brazil...224
  Chile..370
  Colombia...................................486
  Ecuador.....................................565
  Guianas, the 700
  Paraguay...................................688
  Peru...713
  Uruguay....................................830
  Venezuela.................................856
climate change........................... 30
Chuí (Br)..367

estancias 69, 126, 832
Esteros del Iberá (A).....................85
etiquette 36
exchange rates..........................**40**
Argentina...................................53
Bolivia......................................164
Brazil.......................................235
Chile...380
Colombia...................................495
Ecuador.....................................570
French Guiana............................673
Guyana......................................648
Paraguay...................................693
Peru..723
Suriname...................................662
Uruguay....................................834
Venezuela...........................858, 864

F

Fernando de Noronha (Br) 298
Festival de los Diablos
    Danzantes (V) 877
Festival del Chamamé (A).........84
festivals 14
Fiesta de San Juan (Pe)...........816
Filadelfia (Pe).............................709
fishing (U).................................834
Florianópolis (Br) 356–358
food and drink
Argentina...................................49
Bolivia......................................160
Brazil.......................................230
Chile...375
Colombia...................................490
Ecuador.....................................567
French Guiana............................671
Guyana......................................646
Paraguay...................................689
Peru..718
Suriname...................................660
Uruguay....................................832
Venezuela..................................861
football............232, 377, 492, 568,
    690, 834, 862
football World Cup (Br)............232
Fort Nieuw Amsterdam (S) 667
Fortaleza (Br) 298–303
Fortaleza............................... **299**
Fortín Infante Rivarola (P).......710
Foz do Iguaçu (Br)........ 351–353
FRENCH GUIANA.......... 669–684
Futaleufú (Ch)............................456
Fuya Fuya (E) 585

G

Gaiman (A) 131
Galápagos Islands, the (E)
    .... **631–640**
Galibi Nature Reserve (S).......669
gaucho festival, San Antonio
    de Areco (A)...........................69
gay travellers.............................39
GEORGETOWN (G) 649–654
Georgetown 650–651
accommodation.........................652
airport....................................652
arrival and departure 652
banks.......................................653
bars...653
Bourda Market..........................650
buses.......................................652
clubs.......................................653
consulates................................653
embassies.................................653
exchange..................................653
flights......................................652
guesthouses 652
hospitals..................................654
hotels......................................652
internet....................................654
minibuses.................................652
National Art Gallery 650
National Museum 649
nightlife...................................653
pharmacies...............................654
restaurants...............................652
St George's Cathedral...............649
Seawall....................................652
Stabroek Market.......................649
taxis...652
tours.......................................654
Walter Roth Museum of
    Anthropology.......................649
geysers, El Tatio (Ch)................415
Girón (C)....................................512
Glaciar Martial (A)....................148
Glaciar Perito Moreno (A)......142
Glaciar Upsala (A) 142
Glacier Grey (Ch)......................471
Gramado (Br).............................364
Gran Sabana, La (V)...............908
Guajira Peninsula, the (C)......531
Gualaceo (E).............................604
Guatapé (C)...............................540
Guayana (V) 896–909
Guayaquil (E) 621–625
Guayaquil **622**
Guayaramerín (B)....................221
Guevara, Ernesto "Che".......75, 81,
    214
GUIANAS, THE 641–684
Guianas, the 644–655
Guicán (C)..................................514
GUYANA......................... 643–658

H

haciendas....................................33
Hanga Roa (Ch) 477
Hanga Roa **480**
health......................................**34**
Argentina...................................52
Bolivia......................................163
Brazil.......................................234
Chile...379
Colombia...................................493
Ecuador.....................................570
French Guiana............................672
Guyana......................................647
Paraguay...................................692
Peru..723
Suriname...................................661
Uruguay....................................834
Venezuela..................................864
heat stroke.................................34
hiking....................... see trekking
hitchhiking.....................33, 374

hospedajes.................................33
hostales......................................33
hosterías....................................33
hot springs (Ch)........................439
hotels...33
Huaca Cao Viejo (Pe)...............798
Huaca de la Luna (Pe)..............797
Huaca del Sol (Pe) 797
Huaca Rajada (Pe).....................801
Huacachina (Pe)........................769
Huacas del Moche (Pe).............796
Huanchaco (Pe).........................795
Huaquillas (Pe)..........................630
Huaraz (Pe)................... 786–791
Huaraz **787**
Huascarán (Pe)..........................790
Huascarán National Park (Pe)
   790
Humahuaca (A)............................98
Humberstone (Ch) 419

I

Ibarra (E)....................................586
Ica (Pe)......................................768
Iguaçu Falls (Br).......................353
Iguazú Falls (A) 88
Îles du Salut (FG)......................680
Îlet la Mère (FG)........................677
Ilha Bela (Br) 344
Ilha de Fernando de Noronha (Br)
   298
Ilha de São Francisco do Sul (Br)
   354
Ilha do Mel (Br).........................350
Ilha de Marajó (Br)...................310
Ilha Grande (Br) 256
Ilha Santa Catarina (Br)
    .... **356–360**
Imbabura (E)...............................585
Iñak Uyu (B) 181
Inca sites (Pe) 749
Inca Trail (E)..............................600
Inca Trail, the (Pe) 754–757
Inca Trails, alternative 765
indigenous people (Pe).812, 818
Ingapirca (E)..................599, 600
Inhotim Instituto Cultural 264
Inka Jungle Trail (Pe) 766
inoculations................................34
insect repellent 35
insurance....................................40
internet.......................................40
Inti Raymi festival (Pe) 750
Iquique (Ch) 416–418
Iquique **416**
Iquitos (Pe)..................... 813–818
Iquitos area **819**
Central Iquitos **815**
Isla de la Luna (B)....................181
Isla de la Plata (E).....................630
Isla de Margarita (V).... 914–917
Isla del Sol (B)...........................179
Isla Grande de Chiloé (Ch)......466
Isla Isabela, Galápagos (E) 638
Isla Magdalena (Ch)..................467
Isla Navarino (Ch) 476

Isla Negra (Ch) 400
Isla San Cristóbal,
    Galápagos (E).........................636
Isla Santa Cruz, Galápagos (E)
   632
Island of the Sun (Pe)................786
Islas Ballestas (Pe).....................767
Islas de Rosario (C) 519
Islas de San Bernardo (C).........522
Islas Palomino (Pe).....................738
Itaimbézinho (Br).......................366
Itaipú Dam (P)............................707
itineraries 22–27
Iwokrama Rainforest (G) 655

J & K

Jequitinhonha Valley (Br)........275
Jesuit Missions (Br)....................367
Jesuit Missions (B) 215
Jesuit Missions (P) 702
Joaquina (Br)..............................360
Jodensavanne (S) 667
Jonestown Massacre (G) 649
jungle lodges 611, 820, 825
jungle tours ...314, 609, 614, 648,
    820, 825, 898
Jungle, the (Pe) 813–828
Junín de los Andes (A) 112
Kaieteur Falls (G) 653
Karaijía (Pe)................................813
Kaw (FG) 678
kidnappings (C)..........................493
kite-surfing (Pe)..........................803
Kogi Indians, the.......................530
Kourou (FG) 678
Kuelap (Pe).................................812

L

La Chaquira (C).............................555
La Higuera (B) 215
La Payunia (A) 108
LA PAZ (B).................... 165–175
Central La Paz 167
Sopocachi............................. 171
    accommodation..............................171
    arrival and departure 170
    banks...174
    bars..174
    buses 170
    cafés..173
    Calle Jaén..166
    Calle Sagárnaga...........................168
    car rental...174
    Cárcel de San Pedro.....................169
    Catedral 165
    cinemas 174
    clubs 174
    consulates..175
    cycling the Death Road................169
    drinking..174
    eating 173
    El Alto...165
    embassies 175
    exchange..175
    Feria de Alasitas...........................168
    flights 170
    Iglesia de San Francisco.............168
    Iglesia Santo Domingo................166
    immigration.....................................175
    information 170
    internet cafés..................................175
    Mercado Buenos Aires 168
    Mercado de Hechicería................168
    micros..170
    Mount Illimani...............................165
    Museo Casa Murillo.......................166
    Museo Costumbrista Juan de
        Vargas..166
    Museo de Ethnografía y
        Folklore 166
    Museo de Instrumentos
        Musicales....................................166
    Museo de Metales Preciosos 166
    Museo de Textiles Andinos 190
    Museo del Litoral Boliviano 166
    Museo de la Coca...........................168
    Museo Nacional de Arqueología169
    Museo Nacional de Arte...............166
    Museo Tambo Quirquincho 168
    nightclubs..174
    outdoor equipment.......................195
    Palacio Legislativo........................165
    Palacio Presidencial.....................165
    peñas...174
    pharmacy..175
    phones..175
    Plaza Murillo...................................165
    Plaza San Fransisco......................166
    Plaza San Pedro.............................169
    Plaza Sucre......................................169
    police..175
    post office..175
    restaurants......................................173
    San Pedro Prison 169
    shopping...175
    Sopocachi...169
    taxis...170
    telephones.......................................175
    tourist information........................170
    transport..170
    trufis..170
La Pelota (C)...............................555
La Plata (A) 70
La Portada (Ch)...........................410
La Punta (Pe)...............................738
La Quebrada del Toro (A)............93
La Serena (Ch).............................401
La Serena, downtown........ 402
Lago Agrio (E).............................610
Lago Argentino (A) 138
Lago Buenos Aires (A)...............133
Lago Chungará (Ch) 423
Lago Grey (Ch) 471
Lago Huechulafquen (A)...........112
Lago Lácar (A) 114
Lago Llanquihue (Ch) 442
Lago Nahuel Huapi (A) 116
Lago Pehoé (C) 513
Lago Sandoval (Pe) 826
Lago Todos Los Santos (Ch)......445
Lago Valencia (Pe)......................826
Lago Ypacaraí (P)........................693
Lagoa da Conceição (Br)...........358
Laguna Blanca (P).......................691
Laguna de Llancanelo (A)..........108
Laguna Mucubají (V)..................893
Laguna Nimez (A).......................140
Laguna Quilotoa (E)...................590

Laguna San Rafael (Ch) ... 457, 460
Laguna Verde (Ch)......................408
Lake District, the (A).... 111–126
Lake District, the................ 113
Lake District, the (Ch) 431–448
Lake Quilotoa (E) 590
Lake Titicaca (B).........................176
Lake Titicaca, Cordillera Real
    and the Yungas 177
Lake Titicaca (Pe) 785
Lake Titicaca 785
Lambayeque (Pe)........................801
language......................................919
language schools 37
Lares (Pe) 764
Las Leñas (A)..............................106
Latacunga (E) 589
Lençois (Br)................................286
lesbian travellers.......................39
Lethem (G) 657
Leticia (C) 560
LIMA (Pe) 724–738
Lima 726–727
Central Lima 729
Miraflores 731
    accommodation..............................734
    airports...732
    arrival and departure 732
    banks...738
    Barranco 730
    bars..737
    boat tours...734
    buses 733
    catacombs 725
    Cathedral 725
    Chinatown 725
    Circuito Mágico del Agua.............730
    clubs 737
    colectivos..733
    consulates..738
    dance..737
    drinking..736
    eating 735
    embassies 738
    exchange..738
    flights 732
    food...735
    huacas...732
    information 734
    internet...738
    Jirón de la Unión...........................728
    Jirón Ucayali...................................728
    La Merced 728
    La Mistura food festival...............730
    Larcomar...730
    Las Nazarenas.................................728
    live music 737
    Mercado Central.............................725
    Metropolitano bus service 733
    Miraflores...730
    Museo Banco Central de Reserva
        del Perú 728
    Museo de Arte Lima.......................730
    Museo de Arte Religioso...............725
    Museo de la Iglesia y Convento
        San Francisco............................725
    Museo de la Inquisición...............725
    Museo de la Nación.......................730
    Museo Nacional de
        Arqueología...............................732
    Museo Pedro de Osma...................731
    Museo Rafael Larco.......................732
    nightlife..736

Palacio del Gobierno 725
Parque Kennedy 730
Parque Universitario 729
Plaza Grau 729
Plaza Mayor 725
Plaza San Martín 728
police 738
postal services 738
Pueblo Libre 732
restaurants 735
San Isidro 725
San Pedro 728
Santa Rosa de Lima 728
shopping 737
taxis 733
tourist information 734
tours 734
transport 733
Llama Chaqui (B) 207
Llanganuco Lakes (Pe) 790
Loja (E) 604–607
Loja 605
Loma Plata (P) 710
Los Altos de Sucre (V) 910
Los Antiguos (A) 133
Los Llaneros 895
Los Llanos (V) 891, 894–896
Los Penitentes (A) 104
Los Roques (V) 877

M

Macapá (Br) 310
Macas (E) 615
Machala (E) 630
Machu Picchu (Pe) 757–762
Machu Picchu 759
Machu Picchu Pueblo ...see Aguas
    Calientes
Madre de Dios (Pe) 822–826
Madre de Dios 822
mail 40
Malargüe (A) 107
malaria 35
Mamiraua Sustainable
    Development Reserve 316
Manaus (Br) 310–317
Manaus 311
Máncora (Pe) 802–804
Manizales (C) 541–543
Manta (E) 621
Manu Biosphere Reserve (Pe)
    826–828
Manu Biosphere Reserve 827
Manzana Jesuítica, Córdoba ... 71
maps, information and 40
Mar del Plata (A) 70
Mariana (Br) 270
marijuana 38
markets 36
Maroni River (FG) 683
Márquez, Gabriel Garcia 522
mate 38, 833
Mazaruni River (G) 654
Mbaracayú Forest Reserve (P) ......
    691
Medellín (C) 535–540
Medellín 536

Mendoza (A) 100–104
Mendoza 101
Mendoza and San Juan 99
Mendoza tours 102
Mennonite colonies (P) 709
Mérida (V) 888–893
Mérida 888
Military Museum, Callao 738
Mina da Passagem, Mariana ... 270
Minas (U) 846
Minas Gerais (Br) 260–275
Minas Gerais 261
Mindo (E) 581
Mindo 582
Miñiques, Laguna (Ch) 415
Miscanti, Laguna (Ch) 415
Mission Route (Br) 367
Mitad del Mundo, La (E) 580
Moai, Easter Island (Ch) 479
Mochima (V) 913
Molinos (A) 95
Mompiche (E) 618
Mompox (C) 522
Monasterio de Santa Teresa,
    Córdoba (A) 73
money 40
    Argentina 53
    Bolivia 164
    Brazil 234
    Chile 379
    Colombia 494
    Ecuador 570
    French Guiana 672
    Guyana 648
    Paraguay 692
    Peru 723
    Suriname 662
    Uruguay 834
    Venezuela 864
Montañita (E) 627, 628
Monte Fitz Roy (A) 134
Montevideo (U) 835–842
Montevideo 837
Moronacocha (Pe) 820
Morro de São Paulo (Br) 285
mosquito-borne diseases ... 35
Museo de Bellas Artes, Córdoba
    (A) 73
Museo del Ejército, Callao (Pe)
   738
Museo Superior de Bellas
    Artes Palacio Ferreyra,
    Córdoba (A) 81

N

Nappi (G) 657
Nariz del Diablo (E) 597, 598
national parks information (A) 50
Nazca (Pe) 770–773
Nazca 771
Nazca Lines, flying over (Pe) ..744
Nazca Lines, the (Pe) 773
Neruda, Pablo 394
Neu Halbstadt (P) 710
Nevado del Cachi (A) 94
Nieuw Nickerie (S) 668
Niterói (Br) 254

Norte Chico (Ch) 401–409
Norte Grande (Ch) 409–424
Nueva Córdoba (A) 73
Nuevo Rocafuerte (E) 615

O

Observatorio Cerro
    Mamalluca (Ch) 405
Ocumare de la Costa (V) 881
offset schemes 30
Oiapoque (Br) 310
Ojos de Salado, Volcán (Ch) ...408
Ojos del Caburgua (Ch) 438
Oktoberfest (Br) 356
Old Patagonian Express (A) ...124
Olinda (Br) 295–298
Olinda 296
Ollantaytambo (Pe) 753, 762
Olón (E) 628
Ongamira (A) 78
Oriente, the (E) 609–615
Orinoco Delta (V) 908
Orongo (Ch) 480
Oruro (B) 186–189
Oruro 188
Otovalo (E) 584
Otovalo 584
Ouro Preto (Br) 267–270
Ouro Preto 268
Ovahe Beach (Ch) 481

P

Pacaya Samiria National
    Reserve (Pe) 820
Pacific coast (E) 559
Palafitos (Ch) 452
Palumeu (S) 668
Panama (C) 489
Pantanal, the (B) 215
Pantanal, the (Br) 326–331
Pantanal, the 327
Pantanal, the, tours (Br) 329
Papallacta (E) 581
Paracas Reserve (Pe) 767
Paracas, Ica & Nazca 768
Paraguachón (V) 886
PARAGUAY 23, 685–710
Paraguay 687
Paramaribo (S) 662–667
Paramaribo 663
Paraná (Br) 345
Paraná River (A) 68
Paranaguá (Br) 348
Paraty (Br) 257–259
Paredones (Pe) 774
Pariniacota (Ch) 423
Parque Amazónico La Isla (E) .. 612
Parque Arqueológico (C) 555
Parque Arví (C) 538
Parque Ecológico Piedras
    Blancas (C) 540
Parque Estadual do Caracol (Br)
   365

Parque Estadual do
  Itacolomi (Br).........................269
parques nacionales
  Amacayacú (C)........................561
  Amboró (B)..............................212
  Bahuaja-Sonene (Pe).............826
  Canaima (V)............................903
  Chiloé (Ch).............................455
  Conguillío (Ch).......................432
  Cotopaxi (E)...........................588
  de Chichamocha (C)...............511
  de los Arrayanes (A)...............116
  do Itatiaia (Br).......................257
  dos Aparados da Serra (Br)....366
  El Ávila (V).............................876
  El Cajas (E)............................604
  El Cocuy (C)............................513
  El Palmar (A)............................83
  El Rey (A)..................................93
  Henri Pittier (V)......................878
  Huerquehue (Ch).....................438
  Iguazú (A).................................88
  Kaa-lya del Gran Chaco (B).....216
  Lanín (A)................................112
  Los Alerces (A)........................125
  Los Cardones (A).......................94
  Los Glaciares (A).....................134
  Los Glaciares.........................135
  Los Nevados (C).......................543
  Luaca (Ch).............................423
  Machalilla (E).........................629
  Madidi (V)..............................218
  Médanos de Coro (V)..............884
  Mochima (V)...........................911
  Morrocoy (V)..........................882
  Nahuel Huapi (A)....................122
  Nahuel Huapi.........................123
  Nahuelbuta (Ch).....................431
  Natural Ensenada de Utría (C)...559
  Natural Puracé (C)..................554
  Nevado de Tres Cruces (Ch)....408
  Pan de Azúcar (Ch).................409
  Perito Moreno (A)...................133
  Queulat (Ch)...........................457
  Radal Siete Tazas (Ch)............427
  Rapa Nui (Ch).........................480
  Sajama (B)..............................185
  San Rafael (P).........................691
  Serra dos Órgãos (Br).............259
  Sierra Nevada (V)....................893
  Talampaya (A).........................111
  Tayrona (C)............................528
  Teniente Enciso (P).................691
  Tierra del Fuego (A)................151
  Tierra del Fuego....................151
  Torotoro (B)............................207
  Torres del Paine (Ch).......470–475
  Torres del Paine...............472–473
  Vicente Pérez Rosales (Ch).....444
  Villarrica (Ch).........................438
  Volcán Isluga (Ch)..................424
  Yasuní (E)...............................612
Parque Provincial
  Aconcagua (A)........................104
Parque Provincial
  Ischigualasto (A)....................110
Parque Tantauco (Ch)................455
Paso Cardenal Samoré (A)........122
Pasto (C)..................................558
Patagonia (A)..............126–144
Patagonia, Southern (Ch)
  ...462–475
Peguche (E)..............................585
penguins (Ch).........406, 451, 467

Península Valdés (A).................130
Península Valdés tours (A)........130
Pereira (C)................................543
Perito Moreno (A).....................132
Perito Moreno Glacier (A).........142
PERU..........................25, 711–828
Peru..................................714–715
Petrópolis (Br)..........................259
phone codes..............................41
phones.....................................41
Pica (Ch).................................419
Pichilemu (Ch)........................425
Pichinchas, the (E)..................581
Pico Bolívar (V)........................894
Pico Humboldt (V)...................894
Piedra del Peñol (C).................540
Pikillaqta (Pe)..........................751
Piñihuil (Ch)............................451
Pisac (Pe).................................751
pisco...............................405, 722
Pisco (Pe)................................766
Pisco Elqui (Ch).......................406
Plage les Hattes (FG)...............683
Plan Colombia.........................494
Playa Colorada (V)...................911
Playas (E)................................626
Podocarpus (E)........................608
police......................................38
Popayán (C)...................551–553
Popayán.................................551
Porlamar (V).............................914
Porlamar.................................916
porters, Inca Trail.....................756
Porto Allegre (Br).........361–364
Porto Allegre..........................361
Portuguese language................924
post...40
Potosí (B)......................189–193
Potosí.....................................191
Praia Mole (Br)........................360
Providencia (C)........................534
public holidays........................36
  Argentina...............................53
  Bolivia.................................164
  Brazil...................................235
  Chile....................................380
  Colombia..............................494
  Ecuador................................571
  French Guiana.......................673
  Guyana.................................648
  Paraguay..............................693
  Peru.....................................724
  Suriname..............................662
  Uruguay................................835
  Venezuela.............................864
Pucón (Ch)..............................435
Pucón....................................435
Pudeto (Ch).............................470
Pueblito (C).............................529
Pueblo de los Muertos (Pe)......813
Puente del Inca (A)..................104
Puerto Ayachucho (V)...897–899
Puerto Ayachucho..................897
Puerto Ayora (E).......................632
Puerto Ayora.........................633
Puerto Aysén (Ch)....................460
Puerto Baquerizo Moreno (E)
 636
Puerto Baquerizo
  Moreno.............................637

Puerto Carreño (V)...................886
Puerto Chacabuco (Ch)............460
Puerto Colombia (V)................879
Puerto Colombia....................879
Puerto El Morro (E)..................626
Puerto Iguazú (A).......................87
Puerto La Cruz (V)......909–911
Puerto La Cruz.......................910
Puerto López (E)......................628
Puerto Madryn (A)......126–130
Puerto Madryn.......................128
Puerto Maldonado (Pe)...........822
Puerto Maldonado.............823
Puerto Montt (Ch)...................445
Puerto Montt.........................447
Puerto Nariño (C)....................562
Puerto Natales (Ch).................467
Puerto Natales.......................468
Puerto Ordáz (V).....................899
Puerto Pañuelo (A)..................121
Puerto Pirámides (A)...............130
Puerto Rico Tranquilo (Ch).....457
Puerto Varas (Ch)....................442
Puerto Varas..........................443
Puerto Villamil (E)..................638
Puerto Williams (Ch)..............475
Pukapukara (E).......................570
Pululahua Crater and
  Reserve (E)..........................580
Puno (Pe)......................782–785
Puno......................................783
Punta Arenas (Ch)........462–466
Punta Arenas.........................463
Punta del Diablo (U)................853
Punta del Este (U)......848–852
Punta del Este.......................849
Punta Gallinas (C)...................532
Punta Tombo (A).....................132
Punta Walichu (A)...................140
Purmamarca (A)........................97
Putre (Ch)...............................422
Puyo (E).........................594, 614
Puyuhuapi (Ch).......................457

Q

Q'enqo (Pe)..............................750
Quebrada de Humahuaca (A)
 97
Quebrada de las Flechas (A)....95
Quilotoa (E).............................591
Quilotoa Loop........................590
Quiocta, Caverna de (Pe)........813
QUITO (E).....................571–581
Quito New Town......................574
Quito Old Town.......................573
  accommodation.....................577
  airport..................................576
  arrival and departure.............576
  banks...................................579
  bars......................................579
  Basílica del Voto Nacional....574
  books...................................579
  Botanical Gardens................574
  buses....................................576
  Capilla del Hombre...............574
  cars......................................577
  Casa de la Cultura................574

Catedral 572
Centro Cultural Metropolitano ...572
climbing 580
consulates....................................579
cycling..580
drinking 579
driving 577
eating 578
El Panecillo 574
embassies 579
exchange 579
flights 576
Guápulo..576
hiking 580
horseriding...................................580
hospitals.......................................579
Iglesia de San Francisco..............572
Iglesia Santo Domingo................573
information 576
internet...579
Itchimbia Park and Cultural
    Centre 574
kayaking 580
La Compañía de Jesús..................572
La Ronda 573
Museo Alberto Mena Caamaña...572
Museo de Ciencias Naturales 574
Museo de la Ciudad 572
Museo de San Francisco..............572
Museo del Banco Central............574
Museo Fundación Guayasamín ...574
New Town 572
nightlife..579
Old Town 571
Palacio del Gobierno 572
Parque Carolina 574
Parque Metropolitano..................574
phones..579
Plaza Grande 572
Plaza San Francisco 572
Plaza Santa Domingo 573
police..579
post offices...................................579
rafting...580
restaurants....................................578
shopping 579
taxis..577
Teleférico 576
telephones 579
tourist information 576
tours..580
trains...576
Trole, El...576
Vivarium, The...............................574

Rancagua (Ch) 424
Rano Kau crater (Ch) 480
Rano Raraku (Ch).........................481
Recife (Br) 288–295
Recife 290
Recife Antigo (Br)........................288
Régina (FG) 678
Reserva de Biosfera y Territorio
    Indígena Pilón Lajas (B).......218
Reserva de la Biosfera del
    Beni (B) 216
Reserva Ecológica Río
    Blanco (C) 541
Reserva Faunística
    Cuyabeno (E)...........................610

Reserva Nacional las
    Vicuñas (Ch)............................423
Reserva Nacional Pingüino de
    Humbolt (Ch) 406
Reserva Nacional Río
    Simpson (Ch).............................457
Reserva Natural del Iberá (A).......85
Reservar de Fauna Andina
    Eduardo Avaroa (B)...............195
Ribeirão da Ilha (Br) 360
Riberalta (B) 221
RÍO DE JANEIRO (Br).... 236–254
Rio de Janeiro 236
Rio de Janeiro Centro ...240–241
Rio Zona Sul 242–243
accommodation 249
airports....................................248
Arco de Teles..........................238
Arpoador.................................245
banks.......................................254
Barra da Tijuca.......................246
bars 252
Biblioteca Nacional 239
bonde 242
Botafogo 244
buses 248, 249
car rental 254
Carnaval..................................237
Catete......................................243
Centro Cultural Banco do Brasil....238
Cinelândia..............................239
clubs 252
consulates...............................254
Copacabana............................245
Corcovado 247
Cristo Redentor.......................247
cycling.....................................247
drinking...................................250
eating 250
Escadaria Selarón...................239
exchange 254
favela accommodation...........250
ferries.......................................249
Flamengo 244
flights 248
football stadium......................247
Gávea......................................246
gay nightlife............................253
Girl from Ipanema...................245
Glória.......................................243
hang-gliding............................247
hiking 247
hospitals..................................254
Igreja de Nossa Senhora da Glória
    do Outeiro.............................243
Igreja de Nossa Senhora do Carmo
    do Antigá Sé.........................238
Igreja de São Francisco de
    Paula.....................................238
Igreja e Convento de Santo
    Antônio.................................238
Igreja e Mostero de São Bento...238
information 249
Ipanema..................................245
Jardim Botânico......................246
Jockey Club.............................246
Lagoa......................................246
Lapa 239
Largo da Carioca....................238
Largo do Guimarães 242
Leblon 245
Leme 245
lesbian nightlife......................253
Maracaná................................247
metrô.......................................249

Museu Carmen Miranda.............244
Museu Chácara do Céu...............269
Museu da República 243
Museu de Arte Moderna 239
Museu do Índio 244
Museu Histórico Nacional...........238
Museu Nacional 275
Museu Nacional das Belas
    Artes......................................239
nightclubs...................................252
Nova Catedral Metropolitana......239
Olympic Games 246
Paço Imperial...............................237
Palácio Tiradentes........................238
Pão de Açúcar 244
Parque das Ruínas........................243
Parque do Flamengo 244
Parque Lage 246
Parque Nacional de Tijuca 247
police...254
post office....................................254
Praça XV de Novembro................237
Quinta da Boa Vista....................248
Real Gabinete Português de
    Leitura....................................239
restaurants...................................250
Saara 238
samba..239
samba schools 253
Sambódromo................................237
Santa Cruz dos Militares 238
Santa Teresa 229
shopping 254
Sugarloaf 244
taxis..249
Theatro Municipal 239
tourist information 249
tours..248
trams..242
transport 249
Urca..244
visa extensions.............................254
Zona Norte...................................237
Zona Sul 236
Río Gallegos (A)..........................142
Río Grande (A) 152
Rio Grande do Sul (Br) ... 345, 361
Rio Solimões, the (Br)................316
Río Yacuma (B)............................218
Riobamba (E) 596–598
Riobamba 597
Riohacha (C) 531
riverboats, Manaus 314
rodeo (C)......................................377
rodeo (G)......................................647
Roraima, Mount (V)......................908
Rosario (A)........................80–83
Rosario: 81
Rota Missões (Br) 367
round-the-world tickets...........30
Roura (FG) 678
rum (G)..647
rum (S)..660
Rumicolca (Pe).............................751
Runtun (E) 594
Rupertee (G).................................656
Rupununi Savannah (G)..........655
Rurrenabaque (B) 218
Rurrenabaque 219
Ruta 40 (A)...................................132
Ruta de los Siete Lagos (A) ...116
Ruta Humboldt (V) 898
Ruta Jesuítica (P).........................702

R

S

**Sacred Valley of the Incas,
the (Pe)** **751–766**
Sacred Valley of the Incas,
the................................. **752–753**
Sacsaywamán (Pe)....................749
safety.. 38
Saint Laurent du
Maroni (FG)................ **681–683**
Saint Laurent du Maroni ... 682
Salar de Atacama (Ch).............415
Salar de Surire (Ch)..................423
Salar de Uyuni (B)....................195
Salasaca (E).................................592
Salcantay (Pe)............................764
Salento (C)..................................546
Salento **546**
Salinas (E)...................................626
Salta (A).............................**89–93**
Salta Microcentro **92**
Saltos de Petrogué (Ch).........444
SALVADOR (Br) **276–284**
Salvador **277**
   accommodation........................381
   airports......................................280
   banks..284
   bars...283
   beaches......................................279
   boats...280
   buses................................280, 281
   cafés...283
   Câmara Municipal.....................276
   Carnaval.....................................276
   Catedral Basílica.......................278
   Cidade Alta.................................276
   Cidade Baixa..............................276
   comida Baiana.........................282
   consulates..................................284
   crime...280
   drinking......................................282
   eating..282
   embassies...................................284
   exchange....................................284
   fita..278
   flights...280
   forts..279
   Fundação Casa da Cultura Jorge
     Amado....................................279
   hospitals.....................................284
   Igreja da Nossa Senhora dos
     Pretos.....................................279
   Igreja da Ordem Terceira de São
     Francisco................................279
   Igreja do Bonfim.......................380
   information.................................281
   internet cafés............................284
   Largo do Pelourinho.................279
   laundries....................................284
   left luggage................................284
   Mem da Sá..................................278
   Memorial dos Governadores......276
   Mercado Modelo........................279
   Museu Afro-Brasileiro..............278
   Museu da Misericórdia.............276
   Museu dos Ex-Votos do Senhor
     do Bonfim..............................280
   Museu Náutico da Bahia...........279
   nightlife.....................................283
   Palácio do Rio Branco...............276
   Pelourinho.................................278
   pharmacies.................................284

police..284
post office...................................284
capoeira....................................284
Praça da Sé................................278
Praça Municipal........................276
restaurants.................................282
robberies....................................280
safety..280
São Francisco.............................378
shopping.....................................284
taxis..281
Terreiro de Jesus.................... 3278
tourist information....................281
tours..281
transport.....................................281
Samaipata (B).............................213
San Agustín (C)..........................554
San Andrés (C)...........................532
San Antonio de Areco (A).........68
San Antonio de los Cobres (A)
....93
San Augustín de Valle Fértil (A)
....110
San Bartolome (E).....................604
San Bernadino (P).....................699
San Cipriano (C)........................551
San Cosme y San Damián (P) 703
San Fernado de Apure (V)......895
San Francisco de Yare (V) 877
San Gil (C)...................................510
San Ignacio (A)............................86
San Juan (A)...............................108
**San Martín de los
Andes (A)**.................. **114–116**
San Martín de los Andes ... 115
San Pedro de Atacama (Ch)...411
San Pedro de Atacama 412
San Pedro, around 414
San Rafael (A).............................105
San Rafael National Park (P) ..691
San Salvador de Jujuy (A) 96
sandboarding (Pe).........721, 769,
773
Santa Catarina (Br) 345
Santa Clara (Pe)........................820
Santa Cruz (B) **209–212**
Santa Cruz **209**
Santa Cruz (Ch)..........................424
Santa Elena de Uairén (V)
.... **905–908**
Santa Elena de Uairén **906**
Santa Fe (V)................................912
Santa María (Pe)........................766
Santa Marta (C)..........................525
Santa Mission (G)......................654
Santa Rosa de Tastil (A) 93
Santa Teresa (Pe)......................766
Santana do Livramento (Br)...367
SANTIAGO (Br).............. **380–392**
Santiago **382–383**
Bellavista **386**
Downtown Santiago.......... **385**
   accommodation........................387
   airport..387
   arrival and departure 387
   ATMs...425
   banks..391
   Barrio Bellavista.......................384
   Barrio Brasil...............................386
   buses..387
   Catedral de Metropolitana......381

Cerro San Cristóbal..................384
Cerro Santa Lucía......................383
colectivos.................................387
consulates..................................391
Correo Central...........................381
drinking......................................390
eating..388
embassies...................................391
entertainment...........................390
exchange....................................391
flights...387
hospitals.....................................392
information.................................387
internet.......................................392
La Moneda..................................381
La Vega.......................................381
language schools.......................392
laundry..392
Mercado Central........................381
metrô..387
Museo Chileno de Arte
   Precolombino..........................381
Museo de Arte Contemporáneo
   (MAC).......................................384
Museo de Bellas Artes..............384
Museo de la Memoria y los
   Derechos Humanos................384
Neruda, Pablo............................384
nightlife.....................................390
Ñuñoa...386
Palacio de la Real Audiencia.......381
Parque Forestal..........................384
pharmacies.................................392
Pinochet, Augusto.....................384
Piscina Tupahue........................384
Plaza de Armas..........................381
post offices................................392
restaurants.................................388
skiing..392
telephone centres.....................392
tour operators...........................391
tourist information....................387
trains...387
transport.....................................387
Villa Grimaldi.............................384
Santo Angelo (Br) 368
Santo Antônio (Br) 317
Santo Antônio de Lisboa (Br)...360
Santo Domingo de los
Colorados (E) 616
Santo Tomás (Pe)......................820
Santos (Br) 344
São Francisco do Sul (Br) 354
São João del Rei (Br)................271
São Miguel Arcanjo (Br) 368
SÃO PAULO (Br) **332–345**
São Paulo...................... **332–333**
Central São Paulo **335**
**Vila Madelena and
Jardins** **338**
   accommodation........................340
   airports......................................339
   Avenida Paulista.......................337
   banks..343
   Barra Funda...............................336
   bars...342
   Bixiga...336
   buses..................................339, 340
   Butantã......................................339
   car rental...................................343
   Casas das Rosas........................337
   Catedral Metropolitana 334
   clubs...343
   consulates..................................344

crime..344
eating..341
Edifício Banespa.....................334
Edifício Copan.........................336
Edifício Itália...........................336
Edifício Martinelli...................334
exchange..................................343
flights..339
food..341
hospitals...................................344
Igreja de São Fransisco.........334
information...............................340
Ipiranga....................................339
Itaim Bibi..................................337
Jardins......................................337
laundries...................................344
left luggage..............................344
Liberdade..................................336
Luz...334
Memorial de América Latina....336
Mercado Municipal.................334
metrô...340
Moema......................................339
Morumbi...................................339
Mosteiro São Bento................334
Museu da Imigração Japonesa....336
Museu Afro-Brasil....................339
Museu Brasileiro da Escultura....337
Museu da Língua Portuguesa....336
Museu de Arte
    Contemporânea.................339
Museu de Arte de São Paulo
    (MASP)................................337
Museu de Arte Moderna........339
Museu do Futebol....................337
Museu Lasar Segall.................339
Museu Memória do Bixiga.....336
Museu Padre Anchieta............334
Museu Paulista.........................339
nightlife....................................342
Pacaembu.................................336
Parque da Luz...........................336
Parque do Ibirapuera.............339
Pinacoteca do Estado............336
Pinheiros...................................337
police...344
post offices...............................344
Praça da República..................336
Praça da Sé...............................334
pubs...342
restaurants...............................341
Sala São Paulo.........................336
taxis...340
Teatro Municipal.....................336
tourist information..................340
tours..340
transport...................................340
Triângulo...................................334
Vila Madalena..........................337
Vila Mariana.............................339
visa extensions........................344
São Sebastião (Br)..................344
Saquisili (E).............................589
scuba-diving (C).....492, 533, 527
scuba-diving (E).....................569
scuba-diving (V).....................877
Seno Otway (Ch).....................467
Serra do Cipó National
    Park (Br)..............................266
Serra Verde Express (Br).......349
Seven Lakes Route (A).........116
shopping.....................................36
Shulinab (G)............................657
Silvia (C).................................554

skiing (A)...........................51, 107
skiing (Ch)...............................378
Skype...41
slang (C)...................................492
snakes...34
Sorata (B).................................182
soroche......35, 422, 494, 744, 790
Soure (Br).................................310
South American Explorers'
    Club....................................723
Southern Altiplano,
    the (B)....................185–199
Southern Altiplano, the.... 186
Spanish language.......919–923
spiders.................................34, 379
stargazing (Ch)........................403
student discounts.......42, 53, 379
study..37
Sucre (B)......................200–204
Sucre................................. 201
Sucre tours (B).........................202
Suesca (C)................................505
Surama Village (G)..................656
surfing
    Brazil..................................285
    Chile...........................377, 426
    Ecuador...............................569
    Peru...........................721, 803
    Uruguay.......................834, 848
SURINAME....................658–669
Suriname River (S)...................667

T

Tabatinga (Br)..........................316
Taganga (C)..............................527
Talca (Ch).................................428
Tambo Quemado (B)..............187
Tambomachay (Pe).................750
Tambopata National
    Reserve (Pe)......................826
Taquile (Pe)......................784, 786
Tarabuco (B).............................204
Tarija (B)......................197–199
Tastil (A).....................................93
Tatacoa Desert (C)..................556
teaching English........................37
Tefé (Br)....................................316
temperature...............................12
Temuco (Ch).............................431
Tena (E)......................612–614
Tena 613
Teresópolis (Br).......................259
Termales San Vicente (C)........545
Termales Santa Rosa (C)..........545
Termas de Chillán (Ch)............429
thermal springs (C).................554
Tierra del Fuego (Ch)..............475
Tierra del Fuego (A)....144–152
Tierra del Fuego....146–147
Tierra Paisa (C)....... 535–548
Tierradentro (C)....... 557–559
Tigre and the Delta (A)...........68
Tigua (E)...................................591
Tilcara (A)...................................97
time zones..................................42
Tinharé (Br)..............................285

Tipón (Pe).................................750
Tiradentes (Ch)........................372
Titicaca, Lake (Pe)...................785
Tiwanaku (B).............................175
Tocanao (Ch)............................415
Tolú (C).....................................522
Torotoro (B)..............................207
tour operators............................30
tourist agencies.........................30
tourist information...............41
    Argentina..............................53
    Bolivia.................................164
    Brazil...................................234
    Chile....................................379
    Colombia.............................494
    Ecuador...............................570
    French Guiana....................672
    Guyana................................648
    Paraguay.............................692
    Peru.....................................723
    Suriname.............................661
    Uruguay..............................834
    Venezuela...........................864
trains...32
travel agents..............................30
travel insurance.........................40
trekking
    Argentina............. 78, 51, 105
    Argentina–Chile..................134
    Bolivia.................................161
    Chile....... 377, 436, 445, 470, 471
    Colombia.............................530
    Cordillera Real....................181
    Ecuador...............................568
    Nahuel Huapi......................122
    Peru.........721, 777, 788, 790
    Venezuela...........................890
Trelew (A).................................131
Tren a las Nubes (A)...............93
Trindade (Br)............................258
Trinidad (P)..............................702
Trinidad (B)..............................216
Trujillo (Pe)............... 791–796
Trujillo 792
Trujillo, around 797
Tulcán (E).................................587
Tumbes (Pe)............... 804–806
Tunja (C)...................................506
Tupiza (B).................................196
turtles (FG)...............................684
turtles (G).................................716

U

Ubatuba (Br)............................345
UFOs (A).....................................78
Umajallanta (B).......................207
Upsala Glacier (A)...................142
Uribe, Álvaro............................494
Uros Floating Islands (Pe)......784,
    786
Urubamba (Pe).........................752
Uruguaiana (Br).......................367
URUGUAY 23, 829–854
Uruguay.............................. 831
Ushuaia (A)................ 144–151
Ushuaia.............................. 145
Uyuni (B)..................................193
Uyuni 193

V

vaccinations............................ 34
Valdiva (Ch).........................439
Valdivia.............................. 440
Vale do Capão (Br)............286
Valle de Chepu (Ch)..................451
Valle de Cocora (C)...............547
Valle de la Luna (Ch).........415
Valle de la Luna (A) 110
Valle de la Muerte (Ch) 415
Vallegrande (B) 214
Valles Calhaquíes (A) 94
Valparaíso (Ch) 393–398
Valparaíso 394–395
vegetarians (A) 49
VENEZUELA........26, 856–917
Venezuela 857
Vicuña (Ch)...........................404
Vila do Abraão (Br)............283
Vilcabamba (E)..................607
Vilcabamba 607
Vilcabamba (Pe)..................766
Villa Catedral (A)...............121
Villa Cerro Castillo (Ch) 457
Villa de Leyva (C) 507–509
Villa de Leyva 507

Villa General Belgrano (A) 77
Villa la Angostura (A)........116
Villa O'Higgins (Ch).............461
Villa Tunari (B) 208
Villamontes (B) 216
Villarrica (Ch) 432
Lago Villarrica and around... 433
Villavieja (C) 556
Viña del Mar (Ch) 398
Viña del Mar 399
Visa Waiver Program..............29
visas
  Argentina.................................... 47
  Bolivia......................................158
  Brazil..228
  Chile...373
  Colombia.................................489
  Ecuador....................................565
  French Guiana.........................670
  Guyana.....................................645
  Paraguay..................................687
  Peru..713
  Suriname..................................659
  Uruguay...................................831
  Venezuela................................859
Volcan Cayambe (E)...........583
Volcán Chimborazo (E).......598
Volcán Cotopaxi (E)............588
Volcán de Lodo El Totumo (C)
....519

Volcán Sierra Negra (E).............638
Volcán Tungurahua (E)..... 593, 596
Volcán Vilarrica (Ch)..................435
volunteering................................ 37

W

weather .... 12, *see also* climate
whale-watching (Ch)..............451
whale-watching (E)............626
wildlife, top ten places 10
winery visits (A) 96, 100, 104
women travellers.........................38
work... 37

Y & Z

Yacuiba (B) 216
Yasuní National Park (E) 612
yellow fever 35
Yumani (B) 180
Yungas, the (B) 183
Yungay (Pe)........................790
Zipaquirá (C)......................505
Zumbahua (E) 591

Map symbols

The symbols below are used on maps throughout the book

✈	Airport	⚿	Campsite	🕴	Waterfall	- - - -	Path
★	Bus/taxi	☉	Statue	⚐	Swimming pool	🕆	Church
@	Internet café/access	✡	Synagogue	/⋀	Volcano		Building
⊠	Post office	⚞	Ski area	▲	Mountain peak		Market
(i)	Tourist office	♦	Museum		Gorge	◯	Stadium
(C)	Telephone office		Vineyard		Mountain range		Park/national park
⊞	Hospital		Petrol station		Bridge		Beach
♦	Place of interest	⚓	Harbour/port	●-●	Cable car		Christian Cemetery
◠	Cave	(M)	Metro/subway stop	⊠–⊠	Gate		Jewish cemetery
∴	Ruins	⋂	Arch		Steps		Marsh/swamp
₩	Fortress	⚲	Lighthouse	▬	Wall		Glacier
▮	Tower	⬥	Mountain refuge/lodge		Funicular		Salt flats
⚓	Viewpoint	⛫	Park ranger		River		
⚑	Mosque	∿	Spring		Ferry route		

Listings key

■ Accommodation

● Eating/drinking/nightlife

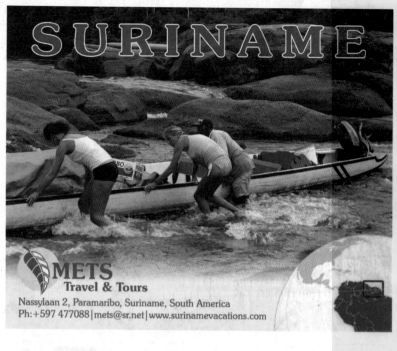